Universal Command Guide for Operating Systems

Guy Lotgering and the UCG Training Team

Hungry Minds, Inc.

Best-Selling Books • Digital Downloads • e-Books • Answer Networks • e-Newsletters
Branded Web Sites • e-Learning

New York, NY ♦ Cleveland, OH ♦ Indianapolis, IN

Universal Command Guide for Operating Systems

Published by
Hungry Minds, Inc.
909 Third Avenue
New York, NY 10022
www.hungryminds.com

Library of Congress Catalog Control Number: 2001099737

ISBN: 0-7645-4833-6

Printed in the United States of America

10 9 8 7 6 5 4 3 2 1

1P/SQ/QT/QS/IN

Distributed in the United States by Hungry Minds, Inc.

Distributed by CDG Books Canada Inc. for Canada; by Transworld Publishers Limited in the United Kingdom; by IDG Norge Books for Norway; by IDG Sweden Books for Sweden; by IDG Books Australia Publishing Corporation Pty. Ltd. for Australia and New Zealand; by TransQuest Publishers Pte Ltd. for Singapore, Malaysia, Thailand, Indonesia, and Hong Kong; by Gotop Information Inc. for Taiwan; by ICG Muse, Inc. for Japan; by Intersoft for South Africa; by Eyrolles for France; by International Thomson Publishing for Germany, Austria, and Switzerland; by Distribuidora Cuspide for Argentina; by LR International for Brazil; by Galileo Libros for Chile; by Ediciones ZETA S.C.R. Ltda. for Peru; by WS Computer Publishing Corporation, Inc., for the Philippines; by Contemporanea de Ediciones for Venezuela; by Express Computer Distributors for the Caribbean and West Indies; by Micronesia Media Distributor, Inc. for Micronesia; by Chips Computadoras S.A. de C.V. for Mexico; by Editorial Norma de Panama S.A. for Panama; by American Bookshops for Finland.

For general information on Hungry Minds' products and services please contact our Customer Care department within the U.S. at 800-762-2974, outside the U.S. at 317-572-3993 or fax 317-572-4002.

For sales inquiries and reseller information, including discounts, premium and bulk quantity sales, and foreign-language translations, please contact our Customer Care department at 800-434-3422, fax 317-572-4002 or write to Hungry Minds, Inc., Attn: Customer Care Department, 10475 Crosspoint Boulevard, Indianapolis, IN 46256.

For information on licensing foreign or domestic rights, please contact our Sub-Rights Customer Care department at 212-884-5000.

For information on using Hungry Minds' products and services in the classroom or for ordering examination copies, please contact our Educational Sales department at 800-434-2086 or fax 317-572-4005.

For press review copies, author interviews, or other publicity information, please contact our Public Relations department at 317-572-3168 or fax 317-572-4168.

For authorization to photocopy items for corporate, personal, or educational use, please contact Copyright Clearance Center, 222 Rosewood Drive, Danvers, MA 01923, or fax 978-750-4470.

About the Author

Guy Lotgering began using computers in 1979 with an Apple II. His first IBM PC computer was built by his father, but Guy continued using and building his own computers throughout the '80s during the IBM PC revolution. In the early '90s Guy studied programming, but ended up working in networking. He installed Novell NetWare and Windows NT networking systems and related network services for companies and government agencies throughout the United States. Guy has over 20 years experience with computers and is certified in many technologies including certificates in programming (C, C+, COBOL, RPG), Microsoft (MCSE), Novell (CNE3, CNE4, CNE5), and A+. In 1999, Guy moved to Sweden to continue his career in networking and specialized with UNIX systems. Guy had experience with UNIX and Linux in the past but needed more knowledge to be as comfortable in UNIX as he is with Novell and Microsoft products. There was no tool that documented the similarities of the many different operating systems. This was the motivation for writing the *Universal Command Guide for Operating Systems.* Guy had never written a book before, but has always had a passion for teaching people about computers and networking technologies. Guy, on his own personal time, has taught and helped over 25 people to become certified Microsoft and Novell engineers. Guy is a gifted teacher who has the ability to break down complicated networking topics, making then easier to understand and more fun to learn. It was Guy's technical background and his passion for teaching that gave him the desire to write this book. Guy and the entire UCG team sincerely hope that this book will help you learn and conquer the many operating systems of our time.

The UCG Team

The UCG team is collection of highly skilled individuals from different technical backgrounds with experience in many operating systems. Combined, the UCG team has over 200 years of technical experience and is certified in most of today's operating system platforms. The UCG team is highly educated and has certificates in Sun Solaris (Solaris 7 Administrator), IBM AIX (System Administration and System Support), programming (C/C++, Java), Microsoft (MCSE, MCP), and Novell (CNE, CNA). Some members of the UCG team are responsible for maintaining large networks at their places of employment, and other members work as consultants for the many computer companies in the north of Sweden. The many consultants who form this team install large backup solutions, Internet solutions, Linux-based firewalls, and configure networking infrastructures for many large and small companies throughout Sweden. The UCG team also includes many programmers who write software programs for their companies and develop new Web-based applications. In Europe, Sweden is known for its commitment to education and technology. Almost every member of the UCG team has attended one of the many technical universities in Sweden, and many are currently enrolled and are taking additional classes. This team of trained professionals has poured their real-life knowledge and experience into every command in this book.

The following people have worked together to make this book a reality. The following descriptions introduce the professional and technical sides of each team member. For a more personal look at each team member, please see the UCG CD-ROM.

Myles Dean (Project Manager) is a Quality Assurance Coordinator for Technia AB, the leading supplier of global business-to-business and eCommerce applications in Scandinavia. He spent six years in the U.S. Navy and developed a strong background in communications working as an internal communications technician aboard submarines. He has worked with 3D-CAD systems for six years and has a total of fifteen years experience with computers. Myles also has worked as facilities manager for Omega/Omicron, a world supplier of optical filters, and later worked as project engineer for Emhart Sweden.

Anders Eriksson has been working with computers for over eleven years and is currently a consultant for Eterra AB, where he is responsible for installing and configuring RS6000 servers running IBM AIX. Anders also works with Solaris 7 and 8, and from time to time he even installs and configures Linux and Windows 2000 servers. His primary focus is high-end backup solutions using Tivoli Storage Manager.

Andreas Svahn also is a consultant from Eterra AB and is a colleague of Anders Eriksson. He is a communications expert and primarily works with configuring Cisco routers and switches for companies in the north of Sweden. Andreas also works with Windows NT and Windows 2000 and is responsible for administrating and maintaining Eterra's local NT network.

Bengt Larsson is currently a student at a local university where he is studying to become a network engineer. He has been using computers for over six years and has primarily used Microsoft Windows and office applications. Over the past year, Bengt has been studying many different operating systems, mostly Linux. He also has worked with computer hardware and is a certified A+ technician.

Bobo Häggström is currently working as a system developer for Easit Internet Solutions. Bobo is a gifted programmer who began writing programs when he was only 9 years old. He works with Linux and Microsoft operating systems. He writes applications in C/C++, Java, Perl, and PHP, and develops applications for SQL databases. Currently he primarily develops Web-based applications.

David Johansson has worked with computers for over ten years; his first computer was a Commodore 64. He continued working with computers through the DOS revolution. He is familiar with every Microsoft operating system from DOS through Windows XP. David is certified in Windows NT, but primarily works with Windows 2000 and terminal services. He is further developing his knowledge of Citrix and ASP.

Eric Bohlin is a UNIX system engineer for Telia AB, the largest telecommunication company in Sweden. Eric primarily works with Solaris 7.0 and 8.0 operating systems, but also works with Linux in his free time. He is certified in Solaris as a system administrator. Eric's primary responsibility for Telia is maintaining the large phone database, including the management of the many Solaris servers.

Joachim Sehlstedt comes from a strong Linux and programming background. He began working with Linux six years ago, and now he develops applications for the Linux platform. Currently Joachim is a teacher; he instructs students about Microsoft applications as well as programming languages. Joachim is a skilled database developer and develops SQL-powered Web sites for local companies.

Jonas Nilsson has extensive experience with the Macintosh. He currently works as a Web Designer and assistant Art Director for ReklamMakarna in Sundsvall, Sweden. Jonas has worked with the Macintosh for over ten years and uses the Macintosh in a network environment at his job. He uses the Macintosh when creating the high-end Web sites and developing graphics for customers.

Håkan Sislegård has a broad working knowledge of UNIX-based operating systems and also has experience working with AIX, Solaris, and Linux. Håkan currently works for Metso, a large engineering company in Sweden. He is the system manager for the UNIX network as well as the IP network, which is primarily Novell, but also includes many Microsoft Windows NT servers and Windows clients.

Lars Wiklund has worked extensively with high-end mainframe and UNIX-based 3D-CAD systems for over 15 years. He was responsible for managing a variety of CAD platforms including IRIX from SGI, Solaris from Sun Microsystems, and AIX from IBM. Today Lars is in charge of managing a large PC-based network using Novell file servers as well as the 3D-CAD systems now based on Windows 2000.

Leif Andersson is an experienced UNIX consultant who has worked professionally with UNIX for over 13 years. Leif has worked with just about all types of UNIX platforms including Solaris, HP/UX, Ultrix, Dnix, Digital UNIX, and AIX. Today, Leif works only with Sun Solaris.

Lollo Hartelius has over 18 years experience working with computers and Microsoft-based operating systems. She has extensive knowledge of user applications. Lollo works for Metso. She is responsible for installing management applications on Windows-based computers. Previously, she was in charge of the telephone switchboard and had the responsibility of routing messages for 500 users using Lotus Notes.

Martin Sislegård is a network consultant for ÅF-SPEAB AB, a consulting company for various industries. He is currently part of a team called TACDIS (Truck And Car Dealer Information System) developing a large database for Volvo to be used throughout Sweden and Norway. Martin has extensive knowledge of Microsoft products and is certified in Windows 2000. Previously, Martin worked at Metso, where he earned his certification in Novell and maintained the NetWare servers.

Micael Belin is a programmer who writes applications in many languages, but prefers C/C++. He has over 11 years experience with computers, and has written applications and games for Microsoft operating systems. Currently he is a student at Linköping University's Institute of Technology, where he hopes to receive his master's degree in computer science in a couple of years.

Ove Thomasson is skilled in many Linux distributions. He primarily works with Debian Linux, but also works with Red Hat, SuSE, and Slackware. Ove also has worked with many varieties of BSD. Currently Ove is working as a consultant for Arrowhead AB, one of the largest Internet service providers in Sweden. He is responsible for the Linux-based e-mail and Web servers, and he configures Linux firewalls.

Peter Bonivart is a high-level UNIX system engineer who has been working professionally with UNIX-based servers for over ten years. He has been using computers since the early '80s, starting with the PC revolution. Peter has worked with Linux, HP/UX, AIX, and Solaris.

Peter Söderström is currently a student at Luleå University of Technology, where he plans to earn a master's degree in space engineering. One day he hopes to work at the NASA space center. Peter has been working with computers for over six years. He has primarily used Microsoft Windows-based operating systems, but also is familiar with Sun Solaris and over the past year has been working with Linux.

Rolf Sundin currently works in the laboratory at SCA Grapic AB, one of the world's largest suppliers of paper products. He tests the quality of paper products using Windows NT. He has studied chemistry and natural science and has been using computers for over 10 years. Rolf primarily has used Microsoft operating systems at home and at work, but has studied UNIX for the past year.

Credits

Acquisitions Editors
Greg Croy
Nancy Maragioglio

Project Editor
Pat O'Brien

Technical Editor
Greg Stephens

Copy Editors
Dennis Weaver
Brian MacDonald

Editorial Managers
Kyle Looper
Ami Frank Sullivan

Vice President and Executive Group Publisher
Richard Swadley

Vice President and Executive Publisher
Bob Ibsen

Editorial Director
Mary Bednarek

Project Coordinator
Dale White

Graphics and Production Specialists
Steve Arany, Kathie S. Schutte

Quality Control Technicians
Laura Albert, Dave Faust,
Andy Hollandbeck, Linda Quigley

Permissions Editor
Laura Moss

Media Development Editor
Travis Silvers

Proofreading and Indexing
Christine Pingleton, Anne Leach

To my lovely wife Jeanette, my son Christian, and my daughter Sara. Your patience with me was second to none. You have been my strength throughout this entire project. Thank you for letting me pursue my dream of uniting our world of operating systems. I am just sorry that it took so long, and for working so much.

I love you.

To our father in heaven who gave me wisdom, courage, and strength to accomplish this project.
"I can do all things through Christ who strengthens me" Philippians 4:13

Foreword

Much has been said in the past about "proprietary" vs. "open" systems, but much has been lost in the context of time. While open systems promised IT managers' freedom to choose "best of breed," doing so and accepting the value-add of these selections tend to lock companies into those decisions for many generations.

Not that this is necessarily a bad thing. Many vendors, my own employer included, bring to the table value-add that is significant in allowing customers to significantly leverage their infrastructure, saving hundreds of millions of dollars or more in time and related business gains.

But choosing to adopt such value-add comes with a price. Not just the lock-in, but also the difficulties of retooling should business or infrastructure needs change.

Indeed today, it's extremely rare to find a data center that deploys only one operating system, as the evolution of different platform and operating system strengths have led to mass deployment of specific system types in different aspects of the data center, whether mainframe, different variants of open systems, Windows, or Linux. Even the many customers I've met with, who've claimed to have only one platform, tend to have at least two or three — often a mainframe or large scale open server for OLTP and/or ERP; large or parallel open servers for data collection, inventory, or perhaps Decision Support; Windows for Email and file sharing, or Linux for a Web server. In some cases, such customers don't even realize the significance or mission-critical nature of the second platform; in fact, most don't until it becomes unavailable.

Good technical people already understand the concepts of operating systems and can already adapt to changes within an operating environment; in fact, they've no doubt already been exposed to various evolution and de-evolution of their primary Operating System and it's surrounding environment. Many of them may also be exposed to several operating environments, whether several different UNIX variants, or perhaps UNIX and Windows (although perhaps not as an administrator).

Qualified technical administrators are not necessarily *experts*. Good technical administrators are flexible and understand the application of the technology to their business. Experts, on the other hand, drive deep into a platform's inner workings but are often limited by how much of their expertise they use on a day-to-day basis; it's nearly impossible to keep an expert challenged in an administrative role. This doesn't mean that good administrators can't become experts in their own right, but such experts, if indeed good at understanding your business, should be ripe for recycling to give them newer and broader challenges.

Indeed the costs of expertise can be extraordinary. In fact, recent industry analyst reports show the worldwide IT spending at nearly one trillion with 10 to 15 percent of that spent on interoperability alone.

Wise IT heads have been working to diminish this cost by working closely with trusted vendors, such as EMC, who maintain such expertise internally and who can help solve the critical technical integration challenges, leaving the customer's IT expertise to their business needs.

Another major factor to be considered is consolidation. The microcomputer explosion of the 1970s and 1980s led to massive decentralization of systems. Unfortunately, this led to decentralization of the core business intelligence, so the trends of the late 1980s and 1990s was to re-centralize to capture control over the business "crown jewels" information. Today, more powerful systems, networks, and expanded infrastructure capabilities allow movement of data between systems to where systems can be both centralized for information repository, but distributed for application presence at the point of data capture or dissemination. Savvy application architects will leverage the capabilities of different systems to leverage the strengths of that platform and operating system for the specific need.

Consolidated environments are another place where the heterogeneous server support of EMC storage systems can help because they can be leveraged, regardless of the number or type of systems being attached. EMC storage technologies can also help distribute the data while leaving the servers free to service the business applications.

Which then leaves only the question of how to best leverage the people resource. We've already established the need to recycle the people resources, but how do you get them up to speed quickly, without significant costly investment in retraining? At some point, training may be necessary, but again, good technical administrators are flexible and understand the concepts and semantics behind what they're doing, not just the syntax. This book, the *Universal Command Guide for Operating Systems*, can significantly reduce the extent of retraining by providing a solid cross-reference between command sets on a wide variety of operating systems, allowing the administrator to think in their own terms, yet make effective use of the new platform's administrative tools.

Doc D'Errico
Director, eLab
EMC_ Engineering
EMC Corporation
Hopkinton, MA USA
doc@emc.com

Preface

Welcome to *The Universal Command Guide*, a book that took almost three years to write. This book contains comprehensive documentation for each and every command from every major operating system available today. Every command documented in this book includes all of the command's options. The commands are documented using a command template that organizes the information consistently, presents it in one standard format, and provides a consistent guide to the location of the information — regardless of the operating system it comes from. The documentation is designed to be clear and easy to read. This book contains 8,232 commands (4, 575 UNIX, 2,403 Microsoft, 1,118 NetWare, 113 Macintosh) and over 57,000 command options from over 20 different operating systems. The "How this book is organized," on the following pages sum up the operating systems and versions included in this book:

The Universal Command Guide for Operating Systems also includes 3,608 command cross-references. The "Quick Command Index" — an exhaustive cross-referencing index — quickly shows you any command's equivalent functionality in all the other major operating systems. Throughout the book, additional cross-reference tables show command functionality in many different platforms. Using this unique cross-referencing feature, you will be able to navigate and manage any operating system — using knowledge from a *different* operating system. In this book, cross-referencing is a way of recycling knowledge from one operating system to another, quickly enabling you to use a foreign or an unfamiliar operating system. Recycling is not a new idea (we have been recycling cans, bottles, and newspapers for many years), but never before have we recycled this type of knowledge in this handy way. By using this book to forge meaningful links with what you already know, you can learn more about a *range* of operating systems in much less time than it takes to learn one from the ground up.

Who should use this book

This book is for anyone who desires more information about managing, using, administrating, or configuring different operating systems. This book is a must for all network and system administrators, but is also helpful as a basic reference for the beginning computer user or student. Perhaps you are familiar with Microsoft Windows and have a need (or a desire) to manage a Linux or NetWare system. You know what task you want to perform, but don't yet know which command to use. You might come from a Novell background and want learn how to perform Novell-type commands on a UNIX-based OS, or maybe you want to learn more about the Macintosh from the Microsoft perspective to help your users migrate from one system to another. You also can manage the many different versions of Microsoft Windows as it continues to evolve and change — often using powerful commands that even power users have never seen or used before. If you want to learn another OS but are afraid to dive right in (or simply want to know more about the operating systems that you use today), you will not find a better resource than the one you are holding right now. This book is designed to help you explore the world of operating systems. When you are free to explore it, you can select an OS according to your needs rather than your previous knowledge. The doors are open; the barriers are gone. The rest is up to you.

How the book was created

To create *The Universal Command Guide*, we installed each and every operating system we cover on over 20 separate computers. We performed a complete installation for every operating system, including all standard applications, services, and packages that come with it. We did not install third-party applications on any of our test servers. Before we documented any command in this book, it had to exist on one of our test servers. After finding the commands, we used a variety of resources (including our own experience) to document and test the commands. We wanted to physically run and test each and every command and report the results of our research in this book.

Our goal was to document literally *every* command from every major operating system. To accomplish this, we created scripts to scan the entire file system and create a list of every executable file. Next, we typed in the filename of every executable file, one by one, to determine whether it could be documented — and if it could, we documented it. If any command is missing from this book, that simply means we did not find it on one of our test servers. In effect, we allowed the operating systems to speak for themselves.

Is this really every command from every operating system? The answer may surprise you, but before giving you the answer, I would like explain the mentality and attitude of the UCG team while this book was in development. We never judged a command by its code; we truly wanted to create the first comprehensive book to include all commands from all operating systems. Some of you may test us to see whether we are telling the truth, and we accept all challengers.

Completists should be aware that we did leave off some specific commands, but only because we felt they had no value at this time. For example, commands that convert BMP files to Atari format are missing, and, for that matter most games are not included. We did not include the 50+ DigiBoard drivers for NetWare because this is a book of commands, not drivers. So are we missing any commands from this book? Technically, yes, but we are confident that any command you need *is* in this book. So (getting back to our question), is this *really* every command from every operating system? Yes — all the ones you're likely to find a use for in the real world. What more do you need?

How the book is organized

I - Cross-References

This is a bird's-eye view of the commands as we cross-reference them at the platform level for the four major platforms of operating systems: Microsoft, NetWare, UNIX/Linux, and Macintosh

Quick Command Index

This is a quick way to find any command's functionality in 14 different operating-system platforms. All cross-referenced commands are listed in alphabetical order.

This feature, used together with the QCI, shows a list of actions that perform the same task as a command used in another operating system (when a suitable equivalent command could not be found).

II - Novell Systems

Here you can look up any NetWare commands.

Universal NetWare Commands

A collection of commands that all NetWare versions, from 3 to 6, have in common.

Shared NetWare 4, 5, and 6 Commands

A collection of commands that NetWare 4, NetWare 5, and NetWare 6 have in common.

Other NetWare Commands

A complete list of all remaining NetWare commands (from NetWare 3, 4, 5, and 6) not listed in the "Universal NetWare Command" section or in the "Shared NetWare 4, 5, and 6 Commands" section.

III - Microsoft Systems

Here you can look up any Microsoft Windows or DOS command.

Universal Windows Commands

A list of common Windows commands for versions from Windows 95 through Windows XP.

Other Windows Commands

A complete listing of all remaining Windows commands (not listed in the "Universal Windows Commands" section) for versions from Windows 95 through Windows XP.

Windows Control Panel Cross-Reference

The functionality of the Windows Control Panel from four Windows versions (Windows 95, Windows NT, Windows 2000, and Windows XP) is cross-referenced here from version to version — *and* to equivalents in other major operating systems.

DOS 6.22 Commands

A complete listing of all DOS commands.

IV – UNIX and Linux Systems

This part covers the major UNIX and Linux families.

Universal UNIX Commands

Common commands from AIX, Solaris 7, Solaris 8, OpenBSD, and Linux are combined to create the "Universal UNIX Commands" section.

AIX Commands

A complete listing of any AIX commands not listed in the "Universal UNIX Commands" section.

Red Hat Linux Commands

A complete listing of Red Hat Linux commands not listed in the "Universal UNIX Commands" section.

OpenBSD Commands

A complete listing of OpenBSD commands not listed in the "Universal UNIX Commands" section.

Solaris 7 Commands

A complete listing of Solaris 7 commands not listed in the "Universal UNIX Commands" section.

Solaris 8 Commands

A listing of all new commands from Solaris 8 that are not found in Solaris 7 or in the "Universal UNIX Commands" section.

V - Macintosh Systems

Macintosh Commands

A complete listing of commands from the Macintosh OS system 9.1 operating system.

Appendix- About the CD-ROM

Describes the software and other cool things on the CD-ROM.

The UCG Syntax

We have developed our very own *Universal Command Guide* syntax, which works with *every operating system in this book.* The command syntax is easy enough for a beginner, specific enough to help the expert, and very simple to learn. The Syntax Toolbox shown here describes the various items you will find in our syntax.

The items listed in the Syntax Toolbox can be and are combined in many creative ways. As you use the book you will want to return here to help you understand the command syntax.

The basic format for the syntax is: `command [ options... ] { operand }`

Syntax Definition

`Commands`	This is the first field in the syntax.
`Option`	Anoption is a command modifier that changes the functionality of the command. Options normally look like -a, -f, --help, etc....
`operand`	An *operand* is a variable for which you must supply specific information; it is always shown in *italics*. Operands normally look like *file*, *servername*, *devicename*, *IP address*, and so on.
[ ]	Square brackets are only used around options; they indicate that the enclosed item is optional. You can use the command with or without the enclosed [option].
{ }	Italic curly brackets are only used around operands and indicate that the enclosed item is optional. You can use the command with or without the enclosed {operand}.
...	The ellipsis can be used with either options or operands; it indicates that multiple options or operands can be combined. An `s` is always added to the word `option` or to the specific operand to indicate the plural form (for example, `options...`, `files...`, `devices...`).
italics	Indicates that whatever is italicized requires specific information that you must supply. If the italicized item is nested in curly brackets, it is optional; otherwise it is required.
option	Indicates that a single option must be used before the command will function normally.
[option]	Indicates that a single option can be used but is not necessary for the command to function properly.
[options...]	Indicates that multiple options can be used but are not necessary for the command to function properly.
operand	Indicates that the specified operand requires specific information; you must supply the information before the command will function normally.
{ operand }	Indicates that the specified operand requires specific information that you must supply; it is optional (not required for the command to function).
option *operand*	Indicates that a single option is required and that it requires specific information. You must supply the information before the command will function normally.
[option *operand*]	Indicates that a single option can be used, but it's optional (not required for the command to function properly). If used, it requires specific information that you must supply.
ACTION	Indicates that an operand is required for the command to function, but there is more than one operand that can be used. Every time you see an italicized and capitalized *ACTION* in the syntax field, you will always find a bold **ACTION** in one of the option fields that shows the different operands you can use for the command.
{ ACTION }	Same as above, but optional (not required for the command to function).

Contents at a Glance

Your feedback

Tell us what is good, and what is bad. You can be sure your feedback will have a direct impact on future editions. You can let us know by e-mailing us at feedback@ucgbook.com, by visiting our Web site at www.ucgbook.com, or e-mailing directly at guy@ucgbook.com. You also can e-mail anyone of our UCG team members whose e-mail addresses are located on the CD-ROM.

This book is the start of a new era in Open Source; therefore, we call it the "Open Book." We want you, the reader, to take an active part in future editions. New operating systems are popping up every day; we want to add more operating systems to the next edition — such as HP/UX, BeOS, VMS, and whatever operating system(s) demand to be included at that time. We will list operating systems on our Web site and ask our readers to vote for those we should include in the next edition. This is your chance to be part of writing a book, be listed as a contributor, and even share in the book's royalties. For more information, please see our Web site: improve.ucgbook.com

Acknowledgments

We would like to give our special gratitude to the following people who contributed to the creation of this book. Some of them donated hardware, some of them gave their time, while others did both.

Anders Dahlqvist, the Linux Guru. Anthony Whitehead, "Mr. Knowledgeable." Carina Lundqvist and Henrik Wikman, thanks for all your hard work and commitment. Eric Bohlin, without your 1.4 Gigahertz computer, this book would still be in production. Jens Fristam, thanks for putting up with my dumb questions. Jonas Sundling, thanks for your hard work on the CD-ROM; your graphics take my breath away. Josef Höök, so much knowledge in only one brain; thank you, my friend. Karl-Erik Svedin, thanks for your laugh, your smile, and your work; you were a pleasure to work with. Kenth Näsström, thanks for your database programming and for inspiring me to continue with the book. Lars-Erk Olsson (LEO), the "Macro Man," thank you for writing those incredible macros that were instrumental in the creation of this book. Lars Nyberg, thanks for the Macintosh and for answering the many late-night questions on how to use it. Liiza Falk, she came, she worked, she left, and I never had time to thank her. Thanks for your help. Mattias Kovacic, thanks for your help and for the server; it is in good hands. Topias Kinnunen, the man, the myth, the legend. Thanks for your tremendous imagination when creating the CD-ROM. The Families: I would like to thank the many families of the people who worked on this book. They sacrificed personal time away from their loved ones while these people worked evenings and weekends. Thank you for supporting them by allowing them to work on this book.

I would also like to acknowledge the following people and companies who have also contributed to the creation of this book:

Anders Agren from Novell Sweden, thanks for keeping us up-to-date with NetWare 6 and for your support. CADSOL AB, thanks for the use of the RS6000 machine; I really appreciate it. Eterra AB, my previous employer, thank you for helping me with hardware, and for your support. I really enjoyed working with all of you. Judy Brief from Hungry Minds, thank you so much for listening and understanding the idea, and then for your passion when presenting the book to Hungry Minds, Inc. Lennart Lindkvist, my neighbor, thanks for providing the UCG team with the needed additional parking. Lou Lotgering and Sally Empry, thank you for editing the CD-ROM team biographies and fixin' all them words that ain't sounding so good. Nancy Maragioglio from Hungry Minds, Inc., thanks for putting up with me and for showing me how hard being an author really is. You were patient and kind, and I thank you. Pat O'Brien from Hungry Minds, Inc., thanks for all of your wisdom about books and for teaching me how to write one. You had many great ideas and contributed so much to the book. Thanks for putting up with me. Roger Gustavssson, thanks for your assistance and support with AIX. Telecomputing AB, my current employer, thanks for giving me the time to finish the book and for your support. To my mother, for her encouragement and showing me that anything is possible and teaching me that I could be anything I want; now I am an author.

When I was seeking a publisher, I hoped the publisher that accepted the book would not try to change the style and vision of the book. I wanted a publisher that would improve upon what we had already developed and see this as an opportunity to create a different style of book. Hungry Minds, Inc. fulfilled all my hopes and expectations and had the courage to take a chance on a new idea for a book, even though it presented many difficult design challenges. I would like to thank the entire staff of Hungry Minds, Inc. for having the courage to publish this unique book and for allowing the book to be what it is.

In This Part

Chapter 1
Command Indexes

This part helps you find equivalents to every command or procedure in every operating system the book covers.

Chapter 1

Quick Command Index

Welcome to Quick Command Index (QCI). Here you find over 1,300 cross-references that link commands to 14 different operating-system versions. All commands that are cross-referenced are listed in alphabetical order.

When using the QCI, you will find cross-reference fields that contain an Action number. These actions describe the tasks needed to match a single command in another operating system.

	AIX	Linux	OpenBSD	Solaris	NetWare 3	NetWare 4	NetWare 5	NetWare 6
#	#	#	#	#	# ;	# ;	# ;	# ;
/etc/defaultrouter	/etc/gateways	/etc/sysconfig/network	/etc/mygate	**/etc/defaultrouter**	\etc\gateways	\etc\gateways	\etc\gateways	\etc\gateways
/etc/gateways	**/etc/gateways**	/etc/sysconfig/network	/etc/mygate	/etc/defaultrouter	\etc\gateways	\etc\gateways	\etc\gateways	\etc\gateways
/etc/inetd.conf	**/etc/inetd.conf** chsubserver	/etc/xinetd.conf	**/etc/inetd.conf**	**/etc/inetd.conf**	install.nlm	inetcfg.nlm	inetcfg.nlm	inetcfg.nlm
/etc/inittab	**/etc/inittab**	**/etc/inittab**	**/etc/rc.conf**	**/etc/inittab**	autoexec.ncf	autoexec.ncf	autoexec.ncf	autoexec.ncf
/etc/mygate	/etc/gateways	/etc/sysconfig/network	**/etc/mygate**	/etc/defaultrouter	\etc\gateways	\etc\gateways	\etc\gateways	\etc\gateways
/etc/myname	hostname	hostname	**/etc/myname**	/etc/nodename	file server name	file server name	file server name	file server name
/etc/nodename	hostname	hostname	/etc/myname	**/etc/nodename**	file server name	file server name	file server name	file server name
/etc/nologin	**/etc/nologin** pdisable	**/etc/nologin**	**/etc/nologin**	**/etc/nologin**	disable login	disable login	disable login	disable login
/etc/printcap	smit print	**/etc/printcap** lpc	**/etc/printcap** lpc	lpset lpadmin	psc.exe pconsole.exe	psc.exe pconsole.exe	nwpmw32.exe nwadmn32.exe ndpsm.nlm	nwadmn32.exe ndpsm.nlm
/etc/rc.conf	/etc/inittab	/etc/inittab	**/etc/rc.conf**	/etc/inittab	autoexec.ncf	autoexec.ncf	autoexec.ncf	autoexec.ncf
/etc/resolv.conf	**/etc/resolv.conf**	**/etc/resolv.conf**	**/etc/resolv.conf**	**/etc/resolv.conf**	tcpcon.nlm	\etc\resolv.cfg	\etc\resolv.cfg	\etc\resolv.cfg
/etc/sysconfig/network	/etc/gateways	**/etc/sysconfig/network**	/etc/mygate	/etc/defaultrouter	\etc\gateways	\etc\gateways	\etc\gateways	\etc\gateways
/etc/xinetd.conf	/etc/inetd.conf chsubserver	**/etc/xinetd.conf**	/etc/inetd.conf	/etc/inetd.conf	install.nlm	inetcfg.nlm	inetcfg.nlm	inetcfg.nlm
;	#	#	#	#	# ;	# ;	# ;	# ;
\etc\gateways	/etc/gateways	/etc/sysconfig/network	/etc/mygate	/etc/defaultrouter	**\etc\gateways**	**\etc\gateways**	**\etc\gateways**	**\etc\gateways**
\etc\hosts	**/etc/hosts**	**/etc/hosts**	**/etc/hosts**	**/etc/hosts**	**\etc\hosts**	**\etc\hosts**	**\etc\hosts**	**\etc\hosts**
\etc\resolv.cfg	vi /etc/resolv.conf chnamsv	vi /etc/resolv.conf	vi /etc/resolv.conf	vi /etc/resolv.conf	**\etc\resolv.cfg**	**\etc\resolv.cfg**	**\etc\resolv.cfg**	**\etc\resolv.cfg**
2xupgrde					**2xupgrde.nlm**		ipcu.nlm	ipcu.nlm
Abort Remirror	unmirrorvg		raidctl -u		**abort remirror**	**abort remirror**	**abort remirror**	**abort remirror**
About This Computer	uname -a svmon	uname -a free	uname -a top	uname -a prtcon	version memory	version memory	version memory	version memory
About Windows, winver	uname -a	uname -a kernelversion	uname -a	uname -a wsinfo	version nver.exe netbios I	version nver.exe	version nver.exe	version

DOS	Windows 9x	NT 4.0	NT 2000	Windows XP	Macintosh	
rem	rem	rem	rem	rem		**#**
	Action: 141	Action: 197	Action: 198	Action: 198	Control Panel > TCPIP	**/etc/defaultrouter**
	Action: 141	Action: 197	Action: 198	Action: 198	Control Panel > TCPIP	**/etc/gateways**
		Control Panel > Services	inetmgr.exe	inetmgr.exe		**/etc/inetd.conf**
autoexec.bat	autoexec.bat	autoexec.bat	autoexec.bat	autoexec.bat	Apple Menu > Control Panels > Extensions Manager *selections...*	**/etc/inittab**
	Action: 141	Action: 197	Action: 198	Action: 198	Control Panel > TCPIP	**/etc/mygate**
	Action: 204	Control Panel > Network	Action: 205	Action: 205		**/etc/myname**
	Action: 204	Control Panel > Network	Action: 205	Action: 205		**/etc/nodename**
		chglogon /DISABLE	chglogon /DISABLE	chglogon /DISABLE		**/etc/nologin**
	Control Panel > Printers net print	Control Panel > Printers net print	Control Panel > Printers net print	Control Panel > Printers and Faxes net print	Action: 115	**/etc/printcap**
autoexec.bat	autoexec.bat	autoexec.bat	autoexec.bat	autoexec.bat	Apple Menu > Control Panels > Extensions Manager *selections...*	**/etc/rc.conf**
	Action: 139	Action: 192	Action: 191	Action: 191	Control Panel > TCPIP	**/etc/resolv.conf**
	Action: 141	Action: 197	Action: 198	Action: 198	Control Panel > TCPIP	**/etc/sysconfig/network**
		Control Panel > Services	inetmgr.exe	inetmgr.exe		**/etc/xinetd.conf**
rem	rem	rem	rem	rem		**;**
	Action: 141	Action: 141	Action: 140	Action: 140	Apple Menu > Control Panels > TCP/IP	**\etc\gateways**
	\windows\hosts	\winnt\system32\driver\etc\hosts	\winnt\system32\driver\etc\hosts	\windows\system32\driver\etc\hosts		**\etc\hosts**
	Action: 139	Action: 192	Action: 191	Action: 191	Control Panel > TCPIP	**\etc\resolv.cfg**
	cvt1.exe cvt.exe	convert.exe	convert.exe	convert.exe		**2xupgrde**
						Abort Remirror
ver mem.exe	winver.exe mem.exe	winver.exe mem.exe	winver.exe mem.exe	winver.exe mem.exe	**Apple Menu > About This Computer**	**About This Computer**
ver	**winver.exe** ver Control Panel > System	**winver.exe** ver Control Panel > System	**winver.exe** ver Control Panel > System	**winver.exe** ver Control Panel > System	Apple Menu > About This Computer	**About Windows, winver**

	AIX	Linux	OpenBSD	Solaris	NetWare 3	NetWare 4	NetWare 5	NetWare 6
accept	Enable	lpc enable *printer*	lpc enable *printer*	Accept enable	Pconsole.exe psc.exe	Pconsole.exe psc.exe	Nwpmw32.exe nwadmn32.exe ndpsm.nlm	Nwadmn32.exe ndpsm.nlm
Accessibility Wizard				accessx				
accessx				**accessx**				
acctcms	**acctcms** acctcom		sa	**acctcms** acctcom	paudit.exe atotal.exe	atotal.exe	atotal.exe	atotal.exe
acctcom	**acctcom** acctcms		sa	**acctcom** acctcms	paudit.exe atotal.exe	atotal.exe	atotal.exe	atotal.exe
acctcon2	**acctcon2**			**acctcon2**	atotal.exe paudit.exe	atotal.exe	atotal.exe	atotal.exe
acctdisk	**acctdisk** quotaon	quotaon	sa quotaon	**acctdisk** quotaon	syscon.exe atotal.exe	atotal.exe	atotal.exe	atotal.exe
acfgd	**acfgd**	cardctl						
acledit	**acledit** chmod	chmod	chmod	chmod setfacl	rights.exe syscon.exe sysconW.exe	rights.exe netadmin.exe nwadmn32.exe	rights.exe nwadmn32.exe consoleone.exe	rights.exe nwadmn32.exe consoleone.exe
aclget	**aclget**	ls -l	ls -l	getfacl	ndir.exe	ndir.exe	ndir.exe	ndir.exe
aclput	**aclput** acledit chmod	chmod	chmod	setfacl chmod	rights.exe	rights.exe	rights.exe	rights.exe
Active Directory Domains and Trust Manager	smit smitty			admintool	syscon.exe sysconW.exe	netadmin.exe nwadmn32.exe	nwadmn32.exe consoleone.exe	nwadmn32.exe consoleone.exe
Active Directory Users and Computers Manager	smit smitty mkuser mkgroup	userconf useradd groupadd	adduser groupadd	admintool useradd groupadd	syscon.exe sysconW.exe	netadmin.exe nwadmn32.exe	nwadmn32.exe consoleone.exe consoleonedos. exe	nwadmn32.exe consoleone.exe consoleonedos. exe
adb	**adb** dbx	gdb	gdb	**adb**				
Add User Account Wizard	mkuser smit smitty	adduser useradd userconf	adduser	useradd admintool	syscon.exe sysconW.exe	netadmin.exe nwadmn32.exe	nwadmn32.exe consoleone.exe consoleonedos. exe	nwadmn32.exe consoleone.exe consoleonedos. exe
add_drv	cfgmgr	insmod	modload	**add_drv**	load startup.ncf	load startup.ncf	load startup.ncf	load startup.ncf
Adduser	mkuser smit	**adduser** useradd	**adduser**	useradd admintool	syscon.exe sysconW.exe	netadmin.exe nwadmn32.exe	nwadmn32.exe consoleone.exe	nwadmn32.exe consoleone.exe
Administrating Wizards	smit smitty	linuxconf		admintool	install.nlm	install.nlm	nwconfig.nlm	nwconfig.nlm
Admintool	smit smitty	linuxconf		**admintool**	syscon.exe sysconW.exe	netadmin.exe nwadmn32.exe	nwadmn32.exe consoleone.exe consoleonedos. exe	nwadmn32.exe consoleone.exe consoleonedos. exe
afbconfig		xf86config	xf86config	**afbconfig** ffbconfig				
afp					**afp.nlm**	**afp.nlm**		

DOS	Windows 9x	NT 4.0	NT 2000	Windows XP	Macintosh	
	net print	net print	net print	net print		**accept**
	accwiz.exe	Control Panel > Accessibility Options	**accwiz.exe**	**accwiz.exe**	Apple Menu > Control Panels > Speech	**Accessibility Wizard**
	accwiz.exe	Control Panel > Accessibility Options	accwiz.exe	accwiz.exe	Apple Menu > Control Panels > Easy Access	**accessx**
		eventvwr.exe	eventvwr.exe	eventvwr.exe		**acctcms**
		eventvwr.exe	eventvwr.exe	eventvwr.exe		**acctcom**
						acctcon2
						acctdisk
	Control Panel > PC Card (PCMCIA)	Control Panel > PC Card (PCMCIA)	Control Panel > PC Card (PCMCIA)	Control Panel > PC Card (PCMCIA)		**acfgd**
		cacls.exe	cacls.exe	cacls.exe		**acledit**
		cacls.exe	cacls.exe	cacls.exe		**aclget**
		cacls.exe	cacls.exe	cacls.exe		**aclput**
		usrmgr.exe musrmgr.exe	**domain.msc** compmgmt. msc	**domain.msc** compmgmt. msc		**Active Directory Domains and Trust Manager**
	Control Panel > Users	usrmgr.exe musrmgr.exe net user	**dsa.msc** compmgmt. msc wizmgr.exe net user	**dsa.msc** compmgmt. msc net user	Apple Menu > Control Panels > File Sharing > Users & Groups	**Active Directory Users and Computers Manager**
debug.exe	debug.exe	debug.exe	debug.exe	debug.exe		**adb**
	Control Panel > Users	**addusrw.exe** usrmgr.exe net user	compmgmt. msc net user wizmgr.exe	compmgmt. msc net user wizmgr.exe	Apple Menu > Control Panels > Multiple Users	**Add User Account Wizard**
config.sys	Action: 62	Control Panel > Devices	Control Panel > Add/Remove Hardware	Control Panel > Add/Remove Hardware	Apple Menu > Control Panels > Extensions Manager *selections...*	**add_drv**
	Control Panel > Users	addusrw.exe usrmgr.exe	compmgmt. msc wizmgr.exe	compmgmt. msc wizmgr.exe	Apple Menu > Control Panels > Multiple Users	**adduser**
		wizmgr.exe	**wizmgr.exe** compmgmt. msc	**wizmgr.exe** compmgmt. msc		**Administrating Wizards**
	control.exe	control.exe	control.exe	control.exe	Apple Menu > Control Panels	**Admintool**
	Action: 250	Action: 250	Action: 250	Action: 250	Apple Menu > Control Panels > Monitors	**afbconfig**
		macfile.exe	macfile.exe	macfile.exe	Apple Menu > Control Panels > File Sharing	**afp**

	AIX	Linux	OpenBSD	Solaris	NetWare 3	NetWare 4	NetWare 5	NetWare 6
aixterm	**aixterm**	xterm	xterm	xterm				
alert	mesg	mesg	mesg	mesg			**alert**	**alert**
alias	**alias**	**alias**	**alias**	**alias**		**alias**	**alias**	**alias**
alloc	svmon	**alloc** free	top	**alloc** prtconf	memory	memory	memory	memory
allow	umask ls -al	umask ls -al	umask ls -al	umask ls -al	**allow.exe**	rights /F rights *filename*	rights /F rights *filename*	rights /F rights *filename*
alog	**alog** strclean	logrotate	newsyslog	strclean newsyslog	load edit /system/sys$log. err	nwadmn32.exe load view /system/sys$log. err	nwadmn32.exe view /system/sys$log. err	nwadmn32.exe view /system/sys$log. err
anacron	at crontab	**anacron** crontab at	at crontab	at crontab	cron.nlm wmsched.exe	cron.nlm wmsched.exe	cron.nlm wmsched.exe	cron.nlm wmsched.exe
answerbook	docsearch man *command*	man *command*	man *command*	**answerbook** man *command*		help	help	help
answerbook2	man *command*	man *command*	man *command*	**answerbook2** man *command*		help	help	help
apm	pmctrl	**apm**	**apm**	pmconfig				
apmsleep	pmctrl	**apmsleep** apm	zzz apm	powerd sys-suspend				
Appearance Control Panel	**xsetroot**	**xsetroot**	**xsetroot**	**xsetroot**			Action: 123	Action: 123
append								
AppleCD Audio Player		cdp cdplay	cdio	audioplay audiotool				
AppleTalk Console					**atcon.nlm**	**atcon.nlm** atconfig.nlm	**atcon.nlm**	**atcon.nlm**
appletviewer, applet				**appletviewer**			**appletviewer** **applet**	**appletviewer** **applet**
apropos	**apropos** man whatis	**apropos** man info	**apropos** man info	**apropos** man whatis		help	help	help
arch	uname -M	**arch**	**arch** machine	**arch** mach	cpucheck.nlm	cpucheck.nlm	cpucheck.nlm	cpucheck.nlm
arp	**arp**	**arp**	**arp**	**arp** netstat -p	Action: 116	Action: 116	Action: 116	Action: 116
Arrange								
As Icons								
As List								
As Pop-up Window								
As Windows								
aset	tcbck Action: 80	rpm -V Action: 80	Action: 80	**aset** Action: 80	security.exe			
aset.restore	tcbck	rpm -V		aset.restore				
ash, bsh	bsh ksh sh csh	ash **bsh** **bash** sh sash tcsh	csh ksh rksh sh	csh jsh ksh rksh sh rsh		netbasic.nlm	netbasic.nlm	netbasic.nlm
aspppd	pppcontrold	pppd	pppd	**aspppd**			nwccon.nlm	
Asynchronous Remote Console	pppcontrold	pppd	pppd	aspppd	**aconsole.exe**	rconsole.exe	rconsole.exe	rconj.exe

DOS	Windows 9x	NT 4.0	NT 2000	Windows XP	Macintosh	
	command.com	cmd.exe	cmd.exe	cmd.exe		**aixterm**
						alert
doskey.com	doskey.com	doskey.exe	doskey.exe	doskey.exe		**alias**
mem	mem	mem winver.exe	mem winver.exe	mem winver.exe	Apple Menu > About This Computer	**alloc**
	Action: 159	Action: 159	Action: 159	Action: 159		**allow**
	wbemcntl.exe	eventvwr.exe	eventvwr.exe	eventvwr.exe		**alog**
	sysagent.exe	at.exe	at.exe	at.exe schtasks.exe		**anacron**
	winhelp.exe helpctr.exe	winhlp32.exe help.exe ntbooks.exe	winhelp.exe help.exe ntbooks.exe	winhelp.exe help.exe helpctr.exe	help menu	**answerbook**
	winhelp.exe helpctr.exe	winhlp32.exe help.exe ntbooks.exe	winhelp.exe help.exe ntbooks.exe	winhelp.exe help.exe helpctr.exe	help menu	**answerbook2**
power.exe	pmres.exe		Control Panel > Power Options	Control Panel > Power Options	Apple Menu > Control Panels > Energy Saver	**apm**
power.exe	pmres.exe		Control Panel > Power Options	Control Panel > Power Options	Apple Menu > Control Panels > Energy Saver	**apmsleep**
	Action: 122	Action: 122	Action: 122	Action: 122	**Apple Menu > Control Panels > Appearance**	**Appearance Control Panel**
append.exe		**append.exe**	**append.exe**	**append.exe**		**append**
	mplayer2.exe mplayer.exe	mplayer2.exe	mplayer2.exe	mplayer2.exe	**Double click the AppleCD Audio Player icon**	**AppleCD Audio Player**
					Apple Menu > Control Panels > AppleTalk	**AppleTalk Console**
						appletviewer, applet
fasthelp.exe help.com	winhelp.exe helpctr.exe	winhlp32.exe help.exe ntbooks.exe	winhelp.exe help.exe	winhelp.exe help.exe helpctr.exe	command + ? Help > Mac Help	**apropos**
msd.exe	Control Panel > System	Control Panel > System	Control Panel > System	Control Panel > System	Apple Menu > Apple System Profiler	**arch**
	arp.exe	**arp.exe**	**arp.exe**	**arp.exe**		**arp**
	Action: 44	Action: 44	Action: 44	Action: 44	**View > Arrange**	**Arrange**
	Action: 45	Action: 45	Action: 45	Action: 45	View > As Icons <control> + Click in window > View > As icons	**As Icons**
	Action: 45	Action: 45	Action: 45	Action: 45	**View > As List**	**As List**
	Action: 52	Action: 52	Action: 52	Action: 52	**View > As Pop-up Window**	**As Pop-up Window**
	Action: 53	Action: 53	Action: 53	Action: 53	**View > As Window**	**As Windows**
			secedit.exe	secedit.exe		**aset**
	sfc.exe		**sfc.exe**	**sfc.exe**		**aset.restore**
command.com	command.com	cmd.exe command.com	cmd.exe command.com	cmd.exe command.com		**ash, bsh**
	My Computer > Dial-Up Networking	rasdial.exe	rasdial.exe	rasdial.exe	Apple Menu > Control Panel > Remote Access	**aspppd**
		rasdial.exe	rasdial.exe	rasdial.exe		**Asynchronous Remote Console**

	AIX	Linux	OpenBSD	Solaris	NetWare 3	NetWare 4	NetWare 5	NetWare 6
at	**at** crontab cron	**at** crontab crond	**at** crontab cron	**at** crontab cron	cron.nlm wmsched.exe	cron.nlm wmsched.exe	cron.nlm wmsched.exe	cron.nlm wmsched.exe
atconfig					atcon.nlm	**atconfig.nlm** atcon.nlm	atcon.nlm	atcon.nlm
atd	at cron	**atd** crond sched	at cron	cron sched at	cron.nlm wmsched.exe	cron.nlm schdelay.nlm wmsched.exe	cron.nlm wmsched.exe	cron.nlm wmsched.exe
ate	**ate**	minicom	cu	cu				
ATM Administrator	atmstat fddistat tokstat netstat -I *interface*	ipppstats pppstats netstat -I *interface*	pppstats slstats netstat -I *interface*	syncstat netstat -I *interface*	tcpcon.nlm	ipxcon.nlm tcpcon.nlm	ipxcon.nlm tcpcon.nlm	ipxcon.nlm tcpcon.nlm
ATM Console	atmstat fddistat tokstat netstat -I *interface*	ipppstats pppstats netstat -I *interface*	pppstats slstats netstat -I *interface*	syncstat netstat -I *interface*	tcpcon.nlm	ppptrace.nlm tcpcon.nlm	**atmcon.nlm**	ppptrace.nlm tcpcon.nlm
atmstat	**atmstat** fddistat	pppstats netstat -I *interface*	pppstats netstat -I *interface*	syncstat netstat -I *interface*	tcpcon.nlm	tcpcon.nlm ppptrace.nlm	tcpcon.nlm ppptrace.nlm	tcpcon.nlm ppptrace.nlm
atotal	acctcon2			acctcon2	**atotal.exe** paudit.exe	**atotal.exe**	**atotal.exe**	
atq	**atq** crontab cron at	**atq** crontab cron at	**atq** crontab cron at	**atq** crontab cron at	cron.nlm wmsched.exe	cron.nlm wmsched.exe	cron.nlm wmsched.exe	cron.nlm wmsched.exe
atrm	**atrm** crontab cron at	**atrm** crontab cron at	**atrm** crontab cron at	**atrm** crontab cron at	cron.nlm wmsched.exe	cron.nlm wmsched.exe	cron.nlm wmsched.exe	cron.nlm wmsched.exe
atrun	at crontab cron	at crontab crond	**atrun** at crontab cron	at crontab cron	cron.nlm wmsched.exe	cron.nlm wmsched.exe	cron.nlm wmsched.exe	cron.nlm wmsched.exe
attrib	ls -l chmod	ls -l chmod chattr	ls -l chmod	ls -l chmod	syscon.exe rights.exe	flag.exe nwadmn32.exe rights.exe	flag.exe nwadmn32.exe rights.exe	flag.exe nwadmn32.exe rights.exe
audiotool		mpg123 rec	cdio	**audiotool** audioplay				
auditcon	accton *file* quotaon	quotaon	accton *file* quotaon	accton *file* quotaon		**auditcon.exe**	**auditcon.exe** nwadmn32.exe	nwadmn32.exe
auditpr	**auditpr**			praudit			csaudit.nlm	csaudit.nlm
autoexec.bat	/etc/inittab	/etc/inittab	/etc/rc.conf	/etc/inittab	autoexec.ncf	autoexec.ncf	autoexec.ncf	autoexec.ncf
autoexec.ncf	/etc/inittab	/etc/inittab	/etc/rc.conf	/etc/inittab	**autoexec.ncf**	**autoexec.ncf**	**autoexec.ncf**	**autoexec.ncf**
backup	**backup**	dump rdump	dump rdump	ufsdump	sbackup.nlm	sbackup.nlm	nwback32.exe sbcon.nlm	nwback32.exe sbcon.nlm
badblocks	fsck	**badblocks** mbadblocks fsck	fsck	fsck Action: 43	vrepair.nlm	vrepair.nlm	vrepair.nlm nss /rebuild nss /menu	vrepair.nlm ConsoleOne > Server > Media
bash	ksh sh csh bsh	bash sh ash bsh sash tcsh	csh ksh rksh sh	**bash** csh jsh ksh rksh sh rsh		netbasic.nlm	netbasic.nlm	netbasic.nlm

DOS	Windows 9x	NT 4.0	NT 2000	Windows XP	Macintosh	
	sysagent.exe	**at.exe**	**at.exe**	**at.exe** schtasks.exe		**at**
					Apple Menu > Control Panels > AppleTalk	**atconfig**
	sysagent.exe Action: 9	at.exe	at.exe Action: 9	at.exe schtasks.exe		**atd**
	hypertrm.exe	hypertrm.exe	hypertrm.exe	hypertrm.exe		**ate**
	atmadm.exe	netmon.exe	**atmadm.exe**	**atmadm.exe**		**ATM Administrator**
	atmadm.exe	netmon.exe	atmadm.exe	atmadm.exe		**ATM Console**
	atmadm	netmon.exe	netmon.exe	netmon.exe		**atmstat**
						atotal
	sysagent.exe Action: 9	at.exe	at.exe	schtasks.exe at.exe		**atq**
	sysagent.exe Action: 9	at.exe	at.exe	schtasks.exe at.exe		**atrm**
	sysagent.exe	at.exe	at.exe	at.exe		**atrun**
attrib.exe	**attrib.exe**	**attrib.exe**	**attrib.exe**	**attrib.exe**	Select icon > command + i	**attrib**
	mplayer2.exe mplayer.exe sndrec32.exe	mplayer2.exe sndrec32.exe	mplayer2.exe mplay32.exe sndrec32.exe	mplayer2.exe mplay32.exe sndrec32.exe	AppleCD Audio Player QuickTime Player	**audiotool**
			Action: 158	Action: 158		**auditcon**
						auditpr
autoexec.bat	**autoexec.bat**	**autoexec.bat**	**autoexec.bat**	**autoexec.bat**	Apple Menu > Control Panels > Extensions Manager *selections...*	**autoexec.bat**
autoexec.bat	autoexec.bat	autoexec.bat	autoexec.bat	autoexec.bat	Apple Menu > Control Panels > Extensions Manager *selections...*	**autoexec.ncf**
msbackup.exe	backup.exe msbackup.exe	**backup.exe** ntbackup.exe	ntbackup.exe	ntbackup.exe		**backup**
scandisk.exe chkdsk.exe	scandisk.exe chkdsk.exe	chkntfs.exe chkdsk.exe	chkntfs.exe chkdsk.exe	chkntfs.exe chkdsk.exe	Action: 101	**badblocks**
command.com	command.com	cmd.exe command.com	cmd.exe command.com	cmd.exe command.com		**bash**

	AIX	Linux	OpenBSD	Solaris	NetWare 3	NetWare 4	NetWare 5	NetWare 6
bash, sh	**sh** ksh csh bsh	**bash** **sh** ash bsh sash tcsh	**sh** csh ksh rksh	**sh** csh jsh ksh rksh rsh		netbasic.nlm	netbasic.nlm	netbasic.nlm
bashbug	sendbug bugfiler	**bashbug** cvsbug	cvsbug sendbug	perlbug -a				
batch	**batch**	**batch**	**batch**	**batch**	cron.nlm wmsched.exe	cron.nlm wmsched.exe	cron.nlm wmsched.exe	cron.nlm wmsched.exe
battery	**battery** pmctrl	apm	apm	pmconfig				
bc	**bc** dc	**bc** dc	**bc** dc	**bc** calctool				
bdiff	**bdiff** diff	diff	diff	**bdiff** diff				
bellmail	**bellmail**	mail	mail	rmail				
biff	**biff**	rcvtty	**biff**	**biff**				
bind	ifconfig	ifconfig	ifconfig	ifconfig	**bind**	**bind**	**bind**	**bind**
binder				**binder**				
Books Online	man apropos whatis	man info apropos	man info apropos	man apropos whatis		help	help	help
Boot from a CD	Action: 99	Action: 48	Action: 48	Action: 47	Action: 48	Action: 48	Action: 48	Action: 48
Boot from a specified partition	bootlist	lilo		eeprom				
Boot from a specified SCSI-number	bootlist			eeprom				
Boot from network	bootlist			eeprom				
bootcfg	Action: 99	vi /etc/lilo.conf						
bootdisk		Action: 69 mkbootdisk	Action: 69					
bootlist	**bootlist**	lilo		eeprom				
bootpd	**bootpd**	dhcpd	**bootpd**	in.dhcpd -b *mode*	rpl.nlm	rpl.nlm	rpl.nlm	rpl.nlm
bootpfwd	dhcprd	dhcrelay	bootpgw dhcrelay	in.dhcpd -r *relaylist*		**bootpfwd.nlm**	**bootpfwd.nlm**	**bootpfwd.nlm**
bootpgw	dhcprd	dhcrelay	**bootpgw** dhcrelay	in.dhcpd		bootpfwd.nlm	bootpfwd.nlm	bootpfwd.nlm
break	stty ignbrk	stty ignbrk	stty ignbrk	stty ignbrk	**break**	**break**	**break**	**break**
broadcast	wall	wall	wall	wall	**broadcast**	**broadcast**	**broadcast**	**broadcast**
bsh	**bsh** ksh sh csh	ash bsh bash sh sash tcsh	csh ksh rksh sh	csh jsh ksh rksh sh rsh		netbasic.nlm	netbasic.nlm	netbasic.nlm
buffers	ulimit limit	ulimit limit	ulimit limit	ulimit limit				
bugfiler	**bugfiler** sendbug errpt	cvsbug bashbug perlbug -a	sendbug cvsbug perlbug -a	perlbug -a				
bunzip2	uncompress	**bunzip2** uncompress unzip gunzip	uncompress gunzip	**bunzip2** uncompress unzip gunzip	nlunpack.exe nwxtract.exe	nwxtract.exe	unzip.nlm tar.nlm	unzip.nlm tar.nlm
bye	exit logout	exit logout	exit logout	**bye** exit logout	exit	exit		

DOS	Windows 9x	NT 4.0	NT 2000	Windows XP	Macintosh	
command.com	command.com	cmd.exe command.com	cmd.exe command.com	cmd.exe command.com		**bash, sh**
	winrep.exe	Action: 19	winrep.exe	Action: 18		**bashbug**
	sysagent.exe Action: 9	at.exe	at.exe	at.exe schtasks.exe		**batch**
power.exe	pmres.exe		Control Panel > Power Options	Control Panel > Power Options	Apple Menu > Control Panels > Energy Saver	**battery**
	calc.exe	calc.exe	calc.exe	calc.exe	Apple Menu > Calculator	**bc**
fc.exe	fc.exe	comp.exe fc.exe	comp.exe fc.exe	comp.exe fc.exe		**bdiff**
	msimn.exe		msimn.exe	msimn.exe	Action: 199	**bellmail**
	Action: 157	Action: 157	Action: 157	Action: 157	Mail > Edit > Preferences > Notification	**biff**
	net start NETBIND Action: 193	Action: 193	Action: 195	Action: 194		**bind**
	Action: 271	Action: 271	Action: 272	Action: 272		**binder**
fasthelp.exe help.com	winhelp.exe helpctr.exe	**ntbooks.exe** winhlp32.exe help.exe	**ntbooks.exe** winhelp.exe help.exe	winhelp.exe help.exe helpctr.exe	command + ? Help > Mac Help	**Books Online**
	Action: 48	Action: 48	Action: 48	Action: 48	**Hold down the key c during startup**	**Boot from a CD**
		boot.ini	boot.ini	boot.ini	**Hold down the keys command + alt + e + *1 or 0* during startup.**	**Boot from a specified partition**
		boot.ini	boot.ini	boot.ini	**Action: 226**	**Boot from a specified SCSI-number**
		boot.ini	boot.ini	boot.ini	**Hold down the key n during startup.**	**Boot from network**
		Action: 125	Action: 125	**bootcfg.exe**	Apple Menu > Control Panels > Startup Disk	**bootcfg**
sys.com format a: /s	**bootdisk.bat** sys.com format a: /s	winnt /xo	makeboot.exe	makeboot.exe		**bootdisk**
		Action: 125	Action: 125	bootcfg.exe	Apple Menu > Control Panels > Startup Disk	**bootlist**
		rplcmd .exe rplmgr.exe				**bootpd**
		Action: 145	Action: 146	Action: 146		**bootpfwd**
		Action: 145	Action: 146	Action: 146	x§	**bootpgw**
break	**break**					**break**
	winpopup.exe	msg.exe	msg.exe	msg.exe		**broadcast**
command.com	command.com	cmd.exe command.com	cmd.exe command.com	cmd.exe command.com		**bsh**
buffers						**buffers**
	winrep.exe	Action: 19	winrep.exe	Action: 18		**bugfiler**
expand.exe		expand.exe	expand.exe	expand.exe	Action: 79	**bunzip2**
exit	exit	exit	exit	exit		**bye**

	AIX	Linux	OpenBSD	Solaris	NetWare 3	NetWare 4	NetWare 5	NetWare 6
bzip2	compress pack	**bzip2** compress gzip zip	compress gzip	compress gzip pack zip **SOL8** **bzip2 SOL8** gzip **SOL8**		flag *files* Ic	flag *files* Ic	flag *files* Ic
cabbit	compress pack	compress bzip2 gzip zip	compress gzip	compress gzip pack zip **SOL8** bzip2 **SOL8** gzip **SOL8**		flag *files* ic	flag *files* ic	flag *files* ic
cachefsstat	cachefswssize			**cachefsstat** cachefswssize				
cachefswssize	**cachefswssize**			**cachefswssize** cachefsstat				
cacls	chmod acledit	chmod	chmod	chmod setfacl	rights.exe syscon.exe sysconW.exe	rights.exe netadmin.exe nwadmn32.exe	rights.exe nwadmn32.exe consoleone.exe	rights.exe nwadmn32.exe consoleone.exe
calctool	dc bc	dc bc	dc bc	**calctool** dc				
Calculator	dc bc	dc bc	dc bc	bc calctool				
call	source	source	source	source	Action: 93	Action: 93	Action: 93	Action: 93
cancel	**cancel** lprm	**cancel** lprm	lprm	**cancel** lprm	pconsole.exe psc.exe	pconsole.exe psc.exe	nwpmw32.exe nwadmn32.exe ndpsm.nlm	nwadmn32.exe ndpsm.nlm
Cancel Operation	kill <CTRL> + <C>	kill <CTRL> + <C>	kill <CTRL> + <C>	kill <CTRL> + <C>	unload *module*	unload *module*	unload *module*	unload *module*
capture					**capture.exe**	**capture.exe**	**capture.exe**	**capture.exe**
capture	**capture**	screendump		snapshot	CONLOG entire=yes	CONLOG entire=yes	CONLOG entire=yes	CONLOG entire=yes
cardctl	acfgd pcmciastat	**cardctl** cardmgr						
cardmgr	acfgd xpcmcia	**cardmgr** cardctl						
castoff	mesg n	mesg n	mesg n	mesg n	**castoff.exe**	send /a=c	set disable broadcast notifications process = on	set disable broadcast notifications process = on
caston	mesg y	mesg y	mesg y	mesg y	**caston.exe**	send /a	set disable broadcast notifications process = off	set disable broadcast notifications process = off
cat	**cat** more	**cat** more	**cat** more	**cat** more	edit.nlm	view.nlm	view.nlm	view.nlm
cd				vold	**cd**	**cd**	**cd**	**cd**
cd, chdir	**cd** **chdir**	**cd** **chdir**	**cd** **chdir**	**cd** **chdir**				
cdinst	mount	mount	mount	mount	cdrom.nlm	cdrom.nlm	**cdinst.nlm**	**cdinst.nlm**
cdio		cdp cdplay	**cdio**	audioplay audiotool				
cdp, cdplay		**cdp** **cdplay**	cdio	audioplay audiotool				
cdrecord		**cdrecord**						
cdrom	mount	mount	mount	mount	**cdrom.nlm** cd	**cdrom.nlm** hfscd.nlm npams.nlm cd	**cdrom.nlm** cdinst.nlm cd	**cdrom.nlm** cdinst.nlm cd
Certificates Manager		openssl	openssl				keytool.exe	keytool.exe keytool

DOS	Windows 9x	NT 4.0	NT 2000	Windows XP	Macintosh	
	cabbit	compact	compact makecab	compact makecab	StuffIt Expander	**bzip2**
	cabbit	compact	compact makecab	compact makecab	Action: 79	**cabbit**
smartdrv /s						**cachefsstat**
smartdrv /s						**cachefswssize**
		cacls.exe	**cacls.exe**	**cacls.exe**		**cacls**
	calc.exe	calc.exe	calc.exe	calc.exe	Apple Menu > Calculator	**calctool**
	calc.exe	**calc.exe**	**calc.exe**	**calc.exe**	**Apple Menu > Calculator**	**Calculator**
call	**call**	**call**	**call**	**call**		**call**
	net print /delete	net print /delete	net print /delete	net print /delete	Action: 107	**cancel**
<CTRL> + <C>	<ALT> + <F4> Action: 212	<ALT> + <F4> Action: 212	<ALT> + <F4> Action: 212	<ALT> + <F4> Action: 212	**<command> + <dot>**	**Cancel Operation**
	net use *device:*	net use *device:*	net use *device:*	net use *device:*		**capture**
	<Print Screen>	<Print Screen>	<Print Screen>	<Print Screen>	<Caps Lock>= on + <command> + <shift> + <4> + click in window	**capture**
	Control Panel > PC Card (PCMCIA)	Control Panel > PC Card (PCMCIA)	Control Panel > PC Card (PCMCIA)	Control Panel > PC Card (PCMCIA)		**cardctl**
	Control Panel > PC Card (PCMCIA)	Control Panel > PC Card (PCMCIA)	Control Panel > PC Card (PCMCIA)	Control Panel > PC Card (PCMCIA)		**cardmgr**
						castoff
						caston
more.com type	more.com type	more.com type	more.com type	more.com type	Action: 82	**cat**
			rsm.exe ntmsmgr.msc	rsm.exe ntmsmgr.msc		**cd**
cd **chdir**	**cd** **chdir**	**cd** **chdir**	**cd** **chdir**	**cd** **chdir**	Action: 51	**cd, chdir**
mscdex.exe	mscdex.exe	mscdexnt.exe	mscdexnt.exe	mscdexnt.exe		**cdinst**
	mplayer2.exe mplayer.exe	mplayer2.exe	mplayer2.exe	mplayer2.exe	Double click the AppleCD Audio Player icon	**cdio**
	mplayer2.exe mplayer.exe	mplayer2.exe	mplayer2.exe	mplayer2.exe	Double click the AppleCD Audio Player icon	**cdp, cdplay**
				Action: 264		**cdrecord**
mscdex.exe	mscdex.exe Action: 90	windisk.exe mscdexnt.exe	diskmgmt.msc mscdexnt.exe	diskmgmt.msc mscdexnt.exe		**cdrom**
			certmgr.msc	**certmgr.msc**		**Certificates Manager**

	AIX	Linux	OpenBSD	Solaris	NetWare 3	NetWare 4	NetWare 5	NetWare 6
certutil		openssl	openssl				keytool.exe	keytool.exe keytool
cfdisk	smitty storage	**cfdisk**	fdisk	fdisk	install.nlm	install.nlm	nwconfig.nlm	ConsoleOne > Tools > Disk Management
cfgif	**cfgif** ifconfig	ifcfg ifconfig	ifconfig	ifconfig	install.nlm	inetcfg.nlm	inetcfg.nlm	inetcfg.nlm
cfginet	**cfginet** smit ifconfig	netconf ifconfig	ifconfig	admintool ifconfig	install.nlm	inetcfg.nlm	inetcfg.nlm	inetcfg.nlm
cfgmgr	**cfgmgr**	isapnp		drvconfig	load *disk_driver*	load *disk_driver*	hdetect.nlm load *disk_driver*	hdetect.nlm load *disk_driver*
cfsadmin	**cfsadmin**			**cfsadmin**				
chage	chuser	**chage**		passwd		nwadmn32.exe	nwadmn32.exe	nwadmn32.exe
Change IP Address	Type smitty > Communications Applications and Services > TCP/IP > Minimum Configuration & Startup	ifconfig *interface new IPaddress subnet mask* vi icfg-*interface*	ifconfig *interface new IPaddress subnet mask* vi hostname.ep0	ifconfig *interface new IPaddress subnet mask* vi /etc/hosts	install.nlm	inetcfg.nlm	inetcfg.nlm	inetcfg.nlm
Change Logon, chglogon	Action: 117 pdisable	passwd -l *user* Action: 117	Action: 117	passwd -l *user* Action: 117	disable login	disable login	disable login	disable login
Change Name	mv	mv	mv	mv	rendir.exe filer.exe	rendir.exe filer.exe	filer.exe nwadmn32.exe	filer.exe nwadmn32.exe
charset	chkbd lskbd	loadkeys setxkbmap kbdconfig	kbd setxkbmap	kbd loadkeys	keyb.nlm	keyb.nlm	**charset.nlm** keyb.nlm	**charset.nlm** keyb.nlm
chat	talk	**chat** talk	**chat** talk	talk	send.exe send	send.exe send	Action: 36 send	Action: 36 send
Chat	talk confer	talk	talk	talk	send	send	Action: 36 send	Action: 36 send
chattr	chmod	**chattr** chmod	chflags chmod	chmod	flag.exe syscon.exe rights.exe	flag.exe nwadmn32.exe rights.exe	flag.exe nwadmn32.exe rights.exe	flag.exe nwadmn32.exe rights.exe
chcp	chkbd lskbd	loadkeys setxkbmap kbdconfig	kbd setxkbmap	kbd loadkeys	keyb.nlm	keyb.nlm	keyb.nlm charset.nlm	keyb.nlm charset.nlm
chflags	chmod	chattr chmod	**chflags** chmod	chmod	flag.exe syscon.exe rights.exe	flag.exe nwadmn32.exe rights.exe	flag.exe nwadmn32.exe rights.exe	flag.exe nwadmn32.exe rights.exe
chfn	**chfn**	**chfn** userinfo	**chfn**	usermod -c "*name*" *user*	syscon.exe sysconW.exe	netadmin.exe nwadmn32.exe	nwadmn32.exe consoleone.exe consoleonedos.exe	nwadmn32.exe consoleone.exe consoleonedos.exe
chgif	**chgif** ifconfig	ifcfg ifconfig	ifconfig	ifconfig	install.nlm	inetcfg.nlm	inetcfg.nlm	inetcfg.nlm
chginet	**chginet** smit ifconfig	netconf ifconfig	ifconfig	admintool ifconfig	install.nlm	inetcfg.nlm	inetcfg.nlm	inetcfg.nlm
chgroup	**chgroup** smit group	groupmod	groupmod	groupmod	syscon.exe	nwadmn32.exe	nwadmn32.exe	nwadmn32.exe
chgrp	**chgrp** chown	**chgrp** chown	**chgrp** chown	**chgrp** chown		**chgrp.exe**		

DOS	Windows 9x	NT 4.0	NT 2000	Windows XP	Macintosh	
			certutil.exe	**certutil.exe**		**certutil**
fdisk	fdisk.exe	windisk.exe	diskmgmt.msc	diskmgmt.msc	Action: 64	**cfdisk**
	Control Panel > Network	Control Panel > Network	Control Panel > Network and Dial Up Connections	Control Panel > Network Connections	Apple Menu > Control Panels > TCP/IP	**cfgif**
	Control Panel > Network	Control Panel > Network	Control Panel > Network Connections	netsetup.exe Control Panel > Network Connections	Apple Menu > Control Panel > TCP/IP	**cfginet**
	Control Panel > Add New Hardware	Control Panel	Control Panel > Add/Remove Hardware	Control Panel > Add Hardware		**cfgmgr**
smartdrv						**cfsadmin**
		usrmgr.exe				**chage**
	Action: 196	Action: 197	Action: 198	Action: 198	Apple Menu > Control Panel > TCP/IP	**Change IP Address**
		chglogon /DISABLE change LOGON /DISABLE Action: 118	**chglogon /DISABLE change LOGON /DISABLE** Action: 118	**chglogon /DISABLE change LOGON /DISABLE** Action: 118		**Change Logon, chglogon**
rename move.exe label	rename move.exe label	rename move.exe label	rename move.exe label	rename move.exe label	**Action: 113**	**Change Name**
chcp keyb.com	chcp.com keyb.com Control Panel > Keyboard	kb16.com chcp.com Control Panel > Keyboard	kb16.com chcp.com Control Panel > Keyboard	kb16.com chcp.com Control Panel > Keyboard	Apple Menu > Control Panels > Keyboard	**charset**
	winpopup.exe	winchat.exe	winchat.exe	winchat.exe		**chat**
	winpopup.exe	**winchat.exe**	**winchat.exe**	**winchat.exe**		**Chat**
attrib.exe	attrib.exe	attrib.exe	attrib.exe	attrib.exe	Select icon > <command> + I	**chattr**
chcp keyb.com	**chcp.com** keyb.com Control Panel > Keyboard	**chcp.com** keyb.com kb16.com Control Panel > Keyboard	**chcp.com** kb16.com Control Panel > Keyboard	**chcp.com** kb16.com Control Panel > Keyboard	Apple Menu > Control Panels > Keyboard	**chcp**
attrib.exe	attrib.exe	attrib.exe	attrib.exe	attrib.exe	Select icon > <command> + i	**chflags**
	Control Panel > Users	usrmgr.exe musrmgr.exe	compmgmt.msc	compmgmt.msc	Apple Menu > Control Panels > Multiple Users	**chfn**
	Control Panel > Network	Control Panel > Network	Control Panel > Network and Dial Up Connections	Control Panel > Network Connections	Control Panel > TCP/IP	**chgif**
	Control Panel > Network	Control Panel > Network	Control Panel > Network Connections	Control Panel > Network Connections netsetup.exe	Apple Menu > Control Panels > TCP/IP	**chginet**
		net group usrmgr.exe	net group compmgmt.msc	net group compmgmt.msc		**chgroup**
						chgrp

	AIX	Linux	OpenBSD	Solaris	NetWare 3	NetWare 4	NetWare 5	NetWare 6
chgrpmem	**chgrpmem** smit group	userconf	groupmod	groupmod admintool	syscon.exe	nwadmn32.exe	nwadmn32.exe	nwadmn32.exe
chitab	**chitab**	vi /etc/inittab	vi /etc/rc.conf	vi /etc/inittab	Action: 214	Action: 215	Action: 215	Action: 215
chkbd	**chkbd** lskbd	loadkeys setxkbmap kbdconfig	kbd setxkbmap	kbd loadkeys	keyb.nlm	keyb.nlm	keyb.nlm charset.nlm	keyb.nlm charset.nlm
chkconfig	who -r Action: 72	**chkconfig** ntsysv runlevel	Action: 67	who -r Action: 65			list stage	list stage
chkdir	df	df	df	df	**chkdir.exe**	ndir *path* /spa	ndir *path* /spa	ndir *path* /spa
chkdsk	fsck	fsck	fsck	fsck	vrepair.nlm	vrepair.nlm	vrepair.nlm nss /menu	vrepair.nlm consoleone.exe c1start.ncf
chkey	**chkey** newkey	ssh-keygen dnskeygen	ssh-keygen	newkey chkey			keytool -genkey	keytool -genkey
chkntfs	fsck	fsck	fsck	fsck	vrepair.nlm	vrepair.nlm	nss /rebuild nss /menu vrepair.nlm	ConsoleOne > Server > Media vrepair.nlm
chkroot	chroot	chroot	chroot	chroot				
chkvol	df	df	df	df	**chkvol.exe**	ndir *drive:* /vol	ndir *drive:* /vol	ndir *drive:* /vol
chlang	**chlang** LANG=*language*	LANG=*language*	LANG=*language*	LANG=*language*				
chlicense	**chlicense**					install.nlm	licmaint.nlm nwucutil.nlm nwconfig.nlm	licmaint.nlm nwucutil.nlm nwconfig.nlm
chmod	**chmod** acledit	**chmod**	**chmod**	**chmod** setfacl	rights.exe syscon.exe sysconW.exe	**chmod.exe** rights.exe netadmin.exe nwadmn32.exe	rights.exe nwadmn32.exe consoleone.exe	rights.exe nwadmn32.exe consoleone.exe
chnfsmnt	**chnfsmnt**	mount	mount	mount	map.exe	map.exe	map.exe	map.exe
choice		dialog		ckyorn				
Chooser	smit print	lpc /etc/printcap	lpc /etc/printcap	lpadmin admintool	capture.exe	capture.exe	capture.exe	capture.exe
chown	**chown**	**chown**	**chown**	**chown**	flag *file* /name=*user*	**chown.exe** flag *file* /name=*user*	flag *file* /name=*user*	flag *file* /name=*user*
chpass, chfn, chsh	chfn	chfn userinfo	**chpass** **chfn** **chsh**	usermod -c "*name*" *user*	syscon.exe sysconW.exe	netadmin.exe nwadmn32.exe	nwadmn32.exe consoleone.exe consoleonedos.exe	nwadmn32.exe consoleone.exe consoleonedos.exe
chprtsv	**chprtsv**	lpc	lpc	lpadmin	psc.exe pconsole.exe	psc.exe pconsole.exe	nwpmw32.exe nwadmn32.exe ndpsm.nlm	nwadmn32.exe ndpsm.nlm
chps	**chps** mkps rmps swapon	swapon swapoff	swapctl	swap			swap	swap
chpv	**chpv**	fdisk	fdisk	format fdisk	install.nlm	install.nlm	nwconfig.nlm	nwconfig.nlm
chquedev	**chquedev**	lpstat	lpq	lpstat dtprintinfo	pconsole.exe	pconsole.exe	nwpmw32.exe nwadmn32.exe ndpsm.nlm	nwpmw32.exe nwadmn32.exe ndpsm.nlm
chroot	**chroot**	**chroot**	**chroot**	**chroot**				
chservices	**chservices**	vi /etc/services	vi /etc/services	vi /etc/services	\etc\services	\etc\services	\etc\services	\etc\services

DOS	Windows 9x	NT 4.0	NT 2000	Windows XP	Macintosh	
	Control Panel > Users	usrmgr.exe musrmgr.exe	compmgmt.msc	compmgmt.msc	Apple Menu > Control Panels > File Sharing > Users & Groups	**chgrpmem**
edit autoexec.bat	edit autoexec.bat	Control Panel > Services	services.msc	services.msc	Apple Menu > Control Panels > Extensions Manager *selections...*	**chitab**
chcp keyb.com	chcp.com keyb.com Control Panel > Keyboard	chcp.com keyb.com Control Panel > Keyboard	chcp.com kb16.com Control Panel > Keyboard	chcp.com kb16.com Control Panel > Keyboard	Apple Menu > Control Panels > Keyboard	**chkbd**
						chkconfig
dir	dir	dir	dir	dir	Action: 165	**chkdir**
chkdsk.exe scandisk.exe	**chkdsk.exe** scandisk.exe scandskw.exe	**chkdsk.exe** chkntfs.exe	**chkdsk.exe** chkntfs.exe	**chkdsk.exe** chkntfs.exe	Action: 101	**chkdsk**
						chkey
scandisk.exe chkdsk.exe	scandisk.exe chkdsk.exe	**chkntfs.exe** chkdsk.exe	**chkntfs.exe** chkdsk.exe	**chkntfs.exe** chkdsk.exe	Action: 101	**chkntfs**
		chkroot.cmd	**chkroot.cmd**			**chkroot**
chkdsk.exe	chkdsk.exe	chkntfs.exe chkdsk.exe	chkntfs.exe chkdsk.exe	chkntfs.exe chkdsk.exe	Action: 165	**chkvol**
country nlsfunc.exe	nlsfunc.exe Control Panel > Regional Settings	nlsfunc.exe Control Panel > Regional Settings	nlsfunc.exe Control Panel > Regional Options	nlsfunc.exe Control Panel > Regional/Langua ge Options	Apple Menu > Control Panels > Numbers	**chlang**
		Control Panel > Licensing	Control Panel > Licensing	Control Panel > Licensing		**chlicense**
		cacls.exe	cacls.exe	cacls.exe		**chmod**
	net use	net use	net use	net use	Control Panel > File Sharing	**chnfsmnt**
choice.com	**choice.com**					**choice**
	Control Panel > Printers net use Action: 58	Control Panel > Printers net use Action: 58	Control Panel > Printers net use Action: 58	Control Panel > Printers and Faxes net use Action: 58	**Apple Menu > Chooser**	**Chooser**
		cacls.exe Action: 63	cacls.exe Action: 111	cacls.exe Action: 111		**chown**
	Control Panel > Users	usrmgr.exe musrmgr.exe	compmgmt.msc	compmgmt.msc	Apple Menu > Control Panels > Multiple Users	**chpass, chfn, chsh**
	Control Panel > Printers	Control Panel > Printers	Control Panel > Printers	Control Panel > Printers and Faxes	Action: 115	**chprtsv**
	Action: 149	Action: 148	Action: 147	Action: 147		**Chps**
fdisk.exe	fdisk.exe	windisk.exe	diskmgmt.msc	diskmgmt.msc diskpart.exe	Action: 64	
	Control Panel > Printers	Control Panel > Printers	Control Panel > Printers	Control Panel > Printers and Faxes	Action: 115	**chquedev**
		chkroot.cmd	chkroot.cmd			**chroot**
	edit \windows\service s	Action: 216	Action: 216	Action: 217		**chservices**

	AIX	Linux	OpenBSD	Solaris	NetWare 3	NetWare 4	NetWare 5	NetWare 6
chsh	**chsh**	**chsh**	**chsh** chpass -s	usermod -s *shell* admintool > User Managment				
chsubserver	**chsubserver** /etc/inetd.conf	/etc/xinetd.conf	/etc/inetd.conf	/etc/inetd.conf	install.nlm	inetcfg.nlm	inetcfg.nlm	inetcfg.nlm
chtz	**chtz**	timeconfig zdump tzselect	zdump	zdump Action: 186	set time zone	set time zone	set time zone	set time zone
chuser	**chuser** smit user	userconf	usermod	admintool	syscon.exe sysconW.exe	netadmin.exe nwadmn32.exe	nwadmn32.exe consoleone.exe consoleonedos.ex e	nwadmn32.exe consoleone.exe consoleonedos.ex e
ckkeywd		dialog		**ckkeywd**				
cksum	**cksum**	**cksum**	**cksum**	**cksum**	version			
ckyorn		dialog		**ckyorn**				
Clean Up								
cleanmgr		nwpurge			purge /a	filer > Purge Deleted Files purge /a	filer > Purge Deleted Files purge /a	filer > Purge Deleted Files
clear	**clear**	**clear**	**clear**	**clear**	cls off	cls off	cls off	cls off
Clear Station	kill	kill	kill	kill	**Clear Station**	**Clear Station**	**Clear Station**	**Clear Station**
Client Connection Manager								
Clipbook Viewer								
Close foremost window								
Close pop-up window								
Close Window								
cls	clear	clear	clear	clear	**cls** off	**cls** off	**cls** off	**cls** off
clspack				jar			jar	jar
cmd	ksh sh csh bsh	ash bsh bash sh sash tcsh	csh ksh rksh sh	csh jsh ksh rksh sh rsh		netbasic.nlm	netbasic.nlm	netbasic.nlm
cmdtool	xterm	xterm	xterm	**cmdtool**				
cmp	**cmp**	**cmp**	**cmp**	**cmp**				
colorpal					**colorpal.exe**	**colorpal.exe**	Action: 123	Action: 123
command	ksh sh csh bsh	ash bsh bash sh sash tcsh	csh ksh rksh sh	csh jsh ksh rksh sh rsh		netbasic.nlm	netbasic.nlm	netbasic.nlm
Communication Port Configuration	stty	stty setserial	stty	stty syncinit	rs232.nlm	rs232.nlm	**aiocon.nlm** rs232.nlm	**aiocon.nlm**
comp	diff cmp	diff cmp	diff cmp	diff cmp				
compact						Action: 109	Action: 109	Action: 109
compress	**compress** pack	**compress** gzip	**compress** gzip	**compress** pack		flag *files* Ic	flag *files* Ic	flag *files* Ic
Computer Management	smit smitty	linuxconf		admintool	fconsole.exe	servman.nlm	NetWare Management Portal	NetWare Remote Manager
config	ifconfig	ifconfig	ifconfig	ifconfig	**config**	**config**	**config**	**config**

DOS	Windows 9x	NT 4.0	NT 2000	Windows XP	Macintosh	
shell						**chsh**
		Control Panel > Services	inetmgr.exe	inetmgr.exe		**chsubserver**
	Control Panel > Date/Time	Control Panel > Date/Time	Control Panel > Date/Time	Control Panel > Date and Time	Apple Menu > Control Panels > Date & Time	**chtz**
	Control Panel > Users	usrmgr.exe musrmgr.exe	compmgmt.msc	compmgmt.msc	Apple Menu > Control Panels > File Sharing > Users & Groups	**chuser**
choice.com						**ckkeywd**
						cksum
choice.com						**ckyorn**
	Action: 59	Action: 59	Action: 59	Action: 59	**View > Clean up**	**Clean Up**
	cleanmgr Action: 17	Action: 17	**cleanmgr** Action: 17	**cleanmgr** Action: 17	Special > Empty Trash	**cleanmgr**
cls	cls Action: 103	cls Action: 103	cls Action: 103	cls Action: 103	Application Menu > Hide Others	**clear**
		srvmgr.exe	srvmgr.exe	srvmgr.exe		**Clear Station**
		conman.exe mstsc.exe	**conman.exe** mstsc.exe	**conman.exe** mstsc.exe		**Client Connection Manager**
	clipbrd.exe	**clipbrd.exe**	**clipbrd.exe**	**clipbrd.exe**	Apple Menu > Scrapbook	**Clipbook Viewer**
	<ALT> + <F4>	<ALT> + <F4>	<ALT> + <F4>	<ALT> + <F4>	**command + w**	**Close foremost window**
	<ALT>+<F4>	<ALT>+<F4>	<ALT>+<F4>	<ALT>+<F4>	**command + shift + w**	**Close pop-up window**
	<ALT> + <F4>	<ALT> + <F4>	<ALT> + <F4>	<ALT> + <F4>	**<command> + <W>** **Click the close window box**	**Close Window**
cls	**cls** Action: 103	**cls** Action: 103	**cls** Action: 103	**cls** Action: 103	Application Menu > Hide Others	**cls**
	clspack.exe		**clspack.exe**	**clspack.exe**		**clspack**
command.com	command.com	**cmd.exe** command.com	**cmd.exe** command.com	**cmd.exe** command.com		**cmd**
	command.com	cmd.exe	cmd.exe	cmd.exe		**cmdtool**
fc.exe	fc.exe	fc.exe	fc.exe	fc.exe		**cmp**
	Action: 122	Action: 122	Action: 122	Action: 122	Apple Menu > Control Panels > Appearance	**colorpal**
command.com	**command.com**	**command.com** cmd.exe	**command.com** cmd.exe	**command.com** cmd.exe		**command**
mode.com	Action: 167 mode.com	Control Panel > Ports mode.com	Action: 166 mode.com	Action: 166 mode.com		**Communication Port Configuration**
fc.exe	fc.exe	**comp.exe** fc.exe	**comp.exe** fc.exe	**comp.exe** fc.exe		**comp**
drvspace.exe	cmpagent.exe drvspace.exe	**compact.exe**	**compact.exe**	**compact.exe**		**compact**
	cabbit.exe	compact.exe	makecab compact.exe	makecab compact.exe	Action: 79	**compress**
		usrmgr.exe windisk.exe	**compmgmt. msc**	**compmgmt. msc**		**Computer Management**
	winipcfg	ipconfig	ipconfig	ipconfig	Apple Menu > Control Panels > TCP/IP	**config**

	AIX	Linux	OpenBSD	Solaris	NetWare 3	NetWare 4	NetWare 5	NetWare 6
config.sys	smit smitty	/etc/modules.conf	config -e -o bsd.new /bsd	touch /reconfigure	startup.ncf	startup.ncf	startup.ncf	startup.ncf
Configuration Manager Console	smit devices	scanpci	scanpci	prtdiag		**ncmcon.nlm**	**ncmcon.nlm**	**ncmcon.nlm**
Configure Print Jobs	chprtsv	vi /etc/lpd.conf		lpadmin	**printcon.exe**	**printcon.exe**	nwadmn32.exe	nwadmn32.exe
connect	tip	rlogin	rlogin tip	tip				
Connection Manager Administration Kit Wizard								
Console Log	script	script	script	script	**conlog.nlm**	**conlog.nlm**	**conlog.nlm**	**conlog.nlm**
consolechars	chfont	**consolechars**						
ConsoleOne (Client)	smit smitty mkuser mkgroup	userconf useradd groupadd	adduser groupadd	admintool useradd groupadd	syscon.exe sysconW.exe	netadmin.exe nwadmn32.exe	**consoleone.exe** consoleonedos.exe c1start.ncf nwadmn32.exe	**consoleone.exe** consoleonedos.exe c1start.ncf nwadmn32.exe
ConsoleOneDos	smit smitty mkuser mkgroup	userconf useradd groupadd	adduser groupadd	admintool useradd groupadd	syscon.exe sysconW.exe	netadmin.exe nwadmn32.exe	**consoleonedos.exe** consoleone.exe c1start.ncf nwadmn32.exe	**consoleonedos.exe** consoleone.exe c1start.ncf nwadmn32.exe
Control Panel	smit smitty	linuxconf		admintool	install.nlm	install.nlm	nwconfig.nlm	nwconfig.nlm
convert					2xupgrde.nlm		ipcu.nlm	ipcu.nlm
copy	cp dtfile	cp mc mcopy	cp	cp dtfile	ncopy.exe filer.exe	ncopy.exe filer.exe	ncopy.exe filer.exe	ncopy.exe filer.exe
Copy File	cp	cp	cp	cp	ncopy.exe filer.exe	ncopy.exe filer.exe	ncopy.exe filer.exe	ncopy.exe filer.exe
Copy Text								
country	LANG=*language* chlang	LANG=*language*	LANG=*language*	LANG=*language*				
cp	**cp** dtfile	**cp** mc	**cp**	**cp** dtfile	ncopy.exe filer.exe	ncopy.exe filer.exe	ncopy.exe filer.exe	ncopy.exe filer.exe
cpucheck		cat /proc/cpuinfo	top	prtdiag	**cpucheck.nlm**	**cpucheck.nlm**	**cpucheck.nlm**	**cpucheck.nlm**
cpustat	tprof	vmstat top	top	**cpustat**	monitor.nlm	monitor.nlm	monitor.nlm	monitor.nlm
Create Bootdisk		Action: 69 mkbootdisk	Action: 69					
Create New Folder	mkdir	mkdir	mkdir	mkdir	filer.exe	filer.exe nwadmn32.exe	filer.exe nwadmn32.exe	filer.exe nwadmn32.exe
Create Shared Folder	smit mknfsexp	vi /etc/exports	vi /etc/exports	vi /etc/dfs/dfstab	syscon.exe grant.exe	nwadmn32.exe rights.exe	nwadmn32.exe rights.exe	nwadmn32.exe rights.exe
cron	cron at	crond at atd sched	cron at	cron sched at	**cron.nlm** wmsched.exe	**cron.nlm** schdelay.nlm wmsched.exe	**cron.nlm** wmsched.exe	**cron.nlm** wmsched.exe
cron, crond	cron at	**crond** at atd sched	cron at	cron sched at	cron.nlm wmsched.exe	cron.nlm schdelay.nlm wmsched.exe	cron.nlm wmsched.exe	cron.nlm wmsched.exe

DOS	Windows 9x	NT 4.0	NT 2000	Windows XP	Macintosh	
config.sys	Action: 62	Control Panel > Devices	Control Panel > Add/Remove Hardware	Control Panel > Add/Remove Hardware	Apple Menu > Control Panels > Extensions Manager *selections...*	**config.sys**
			Action: 177	Action: 177		**Configuration Manager Console**
	Control Panel > Printers	Control Panel > Printers	Control Panel > Printers	Control Panel > Printers	Apple Menu > Chooser > Printer	**Configure Print Jobs**
		connect.exe	tscon.exe	tscon.exe		**connect**
	inetwiz.exe netconn.exe		inetwiz.exe	**cmak.exe** inetwiz.exe	Action: 96	**Connection Manager Administration Kit Wizard**
						Console Log
	Action: 122	Action: 122	Action: 122	Action: 122	Apple Menu > Control Panels > Appearance > Fonts	**consolechars**
	Control Panel > Users	addusrw.exe usrmgr.exe musrmgr.exe net user	compmgmt.msc wizmgr.exe net user	compmgmt.msc wizmgr.exe net user	Apple Menu > Control Panels > File Sharing > Users & Groups	**ConsoleOne (Client)**
	Control Panel > Users	addusrw.exe usrmgr.exe musrmgr.exe net user	compmgmt.msc wizmgr.exe net user	compmgmt.msc wizmgr.exe net user	Apple Menu > Control Panels > File Sharing > Users & Groups	**ConsoleOneDos**
	control.exe	**control.exe**	**control.exe**	**control.exe**	Apple Menu > Control Panels	**Control Panel**
	cvt.exe cvt1.exe	**convert.exe**	**convert.exe**	**convert.exe**		**convert**
copy xcopy.exe	**copy** xcopy.exe Action: 1	**copy** xcopy.exe Action: 1	**copy** xcopy.exe Action: 1	**copy** xcopy.exe Action: 1	alt + Drag a file command + d	**copy**
copy xcopy.exe	copy xcopy.exe	copy xcopy.exe	copy xcopy.exe	copy xcopy.exe	**alt + Drag a file**	**Copy File**
	<CTRL> + <C>	<CTRL> + <C>	<CTRL> + <C>	<CTRL> + <C>	**<command> + <C>** **Edit > Copy**	**Copy Text**
country nlsfunc.exe	nlsfunc.exe Control Panel > Regional Settings	nlsfunc.exe Control Panel > Regional Settings	nlsfunc.exe Control Panel > Regional Options	nlsfunc.exe Control Panel > Regional/Langua ge Options	Apple Menu > Control Panels > Numbers	**country**
copy xcopy.exe	xcopy.exe copy Action: 1	xcopy.exe copy Action: 1	xcopy.exe copy Action: 1	xcopy.exe copy Action: 1	alt + Drag a file command + d	**cp**
	Control Panel > System	Control Panel > System	Control Panel > System	Control Panel > System	Apple Menu > Apple System Profiler	**cpucheck**
		perfmon.exe	perfmon.exe	perfmon.exe	Apple Menu > About This Computer	**cpustat**
sys.com format a: /s	bootdisk.bat sys.com format a: /s	winnt /xo	**makeboot.exe**	**makeboot.exe**		**Create Bootdisk**
md mkdir	md mkdir	md mkdir	md mkdir	md mkdir	**<command> + N**	**Create New Folder**
	Action: 23	shrpubw.exe Action: 23	**shrpubw.exe** Action: 23	**shrpubw.exe** Action: 23	Apple Menu > Control Panels > File Sharing	**Create Shared Folder**
	sysagent.exe Action: 9	at.exe	at.exe Action: 9	at.exe schtasks.exe		**cron**
	sysagent.exe Action: 9	at.exe	at.exe Action: 9	at.exe schtasks.exe		**cron, crond**

	AIX	Linux	OpenBSD	Solaris	NetWare 3	NetWare 4	NetWare 5	NetWare 6
cronadm	**cronadm** at crontab cron	at crontab crond	at crontab cron	at crontab cron	cron.nlm wmsched.exe	cron.nlm wmsched.exe	cron.nlm wmsched.exe	cron.nlm wmsched.exe
crontab	**crontab** at cron	**crontab** at cron	**crontab** at cron	**crontab** at cron	cron.nlm wmsched.exe	cron.nlm wmsched.exe	cron.nlm wmsched.exe	cron.nlm wmsched.exe
cscript		perl tclsh wish	perl	perl			perl.nlm	perl.nlm
csh	**csh** ksh sh bsh	ash bsh bash sh sash tcsh	**csh** ksh rksh sh	**csh** jsh ksh rksh sh rsh		netbasic.nlm	netbasic.nlm	netbasic.nlm
cssysmsg	vi /etc/syslog.conf	vi /etc/syslog.conf	vi /etc/syslog.conf	vi /etc/syslog.conf	conlog.nlm	conlog.nlm	**cssysmsg.nlm** conlog.nlm	**cssysmsg.nlm** conlog.nlm
csvde				ldapadd ldapdelete		uimport.exe	uimport.exe	ice.exe
ct	**ct** ate	minicom	cu	**ct** cu				
ctty	getty		getty	getty	rs232.nlm	rs232.nlm	aiocon.nlm rs232.nlm	aiocon.nlm
cu	**cu**	minicom	**cu**	**cu**				
Cut								
cvsbug	sendbug bugfiler	**cvsbug** bashbug	**cvsbug** sendbug	perlbug -a				
cvt					2xupgrde.nlm		ipcu.nlm	ipcu.nlm
cvt1					2xupgrde.nlm		ipcu.nlm	ipcu.nlm
dadmin	**dadmin** dhcpsconf	dhcpd.conf	dhcpd.conf	dhcpmgr dhcpconfig		dhcpcfg.nlm	dnsdhcp.exe	dnsdhcp.exe
date	**date**	**date** hwclock clock	**date**	**date**	time set time	time set time	time set time	time set time
Date & Time Control Panel	date	date	date	date	set time	set time	set time	set time
dbx	**dbx**	gdb	gdb	adb				
dc	**dc** bc	**dc** bc	**dc** bc	**dc** bc				
debug	dbx	gdb	gdb	adb				
defaultbrowser	**defaultbrowser**	lynx netscape	lynx	netscape				
defrag	defragfs	Action: 74			Action: 73	Action: 73	Action: 73	Action: 73
defragfs	**defragfs**				Action: 73	Action: 73	Action: 73	Action: 73
del, erase	rm unlink	rm	rm	rm unlink	filer.exe	filer.exe nwadmn32.exe	filer.exe nwadmn32.exe	filer.exe nwadmn32.exe
deltree	rm -r	rm -r mdeltree	rm -r	rm -r	filer.exe	filer.exe	filer.exe	filer.exe
devattr	lsattr			**devattr**	list devices	list devices	list devices	list devices
device	smit > Devices > Install / Configure Devices	insmod	modload	modload	install.nlm	install.nlm	hdetect.nlm nwconfig.nlm	hdetect.nlm nwconfig.nlm
Device Management Console	smit smitty	linuxconf		admintool	install.nlm	install.nlm	nwconfig.nlm	nwconfig.nlm
devinfo	lsdev			**devinfo**	list devices	list devices	list devices	list devices
df	**df**	**df**	**df**	**df**	chkdir.exe	ndir *path* /spa	ndir *path* /spa	ndir *path* /spa

DOS	Windows 9x	NT 4.0	NT 2000	Windows XP	Macintosh	
	sysagent.exe	at.exe	at.exe	at.exe schtasks.exe		**cronadm**
	sysagent.exe	at.exe	at.exe	at.exe schtasks.exe		**crontab**
	cscript.exe wscript.exe	**cscript.exe** wscript.exe	**cscript.exe** wscript.exe	**cscript.exe** wscript.exe	Action: 7	**cscript**
command.com	command.com	cmd.exe command.com	cmd.exe command.com	cmd.exe command.com		**csh**
	wbemcntl.exe	eventvwr.exe	eventvwr.exe	eventvwr.exe		**cssysmsg**
			csvde.exe ldifde.exe	**csvde.exe** ldifde.exe		**csvde**
	hypertrm.exe	hypertrm.exe	hypertrm.exe	hypertrm.exe		**ct**
ctty	**ctty**					**ctty**
	hypertrm.exe	hypertrm.exe	hypertrm.exe	hypertrm.exe		**cu**
	<CTRL> + <X>	<CTRL> + <X>	<CTRL> + <X>	<CTRL> + <X>	**<command> + <X>** **Edit > Cut**	**Cut**
	winrep.exe	Action: 19	winrep.exe	Action: 18		**cvsbug**
	cvt.exe cvt1.exe	convert.exe	convert.exe	convert.exe		**cvt**
	cvt1.exe cvt.exe	convert.exe	convert.exe	convert.exe		**cvt1**
		dhcpadmn.exe	dhcpmgmt.msc	dhcpwiz.exe dhcpmgmt.msc		**dadmin**
date time	**date** time	**date** time	**date** time	**date** time	Apple Menu > Control Panels > Date & Time *selections...*	**date**
date time	date time	date time	date time	date time	**Apple Menu > Control Panels > Date & Time**	**Date & Time Control Panel**
debug.exe	debug.exe	debug.exe	debug.exe	debug.exe		**dbx**
	calc.exe	calc.exe	calc.exe	calc.exe	Apple Menu > Calculator	**dc**
debug.exe	**debug.exe**	**debug.exe**	**debug.exe**	**debug.exe**		**debug**
	netscape.exe iexplore.exe	netscape.exe iexplore.exe	netscape.exe iexplore.exe	netscape.exe iexplore.exe	Action: 81	**defaultbrowser**
defrag.exe	**defrag.exe**	Action: 16	compmgmt.msc	**defrag.exe** compmgmt.msc	Action: 70	**defrag**
defrag.exe	defrag.exe	Action: 16	compmgmt.msc	defrag.exe compmgmt.msc	Action: 70	**defragfs**
del **erase**	**del** **erase**	**del** **erase**	**del** **erase**	**del** **erase**	command + Backspace	**del, erase**
deltree.com	**deltree.com**	Action: 15	Action: 15	Action: 15	command + Backspace	**deltree**
	Action: 172	Control Panel > SCSI Adapters	Action: 171	Action: 171	Apple Menu > Apple System Profiler > Devices and Volumes	**devattr**
device=*device* devicehigh= *device*	Control Panel > Add New Hardware	Control Panel > Devices	Control Panel > Add/Remove Hardware	Control Panel > Add Hardware	Control Panels > Extensions Manager	**device**
	Action: 211		**devmgmt.msc** Action: 190	**devmgmt.msc** Action: 190	Apple Menu > Control Panels > Extension Manager	**Device Management Console**
	Action: 190	Control Panel > Devices	Action: 210	Action: 210		**devinfo**
dir	dir	dir	dir	dir	Action: 165	**df**

	AIX	Linux	OpenBSD	Solaris	NetWare 3	NetWare 4	NetWare 5	NetWare 6
dfmounts	showmount	showmount	showmount	**dfmounts** showmount	map.exe	map.exe	map.exe	map.exe
dfshares	lsnfsexp	showmount -e	showmount -e	**dfshares** showmount -e	display servers	display servers	display servers	display servers
dhclient	dhcpcd	dhcpcd pump	**dhclient**	dhcpagent				
DHCP Manager	dhcpd.conf	dhcpd.conf	dhcpd.conf	dhcpconfig dhcpmgr dhtadm pntadm		dhcpcfg.nlm	dnsdhcp.exe	dnsdhcp.exe
DHCP Wizard	dhcpsconf dadmin	dhcpd.conf	dhcpd.conf	dhcpconfig dhcpmgr dhtadm pntadm		dhcpcfg.nlm	dnsdhcp.exe	dnsdhcp.exe
dhcpaction	**dhcpaction** nsupdate8 nsupdate	nsupdate		nsupdate		named.nlm	named.nlm	named.nlm
dhcpagent	dhcpcd	dhcpcd pump	dhclient	**dhcpagent**				
dhcpcd	**dhcpcd**	**dhcpcd** pump	dhclient	dhcpagent				
dhcpcfg	dhcpsconf dadmin	dhcpd.conf	dhcpd.conf	dhcpconfig dhtadm		**dhcpcfg.nlm**	dnsdhcp.exe	dnsdhcp.exe
dhcpconfig	dhcpsconf dadmin	dhcpd.conf	dhcpd.conf	**dhcpconfig** dhcpmgr		dhcpcfg.nlm	dnsdhcp.exe	dnsdhcp.exe
dhcpd	dhcpsd	**dhcpd**	**dhcpd**	in.dhcpd		dhcpcfg.nlm	dhcpsrvr.nlm	dhcpsrvr.nlm
dhcpmgr	dhcpsconf dadmin	dhcpd.conf	dhcpd.conf	**dhcpmgr** dhcpconfig		dhcpcfg.nlm	dnsdhcp.exe	dnsdhcp.exe
dhcprd	**dhcprd**	dhcrelay	dhcrelay	in.dhcpd -r *relaylist*		bootpfwd.nlm	bootpfwd.nlm	bootpfwd.nlm
dhcpsconf	**dhcpsconf**	dhcpd.conf	dhcpd.conf	dhcpconfig dhcpmgr		dhcpcfg.nlm	dnsdhcp.exe	dnsdhcp.exe
dhcpsd	**dhcpsd**	dhcpd	dhcpd	in.dhcpd		dhcpcfg.nlm	dhcpsrvr.nlm	dhcpsrvr.nlm
dhcrelay	dhcprd	**dhcrelay**	**dhcrelay**	in.dhcpd -r *relaylist*		bootpfwd.nlm	bootpfwd.nlm	bootpfwd.nlm
dhtadm	dhcpsconf dadmin	dhcpd.conf	dhcpd.conf	**dhtadm** dhcpconfig dhcpmgr		dhcpcfg.nlm	dnsdhcp.exe	dnsdhcp.exe
dialog		**dialog**		ckyorn				
Dial-up Networking	pppdial	wvdial	ppp	aspppd		Action: 121	niascfg.nlm	Action: 121
diff	**diff** cmp	**diff** cmp	**diff** cmp	**diff** cmp				
dig	nslookup host	**dig** nslookup	**dig** nslookup	nslookup		Action: 201	Action: 201	Action: 201
dip	pppdial	**dip**	pppd				nwccon.nlm	
dir	ls	**dir** ls nwdir	ls	ls	ndir.exe	ndir.exe	ndir.exe	ndir.exe
dircmp	**dircmp** diff -r	gendiff diff –r	diff -r	**dircmp** diff -r	filer.exe	filer.exe	filer.exe	filer.exe
Direct Cable Connection	tip		tip	tip				
dirs	pwd	**dirs** pwd	pwd	pwd				
disable	**disable**	lpc enable *printer*	lpc enable *printer*	**disable**	pconsole.exe psc.exe	pconsole.exe psc.exe	nwpmw32.exe nwadmn32.exe ndpsm.nlm	nwadmn32.exe ndpsm.nlm
Disable Login	Action: 117 pdisable	passwd -l *user* Action: 117	Action: 117	passwd -l *user* Action: 117	**disable login**	**disable login**	**disable login**	**disable login**

DOS	Windows 9x	NT 4.0	NT 2000	Windows XP	Macintosh	
	Windows Explorer > My Computer	Windows NT Explorer > My Computer	Windows Explorer > My Computer	Windows Explorer > My Computer		**dfmounts**
	net view *server*	net view *server*	net view *server*	net view *server*	Apple Menu > Network Browser	**dfshares**
	Action: 234	Action: 235	Action: 233	Action: 233	Apple Menu > Control Panels > TCP/IP	**dhclient**
		dhcpadmn.exe	dhcpmgmt.msc	dhcpmgmt.msc dhcpwiz.exe		**DHCP Manager**
		dhcpadmn.exe	dhcpmgmt.msc	**dhcpwiz.exe** dhcpmgmt.msc		**DHCP Wizard**
						dhcpaction
	Action: 234	Action: 235	Action: 233	Action: 233	Apple Menu > Control Panels > TCP/IP	**dhcpagent**
	Action: 234	Action: 235	Action: 233	Action: 233	Apple Menu > Control Panels > TCP/IP	**dhcpcd**
		dhcpadmn.exe	dhcpmgmt.msc	dhcpmgmt.msc		**dhcpcfg**
		dhcpadmn.exe	dhcpmgmt.msc	dhcpwiz.exe dhcpmgmt.msc		**dhcpconfig**
		dhcpadmn.exe	dhcpmgmt.msc	dhcpwiz.exe dhcpmgmt.msc		**dhcpd**
		dhcpadmn.exe	dhcpmgmt.msc	dhcpwiz.exe dhcpmgmt.msc		**dhcpmgr**
		Action: 145	Action: 146	Action: 146		**dhcprd**
		dhcpadmn.exe	dhcpmgmt.msc	dhcpwiz.exe dhcpmgmt.msc		**dhcpsconf**
		dhcpadmn.exe	dhcpmgmt.msc	dhcpwiz.exe dhcpmgmt.msc		**dhcpsd**
		Action: 145	Action: 146	Action: 146		**dhcrelay**
		dhcpadmn.exe	dhcpmgmt.msc	dhcpwiz.exe dhcpmgmt.msc		**dhtadm**
choice.com	choice.com					**dialog**
	Action: 124	**rasautou.exe**	rasautou.exe	rasphone.exe	Control Panel > Remote Access	**Dial-up Networking**
fc.exe	fc.exe	fc.exe comp.exe	fc.exe comp.exe	fc.exe comp.exe		**diff**
		nslookup	nslookup	nslookup		**dig**
	Action: 22	rasphone.exe	rasphone.exe rasdial	rasphone.exe	Apple Menu > Control Panels > Remote Access	**dip**
dir	**dir**	**dir**	**dir**	**dir**		**dir**
diskcomp.com		diskcomp.com	diskcomp.com	diskcomp.com		**dircmp**
interlnk.exe intersvr.exe	**directcc.exe**					**Direct Cable Connection**
cd	cd	cd	cd	cd	<command> + click the name in title bar	**dirs**
	net print /delete	net print /delete	net print /delete	net print /delete		**disable**
		Action: 118 chglogon /DISABLE change LOGON /DISABLE	Action: 118 chglogon /DISABLE change LOGON /DISABLE	Action: 118 chglogon /DISABLE change LOGON /DISABLE		**Disable Login**

	AIX	Linux	OpenBSD	Solaris	NetWare 3	NetWare 4	NetWare 5	NetWare 6
Disk Administrator	chpv	fdisk	fdisk	format fdisk	install.nlm	install.nlm	nwconfig.nlm	nwconfig.nlm
Disk Cleanup	Action: 202	nwpurge		Action: 202	purge /a	purge /a filer > Purge Deleted Files	purge /a filer > Purge Deleted Files	filer > Purge Deleted Files Action: 4
Disk Copy	dd if=*device* of=*outfile*	dd if=*device* of=*outfile* mkisofs mount -o loop *file destination*	dd if=*device* of=*outfile* mkisofs	dd if=*device* of=*outfile* mkisofs				
Disk Defragmenter Console	defragfs	Action: 74			Action: 73	Action: 73	Action: 73	Action: 73
Disk First Aid	fsck	fsck	fsck	fsck	vrepair.nlm	vrepair.nlm	nss /rebuild nss /menu vrepair.nlm	ConsoleOne > Server > Media vrepair.nlm
Disk Management	chpv	fdisk	fdisk	format fdisk	install.nlm	install.nlm	nwconfig.nlm	nwconfig.nlm
Disk Management Console	smitty storage	cfdisk	fdisk	fdisk	install.nlm	install.nlm	nwconfig.nlm	ConsoleOne > Tools > Disk Management
Disk Usage Utility	edquota	setquota edquota	edquota	edquota	**dspace.exe**	Action: 247	Action: 247	Action: 247
diskcomp	dircmp diff -r	diff -r gendiff	diff -r	dircmp diff -r	filer.exe	filer.exe	filer.exe	filer.exe
diskcopy	flcopy	mcat						
disklabel	chpv lspv	e2label	**disklabel**	labelit prtvtoc	volume	volume	volume	volume
diskpart	chpv	fdisk	fdisk	fdisk format	install.nlm	install.nlm	nwconfig.nlm	nwconfig.nlm
diskperf	iostat	iostat	iostat	iostat			Action: 127	Action: 128
diskusg	**diskusg** acctdisk sa	quotaon	sa quotaon	acctdisk dodisk quotaon	atotal.exe paudit.exe	atotal.exe	atotal.exe	atotal.exe
dismount	umount	umount	umount	umount	**dismount**	**dismount**	**dismount**	**dismount**
disown	kill %*jobID*	**disown**	kill %*jobID*	**disown**				
dispgid	lsgroup cat /etc/group	cat /etc/group	cat /etc/group	**dispgid** cat /etc/group	syscon.exe sysconW.exe	netadmin.exe nwadmn32.exe	nwadmn32.exe consoleone.exe consoleonedos.exe	nwadmn32.exe consoleone.exe consoleonedos.exe
display		**display**						
Display Environment	env	env	env	env		search	**display environment**	**display environment**
Display Interrupts		cat /proc/interrupts	Action: 163				**display interrupts**	**display interrupts**
Display Processors	cpu_state -l			psrinfo mpstat		mpdetect.nlm	**display processors**	**display processors**
Display Servers		slist			**display servers**	**display servers**	**display servers**	**display servers**
dispuid	Action: 29	Action: 29	Action: 29	**dispuid**	syscon.exe sysconW.exe	netadmin.exe nwadmn32.exe	nwadmn32.exe consoleone.exe consoleonedos.exe	nwadmn32.exe consoleone.exe consoleonedos.exe
Distributed File System Manager	smit mknfsexp	vi /etc/exports	vi /etc/exports	vi /etc/dfs/dfstab	syscon.exe grant.exe	nwadmn32.exe rights.exe	nwadmn32.exe rights.exe	nwadmn32.exe rights.exe
dmesg	lscfg svmon	**dmesg** free	**dmesg** top	**dmesg** prtconf	monitor.nlm display interrupts	monitor.nlm display interrupts	monitor.nlm display interrupts	monitor.nlm display interrupts
DNS Manager	named4 named8	named	named	in.named		named.nlm	named.nlm	named.nlm
DNS Wizard	named4 named8	named	named	in.named		named.nlm	named.nlm	named.nlm

DOS	Windows 9x	NT 4.0	NT 2000	Windows XP	Macintosh	
fdisk.exe	fdisk.exe	**windisk.exe**	diskmgmt.msc	diskmgmt.msc diskpart.exe	Action: 64	**Disk Administrator**
	cleanmgr.exe Action: 17	Action: 17	**cleanmgr.exe** Action: 17	**cleanmgr.exe** Action: 17	command + backspace Special > Empty Trash	**Disk Cleanup**
					Action: 110	**Disk Copy**
defrag.exe	defrag.exe	Action: 16	**dfrg.msc**	**dfrg.msc** defrag.exe	Action: 70	**Disk Defragmenter Console**
scandisk.exe chkdsk.exe	scandisk.exe scandskw.exe chkdsk.exe	chkdsk.exe chkntfs.exe	chkdsk.exe chkntfs.exe	chkdsk.exe chkntfs.exe	**Action: 101**	**Disk First Aid**
fdisk.exe	fdisk.exe	windisk.exe	**diskmgmt.msc**	**diskmgmt.msc** diskpart.exe	Action: 64	**Disk Management**
fdisk.exe	fdisk.exe	windisk.exe	**diskmgmt.msc**	**diskmgmt.msc**	Action: 64	**Disk Management Console**
			Action: 158	Action: 158		**Disk Usage Utility**
diskcomp.com		**diskcomp.com**	**diskcomp.com**	**diskcomp.com**		**diskcomp**
diskcopy.com	**diskcopy.com**	**diskcopy.com**	**diskcopy.com**	**diskcopy.com**	Action: 110	**diskcopy**
vol label	vol label	vol label	vol label	vol label	Apple Menu > Apple System Profiler	**disklabel**
fdisk.exe	fdisk.exe	windisk.exe	diskmgmt.msc	**diskpart.exe** diskmgmt.msc	Action: 64	**diskpart**
		diskperf.exe	**diskperf.exe**	**diskperf.exe**		**diskperf**
						diskusg
						dismount
<CTRL> + <C>	Action: 212	Action: 212	Action: 212	Action: 212	<command> + <dot>	**disown**
		net group usrmgr.exe musrmgr.exe	net group compmgmt.msc	net group compmgmt.msc		**dispgid**
	iexplore.exe	iexplore.exe	iexplore.exe	iexplore.exe	Action: 82	**display**
set	set	Action: 154	Action: 155	Action: 155		**Display Environment**
	msinfo32.exe	winmsd.exe msinfo32.exe	winmsd.exe msinfo32.exe	winmsd.exe msinfo32.exe		**Display Interrupts**
						Display Processors
	net view	net view	net view	net view	Apple Menu > Chooser Apple Menu > Network Browser	**Display Servers**
	Control Panel > Users	net user usrmgr.exe musrmgr.exe	net user compmgmt.msc	net user compmgmt.msc	Apple Menu > Control Panels > Multiple Users	**dispuid**
	Action: 23	Action: 23 shrpubw.exe	**dfsgui.msc** Action: 23 shrpubw.exe	**dfsgui.msc** Action: 23 shrpubw.exe	Apple Menu > Control Panels > File Sharing	**Distributed File System Manager**
msd.exe	msinfo32.exe Control Panel > System	msinfo32.exe winmsd.exe	msinfo32.exe winmsd.exe	msinfo32.exe winmsd.exe	Apple System Profiler	**dmesg**
		dnsadmin.exe	Action: 21	Action: 21		**DNS Manager**
			dnsmgmt.msc Action: 131	**dnswiz.exe** dnsmgmt.msc		**DNS Wizard**

	AIX	Linux	OpenBSD	Solaris	NetWare 3	NetWare 4	NetWare 5	NetWare 6
DNS/DHCP Managment Console	dhcpsconf dadmin	dhcpd.conf	dhcpd.conf	dhcpconfig dhtadm		dhcpcfg.nlm	**dnsdhcp.exe**	**dnsdhcp.exe**
dnsdomainname	domainname	**dnsdomainnam e** domainname nisdomainname	domainname	domainname	\etc\resolv.cfg	\etc\resolv.cfg	\etc\resolv.cfg	\etc\resolv.cfg
docsearch	**docsearch** man *command*	man *command*	man *command*	answerbook man *command*		help	help	help
docviewer	man apropos whatis	man info apropos	man info apropos	**docviewer** navigator		help	help	help
dodisk	**dodisk** quotaon	quotaon	sa quotaon	**dodisk** quotaon	syscon.exe atotal.exe	atotal.exe	atotal.exe	atotal.exe
Domain Controller Security Policy Manager	smit smitty	userconf	usermod	admintool	syscon.exe sysconW.exe	netadmin.exe nwadmn32.exe	nwadmn32.exe consoleone.exe	nwadmn32.exe consoleone.exe
Domain Security Policy Manager	smit smitty	userconf	usermod	admintool	syscon.exe sysconW.exe	netadmin.exe nwadmn32.exe	nwadmn32.exe consoleone.exe	nwadmn32.exe consoleone.exe
domainname	**domainname**	**domainname** dnsdomainname	**domainname**	**domainname**	\etc\resolv.cfg	\etc\resolv.cfg	\etc\resolv.cfg	\etc\resolv.cfg
dos set	set setenv variable=value	set setenv variable=value	set setenv variable=value	set setenv variable=value	**dos set**	**dos set**	**dos set**	**dos set**
dosdel	**dosdel** rm unlink	mdel rm	rm	rm unlink	filer.exe	filer.exe nwadmn32.exe	filer.exe nwadmn32.exe	filer.exe nwadmn32.exe
dosdir	**dosdir** ls	mdir dir ls	ls	ls	ndir.exe	ndir.exe	ndir.exe	ndir.exe
dosformat	**dosformat**	mformat		fdformat -d				
dosfsck, fsck.msdos	fsck	**dosfsck** **fsck.msdos**	fsck_msdos fsck	fsck	vrepair.nlm	vrepair.nlm	nss /rebuild nss /menu vrepair.nlm	ConsoleOne > Server > Media vrepair.nlm
dosgen	nimconfig			re-preinstall	**dosgen.exe**	**dosgen.exe**	**dosgen.exe**	**dosgen.exe**
doskey	history Action: 126	bash -o history	ksh	bash -o history Action: 126	Action: 102	Action: 102	Action: 102	Action: 102
dosshell		mc		dtfile		filer.exe	filer.exe	filer.exe
down	shutdown halt	shutdown halt	shutdown halt	shutdown init 5	**down**	**down**	**down**	**down**
Drive Setup	chpv	cfdisk	fdisk	format fdisk	install.nlm	install.nlm	nwconfig.nlm	nwconfig.nlm
DriveSpace 3						Action: 109	Action: 109	Action: 109
Dropdown Path	pwd	pwd	pwd	pwd				
DS Repair						**dsrepair.nlm**	**dsrepair.nlm**	**dsrepair.nlm**
dsadd				ldapadd		nwadmn32.exe netadmin.exe	nwadmn32.exe	nwadmn32.exe
dtfile	**dtfile**	mc		**dtfile** filemgr	filer.exe	filer.exe	filer.exe	filer.exe
dtmail	mhmail mail, Mail, mailx	mutt mail, Mail, mailx pine	mail, Mail, mailx	**dtmail** mail, Mail, mailx				
dtpad	vi	emacs	vi	**dtpad**	edit.nlm	edit.nlm	edit.nlm	edit.nlm
dtpower	pmctrl	apm	apm zzz	**dtpower** pmconfig				
[illegible]tinfo	qchk lpstat	lpstat	lpq	**dtprintinfo**	pconsole.exe	pconsole.exe	nwpmw32.exe nwadmn32.exe ndpsm.nlm	nwadmn32.exe ndpsm.nlm

DOS	Windows 9x	NT 4.0	NT 2000	Windows XP	Macintosh	
		dhcpadmn.exe	dhcpmgmt.msc	dhcpmgmt.msc		**DNS/DHCP Managment Console**
	winipcfg > More Info	ipconfig /all	ipconfig /all	ipconfig /all	Apple Menu > Apple System Profiler	**dnsdomainname**
	winhelp.exe helpctr.exe	winhlp32.exe help.exe ntbooks.exe	winhelp.exe help.exe ntbooks.exe	winhelp.exe help.exe helpctr.exe	help menu	**docsearch**
fasthelp.exe help.com	winhelp.exe helpctr.exe	winhlp32.exe help.exe ntbooks.exe	winhelp.exe help.exe	winhelp.exe help.exe helpctr.exe	**command + ?** **Help > Mac Help**	**docviewer**
						dodisk
		poledit.exe	**dcpol.msc** dompol.msc secpol.msc poledit.exe	**dcpol.msc** dompol.msc secpol.msc poledit.exe		**Domain Controller Security Policy Manager**
		poledit.exe	**dompol.msc** dcpol.msc secpol.msc poledit.exe	**dompol.msc** dcpol.msc secpol.msc poledit.exe		**Domain Security Policy Manager**
	winipcfg > More Info	ipconfig /all	ipconfig /all	ipconfig /all	Apple Menu > Apple System Profiler	**domainname**
set	set	set Action: 77	set Action: 78	set Action: 78		**dos set**
del erase	del erase	del erase	del erase	del erase	<COMMAND> + <BACKSPACE>	**dosdel**
dir	dir	dir	dir	dir		**dosdir**
format a:	format a:	format a:	format a:	format a:	Special > Erase Disk	**dosformat**
scandisk.exe chkdsk.exe	scandisk.exe scandskw.exe chkdsk.exe	chkdsk.exe chkntfs.exe	chkdsk.exe chkntfs.exe	chkdsk.exe chkntfs.exe	Action: 101	**dosfsck, fsck.msdos**
		ncadmin.exe	rbfg.exe	rbfg.exe		**dosgen**
doskey.com	**doskey.com**	**doskey.exe**	**doskey.exe**	**doskey.exe**		**doskey**
dosshell.exe	explorer.exe winfile.exe	explorer.exe winfile.exe	explorer.exe	explorer.exe		**dosshell**
	Start > Shut down	shutdown.exe Start > Shut down	Start > Shut down	shutdown.exe Start > Shut down	Power Button > Shut Down Special > Shut Down	**down**
fdisk.exe	fdisk.exe	windisk.exe	diskmgmt.msc	diskmgmt.msc diskpart.exe	**Action: 64**	**Drive Setup**
drvspace.exe	**drvspace.exe** cmpagent.exe	compact.exe	compact.exe	compact.exe		**DriveSpace 3**
cd	cd	cd	cd	cd	**command + click the name in title bar**	**Dropdown Path**
			ntdsutil.exe	ntdsutil.exe		**DS Repair**
			Action: 136	**dsadd.exe**		**dsadd**
dosshell	winfile.exe explorer.exe	winfile.exe explorer.exe	explorer.exe	explorer.exe	Finder	**dtfile**
	msimn.exe		msimn.exe	msimn.exe	Action: 199	**dtmail**
edit.com	notepad.exe	notepad.exe	notepad.exe	notepad.exe	Action: 82	**dtpad**
power.exe	pmres.exe		Control Panel > Power Options	Control Panel > Power Options	Apple Menu > Control Panels > Energy Saver	**dtpower**
	Control Panel > Printers net print	Control Panel > Printers net print	Control Panel > Printers net print	Control Panel > Printers and Faxes net print	Action: 115	**dtprintinfo**

	AIX	Linux	OpenBSD	Solaris	NetWare 3	NetWare 4	NetWare 5	NetWare 6
dtscreen	xss		xautolock	**dtscreen**	monitor.nlm	monitor.nlm	scrsaver.nlm	scrsaver.nlm
dtstyle				**dtstyle**	**colorpal.exe**	**colorpal.exe**	Action: 123	Action: 123
dtterm	xterm	xterm	xterm	**dtterm**				
dtwm	mwm	fvwm2	fvwm	**dtwm**	<CTRL> + <ESC>	<CTRL> + <ESC>	<CTRL> + <ESC>	<CTRL> + <ESC>
du	**du**	**du**	**du**	**du**	ndir.exe	ndir.exe	ndir.exe	ndir.exe
dump, rdump	**rdump** backup	**rdump** **dump**	**rdump** **dump**	ufsdump	sbackup.nlm	sbackup.nlm	nwback32.exe sbcon.nlm	nwback32.exe sbcon.nlm
dumpe2fs	lsfs	**dumpe2fs**	dumpfs	fstyp	volume volumes	vmvolumes volume volumes	vmvolumes volume volumes	vmvolumes volume volumes
dumpfs	lsfs	dumpe2fs	**dumpfs**	fstyp	volume volumes	vmvolumes volume volumes	vmvolumes volume volumes	vmvolumes volume volumes
Duplicate	cp	cp	cp	cp	ncopy.exe filer.exe	ncopy.exe filer.exe	ncopy.exe filer.exe	ncopy.exe filer.exe
e2fsck, fsck.ext2	fsck	**e2fsck** **fsck.ext2** fsck	fsck_ext2fs fsck	fsck	vrepair.nlm	vrepair.nlm	vrepair.nlm nss /menu	vrepair.nlm ConsoleOne > Server > Media
e2label		**e2label**	disklabel	labelit		install.nlm	nwconfig.nlm	c1start > Tools > Disk Management
echo	**echo** print	**echo**	**echo**	**echo**			**echo**	**echo**
echo off					**echo off**	**echo off**	**echo off**	**echo off**
echo on					**echo on**	**echo on**	**echo on**	**echo on**
edit	**edit** vi tvi	vi emacs	vi	**edit** vi dtpad	**edit.nlm**	**edit.nlm**	**edit.nlm**	**edit.nlm**
edlin	vi ex red	vi ex	vi ex	vi ex red	edit.nlm	edit.nlm	edit.nlm	edit.nlm
edquota	**edquota**	**edquota** setquota	**edquota**	**edquota**	dspace.exe	Action: 247	Action: 247	Action: 247
eeprom	bootlist			**eeprom**				
egrep	**egrep** grep fgrep strings	**egrep** grep	**egrep** grep fgrep strings	**egrep** grep				
eject		**eject**	**eject**	**eject**	cd dismount *device* /eject	cd dismount *device* /eject	cd dismount *device* /eject	cd dismount *device* /eject
Eject Disks		eject	eject	eject	cd dismount *device* /eject	cd dismount *device* /eject	cd dismount *device* /eject	cd dismount *device* /eject
elm	mhmail mail mailx	**elm** mutt pine	mail mailx	dtmail mail mailx				
emacs	vi tvi	**emacs** vi	vi	vi dtpad	edit.nlm	edit.nlm	edit.nlm	edit.nlm
emm386								
Empty Trash	Action: 202			Action: 202	purge.exe	purge.exe filer > Purge Deleted Files	purge.exe filer > Purge Deleted Files	filer > Purge Deleted Files Action: 4
emulate				**emulate**		netbasic.nlm	netbasic.nlm	netbasic.nlm
enable	**enable**	lpc enable *printer*	lpc enable *printer*	**enable** accept	pconsole.exe psc.exe	pconsole.exe psc.exe	nwpmw32.exe nwadmn32.exe ndpsm.nlm	nwadmn32.exe ndpsm.nlm
Enable Login	Action: 187	Action: 187	Action: 187	Action: 187	**enable login**	**enable login**	**enable login**	**enable login**
endcap					**endcap.exe**	capture /endcap	capture /endcap	capture /endcap

DOS	Windows 9x	NT 4.0	NT 2000	Windows XP	Macintosh	
	Action: 150	Action: 150	Action: 150	Action: 150		**dtscreen**
	Action: 213	Action: 213	Action: 213	Action: 213	Apple Menu > Control Panels > Appearance	**dtstyle**
	command.com	cmd.exe	cmd.exe	cmd.exe		**dtterm**
	progman.exe	progman.exe	progman.exe	progman.exe	Finder	**dtwm**
dir	dir	dir	dir	dir	Select folder or file and press <command> + I	**du**
msbackup.exe	backup.exe msbackup.exe	ntbackup.exe backup.exe	ntbackup.exe	ntbackup.exe		**dump, rdump**
chkdsk.exe	Action: 261	Action: 261	Action: 261	Action: 261	Select harddrive and press <COMMAND> + I	**dumpe2fs**
chkdsk.exe	Action: 261	Action: 261	Action: 261	Action: 261	Select harddrive and press <command> + I	**dumpfs**
copy xcopy.exe	xcopy.exe copy Action: 1	xcopy.exe copy Action: 1	xcopy.exe copy Action: 1	xcopy.exe copy Action: 1	**<command> + <D>** **File > Duplicate**	**Duplicate**
chkdsk.exe scandisk.exe	chkdsk.exe scandisk.exe	chkdsk.exe chkntfs.exe	chkdsk.exe chkntfs.exe	chkdsk.exe chkntfs.exe	Action: 101	**e2fsck, fsck.ext2**
label.exe	label.exe	label.exe	label.exe	label.exe	Action: 112	**e2label**
echo	**echo**	**echo**	**echo**	**echo**		**echo**
echo off	echo off	echo off	echo off	echo off		**echo off**
echo on	echo on	echo on	echo on	echo on		**echo on**
edit.com	**edit.com** notepad.exe wordpad.exe	**edit.com** notepad.exe wordpad.exe	**edit.com** notepad.exe wordpad.exe	**edit.com** notepad.exe wordpad.exe	Action: 82	**edit**
edit.com	notepad.exe edit.com	**edlin.exe** notepad.exe edit.com	**edlin.exe** notepad.exe edit.com	**edlin.exe** notepad.exe edit.com	Action: 82	**edlin**
			Action: 158	Action: 158		**edquota**
		Action: 125	Action: 125	bootcfg.exe	Apple Menu > Control Panels > Startup Disk	**eeprom**
find.exe	find.exe	findstr.exe find.exe	findstr.exe find.exe	findstr.exe find.exe		**egrep**
	Action: 68	Action: 68	Action: 68	Action: 68	command + e Drag disk icon to the trash.	**eject**
	Action: 68	Action: 68	Action: 68	Action: 68	**command + e** **Drag disk icon to the trash.**	**Eject Disks**
	msimn.exe		msimn.exe	msimn.exe	Action: 199	**elm**
edit.com	edit.com notepad.exe	edit.com notepad.exe	edit.com notepad.exe	edit.com notepad.exe	Action: 82	**emacs**
emm386.exe	**emm386.exe**					**emm386**
	Action: 17 cleanmgr.exe	Action: 17	Action: 17 cleanmgr.exe	Action: 17 cleanmgr.exe	**command + backspace** **Special > Empty Trash**	**Empty Trash**
						emulate
	net print	net print	net print	net print		**enable**
		Action: 188 chglogon /ENABLE	Action: 188 chglogon /ENABLE	Action: 188 chglogon /ENABLE		**Enable Login**
	net print /delete	net print /delete	net print /delete	net print /delete		**endcap**

	AIX	Linux	OpenBSD	Solaris	NetWare 3	NetWare 4	NetWare 5	NetWare 6
Energy Saver Control Panel	pmctrl	apm	apm	pmconfig				
Enlarge a window								
Enterprise - Licensing	ls_admin					install.nlm	nwconfig.nlm licmaint.nlm	nwconfig.nlm licmaint.nlm
entstat	**entstat**	netstat	netstat	netstat	monitor.nlm	monitor.nlm	monitor.nlm	monitor.nlm
env	**env**	**env**	**env**	**env**		search	display environment	display environment
envset	setenv set variable=value	setenv set variable=value	setenv set variable=value	setenv set variable=value	dos set	dos set	**envset** dos set	**envset** dos set
Erase Disk	fdformat mkfs	fdformat mkfs	fdformat newfs	fdformat mkfs	install.nlm	install.nlm	nwconfig.nlm	ConsoleOne
errdemon	**errdemon** syslogd	klogd sysklogd syslogd	syslogd	syslogd	conlog.nlm	conlog.nlm	conlog.nlm	conlog.nlm
Event Viewer	smit > alog	cat /var/log/messages	cat /var/log/messages	cat /var/adm/messages	load edit /system/sys$log.err	view /system/sys$log.err	view /system/sys$log.err	view /system/sys$log.err
Event Viewer Console	smit > alog	cat /var/log/messages	cat /var/log/messages	cat /var/adm/messages	load edit /system/sys$log.err	view /system/sys$log.err	view /system/sys$log.err	view /system/sys$log.err
ex, e	**ex** **e**	**ex** **e**	**ex** **e**	**ex** **e**	edit.nlm	edit.nlm	edit.nlm	edit.nlm
exit	**exit** logout	**exit** logout	**exit** logout	**exit** logout	**exit**	**exit**		
expand	uncompress tar	uncompress unzip tar	uncompress gunzip tar	uncompress unzip tar	nwxtract.exe nlunpack.exe	nwxtract.exe	tar.nlm unzip.nlm jar	tar.nlm unzip.nlm jar
Expand Content								
exportfs	**exportfs**	**exportfs**	Cross Reference Note: 8	**exportfs** share	flag *file* -sh	flag *file* +sh /FO	flag *file* +sh /FO	flag *file* +sh /FO
Extension Manager	/etc/inittab	/etc/inittab	/etc/rc.conf	/etc/inittab	autoexec.ncf	autoexec.ncf	autoexec.ncf	autoexec.ncf
f	**f** finger	finger	finger	finger	userlist.exe	nlist user	nlist user	nlist user
fastboot	**fastboot** reboot	reboot	reboot	**fastboot** reboot	down server.exe	restart server	restart server reset server	restart server reset server
fasthalt	**fasthalt**	halt	halt	**fasthalt**	down fconsole	down	down	down
fasthelp	man apropos whatis	man info apropos	man info apropos	man apropos whatis		help	help	help
fastopen								
fbconfig		xf86config	xf86config	**fbconfig** afbconfig				
fc	diff cmp	diff cmp	diff cmp	diff cmp				
fdformat	**fdformat**	**fdformat**	**fdformat**	**fdformat**	install.nlm	install.nlm	nwconfig.nlm	ConsoleOne
fdisk	chpv	**fdisk**	**fdisk**	**fdisk** format	install.nlm	install.nlm	nwconfig.nlm	nwconfig.nlm
fetchmail	Action: 76	**fetchmail**	Action: 76	dtmail				
ffbconfig, SUNWffb_config		xf86config	xf86config	**ffbconfig** afbconfig				

DOS	Windows 9x	NT 4.0	NT 2000	Windows XP	Macintosh	
	pmres.exe Control Panel > Power Management		Control Panel > Power Options	Control Panel > Power Options	**Apple Menu > Control Panels > Energy Saver**	**Energy Saver Control Panel**
	Action: 60	Action: 60	Action: 60	Action: 60	**Click zoom box**	**Enlarge a window**
		llsmgr.exe	**llsmgr.exe**	**llsmgr.exe**		**Enterprise - Licensing**
			Action: 218	Action: 219		**entstat**
set	set	Action: 154	Action: 155	Action: 155		**env**
set	set	set Action: 77	set Action: 78	set Action: 78		**envset**
format.com	format.com	format.com	format.com diskmgmt.msc	format.com diskmgmt.msc	**Special > Erase Disk**	**Erase Disk**
	wbemcntl.exe	eventvwr.exe	eventvwr.exe	eventvwr.exe		**errdemon**
	wbemcntl.exe	**eventvwr.exe**	**eventvwr.exe**	**eventvwr.exe**		**Event Viewer**
	wbemcntl.exe	eventvwr.exe	**eventvwr.msc** eventvwr.exe	**eventvwr.msc** eventvwr.exe		**Event Viewer Console**
edit.com	edit.com notepad.exe	edit.com notepad.exe	edit.com notepad.exe	edit.com notepad.exe	Action: 82	**ex, e**
exit	**exit**	**exit**	**exit**	**exit**		**exit**
expand.exe		**expand.exe**	**expand.exe**	**expand.exe**	Action: 79	**expand**
	<RIGHT ARROW> Click on the plus left to the folder.	<RIGHT ARROW> Click on the plus left to the folder.	<RIGHT ARROW> Click on the plus left to the folder.	<RIGHT ARROW> Click on the plus left to the folder.	**<command> + <right arrow>** **Click on the arrows left to the folder.**	**Expand Content**
share	Cross Reference Note: 119 net share	Cross Reference Note: 119 net share	Cross Reference Note: 119 net share	Cross Reference Note: 119 net share	Apple Menu > Control Panels > File Sharing	**exportfs**
autoexec.bat	autoexec.bat	autoexec.bat	autoexec.bat	autoexec.bat	**Apple Menu > Control Panels > Extensions Manager**	**Extension Manager**
		finger.exe	finger.exe	finger.exe		**f**
<CTRL> + <ALT> + <DELETE>	Action: 153	Action: 153	Action: 153	Action: 153	<command> + <control> + <power button>	**fastboot**
	Start > Shut down	shutdown Start > Shut down	Start > Shut down	shutdown Start > Shut down	Power Button > Shut Down Special > Shut Down	**fasthalt**
fasthelp.exe help.com	winhelp.exe helpctr.exe	winhlp32.exe help.exe ntbooks.exe	winhelp.exe help.exe	winhelp.exe help.exe helpctr.exe	command + ? Help > Mac Help	**fasthelp**
fastopen.exe		**fastopen.exe**	**fastopen.exe**	**fastopen.exe**		**fastopen**
	Action: 250	Action: 250	Action: 250	Action: 250	Apple Menu > Control Panels > Monitors	**fbconfig**
fc.exe	**fc.exe**	**fc.exe** comp.exe	**fc.exe** comp.exe	**fc.exe** comp.exe		**fc**
format.com	format.com	format.com	format.com	format.com	Action: 129	**fdformat**
fdisk.exe	**fdisk.exe**	windisk.exe	diskmgmt.msc	diskmgmt.msc diskpart.exe	Action: 64	**fdisk**
	msimn.exe		msimn.exe	msimn.exe		**fetchmail**
	Action: 250	Action: 250	Action: 250	Action: 250	Apple Menu > Control Panels > Monitors	**ffbconfig, SUNWffb_config**

	AIX	Linux	OpenBSD	Solaris	NetWare 3	NetWare 4	NetWare 5	NetWare 6
fgrep	**fgrep** grep	**fgrep** grep	**fgrep** grep	**fgrep** grep				
File Maintenance		mc		dtfile		**filer.exe**	**filer.exe**	**filer.exe**
File Manager	dtfile	mc		dtfile filemgr	filer.exe	filer.exe	filer.exe	filer.exe
File Salvage Utility		Action: 54			**salvage.exe**	filer > salvage deleted files	filer > salvage deleted files	filer > salvage deleted files
File Server Console	smitty system				**fconsole.exe**	servman.nlm	NetWare Management Portal	NetWare Remote Manager
File Server Name	hostname	hostname	hostname	hostname	**file server name**	**file server name**	**file server name**	**file server name**
File Sharing Control Panel	smit exportfs	userconf exportfs	adduser groupadd Action: 8	admintool share	syscon.exe sysconW.exe	netadmin.exe nwadmn32.exe	nwadmn32.exe consoleone.exe	nwadmn32.exe consoleone.exe
filemgr		mc		**filemgr** dtfile	filer.exe	filer.exe	filer.exe	filer.exe
filemon	**filemon** netpmon topas	top	top	perfmeter top	monitor.nlm	monitor.nlm	monitor.nlm	monitor.nlm
files	ulimit -n	ulimit -n	ulimit -n	ulimit -n				
filesync		rsync		**filesync**				
filtcfg	chfilt genfilt	ipchains iptables	ipf			**filtcfg.nlm**	**filtcfg.nlm**	**filtcfg.nlm**
find	grep	grep	grep	grep				
Find File	find / -name *file* which *file* whence *file*	where *file* find / -name *file* which *file*	find / -name *file* which *file* whence *file*	where *file* find / -name *file* which *file* whence *file*	ndir *file* /s filer.exe	ndir *file* /s filer.exe	ndir *file* /s filer.exe	ndir *file* /s filer.exe
findsmb		**findsmb** slist			display servers	display servers	display servers	display servers
findstr	grep egrep fgrep strings	grep egrep	grep egrep fgrep strings	grep egrep				
finger	**finger**	**finger**	**finger**	**finger**	userlist.exe	nlist user	nlist user	nlist user
flag	chmod ls -l	chmod ls -l	chmod ls -l	chmod ls -l	**flag.exe** syscon.exe rights.exe	**flag.exe** nwadmn32.exe rights.exe	**flag.exe** nwadmn32.exe rights.exe	**flag.exe** nwadmn32.exe rights.exe
flagdir	ls -l chmod	ls -l chmod	ls -l chmod	ls -l chmod	**flagdir.exe** syscon.exe	flag /do nwadmn32.exe	flag /do nwadmn32.exe	flag /do nwadmn32.exe
flcopy	**flcopy**	mcat						
fmthard	bosboot mkboot	lilo	installboot	**fmthard** installboot				
fontview								
for	**for** foreach	**for** foreach	**for** foreach	**for** foreach				
Force Quit	kill -9 <CTRL> + <C>	kill -9 <CTRL> + <C>	kill -9 <CTRL> + <C>	kill -9 <CTRL> + <C>	unload *module*	unload *module*	unload *module*	unload *module*
Force Restart	reboot	reboot	reboot	reboot	down server.exe	restart server	restart server reset server	restart server reset server
foreach	**foreach** for	**foreach** for	**foreach** for	**foreach** for				
format	chpv	fdisk	fdisk	**format** fdisk	install.nlm	install.nlm	nwconfig.nlm	nwconfig.nlm
format	mkfs	mkfs	newfs	mkfs	install.nlm	install.nlm	nwconfig.nlm	ConsoleOne
format_floppy	fdformat format	fdformat	fdformat	**format_floppy** fdformat	install.nlm	install.nlm	nwconfig.nlm	ConsoleOne
free	svmon vmstat	**free** alloc vmstat	top vmstat	prtconf alloc vmstat	memory monitor.nlm	memory monitor.nlm	memory monitor.nlm NetWare Management Portal	memory monitor.nlm NetWare Remote Manager

DOS	Windows 9x	NT 4.0	NT 2000	Windows XP	Macintosh	
find.exe	find.exe	findstr.exe find.exe	findstr.exe find.exe	findstr.exe find.exe		**fgrep**
dosshell.exe	explorer.exe winfile.exe	explorer.exe winfile.exe	explorer.exe	explorer.exe	Finder	**File Maintenance**
dosshell	**winfile.exe** explorer.exe	**winfile.exe** explorer.exe	explorer.exe	explorer.exe	Finder	**File Manager**
undelete	Action: 56	Action: 56	Action: 56	Action: 56	Action: 169	**File Salvage Utility**
		srvmgr.exe	srvmgr.exe	srvmgr.exe		**File Server Console**
	Action: 204	Control Panel > Network	Action: 205	Action: 205		**File Server Name**
	Control Panel > Users Action: 23	usrmgr.exe Action: 23	compmgmt.msc Action: 23	compmgmt.msc Action: 23	**Apple Menu > Control Panels > File Sharing**	**File Sharing Control Panel**
dosshell.exe	winfile.exe explorer.exe	winfile.exe explorer.exe	explorer.exe	explorer.exe	Finder	**filemgr**
		perfmon.exe	perfmon.exe	perfmon.exe	Apple Menu > About This Computer	**filemon**
files	**files**					**files**
	mobsync.exe		mobsync.exe	mobsync.exe		**filesync**
			rrasmgmt.msc	rrasmgmt.msc		**filtcfg**
find	**find**	**find**	**find**	**find**		**find**
dir *file* /s	dir *file* /s Action: 182	dir *file* /s Action: 182	dir *file* /s Action: 182	dir *file* /s Action: 182	**command + f** **File > Find**	**Find File**
	net view Action: 222	net view Action: 222	net view Action: 223	net view Action: 223	Apple Menu > Network Browser	**findsmb**
find.exe	find.exe	**findstr.exe** find.exe	**findstr.exe** find.exe	**findstr.exe** find.exe		**findstr**
		finger.exe	**finger.exe**	**finger.exe**		**finger**
attrib.exe	attrib.exe	attrib.exe	attrib.exe	attrib.exe	Select icon > command + i > Locked	**flag**
	attrib.exe	attrib.exe	attrib.exe	attrib.exe	Select icon > command + i	**flagdir**
diskcopy.com	diskcopy.com	diskcopy.com	diskcopy.com	diskcopy.com	Action: 110	**flcopy**
sys.com format a: /s	sys.com format a: /s	winnt /ox winnt32 /ox	makeboot.exe	makeboot.exe		**fmthard**
	fontview.exe	**fontview.exe**	**fontview.exe**	**fontview.exe**	Action: 135	**fontview**
for	**for**	**for**	**for**	**for**		**for**
<CTRL> + <C>	<ALT> + <F4> Action: 212	<ALT> + <F4> Action: 212	<ALT> + <F4> Action: 212	<ALT> + <F4> Action: 212	**<command> + <ALT> + <ESC>**	**Force Quit**
<CTRL> + <ALT> + <DELETE>	Action: 153	Action: 153	Action: 153	Action: 153	**<command> + <control> + <power button>**	**Force Restart**
for	for	for	for	for		**foreach**
fdisk.exe	fdisk.exe	windisk.exe	diskmgmt.msc	diskmgmt.msc diskpart.exe	Action: 64	**format**
format.com	**format.com**	**format.com**	**format.com**	**format.com**	Action: 129	**format**
format.com	format.com	format.com	format.com	format.com	Action: 129	**format_floppy**
mem	mem	mem winver.exe winmsd.exe	mem winver.exe winmsd.exe	mem winver.exe winmsd.exe	Apple Menu > About This Computer	**free**

	AIX	Linux	OpenBSD	Solaris	NetWare 3	NetWare 4	NetWare 5	NetWare 6
from	**from** mail, Mail, mailx sendmail -bp	mail, Mail, mailx sendmail –bp	**from** mail, Mail, mailx sendmail -bp	**from** mail, Mail, mailx sendmail -bp				
fsck	**fsck**	**fsck**	**fsck**	**fsck**	vrepair.nlm	vrepair.nlm	vrepair.nlm nss /menu	vrepair.nlm ConsoleOne > Server > Media
fsck.minix	fsck	**fsck.minix** fsck	fsck	fsck	vrepair.nlm	vrepair.nlm	vrepair.nlm nss /menu	vrepair.nlm ConsoleOne > Server > Media
fsck_ext2fs	fsck	e2fsck fsck.ext2 fsck	**fsck_ext2fs** fsck	fsck	vrepair.nlm	vrepair.nlm	vrepair.nlm nss /menu	vrepair.nlm ConsoleOne > Server > Media
fsck_ffs	fsck	fsck	**fsck_ffs** fsck	fsck	vrepair.nlm	vrepair.nlm	nss /rebuild nss /menu vrepair.nlm	ConsoleOne > Server > Media vrepair.nlm
fsck_msdos	fsck	fsck	**fsck_msdos** fsck	fsck	vrepair.nlm	vrepair.nlm	nss /rebuild nss /menu vrepair.nlm	ConsoleOne > Server > Media vrepair.nlm
fslsfonts	lsfont	**fslsfonts**	**fslsfonts**	**fslsfonts**				
fstat	fuser	lsof fuser	**fstat**	fuser	monitor > File open / Lock activity	monitor > File open/lock activity	monitor > File open/lock activity	monitor > File open/lock activity
fstyp	lsfs	dumpe2fs	dumpfs	**fstyp**	volume volumes	vmvolumes volume volumes	vmvolumes volume volumes	vmvolumes volume volumes
ftp	**ftp**	**ftp**	**ftp**	**ftp**				
ftpcount		**ftpcount**					/etc/ftpstat.log	/etc/ftpstat.log
ftpshut		**ftpshut**					unload nwftpd.nlm	unload nwftpd.nlm
ftpwho		**ftpwho**					/etc/ftpstat.log	/etc/ftpstat.log
fuser	**fuser**	**fuser** lsof	fstat	**fuser**	monitor > File open / Lock activity	monitor > File open/lock activity	monitor > File open/lock activitymonitor > File open/lock activity	monitor > File open/lock activity
fvwm	mwm	fvwm2	**fvwm**	dtwm	<CTRL> + <ESC>	<CTRL> + <ESC>	<CTRL> + <ESC>	<CTRL> + <ESC>
fvwm2	mwm	**fvwm2**	fvwm	dtwm	<CTRL> + <ESC>	<CTRL> + <ESC>	<CTRL> + <ESC>	<CTRL> + <ESC>
gated	**gated** routed	in.routed	routed	in.routed		inetcfg > Protocols > TCP/IP	inetcfg > Protocols > TCP/IP	inetcfg > Protocols > TCP/IP
gdb	dbx	**gdb**	**gdb**	adb				
gendiff	dircmp diff -r	**gendiff** diff -r	diff -r	dircmp diff -r	filer.exe	filer.exe	filer.exe	filer.exe
Get Info	file *filename* ls -l	file *filename* ls -l	file *filename* ls -l	file *filename* ls -l	ndir.exe	ndir.exe	ndir.exe	ndir.exe
getdev	lsdev			**getdev** devinfo	list devices	list devices	list devices	list devices
getfacl	aclget	ls -l	ls -l	**getfacl**	ndir.exe	ndir.exe	ndir.exe	ndir.exe
getmac	arp	arp	arp	arp	Action: 116	Action: 116	Action: 116	Action: 116
getty	**getty**		**getty**	**getty**	rs232.nlm	rs232.nlm	aiocon.nlm rs232.nlm	aiocon.nlm
gnubc	bc	bc	**gnubc**	bc				
goto	**goto**	**goto**	**goto**	**goto**				
grant	chmod acledit	chmod	chmod	chmod setfacl	**grant.exe** syscon.exe	rights.exe netadmin.exe nwadmn32.exe	rights.exe nwadmn32.exe consoleone.exe	rights.exe nwadmn32.exe consoleone.exe
graphics								

DOS	Windows 9x	NT 4.0	NT 2000	Windows XP	Macintosh	
	msimn.exe		msimn.exe	msimn.exe	Action: 199	**from**
chkdsk.exe scandisk.exe	chkdsk.exe scandisk.exe	chkdsk.exe chkntfs.exe	chkdsk.exe chkntfs.exe	chkdsk.exe chkntfs.exe	Action: 101	**fsck**
chkdsk.exe scandisk.exe	chkdsk.exe scandisk.exe	chkdsk.exe chkntfs.exe	chkdsk.exe chkntfs.exe	chkdsk.exe chkntfs.exe	Action: 101	**fsck.minix**
chkdsk.exe scandisk.exe	chkdsk.exe scandisk.exe	chkdsk.exe chkntfs.exe	chkdsk.exe chkntfs.exe	chkdsk.exe chkntfs.exe	Action: 101	**fsck_ext2fs**
scandisk.exe chkdsk.exe	scandisk.exe scandskw.exe chkdsk.exe	chkdsk.exe chkntfs.exe	chkdsk.exe chkntfs.exe	chkdsk.exe chkntfs.exe	Action: 101	**fsck_ffs**
scandisk.exe chkdsk.exe	scandisk.exe scandskw.exe chkdsk.exe	chkdsk.exe chkntfs.exe	chkdsk.exe chkntfs.exe	chkdsk.exe chkntfs.exe	Action: 101	**fsck_msdos**
	Control Panel > Fonts	Control Panel > Fonts	Control Panel > Fonts	Control Panel > Fonts	Apple Menu > Control Panels > Appearance > Fonts	**fslsfonts**
	netwatch.exe	srvmgr.exe	srvmgr.exe	srvmgr.exe		**fstat**
chkdsk.exe	Action: 261	Action: 261	Action: 261	Action: 261	Select harddrive and press <COMMAND> + I	**fstyp**
	ftp.exe	**ftp.exe**	**ftp.exe**	**ftp.exe**		**ftp**
			Action: 209	Action: 209		**ftpcount**
		Control Panel > Services	inetmgr.exe	inetmgr.exe		**ftpshut**
			Action: 209	Action: 209		**ftpwho**
	netwatch.exe	srvmgr.exe	srvmgr.exe	srvmgr.exe	Apple > Control Panel > File Sharing	**fuser**
	progman.exe	progman.exe	progman.exe	progman.exe	Finder	**fvwm**
	progman.exe	progman.exe	progman.exe	progman.exe	Finder	**fvwm2**
		Action: 255	Action: 254	Action: 254		**gated**
debug.exe	debug.exe	debug.exe	debug.exe	debug.exe		**gdb**
diskcomp.com		diskcomp.com	diskcomp.com	diskcomp.com		**gendiff**
dir.exe	dir.exe Action: 189	dir.exe Action: 189	dir.exe Action: 189	dir.exe Action: 189	**Select icon > <command> + i**	**Get Info**
	Control Panel > System > Device Manager	Control Panel > Devices	Control Panel > System > Hardware > Device Manager	Control Panel > System > Hardware > Device Manager		**getdev**
		cacls.exe	cacls.exe	cacls.exe		**getfacl**
	arp.exe	arp.exe	arp.exe	**getmac.exe**		**getmac**
ctty	ctty					**getty**
	calc.exe	calc.exe	calc.exe	calc.exe	Apple Menu > Calculator	**gnubc**
goto	**goto**	**goto**	**goto**	**goto**		**goto**
		cacls.exe	cacls.exe	cacls.exe		**grant**
graphics.com	**graphics.com**	**graphics.com**	**graphics.com**	**graphics.com**		**graphics**

	AIX	Linux	OpenBSD	Solaris	NetWare 3	NetWare 4	NetWare 5	NetWare 6
grep	**grep** egrep	**grep** egrep	**grep** egrep	**grep** egrep				
Group Management Wizard	mkgroup smit	userconf groupadd	groupadd	admintool groupadd	syscon.exe sysconW.exe	netadmin.exe nwadmn32.exe	nwadmn32.exe	nwadmn32.exe
Group Policy Manager	smit smitty	userconf	usermod	admintool	syscon.exe sysconW.exe	netadmin.exe nwadmn32.exe	nwadmn32.exe consoleone.exe	nwadmn32.exe consoleone.exe
groupadd	mkgroup	**groupadd**	**groupadd**	**groupadd**	syscon.exe	netadmin.exe nwadmn32.exe	nwadmn32.exe consoleone.exe consoleonedos.ex e c1start.ncf	nwadmn32.exe consoleone.exe c1start.ncf consoleonedos.ex e
groupdel	smitty group	**groupdel**	rmgroup	**groupdel**	syscon.exe	nwadmn32.exe	nwadmn32.exe	nwadmn32.exe
groupmod	smitty group	**groupmod** groupadd groupdel	**groupmod** groupadd rmgroup	**groupmod** admintool	syscon.exe	nwadmn32.exe	nwadmn32.exe	nwadmn32.exe
groups	**groups**	**groups**	**groups**	**groups**	session.exe	netuser.exe	Action: 239	Action: 239
gunzip	uncompress	**gunzip** unzip uncompress	**gunzip** bunzip2 uncompress	**gunzip** unzip uncompress	nwxtract.exe nlunpack.exe	nwxtract.exe	unzip.nlm jar tar.nlm	unzip.nlm jar tar.nlm
gzcat	pcat uncompress -c *file* zcat	uncompress -c *file* bzcat zcat	**gzcat** uncompress -c *file*	**gzcat** pcat uncompress -c *file* zcat			tar -t *file* unzip -l *file* jar -t *file*	tar -t *file* unzip -l *file* jar -t *file*
gzip	pack compress	**gzip** compress	**gzip** compress	**gzip** compress			tar.nlm jar	tar.nlm jar
halt	**halt** shutdown -F	**halt** shutdown -h now	**halt** shutdown -h now	**halt** init 5	down fconsole	down	down	down
hdparm		**hdparm**			set (Disk)	set (Disk)	set (Disk)	set (Disk)
Help	**help** man apropos whatis	**help** man apropos info	man apropos info	**help** man apropos whatis		**help**	**help**	**help**
Help and Support Center	man apropos whatis	man info apropos	man info apropos	man apropos whatis		help	help	help
Hide Others	clear	clear	clear	clear	cls off	cls off	cls off	cls off
history	**history**	**history**	**history**	**history**	Action: 102	Action: 102	Action: 102	Action: 102
Home Networking Wizard	smit tcpip							
host	**host** nslookup	**host** nslookup dig	**host** nslookup dig	nslookup				
hostconfig	dhcpcd	dhcpcd pump	dhclient	**hostconfig** dhcpagent				
hostent	**hostent**	vi /etc/hosts	vi /etc/hosts	vi /etc/hosts	edit \etc\hosts	edit \etc\hosts	edit \etc\hosts	edit \etc\hosts
hostname	**hostname**	**hostname**	**hostname**	**hostname**	name	name	name	name
httpbind		Action: 164	Action: 164	Action: 164				**httpbind**
httpd		**httpd**	**httpd**	**httpd**			nsweb.ncf nvxwebup.ncf	nsweb.ncf nvxwebup.ncf
hwclock, clock	date	**hwclock** **clock** setclock date	date	date	set time	set time	set time	set time
HyperTerminal	ate	minicom	cu	cu				

DOS	Windows 9x	NT 4.0	NT 2000	Windows XP	Macintosh	
find.exe	find.exe	findstr.exe find.exe	findstr.exe find.exe	findstr.exe find.exe		**grep**
		addgrpw.exe usrmgr.exe	compmgmt.msc wizmgr.exe	compmgmt.msc wizmgr.exe	Apple Menu > Control Panels > File Sharing > Users & Groups	**Group Management Wizard**
		poledit.exe	**gpedit.msc** poledit.exe	**gpedit.msc** poledit.exe		**Group Policy Manager**
		usrmgr.exe musrmgr.exe addgrpw.exe net group	compmgmt.msc wizmgr.exe net group	compmgmt.msc wizmgr.exe net group	Apple Menu > Control Panels > File Sharing > Users & Groups	**groupadd**
		net group /DELETE	net group /DELETE	net group /DELETE		**groupdel**
		net group	net group wizmgr.exe	net group wizmgr.exe		**groupmod**
		Action: 237	Action: 238	Action: 238	Apple Menu > Control Panels > File Sharing > Users & Groups	**groups**
	Action: 143	Action: 143 expand.exe	Action: 143 expand.exe	Action: 143 expand.exe	Action: 79	**gunzip**
	Action: 143	expand -D *file* Action: 143	expand -D *file* Action: 143	expand -D *file* Action: 143		**gzcat**
	Action: 143	Action: 143	Action: 143	Action: 143		**gzip**
	Start > Shut down	shutdown Start > Shut down	Start > Shut down	shutdown Start > Shut down	Power Button > Shut Down Special > Shut Down	**halt**
						hdparm
help.com fasthelp.exe	winhelp.exe helpctr.exe	**help.exe** winhlp32.exe ntbooks.exe	**help.exe** winhelp.exe	**help.exe** winhelp.exe helpctr.exe	command + ? Help > Mac Help	**Help**
help.com fasthelp.exe	**helpctr.exe** winhelp.exe	winhlp32.exe help.exe ntbooks	winhelp.exe help.exe	**helpctr.exe** winhelp.exe help.exe	command + ? Help > Mac Help	**Help and Support Center**
cls	cls Action: 103	cls Action: 103	cls Action: 103	cls Action: 103	**Application Menu > Hide Others**	**Hide Others**
doskey.com	doskey.com	doskey.exe	doskey.exe	doskey.exe		**history**
	inetwiz.exe netconn.exe	icwconn1.exe	**inetwiz.exe** icwconn1.exe	**inetwiz.exe** cmak.exe	Action: 96	**Home Networking Wizard**
		nslookup	nslookup	nslookup		**host**
	Action: 234	Action: 235	Action: 233	Action: 233	Apple Menu > Control Panels > TCP/IP	**hostconfig**
	edit \windows\hosts	edit \winnt\system32\driver\etc\hosts	edit \winnt\system32\driver\etc\hosts	edit \winnt\system32\driver\etc\hosts		**hostent**
	Control Panel > System	**hostname.exe**	**hostname.exe**	**hostname.exe**		**hostname**
			inetmgr.exe	inetmgr.exe		**httpbind**
			inetmgr.exe	inetmgr.exe	Apple Menu > Control Panels > Web Sharing	**httpd**
date time	date time	date time	date time	date time	Apple Menu > Control Panels > Date & Time *selections...*	**hwclock, clock**
	hypertrm.exe	**hypertrm.exe**	**hypertrm.exe**	**hypertrm.exe**		**HyperTerminal**

	AIX	Linux	OpenBSD	Solaris	NetWare 3	NetWare 4	NetWare 5	NetWare 6
IBM Redundant NIC Utility							**ibmrnic.nlm**	**ibmrnic.nlm**
ice								ice
id	**id** whoami	**id** whoami	**id** whoami	**id** whoami	whoami.exe Action: 5	whoami.exe Action: 5	Action: 5	Action: 5
if	**if**	**if**	**if**	**if**	**if**	**if**	**if**	**if**
ifcfg	cfgif ifconfig	**ifcfg** ifconfig	ifconfig	ifconfig	install.nlm	inetcfg.nlm	inetcfg.nlm	inetcfg.nlm
ifconfig	**ifconfig**	**ifconfig**	**ifconfig**	**ifconfig**	install.nlm	inetcfg.nlm	inetcfg.nlm	inetcfg.nlm
ifdown	ifconfig *interface* down	**ifdown** usernetctl down ifconfig *interface* down	ifconfig *interface* down	ifconfig *interface* down		Action: 208	Action: 208	Action: 208
ifport		**ifport**				inetcfg > Boards	inetcfg > Boards	inetcfg > Boards
ifup	ifconfig *interface* up	**ifup**	ifconfig *interface* up	ifconfig *interface* up		Action: 208	Action: 208	Action: 208
imagetool				**imagetool**				
import		**import**		snapshot	CONLOG entire=yes	CONLOG entire=yes	CONLOG entire=yes	CONLOG entire=yes
in.dhcpd	dhcpsd	dhcpd	dhcpd	**in.dhcpd**		dhcpcfg.nlm	dhcpsrvr.nlm	dhcpsrvr.nlm
in.ftpd, ftpd	**ftpd**	**in.ftpd**	**ftpd**	**in.ftpd**			nwftpd.nlm	nwftpd.nlm
in.rlogind, rlogind	**rlogind**	**in.rlogind**	**rlogind**	**in.rlogind**	Action: 252	Action: 252	rconag6.nlm Action: 252	rconag6.nlm Action: 252
in.routed, routed	routed gated		routed	**in.routed**		load inetcfg > Protocols > TCP/IP	inetcfg > Protocols > TCP/IP	inetcfg > Protocols > TCP/IP
in.rshd, rshd	**rshd**	**in.rshd**	**rshd**	**in.rshd**	Action: 252	Action: 252	rconag6.nlm Action: 252	rconag6.nlm Action: 252
inetd	**inetd**	xinetd	**inetd**	**inetd**	autoexec.ncf	autoexec.ncf	**inetd.nlm** autoexec.ncf	**inetd.nlm** autoexec.ncf
info	man	man	**info** man	man		help	help	help
init, telinit	**init**	**init**	**init**	**init**			loadstage	loadstage
In-Place Upgrade					2xupgrde.nlm		**ipcu.nlm**	**ipcu.nlm**
insmod	smit > Devices > Install / Configure Devices	**insmod**	modload	modload	install.nlm	install.nlm	hdetect.nlm nwconfig.nlm	hdetect.nlm nwconfig.nlm
Install (Installation CD)					**install.bat**	**install.bat**	**install.bat**	**install.bat**
installboot	bosboot mkboot	lilo	**installboot**	**installboot**				
installp	**installp** smit install	rpm	pkg_add	pkgadd	install > product options	install > product options	nwconfig > product options	nwconfig > product options
integer	*variable=value* typeset, declare	*variable=value* typeset, declare	*variable=value* ttypeset, declare	**integer** *variable=value* typeset, declare	dos set	dos set	envset dos set	envset setenv dos set
interlnk								
Internet Access Server	vi /etc/gated.conf	ipchains iptables	ipnat	vi /etc/networks			**niascfg.nlm**	
Internet Connection Wizard								
Internet Control Panel								
Internet Information Services	chsubserver vi /etc/inetd.conf	vi /etc/xinetd.conf	vi /etc/inetd.conf	vi /etc/inetd.conf	install.nlm	inetcfg.nlm	inetcfg.nlm	inetcfg.nlm

DOS	Windows 9x	NT 4.0	NT 2000	Windows XP	Macintosh	
			Action: 162	Action: 162		**IBM Redundant NIC Utility**
			ldifde.exe	ldifde.exe		**ice**
						id
if	**if**	**if**	**if**	**if**		**if**
	Control Panel > Network	Control Panel > Network	Control Panel > Network and Dial Up Connections	Control Panel > Network Connections	Apple Menu > Control Panels > TCP/IP	**ifcfg**
	Control Panel > Network	Control Panel > Network	Control Panel > Network and Dial Up Connections	Control Panel > Network Connections	Apple menu > Control Panels > TCP/IP	**ifconfig**
	Action: 207		Action: 206	Action: 206		**ifdown**
	Action: 266	Action: 267	Action: 265	Action: 265		**ifport**
	Action: 224		Action: 206	Action: 206		**ifup**
		Action: 134	kodakimg.exe		Action: 133	**imagetool**
	<Print Screen>	<Print Screen>	<Print Screen>	<Print Screen>	<command> + <shift> + <3>	**import**
		dhcpadmn.exe	dhcpmgmt.msc	dhcpwiz.exe dhcpmgmt.msc		**in.dhcpd**
			inetmgr.exe	inetmgr.exe		**in.ftpd, ftpd**
			Action: 251	Action: 251		**in.rlogind, rlogind**
		Action: 255	Action: 254	Action: 254		**in.routed, routed**
			Action: 251	Action: 251		**in.rshd, rshd**
						inetd
fasthelp.exe help.com	winhelp.exe helpctr.exe	winhlp32.exe help.exe	winhelp.exe help.exe	winhelp.exe helpctr.exe	command + ? Help > Mac Help	**info**
						init, telinit
	cvt.exe cvt1.exe	convert.exe	convert.exe	convert.exe		**In-Place Upgrade**
device=*device* devicehigh=*device*	Control Panel > Add New Hardware	Control Panel > Devices	Control Panel > Add/Remove Hardware	Control Panel > Add Hardware	Apple Menu > Control Panels > Extensions Manager	**insmod**
setup.exe	setup.exe	winnt /b	sysocmgr.exe	sysocmgr.exe		**Install (Installation CD)**
sys.com format a: /s	sys.com format a: /s	winnt /ox winnt32 /ox	makeboot.exe	makeboot.exe		**installboot**
	Control Panel > Add/Remove Programs	Control Panel > Add/Remove Programs	Control Panel > Add/Remove Programs	Control Panel > Add/Remove Programs		**installp**
set	set	set	set	set		**integer**
interlnk.exe	directcc.exe					**interlnk**
			Action: 170	Action: 170		**Internet Access Server**
	inetwiz.exe netconn.exe		**inetwiz.exe**	**inetwiz.exe** cmak.exe	Action: 96	**Internet Connection Wizard**
	Control Panel > Internet Options	Control Panel > Internet Options	Control Panel > Internet Options	Control Panel > Internet Options	**Apple Menu > Control Panels > Internet**	**Internet Control Panel**
		Control Panel > Services	**inetmgr.exe**	**inetmgr.exe**		**Internet Information Services**

	AIX	Linux	OpenBSD	Solaris	NetWare 3	NetWare 4	NetWare 5	NetWare 6
Internet Setup Assistant								
Internetworking Configuration	ifconfig	ifconfig	ifconfig	ifconfig	install.nlm	**inetcfg.nlm**	**inetcfg.nlm**	**inetcfg.nlm**
intersvr	mount	mount	mount	mount	map.exe	map.exe	map.exe	map.exe
IP Configuration	ifconfig -a	ifconfig -a	ifconfig -a	ifconfig -a	config	config	config	config
IP Security Monitor	ipsectrcbuf			ipseckey monitor				
ipchains	chfilt genfilt	**ipchains** iptables	ipf			filtcfg.nlm	filtcfg.nlm	filtcfg.nlm
ipconfig	ifconfig	ifconfig	ifconfig	ifconfig	install.nlm	inetcfg.nlm	inetcfg.nlm	inetcfg.nlm
ipf	chfilt genfilt	ipchains iptables	**ipf**			filtcfg.nlm	filtcfg.nlm	filtcfg.nlm
ipfstat	lsfilt	iptables	**ipfstat**	ipsecconf		filtcfg.nlm	filtcfg.nlm	filtcfg.nlm
ipnat		ipchains iptables	**ipnat**			Action: 232	Action: 232	Action: 232
ipppstats	netstat -I *interface*	**ipppstats** pppstats	pppstats	netstat -I *interface*		ppptrace.nlm	pppcon.nlm ppptrace.nlm	
ipsecadm	chtun		**ipsecadm**	ipsecconf				
ipseccmd	chtun		ipsecadm	ipsecconf				
ipsecconf	chtun		ipsecadm	**ipsecconf**				
iptables	chfilt genfilt	**iptables** ipchains	ipf			filtcfg.nlm	filtcfg.nlm	filtcfg.nlm
iptrace	**iptrace** traceroute	traceroute	traceroute	traceroute		**iptrace.nlm**	**iptrace.nlm**	**iptrace.nlm**
ipv6	ifconfig	ifconfig	ifconfig	ifconfig		inetcfg.nlm	inetcfg.nlm	inetcfg.nlm
IPX Console		ipx_route				**ipxcon.nlm**	**ipxcon.nlm**	**ipxcon.nlm**
IPX Ping					**ipxping.nlm**	**ipxping.nlm**	**ipxping.nlm**	**ipxping.nlm**
ipx_configure		**ipx_configure**			ipxs.nlm	ipxs.nlm	ipxs.nlm	ipxs.nlm
ipx_interface		**ipx_interface**			ipxs.nlm	ipxs.nlm	ipxs.nlm	ipxs.nlm
ipx_route		**ipx_route**				ipxcon.nlm	ipxcon.nlm	ipxcon.nlm
ipxroute		ipx_route				ipxcon.nlm	ipxcon.nlm	ipxcon.nlm
ISDN Configuration Wizard		isdnctrl eiconctrl				inetcfg.nlm	inetcfg.nlm	inetcfg.nlm
isdnctrl		**isdnctrl**						
jar				jar			**jar**	**jar**
java	**java** jre			**java** java_g jre			java.nlm java.exe	java.nlm java.exe
java (Server)	java jre			java java_g jre			**java.nlm** java.exe	**java.nlm** java.exe
java (Client)	java jre			java java_g			**java.exe** java.nlm	**java.exe** java.nlm
java, java_g	**java** **java_g** jre			**java** java_g jre			java.nlm java.exe	java.nlm java.exe
java_g	java_g java jre			**java_g** java jre			java.nlm java.exe	java.nlm java.exe
javac				**javac**			**javac**	**javac**

DOS	Windows 9x	NT 4.0	NT 2000	Windows XP	Macintosh	
	inetwiz.exe netconn.exe		inetwiz.exe	inetwiz.exe cmak.exe	**Action: 96**	**Internet Setup Assistant**
	Control Panel > Network	Action: 178	Action: 180	Action: 180	Apple Menu > Control Panels > TCP/IP	**Internetworking Configuration**
intersvr.exe	net use	net use	net use	net use		**intersvr**
	winipcfg ipconfig	ipconfig	ipconfig	ipconfig	Apple Menu > Control Panel > TCP/IP	**IP Configuration**
			ipsecmon.exe	Action: 161		**IP Security Monitor**
			rrasmgmt.msc	rrasmgmt.msc		**ipchains**
	winipcfg.exe	**ipconfig.exe**	**ipconfig.exe**	**ipconfig.exe**	Apple Menu > Control Panels > TCP/IP	**ipconfig**
			rrasmgmt.msc	rrasmgmt.msc		**ipf**
		Action: 228	Action: 227	Action: 227		**ipfstat**
			Action: 231	Action: 231		**ipnat**
		rasadmin.exe	rasadmin.exe	rraswiz.exe		**ipppstats**
			secpol.msc	ipseccmd.exe secpol.msc ipsec6		**ipsecadm**
			secpol.msc	**ipseccmd.exe** secpol.msc ipsec6		**ipseccmd**
			secpol.msc	ipseccmd.exe secpol.msc ipsec6		**ipsecconf**
			rrasmgmt.msc	rrasmgmt.msc		**iptables**
	tracert.exe	tracert.exe	tracert.exe	tracert.exe	Action: 120	**iptrace**
				ipv6.exe		**ipv6**
		ipxroute.exe	ipxroute.exe	ipxroute.exe		**IPX Console**
	net diag					**IPX Ping**
		vwipxspx.exe	vwipxspx.exe	vwipxspx.exe		**ipx_configure**
	Control Panel > Network	Control Panel > Network	Control Panel > Network Connections	Control Panel > Network Connections		**ipx_interface**
		ipxroute.exe	ipxroute.exe	ipxroute.exe		**ipx_route**
		ipxroute.exe	**ipxroute.exe**	**ipxroute.exe**		**ipxroute**
	cfgwiz32	Control Panel > Network	Control Panel > Network Connections	**netsetup.exe**		**ISDN Configuration Wizard**
	cfgwiz32.exe					**isdnctrl**
	clspack.exe		clspack.exe	clspack.exe		**jar**
	jview.exe wjview.exe		jview.exe wjview.exe	jview.exe wjview.exe		**java**
	jview.exe wjview.exe		jview.exe wjview.exe	jview.exe wjview.exe		**java (Server)**
	jview.exe wjview.exe		jview.exe wjview.exe	jview.exe wjview.exe		**java (Client)**
	jview.exe wjview.exe		jview.exe wjview.exe	jview.exe wjview.exe		**java, java_g**
	jview.exe wjview.exe		jview.exe wjview.exe	jview.exe wjview.exe		**java_g**
						javac

	AIX	Linux	OpenBSD	Solaris	NetWare 3	NetWare 4	NetWare 5	NetWare 6
javadoc				**javadoc**			**javadoc**	**javadoc**
javah	**javah**			**javah**			**javah**	**javah**
javakey				**javakey**			**javakey**	
javap				**javap**			**javap**	**javap**
jdb				**jdb**				
jre	**jre** java			**jre** java java_g			java.nlm java.exe	java.nlm java.exe
jsh	ksh sh	sh tcsh	csh ksh	**jsh** sh		netbasic.nlm	netbasic.nlm	netbasic.nlm
jview	java jre			java java_g jre			java.nlm java.exe	java.nlm java.exe
kb16	chkbd lskbd	loadkeys setxkbmap kbdconfig	kbd setxkbmap	kbd loadkeys	keyb.nlm	keyb.nlm	keyb.nlm charset.nlm	keyb.nlm charset.nlm
kbd	chkbd lskbd	loadkeys setxkbmap kbdconfig	**kbd** setxkbmap	**kbd** loadkeys	keyb.nlm	keyb.nlm	keyb.nlm charset.nlm	keyb.nlm charset.nlm
kbdconfig	chkbd lskbd	**kbdconfig** setxkbmap loadkeys	setxkbmap kbd	kbd loadkeys	keyb.nlm	keyb.nlm	keyb.nlm charset.nlm	keyb.nlm charset.nlm
kbdrate		**kbdrate**						
kernelversion	uname -r	**kernelversion** uname -r	uname -r	uname -r	version nver.exe netbios I	version nver.exe	version nver.exe	version
Key Caps								
keyb	chkbd lskbd	loadkeys setxkbmap kbdconfig	kbd setxkbmap	kbd loadkeys	**keyb.nlm**	**keyb.nlm**	**keyb.nlm** charset.nlm	**keyb.nlm** charset.nlm
Keyboard Control Panel	chkbd lskbd	loadkeys setxkbmap kbdconfig	kbd setxkbmap	kbd loadkeys	keyb.nlm	keyb.nlm	keyb.nlm charset.nlm	keyb.nlm charset.nlm
Keyboard Properties	chkbd lskbd	loadkeys setxkbmap kbdconfig	kbd setxkbmap	kbd loadkeys	keyb.nlm	keyb.nlm	keyb.nlm charset.nlm	keyb.nlm charset.nlm
keytool		openssl	openssl				**keytool**	**keytool**
kill	**kill**	**kill** killall	**kill**	**kill**	unload	unload	unload	unload
killall	**killall** kill	**killall** skill kill	kill	**killall** kill	unload	unload	unload	unload
killall5	killall kill	**killall5** killall	kill	killall kill	unload	unload	unload	unload
klogd	errdemon syslogd	**klogd** sysklogd syslogd	syslogd	syslogd	conlog.nlm	conlog.nlm	conlog.nlm	conlog.nlm
ksh	**ksh** sh csh bsh	ash bsh bash sh sash tcsh	**ksh** rksh csh sh	**ksh** rksh csh jsh sh rsh		netbasic.nlm	netbasic.nlm	netbasic.nlm
kstat	lockstat			**kstat** lockstat			NetWare Management Portal	NetWare Remote Manger

DOS	Windows 9x	NT 4.0	NT 2000	Windows XP	Macintosh	
						javadoc
						javah
						javakey
						javap
	setdebug.exe					**jdb**
	jview.exe wjview.exe		jview.exe wjview.exe	jview.exe wjview.exe		**jre**
command.com	command.com	cmd.exe command.com	cmd.exe command.com	cmd.exe command.com		**jsh**
	jview.exe wjview.exe		**jview.exe** wjview.exe	**jview.exe** wjview.exe		**jview**
chcp keyb.com	chcp.com keyb.com Control Panel > Keyboard	**kb16.com** chcp.com Control Panel > Keyboard	**kb16.com** chcp.com Control Panel > Keyboard	**kb16.com** chcp.com Control Panel > Keyboard	Apple Menu > Control Panels > Keyboard	**kb16**
chcp keyb.com	chcp.com keyb.com Control Panel > Keyboard	chcp.com keyb.com Control Panel > Keyboard	chcp.com kb16.com Control Panel > Keyboard	chcp.com kb16.com Control Panel > Keyboard	Apple Menu > Control Panels > Keyboard	**kbd**
chcp keyb.com	chcp.com keyb.com Control Panel > Keyboard	chcp.com keyb.com Control Panel > Keyboard	chcp.com kb16.com Control Panel > Keyboard	chcp.com kb16.com Control Panel > Keyboard	Apple Menu > Control Panels > Keyboard	**kbdconfig**
	Control Panel > Keyboard	Control Panel > Keyboard	Control Panel > Keyboard	Control Panel > Keyboard	Apple Menu > Control Panels > Keyboard	**kbdrate**
ver	ver winver Control Panel > System	ver winver Control Panel > System	ver winver Control Panel > System	ver winver systeminfo Control Panel > System	Apple Menu > About This Computer	**kernelversion**
	osk.exe		osk.exe	osk.exe	**Apple Menu > Key Caps**	**Key Caps**
keyb.com chcp.com	**keyb.com** chcp.com Control Panel > Keyboard	**keyb.com** kb16.com chcp.com Control Panel > Keyboard	kb16.com chcp.com Control Panel > Keyboard	kb16.com chcp.com Control Panel > Keyboard	Apple Menu > Control Panels > Keyboard	**keyb**
chcp keyb.com	chcp.com keyb.com Control Panel > Keyboard	chcp.com keyb.com Control Panel > Keyboard	chcp.com keyb.com Control Panel > Keyboard	chcp.com keyb.com Control Panel > Keyboard	**Apple Menu > Control Panels > Keyboard**	**Keyboard Control Panel**
chcp keyb.com	**internat.exe** chcp.com keyb.com	**internat.exe** chcp.com keyb.com	**internat.exe** chcp.com keyb.com	**internat.exe** chcp.com keyb.com	Apple Menu > Control Panels > Keyboard	**Keyboard Properties**
			certutil.exe	certutil.exe		**keytool**
	taskman.exe	**kill.exe**	tskill.exe	taskkill.exe tskill.exe	command + alt + esc command + q	**kill**
	taskman.exe	kill.exe	tskill.exe	taskkill.exe tskill.exe	<command> + <alt> + <esc> <command> + <q>	**killall**
	taskman.exe	kill.exe	tskill.exe	taskkill.exe tskill.exe	<command> + <alt> + <esc> <command> + <q>	**killall5**
	wbemcntl.exe	eventvwr.exe	eventvwr.exe	eventvwr.exe		**klogd**
command.com	command.com	cmd.exe command.com	cmd.exe command.com	cmd.exe command.com		**ksh**
						kstat

	AIX	Linux	OpenBSD	Solaris	NetWare 3	NetWare 4	NetWare 5	NetWare 6
label		e2label	disklabel	labelit		install.nlm	nwconfig.nlm	c1start > Tools > Disk Management
labelit		e2label	disklabel	**labelit**		install.nlm	nwconfig.nlm	c1start > Tools > Disk Management
LANG=*language*	**LANG=*languag e***	**LANG=*languag e***	**LANG=*languag e***	**LANG=*languag e***				
lastcomm	**lastcomm** history	history	**lastcomm** history	**lastcomm** history	Action: 102	Action: 102	Action: 102	Action: 102
lb_find	**lb_find**	slist nwsfind			slist.exe display servers	nlist server /B display servers	nlist server /B display servers	nlist server /B display servers
ldapadd				**ldapadd**		nwadmn32.exe netadmin.exe	nwadmn32.exe	nwadmn32.exe
ldifde				ldapadd ldapdelete		uimport.exe	uimport.exe	ice.exe
less	cat more	**less** cat more	cat more	**less** cat more	edit.nlm	view.nlm	view.nlm	view.nlm
less, page	pg more	less more	**less** **page**	pg	edit.nlm	view.nlm	view.nlm	view.nlm
License Maintenance Utility	ls_admin chlicense					install.nlm	**licmaint.nlm** nwconfig.nlm	**licmaint.nlm** nwadmn32.exe
License Manager	ls_admin					install.nlm	nwconfig.nlm licmaint.nlm	nwconfig.nlm licmaint.nlm
lilo	bootlist	**lilo**		bootlist				
limit	**limit**	**limit**	**limit**	**limit**				
link	**link** ln	ln lndir	ln lndir	**link** ln				
linuxconf	smit smitty	**linuxconf**		admintool	syscon.exe sysconW.exe	netadmin.exe nwadmn32.exe	nwadmn32.exe consoleone.exe consoleonedos. exe	nwadmn32.exe consoleone.exe consoleonedos. exe
list devices	lspv	sfdisk -s	df -k	format	**list devices**	**list devices**	**list devices**	**list devices**
list stage	who -r	chkconfig --list runlevel		who -r			**list stage**	**list stage**
List Storage Adapters	smitty lsdev	lspci		prtdiag			**List Storage Adapters**	**List Storage Adapters**
listdir	ls -al | grep ^d	ls -al | grep ^d	ls -al | grep ^d	ls -al | grep ^d	**listdir** *path*	ndir *path* /do	ndir *path* /do	ndir *path* /do
listusers	Action: 29	Action: 29	Action: 29	**listusers** dispuid logins Action: 29	syscon.exe sysconW.exe	netadmin.exe nwadmn32.exe	nwadmn32.exe consoleone.exe consoleonedos. exe	nwadmn32.exe consoleone.exe consoleonedos. exe
ln	**ln** link	**ln** lndir	**ln** lndir	**ln** link				
lndir	link ln	**lndir** ln	**lndir** ln	link ln				
load *disk_driver*	cfgmgr			drvconfig	**load *disk_driver***	**load *disk_driver***	**load *disk_driver***	**load *disk_driver***
loadfix								
loadkeys	chkbd lskbd	**loadkeys** setxkbmap kbdconfig	kbd setxkbmap	kbd loadkeys	keyb.nlm	keyb.nlm	keyb.nlm charset.nlm	keyb.nlm charset.nlm
Loadstage	Init	Init	Init	Init			Loadstage	loadstage
Local Users and Groups Manager	smit smitty mkuser mkgroup	userconf useradd groupadd	adduser groupadd	admintool useradd groupadd	syscon.exe sysconW.exe	netadmin.exe nwadmn32.exe	nwadmn32.exe consoleone.exe consoleonedos. exe	nwadmn32.exe consoleone.exe consoleonedos. `exe

DOS	Windows 9x	NT 4.0	NT 2000	Windows XP	Macintosh	
label.exe	**label.exe**	**label.exe**	**label.exe**	**label.exe**	Action: 112	label
label.exe	label.exe	label.exe	label.exe	label.exe	Action: 112	labelit
country	Control Panel > Regional Settings	Control Panel > Regional Settings	Control Panel > Regional Options	Control Panel > Regional/Language Options	Apple Menu > Control Panels > Numbers	LANG=*language*
doskey.com	doskey.com	doskey.exe	doskey.exe	doskey.exe		lastcomm
	net view	net view	net view	net view	Apple Menu > Chooser Apple Menu > Network Browser	lb_find
			Action: 136	dsadd.exe		ldapadd
			ldifde.exe csvde.exe	**ldifde.exe** csvde.exe		ldifde
type more.com	type more.com	type more.com	type more.com	type more.com	Action: 82	less
type	type	type	type	type	Action: 82	less, page
		llsmgr.exe	llsmgr.exe	llsmgr.exe		License Maintenance Utility
		llsmgr.exe	llsmgr.exe	llsmgr.exe		License Manager
		Action: 125	Action: 125	bootcfg.exe	Hold down the keys command + alt + e + *1 or 0* during startup.	lilo
buffers						limit
	right-click > Create Shortcut	right-click > Create Shortcut	right-click > Create Shortcut	right-click > Create Shortcut	**alt + command + Drag the file or folder you want to make an alias of**	link
	control.exe	control.exe	control.exe	control.exe	Apple Menu > Control Panels	linuxconf
fdisk.exe	fdisk.exe	windisk.exe	compmgmt.msc	compmgmt.msc	Apple Menu > Apple System Profiler	list devices
						list stage
	Action: 172	Control Panel > SCSI Adapters	Action: 171	Action: 171		List Storage Adapters
dir *. dir /ad	dir *. dir /ad	dir *. dir /ad	dir *. dir /ad	dir *. dir /ad		listdir
	Control Panel > Users	net user	net user wizmgr.exe	net user wizmgr.exe	Apple Menu > Control Panels > Multiple Users	listusers
	right-click > Create Shortcut	right-click > Create Shortcut	right-click > Create Shortcut	right-click > Create Shortcut	**alt + command + Drag the file or folder you want to make an alias of**	ln
	right-click > Create Shortcut	right-click > Create Shortcut	right-click > Create Shortcut	right-click > Create Shortcut	**alt + command + Drag the file or folder you want to make an alias of**	lndir
	Control Panel > Add New Hardware	Control Panel > SCSI Adapters	Control Panel > Add/Remove Hardware	Control Panel > Add/Remove Hardware		load *disk_driver*
loadfix.com		**loadfix.com**	**loadfix.com**	**loadfix.com**		loadfix
chcp keyb.com	chcp.com keyb.com Control Panel > Keyboard	chcp.com keyb.com Control Panel > Keyboard	chcp.com kb16.com Control Panel > Keyboard	chcp.com kb16.com Control Panel > Keyboard	Apple Menu > Control Panels > Keyboard	loadkeys
	Control Panel > Users	usrmgr.exe musrmgr.exe	**lusrmgr.msc** compmgmt.msc	**lusrmgr.msc** compmgmt.msc	Apple Menu > Control Panels > File Sharing > Users & Groups	Local Users and Groups Manager

	AIX	Linux	OpenBSD	Solaris	NetWare 3	NetWare 4	NetWare 5	NetWare 6
locale	**locale**	**locale**		**locale**				
lock	**lock** xlock		**lock** xlock	xlock	monitor.nlm	monitor.nlm	scrsaver.nlm	scrsaver.nlm
lockstat	**lockstat**			**lockstat** kstat			NetWare Management Portal	NetWare Remote Manager
log	users	**log** users nwuserlist	users	**log** users	userlist.exe	nlist user /A /B	nlist user /A /B	nlist user /A /B
login	**login**	**login**	**login**	**login**	**login**	**login**	**login**	**login**
logins	who	who	who	**logins**	syscon.exe sysconW.exe	netadmin.exe nwadmn32.exe	nwadmn32.exe	nwadmn32.exe
logname	**logname** whoami	**logname** whoami	**logname** whoami	**logname** whoami	whoami.exe Action: 5	whoami.exe Action: 5	Action: 5	Action: 5
logoff	logout exit	logout exit	logout exit	logout exit	**logoff.exe**	**logoff.exe**	**logoff.exe**	**logoff.exe**
logout	**logout** exit	**logout** exit	**logout** exit	**logout** exit	**logout.exe**	**logout.exe**	**logout.exe**	**logout.exe**
Logview	smit alog	cat /var/log/messages	cat /var/log/messages	cat /var/adm/ messages	load edit /system/sys$log. err	view /system/sys$log. err	view /system/sys$log. err	view /system/sys$log. err
lp	**lp**	**lp** lpr	lpr	**lp** lpr	nprint.exe	nprint.exe	nprint.exe	
lpadmin	smitty print	lpc	lpc	**lpadmin**	psc.exe pconsole.exe	psc.exe pconsole.exe	nwpmw32.exe nwadmn32.exe ndpsm.nlm	nwadmn32.exe ndpsm.nlm
lpc	smitty print	**lpc**	**lpc**	lpadmin	psc.exe pconsole.exe	psc.exe pconsole.exe	nwpmw32.exe nwadmn32.exe ndpsm.nlm	nwadmn32.exe ndpsm.nlm
lpd	**lpd**	**lpd**	**lpd**	lpsched	pconsole.exe psc.exe	pconsole.exe psc.exe	nwpmw32.exe nwadmn32.exe ndpsm.nlm	nwadmn32.exe ndpsm.nlm
lpmove	qmov smit print	lpc		**lpmove**	pconsole.exe psc.exe	pconsole.exe psc.exe	nwpmw32.exe nwadmn32.exe ndpsm.nlm	nwpmw32.exe nwadmn32.exe ndpsm.nlm
lpq	**lpq**	**lpq**	**lpq**	**lpq**	pconsole.exe	pconsole.exe	nwpmw32.exe ndpsm.nlm	nwadmn32.exe ndpsm.nlm
lpr	**lpr** lp	**lpr** lp	**lpr**	**lpr** lp	nprint.exe	nprint.exe	nprint.exe	
lprm	**lprm** cancel	**lprm** cancel	**lprm**	**lprm** cancel	pconsole.exe psc.exe	pconsole.exe psc.exe	nwpmw32.exe nwadmn32.exe ndpsm.nlm	nwadmn32.exe ndpsm.nlm
lpsched	lpd	lpd	lpd	**lpsched**	pserver.exe	nptwin95.exe	nptwin95.exe	nptwin95.exe
lpset	smit print	/etc/printcap lpc	/etc/printcap lpc	**lpset** lpadmin printmgr	psc.exe pconsole.exe	psc.exe pconsole.exe	nwpmw32.exe nwadmn32.exe ndpsm.nlm	nwadmn32.exe ndpsm.nlm
lpstat	**lpstat** qchk	**lpstat**	lpq	**lpstat**	pconsole.exe	pconsole.exe	nwpmw32.exe nwadmn32.exe ndpsm.nlm	nwadmn32.exe ndpsm.nlm
lptest	**lptest**		**lptest**	**lptest**				
lpusers	qpri			**lpusers**	pconsole.exe psc.exe	pconsole.exe psc.exe	nwpmw32.exe nwadmn32.exe ndpsm.nlm	nwadmn32.exe ndpsm.nlm
ls	**ls**	**ls** dir nwdir	**ls**	**ls**	ndir.exe	**ls.exe** ndir.exe	ndir.exe	ndir.exe

DOS	Windows 9x	NT 4.0	NT 2000	Windows XP	Macintosh	
	Control Panel > Regional Settings	Control Panel > Regional Settings	Control Panel > Regional Options	Control Panel > Regional and Language Options	Apple Menu > Control Panels > Numbers	**locale**
	Action: 150	CTRL+ALT+DELETE > lock workstation Action: 150	CTRL+ALT+DELETE > lock workstation Action: 150	CTRL+ALT+DELETE > lock workstation Action: 150		**lock**
						lockstat
		quser.exe	quser.exe	quser.exe		**log**
	Action: 175	Action: 174	Action: 176	Action: 176		**login**
		net user	net user	net user		**logins**
						logname
	net logoff	**logoff.exe**	**logoff.exe**	**logoff.exe**	<command> + <Y>	**logoff**
	net logoff	logoff.exe	logoff.exe	logoff.exe	<command> + <Y>	**logout**
		logview.exe eventvwr.exe	eventvwr.exe	eventvwr.exe		**Logview**
print.exe	type *file* > LPT1	print.exe lpr.exe	print.exe lpr.exe	print.exe lpr.exe	<command> + <p> File > Print	**lp**
	Control Panel > Printers	Control Panel > Printers	Control Panel > Printers	Control Panel > Printers and Faxes	Action: 115	**lpadmin**
	Control Panel > Printers	Control Panel > Printers	Control Panel > Printers	Control Panel > Printers and Faxes	Action: 115	**lpc**
	Action: 168	Action: 168	Action: 168	Action: 168	Apple Menu > Chooser	**lpd**
					Action: 115	**lpmove**
	Conrtol Panel > Printers net print	**lpq.exe** Conrtol Panel > Printers net print	**lpq.exe** Conrtol Panel > Printers net print	**lpq.exe** Conrtol Panel > Printers net print	Action: 115	**lpq**
print.exe	type *file* > LPT1	**lpr.exe** print.exe	**lpr.exe** print.exe	**lpr.exe** print.exe	command + p File > Print	**lpr**
	net print /delete	net print /delete	net print /delete	net print /delete	Action: 107	**lprm**
	Action: 168	Action: 168	Action: 168	Action: 168	Action: 179	**lpsched**
	Control Panel > Printers	Control Panel > Printers	Control Panel > Printers	Control Panel > Printers and Faxes	Action: 115	**lpset**
	Control Panel > Printers net print	Control Panel > Printers net print	Control Panel > Printers net print	Control Panel > Printers and Faxes net print	Action: 115	**lpstat**
	Action: 236	Action: 236	Action: 236	Action: 236		**lptest**
		Action: 257	Action: 258	Action: 258		**lpusers**
dir	dir	dir	dir	dir		**ls**

	AIX	Linux	OpenBSD	Solaris	NetWare 3	NetWare 4	NetWare 5	NetWare 6
lsallq	**lsallq**	lpstat	lpq	lpstat dtprintinfo	pconsole.exe	pconsole.exe	nwpmw32.exe nwadmn32.exe ndpsm.nlm	nwadmn32.exe ndpsm.nlm
lsattr	**lsattr**			devattr	list devices	list devices	list devices	list devices
lscfg	**lscfg** topas svmon	top dmesg	top dmesg	dmesg prtconf	monitor.nlm Display Interrupts	monitor.nlm Display Interrupts	monitor.nlm Display Interrupts	monitor.nlm Display Interrupts
lsdev	**lsdev**			devinfo	list devices	list devices	list devices	list devices
ls-F	ls	**ls-F** ls	ls	**ls-F** ls	ndir.exe	ndir.exe ls.exe	ndir.exe	ndir.exe
lsfilt	**lsfilt**	iptables	ipf	ipsecconf		filtcfg.nlm	filtcfg.nlm	filtcfg.nlm
lsfont	**lsfont**	fslsfonts	fslsfonts	fslsfonts				
lsfs	**lsfs**	dumpe2fs	dumpfs	fstyp	volume volumes	vmvolumes volume volumes	vmvolumes volume volumes	vmvolumes volume volumes
lsgroup	**lsgroup** cat /etc/group	cat /etc/group	cat /etc/group	dispgid cat /etc/group	syscon.exe sysconW.exe	netadmin.exe nwadmn32.exe	nwadmn32.exe consoleone.exe consoleonedos. exe	nwadmn32.exe consoleone.exe consoleonedos. exe
lsitab	**lsitab**	cat /etc/inittab	cat /etc/rc.conf	cat /etc/inittab	edit autoexec.ncf	edit autoexec.ncf	edit autoexec.ncf	edit autoexec.ncf
lskbd	**lskbd**	kbdconfig	kbd -l	kbd -t	keyb.nlm	keyb.nlm	keyb.nlm	keyb.nlm
lslicense	**lslicense**				version	version install.nlm	version nwconfig.nlm	version nwconfig.nlm
lslpp	**lslpp** sysck	rpm	pkg_info	pkginfo	install > product options	install > product options	nwconfig > product options	nwconfig > product options
lsmod		**lsmod**	modstat	modinfo	modules	modules	modules	modules
lsnamsv	**lsnamsv**	cat /etc/resolv.conf	cat /etc/resolv.conf	cat /etc/resolv.conf	edit \etc\resolv.cfg	edit \etc\resolv.cfg	edit \etc\resolv.cfg	edit \etc\resolv.cfg
lsnfsexp	**lsnfsexp** lsnfsmnt	showmount -e	showmount -e	dfshares showmount -e	display servers	display servers	display servers	display servers
lsnfsmnt	**lsnfsmnt** lsnfsexp	showmount -e	showmount -e	dfshares showmount -e	map.exe	map.exe	map.exe	map.exe
lsof	fuser	**lsof** fuser	fstat	fuser	monitor > File open / Lock activity	monitor > File open/lock activity	monitor > File open/lock activity	monitor > File open/lock activity
lspci	smit devices	**lspci** scanpci	scanpci	prtdiag		ncmcon.nlm	ncmcon.nlm	ncmcon.nlm
lsps	**lsps**	swapon swapoff mkswap	swapctl	swap			swap	swap
lspv	**lspv**	sfdisk -s	df -k	format	list devices	list devices	list devices	list devices
lsuser	**lsuser**	cat /etc/passwd	userinfo	cat /etc/passwd admintool	syscon.exe sysconW.exe	netadmin.exe nwadmn32.exe	nwadmn32.exe consoleone.exe consoleonedos. exe	nwadmn32.exe consoleone.exe consoleonedos. exe
lynx	defaultbrowser	**lynx** netscape	**lynx**	netscape				
m64config		xf86config	xf86config	**m64config**				
Mac Help	man apropos whatis	man info apropos	man info apropos	man apropos whatis		help	help	help
macfile					afp.nlm	afp.nlm		
mach	uname -M	arch	arch machine	**mach** arch	cpucheck.nlm	cpucheck.nlm	cpucheck.nlm	cpucheck.nlm

DOS	Windows 9x	NT 4.0	NT 2000	Windows XP	Macintosh	
	Control Panel > Printers net print	Control Panel > Printers net print	Control Panel > Printers net print	Control Panel > Printers and Faxes net print	Action: 115	**lsallq**
	Action: 172	Control Panel > SCSI Adapters	Action: 171	Action: 171	Apple Menu > Apple System Profiler > Devices and Volumes	**lsattr**
msd.exe	msinfo32.exe Control Panel > System	msinfo32.exe Control Panel > System winmsd.exe	msinfo32.exe Control Panel > System winmsd.exe	systeminfo.exe Control Panel > System winmsd.exe	Apple Menu > Apple System Profiler	**lscfg**
	Action: 190	Control Panel > Devices	Action: 210	Action: 210		**lsdev**
dir	dir	dir	dir	dir		**ls-F**
		Action: 228	Action: 227	Action: 227		**lsfilt**
	Control Panel > Fonts	Control Panel > Fonts	Control Panel > Fonts	Control Panel > Fonts	Apple Menu > Control Panels > Appearence > Fonts	**lsfont**
chkdsk.exe	Action: 261	Action: 261	Action: 261	Action: 261	Select harddrive and press <command> + I	**lsfs**
		net group	net group wizmgr.exe	net group wizmgr.exe	Apple Menu > Control Panels > File Sharing > Users & Groups	**lsgroup**
type autoexec.bat	type autoexec.bat	type autoexec.bat	type autoexec.bat	type autoexec.bat	Apple Menu > Control Panels > Extensions Manager *selections...*	**lsitab**
keyb.com	keyb.com	keyb.com	kb16.com	kb16.com	Apple Menu > Control Panels > Keyboard	**lskbd**
		Control Panel > Licensing	Control Panel > Licensing	Control Panel > Licensing		**lslicense**
	Control Panel > Add/Remove Programs	Control Panel > Add/Remove Programs	Control Panel > Add/Remove Programs	Control Panel > Add/Remove Programs		**lslpp**
	Action: 211	Control Panel > Services	Action: 210	Action: 210	Apple menu > Control Panels > Extensions Manager	**lsmod**
	Action: 139	Action: 192	Action: 191	Action: 191	Control Panel > TCPIP	**lsnamsv**
	net view *server*	net view *server*	net view *server*	net view *server*	Apple Menu > Network Browser	**lsnfsexp**
	net share	net share	net share	net share	Apple Menu > Network Browser	**lsnfsmnt**
	netwatch.exe	srvmgr.exe	srvmgr.exe	srvmgr.exe		**lsof**
	Action: 190		Action: 177	Action: 177		**lspci**
	Action: 149	Action: 148	Action: 147	Action: 147		**lsps**
fdisk.exe	fdisk.exe	windisk.exe	compmgmt.msc	compmgmt.msc	Apple Menu > Apple System Profiler	**lspv**
	Control Panel > Users	usrmgr.exe musrmgr.exe	compmgmt.msc	compmgmt.msc	Apple Menu > Control Panels > Multiple Users	**lsuser**
	netscape.exe iexplore.exe	netscape.exe iexplore.exe	netscape.exe iexplore.exe	netscape.exe iexplore.exe	Action: 81	**lynx**
	Action: 250	Action: 250	Action: 250	Action: 250	Apple Menu > Control Panels > Monitors	**m64config**
help.com fasthelp.exe	winhelp.exe helpctr.exe	winhlp32.exe help.exe ntbooks.exe	winhelp.exe help.exe ntbooks.exe	winhelp.exe help.exe helpctr.exe	**command + ?** **Help > Mac Help**	**Mac Help**
		macfile.exe	**macfile.exe**	**macfile.exe**		**macfile**
msd.exe	Control Panel > System	Control Panel > System	Control Panel > System	Control Panel > System	Apple Menu > Apple System Profiler	**mach**

	AIX	Linux	OpenBSD	Solaris	NetWare 3	NetWare 4	NetWare 5	NetWare 6
machine	uname	arch uname	**machine** arch uname	arch mach uname	cpucheck.nlm	cpucheck.nlm	cpucheck.nlm	cpucheck.nlm
Magnifier		xmag	xmag	xmag				
mail, Mail, mailx	**mail, Mail, mailx** sendmail post	**mail, Mail, mailx** sendmail post	**mail, Mail, mailx** sendmail	**mail, Mail, mailx** sendmail rmail				
mailq	**mailq** sendmail -bs folders	**mailq** sendmail -bs messages folders	**mailq** sendmail -bs msgs -l	**mailq** sendmail -bs				
mailwrapper	sendmail spost	**mailwrapper** sendmail spost	sendmail smtpd	sendmail				
Make Alias	ln	ln	ln	ln				
Make Compatible								
makecab	compress pack	compress bzip2 gzip zip	compress gzip	compress gzip zip bzip2		flag *files* lc	flag *files* lc	flag *files* lc
makeuser	mkuser	useradd	adduser	useradd	**makeuser.exe**	Action: 277	Action: 277	Action: 277
man	**man** whatis	**man** info	**man** info	**man** whatis		help	help	help
Managing Folder and File Access Wizard	smit mknfsexp	vi /etc/exports	vi /etc/exports	vi /etc/dfs/dfstab	syscon.exe grant.exe	nwadmn32.exe rights.exe	nwadmn32.exe rights.exe	nwadmn32.exe rights.exe
Managing Security Settings console	smit smitty	userconf	usermod	admintool	syscon.exe sysconW.exe	netadmin.exe nwadmn32.exe	nwadmn32.exe consoleone.exe	nwadmn32.exe consoleone.exe
map	mount	mount ncpmount smbmount	mount	mount	**map.exe**	**map.exe**	**map.exe**	**map.exe**
mattrib	chmod	**mattrib** chmod	chmod	chmod	flag.exe syscon.exe rights.exe	flag.exe nwadmn32.exe rights.exe	flag.exe nwadmn32.exe rights.exe	flag.exe nwadmn32.exe rights.exe
mbadblocks	fsck	**mbadblocks** badblocks fsck	fsck	fsck Action: 43	vrepair.nlm	vrepair.nlm	vrepair.nlm nss /rebuild nss /menu	vrepair.nlm ConsoleOne > Server > Media
mc		**mc**		dtfile	filer.exe	filer.exe	filer.exe	filer.exe
mcat	flcopy	**mcat**						
mcd	cd chdir	**mcd** cd chdir	cd chdir	cd chdir				
mcedit	vi tvi	**mcedit** vi emacs	vi	vi dtpad	edit.nlm	edit.nlm	edit.nlm	edit.nlm
mcopy	cp dtfile	**mcopy** cp mc	cp	cp dtfile	ncopy.exe filer.exe	ncopy.exe filer.exe	xcopy.exe copy.exe Action: 1	ncopy.exe filer.exe
md, mkdir	mkdir mkdirhier	mkdir mkdirhier	mkdir mkdirhier	mkdir mkdirhier				
mdb	dbx	gdb	gdb	**mdb** adb				
mdel	dosdel rm unlink	**mdel** rm	rm	rm unlink	filer.exe	filer.exe nwadmn32.exe	filer.exe nwadmn32.exe	filer.exe nwadmn32.exe
mdeltree	rm -r	**mdeltree**	rm -r	rm -r	filer.exe	filer.exe	filer.exe	filer.exe
mdir	dosdir ls	**mdir** dir ls	ls	ls	ndir.exe	ndir.exe	ndir.exe	ndir.exe

DOS	Windows 9x	NT 4.0	NT 2000	Windows XP	Macintosh	
msd.exe	Control Panel > System	Control Panel > System	Control Panel > System	Control Panel > System	Apple Menu > Apple System Profiler	**machine**
	magnify.exe		**magnify.exe**	**magnify.exe**		**Magnifier**
	msimn.exe	msimn.exe	msimn.exe	msimn.exe	Action: 199	**mail, Mail, mailx**
	msimn.exe		msimn.exe	msimn.exe	Action: 199	**mailq**
			services.msc	services.msc		**mailwrapper**
	right-click > Create Shortcut	right-click > Create Shortcut	right-click > Create Shortcut	right-click > Create Shortcut	**alt + command + Drag the file or folder you want to make an alias of**	**Make Alias**
setver.exe	**mkcompat.exe** setver.exe	setver.exe	setver.exe	setver.exe		**Make Compatible**
	cabbit.exe	compact.exe	**makecab** compact.exe	**makecab** compact.exe	Action: 79	**makecab**
						makeuser
fasthelp.exe help.com	winhelp.exe helpctr.exe	winhlp32.exe help.exe	winhelp.exe help.exe	winhelp.exe helpctr.exe	command + ? Help > Mac Help	**man**
	Action: 23	**shrpubw.exe** Action: 23	shrpubw.exe Action: 23	shrpubw.exe Action: 23	Apple Menu > Control Panels > File Sharing	**Managing Folder and File Access Wizard**
		poledit.exe	**secpol.msc** dcpol.msc poledit.exe	**secpol.msc** dcpol.msc poledit.exe		**Managing Security Settings console**
	net use	net use	net use	net use	Apple Menu > Network Browser	**map**
attrib.exe	attrib.exe	attrib.exe	attrib.exe	attrib.exe	Select icon > <command> + i	**mattrib**
scandisk.exe chkdsk.exe	scandisk.exe chkdsk.exe	chkntfs.exe chkdsk.exe	chkntfs.exe chkdsk.exe	chkntfs.exe chkdsk.exe	Action: 101	**mbadblocks**
dosshell.exe	explorer.exe	explorer.exe	explorer.exe	explorer.exe		**mc**
diskcopy.com	diskcopy.com	diskcopy.com	diskcopy.com	diskcopy.com	Action: 110	**mcat**
cd chdir	cd chdir	cd chdir	cd chdir	cd chdir	Action: 51	**mcd**
edit.com	edit.com notepad.exe	edit.com notepad.exe	edit.com notepad.exe	edit.com notepad.exe	Action: 82	**mcedit**
copy xcopy.exe	copy xcopy.exe Action: 1	copy xcopy.exe Action: 1	copy xcopy.exe Action: 1	copy xcopy.exe Action: 1	alt + Drag a file command + d	**mcopy**
md mkdir	**md mkdir**	**md mkdir**	**md mkdir**	**md mkdir**	command + n	**md, mkdir**
debug.exe	debug.exe	debug.exe	debug.exe	debug.exe		**mdb**
del erase	del erase	del erase	del erase	del erase	<command> + <Backspace>	**mdel**
deltree.exe	deltree.exe	Action: 15	Action: 15	Action: 15	<command> + <Backspace>	**mdeltree**
dir	dir	dir	dir	dir		**mdir**

	AIX	Linux	OpenBSD	Solaris	NetWare 3	NetWare 4	NetWare 5	NetWare 6
mdu	du	**mdu** du	du	du	ndir.exe	ndir.exe	ndir.exe	ndir.exe
Media Player 32		cdp cdplay mpg123 xplaycd	cdio	audioplay audiotool				
mem	svmon	free alloc	top	prtconf alloc	memory	memory	memory	memory
memory	svmon	free alloc	top	prtconf alloc	**memory**	**memory**	**memory**	**memory**
Memory Control Panel	swapon lsps mkps rmps	swapon swapoff mkswap	swapctl	swap			swap	swap
mesg	**mesg**	**mesg**	**mesg**	**mesg**	caston.exe castoff.exe	send /a send /a=c	set disable broadcast notifications process	set disable broadcast notifications process
messages	sendmail -bp mailq folders	**messages** sendmail -bp mailq folders	sendmail -bp mailq msgs -l	sendmail -bp mailq				
mformat	dosformat	**mformat**	newfs	fdformat -d	install.nlm	install.nlm	nwconfig.nlm	ConsoleOne
mhmail	**mhmail**	**mhmail**	mail Mail mailx	mail Mail mailx				
Microsoft Backup	backup rdump	dump rdump	dump rdump	ufsdump	sbackup.nlm	sbackup.nlm	nwback32.exe	nwback32.exe
Microsoft File Transfer	xmodem	sx sz sb						
Microsoft Script Debugger	csh -n	tcsh -n	csh -n	csh -n				
Microsoft System Information	lscfg svmon	dmesg free	dmesg top	dmesg prtconf	monitor.nlm Display Interrupts	monitor.nlm Display Interrupts	monitor.nlm Display Interrupts	monitor.nlm Display Interrupts
midiplay		playmidi	**midiplay**	audioplay				
minicom	ate	**minicom**	cu	cu				
mkboot	**mkboot** bosboot	mkbootdisk Action: 69	Action: 69	Action: 69				
mkbootdisk	mkboot bosboot	**mkbootdisk** Action: 69	Action: 69	Action: 69				
mkdev	**mkdev**	MAKEDEV	MAKEDEV	devfsadm	install.nlm	install.nlm	hdetect.nlm nwconfig.nlm	hdetect.nlm nwconfig.nlm
mkdir	**mkdir** mkdirhier	**mkdir** mkdirhier	**mkdir** mkdirhier	**mkdir** mkdirhier				
mkdirhier	**mkdirhier** mkdir	**mkdirhier** mkdir	**mkdirhier** mkdir	**mkdirhier** mkdir				
mkdosfs, mkfs.msdos	mkfs	**mkdosfs** **mkfs.msdos** mkfs	newfs_msdos mkfs	mkfs	install.nlm	install.nlm	nwconfig.nlm	ConsoleOne
mke2fs, mkfs.ext2	mkfs	**mke2fs** **mkfs.ext2** mkfs	mkfs	mkfs	install.nlm	install.nlm	nwconfig.nlm	nwconfig.nlm
mkfs	**mkfs**	**mkfs**	newfs	**mkfs**	install.nlm	install.nlm	nwconfig.nlm	ConsoleOne
mkfs.minix	mkfs	**mkfs.minix** mkfs	mkfs	mkfs	install.nlm	install.nlm	nwconfig.nlm	nwconfig.nlm
mkgroup	**mkgroup**	groupadd	groupadd	groupadd	syscon.exe sysconW.exe	netadmin.exe nwadmn32.exe	nwadmn32.exe consoleone.exe consoleonedos. exe c1start.ncf	nwadmn32.exe consoleone.exe consoleonedos. exe c1start.ncf

DOS	Windows 9x	NT 4.0	NT 2000	Windows XP	Macintosh	
dir	dir	dir	dir	dir		**mdu**
	mplayer2.exe mplayer.exe	mplayer2.exe	**mplay32.exe** mplayer2.exe	**mplay32.exe** mplayer2.exe	Action: 2	**Media Player 32**
mem	**mem**	**mem** winver.exe	**mem** winver.exe	**mem** winver.exe	Apple Menu > About This Computer	**mem**
mem	mem	mem winver.exe	mem winver.exe	mem winver.exe	Apple Menu > About This Computer	**memory**
	Action: 149	Action: 148	Action: 147	Action: 147	**Apple Menu > Control Panels > Memory**	**Memory Control Panel**
						mesg
	msimn.exe	msimn.exe	msimn.exe	msimn.exe	Action: 199	**messages**
format.com	format.com	format.com	format.com	format.com	Action: 129	**mformat**
	msimn.exe		msimn.exe	msimn.exe	Action: 199	**mhmail**
msbackup.exe restore.exe	**msbackup.exe** backup.exe	ntbackup.exe backup.exe	ntbackup.exe	ntbackup.exe		**Microsoft Backup**
	filexfer.exe					**Microsoft File Transfer**
	wscript //X cscript //X	wscript //X cscript //X	**msscrdbg.exe** wscript //X	wscript //X cscript //X		**Microsoft Script Debugger**
msd.exe	**msinfo32.exe** Control Panel > System	**msinfo32.exe** winmsd.exe	**msinfo32.exe** winmsd.exe	**msinfo32.exe** winmsd.exe	Apple Menu > Apple System Profiler	**Microsoft System Information**
	mplayer.exe mplayer2.exe	mplayer2.exe	mplay32.exe mplayer2.exe	mplay32.exe mplayer2.exe	Double click the QuickTime Player icon.	**midiplay**
	hypertrm.exe	hypertrm.exe	hypertrm.exe	hypertrm.exe		**minicom**
sys.com format a: /s	sys.com format a: /s	winnt /ox winnt32 /ox	makeboot.exe	makeboot.exe		**mkboot**
sys.com format a: /s	sys.com format a: /s	winnt /ox winnt32 /ox	makeboot.exe	makeboot.exe		**mkbootdisk**
device=*device* devicehigh= *device*	Control Panel > Add New Hardware	Control Panel > Devices	Control Panel > Add/Remove Hardware	Control Panel > Add Hardware	Apple Menu > Control Panels > Extensions Manager	**mkdev**
md mkdir	md mkdir	md mkdir	md mkdir	md mkdir	<command> + n	**mkdir**
md mkdir	md mkdir	md mkdir	md mkdir	md mkdir	command + n	**mkdirhier**
format.com	format.com	format.com	format.com	format.com	Action: 129	**mkdosfs, mkfs.msdos**
format.com	format.com	format.com	format.com	format.com	Action: 129	**mke2fs, mkfs.ext2**
format.com	format.com	format.com	format.com	format.com	Action: 129	**mkfs**
format.com	format.com	format.com	format.com	format.com	Action: 129	**mkfs.minix**
		usrmgr.exe musrmgr.exe addgrpw.exe net group	compmgmt.msc wizmgr.exe net group	compmgmt.msc wizmgr.exe net group	Apple Menu > Control Panels > File Sharing > Users & Groups	**mkgroup**

	AIX	Linux	OpenBSD	Solaris	NetWare 3	NetWare 4	NetWare 5	NetWare 6
mkhosts	**mkhosts**	vi /etc/hosts	vi /etc/hosts	vi /etc/hosts	edit \etc\hosts	edit \etc\hosts	edit \etc\hosts	edit \etc\hosts
mkitab	**mkitab**	vi /etc/inittab	vi /etc/rc.conf	vi /etc/inittab	edit autoexec.ncf	edit autoexec.ncf	edit autoexec.ncf	edit autoexec.ncf
mknamsv	**mknamsv**	vi /etc/resolv.conf	vi /etc/resolv.conf	vi /etc/resolv.conf	edit \etc\resolv.cfg	edit \etc\resolv.cfg	edit \etc\resolv.cfg	edit \etc\resolv.cfg
mknfsexp	**mknfsexp**	exportfs	Cross Reference Note: 8	exportfs share	flag *file* -sh	flag *file* +sh /FO	flag *file* +sh /FO	flag *file* +sh /FO
mknfsmnt	**mknfsmnt**	mount	mount	mount	mount	vmmount mount	vmmount mount	vmmount mount
mkprtsv	**mkprtsv**	lpc	lpc	lpadmin	pconsole.exe psc.exe	pconsole.exe psc.exe	nwpmw32.exe nwadmn32.exe ndpsm.nlm	nwadmn32.exe ndpsm.nlm
mkps	**mkps**	swapon swapoff mkswap	swapctl	swap			swap	swap
mkque	**mkque**	lpc	lpc	lpadmin	pconsole.exe psc.exe	pconsole.exe psc.exe	nwpmw32.exe nwadmn32.exe ndpsm.nlm	nwadmn32.exe ndpsm.nlm
mkquedev	**mkquedev**			lpadmin	pconsole.exe psc.exe	pconsole.exe psc.exe	nwpmw32.exe nwadmn32.exe ndpsm.nlm	nwadmn32.exe ndpsm.nlm
mkswap	mkps lsps rmps	**mkswap**	swapctl	swap			swap	swap
mktcpip	**mktcpip** smit	netconf ifconfig	ifconfig	admintool ifconfig	install.nlm	inetcfg.nlm	inetcfg.nlm	inetcfg.nlm
mkuser	**mkuser** smit	adduser useradd	adduser	useradd admintool	syscon.exe sysconW.exe	netadmin.exe nwadmn32.exe	nwadmn32.exe consoleone.exe	nwadmn32.exe consoleone.exe
mlabel		**mlabel** e2label	disklabel	labelit		install.nlm	nwconfig.nlm	c1start > Tools > Disk Management
mmd	mkdir	**mmd** mkdir	mkdir	mkdir	filer.exe	filer.exe nwadmn32.exe	filer.exe nwadmn32.exe	filer.exe nwadmn32.exe
mmount	mount	**mmount** mount	mount_msdos mount	mount	mount	mount	mount	mount
mmove	mv	**mmove** mv	mv	mv	filer.exe	filer.exe	filer.exe	filer.exe
Mobile Synchronize		rsync		filesync				
mode	stty	stty	stty	stty				
Modem Control Panel							cpecfg.nlm	cpecfg.nlm
modinfo		lsmod	modstat	**modinfo**				
modload	smit > Devices > Install / Configure Devices	insmod	**modload**	**modload**	install.nlm	install.nlm	hdetect.nlm nwconfig.nlm	hdetect.nlm nwconfig.nlm
modstat		lsmod	**modstat**	modinfo				
modules		lsmod	modstat	modinfo	**modules**	**modules**	**modules**	**modules**
modules.conf	smit device	**modules.conf**	config -e -o bsd.new /bsd	touch /reconfigure	startup.ncf	startup.ncf	startup.ncf	startup.ncf
mofcomp				**mofcomp**				
monitor	ps gv	ps -ef	ps -auxw	ps -ef	**monitor.nlm** modules	**monitor.nlm** modules	**monitor.nlm** modules	**monitor.nlm** modules
Monitors Control Panel		xf86config	xf86config	afbconfig ffbconfig				

DOS	Windows 9x	NT 4.0	NT 2000	Windows XP	Macintosh	
	edit \windows\hosts	edit \winnt\system32\driver\etc\hosts	edit \winnt\system32\driver\etc\hosts	edit \windows\system32\driver\etc\hosts		**mkhosts**
edit autoexec.bat	edit autoexec.bat	edit autoexec.bat	edit autoexec.bat	edit autoexec.bat	Apple Menu > Control Panels > Extensions Manager *selections...*	**mkitab**
	Action: 139	Action: 192	Action: 191	Action: 191	Apple Menu > Control Panels > TCP/IP	**mknamsv**
share	Cross Reference Note: 119 net share	Cross Reference Note: 119 net share	Cross Reference Note: 119 net share	Cross Reference Note: 119 net share	Apple Menu > Control Panels > File Sharing	**mknfsexp**
	net use	net use	net use	net use		**mknfsmnt**
	Control Panel > Printers	Control Panel > Printers	Control Panel > Printers	Control Panel > Printers	Action: 115	**mkprtsv**
	Action: 149	Action: 148	Action: 147	Action: 147		**mkps**
	Control Panel > Printers	Control Panel > Printers	Control Panel > Printers	Control Panel > Printers and Faxes	Action: 115	**mkque**
	Control Panel > Printers	Control Panel > Printers	Control Panel > Printers	Control Panel > Printers	Apple Menu > Chooser Application Menu > PrintMonitor	**mkquedev**
	Action: 149	Action: 148	Action: 147	Action: 147		**mkswap**
	Control Panel > Network	Control Panel > Network	Control Panel > Network Connections	Control Panel > Network Connections netsetup.exe	Apple Menu > Control Panels > TCP/IP	**mktcpip**
	Control Panel > Users	addusrw.exe usrmgr.exe	compmgmt.msc wizmgr.exe	compmgmt.msc wizmgr.exe	Apple Menu > Control Panels > Multiple Users	**mkuser**
label.exe	label.exe	label.exe	label.exe	label.exe	Action: 112	**mlabel**
md mkdir	md mkdir	md mkdir	md mkdir	md mkdir	<command> + N	**mmd**
	net use	net use	net use	net use		**mmount**
move.exe	move.exe	move.exe	move.exe	move.exe	Select file or folder > Drag the file or folder	**mmove**
	mobsync.exe		**mobsync.exe**	**mobsync.exe**		**Mobile Synchronize**
mode.com	**mode.com**	**mode.com**	**mode.com**	**mode.com**	Apple > Control Panels > Keyboard	**mode**
	Control Panels > Modems	Control Panels > Modems	Control Panels > Modems	Control Panels > Modems	**Apple Menu > Control Panels > Modem**	**Modem Control Panel**
	Action: 211	Control Panel > Services	Action: 210	Action: 210	Apple menu > Control Panels > Extentions Manager	**modinfo**
device=*device* devicehigh=*device*	Control Panel > Add New Hardware	Control Panel > Devices	Control Panel > Add/Remove Hardware	Control Panel > Add Hardware	Apple Menu > Control Panels > Extensions Manager	**modload**
	Action: 211	Control Panel > Services	Action: 210	Action: 210	Apple menu > Control Panels > Extentions Manager	**modstat**
	Action: 211	Control Panel > Services	Action: 210	Action: 210	Apple menu > Control Panels > Extentions Manager	**modules**
config.sys	Action: 62	Control Panel > Devices	Control Panel > Add/Remove Hardware	Control Panel > Add/Remove Hardware	Apple Menu > Control Panels > Extensions Manager *selections...*	**modules.conf**
	mofcomp.exe		**mofcomp.exe**	**mofcomp.exe**		**mofcomp**
	taskmgr.exe	query.exe taskmgr.exe	query.exe taskmgr.exe	query.exe taskmgr.exe		**monitor**
	Control Panel > Display > Settings	Control Panel > Display > Settings	Control Panel > Display > Settings	Control Panel > Display > Settings	**Apple Menu > Control Panels > Monitors**	**Monitors Control Panel**

	AIX	Linux	OpenBSD	Solaris	NetWare 3	NetWare 4	NetWare 5	NetWare 6
more	**more** cat	**more** cat	**more** cat	**more** cat	edit.nlm	view.nlm	view.nlm	view.nlm
mount	**mount**	**mount**	**mount**	**mount**	**mount**	**mount**	**mount**	**mount**
mount_ext2fs	mount	mount	**mount_ext2fs** mount	mount	mount	mount	mount	mount
mount_msdos	mount	mmount mount	**mount_msdos** mount	mount	mount	mount	mount	mount
mount_ufs	mount	mount	**mount_ufs** mount	mount	mount	mount	mount	mount
mountvol	mount	mount	mount	mount	map.exe	map.exe	map.exe	map.exe
Mouse Control Panel		mouseconfig						
mouseconfig		**mouseconfig**						
move	mv	mv mc	mv	mv	filer.exe	filer.exe	filer.exe	filer.exe
Move File	mv	mv mc	mv	mv	filer.exe	filer.exe	filer.exe	filer.exe
Move From Trash		Action: 54			salvage.exe	filer.exe > Salvage Deleted Files	filer.exe > Salvage Deleted Files	filer.exe > Salvage Deleted Files
Move To Trash	rm	rm	rm	rm	filer.exe	filer.exe nwadmn32.exe	filer.exe nwadmn32.exe	filer.exe nwadmn32.exe
mpartition	chpv	**mpartition** fdisk	fdisk	format fdisk	install.nlm	install.nlm	nwconfig.nlm	nwconfig.nlm
mpdetect	cpu_state -l			psradm -a mpstat		**mpdetect.nlm**	display processors	display processors
mpdriver	cpu_state			psradm		**mpdriver.nlm**	start processors stop processors	start processors stop processors
mpg123		**mpg123** cdp, cdplay xplaycd	cdio	audioplay audiotool				
mrd	rmdir	**mrd** rmdir	rmdir	rmdir	filer.exe	filer.exe	filer.exe	filer.exe
mren	mv	**mren** mv	mv	mv	rendir.exe filer.exe	rendir.exe filer.exe	filer.exe nwadmn32.exe	filer.exe nwadmn32.exe
mrinfo			**mrinfo**					
msbackup.exe	backup rdump	dump rdump	dump rdump	ufsdump	sbackup.nlm	sbackup.nlm	nwback32.exe	nwback32.exe
mscdex	mount	mount	mount	mount	map.exe	map.exe	map.exe	map.exe
mscdexnt	mount	mount	mount	mount	cdrom.nlm cd	cdrom.nlm cd	cdrom.nlm cdinst.nlm cd	cdrom.nlm cdinst.nlm cd
msd	lscfg svmon	dmesg free	dmesg top	dmesg prtconf	monitor.nlm	monitor.nlm	monitor.nlm Display Interrupts	monitor.nlm Display Interrupts
msg	write wall	write wall	write wall	write wall	send broadcast	send broadcast	send broadcast	send broadcast
mtype	cat more	**mtype** cat more	cat more	cat more	edit.nlm	view.nlm	view.nlm	view.nlm
Multiple Users Control Panel	smit	userconf useradd	adduser	admintool useradd	syscon.exe sysconW.exe	netadmin.exe nwadmn32.exe	nwadmn32.exe consoleone.exe consoleonedos.exe	nwadmn32.exe consoleone.exe consoleonedos.exe
mutt	mhmail mail mailx	**mutt** pine mailx	mail mailx	dtmail mail mailx				
mv	**mv**	**mv**	**mv**	**mv**	filer.exe	filer.exe	filer.exe	filer.exe

DOS	Windows 9x	NT 4.0	NT 2000	Windows XP	Macintosh	
more.com type edit.exe	**more.com** type	**more.com** type	**more.com** type	**more.com** type	Action: 82	**more**
	net use	net use	net use	net use		**mount**
	net use	net use	net use	net use		**mount_ext2fs**
	net use	net use	net use	net use		**mount_msdos**
	net use	net use	net use	net use		**mount_ufs**
			mountvol.exe	**mountvol.exe**		**mountvol**
	Control Panel > Mouse	Control Panel > Mouse	Control Panel > Mouse	Control Panel > Mouse	**Apple Menu > Control Panels > Mouse**	**Mouse Control Panel**
	Control Panel > Mouse	Control Panel > Mouse	Control Panel > Mouse	Control Panel > Mouse	Apple Menu > Control Panels > Mouse	**mouseconfig**
move.exe	**move.exe** explorer.exe	**move.exe** explorer.exe	**move.exe** explorer.exe	**move.exe** explorer.exe	Select file or folder > Drag the file or folder	**move**
move.exe	move.exe	move.exe	move.exe	move.exe	**Select file or folder > Drag the file or folder**	**Move File**
undelete	Action: 56	Action: 56	Action: 56	Action: 56	**Double-click on trashcan and drag the files to the desktop**	**Move From Trash**
del erase	del erase	del erase	del erase	del erase	**command + Backspace**	**Move To Trash**
fdisk.exe	fdisk.exe	windisk.exe	diskmgmt.msc	diskmgmt.msc diskpart.exe	Action: 64	**mpartition**
						mpdetect
						mpdriver
	mplayer2.exe mplayer.exe	mplayer2.exe	mplayer2.exe mplay32.exe	mplayer2.exe mplay32.exe	AppleCD Audio Player Action: 132	**mpg123**
rd rmdir	rd rmdir	rd rmdir	rd rmdir	rd rmdir	command + Backspace	**mrd**
rename move.exe label	rename move.exe	rename move.exe	rename move.exe	rename move.exe	Action: 113	**mren**
			mrinfo.exe	**mrinfo.exe**		**mrinfo**
msbackup.exe restore.exe	msbackup.exe backup.exe	ntbackup.exe backup.exe	ntbackup.exe	ntbackup.exe		**msbackup.exe**
mscdex.exe	**mscdex.exe** Action: 90	windisk.exe	diskmgmt.msc	diskmgmt.msc		**mscdex**
mscdex.exe	mscdex.exe	**mscdexnt.exe** mscdex.exe	**mscdexnt.exe** mscdex.exe	**mscdexnt.exe** mscdex.exe		**mscdexnt**
msd.exe	Control Panel > System msinfo32.exe	winmsd.exe	winmsd.exe	winmsd.exe	Apple Menu > Apple System Profiler	**msd**
	winpopup.exe	**msg.exe** net send	**msg.exe** net send	**msg.exe** net send		**msg**
type more.com	type more.com	type more.com	type more.com	type more.com	Action: 82	**mtype**
	Control Panel > Users	usrmgr.exe musrmgr.exe	compmgmt.msc	compmgmt.msc	**Apple Menu > Control Panels > Multiple Users**	**Multiple Users Control Panel**
	msimn.exe	msimn.exe	msimn.exe	msimn.exe	Action: 199	**mutt**
move.exe	move.exe explorer.exe	move.exe explorer.exe	move.exe explorer.exe	move.exe explorer.exe	Select file or folder > Drag the file or folder	**mv**

	AIX	Linux	OpenBSD	Solaris	NetWare 3	NetWare 4	NetWare 5	NetWare 6
mvdir	**mvdir** mv	mv	mv	**mvdir** mv	filer.exe	filer.exe	filer.exe	filer.exe
mwm	**mwm**	fvwm2	fvwm	fvwm2	<CTRL> + <ESC>	<CTRL> + <ESC>	<CTRL> + <ESC>	<CTRL> + <ESC>
name	hostname	hostname	hostname	hostname	**name**	**name**	**name**	**name**
named	**named**	**named**	**named**	**in.named**		**named.nlm**	**named.nlm**	**named.nlm**
named.reload		ndc reload	**named.reload**			named.nlm	named.nlm	named.nlm
named.restart		ndc restart	**named.restart**			named.nlm	named.nlm	named.nlm
named4	**named4**	named	named	named		named.nlm	named.nlm	named.nlm
named8	**named8**	named	named	named		named.nlm	named.nlm	named.nlm
namerslv	**namerslv**	vi /etc/resolv.conf	vi /etc/resolv.conf	vi /etc/resolv.conf	edit \etc\resolv.cfg	edit \etc\resolv.cfg	edit \etc\resolv.cfg	edit \etc\resolv.cfg
native2ascii				**native2ascii**			**native2ascii**	**native2ascii**
navigator	man apropos whatis	man info apropos	man info apropos	**navigator** docviewer		help	help	help
ncftp	ftp	**ncftp** ftp	ftp	ftp				
ncftpget	rcp	**ncftpget** ncftpput scp rcp	scp rcp	rcp	ncopy.exe	ncopy.exe	ncopy.exe	ncopy.exe
ncftpput	Li	**ncftpput** ncftpget scp rcp	scp rcp	rcp	ncopy.exe	ncopy.exe	ncopy.exe	ncopy.exe
ncopy	cp dtfile	**ncopy** cp mc	cp	cp dtfile	**ncopy.exe** filer.exe	**ncopy.exe** filer.exe	**ncopy.exe** filer.exe	**ncopy.exe** filer.exe
ncpmount	mount	**ncpmount**	mount	mount	map.exe	map.exe	map.exe	map.exe
ncpumount	umount	**ncpumount** smbumount umount	umount	umount	dismount	dismount	dismount	dismount
ndc	named4 named8	**ndc** named	**ndc** named	in.named		named.nlm	named.nlm	named.nlm
ndir	ls	nwdir ls	ls	ls	**ndir.exe**	**ndir.exe**	**ndir.exe**	**ndir.exe**
NDS Maintenance						**dsmaint.nlm**	Action: 41	Action: 41
NDS Manager						**ndsmgr32.exe**	**ndsmgr32.exe**	consoleone.exe
net accounts	pwdadm passwd	vi /etc/login.defs chage passwd	passwd	vi /etc/default/pass wd passwd	syscon.exe	nwadmn32.exe	nwadmn32.exe	nwadmn32.exe
net continue	kill -CONT	kill -CONT	kill -CONT	kill -CONT				
net diag					ipxping.nlm	ipxping.nlm	ipxping.nlm	ipxping.nlm
net file				clear_locks	flag.exe	flag.exe nwadmn32.exe	flag.exe nwadmn32.exe	flag.exe nwadmn32.exe
net group	smitty group	groupmod groupadd groupdel	groupmod groupadd rmgroup	groupmod admintool	syscon.exe	nwadmn32.exe	nwadmn32.exe	nwadmn32.exe
net localgroup	mkgroup smit	userconf groupadd	groupadd	admintool groupadd	syscon.exe sysconW.exe	netadmin.exe nwadmn32.exe	nwadmn32.exe	nwadmn32.exe
net logoff	logout exit	logout exit	logout exit	logout exit	logout.exe	logout.exe	logout.exe	logout.exe
net name	hostname	hostname	hostname	hostname	name	name	name	name
net password	passwd yppasswd	passwd yppasswd	passwd	passwd yppasswd nispasswd	setpass.exe Action: 37	setpass.exe Action: 37	setpass.exe Action: 37	Action: 37
net print	lpq lprm cancel	lpq pqrm lprm	lpq lprm	lpq lprm cancel	pconsole.exe psc.exe	pconsole.exe psc.exe	nwpmw32.exe nwadmn32.exe ndpsm.nlm	nwadmn32.exe ndpsm.nlm

DOS	Windows 9x	NT 4.0	NT 2000	Windows XP	Macintosh	
move	move	move	move	move	Select file or folder > Drag the file or folder	**mvdir**
	progman.exe	progman.exe	progman.exe	progman.exe	Finder	**mwm**
	Control Panel > System	hostname.exe	hostname.exe	hostname.exe		**name**
		dnsadmin.exe	Action: 21	Action: 21		**named**
		dnsadmin.exe	Action: 21	Action: 21		**named.reload**
		dnsadmin.exe	Action: 21	Action: 21		**named.restart**
		dnsadmin.exe	Action: 21	Action: 21		**named4**
		dnsadmin.exe	Action: 21	Action: 21		**named8**
	Action: 139	Action: 192	Action: 191	Action: 191	Apple Menu > Control Panels > TCP/IP	**namerslv**
						native2ascii
fasthelp.exe help.com	winhelp.exe helpctr.exe	winhlp32.exe help.exe ntbooks.exe	winhelp.exe help.exe	winhelp.exe help.exe helpctr.exe	command + ? Help > Mac Help	**navigator**
	ftp.exe	ftp.exe	ftp.exe	ftp.exe		**ncftp**
	robocopy.exe ftp.exe	rcp.exe ftp.exe	rcp.exe ftp.exe	rcp.exe ftp.exe		**ncftpget**
	robocopy.exe ftp.exe	rcp.exe ftp.exe	rcp.exe ftp.exe	rcp.exe ftp.exe		**ncftpput**
copy xcopy.exe	copy xcopy.exe	copy xcopy.exe	copy xcopy.exe	copy xcopy.exe	alt + Drag a file command + d	**ncopy**
	net use	net use	net use	net use	Apple Menu > Network Browser	**ncpmount**
	net use *drive* /delete	net use *drive* /delete	net use *drive* /delete	net use *drive* /delete		**ncpumount**
		Control Panel > Services	dnsmgmt.msc Action: 131	dnsmgmt.msc dnswiz.exe		**ndc**
dir	dir	dir	dir	dir		**ndir**
			ntdsutil.exe	ntdsutil.exe		**NDS Maintenance**
			ntdsutil.exe	ntdsutil.exe		**NDS Manager**
	net accounts	**net accounts**	**net accounts**	**net accounts**		**net accounts**
		net continue	net continue	net continue		**net continue**
	net diag					**net diag**
		net file	**net file**	**net file**		**net file**
		net group addgrpw.exe	**net group** wizmgr.exe	**net group** wizmgr.exe		**net group**
		net localgroup addgrpw.exe usrmgr.exe	**net localgroup** compmgmt.msc wizmgr.exe	**net localgroup** compmgmt.msc wizmgr.exe	Apple Menu > Control Panels > File Sharing > Users & Groups	**net localgroup**
	net logoff	logoff.exe	logoff.exe	logoff.exe	command + y	**net logoff**
	Control Panel > System	**net name** hostname.exe	**net name** hostname.exe	**net name** hostname.exe		**net name**
	net password Control Panel > passwords	usrmgr.exe Action: 229	compmgmt.msc Action: 229	compmgmt.msc Action: 229	Action: 200	**net password**
	net print Control Panel > Printers	**net print** Control Panel > Printer	**net print** Control Panel > Printer	**net print** Control Panel > Printers and Faxes	Action: 107	**net print**

	AIX	Linux	OpenBSD	Solaris	NetWare 3	NetWare 4	NetWare 5	NetWare 6
net send	write wall	write wall	write wall	write wall	send.exe send broadcast	send.exe send broadcast	broadcast send	broadcast send
net session	finger	finger	finger	finger	userlist.exe	nlist user /A /B	nlist user /A /B	nlist user /A /B
net share	exportfs	exportfs	Cross Reference Note: 8	share exportfs	flag *file* -sh	flag *file* +sh /FO	flag *file* +sh /FO	flag *file* +sh /FO
net start	inetd	xinetd	inetd	inetd	load	load	load	load
net statistics	ifconfig	ifconfig	ifconfig	ifconfig	monitor > LAN/WAN Drivers	monitor > LAN/WAN Drivers	monitor > LAN/WAN Drivers	monitor > LAN/WAN Drivers
net stop	kill	kill	kill	kill	unload	unload	unload	unload
net time	ntpq	Action: 50	Action: 50	ntpq	systime.exe	systime.exe timesync.nlm	timesync.nlm	timesync.nlm
net use	mount	mount	mount	mount	map.exe	map.exe	map.exe	map.exe
net user	mkuser smit smitty	adduser useradd userconf	adduser	useradd admintool	syscon.exe sysconW.exe	netadmin.exe nwadmn32.exe	nwadmn32.exe consoleone.exe consoleonedos.exe	nwadmn32.exe consoleone.exe consoleonedos.exe
net view					display servers	display servers	display servers	display servers
netadmin	smit smitty mkuser mkgroup	userconf useradd groupadd	adduser groupadd	admintool useradd groupadd	syscon.exe sysconW.exe	**netadmin.exe** nwadmn32.exe	nwadmn32.exe consoleone.exe consoleonedos.exe	nwadmn32.exe consoleone.exe consoleonedos.exe
netbasic	ksh sh csh bsh	ash bsh bash sh sash tcsh	csh ksh rksh sh	csh jsh ksh rksh sh rsh		**netbasic.nlm**	**netbasic.nlm**	**netbasic.nlm**
netconf	cfginet smit ifconfig	**netconf** ifconfig	ifconfig	admintool ifconfig	install.nlm	inetcfg.nlm	inetcfg.nlm	inetcfg.nlm
netconfig	ifconfig	**netconfig** ifconfig	ifconfig	ifconfig	install.nlm	inetcfg.nlm	inetcfg.nlm	inetcfg.nlm
netpmon	**netpmon** topas filemon	top	top	perfmeter top	monitor.nlm	monitor.nlm	monitor.nlm	monitor.nlm
netscape	defaultbrowser	**netscape** lynx	lynx	**netscape** lynx				
netstat	**netstat**	**netstat**	**netstat**	**netstat**	tcpcon.nlm	tcpcon.nlm	tcpcon.nlm	tcpcon.nlm
NetWare Administrator	smit smitty mkuser mkgroup	userconf useradd groupadd	adduser groupadd	admintool useradd groupadd	syscon.exe sysconW.exe	**nwadmn32.exe** netadmin.exe	**nwadmn32.exe** consoleone.exe consoleonedos.exe	**nwadmn32.exe** consoleone.exe consoleonedos.exe
NetWare Backup/Restore	backup rdump	backup rdump	backup rdump	ufsdump	sbackup.nlm	sbackup.nlm	**sbcon.nlm** nwback32.exe	**sbcon.nlm** nwback32.exe
NetWare Configuration	smit smitty	linuxconf		admintool	install.nlm	install.nlm	**nwconfig.nlm**	**nwconfig.nlm**
NetWare Enterprise Web Server		httpd	httpd	httpd			**nsweb.ncf** nvxwebup.ncf	**nsweb.ncf** nvxwebup.ncf
Netware Installation	cfgmgr devinstall	isapnp		drvconfig			**hdetect.nlm**	**hdetect.nlm**
NetWare Login	login	login	login	login	**loginw31.exe** **loginw95.exe** **loginw32.exe**	**loginw31.exe** **loginw95.exe** **loginw32.exe**	**loginw31.exe** **loginw95.exe** **loginw32.exe**	**loginw31.exe** **loginw95.exe** **loginw32.exe**
NetWare Management Portal	topas netpmon	top linuxconf	top	perfmeter top	fconsole.exe	servman.nlm	**NetWare Management Portal**	NetWare Remote Manager

DOS	Windows 9x	NT 4.0	NT 2000	Windows XP	Macintosh	
	winpopup.exe	**net send** msg.exe	**net send** msg.exe	**net send** msg.exe		**net send**
		net session	**net session**	**net session**	Apple Menu > Control Panels > File Sharing > Activity Monitor	**net session**
share	**net share** Cross Reference Note: 119	**net share** Cross Reference Note: 119	**net share** Cross Reference Note: 119	**net share** Cross Reference Note: 119	Control Panel > File Sharing	**net share**
		net start	**net start**	**net start**		**net start**
		net statistics	**net statistics**	**net statistics**		**net statistics**
	net stop	**net stop**	**net stop**	**net stop**		**net stop**
	net time	**net time**	**net time** w32tm.exe	**net time** w32tm.exe	Apple Menu >Control Panels > Date & Time	**net time**
	net use	**net use**	**net use**	**net use**		**net use**
	Control Panel > Users	**net user** addusrw.exe usrmgr.exe	**net user** wizmgr.exe compmgmt.msc	**net user** wizmgr.exe compmgmt.msc	Apple Menu > Control Panels > Multiple Users	**net user**
	net view	**net view**	**net view**	**net view**	Apple Menu > Chooser Apple Menu > Network Browser	**net view**
	Control Panel > Users	addusrw.exe usrmgr.exe musrmgr.exe net user	compmgmt.msc wizmgr.exe net user	compmgmt.msc wizmgr.exe net user	Apple Menu > Control Panels > File Sharing > Users & Groups	**netadmin**
command.com	command.com	cmd.exe command.com	cmd.exe command.com	cmd.exe command.com		**netbasic**
	Control Panel > Network	Control Panel > Network	Control Panel > Network Connections	netsetup.exe	Apple Menu > Control Panel > TCP/IP	**netconf**
	Control Panel > Network	Control Panel > Network	Control Panel > Network and Dial Up Connections	Control Panel > Network and Dial Up Connections	Apple Menu > Control Panels > TCP/IP	**netconfig**
	sysmon.exe	perfmon.exe	perfmon.exe	perfmon.exe	Apple Menu > About This Computer	**netpmon**
	netscape.exe iexplore.exe	netscape.exe iexplore.exe	netscape.exe iexplore.exe	netscape.exe iexplore.exe	Action: 81	**netscape**
	netstat.exe	**netstat.exe**	**netstat.exe**	**netstat.exe**		**netstat**
	Control Panel > Users	addusrw.exe usrmgr.exe musrmgr.exe net user	compmgmt.msc wizmgr.exe net user	compmgmt.msc wizmgr.exe net user	Apple Menu > Control Panels > File Sharing > Users & Groups	**NetWare Administrator**
msbackup.exe restore.exe	msbackup.exe backup.exe	msbackup.exe backup.exe	ntbackup.exe	ntbackup.exe		**NetWare Backup/Restore**
		wizmgr.exe	wizmgr.exe compmgmt.msc	wizmgr.exe compmgmt.msc		**NetWare Configuration**
			inetmgr.exe	inetmgr.exe	Apple Menu > Control Panels > Web Sharing	**NetWare Enterprise Web Server**
	Control Panel > Add New Hardware	Control Panel	Control Panel > Add/Remove Hardware	Control Panel > Add Hardware		**Netware Installation**
	Action: 175	Action: 174	Action: 176	Action: 176		**NetWare Login**
		perfmon.exe	perfmon.exe	perfmon.exe	Apple Menu > About This Computer	**NetWare Management Portal**

	AIX	Linux	OpenBSD	Solaris	NetWare 3	NetWare 4	NetWare 5	NetWare 6
NetWare Remote Manager	topas netpmon	top linuxconf	top	perfmeter top	fconsole.exe	servman.nlm	NetWare Management Portal	**NetWare Remote Manager**
NetWatcher	fuser	lsof fuser	fstat	fuser	monitor > connections	monitor > connections	monitor > connections	monitor > connections
Network and Dial-up Connections	pppdial cu	dip wvdial pppd	ppp pppd	aspppd		Action: 121	niascfg.nlm nwccon.nlm	Action: 121
Network Browser					display servers	display servers	display servers	display servers
Network Client Administrator					dosgen.exe	dosgen.exe	dosgen.exe	dosgen.exe
Network Monitor	atmstat fddistat tokstat netstat -I *interface*	ipppstats pppstats netstat -I *interface*	pppstats slstats netstat -I *interface*	syncstat netstat -I *interface*	tcpcon.nlm	tcpcon.nlm ipxcon.nlm	tcpcon.nlm ipxcon.nlm	tcpcon.nlm ipxcon.nlm
Network Setup Wizard	cfginet smit	netconf		admintool	install.nlm	inetcfg.nlm	inetcfg.nlm	inetcfg.nlm
newfs	mkfs	mkfs	**newfs**	**newfs**	install.nlm	install.nlm	nwconfig.nlm	nwconfig.nlm
newfs_msdos	mkfs	mkdosfs mkfs.msdos mkfs	**newfs_msdos** mkfs	mkfs	install.nlm	install.nlm	nwconfig.nlm	ConsoleOne
newgrp	**newgrp**	**newgrp**	groupmod	**newgrp**	syscon.exe	nwadmn32.exe	nwadmn32.exe	nwadmn32.exe
newkey	**newkey** chkey	ssh-keygen dnskeygen	ssh-keygen	**newkey** chkey			keytool -genkey	keytool -genkey
newsyslog	alog strclean	logrotate	**newsyslog**	**newsyslog** strclean	conlog.nlm	conlog.nlm	conlog.nlm	conlog.nlm
newusers		**newusers**	adduser -batch		userdef.exe			
nice	**nice**	**nice**	**nice**	**nice**	load	load	load	load
nimconfig	**nimconfig**			re-preinstall	dosgen.exe	dosgen.exe	dosgen.exe	dosgen.exe
nlist	smit smitty	linuxconf		admintool		**nlist**	**nlist**	**nlist**
NLS Setup utility	ls_admin chlicense					**setupnls.nlm**	**setupnls.nlm**	**setupnls.nlm**
nlsfunc	Action: 63	Action: 63	Action: 63	Action: 63				
nlunpack	uncompress tar	uncompress unzip tar	uncompress gunzip tar	uncompress unzip tar	**nlunpack.exe** nwxtract.exe	nwxtract.exe	tar.nlm unzip.nlm jar	tar.nlm unzip.nlm jar
nmbd		**nmbd**			netbios.exe			
Notepad	vi tvi	vi emacs	vi	vi dtpad	edit.nlm	edit.nlm	edit.nlm	edit.nlm
Novell Licensing Services Manager	ls_admin chlicense					**nlsman32.exe** nwadmn32	**nlsman32.exe** nwadmn32	**nlsman32.exe** nwadmn32
Novell Printer Manager	lpq	lpq	lpq	lpq	pconsole.exe psc.exe	pconsole.exe psc.exe	**nwpmw32.exe** nwadmn32.exe ndpsm.nlm	nwadmn32.exe ndpsm.nlm
npath	env	env	env	env	search	**npath.exe** search	search display environment	search display environment
nprint	lp lpr	**nprint** lp lpr	lpr	lp lpr	**nprint.exe**	**nprint.exe**	**nprint.exe**	
nprinter	lpd	lpd	lpd	lpsched	pserver.exe **nprinter.nlm**	**nprinter.exe** **nprinter.nlm**	**nprinter.exe** **nprinter.nlm**	**nprinter.exe** **nprinter.nlm**
Nprinter Manager	lpd	lpd	lpd	lpsched	pserver.exe	**nptwin95.exe**	**nptwin95.exe**	**nptwin95.exe**
nsend	write wall	**nsend** write wall	write wall	write wall	send broadcast	send broadcast	send broadcast	send broadcast

DOS	Windows 9x	NT 4.0	NT 2000	Windows XP	Macintosh	
		perfmon.exe	perfmon.exe	perfmon.exe		**NetWare Remote Manager**
	netwatch.exe	srvmgr.exe	srvmgr.exe	srvmgr.exe	Apple > Control Panel > File Sharing	**NetWatcher**
	Action: 22	**rasphone.exe**	**rasphone.exe** rasdial.exe	**rasphone.exe**	Apple Menu > Control Panels > Modem	**Network and Dial-up Connections**
	net view	net view	net view	net view	**Apple Menu > Network Browser**	**Network Browser**
		ncadmin.exe	rbfg.exe	rbfg.exe		**Network Client Administrator**
	atmadm.exe	**netmon.exe**	**netmon.exe**	**netmon.exe**		**Network Monitor**
	Control Panel > Network	Control Panel > Network	Control Panel > Network Connections	**netsetup.exe** Control Panel > Network Connections	Apple Menu > Control Panels > TCP/IP	**Network Setup Wizard**
format.com	format.com	format.com	format.com	format.com	Action: 129	**newfs**
format.com	format.com	format.com	format.com	format.com	Action: 129	**newfs_msdos**
		net group	net group	net group		**newgrp**
						newkey
	wbemcntl.exe	eventvwr.exe	eventvwr.exe	eventvwr.exe		**newsyslog**
		addusers.exe	addusers.exe			**newusers**
		start	start	start		**nice**
		ncadmin.exe	rbfg.exe	rbfg.exe		**nimconfig**
		quser.exe	quser.exe	dsget *object* dsquery *object*		**nlist**
		llsmgr.exe	llsmgr.exe	llsmgr.exe		**NLS Setup utility**
nlsfunc.exe country	**nlsfunc.exe** Control Panel > Regional Settings	**nlsfunc.exe** Control Panel > Regional Settings	**nlsfunc.exe** Control Panel > Regional Options	**nlsfunc.exe** Control Panel > Regional/Language Options	Numbers Control Panel	**nlsfunc**
expand.exe		expand.exe	expand.exe	expand.exe	Action: 79	**nlunpack**
	net start	net start	net start	net start		**nmbd**
edit.com	**notepad.exe** edit.com wordpad.exe	**notepad.exe** edit.com wordpad.exe	**notepad.exe** edit.com wordpad.exe	**notepad.exe** edit.com wordpad.exe	Action: 82	**Notepad**
		llsmgr.exe	llsmgr.exe	llsmgr.exe		**Novell Licensing Services Manager**
	Conrtol Panel > Printers	lpq.exe Conrtol Panel > Printers	lpq.exe Conrtol Panel > Printers	lpq.exe Conrtol Panel > Printers	Action: 115	**Novell Printer Manager**
path	path	path	path	path		**npath**
print.exe	type *file* > LPT1	print.exe lpr.exe	print.exe lpr.exe	print.exe lpr.exe	command + p File > Print	**nprint**
	Action: 168	Action: 168	Action: 168	Action: 168	Action: 179	**nprinter**
	Action: 168	Action: 168	Action: 168	Action: 168	Action: 179	**Nprinter Manager**
	winpopup.exe	msg.exe net send	msg.exe net send	msg.exe net send		**nsend**

	AIX	Linux	OpenBSD	Solaris	NetWare 3	NetWare 4	NetWare 5	NetWare 6
nslookup	**nslookup** host	**nslookup** dig host	**nslookup** dig host	**nslookup**		Action: 201	Action: 201	Action: 201
nstest	nslookup host	nslookup dig host	nslookup dig host	**nstest** nslookup		Action: 201	Action: 201	Action: 201
nsupdate	**nsupdate** dhcpaction nsupdate8	**nsupdate**		**nsupdate**			named.nlm	named.nlm
nsupdate8	**nsupdate8** nsupdate	nsupdate		nsupdate			named.nlm	named.nlm
ntbackup	backup	dump rdump	dump rdump	ufsdump	sbackup.nlm	sbackup.nlm	nwback32.exe sbcon.nlm	nwback32.exe sbcon.nlm
ntbooks	man apropos whatis	man apropos info	man apropos info	man apropos whatis		help	help	help
ntpdate	**ntpdate**	rdate	rdate	**ntpdate** rdate		timesync.nlm	timesync.nlm	timesync.nlm
ntpq	**ntpq**	Action: 50	Action: 50	**ntpq**	systime.exe	systime.exe timesync.nlm	timesync.nlm	timesync.nlm
ntsysv	Action: 72	**ntsysv**	Action: 67	Action: 65	autoexec.ncf	autoexec.ncf	autoexec.ncf	autoexec.ncf
Numbers Control Panel	LANG=*language*	LANG=*language*	LANG=*language*	LANG=*language*				
numlock	xset led 1 xset -led 1	setleds +num setleds -num	xset led 1 xset -led 1	xset led 1 xset -led 1				
nver	uname -a	uname -a kernelversion	uname -a	uname -a wsinfo	**nver.exe** version netbios I	**nver.exe** version	**nver.exe** version	version
nvxnew							**nvxnewup.ncf** **nvxnewdn.ncf**	**nvxnewup.ncf** **nvxnewdn.ncf**
nvxweb		httpd	httpd	httpd			**nvxwebup.ncf** nsweb.ncf	**nvxwebup.ncf** nsweb.ncf
nwauth		**nwauth**			login	login	login	login
nwbocreate		**nwbocreate**			syscon.exe sysconW.exe	netadmin.exe nwadmn32.exe	nwadmn32.exe consoleone.exe	nwadmn32.exe consoleone.exe
nwbols		**nwbols**			syscon.exe sysconW.exe	netadmin.exe nwadmn32.exe	nwadmn32.exe consoleone.exe	nwadmn32.exe consoleone.exe
nwboprops		**nwboprops**			syscon.exe sysconW.exe	netadmin.exe nwadmn32.exe	nwadmn32.exe consoleone.exe	nwadmn32.exe consoleone.exe
nwborm		**nwborm**			syscon.exe sysconW.exe	netadmin.exe nwadmn32.exe	nwadmn32.exe consoleone.exe	nwadmn32.exe consoleone.exe
nwbpadd		**nwbpadd**			syscon.exe sysconW.exe	netadmin.exe nwadmn32.exe	nwadmn32.exe consoleone.exe	nwadmn32.exe consoleone.exe
nwbprm		**nwbprm**			syscon.exe sysconW.exe	netadmin.exe nwadmn32.exe	nwadmn32.exe consoleone.exe	nwadmn32.exe consoleone.exe
nwbpset		**nwbpset**			syscon.exe sysconW.exe	netadmin.exe nwadmn32.exe	nwadmn32.exe consoleone.exe	nwadmn32.exe consoleone.exe
nwbpvalues		**nwbpvalues**			syscon.exe sysconW.exe	netadmin.exe nwadmn32.exe	nwadmn32.exe consoleone.exe	nwadmn32.exe consoleone.exe
nwcstat	netstat -I *interface*	ipppstats	pppstats	netstat -I *interface*		**nwcstat.nlm**	**nwcstat.nlm**	
nwdetect				server_upgrade	Action: 40	nwdetect.exe Action: 40	Action: 40	Action: 40
nwdir	ls	**nwdir** ls	ls	ls	ndir.exe	ndir.exe	ndir.exe	ndir.exe
nwfsctrl	rexec rpc.rexd	**nwfsctrl** xon rexec	xon rexec	rpc.rexd				
nwfsinfo		**nwfsinfo** slist			slist.exe	nlist server /B	nlist server /B	nlist server /B
nwfstime	date	**nwfstime** date hwclock	date	date	time set time	time set time	time set time	time set time

DOS	Windows 9x	NT 4.0	NT 2000	Windows XP	Macintosh	
		nslookup.exe	**nslookup.exe**	**nslookup.exe**		**nslookup**
		nslookup	nslookup	nslookup		**nstest**
						nsupdate
			dnsmgmt.msc	dnsmgmt.msc		**nsupdate8**
msbackup.exe	backup.exe msbackup.exe	**ntbackup.exe** backup.exe	**ntbackup.exe**	**ntbackup.exe**		**ntbackup**
help.com fasthelp.exe	winhelp.exe helpctr.exe	**ntbooks.exe** help.exe winhlp32.exe	**ntbooks** help.exe winhelp.exe	help.exe winhelp.exe helpctr.exe	<command> + <?> Help > Mac Help	**ntbooks**
	net time	net time	w32tm.exe net time	w32tm.exe net time	Control Panel > Date & Time	**ntpdate**
*	net time	net time	net time w32tm.exe	net time w32tm.exe	Apple Menu > Control Panels > Date & Time	**ntpq**
autoexec.bat	autoexec.bat	Control Panel > Services	services.msc	services.msc	Apple Menu > Control Panels > Extensions Manager *selections...*	**ntsysv**
country	Control Panel > Regional Settings	Control Panel > Regional Settings	Control Panel > Regional Options	Control Panel > Regional/Langua ge Options	**Apple Menu > Control Panels > Numbers**	**Numbers Control Panel**
numlock						**numlock**
ver	ver winver Control Panel > System	ver winver Control Panel > System	ver winver Control Panel > System	ver winver systeminfo Control Panel > System	Apple Menu > About This Computer	**nver**
			inetmgr.exe	inetmgr.exe		**nvxnew**
			inetmgr.exe	inetmgr.exe	Apple Menu > Control Panels > Web Sharing	**nvxweb**
						nwauth
						nwbocreate
						nwbols
						nwboprops
						nwborm
						nwbpadd
						nwbprm
						nwbpset
						nwbpvalues
		rasadmin.exe	rasadmin.exe	rraswiz.exe		**nwcstat**
						nwdetect
dir	dir	dir	dir	dir		**nwdir**
		rexec.exe	rexec.exe	rexec.exe		**nwfsctrl**
	net view	net view	net view	net view		**nwfsinfo**
date time	date time	date time	date time	date time	Apple Menu > Control Panels > Date & Time *selections...*	**nwfstime**

	AIX	Linux	OpenBSD	Solaris	NetWare 3	NetWare 4	NetWare 5	NetWare 6
nwpasswd	passwd yppasswd	**nwpasswd** yppasswd passwd	passwd	passwd yppasswd nispasswd	setpass.exe Action: 37	setpass.exe Action: 37	setpass.exe Action: 37	Action: 37
nwpurge		**nwpurge**			purge.exe	purge.exe filer > Purge Deleted Files	purge.exe filer > Purge Deleted Files	filer > Purge Deleted Files Action: 4
nwrights	chmod	**nwrights** chattr chmod	chflags chmod	chmod	rights.exe flag.exe	rights.exe flag.exe	rights.exe flag.exe	rights.exe flag.exe
nwsfind		**nwsfind** slist			display servers	display servers	display servers	display servers
nwucinit	chlicense					install.nlm	**nwucinit.nlm** licmaint.nlm	**nwucinit.nlm** licmaint.nlm
nwucutil	chlicense					install.nlm	**nwucutil.nlm** licmaint.nlm	**nwucutil.nlm** licmaint.nlm
nwuserlist	who w	**nwuserlist** who w	who w	whodo who w	userlist.exe	nlist user /A /B	nlist user /A /B	nlist user /A /B
nwvolinfo	df	**nwvolinfo** df	df	df	volinfo.exe	filer.exe ndir /VOL	filer.exe ndir /VOL	filer.exe ndir /VOL
nwxtract	uncompress	unzip gunzip uncompress	gunzip bunzip2 uncompress	unzip gunzip uncompress	**nwxtract.exe** nlunpack.exe	**nwxtract.exe**	unzip.nlm jar tar.nlm	unzip.nlm jar tar.nlm
odbcjoin							**odbcjoin.exe**	
off	clear	clear	clear	clear	**off** cls	**off** cls	**off** cls	**off** cls
oldps	ps	**oldps** ps	ps	ps	monitor.nlm	monitor.nlm	monitor.nlm	monitor.nlm
on	**on** rexec rpc.rexd	xon rexec	xon rexec	**on** rpc.rexd				
On-Screen Keyboard								
Open								
openfiles		lsof smbstatus	fstat		monitor.nlm	monitor.nlm	monitor.nlm	monitor.nlm
openwin	X	X startx	X startx	**openwin** X			startx.ncf	startx.ncf
oslevel	**oslevel**	uname -r	uname -r	uname -r	version	version	version	version
Outlook Express	mhmail mail	mutt pine	mail mailx	dtmail mail				
pack	**pack** compress	compress gzip	compress gzip	**pack** compress		flag *files* Ic	flag *files* Ic	flag *files* Ic
page	**page** more	less more	less more	**page** pg	edit.nlm	view.nlm	view.nlm	view.nlm
passmgmt	smit user smitty user	vi /etc/passwd	vi /etc/passwd	**passmgmt** admintool	syscon.exe	nwadmn32.exe	nwadmn32.exe	nwadmn32.exe
passwd	**passwd** yppasswd	**passwd** yppasswd nwpasswd	**passwd**	**passwd** yppasswd nispasswd	setpass.exe Action: 37	setpass.exe Action: 37	setpass.exe Action: 37	Action: 37
Paste								
patchadd	smit install_update	rpm	pkg_add	**patchadd**	install > product options	install > product options	nwconfig > product options	nwconfig > product options
path	$PATH	$PATH	$PATH	$PATH	search	search	search	search
Pathping	ping traceroute	ping traceroute	ping traceroute	ping traceroute	ping	ping	ping iptrace.nlm	ping iptrace.nlm

DOS	Windows 9x	NT 4.0	NT 2000	Windows XP	Macintosh	
	net password Control Panel > passwords	usrmgr.exe Action: 229	compmgmt.msc Action: 229	compmgmt.msc Action: 229	Action: 200	**nwpasswd**
	Action: 17 cleanmgr.exe	Action: 17	Action: 17 cleanmgr.exe	Action: 17 cleanmgr.exe	Special > Empty Trash	**nwpurge**
attrib.exe	attrib.exe	attrib.exe	attrib.exe	attrib.exe	Select icon > command + i	**nwrights**
	net view	net view	net view	net view	Apple Menu > Chooser Apple Menu > Network Browser	**nwsfind**
		llsmgr.exe	llsmgr.exe	llsmgr.exe		**nwucinit**
		llsmgr.exe	llsmgr.exe	llsmgr.exe		**nwucutil**
		quser.exe query user	quser.exe query user	quser.exe query user		**nwuserlist**
chkdsk.exe	chkdsk.exe	chkdsk.exe	chkdsk.exe	chkdsk.exe	Action: 165	**nwvolinfo**
	Action: 143	Action: 143 expand.exe	Action: 143 expand.exe	Action: 143 expand.exe	Action: 79	**nwxtract**
	Control Panel > ODBC	Control Panel > ODBC	Action: 114	Action: 114		**odbcjoin**
cls	cls Action: 103	cls	cls Action: 103	cls Action: 103	Application Menu > Hide Others	**off**
	taskman.exe	qprocess.exe	qprocess.exe	tasklist qprocess.exe		**oldps**
		rsh	rsh	rsh		**on**
	osk.exe		**osk.exe**	**osk.exe**	Apple Menu > Key Caps	**On-Screen Keyboard**
	Action: 203	Action: 203	Action: 203	Action: 203	**command + o** **Double click**	**Open**
	netwatch.exe	srvmgr.exe Control Panel > Server	compmgmt.msc	**openfiles.exe** compmgmt.msc	Apple Menu > Control Panels > File Sharing	**openfiles**
	win.com					**openwin**
ver	Control Panel > System	Control Panel > System	Control Panel > System	Control Panel > System	Apple Menu > About This Computer	**oslevel**
	msimn.exe		**msimn.exe**	**msimn.exe**	Action: 199	**Outlook Express**
	cabbit.exe	compact.exe	makecab compact.exe	makecab compact.exe	Action: 79	**pack**
more.com type	more.com type	more.com type	more.com type	more.com type	Action: 82	**page**
	Control Panel > Users	usrmgr.exe	compmgmt.msc	compmgmt.msc	Apple Menu > Control Panels > File Sharing > Users & Groups	**passmgmt**
	net password Control Panel > passwords	usrmgr.exe Action: 229	compmgmt.msc Action: 229	compmgmt.msc Action: 229	Action: 200	**passwd**
	<CTRL> + <V>	<CTRL> + <V>	<CTRL> + <V>	<CTRL> + <V>	**<command> + <V>** **Edit > Paste**	**Paste**
	qfecheck.exe wupdmgr.exe	Control Panel > Add/Remove Programs	wupdmgr.exe	wupdmgr.exe		**patchadd**
path	**path**	**path**	**path**	**path**		**path**
	ping.exe tracert.exe	ping.exe tracert.exe	**pathping.exe** ping.exe tracert.exe	**pathping.exe** ping.exe tracert.exe	Action: 120	**Pathping**

	AIX	Linux	OpenBSD	Solaris	NetWare 3	NetWare 4	NetWare 5	NetWare 6
paudit	sa acctcon1		sa	acctcon1	**paudit.exe** atotal.exe	atotal.exe	atotal.exe	
pause	read	read	read	read	**pause**	**pause**	**pause**	**pause**
pcat	**pcat** uncompress -c *file* zcat	uncompress -c *file* bzcat zcat	uncompress -c *file* gzcat	**pcat** uncompress -c *file* zcat			tar -t *file* unzip -l *file* jar -t *file*	tar -t *file* unzip -l *file* jar -t *file*
pcmciastat	**pcmciastat**	cardctl						
pdisable	**pdisable**	nologin	nologin	nologin	disable login	disable login	disable login	disable login
penable	**penable** pstart	Action: 100	Action: 100	Action: 100	enable login	enable login	enable login	enable login
pentnt		cat /proc/cpuinfo						
perfmeter	topas	top	top	**perfmeter** top	monitor.nlm	monitor.nlm	monitor.nlm	monitor.nlm
Performance Monitor	topas netpmon	top	top	perfmeter top	monitor.nlm	monitor.nlm	monitor.nlm	monitor.nlm
Performance Monitor Console	topas netpmon	top	top	perfmeter top	monitor.nlm	monitor.nlm	monitor.nlm	monitor.nlm
perl		**perl**	**perl**	**perl**			**perl.nlm**	**perl.nlm**
perlbug	sendbug bugfiler	**perlbug** bashbug	**perlbug** sendbug	**perlbug**				
pfexec, pfsh, pfcsh, pfksh	Action: 66	Action: 66	Action: 66	**pfexec** **pfsh** **pfcsh** **pfksh**				
pg	**pg** more	less more	less more	**pg** page	edit.nlm	view.nlm	view.nlm	view.nlm
phold	**phold** pdisable	Action: 117	Action: 117	Action: 117	disable login	disable login	disable login	disable login
ping	**ping**	**ping**	**ping**	**ping**	**ping.nlm** tping.nlm	**ping.nlm** tping.nlm	**ping.nlm** tping.nlm	**ping.nlm** tping.nlm
ping6				ping -A inet6				
pinky	finger	**pinky** finger	finger	finger	userlist.exe	nlist user	nlist user	nlist user
pkg_add	installp smit install	rpm	**pkg_add**	pkgadd	install > product options	install > product options	nwconfig > product options	nwconfig > product options
pkg_delete	smit remove	rpm -e	**pkg_delete**	pkgrm	install > product options	install > product options	nwconfig > product options	nwconfig > product options
pkg_info	sysck lslpp	rpm -qa	**pkg_info**	showrev -p pkginfo	install > product options	install > product options	nwconfig > product options	nwconfig > product options
pkgadd	installp	rpm	pkg_add	**pkgadd**	install > product options	install > product options	nwconfig > product options	nwconfig > product options
pkginfo	lslpp sysck	rpm -qa	pkg_info	**pkginfo** showrev	install > product options	install > product options	nwconfig > product options	nwconfig > product options
pkgrm	smit remove	rpm -e	pkg_delete	**pkgrm**	install > product options	install > product options	nwconfig > product options	nwconfig > product options
pkill	kill	**pkill** killall	kill	**pkill**	unload	unload	unload	unload
pmconfig	pmctrl	apm	apm	**pmconfig**				
pmctrl	**pmctrl**	apm	apm	pmconfig				
pntadm	dhcpsconf dadmin	dhcpd.conf	dhcpd.conf	**pntadm** dhcpconfig dhcpmgr		dhcpcfg.nlm	dnsdhcp.exe	dnsdhcp.exe

DOS	Windows 9x	NT 4.0	NT 2000	Windows XP	Macintosh	
		eventvwr.exe	eventvwr.exe	eventvwr.exe		**paudit**
pause	**pause**	**pause**	**pause**	**pause**		**pause**
	Action: 143	expand -D *file* Action: 143	expand -D *file* Action: 143	expand -D *file* Action: 143		**pcat**
	Control Panel > PC Card (PCMCIA)	Control Panel > PC Card (PCMCIA)	Control Panel > PC Card (PCMCIA)	Control Panel > PC Card (PCMCIA)		**pcmciastat**
		chglogon /DISABLE	chglogon /DISABLE	chglogon /DISABLE		**pdisable**
		chglogon /ENABLE	chglogon /ENABLE	chglogon /ENABLE		**penable**
		pentnt.exe	pentnt.exe	pentnt.exe		**pentnt**
	taskman.exe	taskmgr.exe	taskmgr.exe	taskmgr.exe	Apple Menu > About This Computer	**perfmeter**
		perfmon.exe	**perfmon.exe**	**perfmon.exe**	Apple Menu > About This Computer	**Performance Monitor**
		perfmon.exe	**perfmon.msc** perfmon.exe	**perfmon.msc** perfmon.exe	Apple Menu > About This Computer	**Performance Monitor Console**
	cscript.exe wscript.exe	cscript.exe wscript.exe	cscript.exe wscript.exe	cscript.exe wscript.exe	Action: 7	**perl**
	winrep.exe	Action: 19	winrep.exe	Action: 18		**perlbug**
			runas.exe	runas.exe		**pfexec, pfsh, pfcsh, pfksh**
more.com	more.com	more.com	more.com	more.com	Action: 82	**pg**
		chglogon /DISABLE	chglogon /DISABLE	chglogon /DISABLE		**phold**
	ping.exe	**ping.exe**	**ping.exe**	**ping.exe**		**ping**
				ping6.exe		**ping6**
		finger.exe	finger.exe	finger.exe		**pinky**
	Control Panel > Add/Remove Programs	Control Panel > Add/Remove Programs	Control Panel > Add/Remove Programs	Control Panel > Add/Remove Programs		**pkg_add**
	Control Panel > Add/Remove Programs	Control Panel > Add/Remove Programs	Control Panel > Add/Remove Programs	Control Panel > Add/Remove Programs		**pkg_delete**
	qfecheck.exe wupdmgr.exe	Control Panel > Add/Remove Programs	wupdmgr.exe	wupdmgr.exe		**pkg_info**
	Control Panel > Add/Remove Programs	Control Panel > Add/Remove Programs	Control Panel > Add/Remove Programs	Control Panel > Add/Remove Programs		**pkgadd**
	qfecheck.exe	Control Panel > Add/Remove Programs	wupdmgr.exe	wupdmgr.exe		**pkginfo**
	Control Panel > Add/Remove Programs	Control Panel > Add/Remove Programs	Control Panel > Add/Remove Programs	Control Panel > Add/Remove Programs		**pkgrm**
	taskman.exe	kill.exe	tskill.exe	taskkill.exe tskill.exe	<command> + <alt> + <esc> <command> + <q>	**pkill**
power.exe	pmres.exe		Control Panel > Power Options	Control Panel > Power Options	Apple Menu > Control Panels > Energy Saver	**pmconfig**
power.exe	pmres.exe		Control Panel > Power Options	Control Panel > Power Options	Apple Menu > Control Panels > Energy Saver	**pmctrl**
		dhcpadmn.exe	dhcpmgmt.msc	dhcpwiz.exe dhcpmgmt.msc		**pntadm**

	AIX	Linux	OpenBSD	Solaris	NetWare 3	NetWare 4	NetWare 5	NetWare 6
post	**post** sendmail mail, Mail, mailx	**post** sendmail mail, Mail, mailx	sendmail mail, Mail, mailx	sendmail mail, Mail, mailx rmail				
power	pmctrl	apm	apm zzz	dtpower pmconfig				
Power Management	pmctrl	apm apmsleep	apm zzz	pmconfig sys-suspend				
powerd	pmctrl	apmsleep apm	zzz apm	**powerd** sys-suspend				
poweroff	halt shutdown	**poweroff** shutdown	halt shutdown	**poweroff** init 5	down	down	down	down
PPP Console	netstat -I *interface*	ipppstats	pppstats	netstat -I *interface*		ppptrace.nlm	**pppcon.nlm** ppptrace.nlm	
PPP Trace Utility	pppstat netstat -I *interface*	pppstat ipppstats	pppstats	netstat -I *interface*		**ppptrace.nlm**	**ppptrace.nlm** spfcon.nlm pppcon.nlm	
pppcontrold	**pppcontrold**	pppd	pppd	aspppd		Action: 121	niascfg.nlm	Action: 121
pppd	pppcontrold	**pppd**	**pppd**	aspppd		Action: 121	niascfg.nlm nwccon.nlm	Action: 121
pppdial	**pppdial**	pppd dip	pppd	aspppd				
pppstat	**pppstat** netstat -I *interface*	pppstats ipppstats	pppstats	netstat -I *interface*		ppptrace.nlm	ppptrace.nlm spfcon.nlm pppcon.nlm	
pppstats	pppstat netstat -I *interface*	**pppstats** ipppstats	**pppstats**	netstat -I *interface*		ppptrace.nlm	ppptrace.nlm spfcon.nlm pppcon.nlm	
pprof	**pprof**	top	top	perfmeter top	monitor.nlm	monitor.nlm	monitor.nlm	monitor.nlm
pqlist	lpstat qchk	**pqlist** lpstat pqstat	lpq	lpstat dtprintinfo	pconsole.exe	pconsole.exe	nwpmw32.exe nwadmn32.exe ndpsm.nlm	nwadmn32.exe ndpsm.nlm
pqrm	lprm cancel	**pqrm** lprm cancel	lprm	lprm cancel	pconsole.exe psc.exe	pconsole.exe psc.exe	nwpmw32.exe nwadmn32.exe ndpsm.nlm	nwadmn32.exe ndpsm.nlm
pqstat	qchk lpstat	**pqstat** lpstat	lpq	dtprintinfo	pconsole.exe	pconsole.exe	nwpmw32.exe nwadmn32.exe ndpsm.nlm	nwadmn32.exe ndpsm.nlm
praudit	auditpr			**praudit**			csaudit.nlm	csaudit.nlm
Print	lp lpr	lp lpr	lpr	lp lpr	nprint.exe	nprint.exe	nprint.exe	
Print Console	lpq	lpq	lpq	lpq	**pconsole.exe** psc.exe	**pconsole.exe** psc.exe	nwpmw32.exe nwadmn32.exe ndpsm.nlm	nwadmn32.exe ndpsm.nlm
Print Server	lpd	lpd	lpd	lpsched	**pserver.nlm**	**pserver.nlm** nprinter	**pserver.nlm** nprinter	**pserver.nlm** nprinter
print	echo	echo	**print** echo	echo			echo	echo
printenv	**printenv** env	**printenv** env	**printenv** env	**printenv** env		search	display environment	display environment
Printer Definition	chprtsv	lpc	lpc	lpadmin	**printdef.exe**	**printdef.exe**	Action: 27	Action: 27
printmgr	piomkpq smit print	/etc/printcap	/etc/printcap	**printmgr** lpadmin lpset	pconsole.exe psc.exe	pconsole.exe psc.exe	nwpmw32.exe nwadmn32.exe ndpsm.nlm	nwadmn32.exe ndpsm.nlm
PrintMonitor	cancel lprm	cancel lprm	lprm	cancel lprm	pconsole.exe psc.exe	pconsole.exe psc.exe	nwpmw32.exe nwadmn32.exe ndpsm.nlm	nwadmn32.exe ndpsm.nlm
printtool	smitty print			**printtool**	psc.exe pconsole.exe	psc.exe pconsole.exe	nwpmw32.exe nwadmn32.exe ndpsm.nlm	nwpmw32.exe nwadmn32.exe ndpsm.nlm

DOS	Windows 9x	NT 4.0	NT 2000	Windows XP	Macintosh	
	msimn.exe		msimn.exe	msimn.exe	Action: 199	**post**
power.exe	pmres.exe		Control Panel > Power Options	Control Panel > Power Options	Apple Menu > Control Panels > Energy Saver	**power**
power.exe	**pmres.exe**		Control Panel > Power Options	Control Panel > Power Options	Apple Menu > Control Panels > Energy Saver	**Power Management**
power.exe	pmres.exe		Control Panel > Power Options	Control Panel > Power Options	Apple Menu > Control Panels > Energy Saver	**powerd**
	Start > Shut down	shutdown Start > Shut down	Start > Shut down	shutdown Start > Shut down	Power Button > Shut Down Special > Shut Down	**poweroff**
		rasadmin.exe	rasadmin.exe	rraswiz.exe		**PPP Console**
		netmon.exe	netmon.exe	netmon.exe		**PPP Trace Utility**
		rasadmin.exe	rasadmin.exe	rraswiz.exe	Apple Menu > Control Panels > Remote Access	**pppcontrold**
	My Computer > Dial-Up Networking	rasdial.exe	rasdial.exe	rasdial.exe	Apple Menu > Control Panel > Remote Access	**pppd**
		rasdial.exe	rasdial.exe	rasdial.exe	Apple Menu > Control Panels > Remote Access	**pppdial**
		rasadmin.exe	rasadmin.exe	rraswiz.exe		**pppstat**
		rasadmin.exe	rasadmin.exe	rraswiz.exe		**pppstats**
		perfmon.exe	perfmon.exe	perfmon.exe	Apple Menu > About This Computer	**pprof**
	Control Panel > Printers net print	Control Panel > Printers net print	Control Panel > Printers net print	Control Panel > Printers and Faxes net print	Action: 115	**pqlist**
	net print /delete	net print /delete	net print /delete	net print /delete	Action: 107	**pqrm**
	Control Panel > Printers net print	Control Panel > Printers net print	Control Panel > Printers net print	Control Panel > Printers and Faxes net print	Action: 115	**pqstat**
						praudit
print.exe	type *file* > LPT1	**print.exe** lpr.exe	**print.exe** lpr.exe	**print.exe** lpr.exe	**command + p** **File > Print**	**Print**
	Conrtol Panel > Printer	lpq.exe Conrtol Panel > Printer	lpq.exe Conrtol Panel > Printers	lpq.exe Conrtol Panel > Printers	Action: 115	**Print Console**
	Action: 168	Action: 168	Action: 168	Action: 168	Action: 179	**Print Server**
echo	echo	echo	echo	echo		**print**
set	sysedit	Action: 154	Action: 155	Action: 155		**printenv**
	Control Panel > Printers	Control Panel > Printers	Control Panel > Printers	Control Panel > Printers and Faxes	Action: 115	**Printer Definition**
	Control Panel > Printers	Control Panel > Printers	Control Panel > Printers	Control Panel > Printers	Apple Menu > Chooser	**printmgr**
	net print /delete	net print /delete	net print /delete	net print /delete	**Action: 107**	**PrintMonitor**
	Action: 57	Action: 57	Action: 57	Action: 57	Action: 115	**printtool**

	AIX	Linux	OpenBSD	Solaris	NetWare 3	NetWare 4	NetWare 5	NetWare 6
priocntl	nice renice	nice renice	nice renice	**priocntl** nice renice	load	load	load	load
Program Manager	mwm	fvwm2	fvwm	dtwm	<CTRL> + <ESC>	<CTRL> + <ESC>	<CTRL> + <ESC>	<CTRL> + <ESC>
prompt	PS1	PS1	PS1	PS1				
protocol	cat /etc/protocols	cat /etc/protocols	cat /etc/protocols	cat /etc/protocols	**protocol**	**protocol**	**protocol**	**protocol**
Protocol Explorer	cat /etc/protocols	cat /etc/protocols	cat /etc/protocols	cat /etc/protocols	**proto.nlm** protocols tcpcon.nlm ipxcon.nlm	protocols tcpcon.nlm ipxcon.nlm	protocols tcpcon.nlm ipxcon.nlm	protocols tcpcon.nlm ipxcon.nlm
prtconf	lscfg svmon	dmesg free	dmesg	**prtconf** dmesg	monitor.nlm	monitor.nlm	monitor.nlm Display Interrupts	monitor.nlm Display Interrupts
prtdiag	lscfg svmon	dmesg top	dmesg top	**prtdiag** prtconf dmesg	monitor.nlm display interrupts	monitor.nlm display interrupts	monitor.nlm display interrupts	monitor.nlm display interrupts
prtvtoc	chpv lspv	e2label	disklabel	**prtvtoc** labelit	volume	volume	volume	volume
ps	**ps**	**ps**	**ps**	**ps**	monitor.nlm	monitor.nlm	monitor.nlm	monitor.nlm
psc	chprtsv	lpc	lpc	lpadmin	**psc.exe** pconsole.exe	**psc.exe** pconsole.exe	nwpmw32.exe nwadmn32.exe ndpsm.nlm	nwadmn32.exe ndpsm.nlm
pserver	lpd	lpd	lpd	lpsched	**pserver.exe**	nprinter.exe	nprinter.exe	nprinter.exe
pstart	**pstart** penable	Action: 100	Action: 100	Action: 100	enable login	enable login	enable login	enable login
pump	dhcpcd	**pump** dhcpcd	dhclient	dhcpagent				
purge		nwpurge			**purge.exe**	**purge.exe** filer > Purge Deleted Files	**purge.exe** filer > Purge Deleted Files	filer > Purge Deleted Files Action: 4
putdev	smit devices	/etc/modules.conf	config -e -o bsd.new /bsd	**putdev** touch /reconfigure	startup.ncf	startup.ncf	startup.ncf	startup.ncf
pwck	pwdck	**pwck**		**pwck**	security syscon.exe	nwadmn32.exe	nwadmn32.exe	nwadmn32.exe
pwconv		**pwconv**		**pwconv**		Action: 55	Action: 55	Action: 55
pwd	**pwd**	**pwd**	**pwd**	**pwd**				
pwdadm	**pwdadm** passwd	passwd	passwd	passwd admintool	setpass.exe Action: 37	setpass.exe Action: 37	setpass.exe Action: 37	Action: 37
pwdck	**pwdck**	pwck		pwck	security syscon.exe	nwadmn32.exe	nwadmn32.exe	nwadmn32.exe
qadm	**qadm**	lpc	lpc	lpadmin	pconsole.exe	pconsole.exe	nwadmn32.exe	nwadmn32.exe
qbasic								
qcan	**qcan**	lprm cancel	lprm	lprm cancel	pconsole.exe	pconsole.exe	nwadmn32.exe	nwadmn32.exe
qchk	**qchk**	lpstat	lpq	lpstat	pconsole.exe	pconsole.exe	nwadmn32.exe	nwadmn32.exe
qhld	**qhld**	lpc	lpc	lpc	pconsole.exe	pconsole.exe	nwadmn32.exe	nwadmn32.exe
qmov	**qmov**	lpc		lpmove	pconsole.exe	pconsole.exe	nwadmn32.exe	nwadmn32.exe
QoS Admission Control Manager	cfgqos						wtm.nlm	wtm.nlm

DOS	Windows 9x	NT 4.0	NT 2000	Windows XP	Macintosh	
		start	start	start		priocntl
	progman.exe	**progman.exe**	**progman.exe**	**progman.exe**		Program Manager
prompt	**prompt**	**prompt**	**prompt**	**prompt**		prompt
	Control Panel > Network	Action: 178	Action: 180	Action: 180		protocol
						Protocol Explorer
msd.exe	Control Panel > System msinfo32.exe	winmsd.exe	winmsd.exe	winmsd.exe	Apple Menu > Apple System Profiler	prtconf
msd.exe	msinfo32.exe Control Panel > System	msinfo32.exe winmsd.exe	msinfo32.exe winmsd.exe	msinfo32.exe winmsd.exe	Apple Menu > Apple System Profiler	prtdiag
vol label	fdisk label	windisk.exe label	diskmgmt.msc label	diskmgmt.msc label	Apple Menu > Apple System Profiler	prtvtoc
	taskman.exe	taskmgr.exe	taskmgr.exe	taskmgr.exe	Finder	ps
	Control Panel > Printers	Control Panel > Printers	Control Panel > Printers	Control Panel > Printers and Faxes	Action: 115	psc
	Action: 168	Action: 168	Action: 168	Action: 168	Action: 179	pserver
		chglogon /ENABLE	chglogon /ENABLE	chglogon /ENABLE		pstart
	Action: 234	Action: 235	Action: 233	Action: 233	Apple Menu > Control Panels > TCP/IP	pump
	Action: 17 cleanmgr.exe	Action: 17	Action: 17 cleanmgr.exe	Action: 17 cleanmgr.exe	shift + command + delete Special > Empty Trash	purge
config.sys	Action: 62	Control Panel > Devices	Control Panel > Add/Remove Hardware	Control Panel > Add/Remove Hardware	Apple Menu > Control Panels > Extensions Manager *selections...*	putdev
	Control Panel > Users	usrmgr.exe musrmgr.exe	compmgmt.msc	compmgmt.msc		pwck
			syskey.exe	syskey.exe		pwconv
cd	cd	cd	cd	cd	command + click the name in title bar	pwd
net password	net password Control Panel > Users	usrmgr.exe	compmgmt.msc	compmgmt.msc		pwdadm
	Control Panel > Users	usrmgr.exe musrmgr.exe	compmgmt.msc	compmgmt.msc		pwdck
	Control Panel > Printers net print	Control Panel > Printers net print	Control Panel > Printers net print	Control Panel > Printers and Faxes net print	Apple Menu > Chooser Application Menu > PrintMonitor	qadm
qbasic.exe		**qbasic.exe**				qbasic
	net print *jobnr* /DELETE	net print *jobnr* /DELETE	net print *jobnr* /DELETE	net print *jobnr* /DELETE		qcan
	Control Panel > Printers net print	Control Panel > Printers net print	Control Panel > Printers net print	Control Panel > Printers and Faxes net print		qchk
	net print *jobnr* /HOLD net print *jobnr* /RELEASE	net print *jobnr* /HOLD net print *jobnr* /RELEASE	net print *jobnr* /HOLD net print *jobnr* /RELEASE	net print *jobnr* /HOLD net print *jobnr* /RELEASE		qhld
						qmov
			acssnap.msc	**acssnap.msc**		QoS Admission Control Manager

	AIX	Linux	OpenBSD	Solaris	NetWare 3	NetWare 4	NetWare 5	NetWare 6
qpri	**qpri**			lpusers	pconsole.exe psc.exe	pconsole.exe psc.exe	nwpmw32.exe nwadmn32.exe ndpsm.nlm	nwadmn32.exe ndpsm.nlm
qprocess	ps	ps	ps	ps	monitor.nlm	monitor.nlm	monitor.nlm	monitor.nlm
qprt	**qprt** lp	lp	lp	lp	nprint.exe	nprint.exe	nprint.exe	
qstatus	**qstatus**	lpq	lpq	lpq	pconsole.exe	pconsole.exe	nwpmw32.exe ndpsm.nlm	nwadmn32.exe ndpsm.nlm
query	ps gv	ps –ef	ps –auxw	ps –ef	monitor.nlm modules	monitor.nlm modules	monitor.nlm modules	monitor.nlm modules
QuickTime PictureViewer				imagetool				
QuickTime Player		cdp cdplay mpg123	cdio	audioplay audiotool				
Quit	<CTRL> + <C>	<CTRL> + <C>	<CTRL> + <C>	<CTRL> + <C>	unload *module*	unload *module*	unload *module*	unload *module*
quota	**quota**	**quota**	**quota**	**quota**	dspace.exe	Action: 247	Action: 247	Action: 247
quotaoff	**quotaoff**	**quotaoff**	**quotaoff**	**quotaoff**		Action: 246	Action: 246	Action: 246
quotaon	**quotaon**	**quotaon**	**quotaon**	**quotaon**		Action: 246	Action: 246	Action: 246
quser	w who	w who	w who	w who	userlist.exe	nlist user /A /B	nlist user /A /B	nlist user /A /B
r		<UPARROW>	<UPARROW>	**r**	<UPARROW>	<UPARROW>	<UPARROW>	<UPARROW>
raidctl	unmirrorvg		**raidctl –u**		abort remirror	abort remirror	abort remirror	abort remirror
rasdial	pppdial	pppd dip	pppd	aspppd				
rc	**rc** init	**rc** init	**rc** init	Action: 46 init			loadstage	loadstage
rconag, rconag6	telnet	telnet ssh	telnet ssh	telnet	rconsole.exe	rconsole.exe	**rconag** **rconag6** rconsole.exe	**rconag6**
rconsole	pppcontrold	pppd	pppd	aspppd	**rconsole.exe** aconsole.exe	**rconsole.exe**	**rconsole.exe**	rconj.exe
RconsoleJ	pppcontrold	pppd	pppd	aspppd	aconsole.exe	rconsole.exe	**rconj.exe**	**rconj.exe**
rcp	**rcp** ftp	**rcp** ftp	**rcp** ftp	**rcp** ftp	ncopy.exe	ncopy.exe	ncopy.exe	ncopy.exe
rd, rmdir	rmdir	rmdir	rmdir	rmdir	filer.exe	filer.exe	filer.exe	filer.exe
rdate	ntpdate	**rdate**	**rdate**	**rdate** ntpdate		timesync.nlm	timesync.nlm	timesync.nlm
rdist	**rdist** rcp ftp	**rdist** rcp ftp	**rdist** rcp ftp	**rdist** rcp ftp	ncopy.exe	ncopy.exe	ncopy.exe	ncopy.exe
read	**read**	**read**	**read**	**read**	pause	pause	pause	pause
reboot	**reboot**	**reboot**	**reboot**	**reboot**	down	restart server	reset server restart server	reset server restart server
rec		**rec**		audiotool				
recover	fsck	fsck	fsck	fsck	vrepair.nlm	vrepair.nlm	nss /rebuild vrepair.nlm	ConsoleOne > Server > Media vrepair.nlm
red	**red** vi	**red** vi	vi	**red** vi	edit.nlm	edit.nlm	edit.nlm	edit.nlm
reg					set	set	set	set
Registration Wizard				solregis				
Registry Editor					set	set	set	set
reject	disable	lpc	lpc	**reject** lpc	pconsole.exe psc.exe	pconsole.exe psc.exe	nwpmw32.exe nwadmn32.exe ndpsm.nlm	nwadmn32.exe ndpsm.nlm

DOS	Windows 9x	NT 4.0	NT 2000	Windows XP	Macintosh	
		Action: 257	Action: 258	Action: 258		**qpri**
	taskman.exe	**qprocess.exe**	**qprocess.exe**	**qprocess.exe** tasklist		**qprocess**
print.exe	type *file* > LPT1	print.exe	print.exe	print.exe	<command> + <p> File > Print	**qprt**
		lpq.exe	lpq.exe	lpq.exe	Action: 115	**qstatus**
	taskmgr.exe	**query.exe** taskmgr.exe	**query.exe** taskmgr.exe	**query.exe** taskmgr.exe		**query**
		Action: 134	Action: 134		**Action: 133**	**QuickTime PictureViewer**
	mplayer2.exe mplayer.exe	mplayer2.exe	mplayer2.exe mplay32.exe	mplayer2.exe mplay32.exe	**Action: 132**	**QuickTime Player**
	<ALT> + <F4> Action: 105 Action: 212	<ALT> + <F4> Action: 105 Action: 212	<ALT> + <F4> Action: 105 Action: 212	<ALT> + <F4> Action: 105 Action: 212	**<command> + <Q>** **File> Quit**	**Quit**
			Action: 158	Action: 158		**quota**
			Action: 241	Action: 241		**quotaoff**
			Action: 240	Action: 240		**quotaon**
		quser.exe query user	**quser.exe** query user	**quser.exe** query user		**quser**
<F3>	<F3>	<F3>	<F3>	<F3>		**r**
						raidctl
		rasdial.exe	**rasdial.exe**	**rasdial.exe**	Apple Menu > Control Panel > Remote Access	**rasdial**
						rc
	telnet	telnet	telnet Action: 173	telnet Action: 173		**rconag, rconag6**
		rasdial.exe	rasdial.exe	rasdial.exe		**rconsole**
		rasdial.exe	rasdial.exe	rasdial.exe		**RconsoleJ**
	robocopy.exe ftp.exe	**rcp.exe** ftp.exe	**rcp.exe** ftp.exe	**rcp.exe** ftp.exe		**rcp**
rd **rmdir**	**rd** **rmdir**	**rd** **rmdir**	**rd** **rmdir**	**rd** **rmdir**	command + Backspace	**rd, rmdir**
	net time	net time	w32tm.exe net time	w32tm.exe net time		**rdate**
	robocopy.exe ftp.exe	rcp.exe ftp.exe	rcp.exe ftp.exe	rcp.exe ftp.exe		**rdist**
pause	pause	pause	pause	pause		**read**
	Action: 153	Action: 153	Action: 153	Action: 153	Special > Restart	**reboot**
	sndrec32.exe	sndrec32.exe	sndrec32.exe	sndrec32.exe	SimpleText > sound > recorder	**rec**
scandisk.exe	scandisk.exe	**recover.exe**	**recover.exe**	**recover.exe**	Action: 101	**recover**
edit.com	edit.com notepad.exe	edit.com notepad.exe	edit.com notepad.exe	edit.com notepad.exe	Action: 82	**red**
	regedit.exe	regedt32.exe regedit.exe	regedt32.exe regedit.exe	**reg.exe** regedit.exe		**reg**
	regwiz.exe		**regwiz.exe**	**regwiz.exe**		**Registration Wizard**
	regedit.exe	**regedit.exe** regedt32.exe	**regedit.exe** regedt32.exe	**regedit.exe** reg.exe		**Registry Editor**
	Action: 142	Action: 259	Action: 259	Action: 259	Action: 115	**reject**

	AIX	Linux	OpenBSD	Solaris	NetWare 3	NetWare 4	NetWare 5	NetWare 6
rem	#	#	#	#	**REM** # ;	**REM** # ;	**REM** # ;	**REM** # ;
rem_drv	rmdev	rmmod	mounload	**rem_drv**	unload *driver*	unload *driver*	unload *driver*	unload *driver*
rembak	**rembak**	lpr	lpr	lpr	nprint.exe	nprint.exe	nprint.exe	
remote	telnetd	telnetd	telnetd	telnetd	**remote.nlm**	**remote.nlm**	**remote.nlm**	**remote.nlm**
Remote Access Admin	pppcontrold	pppd	pppd	aspppd		Action: 121	niascfg.nlm	Action: 121
Remote Access Configuration	vi /etc/ppp/lcp_config	vi /etc/ppp/options	vi /etc/ppp/options	vi /etc/asppp.cf		**nwccon.nlm**	**nwccon.nlm**	
Remote Access Control Panel	pppcontrold	pppd	pppd	aspppd				
Remote Boot Disk Generator	nimconfig xnim			re-preinstall	dosgen.exe	dosgen.exe	dosgen.exe	dosgen.exe
Remoteboot Manager	vi /etc/bootparams		vi /etc/bootparams	vi /etc/bootparams	rpl.nlm	rpl.nlm	rpl.nlm	rpl.nlm
Removable Storage Manager				vold	cd	cd	cd	cd
remove	chmod acledit	chmod	chmod	setfacl chmod	**revoke.exe**	rights *path* REM /name=*user*	rights *path* REM /name=*user*	rights *path* REM /name=*user*
Remove Network Adapter	ifconfig *italics* detach			ifconfig *italics* unplumb		**Remove Network Adapter**	**Remove Network Adapter**	**Remove Network Adapter**
Remove Network Interface	ifconfig *adapter* detach			ifconfig *adapter* unplumb		**remove network adapter**	**remove network adapter**	**remove network adapter**
ren, rename	mv	**rename** mv mc	mv	mv	filer.exe	filer.exe	filer.exe	filer.exe
rendir	mvdir mv	mv	mv	mvdir mv	**rendir.exe** filer.exe	**rendir.exe** filer.exe	filer.exe	filer.exe
renice	**renice** nice	**renice** snice nice	**renice** nice	**renice** nice	load	load	load	load
replace	cp -f	cp -f	cp -f	cp -f	ncopy.exe	ncopy.exe	ncopy.exe	ncopy.exe
Replace File	cp -f	cp -f	cp -f	cp -f	ncopy.exe	ncopy.exe	ncopy.exe	ncopy.exe
repquota	**repquota**	**repquota**	**repquota**	**repquota**	dspace.exe	Action: 247	Action: 247	Action: 247
reset	unsetenv unset	**reset** unsetenv unset	unsetenv unset	unsetenv unset unsetopt	set *variable=original value*	set *variable=original value*	Reset Environment	Reset Environment
Reset Environment		sys-unconfig		sys-unconfig			**reset environment**	**reset environment**
Reset Network Adapter	ifconfig *interface* down	ifconfig *interface* down	ifconfig *interface* down	ifconfig *interface* down		**Reset Network Adapter**	**Reset Network Adapter**	**Reset Network Adapter**
Reset Network Interface	ifconfig *interface* down ifconfig *interface* up	ifconfig *interface* down ifconfig *interface* up	ifconfig *interface* down ifconfig *interface* up	ifconfig *interface* down ifconfig *interface* up		**Reset Network Interface**	**Reset Network Interface**	**Reset Network Interface**
reset server	reboot	reboot	reboot	reboot	down	restart server	**reset server** restart server	**reset server** restart server
Restart Server	reboot	reboot	reboot	reboot	down server.exe	**restart server**	**restart server** reset server	**restart server** reset server
restore	restore	restore rrestore	restore rrestore	ufsrestore	sbackup.nlm	sbackup.nlm	sbcon.nlm nwback32.exe smdr.nlm	sbcon.nlm nwback32.exe smdr.nlm
revoke	chmod acledit	chmod	chmod	setfacl chmod	**revoke.exe**	rights *path* - attributes /name=*user*	rights *path* - attributes /name=*user*	rights *path* - attributes /name=*user*
rexec	**rexec** rpc.rexd	**rexec** rexecd	rexecd xon	rpc.rexd				
rights	chmod ls -l	chmod ls -l	chmod ls -l	chmod ls -l	**rights.exe** flag.exe	**rights.exe** flag.exe	**rights.exe** flag.exe	**rights.exe** flag.exe

DOS	Windows 9x	NT 4.0	NT 2000	Windows XP	Macintosh	
REM	**REM**	**REM**	**REM**	**REM**		**rem**
	Action: 62	Action: 249	Action: 248	Action: 248		**rem_drv**
		lpr.exe	lpr.exe	lpr.exe		**rembak**
			tlntadmn.exe	tlntadmn start		**remote**
		rasadmin.exe	**rasadmin.exe**	rraswiz.exe	Control Panel > Remote Access	**Remote Access Admin**
		rasadmin.exe	rasadmin.exe	rraswiz.exe		**Remote Access Configuration**
		rasdial.exe	rasdial.exe	rasdial.exe	**Apple Menu > Control Panel > Remote Access**	**Remote Access Control Panel**
		ncadmin.exe	**rbfg.exe**	**rbfg.exe**		**Remote Boot Disk Generator**
		rplmgr.exe rplcmd .exe				**Remoteboot Manager**
			ntmsmgr.msc rsm.exe	**ntmsmgr.msc** rsm.exe		**Removable Storage Manager**
		cacls *path* /E /R *user*	cacls *path* /E /R *user*	cacls *path* /E /R *user*		**remove**
	Action: 185	Action: 184	Action: 181	Action: 181		**Remove Network Adapter**
	Action: 185	Action: 184	Action: 181	Action: 181		**Remove Network Interface**
ren rename	**ren rename**	**ren rename**	**ren rename**	**ren rename**	Action: 113	**ren, rename**
move	move	move	move	move	Move	**rendir**
		start	start	start		**renice**
replace.exe	copy /Y	**replace.exe**	**replace.exe**	**replace.exe**	alt + Drag a file	**replace**
replace.exe	copy /Y	replace.exe	replace.exe	replace.exe	**Replace File**	**Replace File**
			Action: 158	Action: 158		**repquota**
set *variable=*	set *variable=*	set *variable=*	set *variable=*	set *variable=*		**reset**
						Reset Environment
			Action: 160	Action: 160		**Reset Network Adapter**
			Action: 160 Action: 183	Action: 160 Action: 183		**Reset Network Interface**
	Action: 153	Action: 153	Action: 153	Action: 153	Special > Restart	**reset server**
	Action: 153	Action: 153	Action: 153	Action: 153	Special > Restart	**Restart Server**
restore.exe msbackup.exe	srw.exe msbackup.exe	**restore.exe** ntbackup.exe	ntbackup.exe	ntbackup.exe asr_fmt.exe		**restore**
		cacls *path* /E /R *user*	cacls *path* /E /R *user*	cacls *path* /E /R *user*		**revoke**
		rexec.exe	**rexec.exe**	**rexec.exe**		**rexec**
attrib.exe	attrib.exe	attrib.exe	attrib.exe	attrib.exe	Select icon > command + i	**rights**

	AIX	Linux	OpenBSD	Solaris	NetWare 3	NetWare 4	NetWare 5	NetWare 6
rlogin	**rlogin** telnet	**rlogin** telnet ssh	**rlogin** telnet ssh	**rlogin** telnet	rconsole.exe	rconsole.exe	rconsole.exe	rconj.exe
rm	**rm**	**rm**	**rm**	**rm**	filer.exe	filer.exe nwadmn32.exe	filer.exe nwadmn32.exe	filer.exe nwadmn32.exe
rmdev	**rmdev**	rmmod	modunload	rem_drv	unload *driver*	unload *driver*	unload *driver*	unload *driver*
rmdir	**rmdir**	**rmdir**	**rmdir**	**rmdir**	filer.exe	filer.exe	filer.exe	filer.exe
rmfs	**rmfs**	umount	umount	umount	install.nlm	install.nlm	nwconfig.nlm	nwconfig.nlm
rmgroup	**rmgroup** smitty group	groupdel	**rmgroup**	admintool	syscon.exe	nwadmn32.exe	nwadmn32.exe	nwadmn32.exe
rmic				**rmic**			**rmic**	**rmic**
rmiregistry (Client)				**rmiregistry**			**rmiregistry.exe**	**rmiregistry.exe**
rmiregistry (Server)				**rmiregistry**			**rmiregistry**	**rmiregistry**
rmitab	**rmitab**	vi /etc/inittab	vi /etc/rc.conf	vi /etc/inittab	Action: 214	Action: 215	Action: 215	Action: 215
rmmount	mount	mount	mount	**rmmount**	cdrom.nlm	cdrom.nlm	cdinst.nlm	cdinst.nlm
rmnamsv	**rmnamsv**	vi /etc/resolv.conf	vi /etc/resolv.conf	vi /etc/resolv.conf	edit \etc\resolv.cfg	edit \etc\resolv.cfg	edit \etc\resolv.cfg	edit \etc\resolv.cfg
rmnfsexp	**rmnfsexp**	exportfs -u	Action: 8	unshare	syscon.exe flag *file* -sh	nwadmn32.exe flag *file* +sh /FO	nwadmn32.exe flag *file* +sh /FO	nwadmn32.exe flag *file* +sh /FO
rmnfsmnt	**rmnfsmnt**	umount	umount	umount	map.exe	map.exe	map.exe	map.exe
rmprtsv	**rmprtsv**			lpshut	pconsole.exe	pconsole.exe	nwadmn32.exe	nwadmn32.exe
rmps	**rmps**	swapoff	swapctl	swap			swap	swap
rmque	**rmque**	lpc	lpc	lpadmin	pconsole.exe	pconsole.exe	nwadmn32.exe	nwadmn32.exe
rmquedev	**rmquedev**	lpc	lpc	lpadmin	pconsole.exe	pconsole.exe	nwadmn32.exe	nwadmn32.exe
rmuser	**rmuser**	userdel	**rmuser**	userdel	syscon.exe sysconW.exe	netadmin.exe nwadmn32.exe	nwadmn32.exe consoleone.exe consoleonedos. exe	nwadmn32.exe consoleone.exe consoleonedos. exe
robocopy	ftp uucp rcp	ftp ncftpget rcp	ftp rcp uucp	ftp uucp rcp	ncopy.exe	ncopy.exe	ncopy.exe	ncopy.exe
rotatelogs	alog strclean	**rotatelogs** logrotate	**rotatelogs** newsyslog	**rotatelogs** newsyslog strclean	load edit /system/sys$log. err	nwadmn32.exe load view /system/sys$log. err	nwadmn32.exe view /system/sys$log. err	nwadmn32.exe view /system/sys$log. err
route	**route**	**route**	**route**	**route**	tcpcon.nlm	tcpcon.nlm	tcpcon.nlm Action: 130	tcpcon.nlm Action: 130
Routing and Remote Access Server Setup Wizard	pppcontrold	pppd	pppd	aspppd		Action: 121	niascfg.nlm	Action: 121
rpc.rexd	**rpc.rexd**	rexec rexecd	rexecd	**rpc.rexd**				
rpl	vi /etc/bootparams bootparamd		vi /etc/bootparams bootparamd	vi /etc/bootparams bootparamd	**rpl.nlm**	**rpl.nlm**	**rpl.nlm**	**rpl.nlm**
rplcmd	vi /etc/bootparams		vi /etc/bootparams	vi /etc/bootparams	rpl.nlm	rpl.nlm	rpl.nlm	rpl.nlm
rpld	bootpd	dhcpd	bootpd	**rpld**	rpl.nlm	rpl.nlm	rpl.nlm	rpl.nlm
rpm	installp	**rpm**	pkg_add	pkgadd	install > product options	install > product options	nwconfig > product options	nwconfig > product options
rs232	getty		getty	getty	**rs232.nlm**	**rs232.nlm**	**rs232.nlm** aiocon.nlm	aiocon.nlm

DOS	Windows 9x	NT 4.0	NT 2000	Windows XP	Macintosh	
	telnet	telnet	telnet Action: 173	telnet Action: 173		**rlogin**
del erase	del erase	del erase	del erase	del erase	<command> + <Backspace>	**rm**
	Action: 62	Action: 249	Action: 248	Action: 248		**rmdev**
rd rmdir	rd rmdir	rd rmdir	rd rmdir	rd rmdir	<command> + <Backspace>	**rmdir**
fdisk.exe	fdisk.exe	windisk.exe	diskmgmt.msc	diskmgmt.msc diskpart.exe	Action: 64	**rmfs**
		net group /DELETE	net group /DELETE	net group /DELETE		**rmgroup**
						rmic
						rmiregistry (Client)
						rmiregistry (Server)
edit autoexec.bat	edit autoexec.bat	Control Panel > Services	services.msc	services.msc	Apple Menu > Control Panels > Extensions Manager *selections...*	**rmitab**
mscdex.exe	mscdex.exe	mscdexnt.exe	diskmgmt.msc mscdexnt.exe	diskmgmt.msc mscdexnt.exe		**rmmount**
	Action: 139	Action: 192	Action: 191	Action: 191	Apple Menu > Control Panels > TCPIP	**rmnamsv**
	Action: 242 net share	Action: 242 net share	Action: 242 net share	Action: 242 net share	Apple Menu > Control Panels > File Sharing	**rmnfsexp**
	net use /delete	net use /delete	net use /delete	net use /delete	Apple Menu > Network Browser	**rmnfsmnt**
		Action: 220	Action: 221	Action: 221		**rmprtsv**
						rmps
	Control Panel > Printers	Control Panel > Printers	Control Panel > Printers	Control Panel > Printers and Faxes	Application Menu > PrintMonitor	**rmque**
	Control Panel > Printers	Control Panel > Printers	Control Panel > Printers	Control Panel > Printers and Faxes	Application Menu > PrintMonitor	**rmquedev**
	Control Panel > Users	usrmgr.exe musrmgr.exe	compmgmt.msc	compmgmt.msc		**rmuser**
	robocopy.exe ftp.exe	rcp.exe ftp.exe	rcp.exe ftp.exe	rcp.exe ftp.exe		**robocopy**
	wbemcntl.exe	eventvwr.exe	eventvwr.exe	eventvwr.exe		**rotatelogs**
	route.exe	**route.exe**	**route.exe**	**route.exe**		**route**
		rasadmin.exe	rasadmin.exe	**rraswiz.exe**	Apple Menu > Control Panels > Remote Access	**Routing and Remote Access Server Setup Wizard**
		rexec.exe	rexec.exe	rexec.exe		**rpc.rexd**
		rplmgr.exe rplcmd .exe				**rpl**
		rplcmd .exe rplmgr.exe				**rplcmd**
		rplcmd .exe rplmgr.exe				**rpld**
	Control Panel > Add/Remove Programs	Control Panel > Add/Remove Programs	Control Panel > Add/Remove Programs	Control Panel > Add/Remove Programs		**rpm**
ctty	ctty					**rs232**

	AIX	Linux	OpenBSD	Solaris	NetWare 3	NetWare 4	NetWare 5	NetWare 6
rsh, remsh	**rsh** **remsh**	**rsh** **remsh**	**rsh** **remsh**	**rsh** **remsh**				
rsm				vold	cd	cd	cd	cd
rsync		**rsync**		filesync				
runas	Action: 66	suexec Action: 66	suexec Action: 66	Action: 66				
runlevel	who -r	**runlevel**		who -r			list stage	list stage
rusers	**rusers** finger	**rusers** finger	**rusers** finger	**rusers** finger		nlist user	nlist user	nlist user
rwall	**rwall**	wall	**rwall**	**rwall**	broadcast send.exe Action: 36	broadcast send.exe Action: 36	broadcast Action: 36	broadcast Action: 36
rwho	**rwho** finger	**rwho** finger	**rwho** finger	**rwho** finger		nlist user	nlist user	nlist user
sa	**sa** accton		**sa** accton	accton	atotal.exe paudit.exe	atotal.exe	atotal.exe	atotal.exe
sadc	**sadc**	**sadc**		**sadc**	monitor.nlm	monitor.nlm	monitor.nlm	monitor.nlm
sag	topas netpmon	top	top	**sag** perfmeter top	monitor.nlm	monitor.nlm	monitor.nlm	monitor.nlm
sar	**sar** topas	**sar** top	top	**sar** top	monitor.nlm	monitor.nlm	monitor.nlm	monitor.nlm
sash	ksh sh csh bsh	**sash** ash bsh bash sh tcsh	csh ksh rksh sh	csh jsh ksh rksh sh rsh		netbasic.nlm	netbasic.nlm	netbasic.nlm
Scan All	cfgmgr			Action: 151	scan for new devices	scan for new devices	**scan all** scan for new devices	**scan all** scan for new devices
Scan For New Devices	cfgmgr			touch /reconfigure Action: 151	**scan for new devices**	**scan for new devices**	**scan for new devices** scan all	**scan for new devices** scan all
scandisk	fsck	fsck	fsck	fsck	vrepair.nlm	vrepair.nlm	nss /rebuild nss /menu vrepair.nlm	ConsoleOne > Server > Media vrepair.nlm
scanpci	smit devices	**scanpci**	**scanpci**	prtdiag		ncmcon.nlm	ncmcon.nlm	ncmcon.nlm
schdelay	at cron	crond sched at	at cron	at cron sched	cron.nlm wmsched.exe	**schdelay.nlm** cron.nlm wmsched.exe	cron.nlm wmsched.exe	cron.nlm wmsched.exe
sched	at cron	**sched** crond at	at cron	**sched** cron at	cron.nlm wmsched.exe	cron.nlm schdelay.nlm wmsched.exe	cron.nlm wmsched.exe	cron.nlm wmsched.exe
Scheduled Tasks	at cron	crond sched at	at cron	cron sched at	cron.nlm wmsched.exe	cron.nlm wmsched.exe schdelay.nlm	cron.nlm wmsched.exe	cron.nlm wmsched.exe
schtasks	crontab cron at	crontab cron at	crontab cron at	crontab cron at	cron.nlm wmsched.exe	cron.nlm wmsched.exe	cron.nlm wmsched.exe	cron.nlm wmsched.exe
scp	rcp ftp	**scp** rcp ftp	**scp** rcp ftp	rcp ftp	ncopy.exe	ncopy.exe	ncopy.exe	ncopy.exe
Scrapbook								
Screen Saver				dtscreen	monitor.nlm	monitor.nlm	**scrsaver.nlm**	**scrsaver.nlm**
Screen Shot		screendump		snapshot	CONLOG entire=yes	CONLOG entire=yes	CONLOG entire=yes	CONLOG entire=yes
Screen shot of window		screendump		snapshot	CONLOG entire=yes	CONLOG entire=yes	CONLOG entire=yes	CONLOG entire=yes
screendump	capture	**screendump**		snapshot	CONLOG entire=yes	CONLOG entire=yes	CONLOG entire=yes	CONLOG entire=yes
script	**script**	**script**	**script**	**script**	conlog.nlm	conlog.nlm	conlog.nlm	conlog.nlm
sdiff	**sdiff**	**sdiff**	**sdiff**	**sdiff**				
search	$PATH	$PATH	$PATH	$PATH	**search**	**search**	**search**	**search**

DOS	Windows 9x	NT 4.0	NT 2000	Windows XP	Macintosh	
		rsh	**rsh**	**rsh**		**rsh, remsh**
			rsm.exe ntmsmgr.msc	**rsm.exe** ntmsmgr.msc		**rsm**
	mobsync.exe		mobsync.exe	mobsync.exe		**rsync**
			runas.exe	**runas.exe**		**runas**
						runlevel
		finger.exe	finger.exe	finger.exe		**rusers**
	net send	net send	net send	net send		**rwall**
		finger.exe	finger.exe	finger.exe		**rwho**
		eventvwr.exe	eventvwr.exe	eventvwr.exe		**sa**
		perfmon.exe	perfmon.exe	perfmon.exe	Apple Menu > About This Computer	**sadc**
		perfmon.exe	perfmon.exe	perfmon.exe	Apple Menu > About This Computer	**sag**
	taskman.exe	taskmgr.exe	taskmgr.exe	taskmgr.exe		**sar**
command.com	command.com	cmd.exe command.com	cmd.exe command.com	cmd.exe command.com		**sash**
	Action: 152	Action: 152	Action: 152	Action: 152		**Scan All**
	Action: 152	Action: 152	Action: 152	Action: 152		**Scan For New Devices**
scandisk.exe chkdsk.exe	**scandisk.exe** scandskw.exe chkdsk.exe	chkdsk.exe chkntfs.exe	chkdsk.exe chkntfs.exe	chkdsk.exe chkntfs.exe	Action: 101	**scandisk**
	Action: 190		Action: 177	Action: 177		**scanpci**
	sysagent.exe Action: 9	at.exe	at.exe Action: 9	at.exe schtasks.exe		**schdelay**
	sysagent.exe Action: 9	at.exe	at.exe Action: 9	at.exe schtasks.exe		**sched**
	sysagent.exe Action: 9	at.exe	at.exe Action: 9	at.exe schtasks.exe		**Scheduled Tasks**
	sysagent.exe Action: 9	at.exe	at.exe	**schtasks.exe** at.exe		**schtasks**
	robocopy.exe ftp.exe	rcp.exe ftp.exe	rcp.exe ftp.exe	rcp.exe ftp.exe		**scp**
	clipbrd.exe	clipbrd.exe	clipbrd.exe	clipbrd.exe	**Apple Menu > Scrapbook**	**Scrapbook**
	Action: 150	Action: 150	Action: 150	Action: 150		**Screen Saver**
graphics	<Print Screen>	<Print Screen>	<Print Screen>	<Print Screen>	**command + shift + 3** **command + shift + 4**	**Screen Shot**
	<ALT> + <Print Screen>	<ALT> + <Print Screen>	<ALT> + <Print Screen>	<ALT> + <Print Screen>	**<Caps Lock>= on + <command> + <shift> + <4> + click in window**	**Screen shot of window**
	<Print Screen>	<Print Screen>	<Print Screen>	<Print Screen>	<command> + <shift> + <3>	**screendump**
						script
fc.exe	fc.exe	comp.exe fc.exe	comp.exe fc.exe	comp.exe fc.exe		**sdiff**
path	path	path	path	path		**search**

	AIX	Linux	OpenBSD	Solaris	NetWare 3	NetWare 4	NetWare 5	NetWare 6
Search Internet								
secedit	tcbck	rpm -V		aset	security.exe			
securetcpip	**securetcpip**	iptables	ipf			filtcfg.nlm	filtcfg.nlm	filtcfg.nlm
Securing NT Account Database		pwconv		pwconv		Action: 55	Action: 55	Action: 55
security	tcbck	rpm -V		aset	**security.exe**			
Select All								
send (Client)	rwall write wall	write wall	rwall write wall	rwall write wall	**send.exe** Action: 36	**send.exe** Action: 36	Action: 36	Action: 36
send (Server)	write wall	write wall	write wall	write wall	**send** broadcast	**send** broadcast	**send** broadcast	**send** broadcast
sendbug	**sendbug** bugfiler errpt	cvsbug bashbug perlbug -a	**sendbug** cvsbug perlbug -a	perlbug -a				
sendmail	**sendmail** spost post	**sendmail** spost post	**sendmail** smtpd	**sendmail** rmail				
Server Backup Utility	backup rdump	backup rdump	backup rdump	ufsdump	**sbackup.nlm**	**sbackup.nlm**	nwback32.exe	nwback32.exe
Server Installation	smit lvm	fdisk	fdisk	format	**install.nlm**	**install.nlm**	nwconfig.nlm	nwconfig.nlm
Server Manager	smit smitty	linuxconf		admintool	fconsole.exe	**servman.nlm**	NetWare Management Portal cset	NetWare Remote Manger cset
server_upgrade			supfilesrv sup	**server_upgrad e**	setup /ACU	setup /ACU	setup /ACU	setup /ACU
set	**set** setenv variable=value	**set** setenv variable=value	**set** setenv variable=value	**set** setenv variable=value	dos set	dos set	dos set envset	dos set envset setenv
set (Time)	date	date	date	date	**set time** time	**set time** time	**set time** time	**set time** time
Set Time	date	date hwclock	date	date	**set time**	**set time**	**set time**	**set time**
Set Time Zone	chtz	zdump timeconfig tzselect	zdump	zdump Action: 186	**Set Time Zone**	**Set Time Zone**	**Set Time Zone**	**Set Time Zone**
setclock	**setclock** date	**setclock** clock hwclock date	date	date	set time	set time	set time	set time
setdebug				jdb				
setenv	**setenv**	**setenv** nwfsctrl set *variable = value*	**setenv**	**setenv**	dos set	dos set	dos set	**setenv**
setfacl	chmod acledit	chmod	chmod	**setfacl** chmod	rights.exe syscon.exe sysconW.exe	rights.exe netadmin.exe nwadmn32.exe	rights.exe nwadmn32.exe consoleone.exe	rights.exe nwadmn32.exe consoleone.exe
setleds	xset	**setleds**	xset	xset				
setopt		shopt set shellopt=*value*		**setopt** shopt set shellopt=*value*	dos set	dos set	envset dos set	envset setenv dos set
setpass	passwd yppasswd	passwd yppasswd nwpasswd	passwd	passwd yppasswd nispasswd	**setpass.exe** Action: 37	**setpass.exe** Action: 37	**setpass.exe** Action: 37	Action: 37
setquota	edquota	**setquota** edquota	edquota	edquota	dspace.exe	Action: 247	Action: 247	Action: 247
setserial	stty	**setserial** stty	stty	syncinit stty	rs232.nlm	rs232.nlm	aiocon.nlm rs232.nlm	aiocon.nlm

DOS	Windows 9x	NT 4.0	NT 2000	Windows XP	Macintosh	
	Action: 104	Action: 104	Action: 104	Action: 104	**<command> + <H>** **File > Search internet**	**Search Internet**
			secedit.exe	**secedit.exe**		**secedit**
			rrasmgmt.msc	rrasmgmt.msc		**securetcpip**
			syskey.exe	**syskey.exe**		**Securing NT Account Database**
			secedit.exe	secedit.exe		**security**
	CTRL + A	CTRL + A	CTRL + A	CTRL + A	**command + a** **Edit > Select All**	**Select All**
	net send	net send	net send	net send		**send (Client)**
	winpopup.exe	msg.exe net send	msg.exe net send	msg.exe net send		**send (Server)**
	winrep.exe	Action: 19	winrep.exe	Action: 18		**sendbug**
			services.msc	services.msc		**sendmail**
msbackup.exe restore.exe	msbackup.exe backup.exe	ntbackup.exe backup.exe	ntbackup.exe	ntbackup.exe		**Server Backup Utility**
fdisk.exe	fdisk.exe	windisk.exe	diskmgmt.msc	diskmgmt.msc	Action: 64	**Server Installation**
		usrmgr.exe windisk.exe	compmgmt.msc	compmgmt.msc		**Server Manager**
						server_upgrade
set	**set**	**set** Action: 77	**set** Action: 78	**set** Action: 78		**set**
date time	date time	date time	date time	date time	Apple Menu > Control Panels > Date & Time	**set (Time)**
date time	date time	date time	date time	date time	Apple Menu > Control Panels > Date & Time *selections...*	**Set Time**
	Control Panel > Date/Time	Control Panel > Date/Time	Control Panel > Date/Time	Control Panel > Date and Time	Apple Menu > Control Panels > Date & Time	**Set Time Zone**
date time	date time	date time	date time	date time	Apple Menu > Control Panels > Date & Time *selections...*	**setclock**
	setdebug.exe					**setdebug**
set	set	set Action: 77	set Action: 78	set Action: 78		**setenv**
		cacls.exe	cacls.exe	cacls.exe		**setfacl**
numlock						**setleds**
set	set	set	set	set		**setopt**
	net password Control Panel > passwords	usrmgr.exe Action: 229	compmgmt.msc Action: 229	compmgmt.msc Action: 229	Action: 200	**setpass**
			Action: 158	Action: 158		**setquota**
mode.com	Action: 167 mode.com	Control Panel > Ports mode.com	Action: 166 mode.com	Action: 166 mode.com		**setserial**

	AIX	Linux	OpenBSD	Solaris	NetWare 3	NetWare 4	NetWare 5	NetWare 6
setup	smit smitty	**setup** linuxconf		admintool	syscon.exe sysconW.exe	netadmin.exe nwadmn32.exe	nwadmn32.exe consoleone.exe consoleonedos.ex e	nwadmn32.exe consoleone.exe consoleonedos.ex e
Setup DNS/DHCP Managment Console	dhcpsconf dadmin	dhcpd.conf	dhcpd.conf	dhcpconfig dhcpmgr dhtadm pntadm		dhcpcfg.nlm	**\public\dnsdhc p\setup.exe**	**\public\dnsdhc p\setup.exe**
setvar	setenv set variable=value	**setvar** setenv set variable=value	setenv set variable=value	setenv set variable=value	dos set	dos set	envset dos set	envset dos set
setver								
setxkbmap	chkbd lskbd	**setxkbmap** loadkeys kbdconfig	**setxkbmap** kbd	kbd loadkeys	keyb.nlm	keyb.nlm	keyb.nlm charset.nlm	keyb.nlm charset.nlm
sfc	tcbck	rpm -V		aset.restore				
sfdisk	chpv	**sfdisk** fdisk	fdisk	fdisk format	install.nlm	install.nlm	nwconfig.nlm	nwconfig.nlm
sh	bsh ksh sh csh	**sh** ash bsh bash sash tcsh	**sh** csh ksh rksh	**sh** **rsh** csh jsh ksh rksh		netbasic.nlm	netbasic.nlm	netbasic.nlm
share	exportfs	exportfs	Cross Reference Note: 8	**share** exportfs	flag *file* -sh	flag *file* +sh /FO	flag *file* +sh /FO	flag *file* +sh /FO
Shared Folders overview Manager	smit mknfsexp	vi /etc/exports	vi /etc/exports	vi /etc/exports	syscon.exe grant	nwadmn32.exe rights	nwadmn32.exe rights	nwadmn32.exe rights
shell	chsh	chsh	chpass -s	admintool > User Managment				
shift	**shift**	**shift**	**shift**	**shift**	**shift**	**shift**	**shift**	**shift**
shopt		**shopt** set shellopt=*value*		**shopt** setopt set shellopt=*value*	dos set	dos set	envset dos set	envset setenv dos set
Show Clipboard								
Show Original	file	readlink file	readlink file	file				
showfont		**showfont**	**showfont**	**showfont**				
showmount	**showmount**	**showmount**	**showmount**	**showmount** dfmounts	map.exe	map.exe	map.exe	map.exe
showrev	lslpp sysck	rpm -qa	pkg_info	**showrev** pkginfo	install > product options	install > product options	nwconfig > product options	nwconfig > product options
shred		**shred**	rm -P		purge.exe	purge.exe filer > Purge Deleted Files	purge.exe filer > Purge Deleted Files	filer > Purge Deleted Files Action: 4
Shut Down	shutdown -F halt	shutdown -h now halt	shutdown -h now halt	init 5 shutdown -i 5 -g 1	down fconsole	down	down	down
shutacct	**shutacct** accton turnacct off		accton	**shutacct** accton turnacct off	syscon.exe			
shutdown	**shutdown -F** halt	**shutdown -h now** halt	**shutdown -h now** halt	**shutdown -i 5 -g 1** init 5	down fconsole	down	down	down
Shutdown Network Interface	ifconfig *interface* down	ifconfig *interface* down	ifconfig *interface* down	ifconfig *interface* down		**Shutdown Network Interface**	**Shutdown Network Interface**	**Shutdown Network Interface**

DOS	Windows 9x	NT 4.0	NT 2000	Windows XP	Macintosh	
	control.exe	control.exe	control.exe	control.exe	Apple Menu > Control Panels	**setup**
		dhcpadmn.exe	dhcpmgmt.msc	dhcpwiz.exe dhcpmgmt.msc		**Setup DNS/DHCP Managment Console**
set	set	set Action: 77	set Action: 78	set Action: 78		**setvar**
setver.exe	**setver.exe** mkcompat.exe	**setver.exe**	**setver.exe**	**setver.exe**		**setver**
chcp keyb.com	chcp.com keyb.com Control Panel > Keyboard	chcp.com keyb.com Control Panel > Keyboard	chcp.com kb16.com Control Panel > Keyboard	chcp.com kb16.com Control Panel > Keyboard	Apple Menu > Control Panels > Keyboard	**setxkbmap**
	sfc.exe		**sfc.exe**	**sfc.exe**		**sfc**
fdisk.exe	fdisk.exe	windisk.exe	diskmgmt.msc	diskmgmt.msc diskpart.exe	Action: 64	**sfdisk**
command.com	command.com	cmd.exe command.com	cmd.exe command.com	cmd.exe command.com		**sh**
share	Cross Reference Note: 119 net share	Cross Reference Note: 119 net share	Cross Reference Note: 119 net share	Cross Reference Note: 119 net share	Control Panel > File Sharing	**share**
	Action: 23	Action: 23	**fsmgmt.msc** Action: 23	**fsmgmt.msc** Action: 23	Apple Menu > Control Panels > File Sharing	**Shared Folders overview Manager**
shell						**shell**
shift	**shift**	**shift**	**shift**	**shift**		**shift**
set	set	set	set	set		**shopt**
	clipbrd.exe	clipbrd.exe	clipbrd.exe	clipbrd.exe	**Edit > Show Clipboard**	**Show Clipboard**
	Action: 91	Action: 92	Action: 91	Action: 91	**Select shortcut icon > command + r**	**Show Original**
	Control Panel > Fonts	Control Panel > Fonts	Control Panel > Fonts	Control Panel > Fonts		**showfont**
	Windows Explorer > My Computer	Windows NT Explorer > My Computer	Windows Explorer > My Computer	Windows Explorer > My Computer		**showmount**
	qfecheck.exe wupdmgr.exe	Control Panel > Add/Remove Programs	wupdmgr.exe	wupdmgr.exe		**showrev**
						shred
	Start > Shut down	shutdown.exe Start > Shut down	Start > Shut down	shutdown.exe Start > Shut down	**Power Button > Shut Down** **Special > Shut Down**	**Shut Down**
						shutacct
	Start > Shut down	**shutdown.exe** Start > Shut down	Start > Shut down	**shutdown.exe** Start > Shut down	Power Button > Shut Down Special > Shut Down	**shutdown**
			Action: 160	Action: 160		**Shutdown Network Interface**

	AIX	Linux	OpenBSD	Solaris	NetWare 3	NetWare 4	NetWare 5	NetWare 6
SimpleText	vi tvi	vi emacs	vi	vi dtpad	edit.nlm	edit.nlm	edit.nlm	edit.nlm
skill	kill killall	**skill** kill killall	kill killall	kill killall	unload	unload	unload	unload
slist	lb_find	**slist** nwsfind			**slist.exe** display servers	nlist server /B display servers	nlist server /B display servers	nlist server /B display servers
slstats	atmstat fddistat tokstat netstat -I *interface*	ipppstats pppstats netstat -I *interface*	**slstats** pppstats netstat -I *interface*	syncstat netstat -I *interface*	tcpcon.nlm	ppptrace.nlm tcpcon.nlm	atmcon.nlm	ppptrace.nlm tcpcon.nlm
smartdrv					set read ahead enabled = ON	set read ahead enabled = ON	set read ahead enabled = ON	set read ahead enabled = ON
smbclient		**smbclient**			map.exe	map.exe	map.exe	map.exe
smbmnt	mount	**smbmnt** smbmount mount ncpmount	mount	mount	map.exe	map.exe	map.exe	map.exe
smbmount	mount	**smbmount** smbmnt mount ncpmount	mount	mount	map.exe	map.exe	map.exe	map.exe
smbpasswd	yppasswd	**smbpasswd** yppasswd		yppasswd	**setpass.exe** Action: 37	**setpass.exe** Action: 37	**setpass.exe** Action: 37	Action: 37
smbspool	lp lpr	**smbspool** lp lpr	lpr	lp lpr	nprint.exe	nprint.exe	nprint.exe	
smbstatus		**smbstatus**			monitor > connections	monitor > connections	monitor > connections	monitor > connections
smbumount	umount	**smbumount** ncpumount umount	umount	umount	dismount	dismount	dismount	dismount
smit, smitty	**smit** **smitty**	linuxconf		admintool	syscon.exe sysconW.exe	netadmin.exe nwadmn32.exe	nwadmn32.exe consoleone.exe consoleonedos.exe	nwadmn32.exe consoleone.exe consoleonedos.exe
smtpd	sendmail spost	sendmail spost	**smtpd** sendmail	sendmail				
snapshot	capture	screendump		**snapshot**	CONLOG entire=yes	CONLOG entire=yes	CONLOG entire=yes	CONLOG entire=yes
snice	renice nice	**snice** renice nice	renice nice	renice nice	load	load	load	load
snmplog		snmptrapd			**snmplog.nlm**	**snmplog.nlm**	**snmplog.nlm**	**snmplog.nlm**
solregis				**solregis**				
sort	**sort** tsort	**sort** tsort	**sort** tsort	**sort** tsort				
Sound Control Panel								
Sound Recorder		rec		audiotool				
source	**source**	**source**	**source**	**source**	Action: 93	Action: 93	Action: 93	Action: 93
Speech Control Panel				accessx				
splp	**splp**	lpc	lpc	lpadmin	pconsole.exe	pconsole.exe	nwpmw32.exe nwadmn32.exe ndpsm.nlm	nwadmn32.exe ndpsm.nlm
Spoofer Console	hostname uptime uname -a	hostname uptime uname -a	hostname uptime uname -a	hostname uptime uname -a	monitor.nlm version	monitor.nlm version	**spfcon.nlm** monitor.nlm	monitor.nlm version

DOS	Windows 9x	NT 4.0	NT 2000	Windows XP	Macintosh	
edit.com	notepad.exe wordpad.exe	notepad.exe wordpad.exe	notepad.exe wordpad.exe	notepad.exe wordpad.exe	**Action: 82**	SimpleText
	taskman.exe	kill.exe	tskill.exe	tskill.exe taskkill.exe	<command >+ <alt> + <esc> <command> + <q>	skill
	net view	net view	net view	net view	Apple Menu > Chooser Apple Menu > Network Browser	slist
	atmadm.exe	netmon.exe	atmadm.exe	atmadm.exe		slstats
smartdrv.exe	**smartdrv.exe**					smartdrv
	net use	net use	net use	net use		smbclient
	net use	net use	net use	net use	Apple Menu > Network Browser	smbmnt
	net use	net use	net use	net use	Apple Menu > Network Browser	smbmount
	net password Control Panel > passwords	usrmgr.exe Action: 229	compmgmt.msc Action: 229	compmgmt.msc Action: 229	Action: 200	smbpasswd
print.exe	type *file* > LPT1	print.exe lpr.exe	print.exe lpr.exe	print.exe lpr.exe	command + p File > Print	smbspool
	netwatch.exe	srvmgr.exe	srvmgr.exe	srvmgr.exe	Apple > Control Panels > File Sharing	smbstatus
	net use *drive* /delete	net use *drive* /delete	net use *drive* /delete	net use *drive* /delete		smbumount
	control.exe	control.exe	control.exe	control.exe	Apple Menu > Control Panels	smit, smitty
			services.msc	services.msc		smtpd
	<Print Screen>	<Print Screen>	<Print Screen>	<Print Screen>	<Caps Lock>= on + <command> + <shift> + <4> + click in window	snapshot
		start	start	start		snice
						snmplog
	regwiz.exe		regwiz.exe	regwiz.exe		solregis
sort.exe	**sort.exe**	**sort.exe**	**sort.exe**	**sort.exe**		sort
	Control Panel > Multimedia	Control Panel > Multimedia	Control Panel > Sounds And Multimedia	Control Panel > Sounds And Multimedia	**Apple Menu > Control Panels > Sound**	Sound Control Panel
	sndrec32.exe	**sndrec32.exe**	**sndrec32.exe**	**sndrec32.exe**	simpletext > sound > recorder	Sound Recorder
call	call	call	call	call		source
	accwiz.exe	Control Panel > Accessibility Options	accwiz.exe	accwiz.exe	**Apple Menu > Control Panels > Speech**	Speech Control Panel
	Action: 256	Action: 256	Action: 256	Action: 256	Action: 115	splp
msd.exe	Action: 156 winver.exe	hostname winver.exe	hostname winver.exe	hostname winver.exe	Apple Menu > Apple System Profiler	Spoofer Console

	AIX	Linux	OpenBSD	Solaris	NetWare 3	NetWare 4	NetWare 5	NetWare 6
spool	lprm qadm qmov lpr	lprm	lprm	lprm	**spool**	**spool**	**spool**	**spool**
SQL Server Client Network Utility							\public\sqlc\client\odbc\disk1\setup.exe	odbc.exe
ssh, slogin		**ssh** **slogin**	**ssh** **slogin**		remote encrypt	remote encrypt	rconag6 -e	rconag6 -e
sshd	telnetd	**sshd** telnetd	**sshd** telnetd	telnetd		telnetd.nlm	telnetd.nlm	telnetd.nlm
Start Internet Explorer	defaultbrowser	lynx netscape	lynx	netscape				
Start Processors	cpu_state -e			psradm -n		mpdriver.nlm	**start processors**	**start processors**
Start without extensions	Action: 99	linux single linux init=/bin/bash	boot -s	boot -s	server -na -ns	server -na -ns	server -na -ns	server -na -ns
startsrc	**startsrc**	Action: 71	vi /etc/rc.conf	Action: 53	load	load	load	load
Startup Disk Control Panel	Action: 99	vi /etc/lilo.conf						
startup.ncf	smit smitty	/etc/modules.conf	config -e -o bsd.new /bsd	touch /reconfigure	**startup.ncf**	**startup.ncf**	**startup.ncf**	**startup.ncf**
startx	**startx** X	**startx** X	**startx** X	X openwin			startx.ncf	startx.ncf
stat	istat	**stat**	ls -ali	ls -ali	ndir.exe	ndir.exe	ndir.exe	ndir.exe
statserial		**statserial** setserial		syncinit	rs232.nlm	rs232.nlm	rs232.nlm aiocon.nlm	aiocon.nlm
stop	**stop**	**stop**	**stop**	**stop**	unload	unload	unload	unload
Stop Processors	cpu_state -d			psradm -f		unload mpdriver.nlm	**stop processors**	**stop processors**
stopsrc	**stopsrc**	Action: 270	Action: 269	Action: 270	unload	unload	unload	unload
Storage Management Service	backup rdump	backup rdump	backup rdump	ufsdump	sbackup.nlm	sbackup.nlm	**nwback32.exe** sbcon.nlm	**nwback32.exe** sbcon.nlm
stty	**stty**	**stty**	**stty**	**stty**	rs232.nlm	rs232.nlm	aiocon.nlm rs232.nlm	aiocon.nlm
StuffIt Expander	uncompress	uncompress unzip gunzip	uncompress gunzip	uncompress unzip gunzip	nlunpack.exe nwxtract.exe	nwxtract.exe	unzip.nlm tar.nlm	unzip.nlm tar.nlm
su	**su**	**su** suexec	**su** suexec	**su**				
subst	ln –s	ln -s	ln -s	ln -s	map root	map root	map root	map root
swap	lsps mkps rmps	swapon swapoff mkswap	swapctl	**swap**			**swap**	**swap**
swapctl	swapon lsps mkps rmps	swapon swapoff mkswap	**swapctl**	swap			swap	swap
swapdev	lsps mkps rmps	**swapdev**	swapctl	swap			swap	swap
swapoff	mkps rmps	**swapoff** swapon	swapctl	swap			swap	swap
swapon	**swapon** mkps rmps chps	**swapon** swapoff mkswap	swapctl	swap			swap	swap
swcons	**swcons**							

DOS	Windows 9x	NT 4.0	NT 2000	Windows XP	Macintosh	
	net print	net print	net print	net print		**spool**
	cliconfg.exe Control Panel > ODBC Data Sources (32-bit)	Control Panel > ODBC Data Sources	**cliconfg.exe** Action: 114	**cliconfg.exe** Action: 114		**SQL Server Client Network Utility**
						ssh, slogin
			tlntadmn.exe	tlntadmn start		**sshd**
	netscape.exe iexplore.exe	netscape.exe iexplore.exe	netscape.exe iexplore.exe	netscape.exe iexplore.exe	**Action: 81**	**Start Internet Explorer**
						Start Processors
Action: 86	Action: 89		Action: 89	Action: 89	**Hold down the key `shift` during startup.**	**Start without extensions**
		Action: 274	Action: 275	Action: 275		**startsrc**
		Action: 125	Action: 125	bootcfg.exe	**Apple Menu > Control Panels > Startup Disk**	**Startup Disk Control Panel**
config.sys	Action: 62	Control Panel > Devices	Control Panel > Add/Remove Hardware	Control Panel > Add/Remove Hardware	Apple Menu > Control Panels > Extensions Manager *selections...*	**startup.ncf**
	win.com					**startx**
dir	Action: 260	Action: 260	Action: 260	Action: 260	Select harddrive and press <command> + I	**stat**
mode.com	Action: 167 mode.com	Control Panel > Ports mode.com	Action: 166 mode.com	Action: 166 mode.com		**statserial**
	taskman.exe	kill.exe	tskill.exe	tskill.exe	<COMMAND> + <ALT> + <ESC> <COMMAND> + <Q>	**stop**
						Stop Processors
		Action: 124	Action: 268	Action: 268		**stopsrc**
msbackup.exe restore.exe	msbackup.exe backup.exe	msbackup.exe backup.exe	ntbackup.exe	ntbackup.exe		**Storage Management Service**
mode.com	Action: 167 mode.com	Control Panel > Ports mode.com	Action: 166 mode.com	Action: 166 mode.com		**stty**
expand.exe		expand.exe	expand.exe	expand.exe	**Action: 79**	**StuffIt Expander**
			runas.exe	runas.exe		**su**
subst.exe	**subst.exe**	**subst.exe**	**subst.exe**	**subst.exe**		**subst**
	Action: 149	Action: 148	Action: 147	Action: 147		**swap**
	Action: 149	Action: 148	Action: 147	Action: 147		**swapctl**
	Action: 149	Action: 148	Action: 147	Action: 147		**swapdev**
	Action: 149	Action: 148	Action: 147	Action: 147		**swapoff**
	Action: 149	Action: 148	Action: 147	Action: 147		**swapon**
mode.com	mode.com	mode.com	mode.com	mode.com		**swcons**

	AIX	Linux	OpenBSD	Solaris	NetWare 3	NetWare 4	NetWare 5	NetWare 6
swmtool	smit	rpm	pkg_add pkg_delete	**swmtool**	install > product options	install > product options	nwconfig > product options	nwconfig > product options
syncinit	stty	setserial stty	stty	**syncinit** stty	rs232.nlm	rs232.nlm	rs232.nlm aiocon.nlm	aiocon.nlm
syncstat	atmstat fddistat tokstat netstat -I *interface*	ippstats pppstats netstat -I *interface*	pppstats slstats netstat -I *interface*	**syncstat** netstat -I *interface*	tcpcon.nlm	tcpcon.nlm ipxcon.nlm	tcpcon.nlm ipxcon.nlm	tcpcon.nlm ipxcon.nlm
sys	mkboot bosboot	mkbootdisk Action: 69	Action: 69	Action: 69				
sysck	**sysck** lslpp	rpm -qa	pkg_info -a	showrev -p pkginfo	install > product options	install > product options	nwconfig > product options	nwconfig > product options
syscon	smit smitty mkuser mkgroup	userconf useradd groupadd	adduser groupadd	admintool useradd groupadd	**syscon.exe** sysconW.exe	netadmin.exe nwadmn32.exe	nwadmn32.exe consoleone.exe consoleonedos. exe	nwadmn32.exe consoleone.exe consoleonedos. exe
sysconW	smit smitty mkuser mkgroup	userconf useradd groupadd	adduser groupadd	admintool useradd groupadd	**sysconW.exe** syscon.exe	netadmin.exe nwadmn32.exe	nwadmn32.exe consoleone.exe consoleonedos. exe	nwadmn32.exe consoleone.exe consoleonedos. exe
sysdef	lscfg svmon	dmesg free	dmesg top	**sysdef**	monitor.nlm display interrupts	monitor.nlm display interrupts	monitor.nlm display interrupts	monitor.nlm display interrupts
sysidconfig	smit smitty	linuxconf		**sysidconfig** admintool	install.nlm	install.nlm	nwconfig.nlm	nwconfig.nlm
sysidtool	smit smitty	linuxconf		**sysidtool**	syscon.exe sysconW.exe	netadmin.exe nwadmn32.exe	nwadmn32.exe consoleone.exe consoleonedos. exe	nwadmn32.exe consoleone.exe consoleonedos. exe
sysklogd	errdemon syslogd	**sysklogd** klogd syslogd	syslogd	syslogd	conlog.nlm	conlog.nlm	conlog.nlm	conlog.nlm
syslogd	**syslogd** errdemon	**syslogd** sysklogd klogd	**syslogd**	**syslogd**	conlog.nlm	conlog.nlm	conlog.nlm	conlog.nlm
sys-suspend	pmctrl	apmsleep apm	zzz apm	**sys-suspend** powerd				
systat	topas vmstat dmesg	top vmstat dmesg	**systat** top vmstat	prstat vmstat dmesg	monitor.nlm	monitor.nlm	monitor.nlm	monitor.nlm
System Configuration Editor	smit smitty	linuxconf	rc.conf	admintool	install > System Options	install > NCF files Options	nwconfig > NCF files Options	nwconfig > NCF files Options
System Configuration Utility	smit /etc/inittab	linuxconf /etc/inittab	/etc/rc.conf	/etc/inittab	install > System Options	install > NCF files Options	nwconfig > NCF files Options	nwconfig > NCF files Options
System File Checker	tcbck	rpm -V		aset.restore				
System Information	lscfg svmon	dmesg free	dmesg top	dmesg prtconf	monitor.nlm Display Interrupts	monitor.nlm Display Interrupts	monitor.nlm Display Interrupts	monitor.nlm Display Interrupts
System Information Console	lscfg svmon	dmesg free	dmesg top	dmesg prtconf	monitor.nlm display interrupts	monitor.nlm display interrupts	monitor.nlm display interrupts	monitor.nlm display interrupts
System Monitor	topas vmstat	top vmstat	top vmstat systat	perfmeter top prstat	monitor.nlm	monitor.nlm	monitor.nlm	monitor.nlm
System Policy Editor	smit smitty	userconf	usermod	admintool	syscon.exe sysconW.exe	netadmin.exe nwadmn32.exe	nwadmn32.exe consoleone.exe	nwadmn32.exe consoleone.exe
systeminfo	topas lscfg svmon	top dmesg	top dmesg	dmesg prtconf	monitor.nlm Display Interrupts	monitor.nlm Display Interrupts	monitor.nlm Display Interrupts	monitor.nlm Display Interrupts

DOS	Windows 9x	NT 4.0	NT 2000	Windows XP	Macintosh	
	Control Panel > Add/Remove Programs	Control Panel > Add/Remove Programs	Control Panel > Add/Remove Programs	Control Panel > Add/Remove Programs		**swmtool**
mode.com	Action: 167 mode.com	Control Panel > Ports mode.com	Action: 166 mode.com	Action: 166 mode.com		**syncinit**
	atmadm.exe	netmon.exe	netmon.exe	netmon.exe		**syncstat**
sys.com format a: /s	**sys.com** format a: /s bootdisk.exe	winnt /ox winnt32 /ox	bootdisk.exe	bootdisk.exe		**sys**
	qfecheck.exe wupdmgr.exe	Control Panel > Add/Remove Programs	wupdmgr.exe	wupdmgr.exe		**sysck**
	Control Panel > Users	addusrw.exe usrmgr.exe musrmgr.exe net user	compmgmt.msc wizmgr.exe net user	compmgmt.msc wizmgr.exe net user	Apple Menu > Control Panels > File Sharing > Users & Groups	**syscon**
	Control Panel > Users	addusrw.exe usrmgr.exe musrmgr.exe net user	compmgmt.msc wizmgr.exe net user	compmgmt.msc wizmgr.exe net user	Apple Menu > Control Panels > File Sharing > Users & Groups	**sysconW**
msd.exe	msinfo32.exe Control Panel > System	msinfo32.exe winmsd.exe	msinfo32.exe winmsd.exe	msinfo32.exe winmsd.exe	Apple Menu > Apple System Profiler	**sysdef**
		wizmgr.exe	wizmgr.exe compmgmt.msc	wizmgr.exe compmgmt.msc		**sysidconfig**
	control.exe	control.exe	control.exe	control.exe	Apple Menu > Control Panels	**sysidtool**
	wbemcntl.exe	eventvwr.exe	eventvwr.exe	eventvwr.exe		**sysklogd**
	wbemcntl.exe	eventvwr.exe	eventvwr.exe	eventvwr.exe		**syslogd**
power.exe	pmres.exe		Control Panel > Power Options	Control Panel > Power Options	Apple Menu > Control Panels > Energy Saver	**sys-suspend**
msd.exe	sysmon.exe Control Panel > System	perfmon.exe winmsd.exe Control Panel > System	perfmon.exe winmsd.exe Control Panel > System	perfmon.exe winmsd.exe Control Panel > System	Apple Menu > About This Computer	**systat**
	sysedit.exe msconfig.exe	**sysedit.exe**	**sysedit.exe**	**sysedit.exe** msconfig.exe		**System Configuration Editor**
autoexec.bat	**msconfig.exe** sysedit.exe	sysedit.exe	sysedit.exe	**msconfig.exe** sysedit.exe		**System Configuration Utility**
	sfc.exe		**sfc.exe**	**sfc.exe**		**System File Checker**
msd.exe	Control Panel > System msinfo32.exe	**winmsd.exe**	**winmsd.exe** msinfo32.exe	**winmsd.exe** msinfo32.exe	Apple Menu > Apple System Profiler	**System Information**
msd.exe	msinfo32.exe Control Panel > System	msinfo32.exe winmsd.exe	msinfo32.exe winmsd.exe	**msinfo32.msc** msinfo32.exe winmsd.exe	Apple Menu > Apple System Profiler	**System Information Console**
mem.exe msd.exe	**sysmon.exe** Control Panel > System	perfmon.exe winmsd.exe	perfmon.exe winmsd.exe	perfmon.exe winmsd.exe	Apple Menu > About This Computer	**System Monitor**
		poledit.exe	**poledit.exe** secpol.msc	**poledit.exe** secpol.msc		**System Policy Editor**
msd.exe	msinfo32.exe Control Panel > System	msinfo32.exe Control Panel > System	msinfo32.exe Control Panel > System	**systeminfo.exe** Control Panel > System	Apple Menu > Apple System Profiler	**systeminfo**

	AIX	Linux	OpenBSD	Solaris	NetWare 3	NetWare 4	NetWare 5	NetWare 6
systime	ntpq	Action: 50	Action: 50	ntpq	**systime.exe**	**systime.exe** timesync.nlm	timesync.nlm	timesync.nlm
sys-unconfig		**sys-unconfig**		**sys-unconfig**			reset environment	reset environment
talk	**talk** confer wall	**talk** wall	**talk** wall	**talk** wall	send broadcast	send broadcast	send broadcast	send broadcast
tapes	**tapes**			**tapes**	list devices	list devices	list devices	list devices
tar	**tar**	**tar**	**tar**	**tar**			**tar.nlm**	**tar.nlm**
Task Manager	topas	top	top	perfmeter	monitor.nlm	monitor.nlm	monitor.nlm	monitor.nlm
taskkill	kill	kill	kill	kill	unload	unload	unload	unload
tasklist	topas	top	top	perfmeter	monitor.nlm	monitor.nlm	monitor.nlm	monitor.nlm
Tasks	topas	top	top	perfmeter	monitor.nlm	monitor.nlm	monitor.nlm	monitor.nlm
tcbck	**tcbck**	rpm -V		aset	security.exe			
tclsh	perl	**tclsh** wish perl	perl	perl				
TCP/IP Console	netstat	netstat	netstat	netstat	**tcpcon.nlm**	**tcpcon.nlm**	**tcpcon.nlm**	**tcpcon.nlm**
TCP/IP Control Panel	cfginet ifconfig	netconf ifconfig	ifconfig	ifconfig	install.nlm	inetcfg.nlm	inetcfg.nlm	inetcfg.nlm
TCP/IP Control Panel	ifconfig -a	ifconfig -a	ifconfig -a	ifconfig -a	config	config	config	config
tcsh	ksh sh csh bsh	**tcsh** ash bsh bash sh sash	csh ksh rksh sh	**tcsh** csh jsh ksh rksh sh rsh		netbasic.nlm	netbasic.nlm	netbasic.nlm
telnet	**telnet**	**telnet**	**telnet**	**telnet**		Action: 201	Action: 201	Action: 201
telnetd	**telnetd**	**in.telnetd**	**telnetd**	**in.telnetd**		**telnetd.nlm**	**telnetd.nlm**	**telnetd.nlm**
Text Editor	vi tvi	vi emacs	vi	vi dtpad	**edit.nlm**	**edit.nlm**	**edit.nlm**	**edit.nlm**
tftp	**tftp** utftp	**tftp**	**tftp**	**tftp**				
time	date ntpq	date	date	date ntpq	**time**	**time**	**time**	**time**
timeconfig	chtz	**timeconfig** zdump tzselect	zdump	zdump Action: 186	set time zone	set time zone	set time zone	set time zone
timed	**timed**		**timed**	xntpd -b	systime.exe	systime.exe timesync.nlm servman.nlm	timesync.nlm	timesync.nlm
timesync	ntpq	Action: 50	Action: 50	ntpq	systime.exe	**timesync.nlm** systime.exe	**timesync.nlm**	**timesync.nlm**
tip	**tip**		**tip**	**tip**				
tlist	ls -al	ls -al	ls -al	ls -al	**tlist.exe** *path*	rights *path* /T	rights *path* /T	rights *path* /T
tload		**tload** xload	xload systat	xload				
tokstat	**tokstat**	netstat -I *interface*	netstat -I *interface*	netstat -I *interface*	tcpcon.nlm	tcpcon.nlm	tcpcon.nlm	tcpcon.nlm
top	topas lscfg svmon	**top** dmesg	**top** dmesg	dmesg prtconf	monitor.nlm Display Interrupts	monitor.nlm Display Interrupts	monitor.nlm Display Interrupts	monitor.nlm Display Interrupts
topas	**topas** lscfg svmon	top dmesg	top dmesg	dmesg prtconf	monitor.nlm Display Interrupts	monitor.nlm Display Interrupts	monitor.nlm Display Interrupts	monitor.nlm Display Interrupts
tping	ping	ping	ping	ping	**tping.nlm** ping.nlm	**tping.nlm**	**tping.nlm** ping.nlm	**tping.nlm** ping.nlm

DOS	Windows 9x	NT 4.0	NT 2000	Windows XP	Macintosh	
	net time	net time	net time w32tm.exe	net time	Apple Menu > Control Panel > Date & Time	**systime**
						sys-unconfig
	winpopup.exe	winchat.exe	winchat.exe	winchat.exe		**talk**
		Control Panel > Tape Devices	compmgmt.msc	compmgmt.msc		**tapes**
						tar
	taskman.exe	**taskmgr.exe**	**taskmgr.exe**	**taskmgr.exe**		**Task Manager**
	taskman.exe	kill.exe	tskill.exe	**taskkill.exe** tskill.exe	command + alt + esc command + q	**taskkill**
	taskman.exe	taskmgr.exe	taskmgr.exe	**tasklist.exe**		**tasklist**
	taskman.exe	taskmgr.exe	taskmgr.exe	taskmgr.exe		**Tasks**
			secedit.exe	secedit.exe		**tcbck**
	cscript.exe wscript.exe	cscript.exe wscript.exe	cscript.exe wscript.exe	cscript.exe wscript.exe	Action: 7	**tclsh**
	netstat.exe	netstat.exe	netstat.exe	netstat.exe		**TCP/IP Console**
	Control Panel > Network	Control Panel > Network	Control Panel > Network Connections	Control Panel > Network Connections	**Apple Menu > Control Panel > TCP/IP**	**TCP/IP Control Panel**
	winipcfg	ipconfig	ipconfig	ipconfig	**Apple Menu > Control Panel > TCP/IP**	**TCP/IP Control Panel**
command.com	command.com	command.com cmd.exe	command.com cmd.exe	command.com cmd.exe		**tcsh**
	telnet.exe	**telnet.exe**	**telnet.exe**	**telnet.exe**		**telnet**
			tlntadmn.exe	tlntadmn start		**telnetd**
edit.com	edit.com notepad.exe	edit.com notepad.exe	edit.com notepad.exe	edit.com notepad.exe	Action: 82	**Text Editor**
		tftp	**tftp**	**tftp**		**tftp**
time	**time**	**time**	**time**	**time**	Apple Menu > Control Panels > Date & Time	**time**
	Control Panel > Date/Time	Control Panel > Date/Time	Control Panel > Date/Time	Control Panel > Date and Time	Apple Menu > Control Panels > Date & Time	**timeconfig**
	net time	net time	net time services.msc w32tm	net time services.msc		**timed**
	net time	net time	net time w32tm.exe	net time w32tm.exe	Apple Menu > Control Panels > Date & Time	**timesync**
interlnk.exe intersvr.exe	directcc.exe					**tip**
		Action: 152	Action: 152	Action: 152		**tlist**
		taskmgr.exe	taskmgr.exe	taskmgr.exe		**tload**
	atmadm	netmon.exe	netmon.exe	netmon.exe		**tokstat**
msd.exe	msinfo32.exe Control Panel > System	msinfo32.exe Control Panel > System	msinfo32.exe Control Panel > System	systeminfo.exe Control Panel > System	Apple Menu > Apple System Profiler	**top**
msd.exe	msinfo32.exe Control Panel > System	msinfo32.exe Control Panel > System	msinfo32.exe Control Panel > System	systeminfo.exe Control Panel > System	Apple Menu > Apple System Profiler	**topas**
	ping.exe	ping.exe	ping.exe	ping.exe		**tping**

	AIX	Linux	OpenBSD	Solaris	NetWare 3	NetWare 4	NetWare 5	NetWare 6
tprof	**tprof**	vmstat top	top	cpustat	monitor.nlm	monitor.nlm	monitor.nlm	monitor.nlm
tracepath	traceroute	tracepath traceroute	traceroute	traceroute	Action: 201	Action: 201	Action: 201	Action: 201
traceroute	**traceroute**	**traceroute**	**traceroute**	**traceroute**		iptrace.nlm	iptrace.nlm	iptrace.nlm
tracert	traceroute	traceroute	traceroute	traceroute		iptrace.nlm	iptrace.nlm	iptrace.nlm
tree								
tsh	**tsh** ksh sh csh bsh	ash bsh bash sh sash tcsh	ksh rksh csh sh	ksh rksh csh jsh sh rsh		netbasic.nlm	netbasic.nlm	netbasic.nlm
tskill	kill	skill kill	kill	kill	unload	unload	unload	unload
tsort	**tsort** sort	**tsort** sort	**tsort** sort	**tsort** sort				
ttyadm	getty		getty	**ttyadm** getty	rs232.nlm	rs232.nlm	aiocon.nlm rs232.nlm	aiocon.nlm
ttymon	getty		getty	**ttymon**	rs232.nlm	rs232.nlm	aiocon.nlm rs232.nlm	aiocon.nlm
tvi	**tvi** vi	vi emacs	vi	vi dtpad	edit.nlm	edit.nlm	edit.nlm	edit.nlm
type	cat more	cat more	cat more	cat more	edit.nlm	view.nlm	view.nlm	view.nlm
typeperf	iostat	iostat	iostat	iostat	monitor.nlm	monitor.nlm	monitor.nlm NetWare Management Portal	monitor.nlm NetWare Remote Manager
tzselect	chtz	**tzselect** zdump timeconfig	zdump	zdump Action: 186	set time zone	set time zone	set time zone	set time zone
ufsdump	backup rdump	backup rdump	backup rdump	**ufsdump**	sbackup.nlm	sbackup.nlm	nwback32.exe sbcon.nlm	nwback32.exe sbcon.nlm
ufsrestore	restore	restore	restore	**ufsrestore**	sbackup.nlm	sbackup.nlm	sbcon.nlm nwback32.exe smdr.nlm	sbcon.nlm nwback32.exe smdr.nlm
uimport						**uimport.exe**	**uimport.exe**	ice.exe
umask	**umask**	**umask**	**umask**	**umask**	allow.exe	rights.exe	rights.exe	rights.exe
umount, unmount	**umount** unmount	**umount**	**umount**	**umount**	dismount	dismount	dismount	dismount
unalias	**unalias**	**unalias**	**unalias**	**unalias**		alias	alias	alias
uname	**uname**	**uname** kernelversion	**uname**	**uname** wsinfo	version nver.exe netbios I	version nver.exe	version nver.exe	version
unbind	ifconfig	ifconfig	ifconfig	ifconfig	**unbind**	**unbind**	**unbind**	**unbind**
uncompress	**uncompress**	**uncompress** gunzip unzip	**uncompress** gunzip bunzip2	**uncompress** gunzip unzip	nwxtract.exe nlunpack.exe	nwxtract.exe	unzip.nlm	unzip.nlm
undelete		Action: 54			salvage.exe	filer.exe > Salvage Deleted Files	filer.exe > Salvage Deleted Files	filer.exe > Salvage Deleted Files
Undo								
unlink	**unlink** rm	rm	rm	**unlink** rm	filer.exe	filer.exe nwadmn32.exe	filer.exe nwadmn32.exe	filer.exe nwadmn32.exe
unload	kill	kill	kill	kill	**unload**	**unload**	**unload**	**unload**
unmirrorvg	**unmirrorvg**		raidctl -u		abort remirror	abort remirror	abort remirror	abort remirror
unpack	**unpack** uncompress	uncompress gunzip unzip	uncompress gunzip bunzip2	**unpack** uncompress gunzip	nwxtract.exe nlunpack.exe	nwxtract.exe	unzip.nlm	unzip.nlm

DOS	Windows 9x	NT 4.0	NT 2000	Windows XP	Macintosh	
		perfmon.exe	perfmon.exe	perfmon.exe	Apple Menu > About This Computer	**tprof**
	tracert.exe	tracert.exe	tracert.exe pathping.exe	tracert.exe pathping.exe	Action: 120	**tracepath**
	tracert.exe	tracert.exe	tracert.exe	tracert.exe	Action: 120	**traceroute**
	tracert.exe	**tracert.exe**	**tracert.exe**	**tracert.exe**	Action: 120	**tracert**
tree.com		**tree.com**	**tree.com**	**tree.com**		**tree**
command.com	command.com	cmd.exe command.com	cmd.exe command.com	cmd.exe command.com		**tsh**
	taskman.exe	kill.exe	**tskill.exe**	**tskill.exe** taskkill.exe	command + alt + esc command + q	**tskill**
sort.exe	sort.exe	sort.exe	sort.exe	sort.exe		**tsort**
ctty	ctty					**ttyadm**
ctty	ctty					**ttymon**
edit.com	edit.com notepad.exe	edit.com notepad.exe	edit.com notepad.exe	edit.com notepad.exe	Action: 82	**tvi**
type more.com	**type** more.com	**type** more.com	**type** more.com	**type** more.com	Action: 82	**type**
		perfmon.exe	perfmon.exe	**typeperf.exe** perfmon.exe		**typeperf**
	Control Panel > Date/Time	Control Panel > Date/Time	Control Panel > Date/Time	Control Panel > Date and Time	Apple Menu > Control Panels > Date & Time	**tzselect**
msbackup.exe restore.exe	msbackup.exe backup.exe	msbackup.exe backup.exe	ntbackup.exe	ntbackup.exe		**ufsdump**
restore.exe msbackup.exe	backup.exe msbackup.exe	backup.exe restore.exe ntbackup.exe	ntbackup.exe	ntbackup.exe		**ufsrestore**
			ldifde.exe csvde.exe	ldifde.exe csvde.exe		**uimport**
		Action: 152	Action: 152	Action: 152		**umask**
						umount, unmount
doskey.com	doskey.com	doskey.com	doskey.com	doskey.com		**unalias**
ver	ver winver Control Panel > System	ver winver Control Panel > System	ver winver Control Panel > System	ver winver Control Panel > System	Apple Menu > About This Computer	**uname**
	Action: 193	Action: 193	Action: 195	Action: 194		**unbind**
	Action: 143	Action: 143 expand.exe	Action: 143 expand.exe	Action: 143 expand.exe	Action: 79	**uncompress**
undelete	Action: 56	Action: 56	Action: 56	Action: 56	Double click on trashcan and drag files to desktop.	**undelete**
	CTRL + Z	CTRL + Z	CTRL + Z	CTRL + Z	**command + z**	**Undo**
del erase	del erase	del erase	del erase	del erase	command + Backspace	**unlink**
	taskman.exe	kill.exe	tskill.exe	taskkill.exe tskill.exe	command + alt + esc command + q	**unload**
						unmirrorvg
	Action: 143	Action: 143 expand.exe	Action: 143 expand.exe	Action: 143 expand.exe	Action: 79	**unpack**

	AIX	Linux	OpenBSD	Solaris	NetWare 3	NetWare 4	NetWare 5	NetWare 6
unset	**unset** unsetenv	**unset** unsetenv reset	**unset** unsetenv	**unset** unsetenv unsetopt	set *variable=original value*	set *variable=original value*	Reset Environment	Reset Environment
unsetenv	**unsetenv** unset	**unsetenv** unset reset	**unsetenv** unset	**unsetenv** unset unsetopt	set *variable=original value*	set *variable=original value*	Reset Environment	Reset Environment
unsetopt	unset unsetenv	unset unsetenv reset	unset unsetenv	**unsetopt** unset unsetenv	set *variable=original value*	set *variable=original value*	Reset Environment	Reset Environment
unshare	exportfs -u rmnfsexp	exportfs -u	Action: 8	**unshare**	flag *file* -sh	flag *file* +sh /FO	flag *file* +sh /FO	flag *file* +sh /FO
unzip	uncompress	**unzip** gunzip uncompress	gunzip bunzip2 uncompress	**unzip** gunzip uncompress	nwxtract.exe nlunpack.exe	nwxtract.exe	**unzip.nlm** jar tar.nlm	**unzip.nlm** jar tar.nlm
Update Information Tool	lslpp sysck	rpm -qa	pkg_info -a	showrev -p	install > product options	install > product options	nwconfig > product options	nwconfig > product options
uprintfd	**uprintfd** syslogd	klogd sysklogd syslogd	syslogd	syslogd	conlog.nlm	conlog.nlm	conlog.nlm	conlog.nlm
uptime	**uptime**	**uptime**	**uptime**	**uptime**	monitor.nlm	monitor.nlm	monitor.nlm	monitor.nlm
User Manager	smit smitty mkuser mkgroup	userconf useradd groupadd	adduser groupadd	admintool useradd groupadd	syscon.exe sysconW.exe	netadmin.exe nwadmn32.exe	nwadmn32.exe consoleone.exe consoleonedos.exe	nwadmn32.exe consoleone.exe consoleonedos.exe
useradd	smit smitty mkuser mkgroup	userconf useradd groupadd	adduser groupadd	**useradd** admintool groupadd	syscon.exe sysconW.exe	netadmin.exe nwadmn32.exe	nwadmn32.exe consoleone.exe consoleonedos.exe	nwadmn32.exe consoleone.exe consoleonedos.exe
userconf	smit smitty	**userconf**	usermod	admintool	syscon.exe sysconW.exe	netadmin.exe nwadmn32.exe	nwadmn32.exe consoleone.exe	nwadmn32.exe consoleone.exe
userdef		newusers			**userdef.exe**			
userdel	rmuser	**userdel**	rmuser	**userdel**	syscon.exe sysconW.exe	netadmin.exe nwadmn32.exe	nwadmn32.exe consoleone.exe consoleonedos.exe	nwadmn32.exe consoleone.exe consoleonedos.exe
userhelper	smit user	**userhelper**	usermod	usermod	syscon.exe sysconW.exe	netadmin.exe nwadmn32.exe	nwadmn32.exe consoleone.exe consoleonedos.exe	nwadmn32.exe consoleone.exe consoleonedos.exe
userinfo	chfn	**userinfo** chfn	chfn	usermod -c "*name*" *user*	syscon.exe sysconW.exe	netadmin.exe nwadmn32.exe	nwadmn32.exe consoleone.exe consoleonedos.exe	nwadmn32.exe consoleone.exe consoleonedos.exe
userlist	w who	w who	w who	w who	**userlist.exe**	nlist user /A /B	nlist user /A /B	nlist user /A /B
usermod	smit user	**usermod**	usermod	admintool	syscon.exe sysconW.exe	netadmin.exe nwadmn32.exe	nwadmn32.exe consoleone.exe consoleonedos.exe	nwadmn32.exe consoleone.exe consoleonedos.exe
usermount	mount	**usermount**	mount	mount	mount	mount	mount	mount
usernetctl	smit	**usernetctl** ifconfig	ifconfig	admintool ifconfig	install.nlm	inetcfg.nlm	inetcfg.nlm	inetcfg.nlm
userpasswd	passwd yppasswd	**userpasswd** passwd yppasswd	passwd	passwd yppasswd nispasswd	setpass.exe Action: 37	setpass.exe Action: 37	setpass.exe Action: 37	Action: 37
users	**users**	**users** log nwuserlist	**users**	**users** log	userlist.exe	nlist user /A	nlist user /A	nlist user /A
usrck	**usrck**	cat /etc/passwd	cat /etc/passwd	cat /etc/passwd	syscon.exe	nwadmn32.exe	nwadmn32.exe	nwadmn32.exe

DOS	Windows 9x	NT 4.0	NT 2000	Windows XP	Macintosh	
set *variable*=	set *variable*=	set *variable*=	set *variable*=	set *variable*=		**unset**
set *variable*=	set *variable*=	set *variable*=	set *variable*=	set *variable*=		**unsetenv**
set *variable*=	set *variable*=	set *variable*=	set *variable*=	set *variable*=		**unsetopt**
	Action: 242 net share	Action: 242 net share	Action: 242 net share	Action: 242 net share	Apple Menu > Control Panels > File Sharing	**unshare**
	Action: 143	Action: 143 expand.exe	Action: 143 expand.exe	Action: 143 expand.exe	Action: 79	**unzip**
	qfecheck.exe wupdmgr.exe	Control Panel > Add/Remove Programs	wupdmgr.exe	wupdmgr.exe		**Update Information Tool**
	wbemcntl.exe	eventvwr.exe	eventvwr.exe	eventvwr.exe		**uprintfd**
						uptime
	Control Panel > Users	**usrmgr.exe** **musrmgr.exe** net group net user addgrpw.exe	compmgmt.msc wizmgr.exe net group net user	compmgmt.msc wizmgr.exe net group net user	Apple Menu > Control Panels > File Sharing > Users & Groups	**User Manager**
	Control Panel > Users	usrmgr.exe musrmgr.exe net user	dsa.msc compmgmt.msc wizmgr.exe net user	dsa.msc compmgmt.msc net user	Apple Menu > Control Panels > File Sharing > Users & Groups	**useradd**
		poledit.exe	secpol.msc poledit.exe	secpol.msc poledit.exe		**userconf**
		addusers.exe	addusers.exe			**userdef**
	Control Panel > Users	usrmgr.exe musrmgr.exe	compmgmt.msc	compmgmt.msc		**userdel**
	Control Panel > Users	usrmgr.exe	compmgmt.msc	compmgmt.msc	Apple Menu > Control Panels > File Sharing > Users & Groups	**userhelper**
	Control Panel > Users	usrmgr.exe musrmgr.exe	compmgmt.msc	compmgmt.msc	Apple Menu > Control Panels > Multiple Users	**userinfo**
		quser.exe query user	quser.exe query user	quser.exe query user		**userlist**
	Control Panel > Users	usrmgr.exe musrmgr.exe	compmgmt.msc	compmgmt.msc	Apple Menu > Control Panels > File Sharing > Users & Groups	**usermod**
	net use	net use	net use	net use		**usermount**
	Control Panel > Network	Control Panel > Network	Control Panel > Network Connections	Control Panel > Network Connections netsetup.exe	Apple Menu > Control Panel > TCP/IP Apple Menu > Control Panel > AppleTalk	**usernetctl**
	net password Control Panel > passwords	usrmgr.exe Action: 229	compmgmt.msc Action: 229	compmgmt.msc Action: 229	Action: 200	**userpasswd**
		quser.exe	quser.exe	quser.exe		**users**
	Control Panel > Users	usrmgr.exe musrmgr.exe	compmgmt.msc	compmgmt.msc		**usrck**

	AIX	Linux	OpenBSD	Solaris	NetWare 3	NetWare 4	NetWare 5	NetWare 6
vdir	ls	**vdir** ls	ls	ls	ndir.exe	ls.exe ndir.exe	ndir.exe	ndir.exe
vedit	**vedit**	**vedit**	**vedit**	**vedit**	edit.nlm	edit.nlm	edit.nlm	edit.nlm
ver	uname -a	uname -a kernelversion	uname -a	uname -a wsinfo	version nver	version nver	version nver	version
verify					set enable disk read after write verify	set enable disk read after write verify	set enable disk read after write verify	set enable disk read after write verify
version (server)	uname -a	uname -a kernelversion	uname -a	uname -a wsinfo	**version** nver	**version** nver	**version**	**version**
vi, view	**vi** tvi	**vi** emacs	**vi**	**vi** dtpad	edit.nlm	edit.nlm	edit.nlm	edit.nlm
view	cat more	cat more	cat more	cat more	edit.nlm	**view.nlm**	**view.nlm**	**view.nlm**
View Options								
viewtrc	trcrpt						**viewtrc.exe**	
vmdismount	umount	umount	umount	umount	dismount	**vmdismount** dismount	**vmdismount** dismount	**vmdismount** dismount
vmmount	mount	mount	mount	mount	mount	**vmmount** mount	**vmmount** mount	**vmmount** mount
vmstat	**vmstat** svmon	**vmstat** free alloc	**vmstat** top	**vmstat** prtconf alloc	memory	memory	memory	memory
vmvolumes	mount	mount	mount	mount	volume volumes	**vmvolumes** volume volumes	**vmvolumes** volume volumes	**vmvolumes** volume volumes
vol	lspv	e2label	disklabel	labelit	volume	volume	volume	volume
volcheck				**volcheck**				
volrmmount	mount umount	mount umount	mount umount	**volrmmount** mount umount	mount dismount	mount dismount	mount dismount	mount dismount
Volume Information	df	df	df	df	**volinfo.exe**	filer.exe ndir /VOL	filer.exe ndir /VOL	filer.exe ndir /VOL
Volume Repair Utility	fsck	fsck	fsck	fsck	**vrepair.nlm**	**vrepair.nlm**	**vrepair.nlm**	**vrepair.nlm**
volume, volumes	mount	mount	mount	mount	**volume** **volumes**	**volume** **volumes**	**volume** **volumes**	**volume** **volumes**
vwipxspx		ipx_configure			ipxs.nlm	ipxs.nlm	ipxs.nlm	ipxs.nlm
w	**w** who	**w** who	**w** who	**w** who	userlist.exe	nlist user /A /B	nlist user /A /B	nlist user /A /B
w32tm	ntpdate	rdate Action: 50	rdate Action: 50	ntpdate rdate		timesync.nlm	timesync.nlm	timesync.nlm
wall	**wall**	**wall**	**wall**	**wall**	broadcast	broadcast	broadcast	broadcast
Web Sharing Control Panel		httpd	httpd	httpd			nsweb.ncf nvxwebup.ncf	nsweb.ncf nvxwebup.ncf
whatis	**whatis**	**whatis**	**whatis**	**whatis**		help	help	help
WhatRoute	traceroute	traceroute	traceroute	traceroute		iptrace.nlm	iptrace.nlm	iptrace.nlm
whence	**whence *command*** which *command* find / -name *command*	which *command* where *command* find / -name *command*	**whence *command*** which *command* find / -name *command*	**whence *command*** which *command* where *command* find / -name *command*	ndir *command* /s filer.exe	ndir *command* /s filer.exe	ndir *command* /s filer.exe	ndir *command* /s filer.exe
where	find / -name *command* which *command* whence *command*	**where *command*** find / -name *command* which *command*	find / -name *command* which *command* whence *command*	**where *command*** find / -name *command* which *command* whence *command*	ndir *command* /s filer.exe	ndir *command* /s filer.exe	ndir *command* /s filer.exe	ndir *command* /s filer.exe

DOS	Windows 9x	NT 4.0	NT 2000	Windows XP	Macintosh	
set *variable*=	set *variable*=	set *variable*=	set *variable*=	set *variable*=		**unset**
set *variable*=	set *variable*=	set *variable*=	set *variable*=	set *variable*=		**unsetenv**
set *variable*=	set *variable*=	set *variable*=	set *variable*=	set *variable*=		**unsetopt**
	Action: 242 net share	Action: 242 net share	Action: 242 net share	Action: 242 net share	Apple Menu > Control Panels > File Sharing	**unshare**
	Action: 143	Action: 143 expand.exe	Action: 143 expand.exe	Action: 143 expand.exe	Action: 79	**unzip**
	qfecheck.exe wupdmgr.exe	Control Panel > Add/Remove Programs	wupdmgr.exe	wupdmgr.exe		**Update Information Tool**
	wbemcntl.exe	eventvwr.exe	eventvwr.exe	eventvwr.exe		**uprintfd**
						uptime
	Control Panel > Users	**usrmgr.exe** **musrmgr.exe** net group net user addgrpw.exe	compmgmt.msc wizmgr.exe net group net user	compmgmt.msc wizmgr.exe net group net user	Apple Menu > Control Panels > File Sharing > Users & Groups	**User Manager**
	Control Panel > Users	usrmgr.exe musrmgr.exe net user	dsa.msc compmgmt.msc wizmgr.exe net user	dsa.msc compmgmt.msc net user	Apple Menu > Control Panels > File Sharing > Users & Groups	**useradd**
		poledit.exe	secpol.msc poledit.exe	secpol.msc poledit.exe		**userconf**
		addusers.exe	addusers.exe			**userdef**
	Control Panel > Users	usrmgr.exe musrmgr.exe	compmgmt.msc	compmgmt.msc		**userdel**
	Control Panel > Users	usrmgr.exe	compmgmt.msc	compmgmt.msc	Apple Menu > Control Panels > File Sharing > Users & Groups	**userhelper**
	Control Panel > Users	usrmgr.exe musrmgr.exe	compmgmt.msc	compmgmt.msc	Apple Menu > Control Panels > Multiple Users	**userinfo**
		quser.exe query user	quser.exe query user	quser.exe query user		**userlist**
	Control Panel > Users	usrmgr.exe musrmgr.exe	compmgmt.msc	compmgmt.msc	Apple Menu > Control Panels > File Sharing > Users & Groups	**usermod**
	net use	net use	net use	net use		**usermount**
	Control Panel > Network	Control Panel > Network	Control Panel > Network Connections	Control Panel > Network Connections netsetup.exe	Apple Menu > Control Panel > TCP/IP Apple Menu > Control Panel > AppleTalk	**usernetctl**
	net password Control Panel > passwords	usrmgr.exe Action: 229	compmgmt.msc Action: 229	compmgmt.msc Action: 229	Action: 200	**userpasswd**
		quser.exe	quser.exe	quser.exe		**users**
	Control Panel > Users	usrmgr.exe musrmgr.exe	compmgmt.msc	compmgmt.msc		**usrck**

	AIX	Linux	OpenBSD	Solaris	NetWare 3	NetWare 4	NetWare 5	NetWare 6
whereis	**whereis** which *command* find / -name *command*	**whereis** which *command* where *command* find / -name *command*	**whereis** which *command* find / -name *command*	**whereis** which *command* where*command* find / -name *command*	ndir *command* /s filer.exe	ndir *command* /s filer.exe	ndir *command* /s filer.exe	ndir *command* /s filer.exe
which	**which** ***command*** find / -name *command* whence *command*	**which** ***command*** where *command* find / -name *command*	**which** ***command*** find / -name *command* whence *command*	**which** ***command*** where*command* find / -name *command* whence *command*	ndir *command* /s filer.exe	ndir *command* /s filer.exe	ndir *command* /s filer.exe	ndir *command* /s filer.exe
who	**who** w	**who** w	**who** w	**who** w	userlist.exe	nlist user /A /B	nlist user /A /B	nlist user /A /B
who am i	**who am i**	**who am i**	**who am i**	**who am i**	userlist.exe	nlist user /A /B	nlist user /A /B	nlist user /A /B
whoami	**whoami** id	**whoami** id	**whoami** id	**whoami** id	**whoami.exe** Action: 5	**whoami.exe** Action: 5	Action: 5	Action: 5
whodo	who w	who w	who w	**whodo** who w	userlist.exe	nlist user /A /B	nlist user /A /B	nlist user /A /B
Windows	X	X startx	X startx	X openwin			startx.ncf	startx.ncf
Windows 2000/XP Setup					install.bat	install.bat	install.bat	install.bat
Windows Automated System Recovery	smitty mksysb	dump restore	dump restore	ufsdump ufsrestore	sbackup.nlm	sbackup.nlm	smdr.nlm tsa500.nlm	smdr.nlm tsa500.nlm
Windows Help	man apropos whatis	man apropos info	man apropos info	man apropos whatis		help	help	help
Windows Media Player		cdp, cdplay mpg123 xplaycd	cdio	audioplay audiotool				
Windows NT Diagnostics	lscfg svmon	dmesg free	dmesg top	dmesg prtconf	monitor.nlm Display Interrupts	monitor.nlm Display Interrupts	monitor.nlm Display Interrupts	monitor.nlm Display Interrupts
Windows Report Tool	sendbug	bashbug	sendbug	perlbug				
Windows Script Host		perl	perl	perl			perl.nlm	perl.nlm
Windows Setup				boot cdrom	install.bat	install.bat	install.bat	install.bat
winpopup	write wall	write wall	write wall	write wall	send broadcast	send broadcast	send broadcast	send broadcast
wish		**wish** tclsh perl	perl	perl			perl.nlm	perl.nlm
wjview	java jre			java java_g jre			java.nlm java.exe	java.nlm java.exe
wm2	mwm	fvwm2	**wm2**	dtwm	<CTRL> + <ESC>	<CTRL> + <ESC>	<CTRL> + <ESC>	<CTRL> + <ESC>
wmic	smit smitty	linuxconf		admintool	install.nlm	install.nlm	nwconfig.nlm	nwconfig.nlm
WordPad	vi tvi	vi emacs	vi	vi dtpad	edit.nlm	edit.nlm	edit.nlm	edit.nlm
Workstation Scheduler	cron at	crond at sched	cron at	cron sched at	**wmsched.exe** cron.nlm	**wmsched.exe** cron.nlm	**wmsched.exe** cron.nlm	**wmsched.exe** cron.nlm
write	**write** walll	**write** wall	**write** wall	**write** wall	send broadcast	send broadcast	send broadcast	send broadcast
wsinfo	uname –a	uname –a	uname –a	**wsinfo**	version never.exe netbios I	version never.exe	version never.exe	version

DOS	Windows 9x	NT 4.0	NT 2000	Windows XP	Macintosh	
dir *command* /s	dir *command* /s Action: 182	dir *command* /s Action: 182	dir *command* /s Action: 182	dir *command* /s Action: 182	command + f File > Find	**whereis**
dir *command* /s	dir *command* /s Action: 182	dir *command* /s Action: 182	dir *command* /s Action: 182	dir *command* /s Action: 182	command + f File > Find	**which**
		quser.exe query user	quser.exe query user	quser.exe query user		**who**
		quser.exe	quser.exe	quser.exe		**who am i**
						whoami
		quser.exe query user	quser.exe query user	quser.exe query user		**whodo**
	win.com					**Windows**
setup.exe	setup.exe	winnt /b	**sysocmgr.exe**	**sysocmgr.exe**		**Windows 2000/XP Setup**
	srw.exe			**asr_fmt.exe**		**Windows Automated System Recovery**
help.com fasthelp.exe	**winhelp.exe** helpctr.exe	**winhlp32.exe** help.exe ntbooks.exe	**winhelp.exe** help.exe	**winhelp.exe** help.exe helpctr.exe	command + ? Help > Mac Help	**Windows Help**
	mplayer2.exe **mplayer.exe**	**mplayer2.exe**	**mplayer2.exe** mplay32.exe	**mplayer2.exe** mplay32.exe	Action: 2	**Windows Media Player**
msd.exe	msinfo32.exe Control Panel > System	**winmsd.exe** msinfo32.exe	msinfo32.exe winmsd.exe	msinfo32.exe winmsd.exe	Apple Menu > Apple System Profiler	**Windows NT Diagnostics**
	winrep.exe	Action: 19	**winrep.exe**	Action: 18		**Windows Report Tool**
	wscript.exe cscript.exe	**wscript.exe** cscript.exe	**wscript.exe** cscript.exe	**wscript.exe** cscript.exe	Action: 7	**Windows Script Host**
setup.exe	**setup.exe**	winnt.exe winnt32.exe	winnt.exe winnt32.exe	winnt.exe winnt32.exe		**Windows Setup**
	winpopup.exe	net send msg.exe	net send msg.exe	net send msg.exe		**winpopup**
	cscript.exe wscript.exe	cscript.exe wscript.exe	cscript.exe wscript.exe	cscript.exe wscript.exe	Action: 7	**wish**
	wjview.exe jview.exe		**wjview.exe** jview.exe	**wjview.exe** jview.exe		**wjview**
	progman.exe	progman.exe	progman.exe	progman.exe	Finder	**wm2**
	control.exe	control.exe	control.exe	**wmic.exe** control.exe	Apple Menu > Control Panels	**wmic**
edit.com	**wordpad.exe** notepad.exe	**wordpad.exe** notepad.exe	**wordpad.exe** notepad.exe	**wordpad.exe** notepad.exe	**Action: 82**	**WordPad**
	sysagent.exe Action: 9	at.exe	at.exe Action: 9	at.exe schtasks.exe		**Workstation Scheduler**
	winpopup.exe	msg.exe net send	msg.exe net send	msg.exe net send		**write**
ver	ver winver Control Panel > System	ver winver Control Panel > System	ver winver Control Panel > System	ver winver systeminfo Control Panel > System	Apple Menu > About This Computer	**wsinfo**

	AIX	Linux	OpenBSD	Solaris	NetWare 3	NetWare 4	NetWare 5	NetWare 6
wvdial	pppdial	**wvdial**	ppp	aspppd		Action: 121	niascfg.nlm	Action: 121
X	**X**	**X** startx	**X** startx	**X** openwin			startx.ncf	startx.ncf
X Server	**startx**	**startx**	**startx**	openwin dtwm			**startx.ncf**	**startx.ncf**
xautolock	xss xlock		**xautolock** xlock	xlock	monitor.nlm	monitor.nlm	scrsaver.nlm	scrsaver.nlm
xconsole	telnet	telnet ssh	telnet ssh	telnet	rconsole.exe	**xconsole.nlm** rconsole.exe	**xconsole.nlm** rconsole.exe	**xconsole.nlm** rconsole.exe
xcopy	cp dtfile	cp mc mcopy	cp	cp dtfile	ncopy.exe filer.exe	ncopy.exe filer.exe	ncopy.exe filer.exe	ncopy.exe filer.exe
xcopy32	cp dtfile	cp mc	cp	cp dtfile	ncopy.exe filer.exe	ncopy.exe filer.exe	ncopy.exe filer.exe	ncopy.exe filer.exe
xinetd	inetd	**xinetd**	inetd	inetd	autoexec.ncf	autoexec.ncf	inetd.nlm autoexec.ncf	inetd.nlm autoexec.ncf
xkill		**xkill**	**xkill**	**xkill**				
xload		**xload** tload	**xload** systat	**xload**				
xlock	**xlock** xss		**xlock** xautolock	**xlock**	monitor.nlm	monitor.nlm	scrsaver.nlm	scrsaver.nlm
xmag	O	**xmag**	**xmag**	**xmag**				
xman	man whatis	**xman** info	**xman** info	**xman** whatis		help	help	help
xmodem	**xmodem**	sx sz sb						
xmodmap	**xmodmap** chkbd lskbd	**xmodmap** loadkeys setxkbmap kbdconfig	**xmodmap** kbd setxkbmap	**xmodmap** kbd loadkeys	**keyb.nlm**	keyb.nlm	keyb.nlm charset.nlm	keyb.nlm charset.nlm
xntpd	date ntpdate	date hwclock	date	**xntpd** date ntpdate	set time	set time	set time	set time
xon	on rexec rpc.rexd	**xon** rexec	**xon** rexec	on rpc.rexd				
xpcmcia	**xpcmcia** acfgd	cardmgr						
xpowerm	**xpowerm** pmctrl	apm	apm	pmconfig				
xsetroot	**xsetroot**	**xsetroot**	**xsetroot**	**xsetroot**			Action: 123	Action: 123
xss	**xss** xlock		xautolock xlock	xlock dtscreen	monitor.nlm	monitor.nlm	scrsaver.nlm	scrsaver.nlm
xterm	**xterm**	**xterm**	**xterm**	**xterm**				
ypchfn	chfn	**ypchfn** chfn userinfo	chfn	usermod –c "*name*" *user*	syscon.exe sysconW.exe	netadmin.exe nwadmn32.exe	nwadmn32.exe consoleone.exe consoleonedos. exe	nwadmn32.exe consoleone.exe consoleonedos. exe
ypchsh	chsh	**ypchsh** chsh	chsh chpass –s	usermod –s *shell* admintool > User Management				
yppasswd	**yppasswd** passwd	**yppasswd** passwd userpasswd	passwd	**yppasswd** passwd nispasswd	Action: 37 setpass.exe	Action: 37 setpass.exe	Action: 37 setpass.exe	Action: 37
zcat	**zcat** uncompress –c *file* pcat	**zcat** uncompress –c *file* bzcat	uncompress –c *file* gzcat	**zcat** pcat uncompress –c *file*			tar –t *file* unzip –l *file* jar –t *file*	tar –t *file* unzip –l *file* jar –t *file*
zdump	chtz	**zdump**	**zdump**	**zdump**	set time zone	set time zone	set time zone	set time zone

DOS	Windows 9x	NT 4.0	NT 2000	Windows XP	Macintosh	
	Action: 124	rasautou.exe	rasautou.exe	rasphone.exe	Control Panel > Remote Access	**wvdial**
	win.com					**X**
						X Server
	Action: 150	Action: 150	Action: 150	Action: 150		**xautolock**
	telnet	telnet	telnet Action: 173	telnet Action: 173		**xconsole**
xcopy.exe copy	**xcopy.exe** copy Action: 1	**xcopy.exe** copy Action: 1	**xcopy.exe** copy Action: 1	**xcopy.exe** copy Action: 1	alt + Drag a file command + d	**xcopy**
copy xcopy.exe	**xcopy32.exe** xcopy.exe copy	xcopy.exe copy	xcopy.exe copy	xcopy.exe copy	alt + Drag a file command + d	**xcopy32**
						xinetd
	Action: 225	Action: 225	Action: 225	Action: 225	<command> + <w>	**xkill**
		taskmgr.exe	taskmgr.exe	taskmgr.exe		**xload**
	Action: 150	Action: 150	Action: 150	Action: 150		**xlock**
	magnify.exe		magnify.exe	magnify.exe		**xmag**
fasthelp.exe help.com	winhelp.exe helpctr.exe	winhlp32.exe help.exe ntbooks.exe	winhelp.exe help.exe ntbooks.exe	winhelp.exe helpctr.exe	command + ? Help > Mac Help	**xman**
	filexfer.exe					**xmodem**
keyb.com chcp.com	Control Panel > Keyboard keyb.com chcp.com	Control Panel > Keyboard keyb.com kb16.com	Control Panel > Keyboard kb16.com chcp.com	Control Panel > Keyboard kb16.com chcp.com	Apple Menu > Control Panels > Keyboard	**xmodmap**
time	net time	net time	w32tm.exe net time	w32tm.exe net time	Apple Menu > Control Panels > Date & Time	**xntpd**
		rexec.exe	rexec.exe	rexec.exe		**xon**
	Control Panel > PC Card (PCMCIA)	Control Panel > PC Card (PCMCIA)	Control Panel > PC Card (PCMCIA)	Control Panel > PC Card (PCMCIA)		**xpcmcia**
power.exe	pmres.exe		Control Panel > Power Options	Control Panel > Power Options	Apple Menu > Control Panels > Energy Saver	**xpowerm**
	Action: 122	Action: 122	Action: 122	Action: 122	Apple Menu > Control Panels > Appearance	**xsetroot**
	Action: 150	Action: 150	Action: 150	Action: 150		**xss**
	command.com	cmd.exe	cmd.exe	cmd.exe		**xterm**
	Control Panel > Users	usrmgr.exe musrmgr.exe	compmgmt.msc	compmgmt.msc	Apple Menu > Control Panels > Multiple Users	**ypchfn**
shell						**ypchsh**
	net password Control Panel > passwords	usrmgr.exe Action: 229	compmgmt.msc Action: 229	compmgmt.msc Action: 229	Action: 200	**yppasswd**
	Action: 143	expand –D *file* Action: 143	expand –D *file* Action: 143	expand –D *file* Action: 143		**zcat**
	Control Panel > Date/Time	Control Panel > Date/Time	Control Panel > Date/Time	Control Panel > Date/Time	Apple Menu > Control Panels > Date & Time	**zdump**

	AIX	Linux	OpenBSD	Solaris	NetWare 3	NetWare 4	NetWare 5	NetWare 6
zip	pack compress	**zip** gzip compress	gzip compress	**zip** gzip compress			tar.nlm jar	tar.nlm jar
zsh	ksh sh csh bsh	ash bsh bash sh sash tcsh	csh ksh rksh sh	**zsh** csh jsh ksh rksh sh rsh		netbasic.nlm	netbasic.nlm	netbasic.nlm
zzz	pmctrl	apmsleep apm	**zzz** apm	powerd sys-suspend				

DOS	Windows 9x	NT 4.0	NT 2000	Windows XP	Macintosh	
	Action: 143	Action: 143	Action: 143	Action: 143		**zip**
command.com	command.com	cmd.exe command.com	cmd.exe command.com	cmd.exe command.com		**zsh**
power.exe	pmres.exe		Control Panel > Power Options	Control Panel > Power Options	Apple Menu > Control Panels > Energy Saver	**zzz**

ID	ACTION
1	Right-click on a file in Explorer and select copy from the context menu or select Copy from the Edit drop down menu.
2	Use Macintosh HD > Applications > AppleCD Audio Player > `AppleCD Audio Player`.
3	Right-click on the Novell Icon in the Windows task bar and select Novell Client Properties.
4	Right-click on the Novell Icon in the Windows task bar and select NetWare Utilities > Purge.
5	If you have Novell client for Windows installed, right-click on the Tree icon in Network Neighborhood and select WhoAmI…
6	Use `dd if=/dev/zero of=`*`outfile`* `bs=1024 count=`*`size`* to create large files.
7	Double-click on the script that you want to execute.
8	Edit the file /etc/exports.
9	Use Start > Programs > Accessories > System Tools > Schedule Tasks.
10	Use Control Panel > Internet Options > Connections > LAN Settings.
11	Change the option "Message Timeout" to 1 in the Novell Client under Advanced Settings.
12	Use Received Broadcast Messages in the Novell Client under Advanced Settings.
13	Use Control Panel > System > Hardware > Device Manager > Modems > *modem* > Diagnostic > Query Modem.
14	Use Control Panel > Modems > Diagnostics > *modem to test* > More info…
15	Right-click on a folder in Explorer or My Computer and select delete from the context menu.
16	There is no built-in defrag utility for NT 4.0, however there are many 3rd party defrag utilities to use.
17	Right-click on the Recycle Bin and select Empty Recycle Bin from the context menu.
18	Appears automaticly when an error occurs.
19	Use Control Panel > System > Advanced > Error Reporting.
20	Use Control Panel > Network > Identification.
21	Use Control Panel > Administrative Tools > DNS.
22	Use Start > Programs > Accessories > Communications > Dial-Up Networking.
23	Right-click on the folder you want to share and select Sharing from the context menu.
24	Is available for download from www.novell.com.
25	Right-click on the Novell Icon in the Windows task bar and select NetWare Utilities > Salvage.
26	To customize a folder select Customize this folder from the View menu.
27	You can create printer forms using the NetWare Administrator. Right-click on a OU and choose Printer Forms.
28	Use `more /etc/group`.
29	Use `more /etc/passwd`.
30	Should be automatically detected. To manually add it use `config e /bsd` followed by `add sb0`.
31	Use `smitty` > Devices > Multimedia > Audio.
32	Load `servman` then select Network Information.
33	You can also use network cards with boot proms if the `rpl.nlm` is loaded and bound to the server network card.
34	Raid tools are available in the Solstice Disksuite available from Sun.
35	Load `inetcfg` then select Manage Configuration > Configure Remote Access To This Server.
36	Right-click on the Novell Icon in the Windows task bar and select NetWare Utilities > Send Message.
37	Right-click on the Novell Icon and then select User Administration > Novell Password Administration > Change Password.
38	Open the NetWare Administrator select an OU container and press <INSERT> to add a new Template Object.
39	Mount the MS-DOS filesystem then use `cat` on the file.
40	Use `setup /ACU` when installing the Novell Client. Automcatially updates clients if used inside login scripts.
41	Load `nwconfig` then select Directory Options > Directory Backup and Restore Options.
42	LDAP functions is available in the third party product OpenLDAP available at www.openldap.com.

continued

43	Use `format` then choose the disk you want to analyze then type analyze.
44	Right-click in an opened folder and select Arrange Icons from the context menu.
45	Select Large Icons or Small Icons from the View menu in the folder.
46	The commands to change runlevels are: rcS, rc0, rc1, rc2, rc3, rc4, rc5, and rc6.
47	Type "boot cdrom" at the boot prompt.
48	Will automatically boot from the CD-ROM if the CD-ROM is bootable and the BIOS supports it and is configured.
49	Press the button on the CD-ROM drive to eject CD.
50	Network time protocol can be found at http://www.eecis.udel.edu/~ntp/ntp_spool/html/.
51	Double-click on the folder you want to change to.
52	Click on the minimize icon in the window.
53	Use the start scripts in /etc/init.d/
54	Start `mc` then press F9 and select Undelete files from the Command menu.
55	You can download NICI (Novell International Cryptographic Infrastructure) from Novell.com.
56	Open the Recycle Bin and right-click on a file you want to undelete and select restore from the context menu.
57	Drag and drop a file on a printer located in Control Panel > Printers or select print from the file menu.
58	Double-click the `Network Neighborhood` icon on the desktop to browse the network.
59	Select Line Up Icons from the View menu.
60	Click on the maximize icon in the window.
61	Press <stop> + <a> locally and type boot.
62	Use Control Panel > System > Device Manager.
63	Right-click on a file and select Properties > Security > Ownership > Take Ownership. Used on NTFS filesystems only.
64	Use Macintosh HD > Applications > Utilities > Drive Setup > `Drive Setup`.
65	Enables services prefixed with S and disables services prefixed with K found in /etc/rc*runlevel*.d/.
66	Use su *user* -c *command*.
67	All services are enabled or disabled in the /etc/rc.conf file.
68	Right-click on the CD-ROM drive in My Computer or Explorer and select Eject from the context menu.
69	Use `dd if=`*`kernel`* `of=`*`dev`*.
70	A defrag utility is available in Norton Utilities available from Symantec.
71	Use the start scripts found in /etc/rc.d/init.d
72	Services are started from the /etc/rc* files.
73	The NetWare filesystem automatically organizes files for optimal performance therefore defrag is unnecessary.
74	A defrag utility for Linux is available at www.freshmeat.net.
75	In `explorer` select Folder options from the View menu.
76	There is no native email client to retrieve messages from POP or IMAP servers. 3rd party clients are available
77	Use Control Panel > System > Environment.
78	Use Control Panel > System > Advanced > Environment Variables.
79	Use Macintosh HD > Applications > Internet Utilities > Alladin Folder > `Stuffit Expander`.
80	Security functions is available in the third party product Tripwire available at www.tripwire.com.
81	Use Macintosh HD > Applications > Internet Explorer > `Internet Explorer`.
82	Use Macintosh HD > Applications > `SimpleText`.
83	Edit the file /etc/rc.conf, modify the line nfs_server. Valid modification is YES or NO.
84	Edit /etc/fstab.
85	Edit /etc/vfstab.
86	Press the <F5> key to bypass both the config.sys and autoexec.bat when DOS begins to startup.
87	Edit /etc/rc
88	Edit /etc/inittab
89	Press the <F8> key when Windows begins to startup and select Safe Mode from the boot menu.
90	Use Control Panel > System > Device Manger > CDROM > Settings.
91	Right-click on shortcut and select Properties > Find Target.
92	Right-click on shortcut and select Properties > Shortcut > Find Target.
93	Create a file with the .NCF extension that contains commands which can then be called from other .NCF files.
94	Run `ps -auxw | grep rpc.yppasswdd`, note the processID and run `kill 9` on that processID.
95	To configure audit, edit appropriate files in /etc/security/audit.
96	Use Macintosh HD > Applications > Utilities > Assistants > Internet Setup > `Internet Setup Assistant`.
97	Use `env LANG=`*`language code`*.
98	Use `export LANG=`*`language code`*.
99	Press the <F5> key on the keyboard or the <5> key on a terminal keyboard when you hear the startup sound.
100	Remove the `/etc/nologin` file.
101	Use Macintosh HD > Applications > Utilities > `Disk First Aid`.
102	Press the <UPARROW> key on the keyboard from the server console.
103	Click on the icon Show Desktop next to the Start button on the taskbar, or press <WINDOWS BUTTON> + <D>.

continued

104	Click Start menu and select Search (Win2000, WinXP) or Find (Win98, WinNT) > On the Internet.
105	Select Exit from the File menu or press <ALT> + <F4>.
106	Use `dd if=`*`filesystem`*` of=`*`file`*.
107	After submitting a print job select PrintMonitor from the Finder Menu at top right-hand corner of the screen.
108	Use `telnet` *`host`* `25`.
109	Compression is configured when the NetWare volumes are initially created.
110	Use Macintosh HD > Applications > Utilities > `Disk Copy`.
111	Right-click on a file select Properties > Security > Advanced > Owner.
112	Click on the volumes icon title bar once, wait until text is selected, then type in the new label.
113	Click on the filename or directory to rename and wait until text is selected, then type in the new name.
114	Use Control Panel > Administrative Tools > Data Sources (ODBC).
115	Double-click on the printer Icon located on the desktop.
116	Load `tcpcon.nlm` on the server and select Protocol Information > IP > IP Address Translations.
117	Create the file `nologin` in the /etc directory (i.e. touch /etc/nologin).
118	Stop the `Net Logon` service found under Control Panel > Services on Domain Controllers.
119	Right-click on the folder to share in `explorer` and select Sharing > Share this folder.
120	Use Macintosh HD > Applications > Utilities > `WhatRoute`.
121	Novell Intenet Access Services (NIAS) is available for download from www.novell.com.
122	Use Control Panel > Display > Appearance
123	Click on the Novell button in ConsoleOne then select Settings > Backgrounds.
124	Use Control Panel > Services > *service* > Stop.
125	Edit the boot.ini file located in the root of the system boot up device.
126	Use `ksh`, `alias __A=^P`, `alias __B=^N` then `set -o emacs`.
127	Use NetWare Management Portal > Server Management > System Statistics > Media Manager > Data Transfer Rate.
128	Use `NetWare Remote Manager` > Manage Server > View Statistics > Media Manager > Data Transfer Rate.
129	Use Macintosh HD > Applications > Utilities > `Drive Setup`.
130	Use `inetcfg.nlm` > Protocols > TCP/IP > LAN Static Routing Table and then press the Insert button.
131	Use Control panel > Add/Remove Programs > Add/Remove Windows Components > Network Services > DNS.
132	Use Macintosh HD > Applications > Quicktime > `QuickTime Player`.
133	Use Macintosh HD > Applications > Quicktime > `Picture Viewer`.
134	Use Start Menu > Programs > Accesories > Imaging.
135	Use Macintosh HD > System Folder > Fonts and then double-click on the font you want to view.
136	Use Control Panel > Administrative Tools > Active Directory Users and Computers.
137	Use Control Panel > Network Connections> *connection*.
138	Use Control Panel > Network.
139	Use Control Panel > Network > TCP/IP > DNS Configuration.
140	Use Control Panel > Network Connections> *connection* > TCP/IP.
141	Use Control Panel > Network > TCP/IP.
142	Use Control Panel > Printers > *printer* > Printer > Pause Printing.
143	Go to www.winzip.com and download a free evaluation version of the program WinZip.
144	In `explorer`, press F5 to see if new media has been inserted into any removable media device.
145	Right-click on the Network Neighborhood > Properties > Services > Add, and install the DHCP Relay Agent service.
146	Install DHCP Relay Agent from inside the Routing and Remote Access found under Administrative Tools.
147	Use Control Panel > System > Advanced > Performance Options.
148	Use Control Panel > System > Performance.
149	Use Control Panel > System > Performance > Virtual Memory.
150	Use Control Panel > Display > Screen Saver.
151	Press <Stop> + <A> and type probe-scsi-all.
152	Right-click on a file or folder and select Properties > Security.
153	Use Start > Shut Down > Restart the Computer.
154	Use Control Panel > System > Environment.
155	Use Control Panel > System > Advanced > Environment Variables.
156	Use Control Panel > Netwok > Identification.
157	Start Outlook Express (if installed). Select Play sound when new message arrives from Tools > General.
158	Right-click on the drive to limit disk usage on and select the quota tab.
159	Right-click on a shared folder and select Properties > Security or Sharing.
160	Use Control Panel > Network Connections. Right-click on the connection to disable and choose disable.
161	Start Microsoft Management Console and add the IP Security Monitor using Console > Add/Remove Snap-in > Add.
162	Use Control Panel > Network Connections > *connection*, and install the Network Load balancing service.
163	Run `config -e /bsd` and use the internal command list to view found hardware and their interrupt.
164	Edit the configuration file for the webserver (httpd.conf).

continued

165	Select drive and press <COMMAND> + .
166	Use Control Panel > System > Hardware > Device Manager > Ports > Properties.
167	Use Control Panel > System > Hardware > Ports > Properties.
168	Install File and Printer sharing for Microsoft Networks and right-click on a printer and select Sharing.
169	Double-click on trashcan and drag the files or folders you want to undelete to the desktop.
170	Use Control Panel > Network connections > *connection* > Properties > Sharing > Enable Internet sharing.
171	Use Control Panel > System > Hardware > Device Manager > SCSI and Raid Controllers.
172	Use Control Panel > System > Device manager > SCSI Controllers.
173	Install Terminal Services in remote administration mode.
174	Use Start > Shut Down > Close all programs and log on as a different user.
175	Use Start > Log off.
176	Use Start > Shut Down > Log off.
177	Use Control Panel > System > Hardware > Device Manager > choose adapter type.
178	Use Contorl Panel > Network > Protocols.
179	Use Apple Menu > Chooser > *printer* > Setup and click on Share This Printer.
180	Use Control Panel > Network Connections > *connection* > Properties.
181	Use Control Panel > System > Device Manager. Click on the network adapter choose Properties and click uninstall.
182	Click on the Start Menu and select Find or Search and choose Files or Folders.
183	Use Control Panel > Network Connections, right-click on the connection to enable, and choose enable.
184	Use Control Panel > Network > Adapters and choose the adapter and click uninstall.
185	Use Control Panel > Network choose the adapter and click remove.
186	Edit the file /etc/TIMEZONE and change the TZ variable to the new timezone.
187	Remove the file `nologin` in the /etc directory (i.e. rm /etc/nologin).
188	Start the `Net Logon` service found under Control Panel > Services on Domain Controllers.
189	Right-click on the icon you want information about and select Properties, then click the General tab.
190	Use Control Panel > System > Hardware > Device Manager.
191	Use Control Panel > Network Connections > Local Area Connection > Properties > TCP/IP > Advanced > DNS.
192	Use Control Panel > Network > Protocols > TCP/IP Protocol > DNS.
193	Use Control Panel > Network > Configuration > *protocol* > Properties > Bindings.
194	Use Control Panel > Network Connections > Properties > Local Area Connection > Properties > General.
195	Use Control Panel > Network > Local Area Connection > Properties > General.
196	Use Control Panel > Network > TCP/IP > Properties > IP Address.
197	Use Control Panel > Network > Protocols > TCP/IP > Properties.
198	Use Control Panel > Network Connections > Local Area Connection > Properties > TCP/IP > Properties.
199	Use Macintosh HD > Applications > Outlook Express > `Outlook Express`.
200	Use Macintosh HD > System Folder > Control Panels > Multiple Users
201	Use the command UNICON.NLM. For more information please search for document ID# 2912429 on www.novell.com.
202	From the Main Panel in the CDE Windows environment select Trash, then Empty Trash Can.
203	Double-click on the file or folder you want to open.
204	Use Control Panel > Network > Identification.
205	Use Control Panel > System > Network Idenfication.
206	Use Control Panel > Network Connections > Local Area Connection > Properties > Configure > Device usage.
207	Use Control panel > System Properties > Device Manager > Network Adapters > Disable.
208	Use `Internetworking Configuration` > boards, then hit the <tab> key on your keyboard.
209	Start inetmgr.exe, then choose server > default ftp site > properties > current sessions.
210	Use Control Panel > System > Hardware > Device Manager
211	Use Control Panel > System > Device Manager
212	Start Task Manager with <CTRL> + <ALT> + <DEL>, select the process that you want to remove, then End Task.
213	Use Control Panel > Display.
214	Use `Install.nlm` > System Options > Edit AUTOEXEC.NCF
215	Use `nwconfig` > NCF Files Options > Edit AUTOEXEC.NCF
216	Edit \winnt\system32\drivers\etc\services.
217	Edit \windows\system32\drivers\etc\services.
218	Use Control Panel > Network and Dialup Connections > *connection.*
219	Use Control Panel > Network Connections > *connection.*
220	Use Control Panel > Services > Spooler > Stop.
221	Use Control Panel > Administrative Tools > Services > Print Spooler > Stop.
222	Double-click on the Network Neighborhood icon on the desktop.
223	Double-click on the My Network Places icon on the desktop.
224	Use Control Panel > System > Device Manager > Network adapters > Enable.
225	Select current window and press <ALT> + <F4>.
226	Hold down the keys `<command> + <alt> + <shift> + <delete> + the SCSI-ID` during startup.

continued

227	Use Control Panel > Network Connections > Local Area Connection > Properties > TCP/IP > Advanced > Options.
228	Use Control Panel > Network > Protocols > TCP/IP > Advanced > Enable Security > Configure.
229	Press <CTRL> + <ALT> + <DELETE> and choose change password.
230	Use Control Panels > multiple users > select user and open to change password.
231	Use Control Panel > Network Connections > Local Area Connection > Advanced > Internet Connection Sharing.
232	You may use Border Manager available from Novell.
233	Use Control Panel > Network Connections > Local Area Connection > Properties > Internet Protocol > Properties.
234	Use Control Panel > Network > TCP/IP > Properties.
235	Use Control Panel > Network > Protocols > TCP/IP Protocol > Properties...
236	Use Control Panel > Printers > printer > Printer > Properties > Print Test Page.
237	Use `usrmgr.exe` > *user* > Groups.
238	Use `compmgmt.msc` > Local Users and Groups > Users > *user* > Member of.
239	Right-click on the Novell Icon in the Windows task bar and select User Administration > Group Memberships...
240	Right-click on the harddrive to enable quota for and select Properties > Quota > Enable quota management.
241	Right-click on the harddrive to disable quota for and select Properties > Quota > Uncheck Enable quota management.
242	To unshare a folder right-click on the folder you want to unshare and select Sharing from the context menu.
243	Use Control Panel > Network > TCP/IP > DNS Configuration > Disable DNS.
244	Use Control Panel > Network > Protocol > TCP/IP > DNS then remove DNS addresses.
245	Start `cmd.exe` or `command.com`. Then right-click up on the top of the window and choose properties.
246	Start `nwadmn32`, select servername, rightclick and then select Properties > Accounting.
247	Start `nwadmn32`, right-click on volume > Properties > User Space Limits, specify context. Select user > Modify.
248	Use Control Panel > System > Hardware > Device Manager, right-click on device and choose uninstall.
249	Use Control Panel > Devices > *device* > Stop.
250	Use Control Panel > Display > Settings.
251	Install terminal services in Remote administration mode, using Control Panel > Add/Remove Programs.
252	Load `remote.nlm` and enter password to use then load `rspx.nlm`.
253	First install NIS by using `ypinit` then set up the NIS server by running `ypserv` and modifing /etc/yp.conf.
254	Use Control Panel > AdministrativeTools > Services > Routing and Remote Access.
255	Use Control Panel > Network > Services > Add...
256	Use Control Panel > Printers, right-click on printer and choose properties.
257	Use Control Panel > Printers > *printer* > Properties > Scheduling.
258	Use Control Panel > Printers > *printer* > Properties > Advanced.
259	Use Control Panel > Printers > *printer* > Pause Printing.
260	Right-click on a file in `explorer` and select properties.
261	Right-click on a harddrive in `explorer` and select properties.
262	Use Control Panel > Accessibility Options > General tab > SerialKey devices.
263	Use Program > Accessories > Communications > Dial-up Networking.
264	Insert a blank CD-ROM. Right-click on the CD-recorder > Properties > Recording. Drag files to CD-recorder.
265	Use Control Panel > Network Connections > Local area connection > Properties > Configure > Advanced.
266	Use Control Panel > Network Connections > *connection* > Properties > Advanced.
267	Use Control Panel > Network Connections > *connection* > Properties.
268	Use Control Panel > Administrative Tools > Services > *service* > Stop.
269	Use `ps -aux | grep` *`daemonname`*, note the processID and run `kill` on that processed.
270	Use `ps -ef | grep` *`daemonname`*, note the processID and run `kill` on that processID.
271	Open My Computer and select View > Options > File Types to view or edit file types.
272	Open My Computer and select Tools > Folder Options > File Types to view or edit file types.
273	Type in the name of the daemon to start and press enter.
274	Use Control Panel > Services > *service* > Start.
275	Use Control Panel > Administrative Tools > Services > *service* > Start.
276	To change viewing options for files and folders select view option from the View menu.
277	Please search on www.novell.com for document # 2925549 for information on creating users using a script.
278	Use Control Panel > Network > Protocols > TCP Protocol > Properties.
279	Start `cmd.exe` or `command.com`. Then right-click up on the top of the window and choose properties.
280	Use Control Panel > Display > Settings.
281	In `explorer`, press F5 to see if new media has been inserted into any removable media device.
282	In `explorer` select Folder options from the View menu.
283	Start explorer.exe then select file > properties from the context menu.
284	Use the start scripts in `/etc/init.d/`.

In This Part

This part brings together the commands for Novell NetWare and helps you spot the differences from version to version.

Chapter 2

Universal NetWare Commands

The commands in this section are common in all four versions of NetWare: NetWare 3, NetWare 4, NetWare 5 and NetWare 6. The commands are all listed in alphabetical order by the command name.

Even though these commands are available in every version of NetWare, many of the options are different and the commands may have a different syntax as well. Look carefully at the syntax field: you may see a bold NW6, NW5, NW4, or NW3, indicating that the following are unique to that version of NetWare.

Remember, for NLM commands you must type the command "load" in front of the NLM for NetWare 3 and 4. This step is optional in NetWare 5 and 6.

For cross-references to other operating systems, please see Chapter 1, the "Quick Command Index."

#, ;

OS: NetWare Common

Function	Creates a comment in an NCF file or prevents a line from being executed for troubleshooting purposes.
Syntax	# *text* ; *text*

text	Specifies the comment to make or the line of text to prevent execution.

# The next line loads the network driver.	Specifies a comment.
; load portal.nlm	Prevents the loading of the portal.nlm.

\etc\gateways

OS: NetWare Common

Function	Adds gateways that aren't normally found by standard routing protocols.
Syntax	net *network* gateway *gateway* [metric *cost*] { *type* } host *host* gateway *gateway* [metric *cost*] { *type* }

net *network*	Specifies network number or name for the target network.
/*networkmask*	Specifies an optional network mask for the network.
host *host*	Specifies a host to setup route to.
gateway *gateway*	Specifies the gateway to use.
metric *cost*	Specifies the cost for the route.
type	Specifies the type of route can be active or passive.

File Name:	`gateways`	**Directory:**	\etc	**Type:**	Text File
Note:	If network names are used they must be specified in \etc\networks.				

\etc\hosts

OS: NetWare Common

Function	Configures names and aliases of IP-addresses. Fields should be separated with tab or space.
Syntax	*IP-address hostname { aliases... }* # *{ comment }*

IP-address	Specifies the IP-address of the hostname or alias.
hostname	Specifies the hostname of the IP-address or alias.
aliases...	Specifies aliases for the IP-address or hostname.
comment	Specifies a comment in the configuration file.

File Name:	`hosts`	**Directory:**	\etc	**Type:**	Text File

Abort Remirror

OS: NetWare Common

Function	Stops remirroring the specified logical partition.
Syntax	abort remirror *number*

number	Specifies the logical partition number for the partition to abort remirroring on.
Tip:	Use the command `mirror status` to see a list of mirrored partitions and partition number.
abort remirror 3	Stops remirroring partition 3.

Add Name Space

OS: NetWare Common

Function	Usually used to support long filenames (greater the 8 characters) for Windows-based computers. Is also used to support Unix and Macintosh clients to enable them to save and retrieve files.
Syntax	add name space *name* [TO] *volume*

name	Specifies the name space to apply to a volume. Please see Name Spaces below.
volume	Specifies the name of the volume where the name space will be applied.
[TO]	Is optional.
Name spaces	**The following is a listing of available name spaces and their purpose.**
OS2	**NW3 Only:** Provides support for long filenames and OS2 clients.
LONG	Replaces OS2 and supports long files for OS2, Windows and NT clients.
MAC	Provides support for Macintosh clients to enable them to retrieve and save files.
NFS	Provides support for NFS usually used by UNIX clients.
FTAM	Provides support for the FTAM file system and must be purchased separately.
Tip:	Before you can add a name space, load the name space (i.e. load MAC or load LONG).
add name space OS2 to VOL1	Adds long name space support and OS/2 support for VOL1.
and name space LONG SYS	Adds the long name space to volume sys.

aiocomx

OS: NetWare Common

Function	Installs the aiocomx communication driver. If loaded without options it attempts to detect the correct configuration.
Syntax	load aiocomx [options...]

port=*port*	Specifies the I/O port number for the com port.
int=*value*	Specifies the interrupt for the com port.
name=*name*	Specifies a name to assign the port.
node=*value*	Overrides the board number if the board was configured with one.
force	Accepts the specified options without verifying the communication hardware.
nofifo	Overrides the FIFO (16550) device to function as non-FIFO (16450/8250) device.
rxt=*value*	The 16550 FIFO receiver trigger. Values are 1 (non-FIFO), 4 (FIFO only), 8, or 14.
txq=*value*	The 16550 FIFO transmit queue. Values are 1 (non-FIFO), 4, 8,12, or 16 (FIFO only).
NW4, NW5, NW6:	
maxrate=*speed*	Sets maximum baud rate for high-speed devices.

File Name:	`aiocomx.nlm`	**Directory:**	\system	**Type:**	External
load aiocomx	Loads the aiocomx driver and automatically configures it.				

AppleTalk Console

OS: NetWare Common

Function	Monitors AppleTalk activity, shows the local AppleTalk router configuration, diagnoses operational problems, verifies the connectivity of an AppleTalk router to the rest of the network, and monitors AURP status.
Syntax	load atcon

File Name:	`atcon.nlm`	**Directory:**	\system	**Type:**	External
NOTE:	The module APPLETLK.NLM is automatically loaded.				

AppleTalk Stack/Router

OS: NetWare Common

Function	Loads the AppleTalk protocol stack to provide network resources to Macintosh clients.
Syntax	load appletlk [options...] net=*NR* [zone= *"name"*]

-c	Enables transition routing and checks for blocked AppleTalk ranges and zone lists.
-t	Reads the AppleTalk zone configuration from the `sys:system\atzones.cfg` file.
-z	Enables DDP packet checksums and forces the server to calculate or compare checksums.

continued

net=*NR* zone= "*name*"	Specifies the internal network between number 1 and 65279 for the AppleTalk network. Specifies the AppleTalk zone name that the AFP file services will be broadcasted.
File Name: `appletlk.nlm`	**Directory:** \system **Type:** External
Warning:	AppleTalk is a broadcast protocol and should be used on an isolated network or VPN.

autoexec.ncf

OS: NetWare Common

Function	The startup file that contains commands for the OS to execute to complete the boot process and configure the server. It is executed after the STARTUP.NCF file has been executed and the SYS: volume has been mounted.
Syntax	autoexec.ncf

	The following is a list of tasks normally performed inside the autoexec.ncf.
file server name Neptune	Names the file server Neptune.
ipx internal net dad2be	Assigns the internal IPX network to be dad2be.
load sn2000.lan *parameter*	Loads the network card with the parameters you specify (see the `load` command).
load tcpip	Loads the tcpip protocol.
bind IP to *networkcard*	Binds IP to the network card or name you specify (see the `bind` command).
mount all	Mounts all NetWare volumes.
load monitor	Loads the `monitor` NLM
File Name: `autoexec.ncf`	**Directory:** \system **Type:** External

bind

OS: NetWare Common

Function	Binds a network protocol to a network card and enables the specified protocol for use throughout the network.
Syntax	bind *protocol* [to] *name* { *driverparameters...* } { *protocolparameters...* }

protocol	Specifies the protocol that is used.
name	Specifies the LAN driver name or the name assigned by the `load` command.
driverparameters...	Specifies the driver parameters if more than one network board is of the same type.
	If you use name when loading the driver these parameters aren't needed.
DMA=*values*	Specifies the DMA channel for the network card to use.
FRAME=*number*	Specifies the frame type the protocol will use.
INT=*value*	Specifies the interrupt the network card is configured for.
MEM=*address*	Specifies the memory address that the network card will use.
PORT=*port*	Specifies the I/O port for the network card.
SLOT=*number*	Specifies the SLOT where the card is installed. Only used for EISA and Micro channel.
protocolparameters...	**The following protocol parameters explain only the IPX and IP parameters:**
net=*number*	Specifies a unique network number for IPX. Don't use the same number as the internal.
addr=*IPaddress*	Sets the TCP/IP address for the server to use (i.e. 192.168.1.246).
mask=*subnet*	Sets the TCP/IP subnet mask in Hexadecimal format (i.e. FF.FF.FF.0 = 255.255.255.0).
gate=*number*	Sets the TCP/IP default gateway for the server to use.
Warning:	You must `load` a network driver before you can `bind` to it.
bind ipx to 802.2 net=50	Binds the IPX protocol to the name 802.2 that was named by the `load` command and assigns a network number of 50.
bind tcpip to II addr=192.168.1.246 mask=FF.FF.FF.0	Binds the IP protocol to the name II that was named by the `load` command and assigns an IP address, subnet mask, and gateway.

break

OS: NetWare Common

Function	Enables or disables extended CTRL+C checking.
Syntax	break [option] break=[option]

ON	Is used to enable extended CTRL+C checking.
OFF	Is used to disable extended CTRL+C checking.

broadcast

OS: NetWare Common

Function	Sends a broadcast message to all users currently logged into the server or to a specific user specified by destination. The message can't be longer than 55 characters.
Syntax	broadcast "*message*" [TO] { *destination* } [AND or ,] { *destination* }

"*message*"	The message that you want to send to users logged into the server.
destination	Specifies the username or connection number to send the message.
TO	Is optional.
AND	Separates destinations if sending a message to specific users.
,	Is also used to separate destinations and is used as a replacement for AND.

Note: Users who have typed `castoff` or logged in remotely don't receive broadcast messages.

broadcast "The UCG book is DONE!, The UCG book is done!"	Sends a great message to everyone working on this book.
broadcast "Please logout of the server" guy, myles, 3, 12	Sends the message "Please logout of the server" to users guy and myles and connections 3 and 12.

Btrieve Message Router

OS: NetWare Common

Function	The default Message Router for Btrieve. This must be loaded by using NetWare `INSTALL`.
Syntax	load brouter

File Name:	`brouter.nlm`	**Directory:**	\system	**Type:**	External

Tip: For an overview of the Btrieve server-based Record Manager, see the command `btrieve.nlm`.

Btrieve Rebuild Utility

OS: NetWare Common

Function	Converts Btrieve 5.x files into Btrieve 6.x file format. This may be run from the command line or via the Btrieve Setup Utility `bsetup`
Syntax	load brebuild [options...] *file* load brebuild @*buildfile*

-c	Continues onto the next file if an error occurs.
-p { *NR* }	Specifies the page size of the new file or, if not given, selects an optimal size.
-b *directory*	Specifies where to place the new files.
-m0	Copies files but doesn't remove or replace any indexes.
-m2	Removes target file indexes before a copy is done but rebuilds them later (default).
-k *NR*	Navigates through the input file using the specified key number (default is step-thru).
-t	Doesn't save the Transaction Tracking bit of the input file.
-d	Assigns duplicate linkages for those supplemental keys that allow duplicates.
file	Specifies the File Mask to use. One or more files may be specified by using wildcards.
@*buildfile*	Specifies the plain text file that contains valid `brebuild` commands.

File Name:	`brebuild.nlm`	**Directory:**	\system	**Type:**	External

Tip: For an overview of the Btrieve server-based Record Manager, see the command `btrieve.nlm`.

load brebuild -c -m0 -b c:\temp U:\ucg*.jpg	Rebuilds the jpg files in the ucg directory, without index removal to the c:\temp directory, and ignores any errors.
load brebuild @ucgbrebuild.txt	Reads from the ucgbrebuild.txt file for valid brebuild commands.

Btrieve Request Manager

OS: NetWare Common

Function	Manages incoming requests to `btrieve` from remote sources. An example is a workstation requester or a Message Router. This is required on servers supporting remote requests.
Syntax	load bspxcom

File Name:	`bspxcom.nlm`	**Directory:**	\system	**Type:**	External

Tip: For an overview of the Btrieve server-based Record Manager, see the command `btrieve.nlm`.

Btrieve SPX Communications Stub

OS: NetWare Common

Function	Loads the Btrieve SPX communications stub that resolves external references for Btrieve for local server access. Is used when `bspxcom` isn't loaded.
Syntax	load bspxstub
File Name:	`bspxstub.nlm` **Directory:** \system **Type:** External

Btrieve Workstation Requester

OS: NetWare Common

Function	Relays Btrieve requests between applications and the Btrieve server - DOS version. The file `btrcalls.dll` is for OS2, and `wbtrcall.dll` is for MS Windows.
Syntax	brequest [options...]

NW Common	
/d:*buffer*	Specifies the largest buffer length that may be received or sent.
/c:0	Disables the runtime server.
/c:1	Enables the runtime server and allows for login parameters.
{ *login* }	Specifies the login name.
{ *password* }	Specifies the password.
/o	Activates on-the-fly data compression.
NW6	
/s:*NR*	Sets maximum number of connected servers.
/l:*NR*	Specifies how many times a DOS session load will be done (default is once).
/t:*NR*	Sets the client ID maximum (default is 0).
/u	Unloads `brequest` from memory.
File Name: `brequest.exe`	**Directory:** \public **Type:** External
Tip:	For an overview of the Btrieve server-based record manager, please see `btrieve.nlm`.
No Example	Sets the send/receive buffer length to 255.

butil (server)

OS: NetWare Common

Function	The Btrieve Maintenance Utility, which allows for import/export of Btrieve file data or to move it from one Btrieve file to another. Also enables/disables use of Btrieve continuous operation.
Syntax	load butil *ACTION* { *parameters* } load butil @*file*

/O*owner*	Specifies the owner name of the Btrieve original. (Can't be used with create, endbu, startbu, and ver.)
ACTION	**Specify only one of the following Actions:**
-clone *clone bfile* [/O*owner*]	Creates an empty copy of an existing Btrieve file with the same specs and keys.
-clrowner *bfile* [/O*owner*]	Removes the owner name that is associated with the Btrieve file.
-copy *bfile1 bfile2* [/O*owner1*] [/O*owner2*]	Copies one Btrieve file's contents to another, with the specified owner names.
-create *bfile dfile*	Creates a Btrieve file based upon a description file.
-drop *bfile NR* [/O*owner*]	Removes a specified key index number from the specified Btrieve file.
-endbu { *bfile* } | [@*file*]	Stops continuous operation on a specified file or a specified command file. (If no files are specified then this will act upon all Btrieve files.)
-load *ascii bfile* [/O*owner*]	Loads a sequential file's contents (ASCII) into a Btrieve file.
-recover *bfile ascii* [/O*owner*]	Reads from a Btrieve file and creates a sequential file (ASCII).
-salvage *bfile* [/O*owner*]	Views the specified files' contents for PAT corruption and informs if a fix is needed.
-save *bfile ascii* [Y*index*] [N*key*]	Reads from the Btrieve file and then saves data to the specified sequential file.
Y*index*	Specifies to use an external index file for saving records.
N*key*	Specifies a key number that is used for save records (default is 0).
-setowner *bfile* /O*owner level*	Assigns a specific owner to the specified Btrieve file with a specific access level.
0	Requires a specified owner name for an access mode. Doesn't use data encryption.
1	Allows read access without a specified owner name. Doesn't use data encryption.
2	Requires a specified owner name for an access mode. Uses data encryption.
3	Allows read access without a specified owner name. Uses data encryption.
-sindex *bfile dfile* [/O*owner*]	Creates an index for the specified file as directed by the description file.
-startbu { *bfile* } | [@*file*]	Starts continuous operation on a specified file or a specified command file. (This allows the backing up of files that are in use by Btrieve.)

continued

-stat *bfile* [/O*owner*]	Reports file attribute and size information about Btrieve files to the user.
-ver	Shows version information.
@*file*	Specifies the name and full path to a command file to be used by `butil`.
clone	Specifies the clone output file, which includes the full path.
bfile	Specifies the Btrieve original.
ifile	The index file where Btrieve will store external index information.
File Name: `butil.nlm`	**Directory:** \system **Type:** External
load butil @ucg.cmd	Loads the command file ucg, which contains butil commands that are too long to be entered from the command line.

capture

OS: NetWare Common

Function	Redirects LPT ports to network printers. This allows DOS and OS/2 programs that are designed to use a parallel port to print to a network printer.
Syntax	capture [options...]

	The following two options can't be combined.
P=*printer*	Specifies the name of the printer to connect to.
Q=*queue*	Specifies the name of the printer queue to connect to.
L=*NR*	Sets the number of the printer port to capture to the specified queue or printer.
ALL	Is used with EC to end the capture of all LPT ports or with /?.
AU	Closes captured data and sends it to the printer when exiting an application.
B="*string*"	Specifies the text to include in the lower half of the banner page (max is 12 characters).
CA	Is used with the EC options to discard the captured data.
C=*NR*	Sets the number of copies to print. The maximum for NW4 and above is 65000.
	The following option can only be combined with the TI, AU, or NA options:
CR=*file*	Specifies the name and path of a file in which the printed data is stored.
D	Shows the printing parameters for a capture.
EC	Ends capture to the LPT port specified with L= or to all ports if used with ALL.
F=*form*	Specifies the name or number of the form the printer will use.
HOLD	Sends a print job to a queue without printing it. (Use NetWare Administrator to release the hold.)
J=*name*	Sets the job configuration to use.
K	Ensures that the server keeps all received data and prints it if the computer hangs.
NAM=*text*	Specifies the text to include in the upper half of the banner page (max is 12 characters).
NA	Doesn't close captured data and send it to the printer when exiting an application.
NB	Doesn't print the banner page.
NFF	Doesn't use form feed at the end of a print job.
NNOTI	Doesn't notify the user when the print job is done.
NT	Doesn't convert tabs to spaces.
NOTI	Notifies the user when the print job is completed.
S=*name*	Sets the name of the server if the print job is to be sent to a binary print queue.
	The following option can only be used alone.
SH	Shows the status of all LPT ports.
T=*NR*	Sets the number of spaces to use instead of each tab in a print job (default is 8).
TI=*NR*	Sets number of seconds to wait after the last data is received before closing the job.
/VER	Shows version information.
/?	Shows help information.
File Name: `capture.exe`	**Directory:** \public **Type:** External
capture Q=printer01 L=1	Redirects the LPT 1 port to the specified print queue.
capture Q=printer01 L=1 NB NFF	Doesn't print the banner page or use a form feed.

cd

OS: NetWare Common

Function	Manages and monitors CD-ROM devices used as a NetWare volume. This command is only available after loading `cdrom.nlm` in NW3 and NW4 and `cdinst.nlm` in NW5 and NW6.
Syntax	cd *command* [options...]

help	Shows help information.
device list	Lists devices that have been registered, and their list number.
volume list	Lists CD-ROM volumes that are found on registered devices.
dir *device*	Shows a directory listing for specified CD-ROM device. Use volume name or list NR.
mount *device* [options...]	Mounts the CD-ROM specified by device where device is the volume name or list NR.
change *device* [options...]	Changes the CD-ROM specified by device. Values for device are volume name or list NR.
	The following options are used by the mount and the change commands:
/mac	Adds the MAC name space to the CD-ROM volume (can be used with /nfs).
/nfs	Adds the NFS name space to the CD-ROM volume (can be used with /mac).
/dup	Checks for duplicate filenames in current directory.
/G=*NR*	Assigns a group access to the NetWare volume. Range is 1–9 (default is 0 = Everyone).
/r	Rebuilds the index for the CD-ROM drive.
/x=*directory*	Excludes access to the specified directory when mounting the CD-ROM.
	The following caching options provide for faster recall. You may use only one. The size of the cache is in MB specified by NR. Be sure you have enough disk space.
/DNVC=*NR*	Uses direct map caching for CD volumes. Information is cached a short time (fastest).
/ANVC=*NR*	Uses associative caching for CD volumes. Information is cached longer (medium speed).
/LNVC=*NR*	Uses associative LRU caching for CD volumes. Information is cached longest (slowest).
/purge	Removes the index from the volume when the CD-ROM is dismounted. (This option is only available with the change command.)
dismount *device* [option]	Dismounts the CD volume specified by device. You can use the next two options.
/eject	Ejects the CD-ROM after being dismounted.
/purge	Removes the index from the volume when the CD-ROM is dismounted.
image	Allows you to mount and test a CD image before creating (burning) a master image.
path:filename	Adds the specified image file to list of active images.
list	Lists of all active CD images.
del *NR*	Deletes the image number specified by NR from active list of images.
mount *NR*	Mounts a CD image specified by NR as a CD. Use `cd image list` to find image NR.
dismount *NR*	Dismount a CD image specified by NR. Use `cd image list` to find image NR.
rename [/d=*NR*] *newname*	Renames an umounted CD device specified by the device number followed by new name.
group	Lists of groups and their group ID numbers.
{ group } { groupID }	Specifies the name of the group to assign a groupID (valid values for groupID are 1 to 9). (You must first create a group using the NetWare Administrator.)
del *groupID*	Removes the group specified by groupID.

cd mount UCG /mac /nfs	Mounts the UCG cdrom and adds MAC and NFS name space to the CD volume.
cd dismount 2 /purge	Dismounts the CD with ID 2 and purges the indexes from the hard disk.

Clear Station

OS: NetWare Common

Function	Removes all file server resources allocated to a specific workstation.
Syntax	clear station *destination*

destination	
stationnumber	Specifies the workstation number to clear the connection for.
all	Removes all connections to the server. (This isn't a very nice thing to do.) (The above option doesn't work in NetWare 3.)

Tip:	To find the connection number to clear, use the option `Connections` found in `Monitor`.
clear station 5	Clears the specified station number 5.

cls

OS: NetWare Common

Function	Clears the console screen.
Syntax	cls

config

OS: NetWare Common

Function	Shows the server name, server up time, NDS Tree, IP address and subnet mask, and IPX internal net number.
Syntax	config

config

OS: NetWare Common

Function	Creates a configuration file called `config.txt` in `sys:system` containing configuration for the server it was run on.
Syntax	load config [options...]

/a	Appends to the `config.txt` file in `sys:system` instead of overwriting it.
/d	Creates list of all files in the `sys:system` and `c:\nwserver` directories
/s	Adds all of the set parameters for the server in the file as well.
/ads	Performs all the above options when creating the config.txt file.
File Name: `config.nlm`	**Directory:** \system — **Type:** External
Tip:	This file doesn't come with the OS (WHY???) but you can download it from http://support.novell.com.
load config /ads	Adds to the config.txt file containing the server's current configuration including set parameters and a file listing.

Console Log

OS: NetWare Common

Function	Captures all console messages or anything typed in the server console and save the results to a file.
Syntax	load conlog [options...]

file=*logfile*	Specifies an alternate console log file (default is `sys:\etc\consloe.log`).
save=*backupfile*	Saves the current console.log file using the name specified by backupfile.
maximum=*size*	Specifies the maximum size for the console.log file.
archive=yes	Saves old log files in numeric order beginning with console.000, console.001, etc.
next=*{ hh:mm }*	Saves the log file when the log becomes full or at the specified time (if specified).
entire=yes	Captures all information currently on the server console and continues logging.
help	Shows help information.
File Name: `conlog.nlm`	**Directory:** \system — **Type:** External
Tip:	Use in the autoexec.ncf file to be sure all NLMs were loaded without errors.
load conlog save=console.old	Loads conlog but saves the existing file first.
load conlog entire=yes maximum=50	Loads conlog, captures all current information on the console, and sets the maximum size to 50.

cpucheck

OS: NetWare Common

Function	Verifies the processor type for the system and shows it on the screen.
Syntax	load cpucheck *{ number }*

number	Specifies the processor to show information about.
File Name: `cpucheck.nlm`	**Directory:** \nwserver, **NW3:** \server.312 — **Type:** External

cron

OS: NetWare Common

Function	Starts the cron utility used to execute commands at scheduled dates and times that are specified in the `crontab` file. You must create the `crontab` file yourself and place it in the `\etc` directory.
Syntax	load cron *{ size }*

size	Specifies the maximum size for the log file before restarting (default is 5000000).
File Name: `cron.nlm`	**Directory:** \system — **Type:** External
Tip:	Please see `crontab` in the Unix Common chapter to see how to create a `crontab` file.

Disable Login

OS: NetWare Common

Function	Prevents users from logging in to the system.
Syntax	disable login

Disable TTS

OS: NetWare Common

Function	Disables the NetWare Transaction Tracking System on the server.
Syntax	disable tts
Note:	This is typically used by application developers to debug their programs on a NetWare server.

dismount

OS: NetWare Common

Function	Allows volume maintenance or repairs while the file server is up by making a volume unavailable to users
Syntax	dismount *volume*
volume	Specifies volume to disable for users.
dismount sys	Prevents users from accessing the system volume.

Display Networks

OS: NetWare Common

Function	Shows all network numbers the internal router knows.
Syntax	display networks

Display Servers

OS: NetWare Common

Function	Shows all known servers on the network or just the servers matching the wildcard.
Syntax	display servers *{ wildcard }*
wildcard	Show all servers matching the specified wildcard (i.e. S*, or Ven*). (NetWare 3 doesn't support wildcards.)
display servers v*	Shows all servers beginning with the letter v.

dos set

OS: NetWare Common

Function	Sets, shows, or removes DOS environment variables while running the NetWare login script.
Syntax	dos set *{ variable }={ string }*
variable	The variable to set or modify.
string	The string to associate with the specified variable.
Tip:	Can also be used to set NetWare variables.
dos set user="%UCG"	Creates the variable for the user name called UCG.

dosgen

OS: NetWare Common

Function	Used to create remote boot images on the server for DOS clients to boot from instead of booting from local hard disk.
Syntax	dosgen [options...] *{ path }*
/u	Copies a disk image from the server to the floppy.
/?	Shows help information.
path	Specifies the complete path- and filename where the boot image will be created. (The default path- and filename is sys:system\net$dos.sys.)
File Name:	`dosgen.exe`
Directory:	\system, **NW4:** \public
Type:	External
dosgen sys:\boot\boot.dos	Creates a boot image from floppy in a directory called boot.dos in the boot directory.

down

OS: NetWare Common

Function	Ensures data integrity before powering down or restarting the server. In NetWare versions 5 and 6, the file `shutdown.ncf` is executed if present.
Syntax	down

echo off

OS: NetWare Common

Function	Tells the system not to show commands that are executed in a .NCF file
Syntax	Echo Off

echo on

OS: NetWare Common

Function	Tells the system to show commands that are executed in a .NCF file
Syntax	echo on

Enable Login

OS: NetWare Common

Function	Enables users to log on to the system that has previously been logged out.
Syntax	enable login

Enable TTS

OS: NetWare Common

Function	Enables the NetWare Transaction Tracking System on the server.
Syntax	enable tts

File Maintenance

OS: NetWare Common

Function	Copies, moves, and deletes files and directories. Is also used to recover files that have been deleted or purge deleted files so they can't be recovered.
Syntax	filer

NW4, NW5, NW6:	
Manage Files and Directories	Copies, moves, or changes file and directory data.
Manage according to search pattern	Searches for specific file or directory.
Select Current Directory	Manages the selected files and directories.
View Volume Information	Shows volume information.
Salvage Deleted Files	Restores files that haven't been purged.
Purge Deleted Files	Permanently removes purged files.
Set Default Filer Options	Sets default settings regarding how files are copied.
NW3:	
Current Directory Information	Shows information of the directory.
Directory Contents	Shows files and subdirectories of the current directory.
Select Current Directory	Selects the current directory.
Set Filer Options	Changes the *Directory Information* default.
Volume Information	Shows the volume information.

File Name:	`filer.exe`	**Directory:**	\public	**Type:**	External

File Server Name

OS: NetWare Common

Function	Sets the server name. Updates `AUTOEXEC.NCF` and the DNS.
Syntax	file server name *servername*
servername	Specifies the server name.
file server name neptune	Sets the server name to neptune.

Install (Installation CD)

OS: NetWare Common

Function	Starts the NetWare installation from the installation CD.
Syntax	install

File Name:	`install.bat`	**Directory:**	Netware Installation CD	**Type:**	External

IPX Internal Net

OS: NetWare Common

Function	Assigns the server a unique IPX internal network number and is set in the `AUTOEXEC.NCF` file.
Syntax	IPX Internal Net = *HEXNR*
HEXNR	A hexadecimal number and supports numbers (0-9) and characters (A-F).
Tip:	Have some fun HEX. You can make some interesting network numbers using Hexadecimal.
ipx internal net = dad2be	My wife was expecting a baby when I built this server.
ipx internet net = c0ffee	Giving the server a name with coffee will help keep it up longer.
ipx internal net = f00d	Your server will work for food.

IPX Ping				OS:	NetWare Common
Function	Checks IPX connectivity to another server running IPX. The same as `ping` for IP.				
Syntax	load ipxping				
File Name:	`ipxping.nlm`	Directory:	\system	Type:	External
Tip:	A great utility when you are having connection problems to another server over a WAN link.				

ipxs				OS:	NetWare Common
Function	Provides IPXTM protocol to NLMTM applications that require STREAM-based IPX.				
Syntax	load ipxs [LDFILE=*name*]				
LDFILE=*name*	Specifies a file containing SAP filtering, SAP and RIP timers, and IPX parameters.				
File Name:	`ipxs.nlm`	Directory:	\system	Type:	External

keyb				OS:	NetWare Common
Function	Changes the type of keyboard layout to use for the server console.				
Syntax	load keyb *{ country name }*				
country name	Specifies the name of the country for the keyboard type to use. **The following country names are available in all versions of NetWare.** France Italy Spain United States **The following country names are available in NW4, NW5 and NW6 only.** Belgium Canadian French Denmark Latin America Netherlands Norway Portugal Russia Sweden Swiss French Swiss German United Kingdom				
File Name:	`keyb.nlm`	Directory:	\system	Type:	External
Note:	To change to a different keyboard type you must first unload `keyb.nlm` and then reload it.				
load keyb Sweden	Sets the keyboard type for Sweden.				
load keyb United States	Sets the keyboard type for United States				

List Devices		OS:	NetWare Common
Function	Lists all physical storage devices on the server system.		
Syntax	list devices		

load		OS:	NetWare Common
Function	Loads loadable modules (NLM) to the system. In NW5 and NW6, load is optional.		
Syntax	NW3, NW4: load *{ path }module { arguments... }* NW5, NW6: [load] [options...] *{ path }module { arguments }*		
path	Specifies the path where the module is located.		
module	Specifies the module to load.		
arguments...	Specifies arguments to be used by the module.		
NW5, NW6:			
load	Is optional in NetWare 5 and NetWare 6.		
protected	Loads the module into a separate protected address-space.		
restart	Loads the module into a separate address-space. If it abends, it will be restarted.		
address space=*name*	Loads the module into the specified address space		
load SYS:\extra\somemodule	Loads somemodule that is located in SYS:\extra.		
load protected db	Loads module db into a separate address space (NW5 and NW6).		

load *disk_driver*		OS:	NetWare Common
Function	Loads a hard disk controller driver to enable the operating system to see available hard disks in the server.		
Syntax	load *{ path } disk_driver { parameters... }*		
path	Specifies the path to the location of the disk driver. This is usually on drive C:.		
disk_driver	The filename of the disk driver .DSK NLM file.		

continued

parameters...	These are used for drivers that can't read directly from the controller card.
DMA=*values*	Specifies the DMA channel for the disk controller card to use.
PORT=*port*	Specifies the I/O port for the disk controller card. The value for port is: 1F0 or 170
INT=*value*	The hexadecimal value for the interrupt (i.e. A=10, B=11, C=12, D=13, E=14, F=15).
MEM=*address*	Specifies the memory address for the driver to use.
SLOT=*number*	Specifies the SLOT where the card is installed. Only used for EISA and Micro channel.
load IDE PORT=1F0 INT=E	Loads the IDE driver on port 1F0 and on interrupt 14.

login — OS: NetWare Common

Function	Logs in to a NetWare server.
Syntax	NW3: login [options...] *{ server/*[*user }*] *{ scriptparameter }* NW4, NW5, NW6: login *{ server/*] [*user }* [options...] NW4, NW5, NW6: login *{ tree/*] [*user }* [options...]

server	Specifies the server to log in to.
user	Specifies the name of the user to login as.
NW3:	
/script *script*	Specifies a script to be run instead of the login script. Use with /noattach.
/noattach	Doesn't log out from the current server.
/clearscreen	Clears the screen after login is finished.
scriptparameters	Specifies parameters to the login script.
NW4, NW5, NW6:	
/NS	Doesn't run any login script and doesn't log out from current server.
/NB	Hides the welcome to NetWare messages.
/S *path*	Specifies a script to be run.
/S *object name*	Specifies an object name from where to run a script.
/B	Uses bindery login.
/PR=*object*	Runs the script from the specified profile object.
/NOSWAP	Forbids login to swap between expanded memory, extended memory, or disk.
/SWAP *{ path }*	Swaps login to expanded, extended-memory, current disk, or specified path.
/TREE	Logs in to a tree.
/VER	Shows version information.
/?	Shows help information.
/CLS	Clears the screen before logins scripts run.
tree	Specifies a tree to login to.

File Name:	`login.exe`	**Directory:**	\login	**Type:**	External

login venus/ucg	Logs in user ucg into server venus.
login saturn/ucg /NS	Also logs in to server saturn without logout from the other servers (not NW3).

logout — OS: NetWare Common

Function	Logs out from a specified NetWare server or from all. In NetWare 4, 5, and 6, wildcards can be used.
Syntax	NW3: logout *{ server }* NW4, NW5, NW6: logout *{ server }* [option]

server	Specifies a server to log out from. (In NW4, 5, and 6, wildcards can be used.)
NW4, NW5, NW6:	
/T	Logs out from the NDS tree but not from bindery servers.
/?	Shows help information.
/VER	Shows version information.

File Name:	`logout.exe`	**Directory:**	/public	**Type:**	External

logout venus	Logs out from the server venus.
logout v*	Logs out from all servers that begin with s (NW4-6).

magazine

OS: NetWare Common

Function	Is used in response to magazine requests like Insert Magazine and Remove Magazine.
Syntax	magazine *ACTION*

ACTION	The following actions can be used:
Inserted	Confirms that the media magazine was inserted.
Not Inserted	Confirms that the media magazine was not inserted.
Not Removed	Confirms that the media magazine was not removed.
Removed	Confirms that the media magazine was removed.
magazine inserted	Confirms that the media magazine was inserted.

map

OS: NetWare Common

Function	Shows, creates, or changes network or search drive mapping.
Syntax	map [options...] { *drive*:= } { *path* }

	The following two options can't be combined and must be used first.
P	Maps to a physical volume.
NP	Overwrites local or search drives without prompting.
C	Changes a regular drive to a search drive or a search drive to a regular drive.
DEL	Deletes the specified drive mapping.
INS	Inserts a search drive without replacing an existing one.
N	Maps the specified path to the next available drive letter.
ROOT	Maps a drive to a fake root directory.
W	Doesn't change master environment.
/VER	Shows version information.
/?	Shows help information.
drive	Specifies the drive letter or search drive to change.
path	Specifies the network path to map to the specified drive letter.

File Name:	`map.exe`	**Directory:**	\public	**Type:**	External

map x:=neptune/sys:public	Maps the public directory on the volume sys on the server neptune to x:.
map del x:	Deletes the mapping to the x: drive.

media

OS: NetWare Common

Function	Is used in response to media requests like Insert Media and Remove Media.
Syntax	media *ACTION*

ACTION	The following actions can be used:
Inserted	Confirms that the specified media was inserted.
Not Inserted	Confirms that the specified media was not inserted.
Not Removed	Confirms that the specified media was not removed.
Removed	Confirms that the specified media was removed.
media inserted	Confirms that the specified media was inserted.

memory

OS: NetWare Common

Function	Shows the total amount of server RAM memory.
Syntax	memory

memory map

OS: NetWare Common

Function	Shows where the RAM memory is used on the server.
Syntax	memory map

Mirror Status — OS: NetWare Common

Function	Shows status information of mirrored disk partitions. Also shows the percentage of mirrored data on each disk partition and the partition's physical device number.
Syntax	mirror status *{ partitionNR }*
partitionNR	Specifies which partition to show mirror status information on.
Note:	Mirror status must be executed from the MSEngine on a SFTIII system and doesn't work from IOEngine.
mirror status 2	Shows mirror status of the partition 2.

modules — OS: NetWare Common

Function	Lists of currently loaded modules (NLMs), including the date and version of the module. Can specify a specific module to show modules that match the specified wildcard.
Syntax	modules *{ wildcard }*
wildcard	Specifies the name of a module or a wildcard showing modules matching the wildcard. (NetWare 3 doesn't support wildcards.)
	These color codes are used in NW5 and NW6 and show how the module was loaded.
Cyan	Shows that the module was loaded by server.exe.
Red	Shows that the module was loaded from the startup directory.
White	Shows that the module was loaded from the `autoexec.ncf` file.
Purple	Shows that the module was autoloaded by other modules.
Tip:	Use this command to insure that your system is current and up to date.
modules T*	Shows all loaded modules beginning with the letter T.
module clib	Shows the date, version of the currently loaded clib.nlm.

monitor — OS: NetWare Common

Function	Shows server-related information.
Syntax	NW3, NW4: load monitor [options...] NW5, NW6: monitor
NW3	
ns	Disables the screen saver.
nh	Doesn't load the help functions.
-p	Enables the Processor Utilization option. (Unload monitor after use.)
NW4	
L	Locks the console when MONITOR loads. Use the supervisor password to unlock.
N	Disables the screen saver.
T*NR*	Specifies the number of seconds to wait before starting the screen saver.
M	Starts only the screen saver if the MONITOR window is shown on the screen.
File Name:	`monitor.nlm` — **Directory:** \system\ — **Type:** External
Tip:	Don't leave monitor running with -p option in NW3. It could cause your server problems.

mount — OS: NetWare Common

Function	Makes all or just one volume available for users.
Syntax	mount *volume* mount all
volume	Specifies the volume to mount.
all	Mounts all available volumes.
mount all	Mounts all available volumes.

name — OS: NetWare Common

Function	Shows the name of the current server.
Syntax	name

ncopy			**OS:** NetWare Common		
Function	Copies files between different network drives. It will preserve the attributes for files.				
Syntax	ncopy *file { directory }* [options]				
/a	Copies files with archive bit set. Don't alter the archive bit on the source file.				
/m	Copies files with archive bit set. Clears the archive bit on source file.				
/s	Copies subdirectories.				
/e	Copies empty directories (used with /s).				
/f	Copies sparse files.				
/c	Preserves file attributes.				
/l	Shows messages when non-dos information will be lost.				
/v	Verifies the file after copy.				
/?	Shows help information.				
file	Specifies a file to copy. Wildcards can copy multiple files.				
directory	Specifies the destinations directory. If not given, use the default directory.				
NW4, NW5, NW6					
/ver	Shows version information.				
/r	Keeps compression on supported devices.				
/u	Keeps compression on unsupported devices (used with /r).				
File Name:	ncopy.exe	**Directory:**	\public	**Type:**	External
ncopy e:\ucg\book.txt f:/newucg			Copies the file book.txt to the directory f:/newucg		
ncopy e:\data\ucg*.* /s /e			Copies all files and subdirectory from e:/data to current directory.		

ndir	**OS:** NetWare Common
Function	Shows files and directories with information about owner and permissions.
Syntax	ndir *{ directory }* [options...]
	Use the following to specify what to show:
/not	Shows the opposite of the specified option.
/ro	Shows files that are read only.
/sy	Shows system files.
/h	Shows files that are hidden.
/a	Shows file that has the archive bit.
/x	Shows files that are execute only.
/t	Shows files that are transactional.
/p	Shows all purge files.
/i	Shows files that are indexed.
/ci	Shows files that have the copy inhibit bit set.
/di	Shows files that have the delete inhibit bit set.
/ri	Shows files that have the rename inhibit bit set.
/ow [not] eq *name*	Shows files which owner is name.
/si [not] *op size*	Shows files that are greater that (GE), equal (EQ), or less than (LE) size. (op is one of GE, EQ or LE.)
/up [not] *op mm-dd-yy*	Shows files that are updated before, after, or on the specified date.
/cr [not] *op mm-dd-yy*	Shows files that are created before, after, or on the specified date.
/ac [not] *op mm-dd-yy*	Shows files that are accessed before, after, on the specified date.
/ar [not] *op mm-dd-yy*	Shows files that are archived before, after, on the specified date. (op is one of BEF (before), EQ (equal), or AFT (after)).
/FO	Shows only files.
/DO	Shows only directories.
NW4, NW5, NW6:	
/[rev]sort *type*	Specifies how to sort.
ow	Sorts by owner.
si	Sorts by size.
up	Sorts by last update.

continued

cr	Sorts by creation date.
ac	Sorts by last access.
ar	Sorts by last archive.
un	Doesn't sort.
rev	Reverses the sorting. Used with /sort.
	Use one of the following to specify how to show the result.
/da	Shows information about dates (created, modified, accessed, and archived).
/r	Shows filters and rights.
/mac	Shows apple Macintosh filenames.
/l	Shows long filenames.
/d	Shows detailed file information.
/comp	Shows file compression information.
	Use the following to specify what to show:
/rw	Shows files that are readable and writeable.
/ds	Shows files that are not allowed to suballocate.
/sh	Shows files that are sharable.
/co	Shows files that are compressed.
/ic	Shows files that have the immediate compress bit set.
/dc	Shows files that have the don't compress bit set.
/cc	Shows files that can't be compressed.
/dm	Shows files that have the don't migrate bit set.
/m	Shows files that are migrated.
/nam [not] eq *namespace*	Shows files that have the specified name space.
/s	Shows subdirectories.
/c	Shows a continuous list, doesn't stop for a page break.
/vol	Shows information about volumes.
/spa	Shows information about directory space.
/fi	Shows where files are find on a search drive.
/ver	Shows version information.
NW3:	
\sort *type*	Specifies how to sort.
ow	Sorts by owner.
si	Sorts by size.
up	Sorts by last update.
cr	Sorts by creation date.
ac	Sorts by last access.
ar	Sorts by last archives.
un	Doesn't sort.
/rev	Reverses the sorting. Used with /sort.
	Use one of the following to specify how to show the result.
/dates	Shows information about dates (created, modified, accessed, and archived).
/rights	Shows filters and rights.
/mac	Shows Apple Macintosh filenames.
/long	Shows long filenames.
	Use the following to specify what to show:
/s	Shows files that are sharable.
/ra	Shows files that are Read Audit.
/wa	Shows files that are Write Audit.
/SUB	Shows subdirectories.
directory	Specifies the directory to show information for.

File Name:	`ndir.exe`	**Directory:**	\public	**Type:**	External
ndir f:\system /ro			Shows all files in a read only system directory.		
ndir f:\system /cr bef 01-01-97			Shows all files created before 01-01-97.		

NetWare Login

NetWare Login				**OS:**	NetWare Common
Function	Logs in to a NetWare server or NDS tree and executes automatically when Windows is started.				
Syntax	loginw32 [/a]				
/a	Shows the advanced tab in the NetWare Login dialog box.				
	The following login programs are designed for different versions of Windows.				
loginw31.exe	The login utility optimized for use by Windows 3x clients.				
loginw95.exe	The login utility optimized for use by Windows 9x/ME clients.				
loginw32.exe	The login utility optimized for use by Windows NT, 2000 and XP clients.				
File Name:	`loginw31.exe, loginw95.exe, loginw32.exe`	**Directory:**	\novell\client32	**Type:**	External
Tip:	Keep your NetWare client updated from `http://download.novell.com.`				

Novell Client Setup

Novell Client Setup				**OS:**	NetWare Common
Function	Installs the Novell Client				
Syntax	setup [options...]				
/U	Uses the settings given in the `unattend.txt` file when running setup.				
/U:*directory*	Specifies the path where the `unattend.txt` is located.				
/SL	Writes to the default status log file `status.log`.				
/SL:*directory*	Specifies the path where the `status.log` is located.				
/ACU	Automatically upgrades the client if it is an older version.				
/RB	Rolls back the installation to the previous installation if something goes wrong.				
/NCF	Ignores the CAB overwrite protection fix. Allows for CAB file overwrites.				
/508	Enables the Workforce Investment Act of 1998 - section 508 interface enhancements.				
/?	Shows help information.				
File Name:	`setup.exe`	**Directory:**		**Type:**	External
Tip:	Remember to download the latest Novell Client available for free from `www.novell.com.`				
setup /ACU	Automatically upgrades the client.				

nprinter

nprinter				**OS:**	NetWare Common
Function	A printer server that connects printers that are attached to local or remote NetWare servers to the network. At least one NetWare server must be running the print server (`pserver.nlm`) before nprinter will load.				
Syntax	load nprinter *printserver NR* NW4, NW5, NW6: load nprinter *NDSprintername*				
printserver	The name of the print server assigned when it was created.				
NR	The printer number that was assigned when the print server was created.				
NW3, NW4, NW5:					
NDSprintername	The complete NDS name for the printer including the context. (.printer.sales.ucg)				
File Name:	`nprinter.nlm`	**Directory:**	\system	**Type:**	External
nprinter color 3	Loads the print server color with printer number 3.				
nprinter .laser.planets.galaxy	Loads the print server laser in OU planets and tree galaxy.				

off

off		**OS:**	NetWare Common
Function	Clears the console screen. Does the same as `cls`.		
Syntax	off		

pause

pause		**OS:**	NetWare Common
Function	Pauses the execution of login scripts. Waits for a keystroke before continuing.		
Syntax	pause		
pause	Shows "Strike any key when ready..." and then waits for a key to be pressed.		

ping

OS: NetWare Common

Function	Starts the PING utility that can check for TCP/IP connectivity. Also has a very useful interface where you can ping multiple IP addresses simultaneously and show PING statistics and trends.				
Syntax	load ping *{ address... }*				
address...	Specifies IP-addresses to PING.				
File Name:	`ping.nlm`	**Directory:**	\system	**Type:**	External
Tip:	Press INS to insert an additional host to ping and DEL to delete a host from the ping list.				

Print Server

OS: NetWare Common

Function	Monitors, manages, and enables print services on the network. You must first create a print server before loading.				
Syntax	load pserver .CN=*printserver*.OU=*container*.O=*container* NW3: load pserver *printserver*				
printserver	The name of the print server to load.				
NW4, NW5, NW6: *container*	Specifies the name of the container in which the printer object is located.				
	To create a print server use one of the following utilities.				
NW3:	Uses the utility `pconsole` to create printers and queues.				
NW4:	You may use `pconsole` or NetWare Administrator to create printers and queues.				
NW5, NW6:	Uses the utility NetWare Administrator to create printers and queues.				
File Name:	`pserver.nlm`	**Directory:**	\system	**Type:**	External

load pserver .CN=color.OU=planets.O=galaxy	Loads the print server color in the specified NDS directory context.
NW3: load pserver color	NW3: Loads the print server color.

protocol

OS: NetWare Common

Function	Shows all protocols that are registered and running on the server.
Syntax	protocol

Protocol Register

OS: NetWare Common

Function	Shows all registered protocols on the server; also adds new protocols and frame types.
Syntax	protocol register *protocol frame ID*
protocol	Specifies the name of the protocol to register.
frame	Specifies the name of the frame type to be used by the protocol.
ID	Specifies the protocol ID that corresponds to the selected frame type. (The protocol doesn't register if the frame type isn't bound to a NIC.)
Note:	Protocols are automatically registered with the correct protocol ID when the system is started.
protocol register ARP Ethernet_II 806	Registers the ARP protocol if the Frame type is in use by a Network adapter.

register memory

OS: NetWare Common

Function	Registers installed memory that was not automatically registered.
Syntax	register memory *startaddress amount*
startaddress	Specifies the start address of memory to register.
amount	Specifies the amount of memory to register after the start address.
register memory 1000000 F000000	Registers memory from 16Mb to 256Mb.

REM

OS: NetWare Common

Function	Is used for putting comments into login scripts that aren't shown on the user's screen.
Syntax	rem *remark*
remark	Specifies the remark, e.g. date, version, change, etc.
rem 2001-08-12/PB Changed some stuff	The remark isn't shown but can remind you of changes.

Remirror Partition

OS: NetWare Common

Function	Starts or restarts the remirroring of a mirrored disk partition on the server.
Syntax	remirror partition *NR*
NR	Specifies the number of the partition to remirror.
Note:	Remirroring is done automatically on the server but can be shut off with the command `abort remirror`.

remote

OS: NetWare Common

Function	Enables the ability to control the server's console screen remotely from a workstation using `rconsole`.
Syntax	load remote [options...]

password	Specifies the password to use to gain access to the server using rconsole.
NW4, NW5, NW6:	
lock out	Stops any new connections to the server.
unlock	Allows new remote connections to the server.
help	Shows help information.
encrypt	Prompts for a password to encrypt that you can use with the following option.
-E *Epassword*	Specifies an encrypted password that was generated using the encrypt option.

File Name:	`remote.nlm`	**Directory:**	\system	**Type:**	External

load remote himom	Loads the remote.nlm with the password himom.
load remote lock out	Prevents any new connections to the server.
load remote -E J1E2A2N9E6T8TE	Loads remote using an encrypted password.

Reset Router

OS: NetWare Common

Function	Resets and updates the server's internal router table when it becomes invalid or corrupted.
Syntax	reset router
Tip:	Is normally used when problems with other servers, routers, and bridges occur.
reset router	Updates router tables on an active server.

rights

OS: NetWare Common

Function	Shows or modifies group or user rights for files, directories, and volumes.
Syntax	rights *path { rights }* [options...]

/?	Shows help information.
/? all	Shows help information by stepping through all of the help screens.
path	Specifies the file or directory to show or change the rights on.
NW4, NW5, NW6:	
/C	Scrolls continuously through output.
/F	Shows the Inherited Rights Filter (IRF).
/I	Shows the trustee and group rights that created the inherited rights.
/NAME=*name*	Specifies the user or group to show or modify the rights for.
/S	Applies the changes to all subdirectories.
/T	Shows trustee assignments in a directory.
/VER	Shows version information.
[+ | -]*rights*	Adds or removes the specified rights. See available rights below.
rights	Replaces the current rights with the specified rights. See available rights below.
rights	**The following are the available `rights`.**
S	Specifies supervisor rights.
R	Specifies read access.
W	Specifies write access.
C	Specifies create access.
E	Specifies erase access.
M	Specifies modify access.
F	Specifies file scan access.
A	Adds or removes trustees and changes trustee rights to files and directories.

continued

N	Removes all rights.				
REM	Removes the user or group as a trustee of the specified file or directory.				
ALL	Adds all rights except supervisor.				
File Name:	`rights.exe`	**Directory:**	\public	**Type:**	External
Tip:	In NW 3 this command can only show group or user rights.				
rights neptune/sys:public R W F /name=users	Adds the read, write, and file scan rights replacing any existing rights.				
rights neptune/sys:public N /name=users	Removes all rights for the specified group.				

route (Server) — OS: NetWare Common

Function	Tells the server how to pass frames via an IBM-compatible source bridge route on a T/R-network.
Syntax	load route [options...]

board=*NR*	Specifies the T/R-card to configure.				
clear	Clears the routing table.				
def	Sends Unknown Unicast frames as All Routes Broadcast frames.				
gbr	Sends General Broadcast frames as All Routes Broadcast frames.				
remove=*addr*	Removes a specified node from the routing table. (addr is a 12-digit address (hex.) If fewer than 9 digits are used, the address is prefixed with 4000 (0002 becomes 400000000002).				
rsp=*opt*	Specifies how to responds to a broadcast.				
nr	Responds directly (default).				
ar	Responds with All Routes Broadcast frames.				
sr	Responds with a Single Route Broadcast frame. **(NW3 only.)**				
time=*sec*	Specifies how often to update the source routing table.				
NW4, NW5, NW6					
name=*name*	Specifies the board name.				
mbr	Sends Multicast frames as All Routes Broadcast frames.				
xtx=*NR*	Specifies how many times to retransmit when a route is timed-out.				
unload [board=*NR*]	Disables routing for the specified network card, or card nr 1 if not specified.				
NW3					
[board=*NR*] unload	Disables routing for the specified network card, or card nr 1 if not specified.				
File Name:	`route.nlm`	**Directory:**	\system	**Type:**	External
Note:	The command `inetcfg` can configure and load route.				
load route board=01	Loads source route for network board 1.				
load route board=02 time=20	Changes the time parameter for the second board.				

rpl — OS: NetWare Common

Function	Enables diskless workstations to remote boot from the network.				
Syntax	load rpl				
File Name:	`rpl.nlm`	**Directory:**	\system	**Type:**	Internal

rplfix — OS: NetWare Common

Function	Repairs boot disk images files for diskless DOS-based workstations.				
Syntax	rplfix *bootfile*				
bootfile	Specifies the name of the boot image file to repair.				
File Name:	`rplfix.com`	**Directory:**	\login	**Type:**	External

rspx — OS: NetWare Common

Function	Allows RCONSOLE to connect to the server by controlling client packets.
Syntax	load rspx [options...]

SIGNATURES OFF	Allows RCONSOLE client packets without signatures.
	The following two options can only be used when the module is already loaded.
SIGNATURES ON	Requires all RCONSOLE client packets to contain signatures.

continued

HELP		Shows help information.			
File Name:	`rspx.nlm`	**Directory:**	\system	**Type:**	External
Note:	The REMOTE module must be loaded in NW3 before loading the RSPX module.				

Scan For New Devices — OS: NetWare Common

Function	Searches for new storage devices and makes them available to the system without rebooting.
Syntax	scan for new devices

scan for new devices	If you have added or removed devices since you last booted the server, this will update the system.

search — OS: NetWare Common

Function	Shows the current search paths, adds a search path to the search list, or removes a search path from the search list.
Syntax	search [add] [del] *NR { path }* search add *{ NR } path* search del *NR*

add	Adds a search path.
del	Erases a search path by specified number.
NR	Specifies search path line to use.
path	Specifies a search path to add to the search list using the add command.

search add 6 c:\nlms	Adds the c:\nlms path to the search list on the sixth place.
search del 1	Removes the first search path in the list.

Secure Console — OS: NetWare Common

Function	Limits the loading of NLMs from search paths only and prevents access into the internal debugger.
Syntax	secure console

send (Server) — OS: NetWare Common

Function	Sends a message to all users currently logged into the server or to a specific user specified by destination.
Syntax	send "*message*" [TO] *{ destination }* [AND or ,] *{ destination }*

"*message*"	The message that you want to send. Max 55 characters.
destination	Specifies the username or connection number to send the message.
TO	Is optional.
AND	Is used to separate destinations if sending a message to specific users.
,	Separates destinations and is used as a replacement for AND.

send "The server will be down in 10 minutes"	Sends the message to all connected users.
send "Your files has been restored" guy	Sends the message to the user guy.

server — OS: NetWare Common

Function	Starts the NetWare operating system environment and executes the startup.ncf and autoexec.ncf configuration files.
Syntax	server [options...]

-s *path*	Specifies an alternate path and filename for the startup.ncf configuration file.
-na	Starts the server without executing the autoexec.ncf configuration file.
-ns	Starts the server and executes the startup.ncf configuration file.
-na -ns	Starts the server without either the startup or autoexec.ncf files.
NW3:	
-C *cachesize*	Specifies the cache buffer block size. Values are 4, 8, or 16 (default is 4).
NW5, NW6:	
-nl	Starts the server without the splash screen and enables viewing of loading NLMs.

File Name:	`server.exe`	**Directory:**	c:\nwserver, **NW3:** c:\server.312	**Type:**	External
Tip:	The -na option is great for troubleshooting purposes. You can then manually type each entry in the Autoexec.ncf to pinpoint which NLM is giving you trouble.				

Server Based Record Manager

OS: NetWare Common

Function	The server-based record manager that provides a wide range of utilities such as integrity and concurrency control, logging file changes, and disk I/Os.
Syntax	load btrieve

	The following components may be loaded after Btrieve:
bspxcom.nlm	Manages incoming requests to `btrieve` from remote sources. (This is required on servers that need to support remote requests.)
	Btrieve Message Routers:
brouter.nlm	The default Message Router that must be loaded by using NetWare `INSTALL`.
bdrouter.nlm	The Message Router that provides Directory Services support for Btrieve 6.x.
	Btrieve Utilities:
bsetup.nlm	Alters the settings for `btrieve`'s configuration options.
brebuild.nlm	Converts existing `btrieve` 5.x files to 6.x format.
btrmon.nlm	Monitors all activity of the `btrieve` process at the server.
mutil.nlm	Imports/exports `btrieve` data, transfers data between files, and enables automode.
	If you have not loaded `bspxcom` but need `btrmon`, load one of these:
bspxstub.nlm	Resolves external references for Btrieve for local server access. Load this locally.
rspxstub.nlm	Monitors outgoing requests for Btrieve for remote server activity. Load this locally.
	Btrieve Roll Forward Work Station Utilities:
brollfwd.exe	Recovers changes to Btrieve files between system failures and backups. DOS version.
pbroll.exe	Recovers changes to Btrieve files between system failures and backups. OS/2 version.
wbroll.exe	Recovers changes to Btrieve files between system failures and backups. MS-Windows version.
	NetWare Directory Services Support Utility:
bdirect.nlm	Allows you to install/remove Btrieve server objects by registering Btrieve in NDS. (May be run from the command line or via the Btrieve setup utility.)
	Btrieve Work Station Requesters:
brequest.exe	Relays Btrieve requests between applications and the Btrieve server. Written for DOS.
btrcalls.dll	Same as above but is written for OS/2.
wbtrcall.dll	Same as above but is written for MS-Windows.

File Name:	`btrieve.nlm`	**Directory:**	\system	**Type:**	External

set

OS: NetWare Common

Function	Shows many parameters relating to the NetWare server's operation and performance. The list below is a listing of the many categories of set parameters. Each category is documented separately showing available settings.
Syntax	None

Category Names:	**The following categories of set parameters exist in all versions of NetWare.**
Communications	Sets receive buffers, watchdogs, checksums, and filters.
Memory	Controls cache buffer blocks, garbage collection, and corruption checking.
File Caching	Alters the read-ahead, dirty disk and concurrent disk cache settings.
Directory Caching	Sets directory cache and directory handle values.
File System	Sets disk warning message usage, volume settings, and delete wait states.
Locks	Sets how many record and file locks are allowed for each connection.
Transaction Tracking	Controls concurrent, aborted, and backout transactions.
Disk	Sets various disk read/write controls and remirror requests to logical partitions.
Miscellaneous	Sets IPX alerts, thread auto-grow stack values, command-line prompt timeouts, etc.
	These categories of set parameters exist in NW4, NW5, and NW6.
Time	Sets the date and time of the server.
NCP	Specifies various NCP settings such as IP addresses, TCP delay, NCP/UDP checksum, etc.
Error Handling	Controls VOLLOG, TTSLOG, and BOOT$LOG file sizes and various wait states.
Directory Services	Alters DS and NDS paths, traces, and events.
	These categories of set parameters exist in NW5 and NW6.
Multiprocessor	Controls system threshold, Interrupt statistics and auto processor startup modes.
Service Location Protocol	Sets SLP cache and scope list, SLP/UA multicast, and SLP debug mode.
Licensing Services	Allows storing NetWare 5 SCL MLA usage within NDS.
	These categories of set parameters exist only in NW6.
NSS - Novell Storage Services	Sets auto-locks and updates, Cache balancing, buffers and flush times for NSS.

set (Communications) OS: NetWare Common

Function	Sets receive buffers, watchdogs, checksums, and filters.
Syntax	set *parameter* [= *value*]

	Parameters that can only be set in the STARTUP.NCF file are marked by a (*).
allow IP address duplicates = on | off	Allows setting IP addresses that are already in use if value is set to on.
console display watchdog logouts = on | off	Shows the watchdog connection failures if value is set to on.
delay between watchdog packets = *seconds*	Specifies the interval for checking a workstation (range is 9.9 to 626.2).
IP wan client validation = on | off	Enables client validation when dialing with NetWare Connect if value is set to on.
reply to get nearest server = on | off	Informs where the nearest workstation's server is located when asked.
new packet receive buffer wait time = *seconds*	Specifies how long to wait for a new packet received buffer (range is 0.1 to 20).
number of watchdog packets = *NR*	Ends connection if none of the watchdog packets returns (range is 5 to 100).
spx maximum window size = *size*	Specifies the SPXS window maximum size (range is 0 to 16).
NW3:	
allow LIP = on | off	Uses Large Internet Packet support if value is set to on.
delay before first watchdog packet = *seconds*	The time before checking if workstation is up (range is 15.7 to 1252.3).
enable packet burst statistics screen = on | off	Shows packet bursts for NCP on the monitor if value is set to on.
enable ipx checksums = *value*	Specifies if checksumming should be used on IPX packets. Valid values below:
0	Doesn't checksum.
1	Uses checksumming if the client has it enabled.
2	Requires checksum.
maximum packet receive buffers = *buffers*	Specifies available packet receive buffers (range is 50 to 2000).
maximum physical receive packet size = *size*	Sets maximum packet size for a MILD (range is 618 to 24682). (*)
minimum packet receive buffers = *buffers*	Specifies the minimum packet receive buffers (range is 10 to 1000). (*)
ncp packet signature option = *value*	Uses NCP packet signatures. Valid values below:
0	Doesn't use packet signatures.
1	Uses packet signatures if client requires them.
2	Uses packet signatures if the client supports them; otherwise, doesn't use signatures.
3	Uses packet signatures.
NW4:	
delay before first watchdog packet = *seconds*	The time before checking if workstation is up (range is 15.7 to 1209600).
ipx netbios replication option = *value*	Specifies how the IPX router should handle NetBIOS broadcasts.
0	Doesn't replicate.
1	Copies using the old way.
2	Copies using the new way.
3	Copies using the new way, except that replications to WAN links don't work.
load balance local LAN = on | off	Enables load balancing if value is set to on.
maximum pending tcp connection requests = *connections*	Sets the number of pending TCP connections there can be (range is 128 to 4096).
maximum packet receive buffers = *buffers*	Specifies available packet receive buffers (range is 50 to 4294967295).
minimum packet receive buffers = *buffers*	Specifies the minimum packet receive buffers (range is 10 to 4294967295). (*)
maximum interrupt events = *interrupts*	Specifies how many interrupt time events are allowed (range is 1 to 1000000).
maximum physical receive packet size = *size*	Sets maximum packet size for a MILD (range is 618 to 24682). (*)
tcp defend syn attacks = on | off	Enables the protection against SYN attacks if value is set to on.
tcp defend land attacks = on | off	Enables the protection against LAN attacks if value is set to on.
use old watchdog packet type = on | off	Uses watchdog packet type 0 if off and watchdog packet type 4 if on.
NW5:	
delay before first watchdog packet = *seconds*	The time before checking if workstation is up (range is 15.7 to 1209600).
discard oversized ping packets = on | off	Drops PING packets larger than the largest ping packet size setting.
discard oversized udp packets = on | off	Drops UDP packets larger than the largest udp packet size setting.
ipx cmd mode routing = on | off	Enables the IPX CMD mode routing if value is set to on.
nwc login update interval = *minutes*	Sets update interval for remote connections (range is 1 to 1440).
nwc ds search level = *levels*	Specifies how many DS tree levels use for user configuration (range is 0 to 10).
tcp defend syn attacks = on | off	Enables the protection against SYN attacks.
snmp trap logging = on | off	Enables SNMP trap logging if value is set to on.
filter packets with ip header options = on | off	Enables the filtering of packets with IP Header options if value is set to on.

continued

filter log packets without matching rule = on | off	Logs packets without matching rule or not if value is set to on.
filter local loopback packets = on | off	Turns on filter loopback packets if value is set to on.
shutdown public interface on log failure = on | off	Disables the public interface if logging fails if its turned on.
filter subnet broadcast packets = on | off	Turns on subnet broadcast packets if value is set to on.
largest udp packet size = *size*	Specifies the maximum size of the udp packets (range is 0 to 65535).
largest ping packet size = *size*	Specifies the maximum size of the ping packets (range is 0 to 65535).
tcp udp diagnostic services = on | off	Enables or disables the diagnostic servers over the TCP and UDP protocols.
tcp max port limit = *port*	Specifies the highest TCP ephemeral port in a port range (range is 4999 to 54999).
ipx router broadcast delay = *value*	Specifies how long to wait between SAP/RIP broadcast packets.
0	Adjusts the delay to the size of SAP/RIP tables.
1	Delays one tick.
2	Delays two ticks.
maximum packet receive buffers = *buffers*	Specifies available packet receive buffers (range is 50 to 3303820).
minimum packet receive buffers = *buffers*	Specifies the minimum packet receive buffers (range is 10 to 32768).
maximum physical receive packet size = *size*	Sets maximum packet size for a MILD (range is 618 to 65642). (*)
ipx netbios replication option = *value*	Specifies how the IPX router should handle NetBIOS broadcasts.
0	Doesn't replicate.
1	Copies using the old way.
2	Copies using the new way.
3	Copies using the new way, except that replications to WAN links don't work.
load balance local LAN = on | off	Enables load balancing if value is set to on.
tcp defend land attacks = on | off	Enables the protection against LAN attacks if value is set to on.
maximum pending tcp connection requests = *connections*	Sets the number of pending TCP connections there can be (range is 128 to 4096).
maximum interrupt events = *interrupts*	Specifies how many interrupt time events are allowed (range is 1 to 1000000).
use old watchdog packet type = on | off	Uses watchdog packet type 0 if off and watchdog packet type 4 if on.
NW6:	
ipx netbios replication option = *value*	Specifies how the IPX router should handle NetBIOS broadcasts.
0	Doesn't replicate.
1	Copies using the old way.
2	Copies using the new way.
3	Copies using the new way, except that replications to WAN links don't work.
load balance local LAN = on | off	Enables load balancing if value is set to on.
tcp defend land attacks = on | off	Enables the protection against LAN attacks if value is set to on.
maximum pending tcp connection requests = *connections*	Sets the number of pending TCP connections there can be (range is 128 to 4096).
maximum interrupt events = *interrupts*	Specifies how many interrupt time events are allowed (range is 1 to 1000000).
delay before first watchdog packet = *seconds*	The time before checking if workstation is up (range is 15.7 to 1209600).
use old watchdog packet type = on | off	Uses watchdog packet type 0 if off and watchdog packet type 4 if on.
ipx cmd mode routing = on | off	Enables the IPX CMD mode routing if value is set to on.
snmp trap logging = on | off	Enables SNMP trap logging if value is set to on.
filter packets with ip header options = on | off	Enables the filtering of packets with IP Header options if value is set to on.
filter log packets without matching rule = on | off	Logs packets without matching rule if value is set to on.
filter local loopback packets = on | off	Enables filter loopback packets if value is set to on.
shutdown public interface on log failure = on | off	Disables the public interface if logging fails if value is set to on.
filter subnet broadcast packets = on | off	Turns on filter subnet broadcast packets if value is set to on.
discard oversized udp packets = on | off	Drops UDP packets larger than the largest UDP packet size setting.
discard oversized ping packets = on | off	Drops PING packets larger than the largest PING packet size.
largest udp packet size = *size*	Specifies the maximum size of the udp packets (range is 0 to 65535).
largest ping packet size = *size*	Specifies the maximum size of the ping packets (range is 0 to 65535).
tcp udp diagnostic services = on | off	Enables the diagnostic servers over the TCP and UDP protocols if value is set to on.
tcp max port limit = *port*	Specifies the highest TCP ephemeral port in a port range (range is 4999 to 54999).
ipx router broadcast delay = *value*	Specifies how long to wait between SAP/RIP broadcast packets.

continued

0	Adjusts the delay to the size of SAP/RIP tables.
1	Delays one tick.
2	Delays two ticks.
maximum packet receive buffers = *buffers*	Specifies available packet receive buffers (range is 50 to 3303820).
minimum packet receive buffers = *buffers*	Specifies the minimum packet receive buffers (range is 10 to 32768).
maximum physical receive packet size = *size*	Sets maximum packet size for a MILD (range is 618 to 65642). (*)
bsd socket default buffer size in bytes = *bytes*	Specifies the BSD socket send and receive buffer size (range is 4096 to 65536).
tos for IP packets = *tos*	Sets default TOS for all outgoing IP headers (range is 0 to 127).
arp entry update time = *seconds*	Specifies how often to update the Arp Entries (range is 240 to 14400).
arp entry expiry time = *seconds*	Specifies how long to hold an Arp Entry (range is 240 to 14400).
tcp sack option = on | off	Enables sack support if value is set to on.
tcp large window option = on | off	Enables large window support if value is set to on.
icmp redirect timeout = *timeout*	Specifies the ICMP redirect timeout to use (range is 0 to 525600).
maximum rip/sap events = *times*	Specifies the maximum number of RIP/SAP time events (range is 1 to 100000).

set (Directory Caching) — OS: NetWare Common

Function	Sets directory cache and directory handle values.
Syntax	set *parameter* [= *value*]

NW3:	
dirty directory cache delay time = *seconds*	Sets minimum wait time for dirty directory cache buffer writes (range is 0 to 10).
maximum concurrent directory cache writes = *NR*	Specifies maximum concurrent writes of directory cache buffers (range is 5 to 50).
directory cache allocation wait time = *seconds*	The time to wait between directory cache buffer allocations (range is 0.5 to 120).
directory cache buffer nonreferenced delay = *seconds*	Waits set time before re-using a directory cache buffer (range is 1 to 300).
maximum directory cache buffers = *buffers*	Specifies the maximum number of directory cache buffers (range is 20 to 400).
minimum directory cache buffers = *buffers*	Specifies the minimum number of directory cache buffers (range is 10 to 1000).
NW4:	
dirty directory cache delay time = *seconds*	Sets minimum wait time for dirty directory cache buffer writes (range is 0 to 10).
maximum concurrent directory cache writes = *NR*	Specifies maximum concurrent writes of directory cache buffers (range is 5 to 100).
directory cache allocation wait time = *seconds*	The time to wait between directory cache buffer allocations (range is 0.1 to 120).
directory cache buffer nonreferenced delay = *seconds*	Waits set time before re-using a directory cache buffer (range is 1 to 3600).
maximum directory cache buffers = *buffers*	Specifies the maximum number of directory cache buffers (range is 20 to 200000).
minimum directory cache buffers = *buffers*	Specifies the minimum number of directory cache buffers (range is 10 to 100000).
maximum number of internal directory handles = *NR*	Sets the amount of directory handles retained for NLMs (range is 40 to 1000).
maximum number of directory handles = *NR*	Sets the amount of directory handles retained per connection (range is 20 to 1000).
NW5:	
dirty directory cache delay time = *seconds*	Sets minimum wait time for dirty directory cache buffer writes (range is 0 to 10).
maximum concurrent directory cache writes = *NR*	Specifies maximum concurrent writes of directory cache buffers (range is 5 to 500).
directory cache allocation wait time = *seconds*	The time to wait between directory cache buffer allocations (range is 0.1 to 120).
directory cache buffer nonreferenced delay = *seconds*	Waits set time before re-using a directory cache buffer (range is 1 to 3600).
maximum directory cache buffers = *buffers*	Specifies the maximum number of directory cache buffers (range is 20 to 200000).
minimum directory cache buffers = *buffers*	Specifies the minimum number of directory cache buffers (range is 10 to 100000).
maximum number of internal directory handles = *NR*	Sets the amount of directory handles retained for NLMs (range is 40 to 1000).
maximum number of directory handles = *NR*	Sets the amount of directory handles retained per connection (range is 20 to 1000).
NW6:	
dirty directory cache delay time = *seconds*	Sets minimum wait time for dirty directory cache buffer writes (range is 0 to 10).
maximum concurrent directory cache writes = *NR*	Specifies maximum concurrent writes of directory cache buffers (range is 5 to 500).
directory cache allocation wait time = *seconds*	The time to wait between directory cache buffer allocations (range is 0.1 to 120).

continued

directory cache buffer nonreferenced delay = *seconds*	Waits set time before re-using a directory cache buffer (range is 1 to 3600).
maximum directory cache buffers = *buffers*	Specifies the maximum number of directory cache buffers (range is 20 to 200000).
minimum directory cache buffers = *buffers*	Specifies the minimum number of directory cache buffers (range is 10 to 100000).
maximum number of internal directory handles = *NR*	Sets the amount of directory handles retained for NLMs (range is 40 to 1000).
maximum number of directory handles = *NR*	Sets the amount of directory handles retained per connection (range is 20 to 1000).

set (Disk)

OS: NetWare Common

Function	Sets various disk read/write controls and remirror requests to logical partitions.
Syntax	set *parameter* [= *value*]

	Parameters that can only be set in the STARTUP.NCF file are marked by an (*).
NW3:	
enable disk read after write verify = on | off	Reads all data on disk to verify correctness if value is set to on.
concurrent remirror requests = *NR*	Sets allowed remirror requests on logical partitions (range is 2 to 30). (*)
NW4, NW5, NW6:	
remirror block size = *NR*	Specifies the block size for remirrors (range is 1 to 8). (Each number represents a block size, e.g., 1=4K, 2=8K ... 8=32K.)
concurrent remirror requests = *NR*	Sets amount of allowed remirror requests on logical partitions (range is 2 to 32).
mirrored devices are out of sync message frequency = *NR*	Sets the interval to check for devices that are out of sync (range is 5 to 9999).
sequential elevator depth = *depth*	Sets maximum depth of elevator for sequential requests (range is 0 to 4294967295).
ignore disk geometry = on | off	Allows system to create non-standard partitions if value is set to on.
enable IO handicap attribute = on | off	Allows drivers to set attributes to inhibit read requests from devices if set to on.
enable disk read after write verify = on | off	**NW4 only:** Reads all data on disk to verify correctness. (*)
ignore partition ownership = on | off	**NW5, NW6 only:** Allows partitions on other servers to be activated.
enable hardware write back = on | off	**NW5, NW6 only:** Allows drivers to use hardware write back.
enable disk read after write verify = on | off	**NW5, NW6 only:** Reads all data on disk to verify correctness.

set (File Caching)

OS: NetWare Common

Function	Alters the read-ahead, dirty disk and concurrent disk cache settings.
Syntax	set *parameter* [= *value*]

	Parameters that can only be set in the STARTUP.NCF file are marked by an (*).
read ahead enabled = on | off	Reads blocks into the cache in the background during sequential file access.
read ahead LRU sitting time threshold = *seconds*	If Cache LRU sitting time is lower than threshold read it ahead (range is 0 to 3600).
dirty disk cache delay time = *seconds*	No completely dirty disk cache buffer will occur before time (range is 0.1 to 10).
NW3:	
reserved buffers below 16 meg = *buffers*	Saves cache buffers to drivers unable to use memory +16Mb (range is 8 to 300). (*)
maximum concurrent disk cache writes = *NR*	The amount of concurrent writes of dirty disk buffers used (range is 10 to 1000).
minimum file cache report threshold = *threshold*	Sends warnings if the amount of cache buffer matches threshold (range is 0 to 1000).
minimum file cache buffers = *buffers*	Specifies how many file cache buffers to keep for the server (range is 20 to 1000).
NW4, NW5, NW6:	
maximum concurrent disk cache writes = *NR*	The amount of concurrent writes of dirty disk buffers used (range is 10 to 4000).
minimum file cache report threshold = *threshold*	Sends warnings if the amount of cache buffer matches threshold (range is 0 to 2000).
minimum file cache buffers = *buffers*	Specifies how many file cache buffers to keep for the server (range is 20 to 2000).

set (File System)

OS: NetWare Common

Function	Sets disk warning message usage, volume settings and delete wait states.
Syntax	set *argument* [= *value*]

	Parameters that can only be set in the STARTUP.NCF file are marked by an (*).
maximum percent of volume space allowed for extended attributes = *NR*	Allows extended attributes to use specified percent of a volume (range is 5 to 50).
maximum extended attributes per file or path = *NR*	Allows the number of extended attributes per files or paths (range is 4 to 512).
immediate purge of deleted files = on | off	Purges all files as they were deleted if value is set to on.
volume low warn all users = on | off	Sends out warnings to all users when volume is low if value is set to on.
volume low warning reset threshold = *blocks*	Resets warning trigger if disk blocks get above threshold (range is 0 to 100000).
volume low warning threshold = *level*	Sends warnings if the disk allocation units reaches level (range is 0 to 1000000).
turbo fat re-use wait time = *seconds*	Sets the minimum time to wait before re-using a Turbo FAT (range is 0.3 to 3954.6).
minimum file delete wait time = *seconds*	Sets the minimum time to wait before purging a deleted file (range is 0 to 604800).
file delete wait time = *seconds*	Sets the normal time to wait before purging a deleted file (range is 0 to 604800).
NW3:	
maximum percent of volume used by directory = *percentage*	Allows the directory to use specified percent of a volume (range is 5 to 50).
maximum subdirectory tree depth = *levels*	Specifies available levels of subdirectories (range is 10 to 100). (*)
ncp file commit = on | off	All applications can flush the pending file writes to disk if value is set to on.
NW4, NW5, NW6:	
allow deletion of active directories = on | off	Lets directories be deleted when it is mapped to some computer if value is on.
fast volume mounts = on | off	Performs fast mounting of volumes if value is set to on.
maximum percent of volume used by directory = *percentage*	Allows the directory to use specified percent of a volume (range is 5 to 85).
compression daily check stop hour = *hour*	Makes the file compressor end scanning at the specified hour (range is 0 to 23).
compression daily check starting hour = *hour*	Makes the file compressor start scanning at the specified hour (range is 0 to 23).
minimum compression percentage gain = *percentage*	Sets compression percentage that is allowed (range is 0 to 50).
enable file compression = on | off	Makes file compressions on compression-enabled volumes if value is set to on.
maximum concurrent compressions = *NR*	Specifies how many simultaneous compressions there can be (range is 1 to 8).
convert compressed to uncompressed option = *value*	Sets action with the uncompressed file when uncompressing. Valid values below:
0	Leaves the compressed version.
1	Leaves the compressed file if it is read only once.
2	Changes the uncompressed version.
decompress percent disk space free to allow commit = *percentage*	Sets the needed free volume to perform a decompression (range is 0 to 75).
decompress free space warning interval = *seconds*	Sets warning interval when the free space is too low (range is 0 to 2562603.8).
deleted files compression option = *value*	Specifies how to compress deleted files.
0	Doesn't compress files.
1	Compresses files the next day.
2	Compresses now.
days untouched before compression = *days*	Compresses files that have not been used for specified time (range is 0 to 100000).
allow unowned files to be extended = on | off	Allows unowned files to be extended if value is set to on.
maximum subdirectory tree depth = *levels*	**NW4 only:** Levels of subdirectories allowed (range is 10 to 100). (*)
maximum subdirectory tree depth = *levels*	**NW5, NW6 only:** Levels of subdirectories allowed (range is 10 to 100).
purge files on dismount = on | off	**NW5, NW6 only:** Purges removed files on volumes when dismounting.
automatically repair bad volumes = on | off	**NW5, NW6 only:** Attempts to repair a broken volume when mounting.
auto mount mirrored volume containing inactive device = on | off	**NW6 only:** If on volumes with inactive device will be automatically mounted.

set (Locks)

OS: NetWare Common

Function	Sets how many record and file locks are allowed for each connection.
Syntax	set *attributes* [= *value*]

NW3:	
maximum record locks per connection = *NR*	Specifies how many record locks per connection there can be (range is 10 to 10000).
maximum file locks per connection = *NR*	Specifies how many file locks per connection there can be (range is 10 to 1000).
maximum record locks = *NR*	Specifies how many record locks there can be on the system (range is 100 to 200000).
maximum file locks = *NR*	Specifies how many file locks there can be on the system (range is 100 to 100000).
NW4:	
maximum record locks per connection = *NR*	Specifies how many record locks per connection there can be (range is 10 to 100000).
maximum file locks per connection = *NR*	Specifies how many file locks per connection there can be (range is 10 to 1000).
maximum record locks = *NR*	Specifies how many record locks there can be on the system (range is 100 to 400000).
maximum file locks = *NR*	Specifies how many file locks there can be on the system (range is 100 to 100000).
NW5, NW6:	
maximum record locks per connection = *NR*	Specifies how many record locks per connection there can be (range is 10 to 100000).
maximum file locks per connection = *NR*	Specifies how many file locks per connection there can be (range is 10 to 10000).
maximum record locks = *NR*	Specifies how many record locks there can be on the system (range is 100 to 400000).
maximum file locks = *NR*	Specifies how many file locks there can be on the system (range is 100 to 2000000).

set (Memory)

OS: NetWare Common

Function	Controls cache buffer blocks, garbage collection, and corruption checking.
Syntax	set *parameter* [= *value*]

	Parameters that can only be set in the STARTUP.NCF file are marked by an (*).
NW3:	
auto register memory above 16 megabytes = on | off	Automatically detects memory above 16Mb on EISA machines if value is set to on. (*)
cache buffer size = *bytes*	Specifies the buffer size of the cache (range is 4096 to 16384). (*)
maximum alloc short term memory = *memory*	Specifies how big the dynamic memory pool can be (range is 50000 to 33554432).
NW4:	
allow invalid pointers = on | off	Specifies whether to allow invalid pointers.
alloc memory check flag = on | off	Performs a corruption check in the alloc memory nodes if value is set to on.
auto register memory above 16 megabytes = on | off	Automatically detects memory above 16Mb on EISA machines if value is set to on.
garbage collection interval = *seconds*	The time between each garbage collection (range is 60 to 3600).
minimum free memory for garbage collection = *bytes*	The bytes needed for the garbage collection to run (range is 1000 to 1000000).
number of frees for garbage collection = *frees*	The amount of frees to use for the garbage collection (range is 100 to 100000).
read fault emulation = on | off	Emulates a read when reading from a non-existing page if value is set to on.
read fault notification = on | off	Shows emulated read page faults if value is set to on.
reserved buffers below 16 Meg = *buffers*	Saves cache buffers to drivers unable to use memory +16Mb (range is 8 to 300). (*)
write fault emulation = on | off	Emulates a write when writing occurs to a non-existing page if value is set to on.
write fault notification = on | off	Shows emulated write page faults if value is set to on.
NW5:	
alloc memory check flag = on | off	Performs a corruption check in the alloc memory nodes if value is set to on.
garbage collection interval = *seconds*	The time between each garbage collection (range is 60 to 3600).
memory protection restart count = *NR*	The amount of restarts allowed during the restart interval (range is 0 to 1000).
memory protection no restart interval = *minutes*	The time to track restarts before resetting counters (range is 0 to 525600).
reserved buffers below 16 Meg = *buffers*	Saves cache buffers to drivers unable to use memory +16Mb (range is 8 to 2000). (*)
NW6:	
average page in alert threshold = *level*	If level reached, send message to the console (range is 1 to 4294967295).
alloc memory check flag = on | off	Performs a corruption check in the alloc memory nodes if value is set to on.

continued

garbage collection interval = *seconds*	The time between each garbage collections must happen (range is 60 to 3600).
interactive screen timeout = *seconds*	Screen is interactive until the timeout is reached (range is 0 to 235903197).
memory protection abend after restart count = on | off	Abends server after address space restarts more than restart option (below) allows.
memory protection restart count = *NR*	Specifies number of memory restarts allowed while memory is protected (range is 0 to 1000).
memory protection fault cleanup = on | off	Cleans up memory protection faults in user address space if value is set to on.
memory protection restart count = *NR*	The amount of restarts allowed during the restart interval (range is 0 to 1000).
memory protection no restart interval = *minutes*	The time to track restarts before resetting counters (range is 0 to 525600).
vm garbage collector looks = *pages*	The amount of pages the garbage collector should examine (range is 1 to 1048576).
vm garbage collector period = *seconds*	The interval to run the VM garbage collector (range is 10 to 86369.2).
reserved buffers below 16 Meg = *buffers*	Saves cache buffers to drivers unable to use memory +16Mb (range is 8 to 2000). (*)

set (Miscellaneous) — OS: NetWare Common

Function	Sets IPX alerts, thread auto-grow stack values, command-line prompt timeouts, etc.
Syntax	set *parameter* [= *value*]

allow unencrypted passwords = on | off	Allows requests with unencrypted passwords if value is set to on.
new service process wait time = *seconds*	Waits time before starting a request servicing process (range is 0.3 to 20).
display spurious interrupt alerts = on | off	Shows warnings when spurious hardware interrupt is detected if value is set to on.
display lost interrupt alerts = on | off	Shows warnings when the interrupt controller finds a lost interrupt if value is on.
display relinquish control alerts = on | off	Shows warnings when a process doesn't relinquish control frequently if set to on.
replace console prompt with server name = on | off	Uses the server name as the console prompt if value is set to on.
display incomplete ipx packet alerts = on | off	Warnings will show when incomplete IPX packets are received if value is set to on.
display old api names = on | off	Shows names of the modules when loading an old API module if value is set to on.
NW3:	
maximum outstanding ncp searches = *NR*	Sets how many simultaneous NCP directory searches allowed (range is 10 to 1000).
pseudo preemption time = *NR*	Gives NLMs the amount of time before relinquishing (range is 1000 to 10000). (One time number is 0.84 microsecond.)
display disk device alerts = on | off	Warnings will show when disk device is added, deleted, or activated if set to on.
maximum service processes = *NR*	Specifies how many request servicing processes there can be (range is 5 to 40).
allow change to client rights = on | off	Makes the print/job server think that it has the rights of a queue job's submitter.
NW4, NW5, NW6:	
command line prompt default choice = on | off	Sets the default input for questions. Values are: On = "Y" and OFF = "N".
command line prompt time out = *seconds*	Specifies how long to wait before answering a question (range is 0 to 4294967295). (The system will answer with the default answer that you have set.)
sound bell for alerts = on | off	Makes the computer beep when an alert message is shown on console if set to on.
alert message nodes = *NR*	Sets how many alert message nodes should be pre-allocated.
worker thread execute in a row count = *NR*	Dispatches new work NR times before running other threads (range is 1 to 20).
halt system on invalid parameters = on | off	Stops the system when an invalid parameter is detected if value is set to on.
cpu hog timeout amount = *seconds*	Process gets amount of time to relinquish control of the CPU (range is 0 to 3600).
developer option = on | off	Uses options that are fit for developer environments if value is set to on.
pseudo preemption count = *NR*	Relinquish after threads made amount of read/write calls (range is 1 to 4294967295).
global pseudo preemption = on | off	Makes all threads use pseudo preemptions if value is set to on.
minimum service processes = *NR*	How many service processes allowed without new service time (range is 10 to 500).
enable secure.ncf = on | off	Executes the `secure.ncf` when the server boots if value is set to on.
allow audit passwords = on | off	Enables the auditing of passwords if value is set to on.
maximum service processes = *NR*	**NW4 only:** Amount of allowed request servicing processes (range is 5 to 1000).
automatically repair bad volumes = on | off	**NW4 only:** Attempts to repair a broken volume when mounting.
update low priority threads = on | off	**NW4 only:** Gives low priority threads normal priority if value is set to on.
maximum service processes = *NR*	**NW5, NW6 only:** Amount of request servicing processes (range is 50 to 1000).
ipxflt log errors to disk = on | off	**NW5, NW6 only:** Enables the logging of ipx filter errors if value is set to on.

continued

classic work to do pre check flag = on | off display spurious interrupt alerts threshold = *NR* display lost interrupt alerts threshold = *NR* force auto grow stacks = on | off	**NW5, NW6 only:** Warps the OS if classic work to do is already scheduled. **NW5, NW6 only:** Spurious interrupts before alert (range is 1 to 1000000). **NW5, NW6 only:** Lost interrupts before alert (range is 1 to 1000000). **NW6 only:** Creates thread stacks with the auto-grow option if set to on.

set (Transaction Tracking)

OS: NetWare Common

Function	Controls concurrent, aborted, and backout transactions.
Syntax	set *argument* [= *value*]

	Parameters that can only be set in the STARTUP.NCF file are marked by an (*).
auto tts backout flag = on | off	Performs TTS backouts when rebooting if value is set to on. (*)
tts abort dump flag = on | off	Sends data from aborted transactions to log file if value is set to on.
maximum transactions = *NR*	Is amount of allowed concurrent transactions on the system (range is 100 to 10000).
tts unwritten cache wait time = *seconds*	Specifies how long the TTL can delay a cache buffer write (range is 11 to 659.1).
tts backout file truncation wait time = *seconds*	Sets the minimum time to allow a TTS backout file to exist (range is 65.9 to 104911.3).

Set Time

OS: NetWare Common

Function	Sets the date and time of the server.
Syntax	set time *{ month/day/year } { hour:minute:second }*

month/day/year	Specifies the date, e.g. `08/12/01` or `august 12, 2001`.
hour:minute:second	Specifies the time, e.g. `15:24:00` or `3:24:00 pm`
set time 08/12/01 15:24:00	Sets the date to August 12, 2001 and the time to 15:24:00.

Set Time Zone

OS: NetWare Common

Function	Shows the current time zone with the first syntax or sets the time zone of the server using the second syntax.
Syntax	set time zone set time zone *zone*[+ or -] *time{ daylight }*

zone	Sets the time zone where the server is located. Examples include:
EST	Sets the time zone for Eastern Standard Time.
CST	Sets the time zone for Central Standard Time.
MST	Sets the time zone for Mountain Standard Time.
PST	Sets the time zone for Pacific Standard Time.
MET	Sets the time zone for Middle European Time.
+ or -	Specifies the number of hours plus + or minus - from Greenwich Mean Time (GMT).
time	Specifies the time difference from (GMT) and local time in the format hh:mm:ss:.
daylight	Sets the daylight time zone where the server is located. Examples include:
EDT	Sets the daylight time zone for Eastern Daylight Time.
CDT	Sets the daylight time zone for Central Daylight Time.
MDT	Sets the daylight time zone for Mountain Daylight Time.
PDT	Sets the daylight time zone for Pacific Daylight Time.
set time zone MET	Sets the time zone to MET.
set time zone PST9PDT	Sets the time and daylight saving time zones for Pacific Time 9 hours from GMT.

snmp

OS: NetWare Common

Function	Loads and configures SNMP (Simple Network Management Protocol) support used by management applications.
Syntax	load snmp [options...]

AuthenticationTraps=Yes | No	Turns on or off generating an authentication fail trap.
ControlCommunity=*name*	Specifies the read and write community name.
MonitorCommunity=*name*	Specifies a name of a community to monitor.
TrapCommunity=*name*	Sets the community name for SNMP traps (default is public).
Verbose=Yes | No	Enables or disables showing of verbose information.
Configuration=*volume:path*	Specifies a volume and path to an alternative configuration file (default is SYS:ETC).

File Name:	`snmp.nlm`	**Directory:**	\system	**Type:**	External

load snmp trapcommunity=ucg	Loads SNMP and sets the community string to be UCG.

snmplog

snmplog			**OS:**	NetWare Common	
Function	Starts logging of SNMP traps to disk. A binary file called `SYS:ETC\SNMP$LOG.BIN` will be created.				
Syntax	load snmplog				
File Name:	`snmplog.nlm`	**Directory:**	\system	**Type:**	External
load snmplog		Starts the SNMP Log.			

speed

speed	**OS:**	NetWare Common
Function	Checks the processor speed on the server to check if the processor is being fully utilized.	
Syntax	speed	
speed	Shows processor speed.	

spool

spool	**OS:**	NetWare Common
Function	Creates, modifies, and shows spooler mappings.	
Syntax	spool *NR* [to] [queue] *name*	
NR	Specifies the number of the spool; can be between 0 and 4.	
name	Specifies the printer queue name.	
spool 0 to queue UCGQUEUE	Adds spool number 0 to the printer queue UCGQUEUE.	
spool 4 UCGQUEUE	Adds spool number 4 to the printer queue UCGQUEUE.	

spxconfg

spxconfg			**OS:**	NetWare Common	
Function	Configures SPX parameters. If options aren't specified, a configuration menu will start.				
Syntax	load spxconfg [options...]				
A=*value*	Sets the abort timeout for SPX Watchdog in seconds (range is 540 to 5400).				
V=*value*	Sets the verify timeout for SPX Watchdog in seconds (range is 10 to 255).				
W=*value*	Sets the wait timeout for SPX acknowledgements in ticks (range is 10 to 3240).				
R=*value*	Sets the SPX default retry count (range is 1 to 255).				
S=*value*	Sets the maximum concurrent SPX sessions (range is 100 to 2000).				
Q=1	Quiet mode.				
H	Shows help information.				
NW4, NW5, NW6					
I=*value*	Sets the maximum open socket tables for IPX (range is 120 to 65520).				
File Name:	`spxconfg.nlm`	**Directory:**	\system	**Type:**	External
Tip:	You can use INETCFG to configure the same parameters.				
load spxconfg A=1000	Sets the SPX watchdog abort time to 1000 ticks.				

spxs

spxs			**OS:**	NetWare Common	
Function	Provides STREAM-based SPX protocol services.				
Syntax	load spxs [LDFILE=*name*]				
LDFILE=*name*	Specifies a file that contains the SPX timer defaults and physical packet size tables.				
File Name:	`spxs.nlm`	**Directory:**	\system	**Type:**	External

startup.ncf

startup.ncf			**OS:**	NetWare Common	
Function	The first file that loads after `server.exe` and contains the NLMs for disk drivers and name spaces. It also contains various set parameters that can't be set elsewhere (please see the `set` command).				
Syntax	None				
File Name:	`startup.ncf`	**Directory:**	\nwserver	**Type:**	Text File
Note:	This command is located on the DOS partition where server.exe can be found.				

streams

OS: NetWare Common

Function	Is used when an application requires CLIB loadable module or STREAMS-based services, which enable the application to submit requests to the NetWare server using a common interface.
Syntax	load *{ path }* streams *{ size }*

path	Specifies the path to STREAMS if it has been moved to another directory.
size	The maximum size in messages in bytes. The range for size is 4096–65535 bytes. (The option above isn't available in NetWare 3.)

File Name:	`streams.nlm`	**Directory:**	\system	**Type:**	External

TCP/IP Console

OS: NetWare Common

Function	Manages, configures, and monitors many TCP/IP protocols and manages the server's routing table.
Syntax	load tcpcon

SNMP Access Configuration	Configures the SNMP community string, timeout, poll interval, and transport protocol.
Protocol Information	Shows and changes TCP/IP protocol information.
EGP	Shows information and configures the Exterior Gateway Protocol.
ICMP	Shows information and configures the Internet Control Message Protocol.
IP	Shows information and configures the Internet Protocol.
OSPF	Shows information and configures the Open Shortest Path First routing protocol.
TCP	Shows information and configures the Transmission Control Protocol.
UDP	Shows information and configures the User Datagram Protocol.
IP Routing Table	Shows and manages the IP routing table. Can also flush routing tables.
Statistics	Used to select which TCP/IP protocol you want to see statistical information on.
EGP	Shows statistics for Exterior Gateway Protocol.
ICMP	Shows statistic for Internet Control Message Protocol.
IP	Shows statistic for Internet Protocol.
OSPF	Shows statistic for Internet Open Shortest Path First routing protocol.
TCP	Shows statistic for Transmission Control Protocol.
UDP	Shows information for User Datagram Protocol.
Interfaces	Shows current statistics for TCP/IP for network interfaces on the server.
Display Local Traps	Shows the local SNMP trap log that contains significant TCP/IP events.

File Name:	`tcpcon.nlm`	**Directory:**	\system	**Type:**	External

Text Editor

OS: NetWare Common

Function	Starts a text editor to create or edit text or configuration files on the server.
Syntax	edit *{ path } { file }*

	Use these keys to navigate in the text file.
<Arrow Keys>	Moves around in the text file.
<PG DN>	Moves one page down.
<PG UP>	Moves one page up.
<CTRL + PG UP>	Moves to the beginning of the file.
<CTRL + PG DN>	Moves to the end of the file.
<HOME>	Moves to the beginning of the line.
<END>	Moves to the end of the line.
<Back Space>	Deletes the character to the left of the cursor.
<Delete>	Deletes the character under the cursor.
<Tab>	Adds four spaces.
<F5>	Starts or stops highlighting a text for a selection.
<F6>	Copies the selection.
<Insert>	Inserts the previous copied text.
<F1>	Shows help information.
<ESC>	Stops the edit and asks if the file should be saved.
path	Specifies the path to the file edit.nlm if it isn't in its default directory.

continued

file	Specifies the path and name of the file to edit.				
File Name:	`edit.nlm`	**Directory:**	**NW3, NW4:** \system **NW5, NW6:** c:\nwserver	**Type:**	External

time

OS: NetWare Common

Function	Shows the server's current date and time, daylight saving time, and time synchronization information.
Syntax	time

tli

OS: NetWare Common

Function	Provides Transport Level Interface (TLI) communication services. This command requires that SPXS or IPXS is loaded. It also requires STREAMS and CLIB which are auto loaded by NW4 and above.
Syntax	load tli

File Name:	`tli.nlm`	**Directory:**	\system	**Type:**	External
Note:	The modules STREAMS and CLIB must be manually loaded in NW3.				

tping

OS: NetWare Common

Function	Sends an ICMP packet to a host. This is used to check if the host is reachable.
Syntax	load tping.nlm *host* { *size* [*retry*] }

host	Specifies the hostname or IP-address to send the ping to.				
size	Specifies the size in bytes for the ICMP packet.				
retry	Specifies the number of retries before giving up (default is 5).				
File Name:	`tping.nlm`	**Directory:**	\system	**Type:**	External
load tping 192.168.1.254	Sends a ping to the specified host.				

Track Off

OS: NetWare Common

Function	Stops showing the Router Information Protocol (RIP) traffic on the server.
Syntax	track off

Track On

OS: NetWare Common

Function	Starts the RIP Tracking Screen that shows Router Information Protocol traffic.
Syntax	track on

track on	Shows incoming and outgoing packets on the RIP Tracking Screen.

unbind

OS: NetWare Common

Function	Unbinds a network protocol from a network card.
Syntax	unbind *protocol* [from] *name* { *driverparameters...* }

protocol	Specifies which protocol to unbind.
name	Specifies which LAN driver or board name to unbind the protocol from.
driverparameters...	Specifies the driver parameters if more than one network board is of the same type.
DMA=*values*	Specifies the DMA channel for the network card to use.
FRAME=*number*	Specifies the frame type the protocol will use.
INT=*value*	Specifies the interrupt the network card is configured for.
MEM=*address*	Specifies the memory address that the network card will use.
PORT=*port*	Specifies the I/O port for the network card.
SLOT=*number*	Specifies the SLOT where the card is installed. Only used for EISA and Micro channel.
NODE=*number*	Specifies node number for the board.
Note:	When unbinding driver parameters use the same values used when loading the driver.
unbind ipx from 3c509_802.2	Unbinds the ipx protocol from the board named 3c509_802.2.
unbind ip from 3c509_II	Unbinds the ip protocol from the board named 3c509_II.

unload

OS: NetWare Common

Function	Unloads NLMs that have been previously loaded using the `load` command or autoloaded by the server.
Syntax	unload *module*

module	Specifies the module to unload.

unload monitor	Unloads the monitor.
unload kill address space=adress_space1	Shuts down an address space.

version (server)

OS: NetWare Common

Function	Is used on the server to show version, license, and copyright information.
Syntax	version

Volume Repair Utility

OS: NetWare Common

Function	Corrects volume problems and removes name space entries from the Directory tables. If parameters aren't specified, it will start a text GUI.
Syntax	load vrepair *{ volume } { logfile }*

volume	Specifies the volume to check for errors and corrects them.
logfile	Specifies a file to log errors to.

File Name:	`vrepair.nlm`	**Directory:**	\system	**Type:**	External
Note:	You can't run `vrepair` on volumes that are currently mounted.				

load vrepair vol2	Runs the vrepair utility on a volume name vol2.

volume, volumes

OS: NetWare Common

Function	Shows volumes currently mounted, volume attributes specified by flag, and the name spaces added to the volume. Shows more detailed information for a volume when the volume name is specified.
Syntax	volume *{ name }*

	The following are the flags for the attributes that will show in information.
Cp	Shows that file compression is enabled on the volume.
Sa	Shows that block suballocation is enabled on the volume.
Mg	Shows that migration is enabled on the volume.
NSS	Shows that it is a NetWare server system volume.
NSS P	Shows that it is the NSS provider volume.
name	Specifies the name of the volume to show more information about.

wndbcnvt

OS: NetWare Common

Function	A btrieve DLL converter for Microsoft Windows that converts the`wbtrcall.dll` to `wbtrlocl.dll`.
Syntax	wndbcnvt

File Name:	`wndbcnvt.exe`	**Directory:**	\public	**Type:**	External

Workstation Scheduler

OS: NetWare Common

Function	Schedules applications, utilities, or tasks from a workstation and assigns them a priority. You can schedule .EXE, .DLL, ActiveX, or Java files, which can be located on the local workstation or on the network.
Syntax	wmsched

File Name:	`wmsched.exe`	**Directory:**	\novell\client32	**Type:**	External
Tip:	On Windows NT, 2000, and XP, the action can run in the background without being logged in to the server.				

Chapter 3

Shared NetWare 4, 5, and 6 Commands

The commands in this section are in NetWare 4, NetWare 5, and NetWare 6, but are not in NetWare 3. The commands are all listed in alphabetical order by the command name.

Even though these commands are available in many versions of NetWare, many of the options are different and the commands may have a different syntax as well. Look carefully at the syntax field: you may see a bold NW6, NW5, or NW4, indicating that the following options are unique to that version of NetWare.

Remember, for NLM commands you must type the command "load" in front of the NLM for 4. This step is optional in NetWare 5 and 6.

Other commands for your NetWare system are in Chapter 2 and Chapter 4. For cross-references to other operating systems, please see Chapter 1, "Quick Command Index."

\etc\resolv.cfg

OS: NetWare 4,5,6

Function	Configures name servers to use for hostname lookups. Separate keywords and their values with a single space. A normal text editor works just fine.
Syntax	*keyword value*

nameserver *IP-address*	Specifies one name server to use. This can be used three times.
domain *domain*	Specifies the system's, domain name; this is everything after the first dot.

File Name: `resolv.cfg` **Directory:** \etc **Type:** Text File

name server 192.168.1.245	Specifies the name server as 192.168.1.245
domain ucgbook.com	Specifies the system's domain name as ucgbook.com

alias

OS: NetWare 4,5,6

Function	Shows or defines keywords to represent console commands for use at the server console. When alias is used alone it lists defined aliases.
Syntax	alias *{ keyword command }* alias *keyword*

keyword	The alias to assign a console command. Removes alias when no command is specified.
command	The console command that you want to create an alias for.
alias mynet Display Networks	Creates an alias called mynet for Display Networks.
alias mynet	Removes the alias mynet.

bindery

OS: NetWare 4,5,6

Function	Adds or deletes bindery contexts for the server where the command is used. The bindery contexts are stored in a list on the server and allow users to perform a bindery login to the server instead of logging into NDS.
Syntax	bindery option context=*NDS context*

add	Adds the specified context to the list of contexts stored on the server.
delete	Deletes the specified context from the list of contexts stored on the server.
NDS context	Specifies the NDS context where the server object exists.
bindery add context= .OU=sales O=US	Allows users in the sales context to login directly to the server.
bindery delete context .OU=sales O=US	Denies users in the sales context to login directly to the server.

bootpfwd

OS:	NetWare 4,5,6
Function	Forwards BOOT/DHCP request to a server on another network.
Syntax	load bootpfwd options...

Server=*servername*	Specifies the server to forward BOOT/DHCP requests to.
log=yes or no	Tells if a log will be created. If no filename is given, shows log on screen.
file=*filename*	Specifies a log file to use.
NW5, NW6:	
Info	Shows current operation status.

File Name:	`bootpfwd.nlm`	**Directory:**	`\system`	**Type:**	External

load bootpfwd server=192.2.34.15	Sends BOOTP/DHCP request to server 192.2.34.15.

Bridge Console

OS:	NetWare 4,5,6
Function	Shows and manages bridge information from the server console when using the server as a bridge.
Syntax	brgcon

SNMP Access Configuration	Shows and edits settings for the function of the command.
Spanning Tree Information	Shows spanning tree information.
Transparent Bridging Information	Shows and edits settings for transparent bridging.
Ports	Shows information about local ports.
Interfaces	Shows information about local interfaces.

File Name:	`brgcon.nlm`	**Directory:**	\system	**Type:**	External

Btrieve DS Message Router

OS:	NetWare 4,5,6
Function	The Message Router that provides Directory Services support for Btrieve 6.x. Allows an NLM application on a server to talk with a remote server containing other loaded Btrieve NLMs.
Syntax	load bdrouter

File Name:	`bdrouter.nlm`	**Directory:**	\system	**Type:**	External
Tip:	For an overview of the Btrieve server-based Record Manager, please see `btrieve.nlm`.				

Configuration Manager Console

OS:	NetWare 4,5,6
Function	Lists all PCI adapters, including the adapter name, current status, and whether the adapter is hot pluggable. Deactivates or activates hot pluggable PCI adapters for removal and installation.
Syntax	load ncmcon

File Name:	`ncmcon.nlm`	**Directory:**	\system	**Type:**	External

convinet

OS:	NetWare 4,5,6
Function	Converts configuration files from Multi Protocol Router (MPR) version 2.x to version 3.0.
Syntax	load convinet

File Name:	`convinet.nlm`	**Directory:**	\system	**Type:**	External

cx

OS:	NetWare 4,5,6
Function	Changes or shows the current context, or to show containers and leaf objects.
Syntax	cx *{ context }* [options...]

/R	Shows containers at the root level or change context in relation to the root.
/T	Shows containers below the current or specified context.
/CONT	Shows containers at the current or specified context in a vertical list.
/A	Includes all objects when used with /T or /CONT.
/C	Doesn't pause after each screen of output.
.	Returns one level back in the context.
context	The context to change to. For example .ucg.marketing.

File Name:	`cx.exe`	**Directory:**	\public\	**Type:**	External

cx .	Backs up one level in the NDS tree.
cx .ucg.marketing	Changes to the specified context.

DS Repair

OS: NetWare 4,5,6

Function	Corrects problems in the NDS database such as bad record, schema mismatches, bad server addresses, and external references. It can also make advanced changes to the NDS schema.
Syntax	load dsrepair [options...]

-U	Performs a full unattended repair, then exits and unloads `dsrepair`.
	The following five options are used inside the GUI.
Unattended full repair	Performs a full unattended repair.
Time synchronization	Gathers server status and time synchronization information.
Report synchronization status	Gathers synchronization status on all partitions from all servers that have a replica.
View repair log file	Shows and edits the repair log file.
Advanced options menu	Allows manual control of all repair options.
NW5, NW6:	
-A	Enables the advanced replica and partition options in the `dsrepair` menu.
NW6:	
	The following option is used inside the GUI.
Single object repair	Attempts to repair faults on the given object entry id.
File Name: `dsrepair.nlm`	**Directory:** \system\ **Type:** External

dsmerge

OS: NetWare 4,5,6

Function	Is used to merge two separate NDS trees, check that all servers in the NDS tree are responding and have the same tree name, and show time synchronization information.
Syntax	load dsmerge

Check servers in this tree	Checks whether every server in this tree has the correct tree name.
Check time synchronization	Checks whether every server in the tree has the proper time synchronization.
Merge two trees	Merges the current NDS tree into another tree.
Rename this tree	Renames the NDS tree.
NW5, NW6:	
Graft a single server tree	Merges a single server NDS into another tree at the specified container.
File Name: `dsmerge.nlm`	**Directory:** \system **Type:** External

filtcfg

OS: NetWare 4,5,6

Function	Sets and configures filters for IPX, TCP/IP, and AppleTalk protocols. The available filters are Packet forwarding (not with AppleTalk), Service information (not with TCP/IP), and Routing information.
Syntax	filtcfg
File Name: `filtcfg.nlm`	**Directory:** \system **Type:** External

flag

OS: NetWare 4,5,6

Function	Shows or modifies file and directory attributes, the owner of files and directories, and search modes for executable files.
Syntax	flag *file* { *attributes...* } [options...] flag *file* [options...] [/name=*user*] [/owner=user]

- *attributes...*	Removes the specified attributes from a file or directory.
+ *attributes...*	Adds the specified attributes to the file or directory.
File Attributes	
ALL	Specifies the A, Ci, Di, H, Ic, P, Ri, Ro, Sh, Sy and T attributes.
A	Sets that the file has been modified since the last backup.
Ci	Secures the file from being copied (only for MAC files).
Dc	Secures the file from being compressed.
Di	Secures the file from being deleted or copied over.
Dm	Secures the file from being migrated to secondary backup system.
Ds	Secures a specified file from being sub allocated.
H	Secures a file from being seen by the DOS command `dir`.
Ic	Compresses the file as soon as possible.
N	Sets the Read and Write attributes to default.
Ri	Secures the file from being renamed.

continued

Ro	Sets the Read Only attribute to the file.
Rw	Sets the Read and Write attributes to the file.
Sh	Sets the Share attribute to the file allowing many users at the same time.
Sy	Same as /H and also sets prevention from being copied or deleted.
T	Secures the file by use of the Transaction Tracking System.
X	Sets the Execute only attribute to the file. **This attribute can't be removed**. (The X attribute can only be set to .exe and .com files.)
	The following are status flags that show information and can't be changed.
Cc	Shows that the file can't be compressed because of limited space savings.
Co	Shows that the file is compressed.
M	Shows that the file is migrated.
Directory Attributes	
ALL	Specifies the Di, H, Ic, P, Ri, and Sy attributes.
Di	Secures the directory from being deleted.
Dc	Secures the directory from being compressed.
Dm	Secures the directory from being migrated to secondary backup system.
H	Secures the directory from being seen by the DOS command `dir`.
Ic	Compresses the directory as soon as possible.
N	Sets directory to no attributes (default mode).
P	Purges the directory immediately when it is deleted.
Ri	Secures the directory from being renamed.
Sy	Same as /H and also sets prevention from being copied or deleted.
/m=*NR*	Alters the search modes of executable files. The modes are as follows:
0	Searches for instructions in the file NET.CFG (default mode).
1	Searches the path specified in the file. If no path is given, the file searches the default directory, then all search drives.
2	Searches the path specified in file. If no path is given, the default directory.
3	Searches the path specified in file. If no path is given, the default directory. If the request is read only it will then search the search drives also.
4	Is reserved and not to use.
5	Searches first the specified path, then all search drivers. If no path is given it will search the default directory and then all search drivers.
6	Is reserved and not to use.
7	Searches the path specified, then, if the request is read only, the search drivers. If no path is given it will search the default directory and then all search drivers.
/c	Scrolls continuously.
/d	Shows information detail about a file or directory.
/do	Specifies to show or modify only directories in the path.
/fo	Specifies to show or modify only files in the path.
/s	Searches the subdirectory and below in the specified path.
/owner=*name*	Shows information about files and directories owned by the specified user.
/name *name*	Sets the owner for a file to a user specified by name.
/group *name*	Sets the owner for a file to a group specified by name.
/?	Shows help information.
/ver	Shows version information.
file	Specifies the file or directory to alter the attributes for.

File Name:	`flag.exe`	**Directory:**	\public	**Type:**	External

flag *.doc +RW	Sets the reading and writing attributes for all doc files in current directory.
flag *.exe +X	Makes all files in the directory executable only.

help

OS: NetWare 4,5,6

Function	Shows command syntax, description, and usage information.
Syntax	help *{ command }* help all

command	Specifies which command to get help information on.
all	Shows help information for all console commands one by one.

continued

NOTE:	If no parameter is entered, help lists all console commands.
help unbind	Shows description and usage information of the command unbind.

initialize system

OS: NetWare 4,5,6

Function	Executes all of the commands in the `sys:\etc\netinfo.cfg` file that is created by the inetcfg utility. The `netinfo.cfg` file contains all of the network and multiprotocol router information for the server.
Syntax	initialize system

Internetworking Configuration

OS: NetWare 4,5,6

Function	Configures the network settings like network cards, interface, protocols.
Syntax	load inetcfg

Boards	Configures, adds, and removes network cards.
Network Interfaces	Configures the network interface.
WAN Call Directory	Creates new destinations in the wan caller directory.
Protocols	Configures the different network protocols.
Bindings	Sets the different bindings like network number and ip-address.
IPX	Used to set the IPX external network number and the IPX frame type.
IP	Used to set the IP Address, subnet mask, and other TCP/IP options.
Manage Configuration	Configures SNMP, edit system files, or copy configuration files to or from a floppy.
Configure SNMP Parameters.	Configures the SNMP settings.
Configure SNMP Information	Sets information about the server used by SNMP.
Export To Diskette	Exports X.25 profiles, call destination, and Authentication files to a diskette.
Import From Diskette	Imports X.25 profiles, call destination, and Authentication files from a diskette.
Configure Remote Access to This Server	Configures remote access like rconsole, aconsole, and telnet.
Edit AUTOEXEC.NFS	Edits the autoexec.ncf file.
View Configuration	Shows various configurations information.
NW5 and NW6	
Reinitialize System	Activates the changes in the configuration without rebooting the server.

File Name:	`inetcfg.nlm`	**Directory:**	\system	**Type:**	External

IPX Console

OS: NetWare 4,5,6

Function	Troubleshoots IPX, shows status and path, and locates routers.
Syntax	ipxcon [option]

/P	Views the LSPs received by the router, if the router is running NLSP. (The following options are available inside the console:)
IPX Information	Shows information about incoming, forwarded, and outgoing packets.
Detailed IPX Information	Shows more detailed information about incoming and outgoing packets.
IPX Router Information	Shows information about NLSP, RIP, and SAP on the selected router.
NLSP Information	Shows information about the NLSP network and the NLSP system.
System Information	Shows operational information.
Detailed NLSP System Information	Shows detailed information about NLSP.
Area Addresses	Shows all the configured area addresses.
Neighbors	Shows all the neighbors in the NLSP system.
Routers	Shows all routes that are combined in the NLSP system.
LANs	Shows all LANs that are known in the NLSP system.
Mobile IPX Information	Shows mobile IPX information.
Address Mapping Gateway Information	Shows information about address mapping gateway.
Circuits	Shows a list of all NLSP circuits in the system.
Forwarding	Lists all IPX destination networks and shows information about the first hop router.

File Name:	`ipxcon.nlm`	**Directory:**	\system	**Type:**	External

IPX Static Routing Configuration

OS: NetWare 4,5,6

Function	Manages static routes and services on a remote IPX router.
Syntax	load staticon

Dynamically Configure Static Routing Tables	Starts the configuration of the router.

continued

Configure Services from Gatekeepers Configure Local Static Services Configure Local Static Routes Write Static Routing Tables to Permanent Storage Restore Static Routing Tables from Permanent Storage	Uses bindery information on remote routers to manage static services. Lists configurable static services in the local router. Lists configurable static routes in the local router. Stores all information about static routes and services in storage. Restores all information about static routes and services from storage.
File Name: `staticon.nlm`	**Directory:** \system **Type:** External

language

OS: NetWare 4,5,6

Function	Sets language for subsequently loaded modules.
Syntax	language [options...]

language_name | number	Specifies language to use by name or number.
list	Lists of all language names and numbers.
REN *number new_name*	Allows user to rename a language specified by a language number.
Note:	If parameters aren't entered, language will show language setting for current module.
language REN 4 Spanish	Renames English to Spanish.

named

OS: NetWare 4,5,6

Function	Starts the DNS server that resolves hostnames to IP addresses. Also creates, deletes, and modifies DNS zones.
Syntax	named [options...]

-a	Activates newly created zone autodetect (default).
-b	Turns auto-detect off.
-f *script { content }*	Creates multiple zones by using the specified script and any given zone context.
-h	Shows help information.
-l	Allows the DNS to log on as an administrator to create/delete zones.
-m *file { context }*	Imports the specified `.dat` file and then creates a new zone with any context.
-q	Disables debug message verbose mode.
-r *zone*	Specifies the zone that is deleted and removed from the database.
-rp *characters*	Specifies which character is replaced by a dash (-).
-s *{ zone }*	Shows the status of the active zone or a specified one.
-u *file*	Imports the specified `.dat` file and then updates the previously created zone.
-v	Verbose mode. Shows more information for debug messages.
-zi *zone*	Forces a named zone for the zone-in transfer.
File Name: `named.nlm`	**Directory:** \system **Type:** External
Tip:	You can run `named` repeatedly to start different command-line activities. The actual `named.nlm` software is only loaded the first time it is invoked.

ndssch

OS: NetWare 4,5,6

Function	A utility used to manually extend the schema for the NDS database. Schema files have the extension .SCH
Syntax	ndssch *schemafile*

schemafile	Specifies the complete path to the .SCH schema file containing the schema information
File Name: `ndssch.exe`	**Directory:** \public **Type:** External
Tip:	Most of the schema files are found in the directory `sys:\system\schema`.
ndssch v:\system\schema\auditing.sch	Manages the auditing objects in NDS.

netbasic

OS: NetWare 4,5,6

Function	A basic interpreter that is used to run basic scripts on the server, which can manage the server via scripts.
Syntax	load netbasic

	When loaded, the following extra console commands are available:
shell	Starts the interactive shell. See `netbasic shell` for a complete description.
NW5, NW6	
nblibload *component { timeout }*	Loads an NMX component.
component	Specifies an NMX component.
timeout	Sets the timeout used to determine when to unload the component (-1 = don't unload).
nblibunload *component*	Unloads the specified component.

continued

nblibdelay *component timeout*	Sets a new timeout for the specified component.
	The following directories are used by netbasic:
/netbasic/include	Contains include files.
/netbasic/user	Contains any user scripts. Add scripts here.
/netbasic/web	Contains web scripts.
/system/nmx	Contains all other net2000 components.

File Name:	`netbasic.nlm`	**Directory:**	/system	**Type:**	External

netbasic shell

OS: NetWare 4,5,6

Function	Starts an interactive shell that is used to run basic scripts. The `netbasic.nlm` must be loaded to use this command.
Syntax	shell

	The following standard utilities are available in the shell.
cd *directory*	Changes to a directory.
cls	Clears the screen.
copy *from to*	Copies files.
{ server|] [*volume*:] [*path*] *file*	The syntax for from and to
server	Specifies the server to use.
volume	Specifies a volume to use.
path	Specifies a directory path to use.
file	Specifies the file to copy.
del *file*	Deletes a file.
dir [*directory }*	Shows the contents of the specified or current directory.
exit	Leaves the shell.
md *directory*	Creates a directory.
netmon	A simple server monitor. Shows cup usage, disk access.
partsync	Syncs partitions.
rd *directory*	Removes a directory.
ren *file1 file2*	Renames file1 to file2
set *{ variable* [*=value }*]	shows, sets, or removes shell variables.
type *filename*	Shows the file on the screen.
volinfo	Shows a window containing volume information.
NW5, NW6:	
broadcst	Allows you to send broadcast messages to bindery users and groups.
fconsole	Shows status and connections information. Can also send broadcast.
ver	Shows version information.

dir \public*.exe	Shows all files in public that end with .exe
cd \public	Changes to the \public directory.
copy \etc\crontab \tmp\crontab	Makes a copy of the crontab file.

NetWare Administrator

OS: NetWare 4,5,6

Function	Creates, deletes, and manages user and group accounts, assigns permissions to files, directories and other NDS objects. Also used to set up printing and licensing services, and create, move, and rename NDS objects.
Syntax	nwadmn32 [option]

/N	Saves your preferences in your NDS user object instead of updating the local registry.
/F *file*	Saves your preferences in the filename specified.
	The following are older versions of the Netware Administrator available in NW4.
nwadmn3x.exe	Is located in sys:\public\ and has been replaced by nwadmin32.exe
nwadmn95.exe	Is located in sys:\public\win95 and was an optimized version for Windows 95.

File Name:	`nwadmn32.exe`	**Directory:**	\public\win32	**Type:**	External
Tip:	If some NDS object types are unrecognized, simply copy the supporting DLLs into the same directory as nwadmn32.exe.				

nlist

OS: NetWare 4,5,6

Function	Shows information regarding NDS objects like user, server, printers, etc.
Syntax	nlist *class*[=*name*] [where *property logic value*] [show { *property* }] [options...] nlist [options...]

where	Selects information to show.
property	Specifies the property to select from.
logic	Specifies the logical expression to use on the select objects.
EQ	Equal.
NE	Not equal.
LT	Less than.
LE	Less or equal.
GT	Greater than.
GE	Greater or equal.
EXSISTS	True if the property exists.
NEXISTS	True if the property does not exist.
value	Specifies a value to compare against.
show	Shows a specified property.
property	Specifies property to show.
/a	Shows active users or servers.
/s	Shows objects throughout all subordinate contexts.
/co *context*	Shows objects from the specified context.
/r	Shows objects at the root context.
/c	Shows a continuous list, doesn't stop for a page break.
/b	Shows bindery information.
/ver	Shows version information.
/tree	Shows tree information. (Use alone.)
/d	Shows detailed information.
/n	Shows only the object name.

File Name:	`nlist.exe`	**Directory:**	\public	**Type:**	External

nlist user show "Given Name"	Shows information about users' given names.
nlist user where "Group membership" EQ "UCG Team"	Shows users who belong to UCG Team.

NLS Setup utility

OS: NetWare 4,5,6

Function	Creates the Novell License Services object in the NDS tree.
Syntax	setupnls

File Name:	`setupnls.nlm`	**Directory:**	\system	**Type:**	External

Novell Licensing Services Manger

OS: NetWare 4,5,6

Function	Was used to manage NetWare licensing but its functionality has now been migrated into the NetWare Administrator.
Syntax	nlsman32

File Name:	`nlsman32.exe`	**Directory:**	\public\win32	**Type:**	External

nprinter

OS: NetWare 4,5,6

Function	Installs a print server on a DOS or Windows 3.x host. If on options is given it starts a menu utility.
Syntax	nprinter *printer* [options...] nprinter *printserver NR* [options...] nprinter [options...]

/s	Shows the status of the loaded nprinter.
/u	Unloads the loaded nprinter.
/?	Shows help information.
/t=*NR*	Sets the timing interval for the print server from 1 - fast to 9 - slow.
/b=*kbyte*	Sets the data block size (3-60).
printer	Specifies the printer to use.

continued

printserver	Specifies the print server name to use.
NR	Specifies the printer number.

File Name:	`nprinter.exe`	**Directory:**	\public	**Type:**	External

nprinter printer_one	Starts nprinter for printer printer_one
nprinter pserv_one 1	Starts nprinter for print server pserv_one printer 1.

Nprinter Manager

OS: NetWare 4,5,6

Function	A nprinter print server for Windows 95 and is used to share a printer that is physically attached to a Windows 95/98 or Millennium workstation and make the printer available to other users on the network.
Syntax	nptwin95

File Name:	`nptwin95.exe`	**Directory:**	\public	**Type:**	External
Note:	You must have the Novell Client installed on the workstation before you can use this utility.				

reinitialize system

OS: NetWare 4,5,6

Function	Compares the current `NETINFO.CFG` with the old one; if new commands are found, they are executed.
Syntax	reinitialize system

reinitialize system	Executes changes in `NETINFO.CFG`.

Remove Network Adapter

OS: NetWare 4,5,6

Function	Unloads an instance of a LAN driver that has been loaded several times to support multiple boards.
Syntax	remove network adapter *driver* [, *board*]

driver	Specifies the driver name.
board	Specifies the instance number if there is more than one board of the same type.

remove network adapter NE2000	Unloads the NE2000 adapter.
remove network adapter NE2000, 2	Unloads the second NE2000 adapter.

Remove Network Interface

OS: NetWare 4,5,6

Function	Removes one of the logical boards when there are several frame types loaded with a LAN driver.
Syntax	remove network interface *board*

board	Specifies the logical board name or number.

remove network interface 2	Removes the second logical board.

Reset Network Adapter

OS: NetWare 4,5,6

Function	Stops everything the specified adapter is currently doing and resets it.
Syntax	reset network adapter *driver* [, *board*]

driver	Specifies the driver name.
board	Specifies the instance number if there is more than one board of the same type.

reset network adapter NE2000	Resets the NE2000 adapter.
reset network adapter NE2000, 2	Resets the second NE2000 adapter.

Reset Network Interface

OS: NetWare 4,5,6

Function	Restarts a logical network board that has been shut down with `Shutdown Network Interface`.
Syntax	Resets network interface *board.*

board	Specifies the logical board name or number.

reset network interface 2	Restarts the second logical board.

Restart Server

OS: NetWare 4,5,6

Function	Downs the server and then restarts it.
Syntax	restart server *{ option }*

-ns	Restarts the server without using the STARTUP.NCF file.
-na	Restarts the server without using the AUTOEXEC.NCF file.

restart server -na	Restarts the server without using the AUTOEXEC.NCF file.

scmd

OS: NetWare 4,5,6

Function	Starts the Compatibility Mode Device server which connects IPX segments to IP segments and allows for a migration path when used with /ma option from IPX to IP by connecting IPX services to the IP backbone.
Syntax	load scmd [options...]

/ma	Forces `scmd` to act as an IP backbone-supported Migration Agent.
/nat	Allows support for NAT if the Migration Agent is in a public realm.
/filter	Filters predefined IPX services between agents. Must run `filtcfg` utility first.
/net=*NR*	Loads `scmd` with the specified network number.
/prefip=*address*	Changes the preferred IP address while loading `scmd`.
/noslp	Specifies that SLP independent mode will be used.
/synctime=*minutes*	Sets the Migration Agent communication time for SLP in minutes.
/MAADDR=*agents...*	Specifies a semi-colon separated list of IP addresses that Migration Agent nodes use.
/MAlist	Shows any Migration Agents that the CMD server thinks are active.
/Sync	Updates the SAP and RIP router table.
/stat	Shows the current status of the Migration Agent or CMD server.
[/dump]	Sends the status output to the file `cmdstat.dat` in the \sys\etc\ directory.
/search	Shows any services that CMD or the Migration Agent finds.
[NAME=*service*]	Specifies the service name to look for. Use an asterisk here for finding all services.
[NET=*NR*]	Specifies the network number to look for. Use `FFFFFFF` for all network services.
[/dump]	Dumps the output of the search to a file.

File Name:	`scmd.nlm`	**Directory:**	\system	**Type:**	External

load scmd /ma	Starts the compatibility mode device server and enables the migration agent.

set (Directory Services)

OS: NetWare 4,5,6

Function	Alters DS and NDS paths, traces, events
Syntax	set *attribute* [= *value*]

nds trace to screen = on | off	Enables the directory service trace screen if value is set to on.
nds trace to file = on | off	Traces the directory service events and put them in the NDS trace file if on.
nds trace filename = *path*	Specifies the filename path to the NDS trace file on the sys volume.
nds external reference life span = *hours*	Allows external references for specified time before removing (range is 1 to 384).
nds inactivity synchronization interval = *minutes*	Performs full synchronization of replicas with set interval (range is 2 to 1440).
nds synchronization restrictions = on | off	Enables synchronization with specified versions of directory service. (DS versions are specified after the on value separated by commas. If off is specified all versions will be accepted.)
nds servers status = up | down	Changes the status for the server objects in the local namebase to up or down.
nds janitor interval = *minutes*	Specifies an interval to run the NDS janitor process (range is 1 to 10080).
nds backlink interval = *minutes*	Runs the NDS backlink consistency checking with this interval (range is 2 to 10080).
nds trace file length to zero = on | off	Clears the NDS trace file, and then returns to off if value is changed to on.
bindery context = *context*	Sets the NetWare directory services container. Multiple contexts are separated by ;.
NW4:	
nds do not synchronize with = on | off	Disables synchronization with specified versions of directory service. (DS versions are specified after the on value, separated by commas. If off is specified, all versions will be accepted.)
additional security checks = on | off	Runs security checks that aren't compatible with previous NDS versions if on.
check equivalent to me = on | off	Enables checking of equivalent to me attribute when authenticating if set to on.
nds client ncp retries = *NR*	Retries the number of times before the NDS client disconnects.
NW5, NW6:	
nds bindery qos mask = *mask*	Objects that are subjected to bindery QOS delay (range is 0 to 4294967295).
nds bindery qos delay = *milliseconds*	Specifies the delay in milliseconds after finding bindery (range is 0 to 60000).
nds distributed reference link interval =	Runs the NDS consistency checking with this interval (range is 2 to 10080).
nds bootstrap address = *server*	Specifies a server that can perform tree connectivity operations.

set nds synchronization restrictions = on, 421	Allows synchronizations with directory service version 421.

set (Error Handling) — OS: NetWare 4,5,6

Function	Controls SYSLOG, VOLLOG, TTS$LOG and BOOT$LOG file sizes and various wait states.
Syntax	set *attribute* [= *value*]

server log file state = *value*	Sets action for the `sys$log.err` file if it grows larger than size limit. (Valid values are: 0 = nothing, 1 = remove or 2 = rename.)
volume log file state = *value*	Sets action for the `var$log.err` file if it grows larger than size limit. (Valid values are: 0 = nothing, 1 = remove or 2 = rename.)
volume tts log file state = *value*	Sets action for the `tts$log.err` file if it grows larger than size limit. (Valid values are: 0 = nothing, 1 = remove or 2 = rename.)
server log file overflow size = *size*	Specifies how big the `sys$log.err` can be (range is 65536 to 4294967295).
volume log file overflow size = *size*	Specifies how big the `var$log.err` can be (range is 65536 to 4294967295).
volume tts log file overflow size = *size*	Specifies how big the `tts$log.err` can be (range is 65536 to 4294967295).
auto restart after abend delay time = *minutes*	Waits specified time before going down when abend occurs (range is 2 to 60).
enable deadlock detection = on | off	**NW4 only:** Enables the deadlock detection in the smp spin lock code.
auto restart after abend = *value*	**NW4 only:** Specifies action after an abend.
0	Doesn't make attempts to recover from the abend.
1	Attempts to recover from software abend by downing server and restarting OS.
2	Attempts to recover from software/hardware abend by downing server and restarting OS.
NW5, NW6:	
boot error log file state = *value*	Sets action for the `boot$log.err` file if it grows larger than size limit. (values: 0 = nothing, 1 = remove, 2 = rename or 3 = create new on boot.)
boot error log file overflow size = *size*	Specifies how big the `boot$log.err` can be (range is 65536 to 4294967295).
boot error log = on | off	Saves all console messages to the `boot$log.err` file if value is set to on.
hung unload wait delay = *seconds*	Specifies how long to wait for a nlm to unload when hung (range is 0 to 118.3).
auto restart after abend = *value*	Specifies action after an abend.
0	Doesn't make attempts to recover from the abend.
1	Attempts to recover from software abend by downing server and restarting OS.
2	Attempts to recover from software/hardware abend by downing server and restarting OS.
3	Attempts to recover from software/hardware abend by restarting server directly.

set (NCP) — OS: NetWare 4,5,6

Function	Specifies various NCP settings such as IP addresses, TCP delay, NCP/UDP checksum, etc.
Syntax	set *argument* [= *value*]

ncp file commit = on | off	Lets applications flush all pending file writes to disk if value is set to on.
display ncp bad component warnings = on | off	Enables NCP bad component warnings if value is set to on.
reject ncp packets with bad components = on | off	Denies NCP packets that fail component checking if value is set to on.
display ncp bad length warnings = on | off	Shows warnings about NCP bad lengths if value is set to on.
reject ncp packets with bad lengths = on | off	Denies NCP packets that fail boundary checking if value is set to on.
maximum outstanding ncp searches = *NR*	Allows number of NCP directory searches for one connection (range is 10 to 1000).
ncp packet signature option = *value*	Uses of NCP packet signatures. Valid values below:
0	Doesn't use packet signatures.
1	Uses packet signatures if client requires them.
2	Uses packet signatures if client supports them; otherwise doesn't use signatures.
3	Uses packet signatures.
enable ipx checksums = *value*	Specifies if checksumming should be used on IPX packets. Valid values below:
0	Doesn't checksum.
1	Uses checksumming if the client has it enabled.
2	Requires checksum.
allow change to client rights = on | off	Makes the print/job server think that it has the rights of a queue job's submitter.
allow LIP = on | off	Uses Large Internet Packet support if value is set to on.
NW5, NW6:	
ncp exclude IP addresses = *IPaddresses*	Denies IP addresses specified for NCP. Values can be IP address, NONE or ALL.

continued

ncp include IP addresses =	Allows IP addresses specified for NCP. Values can be IP address, NONE or ALL.
ncp over udp = on | off	Enables NCP to go over UDP if value is set to on.
ndc tcp keep alive interval = *seconds*	Disconnects idle NCP connections after specified time (range is 0 to 57593.2).
minimum ncp tcp receive window to advertise = *NR*	Specifies minimum receive window for NCP connections (range is 256 to 16384).
ncp tcp receive window = *NR*	Specifies the receive window for NCP connections (range is 1400 to 65535).
enable udp checksums on ncp packets = *value*	Controls the checksumming of NCP UDP packets. Valid values below:
0	Doesn't checksum.
1	Performs checksumming if it is enabled on the client.
2	Requires checksumming.
client file caching enabled = on | off	Enables client side caching of open files if value is set to on.
ncp protocol preferences = *protocols*	Sets preferred protocols separated by a space. Valid protocols: ipx, TCP, and UDP.
ncp enable ipx address = on | off	**NW5 only:** Makes NDS advertise the server's IPX address.

set (Time) OS: NetWare 4,5,6

Function	Sets the date and time of the server.
Syntax	set *argument* [= *value*]

timesync configuration file = *file*	Specifies path to the timesync configuration file.
timesync configured sources = on | off	Contacts only sources explicitly marked as time source if value is set to on.
timesync directory tree mode = on | off	Ignores SAP packets from other trees than current one if value is set to on.
timesync hardware clock = on | off	Enables clock synchronization on each polling loop if value is set to on.
timesync polling count = *NR*	Specifies the amount of time packets to transfer when polling (range is 1 to 1000).
timesync polling interval = *seconds*	Specifies the polling interval to use (range is 10 to 2678400).
timesync reset = on | off	Enables timesync reset if value is set to on.
timesync restart flag = on | off	Restarts the `timesync.nlm` if set to on, value goes back to off when done.
timesync service advertising = on | off	Enables the time source to advertise using SAP if value is set to on.
timesync synchronization radius = *milliseconds*	Handles adjustment synchronized (range is 0 to 2147483647).
timesync time adjustment = *adjustment*	Specifies the time adjustment. (The adjustment is issued with either +HH:MM:SS or -HH:MM:SS.)
timesync type = *type*	Specifies type of time source to use. (Valid types are: single, reference, primary, or secondary.)
time zone = *zone*	Specifies time zone to use.
default time server type = *type*	Specifies the default type of time synchronization server. (Valid types are: secondary, primary, reference, or single.)
start of daylight savings time = (*date*)	Specifies when to switch to daylight saving time. (Date is specified as month day year hh:mm:ss am (or pm).)
end of daylight savings time = *date*	Specifies when to switch off of daylight saving time. (Date is specified as month day year hh:mm:ss am (or pm).)
daylight savings time offset = *offset*	Sets the offset that is used in time calculations when using daylight saving. (Offset is specified as +hh:mm:ss or -hh:mm:ss.)
daylight savings time status = on | off	Shows if daylight saving time is in use if value is set to on.
new time with daylight savings time status = on | off	Shows if daylight saving time is in use and an offset is used in time calculations.
timesync add time source = *server*	**NW4 only:** Sets a server to add to the configured list of servers to contact.
timesync remove time source = *server*	**NW4 only:** Removes server from the configured list of servers to contact.
timesync time source = *server*	**NW4 only:** A server to add to the configured list of servers to contact.
timesync write parameters = on | off	**NW4 only:** Allows parameters to be written to the configuration file.
timesync write value = *value*	**NW4 only:** Sets what parameters can be written to the configuration file.
1	Allows only internal parameters.
2	Allows only configured time sources.
3	Allows both parameters and configured sources.
timesync time sources = *servers*	**NW5, NW6 only:** Specifies the servers to contact as time sources. (Servers are separated and ended by a semicolon ; NTP servers are marked with an ending :123.)

Shutdown Network Interface

OS: NetWare 4,5,6

Function	Shuts down a logical network board without releasing its resources. After the shutdown, you can restart the board with `Reset Network Interface` without reloading the LAN driver.
Syntax	shutdown network interface *board*
board	Specifies the logical board name or number.
shutdown network interface 2	Shuts down the second logical board.

techwalk

OS: NetWare 4,5,6

Function	Records the NetWare configuration information. Saves configuration information for INETCFG or specified NLM program to a filename sys:etc\TECHWALK.OUT.				
Syntax	load techwalk *{ name }*				
name	Specifies a NLM program to record information configuration.				
File Name:	`techwalk.nlm`	**Directory:**	\system	**Type:**	External
load techwalk clib.nlm	Records the configuration of the clib.nlm module.				

telnetd

OS: NetWare 4,5,6

Function	Starts the telnet daemon used by xconsole and tn3270 to access the server via telnet or X-window.				
Syntax	load telnetd				
File Name:	`telnetd.nlm`	**Directory:**	\system	**Type:**	External
Note:	You must load `xconsole` to be able to connect.				

timesync

OS: NetWare 4,5,6

Function	Shows the current time on the server and is used to control synchronization between servers.				
Syntax	load timesync				
File Name:	`timesync.nlm`	**Directory:**	\system	**Type:**	External
Note:	The `timesync` parameters are specified in the configuration file `TIMESYNC.CFG` or with the `SET` and `SERVMAN` utilities.				

ups_aio

OS: NetWare 4,5,6

Function	Configures the interface between a UPS and the server.				
Syntax	load ups_aio *{ parameters... }*				
downtime=*NR*	Specifies number of seconds to run on battery before taking down the server.				
msgdelay=*NR*	Specifies number of seconds before sending out a message to all users.				
msginterval=*NR*	Specifies number of seconds between repeated messages.				
drivertype=*NR*	Specifies a number that represents the type of driver for the AIO device.				
board=*NR*	Specifies the number of the AIO board.				
port=*NR*	Specifies the number of the port.				
signal_high	Sets the signal from the UPS as high (default is low).				
?	Shows version number and a short description of the parameters.				
File Name:	`ups_aio.nlm`	**Directory:**	\system	**Type:**	External
Tip:	Before loading `ups_aio,` you must first load a com port driver like `aiocomx`.				
load ups_aio	Loads the ups_aio utility using defaults.				

view

OS: NetWare 4,5,6

Function	Shows the content of a file to view in read only mode. A good way to look at configuration files.				
Syntax	load view *{ file }*				
file	Specifies file to show, if omitted the command will prompt for which file to show.				
File Name:	`view.nlm`	**Directory:**	\system	**Type:**	External
load view sys:system\autoexec.ncf	Shows the contents of the autoexec.ncf file.				

vmdismount

vmdismount	OS: NetWare 4,5,6
Function	Dismounts NetWare volumes so they can be checked for errors and repaired by `dsrepair` or `rebuild`.
Syntax	vmdismount option

volumename	Specifies the name of the NetWare volume to dismount.
volumenumber	Specifies the number of the NetWare volume to dismount.

vmdismount sys	Dismounts volume sys to check for and repair errors.
vmdismount 0	Also dismounts volume sys to check for and repair errors.

vmmount

vmmount	OS: NetWare 4,5,6
Function	Mounts NetWare volumes after they have been checked for errors and repaired by `dsrepair` or `rebuild`.
Syntax	vmmount option

volumename	Specifies the name of the NetWare volume to mount.
volumenumber	Specifies the number of the NetWare volume to mount.
vmmount sys	Mounts volume sys after checking for and repairing the volume errors.
vmmount 0	Also mounts volume sys after checking for and repairing the volume errors.

vmvolumes

vmvolumes	OS: NetWare 4,5,6
Function	Shows the current status of all NetWare volumes whether they are mounted or dismounted, whereas the command `volumes` only shows volumes that are mounted. Vmvolumes also shows the volume number and volume name.
Syntax	vmvolumes

xconsole

xconsole	OS: NetWare 4,5,6
Function	Allows remote access to the server via telnet vt100/vt220 terminal or X-window.
Syntax	load xconsole [options...]

s=*NR*	Specifies the maximum number of sessions allowed at the same time.
e=*msec*	Sets the timeout used to distinguish between user input <Esc> and vt220 commands.
/24	Uses lines 2 to 25 on a 24-line display.
	The following key emulation is used in a telnet or X session.
Ctrl-a	Emulates the Alt key.
Ctrl-h	Emulates the Home key.
Ctrl-b	Emulates the backspace key.
Ctrl-g	Emulates the Del key.
Ctrl-d	Emulates down arrow.
Ctrl-e	Emulates the End key.
Ctrl-[	Emulates Escape.
Ctrl-x	Stops the session.
Ctrl-o	Emulates the insert key.
Ctrl-l	Emulates left arrow.
Ctrl-p	Emulates page up.
Ctrl-n	Emulates page down.
Ctrl-r	Emulates right arrow.
Ctrl-z	Selects a screen.
Ctrl-f	Switches screen forward.
Ctrl-u	Emulates up arrow.
Ctrl-w	Shows help information.

File Name:	**Directory:**	**Type:**
`xconsole.nlm`	\system	External

Chapter 4

Other NetWare Commands

The commands in this section are not in all versions of NetWare. The commands are listed in alphabetical order by the command name.

Even though these commands may be available in many versions of NetWare, many of the options are different and the commands may have a different syntax as well. Look carefully at the syntax field: you may see a bold NW3, NW6, NW5, or NW4, indicating that the following options are unique to that version of NetWare.

Remember, for NLM commands you must type the command "load" in front of the NLM for NetWare 3 and NetWare 4. This step is optional in NetWare 5 and 6.

Other commands for your NetWare system are in Chapter 2. Chapter 3 also contains more commands for NetWare 4, NetWare 5, and NetWare 6. For cross-references to other operating systems, please see Chapter 1, the "Quick Command Index."

2xupgrde		**OS:**	NetWare 3
Function	Upgrades the file system from v2.1x and v2.2 to NetWare v3.1x.		
Syntax	load 2Xupgrde [options...]		
/B	Starts the upgrade in batch mode.		
/BATCH	Starts the upgrade in batch mode.		
/BATCH2	Starts the upgrade in batch mode ignoring errors.		
/BINDERY	Jumps to Phase #4 to upgrade the 286 Bindery only.		
/F	Jumps to Phase #1's lengthy memory and disk resource check.		
/FAST	Jumps to Phase #1's lengthy memory and disk resource check.		
/H	Shows help information.		
/HELP	Shows help information.		
/?	Shows help information.		
/P0	Disables creation of space for a DOS partition.		
/P*size*	Creates a DOS partition with the specified space in megabytes, size can be 0 to 32.		
/R	Sets random passwords.		
/R+	Sets random passwords.		
/R-	Disables creation of random passwords, this is the default.		
File Name: 2xupgrde.nlm	**Directory:** \system	**Type:**	External

3cboot		**OS:**	NetWare 3
Function	Loads the 3Com RPL Protocol Stack, which allows for a remote boot of a 3COM workstation.		
Syntax	load 3cboot		
File Name: 3cboot.nlm	**Directory:** \system	**Type:**	External

Activate Server — OS: NetWare 4

Function	Manages different tasks regarding the SFT III server in NetWare. Loads the MSEngine, synchronizes between the two servers, remirrors two servers, and runs `msstart.ncf` and `msauto.ncf`.
Syntax	activate server [option]

-na	Doesn't execute the `msauto.ncf` file while starting the MSEngine.
-ns	Doesn't execute the `msstart.ncf` file while starting the MSEngine.
-na-ns	Executes either the `msauto.ncf` or `msstart.ncf` files while starting the MSEngine.

adaptec — OS: NetWare 3

Function	Installs the Adaptec DIBI-2 tape drivers for use with Cheyenne backup software.
Syntax	load adaptec port=*port* buffer=*value*

port=*port*	Specifies the port number for Adaptec SCSI host adapter (default is 330).				
buffer=*value*	Specifies the number of buffers to allocate. Each buffer is 64k (default is 6).				
File Name:	`adaptec.nlm`	**Directory:**	\system	**Type:**	External

addicon — OS: NetWare 4

Function	Adds icons to Windows 3.1x Program Manager groups.
Syntax	addicon *{ parameters... }* [*@scriptfile*] [option]

icon=*filename*	Specifies an .exe file containing an icon (default is EXE file).				
exe=*filename*	Specifies the .exe file.				
desc=*text*	Specifies the description to the executable file (default is the EXE file).				
cmd=*parameters*	Specifies command-line parameters.				
work=*directory*	Specifies the working directory of the file.				
min=*yes / no*	Sets the minimize flag (default is NO).				
group=*groupname*	Specifies which program group to modify (default is Startup).				
windows=*path*	Specifies the path to the Windows directory. (If not specified, addicon searches for win.com.)				
groupfile=*filename*.GRP	Specifies which .GRP file to update.				
@scriptfile	Specifies a file that contains parameters. (If scriptfile is specified, all other parameters are ignored.)				
/H	Shows help information.				
/S	Quiet mode. Doesn't dump any messages.				
File Name:	`addicon.exe`	**Directory:**	\public	**Type:**	External

afp — OS: NetWare 3,4

Function	Allows Macintosh users to share files and applications with users on other platforms. After loading `AFP`, load the `AFPCON` utility to configure the AppleTalk filing protocol.
Syntax	load afp

File Name:	`afp.nlm`	**Directory:**	\system	**Type:**	External

afpcon — OS: NetWare 4

Function	Configures the AppleTalk Filing Protocol module.
Syntax	load afpcon

Quick Configuration	Configures AppleTalk Filing Protocol to default values.				
Detailed Configuration	Shows and specifies all AppleTalk Filing Protocol parameters.				
Maintenance and Status	Starts and stops the AppleTalk Filing Protocol services.				
File Name:	`afpcon.nlm`	**Directory:**	\system	**Type:**	External

AIOPAD Profile Config — OS: NetWare 5

Function	Creates and modifies Packet Assembler Disassembler (PAD) profiles used to configure X.25 WAN connections.
Syntax	aiopdcon

File Name:	`aiopdcon.nlm`	**Directory:**	\system	**Type:**	External

alert

OS: NetWare 5,6

Function	Enables or disables specific aspects of alert messages. User can limit the amount of information displayed with an alert message.
Syntax	alert *nmID command ON or OFF*

nmID	Specifies nmID number of an alert to manage.
command	Specifies which command to use. Use one of the following:
event	Generates an event when the alert is created.
log	Sends the alert to a log file.
everyone	Sends the alert to everyone on the network.
console	Shows the alert on the server console.
bell	Makes an alert bell sound when the alerts are generated.
id	Shows ID information. Appears in some older alerts, but is no longer used.
locus	Shows locus information. Appears in some older alerts, but is no longer used.
alert	Generates the alert.
nmID	Shows the alert's nmID in the alert message.
all	Enables or disables the log, everyone, consoles, and bell commands at the same time.
ON or OFF	Specifies whether to turn the alert ON or OFF for the specified command.
Tip:	Use `alert` to disable less important alert messages.
alert 40018 all on	Enables the log, everyone, console, and bell commands on all alerts with nmID 40018.

allow

OS: NetWare 3

Function	Shows, sets, or modifies the Inherited Rights Mask for a specified file or directory.
Syntax	allow *{ path } rights*

path	Specifies the path to the directory.
rights	Specifies the rights for the directory.
	The following rights can be combined separated by spaces.
All	Sets the rights to all eight trustee rights.
N	Sets the rights to no rights.
S	Allows users all rights to directories, files, and subdirectories.
R	Allows users to open and read files.
W	Allows users to open and write to files.
C	Allows users to create and write to files.
E	Allows users to erase directories, files, and subdirectories.
M	Allows users to rename and alter the attributes of directories and files.
F	Allows users to see files in a directory.
A	Allows users to alter the trustee assignments and Inherited Rights Masks of files.

File Name:	`allow.exe`	**Directory:**	\public	**Type:**	External

Note:	Remember to use a space between each option.
allow UCG.* R W E M	Sets the rights of all files beginning with UCG to Read, Write, Erase and Modify.

appletviewer, applet

OS: NetWare 5, 6

Function	Runs Java applets on the NetWare server console.
Syntax	appletviewer [options...] *applet*

-debug	Shows debug information.
-J*flags*	Specifies Java runtime flags.
Applet	Specifies the applet as a file or a URL address.
NW6	
-encoding *type*	Specifies the character encoding type to use.
Note:	The `java.nlm` must be loaded to use this command.

Arascon

OS: NetWare 5

Function	Configures AppleTalk remote access connections to a NetWare network for Macintosh clients.
Syntax	arascon

File Name:	`arascon.nlm`	**Directory:**	\system	**Type:**	External

Asynchronous Remote Console

OS: NetWare 3

Function	A remote console that uses a modem connection to manage a remote server.

continued

Syntax	aconsole
Connect To Remote Location Configure Modem	Connects to the remote server. Configures the modem settings.
File Name: aconsole.exe	Directory: \public — Type: External

atconfig
OS: NetWare 4

Function	Configures the AppleTalk protocol on the NetWare server after AppleTalk has been implemented.
Syntax	load atconfig
File Name:	atconfig.nlm — Directory: — Type: External

ATM Console
OS: NetWare 5

Function	Starts a tool used for troubleshooting and monitoring ATM network traffic.
Syntax	atmcon
Link/ATM Network Interfaces	Shows a list of ATM networks.
File Name: atmcon.nlm	Directory: \system — Type: External

atotal
OS: NetWare 3,4,5

Function	Compiles accounting information and shows daily and weekly totals for connection time, service requests, number of blocks read and written, and the disk storage utilized per day.
Syntax	atotal [> *file*] [options...]
/c	Doesn't pause after each screen. Scrolls continuously.
/?	Shows help information.
file	Specifies the path- and filename to redirect the accounting information.
NW4, NW5:	
/ver	Shows utility version number and a list of all files it uses to execute.
File Name: atotal.exe	Directory: **NW3:** \system, **NW4, NW5:** \public — Type: External
Note:	Accounting services must be active on server for `atotal` to work.
atotal >n:\ucg	Redirects the output of atotal to the file ucg on n:.

atpscon
OS: NetWare 4

Function	Configures the AppleTalk printing service on NetWare server.
Syntax	load atpscon
Quick Configuration	Creates spooler, queue, and print server with default values.
Configure Printer Servers	Specifies a print server on AppleTalk that connects to a print server in NetWare.
Define Printer Models	Specifies printers of a new type.
Log Options	Shows and configures system and printer logs.
Management Options	Configures AppleTalk Printing Service regarding fonts and internal files.
Change Context	Changes the position in the NDS tree.

attach
OS: NetWare 3

Function	Connects to another file server and still remains logged on to your current file server.
Syntax	attach *{ server }/{ username }*
server	Specifies the name of the file server to attach to.
username	Specifies the username to use on the file server.
File Name: attach.exe	Directory: \public — Type: External
attach UCG/Myles	Attaches to the file server UCG as user Myles.

atxrp
OS: NetWare 4

Function	Connects a driver to `pserver` that lets users connected to the NetWare server print on AppleTalk printers.
Syntax	load atxrp

auditcon		OS:	NetWare 4,5
Function	Tracks a user's activity on the server regarding applications, files transferred, or printers the user has used and produces a report that can be submitted for billing purposes.		
Syntax	auditcon [/VER]		
/VER	Shows version information.		
File Name: `auditcon.exe`	Directory: \public	Type:	External

bindfix		OS:	NetWare 3
Function	Corrects the data in the bindery files if the file has been corrupted. It creates new versions of the files `NET$OBJ.SYS`, `NET$PROP.SYS`, and `NET$VAL.SYS`. The old files are saved with .old extension.		
Syntax	bindfix		
File Name: `bindfix.exe`	Directory: \system	Type:	External

bindrest		OS:	NetWare 3
Function	Restores the bindery files `NET$OBJ.OLD`, `NET$PROP.OLD`, and `NET$VAL.OLD` created with `bindfix.`		
Syntax	bindrest		
File Name: `bindrest.exe`	Directory: \system	Type:	External
Warning:	If a `bindfix` run fails, the old settings can be restored immediately if the .old files have not been deleted.		

breqnt		OS:	NetWare 5,6
Function	Starts the Btrieve requester for Btrieve databases on an NT client.		
Syntax	breqnt [options...]		
/d:*length*	Specifies the maximum data message length (default is 4096).		
/c:1 or 0	Enables or disables NetWare runtime server support (default is enabled).		
/o:1 or 0	Enables or disables real-time data compression (default is disabled).		
/l	Allows Btrieve to be loaded multiple times.		
/s:*NR*	Specifies the maximum number of connected servers (default is 8).		
/t:*NR*	Specifies the maximum number of client IDs (default is 0).		
/u	Unloads Btrieve from memory.		
File Name: `breqnt.exe`	Directory: \pvsw\clients	Type:	External
breqnt /c:0 /o:1	Disables the NetWare runtime server support and enables real-time data compression.		

breqtcp		OS:	NetWare 5,6
Function	Is used as the Btrieve requester to gain access to data that is stored on a Windows 2000 or NT4 Citrix server. This may be loaded from the command line or from within the autoexec file.		
Syntax	breqtcp [options...]		
/c:*server*	Specifies the runtime server that is used.		
/d:*length*	Specifies the maximum message length that is used (default is 4096 bytes).		
/l:*value*	Specifies how many times the DOS session is loaded (default is only once).		
/o:*value*	Enables real-time data compression (default is disabled).		
/s:*server*	Sets the maximum allowable number of connected servers (default is 8).		
/t:*NR*	Sets the maximum allowable number of client IDs (default is 0).		
/u:*object*	Unloads the specified Btrieve object from memory.		
File Name: `breqtcp.exe`	Directory: \pvsw\clients\dos	Type:	External
breqtcp /s:3	Sets the maximum allowable number of connected servers to 3.		

brequtil

OS:	NetWare 3,4,5
Function	A utility for Btrieve databases used to unload the brequester `brequest.exe` from the client workstation.
Syntax	brequtil option

-ver	Shows version information.
-stop	Unloads the brequester `brequest.exe` from the client workstation.
NW4, NW5:	
-reset *ID*	Resets the Btrieve connection specified by the connection *ID*.

File Name:	`brequtil.exe`	**Directory:**	\public	**Type:**	External
Tip:	You must load the brequester `brequest.exe` before this command works.				

Btrieve Monitor

OS:	NetWare 3,4
Function	Monitors all activity of the Btrieve process at the server. Includes monitoring active files and users as well as current, peak, and maximum values for files.
Syntax	load btrmon

Active Resources	Shows active files, and their users and owners.
User Information	Shows Btrieve users and files they are using.
Resource Usage	Shows current, maximum, and peak values for files, handles, locks, and active users.
Communication Statistics	Shows statistics for the loaded SPX protocol module.
Files	Shows listing over active files.
Handles	Shows how often files have been opened and any lock usage.
Transactions	Shows active transactions.
Clients	Shows the number of clients.
Threads	Shows the number of consecutive Btrieve processes.

File Name:	`btrmon.nlm`	**Directory:**	\system	**Type:**	External
Tip:	Great utility for monitoring your Btrieve database server.				

Btrieve NDS Support Utility

OS:	NetWare 4
Function	Allows you to install or remove Btrieve server objects by registering Btrieve in NDS. This may be run from the command line (which starts a menu) or via the Btrieve setup utility `bsetup`.
Syntax	load bdirect

File Name:	`bdirect.nlm`	**Directory:**	\system	**Type:**	External
Tip:	For an overview of the Btrieve server-based Record Manager, see the command `btrieve.nlm`.				

Btrieve Roll Forward (DOS)

OS:	NetWare 3,4,5
Function	Recovers changes to Btrieve files from the time between a system failure and the latest backup. DOS version. The OS/2 version is `pbroll.exe` and the MS-Windows version is `wbroll.exe`.
Syntax	brollfwd *file* [options...] brollfwd /a [options...]

/a	Recovers all Btrieve files in the `BLOG.GFG` file.
/d:*kbytes*	Sets the size of the data buffer in kilobytes (default is 8KB, min is 1KB, max is 64KB).
/t:*bytes*	Sets the length of the data that is in the operation list file in bytes.
/k:*bytes*	Sets the key length for the operation list file in bytes.
/h	Shows the operations in the list file in hexadecimal form (default is decimal).
/v	Adds information about user, address, source, time, and so forth to the log file.
/l	Lists the operations that would be executed on STDOUT without doing them.
/o	Specifies the name of the owner of the Btrieve file.
file	Specifies the single Btrieve file or a text file containing a list of Btrieve files.

File Name:	`brollfwd.exe`	**Directory:**	\public	**Type:**	External
Tip:	For an overview of the Btrieve server-based record manager, please see `btrieve.nlm`.				

Btrieve Roll Forward (Windows)

OS:	NetWare 3,4,5
Function	Recovers changes to Btrieve files from the time between a system failure and the latest backup. MS-Windows version. The OS/2 version is `pbroll.exe` and the DOS version is `brollfwd.exe`.
Syntax	wbroll
File Name:	`wbroll.exe`
Directory:	\public
Type:	External
Tip:	For an overview of the Btrieve server-based record manager, please see `btrieve.nlm`.

Btrieve Setup Utility

OS:	NetWare 3,4
Function	The main interface for altering the settings for Btrieve's configuration options. Allows viewing and altering current settings, rebuilding or setting up directory services, or installing/removing Btrieve objects.
Syntax	load bsetup
Set Btrieve Configuration	Shows the current configuration settings for Btrieve.
Set Rebuild Configuration	Shows or alters the rebuild configuration settings and shows the rebuild log file.
Set Directory Services	Installs or removes a specified Btrieve server object from a specified directory.
File Name:	`bsetup.nlm`
Directory:	\system
Type:	External

Btrieve SPX Remote Communication

OS:	NetWare 3,4
Function	Loads the Btrieve SPX Communications stub, which monitors outgoing requests for Btrieve for remote server activity. Load this locally. Is used when `bspxcom` isn't loaded.
Syntax	load rspxstub
File Name:	`rspxstub.nlm`
Directory:	\system
Type:	External

butil (client)

OS:	NetWare 5,6
Function	Detects damaged Btrieve files and can also repair or rebuild corrupted files.
Syntax	butil [option]
-clone *outfile infile*	Creates a new file with the same properties, including indexes.
/oowner	Specifies the owner name of the Btrieve original.
-clrowner *infile /oowner*	Removes the owner name that is associated with the Btrieve file.
@commandfile outfile	Specifies the name and full path to a command file to be used by `butil`.
-copy *infile outfile*	Copies one Btrieve file's contents to another one with the specified owner names.
/oowner1	Specifies the owner name of the Btrieve original.
/oowner2	Specifies the owner name of the Btrieve copy.
-create *outfile file* [y | n]	Creates a new Btrieve file based upon a description file.
-drop *infile { keyNR } { syskey }*	Removes a specified key index number from the specified Btrieve file.
/oowner	Specifies the owner name of the Btrieve original.
-index *infile indexfile file*	Creates an external index from a Btrieve file as described by a description file.
/oowner	Specifies the owner name of the Btrieve original.
-load *unfile outfile*	Loads a sequential file's contents (ASCII) into a Btrieve file.
/oowner	Specifies the owner name of the Btrieve original.
-recover *infile unfile*	Reads from a Btrieve file and creates a sequential file (ASCII).
/oowner	Specifies the owner name of the Btrieve original.
-reset [processID]	Resets the specified process.
-save *infile unfile*	Reads from the Btrieve file and then saves data to the specified sequential file.
	Choose only one of the following two:
y *ifile*	Specifies the index file instead of lowest key number.
n *keyNR*	Specifies the key number by which to save records (default is 0).
/oowner1	Specifies the owner name of the Btrieve original.
/oowner2	Specifies the owner name of the Btrieve copy.
-setowner *infile*	Assigns a specific owner to the specified Btrieve file with a specific access level.
/oowner1	Specifies the owner name of the Btrieve original.
level	Specifies the restriction level. Value can be 0, 1, 2, or 3.

continued

-sindex *infile { defile } { syskey }*	Creates an index for the specified file as directed by the description file.
keyNR	Specifies the key number by which to save records.
/oowner	Specifies the owner name of the Btrieve original.
-stat *infile*	Reports file attribute and size information about Btrieve files to the user.
/oowner	Specifies the owner name of the Btrieve original.
-ver	Shows version information.

File Name: `butil.exe` **Directory:** \pvsw\clients\dos **Type:** External

Call Connection Manager — OS: NetWare 5

Function	Shows information about current calls, as well as initiating and terminating calls.
Syntax	callmgr

File Name: `callmgr.nlm` **Directory:** \system **Type:** External

CAPI Tracer — OS: NetWare 5

Function	Traces and monitors negotiations between the CAPI manager and CAPI driver for PPP and ISDN connections.
Syntax	capitrce

File Name: `capitrce.nlm` **Directory:** \system **Type:** External

Note: You must load `capimgr.nlm` before this trace utility can be used.

castoff — OS: NetWare 3

Function	Disables network messages from other workstations and from the server console if the ALL option is used.
Syntax	castoff [ALL]
ALL	Disables all network messages from workstations and server consoles.

File Name: `castoff.exe` **Directory:** \public **Type:** External

Tip: You may also use an "A" instead of "ALL" to accomplish the same thing.

caston — OS: NetWare 3

Function	Enables network messages from other workstations and the server console that were disabled by `castoff`.
Syntax	caston

File Name: `caston.exe` **Directory:** \public **Type:** External

Catalog Services — OS: NetWare 5

Function	Creates a flat database catalog file containing frequently accessed NDS objects, giving them faster access.
Syntax	dscat
	The catalog services consists of the following components:
dscat.nlm	Identifies the engine that provides extended searching capabilities for the NDS database.
dscqry16.dll	Identifies the 16-bit version of the query engine used by NetWare Administrator.
dscqry32.dll	Identifies the 32-bit version of the query engine used by NetWare Administrator.
dscatmgr.dll	Identifies the NetWare Administrator snap-in used to manage the catalog services.

File Name: `dscat.nlm` **Directory:** \system **Type:** External

cdinst — OS: NetWare 5,6

Function	Loads legacy support for CD-ROMs and enables them to be mounted as traditional NetWare volumes.
Syntax	cdinst [option]
/? or /H	Shows help information.
/V=*volume*	Specifies the volume to store the CD-ROM index files (default is SYS:).
/DISPLAYON	Shows directory, filenames, and total file count while the volume is being mounted.

File Name: `cdinst.nlm` **Directory:** \system **Type:** External

Note: This is the same command as `cdrom.nlm` found in NW3 and NW4.

cdrom

OS: NetWare 3,4

Function	Loads support for CD-ROMs and enables them to be mounted as NetWare volumes.
Syntax	load cdrom [option]

/? or /H	Shows help information.
/V=*volume*	Specifies the volume to store the CD-ROM index files (default is SYS:).
/DISPLAYON	Shows directory, filenames, and total file count while the volume is being mounted.

File Name:	`cdrom.nlm`	**Directory:**	\system	**Type:**	External

Tip: After loading the `cdrom.nlm`, use the command `cd` to manage the CD-ROM.

cdrom (nss)

OS: NetWare 5,6

Function	Enables support for CD-ROMs and automatically mounts or remounts CD-ROMs as NSS volumes.
Syntax	cdrom

File Name:	`cdrom.nlm`	**Directory:**	\system	**Type:**	External

charset

OS: NetWare 5,6

Function	Sets the code page support for keyboard characters for different countries.
Syntax	charset *codepage* [stay]

codepage	Specifies the code page to use — for example, CP850.
stay	Keeps the `charset` resident instead of unloading after changing the code page.
	The following is a listing of code pages, their region, and language support:.
CP852, CP775	Keyboard code pages for Central Europe — Extended Latin.
CP437, CP850, CP860, CP863, CP865	Keyboard code pages for Western Europe — Extended Latin.
CP932, CP936, CP949, CP950	Keyboard code pages for the Far East.
CP737	Keyboard code pages for Greece — Greek.
CP862	Keyboard code pages for Israel — Hebrew.
CP949	Keyboard code pages for Korea — Hangul.
CP864	Keyboard code pages for Middle East — Arabic.
CP855, CP866	Keyboard code pages for Russia — Cyrillic.

File Name:	`charset.nlm`	**Directory:**	c:\nwserver	**Type:**	External

charset cp850	Changes the code page to 850.

chgrp

OS: NetWare 4

Function	Changes the group ownership of a file in an NFS file system. Must own the file and belong to the same group.
Syntax	chgrp [-f] *group file*

-f	Shows no output if the command fails.
group	Specifies a group name or a group ID number.
file	Specifies the path to the file to change group permissions for.

File Name:	`chgrp.exe`	**Directory:**	\public	**Type:**	External

chgrp team testfile	Gives a new group membership to team for testfile.
chgrp team f:\nfs\asd.txt	Specifies team as new group for the file `asd.txt` in `f:\nfs`.

chkdir

OS: NetWare 3

Function	Shows some information like available space, usage, and capacity about the specified volume or directory.
Syntax	chkdir *{path }*

path	Specifies either a volume or a directory to show information about.

File Name:	`chkdir.exe`	**Directory:**	\public	**Type:**	External

chkdir u:	Shows information about the specified volume.

chkvol

OS: NetWare 3

Function	Shows volume information, such as free space, space usage, deleted files usage, and user available space.
Syntax	chkvol *{ volume }* [/C]

continued

volume		Specifies which volume to show information on. (Specify a question mark ? to show all valid volumes.)			
/C		Shows information about volumes continuously without pausing after every page.			
File Name:	`chkvol.exe`	**Directory:**	\public	**Type:**	External
Tip:	Use an asterisk * to show information on all volumes connected to the computer.				
chkvol ? /C		Shows information about all volumes in one list.			
Chkvol UCG/vol1: UCG/vol2:		Shows information of the volumes vol1 and vol2 on server UCG.			

chmod — OS: NetWare 4

Function	Changes the access rights of a file in an NFS file system.
Syntax	chmod [-f] *mode file*

-f	Shows no output if the command fails.
mode	Sets the new access rights of the file.
file	Specifies the entire path to the file to change the access rights for.
	The following are `modes` that can be used. Combines into permissions. Type in three digits, these are for owner, group, and other, respectively.
1	Specifies execute rights.
2	Specifies write rights.
3	Specifies write and execute rights.
4	Specifies read rights.
5	Specifies read and execute rights.
6	Specifies read and write rights.
7	Specifies read, write, and execute rights.

File Name:	`chmod.exe`	**Directory:**	\public	**Type:**	External
Note:	Requires the NetWare NFS services.				
chmod 654 testfile	Sets the access rights read and write for owner, read and execute for group, and read for others.				

chown — OS: NetWare 4

Function	Changes the ownership of a file in an NFS file system.
Syntax	chown [-f] *owner file*

-f		Shows no output if the command fails.			
owner		Sets the new owner of the file.			
file		Specifies the complete path to file to change the ownership for.			
File Name:	`chown.exe`	**Directory:**	\public	**Type:**	External
Note:	Requires the NetWare NFS services.				
chown bratton testfile		Changes the ownership for the file testfile in current directory to user bratton.			

colorpal — OS: NetWare 3,4

Function	Changes the color palette for the NetWare menu-based utilities.				
Syntax	colorpal				
File Name:	`colorpal.exe`	**Directory:**	\public	**Type:**	External

Communication Port Configuration — OS: NetWare 5,6

Function	Configures, modifies, and traces communication ports or port groups used for remote access to the network.
Syntax	aiocon

Configures Ports		Used to modify existing ports by pressing Enter or add a new port by pressing Insert.			
Configures Port Groups		Used to create or modify groups of communication ports.			
Manage Ports		Used for tracing communication ports to assist in troubleshooting.			
File Name:	`aiocon.nlm`	**Directory:**	\system	**Type:**	External

Configure Print Jobs — OS: NetWare 3,4

Function	Configures, creates, or deletes print job configurations.
Syntax	printcon

Edit Print Job Configurations	Edits, creates, or deletes print job configurations.
Select Default Print Job	Selects the default print job.

continued

Change Current Object Change Current NetWare Server	**The following option is used in NDS mode (use F4 to change mode):** Changes the current object. **The following option is used in bindery mode (use F4 to change mode):** Changes the server that is administered.				
File Name:	`printcon.exe`	**Directory:**	/public	**Type:**	External
Note:	This command is used with `capture`, `nprint`, `netuser`, and `pconsole`.				

ConsoleOne (Client) — OS: NetWare 5,6

Function	The Java-based management console that allows you to manage NDS objects, permissions, and schemas.				
Syntax	consoleone				
File Name:	`consoleone.exe`	**Directory:**	\public\mgmt\consoleone\1.2\bin	**Type:**	External

ConsoleOne (Server) — OS: NetWare 5,6

Function	A script that loads Java, the X-window server, and ConsoleOne, used to manage NDS objects and permissions.				
Syntax	c1start				
File Name:	`c1start.ncf`	**Directory:**	\system	**Type:**	Script

ConsoleOneDos — OS: NetWare 5,6

Function	The Java-based management console that allows you to manage NDS objects, permissions, and schemas. This command can also be executed from DOS and provides all the functionality found in ConsoleOne.				
Syntax	consoleonedos				
File Name:	`consoleonedos.exe`	**Directory:**	\public\mgmt\consoleone\1.2\bin	**Type:**	External

CPE Configuration Console — OS: NetWare 5,6

Function	A menu utility used to configure devices (modems and so forth) on the serial port (COM1) on the server.				
Syntax	cpecfg				
Configure Async Port CPE Communication Screen Upload Command File	Configures communication parameters for the COM1 port. Opens a terminal window connected to the COM1 port. Uploads a configuration file to the device on the port.				
File Name:	`cpecfg.nlm`	**Directory:**	\system	**Type:**	External
Note:	`Aiocomx.nlm` must be loaded to use this tool.				

cset — OS: NetWare 5,6

Function	Configures set parameters relating to the NetWare server's operation and performance. Specifies the category, walks you through all available settings. For a complete list of categories, see `set`.
Syntax	cset *category*
category	Specifies the set category that you need to walk through and set values for. (The categories are found in the command set.)
cset memory	Steps through the cache buffer blocks, garbage collection, and corruption checking settings.
cset file system	Steps through the disk warning message usage, volume settings, and delete wait state settings.

CSLIB Audit Trail Utility — OS: NetWare 5,6

Function	Configures the global parameters for the audit trail database and can enable or disable audit trail logging for specific products or groups of products.				
Syntax	csaudit				
Audit Trail Configuration Display Audit Trail Records Exit Audit Trail Utility	Configures the global parameters for the audit trail database. Shows the contents of the current or archived audit trail log files. Exits the utility.				
File Name:	`csaudit.nlm`	**Directory:**	\system	**Type:**	External

cssysmsg

OS: NetWare 5,6

Function	The CSLIB system messages facility used for enabling or disabling various system messages and initiating system message logging.
Syntax	cssysmsg *{ ACTION }*

ACTION	**You may specify only one of the following actions:**
cedbgflush	Flushes any wrap files from their targets.
cedbgfmtmblkdetailoff	Disables the global formatting of the `mblk_t` control structure.
cedbgfmtmblkdetailon	Enables the global formatting of the `mblk_t` control structure.
cedbgfmttimeoff	Disables the output of any timestamp that uses formatted hex dumps.
cedbgfmttimeon	Enables the output of any timestamp that uses formatted hex dumps.
cedbdintoff	Disables the CeLib-supported internal debugging commands.
cedbdinton	Enables the CeLib-supported internal debugging commands.
cedbglist	Shows a list of any current files that are being managed.
cedbgoff	Ends the SysMsg-to-CsSysMsg logging process.
cedbgon	Starts the SysMsg-to-CsSysMsg logging process.
cememmanlist	Shows any CeLib memory manager clients that are currently active.
cememstats	Toggles memory statistic recording.
ceresourcecheck	Toggles the memory resource check for CeLib.
cssysmsg	Shows help information for CeLib.
sysmsg	Shows any registered system messages.
sysmsgflush	Clears the `cssysmsg.log` file.

File Name:	`cssysmsg.nlm`	**Directory:**	\system	**Type:**	External

cssysmsg cedbgfmtmblkdetailon	Enables the global formatting of the `mblk_t` control structure.

dhcpcfg

OS: NetWare 4

Function	Configures and manages the DHCP from the server console.
Syntax	load dhcpcfg

File Name:	`dhcpcfg.nlm`	**Directory:**	\system	**Type:**	External

dilog

OS: NetWare 5

Function	Creates a trace log file for ISDN connections to troubleshoot connection problems.
Syntax	dilog *logfile*

logfile	Specifies the name of the file to store trace information.

File Name:	`dilog.nlm`	**Directory:**	\system	**Type:**	External

Disk Usage Utility

OS: NetWare 3

Function	A utility that is used to limit a user's disk space on a volume or a directory.
Syntax	dspace [option]

Change File Server	Selects the server to work with.
User Restrictions	Limits the disk space for a user.
Directory Restrictions	Limits the disk space in a directory.

File Name:	`dspace.exe`	**Directory:**	\public	**Type:**	External

Display Environment

OS: NetWare 5,6

Function	Shows current search paths and current values of the settable server parameters.
Syntax	display environment

Display Interrupts

OS: NetWare 5,6

Function	Shows hardware interrupts, interrupt handlers, and interrupt statistics. If no option is specified, it shows interrupts currently in use.
Syntax	display interrupts [option]

number	Shows information on a specific interrupt or multiple interrupts separated by a space.

continued

all proc alloc real	Shows information about all interrupts. Shows interrupt information per-processor in multi-processor servers. Shows allocated interrupts. Shows real-mode interrupts that have returned for processing in protected mode.
display interrupts 5 10	Shows information on interrupts 5 and 10.

Display IPX Networks

OS: NetWare 5,6

Function	Shows all available IPX networks that the server knows about.
Syntax	display ipx networks

Display IPX Servers

OS: NetWare 5,6

Function	Shows IPX servers. Can show a specified server or multiple servers using wildcards or all with no option.
Syntax	display IPX servers { *server* }
server	Specifies a server to show. Wildcards (*) can select multiple servers.
display ipx server v*	Shows all servers that start with "v".

Display Modified Environment

OS: NetWare 5,6

Function	Shows current and default settings for the server's environment. An easy way to see which settings have changed.
Syntax	display modified environment

Display Processors

OS: NetWare 5,6

Function	Shows the status of all processors installed in the server computer.
Syntax	Display Processors { *number* }

Display SLP Addresses

OS: NetWare 6

Function	Shows all SLP (Service Location Protocol) network service addresses.
Syntax	display slp addresses

Display SLP Attributes

OS: NetWare 5,6

Function	Shows active SLP (Service Location Protocol) attributes that are available on the network.
Syntax	display slp attributes *url* { *attributes...* }
url *attributes...*	Shows all attributes that are registered with the specified service. Specifies a comma-separated list of attributes to show for the specified service.

Display SLP Services

OS: NetWare 5,6

Function	Shows active SLP (Service Location Protocol) services available on the network.
Syntax	display slp services { *type/scope/query* }
type *scope* *query*	Specifies the service type to show information about. Specifies the scope of services to show. Shows services that match the query restriction. Supports operators: ==, <=, and >=.

dnipinst

OS: NetWare 5,6

Function	Extends the NDS schema for DNS/DHCP objects after installing the DNS/DHCP server.				
Syntax	dnipinst [-r]				
-r		Removes the DNS/DHCP extensions from the NDS schema.			
File Name:	`dnipinst.nlm`	**Directory:**	\system	**Type:**	External

DNS/DHCP Managment Console

OS: NetWare 5,6

Function	Manages the DNS/DHCP services for the network. Creates services, import/export & global DHCP preferences.				
Syntax	dnsdhcp				
File Name:	`dnsdhcp.exe`	**Directory:**	\Program Files\Novell\DNSDHCP	**Type:**	External

dnscnvrt

OS: NetWare 5,6

Function	Converts the Btrieve DNS files used in NW 4.x into a BIND file format, to be imported into the new DNS.
Syntax	dnscnvrt
File Name:	`dnscnvrt.nlm` **Directory:** \system **Type:** External

dosnp

OS: NetWare 3

Function	The Named Pipe Extender for DOS, which allows the user to run DOS Named Pipe applications.
Syntax	dosnp [option] *{ ACTION }*
-	Loads the Extender into memory.
/	Same as –.
	Specifies which DOS extender Action to take. Only one may be selected.
i	Shows version information.
u	Unloads the Extender if it is loaded.
?	Shows help information.
File Name:	`dosnp.exe` **Directory:** \public\client **Type:** External
Note:	In order to use DOSNP with MS-Windows, you must load these commands in order: IPX, DOSNP, NETx (ems or xms can also be loaded here), and finally TBMI if needed.
dosnp -	Loads the DOS Extender into memory.

DS Diagnostics

OS: NetWare 5,6

Function	Shows current NDS configuration, checks the status of the NDS tree, and diagnoses problems.
Syntax	dsdiag
Generate Report	Specifies the kind of report the user wants to generate.
Check The NDS Versions	Shows information about each server in the user's tree of NDS.
Check NDS Background Process Status	Shows status on each server, based on the user's selection in General Options.
List Server Partition Table	Shows the server's NDS partitions and generates a report that documents the servers.
List Replica Rings	Shows a list of replica rings and reports unreachable partitions.
Check Partition Status	Shows information about the server's partitions.
Compare Replica Rings	Generates a report to compare for each partition found with other replicas.
Return To Previous Menu	Returns to the previous menu.
Distributed Repair	Specifies certain repair options on portions.
Remove Monitored Network Addresses	Removes user's properties and scans certain parts of the directory tree.
Return To Previous Menu	Returns to the previous menu.
Preferences	Generates diagnostic reports and sets up defaults for DSDIAG.
Manage Naming Conventions	Specifies the object name the user wants to use.
Manage Identities	Enters a new NDS object.
Preferences	Configures the display and format values in the generated reports.
Return To Previous Menu	Returns to the previous menu.
Exit	Exits the DSDIAG interface.
File Name:	`dsdiag.nlm` **Directory:** \system **Type:** External

DSMigrate

OS: NetWare 4

Function	The utility used to migrate the directory structure from NW3.1x to the NDS directory tree of NW4.11.
Syntax	dsmigrat
File Name:	`dsmigrat.exe` **Directory:** \system\dsmigrat **Type:** External
Note:	This is usually started from the NWAdmin utility, but may be started from the directory if you have read/write privileges of the Dsmigrate directory.

dstrace

OS: NetWare 5,6

Function	Traces Novell Directory Services events. Used with no option, it shows current status and all tags.
Syntax	dstrace [options...] *{ tags... }*
on	Starts tracing.

continued

off	Ends tracing.
file	Logs to a file.
screen	Shows log messages on the screen.
inline	Shows log messages inline.
journal	Shows log messages on a separate screen.
fmax=*size*	Specifies the max log file size.
fname=*name*	Specifies the log filename.
tags...	Specifies a list of event tags to trace. Use dstrace alone to show tags. (Use -tag to switch off tracing or +tag to switch on tracing.)
File Name: `dstrace.nlm`	**Directory:** \system **Type:** External
dstrace screen on +sync	Starts tracing on the screen and switches on tracing for sync.

dtrace

OS: NetWare 5

Function	A menu-based utility used to monitor and trace ISDN connections using U.S. Riobotics ISDN adapters.
Syntax	dtrace
File Name: `dtrace.nlm`	**Directory:** \system **Type:** External

echo

OS: NetWare 5,6

Function	Shows messages on the screen that are specified by text.
Syntax	echo *text*
text	Specifies the text messages to show.
File Name: `echo.nlm`	**Directory:** \system **Type:** External
echo Over 6,000 commands in the Universal Command Guide.	Shows Over 6,000 commands in the Universal Command Guide.

Emergency Console

OS: NetWare 5,6

Function	Allows the user to down the file server, cancel the volume mount, or start a new command-line process.
Syntax	Ctrl + Alt + Escape
	Starts a menu where you must select one of these four actions:
1	Downs the file server and then exits to DOS.
2	Cancels the volume mount.
3	Creates a new process from the command line.
Escape	Exits the menu.

endcap

OS: NetWare 3

Function	Terminates the capture of your workstation's LPT ports. This is used after the program capture has been used.
Syntax	endcap [options...]
/ALL	Cancels the capture on all LPT ports.
/Local=*NR*	Specifies which LPT port to end the capture on.
/Cancel	Cancels capture and discards any data without printing it.
/CancelLocal=*NR*	Cancels capture on the specified LPT port and discards any data without printing it.
/CancelALL	Cancels capture on all LPT ports and discards any data without printing it.
File Name: `endcap.exe`	**Directory:** \public **Type:** External

Enhanced SBACKUP

OS: NetWare 5,6

Function	These are the NLMs needed to configure SBACKUP on the server as well as their loading order.
Syntax	The NLM loading order: `smdr, tsa500, smsdi, qman, sbsc, sbcon.`
	The bold NLMs have been documented separately and contain more information:
smdr.nlm	Identifies the SMS data requester used to submit jobs and communicate with the TSA.
tsa500.nlm	Identifies the target service agent that registers with the SMDR.
smsdi.nlm	Identifies the SMS storage device interface used to communicate with backup devices.
qman.nlm	Identifies the job queue manager.
sbsc.nlm	Identifies the SBACKUP communication manager.
sbcon.nlm	Identifies the SBACKUP console used to create and monitor backup jobs.
File Name: `smdr.nlm, tsa500.nlm, smsdi.nlm, qman.nlm, sbsc.nlm, sbcon.nlm`	**Directory:** \system **Type:** External

env

OS: NetWare 5,6

Function	Shows the environment variables for the Java environment.
Syntax	env

envset

OS: NetWare 5,6

Function	Sets and shows variables for the Java environment.
Syntax	envset *{ variable }* [=*value*]

variable	Shows the specified variable.
variable=	Erases the specified variable.
value	Specifies what to assign to the variable.
string	Assigns string to variable.
$var2;string	Adds variable var2 and string together and assigns them to variable.

Note: Java.nlm must be loaded to use this command.

envset path1=/dir1	Sets path1 to /dir1.
envset path2=path1;/dir2	Sets path2 to /dir1;/dir2.

EpsonNet NDPS DriverSetup

OS: NetWare 5,6

Function	Starts a GUI that allows you to upload printer drivers to the broker service so the drivers become available to other users. You can browse for printer drivers and then choose to add them to the broker.
Syntax	slctdrv

File Name: `slctdrv.exe` **Directory:** \public\win32 **Type:** External

exit

OS: NetWare 3,4

Function	Exits to DOS after the server shuts down.
Syntax	exit

Tip: To cause the server to reboot after you exit, type `remove dos`.

extcheck

OS: NetWare 6

Function	Checks a Java archive for any title and version conflicts with the installed Java environment.
Syntax	extcheck [-verbose] *jararchive*

-verbose	Verbose mode. Shows more information.
jararchive	Specifies the .jar file to check.

extcheck ucg.jar	Checks the ucg.jar file for conflicts.

File Migration

OS: NetWare 4

Function	Migrates files from a NetWare 3.x server to a Netware 4.11 server.
Syntax	migwin3x

File Name: `migwin3x.exe` **Directory:** \public **Type:** External

File Salvage Utility

OS: NetWare 3

Function	Used to recover files that have been deleted or simply view deleted files.
Syntax	salvage

Salvage From Deleted Directories	Restores files when the parent directory also is erased.
Select Directories	Changes the current directory.
Set Salvage Options	Changes the sorting order of file lists.
View/Recover Deleted Files	Restores files from directories that still exist.

File Name: `salvage.exe` **Directory:** \public\ **Type:** External

File Server Console

OS: NetWare 3

Function	A menu tool used to show server status, send messages, and shut down the server.
Syntax	fconsole

Broadcast Console Message	Is used by supervisors to send messages to all users logged on to the server.
Change Current File Server	Alters the default file server.
Connection Information	Shows active server connection.
Down File Server	Shuts the file server down.

continued

Status	Shows the current server status.
Version Information	Shows version information for the server.
File Name: `fconsole.exe`	**Directory:** \public **Type:** External

flag

OS: NetWare 3

Function	Shows or modifies NetWare attributes for files and directories.
Syntax	flag *file* { *attributes...* } [options...] flag *file* [options...] [/name=*user*] [/owner=user]

- *attributes...*	Removes the specified attributes from a file or directory.
+ *attributes...*	Adds the specified attributes to the file or directory.
ALL	Sets all available attributes on the file or directory.
A	Sets that the file has been modified since the last backup.
Ci	Secures the files from being copied. (Only for MAC files.)
Di	Secures the file from being deleted or copied over.
H	Secures a file from being seen by the DOS command `dir`.
N	Sets the Read and Write attributes to default.
P	Purges the file immediately when it is deleted.
RA	Sets the read auditing on the file or directory. Tracks when a file is read.
Ri	Secures the file from being renamed.
Ro	Sets the Read Only attribute to the file.
Rw	Sets the Read and Write attributes to the file.
S	Sets the Share attribute to the file allowing many users at the same time.
Sy	Same as /H and also sets prevention from being copied or deleted.
T	Secures the file by use of the Transaction Tracking System.
WA	Sets the write auditing on the file or directory. Tracks when a file is written to.
X	Sets the Execute only attribute to the file. This attribute can't be removed. (The X attribute can only be set to .exe and .com files.)
/?	Shows help information.
SUB	Sets or views attributes in all subdirectories.
file	Specifies the file or directory to alter the attributes for.
File Name: `flag.exe`	**Directory:** \public **Type:** External
Note: The `filer` command also sets and views file attributes.	
flag ucgbook.mdb +s	Makes the file ucgbook.mdb shareable over the network.

flagdir

OS: NetWare 3

Function	Alters attributes for subdirectories in a specified directory.
Syntax	flagdir { *path flags* }

flags	Specifies flags to set to the directories. Below are the valid flags.
Normal	Removes all directory attributes that have been set.
System	Specifies the directory is used by the system.
Hidden	Hides the specified directory from DOS.
Deleteinhibit	Users with erase rights can't remove the directory.
Purge	Purges the directory files when they have been deleted.
Renameinhibit	Disables the feature that lets remote users rename directories.
path	Specifies the path to the directory that you want to view or change.
File Name: `flagdir.exe`	**Directory:** \public **Type:** External
flagdir u:\data hidden	Hides the specified directory from the dos dir command.

Frame Relay Console

OS: NetWare 5

Function	A management console that shows frame relay configuration and statistics using SNMP.
Syntax	frcon

	The main menu consists of these four items:
SNMP Access Configuration	Used to configure SNMP including the community string, poll interval, and timeout.
Frame Relay Interfaces	Shows a list of the frame relay interfaces.
Frame Relay Virtual Circuits	Shows a list of frame relay private virtual circuits (PVCs).
Displays Traps	Shows and optionally deletes messages in the SNMP trap log.
File Name: `frcon.nlm`	**Directory:** \system **Type:** External

Frame Relay Trace

OS:	NetWare 5
Function	A tracing utility used to monitor, capture, and show real-time statistics for frame relay interfaces.
Syntax	frtrace

Network Interface Information	Shows the IRQ, MEM address, I/O address, and channel for frame relay interfaces.
Network Interface Statistics	Shows many statistics regarding packets received and transmitted for an interface.
Real-Time Monitor	Monitors the data frames in real-time and shows the results.
Playback	Shows a captured session from disk or RAM.
Configuration	Configures the protocol, measurement time, and capture device for the trace.

File Name:	**Directory:**	**Type:**
`frtrace.nlm`	\system	External

frdisp

OS:	NetWare 5
Function	Reads the input trace file generated by `frtrace.nlm` and creates an output file in ASCII format.
Syntax	frdisp *inputfile* { *outputfile* }

/d	Translates the input file for the link management protocol and RFC 1490.
inputfile	Specifies the input trace filename that was created by `FRtrace`.
outputfile	Specifies the filename used for the ASCII output instead of showing on the screen.

File Name:	**Directory:**	**Type:**
`frdisp.exe`	\system\utils	External

grant

OS:	NetWare 3
Function	Adds trustee rights to users or groups on a file or a directory.
Syntax	grant *rights* [for *path*] to [USER] *username* [options...] grant *rights* [for *path*] to [GROUP] *groupname* [options...]

/SubDirectories	Uses subdirectories when setting trustees.
/Files	Uses files when setting trustees.
rights	Specifies rights to set for the specified user or group. (Separate multiple rights with spaces, e.g., For read and write: "R W".)
ALL	Gives all rights to the specified name. Supervisor rights are not included.
N	Gives no access to the specified name. (The following options can be prepended with ONLY or ALL BUT strings.)
S	Gives the specified name all rights for the specified directory and its files.
R	Gives the specified name access to read files.
W	Gives the specified name access to write to files.
C	Gives the specified name access to create directories and write to files.
E	Gives the specified name access to remove the directory and its content.
M	Gives the specified name access to modify file attributes.
F	Gives the specified name access to show directory content.
A	Gives the specified name access to modify file and directory trustees.
for *path*	Specifies the path to the volume, directory, subdirectory, or file to use.
username	Specifies the name of the user to grant rights for.
groupname	Specifies the name of the group that you want to set rights for.

File Name:	**Directory:**	**Type:**
`grant.exe`	\public	External

grant s for u:\public to user speed	Gives the user speed supervisor rights on u:\public.
grant r w f u:\data to group users	Gives the group users access to read, write, and show contents in u:\data.

halt

OS:	NetWare 4
Function	Used on one of the mirrored NetWare 4.11 SFT III server's IOEngines to bring that down. If you halt the primary IOEngine, the secondary IOEngine automatically becomes primary.
Syntax	halt

Hewlett-Packard NDPS Gateway

OS:	NetWare 5,6
Function	Configures gateways and public access printing settings for HP printers connected through HP JetDirect print servers. Also shows statistics information for those printers.
Syntax	hpgate

Printer gateways	Lists currently loaded printer gateways.

continued

Global gateway statistics	Shows printer gateway statistics, and job and process information.
Configuration	Configures gateways, search intervals, methods, and public access printers.
Exit gateway	Exits the console and unloads the module.

File Name: `hpgate.nlm` **Directory:** \system **Type:** External

HFS CD-ROM

OS: NetWare 4

Function	Mounts an HFS CD-ROM so it can be shared with Macintosh clients. Buffers data from the CD-ROM on the NetWare server to improve access time and transfer rate.
Syntax	load hfscd

File Name: `hfscd.nlm` **Directory:** \system **Type:** External

HFS CD-ROM Console Utility

OS: NetWare 4

Function	Configures the HFS CD-ROM module used by Macintosh clients.
Syntax	load hfscdcon

Disk List	Shows a list of scanned discs, shows status, mounts discs.
Migrator States	Shows the status of the migration process.
Manual Migrator Start	Removes files from the hard disk volume manually.
Setup	Sets up the driver, including mounting, scanning, migration, and disk space.
Exit	Exits the utility.

File Name: `hfscdcon.nlm` **Directory:** \system **Type:** External

httpbind

OS: NetWare 6

Function	Binds an IP address to the Web server. By default, only the first IP address for each network interface is bound.
Syntax	httpbind *ip-address* [/keyfile:"*certificate*"]

ip-address	Specifies the IP address to bind to the server.
/keyfile:"*certificate*"	Specifies an SSL certificate to use for the specified IP address.

httpbind 192.2.234.234	Binds the given IP address to the Web server.

httpcloseport

OS: NetWare 6

Function	Closes a specified TCP port on all addresses that are bound to HTTPSTK.
Syntax	httpcloseport *port*

port	Specifies the TCP port that is closed on all addresses that are bound to HTTPSTK

httpcloseport 22	Closes the TCP Port 22 if bound to HTTPSTK.

httpopenport

OS: NetWare 6

Function	Opens a specified TCP port or the port's SSL on all addresses that are bound to HTTPSTK.
Syntax	httpopenport *port* [/SSL]

/SSL	Enables the SSL on the specified TCP port.
port	Specifies the TCP port that is opened on all addresses that are bound to HTTPSTK

httpopenport 631 /SSL	Opens TCP port 631 and enables the port's SSL.

httpunbind

OS: NetWare 6

Function	Unbinds an IP address to the Web server.
Syntax	httpbind *ip-address*

ip-address	Specifies an IP address to remove from the Web server.

httpunbind 192.2.234.234	Unbinds the given IP address.

IBM Class of Service Set Manager

OS: NetWare 5,6

Function	A tool used to configure class of service. It defines TCP and UDP ports and sets priority for them.
Syntax	ibmcos

File Name: `ibmcos.nlm` **Directory:** \system **Type:** External

IBM Redundant NIC Utility

OS:	NetWare 5,6
Function	Manages redundant network interfaces.
Syntax	ibmrnic
File Name:	`ibmrnic.nlm`
Directory:	\system
Type:	External

ice

OS:	NetWare 6
Function	Imports and exports LDIF or comma-separated data files and exchanges data between two LDAP servers.
Syntax	ice [options...] -*SACTION* [options...] -*DACTION* [options...]

	These options may be used globally, but must come first:
-e *file*	Specifies the output file to receive any failed records.
-o	Overwrites any existing log file.
-l *file*	Specifies the log file to use.
-v	Verbose mode. Shows more information.
-c *URL*	Specifies the XML creation rule using the format: URL=`file://file`.
-s *URL*	Specifies the XML schema rule. Uses the same format as `-c` above.
-p *URL*	Specifies the XML placement rule. Uses the same format as `-c` above.
-?	Shows help information.
	These are the Actions available for the Source option `-s`:
LDAP [options...]	Specifies the source is an LDAP server.
-s *server*	Specifies the server to export from (default is the local host).
-p *port*	Specifies the port to export from (default is port 389).
-d *user*	Specifies the user to export from (default is `anonymous bind`).
-w *password*	Specifies the password to export (default is an empty string).
-F *value*	Uses the specified RFC-1558 LDAP search filter (default is `objectclass=*`).
-n	Shows the display operation, but doesn't run anything.
-a *{ value }*	Grabs a list of attributes according to the specified value.
1.1	Includes only entry names.
*	Includes all of the user attributes.
-R	Doesn't follow any referrals automatically.
-e *level*	Sets the debug level for LDAP.
-b *name*	Specifies the base DN for searching (default is an empty string).
-c *value*	Sets the total scope of the search. Values are: base, one, or sub (default is one).
-r *value*	Sets the alias differencing. Values are never, always, search, or find (default is never).
-l *NR*	Sets the maximum search time in seconds. A zero (0) means unlimited.
-z *NR*	Sets the maximum number of entries for each search. A zero (0) means unlimited.
-V *value*	Specifies the version of the protocol. Values are 2 or 3 (default is 3).
-v	Verbose mode. Shows more information.
-L *file*	Specifies the DER file that holds the SSL communication server key.
-A	Grabs only the attribute names, not the values.
-o *file*	Specifies which attributes to exclude. Use a comma-separated list.
LDIF [options...]	Specifies the source is a LDIF file.
-f *file*	Specifies the LDIF filename to export from.
-a	Adds records without specifying a change type.
-c	Stops the LDIF handler from halting whenever an error occurs.
-n	Shows what is done without executing it.
-v	Verbose mode. Shows more information.
DLIM [options...]	Specifies the source is a comma-separated data file.
-f *file*	Specifies the file that holds the comma-separated list that is used as a source.
	Either of these two options may be used:
-F *file*	Specifies the file that holds the order of the attributes to be used with `-f`.
-t *list*	Specifies a list containing the order of the attributes to be used with `-f`.
-c	Stops the LDIF handler from halting whenever an error occurs.
-n *attribute*	Sets the LDAP attribute name for the new object.
-l *path*	Sets the path that is appended to the RDN.
-o *list*	Specifies a comma-separated list of object classes.

continued

-i *list*	Specifies a comma-separated list of columns that are skipped. Integer values only.
-d *separator*	Sets the type of separator that is used instead of a comma (`,`).
-q *separator*	Sets the second separator that is used instead of double quotes (`"`).
	These are the Actions available for Destination option `-D`:
LDAP [options...]	Specifies the destination is an LDAP server.
-s *server*	Specifies the server to import from (default is the local host).
-p *port*	Specifies the port to import from (default is port 389).
-d *user*	Specifies the user to import from (default is `anonymous bind`).
-w *password*	Specifies the password to import (default is an empty string).
-e *level*	Sets the debug level for LDAP.
-V *value*	Specifies the version of the protocol. Values are 2 or 3 (default is 3).
-v	Verbose mode. Shows more information.
-B	Disables LBURP.
-F	Allows forward referencing.
-l	Adds hashed passwords.
-L *file*	Specifies the DER file that holds the SSL communication server key.
LDIF [options...]	Specifies the destination is a LDIF file.
-f *file*	Specifies the filename to import from.
-v	Verbose mode. Shows more information.
-B	Allows binary value output.
DLIM [options...]	Specifies the destination is a comma-separated data file.
-f *file*	Specifies the file that holds the comma-separated list that is stored.
	Either of these two options may be used:
-F *file*	Specifies the file that holds the order of the attributes to be used with `-f`.
-t *list*	Specifies a list containing the order of the attributes to be used with `-f`.
-v	Verbose mode. Shows more information.
-l *value*	Tells the driver to put the DN or RDN in the data (default is RDN).
-d *separator*	Sets the type of separator that is used instead of a comma (,).
-q *separator*	Sets the second separator that is used instead of double quotes (").
-n *value*	Sets the attribute name convention to append when importing.

File Name:	`ice.exe`	**Directory:**	\public\mgmt\consoleone\1.2\bin	**Type:**	External

idlj

OS: NetWare 6

Function	Starts the Interface Definition Language to Java compiler, which creates Java bindings from a specified IDL file.
Syntax	idlj [options...] *file*

-fclient	Creates client-side bindings of the specified file.
-fserver	Creates server-side bindings.
-fall	Creates both server and client-side bindings.
-fallTIE	Creates Tie Model bindings (a specific server-side model).
-td *directory*	Directs the created files to the specified directory instead of the current directory.
-i *directory*	Specifies the directory where an included file of the specified file is located.
-emitAll	Creates all types of the specified IDL file and any types that the IDL file includes.
-pkgPrefix *type* com.*prefix*	Specifies that the package type will contain the specified prefix.
type	Specifies the package type.
prefix	Specifies the prefix name.
-d *symbol*	Specifies a symbol to use for compilation other than those already defined in the IDL.
-keep	Prevents the compiler from overwriting any Java bindings that already exist.
-v	Verbose mode. Shows more information.
-version	Shows version information.
file	Specifies the IDL file that is used as the source for creating the Java bindings.

inetd

OS: NetWare 5,6

Function	Starts IP services (like FTP, telnet...) when they are requested. Configuration file is `SYS:\etc\inetd.cfg`.
Syntax	inetd *{ cfgfile }*

cfgfile	Specifies a different configuration file to use instead of `SYS:\etc\inetd.cfg`

File Name:	`inetd.nlm`	**Directory:**	\system	**Type:**	External

initd SYS:\new\etc\initd.cfg	Starts `inetd` with a different configuration file.

In-Place Upgrade

OS:	NetWare 5,6
Function	Upgrades a legacy NetWare volume to a new NSS volume by copying or moving files between the volumes.
Syntax	Syntax1: ipcu *NWvolume* Syntax2: ipcu *NWvolume NSSvolume* Syntax3: ipcu -d *NWvolume NSSvolume*

Syntax1:	Moves the contents of a NetWare volume to a new NSS volume
Syntax2:	Copies the contents of a NetWare volume to a new NSS volume.
Syntax3:	Moves the contents of a NetWare volume to a new NSS volume.
NWvolume	Specifies the name of legacy volume name to upgrade to NSS.
NSSvolume	Identifies the name of the NSS volume to create. The extension _NSS is added to the name.

File Name:	`ipcu.nlm`	**Directory:**	\system	**Type:**	External
Note:	You can't perform an in-place upgrade on volume SYS.				

install (dos client)

OS:	NetWare 3
Function	Installs the NetWare client on a host. It allows you to select directory, select and configure networks card, decide if Windows support is to be added and if autoexec.bat and config.sys should be updated.
Syntax	install

File Name:	`install.bat`	**Directory:**	\public\client	**Type:**	External

Internet Access Server

OS:	NetWare 5
Function	Configures and shows different protocols, settings, and statuses by calling many other network utilities.
Syntax	niascfg

Configure NIAS	Configures remote access and calls `inetcfg` to configure protocols and routing.
View Status for NIAS	Shows status for remote access and many different protocols.

The following applications are called by niascfg to show current status:

AppleTalk console (atcon.nlm) IPX console (ipxcon.nlm) TCP/IP console (tcpcin.nlm)
X.25 console (x25con.nlm) ATM console (atmcon.nlm) PPP console (pppcon.nlm)
Frame Relay Console (frcon.nlm).

File Name:	`niascfg.nlm`	**Directory:**	\system	**Type:**	External

iptrace

OS:	NetWare 5,6
Function	Traces IP traffic over the net and shows each router hop for a host.
Syntax	iptrace *host* [options...]

NW5, NW6	
hops=*NR*	Specifies the maximum number of hops (default is 30).
wait=*sec*	Specifies the timeout (default is 5 seconds).
port=*port*	Specifies that destination ports must be greater than 5999 (default is 40001).
noresolv	Doesn't resolve any names - useful when no DNS is configured.
newlog	Restarts the IPtrace log file `iptrace.log`.
host	Specifies hostname or IP address to do a trace to.
NW6	
starthop=*ttl*	Specifies the starting TTL hop value (default is 1).
pkt=*NR*	Specifies the number of packets to be sent with each hop (default is 3).
pmtubhr	Uses the MPTU Black Hole Router detection when tracing IP traffic.
source=*address*	Specifies the source address of the outgoing interface.

File Name:	`iptrace.nlm`	**Directory:**	\system	**Type:**	External
iptrace www.ucgbook.com		Shows router hops to the Universal Command Guide web site.			

jar

OS:	NetWare 6
Function	Creates, shows, and extracts files form a Java archive.
Syntax	jar [options...] *{ jarfile } { manifest }* [-C *directory*] *files...*

	One of the following four options must be specified.
-c	Creates an archive.
-t	Lists the contents of an archive.
-x	Extracts the specified files or all files.

continued

-u	Updates an archive.
-v	Verbose mode. Shows more information.
-f	Specifies that a jar file has been specified.
-m	Specifies that a manifest file has been specified.
-0	Doesn't use zip compression.
-M	Doesn't create a manifest file.
-C *directory*	Changes to the specified directory, used as root for the specified files.
jarfile	Specifies the jar file to create or extract from.
manifest	Specifies a file containing a manifest to include. (The jarfile and manifest must have the same order as -f and -m.)
files...	Specifies files to add to an archive or extract from an archive.
Note:	Java.nlm must be loaded to use this command.
jar cvf ucg.jar ucg.class print.class	Creates an archive named ucg.jar with two files.
jar cvfm ucg.jar manifest ucg.class print.class	Adds a manifest to the archive.

jar

OS: NetWare 5

Function	Creates, shows, and extracts files from a Java archive.
Syntax	jar [options...] *{ jarfile } { manifest } files...*
	The following three options can't be combined:
c	Creates an archive.
t	Lists the contents of an archive.
x	Extracts the specified files or all files.
v	Verbose mode. Shows more information.
f	Uses a jar file.
m	Uses a manifest file.
0	Doesn't use zip compression.
M	Doesn't create a manifest file.
jarfile	Specifies the jar file to create or extract from.
manifest	Specifies a file containing a manifest to include. (The jar file and manifest file must have the same order as -f and -m.)
files...	Specifies files to add to an archive or extract from an archive.
Note:	Java.nlm must be loaded to use this command.
jar cvf ucg.jar ucg.class print.class	Creates an archive named ucg.jar with two files.
jar cvfm ucg.jar manifest ucg.class print.class	Adds a manifest to the archive.

jarsigner

OS: NetWare 6

Function	Signs or verifies Java archive files (.jar). When used to sign, two files are added in the meta-inf directory. The files are a signature file (.sf) and a signature block file (.dsa).
Syntax	jarsigner [options...] *jarfile alias* jarsigner -verify [options...] *jarfile*
-verify	Verifies the specified jar-file.
-keystore *url*	Specifies a location for the keystore.
-storetype *type*	Specifies the type of the keystore.
-storepass *password*	Specifies the password for the keystore.
-keypass *password*	Specifies the password for the key.
-sigfile *filename*	Specifies a base name for the signature files (default is first eight characters, from alias).
-signedjar *filename*	Specifies the name of the signed jar file.
-certs	Shows certificate information together with -verify and -verbose.
-verbose	Verbose mode. Shows more information.
-internalsf	Includes the information from the .sf file in the .dsa file.
-sectionsonly	Includes only section information in the .sf file, not any header.
-J*javaoptions*	Specifies options to the Java interpreter.
jarsigner ucg.jar anna	Signs the ucg.jar file
jarsigneg -verify ucg.jar	Checks the signed jarfile ucg.jar.

java (Client)

OS: NetWare 6

Function	Starts the Novell JVM module that enables the use of Java products, including ConsoleOne and X-window.
Syntax	java [options...] *class* { *arguments...* } java -jar [options...] *jfile* { *arguments...* }

-cp*directories...*	Sets the Java search path for application resources and classes.
-D*name=value*	Sets the specified property name to the specified value.
-verbose[:*type*]	Verbose mode. Shows more information for the specified type.
class	Verbose mode. Shows more information for the class.
gc	Verbose mode. Shows more information for garbage collection.
jni	Verbose mode. Shows more information for the Java Native Interface.
-version	Shows version information and then exits.
-showversion	Shows version information and then continues.
-help	Shows help information.
-X	Shows a listing of non-standard options.
class	Specifies the Java class to execute.
jfile	Specifies the jar file that is used.
arguments...	Specifies one or more arguments that are class or jar file specific.
	The following are non-standard options that may become invalid at any time:
-Xmixed	Uses mixed mode execution.
-Xint	Uses interpreted mode execution.
-Xbootclasspath:*directories...*	Specifies the search path for bootstrap resources and classes.
-Xbootclasspath/a:*directories...*	Adds the specified directory for the bootstrap class to the end of the search path.
-Xbootclasspath/p:*directories...*	Adds the specified directory for the bootstrap class to the start of the search path.
-Xnoclassgc	Turns off class garbage collection.
-Xincgc	Starts incremental garbage collection.
-Xms*size*	Sets the initial Java heap to the specified size.
-Xmx*size*	Sets the maximum Java heap to the specified size.
-Xprof	Shows CPU profile data.
-Xrunhprof:[option]	Initiates or modifies a JVMPI heap, monitor, or CPU profile, or shows help information.
help	Shows help information.
type=value	Specifies the type to modify and sets any appropriate values. Please see `help` above.
-Xdebug	Starts remote debug mode.

File Name:	`java.exe`	**Directory:**	\public\mgmt\consoleone\1.2\jre\bin	**Type:**	External

Note: When listing more than one directory path, separate each one with a semi-colon (;).

java -Xrunhprof:help	Shows the options that are available when selecting the `type=value` option.

java (Server)

OS: NetWare 5,6

Function	Starts the Novell JVM module that enables the use of Java products, including ConsoleOne and X Window.
Syntax	java [options...] *class*

-help	Shows help information.
-nwhelp	Shows help information for options that are specific for NetWare.
-version	Shows version information.
-v	Verbose mode. Shows more information.
-debug	Starts debug mode.
-noasyncgc	Doesn't use asynchronous garbage collection.
-verbosegc	Forces the garbage collector to show the amount of memory that is available.
-noclassgc	Disables garbage collection.
-ss*size*	Specifies the C stack size for a process.
-oss*size*	Specifies the maximum Java stack size for any thread.
-ms*initsize*	Specifies the initial size for the Java heap.
-mx*maxsize*	Specifies the maximum size for the Java heap.
-classpath *directories...*	Specifies a colon-separated list of directories to look for in classes.
-prof	Outputs profile data to the `./java.prof` file.
-verify	Verifies any classes when loaded.
-verifyremote	Verifies classes that are loaded over the network.

continued

-noverify -d *name=value* -nojit -autounload -env*variable* -exit -kill*ID* -mp*processor* -ns -nsac -show -sn*name* -vm*size* *class*	Doesn't verify any classes. Sets the specified property name to the specified value. Deactivates the JIT compiler. **The following options are specific for NetWare 5:** Unloads the native NLM automatically if no dependencies are attached to it. Sets the specified environment variable to the Java application. Exits and unloads all Java applications presents in the system. Kills the specified Java application ID. Forces the application to run on the specified processor. Sets up a new Java application window. Closes any screen that was created when an application started when terminating. Shows any active Java applications. Specifies the screen name that the application runs in. Specifies the size of the virtual memory pool for any nonheap allocations. Specifies the Java class to execute.
File Name: `java.nlm`	**Directory:** **Type:** External
java -kill185	Kills the Java process with process ID of 185.

java (Client) — OS: NetWare 5

Function	Starts the Novell JVM module that enables usage of Java products, including ConsoleOne and X Windows.
Syntax	java [options...] *class { arguments... }* java -jar [options...] *jfile { arguments... }*

-cp*directories...*
-D*name=value*
-verbose[:*type*]
  class
  gc
  jni
-version
-help
-X
class
jfile
arguments...
 	
-Xbootclasspath:*directories...*
-Xnoclassgc
-Xms*size*
-Xmx*size*
-Xrs
-Xcheck:jni
-Xrunhprof:[option]
  help
  type=value
-Xdebug
-Xfuture
	Sets the Java search path for application resources and classes.
	Sets the specified property name to the specified value.
	Verbose mode. Shows more information for the specified type.
	Verbose mode. Shows more information for the class.
	Verbose mode. Shows more information for garbage collection.
	Verbose mode. Shows more information for the Java Native Interface (JNI).
	Shows version information and then exits.
	Shows help information.
	Shows a listing of non-standard options.
	Specifies the Java class to execute.
	Specifies the jar file that is used.
	Specifies one or more arguments that are class or jar file specific.
	The following are non-standard options that may become invalid at any time:
	Specifies the search path for bootstrap resources and classes.
	Turns off class garbage collection.
	Sets the initial Java heap to the specified size.
	Sets the maximum Java heap to the specified size.
	Limits OS signal usage.
	Starts JNI function tests.
	Initiates or modifies a JVMPI heap, monitor, or CPU profile or shows help information.
	Shows help information.
	Specifies the type to modify and sets any appropriate values. See `:help` above.
	Starts remote debug mode.
	Enables strict Java testing while anticipating any future default settings.

File Name: `java.exe`	**Directory:** \public\mgmt\consoleone\1.2\jre\bin **Type:** External
java -Xrunhprof:help	Shows the options that are available when selecting the `type=value` option.

javac — OS: NetWare 5

Function	A Java compiler that compiles byte code or machine code into Java class files, which allows any computer running Java virtual machine to interpret and run the Java code.
Syntax	javac [options...] *file*

-g -O -debug -depend	Creates debugging tables. Optimizes the Java code and makes it run faster. However the .class files are larger. Enables remote Java debugging. Recompiles classes that have other class files as a source.

continued

-nowarn	Disables warning messages.
-verbose	Verbose mode. Shows more information.
-classpath *path*	Specifies the path to the Java classes.
-nowrite	Reads .java files; doesn't create a .class file. Checks the syntax.
-depreciation	Warns for every code line that has the @deprecated tag.
-d *directory*	Specifies where to put compiled Java classes.
-J*javaflag*	Passes any given java flags along to the Java interpreter.
files...	Specifies .java file or files that contain Java source code.

javac

OS: NetWare 6

Function	A Java compiler that compiles byte code or machine code into Java class files, which allows any computer running Java Virtual Machine to interpret and run the Java code.
Syntax	javac [options...] *files...*

-g	Creates all debugging information.
-g:lines	Generates debug information for line numbers.
-g:vars	Generates debug information for local variables.
-g:source	Generates debug information for the source code.
-g:none	Doesn't create debug information.
-O	Optimizes the Java code and makes it run faster. However, the .class files are larger.
-debug	Enables remote Java debugging.
-depend	Recompiles classes that have other class files as a source.
-nowarn	Disables warning messages.
-verbose	Verbose mode. Shows more information.
-classpath *path*	Specifies the path to the Java classes.
-sourcepath *path*	Specifies the path to the Java classes.
-bootclasspath *path*	Sets new path for bootstrap class files.
-extdirs *directories...*	Sets new path for installed extensions.
-nowrite	Reads .java files but doesn't create a .class file. Is used to check the syntax.
-depreciation	Warns for every code line that has the @deprecated tag.
-d *directory*	Specifies where to put compiled Java classes.
-J*javaoption*	Passes any given Java options along to the Java interpreter.
-encoding *encoding*	Specifies the type of character encoding to use. Possible values are: EUCJIS and SJIS.
-target *version*	Compiles and creates the .class file for the version specified.
files...	Specifies .java file or files that contain Java source code.

javadoc

OS: NetWare 5

Function	Creates documentation about classes, interfaces, and methods in HTML format.
Syntax	javadoc [options...] *{ file }*

-author	Includes @author tags.
-classpath *path*	Specifies path to the Java class files.
-d *directory*	Specifies the destination directory to receive the HTML output files.
-docencoding *name*	Specifies the encoding name of the output files.
-encoding *name*	Specifies the encoding name of the source files.
-J *flag*	Passes options directly to the runtime system.
-nodeprecated	Excludes @deprecated tags.
-noindex	Disables package indexing.
-notree	Disables class and interface hierarchy.
-package	Shows package, protected, and public classes and their members.
-private	Shows all classes and their members.
-protected	Shows public and protected classes and their members.
-public	Shows public classes and their members.
-sourcepath *path*	Specifies path to the Java source files.
-verbose	Verbose mode. Shows more information in the output.
-version	Includes @version tags.
file	Specifies a Java package or source file to generate HTML description about.

javadoc

OS: NetWare 6

Function	Creates documentation about classes, interfaces, and methods in HTML format.
Syntax	javadoc [options...] *{ file }*

-d *directory*	Specifies the destination directory to receive the HTML output files.
-use	Creates a usage page for each documented class and package.
-version	Includes @version tags.
-author	Includes @author tags.
-splitindex	Splits the index file into multiple index files, creating one for each letter.
-windowtitle *text*	Specifies the name of the HTML window when browsing the documentation.
-doctitle *html*	Identifies the document title in HTML code - white spaces must be surrounded using "quotes".
-header *html*	Identifies the document header in HTML code - white spaces must be surrounded using "quotes".
-footer *html*	Identifies the document footer in HTML code - white spaces must be surrounded using "quotes".
-bottom, *html*	Is text for the bottom in HTML code - white spaces must be surrounded using "quotes".
-link *url*	Creates HTML links to previously created documentation.
-linkoffline *docurl pkgurl*	Links the document specified by docurl to the package list specified by pkgurl.
-group *heading packages...*	Specifies the group heading and which packages should be included under the heading.
-nodeprecated	Excludes @deprecated tags.
-nodeprecatedlist	Doesn't create the file deprecated-list.html containing a list of depreciated APIs.
-notree	Disables class and interface hierarchy.
-noindex	Disables package indexing.
-nohelp	Doesn't create the help link in the navigation bar.
-nonavbar	Doesn't create the navigational bars at the header and footer of the document.
-helpfile *file*	Specifies an alternate help file that is linked in the navigational bars.
-stylesheetfile *file*	Specifies the path and filename to customized style sheet other then stylesheet.css.
-docencoding *name*	Specifies the encoding name of the output files.
file	Specifies a Java package or source file to generate an HTML description about.

javah

OS: NetWare 5,6

Function	Creates header files to be used by C language compilers.
Syntax	javah [options...] *classnames...*

-classpath *path*	Specifies the path where the system can find Java classes.
-d *directory*	Specifies where to save output files.
-help	Shows help information.
-jni	Outputs prototypes with JNI native methods.
-o *outfile*	Outputs a list of headers and source files to an output file.
-stubs	Creates C declarations from Java object files.
-td *directory*	Specifies where to place temporary files.
-trace	Adds tracing information to the files created with `-stubs`.
-v	Verbose mode. Shows more information.
-version	Shows version information.
classnames...	Specifies either a Java class or a package to use as input.

javakey

OS: NetWare 5

Function	A security tool that is used to generate digital signatures for Java archive files.
Syntax	javakey [options...]

-l	Shows the usernames of all signers and identities.
-c *user* [trusted]	Creates an identity with a specific username that is trusted or not trusted.
-cs *user* [trusted]	Creates a signer with a specific username that is trusted or not trusted.
-r *user*	Removes the specified identity.
-ic *ID cert*	Imports a certificate from the specified ID file.
-ik *ID key*	Imports a public key from the specified ID file.
-ikp *ID key1 key2*	Imports a combined key pair from the two specified key files.
-g	Creates a key pair for a signer.
-dc *file*	Shows the certificates that are stored in the specified file.

javap

OS: NetWare 5,6

Function	Disassembles Java class files.
Syntax	javap [options...] *classes...*

-b	Uses backward compatibility.
-c	Shows disassembled code for methods in the class file.
-classpath *pathlist*	Sets the class path for `javap`.
-extdirs *directories...*	Sets new path for installed extensions.
-help	Starts the verifier.
-J*javaflag*	Passes any given Java flags along to the Java interpreter.
-l	Shows the tables of local and line variables.
-public	Shows public classes and their members.
-protected	Shows public and protected classes and their members.
-package	Shows protected, public, and package classes and their members.
-private	Shows all classes and their members.
-s	Shows the internal-type signs.
-bootclasspath *pathlist*	Sets new path for bootstrap class files.
classes...	Specifies the Java class files to disassemble.

java-rmi.cgi

OS: NetWare 5

Function	Used to tunnel HTTP packets through a firewall, providing access to distributed Java applications using RMI.
Syntax	java-rmi.cgi

keytool

OS: NetWare 5,6

Function	Starts the key and certificate management tool that is used to create and issue certificate requests, public and private key pairs, import certificate replies, designate public keys, and manage keystores.
Syntax	keytool option [options...]

	The following five suboptions exist in all options except the help option:
-keystore *keystore*	Specifies the location of the keystore file.
-storepass *password*	Specifies the keystore password, which is used to protect the integrity.
-storetype *type*	Specifies the type of keystore to be instantiated.
-v	Verbose mode. Shows more information.
-provider *classnames...*	**NW6 only:** Identifies the master class file from a cryptographic service provider.
-certreq [options...]	Creates a CSR that can be sent to a certification authority.
-alias *alias*	Specifies the alias that is associated with a public key and a distinguished name.
-sigalg *algorithm*	Specifies which algorithm is used when signing the CSR.
-file *file*	Specifies the file to store the CSR. If none is given, then STDOUT is used.
-keypass *password*	Specifies the password to get access to the private key.
-delete [options...]	Deletes the keystore entry that is specified.
-alias *alias*	Specifies the alias that is associated with a public key and a distinguished name.
-export [options...]	Exports the public key found in the specified entry to a specified file.
-rfc	Shows the certificate in printable encoding format.
-alias *alias*	Specifies the alias that is associated with a public key and a distinguished name.
-file *file*	Saves the certificate associated with the alias in the specified file.
-keystore *keystore*	Specifies the location of the keystore file.
-storepass *password*	Specifies the keystore password, which is used to protect the integrity.
-storetype *type*	Specifies the type of keystore to be instantiated.
-genkey [options...]	Creates a keystore entry that contains the private and public keys.
-alias *alias*	Specifies the alias that is associated with a public key and a distinguished name.
-keyalg *algorithm*	Specifies the algorithm to be used to create the key pair.
-keysize *size*	Specifies the size of each key to be created.
-sigalg *algorithm*	Specifies the algorithm that is used to sign the self-signed certificate.
-dname *name*	Specifies the distinguished name.
-validity *duration*	Specifies the number of days the certificate should be valid.
-keypass *password*	Specifies the password to get access to the private key.
-help	Shows help information.

continued

-identitydb [options...]	Imports JDK 1.1.x-style database information.
-file *idbfile*	Imports the specified file and adds its entries to the keystore (default is STDIN).
-import [options...]	Imports a certificate that is trusted or imports a certificate reply from a CA.
-alias *alias*	Specifies the alias that is associated with a public key and distinguished name.
-keypass *password*	Specifies the password to get access to the private key.
-file *certfile*	Specifies the file or a chain of files to import the certificates from.
-nopromt	Doesn't interact with the user.
-trustcacerts	Imports trusted CA cert file from a third-party certification company (for example, VeriSign).
-keyclone [options...]	Creates a keystore entry that uses the same key and certificate as the original entry.
-alias *alias*	Specifies the alias that is associated with a public key and distinguished name.
-dest *destalias*	Specifies the name of the new entry.
-keypass *password*	Specifies the password to get access to the private key.
-new *newpassword*	Specifies the new (cloned) entry's password.
-keypasswd [options...]	Assigns a private key password within a key or certificate entry.
-alias *alias*	Specifies the alias that is associated with a public key and distinguished name.
-keypass *oldpassword*	Specifies the valid password for the private key.
-new *newpassword*	Specifies the new password for the private key.
-list [options...]	Shows keystore entries.
-alias *alias*	Shows the contents (on STDOUT) of the specified entry.
-v | -rfc	Verbose mode or shows the certificate in printable encoding format.
-printcert [options...]	Shows a specified file's certificate information.
-file *certfile*	Shows the contents of the specified file in human-readable format.
-selfcert [options...]	Creates a X.509 v.1 self-signed certificate by using existing keystore information.
-alias *alias*	Specifies the alias that is associated with a public key and distinguished name.
-sigalg *algorithm*	Specifies the algorithm that is used to sign the certificate.
-dname *name*	Specifies the distinguished name to use for the issuer and subject of the certificate.
-validity *duration*	Specifies the number of days the certificate should be valid.
-keypass *password*	Specifies the password to get access to the private key.
-storepasswd [options...]	Assigns a specified password to the keystore.
-new *password*	Specifies the new keystore password, which is used to protect the integrity.

File Name:	`keytool.exe`	**Directory:**	\public\mgmt\consoleone\1.2\jre\bin	**Type:**	External

keytool (Server)

OS: NetWare 6

Function	Starts the key & certificate management tool that is used to create and issue certificate requests, and public and private key pairs, import certificate replies, designate public keys, and manage keystores.
Syntax	keytool option [options...]

	The following five suboptions exist in all options except the help option:
-keystore *keystore*	Specifies the location of the keystore file.
-storepass *password*	Specifies the keystore password, which is used to protect the integrity.
-storetype *type*	Specifies the type of keystore to be instantiated.
-v	Verbose mode. Shows more information.
-provider *classnames...*	**NW6 only:** The master class file from a cryptographic service provider.
-certreq [options...]	Creates a CSR that can be sent to a certification authority.
-alias *alias*	Specifies the alias that is associated with a public key and distinguished name.
-sigalg *algorithm*	Specifies which algorithm is used when signing the CSR.
-file *file*	Specifies the file to store the CSR. If none is given, STDOUT is used.
-keypass *password*	Specifies the password to get access to the private key.
-delete [options...]	Deletes the keystore entry that is specified.
-alias *alias*	Specifies the alias that is associated with a public key and distinguished name.
-export [options...]	Exports the public key found in the specified entry to a specified file.
-rfc	Shows the certificate in printable encoding format.
-alias *alias*	Specifies the alias that is associated with a public key and distinguished name.
-file *file*	Saves the certificate associated with alias in the specified file.
-keystore *keystore*	Specifies the location of the keystore file.
-storepass *password*	Specifies the keystore password, which is used to protect the integrity.
-storetype *type*	Specifies the type of keystore to be instantiated.
-genkey [options...]	Creates a keystore entry that contains the private and public keys.
-alias *alias*	Specifies the alias that is associated with a public key and distinguished name.

continued

-keyalg *algorithm*	Specifies the algorithm to be used to create the key pair.
-keysize *size*	Specifies the size of each key to be created.
-sigalg *algorithm*	Specifies the algorithm that is used to sign the self-signed certificate.
-dname *name*	Specifies the distinguished name.
-validity *duration*	Specifies the number of days the certificate should be valid.
-keypass *password*	Specifies the password to get access to the private key.
-help	Shows help information.
-identitydb [options...]	Imports JDK 1.1.x-style database information.
-file *idbfile*	Imports the specified file and adds its entries to the keystore (default is STDIN).
-import [options...]	Imports a certificate that is trusted or imports a certificate reply from a CA.
-alias *alias*	Specifies the alias that is associated with a public key and distinguished name.
-keypass *password*	Specifies the password to get access to the private key.
-file *certfile*	Specifies the file or a chain of files to import the certificates from.
-nopromt	Doesn't interact with the user.
-trustcacerts	Imports trusted CA cert file from a third-party certification company (for example, VeriSign).
-keyclone [options...]	Creates a keystore entry that uses the same key and certificate as the original entry.
-alias *alias*	Specifies the alias that is associated with a public key and distinguished name.
-dest *destalias*	Specifies the name of the new entry.
-keypass *password*	Specifies the password to get access to the private key.
-new *newpassword*	Specifies the new (cloned) entry's password.
-keypasswd [options...]	Assigns a private key password within a key or certificate entry.
-alias *alias*	Specifies the alias that is associated with a public key and distinguished name.
-keypass *oldpassword*	Specifies the valid password for the private key.
-new *newpassword*	Specifies the new password for the private key.
-list [options...]	Shows keystore entries.
-alias *alias*	Shows the contents (on STDOUT) of the specified entry.
-v | -rfc	Verbose mode or shows the certificate in printable encoding format.
-printcert [options...]	Shows a specified file's certificate information.
-file *certfile*	Shows the contents of the specified file in human-readable format.
-selfcert [options...]	Creates a X.509 v.1 self-signed certificate by using existing keystore information.
-alias *alias*	Specifies the alias that is associated with a public key and distinguished name.
-sigalg *algorithm*	Specifies the algorithm that is used to sign the certificate.
-dname *name*	Specifies the distinguished name to use for the issuer and subject of the certificate.
-validity *duration*	Specifies the number of days the certificate should be valid.
-keypass *password*	Specifies the password to get access to the private key.
-storepasswd [options...]	Assigns a specified password to the keystore.
-new *password*	Specifies the new keystore password that is used to protect the integrity.

License Maintenance Utility

OS: NetWare 5,6

Function	Shows licenses currently installed on server. Use Insert key to add licenses.
Syntax	licmaint

File Name:	`licmaint.nlm`	**Directory:**	\system	**Type:**	External

list stage

OS: NetWare 5,6

Function	Shows which NLMs are loaded for each stage in the boot process.
Syntax	list stage *{ stage }*

stage	Shows NLMs loaded for the specified stage (0 - 5).

show stage 4	Shows NLMs loaded in the fourth stage.

List Storage Adapters

OS: NetWare 5,6

Function	Shows a list of storage adapters and the interface they are using.
Syntax	list storage adapters

List Storage Device Bindings

OS: NetWare 5,6

Function	Shows a list of all CDMs and HAMs bound to a specified storage device.
Syntax	list storage device bindings *NR*

listdir

OS: NetWare 3

Function	Shows short information about directories found in the current or specified directory.
Syntax	listdir *{ path }* [options...]

/All	Uses all the below options.
/Rights	Shows the Inherited Rights for the subdirectories.
/Effective Rights	Shows the effective rights that the current user has in the subdirectories.
/Date	Shows the creation date of the subdirectories.
/Time	Shows the creation time of the subdirectories.
/Subdirectory	Shows the directories in the subdirectories.
path	Specifies the path to the volume, directory to show.

File Name:	`listdir.exe`	**Directory:**	\public	**Type:**	External

listdir u:\public /Date	Shows the creation time for all directories in u:\public.

loadstage

OS: NetWare 5,6

Function	Starts a NetWare server at various levels by loading the specified stage of NLMs for troubleshooting device drivers. To use the loadstage command, you must bring the server up clean by typing `server -na -ns -nl`.
Syntax	loadstage *stage*

Steps	**The following steps are a quick guide to start the server in various levels:**
Step 1	Bring the server up clean by typing `server -na -ns -nl` from the DOS prompt.
Step 2	Type `c:\nwserver\startup.ncf` to load the disk drivers.
Step 3	Then, you may begin loading the stage levels listed below:
Stage Level	**While loading each stage, be sure to watch carefully for any errors.**
1	Volume SYS is mounted. Be sure to check for any errors.
2	Prepares the Novell International Cryptography Infrastructure (NICI) services.
3	Prepares Novell Directory Service (NDS) and starts the NICI services. (This is the most important stage. If NICI doesn't start, NDS can't load.)
4	Loads and opens the NDS.
	Type `autoexec.ncf` to initialize the network before loading stage 5.
5	Loads the final stage of NLMs and should load without problem.
ALL	Loads the entire sequence of stages as listed here.

loadstage 1	Mounts the SYS volume.

ls

OS: NetWare 4

Function	Shows files and information about them.
Syntax	ls [options...] *{ drive } { directory } { file }*

-a	Lists hidden files also.
-c	Shows when the file was last changed. Used with -l option.
-n	Shows the NetWare names. Used with -l option.
-g	Shows the group ID.
-l	Shows in long output format.
-u	Shows when the file was last accessed. Used with -l option.
-8	Finds the 8.3 name from the long name.
-s	Sorts the list by filename.
-t	Sorts the list by time.
drive	Specifies a hard disk letter.
directory	Specifies a directory.
file	Specifies a file.

File Name:	`ls.exe`	**Directory:**	\public	**Type:**	External

makeuser

OS: NetWare 3

Function	Adds and deletes users using a script file that automates the process.
Syntax	makeuser

Create New USR File	Creates a USR file.
Edit USR File	Edits the USR file.
Process USR file	Processes the USR file, which will add and delete the users described in the file.

File Name:	`makeuser.exe`	**Directory:**	\public	**Type:**	External

menucnvt

OS: NetWare 3,4

Function	Converts old NetWare menu files (*.nmu) to Saber menu files (*.sbr).
Syntax	menucnvt *sourcefile { outputfile }* [options...]

/l*text*	Specifies list of title trimming characters.
/M*NR*	Specifies item trim margin.
/H	Shows help information.
sourcefile	Specifies the NetWare menu file to convert.
outputfile	Specifies a name for the new Saber menu file.

File Name:	`menucnvt.exe`	**Directory:**	\public	**Type:**	External

menucnvt util.mnu	Converts `util.mnu` to `util.sbr`.

menuexe

OS: NetWare 3,4

Function	Shows the specified menu file on the screen.
Syntax	menuexe *menufile*

menufile	Specifies the menu file to show.

File Name:	`menuexe.exe`	**Directory:**	\public	**Type:**	External

menuexe util	Shows the util menu.

menumake

OS: NetWare 3,4

Function	Compiles source script files to menu files.
Syntax	menumake *scriptfile* [/h]

/h	Shows help information.
scriptfile	Specifies the script file to compile. Wildcards can be used.

File Name:	`menumake.exe`	**Directory:**	\public	**Type:**	External

menumake util	Compiles the specified script source file to a menu file.
menumake *.src	Compiles all *.src files in the current directory.

menurset

OS: NetWare 3,4

Function	Shows the specified menu file on the screen.
Syntax	menurset *menufile*

menufile	Specifies the menu file to show.

File Name:	`menurset.exe`	**Directory:**	\public	**Type:**	External

menurset util	Shows the util menu.

migprint

OS: NetWare 4

Function	Migrates printers, print queues, print job configurations, and print servers from NW 2 and 3 servers to NW 4. To be used after `Migrate`.
Syntax	migprint /S=*source* /D=*destination* [/VOL=*queue*] [/O=*file*]

/S=*source*	Specifies the NetWare 3 bindery server.
/D=*destination*	Specifies the NetWare 4 server.
/VOL=*queue*	Specifies the name of the print queue volume (default is SYS:).
/O=*file*	Specifies the name of the output file (default is MPxxx.RPT).

File Name:	`migprint.exe`	**Directory:**	\public	**Type:**	External

migprint /S=neptune /D=saturn	Migrates printers from neptune to saturn.

migrate

OS: NetWare 4

Function	Imports the bindery information from NetWare 2 or 3 into NDS in NetWare 4.
Syntax	migrate

Across-The-Wire migration	Is used to migrate when the NetWare 2 or 3 servers are on the same network.
Same-Server migration	Is used to migrate when the server is upgraded from NetWare 2 and 3 to NetWare 4.

File Name:	`migrate.exe`	**Directory:**	\products\migrate On the installation CD	**Type:**	External

migrate	Starts the interface for migrating to NDS.

Modem Script Manager Application

OS:	NetWare 5,6
Function	A Windows-based tool to manage modem scripts for Novell Internet Access Server (NIAS) 4.1.
Syntax	wmdmmgr
File Name:	`wmdmmgr.exe`
Directory:	\system\utils
Type:	External

mpdetect

OS:	NetWare 4
Function	Searches for additional processors in the system. If more than one processor is found, SMP can be installed and the most appropriate PSM is highlighted. Normally run during installation of the server.
Syntax	mpdetect
File Name:	`mpdetect.nlm`
Directory:	\system
Type:	External

mpdriver

OS:	NetWare 4
Function	Enables multiple processors installed in a NetWare server.
Syntax	load mpdriver *{ NR }*
NR	Specifies the number of processors to enable. Use `ALL` to enable all processors.
File Name:	`mpdriver.nlm`
Directory:	\system
Type:	External
Note:	Installation of NetWare SMP (Symmetric Multi Processing) is required before using this command.
load mpdriver 2	Enables two processors in the server.
load mpdriver all	Enables all processors that there are licenses for.

mserver

OS:	NetWare 4
Function	Loads the IOEngine on NetWare 4 SFT III servers.
Syntax	mserver [options...]
-ns	Doesn't run `IOSTART.NCF`.
-na	Doesn't run `IOAUTO.NCF`.
mserver	Loads the IOEngine.
mserver -ns -na	Loads the IOEngine without running `IOSTART.NCF` or `IOAUTO.NCF`.

Native2ASCII

OS:	NetWare 5,6
Function	Is used by Java programmers to convert Java files containing non-ASCII characters or files not written using the Latin-1 or Unicode encoded characters into a 7-bit ASCII file that can be compiled by the Java compiler.
Syntax	native2ascii *filename*
filename	Specifies the filename that contains non-ASCII characters to convert.

NCP Addresses

OS:	NetWare 5,6
Function	Shows a list of NCP (NetWare Core Protocol) addresses and ports currently in use on the server.
Syntax	ncp addresses

NCP Dump

OS:	NetWare 5,6
Function	Dumps NCP deviation statistics in the file specified. NCP trace must be active before using this command.
Syntax	ncp dump *filename*
filename	Specifies the filename to save deviation statistics and is stored in the root of SYS.
ncp dump venus.dump	Enables NCP dump and saves deviation statistics in a filenamed venus.dump at the root of volume SYS.

NCP Stats

OS:	NetWare 5,6
Function	Shows and resets statistics on the number and type of NCP incoming packets received and processed.
Syntax	ncp stats [reset]
reset	Resets all of the NCP counters

NCP Trace

OS:	NetWare 5,6
Function	Enables or disables tracing of NCP (NetWare Core Protocol). If no filename is used, results are shown on console.
Syntax	ncp trace option *{ filename }*
on	Enables tracing of NCP packets.

continued

off *filename*	Disables tracing of NCP packets. Specifies the filename to save the trace results in and stores them in the root of SYS.
ncp trace on venus.trace	Enables NCP tracing and stores the results in a file named venus.trace at the root of volume SYS.
ncp trace off	Disables NCP tracing.

NCS Configuration

OS: NetWare 5

Function	Configures the Novell Connection Services (NCS).
Syntax	ncscon
Configure NCS Generate NCS Configuration Report	Configures NCS options. Specifies for output report (default path and filename: sys:system\ncsrpt.txt).
File Name: `ncscon.nlm`	**Directory:** \system — **Type:** External

NCS Status

OS: NetWare 5

Function	Shows NCS connection status information regarding current sessions.
Syntax	ncsstat
File Name: `ncsstat.nlm`	**Directory:** \system — **Type:** External

ncupdate

OS: NetWare 4

Function	Updates the user's `NET.CFG` files with a new name context. Usually run from a login script.
Syntax	ncupdate [options...]
/np /ver /?	Doesn't prompt for updating the name context. Shows version information. Shows help information.
File Name: `ncupdate.exe`	**Directory:** \public — **Type:** External
ncupdate /np	Updates the user's `NET.CFG` files without prompting.

NDPS Broker

OS: NetWare 5,6

Function	Starts the broker to provide service registry service, event notification service, and resource management service.
Syntax	broker *{ broker }*
broker	Specifies the name and context of the broker.
File Name: `broker.nlm`	**Directory:** \nwserver — **Type:** External
broker "venus_broker.planets"	Loads the NDPS broker on server venus.

NDPS Manager

OS: NetWare 5,6

Function	Starts the NDPS manager to manage broker objects.
Syntax	ndpsm *{ object }*
object	Specifies the name of the broker to manage.
File Name: `ndpsm.nlm`	**Directory:** \nwserver — **Type:** External
ndpsm	Loads the NDPS manager.
ndpsm venus_broker.planets	Starts the GUI and manager venus_broker.planets.

NDS Browser

OS: NetWare 6

Function	Examines NDS objects, NDS schema classes, and the attributes for these.
Syntax	dsbrowse
Tree browse Schema browse Partition browse Object search Exit	Examines NDS objects and attributes values. Examines NDS schema classes and attributes values. Examines NDS objects and attributes values. Searches for NDS objects and attributes after specified criteria. Exits the NDS browser.
File Name: `dsbrowse.nlm`	**Directory:** \system — **Type:** External

NDS Maintenance

OS: NetWare 4

Function	Repairs or restores the NDS when performing a hardware upgrade or restores the NDS after a hardware failure.
Syntax	load dsmaint

Prepare NDS for hardware upgrades	Prepares the local directory information for a hardware upgrade.
Restore NDS following hardware upgrades	Restores directory information from a file created with the previous option.
Replaces server references	Replaces all references to this server in other servers that point to current server.
Restore server references	Searches the DS tree and replaces the temporary object with this server's object.
Restore local server information after hardware failure	Restores directory information using the file `SERVDATA.NDS`.
Log file options	Configures options for DSMaintenance log file.

File Name: `dsmaint.nlm` **Directory:** \system **Type:** Internal

NDS Manager

OS: NetWare 4,5

Function	Creates, deletes, and manages NDS partitions and replicas, checks partition continuity and checks synchronization of the NDS database. Is also used to launch the Schema Manager where you can manage schema classes.
Syntax	ndsmgr32

File Name: `ndsmgr32.exe` **Directory:** \public\win32 **Type:** External

Tip: Don't worry about the yellow circles with question marks next to NDS objects. NDS Manger can only read information on replicas and partitions.

NDS Manager (16-bit)

OS: NetWare 4

Function	Repairs the NDS database, updates Directory Services NLMs to newer version, shows a list of partitions in the directory tree, and provides diagnostic features and partitioning and replication services for NDS.
Syntax	ndsmgr16

File Name: `ndsmgr16.exe` **Directory:** \public **Type:** External

netadmin

OS: NetWare 4

Function	Adds, moves, renames, or edits NDS objects. This is a simple DOS version of Network Administrator.
Syntax	netadmin [/ver]

/ver	Shows version information.
	The following menu options are available in the text base GUI:
Manage objects	Adds, moves, renames, or edits NDS objects.
Manage according to search pattern	Filters specific information to show.
Change context	Changes the location in the directory tree.
Search	Searches for specific objects in the selected container.

File Name: `netadmin.exe` **Directory:** \public **Type:** External

netbios

OS: NetWare 3

Function	Shows NetWare version information, status of NETBIOS, which interrupts in use. Also used to unload NETBIOS.
Syntax	netbios [option]

I	Shows the NW version information, status of the NETBIOS, and the interrupts in use.
U	Unloads the NETBIOS v3.01 and only that version.

File Name: `netbios.exe` **Directory:** \public\client **Type:** External

netbios I	Shows the NW version information, the status of the NETBIOS, and the interrupts in use.

netsync3

OS: NetWare 3,4

Function	Enables synchronization of bindery information in NetWare 3 to the NDS in NetWare 4.
Syntax	load netsync3

File Name: `netsync3.nlm` **Directory:** \system\netsync **Type:** External

Note: This module should be loaded on the NetWare 3 server before loading netsync4 on the NetWare 4 server.

load netsync3	Enables the NetWare 4 server to load netsync4.

netsync4

OS: NetWare 4

Function	Enables synchronization of bindery information in NetWare 3 to the NDS in NetWare 4.
Syntax	load netsync4

View Active Log	Shows a listing of previous and current synchronization actions.
Log File Options	Shows and edits current logging settings.
Edit Server List	Edits the list of NetWare 3 servers to synchronize.
Configuration Options	Edits synchronization settings.
Unload Netsynq	Disable synchronization.

File Name:	`netsync4.nlm`	**Directory:**	\system	**Type:**	External
Note:	Netsync3 must first be loaded on the NetWare 3 server, but it is automatically loaded when loading netsync4.				

NetUser

OS: NetWare 4

Function	Is used from a workstation to perform common network tasks.
Syntax	netuser [/ver]

/ver	Shows version information.
	The main menu consists of these items:
Printing	Redirects ports to printers and manages print jobs.
Messages	Sends messages to other users or groups, and disables or enables incoming messages.
Drives	Manages drive or search mappings, and shows effective rights.
Attachments	Shows server information, and changes login script, password, and network attachments.
Change Context	Sets the context if you are logged in to a directory tree.

File Name:	`netuser.exe`	**Directory:**	\public	**Type:**	External

NetWare Backup/Restore

OS: NetWare 5,6

Function	Manages the backup configuration.
Syntax	sbcon

Job Administration	Creates jobs and administers them.
Backup	Specifies data from a target and backs up to a tape device on the server.
Restore	Restores data from a tape device on the server from a specified target.
Verify	Verifies the backup data.
Create Session Files	Creates a log file from the data on the tape.
Current Job List	Administers jobs in the queue.
Storage Device Administration	Lets the user select the media to administer.
Log File Administration	Administers error and log files generated during a job execution.
View a log file	Shows a log file.
View an error file	Shows an error file.
Set location of Log and Error Files	Specifies location of log and error files.
Change target to Backup From or Restore to	Shows name server tree. Also changes the target for the backup or restores session.
Exit	Closes the user interface.

File Name:	`sbcon.nlm`	**Directory:**	\system	**Type:**	External

NetWare Configuration

OS: NetWare 5,6

Function	Configures the NetWare server, including creating traditional and NSS disk partitions and volumes, installing NetWare licenses, installing and removing NDS, and editing the `startup` and `autoexec` NCF files.
Syntax	nwconfig

	The main menu consists of these items:
Driver Options	Loads or unloads disk and network drivers.
Standard Disk Options	Creates partitions, initializes disks, scans for new devices, mounts volumes, and so forth.
NSS Disk Options	Configures Novell storage services.
License Options	Installs or removes licenses (number of connections) on the server.
Copy Files Options	Installs NetWare system files.
Directory Options	Installs or removes NDS, upgrades bindery to NDS, backs up or restores NDS.
NCF files Options	Creates or edits the startup files.

continued

Multi CPU Options	Installs or uninstalls support for multiprocessing.
Product Options	Installs, configures, or removes NetWare and third-party products.
Exit	Exits NetWare configuration.
File Name: `nwconfig.nlm`	**Directory:** \nwserver **Type:** External

NetWare Enterprise Web Server

OS: NetWare 5,6

Function	Starts and stops the NetWare Enterprise Web server and Web manager. Use nsweb to start and nswebdn to stop.
Syntax	nsweb nswebdn
File Name:	`nsweb.ncf, nswebdn.ncf` **Directory:** \system **Type:** External

Netware Installation

OS: NetWare 5,6

Function	Auto-detects hardware and installs the appropriate software drivers.
Syntax	hdetect

Continue	Continues the configuration and shows a list of drivers for specific devices.
Modify	Modifies storage adapters, hot plugs, and platform support modules.
File Name: `hdetect.nlm`	**Directory:** \ni\update\source\ **Type:** External

NetWare Remote Manager

OS: NetWare 6

Function	Manages volumes, servers, applications, remote server access, hardware, and health monitoring.
Syntax	http://*ipaddress*:8008

	Volume management
Volumes	Shows advanced volume information like migration status and salvage system settings.
Partition Management	Configures disk partition operations and adds or dismounts system volumes.
	Health monitoring
Server Health Monitoring	Shows performance related statistics like memory and thread usage, LAN traffic, etc.
Configure Health Thresholds	Specifies monitor thresholds like allocated and available processes, CPU usage, etc.
Mail Control Panel	Sets mail notification lists, mail server name, etc.
	Configuration
NetWare Remote Manager Configuration Options	Shows hidden files, folders, and system files and enables the emergency account (SADMIN).
HTTP Logging Controls	Manages HTTP logging, for example log file sizing and turning the logger on or off.
HTTP Interface Management	Changes the default or alternate port, the SSL port, or the minimum startup threads.
	Server diagnostics
Health Monitor	See `Server health monitoring` above.
Profile/Debug	Shows thread information, CPU execution profiling and selects debug operation.
Run Config Report	Executes a configuration report of the server.
	Server management
Volumes	See `Volumes` above.
Console Screens	Manages current & HTML-based screen pages by setting page refresh rates, etc.
Connections	Configures connection slots, signing level, and login states.
Set Parameters	Defines set parameters for error handling, memory, NCP, disk, NSS, time, etc.
Schedule Tasks	Shows current scheduled tasks and creates new ones.
Console Commands	Shows a list of console commands and allows you to start a console screen online.
View Memory Configuration	Shows system, cache, file system, swap, NLM and virtual memory usage and settings.
View Statistics	Shows Network Management, Kernel, LSL, and Media Manager statistics.
Down / Restart	Shuts down, restarts, or shuts down and warm boots the server.
	Application Management
Module List	Shows loadable modules information and module load search paths.
Protected Memory	Sets Memory Protection parameters, address space, and protection console interfaces.
System Resources	Sets media manager, NCP, service, Winsock, cache, connection, debug, etc. resources.
NetWare Registry	Configures registry keys and values, and runs registry consistence checks, etc.
Winsock 2.0	Shows active Winsock providers, resources, applications, and protocols.
Protocol Information	Shows detailed information on IP, TCP, UDP, ICMP, OSPF, SNMP, and NCP protocols.
Java Application Information	Shows information on the Java environment or resources, and starts or ends applications.

continued

	Hardware Management
Processors Information	Shows detailed processor information like Stepping technology, feature flags, etc.
LAN/Disk Adapters	Manages storage adapters (SCSI, IDE) and network adapters (Ethernet, TokenRing).
PCI Devices	Shows PCI device information like sub class, interrupts, base class and MAX_LAT.
Hardware Resources	Shows interrupt, slot, port, DMA, and shared memory resources.
	Manage e-directory
Access Tree Walker	Is used to transverse the NDS Tree.
View eDirectory Partitions	Shows the e-directory partitions showing name, type, state, and server.
NDS iMonitor	Allows monitoring of partition synchronization, agent process status, etc.
DS Trace	Configures tracing and trace triggers.
	Use Server Groups
Build Group	Selects which servers are included into a new server group.
Load Group File	Specifies a server group configuration file to be used.
	Access Other Servers
Managed Portal Servers	Starts the Netware Management Portal for any of the connected servers.
Basic File Access	Allows Netware servers running on the same NDS tree to access remote file systems.
	NetWare Usage
Usage Information	Allows selection of information and which date periods are searched.
Configuration	Configures collector server, collector push, IP port communication and data range.

NetWare Web Manager

OS: NetWare 5,6

Function	Administers or accesses the entire range of Web Management tools for NDS, Remote Manager, FTP Server, Web Search Server, Enterprise Web Server, eDirectory/iManage and iFolder StorageServices.
Syntax	https://*ip address*:2200

	Network Settings
Log Settings	Sets access and error log paths.
View Access Log	Shows the most recent accesses. You may select how many records to show.
View Error Log	Shows the most recent errors. You may select how many records to show.
	Enterprise Web Server
Server Preferences	Manages settings, configuration, performance, MIME, errors, access, and encryption.
Programs	Creates CGI directories, starts CGI file type, Query Handler & Server Side JavaScripts.
Server Status	Views error & archive logs, current activity, preferences, reports and SNMP Subagents.
Styles	Creates, removes, and edits Styles and lists Style assignments.
Content Management	Shows document directories, preferences, URL forwarding, Virtual Servers & Parse HTML.
Users and Groups	Shows NDS object content, creates Users & Groups, and configures Directory Services.
WebDAV state	Starts or stops the WebDAV state.
	NDS
Contents	Shows the current NDS object contents.
New Organization	Creates a new NDS object Organization.
New Country	Creates a new NDS object Country.
	Remote Manager
Diagnose Server	Allows activation and operation of the Health Monitor, Profile/Debug & Config Report.
Manage Server	Manages volumes, consoles, connections, parameters, tasks, memory, and statistics.
Manage Applications	Lists modules, manages memory and resources, and shows the Registry, Winsock and protocol.
Manage Hardware	Manages processors, Disk and LAN adapters, PCI devices, Interrupts, slots and ports.
Manage eDirectory	Starts Tree Walker, shows eDirectory partitions and starts NDS iMonitor and DS Tracing.
Use Server Groups	Builds Groups and loads Group files.
Access Other Servers	Shows the managed Server list and enables/disables basic file access.
NetWare Usage	Shows usage information and configuration settings.
	FTP Server
On/Off	Turns the FTP Server on or off.
Server Settings	Sets Welcome banner, message file, max FTP sessions, idle time, system timeout, etc.
Security	Sets up Host Intruder Detection and User Intruder Detection.
User Setting	Sets default home directory, Ignores NDS, sets FTP restrictions and Anonymous settings.
Log Settings	Defines what will be logged and gives audit trail, Intruder and Statistic filenames.

continued

	Web Search Server
Search Sites	Shows the site list and allows you to add sites.
Default Site Settings	Defines general, search, print, index, and security settings.
Services Settings	Sets general, search, and print service settings.
	eDirectory / iManage
	Accesses the eDirectory or iManage services.
	iFolder Storage Services
	Accesses personal files via a Web browser without being connected to a network.

nliclear

OS: NetWare 3

Function	Monitors connections to the server and will clear unused connections making them available to other users.
Syntax	load nliclear [options...]

notify	Notifies the administrator.
conn=*NR*	Specifies the number of connections (default is 50).
poll=*sec*	Specifies the poll interval in seconds (default is 60).
File Name: nliclear.nlm	**Directory:** \system **Type:** External
load nliclear notify	Activates administrator notification.
load nliclear conn=26	Sets the number of connections to monitor to 26.
load nliclear poll=20	Sets the poll interval to 20 seconds.

nlslsapi

OS: NetWare 4

Function	A TSR program for NetWare Licensing Services that provides license resource access for DOS clients.
Syntax	nlslsapi [-u]

-u	Unloads the TSR from memory.
File Name: nlslsapi.exe	**Directory:** \public **Type:** External

nlunpack

OS: NetWare 3

Function	Unpacks compressed files.
Syntax	nlunpack *file { directory }*

file	Specifies the file to uncompress.
directory	Specifies the destination directory.
File Name: nlunpack.exe	**Directory:** \public\client **Type:** External

nmagent

OS: NetWare 3

Function	Enables the management agent of LAN drivers. Must be loaded in `autoexec.ncf` before the LAN drivers.
Syntax	load nmagent

File Name: nmagent.nlm	**Directory:** \system **Type:** External

nmenu

OS: NetWare 3,4

Function	Shows customized menus to help the user find applications and data on the network.
Syntax	nmenu *menu* [option]

menu	Specifies the name of the menu to show.
/?	Shows help information.
File Name: nmenu.bat	**Directory:** \public **Type:** External

Novell Printer Manager

OS: NetWare 5

Function	A graphical application used from a workstation to manage your printers and print jobs. Shows the default printer, lets you add and remove printers, makes them default, and more.
Syntax	nwpmw32

File Name: nwpmw32.exe	**Directory:** \public\win32 **Type:** External
nwpmw32	Starts Novell printer manager.

Novell Upgrade Wizard

OS: NetWare 5,6

Function	Imports the bindery information from NW3 or upgrades the NDS from NW4 when upgrading to NW5 or NW6.
Syntax	upgrdwzd
File Name:	`upgrdwzd.exe` **Directory:** \products\upgrdwzd On the installation CD **Type:** External
Note:	The filename of the wizard is MigWin32.exe located in \Program Files\Novell\Upgrade Wizard.
upgrdwzd	Installs the software that runs the migration wizard.

npams

OS: NetWare 4

Function	Enables mounting of a CD-ROM as a NetWare SFT III volume.
Syntax	load npams
File Name:	`npams.nlm` **Directory:** **Type:** External

npath

OS: NetWare 4

Function	Shows the NetWare search sequence for a file and troubleshoots the station's files if there are problems.
Syntax	load npath *{ nameutility } { file }* [options...]
A	Shows all the paths to all occurrences of the file the user specifies.
D	Shows the version number, language, time, and date of the file the user specifies.
/Uni /D	Shows settings for page and country code. Filename isn't required.
Uni	Shows all paths to Unicode files.
/?	Shows help information.
nameutility	Specifies the utility the user is trying to execute.
file	Is used to specify the file the workstation can't find or to find correct file version.
File Name:	`npath.exe` **Directory:** \public **Type:** External

nprint

OS: NetWare 3,4,5

Function	A command-line utility that is used for printing ASCII text files to a network printer.
Syntax	nprint *file* [options...]
	The following two options can't be combined:
P=*printer*	Specifies the printer to use.
Q=*queue*	Specifies the print queue to use.
ALL	Is used with the /? option to show all help information.
B="*string*"	Specifies the text to include in the lower half of the banner page (max is 12 characters).
C=*NR*	Sets the number of copies to print. The maximum for NW4 and above is 65000.
DEL	Deletes the file after it was printed.
D	Shows the printing parameters for the job to be printed.
F=*form*	Specifies the name or number of the form the printer uses.
FF	Enables form feed at the end of a print job.
HOLD	Sends a print job to a queue without printing it. (Use NetWare Administrator or pconsole to release the hold.)
J=*name*	Sets the job configuration to use.
NAM=*text*	Specifies the text to include in the upper half of the banner page (max is 12 characters).
NB	Doesn't print the banner page.
NFF	Doesn't use form feed at the end of a print job.
NNOTI	Doesn't notify the user when the print job is done.
NT	Doesn't convert tabs to spaces.
NOTI	Notifies the user when the print job is completed.
S=*name*	Sets the name of the server if the print job is to be sent to a binary print queue.
T=*NR*	Sets the number of spaces to use instead of each tab in a print job (default is 8).
/VER	Shows version information.
/?	Shows help information.
file	Specifies the file to print.

continued

File Name:	nprint.exe	Directory:	\public	Type:	External
nprint autoexec.bat q=hplj5simx			Prints the file `autoexec.bat` on the specified print queue.		
nprint autoexec.bat q=hplj5simx NFF NB			Doesn't use form feed and doesn't print the banner page.		
nprint report.txt q=hplj5simx C=10			Prints ten copies of the specified file.		

nss

OS: NetWare 5

Function	The command-line interface to Novell storage services. It can unload NSS, show module and volume information, tune system parameters, and verify and rebuild volumes.
Syntax	nss [options...]

exit	Unloads NSS and all loaded NSS modules.
version	Shows version information.
modules	Shows information about all of the modules loaded into NSS.
help	Shows help information.
menu	Starts the NSS configuration menu.
	The following 13 options can only be used while loading the `nss.nlm`:
/skiploadmodules	Doesn't autoload the NSS support modules.
/noskiploadmodules	Autoloads the NSS support modules.
nolss	Doesn't load any LSS modules.
alllss	Loads all LSS modules.
knownlss	Loads all available LSS modules, including the debug ones.
defaultnlms	Loads the default LSS NLMs and any others specified at the command line.
cd9660	Is used to only load the modules needed for CD9660 support.
cdhfs	Is used to only load the modules needed for CDHFS support.
cdrom	Is used to only load the modules needed for CD9660 and CDHFS support.
dosfat	Is used to only load the modules needed for DOSFAT support.
udf	Is used to only load the modules needed for UDF support.
zlss	Is used to only load the modules needed for ZLSS support.
nwprv	Loads NWPRV and any LSS specified at the command prompt.
	The following options are used by the mbCOMN module:
status	Shows current NSS status information.
volumes	Shows all available NSS volumes.
/activate=*volume*	Activates the specified volume.
/deactivate=*volume*	Deactivates the specified volume.
/maintenance=*volume*	Switches the specified volume to maintenance mode.
/forceactivate=*volume*	Forces the specified volume to activate.
/forcedeactivate=*volume*	Forces the specified volume to deactivate.
/verifyvolume[=*volume*]	Verifies the specified or selected volume's physical integrity.
/rebuildvolume[=*volume*]	Rebuilds the specified or selected volume.
/autoactivatevolume=*volume*	Is used to activate the specified volume at volume load time.
/autodeactivatevolume=*volume*	Is used to not activate the specified volume at volume load time.
/autoverifyvolume=*volume*	Verifies the specified volume's physical integrity at startup time.
/storagealarmthreshold=*limit*	Sets the low storage space warning limit in megabytes (range is 0 to 1000000).
/storageresetthreshold=*limit*	Specifies the limit in megabytes that resets a low storage space warning.
/nostoragealertmessages	Doesn't send low storage space messages.
/storagealertmessages	Sends low storage space messages.
/namecachestats	Shows name caching statistics.
/closedfilecachesize=*NR*	Specifies the number of closed files that can be cached (range is 1 to 1000000).
/fileflushtimer=*time*	Specifies the flush time in seconds for modified open files (range is 1 to 3600).
/minbuffercachesize=*NR*	Specifies the minimum number of NSS buffer cache entries (range is 256 to 1048576).
/minosbuffercachesize=*NR*	Specifies the minimum number of Novell buffer cache entries (range is 1024 to 1048576).
/bufferflushtimer=*sec*	Specifies the flush time for cache buffers that are modified.
/cachebalance	Turns on the dynamic balancing of free memory.
/nocachebalance	Turns off the dynamic balancing of free memory.
/cachebalance=*percentage*	Specifies the amount of free memory used for buffer cache (range is 1 to 99).
/cachebalancetimer=*sec*	Sets the cache balance timer (range is 1 to 3600).
/cachestats	Shows statistics for the buffer caching.
/resetstats	Resets statistics for file and caching.
/salvage=*volume*	Turns on salvage of deleted files for the specified volume.

continued

/nosalavge=*volume*	Turns off salvage of deleted files for the specified volume.
/userspacerestrictions=*volume*	Turns on space restrictions for users on the specified volume.
/nouserspacerestrictions=*volume*	Turns off space restrictions for users on the specified volume.
/filecopyonwrite=*volume*	Creates copy of files open for writing on the specified volume.
/nofilecopyonwrite=*volume*	Doesn't create copy of files open for writing on the specified volume.
	The following nine options can only be used while loading the `nss.nlm`:
/namecachesize=*NR*	Specifies the number of name cache entries (range is 3 to 65521).
/namecache	Turns on name caching.
/nonamecache	Turns off name caching.
/authcachesize=*NR*	Specifies the number of authorization cache entries (range is 16 to 50000).
/openfilehashshift=*size*	Specifies the size of the open file hash table (range is 8 to 20).
/mailboxsize=*size*	Specifies the size of the mailbox (range is 64 to 65536).
/numasyncios=*NR*	Sets how many asyncio entries are allocated (range is 4 to 65536).
/numbonds=*NR*	Sets how many bond entries are allocated (range is 512 to 2097152).
/numworktodos=*NR*	Sets how many WorkToDo entries are concurrently executing (range is 5 to 100).
	The following option is used by the mbMMPRV module:
pendingmmrequests	Shows the number of pending IO requests to the MM.
	The following options are used by the CD9660 module:
/update9660tonds	Updates the NDS object for the CD volumes when they are created or removed.
/noupdate9660tonds	Doesn't update the NDS object for the CD volumes when they are created or removed.
/lock9660mediain	Locks/unlocks the media in the drive when CD volumes are created or removed.
/nolock9660mediain	Doesn't lock/unlock the media in the drive when CD volumes are created or removed.
	The following options are used by the CDHFS module:
/updatehfstonds	Updates the NDS object for the CD volumes when they are created or removed.
/noupdatehfstonds	Doesn't update the NDS object for the CD volumes when they are created or removed.
/lockhfsmediain	Locks/unlocks the media in the drive when CD volumes are created or removed.
/nolockhfsmediain	Doesn't lock/unlock the media in the drive when CD volumes are created or removed.

File Name:	`nss.nlm`	**Directory:**	\system	**Type:**	External

nss modules	Shows which modules are loaded.
nss volumes	Shows the volumes managed by NSS.
nss status	Shows the current status.

nss

OS: NetWare 6

Function	The command-line interface to Novell storage services. It can unload NSS, show module and volume information, tune system parameters, and verify and rebuild volumes.
Syntax	nss [options...]

version	Shows version information.
modules	Shows information about all of the modules loaded into NSS.
help	Shows help information.
menu	Starts the NSS Configuration menu.
/errorcode=*code*	Shows the string that corresponds to the given error code.
/ignoretimezone	Doesn't adjust DOS/UTC time for timezone.
/noignoretimezone	Adjusts DOS/UTC time for timezone.
	The following 12 options can only be used at startup:
/skiploadmodules	Doesn't autoload the NSS support modules.
/noskiploadmodules	Autoloads the NSS support modules.
nolss	Doesn't load any LSS modules.
alllss	Loads all LSS modules.
defaultnlms	Loads only the default LSS NLMs and any other specified at the command line.
cd9660	Loads only the modules needed for CD9660 support.
cdhfs	Loads only the modules needed for CDHFS support.
cdrom	Loads only the modules needed for CD9660 and CDHFS support.
dosfat	Loads only the modules needed for DOSFAT support.
udf	Loads only the modules needed for UDF support.

continued

zlss	Loads only the modules needed for ZLSS support.
nwprv	Loads NWPRV and any LSS specified at the command prompt.
	The following options are used by the COMN module:
status	Shows current NSS status information.
volumes	Shows all available NSS volumes.
/volumeactivate=*volume*	Activates the specified volume.
/volumedeactivate=*volume*	Deactivates the specified volume.
/volumemaintenance=*volume*	Switches the specified volume to maintenance mode.
/forceactivate=*volume*	Forces the specified volume to activate.
/forcedeactivate=*volume*	Forces the specified volume to deactivate.
/poolverify[=*pool*]	Verifies the specified or selected pool physical integrity.
/poolrebuild[=*pool*]	Rebuilds the specified or selected pool.
/volumeautoactivate=*volume*	Activates the specified volume at volume load time.
/volumeautodeactivate=*volume*	Doesn't activate the specified volume at volume load time.
/logicalvolumepurgedelay=*sec*	Specifies the delay for purging on logical volumes after a delete.
/logicalvolumepurgedelayaftercontinue=*sec*	Specifies the delay for purging on logical volumes after a continue.
/logicalvolumepurgedelayafterload=*sec*	Specifies the delay for purging on logical volumes after loading NSS.
/includetype=*type*	Includes local and/or shared pools in the command.
/overridetype=*type*	Overrides options in the specified command. Can be shared, corrupt and questions.
/storagealarmthreshold=*Mbyte*	Sets the threshold for low space warning (range is 0 to 1000000).
/storageresetthreshold=*Mbyte*	Sets the threshold to reset a low space warning (range is 0 to 1000000).
/nostoragealertmessages	Doesn't send low storage space messages.
/storagealertmessages	Sends low storage space messages.
/namecachestats	Shows statistics for name caching.
/closedfilecachesize=*NR*	Specifies the number of closed files that can be cached (range is 1 to 1000000).
/fileflushtimer=*sec*	Specifies the flush time in seconds for modified open files (range is 1 to 3600).
/minbuffercachesize=*NR*	Specifies the minimum number of NSS buffer cache entries (range is 256 to 1048576).
/minosbuffercachesize=*NR*	Specifies the minimum number of Novell buffer cache entries (range is 1024 to 1048576).
/bufferflushtimer=*sec*	Specifies the flush time for cache buffers that are modified.
/cachebalance	Turns on the dynamic balancing of free memory.
/nocachebalance	Turns off the dynamic balancing of free memory.
/cachebalance=*percentage*	Specifies the amount of free memory used for buffer cache (range is 1 to 99).
/cachebalancetimer=*sec*	Sets the cache balance timer (range is 1 to 3600).
/cachebalancemaxbufferspersession=*NR*	Specifies what to limit num buffers for each cache balance (range is 16 to 1048576).
/filecopyonwrite=*volume*	Makes a copy of files when they are open for write.
/nofilecopyonwrite=*volume*	Doesn't make a copy of files when they are open for write.
/upgradeobjectsonvolume=*volume*	Upgrades objects on the specified volume.
/compscreen	Shows compression statistics on the screen.
/poolautomaintenance=*pool*	Switches the specified pool to maintenance mode.
/poolautoverify=*pool*	Checks the specified pool at startup.
VolumeAutoDisplay	Shows current volume load time policies.
/cachestats	Shows statistics for the buffer caching.
/resetstats	Resets statistics for file and caching.
/salvage=*volume*	Turns on salvage of deleted files for the specified volume.
/nosalavge=*volume*	Turns off salvage of deleted files for the specified volume.
/userspacerestrictions=*volume*	Turns on space restrictions for users on the specified volume.
/nouserspacerestrictions=*volume*	Turns off space restrictions for users on the specified volume.
/directoryquotas=*volume*	Turns on directory quotas for the specified volume.
/nodirectoryquotas=*volume*	Turns off directory quotas for the specified volume.
/datashredding=*volume*[:*NR*]	Turns on data shredding for the specified volume. Shred NR time (range is 1 to 7).
/nodatashredding=*volume*	Turns off data shredding for the specified volume.
/flushfilesimmediately=*volume*	Flushes files immediate after a write on the specified volume.
/noflushfilesimmediately=*volume*	Doesn't flush files after a write on the specified volume.
/transaction=*volume*	Turns on file transaction on the specified volume.
/notransaction=*volume*	Turns off file transaction on the specified volume.
/migration=*volume*	Turns on migration on the specified volume.
/nomigration=*volume*	Turns off migration on the specified volume.

continued

/allocaheadblks=*blocks*	Specifies the number of blocks to allocate ahead on writes (range is 0 to 63).
/compression=*volume*	Turns on compression on the specified volume.
/nocompression=*volume*	Turns off compression on the specified volume.
/bgcompression	Turns on background compression.
/nobgcompression	Turns off background compression.
pools	Shows all available nss pools.
/poolautoactivate=*pool*	Places the pool in active stage when loaded.
/poolautodeactivate=*pool*	Leaves the pool in deactivated stage when loaded.
/poolautoverify=*pool*	Verifies the specified pool for physical integrity at startup time.
/mfl=*volume*	Turns on MFL maintenance on the specified volume.
/nomfl=*volume*	Turns off MFL maintenance on the specified volume.
/mflverify=*volume*	Shows the status of the MFL maintenance.
/fixmfl=*volume*	Shows the status of the MFL maintenance.
/getmflstatus=*volume*	Shows the status of the MFL maintenance.
/zidnamespace=*namespace*	Specifies the namespace for ZIDfilename to use. Can be DOS, LONG, MAC, or UNIX.
/zidvolumename=*volume*	Specifies the volume to be used by ZIDfilemname.
/zidtofilename=*name*	Converts ZID into its full path.
	The following 11 options can be used only while loading the NSS.NLM:
/namecachesize=*NR*	Specifies the number of Name Cache entries (range is 3 to 65521).
/namecache	Turns on name caching.
/nonamecache	Turns off name caching.
/asciinamecache	Turns on ASCII name caching.
/noasciinamecache	Turns off ASCII name caching.
/authcachesize=*NR*	Specifies the number of Authorization Cache entries (range is 16 to 50000).
/openfilehashshift=*size*	Specifies the size of the open file hash table (range is 8 to 20).
/mailboxsize=*size*	Specifies the size of the mailbox (range is 64 to 65536).
/numasyncios=*NR*	Sets how many Asyncio entries are allocated (range is 4 to 65536).
/numbonds=*NR*	Sets how many Bond entries are allocated (range is 512 to 2097152).
/numworktodos=*NR*	Sets how many WorkToDo entries are concurrently executing (range is 5 to 100).
	The following option is used by the ZLSS module:
zlssiostatus	Shows current NSS IO status.
/zlsspendingwritelos=*NT*	Specifies number of IOs dropped to the storage subsystem (range is 0 to 3000).
/lvscan=*pool*	Scans for logical volumes in the pool (must be active).
zlsspoolscan	Scans and load all zlss pools.
/zlssvolumeupgrade=*pool*	Upgrades the pool to NSS version 3.0.
/poolactivate=*pool*	Sets the specified pool to active state.
/pooldeactivate=*pool*	Sets the specified pool to deactivate state.
/poolmaintenance=*pool*	Sets the specified pool to maintenance state.
lvdeletestatusbasic	Shows information about deleted volumes.
lvdeletestatussalvageble	Shows information about salvageable logical volumes.
	The following options are used by the NWSA module:
/classicdirectoryquotas	Turns on classic NetWare quotas emulation.
/noclassicdirectoryquotas	Turns off classic NetWare quotas emulation.
	The following option is used by the NWSA module:
/setacondition=*condition*	Sets the specified condition.
	The following options can only be used at startup:
/setvalue	Turns on jstcpValue.
/nosetvalue	Turns off jstcpValue.
/resetdostimes	Resets DOS time conversions cache.
nss modules	Shows which modules are loaded.
nss volumes	Shows the volumes managed by NSS.
nss status	Shows the current status.

nvaltdb

OS: NetWare 5

Function	Converts Open NetView `nvaltgen` output files from DOS into the Btrieve file format so that NWSAA alert information may be monitored. It also remaps code points if there are conflicts.
Syntax	load nvaltdb *source destination { remapfile }*
source	Specifies the volume, full path, and the `cpg` filename that is converted.
destination	Specifies the volume and path to the Btrieve formatted file placement.
remapfile	Specifies the file containing the code point remappings.
File Name:	`nvaltdb.nlm`
Directory:	\system
Type:	External

nver

OS: NetWare 3,4,5

Function	Shows version information about the operating system and NetWare drivers.
Syntax	nver [options...]
/C	Doesn't pause after each help screen.
/VER	Shows version information.
/?	Shows help information.
File Name:	`nver.exe`
Directory:	\public
Type:	External
nver	Shows the version information.
nver /C > versions.txt	Outputs the version information to the file `versions.txt`.

nvxadm

OS: NetWare 5,6

Function	Starts and stops the NetWare Web manager. Use `nvxadmup` to start and `nwxadmdn` to stop.
Syntax	nvxadmup nvxadmdn
File Name:	`nvxadmup.ncf, nvxadmdn.ncf`
Directory:	\system
Type:	External

nvxnew

OS: NetWare 5,6

Function	Starts and stops the NetWare news server. Use `nvxnewup` to start and `nvxnewdn` to stop.
Syntax	nvxnewup nvxnewdn
File Name:	`nvxnewup.ncf, nvxnewdn.ncf`
Directory:	\system
Type:	External

nvxweb

OS: NetWare 5,6

Function	Starts and stops the NetWare Web server. Use `nvxwebup` to start and `nwxwebdn` to stop.
Syntax	nvxwebup nvxwebdn
File Name:	`nvxwebup.ncf, nvxwebdn.ncf`
Directory:	\system
Type:	External

nwcrpair

OS: NetWare 5

Function	Repairs Btrieve file corruption normally caused by a remote access server abend or other server problem.
Syntax	nwcrpair
File Name:	`nwcrpair.nlm`
Directory:	\system
Type:	External
Tip:	Run this utility if you are having trouble starting the remote access server with `nwcstat`.

nwcstat

OS: NetWare 4,5

Function	Shows the current port status, server status, and alerts for the remote access server.
Syntax	nwcstat
File Name:	`nwcstat.nlm`
Directory:	\system
Type:	External

nwcterm

OS: NetWare 5

Function	Sends ASCII characters to any port initialized by `aio.nlm` and shows the response.
Syntax	nwcterm
File Name: `nwcterm.nlm`	**Directory:** \system — **Type:** Internal

nwdetect

OS: NetWare 4

Function	Compares the version and type of the client with the information specified on the command line of the command. The command returns a 1 if the client should be upgraded and a 0 if it's not necessary.
Syntax	nwdetect *{ name } { version1 } { version2 }* [options]
/t *clienttype*	Specifies the type of client to detect. Valid types are NETX, VLM, and NIOS.
/p *text*	Specifies a text to show if the command returns a 1.
/dt	Specifies the default action to be 0 or false.
/c *file*	Specifies the full path and file where to read the install stamp (default is `net.cfg`).
/ns	Searches in net.cfg for a NO STAMP set.
/h	Shows help information and the version number of the command.
string	Specifies a string to detect.
version1	Specifies the version to detect or starting version when used with version2.
version2	Specifies the ending version to detect. (The format for the version is NR.NR.NR.)
File Name: `nwdetect.exe`	**Directory:** \public — **Type:** External

nwipcfg

OS: NetWare 4

Function	Performs three tasks: configures server as a DNS client, configures IP software on server, and starts the IP service.
Syntax	load nwipcfg
Configures DNS Client	Configures a NetWare server as a DNS client.
DNS Domain	Specifies the DNS domain name for the server.
Name Servers...	Identifies the name or IP address of the host of the first, second, and third name servers.
Configures NetWare/IP Server	Configures the software on an IP server.
NetWare/IP Domain	Specifies the name of the NetWare/IP domain.
Preferred DSSes	Sets the preferred DSS servers, select by pressing the Enter key.
Initial DSS Contact Retries	Identifies the number of retries to the DSS server. The range is 0 – 50 (default is 1).
Retry Interval	Identifies the number of seconds between retries. The range is 5 – 100 (default is 10).
Timeout for NWIP Read/Write	Identifies the number of seconds before a TCP socket opened or closed for translation.
Slow Link Customizations	Sets the network name and host to other servers that operate via slow links.
Forward IPX Information to DSS?	Specifies if the NetWare server should act as a forwarding gateway.
Start NetWare/IP Server	Starts the NetWare/IP server.
File Name: `nwipcfg.nlm`	**Directory:** \system — **Type:** External
load nwipcfg	Starts the interface for nwipcfg.

nwlog

OS: NetWare 4

Function	Shows the date, time, user, network number, and MAC address.
Syntax	nwlog [options]
/f *file*	Writes the information on the last line in a file.
/m *message*	Appends a message after the information.
/r *NR*	Specifies the number of retries for opening the log file.
/h	Shows help information.
File Name: `nwlog.exe`	**Directory:** \public — **Type:** External
Tip:	Useful when writing login scripts.
nwlog	Shows the information on STDOUT.
nwlog /f file.log	Appends the information in `file.log`.
nwlog /m "Hello world"	Appends the message "Hello World" after the information.

nwstamp

OS:	NetWare 4
Function	Sets the version of NetWare release in the `net.cfg` file.
Syntax	nwstamp *name version* [options]

/B *name*	Specifies the name and the directory of the old `net.cfg` file.
/C *name*	Specifies the name and the directory of the `net.cfg` file.
/H	Shows help information.
name	Specifies the name in the `net.cfg` file.
version	Specifies the version to put in the `net.cfg` file.

File Name:	`nwstamp.exe`	**Directory:**	\public	**Type:**	External

nwucinit

OS:	NetWare 5,6
Function	Configures the trial versions and add licenses.
Syntax	nwucinit [options...]

-C*NR*	Specifies the product code.
-Q*dir*	Installs `ucmgr.key` located in the path `dir`.
-U*NR*	Installs and removes all licenses for product code.

File Name:	`nwucinit.nlm`	**Directory:**	\system	**Type:**	External

NWUCINIT -C11 -Q sys:\ucg\license	Adds a license.

nwucutil

OS:	NetWare 5,6
Function	Shows information about installed products and adds licenses.
Syntax	nwucutil [options...]

-D*driver*	Adds a license from disk in drive.
-G*NR*	Specifies the user's count for product code.
-K*NR*	Specifies key number.
-S	Shows serial number.
-T*dir*	Enters target directory. Used when pervasive database is installed.

File Name:	`nwucutil.nlm`	**Directory:**	\system	**Type:**	External

nwxtract

OS:	NetWare 3,4
Function	Extracts a file or a group of files directly from the installation CD-ROM or disks to the local or network drive.
Syntax	nwxtract *sourcedrive file { destination }* [options...]

/s=*server*	Specifies the name of the server to extract the files to.
/t=*type*	Identifies the type of file to extract. Types are DOS, MAC, OS2, SER (server), UNX, and WIN.
/?	Shows help information.
/ver	Shows version information.
sourcedrive	Specifies the drive letter where the source files are located.
file	Specifies the filename or file group to be extracted.
destination	Specifies an alternate destination instead of the original location.

File Name:	`nwxtract.exe`	**Directory:**	Installation directory on the installation CD-ROM.	**Type:**	External

nwxtract e: flag.exe /t=dos	Extracts DOS version of `flag.exe` to its original location on current server.
nwxtract e: ndir.exe /t=dos /s=neptune	Extracts DOS version of `ndir.exe` to its original location on server neptune.
nwxtract e: filer.exe c:\nwtemp /t=dos	Extracts DOS version of `filer.exe` to the local c: drive in the directory `nwtemp`.

ODBC Driver for NDS

OS:	NetWare 6
Function	Installs the Novell ODBC driver for NDS on a workstation.
Syntax	odbc

File Name:	`odbc.exe`	**Directory:**	\public\mgmt\consoleone\1.2\reporting\bin	**Type:**	External

odbcjoin

OS:	NetWare 5
Function	Establishes a connection to a database.
Syntax	odbcjoin *database user password*

database	Specifies a database name.

continued

user	Specifies a username in the database.
password	Specifies the password.
File Name: odbcjoin.exe	**Directory:** \public **Type:** External

odbcping

OS: NetWare 5

Function	Tests the connection to a database.
Syntax	odbcping *database user password*

database	Specifies a database name.
user	Specifies a username in the database.
password	Specifies the password.
File Name: odbcping.exe	**Directory:** \public **Type:** External

orbcmd

OS: NetWare 5,6

Function	Enables the object request broker (ORB) on the NetWare server.
Syntax	orbcmd
File Name:	orbcmd.nlm **Directory:** \java\bin **Type:** External
Note:	Smart agent is also needed to run ORB commands on the NetWare server.
orbcmd	Loads the ORB module.

osagent

OS: NetWare 5,6

Function	Registers CORBA objects that are used with the ZENworks 2 system. The client uses this naming service to help locate CORBA objects.
Syntax	osagent [options...]

-p *port*	Sets the UDP port number to use (instead of what is set by `OSAGENT_PORT`).
-v	Shows debug information.
-?	Shows help information.
File Name: osagent.nlm	**Directory:** \java\bin **Type:** External

partmgr

OS: NetWare 4

Function	Creates, shows, and manages NDS partitions and replicas.
Syntax	partmgr [/ver]

/ver	Shows the version level and the files it requires.
Manage partitions	Edits partitions. Creates, modifies, and deletes partitions.
Change context	Specifies the context to act from.
File Name: partmgr.exe	**Directory:** \public **Type:** External

paudit

OS: NetWare 3

Function	Lists the system's accounting records.
Syntax	paudit [/C]

/C	Shows the list in a continuous list, doesn't stop for each page.
File Name: paudit.exe	**Directory:** \public **Type:** External
paudit /C	Shows the list in a continuous list.

P-Class Trace Console

OS: NetWare 5,6

Function	Captures trace data for EiconCard P-Class adapters (P62, P92) when running the SDLC protocol.
Syntax	ptrace
File Name:	ptrace.nlm **Directory:** \system **Type:** External

perl

OS: NetWare 5,6

Function	Runs Perl (Practical Extraction and Report Language) scripts on the server.
Syntax	perl *{ script }*

script	Specifies the script to run. If not given, starts an interactive shell.
File Name: perl.nlm	**Directory:** \system **Type:** External
perl SYS:\tmp\perlscript	Run the specified perlscript.

Policy Tool (Client)

OS:	NetWare 5,6
Function	A Java tool that is used to manage and create external policy configurations to manage Java security. The policy file `.java.policy` containing the Java policies must be located in the \windows directory.
Syntax	policytool
File Name:	`policytool.exe`
Directory:	\public\mgmt\consoleone\1.2\jre\bin
Type:	External

Policy Tool (Server)

OS:	NetWare 6
Function	A graphical tool to manage Java security where you can add, edit and remove permissions to Java policies. The policy file `.java.policy` containing the Java policies must be located at the root of the SYS volume.
Syntax	policytool

PPP Console

OS:	NetWare 5
Function	A monitor tool that is used to show PPP protocol information for the local server or a remote server over SNMP.
Syntax	pppcon

SNMP Access Configuration	Sets SNMP parameters. A local or a remote host can be specified.
PPP Interfaces	Shows the PPP interfaces.
Network Addresses	Shows used network addresses for IP or IPX.
Display Traps	Shows the traps that have been specified.

File Name:	`pppcon.nlm`
Directory:	\system
Type:	External

PPP Trace Utility

OS:	NetWare 4,5
Function	A tracing utility used to monitor and capture frames and show real time statistics for PPP connections.
Syntax	load ppptrace

Network Interface Information	Lists of available PPP-interface.
Real-Time Monitor	Shows the real-time monitor screen.
Playback	Shows a previously saved trace.
Configuration	Configures which device to store data in (ram or disk).

File Name:	`ppptrace.nlm`
Directory:	\system
Type:	External

pppdisp

OS:	NetWare 5
Function	Reads the input trace file generated by `PPPtrace.nlm` and creates an output file in ASCII format.
Syntax	pppdisp *inputfile { outputfile }*

inputfile	Specifies the input trace filename that was created by `PPPtrace`.
outputfile	Specifies the filename used for the ASCII output instead of showing on the screen.

File Name:	`pppdisp.exe`
Directory:	\system\utils
Type:	External

PPPRNS Configuration

OS:	NetWare 5
Function	Configures PPPRNS that are used to connect remote workstations to corporate networks over analog or ISDN lines.
Syntax	ppprncon
File Name:	`ppprncon.nlm`
Directory:	\system
Type:	External

Print Console

OS:	NetWare 3,4
Function	Administers printers, print servers, and print queue.
Syntax	pconsole

	The following options are used in NDS mode (use F4 to change mode):
Print Queues	Shows, edits, creates, or deletes print queues.
Printers	Shows, edits, creates, or deletes printers.
Print Servers	Shows, edits, creates, or deletes printer servers.
Change Context	Changes the current context.
	The following options are used in bindery mode (use F4 to change mode):
Print Queues	Shows, edits, creates, or deletes print queues.
Print Servers	Shows, edits, creates, or deletes printer servers.
Quick Setup	Opens a quick setup window to set up a printer.
Change Current NetWare Server	Changes the server that is administered.

continued

File Name:	`pconsole.exe`	**Directory:**	\public	**Type:**	External
Warning:	Doesn't set up printers in bindery mode on a server that has NDS.				

Print Upgrade Utility

OS: NetWare 4

Function	Upgrades printers and print servers from NetWare 3 into NDS. Also able to convert printcon and printdef databases.
Syntax	load pupgrade

Upgrade PRINTCON Database	Converts the configuration for print jobs.
Upgrade PRINTDEF Database	Converts the forms and printer definitions.
Upgrade Print Server and Printers	Creates NDS objects of the NetWare printers and print servers.
Exit PUPGRADE	Exits and unloads the pupgrade.nlm.

File Name:	`pupgrade.nlm`	**Directory:**	\system	**Type:**	External

Printer Definition

OS: NetWare 3,4

Function	Shows, creates, modifies, or deletes printer definitions.
Syntax	printdef

Print Devices	Creates, edits, or changes printer device options.
Printer Forms	Creates, edits, or changes printer forms.
	The following option is used in NDS mode (use F4 to change mode):
Change Current Context	Changes the current context.
	The following option is used in bindery mode (use F4 to change mode):
Change Current Server	Changes the server that is administered.

File Name:	`printdef.exe`	**Directory:**	\public	**Type:**	External

Protect

OS: NetWare 5,6

Function	Loads NLM modules into a protected memory address space.
Syntax	protect *NLM*

NLM	Specifies the NLM module to load into the protected memory address space.

Protection

OS: NetWare 5,6

Function	Shows a list of protected address spaces or adds or removes restart functionality to or from them.
Syntax	protection [options...]

restart *address*	Adds restart functionality to the specified address space.
No restart *address*	Removes restart functionality from the specified address space.

Protocol Explorer

OS: NetWare 3

Function	Shows information about current protocol stacks on the server and the frame types they are using.
Syntax	load proto

File Name:	`proto.nlm`	**Directory:**	\system	**Type:**	External

psc

OS: NetWare 3,4

Function	Controls and shows information about print servers and printers.
Syntax	psc [options...]

	The following two options are required:
ps=*printserver*	Specifies the print server to use.
p=*printernumber*	Specifies the printer to use.
ab	Aborts the current print job and removes it from the print queue.
cd	Cancels the Going down after current jobs option.
ff	Advances printer to top of next page.
/?	Shows help information. Not available in NW3.
l	Shows a layout of the printing setup. Not available in NW3.
m*character*	Prints a line of the specified character.
mo f=*number*	Uses a new form mounted on the printer.
pau	Pauses the printer.
pri	Removes the printer from the list of network printers.
sha	Makes the network printer available to the print server.
star	Restarts the printer after you have stopped or paused it.

continued

stat	Displays the status, for example, prints job name, ID, and percent complete.
sto	Stops the printer and returns the print job to the print queue.
s=*server*	Sets which NW server has the print server you want to manage. Not available in NW3.
/ver	Shows version information. Not available in NW3.
File Name: psc.exe	**Directory:** \public **Type:** External
psc ps=ps-ucg p=1 pau	Pauses printer 1 on print server ps-ucg.
psc l	Shows a layout of the printing setup.
psc ps=ps-ucg p=1 ab	Aborts the current print job on printer 1 on print server ps-ucg.

pserver

OS: NetWare 3

Function	Installs a print server and establishes print services over the network using a dedicated workstation. Before executing pserver, you must first create a print server using the **pconsole** utility.
Syntax	pserver *{ file server/ } printserver*
file server	Specifies the file server name where the print server was created.
printserver	Specifies the name of the print server to initialize.
File Name: pserver.exe	**Directory:** \public **Type:** External
pserver laser	Loads the pserver and installs a printer named laser.
pserver saturn/color	Loads the pserver and installs a printer name color created on server saturn.

PSM

OS: NetWare 5,6

Function	Shows platform support modules (PSM) information supported by your hardware.
Syntax	psm option
?	Shows a list of PSM commands available on your server.
show pic	Shows the server interrupt table and mask status for protected and real modes.
psm show pic	Shows a list of server interrupts and the mask status.

purge

OS: NetWare 3,4,5

Function	Removes files permanently that have been deleted. Files that are purged can't be recovered.
Syntax	purge *{ file }* [options]
/a	Deletes files in all subdirectories of the current or the specified directory.
/?	Shows help information.
file	Specifies file or directory to purge. Wildcards can be used.
NW4, NW5:	
/ver	Shows the version number of the command.
File Name: purge.exe	**Directory:** \public **Type:** External
Tip:	To recover files that have been deleted, use `salvage` or `filer`.
purge	Purges files in the current directory only.
purge /home/ucg	Purges files in the directory `/home/ucg`.
purge /a	Purges all files in current directory and its subdirectories.

pver

OS: NetWare 6

Function	Shows products version information for NetWare.
Syntax	pver

qman

OS: NetWare 5,6

Function	Loads the SMS queue manager or configures new SMS job queues in the NDS tree.
Syntax	qman [new]
new	Starts the configuration manager to configure or reconfigure the job queue. (The old configuration is overwritten, if one exists.)
File Name: qman.nlm	**Directory:** \system **Type:** External
Note:	You must first configure the SMS data requester using the server command `smdr`.
qman new	Starts the SMS queue manger in interactive mode.

rconag, rconag6

OS: NetWare 5,6

Function	Enables the ability to control the server's console screen remotely from a workstation using `RConsoleJ`.
Syntax	rconag6 [option] *{ password } { tcpport } { spxport }*

encrypt	Encrypts a password and creates a sys:system\ldrconag.ncf if desired.
-e	Encrypts the given password.
password	Specifies the password in clear text or encrypted when used with -e.
tcpport	Specifies the TCP port to use (default is 2034).
spxport	Specifies the TCP port to use (default is 16800). (For tcpport and spxport, use -1 to disable or 0 to use a dynamic port.)

File Name:	`rconag.nlm, rconag6.nlm`	**Directory:**	\system	**Type:**	External
Tip:	Use rconag6 to make a sys:system\ldrconag.ncf file and use that one in autoexec.ncf for startup.				

rconag6 thepass	Loads rconag6 with the password "thepass" and default port configuration.

rconprxy

OS: NetWare 5,6

Function	A proxy server that is used to let RConsoleJ communicate with an IPX-only NetWare server.
Syntax	rconprxy *tcpport*

tcpport	Specifies the TCP port. Use 0 to allow dynamic ports (default is 2035).

File Name:	`rconprxy.nlm`	**Directory:**	\system	**Type:**	External

rconprxy 2035	Loads a proxy server using port 2035.

rconsole

OS: NetWare 3,4,5

Function	Controls a server's console from a workstation, if no server is specified a list will be shown.
Syntax	rconsole *{ server }*

	The following keys are available when using rconsole on NW4, NW5 and NW6:
<ALT-F1>	Shows Available options menu used to transfer files to/from server and other options.
<ALT-F2>	Quits the rconsole session.
<ALT-F3>	Cycles forward through the various console screens.
<ALT-F4>	Cycles backward through the various console screens.
<ALT-F5>	Shows the workstations network address (MAC address).
	The following keys are available when using rconsole on NW3:
*	Shows Available options menu used to transfer files to/from server and other options.
+	Cycles forward through the various console screens.
-	Cycles backward through the various console screens.
<SHIFT-ESC>	Quits the rconsole session.

File Name:	`rconsole.exe`	**Directory:**	\public	**Type:**	External
Tip:	You must load the NLM's rspx.nlm and remote.nlm on the server before you can run rconsole.				

rconsole nucleus	Connects directly to the server Nucleus.

RConsoleJ

OS: NetWare 5,6

Function	A Java-based remote control utility that is used to control a NetWare server console over TCP/IP. It is possible to control a server's console over IPX using `RConsoleJ` through a NetWare proxy server.
Syntax	rjconj

File Name:	`rconj.exe`	**Directory:**	\public\mgmt\consoleone\1.2	**Type:**	External
Tip:	You must load the NLM rcong6.nlm on the server before you can run RConsoleJ.				

rebuild

OS: NetWare 5

Function	Recovers, rebuilds, and verifies NSS volumes or NSS pools that have become corrupt or are suspected of corruption.
Syntax	nss option

/me	Starts NSS with the administration menus.
/rebuild	Shows a menu of NSS volumes that you can select and rebuild.
/rebuild = *NSSvolume*[,*NSSvolumes...*]	Specifies an NSS volume or volumes to rebuild, multiple volumes separated by commas.
/verify	Shows a menu of NSS volumes that you can select and verify.
/verify = *{ NSSvolume }*	Specifies an NSS volume to verify.

continued

File Name:	nss.nlm	**Directory:**	\system	**Type:**	Internal
Warning:	You must run the verify utility after you have performed a rebuild of an NSS volume.				

nss /me	Starts the menu-based NSS administration utility.
nss /rebuild	Shows a list of NSS volumes that you can choose to rebuild.
nss /verify=vol2	Verifies the NSS volume VOL2 after it was rebuilt.

Remote Access Configuration

OS: NetWare 4,5

Function	Configures the communication server used for remote access for inbound and outbound communications.
Syntax	nwccon

Configure Ports	Used to modify existing ports by pressing Enter or add a new port by pressing Insert.
Configure Port Groups	Creates or modifies groups of communication ports.
Configure Synchronize Interfaces	Launches `Inetcfg` to configure a communication device.
Configure Security	Used to restrict port access, set passwords for dialing out, and set dialback options.
Configure Services	Configures ARAS, NCS, and PPPRNS services.
Set Up...	Sets up, configures, and adds drivers for communication ports.
Generate Configuration Report	Shows the current configuration.

File Name:	nwccon.nlm	**Directory:**	\system	**Type:**	External

remove

OS: NetWare 3

Function	Removes the trustees on a file or directory for a user or a group.
Syntax	remove [USER] *username* [from *path*] [options...] remove [GROUP] *groupname* [from *path*] [options...]

/subdir	Removes trustees from subdirectories.
/files	Removes trustees from files.
from *path*	Specifies the path to the volume, directory, or file to remove trustees from.
username	Specifies the name of the user to grant rights for.
groupname	Specifies the name of the group that you want to set rights for.

File Name:	remove.exe	**Directory:**	\public	**Type:**	External

remove USER speed from u:\data	Removes trustees for user speed in the u:\data directory.
remove GROUP users from u:\public /Subdirs	Removes trustees for group users in the u:\public and its subdirectories.

Remove DNS/DHCP Management Console

OS: NetWare 5,6

Function	Uninstalls the DNS/DHCP management console from the client workstation.
Syntax	uninst

File Name:	uninst.exe	**Directory:**	\public\dnsdhcp\english	**Type:**	External

remove dos

OS: NetWare 3,4

Function	Removes DOS from the file server's memory and gives the memory back to NetWare to use.
Syntax	remove dos

Remove Storage Adapter

OS: NetWare 5,6

Function	Removes the specified storage adapter.
Syntax	remove storage adapter *adapter*

adapter	Specifies the adapter to remove.

remove storage adapter A0	Removes storage adapter A0.

rendir

OS: NetWare 3,4

Function	Renames a directory.
Syntax	rendir *path name* [option]

path	Specifies the path to the directory you want to rename.
name	Specifies the new name for the directory.
NW4	
/ver	Shows the version number and list of files it uses to execute.

File Name:	rendir.exe	**Directory:**	\public	**Type:**	External

rendir m:\test temp	Renames the directory `m:\test` to `temp`.

Reset Environment

OS: NetWare 5,6

Function	Resets server parameters to their default values.
Syntax	reset environment

reset server

OS: NetWare 5,6

Function	Downs the server and then restarts it. Is similar to the `restart server` command, but without the options.
Syntax	reset server

reset server	Downs the server and then restarts it.

restart

OS: NetWare 4

Function	Reloads the IOEngine on one NW SFT III server while leaving the other server running.
Syntax	restart
Warning:	Disks should be mirrored before you run this command on the primary IOEngine.

revoke

OS: NetWare 3

Function	Revokes trustee rights from users or groups on a file or a directory.
Syntax	revoke *rights* [for *path*] from [USER] *username* [options...] revoke *rights* [for *path*] from [GROUP] *groupname* [options...]

/subdirectories	Uses subdirectories when revoking trustees.
/files	Uses files when revoking trustees.
ALL	Revokes all rights from the specified name.
S	Revokes all rights from the specified name on the specified directory and its files.
R	Revokes access to read files for the specified name.
W	Revokes access to write to files for the specified name.
C	Revokes access to create directories and write to files for the specified name.
E	Revokes access to remove the directory and its content for the specified name.
M	Revokes access to modify file attributes for the specified name.
F	Revokes name access to show directory content for the specified name.
A	Revokes name access to modify file and directory trustees for the specified name.
rights	Specifies rights to revoke from the specified user or group. (Separate multiple rights with spaces.)
path	Specifies the path to the volume, directory, subdirectory, or file to use.
username	Specifies the name of the user to revoke rights for.
groupname	Specifies the name of the group to revoke rights for.

File Name:	`revoke.exe`	**Directory:**	\public	**Type:**	External

revoke s for u:\public from user speed	Removes the Supervisor rights from the user speed on u:\public.
revoke r w f u:\data from group users	Removes the access to read, write and show contents of u:\data.

rmic

OS: NetWare 5,6

Function	Runs the Java Remote Invocation Compiler, which can create stubs and skeletons.
Syntax	rmic [options...] *{ classnames... }*

-keep	Saves source files of stubs and skeletons to the directory specified by -d.
-v1.1	Creates stubs and skeletons in the 1.1 version of the JDK stub protocol.
-vcompat	Creates stubs and skeletons that are compatible with both 1.1 and 1.2.
-v1.2	Creates stubs and skeletons in the 1.2 version of the JDK stub protocol.
-g	Creates debugging information.
-depend	Recompiles classes that are out-of-date.
-nowarn	Doesn't give warnings.
-verbose	Shows information on what happens during compiling.
-classpath *directory*	Specifies the directory where the compiler finds source and class files.
-d *directory*	Specifies the directory where the compiler creates the class files.
-J*runtimeflag*	Sends argument to the Java interpreter.
classnames...	Specifies the class names to use.

File Name:		**Directory:**	\java\lib\	**Type:**	Internal

rmid

OS:	NetWare 5,6
Function	Enables the Java Remote Method Invocation Daemon that lets objects be registered and activated in a Java Virtual Machine. Must be started to allow objects to be activated in a JVM or registered with activation system.
Syntax	rmid [options...]

-port *NR*	Specifies the number of the port that the command uses for its registry.
-log *directory*	Specifies the directory where the database and related information are created.
-stop	Stops the current session of rmid.
-C*option*	Specifies an option sent to a child process.

File Name:	`rmid.exe`	**Directory:**	\public\mgmt\consoleone\1.2\jre\bin\	**Type:**	External

rmid

OS:	NetWare 6
Function	Enables the Java remote method invocation daemon that lets objects be registered and activated in a Java virtual machine. Must be started to allow objects to be activated in a JVM or registered with activation system.
Syntax	rmid [options...]

-port *NR*	Specifies the number of the port that the command uses for its registry.
-log *directory*	Specifies the directory where the database and related information are created.
-stop	Stops the current session of rmid.
-C*option*	Specifies an option sent to a child process.

rmiregistry (Client)

OS:	NetWare 5,6
Function	Creates and starts a remote object registry that is used by Java RMI servers to bind remote object names.
Syntax	rmiregistry [-J*argument*] *port*

-J*argument*	Specifies the runtime flag argument to pass to the Java interpreter.
port	Specifies a new port to use instead of the default one, which is 1099. (Remember to tell the other clients the change of the port number!)

File Name:	`rmiregistry.exe`	**Directory:**	\public\mgmt\consoleone\1.2\jre\bin	**Type:**	External
Tip:	Use `start rmiregistry` to start it in a new window.				

rmiregistry 1109	Starts RMI registry on port 1109 instead of port 1099.

rmiregistry (Server)

OS:	NetWare 5,6
Function	Creates and starts a remote object registry that is used by Java RMI servers to bind remote object names.
Syntax	rmiregistry *{ port }*

port	Specifies a new port to use instead of the default one, which is 1099. (Remember to tell the other clients that you have changed the port number!)

rmiregistry 1520	Starts RMI registry on port 1520 instead of port 1099.

route (Client)

OS:	NetWare 3
Function	Configures a Source Router that will be loaded or changes one that has been loaded.
Syntax	route [options...]

u	Unloads any preexisting Source Router from the memory.
board=*NR*	Specifies the board number as assigned by the ODI. Don't use with an old IPX driver.
clear	Clears any nodes from a source router that has already been loaded.
def	Sends an unknown (default) node address to ALL ROUTES broadcasts.
gbr	Sends the broadcast FFFF FFFF FFFF address to ALL ROUTES broadcast.
hops=*NR*	Specifies the number of bridge hops that are configured (default is 07, max is 13).
mbr	Sends a multicast COOO xxxx xxxx address to ALL ROUTES broadcast.
nodes=*NR*	Specifies the number of supported NODEs (default is 16, max is 1000).
time=*NR*	Specifies the number of seconds before a route is timed out (default is 10, max is 255).
tra=*NR*	Specifies the number of THIS RING ALTERNATE for broadcasts (default is 00, max is 255).
tro=*NR*	Specifies the number of THIS RING ONLY for broadcasts (default is 00, max is 255). (Separate multiple options with comma.)

continued

File Name: `route.com`	**Directory:** \public\client		**Type:** External
Note:	For the options `def`, *gbr*, `mbr` the default broadcast is SINGLE ROUTES.		
route time=30	Sets the route timeout to 30 seconds.		
route u	Unloads any routers from memory.		
route clear	Clears any loaded nodes on a router.		

rpl (Client) — OS: NetWare 3

Function	Attempts to boot from the preferred server or other server that has loaded the `rpl.nlm`.
Syntax	rpl [options...]

ps=*server*	Specifies the server that the bootstrap connects to.
tro	Forces a `This Ring Only` count of (3) on all broadcast frames on the bootstrap.
wait time=*NR*	Specifies how long the bootstrap must wait (in seconds) before selecting a disk image. (Ranges: 0000 - 65535 (default is 0000 which is the same as infinite).)
File Name: `rpl.com`	**Directory:** \public\client **Type:** External
rpl ps=neptune	Specifies the bootstrap program connects to the server called Neptune.
rpl wait time=333	Makes the bootstrap program wait 333 seconds before selecting a cursored disk image.

rprinter — OS: NetWare 3

Function	Connects or disconnects a remote printer to or from a print server.
Syntax	rprinter *{ printerserver printerNR }* [-r]

-r	Disconnects the specified printer from the specified printerserver.
printerserver printerNR	Connects the specified printer to the specified printerserver.
File Name: `rprinter.exe`	**Directory:** \public **Type:** External
rprinter	Lists all available printservers and printers.
rprinter UCG A123	Connects the printer A123 to the UCG printerserver.

rs232 — OS: NetWare 3,4,5

Function	Sets up a communication port to use for remote management over a null modem cable or modem.
Syntax	NW3: load rs232 *{ port } { speed }* NW4, NW5: load rs232 *{ port } { speed }* [options..]

port	Specifies the COM port to use. Valid values are 1 or 2.
speed	Specifies the baud rate of the modem. Valid values are 2400, 4800, and 9600.
NW4, NW5:	
N	Specifies that a null modem cable is used.
C	Enables call back functions.
File Name: `rs232.nlm`	**Directory:** \system **Type:** External
Note:	A communication port driver such as AIOCOMX must first be loaded.
rs232 1 9600	Uses COM port 1 and sets the baud rate to 9,600.
rs232	Shows the current rs232 settings.
rs232 1 9600 C	Enables call back functions (can't be used in NW3).

Scan All — OS: NetWare 5,6

Function	Scans all LUNs of a SCSI adapter to find any SCSI devices.
Syntax	scan all *adapter*

adapter	Specifies the name of the SCSI adapter to scan for SCSI devices.

schdelay — OS: NetWare 4

Function	Prioritizes server processes, schedules processes to use less CPU power, and slows down processes.
Syntax	load schdelay *{ process_name = NR }*

process_name =	Specifies which process uses scheduling delay. (Valid processes are the ones that access the server CPU.)
NR	Specifies process frequency. Use 0 or a number between 2 and 10000. (0 = run every cycle, 2 means that it runs every second cycle.)

continued

File Name: `schdelay.nlm`	**Directory:** \system	**Type:**	External
load schdelay	Shows a list of valid process names and their current schdelay value.		
load schdelay all processes = 0	Undoes schdelay values for all processes.		

Schema Manager

OS: NetWare 4,5

Function	Is built-in to the NDS Manager and is used to extend the NDS schema by adding new classes, and attributes. Also used to delete unused classes and attributes and find and fix potential problems in the schema and more.
Syntax	ndsmgr32 > Object > Schema Manager

File Name: `ndsmgr32.exe`	**Directory:** \public\win32	**Type:**	Internal

Screen Saver

OS: NetWare 5,6

Function	Locks the server console and activates the screen saver. A colored tail appears for every installed processor - P0 = red, P1 = blue, P2 = yellow, P3 = green. The tail becomes longer as the processor activity increases.
Syntax	scrsaver *{ options... }*

DEFAULT	If no options are specified, the default settings are used.
activate	Activates immediately and overrides `disable` and `enable` modes.
auto clear delay=*seconds*	Sets seconds (1 to 300) to wait before clearing the unlock dialog box (default is 60).
delay=*seconds*	Sets seconds (1 to 7000) to wait before activating screen saver (default is 600).
disable	Disables the screen saver.
disable auto clear	Disables the automatic clearing of the unlock dialog box.
disable lock	Disables the console lock. When the console is unlocked, anyone can access it.
enable	Enables the screen saver. Activates after a set time in the `delay` option.
enable auto clear	Automatically clears the unlock dialog box. Activates after the auto clear delay time.
enable lock	Enables the console lock. Requires username and password before restoring.
no password	Unlocks the console without a password and must be set when loading scrsaver.
status	Shows the current features and options for the screen saver.
help *{ option }*	Shows help information or help on using one of the scrsaver options listed here.

File Name: `scrsaver.nlm`	**Directory:** \system	**Type:**	External
Note:	These options can be combined if they are separated by a semi colon (;) and a blank space.		
scrsaver auto clear delay=40	Sets the autoclear delay time to 40 seconds.		

security

OS: NetWare 3

Function	Shows a listing of security issues. Reads the bindery for passwords, login scripts, and rights in standard directories.
Syntax	security [/c]

/c	Scrolls the whole listing without interruption.

File Name: `security.exe`	**Directory:** \system\	**Type:**	External
security	Starts the listing of security information.		
security > myfile	Creates the file myfile containing the security information.		

send (Client)

OS: NetWare 3,4

Function	Sends a message to all users currently logged into the server or to a specific user specified by destination.
Syntax	send "*message*" [TO] *{ destination }* [AND or ,] *{ destination }* [options...] send "*message*" [TO] *{ server/*]CONSOLE or EVERYBODY [options...]

"*message*"	Identifies the message that you want to send (max 44 characters).
destination	Specifies the username or connection number to send the message.
server	Specifies the server to send the message to.
TO	Is optional.
AND	Separates destinations if sending a message to specific users.
,	Is also used to separate destinations and is used as a replacement for AND.
CONSOLE	Sends the message to the console of the current or specified server.
EVERYBODY	Sends the message to all users connected to the specified server.
NW4:	
/A	Accepts all messages.
/A=C	Accepts only messages from the server console.
/A=N	Doesn't accept any messages.
/A=P	Stores the last message until the user polls to receive it.

continued

/P	Polls for the last stored message.
/S	Shows the current broadcast mode.
/B	Sends across a bindery connection when logged in to NDS.
/?	Shows help information.
/VER	Shows version information.

File Name:	send.exe	**Directory:**	\public\	**Type:**	External

send "Please logout of the server" guy, myles, 3, 12	Sends the message "Please logout of the server" to users guy, myles, and connections 3 and 12.
send "Please wait saving data" CONSOLE	Sends the message to the console of the default server.

senlm

OS: NetWare 5

Function	Executes scripts written in the ScriptEase programming language or starts the ScriptEase command prompt.
Syntax	senlm { /secure=*file* } { *file* } ["*code*"]

/secure=*file*	Uses the specified file for security filtering.
	The following two parameters can't be combined:
file	Specifies the script file to execute and any parameters it might require.
code	Specifies script source text.
	The following command can be used at the ScriptEase command prompt:
alias { *name=string* }	Creates or, if no parameters are used, shows all currently defined aliases.
name	Specifies the name of the new alias.
string	Specifies a string of commands the alias should execute.
cd { *path* }	Changes or shows the current directory.
name	Identifies the directory to change to.
cls	Clears the screen.
echo { *string* }	Prints the specified text to the screen.
string	Specifies the text to print to the screen.
help { *command* }	Shows help on the specified command or shows all available commands.
prompt	Changes the prompt or, if used by itself, changes it back to the default.
pwd	Shows the current directory.
rem	Specifies the following text is a remark.
start *file*	Starts an executable or NLM running asynchronously.
file	Identifies the executable or NLM to start.
type *file*	Shows the specified file on the screen.
exit	Exits the ScriptEase command prompt.

File Name:	senlm.nlm	**Directory:**	\system	**Type:**	External

senlm myscript.jse	Executes the specified script.

serialver

OS: NetWare 5,6

Function	Shows the serial version UID for Java class files.
Syntax	serialver *classfiles...* serialver -show

classfiles...	Specifies the Java class files to show serial version information for.
-show	Starts a Java user interface where you can type in the class files.
serialver -show	Starts the Java user interface where you can enter class filenames.

Server Backup Utility

OS: NetWare 3,4

Function	Manages backup and restore of data on the NetWare server.
Syntax	load sbackup size=*KB* buffer=*NR*

size=*KB*	Specifies the buffer size in kilobytes. Values can be 16, 32, 64, 128, 256.
buffer=*NR*	Specifies the number of buffers. Value can be between 2 and 10 (default is 4).

File Name:	sbackup.nlm	**Directory:**	\system\	**Type:**	External

load sbackup size=128 buffer=5	Loads sbackup using five buffers of 128 kilobytes each.

Server Installation

OS: NetWare 3

Function	Assists in setting up a NetWare 386 file server by providing disk formatting, partition table facilities, and volume creation and management and by managing system and public files.

continued

Syntax	load install		
Disk Options	Manages disks.		
Format	Formats a specific disk drive.		
Partition Table	Creates and deletes partitions and alters the partition's Hot Fix.		
Mirroring	Creates mirrored partitions or removes specified partitions from the set.		
Surface Test	Tests the disk drive partition for bad blocks.		
Volume Options	Manages volumes.		
System Options	Installs additional system files and edit startup files.		
Copy System & Public files	Allows the user to copy the system and public files to a floppy disk or storage device.		
Create AUTOEXEC.NCF File	Allows the user to create the `autoexec.ncf` file.		
Create STARTUP.NCF File	Allows the user to create the `startup.ncf` file.		
Edit AUTOEXEC.NCF File	Allows the user to alter the `autoexec.ncf` file.		
Edit STARTUP.NCF File	Allows the user to alter the `startup.ncf` file.		
Product Options	Installs additional functions to the server.		
Ins	Press `Ins` to install a new NLM-based product.		
Del	Press `Del` to uninstall a new NLM-based product.		
Enter	Press `Enter` to configure any options in the installed product.		
File Name: `install.nlm`	**Directory:** /system	**Type:**	External

Server Installation — OS: NetWare 4

Function	Installs and configures the server.		
Syntax	load install		
Driver options	Configures, loads, and unloads network and disk drivers.		
Disk options	Manages disks.		
Modify disk partitions and Hot Fix	Manages disk partitions.		
Mirror/Unmirror disk partitions	Manages disk mirrors.		
Perform surface test	Checks a disk for bad blocks.		
Scan for additional devices	Adds new disk that was added when the system was up and running.		
Volume options	Manages volumes.		
License option	Adds and removes licenses.		
Copy files option	Copies system files.		
Directory options	Installs and removes. Backs up and restores data for directory service.		
Install Directory Services	Installs directory service from the server.		
Remove Directory Services	Removes directory service from the server.		
Upgrade NetWare 3.x bindery	Upgrades any bindery information from Novell 3.x.		
Upgrade mounted volumes	Upgrades any mounted volumes to be in the directory service.		
Directory backup and restore	Backs up and restores directory service data.		
NCF files options	Creates and edits the startup files `autoexec.ncf` and `startup.ncf`.		
Multi CPU options	Installs or removes support for multiple CPUs.		
Product options	Installs additional functions to the server.		
File Name: `install.nlm`	**Directory:** \system	**Type:**	External

Server Manager — OS: NetWare 4

Function	Shows volume, storage, network, adapter, device, disk, and system parameters information. Is also used to configure system parameters in the `autoexec.ncf, startup.ncf`, and `timesync.cfg` files.
Syntax	load servman
Server parameters	
Communications	Configures the settings for packet receive buffers.
Directory caching	Holds entries from the directory table in the memory.
Directory services	Configures the NDS trace file, various NDS processes, and the bindery contexts.
Disk	Configures the Hot Fix redirection and mirroring parameters.
Error handling	Configures the error log file size and the handling of too-big error log files.
File caching	Configures the file-caching buffers. It holds files in the memory for faster access.
File system	Configures the reuse of FAT files, system warnings about full disks, and file purging.
Locks	Configures number of open files and record locks each station and system can handle.
Memory	Configures the dynamic memory pool and cache buffer size. (Also handles the automatic registering of memory on EISA computers.)
Miscellaneous	Configures encrypted passwords, alerts, and server processes.

continued

NCP	Configures the checking of boundary and NCP packets.
Time	Configures the time synchronization, `timesync.cfg` file, and time zone settings.
Transaction tracking	Configures the Transaction Tracking System (TTS). Don't change some of these commands.
Storage information	Shows adapter, device, and partition information.
Volume information	Shows volume information from selected volume.
Network information	Shows network information about packets , buffers, LANs, and stacks.

File Name:	`servman.nlm`	**Directory:**	\system	**Type:**	External
Note:	This program has the same functionality as the `set` command.				

Session Manager

OS: NetWare 3

Function	Manages mapped drives and search paths. It can also list user information or send messages to users.
Syntax	session

Change Current Server	Shows servers to log in to.
Drive Mappings	Manages mapping of drives. Choose add, modify, or delete.
Group List	Lists groups to send a message to.
Search Mappings	Manages the search path for local or remote file systems.
Select Default Drive	Sets the default drive.
User List	Lists user logged on to the network, to which a message can be sent.

File Name:	`session.exe`	**Directory:**	\public	**Type:**	External

set (Licensing Services)

OS: NetWare 5,6

Function	Allows storing NetWare 5 SCL MLA usage within NDS. In NW5, this can also specify the type of NLS search to run (from the tree root or the partition root).
Syntax	set *argument* [= *value*]

store netware 5 conn scl mla usage in nds = on | off	Stores NW5 SCL MLA usage in NDS when ON is selected.
nls search type = *value*	**NW5 only:** Specifies the type of NLS search that is performed.
0	Stops any upward search at the tree root when looking for license certificates.
1	Stops upward searches at the partition root when looking for license certificates.

set (Multiprocessor)

OS: NetWare 5,6

Function	Controls system threshold, interrupt statistics, and auto processor startup modes.
Syntax	set *parameter* [= *value*]

system threshold = *value*	Sets the calculation value for thread-shedding load balancing (range is 0 to 102400).
auto clear interrupt statistics = on | off	Saves interrupt handler statistics for off-line processors when OFF is selected.
auto start processors = on | off	Starts secondary processors automatically once the PSM is loaded if ON is selected.

set (NSS)

OS: NetWare 6

Function	Sets auto-locks and updates, cache balancing, buffers and flush times for NSS.
Syntax	set *argument* [= *value*]

	Parameters that can only be set in the STARTUP.NCF file are marked by an (*).
nss auto locks hfs cd-rom disc in device = on | off	Locks/unlocks hfs CD-ROMs in the drive if value is set to ON.
nss auto update cdhfs volume objects to nds = on | off	Updates the NDS object for hfs CD-ROMs if value is set to ON.
nss auto locks cd-rom disc in device = on | of	Locks/unlocks CD-ROMs in the drive if value is set to ON.
nss auto update cd9660 volume object to nds = on | off	Updates the NDS object for cd9660 CD-ROMs if value is set to ON.
nss work to do count = *NR*	Sets number of WorkToDo entries to be executed concurrently (range is 5 to 100). (*)
nss maximum cache balance buffers per session = *NR*	Specifies what to limit num buffers to for each cache balance (range is 16 to 1048576).
nss cache balance timer = *seconds*	Sets the cache balance timer (range is 1 to 3600).
nss cache balance percent = *percentage*	Specifies the amount of free memory used for buffer cache (range is 1 to 99).
nss cache balance enable = on | off	Uses the dynamic balancing of free memory if value is set to ON.
nss buffer flush timer = *seconds*	Specifies the flush time for cache buffers that are modified (range is 1 to 3600).

continued

nss minimum os cache buffers = *NR*	Specifies the minimum number of NW buffer cache entries (range is 1024 to 1048576).
nss minimum cache buffers = *NR*	Specifies the minimum number of NSS buffer cache entries (range is 256 to 1048576).
nss file flush timer = *seconds*	Specifies the flush time for modified open files (range is 1 to 3600).
nss closed file cache size = *NR*	Specifies the maximum number of closed files in memory (range is 0 to 1000000) .(*)
nss open file hash shift = *size*	Sets the open file hash table size in power of 2 (range is 8 to 20). (*)
nss auth cache size = *NR*	Specifies number of Authorization Cache entries (range is 16 to 50000). (*)
nss ascii name cache enable = on | off	Uses ASCII name caching if value is set to ON. (*)
nss name cache enable = on | off	Uses name caching if value is set to ON. (*)
nss name cache size = *NR*	Specifies the number of name cache entries (range is 3 to 65521). (*)
nss low volume space alerts = on | off	Sends messages to all users when low on storage if value is set to ON.
nss low volume space warning reset threshold = *Mbytes*	Sets the threshold to reset a low space warning (range is 0 to 1000000).
nss low volume space warning threshold = *Mbytes*	Sets the threshold for low space warning (range is 0 to 1000000).

set nss auto update cdhfs volume objects to nds = on	Tells NSS to update NDS objects for CD-ROM.

set (Service Location Protocol) — OS: NetWare 5,6

Function	Sets SLP cache and scope list, SLP/UA multicast, and SLP debug mode.
Syntax	set *attribute* [= *value*]

SLP cache timeout = *seconds*	Makes the UA cache keep information for specified time (range is 0 to 4294967295).
SLP enable UA multicast = on | off	Enables the user agent multicast packets if value is set to ON.
SLP register nwserver = on | off	Enables the nwserver.novell service registration if value is set to ON.
SLP maximum WTD = *NR*	Allows specified number of controlled work to do (range is 1 to 64).
SLP reset = on | off	Sends new service registers from SA and makes DA to advertise if set to ON.
SLP scope list = *string*	Specifies the SA scope list in a comma-separated way.
SLP close idle tcp connections time = *seconds*	Identifies the time before terminating idle TCP connections (range is 0 to 86400).
SLP DA heart beat time = *seconds*	Specifies the DA heart beat packet send interval (range is 0 to 65535).
SLP DA event timeout = *seconds*	Waits for a DA packet to return for specified time (range is 0 to 120).
SLP SA default lifetime = *seconds*	Specifies how long the service registers live (range is 129 to 65535).
SLP retry count = *NR*	Specifies how many retries there are (range is 1 to 128).
SLP debug = *NR*	Enables the SLP debug mode (range is 0 to 4294967295).
SLP rediscover inactive directory agents = *seconds*	Starts re-discovering inactive DAs after specified time (range is 0 to 86400).
SLP multicast radius = *NR*	Specifies how to describe multicast radius (range is 0 to 32).
SLP DA discovery options = *NR*	Specifies what discovery options to use (range is 0 to 16).
SLP MTU size = *NR*	Specifies the maximum transfer unit size (range is 0 to 24682).
SLP broadcast = on | off	Enables broadcast packets instead of multicast packets if value is set to ON.

setenv — OS: NetWare 6

Function	Sets and shows environment variables.
Syntax	setenv *variable* [= *value*]

variable	Identifies the name of the environment variable to set or show.
value	Identifies the value to assign to the specified environment variable.

setpass — OS: NetWare 3,4,5

Function	Changes network or user password on a server.
Syntax	setpass *{ servername/ } { username }* [option]

/ver	Shows utility version number and a list of all files it uses to execute. (When using the /ver option, all other options are ignored.)
/?	Shows help information.
servername/	Specifies which server to change password on.
username	Specifies which user to change password on.

continued

File Name:	setpass.exe	Directory:	\public	Type:	External
setpass			Changes your password on the network.		
setpass Lou			Changes user Lou's password.		
setpass ucg/Bill			Changes user Bill's password on server ucg.		

settts

OS: NetWare 3,4

Function	Ensures that Transaction Tracking System (TTS) works in harmony with your application in tracking a transaction.
Syntax	settts *{ logical [physical] }* [options...]

logical	Defines the number of TTS logical record locks to ignore.
physical	Defines the number of TTS physical record locks to ignore.
NW4:	
/c	Scrolls through the report of accounting charges.
/n	Sets the logical and physical level to normal.
/d	Disables the logical and physical level.

File Name:	settts.exe	Directory:	\public\os	Type:	External
settts 2 2			Sets TTS to 2 for both logical and physical levels.		

Setup Certification Console

OS: NetWare 5,6

Function	Installs the certification console on the client that shows details and status of user certificates.
Syntax	setup

File Name:	setup.exe	Directory:	\public\mgmt\certconsole	Type:	External

Setup DNS/DHCP Management Console

OS: NetWare 5,6

Function	Installs the DNS/DHCP management console on the client that allows configuration and management of DNS/DHCP.
Syntax	setup

File Name:	setup.exe	Directory:	\public\dnsdhcp	Type:	External

Setup Novell SQL Connector

OS: NetWare 5

Function	Installs the Novell SQL ODBC database connector on an NT server or workstation.
Syntax	setup

File Name:	setup.exe	Directory:	\public\sqlc\drivers\nt\odbc-out\disk1	Type:	External

Setup Pervasive.SQL 2000 Client

OS: NetWare 5,6

Function	Installs the Pervasive SQL 2000 client on the workstation used to connect to Pervasive SQL databases.
Syntax	setup

File Name:	setup.exe	Directory:	\pvsw\clients\win	Type:	External
Note:	When installing SQL on an NW4/5.x server using NDS, you must have the bindery context correctly set to an NDS context (please see `autoexec.ncf` for the line SET BINDERY CONTEXT=xx).				

Setup SQL Connector for NDS

OS: NetWare 5

Function	Installs the Novell SQL ODBC connector into NDS enabling administration of ODBC for individual users or groups.
Syntax	setup

File Name:	setup.exe	Directory:	\public\sqlc\netware\ndsadmin\disk1	Type:	External

Setup SQL Connector JDBC driver

OS: NetWare 5

Function	Installs the Novell SQL JDBC database connector on a Windows 95/98 or ME workstation.
Syntax	setup

File Name:	setup.exe	Directory:	\public\sqlc\client\jdbc	Type:	External

Setup SQL Connector ODBC driver

OS: NetWare 5

Function	Installs the Novell SQL ODBC database connector on a Windows 95/98 or ME workstation.
Syntax	setup

File Name:	setup.exe	Directory:	\public\sqlc\client\odbc\disk1	Type:	External

slist

OS: NetWare 3

Function	Shows the name, the network address, and status of all file servers or the specified one. Wildcards are allowed.
Syntax	slist [options...]

file server	Specifies the file server to show the name, the network address, and status for.
/C	Lists of file servers scrolling down without stopping.
/?	Shows help information.

File Name:	`slist.exe`	**Directory:**	\login and \public	**Type:**	External

slist	Lists information about all file servers.
slist U*	Shows information about all file servers starting with a U.
slist FS01	Lists information on the specified file server.

smdr

OS: NetWare 5,6

Function	Configures the SMS data requester and creates SMS NDS objects used by SBACKUP or `nwback32.exe` backup.
Syntax	smdr [options...] smdr new *SMDRGroupContext SMDRContext user password* [SAP/SLP options...] smdr new ndsdisable [SAP/SLP options...]

new	Starts `smdr` in interactive mode, providing step-by-step configuration.
SMDRGroupContext	Specifies where in NDS to create the SMDR group object (default is current context).
SMDRContext	Specifies where in NDS to create the SMDR object (default is current context).
user	Specifies the username with object creation permissions.
password	Specifies the user password for the above user.
ndsdisable	Doesn't create NDS objects.
SAP/SLP options...	
slpdisable	Disables SLP (Service Location Protocol) used in TCP/IP networks.
sapdisable	Disables SAP (Service Address Protocol) used in IPX networks.

File Name:	`smdr.nlm`	**Directory:**	\system	**Type:**	External

smdr new	Loads SMDR in interactive mode.
smdr new .planets .planets .admin.planets adminpass sapdisable	Loads SMDR and creates SMDR objects.
smdr	Loads the SMS data requester if it was previously configured.

SMDR Configuration

OS: NetWare 5,6

Function	Configures the SMDR client configuration and creates (w32smdr.exe) or updates (sbconfig.exe) the key in the local registry key to perform backups using `nwback32.exe` after configuring `smdr` on the server.
Syntax	sbconfig

File Name:	`sbconfig.exe, w32smdr.exe`	**Directory:**	\public	**Type:**	External

smode

OS: NetWare 3

Function	Specifies how search drivers should act when searching for a data file.
Syntax	smode *{ path } { mode }* [/sub]

/sub	Includes subdirectories in the search mode assignment. A path must be specified.
path	Specifies the file to view or change search modes for.
mode	Specifies search mode to set on the specified file. Valid modes below:
0	Doesn't use any search instructions.
1	Searches the direct path first, then the default directory, and last the other drives.
2	Searches the direct path first then the other drives.
3	Works as mode 1 except that drives will be searched if the open request is read only.
5	Uses the path if it exists, else uses default directory. Then searches drives.
7	Checks the path first. If open request is read only, searches drives. (If no path is given, begins searching in the default directory.)

File Name:	`smode.exe`	**Directory:**	\public	**Type:**	External

smode acc.exe 5	Changes the search mode for the specified file.
smode *.* 3	Changes the search mode on all files in the current directory.

smtlogin

OS: NetWare 5,6

Function	Specifies a username and password with permission on the SMDR Group object in the NDS tree.
Syntax	smtlogin

File Name:	`smtlogin.exe`	**Directory:**	\public	**Type:**	External

Spoofer Console

OS: NetWare 5

Function	Shows the hostname for the server, uptime since last initialization, and NetWare version information. Also shows the PPP interface list and current SPX and NCP connections.
Syntax	spfcon

Interfaces	Shows a list of available PPP-type interfaces.
Connections	Shows a list of all SPX and NCP connections.

File Name:	`spfcon.nlm`	**Directory:**	\system	**Type:**	External

Start Processors

OS: NetWare 5,6

Function	Starts all secondary processors or a specified processor on the server.
Syntax	start processors *{ NR }*

NR	Specifies the secondary processor to start.
Note:	The primary processor (the one that NetWare is running on) is called 0.
start processors	Starts all secondary processors.
start processors 1	Starts the secondary processor number 1.

Stop Processors

OS: NetWare 5,6

Function	Stops processors on servers with multiple processors.
Syntax	stop processors *{ NR }*

NR	Specifies the processor to stop.
stop processors	Stops all extra processors.
stop processors 2 4	Stops processors 2 and 4.

Storage Management Service

OS: NetWare 5,6

Function	Starts a tool used to backup and restore data in a Novell network like NDS, volumes, disks, workstations, and so forth.
Syntax	nwback32

File Name:	`nwback32.exe`	**Directory:**	\public	**Type:**	External

swap

OS: NetWare 5,6

Function	Creates, removes, configures, or shows information regarding swap files.
Syntax	swap [options...]

add *volume { volume parameter = value }*	Adds a swap file on the specified volume and can specify additional parameters.
del *volume*	Deletes the swap file from the specified volume.
parameter *volume parameter = value*	Changes or adds parameters for an existing swap file on the specified volume.
Parameters	The following parameters can be used with options add and parameter:
MIN	Specifies the minimum size of the swap file.
MAX	Specifies the maximum size of the swap file.
MIN FREE	Specifies the minimum size that has to be left on the device.
swap add SYS max=100	Adds the swap file on the SYS device.
swap parameter SYS min free=50	Sets the minimum free space on volume SYS:
swap del SYS	Deletes the swap file on the SYS device.

syscon

OS: NetWare 3

Function	Creates and modifies user and group accounts and maintains login scripts.
Syntax	syscon

Accounting	Manages accounting used to charge users for resources.
Change Current Server	Manages server tasks, logs in or out of servers, or lists servers.
File Server Information	Shows information about file servers available, configuration, users, or versions.

continued

Group Information		Manages group information. Shows or configures groups and their configurations.			
Supervisor Options		Shows available options for a user with supervisor rights.			
User Information		Manages user information. Shows or configures users and their configurations.			
File Name:	syscon.exe	**Directory:**	\public	**Type:**	External

sysconW — OS: NetWare 3

Function	Creates and modifies user and group accounts and edits login scripts. The GUI version of `syscon`.
Syntax	sysconw

File Name:	sysconw.exe	**Directory:**	\public	**Type:**	External

systime — OS: NetWare 3,4

Function	Synchronizes your workstation's time with a server's time.
Syntax	systime *{ server }* [options...]

server		Specifies the server to use.			
/?		Shows help information.			
/ver		Shows version information.			
File Name:	systime.exe	**Directory:**	\public	**Type:**	External
systime			Synchronizes with the default server.		
systime neptune			Synchronizes with the server neptune.		

tar — OS: NetWare 5,6

Function	Manages tar archive. Can create, extract, list contents, and check the archive.
Syntax	tar option [options...] *{ arguments... } { files... }*

	One of the following options must be specified:
-c	Creates a new archive.
-r	Appends files to the archive.
-t	Shows the contents of the archive.
-x	Extracts all files, or the specified files, from the tar file.
-A	Appends a tar file to an archive.
-d	Shows the difference between the archive and files.
-u	Updates the archive with files that are newer.
--delete	Deletes files from an archive.
	The following options can be combined:
-W	Verifies the archive after storing the files.
--remove-files	Removes the files after adding them.
-k	Doesn't replace existing files.
--overwrite	Overwrites existing files.
-U	Removes files before replacing them with an extracted file.
--recursive-unlink	Removes directory contents before extracting to it.
-S	Handles sparse files efficiently.
-O	Extracts files to STDOUT.
-G	Uses old GNU format.
-g	Uses new GNU format.
--ignore-failed-read	Doesn't stop on error.
--owner=*user*	Sets the owner for extracted files.
--group=*group*	Sets the group for extracted files.
--mode=*change*	Changes the mode for extracted files using symbols mode.
--atime-preserve	Preserves the access times on dumped files.
-m	Doesn't extract file modified time.
--same-owner	Preserves the owner of the files if possible.
--no-same-owner	Extracts files as yourself.
--numeric-owner	Uses numeric user/group instead of symbolic.
-p	Extracts permission information.
--no-same-permissions	Doesn't extract permission.
-s	Sorts names to be extracted to match archive.
--preserve	Identifies the same as -p and -s together.
-f *archive*	Specifies the archive to use.

continued

--force-local	Specifies that an archive is local.
--rsh-command=*command*	Specifies remote command to use instead of rsh.
-*decity*	Specifies the density of the drive - can be 0 - 7, l, m, or h.
-M	Uses multi volumes for creating/listing/extracting archives.
-L *NR*	Specifies that tape will be changed after writing NR * 1024 bytes.
-F *file*	Runs the specified script at the end of each tape (implies -M).
--volno-file=*file*	Uses/updates the volume number in file.
-b *blocks*	Sets the record size to blocks * 512 bytes.
--record-size=*bytes*	Sets the record size (use multiple of 512 bytes).
-i	Ignores zeroed blocks in archive (means EOF).
-B	Reads only reblock (for 4.2 BSD pipes).
-V *name*	Gives the archive the volume name.
-o	Uses V7 format archive.
--posix	Uses POSIX format archive.
-I	Uses bzip2 to compress archive.
-z	Uses gzip to compress archive.
-Z	Uses compress to compress archive.
--use-compress-program=*prog*	Specifies program to use for compression (must accept -d).
-C *directory*	Changes to directory before starting any operations.
-T *file*	Specifies a file with a list of files to extract or create.
--null	Specifies that null-terminated names are used with -T, disables -C.
--exclude=*pattern*	Uses the globbing pattern to exclude files.
-X *file*	Specifies a file with a list of files, excluded from using file globbing.
-P	Uses absolute filenames.
-h	Stores the file a symbolic link points to.
--no-recursion	Doesn't descend into directories.
-l	Stays in the same file system.
-K *name*	Starts at filename in the archive.
-N *date*	Stores files newer than date.
--newer-mtime	Uses file modification time instead of creation time.
--backup[=*control*]	Backs up before removal, chooses version control.
--suffix=*suffix*	Does a backup before removal, uses suffix instead of the default.
--help	Shows help information.
--version	Shows help information.
-v	Verbose mode. Shows more information.
--checkpoint	Shows directory names while reading the archive.
--totals	Shows the total number of bytes written.
-R	Shows the block number for each message.
-w	Requests user confirmation for every action.
arguments...	Specifies a list of the operands to the one-character options in the same order.
files...	Specifies files to store, extract, list. File globbing can be used.

File Name:	`tar.nlm`	**Directory:**	\system	**Type:**	External

tar -cvf SYS:\tmp\dns.tar -C SYS:\etc\dns .	Creates an archive.
tar -tvf SYS:\tmp\dns.tar	Lists contents of an archive.
tar -xvf SYS:\tmp\dns.tar -C SYS:\tmp	Extracts files from an archive.

tbackup — OS: NetWare 3

Function	Creates a batch filenamed trestore.bat that can be used for restoring trustees and IRFs for files and directories.
Syntax	tbackup [/s]

/S	Uses the files and directories below the current directory.
/?	Shows help information.

File Name:	`tbackup.exe`	**Directory:**	\system\tools	**Type:**	External

tcopy

OS:	NetWare 3				
Function	Copies trustee assignments from the source directory to the current or the specified destination directory.				
Syntax	tcopy *source* { *destination* } [/S]				
/S	Copies trustees including subdirectories.				
source	Specifies a directory that contains the trustee information.				
destination	Specifies a directory to copy all the trustee information to.				
File Name:	`tcopy.exe`	**Directory:**	\system\tools	**Type:**	External
tcopy e: /S	Copies the trustee information from e:, including its subdirectories, to the current working directory.				
tcopy e: f:	Copies the trustee information from e: to f:.				

tlist

OS:	NetWare 3				
Function	Lists all the users or groups and their rights for a directory.				
Syntax	tlist [/c] { *path object* }				
/c	Set to continuously scroll information.				
path	Specifies the path to the directory. (Wildcards are allowed when selecting path.)				
object	Specifies to show information about. Valid values are: `users` or `groups`.				
File Name:	`tlist.exe`	**Directory:**	\public	**Type:**	External
Tip:	Use Periods (..) to search in directories above the current one.				
tlist *.exe	Shows rights information about all .exe files in the current directory.				
tlist u*	Shows rights information about all directories beginning with a u in the current directory.				
tlist . users	Shows information about all users rights in your default directory.				

tnameserv (Client)

OS:	NetWare 5,6				
Function	An IDL transient name server that provides Java applications or applets access to object request brokers (ORB).				
Syntax	tnameserv [-ORBInitialPort *port*]				
-ORBInitialPort *port*	Allows you start the transient name server on a different port (default is 900).				
File Name:	`tnameserv.exe`	**Directory:**	\public\mgmt\consoleone\1.2\jre\bin\	**Type:**	External
Note:	This is used by many ConsoleOne and other Java-based applications.				
tnamserv -ORBInitialPort 1100	Starts the transient name server on port 1100.				

tnameserv (Server)

OS:	NetWare 6
Function	An IDL transient name server that provides Java applications or applets access to ORB (object request broker).
Syntax	tnameserv [-ORBInitialPort *port*]
-ORBInitialPort *port*	Allows you to start the transient name server on a different port (default is 900).
tnamserv -ORBInitialPort 1100	Starts the transient name server on port 1100.

tracer

OS:	NetWare 6				
Function	Starts the Java Virtual Machine debug tracer.				
Syntax	tracer				
File Name:	`tracer.nlm`	**Directory:**	\java\bin	**Type:**	External

uimport

OS:	NetWare 4,5				
Function	Imports user information from an external database in ASCII format on a workstation to the NDS database.				
Syntax	uimport { *controlfile* } { *datafile* } [options...]				
/c	Shows the output on the screen without pausing between full screens.				
/ver	Shows version information and the programs that it uses.				
/?	Shows help information.				
controlfile	Specifies the file that controls how to load user data to the directory.				
datafile	Specifies the ASCII file that contains the user attributes.				
File Name:	`uimport.exe`	**Directory:**	\public	**Type:**	External

unzip

OS: NetWare 5,6

Function	Extracts files from a zip archive or to show the contents of a zip archive.
Syntax	unzip [options...] *file* { *list* }

-p	Extracts the files to pipe without showing messages.
-f	Updates existing files with files in the archive and doesn't create new files.
-u	Updates existing files with files in the archive and creates new files if needed.
-x *list*	Doesn't extract the files specified in the list.
-l	Shows all files in the archive using a short format.
-t	Tests the archive.
-z	Shows archive comments.
-d *directory*	Extracts the files to the specified directory.
-n	Doesn't overwrite existing files.
-o	Overwrites files without prompting.
-j	Doesn't re-create directories.
-C	Matches filenames case-insensitively.
-M	Pipes through "more" pager.
-q	Uses quiet mode.
-qq	Uses quieter mode.
-a	Autoconverts any text files.
-aa	Handles every file as a text file.
-v	Verbose mode. Shows more information.
-L	Makes names lowercase.
-V	Keeps VMS version numbers.
	The following option can only be used alone:
-Z	Activates ZipInfo mode, which is used to show the contents of an archive.
	The following options are for use with the -Z option:
-1	Shows only one filename per line. Can't be used with the -h, -t, or -z options.
-2	Shows only one filename per line. Can be used with the -h, -t, or -z options.
-s	Shows the contents of the archive using short UNIX "ls -l" format.
-m	Shows the contents of the archive using medium UNIX "ls -l" format.
-l	Shows the contents of the archive using long UNIX "ls -l" format.
-v	Verbose mode. Multiple pages format.
-h	Shows header line.
-z	Shows zip file comment.
-C	Is case-insensitive.
-x *list*	Excludes the files specified in the list.
-t	Shows totals for listed files or for all.
-T	Prints the file times in storable decimal format.
-M	Outputs through the built-in "more".
file	Identifies the file to extract or show the contents of.
list	A list of files to extract from the specified archive.

File Name:	`unzip.nlm`	**Directory:**	\system	**Type:**	External

unzip archive.zip	Extracts all files from the specified archive.
unzip archive.zip -x ucg.txt	Extracts all files except the file `ucg.txt`.

ups

OS: NetWare 3,4

Function	Identifies the software used to connect a UPS to the server.
Syntax	load ups [parameters...]

type=*type*	Sets the name of the hardware interface for the UPS. (Interfaces are DCB, standalone, keycard, mouse, and other.)
port=*port*	Sets the hexadecimal number corresponding to the jumper setting on the board. (Ports are DCB: 346, 34E, 326, 32E, 386, 38E; standalone: 240, 231; keycard: 230, 238; mouse: no number required; other: see board documentation.)
discharge=*minutes*	Sets an estimate of the battery depletion time (default is 20).
recharge=*minutes*	Sets an estimate of the time the battery needs to fully charge (default is 60).

continued

wait=*seconds*	Time to wait following a power interruption before activation (default is 15). (The wait option isn't available in NW3.)				
File Name:	ups.nlm	**Directory:**	\system	**Type:**	External
load ups	Prompts for parameters to use.				
load ups time discharge=30 recharge=120 wait=5	Sets discharge to 30 minutes, recharge to 120 minutes, and wait to 5 seconds.				

ups status

OS: NetWare 3,4

Function	Shows information regarding the UPS like type, power source, current status, and more.
Syntax	ups status
ups status	Shows information about the UPS.

ups time

OS: NetWare 3,4

Function	Adjusts such UPS parameters as activation, charge, and depletion times.
Syntax	ups time [parameters...]
discharge=*minutes*	Sets an estimate of the battery depletion time (default is 20).
recharge=*minutes*	Sets an estimate of the time the battery needs to fully charge (default is 60).
wait=*seconds*	Time to wait following a power interruption before activation (default is 15). (The wait option isn't available in NW3.)
ups time discharge=30 recharge=120 wait=5	Sets discharge to 30 minutes, recharge to 120 minutes, and wait to 5 seconds.

userdef

OS: NetWare 3

Function	Adds multiple users and edits login parameters and script templates. Alters user access on specified volumes.				
Syntax	userdef				
Add Users	Adds multiple users using the selected template.				
Edit/View Templates	Adds, edits, and shows user templates. You can just show the default template.				
Restrict User	Specifies users available disk space for current users.				
File Name:	userdef.exe	**Directory:**	\public	**Type:**	External

userlist

OS: NetWare 3

Function	Shows some information about the currently logged in user or users on the current server or on the specified server.				
Syntax	userlist *{ file server/ } { user }* [options...]				
/A	Shows the network address and node address for every user. Cannot be used with /O.				
/O	Shows the object type for every user. Cannot be used with /A.				
/C	Shows users directly on the screen without pausing between full-screens.				
file server/	Specifies file server to show logged in users on.				
user	Specifies user to match.				
File Name:	userlist.exe	**Directory:**	\public	**Type:**	External
userlist ucgserver/ /C	Shows the list of users logged in on the ucgserver.				
userlist ucgserver/ucg /A	Shows the ucg users information on the specified server, including MAC address and node address.				

version (client)

OS: NetWare 3

Function	Shows version information for a NetWare executable file and its checksum. For non-NetWare files it will only produce a checksum.				
Syntax	version *executable*				
executable	Specifies the path- and filename to a NetWare-executable file to check the version for.				
File Name:	version.exe	**Directory:**	\public	**Type:**	External
version rconsole	Shows version and checksum information for the file rconsole.exe.				
version sys:\public\ncopy.exe	Shows version and checksum information for the file ncopy.exe.				

viewtrc

OS: NetWare 5

Function	Converts trace files into a readable format by reading input trace files, and creates an output file in ASCII format.
Syntax	viewtrc *inputfile* { *outputfile* }

?	Shows help information.
inputfile	Specifies which binary trace file to convert.
outputfile	Specifies a file with readable translation.

File Name:	`viewtrc.exe`	**Directory:**	\system\utils	**Type:**	External

Volume Information

OS: NetWare 3

Function	Shows a window with usage information for available file system volumes.
Syntax	volinfo

Change servers	Specifies server to show volume usage for.
Update interval	Specifies how often to update disk usage information.

File Name:	`volinfo.exe`	**Directory:**	\public	**Type:**	External

WAN Traffic Manager

OS: NetWare 5

Function	Manages the type of network traffic that is sent over WAN links as well as defining specific times when the network traffic should be sent to help minimize the network costs of transmitting data over WAN links.
Syntax	wtm

	The WAN traffic manger reads policy information from the following NDS objects:
Server Object	Selects WAN policies inside server object to configure and edit the server policies.
Lan Area Object	Creates and edits the object LAN area to create policies for the entire network.

File Name:	`wtm.nlm`	**Directory:**	\system	**Type:**	External

Note: After defining or editing the server or LAN policies, load the wtm.nlm on the server console to make the policies active.

whoami

OS: NetWare 3,4

Function	Shows information about your user account, what servers you are logged in to, and who you are logged in as.
Syntax	whoami { *server* } [options...]

server	Specifies the file server (default is current server).
/s	Shows your security equivalences.
/g	Shows your membership in groups.
/r	Shows your effective rights.
/o	Shows object supervisor information as well as the users and groups being supervised.
/w	Shows workgroup manager information.
/a	Shows all the information available.
/c	Specifies continuous scrolling instead of pausing after every page.
	The following option is only available in NW3:
/system	Shows general system information.
	The following option is only available in NW4:
/?	Shows help information.
/ver	Shows version information.

File Name:	`whoami.exe`	**Directory:**	\public	**Type:**	External

whoami	Shows who you are, the server you are on, NetWare version, and the date.
whoami neptune /groups	Shows which groups you belong to on server neptune.

wsupdate

OS: NetWare 3,4

Function	Updates any specified files if the source file is more current than the destination file and allows for renaming them.
Syntax	wsupdate *sourcefile* *destinationfile* [options...]

/f=*file*	Specifies a file containing commands to execute.
/c	Copies the new file over the old one automatically — no backup copy is left.
/r	Renames the old file to .old and copies the new file.
/s	Searches for old files in all subdirectories in the destination file or driver.
/l=*file*	Specifies a log file and starts logging to that file.

continued

/n	Creates the destination path and file and copies the source file there.
/v={ *drivername* }	Updates the `config.sys` backup to `config.311`. Specifies drive if the file is not on C:.
/o	Updates all files. Must be specified if updating read-only files.
/?	Shows help information.
/ver	Shows version information.
NW3:	
/i	Prompts for action to take on all files older than the source file.
NW4:	
/all	Searches all mapped drives. A drive letter can't be specified with this option.
/con	Continuous. Doesn't pause between each screen.
/e	Erases the existing log file. Is used with the L option.
/local	Searches all local drives. A drive letter can't be specified with this option.
/p	Prompts user for approval.
sourcefile	Specifies the path and name of the new file.
destinationfile	Specifies the driver and name of the destination file. (Specify drive as A:, B:, C:, all, or all_local for automatic search.)
File Name: `wsupdate.exe`	**Directory:** **NW3:** \system **NW4:** \public **Type:** External
wsupdate f:net.bat c:net.bat	Updates the `net.bat` file on drive `c:`.

X Server — OS: NetWare 5,6

Function	Loads Java if it isn't already loaded and starts the X-window server where you can run Java applications.
Syntax	startx
File Name:	`startx.ncf` **Directory:** \system **Type:** External

X.25 Console — OS: NetWare 5

Function	A management console that shows X.25 configuration and statistics using SNMP.
Syntax	x25con

	The main menu consists of these six items:
SNMP Access Configuration	Used to configure SNMP, including the community string, poll interval, and timeout.
X.25 Interfaces	Shows interface summary information.
X.25 Call Target Summary	Shows the call target's configuration information.
Cleared Circuit Summary	Shows the cleared circuit's summary information.
Ping Remote System	Tests a remote system from a local by ping.
Display Traps	Accesses the log written by `snmplog.nlm`.
File Name: `x25con.nlm`	**Directory:** \system **Type:** External

X25 Network Monitor — OS: NetWare 4,5

Function	Shows and captures real time incoming and outgoing data frames.
Syntax	x25trace

Network Interface Information	Shows information about available x.25 interfaces.
Real-Time Monitor	Shows the real-time monitor.
Play-Back	Shows and edits settings for the playback device.
Configuration	Specifies capture device and filename on disk.
File Name: `x25trace.nlm`	**Directory:** \system **Type:** External

X25disp — OS: NetWare 5

Function	Reads the input trace file generated by `x25trace.nlm` and shows or converts the results into a variety of formats.
Syntax	x25disp -i*inputfile* [-o*outputfile*] [options...]

-a	Shows the contents of the input trace file in ASCII format.
-c	Shows the contents of the input trace file in complete mode.
-h	Shows the contents of the input trace file in hexadecimal format.
-s	Shows the contents of the input trace file in short mode.
-mo	Interprets the input trace using RAW mode.

continued

-m1 -m2 -i*inputfile* -o*outputfile*		Interprets the input trace using frame mode. Interprets the input trace using packet mode. Specifies the input trace file created by the `x25trace.nlm`. Specifies the filename used for the formatted output instead of showing on the screen.			
File Name:	`x25disp.exe`	**Directory:**	\system\utils	**Type:**	External
x25disp -ivenus.in -a		Shows the content of the venus.in trace file in ASCII format on the screen.			
x25disp -ivenus.in -ovenus.out -a -c -m2		Reads the venus.in file in ASCII format, using complete and packet mode, and saves the results to `venus.out`.			

xlog

OS: NetWare 5,6

Function	Logs ISDN activity for troubleshooting Eicon ISDN connection problems and optionally saves the results in a log file.				
Syntax	xlog [options...] *{ logfile }*				
adapter		Specifies the name of the ISDN adapter as it is configured in `niascfg`.			
+		Writes log information to the specified log file continuously until a key is pressed.			
-		Shows log information to the console screen continuously until a key is pressed.			
s		Specifies to only log SIG events.			
d		Specifies to only log channel events.			
		This is a list of possible ISDN events and their descriptions logged by xlog:			
B1-X, B1-R		Reports that the first ISDN channel is sending and receiving data.			
B2-X, B2-R		Reports that the second ISDN channel is sending and receiving data.			
D-X, D-R		Reports that the D channel is sending and receiving data.			
EVENT:Layer-2 Failed, resend SPID		Reports that an invalid SPID was used and you should check SPID configuration.			
EVENT:SPID Accepted		Reports that the switch has accepted the SPID.			
L1_UP		Reports that layer 1 is active and is sending LAPD RR frames.			
Q.931 ... SETUP		Reports that a call is currently in progress.			
SIG-r		Reports that a TEI number is received from the switch.			
SIG-R ... CALL_PROC		Reports that the call is still in process.			
SIG-R ... CONN		Reports that a connection was established.			
SIG-R ... CONN_ACK		Reports that local acknowledgement was received.			
SIX-x ... SPID		Reports that the SPID was sent to the service provider.			
Sync_Gained		Reports that a physical link was established.			
File Name:	`xlog.nlm`	**Directory:**	\system	**Type:**	External
Note:	You must first load the `didd.nlm` before you use xlog.				
xlog + isdn.log		Logs continuously to the log file isdn.log until a key is pressed.			

In This Part

This part provides the commands you need for controlling the Microsoft Windows operating system and its command-line ancestor, MS-DOS.

Chapter 5

Universal Windows Commands

The commands in this section are common in all versions of Microsoft Windows. The commands are listed in alphabetical order by command name. Even though these commands are available in every version of Windows, many of the options are different and the commands may have a different syntax as well.

Be sure to look carefully at the syntax and directory and option fields for OS abbreviations. Please see "Abbreviations used in this book" in the Preface for a complete explanation.

Any options that are common to all of the other Windows versions are listed at the top of the options field and become more specific to the different versions of Windows as you read down the template. Anytime you see a bold Windows OS abbreviation in the options field, the options that follow it are unique to that version of Windows.

For cross-references outside the Windows environment, please see Chapter 1, the "Quick Command Index."

The versions of Windows in this section are:

- Windows 95
- Windows 98
- Windows ME
- Windows NT 4.0 Workstation
- Windows NT 4.0 Server
- Windows NT 4.0 Terminal Server
- Windows 2000 Professional
- Windows 2000 Server
- Windows 2000 Advanced Server
- Windows XP

About Windows, winver

OS: Microsoft Common

Function	Shows the version of Windows you're using.
Syntax	winver

File Name:	`winver.exe`	**Directory:**	\windows, **NT4, 2000:**\winnt\system32, **XP:**\windows\system32	**Type:**	External
Tip:	In Windows 9x/ME, you can also see the build number and memory information by right-clicking on My Computer.				

arp

OS: Microsoft Common

Function	Shows and modifies the ARP cache table, which maps IP addresses to physical MAC addresses.
Syntax	arp [options...] *{ IPaddress } { MACaddress } { interfaceIP }*

-a	Shows current ARP entries by interrogating the current protocol data.
-g	Shows current ARP entries by interrogating the current protocol data.
-N *interfaceIP*	Shows the ARP entries for the specified interface. Requires the -a option.
-d	Deletes ARP entries for the specified IP address(es). Wildcard * can be used.
-s	Associates the IP address with the physical MAC address.
IPaddress	Specifies the IP address to show, add, or remove from the ARP cache.
MACaddress	Specifies a physical address.
interfaceIP	Specifies the IP address of the interface to update the ARP cache for.

File Name:	`arp.exe`	**Directory:**	\windows, **NT4, 2000:** \winnt\system32, **XP:** \windows\system32	**Type:**	External

arp -d 211.135.*	Deletes all ARP entries starting with 211.135.

attrib

OS: Microsoft Common

Function	Modifies attributes for files and directories. If used with no options, shows attributes for files in current directory.
Syntax	attrib [options...] *{ file }*

/s	Applies changes to all files in every subdirectory. Directories aren't affected.
+R or -R	Sets or removes the read-only file attribute.
+A or -A	Sets or removes the archive file attribute.
+S or -S	Sets or removes the system file attribute.
+H or -H	Sets or removes the hidden file attribute.
/?	Shows help information.
file	Specifies the name or directory for which the attribute should be modified or shown.

File Name:	`attrib.exe`	**Directory:**	\windows\command **NT4, 2000:** \winnt\system32, **XP:** \windows\system32	**Type:**	External

attrib -a *.*	Removes the archive attribute from all the files in the current directory.

Calculator

OS: Microsoft Common

Function	A graphical calculator that can be used in two different modes: Standard or Scientific.
Syntax	calc

File Name:	`calc.exe`	**Directory:**	\windows\ **NT4, 2000:** \winnt\system32, **XP:** \windows\system32\	**Type:**	External

call

OS: Microsoft Common

Function	Calls another batch file or program and executes it, then returns to the original batch file or where it was called from.
Syntax	call *{ drive:path } file* call *:label*

drive:path	Specifies the drive letter and full path of the batch file or program to call.
file	Specifies the name of the batch file or program to call.
:label	Calls or jumps to a specific section of a batch file with the label specified.

cd, chdir

OS: Microsoft Common

Function	Changes or shows the current directory. If no path is given, shows the current directory.
Syntax	cd [..] [["]*path*] cd [..]

path	Identifies the name or full path of the directory to change to.
..	Changes to the parent directory.
"	Used before a directory that has spaces in the name. (Unnecessary when running the cmd.exe shell under Windows NT/2000/XP.)

chcp

OS: Microsoft Common

Function	Shows or changes the number of the active code page for keyboard extensions.
Syntax	chcp *{ NR }* ME: chcp

NR	Specifies the three-digit code page for a specific country.
437	United States, Australia.
737	Greek II.
850	(Multilingual) Latin America, Europe, Sweden, Denmark, Germany, and so forth.
852	Eastern European, Czech, Croatia, Hungary, Poland, Romania, Slavic, Serbia.
855	Cyrillic I, Macedonia.
857	Turkish.
860	Portuguese.
861	Greek.
862	Israel.
863	Canadian-French.
864	Arabic.
865	Nordic.
866	Russian (Cyrillic II).
932	Japan.

File Name:	`chcp.com`	**Directory:**	**9x/ME:** INTERNAL, **NT4, 2000:** \winnt\system32, **XP:** \windows\system32	**Type:**	Internal and External

chcp	Shows the active code page.

chkdsk

OS: Microsoft Common

Function	Shows status or repairs a disk. It can also be used to check a file for fragmentation.
Syntax	chkdsk *{ drive:*] [*files... }* [options...]

/F	Fixes errors on the selected disk.
/V	Shows the files and directories while the check is performed.
/R	Finds and recovers readable information from bad sectors.
/?	Shows help information.
	The following three options are only used with the NTFS file system:
/L:*size*	Sets the size of the log file. If no size given, the current one is shown.
/I	Causes the check of index entries to be less forceful.
/C	Skips the check of cycles within the directory tree.
drive:	Specifies the drive to check. If not given, uses the current drive.
files...	Specifies the files to check for fragmentation. Used only with FAT.

File Name:	`chkdsk.exe`	**Directory:**	\windows\command, **NT4, 2000:** \winnt\system32, **XP:** \windows\system32	**Type:**	External

Note:	Only members of the Administrators group can use this command on a fixed disk.
chkdsk c: /F	Searches for and tries to repair any errors on the c: disk.
chkdsk *.*	All the files in the current directory are checked for fragmentation.

Clipbook Viewer

OS:	Microsoft Common
Function	Shares pictures or documents over the network by pasting them in your clipbook viewer.
Syntax	clipbrd
File Name:	`clipbrd.exe`
Directory:	\windows, **NT, 2000:** \winnt\system32, **XP:** \windows\system32
Type:	External

cls

OS:	Microsoft Common
Function	Clears the screen.
Syntax	cls

command

OS:	Microsoft Common
Function	Starts a new copy of the Windows command interpreter.
Syntax	command *{ path }* *{ device }* [options...]

/E:*bytes*	Specifies the initial environment size.
/P	Makes the new command interpreter permanent.
/MSG	Stores all error messages in memory — requires the /P option.
/c *command*	Executes a specified command and then return.
path	Identifies the directory that contains the command.com file.
device	Identifies the device used for command input and output.
9x/ME	
/L*buffer*	Specifies internal buffer size.
/U*buffer*	Specifies input buffer size.
/LOW	Forces command to store all data in low memory.
/y	Steps through the batch program.
/k*command*	Executes a specified command and then continues running.

File Name:	`command.com`
Directory:	\windows, **NT4, 2000:** \winnt\system32, **XP:** \windows\system32
Type:	External

command /C print autoexec.nt	Starts the command interpreter and prints the file autoexec.nt and then stops.
command /E:4096	Starts the command interpreter with an environment size of 4096 bytes.

Control Panel

OS:	Microsoft Common
Function	Is used to access various computer settings.
Syntax	control

Accessibility Options	Configures accessibility options. **Win95, Win98:** Not available.
Add/Remove Programs	Is used to install and uninstall programs. **WinNT:** Not available.
Date/Time	Is used to set the date and time and select the time zone to use.
Display	Changes screen resolution, desktop appearance, background picture, and screen saver.
Fonts	Manages and shows fonts installed on the computer.
Internet Options	Configures Internet display and connection settings.
Keyboard	Configures settings for the keyboard like keyboard layout.
Mouse	Configures various mouse settings.
Printers	Is used to add, remove, and change printer settings. **WinXP:** Not available.
Game Controllers	Adds, removes, or changes game controller settings. **WinNT:** Not available.
Win9x	
Add New Hardware	Is used to install new hardware.
Modems	Configures installed modems or installs new modems.
Network	Is used to configure network software and hardware.
ODBC Data Source	Manages ODBC connections.
Passwords	Manages passwords and security settings.
Regional Settings	Is used to change regional-specific settings.
Sound	Associates sounds to events. **WinME:** Not available.

continued

Telephony	Is used to configure dialing properties. **Win95:** Not available.
Users	Is used to manage multiple users on the computer. **Win95:** Not available.
	The following option is only available in Windows 95.
Power	Is used to manage the settings for power management.
	The following option is only available in Windows 98.
Power Management	Is used to manage the settings for power management.
	The following options are only available in Windows ME.
Dial-Up Networking	Is used to setup Internet connections and file shares using a modem.
Folder Options	Is used to change the appearance of the display of files and folders.
Power Options	Is used to manage the settings for power management.
Scanners and Cameras	Is used to configure any installed cameras and scanners.
Scheduled Tasks	Is used to schedule tasks to run automatically.
Sound and Multimedia	Associates sounds to events and configures the sound hardware.
Automatic Updates	Changes the settings for automatic updates.
Taskbar and Start Menu	Is used to customize the Taskbar and Start Menu.
WinNT:	
Add/Remove Hardware	Is used to install or uninstall hardware.
Console	Configures the settings for the DOS console.
Devices	Is used to start or stop device drivers.
MS Licensing	Manages licensing options. (Only available on servers.)
Modems	Configures installed modems or installs new modems.
Multimedia	Is used to change multimedia settings.
Network	Is used to configure network software and hardware.
ODBC Data Sources	Manages ODBC connections.
PC Card (PCMCIA)	Is used to enable PCMCIA sockets and change PC-Card settings.
Ports	Manages serial port settings.
SCSI Adapter	Is used to add or remove SCSI adapters and show their settings.
Server	Configures local server settings.
Services	Is used to start, stop and configure services.
Sound	Associates sounds to events.
Tape Devices	Is used to detect tape devices and show their settings.
Telephony	Is used to configure dialing properties.
UPS	Is used to configure the Uninterruptible Power Supply.
Regional Options	Is used to change regional-specific settings.
Win2k:	
Add/Remove Hardware	Is used to install or uninstall hardware.
Administrative Tools	Shows all available administrative tools.
Folder Options	Is used to change the appearance of the display of files and folders.
Licensing	Manages licensing options. (Only available on servers.)
Network and Dial-up Connections	Is used to set up connections to other computers, networks, and the internet.
Phone and Modem Options	Configures dialing rules and modem settings.
Regional Options	Is used to change regional-specific settings.
Scanners and Cameras	Is used to configure any installed cameras and scanners.
Scheduled Tasks	Is used to schedule tasks to run automatically.
Sound and Multimedia	Associates sounds to events and configures the sound hardware.
WinXP:	
Add Hardware	Is used to install new hardware.
Administrative Tools	Shows all available administrative tools.
Folder Options	Is used to change the appearance of the display of files and folders.
Network Connections	Is used to set up connections to other computers, networks, and the Internet.
Power Options	Is used to manage the settings for power management.
Printers and Faxes	Shows and installs printers and fax printers.
Regional and Language Options	Is used to change regional-specific settings.
Scanners and Cameras	Is used to configure any installed cameras and scanners.
Scheduled Tasks	Is used to schedule tasks to run automatically.

continued

Speech	Configures the text to speech settings.
Sounds and Audio Devices	Associates sounds to events and configures the sound hardware.
Taskbar and Start Menu	Is used to customize the Taskbar and Start Menu.
User Accounts	Is used to manage multiple users on the computer.
Wireless Link	Is used to configure infrared file transfer and hardware settings.

File Name:	`control.exe`	**Directory:**	\windows, **NT4, 2000:** \winnt\system32, **XP:** \windows\system32	**Type:**	External

copy

OS: Microsoft Common

Function	Copies one or more files to a specified location or combines two or more files into one.
Syntax	copy *source* { *destination* } [options...]

	The following two options can't be combined:
/A	Indicates an ASCII text file.
/B	Indicates a binary file.
/V	Verifies the files being copied.
/N	Uses short filename when copying.
/Z	Copies network files in restartable mode.
source	Specifies the source file or files.
destination	Specifies the destination directory or file.
9x/ME:	
/Y	Shows no overwrite warning prompt.
/-Y	Shows overwrite warning prompt (is the default). (/Y can be placed in the variable copycmd. To override, use /-Y.)

copy *.* a:	Copies all files in the current directory to a:.
copy 1.txt + 2.txt + 3.txt 123.txt	Combines the files 1.txt, 2.txt, and 3.txt to the file 123.txt.

CTRL-ALT-DEL

OS: Microsoft Common

Function	Allows the user to reboot the computer.
Syntax	<CTRL> + <ALT> + <DEL>

date

OS: Microsoft Common

Function	Shows or sets the current date. Prompts for a new one if no date is specified.
Syntax	date { *mm-dd-yy* }

mm	Specifies the month. Valid values are 1 through 12.
dd	Specifies the day in the month. Valid values are 1 through 31.
yy	Specifies the year. Valid values are 80 through 99 or 1980 through 2099.
NT, 2000, XP:	
/t	Doesn't ask for a new date.

debug

OS: Microsoft Common

Function	Tests and debugs MS-DOS-executable files.
Syntax	debug *file* { *arguments...* }

/?	Shows help information.
file	Identifies the file to debug, including any arguments it may require.
	The following command is available in the program:
A { *address* }	Enters assembly code directly into memory at the specified address.
address	Specifies the address. If not given, it starts assembling where it last stopped.
C *range address*	Compares two portions of memory.
range	The starting address and length or the starting and ending address.
address	Identifies the starting address of the second area of memory.
D { *range* }	Shows the specified range of memory addresses.
range	Sets the starting address and length or the starting and ending address to show.
E *address* { *list* }	Enters data into memory at the specified address.

continued

address	Identifies the first memory location where the data is inserted.
list	Identifies the data to enter.
F *range list*	Fills specified memory area with values — hexadecimal or ASCII is allowed.
range	Sets the starting address and length or the starting and ending address to fill.
list	Identifies the data to fill the specified memory area.
G [=*address*] [breakpoints]	Runs the program currently in memory.
address	Sets the address to start at. If no address is given, it starts at current address.
breakpoint	Sets 1 to 10 temporary breakpoints.
H *value1 value2*	Performs hexadecimal arithmetic on the two specified values.
value1	Specifies any hexadecimal number (valid range is 0 to FFFFh).
value2	Specifies any hexadecimal number (valid range is 0 to FFFFh).
I *port*	Reads and shows 1-byte value from the specified port.
L *{ address }*	Loads a file into memory.
address	Sets memory location where the file is loaded (default is address in CS register).
M *range address*	Copies a block of memory to another location.
range	Sets the starting address and length or the starting and ending address to copy.
address	Identifies the destination address.
N *filename* | *parameters*	Specifies a filename for the L and W commands or parameters for the current one.
O *port value*	Sends a byte value to the specified port.
P [=*address*] *{ NR }*	Runs a loop, a repeated string instruction, a software interrupt, or a subroutine.
address	Sets the location of the first instruction. If not given, the one in CS:IP is used.
NR	Identifies the number of instruction to run (default is 1).
Q	Exits the debugger.
R *{ name }*	Shows or edits the contents of one or more registers.
name	Identifies the CPU register to show or edit.
S *range list*	Searches the specified range of addresses for a pattern of one or more values.
range	Sets the starting address and length or the starting and ending address to search.
list	Identifies the pattern to search for.
T [=*address*] *{ NR }*	Runs on instruction and shows the status of the register, flags, and the instruction.
address	Specifies the starting address.
NR	Specifies the number of instructions to trace.
U *{ range }*	Disassembles the specified address range (default is 20h).
W *{ address }*	Writes the specified number of bytes to a file.
address	Identifies the starting address of the file to write to a file.
XA *{ count }*	Allocates the specified number of 16-kilobyte pages of expanded memory.
XD *{ handle }*	Deallocates the specified handle to expanded memory.
XM *{ lpage } { ppage }* [handle]	Maps a logical page of expanded memory.
lpage	Identifies the number of logical pages of expanded memory to map to a physical ppage.
ppage	Identifies the number of physical pages to which lpage is mapped.
handle	Specifies the handle.
XS	Shows information about the expanded memory.
arguments...	Specifies arguments to the command.

File Name:	`debug.exe`	**Directory:**	\windows\command, **NT4, 2000:** \winnt\system32, **XP:** \windows\system32	**Type:**	External
debug c:\myprogram\ucg.exe			Starts debug with the file ucg.exe.		

del, erase

OS: Microsoft Common

Function	Deletes one or more files.
Syntax	del [options...] *files...* erase [options...] *files...*

/P	Prompts before deleting each file.
files...	Specifies the files to delete. Separate files with semicolon (;).
NT, XP	
/F	Forces the deleting of read-only file.
/S	Deletes the specified file from all subdirectories.

continued

/Q	Doesn't ask before deleting when using a global wildcard.
/A[:*attribute*]	Deletes files according to file attributes. Use one or more of R, H, S, or A. (R - Read-only, H - Hidden, S - System, A - Archive.) Place a - (minus) before an attribute to not delete if set.
/?	Shows help information.

del *.*	Deletes all the files in the current directory.
erase c:\temp	Deletes all files in the directory c:\temp.

dir

OS: Microsoft Common

Function	Lists the files and subdirectories.
Syntax	dir *{ name }* [options...]

/P	Shows the output one screen at a time.
/W	Shows the listing in wide format sorted by row.
/S	Displays files in the specified directory and all subdirectories.
/B	Shows only the name of each directory or file without other information.
/L	Shows unsorted directory names and filenames in lowercase.
/A[[:] *attribute*]	Shows files or directories with the specified attribute. Use D, H, S, R, or A. (Place a - (minus) before an attribute to hide if set.)
/O[[:] *sortorder*]	Sorts the output.
N	Sorts in alphabetic order by name.
E	Sorts in alphabetic order by extension.
D	Sorts by date and time starting with the newest.
S	Sorts by size starting with the smallest.
G	Lists directories before files.
C	Sorts by compression ratio, lowest first. (Place a - (minus) before the sort option to reverse the order.)
name	Specifies the file or directory to see a listing on.
9x/ME:	
/V	Verbose mode. Shows more information.
/4	Shows year with four digits.
NT, XP:	
/T *field*	Specifies which time field is shown or used for sorting.
C	Specifies that the creation time should be used.
A	Specifies that the last access time should be used.
W	Specifies that the last written time should be used.
/N	Shows the filenames on the far right.
/X	Shows the short names for long-name files.
/C	Shows the thousand separator in file size (is the default).
/-C	Doesn't show the thousand separator in file size.
/D	Shows the listing in wide format sorted by column.

dir *.exe	Shows all files with the extension EXE in the current directory.
dir /O:n	Sorts the output in alphabetic order by name.

diskcopy

OS: Microsoft Common

Function	Copies the contents of one floppy disk to another.
Syntax	diskcopy *{ drive1*: [*drive2*:]] [options...]

/V	Verifies the copy.
drive1:	Specifies the source drive.
drive2:	Specifies the target drive. This can be the same as the source drive.
9x/ME:	
/M	Enables a multipass copy using only the memory.
/1	Copies only the first side of the disk.

File Name:	`diskcopy.com`	**Directory:**	\windows\command **NT4, 2000:** \winnt\system32, **XP:** \windows\system32	**Type:**	External

diskcopy a: a:	Copies information from drive a: and prompts for a new floppy to copy information to.

doskey

OS: Microsoft Common

Function	Recalls Windows commands and edits previously typed command lines, as well as creating macros.
Syntax	doskey [options...]

/reinstall	Clears the command history buffer.
/history	Shows the command history.
/listsize=*size*	Sets the number of commands to store in the history buffer (default is 128).
/insert	Inserts new characters in the command line.
/overstrike	Overwrites old text.
/exename=*exename*	Specifies the program in which the `doskey` macro runs.
/macrofile=*file*	Specifies a file that contains macros to install.
macroname=[*macro* }	Creates a new macro.
macroname=	Identifies the macro to create or delete.
macro	Identifies the commands that the macro should perform (separate commands with $t).
	The following special characters are available when creating macros:
$G	Redirects the output to a device or a file.
GG	Appends the output to a file instead of replacing it.
$L	Specifies the input to be read from a device or a file instead of the keyboard.
$B	Sends the output to a command.
$T	Separates multiple commands.
$$	Specifies the dollar $ character.
$*NR*	Represents options passed to the macro ($1-$9 is valid - see example).
$*	Represents all options pasted to the macro.
	The following hot keys are available:
UP ARROW	Recalls the command used before the current one.
DOWN ARROW	Recalls the command used after the current one.
PAGE UP	Recalls the oldest command used.
PAGE DOWN	Recalls the newest command used.
LEFT ARROW	Moves the cursor back one character.
RIGHT ARROW	Moves the cursor forward one character.
CTRL + LEFT ARROW	Moves the cursor back one word.
CTRL + RIGHT ARROW	Moves the cursor forward one word.
HOME	Moves the cursor to the beginning of the line.
END	Moves the cursor to the end of the line.
ESC	Clears the command line.
F1	Copies one character from the beginning of the last command in the history.
F2	Copies characters before the one specified after pressing F2 from the last command.
F3	Copies remaining characters from the last command beginning at the current position.
F4	Deletes all characters between the cursor and the one specified after pressing F4.
F5	Copies the last command to the command line.
F6	Places an end-of-file character at the current position.
F7	Shows all commands in the history.
ALT + F7	Deletes the command history.
*char*F8	Shows all commands beginning with the characters in the command line.
F9	Makes it possible to enter the history number of the command to show.
ALT + F10	Deletes all defined macros.
9x/ME:	
/echo: on | off	Enables or disables echo for macros.
/file:*macrolist*	Specifies a file that contains predefined macros.
/macros	Shows all defined `doskey` macros.
NT, 2000, XP:	
/macros[:all | :*exename*]	Shows all macros or all macros for the specified .EXE file.

File Name:	`doskey.com` `doskey.exe`	**Directory:**	\windows\command, **NT4, 2000:** \winnt\system32, **XP:** \windows\system32	**Type:**	External

doskey QF=format $1 /q	Creates a macro called QF that quick formats the specified drive.
doskey /listsize=50	Sets the number of commands stored to 50.

Dr. Watson

OS: Microsoft Common

Function	Configures the Dr. Watson utility, a diagnostics tool used to debug program errors and show any errors found.				
Syntax	9x/ME, NT, 2000, XP: drwatson NT, 2000, XP: drwtsn32				
File Name:	`drwatson.exe`, `drwtsn32.exe`	**Directory:**	\windows, **NT4, 2000:** \winnt\system32, **XP:** \windows\system32	**Type:**	External
Tip:	To configure Dr. Watson in Windows 95/98/ME, simply right-click the icon in the system tray.				

echo

OS: Microsoft Common

Function	Shows text on the screen. It can also alter the command-echoing mode.
Syntax	echo [option] echo { *message* }

ON | OFF	Enables or disables the command echoing feature.
message	Specifies a message to echo to the screen.

echo on	Turns on the echoing feature.
echo Hello World!	Shows the specified message "Hello World!" on the screen.

edit

OS: Microsoft Common

Function	An editor for text files. If no parameters are given, the editor starts with a new file.
Syntax	edit { *file* } [options...]

/B	Starts the editor in black and white mode.
/H	Shows the maximum number of lines possible for your monitor.
/?	Shows help information.
file	Specifies the file to open or create with the editor.
NT:	
/G	Uses the fastest screen updating possible for CGA monitors.
/NOHI	Allows an eight-color monitor.
9x/ME, 2000, XP	
/R	Loads all files as read-only.
/S	Disables usage of long filenames.
/*value*	Starts the editor in binary file mode, allowing value characters on each line.

File Name:	`edit.com`	**Directory:**	\windows\command, **NT4, 2000:** \winnt\system32, **XP:** \windows\system32	**Type:**	External

edit autoexec.bat	Opens the file autoexec.bat in the current directory.
edit c:\dos\autoexec.bat	Opens the file autoexec.bat in the c:\dos directory.

exit

OS: Microsoft Common

Function	Exits the command interpreter or a bat script.
Syntax	exit

explorer

OS: Microsoft Common

Function	Starts a new Explorer window used to navigate through directories, and if supplied, opens the specified path.
Syntax	explorer { *path* }

path	Identifies the directory to open in the new Explorer window.

File Name:	`explorer.exe`	**Directory:**	\windows, **NT4, 2000:** \winnt\	**Type:**	External

explorer d:	Explores the drive d:.

fc

OS: Microsoft Common

Function	Compares two files and shows the differences between them.
Syntax	fc [options...] *file1 file2*

/A	Shows only first and last lines for each set of differences.
/B	Performs a binary comparison.

continued

/C	Disregards the case of letters.
/L	Compares files as ASCII text.
/LB*NR*	Sets the maximum number of lines that can differ before fc cancels the comparison.
/N	Shows the line numbers when performing an ASCII comparison.
/T	Doesn't expand tabs to spaces.
/W	Handles consecutive spaces and tabs as one space during the comparison.
/*NR*	Specifies the number of lines that has to be the same after a mismatch.
file1	Identifies the name and location of the first file to compare.
file2	Identifies the name and location of the second file to compare.
NT, 2000, XP:	
/U	Compares files as Unicode text files.

File Name:	`fc.exe`	**Directory:**	\windows\command, **NT4, 2000:** \winnt\system32, **XP:** \windows\system32	**Type:**	External

fc autoexec.bat c:\winnt\system32\autoexec.nt	Compares the two specified files and shows the difference.
fc progg.exe c:\dos\progg.exe /B	Performs a binary comparison of the two specified files.

find

OS: Microsoft Common

Function	Searches for text strings in a file or files.
Syntax	find [options...] "*string*" *file*

/V	Shows the lines that don't contain the specified string.
/C	Counts the lines that contain the string, or don't contain it if it's used with /V.
/N	Shows the number of the line that contains the string. Ignored if used with /C.
/I	Specifies the search to be case-insensitive.
/?	Shows help information.
string	Specifies the text string to find.
file	Specifies the file or files to search in.

File Name:	`find.exe`	**Directory:**	\windows\command, **NT4, 2000:** \winnt\system32, **XP:** \windows\system32	**Type:**	External

find /V "LH" autoexec.bat	Shows all the lines that don't contain the string "LH".
find "test" *.*	Searches for the string "test" in all files in the current directory.

fontview

OS: Microsoft Common

Function	Shows the specified font in a window.
Syntax	fontview *font.ttf*

font.ttf	Specifies the name of the font you want to show.

File Name:	`fontview.exe`	**Directory:**	\windows, **NT4, 2000:** \winnt\system32, **XP:** \windows\system32	**Type:**	External

fontview arial.ttf	Shows the font Arial in a window.

for

OS: Microsoft Common

Function	Runs a specified command for each file in a set of files.
Syntax	for %*var* in (*list*) do *cmd*

%*var*	Represents a replaceable variable. (In batch file, the variable uses the syntax %%var instead of %var.)
(*list*)	Specifies one or more files or text strings to process.
cmd	Identifies the command and any parameters it might require for each file.
NT, 2000, XP:	
	Syntax for /d %*var* in (*list*) do *cmd*
/d	Specifies that any wildcards in list match directories instead of files.
	Syntax for /r *{ path }* %*var* in (*list*) do *cmd*
/r	Walks the directory tree specified by *path*, or from current if unspecified.
path	Specifies the path to start in.
list	If the list is . (single dot), go through all directories.
	Syntax for /l %*var* in (*start,step,end*) do *cmd*
/l	Makes a loop from start to end in steps.
start	Specifies the start for the loop.

continued

step	Specifies step size.
end	Specifies the end.
	Syntax for /f ["*opt*"] %*var* in (*list*) do *cmd*
/b	Opens and processes each file in list.
opt	Specifies extra options. These have to be inside quotes (").
eol=*c*	Specifies one character to use as end-of-line marker.
skip=*n*	Specifies number of lines that are skipped in the beginning of a file.
delims=*nnn*	Specifies a delimiter to use to divide the field (default is Tab and Space).
tokens=x,y,m-n	Specifies what field to be passed to the command.
Example:	**Syntax** for /f "delims=1,2,3" %i in (onefile.txt) echo %i %j %k
	Opens one file.txt and sets i = filed1, j = fild2, and k = fild3.

FOR %x IN (*.doc *.txt) DO print %x	Prints all files, in the current directory, of the type DOC and TXT.

format

OS: Microsoft Common

Function	Formats the specified disk.
Syntax	format *disk*: [options...]

/V:*label*	Specifies the volume label. If unused, you're prompted.
/Q	Performs a quick format.
/F:*size*	Specifies the size of the floppy to format.
/T:*tracks*	Specifies the number of tracks per disk side.
/N:*sectors*	Specifies the number of sectors per track.
/1	Formats a single side of a floppy disk.
/4	Specifies a 5.25-inch 360K floppy disk to be formatted in a high-density drive.
/8	Formats a 5.25-inch floppy disk with eight sectors per track.
/?	Shows help information.
disk	Specifies the disk to be formatted.
9x/ME:	
/C	Tests clusters that are currently marked as bad.
/B	Allocates space for the system files in the formatted disk.
/S	Copies the system files (makes the disk bootable) to the disk.
NT, 2000, XP:	
/FS:*filesystem*	Specifies the file system to use. Valid selections are FAT and NTFS.
/C	Causes the files on the new volume to be compressed by default (only NTFS).
/A:*size*	Overrides the default allocation size.

File Name:	`format.com`	**Directory:**	\windows\command, **NT4, 2000:** \winnt\system32, **XP:** \windows\system32	**Type:**	External
Note:	You must be a member of the Administrators group to format a fixed disk.				

format c: /V:SYSTEM	Formats the c: drive and sets the label to SYSTEM.
format a: /Q	Performs a quick format of the floppy disk in drive a:.

ftp

OS: Microsoft Common

Function	An FTP client that allows you to transfer files from an FTP server using the file transfer protocol.
Syntax	ftp [options...] { *host* }

-v	Hides response messages from the remote server.
-n	Doesn't log in to the specified server when the client is started.
-i	Specifies interactive prompting to be turned off during multiple file transfers.
-d	Shows all commands that are passed between the client and server.
-g	Specifies filename globbing to be disabled.
-s:*file*	Specifies a text file containing FTP commands to execute when connected.
-a	Specifies the use of any local interface when binding data connection.
-A	Tries to log in to the server as anonymous.
-w:*size*	Overrides the default transfer buffer size of 4096.
host	Specifies the name or the IP address for the computer to connect to.
	The following commands are available inside the client's interactive shell:
!	Switches to the shell - type exit to return to the client prompt.

continued

? *{ command }*	Shows help information.
append *localfile { remotefile }*	Appends the local file to the remote host.
ascii	Sets the file transfer mode to ASCII (is the default).
bell	When a file completes, a bell sounds.
binary	Sets the file transfer mode to BINARY.
bye	Terminates the FTP session and quits.
cd *directory*	Changes the remote directory.
close	Terminates the FTP session.
debug	Shows all commands that are passed between the client and server.
delete *file*	Deletes the specified file on remote host.
dir *{ directory } { localfile }*	Shows the content of the remote directory. Optionally puts it in localfile.
disconnect	Same as close.
get *remotefile { localfile }*	Specifies file to download and saves it on local host.
glob	Enables filename expansion for mdelete, mget, and mput.
hash	Enables a # hash sign for every data block transferred.
help *{ command }*	Shows help information of the specified FTP command.
lcd *{ directory*	Changes directory on the local host.
literal *args...*	Specifies arguments to send to remote FTP server.
ls [*directory } { localfile }*	Same as `dir`.
mdelete *files...*	Deletes the specified files on the remote host.
mdir *remotefiles... localfile*	Shows list of multiple remote files, and puts the result in the local file.
mget *files...*	Downloads the selected files, wildcards can be used.
mkdir *directory*	Creates a directory on the remote host.
mls *remotefiles... localfile*	Lists multiple remote files and puts the information in the specified local file.
mput *{ files... }*	Specifies multiple files together with wildcards, and continues to upload next file.
open *host { port }*	Specifies the host and port to connect to.
prompt	Enables or disables interactive prompting.
put *localfile { remotefile }*	Uploads a file onto the remote host.
pwd	Shows current directory of the remote host.
quit	Terminates the FTP session and quits.
quote *arg1 arg2*	Specifies arguments to send to remote FTP server.
recv *remotefile { localfile }*	Specifies file to download and saves it on local host.
remotehelp *{ command }*	Shows help from the remote host.
rename *{ from } { to }*	Specifies a file to rename.
rmdir *{ directory }*	Deletes a directory on the remote host.
send *localfile { remotefile }*	Uploads a file onto the remote host.
status	Shows status for FTP.
trace	Toggles to trace packets or not.
type *{ type }*	Sets file transfer type to either ASCII or binary (default is ASCII).
user *user { password } { account }*	Logs in to the remote FTP server.
verbose	Verbose mode. Shows more information.

File Name:	`ftp.exe`	**Directory:**	\windows, **NT4, 2000:** \winnt\system32, **XP:** \windows\system32	**Type:**	External

Tip: Type bin for binary when copying executable files, and use hash; it shows the progress.

ftp -d 192.168.1.250	Enables debugging.
ftp -v ftp.ucg.com	Shows all responses.

goto

OS: Microsoft Common

Function	Jumps to the specified label. Goto is used inside scripts to control the program flow.
Syntax	goto *label*

label	Specifies the label to go to. (A label is a single string on a line beginning with a colon.)

goto ucgbook	Goes to the label ucgbook.
:ucgbook	This is the label ucgbook.

HyperTerminal

OS: Microsoft Common

Function	Starts the HyperTerminal. Use this to connect to other computers, Internet telnet sites, bulletin board, and so forth.
Syntax	hypertrm *{ sessionfile }*

sessionfile	Identifies the name of the file containing the session to connect to.

File Name:	`hypertrm.exe`	**Directory:**	\Program Files\Accessories\, **NT4, 2000, XP:** \Program Files\Windows NT	**Type:**	External

hypertrm ucg.ht	Uses the configuration in ucg.ht to connect to ucg.

if

OS: Microsoft Common

Function	Performs conditional processing in batch programs.
Syntax	9x/ME, NT, 2000, XP: if [NOT] *test command* 2000, XP: if [NOT] *condition* (*command*) else (*command*)

NOT	Executes the command only if the condition is false.
test	The following specifies what to test:
ERRORLEVEL *NR*	Executes the command only if the previously returned exit code is equal or greater.
string1==string2	Executes the command only if the two specified strings are the same.
EXIST *file*	Executes the command only if the specified file exists.
command	Identifies the command to run.
NT, 2000, XP:	
DEFINED *variable*	Executes the command only if the specified variable exists.
CMDEXTVERSION *NR*	Executes the command only if the command extension version is equal or greater.
[/I] *str1 cmp str2*	Executes the command only if the test is true. Test is one of the following:
EQU	Is true if str1 is equal to str2.
NEQ	Is true if str1 isn't equal to str2.
LSS	Is true if str1 is less than str2.
LEQ	Is true if str1 is less than or equal to str2.
GTR	Is true if str1 is greater than str2.
GEQ	Is true if str1 is greater than or equal to str2.
/I	Makes the compare case sensitive. (In Windows 2000 and XP you can use else.)
	The parentheses are used to separate the commands.

IF EXIST c:\autoexec.bat type autoexec.bat	Runs the command if the file exists.
IF NOT EXIST c:\names.dat echo Can't find data file.	Runs the command if the file doesn't exist.

ipconfig

OS: Microsoft Common

Function	Shows the current TCP/IP network configuration. It also releases or renews DHCP IP addresses.
Syntax	ipconfig [option]

/all	Shows all configuration information (by default only IP address, subnet, and gateway).
/?	Shows help information.
9x/ME:	
/release_all	Releases the current DHCP configuration data for all adapters.
/renew_all	Renews the DHCP configuration data for all adapters.
/release *adapter*	Releases the current DHCP configuration data for the specified adapter.
/renew *adapter*	Renews the DHCP configuration data for the specified adapter.
/batch *file*	Writes to the specified file or, if unspecified, to `./winipcfg.out`.
NT:	
/release *{ adapter }*	Releases the current DHCP configuration for the specified adapter or for all.
/renew *{ adapter }*	Renews the DHCP configuration data for the specified adapter or for all.
2000, XP:	
/release *{ adapter }*	Releases the current DHCP configuration for the specified adapters or for all.
/renew *{ adapter }*	Renews the DHCP configuration data for the specified adapter or for all.
/flushdns	Purges the DNS resolver cache.
/registerdns	Reregisters DNS names and refreshes all DHCP leases.
/displaydns	Shows the DNS resolver cache.
/showclassid *adapter*	Shows all allowed DHCP class IDs for the specified adapter.
/setclassid *adapter { classid }*	Modifies the DHCP class ID for the specified adapter.

continued

File Name:	ipconfig.exe	**Directory:**	\windows, **NT4, 2000:** \winnt\system32, **XP:** \windows\system32	**Type:**	External
ipconfig			Shows IP address, subnet mask, and default gateway for all TCP/IP adapters.		
ipconfig /release_all			Releases DHCP configuration data for all TCP/IP adapters.		

isuninst

OS: Microsoft Common

Function	Uninstalls Microsoft's Internet Explorer. You are prompted to confirm before uninstallation takes place.
Syntax	isuninst

File Name:	isuninst.exe	**Directory:**	\windows, \winnt	**Type:**	External

Keyboard Properties

OS: Microsoft Common

Function	Starts the keyboard properties and keyboard language selector and adds it to the system tray.
Syntax	internat

File Name:	internat.exe	**Directory:**	\windows\system, **NT4, 2000:** \winnt\system32, **XP:** \windows\system32	**Type:**	External

label

OS: Microsoft Common

Function	Creates, names, or erases a volume label on disks.
Syntax	label *{ drive: } { label }*

drive	Specifies the drive to modify the label on.
label	Specifies the new volume label.

File Name:	label.exe	**Directory:**	\windows\command, **NT4, 2000:** \winnt\system32, **XP:** \windows\system32	**Type:**	External
label c:UCG			Changes the label of c: to UCG.		

md, mkdir

OS: Microsoft Common

Function	Creates a new directory.
Syntax	md *directory* mkdir *path*

directory	Specifies the name and location of the new directory.

md mydir	Creates the specified directory in the current directory.
md c:\windows\mydir	Creates the mydir directory in the c:\windows directory.

mem

OS: Microsoft Common

Function	Shows how much free memory exists and how memory is used.
Syntax	mem [options...]

/C	Shows memory usage for programs and classifies them.
/D	Shows all modules and drivers in the memory and their status.
/?	Shows help information.
9x/ME:	
/F	Shows how much free memory remains.
/M	Shows more detailed memory usage listings for specified module.
/P	Shows information one screen at a time.
NT, 2000, XP:	
/p	Shows the amount of memory the currently loaded programs are using.

File Name:	mem.exe	**Directory:**	\windows\command, **NT4,2000:** \winnt\system32, **XP:** \windows\system32	**Type:**	External
MEM /C			Shows memory usage for programs.		

mode

OS: Microsoft Common

Function	Shows, changes, or configures system devices. If used without parameters, status of all devices is shown.
Syntax	mode *{ device }* [options...] mode [option]

/?	Shows help information.
/STATUS	Shows the status for all devices or a specified device.
device	Specifies the device to use.
COM*n*[:]	Specifies a serial port.
LPT*n*[:]	Specifies a parallel port.
CON[:]	Specifies the console.
	The following options are used for COM device:
BAUD=*value*	Specifies the baud rate to use.
PARITY=*value*	Sets the parity check type; n (none), e (even), o (odd), m (mark), or s (space).
DATA=*value*	Sets the number of data bits in a character (default is 7).
STOP=*value*	Sets the number of stop bits that define the end of a character (default is 1).
	The following option can be used with LPT ports:
=COM*n*[:]	Redirects outputs from the specified LPT port to the specified COM port.
	The following options are used with the CON device:
cols=*NR*	Sets the number of characters per line in the command prompt screen buffer.
lines=*NR*	Sets the number of lines in the command prompt screen buffer.
	The following two options can't be combined with the two above:
rate=*rate*	Sets the rate for which characters are repeated when holding down a key.
delay=*seconds*	Sets the time that must elapse before characters are repeated (default is 2).
9x/ME:	
	The following option can be used with all devices:
CP PREPARE=((*nnn...*) (*file*))	Specifies a code page to prepare.
nnn...	Specifies one or more code pages.
file	Specifies the coinage information file.
CP SELECT=*NR*	Selects the specified code page.
CP REFRESH	Refreshes the code page.
CP [/STATUS]	Shows the status for the code page.
	The following option is used for the COM device:
RETRY=*NR*	Specifies the number of retries before giving up.
	The following options can be used with LPT ports:
cols=*NR*	Sets the number of characters per line. Valid numbers are 80 or 132 (default is 80).
lines=*NR*	Sets vertical spacing and number of lines per inch (default is 6, valid are 6 or 8).
RETRY=*NR*	Specifies the number of retries before giving up.
NT, 2000, XP:	
	The following options are used for COM device:
to=on | off	Turns infinite timeout processing on or off (default is off).
xon=on | off	Turns the Xon or Xoff protocol for data-flow control on or off.
odsr=on | off	Turns the output handshaking that uses data set ready (DSR) circuit on or off.
octs=on | off	Turns the output handshaking that uses clear to send (CTS) circuit on or off.
dtr=*ACTION*	**Action can be one of the following three:**
on	Turns the DTR circuit on.
off	Turns the DTR circuit off.
hs	Sets the DTR circuit to handshake.
rts=*ACTION*	**Action can be one of the following four:**
on	Turns the RTS circuit on.
off	Turns the RTS circuit off.
hs	Sets the RTS circuit to handshake.
tg	Sets the RTS circuit to toggle.
idsr=on | off	Turns DSR circuit sensitivity on or off.

continued

CP SELECT=*NR* CP [/STATUS]		**The following options are used with the CON device:** Selects the specified code page. Shows the status for the code page.			
File Name:	`mode.com`	**Directory:**	\windows\command, **NT4, 2000:** \winnt\system32, **XP:** \windows\system32	**Type:**	External
mode con cols=100 lines=120			Sets the prompt screen buffer to 100 characters per line and 120 lines.		
mode lpt1=com1			Maps lpt1 to com1.		

more

OS: Microsoft Common

Function	Shows a text file one page at a time. If no file is specified it reads from STDIN.
Syntax	9x/ME: more *files...* NT, 2k, XP: more /e [options...] *files...* NT, 2k, XP: more [options...] *file*

file **NT, 2000, XP:**		Specifies files to show. **more doesn't read a file on the command line without /e or < .**			
/c		Specifies the screen to be cleared before showing the page.			
/p		Expands form-feed characters.			
/s		Shows multiple blank lines as one blank line.			
/t*NR*		Replaces tabs with the specified number of spaces.			
+*NR*		Specifies which line number to start showing the file from.			
/e		Enables the extended feature commands that are used inside the more command. **The following extended feature commands are used at the more prompt:**			
P *NR*		Shows a prompt that enables you to type in the number of lines to show next.			
S *NR*		Shows a prompt that enables you to type in the number of lines to skip.			
F		Shows the next file.			
Q		Exits			
=		Shows the current line number.			
?		Lists available commands.			
<Space>		Shows the next page.			
<Enter>		Shows the next line.			
File Name:	`more.com`	**Directory:**	\windows\command, **NT4, 2000:** \winnt\system32, **XP:** \windows\system32	**Type:**	External
more < textfile.txt			Shows the file textfile.txt one page at a time. Use < when specifying a single file.		
dir | more			Shows the output of `dir` one page at a time.		

move

OS: Microsoft Common

Function	Moves files or renames directories. The command is internal in Windows NT, 2000, and XP.
Syntax	move [option] *source destination* NT: move *source destination*

source		Identifies the file or files to move or the directory to rename.			
destination **9x/ME, 2000, XP:**		Identifies the destination path or the new name of the directory.			
/Y		Doesn't prompt before overwriting or creating a directory or file.			
/-Y		Causes prompting if /Y is pre-set in the COPYCMD environment variable.			
File Name:	`move.exe`	**Directory:**	\windows\command, **NT4, 2000, XP:** INTERNAL	**Type:**	External Internal
move c:\windows\temp*.tmp c:\tmp			Moves all files with extension .tmp in c:\windows\temp to c:\tmp\.		

nbtstat

OS: Microsoft Common

Function	Shows protocol information and TCP/IP connections using NetBIOS over TCP/IP.
Syntax	nbtstat [options...] *{ interval }*

-a *name*	Shows the specified remote computer's name table using its name.
-A *address*	Shows the specified remote computer's name table using its IP address.

continued

-c	Shows the NetBIOS remote name cache table. The IP address is given for each name.
-C	Shows the NetBIOS remote name cache with IP addresses on a per-device basis.
-n	Shows the local NetBIOS names.
-r	Shows information on names resolved by broadcast and via WINS.
-R	Purges all names from the NetBIOS name cache and reloads the `LMHOSTS` file.
-S	Shows client and server sessions. For remote computers, the IP address is shown.
-s	Shows sessions and converts remote IP address to a name using the `HOSTS` file.
interval	Redisplays the information with the specified interval in seconds. (When options are combined, only the last is used; the rest are ignored.)
NT, 2k, XP:	
-RR	Starts refresh after sending name release packets to WINs.

File Name:	`nbtstat.exe`	**Directory:**	\windows, **NT4, 2000:** \winnt\system32, **XP:** \windows\system32	**Type:**	External
Note:	This command is only available if the TCP/IP protocol is installed.				

nbtstat -a jupiter	Shows the name table of the remote host "jupiter".
nbtstat -R	Purges the name cache and reloads the `LMHOSTS`.

net

OS: Microsoft Common

Function	A text-based network configuration utility.
Syntax	net *ACTION* [/?]

/?	Shows help information.
ACTION	**The following are the available actions that may be used:**
config	Configures, for example, the server and workstation services.
help	Gives some information on how to use the NET command.
print	Shows or controls print jobs/queues.
start	Starts a service or shows a list of services already started.
stop	Stops a network service.
time	Synchronizes the clock with another computer.
use	Connects or disconnects to a shared resource.
view	Lists domains, computers, or resources shared by specified computer.
9x/ME:	
diag	Checks the connection between two computers or shows info on a single computer.
init	Loads protocols and network adapters without binding them to Protocol Manager.
logoff	Breaks connections to other computers.
logon	Logs on to another computer.
password	Changes the logon password.
ver	Shows the version of the workgroup redirector.
NT, 2k, XP:	
accounts	Configures the accounts policies
computer	Adds or deletes a computer account (only on a Windows NT domain controller).
continue	A command to use for a service.
file	Gives you the ability to close a file given its ID.
group	Manages groups (only on Windows NT domain controller).
helpmsg	Explains an error number's message.
localgroup	Shows the local groups and manages new local groups.
name	Shows, adds, or deletes a messaging name. Messenger service must run.
pause	Pauses a service given its name.
send	Sends a message over the network to a chosen computer name.
session	Shows or disconnects a session between local computer and clients connected.
share	Controls sharing.
statistics	Shows the statistics log for the server or local workstation service.
user	Adds, modifies, or shows information on user accounts.

File Name:	`net.exe`	**Directory:**	\windows, **NT4, 2000:** \winnt\system32, **XP:** \windows\system32	**Type:**	External

net view	Shows all computers in your workgroup.

net config

OS: Microsoft Common

Function	Shows or modifies running services that are configurable.
Syntax	net config *{ service }* [options...]

NT, 2k, XP:	
service	**The only services available are server and workstation:**
server	**The following options are available for the Server service:**
/autodisconnect:*time*	Sets the maximum number of minutes inactive users can be connected.
/srvcomment:"*text*"	Sets a server comment.
/hidden:yes | no	Specifies if the server should show up on the server list.
workstation	Shows the current settings for the workstation service.

File Name:	`net.exe`	**Directory:**	\windows, **NT4, 2000:** \winnt\system32, **XP:** \windows\system32	**Type:**	External

net config Server /srvcomment:"File Server"	Sets the server comment.
net config Workstation	Shows the current settings for the workstation service.

net help

OS: Microsoft Common

Function	Shows help information on the specified command.
Syntax	net help *{ command }*

command	Specifies the command to show help for.
9x/ME:	
errorNR	Identifies the number of the error messages to show help about.

File Name:	`net.exe`	**Directory:**	\windows, **NT4, 2000:** \winnt\system32, **XP:** \windows\system32	**Type:**	External

net help accounts	Shows help for the net accounts command.

net print

OS: Microsoft Common

Function	Shows and controls printer queues and print jobs.
Syntax	net print *host**printer* net print [*host*] *job* [option]

/delete	Deletes the specified print job.
job	Specifies the number of the print job.
host	Identifies the computer with the printer share.
printer	Identifies the printer share.
9x/ME:	
port	Specifies the printer port where the printer is connected. (This option can't be combined with the host parameter.)
/pause	Pauses the specified print job.
/resume	Resumes the specified print job.
/yes	Doesn't prompt for confirmation.
NT, 2k, XP:	
/hold	Holds the specified print job.
/release	Releases the specified print job.

File Name:	`net.exe`	**Directory:**	\windows, **NT4, 2000:** \winnt\system32, **XP:** \windows\system32	**Type:**	External

net print \\\\server\HPLJ5	Shows all print jobs for the HPLJ5 printer on the server computer.
net print \\\\server 45 /delete	Deletes print job 45 on the server computer.

net start

OS: Microsoft Common

Function	Starts a service. If used without any parameters, it shows all started services (not for Windows 9x/ME).
Syntax	9x/ME: net start [options...] NT, 2k, XP: net start { *name* }

9x/ME:	**The following six options can't be combined:**
BASIC	Starts the basic redirector.
NWREDIR	Starts the Microsoft Novell-compatible redirector.
WORKSTATION	Starts the default redirector.
NETBIND	Binds protocols and network adapter drivers.
NETBEUI	Starts the NetBIOS interface.
NWLINK	Starts the IPX/SPX-compatible protocol.
/LIST	Shows all running services.
/YES	Doesn't prompt for information.
/VERBOSE	Verbose mode. Shows more information.
NT, 2k, XP:	
name	Specifies the name of the service to start.

File Name:	`net.exe`	**Directory:**	\windows, **NT4, 2000:** \winnt\system32, **XP:** \windows\system32	**Type:**	External

net start alerter	Starts the alerter service (not for Windows 9x/ME).
net start "computer browser"	Starts the computer browser service (not for Windows 9x/ME).

net stop

OS: Microsoft Common

Function	Stops a Windows network service.
Syntax	9x/ME: net stop [options...] NT, 2k, XP: net stop *service*

9x/ME:	**The following six options can't be combined:**
BASIC	Stops the basic redirector.
NWREDIR	Stops the Microsoft Novell-compatible redirector.
WORKSTATION	Stops the default redirector.
NETBEUI	Stops the NetBIOS interface.
NWLINK	Stops the IPX/SPX-compatible protocol.
/YES	Doesn't prompt for confirmation.
NT, 2k, XP:	
service	Specifies the service to stop.

File Name:	`net.exe`	**Directory:**	\windows, **NT4, 2000:** \winnt\system32, **XP:** \windows\system32	**Type:**	External

net stop alerter	Stops the alerter service (not for Windows 9x/ME).
net stop "computer browser"	Stops the computer browser service (not for Windows 9x/ME).

net time

OS: Microsoft Common

Function	Synchronizes the time with another computer or domain.
Syntax	net time [*host*] [options...]

9x/ME:	**The following option can't be combined with the `computer` parameter:**
/WORKGROUP:*name*	Specifies that the computer is located in the specified workgroup.
/SET	Synchronizes the clock with the specified workgroup or computer.
/YES	Doesn't prompt for confirmation or other information.
host	Specifies the computer to synchronize with. Can't be used with the /workgroup option.
NT, 2k, XP:	
/set	Synchronizes the clock with the specified domain or computer.
/domain[:*name*]	Specifies the domain to synchronize or check.
/rtsdomain[:*name*]	Specifies the domain of a reliable time server to synchronize with.

continued

/querysntp /setsntp[:*ntpserverlist*] *host*	**The following two options can't be combined with the three above:** Shows the name of the NTP server configured for the local or specified computer. Specifies NTP time servers to use with the local computer. Specifies the computer to synchronize with. Can't be used with the /domain option.				
File Name:	`net.exe`	**Directory:**	\windows, **NT4, 2000:** \winnt\system32, **XP:** \windows\system32	**Type:**	External
net time /domain:CORP /set	Synchronizes the time with the CORP domain (not for Windows 9x/ME).				
net time \\server	Shows the current time of the server computer.				

net use

OS: Microsoft Common

Function	Connects and disconnects network shared resources such as drives or printers to your local computer.
Syntax	net use *{ device: }* *server**sharename* [options...] net use *{ device: } { password }* [/home] net use *device:* /delete

device:	The drive letter or port to map the resource to. Use * for next drive letter.				
*server**sharename*	Specifies the server and the shared resource name or name of the volume. (Use quotes around "server name" if the server name has blanks.)				
password	Specifies the password to access the shared resources.				
/user:*{ domain\ }user*	Specifies the username to connect as, and domain if the account isn't local.				
/user:*{ user@domain\ }user*	Specifies the username to connect as, and domain if the account isn't local.				
/home	Specifies to use the user's home directory to connect to.				
/delete	Disconnects and removes persistent connections.				
/persistent:*yes*	Saves all connections and restores them at next logon.				
/persistent:*no*	Doesn't save connections, but restores the existing connections at next logon.				
File Name:	`net.exe`	**Directory:**	\windows, **NT4, 2000:** \winnt\system32, **XP:** \windows\system32	**Type:**	External
net use lpt3:/delete	Disconnects from the LPT3: printer queue.				
net use /persistent:yes	Restores the current connections at each logon.				

net view

OS: Microsoft Common

Function	Lists domains, computers, or resources being shared by the specified computer.
Syntax	net view [*host*] [option...] net view /network:nw [*host*]

host	Specifies the computer for which to show shared resources.				
9x/ME:					
/WORKGROUP:*name*	Shows computers with shared resources in the specified workgroup.				
/YES	Doesn't prompt for confirmations.				
NT, 9x/ME, XP:					
/network:nw	Shows all servers on a NetWare network or resources on a specified computer.				
/domain[:*name*]	**The following option can't be combined with the `host` operand:** Shows all available computers in a specified domain or shows all available domains.				
File Name:	`net.exe`	**Directory:**	\windows, **NT4, 2000:** \winnt\system32, **XP:** \windows\system32	**Type:**	External
net view /domain	Shows all available domains (not for Windows 9x/ME).				
net view /domain:world	Shows all available computers in the world domain (not for Windows 9x/ME).				
net view \\server	Shows all shared resources of the server computer.				

netstat

OS: Microsoft Common

Function	Shows protocol statistics and current TCP/IP network connections.
Syntax	netstat [options...] *{ interval }*

-a	Shows all connections and listening ports.
-e	Shows Ethernet statistics.
-n	Shows addresses and port numbers in numerical form.
-p *protocol*	Shows connections for the specified protocol. Valid values are TCP, UDP, or IP.
-r	Shows the routing table.
-s	Shows information per protocol.
interval	Shows the selected statistic with the specified interval in seconds. (Use Ctrl+C to abort.)

File Name:	`netstat.exe`	**Directory:**	\windows, **NT4, 2000:** \winnt\system32, **XP:** \windows\system32	**Type:**	External

netstat -a	Shows all connections.
netstat -r 2	Shows the routing table every 2 seconds.

nlsfunc

OS: Microsoft Common

Function	Loads country-specific information for national language support. Used for compatibility with MS-DOS.
Syntax	nlsfunc *{ file }*

file	Specifies the location and name of the file containing country-specific information.

File Name:	`nlsfunc.exe`	**Directory:**	\windows\command, **NT4, 2000:** \winnt\system32, **XP:** \windows\system32	**Type:**	External

nlsfunc cp_850.nls	Loads the information from cp_850.nls.

Notepad

OS: Microsoft Common

Function	Creates or edits simple text files.
Syntax	notepad *{ file }*

file	Specifies the name and path of the file to open.

File Name:	`notepad.exe`	**Directory:**	\windows **NT4, 2000:** \winnt\	**Type:**	External

ODBC Data Source Administrator

OS: Microsoft Common

Function	Adds, deletes, or sets up ODBC data sources.
Syntax	odbcad32

File Name:	`odbcad32.exe`	**Directory:**	\windows\system, **NT4, 2000:** \winnt\system32, **XP:** \windows\system32	**Type:**	External

path

OS: Microsoft Common

Function	Creates a list of directories that is used to search for executable files. If no path is given, it shows the loaded paths.
Syntax	PATH *{ path }*

path	Specifies a semicolon (;) separated list of full path directories. (A semicolon (;) alone removes the list.)
%path%	A variable that represents the current path list.

path c:\dos;c\windows;c:\data	Includes the specified directories in the search path.
path %path%;c:\mydir	Appends c:\mydir to the current path list.

pause

OS: Microsoft Common

Function	Pauses the processing of a batch file. It shows `press any key to continue`, and waits.
Syntax	pause

ping

ping	OS: Microsoft Common
Function	Verifies connection to remote host or hosts. Only available with TCP/IP protocol installed.
Syntax	ping [options...] *address*

-t	Pings the specified computer until interrupted by Ctrl+C.
-a	Determines the hostname from the specified address.
-n *count*	Specifies the number of ECHO requests to send (default is 4).
-l *size*	Specifies the size of ECHO data (default is 32 bytes).
-f	Packets aren't fragmented by gateways on the route.
-i *ttl*	Specifies the time to live.
-v *tos*	Specifies the type of service.
-r *count*	Shows the route for count hops. Count can be between 1-9.
-s *count*	Sets timestamp for the number of hops.
-w *timeout*	Sets the timeout in milliseconds.
	The following two options can't be combined:
-j *host-list*	Specifies the use of loose route along host list. Can't be used together with -k.
-k *host-list*	Specifies the use of strict route along host list. Can't be used together with -j.
address	Specifies IP address or DNS name to ping.

File Name:	`ping.exe`	**Directory:**	\windows, **NT4, 2000:** \winnt\system32, **XP:** \windows\system32	**Type:**	External

ping -n 2 127.0.0.1	Pings 127.0.0.1 2 times.
ping -n 3 -l 4096 127.0.0.1	Pings 127.0.0.1 3 times with a data size of 4096 bytes.

Program Manager

Program Manager	OS: Microsoft Common
Function	Starts the classic Windows shell Program Manager from Windows 3.1.
Syntax	progman

File Name:	`progman.exe`	**Directory:**	\windows, **NT4, 2000:** \winnt\system32, **XP:** \windows\system32	**Type:**	External

Program Manager Group Converter

Program Manager Group Converter	OS: Microsoft Common
Function	Converts program groups from the old Program Manager last seen in Windows 3.11 and Windows NT 3.51.
Syntax	grpconv *file*

file	Specifies the filename of the group to be converted.

File Name:	`grpconv.exe`	**Directory:**	\windows, **NT4, 2000:** \winnt\system32, **XP:** \windows\system32	**Type:**	External

prompt

prompt	OS: Microsoft Common
Function	Changes the appearance of the command prompt.
Syntax	prompt *{ text }*

text	Specifies any text to be included in the prompt.
	The following text combinations can be used in or instead of the text string:
$Q	Uses an equal (=) sign.
$$	Uses a dollar ($) sign.
$T	Uses the current time.
$D	Uses the current date.
$P	Uses the current drive and path.
$V	Uses the Windows version.
$N	Uses the current drive.
$G	Uses a greater than (>) sign.
$L	Shows a less than (<) sign.
$B	Uses a pipe (|) sign.
$_	Adds a new line to the command prompt.
$E	Adds ASCII escape code.
$H	Deletes a character that has been written to the prompt.

continued

NT, 2k, XP:	
$A	Uses an ampersand (&).
$C	Uses left parenthesis.
$F	Uses right parenthesis.
$S	Uses a space.

prompt PG	Makes the prompt include the current path and a greater than (>) sign.

rd, rmdir

OS: Microsoft Common

Function	Removes an empty directory. rmdir has the same function.
Syntax	9x/ME: rd *directory* NT, 2k, XP: rd [options..] *path*

directory	Specifies the location and name of the directory to remove.
NT, 2k, XP:	
/s	Removes all directories and files in the specified directory.
/q	Doesn't ask for permission to remove the directory tree with /s.

rd c:\files\mydir	Removes the directory named mydir located in the c:\files directory.
rd mydir	Removes the specified directory from the current directory.

Registry Editor

OS: Microsoft Common

Function	A utility for modifying system settings in the Windows registry.
Syntax	regedit

File Name:	`regedit.exe`	**Directory:**	\windows **NT4, 2000:** \winnt\	**Type:**	External
Warning:	Changing the wrong settings in the registry can render the computer useless.				

regsvr32

OS: Microsoft Common

Function	Registers or unregisters .DLL files as command components in the registry.
Syntax	regsvr32 [options...] *file*

/u	Unregisters the specified .DLL file.
/s	Doesn't show any messages.
/n	Doesn't call DLLRegisterServer. This option can only be used together with /i.
/i:*cmd*	Calls DLLInstall and passes the specified command line to it.
/?	Shows help information.
file	Specifies the name of the .DLL file to register or unregister.

File Name:	`regsvr32.exe`	**Directory:**	\windows\system, **NT4, 2000:** \winnt\system32, **XP:** \windows\system32	**Type:**	External

regsvr32 driver.dll	Registers the specified .DLL file in the registry.
regsvr32 /u driver.dll	Unregisters the specified .DLL file from the registry.

rem

OS: Microsoft Common

Function	Makes comment in a batch file or in config.sys.
Syntax	rem { *comment* }

comment	Specifies the comment.

rem This is a comment	Specifies the text to use as a comment.

ren, rename

OS: Microsoft Common

Function	Renames a file.
Syntax	ren *oldname newname*

oldname	Specifies the name and location of the file to rename.
newname	Specifies the new name of the file. (The new file has to be on the same directory.)

rename *.log *.txt	Changes the extension of .log file to .txt.
ren myfile.txt yourfile.txt	Changes the name from myfile.txt to yourfile.txt.

route

OS: Microsoft Common

Function	Edits the network routing table. If used without parameters, help information is shown.
Syntax	route [option] *{ ACTION } { host }* [MASK *netmask*] *{ gateway }* [METRIC *NR*] [IF *interfaceNR*]

-f	Clears routing tables from all gateway entries. Overrules other options.
ACTION	**The following actions can be used:**
ADD	Adds a route.
DELETE	Deletes a route.
CHANGE	Changes a route.
PRINT	Shows the routing table.
host	Specifies the computer to send one of the four commands above.
MASK *netmask*	Specifies the subnetmask (default is 255.255.255.255).
gateway	Specifies a gateway.
METRIC *NR*	Assigns a number from 1 to 9999 to calculate the most cost-effective route.
IF *interfaceNR*	Specifies the interface number for the route. If not given, it tries to find the best.
NT, 2k, XP:	
-p	Used with the ADD action, it makes the route persistent on both systems.

File Name:	`route.exe`	**Directory:**	\windows, **NT4, 2000:** \winnt\system32, **XP:** \windows\system32	**Type:**	External

route -f	Clears the routing table.
route print	Shows the routing table.

set

OS: Microsoft Common

Function	Sets, shows, or removes environment variables.
Syntax	9x/ME, NT, 2k, XP: set *{ variable=[string] }* NT, 2k, XP: set /A *{ variable=[expression] }*

variable	Specifies the variable to set or modify.
string	Specifies the string to associate with the specified variable.
NT, 2k, XP:	**The following options are only available in cmd.exe, not in command.com:**
/A	Evaluates the expression given.
expression	Specifies an expression to evaluate. The following operands can be used.
( )	Is used for grouping.
* / %	Is used for arithmetic operations.
+ -	Is used for arithmetic operations.
<< >>	Is used to logical shift.
&	Is used for bitwise and.
^	Is used for bitwise exclusive or.
|	Is used for bitwise or.
= += /= %= += -=	Is used for assignment.
&= ^= <<= >>=	Is used for assignment.
,	Separates expression.
Example:	
set /a x+=10	Adds 10 to the variable x.
set /a a=b+c	Gives a the value of b + c.

set	Shows all environment variables.
set temp=c:\dos	Sets the temp variable to c:\dos.
set temp=	Removes the variable with the name temp.

setver

OS: Microsoft Common

Function	Reports a different MS-DOS version to a program than the one currently running.
Syntax	setver *{ drive:directory } { command version }* [options...]

/d	Removes an entry from the version table.
/quiet	Hides messages when deleting entries from the version table.
/?	Shows help information.
drive:directory	Specifies the location of the setver.exe file.

continued

command *version*		Specifies the command name to report a different MS-DOS version to. Specifies which MS-DOS version to report.			
File Name:	`setver.exe`	**Directory:**	\windows, **NT4, 2000:** \winnt\system32, **XP:** \windows\system32	**Type:**	External
setver c:\utility\blast.com 5.00		Adds the command blast.com dependent on DOS 5.00 to setver.			
setver c:\utility\blast.com /delete		Erases the command blast.com from the setver table.			

sort

OS: Microsoft Common

Function	Sorts input data and writes the result to a file, a screen, or a device
Syntax	sort [options...] < *file1* [> *file2*] *command* | sort [options...] [> *file2*]

/R */+NR* *file1* *file2* *command*		Reverses the sort order; Z to A, 9 to 0. Sorts the file according to the first character in the specified column. Specifies the file, including the full path, that contains the contents to sort. Specifies the file, including the full path, to output the sorted contents to. Specifies the command as to which output should be sorted.			
File Name:	`sort.exe`	**Directory:**	\windows\command, **NT4, 2000:** \winnt\system32, **XP:** \windows\system32	**Type:**	External
sort < myfile.txt > sort.txt		Sorts the file myfile.txt and saves the output in the file sort.txt.			
type autoexec.bat | sort /R		Sorts the output from the type command in reverse order.			

subst

OS: Microsoft Common

Function	Creates a virtual drive mapping to a directory. If no parameters are given, it shows all active mappings.
Syntax	subst *{ drive } { path }* [/d]

/d *drive* *path*		Deletes the specified virtual drive mapping. Specifies the drive letter to which a virtual path is created. Specifies the directory path.			
File Name:	`subst.exe`	**Directory:**	\windows\command, **NT4, 2000:** \winnt\system32, **XP:** \windows\system32	**Type:**	External
subset z: c:\temp		Creates a virtual drive mapping to c:\temp named z:			
subset z: /d		Deletes the virtual drive mapping z:			

System Configuration Editor

OS: Microsoft Common

Function	Starts the System Configuration Editor that allows editing of autoexec.bat, config.sys, system.ini, and win.ini
Syntax	sysedit

File Name:	`sysedit.exe`	**Directory:**	\windows\system, **NT4, 2000:** \winnt\system32, **XP:** \windows\system32	**Type:**	External

telnet

OS: Microsoft Common

Function	Starts the telnet client used to connect to a remote computer and interact with that computer via a terminal window.
Syntax	9x/ME, NT, 2k: telnet *{ host [:portNR] }* XP: telnet [options...] *{ host [:portNR] }*

host *:portNR* **XP** -a -e *char* -f *file* -l *user* -t *term* /? **2k, XP:** open *{ host }* close	Specifies the hostname or IP address of the DNS name to connect to. Specifies the port number or service name. Tries to login automatically using the current username. Specifies the escape character to use to enter the telnet client prompt. Specifies a filename for client-side logging. Specifies a user to use when logging in. Specifies the terminal type to use. Supported types are VT100, VT52, ANSI, VTNT. Shows help information. **The following commands are used inside the telnet program:** Opens a new telnet connection. The host can be the hostname or IP address. Closes your current telnet session.

continued

display	Shows your current telnet configuration.
status	Shows your current connection status.
set	Sets parameters for your telnet session. See the list of available parameters below.
ntlm	Enables NTLM authentication.
local_echo	Enables ECHO on your local computer.
term *type*	Sets the terminal type. Valid choices for type are ANSI, VT100, VT52, VTNT.
crlf	Sends control and line feed characters to the remote server.
	The next six set parameters are only available in Windows XP:
bsasdel	Sends the backspace character as a delete character.
delasbs	Sends the delete character as a backspace character.
escape *char*	Specifies a character to use as an escape character.
logfile *file*	Creates a log file with the name specified by file.
logging	Enables logging.
mode *value*	Specifies the mode to be `console` or `stream`.
unset	Unsets parameters previously set by the set option.
send	**Windows XP only:** Sends strings to the telnet server.
?	Shows help information.
quit	Quits the telnet program.

File Name:	`telnet.exe`	**Directory:**	\windows, **NT4, 2000:** \winnt\system32, **XP:** \windows\system32	**Type:**	External

telnet 192.168.1.1	Starts telnet and tries to connect to 192.168.1.1.
telnet router 56	Starts telnet and tries to connect to router on port 56.

time

OS: Microsoft Common

Function	Shows the current time or sets the computers internal clock.
Syntax	time { *HR*[:*MM*[:*SS*[.*HH* }]]option]

A	Specifies A.M.
P	Specifies P.M.
HR[:*MM*[:*SS*[.*HH*]]]	Specifies the time. The format is: hours:minutes:seconds:hundredths.
NT, 2k, XP:	
/t	Doesn't ask for a new time.

time 12:30:00.00	Sets the time to 12:30:00.00.
time 1:15:00P	Sets the time to 15 minutes past one in the afternoon.

tracert

OS: Microsoft Common

Function	Determines the route to the specified target.
Syntax	tracert [options...] *host*

-d	Specifies addresses to not resolve to computer names.
-h *hops*	Specifies the maximum number of hops when tracing the route.
-j *list*	Specifies a list of computers to use loose source route along.
-w *timeout*	Sets the timeout in milliseconds for each reply.
host	Specifies the name of the computer to trace.

File Name:	`tracert.exe`	**Directory:**	\windows, **NT4, 2000:** \winnt\system32, **XP:** \windows\system32	**Type:**	External

tracert 10.0.20.4	Traces 10.0.20.4.
tracert -h 2 10.0.20.4	Traces 10.0.20.4 but only goes through two routers.
tracert -w 30 10.0.20.4	Traces 10.0.20.4 but only waits 30 milliseconds for each reply.

type

OS: Microsoft Common

Function	Shows the specified text file on the screen.
Syntax	type *file*

file	Specifies the file to show.

type c:\windows\support.txt	Shows the specified file.

ver

OS: Microsoft Common

Function	Shows the version for windows.
Syntax	ver

vol

OS: Microsoft Common

Function	Shows the volume name and serial number of the drive specified.
Syntax	vol *drive:*
drive:	Specifies the drive to show information about.
vol c:	Shows information about drive c:

Windows Help

OS: Microsoft Common

Function	Shows and searches Windows Help files.
Syntax	winhelp *{ helpfile }*
helpfile	Specifies the help file to open.

File Name:	**Directory:**	**Type:**
`winhelp.exe`, `winhlp32.exe`	\windows **NT4, 2000:** \winnt\	External

winhelp help.hlp	Starts Windows Help and opens the help file help.hlp.

Windows Update

OS: Microsoft Common

Function	Is used to update the operating system with the newest patches over the Internet.
Syntax	wupdmgr

File Name:	**Directory:**	**Type:**
`wupdmgr.exe`	**9x, XP:** \windows\system32 **NT4, 2000:** \winnt\system32	External

WordPad

OS: Microsoft Common

Function	An enhanced text editor that supports complex formatting.
Syntax	write OR wordpad

File Name:	**Directory:**	**Type:**
`write.exe`, `wordpad.exe`	\windows, **NT4, 2000:** \winnt\system32, **XP:** \windows\system32	External

xcopy

OS: Microsoft Common

Function	Copies files, directories, and subdirectories, and has many more features over the normal copy program.
Syntax	xcopy *source* *{ destination }* [options...]

/w	Waits for the user to press a key before starting to copy.
/p	Prompts for confirmation before copying each file.
/c	Continues to copy even if errors occur.
/v	Specifies that each file should be verified.
/q	Suppresses any messages.
/f	Shows source and target filenames while copying.
/l	Lists files that would be copied. No files are copied.
/d[:*date*]	Copies files newer than date; if no date is specified, only newer files are copied.
/u	Copies only files that already exist in the destination directory.
/i	Assumes the specified target to be a directory and if it doesn't exist, creates it.
/s	Copies all directories and subdirectories except if they are empty.
/e	Copies all directories and subdirectories even if they are empty.
/t	Copies only the directory structure, not the files. Requires the /e option.
/k	Keeps the read-only attribute if it is present on the source (default it is removed).
/r	Overwrites files with the read-only attribute set.
/h	Copies files with the hidden or system attribute (default they are ignored).
/n	Copies files and directories using NTFS short names.

continued

/exclude:*name* /z /a /m *source* *destination*		Doesn't copy files listed in the specified file. Specifies the use of restartable mode when copying over a network. **The following options can't be combined:** Copies only files with the archive file attribute. Copies only files with the archive attribute and then removes them from the source. Specifies the source path or file. Specifies the target path or file. If none is given, the current path is used.			
File Name:	`xcopy.exe`	**Directory:**	\windows\command, **NT4, 2000:** \winnt\system32, **XP:** \windows\system32	**Type:**	External

xcopy c:\temp*.* d:\temp /s	Copies all files and subdirectories from c:\temp to d:\temp.
xcopy c:\temp*.* d:\temp /d	Copies all files from c:\temp to d:\temp that are newer.

Chapter 6

Other Windows Commands

The commands in this section cover all of the remaining commands from Windows that are not listed in the Universal Windows Commands section (Chapter 5).

For cross-references outside the Windows environment, please see Chapter 1, the "Quick Command Index."

The versions of Windows in this section are:

- Windows 95
- Windows 98
- Windows ME
- Windows NT4 Workstation
- Windows NT4 Server
- Windows NT4 Terminal Server
- Windows 2000 Professional
- Windows 2000 Server
- Windows 2000 Advanced Server
- Windows XP

Accessibility Wizard		OS:	Windows ME, 2000, XP		
Function	Configures Windows to provide help for users who have visual, hearing, or physical disabilities.				
Syntax	Accwiz				
File Name:	accwiz.exe	Directory:	**ME:** \windows\system, **2000:** \winnt\system32, **XP:** \windows\system32	Type:	External

Aciniupd		OS:	Windows 2000 Server, NT4 Terminal Server		
Function	Modifies, creates or updates program `.ini` files.				
Syntax	aciniupd options... *ini-file section key newvalue*				
/e		Updates the value for the key in the section specified.			
/k		Updates the key name with the new key name in the specified section.			
/u		Alters ini-files in the user home directories instead of the system directory.			
/v		Verbose mode. Shows more information.			
ini-file		Specifies the ini-file to update or create.			
section		Specifies the section in the ini-file to update.			
key		Specifies the key to update.			
newvalue		Specifies a new value for the key or a new name for the key.			
File Name:	aciniupd.exe	Directory:	\winnt\Application Compatibility Scripts	Type:	External
aciniupg /e ucg.ini ucgbook ver 1			Updates or adds a key named ver in section ucgbook.		

Active Directory Domains and Trusts		OS:	Windows 2000 Server		
Function	Manages domain modes, user principal name suffixes, and domain trusts.				
Syntax	domain.msc				
File Name:	domain.msc	Directory:	\winnt\system32	Type:	External

Active Directory Install Wizard		OS:	Windows 2000 Server		
Function	Installs or removes Active Directory from a Windows 2000 server.				
Syntax	dcpromo				
File Name:	dcpromo.exe	Directory:	\winnt\system32	Type:	External

Active Directory Users and Computers		OS:	Windows 2000 Server		
Function	Manages the information in published resources in your organization's directory, security and distribution groups, and user and computer accounts.				
Syntax	dsa.msc				
File Name:	dsa.msc	Directory:	\winnt\system32	Type:	External

AD Sites and Services		OS:	Windows 2000 Server		
Function	Manages the configuration of services, sites, and the replication of directory data.				
Syntax	dssite.msc				
File Name:	dssite.msc	Directory:	\winnt\system32	Type:	External

Add User Account Wizard		OS:	Windows NT4 Server		
Function	Creates a User Account in a domain.				
Syntax	addusrw				
File Name:	addusrw.exe	Directory:	\winnt\system32, **TS:** \wtsrv\system32	Type:	External

Address Book		OS:	Windows 2000, XP		
Function	Starts the Address Book. Manages such information as addresses and phone numbers.				
Syntax	wab *{ file }*				
file		Specifies an alternative address book to use. File is created if it doesn't exist.			
File Name:	wab.exe	Directory:	\Program Files\Outlook Express	Type:	External
wab ucg.wab			Opens the address book with the specified address book.		

Address Book Import Tool

OS: Windows 9x/ME, 2000, XP

Function	Merges address books from other e-mail packages into the Windows address book.
Syntax	wabmig [e]

e	Exports from the address book instead of importing into it.

File Name: `wabmig.exe` **Directory:** \Program Files\Outlook Express **Type:** External

Administrating Wizards

OS: Windows 2000 Server, NT4 Server

Function	Simplifies such administration tasks as adding printers, managing users, and managing groups.
Syntax	wizmgr

File Name: `wizmgr.exe` **Directory:** \winnt\system32, **NT4 TS:** \wtsrv\system32 **Type:** External

append

OS: Windows XP

Function	Allows applications to open files in different directories as if they are in the current directory.
Syntax	append *{ paths... }* [options...]

paths...	Specifies the drive and directory to append. Separate multiple entries with semicolon.
/X:ON	Searches in directories that have been appended. `:OFF` will not search.
/PATH:ON	Searches appended directories for a file. `:OFF` will not search.
/E	Copies the appended directory list in the file `APPEND`. (This is used only once after system startup.)
;	Cancels the appended directory list.

File Name: `append.exe` **Directory:** \windows\system32 **Type:** External

append ;	Clears the append list.
append c:\mydir;d:\yourdir	Adds the specified directories to the append list.

at

OS: Windows NT4, 2000, XP

Function	Schedules programs and commands to run on the specified computer at a specified time and date.
Syntax	at [*host*] *{ id } { time }* [options...] ["*command*"]

/delete	Removes a command from the schedule, if no id is given, all commands are removed.
/yes	Answers yes to all questions.
/interactive	Allows the job to interact with the desktop of the current user.
/every:*{ date }*	Runs the command on the specified day of the week or the month.
/next:*{ date }*	Runs the command the next specified day, current day is used if not given. (The date is specified with number (1–31) or days [M,T,W,Th,F,S,Su].)
host	Specifies the computer to run the command on. If not given, it runs on the local.
id	Specifies the identification number for a scheduled command.
time	Specifies time when the command should run.
"*command*"	Specifies the command or batch file to run.

File Name: `at.exe` **Directory:** **NT4, 2000:**\winnt\system32, **XP:** \windows\system32 **Type:** External

at 21:30 /every:M,W,F "copy c:\doc*.* c:\backup"	Runs the command the specified days every month.
at 21:30 /next: "copy c:\doc*.* c:\backup"	Runs the command the next month the same date as the current.

ATM Administrator

OS: Windows ME, 2000, XP

Function	Shows statistics for outgoing and incoming calls on an ATM (Asynchronous Transfer Mode) adapter.
Syntax	atmadm [options...]

-c	Shows call information for all connections to the ATM adapter.
-a	Shows, for each adapter installed, the registered ATM network service access point.
-s	Shows statistics on active ATM connections.

File Name: `atmadm.exe` **Directory:** **ME:** \windows,**2000:** \winnt\system32, **XP:** \windows\system32 **Type:** External

atmadam -c	Checks the information of the current ATM connections.

Authorized Application

OS:	Windows NT4 Terminal Server
Function	Lists authorized applications and enables or disables security for selected application.
Syntax	appsec
File Name:	`appsec.exe`
Directory:	\wtsrv\system32
Type:	External

autoexec.bat

OS:	Windows NT4
Function	Specifies the startup file that runs each time your computer is started and executes any commands specified from the top down.
Syntax	autoexec.bat
File Name:	`autoexec.bat`
Directory:	\
Type:	Script

Automatic Skip Driver

OS:	Windows 98/ME
Function	Shows critical errors that caused Windows to stop responding and shows information on device failures.
Syntax	asd
File Name:	`asd.exe`
Directory:	\windows
Type:	Internal

backup

OS:	Windows NT4
Function	Backs up files to the specified disk.
Syntax	backup *source destination* [options...]

/S	Includes all subdirectories in the backup.
/M	Backs up only new or changed files, it removes the archive attribute.
/A	Adds files to a backup disk without deleting the existing ones.
/F[:*size*]	Formats the disk in the specified size. If no size given, the default is used.
/D:*date*	Specifies that only files changed on or after the specified date will be backed up.
/T:*time*	Specifies that only files changed on or after the specified time will be backed up.
/L[:*logfile*]	Creates a log file at the specified location.
/?	Shows help information.
source	Specifies the source path and/or files.
destination	Specifies the target drive.

File Name:	`backup.exe`
Directory:	\winnt\system32
Type:	External

backup c:\dos*.* a: /M	Only new or changed files are backed up.
backup c:\dos*.* a: /L:C:\BACKUP.LOG	Backs up the files and creates a log file in the c:\ root.

Books Online

OS:	Windows NT4, 2000
Function	Starts the Books Online utility in Windows NT, which shows Windows NT manuals from the last used location.
Syntax	ntbooks [options...]

/s	Accesses NT Server manuals from an NT Workstation.
/w	Accesses NT Workstation manuals from an NT Server.
/n:*path*	Specifies a path to search for manuals.

File Name:	`ntbooks.exe`
Directory:	**NT4, 2000:** \winnt\system32, **NT4 TS:** \wtsrv\system32
Type:	External

ntbooks /w	Accesses manuals for Windows NT Server while used from a Workstation.

bootcfg

OS:	Windows XP
Function	Shows, changes, and configures the BOOT.INI file settings.
Syntax	bootcfg *ACTION*

	The following four options are common to all actions:
/s *host*	Specifies the remote computer to connect to.
/u *{ domain\ }user*	Specifies the user to run the command with. Default is the current user.
/p *{ password }*	Specifies the password for the specified user. Prompts for input if skipped.
/?	Shows help information.
ACTION	
/addsw options...	Adds operating system load options for the specified OS entry.

continued

	The following option is required:
/id *lineNR*	Specifies the number of the OS entry to which options should be added.
/mm *maxram*	Adds the /maxmem option and sets most RAM the OS can use.
/bv	Adds the /basevideo option, directing the OS to use standard VGA mode.
/so	Adds the /sos option, directing the OS to show the namse of all drivers when loading.
/ng	Adds the /noguiboot option. This disables the progress bar showed at startup.
/copy options...	Makes another OS instance copy.
	The following option is required:
/id *lineNR*	Specifies the number of the OS entry to copy.
/d *string*	Describes the new OS entry.
/dbq1394 options...	Configures 1394 port debugging for the specified OS entry.
	The following option is required:
/id *lineNR*	Specifies the number of the OS entry.
	The following three options can't be combined:
ON	Adds the /dbg1394 option, which enables remote debugging support.
OFF	Removes the /dbg1394 option, which disables remote debugging support.
EDIT	Allows changes to baud rate and port settings.
/ch *channel*	Specifies the channel to use for debugging.
/debug options...	
	The following option is required:
/id *lineNR*	Specifies the number of the OS entry.
	The following three options can't be combined but one is required:
ON	Adds the /debug option, which enables remote debugging support.
OFF	Removes the /debug option, which disables remote debugging support.
EDIT	Allows changes to baud rate and port settings.
/port *port*	Specifies the COM port to use for debugging. Valid are COM1 - COM4.
/baud *rate*	Specifies the baud rate to use. Valid are 9600, 19200, 38400, 57600, 115200.
/default /id *lineNR*	Sets the specified OS entry to default.
/delete /id *lineNR*	Deletes the specified OD entry.
/ems options...	Adds or changes settings for redirection of the EMS console.
	The following option is required:
/id *lineNR*	Specifies the number of the OS entry.
	The following three options can't be combined but one is required:
ON	Enables remote output for the specified OS entry.
OFF	Disables remote output for the specified OS entry.
EDIT	Allows changes to port settings.
/port *port*	Specifies the COM port to use for redirection. Valid are COM1 – COM4.
/baud *rate*	Specifies the baud rate to use. Valid are 9600, 19200, 38400, 57600, 115200.
/query [options...]	Shows the [boot loader] and [operating system] sections from the boot.ini file.
/raw "*string*" options...	Adds a string of options to the specified OS entry.
	The following option is required:
/id *lineNR*	Specifies the number of the OS entry where the options should be added.
string	Specifies a string containing load option to add to the specified OS entry. (Replaces all existing options.)
/rmsw options...	Removes operating system load options for the specified OS entry.
	The following option is required:
/id *lineNR*	Specifies the number of the OS entry from which to remove the options.
/mm	Removes the /maxmem option.
/bv	Removes the /basevideo option.
/so	Removes the /sos option.
/ng	Removes the /noguiboot option.
/time *timeout*	Sets the OS timeout value to the specified number of seconds.

File Name:	`bootcfg.exe`	**Directory:**	\windows\system32	**Type:**	External
bootcfg /addsw /ng /id 1			Adds the /noguiboot option to the specified OS entry.		
bootcfg /copy /d "New Entry" /id 2			Makes a copy of the specified OS entry.		

bootdisk

OS: Windows 98

Function	Creates a startup floppy for Windows 98. Requires a directory named EBD before it will run.
Syntax	bootdisk
File Name:	`bootdisk.bat`
Directory:	\windows\command
Type:	External

break

OS: Windows Common

Function	Is used to enable or disable extended Ctrl+C checking. The second syntax is for use in the CONFIG.SYS file.
Syntax	break [option] break=[option]

ON	Is used to enable extended <Ctrl+C> checking.
OFF	Is used to disable extended <Ctrl+C> checking. (If none of the above are specified, break will show current settings.)

break off	Disables the usage of Ctrl+C

cabbit

OS: Windows ME

Function	Compresses files and creates CAB files.
Syntax	cabbit [files...] [options...]

/f: *filename*	Specifies the filename for the CAB file that you want to create.
/a: *suffix*.CAB	Adds the specified `suffix`.CAB to the specified filename.
/w *waittime*	Specifies the time wait for InitChglogAPI in milliseconds. (Requires /f or /a option.)
File Name:	`cabbit.exe`
Directory:	\windows\system\restore
Type:	External
Note:	Creates the CAB file: <COMPUTERNAME>_ddmmyyHHMMSS.CAB if no options are specified.

cabbit /f: ucg.cab	Creates a CAB file named ucg.cab.

cacls

OS: Windows NT4, 2000, XP

Function	Manages access control lists (ACLs) of specified files.
Syntax	cacls *files...* [options...]

/t	Modifies the specified files in the current directory and all subdirectories.
/e	Edits the ACL instead of replacing it.
/c	Ignores errors.
/g *user.perm*	Grants the specified user access rights, perm can be the following:
r	Read.
w	Write. (This option isn't available in Windows NT 4.0.)
c	Change.
f	Full control.
/r *users...*	Revokes the specified user access rights.
/p *user.perm*	Replaces the specified user access rights; permission can be the following:
n	None.
r	Read.
w	Write. (This option isn't available in Windows NT 4.)
c	Change.
f	Full control.
/d *users...*	Denies the specified user(s) access.
files...	Specifies the file or files to show or modify the ACL for.
File Name:	`cacls.exe`
Directory:	**NT4, 2000:** \winnt\system32, **XP:** \windows\system32
Type:	External

cacls *.* /g guest:f	Grants the user guest Full Control of all files in the current directory.
cacls *.* /p guest:r	Changes the user guest rights to read for all files in current directory.
cacls *.* /d guest	Denies the user guest all rights of all files in the current directory.

Certificates

OS: Windows 2000 Server

Function	Manages the certificates for services, computers, and users.
Syntax	certmgr.msc
File Name:	`certmgr.msc`
Directory:	\winnt\system32
Type:	External

certreq

OS: Windows 2000 Server

Function	Requests certificates from a certification authority from the command prompt.
Syntax	certreq [options...] *{ requestID [certfile [certchainfile]]}*

-attrib *string*	Retrieves a certificate that the server already has issued.
-binary	Outputs files in binary format.
-config *string*	Specifies a certification authority server string. Use – for default configuration.
-rpc	Connects with RPC instead of DCOM.
	The following option must be used first and can't be combined with -attrib:
-retrieve	Retrieves a certificate that the server issued.
-?	Shows help information.
requestID	Specifies the request identifier to use. It can be either an ID or a file.
certfile	Specifies a name for the Base64-encoded, X-509 output file.
certchainfile	Specifies a name for the Base64-encoded, PKCS #7 output file.

File Name:	`certreq.exe`	**Directory:**	\winnt\system32\dllcache	**Type:**	External

certsrv

OS: Windows 2000 Server

Function	Starts the Certificate Services as a stand-alone application instead of as a service.
Syntax	certsrv -z

-z	Starts the Certification Services in stand-alone mode.

File Name:	`certsrv.exe`	**Directory:**	\winnt\system32\dllcache	**Type:**	External

certsrv -z	Starts the Certificate Service in stand-alone mode.

certutil

OS: Windows 2000 Server

Function	Manages and troubleshoots Certificate Services (CS) for the default or specified Certification Authority (CA).
Syntax	certutil [options...] *{ ACTION }*

	The following options may be used with or without an appending action:
-?	Shows help information.
-7f *{ file }*	Checks the specified certificate file for encoding that is 0x7f long.
-decode *file1 file2*	Decodes the first file (Base64-encoded) and sends output to the second file.
-decodehex *file1 file2*	Decodes the first file (hexadecimal encoded) and sends output to the second file.
-ds *name*	Lists any (or the specified) CA-related objects to the active directory.
-dump	Dumps the active CA configuration information to the screen.
-encode *file1 file2*	Encodes the first file (Base64-encoded) and sends output to the second file.
-error *errorcode*	Specifies the error code to be used with the localized error message.
-f	Forces overwrite mode.
-getconfig	Shows the CA default configuration string.
-gmt	Shows all times in GMT format.
-idispatch	Uses the IDispatch method of operation instead of the COM method.
-setreg policy*type* [+ or -] *aspenable*	Verifies that the CA issued serial number or identity has not been revoked.
type	Specifies the registry controlled value type to be checked.
[+ or -]	Adds Netscape-compatible revocation checking or removes checking from certificates.
aspenable	Specifies the actual registry value for the specified value type.
-store *name { index } { file }*	Shows any certificates in the local or specified store name.
name	Specifies the store name to look for certificates in.
index	Specifies that the indexed certificate will be shown and nothing else.
file	Writes the indexed certificate information into the specified file.
-user	Uses the key in HKEY_CURRENT_USER or the certificate store in the register.
-v	Verbose mode. Shows more information.
-verify *file { cafile }*	Verifies the specified certification file was issued by the local or specified CA.
file	Specifies the file that contains the certificate to check.
cafile	Specifies the CA file that supposedly issued the certificate.
-verifykeys *keyname cafile*	Verifies the private/public key set by using the CA certificate stored in the CA file.
name	Specifies the key container that contains the private/public key set.
cafile	Specifies the CA certificate file that points to the CA certificate.
-verifystore *storename index*	Same as -store but it also verifies any private keys and each certificate.
name	Specifies the store name to verify.
index	Specifies the Certification Index to use.

continued

-vroot [delete]	Creates a standard set of virtual roots with file shares for the CS Web server.
delete	Deletes the standard set of virtual roots and the file shares.
	The following option may only be used with an action and must precede it.
-config *{ ca }*	Uses the specified CA to process the `certutil` command.
ACTION	**The following actions must be used with at least the `-config:` option:**
-backup *directory* [options...]	Specifies the CA database, keys, and certificates that are backed up.
directory	Specifies the backup directory that the files are stored into.
password	Specifies the PFX password file to use.
incremental	Runs the backup incrementally.
keeplog	Saves a backup logfile instead of overwriting it.
-backupDB *directory* [options...]	Specifies the CA database that is backed up.
directory	Specifies the backup directory that the files are stored into.
incremental	Runs the backup incrementally.
keeplog	Saves a backup logfile instead of overwriting it.
-backupkey *directory { password }*	Specifies the CA keys and certificates that are backed up.
directory	Specifies the backup directory that the files are stored into.
password	Specifies the PFX password file to use.
-ca.cert *file*	Retrieves the CA certificate used for signing and sends it to the specified file.
-ca.chain *file*	Retrieves the CA certificate and chain and sends it to the specified PKCS#7 file.
-ConvertMDB	Migrates the old NT4.0 CS db records to the newer Windows 2000 CS.
-CRL *file*	Publishes the Certificate Revocation List (CRL) to the specified file.
-databaselocations	Lists of any tagged db files and databases.
-deny *ID*	Denies the use of a pending certificate request matching the specified Request ID.
-dynamicfilelist	Lists of any dynamic files that need to be backed up separately.
-GetCRL *file*	Gets the CRL that was published last and sends it to the specified file.
-getreg policy*type*	Shows CA registry values.
type	Specifies the registry controlled value type that is shown.
-importcert *file { flags... }*	Imports certificates to the server database.
file	Specifies the certificate file to import.
flags...	Specifies which flags to use. All flags must be equal to zero (0).
-installcert *file*	Installs subordinate CA certificates upon request.
file	Specifies the PKCS#7 or X.509 path CA certification file.
-isvalid *NR*	Verifies that the specified Serial number for the certificate is valid.
-ping	Verifies that the server is available through the ICertRequest interface.
-pingadmin	Same as -ping, but also verifies that the user has admin access to the server.
-renewCert *file*	Initiates the request for CA certificate renewal from the specified Request file.
-restore *directory { password }*	Restores the CA database, keys, and certificates from the backup directory.
directory	Specifies the backup directory that the files are extracted from.
password	Specifies the PFX password file to use.
-restoreDB *directory*	Restores the CA database from the backup directory. The server must not be active.
directory	Specifies the backup directory that the files are extracted from.
-restorekey *object*	Restores the CA keys and certificates from the specified object.
directory	Specifies the backup directory that the files are extracted from.
file { password }	Specifies the PKCS#12 file and any password that the backup will be extracted from.
-resubmit *ID*	Resubmits any pending certificate request using the specified Request ID.
-revoke *NR*	Revokes the specified certificate by indicating its Serial Number.
-schema	Dumps any CA database schemas to the screen.
-setattributes *ID string*	Sets attributes in the attribute string specified by the Request ID.
-setextension *ID name flags... value*	Sets the extension in a certificate request specified by the ID.
ID	Specifies the certificate request that is used when using this Request ID.
name	Specifies the extension name that is set.
flags...	Specifies which flags to use. All flags must be equal to zero (0).
value	Specifies the value (string format) to set the extension to.
-shutdown	Shuts down the CA server regardless of which mode was used to start it.

continued

File Name:	certutil.exe	Directory:	\winnt\system32\dllcache	Type:	External
certutil -ds			Lists of any CA related objects to the active directory.		
certutil -?			Shows help information showing the various syntax forms and their meanings.		

change

OS: Windows NT4 Terminal Server, 2000 Server

Function	Changes system attributes, such as mapping ports and clients, enable/disable user login, and set the application mode.
Syntax	change *ACTION*

ACTION	**Specifies the action to change.**
LOGON option	Changes configuration on login from sessions.
/QUERY	Shows the current setting.
/ENABLE	Enables login from sessions.
/DISABLE	Disables login from sessions.
PORT *{ port = device }*	Shows the current port mappings, or sets the specified port with the device.
USER option	Changes the user application mode.
/EXECUTE	Sets the application mode to execute.
/INSTALL	Sets the application mode to install.
/QUERY	Shows the current setting.
2000:	
CLIENT *{ hostdrive = clientdrive }*	Shows the current client mapping, or sets a host to client mapping.
hostdrive	Specifies the source drive.
clientdrive	Specifies the target drive.

File Name:	change.exe	Directory:	**NT4 TS:** \wtsrv\system32, **2000:** \winnt\system32	Type:	External
change user /install			Prepares the server for the installation of new applications.		
change logon /disable			Disables logon to the terminal server.		

change client

OS: Windows 2000 Server

Function	Changes the client mappings for user connected to the terminal server.
Syntax	change client [options...] *{ server_device } { client_device }*

/view	Lists all client devices currently available.
/flush	Flushes client drive mappings that are in cache.
/current	Shows current device mappings for current client.
/default	Resets both the client drives and printer mappings to the default settings.
/default_drives	Resets only the client drives to default.
/default_printers	Resets only the client printers to default.
/ascending	Specifies the search order to be ascending. (Default is descending.)
/noremap	Doesn't map drive letters that currently exist on the server.
/persistent	Saves the client's current drive and printer mapping in their user profile.
/force_prt_todef	Assigns the session printer to be the client's default printer.
/delete *device*	Removes the specified client device.
server_device	Specifies the name to assign to a mapped client device.
client_device	Specifies the client device to be mapped to the server device.

File Name:	change.exe	Directory:	\winnt\system32	Type:	External
change client /view			Shows all available client devices.		
change client /default			Resets the client settings to default.		

change logon, chglogon

OS: Windows NT4 Terminal Server, 2000 Server

Function	Enables or disables logon capabilities for terminal sessions.
Syntax	chglogon option change logon option

/QUERY	Shows the status of the current login mode for terminal sessions.
/DISABLE	Alters login mode to not allow users to log in from a terminal session.
/ENABLE	Alters login mode to allow users to log in from a terminal session

File Name:	change.exe, chglogon.exe	Directory:	**NT4 TS:** \wtsrv\system32, **2000:** \winnt\system32	Type:	External
chglogon /disable			Disables logon for terminal sessions.		

change port, chgport

OS: Windows NT4 Terminal Server, 2000 Server

Function	Shows or alters the mapping for COM port for DOS application compatibility.				
Syntax	chgport [option] { *port1=port2* } change port [option] { *port1=port2* }				
/QUERY /D *port* *port1=port2*	Shows the current mapping. Removes the mapping for a port. Maps port1 to port2.				
File Name:	`chgport.exe`	**Directory:**	**NT4 TS:** \wtsrv\system32, **2000:** \winnt\system32	**Type:**	External
chgport COM2=COM1	Maps port COM2 to port COM1.				

Change User, chgusr

OS: Windows NT4 Terminal Server, 2000 Server

Function	Alternates between execution and installation mode for applications on terminal server.				
Syntax	chgusr option change user option				
/QUERY /EXECUTE /INSTALL	Shows the current mode. Places the computer in execute mode used to execute applications on terminal server. Places the computer in install mode used to install applications on terminal server.				
File Name:	`chgusr.exe`	**Directory:**	**NT4 TS:** \wtsrv\system32, **2000:** \winnt\system32\dllcache	**Type:**	External
chgusr /EXECUTE	Puts the terminal server in execute mode.				

Character Map

OS: Windows 2000, XP

Function	Shows the character table for all fonts in the system.				
Syntax	charmap				
File Name:	`charmap.exe`	**Directory:**	**2000:** \winnt\system32,**XP:** \windows\system32	**Type:**	External

Chat

OS: Windows NT4, 2000, XP

Function	Communicates with another user on the same network.				
Syntax	winchat				
File Name:	`winchat.exe`	**Directory:**	**NT4, 2000:** \winnt\system32, **XP:** \windows\system32	**Type:**	External

chkntfs

OS: Windows NT4, 2000, XP

Function	Manages automatic system checking scheduling on the specified harddisk at next boot.				
Syntax	chkntfs [option] *volumes...*				
/D /X /C *volumes...* **2000, XP:** /T[:*time*]	Restores the computer to the default setting, which means that all drives are checked. Excludes the specified drive from the boot time check. Schedules the specified drive to be checked at boot time. Specifies the drive letter, mount point, or volume name to check. Separate with a colon. Manages the countdown time for the autochk initiation.				
File Name:	`chkntfs.exe`	**Directory:**	**NT4, 2000:** \winnt\system32, **NT4 TS:** \wtsrv\system32, **XP:** \windows\system32	**Type:**	External
chkntfs /T:10 c:	Sets the countdown time for the c: drive to 10 seconds.				
chkntfs /X d:	Excludes the specified from the boot time check.				

chkroot

OS: Windows NT4 Terminal Server, 2000 Server

Function	Sets the root drive letter that is mapped to the user's home directory, which is used for mapping applications.				
Syntax	chkroot.cmd				
File Name:	`chkroot.cmd`	**Directory:**	**NT4 TS:** \wtsrv\application compatibility scripts, **2000:** \winnt\Application Compatibility Scripts	**Type:**	External

choice

OS: Windows Common

Function	Is commonly used in batch files to prompt the user to make a choice. When used without any parameters it will prompt for yes (Y) or no (N). The ERRORLEVEL is set to the offset of the pressed key.
Syntax	choice [options...] { *text* }
/C[:]*keys*	Specifies the choices the user has. (Default is YN.)

continued

/N /S /T[:]*c,nn* *c* *nn* *text*		Shows only the specified text, not the available keys. Is used to specify that the choices should be case-sensitive. Waits the specified number of seconds before defaulting to a specified key. The character to default to after the specified number of seconds. The number of seconds to wait. The text string to be shown before the prompt.			
File Name:	choice.com	**Directory:**	\windows\command	**Type:**	External
choice /CABC Select one of the following.		Shows the following: Select one of the following. [A,B,C]?			

cipher

OS: Windows 2000, XP

Function	Manages the encryption of directories and files on NTFS partitions.
Syntax	cipher [options...] { *path* }

/E /D /S:*directory* /A /I /F /Q /H /K /? *path* **XP:** /R /U /W		Encrypts the specified directory. Files added to directory will be encrypted. Decrypts the specified directory. Runs all operations on the specified directory and its subdirectories. Runs operation on both directories and its files. Ignores errors. Forces encryption or decryption. Show only the most important information. Shows files with hidden or system attributes. Creates a new encryption key for the user running CIPHER. Shows help information. Specifies the path to encrypt or decrypt. Separate multiple entries with spaces. Generates an EFS recovery agent key and certificate. Updates user's file encrypted key or recovery agent's key. Removes data from unused disk space that are unused on the entire volume.			
File Name:	cipher.exe	**Directory:**	**2000:** \winnt\system32, **XP:** \ windows\system32	**Type:**	External
cipher c:\winnt c:\data		Shows the current encryption state of the specified directories.			
cipher /E c:\data		Encrypts the specified directory.			

Class pack

OS: Windows 98/ME, 2000

Function	Is used to pack Java Class files into zip files.
Syntax	clspacks [option] *zipfile listfile* clspack [option]

 -auto -dump *file* *zipfile* *listfile*		**The following options can't be combined.** Copies all class files in the system to \java\classes\classes.zip in the Windows dir. Creates the file containing a list of all class files found in the system. Specifies the zip file to create. Specifies the file containing the list of class files to include in the zip file.			
File Name:	clspack.exe	**Directory:**	**98/ME:** \windows, **2000:** \winnt\system32	**Type:**	External
clspack -dump c:\temp\clslist.txt		Creates a list of all class files in the system and writes it to the file.			

Client Connection Manager

OS: Windows NT4 Terminal Server, 2000 Server

Function	Starts the client connection manager, which can make rapid connections to a terminal server or program.
Syntax	conman

File Name:	conman.exe	**Directory:**	**2000:** \winnt\system32\clients\tsclient\win32\disks\disk1, **NT4 TS:** \wtsrv\system32\clients\tsclient	**Type:**	External

cluster

OS: Windows 2000

Function	Administers clusters from the command prompt.
Syntax	cluster [[cluster:] *cluster*] [options...]

/rename:*newcluster* /version /quorum[:*resource*] [/path:*path*] [/maxlogsize:*size*]	Renames the cluster. Shows version information. Alters the name or location of the quorum resource or the size of the quorum log.

continued

/regadminext:*dll-files...* /unregadminext:*dll-files...* /list*{ :domain }* /properties *{ properties }* /privproperties *{ properties }* /? /help		Registers Cluster Administrator extension DLL:s with the cluster. Unregisters Cluster Administrator extension DLL:s from the cluster. Lists of clusters in the specified domain. Don't specify cluster name. Shows or sets the common properties. Shows or sets the private properties. Shows help information. Same as /?. (Is default)			
File Name:	`cluster.exe`	**Directory:**	\winnt\system32	**Type:**	External
cluster /list			Shows the clusters in the computer's domain.		
cluster mycluster /rename:yourcluster			Renames the cluster from mycluster to yourcluster.		

cmd (2000, XP)

OS: Windows 2000, XP

Function	Starts the command interpreter that lets the user run text-based commands.
Syntax	cmd [options...] *{ string }*

		The following two options can't be combined.			
/C		Terminates after running the command specified by the string parameter.			
/K		Continues after running the command specified by the string parameter.			
/S		Doesn't preserve quoted characters on the command line.			
/Q		Sets echo to OFF.			
/D		Disables the execution of AutoRun commands from the registry.			
/A		Causes the output of internal commands to a pipe or file to be ANSI.			
/U		Causes the output of internal commands to a pipe or file to be Unicode.			
/T:*fg*		Allows you to change foreground and background color.			
/E:ON | OFF		Enables or disables command extensions.			
/F:ON | OFF		Enables or disables directory and file name completion characters. (Use Ctrl-D for directories and Ctrl-F for files.)			
/V:ON | OFF		Enables or disables delayed environment expansion.			
string		The command to run.			
File Name:	`cmd.exe`	**Directory:**	**2000:** \winnt\system32, **XP:** \windows\system32	**Type:**	External
cmd			Starts a Windows 2000 Command Interpreter.		
cmd /F:on			Starts a cmd session with file and catalog completion.		

cmd (NT40)

OS: Windows NT4

Function	Starts a command interpreter window on the screen that allows you to run features from command lines.
Syntax	cmd [options...]

/C		Terminates after running a command specified by a string.			
/K		Continues after running a command specified by a string.			
/Q		Sets echo to OFF.			
/A		Causes the output of internal commands to a pipe or file to be ANSI.			
/U		Causes the output of internal commands to a pipe or file to be Unicode.			
/T:*fg*		Changes foreground and background color.			
/X		Enables an extension for Windows NT version of CMD.EXE.			
/Y		Disables an extension for Windows NT version of CMD.EXE.			
File Name:	`cmd.exe`	**Directory:**	\winnt\system32	**Type:**	External
cmd Q			Starts CMD.EXE with the echo turned off.		

cnvrtuc

OS: Windows NT4 Terminal Server

Function	Converts registry-based user configurations to replicated SAM database.
Syntax	cnvrtuc options...

/ALL	Converts all users.
/USER *name*	Converts the specified user.
/DOMAIN *name*	Converts user from the specified domain. (Can be used with /ALL and /USER)

continued

File Name:	cnvrtuc.exe	Directory:	\wtsrv\system32	Type:	External
cnvrtuc /USER ucg /DOMAIN planets		Converts the user ucg in the domain planets.			

comp

OS: Windows NT4, 2000, XP

Function	Performs a byte-by-byte comparison of two files or sets of files.
Syntax	comp *file1* *file2* [options...]

/D	Shows the difference in decimal format instead of hexadecimal.
/A	Shows the difference with ASCI characters.
/L	Shows the number of the line with the difference instead of the byte offset.
/N=*NR*	Compares only the first specified number of lines.
/C	Specifies the comparison to be case-insensitive.
/?	Shows help information.
file1	Specifies the location of the first file or sets of files.
file2	Specifies the location of the second file or set of files.

File Name:	comp.exe	Directory:	**NT4, 2000:** \winnt\system32, **XP:** \windows\system32	Type:	External
comp autoexec.bat c:\winnt\system32\autoexec.nt		Compares the two files and shows the difference.			

compact

OS: Windows NT4, 2000, XP

Function	Shows or manages compression of files on NTFS partitions.
Syntax	compact [options...] *{ file }*

	The two following options can't be combined:
/C	Compresses the specified files.
/U	Uncompresses the specified files.
/S[:*directory*]	Performs action on all subdirectories of specified directory, current if none given.
/A	Shows the files with the hidden or system file attribute.
/I	Causes errors to be ignored.
/F	Forces the requested action on the specified directory or file.
/Q	Shows only the most important information.
/?	Shows help information.
file	Specifies the file or directory. Multiple files can be used if separated with spaces.

File Name:	compact.exe	Directory:	**NT4, 2000:** \winnt\system32, **XP:** \windows\system32	Type:	External
Tip:	With this command you can compress files that you may not use so often to free disk space.				
compact /c c:\temp		Compresses all files in the temp directory.			
compact /U *.*		All files in the current directory will be uncompressed.			

Compression Agent

OS: Windows 95/98

Function	Recompresses files on a DriveSpace 3 drive. If DriveSpace 3 isn't used, it prompts to upgrade or install.
Syntax	cmpagent

File Name:	cmpagent.exe	Directory:	\Program Files\PLUS!	Type:	External

Computer Management

OS: Windows 2000 Server

Function	Manages local or remote computers. Combines all administration tools into a single console.
Syntax	compmgmt.msc

File Name:	compmgmt.msc	Directory:	\winnt\system32	Type:	External

comrepl

OS: Windows 2000, XP

Function	Replicates COM+ Applications from one computer to other computers.
Syntax	comrepl *source* *targetlist* [options...]

/n	Doesn't prompt for confirmation.
/v	Echos log outputs to the console.
source	Specifies the name of the source computer.
targetlist	Specifies computers to replicate to. Separate multiple entries with spaces.

File Name:	comrepl.exe	Directory:	**2000:** \winnt\system32\Com, **XP:** \windows\system32\Com	Type:	External
comrepl ucgcomputer comp1 comp2		Replicates ucgcomputer to comp1 and comp2.			

connect

OS: Windows NT4 Terminal Server

Function	Connects a user session to a specified terminal session.
Syntax	connect *session* [options...]

/SERVER:*name*	Specifies the server to connect to. (Default is current.)
/DEST:*session*	Specifies the destination session.
/PASSWORD:*pass*	Specifies the password for the user owning the session.
/V	Verbose mode. Shows more information.
session	Specifies the name or number of the session.
File Name: `connect.exe`	**Directory:** \wtsrv\system32 — **Type:** External
connect 7	Connects session 7.

Connection Manager Profile Installer

OS: Windows 98/ME, 2000, XP

Function	A command-line-based profile installer for Connection Manager.
Syntax	cmstp [options...] *file*

/?	Shows help information.
/s	Runs a quiet installation or uninstallation. User action isn't needed.
	The following options can't be combined with the -u or -x options.
/ns	Doesn't create a shortcut in the "Network and Dial-up connections" folder.
/nf	Doesn't install .dll support files.
/i	Combines option /nf and /s.
/su	Installs Connection Manager for a single user. Only in Windows 2000.
	The following options can't be combined with any command except -s.
/x	Uninstalls the Connection Manager.
/u	Uninstalls the service profile.
file	Specifies the full pathname for the file created with the CMAK wizard.
File Name: `cmstp.exe`	**Directory:** **98/ME:** \windows\system, **2000:** \winnt\system32, **XP:** \windows\system32 — **Type:** External

convert

OS: Windows NT4, 2000, XP

Function	Converts FAT partitions to NTFS partitions.
Syntax	convert *volume* /FS:NTFS [options...]

/FS:NTFS	Converts the volume to NTFS.
/V	Verbose mode. Shows more information.
/?	Shows help information.
volume	Specifies the drive, volume name, or mount point to convert.
XP:	
/cvtarea:*file*	Specifies a placeholder file for the NTFS system file in the root directory.
/nosecurity	Makes the converted files and directories accessible to everyone.
/X	Forces the volume to dismount.
File Name: `convert.exe`	**Directory:** **NT4, 2000:** \winnt\system32, **XP:** \windows\system32 — **Type:** External
convert c: /FS:NTFS	Converts the c: drive to the NTFS file system.

convlog

OS: Windows 2000, XP

Function	Converts log files created by Microsoft Internet Information server to the NCSA common log file format.
Syntax	convlog.exe [options...] *logfile*

-i*type*	Specifies the input file type; i = Microsoft (standard), n = NCSA (common), or e = W3C (extended).
-t *NCSA:GMToffset*	Converts the time in NCSA format and the GMToffset.
-o *directory*	Specifies the output directory for the converted file (default is current directory).
-x	Saves any entries that aren't web entries to a dump file.
-d	Converts all IP addresses to DNS host names during conversion.
-l*format*	Specifies the date format to use and is used together with the 0, 1, or 2 option.
0	Specifies the United States date format MM/DD/YY (is the default).

continued

1	Specifies the ISO standard date format YY/MM/DD.
2	Specifies the Germany date1 format DD.MM.YY.
logfile	Specifies the converted log file.
XP:	
-c	Continues even if a bad line is found.
File Name: `convlog.exe`	**Directory:** **2000:** \winnt\system32, **XP:** \windows\system32 — **Type:** External
convlog.exe -ii in*.log -d -t ncsa:+0200 newfile	Converts all IIS log files to NCSA format and adjusts the time 2 hours from GMT.

cprofile

OS: Windows NT4 Terminal Server, 2000 Server

Function	Removes unused profiles and removes user-specific associations from the registry.
Syntax	cprofile [options...] *{ filelist }*

/l	Cleans all local profiles.
/i	Asks the users about each profile.
/v	Shows information about the actions being performed.
filelist	Specifies files to remove.
File Name: `cprofile.exe`	**Directory:** **NT4 TS:** \wtsrv\system32, **2000:** \winnt\system32 — **Type:** External

Create Bootdisk

OS: Windows 2000

Function	Creates boot disks that can be used to start the system from the 3.5-inch drive. The disks are created from the Win 2000 CD-ROM. Four formatted, blank, 3.5-inch, 1.44-MB disks are needed.
Syntax	*cdromdrive*: \bootdisk\makeboot a:
File Name: `makeboot.exe`	**Directory:** \bootdisk — **Type:** External

Create Shared Folder

OS: Windows NT4 Server, 2000, XP

Function	Starts the Create Shared Folder wizard, which shares a folder over the network.
Syntax	shrpubw
File Name: `shrpubw.exe`	**Directory:** **NT4, 2000:** \winnt\system32, **NT4 TS:** \wtrsv\system32, **XP:** \windows\system32 — **Type:** External

cscript

OS: Windows 98/ME, 2000, XP

Function	Runs Java and VB scripts on a Windows computer.
Syntax	cscript *file* [options...]

//B	Hides prompts and script errors (batchmode).
//D	Enables active debugging.
//E:*engine*	Specifies the engine to use when executing the script.
//H:CScript	Changes the default script host to CScript.exe.
//H:WScript	Changes the default script host to WScript.exe.
//I	Shows prompt and script errors (interactivemode).
//Job:*NR*	Runs the specified job.
//Logo	Shows logo (is the default).
//Nologo	Hides logo.
//S	Saves the current command line options for the current user.
//T:*time*	Specifies the script time out in seconds.
//X	Executes the script in debugger.
//U	Uses Unicode for redirected I/O from the console.
file	Specifies the script to run including any parameters it requires.
File Name: `cscript.exe`	**Directory:** **98/ME:** \windows\command, **2000:** \winnt\system32, **XP:** \windows\system32 — **Type:** External
cscript script.vbs //D	Runs the specified script with active debugging.

csvde

OS: Windows 2000 Server

Function	Imports or exports users from the Active Directory.
Syntax	csvde [options...]

	The following options are general:
-i	Uses import mode. Default is the export mode.
-f *filename*	Specifies the input or output file.

continued

-s *server*	Specifies the server to connect to.				
-v	Verbose mode. Shows more information.				
-c *fromDN toDN*	Replaces any occurrence of fromDN with toDN.				
-j	Logs file location.				
-t *port*	Specifies a port to use. (Default is 389.)				
-u	Uses Unicode format.				
-?	Shows version information.				
	These options are in export mode:				
-d *root*	Specifies the root to start.				
-r *filter*	Specifies a search filter for LDAP.				
-p *scope*	Specifies the search scope. Can be Base, One Level or Sub tree.				
-l *list*	Specifies a comma-separated list of attributes to look for in a search.				
-o *list*	Specifies a comma-separated list of attributes not to show in the output.				
-g	Doesn't do a page search.				
-m	Uses SAM logic on export.				
-n	Doesn't export binary values.				
	This option is used in import mode.				
-k	Ignores Constraint Violation and Object Already Exists errors.				
File Name:	`csvde.exe`	**Directory:**	\winnt\system32	**Type:**	External
csvde -f /temp/outfile.txt	Exports information to outfile.txt.				

ctty

OS: Windows Common

Function	Is used to change the standard device used for input/output.				
Syntax	ctty *device*				
device	Specifies device name. Valid values: LPT1, LPT2, LPT3, COM1, COM2, PRN, CON and AUX.				
CTTY com1	Specifies that com1 should be used for input.				

Customize This Folder Wizard

OS: Windows 98/ME, 2000

Function	Used to alter the appearance of a folder by selecting or editing a specified HTML template.				
Syntax	ieshwiz				
File Name:	`ieshwiz.exe`	**Directory:**	**98/ME:** \windows\system, **2000:** \winnt\system32	**Type:**	External

cvt

OS: Windows 98/ME

Function	Starts DOS version of the file system converter, which converts FAT16 file systems to FAT32 file systems.				
Syntax	cvt *drive*:				
drive:	Specifies the drive to convert.				
File Name:	`cvt.exe`	**Directory:**	\windows\command	**Type:**	External

cvt1

OS: Windows 98

Function	A graphical wizard that converts FAT16 file systems to FAT32 file systems.				
Syntax	cvt1				
File Name:	`cvt1.exe`	**Directory:**	\windows	**Type:**	External

dbgtrace

OS: Windows NT4 Terminal Server, 2000 Server

Function	Enables and disables debug tracing of terminal sessions.
Syntax	dbgtrace *{ name }* [options...]
/SYSTEM	Runs the trace on all sessions.
/ALL	Runs the trace on all classes and types.
/C:*class*	Specifies a class value.
/E:*type*	Specifies a type value.
/D	Specifies that trace results are debugged.
/T	Runs tracing until interrupted.
/O:*string*	Specifies the driver options that you can use to limit tracing.
/?	Shows help information.
name	Specifies a name or an id of the session to debug.

continued

File Name:	`dbgtrace.exe`	**Directory:**	**NT4 TS:** \wtsrv\system32, **2000:** \winnt\system32	**Type:**	External
dbgtrace 12			Shows trace information about session 12.		

DDE Share

OS: Windows NT4, 2000, XP

Function	Manages dynamic data exchange (DDE) conversation over a network by creating, modifying, and deleting DDE shares.
Syntax	ddeshare

File Name:	`ddeshare.exe`	**Directory:**	**NT4, 2000:** \winnt\system32, **NT4 TS:** \wtsrv\system32, **XP:** \windows\system32	**Type:**	External

dectohex

OS: Windows NT4 Server

Function	Converts decimal numbers to hexadecimal numbers. If number not specified, it starts an interactive mode.
Syntax	dectohex *{ number }*

number		Specifies a decimal number to convert.			
File Name:	`dectohex.exe`	**Directory:**	\winnt\rpl\rplfiles\binfiles\binr\	**Type:**	External
dectohex 7356			Shows that it is 1CBC in hexadecimal.		

defrag

OS: Windows 9x/ME, XP

Function	Starts the disk defragmenter tool to reorganize the data on hard and floppy disks and increase the performance.
Syntax	defrag *drive* [options...]

/a		Analyzes and shows the current level of fragmentation.			
/f		Defragments even if free disk space is low.			
/v		Verbose mode. Shows more information.			
/?		Shows help information.			
drive		Specifies the drive to defrag.			
File Name:	`defrag.exe`	**Directory:**	**9x/ME:** \windows, **XP:** \windows\system32	**Type:**	External

deltree

OS: Windows Common

Function	Is used to delete a directory including any files or subdirectories it might contain.
Syntax	deltree [/Y] *{ path }*

/Y		Doesn't prompt before deleting directories or subdirectories.			
path		Is used to specify the full path of the directory to delete.			
File Name:	`deltree.exe`	**Directory:**	\windows\command	**Type:**	External
deltree c:\test			Prompts if you wish to delete the directory c:\test and if yes it will.		
deltree c:\windows /Y			Skips prompting and immediately deletes the directory c:\windows and its subdirectories.		

Device Manager

OS: Windows 2000 Server

Function	Manages the system's hardware configuration and the interaction with the processor.
Syntax	devmgmt.msc

File Name:	`devmgmt.msc`	**Directory:**	\winnt\system32	**Type:**	External

dfscmd

OS: Windows 2000 Server

Function	Manages the configuration of a Distributed File System tree.
Syntax	dfscmd [options...]

/help		Shows help information.			
/map \\dfsname\dfsshare\path \\server\share\path		Creates a Distributed File System volume.			
/unmap \\dfsname\dfsshare\path		Removes a Distributed File System volume.			
/add \\dfsname\dfsshare\path \\server\share\path		Creates a replica of the Distributed File System.			
/remove \\dfsname\dfsshare\path \\server\share\path		Removes a replica of the Distributed File System.			
/view \\dfsname\dfsshare\		Shows volumes in the Distributed File System.			
/partial		Shows comments.			
/full		Shows volume names.			
/batch		Outputs to a batch file to re-create the Distributed File System volume.			
/batchrestore		Outputs to a batch file to re-create the DFS volume with the /restore option.			
/restore		Doesn't check destination server.			
File Name:	`dfscmd.exe`	**Directory:**	\winnt\system32	**Type:**	External

DHCP Manager

OS: Windows NT4 Server

Function	Manages DHCP Servers and clients and IP addresses.				
Syntax	dhcpadmn				
File Name:	`dhcpadmn.exe`	**Directory:**	\winnt\system32, **TS:** \wtsrv\system32	**Type:**	External

Dial-up Networking

OS: Windows NT4

Function	Dials up a remote network specified in the phone book.				
Syntax	rasautou *entry*				
entry		Specifies an entry in the phone book to dial.			
File Name:	`rasautou.exe`	**Directory:**	\winnt\system32	**Type:**	External
rasautou UCG			Dials up entry UCG in the phone book.		

Direct Cable Connection

OS: Windows Common

Function	A wizard to help configure a direct cable connection between two computers via a serial or parallel cable.				
Syntax	directcc				
File Name:	`directcc.exe`	**Directory:**	\windows	**Type:**	External

Direct X Diagnostic Tool

OS: Windows 98/ME, 2000, XP

Function	Starts the Direct X Diagnostics Tool, which will show information about DirectX drivers.				
Syntax	dxdiag				
File Name:	`dxdiag.exe`	**Directory:**	**98/ME:** \windows\system, **2000:** \winnt\system32, **XP:** \windows\system32	**Type:**	External

discover

OS: Windows 2000 Professional

Function	Prompts you for the Window 2000 CD-ROM and shows the new features.				
Syntax	discover				
File Name:	`discover.exe`	**Directory:**	\winnt	**Type:**	External

Disk Administrator

OS: Windows NT4

Function	A graphical tool to manage partitions and volumes on local hard disks.				
Syntax	windisk				
File Name:	`windisk.exe`	**Directory:**	\winnt\system32	**Type:**	External

Disk Cleanup

OS: Windows 98/ME, 2000, XP

Function	Starts the Disk Cleanup manager, which removes unnecessary files such as temporary files.				
Syntax	cleanmgr				
File Name:	`cleanmgr.exe`	**Directory:**	**98/ME:** \windows,**2000:** \winnt\system32, **XP:** \windows\system32	**Type:**	External

Disk Defragmenter

OS: Windows 2000 Server

Function	Consolidates fragmented files and folders on the local drives.				
Syntax	dfrg.msc				
File Name:	`dfrg.msc`	**Directory:**	\winnt\system32	**Type:**	External

Disk Management

OS: Windows 2000

Function	Manages and creates disk partitions, configures disk mirroring, and modifies drive letters for local hard disks.				
Syntax	diskmgmt.msc				
File Name:	`diskmgmt.msc`	**Directory:**	\winnt\system32	**Type:**	External

diskcomp

OS: Windows XP

Function	Compares the contents of two floppy disks.
Syntax	diskcomp *{ drive1: } {drive2: }*
/?	Shows help information.

continued

drive1: *drive2*:		Specifies the drive containing the first floppy disk. Specifies the drive containing the second floppy disk.			
File Name:	diskcomp.com	**Directory:**	\windows\system32	**Type:**	External
diskcomp a: b:		Compares the disk in drive a: with the disk in drive b:.			
diskcomp a: a:		If you only have one floppy drive you can do this.			

diskpart

OS: Windows XP

Function	Handles disks, partitions, and volumes. Runs in interactive mode.
Syntax	diskpart [options...]

/?		Shows help information.			
/s *file*		Reads input from the specified file instead of the interactive prompt.			
		The following is a list of commands to use.			
ADD		Adds a mirror to the specified volume.			
ACTIVE		Makes the selected partition active.			
ASSIGN		Assigns a letter or mount point to the selected volume.			
BREAK		Breaks a mirror set.			
CLEAN		Clears the configuration information on the selected disk.			
CONVERT		Converts the selected disk to a different format.			
CREATE		Creates a new volume or partition.			
DELETE		Deletes a disk, partition, or volume.			
DETAIL		Shows detailed information on a disk, partition, or volume.			
EXIT		Exits the program.			
EXTEND		Extends a volume.			
HELP		Shows help information on the internal commands.			
IMPORT		Imports a disk group.			
LIST		Lists all disks, volumes, or partitions.			
ONLINE		Marks the selected disk as online.			
REM		Marks comments that aren't executed as commands.			
REMOVE		Removes a drive letter or mount point assignment.			
RESCAN		Scans the computer for disks, partitions, and volumes.			
SELECT		Selects a disk, partition, or volume.			
File Name:	diskpart.exe	**Directory:**	\windows\system32	**Type:**	External
diskpart /s script.txt		Runs the command by reading from script.txt.			

diskperf

OS: Windows NT4, 2000, XP

Function	Starts and stops the disk performance counters. If used without an option, it shows whether disk performance counters are enabled.
Syntax	diskperf [option] [*host* }

-Y		Specifies the disk performance counters to start when the system is rebooted.			
-N		Specifies the disk performance counters to be stopped when the system is rebooted.			
/?		Shows help information.			
computer		Specifies the computer on which to show or set disk performance counters.			
2000, XP:					
-YD		Enables the disk performance counter for physical drives after rebooting.			
-YV		Enables the disk performance counter for logical drives after rebooting.			
-ND		Disables the disk performance counter for physical drives after rebooting.			
-NV		Disables the disk performance counter for logical drives after rebooting.			
File Name:	diskperf.exe	**Directory:**	**NT4, 2000:** \winnt\system32, **XP:** \windows\system32	**Type:**	External
diskperf -Y		Starts disk performance counters on the local computer after a rebooting.			
diskperf -N		Stops disk performance counters on the local computer after a rebooting.			

Distributed COM Properties

OS: Windows NT4, 2000, XP

Function	Enables the use of distributed programs consisting of multiple processes working to accomplish a single task.
Syntax	dcomcnfg

File Name:	dcomcnfg.exe	**Directory:**	**NT4, 2000:** \winnt\system32, **NT4 TS:** \wtsrv\system32, **XP:** \windows\system32	**Type:**	External

Distributed File System

OS: Windows 2000 Server

Function	Manages and organizes distributed file systems.
Syntax	dfsgui.msc

File Name:	`dfsgui.msc`	**Directory:**	\winnt\system32	**Type:**	External

Distributed Transaction Coordinator

OS: Windows 2000

Function	Starts the installation of Microsoft Distributed Transaction Coordinator.
Syntax	dtcsetup [options...]

/Q	Hides any output.
/T:*directory*	Specifies a directory for temporary files.
/C	Places extra files only in the directory specified with /T.
/C:*command*	Uses command instead of the default.

File Name:	`dtcsetup.exe`	**Directory:**	\winnt\system32	**Type:**	External

dctsetup /Q	Runs with quiet mode for packages.

DNS Manager

OS: Windows NT4 Server

Function	Starts the Domain Name Service Manager.
Syntax	dnsadmin

File Name:	`dnsadmin.exe`	**Directory:**	\winnt\system32, **TS:** \wtsrv\system32	**Type:**	External

Domain Controller Security Policy

OS: Windows 2000 Server

Function	Manages the security level settings for groups, objects, or the local computer security policy.
Syntax	dcpol.msc

File Name:	`dcpol.msc`	**Directory:**	\winnt\system32	**Type:**	External

Domain Security Policy

OS: Windows 2000 Server

Function	Configures the security levels assigned to a local computer policy or a group policy.
Syntax	dompol.msc

File Name:	`dompol.msc`	**Directory:**	\winnt\system32	**Type:**	External

doskbd

OS: Windows NT4 Terminal Server

Function	Changes DOS keyboard polling detection algorithm for a specific DOS window.
Syntax	doskbd [options...]

/detectprobationcount *NR*	Specifies number of peeks to force an application into probation state.
/inprobationcount *NR*	Specifies number of peeks to put an application to sleep when in probation state.
/msallowed *msec*	Puts the application to sleep in this time if in probation state.
/mssleep *msec*	Specifies the time before an application is put to sleep.
/busymallowed *msec*	Isn't to be set to probation state if the application is busy in this time.
/msprobationtrial *ms*	Uses detectprobationcount instead of inprobationcount every msec in probation.
/msgoodprobationend *msec*	Specifies the time an application must avoid being put to sleep to end probation.
/detectioninterval *tics*	Specifies the time for the polling loop to count polling events.
/startmonitor *{ name }*	Starts to monitor polling statistic for the named application if specified or all.
/stopmonitor	Stops the monitor and shows the result.
/q	Hides any information
/default	Sets all parameters to its default value.

File Name:	`doskbd.exe`	**Directory:**	\wtsrv\system32	**Type:**	External

Tip:	The option */msprobationtrial* is also used when detectprobationcount is used instead of inprobationcount.
doskbd	Shows the current settings.

dpnsvr

OS: Windows XP

Function	A server that allows multiple processes to share an IP or IPX port.
Syntax	dpnsvr [/kill]

/kill	Kills the server.

File Name:	`dpnsvr.exe`	**Directory:**	\windows\system32	**Type:**	External

driverquery

OS:	Windows XP
Function	Shows all device drivers and their properties on the local computer or a remote computer.
Syntax	driverquery [options...]

/s *host*	Specifies the remote computer to connect to.
/u { *domain* }*user*	Specifies the user to run the command with. Default is the current user.
/p { *password* }	Specifies the password for the specified user. Prompts for input if skipped.
/fo *format*	Specifies the output format to use. Valid are: TABLE, LIST, CSV.
/nh	Hides column header. Can only be used with the TABLE and CSV format.
/v	Verbose mode. Shows more information.
/si	Shows digital signature information for signed and unsigned device drivers.
/?	Shows help information.

File Name:	`driverquery.exe`	**Directory:**	\windows\system32	**Type:**	External

driverquery /fo list	Shows all installed device drivers in a list format.
driverquery /si	Shows digital signature information for all device drivers.

DriveSpace 3

OS:	Windows Common
Function	Initiates the Drive Space compression utility that can compress/decompress selected drives, mount compressed volume files, and create a Compression Agent to assist with `smart` compression schemes.
Syntax	drvspace

File Name:	`drvspace.exe`	**Directory:**	\windows	**Type:**	External

DVD Player

OS:	Windows ME, 2000, XP
Function	Plays DVD movies. To be able to use the DVD Player a software or hardware DVD decoder must be installed.
Syntax	dvdplay

File Name:	`dvdplay.exe`	**Directory:**	**ME:** \windows, **2000:** \winnt\system32, **XP:** \windows	**Type:**	External

edlin

OS:	Windows NT4, 2000, XP
Function	A line-oriented text editor
Syntax	edlin *file* [option]

/B	Ignores end of file (Ctrl-Z) characters.
/?	Shows help information.
	The following commands can be used on the prompt inside edlin.
line	Shows and edits the specified line.
NRA	Loads the specified number of lines into memory.
{ *line1* }, { *line2* }, *line3* , { *count* } C	Copies a block of text lines to a specified location in the file.
line1	Specifies the first line to copy.
line2	Specifies the last line to copy.
line3	Inserts text before this line number
count	Specifies the number of times the line should be copied.
{ *line1* }, { *line2* } D	Deletes a block of lines.
line1	Specifies the first line to delete.
line2	Specifies the last line to delete.
E	Writes the file to disk and exits.
*line*I	Inserts text before the specified line. To abort, press Ctrl-C.
{ *line1* }, { *line2* } L	Shows the specified lines of text.
{ *line1* }, { *line2* }, { *line3* } M	Moves a block of lines.
line1	Specifies the first line to move.
line2	Specifies the last line to move. Use +*NR* to move a specified number of lines.
line3	Inserts text before this line number
{ *line1* }, { *line2* } P	Shows all or a part of a file one page at a time.
line1	Specifies the first line to show.
line2	Specifies the last line to show.
Q	Exits the editor without saving.

continued

{ line1 }, { line2 } [?] R [string1] [separator string2]	Finds and replaces text strings.
line1	Specifies the first line to search.
line2	Specifies the last line to search.
?	Prompts the user before replacing a line.
string1	Searches for this string.
separator	Separates the two strings. Only valid entry is the end-of-file (Ctrl-Z) character.
string2	Specifies the new string.
{ line1 }, { line2 } [?] S *{ string }*	Searches for a string.
line1	Specifies the first line to search.
line2	Specifies the last line to search.
?	Prompts the user when the first occurrence is found.
string	Searches for this string.
{ NR } T *file*	Appends a file read from disk to the one currently in memory.
NR	Inserts text before this line number.
file	Specifies the full path to the file that contains the text to insert.
{ NR } W	Writes the first part of the file to disk.
NR	Specifies the number of lines to write starting with the first.
File Name: `edlin.exe`	**Directory:** **NT4, 2000:** \winnt\system32, **XP:** \windows\system32 **Type:** External
edlin autoexec.bat	Starts the editor and opens the file autoexec.bat.

emm386 — OS: Windows Common

Function	Is used to enable or disable expanded memory support for the expanded memory manager.
Syntax	emm386 [options...]

-on | off	Enables or disables the emm386 expanded memory support.
-auto	Sets the emm386 to automatic mode.
w=on | off	Enables or disables support for Weitec coprocessor.
File Name: `emm386.exe`	**Directory:** \windows **Type:** External
emm386 -auto	Sets the emm386 in automatic mode.

esentutl — OS: Windows 2000, XP

Function	Repairs, checks, defragments, recovers, and restores Microsoft Windows 2000 databases.
Syntax	esentutl /d *database* [options...] esentutl /r [options...] esentutl /g *database* [options...] esentutl /m*{ mode } file* esentutl /p *database* [options...] esentutl /c*mode directory* [options...]

	The following options can't be combined:
/d	Defragments a database.
/r	Recovers Microsoft Windows 2000 databases.
/g	Checks integrity.
/m*{ mode }*	Exports different types of information.
h	Dumps the database header (Is default).
k	Dumps the checkpoint file.
l	Dumps the log files.
m	Dumps the metadata.
s	Dumps any space usage.
/p	Fixes a corrupted database.
/c*mode*	Restores information to the database.
m	Dumps restore.env.
c	Starts a recover on `restore.env`.
	These options are used with each of the above options:
/o	Hides the logo.
database	Specifies the database to use.

continued

	These options are used with the /d option:
/s*file*	Specifies the streaming file.
/t*database*	Specifies the temporary database to use.
/f*file*	Specifies the temporary streaming file.
/i	Doesn't defragment the streaming file.
/p	Keeps the temporary database.
/b*database*	Creates a backup of the database.
	These options are used with the /r option:
/l*path*	Specifies the path for the log file.
/s*path*	Specifies the path for the system files.
/i	Ignores mismatched or missing database attachments.
	These options are used with the /g option:
/s*file*	Specifies the streaming file.
/t*database*	Specifies the temporary database to use.
/f*prefix*	Specifies the prefix for the report file.
	These options are used with the /m option:
/s*file*	Specifies the streaming file.
/t*table*	Specifies the table to dump.
/v	Verbose mode. Shows more information.
file	Specifies the file to dump.
	These options are used with the /p option:
/s*file*	Specifies the streaming file.
/t*database*	Specifies the temporary database to use.
/f*prefix*	Specifies the prefix for the report file.
	These options are used with the /p option:
/t*instance*	Specifies where to start within the play forward log file (default is from backup).
/k	Keeps the log file.
directory	Specifies the directory where `restore.env` is located.

File Name:	`esentutl.exe`	**Directory:**	**2000:** \winnt\system32, **XP:** \windows\system32	**Type:**	External
Tip:	A database power-tool that every host owner shouldn't be without.				

esentutl /p ucgdatabase /d	Scans for errors in ucgdatabase.
esentutl /d ucgdatabase /l c:\logfiles	Compacts the ucgdatabase and puts log files in c:\logfiles.

Event To Trap Translator

OS: Windows 2000, XP

Function	Traps selected events whenever they occur.
Syntax	evntwin *{ host }*

host	Specifies which computer network name to run trap on.

File Name:	`evntwin.exe`	**Directory:**	**2000:** \winnt\system32\dllcache, **XP:** \windows\system32\dllcache	**Type:**	External

Event Viewer

OS: Windows NT4, 2000, XP

Function	Shows Application, Security, and System event logs.
Syntax	eventvwr

File Name:	`eventvwr.exe`, `eventvwr.msc`	**Directory:**	**NT4, 2000:** \winnt\system32, **NT4 TS:** \wtsrv\system32, **XP:** \windows\system32	**Type:**	External

eventcreate

OS: Windows XP

Function	Creates an event in the specified event log.
Syntax	eventcreate options...

	The following three options are required:
/t *type*	Specifies the event type to create: ERROR, INFORMATION, WARNING, or SUCCESSAUDIT.
/id *id*	Specifies the ID of the event.
/d *string*	Specifies a description.
/s *host*	Specifies the remote computer to connect to.
/u *{ domain\ }user*	Specifies the user to run the command with. Default is the current user.
/p *{ password }*	Specifies the password for the specified user. Prompts for input if skipped.
	The following two options can't be combined:
/l *{ type }*	Specifies the event log where the event is saved. Valid types are: APPLICATION or SYSTEM.

continued

/so *string*	Specifies which component or application generates the event.
/?	Shows help information.
File Name: eventcreate.exe	**Directory:** \windows\system32 **Type:** External
eventcreate /t error /id 12 /d "Created Event"	Creates an Error in the Application event log.
eventcreate /l system /t warning /id 13 /d "My system event"	Creates a Warning in the system event log.

eventtriggers

OS: Windows XP

Function	Shows, creates, and deletes event triggers on local or remote computer.
Syntax	eventtriggers *ACTION*

	The following four options are common to all actions:
/s *host*	Specifies the remote computer to connect to.
/u *{ domain\ ]user*	Specifies the user to run the command with. Default is the current user.
/p *[password }*	Specifies the password for the specified user. Prompts for input if skipped.
/?	Shows help information.
ACTION	**The following three actions are available.**
/create [options...]	Creates a new event trigger.
	The following two options are required.
/tr *name*	Specifies the new trigger.
/tk *name*	The task or command to execute when the event trigger conditions are met.
/l *{ types ... }*	Specifies the event log to monitor. Wildcards (*) can be used. (Valid types are: APPLICATION, SYSTEM, SECURITY, "DNS Server", LOG and DirectoryLogName.)
	The following three options can't be combined.
/eid *id*	Specifies an event id that the event trigger should monitor.
/t *type*	Specifies the event type the event trigger should monitor. (Valid types are: ERROR, INFORMATION, WARNING, SUCCESSAUDIT, FAILUREAUDIT.)
/so *source*	Specifies an event source that the event trigger should monitor.
/d *string*	Specifies a description.
/ru *user*	Specifies the user account under which the tasks will run. (Specify "System" to use the NT Authority\System account.)
/rp *password*	Specifies the password for the user account.
/delete [options...]	Deletes an event trigger using the event trigger ID.
/tid *id*	Specifies the ID of the event trigger to delete.
/query [options...]	Shows the system's event trigger properties and settings.
/fo *format*	Specifies the output format to use. Valid are: TABLE, LIST, CSV.
/nh	Hides column header. Can only be used with the TABLE and CSV format.
/v	Verbose mode. Shows more information.
File Name: eventtriggers.exe	**Directory:** \windows\system32 **Type:** External
eventtriggers /create /tr Trigger1 /l system /t error /tk c:\apps\myapp.exe	Creates a trigger with the specified name.
eventtriggers /query /fo list	Shows all event triggers in a list format.

evntcmd

OS: Windows 2000, XP

Function	Translates snmp events to snmp traps.
Syntax	evntcmd [options...] *file*

-?	Shows help information.
-s *sysname*	Specifies the target system.
-v *NR*	Specifies the verbose level (0-none to 10-high).
-n	Doesn't restart the snmp service if a snmp trap is changed.
file	Specifies a file with events to translate.
File Name: evntcmd.exe	**Directory:** **2000:** \winnt\system32\dllcache, **XP:** \windows\system32 **Type:** External

exe2bin

OS: Windows NT4, 2000, XP

Function	Converts an executable .EXE file to binary format. If no target is specified, the source file name is used.
Syntax	exe2bin *source { destination }* [/?]

/?	Shows help information.
source	Specifies the source-executable .EXE file to convert.
destination	Specifies the target binary file. The default extension is .BIN.

File Name:	`exe2bin.exe`	**Directory:**	**NT4, 2000:** \winnt\system32, **XP:** \windows\system32	**Type:**	External

expand

OS: Windows XP

Function	Expands compressed files.
Syntax	expand [-r] *file { destination }* expand -D *cabfile* [-F:*files*] expand *cabfile* -F:*files destination*

-D	Shows the contents of the source file.
-F:*file*	Specifies the file to expand from a .CAB file.
/r	Renames expanded files automatically.
file	Specifies the file to expand.
cabfile	Specifies the .CAB file to expand files from.
destination	Specifies the destination directory or file.

File Name:	`expand.exe`	**Directory:**	\windows\system32	**Type:**	External

expand driver.cab -F:1394bus.sys C:\temp	Expands the specified file to the c:\temp directory.
expand driver.cab -F:*.* c:\temp	Expands all the files in the specified .CAB file to the c:\temp directory.

extract

OS: Windows Common

Function	Extracts individual files from .CAB files (cabinet files), can also be used to extract entire cabinet files.
Syntax	extract [options...] *cabfile { filename } { destination }*

/A	Follows the cabinet chain and extracts them all.
/C	Copies the file from within the cabinet. Can only be used with `destination`.
	The following two options can't be combined:
/D	Shows the contents of the file. Does not extract anything.
/E	Extracts the whole cabinet file instead of a specified file.
/L *directory*	Specifies where extracted files should be put. (Default is current directory.)
/Y	Skips prompting before overwriting existing files.
cabfile	Specifies the cabfile to extract or copy from.
filename	Specifies file to extract, or, if only one file exists in cabinet, this names the file.
destination	Specifies the destination for a file being copied from cabinet. (The destination can only be used with /C and no other option.)

File Name:	`extract.exe`	**Directory:**	\windows\command	**Type:**	External

extract d:\win95\mini.cab /d	Shows the contents of mini.cab on the Windows CD-ROM.

fastopen

OS: Windows NT4, 2000, XP

Function	Improves performance on computers with large directories. Only used for compatibility with MS-DOS files.
Syntax	fastopen

File Name:	`fastopen.exe`	**Directory:**	**NT4, 2000:** \winnt\system32, **NT4 TS:** \wtsrv\system32, **XP:** \windows\system32	**Type:**	External

Fax Service Management

OS: Windows 2000 Server

Function	Configures the group policy applied to user groups or computers. It defines the environment on users' systems.
Syntax	faxserv.msc

File Name:	`faxserv.msc`	**Directory:**	\winnt\system32	**Type:**	External

fdisk

OS: Windows Common

Function	Creates, removes, manages, and shows disk partitions on your hard disk. A menu-based utility.
Syntax	fdisk [options...]

/STATUS	Shows current partition information.
/X	Ignores extended disk-access support.
/MBR	A hidden switch for the Master Boot Record. Is great to remove a boot sector virus.

File Name:	`fdisk.exe`	**Directory:**	\windows\command	**Type:**	External

fdisk /status	Shows partition information of current disks.

File Manager

OS: Windows 9x/ME, NT4

Function	Starts the "Classic" file manager that was originally in Windows 3.x. It is the older version of `explorer.exe`.
Syntax	winfile *{ path }*

path	Specifies path to a directory to open or a file to execute.

File Name:	`winfile.exe`	**Directory:**	**9x/ME:** \windows, **NT4:** \winnt\system32	**Type:**	External

File Signature Verification

OS: Windows 98/ME, 2000, XP

Function	Identifies whether files have the Microsoft signature.
Syntax	sigverif

File Name:	`sigverif.exe`	**Directory:**	**98/ME:** \windows, **2000:** \winnt\system32, **XP:** \windows\system32	**Type:**	External

Files and Settings Transfer Wizard

OS: Windows XP

Function	Transfers files and settings to another computer.
Syntax	migwiz

File Name:	`migwiz.exe, migload.exe`	**Directory:**	\windows\system32\usmt	**Type:**	External

findramd

OS: Windows 98/ME

Function	Searches all available drive letters for RAM drives.
Syntax	findramd

File Name:	`findramd.exe`	**Directory:**	\windows\command\ebd	**Type:**	External

findstr

OS: Windows NT4, 2000, XP

Function	Searches for strings in files using regular expressions or literal text.
Syntax	findstr [options...] *strings files...*

/B	Matches pattern if at the beginning of a line.
/E	Matches pattern if at the end of a line.
/L	Uses search strings literally.
/R	Searches strings as regular expressions.
/S	Searches for matching files in the current directory and all subdirectories.
/I	Makes the search not case-sensitive.
/X	Shows lines that match exactly.
/V	Shows only lines that don't contain a match.
/N	Shows the line number before every line that matches.
/M	Shows only files that contain a match.
/O	Shows seek offset before every matching line.
/P	Skips files with non-printable characters.
/F:*file*	Specifies a file to read a file list from.
/C:*string*	Specifies a string to be used as a literal search string.
strings	Specifies the string to search for.
files...	Specifies the files to search in.

continued

2000, XP:	
/A:*attr*	Specifies a color attribute with two hex digits.
/D:*dir*	Searches the semicolon-separated list of directories.
/G:*file*	Specifies a string to be used as a literal search string.
File Name: `findstr.exe`	**Directory:** **NT4, 2000:** \winnt\system32, **XP:** \windows\system32 **Type:** External
findstr "Hi There" *.*	Searches for "Hi" or "There" in all files in the current directory.
findstr /c:"Hi There" *.*	Searches for "Hi There" in all files in the current directory.

finger

OS: Windows NT4, 2000, XP

Function	Shows information about a user on the specified system running the Finger service.
Syntax	finger [-l] *{ user }@host*
-l	Shows the information in a long list format.
user	Specifies the user to show information about. Skip this to show all users.
host	Specifies the server where the user is located.
File Name: `finger.exe`	**Directory:** **NT4, 2000:** \winnt\system32, **XP:** \windows\system32 **Type:** External
finger @192.168.11.1	Shows information about all users on the specified computer.
finger admin@192.168.11.1	Shows information about the admin user.

flattemp

OS: Windows NT4 Terminal Server, 2000 Server

Function	Enables or disables flat temporary directories.
Syntax	flattemp [option]
/QUERY	Shows the current settings.
/ENABLE	Enables the use of flat temporary directories.
/DISABLE	Disables the use of flat temporary directories.
File Name: `flattemp.exe`	**Directory:** **NT4 TS:** \wtsrv\system32, **2000:** \winnt\system32 **Type:** External

forcedos

OS: Windows NT4, 2000, XP

Function	Starts a program in the MS-DOS subsystem. This is only necessary if Windows doesn't recognize it as an MS-DOS program.
Syntax	forcedos [option] *file { parameters }*
/D *directory*	Specifies the directory the program should use.
/?	Shows help information.
file	Specifies the program to start.
parameters	Specifies any parameters to use with the specified program.
File Name: `forcedos.exe`	**Directory:** **NT4, 2000:** \winnt\system32, **XP:** \windows\system32\ **Type:** External
forcedos myapp.exe	Forces myapp.exe to start in the MS-DOS subsystem.

fortutil

OS: Windows 2000

Function	Accesses Fortezza certificate cards containing SSL certificate and moves them to the IIS.
Syntax	fortutil options...
-o:*action*	Specifies what to do.
create	Copies a certificate from the card to the server.
delete	Removes a certificate from the server.
check	Checks a certificate.
-l:*NR*	Specifies the instance number.
-n:*PIN*	Specifies the pin-code.
-s:*serial*	Specifies the serial number for the card.
-p:*personality*	Specifies the personality of the card.
-?	Shows help information.
File Name: `fortutil.exe`	**Directory:** \winnt\system32\inetsrv **Type:** External

fpremadm

OS: Windows 2000, XP

Function	Administrates a remote FrontPage server extension.
Syntax	fpremadm options... { *-command option* } ...

-targetserver *server*	Specifies the full URL to the target server administration program. (This is fpadmdll.dll on an IIS and fpadmcgi.exe on other servers.)
	If Response/challenge is used, the following two options aren't used:
-adminusername *name*	Specifies the username used for administration of FrontPage.
-adminpassword *password*	Specifies the password for the user.
-command option	Specifies commands for the FrontPage administration program.

File Name:	`fpremadm.exe`	**Directory:**	**2000:** \winnt\system32\dllcache, **XP:** \windows\system32\dllcache	**Type:**	External

fpremadm -targetserver https:\\www.ucg.com\cgibin\fpadmdll.dll ...	This shows how the server is specified.

fpsrvadm

OS: Windows XP

Function	Installs, uninstalls, and manages FrontPage extensions for many types of web servers.
Syntax	fpsrvadm -o *install* -t *type* -m *mhost* -u *user* -pw *password* -s *config* fpsrvadm -o *operation* -p *port* [-w *webname*] [options...]

-o	Specifies the operation to perform.
install	Installs FrontPage extensions for the server type specified by the -t option.
	The following operations require the -p and -w options described below:
create	Creates a sub web with the specified name. (Requires -p and -w options.)
merge	Merges a parent web and child web together.
recalc	Recalculates the links contained in the web page.
delete	Removes the web page.
	The following operations require the -p option described below:
upgrade	Upgrades the FrontPage extensions on the web server.
uninstall	Uninstalls FrontPage extensions for the server type specified by the -t option.
fulluninstall	Uninstalls all FrontPage information from the server specified.
check	Checks and repairs the web page extensions on the port specified.
enable	Enables modifications of the web page.
disable	Disables modifications of the web page.
	The following operations require the -p, -w, and -d options described below:
setDirExec	Enables execution in the directory specified.
setDirNoExec	Disables execution in the directory specified.
recalcfile	Recalculates the web with the URL specified.
rename	Renames the web.
	The following operation requires the -p, -w, -d, and -f options described below:
putfile	Copies a file specified to the web name and directory specified.
-f *file*	Specifies the file name to copy to the web server.
security	Changes the security settings. (Requires the -p, -w, -a, -u, -pw, and -i options).
-p *port*	Specifies the port the web server is running on. (Default is 80.)
-w *name*	Specifies the web page.
-t *type*	Specifies web server type: msiis, FrontPage, Netscape-enterprise, Netscape-fastrack
-s *config*	Specifies the location to the configuration file.
-m *mhost*	Specifies the hostname or IP address for multi-host web servers.
-u *user*	Specifies the username with access to the web server.
-pw *password*	Specifies the password for the above username.
-i *IPaddress*	Specifies the hostname or IP address of the web server. (Default is local.)
-a *group*	Specifies access group. Values for group are: remove, administrators, authors, users.
-d *destination*	Specifies the destination. The destination could be a file, a folder, or a URL.

File Name:	`fpsrvadm.exe`	**Directory:**	\Program Files\Common Files\Microsoft Shared\Web Server Extensions\40\bin	**Type:**	External

fpsrvadm -o install -p 80 ucg	Installs FrontPage extensions for the web ucg.
fpsrvadm -d disable -p 80	Disables updates to the web page.

FrontPage TCP/IP Test	OS: Windows 2000, XP
Function	Checks the status on the TCP/IP protocol.
Syntax	tcptest

File Name:	`tcptest.exe`	**Directory:**	**2000:** \winnt\system32\dllcache, **XP:** \windows\system32	**Type:**	External

fsutil	OS: Windows XP
Function	Performs FAT and NTFS file system tasks, such as managing reparse points and sparse files.
Syntax	fsutil *ACTION*

ACTION	**Use one of the following actions:**
behavior *ACTION*	Is used with one of the following two actions.
query *behavior*	Shows the current setting for the specified behavior.
set *behavior value*	Changes the setting of the specified behavior.
	The following 5 behaviors are available:
disable8dot3	Prevents the creation of 8.3 file names.
allowextchar	Determines if extended characters can be used.
disablelastaccess	Determines if last access timestamp is used when listing directories. (The last three behaviors can have the value of 1 or 0.)
quotanotify	Specifies how often quota notification should occur in the system log. (The value for the option above is in seconds.)
mftzone	Configures the master file table zone. Valid values are 1 through 4.
dirty *ACTION*	Is used together with one of the following two actions:
query *drive*	Shows the state of the dirty-bit for the specified volume.
set *drive*	Sets the dirty-bit for the specified volume
file *ACTION*	Is used together with one of the following six actions:
creatnew *file size*	Creates a new empty file with the specified name and size.
findbysid *user volume*	Finds a specific user's files on an NTFS volume.
user	Shows the files for the specified user.
volume	Specifies the drive letter, mount point, or volume name to search.
queryallocranges	Queries the allocated range for a file on a NTFS volume. Use syntax below.
offset=*value*	Specifies the start of the range.
length=*value*	Specifies the length of the range.
file	Specifies the file.
	SYNTAX: queryallocranges offset=*offset* length=*value file*
setshortname *file name*	Changes the short name of the specified file to the specified name.
setvaliddata *file length*	Sets the valid data length for the specified file.
setzerodata	Sets a range of a file to zeroes. Use syntax below.
offset=*value*	Specifies the start of the range.
length=*value*	Specifies the length of the range.
file	Specifies the file.
	SYNTAX: setzerodata offset=*offset* length=*value file*
fsinfo *ACTION*	Is used together with one of the following five actions.
drives	Shows all drives in the computer.
drivetype *path*	Shows the type of the specified drive.
ntfsinfo *volume*	Shows NTFS information on the specified volume.
statistics *volume*	Shows statistics for the specified volume.
volumeinfo *volume*	Shows information on the specified volume.
hardlink *ACTION*	Is used together with the following action.
create *newname file*	Creates a new hard link to a file.
newname	Specifies the new hard link (file name).
file	Specifies an existing file from which to create the hard link.
objectid *ACTION*	Is used together with one of the following four actions.
create *file*	Creates an object identifier for the specified file if none exists.
delete *file*	Deletes the object identifier for the specified file.
query *file*	Shows the object identifier for the specified file.
set	Is used specify set identifiers for the specified file. Use syntax below.
oid	Specifies the 16-byte hexadecimal object id.
bvid	Specifies the 16-byte hexadecimal birth volume id.

continued

boid	Specifies the 16-byte hexadecimal birth object id.
did	Specifies the 16-byte hexadecimal domain id. (Not used, set to zero.)
file	The file to set identifiers for.
	SYNTAX: set *oid bvid boid did file*
quota *ACTION*	Is used together with one of the following actions:
disable *volume*	Disables quota on the specified volume.
enforce *volume*	Enables quota on the specified volume.
modify	Creates or modifies disk quota. Use syntax below.
volume	The volume on which to create or modify the quota.
wlimit	Specifies the warning level.
limit	Specifies the maximum amount of allowed disk space.
user	The user the quota should apply to.
	SYNTAX: quota *volume wlimit limit user*
reparsepoint *ACTION*	Is used together with one of the following two actions.
query *path*	Shows the reparse point data for the specified file or directory.
delete *path*	Deletes the reparse point data for the specified file or directory.
sparse *ACTION*	Is used together with one of the following four actions.
queryflag *file*	Shows whether a file has the sparse flag set.
queryrange *file*	Scans the specified file for ranges that contain nonzero data.
setflag *file*	Sets the sparse flag for the specified file.
setrange	Fills the specified range of the file with zeroes. Use syntax below.
file	Specifies the file to fill with zeroes.
offset	Specifies the beginning offset.
range	Specifies the length to fill.
usn *ACTION*	Is used together with one of the following five actions.
creatjournal	Creates an update sequence number (USN) change journal. Use syntax below.
m=*maxsize*	Specifies the maximum number of bytes to use for the change journal.
a=*allocdelta*	Specifies the number of bytes to remove from the start and add to the end of the journal.
volume	Specifies the volume.
	SYNTAX: usn *maxsize allocdelta volume*
deletejournal	Deletes or disables an active USN change journal. Use syntax below.
	The following two options can't be combined but one is required:
/D	Disables an active journal and returns I/O control while the operation is performed.
/N	Disables an active journal and returns I/O control when the operation is completed.
volume	Specifies the volume.
	SYNTAX: deletejournal /D /N *volume*
enumdata	Is used to enumerate and show the USN change journal entries. Use syntax below.
fileref	Specifies ordinal position within the files from which the enumeration is to begin.
lowusn	Specifies the lower boundary of the USN value filter range.
highusn	Specifies the upper boundary of the USN value filter range.
volume	Specifies the volume.
	SYNTAX: enumdata *fileref lowusn highusn volume*
queryjournal *volume*	Shows information on the USN change journal on the specified volume.
readdata *file*	Reads the USN data for the specified file.
volume *ACTION*	Is used together with one of the following two actions.
diskfree *drive*:	Shows the amount of free space on the specified volume.
dismount *volume*	Dismounts the specified volume.

File Name:	`fsutil.exe`	**Directory:**	\windows\system32	**Type:**	External
fsutil file creatnew file.bin 1000			Creates a file with the specified name and makes it 1000 bytes big.		
fsutil hardlink create c:\data\file.bin file.bin			Creates a hard link named c:\data\file.bin to the specified file.		

getmac

OS: Windows XP

Function	Returns the MAC address and a list of protocols for all network cards in the local or remote computer.
Syntax	getmac [options...]

/s host	Specifies a remote computer either by its IP address or its hostname.
/u user	Runs the command with the specified user.
/p password	Specifies the password for the user.

continued

/fo *format*	Specifies the output format to use. Valid are: TABLE, LIST, CSV.
/nh	Hides column header. Can only be used with the TABLE and CSV format.
/v	Verbose mode. Shows more information.
/?	Shows help information.
File Name: `getmac.exe`	**Directory:** \windows\system32 **Type:** External
getmac /s fs01 /u admin /p gY53Kj	Shows the information for the specified computer.
getmac /fo list	Shows the information in a list format.

gpresult

OS: Windows XP

Function	Shows Resultant Set of Policy (RSOP) and Group Policy settings for a computer or user.
Syntax	gpresult [options...]

/s *host*	Specifies a remote computer either by its IP address or its hostname.
/u *user*	Runs the command with the specified user.
/p *password*	Specifies the password for the user.
/user *name*	Specifies the name of the user whose RSOP data is to be shown.
/scope user | computer	Shows either user or computer results; by default, results for both are shown.
/v	Verbose mode. Shows more information.
/z	Shows all available information about Group Policy.
/?	Shows help information.
File Name: `gpresult.exe`	**Directory:** \windows\system32 **Type:** External
gpresult /z > result.txt	Saves all available information in the file result.txt.

gpupdate

OS: Windows XP

Function	Refreshes Group Policy settings.
Syntax	gpupdate [options...]

/target:computer | user	Specifies the settings to process, user or computer. Default is both.
/force	Ignores all processing optimization.
/wait:*value*	The number of seconds the policy processing waits to finish.
/logoff	Logs off after the operation is completed.
/boot	Reboots after the operation is completed.
/?	Shows help information.
File Name: `gpupdate.exe`	**Directory:** \windows\system32 **Type:** External
gpupdate /boot	Refreshes all Group Policy settings and then reboots.

graftabl

OS: Windows NT4, 2000, XP

Function	Enables Windows NT to show the extended characters of the specified code page in full-screen mode. If no parameters are given, the current code page is shown.
Syntax	graftabl *{ codepage }* [option]

/STATUS	Shows the current code page number used.
codepage	Specifies the code page number.
File Name: `graftabl.com`	**Directory:** **NT4, 2000:** \winnt\system32, **XP:** \windows\system32 **Type:** External
graftabl /status	Shows the active code page.
graftabl 437	Sets the code page 437 to be used.

graphics

OS: Windows XP

Function	Loads a program into memory that allows Windows NT to print the contents of the screen when using a color or graphics adapter.
Syntax	graphics *{ type } { file }* [options...]

/r	Prints the text as it appears on the screen, white text on a black background.
/b	Prints the background in color. Valid for color4 and color8 printers.
/lcd	Specifies to print by using the LCD aspect ratio instead of the CGA aspect ratio.
/printbox:*size*	Selects the print box size. Valid options are either STD or LCD.
type	Specifies the type of printer.
file	Specifies the full path and name of the printer profile.

continued

File Name:	graphics.com	**Directory:**	\windows\system32	**Type:**	External

Group Management Wizard

OS: Windows NT4 Server

Function	Creates and alters groups.
Syntax	addgrpw

File Name:	addgrpw.exe	**Directory:**	\winnt\system32, **TS:** \wtsrv\system32	**Type:**	External

Group Policy

OS: Windows 2000 Server

Function	Configures the group policy applied to user groups or computers. It defines the environment on the user's system.
Syntax	gpedit.msc

File Name:	gpedit.msc	**Directory:**	\winnt\system32	**Type:**	External

Help

OS: Windows NT4, 2000, XP

Function	Shows help information about NT commands.
Syntax	help *{ command }* [/?]

/?	Shows help information.
command	Specifies the command to show help about.

File Name:	help.exe	**Directory:**	**NT4, 2000:** \winnt\system32, **XP:** \windows\system32	**Type:**	External

help	Lists all commands in NT.
help format	Shows help information about format.

Help and Support Center

OS: Windows ME, XP

Function	Answers many questions about Windows.
Syntax	helpctr

File Name:	helpctr.exe	**Directory:**	\windows\pchealth\helpctr\binaries	**Type:**	External

Home Networking Wizard

OS: Windows ME

Function	Guides you in configuring your Internet connection and sharing files.
Syntax	netconn

File Name:	netconn.exe	**Directory:**	\windows	**Type:**	External

hostname

OS: Windows NT4, 2000, XP

Function	Shows the hostname on the current computer.
Syntax	hostname

File Name:	hostname.exe	**Directory:**	**NT4, 2000:** \winnt\system32, **XP:** \windows\system32	**Type:**	External

iextract

OS: Windows 98/ME

Function	Extracts Internet Explorer Backup Information.
Syntax	iextract [option] *datafile { files... }*

/W	Notifies before it overwrites a file.
/L *directory*	Saves the extracted files in the specified directory.
datafile	Specifies the full path to the backup information .dat file.
files...	Specifies the files to extract from the backup information file. (Use blanks to separate multiple filenames.)

File Name:	iextract.exe	**Directory:**	\windows\command	**Type:**	External

iissync

OS: Windows 2000, XP

Function	Replicates metabase between hosts running IIS.
Syntax	iissync

File Name:	iissync.exe	**Directory:**	**2000:** \winnt\system32\inetsrv, **XP:** \windows\system32\inetsrv	**Type:**	External

Image Preview

OS:	Windows 2000
Function	Previews, zooms, and rotates pictures.
Syntax	kodakprv

File Name:	Directory:	Type:
`kodakprv.exe`	\Program Files\Windows NT\Accessories\Imagevue	External

Imaging

OS:	Windows 2000
Function	Starts the `Imaging` application. Use this to retrieve pictures from a scanner or a digital camera. Can also print or e-mail a picture.
Syntax	kodakimg

File Name:	Directory:	Type:
`kodakimg.exe`	\Program Files\Windows NT\Accessories\ImageVue	External

Indexing Service

OS:	Windows 2000 Server
Function	Creates a catalog with an index of documents and their properties from the drivers in your system. The created file can be searched from the search function or from a web browser.
Syntax	ciadv.msc

File Name:	Directory:	Type:
`ciadv.msc`	\winnt\system32\	External

Install Windows Messaging

OS:	Windows NT4
Function	Installs the Windows Messaging client. May also prompt you to insert your CD-ROM.
Syntax	mlset32

File Name:	Directory:	Type:
`mlset32.exe`	\Program Files\Windows NT\Windows Messaging	External

Internet Authentication Service

OS:	Windows 2000 Server
Function	Manages authentication, authorization, and accounting for users who connect to a network from a virtual private network through dial-up technology.
Syntax	ias.msc

File Name:	Directory:	Type:
`ias.msc`	\winnt\system32	External

Internet Connection Wizard

OS:	Windows 9x/ME, 2000, XP
Function	Starts the Internet Connection Wizard, which allows for automatic configuration of a connection to the Internet via the Local Area Network or a service provider through a modem connection.
Syntax	**2000, XP:** inetwiz **9x/ME:** icwconn1

File Name:	Directory:	Type:
`inetwiz.exe`, `icwconn1.exe`	**9x/ME, XP:** \Program Files\Internet Explorer\Connection Wizard, **2000:** \winnt\system32\dllcache	External

Internet Information Services

OS:	Windows 2000, XP
Function	Manages the Internet information services server. Can add, remove, and alter web and ftp services.
Syntax	inetmgr

File Name:	Directory:	Type:
`inetmgr.exe`	**2000:** \winnt\system32\inetsrv, **XP:** \windows\system32\inetsrv	External

IP Configuration

OS:	Windows Common
Function	Shows the current TCP/IP network configuration values for all available network adapters. It is also used to release or renew the configuration values from the DHCP server. This command is GUI based.
Syntax	winipcfg [options...]

/all	Shows all configuration information (by default, only IP-Address, Subnet, and Gateway).
/batch *{ file }*	Writes to the specified file or, if not specified, to ./winipcfg.out.
/renew_all	Is used to renew the DHCP configuration data for all adapters.
/release_all	Is used to release the current DHCP configuration data for all adapters.
/renew *adapterNr*	Is used to renew the DHCP configuration data for the specified adapter.
/release *adapterNr*	Is used to release the current DHCP configuration data for all adapters.

continued

File Name:	winipcfg.exe	Directory:	\windows	Type:	External
winipcfg /all			Shows detailed network adapter information.		
winipcfg /release 0			Releases DHCP configuration data for all TCP/IP adapters.		

IP Security Monitor

OS: Windows 2000

Function	Starts the IP Security Monitor in Windows.
Syntax	ipsecmon

File Name:	ipsecmon.exe	Directory:	\winnt\system32	Type:	External

iprop

OS: Windows NT4

Function	Installs or uninstalls the Microsoft OLE property set implementation.
Syntax	iprop [options...]

/i	Installs Microsoft OLE property set implementation.
/u	Uninstalls Microsoft OLE property set implementation.
/c	Verbose mode. Shows more information.

File Name:	iprop.exe	Directory:	\winnt\system32	Type:	External
iprop /i			Installs Microsoft OLE property set implementation.		

ipsec6

OS: Windows XP

Function	Manipulates IPv6 IPsec security policies and associations.
Syntax	ipsec6 option

SP *{ interface }*	Shows security policies.
SA	Shows security associations.
L *file*	Loads security policies and associations from the specified file.
S *file*	Saves security policies and associations to the specified file.
D SP *index*	Deletes the specified security policy.
D SA *index*	Deletes the specified security association.
M *switch*	Enables or disables mobile IPv6 security checks. (Can be either ON or OFF.)

File Name:	ipsec6.exe	Directory:	\windows\system32	Type:	External

ipseccmd

OS: Windows XP

Function	Configures Internet Protocol Security (IPsec) policies in a directory service or in a local or remote registry.
Syntax	ipseccmd [*computer*] [options...] ipseccmd [*computer*] mode [option]

	The following options and parameters are for use with Dynamic and Static mode. (Adds anonymous rules to the existing IPsec policy.)
	The following option is required:
-f *FilterList*	Specifies one or more filter specifications for quick mode security associations (SA).
-n *NegotiationPolicyList*	Specifies a list of security methods for securing traffic defined by the filter list.
-t *TunnelAddr*	The tunnel endpoint for tunnel mode. Specify either a DNS name or IP address.
-a *AuthMethodList*	Specifies a list of authentication methods.
-1s *SecurityMethodList*	Specifies a list of key exchange security methods.
-1k *MainModeRekeySettings*	Specifies the main mode SA rekey settings.
-1p	Enables master key perfect forward secrecy.
-1f *MMFilterList*	Specifies a list of filter specifications for main mode SAs.
-1e *SoftSAExpirationTime*	Sets the expiration time for soft SAs in seconds.
-soft	Enables soft SAs.
-confirm	Prompts for confirmation before adding the rule.
	The following two options can't be combined:
-dialup	Specifies that the rule only applies to remote access or dial-up connections.
-lan	Specifies that the rule only applies to network connections.
	The following option can only be used alone:
-u	Deletes all dynamic rules.
/?	Shows help information.

continued

computer	The computer to add the rule to.
	The following options and parameters are for use with the Static mode (creates named policies and named rules):
	The following three options are required:
-w *Type*[:*Location*]	Specifies where the policies and rules are written.
Type	Is where the policies and rules are written. Use "reg" for registry or "ds" for AD.
Location	Specifies the remote computer where the policies and rules should be written.
-p *Name*[:*Interval*]	Specifies the policy and how often it is check for changes. (The interval is specified in minutes.)
-r *Name*	Specifies the rule.
	The following two options can't be combined:
-x	Specifies that the local registry policy is assigned.
-y	Specifies that the local registry policy is unassigned.
-o	Deletes the rule or policy
	The following options and parameters are for use with the Query mode (the Query mode shows information from the IPsec database):
filters	Shows main mode and quick mode filters.
policies	Shows main mode and quick mode policies.
auth	Shows main mode authentication methods.
stats	Shows statistics on Internet Key Exchange (IKE) and IPsec.
sas	Shows main mode and quick mode security associations (SAs).
all	Shows all of the data types.
File Name: `ipseccmd.exe`	**Directory:** \windows\system32 **Type:** External

ipv6

OS: Windows XP

Function	Installs, uninstalls, configures, and shows information for the IP version 6 protocol.
Syntax	ipv6 options...

install	Installs IPv6 on the computer.
uninstall	Removes IPv6 from the computer.
if *{ number }* [-v]	Shows information in the specified interface number, or all if not specified. (-v gives more information.)
ifc options...	Changes attributes on specified interface.
number	Specifies the interface to change the attributes on.
[[-]forwards]	Turns forwarding on/off.
[[-]advertises]	Turns advertising on/off.
[mtu *size*]	Sets the MTU size in bytes.
[site *identifier*]	Sets the site identifier for the interface.
ifd *number*	Deletes the specified interface.
nc [options...]	Shows the contents of the neighbor cache.
{ number }	Shows only the cache on the specified interface.
{ address }	Shows only the cache on the specified address.
ncf [options...]	Flushes the neighbor cache entries.
{ number }	Flushes only the neighbor cache related to the specified interface.
{ address }	Flushes only the neighbor cache related to the specified address.
rc [option]	Shows the contents of the route cache.
{ number address }	Shows only the route cache for the specified address by the specified interface.
rcf [options...]	Flushes the route cache entries.
{ number }	Flushes the route cache related to the specified interface.
{ address }	Flushes the route cache related to the specified address.
bc	Shows the contents of the binding cache.
adu options...	Adds or removes a unicast or anycast address assignment on an interface.
number/address	Specifies the interface and the address to assign.
{ time }	Specifies the valid lifetime for the assignment. Infinite if not specified. (Set the lifetime to 0 to remove the assignment.)
[*/ptime*]	Specifies the preferred lifetime.
{ mode }	Is either `anycast` or `unicast`.
spt	Shows the current contents of the site prefix table.
spu options...	Adds, removes, or alters the specified prefix.

continued

prefix	Specifies the prefix to use.
number	Specifies the interface to use.
{ time }	Sets the lifetime for the prefix. Set to 0 to remove the prefix.
rt	Shows the current contents of the routing table.
rtu options...	Adds, removes, or alters a route in the routing table.
prefix	Specifies the route prefix to use.
number[/*address*]	Specifies the interface (and address) to use.
{ lifetime }	Specifies the lifetime on the route. Set to 0 to remove the route.
{ preference }	Specifies the preference for the route.
[publish]	Makes the route publish.
[age]	Makes the route to age. If not specified, the lifetime will not count down.
[spl *length*]	Specifies the site prefix length to use with the route.
File Name: `ipv6.exe`	**Directory:** \windows\system32 — **Type:** External

ipxroute (2000,XP) — OS: Windows 2000, XP

Function	Shows and alters information about the routing tables used by the IPX protocol.
Syntax	ipxroute *ACTION*

ACTION	**The following are the IPX Routing actions to use.**
servers [/type=*value*]	Shows the specified server type's Service Access Point (SAP) table.
stats [options...]	Shows or clears the IPX router statistics. (Default is `/show`.)
/show	Shows IPX router interface statistics.
/clear	Clears IPX router interface statistics.
table	Shows the routing table for IPX in a sorted network number order.
ripout *network*	Checks the IPX stack's routing table for the specified network.
resolve *ID name*	Resolves the specified adapter name to either its specified GUID or its ID name.
ACTION	**The following are the Source Routing Actions to use.**
board=*NR* [options...]	Queries or sets the parameters for the network adapter.
NR	Specifies the network adapter to use.
clear	Clears the source routing table.
def	Sends packets sent to an unknown address to the ALL ROUTES broadcast.
gbr	Sends packets sent to address FFFFFFFFFFFF to the ALL ROUTES broadcast.
mbr	Sends packets sent to address C000 xxxx xxxx to the ALL ROUTES broadcast.
remove=*MAC*	Removes the specified MAC address from the routing table.
config	Shows where IPX is bound to.
File Name: `ipxroute.exe`	**Directory:** **2000:** \winnt\system32, **XP:** \windows\system32 — **Type:** External
Tip:	This command is useful for IPX troubleshooting or information about IPX.
ipxroute servers	Shows all server types in the network.
ipxroute ripout 00000050	Checks the IPX stack's routing table for the specified network.

ipxroute (NT4) — OS: Windows NT4

Function	Shows and alters information about the routing tables used by the IPX protocol.
Syntax	ipxroute [options...]

	These three options are for IPX routing. Choose only one.
servers [/type=*NR*]	Specifies the server type and shows the SAP table for it.
stats /*show* | *clear*	Shows (default) or clears the statistic for the IPX router interface.
table	Shows the IPX routing table, sorted by network number. Used standalone.
	These are the options for source routing.
board=*NR*	Specifies the network adapter card to check.
clear	Clears the source routing table.
def	Sends packets with an unknown address to the ALL ROUTES broadcast.
gbr	Sends packets with address FFFF FFFFF FFFFF to the ALL ROUTES broadcast.
mbr	Sends packets with multicast address C000 xxxx xxxx to the ALL ROUTES broadcast.
remove=*address*	Removes the specified MAC address from the source routing table.
config	Shows information on all the bindings for which IPX is configured.
File Name: ipxroute.exe	**Directory:** \winnt\system32 — **Type:** External
ipxroute table	Shows the IPX routing table, sorted by network number.

ISDN Configuration Wizard

OS: Windows 98/ME

Function	Configures your ISDN adapter.
Syntax	cfgwiz32
File Name:	`cfgwiz32.exe`
Directory:	\windows\system
Type:	External

ismserv

OS: Windows 2000 Server

Function	Starts or stops the intersite messaging service.
Syntax	ismserv [options...]
/install	Adds the service to the service control manager database.
/remove	Removes the service from the service control manager database.
/debug	Starts the service as a normal process, not under the service control manager.
File Name:	`ismserv.exe`
Directory:	\winnt\system32
Type:	External

jetpack

OS: Windows NT4 Server, 2000 Server

Function	Fixes or compresses different versions of the DHCP database.
Syntax	jetpack [option] *database1 database2*
-351db	Compresses NTS 3.51 or earlier databases.
database1	Specifies the database that is compressed or fixed.
database2	The temporary database that stores db information while compressing.
2000, XP:	
-40db	Compresses NTS 4.0 databases. (If no option is given, then a NTS 5.0 database is assumed.)
File Name:	`jetpack.exe`
Directory:	**NT4, 2000:** \winnt\system32, **NT4 TS:** \wtsrv\system32
Type:	External
jetpack ucg.mdb ucgtemp.mdb	Compresses the ucg database and uses the temporary database ucgtemp.mdb to store information during compression.

jview

OS: Windows 9x/ME, 2000

Function	Executes java .class files.
Syntax	jview [options..] *classname { arguments... }*
/?	Shows help information.
/cp *path*	Specifies the path to class.
/cp:p *path*	Adds a path before the class path.
/cp:a *path*	Adds a path after the class path.
/n *namespace*	Specifies the namespace to execute in.
/p	Pauses the application if an error occurs.
/v	Verifies all classes.
/d: *name=value*	Defines system properties.
/a	Runs the Applet Viewer.
classname	Specifies the .class file to be executed.
arguments...	Specifies argument to the class file.
File Name:	`jview.exe`
Directory:	**9x/ME:** \windows, **2000:** \winnt\system32
Type:	External
jview /p java.class	Runs java.class and will pause if an error occurs.

kb16

OS: Windows 2000, XP

Function	Configures a keyboard for a specific language. The second syntax is used in the CONFIG.SYS file.
Syntax	kb16 *{ xx [, [yyy } [,file]]]* [options...]
/E	Specifies that an enhanced keyboard is installed.
/ID:*NR*	Specifies the keyboard in use. (Only used for countries with more than one keyboard layout.)
xx	Specifies the code for the keyboard layout.
yyy	Specifies the code page to use. If not used, the current code page is used.
file	Specifies the name and location of the keyboard definition file.
path	Specifies the location of the KEYB.COM file.
File Name:	`kb16.com`
Directory:	**2000:** \winnt\system32, **XP:** \windows\system32
Type:	External
kb16 sv,,c:\winnt\system32\keyboard.sys	Configures the keyboard to use a Swedish keyboard layout.

keyb

OS: Windows Common

Function	Is used to configure a keyboard for a specific language. The second syntax is for use in the CONFIG.SYS file.
Syntax	keyb *{ xx* [, [*yyy }* [*,file*]]] [options...] INSTALL=*{ path }*KEYB.COM *{ xx* [, [*yyy }* [*,file*]]] [options...]

/E	Is used to specify that an enhanced keyboard is installed.
/ID:*NR*	Is used to specify the keyboard in use. (Only used for countries with more then one keyboard layout.)
xx	Is used to specify the code for the keyboard layout.
yyy	The code page to use. If not used, the current code page is used.
file	Is used to specify the name and location of the keyboard definition file.
path	The location of the KEYB.COM file.

File Name:	`keyb.com`	**Directory:**	\windows\command	**Type:**	External

Tip: Please see the command `chcp` for a list of available code pages.

keyb sv,,c:\dos\keyboard.sys	Configures the keyboard to use a Swedish keyboard layout.
INSTALL=c:\dos\keyb.com sv,,c:\dos\keyboard.sys	Configures the keyboard to use a Swedish keyboard layout.

keyb, kb16

OS: Windows NT4

Function	Configures a keyboard for a specific language. If used without a parameter it shows the current code. The install syntax is used in the `CONFIG.NT` file.
Syntax	keyb *{ xx }* kb16 *{ xx* [, [*yyy }* [*,file*]] [/E] [/ID:*NR*] install=*{ path }* KEYB.COM *{ xx } { yyy } { file }* [/E] [/ID:*NR*]

xx	Specifies the keyboard country code.
path	Specifies the location of the KEYB.COM file.
	These options are only used for the kb16 and are ignored by keyb:
yyy	Specifies which code page to use for character set.
file	Specifies the name and location of the keyboard definition file.
/E	Specifies that an enhanced keyboard is installed.
/ID:*NR*	Specifies keyboard. (Only used for countries with more then one keyboard layout.)

File Name:	`keyb.com`	**Directory:**	\winnt\system32	**Type:**	External

kb16 us	Configures the keyboard to use the layout for United States.

kill

OS: Windows NT4 Terminal Server

Function	Kills processes on a terminal server.
Syntax	kill *process* [options...]

/SERVER:*name*	Specifies the server where the process is running. /ID or /A must be used.
/ID:*session ID*	Specifies in which session the process should be killed.
/A	Kills processes in all sessions.
/V	Verbose mode. Shows more information.
process	Specifies the process name or id.

File Name:	`kill.exe`	**Directory:**	\wtsrv\system32	**Type:**	External

ldifde

OS: Windows 2000 Server

Function	Imports or exports information from Active Directory.
Syntax	ldifde options...

-i	Imports information. Default is to export.
-f *file*	Specifies the file to use.
-s *server*	Specifies the domain controller to use
-c *str1 str2*	Replaces str1 with str2. This can move data between different domains.
-v	Verbose mode. Shows more information.
-j *path*	Specifies where the log files are located.
-t *port*	Specifies the LDAP port to use. (Default is 389.)
-u	Specifies that Unicode format is to be used.
-?	Shows help information.

continued

	The following options are used in export mode:		
-d *root*	Specifies the root at which to start LDAP search.		
-r *filter*	Specifies a filter for searching. (Default is (objectClass=*).)		
-p *scope*	Specifies what scope to search. Can be Base, OneLevel, or Subtree.		
-l *list*	Specifies a comma-separated list of attributes to look for.		
-o *list*	Specifies a comma-separated list of attributes to omit.		
-g	Doesn't do page search.		
-m	Uses SAM logic for export.		
-n	Specifies that no binary values are exported.		
	The following options are used in import mode:		
-k	Specifies that error messages are ignored.		
-y	Specifies that lazy commit should increase the perforation.		
	The following option changes credentials:		
-a *d-name password*	Specifies the distinguished username and password of the user to use.		
-b *name domain password*	Specifies the username, domain, and password for the user to use.		
File Name: `ldifde.exe`	**Directory:** /winnt/system32	**Type:**	External
ldifde -f outfile.txt	Exports information to outfile.txt.		

License Compliance Wizard

OS: Windows NT4 Server, 2000 Server

Function	Starts the License Compliance Wizard, which allows the user to search for any unlicensed products within a domain.		
Syntax	lcwiz		
File Name: `lcwiz.exe`	**Directory:** **NT4, 2000:** \winnt\system32, **NT4 TS:** \wtsrv\system32	**Type:**	External
Warning:	One of many tools that can be used by your local Domain Administration Police force to keep you in line.		
lcwiz	Starts the License Compliance Wizard.		

License Manager

OS: Windows NT4 Server, 2000 Server

Function	Starts the License Manager, allowing license management for the specified domain.		
Syntax	llsmgr *{ domain }*		
domain	Specifies the domain from the command line. Use the GUI for search capabilities.		
File Name: `llsmgr.exe`	**Directory:** **NT4, 2000:** \winnt\system32, **NT4 TS:** \wtrsv\system32	**Type:**	External
Warning:	One of many tools available for the Domain Administration Police.		
llsmgr UCGDOMAIN	Starts the License Manager on UCGDOMAIN. This can be re-selected later.		

loadfix

OS: Windows XP

Function	Loads a program above the first 64K of conventional memory, then runs it.		
Syntax	loadfix *program*		
program	Specifies the program to load.		
File Name: `loadfix.com`	**Directory:** \windows\system32	**Type:**	External
Tip:	Use LOADFIX to load a program if you have received the message "Packed file corrupt".		
loadfix c:\program.exe	Loads c:\program.exe above the first 64k and runs it.		

Local Security Settings

OS: Windows 2000 Server

Function	Configures and manages the security settings assigned to a group policy or an object or a local system policy.		
Syntax	secpol.msc		
File Name: `secpol.msc`	**Directory:** \winnt\system32	**Type:**	External

Local Users and Groups

OS: Windows 2000 Server

Function	Manages local users and groups. It's possible to add local and global users and global groups to local groups and also to set their rights and permissions.		
Syntax	lusrmgr.msc		
File Name: `lusrmgr.msc`	**Directory:** \winnt\system32	**Type:**	External

lodctr

lodctr	**OS:** Windows NT4, 2000, XP
Function	Updates the Performance Monitor counter names and explains text for an extensible counter DLL.
Syntax	lodctr [option] *file*

computername	Specifies the computer name. If none given, the local computer is used.
file	Specifies the file that contains the counter name definitions and explain text.
File Name: `lodctr.exe`	**Directory:** **NT4, 2000:** \winnt\system32, **XP:** \windows\system32 **Type:** External

logman

logman	**OS:** Windows XP
Function	Schedules and manages event trace log collections and performance counters on local and remote computers.
Syntax	logman *ACTION* [options...]

ACTION	**The following six actions are available and can't be combined:**
create *type name*	Creates collection queries
type	The type for which the queries should be created. Valid are: counter or trace.
name	Specifies a name for the collection.
start *name*	Starts the specified data collection query.
stop *name*	Stops the specified data collection query.
delete *name*	Deletes the specified data collection query.
query *{ name }*	Queries collection properties. If used alone, all collections are shown. (Use the keyword PROVIDERS to show all registered event trace providers.)
update *name*	Updates the specified collection query.
	The following five options can be used with all actions:
-s *computer*	The remote computer where the command should be executed.
-u *user password*	Specifies the user to run with.
--u	Reverts to using the Performance Logs and Alerts service account.
-config *file*	The name and path of a file containing command options.
-mode *mode*	Specifies the event trace logger mode to use.
	The following 19 options can be used with the CREATE and UPDATE actions:
-y	Overwrites settings without prompting.
-b *time*	The time when the collection should start. The time format is: m/d/yyyy h:mm:ss.
-e *time*	The time when the collection should end. The time format is: m/d/yyyy h:mm:ss.
-rf *time*	Collects data during the specified time. (The time format to use is [[hh:]mm:]ss.)
-m start | -m stop	Starts or stops the collection manually. Can't be combined with -b, -e, -rf options
-f *format*	The format of the output file. Valid formats are BIN, BINCIRC, CSV, TSV or SQL.
-r	Repeats the collection every day at the specified time period.
--r	Disables the repeat option.
-o *output*	The path of the output file or the SQL database where the data will be written.
-a	Appends the file.
--a	Overwrites instead of appending.
-v *NR date*	Adds version control information to the end of the output file.
	The following two parameters can't be combined:
NR	Specifies a numeric format.
datetime	Specifies a date/time format. Use the following format: mmddhhmm.
--v	Disables the version option.
-rc *file*	Runs the specified command when the files are closed.
--rc	Disables the run command option.
-max *value*	Specifies the maximum size of the log file in megabytes.
--max	Disables the maximum file limit.
-cnf *time*	Starts on a new file after the specified time or when the size limit is reached. (The time format to use is [[hh:]mm:]ss.)
--cnf	Disables the create new file option.
	The following six options can be used with the UPDATE action:
-max *value*	Specifies the maximum size of the log file in megabytes.
-o *output*	The path of the output file or the SQL database where the data will be written.
-ft *time*	The flush time interval for data collections. The time format is [[hh:]mm:]ss.
-fd *name*	Flushes all active buffers to a disk.

continued

-f *format*	The format of the output file. Valid formats are BIN, BINCIRC, CSV, TSV, or SQL.
-o *output*	The path of the output file or the SQL database where the data will be written.
	The following 15 options can be used with the CREATE action:
	The following two options can't be combined:
-c *path ...*	Is used to specify the performance counter to collect.
-cf *file*	A file containing a list of counters to collect.
-si *time*	Specifies the time interval used for performance counter collection. (The time format to use is [[hh:]mm:]ss.)
-ln *name*	The name to use for the Event Trace logging session.
-rt	Runs the event trace session in real time and doesn't save to a file.
--rt	Disables real time logging.
	The following two options can't be combined:
-p *provider*	Specifies a single Event Trace provider to enable.
-pf *file*	A file containing a list of Event Trace providers to enable.
-ul	Runs the event trace session in user mode.
--ul	Disables user mode and reverts to kernel mode.
-bs *size*	Specifies the buffer size in kilobytes for the data collection.
-ft *time*	The flush time interval for data collections. The time format is [[hh:]mm:]ss.
-nb *min max*	The minimum and maximum numbers of buffers for data collection.
-fd *name*	Flushes all active buffers to a disk.
-ets	Sends commands directly to the Event Trace session.

File Name:	`logman.exe`	**Directory:**	\windows\system32	**Type:**	External

logoff

OS: Windows NT4 Terminal Server, 2000 Server, XP

Function	Logs the user out of the terminal session specified.
Syntax	logoff *{ session }* [options...]

session	Specifies the session name or session ID to log off.
/SERVER:*servername*	Specifies a terminal server with the user to log off.
/V	Verbose mode. Shows more information.

File Name:	`logoff.exe`	**Directory:**	**NT4 TS:** \wtsrv\sytem32, **2000:** \winnt\System32, **XP:** \windows\system32	**Type:**	External

Logview

OS: Windows NT4 Server

Function	Shows log files.
Syntax	logview

File Name:	`logview.exe`	**Directory:**	\winnt\system32, **TS:** \wtsrv\system32\	**Type:**	External

lpq

OS: Windows NT4, 2000, XP

Function	Shows the status of a print queue on a remote computer running the LPD service.
Syntax	lpq -S *server* -P *printer* [-l]

-S *server*	Specifies the name or IP-Address to the computer running the LPD service.
-P *printer*	Specifies the print queue.
-l	Verbose mode. Shows more information.

File Name:	`lpq.exe`	**Directory:**	**NT4, 2000:** \winnt\system32, **NT4 TS:** \wtrsv\system32, **XP:** \windows\system32	**Type:**	External

lpq -S 192.168.1.2 -P LaserJet	Shows the status of the specified server.
lpq -S 192.168.1.2 -P LaserJet –l	Shows status with more details.

lpr

OS: Windows NT4, 2000, XP

Function	Sends a print job to a computer running the LPD server.
Syntax	lpr [options...] *file*

	The following two options are required:
-S *server*	Specifies the name or IP-Address to the computer running the LPD service.
-P *printer*	Specifies the print queue.
-C *class*	Specifies the contents of the banner page.
-J *job*	Specifies the print job.

continued

-o *option* *file* **2000, XP:** -x -d	Specifies the type of file to print. Default is text. Use -ol for binary file. Specifies the file to print. Maintains compatibility with SunOS 4.1.x and prior. Sends data file first.

File Name:	`lpr.exe`	**Directory:**	**NT4, 2000:** \winnt\system32, **NT4 TS:** \wtrsv\system32, **XP:** \windows\system32	**Type:**	External

lpr -S 192.168.1.2 -P print01 ucg.txt	Prints ucg.txt on 192.168.1.2 print01.
lpr -S ucgserv -P print01 -d ucg.txt	Sends data file first, then prints the file.

macfile

OS: Windows NT4 Server, 2000 Server

Function	Creates, deletes, or manages volumes and directories for Macintosh users.
Syntax	macfile *ACTION* [options...]

ACTION	**The following are the four actions that can be used:**
volume	Manages the volumes.
directory	Alters or creates directories.
forkize	Joins data and resource forks into one file.
server	Configures the SFM server.
	These options are used with the volume action:
/add	Adds a new volume to share.
/remove	Erases a volume.
/set	Alters the settings for a volume.
/name:*name*	Specifies the volume name. This option is required when using volume.
/path:*path*	Specifies the root path for the volume. Requires /add.
/readonly:*true or false*	Specifies whether the volume is read-only. Can be true or false (default is false).
/guestallowed:*true or false*	Specifies whether guest login is allowed. Can be true or false (default is true).
/password:	Specifies the password to use (default is none).
/maxusers:*nr*	Specifies a maximum number of users to allow. Use a number or UNLIMITED.
	These options are used with the directory action:
/path:*path*	Specifies the directory path to alter. This option is required for directory.
/owner:*name*	Specifies the username for the owner of the directory.
/group	Specifies the group name for the directory.
/permission:*string*	Specifies the permission for the directory. This is an 11-bit binary number. (It has the form: 11111010110. Use macfile directory for the value.)
	These options are used with the forkize action:
/type:*type*	Specifies the type name.
/creator:*name*	Specifies the creator.
/datafork:*file*	Specifies the file to use as the data fork.
/resourcefork:*file*	Specifies the file to use as the resource fork.
/targetfile:*file*	Specifies the target file.
	These options are used with the server action:
/maxsessions:*nr*	Specifies the maximum number of sessions allowed. Use a number or UNLIMITED.
/loginmessages:*message*	Specifies a login message to show at login.
/guestallowed:*true or false*	Specifies whether a guest login is allowed. Can be true or false (default is true).
	This may be used with any action:
/server:*name*	Specifies the server name to use (default is local).

File Name:	`macfile.exe`	**Directory:**	\winnt\system32	**Type:**	External

macfile volume /add /name:ucg /path:c:\ucg	Creates a share for the volume ucg with a root in c:\ucg.

Magnifier

OS: Windows ME, 2000, XP

Function	Magnifies a section of the screen to make it easier to read.
Syntax	magnify

File Name:	`magnify.exe`	**Directory:**	**ME:** \windows\system, **2000:** \winnt\system32, **XP:** \windows\system32	**Type:**	External

Maintenance Wizard

OS:	Windows 98/ME				
Function	Increases the computer's performance.				
Syntax	tuneup				
File Name:	`tuneup.exe`	**Directory:**	\windows	**Type:**	External

Make Compatible

OS:	Windows Common				
Function	Enables older applications that are not Windows 95 compatible to run.				
Syntax	mkcompat *{ file }*				
file		Specifies the program to run.			
File Name:	`mkcompat.exe`	**Directory:**	\windows\system	**Type:**	External

makecab

OS:	Windows 2000, XP				
Function	Compresses and adds the file to a new or existing .CAB file. Overwrites any existing files within the .CAB file.				
Syntax	makecab [options...] *{ srcfile } { dstfile }*				
/V{ level }		Shows verbose information. Level can be 1 to 3 and specifies which level to use.			
/D *variable=value*		Defines the specified variable with the given value.			
/L *directory*		Specifies the directory in which to put the created .CAB file.			
/F *file*		Specifies a directive file with information on how to create the .CAB file.			
		The following arguments are required if the /F option isn't specified:			
srcfile		Specifies the files to put in the .CAB file.			
dstfile		Specifies the .CAB file to create.			
File Name:	`makecab.exe, diantz.exe`	**Directory:**	**2000:**\winnt\system32,**XP:** \windows\system32	**Type:**	External
makecab mydata.txt data.cab			Compresses the file mydata.txt to data.cab		
makecab yourdata.txt data.cab			Adds the file yourdata.txt to data.cab		

Management Instrumentation Tester

OS:	Windows ME, 2000, XP				
Function	A graphical utility for program developers to test their own drivers written for new Microsoft WMI standard.				
Syntax	wbemtest				
File Name:	`wbemtest.exe`	**Directory:**	**ME:** \windows\system\wbem, **2000:** \winnt\system32\wbem, **XP:** \windows\system32\wbem	**Type:**	External

Media Player

OS:	Windows 98/ME				
Function	Starts the Microsoft Media Player, which plays MIDI, wave, CD, video, and ActiveMovie files.				
Syntax	mplayer				
File Name:	`mplayer.exe`	**Directory:**	\windows	**Type:**	External

Media Player 32

OS:	Windows 2000, XP				
Function	Starts the 32-bit Media Player in Windows, which allows playing, editing, and embedding multimedia files.				
Syntax	mplay32				
File Name:	`mplay32.exe`	**Directory:**	**2000:** \winnt\system32, **XP:** \windows\system32	**Type:**	External
mplay32			Starts the Media Player.		

Message Queue Service

OS:	Windows 2000, XP				
Function	Starts the Microsoft Message Queue Server.				
Syntax	mqsvc				
File Name:	`mqsvc.exe`	**Directory:**	**2000:** \winnt\system32, **XP:** \windows\system32	**Type:**	External
mqsvc			Starts the Message Queue Server service.		

Microsoft Backup

OS:	Windows 95, 98				
Function	Is used to back up, or restore, data to a tape, floppy, removable media or a file.				
Syntax	**98:** msbackup **95:** backup				
File Name:	`msbackup.exe`	**Directory:**	\Program Files\accessories\backup	**Type:**	External

Microsoft File Transfer

OS:	Windows 95
Function	Transfers and receives files over a modem connection using a wizard.
Syntax	filexfer

File Name:	`filexfer.exe`	Directory:	\windows	Type:	External

Microsoft Management Console (2000)

OS:	Windows 2000
Function	Hosts administrative tools called snap-ins. The utility enables the users to create their own customized administrative tool.
Syntax	mmc { *file* }

file	The name and location of the console to open.
	The following snap-ins are available, depending on the installed software:
Active Directory Domains and Trusts	Manages Active Directory domains and trusts.
Active Directory Sites and Services	Shows and manages Sites and Services.
Active Directory Users and Computers	Manages AD objects, such as users, groups, and organizational units.
ActiveX Control	Adds an ActiveX control to the console.
Certificates	Shows the contents of the certificate stores.
Component Services	Manages COM+ applications.
Computer Management	Manages the computer.
Device Manager	Shows all installed hardware devices and their properties.
DHCP	Manages the DHCP service.
Disk Defragmenter	Defragments disks on the computer.
Disk Management	Manages disks and volumes.
Distributed File System	Builds a single logical namespace using existing files shares.
DNS	Administers the DNS service.
Event Viewer	Shows event logs.
Fax Service Management	Manages the Fax service on the computer.
Group Policy	Configures Group Policy Objects.
Indexing Service	Manages the indexing service.
Internet Authentication Services (IAS)	Configures the IAS.
Internet Information Services	Manages the Internet Information Services.
IP Security Policy Management	Administers IPsec policies for secure communications.
Local Users and Groups	Administers local users and groups.
Performance Logs and Alerts	Configures performance data logs and alerts.
QoS Admission Control	Manages the QoS Admission Control.
Removable Storage Management	Manages removable storage.
Routing and Remote Access	Configures the Routing and Remote Access services.
Security Configuration and Analysis	Provides security configuration and analysis for computers using security templates.
Security Templates	Edits security templates.
Services	Starts, stops, and configures Windows services.
Shared Folders	Shows all shared folders, current sessions, and open files.
System Information	Shows system information, for example, hardware resources.
Telephony	Manages the Telephony service.
Terminal Services Configuration	Manages Terminal service connections.
WINS	Manages the Windows Internet Name Service (WINS).
WMI Control	Manages the Windows Management Instrumentation (WMI) service. (The availability of the snap-ins depends on the installed software.)

File Name:	`mmc.exe`	Directory:	\winnt\system32	Type:	External

mmc c:\windows\system32\compmgmt.msc	Opens the Computer Management snap-in.

Microsoft Management Console (XP)

OS:	Windows XP
Function	A utility used to host different administrative tools called snap-ins. Users can create their own snap-ins.
Syntax	mmc { *file* }

continued

file	The name and location of the console to open. **The following snap-ins are available, depending on the installed software:**
Active Directory Domains and Trusts	Manages Active Directory domains and trusts.
Active Directory Sites and Services	Shows and manages Sites and Services.
Active Directory Users and Computers	Manages AD objects, such as users, groups, and organizational units.
ActiveX Control	Adds an ActiveX control to the console.
Certificate Templates	Manages the certificate templates.
Certificates	Shows the contents of the certificate stores.
Certification Authority	Shows the certificate database and cancels issued certificates.
Component Services	Manages COM+ applications.
Computer Management	Manages the computer.
Device Manager	Shows all installed hardware devices and their properties.
DHCP	Manages the DHCP service.
Disk Defragmenter	Defragments disks on the computer.
Disk Management	Manages disks and volumes.
Distributed File System	Builds a single logical namespace using existing file shares.
DNS	Administers the DNS service.
Event Viewer	Shows event logs.
Fax Server	Manages the Fax service on the computer.
Group Policy	Configures Group Policy Objects.
Indexing Service	Manages the indexing service.
Internet Authentication Services (IAS)	Configures the IAS.
Internet Information Services	Manages the Internet Information Services.
IP Security Monitor	Shows the IP Security status.
IP Security Policy Management	Administers IPsec policies for secure communications.
Local Users and Groups	Administers local users and groups.
Performance Logs and Alerts	Configures performance data logs and alerts.
QoS Admission Control	Manages the QoS Admission Control.
Remote Desktops	Connects to terminal servers.
Remote Storage	Manages secondary storage media.
Removable Storage Management	Manages removable storage.
Routing and Remote Access	Configures the Routing and Remote Access services.
Security Configuration and Analysis	Provides security configuration and analysis for computers using security templates.
Security Templates	Edits security templates.
Services	Starts, stops, and configures Windows services.
Shared Folders	Shows all shared folders, current session, and open files.
System Information	Shows system information (for example, hardware resources).
Telephony	Manages the Telephony service.
Terminal Services Configuration	Manages Terminal service connections.
WINS	Manages the Windows Internet Name Service (WINS).
WMI Control	Manages the Windows Management Instrumentation (WMI) service. (The availability of the snap-ins depends on the installed software.)

File Name:	`mmc.exe`	**Directory:**	\windows\system32	**Type:**	External

mmc c:\windows\system32\compmgmt.msc	Opens the Computer Management snap-in.

Microsoft Script Debugger

OS: Windows 2000

Function	Starts a window-based debugger for scripts.
Syntax	msscrdbg

File Name:	`msscrdbg.exe`	**Directory:**	\Program Files\Microsoft Script Debugger	**Type:**	External

Microsoft System Information

OS: Windows 98/ME, 2000, XP

Function	Starts a graphic interface to show lots of information about the system or start other diagnostic programs.
Syntax	msinfo32

File Name:	`msinfo32.exe`	**Directory:**	\Program Files\Common Files\Microsoft Shared\msInfo	**Type:**	External

migrate

OS: Windows NT4 Terminal Server

Function	Migrates selected parts of ini-files from Windows 3.1.
Syntax	migrate option *{ directory }*

/INI	Migrates information for Windows app, desktop settings, and file associations.
/GROUP	Imports program groups not on the terminal server.
/REGDATA	Imports register information from reg.dat.
directory	Specifies directory of the configuration files (default is current directory).

File Name:	`migrate.exe`	**Directory:**	\wtsrv\system32	**Type:**	External

migrate /GROUP	Imports program groups from Windows 3.11

Migration

OS: Windows NT4 Server

Function	Moves groups, files, and users from NetWare to NT.
Syntax	nwconv

File Name:	`nwconv.exe`	**Directory:**	\winnt\system32, **TS:** \wtsrv\system32\	**Type:**	External

mlset32

OS: Windows NT4

Function	Installs the Windows messaging system.
Syntax	mlset32

File Name:	`mlset32`	**Directory:**	\program file\windows nt\windows messaging	**Type:**	External

Mobile Synchronize

OS: Windows 98/ME, 2000, XP

Function	Synchronizes files between your mobile computer and network server. Can also schedule when to synchronize.
Syntax	mobsync

File Name:	`mobsync.exe`	**Directory:**	**98/ME:** \windows\system, **2000:** \winnt\system32, **XP:** \windows\system32	**Type:**	External

Modem Quicktest

OS: Windows 2000

Function	Tests basic operations on the connected modem.
Syntax	qtest32

File Name:	`qtest32.exe`	**Directory:**	\winnt\system32\dllcache	**Type:**	External

mofcomp

OS: Windows ME, 2000, XP

Function	Verifies and compiles MOF (Meta Object Family) files.
Syntax	mofcomp [options...]

-check	Checks the syntax for accuracy.
-N:*path*	Specifies the path for the default namespace to load.
-class:updateonly	Doesn't create any new classes.
-class:safeupdate	Updates only if there isn't conflict.
-class:forceupdate	Attempts to resolve any conflicts and then performs the update.
-class:createonly	Doesn't modify any classes that currently exist.
-instance:updateonly	Doesn't create any additional instances.
-instance:createonly	Creates only new instances and will not modify any instances currently existing.
-U:*user*	Specifies the username.
-P:*password*	Specifies the password.
-A:*authority*	Specifies the type of authority to use, for example: NTLMDOMAIN:Domain.
-B:*file*	Specifies the Creates a binary MOF file, doesn't add to DB.
-WMI	Checks the WMI syntax checks. (Requires the -B switch.)
-AUTORECOVER	Uses MOF for listing files that were compiled during DB recovery.
-Amendment:*lang*	Creates different language versions for the MOF file specified by lang (such as MS_4??).
-MOF:*path*	Specifies the file for MOF files that aren't language-specific.
-MFL:*path*	Specifies the file for MOF files that are language-specific.

continued

File Name:	mofcomp.exe	**Directory:**	**ME, XP:** \windows\system32\wbem, **2000:** \winnt\system32\wbem	**Type:**	External
mofcomp -N:root\default c:\moffile.mof			Compiles the moffile.mof using the default name space.		
mofcomp -check -N:root\default c:\moffile.mof			Checks the syntax in the c:\moffile.mof.		

mountvol

OS: Windows 2000, XP

Function	Creates, deletes, or lists volume mount points for the system.
Syntax	mountvol *{ drive } { path* option *}*

drive	Specifies the NTFS drive letter to use.
path	Specifies the drive: and path to the NTFS directory where the mountpoint will be.
	Select only one of these three options:
name	Creates the specified volume mount point
/d	Deletes the volume mount point from the specified directory.
/l	Shows the volume name for the specified mount point.
/?	Shows help information including valid volume names and their current mount points.

File Name:	mountvol.exe	**Directory:**	**2000:** \winnt\system32, **XP:** \windows\system32	**Type:**	External
Tip:	Delete the drive letter from the volume before assigning a new one using this command.				
mountvol r:\mount01 /d			Removes the mountpoint from r:\mount01.		
mountvol r:\mount01 /l			Lists mounted volume name in r:\mount01.		

mqbkup

OS: Windows 2000, XP

Function	Makes backup and restores the messages queuing system.
Syntax	mqbkup [options...] *directory*

-b	Backs up to file.
-r	Restores from file.
-y	Answers yes to all questions.
-?	Shows help information.
directory	Specifies the backup directory..

File Name:	mqbkup.exe	**Directory:**	**2000:** \winnt\system32, **XP:** \windows\system32	**Type:**	External
mqbkup -b c:\backup			Creates the backup in c:\backup.		
mqbkup -r c:\backup			Restores the backup from c:\backup.		

mqexchng

OS: Windows 2000

Function	Installs the Microsoft Message Queuing Exchange Connector.
Syntax	mqexchng

/Q	Specifies quiet mode.
/T:*directory*	Specifies a full path to a working directory.
/C	Extracts only the files when used together with /T.
/C:*command*	Overrides the install program.

File Name:	mqexchng.exe	**Directory:**	\winnt\system32	**Type:**	External

mqmig

OS: Windows 2000

Function	Upgrades Microsoft message queuing.
Syntax	mqmig [options...]

/r	Specifies that recover mode is to be used.
/c	Specifies cluster mode.
/s *server*	Specifies the server to recover from (recover mode) or upgrade from (cluster mode).
/u	Tries to upgrade remote MQIS databases.
/?	Shows help information.

File Name:	mqmig.exe	**Directory:**	\winnt\system32\dllcache	**Type:**	External

mrinfo

OS: Windows 2000, XP

Function	Queries a multicast router with an Internet Group Management Protocol (IGMP) message and shows the configuration information about it.
Syntax	mrinfo [options...] *destination*

-n	Shows IP addresses in numeric format.
-i *address*	Sends the mrinfo query from the specified IP address.
-t *sec*	Specifies the seconds to wait for a neighbor query reply.
-r *NR*	Specifies the number of times to retry to do a neighbor query.
-?	Shows help information.
destination	Specifies the address or name of the multicast router.

File Name:	`mrinfo.exe`	**Directory:**	**2000:** \winnt\system32, **XP:** \windows\system32	**Type:**	External

mscdex

OS: Windows Common

Function	Is used to provide access to CD-ROM drives and assigns the CD-ROM a drive letter.
Syntax	mscdex [options...]

/D:*drive*	Is used to specify the drive signature of the CD-ROM device driver.
/E	Is used to allow the use of expanded memory.
/K	Allows MS-DOS to recognize CD-ROM volumes encoded in Kanji.
/S	Is used to enable sharing of CD-ROM drives when using MS-NET or Windows.
/V	Shows memory statistics when starting.
/L:*letter*	Is used to specify the drive letter to assign to the CD-ROM drive.
/M:*NR*	Is used to specify the number of sector buffers.

File Name:	`mscdex.exe`	**Directory:**	\windows\command	**Type:**	External

mscdex /D:MSCD000 /L:D	Gives access to the CD-ROM device MSCD000 and assigns it the letter D:.

mscdexnt

OS: Windows NT4, 2000, XP

Function	Enables the Microsoft CD Extension in Windows.
Syntax	mscdexnt

File Name:	`mscdexnt.exe`	**Directory:**	**NT4, 2000:** \winnt\system32, **NT4 TS:** \wtsrv\system32, **XP:** \windows\system32	**Type:**	External

mscdexnt	Enables CD extensions.

msg

OS: Windows NT4 Terminal Server, 2000 Server, XP

Function	Sends a message to the specified user or users.
Syntax	msg *ACTION* [options...] *message*

ACTION	**You must select one of the following actions:**
username	Specifies the user to receive the message.
sessionname	Specifies the session to receive the message.
sessionid	Specifies the sessionid to receive the message.
@*filename*	Specifies a file with users, session names, and session IDs to receive the message.
*	Sends the message to all users on the system.
	The following options are required and can be combined:
/server: *servername*	Specifies another Terminal Server, if not to use the current.
/time: *seconds*	Specifies time to wait for a confirmation for the user who received the message.
/w	Waits for response from users.
/v	Shows information on current action.
message	Specifies the text to send. If no message is entered it will send STDIN. (To send a text within a file, type (<) and then the filename.)

File Name:	`msg.exe`	**Directory:**	**NT4 TS:** \wtsrv\system32, **2000:**\winnt\system32, **XP:** \windows\system32	**Type:**	External

msg MYLES Let's go and eat.	sends the message "Let's go and eat." to user MYLES.
msg * Let's go and eat.	Sends the message "Let's go and eat." to all users.

Narrator

OS:	Windows 2000, XP
Function	A text-to-speech program that can help people with reduced vision.
Syntax	narrator
File Name:	`narrator.exe`
Directory:	**2000:** \winnt\system32, **XP:** \windows\system32
Type:	External

ndspsvr

OS:	Windows NT4 Terminal Server
Function	Manages settings for preferred NDS server used for logons.
Syntax	ndspsvr option
/QUERY	Shows the current settings.
/ENABLE:*server*	Specifies the NDS server to use.
/DISABLE	Removes the use of the preferred NDS server.
File Name:	`ndspsvr.exe`
Directory:	\wtsrv\system32
Type:	External
ndspsvr /QUERY	Shows the current status.

net accounts

OS:	Microsoft Common
Function	Updates the user accounts database and modifies logon policies.
Syntax	net accounts [options...]
/forcelogoff:*minutes*	Specifies the number of minutes before closing a user's connection. No disables.
/forcelogoff | no	Disables the forcelogoff.
/minpwlen:*length*	Specifies the minimum password length
/maxpwage:*days* | unlimited	Sets the maximum password age. Unlimited doesn't require password changes.
/minpwage:*days*	Sets the minimum password age.
/uniquepw:*number*	Requires the user to select a unique password for specified number of times.
/domain	Performs the operations on the primary domain controller.
File Name:	`net.exe`
Directory:	\windows, **NT, 2k:** \winnt\system32, **XP:** \windows\system32
Type:	External
net accounts /minpwlen:5	Sets the minimum password length to five characters.
net accounts /forcelogoff:no	Disables forced logoffs.

net computer

OS:	Microsoft Common
Function	Adds or a deletes a computer in the domain.
Syntax	net computer *host* option
/add	Adds a computer to the domain.
/del	Removes a computer from the domain.
host	Specifies the computer to add or remove.
File Name:	`net.exe`
Directory:	\windows, **NT, 2k:** \winnt\system32, **XP:**\windows\system32
Type:	External
net computer \\\\DESKTOP /add	Adds the computer named DESKTOP to the domain.

net continue

OS:	Microsoft Common
Function	Reactivates a suspended service.
Syntax	net continue *service*
service	Specifies the service to reactivate.
File Name:	`net.exe`
Directory:	\windows, **NT, 2k:** \winnt\system32, **XP:**\windows\system32
Type:	External
net continue Workstation	Reactivates the workstation service.

net diag

OS:	Windows Common
Function	Tests the network connections between computers and shows the information gathered.
Syntax	net diag *{ /computer }*
/computer	Specifies either a computer to perform a diagnostic on or a diagnostics server name.
File Name:	`net.exe`
Directory:	\windows
Type:	External
net diag ucgcomputer	Specifies ucgcomputer as a diagnostics server if it runs as such or a computer to test.

net file

OS: Microsoft Common

Function	Shows and modifies shared files.				
Syntax	net file *{ id }* [/close]				
/close	Closes the specified file and releases locked records.				
id	Specifies the files identification number.				
File Name:	net.exe	**Directory:**	\windows, **NT, 2k:** \winnt\system32, **XP:** \windows\system32	**Type:**	External

net group

OS: Microsoft Common

Function	Is used to show, add, or modify global groups on Windows Server domains.				
Syntax	net group *{ group } { names... }* [options...]				
/comment:"*text*"	Adds a comment to a new or existing group.				
/add	Adds a group, or adds a user to a group.				
/delete	Deletes a group, or deletes a user from a group.				
/domain	Performs the operation on the primary domain controller.				
group	Specifies the name of the group to add, delete, or expand.				
names...	Specifies a list of users to add to the specified group.				
File Name:	net.exe	**Directory:**	\windows, **NT, 2k:** \winnt\system32, **XP:** \windows\system32	**Type:**	External
net group marketing /add /comment:"Marketing"	Adds the group marketing with the comment "Marketing."				
net group marketing Johan Sara /add	Adds the users Johan and Sara to the marketing group.				

net helpmsg

OS: Microsoft Common

Function	Shows help information on a Windows network error message.				
Syntax	net helpmsg *NR*				
NR	Specifies the number of the error message to get help on.				
File Name:	net.exe	**Directory:**	\windows, **NT, 2k:** \winnt\system32, **XP:** \windows\system32	**Type:**	External

net init

OS: Windows Common

Function	Is used to load network drivers and protocol without tying them to the Protocol Manager; see `net start` for tying them to the Protocol Manager. This can't be run in a MS-DOS window.				
Syntax	net init [/dynamic]				
/dynamic	Initializes the Protocol Manager in dynamical mode.				
File Name:	net.exe	**Directory:**	\windows	**Type:**	External
net init	Loads the protocol and network drivers.				

net localgroup

OS: Microsoft Common

Function	Shows, adds, or modifies local groups. If used without parameters, it shows a list of all the local groups.				
Syntax	net localgroup *{ group } { names... }* [options...]				
/comment:"*text*"	Adds a comment to a new or existing group.				
/add	Adds a group, or adds a group or user to a group.				
/delete	Deletes a group, or deletes a group or user from a group.				
/domain	Performs the operation on the primary domain controller.				
group	Specifies the name of the group to add, delete, or expand.				
names...	Specifies a list of users or global groups to add to the specified group.				
File Name:	net.exe	**Directory:**	\windows, **NT, 2k:** \winnt\system32, **XP:** \windows\system32	**Type:**	External
net localgroup marketing /add /comment:"Marketing"	Adds the group marketing with the comment "Marketing."				
net localgroup marketing Johan Sara /add	Adds the users Johan and Sara to the marketing group.				

net logoff

OS:	Windows Common
Function	Disconnects the computer from the network. Cannot be run from a MS-DOS window.
Syntax	net logoff [/yes]

/yes	Skips prompting before disconnecting.
File Name: net.exe	**Directory:** \windows **Type:** External
net logoff	Disconnects from the network after prompting.

net logon

OS:	Windows Common
Function	Logs on the network as a workgroup member. Cannot be run in a MS-DOS window.
Syntax	net logon *{ user }* [options...]

/domain:*name*	Specifies the Windows NT or LAN Manager domain to log on to.
/savepw:no	Skips prompting for creation of a password list file.
/yes	Skips prompting for verifying or information input.
user	Specifies the user to log on as.
?	Prompts for password.
password	Specifies the password to use.
File Name: net.exe	**Directory:** \windows **Type:** External
net logon	Logs on to default domain and prompts for user and password.

net name

OS:	Microsoft Common
Function	Adds or deletes a messaging name (alias). If no parameters are given, a list is shown of all names currently in use.
Syntax	net name *{ name }* [option]

/add	Adds a name to the computer.
/delete	Deletes a name from the computer.
name	Specifies the name to add.
File Name: net.exe	**Directory:** \windows, **NT, 2k:** \winnt\system32, **XP:** \windows\system32 **Type:** External
Note:	The messenger service must be running to use this command.
net name secretary /add	Adds the name "secretary" to the computer.

net password

OS:	Windows Common
Function	Is used to alter the password on a password list, a server, or a domain.
Syntax	net password *{ oldpass }* net password *{ \\server }* [/domain:*name*] *{ user }*

	The following two can't be combined.
/domain:*name*	Specifies the Windows NT or LAN manager domain to change password on.
server	Specifies the Windows NT or LAN manager server to change password on.
user	Specifies the user to change password for.
useroldpass	Specifies the user's old password.
usernewpass	Specifies the user's new password.
oldpass	Specifies the old password for the password list file.
newpass	Specifies the new password for the password list file.
File Name: net.exe	**Directory:** \windows **Type:** External
net password \\ucgserver PeterS bla blabla	Changes the password for PeterS on ucgserver from bla to blabla.

net pause

OS:	Microsoft Common
Function	Pauses a running service.
Syntax	net pause *service*

service	Specifies the service to pause.
File Name: net.exe	**Directory:** \windows, **NT, 2k:** \winnt\system32, **XP:** \windows\system32 **Type:** External

net send

OS: Microsoft Common

Function	Sends a message to other users, computers, or messaging names.
Syntax	net send *{ name }* [option] *message*

	Only one of the following parameters must be specified:
*	Sends a message to all users in your group.
/domain[:*name*]	Sends a message to all users in your domain/workgroup or the specified one.
/users	Sends a message to all users connected to the server.
name	Specifies the computer to send the message to.
message	Specifies the text to send.

File Name: `net.exe` **Directory:** \windows, **NT, 2k:** \winnt\system32, **XP:** \windows\system32 **Type:** External

net send * Hello Everybody	Sends the message to all users in your group.
net send /domain Hello Everybody	Sends the message to every user in your domain or workgroup.

net session

OS: Microsoft Common

Function	Shows or disconnects sessions between the local computer and the connected clients.
Syntax	net session [*host*] [/delete]

/delete	Ends a computer's session. If no computer is specified, all sessions are ended.
host	Specifies the computer to list or disconnect the sessions from.

File Name: `net.exe` **Directory:** \windows, **NT, 2k:** \winnt\system32, **XP:** \windows\system32 **Type:** External

net session \\desktop /delete	Ends the session for the specified computer.
net session /delete	Ends all sessions.

net share

OS: Microsoft Common

Function	Creates, deletes, or shows shared resources that other users on the network can gain access to.
Syntax	net share *{ sharename=resource }* [options...] net share *sharename* /delete

/users: *NR*	The maximum number of users that are allowed to access the resource simultaneously.
/unlimited	Allows an unlimited number of users to access the resource.
/remark:"*text*"	A small description of the share that users will see when browsing the network.
/delete	Removes the share.
/cache *value*	**Windows 2k Only:** Valid values are: Manual, Automatic, or No
/cache *value*	**Windows XP Only:** Valid values are: Manual, Documents, Programs, or None.
sharename=resource	Specifies the name of share and the full path to the directory or resource to share.

File Name: `net.exe` **Directory:** \windows, **NT, 2k:** \winnt\system32, **XP:** \windows\system32 **Type:** External

net share mp3files /delete	Removes the share mp3files (to the disappointment of many users).
net share	Shows all current resources that you are sharing.

net statistics

OS: Microsoft Common

Function	Shows the statistic log for the local workstation or server service.
Syntax	net statistics [option]

workstation	Shows statistics for the workstation service.
server	Shows statistics for the server service.

File Name: `net.exe` **Directory:** \windows, **NT, 2k:** \winnt\system32, **XP:** \windows\system32 **Type:** External

net user

OS: Microsoft Common

Function	Adds, deletes, or modifies user accounts or shows information on user accounts.
Syntax	net user *{ user } { password }* [options...]

/add [options...]	Adds a user.
/active:no | yes	Selects whether the user account should be active or not (default is active).
/comment:"*test*"	Adds a comment to the user account.
/countrycode:*NR*	Sets the country code for the user; 0 means that the default is used.

continued

/expires:*date* | never	Sets an expiration date for the user account; never means account doesn't expire.
/fullname:"*name*"	Specifies the full name of the user.
/homedir:*path*	Sets the home directory path.
/passwordchg:yes | no	Specifies whether the user can change the password or not; default is yes.
/passwordreq:yes | no	Specifies whether a password is required or not.
/profilepath:*path*	Specifies a path for the user's logon profile.
/scriptpath:*path*	Specifies the path to the user's login script.
/times:*times* | all	Sets the time the user can log in; all means that the user always can log in.
/usercomment:"*test*"	Adds or changes the user comments.
/workstations:*computers...* | *	Specifies on which computer the user can log in; * means all computers.
/delete	Deletes a user account.
/domain	Performs the operation on the primary domain controller.
user	Specifies the username to add, delete, or show information on.
password	Sets the password. Use an asterisk * to be prompted for the password.

File Name:	`net.exe`	**Directory:**	\windows, **NT, 2k:** \winnt\system32, **XP:** \windows\system32	**Type:**	External

net user Johan /add /expires:never /passwordchg:no	Adds the user Johan with some extra options.
net user Johan	Shows information on the user Johan.
net user Johan /delete	Deletes the user account Johan.

net ver

OS: Windows Common

Function	Shows the workgroup redirector's version and type.
Syntax	net ver

File Name:	`net.exe`	**Directory:**	\windows	**Type:**	External

netsh

OS: Windows 2000, XP

Function	The NetShell utility that works as a scripting interface for monitoring and configuring the system.
Syntax	netsh [options...] { *command* }

	Valid options:
?	Shows help information.
-a *file*	Specifies the alias file.
-c *context*	Specifies the context.
-r *host*	Specifies the remote machine.
	Select only one of these two options when specifying an object:
-f *file*	Specifies that the given script file will be used.
command	Specifies that the given command will be used.
	Valid commands:
command ?	Shows help information specific to the listed command such as options and usage.
aaaa	Uses the `aaaa` subcontext.
add	Adds a configuration entry to the list of entries.
delete	Deletes a specified configuration entry from the list of entries.
dhcp	Uses the `dhcp` subcontext.
dump	Shows a specified configuration script.
exec	Runs a specified script file.
help	Shows the list of available commands.
interface	Uses the `interface` subcontext.
ras	Uses the `ras` subcontext.
routing	Uses the `routing` subcontext.
set	Updates the specified configuration.
show	Shows various forms of information based upon the object that is specified.
wins	Uses the `wins` subcontext.
XP:	
bridge	Changes to the "netsh bridge" context. (Only available in XP Professional).

File Name:	`netsh.exe`	**Directory:**	**2000:** \winnt\system32, **XP:** \windows\system32	**Type:**	External

netsh aaaa show version	Shows the version of the subcontext aaaa configuration database.
netsh wins dump	Sends configuration settings to STDOUT.
netsh routing ipx	Uses the ipx routing context.

NetWare user access for TS

OS: Windows NT4 Terminal Server

Function	Gives users on a NetWare server access to the Terminal Server.
Syntax	nw2nt
File Name:	`nw2nt.exe`
Directory:	\wtsrv\system32
Type:	External
Note:	Require Gateway Service for NetWare.

NetWatcher

OS: Windows Common

Function	Monitors and shares network resources and shows the number of open files and connections on your computer.
Syntax	netwatch
File Name:	`netwatch.exe`
Directory:	\windows
Type:	External

Network and Dial-up Connections

OS: Windows NT4, 2000, XP

Function	Starts the Network and Dial-up Connections interface used to handle dial-up networking properties.
Syntax	rasphone [options...]

-v	Forbids entry rename with -a or -e.
-f *file*	Specifies the phonebook file.
	The following options can't be combined with each other.
-a *entry*	Shows the new entry popup dialog.
-e *entry*	Shows the edit entry popup dialog.
-c *entry*	Shows the clone entry popup dialog.
-d *entry*	Shows the dial entry popup dialog.
-h *entry*	Hangs up the entry quietly.
-r *entry*	Deletes the entry quietly.
-l*flag link*	Makes the dial-up shortcut to execute the program with the specified flag.
flag	Specifies one of the commands a, e, v, c, d, h, or r.
link	The shortcut file to change.
	The -s option must be used alone.
-s	Shows the status popup dialog.

File Name:	`rasphone.exe`
Directory:	**NT4, 2000:** \winnt\system32, **XP:** \windows\system32
Type:	External

rasphone -d ucg	Shows the dial entry dialog box for the "ucg" entry.
rasphone -ld c:\temp\dialup.lnk	Makes the shortcut open the dial popup dialog.

Network Client Administrator

OS: Windows NT4 Server

Function	Starts the Network Client Administrator, which can create boot disks or a set of disks for installing network client software while also providing `remoteboot` client information.
Syntax	ncadmin
File Name:	`ncadmin.exe`
Directory:	\winnt\system32, **TS:** \wtsrv\system32
Type:	External

Network DDE agent

OS: Windows NT4

Function	Starts the Network DDE agent, which starts network DDE if it detects DDE network activity on the local computer.
Syntax	nddeagnt
File Name:	`nddeagnt.exe`
Directory:	\winnt\system32, **TS:** \wtsrv\system32
Type:	External
Note:	This doesn't detect a remote computer trying to connect. The network DDE can be initiated with `netdde.exe`.

Network Monitor

OS: Windows NT4, 2000 Server

Function	Starts the monitor for network traffic, clients, and servers.
Syntax	netmon
File Name:	`netmon.exe`
Directory:	**NT4 TS:** \wtsrv\system32\netmon, **2000:** \winnt\system32\dllcache
Type:	External

Network Setup Wizard

OS: Windows XP

Function	Configures the computer to run on a network. The wizard will guide the user through the installation steps.
Syntax	netsetup
File Name:	`netsetup.exe`
Directory:	\windows\system32
Type:	External

nslookup

OS:	Windows NT4, 2000, XP
Function	A diagnostic tool that shows information from Domain Name System (DNS) name servers.
Syntax	nslookup *{ host }* *{ server }* [options...]

-option	Specifies subcommands given as an option; each subcommand must have a - (ex: -querytype=MX -debug).
host	Specifies the host to look for.
server	Specifies the DNS-server to use. - alone shows the used server.
	The following are subcommands used within nslookup:
help	Shows help information.
exit	Exits the program.
finger *{ user }*	Fingers the optional user at current host.
server *name*	Sets the default server to the specified one, using current default server.
lserver *name*	Sets the default server to the specified one, using initial server.
root	Changes the default server to the server for the root of the Domain Name Space.
view *filename*	Sorts and lists the output of previous ls command.
set	Changes configuration in NSLOOKUP. Use set all to view current settings.
all	Shows options, current server, and host.
debug	Shows debug information.
nodebug	Disables debugging information.
d2	Shows exhaustive debugging information.
nod2	Disables exhaustive debugging information.
defname	Appends domain name to each query.
nodefname	Disables append of domain name to each query.
recurse	Asks for recursive answer to query.
norecurse	Disables ask for recursive answer to query.
search	Uses domain search list.
nosearch	Disables domain search list.
vc	Uses a virtual circuit.
novc	Disables a virtual circuit.
domain=*name*	Sets default domain name to the specified one.
srchlist=*name*[/*list...*]	Sets domain to the specified one and search list to the specified one.
root=*name*	Sets root server to the specified one.
retry=*number*	Sets the number of retries.
timeout=*seconds*	Sets initial timeout interval to specified seconds.
type=*type*	Specifies the query type, type can be any of: A, ANY, CNAME, MX, NS, PTR ,SOA, SRV.
querytype=*type*	Same as type.
class=*type*	Specifies the query class.
msxfr	Uses MS fast zone transfer.
nomsxfr	Disables MS fast zone transfer.
ixfrver=*version*	Specifies current version to use in IXFR transfer request.
ls [options...] *domain* [> *filename*]	Shows addresses in the specified domain.
-a	Shows canonical names and aliases.
-d	Shows all records.
-t *type*	Shows all records with the type specified.
filename	Writes output to the specified file.
name	Specifies the host to look for.

File Name: `nslookup.exe`	**Directory:**	**NT4, 2000:** \winnt\system32, **XP:** \windows\system32	**Type:** External
nslookup ucgbook.com		Looks up the address for ucgbook.com.	
nslookup ucgbook.com ns.newstyledata.net		Looks up the address for ucgbook.com using ns.newstyledata.net as server.	

NT File Replication Service Upgrade

OS: Windows 2000 Server

Function	Upgrades the NT File Replication Service directories from the specified share volume.
Syntax	ntfrsupg option *{ volume }*

-D	Handles the upgrade as the first upgrade made.
-RESTORE	Deletes the replicated directories. A volume isn't needed.
-Y	Deletes the directories without prompt. Can only be used with -RESTORE option.
volume	Specifies the share volume to upgrade from.

File Name: `ntfrsupg.exe` **Directory:** \winnt\system32 **Type:** External

ntbackup (2000)

OS: Windows 2000

Function	Starts the GUI-based version of Backup. It can also be used with the command line.
Syntax	ntbackup ntbackup backup [systemstate] [options...]

systemstate	Backs up the System State data.
/J "*jobname*"	Specifies the name to use for the backup in the log file.
/P "*poolname*"	Specifies the media pool to use.
/G "*guidname*"	Overwrites or appends to the specified tape. Can't be combined with /P option.
/T "*tapename*"	Overwrites or appends to the specified tape. Can't be combined with /P option.
/N "*medianame*"	Specifies a new name for the tape. Can't be combined with the /A option.
/F "*file*"	Backs up to the specified file. Can't be combined with /P, /G, and /T options.
/D "*description*"	Is used to specify a name for each backup set.
/DS "*server*"	Backs up the Directory Service file on the specified Microsoft Exchange Server.
/IS "*server*"	Backs up the Information Store file on the specified Microsoft Exchange Server.
/A	Performs an append operation. Requires /G or /T. Not compatible with /P.
/V:yes | no	Specifies whether the data should be verified after the backup.
/R:yes | no	Restricts access to only the owner or Administrators of the file.
/L:*type*	Selects the type of log file to use. Uses f (full), s (summary), or n (none).
/M *type*	Specifies the type of backup to perform: normal, copy, differential, incremental, or daily.
/RS:yes | no	Specifies whether the Removable Storage database should be backed up.
/HC:on | off	Specifies whether hardware compression, if available, should be used.
/UM	Uses the first available media, formats it and uses it for the current backup job.
bksfile	The Backup Selection file (.BKS) to use. Must be created with the GUI interface.

File Name: `ntbackup.exe` **Directory:** \winnt\system32 **Type:** External

ntbackup backup d:\ /j "Job 1" /a /t "TAPE01" /m normal	Creates a normal backup of the d: drive to the specified tape.

ntbackup (NT4)

OS: Windows NT4

Function	Starts the NT Backup. This command can also be controlled by a batch file.
Syntax	ntbackup [/nopoll] [/missingtape] ntbackup *operation path* [options...]

	User input is required with the following parameters:
/nopoll	Erases the tape. Can't be used with any other parameter.
/missingtape	Specifies a missing tape in a backup set including several tapes.
	The following options may be used in a batchfile:
/a	Appends the backup after the last backup set on the tape.
/v	Verifies the operation.
/r	Restricts access.
/d "*text*"	Gives a description to the backup contents.
/b	Backs up the local registry.
/hc:on	Sets the hardware compression on.
/hc:off	Sets the hardware compression off.
/t *type*	Sets the backup type specified with one of the following options:
normal	Backs up all selected items and marks the archive bits accordingly.
copy	Does the same as `normal`, but doesn't mark the archive bit.

continued

incremental		Backs up selected files, modified since last backup, and marks the archive bits.			
differential		Does the same as incremental, but doesn't mark the archive bit.			
daily		Backs up only files that are changed the day the backup is run.			
/l "*filename*"		Specifies the filename to use in the backup log.			
/e		Makes the backup log to only include exceptions.			
/tape: *NR*		Specifies the tape drive to use for backup. The number was assigned during install.			
operation		Specifies whether to `backup` or `eject`.			
path		Specifies what paths of directories are to be backed up.			
File Name:	`ntbackup.exe`	**Directory:**	\winnt\system32	**Type:**	External
Tip:	If you do backups at home this command should be enough. You don't need to buy backup exec.				
ntbackup backup /v /l "backup.log"		As above but also adds a backup.log file.			
ntbackup backup /t NORMAL /d "Full Backup"		Starts a NORMAL backup with description "Full Backup."			

ntbackup (XP)

OS: Windows XP

Function	Starts the GUI-based version of Backup. It can also be used with the command line.
Syntax	ntbackup ntbackup backup [systemstate] [options...]

systemstate		Backs up the System State data.			
/J "*jobname*"		Specifies the name to use for the backup in the log file.			
/P "*poolname*"		Specifies the media pool to use.			
/G "*guidname*"		Overwrites or appends to the specified tape. Can't be combined with /P option.			
/T "*tapename*"		Overwrites or appends to the specified tape. Can't be combined with /P option.			
/N "*medianame*"		Specifies a new name for the tape. Can't be combined with the /A option.			
/F "*file*"		Backs up to the specified file. Can't be combined with /P, /G, or /T options.			
/D "*description*"		Specifies a name for each backup set.			
/A		Performs an append operation. Requires /G or /T not compatible with /P.			
/V:yes | no		Specifies whether the data should be verified after the backup.			
/R:yes | no		Restricts access to the owner or an administrator.			
/L:*type*		Selects the type of log file to use. Use f (full), s (summary), or n (none).			
/M *type*		Specifies the type of backup to perform. (Valid are: normal, copy, differential, incremental, or daily.)			
/RS:yes | no		Specifies whether the Removable Storage database should be backed up.			
/HC:on | off		Specifies whether hardware compression, if available, should be used.			
/UM		Uses the first available media, formats it, and uses it for the current backup job.			
/SNAP:on | off		Specifies whether the backup is a Volume Shadow Copy.			
bksfile		The Backup Selection file (.BKS) to use. Must be created with the GUI interface.			
File Name:	`ntbackup.exe`	**Directory:**	\windows\system32	**Type:**	External
ntbackup backup d:\ /j "Job 1" /a /t "TAPE01" /m normal		Creates a normal backup of the d: drive to the specified tape.			

ntdsutil

OS: Windows 2000

Function	Starts an interactive tool utility to perform database management on an Active directory store.
Syntax	ntdsutil *{ subcommands }*

subcommands	Specifies one command to perform. Takes the same command as the prompt.
	These commands can be used on the prompt:
?	Shows help information.
Authoritative restore	Restores the DIT database.
Domain management	Prepares to make a new domain.
Files	Manages NTDS database files.
Help	Shows help information.
IPDeny List	Alters the LDAP IP Deny List.
LDAP policies	Alters the LDAP protocol policies.
Metadata cleanup	Cleans up objects.
Popups *switch*	Sets whether popup is used.
Quit	Leaves the utility.
Roles	Alters tokens for NTDS role owner.

continued

Security account management Semantic database analysis		Alters the Security Account Database and removes duplicate SID. Checks a semantic database.			
File Name:	`ntdsutil.exe`	**Directory:**	\winnt\system32	**Type:**	External
ntdsutil help			Starts the ntdsutil utility and shows the help..		

ntsd (2000) — OS: Windows 2000

Function	The NT Symbolic Debugger for debug user-mode programs.
Syntax	ntsd [options...]

-?	Shows help information.
-2	Creates a separate screen window for the object being debugged.
-a*name*	Specifies the default extension DLL name.
-c *command*	Runs a specified debugger command.
-d	Sends debug output to the kernel debugger using `DbgPrint`.
-e	Uses hEventToSignal.
-g	Ignores any initial breakpoint in the object being debugged.
-G	Ignores any final breakpoint at the process termination.
-hd	Disables the heap manager validity check.
-i	Ignores any AV generated by the loader fixups on a pre–3.51 Windows NT system.
-lines	Uses line number information when available.
-n	Verbose mode. Shows more information for the symbol handler.
netsyms:[yes|no]	Allows symbol loading from a network path using yes. No prevents it.
-o	Debugs any processes started by the debugger.
-r *level*	Specifies the break error level to show. Valid values are 0–3.
-s	Prevents lazy symbol loads.
-t *level*	Specifies the error level to show. Valid values are 0–3.
-v	Verbose mode. Shows more information.
-w	Debugs 16-bit applications using a separate VDM.
	When using exceptions, select only one of these options:
-x	Deactivates break for AV exceptions.
-xd *{ NR }*	Deactivates stop for the specified exception.
-xe *{ NR }*	Activates stop for specified exception.
-z	Is reserved for OS/2 debug only.
	Only one of these three options may be selected:
--	Same as using `-G -g -o -p -1`.
-p *PID*	Specifies the Process ID to attach to.
command	Specifies the command to run during debug.
	Environment Variables:
_NT_SYMBOL_PATH=[Drive:][Path]	Specifies the symbol image path to use (Default is %SystemRoot%).
_NT_ALT_SYMBOL_PATH=[Drive:][Path]	Specifies an alternative symbol image path to use.
_NT_DEBUG_EXTENSIONS=dllname(s)	Specifies a semicolon separated list of debugger DLL extension names.

File Name:	`ntsd.exe`	**Directory:**	\winnt\system32	**Type:**	External

ntsd (XP) — OS: Windows XP

Function	Debugs user-mode programs.
Syntax	ntsd [options...]

-a*name*	Specifies the default extension DLL name.
-c *command*	Runs a specified debugger command.
-clines *NR*	Specifies the number of lines of history retrieved by a remote client.
-failinc	Causes incomplete modules and symbol loads to fail.
-d	Sends debug output to the kernel debugger using `DbgPrint`.
-g	Ignores any initial breakpoint in the object being debugged.
-G	Ignores any final breakpoint at the process termination.
-hd	Doesn't use the debug heap.
-o	Debugs any processes started by the debugger.
-p *PID*	Specifies the Process ID to attach to.

continued

-pd	Automatically detaches the debugger.
-pe	Specifies that any attach should be to an existing port.
-pn *name*	Specifies the process to attach to.
-pt *NR*	Specifies the interrupt time out.
-pv	Specifies that any attach should be noninvasive.
-r *level*	Specifies the break error level to show. Valid values are 0–3.
-robp	Allows that breakpoint is set in read-only memory.
-t *level*	Specifies the error level to show. Valid values are 0–3.
-w	Debugs 16-bit applications using a separate VDM.
-x	Deactivates break for AV exceptions.
-2	Creates a separate screen window for the object being debugged.
-i	Ignores any AV generated by the loader fixups on a pre-3.51 system.
-lines	Uses line number information when available.
-myob	Ignores any version mismatches in DBGHELP.DLL.
-n	Verbose mode. Shows more information for the symbol handler.
-noio	Disables all I/O for dedicated remoting servers.
-noshell	Disables the .shell command.
-qr *computer*	Queries the specified remote server.
-s	Prevents lazy symbol loads.
-ses	Enables strict symbol loading.
-sfce	Fails critical errors encountered during file searching.
-sicv	Ignores CV record when symbols are loading.
-snul	Disables automatic symbol loading for unqualified names.
-srcpath *path*	Specifies the source search path.
-v	Verbose mode. Shows more information.
-z *file*	Specifies the crash dumb file to debug.
-zp *file*	Specifies the crash dumb file.
-remote	Connects to a debugger session started with the `-server`
-server	Creates a debugger session that users can connect to using `-remote`.
-premote *transport:portid*	Specifies the process server to connect to.

File Name:	`ntsd.exe`	**Directory:**	\windows\system32	**Type:**	External

nw16

OS:	Windows NT4 Server, 2000, XP
Function	Loads the redirector for VDM NetWare. Used by 16-bit programs.
Syntax	nw16

File Name:	`nw16.exe`	**Directory:**	**NT4, 2000:** \winnt\system32, **XP:** \windows\system32	**Type:**	External

nwscript

OS:	Windows NT4 Server, 2000, XP
Function	Runs a NetWare script on your computer only if there is a connection with a NetWare server.
Syntax	nwscript

File Name:	`nwscript.exe`	**Directory:**	**NT4, 2000:** \winnt\system32, **NT4 TS:** \wtsrv\system32, **XP:** \windows\system32	**Type:**	External

odbcconf

OS:	Windows 9x, 2000, XP
Function	Performs MS Data Access Components (MDAC) install actions and configures ODBC drivers data sources.
Syntax	odbcconf [options...] [/A{*ACTION*}]

/C	Continues to execute actions even if a failure occurs.
/E	Removes the response file when actions are complete.
/F *file*	Creates a response file with the name specified by file.
/H	Shows help information.
/L*mode file*	Enables logging for the mode specified (see below) and saves it in the file specified.
mode	Specifies the mode type N, V, or D. N=normal, V=verbose, D=debug.
/R	Executes the actions after the next reboot.
/S	Is silent mode and will not show any error messages.
/A{*ACTION*}	Specifies the action. This option can be used multiple times.
REGSVR *path*	Specifies the path to the DLL files to register.
REGMDACVERSION *ver*	Registers the DLL files and specifies the correct MDAC version.

continued

SETFILEDSNDIR	Sets the default directory for File DSNs.
INSTALLDRVRMGR	Installs a new driver manager.
INSTALLDRIVER *config path*	Specifies a driver configuration and driver path.
INSTALLTRANSLATOR *config path*	Specifies a translator configuration and driver path.
CONFIGDRIVER *driver config*	Configures or reconfigures the specified driver using the driver parameters.
CONFIGDSN *driver value*	Specifies the DSN driver to configure and any attributes for the driver.
CONFIGSYSDSN *driver value*	Specifies the System DSN driver to configure and any attributes for the driver.

File Name:	`odbcconf.exe`	**Directory:**	**9x:** \windows\system, **2000:** \winnt\system32, **XP:** \windows\system32	**Type:**	External

odbcconf /e /f "responsefile.log"	Uses responsefile with odbcconf and deletes responsefile after installation.

On-Screen Keyboard

OS: Windows ME, 2000, XP

Function	Shows a miniature keyboard on your screen where you can click on characters instead of typing them in.
Syntax	osk

File Name:	`osk.exe`	**Directory:**	**ME:** \windows\system, **2000:** \winnt\system32, **XP:** \windows\system32	**Type:**	External

openfiles

OS: Windows XP

Function	Shows or disconnects files opened by network users.
Syntax	openfiles *ACTION* [/?]

	The following option can be used with all actions.
/?	Shows help information.
ACTION	**The following actions are available.**
/disconnect	The remote computer to connect to.
/s *host*	Specifies the user to run the command with. Default is the current user.
/u *{ domain\ }user*	Specifies the user to run the command with. Default is the current user.
/p *{ password }*	The password for the specified user. Prompts for input if skipped.
	The following three options can't be combined
/id *fileid*	Disconnects the file with the specified ID.
/a *user*	Disconnects all files opened by the specified user.
/o *mode*	Disconnects all files with the specified open mode. (Read, Write, or Read/Write)
/op *file*	Disconnects all files opened by the specified file.
/se *session*	Disconnects all files opened by the specified session. (The "*" wildcard can be used with the previous five options.)
/query	Shows the opened files.
/s *host*	Specifies the user to run the command with. Default is the current user.
/u *{ domain\ }user*	Specifies the user to run the command with. Default is the current user.
/p *{ password }*	The password for the specified user. Prompts for input if skipped.
/fo *format*	Specifies the output format to use. Valid are: TABLE, LIST, CSV.
/nh	Hides column header. Can only be used with the TABLE and CSV formats.
/v	Verbose mode. Shows more information.
/local ON | OFF	Enables or disables the system global flag "maintain object list." (A restart is required for the change to take effect.)

File Name:	`openfiles.exe`	**Directory:**	\windows\system32	**Type:**	External

openfiles /disconnect /a caduser1	Disconnects all files opened by the specified user.

os2

OS: Windows NT4, 2000

Function	Runs OS/2 application.
Syntax	os2 [options]

/P *file*	Specifies the application to run.
/C *arguments*	Specifies the arguments for the program.

File Name:	`os2.exe`	**Directory:**	\winnt\system32	**Type:**	External

os2 \P os2app.exe \C infile	Runs the specified application.

osuninst

OS:	Windows XP		
Function	Uninstalls Windows XP and reverts to the previously installed OS.		
Syntax	osuninst		
File Name:	osuninst.exe	**Directory:**	\windows\system32
Type:	External		

Outlook Express

OS:	Windows 2000, XP		
Function	Reads and sends e-mail messages. It can also access news-groups.		
Syntax	msimn		
File Name:	msimn.exe	**Directory:**	\Program Files\Outlook Express
Type:	External		

packager

OS:	Windows 9x, 2000, XP		
Function	Creates a package that can be inserted into a document where it's shown as an icon.		
Syntax	packager		
File Name:	packager	**Directory:**	**9x:** \windows, **2000:** \winnt\system32, **XP:** \windows\system32
Type:	External		

pathping (2000)

OS:	Windows 2000
Function	A route tracing tool that combines features of the ping and tracert commands with additional information.
Syntax	pathping [options...] *address*
-n	Doesn't resolve addresses to hostnames.
-h *number*	Specifies the maximum number of hops when searching.
-g *list*	Specifies a host list for source.
-p *time*	Sets the wait period in milliseconds between pings.
-q *number*	Specifies the number of queries per hop.
-w *time*	Sets the wait timeout in milliseconds for each reply.
-T	Specifies to test connectivity to each hop with Layer-2 priority tags.
-R	Tests if each hop is RSVP aware.
address	Specifies the target IP-address.
File Name: pathping.exe	**Directory:** \winnt\system32 **Type:** External
pathping -n 10.0.0.10	Ping 10.0.0.10 but don't resolve address to hostname.
pathping -h 2 10.0.0.10	Ping 10.0.0.10 if it is closer than or equal to 2 router hops.

pathping (XP)

OS:	Windows XP
Function	A route tracing tool that combines features of the ping and tracert commands with additional information.
Syntax	pathping [options...] *address*
-g *list*	Drops source routes in the specified host list.
-h *number*	Specifies the maximum number of hops when searching.
-i *address*	Uses the specified source address.
-n	Doesn't resolve addresses to hostnames.
-p *time*	Sets the wait period in milliseconds between pings.
-q *number*	Specifies the number of queries per hop.
-w *time*	Sets the wait timeout in milliseconds for each reply.
-P	Tests for RSVP path connectivity.
-R	Tests whether each hop is RSVP aware.
-T	Specifies to test connectivity to each hop with Layer-2 priority tags.
-4	Forces the use of IPv4.
-6	Forces the use of IPv6
File Name: pathping.exe	**Directory:** \windows\system32 **Type:** External
pathping -n 10.0.0.10	Ping 10.0.0.10 but don't resolve address to hostname.
pathping -h 2 10.0.0.10	Ping 10.0.0.10 if it is closer than or equal to 2 router hops.

pentnt

OS:	Windows NT4, 2000, XP
Function	Checks whether the floating-point division error is present in the Pentium chip, disables floating point hardware, and enables emulation.
Syntax	pentnt [option]
-c	Enables error detection. If the error is detected at startup, emulation is forced.
-f	Forces floating-point emulation and disables the floating-point hardware.

continued

-o -?		Enables floating-point hardware. Shows help information. (All options require rebooting.)			
File Name:	pentnt.exe	**Directory:**	**NT4, 2000:** \winnt\system32, **XP:** \windows\system32	**Type:**	External
pentnt -c			Enables error detection.		
pentnt -o			Re-enables the floating-point hardware.		

Performance Monitor (2000, XP)

OS: Windows 2000 Server, XP

Function	Starts the Performance Monitor console that monitors the system load. It will help to observe and test the system or parts of the system and also help to find any problems.				
Syntax	perfmon.msc				
File Name:	perfmon.msc	**Directory:**	**2000:** \winnt\system32, **XP:** \windows\system32	**Type:**	External

Performance Monitor (NT4)

OS: Windows NT4

Function	Monitors the performance of a computer. Including monitor resources used by specific programs and components, helps troubleshoot possible problems, or checks to see if new hardware is required.				
Syntax	perfmon				
		The following views are available in the GUI interface:			
Chart Alert Log Report		Gives you a chart where, for example, you can view the usage of the CPU and memory. Configures alert limits. When a limit is reached a program can be started. Specifies what to log and the log interval. Gives you the ability to create a report.			
File Name:	perfmon.exe	**Directory:**	\winnt\system32	**Type:**	External

peruser

OS: Windows NT4 Terminal Server

Function	Manages per-user file associations.				
Syntax	peruser option				
/QUERY /ENABLE /DISABLE		Shows the current status. Enables the file associations for per-users. Disables the file associations for per-users.			
File Name:	peruser.exe	**Directory:**	\wtsrv\system32	**Type:**	External
peruser /QUERY			Show the current status.		

Phone Dialer (2000, XP)

OS: Windows 2000, XP

Function	Makes voice, video, or conference calls over a network or a phone line via modem.				
Syntax	dialer				
File Name:	dialer.exe	**Directory:**	\Program Files\Windows NT	**Type:**	External

Phone Dialer (Win 98/ME)

OS: Windows 98/ME

Function	Lets you make telephone calls from your computer using your modem and sound card.				
Syntax	tlocmgr [options]				
/i *ID* /n *XXX* /x		Specifies the telephone ID to the location specified. Specifies the name to set for the new Telephony Location. Useful for laptops. Quits the program directly after defining the new Telephony Location.			
File Name:	tlocmgr.exe	**Directory:**	\windows\system	**Type:**	External

ping6

OS: Windows XP

Function	Verifies a connection to remote computer using IPv6.
Syntax	ping [options...] *address*
-t -a -n *count*	Pings the specified computer until interrupted by Ctrl+C. Determines the hostname from the specified address. Specifies the number of ECHO requests to send. Default is 4.

continued

-l *size* -w *timeout* -s *srcaddr* -r		Specifies the size of ECHO data. Sets the timeout in milliseconds. Specifies the source address to use. Tests reverse route, using routing header.			
File Name:	`ping6.exe`	**Directory:**	\windows\system32	**Type:**	External
ping -t IPv6Host		Pings IPv6Host until interrupted by CTRL+C.			
ping -n 3 -l 4096 IPv6Host		Pings IPv6Host 3 times with a data size of 4096 bytes.			

portuas — OS: Windows NT4

Function	Converts a LAN Manager 2.x user account database into an existing Windows NT user account database.				
Syntax	portuas -f *file* [options...]				
-f *file* -u *user* -v -codepage *codepage* -log *file*		Specifies the LAN Manager 2.x NET.ACC file. Specifies a single user or group to be inserted. Verbose mode. Shows more information. Specifies the OEM codepage the LAN Manager 2.x NET.ACC file is in. Creates a log file.			
File Name:	`portuas.exe`	**Directory:**	\winnt\system32	**Type:**	External

posix — OS: Windows NT4, 2000

Function	Runs POSIX-compliant applications.				
Syntax	posix /c *file { arguments }*				
file *arguments*		Specifies the POSIX-application to run. Specifies options to the program.			
File Name:	`posix.exe`	**Directory:**	\winnt\system32	**Type:**	External
posix /c prog		Runs the application in the POSIX environment.			

Power Management — OS: Windows ME

Function	Starts the power management in resident memory and puts the computer in stand-by mode after period.				
Syntax	pmres				
File Name:	`pmres.exe`	**Directory:**	\windows	**Type:**	External

print — OS: Windows XP

Function	Prints a text file to the specified output device. It can be used in the background.				
Syntax	print *file* [option]				
/d:*device* /? *filename*		Specifies the device to print on: LPT1-3 COM1-4. Shows help information. Specifies the file to print.			
File Name:	`print.exe`	**Directory:**	\windows\system32	**Type:**	External
print /d:lpt1 c:\winnt\textfile.txt		Prints the file c:\winnt\textfile.txt using the LPT1 port.			
print /d:com1 c:\data\document.txt		Prints the file c:\data\document.txt using the COM1 port.			

printimg — OS: Windows ME

Function	A quick and easy way to print your digital photos or scanned images.				
Syntax	printimg *picture*				
picture		Specifies the name of the picture you want to print.			
File Name:	`printimg.exe`	**Directory:**	\windows\system	**Type:**	External
Tip:	Be sure that you have color printer installed and load some photo paper if your printer supports it.				
printimg mombday.jpg		Prints a picture called mombday.jpg.			

Private Character Editor — OS: Windows 2000, XP

Function	Creates unique characters (up to 6400) used in the font library.				
Syntax	eudcedit				
File Name:	`eudcedit.exe`	**Directory:**	**2000:** \winnt\system32, **XP:** \windows\system32	**Type:**	External

Properties for Microsoft IME 2000

OS:	Windows 2000				
Function	Converts keystrokes into phonetics and ideographic characters.				
Syntax	imejpuex				
File Name:	`imejpuex.exe`	**Directory:**	\winnt\system32\dllcache	**Type:**	External

proxycfg

OS:	Windows XP				
Function	Configures WinHTTP Proxy. If used without any parameters, the current setting is shown.				
Syntax	proxycfg [options...]				
/d	Specifies that WinHTTP application should not use a proxy.				
/p *server* { *list* }	The proxy server to use and an optional list of servers accessed without a proxy.				
/u	Uses the current user's Internet Explorer settings for proxy. (This option doesn't work if IE automatically detecting proxy settings.)				
/?	Shows help information.				
File Name:	`proxycfg.exe`	**Directory:**	\windows\system32	**Type:**	External
proxycfg /p ucgproxy	Specifies the proxy to use for WinHTTP applications.				
proxycfg /d	Specifies that WinHTTP applications should not use a proxy.				

qappsrv

OS:	Windows NT4 Terminal Server, 2000 Server, XP				
Function	Shows available application terminal servers on the network.				
Syntax	qappsrv { *server* } [options...]				
/DOMAIN:*domain*	Shows information for the specified domain.				
/ADDRESS	Shows network and node addresses.				
/CONTINUE	Specifies that no pause after each screen is to take place.				
server	Specifies a terminal server to query.				
File Name:	`qappsrv.exe`	**Directory:**	**NT4 TS:** \wtsrv\system32, **2000:** \winnt\system32, **XP:** \windows\system32	**Type:**	External

qbasic

OS:	Windows NT4				
Function	An editor and compiler for the Basic computer language.				
Syntax	qbasic [options...] { *file* }				
/b	Starts the editor in black-and-white mode.				
/editor	Starts the MS-DOS editor.				
/g	Optimizes the update on a CGA monitor.				
/h	Shows the maximum number of lines possible on your screen.				
/mbf	Converts MKS$, MKD$, CVS, and CVD to MKSMBF$, MKDMBF$, CVSMBF, and CVDMBF.				
/nohi	Provides support for monitors without high intensity video support.				
/run	Executes the program before starting the editor. A file must be specified.				
/?	Shows help information.				
file	Specifies the file to open in the editor.				
File Name:	`qbasic.exe`	**Directory:**	\winnt\system32	**Type:**	External
qbasic /h c:\gorilla.bas	Opens the file c:\gorilla.bas with the maximum number of lines.				
qbasic /run c:\program.bas	Runs the program c:\program.bas before starting the editor.				

qobject

OS:	Windows NT4 Terminal Server				
Function	Shows information about object manager namespace for the system.				
Syntax	qobject { *object* }				
object	Specifies the name of the object to query or /DEVICE for the device objects.				
File Name:	`qobject.exe`	**Directory:**	\wtsrv\system32	**Type:**	External
qobject /DEVICE	Shows information about the device objects.				

QoS Admission Control

OS:	Windows 2000 Server
Function	Administers the rights on when and how users are allowed to use the subnet resources.
Syntax	acssnap.msc
File Name:	`acssnap.msc`
Directory:	\winnt\system32
Type:	External

qprocess

OS:	Windows NT4 Terminal Server, 2000 Server, XP
Function	Shows processes on a terminal server.
Syntax	qprocess *{ type }* [options...] *{ programname }*

/ID:*number*	Shows all processes running at the specified session.
/SERVER:*servername*	Specifies the terminal server to query.
/SYSTEM	Shows process information for system processes.
type	Specifies the type to query for, type can be *, processid, username or session name.
programname	Shows all processes associated with programname.
File Name: `qprocess.exe`	**Directory:** **NT4 TS:** \wtsrv\system32, **2000:** \winnt\system32, **XP:** \windows\system32 — **Type:** External
qprocess winword.exe	Shows all processes for winword.exe

query

OS:	Windows NT4 Terminal Server, 2000 Server
Function	Shows system information such as current allocation of resources and system status.
Syntax	query [options...]

object	Shows Object Manager Namespace information.
objectname	Specifies an object to query.
/device	Queries only a device object.
process	Shows process information.
processid	Shows processes from specified processid.
username	Shows all processes from specified username.
sessionname	Shows all processes running at the specified sessionname.
programname	Shows all processes associated with the specified programname.
/ID:*number*	Shows all processes running at the specified session number.
/server:*servername*	Specifies which Terminal Server to query.
/system	Shows process information for the system processes.
session	Shows Terminal Session information.
sessionname	Identifies the session with the specified sessionname.
username	Identifies the session with the specified username.
sessionid	Identifies the session with the specified sessionid.
/server:*servername*	Specifies which server to query. (Default is current.)
/mode	Shows the current line settings.
/flow	Shows the current flow control settings.
/connect	Shows the current connect settings.
termserver	Identifies the Terminal Server.
appserver	Specifies which Application Server to query.
/domain:*domain*	Shows information for the specified domain. (Default is current domain.)
/address	Shows network and node addresses.
/continue	Doesn't pause between each screen of information.
user	Shows user information on users logged on to the system.
username	Identifies the specified username.
sessionname	Identifies the session with the specified sessionname.
sessionid	Identifies the session with the specified sessionid.
/server:*servername*	Specifies which server to query. (Default is current.)
/?	Shows available options.
File Name: `query`	**Directory:** **NT4 TS:** \wtsrv\system32, **2000:** \winnt\system32 — **Type:** External
query session /mode	Shows the current line setting.
query termserver /address	Shows network and node addresses of current network.

quser

OS: Windows NT4 Terminal Server, 2000 Server

Function	Shows information about users logged on to the system.
Syntax	quser *{ name }* [/SERVER]

/SERVER:*servername*	Specifies the server to query.
name	Specifies the name to look for. Can be a username, session name, or ID.

File Name:	`quser.exe`	**Directory:**	**NT4 TS:** \wtsrv\system32, **2000:** \winnt\system32	**Type:**	External

qwinsta

OS: Windows NT4 Terminal Server, 2000 Server, XP

Function	Shows information about terminal sessions.
Syntax	qwinsta *{ name }* [options...]

/SERVER:*servername*	Specifies a server to query.
/MODE	Shows current line settings.
/FLOW	Shows current flow control settings
/CONNECT	Shows current connect settings.
name	Specifies the name to look for. Can be a username, session name, or ID.
2000:	
/COUNTER	Shows current terminal service counters information.

File Name:	`qwinsta.exe`	**Directory:**	**NT4 TS:** \wtsrv\system32, **2000:** \winnt\system32, **XP:** \windows\system32	**Type:**	External

qwinsta console /CONNECT	Shows information about connection for the console.

rasdial

OS: Windows NT4, 2000, XP

Function	Makes a remote network connection. If used alone will show the current status of connections.
Syntax	rasdial *name { username [password }]* [options...]

name	Specifies the name of the connection from the current phone book.
username	Specifies the username to use.
password	Specifies the password to use. If a * is given the program asks for a password.
/domain:*domain*	Specifies the domain to dial up into. This isn't necessary in many cases.
/phone:*number*	Specifies the phone number to call, if not already configured in entry name.
/callback:*number*	Specifies the callback phone number.
/phonebook:*file*	Specifies an alternate phonebook file to use.
/prefixsuffix	Specifies the local dialing settings that will be applied to the phone number.
/disconnect	Disconnects the specified connection.

File Name:	`rasdial.exe`	**Directory:**	**NT4, 2000:** \winnt\system32, **XP:** \windows\system32	**Type:**	External

rasdial office /callback:555-0100	Connects to OFFICE 2 entry in Rasphone.pbk and specifies a callback number.
rasdial "office 2" /disconnect	Disconnects the specified entry.

rcp

OS: Windows NT4, 2000, XP

Function	Copies files from an NT Workstation to a computer that runs rshd (remote shell daemon) that normally only exists on UNIX systems.
Syntax	rcp [options...] *{ host.user } sourcefiles... { host.user } destinationfile*

-a	Sets transfer mode to ASCII. Can't be combined with -b option (is the default).
-b	Sets transfer mode to Binary. Can't be combined with -a option.
-h	Transfers files with attribute hidden.
-r	Includes files in subdirectories.
host	Specifies a host to copy files to or from.
user	Specifies a username. An optional operand to host. (Default is current user.)
sourcefiles...	Specifies source files. Use a proceeding (:) if host is used.
destinationfile	Specifies the destination for the files. Use a proceeding (:) if host is used.

File Name:	`rcp.exe`	**Directory:**	**NT4, 2000:** \winnt\system32, **XP:** \windows\system32	**Type:**	External

rcp test.bat pluto:/program/test.bat	Copies test.bat to the host pluto in the directory /program.

recover

recover	OS: Windows NT4, 2000, XP
Function	Recovers data from a bad or defective disk.
Syntax	recover *file*

file	The file, including the full path, to recover.
File Name: `recover.exe`	**Directory:** **NT4, 2000:** \winnt\system32, **XP:** \windows\system32 **Type:** External
recover c:\test\test.exe	Recovers the file test.exe in the directory c:\test\.

redir

redir	OS: Windows NT4, 2000, XP
Function	Loads the VDM Redirector.
Syntax	redir

File Name: `redir.exe`	**Directory:** **NT4, 2000:** \winnt\system32, **XP:** \windows\system32 **Type:** External
redir	Loads the VDM Redirector.

reg

reg	OS: Windows XP
Function	Shows, adds, and changes Registry values and subkey information in Registry entries.
Syntax	reg *ACTION* [/?]

	The following option can be used with all actions:
/?	Shows help information.
ACTION	**The following eleven actions are available:**
add *key* [options...§]	Adds a new entry or subkey to the registry.
	The following two options can't be combined:
/v *entry*	Specifies the entry to add under the specified subkey.
/ve	Specifies that the new entry has a null value.
/t *type*	The data type to use for the new entry value. (Available types: REG_SZ, REG_MULTI_SZ, REG_DWORD_BIG_ENDIAN, REG_DWORD, REG_BINARY, REG_DWORD_LITTLE_ENDIAN, REG_LINK, REG_FULL_RESOURCE_DESCRIPTOR, REG_EXPAND_SZ.)
	The following option is only used with the REG_MULTI_SZ data type:
/s *separator*	The separator character to use with multiple instances of data, default is \0.
/d *value*	The value for the new entry.
/f	Doesn't prompt before adding the new subkey or entry.
key	Specifies the full path to the subkey.
compare *key1* *key2* [options...]	Compares two entries or subkeys. *The following two options can't be combined.*
/v *entry*	Compares the specified entry under the subkey.
/ve	Compares only entries with no values.
	The following four options can't be combined:
/oa	Shows all differences and matches.
/od	Shows only differences. This is the default.
/os	Shows only matches.
/on	Shows nothing.
/s	Compares all subkeys and entries.
key1	Specifies the full path to the first subkey.
key2	Specifies the full path to the second subkey.
copy *key1* *key2* [options...]	Copies an entry to the specified destination.
/s	Copies all subkeys and entries from the source subkey.
/f	Doesn't prompt before copying.
key1	Specifies the full path to the source subkey.
key2	Specifies the full path to the target subkey.
delete *key* [options...]	Deletes a subkey or entry.
	The following three options can't be combined:
/v *entry*	Deletes the specified entry under the subkey.
/ve	Deletes all entries without values.
/va	Deletes every entry under the subkey.
/f	Doesn't prompt before deleting.
key	Specifies the full path of the subkey to delete.

continued

export *key file*	Exports the specified subkey, including all entries and values to a file.
key	The subkey to export.
file	The name and path of the target file.
import *file*	Imports subkeys, including all entries and values from the specified file.
file	The name and the path of the file to import.
load *key file*	Imports subkeys and entries to a different subkey.
key	The full path of the target subkey.
file	The name and the path of the file to import.
unload *key*	Deletes a part of the registry that was loaded using the `load` action.
key	The full path of the subkey.
query *key* [options...]	Returns the next level of subkeys and entries located under the specified subkey.
	The following two options can't be combined:
/v *entry*	Returns the specified entry and its value.
/ve	Returns only entries with no values.
/s	Returns all subkeys and entries in all levels.
key	The full path of the subkey to query.
save *key file*	Saves a copy of the specified subkey, entries, and values to a file.
key	The full path of the subkey to save.
file	The name and path of the target file.
restore *key file*	Restores saved subkeys, entries, and values.
key	The full path of the target subkey.
file	The name and path of the source file.

File Name:	`reg.exe`	**Directory:**	\windows\system32	**Type:**	External

reg add "hkcu\software\ucg" /v Version /t reg_sz /d v1.0	Adds the specified subkey and entry to the registry.
reg query "hkcu\software\ucg"	Shows all entries and values for the specified subkey.

register

OS: Windows NT4 Terminal Server, 2000 Server

Function	Assigns special execution characteristics to a program.
Syntax	register *file* [option]

/system	Registers a system global resource to the file.
/user	Registers a user global resource to the file.
/v	Verbose mode. Shows more information.
file	Specifies the file to register.
NT4:	
/guitext	Registers the file as executable on text-only sessions.
/noguitext	Registers the file as a non-executable file on text-only sessions.

File Name:	`register.exe`	**Directory:**	**NT4 TS:** \wtsrv\system32, **2000:** \winnt\system32	**Type:**	External

Registration Wizard

OS: Windows 9x, 2000, XP

Function	Starts the registration wizard, which will help you to register your software online.
Syntax	regwiz

File Name:	`regwiz.exe`	**Directory:**	**9x:** \windows\system, **2000:** \winnt\system32, **XP:** \windows\system32	**Type:**	External

Registry Editor (32-bit)

OS: Windows NT4, 2000

Function	A 32-bit version of the registry editor used to inspect and edit the Windows NT Registry. The Windows NT Registry is a database containing configuration information about the system.
Syntax	regedt32

File Name:	`regedt32.exe`	**Directory:**	\winnt\system32	**Type:**	External

regedt32	Starts the registry editor.

regtrace, nntp_regtrace, smtp_regtrace

OS: Windows 2000 Server

Function	Enables tracing in the following discount components: Cache Manager, CSFLoadAdvertisement, CSFLoadCampaignsCommon, CSFLoadDiscount, EvalTargetGroups and OrderDiscount.
Syntax	regtrace

File Name:	`regtrace.exe, nntp_regtrace, smtp_regtrace`	**Directory:**	\winnt\system32, \winnt\system32\dllcache	**Type:**	External

relog

OS: Windows XP

Function	Extracts and converts performance counters stored in performance counter logs to BIN, CSV, TSV, or SQL format.
Syntax	relog *files* ... [options...]

/a	Appends the output to an existing binary file.
/c *path* ...	Specifies the performance counter path to log.
/cf *file*	Specifies a text file containing a list of performance counters to include.
/f *format*	The format of the output file. Valid formats are BIN (default), CSV, TSV, and SQL
/t *NR*	Writes only every NRth record to the output file.
/o *output*	The path of the output file or the SQL database where the data will be written.
/b *time*	Specifies the start time for copying first record.
/e *time*	Specifies the end time for copying last record. (The format for the time is: mm/dd/yyyy hh[:mm[:ss]].)
/config *file*	The pathname of the file containing command-line parameters.
/q	Shows the performance counters in the input file.
/?	Shows help information.

File Name:	`relog.exe`	**Directory:**	\windows\system32	**Type:**	External

relog c:\loggs\weekly.blg /cf counters.txt /o c:\logg\logg.csv /f csv	Extracts the counters to the specified file with the CSV format.

Remote Access Admin

OS: Windows NT4, 2000

Function	Starts Remote Access Administrator.
Syntax	rasadmin *{ domain }*

domain	Specifies the domain to administer.

File Name:	`rasadmin.exe`	**Directory:**	\winnt\system32	**Type:**	External

Remote Boot Disk Generator

OS: Windows 2000 Server

Function	Creates a remote boot disk to use with the Windows 2000 Remote Installation Service. Only works with computers that use supported PCI-based network adapters.
Syntax	rbfg

File Name:	`rbfg.exe`	**Directory:**	\winnt\system32\dllcache	**Type:**	External

Remote Desktop Connection

OS: Windows XP

Function	Starts the Microsoft Terminal Server Client
Syntax	mstsc *file* [options...]

/console	Connects to a console session on a server.
/edit *file*	Opens the specified .rdp file for editing.
/f	Runs the client in full screen mode.
-h*height*	Specifies the remote screen height.
-w*width*	Specifies the remote screen width.
/migrate	Migrates legacy connection files to new .rdp connection files.
/v*server { port }*	Specifies the server to connect to.
/?	Shows help information.
file	Specifies the .rpd file for the connection.

File Name:	`mstsc.exe`	**Directory:**	\windows\system32	**Type:**	External

Remote Installation Services Setup

OS:	Windows 2000 Server				
Function	Prepares the current server for remote installation of Windows 2000 Professional on remote boot-enabled computers.				
Syntax	risetup				
File Name:	risetup.exe	Directory:	\winnt\system32\dllcache	Type:	External

Remoteboot Manager

OS:	Windows NT4 Server				
Function	Starts a graphic interface to manage the remote boot services.				
Syntax	rplmgr				
File Name:	rplmgr.exe	Directory:	\winnt\system32	Type:	External

Removable Storage

OS:	Windows 2000 Server				
Function	Manages all your removable storage media such as optical disks and tapes. It makes it possible for several programs to share storage resources.				
Syntax	ntmsmgr.msc				
File Name:	ntmsmgr.msc	Directory:	\winnt\system32	Type:	External

Removable Storage Operator Requests

OS:	Windows 2000 Server				
Function	Manages the jobs in the work queue for the Removable Storage program.				
Syntax	ntmsoprq.msc				
File Name:	ntmsoprq.msc	Directory:	\winnt\system32	Type:	External

Repair Disk Utility

OS:	Windows NT4				
Function	Starts the Repair Disk Utility to create and update an Emergency Repair Disk.				
Syntax	rdisk				
	These are tasks to do in the utility.				
Update Repair Info	Updates repair information or creates Emergency Repair Disk with new repair info.				
Create Repair Disk	Creates an Emergency Repair Disk with current information.				
File Name:	rdisk.exe	Directory:	\winnt\system32	Type:	External
rdisk	Starts the rdisk utility.				

replace

OS:	Windows XP				
Function	Replaces files in the target directory with the files in the source directory that have the same names.				
Syntax	replace *source destination* [options...]				
/a	Adds new files instead of replacing existing ones. Not combinable with /s /u.				
/p	Prompts for confirmation before the file is replaced.				
/r	Specifies that read-only files are overwritten.				
/w	Pauses the replace process until a source disk is inserted.				
/s	Replaces all matching files in all subdirectories. Not combinable with the /a option.				
/u	Replaces only files that are older than the source. Not combinable with /a.				
/?	Shows help information.				
source	Specifies the source files.				
destination	Specifies the target directory.				
File Name:	replace.exe	Directory:	\windows\system32	Type:	External
replace a:*.* c:\program\ucg /u	Only files that are newer than the target are replaced.				
replace a:*.* c:\program\ucg /a	Only files that don't exist in the target are added.				

reset

OS:	Windows NT4 Terminal Server, 2000, XP				
Function	Resets sessions from a terminal server.				
Syntax	reset *session*				
session	Specifies the session to reset.				
File Name:	reset.exe	Directory:	**NT4 TS:** \wtsrv\system32, **2000:** \winnt\system32, **XP:** \windows\system32	Type:	External
reset 10	Resets session 10 on the current terminal server.				

restore

restore		**OS:**	Windows NT4
Function	Restores backup files created with the backup command.		
Syntax	restore *source destination* [options...]		

/S	Restores all subdirectories.
/P	Prompts you before restoring files with the read-only or archive attribute.
/B:*date*	Restores only files with dates on or before specified date.
/A:*date*	Restores only files with dates on or after specified date.
/E:*time*	Restores only files with time at or earlier than specified time.
/L:*time*	Restores only files with time at or later than specified time.
/M	Restores only files that have been modified since the last backup.
/N	Restores only files that don't exist in the target directory.
/D	Shows a list with matching files without restoring files.
/?	Shows help information.
source	Specifies the source disk on which the backup files are located.
destination	Specifies the full path and names of the files to be restored. (The directory path must be the same as used when making the backup.)

File Name:	`restore.exe`	**Directory:**	\winnt\system32	**Type:**	External

restore h: c:\program\ucg /S	Restores all subdirectories.
restore h: c:\dos /B:06/11/2000	Restores only files with dates on or before specified date.

rexec

rexec		**OS:**	Windows NT4, 2000, XP
Function	Authenticates a username to a remote computer running the REXEC service and then executes the specified command.		
Syntax	rexec *host* [options...] *command*		

-l *username*	Specifies the remote user to use, if not used you will be prompted.
-n	Redirects the input to NULL.
/?	Shows help information.
host	The computer to run the command on.
command	The command to run on the remote computer.

File Name:	`rexec.exe`	**Directory:**	**NT4, 2000:** \winnt\system32, **XP:** \windows\system32	**Type:**	External

rexec ucgremote -l ucguser md c:\test	Runs the specified command on the ucgremote computer.

robocopy

robocopy		**OS:**	Windows ME
Function	A robust file copy that supports UNC path names for source and destination and is great for copying large files.		
Syntax	robocopy *sourcedirectory destinationdirectory* [options...]		

/S	Copies subdirectories that contain data.
/E	Copies subdirectories even if they are empty.
/T	Assigns all files in the destination directory a new timestamp, even skipped files.
/R:*num*	Specifies the number of retries for failed copy attempts. (Default is 1 million.)
/W:*seconds*	Specifies the number of seconds between recopy attempts. (Default is 30 seconds.)
/REG	Save the values from the /R and /W options in the Registry as default settings.
/X	Shows a report for all files, even those not copied.
/V	Verbose mode. Shows more information for copied files, even files that were skipped.
/L	Lists information about the files it copies but won't actually copy any files.
/A+:*attributes...*	Adds specified attributes to copied files: R=Read only, A=Archive, S=System, H=Hidden.
/A-:*attributes...*	Removes attributes from copied files: R=Read only, A=Archive, S=System, H=Hidden.
/XA:*attributes...*	Excludes files with specified attributes: R=Read only, A=Archive, S=System, H=Hidden.
/AA:*attributes...*	Copies files with specified attributes: R=Read only, A=Archive, S=System, H=Hidden.
/MA:*attributes...*	Specifies the same as the /AA option but also removes the attributes from the source files.
/XF *pattern*	Doesn't copy the files matching the pattern or wildcards specified.
/XD *pattern*	Doesn't copy the directories matching the pattern or wildcards specified.
/XC	Doesn't copy changed files.
/XN	Doesn't copy newer files.
/XO	Doesn't copy older files.
/XX	Doesn't copy any extra files and directories that the destination doesn't have.
/XL	Doesn't copy lonely files and directories.
/IS	Copies matching filenames only.

continued

/ETA /MOVE /PURGE *sourcedirectory* *destinationdirectory*	Shows the estimated time of arrival for the files that are being copied. Removes all files from the source after the copy is complete. Removes all destination directories that don't exist in the source. Specifies the source directory. Supports both drive letters and UNC pathnames. Specifies the destination directory. Supports both drive letters and UNC pathnames.
File Name: `robocopy.exe`	**Directory:** \windows\options\install **Type:** External
Tip:	This is a great tool to replicate directories throughout the network. (At night of course!)
robocopy c:\documents \\myserver\backup /S /V /ETA	Copies all files in the documents directory to myserver\backup and shows the ETA.

Routing and Remote Access

OS: Windows 2000 Server

Function	Manages the setup and maintenance of routing services for LAN and WAN networks via Internet by use of a Secure Private Network.
Syntax	rrasmgmt.msc
File Name: `rrasmgmt.msc`	**Directory:** \winnt\system32 **Type:** External

rplcmd

OS: Windows NT4 Server

Function	Manages the remote boot service. Manages the local server if computer name isn't given.
Syntax	rplcmd [*computername*]
computername	Specifies a remote computer to run the Remote Boot Service.
File Name: `rplcmd.exe`	**Directory:** \winnt\system32 **Type:** External
rplcmd	Starts the manager.

rplcnv

OS: Windows NT4 Server

Function	Converts databases used by LANMAN Remote boot to Windows NT Remote boot databases.
Syntax	rplcnv *path*
path	Specifies path to the rpl.map and rplmgr.ini files.
File Name: `rplcnv.exe`	**Directory:** \winnt\system32 **Type:** External
rplcnv c:\old\remoteboot	Converts the databases located in c:\old\remoteboot.

rsh

OS: Windows NT4, 2000, XP

Function	Runs a command on a remote computer running the RSH service.
Syntax	rsh *host* [options...] *command*
-l *user* -n *host* *command*	Specifies the remote user to use; if not specified, the current user is used. Redirects the input to NULL. The computer to run the command on. The command to run on the remote computer.
File Name: `rsh.exe`	**Directory:** **NT4, 2000:** \winnt\system32, **XP:** \windows\system32 **Type:** External
rsh ucgremote -l username cd c:\winnt\system32	Runs the specified command on the ucgremote computer.

rsm

OS: Windows 2000, XP

Function	The Removable Storage Manager. Manages removable media.
Syntax	rsm *ACTION*
ACTIONS	**Use one of the following actions:**
ALLOCATE options...	Allocates a piece of available media.
	The following options must be specified:
/m*name*	Specifies the mediapool name to allocate from.
/o*mode*	Specifies the action to do. Mode can be one of the following:
ERRUNAVAIL	Doesn't do an operator request submission if no media was found.
NEW	Allocates the partition of a media that can't be shared with another media.
NEXT	Allocates the next partition of the previous created partition by NEW.
	Only one of the following options must be specified:
/l{ *type* }*mediaID*	Defines the type of the logicalmediapoolID.
/p{ *type* }*partitionID*	Defines the type of the partitionID.
type	Is either: G=Treat the ID as GUID, F=Treat the ID as friendly name.

continued

	The following options are optional:
/t*timeout*	Specifies the timeout, in microseconds. (Default is INFINITE.)
/b	Shows only GUIDS.
	The following options can only be used if working with a logical media object:
/ln*medianame*	Specifies the friendly name to assign to the logical media object of the media.
/ld*mediadescription*	Specifies the description to assign to the logical media object of the media.
	The following options can only be used if working with a partition object:
/pn*partitionname*	Specifies the friendly name to assign to the partition object of the media.
/pd*partitiondescription*	Specifies the description to assign to the partition object of the media.
DEALLOCATE option	Deallocates the specified media.
	The following options can only be used if working with a logical media object:
/l*type mediaID*	Deallocates the logical media ID if supplied as a GUID.
/l*typemediaID*	Deallocates the logical media ID if supplied as a friendly name.
	The following options can only be used if working with a partition object:
/p*typepartitionID*	Deallocates the partition ID if supplied as a GUID.
/p*typepartitionID*	Deallocates the partition ID if supplied as a friendly name.
MOUNT options...	Mounts the specified piece of media.
	The following option is required:
/o *mode*	Specifies the mode to mount the device in. Can be one of the following (specify multiple /o options for multiple modes):
ERRUNAVAIL	Creates an error message if a mount isn't available.
READ	Mounts in read access.
WRITE	Mounts in write access.
DRIVE	Must be specified if drive GUID or name is provided.
OFFLINE	Creates an error message if the media is offline.
	Only one of the following options must be specified:
/l*typemediaID*	Specifies the logical media ID.
/p*typepartitionID*	Specifies the partition ID.
/s*typeslotID*	Specifies the slot ID.
	The following option must be specified only if /s is used:
/c*typechangerID*	Specifies the changer ID.
/d*typedriveID*	Specifies the drive ID.
/t *timeout*	Specifies the timeout in milliseconds. (Default is INFINITE.)
/r *priority*	Specifies the priority for the mounted media (lowest, low, normal, high, highest).
DISMOUNT options...	Releases the specified piece of media from a drive.
	One of the following options must be specified:
/l*typemediaID*	Specifies the logical media ID.
/p*typepartitionID*	Specifies the partition ID.
	The following option is optional:
/o [deferred]	If deferred is typed, dismounts, but keeps the medium in the drive.
EJECT options...	
	Only one of the following options must be specified:
/p*typemediaID*	Specifies the physical media ID.
/s*typeslotID*	Specifies the slot ID.
/l*typelibraryID*	Specifies the library ID.
/d*typedriveID*	Specifies the drive ID. /l is also required with this option.
	The following options are optional:
/a*mode*	Specifies the mode to run. (Can be START to start eject, STOP to stop, QUEUE to queue for ejection.)
/o*operation*	Obtains the GUID when eject is used with the START mode.
/b	Shows the eject operation GUID.
EJECTATAPI /n *number*	Ejects the media from an ATAPI driver. Number specifies the device number to eject.
CREATEPOOL options...	Creates a media pool.
/m*name*	Specifies the media pool to create.
/t*typepooltypeID*	Specifies the pooltypeID.
/a*mode*	Specifies the mode to create the pool.
EXISTING	Opens only existing media pools.
ALWAYS	Opens media pools or creates new pool.
NEW	Creates only new pools. Shows an error if pool already exists.

continued

/d	Lets the media pool draw media from the free pool.
/r	Lets the media pool return media from the free pool.
DELETEPOOL /m *name*	Deletes the specified media pool.
VIEW options...	Shows all instances of the specified object type.
/t*type*	Specifies object type to show. Select one of the following object types: DRIVE, LIBRARY, CHANGER, STORAGESLOT, IEDOOR, IEPORT, MEDIA_POOL, PHYSICAL_MEDIA, PARTITION, LOGICAL_MEDIA, MEDIA_TYPE, DRIVE_TYPE, LIBREQUEST.
/CG*containerID*	Specifies the GUID of a container object.
/GUIDDISPLAY	Shows both the GUIDs and the friendly names.
/b	Shows only the GUIDs.
REFRESH option	Refreshes the specified devices. **Only one of the following options must be specified:**
/l*typelibraryID*	Specifies the library ID.
/p*typemediaID*	Specifies the physical media ID.
/t*typemediatyperID*	Specifies the media type ID.
INVENTORY options...	Runs an inventory to the specified online library. **The following options are required:**
/l*typelibraryID*	Specifies the library ID.
/a*mode*	Specifies the mode to run the inventory in. Can be one of the following:
ALL	Does a full inventory.
FAST	Does a differential inventory or a bar code inventory if bar code reader is installed.
DEFAULT	Uses the inventory method specified in the library object.
NONE	Doesn't do any inventory.
STOP	Stops the inventory on the specified library object.

File Name:	rsm.exe	**Directory:**	**2000:** \winnt\system32, **XP:** \windows\system32	**Type:**	External

rstore — OS: Windows 2000 Server

Function	Restores the jet database from the backup file.
Syntax	rstore *directory*

directory	Specifies the directory to restore to.

File Name:	rstore.exe	**Directory:**	\winnt\system32\dllcache	**Type:**	External

runas (2000) — OS: Windows 2000

Function	Allows a user to run specific tools and programs as another user.
Syntax	runas [options...] *program*

/profile	Loads the user's profile.
/env	Uses the current environment.
/netonly	Specifies that the credentials are for remote access.
/user:*username*	Specifies the user in the form USER@DOMAIN or DOMAIN\USER.
program	Specifies what program to run with other permissions.

File Name:	runas.exe	**Directory:**	\winnt\system32	**Type:**	External
Tip:	No need to log off and on again to run only one small program.				

runas /env /user:ucg@ucg.com "notepad myfile.txt"	Edits the file "my file.txt" with the permissions of the user ucg.

runas (XP) — OS: Windows XP

Function	Allows a user to run specific tools and programs as another user.
Syntax	runas [options...] *program*

/noprofile	Doesn't load the user profile.
/profile	Loads the users' profile.
/env	Uses the current environment.
/netonly	Specifies that the credentials are for remote access.
/savecred	Uses credentials previously saved by the user.
/smartcard	Specifies that credentials are supplied from a smartcard.
/user:*username*	Specifies the user in the form USER@DOMAIN or DOMAIN\USER.
program	Specifies what program to run with other permissions.

continued

File Name:	runas.exe	**Directory:**	\windows\system32	**Type:**	External
runas /env /user:ucg@ucg.com "notepad myfile.txt"			Edits the file "my file.txt" with the permissions of the user ucg.		

rwinsta

OS: Windows NT4 Terminal Server, 2000 Server, XP

Function	Resets session's subsystem hardware and software to its known initial values.
Syntax	rwinsta *{ session }* [options...]

/SERVER:*servername*	Specifies the server that contains the session.
/V	Verbose mode. Shows more information.
session	Specifies the session id or session name to reset.

File Name:	rwinsta.exe	**Directory:**	**NT4 TS:** \wtsrv\system32, **2000:** \winnt\system32, **XP:** \windows\system32	**Type:**	External
rwinsta 16			Resets session 16.		

sc

OS: Windows XP

Function	Communicates with the NT service controller and services.
Syntax	sc [*server*] *{ command }* *{ service }*

query	Asks the service for its status or adds the status for types of services.
type= *value*	Specifies the type to add. Values are drivers, service (is default), and all.
state= *value*	Specifies the state to add. Values are inactive, active (is default), and all.
bufsize=*value*	Specifies the size (in bytes) for the enumerated buffer. (Default is 4096.)
ri= *NR*	Specifies the resume index number at which to start the enumeration. (Default is 0.)
group= *name*	Specifies the service group to enumerate. (Default is all.)
queryex	Asks the service for its extended status or adds the status for types of services.
type= *value*	Specifies the type to add. Values are drivers, service (is default), and all.
state= *value*	Specifies the state to add. Values are inactive, active (is default), and all.
bufsize= *value*	Specifies the size (in bytes) for the enumerated buffer. (Default is 4096.)
ri= *NR*	Specifies the resume index number at which to start the enumeration. (Default is 0.)
group= *name*	Specifies the service group to enumerate. (Default is all.)
start	Starts the service.
pause	Sends a request to pause the service.
interrogate	Sends a request to interrogate the service.
continue	Sends a request to continue the service.
stop	Sends a request to stop the service.
description	Alters the service description: description [service] [description]
{ description }	Adds the description after the service name.
qc	Queries the configuration information for a service.
buffersize	Specifies the buffersize: qc [service] [buffersize]
qdescription	Queries the description for a service.
buffersize	Specifies the buffersize: qdescription [service] [buffersize]
qfailure	Queries the failure actions for the service.
buffersize	Specifies the buffersize: qfailure [service] [buffersize]
delete	Erases the service from the registry.
sdshow	Shows the security descriptor in SDDL format for a service.
sdset	Sets a security descriptor for the service. sdset [service] descriptor
descriptor	Specifies a security descriptor in SDDL format.
getdisplayname	Specifies the service displayname.
buffersize	Specifies the buffersize: getdisplayname [service] [buffersize]
getkeyname	Specifies the service's servicekeyname: getkeyname, service, displayname, and buffersize.
displayname buffersize	Specifies the displayname and buffersize.
enumdepend	Adds Service Dependencies.
buffersize	Specifies the buffersize: enumdepend service buffersize.
config *options...*	Alters the configuration for the service.
type= *value*	Specifies the type. Values are own, share, interact, kernel, filesys, rec, and adapt.
start= *value*	Specifies how to start. Values are boot, system, auto, demand, and disabled.

continued

error= *value*	Specifies the error mode. Values are normal, severe, critical, and ignore.
binPath= *name*	Specifies the binary path name.
group= *name*	Loads the specified order group.
tag= yes | no	Enables or disables tagging.
depend= *dependencies*	Specifies the dependencies separated with a /.
obj= *name*	Specifies the account- or objectname.
displayname= *name*	Specifies the display.
password= *password*	Specifies the password.
failure	Alters the failure action for the service.
reboot= *message*	Specifies the message to broadcast before reboot on a failure.
command= *line*	Specifies the command line to be run on failure.
	These two options must be used together:
reset= *sec*	Specifies the time to reset the failure count to 0 if there isn't a failure.
actions=*values...*	Specifies the actions on failure and the delay time in milliseconds, separated by a /
	Values are: run, restart, and reboot (e.g., run/6000/reboot/9000).
create *options...*	Creates and adds the service to the registry.
type= *value*	Specifies the type. Values are own, share, interact, kernel, filesys and rec.
start= *value*	Specifies how to start. Values are boot, system, auto, demand, and disabled.
error= *value*	Specifies the error mode. Values are normal, severe, critical, and ignore.
binPath= *name*	Specifies the binary pathname.
group= *name*	Loads the specified order group.
tag= yes | no	Enables or disables tagging.
depend= *dependencies*	Specifies the dependencies separated with a /.
obj= *name*	Specifies the account- or objectname. (Default is Localname.)
displayname= *name*	Specifies the display.
password= *password*	Specifies the password.
control	Sends a control code value to the service: control [service] value.
value	Specifies a user or pre-defined value. Select from the following: netbindadd, netbindremove, netbindenable, netbinddisable, or paramchange.
	These commands don't need a service name:
boot *ok* | *bad*	Saves or unsaves the last boot configuration as the last-known-good boot configuration.
lock	Locksets the service database.
querylock	Queries the SCManager database for its lockstatus.
server	Specifies the server to use.
service	Specifies service to modify or check.

File Name:	`sc.exe`	**Directory:**	windows\system32	**Type:**	External
sc query messenger		Shows status for the service messenger.			

ScanDisk

OS: Windows Common

Function	A utility that checks disks for errors. If executed in windows, scandskw.exe will start, rather than scandisk.exe.
Syntax	scandisk *{ drives... }* [options...]

/A	Checks all local drivers.
/N	Is used to start and finish scandisk automatically. (In scandskw.exe, a click on the close button is still required.)
/P	Doesn't correct found errors.
drives...	Specifies the disk drives to scan.

File Name:	`scandisk.exe, scandskw.exe`	**Directory:**	\windows\command	**Type:**	External
scandisk /n /a		Scans all drives automatically.			

Scheduled Tasks

OS: Windows 98/ME

Function	Adds, removes, and modifies scheduled task, which runs programs at a specified time.
Syntax	sysagent

File Name:	`sysagent.exe`	**Directory:**	**Win98:** \Program Files\PLUS! **WinME:** \windows\system	**Type:**	External

schtasks

OS: Windows XP

Function	Manages scheduled tasks on the local computer or on a remote computer.
Syntax	schtasks *ACTION*

	The following four options are common to every action:
/s *host*	The remote computer to connect to.
/u *user*	Specifies the user to run the command with. Default is the current user.
/p *password*	The password for the specified user. Prompts for input if skipped.
/?	Shows help information.
ACTION	**The following six actions are available:**
/create options...	Creates a scheduled task on a local or remote computer.
	The following three options are required:
/sc *schedule*	Specifies the schedule type. (MINUTE, HOURLY, DAILY, WEEKLY, MONTHLY, ONCE, ONSTART, ONLOGON, ONIDLE.)
/tn *name*	A unique name to use for the task.
/tr *taskrun*	The program including the full path to run.
/ru *user*	Specifies the user account under which the tasks will run.
/rp *password*	The password for the user account.
/mo *modifier*	Specifies the time interval for the schedule type. (Use 1–1439 for MINUTE; 1–23 for HOURLY; 1–365 for DAILY; 1–52 for WEEKLY; 1–12 or FIRST, SECOND, THIRD, FOURTH, LAST, LASTDAY for MONTHLY.)
/d *days*	Specifies the day the scheduled task should run on. (Use MON, TUE, WED, THU, FRI, SAT, SUN or, for monthly, 1–31. This option can only be used with the MONTHLY and WEEKLY type. This option requires the FIRST, SECOND, THIRD, FOURTH, LAST modifier.)
/m *month*	The month to run the command. Default is the first day of the month. (Use JAN, FEB, MAR, APR, MAY, JUN, JUL, AUG, SEP, OCT, NOV, DEC. This option is required when using the LASTDAY modifier.)
/i *time*	The number of idle minutes to wait before running a task of the type ONIDLE.
/st *time*	The time when the task should run. The format is: HH:MM:S (24-hour time). (This option is valid for the MINUTE, HOURLY, DAILY, WEEKLY, MONTHLY and required for the ONCE scheduler type.)
/sd *date*	The first date the task should run. The format is: "yyyy/mm/dd." (This option is valid for all and required for the ONCE scheduler type.)
/ed *date*	The last date the task should run. The format is: "yyyy/mm/dd." (This option isn't valid for the ONCE, ONSTART, ONLOGON, ONIDLE type.)
/Run options...	Runs the specified scheduled task at once.
	The following option is required:
/tn *name*	Specifies the name of the task to run.
/End	Stops the specified active scheduled task.
	The following option is required:
/tn *name*	Specifies the task to stop.
/Delete	Deletes a scheduled task.
/tn *name*	Specifies the task to delete.
/f	Deletes the task even if it's currently running.
/Query	Shows all the scheduled tasks.
/fo *format*	Specifies the format to use for the output. Valid are TABLE, LIST, CSV.
/nh	Hides column header. Can only be used with the TABLE and CSV format.
/v	Verbose mode. Shows more information.
/Change	Changes the user account and password used by the task or the program to run.
/ru *user*	Specifies a new user account under which the tasks will run.
/rp *password*	The password for the user account.
/tr *taskrun*	The new program, including the full path to run.
/tn *name*	Specifies the task to change.

File Name:	schtasks.exe	**Directory:**	\windows\system32	**Type:**	External

schtasks /create /sc monthly /tn task1 /tr c:\myapp.exe /mo third /d wed	Runs the specified program the third Wednesday every month.
schtasks /run /tn task1	Runs the specified task at once.

secedit (2000)

OS: Windows 2000

Function	Analyzes, configures, refreshes, exports, or validates the system's security settings.
Syntax	secedit *ACTION*

ACTION	**The following four actions are available:**
/analyze /db *file* [options...]	
/db *file*	The name and path of the database against which the analysis is performed.
/cfg *file*	The name and path of the security template that is imported for analysis.
/log *file*	The name and path of the log file to use; if not given, the default file is used.
/verbose	Verbose mode. Shows more information.
/quiet	Suppresses screen and log output.
/configure /db *file* [options...]	Configures system security by applying a stored template.
/db *file*	Specifies the name and path of the database that contains the security template to apply.
/cfg *file*	Specifies the name and path of the security template that is imported and applied.
/overwrite	Overwrites security template stored in the database.
/areas *area ...*	Specifies the security areas to apply.
/log *file*	The name and path of the log file to use; if not given, the default file is used.
/verbose	Verbose mode. Shows more information.
/quiet	Suppresses screen and log output.
/refreshpolicy	Refreshes system security by reapplying the security settings to the Group Policy.
	The following two options can't be combined:
machine_policy	Refreshes the policies for the local computer.
user_policy	Refreshes the policies for the current user.
/enforce	Refreshes the policies even if no changes have been made.
/export [options...]	Exports stored template from a security database to a template file.
/mergedpolicy [options...]	Merges and exports domain and security settings.
/db *file*	Specifies the database where the templates are exported.
/cfg *file*	Specifies the name of the file where the templates are exported.
/areas *area ...*	Specifies the security areas that are exported.
/log *file*	The name and path of the log file to use; if not given, the default file is used.
/verbose	Verbose mode. Shows more information.
/quiet	Suppresses screen and log output.
/validates *file*	Validates the specified security template.

File Name:	`secedit.exe`	**Directory:**	\winnt\system32	**Type:**	External

secedit (XP)

OS: Windows XP

Function	Analyzes, configures, refreshes, exports, or validates the systems security settings.
Syntax	secedit *ACTION*

ACTION	**The following four actions are available:**
/analyze /db *file* [options...]	
/db *file*	The name and path of the database to analyze.
/cfg *file*	The name and path of the security template that is imported for analysis.
/log *file*	The name and path of the logfile to use; if not given, the default file is used.
/quiet	Suppresses screen and log output.
/configure /db *file* [options...]	Configures system security by applying a stored template.
/db *file*	The name and path of the database that contains the security template to apply.
/cfg *file*	The name and path of the security template that is imported and applied.
/overwrite	Overwrites security template stored in the database.
/areas *area ...*	Specifies the security areas to apply.
/log *file*	The name and path of the log file to use; if not given, the default file is used.
/quiet	Suppresses screen and log output.
/export [options...]	Exports stored template from a security database to a template file.
/mergedpolicy [options...]	Merges and exports domain and security settings.
/db *file*	Specifies the database where the templates are exported.
/cfg *file*	Specifies the file where the templates are exported.
/areas *area ...*	Specifies the security areas that are exported.
/log *file*	The name and path of the log file to use; if not given, the default file is used.

continued

/quiet	Suppresses screen and log output.				
/validates *file*	Validates the specified security template.				
File Name:	secedit.exe	**Directory:**	\windows\system32	**Type:**	External

Securing NT Account Database — OS: Windows 2000, XP

Function	Runs the tool that enables encryption on the account database in your system.
Syntax	syskey
File Name:	syskey.exe — **Directory:** **2000:** \winnt\system32, **XP:** \windows\system32 — **Type:** External
Note:	CAUTION! Once the encryption is enabled, it can't be disabled.

Server Manager — OS: Windows NT4 Server, 2000 Server

Function	Administers Windows NT 4.0 or 3.51 domains and computers.
Syntax	srvmgr
File Name:	srvmgr.exe — **Directory:** \winnt\system32 — **Type:** External

Services — OS: Windows 2000 Server

Function	Manages services on a local or remote system. Enables or disables services for specified hardware profiles. Configures startup and recovery sequences. Creates custom names for services.
Syntax	services.msc
File Name:	services.msc — **Directory:** \winnt\system32 — **Type:** External

setdebug — OS: Windows 98/ME

Function	An ActiveX debugging tool for Java. If no arguments are given, the command asks whether to turn debug on/off.
Syntax	setdebug [option]

-d	Disables ActiveX debugging for Java.
-e	Enables ActiveX debugging for Java.
-p *directory*	Adds the specified directory to the Java source path.
-r *directory*	Removes the specified directory from the Java source path.
/?	Shows help information.
File Name: setdebug.exe	**Directory:** \windows — **Type:** External

setreg — OS: Windows 2000

Function	Alters the Software Publishing State Keys that control the behavior of the certificate behavior process.
Syntax	setreg [options...] *{ choice [value] }*

-q	Specifies quiet mode. Doesn't give any output.
-?	Publishing State Keys
choice	Specifies what to alter.
1	Specifies whether to trust the test root.
2	Specifies whether to use expiration date on certificates.
3	Specifies whether the revocation list is to be checked.
4	Allows offline approval for individual certificates.
5	Allows offline approval for commercial certificates.
6	Allows offline approval for individual certificates for Java.
7	Allows offline approval for commercial certificates for Java.
8	Invalidates objects that are signed with version 1.
9	Checks for Time Stamp Signer in the revocation list.
10	Trusts only items in the trust database.
value	Specifies the value for the choice TRUE or FALSE.
File Name: setreg.exe	**Directory:** \winnt\system32\dllcache — **Type:** External

sfc (2000) — OS: Windows 2000

Function	Searches all protected system files and replaces incorrect versions with the original files from Microsoft.
Syntax	sfc [options...]

/SCANNOW	Scans all protected system files.
/SCANONCE	Scans all protected system files at the next boot.

continued

/SCANBOOT	Specifies that the protected system files should be scanned at every boot.		
/CANCEL	Cancels all pending scans.		
/QUIET	Doesn't prompt before overwriting files.		
/ENABLE	Enables Windows File Protection for normal operation.		
/PURGECACHE	Clears the file cache and scans all protected system files.		
/CACHESIZE=*size*	Specifies the size of the file cache.		
File Name: `sfc.exe`	**Directory:** \winnt\system32	**Type:**	External
sfc /SCANNOW	Scans protected system files.		
sfc /ENABLE	Enables Windows File Protection for normal operation.		

sfc (XP)

OS: Windows XP

Function	Searches all protected system files and replaces incorrect versions with the original files from Microsoft.
Syntax	sfc [options...]

/SCANNOW	Scans all protected system files.		
/SCANONCE	Scans all protected system files at the next boot.		
/SCANBOOT	Specifies that the protected system files should be scanned at every boot.		
/REVERT	Loads default settings.		
/PURGECACHE	Clears the file cache and scans all protected system files.		
/CACHESIZE=*size*	Specifies the size of the file cache.		
File Name: `sfc.exe`	**Directory:** \windows\system32	**Type:**	External
sfc /SCANNOW	Scans protected system files.		
sfc /REVERT	Loads default settings.		

shadow

OS: Windows NT4 Terminal Server, 2000 Server, XP

Function	Monitors another terminal service session.
Syntax	shadow *{ session }* [options...]

/SERVER:*servername*	Specifies the server to query.		
/V	Verbose mode. Shows more information.		
session	Specifies the session name or ID to monitor.		
File Name: `shadow.exe`	**Directory:** **NT4 TS:** \wtsrv\system32, **2000:** \winnt\system32, **XP:** \windows\system32	**Type:**	External
shadow 23 /SERVER:moon	Monitors session 23 on server moon.		

Shared Folders

OS: Windows 2000 Server

Function	Manages and shows the use of shared folders on remote and local systems. Configures services for Macintosh to enable sharing on the same network as personal computers.
Syntax	fsmgmt.msc

File Name: `fsmgmt.msc`	**Directory:** \winnt\system32	**Type:**	External

Sharing Session

OS: Windows XP

Function	Shares applications (work in the same application at the same time) with another computer. It can also be used to share a whiteboard between the computers.
Syntax	rtcshare *{ computer }*

computer	The computer to connect to.		
File Name: `rtcshare.exe`	**Directory:** \windows\system32	**Type:**	External
rtcshare UCGPC	Connects to the specified computer running rtcshare in wait mode.		

shutdown (NT4)

OS: Windows NT4 Terminal Server

Function	Stops the current server or a remote one in a controlled way.
Syntax	shutdown *{ delay }* [options...]

/SERVER:*name*	Specifies the server to shut down (default is the current one).
/REBOOT	Reboots the server after all sessions have been stopped.
/POWERDOWN	Prepares the server for turning off the power.

continued

/DELAY:*sec*		Specifies time to delay the shutdown (default is 30 seconds).		
/V		Verbose mode. Shows more information.		
delay		Specifies how long to wait after the user has been informed (default is 60 seconds).		
File Name:	shutdown.exe	**Directory:** \wtsrv\system32	**Type:**	External
shutdown /REBOOT		Reboots the server after it has been shut down.		

shutdown (XP)

OS: Windows XP

Function	Shuts down the current server, workstation, or a remote computer in a controlled way.
Syntax	shutdown [options...]

		The following five options can't be combined.		
-i		Shows a GUI interface.		
-l		Logs off the current computer. This option can't be used with the -m option.		
-s		Shuts down the computer.		
-r		Shuts down and restarts the computer.		
-a		Aborts a system shutdown.		
-m *computer*		Specifies the remote computer to shut down, restart, or abort.		
-t *NR*		Specifies the number of seconds to wait before shutting down the computer.		
-c "string"		Specifies a shutdown comment of a maximum of 127 characters.		
-f		Forces running application to close without any warnings.		
-d [u][p]:*xx:yy*		Specifies the reason code for the shutdown.		
u		The user code.		
p		The planned shutdown code.		
xx		Specifies the major reason code. Valid values are 0 – 256.		
yy		Specifies the minor reason code. Valid values are 0 – 65536.		
File Name:	shutdown.exe	**Directory:** \windows\system32	**Type:**	External
shutdown -s -t 120 -d up:12:345		Shuts down the computer after 120 seconds and indicates a planned user code.		
shutdown -r -t 60 -m \\\\ucgwork01		Shuts down and restarts the specified computer after 60 seconds.		

smartdrv

OS: Windows Common

Function	Is used to create a disk cache in extended memory to speed up MS-DOS disk operations.
Syntax	smartdrv *{ drive }* [options...] *{ initcachesize } {wincachesize }*

/B:*size*		Is used to specify the size of the read ahead buffer; default is 16K (16384 bytes).		
/E:*size*		Is used to specify the amount of cache data to move at a time; default is 8192 bytes.		
/L		Is used to prevent SMARTDrive from loading into upper memory blocks (UMBs).		
/X		Disables write behind caching for all drives.		
/U		Is used to not load the CD-ROM caching module.		
		The following two options can't be combined.		
/C		Writes all cached data from memory to cached disks.		
/R		Writes all cached data to disk, then clears the cache and restarts SMARTDrive.		
		The following two options can't be combined.		
/F		Writes cached data to disk after the completion of each command; this is default.		
/N		Writes cached data to disk when the system is idle.		
		The following three options can't be combined.		
/V		Verbose mode. Shows status and error messages when starting.		
/Q		Quiet mode. Doesn't show status messages when starting.		
/S		Is used to show additional status information.		
drive[+ | -]		Enables or disables caching for the specified drive or drives.		
initcachesize		Specifies the cache size in kilobytes.		
wincachesize		Specifies the amount of memory to reduce the cache to when Windows starts.		
File Name:	smartdrv.exe	**Directory:** \windows	**Type:**	External
smartdrv 3000		Starts Smart Drive and sets the cache size to 3000K.		
smartdrv c: /S		Enables disk caching on c: showing additional status information.		

smbdpmi

OS:	Windows ME				
Function	Shows the memory address where the System Management BIOS is loaded if it is loaded in base memory.				
Syntax	smbdpmi [options...]				
/a value	Searches for a specific EPS. Possible values are: `SM, DMI, PNP`				
/d	Shows a raw dump of the SMB data and doesn't write to the file.				
/v	Verbose mode. Shows more information.				
File Name:	`smbdpmi.exe`	**Directory:**	\windows\system\wbem	**Type:**	External
Note:	Sometimes the SMB is loaded in high memory and creates a small file `smbios.dat` in the systems folder.				
smbdpmi /a sm /v	Searches for the system management BIOS in memory.				

smi2smir

OS:	Windows XP				
Function	Compiles MIBs (Management Information Bits) and is used by management applications over the SNMP protocol.				
Syntax	smi2smir [options...]				
/merrorlevel	Sets message level 0=none, 1=fatal , 2=fatal, warning, 3=fatal, warning, information.				
/c maximumerror	Sets the maximum error messages to display.				
/v1	Ensures that the MIBs, when compiled, strictly comply with the SNMPv1 SMI standard.				
/v2c	Ensures that the MIBs, when compiled, strictly comply with the SNMPv2 SMI standard.				
/d	Erases the specified module from the SMIR.				
/p	Removes all modules from SMIR.				
/l	Shows a list of all modules in SMIR.				
/lc	Is used to locally check the syntax in the module.				
	The following options have additional modifier options. See modifiers below:				
/ec *{ modifier }*	Checks the module both locally and externally.				
/a *{ modifier }*	Loads the module in the SMIR after a local and external syntax check.				
/sa *{ modifier }*	Works as the /a option but with no error display.				
/g *{ modifier }*	Creates a SMIR MOF file that can be compiled and loaded into CIMOM.				
/gc *{ modifier }*	Creates an inactive MOF file that can be used into CIMOM for particular namespace.				
	The following are modifiers for the options listed above:				
/ch	Includes user, host, and time information in the MOF header. Needs /g or /gc options.				
/t	Creates SnmpNotification classes. Needs /a, /sa, and /g options.				
/ext	Creates SnmpExtendedNotification classes. Needs /a, /sa, and /g options.				
/t /o	Creates only SnmpNotification classes. Needs /a, /sa, and /g options.				
/ext /o	Creates only SnmpExtendedNotification classes. Needs /a, /sa, and /g options.				
/s	Doesn't map the DESCRIPTION clause text. Needs /a, /sa, /g, and /gc options.				
/auto	Completes after the MIB lookup has rebuilt the table.				
/idir	Searches for a dependent MIB module. Needs /ec, /a, /sa, /g, and /gc options.				
/pa	Inserts a directory to the registry. (Current is default.)				
/pd	Removes a directory in the registry. (Current is default.)				
/pl	Shows a list in the registry of MIB lookup directories.				
/r	Reconstructs the total MIB lookup table.				
/n	Shows the ASN.1 name for the module specified.				
/ni	Shows the ASN.1 names for imports modules that the input module references.				
/h	Shows help information.				
/?	Shows help information.				
File Name:	`smi2smir.exe`	**Directory:**	\windows\system32\wbem\snmp	**Type:**	External

Sound Recorder

OS:	Windows 98/ME, NT4, 2000, XP				
Function	Records sounds in the .WAV format. It can add a few simple sound effects to the audio file.				
Syntax	sndrec32				
File Name:	`sndrec32.exe`	**Directory:**	**98/ME:** \windows, **NT4, 2000:** \winnt\system32, **XP:** \windows\system32	**Type:**	External

SQL Server Client Network Utility

OS:	Windows 98/ME, 2000, XP
Function	Starts the SQL Server Client Network Utility, which configures SQL Server connections.
Syntax	cliconfg.exe
File Name:	`cliconfg.exe`
Directory:	**98/ME:** \windows\system, **2000:** \winnt\system32, **XP:** \windows\system32
Type:	External

start

OS:	Windows Common
Function	Runs the specified file. If not executable, it runs the program associated with the file extension.
Syntax	start [options...] *{ file }*
/m	Starts specified program in the background, minimized.
/max	Starts specified program in the foreground, maximized.
/r	Starts specified program restored, normal window size. (Is the default.)
/w	Waits until the started program exits.
file	Specifies the file to start.
File Name:	`start.exe`
Directory:	\windows\command
Type:	External
start /m notepad.exe	Starts notepad in minimized mode.
start start start start winver	An unnecessary way to check the OS version.

Startup Disk Wizard

OS:	Windows 95/98
Function	Creates a special startup diskette to give DOS programs more memory. Used often for DOS-based games.
Syntax	nocomp.exe
File Name:	`nocomp.exe`
Directory:	\Program Files\Plus!\System
Type:	External

sys

OS:	Windows Common
Function	Is used to create a bootable disk by copying the system files to it.
Syntax	sys *{ source } destination*
source	Specifies the location of the system files. (Reads the files from the root directory of the current drive if not specified.)
destination	Specifies the target drive to which root the files should be copied.
File Name:	`sys.com`
Directory:	\windows\command
Type:	External
Note:	The command `format a: /s` is like typing sys a: after the format is done.
sys a:	Copies the system files from the root of the current drive to the floppy drive.

System Configuration Utility

OS:	Windows 98/ME, XP
Function	Modifies the startup procedures and edits configuration files.
Syntax	msconfig
File Name:	`msconfig.exe`
Directory:	\windows\pchealth\helpctr\binaries
Type:	External

System File Checker

OS:	Windows 98
Function	Starts the System File Checker. Searches for altered system files and asks whether to restore them.
Syntax	sfc
File Name:	`sfc.exe`
Directory:	\windows\system
Type:	External

System Information (2000)

OS:	Windows 2000
Function	Starts the MS System Information in Win2000, GUI.
Syntax	winmsd [options...]
/?	Shows the help for the command.
/msinfo_file=*file*	Opens the specified .NFO or .CAB file.
/s	Outputs an NFO to the specified file.
/report *filename*	Outputs a text format file to the specified file.
/computer *name*	Connects to the specified computer.
/categories *name* | ALL	Shows or outputs the specified categories.
/category *name*	Sets focus to the specified category at startup.

continued

File Name: `winmsd.exe`	**Directory:** \winnt\system32\wbem **Type:** External
winmsd /report file.txt	Creates a report into the file.txt.
winmsd /s nfo.txt	Puts the information into nfo.txt.

System Information (XP)

OS: Windows XP

Function	Starts the MS System Information for Windows XP.
Syntax	winmsd *{ file }* [options...]

/?	Displays the help for the command.
/report *filename*	Outputs a text format file to the specified file.
/computer *name*	Connects to the specified computer.
/categories *name* | ALL	Shows or outputs the specified categories.
/category *name*	Sets focus to the specified category at startup.
/pch	Launches the history view.
/nfo *file*	Outputs an NFO to the specified file.
/showcategories	Lists of category names.
file	Opens the specified .NFO, .CAB, or PCHealth XML file.

File Name: `winmsd.exe`	**Directory:** \windows\system32 **Type:** External
winmsd /report file.txt	Creates a report into the file.txt
winmsd /showcategories	Lists category names.

System Monitor

OS: Windows Common

Function	Shows various activities on the computer, like CPU usage, thread count, unused physical memory, etc.
Syntax	sysmon
File Name: `sysmon.exe`	**Directory:** \windows **Type:** External

System Policy Editor

OS: Windows NT4, 2000

Function	Sets Windows NT 4.0 policies for NT 4 clients and NT 4 style policies for Windows 2000 clients.
Syntax	poledit
File Name: `poledit.exe`	**Directory:** \winnt **Type:** External

System Recovery

OS: Windows 98

Function	Restores the system from a full system backup copy. It prompts for registration information and installs drivers.
Syntax	srw
File Name: `srw.exe`	**Directory:** \windows\system **Type:** External

System Restore

OS: Windows ME

Function	Checks that a system restore was the last operation performed and provides an opportunity to undo the changes.
Syntax	checksr
File Name: `checksr.bat`	**Directory:** \windows\command\ebd **Type:** External

systeminfo

OS: Windows XP

Function	Shows system information, such as OS version, security information, hardware properties, and product ID.
Syntax	systeminfo [options...]

/s *host*	The remote computer to connect to.
/u *{ domain\ }user*	Specifies the user to run the command with the default is the current user.
/p *{ password }*	The password for the specified user. Prompt for input if skipped.
/fo *format*	Specifies the output format to use. Valid are: TABLE, LIST, CSV.
/nh	Hides column header. Can only be used with the TABLE and CSV format.
/?	Shows help information.

File Name: `systeminfo.exe`	**Directory:** \windows\system32 **Type:** External
systeminfo /s webserver /u administrator	Shows system information for the specified computer.
systeminfo /fo table /nh	Shows the information in a table format with no column.

Task Manager

OS:	Windows NT4, 2000, XP
Function	This command starts the Windows Task Manager to administer applications that are currently running, or gets some system information.
Syntax	taskmgr

	The following views are available.
Applications	Controls and shows which applications are running.
Processes	Shows all the processes that are currently running.
Performance	Shows a graphic overview of CPU and memory usage.
XP:	
Networking	Shows the current network load.
Users	Shows all connected users.

File Name:	`taskmgr.exe`	**Directory:**	**NT4, 2000:** \winnt\system32, **XP:** \windows\system32	**Type:**	External

taskmgr	Starts the Task Manager, GUI.

taskkill

OS:	Windows XP
Function	Terminates a process (program or service).
Syntax	taskkill [options...]

/s *host*	The remote computer to connect to.
/u { *domain* }*user*	Specifies the user to run the command with. Default is the current user.
/p { *password* }	The password for the specified user. Prompts for input if skipped.
	The following three options can't be combined:
/fi "*filter operator value*"	Filters which processes are stopped.
filter	Specifies the filter to use.
	The following four filters accepts these operators: eq, ne, gt, lt, ge, le:
PID	Filters by PID number.
Session	Filters by session.
CPUTime	Filters by CPU time. For value use the following time format: hh:mm:ss.
Memusage	Filters by mem usage.
	The following six filters accept these operators: eq, ne:
Hostname	Filters by hostname.
Status	Filters by status. For value use RUNNING or NOT RESPONDING.
Imagename	Filters by image name.
Username	Filters by username.
Services	Filters by services.
Windowtitle	Filters by window title.
operator	Specifies which operator to use with the filter. Valid are: eq, ne, gt, lt, ge, le.
value	The value to use with the filter.
/pid *PID*	The PID number of the process to terminate.
/im *name*	The image name of the process to terminate.
/f	Terminates the program or service forcefully.
/t	Terminates all child processes together with the parent.
/?	Shows help information.

File Name:	`taskkill.exe`	**Directory:**	\windows\system32	**Type:**	External

taskkill /pid 800 /pid 1972	Terminates the processes with the specified PID numbers.
taskkill /fi "status eq not responding"	Terminates every process that isn't responding.
taskkill /im wmplayer.exe	Terminates the selected application.

tasklist

OS:	Windows XP
Function	Lists all running programs and services including their Process ID on the local or a remote computer.
Syntax	tasklist [options...]

/s *host*	The remote computer to connect to.
/u { *domain* }*user*	Specifies the user to run the command with. Default is the current user.
/p { *password* }	The password for the specified user. Prompts for input if skipped.

continued

	The following three options can't be combined:
/m *{ module }*	
/svc	Shows services in each process.
/v	Verbose mode. Shows more information.
/fi "*filter operator value*"	Filters which processes are shown. (This option can be used multiple times.)
filter	Specifies the filter to use.
	The following four filters accept these operators: eq, ne, gt, lt, ge, le:
PID	Filters by PID number.
Session	Filters by session.
CPUTime	Filters by CPU time. For value use the following time format: hh:mm:ss.
Memusage	Filters by mem usage.
	The following seven filters accept these operators: eq, ne:
Status	Filters by status. For value use RUNNING or NOT RESPONDING.
Imagename	Filters by image name.
SessionName	Filters by session name.
Username	Filters by username.
Services	Filters by services.
Windowtitle	Filters by window title.
Module	Filters by module.
operator	Specifies which operator to use with the filter. Valid are: eq, ne, gt, lt, ge, le.
value	The value to use with the filter.
/fo *format*	Specifies the output format to use. Valid are: TABLE, LIST, CSV.
/nh	Hides column header. Can only be used with the TABLE and CSV format.
/?	Shows help information.

File Name:	`tasklist.exe`	**Directory:**	\windows\system32	**Type:**	External

tasklist /fo list	Shows the list in a list format.
tasklist /fi "Status ne running"	Shows only programs and services that aren't responding.

Tasks

OS: Windows Common

Function	Shows a list of all running applications and enables the user to select or end an application.
Syntax	taskman

File Name:	`taskman.exe`	**Directory:**	\windows	**Type:**	External

Telephony

OS: Windows 2000 Server

Function	Manages and configures the Telephony Application Programming Interface (TAPI) that unifies the IP protocol and the regular telephone net for both IP and PSTN telephony servers and clients.
Syntax	tapimgmt.msc

File Name:	`tapimgmt.msc`	**Directory:**	\winnt\system32	**Type:**	External

Telephony Client Setup

OS: Windows 98/ME, 2000, XP

Function	Enables or disables your client to communicate with Telephony (TAPI) server.
Syntax	tcmsetup /C *servers...* [options...]

/C *servers...*	Sets up the client to use the specified server.
/D	Disables the settings for the specified server.
/Q	Hides message boxes.
2000, XP:	
/X	Uses connection-oriented callbacks.

File Name:	`tcmsetup.exe`	**Directory:**	**98/ME:** \windows\system, **2000:** \winnt\system32, **XP:** \windows\system32	**Type:**	External

tcmsetup /C myserver	Sets up the client to use the specified server.
tcmsetup /C myserver /D	Disables the settings for the specified server.

Telnet Server Admin Utility (2000)	OS: Windows 2000
Function	Starts the Telnet Server Admin Utility that can edit the Telnet Server preferences.
Syntax	tlntadmn
File Name: `tlntadmn.exe`	Directory: \winnt\system32 — Type: External

Telnet Server Admin Utility (XP)	OS: Windows XP
Function	Starts the Telnet Server Admin Utility that can edit the telnet server preferences.
Syntax	tlntadmn *{ host }* [options...] *ACTION*
-u *user*	Specifies the identity of the user.
-p *password*	Specifies the password for the user.
ACTION	**Use one of the following actions.**
start	Starts the Telnet Server Admin Utility.
stop	Stops the Telnet Server Admin Utility.
pause	Pauses the Telnet Server Admin Utility.
contin	Continues the Telnet Server Admin Utility after a pause.
-s *sessionid*	Shows information about the session. Use `-s all` to show all sessions.
-k *sessionid*	Stops the specified session.
-m *sessionid*	Sends a message to the specified session.
config	Is used to configure the Telnet Server parameters with the following options.
dom	Sets the default domain name for an unqualified user.
ctrlakeymap = yes | no	Specifies the mapping of the Alt key.
timeout = *time*	Specifies the idle session timeout in hh:mm:ss.
timeoutactive = yes | no	Starts or stops the timeout function.
maxfail = *number*	Sets the max number of failed login attempts before disconnecting.
maxconn = *number*	Sets the max number of possible connections.
port = *number*	Specifies the number of the port to use.
killall = yes | no	Enables the termination applications started from telnet while disconnecting.
sec = [+ | -]NTLM [+ | -]password	Sets the mechanism of the authentication.
fname = *file*	Specifies the audit file to use.
fsize = *MB*	Specifies the max size of the audit file.
mode = console | stream	Sets the operation mode.
auditlocation = LOCATION	Specifies the place where to save the log.
eventlog	Saves the log in `eventlog`.
file	Saves the log in the file specified with `fname`.
both	Saves the log in both the eventlog and the file.
audit = [+ | -]user [+ | -]fail [+ | -]admin	Specifies the event to log.
host	Specifies another system to run the command on.
File Name: tlntadmn.exe	Directory: \windows\system32 — Type: External

Terminal Services Client (2000)	OS: Windows 2000 Server
Function	Accesses a specified server running Terminal Services, which can then be connected, disconnected, or verified.
Syntax	mstsc
File Name: `mstsc.exe`	Directory: \winnt\system32\clients\tsclient\net — Type: External
mstsc	Starts the GUI interface for Terminal Service overview.

Terminal Services Client (NT4)	OS: Windows NT4 Terminal Server
Function	Starts the Windows-based program Microsoft Terminal Server Client.
Syntax	mstsc
File Name: `mstsc.exe`	Directory: \wtsrv\system32\clients\tsclient — Type: External

Terminal Services Client Creator	OS: Windows 2000 Server
Function	Creates terminal services clients.
Syntax	clcreate
File Name: `clcreate.exe`	Directory: \winnt\system32\clients — Type: External

Terminal Services Client Setup

OS: Windows 2000 Server

Function	The Terminal Services Client installer program.				
Syntax	setup				
File Name:	`setup.exe`	**Directory:**	\winnt\system32\clients\tsclient	**Type:**	External
Tip:	Comes in two flavors, a 16- and 32-bit version.				
setup	Starts the Terminal Services installer program.				

Terminal Services Configuration

OS: Windows 2000 Server

Function	Configures and administers connections for terminal services to remote hosts and systems. It will also configure settings for a Terminal server, including default connection security.				
Syntax	tscc.msc				
File Name:	`tscc.msc`	**Directory:**	\winnt\system32	**Type:**	External

Terminal Services License Manager

OS: Windows NT4 Terminal Server, 2000 Server

Function	Manages licenses for terminal services.				
Syntax	licmgr				
File Name:	`licmgr.exe`	**Directory:**	**NT4 TS:** \wtsrv\system32, **2000:** \winnt\system32\dllcache	**Type:**	External

Terminal Services Manager

OS: Windows NT4 Terminal Server, 2000 Server

Function	Starts the Terminal Services manager used to administrate users and terminal servers.				
Syntax	tsadmin				
File Name:	`tsadmin.exe`	**Directory:**	**NT4 TS:** \wtsrv\system32, **2000:** \winnt\system32	**Type:**	External

tftp

OS: Windows NT4, 2000, XP

Function	Copies files to and from a computer running the TFTP service.				
Syntax	tftp [-i] *host { command } source { destination }*				
-i	Enables binary transfer mode instead of ASCII, which is the default.				
command	**The following two commands are available:**				
GET	Copies the file destination from the remote host to the file source on the local.				
PUT	Copies the file source from the local host to the file destination on the remote.				
host	Copies the file source from the local host to the file destination on the remote.				
destination	Specifies the destination file.				
File Name:	`tftp.exe`	**Directory:**	**NT4, 2000:** \winnt\system32, **XP:** \windows\system32	**Type:**	External
tftp -i ucghost get c:\downloads song.mp3	Copies the file song.mp3 to c:\download on the local host.				
tftp ucghost put textfile.txt c:\documents	Copies the file textfile.txt to c:\documents on the remote host.				

Tour

OS: Windows XP

Function	Starts the Multimedia tour of Microsoft Windows XP.				
Syntax	tour				
File Name:	`tour.exe`	**Directory:**	\windows\help\tours\mmtour	**Type:**	External

tracerpt

OS: Windows XP

Function	Creates trace analysis reports by processing event trace logs or real-time data from event trace providers.				
Syntax	tracerpt *{ file ... }* [options...]				
/?	Shows help information.				
/o *{ file }*	Specifies a CSV (comma delimited) file for output. Default is dumpfile.csv				
/rt *sessions ...*	Collects the data from the real-time data source. Specify event trace session(s).				
/summary *{ file }*	Specifies a summary output file. Default is summary.txt.				
/config *file*	Specifies a file containing command line parameters.				
	The following two parameters can't be combined but one is required:				
/rt *sessions ...*	Collects the data from the real-time data source. Specifies event trace sessions.				
file ...	Specifies event trace log files to process.				
File Name:	`tracerpt.exe`	**Directory:**	\windows\system32	**Type:**	External
tracerpt logg.etl /report	Creates a report from the specified log file and outputs it to workload.txt.				
tracerpt event_session -o logg.csv	Creates the report from the specified real-time data source.				

tracert6

tracert6	OS: Windows XP
Function	Determines the route to the specified target, using IPv6.
Syntax	tracert6 [options...] *host* tracert6 [options...] *IPv6addr*[%*scopeid*]

-d	Specifies addresses to not be resolved to computer names.
-h *hops*	Specifies the maximum number of hops when tracing the route.
-w *timeout*	Sets the timeout in milliseconds for each reply.
-s *srcaddr*	Specifies the source address to use.
-r	Tests reverse route using routing header.
host	Specifies the host name of the computer to trace.
IPv6addr	The IPv6 address to the remote computer.
scopeid	Specifies the scope id for the target address. Not required for global addresses.

File Name:	`tracert6.exe`	**Directory:**	\windows\system32	**Type:**	External
tracert6 server01		Traces the route to the specified host.			

trcdlc

trcdlc	OS: Windows 95/98
Function	Enables and configures tracing of DLC applications. Can store the trace results in a file.
Syntax	trcdlc [options...]

-d*name*	Specifies the DLC VxD name to trace. (Default is DLC)
-f*name*	Specifies the file to store the trace results.
-i A | S	Specifies I/O method to use. Use A for asynchronous (Default) or S for synchronous.
-q	Hides the trace information to the screen.
-t*value*	Sets the size for the trace file. You must use increments of 1024.
-w	Forces writing to the disk.
-c	Sends a close request to the application.
-l*value*	Sets the maximum size for message length to the value specified.
-n*XXXX*	Sets the adapter mask to the specified value.
-p	Shows configuration parameters.
-r	Resets and flushes all trace pointer buffers.
-s	Reads the current status from the driver.
-m*XXXX*	Sets the trace mask to one of the following values:

8000 = Enables snapshot	4000 = Activates snapshot	2000 = Debugs INT3.
1000 = State Machine	0080 = Enables CCB2's	0040 = Not currently used
0020 = Enables Debug	0010 = Command done	0800 = Enables I/O Controls
0400 = DLC Buffer pool	0200 = Traces received data	0100 = Traces transmit data.
0008 = Traces configuration	0004 = Initialization	0002 = Session
0001 = Traces overflow continue		

File Name:	`trcdlc.exe`	**Directory:**	\windows\system	**Type:**	External
trcdlc -m0001		Creates a trace driver and enables overflow.			

tree

tree	OS: Windows XP
Function	Shows a graphical representation of a directory structure. If no parameters are used, the current directory structure is shown.
Syntax	tree { *path* } [options...]

/f	Specifies that the files also should be shown.
/a	Specifies that ASCII characters should be used instead of graphics.
/?	Shows help information.
path	Specifies the path to the drive or directory for which you want the structure shown.

File Name:	`tree.com`	**Directory:**	\windows\system32	**Type:**	External
tree c:\windows		Shows the directory structure of c:\windows.			
tree c:\windows /f		Shows the file and directory structure of c:\windows.			

TS Connection Configuration

OS: Windows NT4 Terminal Server

Function	Manages connections for the terminal server.				
Syntax	tscfg				
File Name:	`tscfg.exe`	**Directory:**	\wtsrv\system32	**Type:**	External

tscon

OS: Windows 2000, XP

Function	Connects, reconnects, or sends a user session or a terminal session to another terminal session.
Syntax	tscon *session* [/SERVER:*servername*] /DEST:*sessionname* [options...]

/SERVER:*servername*	Specifies another server if session isn't located on current server.
/DEST:*sessionname*	Specifies the session NAME of the session that you want to connect TO.
/PASSWORD:*pw*	Specifies the user password for the destination session.
/V	Verbose mode. Shows more information during the connection process.
session	Specifies the session ID or session name that you want to connect FROM.

File Name:	`tscon.exe`	**Directory:**	**2000:** \winnt\system32, **XP:** \windows\system32	**Type:**	External
Tip:	Use the commands *query session* or *query users* to help identify sessions.				

tscon rdp-tcp#47 /DEST:rdp-tcp#59	Sends session rdp-tcp#47 /DEST:rdp-tcp#59

tsdiscon

OS: Windows 2000, XP

Function	Disconnects a terminal session that you can later reconnect to and allows any current processes to continue to run.
Syntax	tsdiscon { *session* } [/SERVER:*servername*] [/V]

/SERVER:*servername*	Specifies another server if session isn't located on current server.
/V	Verbose mode. Shows more information during the connection process.
session	Specifies the session ID or session name that you want to disconnect.

File Name:	`tsdiscon.exe`	**Directory:**	**2000:** \winnt\system32, **XP:** \windows\system32	**Type:**	External

tsdiscon rdp-tcp#47	Disconnects the session rdp-tcp#47 from current server.

tskill

OS: Windows 2000, XP

Function	Stops a process ID (PID) or a process name specified by process.
Syntax	tskill *process* [options...]

/SERVER:*servername*	Specifies another server if the process isn't located on current server.
	The following two options can't be combined:
/ID:*sessionID*	Stops all processes that are connected to the specified session ID.
/A	Stops all processes in ALL active sessions
/V	Verbose mode. Shows more information.
process	Specifies the process ID (PID) or process name that you want to terminate.

File Name:	`tskill.exe`	**Directory:**	**2000:** \winnt\system32, **XP:** \windows\system32	**Type:**	External
Tip:	To show running processes, use the command `query process`.				

tskill 2943 /SERVER:star	Stops the PID number 2943 on server star.

tsprof

OS: Windows NT4 Terminal Server, 2000 Server

Function	Copies or updates the terminal server user configuration information.
Syntax	tsprof *ACTION* [option] [/PROFILE:*path*] *user* tsprof /COPY [option] [/PROFILE:*path*] *srcuser destuser*

ACTION	**One of the following 3 actions must be specified:**
/UPDATE	Updates the profile path information for the specified user.
/COPY	Copies the user configuration information from `srcuser` to `user`.
/Q	Shows the current profile path for the specified user.
	The following 2 options can't be combined:
/DOMAIN:*domain*	Specifies the domain to work in.
/LOCAL	Works on the local computer.

continued

	The following option is only required with /update and is optional with /COPY:
/PROFILE:*file*	Specifies the profile path to use.
user	Specifies the user to work on.
srcuser	Specifies the user to copy the configuration information from.
destuser	Specifies the user to copy the configuration information to.
File Name: `tsprof`	**Directory:** **NT4 TS:** \wtsrv\system32, **2000:** \winnt\system32 **Type:** External

tsshutdn

OS: Windows 2000, XP

Function	Stops terminal services after a wait delay and can reboot or shut down the server.
Syntax	tsshutdn *{ time }* [options...]

time	The amount of time before terminal services are shut down. (Default is 60 sec.)
/SERVER:*servername*	Specifies the server name to shut down terminal services on. (Default is current server.)
/REBOOT	Reboots the server after terminal services have been shut down.
/POWERDOWN	Stops the server and power the server off if possible.
/DELAY:*time*	The time delay before REBOOT or SHUTDOWN after terminal services are shut down.
/V	Verbose mode. Shows more information.
File Name: `tsshutdn.exe`	**Directory:** **2000:** \winnt\system32, **XP:** \windows\system32 **Type:** External
tsshutdn 300 /SERVER:star /REBOOT	Stops terminal services on server star in 5 min. and then reboots.

typeperf

OS: Windows XP

Function	Shows or saves performance counter data. Abort the command with Ctrl+C.
Syntax	typeperf ["*counter ...*"] [options...]

/f *format*	Specifies the file format to use. Valid selections are CSV (default), TSV, BIN, SQL.
/si *time*	Sets the time between samples. Default is 1 second. Use this format: [[hh:]mm:]ss.
/o *file*	Specifies the path to the output file or SQL database. Default is STDOUT.
/sc *NR*	Sets the number of samples to collect. Default is to run until CTRL+C is pressed.
/config *file*	A file containing command options.
/s *computer*	Specifies the server to monitor if none is specified in the counter path.
/y	Answers yes to all questions.
/?	Shows help information.
	The following four parameters can't be combined but one is required:
/cf *file*	Specifies a file containing performance counters to monitor.
/q ["*object*"]	Shows all installed counters (no instances) or for the specified object.
/qx ["*object*"]	Shows all installed counters with instances or for the specified object.
counter ...	The counter or counters to monitor.
File Name: `typeperf.exe`	**Directory:** \windows\system32 **Type:** External
typeperf "\processor(*)\% User Time"	Monitors the specified counter and shows the information.
typeperf "\processor(*)\% User Time" /sc 10	Shows ten samples of the specified counter.

unlodctr

OS: Windows NT4, 2000, XP

Function	Removes counter names and explains text for the specified counter.
Syntax	unlodctr [*host*] *driver*

host	Specifies a remote computer; the local is used if not specified.
driver	Specifies the driver that name definition and explain text should be removed from.
File Name: `unlodctr.exe`	**Directory:** **NT4, 2000:** \winnt\system32, **XP:** \windows\system32 **Type:** External
unlodctr \\ucghost driver	Removes the name and text for driver from the ucghost host.

Update Information Tool (95)

OS: Windows 95

Function	Shows registered system files that have been updated and registered updates.
Syntax	qfecheck
File Name: `qfecheck.exe`	**Directory:** \windows **Type:** External

Update Information Tool (ME)

OS: Windows ME

Function	Shows registered system files that have been updated and registered updates.
Syntax	qfecheck
File Name: `qfecheck.exe`	**Directory:** \windows **Type:** External

Update Wizard Uninstall

OS:	Windows 98/ME, 2000
Function	Uninstalls device drivers that have been updated from the Windows Update web program.
Syntax	upwizun
File Name:	upwizun.exe
Directory:	**98/ME:** \windows, **2000:** \winnt
Type:	External

upg351db

OS:	Windows NT4 Server, 2000 Server
Function	Converts the DHCP or Wins database from a Windows 3.51 server to a Windows 2000 or NT 4.0 server.
Syntax	upg351db *{ db }* /e*type* [options...]

/e*type*	Selects the type. Valid choices are 1 (DHCP), 2 (Wins) and 3 (RPL).
/d*file*	Specifies the name and path of the 200 series .DLL.
/y*file*	Specifies the name and path of the 200 series system database.
/l*path*	The path to the old log files.
/b*path*	The path to the backup database that is used if the main isn't consistent.
/i	Saves the conversion stats to UPGDINFO.TXT
/p*directory*	Saves the database files in the specified directory.
/r	Removes the backup database when the conversion is done.
db	Specifies the database to convert.

File Name:	upg351db.exe
Directory:	\winnt\system32
Type:	External
Note:	The file JET.DLL is needed from the Windows 3.51 server.

upg351db dhcp.mdb /e1 /djet.dll	Converts the old DHCP database to the new format.
upg351db wins.mdb /e2 /djet.dll	Converts the old Wins database to the new format.

User Manager

OS:	Windows NT4
Function	Administers users, groups, and policies on the computer, including the ability to change, add, or delete. Only members of the administrators group are allowed to make changes.
Syntax	**Server:** usrmgr **Workstation:** musermgr
File Name:	usrmgr.exe, musrmgr.exe
Directory:	\winnt\system32
Type:	External

User Manager for Domains

OS:	Windows 2000 Server
Function	Administers Windows NT domains. Can't administer Windows 2000 or newer domains.
Syntax	usrmgr
File Name:	usrmgr.exe
Directory:	\windows\system32\dllcache
Type:	External

userinit

OS:	Windows NT4, 2000, XP
Function	Initializes the user interface for the client by running logon scripts, establishing any network connections, and then starts Windows Explorer (containing the user's personalized settings).
Syntax	userinit
File Name:	userinit.exe
Directory:	**NT4, 2000:** \winnt\system32, **XP:** \windows\system32
Type:	External

userinit	Starts the initialization process and starts the Windows Explorer.

verifier

OS:	Windows 2000, XP
Function	A graphical utility used to verify device drivers, show device status, and verify I/O addresses.
Syntax	verifier
File Name:	verifier.exe
Directory:	**2000:** \winnt\system32, **XP:** \windows\system32
Type:	External

Version Conflict Manager

OS:	Windows 98
Function	Shows a list of files from a previous version of Windows that were updated in Windows 98 that can be restored.
Syntax	vcmui
File Name:	vcmui.exe
Directory:	\windows
Type:	External

vssadmin

OS:	Windows XP		
Function	Shows all installed snapshot providers and writers and shows current volume snapshot backups.		
Syntax	vssadmin list *ACTION*		

ACTION	**The following actions are available:**
snapshots [-set=*GUID*]	Shows every snapshot in the system, and groups them by id.
writers	Shows all available writers.
providers	Shows every installed snapshot provider.

File Name:	`vssadmin.exe`	**Directory:**	\windows\system32	**Type:**	External

vssadmin list providers	Shows all installed snapshot providers.

vwipxspx

OS:	Windows NT4 Server, 2000, XP				
Function	Loads the VDM IPX/SPX support.				
Syntax	vwipxspx				
File Name:	`vwipxspx.exe`	**Directory:**	**NT4, 2000:** \winnt\system32, **XP:** \windows\system32	**Type:**	External

w32tm

OS:	Windows 2000
Function	This command is used for time synchronization.
Syntax	w32tm [options]

-tz	Shows local time zone information.
-s *computer*	Forces synchronization on the specified computer.
-adj	Resets system clock to the last known synchronization.
-adjoff	Resets the system clock to the system's default values.
-once	Synchronizes time one time only.
-test	Doesn't change the local system clock.
-v	Verbose mode. Shows more information.
-p *port*	Specifies the server port.
-period *freq*	Specifies the sync period.
freq	**Frequency can be one of the following:**
0	Synchronizes once a day.
65535	Synchronizes every second day.
65534	Synchronizes every third day.
65533	Synchronizes every seventh day.
65532	Synchronizes every 45 min. until three accepted synchronizations, then once every 8 hours.
65531	Synchronizes every 45 min. until one accepted synchronizations, then once every day.

File Name:	`w32tm.exe`	**Directory:**	\winnt\system32	**Type:**	External
Note:	Time synchronization is commonly used in networks. –AS				

w32tm -tz	Shows local time zone information.

wb16off

OS:	Windows ME				
Function	Prevents your computer from locking up if you are using a Cyrix processor with an ACC2066 chip set.				
Syntax	wb16off				
File Name:	`wb16off.exe`	**Directory:**	\windows\options\install	**Type:**	External
Note:	Normally the ACC2066 chipset is used in laptop computers.				

Welcome

OS:	Windows 95/98, NT4				
Function	Shows a welcome window with a new tip every time it is started. In Windows 95/98 it offers a guided tour.				
Syntax	welcome				
File Name:	`welcome.exe`	**Directory:**	**95/98:** \windows, **NT4:** \winnt	**Type:**	External

win95clt

OS: Windows NT4 Server

Function	Moves the workstation boot files from the workstation home directory to the profiles directory.
Syntax	win95clt *directory* *server* *profile*

directory	Specifies the home directory for the workstation.
server	Specifies the name of the remote boot server.
profile	Specifies the name of the workstation profile.
File Name: `win95clt.bat`	**Directory:** \winnt\rpl\bin **Type:** Script
win95clt h:\directory1 \\ucgrplserver Win95IP	Moves the boot file from the directory into the profile.

Windows

OS: Windows Common

Function	Starts Windows. The parameters are good for troubleshooting when Windows doesn't start correctly.
Syntax	win [/D]

/D	Debug mode. Useful for troubleshooting.
:F	Disables access for 32-bit disks.
:M	Is used to run Windows in safe mode.
:N	Is used to run Windows in safe mode with the network enabled.
:S	Disables usage of ROM address space between F000:0000 and 1MB for a breakpoint.
:V	Manages interrupts from hard disk controller using the ROM routine.
:X	Finds unused space by excluding all adapter area from memory that Windows scans.
File Name: `win.com`	**Directory:** \windows **Type:** External
win /D:N	Starts Windows in safe mode with networking.

Windows 2000/XP Setup

OS: Windows 2000

Function	A graphical user interface that guides the user through the setup of Windows 2000.
Syntax	sysocmgr [options...]

/i:*master_oc_inf*	Specifies the master inf file to use.
/u:*unattend_spec*	Specifies parameters so that installation can be unattended.
/r	Doesn't reboot the computer during installation.
/z	Specifies that the following arguments should be passed to components.
/n	Forces the master inf file to be treated as new.
/f	Resets all component installation states.
/c	Disables the cancel feature during final installation phase.
/x	Suppresses the initializing banner.
/q	Runs an unattended installation without a User Interface. Only used with /u.
/w	Prompts the user before rebooting. Only used with /u.
/l	Uses multi-language support during installation.
File Name: `sysocmgr.exe`	**Directory:** \winnt\system32 **Type:** External
sysocmgr /r	Starts the installer with suppression of reboots.

Windows Automated System Recovery

OS: Windows XP

Function	Performs a system backup or restores the system from the backup file.
Syntax	asr_fmt options...

/backup /context=*context*	Runs a backup with the specified context.
/restore /sifpath=*file*	Runs a restore from the specified .SIF file.
File Name: `asr_fmt.exe`	**Directory:** \windows\system32 **Type:** External

Windows Help

OS: Windows XP

Function	Starts Windows Help and optionally opens a help file.
Syntax	winhelp { *helpfile* }

helpfile	Specifies the help file to open.
File Name: `winhelp.exe`	**Directory:** \windows **Type:** External
winhelp help.hlp	Starts Windows Help and opens the help file help.hlp.

Windows Management Infrastructure (WMI)

OS: Windows 2000 Server

Function	Configures the WMI settings on a local or remote system.
Syntax	wmimgmt.msc
File Name:	`wmimgmt.msc`
Directory:	\winnt\system32
Type:	External

Windows Media Player

OS: Windows 98/ME, NT4, 2000, XP

Function	Starts the Windows Media Player used to play many different types of audio and video files.
Syntax	mplayer2.exe
File Name:	`mplayer2.exe`
Directory:	**98/ME, 2000, XP:** \Program Files\Windows Media Player, **NT4:** \windows\system32
Type:	External

Windows NT Diagnostics

OS: Windows NT4

Function	Shows information on Services, Resources, Environment, Network, Version, System, Display, Drives, and Memory.
Syntax	winmsd [*host*] [options...]

/a	Generates a complete system report. Can't be combined with the /s option.
/s	Generates a summary system report. Can't be combined with the /a option.
/f	Sends the report to a file. Can't be combined with the /p option.
/p	Sends the system report to the current printer. Not combinable with the /f option.
/?	Shows help information.
	The following hot keys are available in the program:
F2	Copies a summary of the current tab to the clipboard.
Shift-F2	Copies all details of the current tab to the clipboard.
host	Specifies the Windows NT host to show information about.
File Name:	`winmsd.exe`
Directory:	\winnt\system32
Type:	External
winmsd \\\\ucghost /a	Creates a complete system report on the ucghost host.

Windows Registry Checker

OS: Windows 98/ME

Function	Scans the Windows system Registry for errors and creates or restores backups of the registry. When the program is executed from within Windows with no options, the GUI version `scanregw.exe` will be executed.
Syntax	scanreg [option] scanregw

/?	Shows help information.
/backup	Makes a backup of the register and system configuration files.
/restore	Restores a backup.
/fix	Repairs the registry.
/comment= *comment*	Adds a comment to the CAB-file when making the backup. No spaces allowed in comment.
/autorun	Scans the Registry with no questions asked.
File Name:	`scanreg.exe, scanregw.exe`
Directory:	\windows\command
Type:	External
Note:	This command runs every time the computer starts and makes a backup of the system registry.
scanreg /comment="Before_installing_office"	Creates a backup of the Registry and adds the comment "Before_installing_office."

Windows Report Tool

OS: Windows 98, 2000

Function	The Windows Report Tool. Collects information about the computer and creates a report to send to the help desk.
Syntax	winrep
File Name:	`winrep.exe`
Directory:	**98:** \windows, **2000:** \winnt
Type:	External

Windows Script Host

OS: Windows 98/ME, 2000

Function	Starts a graphic window for a different script language on a Windows computer.
Syntax	wscript [options...] *script*

//B	Hides prompts and script errors (Batch Mode).
//D	Enables active debugging.
//E:*engine*	Specifies the engine to use when executing the script.

continued

//H:CScript	Changes the default script host to CScript.exe.				
//H:WScript	Changes the default script host to WScript.exe.				
//I	Shows prompt and script errors. (Interactive Mode.)				
//Job:*NR*	Runs the specified job.				
//Logo	Shows logo. (Default.)				
//Nologo	Hides logo.				
//S	Saves the current command line options for the current user.				
//T:*time*	Specifies the script timeout in seconds.				
//X	Executes the script in debugger.				
//U	Uses Unicode for redirected I/O from the console.				
file	Specifies the script to run including any parameters it requires.				
File Name: `wscript.exe`	**Directory:**	**98/ME:** \windows, **2000:** \winnt\system32	**Type:**	External	
wscript file.vbs //D	Runs the specified script with active debugging.				
wscript file.vbs //I	Run file.vbs in interactive mode.				

Windows Setup (ME)

OS: Windows ME

Function	Starts the Windows ME setup program.
Syntax	setup *{ file }* [options...]

/ie	Doesn't create a startup disk.			
/ih	Runs Scandisk in the foreground.			
/im	Doesn't check if there is enough free conventional memory.			
/is	Doesn't run Scandisk.			
/iv	Hides billboard during setup.			
/F:*tmp*	Specifies the temp directory to use. (The directory must exist and all files in it will be deleted.)			
File Name: `setup.exe`	**Directory:**	\windows	**Type:**	External

Windows Setup (XP)

OS: Windows XP

Function	A graphical user interface that guides the user through the setup of Windows XP.
Syntax	sysocmgr [options]

/i:*master_oc_inf*	Specifies the master inf file to use.			
/u:*unattend_spec*	Specifies parameters so that installation can be unattended.			
/r	Doesn't reboot the computer during installation.			
/z	Specifies that the following arguments should be passed to components.			
/n	Forces the master inf file to be treated as new.			
/f	Resets all component installation states.			
/c	Disables the cancel feature during final installation phase.			
/x	Suppresses the initializing banner.			
/q	Runs an unattended installation without a User Interface. Only used with /u.			
/w	Prompts the user before rebooting. Only used with /u.			
/l	Uses multi language support during installation.			
File Name: `sysocmgr.exe`	**Directory:**	\windows\system32	**Type:**	External
sysocmgr /r	Starts the installer with suppression of reboots.			

Windows XP Tour

OS: Windows XP

Function	Welcomes the user to the Windows XP Tour and lets the user select between the animated and non-animated tours.				
Syntax	tourstart				
File Name:	`tourstart.exe`	**Directory:**	\windows\system32	**Type:**	External

WinMgmt

OS: Windows ME

Function	Starts the Windows Management tool.
Syntax	winmgmt [options...]

/kill	Causes the service to stop any running copies, even if running copy is an NT service.
/Regserver	Invokes the self registration.
/Unregserver	Removes registry entries.
/backup <*file*>	Backs up the repository to the specified file.

continued

/restore <*file*> <*flag*> flag = 1 flag = 0 /resyncperf <*winmgmt service PID*> /clearadap	Restores the repository from the specified file. Disconnects users and restore the repository. Restores if no users are connected. Registers the system's performance libraries with WMI. Clears prior WMI /resyncperf information from the registry.				
File Name:	`winmgmt.exe`	**Directory:**	\windows\system\wbem	**Type:**	External

WinPopup

OS: Windows Common

Function	A popup messaging system used to send and receive messages to other users, computers, or workgroups.
Syntax	winpopup

File Name:	`winpopup.exe`	**Directory:**	\windows	**Type:**	External

WINS Manager

OS: Windows NT4 Server

Function	Manages WINS servers.
Syntax	winsadm

File Name:	`winsadmn.exe`	**Directory:**	\winnt\system32	**Type:**	External

Wireless link

OS: Windows 2000, XP

Function	Sends files using an infrared link.
Syntax	irftp [options...] *{ files... }*

/h	Sends files using quiet mode.
/s	Shows preferences for Wireless link.
files...	Specifies which files to send.

File Name:	`irftp.exe`	**Directory:**	**2000:** \winnt\system32, **XP:** \windows\system32	**Type:**	External

wjview

OS: Windows 98/ME, 2000

Function	Starts a graphical interface used to load Java command in .class files.
Syntax	wjview [options...] *file { arguments... }*

/?	Shows help information.
/cp *path*	Specifies the path to class.
/cp:p *path*	Adds a path before the class path.
/cp:a *path*	Adds a path after the class path.
/n *namespace*	Specifies the namespace to execute in.
/p	Pauses the application if an error occurs.
/v	Verifies all classes.
/d: *name=value*	Defines system properties.
/a	Runs the Applet Viewer.
/vst	Verbose mode. Shows stack trace information.
file	Specifies the .CLASS file to be executed.
arguments...	Specifies command-line arguments to be passed on to the .CLASS file.

File Name:	`wjview.exe`	**Directory:**	**98/ME:** \windows, **2000:** \winnt\system32	**Type:**	External

wjview /p java.class	Runs java.class and will pause if an error occurs.
wjview /a	Runs the appletviewer.

wlbs

OS: Windows 2000 Server

Function	Manages a network load-balancing cluster. This is only available in Windows 2000 Advanced Server.
Syntax	wlbs option *{ cluster}{ :host }* [options...]

	The following options can't be combined
help	Shows help information.
ip2mac *cluster*	Converts cluster IP-address to cluster MAC addresses for the cluster.
reload	Reloads the parameters from the register.
query	Shows hosts that belong to the cluster.
display	Shows configuration, status, and some of the most recent events from the log.
suspend	Suspends the control of the cluster.
resume	Resumes control of the cluster.
start	Starts the cluster.

continued

stop	Stops the cluster.
drainstop	Finishes all existing connections and stops the cluster.
enable *port*	Specifies port to enable traffic for, (or if ALL is specified) all ports.
disable *port*	Specifies port to disable traffic for, (or if ALL is specified) all ports.
drain *port*	Specifies port to disable new traffic for, (or if ALL is specified) all ports.
	The following options shall be at the end:
/PASSW *{ password }*	Specifies the remote password default is NONE and a blank will give console prompt.
/PORT *port*	Specifies the control UDP port to use.
cluster	Specifies cluster name or IP-address.
host	Specifies hostname, IP-address, priority ID or 0 for current. (Default is all.)

File Name:	`wlbs.exe`	**Directory:**	\winnt\system32	**Type:**	External
Note:	This is the only executable file added to 2000 Advanced Server from 2000 Server.				

WMI Control — OS: Windows ME

Function	Connects to the WMI service on local or other computers and provides general information about the computer's configuration. Can also set up security, logging, and perform backup and restore functions of the WMI repository.
Syntax	wbemcntl

File Name:	`wbemcntl.exe`	**Directory:**	\windows\system\wbem	**Type:**	External

wmic — OS: Windows XP

Function	Handles almost all configurations on the computer. Can be command- or interactive-based.
Syntax	wmic [options...] *ACTION { ACTION2 }*

/namespace:*namespace*	Specifies the namespace to use the alias on. (Default is \\root\cli.)
/role:*namespace*	Specifies the role containing the alias definitions to use with the utility session.
/node:*list*	Specifies the servers the alias will operate against.
/implevel:*level*	Specifies the impersonal level to use. (Can be Anonymous, Identify, Impersonate, or Delegate.)
/authlevel:*level*	Specifies the authlevel to use. (Can be Default, None, Connect, Call, Pkt, Pktintegrity, Pktprivacy.)
/locale:*ID*	Specifies which language ID the command should use. ID is the syntax `MS_xxx`.
/privileges:*mode*	Enables or disables all privileges. Mode can be ENABLE or DISABLE.
/trace:*switch*	Shows debug information if turned on. Switch can be either ON or OFF.
/record:*file*	Logs all events occurred during the use of the command to the specified file.
/interactive:*switch*	Sets or resets the interactive mode.
/failfast:*switch*	Sets or resets the failfast mode.
/output:*output*	Sets output redirection.
/append:*output*	Sets output redirection.
output	Can either be STDOUT, CLIPBOARD, or a file.
/user:*user*	Specifies the user to use. Syntax is `domain\user.`
/aggregate:*switch*	Determines the mode of showing results. Can be either TRUE or FALSE.
/password:*password*	Specifies the password for the user to use.
/? [`:mode`]	Shows help information. Can be used everywhere to show help at current position.
mode	Can either be BRIEF or FULL. (Type a /? after ACTION2 to view a list of all parameters to use.)
ACTION	Specifies which category to view or alter. If ACTION2 not used, shows default values.
ALIAS	Gives access to all aliases available on the local system.
BASEBOARD	Handles the baseboard configuration. (Motherboard.)
BIOS	Handles the BIOS configuration.
BOOTCONFIG	Handles the Boot configuration.
CDROM	Handles CD-ROM configuration.
COMPUTERSYSTEM	Handles general computer configuration.
CPU	Handles CPU configuration.
CSPRODUCT	Handles computer system product information.
DCOMAPP	Handles DCOM application management.

continued

DESKTOP	Handles desktop properties.
DESKTOPMONITOR	Handles monitor properties.
DEVICEMEMORYADDRESS	Handles device memory address configuration.
DIR	Handles the filesystem directory entry.
DISKDRIVE	Handles the physical disk drives configuration.
DISKQUOTA	Handles disk space quotas on NTFS system.
DMACHANNEL	Handles DMA channel configuration.
ENVIRONMENT	Handles system environment configuration.
GROUP	Handles group accounts.
IDECONTROLLER	Handles the IDE controller configuration.
IRQ	Handles IRQ configuration.
JOB	Handles scheduled jobs from the schedule service.
LOADORDER	Handles execution dependencies of system services.
LOGICALDISK	Handles local storage device configuration.
LOGON	Handles logon session configuration.
MEMCACHE	Handles cache memory configuration.
MEMLOGICAL	Handles system memory configuration.
MEMPHYSICAL	Handles physical system memory configuration.
NETCLIENT	Handles network client configuration.
NETLOGIN	Handles configuration of network login information for the specified user.
NETPROTOCOL	Handles network protocol configuration.
NETUSE	Handles active network connection configuration.
NIC	Handles network interface controller configuration.
NICCONFIG	Handles network adapter configuration.
NTDOMAIN	Handles the NT domain configuration.
NTEVENT	Handles entries in the NT event log.
NTEVENTLOG	Handles configuration on the NT eventlog file.
ONBOARDDEVICE	Handles adapters built into the motherboard.
OS	Handles information on installed operating systems.
PAGEFILE	Handles virtual memory swap file configuration.
PAGEFILESET	Handles page file settings.
PARTITION	Handles partition configuration on a physical disk.
PORT	Handles I/O port configuration.
PORTCONNECTOR	Handles physical port connection configuration.
PRINTER	Handles printer devices.
PRINTERCONFIG	Handles printer device configuration.
PRINTJOB	Handles printer jobs.
PROCESS	Handles processes running on the system.
PRODUCT	Handles the installation package tasks.
QFE	Handles quick fix engineering.
QUOTASETTING	Handles settings for disk quotas on a volume.
RECOVEROS	Handles crash dump configuration.
REGISTRY	Handles computer registry configuration.
SCSICONTROLLER	Handles SCSI controller configuration.
SERVER	Handles server information.
SERVICE	Handles service application configuration.
SHARE	Handles shared resource configuration.
SOFTWAREELEMENT	Handles the elements of a software product installed on the system.
SOFTWAREFEATURE	Handles software product subset of software elements.
SOUNDDEV	Handles sound device configuration.
STARTUP	Handles applications that autostart when the user logs in.
SYSACCOUNT	Handles system account configuration.
SYSDRIVER	Handles the system driver for base services.
SYSTEMCLOSURE	Handles physical system enclosures.
SYSTEMSLOT	Handles physical connection points.
TAPEDRIVE	Handles tape drive configuration.
TEMPERATURE	Handles temperature sensor configuration.
TIMEZONE	Handles timezone configuration.

continued

UPS	Handles uninterruptible power supply configuration.
USERACCOUNT	Handles user account configuration.
VOLTAGE	Handles voltage sensor configuration.
WMISET	Handles WMI service operational parameters.
	The following actions uses private syntaxes, and don't use ACTION2:
CLASS *classpath { verb } { verbdescription }*	Escapes to full WMI schema.
PATH *path* [WHERE *clause*] *{ verb }*	Escapes to full WMI object paths.
CONTEXT	Shows the values on all command flags.
EXIT/QUIT	Exits the program. (Is only used in interactive mode.)
ACTION2	The subaction to do on the specified action.
ASSOC[:*format*] [options...]	Shows associations for the current object.
/RESULTCLASS:*class*	Shows only result classes that belong to (or derive from) the specified class.
/RESULTROLE:*role*	Shows only results that play a role for the object.
/ASSOCCLASS:*class*	Shows only result classes that are associated with the specified class and the object.
format	Is either an xsl file, TABLE or MOF. (Default is TABLE.)
TABLE	Shows all associations in a brief description.
MOF	Shows more detailed information on all associations.
CREATE *property=definition*	Creates a new instance on the current object. Use CREATE /? for a list of variables. (Use a comma-separated list for multiple assignments.)
DELETE	Prompts for a verification for each instance in the object whether to delete.
GET *{ property }* [options...]	Retrieves values on specified properties, separated by commas. (Use GET /? for a list of properties to use.)
/VALUE	Retrieves the value only.
/ALL	Retrieves data and metadata for the properties. (Is default.)
/TRANSLATE:*name*	Translates the values through the table name, specified in the alias namespace.
/EVERY:*interval* [/REPEAT:*value*]	Runs the command `value` number of times, with the specified interval. (If /REPEAT isn't specified, the command runs in an infinite loop.)
/FORMAT:*file*	Specifies the XSL file to process the XML results.
LIST *{ format }* [options...]	Shows properties on the current object.
/TRANSLATE:*name*	Translates the values through the table name, specified in the alias namespace.
/EVERY:*interval* [/REPEAT:*value*]	Runs the command `value` number of times, with the specified interval. (If /REPEAT isn't specified, the command runs in an infinite loop.)
/FORMAT:*file*	Specifies the XSL file to process XML results.
format	Depends on which object is the current one. Use LIST /? to view a list of them.

File Name:	`wmic.exe`	**Directory:**	\windows\system32	**Type:**	External
Note:	Who would ever need a mouse or graphical interface in windows? This command has everything!				

wmic GROUP CREATE caption=newgroup,Description="The new group"	Creates a new user group on the system.

xcopy32		OS:	Windows Common		
Function	Is used to copy files, directories, and subdirectories. Is intended to be run as a helper from the `xcopy` program.				
Syntax	xcopy *source* { *destination* } [options...]				

	The following two options can't be combined:
/a	Copies only files with the archive file attribute.
/m	Only copies files with the archive attribute and then removes them from the source.
/d:{ *date* }	Copies files newer than date. If no date is specified, only newer file is copied.
/p	Is used to prompt for confirmation before copying each file.
/s	Copies all directories and subdirectories except if they are empty.
/e	Copies all directories and subdirectories even if they are empty.
/w	Waits for the user to press a key before starting to copy.
/c	Forces xcopy to continue copying when errors occur.
/i	Assumes that the destination is a directory if it doesn't exist.
/y	Replaces existing files without prompting.
/-y	Prompts before replacing existing files.
/h	Enables copying of hidden and system files.
/r	Enables xcopy to overwrite read-only files.
/t	Skips copying files and creates directory structure.
/n	Uses generated short filenames when copying.
/u	Updates existing files in the destination.
/q	Quiet mode.
/f	Shows full path of both source and destination file when copying.
/l	Shows files that are going to be copied.
/k	Copies files including their current attributes.
source	Specifies which directory or file to copy.
destination	Specifies where to copy files or name of new file.

File Name:	`xcopy32.exe`	**Directory:**	\windows\command	**Type:**	External
xcopy32 c:\temp*.* d:\temp /s		Copies all files and subdirectories from c:\temp to d:\temp.			

Chapter 7

Windows Control Panel Cross-Reference

The functionality of the Windows Control from Windows 95, Windows NT, Windows 2000 and Windows XP has been cross-referenced to each other and other major operating systems.

The Windows Control Panel is a very powerful tool and many people are very familiar with the functionality of the Control Panel. Using this table, you can find equivalent commands on Novell, UNIX, and Macintosh systems.

Windows XP Control Panel	AIX	OpenBSD	Linux	Solaris	NetWare 3	NetWare 4	NetWare 5	NetWare 6
Accessibility Options				accessx				
Add Hardware	smit > Devices > Install	insmod	modload	touch /reconfig	install.nlm	install.nlm	hdetect.nlm nwconfig.nlm	hdetect.nlm nwconfig.nlm
Add/Remove Programs	installp	rpm	pkg_add	pkgadd	install > product options	install > product options	install > product options	install > product options
Administrative Tools	smit	linuxconf		admintool	syscon.exe sysconW.exe	netadmin.exe nwadmn32. exe	nwadmn32. exe consoleone. exe	nwadmn32. exe consoleone. exe
Date/Time	chtz date	timeconfig zdump tzselec	zdump date	Action: 186 zdump	Set Time Zone	Set Time Zone	Set Time Zone	Set Time Zone
Display		xf86config	xf86config	afbconfig ffbconfig	monitor.nlm	monitor.nlm	monitor.nlm	monitor.nlm
Folder Options								
Fonts	lsfont	fslsfonts	fslsfonts	fslsfonts				
Game Controllers		insmod						
Internet Options								
Keyboard	xmodmap chkbd lskbd	xmodmap setxkbmap kbdconfig	xmodmap setxkbmap kbd	xmodmap kbd loadkey	keyb.nlm	keyb.nlm	keyb.nlm charset.nlm	keyb.nlm charset.nlm
Licensing	chlicense					install.nlm	licmaint.nlm nwucutil.nlm nwconfig.nlm	licmaint.nlm nwucutil.nlm nwconfig.nlm
Mouse		mouseconfig						
Network Connections	smit chginet ifconfig	netconf ifconfig	ifconfig	admintool ifconfig	install.nlm	inetcfg.nlm	inetcfg.nlm	inetcfg.nlm
Phone and Modem Options		wvdialconf					cpecfg	cpecfg
Power Options	pmctrl	apm	apm	pmconfig				
Printers and Faxes	piomkpq smit print	/etc/printcap	/etc/printcap	printmgr lpadmin lpset	pconsole.exe psc.exe	pconsole.exe psc.exe	nwpmw32. exe nwadmn32. exe ndpsm.nlm	nwadmn32. exe ndpsm.nlm
Regional and Language Options	LANG= *language* chlang	LANG= *language*	LANG= *language*	LANG= *language*				

DOS	Windows 9x	NT 4.0	NT 2000	Windows XP	Macintosh	Windows XP Control Panel
	Accessibility Options	Accessibility Options	Accessibility Options	Accessibility Options	Apple Menu > Control Panels > Speech	Accessibility Options
	Add New Hardware		Add/Remove Hardware	Add Hardware	Apple Menu > Control Panels > Extensions	Add Hardware
	Add/Remove Programs	Add/Remove Programs	Add/Remove Programs	Add or Remove Programs		Add/Remove Programs
		Program > Administrative Tools	Administrative Tools	Administrative Tools	Apple Menu > Control Panels	Administrative Tools
date time	Date/Time	Date/Time	Date/Time	Date and Time	Apple Menu > Control Panels > Date & Time	Date/Time
	Display	Display	Display	Display	Apple Menu > Control Panels > Monitors	Display
	Action: 75	Action: 260	Folder Options	Folder Options		Folder Options
	Fonts	Fonts	Fonts	Fonts	Apple menu > Control Panels > Appearance > Fonts	Fonts
	Game Controllers		Game Controllers	Game Controllers		Game Controllers
	Internet Options	Internet Options	Internet Options	Internet Options	Apple Menu > Control Panels > Internet	Internet Options
keyb.com chcp.com	Keyboard	Keyboard	Keyboard	Keyboard	Apple Menu > Control Panels > Keyboard	Keyboard
		Licensing	Licensing	Licensing		Licensing
	Mouse	Mouse	Mouse	Mouse	Apple Menu > Control Panels > Mouse	Mouse
	Network	Network	Network and Dial-Up Connections	Network Connections	Apple Menu > Control Panels > TCP/IP	Network Connections
	Modems	Modems	Phone and Modem Options	Phone and Modem Options	Apple Menu > Control Panels > Modem	Phone and Modem Options
	Power Management		Power Options	Power Options	Apple Menu > Control Panels > Energy Saver	Power Options
	Printers	Printers	Printers	Printers and Faxes	Apple Menu > Chooser	Printers and Faxes
country nlsfunc.exe	Regional Settings	Regional Settings	Regional Options	Regional and Language Options	Apple Menu > Control Panels > Numbers	Regional and Language Options

Windows XP Control Panel	AIX	OpenBSD	Linux	Solaris	NetWare 3	NetWare 4	NetWare 5	NetWare 6
Scanners and Cameras								
Scheduled Tasks	at crontab cron	at crontab crondat crontab cron	at crontab cron	at crontab cron	cron.nlm wmsched.exe	cron.nlm wmsched.exe	cron.nlm wmsched.exe	cron.nlm wmsched.exe
Sounds and Audio Devices		sndconfig						
System	smitty topas lscfg svmon	linuxconf top dmesg	top dmesg	admintool dmesg prtconf	monitor.nlm syscon.exe sysconW.exe	monitor.nlm netadmin.exe nwadmn32. exe	monitor.nlm nwadmn32. exe consoleone. exe	monitor.nlm nwadmn32. exe consoleone. exe

Windows 2000 Control Panel	AIX	OpenBSD	Linux	Solaris	NetWare 3	NetWare 4	NetWare 5	NetWare 6
Accessibility Options				accessx				
Add/Remove Hardware	smit > Devices > Install	insmod	modload	touch /reconfig	install.nlm	install.nlm	hdetect.nlm nwconfig.nlm	hdetect.nlm nwconfig.nlm
Add/Remove Programs	installp	rpm	pkg_add	pkgadd	install > product options	install > product options	install > product options	install > product options
Administrative Tools	smit	linuxconf		admintool	syscon.exe sysconW.exe	netadmin.exe nwadmn32. exe	nwadmn32. exe consoleone. exe	nwadmn32. exe consoleone. exe
Date/Time	chtz date	timeconfig zdump tzselec	zdump date	Action: 186 zdump	Set Time Zone	Set Time Zone	Set Time Zone	Set Time Zone
Display		xf86config	xf86config	afbconfig ffbconfig	monitor.nlm	monitor.nlm	monitor.nlm	monitor.nlm
Folder Options								
Fonts	lsfont	fslsfonts	fslsfonts	fslsfonts				
Game Controllers		insmod						
Internet Options								
Keyboard	xmodmap chkbd lskbd	xmodmap setxkbmap kbdconfig	xmodmap setxkbmap kbd	xmodmap kbd loadkey	keyb.nlm	keyb.nlm	keyb.nlm charset.nlm	keyb.nlm charset.nlm
Licensing	chlicense					install.nlm	licmaint.nlm nwucutil.nlm nwconfig.nlm	licmaint.nlm nwucutil.nlm nwconfig.nlm

DOS	Windows 9x	NT 4.0	NT 2000	Windows XP	Macintosh	Windows XP Control Panel
			Scanners and Cameras	Scanners and Cameras		**Scanners and Cameras**
	sysagent.exe	at.exe	Scheduled Tasks	Scheduled Tasks		**Scheduled Tasks**
	Multimedia	Multimedia	Sounds and Multimedia	Sounds and Audio Devices	Apple Menu > Control Panels > Sound	**Sounds and Audio Devices**
	System	System	System	System	Apple Menu > Apple System Profiler	**System**

DOS	Windows 9x	NT 4.0	NT 2000	Windows XP	Macintosh	Windows 2000 Control Panel
	Accessibility Options	Accessibility Options	Accessibility Options	Accessibility Options	Apple Menu > Control Panels > Speech	**Accessibility Options**
	Add New Hardware		Add/Remove Hardware	Add Hardware	Apple Menu > Control Panels > Extensions	**Add/Remove Hardware**
	Add/Remove Programs	Add/Remove Programs	Add/Remove Programs	Add or Remove Programs		**Add/Remove Programs**
		Program > Administrative Tools	Administrative Tools	Administrative Tools	Apple Menu > Control Panels	**Administrative Tools**
date time	Date/Time	Date/Time	Date/Time	Date and Time	Apple Menu > Control Panels > Date & Time	**Date/Time**
	Display	Display	Display	Display	Apple Menu > Control Panels > Monitors	**Display**
	Action: 75	Action: 260	Folder Options	Folder Options		**Folder Options**
	Fonts	Fonts	Fonts	Fonts	Apple menu > Control Panels > Appearance > Fonts	**Fonts**
	Game Controllers		Game Controllers	Game Controllers		**Game Controllers**
	Internet Options	Internet Options	Internet Options	Internet Options	Apple Menu > Control Panels > Internet	**Internet Options**
keyb.com chcp.com	Keyboard	Keyboard	Keyboard	Keyboard	Apple Menu > Control Panels > Keyboard	**Keyboard**
		Licensing	Licensing	Licensing		**Licensing**

Windows 2000 Control Panel	AIX	OpenBSD	Linux	Solaris	NetWare 3	NetWare 4	NetWare 5	NetWare 6
Mouse		mouseconfig						
Network and Dial-Up Connections	smit chginet ifconfig	netconf ifconfig	ifconfig	admintool ifconfig	install.nlm	inetcfg.nlm	inetcfg.nlm	inetcfg.nlm
Phone and Modem Options		wvdialconf					cpecfg	cpecfg
Power Options	pmctrl	apm	apm	pmconfig				
Printers	piomkpq smit print	/etc/printcap	/etc/printcap	printmgr lpadmin lpset	pconsole.exe psc.exe	pconsole.exe psc.exe	nwpmw32. exe nwadmn32. exe ndpsm.nlm	nwadmn32. exe ndpsm.nlm
Regional Options	LANG= *language* chlang	LANG= *language*	LANG= *language*	LANG= *language*				
Scanners and Cameras								
Scheduled Tasks	at crontab cron	at crontab crondat crontab cron	at crontab cron	at crontab cron	cron.nlm wmsched.exe	cron.nlm wmsched.exe	cron.nlm wmsched.exe	cron.nlm wmsched.exe
Sound and Multimedia		sndconfig						
System	smitty topas lscfg svmon	linuxconf top dmesg	top dmesg	admintool dmesg prtconf	monitor.nlm syscon.exe sysconW.exe	monitor.nlm netadmin.exe nwadmn32. exe	monitor.nlm nwadmn32. exe consoleone. exe	monitor.nlm nwadmn32. exe consoleone. exe

Windows NT Control Panel	AIX	OpenBSD	Linux	Solaris	NetWare 3	NetWare 4	NetWare 5	NetWare 6
Accessibility Options				accessx				
Add/Remove programs	installp	rpm	pkg_add	pkgadd	install > product options	install > product options	install > product options	install > product options
Console	chfont	setfont consolechars						
Date/Time	chtz date	timeconfig zdump tzselec	zdump date	Action: 186 zdump	Set Time Zone	Set Time Zone	Set Time Zone	Set Time Zone
Devices	lsdev			getdev devinfo	list devices	list devices	list devices	list devices

DOS	Windows 9x	NT 4.0	NT 2000	Windows XP	Macintosh	Windows 2000 Control Panel
	Mouse	Mouse	Mouse	Mouse	Apple Menu > Control Panels > Mouse	**Mouse**
	Network	Network	Network and Dial Up Connections	Network Connections	Apple Menu > Control Panels > TCP/IP	**Network and Dial-Up Connections**
	Modems	Modems	Phone and Modem Options	Phone and Modem Options	Apple Menu > Control Panels > Modem	**Phone and Modem Options**
	Power Management		Power Options	Power Options	Apple Menu > Control Panels > Energy Saver	**Power Options**
	Printers	Printers	Printers	Printers and Faxes	Apple Menu > Chooser	**Printers**
country nlsfunc.exe	Regional Settings	Regional Settings	Regional Options	Regional and Language Options	Apple Menu > Control Panels > Numbers	**Regional Options**
			Scanners and Cameras	Scanners and Cameras		**Scanners and Cameras**
	sysagent.exe	at.exe	Scheduled Tasks	Scheduled Tasks		**Scheduled Tasks**
	Multimedia	Multimedia	Sounds and Multimedia	Sounds and Audio Devices	Apple Menu > Control Panels > Sound	**Sound and Multimedia**
	System	System	System	System	Apple Menu > Apple System Profiler	**System**

DOS	Windows 9x	NT 4.0	NT 2000	Windows XP	Macintosh	Windows NT Control Panel
	Accessibility Options	Accessibility Options	Accessibility Options	Accessibility Options	Apple Menu > Control Panels > Speech	**Accessibility Options**
	Add/Remove Programs	Add/Remove Programs	Add/Remove Programs	Add/Remove Programs		**Add/Remove programs**
	Action: 245 Action: 122	console Action: 279	Action: 245 Action: 122	Action: 245 Action: 122	Apple Menu > Control Panels > Appearance > Fonts	**Console**
date time	Date/Time	Date/Time	Date/Time	Date and Time	Apple Menu > Control Panels > Date & Time	**Date/Time**
	Cross Reference Note: 211	Cross Reference Note: 211	Action: 190	Action: 190		**Devices**

Windows NT Control Panel	AIX	OpenBSD	Linux	Solaris	NetWare 3	NetWare 4	NetWare 5	NetWare 6
Display		xf86config	xf86config	afbconfig ffbconfig	monitor.nlm	monitor.nlm	monitor.nlm	monitor.nlm
Find Fast	find / -name *file* which *file* whence *file*	where *file* find / -name *file* which *file*	find / -name *file* which *file* whence *file*	where *file* find / -name *file* which *file*	ndir *file* /s filer.exe	ndir *file* /s filer.exe	ndir *file* /s filer.exe	ndir *file* /s filer.exe
Fonts	lsfont	fslsfonts	fslsfonts	fslsfonts				
Internet Options								
Keyboard	xmodmap chkbd lskbd	xmodmap setxkbmap kbdconfig	xmodmap kbd setxkbmap	xmodmap kbd loadkey	keyb.nlm	keyb.nlm	keyb.nlm charset.nlm	keyb.nlm charset.nlm
Licensing	chlicense					install.nlm	licmaint.nlm nwucutil.nlm nwconfig.nlm	licmaint.nlm nwucutil.nlm nwconfig.nlm
Modems		wvdialconf					cpecfg	cpecfg
Mouse		mouseconfig						
Multimedia		sndconfig						
Network	smit chginet ifconfig	netconf ifconfig	ifconfig	admintool ifconfig	install.nlm	inetcfg.nlm	inetcfg.nlm	inetcfg.nlm
ODBC Data Sources							odbcjoin.exe	odbc.exe
PC Card (PCMCIA)	xpcmcia acfgd	cardmgr cardctl						
Ports	stty	stty statserial setserial	stty	stty syncinit	rs232.nlm	rs232.nlm	rs232.nlm aiocon.nlm	aiocon.nlm
Printers	piomkpq smit print	/etc/printcap	/etc/printcap	printmgr lpadmin lpset	pconsole.exe psc.exe	pconsole.exe psc.exe	nwpmw32.exe nwadmn32.exe ndpsm.nlm	nwadmn32.exe ndpsm.nlm
Regional Settings	LANG=*language* chlang	LANG=*language*	LANG=*language*	LANG=*language*				
SCSI Adapters	smitty	scsi_info		prtdiag	list devices	list devices	List Storage Adapters list devices	list devices
Server		lsof smbstatus	fstat		monitor.nlm	monitor.nlm	monitor.nlm	monitor.nlm

DOS	Windows 9x	NT 4.0	NT 2000	Windows XP	Macintosh	Windows NT Control Panel
	Display	Display	Display	Display	Apple Menu > Control Panels > Monitors	**Display**
dir *file* /s	Action: 182	Find Fast	Action: 182	Action: 182	command + f File > Find	**Find Fast**
	Fonts	Fonts	Fonts	Fonts	Apple menu > Control Panels > Appearance > Fonts	**Fonts**
	Internet Options	Internet Options	Internet Options	Internet Options	Apple Menu > Control Panels > Internet	**Internet Options**
keyb.com chcp.com	Keyboard	Keyboard	Keyboard	Keyboard	Apple Menu > Control Panels > Keyboard	**Keyboard**
		Licensing	Licensing	Licensing		**Licensing**
	Modems	Modems	Phone and Modem Options	Phone and Modem Options	Apple Menu > Control Panels > Modem	**Modems**
	Mouse	Mouse	Mouse	Mouse	Apple Menu > Control Panels > Mouse	**Mouse**
	Multimedia	Multimedia	Sounds and Multimedia	Sounds and Audio Devices	Apple Menu > Control Panels > Sound	**Multimedia**
	Network	Network	Network and Dial-Up Connections	Network Connections	Apple Menu > Control Panels > TCP/IP	**Network**
	ODBC data sources (32bit)	ODBC data sources	Action: 114	Action: 114		**ODBC Data Sources**
		PC Card (PCMCIA)				**PC Card (PCMCIA)**
mode.com	Action: 167	Ports	Action: 166	Action: 166		**Ports**
	Printers	Printers	Printers	Printers and Faxes	Apple Menu > Chooser	**Printers**
country nlsfunc.exe	Regional Settings	Regional Settings	Regional Options	Regional and Language Options	Apple Menu > Control Panels > Numbers	**Regional Settings**
	Action: 171	SCSI Adapters	Action: 171	Action: 171	Apple Menu > Apple System Profiler > Devices and Volumes	**SCSI Adapters**
	netwatch.exe	Server	compmgmt. msc	compmgmt. msc openfiles.exe		**Server**

Windows NT Control Panel	AIX	OpenBSD	Linux	Solaris	NetWare 3	NetWare 4	NetWare 5	NetWare 6
Services	chsubserver /etc/inetd. conf	/etc/xinetd. conf	/etc/inetd. conf	/etc/inetd. conf	install.nlm	inetcfg.nlm	inetcfg.nlm	inetcfg.nlm
Sounds		sndconfig						
System	smitty topas lscfg svmon	linuxconf top dmesg	top dmesg	admintool dmesg prtconf	monitor.nlm	monitor.nlm	monitor.nlm nwadmn32. exe consoleone. exe	monitor.nlm
Tape Devices	tapes			tapes	list devices	list devices	list devices	list devices
Telephony								

Windows 95 Control Panel	AIX	OpenBSD	Linux	Solaris	NetWare 3	NetWare 4	NetWare 5	NetWare 6
Accessibility Options				accessx				
Add New Hardware	smit > Devices > Install	insmod	modload	touch /reconfig	install.nlm	install.nlm	install.nlm	install.nlm
Add/Remove Programs	installp	rpm	pkg_add	pkgadd	install > product options	install > product options	install > product options	install > product options
Automatic Updates	smit install_ update	rpm	pkg_add	patchadd	nwconfig > product options	nwconfig > product options	nwconfig > product options	nwconfig > product options
Date/Time	chtz date	timeconfig zdump tzselec date	zdump date	Action: 186 zdump date	Set Time Zone	Set Time Zone	Set Time Zone	Set Time Zone
Display		xf86config	xf86config	afbconfig ffbconfig	monitor.nlm	monitor.nlm	monitor.nlm	monitor.nlm
Find Fast	find / -name *file* which *file* whence *file*	where *file* find / -name *file* which *file*	find / -name *file* which *file* whence *file*	where *file* find / -name *file* which *file*	ndir *file* /s filer.exe	ndir *file* /s filer.exe	ndir *file* /s filer.exe	ndir *file* /s filer.exe
Fonts	lsfont	fslsfonts	fslsfonts	fslsfonts				
Game Controllers		insmod						
Internet Options								
Keyboard	xmodmap chkbd lskbd	xmodmap setxkbmap kbdconfig	xmodmap kbd setxkbmap	xmodmap kbd loadkey	keyb.nlm	keyb.nlm	keyb.nlm charset.nlm	keyb.nlm charset.nlm

DOS	Windows 9x	NT 4.0	NT 2000	Windows XP	Macintosh	Windows NT Control Panel
		Services	services.msc	services.msc		**Services**
	Sounds	Sounds	Sounds And Multimedia	Sounds and Audio Devices	Apple Menu > Control Panels > Sound	**Sounds**
	System	System	System	System	Apple Menu > Apple System Profiler	**System**
		Tape Devices	compmgmt. msc	compmgmt. msc		**Tape Devices**
	Telephony	Telephony	Phone and Modem Options	Phone and Modem Options		**Telephony**

DOS	Windows 9x	NT 4.0	NT 2000	Windows XP	Macintosh	Windows 95 Control Panel
	Accessibility Options	Accessibility Options	Accessibility Options	Accessibility Options	Apple Menu > Control Panels > Speech	**Accessibility Options**
	Add New Hardware		Add/Remove Hardware	Add/Remove Hardware	Apple Menu > Control Panels > Extensions	**Add New Hardware**
	Add-Remove Programs	Add/Remove Programs	Add/Remove Programs	Add or Remove Programs		**Add/Remove Programs**
	wupdmgr.exe qfecheck.exe		wupdmgr.exe	wupdmgr.exe		**Automatic Updates**
date time	Date/Time	Date/Time	Date/Time	Date and Time	Apple Menu > Control Panels > Date & Time	**Date/Time**
	Display	Display	Display	Display	Apple Menu > Control Panels > Monitors	**Display**
dir *file* /s	Find Fast Action: 182	Find Fast Action: 182	Action: 182	Action: 182	command + f File > Find	**Find Fast**
	Fonts	Fonts	Fonts	Fonts	Apple menu > Control Panels > Appearance > Fonts	**Fonts**
	Game Controllers		Game Controllers	Game Controllers		**Game Controllers**
	Internet Options	Internet Options	Internet Options	Internet Options	Apple Menu > Control Panels > Internet	**Internet Options**
keyb.com chcp.com	Keyboard	Keyboard	Keyboard	Keyboard	Apple Menu > Control Panels > Keyboard	**Keyboard**

Windows 95 Control Panel	AIX	OpenBSD	Linux	Solaris	NetWare 3	NetWare 4	NetWare 5	NetWare 6
Modems		wvdialconf					cpecfg	cpecfg
Mouse		mouseconfig						
Multimedia		sndconfig						
Network	smit chginet ifconfig	netconf ifconfig	ifconfig	admintool ifconfig	install.nlm	inetcfg.nlm	inetcfg.nlm	inetcfg.nlm
ODBC Data Sources (32bit)							odbcjoin.exe	odbc.exe
Passwords	passwd yppasswd	passwd yppasswd	passwd	passwd yppasswd nispasswd	setpass.exe Action: 37	setpass.exe Action: 37	setpass.exe Action: 37	Action: 37
Power Management	pmctrl	apm	apm	pmconfig				
Printers	piomkpq smit print	/etc/printcap	/etc/printcap	printmgr lpadmin lpset	pconsole.exe psc.exe	pconsole.exe psc.exe	nwpmw32. exe nwadmn32. exe ndpsm.nlm	nwadmn32. exe ndpsm.nlm
Regional Settings	LANG= *language* chlang	LANG= *language*	LANG= *language*	LANG= *language*				
Sounds		sndconfig						
System	smitty topas lscfg svmon	linuxconf top dmesg	top dmesg	admintool dmesg prtconf	monitor.nlm syscon.exe sysconW.exe	monitor.nlm netadmin.exe nwadmn32. exe	monitor.nlm nwadmn32. exe consoleone. exe	monitor.nlm nwadmn32. exe consoleone. exe
Telephony								
Users	smit smitty mkuser mkgroup	userconf useradd groupadd	adduser groupadd	admintool useradd groupadd	syscon.exe sysconW.exe	netadmin.exe nwadmn32. exe	nwadmn32. exe consoleone. exe consoleone dos.exe	nwadmn32. exe consoleone. exe consoleone dos.exe

DOS	Windows 9x	NT 4.0	NT 2000	Windows XP	Macintosh	Windows 95 Control Panel
	Modems	Modems	Phone and Modem Options	Phone and Modem Options	Apple Menu > Control Panels > Modem	**Modems**
	Mouse	Mouse	Mouse	Mouse	Apple Menu > Control Panels > Mouse	**Mouse**
	Multimedia	Multimedia	Sounds and Multimedia	Sounds and Audio Devices	Apple Menu > Control Panels > Sound	**Multimedia**
	Network	Network	Network and Dial Up Connections	Network Connections	Apple Menu > Control Panels > TCP/IP	**Network**
	Control Panel > ODBC Data Sources (32bit)	Control Panel > ODBC Data Sources	Action: 114	Action: 114		**ODBC Data Sources (32bit)**
	Passwords	Action: 229	Action: 229	Action: 229	Action: 200	**Passwords**
	Power Management		Power Options	Power Options	Apple Menu > Control Panels > Energy Saver	**Power Management**
	Printers	Printers	Printers	Printers and Faxes	Apple Menu > Chooser	**Printers**
country nlsfunc.exe	Regional Settings	Regional Settings	Regional Options	Regional and Language Options	Apple Menu > Control Panels > Numbers	**Regional Settings**
	Sounds	Sounds	Sounds and Multimedia	Sounds and Audio Devices	Apple Menu > Control Panels > Sound	**Sounds**
	System	System	System	System	Apple Menu > Apple System Profiler	**System**
	Telephony	Telephony	Phone and Modem Options	Phone and Modem Options		**Telephony**
	Users	addusrw.exe usrmgr.exe musrmgr.exe net user	wizmgr.exe net user	wizmgr.exe net user	Apple Menu > Control Panels > File Sharing > Users & Groups	**Users**

Chapter 8

DOS 6.22 Commands

The commands in this section cover all of the commands from Microsoft DOS 6.22. For cross-references from DOS to other operating systems, please see Chapter 1, the "Quick Command Index."

ansi.sys

Function	Defines functions that control cursor movement, reassign keys, and change display graphics. This command can only be used in the CONFIG.SYS file.
Syntax	DEVICE=*path*ANSI.SYS [options...] DEVICEHIGH=*path*ANSI.SYS [options...]

/X	Remaps extended keys separately on 101-key keyboards.
/K	Handles a 101-key keyboard like an 84-key keyboard.
/R	Improves readability when used with screen-reading programs.
path	Specifies the location for the `ansi.sys` driver.

File Name:	`ansi.sys`	**Directory:**	\dos	**Type:**	External

device=c:\dos\ansi.sys	Loads the device driver.
devicehigh=c:\dos\ansi.sys	Loads the device driver into the upper memory area.

append

Function	Allows programs to open files in different directories as if they are in the current directory.
Syntax	append *{ paths... }* [options...]

paths...	Specifies which drive and directory to append. Separate multiple entries with semicolon.
/X:ON	Searches in directories that have been appended. Don't search using `:OFF`.
/PATH:ON	Searches appended directories for a file. Don't search using `:OFF`.
/E	Copies the appended directory list in the file `APPEND.` (This is used only once after system startup.)
;	Cancels the appended directory list.

File Name:	`append.exe`	**Directory:**	\dos	**Type:**	External

append c:\mydir;d:\yourdir	Adds the specified directories to the append list.

attrib

Function	Modifies the file or directory attribute. If used with no parameters, the file attributes are shown for all the files in the current directory.
Syntax	attrib [options...] *{ file }*

/s	Applies changes to all files in every subdirectory. Directories aren't affected.
+R or -R	Sets or removes the Read-only file attribute.
+A or -A	Sets or removes the Archive file attribute.
+S or -S	Sets or removes the System file attribute.
+H or -H	Sets or removes the Hidden file attribute.
/?	Shows help information.
file	Specifies the name or directory for which the attribute should be modified or shown.

File Name:	`attrib.exe`	**Directory:**	\dos	**Type:**	External

attrib +a -s io.sys	Adds the archive attribute and removes the system attribute from the file io.sys.
attrib -s -h msdos.sys	Removes the system and hidden attribute from the file msdos.sys.

autoexec.bat

Function	The startup file that runs when your computer is started and executes any commands specified from the top down.				
Syntax	autoexec.bat				
File Name:	`autoexec.bat`	**Directory:**	\	**Type:**	Text File

break

Function	Enables or disables extended Ctrl+C checking. The second syntax is used in the CONFIG.SYS file.
Syntax	break [option] break=[option]
ON	Enables extended Ctrl+C checking.
OFF	Disables extended Ctrl+C checking.

buffers

Function	Allocates memory for a specified number of disk buffers. This command only works in the CONFIG.SYS file.
Syntax	BUFFERS=*NR*[,*m*]
NR	The number of disk buffers. Valid values are 1 through 99.
m	The number of buffers in the secondary buffer cache. Valid values are 0 through 8.
buffers=30,5	Sets the number of disk buffers to 30 and the number of secondary to 5.

cd, chdir

Function	Changes or shows the current directory.
Syntax	cd *{ path }* cd [..]
path	The name or full path of the directory to change to.
..	Changes to the parent directory.
cd ..	Changes to parent directory.
cd \dos	Changes to the \dos directory on the current drive.

chcp

Function	Shows or changes the number of the active code page.
Syntax	chcp *{ NR }*
NR	Specifies the number of a prepared code page.
Note:	The NLSFUNC program must be installed to use this command.
chcp	Shows the active code page.
chcp 437	Changes the active code page to 437.

chkdsk

Function	Shows a status report for a disk. It can also find and repair errors. If no parameters are given, the status of the current drive is shown.				
Syntax	chkdsk *{ driveletter: } { file }* [options...]				
/F	Fixes errors on the selected disk.				
/V	Shows the files and directories while checking.				
/?	Shows help information.				
driveletter:	Specifies the drive to check.				
file	Specifies the file or files to check for fragmentation.				
File Name:	`chkdsk.exe`	**Directory:**	\dos	**Type:**	External
chkdsk c: /F	Repairs any errors on the c: disk.				

choice

Function	Is used in batch program to prompt the user to make a choice. If used without any parameters it will prompt for yes (Y) or no (N). ERRORLEVEL is set to the offset of the presses key.
Syntax	choice [options...] *{ text }*

/C[:]*keys*	Specifies the choices the users have. Default is YN.
/N	Shows only the specified text, not the available keys.
/S	Specifies that the choices should be case-sensitive.
/T[:]*c,nn*	Waits the specified number of seconds before defaulting to a specified key.
c	The character to default to after the specified number of seconds.
nn	The number of seconds to wait.
text	The text string to be shown before the prompt.
File Name: `choice.com`	**Directory:** \dos **Type:** External
choice Continue	Shows the following: Continue [Y,N]?
choice /CABC Select one of the following.	Shows the following: Select one of the following. [A,B,C]?
choice /C:CA /T:C,10	Selects automatically select C after 10 seconds.

cls

Function	Clears the screen.
Syntax	cls [/?]

/?	Shows help information.

command

Function	Starts a new instance of the MS-DOS command interpreter. The second syntax is used in the CONFIG.SYS file.
Syntax	command *{ path } { device }* [options...] SHELL=*{ path }*COMMAND.COM *{ device }* [options...]

/E:*bytes*	Specifies the initial environment size.
/P	Makes the new command interpreter permanent.
/MSG	Stores all error messages in memory, requires the /P option.
/Y	Steps through the batch file specified with the /C or /K option.
	The following two options can't be combined and must be at the end.
/C *command*	Runs the command specified and then exits.
/K *command*	Runs the command specified and then shows the MS-DOS command prompt.
path	The directory that contains the COMMAND.COM file.
device	Specifies a different device for command input and output.
File Name: `command.com`	**Directory:** \dos **Type:** External
command /C print autoexec.nt	Starts the command interpreter and prints the file autoexec.nt and then stops.
command /E:4096	Starts the command interpreter with an environment size of 4096 bytes.

config.sys

Function	A text file used to add device drivers to the operating system and configure how the operating system performs.
Syntax	none
File Name: `config.sys`	**Directory:** \ **Type:** Text File

copy

Function	Copies one or more files to a specified location or combines several files into one.
Syntax	copy *source { destination }* [options...]

	The following two options can't be combined.
/A	Indicates an ASCII text file.
/B	Indicates a binary file.
/V	Verifies the files being copied.

continued

	The following two options can't be combined.
/Y	Doesn't prompt before overwriting files.
/-Y	Prompts before overwriting files. This is default.
source	Specifies the source file or files.
destination	Specifies the destination directory or file.

copy *.* a:	Copies all files in the current directory to a:.
copy c:\dos\readme.txt	Copies the file c:\dos\readme.txt to the current directory.

country

Function	Enables the use of country-specific conventions for showing times, dates, and currency. This command can only be used in the CONFIG.SYS file.
Syntax	COUNTRY=*xxx* [,{ *yyy* } [,*name*]]

xxx	Specifies the country code.
yyy	Specifies the character set for the country.
name	The full path and name of the file containing country information.

Country=046,850,c:\dos\country.sys	Sets the country to Sweden and the codepage to multilingual.

ctty

Function	Changes the terminal device used to control the computer.
Syntax	ctty *device*

device	The device to use as input. Valid values are: LPT1-3, COM1-4, PRN, CON and AUX.

date

Function	Shows the current date and prompts for a new date if no date is specified.
Syntax	date { *mm-dd-yy* }

mm	Specifies the month. Valid values are 1 through 12.
dd	Specifies the day in the month. Valid values are 1 through 31.
yy	Specifies the year. Valid values are 80 through 99 or 1980 through 2099.

date 10-19-2001	Sets the date to the one specified.

debug

Function	Tests and debugs MS-DOS-executable files, when the program starts a command prompt is invoked where the debug commands are typed in.
Syntax	debug *file*

file	The full path to the file to debug including any options it may require.
	The following command is available in the program.
A	Enters assembly code directly into memory at the specified address.
{ *address* }	Specifies the address, if not given it starts assembling where it last stopped.
C	Compares two portions of memory.
range	The starting address and length or the starting and ending address.
address	The starting address of the second area of memory.
D	Shows the specified range of memory addresses.
{ *range* }	The starting address and length or the starting and ending address to show.
E	Enters data into memory at the specified address.
address	The first memory location where the data is inserted.
{ *list* }	The data to enter.
F	Fills specified memory area with values, hexadecimal or ASCII is allowed.
range	The starting address and length or the starting and ending address to fill.
list	The data to fill the specified memory area with.
G	Runs the program currently in memory.
[=*address*]	The address to start at, if no address is given it starts at current address.
{ *breakpoint* }	Sets 1 to 10 temporary breakpoints.
H	Performs hexadecimal arithmetic on the two specified values.
value1	Specifies any hexadecimal number; valid range is 0 to FFFFh
value2	Specifies any hexadecimal number; valid range is 0 to FFFFh

continued

I *port*	Reads and shows one byte value from the specified port.
L	Loads a file into memory.
{ address }	The memory location where the file is loaded. Default is address in CS register.
M	Copies a block of memory to another location.
range	The starting address and length or the starting and ending address to copy.
address	The destination address.
N *filename* | *parameters*	Specifies a filename for the L and W commands or parameters for the current.
O *port value*	Sends a byte value to the specified port.
P	Runs a loop, a repeated string instruction, a software interrupt, or a subroutine.
[=*address*]	The location of the first instruction to run, if not given the one in CS:IP is used.
{ NR }	The number of instruction to run. Default is 1.
Q	Exits the debugger.
R	Shows or edits the contents of one or more registers or shows contents of all registers.
{ name }	Specifies the CPU register to show or edit.
S	Searches the specified range of address for a pattern of values.
range	The starting address and length or the starting and ending address to search.
list	The pattern to search for.
T	Runs on instruction and shows the status of the register, flags, and the instruction.
[=*address*]	Specifies the starting address.
{ NR }	Specifies the number if instruction to trace.
U *{ range }*	Disassembles the specified address range. Default is 20h.
W	Writes the specified number of bytes to a file.
{ address }	The starting address of the file to write to a file.
XA *{ count }*	Allocates the specified number of 16-kilobyte pages of expanded memory.
XD *{ handle }*	Deallocates the specified handle to expanded memory.
XM	Maps a logical page of expanded memory.
{ lpage }	The number of logical page of expanded memory to map to a physical page.
{ ppage }	The number of physical page to which lpage is mapped.
{ handle }	Specifies the handle.
XS	Shows information about the expanded memory.
File Name: `debug.exe`	**Directory:** \dos **Type:** External

defrag

Function	Reorganizes the files to optimize disk performance.
Syntax	defrag *{ drive: }* [options...]

	The following two options can't be combined.
/F	Defragments files and ensures that there are no empty space between them.
/U	Defragments files and leaves any empty spaces between them.
/S *order...*	Controls how the files are sorted, if not used the current order is used.
N	Sorts in alphabetic order by name.
N-	Sorts in reverse alphabetic order by name.
E	Sorts in alphabetic order by extension.
E-	Sorts in reverse alphabetic order by extension.
D	Sorts by date and time starting with the earliest.
D-	Sorts by date and time starting with the latest.
S	Sorts by size starting with the smallest.
S-	Sorts by size starting with the largest.
/B	Restarts the computer after the files have been reorganized.
/SKIPHIGH	Loads DEFRAG into conventional memory. By default it's loaded into upper memory.
	The following three options can't be combined.
/LCD	Uses an LCD color scheme.
/BW	Uses a black-and-white color scheme.
/G0	Disables the graphic mouse and graphic characters.
/H	Moves hidden files.
/?	Shows help information.
drive	The drive to optimize.

continued

File Name:	defrag.exe	Directory:	\dos	Type:	External
defrag c: /F			Optimizes the c: drive ensuring that no spaces exist between files.		

del, erase

Function	Deletes one or more files.
Syntax	del *file* [option]

/P	Prompts before deleting each file.
/?	Shows help information.
file	The file to delete.

del *.*	Deletes all the files in the current directory.
del c:\temp	Deletes all files in the directory c:\temp.

deltree

Function	Deletes a directory, including any file or directory it contains.
Syntax	deltree [/Y] { *path* }

/Y	Doesn't prompt before deleting.
path	Specifies the full path of the directory to delete.

File Name:	deltree.exe	Directory:	\dos	Type:	External
deltree c:\tmp			Deletes the specified directory after prompting for confirmation.		
deltree /Y c:\tmp			Deletes the specified directory without prompting for confirmation.		

device

Function	Loads a device driver into memory. This command can only be used in the CONFIG.SYS file.
Syntax	device=*name*

name	Specifies the name and location of the driver to load and any parameters it requires.

device=c:\dos\ansi.sys	Loads the device driver ansi.sys into memory.

devicehigh

Function	Loads a device driver into the upper memory area.
Syntax	DEVICEHIGH= [options...] *name*

/L:*region*[,*minsize*]	Specifies regions of memory into which to load the driver. NOTE: Separate multiple entries with a ; semicolon.
/S	Shrinks the UMB to its minimum size while the driver is loading.
name	Specifies the name and location of the driver to load and any parameters it requires.

devicehigh=c:\dos\ansi.sys	Loads the driver ANSI.SYS into the upper memory.
devicehigh= /L:2 c:\dos\ansi.sys	Loads the driver into the upper memory area in region 2.

dir

Function	Lists of the files and subdirectories.
Syntax	dir { *name* } [options...]

/P	Shows the output one screen at a time.
/W	Shows the listing in wide format.
/A[[:] *attrib*]	Shows only the files or directories with the specified attribute.
/O[[:] *sortorder*]	Sorts the output.
N	Sorts in alphabetic order by name.
-N	Sorts in reverse alphabetic order by name.
E	Sorts in alphabetic order by extension.
-E	Sorts in reverse alphabetic order by extension.

continued

D	Sorts by date and time starting with the newest.
-D	Sorts by date and time staring with the oldest.
S	Sorts by size starting with the smallest.
-S	Sorts by size starting with the largest.
G	Lists directories before files.
-G	Lists directories after files.
C	Sorts by compression ratio, lowest first.
-C	Sorts by compression ratio, highest first.
/S	Shows all files in the specified directory and all subdirectories.
/B	Shows only the name of each directory or file without any other information.
/L	Shows unsorted directory names and filenames in lowercase.
/C[H]	Shows the compression ratio of files compressed using DoubleSpace.
name	Specifies the name, including the full path, of the file or directory to see a listing on.
dir *.exe	Shows all files with the extension EXE in the current directory.

diskcomp

Function	Compares the contents of two floppy disks. If no parameter is given, the active drive is used; if only the first drive is specified, the active drive is used as the second drive.
Syntax	diskcomp *{ drive1: } { drive2: }* [options...]

/1	Compares the first side of the disk.
/8	Compares only the first 8 sectors per track.
/?	Shows help information.
drive1:	Specifies the drive containing the first floppy disk.
drive2:	Specifies the drive containing the second floppy disk. Can be `drive1`.
File Name: `diskcomp.com`	**Directory:** \dos — **Type:** External
diskcomp a: b:	Compares the disk in drive a: with the disk in drive b:

diskcopy

Function	Copies the contents of one floppy disk to another. If no parameters are given, the current drive is used as both or if only the first is specified, the current is used as the second.
Syntax	diskcopy *{ drive1: } { drive2: }* [options...]

/V	Verifies the copy.
/1	Copies only the first side of the disk.
/?	Shows help information.
drive1:	Specifies the source drive.
drive2:	Specifies the target drive. This can be the same as the source drive.
File Name: `diskcopy.com`	**Directory:** \dos — **Type:** External
diskcopy a: b:	Copies the floppy disk in drive a: to the drive b:.

DOS

Function	Loads parts of MS-DOS into the High Memory Area (HMA) and/or maintains a link to the Upper Memory Block (UMB). This command can only be used in the CONFIG.SYS file.
Syntax	DOS=[option],[option]

	The following two options can't be combined.
HIGH	Tries to load a part of MS-DOS into the high memory area.
LOW	Keeps all of MS-DOS in conventional memory.
	The following two options can't be combined.
UMB	Specifies that MS-DOS should manage upper memory blocks.
NOUMB	Specifies that MS-DOS should not mange upper memory blocks.
DOS=HIGH,UMB	Tries to load MS-DOS into HMA and manage UMB.

doskey

Function	Recalls and edits command lines previously written. Also used to create macros.
Syntax	Doskey [options.]

/reinstall	Clears the command history buffer.
/bufsize=*size*	Specifies the size of the command buffers. Default is 512 bytes.
/macros	Lists all macros.
/history	Shows the command history.
/?	Shows help information.
	The following two options can't be combined.
/insert	Doesn't overwrite old text.
/overstrike	Overwrites old text. This is the default setting.
macroname = { macro }	Creates a new macro.
macroname=	Specifies the macro to create or delete.
macro	Specifies the commands that the macro should perform. Separate commands with $t.
	The following special characters are available when creating macros.
$T	Separates multiple commands.
$*NR*	Represents options passed to the macro. $1 - $9 is valid.
$*	Represents all options passed to the macro.
	The following Hot Keys are available:
UP ARROW	Recalls the previously used command.
DOWN ARROW	Recalls the command used after the current.
ESC	Clears the command line.
F7	Shows all commands in the history.
ALT + F7	Deletes the command history.
F8	Shows all commands beginning with the characters in the command line.
F9	Makes it possible to enter the history number of the command to show.
ALT + F10	Deletes all defined macros.

File Name:	`doskey.com`	**Directory:**	\dos	**Type:**	External

doskey QF=format $1 /q	Creates a macro called QF that will quick format the specified drive.
doskey /reinstall	Clears the command history.

dosshell

Function	Starts the MS-DOS Shell in either graphic or text mode.
Syntax	dosshell [options...]

	The following two parameters are for use with the /T and /G option.
res	Specifies the screen resolution category. Valid are L (low), M (medium), H (high).
n	Specifies the screen resolution.
/T[:*res*{ *n* }]	Starts the MS-DOS Shell in text mode.
/G[:*res*{ *n* }]	Starts the MS-DOS Shell in graphic mode.
/B	Start the MS-DOS Shell in monochrome.

File Name:	`dosshell.exe`	**Directory:**	\dos	**Type:**	External

driver.sys

Function	Creates a logical drive that can refer to a physical floppy disk. This driver must be loaded in the CONFIG.SYS file.
Syntax	DEVICE={ *path* }DRIVER.SYS [options...]

/D:*NR*	Specifies the number of the physical floppy drive.
/C	Specifies that the physical drive can detect if the drive door is closed.

continued

/F*factor*	Specifies the type of disk drive.
0	Specifies 160K/180K or 320K/360K.
1	Specifies 1.2MB.
2	Specifies 720K. This is default.
7	Specifies 1.44MB.
9	Specifies 2.88MB.
/H:*heads*	Specifies the number of heads in the disk drive. Valid are 1 through 99.
/S:*sectors*	Specifies the number of sectors per track. Valid are 1 through 99.
/T:*tracks*	Specifies the number of tracks per side. Valid are 1 through 999.
path	Specifies the full path to the DRIVER.SYS file.

File Name:	driver.sys	**Directory:**	\dos	**Type:**	External

drivparm

Function	Defines parameters for devices (such as disk and tape drives) when MS-DOS starts. This command can only be used in the CONFIG.SYS file.
Syntax	DRIVPARM=[options...]

/D:*NR*	Specifies the number of the physical drive.
/C	Specifies that the drive can detect whether the drive door is closed.
/F:*factor*	Specifies the type of the drive.
0	Specifies 160K/180K or 320K/360K.
1	Specifies 1.2MB.
2	Specifies 720K. This is default.
5	Specifies Hard disk.
6	Specifies Tape.
7	Specifies 1.44MB.
8	Specifies Read/Write optical disk.
9	Specifies 2.88MB.
/H:*heads*	Specifies the number of heads in the disk drive. Valid are 1 through 99.
/I	Specifies an electronically compatible 3.5-inch floppy disk drive.
/N	Specifies a non-removable block device.
/S:*sectors*	Specifies the number of sectors per track. Valid are 1 through 99.
/T:*tracks*	Specifies the number of tracks per side. Valid are 1 through 999.

DRIVPARM=/D:3 /F:6 /H:1 /S:99 /T:10	Sets the parameters for physical drive number 3.

drvspace

Function	Drvspace is used to compress or configure hard drives or floppy disks that were compressed by DriveSpace.
Syntax	Drvspace.exe

File Name:	drvspace.exe	**Directory:**	\dos	**Type:**	External

echo O

Function	Shows or hides text in batch programs.
Syntax	echo [option] echo *{ message }*

ON	Enables the command-echoing feature.
OFF	Disables the command-echoing feature.
message	Specifies a message to echo to the screen.

echo Hello World!	Shows the specified message on the screen.

edit

Function	An ASCII editor that creates and edits ASCII files. If no parameters are given, the editor starts with a blank document.
Syntax	edit *{ file }* [options...]

/B	Starts the editor in monochrome mode.
/G	Uses the fastest screen updating possible for CGA monitors.
/H	Shows the maximum number of lines possible for your monitor.
/NOHI	Enables the use of an 8-color monitor.
/?	Shows help information.
file	Specifies the file to open or create with the editor.

File Name:	`edit.com`	**Directory:**	\dos	**Type:**	External

edit autoexec.bat	Opens the file autoexec.bat in the current directory.
edit c:\dos\autoexec.bat	Opens the file autoexec.bat in the c:\dos directory.

emm386

Function	Provides access to the upper memory area and simulates expanded memory with extended memory. Must be loaded with syntax 1 in CONFIG.SYS before it can be used at the command line.
Syntax	DEVICE=*{ path }*EMM386.EXE *{ mode } { memory }* [options...] emm386 *{ mode }* [W=*state*]

MIN=*size*	Specifies the minimum amount of EMS/VCPI memory, in kilobytes, to provide.
W=*state*	Enables or disables support for the Weitec coprocessor. Valid is ON or OFF.
	The following three options can't be combined.
M*x*	Specifies the address of the page frame. Valid values are 1 through 14.
FRAME=*address*	Specifies the page frame segment base directly.
/P*mmmm*	Specifies the address of the page frame.
P*n*=*address*	Specifies a segment address of a page.
X=*mmmm-nnnn*	Prevents the use of a range of segment addresses for an EMS page or UMBs.
I=*mmmm-nnnn*	Specifies a range of segment addresses for an EMS page or UMBs.
B=*address*	Specifies the lowest segment address available for EMS banking.
I=*minXMS*	Specifies the amount of extended memory that should be available after EMM386 loads.
A=*altregs*	Specifies the number of fast alternate register sets to allocate to EMM386.
H=*handles*	Specifies the number of handles EMM386 can use. Valid are 2 through 255. Default is 64.
D=*nnn*	Specifies the amount of memory that should be reserved for DMA.
RAM=*mmmm-nnnn*	Specifies a range of segment addresses for UMBs and also enables EMS support.
NOEMS	Prevents access to expanded memory but provides access to the upper memory area.
NOVCPI	Disables support for VCPI applications. Can only be used with the NOEMS option.
HIGHSCAN	Uses an additional check to determine the availability of upper memory.
VERBOSE	Shows status and error messages while loading.
WIN=*mmmm-nnnn*	Reserves the specified range of segment addresses for Windows.
NOHI	Prevents EMM386 from loading into upper memory area.
ROM=*mmmm-nnnn*	Specifies a range of segment addresses to use for shadow RAM.
NOMOVEXBDA	Prevents EMM386 from moving the extended BIOS data to upper memory.
ALTBOOT	Enables the use of an alternate handler to restart the computer using Ctrl+Alt+Del.
path	Specifies the path to the EMM386.EXE file.
mode	Specifies the mode of the EMM386 device driver.
ON	Activates the driver. This is the default mode.
OFF	Disables the driver.
AUTO	Enables expanded memory and upper memory block support only when needed.
memory	Specifies the maximum amount of memory to provide as EMS/VCPI memory.

continued

File Name:	emm386.exe	**Directory:**	\dos	**Type:**	External
DEVICE=c:\dos\emm386.exe			Loads the driver with default settings.		
emm386 AUTO			Enables expanded memory and upper memory block support only when needed.		

exit

Function	Exits the MS-DOS command interpreter and returns to the program that started it.
Syntax	exit

expand

Function	Expands compressed files.
Syntax	expand [-r] *file destination* expand -r *file { destination }*

-r	Renames expanded files automatically, only valid for files compressed with -r.				
file	Specifies the file or files to expand.				
destination	Specifies the destination directory or file.				
File Name:	expand.exe	**Directory:**	\dos	**Type:**	External
expand emm386.ex_ c:\dos	Expands the file emm386.ex_ to the c:\dos directory.				

fasthelp

Function	Shows help on the specified command. If no command is specified, all commands in MS-DOS are shown.
Syntax	fasthelp *{ command }*

command	Specifies the command to show help on.				
File Name:	fasthelp.exe	**Directory:**	\dos	**Type:**	External
fasthelp	Lists of all available commands.				
fasthelp doskey	Shows help on the DOSKEY command.				

fastopen

Function	Improves performance on computer with large directories. This is done by monitoring the location of files stored on the hard disk, and storing that information.
Syntax	fastopen *drive*:[[=] *n*] [/X] INSTALL=*path*FASTOPEN.EXE *drive*:[[=] *n*] [/X]

/X	Uses expanded memory instead of conventional to store the name cache.				
path	Specifies the location of the FASTOPEN.EXE file.				
drive	Specifies the drive to monitor.				
n	Specifies the number of files that can be worked with at the same time.				
File Name:	fastopen.exe	**Directory:**	\dos	**Type:**	External
Note:	The second syntax is for use in the CONFIG.SYS file				
fastopen c:	Improves performance of the c: drive.				
INSTALL=c:\dos\fastopen.exe c: /X	Loads FASTOPEN into expanded memory.				

fc

Function	Identifies the difference between two files.
Syntax	fc [options...] *file1 file2*

/A	Shows only first and last lines for each set of differences.
/B	Performs a binary comparison. This option can only be used alone.
/C	Disregards the case of letters.
/L	Compares files as ASCII text.

continued

/LB*NR*	Sets the maximum number of lines that can differ before fc cancels the comparison.
/N	Shows the line numbers when performing an ASCII comparison.
/T	Doesn't expand tabs to spaces.
/W	Handles many spaces and tabs as one space during the comparison.
/*NR*	Specifies the number of line that has to be the same.
file1	Specifies the name and location of the first file to compare.
file2	Specifies the name and location of the second file to compare.
File Name: `fc.exe`	**Directory:** \dos **Type:** External
fc file1 file2	Compares the two specified files and shows the difference.
fc progg.exe /B c:\dos\progg.exe	Performs a binary comparison of the two specified files.

fcbs

Function	Specifies the number of file control blocks (FCBs) that MS-DOS can have open at the same time. This command can only be used in the CONFIG.SYS file.
Syntax	FCBS=*NR*
NR	Specifies the number of FCBs. Default is 4 and valid values are 1–255.
FCBS=25	Specifies that MS-DOS can have 25 FCBs open at the same time.

fdisk

Function	A disk partition utility. It can create or delete a partition, set active partition, or show partition information.
Syntax	fdisk [option]
/STATUS	Shows partition information without starting the FDISK program.
/MBR	Runs fdisk on the Master Boot Record only. Great way to eliminate a boot sector virus.
File Name: `fdisk.exe`	**Directory:** \dos **Type:** External

files

Function	Specifies how many files MS-DOS can access at one time. This command can only be used in the CONFIG.SYS file.
Syntax	FILES=*NR*
NR	Specifies how many files MS-DOS can access at one time. Valid are 8 – 255.
FILES=30	Specifies that MS-DOS can access 30 files at a time.

find

Function	Searches for text strings in a file or files.
Syntax	find [options...] "*string*" *file*
/V	Shows the lines that do NOT contain the specified string.
/C	Counts the lines that contain the string. Counts lines not containing the string if it is used with /V.
/N	Shows the number of the line that contains the string.
/I	Specifies the search to be case-insensitive.
/?	Shows help information.
"*string*"	Specifies the text string to find.
file	Specifies the file or files to search in.
File Name: `find.exe`	**Directory:** \dos **Type:** External
find /V "LH" autoexec.bat	Shows all the lines that don't contain the string "LH".
find "test" *.*	Searches for the string "test" in all files in the current directory.

for

Function	Runs a specified command for each file in a set of files. Syntax 1 is for use at the command prompt and syntax 2 is used in a batch program.
Syntax	FOR %*var* IN (*set*) DO *command* FOR %%*var* IN (*set*) DO *command*
var	Represents a replaceable variable.

continued

(set)	Specifies one or more files or text strings to process.
command	The command and any parameters it requires for each file.
FOR %x IN (*.doc *.txt) DO print %x	Prints all files, in the current directory, of the type DOC and TXT.

format

Function	Formats the specified disk.
Syntax	format *drive:* [options...]

/V:*label*	Specifies the volume label. If not used you are prompted.
/Q	Performs a quick format.
/U	Performs an unconditional format.
/F:*size*	Specifies the size of the floppy to format.
/B	Allocates space for the system files in the formatted disk.
/S	Copies the system files (make the disk bootable) to the disk.
/T:*tracks*	Specifies the number of tracks per disk side.
/N:*sectors*	Specifies the number of sectors per track.
/1	Formats a single side of a floppy disk.
/4	Specifies a 5.25-inch 360K floppy disk to be formatted in a high-density drive.
/8	Formats a 5.25-inch floppy disk with 8 sectors per track.
/C	Tests clusters that are marked as bad.
/?	Shows help information.
drive:	Specifies the disk to be formatted.

File Name:	`format.com`	**Directory:**	\dos	**Type:**	External

format a:	Formats the a: drive.
format c: /V:SYSTEM	Formats the c: drive and sets the label to SYSTEM.

goto

Function	Jumps to the location marked by the specified label. This command can only be used in a batch program.
Syntax	goto *label*

label	Specifies the label in a batch program to jump to.

goto end	Jumps to the location labeled end.

graphics

Function	Loads a program into memory that will allow MS-DOS to print the contents of the screen when using a color or graphics adapter.
Syntax	graphics *{ type } { file }* [options...]

/r	Prints the text as it appears on the screen, white text on a black background.
/b	Prints the background in color. Valid for color4 and color8 printers.
/lcd	Specifies to print by using the LCD aspect ratio instead of the CGA aspect ratio.
/printbox:*size*	Selects the print box size. Valid options are STD or LCD.
type	Specifies the type of printer.
file	Specifies the full path and name of the printer profile.

File Name:	`graphics.com`	**Directory:**	\dos	**Type:**	External

help

Function	Starts MS-DOS Help and shows help on the specified command or, if none given, shows all available topics.
Syntax	help [options...] *{ command }*

/B	Allows the use of a monochrome screen with a color adapter.
/G	Provides the fastest update for a CGA screen.

continued

/H /NOHI /? *command*	Starts using the maximum number of lines supported by the current hardware. Allows the use of a screen without high intensity support. Shows help information. Specifies the command to show help about.				
File Name:	`help.com`	**Directory:**	\dos	**Type:**	External
help expand	Shows the help topic of the EXPAND command.				

himem.sys

Function	An extended memory manager that coordinates the use of the computer's extended memory, including the high memory area (HMA). This driver can only be loaded in CONFIG.SYS.
Syntax	DEVICE=*path*HIMEM.SYS [options...]

/A20CONTROL:ON | OFF /CPUCLOCK:ON | OFF /EISA /HMAMIN=*m* /INT15=*xxxx* /NUMHANDLES=*n* /MACHINE:*xxxx* /SHADOWRAM:ON | OFF /TESTMEM:ON | OFF /VERBOSE *path*	Specifies whether HIMEM should take control of the A20 line even if A20 was on. Specifies whether HIMEM should affect the clock speed of the computer. Allocates all available extended memory. The minimum amount of memory a program must use before being allowed to use HMA. Specifies the amount of memory to allocate for the Interrupt 15h interface. Specifies the maximum number of extended memory blocks used simultaneously. Specifies the type of computer. Specifies whether to disable shadow RAM. Specifies whether the memory should be tested at startup. Shows status and error messages while loading. Specifies the path to the HIMEM.SYS file.				
File Name:	`himem.sys`	**Directory:**	\dos	**Type:**	External
device=c:\dos\himem.sys	Loads with default settings.				
device=c:\dos\himem.sys /TESTMEM:OFF	Loads without testing the memory.				

if

Function	Performs conditional processing in batch programs.
Syntax	IF [NOT] option *command*

NOT ERRORLEVEL *NR* *string1==string2* EXIST *file* *command*	Performs the command only if the condition is false. Carries out the command only if the previous returned exit code is equal or greater. Carries out the command only if the two specified strings are the same. Carries out the command only if the specified file exists. Specifies the command to run.
IF EXIST c:\autoexec.bat type autoexec.bat	Runs the command if the specified file exists.
IF NOT EXIST c:\names.dat echo Can't find data file.	Runs the command if the file doesn't exist.

include

Function	Includes the content of one configuration block within another. This command can only be used in CONFIG.SYS.
Syntax	INCLUDE=*blockname*

blockname	Specifies the configuration block to include.

install

Function	Installs a memory resident program into memory when MS-DOS starts. This command can only be used in the CONFIG.SYS file.
Syntax	INSTALL=*name*

name	The name and location of the program to load and any parameters it might require.

interlnk

Function	Shares disks and printer ports between two computers using parallel or serial ports. The INTERLNK.EXE driver must be installed using the second syntax in the CONFIG.SYS file.
Syntax	interlnk *{ client* [:] *}*]=[*server* [:]] [/?] DEVICE=*path*interlnk.exe [options...]

/DRIVES:*NR*	Specifies the number of redirected drives, default is 3.
/NOPRINTER	Doesn't redirect printers.
/COM[:]*{NR* | *address }*	Specifies a serial port to use for data transfer.
NR	Specifies the number of the serial port to use.
address	Specifies the address of the serial port to use.
	NOTE: If /COM is used alone the first connected port found is used.
/LPT[:]*{ NR* | *address }*	Specifies a parallel port to use for data transfer.
NR	Specifies the number of the parallel port to use.
address	Specifies the address of the parallel port to use.
	NOTE: If /LPT is used alone the first connected port found is used.
/AUTO	Installs the driver only if a connection can be established.
/NOSCAN	Installs the driver but prevents establishing a connection during setup.
/LOW	Loads the driver into conventional memory.
/BAUD:*rate*	Specifies the maximum baud rate for serial communication.
/V	Prevents conflicts with a computer's timer.
/?	Shows help information.
client	Specifies the drive of the client that is redirected to a drive on the Interlink server.
server	Specifies the driver letter of the drive on the Interlink server that is redirected.

File Name:	interlnk.exe	**Directory:**	\dos	**Type:**	External

interlnk g=c	Redirects the drive G on the client to the C drive on the server.
device=c:\dos\interlnk.exe /lpt	Loads the Interlnk driver using the first connected parallel port.

intersvr

Function	Starts the Interlink server that redirects drives.
Syntax	intersvr *{ drive: }* [options...]

/X=*drive:*	Specifies the drive or drives that should not be redirected.
/LPT[:]*{ NR* | *address }*	Specifies a parallel port to use for data transfer.
NR	Specifies the number of the parallel port to use.
address	Specifies the address of the parallel port to use.
	NOTE: If /LPT is used alone the first connected port found is used.
/COM[:]*{ NR* | *address }*	Specifies a serial port to use for data transfer.
NR	Specifies the number of the serial port to use.
address	Specifies the address of the serial port to use.
	NOTE: If /COM is used alone the first connected port found is used.
/BAUD:*rate*	Specifies the maximum baud rate for serial communication.
/B	Shows the server screen in monochrome mode.
/V	Prevents conflicts with a computer's timer.
	The following option isn't combinable.
/RCOPY	Copies Interlnk files from one computer to another using a null-modem cable.
/?	Shows help information.
drive:	Specifies what drive(s) to be redirected.

File Name:	intersvr.exe	**Directory:**	\dos	**Type:**	External

intersvr c: a: b:	Starts the Interlnk server and redirects the c:, a:, and b: drives.
intersvr /COM1	Starts the Interlnk server using the COM1 port.

keyb

Function	Configures a keyboard for a specific language. The second syntax is used in the CONFIG.SYS file.
Syntax	keyb *{ xx }* , *{ yyy }* , *{ file }* [options...] INSTALL=*{ path }* KEYB.COM *{ xx }* , *{ yyy }* , *{ file }* [options...]

/E	Specifies that an enhanced keyboard is installed.
/ID:*NR*	Specifies the keyboard in use. NOTE: Only used for countries with more than one keyboard layout.
xx	Specifies the code for the keyboard layout.
yyy	Specifies the code page to use. If not used, the current code page is used.
file	Specifies the name and location of the keyboard definition file.
path	Specifies the location of the KEYB.COM file.

File Name:	`keyb.com`	**Directory:**	\dos	**Type:**	External

keyb us	Configures the keyboard to use the layout for United States.
INSTALL=c:\dos\keyb.com sv,,c:\dos\keyboard.sys	Configures the keyboard to use a Swedish keyboard layout.

label

Function	Creates, renames, or erases a volume label.
Syntax	label *{ drive: } { label }*

drive:	Specifies the drive to modify label on.
label	Specifies the new volume label.

File Name:	`label.exe`	**Directory:**	\dos	**Type:**	External

label c: mydisk	Sets the volume label to "mydisk" on the c: drive.

lastdrive

Function	Specifies the maximum numbers of drives that can be accessed. This command can only be used in CONFIG.SYS.
Syntax	LASTDRIVE=*letter*

letter	Specifies the last valid drive letter to use, valid values are A through Z.
LASTDRIVE=Z	Sets the last valid drive letter to Z.

lh, loadhigh

Function	Loads a program into the upper memory area.
Syntax	LH = [options...] *name*

/L:*region*[,*minsize*]	Specifies regions of memory into which to load the program. NOTE: Separate multiple entries with a ; semicolon.
/S	Shrinks the UMB to its minimum size while the driver is loading.
name	Specifies the name and location of the program to load and any parameters it requires.

LH c:\dos\doskey.exe	Loads the program doskey.exe into upper memory.
LH /L:2;4 c:\dos\doskey.exe	Loads doskey.exe into upper memory area in regions 2 and 4.

loadfix

Function	Loads a program above the first 64K of conventional memory and then runs it.
Syntax	loadfix *program*

program	Specifies the program, including the full path, to load.

File Name:	`loadfix.com`	**Directory:**	\dos	**Type:**	External
Tip:	Use loadfix if you receive the message "Packed file corrupt."				

loadfix c:\ucg\progg.exe	Loads c:\ucg\progg.exe above the first 64k and runs it.

md, mkdir

Function	Creates a new directory.
Syntax	md *path*

path	Specifies the name and location of the new directory.

md mydir	Creates the specified directory in the current directory.
md c:\windows\mydir	Creates the mydir directory in the c:\windows directory.

mem

Function	Shows the amount of used and free memory in your system. If used without an option it will display the status of the MS-DOS subsystem's memory usage.
Syntax	mem [options...]

	The following four options can't be combined.
/C	Shows memory usages of programs loaded into the upper and conventional memory area.
/D	Shows memory usages of programs, internal drivers, and other information.
/F	Shows the amount of free memory in the conventional and upper memory area.
/M *modulename*	Shows how a program module uses memory.
/P	Pauses after each screen of output.
/?	Shows help information.

File Name:	`mem.exe`	**Directory:**	\dos	**Type:**	External

memmaker

Function	A memory optimization program that optimizes the computer's memory by moving memory-resident programs and device drivers to upper memory.
Syntax	memmaker [options...]

/B	Shows MemMaker in monochrome.
/BATCH	Runs MemMaker in unattended mode.
/SESSION	Is used exclusively by MemMaker during optimization.
/SWAP:*drive*	Specifies the drive letter of the original startup disk. Used if the letter has changed.
/T	Disables detection of IBM Token-Ring networks.
/UNDO	Undoes the last changes.
/W:*size1,size2*	Specifies how much upper memory to reserve for Windows translation buffers.
/?	Shows help information.

File Name:	`memmaker.exe`	**Directory:**	\dos	**Type:**	External

memmaker /UNDO	Reverses the last changes done by MemMaker.
memmaker /BATCH	MemMaker selects default values at all prompts.

menucolor

Function	Sets the text and background color for the startup menu. This command can only be used within a menu block in the CONFIG.SYS file.
Syntax	MENUCOLOR=*x* [,*y*]

x	Specifies the color of the menu text. Valid values are 0 through 15.
y	Specifies the color of the screen background. Valid values are 0 through 15.

MENUCOLOR=15,1	Sets the text color to 15 and the screen color to 1.

menudefault

Function	Specifies the default menu item on the startup menu and sets the time to wait before using this menu item, can only be used within a menu block in the CONFIG.SYS file.
Syntax	MENUDEFAULT=*blockname*[,*timeout*]

blockname	Specifies the default menu item by its associated configuration block.
timeout	Defines how many seconds to wait before starting the computer.

MENUDEFAULT=DOS, 10	Sets the default menu item to DOS and the timeout to 10 seconds.

menuitem

Function	Defines an item on the startup menu. This command can only be used within a menu block in the CONFIG.SYS file.
Syntax	MENUITEM=*blockname*[,*text*]

blockname	Specifies the associated configuration block.
text	Specifies the text to show for this menu item.

menuitem=DOS,Will start DOS	Creates a menu item called DOS with the specified text.
menuitem=WIN, Will start Windows	Creates a menu item called WIN with the specified text.

mode

Function	Shows, changes, or configures system devices. If used without parameters status of all devices is shown or if any actions are used without options the status for that device is shown.
Syntax	mode *{ ACTION }* [/?]

/?	Shows help information.
ACTION	**Specifies the action to use.**
COM*NR*[:] [options...]	Sets properties for the specified COM port. Shows information if no argument is used.
BAUD=*value*	Specifies the first two digits for the baud rate to use.
PARITY=*value*	Sets the parity check type. Can be n (none), e (even), o (odd), m (mark), s (space).
DATA=*value*	Sets the number of data bits in a character. Default is 7 and valid are 5 through 8.
STOP=*value*	Sets the number of stop bits that defines the end of a character. Default is 1.
RETRY=*r*	Sets the action to take if a timeout occurs.
LPT*NR*[:] [options...]	Configures a printer connected to the specified parallel port.
COLS=*NR*	Sets the number of characters per line. Valid numbers are 80 or 132. Default is 80.
LINES=*NR*	Sets vertical spacing and number of lines per inch. Default is 6. Valid are 6 or 8.
RETRY=*r*	Sets the action to take if a timeout occurs.
LPT*NR*[:]=COM*NR*[:]	Redirects outputs from the specified LPT port to the specified COM port.
CON[:] [options...]	Sets the number of columns and lines shown or the keyboard repeat rate.
cols=*NR*	Sets the number of characters per line. Valid numbers are 80 or 132. Default is 80.
lines=*NR*	Sets vertical spacing and number of lines per inch. Default is 6. Valid are 6 or 8.
	The following two options can't be combined with the two above.
rate=*rate*	Sets the rate for which characters are repeated when holding down a key.
delay=*seconds*	Sets the time that must elapse before characters are repeated. Default is 2.
device CP PREPARE=((*NR*) *file*)	Prepares a codepage for the specified device.
device	Specifies the device for which the codepage should be prepared.
NR	Specifies the number of the codepage to prepare.
file	Specifies the .CPI file, including the full path, to use.
device CP SELECT=*NR*	Selects a codepage to use with the specified device.
device	Specifies the device for which the codepage should be selected.
NR	Specifies the number of the codepage to select.
device CP REFRESH	Reinstates the codepages in case they are lost due to a hardware problem.
device CP [/STATUS]	Shows the numbers of the codepages that are prepared or selected.
/STATUS	Shows the numbers of the codepages that are prepared or selected.

continued

File Name:	mode.com	**Directory:**	\dos	**Type:**	External
mode con cp select=437			Specifies the use of code page number 437.		
mode con rate=1			Sets the repeat rate for the keyboard to 1.		

more

Function	Shows one screen of information at a time.
Syntax	more < *file* *command* | more

file	Specifies the file, including the full path, to show one screen at a time.
command	Specifies the command to run which will then show the output one screen at a time.

File Name:	more.com	**Directory:**	\dos	**Type:**	External
more < c:\autoexec.bat			Shows the file autoexec.bat one screen at a time.		
type autoexec.bat | more			Shows the output from the specified command one screen at a time.		

move

Function	Moves files or renames directories.
Syntax	move [option] *source destination* move *oldname newname*

/Y	Doesn't prompt before overwriting or creating a directory or file.
/-Y	Prompts before overwriting or creating a directory.
source	Specifies the file or files to move.
destination	Specifies the destination path.
oldname	Specifes the directory to rename.
newname	Specifies the new name of the directory.

File Name:	move.exe	**Directory:**	\dos	**Type:**	External
move c:\data\file.txt c:\data\textfiles			Moves the specified file to the c:\data\textfiles\ directory.		
move *.* c:\data			Moves all files in the current directory to c:\data.		

msav

Function	Scans the computer for viruses.
Syntax	msav *{ drive: }* [options...]

	The following two options can't be combined.
/S	Scans the drive without removing any found viruses.
/C	Scans the drive and removes any found viruses.
/R	Creates a report file, MSAV.RPT, which is stored in the root directory.
	The following two options can't be combined.
/A	Scans all drives except drives a: and b:.
/L	Scans all local drives except network drives.
/N	Shows the file MSAV.TXT and then scans the selected drive without using the GUI.
/P	Runs with a command-line interface.
/F	Hides scanned files. Can only be used with the /N or /P option.
/?	Shows help information.
/VIDEO	Lists options that affect the way MSAV is shown.
	The following options are shown when the option /VIDEO is used.
/25	Sets the display to 25 lines. This setting is the default.
/28	Sets the display to 28 lines. Only use this with a VGA adapter.
/43	Sets the display to 43 lines. Use this option with EGA and VGA adapters.
/50	Sets the display to 50 lines. Only use this with a VGA adapter.

continued

/60	Sets the display to 60 lines. Only use this with a Video 7 adapter.
/IN	Uses a color scheme even if a color adapter isn't detected.
/BW	Uses a black-and-white color scheme.
/MONO	Uses a monochromatic color scheme.
/LCD	Uses an LCD color scheme.
/FF	Uses the fastest display updating on the computer with a CGA adapter.
/BF	Uses the computer's BIOS to show video.
/NF	Uses alternate fonts.
/BT	Allows the use of a graphic mouse in Windows.
/NGM	Shows the default mouse character instead of the graphic character.
/LF	Exchanges the left and right mouse buttons.
/PS2	Resets the mouse cursor. Use this if the cursor locks up or disappears.
drive:	Specifies the drive to scan for viruses. If not used the current drive is scanned.

File Name:	`msav.exe`	**Directory:**	\dos	**Type:**	External

msav c:	Scans the c: drive for viruses.
msav /L /C	Scans all local drives and removes any found viruses.

msbackup

Function	Starts Microsoft Backup, which backs up or restores files.
Syntax	msbackup *{setupfile }* [option]

/BW	Starts while using a black-and-white color scheme.
/LCD	Starts while using a video mode compatible with laptop screens.
/MDA	Starts while using a monochrome display adapter.
setupfile	Specifies the setup file that includes all settings.

File Name:	`msbackup.exe`	**Directory:**	\dos	**Type:**	External

mscdex

Function	Provides access to CD-ROM drives.
Syntax	mscdex [options...]

/D:*drive*	Specifies the drive signature of the CD-ROM device driver.
/E	Allows the use of expanded memory.
/K	Allows MS-DOS to recognize CD-ROM volumes encoded in Kanji.
/S	Enables sharing of CD-ROM drives when using MS-NET or Windows.
/V	Shows memory statistics when starting.
/L:*letter*	Specifies the drive letter to assign to the CD-ROM drive.
/M:*NR*	Specifies the number of sector buffers.

File Name:	`mscdex.exe`	**Directory:**	\dos	**Type:**	External

mscdex /D:MSCD000 /L:D	Gives access to the CD-ROM device MSCD000 and assigns it the letter D:.

msd

Function	Shows technical information about the computer or writes the information to a file.
Syntax	msd [options...]

/B	Runs MSD in black-and-white mode.
/I	Doesn't initially detect hardware.

continued

/F *file* /P *file* /S *file*		Prompts for user information, and then writes a full report to the specified file. Writes a complete report to the specified file. Writes a summary report to the specified file.			
File Name:	`msd.exe`	**Directory:**	\dos	**Type:**	External
msd /P c:\windows\report\system.txt		Writes a complete report to the specified file.			
msd /S c:\windows\report\system.txt		Writes a summary report to the specified file.			

nlsfunc

Function	Loads country-specific information for national language support. Uses the second syntax in the CONFIG.SYS file.
Syntax	nlsfunc *{ file }* INSTALL=*{ path }*NLSFUNC.EXE *{ file }*

path *file*		Specifies the location of the NLSFUNC.EXE file. Specifies the location and name of the file containing country-specific information.			
File Name:	`nlsfunc.exe`	**Directory:**	\dos	**Type:**	External
nlsfunc ndpg.sys		Loads the country-specific information from the specified file.			
INSTALL=c:\dos\nlsfunc.exe c:\dos\ndpg.sys		Loads the country-specific information from the specified file.			

numlock

Function	Specifies whether the NUM LOCK key is set to ON or OFF when the computer starts. This command can only be used in the CONFIG.SYS file.
Syntax	NUMLOCK = [option]

ON OFF	Enables the NUM LOCK key. Disables the NUM LOCK key.

path

Function	Lists of directories that MS-DOS should search for executable files.
Syntax	PATH *path*

path	Specifies the full path of the directory or directories to search in. NOTE: Multiple directories can be specified with a ; semicolon as separator.
path c:\dos;c\windows;c:\data	Includes the specified directories in the search path.

pause

Function	Pauses a batch file processing. A message prompts the user to press any key to continue. This command can only be used in a batch program.
Syntax	pause

power

Function	Reduces the power used by the computer. If used without any option, the current setting is shown.
Syntax	power [option]

ADV:*type* MAX REG MIN STD OFF		Conserves power when applications and hardware devices are idle. Uses maximum power conservation. Balances power conservation with application and device performance. Uses minimum power conservation. Uses the computer's hardware base power management, the computer must support APM. Disables power management.			
File Name:	`power.exe`	**Directory:**	\dos	**Type:**	External
power ADV:MAX		Uses maximum power conservation.			

print

Function	Prints a text file while you are using other MS-DOS commands.
Syntax	print [options...] *files...*

/D:*device*	Specifies the device to print on: LPT1-3 or COM1-4. Default is LPT1.
/B:*size*	Specifies the size of the internal buffer.
/U:*ticks1*	Specifies the maximum number of clock ticks to wait for the printer to be available.
/M:*ticks2*	Specifies the maximum number of clock ticks it takes to print a character.
/S:*ticks3*	Allocates specified number of clock ticks for background printing to the scheduler.
/Q:*qsize*	Specifies the maximum number of files allowed in the print queue.
/T	Removes every file from the print queue.
	Use the following two options after the `file` operand.
/C	Cancels the printing of the preceding filename and subsequent filenames.
/P	Adds the preceding filename and subsequent filenames to the print queue.
/?	Shows help information.
files...	Specifies the file or file to print.

File Name:	`print.exe`	**Directory:**	\dos	**Type:**	External

print /D:LPT1 myfile.txt	Prints the specified file on the LPT1 device.

prompt

Function	Changes the appearance of the command prompt.
Syntax	PROMPT *{ text }*

text	Specifies any text to be included in the prompt.
	The following text combinations can be used in or instead of the text string.
$Q	Shows a = equal sign.
$$	Shows a $ dollar sign.
$T	Shows the current time.
$D	Shows the current date.
$P	Shows the current drive and path.
$V	Shows the MS-DOS version.
$N	Shows the current drive.
$G	Shows a > greater than sign.
$L	Shows a < less than sign.
$B	Shows a | pipe sign.
$_	Adds a new line to the command prompt.
$E	Adds ASCII escape code.
$H	Deletes a character that has been written to the prompt.

prompt PG	Includes the current path and a > sign in the prompt.

qbasic

Function	An editor and compiler for the Basic computer language.
Syntax	qbasic [options...] *{ file }*

/b	Starts the editor in monochrome mode.
/editor	Starts the MS-DOS editor.
/g	Optimizes the update on a CGA monitor.
/h	Shows the maximum number of lines possible on your screen.
/mbf	Converts MKS$, MKD$, CVS, and CVD to MKSMBF$, MKDMBF$, CVSMBF, and CVDMBF.
/nohi	Allows display on a screen without high intensity video support.
/run	Executes the program before starting the editor. A file must be specified.
/?	Shows help information.
file	Specifies the file to open in the editor.

continued

File Name:	qbasic.exe	Directory:	\dos	Type:	External
qbasic /h c:\program.bas			Opens the file c:\program.bas with the maximum number of lines.		
qbasic /run c:\program.bas			Runs the program c:\program.bas before starting the editor.		

ramdrive.sys

Function	Ramdrive.sys uses part of the system's memory (RAM) to simulate a hard disk drive, must be loaded by device in CONFIG.SYS.
Syntax	DEVICE=*{ path }* RAMDRIVE.SYS *{ disksize* [*sectorsize }*] [option] DEVICE=*{ path }* RAMDRIVE.SYS *{ disksize sectorsize* [*NRentries }*] [option]

/E	Creates the RAM drive in extended memory.
/A	Creates the RAM drive in expanded memory.
path	Specifies the path to the RAMDRIVE.SYS file.
disksize	Specifes the number of kilobytes of memory to use for the RAM drive.
sectorsize	Specifies the disk sector size in bytes. Valid values are: 128, 256, or 512.
NRentries	Specifies the maximum number of files and directories in the root directory.

File Name:	ramdrive.sys	Directory:	\dos	Type:	External
device=c:\dos\ramdrive.sys			Creates a RAM drive with the default size, 64K.		
device=c:\dos\ramdrive.sys 4096 /A			Creates the RAM drive in expanded memory.		

rd, rmdir

Function	Removes an empty directory.
Syntax	rd *path*

path	Specifies the location and name of the directory to remove.

rd myfiles	Removes the specified directory from the current directory.

rem

Function	Adds comments or disables commands in a batch file.
Syntax	rem *{ string }*

string	Specifies the comment to add or the command to disable.

rem lastdrive=z	Disables the command lastdrive=z.
rem This is my new copy program	Adds the specified comment.

ren, rename

Function	Renames a file.
Syntax	ren *oldname newname*

oldname	Specifies the name and location of the file to rename.
newname	Specifies the new name of the file.

ren *.log *.txt	Changes the extension of .log file to txt
ren myfile.txt yourfile.txt	Changes the name from myfile.txt to yourfile.txt

replace

Function	Replaces files in the target directory with the files in the source directory that have the same names.
Syntax	replace *source destination* [options...]

/a	Adds new files instead of replacing existing files. Not combinable with /s /u.
/p	Prompts for confirmation before the file is replaced.
/r	Specifies that read-only files are overwritten.
/w	Pauses the replace process until a source disk is inserted.
/s	Replaces all matching files in all subdirectories. Not combinable with the /a option.
/u	Replaces only files that are older than the source. Not combinable with /a.
/?	Shows help information.
source	Specifies the source files.
destination	Specifies the target directory.

continued

File Name:	`replace.exe`	**Directory:**	\dos	**Type:**	External
replace a:\update.exe c:\program\ucg			If the file update.exe exists in the target it is replaced.		
replace a:*.* c:\program\ucg /u			Only files that are newer than the target is replaced.		

restore

Function	Restores backup files created with the backup command.
Syntax	restore *source destination* [options...]

/S	Restores all subdirectories.
/P	Prompts you before restoring files with the read-only or archive attribute.
/B:*date*	Restores only files with dates on or before specified date.
/A:*date*	Restores only files with dates on or after specified date.
/E:*time*	Restores only the files with a time stamp equal to, or earlier than, the time specified.
/L:*time*	Restores only the files with a time stamp later then the time specified.
/M	Restores only files that were modified after the last backup.
/N	Restores only the files that currently don't exist in the destination directory.
/D	Shows a list with matching files without restoring files.
/?	Shows help information.
source	Specifies the source disk where the backup files are located.
destination	Specifies the full path and names of the files to be restored.
	NOTE: The directory path must be the same as used when making the backup.

File Name:	`restore.exe`	**Directory:**	\dos	**Type:**	External
restore a: c:\dos*.*			Restores files from the h: drive to the specified directory.		
restore h: c:\dos /B:06/11/2000			Restores only files with dates on or before the specified date.		

scandisk

Function	Checks a drive for errors and then corrects them. If used without any parameters, the current drive is checked for errors.
Syntax	scandisk { *drive:* } [options...] scandisk *volume* [options...] scandisk /UNDO { *drive* } [/MONO]

/ALL	Checks and repairs all local drives.
	The following three options can't be combined.
/AUTOFIX	Doesn't prompt before fixing errors.
/CHECKONLY	Checks the drive without correcting errors.
/CUSTOM	Uses the settings found in the SCANDISK.INI file.
/NOSAVE	Deletes any lost cluster found, can only be used together with the /AUTOFIX option.
/NOSUMMARY	Hides a summary after checking each drive.
/SURFACE	Performs a surface scan automatically.
/MONO	Starts while using a monochrome display.
	The following option isn't combinable.
/FRAGMENT *file*	Checks the specified file or files for fragmentation.
/UNDO { *drive* }	Undoes changes made with `scandisk`.
drive:	Specifies the drive to check.
volume	Specifies an unmounted DoubleSpace volume to check and repair.

File Name:	`scandisk.exe`	**Directory:**	\dos	**Type:**	External

set

Function	Sets, shows, or removes MS-DOS environment variables.
Syntax	set { *variable*=[*string* }]

variable	Specifies the variable to set or modify.
string	Specifies the string to associate with the specified variable.

continued

set temp=c:\dos	Sets the temp variable to c:\dos.
set temp=	Removes the variable with the name temp.

setup

Function	Setup installs MS-DOS 6.22
Syntax	setup [options...]

/B /E /F		Displays setup screen in monochrome instead of color. Configures Windows optional programs. Installs a minimal MS-DOS 6.22 system on a floppy disk.			
File Name:	`setup.exe`	**Directory:**	\dos	**Type:**	External

setver

Function	Reports a different MS-DOS version to a program than the one currently running. If used without any parameters, the current setver table is shown.
Syntax	setver *{ drive:directory } { command version }* [options...]

/d /quiet /? *drive:directory* *command* *version*		Removes an entry from the version table. Hides messages when deleting entries from the version table. Shows help information. Specifies the location of the setver.exe file. Specifies the command name to report a different MS-DOS version to. Specifies which MS-DOS version to report.			
File Name:	`setver.exe`	**Directory:**	\dos	**Type:**	External
Note:	For setver to work, it has to be loaded in the CONFIG.SYS file.				

setver c:\utility\blast.com 5.00	Adds the command blast.com dependent on DOS 5.00 to setver.
setver c:\utility\blast.com /delete	Erases the command blast.com from the setver table.

share

Function	Enables file sharing and file locking capabilities. The second syntax is used in the CONFIG.SYS file.
Syntax	share [options...] INSTALL=*path*SHARE.EXE [options...]

/F:*space* /L:*locks* /? *path*		Allocates space for the MS-DOS storage used to record file-sharing info. Specifies the number of files that can be locked at the same time. Default is 20. Shows help information. Specifies the path to the SHARE.EXE executable. Only used in the CONFIG.SYS file.			
File Name:	`share.exe`	**Directory:**	\dos	**Type:**	External

install=c:\dos\share.exe	Installs SHARE.EXE using the CONFIG.SYS file.
share /L:30	Installs SHARE.EXE and allows 30 files to be locked.

shell

Function	Specifies the name and location of the command interpreter to use. This command can only be used in CONFIG.SYS.
Syntax	SHELL=*name*

name	Specifies the name and location of the interpreter to use and any required parameters.

SHELL=c:\command.com	Uses command.com as the command interpreter.

shift

Function	Shifts the command-line argument one step to the left.
Syntax	shift

shift	Shifts the command line one step to the left.

smartdrv

Function	Creates a disk cache in extended memory to accelerate MS-DOS disk operations.
Syntax	smartdrv *{ drive }* [options...] *{ initcachesize* [*wincachesize }*]

/X	Disables write behind caching for all drives.
/U	Doesn't load the CD-ROM caching module.
	The following two options can't be combined.
/C	Writes all cached data from memory to cached disks.
/R	Writes all cached data to disk, then clears the cache and restarts SMARTDrive.
	The following two options can't be combined.
/F	Writes cached data to disk after the completion of each command. This is the default.
/N	Writes cached data to disk when the system is idle.
/L	Prevents SMARTDrive from loading into upper memory blocks (UMBs).
	The following three options can't be combined.
/V	Shows status and error messages when starting.
/Q	Hides status messages when starting.
/S	Shows additional status information.
/E:*size*	Specifies the amount of cache data to move at a time, default is 8192 bytes.
/B:*size*	Specifies the size of the read ahead buffer, default is 16K (16384 bytes).
drive[+ | -]	Enables or disables caching for the specified drive or drives.
initcachesize	Specifies the cache size in kilobytes.
wincachesize	Specifies the amount of memory to reduce the cache to when Windows starts.

File Name:	`smartdrv.exe`	**Directory:**	\dos	**Type:**	External

smartdrv 3000	Starts SMARTDrive and sets the cache size to 3000K.

sort

Function	Sorts input data and writes the result to a file, screen, or device.
Syntax	sort [options...] < *file1* [> *file2*] *command* | sort [options...] [> *file2*]

/R	Reverses the sort order.
/+*NR*	Sorts the file according to the first character in the specified column.
file1	The file, including the full path, to sort.
file2	The file, including the full path, to receive the sorted contents.
command	Specifies the command to run which will then send the output to sort.

File Name:	1	**Directory:**	\dos	**Type:**	External

sort < myfile.txt > sort.txt	Sorts the file myfile.txt and saves the output in the file sort.txt.
type autoexec.bat | sort /R	Sorts the output from the TYPE command in reverse order.

stacks

Function	Supports the dynamic use of data stacks to handle hardware interrupts. Can only be used in the CONFIG.SYS file.
Syntax	STACKS=*NR,size*

NR	Specifies the numbers of stacks. Valid values are 0 and 8 – 64.
size	Specifies the size in bytes for each stack. Valid values are 0 and 32 – 512.

stacks=8,512	Specifies 8 stacks with the size of 512 bytes each.

submenu

Function	Creates a submenu in a startup menu. This command can only be used within a menu block in the CONFIG.SYS file.
Syntax	SUBMENU=*blockname*[,*text*]

blockname	Specifies the associated configuration block.
text	Specifies the text to show for this submenu.

SUBMENU=DOS, Different DOS choices.	Creates a submenu with the specified description.

subst

Function	Maps a virtual drive to a directory. If used without any parameters, all the active mappings are shown.				
Syntax	subst *{ drive }* *{ path }* [/d]				
/d	Deletes the specified virtual drive mapping.				
drive	Specifies the drive letter to which a virtual path will be created.				
path	Specifies the directory path that is mapped to the specified drive letter.				
File Name:	`subst.exe`	**Directory:**	\dos	**Type:**	External
subst z: c:\temp	Creates a virtual drive mapping to c:\temp named z:.				
subst z: /d	Deletes the virtual drive mapping z:.				

switches

Function	Specifies special MS-DOS options. This command can only be used in the CONFIG.SYS file.
Syntax	SWITCHES= [options...]
/F	Skips the two-second delay after showing the "Starting MS-DOS ..." message.
/K	Forces an enhanced keyboard to act like a standard keyboard.
/N	Prevents the user from using the F5 or F8 keys to bypass startup commands.
/W	Specifies that the file WINA20.386 has been moved from the root directory.

sys

Function	Creates a bootable disk by copying the system files to it.				
Syntax	sys *{ source }* *destination*				
source	Specifies the location of the system files. NOTE: If not used, MS-DOS searches the root of the current drive for the files.				
destination	Specifies the target drive to which root the files should be copied.				
File Name:	`sys.com`	**Directory:**	\dos	**Type:**	External
sys a: c:	Copies the system files from a: to c:.				
sys d:\sysfiles c:	Copies the system files from the specified directory to the c: drive.				

time

Function	Shows the current time or sets the computer's internal clock.
Syntax	time *{ time }* [option]
	The following two options can't be combined.
A	Specifies A.M.
P	Specifies P.M.
time	Specifies the time. The format is: hours:minutes:seconds.hundredths.
time 12:30:00.00	Sets the time to 12:30:00.00.

tree

Function	Shows a graphical representation of a directory structure.				
Syntax	tree *{ path }* [options...]				
/f	Specifies that the files also should be shown.				
/a	Specifies that text characters should be used instead of graphics.				
path	Specifies the path to the drive or directory for which you want the structure shown.				
File Name:	`tree.com`	**Directory:**	\dos	**Type:**	External
tree c:\winnt /f	Shows the file and directory structure of c:\winnt.				

type

Function	Shows the contents of a text file.
Syntax	type *file*

file	Specifies the name and location of the file to show.

type c:\autoexec.bat	Shows the contents of the file c:\autoexec.bat.

undelete

Function	Restores files that were deleted using the `del` command.
Syntax	undelete *{ file }* [option]

/DT	Restores only files listed in the deletion-tracking file.
/DS	Restores only files listed in the sentry directory.
/DOS	Restores only files that are listed as deleted by MS-DOS.
	The following nine options can't be used with the file operand.
/LIST	Shows all files that can be restored without recovering any files.
/ALL	Restores all deleted files without prompting for confirmation.
/LOAD	Loads the Undelete memory resident program into memory.
/UNLOAD	Unloads the memory resident program from memory.
/PURGE*{ drive }*	Deletes the contents of the sentry directory on the specified or current drive.
/STATUS	Shows the current type of delete protection active for each drive.
/S*{ drive }*	Enables the Delete Sentry protection on the specified or current drive.
/T*drive*[-*entries*]	Enables the Delete Tracker protection on the specified drive.
entries	Specifies the maximum number of entries in the deletion-tracking file, 1 through 999.
/?	Shows help information.
file	Specifies a specific file to restore, including the full path.

File Name:	`undelete.exe`	**Directory:**	\dos	**Type:**	External

undelete /Tc-50	Enables Delete Tracker protection with a maximum of 50 entries.

unformat

Function	Restores a disk that was erased using the FORMAT command or restructured using the RECOVER command.
Syntax	unformat *drive*: [options...] unformat /PARTN [/L]

/L	Shows every file and subdirectory found.
/TEST	Shows only how the data on the disk would be re-created.
/P	Sends output messages to the printer connected to LPT1.
	The following option isn't combinable.
/J	Verifies that the mirror files agree with system information on the disk.
/U	Unformats without using mirror files.
/PARTN	Restores partition tables. This option can only be combined with /L.
drive:	Specifies drive to restore.

File Name:	`unformat.com`	**Directory:**	\dos	**Type:**	External

unformat d:	Restores the data on the d: drive.

ver

Function	Shows the version number of MS-DOS.
Syntax	ver

verify

Function	Specifies that MS-DOS should verify that write operations are done correctly.
Syntax	verify [option]

ON | OFF	Turns write verification on or off.

verify	Shows whether write verification is on or off.

vol

Function	Shows the disk volume label and serial number.
Syntax	vol *{ drive: }*

drive	Specifies the drive. If not used, the current drive is used.
vol d:	Shows volume label and serial number on the d: drive.

vsafe

Function	A memory resident virus scanner that displays a warning when a virus is found.
Syntax	vsafe [options...]

/NR+ | -	Specifies a number listed below followed by a plus sign (+) to enable or minus (-) to disable.
1	Warns if an attempt is made to format the hard disk. Default is ON.
2	Warns if a program tries to stay in memory. Default is OFF.
3	Prevents programs from writing to the disk. Default is OFF.
4	Checks executable files that are opened by MS-DOS for viruses. Default is ON.
5	Checks all drives for boot sector viruses. Default is ON.
6	Warns for attempts to write to the boot sector or partition table. Default is ON.
7	Warns if an attempt is made to write to the boot sector of a floppy. Default is OFF.
8	Warns if an attempt is made to modify an executable file. Default is OFF.
	The following two options can't be combined.
/NE	Prevents VSafe from loading into expanded memory.
/NX	Prevents VSafe from loading into extended memory.
/A*key*	Sets the hot key to Alt plus the specified key.
/C*key*	Sets the hot key to Ctrl plus the specified key.
/N	Monitors for possible viruses on network drives.
/D	Disables checksumming.
/U	Unloads VSafe from memory.

File Name:	`vsafe.com`	**Directory:**	\dos	**Type:**	External

vsafe /1+ /2+ /3+ /4+ /5+ /6+ /7+ /8+	Loads VSafe into memory with all settings on.
vsafe /U	Unloads VSafe from memory.

xcopy

Function	Copies files, directories, and subdirectories, except hidden and system files.
Syntax	xcopy *source { destination }* [options...]

	The two following options can't be combined.
/a	Copies files with the archive file attribute.
/m	Copies only files with the archive attribute set and then removes the files from the source.
/d:*{ date }*	Copies files newer than date. If no date is specified, only newer file is copied.
/p	Prompts for confirmation before copying each file.
/s	Copies all directories and subdirectories except if they are empty.
/e	Copies all directories and subdirectories even if they are empty.
/v	Specifies that each file should be verified.
/w	Waits for the user to press a key before starting to copy.
/y	Replaces existing files without prompting.
/-y	Prompts before replacing existing files.
/?	Shows help information.
source	Specifies which directory or file to copy.
destination	Specifies where to copy files or name of new file.

File Name:	`xcopy.exe`	**Directory:**	\dos	**Type:**	External

xcopy c:*.* d:\temp	Copies all the files from c:\ to d:\temp.

In This Part

This part helps you discern among the various stepchildren of the Unix operating system, including Linux, to make this classic OS more comprehensible (if not always easy to use).

Chapter 9

Universal UNIX Commands

The commands in this section are common in UNIX operating systems.

The commands are all listed in alphabetical order by the command name. Even though these commands are available in each operating system, many of the options are different and the commands may have a different syntax as well. Be sure to look carefully at the syntax field; you may see multiple OS names that specify a different command syntax for that UNIX version. In this case, any options common to all versions are listed at the top of the options field and become more specific to the different versions as you read down the template. A bold OS name in the options field indicates that the options that follow are unique to that operating system.

For cross-references to other operating systems, please see Chapter 1, "Quick Command Index."

The versions of UNIX in this section are:

- ✦ IBM AIX 4.3.3
- ✦ Red Hat Linux 7.0
- ✦ OpenBSD 2.7
- ✦ Sun Solaris 7.0
- ✦ Sun Solaris 8.0

#		**UNIX Shell:**	**Shells (ash, bash, bsh, csh, ksh, sh, tcsh, zsh)**
Function	Used to make comments in a shell script or tells which shell to use as an interpreter for the script.		
Syntax	# { *comment* } #! *shell*		
comment	Is any text that is a comment in the script.		
shell	Specifies the shell to use as interpreter for the script. (This must be the first line in a script.)		
Common:	# This is a comment	A comment in a script.	
Common:	#!/usr/bin/csh	If this is the first line, use csh as the shell interpreter for the script.	

.

UNIX Shell:	Shells (ash, bash, bsh, ksh, sh, zsh)
Function	Reads commands from a script and executes them in your current environment.
Syntax	. *filename* { *arguments...* } sh: . *filename*

filename	Specifies the file containing the commands that you want to execute.
arguments...	Specifies any needed arguments for the file or command. Can't be used in sh.
Common: . .profile	Run the commands in .profile

/etc/hosts

UNIX Shell:	N/A
Function	Configures names and aliases of IP-addresses. Fields should be separated with Tab or white space.
Syntax	*IP-address hostname* { *aliases...* } # { *comment* }

IP-address	Specifies the IP-address of the hostname or alias.
hostname	Specifies the hostname of the IP-address or alias.
aliases...	Specifies aliases for the IP-address or hostname.
comment	Specifies a comment in the configuration file.
Example	**Below is a sample `hosts` file and will work in all flavors of UNIX.** # sample host file comment 192.168.1.1 gw.ucgbook.com gw firewall 192.168.1.3 webserver
File Name: `hosts`	**Directory:** /etc/ **Type:** Text File

/etc/resolv.conf

UNIX Shell:	N/A
Function	Configures DNS name servers to use for hostname lookups.
Syntax	*keyword value*

nameserver *IP-address*	Specifies one name server to use. This can be used three times.
domain *domain*	Specifies the system's domain name; this is everything after the first dot.
search *list*	Searches list for hostname lookup.
sortlist *addresslist*	Causes addresses returned by gethostbyname to be sorted in accordance.
options *options...*	The following options can be used:
debug	Sets RES_DEBUG in _res.options.
ndots:*number*	Sets a threshold of dots which must appear in a name given to res_query().
BSD:	
options *options...*	The following options can be used under BSD only:
inet6	Tries an AAAA query before an A query inside the gethostbyname function.
lookup *list*	Specifies which databases should be searched, and the order in which to do so.
bind	Uses the Domain Name server by querying named.
file	Searches for entries in `/etc/hosts`.
yp	Talks to the YP system if ypbind is running.
Linux	
options *options...*	The following options can be used under Linux only:
timeout:*number*	Sets the amount of time the resolve waits for timeout.

continued

attempts:*number*	Sets the timeout before sending an error to the calling application.
rotate	Causes round robin selection of name servers from among those listed.
no-check-names	Disables the checking of incoming hostnames and mail names for invalid characters.
inet6	Tries an AAAA query before an A query inside the gethostbyname function.
Solaris:	
retry:*number*	Sets the number of attempts made to connect to each name server.
retrans:*number*	Sets the basic retransmit timeout, in seconds.
	Below is a sample `resolv.conf` file and will work in all flavors of UNIX. search ucgbook.com nameserver 192.168.1.10 nameserver 192.169.1.11
File Name: `resolv.conf`	**Directory:** /etc/ **Type:** Text File

a2p

UNIX Shell: Shells (bash,tcsh,sh,ksh,csh,zsh)

Function	Transforms `awk` scripts to `perl` scripts, and shows the result on STDOUT.
Syntax	a2p [options...] *file*

-D*number*	Sets the specified debug flag number.
-F*switch*	Specifies the awk script to always run with the specified switch.
-n*name*	Sets the names of the input fields if input doesn't have to be split into an array.
-o	Uses old awk behavior.
-*number*	Specifies the required amount of arguments for the script.
file	Specifies the input file to use.

File Name:	`a2p`	**Directory:**	/usr/bin/, **AIX:** /usr/opt/perl5/bin/, **Solaris 8:** /usr/perl5/5.00503/bin/	**Type:**	External
Note:	This command only exists in Solaris 8, not in Solaris 7.				
Common:	a2p -3 -ngroup.type.gid group	Transforms the awk script to a perl script with an input of three fields.			
Common:	a2p awk_script.awk > perl_script.pl	As above — writes to perl_script but accepts the entire file.			

alias

UNIX Shell: Shells (bash, ksh, csh, tcsh, zsh)

Function	Creates an alias for a command. If options aren't specified, it will show all aliases.
Syntax	alias [options...]

bash:	
-p	Lists all aliases.
name	Shows the alias for name if it exists.
name=value	Defines the alias name to value.
ksh:	
name	Shows the alias for name if it exists.
name=value	Defines the alias name to value.
-t	Sets and shows tracked aliases.
-x	Sets and shows exported aliases.
csh, tcsh:	
name	Shows the alias for name if it exists.
name value	Defines the alias name to value.
zsh:	
-g	Shows or defines global aliases
-m	Uses patten matching for aliases.
-r	Shows regular aliases.
-L	Shows aliases in a way that can be used in a shell script.
name	Shows the alias for name if it exists.
name=value	Defines the alias name to value.

Note:	It is often used to change the default behavior of commands.	
Common:	alias ls "ls -lia"	Makes an alias for ls to be ls -lia (csh)
Common:	alias df="df -k"	Makes an alias for df to be df -k (ksh)

apropos

apropos	UNIX Shell:	Shells (ash, bash, bsh, csh, ksh, sh, tcsh, zsh)

Function	Shows all manual pages that contain the specified keywords, including the section number and a short description.
Syntax	apropos [options...] *keywords...*

keywords...	Specifies keywords to search for.
AIX:	
-M *path*	Specifies a different search path. Directories must be separated by colons.
BSD:	
-M *path*	Specifies a different search path. Directories must be separated by colons.
-m *path*	Adds to the search path. Directories must be separated by colons.

File Name:	`apropos`	**Directory:**	/usr/bin/	**Type:**	External

Note:	In AIX and Solaris you can run `catman -w` to create the database `apropos` uses.	
Common:	apropos password	Shows manual pages containing the word password.
Common:	apropos apropos man pwd	Shows manual pages containing the words apropos, man and pwd.
AIX:	apropos -M /usr/share/ucgman pwd	Searches only the specified path.

ar

ar	UNIX Shell:	Shells (ash, bash, bsh, csh, ksh, sh, tcsh, zsh)

Function	Creates and updates library files. It combines files into a single archive file.
Syntax	ar option [options...] *{ pos } { archive } { files... }* Linux: ar option [options...] *{ pos } { count } { archive } { files... }*

	The following options can't be combined:
-d	Deletes files from the archive.
-m	Gives the file a new position or moves it to the end of the archive.
-p	Shows the content of an archive on STDOUT.
-q	Appends files to the end of the archive.
-r	Replaces files in archive.
-t	Shows the archive's table of contents.
-x	Extracts files from archive.
	The following options can be combined:
-a	Places new files in the archive after the position specified by `pos`.
-b	Places new files in the archive before the position specified by `pos`.
-c	Doesn't show messages during archive creation.
-i	Places new files in the archive before the position specified by `pos`.
-u	Replaces older files with newer.
-v	Verbose mode. Shows more information.
pos	Names a file in the archive to use relative positioning.
archive	Specifies the path and name of the archive.
files...	Specifies files to add to archive or files inside archive to modify.
AIX:	
-C	Doesn't replace existing files.
-g	Orders the members of the archive for maximum loader efficiency with minimum space.
-h	Sets the modification times in the member headers to the current date and time.
-l	Stores temporary files in the current directory instead of `/tmp`.
-o	Orders the members of the archive for maximum loader efficiency with minimum space.
-s	Restores the symbol table if it has been broken.
-T	Truncates files with unsupported filename length.
-w	Shows the archive symbol table.
-X *mode*	Specifies the type of object file to examine. Modes are 32, 64, or 32_64.
BSD:	
-C	Doesn't replace existing files.
-o	Sets the modification times of extracted files to the times when they were archived.
-T	Truncates files with unsupported filename length.
Linux:	
-f	Truncates name in the archive.
-l	Used for compatibility, is ignored.

continued

-N	Extracts or deletes instances of the given name from the archive, uses count parameter.
-o	Sets the modification times of extracted files to the times when they were archived.
-P	Uses the full pathname when matching names in the archive.
-s	Restores the symbol table if it has been broken.
-S	Doesn't generate the symbol table for the archive. The archive can't be used for linking.
-V	Shows version information.
name	Specifies a file to extract from the archive.
count	Specifies a number to be used with option -N.
Solaris:	
-C	Doesn't replace existing files.
-s	Restores the symbol table if it has been broken.
-T	Truncates files with unsupported filename length.
-V	Shows version information.

File Name:	ar	**Directory:**	/usr/bin/, **Solaris:** /usr/ccs/bin/	**Type:**	External
Common:	ar -r newarchive *		Creates a new archive holding all files in current directory.		
Common:	ar -x archive		Extracts all files from archive.		

arp

UNIX Shell: Shells (ash, bash, bsh, csh, ksh, sh, tcsh, zsh)

Function	Shows and alters the ARP table which is used to map MAC addresses to their assigned IP addresses.
Syntax	arp options... arp *hostname* AIX: arp -t atm options... AIX: arp -t atm *hostname*

hostname	Shows the ARP entry for the specified hostname.
AIX:	
-a	Shows all current ARP entries.
n	Doesn't try to translate the IP-addresses to hostnames.
/dev/kmem	Shows information from the kernel memory.
-d *hostname*	Deletes the the ARP entry for the specified hostname.
-s *type host MAC-address*	Creates a static ARP entry into the ARP table.
	Type can be one of the following four:
ether	Specifies MAC-address to use.
802.3	Specifies 802.3 interface.
fddi	Specifies Fiber Distributed Data interface (FDDI) .
802.5	Specifies Token-Ring (T/R) interface (host is the IP-address or hostname to set.) (MAC-address is the MAC-address to set for the host.)
	The following three options may be used with -s:
Route	Adds a route for a T/R or FDDI interface. As defined in T/R or FDDI header.
temp	Adds an ARP entry to the table temporarily.
pub	Adds an entry that is published for others.
-f *filename { type }*	Reads information from a file to create ARP entries. For type please see -s.
	The following options are used for ATM networks.
-t atm	Specifies that ATM networks option will be altered. Must be used with the following.
-a	Shows all current ARP entries.
n	Doesn't try to translate the IP-addresses to hostnames.
/dev/kmem	Shows information from the kernel memory.
virtual	Specifies which specification to show. Only one can be used of the following two.
pvc	Specifies Permanent Virtual Circuits.
svc	Specifies Switched Virtual Circuits.
-d pvc *vpi:vci* if *ifname*	Deletes PVC ARP. vpi:vci specifies the circuit. ifname is the interface name.
-s *type host ether* [temp]	Creates a static ARP entry for SVC into the arp table. See above for parameters.
-s *type* pvc *vpi:vci* if *ifname aopt*	Creates a static ARP entry for PVC into the arp table. See above for parameters.
vpi:vci	Specifies the circuit.
ifname	Specifies the interface name.
Aopt	Specifies extra options
no–llc	Doesn't use LLC/SNAP encapsulation on this virtual circuit.

continued

no-arp	Doesn't use ARP protocol on this virtual circuit.
temp	Adds an ARP entry to the table temporarily.
BSD:	
-a	Shows all current ARP entries.
-n	Doesn't look up hostnames. Shows only numeric addresses.
-d *hostname*	Deletes the ARP entry for the specified hostname. Superusers only.
-s	Creates a static ARP entry into the arp table.
host	Specifies the hostname or ip-address.
MAC-address	Specifies the Ethernet address in the form xx:xx:xx:xx:xx:xx .
opt	Specifies options when setting entries.
temp	Adds an ARP entry to the table temporarily.
permanent	Adds an ARP entry to the table permanently.
pub	Adds an entry that is published for others.
Linux:	
-a	Shows all current ARP entries, or for the specified host.
-v	Verbose mode. Shows more information.
-n	Shows host ip-address instead of hostnames.
-H *type*	Specifies the class of entries it should check for. (Default is ether.)
-d *hostname*	Deletes the ARP entry for the specified hostname. Superusers only.
-D	Uses the ifa hardware address for the interface.
-i *interface*	Selects an interface to use.
-s *host MAC-address*	Creates a static ARP entry into the arp table.
-f *filename*	Reads information from a file to create ARP entries.
Solaris:	
-a	Shows all current ARP entries.
-d *hostname*	Deletes the ARP entry for the specified hostname. Superusers only.
-s *host MAC-address opt*	Creates a static ARP entry into the arp table.
host	Specifies the hostname or IP-address.
MAC-address	Specifies the Ethernet address in the form xx:xx:xx:xx:xx:xx .
opt	Specifies options.
temp	Adds an ARP entry to the table temporarily.
pub	Adds an entry that is published for others.
trail	Indicates that this host will allow trailer encapsulations.
-f *filename*	Reads information from a file to create ARP entries.

File Name:	arp	**Directory:**	/usr/sbin/, **Linux:** /sbin	**Type:**	External

Tip:	Is very useful for troubleshooting.	
Common:	arp -s sun 08:00:20:7c:4e:29	Sets the specified ether address to host sun.
Common:	arp -d sun	Deletes ARP entry for host sun.
AIX:	arp -t atm -a	Shows arp table for ATM interface.
Solaris:	arp -s sun 08:00:20:7c:4e:29 pub	Sets the specified ether address to host sun and make it public.

as

UNIX Shell: Shells (ash, bash, bsh, csh, ksh, sh, tcsh, zsh)

Function	An assembler that creates object files using assembly language source files as input.
Syntax	as [options...] *file*

AIX:	
-a*mode*	Specifies the mode to operate in, can be 32 or 64 (default is 32).
-o *outfile*	Outputs the assembly to outfile.
-n *name*	Specifies the name that appears in the header of the assembler listing.
-u	Accepts an undefined symbol as an extern so that an error message isn't shown.
-l *{ file }*	Produces an assembler listing to `infile`.lst or file if specified.
-W	Turns all warning messages off.
-w	Turns warning messages on.
-x{file}	Produces cross reference output to infile.xref or file if specified.
-s{file}	Includes a mnemonics cross-reference for POWER and Power PC.
-m *mode*	Specifies the assembly mode, mode can be any of: " , s., com, or g.
file	Specifies the file to assemble.

continued

BSD:	
	Only one of the following 3 options can be used.
-a	Turns on all assembly listing.
-al	Turns on listing only.
-as	Turns on symbol only listing.
-D	Uses for compatibility with calls to other assemblers.
-f	Assumes source is compiler output, skips preprocessing.
-I*path*	Inserts a directory path to the file that is being processed.
-k	Handles position independent code, generated by program `gcc`.
-K	Handles position independent code for ns32k architectures.
-L	Saves all symbols in the symbol table.
-o *outfile*	Outputs the assembly to outfile.
-R	Folds data sections into text section.
-v	Shows version information.
-W	Suppresses warning messages.
	The following option is only available when configured for Intel 960:
-A*var*	Specifies which variant of the 960 architectures is the target.
-b	Adds code to collect statistics about branches taken.
-norelax	Specifies that compare-and-branch instructions for long displacements are disabled.
	The following option is only available when configured for Motorola 68000:
-l	Shortens references to undefined symbols to one word instead of two.
	Only one of the following 3 options can be used.
-mc68000	Specifies the 68000 processor is the target.
-mc68010	Specifies the 68010 processor is the target.
-mc68020	Specifies the 68020 processor is the target, this is the default.
file	Specifies the file or files to assemble.
Linux:	
-a*[options...*	Turns on assembly listing. The following sub option can be specified.
d	Omits debugging directives.
h	Includes the high level source code if available.
l	Includes assembly listing
n	Doesn't process forms.
s	Includes symbol listing.
=*file*	Specifies the file to write to.
-D	Used for compatibility with calls to other assemblers.
--defsym *sym=value*	Defines a symbol sym and sets it to value.
-f	Assumes source is compiler output, skips preprocessing.
-I*path*	Inserts a directory path to the file that is being processed.
--gstabs	Generates stabs debugging information.
-K	Handles position independent code, generated by program `gcc`.
-L	Saves all symbols in the symbol table.
-M	Uses MIR compatibility mode.
-o *outfile*	Outputs the assembly to outfile.
-R	Folds data sections into text section.
--traditional-format	Uses as native assembler format.
-v	Shows version information.
-W	Suppresses warning messages.
--fatal-warnings	Handles a warning as fatal.
--warn	Shows warnings messages.
	The following option is only available when configured for Intel 960:
-A*var*	Specifies which variant of the 960 architectures is the target.
-b	Adds code to collect statistics about branches taken.
-norelax	Specifies that com-pare-and-branche instructions for long displacements are disabled.
	The following option is only available when configured for Motorola 68000:
-l	Shortens references to undefined symbols to one word instead of two.
	Only one of the following 3 options can be used.
-mc68000	Specifies the 68000 processor is the target.
-mc68010	Specifies the 68010 processor is the target.

continued

-mc68020	Specifies the 68020 processor is the target, this is the default.
file	Specifies the file or files to assemble.
Solaris:	
-b	Creates some extra information about symbol tables for the Sun SourceBrowser.
-K PIC	Generates position-independent code.
-L	Saves all symbols in the symbol table.
-m	Runs the m4 macro processor on the input file or files.
-n	Doesn't show messages during processing.
-o *outfile*	Outputs the assembly to outfile.
-P	Runs the C preprocessor on the input file or files.
-D*name=def*	Defines a name to the source file that is being processed.
-I*path*	Inserts a directory path to the file that is being processed.
-U*name*	Removes a defined name from the file that is being processed.
-Q y	Doesn't create any assembler messages in the output file.
-Q n	Creates assembler messages in the output file.
-s	Moves all stabs into the .stabs section to prevent the static linker ld from removing them.
-S[*options*]	Disassembles and show sources code on STDOUT. Use any of these options:
a	Disassembles and shows source code sorted by address. Capital A turns switch off.
b	Disassembles and shows source code from start of file. Capital B turns switch off.
c	Disassembles and shows source code with comments. Capital C turns switch off.
l	Disassembles and shows source code with line numbers. Capital L turns switch off.
-T	Is used for migration between 4.x and 5.x assembly files.
-V	Shows version information.
-xF	Creates some performance information that can be analyzed.
-q	Assembles quick without error check.
-xarch=v7	Accepts instructions from SPARC version 7.
-xarch=v8	Accepts instructions from SPARC version 8.
-xarch=v8a	Accepts instructions from SPARC version 8 without the `fsmuld` instructions.
-xarch=v8plus	Accepts instructions from SPARC version 9.
-xarch=v8plusa	Accepts instructions from SPARC version 9 and VIS.
-xarch=v9	Accepts only SPARC version 9 instruction sets.
-xarch=v9a	Accepts only SPARC version 9 and VIS instruction sets.
file	Specifies the file or files to assemble.

File Name:	`as`	**Directory:**	/usr/bin/, **Solaris:** /usr/ccs/bin/	**Type:**	External
Common:	as -o hello hello.s	Assembles the file hello.s to object file hello.			
Solaris:	as -K PIC -o hello.o hello.s	Assembles the file hello.s to position independent object file hello.o.			

at

UNIX Shell: Shells (ash, bash, bsh, csh, ksh, sh, tcsh, zsh)

Function	Schedules commands to be executed at a later time.
Syntax	AIX, Solaris: at [**SHELL**] [options...] *timespecs* AIX, Solaris: at -l -q *queue jobID* AIX, BSD, Linux, Solaris: at [-q *queue*] [-f *file*] *timespecs* BSD, Linux: at [-V] -c *jobs...*

-m	Reports by mail to the user who sent job when the job has finished.
-f *file*	Is used to specify a file that contains the `job` instead of STDIN.
-q *queue*	Specifies the queue to put the `job` in to.
timespecs	Specifies the time to run the `job`. Time specs can be one of the following:
time	Specifies the time in hours and minutes or now, noon or midnight.
date	Specifies the month and day, today or tomorrow to run the `job`.
increment	Specifies the time to run the `job` by using a + sign as increment from now.
AIX:	
SHELL	**You can choose one of the following shells.**
-c	Uses the C-shell to run the `job`.

continued

-k	Uses the Korn shell to run the `job`.
-s	Uses the Bourne shell to run the `job`.
-r *jobID*	Removes a specific job ID specified by *jobID* from the `at` queue.
-t *time*	Runs the job at a specified time using the format `CCYYMMDDhhmm.ss`.
-n { *user* }	Shows the file queue for the current user. Root can specify another user.
-l	Shows all jobs that are scheduled for the current user.
-l { *jobID* }	Shows a specific `jobID` number.
-o	Shows all scheduled jobs sorted by scheduled time. (Requires the -l option.)
-F	Deletes without asking any questions. Only with -r option.
BSD:	
-V	Shows version information.
-d *job...*	Removes jobs. (Alias for atrm).
-b	Runs jobs when the system isn't so busy. (Alias for batch).
-v	Shows the time the job starts.
-c *jobs...*	Specifies jobs to show information for to STDOUT.
Linux:	
-V	Shows version information.
-d *job...*	Removes jobs. (Alias for atrm).
-b	Runs jobs when the system isn't so busy. (Alias for batch).
-v	Shows the time the job starts.
-c *job...*	Specifies jobs to show information for to STDOUT.
Solaris:	
SHELL	**You can choose one of the following shells.**
-c	Uses the C-shell to run the `job`.
-k	Uses the Korn shell to run the `job`.
-s	Uses the Bourne shell to run the `job`.
-r *jobID*	Removes a specific job ID specified by *jobID* from the `at` queue.
-t *time*	Runs the job at a specified time using the format `CCYYMMDDhhmm.ss`.
-l	Shows all jobs that are scheduled for the current user.
-l { *jobID* }	Shows a specific `jobID` number.

File Name:	`at`	**Directory:**	/usr/bin/ **Type:** External
AIX:	at -f at_example.sh -t now	Runs the specified job now.	
Linux:	at -k -f at_example.ksh -m -t noon	Runs the specified job at 12:00PM and sends an e-mail to the user.	
OpenBSD:	at -f at_example.sh now	Runs the specified job now.	
Solaris:	at -t midnight	Runs a job input from STDIN at 12:00AM.	

atq

UNIX Shell: Shells (ash, bash, bsh, csh, ksh, sh, tcsh, zsh)

Function	Shows any queued `at` jobs for the current user or for a specified user.
Syntax	atq [options...] { *users...* }

users...	Shows jobs that belong to a specific user or users.
AIX:	
-c	Shows the queued jobs sorted by time of creation.
-n	Shows the number of jobs that are in the queue.
BSD:	
-V	Shows version information.
-q *queue*	Uses the specified queue.
-v	Shows completed but not yet deleted jobs.
Linux:	
-V	Shows version information.
-q *queue*	Uses the specified queue.
Solaris:	
-c	Shows the queued jobs sorted by time of creation.
-n	Shows the number of jobs that are in the queue.

continued

File Name:	atq	**Directory:**	/usr/bin	**Type:**	External
Common:	atq root	Shows jobs that belong to root.			
OpenBSD:	atq -v	Shows completed but not yet deleted jobs.			

atrm

UNIX Shell: Shells (ash, bash, bsh, csh, ksh, sh, tcsh, zsh)

Function	Removes jobs from the at or batch queues.
Syntax	AIX, Solaris: atrm [options...] *{ jobs... } { users... }* BSD, Linux: atrm [-V] *{ jobs... }*

jobs...	Specifies jobs to remove.
AIX:	
-f	Removes the job from the queue with force.
-i	Prompts the user for confirmation before removing the job.
users...	Removes all jobs created by the specified user or users.
BSD,Linux:	
-V	Shows version information.
Solaris:	
-a	Removes all at jobs created by the current user.
-f	Removes the job from the queue with force.
-i	Prompts the user for confirmation before removing the job.
users...	Removes all jobs created by the specified user or users.

File Name:	atrm	**Directory:**	/usr/bin/	**Type:**	External
Note:	To remove jobs for other users you must have superuser privileges.				
Common:	atrm 332	Removes job 332.			
Solaris:	atrm -a ove	Remove all jobs created by the user ove.			

banner

UNIX Shell: Shells (ash, bash, bsh, csh, ksh, sh, tcsh, zsh)

Function	Shows the specified strings in large letters on STDOUT.
Syntax	banner *strings...* Linux: banner -w*width strings...*

strings...	Specifies the strings to show. Each string may have up to 10 characters.
Linux:	
-w*width*	Specifies the width of the output.

File Name:	banner	**Directory:**	/usr/bin/, **Linux:** /usr/games/	**Type:**	External
Common:	banner universal command guide	Shows UNIVERSAL COMMAND GUIDE.			

basename

UNIX Shell: Shells (ash, bash, bsh, csh, ksh, sh, tcsh, zsh)

Function	Removes the prefix and suffix from a string and shows the output to STDOUT.
Syntax	basename *string { suffix }* Linux: basename *string { suffix }* [options...]

string	Shows the string without a prefix.
suffix	Deletes the specified suffix from string.
Linux:	
--help	Shows help information.
--version	Shows version information.

File Name:	basename	**Directory:**	**AIX, Linux:** /bin, **BSD, Solaris:** /usr/bin/	**Type:**	External
Tip:	Very useful in shell scripts.				
Common:	basename $HOME	Shows the current user's home directory without the full path.			
Common:	basename /usr/local/bin/gcc.sparc .sparc	Returns the string gcc.			

batch

batch	UNIX Shell:	Shells (ash, bash, bsh, csh, ksh, sh, tcsh, zsh)

Function	Executes commands at a future time when the system load level permits. The command is read from STDIN.
Syntax	AIX, Solaris: batch BSD, Linux: batch [options...] *{ time }*

BSD:	
-V	Shows version information.
-q *queue*	Specifies the queue to use. Valid value is a-z or A-Z. (Default is E.)
-f *file*	Specifies a file to read jobs from instead of STDIN.
-m	Sends mail to the user when the job has completed.
-v	Shows the time the job will be run.
time	Specifies the time when the job will be run.
Linux:	
-V	Shows version information.
-q *queue*	Specifies the queue to use. Valid value is a-z or A-Z. (Default is b.)
-f *file*	Specifies a file to read jobs from instead of STDIN.
-m	Sends mail to the user when the job has completed.
-v	Shows the time the job will be run.
time	Specifies the time when the job will be run.

File Name:	`batch`	**Directory:**	/usr/bin/	**Type:**	External

Tip:	Use the at command to run command on a specified time.	
Common:	batch	Reads a job from STDIN and runs it when the system load permits.
Linux:	batch -m	Reads a job from STDIN and sends an e-mail message when the job is finished.

bc

bc	UNIX Shell:	Shells (ash, bash, bsh, csh, ksh, sh, tcsh, zsh)

Function	Reads a file or STDIN and uses a C-like arithmetic language. Acts as a pre-processor for the command `dc`.
Syntax	bc [options...] *{ files... }*

files...	Reads bc compatible input from a file or files instead of STDIN.
AIX, Solaris:	
-c	Doesn't execute `dc` only compiles and shows `dc` commands.
-l	Uses math functions and a 20 scale instead of the default zero scale.
BSD, Linux:	
-l	Specifies the standard math library should be used.
-w	Shows warnings for extensions to `POSIX` program.
-s	Processes exactly the `POSIX` program language.
-q	Specifies quiet mode, less information is shown.
-v	Shows version information.

File Name:	`bc`	**Directory:**	/usr/bin/	**Type:**	External

Common:	bc	Start the calculator prompt.
Common:	bc bc.cal	Run the calculator on the file `bc.cal`.

bdftopcf

bdftopcf	UNIX Shell:	Shells (ash, bash, bsh, csh, ksh, sh, tcsh, zsh)

Function	Compiles a font for the X server and the font server. It converts BDF-fonts into PCF-fonts.
Syntax	bdftopcf [options...] *file*

-p*n*	Sets the font glyph padding, n has got to be 1, 2, 4, or 8.
-u*n*	Sets the font scanline unit, n has got to be 1, 2, or 4.
-m	Sets the font bit order to the most significant bit first (MSB).
-l	Sets the font bit order to the least significant bit first (LSB).
-M	Sets the font byte order to the most significant bit first (MSB).
-L	Sets the font byte order to the least significant bit first (LSB).
-t	Converts fonts into terminal fonts when possible.
-i	Prevents the computation of ink metrics.

continued

-o *outputfile* *file*	Sends the PCF data to *outputfile* rather than STDOUT. The BDF input file.

File Name:	bdftopcf	**Directory:**	**AIX, Linux:** /usr/bin/X11/, **BSD:** /usr/X11R6/bin/, **Solaris:** /usr/openwin/bin/	**Type:**	External
Note:	The Portable Compiled Format is very global since it can be read with any architecture.				
Common:	bdftopcf -o outfile.pcf fontfile.bdf	Converts fontfile.bdf to outfile.pcf.			
Common:	bdftopcf -i -o outfile.pcf fontfile.bdf	Converts fontfile.bdf to outfile.pcf omitting ink metric data.			

bg

UNIX Shell: Shells (ash, bash, bsh, csh, ksh, sh, tcsh, zsh)

Function	Places the specified job in the background.
Syntax	bg *{ jobids... }*

jobids...	Specifies job id. If not given, uses the current job. **Use one of the following to specify job id.**
%	Specifies the current job. You can also use %% and %+.
%*number*	Specifies job number.
%?*string*	Specifies a command that contains string.
sh, ksh:	
%*string*	Specifies a command that starts with string.
%-	Specifies the previous job.
csh, tcsh:	
%minus;	Specifies the previous job.

Note:	Solaris: Bourn shell (sh) must be started in job control mode by starting it with jsh.	
Common:	bg %5505	Places jobID 5505 in the background.
Common:	bg	Places the current job in the background.
Common:	bg %-	Places the previous job in the background.

break

UNIX Shell: Shells (ash, bash, bsh, csh, ksh, sh, tcsh, zsh)

Function	Exits from a for, foreach, while, select, or until loop.
Syntax	sh, ksh, zsh: break *{ num }* csh, tcsh: break

sh, ksh, zsh: *num*	The following option is only valid in Bourne, Korn, and Z-shell, respectively. Specifies the level you want to break out of. (Default is 1.)

Note:	Csh doesn't support a number of breaks but you can have several breaks on one line for the same effect, e.g. break ; break ; break equals break 3.	
Common:	break	Exits from a loop.
Common:	break 2	Exits from two nested loops.

cal

UNIX Shell: Shells (ash, bash, bsh, csh, ksh, sh, tcsh, zsh)

Function	Shows the calendar for a selected month in the year, or the entire year.
Syntax	cal [options...] [*{ month } year*]

month	Specifies the month to show, 1 - 12.
year	Specifies the year for the calendar you want to show, 1 - 9999.
BSD:	
-j	Shows dates using the julian format (counts days from January 1).
-y	Shows a calendar for the current year.
Linux:	
-m	Shows Monday as the first day of the week (default is Sunday).
-j	Shows dates using the julian format (counts days from January 1).
-y	Shows a calendar for the current year.

continued

File Name:	`cal`	**Directory:**	/usr/bin/	**Type:**	External
Common:	cal		Shows the current month.		
Common:	cal 1970		Shows the year 1970.		
Common:	cal 9 1752		Shows the month of September in year 1752.		
Linux:	cal -m 6 2001		Shows a calendar for June in year 2001 with Monday as the first day of the week.		

captoinfo

UNIX Shell: Shells (ash, bash, bsh, csh, ksh, sh, tcsh, zsh)

Function	Searches file for `termcap` descriptions and shows the equivalent `terminfo` description with any comments.
Syntax	captoinfo [options...] *files...*

-1	Shows the fields one to a line instead of several to a line.
-V	Shows version information.
-w *width*	Specifies the width to be used in the output line.
files...	Specifies the file to search for `termcap` data.

File Name:	`captoinfo`	**Directory:**	/usr/bin/	**Type:**	External
Common:	captoinfo -1 /etc/termcap		Shows the terminfo information in /etc/termcap one to a line.		
Common:	captoinfo -v –w 100		Shows tracking information with 100 characters.		

case

UNIX Shell: Shells (ash, bash, bsh, ksh, sh, zsh)

Function	Matches each pattern successively against the word and runs the commands when the first match is found.
Syntax	case *word* in *pattern*) *commands...* ;; esac

word	A word or variable to find a match for.
pattern)	Specifies the pattern for matching word. (The filename metacharacters * ? [...] may be used in the pattern. More than one pattern can be used by divide them with |.)
commands...	Specifies commands to run when a match is found.
;;	Specifies the end of a match. Continue execution after esac.
esac	Specifies the end of the case statement. It is case spelled backwards.

Tip:	You can use *) to match everything. Use as default.	
Common:	case $a in a) echo 1;; b) echo 2;; esac	Shows 1 if $a=a or 2 if $a=b.
Common:	case $a in [yY])echo 1;;[nN])echo 2;;esac	Shows 1 if $a = y or Y or 2 if $a = n or N.

cat

UNIX Shell: Shells (ash, bash, bsh, csh, ksh, sh, tcsh, zsh)

Function	Shows files and can also combine several files into one file.
Syntax	cat [options...] *{ files... }*

-n	Show each line's line number in the output.
-b	Omits the line numbers from blank lines.
-v	Show non-printing characters except tabs, new-lines, and form-feed characters.
-e	Prints a $ character at the end of each line.
-t	Show tabs as `I` and form-feed as `L` characters.
-	Reads input from STDIN.
files...	Specifies the file(s) to be shown or used. If not specified, reads from STDIN.
AIX:	
-q	Hides any error messages if a file doesn't exist.
-r	Replaces multiple blank lines with one blank line.
-s	Hides any error messages if a file doesn't exist.
-S	Replaces multiple blank lines with one blank line.
-u	Doesn't buffer the output.
BSD:	
-u	Doesn't buffer the output.
-s	Replaces multiple blank lines with one blank line.

continued

Linux:	
-A	Shows all special characters. Same as –vte.
-E	Prints a $ character at the end of each line.
-T	Shows tabs as `I` and form-feed as `L` characters.
-s	Replaces multiple blank lines with one blank line.
--help	Shows help information.
--version	Shows version information.
Solaris:	
-s	Hides any error messages if a file doesn't exist.
-u	Doesn't buffer the output.

File Name:	cat	**Directory:**	**AIX, Solaris:** /usr/bin/, **BSD, Linux:** /bin/	**Type:**	External
Warning:	If you direct the output into one of the files that are being read, you will lose the data in that file.				
Common:	cat -v file1	Shows file1 with non-printing characters.			
Common:	cat file1 file2 >> file3	Appends file1 and file2 to the end of file3.			
Common:	cat -n file1	Shows file1 with line numbering.			

cd, chdir

UNIX Shell: Shells (ash, bash, bsh, csh, ksh, sh, tcsh, zsh)

Function	Changes the working directory. If no directory is specified, $HOME is used.
Syntax	cd [options...] *{ directory }* chdir *{ directory }*

directory	Specifies the path to the directory you want to go to.
bash:	
-L	Follows symbolic links.
-P	Uses physical directory structure instead of symbolic.
ksh:	
old new	Substitutes the word old with new in the current path and changes to that one.
tcsh:	
-p	Shows the directory stack after a change of directory.
-l	Prevents ~ in the output.
-n	Wraps lines longer than the screen.
-v	Shows one entry per line.
zsh:	
-s	Prevents changing current directory if the directory contains symbolic links.
-L	Follows symbolic links.
-P	Uses physical directory structure instead of symbolic.
old new	Substitutes the word old with new in the current path and changes to that one.
+n	Changes to the n:th entry counting from the left.
-n	Changes to the n:th entry counting from the right. (chdir exists only in sh, csh, tcsh and zsh.)

Note:	Use `pwd` to see where you are and `echo $HOME` to show you the directory that is set as home.	
Common:	cd	Changes directory to your home-directory.
Common:	cd /usr/bin	Changes to directory /usr/bin.
Common:	cd ..	Moves you back one step in the directory tree.

chgrp

UNIX Shell: Shells (ash, bash, bsh, csh, ksh, sh, tcsh, zsh)

Function	Sets or changes the group ID for the file or files specified.
Syntax	chgrp [options...] *group files...*

-f	Hides any errors.
-h	Changes the owner of the symbolic link specified.
-R	Alters the ownership on subdirectories recursively through the directory.
group	Specifies the group name or GroupID that the files will get.
files...	Specifies the file or files to be altered.

continued

BSD:	
-H	Follows symbolic links specified on the command line. Used with -R.
-L	Follows all symbolic links. Used with -R.
-P	Doesn't follow symbolic links. Used with -R.
Linux:	
-c	Shows reports when changes are made to a file.
--dereference	Makes changes to the file a symbolic link is pointing to.
--reference=*file*	Specifies a file that has the right owner, instead of using the ones specified.
-v	Verbose mode. Shows more information.
--help	Shows help information.
--version	Shows version information.

File Name:	`chgrp`	**Directory:** /usr/bin/	**Type:** External
Common:	chgrp root mytextfile	Alters the group owner of the file mytextfile to root.	
Common:	chgrp 0 mytextfile	Alters the group owner of the file mytextfile to groupID 0.	
Common:	chgrp -R 0 /var/adm	Alters the group owner of all files and directories in /var/adm to groupID 0.	

chmod

UNIX Shell: Shells (ash, bash, bsh, csh, ksh, sh, tcsh, zsh)

Function	Alters or assigns permissions to a file.
Syntax	chmod [options...] *mode files...*

	There are 2 modes you can use: Absolute or Symbolic.
	The following are `absolute modes` that can be used.
4000	Sets user ID.
20#0	Sets group ID if # = 7, 5, 3, or 1. Enables mandatory locking if # = 6, 4, 2, or 0.
1000	Turns on sticky bit.
0400	Allows read by owner.
0200	Allows write by owner.
0100	Allows execute by owner.
0700	Allows read, write, and execute by owner.
0040	Allows read by group.
0020	Allows write by group.
0010	Allows execute by group.
0070	Allows read, write, and execute by group.
0004	Allows read by others.
0002	Allows write by others.
0001	Allows execute by others.
0007	Allows read, write, and execute by others.
	The following are `symbolic modes` that can be used.
	The form to use in the symbolic list is... [who] operator [permissions].
u	Alters user permissions.
g	Alters group permissions.
o	Alters Others permissions.
a	Alters all permissions (user, group, and other).
	Use one of the following for operator.
+	Adds the following permissions.
-	Removes the following permissions.
=	Assigns the following permissions absolutely.
	Use any of the following for permissions.
r	Alters the read permissions.
w	Alters the write permissions.
x	Alters the execute permissions.
l	Alters mandatory locking.
s	Alters the user or group set-ID.
t	Alters the sticky bit.
u	Takes the permissions from the current user mode.
g	Takes the permissions from the current group mode.

continued

o	Takes the permissions from the current other mode.
	Use these options with both modes.
-R	Alters the permissions on subdirectories recursively through the directory.
files...	Sets the name and path to a file to alter.
AIX:	
-f	Sets force mode. No error messages are reported.
-h	Suppresses a mode change for the file or directory pointed to by the symbolic link.
BSD:	
-H	Specifies that symbolic links that are on the command line should be followed.
-L	Specifies that all symbolic links should be followed.
-P	Doesn't follow symbolic links.
Linux:	
-c	Reports changes only if they are made.
-f	Sets force mode. No error messages are reported.
-v	Shows a diagnostic for every file processed.
--reference=*file*	Uses file's mode instead of specifying a mode.
--help	Shows help information.
--version	Shows version information.
Solaris:	
-f	Sets force mode. No error messages are reported.

File Name:	chmod	**Directory:** **AIX, Solaris:** /usr/bin/, **BSD, Linux:** /bin	**Type:** External
Note:	You can use `getfacl file` to make sure the appropriate permissions are set for all ACL entries.		
Common:	chmod 0644 /UCG_Examples/passwd	Alters permission to rw-r--r-- for the file passwd.	
Common:	chmod go+w /UCG_Examples/passwd	Adds write permission for group/other to passwd.	
Common:	chmod -l /UCG_Examples/passwd	Causes the file passwd to be locked during access.	
AIX:	chmod -h 644 *	Specifies that symbolic links should not be followed and sets mode 644 for regular files and directories.	
Linux:	chmod -v 644 *	Shows diagnostics for all files that are changed and sets mode 644 for regular files and directories.	
OpenBSD:	chmod -L 644 *	Specifies that all symbolic links should be followed and sets mode 644 for regular files and directories.	
Solaris:	chmod -f 644 *	Hides error messages and sets mode 644 to all files and directories.	

chown

UNIX Shell: Shells (ash, bash, bsh, csh, ksh, sh, tcsh, zsh)

Function	Alters the ownership ID of files and also sets the group ID if it is specified.
Syntax	chown [options...] *owner* [:*group*] *files...*

-f	Hides any errors.
-R	Alters the ownership on subdirectories recursively through the directory.
-h	Changes the owner of the symbolic link specified.
owner	Sets the username or user ID to use on the file.
:*group*	Sets the group name or group ID to use on the file.
files...	Specifies the path and name of the file or directory to alter.
BSD:	
-H	Follows symbolic links specified on the command line. Used with -R.
-L	Follows all symbolic links. Used with -R.
-P	Doesn't follow symbolic links. Used with -R.
Linux:	
-c	Shows reports when changes are made to a file.
--dereference	Makes changes to the file a symbolic link is pointing to.
--from=*owner.group*	Changes only those files that are owned by the specified user and/or group.
--reference=*file*	Specifies a file that has the right owner, instead of using the ones specified.
-v	Verbose mode. Shows more information.
--help	Shows help information.
--version	Shows version information.

File Name:	chown	**Directory:** /usr/bin/	**Type:** External
Note:	Only a superuser or owner of the file may change the ownership of files.		
Common:	chown root /etc/passwd	Makes root the owner of /etc/passwd.	

continued

Common:	chown -R root:root /usr/share	Changes the owner of all files under /usr/share
Common:	chown root:sys file1	Changes both owner and group.
Linux:	chown -R --from=speed:users ove:users /	Changes all files owned by speed with group users to ove.

chroot

UNIX Shell: Shells (ash, bash, bsh, csh, ksh, sh, tcsh, zsh)

Function	Alters the root directory for a command.
Syntax	chroot [options...] *directory command*

directory	Sets the path to the new root directory that the command will have.
command	The command that you want to alter the root for. (The new root must contain enough system files to support the command.)
Linux:	
--help	Shows help.
--version	Shows version information.

File Name:	`chroot`	**Directory:**	/usr/sbin/	**Type:**	External
Tip:	Commonly used to limit access to directories on FTP servers for anonymous users.				
Common:	chroot /ftpd /ftpd/bin/ftpd	Runs the specified program in a miniroot file system built at /ftpd.			

cksum

UNIX Shell: Shells (ash, bash, bsh, csh, ksh, sh, tcsh, zsh)

Function	Calculates the checksum (CRC) and number of octets for each input file.
Syntax	cksum [options...] *{ files... }*

files...	Specifies the full path and the name of the file or files that you want to report.
BSD:	
-o	Uses one of the two old algorithms specified below.
1	Uses the old BSD algorithm.
2	Uses the old AT&T algorithm.
Linux:	
--help	Shows help information.
--version	Shows version information.

File Name:	`cksum`	**Directory:**	/usr/bin/	**Type:**	External
Tip:	Use this to check if a file has been modified or if it has changed during a transfer.				
Common:	cksum /etc/services	Shows you the CRC and the number of octets of the file messages.			
Common:	cksum file.tar > file.crc	Creates a checksum file for a tar archive file.			
OpenBSD:	cksum -o 1 /bin/sh	Shows the checksum for /bin/sh with the old BSD algorithm.			

clear

UNIX Shell: Shells (ash, bash, bsh, csh, ksh, sh, tcsh, zsh)

Function	Clears the screen of all information if not disabled by your terminal environment.
Syntax	clear

		Solaris Only:	The command clear is a Bourne shell script.		
File Name:	`clear`	**Directory:**	/usr/bin/	**Type:**	External

cmp

UNIX Shell: Shells (ash, bash, bsh, csh, ksh, sh, tcsh, zsh)

Function	Compares two files of any type and shows the line number and byte where the files differ.
Syntax	cmp [options...] *file1 file2 { skip1 } { skip2 }* AIX: cmp [options...] *file1 file2*

-l	Writes byte numbers in decimal format and the differences in octal format.
-s	Doesn't write the differences, only exits with the return value of 1 if different.
file1	Specifies pathname to the first file to use in comparison.
file2	Specifies pathname to the second file to use in comparison.
BSD, Linux, Solaris:	
skip1	Skips the specified number of bytes in file1 before starting to compare.
skip2	Skips the specified number of bytes in file2 before starting to compare.

File Name:	`cmp`	**Directory:**	/usr/bin/	**Type:**	External
Note:	Also look at the command `diff`. The skip operands are great to use if you, say, want to compare two files with a serial number in the beginning.				

continued

Common:	cmp myfile.txt yourfile.txt	Compares the files and shows if there is a difference.
Common:	cmp -l myfile.txt yourfile.txt	Compares the byte number and the differing bytes.
Linux:	cmp myfile.txt yourfile.txt 0 10	Doesn't include the 10 first bytes in the yourfile.txt file.
Solaris:	cmp myfile.txt yourfile.txt 100 100	Doesn't include the 100 first bytes in the files when comparing the files.

col

UNIX Shell: Shells (ash, bash, bsh, csh, ksh, sh, tcsh, zsh)

Function	Converts spaces to Tabs or Tabs to spaces in text files to create or modify columns.
Syntax	col [options...]

-b	Hides backspace characters.
-f	Accepts half line feeds.
-x	Converts Tabs into spaces instead of converting spaces into Tabs as usual.
AIX:	
-p	Shows unknown escape sequences as regular characters.
-T*name*	Uses the workstation specification indicated by the name variable.
-l *number*	Sends the specified number lines of text in memory to a buffer.
BSD:	
-l *number*	Buffers at least number lines in memory (default is 128 lines).
Linux:	
-p	Shows unknown escape sequences as regular characters.
-l *number*	Buffers at least number lines in memory (default is 128 lines).
Solaris:	
-p	Shows unknown escape sequences as regular characters.

File Name:	`col`	**Directory:**	/usr/bin/	**Type:**	External

Note:	Very useful to filter the output from `rt` or `nroff` and the `tbl` preprocessor.	
Common:	col -x < /etc/hosts > colhosts	Converts the Tabs in `/etc/hosts` to blank characters.
Common:	col < colhosts > tabhosts	Converts the blanks in `colhosts` to Tab spaces.
OpenBSD:	col -l 256 < colhosts > tabhosts	Converts the blanks in `colhosts` to Tab spaces and buffers 256 lines in the memory.

comm

UNIX Shell: Shells (ash, bash, bsh, csh, ksh, sh, tcsh, zsh)

Function	Compares two files and shows you the unique and common lines from both files.
Syntax	comm [options...] *file1 file2*

-1	Hides lines unique to file 1.
-2	Hides lines unique to file 2.
-3	Hides the lines that are common in both files.
file1	Specifies the first file to be compared.
file2	Specifies the second file to be compared.
BSD:	
-f	Specifies that fold case in line comparisons should be used.
Linux:	
--help	Shows help information.
--version	Shows version information.

File Name:	`comm`	**Directory:**	/usr/bin/	**Type:**	External

Tip:	With a – as a filename it will read from STDIN.	
Common:	comm abc.txt def.txt	Shows you all that is unique and common in the files.
Common:	comm -1 abc.txt def.txt	Suppresses lines unique to abc.txt.

command

UNIX Shell: Shells (bash, ksh)

Function	Executes the command and will disable lookup functions in the current shell. Can also give information on how the command will be interpreted by the shell.
Syntax	command [options...] *{ command } { arguments... }*

	The following options can't be combined.
-p	Uses the default path when it searches for the command to run.
-V++	Shows information to STDOUT about the path or command that the shell will use.
-V	Shows information to STDOUT about how the command name is used by the shell.
command	Specifies the command to execute.
arguments...	Is any valid argument associated with the command that you want to run.

Common:	command -p alias	In c-shell it runs the /usr/bin/alias instead of the built-in alias.
Common:	command -V ls	In c-shell it shows that there is an internal alias that leads to the default shell ls.

compress

UNIX Shell: Shells (ash, bash, bsh, csh, ksh, sh, tcsh, zsh)

Function	Compresses the size of a file and replaces the old file with a new file with the extension .Z. The new file will inherit the same permissions and modification times from the original file.
Syntax	compress [options...] *{ files... }*

-c	Uncompresses and shows the contents of the files. No changes will be made.
-f	Is force mode and creates the .Z file even if the .Z already exists.
-v	Verbose mode. Shows more information.
-b *value*	Sets the bit size for compression, 9-16. Low value=low compression (default is 16).
files...	Specifies the path and name of the file that you want to compress.
AIX:	
-C	Makes the compressed file compatible with BSD.
-d	Uncompresses the specified files instead.
-n	Doesn't include the compression header in the compressed file.
-q	Quiet mode. Shows less information.
-V	Shows version information.
BSD:	
-d	Uncompresses the specified files.
-t	Tests the file's integrity.
-g	Uses a better compression method. (By using a deflate scheme.)
-O	Uses an older compression method.
-q	Quiet mode. Shows less information.
-o *file*	Specifies the output file.
Linux:	
-r	Follows specified directories and includes all files contained within.
-V	Shows version information.

File Name:	compress	**Directory:**	/usr/bin/	**Type:**	External

Tip:	The utility *uncompress* will uncompress the compressed file.	
Common:	compress -v bigfile	Compresses file bigfile and shows verbose output.
Common:	compress bigfile	Compresses only the file bigfile.
AIX:	compress -C bigfile	Makes the file compatible with BSD.
Linux:	compress -r /home/micael	Compresses all files included in Micael's home directory.
OpenBSD:	compress -g bigfile	Uses an older compression method.

continue

UNIX Shell: Shells (ash, bash, bsh, csh, ksh, sh, tcsh, zsh)

Function	Doesn't run the remaining commands in the loop and continues to the next iteration. Can be used in the commands `for, while, until, select, and foreach.`
Syntax	continue *{ n }*

continued

n		**This option is used in Bourne, Korn, Bash, and Z-shell (sh, ksh, bash, zsh)** Continues in the n:th level of nested loops.
Common:	continue	Continues with the next iteration of a loop.
Common:	continue 3	Continues with the third nested loop.

cp

UNIX Shell: Shells (ash, bash, bsh, csh, ksh, sh, tcsh, zsh)

Function	Copies files and directories to a new destination.
Syntax	cp [options...] *source destination*

-f	Unlinks the file and continues with copying if the linked file can't be found.
-i	Is interactive mode and will prompt to confirm before overwriting files if they exist.
-p	Saves the permissions, owner, and group information of the file.
-R	Copies all files and directories including special files like FIFO files (pipes).
source	Specifies the source file or a directory that you want to copy.
destination	Specifies the destination file or directory to copy to.
AIX:	
-h	Forces symbolic links to be copied.
-r	Copies the directory and all subdirectories and all of the files contained in them.
BSD:	
-H	Specifies that symbolic links should be followed that are on the command line.
-L	Specifies that all symbolic links should be followed.
-P	Doesn't follow symbolic links.
Linux:	
-a	Specifies that options -d, -p and -R should be used.
--backup=*argument*	Creates a backup of each existing destination file with argument.
-b	Creates a backup of each existing destination file.
-d	Specifies that links should be preserved.
-l	Specifies that files should be linked instead of copied.
-P	Appends source path to directory.
-r	Copies the directory and all subdirectories and all of the files contained in them.
--sparse=*argument*	Controls creation of sparse files.
--strip-trailing-slashes	Removes any trailing slashes from each source argument.
-s	Creates symbolic links instead of copying.
-S=*suffix*	Overrides the usual backup suffix.
-u	Specifies that files should only be copied if the source file is newer.
-v	Shows changes being made.
-x	Specifies that it should stay on this file system.
--help	Shows help information.
--version	Shows version information.
Solaris:	
-r	Copies the directory and all subdirectories and all of the files contained in them.

File Name:	`cp`	**Directory:**	**AIX, Solaris:** /usr/bin/, **BSD, Linux:** /bin/ — **Type:** External
Common:	cp /myfile.txt /home/anders/		Copies the file myfile.txt to the directory /home/anders.
Common:	cp -i /myfile.txt /home/anders/		Asks for confirmation if the target file already exists.
AIX:	cp -h /bin/* /tmp/bin		Copies all files from `/bin` to `/tmp/bin`. Symbolic links are also copied.
Linux:	cp -l /bin/bash /tmp		Creates a symbolic link to `/bin/bash` in `/tmp/bash`.
OpenBSD:	cp -L /bin/* /tmp/bin		Copies all files from `/bin` to `/tmp/bin`. Symbolic links are followed and copied.
Solaris:	cp -r /etc /tmp		Copies all files and subdirectories from `/etc` to `/tmp`.

cpio

UNIX Shell: Shells (ash, bash, bsh, csh, ksh, sh, tcsh, zsh)

Function	Copies files into and out of a cpio archive. It operates in three different modes.
Syntax	cpio -i [options...] *{ pattern } { archive }* cpio -o [options...] *{ namelist } { archive }* cpio -p [options...] *directory { namelist }*

continued

	There are three different modes of operation for this command.
-i	Restore Mode. Reads files from STDIN and copies them into the current directory.
-o	Backup Mode. Reads a list of files from STDIN and copies the files to STDOUT.
-p	Pass Mode. Reads the file list from STDIN.
	These options are used with the -i, Restore Mode.
-b	Reverses the byte order in every word.
-B	Sets the in/out buffer block size to 5120 bytes instead of the default 512 bytes.
-c	Uses ASCII character format to read or write the header information.
-C *bufsize*	Sets the in /out buffer block size to this size in bytes.
-d	Creates the directories if they don't exist.
-f	Excludes the files specified in the `pattern` when copying.
-m	Maintains the copied files modification time in the copy.
-r	Renames files interactively by prompting for names.
-s	Tells the command to swap bytes within each half word.
-S	Tells the command to swap half words within each word.
-t	Shows a table of contents without creating the files.
-u	Forces the copy, copies even if the file is older than the one to replace.
-v	Verbose mode. Shows more information.
pattern	Specifies standard file matching pattern for files to extract.
archive	Specifies the archive file. If not specified, reads from STDIN.
	These options are used with the -o, Backup Mode.
-a	Resets the access time on the new file.
-B	Sets the in/out buffer block size to 5120 bytes instead of the default 512 bytes.
-c	Uses ASCII character format to read or write the header information.
-C *bufsize*	Sets the in /out buffer block size to this size in bytes.
-v	Verbose mode. Shows more information.
namelist	Specifies a list of names to copy. If not specified, reads from STDIN
archive	Specifies the archive file. If not specified, writes to STDOUT.
	These options are used with the -p, Pass Mode.
-a	Resets the access time on the new file.
-d	Creates the directories if they don't exist.
-l	Links files instead of copying them if it is possible.
-m	Maintains the copied files modification times during the copy.
-u	Forces the copy, copies even if the file is older than the one to replace.
-v	Verbose mode. Shows more information.
directory	Specifies directory to copy files to.
namelist	Specifies a list of names to copy. If not specified, reads from STDIN
AIX:	
	These options are used with the -i, Restore Mode.
-6	Specifies the file is a UNIX System Sixth Edition archive format file.
-M	Maintains the copied files modification time in the copy. Also for directories.
	This option is used with the -p, Pass Mode.
-M	Maintains the copied files modification time in the copy. Also for directories.
BSD:	
	These options are used with the -i, Restore Mode.
-E *file*	Specifies the name and path to a file containing a list of files to extract.
-F *archive*	Reads from the archive file. If not specified, read sfrom STDIN.
-H *format*	Uses the format to read or write the header information. For system compatibility.
-I *archive*	Reads from the archive file. If not specified, reads from STDIN.
-z	Uncompresses the archive using gzip format.
-Z	Uncompresses the archive using compress format.
-6	Specifies the file is a UNIX System Sixth Edition archive format file.
	These options are used with the -o, Backup Mode.
-A	Specifies the file is to be appended to an archive.
-H *format*	Uses the format to read or write the header information. For system compatibility.
-L	Specifies that symbolic links are to be followed.
-F *archive*	Specifies archive file to write to instead of STDOUT.
-O *archive*	Specifies archive file to write to instead of STDOUT.

continued

-z	Compresses the archive using gzip format.
-Z	Compresses the archive using compress format.
	This option is used with the -p, Pass Mode.
-L	Specifies that symbolic links are to be followed.
Linux:	
	These options are used for all modes.
--quiet	Hides number of copied blocks.
-V	Shows a dot (.) for each file processed.
--version	Shows version information.
--help	Shows help information.
	These options are used with the -i, Restore Mode.
-0	Uses filename list separated by null character instead of new line.
-E *file*	Specifies the name and path to a file containing a list of files to extract.
-F *archive*	Reads from the archive file. If not specified, reads from STDIN.
-H *format*	Uses the format to read or write the header information. For system compatibility.
-I *archive*	Reads from the archive file. If not specified, reads from STDIN.
-M *message*	Specifies the text message you want to show when media needs to be changed.
-R *ID*	Ownership and group information will be reassigned to this user ID for each file.
--block-size=*blocks*	Sets I/O- block size to blocks*521 bytes.
--force-local	Uses local file even if there is a colon in the name. Used with -I and -F.
-n	Shows numeric userid and groupid instead of names.
--no-preserve-owner	Doesn't preserve ownership for file.
--only-verify-crc	Checks only the crc for each file in the archive. Does not create any files.
	These options are used with the -o, Backup Mode.
-A	Specifies the file is to be appended to an archive.
-H *format*	Uses the format to read or write the header information. For system compatibility.
-L	Specifies that symbolic links are to be followed.
-M *message*	Specifies the text message you want to show when media needs to be changed.
-O *archive*	Specifies archive file to write to instead of STDOUT.
-F *archive*	Specifies archive file to write to instead of STDOUT.
--force-local	Uses local file even if there is a colon in the name. Used with -O and -F.
--sparse	Writes files with large blocks of zeros as sparse files.
	These options are used with the -p, Pass Mode.
-0	Uses filename list separated by null character instead of new line.
-L	Specifies that symbolic links are to be followed.
-R *ID*	Ownership and group information will be reassigned to this user ID for each file.
--no-preserve-owner	Doesn't preserve ownership for file.
--sparse	Writes files with large blocks of zeros as sparse files. (For the -I, -O, and -F option filename can have the form : [[user@]host:]archive to access resources on another host.)
Solaris:	
	This option is used for all modes.
-V	Shows a dot (.) for each file processed.
	These option are used with the -i, Restore Mode.
-E *file*	Specifies the name and path to a file containing a list of files to extract.
-H *format*	Uses the format to read or write the header information. For system compatibility.
-I *file*	Reads the file content as an input archive. Instead of STDIN.
-k	Tries to skip corrupted headers and input/output errors when you create a copy.
-M *message*	Specifies the text message you want to show when media needs to be changed.
-P	Maintains the Access Control Lists when you create a copy.
-R *ID*	Ownership and group information will be reassigned to this user ID for each file.
-6	Specifies the file is a UNIX System Sixth Edition archive format file.
	These options are used with the -o, Backup Mode.
-A	Specifies the files is to be appended to an archive.
-H *format*	Uses the format to read or write the header information. For system compatibility.
-L	Specifies that symbolic links are to be followed.

continued

-M *message* -O *file* -P -L -P -R *ID*		Specifies the text message you want to show when media needs to be changed. Directs the output to this file. Maintains the Access Control Lists when you create a copy. **These options are used with the -p, Pass Mode**. Specifies that symbolic links are to be followed. Maintains the Access Control Lists when you create a copy. Ownership and group information will be reassigned to this user ID for each file.			
File Name:	cpio	**Directory:**	**AIX, Solaris:** /usr/bin/, **BSD, Linux:** /bin/	**Type:**	External
Common:	ls | cpio -o > /tmp/cpio.out	Copies all files in current directory to /tmp/cpio.out .			
Common:	ls /usr/ccs/bin/* | cpio -ov /tmp/cpio.res	Copies all files from /usr/ccs/bin/ and lists the files copied.			
Common:	cpio -iv < /tmp/cpio.res	Copies all files from the archive to the hard drive.			

cpp

UNIX Shell: Shells (ash, bash, bsh, csh, ksh, sh, tcsh, zsh)

Function	A C language preprocessor that inserts include files in the source code of the source file, creating a single file.
Syntax	cpp [options...] *{ inputfile } { outputfile }*

-C	Passes all comments through the preprocessor, except comments on directive lines.
-P	Doesn't produce line control information used by the next pass of the C compiler.
-D*name*	Defines name as 1 (one).
-D*name=def*	Defines name as def.
-I*directory*	Adds directory into the search path for include files not beginning with '/'.
-U*name*	Removes any initial definitions of the specified name.
inputfile	Specifies the file to use.
outputfile	Specifies the file to create.
AIX:	
-q*mode*	Specifies the double-byte character set mode.
-qlanglvl=*language*	Specifies the language level for processing. Can be ANSI, SAA, SAAL2 or extended.
BSD:	
-$	Forbids "$" in identifiers.
-A*name*[(*value*)]	Predicates the specified name with the specified tokenlist value.
-dM	Shows only a list of "#define" directives for all defined macros.
-dD	Shows both "#define" directives and the result of preprocessing.
-H	Shows all header files used.
-I-	Uses only added directories when looking for local include files. ("#include ")
-imacros *file*	Reads macros from the specified file and applies them to the main file.
-include *file*	Processes the specified file and includes it in the main file.
-idirafter *directory*	Specifies secondary directories when searching for include files.
-iprefix *prefix*	Specifies the prefix for the `-iwithprefix` option.
-iwithprefix *directory*	Creates secondary search directories by the directory with the prefix.
-lang-c	Handles the source language as C code.
-lang-c++	Handles the source language as C++ code.
-lang-objc	Handles the source language as C code with Objective C "#import" directive enabled.
-lang-objc++	Handles the source language as C++ code with Objective C "#import" directive enabled.
-lint	Emits comments with #pragma lint `comment`.
-M [-MG]	Shows only rules suitable for `make` how to make dependencies.
-MM [-MG]	Makes only dependencies on local include files ("#include ")
-MG	Assumes that missing headers will be present on future compilations.
-MD *file*	Is like -M, but will write the information to the specified file.
-MMD *file*	Is like -MD, but will only include user header files and exclude system header files.
-nostdinc	Doesn't search the standard system header file directories.
-nostdinc++	Doesn't search the C++ specific standard directories.
-pedantic	Shows warning on ANSI C standard with incorrect typing.
-pedantic-errors	Is like `-pedantic`, but shows the warnings as errors.
-traditional	Imitates the behavior of old-fashioned C, instead of ANSI C.
-trigraphs	Processes ANSI standard trigraph sequences.
-undef	Doesn't predefine non-standard macros.
-Wtrigraphs	Warns if trigraphs are encountered.

continued

-Wall	Is like typing `-Wtrigraphs -Wcomment.`
-Wtraditional	Warns if finding constructs that behave differently than in traditional and ANSI C.
-Wcomment	Warns on comment-start sequences . (1*)
Linux:	
-H	Shows the pathnames of the included files.
-traditional	Imitates the behavior of old-fashioned C, instead of ANSI C.
-trigraphs	Processes ANSI standard trigraph sequences.
-pedantic	Shows warning on ANSI C standard with incorrect typing.
-pedantic-errors	Is like `-pedantic`, but shows the warnings as errors.
-Wcomment	Warns on comment-start sequences. (/*)
-Wtrigraphs	Warns if trigraphs are encountered.
-Wwhite-space	Warns on possible white-space confusion.
-Wall	Is like typing `-Wtrigraphs -Wcomment -Wwhite-space.`
-Wtraditional	Warns if finding constructs that behave differently than in traditional and ANSI C.
-Wundef	Warns if an undefined identifier is evaluated in an #if directive.
-I-	Uses only added directories when looking for local include files ("#include ").
-nostdinc	Doesn't search the standard system header file directories.
-nostdinc++	Doesn't search the C++ specific standard directories.
-remap	Remaps found header files in `header.cpp`, if exist.
-gcc	Defines GNU macros.
-A *name*[(*value*)]	Predicates the specified name with the specified tokenlist value.
-A -*name*[(*value*)]	Removes the specified predicate and its tokenlist value.
-dM	Shows only a list of "#define" directives for all defined macros.
-dD	Shows both "#define" directives and the result of preprocessing.
-dN	Is like -dD, but will only show the macro names, and exclude their expansions.
-dI	Shows "#include" directives.
-M [-MG]	Shows only rules suitable for `make` how to make dependencies.
-MM [-MG]	Makes only dependencies on local include files (" #include ").
-MG	Assumes that missing headers will be present on future compilations.
-MD *file*	Is like -M, but will write the information to the specified file.
-MMd *file*	Is like -MD, but will only include user header files and exclude system header files.
-imacros *file*	Reads macros from the specified file and applies them to the main file.
-include *file*	Processes the specified file and includes it in the main file.
-idirafter *directory*	Specifies secondary directories when searching for include files.
-iprefix *prefix*	Specifies the prefix for the `-iwithprefix` option.
-iwithprefix *directory*	Creates secondary search directories by the directory with the prefix.
-isystem *directory*	Adds an include directory and marks it as a system include directory.
-x *mode*	Specifies the source language for the input file. Mode can be one of the following.
c	Handles the source language as C code.
c++	Handles the source language as C++ code.
objective-c	Handles the source language as C code with Objective C "#import" directive enabled.
assembler-with-cpp	Handles the source language as assembler code.
-undef	Doesn't predefine non-standard macros.
-std=*standard*	Specifies the standard to follow.
c89	The ISO C standard from 1989.
iso9899:199409	The 1990 C standard, as amended in 1994.
c99	IS the revised ISO C standard, published in December 1999.
c9x	IS the revised ISO C standard, published in December 1999.
gnu89	The 1990 C standard with GNU extensions.
gnu99	The 1999 C standard with GNU extensions.
gnu9x	The 1999 C standard with GNU extensions.
-ftabstop=*size*	Specifies the tabstop size.
-$	Forbids "$" in identifiers.
Solaris:	
-B	Supports the C++ comment //.
-H	Shows the pathnames of the included files.
-M	Makes a list of makefile dependencies and shows it on the screen.
-p	Uses only the first eight characters to distinguish preprocessor symbols.

continued

-R -T -undef -Y *directory*		Used to allow recursive macros. Uses only the first eight characters for defining different preprocessor names. Removes initial definitions for all predefined symbols. Uses directory to search for include files. Not the standard list of directories.			
File Name:	cpp	**Directory:**	**AIX, Solaris:** /usr/lib/, **BSD:** /usr/bin/, **Linux:** /usr/bin/	**Type:**	External
Common:	cpp -I /usr/include/myincludes/ hello.c	Searches for header files in the specified directory.			
Common:	cpp hello.c preprocess.c	Saves the output file in preprocess.c.			
OpenBSD:	cpp -H hello.c	Shows all header files used by the source code.			
Solaris:	cpp -M hello.c	Lists of makefile dependencies on the file.			

cron, crond

UNIX Shell: Shells (ash, bash, bsh, csh, ksh, sh, tcsh, zsh)

Function	Starts the cron daemon used to execute commands at scheduled dates and times specified in the `crontab` file.				
Syntax	cron				
File Name:	cron, crond	**Directory:**	/usr/sbin/, **Linux:** /usr/sbin/	**Type:**	External
Note:	Usually the cron process starts and stops when the server is booted and shut down.				
Common:	cron	Starts the cron daemon, reading the crontab.			
Linux:	crond	Starts the cron daemon, reading the crontab.			

crontab

UNIX Shell: Shells (ash, bash, bsh, csh, ksh, sh, tcsh, zsh)

Function	Views, creates, deletes, or edits the crontab file which contains a list of jobs including the time and date they will execute. If option isn't given, reads from STDIN.
Syntax	crontab [options...] *{ file }*

	Use one of the following:
-e	Edits or creates a new crontab file for the current user.
-l	Shows the crontab file for the current user.
-r	Specifies to remove the crontab file for the current user.
file	Specifies a crontab to replace the current one.
AIX:	
-v	Shows status of the cron jobs for the current user.
BSD, Linux:	
-u *user*	Specifies a different user than the current user.
Solaris:	
user	Used with -e, -l, and -r to specify a different user than the current user.
	The following is a list of rules when creating or editing a crontab file.
RULE1:	Crontab files are read left to right and have 6 fields separated by spaces or tabs.
RULE2:	The first 5 fields deal with date and time (see below) and the sixth is the command.
RULE3:	The first 5 fields may contain a comma , a dash -, or an asterisk *. (See below.)
-	A dash - may be used between 2 numbers indicating to include all numbers in between.
,	A comma , may be used between numbers indicating to include only those numbers.
*	An asterisk can indicate any valid number for that field
	The following are the six fields and the formats for using them.
Field1: Minute	Any valid number between (0-59).
Field2: Hour	Any valid number between (0-23).
Field3: Day of month	Any valid number between (1-31).
Field4: Month	Any valid number between (1-12).
Field5: Day of week	Any valid number between (0-6) 0=Sun.
Field6: Command	The command including the argument that you want to execute.
Example	30 8 * * 5 find / -name core | xargs rm -f Removes core files every Friday morning. (By default everyone has access to modify and view the crontab file.)
	To limit permissions to the crontab file you must create the following files.
	Use the following two files for AIX.
To Allow Access	Create a file in /var/adm/cron.allow and add usernames to allow access.

continued

To Deny Access	Create a file in /var/adm/cron.deny and add usernames to deny access.
	Use the following two files for BSD.
To Allow Access	Create a file in /var/cron/allow and add usernames to allow access.
To Deny Access	Create a file in /var/cron/deny and add usernames to deny access.
	Use the following two files for Linux.
To Allow Access	Create a file in /etc/cron.allow and add usernames to allow access.
To Deny Access	Create a file in /etc/cron.deny and add usernames to deny access.
	Use the following two files for Solaris.
To Allow Access	Create a file in /etc/cron.d/cron.allow and add usernames to allow access.
To Deny Access	Create a file in /etc/cron.d/cron.deny and add usernames to deny access. (The environment variable EDITOR is used to specify the editor.)

File Name:	crontab	**Directory:**	/usr/bin/	**Type:**	External
Warning:	If you have started crontab without arguments, don't use Ctrl+D to exit. Use Ctrl+C or you will lose your crontab file.				
Common:	crontab -e	Edits the current user's crontab.			
Common:	crontab -l	Shows the current user's crontab.			
Linux:	crontab -e -u speed	Edits the crontab for the specified user.			

ctags, etags

UNIX Shell:	**Shells (ash, bash, bsh, csh, ksh, sh, tcsh, zsh)**
Function	Inserts tags into programming source code files f that can act as markers making it easier to find section headings quickly and edit them using `ex` or `vi`.
Syntax	ctags [options...] *files...*

	Linux Only: The command `etags` is the same as `ctags`.
-a	Appends the output to another tag file that already exists.
-B	Allows backward pattern searches using `(?...?)`.
-F	Allows forward pattern searches using `(/.../)`.
-w	Hides warning messages.
-x	Lists object names including the filenames and line numbers.
-f *tagfile*	Specifies a different name for the tag file (default is tags).
files...	Specifies source file to process.
AIX, BSD, Solaris:	
-t	Creates tags for use with typedefs.
-u	Appends new values to update the specified files.
-v	Shows index listing, function name, filename, and page number to STDOUT.
-m	**AIX only:** Doesn't create tags for macro definitions.
-o	**AIX only:** Generates line numbers for typedefs.
-d	**BSD only:** Creates tags for #defines that don't take argument also.
Linux:	
-e	Generates a tag file for emacs. To use etags has the same effect.
-h *list*	Specifies a list of file extensions to be interpreted as include, or header, files.
-i *types*	Specifies c/c++ tags to show.
-I *tokenlist*	Specifies a list of tokens to be specially handled in c and c++ source files.
-L *file*	Specifies a file that contains a list of files to process.
-n	Uses only use line numbers for ex commands.
-N	Uses only use search pattern for ex commands.
-o *tagfile*	Specifies a different name for the tag file (default is tags).
-p *path*	Specifies the default path for source files.
-R	Recurses directories.
-u	Doesn't sort the tag file.
-V	Verbose mode. Shows more information.
--append=yes | no	Indicates if tags generated from specified files should be append/replace existing.
--beta-types=*types*	Specifies BETA language tag to included in the tag file.
--c-types=*types*	Specifies C/C++ language tag to include in the tag file.
--eiffel-types=*types*	Specifies Eiffel language tag to include in the tag file.
--etags-include=*file*	Includes a reference to file in the tag file. Only available with -e.

continued

--excmd=*type*	Specifies how the command to EX will be.
number	Uses only line numbers.
pattern	Uses a search pattern.
mixed	Uses search pattern except when it is meaningless (equal source lines).
--file-scope=yes | no	Specifies if tags local to a file should be included in the tag file (default is yes).
--file-tags=yes | no	Specifies if tags should be generated for source filenames.
--filter=yes | no	Specifies if ctags should work as a filter.
--filter-terminator=*string*	Specifies a string to print to STDOUT following tags for each filename.
--format=level	Specifies the format level. Can be 1 or 2. (Not used with –e.)
--fortran-types=*types*	Specifies Fortran language tag to include in the tag file.
--help	Shows help information.
--if0=yes | no	Specifies if code inside a #if 0 branch should be examined.
--java-types=*types*	Specifies Java language tag to include in the tag file.
--kind-long=yes | no	Specifies whether identifier is a verbose name or a single letter.
--lang=*language*	Specifies the language to examine. By default ctags try to select the right language.
--langmap=*maps...*	Specifies language to use for an extension (Ex: --langmap=C:.c.cc,java:+.j
--license	Shows license information.
--line-directives=yes | no	Specifies if a #line directive will be recognized.
--links=yes | no	Specifies if symbolic links will be followed.
--options=*file*	Reads more options from file.
--recurse=yes | no	Specifies if ctag will go into directories recourse.
--sort=yes | no	Specifies if the tag file will be sorted by tag name.
--totals=yes | no	Specifies if statistics will be generated.
--verbose=yes | no	Verbose mode. Shows more information.
--version	Shows version information.

File Name:	`ctags`	**Directory:**	/usr/bin/	**Type:**	External
Note:	Linux: `ctags` can be started with `etags`. This is the same as `ctags -e`				
Common:	ctags truss.c	Creates a tag file from file truss.c.			
Common:	ctags -v truss.h ucg.c | sort -f > index	Creates a sorted output index on STDOUT.			
Linux:	etags truss.c	Creates a tag file from file truss.c in emacs format.			

cut

UNIX Shell: Shells (ash, bash, bsh, csh, ksh, sh, tcsh, zsh)

Function	Selects fields or columns from a text file or a table and shows the result to STDOUT.
Syntax	cut option [options...] *files...*

	The following options can't be combined.
-b *list*	Specifies the number of bytes positions to include in the output. (i.e. b1-50)
-n	Doesn't split the characters.
-c *list*	Uses the specified character positions from this list to cut in the file.
-f *list*	Specifies the number of the field or fields to cut from the file specified.
-d *delimiter*	Specifies a field delimiter to use. (Default is a space.)
-s	Doesn't cut lines that don't contain a field delimiter.
files...	Specifies the file to cut fields or columns from.
list	Contains fields with numbers and can be separated by dashes - to indicate ranges.
Linux:	
--output-delimiter=*string*	Specifies a string to use for output delimiter. Default is same as input delimiter.
--help	Shows help information.
--version	Shows version information.

File Name:	cut	**Directory:**	/usr/bin/	**Type:**	External
Note:	If target file isn't specified it will read from STDIN.				
Common:	who am i | cut -f1 -d' '	Lists the current login names.			
Common:	cut -d: -f1,6 /etc/passwd	Lists the users and their home-library.			
Common:	cut -b5-7 /etc/passwd	Lists the characters in position 5, 6, and 7.			

date

UNIX Shell:	**Shells (ash, bash, bsh, csh, ksh, sh, tcsh, zsh)**
Function	Shows current date and time or sets the date and time on your computer.
Syntax	date [options...] *{ date }*

-u	Sets or shows the Greenwich Mean Time (GMT).
+*format*	Specifies the date format to show the date on.
AIX:	
-n	Sets the local time only, not the global time if in a LAN with synchronized clocks.
date	Sets the new date. Format is mmddHHMM[[cc]yy][.SS]. (mm=month, dd=day, HH=hour, MM=minute, SS=second, cc=century -1, yy=year)
BSD:	
-d *value*	Sets the kernel's value for daylight saving time.
-r *seconds*	Shows the date and time based on the specified seconds from the Epoch.
-t *minutes*	Specifies the number of minutes west of GMT.
-n	Sets the local time only, not the global time if in a LAN with synchronized clocks.
date	Sets the new date. Format is ccyymmddHHMM.SS.
Linux:	
-d *string*	Specifies the time to use, instead of current time.
-f *file*	Specifies a file containing a list of times to use, instead of current time.
-r *file*	Shows the last modification time on the specified file.
-R	Shows the date and time as RFC-822 compliant.
-s *string*	Sets the time to the specified time.
-u	Shows or sets coordinated universal time.
--help	Shows help information.
--version	Shows version information.
date	Sets the new date. Format is mmddHHMM[[cc]yy][.SS].
Solaris:	
-a [-]*sss.fff*	Alters the system time gradually by the specified seconds and fractions of a second.
date	Sets the new date. Format is mmddHHMM[[cc]yy][.SS].

File Name:	date	**Directory:**	**AIX, Solaris:** /usr/bin/ **BSD, Linux:** /bin/	**Type:**	External
Common:	date -u	Shows the time in GMT time zone.			
Common:	date '+TIME: %H:%M'	Shows the time in the format: `TIME: hours:minutes`.			
Common:	date 062319032001.00	Sets the date to June 23 2001 and the time to 19:03:00.			

dc

UNIX Shell:	**Shells (ash, bash, bsh, csh, ksh, sh, tcsh, zsh)**
Function	A calculator that uses reverse-polish notation. It uses a stack to performs calculations.
Syntax	dc *{ file }*

file	Takes the input from the given filename instead of STDIN.
	The following are the constructions that you may use:
number	A string of numbers 0-9. To indicate a negative number, begin with underscore _.
+ - / * % ^	Used for adding, subtracting, dividing, multiplying, remaindering, or exponentiation.
s*x*	Stores the top of the stack into a registry named x. The x could be any character.
l*x*	Pushes the values onto the stack that were stored using the `sx` option.
d	Duplicates the top value of the stack.
p	Prints the top value of the stack.
P	Converts the top of stack into ASCII format, removes the string and prints it.
f	Shows all values in the stack.
q	Exits the program and populates the recurring level by 2 if executing a string.
Q	Exits the program and populates the top value of the stack and executes the string.
x	The top element is treated as a character string and the string will be executed.
X	Replaces the number on top of the stack with scale factor.
{ string }	Pushes the string onto the top of the stack. The brackets ([ ]) must be used.
<x >x =x	Populates the two elements and compares them. Runs the macro in register x if true.
v	Replaces the top element of the stack with its square root.

continued

!	Interprets the rest of the string as a shell command.
c	Clears the stack.
i	Populates the top value of the stack and uses that number for more input.
I	Pushes the input base onto the top of the stack.
o	Only the top of the stack is populated then used as the number radix for more output.
O	Pushes the output base to the top of the stack.
k	The top of the stack is populated and then used as a plus scaling factor.
z	Only the stack level is pushed on the stack.
Z	Replaces the length with the number on the top of the stack.
?	Executes a line of input from the terminal.
; :	Are used when working with arrays.
AIX:	
L*x*	Pops a value from the register stack and pushes it on the stack.
S*x*	Pops a value from the stack and pushes. it on the register stack x.
BSD, Linux:	
n	Pops a value from the stack and shows it without any new line after.
r	Swaps the two top elements on the stack.
L*x*	Pops a value from the register stack and pushes it on the stack.
S*x*	Pops a value from the stack and pushes it on the register stack x.
#	Handles the line as comment.
K	Pushes the current scaling factor that is on top of the stack.
Solaris:	
Y	Shows debug information.
K	Pushes the current scaling factor that is on top of the stack.

File Name:	`dc`	**Directory:**	/usr/bin/	**Type:**	External

dd

UNIX Shell: Shells (ash, bash, bsh, csh, ksh, sh, tcsh, zsh)

Function	Copies and converts an input file to an output file.
Syntax	dd [option=*value*...]

if=*file*	Specifies the path and name of the input file. (Default is STDIN.)
of=*file*	Specifies the path and name of the output file. (Default is STDOUT.)
ibs=*n*	Specifies the block size of the input in bytes. (Default is 512.)
obs=*n*	Specifies the block size of the output in bytes. (Default is 512.)
bs=*n*	Sets both the input and the output block sizes to n. Overrides `ibs` & `obs`
cbs=*n*	Sets the block conversion size for `block` and `unblock` in bytes.
skip=*n*	Skips the specified amount of blocks from the input before copying.
seek=*n*	Skips, starting from the beginning of an output file, n blocks before copying.
count=*n*	Copies only the specified number of input blocks.
conv=*value*[,*value*]	Converts when copying. Where values are the following symbols separated by commas:
ascii	Converts a EBCDIC file into ASCII format.
ebcdic	Converts an ASCII file into EBCDIC format.
ibm	Uses a different ASCII to EBCDIC map when converting.
block	Handles input as EOF or new line variable length records and ignores block limits.
unblock	Converts all fixed-length records into variable length ones.
lcase	Maps all uppercase characters to lowercase.
ucase	Maps all lowercase characters to uppercase.
swab	Swaps each pair of input bytes. Skips the last byte if the input has an odd number.
noerror	Ignores input errors and continues to process.
notrunc	Forbids truncation of the output file.
sync	Expands input blocks to the same size as the `ibs=` buffer.
AIX:	
files=*n*	Terminates after copying and linking together the specified amount of input files.
fskip=*n*	Skips the specified amount of end-of-file characters from the input before copying.
	This is additional option to conv=
iblock	Rereads data in smaller blocks if an error occurs.
oblock	Rewrites data in smaller blocks if an error occurs.

continued

BSD:	
files=*n*	Terminates after copying and linking together the specified amount of input files.
	This is additional option to conv=
oldascii	Converts a EBCDIC file into ASCII format.
oldibm	Uses a different ASCII to EBCDIC map when converting.
oldebcdic	Converts an ASCII file into EBCDIC format.
osync	Pads outputblock to the full output block size.
Linux:	
--help	Shows help information.
--version	Shows version information.
Solaris:	
files=*n*	Terminates after copying and linking together the specified amount of input files.
iseek=*n*	Seeks, starting from the beginning of an input file, n blocks before copying.
oseek=*n*	Seeks, starting from the beginning of an output file, n blocks before copying.
	This is additional option to conv=
asciib	Converts a EBCDIC file into ASCII format using BSD character translations.
ebcdicb	Converts an ASCII file into EBCDIC format using BSD character translations.
ibmb	Uses a different ASCII to EBCDIC map using BSD character translation.

File Name:	dd	**Directory:** **AIX, Solaris:** /usr/bin/, **BSD, Linux:** /bin/	**Type:** External
Warning:	When copying files between two separate file systems that have different block sizes, don't use dd.		
Common:	dd if=resc1440.raw of=/dev/floppy	Writes the specified input raw file to the floppy.	
Common:	dd if=/dev/rmt1/1 of=tape1.raw bs=1024k	Writes a rawfile from the tape, blocksize is set to 1024K.	
Common:	dd if=/dev/zero of=swap bs=1024 count=1024	Makes a 1 Mbyte file called swap.	

df

UNIX Shell: Shells (ash, bash, bsh, csh, ksh, sh, tcsh, zsh)

Function	Shows used and free disk space for all file systems or the one specified.
Syntax	df [options...] *{ filesystem }*

-k	Shows information for all features in kilobytes.
filesystem	Specifies file system. Use one of the following forms.
files...	Shows information about the file system where file is located.
directories...	Shows information about the file system where directory is located.
AIX:	
-t	Verbose mode. Shows more information.
-P	Uses POSIX output format.
-I	Shows the total number of blocks free and used percentage free space and mountpoint.
-M	Shows the mountpoint.
-i	Shows number of free and used i-nodes.
-s	Uses the VFS specific system helper instead of the statfs system call.
-v	Shows all information about the file system.
BSD:	
-h	Shows the output in human readable format.
-i	Shows number of free and used i-nodes.
-n	Shows statistics previously obtained from the file system.
-P	Shows the output in strict format that can be used by scripts.
-t *type*	Specifies the file system type to check.
Linux:	
-a	Includes file systems that have 0 blocks.
--block-size=*size*	Specifies the block size to use.
-h	Shows the output in human readable format.
-H	Shows the output in human readable format. Use 1000 as the base instead of 1024.
-i	Shows number of free and used i-nodes.
-l	Checks only the local file system.
-m	Same as --block-size=1048576
--no-sync	Doesn't sync before reading information from the file system. (Is default.)
-P	Uses the POSIX output format.

continued

--sync	Synchronizes before reading information from the file system.
-t *type*	Specifies the file system type to check.
-x *type*	Specifies the file system type not to check.
--help	Shows help information.
--version	Shows version information.
Solaris:	
-F *FSType*	Specifies an unmounted file system to check.
-a	Creates a report on all file systems and on file systems that have the ignore flag.
-b	Shows how much free space in Kilobytes.
-e	Shows how much free files that exists.
-g	Shows the entire `statvfs` structure, works only on mounted file systems. (Don't use -g with the -o option.)
-k	Shows information for all features in kilobytes.
-l	Checks only the local file system.
-n	Shows only the FSType name. This only works on mounted file systems.
-t	Verbose mode. Shows more information.
-V	Shows the complete set of file system specific command lines, but doesn't run them.
-o *FSTypeSpecific*	Specifies the FSType-specific options separated by commas.
	The following can also specify file system.
blockdevice	Represents a block special device like `/dev/dsk/c0t0d0s7`.
resource	Specifies an NFS resource name.

File Name:	`df`	**Directory:** /usr/bin/	**Type:** External
Common:	df -k	Shows allocation, free space, mount point, etc.	
Common:	df /	Shows available disk space on root partition.	
AIX:	df -i	Show number of free i-nodes	
OpenBSD:	df -h /usr	Shows information in human readable format.	
Solaris:	df -b /	Shows available disk space on root partition.	

diff

UNIX Shell: Shells (ash, bash, bsh, csh, ksh, sh, tcsh, zsh)

Function	Compares two text files in every line.
Syntax	diff [options...] *file1 file2*

-C *lines*	Specifies how many differences to create context lines for.
-e	Creates a script of a, c, and d commands for `ed`. Re-creates file2 from file1.
-f	Creates similar output as -e in reverse order. It isn't for use with `ed.`
-b	Ignores spaces, Tabs, and blank strings.
-i	Ignores capitalization.
-t	Converts Tab characters to spaces to preserve the original style.
-w	Ignores all blanks such as space, Tab, and blank lines.
-c	Creates a three line context differences report.
-h	Does a quick compare on `easy to work on files.`
-n	Creates a similar output to -e but reversed and counts changed lines.
-D *string*	Merges file1 and file 2 and includes C preprocessor controls.
-l	Shows more information in a long list.
-r	Follows subdirectories when comparing directories.
-s	Creates a report also on identical files.
-S *file*	Specifies a file to start the difference on.
file1	Specifies the first filename or directory.
file2	Specifies the second filename or directory.
BSD, Linux:	
-*lines*	Specifies the context line size.
-a	Handles binary files as if they were text files.
-B	Ignores changes that just insert or delete empty lines.
-d	Searches more accurately on the files. Slows the process significantly.
-F *expression*	Shows some of the last preceding line that matches the expression for contexts.
-H	Uses heuristics to speed up handling of large files with numerous small changes.
-I *expression*	Ignores changes matching the expression and that just inserts or deletes empty lines.

continued

-n	Shows the information in RCS format.
-N	Compares files with an empty file if a file only exists in one compare directory.
-p	Shows which C function each change is in.
-T	Inserts a Tab instead of a space before the text of a line.
-u	Uses the unified output format.
-U *{ lines }*	Uses the unified output format, and shows the specified amount of lines of context.
-v	Shows version information.
-w	Ignores white space when comparing files.
-W *columns*	Specifies the column count in side-by-side format.
-x *pattern*	Ignores files and directories matching the specified pattern.
-X *file*	Ignores files and directories matching any pattern contained in the specified file.
-y	Uses the side-by-side output format.
--changed-group-format=*format*	Specifies the format to use to show a line group containing differing lines.
--horizon-lines=*lines*	Specifies the line count not to discard from end of prefix and start of suffix.
--ignore-all-space	Ignores white spaces when comparing lines.
--left-column	Shows the left side only for common lines in side-by-side format.
--sdiff-merge-assist	Shows the information in a format so that `sdiff` can read it.
--show-c-function	Shows which C function each change is in.
--suppress-common-lines	Hides common lines in side-by-side format.
	The following options are only used for the if-then-else format.
--new-group-format=*format*	Specifies the format to show a group of lines from the second file.
--new-line-format=*format*	Specifies the format to show a line from the second file.
--old-group-format=*format*	Specifies the format to show a group of lines from the first file.
--old-line-format=*format*	Specifies the format to show a line from the first file.
--unchanged-group-format=*format*	Specifies the format to show a common group of lines from both files.
--unchanged-line-format=*format*	Specifies the format to show a common line from both files.

File Name:	`diff`	**Directory:**	/usr/bin/ **Type:** External
Common:	diff /etc/passwd /usr/bin/passwd		Shows if files are the same or not.
Common:	diff -e /etc/passwd /etc/passwd		Shows a script for the `ed` command.
Linux:	diff -y /etc/passwd /usr/bin/passwd		Shows the difference in side-by-side format.
OpenBSD:	diff -e -x a* /sbin /usr/sbin		Doesn't compare any files beginning with an a.

diff3

UNIX Shell: Shells (ash, bash, bsh, csh, ksh, sh, tcsh, zsh)

Function	Compares the difference between three files.
Syntax	diff3 [options...] *file1 file2 file3*

-e	Creates a script for ed that will add all changes between file2 and file3 into file1.
-x	Creates a script to add changes from all files.
-E	Same as -e but handles overlapping changes differently.
-X	Creates a script that will add all changes. Close to the -E option.
-3	Creates a script to add changes from file3.
file1	Specifies the first path and filename.
file2	Specifies the second path and filename.
file3	Specifies the third path and filename.
BSD, Linux:	
-a	Handles binary files as text files.
-A	Incorporates all changes from file2 to file3 into file1 and captures conflicts.
--easy-only	Is like -e, but will only show the non-overlapping changes.
-i	Makes the `ed` script System V compatible. Cannot be combined with -m.
-L *label*	Specifies the label for the brackets output by the -A, -E, and -X options.
-m	Applies the edit script to the first file and sends the result to STDOUT.
-T	Shows a Tab instead of two spaces before the text of a line.
-v	Shows version information.

continued

File Name:	`diff3`	**Directory:**	/usr/bin/	**Type:**	Script
Common:	diff3 text1 text2 text3	Compares the three files.			
Common:	diff3 -e text1 text2 text3	Adds all changes between file2 and file3 into file1.			
OpenBSD:	diff3 -a text1 text2 text3	Compares the files as text files, even if they are not.			

dirname

UNIX Shell: Bourne shell (sh)

Function	Shows everything up to the last level of the given pathname.
Syntax	dirname *path*

path	Specifies the path string to use.
Linux:	
--help	Shows help information.
--version	Shows version information.

File Name:	`dirname`	**Directory:**	/usr/bin/	**Type:**	External
Note:	In Solaris it's a script.				
Common:	dirname /export/home/ucg/ucgfile	Shows `/export/home/ucg`.			
Common:	UCGPATH=`dirname $HOME/misc/ucgfile`	Sets UCGPATH to `$HOME/misc`..			

dirs

UNIX Shell: Shells (bash, csh, tcsh, zsh)

Function	Shows the directory stack with the most recent one to the left.
Syntax	dirs [options...]

bash:	
+*n*	Shows the n:th entry counting from the left.
-*n*	Shows the n:th entry counting from the right.
-c	Clears the directory stack.
-l	Prevents ~ in the output.
-p	Shows one entry per line.
-v	Shows one entry per line with the index in the stack.
csh:	
-l	Prevents ~ in the output.
tcsh:	
-l	Prevents ~ in the output.
-n	Wraps lines longer than the screen.
-v	Shows one entry per line.
-S *{ filename }*	Saves the directory stack in file (default is ~/.cshdirs).
-L *{ filename }*	Loads the directory stack from file (default is ~/.cshdirs).
-c	Clears the directory stack.
zsh:	
-v	Shows one entry per line.
directories...	Adds the directories specified to the directory stack.

Note:	Use `popd` and `puchd` to manipulate the directory stack.	
Common:	dirs	Shows the directory stack, e.g. "~ /usr /etc"
Common:	dirs -l	Shows the directory stack, e.g. "/home/ucg /usr /etc"

domainname

UNIX Shell: Shells (ash, bash, bsh, csh, ksh, sh, tcsh, zsh)

Function	Sets or shows the domain your system is configured for.
Syntax	domainname *{ domain }*

domain	Sets a new domain name to use. Can only be set by the superuser.
Linux:	
-v	Verbose mode. Shows more information.
-F *file*	Reads hostname from the specified file.

File Name:	`domainname`	**Directory:**	**AIX, Solaris:** /usr/bin/, **BSD, Linux:** /bin/	**Type:**	External
Common:	domainname ucg.com	Sets the domain name to ucg.com.			
Common:	domainname	Shows the current domain name.			
Linux:	Domainname –F/etc/hostname	Reads hostname from the specified hostname file.			

du

du	UNIX Shell:	Shells (ash, bash, bsh, csh, ksh, sh, tcsh, zsh)

Function	Shows disk usage for a directory and its subdirectories.
Syntax	du [options...] *{ files... }*

-a	Shows the size of every file.
-k	Shows sizes in units of 1024 bytes instead of the default 512 bytes.
-s	Shows only the total sum of each specified file.
files...	One or more files or directories to use. (Default is current directory.)
AIX:	
-l	Blocks will be calculated evenly between links for files with multiple links.
-r	Shows messages when problems occur, e.g., read errors.
-x	Doesn't cross file system limits.
BSD:	
-H	Follows only symbolic links on the command line.
-L	Follows all symbolic links.
-P	Doesn't follow any symbolic links.
-c	Shows a grand total.
-r	Shows messages when problems occur, e.g., read errors.
-x	Doesn't cross file system limits.
Linux:	
--block-size=*size*	Specifies the block size to use.
-b	Shows sizes in bytes.
-c	Shows a grand total.
-D	Follows only symbolic links on the command line.
-h	Shows sizes in a human readable format, e.g., 4G.
-H	Same as -h but uses powers of 1000 instead of 1024.
-l	Counts the sizes of all hard links.
-L	Uses the file a link points at instead of the link itself.
-m	Shows sizes in units of 1048576 bytes instead of the default 512 bytes.
-S	Doesn't add the size of subdirectories to the parent's size.
-x	Doesn't cross file system limits.
-X *file*	Excludes files that match the patterns in the specified file.
--exclude=*pattern*	Excludes files that match the specified pattern.
--max-depth=*n*	Specifies the number of subdirectories that are searched.
--help	Shows help information.
--version	Shows version information.
Solaris:	
-d	Doesn't cross file system limits.
-L	Uses the file a link points at instead of the link itself.
-o	Doesn't add the size of subdirectories to the parent's size.
-r	Shows messages when problems occur, e.g., read errors.

File Name:	du	**Directory:**	/usr/bin/	**Type:**	External

Common:	du -a	Shows the size of every file in current directory.
Common:	du -ks /export/home/*	Shows the sizes of all user's home directories in kilobytes.
Common:	du /etc /var	Shows disk usage for /etc and /var.
AIX:	du -x /	Shows disk usage for all files on the same device as /.
OpenBSD:	du -P /usr/bin	Shows disk usage for /usr/bin. Doesn't follow symbolic links.
Solaris:	du -o	Shows disk usage for current directory but doesn't count subdirectories.

echo

echo	UNIX Shell:	Shells (ash, bash, bsh, csh, ksh, sh, tcsh, zsh)

Function	Copies the written string to the screen. Exists as internal in all shells.
Syntax	echo [options...] *{ strings... }* sh, ksh: echo *{ strings... }* csh: echo [-n] *{ strings... }*

strings...	The text to show on the screen.

continued

BSD:	
-n	Is used to suppress new-line.
Linux:	
-n	Suppresses new-line.
-e	Interprets escape characters. Escape characters are shown below.
-E	Doesn't interpret escape characters.
--help	Shows help information.
--version	Shows version information.
	All shells have internal echo commands.
csh, tcsh:	
-n	Suppresses new-line.
bash, zsh:	
-n	Suppresses new-line.
-e	Interprets escape characters. Escape characters are shown below.
-E	Doesn't interpret escape characters.
	Escaped characters used. See above which echos use them.
\a	Adds an alert character.
\b	Adds a backspace.
\c	Forms a print line without new-line.
\f	Initiates a form-feed.
\n	Adds a new-line.
\r	Initiates a carriage return.
\t	Adds a tab.
\v	Adds a vertical tab.
\\	Adds a backslash.
\0n	Adds an ASCII code character.

File Name:	`echo`	**Directory:**	**AIX, Solaris:** /usr/bin/, **BSD, Linux:** /bin/	**Type:**	External, Internal
Common:	echo UCG has Every Command!	Echo the text string.			
Common:	echo $SHELL	Shows you the shell you are working in.			
Common:	echo $MANPATH	Prints your search path to man pages.			
Linux:	echo -n "enter your name: "	Doesn't make a carrage return after the text string.			

ed

UNIX Shell:	**Shells (ash, bash, bsh, csh, ksh, sh, tcsh, zsh)**
Function	A line-based editor. It is often used to edit files automatically in a script.
Syntax	ed [options...] *{ file }*

-	Reads in the input from STDIN.
-s	Suppresses some character counting and diagnostics.
-p *string*	Specifies a string of text as prompt (default is no string at all).
file	Specifies the file to edit.
BSD, Solaris:	
-x	Uses encryption, tries to figure out if the text is encrypted or not.
-C	**Solaris only:** Uses encryption; assumes the text is encrypted.
Linux:	
-G	Forces backward compatibility.

File Name:	`ed`	**Directory:**	**AIX, Solaris:** /usr/bin/, **BSD, Linux:** /bin/	**Type:**	External
Note:	If the editor input is coming from a command file, the editor exits at the first failure.				
Common:	ed	Starts the ed text editor.			
Linux:	ed -G hello.txt	Forces backward compatibility and opens the file `hello.txt`.			

edquota

edquota		UNIX Shell:	Shells (ash, bash, bsh, csh, ksh, sh, tcsh, zsh)
Function	Manages user quotas for a ufs file system.		
Syntax	Solaris: edquota [-p *protouser*] *user* Solaris: edquota -t AIX, BSD, Linux: edquota [options...] *user* AIX, BSD, Linux: edquota [options...] *group* AIX, BSD, Linux: edquota [options...] -t		

	The following two options can't be used together.
-p *protouser*	Specifies a prototype user to use as template for a specified user.
-t	Alters the soft limit for all file systems.
user	Specifies the user to edit.
AIX, BSD, Linux:	
-u	Edits quota for users. If a user is specified, -t doesn't work.
-g	Edits quota for groups. If a group is specified, -t doesn't work.
-n	**Linux only:** Alters the non-local quota using rpc.rquotad.
group	

File Name:	`edquota`	**Directory:**	/usr/sbin/	**Type:**	External
Common:	edquota -p skeluser ucguser10	Sets quota for ucguser10 to be the same as for skeluser.			
Common:	edquota ucguser11	Sets quota for ucguser11.			
AIX:	edquota -g users	Sets quota for group users.			

egrep

egrep		UNIX Shell:	Shells (ash, bash, bsh, csh, ksh, sh, tcsh, zsh)
Function	Shows lines form the file that matches the given pattern using full regular expressions.		
Syntax	egrep [options...] *{ pattern } { files... }*		

-c	Shows only the count of the lines that matches the specified pattern.
-h	Hides the filenames when searching multiple files.
-i	Ignores upper/lower case distinctions.
-l	Shows only the filenames that contain matching strings.
-n	Shows the line number of each line where a match occurred.
-v	Shows only lines that don't match the pattern.
-e *pattern_list*	Searches for pattern_list of full regular expression.
-f *file*	Uses the list of full regular expression from this file.
pattern	Specifies a single string as the pattern to search for.
files ..	Specifies the file/files to operate on. If none given, uses STDIN.
AIX:	
-b	Shows the block number that the pattern was found in.
-s	Shows only error messages.
-x	Matches only if the input line and the pattern match exactly
-p*{ separator }*	Shows the whole paragraph for a match. Specifies separator (default is blank line).
-q	Shows nothing. Exits with exit status 0 if a match is found.
-w	Searches for a whole word.
-y	Ignores the case of letters when making comparisons.
BSD:	
-s	Hides error about non-existing files.
-x	Matches only if the input line and the pattern match exactly
-*NR*	Shows NR of lines before and after the matched line.
-A *NR*	Shows NR of lines after the matched line.
-B *NR*	Shows NR of lines before the matched line.
-C	Shows 2 lines before and after the matched line.
-V	Shows version information.
-b	Shows the byte offset for the match.
-L	Shows only the filenames that don't contain matching strings.

continued

-o	Shows the filename on each match.
-q	Shows nothing. Exits with exit status 0 if a match is found.
-w	Searches for a whole word.
Linux:	
-s	Hides error about non-existing files.
-*NR*	Shows NR of lines before and after the matched line.
-A *NR*	Shows NR of lines after the matched line.
-B *NR*	Shows NR of lines before the matched line.
-C *{ NR }*	Shows NR lines before and after the matched line (default is 2).
-a	Processes a binary file like a text file.
-b	Shows the byte offset for the match.
--binary-files=*type*	Specifies action with binary files.
binary	Shows only a line saying that a match is found (default).
without-match	Assumes that there aren't matches in binary files.
text	Processes a binary file like a text file.
-d *action*	Specifies action with a directory.
read	Reads the directory like an ordinary file.
skip	Skips the directory.
recurse	Reads all files under directory and its subdirectories recursively.
-H	Shows the filenames for each match.
--help	Shows help information.
-I	Assumes that there aren't matches in binary files.
-L	Shows only the filenames that don't contain matching strings.
--mmap	Uses the mmap systemcal to read files instead of read.
-q	Suppresses normal output. Stops after the first match.
-r	Reads all files under directory and its subdirectories recursively.
-s	Hides error about non-existing files.
-U	Handles the file as binary.
--version	Shows version information.
-w	Searches for a whole word.
-x	Matches only if the input line and the pattern match exactly.
-Z	Uses a ASCII NULL character after filename instead of a new-line character.
Solaris:	
-s	Shows only error messages.
-b	Shows the block number that the pattern was found in.
	Another copy of egrep exists in /usr/xpg4/bin and it has one more option.
-x	Matches only if the input line and the pattern match exactly:

File Name:	`egrep`	**Directory:**	/usr/bin/, **Linux:** /bin/ — **Type:** External
Note:	This is the same thing as using `grep -E`.		
Common:	egrep "^root" /etc/passwd	Searches for a line in `/etc/passwd` starting with root.	
Common:	egrep -c sh /etc/passwd	Shows how many times sh appears in `/etc/passwd`.	
Common:	egrep -l root /etc/*	Shows all filenames where username `root` appears.	

env

UNIX Shell: Shells (ash, bash, bsh, csh, ksh, sh, tcsh, zsh)

Function	Alters the current environment and invokes a utility or shows the current environment.
Syntax	env [options...] *{ utility } { arg }*

-i	Doesn't inherit the environment from the current shell.
variable=value	Specifies a new value for the specified variable.
utility	The name of the utility to invoke. The utility can have arguments.
arg	Specifies the string to pass to the utility.
Linux:	
-u *name*	Removes variable from the environment.

File Name:	env	**Directory:**	/usr/bin/ — **Type:** External
Common:	env	Shows environment variables.	
Common:	env PATH=/usr/sbin:/usr/bin sh	Sets new PATH and starts a new Bourne shell with it.	
Linux:	env -u PATH	Removes environment PATH.	

eqn, geqn

eqn, geqn	UNIX Shell:	Shells (ash, bash, bsh, csh, ksh, sh, tcsh, zsh)
Function	Preprocesses files for troff which contain mathematics equations.	
Syntax	eqn [options...] *{ files... }*	

	Linux Only: The command `geqn` is the same as the command `eqn`.
-d *xy*	Uses characters x and y as the equation delimiters.
-f *value*	Alters the font to the specified one.
-p *size*	Reduces subscripts and superscripts by the specified point size.
-s *size*	Alters the point size to the specified one.
files...	The file to be processed by eqn. (Default is STDIN.)
AIX:	
-T *printer*	Prepares the output for the specified printing device.
BSD,Linux:	
-C	Recognizes .EQ and .EN even when followed by a character other than space or new line.
-N	Disallows new lines within delimiters.
-v	Shows version information.
-r	Specifies that only one size reduction should be used.
-m*number*	Specifies the number of minimum point size.
-T *printer*	Prepares the output for the specified printing device.
-M*directory*	Searches for configuration file in directory.
-R	Specifies the configuration file should not be loaded.

File Name:	`eqn`	**Directory:**	/usr/bin/	**Type:**	External
Note:	Use the command `neqn` for preprocessing `nroff` files.				
Common:	eqn report.roff | troff	Process and pipe `report.roff` into `troff`.			

eval

eval	UNIX Shell:	Shells (ash, bash, bsh, csh, ksh, sh, tcsh, zsh)
Function	Reads the argument as input to the shell and runs the resulting commands.	
Syntax	eval *arguments...*	

arguments...	The argument to read.
Common:	eval "echo UCG is the best book ever" — Runs echo and shows "UCG is the best book ever."
Common:	eval ls — Runs the ls command.

ex, e

ex, e	UNIX Shell:	Shells (ash, bash, bsh, csh, ksh, sh, tcsh, zsh)
Function	A line-based text editor. It is able to work on several files at the same time.	
Syntax	ex [options...] *files...*	

-s	Suppresses all interactive user feedback.
-R	Starts in read-only mode.
-r *file*	Opens file in the editor after an editor or system crash.
-t *tag*	Opens the file and positions the editor at the position for tag.
-v	Uses the `vi` editor.
-C	Uses encryption but assumes the text is encrypted.
-c *command*	Executes the editor command after the file is reading.
files...	Specifies files to edit.
AIX:	
+*command*	Starts an edit with the specified command.
-l	Edits LISP programs.
-V	Verbose mode. Shows more information.
-w*n*	Sets the default window size to n.
BSD:	
-F	Doesn't copy the entire file before starting to edit it.
-S	Runs in secure mode. Disallows any access to external programs.
-w*n*	Sets the default window size to n.
Linux:	
+*NR*	Goes to the specified line.
+/*pattern*	Goes to the specified patterns.

continued

+*command*	Runs the specified command.
-b	Uses binary mode.
-h	Shows help information.
-L	Shows the name of all files saved as the result of an editor or system crash.
-m	Starts in read-only mode.
-n	Doesn't use any swap file. Recover after a crash isn't possible.
-s *file*	Reads commands from the file.
-u *file*	Uses file as in initializations file instead of .vimrc.
-w *file*	Saves all commands entered in file. The file can be used with -s file.
-W *file*	Same as -w but will overwrite any existing file. -w will append to an existing file.
-l	Edits LISP programs.
-V	Verbose mode. Shows more information.
-x	Uses encryption.
Solaris:	**Solaris only:** The command `e` is the same as the command `ex`.
-l	Edits LISP programs.
-L	Shows the name of all files saved as the result of an editor or system crash.
-V	Verbose mode. Shows more information.
-x	Uses encryption, tries to determine if the file is encrypted or not.
-w*n*	Sets the default window size to n.
-C	Uses encryption but assumes the text is encrypted.

File Name:	`ex`	**Directory:**	**AIX, BSD:** /usr/bin/, **Solaris:** /usr/ucb/, **Linux:** /bin/	**Type:**	External
Common:	ex /etc/passwd		Edit /etc/passwd using ex.		
Common:	ex -v /etc/passwd		Edit /etc/passwd using vi.		
Solaris:	ex -L		List editor or system crash files.		

exec

UNIX Shell: Shells (ash, bash, bsh, csh, ksh, sh, tcsh, zsh)

Function	Runs a command in place of the current shell. Usually another shell.
Syntax	exec *command* bash: exec [options...] *command*

command	Specifies a command to execute instead of the current shell.
bash:	
-c	Runs the command in an empty environment.
-l	Runs the command as a login shell.
-a *name*	Passes name as the zeroth argument to the command.

Note:	Remember that if you replace the main shell, your session will end when the new process ends.	
Common:	exec tcsh	Replaces your current shell with tcsh.
Linux:	exec -l bash	Replaces your current bash with a new one, and runs it as login shell.

exit

UNIX Shell: Shells (ash, bash, bsh, csh, ksh, sh, tcsh, zsh)

Function	Exits a shell or shell script with an exit status.
Syntax	exit [option]

sh,ksh,bash,zsh:	
number	The exit status. (Default is the exit status of the last command.)
csh,tcsh:	
(*expression*)	Returns the result of the expression. (Default is the value of status variable.)

Common:	exit	Exits the shell or script.
Common:	exit 5	Exits with status 5.

expand

UNIX Shell: Shells (ash, bash, bsh, csh, ksh, sh, tcsh, zsh)

Function	Replaces Tabs with spaces in text files. If no input files are specified, STDIN will be used.
Syntax	expand [options...] *{ files... }*

files...	Specifies text files to use as input.
AIX:	
-t *tabs*	Specifies the Tab positions. Can be an absolute number or a comma-separated list.

continued

BSD:	
-tabs	Specifies the Tab positions. Can be an absolute number or a comma-separated list.
Linux:	
-i	Doesn't replace Tabs after non-whitespace.
-t *tabs*	Specifies the Tab positions. Can be an absolute number or a comma-separated list.
--help	Shows help information.
--version	Shows version information.
Solaris:	
-tabs	Specifies the Tab positions. Can be an absolute number or a comma-separated list.
-t *tabs*	Specifies the Tab positions. Can be an absolute number or a comma-separated list.

File Name:	expand	**Directory:**	/usr/bin/
Type:	External		
Note:	The default Tab value is 8 spaces apart.		
Common:	expand ucg1	Expands the file ucg1 to STDOUT.	
Common:	expand ucg1 > ucg2	Expands the file ucg1 to ucg2.	
AIX:	expand -t 10 ucg1 > ucg2	Expands the file ucg1 to ucg2 with a tab value set to 10.	
OpenBSD:	expand -10 ucg1 > ucg2	Expands the file ucg1 to ucg2 with a tab value set to 10.	

export

UNIX Shell: Shells (ash, bash, bsh, ksh, sh)

Function	Exports a shell variable to environment.
Syntax	export *{ name }*

name	The name of the variable to export to the environment.
ksh,zsh:	
name=value	Exports the variable name to the environment and sets it to a given value.
bash:	
-f	Specifies that name is a function.
-n	Removes name from the environment.
-p	Shows all exported variables in this shell.
variable=value	Exports the variable name to the environment and sets it to a given value.

Note:	In csh and tcsh use setenv instead.	
Common:	export MANPATH	Exports the MANPATH environment variable.
Common:	export MANPATH=/usr/man	Sets MANPATH to /usr/man and exports it. (ksh, bash).

expr

UNIX Shell: Shells (ash, bash, bsh, csh, ksh, sh, tcsh, zsh)

Function	Evaluates an expression and shows the result to STDOUT.
Syntax	expr *arguments...*

argument	The argument to evaluate. It is built up of terms and operators.
The syntax is:	**arg1 operand arg2 [operand .... argn]. Arg is either an integer or string.**
+, -	Is used for addition, subtraction of integer values.
* , / , %	Is used for multiplication, division, or remainder of integer values.
=, !=, <, <=, >, >=	Is used for comparison of two arguments. Returns 1 if it's true, otherwise 0.
arg1 \\| arg2	Returns arg1 if arg1 not is NULL or 0; otherwise returns arg2.
arg1 \& arg2	Returns arg1 if neither arg1 nor arg2 is NULL or 0; otherwise returns 0.
arg1:arg2	Locks for arg2 in arg1, returns number of matched character.
AIX:	
match *str1 str2*	Locks for arg2 in arg1, returns number of matched character.
index *str1 str2*	Reports the first position if any of the characters in str2 appear in str1.
length *str1*	Reports the length of string str1.
substr *str1 arg1 arg2*	Extracts a substring from str1, starting at position arg1 of arg2.
Linux:	
match *str1 str2*	Locks for arg2 in arg1; returns number of matched character.
index *str1 str2*	Reports the first position of any of the characters if str2 appears in str1.
length *str1*	Reports the length of string str1.
substr *str1 arg1 arg2*	Extracts a substring from str1, starting at position arg1 of arg2.

continued

quote *token* --version --help **Solaris:** index *str1 str2* length *str1* substr *str1 arg1 arg2*	Interprets token as a string even if it is a keyword like index. Shows version information. Shows help information. **The following is used only on x86 for capability.** Reports the first position if any of the characters in str2 appear in str1. Reports the length of string str1. Extracts a substring from str1, starting at position arg1 of arg2.				
File Name:	expr	**Directory:**	/usr/bin/, **BSD:** /bin/	**Type:**	External
Tip:	This is very useful in scripts.				
Common:	foo=`expr $bar * 2`	Multiplies $bar with 2 and places the result in $foo.			
Common:	foo='expr $foo +1'	Increments $foo with one.			

factor

UNIX Shell: Shells (ash, bash, bsh, csh, ksh, sh, tcsh, zsh)

Function	Finds the prime factor of a number. Also shows if the number is a prime factor.
Syntax	factor *number*

number **Linux:** --help --version	Specifies a positive number. Shows help information. Shows version information.				
File Name:	factor	**Directory:**	/usr/bin/, **BSD:** /usr/games/	**Type:**	External
Common:	factor 100	Shows 2,2,5,5, which, when multiplied, will be 100.			

false

UNIX Shell: Shells (ash, bash, bsh, csh, ksh, sh, tcsh, zsh)

Function	Provides a false value in scripts, does nothing but always exits with a non zero-value.
Syntax	false

Linux: --help --version	 Shows help information. Shows version information.				
File Name:	false	**Directory:**	/usr/bin/, **Linux:** /bin/	**Type:**	Script
Common:	while false ; do echo "Noway" ; done	Doesn't show anything, since false is always false.			

fc

UNIX Shell: Shells (bash, ksh, zsh)

Function	Reruns, edits, or lists commands that have recently been used. With no options, edits and runs the last command.
Syntax	fc [options...] *{ command }*

-e *editor*	Uses editor instead of the default one. If editor is - doesn't start any editor.
-l	Lists the commands.
-n	Doesn't show the command numbers when listing with -l.
-r	Shows most recent first.
first last	Selects commands to list or edit from the specified range. Can be a string or a number.
old=new	Modifies the command before it will be run (used with -e -).
command	The command to run again. If not given, use the last one.
bash, ksh:	
-s *{ string }*	Runs the last command used or the last command used beginning with the string.
zsh:	
-d	Shows timestamp for the commands.
-D	Shows elapsed time.
-f	Shows full time and date stamps.
-E	Shows dates as dd.mm.yyyy instead of mm/dd/yyyy.
-i	Shows dates in yyyy-mm-dd instead of mm/dd/yy.
-m	Specifies that command as a pattern that should be quoted.

continued

	The following options can't be used with the above.
-A *file*	Appends the history list to file.
-R *file*	Reads in the history list from file.
-W	Writes the history list to file.
-I	Reads/writes/appends new entries only when used with –R, -W, or -A
Common: fc -lr	Shows the most recent commands, latest first.
Common: fc -e - type	Runs the most recent command that begins with type.

fdformat

UNIX Shell: Shells (ash, bash, bsh, csh, ksh, sh, tcsh, zsh)

Function	Formats new diskettes.
Syntax	AIX: fdformat *{ device }* [-h] BSD: fdformat [options...] *device* Linux: fdformat [-n] *device* Solaris: fdformat [options...] *{ device }*

AIX:	
-h	Uses high-density formatting.
device	Specifies the device containing the diskette (default is `/dev/rfd0`).
BSD:	
-q	Suppresses any normal output from the command.
-v	Verifies the diskette.
-n	Doesn't verify diskette after formatting.
-c *cyls*	Specifies number of cylinders.
-s *secs*	Specifies number of sectors.
-h *heads*	Specifies number of heads.
-t *steps_per_track*	Specifies an alternate method to specify the geometry data for the diskette.
device	Specifies the device containing the diskette. (Default is /dev/rfd0a.)
Linux:	
-n	Doesn't verify diskette after formatting.
device	Specifies the device containing the diskette. (Default is /dev/fd0.)
Solaris:	
-d	Formats an MS-DOS diskette or PCMCIA memory card.
-D	Formats a 720KB (3.5-inch) or 360KB (5.25-inch) double-density diskette.
-e	Ejects the diskette when complete.
-E	Formats a 2.88-megabyte (3.5-inch) extended density diskette.
-f	Doesn't verify before the format starts.
-H	Formats a 1.44-megabyte (3.5-inch) or 1.2-megabyte (5.25-inch) high-density diskette.
-l	Formats a 720KB (3.5-inch) or 360KB (5.25-inch) double-density diskette.
-L	Same as -l.
-m	Writes a 1.2-megabyte (3.5-inch) medium-density format on a high-density diskette.
-M	Same as -m.
-U	Unmounts any file systems before the format.
-q	The Quiet Mode.
-v	Verifies each block of the diskette after the format.
-x	Skips the format, and only writes a SunOS label or an MS-DOS file system.
-b *label*	Specifies the label on the media.
-B *filename*	Installs a special boot loader in `filename` on an MS-DOS diskette.
-t *dos*	Installs an NEC-DOS file system and boot sector on the disk after formatting.
device	Specifies the device containing the diskette or PCMCIA-card (default is diskette).

File Name:	`fdformat`	**Directory:**	**AIX, BSD:** /usr/sbin/, **Linux, Solaris:** /usr/bin/	**Type:**	External

Note:	Solaris: fdformat can also format PCMCIA memory cards.	
AIX:	fdformat -h	Formats a diskette in high-density format.
Linux:	fdformat /dev/fd0H1440	Formats a diskette in 1.44MB format.
OpenBSD:	fdformat /dev/rfd0c	Formats a diskette.
Solaris:	format -H /floppy/floppy0 -b myfloppy	Formats and labels diskette in 1.44 or 1.2 megabyte.

fg

UNIX Shell: Shells (ash, bash, bsh, csh, ksh, sh, tcsh, zsh)

Function	Resumes the execution of a stopped job in the foreground. Without an argument the current job is used.

continued

Syntax	fg *{ jobid }*

jobid	Specifies job id. If not given use the current job.
	Use one of the following to specify job id.
%	Specifies the current job. You can also use %% and %+.
%*number*	Specifies job number.
%?*string*	Specifies a command that contains string.
sh, ksh:	
%*string*	Specifies a command that starts with string
%-	Specifies the previous job.
csh, tcsh:	
%minus;	Specifies the previous job.

Note:	Solaris: Bourn shell (sh) must be started in job control mode by starting it with jsh.	
Common:	fg %5	Brings job number 5 to the foreground.
Common:	fg %" ls -l"	Brings the job that starts with ls -l to the foreground.
Common:	fg %	Brings the current job to the foreground.

fgrep

UNIX Shell:	Shells (ash, bash, bsh, csh, ksh, sh, tcsh, zsh)
Function	Shows lines from the file that match the given pattern.
Syntax	fgrep [options...] *{ pattern } { files... }*

-c	Shows only the count of the lines that match the specified pattern.
-h	Hides the filenames when searching multiple files.
-i	Ignores upper/lower case distinctions.
-l	Shows only the filenames that contain matching strings.
-n	Shows the line number of each line where a match occurred.
-v	Shows only lines that don't match the pattern.
-x	Matches only if the input line and the pattern match exactly.
-e *pattern_list*	Searches for pattern_list of full regular expression.
-f *file*	Uses the list of patterns from this file.
pattern	Specifies a single string as the pattern to find.
files ..	Specifies the file/files to operate on. If none given uses STDIN.
AIX:	
-b	Shows the block number the pattern was found in.
-s	Shows only error messages.
-p*{ separator }*	Shows the whole paragraph for a match. Specifies separator. (Default is blank line).
-q	Shows nothing. Exits with exit status 0 if a match is found.
-w	Searches for a whole word.
-y	Ignores the case of letters when making comparisons.
BSD:	
-s	Hides show error about non-existing files.
-*NR*	Shows NR of lines before and after the matched line.
-A *NR*	Shows NR of lines after the matched line.
-B *NR*	Shows NR of lines before the matched line.
-C	Shows 2 lines before and after the matched line.
-V	Shows version information.
-b	Shows the byte offset for the match.
-L	Shows only the filenames that don't contain matching strings.
-o	Shows the filename on each match.
-q	Shows nothing. Exits with exit status 0 if a match is found.
-w	Searches for a whole word.
Linux:	
-s	Hides error about non-existing files.
-*NR*	Shows NR of lines before and after the matched line.
-A *NR*	Shows NR of lines after the matched line.
-B *NR*	Shows NR of lines before the matched line.

continued

-C *{ NR }*	Shows NR lines before and after the matched line. (Default is 2.)
-a	Processes a binary file like a text file.
-b	Shows the byte offset for the match.
--binary-files=*type*	Specifies action with binary files.
binary	Shows only a line saying that a match is found. (Is default.)
without-match	Assumes that there aren't matches in binary files.
text	Processes a binary file like a text file.
-d *action*	Specifies action with a directory.
read	Reads the directory like an ordinary file.
skip	Skips the directory.
recurse	Reads all files under directory and its subdirectories recursively.
-H	Shows the filenames for each match.
--help	Shows help information.
-I	Assumes that there aren't matches in binary files.
-L	Shows only the filenames that don't contain matching strings.
--mmap	Uses the mmap systemcal to read files instead of read.
-q	Suppresses normal output. Stops after the first match.
-r	Reads all files under directory and its subdirectories recursively.
-s	Hides error about non-existing files.
-U	Handles the file as binary.
--version	Shows version information.
-w	Searches for a whole word.
-Z	Uses a ASCII NULL character after filename instead of a new line character.
Solaris:	
-s	Shows only error messages.
-b	Shows the block number the pattern was found in.
-x	Matches only if the input line and the pattern match exactly.

File Name:	`fgrep`	**Directory:** /usr/bin/, **Linux:** /bin/	**Type:** External
Common:	fgrep -i root /etc/passwd	Searches for root in the file /etc/passwd.	
Common:	ps -ef | fgrep -i daemon	Searches for daemons in the process list.	
Common:	fgrep -v root /etc/passwd	Displays all lines except the ones containing root.	

file

UNIX Shell: Shells (ash, bash, bsh, csh, ksh, sh, tcsh, zsh)

Function	Performs tests on each file that you have specified to determine what file type it is.
Syntax	file [options...] *files...*

-m *mfile*	Specifies an alternative magic file, instead of `/etc/magic.`
-f *file*	Examines the files from the specific file.
files...	Specifies the full path and filename to be tested.
BSD:	
-v	Shows version information.
-c	Searches for format errors in the magic file.
-z	Tries to look inside compressed files.
-L	Specifies that symbolic links should be followed.
Linux:	
-b	Specifies the search path should not be shown on the output.
-c	Searches for format errors in the magic file.
-i	Shows the MIME type.
-n	Forces STDOUT to be flushed after checking a file.
-s	Specifies that special files should be accepted.
-v	Shows version information.
-z	Tries to look inside compressed files.
-L	Specifies that symbolic links should be followed.
Solaris:	
-c	Searches for format errors in the magic file.
-h	Doesn't follow any symbolic links.

continued

File Name:	file	**Directory:**	/usr/bin/	**Type:**	External
Common:	file /etc/hosts		Shows file type for /etc/hosts .		
Common:	file -c		Checks the magic file for format errors.		
Linux:	file -z linux-2.4.5.tar.gz		Tries to check files in the compressed achieve `linux-2.4.5.tar.gz`.		

find

UNIX Shell: Shells (ash, bash, bsh, csh, ksh, sh, tcsh, zsh)

Function	Finds files in the specified directories and subdirectories using the Boolean expression from the input line.
Syntax	find *directories... { options... }*

directories...	Specifies directories search.
	The following is used to define what to find.
-atime *n*	Finds files that were accessed n days ago.
-ctime *n*	Finds files the status of which were changed days ago.
-mtime*n*	Finds files that were modified n days ago. (For n use: +n = more than, n = equal to, -n = less than.)
-size *n[c]*	Finds files n blocks long. If c is used, look for files n bytes long.
-fstype *type*	Finds files that belong to the specified file system type.
-group *group*	Finds files that belong to this group.
-user *user*	Finds files that belong to this user.
-inum *n*	Finds file with inode number n .
-links *n*	Finds files with n links.
-name *pattern*	Finds files with names that match the pattern. Wildcards can be used inside ".
-newer *file*	Finds files that have been modified more recently than the file specified.
-nogroup	Finds files that don't belong to a group in /etc/group.
-nouser	Finds files that don't belong to a user in /etc/passwd file.
-perm [-]*mode*	Finds files with this file mode in octal or symbolic.
-type *x*	Finds files of type `x`. Types are `b,c,d,D,f,l,p, or s`
b	Specifies block file.
c	Specifies special character.
d	Specifies directory.
f	Specifies plain file.
l	Specifies symbolic link.
p	Specifies Named pipe (FIFO).
s	Specifies socket.
-prune	Doesn't examine directory or file in directory structure below patterns that match.
	When a file is found the following will define action on it.
-exec *command* \;	Specifies a command to execute. { } The found file.
-ok *command* \;	Same as -exec but asks user first if he wants to execute the command.
-ls	Shows current pathname with its associated statistics.
-print	Shows the current pathname.
	The expressions can be combined to make more complex search.
(*expression*)	True when expression is true.
!*expression*	Is true when expression is false.
expr1 expr2	Is true when expr1 and expr2 are true.
	This can be used in BSD and Linux.
expr1 -and *expr2*	Is true when expr1 and expr1 are true.
expr1 -or *expr2*	Is true when expr1 or expr1 are true.
	This can be used in AIX, Linux, and Solaris.
expr1 -a *expr2*	Is true when expr1 and expr1 are true.
expr1 -o *expr2*	Is true when expr1 or expr1 is true.
AIX:	
-depth	Descends into hierarchy so entries are acted on before the directory.
-xdev	Searches only in the same file system.
-cpio *device*	Writes the file on the specified device in cpio format.
BSD:	
-H	Shows info and file type for each symbolic link encountered on the command line.
-d	Descends into hierarchy so entries are acted on before the directory.
-h	Shows info and file type for each symbolic link.
-X	Uses find safely with xargs.

continued

-x	Searches only search in the same file system.
-f *file*	Specifies the directory to search.
-w	Considers whiteouts when scanning directories.
-maxdepth levels	Descends most down in a directory structure.
-mindepth levels	Searches only in directory level greater or equal to level.
	The following is used to define what to find.
-follow	Follows symbolic links.
-amin *n*	Finds files that were accessed n minutes ago.
-cmin *n*	Finds files whose status changed n minutes ago.
-empty	Finds files that are empty and are either a regular file or a directory.
-mmin n	Finds files that were modified n minutes ago.
-path *pattern*	Finds files with a pathname that matches the specified pattern.
	When a file is found the following will define action on it.
-execdir *command*	Same as -exec, except that command is run in the found directory.
-print0	Separates filenames with a NULL character instead of a new line character.
Linux:	
-daystart	Measures times from the beginning of the day.
-maxdepth levels	Descends most in a directory structure.
-mindepth levels	Searches only in directory level greater or equal to level.
-noleaf	Doesn't assume that a directory has two hard links.
-version	Shows version information.
	The following is used to define what to find.
-amin *n*	Finds files that were accessed n minutes ago.
-anewer *file*	Finds files that were accessed more recently than file.
-cnewer *file*	Finds files whose status was changed more recently than file.
-cmin *n*	Finds files whose status was changed n minutes ago.
-empty	Finds files that are empty and are either a regular file or a directory.
-false	Specifies a false value.
-gid *n*	Finds files with group ID n.
-ilname pattern	Same as -lname, but the match is case-insensitive.
-iname pattern	Same as -name, but the match is case-insensitive.
-ipath pattern	Same as -path, but the match is case-insensitive.
-iregex pattern	Same as -regex, but the match is case-insensitive.
-lname *pattern*	Finds symbolic links whose contents match pattern.
-mmin n	Finds files that were modified n minutes ago.
-path *pattern*	Finds files with a pathname that matches the specified pattern.
-regex *pattern*	Finds a file that matches the regular expression specified.
-true	Specifies a true value.
-uid *n*	File's numeric user ID is n.
-used *n*	Finds files that were last accessed n days after their status was changed.
-xtype c	Same as -type except that symbolic links are followed.
	When a file is found the following will define action on it.
-fls *file*	Same as -ls except that output is written to file.
-fprint *file*	Same as -print except the output is written to file.
-fprint0 *file*	Same as -print0 except the output is written to file.
-fprintf *file format*	Same as -printd except the output is written to file.
-print0	Separates filenames with a NULL character instead of a new line character.
-printf *format*	Shows filename formatted with format. Uses the same syntax as C-function printf.
-depth	Descends into hierarchy so entries are acted on before the directory.
-follow	Follows symbolic links.
Solaris:	
	The following is used to define what to find.
-depth	Descends into hierarchy so entries are acted on before the directory.
-follow	Follows symbolic links.
-local	Searches for files on the local file system.
-mount	Searches only in the same file system.

continued

-xdev	Searches only in the same file system.
	When a file is found the following will define action on it.
-ncpio *device*	Writes the file on the specified device in cpio -c format.
-cpio *device*	Writes the file on the specified device in cpio format. (Solaris has one more file type (-type), which is D for Door.)

File Name:	find	**Directory:**	/usr/bin/	**Type:**	External
Tip:	Learn to use this command quickly; it is very useful.				
Common:	find / -name "*dsk*"	Finds for dsk from /.			
Common:	find /etc -name "*pass*" -ls	Finds for pass in /etc and do a long listing.			
Common:	find /etc -perm 0444	Finds for files with permission 0444 in /etc.			
Linux:	find /etc \\(-name passwd -o -name group \\) -print	Finds for passwd or group.			

finger, safe_finger

UNIX Shell: Shells (ash, bash, bsh, csh, ksh, sh, tcsh, zsh)

Function	Shows information about logged in users.
Syntax	finger [options...] *{ arguments... }*

-l	Shows a long output.
-m	Matches username arguments.
-p	Hides the .plan file when it shows a long list.
-s	Show a normal short list.
user...	Shows information about the specified user or users.
	When you use this option it only supports the -l option.
username@hostname1	Shows information about the specified user at the specified host.
@hostname	Shows information of all users on the host that you specify.
@hostnames...	Shows information about all users on the hosts that you specify.
AIX,Solaris:	
-b	Doesn't show home path for user and shell when it shows a long format list.
-f	Hides header in the short-print mode.
-h	Hides the .project file when it shows a long format list.
-i	Shows a very short `idle` list.
-q	Shows a brief list of information (the quick format).
-w	Hides the full name when it shows a short list.
BSD:	
-h	Shows only the hostname instead of the office location and office phone.
-M	Matches usernames.
-o	Shows office location and office phone info instead of the remote host.

File Name:	`finger`	**Directory:**	/usr/bin/	**Type:**	External
Warning:	This command is often used by hackers to get user information.				
Common:	finger root@sun	Shows information about root at system sun.			
Common:	finger @192.168.1.244	Shows information about all users at 192.168.1.244.			

fmt

UNIX Shell: Shells (ash, bash, bsh, csh, ksh, sh, tcsh, zsh)

Function	A text formatter. It will take the text from the file and produce output lines that are joined in the correct way.
Syntax	fmt [options...] *{ file }* BSD: fmt [options...] *{ goal } { maximum } { files... }*

AIX:	
-Width	Specifies the width of the file (default is 72 characters).
file	Specifies the input file to use. If not given, uses STDIN.
BSD:	
-c	Specifies the text should be centered.
-m	Tries to format mail header lines contained in the input sensibly.
-p	Specifies that indented paragraphs should be allowed.
-s	Collapses white space inside lines.
-d *chars*	Handles the chars as sentence-ending characters.
-l *number*	Replaces multiple spaces with tabs at the start of each output line, if possible.

continued

-t *number*	Specifies the length of a tab (default is 8).
goal	Specifies the number of lines to process.
maximum	Specifies the maximum lines to override the goal number.
Linux:	
-c	Preserves indentation of first two lines.
-p *string*	Combines only lines having string as prefix.
-s	Splits long lines, but doesn't refill them.
-t	Indentations of first line different from second.
-u	Specifies that one space should be used between each word and two after sentence.
-w *width*	Specifies the width of the text (default is 75 characters).
-*width*	Same as -w width.
--help	Shows help information.
--version	Shows version information.
file	Specifies the input file to use.
Solaris:	
-c	Maintains the indentation of the first two lines within a paragraph.
-s	Doesn't joint short lines to create longer lines.
-w *width*	Specifies the width of the columns.
-*width*	Same as -w width.
file	Specifies the input file to use.

File Name:	`fmt`	**Directory:** /usr/bin/	**Type:** External
Common:	fmt myfile	Fills and joins myfile with width 72 that is the default.	
Linux:	fmt -w 80 myfile	Fills and joins myfile with width 80.	
OpenBSD:	fmt -s myfile	Doesn't join short lines to create longer ones.	

fold

UNIX Shell: Shells (ash, bash, bsh, csh, ksh, sh, tcsh, zsh)

Function	Breaks lines in text files to the specified width.
Syntax	fold [options...] *{ files... }*

-b	Counts width in bytes (default is columns).
-s	Breaks the line after the last blank character within the specified width.
-w *width*	Specifies the maximum line length.
files...	Specifies text files to fold.
Linux:	
--help	Shows help information.
--version	Shows version information.
Solaris:	
-*width*	Specifies the maximum line length.

File Name:	`fold`	**Directory:** /usr/bin/	**Type:** External
Common:	fold -w 25 ucg1 > ucg2	Breaks all lines in ucg1 to ucg2 with a line width of 25.	
Common:	fold ucg	Breaks all lines to a line width of 80.	
Solaris:	fold -60 < ucg1 > ucg2	Breaks all lines in ucg1 to a line width of 60, sending the result to ucg2.	

for

UNIX Shell: Shells (ash, bash, bsh, ksh, sh, zsh)

Function	Is used to go through each word in the list, assign the value to variable, and run the commands.
Syntax	for *variable* [in *words...*]; do *commands...* ; done bash, zsh: for ((*expr1*;*expr2*;*expr3*)); do *commands*; done

variable	The variable that is assigned the value for each variable.
words...	A list of words to go through. If not given, $@ is assumed.
commands...	Commands to run for each loop.
bash, ash:	**bash and zsh has a second form.**
expr1	Evaluates this expression at start. Used to set start variables.
expr2	Checks this expression before each loop. Exits if false.

continued

expr3		Evaluates this expression after each loop.
commands...		Commands to run for each loop.
Common:	for c in red blue; do echo $c; done	Shows: red blue on two rows.
Common:	for f in *; do echo $f; done	Shows every file in the current directory.
Common:	for ((i=1;$i<3;i=$i+1)); do echo $i; done	Shows 1 and 2 on two lines. (bash, zsh)

foreach

UNIX Shell: Shells (csh, tcsh)

Function	Is used to go through each word in the list, assign the value to variable, and run the commands.	
Syntax	foreach *variable* (*words...*) *commands...* end	
variable	The variable that is assigned the value for each variable.	
words...	A list of words to go through.	
commands...	Is commands to run for each loop.	
Note:	Both foreach and end must appear alone on separate lines.	
Common:	foreach color (red blue green) echo $color end	Performs a for loop that shows red blue green on 3 lines. Echoes the color to STDOUT. Marks the end of the loop.

fsck

UNIX Shell: Shells (ash, bash, bsh, csh, ksh, sh, tcsh, zsh)

Function	Checks file systems for inconsistencies and repairs them.
Syntax	fsck [options...] *{ filesystem }*
filesystem	Specifies the file system to check.
AIX:	
-n	Answers no to all questions.
-y	Answers yes to all questions.
-p	Fixes minor problems automatically and without showing them.
-d *block*	Searches for references to a specified disk block.
-f	Checks quickly.
-i *inode*	Searches for references to a specified i-node.
-o *options*	Specifies a comma-separated list of file system specific options.
-t *file*	Specifies a 'file to be used as a scratch file, can't be on the same file system.
-V *Vfsname*	Specifies a description for the virtual file system to be checked.
BSD:	
-d	Specifies debugging mode.
-v	Shows commands before executing them.
-p	Enters preen mode.
-f	Checks file system, even if it is marked clean.
-y	Answers yes to all questions.
-n	Answers no to all questions.
-l *maxparallel*	Specifies maximum number of parallel checks to maxparallel.
-t *fstype*	Specifies a comma-separated list of file system types to check.
-T *fstype:fsoptions*	Specifies a comma-separated list of file system and file system options.
Linux:	
-s	Checks file system in serial mode.
-A	Checks all file systems in /etc/fstab.
-C	Shows a progress bar for the file system check.
-V	Verbose mode. Shows more information.
-R	Doesn't check the root file system. Used with –A.
-T	Hides the title on startup.
-N	Doesn't run any test; just shows what will be done.
-P	Checks the root file system in parallel with the other file systems. Used with –A.
-t *fstype*	Specifies which file system type to check.
-a	Automatically repairs the file system without any questions.

continued

-r	Interactively repairs the file system.
--	Marks the beginning of file system specific options.
Solaris:	
-F *FSType*	Specifies the file system type you want to run fsck on.
-m	Checks but doesn't repair.
-V	Shows the expanded command line but doesn't execute the command.
-n	Responds no to all questions from fsck.
-N	Same as -n.
-y	Responds yes to all questions from fsck.
-Y	Same as -y.
-o *options*	Specifies a combination of commands.
	The following options can be combined with the -o option.
b=*block*	Specifies the super block for the system.
c	Converts old static table format to new dynamic table format and vice versa.
f	Forces a check on the file system.
p	Checks and fixes the file system noninteractively.
w	Checks only writeable file systems.

File Name:	`fsck`	**Directory:**	**AIX, Solaris:** /usr/sbin/, **BSD, Linux:** /sbin/ **Type:** External
AIX:	fsck /dev/hd2		Checks and repairs file system on /dev/hd2.
Linux:	fsck -V /dev/hda3		Runs fsck /dev/hda3 in verbose mode.
OpenBSD:	fsck -y /dev/wd0a		Checks file system on partition /dev/wd0a.
Solaris:	fsck /dev/rdsk/c0t3d0s0		Checks file system on partition /dev/rdsk/c0t3d0s0.

ftp

UNIX Shell: Shells (ash, bash, bsh, csh, ksh, sh, tcsh, zsh)

Function	Transfers files from a remote network. It uses the File Transfer Protocol.
Syntax	ftp [options...] { *hostname* } BSD: ftp [options...] { *url* }

-d	Enables debug.
-g	Disables filename `globbing.`
-i	Disables the interactive prompt when transferring multiple files.
-n	Doesn't make an auto-login when connecting.
-v	Shows all responses from the remote server or host.
hostname	Specifies the host you want to connect to.
AIX:	
-f	Forwards credentials if Kerberos 5 is the current authentication method.
-k *realm*	Specifies the realm for the remote system if Kerberos 5 is used.
BSD:	
-A	Uses active FTP mode.
-a	Logs in as anonymous instead of using normal login sequence.
-e	Disables command line editing.
-m	Causes the progress meter to always be shown.
-o *file*	Uses when fetching a single file to save the contains in file.
-p	Uses passive FTP mode (default).
-P *port*	Specifies the port to use.
-r *sec*	Specifies the time between multiple attempts to connect.
-t	Enables packet tracing.
-V	Disables verbose mode.
url	Specifies a file on a remote host to fetch. URL has one of the following forms:
ftp://[user:password@]host[:port]/file[/]	Specifies a file to get using the FTP protocol.
http://host[:port]/file	Specifies a file to get using the http protocol.
host:[/path/]file[/]	Specifies a file to get using the FTP protocol.
Linux:	
-p	Uses passive FTP mode (default).
-e	Disables command line editing.

continued

Solaris:	
-t	Enables packet tracing.
	The following commands are used inside ftp:
! *{ command [args }]*	Starts an interactive shell and runs the specified commands, if any.
$ *macro { args }*	Runs the specified macro previously defined by macdef.
account *password*	Specifies the password to login with.
append *local-file { remote-file }*	Appends the local file to a file on the remote host.
ascii	Sets the file transfer mode to ASCII (the default).
bell	When a file completes this will sound a bell.
binary	Sets the file transfer mode to BINARY.
bye	Terminates the FTP session and quits.
case	Makes all files from remote host to be copied to local host in lowercase.
cd *remote-directory*	Changes the remote directory.
cdup	Changes the working directory on the remote server to the parent directory.
close	Terminates the FTP session and returns to terminal.
cr	Enables carriage return stripping.
delete *remote-file*	Deletes the specified file on remote host.
dir *{ remote-directory } { local-file }*	Shows the content of the remote directory. Optionally put the information in localfile.
disconnect	Terminates the FTP session and returns to terminal.
form *format*	Specifies format on file transfer form.
get *remote-file { local-file }*	Downloads a file from remote host and gives it a new name if specified.
glob	Enables filename expansion for mdelete, mget, and mput.
help *{ command }*	Shows help information of the specified FTP command.
lcd *{ directory }*	Changes directory on local host. If directory not given, changes to $HOME.
ls *{remote-directory } { local-file }*	Shows contents of directory on remote host. The format is taken from remote host.
macdef *macro-name*	Defines a macro. The following lines is the definition. Ends with a blank line.
mdelete *remote-files...*	Deletes the specified files on remote host.
mdir *remote-files... local-file*	Shows list of multiple remote files, and put the results in the local-file.
mget *remote-files...*	Proceeds to next file and downloads it. * wildcards can be used.
mkdir *directory*	Creates a directory on remote host.
mls *remote-files local-file*	Shows a list of files on the remote server and saves the information in the specified local-file.
mode *{ mode }*	Specifies the transfer mode. The default is stream mode.
mput *{ local-files... }*	Specifies multiple files with * wildcards, and continues to upload next file.
nmap *{ inpattern outpattern }*	Enables or disables the filename mapping.
ntrans *{ inchars [outchars] }*	Enables or disables the filename translate process.
open *host{ port }*	Specifies host and port to connect to.
prompt	Enables or disables interactive prompting.
proxy *ftp-command*	Specifies a FTP-command to execute on secondary control connection.
put *local-file { remote-file }*	Uploads a file onto the remote host. Gives it a new name if specified.
pwd	Shows current directory of remote host.
quit	Terminates the FTP session and quits.
quote *arg1 arg2*	Specifies arguments to send to remote ftp server.
recv *remote-file { local-file }*	Downloads a file from remote host, and gives it a new name if specified.
remotehelp *{ command-name }*	Shows help from remote host.
rename *{ from* [*to }*]	Renames the file from on the remote FTP server.
reset	Clears the reply queue.
rmdir *{ directory-name }*	Deletes a directory on remote host.
runique	Enables or disables to save files on local system with unique filenames.
send *local-file { remote-file }*	Uploads a file onto the remote host.
sendport	Toggles PORT command.
status	Shows status for FTP.
struct *{ struct-name*	Sets file transfer structure. Default is `stream`.
sunique	Enables or disables to save files on remote host under unique files.
tenex	Sets file transfer type to TENEX.
trace	Toggles to trace packets.
type [*type-name }*	Sets file transfer type. Default is ASCII.
user *username { password } { account }*	Logs into the remote FTP server.
verbose	Verbose mode. Shows more information.

continued

? *{ command }*	Shows help information.
AIX:	
block	Mode block.
carriage-control	Sets the file transfer form to carriage-control.
copylocal	Toggles local copy. Default is to check if a file is copied to itself.
debug [1 | 0]	Toggles the debug mode. 1 Show debug information. 0 no debug.
ebcdic	Sets the file transfer mode to ebcdic.
exp_cmd	Toggles between excremental and conventional protocol commands.
file	Sets the data transfer structure type to file.
hash	Shows a # hash sign for every data block transferred.
image	Sets the file transfer mode to image.
local *bits*	Sets the number of image bits used in file transfer mode.
modtime *file*	Shows the modification time for the remote file.
nlist *{ directory } { file }*	Writes the contents of the remote directory to file.
non-print	Sets the file transfer form to non-print.
private	Sets the protection level to private.
protect	Shows the current protection level.
record	Sets the data transfer structure type to record.
reinitialize	Reinitializes the FTP session.
restart *command*	Restarts a transfer from the last checkpoint. Command can be get, put, or append.
safe	Sets the protection level to safe.
site *args...*	Sends arguments to the remote host as SITE commands.
size *remotefile*	Shows the size of the remote file in bytes.
stream	Sets the file transfer mode to stream.
system	Shows the operating system on the remote host.
telnet	Sets the file transfer form to telnet.
BSD:	
chmod *{ mode } { remote-file }*	Changes permission of remote-file.
debug *{ debug-value }*	Shows debug information. If given sets the debug level.
edit	Toggles the command line editing.
exit	Terminates the FTP session and quits.
ftp *host { port }*	Specifies host and port to connect to.
gate *{ host [port }]*	Toggles gate-FTP mode. If host is given, enables gate-FTP mode with host.
hash *{ size }*	Shows a # for every block transferred. Block size can be specified (default is 1024).
idle *{ sec }*	Sets the interactive timer to sec. If sec not given, shows current value.
less *file*	Gets the file from the remote host and show it.
lpwd	Shows the local working directory.
modtime *file*	Shows the modification time for the remote file.
more *file*	Gets the file from the remote host and shows it.
msend	Specifies multiple files with * wildcards, and continues to upload next file.
nlist *{ directory [file }]*	Writes the contents of the remote directory to file.
page *file*	Gets the file from the remote host and shows it.
newer *file*	Gets the file if it is newer than the existing file.
passive	Toggles FTP passive mode.
preserve	Toggles the preservation of the modification time on retrieved files.
progress	Toggles if a progress bar will be shown.
reget *remote-file { local-file }*	Resumes transferring a file after transfer was interrupted.
rstatus *{ file }*	Shows the status of remote host or, if given, remote file.
restart *marker*	Restarts a following put or get on the specified marker.
site *args...*	Sends arguments to the remote host as SITE commands.
size *remotefile*	Shows the size of the remote file in bytes.
system	Shows the operating system on the remote host.
umask *{ umask }*	Sets the umask on remote host. If not given, shows the current one.
Linux	
chmod *{ mode } { remote-file }*	Changes permission of remote-file.
debug *{ debug-value }*	Shows debug information. If given sets the debug level.
hash	Shows a # hash sign every data block transferred.

continued

idle *{ sec }*	Sets the interactive timer to sec. If sec not given show current value.
modtime *file*	Shows the modification time for the remote file.
newer *file*	Gets the file if it is newer than the existing file.
nlist *{ directory } { file }*	Writes the contents of the remote directory to file.
reget *remote-file { local-file }*	Resumes transferring a file after transfer was interrupted.
remotestatus *{ file }*	Shows the status of remote host or, if given, remote file.
restart *marker*	Restarts a following put or get on the specified marker.
site *args...*	Sends arguments to the remote host as SITE commands.
size *remotefile*	Shows the size of the remote file in bytes.
system	Shows the operating system on the remote host.
umask *{ umask }*	Sets the umask on remote host. If not given, shows the current one.
Solaris:	
debug	Shows debug information.
hash	Shows a # hash sign for every data block transferred.

File Name:	ftp	**Directory:**	/usr/bin/	**Type:**	External
Common:	ftp ftp.ucg.com	Connects to ftp.ucg.com.			

function

UNIX Shell: Shells (ash, bash, bsh, ksh, sh, zsh)

Function	Defines function in a shell.
Syntax	bash,zsh: function *name* ( ) { *commands...* ; } ksh,zsh: function *name* { *commands...* ; } ash,sh,bash,ksh,zsh: *name* ( ) { *commands...* ;} ash,zsh: *name* ( ) *command*

name	Specifies the name of the function.
commands...	Specifies a list of commands to be the boby of the function.
command	Specifies the command for the function.

Common:	function print_msg { echo $1 ; }	Defines the function print_msg.
Common:	print_msg hello	Shows hello on the screen.

getconf

UNIX Shell: Shells (ash, bash, bsh, csh, ksh, sh, tcsh, zsh)

Function	Retrieves current configuration values and shows them to STDOUT.
Syntax	AIX, Solaris: getconf [-v *specification*] *pathvar pathname* AIX, Solaris: getconf [-v *specification*] *systemvar* Solaris: getconf -a BSD, Linux: getconf *pathvar { pathname }* BSD: getconf *systemvar*

systemvar	Specifies the system configuration variable to retrieve information from.
pathvar	Specifies the path configuration variable to retrieve information from.
pathname	Specifies the pathname for the `pathvar` variable.
AIX,Solaris:	
-v *specification*	Shows the value of the specification specified.
Solaris:	
-a	Shows the names of all variables currently configured to STDOUT. Must be used alone.
-v *specification*	Shows the value of the specification specified.

File Name:	`getconf`	**Directory:**	/usr/bin/	**Type:**	External
Common:	getconf NAME_MAX /usr	Shows the value for the `NAME_MAX` variable for directory /usr.			
AIX:	getconf USHRT_MAX	Shows the value of the variable USHRT_MAX to STDOUT.			
Solaris:	getconf -a	Write all configuration values.			

getopt

getopt	UNIX Shell:	Shells (ash, bash, bsh, csh, ksh, sh, tcsh, zsh)

Function	Cleans up and checks options given to a shell script. It splits option given together and places each option in its own variable. Any additional arguments are placed after --.
Syntax	set -- `getopt *optstring* $*` getopt *optstring parameter* Linux: [options...] -- *optstring parameter* Linux: getopt [options...] -o *optstring* [options...] [--] *parameter*

optstring	Specifies a string of option letters that is recognized by the script. (If a letter is followed by a colon (:) it will take an argument.)
parameter	Specifies the options to check. (This is often $*, the argument list to the script.)
set --	Sets the argument list $* .
Linux:	
-a	Allows long options to start with a single -.
-h	Shows help information.
-l *longoptions*	Specifies a long option that is recognized.
-n *progname*	Specifies a program to use to report errors.
-o *optstring*	Specifies a list of short options.
-q	Disables error reporting.
-Q	Doesn't generate any output. Errors are reported unless -q is also given.
-s *shell*	Uses quoting conversions of the specified shell (sh, bash, csh or tcsh).
-u	Doesn't quote the output.
-T	Tests if this is the enhanced version.
-V	Shows version information.

File Name:	`getopt`	**Directory:**	/usr/bin/	**Type:**	External

Note:	This is very useful to make easy option check in a shell script.	
Common:	set -- `getopt ab:c $*`	Specifies that a and c don't take an argument but c will.
Common:	If argument is: -ac -b hello	It will be converted to: -a -c -b hello --.
Common:	If argument is: -bhello ucg	It will be converted to: -b hello – ucg.
Linux:	set -- `getopt -l help ab:c $*`	Also recognizes the long option –help.

getopts

getopts	UNIX Shell:	Shells (ash, bash, bsh, ksh, sh, zsh)

Function	Retrieves or sets environment options and processes them from the command line. The values specified by name and the index of the next arguments are placed into the shell variable OPTIND.
Syntax	getopts *string name { arguments... }*

string	Specifies a valid string in the utility that will execute getopts.
name	Specifies the shell variable that getopts will set.
arguments...	The argument that is passed to the shell variable OPTARG.
Note:	The shell variables `OPTARG` and `OPTIND` are used by getopts.

glob

glob	UNIX Shell:	Shells (csh, tcsh)

Function	Performs filename expansion on the words. The result is separated by a NULL-character.
Syntax	glob *words...*

words...	A list of words to do filename expansion on.	
Common:	glob /u*	Shows all directories beginning with /u.
Solaris:	glob /etc/rc?.d	shows: /etc/rc1.d/rc2.d/rc3.d ...

goto

UNIX Shell:	Shells (csh, tcsh)
Function	Jumps to label in a shell script.
Syntax	goto *label*

label	The label to go to. (A label has the form label: and it's placed at beginning of a row.)	
Common:	goto label1	Goes to label1.
Common:	label1:	This is the label label1.

gprof

UNIX Shell:	Shells (ash, bash, bsh, csh, ksh, sh, tcsh, zsh)
Function	Shows an execution (call-graph) profile of a program. It can also create files containing portions of this information.
Syntax	gprof [options...] *{ image-file } { profile-files... }* Solaris: gprof [options...] *{ image-file } { profile-files... }* [-n *count*]

-b	Suppresses all descriptions of every field in the profile.
-s	Creates gmon.sum which contains all profile information in the specified files.
-z	Shows all routines that have not been used. Zero Usage.
-e *funcname*	Hides graph profile entries for routine function names and all descendants.
-E *funcname*	Same as -e but also excludes time spent in the function name and its descendants.
-f *funcname*	Shows the graph profile entry for the specified routine function and its descendants.
-F *funcname*	Same as -f but also includes the times the printed routines were in total time.
image-file	Specifies a specific executable image file. The default is a.out.
profile-file	Specifies a specific call-graph profile file. The default is gmon.out.
AIX:	
-L *directory*	Specifies an alternate directory for shared objects.
BSD:	
-a	Hides static functions such as time samples and calls to/from other functions.
-c	Finds the static call-graph of the program by inspecting the object file's text space.
-C *NR*	Finds minimum set of arcs for cycles with NR or more members.
-k *fromname toname*	Erases any arcs from routine fromname to routine toname.
Linux:	
-a	Hides static functions such as time samples and calls to/from other functions.
-c	Finds the static call-graph of the program by inspecting the object file's text space.
-k *fromname toname*	Erases any arcs from routine fromname to routine toname
-v	Shows version information.
Solaris:	
-a	Hides static functions such as time samples and calls to/from other functions.
-c	Finds the static call-graph of the program by inspecting the object file's text space.
-C	Cleans up C++ symbol names before showing them.
-D	Creates a gmon.sum file that contains the differences between the specified profiles.
-l	Suppresses graph profile entry reporting of any local symbols.
-n *count*	Limits the size of the profile lists to the specified count of offending functions.

File Name:	gprof	**Directory:**	/usr/bin/, **Solaris:** /usr/ccs/bin/	**Type:**	External

grep

UNIX Shell:	Shells (ash, bash, bsh, csh, ksh, sh, tcsh, zsh)
Function	Shows lines from the file that match the given pattern.
Syntax	grep [options...] *{ pattern } { files... }*

-c	Shows only the count of the lines that matches the specified pattern.
-h	Hides the filenames when searching multiple files.
-i	Ignores upper/lower case distinctions.
-l	Shows only the filenames that contain matching strings.
-n	Shows the line number of each line where a match occurred.
-v	Shows only lines that don't match the pattern.
-w	Searches for a whole word.
pattern	Specifies a single string as the pattern to search for.

continued

files...	Specifies the file/files to operate on. If none given, use STDIN.
AIX:	
-b	Shows the block number the pattern was found in.
-s	Shows only error messages.
-x	Matches only if the input line and the pattern match exactly
-p{ *separator* }	Shows the whole paragraph for a match. Specifies separator (default is blank line).
-q	Shows nothing. Exits with exit status 0 if a match is found.
-y	Ignores the case of letters when making comparisons.
-e *pattern_list*	Searches for pattern_list of basic regular expression.
-f *file*	Uses the list of basic regular expression from this file.
-E	Runs grep as egrep.
-F	Runs grep as fgrep.
BSD:	
-s	Hides error about non-existing files.
-x	Matches only if the input line and the pattern match exactly
-*NR*	Shows NR of lines before and after the matched line.
-A *NR*	Shows NR of lines after the matched line.
-B *NR*	Shows NR of lines before the matched line.
-C	Shows 2 lines before and after the matched line.
-V	Shows version information.
-b	Shows the byte offset for the match.
-L	Shows only the filenames that don't contain matching strings.
-o	Shows the filename on each match.
-q	Shows nothing. Exits with exit status 0 if a match is found.
-e *pattern_list*	Searches for pattern_list of basic regular expression.
-f *file*	Uses the list of basic regular expression from this file.
-E	Runs grep as egrep.
-F	Runs grep as fgrep.
Linux:	
-s	Hides error about non-existing files.
-*NR*	Shows NR of lines before and after the matched line.
-A *NR*	Shows NR of lines after the matched line.
-B *NR*	Shows NR of lines before the matched line.
-C { *NR* }	Shows NR of lines before and after the matched line. (Default is 2.)
-a	Processes a binary file like a text file.
-b	Shows the byte offset for the match.
--binary-files=*type*	Specifies action with binary files.
binary	Shows only a line saying that a match is found (Is default.)
without-match	Assumes that there aren't matches in binary files.
text	Processes a binary file like a text file.
-d *action*	Specifies action with a directory.
read	Reads the directory like an ordinary file.
skip	Skips the directory.
recurse	Reads all files under directory and its subdirectories recursively.
-H	Shows the filenames for each match.
--help	Shows help information.
-I	Assumes that there aren't matches in binary files.
-L	Shows only the filenames that don't contain matching strings.
--mmap	Uses the mmap systemcal to read files instead of read.
-q	Suppresses normal output. Stops after the first match.
-r	Reads all files under directory and its subdirectories recursively.
-s	Hides error about non-existing files.
-U	Handles the file as binary.
--version	Shows version information.
-w	Searches for a whole word.
-x	Matches only if the input line and the pattern match exactly
-Z	Uses a ASCII NULL character after filename instead of a new line character.

continued

-e *pattern_list*	Searches for pattern_list of basic regular expression.
-f *file*	Uses the list of basic regular expression from this file.
-E	Runs grep as egrep.
-F	Runs grep as fgrep.
Solaris:	
-s	Shows only error messages.
-b	Shows the block number that the pattern was found in.
	Another copy of grep exists in /usr/xpg4/bin and it has one more option
-x	Matches only if the input line and the pattern match exactly.
-e *pattern_list*	Searches for pattern_list of basic regular expression.
-f *file*	Uses the list of basic regular expression from this file.
-q	Suppresses normal output. Stops after the first match.
-E	Runs grep as egrep.
-F	Runs grep as fgrep.

File Name:	`grep`	**Directory:**	/usr/bin/, **Linux:** /bin/ — **Type:** External
Common:	grep -n root /etc/passwd		Grep for root in passwd, show line.
Common:	ps -ef | grep telnet		Grep for telnet sessions in the processlist.
Common:	grep ipv6 /etc/protocols		Grep for string IPv6 in the protocols file in /etc.

groups

UNIX Shell: Shells (ash, bash, bsh, csh, ksh, sh, tcsh, zsh)

Function	Shows the groups that a user is a member of.
Syntax	AIX, BSD: groups *{ user }* Linux, Solaris: groups [options...] *{ users... }*

AIX:	
user	Shows group membership for the specified user.
BSD:	
user	Shows group membership for the specified user.
Linux:	
--help	Shows help information.
--version	Shows version information.
users...	Shows group membership for specified users.
Solaris:	
users...	Shows group membership for specified users.

File Name:	`groups`	**Directory:**	/usr/bin/ — **Type:** External
Common:	groups		Shows all the groups the current user is a member of.
Common:	groups root		Shows all the groups root is a member of.
Linux:	groups root ucg		Shows all the groups root and ucg are members of.

halt

UNIX Shell: Shells (ash, bash, bsh, csh, ksh, sh, tcsh, zsh)

Function	Writes any remaining data in memory to the disks and then stops the computer.
Syntax	halt [options...]

-n	Doesn't sync the disc.
AIX:	
-l	Doesn't send a message to the system log daemon about who halted the computer.
-p	Halts the system without a power down.
-y	Halts the system, even if a dial-up terminal is used.
-q	Halts quick.
BSD:	
-d	Specifies the system should create a dump before rebooting.
-p	Causes the system to power down.
-q	Halts quick.
Linux:	
-w	Writes reboot information to `/var/log/wtmp`, without rebooting or halting.
-d	Specifies the wtmp entire should not be written.
-f	Forces reboot or halt.

continued

-i	Shuts down all network interfaces just before halt or reboot.
-p	Causes the system to power down.
Solaris:	
-l	Doesn't send a message to the system log daemon about who halted the computer.
-q	Halts quick.
-y	Halts the system, even if a dialup terminal is used.

File Name:	`halt`	**Directory:**	**AIX, Solaris:** /usr/sbin/, **BSD, Linux:** /sbin/	**Type:**	External
Common:	halt	Stops all processes and shuts down the system.			
Common:	halt -n	Specifies the disc should not be synced.			
AIX:	halt -q	Does a quick halt.			
Linux:	halt -p	Specifies the system should power down.			

hash

UNIX Shell: Shells (ash, bash, bsh, ksh, sh, zsh)

Function	Shows or changes information in the internal hash table that stores information about executed commands.
Syntax	sh, bash: hash [options...] *{ name }* ksh: hash *{ name }*

sh:	
name	Adds the utility name to the list or clears the hit count if it exists.
-r	Removes all elements from the list.
bash:	
-r	Removes all element from the list.
-p *file*	Specifies a full path to add to the hash table. No search is done.
name	Adds the utility name to the list.
ksh:	
name	Adds the utility name to the list.
zsh:	
-d	Uses the named directory hash table.
-f	Rebuilds the hash table.
-m	Shows all entries that match the specified pattern should be quoted.
-r	Removes all elements from the list.
name	Adds the utility name to the list.
=path	Specifies a full path to add to the hash table. No search is done.

Note:	Useful if you want to know which commands have been executed.	
Common:	hash	Displays current hash list.
Common:	hash -r	Deletes current hash list.
Common:	hash ls	Adds ls to list.

hashstat

UNIX Shell: Shells (csh, tcsh)

Function	Shows information about how effective the internal hash table is.
Syntax	hashstat

head

UNIX Shell: Shells (ash, bash, bsh, csh, ksh, sh, tcsh, zsh)

Function	Shows lines from the beginning of each file on the screen.
Syntax	head [option...] *{ files... }*

-number	Specifies how many numbers of lines to show from the top of the specified file.
files...	Specify input files.
AIX:	
-c *number*	Specifies the numbers of bytes to display.
Linux:	
-c *number*	Specifies the numbers of bytes to display.
-q	Hides headers.
-v	Verbose mode. Shows more information.

continued

--help --version		Shows help information. Shows version information.			
File Name:	`head`	**Directory:**	/usr/bin/	**Type:**	External
Common:	head -3 /etc/passwd	Shows the first 3 lines of `/etc/passwd`.			
Common:	head /etc/inetd.conf	Shows the first 10 lines of `/etc/inetd.conf`.			
Linux:	head -c 20 /etc/services	Shows the first 20 characters from the specified file.			

history

UNIX Shell: Shells (bash, csh, tcsh, zsh)

Function	Shows a list of previously used commands, and can optionally execute them again.
Syntax	history [option] *{ NR }*

bash:	
-c	Clears the history list
-d *offset*	Removes the entry at offset.
-a *{ file }*	Appends the new lines to the history file or the file specified.
-n *{ file }*	Reads lines from the history file and adds them to the current history list.
-r *{ file }*	Reads lines from the history file and adds them to the current history list.
-w *{ file }*	Writes the current history list to the history file. Overwrites the file.
-p *args...*	Performs history substitution and shows the result.
-s *args...*	Replaces the last argument in the history list with args.
NR	The number of recently used commands to show.
csh:	
-h	Shows the command history list without using leading numbers.
-r	Shows the commands in reverse order.
NR	The number of recently used commands to show.
tcsh:	
-h	Shows the command history list without using leading numbers.
-r	Shows the commands in reverse order.
-T	Shows timestamps in comment form.
-S *{ file }*	Saves the history list to file.
-L *{ file }*	Reads lines from the history file and adds them to the current history list.
-M *{ file }*	Merges lines from the history file into the current history list sorted by time.
-c	Clears the history list.
zsh:	
-n	Shows the command history list without using leading numbers.
-r	Shows the commands in reverse order.
-d	Shows the timestamp for each command.
-D	Shows elapsed times.
-f	Shows full time-date stamps.
-E	Shoes date as dd.mm.yyyy instead of mm/dd/yyyy.
-i	Shows date as yyyy-mm-dd.
-m *arg*	Performs history substitution and shows the result.
old=new	Substitutes old with new on the commands.
first	Specifies the first commands to show or work on.
last	Specifies the last commands to show or work on.
	To repeat a command you have used previously, use the following commands:
!!	Executes the last command you typed in.
!*num*	Executes command number that you specify.
!-*num*	Executes the n:th command from the end of the history list.
!*str*	Executes the most recent command that starts with str.
!?*str*?	Executes the most resent command that contained str.
bash:	
^*str1*^*str2*^	Executes the previous command but will replace str1 with str2.
!!:s/*str1*/*str2*/	Finds the command with str1 and replaces with str2 and re-executes it
csh:	
^*str1*^*str2*^	Executes the previous command but will replace str1 with str2.
!:s/*str1*/*str2*/	Finds the command with str1 and replaces with str2 and re-executes it.
!*num*:s/*str1*/*str2*/	Finds the command with num and replaces with str1 and re-executes it.

continued

tcsh: *^str1^str2^*	Executes the previous command but will replace str1 with str2. (For options listed above you can add an additional argument !! /etc.)

Note:	The length of the history list is specified by variable `history` in csh and tcsh. and with `HISTSIZE` in bash and zsh.	
Common:	history 5	Shows the last five commands.
Common:	history -r 5	As above but in reverse order.
Common:	!5 /etc	Executes command number 5 and adds /etc to it.

hostname

UNIX Shell: Shells (ash, bash, bsh, csh, ksh, sh, tcsh, zsh)

Function	Sets or shows the hostname for the computer.
Syntax	hostname [options...] { *hostname* }

hostname	Specifies the hostname you want to give the computer. Otherwise shows current.
AIX,BSD:	
-s	Removes any domain information from the shown name.
Linux:	
-v	Verbose mode. Shows more information.
-a	Shows the alias name of the host.
-d	Shows the name of the DNS domain.
-f	Shows the Fully Qualified Domain Name (FQDN).
-i	Shows the IP address(es) of the host.
-s	Shows the short hostname.
-y	Shows the NIS domain name.
-n	Shows the DECnet node name.
-F *file*	Reads the hostname from the specified file.
-h	Shows help information.
-V	Shows version information.

File Name:	hostname	**Directory:**	**AIX, Solaris:** /usr/bin/, **BSD, Linux:** /bin/	**Type:**	External

Common:	hostname	Shows the hostname.
Common:	hostname ucgbook	Sets hostname to ucgbook.
AIX:	hostname -s	Removes any domain information from the shown name.
Linux:	hostname -i	Shows the IP address(es) of the host.

id

UNIX Shell: Shells (ash, bash, bsh, csh, ksh, sh, tcsh, zsh)

Function	Shows the userID and groupID of the user that you specify.
Syntax	id [options...] { *user* }

user	Specifies the user you want information about.
AIX:	
-G	Shows `ALL` the different groupID's.
-g	Shows only the effective groupID.
-n	Shows the names instead of the numericID's.
-r	Shows the real userID instead of the effective userID.
-u	Shows the effective userID.
Linux,Solaris:	
-a	Shows the user's name, ID, and groups.
--help	**Linux only:** Shows help information.
--version	**Linux only:** Shows version information.

File Name:	id	**Directory:**	/usr/bin/	**Type:**	External

Common:	id	Shows userID and groupID for the current user.
Common:	id uk	Shows userID and groupID for the user uk.
Common:	id -g	Shows only the effective groupID.
Solaris:	id -a	Shows userID, groupID, and groups for the current user.

if

UNIX Shell: Shells (ash, bash, bsh, csh, ksh, sh, tcsh, zsh)

Function	Makes a decision inside a shell script. If the first expr is true, runs the first commands. If not, checks the next expr and so on. If no expr was true, runs commands after `then`.
Syntax	sh, ksh: if *expr* then *commands...* [elif *expr* then *commands...*]... [else *commands...*] fi csh,tcsh: if (*expr*) *commands...* csh,tcsh: if (*expr*) then *commands...* [else if (*expr*) then *commands...*]... [else *commands...*] endif

ksh,sh:	
expr	A command (if its exit status is 0, the expression is true) or a test inside [ ]. (The syntax for a test inside [ ] is the same as for the test command.)
commands...	Specifies commands to run.
csh,tcsh:	
expr	A standard c-shell expression.
commands...	Specifies commands to run. (if, else if, and else must be first on a line.)

Note:	zsh in Solaris and ash in Linux have the same syntax as sh.	
Common:	if [-f /etc/hosts]; then echo hello; fi	Shows hello if /etc/hosts exist. Hopefully it does (sh, ksh).
Common:	if test $a = y ; then echo YES; fi	Shows YES if $a is equal to y (sh, ksh).
Common:	if ($a == u) echo YES	Shows YES if $a is equal to y (csh,tcsh).

ifconfig

UNIX Shell: Shells (ash, bash, bsh, csh, ksh, sh, tcsh, zsh)

Function	Configures network interface parameters or shows the status for network interface.
Syntax	ifconfig *{ interface } { addressfamily } { address }* [options...] Solaris: ifconfig *interface* dhcp [options...]

up	Activates the specified interface.
down	Deactivates the specified interface.
netmask *mask*	Sets the subnet mask.
broadcast *address*	Sets the broadcast address.
arp	Uses the ARP protocol to map between IP-address and MAC-address.
-arp	Doesn't use the ARP protocol.
metric *n*	Adds hops to a route to make it less preferred.
interface	Specifies the interface to use.
addressfamily	Specifies the address family you want to use. Valid address families for AIX: inet, inet6, and ns. Valid address families for BSD: inet, atalk, iso, ipx or ns. Valid address families for Linux: inet, inet6, ax25, ddp, ipx, and netrom. Valid address families for Solaris: ether and inet.
address	Specifies the address.
destaddress	Specifies the destination address for a point-to-point link.
AIX:	
-a	Shows information about all interfaces on the system.
-d	Shows information about interfaces that are down.
-l	Shows information about all available interfaces on the system.
-u	Shows information about interfaces that are up.

continued

alias	Creates an additional network address for the interface.
allcast	Broadcasts to all rings on a token ring network.
-allcats	Doesn't broadcast to all rings on a token ring network.
-debug	Disables driver-dependent debug code.
delete	Removes a specified address.
detach	Removes a specified interface from the interface list.
group *id*	Adds a group ID to the interface group ID list.
-group *id*	Removes a group ID from the list.
hwloop	Enables a hardware loopback.
-hwloop	Disables a hardware loopback.
ipdst	Specifies a host to receive IP packets encapsulating ns packets to a remote network.
ipv6dst	Specifies a IPv6 host to receive encapsulated IP packaged through a tunnel.
link [0-3]	Uses special processing for the link level of the interface.
-link [0-3]	Doesn't use any special processing for the link level.
mtu *n*	Specifies the maximum IP-packet size.
tcp_nocksum	Disables the verification of checksum for TCP data on local network.
-tcp_nocksum	Enables the verification of checksum for TCP data on local network.
thread	Uses dedicated kernel threads for an interface. Only on SMP hosts.
-thread	Doesn't use separate kernel threads for interface.
rfc1323 [1 | 0]	Enables or disables the RFC1323 TCP extension for high performance.
-rfc1323	Removes any use of ISNO for RFC1323 for this network.
tcp_mssdflt *n*	Sets the default maximum segment size used when communicating with remote networks.
-tcp_mssdflt	Removes the use of ISNO for tcp_mssdflt.
tcp_recvspace	Specifies the default size for the receive socket buffer.
-tcp_recvspace	Removes the use of ISNO for tcp_recvspace.
tcp_sendspace	Specifies the default size for the send socket buffer.
-tcp_sendspace	Removes the use of ISNO for tcp_sendspace .
tcp_nodelay [1 | 0]	Specifies that Nagle algorithm will be used when sending dat.
-tcp_nodelay	Removes the use of ISNO for tcp_nodelay.
	These options are only used with IPv6.
-dad	Doesn't repeat any IPv6 address detection.
eui64	Sets the last 64 bits of the IP-address the same as the interface identifier.
first	Uses an IPv6 address at the first place on an interface.
firstalias	Same as alias but sets the address in front in the interface address list.
site6	Sets the site number for a IPv6 network. (Default is 0.)
	These options are used for ATM network.
device *name*	Specifies a device name for an ATM interface.
pvc	Specifies that PVC (Permanent Virtual Circuit) is used.
svc_c *serveraddr*	Specifies an ATM address for the arp-server.
svc-s	Specifies that this interface is the arp-server for this network.
protocolfamily	Specifies the protocol family to use. Can be tcp, udp, tcp6, udp6, icmp, or icmp6.
	Use this with an IP-address to specify a point-to-point link.
destaddress	Specifies the destination IP-address for a point-to-point link.
BSD:	
	Use one of the following options to show information about interfaces.
-a	Shows information about all interface on the system.
-am	Shows information about all interface on the system with media information.
-A	Shows full interface alias information.
-Am	Shows full interface alias information with media information. (If an address family is specified only show that information.)
alias	Creates an additional network address for the interface.
Debug	Enables driver dependent debug code.
-debug	Disables driver dependent debug code.
Delete	Removes a specified address.
Ipdst	Specifies a host to receive IP packets encapsulating ns packets to a remote network.
Media *type*	Specifies the media to use. Some possible values are AUI, UTP. (See the description for each interface type for a complete list.)
mediaopt *opts*	Specifies media-specific options.
-mediaopt *opts*	Disables specified media-specific options.

continued

instance *minst*	Specifies the media instance to minst.
nsellength *n*	Specifies a trailing number of bytes for a received NSAP (ISO only).
trailers	Uses trailer link level encapsulation when sending (default).
-trailers	Doesn't use use trailer link level encapsulation.
link [0-3]	Uses special processing for the link level of the interface.
-link [0-3]	Doesn't use any special processing for the link level.
	The following two options are used for AppleTalk.
range	Specifies the interface will respond to a netrange of the form startnet-endnet.
phase *n*	Specifies the version of the AppleTalk network (possible values are 1 or 2).
	Use this with an IP-address to specify a point-to-point link.
destaddress	Specifies the destination IP-address for a point-to-point link.
Linux:	
promisc	Enables promiscuous mode for the interface. Receives all packages.
-promisc	Disables promiscuous mode for the interface.
allmulti	Enables all-multicast mode for the interface. Receives all multicast packages.
-allmulti	Disables all-multicast mode for the interface.
mtu *n*	Specifies the maximum IP-packet size.
add *addr/prefixlen*	Adds a IPv6 address to the interface.
del *addr/prefixlen*	Removes a IPv6 address from the interface.
tunnel *ip-address*	Creates a IPv6-in-IPv4 tunnel to the specified address.
media *type*	Specifies the media to use. Some possible values are AUI, 10baseT. (See the description for each interface type for a complete list.) Using auto as the type sets the interface to auto sense.
broadcast	Sets the IFF_BROADCAST flag for the interface.
-broadcast	Clears the IFF_BROADCAST flag for the interface. (See also broadcast in the common section.)
pointopoint *addr*	Specifies the remote address for a point-to-point link.
pointopoint	Sets the IFF_POINTOPOINT flag for the interface.
-pointopoint	Clears the IFF_POINTOPOINT flag for the interface.
hw *class addr*	Sets the hardware address for the interface.
class	Specifies the class. Use one of ether, ax25, ARCnet, or netrom.
addr	Specifies a valid hardware address.
multicast	Sets the multicast flag for the interface.
txqueuelen *length*	Sets the transmit queue length.
	The following option will alter the hardware parameters.
irq *irq*	Sets the interrupt line used by the network card.
io_addr *addr*	Sets the I/O space used by the network card.
mem_start *addr*	Sets the start address for shared memory used by the network card.
Solaris:	
	In Solaris the interface can also be specified in these ways.
-a	Specifies all interfaces.
-ad	Specifies all interfaces that aren't active.
-adD	Specifies interface that isn't active and not configured to use DHCP.
-au	Specifies interfaces that are active.
-auD	Specifies interfaces that are active and not configured to use DHCP.
interface	Specifies the name of the interface (like le0 or le0:2).
	These are the options to be used.
Auto-revarp	Uses the RARP protocol to receive an address automatically.
Mtu *n*	Specifies the MTU to use with the interface.
Trailers	Is ignored. Provided for compatibility only.
-trailers	Disables the trailer option.
Private	Doesn't broadcast an interface.
-private	Is used to broadcast an interface.
Plumb	Creates the interface to be used with TCP/IP.
Unplumb	Disables the TCP/IP functions for the interface.
	The following options are used with dhcp or auto-dhcp.
Dhcp	Uses DHCP to receive an ipaddress for the interface.
Auto-dhcp	Same as dhcp.
Primary	Specifies the interface to be used as the primary interface.

continued

wait *seconds*	Specifies the timeout in seconds for the DHCP configuration to finish.
drop	Erases the DHCP configuration from the interface.
extend	Attempts to extend the lease for the IP-address.
ping	Verifies that the interface uses DHCP, if exit status of 0 = yes and 1 = no.
release	Releases the ipaddress and deactivates the interface.
start	Starts the use of DHCP on the interface.
status	Shows the DHCP status of the interface.
	Use this with an IP-address to specify a point-to-point link.
destaddress	Specifies the destination address for a point-to-point link.

File Name:	`ifconfig`	**Directory:**	**AIX:** /etc/, **BSD, Linux:** /sbin/, **Solaris:** /usr/sbin/	**Type:**	External

Warning:	Be careful if you use this command remotely. You could cut the branch you are sitting on.	
Common:	ifconfig -a	Shows information about all interfaces.
AIX:	ifconfig en0 192.22.15.21 netmask 255.255.255.0	Sets up the interface.
Linux:	ifconfig eth0 192.22.15.23 netmask 255.255.255.0	Sets up the interface.
OpenBSD:	ifconfig ep0 inet 192.22.15.22 netmask 255.255.255.0	Sets up the interface.
Solaris:	ifconfig hme0 plumb	Sets up the interface to use tcp/ip..

in.fingerd, fingerd

UNIX Shell: Shells (ash, bash, bsh, csh, ksh, sh, tcsh, zsh)

Function	The daemon that manages the finger protocol.
Syntax	Solaris: in.fingerd AIX, BSD: fingerd [options...] Linux: in.fingerd [options...]

AIX:	
-s	Turns on socket-level debugging.
-f	Turns on finger forwarding service for this fingerd daemon.
BSD:	
-s	Enables secure mode, forwarding of queries to a remote host is denied.
-l	Enables logging.
-u	Queries without a username are rejected.
-m	Disables matching of usernames.
-M	Enables matching of usernames.
-p	Specifies that `.plan` and `.project` files should not be shown.
-S	Shows user information in short mode.
-P *file*	Specifies an alternate program as the local information provider.
Linux:	
-w	Shows information about the system.
-u	Specifies that queries matching "finger @host" should be denied.
-l	Enables logging.
-f	Enables forwarding.
-p *file*	Specifies an alternate program as the local information provider.
-t *timeout*	Specifies the number of seconds to wait before the connection is timed out.

File Name:	`in.fingerd, fingerd`	**Directory:**	/usr/sbin/, **BSD:** /usr/libexec/	**Type:**	External

Note:	Is usually started by `inetd` daemon in AIX, BSD, and Solaris. Linux uses `xinetd` to start network services.	
AIX:	fingerd -s	Enables socket-level debugging.
Linux:	in.fingerd –w	Gives system information to remote host when queried.
OpenBSD:	fingerd –l	Enables logging.
Solaris:	in.fingerd	Starts the daemon.

in.ftpd, ftpd

UNIX Shell: Shells (ash, bash, bsh, csh, ksh, sh, tcsh, zsh)

Function	The Internet FTP daemon that manages FTP services. It is only started by the `inetd` daemon when requested.
Syntax	AIX, BSD: ftpd [options...] Linux, Solaris: in.ftpd [options...]

-d	Logs debugging information to the system log.
-l	Logs all FTP connections to the system log.

continued

-t *timeout*	Specifies the timeout period for inactive FTP connections.
AIX:	
-k	Enables data transfer to timeout in the event TCP/IP hangs.
-T *timeout*	Logs out inactive client sessions after a maximum number of seconds specified.
-s	Turns on socket-level debugging.
-o *octval*	Sets the daemons umask.
BSD:	
-A	Permits only anonymous FTP connections or accounts listed in `/etc/ftpchroot`.
-D	Forks the daemon to the background.
-h	Uses data ports in the high port range for passive connections.
-M	Enables multihomed mode.
-p	Disables passive mode FTP connections.
-P	Permits illegal port numbers or addresses for PORT command initiated connects.
-S	Logs all anonymous downloads to the file `/var/log/ftpd`.
-U	Logs sessions to the file `/var/run/utmp`.
-T *timeout*	Logs out inactive client sessions after a maximum number of seconds specified.
-u *mask*	Changes the default umask from 027 to the one specified.
Linux:	
-v	Logs debugging messages to `syslog`.
-T *timeout*	Logs out inactive client sessions after a maximum number of seconds specified.
-a	Enables use of the file `ftpaccess`.
-A	Disables use of the file `ftpaccess`.
-L	Enables logging of commands sent to the server.
-i	Logs incoming files to the file `xferlog`.
-I	Disables the use of RFC931.
-o	Logs outgoing file to the file `xferlog`.
-p *ctrlport*	Overrides the port numbers used by the control connections to the server.
-P *dataport*	Overrides the port numbers used by the data connection to the server.
-q	Enables use of the PID files.
-Q	Disables use of the PID files.
-r *rootdir*	Specifies the daemon should chroot to the directory specified.
-s	Starts the daemon in standalone oper mode.
-S	Starts the daemon in standalone oper mode and places it in the background.
-u *mask*	Changes the default umask from 027 to the one specified.
-V	Shows version information.
-w	Enables writing user login and logout information to the `wtmp` file.
-W	Disables writing user login and logout information to the `wtmp` file.
-X	Specifies that output created by the -i and -o options is logged to `syslog`.

File Name:	`in.ftpd, ftpd`	**Directory:**	/usr/sbin/, **BSD:** /usr/libexec	**Type:**	External
Warning:	Remember that anonymous FTP logins are a major security risk!				
AIX:	ftpd -o 007	Starts the daemon with umask 007 as default.			
Linux:	in.ftpd –i	Starts the deamon and logs all incoming files.			
OpenBSD:	ftpd –D	Starts the daemon in the background.			
Solaris:	inetd –s	Starts the FTP service after typing `in.ftpd`.			

in.rexecd, rexecd

UNIX Shell: N/A

Function	A daemon that services remote execution requests and uses username and password authentication. `inetd` will automatically start the daemon when needed.
Syntax	AIX: rexecd [options...] BSD: rexecd Linux, Solaris: in.rexecd

AIX:	
-s	Enables debugging on IP sockets.
-c	Stops reverse name resolution.

File Name:	in.rexecd, rexecd	**Directory:**	/usr/sbin/, **BSD:** /usr/libexec/	**Type:**	External
Note:	This is the daemon that serves the `rexec` command.				
AIX:	rexecd –sc	Starts the rexecd daemon, enables debug mode, and stops reverse name lookup.			

continued

Linux:	in.rexecd	Starts the rexecd daemon.
OpenBSD:	rexecd	Starts the rexecd daemon.
Solaris:	in.rexecd	Starts the rexecd daemon.

in.rlogind, rlogind

UNIX Shell: Shells (ash, bash, bsh, csh, ksh, sh, tcsh, zsh)

Function	The server for the rlogin command. The server looks at client's source port. If port isn't in the range 0-1023, the server will abort the connection.
Syntax	AIX, BSD: rlogind [options...] Linux: in.rlogind [options...] Solaris: in.rlogind

AIX:	
-c	Disables reverse lookup of the hostname.
-l	Doesn't use the user's `$HOME/.rhosts` file for authentication.
-n	Doesn't use keep-alive messages.
-s	Enables socket level debugging.
BSD:	
-a	Prompts for verification of the hostname.
-l	Doesn't use the user's `$HOME/.rhosts` file for authentication.
-n	Doesn't use keep-alive messages.
Linux:	
-a	Prompts for verification of the hostname.
-h	Allows authentication using the superusers `.rhosts` file.
-l	Doesn't use the user's `$HOME/.rhosts` file for authentication.
-L	Disables all authentication from `.rhosts` or `hosts.equiv` files
-n	Doesn't use keep-alive messages.

File Name:	`in.rlogind, rlogind`	**Directory:**	/usr/sbin/, **BSD:** /usr/libexec/	**Type:**	External
Note:	Started by `inetd` or `xinetd` when a remote login connection is created.				

AIX:	rlogind -s	Starts the rlogind daemon and enables socket level debugging.
Linux:	in.rlogind -l	Starts the rlogind daemon without using the users .rhosts file.
OpenBSD:	rlogind -n	Starts the rlogind daemon without using keep-alive messages.
Solaris:	in.rlogind	Starts the remote login daemon on the server.

in.rshd, rshd

UNIX Shell: Shells (ash, bash, bsh, csh, ksh, sh, tcsh, zsh)

Function	The server for rsh (remote shell). Allows clients to execute commands from remote clients. The server accepts connections from the client on any port lower than 1024.
Syntax	AIX, BSD: rshd [options...] Linux: [options...] Solaris: in.rshd *host.port*

AIX:	
-c	Disables reverse hostname lookup.
-s	Enables socket level debugging. Used for troubleshooting.
BSD:	
-a	Requests the host for verification.
-l	Doesn't use the `.rhosts` file for authentication.
-L	Logs successful connections in verbose mode.
-n	Disables keep-alive messages.
Linux:	
-a	Requests the host for verification.
-h	Allows access to superuser accounts.
-l	Doesn't use the `.rhosts` file for authentication.
-L	Logs successful connections in verbose mode.
-n	Disables keep-alive messages.
Solaris:	
host.port	Specifies the client's host address (hexadecimal form) and port number (decimal form).

File Name:	`in.rshd, rshd`	**Directory:**	/usr/sbin/ **BSD:** /usr/libexec/	**Type:**	External

continued

Note:	Started by `inetd` when shell services are requested.	
AIX:	startsrc -t shell	Starts the rshd daemon.
Linux:	in.rshd	Starts the rshd daemon.
OpenBSD:	rshd	Starts the rshd daemon.
Solaris:	in.rshd	Starts the rshd daemon.

In.telnetd, telnetd

UNIX Shell: Shells (ash, bash, bsh, csh, ksh, sh, tcsh, zsh)

Function	Used to process incoming requests on the telnet port. Started by the Internet Server (`inetd`).
Syntax	Linux, Solaris: in.telnetd [options...] AIX, BSD: telnetd [options...]

AIX:	
-n	Disables transport-level keep-alive messages.
-s	Turns on socket-level debugging.
BSD:	
-a *mode*	Specifies the mode to be used for authentication.
-D *mode*	Specifies the debug mode to use.
-debug	Enables debugging on each socket.
-edebug	Enables encryption debugging code.
-g *argument*	Specifies which entry from `/etc/gettytab` should be used to get banner strings.
-h	Disables the printing of host-specific information before login has been completed.
-I *id*	Specifies the ID from `/etc/inittab` to use when init starts login sessions.
-k	Specifies the program will operate in character at a time mode.
-l	Specifies that line mode should be used.
-n	Disables TCP keep-alive.
-r *number-number*	Specifies a range of pseudo-terminal devices to use.
-S *value*	Specifies the Time Of Service value.
-u *length*	Specifies the size of the field in the structure that holds the remote hostname.
-U	Refuses connections from addresses that can't be mapped back into a symbolic name.
-X *type*	Specifies the authentication type to use.
Linux:	
-a *mode*	Specifies the mode to be used for authentication.
-D *mode*	Specifies the debug mode to use.
-edebug	Enables encryption debugging code.
-h	Disables the printing of host-specific information before login has been completed.
-L *program*	Specifies the login program to use (default is `/bin/login`).
-n	Disables TCP keep-alive.
-s	Specifies that SecurID validated logins are allowed, if supported.
-S *value*	Specifies the Time Of Service value.
-X *type*	Specifies the authentication type to use.

File Name:	in.telnetd, telnetd	**Directory:**	/usr/sbin, **BSD:** /usr/libexec/	**Type:**	External

in.tftpd, tftpd

UNIX Shell: Shells (ash, bash, bsh, csh, ksh, sh, tcsh, zsh)

Function	A server that gives you TFTP functionality; it uses the UDP protocol instead of TCP.
Syntax	Linux, Solaris: in.tftpd [options...] *{ directory }* AIX, BSD: tftpd [options...] *{ directory }*

directory	Specifies a home directory for the `TFTP` server.
AIX:	
-c *number*	Specifies the maximum number of concurrent threads per process.
-I	Logs the Ipaddress of the calling server with error messages.
-n	Allows the remote user to create files on your computer.
-p *port*	Specifies the port for incoming connections.
-r	Converts the IP address to the appropriate hostname before it logs messages.
-v	Logs information messages when any file is successfully transferred by the daemon.
-t	Specifies the timeout value for data grams.
-s	Turns on socket-level debugging.
-x	Specifies the maximum of timeouts waiting for a data gram.

continued

-z	Specifies the maximum allowed segment size for transfers.
-d *directory*	Specifies the destination folder.
BSD:	
-c	Allows new files to be created.
-s	Runs the server in secure mode.
Linux:	
-c	Allows new files to be created.
-s	Runs the server in secure mode.
-r *options*	Specifies that RFC 2347 option negotiation should be used.
Solaris:	
-s	Runs the server in secure mode.

File Name:	`in.tftpd, tftpd`	**Directory:**	/usr/sbin/, **BSD:** /usr/libexec	**Type:**	External
Note:	This protocol is often used for remote boot process.				
Common:	in.tftpd /tftpboot	Starts a tftp server with homedir set to /tftpboot.			
AIX:	in.tftpd -c 30	Starts a tftp server with maximum 30 threads per process.			
OpenBSD:	in.tftpd -c	Allows new files to be created.			
Solaris:	in.tftpd -s /tftpboot	Starts a tftp server in secure mode with homedir set to /tftpboot.			

indxbib

UNIX Shell: Bourne shell (sh)

Function	Creates an index for a database file in inverted form. It can be read by the commands `lookbib` and `refer`. An executable in Linux, BSD and a script in AIX, Solaris.
Syntax	AIX, Solaris: indxbib *files...* BSD, Linux: indxbib [options...] *files...*

files...	Specifies the database files to index. Files must be in current directory.
BSD,Linux:	
-v	Shows version information.
-w	Indexes entire files and treats every file as a separate record.
-c*file*	Specifies a file to read common words from. (Default is /usr/share/groff/eign.)
-d*directory*	Specifies the directory to be stored as the current working directory in the index.
-f*file*	Specifies a file with files to be indexed. If file is - read from STDIN.
-i*string*	Doesn't index fields whose names are in string.
-h*n*	Specifies a value for creating the hash table. (Default is 997.)
-k*n*	Specifies maximum numbers of keys per input record. (Default is 100.)
-l*n*	Doesn't use keys shorter than n. (Default is 3.)
-n*n*	Doesn't use the n most common words. (Default is 100.)
-o*name*	Specifies the name of the index. The filename will be name.i.
-t*n*	Truncates keys to n. (Default is 6.)

File Name:	indxbib	**Directory:**	/usr/bin/	**Type:**	External
Common:	indxbib dbfile	Creates an index for the specified database file.			

infocmp

UNIX Shell: Shells (ash, bash, bsh, csh, ksh, sh, tcsh, zsh)

Function	Shows terminal information or compares descriptions between two or more terminals.
Syntax	infocmp [options...] *{ names... }*

-d	Shows the differences between two entries.
-c	Shows all common fields between two entries.
-n	Lists of fields that were in neither entry.
-I	Uses terminfo names.
-L	Uses long C variable names.
-C	Uses termcap names.
-r	Shows capabilities in termcap format. Use with –C.
-u	Makes a terminfo of the first term relative to the sum of the following term.
-s *order*	Specifies the sort order given below.
D	Doesn't sort the fields in the terminfo database.
I	Sorts by terminfo names.
L	Sorts by C variable names.

continued

c	Sorts by termcap names.
-v	Shows trace information on STDERR.
-V	Shows version information.
-1	Shows only one field per line.
-w *width*	Sets the output width in characters.
-A *directory*	Specifies the variable TERMINFO for the first termname.
-B *directory*	Specifies the variable TERMINFO for other termnames.
names...	Specifies the name of the terminfo to show or compare.
AIX, Solaris:	
-v	Shows trace information on STDERR.
BSD, Linux:	
-F *file1 file2*	Compares the two specified terminfo files.
-G	Shows constant literals in decimal form instead of the character.
-R*subset*	Shows only a given subset.
-T	Eliminates the size-restriction for the generated text.
-e	Shows the capabilities of the given terminal as a C initializer.
-E	Shows the capabilities of the given terminal as tables for the C initializer.
-f	Shows complex terminfo strings in a more clear way.
-g	Shows constant character literals in quoted form.
-i	Analyzes the initialization and resets strings in the entry.
-p	Ignores padding specification when comparing strings.
-v *n*	Shows trace information on STDERR. n specifies the level of verbosity.

File Name:	`infocmp`	**Directory:**	/usr/bin/	**Type:**	External
Common:	infocmp vt100		Shows info about the vt100 terminal.		
Common:	infocmp -L		Shows long C variable names.		
Linux:	infocmp -f xterm		Shows info about the xterm in a clearer way.		

init, telinit

UNIX Shell: Shells (ash, bash, bsh, csh, ksh, sh, tcsh, zsh)

Function	Changes run levels for the system. Shuts down or restarts the computer in different modes.
Syntax	init [options] Linux: init [options...]

AIX, Linux, Solaris:	
a	Processes `/etc/inittab` entries that have a as the run level.
b	Processes `/etc/inittab` entries that have b as the run level.
c	Processes `/etc/inittab` entries that have c as the run level.
q	Rereads the `/etc/inittab` file.
s	Switches the system to single-user mode.
S	Switches the system to single-user mode.
AIX:	
	Run levels 0 and 1 are reserved for future use.
2	Switches the system to multi-user mode.
	Run levels 3 to 9 are available for creating a customized run level.
m	Puts the system in maintenance mode.
M	Puts the system in maintenance mode.
N	Sends a signal that stops processes from being respawned.
BSD:	(This system doesn't have the telinit command.)
-1	Puts the system in a permanently insecure mode.
0	Puts the system in an insecure mode.
1	Puts the system in a secure mode.
2	Puts the system in a high secure mode.
Linux:	
0	Halts the system.
1	Puts the system in single-user mode.
2	Switches the system to multi-user mode, without NFS.
3	Switches the system to full multi-user mode (default).
4	Currently unused run level.
5	Puts the system in X11 user mode.
6	Reboots the system.

continued

	The following options are only used by `init`.
-a	Boots the system with default command line.
-s	Boots the system in single-user mode.
-b	Boots directly into a single-user shell without running any other startup scripts.
-z *argument*	Expands the command line a bit, the argument is ignored.
	The following option only applies to `telinit`:
-t *seconds*	Specifies the seconds to wait before sending SIGKILL after SIGTERM is used.
Solaris	
0	Switches the system to PROM mode; it is safe to turn off hardware.
1	Switches the system to single-user mode, no external file systems are mounted.
2	Switches the system to multi-user mode, without NFS server.
3	Switches the system to multi-user mode, with NFS server.
4	Creates a customized run level.
5	Shuts down and powers down the system.
6	Shuts down and reboots the system.

File Name:	`init, telinit`	**Directory:** **AIX, Solaris:** /usr/sbin/, **BSD, Linux:** /sbin/ **Type:** External
AIX:	init N	Sends a signal that stops processes from being respawned.
Linux:	init 6	Shuts down and reboots the system.
OpenBSD:	init 2	Puts the system in high secure mode.
Solaris:	init 5	Shuts down and powers off the system.

install

UNIX Shell: Shells (ash, bash, bsh, csh, ksh, sh, tcsh, zsh)

Function	Manages the installation of files to a specific location or creates directories in a file system.
Syntax	AIX, Solaris: install [options...] *file { dir }* BSD, Linux: install [options...] *file1 file2* BSD, Linux: install [options...] *files... dir* Linux, Solaris: install [options...] *dirs...*

AIX:	
-c *directory*	Installs a file into the specified directory only if the file doesn't exist.
-f *directory*	Tries to force the installation of the file even if the file already exists.
-n *directory*	Installs the file in the specified directory if it isn't found anywhere.
-i	Ignores the directory search list.
-o	Makes a backup copy of the file if it already exists.
-s	Shows only error messages.
-G *group*	Specifies the groupID of the file.
-M *mode*	Specifies the mode of the file.
-O *user*	Specifies the owner of the file.
-m	Moves the file instead of copying it. Can't be used with -c, -f, -i, and -n.
-S	Strips binary after installation.
	These operands can be used: file for -c, -f and –n; dirs for -i.
file	Specifies the file that you want to install.
dirs...	Specifies a list of directories to search before the command executes.
BSD:	
-b	Makes a backup copy of the file if it already exists.
-B *suffix*	Specifies the suffix for backup files (default is .old).
-C	Copies the file. If the target file is the same, don't change the modification time.
-c	Copies the file (is default).
-d	Creates any missing directories.
-f *flag*	Specifies the flags for the target file.
-g *group*	Specifies the groupID of the file.
-o *owner*	Specifies the owner of the file.
-m *mode*	Specifies the mode of the file.
-p	Saves the modification time for files.
-S	Installs the file in a safe mode.
-s	Strips binary after installation.
file1	Specifies the file to install.
file2	Specifies the target filename.

continued

files...	Specifies files to install.
dir	Specifies directory to install in.
Linux:	
--backup[=*control*]	Makes a backup of existing files.
none	Doesn't make any backup.
simple	Makes simple backups.
existing	Makes numbered backups if they exist; otherwise uses simple.
numbered	Makes numbered backups.
-b	Makes a backup of existing files.
-C	Copies the file. If the target file is the same, the modification time doesn't change.
-d	Handles all arguments as directories.
-D	Creates any missing directories.
-o *owner*	Specifies the owner of the file.
-m *mode*	Specifies the mode of the file.
-p	Saves the modification time for files.
-s	Strips binary after installation.
-S *suffix*	Specifies the suffix for backup files (default is ~).
-v	Shows version information.
--help	Shows help information.
--version	Shows version information.
file1	Specifies the file to install.
file2	Specifies the target filename.
files...	Specifies files to install.
dir	Specifies directory to install in.
Solaris:	
	The following options can't be combined.
-c *directory*	Installs a file into the specified directory only if the file doesn't exist.
-f *directory*	Tries to force the installation of the file even if the file already exists.
-n *directory*	Installs the file in the specified directory if it isn't found anywhere.
-d	Creates a directory if it is missing.
-i	Ignores the directory search list.
	The following options can be combined:
-m *mode*	Specifies the mode of the file.
-u *user*	Specifies the owner of the file.
-g *group*	Specifies the groupID of the file.
-o	Makes a backup copy of the file if it already exists.
-s	Shows only error messages.
	These operands can be used: file for -c, -f and –n; dirs for -d and -i ..
file	Specifies the file that you want to install.
dirs...	Specifies a list of directories to search before the command executes.

File Name:	install	**Directory:**	/usr/sbin	**Type:**	Script
Note:	It is often used inside makefiles.				
AIX:	install -c /ucgbook -o ucg.txt	Installs the file ucg.txt in /ucgbook and makes backup.			
Linux:	install --backup=nubered ucg.txt /ucgbook	Installs the file ucg.txt in /ucgbook and makes backup.			
OpenBSD:	install -b ucg.txt /ucgbook	Installs the file ucg.txt in /ucgbook and makes backup.			

iostat

UNIX Shell:	Shells (ash, bash, bsh, csh, ksh, sh, tcsh, zsh)
Function	Shows input and output statistics for disks, terminals, and tapes.
Syntax	AIX, Solaris: iostat [options...] *{ disks... } { interval } { count }* BSD: iostat [options...] *{ disks... }* Linux: iostat [options...] *{ interval } { count }*

AIX:	
-d	Shows only the usage degree of disks. Cannot be combined with -t.
-t	Shows the usage degree of cpu and terminals. Cannot be combined with -d.
disks...	Specifies a disk run to show statistics from.
Interval	Sets the interval to collect statistics. In seconds.
Count	Specifies the number of times to collect statistics.

continued

BSD:	
-c *count*	Specifies the number of times to collect statistics.
-C	Shows the usage degree of cpu.
-d	Shows the transfer rate and number of transfers per second in megabytes for all disks.
-D	Shows number of transfers, kilobytes transferred, and the transfer times.
-I	Shows counts per interval instead of rates.
-M *core*	Specifies a core namelist to extract values from instead of default /dev/mem/.
-N *system*	Specifies system to extract namelist from instead of default /bsd.
-T	Shows the usage degree of terminals.
-w *interval*	Sets the interval to collect statistics. In seconds.
disks...	Specifies a disk run to show statistics from.
Linux:	
-c	Shows the usage degree of cpu and terminals. Cannot be combined with -d.
-d	Shows only the usage degree of disks. Cannot be combined with -c.
-f *file*	Specifies the -o option output file to extract records. Cannot be combined with -o.
-o *file*	Specifies a file to output to. Cannot be combined with -f.
-I	Shows each drive's logical block statistics. Cannot be combined with -p.
-p	Shows Kb/s I/O statistics. Cannot be combined with -I.
-t	Shows each report's time.
-V	Shows version and help information.
interval	Sets the interval to collect statistics. In seconds.
count	Specifies the number of times to collect statistics.
Solaris:	
-c	Shows system usage for user mode, system mode, idle time, I/O waiting in percentages.
-d	Shows transfer rate and number of transfers per second in kilobytes for all disks.
-D	Shows reads and writes per second on all disks, including a usage degree in percent.
-e	Shows error summary for only transport errors and total errors.
-E	Shows a complete error summary for all devices.
-I	Shows counts per interval instead of rates.
-l *n*	Limits the number of disks to show statistics from.
-M	Shows transfer rate in MB/sec instead of KB/sec.
-n	Shows names in a readable format.
-p	Shows statistics for both partitions and devices.
-P	Shows statistics for a partition instead of a device.
-t	Shows the amount of reads and writes to terminals per second.
-x	Shows extended disk statistics.
disks...	Specifies a disk run to show statistics from.
interval	Sets the interval to collect statistics. In seconds.
count	Specifies the number of times to collect statistics.

File Name:	iostat	**Directory:**	/usr/bin/, **BSD:** /usr/sbin/	**Type:**	External
AIX:	iostat -d		Shows usage degree of disks.		
Linux:	iostat -o ucg		Outputs to a record file called ucg.		
OpenBSD:	iostat -C		Shows cpu's usage degree.		
Solaris:	iostat 3 5		Runs iostat with 3 seconds interval, 5 times.		

ipcrm

UNIX Shell: Shells (ash, bash, bsh, csh, ksh, sh, tcsh, zsh)

Function	Releases shared memory by removing identifiers from message queues, semaphores, and shared memory segments that programs or services have left behind.
Syntax	ipcrm [options...]

AIX, BSD, Solaris:	
-m *smid*	Erases the specified shared memory identifier from the system.
-q *mqid*	Erases the specified message queue identifier from the system.
-s *semid*	Erases the specified semaphore identifier from the system.
-M *smkey*	Erases only the shared memory identifier created with the specified key.
-Q *mqkey*	Erases only the message queue identifier created with the specified key.
-S *semkey*	Erases only the semaphore identifier created with the specified key.

continued

Linux: shm *id* msg *id* sem *id*		 Erases the specified shared memory identifier from the system. Erases the specified message queue identifier from the system. Erases the specified semaphore identifier from the system.			
File Name:	ipcrm	**Directory:**	/usr/bin/	**Type:**	External
Tip:	To show active memory segments, use the command `ipcs -m`				
AIX:	ipcrm -m 2	Removes the shared memory segment with the id 2.			
Linux:	ipcrm shm 4	Removes the shared memory segment with the id 4.			
OpenBSD:	ipcrm -m 3	Removes the shared memory segment with the id 3.			
Solaris:	ipcrm -m 5	Removes the shared memory segment with the id 5.			

ipcs

UNIX Shell: Shells (ash, bash, bsh, csh, ksh, sh, tcsh, zsh)

Function	Shows information about inter-process communications currently active in the system, such as shared memory segments, semaphores, and message queues.
Syntax	ipcs [options...]

-a	Joins the options -b, -c, -o, -p, and -t together.
-c	Shows the login and group name of the creator.
-m	Shows information about all active shared memory segments.
-p	Shows the ID of the active processes.
-q	Shows information about all active message queues.
-s	Shows information about all active semaphores.
-t	Shows information about modification time.
AIX:	
-b	Shows the maximum size for shared memory, semaphores and message queues.
-C *file*	Specifies another corefile than the default `/dev/mem`.
-N *kernel*	Specifies another kernel instead of default /usr/lib/boot/unix.
-o	Shows the total number of bytes and messages that are on the queue.
BSD:	
-b	Shows the maximum size for shared memory, semaphores, and message queues.
-C *file*	Specifies another corefile than the default `/dev/kmem`.
-M	Shows shared memory system information.
-N *namelist*	Specifies system namelist files other than the default `/dev/ksyms`.
-o	Shows the total number of bytes and messages that are on the queue.
-Q	Shows message queue system information.
-S	Shows semaphore system information.
-T	Joins the -M and -Q options.
Linux:	
-h	Shows help information.
-i *id*	Shows only the specified resource's information.
-l	Shows a summary of memory, semaphores, and message limits.
-u	Shows a summary of memory, semaphores, and message status.
Solaris:	
-A	Joins the options -b, -c, -i, -o, -p, and -t together.
-b	Shows the maximum size for shared memory, semaphores, and message queues.
-C *file*	Specifies corefile other than the default `/dev/mem` and `/dev/kmem/`.
-i	Shows the number of ISM that are connected to shared memory segments.
-N *namelist*	Specifies system namelist file other than the default `/dev/ksyms`.
-o	Shows the total number of bytes and messages that are on the queue.

File Name:	ipcs	**Directory:**	/usr/bin/	**Type:**	External
Common:	ipcs -c	Shows creator's login and group name.			
Common:	ipcs -m	Shows active shared memory segments.			

jobs

UNIX Shell: Shells (ash, bash, bsh, csh, ksh, sh, tcsh, zsh)

Function	jobs is used to report all jobs that are stopped or executing in the background.
Syntax	jobs [options...]

-l	Shows process id and working directory of the jobs.

continued

sh:	
-p	Shows only the process id of the job.
-x *command*	Replaces any job id with the process id and runs the command.
bash:	
-p	Shows only the process id of the job.
-n	Shows only jobs that have stopped or exited since the last notification.
-r	Shows only running jobs.
-s	Shows only stopped jobs.
-x *command*	Replaces any job id with the process id and runs the command.
ksh:	
-l	Shows the process id.
-n	Shows only jobs that have stopped or exited since the last notification.
-p	Shows only the process id of the job.
% jobid	Shows only information about %jobid.
zsh:	
-d	Shows the directory from which the job was started from.
-p	Shows process groups.
-r	Shows only running jobs.
-s	Shows only stopped jobs.
-Z *string*	Replaces the shells argument and environment space with string.
	Use one of the following to specify job id.
%	Specifies the current job. You can also use %% and %+.
%*number*	Specifies job number.
%?*string*	Specifies a command that contains string.
sh, ksh, bash:	
%*string*	Specifies a command that starts with string
%-	Specifies the previous job.
csh, tcsh:	
%minus;	Specifies the previous job.

Note:	Solaris: Bourne shell (sh) must be started in job control mode by starting it with jsh.	
Common:	jobs	Displays job numbers that are executed or in background.
Common:	jobs -x echo Process: %1	Shows something like Process: 25376 (sh, bash).
Common:	jobs -l	Shows process id and working directory of the jobs (ksh).

join

UNIX Shell: Shells (ash, bash, bsh, csh, ksh, sh, tcsh, zsh)

Function	Compares two files and joins them together where the fields are identical and shows the result to STDOUT.
Syntax	join [option] [options...] *file1 file2*

-a *filenumber*	Creates a line for each unmatching line for the filenumber specified. Value is 1 or 2.
-1 *fieldnumber*	Specifies fieldnumber to join to file1.
-2 *fieldnumber*	Specifies fieldnumber to join to file2.
-j1 *fieldnumber*	Joins on the specified field of file 1.
-j 2*fieldnumber*	Joins on the specified field of file 2.
-j *fieldnumber*	Joins on the specified field of both file 1 and file 2.
file1	Specifies the first input file.
file2	Specifies the second input file.
AIX:	
-v *number*	Creates a single output for line for every mismatch found in the other output file.
-o *list*	Creates an output line to include the specified fields.
-t *character*	Uses the character as the filed separator in the input and output.
BSD:	
-v *number*	Shows a line for each unpairable line in the specified file.
-o *fields...*	Contains a list of fields for creating the output lines.
-e *string*	Replaces empty output fields with string.
-t *char*	Specifies a character to use as a separator.
Solaris:	
-v *number*	Shows a line for each unpairable line in the specified file.
-1 *fieldnumber*	Joins on the specified field of file 1.
-2 *fieldnumber*	Joins on the specified field of file 2.

continued

-o *list* **Linux:** -i		Creates an output line to include the specified fields. Difference in cases is ignored in compared fields.			
File Name:		join			
Common:	join -a 1 file1 file2	**Directory:**	/usr/bin/	**Type:**	External
Common:	join phonebook addressbook		Creates a line for each unmatching line in file 1.		
Linux:	join -i 1 file1 file2		Shows to STDOUT all the fields that are equal in these.		

kill

UNIX Shell: Shells (ash, bash, bsh, csh, ksh, sh, tcsh, zsh)

Function	Stops a process or sends a signal to a processs.
Syntax	kill [option] *{ job ... }*

-l	Lists all signals.
-*signal*	Specifies the signal to send to the process (default is SIGTERM).
job ...	Sends signal to the specified job. Job is process ID or a job ID (see below).
bash:	
-s *signal*	Specifies the signal to send to the process (default is SIGTERM).
-n *signum*	Specifies the signal number to send to the process.
ksh:	
-s *signal*	Specifies the signal to send to the process (default is SIGTERM).
	Use one of the following to specify job ID.
%	Specifies the current job. You can also use %% and %+.
%*number*	Specifies job number.
%?*string*	Specifies a command that contains the specified string.
sh, ksh, bash, zsh:	
%*string*	Specifies a command that starts with the specified string.
%-	Specifies the previous job.
csh, tcsh:	
%minus;	Specifies the previous job. (To use job ID in Solaris, Bourne shell (sh) must be started as jsh.)

Note:	You can only send signal to a process that you own. User root can send signal to all processes.	
Common:	kill -l	Display all supported signals.
Common:	kill -s TERM 5556	Send SIGTERM to pid 5556.
Common:	kill -9 5556	Send KILL to process 5556.

LANG=*language*

UNIX Shell: Shells (ash, bash, bsh, csh, ksh, sh, tcsh, zsh)

Function	Change the regional setting and language translation.
Syntax	LANG=*language*

AIX:	Place in the `/etc/profile` file to set the language variable for all users.
BSD:	Place in the `/etc/csh.login` file to set the language variable for all users.
Linux:	Place in the `/etc/profile` file to set the language variable for all users.
Solaris:	Place in the `/etc/profile` file to set the language variable for all users.
	The following are examples of some common language variables used. *en_US* — English, *sv* — Swedish, *fi* — Finnish, *ru* — Russian *no* — Norwegian, *pl* - Polish, *fr* — French, *nl* — Dutch (You may have to install the language you need.)

Note:	Do not forget to export the variable. For csh and tcsh use setenv LANG language instead.	
Common:	LANG=en_US	Changes the regional settings to English (United States).
Common:	LANG=nl ; export	Changes the regional settings to Dutch and exports the variable.

Last

UNIX Shell: Shells (ash, bash, bsh, csh, ksh, sh, tcsh, zsh)

Function	Shows login information about users, hosts, and terminals.
Syntax	last [options...] *{ users... } { ttys... }* BSD: last [options...] *{ users... }*

-*number*	Limits the number of entries shown to specified number.
-f *file*	Specifies the accounting file to use instead of the default.
Users...	Specifies usernames.

continued

AIX,Solaris:	
-n *number*	**Solaris only:** Limits the number of entries shown to specified number.
ttys...	Specifies terminals.
BSD:	
-c	Shows the total time.
-s	Shows time in seconds since the epoch.
-T	Shows more time information.
-h *host*	Specifies an IP address or hostname.
-t *tty*	Specifies a terminal.
-d *date*	Shows all users logged in at the specified date. Format: [[CC]YY][MMDD]hhmm[.SS] (CC=century, YY=year, MM=month, DD=date, hh=hour, mm=minute, SS=second).
Linux:	
-R	Hides the hostname field.
-n *number*	Limits the number of entries shown to that specified by number.
-a	Shows the hostname in the last column.
-d	Converts the IP address of remote hosts to hostnames.
-i	Shows IP addresses instead of hostnames.
-o	Specifies the old style `wtmp` file to be used.
-x	Shows system shutdowns and runs level changes.
ttys...	Specifies terminals.

File Name:	last	**Directory:**	/usr/bin/	**Type:**	External
Common:	last reboot	Shows all reboots.			
Common:	last -5 root	Shows root's five most recent logins.			
AIX:	last console	Shows all logins on the console.			
Linux:	last -n 10	Shows the ten most recent logins.			
OpenBSD:	last -d 200106241400.00	Shows all users that were logged in June 24th 2001, at 2pm.			
Solaris:	last -n 10 console	Shows the ten most recent logins on the console.			

lbxproxy

UNIX Shell:	**Shells (bash,tcsh,sh,ksh,csh,zsh)**
Function	An X proxy that uses the low bandwidth extension to X (LBX). Some optimizations are made to the connections that increase speed over slow connections. **Solaris 8 only.**
Syntax	lbxproxy [:*port*] [options...]

-help	Shows help information.
-display *address*	Specifies an address to an X server that supports the LBX extension.
-motion *count*	Specifies the number of active motions events at one time (default is 8).
-terminate	Terminates the proxy after last client leaves (default is continue).
-reset	Resets the proxy after last client leaves (default is continue).
-I	Ignores all remaining arguments.
-reconnect	Tries to reconnect to proxy if server connection is broken (default is to exit).
-nolbx	Sets LBX optimizations off.
-nocomp	Sets LBX stream compression off.
-nodelta	Sets substitutions for delta requests off.
-notags	Sets usages of tags off.
-nogfx	Sets graphic re-encoding off.
-noimage	Sets image compression off.
-nosquish	Sets X-events compression off.
-nointernsc	Sets InternAtom short circuit off.
-noatomsfile	Sets atom control file reading off.
-atomsfile *file*	Specifies an atom control file other than default.
-nowinattr	Doesn't group GetWindowAttributes/GetGeometry.
-nograbcmap	Sets color map grabbing off.
-norgbfile	Sets color name to RGB resolution off.
-rgbfile *path*	Specifies a color name to RGB resolution database.
-tagcachesize *size*	Specifies the tag cache size for the proxy in bytes.
-maxservers *number*	Specifies maximum number of servers to use (default is 20).
-zlevel *level*	Specifies Zlib stream compression level. Valid is 1 to 9 where 9 is highest.
-compstats	Shows statistics for stream compression when proxy resets.

continued

-nozeropad	Suppresses writing zeroes in unused space in X requests and replies.
-cheaterrors	Cheats and violates the X protocol rules for errors to improve performance.
-cheatevents	Cheats and violates the X protocol rules for events and errors.
:*port*	Specifies a port address to listen to connections. The port is 60xx, type in xx.
Linux, Solaris:	
-maxservers *number*	Specifies maximum number of servers to use (default is 20).

File Name:	`lbxproxy`	**Directory:**	**AIX:** /usr/bin/X11/, **BSD, Linux:** /usr/X11R6/bin/, **Solaris:** /usr/openwin/bin/	**Type:**	External

ld

UNIX Shell: Shells (ash, bash, bsh, csh, ksh, sh, tcsh, zsh)

Function	A linker for object files used to link executables or shared libraries. Ld operates in two modes, static or dynamic.
Syntax	ld [options...] *file...*

-s	Removes symbolic information from the output file.
-e *epsym*	Sets the symbol epsym to be the entry point address for the output file.
-L *path*	Adds path to the library search directories. Useful only preceding the -l option.
-l *x*	Searches a library libx.so, or libx.a , respectively, in dynamic mode.
-o *outfile*	Produces an output object filenamed outfile.
-r	Combines relocatable object files to produce one relocatable object file.
files...	Specifies object files.
AIX:	
-b*options*	Sets special processing options.
32	Uses 32-bit linking mode.
64	Uses 64-bit linking mode.
asis	Processes external mode in mixed case mode.
autoexp	Exports some symbols automatically.
autoimp	Imports symbols from any shared objects specified as input files.
bigtoc	Generates extra code if a table of contents is greater than 64K.
bindcmds:*file*	Writes a copy of the bind commands to file.
binder:*file*	Specifies a binder program to use.
bindopts:*file*	Writes the binder options to file.
calls:*file*	Writes an address map of the output objects to file.
caps	Processes external symbols in uppercase.
comprld	Combines multiple relocation entries into single RLD when possible.
cror15	Uses the cror 15,15,15 instruction as no-op instruction.
croe31	Uses the cror 31,31,31 instruction as no-op instruction.
dbg:*option*	Specifies debug options.
delcsect	Deletes all symbols in CSSET.
dynamic	Processes shared object in dynamic mode.
E:*file*	Exports external symbols listed in file.
ernotok	Reports error for unresolved external reference.
erok	Produces an output even if there are unresolved external references.
errmsg	Writes error messages to STDERR
	The following options (ex1 - ex5) provide binder option in a file that:
ex1:*file*	Will be read before reading any input file.
ex2:*file*	Will be read before symbol resolution.
ex3:*file*	Will be read after symbol resolution.
ex4:*file*	Will be read before writing the output file
ex5:*file*	Will be read after writing the output file.
expall	Exports all global symbols except imported, unreferenced and start with _ ones.
export:*file*	Exports external symbols listed in file.
gc	Performs garbage collection.
gcbypass	Specifies the number of files to skip when doing garbage collection.
glink:*file*	Uses the global linkage prototype code specified by file.
halt:*NR*	Specifies the highest error level to accept in the binder before aborting.
import:*file*	Imports the symbols listed in file.
initfini:[init] [:term] [:pri)	Specifies the initial, termination routine and the priority values for the module.
ipath	Uses the path component when listing shared object in the loader section.
keepfile:*file*	Doesn't do garbage collection on file.

continued

lazy	Enables lazy loading of a module's dependent modules.
loadmap:*file*	Writes a log of binder commands to file.
libpath:*path*	Specifies a library path to use when writing the loader section.
modtype:*type*	Sets the two-letter module type.
map:*file*	Writes an address map of the output object to file.
maxdata:*number*	Specifies the maximum size of the user data area.
maxstack:*number*	Sets the maximum size in bytes for the user stack.
noloadmap	Doesn't write binder subcommands to a file.
noautoexport	Doesn't automatically export symbols.
noautoimp	Links any unstripped shared objects as ordinary objects files.
nobigtoc	Generates an error if the TOC is greater than 64K.
nobind	Doesn't call the binder.
nocomprld	Doesn't combine multiple relocation entries into single RLD.
nodelcsect	Uses symbols in CSSET during symbol resolution.
noexpall	Exports only symbols specified in an export file.
noentry	Indicates the output file has no entry point.
noerrmsg	Doesn't write any error messages.
nogc	Doesn't do any garbage collection.
noglink	Doesn't insert any global linkage code.
noipath	Uses the null path when listing shared object in the loader section.
nolibpath	Uses the default library path instead of any specified.
nom	Doesn't list the object files used to create the output file.
noobjreorder	Doesn't reorder with the depth-first CSECT recording logic.
nop:*nop*	Specifies the no-op instruction.
noquiet	Shows each binder command and its result to STDOUT.
noreorder	Doesn't reorder CSECTs.
nortl	Disables runtime linking.
nortllib	Doesn't include any reference to the runtime linker.
nostrip	Generates output file that isn't striped.
nosymbolic	Assigns the nosymbolic attribute to most exported symbols.
nosymbolic-	Assigns the nosymbolic- attribute to most exported symbols.
notextro	Doesn't check to ensure that load time relocation entries don't exist in the text section.
notypechk	Doesn't check function-parameter types.
nov	Doesn't write additional information to the load map.
nox	Doesn't make the output file executable.
pD:*addr*	Specifies the address for the beginning of the data section in the file page.
pT:*addr*	Specifies the address for the beginning of the text section in the file page.
quiet	Hides each binder command and its result.
reorder	Reorders the CSECT.
rtl	Enables runtime linking.
rtllib	Includes a reference for the runtime linker.
S:*number*	Sets the maximum size in bytes for the user stack.
scalls:*file*	Writes an address map of the object file to file.
shared	Processes shared object in dynamic mode.
smap:*file*	Writes an address map of the object file to file.
stabcmpct:*level*	Specifies the level of compaction.
static	Makes a static linked output file.
sxref:*file*	Writes an address map of the object file to file.
symbolic	Assigns the symbolic attribute to most exported symbols.
textro	Checks to ensure that load time relocation entries don't exist in the text section.
typechk	Makes a function parameter check between external functions.
x	Makes the output file executable.
xref:*file*	Writes an address map of the object file to file.
-D*addr*	Sets the starting address for the initialized data.
-f*file*	Specifies a file with a list of files to process.
-H*NR*	Begins text, data, and loader section on an offset that is a multiple of NR bytes.
-K	Aligns the beginning of text, data, and loader so it starts at a page start.
-S *NR*	Sets the maximum size in bytes for the user stack.
-T *addr*	Sets the starting address for the text section.
-u *name*	Prevents garbage collection for the specified external name.

continued

-v	Writes more information to the loadmap file about binder command execution.
-z	Aligns the beginning of text, data, and loader so it starts at a page start.
-Z*string*	Prefixes the standard library search with string. Useful for development.
BSD:	
-A *file*	Specifies symbol file to be used as a base for link-editing the object files.
-assert *keywords*	Used for compatibility, is ignored.
-Bdynamic	Performs dynamic linking.
-Bstatic	Performs static linking.
-Bshareable	Builds shared objects.
-Bsymbolic	Resolves all symbolic references in the output.
-Bforcearchive	Loads all members of archives.
-Bsilly	Searches shared objects and locates silly archive (.sa) companions.
-D *size*	Sets the size of the data segment.
-d c	Allocates commons even producing relocatable output.
-d p	Makes alias definitions of procedure calls in non-PIC mode.
-M	Shows link-map information on STDOUT.
-N	Makes an OMAGIC output file.
-n	Makes an NMAGIC output file.
-nostdlib	Doesn't use the standard path to find libraries.
-P	Makes data segment to start on a page boundary.
-Q	Makes a QMAGIC output file.
-R*path*	Specifies a library path to use when writing the loader section.
-S	Strips all debugging information from the output.
-T *addr*	Specifies the start address for the text segment.
-t	Traces input files as they are processed.
-u *symbol*	Marks symbol as undefined.
-V *version*	Sets the version for shared library (default is 8).
-X	Discards local symbols in input files that start with L.
-x	Discards all local symbols in the output file.
-y *symbol*	Traces any manipulations of symbol.
-z	Makes a ZMAGIC output file. (is default).
Linux:	
-A*architecture*	Specifies output target, and warns of incompatible instructions in input file.
-b *input-format*	Specifies the format for input object files.
-Bdynamic	Performs dynamic linking.
-Bstatic	Performs static linking.
-Bsymbolic	Resolves all symbolic references in the output.
-c *file*	Specifies a command file to use read link commands from.
--cref	Outputs a cross-reference table in a map file or on STDOUT.
-d	Assigns space to common symbols even if a relocatable output file is specified.
-defsym *symbol=expression*	Creates a global symbol containing the address given by expression.
--demangle	Tries to present symbol names in error messages.
--no-demangle	Doesn't try to present symbol names in error messages.
-embedded-relocs	Creates a table which can relocate static data at runtime.
-E	Adds all symbols to the dynamic symbol table in an ELF-file.
-f *name*	Sets the internal DT_AUXILIARY field to name in an ELF-shared object.
-F *name*	Sets the internal DT_FILTER field to name in an ELF-shared-object.
-format *input-format*	Specifies the format for input object files.
-g	Used for compatibility, is ignored.
-G *size*	Sets the maximum size for objects to optimize under MIPS ECOFF.
-h *name*	Sets the internal DT_SONAME field to name in an ELF-shared-object.
--help	Shows help information.
-i	Makes an incremental link.
-M	Shows link-map information on STDOUT.
-Map *file*	Writes map-diagnostic information to file.
-m *emulation*	Emulates the emulation linker. Use ld -V to see a list of possible values.
-N	Makes an OMAGIC output file.
-n	Makes an NMAGIC output file.
-noinhibit-exec	Makes an output file even after a non-fatal error.
-no-keep-memory	Optimizes the memory usage.

continued

-no-warn-mismatch	Doesn't warn for mismatching inputfile.
-O*level*	Specifies the optimizing level.
-oformat *oformat*	Specifies the output format of the object file.
-R *file*	Reads symbols and addresses from file.
-relax	Will do global optimizations on some platforms.
-rpath *path*	Adds path to the runtime library search path.
-rpath-link *path*	Specifies a path where to search for library dependent shared libraries.
-S	Strips all debugging information from the output.
-shared	Creates a shared library.
-sort-common	Doesn't sort symbols in the output section.
Solaris:	
-a	Static mode only, creates an executable object file which shows reference errors. (a can't be used with the -r option.)
-b	Dynamic mode only, doesn't special processing for shared objects.
-G	In dynamic mode only, produces a shared object, allows undefined symbols.
-i	Ignores LD_LIBRARY_PATH.
-m	Creates a memory map or shows the input/output sections on the STDOUT.
-t	Turns off the warning about multiply defined symbols with different sizes.
-V	Shows version information of ld in use.
-B dynamic	Governs library inclusion. Accepts shared objects.
-B static	Governs library inclusion. Doesn't accept any shared objects.
-B group	Groups a shared object with all its dependencies.
-B local	Reduces any global symbols, not assigned to a version definition, to be local.
-B eliminate	Eliminates any global symbols, not assigned to a specific version, from symbol table.
-B symbolic	Binds references of global symbols to their definition in the object. For Dynamic mode.
-d *action*	Activate dynamic linking. Action is `yes (y) or no (n).`
-D *tokens...*	Shows debugging information to the STDERR, as specified by each token.
-F *name*	Uses symbol table of shared objects as filter on the shared object specified by name.
-f *name*	Uses symbol table of shared objects as an auxiliary filter on the shared object name.
-h *name*	Records executables names in the object's dynamic section to search for at runtime.
-I *name*	Uses the interpreter name as the path name to be written into the program header.
-M *mapfile*	Reads map file as a text file of directives to ld. Can be used multiple times.
-N *string*	Adds the specific string to the dynamic section of the object being built.
-Qy	Adds an ID string to the comment section to identify the version of the link-editor.
-Qn	Suppresses the version identification.
-R *path*	A colon-separated list of directories used to specify library search directories.
-u *symname*	Adds symname as an undefined symbol in the symbol table.
-Y P,*dirlist*	A path list that changes the default directories used to find libraries.
	Only one of the following three options can be used.:
-z allextract	Extracts all archive members from the archive.
-z defaultextract	Returns archive members to the default archive using former extract options.
-z weakextract	Triggers archive extraction using weak references.
-z combreloc	Combines multiple relocation section; reduces overhead loading objects into memory.
-z defs	Forces fatal error when undefined symbols exist.
-z ignore	Ignores dynamic dependencies that aren't referenced.
-z record	Records dynamic dependencies that aren't referenced.
-z initfirst	Marks the object so its runtime starts before the runtime of any other object.
-z lazyload	Marks dynamic dependencies to be lazily loaded.
-z nolazyload	Doesn't mark dynamic dependencies to be lazily loaded.
-z loadfltr	Binds symbol references to the object and processes the object immediately at runtime.
-z muldefs	Allows multiple symbol definitions and the first symbol definition to be taken.
-z nodefs	Allows undefined symbols. This is default when shared objects is built.
-z nodelete	Marks the object as non-deletable at runtime.
-z nodlopen	Marks the object or any form of dependency as not available to dlopen.
-z nopartial	Expands partially initialized symbols when an output file is generated.
-z noversion	Doesn't record sections having versions or associated *.dynamic* section entries.
-z now	Marks the object to override the default mode of the runtime linker.
-z origin	Marks the object to require immediate `$ORIGIN` processing at runtime.
-z redlocsym	Excludes all local symbols except for the SECT symbols.
-z text	Forces a fatal error if relocations against non-writable, allocatable sections remain

continued

-z textoff -z textwarn	Allows relocations against non-writable, allocatable sections. Dynamic. Shows a warning if any relocations against sections remain. Dynamic.		
File Name: `ld`	**Directory:** /usr/bin/, **Solaris:** /usr/css/bin/	**Type:**	External
Note:	Obsolete options are –zn		

let

UNIX Shell: Shells (bash, ksh, zsh)

Function	Evaluates the arguments. If the result is zero, the exit status is 1; otherwise, 0.	
Syntax	let *arguments...*	
arguments...	Specifies argument to evaluate.	
Common:	let 5-5	Returns 1.
Common:	let 5+5	Returns 0.

lex

UNIX Shell: Shells (ash, bash, bsh, csh, ksh, sh, tcsh, zsh)

Function	Creates C programs to be used in lexical processing of character input. Can be used as an interface to yacc.
Syntax	lex [options...] *{ files... }*

files...	Specifies the pathname of input files.
AIX:	
-C	Generates program suitable for C++ compilers.
-t	Writes the code to STDOUT instead of a file.
-v	Shows statistics summary on one line only. Cannot be used with -n.
-n	Quiet mode. Hides statistics summary information. Cannot be used with -v.
BSD, Linux:	
-b	Creates backup information to the file `lex.backup`.
-c	Is only used as POSIX compliance.
-d	Debug mode. Shows more information.
-f	Scans the input file fast by ignoring table compression and bypass STDIO.
-i	Runs a case-insensitive scanner.
-l	Makes the output as compliant to the original AT&T lex command as possible.
-n	Is only used as POSIX compliance.
-p	Shows performance reports on STDERR.
-s	Aborts on scan errors; doesn't only show it.
-t	Writes the code to STDOUT instead of the a file.
-v	Verbose mode. Shows more information.
-w	Hides warning messages.
-B	Runs the scanner in batch mode.
-F	Is like -f, but will only bypass STDIO operations.
-I	Runs the scanner in interactive mode.
-L	Doesn't create #line directives.
-T	Writes reports to STDERR containing each and every step the command takes.
-V	Shows version information.
-7	Creates a 7-bit scanner.
-8	Creates an 8-bit scanner.
-+	Creates a C++ compliant code.
-?	
-C*{ character }*	Controls degree of table compression and trade-offs between small and fast scanners.
A	Will trade off larger tables in the generated scanner.
E	Constructs equivalence classes.
F	Generates full scanner tables.
F	Uses the alternate fast scanner representation.
M	Constructs meta-equivalence classes.
R	Bypasses STDIO operations.
-o*file*	Specifies the file to create (default is `lex.yy.c`).
-P*prefix*	Specifies the prefix to use (default is yy).
-S*file*	Uses the specified skeleton file instead of the default one.
--help	Shoes help information.
--version	Shows version information.
Solaris:	
-c	Specifies C-language action, it is the default.

continued

-e	Specifies a program that can handle EUC characters. Can't be used with -w.
-n	Suppresses the summary of statistics written with the -v option.
-t	Writes the resulting program to STDOUT instead of lex.yy.c.
-v	Writes a summary of lex statistics to the STDERR. Can't be used with -n.
-w	Generates a program that can handle EUC characters. Can't be used with -e.
-V	Shows version information on STDERR.
-Q	The following options can be used with -Q.
y	Shows version info in lex.yy.c.
n	Hides version info in lex.yy.c (default).

File Name:	`lex`	**Directory:** /usr/bin/ **Solaris:** /usr/ccs/bin/	**Type:** External
Common:	lex file	Generates a C code on the file `file`.	
AIX:	lex -C file	Creates a C++ compliant output.	
Linux:	lex -+ file	Creates a C++ compliant output.	
OpenBSD:	lex -I file	Runs the command in interactive mode.	
Solaris:	lex -e file	Generates output file that handles EUC characters.	

limit

UNIX Shell: Shells (csh, tcsh, zsh)

Function	Sets limitations on the system resources available to the current shell.
Syntax	limit [options...] { *resource* [*limit* }]

-h	Sets hard limits. Only root can change hard limits.
resource	The resource to set limit for. Listed below:
cputime	Specifies maximum CPU time per process.
filesize	Specifies maximum size of a single file allowed.
stacksize	Specifies maximum stack size for the process.
coredumpsize	Specifies maximum core dump file size.
csh:	
descriptors	Specifies maximum number of file descriptors.
memorysize	Specifies maximum virtual memory size.
tcsh:	
memorysize	Specifies maximum virtual memory size.
zsh:	
descriptors	Specifies maximum number of file descriptors.
memorylocked	Specifies maximum memory locked in RAM.
resident	Specifies maximum resident set size.
vmemorysize	Specifies maximum of virtual memory.
addressspace	Specifies maximum address space.
cachedthreads	Specifies maximum cached threads.
limit	The limit to use.
n	Specifies the limit. (Default is number, kilobyte or second.)
*n*k	Kilobytes. Default.
*n*h	Hours for cputime.
mm:ss	Minutes and seconds for cputime.
zsh:	
-s	Sets limit for the current shell. Default is for the children of the shell.

Note:	Use unlimit to remove limits.	
Common:	limit coredumpsize 0	Sets maximum coredumpsize to 0.
Common:	limit filesize unlimited	Sets filesize to unlimited.
Common:	limit	Shows current settings.

ln

UNIX Shell: Shells (ash, bash, bsh, csh, ksh, sh, tcsh, zsh)

Function	Creates a link between the specified source and destination files.
Syntax	ln [options...] *source... { destination }*

-f	Removes existing destination files.
-s	Creates a symbolic link.
source...	Sets file to link to. If more than one, destination must be a directory.
destination	Sets name of link. If not given, the link will have the same name as the source.

continued

Linux:	
--backup=*control*	Make a backup of each existing destination file. **The control string can be one of the following:**
none	Never makes backups.
off	Same as none.
numbered	Makes numbered backups.
t	Same as numbered.
existing	Makes numbered backups if numbered backups exist; otherwise simple.
nil	Same as existing.
simple	Makes simple backups.
never	Same as simple.
-b	Same as --backup but without arguments.
-d	Hard links directories. Only for the superuser.
-f	Removes existing destination files.
-n	Doesn't override the contents of an existing file.
-i	Prompts whether to remove destinations.
-s	Creates symbolic links. Can link to other file systems.
-S=*suffix*	Overrides the usual backup suffix.
--target-directory=*directory*	Specifies the directory in which to create the links.
-v	Verbose mode. Shows more information.
--help	Shows help information.
--version	Shows version information.
Solaris:	
-n	Doesn't override the contents of an existing file.

File Name:	`ln`	**Directory:**	**AIX, Solaris:** /usr/bin/ **BSD, Linux:** /bin — **Type:** External
Common:	ln -s /usr/java1.1.2 /usr/java		Creates a symbolic link to /usr/java1.1.2 named /usr/java.
Common:	ln file1 file2		Creates a hard link to file1 named file2.
Linux:	ln -d /usr /myusr		Creates a hard link to /usr named /myusr.
Solaris:	ln -n ucg1 ucg2		Doesn't overwrite ucg2 if it exists.

logger

UNIX Shell: Shells (ash, bash, bsh, csh, ksh, sh, tcsh, zsh)

Function	Adds messages to the system log from the command line.
Syntax	logger [options...] *{ message }*

-f *file*	Uses the contents of file as the message to log.
-i	Logs the PID of logger with each line.
-p *priority*	Enters the message with the specified priority instead of default.
-t *tag*	Marks and adds each line with the specified tag to the log.
message	Specifies the message that is added to system log.
BSD,Linux:	
-s	Shows also the message on STDERR.
-u *socket*	**Linux only:** Writes to the specified socket instead of `syslog`.
--	**Linux only:** Specifies the end of the options.

File Name:	`logger`	**Directory:**	/usr/bin/ — **Type:** External
Tip:	Add your own messages to the system log.		
Common:	logger Rebooted the system		Adds a message to the system log.
Common:	logger -f ucgmessage		Adds the contents of the file ucgmessage to the system log.
Linux:	logger -- -System Reboot-		Adds the message to the system log.
OpenBSD:	logger -s Reboot		Adds the message and shows it on STDERR.

login

UNIX Shell: Shells (ash, bash, bsh, csh, ksh, sh, tcsh, zsh)

Function	Lets you sign on to the system.
Syntax	login [options...] *{ name }* AIX, Solaris: login [options...] *{ name [environment }]*

continued

-p *name* **AIX, BSD, Linux:** -f *name* -h *hostname* *variable=value* **Solaris:** -h *host [terminal]* -d *device* -r *hostname* *variable=value* **csh:** -p *name*	Passes environment variables to the login shell. Specifies the username to login. Specifies a user that is already authenticated. Passes information about the remote host by telnetd. **AIX Only:** Specifies environment variables and values to set. Passes information about the remote host and terminal type by telnetd. Specifies the path name for the tty port login to operate. Passes information about the remote host in in.rlogind. Specifies environment variables and values to set. **login exists as an internal command in sh, ksh, csh, and tcsh.** **In sh, ksh and tcsh, it's the same as the external login.** Passes environment variables to the login shell. Specifies the username to login.

File Name:	`login`	**Directory:**	/usr/bin/, **Linux:** /bin/	**Type:**	External, Internal
Note:	If login is invoked as a command, it must replace the initial command interpreter (exec login).				
Common:	login root	Login root user; command prompts for password.			
Common:	exec login	Make sure the external login is run.			
Common:	login -p ucg	Login as ucg and preserve the environment.			

logname

UNIX Shell: Shells (ash, bash, bsh, csh, ksh, sh, tcsh, zsh)

Function	Shows your login name.
Syntax	logname

Linux: --help --version	 Shows help information. Shows version information.

File Name:	`logname`	**Directory:**	/usr/bin/	**Type:**	External

logout

UNIX Shell: Shells (bash, csh, tcsh, zsh)

Function	Exits a login shell form in Bash, C, TC, and Z-Shell (bash, csh, tcsh, zsh).
Syntax	logout zsh: logout *{ NR }*

zsh: *NR*	 Specifies the exit code for the shell.

Note:	In all shells you can use exit to logout.	
Common:	logout	Logout from the shell.
Common:	logout 3	Logout from the shell with exit code 3.

look

UNIX Shell:	Shells (ash, bash, bsh, csh, ksh, sh, tcsh, zsh)
Function	Finds words in the system dictionary and shows all lines that begin with the specified string.
Syntax	look [options...] *string { file }*

-d	Specifies dictionary order, only alphanumeric characters are compared.
-f	Doesn't distinguish between uppercase and lowercase letters.
string	Shows all lines that begin with string.
file	Searches for string in specified file.
BSD, Linux, Solaris:	
-t *char*	Ignores all characters in the string after the specified character.
-a	**Linux only:** Specifies an alternate dictionary, `/usr/share/dict/web2`.

File Name:	`look`	**Directory:**	/usr/bin/
Type:	External		
Tip:	Try this one: `look into 'my eye'`. Fun in AIX and Solaris.		
Common:	look -f rockefeller	Searches for Rockefeller in the dictionary. Not case-sensitive.	
Common:	look command	Shows all words beginning with command.	
Linux:	look -t u Linux	Searches for words starting with linu.	
OpenBSD:	look -t c ucg	Searches for words starting with uc.	
Solaris:	look -tu Linux	Searches for words starting with linu.	

lookbib, glookbib

UNIX Shell:	Shells (ash, bash, bsh, csh, ksh, sh, tcsh, zsh)
Function	Finds references in a bibliographic database and recovers records containing the keywords entered at the prompt.
Syntax	AIX: lookbib [-n] *{ database }* BSD, Linux: lookbib [options...] *database* Solaris: lookbib *database*

	Linux Only: The command `glookbib` is the same as `lookbib`.
database	Specifies database to search for indexes.
AIX:	
-n	Disables the prompt for instructions.
BSD,Linux:	
-v	Shows version information.
-i *string*	Doesn't search the contents of the fields whose names are specified.
-t *NR*	Requires only the first NR of characters of keys to be given (default is 6).

File Name:	`lookbib`	**Directory:**	/usr/bin/
Type:	External		
Common:	lookbib bibdb	Searches the bibdb database for the keywords entered at the prompt.	
AIX:	lookbib -n bibdb	Disables the prompt for instruction.	
OpenBSD:	lookbib -i NAME bibdb	Doesn't search the contents of the field named NAME.	

lpq

UNIX Shell:	Shells (ash, bash, bsh, csh, ksh, sh, tcsh, zsh)
Function	Shows the content of a print queue.
Syntax	lpq [options...] *{ jobNR ... } { user ... }* Linux: lpq [options...] *{ jobNR ... }*

-P *destination*	Shows information about printer or class of printers. Uses FNS or POSIX-style.
-l	Shows information in long format, including the name of the host.
jobNR	Specifies the job number associated with a print request.
AIX:	
-w	Shows status information with longer queue names, device names, and job numbers.
+ *interval*	Shows information at specific time intervals. Clears screen before showing queue.
user	Specifies the name of the user whose jobs `lpq` will report.
BSD:	
-a	Shows a report on all printers.
user	Specifies the name of the user whose jobs `lpq` will report.

continued

Linux:	
-a	Shows a report on all printers.
-A	Uses authentication specified by the value of the AUTH environment variable.
-L	Uses maximum verbosity.
-s	Shows a short single line status summary for each queue and subqueue.
-t *sleeptime*	Shows the spool queues repeatedly with the specified time interval.
-V	Shows version information.
-D *debugopt*	Specifies a comma-separated list of debugging settings.
Solaris:	
+ *interval*	Shows information at specific time intervals. Clears screen before showing queue.
user	Specifies the name of the user whose jobs `lpq` will report.

File Name: `lpq` | **Directory:** /usr/bin/ **Solaris:** /usr/ucb/ | **Type:** External

lpr

UNIX Shell: Shells (ash, bash, bsh, csh, ksh, sh, tcsh, zsh)

Function Sends print requests to a printer. Uses STDIN if no file is specified.

Syntax lpr [options...] *{ files... }*

-P *printer*	Prints the file on the specified printer.
-# *number*	Shows a specific number of copies. The default for numbers is 1.
-C *class*	Shows the job classification on the banner page of the STDOUT.
-J *job*	Shows the job name on the banner page of the STDOUT.
-T *title*	Shows a title on the banner page of the output.
-i *indent*	Indents the output a specific number of SPACE characters. (Default is 8.)
-w *cols*	Shows pages of a specific width; cols indicates the number of columns wide.
-m *user*	Sends mail after file has printed. By default no mail is sent after completion.
-h	Suppresses printing of the banner page of the output.
-s	Uses full pathnames to file instead of copying them.
-p	Uses the command `pr`to format the files.
-n	Includes `ditroff` (device independent troff) data in the file.
-g	Specifies the files include plot data.
files...	Specifies the name of the file to be printed.
AIX:	
-f	Interprets the first character of each line as a FORTRAN carriage control character.
-j	Shows a message that shows the job when submitting to a local printer.
-l	Prints control characters and suppresses page breaks.
-r	Removes the file after the file has been completely spooled.
BSD:	
-c	Specifies the file includes data produced by cifplot.
-d	Includes `tex` (DVI format from Stanford) data in the file.
-f	Interprets the first character of each line as a FORTRAN carriage control character.
-l	Prints control characters and suppresses page breaks.
-r	Removes the file after the file has been completely spooled.
-t	Includes troff binary data in the file.
-v	Includes a raster image in the file.
valuefont	Mounts the font to the font position specified by value where the value is 1,2,3, or 4
Linux:	
-A	Uses the value in the `AUTH` variable for authentication.
-c	Includes data produced by cifplot in the file.
-d	Includes `tex` (DVI format from Stanford) data in the file.
-F*filterformat*	Specifies filters and is optional with the filter options (c, d, g, l, n, p, r, t).
b	Specifies a binary file but doesn't perform any processing. Requires the -F option.
l	The same as option –b.
-k	Sends the print job directly to the server without creating any temporary files.
-Q	Adds the name of the queue into the job file.
-r	Removes the file after the file has been completely spooled.
-R *account*	Specifies the account to use when printing your document (for accounting only).
-t	Includes `troff` binary data in the file.

continued

-u *username*	Specifies a username for a specific print job.
-v	Includes a raster image in the file.
-V	Verbose mode. Shows more information with every additional –V.
-Z *zoptions*	Passes any specified options to the print spooler to give it special information.
valuefont	Mounts the font to the font position specified by value where the value is 1, 2, 3, or 4.
Solaris:	
-l	Prints control characters and suppresses page breaks.
-t	Includes troff binary data in the file.
-d	Includes `tex` (DVI format from Stanford) data in the file.
-v	Includes a raster image in the file.
-c	Includes data produced by cifplot in the file.
-f	Interprets the first character of each line as a FORTRAN carriage control character.
valuefont	Mounts the font to the font position specified by value where the value is 1, 2, 3, or 4

File Name:	`lpr`	**Directory:** /usr/bin/ **Solaris:** /usr/ucb/	**Type:** External
Common:	lpr textfile	Prints textfile on the default printer.	
Common:	lpr -P laser	Prints textfile on the printer named laser.	
Common:	lpr -m textfile	Prints textfile and sends a mail when finished.	

lprm

UNIX Shell: Shells (ash, bash, bsh, csh, ksh, sh, tcsh, zsh)

Function	Removes print requests from the print queue and reports the filename of removed request.
Syntax	lprm [options...] *{ jobNR } { user }* Linux: lprm [options...] *{ jobNR }* [-u*user*]

-P *printer*	Specifies the name of the printer or class of printers from which to remove print requests.
-	Removes all print requests owned by that user invoking the command.
jobNR	Specifies the job number and that you want to remove from the queue.
AIX, BSD, Solaris:	
user	Removes print requests related to a specific user. (Used by a superuser only.)
Linux:	
-A	Uses the value in the `AUTH` variable for authentication.
-a	Removes all files from all print queues that the user has access to.
-D*level*	Specifies a number that represents the debug level (1, 2, 3, and so forth).
-u*user*	Removes print requests related to a specific user. (Used by a superuser only.)
-V	Shows version information and enables verbose mode.

File Name:	`lprm`	**Directory:** /usr/bin, **Solaris:** /usr/ucb/	**Type:** External
Note:	Users can only remove print requests they have submitted. Root or superusers can remove all jobs.		
Common:	lprm -	Removes all requests owned by current user on default printer.	
Common:	lprm 27	Removes job 27 from the default printer.	
Linux:	lprm -a all	Remove all jobs in all spool queues.	
Solaris:	lprm -P lp0 jeanette	Removes all jobs submitted by Jeanette from printer lp0.	

ls

UNIX Shell: Shells (ash, bash, bsh, csh, ksh, sh, tcsh, zsh)

Function	Lists the contents of a specified directory and supports wildcards.
Syntax	ls [options...] *{ file... }*

-a	Shows all entries including those that begin with a dot (.).
-A	Like -a but doesn't show working or parent directories (dot and dot dot).
-c	Uses time of last modification of the i-node for sorting with -t or showing with -l.
-C	Shows the entries sorted in multi-columns. The default output format.
-d	When argument is a directory shows only the name, not the content.
-f	Forces each argument to be shown as a directory and to list the names found.
-F	Marks directories with a trailing slash /, doors with >, and executables with *.
-g	Shows the same as -l, except the owner isn't shown (ignored in Linux).
-i	Shows for each file the i-node number in the first column of the report.
-l	Shows in long format, giving mode, ACL indication number of links, owner, group, etc.
-L	Shows the file, directory, or link references rather than the link itself.
-m	Streams the information on STDOUT. Shows files across the page.

continued

-n	Shows the same as -l, and the owner's UID and group's GID numbers.
-o	Shows same as -l, except the group isn't shown.
-p	Adds a slash (/) after each filename if the file is a directory.
-q	Forces non-printable characters in filenames to be shown as a question mark (?).
-r	Reverses the sorting order of a list.
-R	Shows all subdirectories (recursive list).
-s	Shows size for each entry in blocks, including indirect blocks.
-t	Sorts by timestamp by name. Default is the last modification time.
-u	Sorts by time of last access.
-x	Multi-column output with entries sorted across rather than down the page.
-1	Shows one entry per line of output.
file	Specifies the path name of a file to be shown.
AIX:	
-b	Forces non-printable characters to be shown in the octal \ddd notation.
-e	Shows extended information including the mode, number of links, owner, group, etc.
-N	Doesn't follow symbolic links when status of file is being determined.
BSD:	
-k	Alters the -s option and reports the size in kilobytes.
-S	Sorts the files by size from largest to smallest.
-T	Shows the month, day, hour, minute, second, and year for the file (needs -l or -n).
-W	Shows whiteouts when directories are scanned.
Linux:	
-b	Forces non-printable characters to be shown in the octal \ddd notation.
--block-size=*size*	Specifies the block size to use.
-B	Hides files or directory that end with a tilde ~.
--color[=*value*]	Distinguishes file types. The value can be never, always, or auto.
-D	Creates an output suitable for Emac's dired mode.
--format=*value*	Is format to use. Value is verbose, long, commas, horizontal, across, vertical-column.
--full-time	Shows the complete time and date for the files.
-G	Hides group information.
-h	Shows file sizes in an easy-to-understand format, also called human format.
-H	The same as -h but uses powers 1000 instead 1of 024.
-I=*pattern*	Hides file entries matching the pattern specified.
-k	Is kilobytes and is the same thing as using --block-size=1024.
-N	Shows the raw entry names by not formatting special characters.
--show-control-chars	Shows all non-graphic characters without formatting them.
-Q	Shows all file and directories enclosed in double quotes.
--quoting-style=*value*	Specifies the quoting style. Value choices = literal, locale, shell, shell-always, c, escape.
-S	Shows files and directories sorted by size.
--sort=*value*	Specifies how to sort files. Value choices = extension, none, size, time, version.
--time=*value*	Shows the time specified by value. Value choices = atime, access, use, ctime, status.
-T *column*	Sets the Tab size specified by column (default is 8).
-U	Doesn't sort, lists all files and directories by directory order.
-v	Sorts the files by version number.
-w *column*	Specifies the width of the column when listing files.
-X	Sorts the output by extensions and then sorts them in alphabetical order.
--help	Shows help information.
--version	Shows version information.
Solaris:	
-b	Forces non-printable characters to be shown in the octal \ddd notation.

File Name:	`ls`	**Directory:**	**AIX, Solaris:** /usr/bin/, **BSD, Linux:** /bin	**Type:**	External
Note:	Probably the first command I learned in UNIX.				
Common:	ls /etc/i*	Shows files in /etc starting with i.			
Common:	ls -lp	Shows a long listing and marks directories with a /.			
Common:	ls -t	Shows files and sorts by timestamp (latest first).			
AIX:	ls -e	Shows extended information on files and directories.			
Linux:	ls --color=always	Shows files with different colors based on the file type.			

m4

UNIX Shell:	Shells (ash, bash, bsh, csh, ksh, sh, tcsh, zsh)
Function	A front end macro processor that is used for programming languages like C and assembler.
Syntax	m4 [options...] *{ files... }*

-D*name=value*	Sets name to value. If no value given, set it to NULL.
-U *name*	Undefines a name created by the -D option.
AIX:	
-e	Ignores interrupts and doesn't buffer output. Operates interactively.
-l (lower case)	Starts line-numbering output for the assembler.
-s	Starts the line-sync output for the C preprocessor.
-B *number*	Specifies the size of the push-back and parameter collection buffers.
-H *number*	Specifies the size of the symbol table hash array (must be a prime number).
-I *directory* (upper case)	Scans first the specified directory, then on standard list for include files dirs.
-S *number*	Specifies the size of the call stack.
-T *number*	Specifies the size of the token buffer.
file	Specifies the file to be processed.
BSD:	
-I *name*	Adds the specified directory to the include path.
Linux:	
--help	Shows help and exits.
--version	Shows version information and exits.
-e	Works interactively, unbuffers output, and ignores interrupts.
-E	Stops execution after the first warning.
-Q	Silent, doesn't show some warnings for built-ins.
-P	Sets a m4 prefix to all built-ins.
-I *directory*	Scans first standard list for include files dirs., then the specified directory.
-s	Starts the line-sync output for the C preprocessor.
-G	Hides all GNU extensions.
-H *prime*	Sets the size of the symbol lookup hash table.
-L *number*	Alters the artificial nesting limit.
-F *file*	Creates a frozen state on the specified file at end.
- *file*	Specifies the file to be processed.
Solaris:	
-e	Operates interactively.
-s	Syncs the output for the C preprocessor.
-B *int*	Alters the size of the collection buffers.
-H *int*	Changes the size of the symbol table hash array.
-S *int*	Alters the call stack size.
-T *int*	Alters the buffer size of the token.
files...	Specifies the name of the files to process. If none or - is specified, read from STDIN.

File Name:	m4	**Directory:**	/usr/bin/ **Solaris:** /usr/ccs/bin/	**Type:**	External

mail, Mail, mailx

UNIX Shell:	Shells (ash, bash, bsh, csh, ksh, sh, tcsh, zsh)
Function	Reads and sends mail.
Syntax	AIX, Linux, Solaris: mail [options...] *{ recipients... }* BSD: mail [options...] *{ recipients... }* [-sendmailoptions...]

	Linux Only: Only the command `mail` is available.
	These options are used to send mail.
recipient	Specifies a valid username on the server or an e-mail address for each recipient.
	These options are used to read mail.
-f *file*	Reads the messages in the specified file.
AIX:	
-n	Skips reading the /usr/share/lib/Mail.rc file.
-N	Disables headers from being showed.
	These options are used to send mail.
-c *list*	Specifies a list with users to send copies of message to.
-d	Debug mode. Shows debug information.

continued

-i	Ignores tty interrupt signals.
-s *subject*	Specifies the message subject.
-v	Verbose mode. Shows more information.
	These options are used to read mail.
-F	Names the message after the recipient and saves it as a file.
-H	Lists mail headers instead of showing the last message.
-u *userID*	Starts `mail` with the mailbox of the specified user. Requires permissions.
BSD:	
-i	Ignores tty interrupt signals.
-I	Runs `mail` in interactive mode.
-n	Skips reading the `/etc/mail.rc` file.
-v	Verbose mode. Shows more information.
	These options are used to send mail.
-b *list*	Specifies a list of users to send blind carbon copies to, hiding recipient names.
-c *list*	Specifies a list with users to send copies of message to.
-s *subject*	Specifies the message subject.
-sendmailoptions...	Specifies options from the `sendmail` command.
	These options are used to read mail.
-N	Disables headers from being showed.
-u	Starts `mail` with the mailbox of the specified user.
Linux:	
-i	Ignores tty interrupt signals.
-I	Runs `mail` in interactive mode.
-n	Skips reading the /etc/mail.rc file.
-v	Verbose mode. Shows more information.
	These options are used to send mail.
-s *subject*	Specifies the message subject.
-c *list*	Specifies a list with users to send copies of message to.
-b *list*	Specifies a list of users to send blind carbon copies to, hiding recipient names.
	These options are used to read mail.
-N	Disables headers from being showed.
-u *userID*	Starts `mail` with the mailbox of the specified user.
Solaris:	
-x *debug_level*	Saves trace info in a file. 0 gives no debug, -1 always saves file, 1 saves on error.
	These options are used to send mail.
-m *type*	Defines the message type.
-t	Adds a To: line for each recipient to receive the mail.
-w	Sends a letter to a remote recipient and doesn't wait for transfer completion.
	These options are used to read mail.
-e	Checks whether mail exists. If mail exists, will exit with status 0; otherwise 1.
-h	Lists mail headers instead of showing the last message.
-p	Shows all messages.
-P	Shows all messages with all header information.
-q	Quits if interrupted.
-r	Shows the messages in reverse order. The first message in is first message out.

File Name:	`mail`	**Directory:**	/usr/bin/, **Linux:** /bin/	**Type:**	External
Note:	When creating a new mail message, you must end the message with a control-D. Solaris: When using a terminal device, a message is ended by putting a line with a single period at the end.				
Common:	mail -f mbox	Reads the mail in the file mbox.			
Common:	mail Scarloc	Sends a mail to the user Scarloc.			

mailq

mailq		**UNIX Shell:**	Shells (ash, bash, bsh, csh, ksh, sh, tcsh, zsh)
Function	Shows the mail queue. Shows first line for each mail message, host for the message, the size, the date, and the time.		
Syntax	mailq [options...]		

-v	Verbose mode. Shows more information.
Solaris:	
-q *Xstring*	Runs the queue only one time depending on the value of the Xstring argument.
	The following are valid Xstring values:
S*string*	Shows only the `sender` information if the address matches the given string.
R*string*	Shows only the `recipient` information if the address matches the given string.
I*string*	Shows only the `identifier` information if the address matches the given string.

File Name:	`mailq`	**Directory:**	/usr/bin/, **AIX:** /usr/sbin	**Type:**	External
Common:	mailq		Shows the mail queue.		
Common:	mailq -v		Verbose mode. Shows more information.		

mailstats

mailstats		**UNIX Shell:**	Shells (ash, bash, bsh, csh, ksh, sh, tcsh, zsh)
Function	Shows the statistics collected by the program sendmail.		
Syntax	mailstats [options...] *{ file }*		

file	Collects statistics from file instead of the default /etc/mail/sendmail.st.
AIX:	
-S *file*	Specifies a file to use as statistics file. Default is `/etc/sendmail.st`.
-z	Clears the contents of the statistics file.
BSD:	
-o	Hides the name of the mailer in the output.
-C *file*	Specifies a cf file to read instead of the default one.
-f *statistics file*	Specifies a statistics file for the sendmail program.
Linux:	
-o	Hides the name of the mailer in the output.
-p	Shows information in program-readable mode and clears statistics.
-C *file*	Specifies a cf file to read instead of the default one.
-f *statistics file*	Specifies a statistics file for the sendmail program.
Solaris:	
-c *config file*	Specifies a configuration file for the sendmail program.
-f *statistics file*	Specifies a statistics file for the sendmail program.

File Name:	`mailstats`	**Directory:**	/usr/sbin/, **Solaris:** /usr/bin/,	**Type:**	External
Common:	mailstats		Checks mail statistics.		
AIX:	mailstats -z		Clears the statistics file.		
OpenBSD:	mailstats -o		Hides the mailers name on the output.		

make, gmake

make, gmake		**UNIX Shell:**	Shells (ash, bash, bsh, csh, ksh, sh, tcsh, zsh)
Function	Updates a target file and all of its dependencies or repairs missing or invalid target dependency trees.		
Syntax	make [options...] *{ target } { macro=value }*		

	Linux Only: The command `gmake` is the same as `make`.
-e	Lets environmental variables overrule variables in the makefile.
-i	Ignores any reported error codes.
-k	Skips the current target and continues when the target rule has errors or is missing.
-n	No execute. Shows the command line but doesn't execute it.
-q	Query mode. Returns a nonzero or zero status code whether the file is up-to-date or not.
-r	Doesn't read the default makefile /usr/share/lib/make/make.rules.
-s	Silent mode. Doesn't show the command lines before executing them.
-S	Undoes the results of -k. Stops processing when a nonzero exit status exists.
-t	Touches up target files by making them up-to-date instead of executing their rules. (Use -t with caution since files can be maintained by more than one person.)

continued

-f *makefiles...*	Specifies the file that will determine how to bring the target up-to-date. (When multiple files are used, they are linked and executed in order.)
target	Specifies the target section within the makefile to read process information.
[:]	Denotes the end of the list of targets.
{ deplist }	Specifies the list of dependencies that are used for building the target.
[;]	Denotes the start of commands.
{ commands... }	Selects the commands that are executed.
	The following special target functions are supported within a makefile:
.DEFAULT	Processes this target using these rules when there aren't rules elsewhere.
.DONE	Processes this target, including dependents, after the other targets are built.
.FAILED	Processes this target, including dependents, instead of .DONE. Ends with an error.
.GET_POSIX	Provides rules for recovering the current version of a SCCS file. POSIX mode default.
.IGNORE	Ignores any errors. In POSIX mode, a following target's errors would be ignored.
.INIT	This target, including dependents, will be built before any others are processed.
.KEEP_STATE	Updates the .make.state and state file in the current directory and activates dependents. (Does nothing if POSIX mode is active.)
.KEEP_STATE_FILE	Uses a following file or directory as the state file or a source for .make.state.
.MAKE_VERSION: Version	Compares the version of make against the version of the given target function.
.PARALLEL	Does nothing. For future use only.
.POSIX	Activates POSIX mode.
.PRECIOUS	Denotes a list of dependency files that won't be deleted during an interrupt. (If POSIX is active and files aren't listed, then every file is PRECIOUS.)
.SCCS_GET	Contains the rule for recovering the current version of a SCCS file.
.SCCS_GET_POSIX	Same as .SCCS_GET but for POSIX mode.
.SILENT	Suppresses command echoing when executing them. (If POSIX is active, any following targets will be run in silent mode.)
.SUFFIXES	Specifies the list of suffixes that are used for selecting the implicit rules.
.WAIT	Does nothing. For future use only.
macro=value	Overrides regular definitions within the makefile or the environment.
AIX:	
-D*variable*	Sets the specified variable to 1.
-d*{ flags }*	Shows debug information.
A	Shows all debug information.
a	Shows archive search and cache information.
d	Shows directory search information.
g1	Shows input graph information before make.
g2	Shows input graph information after make.
m	Shows target making information.
s	Shows suffix search information.
v	Shows variable assignment information.
-p	Shows a complete set of macro definitions before beginning processing.
BSD:	
-B	Tries to run in backward compatibility.
-P	Compares all different jobs and shows the result after the process.
-D *variable*	Sets the specified variable to 1.
-d *flags*	Shows debug information. See the AIX option for debugging flags.
-I *directory*	Specifies the directory to search for makefiles.
-j *value*	Specifies the maximum number of jobs to run at one time.
-m *directory*	Specifies the directory to search for included makefiles.
-V *variable*	Shows the value of the specifies variable.
Linux:	
-C *directory*	Specifies the directory to change to before processing the makefile.
-d	Shows debug information.
-I *directory*	Specifies the directory to search for included files.
-j *value*	Specifies the maximum number of jobs for make to run at one time.
-l *{ load }*	Sets the valid load average for the command. If above, other jobs don't start. (If no load is set, the option is disabled.)

continued

-o *file*	Doesn't remake the specified file.
-p	Shows rule and variable values within the makefile.
-v	Shows version information.
-w	Shows the working directory before and after processing.
-W *file*	Makes the command believe that the specified file has just been modified.
Solaris:	
-d	Shows the reasons why `make` selects to rebuild a target.
-D	Shows the text in the specified -f *makefile*.
-dd	Shows the dependency check and processing information. A verbose version of -d.
-DD	Shows the *makefile*, make.rules, the state file, and hidden dependency reports.
-p	Prints the complete set of macro and target definitions.
-P	Reports any dependencies instead of building them.
-V	Forces `make` into SysV mode.
-K *statefile*	Overrides implicit rules and predefined macros using the states in the specified file. (This option is only available for the make found in /usr/ccs/bin/.)

File Name:	`make`	**Directory:** /usr/bin/ **Solaris:** /usr/ccs/bin/ **Type:** External
Warning:	When using the options -n, -q, or -t if POSIX mode is active, lines starting with a plus + will be executed.	
Common:	make	Looks for a filenamed makefile or Makefile, and processes it if found.
Common:	make -f mymakefile dep	Searches the section "dep" in mymakefile and processes it according to that section.
AIX:	make -Dsafemode -dv	Sets the safemode variable to 1 and shows variable assignment information.
Linux:	make -l 0.1 -j 100	Allows 100 jobs to run simultaneously, but limits the maximum load to 0.1.
OpenBSD:	make -B	Tries to process the makefile in backward compatibility.
Solaris:	make -V	Runs the command in SysV mode.

makedbm

UNIX Shell: Shells (ash, bash, bsh, csh, ksh, sh, tcsh, zsh)

Function	Creates a DBM file or converts a DBM file to a text file.
Syntax	makedbm [options...] *infile outfile*

-b	Adds the `YP_INTERDOMAIN` into the output.
-i *file*	Creates a special entry for key specified by the input file.
-m *{ name }*	Creates special entry for key for yp master name (default is local hostname).
-o *file*	Creates a special entry for the specified key.
-u *file*	Reverses a DBM file and shows the file in text format. (Cannot be used with any other options or operands.)
infile	Specifies the input file. If dash - is used it reads from STDIN.
outfile	Specifies the output file in ndbm format.
AIX:	
-d *domain*	Creates a special entry for key specified by the domain name.
BSD, Solaris:	
-U *file*	**BSD only:** The same as -u, but will also try db hash format.
-l	Converts all keys to lowercase.
-s	Accepts only connections from secure NIS networks.
-d *domain*	Creates a special entry for key specified by the domain name.
Linux:	
-a	Adds special support for mail aliases. Cannot be use with -r.
-r	Removes all # comments. Cannot be used with -a.
-c	Makes `ypserv` invalidate all cached entries.
-s	Accepts only connections from secure NIS networks.
-l	Converts all keys to lowercase.
--version	Shows version information.

File Name:	`makedbm`	**Directory:** /usr/sbin/, **Linux:** /usr/lib/yp/ **Type:** External
Common:	makedbm database.txt database.dbm	Creates a database from database.txt.
Common:	makedbm -u database.dbm	Converts the database to a pure text file and shows it on STDOUT.

makedepend

makedepend	UNIX Shell:	Shells (ash, bash, bsh, csh, ksh, sh, tcsh, zsh)
Function	Reads each specified source file in the given sequence and then parses it.	
Syntax	makedepend [options...] *file*	

-D*name*[=*def*]	Places a name definition in the symbol table. Not specifying =def the symbol becomes 1.
-I*directory*	Includes the specified directory into the search.
-Y*directory*	Replaces include directories with specified one. Only -Y: reject standard directories.
-a	Attaches, instead of replacing, dependencies to the end of the file.
-f*makefile*	Specifies a different makefile for output.
-o*suffix*	Allows specifying another suffix to an object file other than `.o`, example: .b.
-p*prefix*	Attaches a prefix to the name of an object file.
-s*string*	Permits specifying an alternate string to search for.
-v	Verbose mode. Shows more information.
-w*width*	Specifies the output line width instead of the standard 78 characters.
-m	Allows for multiple inclusion warnings.
--*modifier*--	Ignores the arguments or executes the options found in-between the double hyphens --.
files...	Specifies the files to use.

File Name:	`makedepend`	**Directory:**	**AIX:** /usr/bin/X11/, **BSD, Linux:**, **Solaris:** /usr/openwin/bin/	**Type:**	External
BUG:	Doesn't evaluate SVR4 token list expressions. All expressions are assumed to be true, which may cause incorrect include directives assessment.				
Common:	makedepend helloworld.c	Makes dependencies on helloworld.c.			
Common:	makedepend -fout.c helloworld.c	Writes the output to out.c.			

makewhatis

makewhatis	UNIX Shell:	Shells (ash, bash, bsh, csh, ksh, sh, tcsh, zsh)
Function	Updates the `whatis` database.	
Syntax	AIX, BSD: makewhatis Linux: makewhatis [options...] *{ manpath }* Solaris: makewhatis *manpath*	

Linux:	
-u	Updates the database with new pages.
-v	Verbose mode. Shows more information.
-w	Uses the manpath given by `man --path`.
-c *{ catpath }*	Specifies the top directory of the cat pages to update.
manpath	Specifies the top directory of the man pages to update.
Solaris:	
manpath	Specifies the top directory of the man pages to update.

File Name:	`makewhatis`	**Directory:**	**AIX:** /usr/lbin/, **BSD:** /usr/libexec/, **Linux:** /usr/sbin/, **Solaris:** /usr/lib/	**Type:**	Script
Linux:	makewhatis -v	Updates the whatis database for manpages in verbose mode.			
OpenBSD:	makewhatis	Updates the whatis database for manpages.			
Solaris:	makewhatis /usr/man	Updates the whatis database for manpages under /usr/man.			

man

man	UNIX Shell:	Shells (ash, bash, bsh, csh, ksh, sh, tcsh, zsh)
Function	Shows the manual page of the specified command.	
Syntax	man [options...] *{ section } names...* AIX: man [options...] *{ section }* [options...] *names...*	

AIX:	**The -c and -t options must be set before the section.**
-c	Uses the `cat` command to show information.
-t	Formats the information to fit the `troff` command.

continued

	The following options must be set after the section.
-k	Shows all available man pages about the specified keyword. Cannot be use with -f.
-f	Locates manual pages related to the file. Cannot be use with -k.
-M*path*	Specifies a new search path for manual pages.
section	Specifies a section string telling which sections to search.
C	Specifies commands.
F	Specifies file-types.
L	Specifies library functions.
n	Specifies new.
l	Specifies local.
o	Specifies old.
p	Specifies public.
names...	A keyword or the name of a standard utility.
BSD:	
-a	Shows all pages matching the name (default is to show the first only).
-c	Writes the information raw to STDOUT, instead of using the `more` command.
-h	Shows only the synopsis lines of the matching pages.
-w	Shows the directory where the page was found.
-C *file*	Uses the specified file as configuration file, instead of the default.
-M *directory*	Specifies a new search path for manual pages (separate with : for multiple directories).
-m *directory*	Adds the directory to the default search path (separate with : for multiple directories).
-s *section*	Specifies a section string telling which sections to search.
-S *subsection*	Specifies the machine-dependent subsection.
section	Specifies a section string telling which sections to search.
names...	A keyword or the name of a standard utility.
Linux:	
-a	Shows all pages matching the name (default is to show the first only).
-c	Forces a reformat on the source man page.
-d	Shows debug information.
-f	Makes equivalent to `whatis`.
-F	Formats the page without showing it.
-h	Shows help information.
-k	Makes equivalent to `apropos`.
-K	Searches in all man pages for match.
-t	Runs `groff -Tps -mandoc` to format the page.
-w	Shows only the location of the found page.
-W	Is like -w, but shows more information on each page.
-m *system*	Specifies the system to redirect the search path to the appropriate system.
-p *string*	Specifies preprocess arguments to run before running `nroff` or `troff`.
-C *file*	Specifies the config file to use (default is `/etc/man/config`).
-M *path*	Specifies the list of directories to search for man pages.
-P *pager*	Sets which pager to use.
-S *section*	Specifies a section string telling which sections to search.
section	Specifies a section string telling which sections to search.
name	A keyword or the name of a standard utility.
Solaris:	
-a	Shows all manual pages like `name` in the MANPATH search path.
-d	Shows what a section-specifier asseses, method for searching, and search paths.
-F	Searches all directories specified by MANPATH or the `man.cf` file.
-l	Shows all manual pages found in the search path, matching the given `name`.
-r	Reformats the manual page without showing it.
-t	Arranges the manual pages in a format suitable for the troff editor.
-M *path*	Specifies a new search path for manual pages. Must be first if used with -f or -k.
-T *macro-package*	Uses macro-package instead of the standard macros.
-s *section*	Specifies the section to search for `name` (default is `man.cf` file).
-k *keyword*	Shows all available man pages about the specified keyword.
-f *file*	Locates manual pages related to the file.

continued

- *name*		Pipes output through cat instead of more -s. A keyword or the name of a standard utility.			
File Name:	man	**Directory:**	/usr/bin/	**Type:**	External
Note:	Sorry, man. Now you are only the SECOND best UNIX manual.				
Common:	man printf	Shows the manual page on `printf`.			
Linux:	man -w printf	Tells where the printf documentation is found.			
OpenBSD:	man -C myconfig printf	Configures the man page based on the specified config file.			
Solaris:	man -s3C printf	Shows section 3C of printf `printf(3C)`.			

mesg

UNIX Shell: Shells (ash, bash, bsh, csh, ksh, sh, tcsh, zsh)

Function	Allows or disallows messages to be sent to your terminal.				
Syntax	mesg [option]				
n y		Disallows other users to send or receive messages. Allows other users to send or receive messages.			
File Name:	mesg	**Directory:**	/usr/bin/	**Type:**	External
Tip:	Set mesg to yes if you want to use commands like `talk` and `write`.				
Common:	mesg n	Sets message function to no (deny).			
Common:	mesg y	Sets message function to yes (allow).			
Common:	mesg	Shows current mesg setting.			

mkdir

UNIX Shell: Shells (ash, bash, bsh, csh, ksh, sh, tcsh, zsh)

Function	Creates directories.				
Syntax	mkdir [options...] *directories...*				
-m *mode* -p *directories...* **Linux:** -v --help --version		Sets the permission to the specified mode for the new directories. Creates the directory and all non-existing parent directories. Specifies the name of directories to be created. Shows verbose information. Shows help information. Shows version information.			
File Name:	mkdir	**Directory:**	/usr/bin/, **BSD, Linux:** /bin/	**Type:**	External
Common:	mkdir /export/home/anders	Make the directory /export/home/anders.			
Common:	mkdir -m 644 /anders	Make the directory /anders with permission 644.			

mkdirhier

UNIX Shell: Shells (ash, bash, bsh, csh, ksh, sh, tcsh, zsh)

Function	Creates the specified directories including any unspecified parent directories as well.				
Syntax	mkdirhier *directories...*				
directories...		Specifies the directory and parent directories to create.			
File Name:	mkdirhier	**Directory:**	**AIX:** /usr/bin/X11/, **BSD, Linux:** /usr/X11R6/bin/, **Solaris:** /usr/openwin/bin/	**Type:**	Script
Common:	mkdirhier dir1/dir2	Creates the directories: dir1 and dir2 within the directory dir1.			

mkfifo

UNIX Shell: Shells (ash, bash, bsh, csh, ksh, sh, tcsh, zsh)

Function	Creates the FIFO special files specified by the paths and filenames on the command line.	
Syntax	mkfifo [-m] *{ files... }*	
-m *mode* *files...* **Linux:** --help --version		Specifies the file's permission bits on the created file. Specifies the files to create. Shows help information. Shows version information.

continued

File Name:	mkfifo	**Directory:**	/usr/bin/	**Type:**	External
Common:	mkfifo fifofile		Creates a FIFOfile named fifofile in current directory.		
Common:	mkfifo -m 777 fifo		Creates a FIFOfile named fifo with the mode 777.		

mkfontdir

UNIX Shell: Shells (ash, bash, bsh, csh, ksh, sh, tcsh, zsh)

Function	Creates an index file from any X font files found in a directory. It typically looks for .pcf, .snf, and .bdf fonts and then creates the file `fonts.dir` in the same specified directory.
Syntax	mkfontdir *{ directory }* Linux: mkfontdir [options...] *{ directory }*

directory	Specifies the directory to search for fonts. (For scalable fonts, use the file fonts.scale to create fonts.dir.)
Linux:	
-r	Doesn't convert the directory to its absolute address.
-p *prefix*	Specifies a prefix that is added to the beginning of the encoding file pathname.
-e *name*	Specifies a directory of encoding files.
--	Disables options after these signs.

File Name:	mkfontdir	**Directory:**	**AIX:** /usr/bin/X11/, **BSD, Linux:** /usr/X11R6/bin/, **Solaris:** /usr/openwin/bin/	**Type:**	External
Common:	mkfontdir		Creates a folder named fonts.dir in your home directory.		
Linux:	mkfontdir /usr/share/fonts		Searches the directory /usr/share/fonts for fonts.		

mknetid

UNIX Shell: Shells (ash, bash, bsh, csh, ksh, sh, tcsh, zsh)

Function	Creates the NIS netid map called netid.byname using the contents of the `hosts`, `passwd`, `group` and netid files.
Syntax	mknetid [options...]

-q	Activates quiet mode which suppresses entries.
-h *file*	Specifies the host's file. (Default is /etc/hosts.)
-p *file*	Specifies the password file. (Default is /etc/passwd.)
-g *file*	Specifies the group file. (Default is /etc/group.)
AIX, BSD, Solaris:	
-m *file*	Specifies the netid file. (Default is /etc/netid.)
-d *domain*	**BSD only:** Specifies the domain name to set.
Linux:	
-d *domain*	Specifies the domain name. Use this to specify a new domain or to set the current one.
-n *file*	Specifies the netid file. (Default is /etc/netid.)
--version	Shows version information.

File Name:	mknetid	**Directory:**	/usr/sbin/, **Linux:** /usr/lib/yp/	**Type:**	External
Common:	mknetid		Creates a map with default files.		
Common:	mknetid -h myhosts -g mygroups		Creates a map with other host and group files set.		
Common:	mknetid -q		Hides warning messages if something is wrong.		
AIX:	mknetid -m mynetid		Creates a map with another netid file set.		
Linux:	mknetid -n mynetid		Creates a map with another netid file set.		

mknod

UNIX Shell: Shells (ash, bash, bsh, csh, ksh, sh, tcsh, zsh)

Function	Creates a directory entry for a specified special file.
Syntax	mknod *name* option *{ major minor }*

b *major minor*	Creates a block-type special file.
c *major minor*	Creates a character-type special file.
p	Creates a FIFO special file (named pipe).
major	Specifies the major device number.
minor	Specifies (as a superuser only) the octal or decimal number of the minor device.
name	Specifies the name of the special file to create. (The major and minor numbers are always interpreted by the local kernel.)

continued

BSD:	
-m *mode*	Specifies the mode for the file.
Linux:	
-m *mode*	Specifies the mode for the file.
--help	Shows help information.
--version	Shows version information.

File Name:	`mknod`	**Directory:**	**AIX, Solaris:** /usr/sbin/, **BSD:** /sbin/, **Linux:** /bin/	**Type:**	External
Tip:	It is preferable to create a symbolic link to the physical names of devices.				
Common:	mknod fifofile p	Creates a FIFO file named fifofile.			
Linux:	mknod hda1 b 3 1	Creates the hda1 device with major number 3 and minor number 1.			

more

UNIX Shell: Shells (ash, bash, bsh, csh, ksh, sh, tcsh, zsh)

Function	Shows a text file one page at a time. Continues reading files specified on the command line.
Syntax	more [options...] *{ files... }*

-c	Clears the screen every time a new page is to be shown.
-d	Shows error messages on the screen instead of ringing the terminal bell.
-s	Replaces multiple blank lines with a single blank line.
-u	Doesn't generate escape sequences that might be created for underlining.
-u	Shows backspaces as printable control characters.
files...	Specifies the file or files to show.
AIX:	
-e	Exits automatically after showing the last in the file.
-i	Ignores case mismatch when searching for patterns.
-l	Pauses after detecting a page break in the input.
-N	Hides line numbers.
-v	Doesn't do translations on nonprinting characters.
-z	Translates Tabs, backspaces, and returns to their names.
-n *number*	Specifies the count of lines per page to view.
-p *command*	Specifies a subcommand to run on start.
-t *string*	Shows a page of the file containing the specified tag.
-W *option*	Provides extra options.
notite	Prevents from sending the terminal initialization string.
tite	Sends the terminal initialization string (default).
-x *value*	Sets the Tab space (default is 8).
BSD:	
	To reset options to default values, type a -+ instead of - in the option.
-a	Starts searches on the last shown line (default is to start on first shown line).
-B	Allocates only buffers defined with -b.
-C	Is like -c, but clears the screen before rewriting it.
-e	Exits automatically after showing the last line twice in the file.
-E	Exits automatically after showing the last line in the file.
-f	Forces open files that aren't actually files (like directories or devices).
-g	Highlights only the particular string found in a search and skips other matches.
-G	Doesn't highlight.
-i	Ignores case mismatch when searching for patterns.
-I	Is like -i, but will also ignore cases typed in the search string.
-m	Shows the position in the file in percent.
-M	Verbose mode. Shows more information.
-n	Hides line numbers.
-N	Shows the line number left to each line.
-q	Quiet mode. Doesn't do sound on attempts to scroll beyond end of file.
-Q	Quieter mode. Doesn't do sound at all.
-r	Shows the control characters as readable text.
-S	Truncates lines longer than the screen, instead of making multiple lines.
-U	Shows backspaces and carriage returns as text.
-V	Shows version information.

continued

-w	Shows blank lines after end of file (default is ~).
-X	Doesn't send termcap initialization.
-?	Shows help information.
-b *size*	Specifies the maximum buffer size for each file.
-h *lines*	Specifies the maximum number of lines to scroll backwards.
-j *position*	Specifies the column position to put the target line on.
-k*file*	Opens the specified file as a lesskey file.
-o*file*	Copies the formated input to the specified file.
-p*pattern*	Starts in the file where something matches the specified pattern.
-P*prompt*	Changes the prompt styles for the short prompt. (Begin with m to change the medium prompt, and M for the long.)
-t*tag*	Edits the file containing the specified tag. (Works only if a file called tags exists.)
-T*file*	Specifies an alternate tag file instead of `tags`.
-x*tab*	Specifies the Tab space (default is 8).
-y*lines*	Specifies the maximum number of lines to scroll forward, before rewriting the screen.
-z*lines*	Specifies the amount of lines to show at one time.
+*command*	Specifies a subcommand to run at start.
Linux:	
-l	Doesn't pause on form feeds.
-f	Counts only lines turning to multiple lines as one line.
-p	Doesn't scroll. Rewrites the screen every time a change appears.
-*value*	Specifies the amount of lines to show at one time.
+/ *pattern*	Starts in the file where something matches the specified pattern.
+ *number*	Specifies the line number to begin at on start.
Solaris:	
-f	Prints lines containing nonprinting characters or escape sequences.
-l	Doesn't treat usual formfeed characters as page breaks.
-r	Shows the control characters as readable text.
-w	Doesn't quit before a keypress on end of file.
-*lines*	Shows the count of lines specified as one page.
+ *number*	Starts showing text at the specified line number.
+/*pattern*	Starts showing text from two lines above the line containing the pattern.
	When using `/usr/xpg4/bin/more`, the following options are also available.
-n *number*	Specifies the count of lines per page to view.
-p *command*	Runs the more command specified when you start more.
-t *string*	Shows a page of the file containing the tag specified.
-e	Exits more directly after showing the last in the file.
-i	Ignores case mismatch when searching for patterns.

File Name:	`more`	**Directory:**	/usr/bin/, **Linux:** /bin/	**Type:**	External
Common:	more -c topsecret.txt	Clears screen and shows messages.			
Common:	more topsecret.txt	Shows messages.			
Linux:	more +/ password topsecret.txt	Jumps to the first line containing the string "password."			

mount

UNIX Shell: Shells (ash, bash, bsh, csh, ksh, sh, tcsh, zsh)

Function	Mounts a file system or shows a file system that is already mounted. The file system can be local or remote.
Syntax	mount [options...] *mountpoint* mount -a [options...] mount [options...] *device mountpoint* mount [options...] *host:directory mountpoint*

mountpoint	Specifies where to mount the file system.
AIX:	
-a	Mounts the file systems configured in the `/etc/filesystems` file. (You can't specify a special device when you use -a.)
-f	Forces a mount during system initialization to mount over the root file system.
-n *node*	Uses the specified remote node that contains the directory to be mounted.

continued

-o *fsspecific*	Specifies a comma-separated list of options to use while mounting file systems.
bsy	Doesn't mount directory that is the current working directory of a process.
log=*lvname*	Specifies the path to the file system logging logical volume.
nodev	Disables the possibility to open devices while mounting.
nosuid	Disables set-uid execution.
ro	Mounts read-only.
rw	Mounts read-write.
	The following options are NFS-specific.
bg	Mounts in the background if the first attempt failed.
fg	Mounts in the foreground even if the first attempt failed.
vers=*nfsversion*	Specifies NFS version to use. Valid versions are 2 or 3.
proto=*protocol*	Specifies protocol to use when mounting. Valid protocols are UDP or TCP.
retry=*number*	Tries to mount the specified file system for the specified amount of time.
rsize=*number*	Specifies the read buffer size to use (default is 8192).
wsize=*number*	Specifies the write buffer size to use (default is 8192).
llock	Specifies that files should lock locally at the NFS client.
timeo=*number*	Specifies number of tenths per second for the NFS timeout to use.
retrans=*number*	Specifies how many NFS transmissions to do (default is 3).
port=*port*	Specifies port to connect to on the server.
soft	Shows an error message if the server was unreachable.
hard	Doesn't give up a connect against the NFS server.
intr	Accepts keyboard interrupts on hard mounts.
nointr	Denies keyboard interrupts on hard mounts.
posix	Makes pathconf information available on a NFS version 2 mount.
secure	Uses the DES for NFS transactions.
grpid	The file or directory that created the group ID that the parent directory have.
acl	Uses the AIX Access Control List RPC program when mounting.
noacl	Doesn't use the AIX Access Control List RPC program when mounting.
noac	Doesn't use any attribute or directory caching.
shortdev	Tells the remote server that the client doesn't support 32-bit device special files.
actimeo=*number*	Specifies maximum and minimum times for regular files and directories.
acregmin=*number*	Specifies the minimum time to store cached attributes after a file modification.
acregmax=*number*	Specifies the maximum time to store cached attributes after a file modification.
acdirmin=*number*	Specifies the minimum time to store cached attributes after a directory update.
acdirmax=*seconds*	Specifies the maximum time to store cached attributes after a directory update.
	The following options are CacheFS-specific.
backfstype=*type*	Specifies the back file system type to use.
backpath=*path*	Specifies the mount point of the premounted back file system.
cachedir=*directory*	Specifies the name of the cache directory.
cacheid=*ID*	Specifies the instance of a cache.
write-around	Writes to the back file system and purges the file from the cache.
non-shared	Doesn't write to the cache file system if someone else is writing to it.
noconst	Turns off the cache consistency checking.
local_access	Lets the front file system interpret the mode bits while access checking.
purge	Drops all cached information for the specified file system.
suid	Enables set-uid execution.
-p	Mounts the file system as a removable file system.
-r	Mounts the file system as read-only.
-t *type*	Specifies type attribute to match in `/etc/filesystems` and mount.
-v *vfsname*	Checks in `/etc/vfs` whether the file system is defined by the specified name.
BSD:	
-A	Mounts the file systems configured in the `/etc/fstab` file. (Entries with the option noauto aren't mounted with -A.)
-a	Works like -A except that file system that is already mounted won't be mounted again.
-d	Performs all mount steps but the invocation of the file system specific program.
-f	Revokes the write access when mounting read-write to read-only.
-o *fsspecific*	Specifies a comma-separated list of options to use while mounting file systems.

continued

async	Forces all the I/O to the file system to be done asynchronously.
force	Revokes the write access when mounting read-write to read-only.
noatime	Updates access time on files if modification time or change time has changed.
noaccesstime	Updates access time on files if modification time or change time has changed.
nodev	Disables the possibility to open devices while mounting.
noexec	Disables the possibility to execute binaries on the file system.
nosuid	Disables set-uid execution.
rdonly	Mounts the file system as read-only.
sync	Forces all the I/O to the file system to be done synchronously.
update	Alters the status of a mounted file system.
union	Uses the mount point namespace to appear as the union of the mounted file system root.
-r	Mounts the file system as read-only.
-t *type*	Specifies a comma-separated list of type attribute to match in /etc/fstab and mount.
-u	Alters the status of a mounted file system.
-v	Verbose mode. Shows more information.
-w	Sets the file system option to be read and write.
Linux:	
-a	Mounts the file systems configured in the `/etc/fstab` file.
-F	Mounts the devices in the background so all mounts will be done parallel.
-f	Fakes a mount. Runs all steps but the actual system call.
-l	Shows the ext2 labels when showing the mounted file systems.
-n	Mounts a file system without writing to `/etc/mtab`.
-s	Allows the sloppy options being sent to the file system.
-r	Mounts the file system as read-only.
-w	Sets the file system option to be read and write.
-L *label*	Specifies a label to match on a file system to mount.
-U *UserID*	Specifies a UserID to mount the file system as. (For - U to work you need a kernel version newer than 2.2.116.)
-t *type*	Specifies a comma-separated list of type attribute to match in /etc/fstab and mount.
-o *fsspecific*	Specifies a comma-separated list of options to use while mounting file systems.
async	Forces all the I/O to the file system to be done asynchronously.
atime	Alters the inode access time for each access.
auto	Marks the file system to be mounted with -a.
defaults	Enables default options.
dev	Use character or block special devices on the file system.
exec	Allows execution of binaries found on the file system mounted.
noatime	Doesn't update the inode access time on the mounted file system.
nodev	Disables the possibility to open devices while mounting.
noexec	Disables the possibility to execute binaries on the file system.
nosuid	Disables set-uid execution.
nouser	Doesn't let other users than root mount the specified file system.
remount	Remounts a file system that has already been mounted.
ro	Mounts read-only.
rw	Mounts read-only.
suid	Enables set-uid execution.
sync	Forces all the I/O to the file system to be done synchronously.
user	Lets users other than root mount the specified file system.
	The following options are `ext2`-specific.
bsddf	Shows status for the file system in the bsd default way.
minixdf	Shows status for the file system in the minix way.
check=*level*	Specifies the checking level to use. The levels are listed below:
normal	Checks inodes and blocks bitmaps on mount.
strict	Runs a block deallocation check to free the block in the data zone.
none	Doesn't run any file system checking.
nocheck	Doesn't run any file system checking.
debug	Shows debugging information when mounting or remounting.
errors=*solution*	Specifies action if an error has occurred.

continued

continue	Continues without acting on the error.
remount-ro	Remounts the file system with the read-only flag.
panic	Causes the system to halt.
grpid	Sets the GroupID to the file from the directory it was created in.
resgid=*number*	Specifies groupID that can use the reserved percentage of the file system.
resuid=*number*	Specifies userID that can use the reserved percentage of the file system.
sb=*number*	Specifies which block should be the super block.
	The following options are `FAT`-specific.
blocksize=*size*	Specifies block size to use. Valid block sizes are: 512, 1024 or 2048.
uid=*UserID*	Specifies user that should own the files on the file system.
gid=*GroupID*	Specifies group that should own the files on the file system.
umask=*mask*	Specifies umask to use when mounting.
check=*type*	Specifies pickyness to use.
relaxed	Processes upper- and lowercase. Long names will be truncated.
normal	Works like the relaxed type, except that special characters are rejected.
strict	Works like the normal type, except that long parts or special characters are rejected.
codepage=*codepage*	Specifies codepage to use when converting shortname characters.
debug	Shows debug information.
fat=*number*	Specifies `FAT` bit to use. Valid are: 12, 16, or 32.
quiet	Doesn't return errors when trying to chown or chmod files.
	The following options are `ISO9660`-specific.
norock	Doesn't use Rock Ridge extensions.
uid=*UserID*	Specifies user that should own the files on the file system.
gid=*GroupID*	Specifies group that should own the files on the file system.
unhide	Shows files that are hidden and associated.
block=*number*	Specifies block size to use: Valid block sizes are: 5120, 1024, and 2048.
	The following options are `NFS`-specific.
rsize=*number*	Specifies the read buffer size to use (default is 8192).
wsize=*number*	Specifies the write buffer size to use (default is 8192).
timeo=*number*	Specifies number of tenths per second the `NFS` timeout is to use.
retrans=*number*	Specifies how many `NFS` transmissions to do (default is 3).
acregmin=*number*	Specifies the minimum time to store cached attributes after a file modification.
acregmax=*number*	Specifies the maximum time to store cached attributes after a file modification.
acdirmin=*number*	Specifies the minimum time to store cached attributes after a directory update.
acdirmax=*seconds*	Specifies the maximum time to store cached attributes after a directory update.
actimeo=*number*	Specifies maximum and minimum times for regular files and directories.
retry=*number*	Tries to mount the specified file system for the specified amount of time.
port=*port*	Specifies port to connect to on the server.
soft	Shows an error message if the server was unreachable.
hard	Doesn't give up a connect against the `NFS` server.
nolock	Disables locking.
	The following options are *UFS*-specific.
ufstype=*type*	Specifies type of ufs to mount.
old	Uses the old format of ufs.
44bsd	Uses the BSD ufs.
sun	Uses the SunOS or Solaris implementations on SPARC systems.
sunx86	Uses the SunOS implementations on an x86 system.
nextstep	Uses the NeXTStep implementations on a NeXT station.
nextstep-cd	Uses the NeXTStep CD-ROM's implementations.
openstep	Uses the OpenStep implementations.
	The following option are `LOOP` device-specific.
loop=*device*	Specifies loop device to use when mounting loopback devices.
Solaris:	
-a	Mounts all file systems from `/etc/vfstab` that are marked mount at boot.
-F *fstype*	Specifies the file system type that you want to mount NFS, UFS, HSFS, etc.
-m	Mounts the file system without editing the `/etc/mnttab` file.
-r	Mounts the file system in read-only mode.

continued

-o *fsspecific*	Specifies a comma-separated list of options to use while mounting file systems.
noatime	Doesn't record access time.
f	Creates an entry in the `/etc/mnttab` file but doesn't mount the file system.
intr	Accepts keyboard interrupts on hard mounts.
nointr	Denies keyboard interrupts on hard mounts.
logging	Logs file system changes.
nologging	Doesn't log file system changes.
onerror=*ACTION*	Specifies action if an error occurs. Valid actions are: panic, lock, or umount.
quota	Sets quotas for the file system.
remount	Remounts a read-only file system as a read-write file system.
rq	Sets read-write and quota at the same time.
ro	Mounts read-only.
rw	Mounts read-write.
suid	Enables set-uid execution.
nosuid	Disables set-uid execution.
-O	Mounts the file system over an existing mountpoint.
-V	Shows what the command would do without executing it.
-p	Shows all mounted FS from `/etc/vfstab`.
-v	Verbose mode. Shows more information.

File Name:	mount	**Directory:**	**AIX, Solaris:** /usr/sbin/, **BSD:** /sbin/, **Linux:** /bin/	**Type:**	External

Common:	mount /usr/home	Mounts the home partition. The mountpoint must exist in the file system configuration file.
Common:	mount 192.168.1.10:/usr/home /usr/home	Mounts a remote home directory.
AIX:	mount -o ro /dev/hd1 /usr/home	Mounts the home directory without write access.
Linux:	mount install.iso /mnt -o loop -t iso9660	Mounts an iso file system over the loopback device.
OpenBSD:	mount -A	Mounts all mountable devices specified in `/etc/fstab` except those marked with noauto.
Solaris:	mount -V -v /usr/home	Shows a verbose output of what the program is doing without mounting the directory.

mountd, rpc.mountd

UNIX Shell: Shells (ash, bash, bsh, csh, ksh, sh, tcsh, zsh)

Function	Answers file system mount requests and NFS access information checks.
Syntax	AIX, Linux: rpc.mountd [options...] BSD: mountd [options...] *exportfile* Solaris: mountd [options...]

AIX:	
-n	Provides support for clients using older versions of NFS to be able to connect.
BSD:	
-d	Enables debug mode and sends debug information to STDERR.
-n	Allows clients (usually PCs) to mount requests from non-reserved ports.
exportfile	Specifies a different location for the exports file.
Linux:	
-N	Provides support for clients using older versions of NFS to be able to connect.
-v	Shows version information.
Solaris:	
-v	Verbose mode. Shows more information.
-r	Rejects mount requests from clients that don't have their file systems mounted.

continued

File Name:	mountd, **AIX, Linux:** rpc.mountd	**Directory:**	**AIX, Linux:** /usr/sbin/, **BSD:** /sbin/, **Solaris:** /usr/lib/nfs/	**Type:**	External
Warning:	BSD: If you use the -n option, it creates many security problems. Avoid using it if you can.				
Common:	mountd	Starts the server.			
AIX:	startsrc -s rpc.mountd	Starts the rpc.mountd daemon.			
Linux:	rpc.mountd -N	Starts the rpc.mountd daemon and provides support for older clients.			
OpenBSD:	mountd -d	Starts the mountd daemon.			

mt

UNIX Shell: Shells (ash, bash, bsh, csh, ksh, sh, tcsh, zsh)

Function	Sends commands to a tape device.
Syntax	mt [-f *device*] *commands... { count }*

-f *device*	Specifies the raw tape device to use. If not given, uses the default one.
count	Specifies the number of times a command should be run.
	The following are commands that can be sent to the magnetic tape device.
eof	Writes count of EOF marks at the current position on the tape.
fsf	Jumps over count of EOF marks. Tape will be placed on the first block of file.
fsr	Jumps over count of records.
bsf	Jumps back count of EOF marks. Tape will be placed on the last block of previous file.
bsr	Jumps back count of records.
rewind	Rewinds the specified magnetic tape.
rewoffl	Same as offline command, means rewind then offline.
status	Reports status information about the tape device.
BSD:	
eom	Jumps to the next unused part of the tape.
blocksize	Sets the block size for the tape to count.
density	Sets the density code to count as specified in the SCSI-2 specification.
offline	Rewinds the specified magnetic tape and brings the device offline (ejects the tape).
retension	Adds tension to the tape through rewinding and fast forwarding functions.
erase	Empties the tape of data.
Linux:	
-h	Shows help information.
-v	Shows version information.
fsfm	Jumps over count of EOF marks. Tape will be placed on the last block of previous file.
bsfm	Jumps back count of EOF marks. Tape will be placed on the first block of next file.
asf	Rewinds the tape and jumps count of files.
eod	Moves to the end of valid data.
offline	Rewinds the specified magnetic tape and brings the device offline (ejects the tape).
retension	Adds tension to the tape through rewinding and fast forwarding functions.
erase	Empties the tape of data.
	The following subcommands can only be used with a SCSI tape:
fss	Jumps over count of set marks.
bss	Jumps back count of set marks.
wset	Writes count set marks to the tape.
seek	Moves to the count block on the tape as gotten from an earlier tell command.
tell	Shows the current block on the tape.
setpartition	Changes to the partition count.
partseek	Moves the tape to block count in partition given by argument.
mkpartition	Makes one (count = 0) or two (count = size of second partition in MB) partitions.
load	Loads the tape into the drive.
lock	Locks the drive door.
unlock	Unlocks the drive door.
setblk	Specifies the block size to count bytes per record.
setdensity	Specifies the density code for the drive to count.
densities	Shows explanation of some density codes.

continued

drvbuffer	Specifies the drive buffer code to count.
compression	Specifies the compression.
	The following commands can only be used by superuser.
stoptions	Alters the driver option bits.
buffer-writes	Enables the buffered write.
async-writes	Enables asynchronous writes.
read-ahead	Uses read-ahead for fixed block size.
debug	Shows debug information.
two-fms	Writes two filemarks when closing a file.
fast-eod	Moves fast to eod (will lose file count).
auto-lock	Automatically locks and unlocks the driver door.
def-writes	Specifies the block size and density are for write.
can-bsr	Specifies the drive can space backwards.
no-blklimits	Specifies the drive doesn't support read block limits.
can-partitions	Specifies the drive can handle partitions.
scsi2logical	Uses SCSI-2 logical addresses instead of drive dependent.
sysv	Enables System V semantics.
stsetoptions	Sets the driver option bits. Please see stoptions for options.
stclearoptions	Clears the drive option bits. Please see stoptions for options.
stwrthreshold	Specifies the write threshold to count kilobytes.
defblksize	Sets the default block size to count bytes.
defdensity	Sets the default density code to count.
defdrvbuffer	Sets the default drive buffer code to count.
defcompression	Sets the default drive compression state.
sttimeout	Sets the normal timeout to count seconds.
stlongtimeout	Sets the long timeout to count seconds.
datcompression	Tells if the data compression will be used (count = 0 | OFF to disable).
Solaris:	
nbsf	Jumps back *amount* of files. Tape will be placed on the first block of the file.
asf	Rewinds the tape and jumps `amount` of files.
eom	Jumps to the next unused part of the tape.
offline	Rewinds the specified magnetic tape and brings the device offline (ejects the tape).
reserve	Reserves the tape device after closing it. To use it again it must be released.
release	Releases the tape device after having it reserved.
forcereserve	Breaks other reserves by other hosts and reserves it.
erase	Empties the tape of data.

File Name:	`mt`	**Directory:**	**AIX, Solaris:** /usr/sbin/, **BSD, Linux:**/bin/	**Type:**	External
Tip:	This is a useful command if you use `ufsdump` and `ufsrestore`.				
Common:	mt eof	Writes one end of file mark to the tape.			
Common:	mt rewind	Rewinds the tape in the default tape device.			
Common:	mt fsf 2	Positions the tape at the start of the third tape file.			
AIX:	mt -f /dev/rmt0.1 fsf	Moves one file forward.			
Linux:	mt -f /dev/rmt0 status	Shows the status of the first tape drive.			
OpenBSD:	mt -f /dev/rst retension	Retensions the second tape drive.			
Solaris:	mt -f /dev/rmt/0 erase	Erases the first tape drive.			

mv

UNIX Shell: Shells (ash, bash, bsh, csh, ksh, sh, tcsh, zsh)

Function	Moves or renames files and directories.
Syntax	mv [options...] *files... directory*

-f	Do not prompt even if writing over existing target. This is the default.
-i	Always prompt if target exists.
files...	Specifies the pathname to the file or directory to be moved.
directory	Specifies a new directory for the directory or file to be moved to. (Can also be a file. Can only be used if only one file or dir is used.)

continued

Linux:	
--backup=*string*	Specifies how to back up the files to move.
none	Doesn't make a backup.
numbered	Makes numbered backups.
existing	Makes numbered backups if numbered files already exist, simple if not.
simple	Makes simple backups.
-b	Is like --backup, but without arguments.
--strip-trailing-slashes	Deletes all trailing slashes from the source argument.
-S *suffix*	Specifies the backup suffix to use.
--target-directory=*directory*	Specifies the target directory as an option.
-u	Moves only older or brand-new non-directories.
-v	Verbose mode. Shows more information.
--help	Shows help information.
--version	Shows version information.

File Name:	mv	**Directory:**	/usr/bin/, **BSD, Linux:** /bin/	**Type:**	External
Common:	mv /opt/mytext.txt /ucg_examples/new.txt	Move a file to a different directory with a new name.			
Common:	mv -i /opt/text2.txt /ucg_examples	Move a file and prompt if target exists.			
Common:	mv /opt/*.txt /ucg_examples	Move all *.txt files to a different directory.			

named, in.named

UNIX Shell: Shells (ash, bash, bsh, csh, ksh, sh, tcsh, zsh)

Function	The domain name server that answers DNS requests and resolves hostnames and finds their assigned IP addresses.
Syntax	AIX, BSD: named [options...] Linux: named [options...] *{ config file }* Solaris: in.named [options...]

-b *file*	Specifies the boot file (default is /etc/named.conf).
-d *level*	Sets the level of the debug information. Higher value gives more info.
AIX:	
-p *remoteport*	Specifies the remote port to connect to.
BSD:	
-g *group*	Specifies the server's running group as a group name or a group ID.
-p *remote*/*local-port*	Specifies the remote and the local port to connect to.
-q	Tracks incoming DNS queries.
-r	Accepts DNS query answers from local zones only.
-t *directory*	Specifies a chroot directory the server will change to after startup.
-u *user*	Specifies a user as a username or userID.
Linux:	
-c *file*	Specifies the boot file (default is `/etc/named.conf`).
-f	Runs `named` in the foreground instead of as a daemon.
-g *group*	Specifies the servers running group as a groupname or a group ID.
-p *remoteport*	Specifies the remote port to connect to.
-q	Tracks incoming DNS queries.
-r	Accepts DNS query answers from local zones only.
-t *directory*	Specifies a chroot directory the server will change to after startup.
-u *user*	Specifies a user to run named as.
-v	Shows version information.
-w	Sets a new working directory for the name server.
config file	Specifies config file and overrides any setting of -b or -c options.
Solaris:	
-c *file*	The same as `-b`.
-p *remote/local-port*	Specifies the remote and the local port to connect to.
-q	Tracks incoming DNS queries.
-r	Accepts DNS query answers from local zones only.
-f	Runs `named` in the foreground instead of as a daemon.
-w *directory*	Sets a new working directory for the name server.

continued

File Name:	`named, in.named`	**Directory:**	/usr/sbin/, **Solaris:** /usr/sbin/	**Type:**	External
Note:	Solaris: For the examples below to work, you must replace named with in.named.				
Common:	named -d 11		Starts debugging with maximum debug level.		
Common:	named -b ucg.conf		Starts the name server with configuration as specified in ucg.conf.		
Linux:	named -t /var/named -u named -g named -c /var/named/named.conf		Runs the name server in the specified chrooted directory.		
Solaris:	in.named -q		Starts the name server, tracking incoming DNS queries.		

netstat

UNIX Shell: Shells (ash, bash, bsh, csh, ksh, sh, tcsh, zsh)

Function	Shows statistics and other network information, based on options selected.
Syntax	netstat [options...] netstat [options...]

-a	Shows status for all routing tables and sockets.
-n	Shows network numbers instead of symbols.
-r	Shows the routing tables.
-s	Shows statistics for each protocol.
AIX:	
-A	Shows addresses of protocol control blocks and the sockets they are using.
-c	Shows the status of the network buffer cache.
-D	Shows total number of packets sent, received, and dropped in the network subsystem.
-f *address_family*	Specifies the address family to report statistics on. See below for valid values. **Supported address families are:** inet, inet6, ns, unix
-i	Shows the status of currently configured interfaces.
-I *interface*	Shows the status of the specified interface.
-m	Shows saved statistics generated by memory management routines.
-p *protocol*	Shows network statistics for protocol or protocol alias specified.
-P	Shows statistics for Data Link Provider Interface.
-ss	Shows network statistics for all active protocols in a short, concise display.
-u	Shows domain socket information.
-v	Shows statistics for CDLI communication adapters.
-Zc	Clears network buffer statistics.
-Zi	Clears statistics on network interfaces.
-Zm	Clears statistics for network memory allocation.
-Zs	Clears all protocol statistics. To clear a specific protocol, use the -p option.
-p *protocol*	Clears statistics for a specific protocol (i.e. `netstat -Zs -p udp`).
BSD:	
-A	Shows addresses of protocol control blocks and the sockets they are using.
-d	Shows the number of dropped packets. Must be used with the -i or interval option.
-f *address_family*	Specifies the address family to report statistics on. See below for valid values. **Supported address families are:** inet, ipx, atalk, ns, iso, encap, local, unix.
-g	Shows multicast group membership for all interfaces.
-i	Shows the status of network interfaces that have been configured automatically.
-I *interfaces*	Shows state for a specific interface.
-m	Shows saved statistics generated by memory management routines.
-M *core*	Specifies an alternate core file to read information from. (Default is `/dev/kmem`.)
-N *system*	Specifies an alternate system file to extract the name list instead of `/bsd`.
-p *protocol*	Shows network statistics for protocol or protocol alias specified.
-v	Verbose mode. Shows more information. (This option is currently unavailable.)
-w *time*	Specifies the time interval to show network interface statistics.
Linux:	
-A *address_family*	Specifies the address family to report statistics on. See below for valid values. **Supported address families are:** inet, unix, ipx, ax25, netrom, ddp
-c	Shows continuous network status information updating every second.
-C	Shows routing information from the routing cache.
-e	Shows extended information and will show twice as much information.
-F	Shows routing information from the FIB (Forward Information Base).
-g	Shows multicast group membership for all interfaces.

continued

-i *{ interface }*	Shows the status of all interfaces or just the specified interface.
-L	Shows only ports used for listening. These ports aren't shown by default.
-M	Shows all masqueraded connections.
-o	Shows network timer information.
-p *program*	Shows the PID and the socket for the program specified.
-v	Verbose mode. Shows more information.
Solaris:	
-d	Shows the state for all DHCP interfaces.
-D	Shows status for interfaces that is configured with DHCP.
-f *address_family*	Specifies the address family to report statistics on. See below for valid values. **Solaris 7:** Supported address families are AF_INET, AF_UNIX. **Solaris 8:** Supported address families are AF_INET, AF_INET6, AF_UNIX.
-g	Shows multicast group membership for all interfaces.
-i	Shows the state for TCP/IP interfaces.
interval	Shows information for an interval in seconds; repeats until it gets a break signal.
-I *interfaces*	Shows state for a specific interface.
-m	Shows statistics for STREAMS.
-M	Shows multicast routing tables; multicast routing statistics with -s option.
-p	Shows the ARP tables.
-P *protocol*	Shows statistics of all sockets for protocol specified.
-v	Verbose mode. Shows more information.

File Name:	netstat	**Directory:**	/usr/bin/, **Linux:** /bin	**Type:**	External
Note:	Very useful command to verify network interface status.				
Common:	netstat -a	Shows status of all sockets and routing tables.			
Common:	netstat -r	Shows the routing table.			
AIX:	netstat -D	Shows the totals for packets sent, received, and dropped.			
OpenBSD:	netstat -f inet	Shows all active ip connections.			
Solaris:	netstat -i	Shows status for interfaces that use TCP/IP.			

newaliases

UNIX Shell: Shells (ash, bash, bsh, csh, ksh, sh, tcsh, zsh)

Function	Rebuilds the mail aliases file.				
Syntax	newaliases				
File Name:	newaliases	**Directory:**	/usr/bin/	**Type:**	External
Note:	Automatically invoked by sendmail, but you can use the same options as for the sendmail command.				

nfsd, rpc.nfsd

UNIX Shell: Shells (ash, bash, bsh, csh, ksh, sh, tcsh, zsh)

Function	Manages NFS file system requests for clients.
Syntax	AIX: nfsd [options...] *number* BSD: nfsd [options...] Linux: rpc.nfsd [-p *port*] *number* Solaris: nfsd [options...] *{ number }*

AIX:	
-a	Starts an NFS daemon over all TCP and udp connections. Not usable with -p.
-p *protocol*	Starts an NFS daemon using the specified TCP or udp protocol. Not usable with -a.
-c *maxcon*	Sets the maximum connections for the NFSserver to handle.
-r *value*	Specifies read file request's max size. Maximum and default is 32k. NFS 3 only.
-w *value*	Specifies write file request's max size. Maximum and default is 32k. NFS 3 only.
number	Specifies how many connections the NFSserver can handle.
BSD:	
-n *number*	Specifies how many connections the NFSserver can handle. (Max is 20.)
-r	Uses `portmap` to register the NFS service without creating any servers.
-t	Starts an NFS daemon using the TCP protocol.
-u	Starts an NFS daemon using the udp protocol.

continued

Linux:	
-p *port*	Specifies a port the NFS daemon will listen on instead of default 2049.
number	Specifies how many connections the NFSserver can handle.
Solaris:	
-a	Starts an NFS daemon over all TCP and udp connections. Not usable with -p.
-c *maxcon*	Sets the maximum connections for the NFSserver to handle.
-l *backlog*	Sets the queue length for NFS connections over TCP.
-p *protocol*	Starts an NFS daemon using the specified TCP or UDP protocol. Not usable with -a.
-t *device*	Starts an NFS daemon using the specified device.
number	Specifies how many connections the NFSserver can handle.

File Name:	`nfsd, rpc.nfsd`	**Directory:**	**AIX, Linux:** /usr/sbin/, **BSD:** /sbin/, **Solaris:** /usr/lib/nfs/	**Type:**	External
Note:	You can only run this daemon as root.				
AIX:	nfsd -a 16	Starts the NFS daemon listening on all udp and tcp connections with 16 connections available.			
Linux:	rpc.nfsd 14	Starts the NFS daemon on default port 2049 with 14 connections available.			
OpenBSD:	nfsd -t -n 15	Starts the NFS daemon listening on all tcp connections with 15 connections available.			
Solaris:	nfsd -p udp 12	Starts the NFS daemon listening on all udp connections with 12 connections available.			

nfsstat

UNIX Shell: Shells (ash, bash, bsh, csh, ksh, sh, tcsh, zsh)

Function	Shows NFS and RPC statistics.
Syntax	nfsstat [options...]

-s	Shows information about server.
-c	Shows only client-side NFS and RPC information.
AIX, Solaris:	
-n	Shows client and server NFS information.
-m	Shows statistics information for mounted file systems mounted with NFS.
-r	Shows RPC information.
-z	Sets specific statistics to zero (reset).
BSD:	
-M *core*	Uses the statistics found in the specified core file (default is `/dev/kmem`.)
-N *system*	Uses the name list from the system specified (default is `/bsd`).
-w *seconds*	Monitors the NFS activity under the specified amount of seconds.
Linux:	
-n	Shows client and server NFS information.
-r	Shows RPC information.
-z	Sets specific statistics to zero (reset).
-o *facility*	Specifies facility to show statistics for.
nfs	Show NFS protocol information.
rpc	Shows RPC information.
net	Shows network layer information.
fh	Shows the server's file handle cache information.
rc	Shows the server's request reply cache information.

File Name:	`nfsstat`	**Directory:**	/usr/bin/	**Type:**	External
Common:	nfsstat -c	Shows the NFS and RPC info on the client side.			
Common:	nfsstat -z	Resets statistic counters.			

nice

UNIX Shell: Shells (ash, bash, bsh, csh, ksh, sh, tcsh, zsh)

Function	Starts commands to be run in a different priority.
Syntax	nice [options...] *command { arguments... }*

-n *inc*	Specifies priority level. Lower inc means higher priority.
command	Specifies the command to start.
arguments...	Supplies any argument string to the command.
AIX:	
-inc	Specifies priority level. Lower inc means higher priority.

continued

Linux:	
inc	Specifies priority level. (Priority can be from -20 to 19. The lower number the higher priority.)
--help	Shows help information.
--version	Shows version information.
Solaris:	
-inc	Specifies priority level. Lower inc means higher priority.
csh,tcsh:	
+inc	Sets lower priority level.
-inc	Sets higher priority level. Must be root.
command	Specifies the command to start.
arguments...	Supplies any argument string to the command. (In csh, tcsh command is optional. It alters the shell priority if blank.)

File Name:	`nice`	**Directory:**	/usr/bin/, **Linux:** /bin/	**Type:**	External, Internal
Note:	It's not nice to change your priority.				
Common:	nice +19 find / -name core -print	Runs find command with very low priority. (csh)			
Common:	nice -19 find / -name core -print	Runs find command with very high priority, for superuser only.			

nm

UNIX Shell: Shells (ash, bash, bsh, csh, ksh, sh, tcsh, zsh)

Function	Shows a table of the symbol names used for the specified ELF object file.
Syntax	nm [options...] *{ files... }*

-g	Shows the external symbols.
-p	Shows the symbols as they are, doesn't sort.
-u	Shows the undefined symbols.
files...	Specifies input object files, an executable or an object-file library.
AIX:	
-A	Shows the full path or the library name of an object.
-B	Shows the output in BSD format. Ex. Value Type Name.
-P	Shows symbol information in a portable format.
-C	Organizes C++ symbol names first, then shows them to STDOUT.
-d	Shows the symbol value as a decimal (is default).
-e	Shows only symbols that are external and static.
-f	Shows full output for nonexistent symbols.
-h	Hides heading data in the output.
-o	Shows values in octal format and not in decimal.
-r	Reverses the sorting order.
-T	Truncates the symbol names because of earlier overflow problems.
-t *format*	Uses the format below for numeric values that are shown to output.
d	Shows the symbol value as a decimal.
o	Shows values in octal format and not in decimal.
x	Shows values in hexadecimal format and not in decimal.
-v	Organizes the symbols by value.
-x	Shows values in hexadecimal format and not in decimal.
-X *mode*	Examines using the specified type of object.
32	Uses only 32-bit object files.
64	Uses only 64-bit object files.
32_64	Uses both 32-bit and 64-bit object files.
BSD:	
-a	Shows the symbol tables entries added.
-n	Sorts the results in numerical order.
-o	Shows values in octal format and not in decimal.
-r	Sorts the result in reversed order.
-w	Looks for non-object archive members and reports them.
Linux:	
-o	Shows the path and name of the input file containing the symbol.
-a	Shows the symbols used for debugging only.
-B	Shows the output in BSD format. Ex. Value Type Name.

continued

-C	Organizes C++ symbol names first, then shows them to STDOUT.
-D	Shows dynamic symbols instead of the normal ones.
-f *format*	Specifies format to use in the output. Valid formats are: bsd, sysv, or POSIX.
-n	Sorts the results in numerical order.
-P	Uses the POSIX.2 standard format when listing symbols. As -f posix.
-s	Sorts the results in reverse order.
--size-sort	Sorts the symbols by size.
-t *radix*	Uses the format below for numeric values that are shown to output.
d	Shows the symbol value as a decimal.
o	Shows values in octal format and not in decimal.
x	Shows values in hexadecimal format and not in decimal.
--target=*format*	Uses the specified object code format specified instead of the default.
-l	Shows, for each symbol, the filename and a line number.
-V	Shows version information.
--help	Shows help information.
Solaris:	
-A	Shows the full path or the library name of an object.
-C	Organizes C++ symbol names first, then shows them to STDOUT.
-D	Shows information about the SHT_DYNSYM symbol.
-h	Hides heading data of the symbol.
-l	Adds a * in front of the key letter for WEAK symbols to identify WEAK and GLOBAL.
-n	Organizes external symbols by name before shown on STDOUT.
-o	Shows values in octal format and not in decimal. Same as option -t o.
-P	Shows output information in a portable format.
-r	Adds, for each line of output, the name of the object file or archive.
-R	Shows, when present, the archive name, the object file, and symbol name.
-s	Shows the name and not the index for a section.
-t *format*	Uses the format below for numeric values that are shown to output.
d	Shows the symbol value as a decimal.
o	Shows values in octal format and not in decimal.
x	Shows values in hexadecimal format and not in decimal.
-e	Shows only symbols that are external and static. Will be removed in future releases.
-f	Shows full output for nonexistent symbols. Will be removed in future releases.
-v	Organizes the symbols by value.
-V	Shows version information.
-x	Shows version information.

File Name:	`nm`	**Directory:**	/usr/bin/, **Solaris:** /usr/ccs/bin/	**Type:**	External
Common:	nm -u /usr/lib/libc.so	Shows undefined symbols from the specified shared object file.			

nohup

UNIX Shell: Shells (ash, bash, bsh, csh, ksh, sh, tcsh, zsh)

Function	A way to run a command which will be immune to any hang up signals.
Syntax	nohup *command* { *arguments...* }

command	Specifies the name of a command to start.
arguments...	Provides any arguments that belong to the command.
Linux:	
--help	Shows help information.
--version	Shows version information.
	C- and TC-shell have an internal nuhup with the same function.

File Name:	`nohup`	**Directory:**	/usr/bin/	**Type:**	External, Internal
Note:	Lets you start a command that continues to run even when you log out.				
Common:	nohup prog	Runs the program `prog` and ignores hang-ups.			
Common:	nuhup prog &	Runs the prog in the background and ignores hang-ups.			

notify

UNIX Shell:	Shells (csh, tcsh)
Function	Notifies a user asynchronous when the status of a job is changed. If job isn't given, the current job is used.
Syntax	notify *{ jobids... }*

jobids...	Specifies job id. If not given, use the current job. **Use one of the following to specify the job id:**
%	Specifies the current job. You can also use %% and %+.
%*number*	Specifies job number.
%?*string*	Specifies a command that contains string.
%minus;	Specifies the previous job.
Common: notify	Notifies the user when the current job changes status.
Common: notify %3	Notifies the user when job %3 changes status.

nroff

UNIX Shell:	Shells (ash, bash, bsh, csh, ksh, sh, tcsh, zsh)
Function	Processes a text file and formats the output for use with a letter quality printer or line printer.
Syntax	nroff [options...] *{ file }*

-h	Replaces 8 horizontal spaces with a Tab. This improves the output time.
-i	Continues to read from STDIN after the input file has been processed.
-q	Starts simultaneous input-output mode.
-n*value*	Specifies the starting page number indicated by `n`.
-o*pagelist*	Specifies which pages to print. The format is a comma-separated list (i.e.1, 2, 5-8).
-r*aN*	Sets the register character `a` to equal `N`.
-T*printer*	Prepares the output for the printer name specified.
file	Specifies the input file to process. Type "-" to read from STDIN.
AIX:	
-e	Justifies the lines by spacing the words so they fill up the entire line.
-z	Prints only messages generated by .tm requests.
-u *value*	Sets the bold factor for the third font position to the specified number.
-man	Uses the man macro processing package.
-me	Uses the me macro processing package.
-mm	Uses the mm macro processing package.
-mptx	Uses the mptx macro processing package.
-ms	Uses the ms macro processing package.
-s *number*	Pauses every number pages for paper loading and resumes after every new line.
-q	Starts simultaneous input-output mode.
BSD:	
-m *name*	Uses the macro tmac.`name` found in `/usr/share/`.
Linux:	
-m *name*	Uses the macro tmac.`name` found in `/usr/share/groff/`.
Solaris:	
-e	Justifies the lines by spacing the words so they fill up the entire line.
-q	Starts simultaneous input-output mode.
-s *number*	Pauses every number of pages for paper loading and resumes after every new line.

File Name:	nroff	**Directory:**	/usr/bin/	**Type:**	External

Tip:	Use `troff` if the printer that you are formatting the output for is a laser printer.
Common: nroff -o1 textfile1	Prints page one of the file textfile1.
Common: nroff -T backupprinter textfile1.	Prints the file on backupprinter.

nslookup

UNIX Shell:	Shells (ash, bash, bsh, csh, ksh, sh, tcsh, zsh)
Function	Contacts and sends queries to DNS servers interactively or non-interactively.
Syntax	nslookup [options...] *ACTION { server }*

continued

	The following options can also be set in interactive mode with the set command.
-all	Shows the current settings.
-class=*classname*	Limits search according to the specified class.
-d2	Enables the debug mode to show extensive information.
-nod2	Disables the debug mode to show extensive information.
-debug	Enables debug information.
-nodebug	Disables debug information.
-defname	Enables domain-appending information.
-nodefname	Disables domain-appending information.
-domain=*string*	Creates the attachable domain.
-ignoretc	Ignores packet errors that are truncated.
-noignoretc	Acknowledges packet errors that are truncated.
-srchlst=*list*	Specifies a list, separated by slash /, of domains to lookup in first.
-search	Uses the domains in the domains list when searching.
-nosearch	Doesn't use the domains found in the domain list when searching.
-port=*port*	Specifies the TCP and UDP port to connect to on the remote server.
-recurse	Searches on other domain name servers before dropping the search.
-norecurse	Doesn't search on any other domain name server.
-retry=*number*	Specifies the maximum amount of retries to do before dropping the search.
-root=*host*	Specifies another root server to use. (Default is ns.internic.net).
-timeout=*seconds*	Specifies how long to wait for a request before dropping the search.
-vc	Uses a virtual circuit while sending requests.
-novc	Doesn't use the virtual circuit while sending requests.
-querytype=*type*	Specifies type of information to be returned from the server.
-type=*type*	Specifies type of information to be returned from the server.
	The following commands are used only from the interactive mode.
server *server*	Specifies default server to use. Find that server with the default server.
lserver *server*	Specifies default server to use. Find that server with the server specified.
root	Sets the default server to ns.internic.net.
view *file*	Shows the output of the internal ls command and show one page at the time.
ls [options...] *domain*	Shows the information for the specified domain. Below are the options.
-t *type*	Specifies query type to look for.
-a	Shows the CNAMEs for the specified domain.
-d	Shows all information for the specified domain.
-h	Shows the cpu and other system information for the specified domain.
-s	Shows the well known services for the specified domain.
finger *{ host }*	Communicates with the finger service on the current host.
set *variable* [=*value*]	Changes the value of the specified variable.
ACTION	**You must select one of these two actions:**
host	Specifies the hostname or IP address of the computer. Non-interactive mode.
-	Prompts for more information about hostnames before sending queries. Interactive.
server	Queries go to the specified server instead of `resolv.conf` file.

File Name:	`nslookup`	**Directory:**	/usr/sbin/	**Type:**	External
Common:	nslookup ucgbook.com	Makes a query to the domain ucgbook.com.			
Common:	nslookup -all	Lists the current settings.			
Common:	nslookup -debug - ns.ucgbook.com	Starts nslookup in interactive mode with debugging turned on.			

od

od		**UNIX Shell:**	**Shells (ash, bash, bsh, csh, ksh, sh, tcsh, zsh)**
Function	Reads a file from STDIN or from a specified file and exports the content to STDOUT in octal format.		
Syntax	od [options...] *{ file } { offset }* AIX: od [options...] *{ file } { label }*		

-b	Shows the bytes in octal format.
-c	Shows the bytes in ASCII format.
-d	Shows words which are equal to 16-bit units in unsigned decimal.
-f	Shows long words which are equal to 32-bit units in floating-point format.
-o	Shows the words which are equal to 16-bit units in octal format.
-x	Shows words which are equal to 16-bit units in Hexadecimal.

continued

+	Is required when specifying an offset if a file isn't specified.
file	Specifies the file to be used as input.
offset	The offset in the file where the file output begins. (Is by default read in octals. Begin with 0x for hexadecimal or end with a . for decimal.)
b	Is interpreted in blocks of 512 bytes.
B	Is interpreted in blocks of 1024 bytes.
AIX:	
-A *base*	Specifies the format of the offset n=no, d=decimal, o=octal, or x=hexadecimal.
-N *count*	Formats only the number of bytes specified by count.
-j *skip*	Hops over the number of bytes specified from the start of the input.
-t *string*	Specifies types of output. The following are the valid types.
a *name_character*	\000=nul,\001=soh,\002=stx,\003=etx,\004=eot,\005=enq,\006=ack,\007=bel. \010=bs,\011=ht,\012=lf,\013=vt,\014=ff,\015=cr,\016=so,\017=si,\020=dle. \021=dc1,\022=dc2,\023=dc3,\024=dc4,\025=nak,\026=syn,\027=etb,\030=can. \031=em,\032=sub,\033=esc,\034=fs,\035=gs,\036=rs,\037=us,\040=sp,\177=del.
c *character*	Used for single or multibyte characters. You may use characters d, f, o, u, and x.
f *floatingpoint*	The floating point and can be followed by optional characters F,D, or L.
-a	Shows bytes in characters and interprets in their ASCII names.
-C	Same as -c but will show non-printable characters as C escapes.
-D	Shows long words which are equal to 32-bit units in unsigned decimal.
-e	Shows long words as double precisions.
-F	The same as -e.
-h	Shows 16-bit words as unsigned hexadecimals.
-H	Shows long words as unsigned hexadecimals.
-i	Shows 16-bit words as signed decimals.
-l	Shows long words as signed decimals.
-l	The same as -l.
-L	The same as -l.
-O	Shows the long words which are equal 32-bit units in octal.
-p	Indicates even parity on -a conversions.
-P	Indicates odd parity on -a conversions.
-s	Shows the words which are equal to 16-bit units in signed decimal format.
-v	Writes all input data, not only those converted.
-X	The same as -H.
-S *{ size }*	Searches for null-ended strings to convert.
size	Specifies the minimum string size to recognize.
-w *{ value }*	Specifies the number of input bytes to be read each conversion time (default is 32).
+	Is required when specifying a label if a file isn't specified.
label	Is interpreted as a pseudo-address for the first byte shown.
BSD:	
-a	Shows bytes in characters and interprets in their ASCII names.
-B	Shows the bytes in octal format.
-D	Shows long words which are equal to 32-bit units in unsigned decimal.
-e	Shows long words as double precisions.
-F	The same as -e.
-H	Shows long words as unsigned hexadecimals.
-h	Shows 16-bit words as unsigned hexadecimals.
-i	Shows 16-bit words as signed decimals.
-l	Shows long words as signed decimals.
-l	The same as -l.
-L	The same as -l.
-O	Shows the long words which are equal to 32-bit units in octal.
-v	Writes all input data, not only those converted.
-X	The same as -H.
Linux:	
-a	Shows bytes in characters and interprets in their ASCII names.
-h	Shows 16-bit words as unsigned hexadecimals.

continued

-i	Shows 16-bit words as signed decimals.
-l	Shows long words as signed decimals.
-v	Writes all input data, not only those converted.
-A *base*	Specifies the format of the offset n=no, d=decimal, o=octal, or x=hexadecimal.
-j *skip*	Hops over the number of bytes specified from the start of the input.
-N *count*	Formats only the number of bytes specified by count.
-s *{ size }*	Searches for null-ended strings to convert.
size	Specifies the minimum string size to recognize.
-t *string*	Specifies types of output. The following are the valid types.
-w *{ value }*	Specifies the number of input bytes to be read each conversion time (default is 32).
--traditional	Accepts arguments in pre-posix form.
--help	Shows help information.
--version	Shows version information.
Solaris:	
-A *base*	Specifies the format of the offset n=no, d=decimal, o=octal, or x=hexadecimal.
-C	Same as -c but will show non-printable characters as C escapes.
-D	Shows long words which are equal to 32-bit units in unsigned decimal.
-F	Shows double long words which are equal to 64-bit units in extended precision.
-j *skip*	Hops over the number of bytes specified from the start of the input.
-N *count*	Formats only the number of bytes specified by count.
-O	Shows the long words which are equal to 32-bit units in octal
-s	Shows the words which are equal to 16-bit units in signed decimal format.
-S	Shows the words which are equal to 32-bit units in signed decimal format.
-t *string*	Specifies types of output.
-v	Verbose mode. Shows more information.
-X	Shows long words which are equal to 32-bit units in Hexadecimal.

File Name:	od	**Directory:**	/usr/bin/	**Type:**	External
Note:	Very useful when you want to know what's in a file including non-printable characters.				
Common:	echo "Hello World" | od -c	Prints out character by character and the new line character.			
Common:	od -c readme.txt 256	Reads from the readme.txt file and starts 256 bytes in it.			

onintr

UNIX Shell: Shells (csh, tcsh)

Function	Specifies the shell will do with an interrupt. If option isn't given what normal interrupt handles are restored.
Syntax	onintr [-] onintr *label*

	The following options can't be combined:
-	Disables all interrupts.
label	Jumps to label on an interrupt.
Common: onintr	Restores normal action for interrupt.
Common: onintr handelinterrupt	On an interrupt go to handelinterrup.

passwd

UNIX Shell: Shells (ash, bash, bsh, csh, ksh, sh, tcsh, zsh)

Function	Changes login password and password attributes for the current or the specified user.
Syntax	passwd [options...] [user]

AIX:	
-f	Alters the user information in the GECOS field.
-s	Alters the login shell.
BSD:	
-l	Updates the local password file.
-y	Updates the YP password entry.
-k	Updates the Kerberos database.
-n *name*	Specifies the principal name to use.
-i *instance*	Uses the specified instance.
-r *realm*	Uses the specified realm instead of the local one.
-u *username.instance@realm*	Specifies the fully qualified kerberos principal.

continued

Linux:	
-k	Alters the expired passwords.
-l	Locks the username specified.
-u	Unlocks the username specified.
-f	Causes the -u option to be forced if a password doesn't exist.
-d	Removes the password for the username specified.
-S	Shows some information about the specified user's account.
Solaris:	
-r *database*	Specifies the database to alter. Can be one of files, ldap, NIS, or nisplus.
-e	Prompts for a new shell for the specified user.
-g	Alters the finger information for the user.
-h	Alters the user's home directory.
	The following options can only be used with the files and nisplus databases.
-s { *user* }	Shows the password attributes for the user.
-a	Shows the password attributes for all users. Used with -s without user.
-f	Makes the user change password at the next login.
-l	Locks the user account.
-n *days*	Specifies the time in days the user can't change the password.
-w *days*	Specifies how many days the user will be warned before the password has to change.
-x *days*	Specifies how many days the password the user has will be valid. Not usual days are:
-1	Lets the user keep its password forever.
0	Does the same thing as -f. The user has to change password at next logon.
	The following option can only be used with the files database.
-d	Deletes the password for the user. Used instead of -l.
	The following option can only be used with the nisplus database.
-D *domain*	Specifies the NIS domain to use.
user	The user login name.

File Name:	passwd	**Directory:** /usr/bin/	**Type:** External
Tip:	It is a good idea to have a strong password with numbers.		
Common:	passwd	Changes the password for the current user.	
Common:	passwd ove	Changes the password for the specified user.	
AIX:	passwd -s	Changes the shell interactively, choose from a list of available shells.	
OpenBSD:	passwd -l ucg	Changes the specified users password in the local password file.	
Solaris:	passwd -r NIS -D ucgteam -l ucguser1	Locks the ucguser1 user on the nis domain ucgteam.	

paste

UNIX Shell:	**Shells (ash, bash, bsh, csh, ksh, sh, tcsh, zsh)**
Function	Creates vertical columns of the content in the specified input files.
Syntax	paste [options...] *files...*

-d "*character*"	Specifies the delimiter to use between columns, could be an escape sequence. (To separate columns differently you could use more than one character.)
\t	Inputs a Tab between columns. This is the default.
\n	Inputs a new line for every column.
\\	Inputs a backslash.
\0	Inputs an empty string.
-s	Organizes every line from an input file into columns.
files...	The files that are shown in columns.

File Name:	paste	**Directory:** /usr/bin/	**Type:** External
Common:	paste users userpermissions	Shows the list of users and its permisions.	
Common:	paste -s users userpermissions	Creates a horizontal list.	

patch	UNIX Shell:	Shells (ash, bash, bsh, csh, ksh, sh, tcsh, zsh)

Function	Makes changes to files with patch files.
Syntax	patch [options...] *{ file } { patchfile }* patch [options...] *patchfile*

-p *number*	Specifies the amount of slashes to ignore in the pathname to the file being patched.
-b	Creates a backup of changed files and adds .orig to that filename.
-l	Matches different sized of sequences of black characters instead of being exact.
-N	Ignores changes to files if those changes already have been made to file.
-R	Reverses the way of patching. The patch file was created from new to old version.
-c	Reads the patch file as a context difference.
-e	Reads the patch file as an ed script.
-n	Reads the patch file as a normal difference.
-d *directory*	Changes the current working directory before changing any files.
-D *define*	Marks changes with the C preprocessor construct.
-o *outfile*	Specifies a file to hold the new file content, like files after patch.
-r *rejectfile*	Specifies a file where all the rejected patches go; otherwise .rej will be appended.
AIX:	
-B *prefix*	Specifies a prefix to use on the backup filename.
-f	Doesn't ask any questions and runs a forced patch.
-s	Suppresses all messages except if an error occurred.
-v	Shows revision header and patch level. No other options will be used.
-F *number*	Specifies how many lines to ignore before finding a place to install a hunk.
-i *patchfile*	Specifies the file to read proposed changes from.
-x *number*	Specifies internal debugging flags to use.
BSD:	
-B *prefix*	Specifies a prefix to use on the backup filename.
-C	Performs a patch check to see if any problems would occur, doesn't alter files.
-E	Removes files that becomes empty after applying a patch.
-f	Doesn't ask any questions and runs a forced patch.
-t	Forces a patch but not on patches that can't be found or have the wrong version.
-F *number*	Specifies how many lines to ignore before finding a place to install a hunk.
-s	Suppress all messages except if an error occurred.
-S	Specifies a patch to skip from the patch file.
-u	Interprets the patch as a unified context diff.
-v	Shows revision header and patch level. No other options will be used.
-V	Specifies method to use when creating backups. Valid methods below:
numbered	Creates numbered backups.
existing	Creates numbered backups of files that already have them.
simple	Creates simple backups.
-x *number*	Specifies internal debugging flags to use.
Linux:	
--backup-if-mismatch	Will back up files or which patches don't match exactly.
--no-backup-if-mismatch	Doesn't back up files on which patches don't match exactly.
-B *prefix*	Specifies a prefix to use on the backup filename.
--binary	Reads and writes files only in binary mode.
--dry-run	Fakes a patch and shows the faked results to the screen.
-E	Erases files that become empty after applying a patch.
-f	Doesn't ask any questions and runs a forced patch.
-F *number*	Specifies how many lines to ignore before finding a place to install a hunk.
-g *number*	Will search for, ignore, or ask for a file to patch if it can't be found. (Number can be: 1 search files, 0 ignore files, or -1 ask for files.)
--help	Shows help information.
-i *patchfile*	Specifies the file to read proposed changes from.
--posix	Uses the POSIX standard.

continued

--quoting-style=*style*	Specifies style to show the names in.
literal	Shows names as they are.
shell	Quotes names that contain shell metacharacters.
c	Quotes the names like a C language string.
escape	Quotes the names like a C language string, but without double-quotes."
-s	Suppresses all messages except if an error occurred.
-t	Forces a patch except for patches that aren't found or are the wrong version.
-T	Sets the modification times and access times to the patched files from the patch.
-u	Interprets the patch as a unified context diff.
-v	Shows revision header and patch level. No other options will be used.
-V	Specifies method to use when creating backups. Valid methods below:
numbered	Creates numbered backups.
existing	Creates numbered backups of files that already have them.
simple	Creates simple backups.
--verbose	Verbose mode. Shows more information.
-x *number*	Specifies internal debugging flags to use.
-Y *prefix*	Specifies the prefix to use when generating simple backup filenames.
-z *suffix*	Specifies the suffix to use when generating simple backup filenames.
-Z	Uses the modification times and access times found in the diff headers.
Solaris:	
-i *patchfile*	Specifies the file to read proposed changes from.
file	Specifies the file to patch.
patchfile	Specifies the file to read proposed changes from.

File Name:	patch	**Directory:**	/usr/bin/	**Type:**	External
Tip:	Very useful when a big file needs to be fixed and you don't want to download the whole file again; just grab the patch.				
Common:	patch -p 0 < bigchanges.diff	Patches files specified inside the bigchanges.diff file and uses the full pathname.			
Linux:	patch -p1 < patch-2.2.16	Patching the linux kernel with the 2.2.16 patch. Standing in /usr/src with the original unpacked kernel in /usr/src/linux/.			

perl

perl		**UNIX Shell:**	**Shells (ash, bash, bsh, csh, ksh, sh, tcsh, zsh)**
Function	A programming language. Perl stands for Practical Extraction Report Language.		
Syntax	perl [options...] [--] *{ file } { arguments... }*		

-s	Changes the arguments to variable switches that can be invoked in the program.
-T	Forces taint checks.
-u	Dumps the core after a compile.
-U	Allows unsafe operations.
-v	Shows version information.
-V	Shows Perl configuration values and the current value of @INC.
-V:*configvariable*	Shows the value of specified configuration variable.
-c	Checks the syntax of the script without running it.
-w	Shows warnings on spelling errors and other error-prone constructs in the script.
-d [:*debugger*]	Runs the script in debug mode.
debugger	Specifies the module to control the debug.
-D*flags*	Specifies debugging flags.
-p	Assumes an input loop around the script. Shows the input lines.
-n	Assumes an input loop around the script. Doesn't show the input lines.
-a	Activates autosplit mode. Must be combined either with -n or -p options.
-F*pattern*	Specifies an expression to split on. Must be combined with -a option.
-l*octal*	Specifies line terminator and enables line ending processing.
-0*octal*	Specifies record separator (default is "\0").
-I*dir*	Specifies the directory to look for include files. Must be combined with -p option.
-m[-]*module*[=*argument*]	Runs the specified module before the script.
[-]	Doesn't run the specified module.
argument	Specifies the argument for the module.
-P	Runs the C preprocessor before compile.

continued

-S	Uses the PATH environment variable to search for the script.
-x*directory*	Switches to the specified directory before running the script.
-i{ *suffix* }	Edits the files in their actual places in the construct processor.
suffix	Makes a backup with specified suffix.
-e '*command*'	Runs the specified command. Doesn't look for a script filename.
--	Tells to load script from STDIN, and takes all following operands as parameters.
file	Specifies the script file.
arguments...	Specifies the arguments for the script program.
BSD, Linux:	
-C	Uses the native wide-character APIs on the target system.
-W	Enables all warnings.
-X	Disables all warnings.

File Name:	`perl`	**Directory:**	/usr/bin/	**Type:**	External
Common:	perl -e 'print "UCG\n"'	Shows "UCG" on the screen.			
Linux:	perl -X test.pl	Runs test.pl and disables all the warnings.			

ping

UNIX Shell: Shells (ash, bash, bsh, csh, ksh, sh, tcsh, zsh)

Function	Sends ICMP echo requests to specified hosts. The remote host will, if it can, respond with an ICMP echo reply.
Syntax	AIX: ping [options...] *host { packetsize count }* BSD, Linux: ping [options...] *host* Solaris: ping [options...] *host { timeout packetsize count }*

-d	Enables the SO_DEBUG option for the socket used.
-L	Doesn't loop back the multicast packets.
-n	Shows addresses as numbers instead of hostnames.
-r	Sends requests directly to remote host without passing any router.
-R	Stores the route for the packet in the ip header.
-v	Verbose mode. Shows more information.
host	The hostname or IP address to send the ICMP echo requests to.
AIX:	
-q	Specifies quiet output.
-c *count*	Specifies how many ICMP echo requests you will send out.
-f	Floods the target host with pings.
-i *wait*	Waits the number of seconds between the sending of each packet.
-l *preload*	Sends the number of packets as fast as possible before falling into normal mode.
-p *pattern*	Specifies up to 16 "pad" bytes to fill out the packet you send.
-s *packetsize*	Specifies how big the packet you are sending will be.
-I *address*	Specifies the IP address of the interface to send packets from.
-T *ttl*	Specifies packets Time To Live before the request times out.
packetsize	Specifies how big the packet you are sending will be.
count	Specifies how many ICMP echo requests you will send out.
BSD:	
-c *count*	Specifies how many ICMP echo requests you will send out.
-D	Sets the Don't Fragment bit.
-f	Floods the target host with pings.
-I *address*	Specifies the IP address of the interface to send packets from.
-i *wait*	Waits the number of seconds between the sending of each packet.
-l *preload*	Sends the number of packets as fast as possible before falling into normal mode.
-p *pattern*	Specifies up to 16 "pad" bytes to fill out the packet you send.
-q	Specifies quiet output.
-s *packetsize*	Specifies the how big the packet you are sending will be.
-T *tos*	Specifies the type of service value.
-t *ttl*	Specifies the time to live value.
-w *maxwait*	Specifies the number of seconds to wait for a response to a packet.

continued

Linux:	
-b	Allows pings a broadcast address.
-c *count*	Specifies how many ICMP echo requests you will send out.
-f	Floods the target host with pings.
-i *wait*	Waits the number of seconds between the sending of each packet.
-I *interface address*	Specifies the interface and address to send the ping package from.
-l *preload*	Sends the number of packets as fast as possible before falling into normal mode.
-p *pattern*	Specifies up to 16 "pad" bytes to fill out the packet you send.
-q	Specifies quiet output.
-s *packetsize*	Specifies how big the packet you are sending will be.
-t *ttl*	Specifies the time to live value.
-T *timestampoption*	Specifies the special IP timestamp options.
-U	Shows true user-to-user latency.
-V	Shows version information.
-w *timeout*	Specifies how many seconds to wait before timeout and exit.
Solaris:	
-s	Sends requests every second and prints info about their replies.
-l	Marks packets to go to the specified host and back again.
-i *ipaddress*	Specifies the IP address of the interface to send packets from.
-I *interval*	Specifies another interval for sending ICMP echo requests, in seconds.
-t *ttl*	Specifies packet Time To Live before the request times out.
timeout	Specifies the time to wait for a reply from host. Can't be used with -s.
packetsize	Specifies size of the packet you are sending.
count	Specifies how many ICMP echo request you will send out.

File Name:	ping	**Directory:**	**AIX, Solaris:** /usr/sbin/, **BSD:** /sbin/, **Linux:** /bin/ — **Type:** External
Common:	ping 192.168.1.254		Sends ICMP echo requests to address 192.168.1.254.
Common:	ping -n www.ucgbook.com		Sends ICMP echo requests to host www.ucgbook.com, but only shows numeric addresses.
Common:	ping -r 192.168.1.254		Sends ICMP echo requests to address 192.168.1.254 without passing any routers.
AIX:	ping -c 10 192.168.1.254		Sends ten ICMP echo requests to address 192.168.1.254
Linux:	ping -I eth0 192.168.1.1 192.168.1.254		Sends ICMP echo requests over interface eth0 with address 192.168.1.1 to address 192.168.1.254.
OpenBSD:	ping -f 192.168.1.254		Floods the address 192.168.1.254 with ICMP echo requests.
Solaris:	ping -sn www.ucgbook.com		Returns numeric addresses and continues until ping is terminated.

pod2html

UNIX Shell: Shells (ash, bash, bsh, csh, ksh, sh, tcsh, zsh)

Function	Converts pod to HTML files.
Syntax	pod2html [options...]

--help	Shows help information.
--htmlroot=*name*	Specifies the base URL for the HTML file.
--infile=*name*	Specifies which POD file is to be converted (default is STDIN).
--outfile=*name*	Specifies which HTML file is to be created (default is STDOUT).
--podroot=*name*	Specifies the base directory for searching library pods.
--podpath=*name*:	Specifies the subdirectory that contains pod files.
--libpods=*name*:	Specifies the list of page names that have linkable items.
--netscape	Uses Netscape HTML directives.
--nonetscape	Doesn't use Netscape HTML directives as the default.
--index	Generates an index at the beginning of the HTML file as the default.
--noindex	Doesn't generate an index at the beginning of the HTML file.
--recurse	Recurses into the specified subdirectories in the pod path (is the default).
--norecurse	Doesn't recurse into subdirectories specified in podpath.
--title=*title*	Specifies the title that's used in the created HTML file.
--verbose	Verbose mode. Shows more information.

File Name:	pod2html	**Directory:**	**AIX:** /usr/opt/perl5/bin/, **BSD, Linux:** /usr/bin/, **Solaris:** /usr/perl5/5.00503/bin/	**Type:**	Script

pod2latex

pod2latex		UNIX Shell:	Shells (ash, bash, bsh, csh, ksh, sh, tcsh, zsh)
Function	Converts Perl pod document files into LaTeX document files.		
Syntax	pod2latex		
File Name:	pod2latex	Directory:	**AIX:** /usr/opt/perl5/bin/, **BSD, Linux:** /usr/bin/, **Solaris:** /usr/perl5/5.00503/bin/ — **Type:** Script

pod2man

pod2man		UNIX Shell:	Shells (ash, bash, bsh, csh, ksh, sh, tcsh, zsh)
Function	Generates `*roff` input from a POD source which can then be shown on STDOUT using `nroff` or to a printer using `troff`.		
Syntax	pod2man [options...] *input* { *output* }		

-s=*section*	Sets the section that's used for the `.TH` macro (default is 1).
-r=*release*	Sets a different footer than the default which shows the `perl` version that you are in.
-c *string*	Sets the header: `User Contributed Perl Documentation` if no other text is given.
-d *string*	Sets the footer to the specified value (default is modification date of the input file).
--fixed=*font*	Specifies the fixed-width font to use instead of the default formatter font CW.
--official	Sets the default header to refer to the man page as the standard `perl` release.
--lax	Doesn't react to missing sections. Not used if POD checking isn't used in Pod::Man
-h	Shows help information.
input	Specifies the POD source. This source can even be embedded in code (default is STDIN).
output	Specifies the file to use as output.
BSD, Linux:	
--fixedbold=*font*	Uses a different bold fixed-width font, instead of the default CB.
--fixeditalic=*font*	Uses a different italic fixed-width font, instead of the default CI.
--fixedbolditalic=*font*	Uses a different bold italic fixed-width font, instead of the default CB or CX.

File Name:	pod2man	Directory:	**AIX:** /usr/opt/perl5/bin/, **BSD, Linux:** /usr/bin/, **Solaris:** /usr/perl5/5.00503/bin/	Type:	Script

pod2text

pod2text		UNIX Shell:	Shells (ash, bash, bsh, csh, ksh, sh, tcsh, zsh)
Function	Converts POD files into formatted ASCII text files.		
Syntax	pod2text [options...] { *inputfile* } { *outputfile* }		

-a	Specifies an alternative output format, which may include different headings.
-c	Formats the output in color using ANSI escape sequences.
-i	Specifies the number of spaces to indent (default is 4).
-h	Shows help information.
-l	Places a blank after a line containing the heading `` `=head1' `` is used.
-s	Reserves two spaces at the end of each sentence.
-t	Attempts to determine the screen width from `termcap`.
-w	Specifies the width of the columns before beginning to wrap the text (default is 76).
inputfile	Specifies the perl file to use as input that is converted to an ASCII text file.
outputfile	Specifies the output filename to use.

File Name:	pod2text	Directory:	**AIX:** /usr/opt/perl5/bin/, **BSD, Linux:** /usr/bin/, **Solaris:** /usr/perl5/5.00503/bin/	Type:	Script

popd

popd		UNIX Shell:	Shells (bash, csh, tcsh, zsh)
Function	Pops a directory from the directory stack and changes to it.		
Syntax	popd [+*n*]		

+*n*	Removes the specified element in the directory stack. Numbers starting at 0.
bash:	
-n	Doesn't change directory.
+*n*	Removes the n:th element from the right in the stack.
tcsh:	
-p	Hides the directory stack.
-l	Prevents the use of ~ in the output.

continued

-n	Wraps lines longer than the screen.
-v	Shows one entry per line.
zsh:	
+*n*	Removes the specified element in the directory stack. Numbers starting at 0.

Note:	`puchd` is used to add `element` to the stack and `dirs` is used to show the stack.	
Common:	popd	Removes the first directory in the stack and changes to it.
Common:	popd 4	Removes the 4:th element in the stack.
Common:	popd -p	Hides the resulting directory stack list (tcsh).

pr

UNIX Shell: Shells (ash, bash, bsh, csh, ksh, sh, tcsh, zsh)

Function	Filters printing and pagination, each input file/files are read, formatted and written to STDOUT.
Syntax	pr [options...] *{ file... }*

-*columns*	Specifies the number of columns produced for the output. Can't be used with -m.
-a	Specifies that columns will be filled across the page.
-d	Specifies that output will be double-spaced, appends an extra new line.
-m	Merges files and writes one line from each input file to STDOUT.
-r	Doesn't report failure when opening a file.
-t	Hides header or trailer information for each page.
-h *header*	Specifies the page header.
-l *lines*	Resets page length to the number of lines specified.
-o *offset*	Sets a number of spaces to offset the start of each line.
-w *width*	Specifies line width for the output. Single column lines aren't truncated.
-f	Uses FORMFEED character for new pages.
-i *{ char } { gap }*	Converts number of spaces specified by char to Tabs. Gap is the space between columns.
-n *{ char } { width }*	Makes lines the specified width. Optionally appends value in char to lines.
-e *{ char } { gap }*	Converts Tab characters to space characters specified by gap (i.e. gap+1).
-s *{ char }*	Separates text columns with char (default is Tab character).
file	Specifies the pathname of a file to show. If a file isn't specified, STDIN will be used.
AIX:	
+*page*	Specifies page number to start output of the input file.
-F	Uses FORMFEED character for new pages.
-x	Makes lines the specified width. Optionally appends value in char to lines.
-p	Pauses before beginning each page if STDOUT is sent to a terminal.
BSD:	
+*page*	Specifies page number to start output of the input file.
-F	Uses FORMFEED character for new pages.
Linux:	
+*page*[:*last*]	Specifies the first (and last) page to start (and end) output from the file.
-c	Uses hat and octal backslash notation in the output.
-F	Uses FORMFEED character for new pages.
-J	Merges full lines.
-N *number*	Starts the line numbering with number (used with -number).
-S *{ string }*	Separates text columns with char.
-T	Hides header or trailer information and removes any form feed from the input.
-v	Show non-printing characters with an octal backslash notation.
-W *width*	Specifies line width for the output. Single column lines aren't truncated.
--help	Shows help information.
--version	Shows version information.
Solaris:	
+*page*	Specifies page number to start output of the input file.
-F	Folds the lines of input file to fit the line width, with -a or -m to fit the column.
-p	Pauses before beginning each page if STDOUT is sent to a terminal.

File Name:	pr	**Directory:** /usr/bin/	**Type:** External
Common:	pr -h ucgbook ucg.txt	Prints the file named ucg.txt with header ucgbook.	
Linux:	pr -2:3 ucg.txt	Prints pages 2 and 3 from file ucg.txt	

printenv

UNIX Shell:	Shells (ash, bash, bsh, csh, ksh, sh, tcsh, zsh)				
Function	Shows the variable values in the environment.				
Syntax	printenv *{ variable }*				
variable	Shows the values of the specified variable.				
Linux:					
--help	Shows help information.				
--version	Shows version information.				
	TC-shell (tcsh) has an internal printenv.				
File Name:	`printenv`	**Directory:**	/usr/bin, **Solaris:** /usr/ucb/	**Type:**	External, Internal
Common:	printenv	Shows all environment variables.			
Common:	printenv PATH	Shows the PATH environment variable.			

printf

UNIX Shell:	Shells (ash, bash, bsh, csh, ksh, sh, tcsh, zsh)
Function	Interprets certain characters in the format string.
Syntax	printf "*format*" *{ arguments... }*
"*format*"	Specifies the format string to interpret. Can also be used as a regular string.
arguments...	Specifies the string or number to insert instead of the conversion characters.
	The following characters will be treated as a special character.
\a	Indicates an alert.
\b	Indicates a backspace.
\f	Indicates a formfeed.
\n	Indicates a newline.
\r	Indicates a carriage return.
\t	Indicates a tab.
\v	Indicates a vertical tab.
\c	Tells the command to end the line, even if there remain characters.
\ddd	Shows the character specified by a two- or three-digit octal number.
%*{ flags }{ minwidth }*[*.digits*]*character*	This is the syntax for creating a conversion character in the format string.
minwidth	Sets the minimum width of the field. Fills with space if the width isn't reached.
.precision	Sets the minimum amount of digits. Fills up with zeros if not reached.
	The following flags can be specified:
-	Left-justifies the conversion within the field.
+	Shows a + or - before a signed conversion.
<space character>	Shows a space before a positive signed conversion. If negative, a - will show.
#	**The following conversions are supported:**
o	Adds a zero at the beginning of the conversion.
X, x	Adds a `0x` or `0X` at the beginning of the conversion.
e, E, f, g, G	Makes results always contain a decimal point.
0	Fills the remaining characters in the field width with zeros. Numeric values only.
	Following is a description for each conversion character:
d, i	Shows the integer argument as a signed decimal.
o	Shows the integer argument as an unsigned octal.
u	Shows the integer argument as an unsigned decimal.
x, X	Shows the integer argument as an unsigned hexadecimal.
f	Shows the floating point argument with the amount digits as specified in precision.
e, E	Shows the float argument as one numeric value, 6 digits and a 2 digit exponent.
g, G	The same as e and E, but with the amount digits specified in `precision`.
c	Shows the first character in the string.
s	Inserts the additional string into the format string.
b	The same as s, but converts special characters in the additional string. (This is also an internal command in bash.)

continued

File Name:	printf	**Directory:**	/usr/bin/	**Type:**	External
Note:	If you want to type a backslash \ or percent % character, then type it twice, like \\ or %%.				
Common:	printf "UCG %s, the world\n" unites	Shows the string "UCG unites, the world", ending with a newline.			
Common:	printf "Hexadecimal number: %#.8x" 9928	Shows the string "Hexadecimal number: 0x0000d829"			

proxymngr

UNIX Shell: Shells (ash, bash, bsh, csh, ksh, sh, tcsh, zsh)

Function	The proxy manager service determines client requests, keeping track of available and starting new proxies.
Syntax	proxymngr [options...]

-config *file*	Overrides the default proxy manager config file.
-timeout *time*	Specifies the amount of time, in seconds, between search attempts. Default is 10.
-retries *amount*	Specifies the amount of retries between search attempts. Default is 3.
-verbose	Verbose mode. Shows more information including tracing and debugging records.

File Name:	proxymngr	**Directory:**	**AIX:** /usr/lpp/X11/bin/, **BSD, Linux:** /usr/X11R6/bin/, **Solaris:** /usr/openwin/bin/	**Type:**	External

ps

UNIX Shell: Shells (ash, bash, bsh, csh, ksh, sh, tcsh, zsh)

Function	Shows process ID, execution time, command name, terminal and other information about the active processes.
Syntax	ps [options...]

AIX:	
-A	Shows information for all processes.
-a	Shows processes associated with a terminal and that isn't a session leaders.
-c *clist*	Shows only processes assigned to the workload management classes listed in the clist.
-d	Shows processes that aren't session leaders.
-e	Shows processes that aren't kernel process.
-F *format*	Shows the information in the specified format.
-f	Generates a full list.
-G *glist*	Shows only processes assigned to the process group listed in the glist.
-k	Shows kernel processes.
-l	Generates a long list.
-m	Lists kernel threads with processes.
-N	Hides any thread statistics.
-n *namelist*	Specifies alternative name list file. Only for compatibility, will be ignored.
-o *format*	Shows the information in the specified format.
-p *plist*	Shows only processes with process id listed in plist.
-t *term*	Shows processes associated with the specified terminal.
-U *uidlist*	Shows processes owned by the specified real-user ID number or login name.
-u *uidlist*	Shows processes owned by the specified real-user ID number or login name.
a	Shows processes associated with a terminal.
c	Shows the command name, not the command parameters.
e	Shows the environment and parameters to the command.
ew	Same as e but wrap the line to one more line.
eww	Same as e but wrap the line as many times as needed.
g	Shows all processes.
l	Generates a long listing.
n	Shows numeric output.
s	Shows the size of the kernel stack of each process.
t *tty*	Shows processes associated with the tty. (The same syntax as ps shows.)
u	Shows user-oriented output.
v	Shows PGIN, SIZE, RSS, LIM, TSIZ, TRS, %CPU, %MEM fields.
w	Uses a wide column format—132 instead of 80 characters wide.
x	Shows processes without terminal.

continued

BSD:	
-a	Shows information for all processes.
-c	Shows the command nam not the command parameters.
-C	Changes the way the CPU percentage is calculated.
-e	Shows the environment.
-h	Shows the information header multiple times so it appears on every page.
	The following 3 options shows information associated with the keywords listed.
-j	ser, pid, ppid, pgid, sess, jobc, state, tt, time, and command.
-l	uid, pid, ppid, cpu, pri, nice, vsz, rss, wchan, state, tt, time, and command.
-v	pid, state, time, sl, re, pagein, vsz, rss, lim, tsiz, %cpu, %mem, and command.
-u	user, pid, %cpu, %mem, vsz, rss, tt, state, start, time, and command.
-L	Lists the available keywords.
-M *core*	Extracts information from the name list specified by core and not /dev/kmem.
-m	Sorts the output by memory usage.
-N *system*	Extracts the name list from the specified system instead of /bsd.
-O *format*	Adds information specified in a space or comma-separated list to the header.
-o *format*	Shows information specified in a space or comma-separated list in the header.
-p *pid*	Shows information about processes associated with process id pid.
-r	Sorts by current cpu usage.
-S	Changes the way the CPU time is calculated by add the children's time to the parents.
-T	Shows only processes associated with STDIN.
-t *term*	Shows processes associated with the specified terminal.
-U *username*	Shows processes owned by the specified username.
-W *swap*	Extracts swap information from file instead of /dev/drum.
-w	Uses a wide column format 132 instead of 80 characters wide.
-x	Shows processes without associated terminal.
Linux:	
-A	Shows all processes.
-N	Inverts the selection of other options. Shows processes not selected.
-a	Shows processes associated with a terminal and that isn't a session leaders.
-d	Shows processes that aren't session leaders.
-e	Shows all processes.
T	Shows processes associated with a terminal.
a	Shows all processes associated with a terminal.
g	Shows all processes.
r	Shows only running processes.
x	Shows processes without associated terminal.
--deselect	Inverts the selection of other options. Shows processes not selected.
-C *list*	Shows processes with command name in list.
-G *glist*	Shows only processes assigned to the process group listed in the glist.
-U *list*	Shows processes owned by the specified real-user ID number or login name.
-g *list*	Shows processes specified by session leader OR by group name in list.
-p *list*	Shows only processes with process id listed in list.
-s *session*	Shows processes belonging to the specified session.
-t *term*	Shows processes associated with the specified terminal.
-u *uidlist*	Shows processes owned by the specified real-user ID number or login name.
U *uid*	Shows processes owned by the specified real-user ID number or login name.
P *list*	Shows only processes with process id listed in list.
t *term*	Shows processes associated with the specified terminal.
--Group *list*	Shows only processes assigned to the real group listed in the glist.
--User *uidlist*	Shows processes owned by the specified real-user ID number or login name.
--group *glist*	Shows only processes assigned to the effective group listed in the glist.
--pid *list*	Shows only processes with process ID listed in list.
--sid *list*	Shows processes belonging to the specified session.
--tty *term*	Shows processes associated with the specified terminal.
--user *ulist*	Shows processes owned by the specified real user ID number or login name.
-sid	Shows processes belonging to the specified session.
pid	Shows only processes with the specified process ID.

continued

-O *format*	Specifies the output format.
-c	Shows a different scheduler info for the -l option.
-f	Generates a full list.
-j	Shows the output in job format.
-l	Generates a long list.
-o *format*	Specifies the output format.
-y	Hides any flags.
O *format*	Specifies the output format.
X	Generates old Linux i386 format.
j	Shows the output in job format.
l	Generates a long list.
o *format*	Specifies the output format.
s	Shows the output in signal format.
u	Shows the output in user-oriented format.
v	Shows the output in virtual memory format.
--format *format*	Specifies the output format.
-H	Shows process hierarchy.
-m	Shows threads.
-n	Sets the name list file.
-w	Uses a wide column format—132 instead of 80 characters wide.
C	Uses raw cpu time for %CPU instead of decaying average.
N	Sets the name list file.
S	Includes some dead children processes.
c	Shows the command name, not the command parameters.
e	Shows the environment.
f	Shows process hierarchy.
h	Hides header lines.
m	Shows all threads.
n	Uses numeric output.
w	Uses a wide column format—132 instead of 80 characters wide.
--cols *n*	Sets the screen width to n.
Solaris:	
-a	Shows information for the most frequently requested processes.
-A	Shows information for all processes.
-c	Shows scheduler properties.
-d	Shows information for all processes but session leaders.
-e	Shows information for all processes.
-f	Full listing.
-j	Shows session ID and process group ID.
-l	Long listing.
-L	Shows information for each lightweight process.
-P	Shows the processor ID to which the process or lwp is connected.
-y	Replaces F and ADDR with resident set size of the process (RSS). Used with -l.
-g *grplist*	Only shows processes with the specified group leader ID.
-G *gidlist*	Shows processes owned by the specified real group ID number.
-n *namelist*	Specifies alternative name list file. Only for compatibility, will be ignored.
-o *format*	Shows the information in the specified format.
-p *proclist*	Only shows processes with the specified PID.
-s *sidlist*	Only shows processes with the specified session leader ID.
-t *term*	Only shows processes associated with the specified terminal.
-u *uidlist*	Shows processes owned by the specified effective user ID number or login name.
-U *uidlist*	Shows processes owned by the specified real user ID number or login name.

File Name:	ps	**Directory:**	**AIX, Solaris:** /usr/bin/, **BSD, Linux:** /bin/	**Type:**	External
Tip:	Useful when you want to find problematic processes and then kill them.				
Common:	ps -a	Shows many processes.			
Common:	ps -l	Shows processes in log format.			
AIX:	ps -k	Shows all kernel processes.			

continued

Linux:	ps -ac	Shows only the command name for each process.
OpenBSD:	ps -r	Sorts the output by cpu usage.
Solaris:	ps -ef | grep inetd	Shows info about the inetd process.

pushd

UNIX Shell: Shells (bash, csh, tcsh, zsh)

Function	Changes to a new working directory and places the current working directory into a directory stack.
Syntax	pushd [option]

	Select only one of the following:
+n	Rotates the stack n times and changes to the directory at the top.
directory	Pushes the current directory onto the stack and changes to that directory.
bash:	
-n	Doesn't change the directory
-n	Rotates the stack n times starting from the right and changes to the directory.
tcsh:	
-p	Hides the directory stack.
-l	Prevents the use of ~ in the output.
-n	Wraps lines longer than the screen.
-v	Shows one entry per line.
zsh:	
old new	Substitutes the word old with new in the current path and changes to that one.
-n	Hides the directory stack.

Tip:	Swaps between directory stacks when used without any options.	
Common:	pushd /etc	Changes to /etc and pushes the current dir on the stack.
Common:	pushd +3	Moves the 3rd entry to the top of the stack and then changes its directory to it.
Common:	pushd usr var	Replaces any usr with var in the current path and goes there.

pwd

UNIX Shell: Shells (ash, bash, bsh, csh, ksh, sh, tcsh, zsh)

Function	Shows the absolute path to the current working directory.
Syntax	pwd [option]

Linux:	
--help	Shows help information.
--version	Shows version information.
	It is internal in Bourne, Bash, Korn, and Z-shells (sh, bash, ksh, zsh).
bash:	
-L	Shows the working directory with symbolic links.
-P	Shows the working directory without symbolic links.
zsh:	
-L	Shows the working directory with symbolic links.
-P	Shows the working directory without symbolic links.
-r	The same as -P.

File Name:	pwd	**Directory:**	**AIX, Solaris:** /usr/bin/, **BSD, Linux:** /bin/	**Type:**	External, Internal
Common:	pwd	Shows which directory you are currently in, e.g. `/export/home/ucg`.			
Common:	pwd -L	Shows current directory with any symbolic links.			

quota

UNIX Shell: Shells (ash, bash, bsh, csh, ksh, sh, tcsh, zsh)

Function	Shows the disk usage and limits for a user on mounted file systems.
Syntax	quota [options...] Solaris: quota [-v] *user*

-v	Verbose mode. Shows user's quota on all mounted file systems.
AIX:	
-g *{ group }*	Shows quotas for the specified user group.
-u *{ user }*	Shows quotas for the specified user.
	The following options can't be combined:
-v	Verbose mode. Shows user's quota on all mounted file systems.

continued

-q	Shows message about file systems with usage over quotas.
BSD:	
-u *{ user }*	Shows quotas for the specified user.
-g *{ group }*	Shows quotas for the specified user group.
-q	Shows message about file systems with usage over quotas. Can't be combined with -v.
Linux:	
-u *{ user }*	Shows quotas for the specified user (default).
-g *{ group }*	Shows quotas for the specified user group.
-q	Shows message about file systems with usage over quotas.
Solaris:	
-v	Shows user quota on all mounted file systems with quotas.
user	Specifies the user by name or can be the numeric UID of a user.

File Name:	quota	**Directory:**	/usr/sbin/	**Type:**	External
Note:	Only the superuser is allowed to use the user argument.				
Common:	quota	Shows your disk usage and limits. Only exceeded quotas are shown.			
Common:	quota -v	Shows quotas on all file systems where quotas exist.			
Common:	quota ucg	The superuser can check quotas for the user ucg.			

quotacheck

UNIX Shell: Shells (ash, bash, bsh, csh, ksh, sh, tcsh, zsh)

Function	Checks and updates the quota for mounted file systems.
Syntax	quotacheck [options...] *filesystem*

-a	Checks all the file systems.
AIX:	
-g	Checks group quotas only.
-u	Checks user quotas only.
-v	Shows discrepancies between the calculated and recorded disk quotas.
BSD:	
-d	Enables debugging mode.
-g	Checks group quotas only.
-u	Checks user quotas only.
-l *number*	Limits the number of parallel checks to the specified number.
-v	Shows discrepancies between the calculated and recorded disk quotas.
Linux:	
-d	Enables debug mode.
-g	Checks group quotas only.
-u	Checks user quotas only.
-v	Verbose mode. Shows more information.
-R	Disables checking the root file system.
Solaris:	
-p	Will parallel check the file system's quota. If logging is enabled, you must use -f .
-f	Forces a check if logging is enabled. Must be used with the -p option.
-v	Calculates disk quotas for each user on a file system.

File Name:	quotacheck	**Directory:**	**AIX, Solaris:** /usr/sbin/, **BSD, Linux:** /sbin/	**Type:**	External
AIX:	quotacheck -au	Checks user quotas on all file systems.			
Linux:	quotacheck -ag	Checks group quotas on all file systems.			
OpenBSD:	quotacheck -l 10 /mnt	Checks the file system mounted on `/mnt/` and limits the parallel checks to 10.			
Solaris:	quotacheck -pfa	Checks all file systems parallel.			

quotaoff

UNIX Shell: Shells (ash, bash, bsh, csh, ksh, sh, tcsh, zsh)

Function	Turns off disk quotas for file systems.
Syntax	quotaoff [options...] *{ filesystems... }*

-a	Disables all file systems where quotas are enabled.
-v	Shows a message for every file system with quotas disabled.
filesystem...	Specifies ufs file systems. Can't be used with -a.

continued

AIX, BSD, Linux: -g -u		 Specifies that only group quotas are disabled. Specifies that only user quotas are disabled.			
File Name:	quotaoff	**Directory:**	/usr/sbin/, **Linux:** /sbin/	**Type:**	External
Common:	quotaoff -a	Turns off quota for every file system.			
Common:	quotaoff /ucg	Turns off quota for the file system /ucg.			

quotaon

UNIX Shell: Shells (ash, bash, bsh, csh, ksh, sh, tcsh, zsh)

Function	Enables disk quotas for file systems.
Syntax	quotaon [options...] *{ filesystems... }*

-a -v *filesystems...*		Enables quota for all file systems. Shows a message for every file system with quotas enabled. Specifies file systems. Can't be used with -a.			
File Name:	quotaon	**Directory:**	/usr/sbin/, **Linux:** /sbin/	**Type:**	External
Common:	quotaon -a	Turns on quotas for all file systems with quotas on them.			
Common:	quotaon /ucg	Turns on quotas for /ucg.			

ranlib

UNIX Shell: Shells (ash, bash, bsh, csh, ksh, sh, tcsh, zsh)

Function	Appends a table of contents to archive libraries so that they are linked faster.
Syntax	ranlib [options...] *archive* Solaris: ranlib *archive*

archive **AIX:** -t -X *type* 32 64 32_64 **BSD:** -t **Linux:** -v		Specifies the archive to convert. Touches the archives. No modification is done. Specifies the object file to examine. Processes 32-bit files. Processes 64-bit files. Processes both 32-and 64-bit files. Sets the modification time of the __.SYMDEF file. Shows version information.			
File Name:	ranlib	**Directory:**	/usr/ccs/bin/, **Linux:** /usr/bin/	**Type:**	Script
Note:	The function that ranlib has is now supported in `ar`, so it isn't used so often now.				
Common:	ranlib mybook	Converts mybook to a random-access library.			
AIX:	ranlib -X 32 mybook hisbook herbook	Processes 32-bit archives.			

rcp

UNIX Shell: Shells (ash, bash, bsh, csh, ksh, sh, tcsh, zsh)

Function	Copies files between two computers. The computer can be local or remote.
Syntax	rcp [options...] *sources... destination*

-p	Attempts to give the file same ACLs, access times, and modes as the original file.
-r	Copies a directory and includes all files and subdirectories.
sources...	Specifies the files or directories to copy from.
destination	Specifies the file or directory to copy to. (The format used is: username@hostname.domain:directory/filename.)
AIX:	
-F	Forwards the credentials.
-k *realm*	Specifies the realm for the destination computer.
BSD:	
-K	Doesn't authenticate Kerberos.
-x	Copies the files in encrypted form.

continued

-k *realm*	Specifies the realm for the destination computer.
Linux:	
-x	Copies the files in encrypted form.

File Name:	rcp	**Directory:**	/usr/bin/, **BSD:** /bin/	**Type:**	External
Warning:	This command is a security risk . Use with caution.				
Common:	rcp file1 host1:/tmp	Copies file1 to /tmp at host1.			
Common:	rcp /etc host1:/tmp	Copies /etc and all files to /tmp/etc at host1.			

rdist

UNIX Shell: Shells (ash, bash, bsh, csh, ksh, sh, tcsh, zsh)

Function	Distributes files from one computer to others. Keeps the owner, group, mode, and modification times.
Syntax	rdist [options...] *{ Name... }* Solaris: rdist [options...]

-D	Shows debug information.
-n	Shows commands that would run but doesn't run them. Dummy mode.
	To specify a predefined way of updating files, use the following options.
-d *macroname=value*	Specifies a value to the specified macro.
-f *distfile*	Specifies the distribution file to use.
-m *host*	Specifies the host of the computer to update. You can use -m several times.
	To specify exactly what to update you may use this. Not used with -d, -f or -m
-c *pathnames... [username@]host[:destpath]*	Updates pathnames on the specified host with the given username.
AIX:	
-b	Compares files in a binary format, not by dates and sizes.
-h	Copies linked file instead of the link itself.
-i	Jumps over links that don't have a destination file.
-q	Enables stealth mode. Hides what files are being updated.
-R	Removes files in the remote directory that exist on the local directory while updating.
-v	Checks whether all the files on the remote computers are the most current.
-w	Keeps the file structure with whole pathnames of the files being copied.
-y	Doesn't update files that were created before the current base file.
name	Specifies a subcommand to execute or a file to update.
BSD,Linux:	
-A *amount*	Specifies minimum free inodes that must exist on a file system to perform an update.
-a *amount*	Specifies minimum free space in bytes existing on a file system to perform an update.
-F	Disables forking `rdist` child processes.
-l *options*	Specifies options to use for local logging as option=suboption:option=suboptions.
-L *options*	Runs as above but for remote logging. The following options are valid:
stdout	Outputs to standard out.
file	Outputs to a file. File is specified as file=filename=suboptions.
syslog	Enables the `syslog` daemon.
notify	Enables `rdist`'s internal notify service and messages
	The following sets the type of info logged, should be a comma-separated list.
change	Logs information about changes.
info	Logs general information.
notice	Logs general information about changes.
nerror	Logs normal errors.
ferror	Logs fatal errors.
warning	Logs serious errors which aren't really fatal.
debug	Debug mode. Logs debug information.
all	Logs all of the above except debug information.
-M *amount*	Specifies the max amount of child processes running simultaneously. (Default is 4.)
-o *options...*	Sets `dist` options in a comma-separated list. The following options are valid:
verify	Checks if all the files on the remote computers are the most current.
whole	Keeps the file structure with whole pathnames of the files being copied.
noexec	Skips executable files in `a.out` format.
younger	Doesn't update files that were created before the current base file.

continued

compare	Makes a binary comparison on files to see if they differ, not by dates and sizes.
follow	Copies linked file instead of the link itself.
ignlnks	Ignores links that can't be resolved.
chknfs	Skips host residing on an NFS file system.
chkreadonly	Checks if the specified host is on a read-only file system and skips updating if so.
chksym	Checks if target is a symbolic link but not the source. If so, target is left as it is.
quiet	Enables stealth mode. Don't show files that are being updated.
remove	Removes files in the remote directory that don't exist on the local directory while updating.
nochkowner	Skips checking file user ownership before updating, sets new ownership after update.
nochkgroup	Skips checking file group ownership before updating, sets new ownership after update.
nochkmode	Skips checking permissions before updating, permissions are set after update.
nodescend	Skips the recursive checking of directories.
numchkgroup	Checks group ownership by groupID instead of group name.
numchkowner	Checks user ownership by userID instead of username.
savetargets	Saves files being updated as file.old instead of removing them.
-p *path*	Specifies target host's rdistd server path.
-P *path*	Specifies the transport command's path (efault is `rsh`).
-t *time*	Specifies the time in seconds before process will timeout (default is 900 seconds).
-V	Shows version information.
sparse	Checks for sparse files.
Solaris:	
-b	Makes a binary comparison on files to see if they differ, not by dates and sizes.
-h	Copies linked file instead of the link itself.
-i	Jumps over links that don't have a destination file.
-q	Enables stealth mode. Hides files that are being updated.
-R	Removes files in the remote directory that don't exist on the local directory while updating.
-v	Checks whether all the files on the remote computers are the most current.
-w	Keeps the file structure with whole pathnames of the files being copied.
-y	Doesn't update files that were created before the current base file.

File Name:	rdist	**Directory:**	/usr/bin/	**Type:**	External
Common:	rdist -f /ucg_examples/distfile	Distributes files selected from the description file.			
Common:	rdist -c project/main.c ucgcomputer	Updates main.c on ucgcomputer.			
Linux:	rdist -l stdout=changes:syslog=ferror	Outputs change information to STDOUT and fatal error information to syslog.			
OpenBSD:	rdist -l stdout=all, debug	Outputs all information, including debug to standard output.			

read

UNIX Shell: Shells (sh, bash, ksh, zsh)

Function	Reads a line from STDIN.
Syntax	AIX: read [options...] *{ variable?prompt } { variables... }* Solaris, bash: read [options...] *variables...* sh: read *variables...* ksh: read [options...] *{ variable?prompt } { variables... }*

	read is external in AIX and Solaris and internal in sh, ksh, bash and zsh
variables...	Specifies variables. Place the first word in the first variable and so on. (The last part of the string is placed in the last variable.)
AIX:	
-p	Reads the input from a process spawned using |&
-r	Doesn't treat a backslash character in any special way.
-s	Saves the input in the Korn Shell history file.
-u *{ n }*	Reads from an open one-digit file descriptor (default is 0 ,which is the keyboard).
variable?prompt	Shows prompt on STDERR.
Solaris:	
-r	Doesn't treat a backslash character in any special way.
bash:	
-e	Uses readline to obtain the line.
-r	Doesn't treat a backslash character in any special way.
-s	Specifies silent mode; doesn't echo characters.

continued

-t *time*	Times out after time seconds and returns with an error.
-a *array*	Specifies an array to assign values to starting at position 0.
-p *prompt*	Specifies a prompt to display.
-n *NR*	Returns after NR characters has been read.
-d *delim*	Specifies character that should terminate the input (default is new line).
ksh:	
-p	Reads the input from a process spawned using |&.
-r	Doesn't treat a backslash character in any special way.
-s	Saves the input in the history file.
-u *{ num }*	Reads from an open one-digit file descriptor (default is 0 ,which is the keyboard).
variable?prompt	Shows prompt on STDERR.
zsh:	
-r	Uses raw mode, a \ at the end of a row isn't treated in any special way.
-q	Reads one character. If it is y or Y, sets variable to y; otherwise n.
-k *{ n }*	Reads only one or n character.
-z	Reads one entry from the command stack and places it in the first variable.
-e	Echoes the output to STDOUT, doesn't assign any variables.
-E	Echoes the output to STDOUT.
-A	Specifies the first variable is an array to assign values to.
-c	Reads word of the current command (used inside a function).
-l	Assigns the line as a scalar (used inside a function).
-nc	Gives the number of the word the cursor is on.
-nl	Gives the index of the character the cursor is on.
-u*n*	Reads from file descriptor n.
-p	Reads from the coprocess.

File Name:	`read`	**Directory:**	**AIX, Solaris:** /usr/bin/	**Type:**	External, Internal
Tip:	This command is used with scripts to read input from the user. In C-Shell (csh) use `set variable=$<`.				
Common:	read var1 var2	Places input in two variables.			
Common:	read -r var	Places any \ in the variable.			
AIX:	read var?Choice:	Shows Choice: and waits for an input.			
Linux:	read -p Choice: var	Shows Choice: and waits for an input (bash).			

readonly

UNIX Shell: Shells (ash, bash, bsh, ksh, sh, zsh)

Function	Sets a variable read-only. If no name is given, shows all read-only variables.
Syntax	sh: readonly *{ name... }* ksh: readonly *{ variables... } { variable=value }*

name...	Specifies variables to set to read-only.
bash:	
-a	Specifies that name is an array.
-p	Shows read-only variables.
-f	Specifies that name is a function.
ksh, zsh:	
variable=value	Specifies a variable and assigns value to it.

Common:	readonly ucgbook	Set the variable ucgbook read-only.
Common:	readonly ucgbook=best	Set ucgbook to best and make it read-only (ksh).
Common:	readonly -a func	Set the function func read-only (bash).

reboot

UNIX Shell: Shells (ash, bash, bsh, csh, ksh, sh, tcsh, zsh)

Function	Restarts the operating system.
Syntax	reboot [options...] Solaris: reboot [options...] *{ arguments }*

-n	Doesn't sync the disks.

continued

AIX:	
-l	Doesn't send a message to the system log daemon about the restart.
-q	Performs quick and ungraceful shutdown by not shutting down running processes first.
-t *date*	Specifies the date to set for the next startup. Format is: `mmddHHMM[yy]`.
BSD:	
-d	Creates a dump before rebooting.
-q	Performs quick and ungraceful shutdown by not shutting down running processes first.
Linux:	
-w	Writes only the wtmp record to the `/var/log/wtmp` file. Doesn't reboot.
-d	Doesn't write the wtmp record.
-f	Forces a reboot.
-i	Shuts down all network interfaces just before reboot.
Solaris:	
-d	Creates a dump before rebooting.
-l	Doesn't send a message to the system log daemon about the restart.
-q	Performs quick and ungraceful shutdown by not shutting down running processes first.
arguments	Specifies arguments to pass to the boot process.

File Name:	`reboot`	**Directory:**	/usr/sbin/, **BSD:** /sbin/, **Linux:** /usr/bin/	**Type:**	External
Tip:	Normally you use `shutdown` so the users can log off first.				
Common:	reboot	Restarts the system.			
Solaris:	reboot -- "cdrom -s"	Restarts and boots from CD-ROM into single user mode.			

refer, grefer

UNIX Shell: Shells (ash, bash, bsh, csh, ksh, sh, tcsh, zsh)

Function	Finds and formats references as a preprocessor for nroff or troff.
Syntax	refer [options...] *filenames...*

	Linux Only: The command `grefer` is the same as `refer`.
-b	Doesn't use any flags (numbers or labels) in the text.
-e	Collects references at the end instead of leaving them where they were found.
-n	Doesn't search in the default file.
-a *{ number }*	Specifies the number of authors' names to reverse. Reverses all if no number specified.
-c*list*	Capitalizes the fields that have a key-letter matching one in the list specified.
-k*x*	Labels references with data taken from a field in a database starting with %x.
-l *{ name,year }*	Labels references with the author's last name and the year (see below) when published.
name,year	Specifies how many characters the author's name and the publication year may contain.
-p *filename*	Specifies a file from which to read reference.
-s*key-letters*	Sorts the references field by the key letters specified.
filenames...	Specifies the file or files to format.
AIX:	
-B `label.macro`	Creates a troff command input file and creates .AP macro file with the label variable.
-f *value*	Specifies a new footnote number (default is 1).
-P	Moves the punctuation marks after the reference signal instead of before.
-S	Creates the references in social science format, also known as the natural format.
BSD:	
-C	Recognizes .R1 and .R2 even when the next character isn't a space or a newline.
-f *value*	Specifies a new footnote number (default is 1).
-i *value*	Ignores the specified value when searching for keys in a database without indexes.
-P	Moves the punctuation marks after the reference signal instead of before.
-S	Creates the references in social science format, also known as the natural format.
-t*value*	Limits the number of first characters needing to match when searching for keywords.
Linux:	
-C	Recognizes .R1 and .R2 even when the next character isn't a space or a newline.
-f *value*	Specifies a new footnote number (default is 1).
-P	Moves the punctuation marks after the reference signal instead of before.
-S	Creates the references in social science format, also known as the natural format.
-i *value*	Ignores the specified value when searching for keys in a database without indexes.
-t*value*	Limits the number of first characters needing to match when searching for key words.

continued

File Name:	`refer`	**Directory:**	/usr/bin/	**Type:**	External
Common:	refer -p refs macros.ms	Reads references from refs and format macros.ms.			

rehash

UNIX Shell: Shells (csh, tcsh, zsh)

Function	Recalculates the internal hash table.
Syntax	rehash

renice

UNIX Shell: Shells (ash, bash, bsh, csh, ksh, sh, tcsh, zsh)

Function	Alters the priority of currently running processes.
Syntax	renice *{ priority }* [options...] AIX: renice [options...]

	The following options can't be combined.
-u *userIDs...*	Specifies the username or the userID of user.
-g *groupIDs...*	Specifies the group name or the groupID of the group.
-p *processIDs...*	Specifies the process name or the process ID of the process.
priority	Specifies the priority for the processes.
AIX,Solaris:	
-n*increment*	Specifies a positive or negative number that alters the priority of the process.

File Name:	`renice`	**Directory:**	/usr/bin/	**Type:**	External
Note:	You need to have system privileges to increase scheduling priority.				
Common:	renice -0 -p 30 40	Sets the scheduling priority to 0 for process ID 30 & 40.			
Common:	renice 5 -g 10	Sets the scheduling priority to 19 for groupID 10.			

repeat

UNIX Shell: Shells (csh, tcsh)

Function	Executes a command a specified number of times.
Syntax	repeat *num command*

num	Specifies how many times to repeat the command.
command	Specifies the command to execute.
Common: repeat 5 echo hello	Prints hello 5 times.

repquota

UNIX Shell: Shells (ash, bash, bsh, csh, ksh, sh, tcsh, zsh)

Function	Shows the quota limit and the usage of the file systems.
Syntax	repquota [options...] *{ filesystem }*

-a	Shows file system usage for all registered file systems (see below) with quotas enabled. **AIX:**/etc/filesystems **BSD, Linux:**/etc/fstab **Solaris:**/etc/vfstab
-v	Shows a summary of quota information for every user on the system.
filesystem	Specifies the file system to show information for.
AIX, BSD, Linux:	
-g	Shows only group quotas.
-u	Shows only user quotas.

File Name:	`repquota`	**Directory:**	/usr/sbin/	**Type:**	External
Common:	repquota -v -a	As above, but shows all users regardless of allocated resources.			
Solaris:	repquota /dev/dsk/c0t0d0s3	Shows quota information for the file system specified.			

resize

UNIX Shell: Shells (ash, bash, bsh, csh, ksh, sh, tcsh, zsh)

Function	Shows current size of the xterm window and sets the `TERMCAP` settings to active window.
Syntax	resize [options...]

-u	Creates commands for Bourne shell if the Bourne shell isn't the current shell.
-c	Creates commands for C shell if the C shell isn't the current shell.
-s *{ row col }*	Shows that Sun console escape sequences are used instead of the xterm escape code.
row col	Asks the xterm to resize itself using the rows and columns given.

continued

File Name:	resize	**Directory:**	**AIX:** /usr/bin/X11/, **BSD, Linux:** /usr/X11R6/bin/, **Solaris:** /usr/openwin/bin/	**Type:**	External
Common:	resize -s 35 80	Sets TERM settings to 35 rows and 80 columns.			

return

UNIX Shell: Shells (ash, bash, bsh, sh, ksh, zsh)

Function	Reports from a shell function. If used outside a function, it functions as exit.	
Syntax	return *{ num }*	
num	The report value. If not given, the reported value of the last command is used.	
Common:	return	Returns from a shell function.
Common:	return 4	Returns with 4 as the exit status.

revnetgroup

UNIX Shell: Shells (ash, bash, bsh, csh, ksh, sh, tcsh, zsh)

Function	Reverses the order of host and user listings in the network group `/etc/netgroup` file in NIS maps.
Syntax	revnetgroup option *{ file }*

	You must select between these two options.
-h	Creates an output that creates the netgroup.byhost map.
-u	Creates an output that creates the netgroup.byuser map.
	BSD Only: The file argument requires a preceding -f.
file	Specifies an alternate netgroup file to use instead of the default /etc/netgroup.

File Name:	revnetgroup	**Directory:**	/usr/sbin/, **Linux:** /usr/lib/yp/	**Type:**	External
Tip:	Specifying an alternative file makes it possible to create customized network group maps.				
Common:	revnetgroup -h	Creates an output sorted by hosts.			
Common:	revnetgroup -h /etc/netgroup.old	Uses /etc/netgroup.old as the input file.			
OpenBSD:	revnetgroup -h -f /etc/netgroup.old	Uses /etc/netgroup.old as the input file.			

rlogin

UNIX Shell: Shells (ash, bash, bsh, csh, ksh, sh, tcsh, zsh)

Function	Runs a remote login to a remote computer.
Syntax	rlogin [options...] *hostname*

-8	Uses eight-bit data instead of seven-bit data when passing data across the net.
-e*character*	Specifies an escape character to use when disconnecting from the remote host.
-l *username*	Specifies a different username, instead of your local username, for the remote login.
-L	Allows the rlogin session to be run in "litout" mode.
hostname	Specifies the host to login to.
AIX:	
-f	Forwards the credentials.
-F	Causes the credentials to be forwarded. Marked forwardable.
-k *realm*	Specifies realm of the remote station.
BSD, Linux:	
-E	Doesn't recognize any character as an escape character.
-K	Disables all Kerberos authentications.
-L	Runs the rlogin session in "litout" mode.
-d	Turns debugging on for the TCP sockets communicating with the remote host.
-x	Turns on DES encryption of all data passed during the rlogin session.
-k *realm*	**BSD only:** Specifies realm of the remote station.

File Name:	rlogin	**Directory:**	/usr/bin/	**Type:**	External
Note:	The file .rhosts contains a private list of trusted hostname/username combinations.				
Common:	rlogin -l root sun	Remote login as admin on server sun.			
Linux:	rlogin -x sun	Secures the session with encryption.			
OpenBSD:	rlogin -d sun	Runs the command in debug mode.			

rm

UNIX Shell: Shells (ash, bash, bsh, csh, ksh, sh, tcsh, zsh)

Function	Removes files and directories from the file system.
Syntax	rm [options...] *files...*

continued

-r	Removes all directories and subdirectories including any files they contain.
-R	Same as -r.
-f	Removes all files even if write-protected without prompting for confirmation.
-i	Prompts for confirmation before removing any files.
files...	Specifies files or directories to remove.
AIX:	
-e	Shows a message after each file is removed.
BSD:	
-d	Tries to remove directories.
-P	Overwrites files three times before removing them.
-W	Tries to undelete the specified files.
Linux:	
-d	Removes a directory even if it isn't empty. Only for the superuser.
-v	Verbose mode. Shows more information.
--help	Shows help information.
--version	Shows version information.

File Name:	`rm`	**Directory:**	**AIX, Solaris:** /usr/bin/, **BSD, Linux:** /bin/	**Type:**	External

Common:	rm ucgtest	Removes the file ucgtest.
Common:	rm -rf /export/home/ucgtest/	Removes the directory /export/home/ucgtest/ and all files and subdirectories in it without prompting.
Common:	rm -i ucgtest	Interactively removes the file ucgtest.
AIX:	rm -e *.Z	Removes all compressed files in the current directory and shows a message after each one is removed.
Linux:	rm -d /export/home/ucgtest/	Removes the directory /export/home/ucgtest/ even if it isn't empty. Can only be used by the superuser.
OpenBSD:	rm -P test	Removes the file test by first overwriting it three times.

rmdir

UNIX Shell: Shells (ash, bash, bsh, csh, ksh, sh, tcsh, zsh)

Function	Removes empty directories from the file system.
Syntax	rmdir [options...] *directories...*

-p	Removes the parent directory if it is empty after removing the child directory.
directories...	Specifies directories to be removed.
Linux:	
--ignore-fail-on-non-empty	Ignores errors caused by directories not being empty.
-v	Verbose mode. Shows more information.
--help	Shows help information.
--version	Shows version information.
Solaris:	
-s	Hides messages on STDERR when -p is used.

File Name:	`rmdir`	**Directory:**	**AIX, Solaris:** /usr/bin/, **BSD, Linux:** /bin/	**Type:**	External

Tip: You can use `rm -R` to erase a directory that isn't empty.

Common:	rmdir -p /ucg/ucg	Removes /ucg/ucg and /ucg if they are empty.
Common:	rmdir /export/home/ucg /ucg/ucg	Removes the directories /export/home/ucg and /ucg/ucg if they are empty.

rmt

UNIX Shell: Shells (ash, bash, bsh, csh, ksh, sh, tcsh, zsh)

Function	Allows remote access to magnetic tape devices, normally started from a rexec or rcmd subroutine.
Syntax	rmt

File Name:	`rmt`	**Directory:**	/usr/sbin/, **Linux:** /sbin/	**Type:**	External

route	**UNIX Shell:**	Shells (ash, bash, bsh, csh, ksh, sh, tcsh, zsh)
Function	Manages and shows the routing tables on the host.	
Syntax	AIX, BSD, Solaris: route [options...] *ACTION { type } destination gateway { modifiers... }* Linux: route [options...] *{ ACTION [type } destination { modifiers... }]*	

-n	Hides host and network symbolic.
-v	Verbose mode. Shows more information.
destination	Specifies the destination network or host.
gateway	Specifies the IP-address where to send packets that are to be routed.
AIX:	
-q	Doesn't show output during execution.
ACTION	**Action can be one of the following.**
add	Adds a route.
change	Changes a route.
delete	Deletes a route.
flush	Deletes all gateway entries from a routing table.
get	Shows a route.
monitor	Monitors changes made to the routing table.
type	Specifies the type of destination.
-net	Specifies the destination is a network.
-host	Specifies the destination is a host.
	These arguments have to come between destination and gateway.
-netmask *netmask*	Specifies the network mask.
-prefixlen *n*	Specifies the number of bits in the netmask.
modifiers...	**You can also specify these additional modifiers for the actions**.
-cloning	Clones a new route.
-genmask	Extracts the length of TSEL.
-interface	Manipulates interface routing entries.
-rtt *n*	Sets the round-trip time.
-rttvar *n*	Sets the round-trip time variance.
-sendpipe *n*	Sets the send-window size.
-recvpipe *n*	Sets the receive-window size.
-allowgroup *gid*	Adds gid to the list of groups that are allowed to use the route.
-denygroup *gid*	Adds gid to the list of groups that aren't allowed to use the route.
-mtu *n*	Sets the maximum transmission unit for the route.
-hopcount *n*	Sets the maximum number of gateways in the route.
-expire *n*	Sets the expiration metrics for the routing protocol.
-ssthresh *n*	Sets the outbound gateway buffer limit.
-lock *modifier*	Specifies a meta-modifier that can individually lock a metric modifier.
-lockrest	Specifies a meta-modifier that can lock all subsequent metrics.
BSD	
-d	Shows debug information. Doesn't change the routing table.
-q	Hides everything.
ACTION	**Action can be one of the following.**
add	Adds a route.
change	Changes a route.
delete	Deletes a route.
get	Shows a route.
monitor	Monitors changes made to the routing table.
flush	Deletes all gateway entries from a routing table. (Or flush an address family can be specified to delete those routes. Address family can be: -osi, -xns, -ipx, -link, -encap, -x25, -inet, or -inet6.)
type	Specifies the type of destination.
-net	Specifies the destination is a network.
-host	Specifies the destination is a host.

continued

	These arguments have to come between destination and gateway.
-netmask *netmask*	Specifies the network mask.
-prefixlen *n*	Specifies the number of bits in the netmask.
modifiers...	**You can also specify these additional modifiers for the actions.**
-cloning	Creates a new route that can be used.
-xresolve	Broadcasts messages when executing.
-iface	Specifies that destination is on the same network.
-static	Specifies the route is manually added.
-nostatic	Specifies the route has been added by a daemon or the kernel.
-reject	Disables ICMP requests.
-blackhole	Ignores packets when updates are made.
-proto1	Sets the protocol specific routing flag to 1.
-proto2	Sets the protocol specific routing flag to 2.
-llinfo	Is used for translation between protocol address and link address.
-rtt *n*	Sets the round-trip time.
-rttvar *n*	Sets the round-trip time variance.
-sendpipe *n*	Sets the send-window size.
-mtu *n*	Sets the maximum transmission unit for the route.
-hopcount *n*	Sets the maximum numbers of gateways in the route.
-expire *n*	Sets the expiration metrics for the routing protocol.
-ssthresh *n*	Sets the outbound gateway buffer limit.
-lock *modifier*	Specifies a meta-modifier that can individually lock a metric modifier.
-lockrest	Specifies a meta-modifier that can lock all subsequent metrics.
-ifp *interface*	Specifies the interface.
-ifa *address*	Specifies the interface address.
-interface *interface*	Specifies the interface to use.
Linux:	
-A *family*	Specifies the address family. Use route --help for a list.
-F	Alters the kernel forwarding information base routing table (is default).
-C	Alters the kernel routing cache.
-e	Shows the routing table in netstat format.
--help	Shows help information.
--version	Shows version information.
ACTION	**Action can be one of the following.**
add	Adds a route.
del	Deletes a route.
type	Specifies the type of destination.
-net	Specifies the destination is a network.
-host	Specifies the destination is a host.
modifiers...	**You can also specify these additional modifiers for the actions.**
netmask *netmask*	Specifies the network mask for the target network.
gw *gateway*	Specifies the ip-address where to send packets that are to be routed.
metric *n*	Specifies the metric value in the routing table.
mss *n*	Sets the TCP maximum segment size to n bytes.
window *n*	Sets the TCP window size to n bytes.
irtt *msec*	Sets the initial round trip time to msec milliseconds.
reject	Blocks the route.
mod	Installs a modified route (used by the routing daemon and for diagnostic).
dyn	Installs a dynamic route (used by the routing daemon and for diagnostic).
reinstate	Reinstates a route (used by the routing daemon and for diagnostic).
dev *interface*	Specifies the interface to use.
Solaris:	
-f	Flushes routing tables for all gateways.
-n	Hides host and network symbolic.
-v	Verbose mode. Shows more information.
-q	Doesn't show output during execution.

continued

ACTION		**Action can be one of the following.**			
add		Adds a route.			
change		Changes a route.			
delete		Deletes a route.			
flush		Deletes all gateway entries from a routing table.			
get		Shows a route.			
monitor		Monitors changes made to the routing table.			
type		Specifies the type of destination.			
host		Specifies the destination is a host.			
net		Specifies the destination is a network.			
modifiers...		**You can also specify these additional modifiers for the actions.**			
-cloning		Creates a new route that can be used.			
-xresolve		Broadcasts messages when executing.			
-iface		Specifies that destination is on the same network.			
-static		Specifies the route is manually added.			
-nostatic		Specifies the route has been added by a daemon or the kernel.			
-reject		Disables ICMP requests.			
-blackhole		Ignores packets when updates are made.			
-proto1		Sets the protocol-specific routing flag to 1.			
-proto2		Sets the protocol-specific routing flag to 2.			
-llinfo		Is used for translation between protocol address and link address.			
File Name:	`route`	**Directory:**	**AIX, Solaris:** /usr/sbin/, **BSD, Linux:** /sbin/	**Type:**	External
Note:	A default route can be added by specifying the destination network name to be default.				
AIX:	route add -host star moon	Creates a route for the host star via the host moon.			
Linux:	route -add -net 192.22.15.0 netmask 255.255.255.0 gw moon	Sets up a route to the 192.22.15.0 network via gateway moon.			
OpenBSD:	route -flush	Removes all entries from the routing table.			
Solaris:	route add net default 192.22.15.22	Specifies 192.22.15.22 to be the default router.			

rpc.rstatd

UNIX Shell: Shells (ash, bash, bsh, csh, ksh, sh, tcsh, zsh)

Function	Returns statistics received from the kernel about performance.				
Syntax	rpc.rstatd				
File Name:	`rpc.rstatd`	**Directory:**	**AIX, Linux:** /usr/sbin/, **BSD:** /usr/libexec/, **Solaris:** /usr/lib/netsvc/rstat/	**Type:**	External

rpc.rusersd

UNIX Shell: Shells (ash, bash, bsh, csh, ksh, sh, tcsh, zsh)

Function	The username server that lists users on the host.				
Syntax	rpc.rusersd				
File Name:	`rpc.rusersd`	**Directory:**	**AIX, Solaris:** /usr/lib/netsvc/rusers/, **BSD:** /usr/libexec/, **Linux:** /usr/sbin/	**Type:**	External

rpc.rwalld

UNIX Shell: Shells (ash, bash, bsh, csh, ksh, sh, tcsh, zsh)

Function	The `rwall` server that manages rwall requests. It is applied by using `wall` on all appropriate hosts.				
Syntax	rpc.rwalld				
File Name:	`rpc.rwalld`	**Directory:**	**AIX, Solaris:** /usr/lib/netsvc/rwall/, **BSD:** /usr/libexec/, **Linux:** /usr/sbin/	**Type:**	External

rpc.yppasswdd, yppasswdd

UNIX Shell: Korn shell (ksh)

Function	Handles the requests that comes from yppasswd to set new correct passwords.
Syntax	rpc.yppasswdd *{ passwdfile }* [options...]

AIX, BSD, Solaris:	
-nogecos	Disables altering of the `GECOS` field in the password file.
-noshell	Disables altering of the `shell` field in the password file.

continued

-nopw -m *{ arg1 }* *{ arg2... }* *passwdfile*	Disables the altering of the password file. Uses `make` on /var/yp. Arguments specified are passed to make. Ignored in Linux. Specifies the path to password file you want to change.
AIX: -r	 Updates /var/yp/domainname/passwd.byname and /var/yp/domainname/passwd.byuid directly.
BSD: -d *directory*	 Specifies the directory where passwd, shadow or passwd.adjunct files exist.
Solaris: -D *directory* *adjunctfile*	 Specifies the directory where passwd, shadow or passwd.adjunct files exists. Specifies the adjunctfile and can't be used without the -D option.
Linux: -D *directory* -E *program* -p *passwdfile* -s *shadowfile* -e chsh -e chfn -x *program* -v	 Specifies the directory where passwd, shadow files exist. Specifies the program to edit the passwd file. Specifies a different password file then the default `/etc/passwd/`. Specifies a different password file then the default `/etc/passwd/`. Disables altering of the shell field in the password file. Disables altering of the GECOS field in the password file. Runs the program specified and passes current information to the program. Shows version information.

File Name:	`rpc.yppasswdd`	**Directory:**	**AIX, Solaris:** /usr/lib/netsvc/yp/, **BSD, Linux:** :/usr/sbin/	**Type:**	External
Tip:	Solaris: Make sure you check the PWDIR variable in `/var/yp/Makefile` if you plan to use -D option.				
AIX:	rpc.yppasswdd -m	Starts up and does a make after every modification is done.			
Linux:	rpc.yppasswdd -e chfn	Starts the daemon and doesn't let users change shells and realname, phone or others.			
OpenBSD:	rpc.yppasswdd -nopw -m	Starts up and doesn't let users change their passwords.			
Solaris:	rpc.yppasswdd -noshell -nogecos -m	Starts the daemon and doesn't let users change shells and realname, phone or others.			

rpcgen

rpcgen	**UNIX Shell:**	**Shells (ash, bash, bsh, csh, ksh, sh, tcsh, zsh)**
Function	Creates C code to make an rpc protocol.	
Syntax	rpcgen [options...] *{ infile }*	

-o *outfile*	Specifies the output file. (Can only be used with options that can't be combined.)
	These options can't be combined:
-c	Compiles to XDR routines.
-h	Compiles to C data-definitions. Creates header which supports RPC dispatch tables.
-l	Compiles to client-side stubs.
-m	Compiles to server-side stubs, doesn't create main routine.
-s *nettype*	Specifies class nettype to compile to server-stubs.
tcp	Refers to Internet UDP.
udp	Refers to Internet TCP.
	The following are also available in BSD, Linux, and Solaris
netpath	Specifies the transports which have been specified in the NETPATH env table.
visible	Chooses transports that have the visible flag in the `/etc/netconfig file`.
circuit_n	The same as netpath but it chooses only connection-oriented transports.
circuit_v	The same as visible but it chooses only connection-oriented transports.
datagram_n	The same as netpath but it chooses only connectionless transports.
datagram_v	The same as visible but it chooses only connectionless transports.
infile	Specifies in file to create rpc protocol.
BSD:	
-a	Creates all files, including sample files.
-b	Backward compatibility mode. SunOS4.1.
-C	Generates ANSI C code.
-D*name*[=*value*]	Specifies a symbol name.
-K *seconds*	Specifies seconds for request timeout.
-N	Enables user to use multiple arguments.
-T	Creates code to support RPC dispatch tables.

continued

	These options can't be combined:
-t	Compiles to RPC dispatch table.
-Sc	Creates sample client code that uses remote procedure calls.
-Ss	Creates sample server code that uses remote procedure calls.
-n *netid*	Specifies the transport to compile to server-side stubs.
Linux:	
-a	Creates all files including sample files.
-b	Backward compatibility mode. SunOS4.1.
-C	Generates ANSI C code.
-D*name*[=*value*]	Specifies a symbol name.
-I	Compiles support for `inetd`.
-K *seconds*	Specifies seconds for request timeout.
-N	Enables user to use multiple arguments.
-T	Creates code to support RPC dispatch tables.
-5	Generates SysVr4 style RPC code.
-k	Generates code in K&R C.
	These options can't be combined:
-t	Compiles to RPC dispatch table.
-Sc	Creates sample client code that uses remote procedure calls.
-Ss	Creates sample server code that uses remote procedure calls.
-n *netid*	Specifies the transport to compile to server-side stubs.
Solaris:	
-a	Creates all files including sample files.
-A	Enables automatic MT mode in server main program.
-b	Backward compatibility mode. SunOS4.1.
-C	Generates ANSI C code.
-D*name*[=*value*]	Specifies a symbol name.
-i *size*	Specifies size to start creating inline code.
-I	Compiles support for `inetd`.
-K *seconds*	Specifies seconds for request timeout.
-L	Logs to STDERR with `syslog`.
-M	Creates multithread-safe stubs.
-N	Enables user to use multiple arguments.
-T	Creates code to support RPC dispatch tables.
-V *pathname*	Specifies start directory to search for c preprocessor.
	These options can't be combined:
-t	Compiles to RPC dispatch table.
-Sc	Creates sample client code that uses remote procedure calls.
-Ss	Creates sample server code that uses remote procedure calls.
-Sm	Creates sample `MakeFile` which is used to compile the application.
-n *netid*	Specifies the transport to compile to server-side stubs.

File Name:	`rpcgen`	**Directory:**	/usr/bin/	**Type:**	External
Common:	rpcgen -h prot.x	Creates a header file.			
Solaris:	rpcgen -T prot.x	Creates all five files: prot.h, prot_clnt.c, prot_svc.c, prot_xdr.c, and prot_tbl.i.			

rpcinfo

UNIX Shell: Shells (ash, bash, bsh, csh, ksh, sh, tcsh, zsh)

Function	Creates an RPC call to an RPC server and shows the information on what it finds.
Syntax	rpcinfo [options...] *{ host } { prognum } { versnum }*

-n *portnum*	Specifies port orther than the one given by rpcbind.
	The following options can't be combined with the -n option.
-b	Creates a Broadcast procedure 0 of the specified versnum and prognum.
-d	Deletes the RPC service registration of specified prognum and versnum.
	The following options can only be combined with the -n option.
-u	Creates an RPC call to a host using UDP on procedure 0 of prognum.
-t	Creates an RPC call to a host using TCP on procedure 0 of prognum.
	The following options can't be combined.
-p	Inspects a rpcbind on host using version 2 of the rpcbind protocol.

continued

host	Specifies the hostname. Required for options l, u, t and optional for options p, m, s.
prognum	Specifies the program number. Required for a, b,d, T, l,u and t options.
versnum	Specifies the version number. Required for b, d, l options. Optional for a, T, u,t.
AIX, Solaris:	
-T *transport*	Specifies the transport on which the service is required. Can be used with -b, -d, -l.
-l	Shows the entries with a versnum and prognum on host.
	The following options can't be combined.
-m	Shows statistics of rpcbind operations on the given host.
-s	Shows a short list of all registered RPC programs on the given host.
	This option exists only in Solaris.
-a *server address*	Ping procedure 0 of specified prognum by server address. Requires the -T option.

File Name:	`rpcinfo`	**Directory:** /usr/bin/	**Type:** External
Tip:	A lot of combinations can give you all you want to know about RPC services on a server.		
Common:	rpcinfo	Lists all the RPC services on the local host.	
Common:	rpcinfo -p server1	Lists the RPC programs using version 2 of rpcbind protocol.	
Common:	rpcinfo -l server1 100000 2	Lists entries with prognum 100000 and versnum 2 on server1.	

rsh, remsh

UNIX Shell: Shells (ash, bash, bsh, csh, ksh, sh, tcsh, zsh)

Function	A remote shell which is used to connect to a host and execute one specified command.
Syntax	rsh [options...] *hostname command* rsh *hostname* [options...] *command*

	AIX, Solaris: The command `remsh` is the same as the command `rsh`.
-n	Blocks the shell to start rsh. The input is redirected to `/dev/null`.
-l*username*	Specifies the username to use on the remote server.
hostname	Specifies the hostname or the IP address of the server.
command	Specifies the command to execute on the remote host.
AIX:	
-f	Forwards user credentials if `Kerberos` is the current authentication method.
-F	Forwards user credentials and flags the credentials to forward them to the next host.
-k *realm*	Specifies the realm to receive Kerberos tickets from instead of the local realm.
BSD:	
-d	Enables socket level debugging.
-K	Disables `Kerberos` authentication.
-k *realm*	Specifies the realm to receive Kerberos tickets from instead of the local realm.
-x	Enables DES encryption for all data transmitted. May slow down response time.
Linux:	
-d	Enables socket level debugging.
-K	Disables `Kerberos` authentication.
-x	Enables DES encryption for all data transmitted. May slow down response time.

File Name:	`rsh`	**Directory:** /usr/bin/	**Type:** External
Note:	Command works only if there is a .rhosts file created on the remote computer.		
Common:	rsh orion ls /var/adm	Lists the files in /var/adm in the computer orion.	
Common:	rsh 192.168.1.244 -l root vi /etc/hosts	Runs the vi editor and edits the /etc/hosts file on remote server.	

rup

UNIX Shell: Shells (ash, bash, bsh, csh, ksh, sh, tcsh, zsh)

Function	Shows the status of machines on the network. Similar to `uptime` but for remote computers.
Syntax	rup [options...] *{ hosts... }*

-h	Sorts by hostname.
-l	Sorts by load average.
-t	Sorts by uptime.
hosts...	Specifies a list of hosts to query.

File Name:	`rup`	**Directory:** /usr/bin/	**Type:** External
Common:	rup pluto moon	Shows status for pluto and moon.	
Common:	rup	Shows status for all remote machines that answer the broadcast.	

ruptime

ruptime	UNIX Shell:	Shells (ash, bash, bsh, csh, ksh, sh, tcsh, zsh)
Function	Shows the status of machines on the network. Similar to `uptime` but for remote machines.	
Syntax	ruptime [options...]	

-a	Includes all users, even those who have been idle for more than one hour.
-l	Sorts by load average.
-r	Reverses the sort order. Should be used with -l, -t, or -u.
-t	Sorts by uptime.
-u	Sorts by number of users.

File Name:	`ruptime`	**Directory:** /usr/bin/	**Type:** External
Common:	ruptime -a	Shows status for remote machines, counting all users, even idle ones.	
Common:	ruptime -rt	Shows status for remote machines sorted by uptime in reverse order.	

rusers

rusers	UNIX Shell:	Shells (ash, bash, bsh, csh, ksh, sh, tcsh, zsh)
Function	Lists users logged into the remote server. Similar to `who` but for remote servers.	
Syntax	rusers [options...] *{ hosts... }*	

-a	Shows every host, even those without current users.
-l	Shows a long format listing.
hosts...	Specifies the IP address or the hostname of the server to check.
AIX, Solaris:	
-h	Sorts the list by hostnames.
-i	Sorts the list by idle time.
-u	Sorts the list by number of users.

File Name:	`rusers`	**Directory:** /usr/bin/	**Type:** External
Common:	rusers -l pluto	Shows a long listing about users logged in to pluto.	
Common:	rusers -a	Shows a listing with all users, including idle ones.	
Common:	rusers pluto moon	Shows a listing about users logged in to pluto and moon.	
AIX:	rusers -h	Shows a listing sorted by hostnames.	
Solaris:	rusers -i	Shows a listing sorted by idle time.	

rwho

rwho	UNIX Shell:	Shells (ash, bash, bsh, csh, ksh, sh, tcsh, zsh)
Function	Shows who is logged in to hosts on the local network.	
Syntax	rwho [-a]	

-a	Includes all users, even those idle for more than an hour.		
File Name:	`rwho`	**Directory:** /usr/bin/	**Type:** External
Common:	rwho	Shows who is logged in on the local network.	
Common:	rwho -a	Shows who is logged in even if they have been idle for more than an hour.	

rwhod, in.rwhod

rwhod, in.rwhod	UNIX Shell:	Shells (ash, bash, bsh, csh, ksh, sh, tcsh, zsh)
Function	A system status server for the programs `rwho` and `ruptime`.	
Syntax	AIX, BSD: rwhod Linux: rwhod [options...] Solaris: in.rwhod [-m] *{ ttl }*	

Linux:	
-b	Specifies that only broadcast interfaces like Ethernets should be used.
-p	Specifies that only point-to-point interfaces will be used.
-a	Specifies that all interfaces should be used. The same as setting no options.
Solaris:	
-m	Sends information via the multicast address 224.0.1.3 and sets IP TimeToLive to 1.
ttl	Transmits packets on one interface and sets IP Time-To-Live specified by ttl.

File Name:	`rwhod, in.rwhod`	**Directory:** /usr/sbin/, **Solaris:** /usr/sbin/	**Type:** External

script

script	UNIX Shell:	Shells (ash, bash, bsh, csh, ksh, sh, tcsh, zsh)
Function	Records everything that is shown on the screen during a terminal session and saves the information into a file.	
Syntax	script [-a] { *file* }	

-a	Appends another terminal session to the same file instead of overwriting it.
file	Specifies the filename to save the recording. (If no filename is given, the file `typescript` will be created.)

File Name:	`script`	**Directory:**	/usr/bin/	**Type:**	External
Tip:	Great to use it if you want to document what you do or if you are creating a script.				
Common:	script -a /tmp/script.txt	Appends the script.txt file.			

sdiff

sdiff	UNIX Shell:	Shells (ash, bash, bsh, csh, ksh, sh, tcsh, zsh)
Function	Compares the two files and shows the differences between them, side by side on the screen.	
Syntax	sdiff [options..] *file1 file2* BSD: sdiff -o *file* [options...] *file1 file2* Linux: sdiff -o *file* [options...] *file1 file2*	

-o *file*	Starts `ed` and merges the two files into the specified file.
	When using -o option, the following internal commands are also available.
l	Adds left column to the end of the file specified with -o.
r	Adds right column to the end of the file specified with -o.
s	Hides identical lines.
v	Shows identical lines.
e l	Edits the left column, using the editor `ed`.
e r	Edits the right column, using the editor `ed`.
e b	Links both files together and calls the editor `ed`.
e	Starts the editor without file.
q	Exits the program.
AIX, Solaris:	
-l	Shows the identical lines on the left side of the screen only.
-s	Hides identical lines.
-w *width*	Changes the output to the line length specified (default is 130 characters).
BSD, Linux:	
-a	Handles all files as text files, even if they are not.
-b	Ignores white space changes.
-B	Ignores changes that just insert or delete blank lines.
-d	Searches more precisely. Finds smaller changes and makes the progress slower.
-H	Uses heuristics to speed handling of large files.
-i	Ignores case mismatch.
-I *expression*	Ignores changes that inserts deletes that match the expressions.
-l	Shows only the left column of two common lines.
-s	Doesn't print common lines.
-t	Converts tabs to spaces.
-v	Shows version information.

File Name:	`sdiff`	**Directory:**	/usr/bin/	**Type:**	External
Note:	This command is basically the same as the *diff* command, but with additional features.				
Common:	sdiff -o mergefile /ucg_examples/textfile1 /ucg_examples/textfile2	Compares the two files and puts the merged information to mergefile.			
Linux:	sdiff -o mergefile -d -s /ucg_examples/textfile1 /ucg_examples/textfile2	Searches more accurately and only writes mismatches.			
OpenBSD:	sdiff -o mergefile -a -i /ucg_examples/textfile1 /ucg_examples/textfile2	Ignores case mismatch and treat the files as text files.			

sed	UNIX Shell:	Shells (ash, bash, bsh, csh, ksh, sh, tcsh, zsh)
Function	Edits text files using a script of specified edit commands and shows the result.	
Syntax	sed [options...] *{ script } { files... }*	

-n	Hides the input lines used for processing. Shows only generated text.
-e *script*	Specifies a subcommand to use on the text file.
-f *scriptfile*	Reads the subcommands from specified file, one command per line.
script	Specifies a single edit command to use on the text file.
files...	Specifies the file to edit.
BSD:	
-a	File isn't opened until a command related to the w function is read from a line.
Linux:	
-V	Shows version information.
-h	Shows help information.
Internal commands:	
{ address } [,address2] command { arguments }	This is the syntax on the internal commands.
address	Specifies a line count, telling which line to work on. (Can also be a $ for current line, a regular expression with a delimiter for a pattern of lines, or nothing at all, for all lines.)
address2	Specifies a range of lines, starting from address to address2. Both must be numbers.
command	Specifies the command to run.
arguments	Specifies the arguments, if any, for the command.
	Following are a list of regular expressions besides basic regular expressions.
\n	A new line character.
\c*STRINGc*	Changes the string to STRING only.
c	Is any character besides a backslash or a new line character.
	Following are the subcommands to use.
	A \ character means that the arguments must be typed on the next line.
a \ *text*	Executes the N command or begins a new cycle.
text	Shows the text each time a new line is read.
b *label*	Jumps to the : command matching the label, or to end of file if none specified.
c \ *text*	Deletes the specified line or lines and shows the text.
d	Deletes the specified line or lines.
D	Deletes the text from the specified beginning to the first new line character. (Starts the next cycle.)
g	Replaces the specified line with the contents of the hold space.
G	Adds the contents of the hold space to the specified line.
h	Fills the hold space with the specified line.
H	Adds the specified line to the hold space.
i \ *text*	Shows the specified text.
l	Shows the specified line in a clear sentence.
n	Shows the specified line and moves to the next line.
N	Adds the next line to the current line with a new line character between.
p	Shows the current line.
P	Shows the current line, up to the first new line character.
q	Quits the script.
r *file*	Shows the contents in the file before next attempt to read a line.
s/*substring*/*replacement*/*flags*	Replaces the specified substring in the line with the replacement string.
flags	A list of flags, specified below:
0 - 9	Replaces only the n'th occurrence found in the line.
g	Replaces all matches found, not only the first.
p	Shows the line if a replacement occurred.
w *file*	Appends the line to the specified file, if a replacement occurred.
t *label*	Jumps to the label if any substitutions have been made.
w *file*	Appends the line to the specified file.
x	Swaps the contents of the pattern and hold spaces.

continued

y/string1/string2	Replaces all characters found in string1 with the corresponding position in string2.
!*command*	Runs the command on all lines that aren't in the range of the addresses.
:*label*	A label sign for the b and t commands.
=	Shows the current line number.
#*comment*	A comment, and does nothing else.

File Name:	sed	**Directory:**	/usr/bin/, **Linux:** /bin/	**Type:**	External
Note:	It is possible to supply several -e and -f options.				
Common:	sed s/hello/HELLO/g example.txt	Replaces hello with HELLO in the example.txt file.			
Common:	sed -n "1,5 l" ucgbook	Shows only the first five lines.			

select

UNIX Shell: Shells (bash, ksh, zsh)

Function	Shows words as a menu on STDERR and $PS3 as a prompt wait for user input. Repeats until terminated.
Syntax	select *variable* [in *words...*] ; do *commands...* ; done

variable	The variable that is assigned the value for each variable.
in *words...*	A list of words to use as menu. If not given, $@ is assumed.
do *commands...*	Specifies commands to run for each loop.
done	Ends the select loop.
Common: select a in 1 2 3; do echo $a ; done	Shows a menu and lets the user make a choice.

sendmail

UNIX Shell: Shells (ash, bash, bsh, csh, ksh, sh, tcsh, zsh)

Function	A mail router used to deliver mail messages locally or via the internet.
Syntax	sendmail [options...] { *addresses...* }

-ba	Adds a return-linefeed at the end of all lines.
-bD	Runs the command as a foreground daemon.
-bd	Runs the command as a background daemon.
-bi	Enables use of the mail aliases database.
-bm	Delivers mail as usual.
-bp	Shows mail queue summary.
-bs	Enables use of the SMTP protocol.
-bt	Runs the command in test mode for debugging.
-bv	Verifies names of users.
-B *type*	Specifies the body type. Type can be 7BIT or 8BITMIME.
-N *notification*	Specifies notification level, i.e. success: failure, etc.
-n	Disables the use of aliasing.
-O*option=value*	Specifies processing options.
-o*xvalue*	Specifies processing options.
-p*protocol*	Specifies the protocol.
-q*time*	Specifies time interval to process queued messages.
-q*Xstring*	Runs specified jobs in the queue where `Xstring` can be one of the following:
I	Limits on queue identifier.
R	Limits on recipient.
S	Limits on sender.
-R *ret*	Specifies return information if message fails.
-r *name*	The same as -f.
-t	Scans To:, Cc: and Bcc: for people to send messages to.
-V *envID*	Specifies id on envelope for the message in case of message sending failure.
-v	Verbose mode. Shows more information.
-X *logfile*	Specifies a logfile to log sendmail actions.
addresses...	Specifies recipient address.
AIX, BSD, Linux:	
-bh	Shows the persistent host status database.
-BH	Shows the persistent host status database.
-C*file*	Specifies an alternate configuration file to use.

continued

-d*value* -F*fullname* -f*name* -h*number* -i -U -Mx*value* -- -L *tag*		Specifies the debugging value. Sets the full name of the sender to the specified. Sets the name of the sender to the specified. Sets the hop count to the value specified. Ignores dots alone on lines by themselves in incoming messages. Sets initial user submission. **AIX and Solaris only:** Specifies the macro value. **BSD and Linux only:** Marks the end of command flags. **Linux only:** Sets the identifier used in `syslog` messages to the specified tag.			
File Name:	`sendmail`	**Directory:**	/usr/sbin/, **Solaris:** /usr/lib/	**Type:**	External
Common:	sendmail -bd -q15m		Starts as a background daemon, and process queued messages every 15 minutes.		
Common:	sendmail -bp		Gives you status about the mail queue.		
Common:	sendmail -bi		Enables the mail aliases database.		

sessreg

UNIX Shell: Shells (ash, bash, bsh, csh, ksh, sh, tcsh, zsh)

Function	Manages utmp/wtmp entries for xdm sessions.				
Syntax	sessreg [options...] *user*				
-a -d -w *file* -u *file* -l *linename* -h *host* -s *slotnumber* -x *Xserverfile* -t *ttyfile* *user*		Adds session to utmp/wtmp. Removes session from utmp/wtmp. Specifies an alternative wtmp file. Specifies an alternative utmp file. Specifies the line name of an entry. Specifies the BSD hosts or IP address to notify about the remotely started session. Overrides the default slot number. Sets the slot number to be equal to the number of lines in the ttyfile plus the index. Specifies a file used to count the number of terminal sessions on a host. Specifies username to manage utmp/wtmp entries for.			
File Name:	sessreg	**Directory:**	**AIX:** /usr/lpp/X11/lib/X11/xdm/, **BSD, Linux:** /usr/X11R6/bin, **Solaris:** /usr/openwin/bin/	**Type:**	External

set

UNIX Shell: Shells (ash, bash, bsh, csh, ksh, sh, tcsh, zsh)

Function	Sets a shell variable to value. With no argument it shows all variables. In Bourne, Bash, Korn, and Z-shell (sh, bash, ksh, zsh) set is used to set shell flags.
Syntax	csh, tcsh: set [options...] { *variable[=value]* } csh, tcsh: set [options...] *variable[n] = value* sh, bash, ksh, zsh: set [option] { *argument* } zsh: set option { *array* [*argument* }]
csh: *variable* *variable=value* *variable=(list...)* *variable[n]=value* **tcsh:** *variable* *variable=value* *variable=(list...)* *variable[n]=value* -r -f -l **sh, bash, ksh, zsh:** *option* *argument* **zsh:** -A	csh has no options. Sets variable to an empty (null) value. Sets variable to value. Sets variable to the list specified inside ( ). Alters the element number n in the list of values mentioned above. Sets variable to an empty (null) value. Sets variable to value. Sets variable to the list specified inside ( ). Alters the element number n in the list of values mentioned above. Sets the variable read-only. Uses only the first occurrence of a word in a list. Uses only the last occurrence of a word in a list. Please see the description for Bourne, Bash, Korn, and Z-shell (sh, bash, ksh, zsh). The argument to use for any option. Specifies an array to assign arguments to.

continued

+A *array* *argument*		Specifies an array in which arguments replace the values. (If no name is given, shows all arrays.) Specifies the name of the array. Specifies values for the array.
Common:	set ucg="Great Book"	set the variable ucg to "Great Book."
Common:	set path=($path /home)	Add home to the path list.
Common:	set path[3]=/usr/bin	Changes item number 3 in the list that path holds.

setenv

UNIX Shell: Shells (csh, tcsh)

Function	Sets an environment variable. With no argument, it shows all environment variables.	
Syntax	setenv *{ variable value }*	
variable *variable value*		Sets the environment variable to an empty (null) value. Sets the environment variable to value.
Note:	In the other shells, use export to make an environment variable.	
Common:	setenv book ucg	Sets the environment variable book to ucg.
Common:	setenv	Shows all environment variables.
Common:	setenv MANPATH /usr/man:/usr/local/man	Sets the MANPATH used by the `man` command.

shift

UNIX Shell: Shells (ash, bash, bsh, csh, ksh, sh, tcsh, zsh)

Function	Shifts the command-line argument one (or number) step to the left.	
Syntax	sh, bash, ksh: shift *{ number }* csh, tcsh: shift *{ variable }* zsh: shift *{ number } { variable }*	
sh, bash, ksh: *number* **csh, tcsh:** *variable* **zsh:** *number* *variable*		 Shifts the command-line argument number steps (default is 1). Shifts variable rather than the command-line argument. Shifts the command-line argument number steps (default is 1). Shifts variable rather than the command-line argument.
Common:	shift	Shifts the command line one step to the left.
Common:	shift 4	Shifts the command line 5 times.
Common:	shift ucgbook	Shifts the variable ucgbook one step.

showmount

UNIX Shell: Shells (ash, bash, bsh, csh, ksh, sh, tcsh, zsh)

Function	Shows all clients that have remote mounts from a server.				
Syntax	showmount [options...] *{ server }*				
-a -d -e *server* **BSD:** -3 **Linux:** -h -v --no-headers			Shows mounts in the format `clienthost : directory`. Shows the directories that have been remotely mounted. Shows the file systems that are shared. Specifies a server. Default is the local host. Specifies that mount protocol version 3 should be used. Shows help information. Shows version information. Suppresses the descriptive headings from the output.		
File Name:	`showmount`	**Directory:**	**AIX, BSD:** /usr/bin/, **Linux, Solaris:** /usr/sbin/	**Type:**	External
Common:	showmount -a pluto		Shows all remote mounts from pluto with clients and directories.		
Common:	showmount -e		Shows the file systems shared on the local computer.		
Linux:	showmount --no-headers -d		Shows the directories on the local host that have been remotely mounted without any headers.		

shutdown		UNIX Shell:	Shells (ash, bash, bsh, csh, ksh, sh, tcsh, zsh)
Function	Changes the current run level. Most often to shut the system down.		
Syntax	shutdown [options...] *{ message }*		

AIX:	
-d	Alters the system from distributed mode to multi-user mode.
-F	Shuts down the system as fast as possible, skipping notifying other users.
-h	Stops the system.
-i	Shows interactive information to guide the user through a shutdown.
-k	Avoids any system shutdown.
-m	Puts the system in single-user maintenance mode.
-p	Stops the system without shutting power off.
-r	Restarts the system after a shutdown by the reboot.
-t *mmddHHMM [yy]*	Restarts the system on the specified date.
-v	Stops the whole operating system.
+time(message)	Sets the time to stop the system. (You can add a message).
	The format for future time can be specified as follows:
+number	Specifies the number of minutes to shut down.
+hour:minute	Specifies (as a 24-hour clock) at what time of day to shutdown.
now	Indicates immediate shutdown.
message	Specifies the message to show (only together with the time parameter).
BSD:	
-d	Runs a system crash dump.
-f	Doesn't recheck the file systems on reboot.
-h	Stops the system at the time when shutdown runs halt.
-k	Kicks everyone but superuser off without halting the system.
-r	Runs reboot at the specified time.
-n	Stops the normal sync before stopping.
-p	Powers off the computer if that is supported after shutdown.
-t *mmddHHMM [yy]*	Restarts the system on the specified date.
	The format for future time can be specified as follows:
+number	Specifies the number of minutes to shutdown.
+hour:minute	Specifies (as a 24-hour clock) at what time of day to shut down.
now	Indicates immediate shutdown.
message	Specifies the message to show. (Only with the time parameter.)
message	Provides a message to be added after the standard warning message. (If message is - it will be read from STDIN.)
-t *sec*	Specifies the seconds between warning and kill signal to change run level.
-a	Uses `/etc/shutdown.allow`.
-r	Reboots after shutdown.
-k	Warns everyone but doesn't shut down.
-h	Halts after shutdown.
-n	Doesn't call init to perform shut down.
-c	Cancels a running shutdown.
-f	Doesn't run fsck on reboot.
-F	Runs fsck on reboot.
time	Sets time to shut down.
message	Message for all users.
Solaris:	
-y	Answers yes to the confirmation question in advance.
-g *graceperiod*	Specifies the number of seconds before shutdown (default is 60).
-i *initlevel*	Specifies the new run level (0, 1, s (or S), 5, or 6) (default is s).
message	Provides a message to be added after the standard warning message.

File Name:	`shutdown`	**Directory:**	**AIX, Solaris:** /usr/sbin/, **BSD, Linux:** /sbin/	**Type:**	External
Common:	shutdown -y -g 600 -i 6	Waits 10 minutes before restart; no confirmation needed.			
Common:	shutdown -y -g 0 -i s	Changes to single-user mode immediately, without confirmation.			

size

UNIX Shell: Shells (ash, bash, bsh, csh, ksh, sh, tcsh, zsh)

Function	Shows segment or section size information for each loaded section in object files.
Syntax	size [options...] *files...*

AIX:	
-d	Shows the output in decimal notation.
-o	Shows the output in octal notation.
-x	Writes in hexadecimal notation.
-f	Shows the section size with the section names in parentheses.
-X	A mode that defines which type of object file size to examine. Values are:
32	Processes 32-bit object files.
64	Processes 64-bit object files.
32_64	Processes both 32-bit and 64-bit object files.
-V	Shows version information.
files...	Specifies the file or files to show information from.
BSD:	
-t	Shows a total of the size of all the processed object files at the end of output.
-w	Gives a warning about non-object archive members. (Default is silent.)
files...	Specifies the file or files to show information from.
Linux:	
-A	Shows GNU output resembling output from System V size.
--format=sysv	Shows GNU output resembling output from System V size.
-B	Shows GNU output resembling output from Berkley size.
--format=berkeley	Shows GNU output resembling output from Berkley size.
--help	Shows help information such as arguments and options.
	The following three options can't be combined:
-d	Shows the output in decimal notation.
--radix 10	Shows the output in decimal notation.
-o	Shows the output in octal notation.
--radix 16	Shows the output in octal notation.
-x	Writes in hexadecimal notation.
--radix 8	Writes in hexadecimal notation.
--target=*bfdname*	Specifies an object-code format for object files.
-V	Shows version information.
--version	Shows version information.
files...	Specifies the file to show information from.
Solaris:	
-f	Shows the total size of all allocatable sections and each section's name and size.
-F	Shows the total size of all loadable segments and each segment's permission flags.
-n	Shows the size of all non-loadable segments and non-allocatable sections.
-o	Shows numbers in octal instead of decimal.
-V	Shows version information.
-x	Shows numbers in hexadecimal instead of decimal.
files...	Specifies the object file. Can also be a path to make it read all object files in it.

File Name: size	**Directory:** **AIX, Linux:** /usr/bin/, **BSD:** /usr/bin/inux/usr/bin/, **Solaris:** /usr/ccs/bin/	**Type:**	External

sleep

UNIX Shell: Shells (ash, bash, bsh, csh, ksh, sh, tcsh, zsh)

Function	Puts the system to sleep for a period of time.
Syntax	sleep [option] *time { suffix }*

time	Specifies time in seconds for the system to sleep.
Linux:	
--help	Shows help information.
--version	Shows version information.
time	Specifies time in seconds for the system to sleep.
suffix	Specifies time to be in seconds, minutes, hours or days.

File Name: sleep	**Directory:** /usr/bin/, **BSD, Linux:** /bin/	**Type:**	External

continued

Tip:	Can be useful when you are writing scripts.	
Common:	sleep 30	Sleeps for 30 seconds.
Linux:	sleep 1h	Sleeps for 1 hour.

soelim

UNIX Shell: Shells (ash, bash, bsh, csh, ksh, sh, tcsh, zsh)

Function	Determines and excludes the .so requests from either troff or nroff input.
Syntax	AIX, Solaris: soelim *{ file }* BSD, Linux: soelim [options..] *{ file }*

file	Specifies the input file to use. If - is used, read from STDIN.
BSD, Linux:	
-C	Recognizes .so when followed by characters other than space or newline.
-v	Shows version information.
-I *dir*	Sets a directory to search for files on command line and in .so lines.

File Name:	soelim	**Directory:**	/usr/bin/	**Type:**	External
Common:	soelim nroff.n	Eliminates so requests from nroff.n.			

sort

UNIX Shell: Shells (ash, bash, bsh, csh, ksh, sh, tcsh, zsh)

Function	Sorts and merges lines from the specified files or from STDIN, and prints them to STDOUT.
Syntax	sort [options...] *{ files... }*

-b	Calculates the start and end positions of a sort key after erasing leading blanks.
-c	Checks whether files are sorted as you wanted.
-d	Sorts in dictionary mode. Sort only by letters and digits, no special characters.
-f	Turns off case-sensitivity.
-i	Jumps over the non-printable characters.
-m	Merges the files (instead of sorting them and then merging them).
-n	Sorts by the first numeric string.
-r	Sorts in reversed order.
-u	Erases extra lines that are identical.
+*pos1* [-*pos2*]	Specifies the key to start at pos1 and end at pos2. This is obsolete; use -k instead.
-k *pos1*[,*pos2*]	Specifies the sort key to use starts at pos1 and ends at pos2.
F.[C][type]	Specifies the format for pos1 and pos2.
F	Specifies the filed.
C	Specifies the character in the filed (default is .0).
type	Specifies a type to use. Can be any of b d f i n r with same meaning as the option. (In Linux and Solaris, M is also a valid type.)
-o *output*	Sends output to the output file specified and not to the STDOUT.
-t *delimiter*	Specifies the delimiter to use between fields.
-T *directory*	Stores temporary files in the specified directory.
files...	The file or files to sort or merge. Filename can also be a dash to read from STDIN.
AIX:	
-A	Sorts in a byte-by-byte order using ASCII collection.
-z *recordsize*	Specifies the maximum record size allowed (equal line length) in bytes.
-y *{ kmem }*	Specifies the memory in kilobytes that is used initially.
BSD:	
-H	Sorts files larger than 60MB.
-R *character*	Specifies the record separator (default is new line character).
Linux:	
+*pos1* [-*pos2*]	Specifies the key to start at pos1 and end at pos2. Use -k instead.
-s	Disables the last resort comparison to stabilize the sort.
-z	Ends lines with a NULL character instead of starting a new line.
--help	Shows help information.
--version	Shows version information.
-M	Sorts the first sequence of three non-blank characters as months.

continued

Solaris: -M -y *{ kmem }*		Sorts the first sequence of three non-blank characters as months. Specifies the memory in kilobytes that is used initially.			
File Name:	sort	**Directory:**	/usr/bin/, **Linux:** /bin/	**Type:**	External
Note:	Sort doesn't guarantee preservation of relative line ordering on equal keys.				
Common:	sort -r /etc/passwd	Does a reversed sort of the file passwd.			
Common:	sort -k 3,3 -n -t ":" /etc/passwd	Shows the passwd file sorted by the userIDs.			

source

UNIX Shell: Shells (bash, csh, tcsh, zsh)

Function	Reads commands from a file and runs them in the current shell.
Syntax	csh: source [-h] *file* tcsh: source [-h] *file { arguments... }* bash, zsh: source *file { arguments... }*

file	The file to read command from.
csh:	
-h	Places the commands in the history file without running them.
tcsh:	
-h	Places the commands in the history file without running them.
arguments...	Specifies any needed arguments for the file or command.
bash, zsh:	
arguments...	Specifies any needed arguments for the file or command.

Note:	In Bourne shell (sh) and Korn shell (ksh) use `. file` instead.	
Common:	source .cshrc	Runs the command in .cshrc.
Common:	source -h .cshrc	Placed the commands in .cshrc in the history file (csh, tcsh).

split

UNIX Shell: Shells (ash, bash, bsh, csh, ksh, sh, tcsh, zsh)

Function	Splits a file into a set of smaller files. The output files receive a double letter extension (.aa, .ab, .ac ...).
Syntax	split [options...] *{ file } { name }*

-l *linecount*	Specifies the number of lines in each piece (default is 1000).
-b *NR*	Defines the size of the split files in bytes.
-b *NR* k	Defines the size of the split files, in blocks of Kilobytes.
-b *NR* m	Defines the size of the split files, in blocks of Megabytes.
file	Specifies the file to split (default is STDIN).
name	Specifies the name to use for the divided file segments (default is x).
AIX:	
-a *suffixlength*	Specifies the length of the suffix letters (default is two letters).
BSD:	
-p *pattern*	Splits the file when an input line matches the pattern. Must be used alone.
Linux:	
-b *NR* b	Defines the size of the split files in blocks of 512 bytes.
-C *NR*	Defines the size of the split files in bytes, but doesn't split the text lines.
-C *NR* b	Defines the size of the split files in 512 bytes, but doesn't split the text lines.
-C *NR* k	Defines the size of the split files in Kilobytes, but doesn't split the text lines.
-C *NR* m	Defines the size of the split files in Megabytes, but doesn't split the text lines.
--verbose	Prints information to STDERR.
--help	Shows help information.
--version	Shows version information.
Solaris:	
-a *suffixlength*	Specifies the length of the suffix letters (default is two letters).

File Name:	`split`	**Directory:**	/usr/bin/	**Type:**	External
Tip:	This command is very useful if you want to split a very big file.				
Common:	split -b 2 k /var/adm/messages	Splits /var/adm/messages into 2 Kb pieces.			
Common:	split -l 20 /var/adm/messages splitfile.	Splits the file with the prefix splitfile.aa, splitfile.ab			

stop

stop	**UNIX Shell:** Shells (bsh, csh, ksh, sh, tcsh)
Function	Stops a process.
Syntax	stop *pid* stop *jobid*

pid	The process ID for a job to stop.
jobid	Specifies job ID.
	Use one of the following to specify job id:
%	Specifies the current job. You can also use %% and %+.
%*number*	Specifies job number.
%?*string*	Specifies a command that contains string.
sh, ksh:	
%*string*	Specifies a command that starts with string
%-	Specifies the previous job.
csh, tcsh:	
%minus;	Specifies the previous job.

Note:	Solaris: To use jobid, Bourne shell (sh) must be started in job control mode by starting it with jsh.	
Common:	stop %1	Stops job %1.
Common:	stop 6623	Stops the job with prosessid 6623.

strings

strings	**UNIX Shell:** Shells (ash, bash, bsh, csh, ksh, sh, tcsh, zsh)
Function	Searches for printable strings in object or binary files.
Syntax	strings [options...] *{ files... }*

-a	Searches the whole file for strings.
-	The same as -a.
-n *number*	Specifies the minimum string length (default is 4).
-t *format*	Precedes each string with its byte offset from the start of the file. (Format can be d for decimal, o for octal or x for hexadecimal.)
-o	The same as -t o.
files...	Specifies files (default is STDIN).
AIX:	
-*number*	The same as -n.
BSD:	
-f	Puts the name of the file where the string was found before all strings.
-m *number*	Specifies the maximum string length (default is unlimited).
Linux:	
-f	Puts the name of the file where the string was found before all strings.
--help	Shows help information.
-v	Shows version information.
--target=*bfdname*	Specifies an object code format rather than using the default for the system.
Solaris:	
-*number*	The same as -n.

File Name:	`strings`	**Directory:** /usr/bin/	**Type:** External
Common:	strings /usr/bin/pwd	Searches for printable strings in the file /usr/bin/pwd.	
Common:	strings -o /usr/bin/pwd	Precedes each string with its decimal byte offset from the start of the file.	

strip

strip	**UNIX Shell:** Shells (ash, bash, bsh, csh, ksh, sh, tcsh, zsh)
Function	Strips the symbol table and the information about debugging and line numbers from an object file.
Syntax	strip [options...] *files...*

AIX:	
-l	Strips only line number information.
-V	Shows version information.
-e	Specifies the F_LOADONLY flag in the header of the object file.
-E	Turns off the -e option.
-H	Removes all headers.
-l	Hides the line number information.

continued

-r	Doesn't remove external and static symbols and relocation information.
-t	Doesn't remove function symbols and line number information.
-x	Doesn't remove external and static symbols.
-X *type*	Specifies the type of the file to strip.
32	Specifies to process only 32-bit files (default).
64	Specifies to process only 64-bit files.
32_64	Specifies to process both the 32- and the 64-bit files.
--	Specifies that everything following is filenames.
files...	Specifies the file to strip.
BSD:	
-d	Removes the debugging and empty symbols.
-x	Specifies to remove debugging, compiler identification, and local symbols.
files...	Specifies the file to strip.
Linux:	
--help	Shows help information.
-I *bfdname*	Handles the input file as an object code format bfdname.
-F *bfdname*	Handles the input and output file as an object code format bfdname.
-O *bfdname*	Creates and replaces the input file with a file in the format bfdname.
-R *sectionname*	Removes the specified section.
-s	Removes all symbols.
-S	Specifies to remove the debugging symbols.
--strip-unneeded	Removes all symbols that aren't needed for relocation processing.
-N *symbolname*	Doesn't copy the specified symbol.
-o *file*	Saves the output in the specified file. You can only specify one input file.
-p	Maintains the modification and access dates of the file.
-x	Removes all non-global symbols.
-X	Removes compiler-generated local symbols.
-K *symbolname*	Copies the specified symbols from the input file.
-v	Verbose mode. Shows more information.
-V	Shows version information.
files...	Specifies the file to strip.
Solaris:	
-l	Strips only line number information.
-V	Shows the version number on STDERR.
-x	Specifies to remove the debugging and line number information.
files...	Specifies the file to strip.

File Name:	`strip`	**Directory:**	/usr/bin/, **Solaris:** /usr/ccs/bin/	**Type:**	External
Common:	strip ls		Removes the default information.		

stty

UNIX Shell: Shells (ash, bash, bsh, csh, ksh, sh, tcsh, zsh)

Function	Alters the options for a terminal.
Syntax	stty [options...] *{ modes... }*

modes...	Specifies the tty modes to set.
-a	Shows the current option settings for the terminal.
-g	Shows current settings in a form that can be used as an argument to another stty.
BSD:	
-e	Shows the current settings in traditional BSD formats.
-f *device*	Runs the command by reading from the specified device, instead of STDIN.
Linux:	
-F *device*	Runs the command by reading from the specified device, instead of STDIN.
--help	Shows help information.
--version	Shows version information.
Solaris:	
-a	Shows the current option settings for the terminal.
-g	Shows current settings in a form that can be used as an argument to another stty.

continued

	The following are modes that can be used:
[-]brkint	Will signal/not signal INTR on break.
[-]icrnl	Will map/not map carriage return to new line on input.
[-]ignbrk	Will ignore/not ignore break on input.
[-]igncr	Will ignore/not ignore carriage return on input.
[-]ignpar	Will ignore/not ignore parity errors.
[-]imaxbel	Will echo/not echo BEL when input line is too long.
[-]inlcr	Will map/not map new line to carriage return on input.
[-]inpck	Enables/disables input parity checking.
[-]istrip	Will strip/not strip input characters to 7 bits.
[-]iuclc	Will map/not map uppercase to lowercase on input.
[-]ixany	Will, if enabled, allow any character to restart output, or, if disabled, only XON.
[-]ixoff	Will send/not send START/STOP characters when the queue is nearly empty or full.
[-]ixon	Enables/disables START/STOP output control.
[-]parmrk	Will mark/not mark parity errors.
Output modes	**Modes beginning with [-] can either be enabled or disabled.**
bs0, bs1	Selects style of delay for backspaces.
cr0, cr1, cr2, cr3	Selects style of delay for carriage returns.
ff0, ff1	Selects style of delay for formfeeds.
nl0, nl1	Selects style of delay for linefeeds.
tab0, tab1, tab2, tab3	Selects style of delay for horizontal tabs.
vt0, vt1	Selects style of delay for vertical tabs.
[-]ocrnl	Will map/not map carriage return to new line on-screen.
[-]ofdel	Will, if enabled, set fill character to DEL, or, if disabled, to NULL.
[-]ofill	Will, if enabled, delay output with fill characters, or, if disabled, with timing.
[-]olcuc	Will map/not map lowercase to uppercase on-screen.
[-]onlcr	Will map/not map newline to carriage return-newline on-screen.
[-]onlret	Will perform/not perform carriage return after new line.
[-]onocr	Will show/not show carriage returns at column zero.
[-]opost	Will postprocess/not postprocess output.
Hardware flow control modes	**Type the mode to enable it, or type a dash before the mode to disable it.**
[-]cdxon	Enables/disables CD hardware flow control on output.
[-]ctsxon	Enables/disables CTS hardware flow control on output.
[-]dtrxoff	Enables/disables DTR flow control on input.
[-]isxoff	Enables/disables isochronous hardware flow control on input.
[-]rtsxoff	Enables/Disables RTS hardware flow control on input.
Window size	**The following modes have a required additional operand.**
columns *value*	Sets size to specified columns.
rows *value*	Sets size to specified rows.
xpixels *value*	Sets size to specified pixels horizontally.
ypixels *value*	Sets size to specified pixels vertically.
Control modes	**modes beginning with [-] can either be enabled or disabled.**
baud rate	Sets the baud rate to specified rate. If set to 0, the connection hangs up.
[-]clocal	Enables/disables modem control.
[-]cread	Enables/disables the receiver.
[-]crtscts	Enables/disables output hardware flow control using RTS/CTS.
[-]crtsxoff	Enables/disables input hardware flow control using RTS.
cs5, cs6, cs7, cs8	Selects character size in bits.
[-]cstopb	Will, if enabled, use two stop bits per character, or, if disabled, one stop bit.
defeucw	Sets the widths of multibyte EUC characters to default, specified by LC_CTYPE.
[-]hup	Will hang up/not hang up connection on last close.
ispeed *baud rate*	Sets terminal input baud rate to specified value.
[-]loblk	Will block/not block output from a non-current layer.
ospeed *baud rate*	Sets terminal output baud rate to specified value.
[-]parenb	Enables/disables parity generation and detection.
[-]parext	Enables/disables extended parity generation and detection for mark and space parity.
[-]parodd	Will, if enabled, use odd parity, or if disabled, use even parity.

continued

Local Modes	**Type the mode to enable it, or type a dash before the mode to disable it.**
[-]echo	Will echo/not echo every character typed.
[-]echoctl	Will echo/not echo control characters as ^char and delete as ^?.
[-]echoe	Will echo/not echo ERASE characters as backspace-space-backspace string.
[-]echok	Will echo/not echo new line after KILL character.
[-]echoke	Will [not] erase entire line with backspace-space-backspace characters on linekill.
[-]echonl	Will echo/not echo new line.
[-]echoprt	Will echo/not echo the erase character.
[-]flusho	Will flush/not flush the output.
[-]icanon	Enables/disables canonical input, like ERASE and KILL processing.
[-]iexten	Enables/disables extended functions for input data.
[-]isig	Enables/disables checking of characters against INTR, QUIT, and SWITCH.
[-]noflsh	Will, If `enabled`, `not` flush after INTR, QUIT, and SWITCH.
[-]pendin	Will retype/not retype pending input at next read or input character.
[-]stappl	Uses application mode, or if disabled, line mode, on a synchronous line.
[-]stflush	Enables/disables flush on synchronous line.
[-]stwrap	Will, if enabled, disable truncation on synchronous line.
[-]tostop	Will send/not send SIGTTOU when background processes write to the terminal.
[-]xcase	Will change/not change case on local output.
Control assignments	**Following mode can either be ctab, discard, dsusp, eof, eol, eol2, erase, intr, kill, lnext, quit, reprint, start, stop, susp, swtch or werase.**
control character	Sets specified control character to specified character.
	The following modes have a required additional operand.
min *value*	Sets the minimum number of characters to wait for before a read system call times out
time *value*	Sets the number of tenths of seconds to wait before a read system call times out. (The options min and time are only used when icanon is disabled.)
line *value*	Sets the line discipline to specified number. The value must be between 1 and 126.
Combination modes	**Modes beginning with [-] can either be enabled or disabled.**
async	Sets normal asynchronous communications.
[-]evenp	Sets cs7 and enable/disable parenb.
ek	Resets ERASE and KILL characters to # and @.
[-]lcase	Enables/disables xcase, iuclc, and olcuc.
[-]markp	Sets cs7 and enable/disable parenb,parodd and parext.
[-]nl	Will enable/disable icrnl and onlcr. (nl also disables inlcr, igncr, ocrnl, and onlret.)
[-]raw	Enables/disables raw input and output.
sane	Resets all modes to reasonable values.
[-]spacep	Sets cs7 and enables/disables parenb and parext.
[-]tabs	Will, if enabled, preserve output tabs, or if disabled, expand to spaces.
	The following mode can either be tty33, tty37, tv05, tn300, ti700, or tek:
term	Sets all modes suitable for terminal type term.

File Name:	stty	**Directory:**	/usr/bin/, **BSD, Linux:** /bin/	**Type:**	External
Tip:	Unless you want an advanced configuration, check the combination mode category first.				
Common:	stty sane	Resets all modes to some reasonable values.			
Common:	stty -a	Shows all option settings for terminal.			

su

UNIX Shell: Shells (ash, bash, bsh, csh, ksh, sh, tcsh, zsh)

Function	Switches to another user in the current session.
Syntax	su [options...] *{ user } { arguments... }*

-	Gets the new user's environment.
-c *string*	Executes the string using the shell.
user	Specifies the user you want to become (default is superuser (root) if not specified).
arguments...	Passes the string to the shell.
BSD:	
-K	Disables Kerberos to authenticate the user.
-f	Prevents `csh` from reading the `.cshrc` file.
-l	Simulates a full login.

continued

-m	Leaves the environment unmodified.
-c *string*	Executes the string using the shell.
Linux:	
-l	Makes the shell a login shell.
-c *string*	Executes the string using the shell.
-f	Passes the -f option to the shell, only for `csh` and `tcsh`.
-m	Leaves the environment unmodified.
-p	Same as option -m.
-s *shell*	Runs the specified shell if `/etc/shells` allows it.
--help	Shows help information.
--version	Shows version information.
Solaris:	
-r	Gives the user a restricted shell.

File Name:	`su`	**Directory:**	/usr/bin/, **Linux:** /bin/	**Type:**	External
Note:	You must have a space between the dash and the user you want to become.				
Common:	su	Becomes superuser.			
Common:	su - ucg	Becomes ucg and gets the environment from ucg.			
Common:	su - ucg -c ls	Executes the command `ls` as user ucg.			

sum

UNIX Shell: Shells (ash, bash, bsh, csh, ksh, sh, tcsh, zsh)

Function	Shows a 16-bit checksum and a 512 byte block count for a file.
Syntax	sum [options...] *file...*

-r	Uses an alternate checksum algorithm. This algorithm is server dependent.
file...	Specifies the file to checksum. If a file isn't specified, STDIN is used.
AIX:	
-i	Allows the user to compute the checksum without including header information.
-o	Uses the word-by-word algorithm to compute the checksum.
Linux:	
-s	Uses System V sum algorithm, use 512 bytes blocks.
--help	Shows help information.
--version	Shows version information.

File Name:	`sum`	**Directory:**	/usr/bin/	**Type:**	External
Common:	sum /etc/passwd	Returns the checksum for /etc/passwd.			

suspend

UNIX Shell: Shells (bash, bsh, csh, ksh, sh, tcsh, zsh)

Function	Stops the current shell as if Ctrl-Z has been pressed. Login shell can't be stopped.
Syntax	suspend bash, zsh: suspend [-f]

bash, zsh:	
-f	Suspends a shell even if it's a login shell.
Common: suspend	Stops the current shell.

switch, breaksw

UNIX Shell: Shells (csh,tcsh)

Function	Matches each pattern successively against the word and runs the commands when the first match is found.

Syntax	switch (*words*)
	   case *pattern*:
	      commands...
	   breaksw
	   default:
	      commands...
	   breaksw
	endsw

continued

(*words*)	A string or variable to find a match for.
case *pattern*:	Specifies the pattern for matching word. (The filename metacharacter * ? [...] may be used in the pattern. More case statements can be used after each other to match multiple patterns.)
commands...	Specifies commands to run when a match is found.
breaksw	Used to end current match and continue execution after endsw. If not, used execution continues with the next line, ignores any case.
default:	Matches everything that isn't already matched.
endsw	Ends the case statement. (Both case and default must appear on the beginning of a line.)

sync

UNIX Shell: Shells (ash, bash, bsh, csh, ksh, sh, tcsh, zsh)

Function	Flushes all unwritten file system buffers to disk.
Syntax	sync

Linux:	
--help	Shows help information.
--version	Shows version information.

File Name:	`sync`	**Directory:**	/bin/, **AIX:** /usr/sbin/, **Solaris:** /usr/bin/	**Type:**	External
Common:	sync ; sync ; reboot	Writes buffers to disk before restarting the system.			

syslogd

UNIX Shell: Shells (ash, bash, bsh, csh, ksh, sh, tcsh, zsh)

Function	Logs system messages and saves it into a file.
Syntax	syslogd [options...]

-d	Shows debug information.
-f *configfile*	Specifies an alternate configuration file (default is `/etc/syslogd.conf`).
-m *interval*	Specifies an interval, in minutes, between mark messages (default is 20).
AIX:	
-s	Forwards a "shortened" message to another system.
-r	Suppresses logging of messages received from remote hosts.
BSD:	
-u	Accepts input from the UDP port.
-p *path*	Specifies an alternate log device name (default is `/dev/log`).
-a *path*	Specifies a location to an additional logging socket.
Linux:	
-a *path*	Specifies a location to an additional logging socket.
-h	Enables forwarding of remote messages received.
-l *hostlist...*	Specifies one or more hosts separated with colon to log with its short hostname.
-n	Disables that the daemon is automatically placed in the background.
-p *path*	Specifies an alternate log device name (default is `/dev/log`).
-r	Enables receiving messages from the network using an Internet domain socket.
-s *domainlist...*	Specifies one or more domain names separated with column that should be stripped off.
-v	Shows version information.
Solaris:	
-p *path*	Specifies an alternate log device name (default is `/dev/log`).

File Name:	`syslogd`	**Directory:**	/usr/sbin/	**Type:**	External
Note:	Normally the `syslog` daemon is started when the system boots.				
Common:	syslogd	Starts the daemon.			
Common:	syslogd -m 60	Starts the daemon and tells it to mark the file every 60 minutes.			
Common:	syslogd -f syslogd.conf	Starts the daemon and uses `syslogd.conf` as configuration file.			

tail

UNIX Shell: Shells (ash, bash, bsh, csh, ksh, sh, tcsh, zsh)

Function	Shows the tail end of the file specified to STDOUT. Shows the last 10 entries by default.
Syntax	tail [options...] *{ file }* tail *{ number }* [options...] *{ file }*

continued

	A + before the number variable starts the count in the beginning of the file.
AIX:	
-b *number*	Starts reading the file at the number of 512-byte block location.
-c *number*	Starts reading the file at the number of byte block location.
-k *number*	Starts reading the file at the number of Kilobyte block location.
-m *number*	Starts reading the file at the number of the multibyte character block location.
-n *number*	Starts reading the file at the number of line location.
-f	Shows last 10 lines of the file, sleeps and rereads the file in a loop.
-r	Shows lines in reverse order in the file.
file	Specifies the input file to use.
BSD:	
-b *number*	Starts reading the file at the number of 512-byte block location.
-c *number*	Starts reading the file at the number of byte block location.
-n *number*	Starts reading the file at the number of line location.
-f	Shows last 10 lines of the file and sleeps and rereads the file in a loop.
-r	Shows lines in reverse order in the file.
file	Specifies the input file to use.
Linux:	
-c *number{ suffix }*	Specifies the amount of bytes to show and can specify a suffix type of b, k, or m. Suffix: The suffix b = 512-bytes, k = Kilobytes, or m = Megabytes
-f	Shows appended data as the file grows.
--retry	Forces to try to open the file if it isn't inaccessible. Only used with -f option.
-n *number*	Shows the last number of lines.
--pid=*PID*	Kills the specified PID. Used with -f option.
-q	Hides headers giving filenames.
-s *sec*	Waits the specified time between iterations. Used with -f option.
--verbose	Always shows headers giving filenames.
--help	Shows help information.
--version	Shows version information.
file	Specifies the input file to use.
Solaris:	
-r	Shows lines in reverse order in the file.
-f	Shows last 10 lines of the file and sleeps and rereads the file in a loop.
-l	Shows the number of lines in the file.
-b	Shows the number of blocks in the file.
-c	Shows the number of bytes in the file. You can't use the -r and -f options together.
	These options are only available from the tail found in `/usr/xpg4/bin/`.
-c *number*	Starts reading the file at the number of byte block location.
-n *number*	Starts reading the file at the number of line location.
file	Specifies the input file to use.

File Name:	`tail`	**Directory:**	/usr/bin/	**Type:**	External
Common:	tail -1 /etc/passwd	Shows the last user created on the system.			
Linux:	tail -f /var/log/messages	Looks at the last 10 lines of /var/log/messages and prints out new lines from the file.			
Solaris:	tail -f /var/adm/messages	Prints last 10 lines of messages and doesn't terminate.			

talk

UNIX Shell: Shells (ash, bash, bsh, csh, ksh, sh, tcsh, zsh)

Function	Is used to talk to another user, using the terminal.
Syntax	talk *address { terminal }*

address	Specifies address to the user to contact, most common is user@host.
terminal	Specifies a terminal to contact, e.g. pts/2.

File Name:	`talk`	**Directory:**	/usr/bin/	**Type:**	External
Common:	talk root	Talks to the user root.			
Common:	talk ucg@sun	Talks to the user ucg on host sun.			

talkd, in.talkd, in.ntalkd, ntalkd

talkd, in.talkd, in.ntalkd, ntalkd		UNIX Shell:	Shells (ash, bash, bsh, csh, ksh, sh, tcsh, zsh)
Function	Provides the server function for the `talk` command. Usually started by the Internet Server.		
Syntax	AIX: talkd [-s] BSD: ntalkd Linux: in.talkd [options...] Solaris: in.talkd		

AIX:	
-s	Enables socket-level debugging.
Linux:	
-d	Enables debug mode.
-p	Enables packet-logging mode.

File Name:	`in.talkd`, **BSD:** `ntalkd`	**Directory:**	/usr/sbin/, **BSD:** /usr/libexec/	**Type:**	External

AIX:	talkd -s	Starts the talkd daemon and enables socket debugging.
Linux:	in.talkd -dp	Starts the talkd daemon with debug and packet logging enabled.
OpenBSD:	ntalkd	Starts the talkd daemon.
Solaris:	in.talkd	Starts the talkd daemon.

tar

tar		UNIX Shell:	Shells (ash, bash, bsh, csh, ksh, sh, tcsh, zsh)
Function	Extracts or creates files from or to a tar file, tape by default but can be any media or file.		
Syntax	tar option [options...] *{ files... }*		

	The following options are not combinable and one is required.
c	Creates a new tar file, starting from the beginning.
r	Appends files to the tar file.
t	Shows all files, or the specified files, existing in the table of contents.
u	Updates an existing tar-file with the named files. Adds to the end if missing.
x	Extracts files within the tar file into the directory specified by files in tar file.
	The following options can be combined.
v	Verbose mode. Shows more information.
f *file*	Specifies where the archive is stored.
w	Verifies the actions by asking the user before anything is done.
p	Restores file modes and user/group IDs and ignores current `umask`.
-C *directory file*	Performs a cd to a directory and archives the file.
files...	Specifies one or more files to process.
AIX:	
-B	Forces tar to read the amount of bytes to exactly fill a block.
-d	Makes separate entries for block files.
-o	Sets the ownership of the files extracted to the one who starts it.
-m	Shows the modification time.
-F	Checks the file type before archiving, excludes SCCS, RCS, core, errs, a.out, and .o.
-b *blocks*	Specifies the number of 512 bytes blocks per record.
-h	Specifies that symbolic links followed as normal files. (Default isn't to.)
-i	Ignores directory checksum errors.
-L *inputlist*	Writes the files and directories listed in the inputlist to the archive.
-N *blocks*	Allows use of very large clusters of blocks when streaming tape archives are used.
-s	Tries to create a symbolic link if unsuccessful in its attempt to link two files.
-S *argument*	Specifies the number of 512KB blocks per volume.
BSD:	
-b *blocking factor*	Sets blocking factor to use for the archive.
-e	Exits when an unexpected error arises, and shows a positive exit status.
-h	Specifies that symbolic links are followed as normal files. (Default isn't to.)
-m	Shows the modification time.
-f *archive*	Specifies where the archive is stored.

continued

-O	Writes old-style (non-POSIX) archives.
-o	Disables writing directory information with the older (V7) style.
-s *replstr*	Modifies the file or archive member names that match replstr.
-q	Stops extracting when file is found. (Default is continue.)
-z	Compresses archive using `gzip`.
-P	Suppresses the last slash / for directories in archive.
-H	Follows symlinks given on command line only.
-L	Follows all symlinks.
-T *file*	Includes or extracts the file specified from the archive.
-X	Disables cross mount points in the file system.
-Z	Compresses archive using `compress`.
-*number*	Specifies a number between 0 and 8, which specifies what backup device to use.
blocks	Specifies the number of 512-k blocks for every read and write request. (used with b).
Linux:	
-A	Appends tar files to an archive.
-d	Finds differences between archive and file system.
--delete	Deletes from the archive.
--atime-preserve	Disables changes access times on dumped files.
--checkpoint	Shows directory names while reading the archive.
--force-local	Archive file is local even if has a colon.
-F *script*	Runs the specified script at end of each tape.
-G	Creates, lists, or extracts old GNU-format incremental backup.
-P	Suppresses the last slash / for directories in archive.
-g *file*	Creates, lists, or extracts new GNU-format incremental backup.
-h	Dumps the file a symlink points to.
-i	Ignores blocks of zeros in archive.
-I	Filters the archive through `bzip2`.
--ignore-failed-read	Disables so no exit occurs with non-zero status on unreadable files.
-k	Keeps existing files, doesn't overwrite them from archive.
-K *file*	Begins at the specified file in the archive.
-l	Stays on the local file system when creating an archive.
-L *number*	Changes tapes after writing number*1024 bytes.
-m	Disables extraction of file modified time.
-M	Creates, lists, or extracts multi-volume archive.
-N *date*	Stores only files newer than the date specified.
-o	Disables writing directory information with the older (V7) style.
-O	Extracts files to STDOUT.
--preserve	Invokes -p and -s.
-R	Shows record number within archive with each message.
--remove-files	Removes files after adding them to the archive.
-s	Shows names to extract in sorted to match archive.
--same-owner	Creates extracted files with the same ownership.
-S	Handles sparse files efficiently.
-T *file*	Gets names to extract or create from the file specified.
--null	Reads null-terminated names; use with option –T.
--totals	Shows total bytes written when creating an archive.
-V *name*	Creates archive with the specified volume name.
--version	Shows version information.
-W	Attempts to verify the archive after creating it.
--exclude *file*	Excludes the specified file.
-X *file*	Excludes files that are listed in the specified file.
-Z	Compresses archive using `compress`.
-z	Compresses archive using `gzip`.
--use-compress-program *program*	Filters the archive through the specified program, the program must accept -d flag.

continued

Solaris:	
B	Forces tar to read the amount of bytes to exactly fill a block.
e	Exits when an unexpected error arises, and shows a positive exit status.
F	Checks the file type before archiving, excludes SCCS, RCS, core, errs, a.out, and .o.
h	Specifies that symbolic links are followed as normal files (default isn't to).
i	Ignores directory checksum errors.
k *size*	Specifies an archive of fixed size. Additional data is spanned over new volumes.
l	Specifies that failure to resolve links outputs error (default isn't to).
n	Specifies the file is a non-tape device.
q	Stops extracting when file is found (default is continue).
E	Writes an extended header.
b *number*	Specifies the number of blocks for every read or write operation.
P	Suppresses the last slash / for directories in archive.
X	Specifies the excludefile argument will be used.
m	Shows the modification time.
o	Sets the ownership of the files extracted to the one who starts it.
0-7	Specifies tape device to use (default is 0).
-I *includefile*	Specifies a file that contains all files that should be archived.
blocks	Specifies the number of 512-k blocks for every read and write request (used with b).
excludefile	Specifies a file that contains files to exclude (used with X).

File Name:	`tar`	**Directory:** **AIX:** /usr/bin/, **BSD, Linux:** /bin/, **Solaris:** /usr/sbin/	**Type:** External
Warning:	Avoid using full path for the files to store. This causes problems when restoring them.		
Common:	tar xvf tarfile.tar	Extracts `tarfile.tar` into current directory.	
Common:	tar c dir	Saves the contents of directory dir to the default tape station.	
AIX:	tar cvh tartest.tar *	Creates a file called `tartest.tar` containing all files in the in current directory, and follows symlinks as normal files.	
Linux:	tar cf tartest.tar *	Creates a file called `tartest.tar` containing all files in the current directory.	
OpenBSD:	tar cvzf tartest.tar.gz *	Creates a file called `tartest.tar.gz` containing all files in the current directory.	
Solaris:	tar xvf tarfile	Extracts the tarfile verbosely.	

tbl

UNIX Shell: Shells (ash, bash, bsh, csh, ksh, sh, tcsh, zsh)

Function	Formats tables before to use them in nroff or troff. For BSD and Linux it is only used for troff.
Syntax	tbl [options...] *{ files... }*

-me	Takes the -me macro package and copies it to the start of the output file.
-mm	Takes the -mm macro package and copies it to the start of the output file.
-ms	Takes the -ms macro package and copies it to the start of the output file.
files...	Specifies the input file or files.
AIX:	
-TX	Uses full vertical line motions.
--	Specifies the end of flags.
-	Specifies to read from STDIN.
BSD,Linux:	
-C	Specifies to always recognize .TS and .TE format.
-v	Shows version information.

File Name:	tbl	**Directory:** /usr/bin/	**Type:** External
Common:	tbl textfile	Compiles the textfile containing table macros.	

tee

UNIX Shell: Shells (ash, bash, bsh, csh, ksh, sh, tcsh, zsh)

Function	Copies STDIN to STDOUT as well as to files.
Syntax	tee [options...] *{ files... }*

-a	Appends to the files instead of overwriting them.
-i	Ignores interrupts.
files...	Specifies output files.

continued

Linux:					
--help		Shows help information.			
--version		Shows version information.			
File Name:	tee	**Directory:**	/usr/bin/	**Type:**	External
Tip:	This is good for logging error messages on the screen and in a file at the same time.				
Common:	echo UCG | tee /tmp/ucg	Puts output from echo into /tmp/ucg and to STDOUT.			

telnet, tn

UNIX Shell: Shells (ash, bash, bsh, csh, ksh, sh, tcsh, zsh)

Function	Uses the telnet protocol to communicate with other hosts.
Syntax	telnet [options...] *{ host: port }*

	AIX Only: The command `tn` is the same as the command `telnet`.
-d	Enables debug information.
-l *user*	Specifies the username to connect as.
-n *tracefile*	Records trace information in the file specified.
host	Specifies a hostname or IP address to connect to.
port	Specifies a port to use when connecting (default is 23).
AIX:	
-e *termtype*	Sets the terminal type to the type specified. Valid values are: vt100, 3270, or none.
-p	Saves current tty attributes.
-f	Forwards user credentials if Kerberos is the current authentication method.
-F	Forwards user credentials and flags the credentials to forward them to the next host.
-k *realm*	Specifies the realm or DCE cell if different from the local realm. Requires Kerberos.
-l *user*	Specifies the username to connect as.
BSD, Linux:	
-8	Sets an 8-bit data path for input and output.
-a	Enables automatic login.
-b *hostalias*	Binds the hostalias specified to an alias IP address created by `ifconfig`.
-c	Prevents the users .telnetrc file from being read.
-e *escapechar*	Sets the initial escape character.
-E	Prevents any character from being recognized as an escape character.
-f	Forwards user credentials if `Kerberos` is the current authentication method.
-F	Forwards user credentials and flags the credentials to forward them to the next host.
-k *realm*	Specifies the realm or DCE cell if different from the local realm. Requires Kerberos.
-K	Disables automatic login.
-L	Sets an 8-bit data path for output.
-r	Sets a user interface similar to rlogin.
-S *tos*	**Linux Only:** Specifies the type of service for telnet found in `/etc/iptos`.
-x	Enables data encryption for the data stream.
-X *type*	Disables the authentication type specified.
Solaris:	
-8	Sets an 8-bit data path for input and output.
-c	Prevents the user's .telnetrc file from being read.
-e *escapechar*	Sets the initial escape character.
-E	Prevents any character from being recognized as an escape character.
-L	Sets an 8-bit data path for output.
-r	Sets a user interface similar to rlogin.

File Name:	`telnet`	**Directory:**	/usr/bin/	**Type:**	External
Warning:	During authentication, login names and passwords are sent without encryption.				
Common:	telnet 192.168.1.244 3210	Opens a session to 192.168.1.244 on port 3210.			
Common:	telnet -c pluto	Opens a session, doesn't use the .telnetrc file.			
Common:	telnet -l ucg pluto	Opens a session to pluto as user ucg.			

test, [ ]	UNIX Shell:	Shells (sh, ksh and zsh)
Function	Evaluates conditions. In if structures conditions are often used inside brackets ([ ]).	
Syntax	test *conditions...* *[conditions...]*	

Internal	**Test is internal in Bourne, Korn, and Z-shell.**
-o *option*	Is true when option is on.
-t *n*	Is true when the open file with descriptor number n is associated to a terminal.
	The following conditions are true when the file exists and...
-a *file*	is true when file exists (not available in sh).
-b *file*	is block special file.
-c *file*	is character special file.
-d *file*	is a directory.
-e *file*	is true when file exists (not available in sh).
-f *file*	is regular file.
-g *file*	its set-group ID bit is set.
-h *file*	is symbolic link (not available in ksh).
-k *file*	its sticky bit is set.
-p *file*	is named pipe.
-r *file*	is readable.
-s *file*	has a size greater than zero.
-u *file*	its set-user ID bit is set.
-w *file*	is writable.
-x *file*	is executable.
-G *file*	its group is the same as the group ID of this process (not available in sh).
-L *file*	is symbolic link (not available in sh).
-O *file*	is owned by the user ID of this process.
-S *file*	a socket (not available in sh).
	File comparison. Used in bash, ksh, zsh.
file1 -nt *file2*	True if file1 is newer than file2.
file1 -ot *file2*	True if file1 is older than file2.
file1 -ef *file2*	True if file1 and file2 refer to the same file.
	Algebraic comparison. The following are true when:
int1 -eq *int2*	int1 is equal to int2.
int1 -ne *int2*	int1 is not equal to int2.
int1 -lt *int2*	int1 is less than int2.
int1 -gt *int2*	int1 is greater than int2.
int1 -le *int2*	int1 is less than or equal to int2.
int1 -ge *int2*	int1 is greater than or equal to int2.
	String comparison. The following are true when:
str	str isn't null.
-n *str*	length of str isn't zero.
-z *str*	length of the string is zero.
str1 = str2	str1 identical to str2.
str1 != str2	str1 not identical to and str2.
	String comparison. Used n in Korn, Bash, and Z-shell (ksh, bash, zsh).
str1 == str2	str1 identical to str2.
str1 < str2	the value of str1 is before the value of str2 by ASCII.
str1 > str2	the value of str1 is after the value of str2 by ASCII.
	Logical operators.
! *expr*	Is true when expression is false.
	Logical operators. Used in Bash-shell (bash).
expr1 -a *expr2*	Is true when both expr1 and expr2 is true.
expr1 -o *expr2*	Is true when one of expr1 and expr2 is true.

continued

	Logical operators. Used in Korn and Z-shell (ksh, zsh).
expr1 && *expr2*	Is true when both expr1 and expr2 is true.
expr1 || *expr2*	Is true when one of expr1 and expr2 is true.
	The following is used for Korn shell (ksh) and Z-shell (zsh).
(expr)	Is true when expression is true.
External	
AIX	External test takes the same options as internal test for Bourne shell (sh).
BSD	External test takes the same options as internal test for Bourne shell (sh).
Linux	External test takes the same options as internal test for Bourne shell (sh).
--version	Shows version information.
--help	Shows help information.
Solaris	External test takes the same options as internal test for Korn shell (ksh).

File Name:	`test`	**Directory:**	/usr/bin, **BSD:** /bin	**Type:**	External, Internal
Note:	If < or > is used, you must enclose the condition inside " if test is used. If used inside [ ] in an if structure, use [[ ]] instead.				
Common:	test -f /etc/passwd -a -f /etc/shadow	True if /etc/passwd is readable.			
Common:	test -e /var/adm/messages	True if /var/adm/messages exist.			
Common:	test " ab < cd "	Will be true.			

tftp

UNIX Shell: Shells (ash, bash, bsh, csh, ksh, sh, tcsh, zsh)

Function	Sends files to and from a remote host using the Trivial File Transfer Protocol (TFTP).
Syntax	AIX: tftp [options] *localfile Host:**{ Port }** remotefile { netascii } { image }* BSD, Linux, Solaris: tftp *{ hostname }*

	The following commands are internal to tftp.
ascii	Sets transfer mode to ASCII. The same as `mode netascii`.
binary	Sets transfer mode to binary. The same as `mode image`.
connect *hostname { port }*	Is used to specify a hostname or IP address to a tftp server.
mode *{ netascii* | *image }*	Shows or sets the current mode used to transfer files.
put *file*	Specifies the filename of the file to transfer.
get *file*	Specifies the filename of the file to receive.
timeout *value*	Is used to specify the timeout value for the connection.
verbose	Toggles verbose mode on or off. When on, verbose mode will show more information.
trace	A toggle used to enable or disable packet tracing during file transfer.
status	Shows connection status, mode status, tracing status, and the timeout status.
?	Shows help information on the internal commands.
quit	Exits the interactive mode.
AIX:	
	The following options can only be used one at a time.
-g	Gets remote data from RemoteName from Host and writes to LocalName.
-o	Overwrites an existing local file without prompting.
-p	Puts local data LocalName to file RemoteName.
-r	Reads remote data from RemoteName from Host and writes to LocalName.
-w	Writes local data LocalName to file RemoteName.
localfile	Specifies local file to put or get data to or from.
Host:{ Port }	Specifies remote computer and port to connect to.
remotefile	Specifies remote file to put or get data to or from.
	Use only one of the following modes.
netascii	Transfers the data as 7-bit ASCII characters in 8-bit transfer bytes.
image	Transfers the data as 8-bit binary data bytes in 8-bit transfer bytes.
BSD, Linux, Solaris:	
hostname	Specifies the hostname to connect to.

File Name:	tftp	**Directory:**	/usr/bin/	**Type:**	External

tic

tic	UNIX Shell:	Shells (ash, bash, bsh, csh, ksh, sh, tcsh, zsh)

Function	Compiles a terminfo file. The data is saved in the directory `/usr/share/lib/terminfo` for AIX and Solaris and in the directory `/usr/share/terminfo` for BSD and Linux.
Syntax	tic [options...] *{ file }*

-v *{ n }*	Redirects verbose output to STDERR, n is used to set the detail level (1-10).
-c	Checks the file for incorrect syntax or bad links.
file	Specifies a file containing terminfo terminal descriptions in source format.
BSD,Linux:	
-o*directory*	Specifies the directory to save compiled entries in.
-w*NR*	Sets the output width.
-1	Specifies the output to be in a single column.
-C	Specifies the source translation to be in termcap format.
-G	Shows constant character literals in decimal form.
-I	Specifies the source translation to be in terminfo format.
-L	Translations in terminfo format use the long C variable names listed in term.h.
-N	Disables smart defaults.
-R*subset*	Specifies the subset to use. Values are SVr1, Ultrix, HP, BSD, and AIX.
-T	Doesn't use size-restrictions on the generated text.
-r	Uses entry resolution even when doing a termcap format translation.
-e *terminals...*	Specifies the terminals (separated with a), to make the translations and writes to.
-f	Shows the if/then/else/endif expressions in a terminfo string.
-g	Shows constant character literals in quoted form.
-s	**BSD only:** Shows path to files and the number of entries compiled.
-a	**Linux only:** Uses commented-out capabilities.
-x	**Linux only:** Handles unknown capabilities as user-defined.

File Name:	`tic`	**Directory:**	/usr/bin/	**Type:**	External
Common:	tic -c termfile	Compiles the file termfile and checks the file for correct syntax.			

time

time	UNIX Shell:	C & TC - shell (csh, tcsh)

Function	Starts a program and shows statistics on STDERR about how long it took to run.
Syntax	time [options...] *program { arguments... }* csh, tcsh: time *{ program }*

-p	Shows the output in the POSIX format.
program	Specifies the program to be started.
arguments...	Specifies options to the program.
BSD:	
-l	Shows the contents of the rusage structure.
Linux:	
-o *file*	Writes the output to file.
-a	Appends to the file instead of overwriting it.
-f *string*	Specifies a format string.
--help	Shows help information.
-v	Verbose mode. Shows more information.
-V	Shows version information. (C and TC-Shell (csh, tcsh) have an internal time version with this option.)

File Name:	`time`	**Directory:**	/usr/bin/	**Type:**	External, Internal
Tip:	You can run any program, command, or even an application.				
Common:	time ls -al	Measures how long it takes to run the ls -al command.			

times

times	UNIX Shell:	Shells (bash, ksh, sh, zsh)

Function	Shows accumulated system and user times for processes run from the shell.
Syntax	times

touch

touch	UNIX Shell:	Shells (ash, bash, bsh, csh, ksh, sh, tcsh, zsh)

Function	Gives the file specified a new time and date stamp. If the file doesn't exist it will be created.
Syntax	touch [options...] *files...*

-a	Alters just the access time and won't alter the modification time unless -m is used.
-c	Doesn't create the file if the file doesn't already exist.
-f	Forces a time update and overrides the permissions set on the file. (Ignored in Linux.)
-m	Alters the modification time to the current time.
-r *ref-file*	Uses the time from the specified file instead of current time.
-t *time*	Specifies a time to use instead of current time. Uses the following time format.
[[CC]YY]MMDDhhmm [.SS]	Use specified date-time instead of current time.
MM	Specifies the month using the format [01-12].
DD	Specifies the day of the month using the format [01-31].
hh	Specifies the hour using the format [00-23].
mm	Specifies the minute using the format [00-59].
CC	Specifies the minute using the format [00-59]. The first two digits of the year.
YY	The second two digits of the year.
SS	The second of the minute [00-61].
files...	Specifies the file to change or create.
Linux:	
-d *string*	Parses the string specified and uses it for the time instead of current time.
--time=*time*	Alters the time specified. Values: atime, access (like -a) mtime, modify (like -m).
--help	Shows help information.
--version	Shows version information.

File Name:	`touch`	**Directory:**	/usr/bin/, **Linux:** /bin/	**Type:**	External

Common:	touch -c myfile	Does not create the file if it doesn't exist.
Common:	touch -m myfile	Changes modification time if it exists; otherwise creates it.
Linux:	touch --time=access myfile§	Alters the access time on the file myfile.
Solaris:	touch /reconfigure	Does a reconfigure of machine at next boot.

tput

tput	UNIX Shell:	Shells (ash, bash, bsh, csh, ksh, sh, tcsh, zsh)

Function	This utility is used to initialize a terminal or query a terminfo database.
Syntax	tput [option] *capname { params... }*

-T *type*	Specifies the type of terminal.
-S	Shows more than one capability per invocation.
capname	Specifies capability attributes from the terminfo database.
params...	Specifies parameters to capname.

File Name:	`tput`	**Directory:**	/usr/bin/	**Type:**	External

Tip:	Use the terminfo command to see a list of capabilities and the capname associated with each.	
Common:	tput reset	Resets the terminal.
Common:	tput -T vt220 cols	Prints the number of columns.
Common:	tput cup 12 40	Moves the screen cursor to row 12 and column 40.

tr

tr	UNIX Shell:	Shells (ash, bash, bsh, csh, ksh, sh, tcsh, zsh)

Function	Replaces or deletes characters while copying from STDIN to STDOUT.
Syntax	tr [options...] *string1 { string2 }*

-s	Replaces repeated characters with a single character specified by string1.
-d	Deletes all characters specified by string1.
-c	Complements string1 with string2. Can't be used alone.
string1	String that controls the translation.
string2	String that controls the translation.
	To specify characters the following can be used:
octal	Specifies a character by the octal code, e.g. \012 will be a newline.
\a	Bell.
\b	Backspace.

continued

\f	Form feed.
\n	Newline.
\r	Carriage return.
\t	Tab.
\v	Vertical tab.
{ char1-char2 }	Defines a range of characters, e.g., a-z.
[:*class*:]	Defines a class of characters, e.g., alpha, digit, upper, lower, blank.
*{ char*number }*	Expands a character a number of times, e.g. [Z*5] will be ZZZZZ.
[=*char*=]	Defines all characters equivalent to char, e.g., é is equivalent to e. (The brackets are required.)
-A	Replaces text using the byte-by-byte method instead of the ASCII method.

File Name:	`tr`	**Directory:**	/usr/bin/	**Type:**	External
Common:	tr -d ! < ucg1 > ucg2	Deletes all exclamation marks in ucg1 and copies it to ucg2.			
Common:	tr -s . < ucg1 > ucg2	Removes all repeated occurrences of dots in ucg1 and copies it to ucg2.			
Common:	cat ucg1 | tr ! . > ucg2	Replaces all exclamation marks in ucg1 with dots in ucg2.			

traceroute

UNIX Shell: Shells (ash, bash, bsh, csh, ksh, sh, tcsh, zsh)

Function	Shows you a list of the route a packet takes to reach a network host.
Syntax	traceroute [options...] *host { packetlength }*

-n	Shows the hop addresses only in numeric style, not symbolic and numeric.
-v	Verbose mode. Shows more information.
-r	Sends the packages directly to a host on an attached network.
-m *maxttl*	Specifies the maximum Time To Live value (default is 30).
-p *port*	Specifies the base UDP port number to use in the probes (default is 33434).
-w *waittime*	Specifies the time to wait for a probes response in seconds (default is 5 seconds).
-q *nqueries*	Specifies the number of probe queries (default is 3).
-s *srcaddr*	Specifies the address to use as source address for the outgoing probe packets.
-t *tos*	Specifies the type-of-service value in probe packets 0 - 255 (default is 0).
host	Specifies the receiver of the probe packets.
packetlength	Specifies the probe packet length in bytes (default 40 bytes).
AIX:	
-v	Verbose mode. Shows more information.
BSD:	
-d	Enables socket level debugging.
-D	Shows the packet data on STDERR before transmitting it.
-g *gateway*	Uses the specified loose source route gateway or gateways (-g1, -g2 ...-g8).
-l	Shows the ttl value of the returned packet.
-P *protocol*	Specifies the protocol to use.
Linux, Solaris:	
-d	Enables socket level debugging.
-F	Doesn't fragment the package.
-I	Specifies to use the ICMP ECHO probes, not the UDP datagram protocol.
-f *firstttl*	Specifies the starting Time To Live value (default is 1).
-g *gateway*	Uses the specified loose source route gateway or gateways (-g1, -g2 ...-g8).
-i *interface*	Specifies the network interface to obtain the source IP address for the package.
-x	Doesn't calculate the checksums.

File Name:	traceroute	**Directory:**	/usr/sbin/, **AIX:** /usr/bin/	**Type:**	External
Tip:	Very useful if you have network problems.				
Common:	traceroute pluto	Shows the route of the packets to pluto.			
Common:	traceroute -n pluto	Shows the route to pluto and prints hop addresses numerically.			
Common:	traceroute -m 60 pluto	Shows the route to pluto with maximum ttl 60.			

trap

UNIX Shell: Shells (ash, bash, bsh, ksh, sh, zsh)

Function	Runs the command when the shell receives signal. If command is a null string (''), it resets the signals to their original behavior. Used alone, it shows all traps.

Syntax	trap *{ command } { signals... }*

command	The command to run; enclose in " if it contains SPACE.
signals...	Is signal that triggers the command.
bash:	
-l	Lists of all signals and their numbers.
-p *signal*	Shows any command associated with signal.

Tip:	Is useful to make cleanup function inside a script.	
Common:	trap "echo hello" DEBUG	Shows hello after each command (in Korn shell (ksh)).
Common:	trap	Lists all traps that have been assigned.

troff, gtroff

UNIX Shell: Shells (ash, bash, bsh, csh, ksh, sh, tcsh, zsh)

Function	Formats the text in the specified file for printing or typesetting.
Syntax	troff [options...] *{ files... }*

	Linux Only: The command **gtroff** is the same as `troff`.
-a	Shows an ASCII approximation of the output on STDOUT.
-F*directory*	Searches the directory specified for settings for terminal tables and font files.
-i	Reads the STDIN after the execution of the specified files.
-m*macrofile*	Specifies the macro to process the file. (Please see Examples and MACRO directories.)
	AIX directory: /usr/lib/tmac/ **SOLARIS directory:** /usr/share/lib/tmac/.
EXAMPLES	**BSD directory:** /usr/share/tmac/ **LINUX directory:** /usr/share/groff/tmac/.
-man	Uses the man macro to process the files.
-me	Uses the e macro to process the files.
-ms	Uses the s macro to process the files.
-n*number*	Starts numbering the pages from the number specified.
-o*list*	Prints the pages specified in list either comma-separated 1,2,3, or in a range 1–4.
-r*aN*	Sets the specified register, a, to the specified value, N.
-z	Shows only .tm request and diagnostic messages, no formatted output.
-	Uses the input from STDIN instead of a file.
files...	Specifies the file containing the text to format.
AIX:	
-U	**Linux only:** Disables the use of the `safer` macro.
-M *size*	Specifies the paper size . Values for size are: A4, A5, B5, EXEC, LEGAL, LETTER.
-q	Provides input and output modes simultaneously for .rd requests
-s*value*	Stops the typesetter after every number of pages specified by value.
-T*type*	Specifies the printing device name to use for printing. (Default is ibm3816.)
BSD, Linux	**BSD and Linux use the GNU version of troff as described below.**
-b	Provides line numbers with warning or error messages to backtrack and solve problems.
-C	Enables compatibility mode.
-d*CString*	Specifies a single character `C` to be the string specified by *String.*
-d*name=String*	Specifies a `name` to be the string specified by *String.*
-E	Disables all error messages.
-f*fontfamily*	Specifies the font family to be used by default.
-M*directory*	Searches the specified directory for macro files, then searches the default dir.
-R	Doesn't load `troffrc`.
-T*type*	Specifies the printing device name to use for printing. (Default is `ps`.)
-v	Shows the version number.
-w*warning*	Enables the warning specified by the warning argument (See warnings below.)
-W*warning*	Disables the warning specified by the warning argument (See warnings below.)
	The following is a list of warnings you can use with the -w and -W options.
char	Warns for non-existent characters. This warning is enabled by default.
number	Warns for numeric expressions that are invalid. This warning is enabled by default.
break	Warns when lines are unable to be adjusted to the requested line length.
delim	Warns for missing or unmatched closing delimiters.
el	Warns when there is no matching `ie` for `el` requests.
scale	Warns for scaling indicators.
range	Warns when arguments are out of range.
syntax	Warns when the syntax is uncertain in numeric expressions.

continued

di	Warns when using `di` or `da` macros without an argument.
mac	Warns when undefined macros, strings, and diversions are found.
reg	Warns if undefined number registers are encountered. Automatically uses 0.
tab	Warns for incorrect use of Tab characters.
right-brace	Warns when a \} is found and a number was expected.
missing	Warns when requests don't include required arguments.
input	Warns for illegal input characters.
escape	Warns when escape sequences aren't recognized.
space	Warns when there is no space between an argument and its request or macro.
font	Warns for fonts that are missing.
ig	Warns for escape characters that are ignored by the ig request.
all	Includes all useful warnings. The warnings not included are `di, mac, and reg`.
w	Shows all warnings including `di, mac, and reg`.
Solaris:	
-f	Doesn't print a trailer page after the last page has been printed.
-s*value*	Stops the typesetter after every number of pages specified by value.
-T*type*	Sets the output type to PostScript or Autologic APS-5 . Value is: `post or aps`.
-u*N*	Sets the emboldening factor for the font in position 3 to the specified value.
File Name: `troff`	**Directory:** /usr/bin/ **Type:** External

true

UNIX Shell: Shells (ash, bash, bsh, csh, ksh, sh, tcsh, zsh)

Function	Provides a true value in scripts, does nothing but always exits with a value of 0.
Syntax	true

Linux:	
--help	Shows help information.
--version	Shows version information.
File Name: `true`	**Directory:** /usr/bin/, **Linux:** /bin/ **Type:** Script
Common: while [true] ; do who | grep root ; sleep 60 ; done	Check every 60 seconds to see if root has logged in.

tset

UNIX Shell: Shells (ash, bash, bsh, csh, ksh, sh, tcsh, zsh)

Function	Determines and configures your terminal.
Syntax	tset [options...] *{ type }*

-	Shows the terminal type on STDOUT.
-I	Doesn't send terminal-initialization strings.
-Q	Hides what the kill and erase characters are set to in the messages.
-r	Shows the terminal type in messages.
-s *{ terminal }*	Installs a new terminal to the environment and activates it.
-m *port-id { baudrate }*	Maps the terminal on the specified port.
type	Specifies a terminal type to configure, or to map with the -m option.
AIX, BSD, Linux:	
-e *char*	Specifies the erase character to use on all terminals (default is backspace).
-i *char*	Specifies the interrupt character to use on all terminals (default is Ctrl+C).
-k *char*	Specifies the kill character to use on all terminals (default is Ctrl+U).
-q	**BSD only:** Shows terminal type on STDOUT without initialization.
-S	**BSD only:** Shows the termcap entry and the terminal type on STDOUT.
Solaris:	
-e*char*	Specifies the erase character to use on all terminals (default is BACKSPACE).
-i*char*	Specifies the interrupt character to use on all terminals (default is Ctrl+C).
-k*char*	Specifies the kill character to use on all terminals (default is Ctrl+U).
-n	Uses the new tty driver modes (default).
File Name: tset	**Directory:** /usr/bin, **Solaris:** /usr/ucb/ **Type:** External
Tip:	Do not set erase key to any of the following characters: t, :, e, (t). **Solaris Note**: There is no space between -e, -I, or -k and their operands as in BSD, AIX, and Linux.

continued

Common:	tset -	Shows terminal type on STDOUT.
AIX:	tset -e <CTRL+b>	Sets the erase character to ctrl+b.
Linux:	tset -i N	Sets the interrupt character to N.
OpenBSD:	tset -k g	Sets the kill character to g.
Solaris:	tset -e<CTRL+b>	Sets the erase character to ctrl+b.

tsort

tsort		**UNIX Shell:**	**Shells (ash, bash, bsh, csh, ksh, sh, tcsh, zsh)**
Function	Sorts items from a text file or STDIN and shows on STDOUT an ordered listing of the items.		
Syntax	AIX: tsort [--] *{ file }* BSD, Linux: tsort [options...] *{ file }* Solaris: tsort *{ file }*		

file	Specifies the pathname to a text file to order.
AIX:	
--	Handles all following arguments as filenames.
BSD:	
-l	Searches for the longest cycle and shows it.
-q	Disables showing any cycles information.
Linux:	
--help	Shows help information.
--version	Shows version information.

File Name:	`tsort`	**Directory:**	/usr/bin/, **Solaris:** /usr/ccs/bin	**Type:**	External
AIX:	tsort -- /ucg_examples/sorttest	Sorts the file sorttest.			
Linux:	tsort /ucg_examples/sorttest	Sorts the file sorttest.			
OpenBSD:	tsort -l/ucg_examples/sorttest	Sorts the file sorttest and searches for the longest cycle, which can take a long time.			
Solaris:	tsort /ucg_examples/sorttest	Sorts the file sorttest.			

tty

tty		**UNIX Shell:**	**Shells (ash, bash, bsh, csh, ksh, sh, tcsh, zsh)**
Function	Shows the terminal that is used as STDIN.		
Syntax	tty [options...]		

-s	Hides the terminal on STDOUT. Used for testing exit status.
Linux:	
--help	Shows help information.
--version	Shows version information.
Solaris:	
-l	Shows the synchronous line number the terminal is connected to.

File Name:	`tty`	**Directory:**	/usr/bin/	**Type:**	External
Common:	tty	Shows the current terminal name, e.g. /dev/pts/7.			
Common:	tty -s ; echo $?	No output from tty. If echo shows 0, STDIN is a terminal.			
Solaris:	tty -l	Shows the line number if it is on an active synchronous line.			

type

type		**UNIX Shell:**	**Shells (bash, sh, ksh, zsh)**
Function	Shows a description of a commands type.		
Syntax	type *commands...* bash: type [options...] *commands...*		

command...	Specifies commands to get information about.
bash:	
-a	Shows all possible versions of command.
-t	Shows only the type of command.
-p	Shows only informations about commands that is a file.
zsh:	
-w	Shows only the type of command.
-f	Shows the contents of the function specified.
-p	Searches for command in the search path.
-a	Shows all possible versions of command.
-m	Handles command as a pattern, used quote.

continued

-s		Shows a symlink free pathname.
Common:	type type	Shows a description for the type command.
Common:	type ps	Shows a description for the ps command.
Common:	type -a test	Shows all possible versions of test. (bash)

typeset, declare

UNIX Shell: Shells (bash, ksh, zsh)

Function	Sets values and attributes for variables. A new variable instance is created when used inside functions.
Syntax	typeset [options...] *{ name[=value }*]

-r	Sets the variable read-only.
-x	Exports the variables to the environment.
variable=value	Specifies a value to set to the variable.
ksh:	
-H	When non-UNIX hosts are used, provides UNIX to host-name file mapping.
	In the following, *n* is the width of the field if it's not zero.
-L*{ n }*	Left-justifies value by removing leading space.
-R*{ n }*	Right-justifies value by adding space in the beginning.
-Z*{ n }*	Right-justifies value by adding 0 in the beginning if first character is a digit.
-i*{ n }*	Is used for integer. If n isn't zero, it's the base for the value.
-l	Converts uppercase to lowercase.
-t	Tags the variable.
-u	Converts lowercase to uppercase.
-f	The names refer to a function; the options will now have the following meaning.
-t	Turns on execution trace on this function.
-u	Marks the function undefined.
-x	Keeps the function definition when shell procedures are invoked by the name.
name	The name of the variable or the function if -f is used.
=value	The value to assign to the variable.
bash:	
-a	Specifies that name is an array.
-f	Specifies that name is a function.
-i	Specifies that name is an integer.
-F	Hides the function definition.
-p	Shows attribute and values for each name.
zsh:	
-A	Specifies that name is associative array.
-L*{ n }*	Left-justifies value by removing leading space.
-R*{ n }*	Right-justifies value by adding space in the beginning.
-U	Keeps only the first occurrence of duplicated values in an array.
-Z*{ n }*	Right-justifies value by adding 0 in the beginning if first character is a digit.
-a	Specifies that name is an array.
-i*{ n }*	Is used for integer. If n isn't zero, it's the base for the value.
-l	Converts uppercase to lowercase.
-t	Tags the variable.
-u	Converts lowercase to uppercase.
-f	The names refer to a function, the options will now have the following meaning.
-t	Turns on execution trace on this function.
-u	Marks the function for auto loading.
-U	Marks the function for auto loading and suppresses alias expansion when loading.
-g	Doesn't restrict any resulting parameters to local scope.
-m	Handles the variable names as a pattern to match. (In zsh, the option can have + as prefix instead of - . That will turn off the option.)

Note:	In bash and zsh declare has the same function.	
Common:	typeset -x UCG	Exports the UCG variable.
Common:	typeset -i2 binary=57	Sets $binary to 2#111001 (ksh and zsh)
Common:	typeset -r ucg	Makes the ucg variable read-only.

ul

ul		**UNIX Shell:**	Shells (ash, bash, bsh, csh, ksh, sh, tcsh, zsh)
Function	Reads STDIN or specified files and alters the underscore characters to fit your terminal.		
Syntax	ul [options...] *{ files... }*		

-t *terminal*	Specifies terminal other than your default terminal.
-i	Shows underlines in text by a separate line with dashes or underline characters.
files...	Specifies input files to use.

File Name:	`ul`	**Directory:**	/usr/bin/	**Type:**	External
Common:	ul ucgfile	Shows the file ucgfile with real underlining on the terminal.			
Common:	ul -i ucgfile	Shows underlines in ucgfile by a separate line with dashes or underline characters.			
Common:	ul -t xterm ucgfile	Uses `xterm`.			

ulimit

ulimit		**UNIX Shell:**	Shells (bash, bsh, sh, ksh, zsh)
Function	Sets and shows the size limits used by the shell and its child processes. Shows the current limit if not given.		
Syntax	ulimit [options...] *{ limit }*		

-a	Lists of all of the current size limits.
-H	Shows or sets the hard limit.
-S	Shows or sets the soft limit.
	The following options specify the resource to show or set the limits:
-c	Shows or sets the size limits of the core file in 512 byte blocks.
-d	Shows or sets the size limits of data, the segment, or heap in kilobytes.
-f	Shows or sets the size limits of files in 512 byte blocks.
-n	Shows or sets the maximum amount of open file descriptors.
-s	Shows or sets the size limits of the stack segment in kilobytes.
-t	Shows or sets the limits of CPU time in seconds to use on the processes.
-v	Shows or sets the size limits of the virtual memory in kilobytes.
limit	Specifies a number with the optional scaling factors below:
*n*h	Specifies time in hours (CPU time).
*n*k	Specifies the size in kilobytes. Default value except when using CPU time.
*n*m	Specifies megabytes or minutes (CPU time).
mm:ss	Specifies time in minutes and seconds (CPU time).
bash:	
-l	Shows or sets the maximum size to be locked in memory in kilobytes.
-m	Shows or sets the maximum resident size in physical memory in kilobytes.
-u	Shows or sets the number of available processes for the user.
-p	Shows the pipe size in 512 bytes block (this can't be set).
zsh:	
-l	Shows or sets the maximum size to be locked in memory in kilobytes.
-m	Shows or sets the maximum resident size in physical memory in kilobytes.
-u	Shows or sets the number of available processes for the user.

Tip:	Use ulimit -c if you have a program that generates big core files.	
Common:	ulimit -a	Shows all resource limits.
Common:	ulimit -n 64	Sets the number of file descriptors to 64.
Common:	ulimit -c 1024	Sets the size of the core file to 512 kilobytes.

umask

umask		**UNIX Shell:**	Shells (ash, bash, bsh, csh, ksh, sh, tcsh, zsh)
Function	Alters the file mode creation mask of the current shell execution environment.		
Syntax	sh, csh: umask *{ mask }* ksh, bash, zsh: umask [options...] *{ mask }*		

mask	Specifies the mask to use in absolute (octal) mode. (Symbolic or absolute mode can be used in ksh, bash, and zsh.)
-p	Shows the output in a form that can be used as input.
-S	Shows the umask in symbolic mode.
-S	Shows the umask in symbolic mode.

Tip:	See the command `chmod` for absolute modes. Using the absolute mode is much easier.	
Common:	umask 022	Sets the umask to 022.

Common:	umask u=rwx,g=rx,o=rx	Sets the umask to 022 in ksh, bash, and zsh.
Common:	umask	Shows you the current umask setting.

umount, unmount

UNIX Shell: Shells (ash, bash, bsh, csh, ksh, sh, tcsh, zsh)

Function	Unmounts local or remote file systems. AIX also has an unmount command with the same syntax.
Syntax	umount [options...] *{ special } { directories... }* AIX: unmount [options...] *{ special } { directories... }*

-a	Unmounts all file systems listed or all that aren't used if none listed.
	Use one of these to determine the file system to unmount:
special	Specifies the device on which the file system resides.
directories...	Specifies the mount point to unmount, e.g., /ucg. Combine with -a for multiple mounts.
AIX:	
all	Unmounts all mounted file systems.
allr	Unmounts all remote mounted file systems.
-f	Forces an unmount of a remote file system if the remote host is down.
-n *host*	Unmounts all remote mounts from the remote host.
-t *type*	Unmounts all file systems with type=type in the `/etc/filesystems` file.
BSD:	
-f	Forces an unmount of the file system. (The root file system can't be forced.)
-h *host*	Unmounts file system mounted from the specified host.
-t *type*	Specifies a comma-separated list of file system types to unmount.
-v	Verbose mode. Shows more information.
Linux:	
-V	Shows version information.
-h	Shows help information.
-v	Verbose mode. Shows more information.
-n	Unmounts without updating /etc/mtab.
-r	Tries to remount the file system read only if an unmount fails.
-t *type*	Specifies a comma-separated list of file system types to unmount.
-f	Forces an unmount of a remote file system if the remote host is down.
Solaris:	
-V	Shows the complete command line, but doesn't execute the command.
-o *options*	Specifies file system options, comma-separated if more than one.

File Name:	`umount, unmount`	**Directory:**	**AIX, Solaris:** /usr/sbin/, **BSD:** /sbin/, **Linux:** /bin/	**Type:**	External

Note:	You can't unmount file systems that are in use.	
Common:	umount /ucg	Unmounts the file system mounted on /ucg.
Common:	umount -a	Unmounts all file systems except the required ones, e.g., `/`.
Common:	umount /usg /local	Unmounts the file system mounted on /ucg and /local.
AIX:	umount -f /remotedir	Unmounts the remote file system even if the server is down.
Linux:	umount -t nfs	Unmounts all nfs file systems.
OpenBSD:	umount -h moon	Unmounts the file system from host moon.
Solaris:	umount /dev/dsk/c0t0d0s3	Unmounts the /dev/dsk/c0t0d0s3 file systems.

unalias

UNIX Shell: Shells (csh, bash, ksh, tcsh, zsh)

Function	Erases the definitions of all aliases specified on the command line from the current shell execution environment.
Syntax	csh, tcsh: unalias *aliasnames...* bash, ksh, zsh: unalias [option] *aliasnames...*

aliasnames...	Erases specified alias names.
bash, ksh:	
-a	Erases all alias names.
zsh:	
-m	Uses name as a pattern and removes all alias that match.

Common:	unalias mee	Erases the name specified.
Common:	unalias -a	Erases all the aliases (bash, ksh).
Common:	unalias -m ls*	Erases all aliases that start with ls (zsh).

uname

UNIX Shell:	Shells (ash, bash, bsh, csh, ksh, sh, tcsh, zsh)
Function	Shows information about the current system.
Syntax	uname [options...]

-a	Shows all basic information about the system.
-m	Shows the hardware name, e.g., Sun4u.
-n	Shows the hostname, e.g., ucg.
-r	Shows the operating system release, e.g., 5.7.
-s	Shows the name of the operating system, e.g., SunOS (Is default).
-v	Shows the version of the operating system, e.g., Generic.
AIX:	
-l	Shows the LAN network number, e.g., 1569080652.
-M	Shows the system model name, e.g., IBM PPS Model 7248.
-S *host*	Changes the node name. Can only be used by the superuser.
-T *host*	Changes the system name. Can only be used by the superuser.
-u	Shows the system ID number, e.g., IBM724855D8645.
-x	Same as -a and -l together.
BSD:	
-p	Shows the processor type, e.g., sparc.
Linux:	
-p	Shows the processor type, e.g., sparc.
--help	Shows help information.
--version	Shows version information.
Solaris:	
-i	Shows the name of the platform, e.g. SUNW,Ultra-1.
-p	Shows the processor type, e.g., sparc.
-X	Shows more system information, one record per line. Similar to SCO UNIX.
-S *host*	Changes the hostname. Can only be used by the superuser.

File Name:	`uname`	**Directory:** /usr/bin/, **Linux:** /bin/ — **Type:** External
Common:	uname -a	Shows all basic information about the system.
Common:	uname -r	Shows the release level of the OS.

uncompress

UNIX Shell:	Shells (ash, bash, bsh, csh, ksh, sh, tcsh, zsh)
Function	Uncompresses .Z files. Removes the .Z suffix when it is done.
Syntax	uncompress [options...] *{ files... }*

-c	Expands the file and shows it on STDOUT but doesn't change the file.
-f	Doesn't prompt before overwriting files.
files...	Specifies files to be uncompressed.
AIX:	
-n	Doesn't include the compression header in the compressed file.
-q	Quiet mode. Shows less information.
-V	Shows version information.
BSD:	
-t	Tests the file's integrity.
-0	Uses an older compression method.
-q	Quiet mode. Shows less information.
-v	Verbose mode. Shows more information.
-o *file*	Specifies the output file.
Linux:	
-v	Verbose mode. Shows more information.
-V	Shows version information.
Solaris:	
-v	Verbose mode. Shows more information.

File Name:	`uncompress`	**Directory:** /usr/bin/ — **Type:** External
Note:	Before uncompressing anything, you must compress something.	
Common:	uncompress bigfile.Z	Uncompresses bigfile.Z.
Common:	uncompress -c bigfile.Z	Shows the contents of bigfile.Z without changing the file. Same as `zcat bigfile.Z`.

unexpand

UNIX Shell: Shells (ash, bash, bsh, csh, ksh, sh, tcsh, zsh)

Function	Replaces the spaces in text files created with `expand` with Tab characters.
Syntax	unexpand [options...] *{ files... }*

-a	Replaces all spaces with Tabs if the result is a smaller output file.
files...	Specifies text files to use as input.
AIX, Linux, Solaris:	
-t *tabs*	Specifies the Tab positions. Can be an absolute number or a comma-separated list.
--help	**Linux only:** Shows help information.
--version	**Linux only:** Shows version information.

File Name:	`unexpand`	**Directory:**	/usr/bin/	**Type:**	External

Note:	The default Tab value is 8 spaces apart.	
Common:	unexpand ucg1	Unexpands the file ucg1 to STDOUT.
Common:	unexpand -a ucg1	Unexpands all spaces in ucg1.
AIX:	unexpand -t 10 ucg1 > ucg2	Unexpands the file ucg1 to ucg2 with a tab value set to 10.

unhash

UNIX Shell: Shells (csh, tcsh, zsh)

Function	Disables the internal hash table. In `zsh` it removes names from the internal hash table.
Syntax	unhash zsh: unhash [option] *names...*

zsh:	
-a	Removes aliases.
-d	Removes named directories.
-f	Removes functions.
-m	Uses name as a pattern and removes all elements that match.
names...	Specifies name of elements to remove.

Common:	unhash	The internal hash table will be disabled.

uniq

UNIX Shell: Shells (ash, bash, bsh, csh, ksh, sh, tcsh, zsh)

Function	Filters out adjacent lines that are alike and shows the output on STDOUT or saves it to a file.
Syntax	uniq [options...] *inputfile { outputfile }*

-c	Shows you how many times a line occurred in input.
-d	Shows only the lines that were repeated in the input file.
-f *fields*	Specifies the number of fields to ignore starting from the beginning of the lines.
-s *chars*	Specifies the number of characters to ignore starting from the beginning of the lines.
-u	Hides the lines that were repeated in the input file.
-*fields*	The same as the option `-f fields` with n set to the specified number.
+*chars*	The same as the option `-s` with m set to the specified number.
inputfile	Specifies the path and name of the input file.
outputfile	Specifies the path and name of the output file.
Linux:	
-D	Shows all the lines that were repeated in the input file.
-i	Compares without consideration to upper- or lowercase.
-w	Specifies number of characters to compare in each line starting from the beginning.
--help	Shows help information.
--version	Shows version information.

File Name:	`uniq`	**Directory:**	/usr/bin/	**Type:**	External

Tip:	Use this command in addition to `sort` and you remove all duplicate lines in a text.	
Common:	uniq -c cleartext.txt	Reports how many times every line is repeated.
Common:	uniq cleartext.txt /tmp/test	Saves file cleartext.txt without repeated lines in /tmp/test.
Common:	uniq -d cleartext.txt	Shows only the repeated lines in cleartext.txt.

unlimit

UNIX Shell: Shells (csh, tcsh, zsh)

Function	Removes resource limits. If no options are specified all limits will be erased.
Syntax	unlimit [-h] *{ resource }*

-h	Erases corresponding hard limits.
resource	Specifies the resource for which limits will be erased. The following types are used:
cputime	Maximum CPU time per process.
filesize	Maximum size of a single file allowed.
datasize	Maximum process's heap size.
stacksize	Maximum stack size for the process.
coredumpsize	Maximum core dump file size.
csh:	
descriptors	Specifies maximum number of file descriptors.
memorysize	Specifies maximum virtual memory size.
tcsh:	
memorysize	Specifies maximum virtual memory size.
zsh:	
descriptors	Specifies maximum number of file descriptors.
memorylocked	Specifies maximum memory locked in RAM.
resident	Specifies maximum resident set size.
vmemorysize	Specifies maximum of virtual memory.
maxproc	Specifies maximum of processes.
addressspace	Specifies maximum address space.
cachedthreads	Specifies maximum cached threads.
zsh:	
-s	Removes limit for the current shell. Default is for the children of the shell.

Note:	Use `limit` to set limits.	
Common:	unlimit	Unset all limits.
Common:	unlimit cputime	Erases any limit for cputime.

unset

UNIX Shell: Shells (ash, bash, bsh, csh, ksh, sh, tcsh, zsh)

Function	Removes variable or function from the shell.
Syntax	sh, csh, tcsh: unset *names...* bash, ksh: unset [options] *names...*

names...	Specifies names of variables or functions to remove.
bash:	
-f	Removes functions. (If not used, only variables will be removed.)
-f	Removes shell variables. (Is default.)
ksh:	
-f	Removes functions. (If not used, only variables will be removed.)
zsh:	
-f	Removes functions. (If not used, only variables will be removed.)
-m	Uses name as a pattern and removes all variables that match.

Common:	unset hello	Removes the hello variable.
Common:	unset -f printhello	Removes the function print hello (ksh).
Common:	unset -m "*hello*"	Removes any variable that contains the word hello (zsh).

unsetenv	UNIX Shell:	Shells (csh, tcsh)
Function	Removes environment variables.	
Syntax	unsetenv *variable*	
variable	The name of the variable to remove.	
Warning:	In tcsh unsetenv * removes all environment variables. Use with care!	
Common:	unsetenv TIME	Removes the environment variable TIME.
Common:	unsetenv *	Removes all environment variables (tcsh).

until	UNIX Shell:	Shells (ash, bash, bsh, ksh, sh, zsh)
Function	Repeats the commands until expression is true.	
Syntax	until *expr*; do *commands...*; done	
expr	A command (if its exit status is 0 the expression is true) or a test inside [ ]. (The syntax for a test inside [ ] is the same as for the test command.)	
commands...	Are commands to run.	
done	The end of the until loop.	
Note:	This is the opposite of while.	
Common:	until [$a = y] ; do read $a ; done	Reads from the keyboard. Repeats until `y` is entered.

uptime		UNIX Shell:	Shells (ash, bash, bsh, csh, ksh, sh, tcsh, zsh)		
Function	Shows how long the system has been up, the number of users, and the load average for the last 1, 5, and 15 minutes.				
Syntax	uptime BSD, Linux: uptime [options...]				
BSD:					
-M *core*	Specifies which cores name list to use (default is `/dev/kmem`).				
-N *system*	Specifies the system to use (default is `/bsd`).				
Linux:					
-V	Shows version information.				
File Name:	`uptime`	**Directory:**	/usr/bin/	**Type:**	External
Common:	uptime	Shows how long your system has been up.			
OpenBSD:	uptime -N /ucg	Uses `/ucg` instead of `/bsd`.			

users		UNIX Shell:	Shells (ash, bash, bsh, csh, ksh, sh, tcsh, zsh)		
Function	Shows a one-line list of the users who are logged in on the system.				
Syntax	users [options...] *{ file }* BSD: users				
AIX:					
file	Specifies the file to use. (Default is `/etc/utmp.`)				
Linux:					
--help	Shows help information.				
--version	Shows version information.				
file	Specifies the file to use. (Default is `/var/run/utmp.`)				
Solaris:					
file	Specifies the file to use. (Default is `/var/adm/utmp.`)				
File Name:	`users`	**Directory:**	/usr/bin/, **Solaris:** /usr/ucb/	**Type:**	External
Common:	users	Lists of the currently logged in users on a single line.			
AIX:	users /etc/ucg	Uses `/etc/ucg` instead of `/etc/utmp`.			

uudecode

UNIX Shell:	Shells (ash, bash, bsh, csh, ksh, sh, tcsh, zsh)
Function	Decodes an encoded file created by `uuencode`. The decoded filename is set by `uuencode`.
Syntax	uudecode [options...] *{ file }*

file	Specifies the file to decode. BSD and Linux accept several files.
BSD, Solaris:	
-p	Shows the output on STDOUT instead.
Linux:	
-o *file*	Specifies the decoded filename.

File Name:	`uudecode`	**Directory:**	/usr/bin/	**Type:**	External
Common:	uudecode ucg1	Decodes ucg1 to the name set by `uuencode`.			

uuencode

UNIX Shell:	Shells (ash, bash, bsh, csh, ksh, sh, tcsh, zsh)
Function	Creates an encoded file to use when you send mail.
Syntax	uuencode *{ sourcefile } decodefile*

sourcefile	Specifies the file to encode.
decodefile	Specifies the decoded filename for use by `uudecode`.
Linux:	
-m	Specifies `base64` encoding to be used.

File Name:	`uuencode`	**Directory:**	/usr/bin/	**Type:**	External
Common:	uuencode ucg1 ucg2	Encodes ucg1. The decoded file will be ucg2.			

vi, view

UNIX Shell:	Shells (ash, bash, bsh, csh, ksh, sh, tcsh, zsh)
Function	Edits or views text files.
Syntax	vi [options...] *files...* view [options...] *files...*

-c *command*	Specifies a command to begin edit with.
files...	Specifies file to edit.
AIX:	
-y *size*	Overrides the maximum line setting.
-w *size*	Specifies the window size.
+*command*	Specifies a command to begin edit with.
-v	The same as starting vi.
-t *tag*	Specifies the tag in a file to edit.
-r *file*	Specifies filename to recover after edit or system crash.
-R	The read-only mode.
-l	Edits LISP programs.
BSD:	
-e	Starts editing in `ex` mode.
-F	Disables copy of the entire file when starting to edit.
-S	Doesn't sort tag files, used with the `-t tag` option.
-w *size*	Specifies the window size.
-v	The same as starting vi.
-t *tag*	Specifies the tag in a file to edit.
-r *file*	Specifies file name to recover after edit or system crash.
-R	The read-only mode.
-l	Edits LISP programs.
Linux:	
--	Specifies end of options.
-v	Starts editing in `vi` mode.
-e	Starts editing in `ex` mode.
-s	Starts in silent mode.
-R	Starts in read-only mode.
-Z	Starts in restricted mode.

continued

-m	Specifies that writing files aren't allowed.
-b	Runs in binary mode.
-C	Specifies the program should almost behave as original `vi`.
-N	Specifies the program should not behave as original `vi`.
-V *{ number }*	Specifies the verbose level.
-n	Specifies that no swap file should be used.
-r	Shows swap files.
-r *filename*	Recovers crashed session.
-L	Same as -r option.
-T *terminal*	Sets the terminal type.
-o *{ number }*	Specifies the number of windows to open. Default is one for each file.
+	Starts at end of file.
+*number*	Starts at the specified line number.
-s *script*	Reads commands from the specified script file.
-w *script*	Appends commands from the specified script file.
-W *script*	Writes commands from the specified script file.
-u *configurefile*	Specifies an alternative configuration file to use.
-h	Shows help information.
--version	Shows version information.
Solaris:	
-	Suppresses all interactive user feedback.
-s	Same as -.
-l	Edits LISP programs.
-L	Shows all files saved if editor or system crashes.
-R	The read-only mode.
-r *file*	Specifies filename to recover after edit or system crash.
-S	Doesn't sort tag files, used with the `-t tag` option.
-t *tag*	Specifies the tag in a file to edit.
-v	The same as starting vi.
-V	Verbose mode. Shows more information.
-x	The encryption mode, simulates X commands of ex.
-w *size*	Specifies the window size.
-C	The encryption mode, simulate C commands of ex.
+*command*	Specifies a command to begin edit with.

File Name:	`vi`	**Directory:**	/usr/bin/, **Linux:** /bin/	**Type:**	External
Common:	vi /etc/hosts		Edits the hosts file.		
Common:	view ucgtext.txt		Runs view on the ucgtext.txt file.		

vmstat

UNIX Shell:	**Shells (ash, bash, bsh, csh, ksh, sh, tcsh, zsh)**
Function	Shows various statistics for the system., for example, memory and io usages.
Syntax	vmstat [options...] *{ disks } { interval } { count }* BSD: vmstat [options...] *disks* Linux: vmstat [options...] *{ interval [count }]*

AIX:	
-f	Shows the number of forks since system startup.
-i	Reports number of interrupts per device.
-s	Shows total number of system events since boot.
disks	Specifies which disks are to be given priority in the output.
interval	Specifies the interval in seconds between summaries.
count	Specifies the number of times to repeat the statistics.
BSD:	
-c *count*	Specifies the number of times to repeat the statistics.
-f	Shows the number of forks since system startup.
-i	Reports number of interrupts per device.
-M *core*	Extracts values associated with the name list from the specified core.
-N *system*	Extracts the name list from the specified system.

continued

-m	Shows the usage of kernel dynamic memory.
-s	Shows total number of system events since boot.
-t	Shows the number of page in and page reclaims since system startup.
-w *seconds*	Pauses the specified seconds between each display.
disks	Specifies which disks are to be given priority in the output.
interval	Specifies the interval in seconds between summaries.
count	Specifies the number of times to repeat the statistics.
Linux:	
-n	Shows the header only one time.
-V	Shows version information.
Solaris:	
-c	Reports cache flush statistics.
-i	Reports number of interrupts per device.
-s	Shows total number of system events since boot.
-S	Reports swapping activity.
disks	Specifies which disks are to be given priority in the output.
interval	Specifies the interval in seconds between summaries.
count	Specifies the number of times to repeat the statistics.

File Name:	`vmstat`	**Directory:** /usr/bin/	**Type:** External
AIX:	vmstat -f	Shows the number of forks since system startup.	
Linux:	vmstat -n 2	Shows virtual memory statistics with two-seconds interval and only shows the header one time.	
OpenBSD:	vmstat -c 10	Shows virtual memory statistics ten times.	
Solaris:	vmstat -s	Displays total number of system events.	

w

UNIX Shell: Shells (ash, bash, bsh, csh, ksh, sh, tcsh, zsh)

Function	Shows information about logged in users.
Syntax	w [options...] *{ user }*

-h	Suppresses the heading.
user	Specifies a user to show login information about.
AIX, Solaris:	
-l	Shows a long output. (Is default.)
-s	Shows a short output.
-u	Shows the current time, uptime, number of logged in users, and the load average.
BSD:	
-i	Sorts the output by idle time.
-a	Tries to resolve IP addresses into names.
-M *core*	Specifies which cores name list to use. (Default is `/dev/kmem`.)
-N *system*	Specifies the system to use. (Default is `/bsd`.)
Linux:	
-u	Ignores the username when determining the current process and CPU times.
-s	Shows a short output.
-f	Hides the `FROM` field.
-V	Shows version information.

File Name:	`w`	**Directory:** /usr/bin/	**Type:** External
Note:	The command `w -u` is the same as using `uptime`.		
AIX:	w -u	Shows the current time, uptime, number of logged in users, and the load average.	
Linux:	w -f	Hides the `FROM` field.	
OpenBSD:	w -a	Tries to resolve IP addresses into names.	
Solaris:	w -s	Shows a short output.	

wait

wait	UNIX Shell:	Shells (ash, bash, bsh, csh, ksh, sh, tcsh, zsh)
Function	Waits for a background process to complete. C and TC-Shell wait for all background processes.	
Syntax	sh, bash, ksh, zsh: wait *{ jobid }* csh, tcsh: wait	

sh, bash, ksh, zsh: *jobid*	Specifies the process ID or a job id of a command to wait for.

Note:	Solaris: Bourne-shell must be started in job-control mode (jsh) to use jobid.	
Common:	wait %2	Waits for job ID 2 to complete.
Common:	wait 123	Waits for process 123 to complete.
Common:	wait	Waits for all active child processes.

wall

wall	UNIX Shell:	Shells (ash, bash, bsh, csh, ksh, sh, tcsh, zsh)
Function	Shows a message to all currently logged-in users.	
Syntax	wall [options...] *{ message }* BSD: wall [-g] *{ file }*	

AIX: *message*	Specifies the message string. Default is STDIN.
BSD: -g *group* *file*	Specifies a group to broadcast to. Specifies a file to read the message from. Default is STDIN.
Linux: *message*	Specifies the message string. Default is STDIN.
Solaris: -a -g *group* *message*	Broadcasts the message to the console and all pseudo-terminals. Specifies a group to broadcast to. Specifies a file to read the message from. Default is STDIN.

File Name:	wall	**Directory:**	/usr/sbin/, **BSD, Linux:** /usr/bin/	**Type:**	External

Note:	The sender must be superuser to override any protections the users may have enabled.	
Common:	wall	Starts wall in interactive mode, type the message and terminate with Ctrl-D.
AIX:	wall Hello	Sends "Hello" to all users.
Linux:	wall Hello	Sends "Hello" to all users.
OpenBSD:	wall -g sys /ucgmessage	Sends the message in the file /ucgmessage to all users in the group sys.
Solaris:	wall -a /ucgmessage	Shows the contents of the file /ucgmessage on all terminals, even pseudo-terminals.

wc

wc	UNIX Shell:	Shells (ash, bash, bsh, csh, ksh, sh, tcsh, zsh)
Function	Counts characters, words, and lines in files.	
Syntax	wc [options...] *{ files... }*	

-l -w -c *files...*	Counts lines. Counts words. Counts bytes. Specifies input files. If none given, STDIN will be used.
AIX: -k -m	Specifies that -c counts characters instead of bytes. Counts characters.
BSD: -m	Counts characters.
Linux: -L --help --version	Shows the length of the longest line. Shows help information. Shows version information.

continued

Solaris: -m -C		Counts characters. Same as -m.			
File Name:	`wc`	**Directory:**	/usr/bin/	**Type:**	External
Common:	wc -l /etc/passwd	Counts lines in the file /etc/passwd.			
Common:	wc -w /etc/hosts	Counts words in the file /etc/hosts.			
Common:	wc /etc/passwd	Counts bytes, words, and lines in the file /etc/passwd.			

whatis

UNIX Shell: Shells (ash, bash, bsh, csh, ksh, sh, tcsh, zsh)

Function	Shows the header line from the manual page for a command.
Syntax	whatis [options...] *commands...*

commands... **AIX,BSD:** -M *path* -m *path*		Specifies commands to show a header for. Specifies a search path instead of the default one. Must be a colon-separated list. **BSD only:** Specifies a comma-separated list of search paths to use.			
File Name:	`whatis`	**Directory:**	/usr/bin/	**Type:**	External
Note:	This command is the same as using `man -f`.				
Common:	whatis whatis	Shows the header from the man page for the command whatis.			
Common:	whatis vi	Shows the header from the man page for the text editor vi.			
Common:	whatis catman	Shows the header from the man page for the command catman.			
AIX:	whatis -M /usr/share/ucgman catman	Searches only `/usr/share/ucgman`.			
OpenBSD:	whatis -m /usr/share/ucgman catman	Searches `/usr/share/ucgman` before the standard path.			

whereis

UNIX Shell: Shells (ash, bash, bsh, csh, ksh, sh, tcsh, zsh)

Function	Searches binary, source, and manual page files for the specified command.
Syntax	whereis [options...] *files...* BSD: whereis *files...*

files... **AIX, Linux, Solaris:** -b -m -s -u -B *directory* -M *directory* -S *directory* -f		Specifies the command to search for. * wildcards can be used. Searches for binaries. Searches for manual sections. Searches for sources. Searches for unusual entries. Changes or limits the places where `whereis` searches for binaries. Changes or limits the places where `whereis` searches for manual sections. Changes or limits the places where `whereis` searches for sources. Terminates the last directory and start filenames. (Option -f can only be used with -B, -M, or -S.)			
File Name:	`whereis`	**Directory:**	/usr/bin/, **Solaris:** /usr/ucb/	**Type:**	External
Note:	Since `whereis` uses `chdir` to run faster, pathnames given with -M, -S, or -B must be absolute.				
Common:	whereis whereis	Shows where the command whereis is located.			
AIX:	whereis -b /usr/bin/*	Shows all binaries in /usr/bin/.			
Linux:	whereis -u /usr/bin/*	Shows all unusual files in /usr/bin/.			

which

UNIX Shell: Shells (ash, bash, bsh, csh, ksh, sh, tcsh, zsh)

Function	Shows the path to a command.
Syntax	which [options...] *commands...*

commands... **BSD:** -a **Linux:** --all --read-alias --skip-alias	Specifies the commands to look for. Lists all matches instead of just the first one. Lists all matches instead of just the first one. Reads aliases from STDIN, matching ones are shown on STDOUT. Ignores the option --read-alias.

continued

--skip-dot	Excludes directories that start with a dot.
--skip-tilde	Excludes directories that start with a tilde and executables in the home directory.
--show-dot	Doesn't expand a dot in the path to the full name.
--show-tilde	Shows a tilde instead of the home directory. Not for root.
--tty-only	Doesn't use the options on the right if you aren't on a tty.
--version	Shows version information.
--help	Shows help information.
	It is an internal command in tcsh and zsh.
commands...	Specifies the commands to look for.
zsh:	
-w	Shows if a name is: alias, builtin, command, function, hashed, reserved or none.
-p	Searches the path even if the command is a function, a reserved word or an alias.
-m	Uses the argument as a pattern and shows all matching commands.
-s	Shows the symlink-free pathname if the pathname contains symlinks.
-a	Searches for all occurrences of name.

File Name:	`which`	**Directory:**	/usr/bin/	**Type:**	External, Internal
Note:	It is a C-shell script in AIX and Solaris.				
Common:	which which	Shows the path to the command `which`.			
Linux:	which --tty-only --show-tilde ls	If run from a script, the option --show-tilde isn't used.			
OpenBSD:	which -a ls	Shows all occurrences of the command `ls`.			

while

UNIX Shell: Shells (ash, bash, bsh, csh, ksh, sh, tcsh, zsh)

Function	Repeats the commands while the expression is true.

Syntax	sh, bash, ksh, zsh:
	while *expr*:
	  do *commands...*;
	done
	csh, tcsh:
	while (*expr*)
	  commands....
	end

sh, bash, ksh, zsh:	
expr	A command (if it's exit status is 0 the expression is true) or a test inside [ ]. (The syntax for a test inside [ ] is the same as for the test command.)
commands...	Is commands to run.
csh, tcsh:	
expr	A standard c-shell expression.
commands...	Specifies commands to run.

Note:	This is the opposite of until.	
Common:	while [$a != y) ; do read a ; done	Read from the keyboard. Repeat until y is entered (sh, ksh).

who

UNIX Shell: Shells (ash, bash, bsh, csh, ksh, sh, tcsh, zsh)

Function	Shows who is on the system.
Syntax	who [options...] *{ file }*

-H	Shows headers.
-q	Shows how many currently logged-in users.
file	Specifies a file to substitute for the database of logged-on users.
AIX:	
-a	Processes `/var/adm/utmp` or the named file with -bdlprtTu options enabled.
-b	Shows the time and date of the last reboot.
-d	Shows all processes that have expired but not been respawned by init.
-i	Shows currently logged-in users, same as option -u.
-l	Shows lines on which the system is waiting for someone to log in.

continued

-m	Shows information about the current terminal.				
-p	Shows active processes that have been spawned by init.				
-r	Shows the current run level of the init process.				
-s	Shows the name, line, and time fields. This is default.				
-t	Shows the last change to the system clock.				
-u	Shows currently logged in users.				
-w	Shows name, line, time and state fields, same as option -T.				
-A	Shows all accounting entries in the `/etc/utmp` file.				
-T	Shows name, line, time, and state fields.				
BSD:					
-m	Shows information about the current terminal.				
-T	Shows each user's message status.				
-u	Shows the idle time for each user.				
Linux:					
-i	Shows the idle time for each user, same as option -u.				
-u	Shows the idle time for each user, same as option -i.				
-l	Attempts to canonicalize hostnames via DNS.				
-m	Shows only hostname and user associated with STDIN.				
-s	This option is ignored.				
-T	Shows each user's message status, same as option -w.				
-w	Shows each user's message status, same as option -T.				
--help	Shows help information.				
--version	Shows version information.				
Solaris:					
-a	Processes `/var/adm/utmp` or the named file with -bdlprtTu options enabled.				
-b	Shows the time and date of the last reboot.				
-d	Shows all processes that have expired but not been respawned by init.				
-l	Shows lines on which the system is waiting for someone to log in.				
-m	Shows information about the current terminal.				
-n *x*	Specifies number of users per line to show.				
-p	Shows active processes that have been spawned by init.				
-r	Shows the current run level of the init process.				
-t	Shows the last change to the system clock.				
-T	Shows name, line, time, and state fields.				
-u	Shows currently logged-in users.				
-s	Shows the name, line, and time fields. This is default.				
File Name:	`who`	**Directory:**	/usr/bin/	**Type:**	External
Common:	who	Shows who is on the system			
Common:	who -q	Shows how many currently logged-in users			
Common:	who -H	Shows headers for the information.			

who am i

UNIX Shell: Shells (ash, bash, bsh, csh, ksh, sh, tcsh, zsh)

Function	Is actually the who command but only shows the current user. It takes two arguments that can be anything.				
Syntax	who am i who am I				
File Name:	`who`	**Directory:**	/usr/bin/	**Type:**	External
Note:	This is the command that gave me the idea of this book. I used this command very often in Novell.				
Common:	who am i	Shows who you are logged in as.			
Common:	who mum likes	Shows who you are logged in as.			
Common:	who is best	Shows who you are logged in as.			

whoami

whoami	UNIX Shell:	Shells (ash, bash, bsh, csh, ksh, sh, tcsh, zsh)
Function	Shows the login name of the current effective user.	
Syntax	whoami	

Linux:	
--help	Shows help information.
--version	Shows version information.

File Name:	whoami	**Directory:**	/usr/bin/, **Solaris:** /usr/ucb/	**Type:**	External

whois

whois	UNIX Shell:	Shells (ash, bash, bsh, csh, ksh, sh, tcsh, zsh)
Function	Finds names or handles for an Internet domain name.	
Syntax	whois [options...] *name* AIX: whois [options...] *{ search name }* Linux: whois [options...] *name*[*@server*]:*port*]]	

-h *host*	Specifies the host of the server to search on.
name	Specifies the name or handle you are looking for.
AIX:	
?	Requests help from the ARPANET host.
search	The following search options can be used.
.	Forces a name-only search for the name specified.
!	Shows help information for the nickname or handle ID specified.
*	Shows the entire membership list of a group or organization.
BSD:	
-a	Uses the American Registry for Internet Numbers (ARIN) database.
-d	Uses the (US Military) Defense Data Network (DDN) database.
-m	Uses the Route Arbiter Database (RADB) database.
-p	Uses the Asia/Pacific Network Information Center (APNIC) database.
-q	Constructs the name of a whois server to use from the top-level domain.
-r	Uses the R'eseaux IP Europ'eens (RIPE) database.
Linux:	
-p *port*	Specifies the port to connect on the whois database server.
-r	Forces recursion.
server	Specifies the whois server to connect to.
port	Specifies the port to connect on the whois database server.

File Name:	whois	**Directory:**	/usr/bin/	**Type:**	External

Common:	whois ucg	Searches for the name ucg at whois.internic.net.
Common:	whois -h nic.nu flexxa.nu	Searches for the name flexxa.nu in the nic.nu database.
AIX:	whois ?	Requests help from the ARPANET host.
Linux:	whois flexxa.nu@nic.nu	Searches for the name flexxa.nu in the nic.nu database.
OpenBSD:	whois -a ucgbook.com	Searches for the name ucgbook.com in the American Registry for Internet Numbers database.

write

write	UNIX Shell:	Shells (ash, bash, bsh, csh, ksh, sh, tcsh, zsh)
Function	Writes to another user's screen. The message is read from the console. Can be used to reply in AIX.	
Syntax	write *user { terminal }* AIX: write [options...] *{ user } { terminal }*	

user	Specifies the user to send the message to.
terminal	Specifies the terminal to write to, if multiple terminals are used.
AIX:	
-q	Shows all messages and their handles, sent to the current user.
-n *{ host }*	Specifies the host to act on.

continued

-h*handle, reply* *handle* *reply* -r	Tells whether to reply to messages sent to the current user. Specifies the handle of the message to reply to. Specifies how to reply. Can be ok, cancel, or query. Creates a message handle to send with the message.

File Name:	write	**Directory:**	/usr/bin/	**Type:**	External
Common:	write root	Writes a message to user root.			
Common:	write root pts/4	Writes to user root on terminal pts/4.			
AIX:	write -q	Lists messages waiting to be read.			

X

UNIX Shell:	**Shells (ash, bash, bsh, csh, ksh, sh, tcsh, zsh)**
Function	The X-window system which is a network-transparent GUI system developed by X Consortium, Inc. This is used with bitmap display systems and manages user input to and from various programs.
Syntax	X

-a *number*	Sets the mouse movement with a specified acceleration multiplier.
-auth *file*	Specifies the authorization file.
-co *file*	Specifies the color database file (R,G,B).
-f *number*	Specifies the volume of the beeps from 0 to 100.
-fc *font*	Specifies the font for the cursor.
-fn *font*	Specifies the default text font.
-fp *path*	Specifies the path to the default font.
-help	Shows help information about the usage and options.
-I	Ignores all the following arguments.
-logo	Shows the X-window logo in the screen saver.
-nologo	Hides the logo in the screen saver.
-once	Runs the server only one time and then terminates.
-p *number*	Specifies the time in minutes between changes in the screen saver.
-r	Disables the auto repeat function.
r	Enables the auto repeat function.
-su	Disables the save possibility under support on all screens.
-t *number*	Specifies the threshold for the mouse speed movement.
-to *number*	Specifies the connection timeout in minutes.
-v	Sets screen saver to run without video blanking.
-wm	Forces the WhenMapped value to all windows as default backing store.
-x *name*	Specifies the extension to load at initiation.
-query *address*	Enables XDMCP and sends a query packet to the specified host.
-broadcast	Enables XDMCP and sends a broadcasted query to the network.
-indirect *hostnamename*	Enables XDMCP and sends an IndirectQuery packet to the specified host.
-port *number*	Specifies a port for communication.
-class *name*	Specifies the display class.
	The following options are common in BSD, Linux, and Solaris.
-ac	Disables all access control restrictions.
-audit *number*	Specifies the audit trail level.
-bc	Enables bug compatibility.
-bs	Disables all backing store support.
-c	Disables the key click.
c *number*	Specifies the volume of the key click from 0 to 100.
-cc *number*	Sets the default color visual class.
-core	Saves a core dump when a fatal error occurs.
-dpi *number*	Specifies the screen resolution in dots per inch.
-deferglyphs [none|all|16]	Suspends the loading of the specified glyphs.
-ld *number*	Limits the space for the data to the specified number of Kb.
-lf *number*	Sets the limit of open files.
-ls *number*	Limits the stack space to the specified number of Kb.
-pn	Accepts failure to listen on all ports.
-terminate	Terminates at server reset.
-tst	Disables all testing extensions.
ttyxx	Starts server from init on /dev/ttyxx.

continued

v	Sets video blanking for screen saver
-ar1	Sets the XKB autorepeat delay.
-ar2	Sets the XKB autorepeat interval.
AIX:	
-bc	Toggles the backward compatibility off.
+bc	Toggles the backward compatibility on, = Default.
-bp *color*	Specifies the black pixel color for the screen. Default is screen dependent.
-bs	Enables the backing store support on all screens. Default is = off.
-c *number*	Specifies the volume of the clicks.
-cc *type*[:screen]	Specifies the root windows type of visual on a specified screen.
-D *file*	Specifies the color definition database file. Default is /usr/lib/X11/rgb.
-d *depth*[:Display]	Specifies the root depth on a specified screen.
-layer *number*[:screen]	Specifies the default visual number of layers on a specified screen.
-n *number*	Specifies the connection number.
-nobs	Toggles the backing store support on all screens off.
-PRowColumn *screen*	Specifies the physical positioning of the screen in a multi configuration.
-pbuffer *level* [:display name | :display number]	Specifies the allocation level for the pbuffer memory on a specified screen.
-P *number*	Specifies the interval in minutes between changes of the X logo in screen saver.
-secIP *code*	Sets local access control to the Internet socket.
-secLocal *code*	Sets access control to the UNIX socket.
-secSMT *code*	Sets access control to the shared memory transport socket.
-stereo [:screen]	Configures optimum stereo support for a specified screen.
-T	Disables the Ctrl-Alt-Delete key sequence.
-v	Replaces the screen with the background color after the time specified with -s.
-wp *color*	Specifies the white pixel color for the screen.
-wrap	Wraps the mouse pointer around from top till bottom, left to right on movement.
-wrapx	Keeps the mouse pointer at the position it hit left or right borders.
-wrapy	Keeps the mouse pointer at the position it hit top or bottom borders.
-cookie *XDMAbits*	Specifies the magic cookie for XDMCP.
BSD:	
dpms	Enables VESA DPMS monitor control.
-nolock	Disables the mechanism used for locking.
-nolisten *protocol*	Doesn't listen on the protocol specified.
-nopn	Rejects failure on all available ports.
-sp *file*	Specifies the security policy file to use.
-cookie *XDMAbits*	Specifies the magic cookie for XDMCP.
-kb	Disables the X keyboard extension.
+kb	Enables the X keyboard extension.
-accessx	Disables accessx key sequences.
+accessx	Enables accessx key sequences.
-ar1	Enables XKB autorepeat delay.
-ar2	Enables XKB autorepeat interval.
-noloadxkb	Doesn't load XKB keymap description.
-xkb*db*	Specifies the file containing the default XKB keymaps.
-xkb*map*	Specifies the XKB keyboard description to load at startup.
-probeonly	Probes only for devices, then exits.
-verbose	Verbose mode. Shows more information on startup.
-quiet	Quiet mode. Shows less information on startup.
-gamma *value*	Specifies the gamma value. Value is a float between 0 and 1.
-rgamma *value*	Specifies the red gamma value. Value is a float between 0 and 1.
-ggamma *value*	Specifies the green gamma value. Value is a float between 0 and 1.
-bgamma *value*	Specifies the blue gamma value. Value is a float between 0 and 1.
-weight *type*	Specifies the RGB weighting at 16 bpp. (Default is 565.)
-flipPixels	Inverts the colors on the screen.
-disableVidMode	Disables adjustments with xvidtune.
-allowNonLocalXvidtune	Allows xvidtune to run as non-local client.

continued

-disableModInDev	Disables dynamic modification of input device settings.
-allowMouseOpenFail	Starts the server even if no mouse is present.
-allowNonLocalModin	Allows keyboard and mouse setting changes from non-local clients.
-bestRefresh	Picks the mode with the best refresh rate.
vt*value*	Specifies the VT number to use. (Is between 1 and 12.)
-keeptty	Doesn't detach controlling tty.
Linux:	
+bs	Enables all backing store support.
dpms	Enables the monitor control for VESA DPMS.
nolock	Disables the mechanism for locking.
-nolisten *protocol*	Doesn't listen on the protocol specified.
-nopn	Rejects failure on all ports.
-sp *file*	Specifies the security policy file.
+xinerama	Toggles the XINERAMA extension on.
-xinerama	Toggles the XINERAMA extension off.
-from *address*	Specifies the local address for connections.
-kb	Disables the extension X Keyboard.
+kb	Enables the extension X Keyboard.
+ | -accessx	Toggles the accessx key sequences on (+) or off (-).
-noloadxkb	Suppresses the load of XKB keymap descriptions.
-xkbcomp	Specifies the default keymap compiler.
-xkb*bd*	Specifies the file containing the default XKB keymaps.
-xkbmap	Shows the XKB keyboard description to load on startup.
-probeonly	Probes only for devices, then exits.
-verbose *level*	Verbose mode. Shows more information on startup.
-quiet	Quiet mode. Shows less information on startup.
-gamma *value*	Specifies the gamma value. Value is a float between 0 and 1.
-rgamma *value*	Specifies the red gamma value. Value is a float between 0 and 1.
-ggamma *value*	Specifies the green gamma value. Value is a float between 0 and 1.
-bgamma *value*	Specifies the blue gamma value. Value is a float between 0 and 1.
-weight *number*	Specifies the RGB weighting at 16 bpp. (Default is 565.)
-flipPixels	Inverts the colors on the screen.
-disableVidMode	Disables adjustments with xvidtune.
-allowNonLocalXvidtune	Allows xvidtune to run as non-local client.
-disableModInDev	Disables dynamic modification of input device settings.
-allowMouseOpenFail	Starts the server even if no mouse is present.
-allowNonLocalModInDev	Allows keyboard and mouse setting changes from non-local clients.
-xf86config	Specifies the configuration file.
-modulepath *file*	Specifies the path to the modules.
-logfile *file*	Specifies the log file.
-configure	Creates an XF86Config file.
-scanpci	Runs the scanpci module only.
-logverbose *number*	Saves a verbose log.
-pixmap24	Uses 24bpp pixmaps for depth 24.
-pixmap32	Uses 32bpp pixmaps for depth 24.
-fbbpp *number*	Sets the bpp for the framebuffer. Default is 8.
-depth *number*	Sets the color depth. Default is 8.
-layout *name*	Specifies the name of the ServerLayout section.
-screen *name*	Specifies the name of the Screen section.
-keyboard *name*	Specifies the name of the core keyboard InputDevice.
-pointer *name*	Specifies the name of the core pointer InputDevice.
-nosilk	Disables the Silken Mouse function.
-version	Shows version information.
Solaris:	
-config *file*	Specifies the file to read options from.
-ep *directory*	Specifies the default encodings directory.
-banner	Enables Solaris banner.
-dev *framebuffer*	Specifies the device to open.

continued

-dpsfileops	Enables DPS file operators.
-dur	Enables the use of bell duration.
-flipPixels	Inverts the colors on the screen.
-mden	Enables the pointer acceleration denominator.
-nobanner	Disables the Solaris banner.
-nominexp	Disables the exposure on minimizations.
-pit	Enables the use of bell pitch.
-sharedretainedpath *path*	Specifies a file system path.
	The following are device options to use with –dev.
left, right, top, bottom	Specifies the orientation relative to previous screen.
dpix *value*	Specifies the dpi in the x direction.
dpiy *value*	Specifies the dpi in the y direction.
defclass *{ type }*	Specifies the default visual report. (Can be StaticGray, PseudoColor, StaticColor, DirectColor, or TrueColor.)
defdepth *value*	Specifies the default depth of visual report.
grayvis	Reports GrayScale and StaticGray visuals.

File Name:	X	**Directory:**	**AIX:** /usr/bin/X11, **BSD, Linux:** /usr/X11R6/bin, **Solaris:** /usr/openwin/bin	**Type:**	External
Note:	R.I.P – The last UNIX command documented in this book.				

xargs

UNIX Shell: Shells (ash, bash, bsh, csh, ksh, sh, tcsh, zsh)

Function	Creates a list of arguments, starts a program and runs the arguments.
Syntax	xargs [options...] *{ utility arguments... }*

-t	Enables trace mode.
-n *number*	Starts utility using as many Standard In arguments as possible but less than number.
-x	Stops if a command line doesn't fit in the specified size or number.
-s *size*	Starts utility using as many Standard In arguments as possible but less than size.
utility	Specifies a program to start.
argument	Specifies arguments to the command.
AIX:	
-p	Prompts the user before to run a command.
-e *eofstr*	Specifies the logical end-of-file string. Default is underscore.
-E *eofstr*	Specifies a logical end-of-file string to replace the default.
-I *replstr*	Insert Mode; utility will be executed for each line from STDIN.
-i *replstr*	The same as the -I option.
-L *number*	Runs for each non-empty number lines of arguments from STDIN.
-l *number*	The same as the -L option.
BSD:	
-0	Specifies that input filenames are terminated by a null character.
Linux:	
-0	Specifies that input filenames are terminated by a null character.
-e *eofstr*	Specifies the logical end-of-file string. Default is underscore.
-i*{ replace-str }*	Replaces occurrence of the string specified.
-l*{ max-lines }*	Uses at most the specified number nonblank input lines per command line.
-p	Prompts the user before to run a command.
-r	Specifies that if the stdin is empty the program exits.
-P *number*	Runs the specified number of processes at a time.
--help	Shows help information.
--version	Shows version information.
Solaris:	
-p	Prompts the user before to run a command.
-e *eofstr*	Specifies the logical end-of-file string. Default is underscore.
-E *eofstr*	Specifies a logical end-of-file string to replace the default.
-I *replstr*	Insert Mode, utility will be executed for each line from STDIN.
-i *replstr*	The same as the -I option.
-L *number*	Runs for each non-empty number lines of arguments from STDIN.
-l *number*	The same as the -L option.

continued

File Name:	`xargs`	**Directory:**	/usr/bin/	**Type:**	External
Common:	xargs /bin/ls -al	Runs `ls -al` on all the files you specifiy in the interactive mode.			

xauth

UNIX Shell: Shells (ash, bash, bsh, csh, ksh, sh, tcsh, zsh)

Function	Manages the authorization rules used when connecting to an X-server.
Syntax	xauth [options...] *{ command argument...]*

-f *authfile*	Specifies the authority file to use.
-q	Specifies that xauth should be more quiet and doesn't show error messages.
-v	Verbose mode. Shows more information.
-b	Breaks any authority file locks before proceeding.
-i	Ignores any authority file locks before proceeding.
command	Specifies the command to manage authority files.
argument	Specifies arguments to the command.

File Name:	xauth	**Directory:**	**AIX, Linux:** /usr/bin/X11/, **BSD:** /usr/X11R6/bin/, **Solaris:** /usr/openwin/bin/	**Type:**	External
Common:	xauth	Starts the interactive mode.			
Common:	xauth list	Shows the authority list.			
Common:	xauth remove 192.168.1.14:0	Removes host 192.168.1.14 from the authority list.			

xfindproxy

UNIX Shell: Shells (ash, bash, bsh, csh, ksh, sh, tcsh, zsh)

Function	Finds proxy services to be used with a proxy manager.
Syntax	xfindproxy options...

	Solaris Only: This is only available in Solaris 8.
	The following options are required.
-manager *protocol/hostname:port*	Specifies the proxy manager's network address in an ICE network id.
-name *servicename*	Specifies the proxy service name.
-server *hostname:port*	Specifies target server in a format specific to the proxy service defined with -name.
	The following options are optional.
-auth	Reads 2 lines from STDIN which will be passed to proxy to be used for authorization. (First line is authorization name, the second authorization data in hex.)
-host *hostname*	Passes the host to a newly started or existing proxy.
-options *options*	Specifies options are passed to a newly started or existing proxy.

File Name:	`xfindproxy`	**Directory:**	**AIX:** /usr/bin/X11/, **BSD, Linux:** /usr/X11R6/bin/, **Solaris:** /usr/openwin/bin/	**Type:**	External

xfs

UNIX Shell: Shells (ash, bash, bsh, csh, ksh, sh, tcsh, zsh)

Function	Supplies fonts to X-Window servers.
Syntax	xfs [options...]

-config *file*	Specifies configuration file to use.
-ls *listen-socket*	Specifies a file descriptor that is already set up to be used as listen socket.
-port *tcp-port*	Specifies TCP port number for the server to listen for connections.
	Configuration options, keyword and value pairs, keyword = value
catalogue-list	Shows ordered list of font path element names to the server.
alternate-servers-list	Lists alternate servers for the font server to use.
client-limit	Specifies max number of clients before refusing service.
clone-self	Specify yes if you want the server to attempt cloning if it reaches client limit.
default-point-size	Sets default point size for unspecified fonts in decipoints.
default-resolutions	Specifies resolutions in X,Y pairs in pixels for default support by the server.
error-file string	Specifies the name of the file to write errors and warnings to.
port	Specifies the name of the port that the server will listen to.
use-syslog	Specifies if you want to use the `syslog` to be used for error logging.
deferglyphs	Specifies delayed glyph-fetching and caching mode.

continued

Linux: -daemon -droppriv		Specifies the program should fork and be run in the background. Specifies the program will try to run as user xfs and group xfs.			
File Name:	`xfs`	**Directory:**	**AIX, Linux:** /usr/bin/X11/, **BSD:** /usr/X11R6/bin/, **Solaris:** /usr/openwin/bin/	**Type:**	External
Common:	xfs -port 795	Tells xfs to listen on port 795 for connections.			
Common:	xfs -config /usr/X11/lib/fontserver.cfg	Uses `/usr/X11/lib/fontserver.cfg` as the configuration file.			
Linux:	xfs -daemon	Forks the daemon to the background.			
Solaris:	xfs -config /usr/openwin/lib/X11/fontserver.cfg	Tells xfs to use `/usr/openwin/lib/X11/fontserver.cfg` as the configuration file.			

xhost

UNIX Shell: Shells (ash, bash, bsh, csh, ksh, sh, tcsh, zsh)

Function	Controls access to the X server by keeping a list of allowed hosts and users.				
Syntax	xhost *{options... }*				
+name *name* *-name* + -		Specifies a host or a user who is allowed to access the X server. Same as +name. Specifies a host or a user who isn't allowed to access the X server. Grants everyone access. Only hosts and users added to the list with +name are allowed access.			
File Name:	`xhost`	**Directory:**	/usr/X11R6/bin/, **AIX:** /usr/bin/X11/, **Solaris:** /usr/openwin/bin/	**Type:**	External
Common:	xhost	With no options, the status of whether access control is enabled is returned.			
Common:	xhost +	Everyone can connect to the X server. Handy but not secure.			
Common:	xhost pluto	The host pluto can connect to the X server.			

xinit

UNIX Shell: Shells (ash, bash, bsh, csh, ksh, sh, tcsh, zsh)

Function	Starts the X-Window server specified.				
Syntax	xinit *{ client options }* [-- *server :screen options*]				
client *options...* -- *server* *:screen* *options...*		Specifies the client program to start an X window with. Specifies options to the client program. Starts a specified server on a specified screen. Specifies the server name. Starts a specified server on a specified screen. Specifies options to server and display.			
File Name:	`xinit`	**Directory:**	**AIX:** /usr/bin/X11, **BSD, Linux:** /usr/X11R6/bin, **Solaris:** /usr/openwin/bin	**Type:**	External

xlsfonts

UNIX Shell: Shells (ash, bash, bsh, csh, ksh, sh, tcsh, zsh)

Function	Lists X Window fonts that match a specified pattern.	
Syntax	xlsfonts [options...]	
-display *host:dpy* -l -ll -lll -m -C -1 -w *width* -n *columns* -u -o -fn *pattern*		Specifies which X server to contact. Lists font names and their attributes. Same as -l but lists font properties too. Same as -ll but lists character metrics too. Shows the minimum and maximum boundaries for each font. Specifies the lists use multiple columns. Same as -n 0. Specifies the lists will only use one column. Same as -n 1. Determines how many columns to print by setting the width. (Default is 79.) Specifies how many columns to show. Default is fitting as many as -w allows. Specifies the output will be unsorted. Forces OpenFont or QueryFont instead of the default ListFont. Specifies the font name pattern that is searched for and matched. (Supports the met characters * and ?. Must be quoted.)

continued

File Name:	xlsfonts	**Directory:**	**AIX, Linux:** /usr/bin/X11/, **BSD:** /usr/X11R6/bin/, **Solaris:** /usr/openwin/bin/	**Type:**	External
Common:	xlsfonts -l		Shows font names and their attributes.		
Common:	xlsfonts -C		Shows the list in multiple columns.		
Common:	xlsfonts -n 4		Shows the list in four columns.		

xmkmf

UNIX Shell: Shells (ash, bash, bsh, csh, ksh, sh, tcsh, zsh)

Function	Converts an Imakefile to a Makefile.
Syntax	xmkmf [-a] *{ topdir } { curdir }*

-a	Creates the Makefile in the current directory and runs the make command.
topdir	Specifies a relative pathname from current directory to the top of the build tree.
curdir	Specifies a relative pathname from the top of the build tree to current directory.

File Name:	xmkmf	**Directory:**	**AIX:** /usr/bin/X11, **BSD, Linux:** /usr/X11R6/bin, **Solaris:** /usr/openwin/bin	**Type:**	External
Note:	The topdir and curdir are almost never used.				
Common:	xmkmf	Runs with the arguments configured into xmkmf when X was built and creates the Makefile.			
Common:	xmkmf -a	Builds the Makefile in the current directory and runs all necessary changes.			

xmodmap

UNIX Shell: Shells (ash, bash, bsh, csh, ksh, sh, tcsh, zsh)

Function	Shows and modifies the keymaps in X.
Syntax	xmodmap [options...] *{ file }*

-display *host:dpy*	Specifies the host and screen to use.
-help	Prints help information about the commandline arguments to STDERR.
-grammar	Shows help message about expression.
-verbose	Verbose mode. Shows more information.
-quiet	Suppresses the verbose mode.
-n	Shows but doesn't run changes.
-e *expression*	Specifies an expression to run.
-pm	Shows current modifier map to STDOUT.
-pk	Shows current keymap table to STDOUT.
-pke	Shows current keymap table in form of expressions to STDOUT.
-pp	Shows current pointer map to STDOUT.
file	Specifies a file that contains xmodmap expressions to run.

File Name:	xmodmap	**Directory:**	**AIX:** /usr/bin/X11, **BSD, Linux:** /usr/X11R6/bin, **Solaris:** /usr/openwin/bin/	**Type:**	External
Common:	xmodmap -e "pointer = 3 2 1"		Reverses the buttons on the mouse for a left-handed user.		
Common:	xmodmap -pke		Shows the current keymap table on STDOUT.		
Common:	xmodmap -		Runs the command and uses STDIN as input.		

xrdb

UNIX Shell: Shells (ash, bash, bsh, csh, ksh, sh, tcsh, zsh)

Function	Contains resources for the X server. This program normally runs from an X startup file.
Syntax	xrdb [options...] *{ file }*

-help	Shows help information.
-display *host:dpy*	Specifies display to use.
-all	Makes all resources.
-global	Makes screen-independent resources.
-screen	Makes screen-specific resources for one screen
-screens	Makes screen-specific resources for all screens.
-quiet	Disables warnings about duplicate entries.
-n	Shows changes but doesn't run.
-cpp *file*	Uses preprocessor.
-nocpp	Disables the use of preprocessor.
-query	Queries resources.
-load *file*	Loads resources from file.

continued

-override	Adds resources from file.
-merge	Merges resources from file.
-remove	Specifies the properties to remove from the server.
-retain	Doesn't reset server if xrdb is the first client.
-edit *file*	Edits resources into file.
-backup *string*	Backs up suffix fro -edit (*.bak).
-symbols	Shows preprocessor symbols.
-D*name*[=*value*]	Passes through preprocessor and defines symbols to use with conditionals.
-U*name*	Specifies symbol to remove. It will pass through the preprocessor.
-I*directory*	Specifies directory to search for files that are referenced with #include.
file	Specifies filename of the resource to show.

File Name:	`xrdb`	**Directory:**	**AIX, Linux:** /usr/bin/X11/, **BSD:** /usr/X11R6/bin/, **Solaris:** /usr/openwin/bin/	**Type:**	External
Common:	xrdb -quiet		Disables warnings about duplicate entries.		
Common:	xrdb -nocpp		Disables the use of preprocessor.		
Common:	xrdb -screens		Makes screen-specific resources for all screens.		

xset

UNIX Shell: Shells (ash, bash, bsh, csh, ksh, sh, tcsh, zsh)

Function	Sets the user options for the X display, such as mouse, bell, keys, and much more.
Syntax	xset [options...]

-display *host:dpy*	Specifies the server.
-b	Turns the bell off.
b on | off	Toggles the bell on or off (default is on).
-b *{ volume } { pitch } { duration }*	Specifies the volume (% of max), pitch (in hz), and duration (in milliseconds).
bc	Enables bug compatibility mode. A -bc will disable bug compatibility mode.
c on | off	Sets the key click on/off and the volume. c on 85, = on and 85% volume. -c, = off.
c *{ volume }*	Specifies the volume of the click as a % of maximum i.e., 1-100.
fp=*paths...*	Sets the font path to the server-interpreted entries to the specified path(s).
-fp=*paths...*	Removes the specified path elements from the path list.
+fp=*paths...*	Adds the specified path elements to the path list.
fp default	Resets the font path to the default server's font path.
fp rehash	Resets the font path to the current value, which causes the server to reread the path.
+led *{ NR }*	Turns all of the keyboard LED lights on or only the specified ones (1-3).
-led *{ NR }*	Turns all of the keyboard LED lights off or only the specified ones (1-3).
m *{ accel }* [*/threshold*]	Sets the movement attributes of the mouse.
accel	Sets the acceleration movement of the mouse to the specified amount.
/threshold	Sets the movement of the mouse as a balance between accel and the threshold.
m default	Sets the movement attributes of the mouse to the default values.
p *color*	Sets the pixel color values. Specifies color map number and color specifications.
r *code*	Sets the autorepeat for the specified keycode.
-r	Turns the autorepeat function off.
r on	Turns the autorepeat function on.
s *parameters...*	Sets the screen saver parameters. One or two arguments are acceptable.
blank	Shows a blank screen instead of a pattern.
noblank	Shows a pattern as screen saver.
expose	Allows window exposures.
noexpose	Forbids window exposures if the server can't handle it.
on	Turns the screen saver on.
off	Turns the screen saver off.
activate	Activates the saver even if it is turned off.
reset	Deactivates the saver even if it is turned on.
length	Sets the time of inactivity in seconds before tha saver turns on.
period	Sets the time in seconds between the changes of patterns.
default	Resets the saver to the default values.

continued

q	Shows information about the current settings.
BSD:	
-dpms	Disables DPMS (Energy Star) features.
+dpms	Enables DPMS (Energy Star) features.
dpms *flags...*	Specifies the DPMS parameter; flags can be standby, suspend, or off.
Linux:	
-dpms	Disables DPMS (Energy Star) features.
+dpms	Enables DPMS (Energy Star) features.
dpms *flags...*	Specifies the DPMS parameter; flags can be standby, suspend, or off.

File Name:	`xset`	**Directory:**	**AIX, Linux:** /usr/bin/X11/, **BSD:** /usr/X11R6/bin/, **Solaris:** /usr/openwin/bin/	**Type:**	External
Common:	xset b on	Turns the bell on.			
Common:	xset m default	Sets the movement attributes of the mouse to the default values.			
Linux:	xset +dpms	Enables DPMS features, if your monitor supports them.			
OpenBSD:	xset -dpms	Disables DPMS features, if your monitor supports them.			

xsetroot

UNIX Shell: Shells (ash, bash, bsh, csh, ksh, sh, tcsh, zsh)

Function	Modifies how to view the background window on a workstation that runs X.
Syntax	xsetroot [options...]

-help	Shows help information.
-def	Sets the window or any unspecified attributes to its default state.
-display *host:dpy*	Specifies which server to connect to.
-cursor *cursorfile maskfile*	Changes the pointer cursor.
-cursorname *cursorname*	Changes the pointer cursor to one of the standard ones.
-bitmap *filename*	Uses bitmap to set window pattern.
-mod *x y*	Gives you a plaid-looking grid pattern on the screen.
-gray	Makes the background gray.
-grey	Makes the background grey.
-fg *color*	Specifies the foreground color.
-bg *color*	Specifies the background color.
-rv	Flips the foreground with the background color.
-solid *color*	Specifies color you want for the background of the root window. Color servers only.
-name *string*	Changes name of the root window.
AIX, BSD, Linux:	
-rv	Reverses the foreground and background colors.

File Name:	`xsetroot`	**Directory:**	**AIX:** /usr/bin/X11/, **BSD, Linux:** /usr/X11R6/bin/, **Solaris:** /usr/openwin/bin/	**Type:**	External
Common:	xsetroot -def	Sets the window to its default state.			

xterm

UNIX Shell: Shells (ash, bash, bsh, csh, ksh, sh, tcsh, zsh)

Function	A terminal emulator for X-Window. Provides terminal emulation for programs that can't use X-Window.
Syntax	xterm [options...]

-help	Shows help information.
-132	Ignores escape sequence that switches between 80- and 132-column mode.
-ah	Highlights the text cursor.
+ah	Bases text cursor highlighting on focus.
-b *number*	Specifies the size of the inner border in pixels.
-cc *characterclassrange:value*	Specifies class to use when selecting by words.
-cn	Doesn't cut `newlines` in line-mode selections.
+cn	Cuts `newlines` in line-mode selections.
-cr *color*	Specifies the color for text cursor.
-cu	Works around the `more` bug which causes the leading tabs not to show.
+cu	Doesn't work around the `more` bug.
-e *program*	Specifies which program will be run in the xterm window. (Uses as last option.)
-fb *font*	Specifies font that will show bold text.

continued

-j	Enables jump scrolling.
+j	Disables jump scrolling.
-ls	When run, the shell that starts in the xterm window will be the login shell.
+ls	When run, the shell that starts in the xterm window isn't the login shell.
-mb	Causes xterm to ring a bell when the user is near the right end of a line.
+mb	Disables the margin bell.
-mc *milliseconds*	Specifies maximum time between multi-click selections.
-ms *color*	Specifies color for the pointer cursor.
-nb *number*	Specifies number of characters from the right end of a line when to ring the bell.
-rw	Enables reverse-wraparound.
+rw	Disables allow reverse-wraparound.
-aw	Enables auto-wraparound.
+aw	Disables allow auto-wraparound.
-s	Scrolls xterm asynchronously.
+s	Scrolls xterm synchronously.
-sb	Shows the scrollbar for text scrolled off the window.
+sb	Hides the scrollbar for text scrolled off the window.
-sf	Uses Sun Function Key escape code creation for function keys.
+sf	Uses standard escape code creation for function keys.
-si	Doesn't scroll to the bottom.
+si	Makes the output to a window to scroll the bottom.
-sl *number*	Specifies lines that have been scrolled off the top off screen. (Default is 64.)
-t	Uses the Tektronix mode.
+t	Starts in VT102 mode.
-tm *string*	Specifies terminal setting keywords and the following characters to bound.
-tn *name*	Specifies the name of the terminal to be used in the TERM environment variable.
-ut	Doesn't write a record to the system log file `/etc/utmp`.
+ut	Writes a record to the system log file `/etc/utmp`.
-vb	Uses a visual bell instead of an audible one.
+vb	Doesn't use a visual bell.
-C	Enables this window to receive console output.
-S*ccn*	Specifies pseudo terminal to use in slave mode and also number of file descriptor.
AIX:	
-i	Activates the useInsertMode resource.
+i	Disables the useInsertMode resource.
-sk	Returns to the bottom of the screen while using the scrollbar and presses a key.
+sk	Doesn't return to the bottom of the screen while using the scrollbar and presses a key.
-wf	Waits for the window to be set up before starting sub process.
+wf	Starts sub process without waiting for the window to be set up.
-T *string*	Sets a string as the title of the window.
-n *string*	Sets a string as the icon name of the window.
BSD:	
-version	Shows version information.
-ai	Specifies active icon support off.
+ai	Specifies active icon support on.
-bdc	Shows bold characters as bold.
+bdc	Shows bold characters in a color.
-cb	Sets vt100 cutToBeginningOfLine to false.
+cb	Sets vt100 cutToBeginningOfLine to true.
-cm	Doesn't recognize ANSI color-change escape sequences.
+cm	Recognizes ANSI color-change escape sequences.
-dc	Specifies dynamic change of colors by escape sequence off.
+dc	Specifies dynamic change of colors by escape sequence on.
-fi	Sets the active icon font.
-hc *color*	Specifies the color for background of highlighted text (default is reversed video).
-hf	Specifies the function key output will be into HP escape codes format.
+hf	Specifies the function key output will not be into HP escape codes format.

continued

-im	Activates the useInsertMode resource.
+im	Disables the useInsertMode resource.
-nu1	Shows underlining.
+nu1	Doesn't show underlining.
-pc	Uses PC-style bold colors.
+pc	Doesn't use PC-style bold colors.
-rightbar	Positions the scrollbar at the right side.
-samename	Doesn't send requests for change of icon name or title.
+samename	Sends requests for change of icon name or title.
-sk	Returns to the bottom of the screen while using the scrollbar and presses a key.
+sk	Doesn't return to the bottom of the screen while using the scrollbar and presses a key.
-sp	Specifies use of SUN keyboard map.
+sp	Specifies use of normal keyboard map.
-ti *type*	Sets the terminal type. Examples of valid values are vt100, 100, vt420, 420, etc.
-ulc	Shows characters with underline and not with color.
+ulc	Shows characters with color and not underline.
-wf	Waits for the window to be set up, before start sub process.
+wf	Starts sub process without waiting for the window to be set up.
-ziconbeep *percentage*	Sets the icon beep volume as a percentage.
Linux:	
-version	Shows version information.
-ai	Specifies active icon support off.
+ai	Specifies active icon support on.
-bc	Specifies cursor blink off.
+bc	Specifies cursor blink on.
-bcf *milliseconds*	Specifies the off-time as a delay in the text blink.
-bcn *milliseconds*	Specifies the on-time as a delay in the text blink.
-cb	Sets vt100 cutToBeginningOfLine to false.
+cb	Sets vt100 cutToBeginningOfLine to true.
-cm	Doesn't recognize ANSI color-change escape sequences.
+cm	Recognizes ANSI color-change escape sequences.
-dc	Specifies dynamic change of colors by escape sequence off.
+dc	Specifies dynamic change of colors by escape sequence on.
-fi	Sets the active icon font.
-hc *color*	Specifies the color for background of highlighted text (default is reversed video).
-hf	Specifies the function key output will be into HP escape codes format.
+hf	Specifies the function key output will not be into HP escape codes format.
-hold	Leaves the window open after the shell command completes.
+hold	Closes the window after the shell command completes.
-ie	Lets the pseudo-terminal sense the stty-erase-value.
+ie	Lets the term cap entry set the stty-erase-value.
-im	Activates the useInsertMode resource.
+im	Disables the useInsertMode resource.
-leftbar	Positions the scrollbar at the left side.
-rightbar	Positions the scrollbar at the right side.
-mesg	Denies access to write messages to the terminal.
+mesg	Allows access to write messages to the terminal.
-nul	Shows underlining.
+nul	Hides underlining.
-pc	Uses PC-style bold colors.
+pc	Doesn't use PC-style bold colors.
-rvc	Doesn't show reverse attribute characters as color.
+rvc	Shows reverse attribute characters as color.
-samename	Doesn't send requests for change of icon name or title.
+samename	Sends requests for change of icon name or title.
-sk	Returns to the bottom of the screen while using the scrollbar and presses a key.
+sk	Doesn't return to the bottom of the screen while using the scrollbar and presses a key.
-sp	Specifies use of SUN keyboard map.

continued

+sp	Specifies use of normal keyboard map.
-ti *type*	Sets the terminal type. Examples of valid values are vt100, 100, vt420, 420, etc.
-u8	Translates incoming data as UTF-8.
+u8	Doesn't translate incoming data as UTF-8.
-ulc	Shows characters without underline and not with color.
+ulc	Shows characters with underline and not with color.
-wc	Uses the wide Chars resource, and handles 16-bit characters' internal structures.
+wc	Doesn't use wide Chars resource.
-wf	Waits for the window to be set up before starting sub process.
+wf	Doesn't wait for the window to be set up before starting sub process.
-ziconbeep *percentage*	Sets the icon beep volume as a percentage.
Solaris:	
-cb	Sets vt100 cutToBeginningOfLine to false.
+cb	Sets vt100 cutToBeginningOfLine to true.
-im	Activates the useInsertMode resource.
+im	Disables the useInsertMode resource.
File Name: `xterm`	**Directory:** /usr/openwin/bin/ **Type:** External
Common: xterm	Starts the xterm application.

xwd

UNIX Shell: Shells (ash, bash, bsh, csh, ksh, sh, tcsh, zsh)

Function	Saves window images into a dump file.
Syntax	xwd [options...]

-debug	The debug mode.
-help	Shows help information.
-nobdrs	Doesn't include pixels that compose an X window border in the dump.
-out *file*	Specifies output file; otherwise the default is STDOUT.
-xy	Uses XY format dump instead of Z. Is used only for color screens.
-frame	Includes window manager frame.
-add *value*	Specifies value to add to every pixel.
-root	Selects the root window for the dump.
-id *id*	Specifies ID of a window to use for the dump.
-name *name*	Specifies the name of the window for the dump.
-icmap	Forces to use the first installed color map.
-screen	Uses GetImage to get image on root window.
-display *host:dpy*	Specifies the server that you want to connect to.
File Name: `xwd`	**Directory:** /usr/openwin/bin/ **Type:** External

xwud

UNIX Shell: Shells (ash, bash, bsh, csh, ksh, sh, tcsh, zsh)

Function	Shows an image dump that is saved in a formatted dump file.
Syntax	xwud [options...]

-in *file*	Specifies input file. If no input file is specified, then it uses the STDIN.
-noclick	Prevents an application from terminating when clicking a button in the window.
-geometry *geom*	Specifies the size and position of the window.
-display *host:dpy*	Specifies the server that you want to connect to.
-new	Creates a new color map.
-std *maptype*	Specifies color map to be used by the image.
-raw	Shows image with existing colors on the screen.
-vis *vistype*	Specifies a visual ID or visual class you want to use.
-help	Shows help information.
-rv	Reverses the foreground with the background color.
-plane *number*	Selects a single bit plane of the image that you want to show.
-fg *color*	Specifies color to show for the 1-bits in an image.
-bg *color*	Specifies color to show for the 0-bits in an image.
File Name: `xwud`	**Directory:** /usr/openwin/bin/ **Type:** External

yacc, byacc

UNIX Shell:	Shells (ash, bash, bsh, csh, ksh, sh, tcsh, zsh)
Function	Converts a file containing grammar rules into a C-source file named `y.tab.c`.
Syntax	yacc [options...] *file*

	Linux Only: The command `byacc` is the same as `yacc`.
-b *fileprefix*	Uses the prefix specified for the filename instead of the default filename y.
-d	Creates the file `y.tab.h` that is used to relate token codes with token names.
-l	Specifies the code produced in `y.tab.c` will not contain any #line constructs.
-p *symprefix*	Uses the prefix specified for external names created by `yacc` instead of `yy`.
-t	Compiles runtime debugging code by default generated in the file `y.tab.c`.
-v	Creates a file `y.output` containing errors and conflicts from unclear grammar.
file	Specifies the file containing grammar rules to convert into tables.
AIX:	
-C	Creates the `y.tabC` file to use with a C++ compiler instead of `y.tab.` file.
-Nn*number*	Alters the size of the token array.
-Nm*number*	Alters the size of the memory states array.
-Nr*number*	Alters the size of the internal buffer to handle large grammars.
-s	Splits the yyparse function into many smaller functions.
-y *path*	Uses the specified parser prototype instead of `/usr/lib/yaccpar` file.
BSD:	
-r	Creates a code file named `y.code.c` and a table file named `y.tab.c`.
-o *outputfile*	Sets an explicit name for the output file.
Linux:	
-r	Creates a code file named `y.code.c` and a table file named `y.tab.c`.
Solaris:	
-P *parser*	Specifies a parser to use instead of the default `/usr/ccs/bin/yaccpar`.
Q*y*	Shows the version information regarding `yacc` in the file `y.tab.c`.
Q*n*	Hides version information regarding `yacc` in the file `y.tab.c`.
-V	Shows version information.

File Name:	`yacc`	**Directory:**	/usr/bin, **Solaris:** /usr/ccs/bin/	**Type:**	External

ypbind

UNIX Shell:	Shells (ash, bash, bsh, csh, ksh, sh, tcsh, zsh)
Function	Runs at startup and keeps information about the bindings between NIS clients and servers.
Syntax	ypbind [options...]

-ypset	Lets any user change the binding with `ypset`. (Default is nobody)
-ypsetme	Lets the superuser on the local system change the binding with `ypset`.
AIX:	
-s	Runs the daemon in a secure mode on privileged communications ports.
BSD:	
-insecure	Permits binding to a non-reserved port.
Linux:	
-c	Checks for syntax errors in the config file.
-d	Runs the daemon in debug mode.
-broadcast	Broadcasts for NIS servers on the net (default during startup).
-broken-server	Accepts answers from servers running on an illegal port number.
-no-ping	Disables checking if the binding is dead.
-p *port*	Specifies a port to bind to.
-f *file*	Specifies the config file to use (default is `/etc/yp.conf`).
--version	Shows version information.
Solaris:	
-broadcast	Broadcasts for NIS servers on the net. Default during startup.

File Name:	`ypbind`	**Directory:**	**AIX, Solaris:** /usr/lib/netsvc/yp/, **BSD:** /usr/sbin/, **Linux:** /sbin	**Type:**	External

Warning:	Broadcast isn't secure because it trusts any host that poses as an NIS server.	
Common:	ypbind	Looks for an NIS server by using the list of servers created during client setup.
Common:	ypbind -ypsetme	Lets the superuser change the bindings.
AIX:	ypbind -s	Runs the daemon in a secure mode.
Linux:	ypbind -broken-server	Accepts answers from server running on an illegal port.

continued

OpenBSD:	ypbind -insecure	Permits binding to a non-reserved port.
Solaris:	ypbind -broadcast	Broadcasts for NIS servers on the net.

ypcat

UNIX Shell: Shells (ash, bash, bsh, csh, ksh, sh, tcsh, zsh)

Function	Shows the values in the specified NIS map.
Syntax	ypcat [options...] *map*

-k	Shows the map keys.
-x	Shows nicknames for the maps. Can only be used alone.
-d *domain*	Specifies another domain to use instead of the default.
map	Specifies the NIS map name that you want to query, can also be a nickname.
AIX, BSD, Linux:	
-t	Forbids map nickname translation.

File Name:	`ypcat`	**Directory:**	/usr/bin/	**Type:**	External

Common:	ypcat -x	Shows map nicknames.
Common:	ypcat hosts	Shows the map hosts (nickname for hosts.byname).
AIX:	ypcat -t passwd.byname	Shows the map passwd.byname.
Linux:	ypcat -t hosts.byaddr	Shows the map hosts.byaddr.
OpenBSD:	ypcat -t hosts.byname	Shows the map hosts.byname.

ypinit

UNIX Shell: Shells (ash, bash, bsh, csh, ksh, sh, tcsh, zsh)

Function	Sets up an NIS server or client system.
Syntax	ypinit [options...]

AIX:	
-o	Allows any existing maps for the current NIS domain to be overwritten.
-n	Specifies the program should terminate if errors occurs.
-q	Specifies the -m option can take slave serves as an argument.
-m *{ slaveservers... }*	Makes the local host the NIS master.
-s *mastername*	Copies NIS maps from the server workstation specified.
BSD:	
-m *{ domainname }*	Starts a master YP server, if no domainname is given, default is used.
-s *masterserver { domainname }*	Starts a slave YP server, if no domainname is given, default is used.
-u *{ domainname }*	Updates the ypserver map on a YP master server.
Linux:	
-m	Builds the master ypserver database. Interactive.
-s *masterserver { domainname }*	Sets up the slave database from masterserver.
Solaris:	
-c	Sets up the system as a ypclient.
-m	Builds the master ypserver database. Interactive.
-s *masterserver*	Sets up the slave database.

File Name:	`ypinit`	**Directory:**	/usr/sbin/, **Linux:** /usr/lib/yp/	**Type:**	Script

AIX:	ypinit -o	Allows any existing maps for the current NIS domain to be overwritten.
Linux:	ypinit -m	Builds a master ypserver database.
OpenBSD:	ypinit -m	Starts the daemon with default hostname.
Solaris:	ypinit -c	Sets up the system as a ypclient.

ypmatch

UNIX Shell: Shells (ash, bash, bsh, csh, ksh, sh, tcsh, zsh)

Function	Shows the values of keys from an NIS map.
Syntax	ypmatch [options...] *keys... map*

-x	Shows the map nicknames. Must be used alone.
-k	Shows the key name before the value of the key.
-t	Prevents map nickname conversion.
-d *domain*	Specifies domain to use instead of the default one.
keys...	Specifies keys from an NIS map.

continued

map		NIS map to query. Can be an nickname.			
File Name:	`ypmatch`	**Directory:**	/usr/bin/	**Type:**	External
Common:	ypmatch -x	Shows the map nicknames.			
Common:	ypmatch pluto hosts	Shows the value of the key pluto in the map hosts.			
Common:	ypmatch -d ucg pluto hosts	Same as above but uses the ucg domain.			

yppoll

UNIX Shell: Shells (ash, bash, bsh, csh, ksh, sh, tcsh, zsh)

Function	Uses `ypserv` to get the version number and master NIS server for the specified map.
Syntax	yppoll [options...] *map*

-d *ypdomain*	Specifies a domain to use instead of the default domain.
-h *host*	Specifies the server to use.
map	Specifies the NIS map to query.

File Name:	`yppoll`	**Directory:**	/usr/sbin/	**Type:**	External
Common:	yppoll hosts.byname	Shows the version number and master server for the map hosts.byname.			
Common:	yppoll -d ucg hosts.byname	Same as above but uses the ucg domain.			

yppush

UNIX Shell: Shells (ash, bash, bsh, csh, ksh, sh, tcsh, zsh)

Function	Copies a new NIS map from the master server to the slave servers.
Syntax	yppush [options...] *mapname*

-d *domain*	Specifies the domain.
-v	Verbose mode. Shows more information.
mapname	Specifies the map to copy.
BSD:	
-h *host*	Copies the map only to the specified host.
Linux:	
-h *host*	Copies the map only to the specified host.
-p *number*	Specifies the number of map copies that can be sent at the same time.
-t timeout	Specifies the timeout in seconds. (Default is 90.)
Solaris:	
-h *host*	Copies the map only to the specified host.
-p *number*	Specifies the number of map copies that can be sent at the same time.

File Name:	yppush	**Directory:**	/usr/sbin/, **Solaris:** /usr/lib/netsvc/yp/	**Type:**	External
Common:	yppush hosts	Copies the map hosts to all NIS servers without more than two at the same time.			
Common:	yppush -d ucg hosts	Same as above but uses the ucg domain instead.			
Linux:	yppush -t 360 hosts	Specifies a longer timeout for big maps.			
OpenBSD:	yppush -h pluto hosts	Copies the map hosts to the NIS server pluto only.			
Solaris:	yppush -p 4 hosts	Copies the map hosts to all NIS servers, four at a time.			

ypserv

UNIX Shell: Shells (ash, bash, bsh, csh, ksh, sh, tcsh, zsh)

Function	An NIS server daemon that looks up information requested by other yp commands.
Syntax	ypserv [options...]

BSD:	
-1	Allows ypserv to answer old YP version 1 requests.
-a *file*	Specifies an aclfile to use (default is `/var/yp/securenet`).
-d	Searches the DNS for more information about hosts.
-x	Specifies the server should be terminated after processing the aclfile.
Linux:	
-b	Searches the DNS for more information about hosts.
-d *{ directory }*	Specifies that debugging mode should be used, directory is where to save.
-p *port*	Specifies a port to bind the daemon to.
-v	Shows version information.
Solaris:	
-d	Searches the DNS for more information about hosts.
-v	Verbose mode. Shows more information.

continued

File Name:	ypserv	**Directory:**	/usr/lib/netsvc/yp/, **BSD, Linux:** /usr/sbin/	**Type:**	External
Linux:	ypserv –p 100		Specifies that port 100 should be used.		
OpenBSD:	ypserv –1		Specifies that YP version 1 should be answered.		
Solaris:	ypserv –d		Searches the DNS for more information about hosts.		

Ypset

UNIX Shell: Shells (ash, bash, bsh, csh, ksh, sh, tcsh, zsh)

Function	Tells ypbind to use the specified server for NIS services.
Syntax	ypset [options…] *server*

-d *domain*	Sets the domain to use instead of the default domain.
-h *host*	Sets the ypbind bindings on this host instead of on the local host.
Server	Specifies the NIS server that you want to bind to.
AIX:	
-V1	Binds the server using the old NIS protocol version 1.

File Name:	ypset	**Directory:**	/usr/sbin/	**Type:**	External
Common:	ypset rluto		Binds to the ypserv process on pluto.		
Common:	ypset –h moon rluto		Tells moon to bind to pluto.		
Common:	ypset –d ucg –h moon rluto		Tells moon in the ucg domain to bind to pluto.		
AIX:	ypset –V1 rpluto		Binds to the ypserv process on pluto using NIS protocol version 1.		

Ypwhich

UNIX Shell: Shells (ash, bash, bsh, csh, ksh, sh, tcsh, zsh)

Function	Shows the name of the NIS server that provides the name services to a NIS client.
Syntax	ypwhich [options…] *{ hostname }*

-x	Shows the map nicknames. Can only be used alone.
-d *domain*	Sets the domain to use instead of the default domain.
-t	Prevents nickname conversion.
-m *{ map }*	Shows the NIS server for the specified map or for all maps if not specified.
Hostname	Shows the NIS server for the specified host.
AIX, Linux, Solaris:	
-V*version*	Specifies the Ypbind version, the default is 3.
BSD:	
-h *host*	Specifies a host to use when the –m option is specified.

File Name:	ypwhich	**Directory:**	/usr/bin/	**Type:**	External
Common:	ypwhich		Shows the NIS server for your current system.		
Common:	ypwhich luto		Shows the NIS server for pluto.		
Common:	ypwhich –m hosts		Shows the NIS server for the map hosts (nickname for hosts.byname).		

ypxfr

UNIX Shell: Shells (ash, bash, bsh, csh, ksh, sh, tcsh, zsh)

Function	Manages NIS map transfers between an NIS server and a host.
Syntax	ypxfr [options…] *mapname*

-c	Doesn't send a request to clear the current map.
-d *ypdomain*	Specifies that you want to manage domain other than the default.
-f	Tries to force the transfers.
-h *host*	Retrieves the map from the specified host regardless of the master.
-s *ypdomain*	Specifies the domain to transfer maps from.
Mapname	Specifies the NIS map to transfer.
	The following scripts synchronize NIS maps at different time intervals:
ypxfr_1perday	Executes an NIS check/update daily.
Ypxfr_1perhour	Executes an NIS check/update every hour.
Ypxfr_2perday	Executes an NIS check/update twice daily.
AIX:	
-C *TID program server port*	Used only by ypserv. Calls yppush with specified flags.
-S	Uses privileged ports.

continued

BSD: -C *TID program server port* -b -p *yppath*		Used only by `ypserv`. Calls `yppush` with specified flags. **BSD only:** Uses DNS for hostname resolution. **Linux only:** Changes the directory for the maps.			
File Name:	ypxfr	**Directory:**	/usr/sbin/, **Linux:** /usr/lib/yp/, **Solaris:** /usr/lib/netsvc/yp	**Type:**	External
Common:	ypxfr -f -d ucgmedia hosts		Transfers the hosts map for the domain ucgmedia.		
Common:	ypxfr -s company passwd		Retrieves password map from the company domain.		
Common:	ypxfr -c publickey		Transfers publickey map without clearing the local `ypserv`.		

Chapter 10

AIX Commands

The commands in this section are all of the commands from IBM AIX 4.3.3 that are not listed in the Universal UNIX Commands (Chapter 9). The commands are all listed in alphabetical order by the command name.

For cross-references to other operating systems, please see the Quick Command Index (QCI) in Chapter 1.

/etc/gateways

UNIX Shell:	N/A
Function	Contains all the routes and default gateways for the system.
Syntax	NONE
destinationtype	Specifies the type of the route - can be `net` or `host`.
hostname	Specifies the hostname or IP address for the destination gateway.
gateway *address*	Specifies the address of the gateway.
metric *value*	Specifies the hop count to the destination host or network.
type	Specifies how the gateway should be treated. The type can be active, passive, or external. **The following is an example of a `gateways` file:** net 192.168.1.0 gateway 192.168.1.1 metric 1 passive
File Name:	`gateways`
Directory:	/etc/
Type:	Text File
TIP:	Use the command `smitty route` to add a route for the system.

/etc/inetd.conf

UNIX Shell:	N/A
Function	The Internet services database ASCII file, which contains a list of available network services.
Syntax	inetd.conf
The fields are:	**The database file must follow the following formats, separated by spaces or tabs:** **service endpoint protocol status uid program arguments**
service	Specifies the name of a service that is found in the services file.
endpoint	Specifies the endpoint type which can be only one of the following:
stream	Specifies a stream socket.
dgram	Specifies a datagram socket.
raw	Specifies a raw socket.
seqpacket	Specifies a sequenced packet socket.
tli	Specifies all tli endpoints.
protocol	Specifies a valid protocol that is found in the `/etc/inet/protocols` file.
status	Activates nowait mode for all datagram servers except those that are single-threaded.
uid	Specifies the user ID the servers should run under.
program	Specifies the server program to be started by `inetd`. Specify pathname.
arguments	Invokes a server from the command line using a list of no more than five arguments.
Example	**Below is a sample line for a standard FTP and telnet services:** ftp stream TCP6 nowait root /usr/sbin/ftpd ftpd telnet stream TCP6 nowait root /usr/sbin/telnetd telnetd -a
File Name:	`inetd.conf`
Directory:	/etc
Type:	Text File
TIP:	Use `smitty inetd.conf` when you want to add, change or remove a service.

/etc/inittab

UNIX Shell:	N/A
Function	A script used by `init`. Controls process dispatching.
Syntax	*id:rstate:action:process*

id	Specifies a unique identifier for the entry. 1–14 characters.
rstate	Specifies the run level for which the entry applies.
action	Specifies how to handle the process field. The following are available:
respawn	Starts the process if it does not exist.
wait	Starts the process and waits for it to terminate.
once	Starts the process once.
boot	Starts the process at boot time.
bootwait	Same as `boot` but waits for process to terminate.
powerfail	Starts the process when the power fail signal (SIGPWR) is received.
powerwait	Same as `powerfail` but waits for process to terminate.
off	Sends the process a SIGTERM signal, waits 20 seconds and then sends SIGKILL.
hold	Does not restart the process when it terminates.
ondemand	Same as `respawn` but for run levels a,b, and c.
initdefault	Specifies the default run level of the system.
sysinit	Starts the process before accessing the console. Completes before continuing.
process	Specifies a command.

File Name:	Directory:	Type:
`inittab`	/etc/	Text File

/etc/netsvc.conf

UNIX Shell:	N/A
Function	Specifies how different name resolution services will look up names.
Syntax	*key values...*

hosts = *values*	Specifies the order in which hostnames should be looked up, using a comma-separated list.
bind	Uses DNS for host lookups.
local	Uses the local `/etc/host` file for host lookups.
nis	Uses NIS for host lookups. (Add = auth to make a choice authoritative.)
aliases = *alias*	Specifies the order for aliases lookup, using a comma-separated list.
files	Uses `/etc/aliases` for alias lookup.
nis	Uses NIS for alias lookup.
	The following is a sample of the `netsvc.conf` file: hosts = nis, local aliases = nis (Uses NIS first, then /etc/hosts to look up hosts, and use NIS to look up aliases.)

File Name:	Directory:	Type:
`netsvc.conf`	/etc	Text File

ac

UNIX Shell:	All primary shells (csh, ksh, bsh)
Function	Shows how long a user or users have been logged in.
Syntax	ac [options...] *users...*

-d	Shows the total login time for each day.
-p	Shows the total login time for each individual user.
-w *file*	Reads the time account from specified file, instead of the default `/var/log/wtmp`.
users...	Specifies the users to show login time for. If no user is specified, all users will be listed.

File Name:	Directory:	Type:
`ac`	/usr/sbin/acct/	External

ac programmer1 programmer2	Shows the total login time for users programmer1 and programmer2.

acctcms

UNIX Shell:	All primary shells (csh, ksh, bsh)
Function	Creates a summary of command usage using accounting records. Shows the result to STDOUT.
Syntax	acctcms [options...] *{ files... }*

continued

	You may select only one of the following two options:
-t	Processes all collected records as total accounting records.
-a	Shows output in ASCII format. Select either or both of the following two options:
-o	Shows the non-working hours command summary.
-p	Shows the working hours command summary.
-c	Shows total CPU time.
-n	Sorts commands by number of invocations. When used with the `-c` the `-n`, option takes effect.
-j	Shows all commands invoked only once under the column `***other`.
files...	Specifies one or more files as input.
File Name: `acctcms`	**Directory:** /usr/sbin/ **Type:** External
acctcms -a /var/adm/pacct	Shows a total command summary.

acctcom

UNIX Shell: All primary shells (csh, ksh, bsh)

Function	Reads the specified files, or the file `/var/adm/pacct`, and searches for account information.
Syntax	acctcom [options...] *{ files... }*

-a	Shows the average statistics for the selected processes.
-b	Shows the most recent commands first.
-f	Shows use of the fork command to create a process, and the system exit value.
-h	Shows the portion of the total available CPU time used by the process.
-i	Shows the columns that contain the I/O counts.
-k	Shows the used memory measurement in kilobyte segments per minute of run time.
-m	Shows the mean core size. (Is default).
	The -o and -q options can't be combined with any other options.
-o *outputfile*	Copies the selected records in the input data format to a specified output file.
-q	Shows just the statistics, not the output record.
-r	Shows the CPU factor using the format `user-time/(system-time + user-time)`.
-t	Shows separate user and system CPU times.
-v	Eliminates column headings from the output.
-e *time*	Selects the processes that exist at or before the specified time.
-E *time*	Selects processes that end at or before the specified time.
-g *group*	Shows the processes that belong to group, using the group ID or a group name.
-H *factor*	Shows the processes that exceed the specified CPU time factor.
-I *chars*	Shows the processes that have more characters than the number specified in chars.
-l *line*	Shows the processes that belong to terminal /dev/term/line.
-n *pattern*	Shows the commands that match the specified `pattern`.
-O *sec*	Shows the processes which the CPU system time exceeds `sec` seconds.
-s *time*	Selects the processes that exist at or after time. Uses the format hr[:min[:sec]].
-S *time*	Selects processes starting at or before the specified time.
-u *user*	Shows the processes that belong to the user. User ID, username or ? are allowed.
-C *sec*	Specifies the minimum seconds of CPU-time to show processes for.
files...	Specifies the input files other than the STDIN or `/var/adm/pacct`.
File Name: `acctcom`	**Directory:** /usr/sbin/acct/ **Type:** External
acctcom -O 2 < /var/adm/pacct	Shows CPU system/user-time from /var/adm/pact.
acctcom -l /dev/console -s 17:00	Shows active processes on the console at 17:00.

acctcon1

UNIX Shell: All primary shells (csh, ksh, bsh)

Function	Converts login/logoff records into ASCII output. Uses STDIN or reads from the wtmp file located in /var/adm/.
Syntax	acctcon1 [options...]

-p	Shows the line name, login name, and time in numeric and date/time format.
-t	Uses the last time found in the file instead of the current time for the ending time.
-l *file*	Writes a line-summary file and information on each line.
-o *file*	Writes a file containing an overall record for the accounting period.
File Name: `acctcon1`	**Directory:** /usr/sbin/acct/ **Type:** External

acctcon2

UNIX Shell:	All primary shells (csh, ksh, bsh)
Function	Reads the ASCII records created from `acctcon1` and converts them into total accounting (tacct) records.
Syntax	acctcon2
File Name:	`acctcon2`
Directory:	/usr/sbin/acct/
Type:	External

acctdisk

UNIX Shell:	All primary shells (csh, ksh, bsh)
Function	Reads the output lines from `diskusg` or `acctdusg` from STDIN, to create total accounting records.
Syntax	acctdisk
File Name:	`acctdisk`
Directory:	/usr/sbin/acct/
Type:	External

acctdusg

UNIX Shell:	All primary shells (csh, ksh, bsh)
Function	Calculates disk resource consumption for users. Reads from STDIN.
Syntax	acctdusg [options...]
-u *file*	Creates a `No charge`file that specifies which files no one will be charged for.
-p *file*	Specifies a password file. Cannot be used if the file is `/etc/passwd`.
File Name:	`acctdusg`
Directory:	/usr/sbin/acct/
Type:	External
find . -print | /usr/lib/acct/acctdusg	Makes a summary and shows disk resource usage.

acctmerg

UNIX Shell:	All primary shells (csh, ksh, bsh)
Function	Merges or adds accounting files in the total accounting (tacct) or ASCII format.
Syntax	acctmerg [options...] *{ files... }*
-a	Creates an ASCII version of a tacct file.
-h	Shows column headings.
-i	Specifies the input file is in ASCII format.
-p	Shows the input without performing any processing.
-q *file*	Reads the specified qacct file and outputs records sorted by user ID and name.
-t	Creates a single record that totals all input.
-u	Summarizes by userID only instead of both user ID and username.
-v	Verbose mode. Shows more information.
files...	Specifies the total accounting (tacct) or ASCII file to merge or add.
File Name:	`acctmerg`
Directory:	/usr/sbin/acct/
Type:	External

accton

UNIX Shell:	All primary shells (csh, ksh, bsh)
Function	Outputs process accounting to the specified file. If no filename is given, turns process accounting off.
Syntax	accton *{ file }*
file	Specifies an existing file where the kernel stores process accounting records.
File Name:	`accton`
Directory:	/usr/bin/
Type:	External
accton /var/adm/pacct	Turns on process accounting and uses the specified accounting file.

acctprc1

UNIX Shell:	All primary shells (csh, ksh, bsh)
Function	Converts information created with acct, and adds the login names that correspond with the user IDs.
Syntax	acctprc1 *{ file }*
file	Supplies a list of sessions sorted by user IDs and their login name.
File Name:	`acctprc1`
Directory:	/usr/sbin/acct/
Type:	External

acctprc2

acctprc2	UNIX Shell:	All primary shells (csh, ksh, bsh)
Function	Reads records from STDIN formatted by `acctprc1`, sorts them by ID and name, and shows the result to STDOUT.	
Syntax	acctprc2	
File Name: `acctprc2`	**Directory:** /usr/sbin/acct/	**Type:** External

acctwtmp

acctwtmp	UNIX Shell:	All primary shells (csh, ksh, bsh)
Function	Manages connect-time accounting records by writing a UTMP record to STDOUT.	
Syntax	acctwtmp *reason*	
reason	Specifies the reason to put in the record; can't be longer than 11 characters.	
File Name: `acctwtmp`	**Directory:** /usr/sbin/acct/	**Type:** External

acfgd

acfgd	UNIX Shell:	All primary shells (csh, ksh, bsh)
Function	Manages auto-configuration of PCMCIA devices.	
Syntax	acfgd	
File Name: `acfgd`	**Directory:** /usr/sbin/	**Type:** External

acledit

acledit	UNIX Shell:	All primary shells (csh, ksh, bsh)
Function	An editor used to manage access control list (ACL) for a file.	
Syntax	acledit *{ file }*	
file	Specifies the file to edit access control information for.	
File Name: `acledit`	**Directory:** /usr/bin	**Type:** External

aclget

aclget	UNIX Shell:	All primary shells (csh, ksh, bsh)
Function	Shows the access control information for a specific file.	
Syntax	aclget [-o *outfile*] *file*	
-o *outfile*	Writes output from the command to a file instead of STDOUT.	
file	Specifies the file to show access control information for.	
File Name: `aclget`	**Directory:** /usr/bin	**Type:** External

aclput

aclput	UNIX Shell:	All primary shells (csh, ksh, bsh)
Function	Sets the access control list for a file.	
Syntax	aclput [-i *inputfile*] *file*	
-i *inputfile*	Specifies a file to use as input instead of STDIN.	
file	Specifies the file to alter the access control list for.	
File Name: `aclput`	**Directory:** /usr/bin	**Type:** External

adb

adb	UNIX Shell:	All primary shells (csh, ksh, bsh)
Function	Provides a controlled environment to examine files, and acts as an interactive general-purpose debugger.	
Syntax	adb [options...] *{ objectfile } { corefile }*	
-k	Performs kernel mapping.	
-w	Creates an objectfile and a corefile if needed, and opens them for use by `adb`.	
-l *dir*	Specifies a colon-separated list of directories to read.	
	The following files may be used, and can be combined:	
objectfile	Specifies the executable program file that should contain the symbol table.	
corefile	Specifies the corefile image file produced from the objectfile.	
adb -k /dev/ksyms /dev/mem	Starts adb on the running kernel.	

addbib

UNIX Shell: All primary shells (csh, ksh, bsh)

Function	Creates, modifies, or updates a library database of information. Prompts for necessary information after executing.
Syntax	addbib [options...] *database*

-a	Does not prompt for a summary.
-p *file*	Uses another step-by-step prompting scheme other then the default.
database	Specifies the database to create, modify, or update.

File Name: `addbib` **Directory:** /usr/bin/ **Type:** External

addX11input

UNIX Shell: All primary shells (csh, ksh, bsh)

Function	Collects X11 values and creates an X11 input extension record in the ODM database.
Syntax	addX11input

File Name: `addX11input` **Directory:** /usr/bin/X11 **Type:** External

adfutil

UNIX Shell: All primary shells (csh, ksh, bsh)

Function	Merges MCA driver information from a diskette for PS/2 adapters into the ODM.
Syntax	adfutil [options...]

-d *device*	Specifies the location of the description file for the adapter.
-f *file*	Specifies a path for the adapter description file. Cannot be used with -d.
-a *adapter*	Looks in the ODM for information to create a DOS filename for the description file.
-c *ps2ID*	Specifies the PS/2 card identifier for the adapter. Cannot be used with -a.
-m *files...*	Loads microcode information from files on the diskette.
-q	Shows no output.

File Name: `adfutil` **Directory:** /usr/sbin **Type:** External

admin

UNIX Shell: All primary shells (csh, ksh, bsh)

Function	Manages SCCS history files. SCCS history files have the form s.filename.
Syntax	admin [options...] *files...*

-n	Creates a new history file.
-a *username*	Gives permissions for a specified user to change deltas.
-a *groupID*	Gives permissions for a specified group to change deltas.
-f *flag* [values...]	Sets values for the specified history file flag.
	The following are the flags that can be used:
b	Enables the SCCS-get command to create branch deltas.
c *ceil*	Limits the maximum number of releases that can be checked out.
f *floor*	Sets a limit or a floor for the number of releases the can be checked out.
d *sid*	Specifies the default SID that is the delta number that is used by `SCCS-get`.
i	Handles the message No id keywords (ge6) as an error instead of a warning.
j	Allows multiple simultaneous updates.
l *release*[releases...]	Locks only the release or releases specified against deltas.
n	Creates an empty release or empty delta when a release is skipped over.
q *value*	Specifies the value to expand when a read-only version is retrieved.
m *module*	Specifies the module name to use. The default name is the SCCS file with no leading s.
t *type*	Sets the release level for the delta.
v *{ NR }*	Prompts for a delta modification number when creating a new delta.
-m *mr-list*	Puts modification request numbers into the comments for the first version.
-r *level*	Sets the level for the delta to be created.
-t *file*	Adds additional text for description into the delta from the specified file.
-y *comment*	Adds additional text for comments into the comment field of the delta.
file...	Specifies a file to create or manage.
-e *username*	Removes the ability to make deltas from the specified user.
-e *groupID*	Removes the ability to make deltas from the specified group.
-d *flag*	Erases a specific flag from the history file.

continued

-h	Checks the structure of the old file and compares the checksum with the new s. file.
-z	Recalculates the file's checksum and stores it in the first line of history file.
-i *file*	Uses text from input file to start a new history file.
files...	Specifies a file to create or manage.
File Name: admin	**Directory:** /usr/bin/ **Type:** External

aixterm

UNIX Shell: All primary shells (csh, ksh, bsh)

Function	An enhanced terminal emulator for X-window.
Syntax	aixterm [options...]

-ah	Always highlights the cursor.
-ar	Automatically raises the window when the cursor enters the window.
-autopush	Enables the autopush mode.
-b *numpix*	Specifies the width of the inner border, in pixels.
-bd *color*	Sets the color for the highlighted border.
-bg *color*	Sets the background color.
-bw *numpix*	Sets the border width of the window, in pixels.
-C	Picks up console messages.
-cc *chrange:value*	Changes the character type of a word.
-cr *color*	Specifies the color of the text cursor on color displays.
-csd *chshape*	Sets the default shape of Arabic text: automatic, initial, middle, final, or isolated.
-cu	Shows leading tabs in the correct way.
-display *name:num*	Specifies the host and display number to run aixterm.
-dw	Automatically centers the cursor if the icon window is deiconified.
-e *command*	Specifies a command that you want to execute in the aixterm window.
-f*action*	Specifies the fonts position in the font table. Action is 0-6. Default font is 0.
--f*action fontset*	Specifies names for the font sets in the different positions. Action is 0-6.
-fb *font*	Sets the name for the bold font.
-fg *color*	Sets the foreground color for the text.
-fi *fontset*	Sets the name for the italic font.
-fn *font*	Sets the name for the normal text font.
-fs *font*	Sets the name for the special graphics font.
-fullcursor	Uses a full block cursor.
-geometry *geometry*	Sets the location and size of a window.
#geometry *geometry*	Sets the location for the icon window.
-help	Shows help information.
-ib *file*	Specifies a bitmap for the icon.
-im *inputmet*	Specifies the input method for aixterm.
-j	Uses jump scroll.
-lang *language*	Specifies the language to use.
-l	Puts any output from the window at the end of the log file.
-leftscroll	Puts the scrollbar on the left side.
-lf *file*	Specifies where to save output.
-ls	Uses aixterm as a login shell.
-mb	Enables right margin bell.
-mc *number*	Sets the multiple click time.
-ms *color*	Sets mouse cursor color.
-mn	Ignores event notification.
-n *iconname*	Sets a name for the icon.
-name *app*	Specifies the application to use for the .Xdefaults.
-nb *number*	Sets the margin distance where the bell rings.
-nobidi	Does not use Arabic and Hebrew functions.
-nonulls	Enables nonulls mode.
-nss *nrshape*	Sets the default shape of numerals: bilingual, Hindi, Arabic or passthru.
-orient *orientation*	Specifies the screen orientation: ltr for left-to-right or rtl for right-to-left.
-outline *color*	Sets the color for the outline.

continued

-po *number*	Specifies how many lines to save from the previous screen when scrolling.
-ps	Enables page scroll.
-pt *preedit*	Specifies the pre-edit type for text composing: over, off, root, or none.
-reduced	Uses aixterm with reduced manageability.
-rfb *font*	Sets the name for the reduced bold font.
-rfi *font*	Sets the name for the reduced italic font.
-rfn *font*	Sets the name for the reduced normal font.
-rfs *font*	Sets the name for the reduced special graphics font.
-rf*action font*	Sets name for the reduced fonts in the different font table positions. Action is 0-6.
--rf*action fontset*	Sets name for the fontsets in the different font table positions. Action is 0-6.
-rv	Reverses the foreground and background colors.
-rw	Uses reverse wraparound.
-s	Disables synchronous scrolling.
-sb	Shows the scrollbar.
-sf	Creates Sun function keycodes for to use with VT102 terminals.
-si	Does not reposition the window when using the scrollbar.
-sk	Automatically repositions the window when scrolling.
-sl *numlines*	Saves the specified number of files on top of the window when scrolling.
-sn	Shows the status line in normal video mode.
-st	Shows the status line on startup.
-suppress	Shows no output from IMIoctl calls.
-symmetric	Uses symmetric swapping to handle bi-directional character pairs.
-T *title*	Specifies the title for the title bar.
-text *type*	Specifies the text type for the data streams. implicit or visual.
-ti	Shows the title to the right of the bitmap in the icon window.
-tm *string*	Specifies the terminal settings to use.
-tn *termname*	Sets the terminal environmental variable.
-ut	Does not add login ID to the file /etc/utmp.
-V	Uses VT102 emulation.
-vb	Does not use a visual bell.
-W	Moves the cursor to the middle when the aixterm window is created.
-xrm *string*	Sets aixterm resources using a stream of input commands.
-132	Resizes the aixterm window as you want.
File Name: `aixterm`	**Directory:** /usr/bin/X11 — **Type:** External
NOTE:	Remember to set the DISPLAY variable.

ali

UNIX Shell: All primary shells (csh, ksh, bsh)

Function	Shows addresses for mail aliases.
Syntax	ali [options...] *{ aliases... }*

-alias *aliasfile*	Specifies file to inspect.
-list	Shows one line per address.
-nolist	Shows multiple addresses on the same line (is default).
-normalize	Tracks down the official hostname of the address.
-nonormalize	Disables the -normalize option (is default).
-user	Invert mode; shows aliases that expand to each address.
-nouser	Does not show aliases (is default).
-help	Shows help information.
aliases...	Specifies the alias or aliases to show.
File Name: `ali`	**Directory:** /usr/bin/ — **Type:** External
ali -alias /etc/nmh/MailAliases nisse	Uses /etc/local/aliases as the alias file to list nisse.

alog

alog		**UNIX Shell:**	All primary shells (csh, ksh, bsh)
Function	Manages the systems log files.		
Syntax	alog [options...]		

-f *logfile*	Specifies the name of the log file; if the file does not exist, it is created.
-o	Shows the contents of the specified log file.
-q	Copies STDIN to a log file, but does not show anything on STDOUT.
-s *size*	Specifies the size of the logfile in bytes.
-t *logtype*	Specifies an identifier for the log in the `alog` configuration database.
-V	Shows the value of the verbosity attribute for logtype from the alog database.
-C	Changes the attributes for the logtype. Can only be used with the -f, -s, and -w options.
-w *verbosity*	Alters the verbosity attribute value.
-L	Shows which logtypes are defined in the configuration database for alog.

File Name:	`alog`	**Directory:**	/usr/bin	**Type:**	External
TIP:	Use `smitty alog` to show a system log.				

alog -f /tmp/sample.log -o	Shows the content of the log file /tmp/sample.log.

alt_disk_install

alt_disk_install		**UNIX Shell:**	Korn shell (ksh)
Function	Installs or clones an mksysb image on an alternate disk.		
Syntax	alt_disk_install option [options...] *targetdisks...*		

	The following seven options can't be combined:
-d *device*	Specifies a device or path to a mksysb image.
-C	Clones the root volume group.
-X	Removes an altinst_rootvg definition from the ODM.
-q *disk*	Shows the volume group boot disk name.
-v *newvgname disk*	Renames the alternate disk volume group.
-W *disk*	Activates the volume group.
	The following options can only be used with the -d and -C options:
-i *image.data*	Specifies an image.data file other than the default.
-s *script*	Specifies a script to run at the end of mksysb or cloning.
-R *resconf*	Specifies a resolv.conf file to replace the existing file after execution.
-D	Starts the debug.
-B	Does not run bootlist after either mksysb or cloning.
-V	Verbose mode. Shows more information.
-p *platform*	Specifies the platform used to create the disk boot image name.
-L *mksysblev*	Specifies the boot image OS level name.
-b *bundlename*	Specifies a list of filesets or packages to install after the mksysb or cloning.
-I *installpflags*	Specifies additional installp flags to use.
-l *imagelocation*	Specifies the location of installp updates or images to install after the mksysb or cloning.
-f *fixbundle*	Specifies a file of APARs to install after the mksysb or cloning.
-F *fixes*	Specifies a list of APARs to install after the mksysb or cloning.
-e *excludelist*	Specifies files to be excluded from the mksysb or clone.
-w *filesets*	Specifies a list of filesets to install after the mksysb or cloning.
-n	Keeps all NIM information.
-p *phaseoption*	Specifies the phase order. 1, 2, 3, 12, 23 or all are valid options.
targetdisks...	Specifies the alternate disk or disks to install on.

File Name:	`alt_disk_install`	**Directory:**	/usr/sbin/	**Type:**	Script

apply

apply		**UNIX Shell:**	All primary shells (csh, ksh, bsh)
Function	Applies parameters to a specific command.		
Syntax	apply [options...] *command parameters...*		

-a*char*	Specifies another substitution character or string than the default percent sign.

continued

-nr *command* *parameters...*		Specifies how many parameters to pass to the specified command. Specifies the command to run. Specifies parameters for the command.			
File Name:	`apply`	**Directory:**	/usr/bin	**Type:**	External
apply 'aclget %1' *			Runs aclget on every command in the current directory.		

arithmetic

UNIX Shell: All primary shells (csh, ksh, bsh)

Function	A simple math game that keeps track of progress and shows results after every twenty questions.
Syntax	arithmetic [options...]

+ - x / *range*		Uses addition problems. Uses subtraction problems. Uses multiplication problems. Uses division problems. Specifies the range of numbers to be used in the game (99 is the maximum).			
File Name:	`arithmetic`	**Directory:**	/usr/games/	**Type:**	External
arithmetic +x/ 50			Drills addition, multiplication, and division with the integers 0 to 50.		

asa, fpr

UNIX Shell: All primary shells (csh, ksh, bsh)

Function	Converts FORTRAN carriage control output to an AIX line printer format.
Syntax	asa *{ files... }*

files...		Specifies the pathname and the file to be used for input.			
File Name:	`asa`	**Directory:**	/usr/bin/	**Type:**	External

ate

UNIX Shell: All primary shells (csh, ksh, bsh)

Function	An asynchronous terminal emulation program.
Syntax	ate

		The following are subcommands for the ate program:			
alter l *charleng* s *stopbit* p *parity* r *baudrate* d *device* i *dialprefix* f *dialsuffix* w *second* a *redial* t *transprot* c *pacingtype* break connect directory help modify perform quit receive send terminate		Alters the characteristics for data transmission. Alters the data character length. Alters stop bits. Alters parity bits. Alters the baud rate. Alters the port name. Alters the dial prefix. Alters the dial suffix. Alters the wait time. Alters the redial attempts. Alters the transfer protocol. Alters the pacing character or delay time. Breaks the current activity. Connects to a remote system. Shows the dialing directory. Shows help information. Alters local settings temporarily. Enables the use of operating system commands. Quits the ate program. Receives a file from a remote system. Sends a file to a remote system. Terminates a connection.			
File Name:	`ate`	**Directory:**	/usr/bin/	**Type:**	External
NOTE:	Users must be a member of the uucp group to use ate.				

atmstat

atmstat	UNIX Shell:	All primary shells (csh, ksh, bsh)
Function	Shows the status of ATM adapters.	
Syntax	atmstat [options...] *device*	

-d	Verbose mode. Shows more information.
-r	Resets all statistics.
device	Specifies the ATM device.
File Name: `atmstat`	**Directory:** /usr/bin/ **Type:** External
atmstat -d atm0	Shows verbose status of the atm0 device.

audit

audit	UNIX Shell:	All primary shells (csh, ksh, bsh)
Function	Manages the way the audit daemon auditd performs.	
Syntax	audit *ACTION*	

ACTION	**Select only one of the following actions:**
start	Starts the audit subsystem.
shutdown	Terminates the collection of audit records and resets the configuration information.
on [panic]	Restarts the auditing system after a suspension.
panic	Shuts down the system if bin data can't be written to a bin file.
query	Shows the current status of the audit subsystem.
File Name: `audit`	**Directory:** /usr/sbin/ **Type:** External

auditbin

auditbin	UNIX Shell:	All primary shells (csh, ksh, bsh)
Function	A daemon that manages bin files of audit information.	
Syntax	auditbin	
File Name: `auditbin`	**Directory:** /usr/sbin/	**Type:** External

auditcat

auditcat	UNIX Shell:	All primary shells (csh, ksh, bsh)
Function	The subsystem of the audit command that writes records to trail files.	
Syntax	auditcat [options...] *{ inputfile }*	

-p	Compresses bin files before output.
-u	Uncompresses trail files before output.
-o *outfile*	Specifies an audit trail file where to write records.
-r	Tries to recover a broken bin file. Must be used with the -o option and the inputfile.
inputfile	Specifies the input audit bin file.
File Name: `auditcat`	**Directory:** /usr/sbin/ **Type:** External

auditconv

auditconv	UNIX Shell:	All primary shells (csh, ksh, bsh)
Function	Converts audit records from older OSes to AIX version 4 format.	
Syntax	auditconv *oldfile newfile*	

oldfile	Specifies a file from the older OS.
newfile	Specifies a file in the new OS.
File Name: `auditconv`	**Directory:** /usr/sbin/ **Type:** External

auditmerge

auditmerge	UNIX Shell:	All primary shells (csh, ksh, bsh)
Function	Merges two or more audit trail files into one single trail file.	
Syntax	auditmerge [-q] *files...*	

-q	Shows no output.
files...	Specifies the trail files to merge.
File Name: `auditmerge`	**Directory:** /usr/sbin/ **Type:** External

auditpr

UNIX Shell: All primary shells (csh, ksh, bsh)

Function	Shows or prints audit records.
Syntax	auditpr [options...]

-m *message*	Specifies a message to show with each heading.
-t *action*	Specifies how to show headers. 0=never, 1=before each series, 2=before each record.
-h	Specifies which fields to show and in which order. The following are valid fields.
e	Shows the audit event.
l	Shows the login name.
R	Shows the audit status.
r	Shows the real username.
c	Shows the command name.
h	Shows which host generated the record.
P	Shows the parent process ID.
p	Shows the process ID.
T	Shows the kernel thread ID.
t	Shows the time the record was written.
-r	Does not translate IDs to the symbolic name.
-v	Shows the tail of each audit record.

File Name: auditpr **Directory:** /usr/sbin/ **Type:** External

auditselect

UNIX Shell: All primary shells (csh, ksh, bsh)

Function	Shows all audit records that match the specified criteria.
Syntax	auditselect option *{ trail }*

-e *expression*	Specifies the criteria to use to select audit records.
-f *file*	Specifies a file that contains the selection criteria's that you want to use.
trail	Specifies an audit trail file to search through.

File Name: auditselect **Directory:** /usr/sbin/ **Type:** External

auditstream

UNIX Shell: All primary shells (csh, ksh, bsh)

Function	Copies records from the audit device to STDOUT in binary format.
Syntax	auditstream [options...]

-m	Shows the cpuID in each record.
-c *classes...*	Specifies the audit classes to show on STDOUT.

File Name: auditstream **Directory:** /usr/sbin/ **Type:** External

autoconf6

UNIX Shell: All primary shells (csh, ksh, bsh)

Function	Configures IPv6 network interfaces at startup.
Syntax	autoconf6 [options...] *{ interfaces... }*

-a	Configures all accepted interfaces.
-i	Configures all specified interfaces.
-s	Installs the SIT interfaces IP version 4 compatible programs.
-6	Does not install the SIT interfaces IP version 4 compatible programs.
-M	Does not alter existing IPv6 multicast routes.
-O	Does not configure the loopback interface.
-R	Does not alter the default route.
-c	Used for compatibility if you have a bad LL address.
-v	Verbose mode. Shows more information.
-m *interface*	Specifies the name of the main network interface.
interfaces...	Specifies the network interfaces to configure.

continued

File Name:	`autoconf6`	**Directory:**	/usr/sbin/	**Type:**	External
TIP:	Use `smitty tcpip` to configure a network interface with IPv6.				

automount

UNIX Shell: Korn shell (ksh)

Function	Installs mount points for automatic mounting upon requests from users. Uses automount maps to relate to each mount point that has been installed.
Syntax	automount [options...] *directories... mapnames... { mountoptions... }*

-m	Suppresses initialization of directory-mapname pairs listed in master NIS.
-T	Traces and shows automount activity for diagnostic purposes.
-v	Verbose mode. shows more information.
-D *name=value*	Assigns a value to the indicated automount command environment variable.
-f *masterfile*	Reads the named local file instead of the master NIS map file.
-tl *duration*	Specifies the number of seconds that a lookup name remains cached when not in use.
-tw *interval*	Specifies an interval in seconds between attempts to unmount a file system.
directories...	Specifies the mount point.
mapnames...	Specifies the mapname for the mount point.
mountoptions...	Specifies the mount options to use when automounting.

File Name:	`automount`	**Directory:**	/usr/sbin/	**Type:**	Script

automountd

UNIX Shell: All primary shells (csh, ksh, bsh)

Function	The daemon that manages mount and unmount requests made by the `autofs` kernel extension.
Syntax	automountd [options...]

-T	Gives trace information of each RPC call.
-v	Verbose mode. Shows more information.
-D *name=value*	Sets additional values to the automount map.

File Name:	`automountd`	**Directory:**	/usr/sbin/	**Type:**	External

autopush

UNIX Shell: All primary shells (csh, ksh, bsh)

Function	Configures a list of modules are automatically streamed when a device is opened.
Syntax	autopush [options...]

	The following three options must be used separately and can't be combined:
-f *file*	Creates the autopush configuration for a driver based upon the file.
	Requires a text file that is made up of 4 or more columns separated by spaces.
Example file	minor major last-minor moduleA moduleB moduleC
-g -M *major* -m *minor*	Gets the current setting of the specified major and minor devices.
-r -M *major* -m *minor*	Removes the configuration setting of the specified major and minor devices.

File Name:	`autopush`	**Directory:**	/usr/sbin/	**Type:**	External

awk, nawk

UNIX Shell: All primary shells (csh, ksh, bsh)

Function	Scans the input file or files for lines that match the specified pattern in ' *scriptstr* ', or from a file.
Syntax	awk [options...] [' *scriptstr* '] [-v *var=value*] *{ files... }*

-F*expression*	Specifies the expression to use for a field separator.
-f *file*	Specifies the file that contains the specific pattern action statements to be used.
	The pattern action statements must follow the format: pattern { action }.
pattern { action }	Defines the pattern action statements and must be enclosed in single quotes *' scriptstr '*.
	The following arithmetic functions are supported:
atan2(*x,y*)	Returns the arctangent of y/x.
sin(*x*)	Returns the sine of the specified value. The value must be in radians.
exp(*x*)	Returns the exponential function of the specified value.
log(*x*)	Returns the natural logarithm of the specified value.
sqrt(*x*)	Returns the square root of the specified value.

continued

int(*x*)	Shortens the specified value to an integer. It trims the value when x > 0.
rand()	Returns a value between 0 and 1.
srand(*{ x }*)	Sets the seed value for rand. If no value is specified, the current time is used.
	The following are the supported string functions (string is indicated by s):
sub(*src,repl,s*)	Replaces the first src string found in `s` with the repl string.
gsub(*src,repl,s*)	Replaces all src strings found in `s` with the repl string.
index(*s, sub*)	Gives the position of string `s` where the substring *sub* occurs first.
int(*s*)	Trims `s` to an integer. If no `s` is shown, $0 is used.
length(*s*)	Gives the total length of an argument, or an entire line if there is no argument.
blength(*s*)	Like `length`, but gives the byte length instead of the character length.
match(*s, re*)	Returns the position where the regular expression `re` matches the string `s`.
split(*s, a, fs*)	Splits string s into an array of elements of a, and separates fields with the fs expression.
sprintf(*fmt, expr...*)	Formats listed expressions with `printf` using the format specified by fmt.
substr(*s, m, n*)	Gives the n-character substring of the string s that starts at the m position.
tolower(*s*)	Changes all characters in the string to lowercase.
toupper(*s*)	Changes all characters in the string to uppercase.
-v *var=value*	Specifies a built-in variable and assigns it a value.
	The following are built-in variables that can be used:
FILENAME	Specifies the name of the current file being used for input.
FS	Defines input field separators (defaults is space and tab).
NF	Defines the number of fields in the existing file.
NR	Defines the ordinal number for the current record.
OFMT	Defines the output numbers in a specific format (default is %.6g).
OFS	Defines the output field separators (default is blank).
ORS	Defines the output record separators (default is newline).
RS	Defines the input record separators (default is newline).
	The following are control flow functions:
break	Exits from a *for*/*while*, or *do* loop.
continue	Starts the next loop cycle in a *for*/*while*, or *do* loop.
do *statement*	A loop that executes the specified statement while the condition is true.
while (*condition*)	The statement evaluated by do; runs the do statement if condition is true, and exits if false.
exit *{ exp }*	Executes the end routine if one exists, and exits the script with return value exp.
if (*condition*)	Performs the statement if the condition is true, or else performs the else condition.
else (*condition*)	Performs the else condition when the if condition is false.
while (*condition*)	Performs the condition as long as the condition is true.
for (*exp1; exp2 ; exp3*)	A loop that uses three expressions (see below). Exits when any expr. is false.
exp1	Sets the counter variable to an initial value that counts the number of loops.
exp2	Defines the variable that is read and evaluated before executing the statement.
exp3	A counter that increments each time the loop is true. (The variables exp1, exp2, and exp3 are all optional, and are true if not used.)
for (*arrayvar*)	A loop that executes each variable defined in an array.
next	Reads the input line and begins a new loop or procedure.
	The following input/output functions are supported:
getline *{ variable }*	Reads the next record from the current file and writes it to the specified variable.
expression | getline *{ variable }*	Reads the specified pipe and writes it to the specified variable.
print	Shows the results of the ' *scriptstr* ' and variables to STDOUT.
printf	Same as *print*, but also formats the output.
$*n*	Specifies the field number in the file ($1, $2, $3 etc...) and are separated by FS.
$0	Specifies to use the entire line in the file as input.
	The following general functions are supported:
close*{ file }*	Closes the file once opened by print or printf.
system*{ command }*	Runs the specified command and return its exit status.
function *name* (*parameters...*) *{ statements }*	Creates a user-defined function. When called, runs all functions specified within the braces.
return *value*	The return value for the user-defined function.
exit *value*	Ends the script with the specified return value.

continued

delete *array { position }*	Deletes a variable in an array.		
files...	Specifies the input files to scan for pattern matching.		
' scriptstr '	Contains the pattern action statements, and must be enclosed by singles quotes.		
File Name: awk	**Directory:** /usr/bin/	**Type:**	External
awk 'length >80' foo	Prints every line in foo that is longer then 80 chars.		
awk '/start/' smit.log | wc -l	Counts the number of commands executed by smit.		
ls -latrg | awk '{ print $8 }'	Prints the 8th column from ls -latrg		

backup

UNIX Shell: All primary shells (csh, ksh, bsh)

Function	A backup program that can back up file systems or files to a tape or a diskette.
Syntax	backup [options...]

	The following options are used to backup files by name:		
-i	Reads filenames from STDIN.		
-b *number*	Specifies the number of blocks to write in a single backup operation.		
-p	Compresses the files that are backed up.		
-e *expr*	Specifies a regular expression that matches files that are not to be backed up.		
-f *device*	Specifies the backup device.		
-l *number*	Sets a block limit for a diskette.		
-o	Makes the backup compatible with version 2 systems.		
-v	Verbose mode. Shows more information.		
	The following options are use to back up file systems by inode number:		
-*level*	Specifies the backup level; valid levels are 0-9.		
-c	Specifies the tape is a cartridge.		
-L *length*	Specifies the tape length in bytes.		
-u	Updates the /etc/dumpdates file.		
filesystem	Specifies the file system to backup.		
-w	This option is currently disabled.		
-W	Shows the most recent backup; can only be used alone.		
File Name: backup	**Directory:** /usr/sbin/	**Type:**	External
backup -0 -u -f /dev/rmt0 /	Takes a full backup of the root (/) file system.		

battery

UNIX Shell: All primary shells (csh, ksh, bsh)

Function	Shows battery information.
Syntax	battery [-d]

-d	Discharges the battery.		
File Name: battery	**Directory:** /usr/bin/	**Type:**	External

bdiff

UNIX Shell: All primary shells (csh, ksh, bsh)

Function	Compares files that are too large for the command diff.
Syntax	bdiff *file1 file2 { NR }* [-s]

-s	Silent mode; does not show diagnostics.		
file1	Specifies the first file to compare. This can also be a -, which indicates STDIN.		
file2	Specifies the second file to compare. This can also be a -, which indicates STDIN.		
NR	Sets the number of line segments (default is 3500).		
File Name: bdiff	**Directory:** /usr/bin/	**Type:**	External

bellmail

UNIX Shell: All primary shells (csh, ksh, bsh)

Function	Shows or sends messages to users in the system.
Syntax	bellmail [options...] *users...*

-e	Does not show messages.
-f *file*	Specifies a file to read mail from.

continued

-p	Shows mail without prompting.		
-q -r -t *users...*	Enables the use of Ctrl+C to quit the program. Shows mail sorted by date. Shows all recipients of the mail. Specifies a login name or names to send mail to.		
File Name: `bellmail`	**Directory:** /usr/bin/	**Type:**	External

bf

UNIX Shell: All primary shells (csh, ksh, bsh)

Function	Shows the amount of memory an application is using.
Syntax	bf [options...] -x *program*

-b *buffsize* -W *windowsize* -o *outfile* -p *process* -x *program*	Specifies how many records to save in the kernel buffer. Specifies how many unpinned pages to reference for a new page to be logged. Specifies a file to save the output in. Tracks only the specified processes. Specifies the program to run.		
File Name: `bf`	**Directory:** /usr/bin/	**Type:**	External

bffcreate

UNIX Shell: All primary shells (csh, ksh, bsh)

Function	Creates backup files of an installation image in bff format to support software installations.
Syntax	bffcreate [options...]

-q -S -v -X -d *Device* -w *Directory* -l -f *ListFile*	Suppresses the request for media. Specifies single-volume processing, even if the CD-ROM contains multiple volume set. Writes the name of the backup format file to STDOUT. Automatically extends the file system, if needed. Specifies the device on which the original image resides. Specifies where to create a temporary working directory (default is /tmp). Lists the Package, Level, Image Type, and Part(s) of all packages on media. Reads a list of PackageNames and Levels from ListFile.		
File Name: `bffcreate`	**Directory:** /usr/sbin/	**Type:**	External
bffcreate -d /dev/rmt0.1	Creates an installation image file on rmt0.1.		

bfrpt

UNIX Shell: Korn shell (ksh)

Function	Shows output from the bf command in a readable format.
Syntax	bfrpt [options...]

-r *action* *act* *global* *all* -f *reportfile* -P *process* -N *procnum* -p	Specifies the type of report to create. action can be one of the following three. Shows footprints of each routine in the specified processes. Shows header and table information. Combines the act and global actions. Specifies the name of the reportfile. Specifies the process to report on. Specifies the number of processes to get from the trace file. Makes the report in PostScript format.		
File Name: `bfrpt`	**Directory:** /usr/bin/	**Type:**	Script

bfs

UNIX Shell: All primary shells (csh, ksh, bsh)

Function	Scans big files to identify sections. Supports all command operators from the command `ed`.
Syntax	bfs [-] *file*

- *file*	Does not show sizes. Specifies the file to scan.		
File Name: `bfs`	**Directory:** /usr/bin/bfs	**Type:**	External
Note:	The bfs command is basically a read-only version of the ed command.		

bicheck

bicheck	UNIX Shell:	All primary shells (csh, ksh, bsh)
Function	Checks the syntax for bosinst.data files that have been modified by a user.	
Syntax	bicheck *file*	

file	Specifies the bosinst.data file to check.			
File Name: bicheck	Directory: /usr/bin/		Type:	External

biff

biff	UNIX Shell:	All primary shells (csh, ksh, bsh)
Function	Enables or disables mail notification. If no arguments are used, shows the current status.	
Syntax	biff [option]	

y	Enables mail notification.			
n	Disables mail notification.			
File Name: biff	Directory: /usr/bin/		Type:	External

bindprocessor

bindprocessor	UNIX Shell:	All primary shells (csh, ksh, bsh)
Function	Shows processors, or handles kernel thread bindings of a process.	
Syntax	bindprocessor *process* { *processorNR* } bindprocessor option	

processorNR	Specifies which processor to bind a process on.			
-q	Shows which processors are available.			
-u *process*	Unbinds the threads of the specified process.			
process	Specifies the process to bind or unbind.			
File Name: bindprocessor	Directory: /usr/sbin/		Type:	External

biod

biod	UNIX Shell:	All primary shells (csh, ksh, bsh)
Function	A daemon that manages client requests for files over NFS.	
Syntax	biod *biodNR*	

biodNR	Specifies the number of block I/O daemons to start.			
File Name: biod	Directory: /usr/sbin/		Type:	External

bootinfo

bootinfo	UNIX Shell:	All primary shells (csh, ksh, bsh)
Function	Shows boot information.	
Syntax	bootinfo [options...]	

-P *ppsize*	Specifies the physical partition size to use to calculate defaults.			
-s *disk*	Shows the disk size.			
-b	Shows last boot device.			
-B *disk*	Shows a 1 if the specified disk is bootable, and a 0 if it is not.			
-c	Shows reply packets from the bootp daemon.			
-k	Shows which position the key is in: 1=secure, 2=service, and 3=normal.			
-m	Shows the server model code.			
-q *adapter*	Shows a 1 if the specified adapter is bootable, and a 0 if it is not.			
-r	Shows the real memory in kilobytes.			
-t	Shows the boot category: 1=disk, 2=cdrom, 3=tape, and 4=network.			
-T	Shows the hardware platform of the system.			
-o *disk*	Shows the disk device name or location.			
-z	Shows if the system is multiprocessor-capable.			
File Name: bootinfo	Directory: /usr/sbin/		Type:	External
bootinfo s hdisk0	Shows the size of hdisk0.			

bootlist

UNIX Shell:	All primary shells (csh, ksh, bsh)
Function	Manages the boot order in the system.
Syntax	bootlist [options...] *{ devices... } { attr=value }*

-m *mode*	Specifies the bootlist that you want to manage. mode can be one of the following:
normal	Uses the normal bootlist.
service	Uses the service bootlist.
prevboot	Uses the previous bootlist.
-r	Shows hardware platform information if the bootlist has been altered.
-o	Shows device name information if the bootlist has been altered.
-i	Disables the bootlist specified with the -m option.
-f *file*	Reads device information from the specified file.
devices...	Specifies a device or devices to include in the bootlist.
attr=value	Is used to supply extra attributes to the specified bootdevice.
File Name: `bootlist`	**Directory:** /usr/bin **Type:** External
bootlist -m normal hdisk0 hdisk1	Sets boot order to hdisk0 and hdisk1.

bootparamd

UNIX Shell:	All primary shells (csh, ksh, bsh)
Function	Provides information to diskless clients for booting by searching the bootparams database or the /etc/bootparams file.
Syntax	bootparamd [-d]

-d	Shows debug information.
File Name: `bootparamd`	**Directory:** /usr/bin/ **Type:** External

bootpd

UNIX Shell:	All primary shells (csh, ksh, bsh)
Function	Sets up the Internet Boot Protocol server.
Syntax	bootpd [options...]

-s	Runs `bootp` in a stand-alone configuration.
-t *Integer*	Specifies the timeout value in minutes. The default is 15 minutes; 0 means forever.
-g	Uses the same gateway IP address that is in the bootp request.
configfile	Specifies the configuration file. The default is /etc/bootptab.
dumpfile	Specifies where the bootpd daemon will dump a copy of the bootp server database.
File Name: `bootpd`	**Directory:** /usr/sbin/ **Type:** External

bootptodhcp

UNIX Shell:	All primary shells (csh, ksh, bsh)
Function	Converts between bootp and dhcp, or removes bootp entries from a dhcp configuration file.
Syntax	bootptodhcp [options...]

-d *dhcpfile*	Specifies the dhcp configuration file to put old bootp information into.
-b *bootpfile*	Specifies the bootp configuration file to be converted.
-r *hostname*	Specifies the bootp entry hostname to remove from the dhcp configuration file.
File Name: `bootptodhcp`	**Directory:** /usr/sbin/ **Type:** External

bosboot

UNIX Shell:	All primary shells (csh, ksh, bsh)
Function	Copies or creates a boot image.
Syntax	bosboot option [options...]

	One of the following three options is required, and they can't be combined:
-a	Creates a boot image and device.
-w *file*	Copies the specified device boot image to a device.
-r *file*	Creates a Read Only Storage emulation boot image.
-d *device*	Specifies the boot device.

continued

-p *proto*	Specifies a prototype file to use.
-k *kernel*	Specifies a kernel file to use for the boot image.
-U	Creates an uncompressed boot image.
-I	Loads and starts the low-level debugger.
-D	Only loads the low-level debugger.
-l *lvdev*	Uses the specified boot logical volume as a boot image.
-L	Enables lock instrumentation for multi processor systems.
-M *action*	Specifies the boot mode.
norm	Uses normal boot mode.
serv	Uses service boot mode.
both	Uses both modes.
-O *number*	Specifies an offset from the beginning of a CD-R boot image of CD-R device.
-T *type*	Specifies the type of the hardware platform.
-b *file*	Specifies a name for the boot image.
-q	Simulates the size needed to create a boot image.
File Name: bosboot	**Directory:** /usr/sbin/ **Type:** External

bosdebug

UNIX Shell: All primary shells (csh, ksh, bsh)

Function	Enables, disables, or shows the status of debugging information on the system.
Syntax	bosdebug [options...]

	To enable the status information of the system, select the -I or -D option.
-I	Sets the kernel debug program to be loaded and invoked on each subsequent reboot.
-D	Sets the kernel debug program to be loaded on each subsequent reboot.
-M	Enables the memory overlay detection system; can be used with following options:
-S	Triggers the memory overlay detection to set the next higher multiple of page size.
-s sizelist	Sets memory overlay detection to promote each specified allocation to a full page.
-n sizelist	Same as the -s option, but used for network memory.
-o	Disables all debugging features of the system.
-L	Shows settings for the kernel debug program and the memory overlay detection system.
File Name: bosdebug	**Directory:** /usr/sbin/ **Type:** External

bs

UNIX Shell: All primary shells (csh, ksh, bsh)

Function	Compiles and interprets smaller programs; also used for debugging.
Syntax	bs *{ file } { arguments... }*

file	Specifies a file of program statements.
arguments...	Gives additional instructions to the program. Example: use arg or narg.
File Name: bs	**Directory:** /usr/ccs/bin/ **Type:** External
bs < input.n > ucgteam	Executes the bs command, and directs the result to a file called ucgteam.

bsh

UNIX Shell: Bourne shell (bsh)

Function	Invokes the Bourne shell; also works as an interactive command interpreter and command programming language.
Syntax	bsh [options...] *{ file } { parameter }*

-a	Marks for export all variables to which an assignment is performed.
-c *command*	Runs the specified command.
-e	Exits immediately after receiving conditions from a command.
-f	Disables filename generation.
-h	Finds and remembers commands defined as a function in functions.
-k	Places all keyword parameters in the environment for a command.
-n	Reads commands, but don't run them.
-r	Invokes the restricted shell.
-s	Reads the commands from STDIN.
-t	Reads and runs one command, and then exits.
-u	Exits after finding unset variables when performing variable substitution.

continued

-v	Shows shell input lines when they are being read.
-x	Echoes each command before they are executed. (If + is used instead of -, the flag is turned off.)
file	Specifies a file that contains a bsh script.
parameter	Specifies a parameter to the script.
File Name: bsh	**Directory:** /usr/bin/ **Type:** External

bterm

UNIX Shell: All primary shells (csh, ksh, bsh)

Function	A bidirectional terminal emulator.
Syntax	bterm [options...]

-maps *map*	Specifies a keyboard mapping.
-help	Shows help information.
-keywords	Shows available keywords.
-nobidi	Turns off bidirectional mode.
-symmetric	Turns on the symmetric swapping mode.
-autopush	Turns on the autopush mode.
-or *orientation*	Specifies screen orientation.
-text *texttype*	Specifies the data stream type.
-csd *charshape*	Specifies Arabic character shapes: automatic, isolated, initial, middle, final.
-tail	Writes the Arabic characters seen, sheen, sad, and dad in two cells.
-nonulls	Starts the screen with spaces instead of nulls.
File Name: bterm	**Directory:** /usr/bin/ **Type:** External

bugfiler

UNIX Shell: All primary shells (csh, ksh, bsh)

Function	Stores bug reports in a mail directory.
Syntax	bugfiler [options...] *{ maildir }*

-d	Shows debug information.
-b *user*	Specifies a user other than the one who is logged in.
-m *messagemode*	Specifies protection for the message in one of the following three modes: user, group, or other.
maildir	Specifies a mail directory other than the logged-in user's directory.
File Name: bugfiler	**Directory:** /usr/lib/ **Type:** External

burst

UNIX Shell: All primary shells (csh, ksh, bsh)

Function	Allows a message to be split into several new messages.
Syntax	burst [+folder] *messages...* [options...]

-inplace	Adds a table of contents for each digest instead of the digest.
-noinplace	Maintains the digest and doesn't add a table of contents. (Is default.)
-quiet	Disables message reporting about messages that are not in digest format.
-noquiet	Reports non-digest format messages (Is default.)
-verbose	Verbose mode. Shows more information.
-noverbose	Disables verbose mode (Is default.)
-help	Shows help information.
+folder	Specifies the target folder of the message to burst; the default is the current folder.
messages...	Specifies the messages to divide. This can be single or multiple messages.
File Name: burst	**Directory:** /usr/bin/ **Type:** External

cachefslog

UNIX Shell: All primary shells (csh, ksh, bsh)

Function	Shows where the statistics for CacheFS are being logged. Can also redirects logs to another location, or stop logging.
Syntax	cachefslog [option] *mountpoint*

-f *logfile*	Sets the log file where you want to log the statistics.
-h	Stops logging.
-v	Verbose mode. Shows more information.

continued

mountpoint		Specifies the mount point of a cache file system; all files under the point will be logged.			
File Name:	cachefslog	**Directory:**	/usr/sbin/	**Type:**	External
cachefslog /cache/home		Checks if the directory /cache/home is logged.			
cachefslog -h /cache/home		Stops the logging of /cache/home.			

cachefswssize

UNIX Shell: All primary shells (csh, ksh, bsh)

Function	Shows the workspace size and the total cache size statistics for the specified cache log file.
Syntax	cachefswssize *logfile*

logfile		Specifies the name of the cachefs log file to show statistics for.			
File Name:	cachefswssize	**Directory:**	/usr/sbin/	**Type:**	External

calendar

UNIX Shell: All primary shells (csh, ksh, bsh)

Function	Reads from the calendar file and shows any scheduled events.
Syntax	calendar [-]

-		Reads the calendar file in everyone's login directory and send a mail message.			
File Name:	calendar	**Directory:**	/usr/bin/	**Type:**	External

cancel

UNIX Shell: All primary shells (csh, ksh, bsh)

Function	Kills print requests to the lp command. It stops print requests related to a specified queue or printer.
Syntax	cancel *ACTION*

ACTION		**Select only one of these two ACTIONS:**			
JobIDs...		Cancels the specified print request, even if it is printing out.			
printer		Cancels printing on the specified queue. If the initiator is root, all jobs die.			
File Name:	cancel	**Directory:**	/usr/bin/	**Type:**	External
cancel 101 102		Cancels the print jobs 101 and 102 on the local printer.			

canonls

UNIX Shell: All primary shells (csh, ksh, bsh)

Function	Processes one or more troff command output for the Canon LASER SHOT in LIPS III mode.
Syntax	canonls [options...] *{ files... }*

-eg *File*		Sets the Gothic font for the IBM Japanese extended character set.			
-em *File*		Sets the Mincho font for the IBM Japanese extended character set.			
-F *Directory*		Specifies the directory to find the font files in.			
-ug *File*		Sets the Gothic font for the user-defined characters in Japanese.			
-um *File*		Sets the Mincho font for the user-defined characters in Japanese.			
files...		Specifies the files to act on.			
File Name:	canonls	**Directory:**	/usr/bin/	**Type:**	External

capture

UNIX Shell: All primary shells (csh, ksh, bsh)

Function	Takes a screen dump of a terminal.
Syntax	capture [-a] *{ file }*

-a		Appends the output to the specified file.			
file		Specifies an output file.			
File Name:	capture	**Directory:**	/usr/bin/	**Type:**	External

catman

UNIX Shell: All primary shells (csh, ksh, bsh)

Function	Manages the manual pages and the windex database, which contains a short description of the commands.
Syntax	catman [options...] *{ sections... }*

-n	Does not allow the `windex` database to be created or re-created.
-p	Show what would be done, but do not execute the changes.

continued

-w	Reads the BSD-style man page, then the hypertext base, and creates the whatis database.
-M *directory*	Updates the man pages located in the specified directory.
sections...	Updates the man page section specified. Use whole numbers: 1, 2, 3,...
File Name: `catman`	**Directory:** /usr/sbin/ **Type:** External

cb

UNIX Shell: All primary shells (csh, ksh, bsh)

Function	Reads the C source codes from STDIN or specified files and writes the code in a structured way to STDOUT.
Syntax	cb [options...] *{ files... }*

-s	Formats the source code according to the style of Kernighan and Ritchie.
-l *length*	Splits lines that are longer than Length characters.
-j	Joins split lines; ignored if the -l flag is given.
files...	Specifies the C program files to use as input.
File Name: `cb`	**Directory:** /usr/bin/ **Type:** External

cfgif

UNIX Shell: All primary shells (csh, ksh, bsh)

Function	Manages network interface instances in the system configuration database.
Syntax	cfgif [options...]

-l *interfaceinstance*	Specifies which network interface instance to manage.
-2	Specifies that ifconfig will run in the second phase of the initial program load.
File Name: `cfgif`	**Directory:** /usr/lib/methods/ **Type:** External

cfginet

UNIX Shell: All primary shells (csh, ksh, bsh)

Function	Manages configuration of Internet instances and their interface instances.
Syntax	cfginet [-2]

-2	Configures the device in the second phase of the initial program load.
File Name: `cfginet`	**Directory:** /usr/lib/methods/ **Type:** External

cfgmgr

UNIX Shell: All primary shells (csh, ksh, bsh)

Function	Configures devices and installs device software specified in the Configuration Rules object class.
Syntax	cfgmgr [options...]

-f	Runs the phase 1 configuration rules, but is not valid after system start.
-s	Runs the phase 2 configuration rules.
-i*device*	Specifies the installation medium.
-l *name*	Configures the named device along with its children.
-v	Verbose mode. Shows more information.
File Name: `cfgmgr`	**Directory:** /usr/sbin/ **Type:** External
cfgmgr -l scsi0	Configures only the scsi0 device and its children.

cfgqos

UNIX Shell: All primary shells (csh, ksh, bsh)

Function	Manages the quality of service instances.
Syntax	cfgqos
File Name: `cfgqos`	**Directory:** /usr/lib/methods/ **Type:** External

cflow

UNIX Shell: All primary shells (csh, ksh, bsh)

Function	Analyzes the C and C++ and object files, and generates a flow graph of external references to STDOUT.
Syntax	cflow [options...] *files...*

-d*number*	Specifies with a decimal integer the depth at which the flow graph is cut off.
-I *directory*	Adds a list of directories in which cflow searches for #include files.

continued

-i_	Adds names beginning with an underline character.
-ip	Disables ANSI function prototypes.
-ix	Adds external and static data symbols; the default gives only functions.
-q *option*	Sends the specified option to the preprocessor.
-r	Creates an inverted and sorted listing that shows the callers of each function.
-MA	Specifies ANSI C code mode.
-U *name*	Erases any initial definition of the name parameter.
-Nd *number*	Alters the dimension table size to the number parameter (default is 2000).
-Nl *number*	Alters the number of type nodes to the number parameter (default is 8000).
-Nn *number*	Alters the symbol table size to the number parameter (default is 1500).
-Nt *number*	Alters the number of tree nodes to the number parameter (default is 1000).
-D *name(definition)*	Defines the name parameter, as if by the #define statement (default definition is 1).
files...	Specifies file to act on.
File Name: `cflow`	**Directory:** /usr/bin/ **Type:** External

cfsadmin

UNIX Shell: All primary shells (csh, ksh, bsh)

Function	A disk space administration utility for use with the cache File System (cacheFS).
Syntax	cfsadmin option [options...] *cachedir* cfsadmin -s *action*

	The following options can't be combined:
-c	Creates a cache directory under the specified directory.
-d *option*	Removes a cache directory. The options can be one of the following two:
cacheID	Removes the cache directory that has the specified cacheID.
all	Removes all file systems in the cache directory.
-l	Show the file systems in the cache directory.
-s *action*	Runs a consistency check on mounted file system. Action can be one of the following:
mountpoint	Runs a consistency check on the specified mountpoint only.
all	Runs a consistency check on all cache file systems.
-u	Updates resource parameters for the specified cache directory.
	The following options are file-system-specific, and can only be used with -c and -u:
-o *fstype-specific*	File-system-specific options can be used together, separated with a comma.
maxblocks=*n*	Specifies the maximum space that cacheFS can use, as a percentage.
minblocks=*n*	Specifies the minimum space that cacheFS can use, as a percentage.
threshblocks=*n*	Specifies the maximum number of blocks that cacheFS can use in the front file system.
threshfiles=*n*	Specifies the maximum number of inodes that cacheFS can use in the front file system.
maxfiles=*n*	Specifies the maximum number of files that cacheFS can use, as a percentage of inodes.
minfiles=*n*	Specifies the minimum number of files that cacheFS can use, as a percentage of inodes.
maxfilesize=*n*	Sets the largest allowed file size for the cache directory.
	The following can be used together with the -c, -d, -l and -u options:
cachedir	Specifies the cache directory that you want to manage.
File Name: `cfsadmin`	**Directory:** /usr/sbin/ **Type:** External

chargefee

UNIX Shell: All primary shells (csh, ksh, bsh)

Function	An accounting command used to charge units to a login.
Syntax	chargefee *user NR*

user	Specifies the login name to charge units from.
NR	Specifies the number of units to charge.
File Name: `chargefee`	**Directory:** /usr/sbin/acct/ **Type:** External

chauthent

UNIX Shell: All primary shells (csh, ksh, bsh)

Function	Manages the authentication method for the system.
Syntax	chauthent [options...]

-k5	Changes to the Kerberos 5 authentication method.

continued

-k4	Changes to the Kerberos 4 authentication method.		
-std	Changes to the standard AIX authentication method.		
File Name: chauthent	**Directory:** /usr/bin/	**Type:**	External

chclass

UNIX Shell: All primary shells (csh, ksh, bsh)

Function	Manages workload management classes.
Syntax	chclass -a *attribute=value* [options...] *name*

-a *attribute=value*	Specifies the attribute and its new value; can be repeated.		
-c *keyword=value*	Alters the limit or shares values for the cpu.		
-m *keyword=value*	Alters the limit or shares values for the memory.		
-d *confdir*	Specifies a configuration directory other than the default.		
name	Specifies the class to modify.		
File Name: chclass	**Directory:** /usr/sbin/	**Type:**	External

chcons

UNIX Shell: All primary shells (csh, ksh, bsh)

Function	Redirects the system console to a specified device or file. The change is effective on the next startup of the system.
Syntax	chcons [options...] *file*

-a *login=enable | disable*	Enables or disables login from the screen for all run levels on the next startup.		
-a *console_logname=file*	Specifies a full pathname for the console output log file.		
-a *console_logsize*	Specifies the size of the console output log file, in bytes.		
-a *console_logverb*	Specifies, by a number 1-9, the verbosity level for console output logging; 0=disable.		
-a *console_tagverb=number*	Specifies, by a number 1-9, the verbosity level for console output tagging; 0=disable.		
file	Specifies the device or file to redirect to.		
File Name: chcons	**Directory:** /usr/sbin/	**Type:**	External
Warning:	CAUTION: If the console is the only login terminal on the system, don't use the -a login=disable flag.		
chcons /dev/tty3	Sets /dev/tty3 as the default console.		

chdev

UNIX Shell: All primary shells (csh, ksh, bsh)

Function	Changes the characteristics of a specified device, whether the device is in a defined, stopped, or available state.
Syntax	chdev -l *name* [options...]

-l *name*	Specifies the logical name of device on which the characteristics will be changed.		
-a *attribute=value*	Specifies which device attribute/value pairs to change to.		
-f *file*	Reads the required flags from the specified file.		
-h	Shows the command usage message.		
-p *parentname*	Specifies which new device logical name the parent device will change to.		
-P	Changes the device's characteristics without changing the device.		
-T	Changes the characteristics of the device temporarily. Can't be used with the -P flag.		
-q	Suppresses output messages from STDOUT and STDERR.		
-w *connectionlocation*	Specifies the new connection location on the parent; not supported by all devices.		
File Name: chdev	**Directory:** /usr/sbin/	**Type:**	External
chdev -l scsi0 -a id=6 -P	Changes the id attribute on scsi0.		

chdisp

UNIX Shell: All primary shells (csh, ksh, bsh)

Function	Changes the default display to use with the system.
Syntax	chdisp [options...]

-d *device*	Temporarily changes the display device; it changes back on the next reboot.		
-p *device*	Permanently changes the default display device.		
File Name: chdisp	**Directory:** /usr/bin/	**Type:**	External

chdoclang

chdoclang	UNIX Shell:	All primary shells (csh, ksh, bsh)
Function	Manages documentation language.	
Syntax	chdoclang [options...] *language*	

-d	Removes the default documentation language.
-u *uid*	Modifies settings for a specific userID.
username	Modifies settings for a specific username.
language	Specifies the language to change to.
File Name: `chdoclang`	**Directory:** /usr/bin/ **Type:** External
chdoclang en_US	Changes the default documentation language to English.

chdsmitd

chdsmitd	UNIX Shell:	All primary shells (csh, ksh, bsh)
Function	Manages a domain from the DSMIT member list.	
Syntax	chdsmitd [options...] *domain*	

-a	Adds a host to the specified domain.
-d *domain*	Specifies one or more domain names.
-m *machine*	Specifies one or more hostnames.
-o *os*	Specifies one or more operating systems.
-r	Redefines a member list for a domain.
-s	Removes a host from the domain.
-x	Uses the intersection of a subset of hosts specified by the -d, -m, and -o options.
-?	Shows help information.
domain	Specifies the domain to manage.
File Name: `chdsmitd`	**Directory:** /usr/share/DSMIT/ **Type:** External

checkcw

checkcw	UNIX Shell:	All primary shells (csh, ksh, bsh)
Function	Manages the balance between left and right delimiters and .CW and .CN pairs.	
Syntax	checkcw [options...] *{ files... }*	

-l *delimiter*	Sets the left delimiter as a 1- or 2-character string (default is undefined).
-r *delimiter*	Sets the right delimiter to the specified value.
files...	Specifies file to act on.
File Name: `checkcw`	**Directory:** /usr/bin/ **Type:** External

checkeq

checkeq	UNIX Shell:	All primary shells (csh, ksh, bsh)
Function	Creates a report of wrong or lost delimiters and equation start/end markers (EQ/EN). This is useful when you use the eqn and neqn language processors on a text file.	
Syntax	checkeq *{ files... }*	

files...	Specifies the file to verify.
File Name: `checkeq`	**Directory:** /usr/bin/ **Type:** External

checkmm

checkmm	UNIX Shell:	All primary shells (csh, ksh, bsh)
Function	Checks documents formatted with memorandum macros, checks syntax errors in files prepared for mm or mmt.	
Syntax	checkmm *{ files... }*	

files...	Specifies the file to check.
File Name: `checkmm`	**Directory:** /usr/bin/ **Type:** External

checknr

UNIX Shell:	All primary shells (csh, ksh, bsh)
Function	Checks `nroff` or `troff` files for errors such as missing delimiters and unknown commands.
Syntax	checknr [options...] *files...*

-a *.x.y*	Adds macro pairs to the list of pairs to check.
-c *.x.y*	Defines commands that otherwise would create error messages.
-f	Ignores \f font changes.
-s	Ignores \s size changes.
files...	Specifies the file to verify. The default is STDIN.
File Name: `checknr`	**Directory:** /usr/bin/ **Type:** External

chfilt

UNIX Shell:	All primary shells (csh, ksh, bsh)
Function	Manages filter rule definitions in a filter rule table.
Syntax	chfilt options [options...]

	The following two options are required:
-v *4 | 6*	Specifies the IP version of the filter rule.
-n *fid*	Specifies the ID of the filter rule.
	The following options are optional:
-a *D | P*	Denies or permits traffic.
-s *saddr*	Specifies the source address, either a hostname or an IP address.
-m *mask*	Specifies the subnet mask for the source address.
-d *daddr*	Specifies the destination address, either a hostname or an IP address.
-M *mask*	Specifies the subnet mask for the destination address.
-g *Y | N*	Specifies that filter rules apply to source routed packets.
-c *protocol*	Specifies the protocol: udp, icmp, icmpv6, tcp, tcp/ack, ospf, ipip, esp, ah, or all.
-o *sourceop*	Compares the icmp type and source port with the filter rule values.
-p *sourceport*	Specifies the source port and ICMP type to compare to the IP packet source port.
-O *destop*	Specifies the destination port or operation code for icmp: lt, le, gt, ge, eq, neq, or any.
-P *destport*	Specifies the destination port and icmp code to compare to the destination IP port.
-r *value*	Specifies the rules apply to routed packets. Use one of the following values:
R	Enables the rules on forwarded packets.
L	Enables the rules for packet sent from the localhost or destined for the localhost.
B	Enables the rules for both forwarded packets and packets to or from the localhost.
-w *value*	Specifies the direction where rules apply: I for incoming, O for outgoing, and B for both.
-l *Y | N*	Specifies if you want to log all packets that match the filter's rules.
-f *value*	Specifies how to handle packets that are fragmented. Select one of the following values:
Y	Enables fragmentation control on all packets.
H	Enables fragmentation control only on headers and unfragmented packets.
O	Enables fragmentation control only on headers and fragmented packets.
N	Enables fragmentation control only on unfragmented packets.
-t *ID*	Specifies a tunnel ID for rules. The rules only apply for packets with the same ID.
-i	Specifies the IP device interface to enable the filters on; all, tr0, en0, lo0.
File Name: `chfilt`	**Directory:** /usr/sbin/ **Type:** External

chfn

UNIX Shell:	All primary shells (csh, ksh, bsh)
Function	An interactive utility that changes a user's finger information.
Syntax	chfn *name*

name	Specifies which user's finger information to change.
File Name: `chfn`	**Directory:** /usr/bin/ **Type:** External

chfont

chfont				**UNIX Shell:**	**All primary shells (csh, ksh, bsh)**
Function	Changes the default font selected at boot time. You must have root authority to run this command.				
Syntax	chfont [FontID]				
fontID		Specifies the id of the new font.			
File Name:	chfont	**Directory:**	/usr/bin/	**Type:**	External

chfs

chfs				**UNIX Shell:**	**All primary shells (csh, ksh, bsh)**
Function	Changes specified attributes of a file system.				
Syntax	chfs [option] *{ filesystem }*				
-n *name*		Specifies which node name to change.			
-m *point*		Specifies a new mount point for the node.			
-u *group*		Specifies a mount group for the node.			
-A *yes or no*		Specifies if the file system is automatically mounted at system restart.			
-p *ro or rw*		Sets the permissions for the file system to `read-only` or `read-write`.			
-t *yes or no*		Specifies whether the file system accounting is processed by the accounting subsystem.			
-a *attribute=value*		Specifies Attribute=Value pairs, dependent on virtual file system type.			
-d *attribute*		Deletes the attribute from /etc/filesystems file for the specified file system.			
filesystem		Specifies the name of the file system, expressed as a mount point.			
File Name:	chfs	**Directory:**	/usr/sbin/	**Type:**	External
chfs -a size=+8192 /home			Increases the size of the /home file system.		

chgif

chgif				**UNIX Shell:**	**All primary shells (csh, ksh, bsh)**
Function	Changes the configuration of a network interface instance.				
Syntax	chgif [-d] options...				
-d		Makes the changes in the system configuration database only.			
-l *interfaceinstance*		Specifies the network interface instance to configure.			
-a *attribute=value*		Specifies the attributes and values to configure.			
netaddr		Specifies the IP address of the network card.			
state up | down		Marks the network card activated or deactivated.			
trailers on | off		Enables or disables trailer link level encapsulation.			
arp on | off		Turns the address resolution protocol on or off.			
allcast on | off		Specifies if broadcasts are to go to all of the token-ring network or just the local network.			
hwloop on | off		Turns hardware loopback on or off.			
netmask		Specifies the subnet mask.			
security level		Specifies the security level to configure.			
none		Specifies no security.			
unclassified		Specifies unclassified security.			
confidential		Specifies confidential security.			
secret		Specifies secret security.			
topsecret		Specifies top-secret security.			
authority level		Specifies the authority security level.			
genser		Specifies defense communications agency.			
siop		Specifies department of defense organization of the joint of chiefs of staff.			
dsccs-spintcom		Specifies defense intelligence agency.			
dsccs-criticom		Specifies national security agency.			
mtu		Specifies the maximum packet size for IP packets.			
broadcast		Specifies the broadcast address.			
dest		Specifies the destination address for a ppp link.			
File Name:	chgif	**Directory:**	/usr/lib/methods/	**Type:**	External

chginet

UNIX Shell:	All primary shells (csh, ksh, bsh)

Function	Changes the configuration for Internet instances.
Syntax	chginet [options...]

-d	Makes changes in the system configuration database only.
-a *attribute=value*	Specifies the attribute and the value to reconfigure.
hostname	Specifies the hostname.
gateway	Specifies the address for the default gateway.
route	Specifies the route in the format, route=destination, gateway, metric.
delroute	Specifies a route to be removed in the format route=destination, gateway, metric.

File Name:	chginet	**Directory:**	/usr/lib/methods/	**Type:**	External

chgroup

UNIX Shell:	All primary shells (csh, ksh, bsh)

Function	Changes attributes for groups.
Syntax	chgroup *attribute=values... group*

attribute=values...	Specifies which attribute to change.
adms=*{ loginnames... }*	Specifies users with group administration rights.
admin=*values...*	Specifies the group's administrative status. Select only one of the following values:
true	Sets the group as administrative.
false	Sets the group as a standard group (Is default).
id=*string*	Specifies the group ID; the value is a unique integer string.
users=*users...*	Specifies the users to modify attributes for.
group	Specifies the group to act on.

File Name:	chgroup	**Directory:**	/usr/bin/	**Type:**	External

Warning:	Do not use the chgroup command if you have a NIS database installed on your system. Changing the group ID compromises system security, so be careful changing this attribute.
chgroup users=sam,carol,frank sales	Adds sam and carol to the sales group, which currently only has frank as a member.

chgrpmem

UNIX Shell:	All primary shells (csh, ksh, bsh)

Function	Changes the administrators or members of a group.
Syntax	chgrpmem [options...] *group*

-a	Changes the administrators list for a group.
-m	Changes the members list for a group.
+	Adds a specified user.
-	Erases a specified user.
=	Sets the list administrators or members to the specified user.
group	Specifies the group to act on.

File Name:	chgrpmem	**Directory:**	/usr/bin/	**Type:**	External

chgrpmem -a - jones f612	Removes jones as an administrator of the f612 group.

chhwkbd

UNIX Shell:	All primary shells (csh, ksh, bsh)

Function	Changes keyboard attributes stored in the ODM database.
Syntax	chhwkbd [options...]

-d *delay*	Sets the keyboard repetition delay: 250, 500, 750, or 1000 msec.
-r *repetition*	Sets the rate of repetition to the specified value: 2-30 (default is 11).
-c *value*	Sets the clicker volume to the specified value: 0-3, off, low, medium, high.
-a *value*	Sets the alarm volume to the specified value: 0-3, off, low, medium, high.
-m	Removes extended keyboard identification.
["KR","JP","TW"]	Sets the Korean, Japanese, or Chinese keyboard.
-t	Disables numeric pad emulation.
["nonum"]	Enables numeric pad emulation.

continued

File Name:	chhwkbd	Directory:	/usr/bin/	Type:	External

chitab

UNIX Shell: All primary shells (csh, ksh, bsh)

Function	Changes records in the /etc/inittab file.
Syntax	chitab *{ identifier }* : *{ runlevel }* : *{ action }* : *{ command }*

identifier	Identifies an object. Can be 14 characters long, and must be unique.
runlevel	Defines the run levels where the `identifier` will be processed; maximum 20 characters.
action	Sets the action to be used by the init command; maximum 20 characters.
boot	Reads the /etc/inittab file when the system boots.
bootwait	Does not restart the process when system boots.
initdefault	Used by the init command to identify which run level to enter.
off	Sends a warning and waits 20 seconds before sending SIGKILL to stop the process.
once	Starts the process immediately, but does not restart a stopped process.
ondemand	Sets this action to perform the respawn action when using a, b, or c run levels.
powerwait	Runs the process only if a power fail signal is received, then continues.
respawn	Continues scanning the /etc/inittab file.
sysinit	Starts the process before the init command accesses the screen.
wait	Starts the process and waits for it to stop.
command	Specifies the shell command; can be 1024 characters long.

File Name:	chitab	Directory:	/usr/sbin/	Type:	External

chitab tty002:3:respawn:/usr/sbin/getty /dev/tty	Changes the run level of a record for tty2.

chkbd

UNIX Shell: All primary shells (csh, ksh, bsh)

Function	Changes the software keyboard map to be loaded into the system at the next initial program load.
Syntax	chkbd *name*

name	Specifies the name of the keyboard map.

File Name:	chkbd	Directory:	/usr/bin/	Type:	External

chkey

UNIX Shell: All primary shells (csh, ksh, bsh)

Function	Creates a new encryption key, asks for a password, and updates the `/etc/publickey` file.
Syntax	chkey

File Name:	chkey	Directory:	/usr/bin/	Type:	External

chlang

UNIX Shell: Korn shell (ksh)

Function	Manages language settings for the system or for a user.
Syntax	chlang [options...] *lang*

-d	Deletes the NLSPATH environment variable from the /etc/environment file.
-u *uid*	Specifies a userID to modify settings for.
-u *user*	Specifies a user name to modify settings for.
-m *msgtranslist*	Specifies a colon-separated list of message translations to make to the NLSPATH.
-M	Resets the LC_MESSAGES and NLSPATH environment variables.
lang	Specifies the language locale to use.

File Name:	chlang	Directory:	/usr/bin/	Type:	Script

chlicense

UNIX Shell: All primary shells (csh, ksh, bsh)

Function	Changes the status of user-floating licensing for the system and changes the number of user-fixed licenses.
Syntax	chlicense [options...]

-u *license*	Changes the number of fixed licenses. The value must be greater than 0.
-f *on / off*	Changes the status of the floating licensing; must be on or off.

File Name:	chlicense	Directory:	/usr/bin/	Type:	External

chlv

UNIX Shell:	Korn shell (ksh)
Function	Is used to manage characteristics of a logical volume.
Syntax	chlv [options...] *logicalvolumes...*

-a *position*	Sets the allocation policy for an intraphysical volume. Position values are as follows:
m	Assigns partition in the outer middle section of each volume (Is default).
c	Assigns partitions in the center section of each volume.
e	Assigns partitions in the outer edge section of each volume.
ie	Assigns partitions in the inner edge section of each volume.
im	Assigns partitions in the inner middle section of each volume.
-b *badblocks*	Sets the policy for bad-block relocation. Use one of the following variables:
y	Causes bad block relocation to occur.
n	Stops bad block relocation from occurring.
-d *schedule*	Sets the scheduling policy if multiple partitions are written. Optional variables:
p	Creates a parallel scheduling policy.
s	Creates a sequential scheduling policy.
-e *range*	Sets the allocations policy of the interphysical volume. **range is limited by variables set by -u flag, being one of the following:**
x	Assigns partitions across the maximum number of volumes.
m	Assigns partitions across the minimum number of volumes.
-L *label*	Specifies the logical volume label. Maximum size is 127 characters.
-p*permission*	Changes the access permission between read-write or read-only:
w	Permits read-write access.
r	Permits read-only access.
-r *relocate* y or n	Allows or prevents relocation of the logical volume during reorganization.
-s *strict* y or n	Sets the allocation policy. Copies of a partition can share the same volume or not.
-t *type*	Specifies the logical volume type. Maximum is 31 characters.
-u *upperbound*	Sets the maximum number of volumes for new allocation.
-v *verify* y or no	Specifies whether all writes to the volume will be verified by a follow-up read.
-w *MirrorCons* y or no	Turns mirror write consistency on or off, ensuring data consistency of volume copies.
-x *maximum*	Specifies how many logical partitions can be allocated to the logical volume.
-U *userid*	Defines the user ID for the logical volume special file.
-G *groupid*	Specifies the group ID for the logical volume special file.
	To change the name of a logical volume
-n *NewVolume*	Specifies the new name of the volume; maximum 15 characters long.
logicalvolumes...	Specifies the logical volume to change.

File Name:	Directory:	Type:
`chlv`	/usr/sbin/	Script

chlvcopy

UNIX Shell:	Korn shell (ksh)
Function	Manages mirror copies on a logical volume.
Syntax	chlvcopy [options...] *logicalvol*

-f	Forces split mirror copies.
-B	Deactivates a mirror copy as split mirror copy.
-s	Starts a syncvg for the logical volume in the background.
-b	Activates a mirror copy as a split mirror copy.
-c *copy*	Specifies the number of mirrored copies to create.
-P	Keeps information about online split mirror copies after a reboot.
-l *newlv*	Specifies the new name of the backup logical volume.
-w	Makes split mirror copies writeable.
logicalvol	Specifies the logical volume to work with.

File Name:	Directory:	Type:
`chlvcopy`	/usr/sbin/	Script

chlvcopy -c 3 lv00	Creates three mirrored copies of lv00.

chmaster

UNIX Shell:	Bourne shell (bsh)
Function	Runs the ypinit command and restarts the NIS daemons to change a master server.
Syntax	chmaster [options...]

-s *hosts...*	Specifies the slave hostname, or names for the slave for this master server.
-O	Overwrites existing maps for this domain.
-o	Prevents overwriting of NIS maps (Is default).
-E	Exits from the ypinit and chmaster commands if errors are found (Is default).
-e	Suppresses exiting from ypinit and chmaster if errors are found.
-P	Starts the yppasswdd daemon and the ypserv daemon.
-p	Suppresses the start of the yppasswdd daemon (Is default).
-U	Starts the ypupdated daemon and the ypserv daemon.
-u	Suppresses the start of the ypupdated daemon (Is default).
-C	Starts the ypbind daemon and the ypserv daemon (Is default).
-I	Changes /etc/rc.nfs to start suitable daemons on the next restart.
-B	Updates etc/rc.nfs to start suitable daemons, and invokes ypinit.
-N	Invokes the ypinit command and starts the suitable daemons.

File Name:	Directory:	Type:
`chmaster`	/usr/sbin/	Script

chnamsv

UNIX Shell:	All primary shells (csh, ksh, bsh)
Function	Manages TCP/IP based name service configuration on a host, but does not change the name server database.
Syntax	chnamsv [option]

-a *"attribute=value ..."*	Specifies values for updating server initialization files in the database.
-A *filename*	Specifies the file containing the named server initialization information.

File Name:	Directory:	Type:
`chnamsv`	/usr/sbin/	External

chnfs

UNIX Shell:	Bourne shell (bsh)
Function	Manages how many biod and nfsd daemons to start.
Syntax	chnfs [options...]

-n *number*	Specifies how many nfsd daemons to run on the system.
-b *number*	Specifies how many biod daemons to run on the system.
-I	Changes the source database so the specified daemons will run on next restart.
-B	Momentarily stops the daemons currently running on the system, and modifies the database.
-N	Momentarily stops daemons currently running, and restarts the daemons indicated.

File Name:	Directory:	Type:
`chnfs`	/usr/sbin/	Script

chnfsexp

UNIX Shell:	Bourne shell (bsh)
Function	Manages export settings for directories to NFS clients.
Syntax	chnfsexp -d *directory* [options...]

-d *directory*	Specifies the exported directory to modify settings for.
-f *expfile*	Specifies an export file other than the default.
-t *type*	Specifies the mount access type allowed for clients.
rw	Exports directory in read-write mode.
ro	Exports directory in read-only mode.
rm	Exports directory in read-mostly mode. Must be used with the -h option.
-h *hostnames...*	Specifies the hosts that have read-write access to the directory.
-a *uid*	Uses the specified userID as the effective user.
-r *hostnames...*	Specifies that root users on the specified hosts have access.
-c *hostnames...*	Specifies that all users on the specified hosts have mount access.
-s	Requires clients to use secure protocol to access the directory.
-n	Does not require clients to use secure protocol to access the directory.

continued

-l	Exports the directory after next reboot.
-B	Exports the directory immediately.
-N	Does not modify the /etc/exports file, but run exportfs to change export settings.
-P	Exports the directory as a public directory.
-p	Exports the directory as a non-public directory.
File Name: chnfsexp	**Directory:** /usr/sbin/ **Type:** Script

chnfsmnt

UNIX Shell: All primary shells (csh, ksh, bsh)

Function	Manages mount settings for a directory on an NFS server.
Syntax	chnfsmnt options... [options...]

-f *path*	Specifies the mount point for the NFS directory. This is mandatory.
-d *remotedir*	Specifies the NFS directory to mount. This is mandatory.
-h *remotehost*	Specifies the NFS server to mount from. This is mandatory.
-t *action*	Specifies how to mount the directory:
rw	Mounts the directory as read-write.
ro	Mounts the directory as read-only.
-m *mounttype*	Mounts all specified unmounted directories.
-w *action*	Specifies how the mount should work.
fg	Mounts in the foreground.
bg	Mounts in the background.
-X	Supports long device numbers.
-x	Does not support long device numbers.
-S	Makes the mount a soft mount.
-H	Makes the mount a hard mount.
-Y	Allows suid and sgid program executions.
-y	Does not allow suid and sgid program executions.
-Z	Allows device access through mount.
-z	Does not allow device access through mount.
-E	Allows keyboard interrupts on hard mounts.
-e	Does not allow keyboard interrupts on hard mounts.
-A	Automatically mounts at reboot.
-a	Does not automatically mount at reboot.
-J	Uses ACL's on mount.
-j	Does not use ACL's on mount.
-q	Does not exchange any pathconf information if NFS version 2 is used.
-Q	Does not make POSIX pathconf information available on an NFS version 2 mount.
-G	Makes directories or files inherit the group ID of the parent directory.
-g	Does not make directories or files inherit the group ID of the parent directory.
-s	Uses more secure protocol.
-n	Does not use more secure protocol.
-B	Changes the /etc/filesystems entries and remounts the directory.
-N	Does not allow modification of the /etc/filesystems file.
-R *retrans*	Specifies how many times to make a request.
-b *readbuffsize*	Specifies the size of the read buffer in bytes.
-c *writebuffsize*	Specifies the size of the write buffer in bytes.
-r *tries*	Specifies the number of times to retry a mount.
-o *timeout*	Specifies the length of the NFS time out in tenths of a second.
-u *acregmin*	Sets the minimum seconds to hold cached attributes for file modification.
-U *acregmax*	Sets the maximum seconds to hold cached attributes for file modification.
-v *acdirmin*	Sets the minimum seconds to hold cached attributes for directory updates.
-V *acdirmax*	Sets the maximum seconds to hold cached attributes for directory updates.
-T *actimeo*	Sets the minimum and maximum time values for regular files and directories.
-p *numbiods*	Specifies the maximum number of biod daemons that are allowed on a file system.
-P *portnum*	Specifies the IP port number on the server.
-K *version*	Specifies the NFS version used for this NFS mount. Any, 2, or 3 can be used.

continued

-k *protocol*	Specifies the transport protocol used for the mount.
any	Makes the mount command choose a protocol.
tcp	Uses the TCP protocol.
udp	Uses the UDP protocol.
File Name: `chnfsmnt`	**Directory:** /usr/sbin/ **Type:** External

chprtsv

UNIX Shell: All primary shells (csh, ksh, bsh)

Function	Manages print service configurations.
Syntax	chprtsv option [options...]

	You must specify one of these two options:
-c	Manages print service for a client.
-s	Manages print service for a server.
	You may select one of these two options:
-d	Modifies the system database only.
-i	Modifies the system and the system database.
-h *hosts...*	Specifies the hosts allowed to use the print server.
-H *file*	Specifies a file with a list of hostnames to include.
-x *hosts...*	Specifies the hosts to exclude from the print service.
-X *file*	Specifies a file with a list of hostnames to exclude.
-q *qentry*	Specifies a qconfig file entry to remove.
-v *device*	Specifies a list of device stanzas to change.
-a *attr=value*	Specifies attributes for updating the spooler's qconfig file or object class.
	You may select one of these two options:
-b *attr=value*	Specifies attributes for the device stanza to update the spooler's qconfig or object class.
-A *file*	Specifies the name of the file with qconfig command-related entries.
File Name: `chprtsv`	**Directory:** /usr/sbin/ **Type:** External

chps

UNIX Shell: All primary shells (csh, ksh, bsh)

Function	Changes attributes of a paging space.
Syntax	chps [options...] *pagingspace*

-s *logicalpartitions*	Specifies the number of logical partitions to add.
-a yes | no	Specifies whether to use a paging space at the next system restart.
pagingspace	Specifies which paging space to change.
File Name: `chps`	**Directory:** /usr/sbin/ **Type:** External

chpv

UNIX Shell: All primary shells (csh, ksh, bsh)

Function	Changes the characteristics of a physical volume in a volume group.
Syntax	chpv [options...] *physicalvolumes...*

-a *allocation*	Specifies the allocation permission for additional physical partitions.
-v*availability*	Specifies the availability of the physical volume.
-c	Clears the boot record of the given physical volume.
physicalvolumes...	Specifies the physical volyme(s) to act on.
File Name: `chpv`	**Directory:** /usr/sbin/ **Type:** External

chque

UNIX Shell: All primary shells (csh, ksh, bsh)

Function	Changes the queue name in the config file.
Syntax	chque -q *name* [-a *"attribute=value"*]

-q *name*	Specifies the name of queue and of stanza in the qconfig file to be changed.
-a *"attribute=value"*	Specifies what value to add or replace with the one entered on command line.
File Name: `chque`	**Directory:** /usr/bin/ **Type:** External

chquedev

UNIX Shell:	All primary shells (csh, ksh, bsh)
Function	Changes the queue device names of printer or plotter.
Syntax	chquedev options... [-a *"attribute=value"*]

-q *name*	Specifies the queue name in which to change the device stanza.
-d *name*	Specifies the device name in the queue to be changed.
-a *"attribute=value"*	Specifies what stanza lines to change or add.

File Name:	Directory:	Type:
`chquedev`	/usr/bin/	External

chrole

UNIX Shell:	All primary shells (csh, ksh, bsh)
Function	Manages role attributes.
Syntax	chrole *attribute=value name*

attribute=value	Specifies the attribute to change and the new value.
name	Specifies the role for which to change the attributes.

File Name:	Directory:	Type:
`chrole`	/usr/bin/	External

chsec

UNIX Shell:	All primary shells (csh, ksh, bsh)
Function	Changes the attributes in the security stanza files.
Syntax	chsec [options...]

-f *file*	Specifies the stanza file to alter.
-s *stanza*	Specifies the stanza to alter.
-a *attribute = value*	Specifies the attribute to alter and the new value for that attribute.

File Name:	Directory:	Type:
`chsec`	/usr/bin/	External

chserver

UNIX Shell:	All primary shells (csh, ksh, bsh)
Function	Alters a subserver definition in the subserver object class.
Syntax	chserver -t *oldserver* [options...]

-t *oldserver*	Specifies the old name of the existing subserver.
-c *value*	Specifies the CodePoint integer that identifies the subserver.
-s *newsystem*	Specifies the name for the new subsystem on the subserver.
-t *newserver*	Specifies the new name of the existing subserver.

File Name:	Directory:	Type:
`chserver`	/usr/bin/	External

chservices

UNIX Shell:	Bourne shell (bsh)
Function	Manages the /etc/services file.
Syntax	chservices [-a] options... [-u *aliases...*]

-v *service*	Specifies the name of the service to manage.
-p *protocol*	Specifies the protocol that the service uses.
-n *port*	Specifies the port that the service uses.
-c	Makes changes to the /etc/services file.
-d	Deactivates entries in the /etc/services file.
-V *newservice*	Specifies a new name for the service.
-P *newprotocol*	Specifies a new protocol for the service.
-N *newport*	Specifies a new port for the service.
-u *aliases...*	Specifies a list of aliases to use.
-a	Adds or activates /etc/services entries.

File Name:	Directory:	Type:
`chservices`	/usr/sbin/	Script

chsh

UNIX Shell: All primary shells (csh, ksh, bsh)

Function	Changes the login shell for the current user or for the specified user.
Syntax	chsh *{ user } { shell }*

user	Specifies the user to change the shell for (the default is the current user).
shell	Specifies the shell to set for the specified user.

File Name:	`chsh`	**Directory:**	/usr/bin/	**Type:**	External

chslave

UNIX Shell: Bourne shell (bsh)

Function	Reruns the ypinit command to retrieve maps from a master server and restarts the ypserv daemon to change the slave server.
Syntax	chslave [options...] *master*

	The following two options can't be used together, but can be used with other options:
-C	Adds -n to ypinit (Is default).
-c	Stops the process when errors occur.
	The following two options can't be used together, but can be used with other options:
-O	Overwrites all maps in the domain.
-o	Prevents the overwrite of maps in the domain.
	The following three options can't be used together, but can be used with other options:
-I	Runs only ypinit immediately. Kills and restarts running ypserv daemon.
-B	Starts the ypinit command and the ypserv daemon (Is default).
-N	Starts the ypinit command and restarts the ypserv daemon.
master	Specifies the host of the master server.

File Name:	`chslave`	**Directory:**	/usr/sbin	**Type:**	Script

chssys

UNIX Shell: All primary shells (csh, ksh, bsh)

Function	Manages subsystem definitions in the subsystem object class.
Syntax	chssys -s *oldsubsys* [options...]

-s *oldsubsys*	Specifies the subsystem to modify.
-a *arguments...*	Passes arguments to the subsystem.
-e *stderr*	Specifies a STDERR for the subsystem.
-i *stdin*	Specifies a STDIN for the subsystem.
-o *stdout*	Specifies a STDOUT for the subsystem.
-p *path*	Specifies the absolute path to the subsystem.
-s *newsubsys*	Specifies a new name for the subsystem.
-u *userid*	Specifies the userID for the subsystem.
-O	Does not restart the subsystem if it abends.
-R	Restarts the subsystem if it abends.
-d	Shows inactive subsystems with the command lssrc -a.
-D	Does not show inactive subsystems with the command lssrc -a.
-q	Allows multiple instances to run on the subsystem.
-Q	Does not allow multiple instances to run on the subsystem.
-K	Uses sockets for communication.
-I *messqueue*	Uses message queues for communication.
-m *messtype*	Specifies the `MessageMtype` keys to send from the subsystem to the SRC.
-f *stopforce*	Specifies a stop signal to send to the subsystem when a force stop is requested.
-n *stopnorm*	Specifies a stop signal to send to the subsystem when a normal stop is requested.
-S	Uses signals for communication.
-E *nice*	Sets a nice value for the subsystem.
-G *group*	Specifies which group the subsystem belongs to.
-w *wait*	Specifies the time to wait between SIGTERM and SIGKILL.

File Name:	`chssys`	**Directory:**	/usr/bin/	**Type:**	External

chsubserver

UNIX Shell: All primary shells (csh, ksh, bsh)

Function	Manages the contents of the /etc/inetd.conf file.
Syntax	chsubserver [option] options... [options...] *{ program arguments... }*

	Use this option first if you want to add or activate a server or subserver entry:
-a	Adds or activates an entry in the configuration file; optional.
	Use this option first if you want to change a server entry:
-c	Changes entries in the configuration file.
	Use this option first if you want to deactivate a server entry:
-d	Deactivates entries in the /etc/inetd.conf file.
	You must use these two options in the order that they appear here:
-v *service*	Specifies the service to work with.
-p *protocol*	Specifies the protocol to work with.
-t *sockettype*	Specifies a type of socket to work with.
-w *waitindicator*	Specifies the wait indicator, either wait or nowait.
-u *user*	Specifies a user name to work with.
-g *program*	Specifies which program to start.
-V *newservice*	Specifies a new service name.
-P *newprotocol*	Specifies a new protocol for the service.
-T *newsocket*	Specifies a new socket for the service.
-W *newwaitindicator*	Replaces the existing wait indicator with a new one.
-U *newuser*	Replaces the existing user name.
-G *newprogram*	Replaces the program to start.
-r *server*	Sends a SIGHUP signal to the specified server.
-C *conffile*	Specifies a configuration file other than the /etc/inetd.conf.
program	Specifies the server or subserver to work with.
arguments...	Specifies additional arguments to pass to the server or subserver.

File Name:	chsubserver	**Directory:**	/usr/sbin/	**Type:**	External

chtcb

UNIX Shell: All primary shells (csh, ksh, bsh)

Function	Changes or queries the specified trusted computing base attribute of a file.
Syntax	chtcb [options...] *file*

on	Enables the trusted computing base attribute.
off	Disables the trusted computing base attribute.
query	Shows the value of the trusted computing base attribute.
file	Specifies which file to change or query.

File Name:	chtcb	**Directory:**	/usr/sbin/	**Type:**	External

chtun

UNIX Shell: All primary shells (csh, ksh, bsh)

Function	Changes the tunnel definition between a local host and a partner host.
Syntax	chtun [options...]

	The following options are valid for manual tunnels:
-A *algorithm*	Sets the authentication algorithm used by the destination for IP packet encryption.
-a *algorithm*	Sets the authentication algorithm used by the source host for IP packet authentication.
-B *algorithm*	Specifies destination ESP authentication algorithm (new header format only).
-C *key*	Specifies destination ESP authentication key, as a hexadecimal string starting with Ox.
-c *key*	Specifies source ESP authentication key, as a hexadecimal string starting with Ox.
-E *algorithm*	Sets the encryption algorithm used by the destination for IP packet encryption.
-N *spi*	Specifies the security parameter index for the ESP destination.
-n *spi*	Specifies the security parameter index for the ESP source.
-P *policy*	Specifies how IP packet authentication and/or encryption is used by the destination.
-U *spi*	Specifies the security parameter index for the AH destination.
-u *spi*	Specifies the security parameter index for the AH source.
-y y | n	Sets the reply prevention flag using yes or no; only valid with the new header format.

continued

-z	Sets the new header format flag that allows ESP authentication.
	The following options are valid for IBM tunnels:
-i y | n	Specifies which partner starts the negotiations; y for local host starts, n for target host.
-k *key*	Specifies the key string for the source, used to create a tunnel. Hexadecimal "Ox".
-r *refresh*	Specifies the overlap time of the new key start and an old key expiration, from 1 to -720 minutes.
	The following are general options:
-e *algorithm*	Specifies the encryption algorithm used by the source host for IP packet encryption.
-f *fw*	Specifies the IP address of the firewall between the source and destination hosts.
-m	Uses the default tunnel if -f is specified.
-H *key*	Specifies the destination AH destination key, as a hexadecimal string starting with Ox.
-h *key*	Specifies the destination AH source key, as a hexadecimal string starting with Ox.
-K *key*	Specifies the destination ESP destination key, as a hexadecimal string starting with Ox.
-l *key*	Specifies the lifetime in minutes.
-p *source*	Sets how the source uses IP packet authentication.
-s *address*	Specifies the interface IP address to be used by the tunnel.
-v 4 or 6	Specifies the IP version to create the tunnel for.
-t *tunnelNR*	Specifies the number of the tunnel identifier.

File Name:	`chtun`	**Directory:**	/usr/sbin/	**Type:**	External

chtz

UNIX Shell: Korn shell (ksh)

Function	Manages the TZ environment variable in the /etc/environment file.
Syntax	chtz *TimeZone*

TimeZone	Specifies the time zone variable.

File Name:	`chtz`	**Directory:**	/usr/bin/	**Type:**	Script

chuser

UNIX Shell: All primary shells (csh, ksh, bsh)

Function	Changes the user attribute identified by the name. Manipulates local user data only.
Syntax	chuser *attribute=value... name*

	The following user attributes are only available if you have the proper authority:
account_locked	Shows if the user account is locked. Possible values are:
true	Indicates that the account is locked, denied access to the system.
false	Indicates that the account is not locked, allowed access to the system.
admin	Shows the administrative status of the user. Possible values are:
true	Indicates that the user is an administrator.
false	Indicates that the user is not an administrator (is default).
admgroups	Shows the groups administrated by the user in a comma-separated list.
auditclasses	Shows the user's auditclasses in a comma-separated list.
auth1	Shows the primary methods for authenticating the user in a comma-separated list.

File Name:	chuser	**Directory:**	/usr/bin/	**Type:**	External
Warning:	If you have the NIS database installed on your system, don't use chuser.				

chvfs

UNIX Shell: All primary shells (csh, ksh, bsh)

Function	Changes entries in the /etc/vfs file.
Syntax	chvfs *VFSEntry*

VFS*Entry*	Specifies the field within the VFSEntry parameter to alter.
	Use one of the following parameters:
VFS*Name*	Specifies the new name for the virtual file system.
VFS*Number*	Specifies the internal number of the virtual file system type known by the kernel.
MountHelper	Specifies the back-end used to mount a VFS file system.
FileSystemHelper	Specifies the back-end used by file-system-specific commands for this file system type.

File Name:	`chvfs`	**Directory:**	/usr/sbin/	**Type:**	External

chvg

UNIX Shell:	Korn shell (ksh)
Function	Specifies characteristics of a volume group, and specifies if the group is automatically activated at system startup.
Syntax	chvg [options...] *group*

-a AutoOn n | y	Sets automatic activation of volume group during startup. Select y or n.
-c	Converts the volume group to a Concurrent Capable volume group.
-l	Converts the volume group to a Non-Concurrent Capable volume group.
-Q n | y	Defines if the group is automatically deactivated after losing its quorum of volumes.
-u	Unlocks the volume group if locked by abnormal termination of an LVM operation.
-x	Alters the mode that the Concurrent Capable volume group is varied on.
-t*factor*	Alters the limitation of the number of physical partitions per physical volume.
-B	Sets big vg format. (Holds up to 128 physical and 512 logical volumes.)
VolumeGroup	Specifies which group to change the characteristics of.

File Name:	`chvg`	**Directory:**	/usr/sbin/	**Type:**	Script

chvirprt

UNIX Shell:	All primary shells (csh, ksh, bsh)
Function	Changes the attribute values of a virtual printer.
Syntax	chvirprt [options...]

-d *device*	Specifies the name of the queue device for the virtual printer.
-q *name*	Specifies the name of the print queue for the virtual printer.
-a *attribute=value*	Replaces the specified attribute value with a new one.

File Name:	`chvirprt`	**Directory:**	/usr/sbin/	**Type:**	External

chypdom

UNIX Shell:	Bourne shell (bsh)
Function	Changes the current domain name of the system.
Syntax	chypdom [option] *domain*

	The following options can't be combined:
-B	Specifies the domain name to be changed now, and that /etc/rc.nfs must be updated.
-N	Specifies the domain name to be changed now, but makes no changes to the /etc/rc.nfs file.
domain	Specifies the new domain name for the system.

File Name:	`chypdom`	**Directory:**	/usr/sbin/	**Type:**	Script

ckpacct

UNIX Shell:	All primary shells (csh, ksh, bsh)
Function	Sets the maximum file size for the process accounting file.
Syntax	ckpacct *{ size }*

size	Specifies the maximum size in blocks of the accounting file `/var/adm/pacct.`

File Name:	`ckpacct`	**Directory:**	/usr/sbin/acct/	**Type:**	External

ckprereq

UNIX Shell:	All primary shells (csh, ksh, bsh)
Function	Checks whether the system level is compatible with the software being installed or updated.
Syntax	ckprereq [options...]

-v	Displays a message to STDERR for failure in prerequisite list file.
-O	Specifies the part of file tree of the software product to check.
	Use one of the following operands with -O:
r	Specifies to check the / (root) part of the software.
u	Specifies to check the /usr part of the software.
s	Specifies to check the /usr/share part of the software.
-f *file*	Specifies the name of a prerequisite list file to use.
-l *fileset*	Specifies where to look for the prerequisite information from the SWVPD database.

continued

File Name:	ckprereq	Directory:	/usr/sbin/	Type:	External

colcrt

UNIX Shell: All primary shells (csh, ksh, bsh)

Function	Removes underlines or shows them on new lines when filtering the nroff file for a CRT preview.
Syntax	colcrt [options...] { *files...* }

-	Removes underlines from input.
-2	Shows all underline lines on their own rows.
files...	Specifies a file to act upon.

File Name:	colcrt	Directory:	/usr/bin/	Type:	External

colrm

UNIX Shell: All primary shells (csh, ksh, bsh)

Function	Deletes selected columns from a file reading from STDIN to STDOUT.
Syntax	colrm *startcolumn* { *endcolumn* }

startcolumn	Specifies where to start in the file.
endcolumn	Specifies where to end in the file.

File Name:	colrm	Directory:	/usr/bin/	Type:	External

comb

UNIX Shell: All primary shells (csh, ksh, bsh)

Function	Creates a script that is used to re-create and combine older versions of SCCS files, `s.files`.
Syntax	comb [options...] *file directory* comb [options...] *directory*

-o	Allows you to access the new version `delta` that is to be created.
-s	Does not combine deltas, but creates scripts to show how much space would be saved.
-c*sidlist*	Specify a list of delta identifiers (`SID`'s) to combine.
-p*SID*	Specifies the SID of the oldest delta to keep a copy of.
file	Specifies the `s.file` files that are to be re-created.
directory	Creates scripts for all `s.file` files found in that directory. (Use sccs-get -lp to show a delta table log to STDOUT.)

File Name:	comb	Directory:	/usr/bin/	Type:	External

comp

UNIX Shell: All primary shells (csh, ksh, bsh)

Function	Creates a mail message with a preconfigured form.
Syntax	comp [+*folder*] { *message* } [options...]

-draftfolder +*folder*	Identifies the draft message folder.
-nodraftfolder *folder*	Places the draft in the UserMhDirectory/draft file (is default).
-draftmessage *message*	Identifies a draft message.
-file *file*	Specifies the file to use as the message draft.
-editor *editor*	Specifies the initial editor to use.
-noedit	Suppresses the initial edit.
-form *file*	Uses header fields from the specified file, and treats each line as a format string.
-use	Tells comp to continue editing an already started message.
-nouse	Creates a new message.
-nowhatnowproc	Disables the whatnow program.
-nowwhatproc *program*	Starts a guide to the composing tasks for the specified program.
+*folder*	Specifies a message folder containing a form to use for the new message.
message	Specifies a message containing a form to use for the new message.

File Name:	comp	Directory:	/usr/bin/	Type:	External

comsat

UNIX Shell:	All primary shells (csh, ksh, bsh)
Function	A daemon that listens to the datagram port for any reports of incoming mail, and then notifies any users who have asked to be told of the mail delivery.
Syntax	comsat [-d *directory*]

-d *directory*	Specifies the directory to use as the system mail directory.

File Name:	comsat	**Directory:**	/usr/sbin/	**Type:**	External

confer

UNIX Shell:	All primary shells (csh, ksh, bsh)
Function	Starts an online conferancing system. The participants must type **joinconf** at the command line to join the conferance.
Syntax	confer [options...] { *parameter* }

-n*name*	Joins the specified conference.
-v	Sends conference messages one character at a time.
-~	Specifies the conference is to be off the record. No transcript is recorded.
	You may specify one of these parameters:
user	Specifies the user can join the conference from any workstation
@TTYnumber	Specifies that any user can join the conference from the specified workstation.
user@TTYnumber	Specifies the user only can join the conference from the specified workstation.
	The following are the subcommands to use in the conference:
!excuse { *parameter* }	Excuses the specified computer or host from the conference.
!~	Specifies that all comments from the user are off the record, until the !~~ command is entered.
!~~	Cancels the command !~. (Use the Enter key to get the floor.)

File Name:	confer	**Directory:**	/usr/bin/	**Type:**	External

conflict

UNIX Shell:	All primary shells (csh, ksh, bsh)
Function	Reports conflicts between nmh and the transport system. Reports maildrops that are not owned by a user found on the system, or if a user owns more than one maildrop.
Syntax	conflict [options...] { *aliasfiles...* }

-mail *username*	Specifies which user to send the results to instead of sending it to STDOUT.
-search *directory*	Specifies a directory to check for conflicts.
-version	Shows version information.
-help	Shows help information.
aliasfiles...	Checks conflicts between aliases found in the specified alias file and maildrops. (The default alias file is /etc/mh/MailAliases.)

File Name:	conflict	**Directory:**	/usr/lib/mh/	**Type:**	External

cplv

UNIX Shell:	Korn shell (ksh)
Function	Manages copying from one logical volume to another logical volume.
Syntax	cplv [options...] *source*

	To copy a new logical volume, use following options:
-v *group*	Specifies where the new logical volume resides.
-y *volume*	Specifies the name for the new logical volume.
-Y *prefix*	Specifies a prefix to use in building a generated name for new logical volume.
	To copy to an existing logical volume, use the following two options:
-e	Specifies that destination volume exists and that a new volume should not be created.
-f	Copies to an existing logical volume, may overwrite data if the content is to large.
source	Specifies the logical volume to copy.

File Name:	cplv	**Directory:**	/usr/sbin/	**Type:**	Script

cpu_state

cpu_state	**UNIX Shell:**	**All primary shells (csh, ksh, bsh)**
Function	Manages which processors on a multiprocessor system will be active on the next restart.	
Syntax	cpu_state [option] *{ processorNR }*	

	The following three options can't be combined:
-l	Shows the status of all processors.
-d	Disables the specified processor.
-e	Enables the specified processor.
processorNR	Specifies which processor to work with.

File Name:	`cpu_state`	**Directory:**	/usr/sbin/	**Type:**	External

crash

crash	**UNIX Shell:**	**All primary shells (csh, ksh, bsh)**
Function	Examines the image of the system memory of a currently running or crashed system.	
Syntax	crash [options...] *{ imagefile } { kernelfile }*	

-a	Shows an assortment of data structures without user interaction.
-i *file*	Allows structures declared in this file to be used with the print subcommand.
imagefile	Specifies the file that contains the system image.
kernelfile	Specifies the file that contains the kernel symbol definitions (default is /unix).

File Name:	`crash`	**Directory:**	/usr/sbin/	**Type:**	External

crfs

crfs	**UNIX Shell:**	**All primary shells (csh, ksh, bsh)**
Function	Adds a file system on a logical volume to a previously created volume group.	
Syntax	crfs [options...]	

-v *VfsType*	Specifies the virtual file system type.
-g *VolumeGroup*	Specifies an existing volume group on which to make the file system.
-l *LogPartitions*	Specifies the size of the log logical volume.
-m *MountPoint*	Specifies the mount point.
-n *NodeName*	Specifies the remote hostname where the file system resides.
-u *MountGroup*	Specifies the mount group.
-A	Specifies whether the file system is mounted at each system restart.
-p	Sets the permissions for the file system.
-a *attribute=value*	Specifies an attribute/value pair that is virtual file system-dependent .
	For Journaled File System (JFS) use one of the following attribute/value pairs:
ag=*NR*	Sets the allocation group size in megabytes: can be 8, 16, 32, or 64 (default is 8).
bf=true | false	Specifies whether the system is large-file-enabled.
compress=no | LZ	Specifies compression. LZ sets data compression, no prevents compression.
frag=*NR*	Sets the JFS fragment size in bytes: can be 512, 1024, 2048, or 4096 (default is 4096).
logname=*LVname*	Specifies the logical volume to be the logging device for the new JFS.
nbpi=*NR*	Specifies the number of bytes per i-node, default is 4096.
size=*value*	Sets the size of the JFS in 512-byte blocks.
-t yes | no	Specifies whether the file system is to be processed by the accounting subsystem.

File Name:	`crfs`	**Directory:**	/usr/sbin/	**Type:**	External

crfs -v jfs -g rootvg -m /test -a size=32768	Creates a new file system under rootvg with /test as its mountpoint.

cronadm

cronadm	**UNIX Shell:**	**All primary shells (csh, ksh, bsh)**
Function	Shows or removes crontab or at jobs specified by parameters.	
Syntax	cronadm [options...]	

	To list or remove crontab jobs, use one of the following options:
cron	Mandatory option.
-l [user]	Shows all crontab files. Shows the designated crontab file if `user` is specified.
-v [user]	Shows the status of all crontab jobs. Only designated files are listed verbosely.

continued

-r [user]	Removes crontab files. Removes the designated crontab file if `user` is specified.
	To show or remove at jobs, use one of the following options:
at	Mandatory option.
	You must specify only one of the followings two options.
-l	Shows the at jobs for the specified user.
-r*user or job*	Removes the at job specified by `user` or `job`.
File Name: `cronadm`	**Directory:** /usr/sbin/ **Type:** External

crvfs

UNIX Shell: All primary shells (csh, ksh, bsh)

Function	Creates entries in the /etc/vfs file.
Syntax	crvfs *entry*

	The entry sets a string in the following format, separated by colons:
name	Defines the name of a virtual file system type.
number	Defines the internal number of the virtual file system known by the kernel.
mounthelper	Defines the name of the back-end that is used to mount the specified type of file system.
filesystemhelper	Defines the back-end used by file system commands.
File Name: `crvfs`	**Directory:** /usr/sbin/ **Type:** External

csh

UNIX Shell: C shell (csh

Function	The C-shell command interpreter, which uses a syntax similar to the C language.
Syntax	csh [options...] *{ arguments... }*

-	When used as the first argument, a complete login to the shell is done.
-b	Lets the rest of the options to be passed directly to the scripts.
-c	Runs the first argument from the list and passes the other arguments to csh.
-e	Exits on nonzero exit status or other abnormal terminations.
-f	Does not run .cshrc and .login; used for fast starts.
-i	Forces the command prompt on any type of terminal for interactive use.
-n	Interprets, but does not run the commands; used for debugging scripts.
-s	Reads STDIN to get the commands.
-t	Runs a single command line.
-v	Verbose mode. Shows more information. Sets verbose after reading .cshrc.
-V	Verbose mode. Shows more information. Sets verbose before reading .cshrc.
-x	Echoes each command before they are run. Sets echo after reading .cshrc.
-X	Echoes each command before they are run. Sets echo before reading .cshrc.
arguments...	Specifies one or more arguments to the command.
File Name: `csh`	**Directory:** /usr/bin/ **Type:** External

csplit

UNIX Shell: All primary shells (csh, ksh, bsh)

Function	Splits all or part of a file into other files in the way specified with the arguments.
Syntax	csplit [options...] *file ACTIONS...*

-f *prefix*	Specifies a prefix for the created files.
-k	Does not remove the previously created files if an error occurs.
-n *number*	Specifies how many digits to use as name for created files (default is two digits).
-s	Does not show messages about file sizes.
ACTIONS...	**Specifies the action arguments for splitting the files. Offsets must begin with a + or a -.**
value	Copies up to but not including the specified line number.
/REGEXP/*{ offset }*	Copies up to but not including matching lines.
%REGEXP%*{ offset }*	Skips to, but does not include, a matching line.
{*value*}	Repeats the previous pattern the specified number of times.
{*}	Repeats the previous pattern as many times as possible.
file	Specifies the file to split.

continued

File Name:	csplit	Directory:	/usr/bin/	Type:	External
csplit ucg_txt 1000 {*}			Splits the file ucg_txt into as many 1000-line files as possible.		
csplit ucg_db {4}			Splits the file ucg_db into four equally large files.		

ct

UNIX Shell: All primary shells (csh, ksh, bsh)

Function	Dials up a terminal modem trying each line listed in `/etc/uucp/Devices` until an available line is found, and initiates a login process to that terminal.
Syntax	ct [options...] *phoneNR*

-h	Does not hang up, and waits for process to stop before returning control to the user.
-s*baudrate*	Sets the data baud rate (default is 1200 baud).
-v	Verbose mode; sends information to STDERR.
-w*n*	Specifes how many minutes to wait for a line if no lines are available at the moment.
-x*n*	Sets debug mode with a number from 1 to 9; higher numbers give you more details.
phoneNR	Specifies the telephone number to dial.

File Name:	ct	Directory:	/usr/bin/	Type:	External

cu

UNIX Shell: All primary shells (csh, ksh, bsh)

Function	Connects to a remote computer or acts as a dial-in terminal.
Syntax	cu [options...] *ACTION command*

-d	Shows debugging information.
-e	Uses even parity when sending data.
-h	Uses half-duplex communication mode.
-l *line*	Specifies a device to use for communication; overrides the default search.
-m	Ignores the modem control signal data carrier detect (DCD).
-n	Asks for a telephone number to dial.
-o	Uses odd parity when sending data.
-s *speed*	Sets the transmission baud-rate to use.
-t	Uses appropriate carriage mapping when dialing an auto-answer terminal.
ACTION	**You may use one of the following actions to connect; these can't be combined:**
system	Specifies the system name or hostname to contact.
number	Specifies the telephone number to call.
	The following are internal commands to control the program:
~!	Toggles between local and remote system.
~%break	Transmits a break sequence to the remote system.
~%cd *DirectoryName*	Specifies a new directory on the local system.
~%debug	Turns the debug flag on or off.
~%nostop	Toggles the input control protocol between DC3/DC1 or OFF.
~.	Terminates the connection.
~! *command*	Runs the specified command in a shell.
~$ *command*	Runs the specified command and sends the STDOUT to the remote site.
~l	Shows the TERMIO structure variables values on the remote system.
~t	Shows the TERMIO structure variables values on the local system.
~~ *strings*	Sends the specified strings to the remote system.

File Name:	cu	Directory:	/usr/bin/	Type:	External

custom

UNIX Shell: All primary shells (csh, ksh, bsh)

Function	Enables users to customize X applications.
Syntax	custom [options...] *{ Application }*

-h	Gives command-line help.
-e *browser*	Sets one of the stand-alone browsers using values: color, font, cursor, or picture.
-s *resourcefile*	Sets the resource file to load or save resource settings.

continued

Application		Specifies the application to act on.			
File Name:	custom	**Directory:**	/usr/bin/X11/	**Type:**	External

cw

UNIX Shell: All primary shells (csh, ksh, bsh)

Function	Preprocesses specific troff files containing English language text, for typesetting with the constant width font.
Syntax	cw [options...] *{ files... }*

+t	Sets the transparent mode on (is default).				
-t	Sets the transparent mode off.				
-d	Shows the current flag settings on STDERR; meant for debugging.				
-f *font*	Alters the value of the font variable with the cw command font.				
-l *delimiter*	Specifies the left delimiter as the 1- or 2-character string.				
-r *delimiter*	Specifies the right delimiter. The left and right delimiters can be different.				
{ files... }	Specifies the troff file to process.				
File Name:	cw	**Directory:**	/usr/bin/	**Type:**	External
NOTE:	This command is related to checkcw.				

cxref

UNIX Shell: All primary shells (csh, ksh, bsh)

Function	Creates a C and C++ program cross-reference listing, and writes to STDOUT a listing of all symbols in the processed files.
Syntax	cxref [options...] *files...*

-c	Shows a combined listing of the cross-references in all input files.				
-o *file*	Shows the output in the specified file.				
-q *option*	Sends the defined option to the preprocessor.				
-s	Does not show the input filenames.				
-t	Sets the listing to 80-column width.				
-w *number*	Specifies the column width of the listing; must be greater than or equal to 51.				
-Nd *number*	Specifies the dimension table size (default is 2000).				
-N1 *number*	Specifies the number of type node (default is 8000).				
-Nn *number*	Specifies the symbol table size (default is 1500).				
-Nt *number*	Specifies the number of tree nodes (default is 1000).				
-D *name*	Specifies a #define directive (default is 1).				
-I *directory*	Looks first in directory, then in directories in the standard list.				
-U *name*	Removes the initial definition of name, defined by the preprocessor as a reserved symbol.				
files...	Specifies the files to act on.				
File Name:	cxref	**Directory:**	/usr/bin/	**Type:**	External

dadmin

UNIX Shell: All primary shells (csh, ksh, bsh)

Function	Used by the administrator to locally or remotely query and modify the status of the DHCP servers' databases.
Syntax	dadmin [options...]

-?	Shows the usage syntax.
-v	Runs the command in verbose mode.
-h *host*	Specifies the destination DHCP server.
-f	Erases the lease information for an IP address without prompting; used with -d.
-d *IPaddress*	Erases the lease information associated with the specified IP address.
-x	Connects to Version 1 of the dadmin protocol; only valid for the -i and -s flags.
-i	Reinitializes the DHCP server by restarting and rereading the configuration file.
-s	Returns the status of each address in the DHCP server's configured pools.
-t	Alters the tracing level of the DHCP server, specified by one of the following values:
on	Enables a single bit at a time in the tracing mask.
off	Disables a single bit at a time in the tracing mask.
value	Specifies a decimal or hexadecimal format.
-q *address*	Shows the status of the specified IP address.

continued

-p *address*	Shows the status of each IP address in a subnet.		
-c *clientID*	Shows the status for a specific client that may be known to the DHCP server.		
File Name: `dadmin`	**Directory:** /usr/sbin/	**Type:**	External

dbx

UNIX Shell: All primary shells (csh, ksh, bsh)

Function	A debug program for C, C++, Pascal and FORTRAN.
Syntax	dbx [options...] *{ objectfile } { corefile }*

-a *processid*	Attaches the debug program to a process that is running.		
-c *commandfile*	Runs subcommands in the file before reading from STDIN.		
-d *nestingdepth*	Sets the limit for the nesting of program blocks.		
-I *directory*	Includes the specified directory in the list of directories searched for source files.		
-E *debugenvironment*	Specifies the environment variable for the debug program.		
-k	Maps memory addresses.		
-u	Prefixes filename symbols with an @.		
-r	Runs the object file immediately.		
-x	Disables stripping _ characters from symbols originating in FORTRAN source code.		
objectfile	Specifies the object file to use.		
corefile	Specifies the core file to use.		
File Name: `dbx`	**Directory:** /usr/ccs/bin/	**Type:**	External

defaultbrowser

UNIX Shell: Korn shell (ksh)

Function	Launches the default Web browser and optionally loads a specified URL.
Syntax	defaultbrowser *{ URL } { windowname }*

URL	Specifies the page for the browser to load on startup.		
NSwindowname	Specifies a window to open together with a Netscape browser.		
File Name: `defaultbrowser`	**Directory:** /usr/bin/	**Type:**	Script

defragfs

UNIX Shell: All primary shells (csh, ksh, bsh)

Function	Increases a file system's contiguous free space by reorganizing scattered allocations.
Syntax	defragfs [options] *{ device } { filesystem }*

-q	Shows the current state of the file system.		
-r	Shows the state that would result if defragfs is run without flags.		
device	Specifies the device to act on.		
filesystem	Specifies the file system to act on.		
File Name: `defragfs`	**Directory:** /usr/sbin/	**Type:**	External

deleteX11input

UNIX Shell: All primary shells (csh, ksh, bsh)

Function	Removes an X11 input extension record from the ODM database.
Syntax	deleteX11input *devices...*

devices...	Specifies the name of the X11 input extension device to operate on.		
File Name: `deleteX11input`	**Directory:** /usr/bin/X11/	**Type:**	External

delta

UNIX Shell: All primary shells (csh, ksh, bsh)

Function	Saves the changes made to an original SCCS file and creates a new delta ID for that version.
Syntax	delta [options...] *files...*

-n	Keeps the edited file on screen instead of removing it.
-p	Shows the differences line-by-line on the STDOUT in `diff` format.
-s	Does not show any warnings or confirmation messages.
-g *deltaIDs...*	Excludes the specified deltaIDs from being used when creating this file.
-m *mrlist*	Specifies one or more modification request numbers for the new delta.

continued

-r *deltaID*	Specifies the version to save when two or more versions are checked out.
-y{ *comment* }	Specifies a text string to save as a comment to the version file.
files...	Specifies the file to save and create the delta for.
File Name: `delta`	**Directory:** /usr/bin/ **Type:** External

deroff

UNIX Shell: All primary shells (csh, ksh, bsh)

Function	Removes command constructs made by `nroff, troff, tbl or eqn` from the specified files.
Syntax	deroff [options...] *files...*

-ma	Ignores MA macros in text so that only running text is output.
-me	Ignores ME macros in text so that only running text is output (is default).
-ms	Ignores MS macros in text so that only running text is output.
-mm	Disregards the text in macro lines and shows the plain text of the file to STDOUT.
-ml	The same as -mm, but also deletes all lists associated with -mm macros.
-i	Doesn't process included files.
-l	Doesn't process included files contained in /usr/lib/.
-k	Retains blocks specified to be kept together.
-p	Processes special paragraphs.
-u	Removes the ASCII underline and boldface control sequences.
-w	Shows a column containing one word per line.
files...	Specifies the files to work on.
File Name: `deroff`	**Directory:** /usr/bin/ **Type:** External

devinstall

UNIX Shell: All primary shells (csh, ksh, bsh)

Function	Installs software support for devices added after the initial OS installation.
Syntax	devinstall [options...]

-f *file*	Specifies a file with the list of packages to be installed; mandatory.
-d *device*	Specifies where to find the installation medium; mandatory.
-v	Verbose mode; shows more information.
File Name: `devinstall`	**Directory:** /usr/sbin/ **Type:** External

devnm

UNIX Shell: All primary shells (csh, ksh, bsh)

Function	Shows the location where a device is mounted.
Syntax	devnm *files...*

files...	Specifies devices to show information about. Separate multiple devices with a space.
File Name: `devnm`	**Directory:** /usr/sbin/ **Type:** External
devnm /	Shows on which device / (root) is mounted.

dfsck

UNIX Shell: All primary shells (csh, ksh, bsh)

Function	Checks and fixes two different drives file systems at the same time. Uses different options for each file system.
Syntax	dfsck [options...] *filesystem1* [options...] *filesystem2*

-d*blocks*	Checks for references to the specified block, and outputs i-node and pathname information.
-f	Skips file systems that has been successfully unmounted, giving a faster check.
-i*number*	Searches for references to the i-node with the specified number, and outputs the pathname.
-n	Assumes that all questions are answered with a no.
-o *fsoptions...*	Passes file-system-specific options separated by a comma to the fsck command.
	The following two options are valid for all file systems:
mountable	Checks if the file system is mountable, and if so, returns a value of 0, if not 8.
mytype	Checks if the file system matches with the information in `/etc/filesystems`. (If the -V option is specified, mytype will match that instead.)
-p	Fixes minor problems automatically without showing a message about the problem.
-t*file*	Specifies a scratch file on a file system other than the one being checked.

continued

-V *Vfsname*	Specifies the description of file system instead of using `/etc/filesystems`.
-y	Assumes that all questions are answered with a yes.
-	Is used to separate the file system groups.
filesystem1	Specifies the first file system to act on.
filesystem2	Specifies the second file system to act on.

File Name: dfsck | **Directory:** /usr/sbin/ | **Type:** External

Warning: The dfsck command should not be used to check the root file system.

dhcpaction

UNIX Shell: Korn shell (ksh)

Function Is used as a configurable script that runs every time a client updates its lease.

Syntax dhcpaction *hostname domainname IPaddress leasetime record1 record2*

hostname	Specifies which hostname to try to update in the DNS server.
IPaddress	Specifies which IP address to associate with the hostname in the DNS server.
leasetime	Sets the duration of association between hostname and IP address in the DNS server.
record1	Specifies DNS records to update, using one of the following: A, PTR, BOTH, or NONE.
record2	Specifies which script will act to help NIM and DHCP interact correctly: NONIM, or NIM.

File Name: dhcpaction | **Directory:** /usr/sbin/ | **Type:** Script

dhcpcd

UNIX Shell: All primary shells (csh, ksh, bsh)

Function Requests an IP address from a DHCP server connected to the same network that your system is on.

Syntax dhcpcd [options...]

-f *ConfigurationFile*	Specifies which configuration file to use.
-i *IPAddress*	Specifies an IP address to use when informing the DHCP server.
-t *Seconds*	Specifies time in seconds before dhcpcd places itself in the background.

File Name: dhcpcd | **Directory:** /usr/sbin/ | **Type:** External

dhcprd

UNIX Shell: All primary shells (csh, ksh, bsh)

Function Is used to manage forwarding of BOOTP and DHCP packets off the local network.

Syntax dhcprd [-f *file*]

-f *file*	Specifies the configuration file to use.

File Name: dhcprd | **Directory:** /usr/sbin/ | **Type:** External

dhcpsconf

UNIX Shell: All primary shells (csh, ksh, bsh)

Function A GUI that will help you configure your DHCP server.

Syntax dhcpsconf

File Name: dhcpsconf | **Directory:** /usr/sbin/ | **Type:** External

dhcpsd

UNIX Shell: All primary shells (csh, ksh, bsh)

Function Starts a DHCP server.

Syntax dhcpsd [-f *file*]

-f *file*	Specifies the configuration file to use.

File Name: dhcpsd | **Directory:** /usr/sbin/ | **Type:** External

diag

UNIX Shell: Bourne shell (bsh)

Function A diagnostic program that is used to perform hardware problem determination.

Syntax diag [options...]

-a	Performs changes in the hardware configuration by asking if lost resources have been detached.
-s	Starts diagnostics on all resources.
-d *device*	Shows the device to run diagnostics on.

continued

-v	Starts the diagnostics in System Verification Mode.
-c	Indicates the computer will not be attended.
-e	Runs error log analysis if supported on the chosen device.
-A	Runs advanced mode.
-E *days*	Sets number of days to use when searching error log during Run Error Log Analysis.
-B	Gives orders to diagnostics to run the base system test.
-T *task*	Takes a shortcut to the specified task.
-S *suite*	Performs diagnostics on a suite of devices; specify one of the following numbers:
1	Tests the base system.
2	Tests I/O devices.
3	Tests async devices.
4	Tests graphic devices.
5	Tests SCSI devices.
6	Tests storage devices
7	Tests communication devices.
8	Tests multimedia devices.
File Name: `diag`	**Directory:** /usr/sbin/ **Type:** Script
TIP:	Run the command `lsdev -C` to list available devices for testing.
diag -d scsi0 -c	Runs the diagnostics on the scsi0 device.

diction

UNIX Shell: All primary shells (csh, ksh, bsh)

Function	Is used to highlight messy sentences.
Syntax	diction [options...] *files...*

-ml	Causes the deroff command to skip mm macro lists.
-mm	Overrides the default ms macro package.
-n	Suppresses the use of the default file when used with the -f flag.
files...	Specifies one or more files to search in.
File Name: `diction`	**Directory:** /usr/bin/ **Type:** External

diffmk

UNIX Shell: All primary shells (csh, ksh, bsh)

Function	Compares two versions of a troff input file and then creates a third file.
Syntax	diffmk [options...] *file1 file2 { outfile }*

-ab'*string*'	Specifies the string to mark where added lines begin.
-ae'*string*'	Specifies the string to mark where added lines end.
-b	Ignores differences that are only changes in tabs or spaces on a line.
-cb'*string*'	Specifies the string to mark where changed lines begin.
-ce'*string*'	Specifies the string to mark where changed lines end.
-db'*string*'	Specifies the string to mark where deleted lines begin.
-de'*string*'	Specifies the string to mark where deleted lines end.
file1	Specifies the first file to compare.
file2	Specifies the second file to compare.
outfile	Specifies the file to create. If no file is specified, the output is written to STDOUT.
File Name: `diffmk`	**Directory:** /usr/bin/ **Type:** External

dircmp

UNIX Shell: Bourne shell (bsh)

Function	Compares the differences between two directories and shows a file listing of unique files.
Syntax	dircmp [options...] *directory1 directory2*

-d	Compares files or directories and shows a list of changes needed to make them identical.
-s	Suppresses messages about identical files.
directory1	Specifies the first pathname to compare.
directory2	Specifies the second pathname to compare against the first.
File Name: `dircmp`	**Directory:** /usr/bin/ **Type:** Script

disable

UNIX Shell: All primary shells (csh, ksh, bsh)

Function	Disables the specified printer from receiving additional print jobs sent using the `lp` command.		
Syntax	disable [options...] *printers...*		

-c	Cancels print requests that are currently printing; can't be used with the -w option.
-r{ *reason* }	Sets the reason the printer was disabled, which shows when typing `lpstat -p`.
printer	Specifies the name of printer to disable print requests for.

File Name: `disable` | **Directory:** /usr/bin/ | **Type:** External

diskusg

UNIX Shell: All primary shells (csh, ksh, bsh)

Function	Creates disk accounting data by user ID, and writes one record per user to STDOUT.
Syntax	diskusg [options...]

-U *maxusers*	Specifies the maximum number of users that can be processed (must be less than 5000).
-i *filelistname*	Ignores the data in the specified file system, uses a comma between files.
-p *file*	Uses the specified password file to generate login names.
-u *file*	Shows a record to the specified file, which holds filename, i-node number, user ID.
-v	Shows a list of all files that are owned by no one to the STDERR.
-s *(file)*	Merges all records from input file or from STDIN to a single record.
filesystem	Specifies the file system to act on.

File Name: `diskusg` | **Directory:** /usr/sbin/acct/ | **Type:** External

docsearch

UNIX Shell: All primary shells (csh, ksh, bsh)

Function	Runs a search program for AIX documentation files in the global library through a Web browser window.
Syntax	docsearch [-lang *language*]

-lang *language*	Runs and shows the documents in the specified language only.

File Name: `docsearch` | **Directory:** /usr/bin/ | **Type:** External

NOTE: When a language is specified, both the Web browser window and the document use that language.

dodisk

UNIX Shell: Bourne shell (bsh)

Function	Runs disk accounting functions; normally started by the `cron` command.
Syntax	dodisk [-o] *{ files... }*

-o	Uses the `acctdusg` to perform accounting on the login directory (which is slower).
files...	Runs accounting on the specified filesystems only.

File Name: `dodisk` | **Directory:** /usr/sbin/acct/ | **Type:** Script

dosdel

UNIX Shell: All primary shells (csh, ksh, bsh)

Function	Deletes DOS files.
Syntax	dosdel [options...] *files...*

-v	Writes information to STDOUTt about the format of the disk.
-D *device*	Specifies the name of the DOS device as `/dev/fd0` or `/dev/fd1`.
files...	Specifies one or more DOS files to delete.

File Name: `dosdel` | **Directory:** /usr/bin/ | **Type:** External

dosdir

UNIX Shell: All primary shells (csh, ksh, bsh)

Function	Shows the directory for DOS files.
Syntax	dosdir [options...] *{ file } { directory }*

-l	Shows a list of clusters that includes the creation date, size and attributes.
-e	Uses the -l flag to show the list of clusters allocated to the file.
-a	Shows information on all files, including hidden and system files.
-d	Handles the file value as a file even if a directory is specified. (If used without the -d option, all files in the directory are shown.)

continued

-t	Shows the entire directory tree, starting with the named directory.		
-v	Show information about the format of the disk; used to verify that it's a DOS disk.		
-D*device*	Specifies the name of the DOS device. Use /dev/fd0 (default) or /dev/fd1.		
	The two following operands cannot be combined:		
file	Specifies a file to show information about.		
directory	Specifies a directory to show information about.		
File Name: dosdir	**Directory:** /usr/bin/	**Type:**	External

dosformat

UNIX Shell: All primary shells (csh, ksh, bsh)

Function Formats a DOS diskette.

Syntax dosformat [options...]

-V *label*	Writes the label parameter to the diskette as the DOS volume label.		
-D *device size*	Specifies the disk drive type and size.		
-4	Specifies the lower density for the diskette size.		
File Name: dosformat	**Directory:** /usr/bin/	**Type:**	External

dosread

UNIX Shell: All primary shells (csh, ksh, bsh)

Function Copies files between DOS and AIX.

Syntax dosread [options...] *file1 { file2 }*

-a	Replaces each CR-LF with a new-line character, and Ctrl-Z with the end-of-line character.		
-v	Writes file information about the format of the disk to STDOUT.		
-D*device*	Specifies the name of the DOS device as /dev/fd0 or /dev/fd1.		
file1	Specifies the DOS file to copy.		
file2	Specifies the AIX name of the file.		
File Name: dosread	**Directory:** /usr/bin/	**Type:**	External

doswrite

UNIX Shell: All primary shells (csh, ksh, bsh)

Function Is used to copy files between AIX and DOS.

Syntax doswrite [options...] *file1 file2*

-a	Replaces NL characters with CR-LF, and Ctrl-Z is added at the end of file.		
-v	Writes information to STDOUT about the format of the disk.		
file1	Specifies the AIX file to copy.		
file2	Specifies the name of the DOS file to save.		
File Name: doswrite	**Directory:** /usr/bin/	**Type:**	External

dp

UNIX Shell: All primary shells (csh, ksh, bsh)

Function Converts dates fitting the ARPA Internet standard (822-format).

Syntax dp [options...] *dates...*

	Use only one of the two following options:		
-form *file*	Reformats the specified date to the format specified by the file variable.		
-width *number*	Specifies the maximum number of columns to use for dates and error messages.		
dates...	Specifies the date to parse.		
File Name: dp	**Directory:** usr/lib/mh	**Type:**	External

drm_admin

UNIX Shell: All primary shells (csh, ksh, bsh)

Function Administers servers based on the Data Replication Manager.

Syntax drm_admin [-version]

-version	Shows version information.		
File Name: drm_admin	**Directory:** /usr/lib/ncs/bin/	**Type:**	External

ds_reg

UNIX Shell:	All primary shells (csh, ksh, bsh)
Function	A registration tool for documentation library service files.
Syntax	ds_reg [-q] -l *locale viewset view* ds_reg [-q] [-d] *Locale viewset view file*

-q	Suppresses most warning messages.
-l	Shows a list of information regarding the specified view, set, and locale.
-d	Erases the specified file from the specified view, set, and locale.
locale	Specifies the language that the file is written in.
viewset	Specifies the overall category in which to find the `view` chapter.
view	Specifies under what chapter the file should be.
file	Specifies the document to register or erase.

File Name:	`ds_reg`	**Directory:**	/usr/sbin/	**Type:**	External

dscreen

UNIX Shell:	All primary shells (csh, ksh, bsh)
Function	Enables the physical terminal to connect to multiple screens or virtual sessions. A.K.A the Dynamic Screen utility.
Syntax	dscreen [options...]

-i *file*	Specifies a file containing key mappings other than the default. (Default is the first DSINFO env variable, the second is the /etc/dsinfo file.)
-t *type*	Specifies the name of a terminal type to be read from the file containing key mappings.

File Name:	`dscreen`	**Directory:**	/usr/bin/	**Type:**	External

dspcat

UNIX Shell:	All primary shells (csh, ksh, bsh)
Function	Shows all or specific messages in a message catalog.
Syntax	dspcat [-g] *catalog { SetNR } { messageNR }*

-g	Outputs formatted information usable as input by the `gencat` command.
catalog	Specifies message catalog in which the messages to show exists.
SetNR	Specifies a set of messages.
messageNR	Specifies the message in the set to show. If none is specified, all messages are shown.

File Name:	`dspcat`	**Directory:**	/usr/bin/	**Type:**	External

dspmsg

UNIX Shell:	All primary shells (csh, ksh, bsh)
Function	Shows a specified message from a message catalog or a default message supplied as a parameter, on STDOUT.
Syntax	dspmsg [-s *number*] *file number* ['*defaultmessage*' *{ arguments... }*]

-s *number*	Sets the set number (default is 1).
file	Specifies the name of the catalog to display messages from.
number	Specifies the message number in the message set.
'*defaultmessage*'	Specifies a default message to use if the message can't be recovered.

File Name:	`dspmsg`	**Directory:**	/usr/bin/	**Type:**	External

dtfile

UNIX Shell:	All primary shells (csh, ksh, bsh)
Function	The CDE File Manager. It is used to view, and manage files in the file system.
Syntax	dtfile [options...]

-noview	The Server mode. Shows a window only when client wants to show a folder.
-standalone	Runs with process attributes that are different from the server that run -noview.
-session *sessionfile*	Specifies a session file to run with.
-folder *folders...*	Specifies folders separated by comma to show a window for each folder.
-restricted	Doesn't show folders above the restricted folder.
-reuse	Opens new windows for the specified folders.
-grid *action*	Specifies the grid, action is on or off.
-tree *action*	Specifies the tree, action is on or off.
-title *title*	Specifies the title bar.

continued

-help_volume *helpvolumename*	Specifies help volume to use with File Manager.
-tree_files *action*	Specifies if files will be shown in the folder tree mode.
	Here are the three available actions:
never	Never shows files.
always	Always shows files.
choose	Enables user to choose if files are to be shown.
-order *ordertype*	Specifies the order to show files.
	Here are the available types to show files:
alphabetical	Shows files alphabetically.
file_type	Show files by filetypes together.
date	Show files in order that is based on date file was last modified.
size	Shows files in order by their size.
-view *viewtype*	Shows files in the specified format.
	Here are the view types to specify with -view:
no_icon	Shows files by their name.
large_icon	Shows files by name and with a large icon. (Is default.)
small_icon	Shows files by name and with a small icon.
attributes	Shows files by their attributes.
-direction *direction*	Specifies the direction to show files in.
	Then use these values as directions:
ascending	Shows files in the ascending direction (is default).
descending	Shows files in the descending direction.
-small_icon_width *size*	Specifies the small icon height in pixels (default is 24 pixels).
-large_icon_width *size*	Specifies the large icon width in pixels (default is 38 pixels).
-large_icon_height *size*	Specifies the large icon height in pixels (default is 38 pixels).

File Name:	dtfile	**Directory:**	/usr/dt/bin/	**Type:**	External

dump

UNIX Shell: All primary shells (csh, ksh, bsh)

Function	Takes selected parts of an object, archive, or executable file and dumps them.
Syntax	dump [options...] *files...*

-a	Dumps the archive header for each specified file.
-c	Dumps the string table.
-d	Dumps each section's raw data.
-g	Dumps all the global symbols in the symbol table of the archive.
-h	Dumps section headers.
-l	Dumps line number information.
-n	Dumps loader section information.
-o	Dumps any optional header.
-p	Suppresses the printing of the header.
-r	Dumps re-location information.
-s	Dumps raw data from each section.
-t	Dumps the symbol table entries.
-t *index*	Dumps the symbol table entry of the specified index parameter.
+t *index*	Dumps the symbol entry according to the range that ends with the index parameter.
-u	Underlines the name of the specified file parameter.
-v	Dumps symbolic representation information instead of numeric.
-z *name* [,*number*]	Dumps the line number entries for one or more name parameters.
+z *number*	Dumps all of the line numbers up to the specified number.
	The following three options work only with executable files:
-H	Dumps the loader section header.
-R	Dumps the loader section relocation entries.
-T	Dumps the loader section symbol table entries.
-X *mode*	Specifies which type of file dump should be examined. Select only one of three:
32	Processes 32-bit object files only.
64	Processes 64-bit object files only.

continued

32_64	Processes both 32-bit and 64-bit object files.		
files...	Specifies the filename to dump from.		
File Name: dump	**Directory:** /usr/bin/	**Type:**	External

dumpfs

UNIX Shell: All primary shells (csh, ksh, bsh)

Function	Shows information about a specified device or file system.
Syntax	dumpfs *{ filesystem } { device }*

	The following options can't be combined:		
filesystem	Shows the information about the specified file system.		
device	Shows the information about the specified device.		
File Name: dumpfs	**Directory:** /usr/sbin/	**Type:**	External

e

UNIX Shell: All primary shells (csh, ksh, bsh)

Function	Is used to start the INed full-screen editor.
Syntax	e *{ file }* [options...]

=*widthxheight+row+column*	Specifies the size and placement of the INed window when using an AIX window.		
-b *distance*	Specifies the distance between the INed characters and the border of the AIX window.		
-bw *width*	Specifies the width of the border for an AIX window (default is 2).		
-fb *font*	Sets the name of the bold font.		
-fi *font*	Sets the name of the italic font.		
-rv	Shows the INed window in reverse video.		
-t	Opens INed in the current window.		
file { actions... }	Specifies the file to start the editor in, the editor starts at the first page.		
	You may specify one of these actions:		
line	Specifies the line to start at (default is 1).		
column	Specifies the column to start at.		
searchkey	Specifies the search key to find.		
File Name: e	**Directory:** /usr/share/lib/terminfo/	**Type:**	External

edit

UNIX Shell: All primary shells (csh, ksh, bsh)

Function	Is just a simple line editor.
Syntax	edit [-r] *{ files... }*

-r	Recovers the file being edited after an editor or system malfunction.		
files...	Specifies the file to open or create in the editor.		
File Name: edit	**Directory:** /usr/bin/	**Type:**	External

enable

UNIX Shell: All primary shells (csh, ksh, bsh)

Function	Enables printers to accept print requests from the lp command. Runs only on the print server.
Syntax	enable *printers...*

printers...	Specifies one or more printers to enable.		
File Name: enable	**Directory:** /usr/bin/	**Type:**	External

enq

UNIX Shell: All primary shells (csh, ksh, bsh)

Function	Enqueues and manages requests to a shared resource, such as a printer device.
Syntax	enq [options...] *{ files... }*

	Use these options for file processing:
-	Runs `enq` as a filter. This must be the last declared.
-B *charpair*	Specifies how burst pages should be printed.

continued

	NOTE: The *charpair* is represented by a header character and a trailer character.
	Valid settings for the `header` and `trailer` are as follows:
nn	Shows no headers and no trailers.
na	Shows no headers, but trailer on every file.
ng	Shows no header and trailer at the end of the job.
an	Shows header on every file, but no trailers.
aa	Shows headers or trailers on every file in the job
ag	Shows header on every file and trailer after the job.
gn	Shows header at the beginning of the job, but no trailer.
ga	Shows header at the beginning of the job and trailer after every file.
gg	Shows header at the beginning of the job and trailer at the end of the job.
-c	Copies the filename instead of saving the file until the current copy is shown.
-C	Initiates `enq` to use `mail` instead of `write` for messages.
-j	Shows the message job number in STDOUT if the job is submitted to a local print queue.
-m *text*	Sends an operator message with an `enq` request. text indicates the message.
-M *file*	Sends an operator message with an `enq` request. file indicates the message text.
-n	Alerts you when your job is finished.
-N *NR*	Prints the specified number of copies of the file.
-o *option*	Passes flags specific to the backend to the backend.
-P *queue*	Specifies which queue the job will be sent to.
-r	Erases the file after it has been successfully printed.
-R *NR*	Specifies the priority of the job number.
-t *"user"*	Specifies the name of the output for delivery; the value must be a single word.
-T *title*	Adds a title on the header page and shows it when the -q flag is specified.
	To change the priority of print jobs:
-a *NR*	Alters the priority of the named job.
-# *jobNR*	Sets the job number used by the enq -q command or the enq -a command.
	To show status, you can select one of the following options:
-q	Shows the status of the default queue.
-A	Shows the status for all queues.
-L	Sets the long status; can be used with the -A flag or the -q flag, not the -W flag.
-W	Sets the wide format showing longer queue names, device names, and job numbers.
-e	Excludes status information from queues not controlled by qdaemon.
-# *jobNR*	Specifies the job number used by the enq -q command or the enq -a command.
-u *name*	Specifies which user to print job status for.
-w *seconds*	Sets the time in seconds between status output; stops when the queue is empty.
-s	Receives the status of print queues not listing any files.
	To change the queue and queue daemon options for local print jobs, use the following options:
-d	Runs the digest command on the /etc/qconfig file and reflects any changes into it.
-D	Turns off the device associated with the queue.
-G	Brings the qdaemon process down after all currently running jobs are finished.
-K	Brings the qdaemon process down killing current jobs that are run when the device starts.
-L	Long status, shows multiple files to be printed in a single printjob; used with -A or -q.
-U	Starts the device associated with a queue, sends jobs to it again.
	To cancel print jobs, use the following options:
-X	Cancels printing of your jobs. With root authority, cancels all jobs in the specified queue.
-x *NR*	Cancels printing of the specified job.
-P *printer*	Specifies which printer to cancel jobs on.
	To hold or release a print job option, use the following options:
-# *jobNR*	Specifies which print job to hold or release.
-h	Holds the specified print job.
-H	Holds and queues the specified file.
-p	Releases the specified print job.
-P*queue*	Holds or releases the specified print queue.
-u *user*	Specifies which user's print job to hold or release.

continued

	To move a print job, use the following options:
-# *jobNR*	Specifies which print job to move.
-P*queue*	Moves the specified queue; the value can be a queue name or in form queue: device name.
-Q *newqueue*	Sets the target queue for the print job.
-u *user*	Specified which user's print job to move.
files...	Specifies files to process.
File Name: `enq`	**Directory:** /usr/bin/ **Type:** External

enroll

UNIX Shell: All primary shells (csh, ksh, bsh)

Function	Is used to create a password that can be used to implement a secure communication channel.
Syntax	enroll
File Name: `enroll`	**Directory:** /usr/bin/ **Type:** External

entstat

UNIX Shell: All primary shells (csh, ksh, bsh)

Function	Is used to show statistics from the Ethernet device and its driver.
Syntax	entstat [options...] *device*
-d	Shows all statistics.
-r	Resets all the statistics back to their initial values.
-t	Toggles debug trace in some device drivers.
device	Specifies the Ethernet device.
File Name: `entstat`	**Directory:** /usr/sbin/ **Type:** External

errclear

UNIX Shell: All primary shells (csh, ksh, bsh)

Function	Deletes entries from the error log file that are older than the specified number of days.
Syntax	errclear [options...] *days*
-i *file*	Specifies the error log file to use.
	The following two options cannot be combined:
-J *errorlabel* [,*errorlable*]	Deletes the log entry specified by the error label variable.
-K *errorlabel* [,*errorlable*]	Deletes all the log entries except those specified by the error label variable.
-l *sequenceNR*	Deletes the error log entries with the specified sequence number.
-m *computer*	Deletes error log entries for the specified computer.
-n *node*	Deletes error log entries for the specified node.
	The variables of the five following options are comma-separated lists:
-N *resourcenamelist*	Deletes error log entries for the specified resource names.
-R *resourcetypelist*	Deletes error log entries for the specified resource types.
-S *resourceclasslist*	Deletes error log entries for the specified resource classes.
-T *errortypelist*	Deletes error log entries for the specified error types. (Valid values are: PERM, TEMP, PERF, PEND, INFO and UNKN.)
-d *errorclasslist*	Deletes error log entries for the specified error classes. (Valid values are H (hardware), S (software), O (errlogger msg), and U (unknown).)
-y *file*	Specifies the error record template file to use.
	The following two options can not be combined:
-j *errorid* [,*errorid*]	Deletes the log entry specified by the error ID variable.
-k *errorid* [,*errorid*]	Deletes all the log entries except those specified by the error ID variable.
days	Specifies how old the entries must be to be deleted.
File Name: `errclear`	**Directory:** /usr/bin/ **Type:** External
errclear -d H 0	Deletes all entries with the error class H (hardware).

errdead

UNIX Shell: All primary shells (csh, ksh, bsh)

Function	Extracts error records from a system dump file and adds them to the error log.
Syntax	errdead [-i *file*] *dumpfile*

-i *file*	Specifies the log file to add the records to, if needed, a file is created. (If no file is given, the value from the error log configuration database is used.)
dumpfile	Specifies the dump file to extract error records from.

File Name: `errdead` | **Directory:** /usr/lib/ | **Type:** External

errdemon

UNIX Shell: All primary shells (csh, ksh, bsh)

Function	Starts the error logging daemon.
Syntax	errdemon [options...]

-B *buffersize*	Specifies the number of bytes for the error log device driver's in-memory buffer.
-i *file*	Specifies the error log file to use.
-s *logsize*	Specifies the maximum size of the error log file.
	The following option can only be used alone:
-l	Shows values for log filename, size, and buffer size from the configuration db.

File Name: `errdemon` | **Directory:** /usr/lib/ | **Type:** External

errinstall

UNIX Shell: All primary shells (csh, ksh, bsh)

Function	Is used to add messages into the error logging message sets.
Syntax	errinstall [options...] *file*

-c	Checks the input file parameter for syntax errors.
-f	Replaces messages that have duplicate IDs.
-z *filename*	Uses the error logging message catalog specified.
file	Specifies an input file containing messages to be added or replaced.

File Name: `errinstall` | **Directory:** /usr/bin/ | **Type:** External

errlogger

UNIX Shell: All primary shells (csh, ksh, bsh)

Function	Creates an operator error log entry that contains an operator message.
Syntax	errlogger *message*

message	Specifies the message to write.

File Name: `errlogger` | **Directory:** /usr/bin/ | **Type:** External

errmsg

UNIX Shell: All primary shells (csh, ksh, bsh)

Function	Is used to add a message into the errorlog message catalog.
Syntax	errmsg [options...] { *file* }

-c	Checks the input file for syntax errors.
-z *file*	Specifies the error-logging message catalog.
-w *set_list*	Shows the specified error log message sets.
file	Specifies the input file.

File Name: `errmsg` | **Directory:** /usr/bin/ | **Type:** External

errpt

UNIX Shell: All primary shells (csh, ksh, bsh)

Function	Processes and generates a report from entries in an error log.
Syntax	errpt [options...]

-a	Shows detailed information about errors in the error file.
-c	Formats and shows each of the error entries concurrently at the time they are logged.

continued

-d *class*	Limits the error report to specified types of records set by the following values:
H	Specifies the hardware.
S	Specifies the software.
O	Sets errlogger command messages.
U	Undetermined.
-e *enddate*	Specifies records posted up to and including 'enddate'. Format is mmddhhmmyy.
-g	Shows the ASCII format of unformatted error-log entries.
-i *file*	Specifies the error log file.
-j *errorID*	Specifies which errorlog entries to include.
-k *errorID*	Specifies which errorlog entries to exclude.
-l *number*	Selects a specified unique errorlog entry.
-J *label*	Specifies the errorlog entries to include.
-K *label*	Specifies the errorlog entries to exclude.
-m *computer*	Includes errorlog entries for the specified computer.
-n *node*	Includes errorlog entries for the specified node.
-s *startdate*	Specifies all records posted on and after the start date.
-t	Runs the error-record template repository and shows the templates in report form.
-y *file*	Specifies the error-record template to use.
-z *file*	Specifies the error logging message catalog to use.
-F*flaglist*	Selects error-record template set by the Alert, Log or Report field of the template.
-N *name*	Generates a report of specified resource names.
-R *type*	Generates a report of specified resource types.
-S *class*	Generates a report of specified resource classes.
-T *type*	Limits the error report to specified by valid Error Type List variables. (Valid variables are: INFO, PEND, PERF, PERM, TEMP and UNKN.)

File Name:	errpt	Directory:	/usr/bin/	Type:	External

errstop

UNIX Shell: All primary shells (csh, ksh, bsh)

Function	Stops the error logging daemon.
Syntax	errstop

File Name:	errstop	Directory:	/usr/lib/	Type:	External

errupdate

UNIX Shell: All primary shells (csh, ksh, bsh)

Function	Is used to manage entries in the error record template repository.
Syntax	errupdate [options...] *{ file }*

-c	Checks the input file for syntax errors.
-f	Forces all templates to be updated.
-h	Creates a #define statement for each error ID assigned to an error template.
-n	Suppresses the addition of the error record template.
-p	Adds or updates a template with the Alert field set to true.
-q	Suppresses the creation of an undo file.
-y *filename*	Uses the specified error record template file.
file	Specifies the input file.

File Name:	errupdate	Directory:	/usr/bin/	Type:	External

execerror

UNIX Shell: All primary shells (csh, ksh, bsh)

Function	Writes error messages to STDERR, executed by an exec subroutine when load of a program is unsuccessful.
Syntax	execerror

File Name:	execerror	Directory:	/usr/sbin/	Type:	External

expfilt

UNIX Shell:	All primary shells (csh, ksh, bsh)
Function	Exports filter rules to a text file that can be used by the command impfilt.
Syntax	expfilt [options...]
-v 4 | 6	Specifies the IP version to use.
-f *directory*	Specifies the directory where the exported text files are to be written.
-l *list*	Specifies a list of the filter rule IDs to export.
File Name: `expfilt`	**Directory:** /usr/sbin/ — **Type:** External

explain

UNIX Shell:	Bourne shell (bsh)
Function	An interactive thesaurus for English language phrases.
Syntax	explain
File Name: `explain`	**Directory:** /usr/bin/ — **Type:** Script

exportfs

UNIX Shell:	All primary shells (csh, ksh, bsh)
Function	Translates exportfs options to share/unshare commands. Without options it shows a list of shared NFS file systems.
Syntax	exportfs [options...] { *directories...* }
-a	Exports or unexports all directories.
-v	Verbose mode; shows more information.
-u	Unexports one or more directories.
-i	Ignores the /etc/exports file; only uses default and specified options.
-f*file*	Specifies an export file other than `/etc/exports`.
-o*options...*	Specifies a list of export options.
directories...	Specifies the directory to the filesystem.
File Name: `exportfs`	**Directory:** /usr/sbin/ — **Type:** External

exportvg

UNIX Shell:	Korn shell (ksh)
Function	Is used to export a volume group.
Syntax	exportvg *volumegroup*
volumegroup	Specifies the volume group to export.
File Name: `exportvg`	**Directory:** /usr/sbin/ — **Type:** Script

exptun

UNIX Shell:	All primary shells (csh, ksh, bsh)
Function	Is used to export a tunnel definition.
Syntax	exptun [options...]
-v 4 | 6	Specifies the IP-version to use.
-f *directory*	Specifies the directory where the export files are to be written.
-t *list*	Specifies the list of tunnel IDs to be used for the export files.
-r	Exports all the user-defined filter rules associated with the tunnel.
-l ibm | manual	Specifies the type of tunnel to export.
File Name: `exptun`	**Directory:** /usr/sbin/ — **Type:** External

extendlv

UNIX Shell:	Korn shell (ksh)
Function	Is used to increase the size of a logical volume.
Syntax	extendlv [options...] *partitions* { *volumes...* } extendlv *mapfile* { *volumepartions...* }
-a *position*	Specifies the position of the logical partitions on the physical volume.

continued

	The variable can be one of the following:
m	Allocates logical partitions in the outer middle section of the physical volume.
c	Allocates logical partitions in the center of the physical volume.
e	Allocates logical partitions at the outer edge of the physical volume.
ie	Allocates logical partitions at the inner edge of the physical volume.
im	Allocates logical partitions in the inner middle of the physical volume.
-e *range*	Specifies the number of physical volumes to extend across. Variables are:
x	Allocates logical partitions across the maximum number of physical volumes.
m	Allocates logical partitions across the minimum number of physical volumes.
-u *upperbound*	Specifies the maximum number of physical volumes for new allocation.
-s *strict*	Sets the strict allocation policy; y for yes, n for no, s for superstrict.
logicalvolume	Specifies a logical volume name or a logical volume ID.
partitions	Specifies additional logical partitions.
physicalvolume	Limits the allocation to the specified physical volume.
-m *mapfile*	Defines the exact physical partitions to allocate; partitions are used in given order
File Name: `extendlv`	**Directory:** /usr/sbin/ **Type:** Script

extendvg

UNIX Shell: Korn shell (ksh)

Function	Is used to increase the number of disks in a volume group by adding a physical volume to the volume group.
Syntax	extendvg [-f] *volumegroup physicalvolume*

-f	Forces the physical volume to be added to the specified volume group.
volumegroup	Specifies the volume group to increase.
physicalvolume	Specifies the physical volume to be added to volume group.
File Name: `extendvg`	**Directory:** /usr/sbin/ **Type:** Script

f

UNIX Shell: All primary shells (csh, ksh, bsh)

Function	Shows user information about users currently logged in to a host (same as the finger command).
Syntax	f [options...] *{ ID }*

	Use one of the following options:
-b	Presents a brief, long-form listing.
-h	Doesn't show .project files in long and brief long formats.
-l	Presents a long-form listing.
-p	Doesn't show .plan files in long and brief long formats.
	Use one of the following options:
-i	Presents a quick listing with idle times.
-q	Presents a quick listing.
-w	Presents a narrow, short-format list.
-f	Doesn't show a header line on output.
-m	Interprets a user parameter as a user ID, not a user login name.
ID	Use one of following to specify who to show information about.
user	Specifies a local user ID or login name as specified in the /etc/passwd file.
user@host	Specifies a user ID on the remote host, shown in long format.
@host	Specifies all users logged-in on the remote host.
File Name: `f`	**Directory:** /usr/bin/ **Type:** External

fastboot

UNIX Shell: All primary shells (csh, ksh, bsh)

Function	Restarts the system, but does not take the time to write data in memory to the disks.
Syntax	fastboot [options...]

-l	Doesn't send a message to the system log daemon about who rebooted the system.
-n	Doesn't sync the disks. **WARNING:** This can cause file system damage!
-q	Performs a quick and ungraceful shutdown by not shutting down running processes first.
-t *mmddHHMM[yy]*	Restarts the system on the specified date; month, day, hour, minute, year.
File Name: `fastboot`	**Directory:** /usr/sbin/ **Type:** External

fasthalt

UNIX Shell:	All primary shells (csh, ksh, bsh)
Function	Stops the system immediately, and writes unsaved data to the disks.
Syntax	fasthalt [options...]

-l	Suppresses the message to the system log daemon about who executed halt.
-n	Prevents sync before stopping.
-p	Halts the system without a power down.
-q	Performs a quick halt, without syncronizing the data.
-y	Halts the system, even if a dialup terminal is used.

File Name:	fasthalt	Directory:	/usr/sbin/	Type:	External

fddistat

UNIX Shell:	All primary shells (csh, ksh, bsh)
Function	Shows FDDI device drivers and statistics.
Syntax	fddistat [options...] *device*

-r	Resets all statistics back to their initial values.
-t	Toggles debug trace in some device drivers.
device	Specifies the name of the FDDI device.

File Name:	fddistat	Directory:	/usr/bin/	Type:	External

fdpr

UNIX Shell:	All primary shells (csh, ksh, bsh)
Function	Optimizes a command in three phases. First, it creates an instrumental program that learns the program behavior. Then it starts the program. Finally, it creates an optimized version.
Syntax	fdpr -p *program* [options...]

-p *program*	Specifies the unstripped executable program to optimize.
-M *location*	Sets a location for shared memory to use for profiling (default is 0x30000000).
-*NR*	Specifies the optimization phase; can be 1, 2 or 3 (default is all). Requires -s.
-nl	Disallows branch reversing.
-o *outfile*	Sets a name for the output file (default is program.fdpr).
-armember *list*	Gives a list of the members in the file specified by the -p option (default is all).
-R*NR*	Sets the optimization level: lowest is 0, highest is 3, and n is no (default is 0).
-s	Denies removal of temporary files; is required when the optimization phase is specified.
-v	Verbose mode; shows more information.
-tb	Restructures the traceback tables in reordered code.
-pc	Specifies to preserve CSECT boundaries; with optimization levels 1 and 3 only.
-pp	Specifies to preserve procedure boundaries; with optimization levels 1 and 3 only.
-toc	Enables modifications of the TOC pointer; with optimization levels 0 and 2 only.
-bt	Enables modifications of branch tables; with optimization levels 0 and 2 only.
-inline	Inlines hot functions.
-nop	Cleans the reordered code from NOP instructions.
-opt_fdpr_glue	Uses FDPR Glue to optimize hot BB while reordering code.
-map	Creates a list of old and new addresses in a .map file.
-disasm	Creates a .dis file with the disassembled program.
-profcount	Creates a .counters file that contains the profiling counters.
-x *command*	Specifies a command that starts the command to optimize.

File Name:	fdpr	Directory:	/usr/bin/	Type:	External

feprom_update

UNIX Shell:	All primary shells (csh, ksh, bsh)
Function	Is used to load the systems EPROM with the specified file and then reboots the system.
Syntax	feprom_update [-f] *file*

-f	Forces an update without asking for confirmation.
file	Specifies the file containing the flash EPROM image.

File Name:	feprom_update	Directory:	/usr/sbin/	Type:	External

ff

UNIX Shell:	All primary shells (csh, ksh, bsh)
Function	Shows filenames and statistics for a file system.
Syntax	ff [options...] *filesystem*

-a *n*	Lists files that have been accessed during the past n days.
-c *n*	Lists files whose status has been changed during the past n days.
-i *i-node- list*	Generates names for i-nodes that are specified in i-node-list.
-I	Doesn't print any i-node numbers after each pathname.
-l	Creates an extended list of pathnames for multiply linked files.
-m *n*	Lists files that have been written to or created during the past n days.
-n *file*	Lists files that have been modified more recently than the argument file.
-o *specific_options*	Specifies `FSType` specific options using a comma-separated list.
-p *prefix*	Adds a prefix to each of the new pathnames.
-s	Shows the file size, in bytes, after each of the pathnames.
-u	Shows the owner's login name after each of the pathnames.
-V *VFSName*	Instructs the `ff` command to assume the file system type is VFSName.
filesystem	Specifies the file system.

File Name:	Directory:	Type:
`ff`	/usr/sbin/	External

ffill

UNIX Shell:	All primary shells (csh, ksh, bsh)
Function	A faster version of the command `fill` and will not use `nroff` formatting.
Syntax	ffill [-l*NR*]

-l*NR*	Specifies the right margin at the column. (Default is 65)

File Name:	Directory:	Type:
`ffill`	/usr/bin/	External

fformat

UNIX Shell:	All primary shells (csh, ksh, bsh)
Function	Fills or justifies paragraphs to the right margin, while preserving any left-margin indentation.
Syntax	fformat *{ file }* [options...]

-df	Sets the format mode to fill (is default).
-dj	Sets the format mode to justify.
-l*NR*	Sets the left margin to the specified number, default is 0.
-r*NR*	Sets the right margin to the specified number, default is 65, maximum is 130.
file	Specifies the text file to use the command on.

File Name:	Directory:	Type:
`fformat`	/usr/bin/	External

filemon

UNIX Shell:	All primary shells (csh, ksh, bsh)
Function	Monitors file system performance and report I/O activity, virtual memory segments, physical, and logical volumes.
Syntax	filemon [options...]

-d	Starts the command but doesn't start to trace until the trcon command is used.
-i *file*	Reads the I/O trace from the specified file.
-o *file*	Writes the I/O activity report to the specified file instead to STDOUT.
-O *levels*	Monitors only the specified file system levels. Valid levels are:
lf	Specifies the logical file level.
vm	Specifies the virtual memory level.
lv	Specifies the logical volume level.
pv	Specifies the physical volume level.
all	Specifies all levels.
-P	Holds monitor process in memory for the duration of the monitoring period.
-T *NR*	Sets the trace buffer size to the specified number of bytes (default is 32000).
-u	Reports on files opened before the trace daemon was started.
-v	Verbose mode; shows more information.

File Name:	Directory:	Type:
`filemon`	/usr/bin/	External

fileplace

UNIX Shell: All primary shells (csh, ksh, bsh)

Function	Shows where a specified file is placed within the physical or logical volumes containing the file.
Syntax	fileplace [options...] *file*

	The following two options can't be combined:
-l	Shows file placement in terms of logical volume fragments (is default).
-p	Shows file placement in terms of the underlying physical volume.
-i	Shows the indirect blocks for the specified file, if any.
-v	Verbose mode; shows more information.
file	Specifies the file to use.

File Name: `fileplace` **Directory:** /usr/bin/ **Type:** External

fill

UNIX Shell: All primary shells (csh, ksh, bsh)

Function	Reads text from STDIN, justifies and fills each paragraph, and writes the result to STDOUT.
Syntax	fill [options...] *{ requests... }*

-d	Specifies not to process through the nroff formatter.
-x	Suppresses compression of multiple blanks within input text lines.
requests...	Supplies **nroff** requests.

File Name: `fill` **Directory:** /usr/bin/ **Type:** External

fjust

UNIX Shell: All primary shells (csh, ksh, bsh)

Function	Reads text from STDIN, justifies and fills each paragraph, and writes the result to STDOUT.
Syntax	fjust [-l*number*]

-l*number*	Specifies the right margin of the column (default is 65).

File Name: `fjust` **Directory:** /usr/bin/ **Type:** External

flcopy

UNIX Shell: All primary shells (csh, ksh, bsh)

Function	Copies to and from diskettes.
Syntax	flcopy [options...]

-f *device*	Specifies a drive other than /dev/rfd0.
	The following two options can't be combined:
-h	Opens the floppy file in the current directory and copies it to /dev/rfd0.
-r	Exits after copying the diskette to the floppy file in the current directory.
-t *NR*	Copies only the specified number of tracks.

File Name: `flcopy` **Directory:** /usr/sbin/ **Type:** External

folder, folders

UNIX Shell: All primary shells (csh, ksh, bsh)

Function	Shows the current folder and information about the messages in it.
Syntax	folder [+*folder*] *{ msg }* [options...]

-all	Shows an alphabetical summary for all top-level folders in the `nmh` directory.
-fast	Shows only the folder name; does not read the folders.
-nofast	Shows all information and reads the folders.
-header	Shows the header information.
-recurse	Shows folder information recursively.
-norecurse	Shows folder information as it is stored.
-total	Shows the total count of messages in each folder.
-nototal	Suppresses the total count of messages in folders.
-list	Shows the contents of the folder-stack.
-nolist	Suppresses the show of the folder-stack.
-push	Directs folder to push the current folder onto the folder-stack.
-pop	Directs folder to discard the top of the folder-stack.

continued

-pack	Compresses the message names in the designated folders.		
-nopack	Suppresses the compression of the message names.		
-print	Shows information on STDOUT.		
-noprint	Suppresses the showing of information.		
-help	Shows help information.		
+*folder*	Switches to the specified folder and makes it the current folder.		
msg	Switches to the specified message and makes it the current message.		
File Name: `folder`	**Directory:** /usr/bin/	**Type:**	External

format

UNIX Shell: All primary shells (csh, ksh, bsh)

Function	Formats diskettes or read/write optical media disks.
Syntax	format [options...]

-d *device*	Specifies the device used to format the diskette.		
-f	Formats the diskette without checking for bad tracks.		
-l	Formats a 360KB disk in a 5.25-inch drive and a 720KB disk in a 3.5-inch drive.		
File Name: `format`	**Directory:** /usr/sbin/	**Type:**	External

fortune

UNIX Shell: All primary shells (csh, ksh, bsh)

Function	Shows a fortune from either the fortune.dat file or from the file specified.
Syntax	fortune [options...] *{ files... }*

-	Shows usage summary.		
-a	Shows all type of fortunes.		
-l	Shows only long phrases.		
-s	Shows only short phrases.		
-w	Waits before exiting the program; time to wait is based on the number of characters.		
files...	Specifies one or more files or directories containing fortunes.		
File Name: `fortune`	**Directory:** /usr/games/	**Type:**	External

frcactrl

UNIX Shell: All primary shells (csh, ksh, bsh)

Function	Administers the kernel extension FRCA to use in Web servers.
Syntax	frcactrl *subcommands...* frcactrl *{ subcommands... }*

[load | unload]	Loads or unloads the kernel extension.		
stats	Shows statistics information.		
[reset]	Resets the counters.		
logging	Specifies the HTTP log behavior.		
on | off	Sets logging on or off.		
logfmt	Converts log files from binary to common log format.		
logfile	Specifies the log file in binary format.		
[start | stop]	Starts or stops to serve requests sent to the address and the port.		
IPaddress	Specifies the IPaddress.		
port	Specifies port number.		
loadfile	Loads files manually into cache.		
documentroot	Specifies the document root.		
filelist	Specifies a list of files to load.		
config	Configures FRCA for use with other Web servers other than IBM.		
IPaddress	Specifies the IPaddress.		
port	Specifies the port number.		
servername	Specifies the name of the Web server.		
rootdirectory	Specifies the virtual root directory.		
logfilename	Specifies the name of the log file.		
[bin]	Specifies the log to be in binary format.		
File Name: `frcactrl`	**Directory:** /usr/sbin/	**Type:**	External

from

from	UNIX Shell:	All primary shells (csh, ksh, bsh)
Function	Shows the sender and date of newly arrived mail messages.	
Syntax	from [options...]	
-d *directory*	Specifies the system mailbox directory.	
-s *sender*	Shows headers for mail sent by the specified sender.	
File Name: `from`	**Directory:** /usr/bin/	**Type:** External

fsck_cachefs

fsck_cachefs	UNIX Shell:	All primary shells (csh, ksh, bsh)
Function	Checks the integrity of data cached with the CacheFS command.	
Syntax	fsck_cachefs [options...] *directory*	
-m	Checks but don't repair.	
-o noclean	Forces a check on the cache.	
directory	Specifies the cache directory to check.	
File Name: `fsck_cachefs`	**Directory:** /usr/bin/	**Type:** External

fsdb

fsdb	UNIX Shell:	All primary shells (csh, ksh, bsh)
Function	Debugs a file system.	
Syntax	fsdb *filesystem* [-]	
-	Disables the error checking routines used to verify i-nodes and block addresses.	
filesystem	Specifies the file system to debug.	
File Name: `fsdb`	**Directory:** /usr/sbin/	**Type:** External

fsplit

fsplit	UNIX Shell:	All primary shells (csh, ksh, bsh)
Function	Reads a FORTRAN source code from a file or STDIN and splits the input into separated routine files.	
Syntax	fsplit [-e *SubProgramUnit*] { *file* }	
-e *SubProgramUnit*	Specifies the subprogram units are split into separated files.	
file	Specifies the file to split.	
File Name: `fsplit`	**Directory:** /usr/bin/	**Type:** External

fuser

fuser	UNIX Shell:	All primary shells (csh, ksh, bsh)
Function	Shows the PIDs of processes using the specified files or file systems.	
Syntax	fuser [options...] *files...*	
-c	Logs all files in the file system containing file.	
-d	Reports on any open files that have been unlinked from the file system.	
-f	Reports only on open instances of the specified file.	
-k	Kills all processes accessing the specified file.	
-u	Appends the user name of the process owner to each PID.	
-x	Reports on executable/loadable objects.	
-V	Verbose mode; shows more information.	
files...	Specifies the files to check.	
File Name: `fuser`	**Directory:** /usr/sbin/	**Type:** External

fwtmp

fwtmp	UNIX Shell:	All primary shells (csh, ksh, bsh)
Function	Converts binary records in `wtmp` to readable text records. Reads from STDIN and writes to STDOUT.	
Syntax	fwtmp [options...]	
-i	Accepts ASCII records in the utmp format as input.	
-c	Converts output to utmp-formatted binary records.	

continued

-ic	Specifies that input is readable text and output is binary.		
File Name: `fwtmp`	**Directory:** /usr/sbin/acct/	**Type:**	External

gated

UNIX Shell: All primary shells (csh, ksh, bsh)

Function	Provides gateway routing functions for the following protocols: RIP, RIPng, EGP, BGP, BGP4+, HELLO, IS-IS, ICMP, ICMPv6, and SNMP.
Syntax	gated [options...] { *tracefile* }

-c	Specifies parsing of the configuration file for syntax errors after program exits.
-C	Specifies the configuration file is parsed only for syntax errors.
-n	Specifies the daemon will not modify the kernel's routing table.
-N	Disables background operations; runs in foreground.
-t *traceoptions*	Specifies which trace options are enabled at system startup.
-f *configfile*	Specifies an alternate configuration file, default is /etc/gated.conf.
tracefile	Specifies a trace file, to use for trace output.
File Name: `gated`	**Directory:** /usr/sbin/ **Type:** External

gdc

UNIX Shell: All primary shells (csh, ksh, bsh)

Function	A user interface for gated routing daemon.
Syntax	gdc [options...] *subcommands*

-q	Quiet mode. Messages to STDOUT are not shown. Error messages are logged with `syslog`.
-n	Runs without changes in the kernel-forwarding table.
-c *coresize*	Sets the maximum size for a `gated`-produced core dump run by `gdc`.
-f *filesize*	Sets the maximum size for a `gated`-produced file run by `gdc`.
-m *datasize*	Sets the maximum size for a `gated`-produced data segment run by `gdc`.
-s *stacksize*	Sets the maximum size for a `gated`-produced stack run by `gdc`.
-t *sec*	Sets the time in seconds that gdc waits for gated to complete operations.
subcommands	Specifies signals to gated as follows:
COREDUMP	Sends an abort signal to terminate with a coredump.
dump	Dumps the current state into the file /var/tmp/gated_dump.
interface	Rechecks the interface configuration immediately.
KILL	Terminates ungracefully.
reconfig	Rereads and reconfigures the current state as needed.
term	Terminates after shutting down all operating protocols gracefully.
toggletrace	Toggles tracing on and off.
checkconf	Checks /etc/gated.conf for syntax errors.
checknew	Checks the new configuration file, /etc/gated.conf+.
newconf	Moves the /etc/gated.conf+ file into place as /etc/gated.conf.
backout	Moves the old configuration file to /etc/gated.conf.
BACKOUT	Runs a backout operation even if /etc/gated.conf+ exists and has zero length.
modeconf	Sets configuration files, owner root, and group system, to mode 664.
createconf	Creates a zero-length file with file mode set to 664, if /etc/gated.conf+ is missing.
running	Verifies if gated is currently running.
start	Starts gated, returning an error if it is already running.
stop	Stops gated, returning an error if it is not currently running.
restart	Terminates and starts gated via the same procedures as the start and stop commands.
	To remove files, use the following:
rmcore	Removes any gated core dump file.
rmdump	Removes any gated state dump file.
rmparse	Removes the parse error file generated when syntax errors occurs in config file.
version	Shows version information; can't be used while gated is running.
File Name: `gdc`	**Directory:** /usr/sbin/ **Type:** External

gencat

UNIX Shell:	All primary shells (csh, ksh, bsh)
Function	Formats text from a message file and merges the information into the formatted message database called a catfile.
Syntax	gencat *outputfile inputfiles...*

outputfile	Specifies the database file to create.
inputfiles...	Specifies the message files to read from.

File Name:	gencat	**Directory:**	/usr/bin/	**Type:**	External

genfilt

UNIX Shell:	All primary shells (csh, ksh, bsh)
Function	Adds a filter rule to the filter rule table.
Syntax	genfilt options... [options...]

	The following three options must all be specified:
-v *value*	Specifies the IP version: 4 or 6.
-s *address*	Specifies the source address.
-m *mask*	Specifies the source subnet mask.
	The following options are optional:
-n *filterID*	Specifies the filter ID to give the filter.
-a *action*	Is used to either block traffic (D) or allows traffic (P).
-d *address*	Specifies the destination traffic.
-M *mask*	Specifies the destination subnet mask.
-g *action*	Indicates whether to apply to source routing. (Y or N).
-c *protocol*	Specifies the protocol to use: (udp, icmp, icmpv6, tcp, tcp/ack, ospf, ipip, esp, ah, or all).
-o *operation*	Specifies the source port or ICMP type operation.
-p *port*	Specifies the source port or ICMP type.
-O *operation*	Specifies the destination port or ICMP type operation.
-P *port*	Specifies the destination port or ICMP type.
-r *action*	Specifies how to apply routing: R for forward packets, L for locahost packets, or B for both.
-w *action*	Specifies the rule direction: I for incoming, O for outgoing, or B for both directions.
-i *interface*	Specifies the name of the IP interface to which the filter rule applies.
-l *action*	Toggles filter log on or off (Y or N).
-f	Specifies which kinds of packets the rule will apply to. Y for all, H for headers and unfragmented, O for headers and fragmented, N for unfragmented.
-t	Specifies the tunnel ID to send the packets matching the filter.

File Name:	genfilt	**Directory:**	/usr/sbin/	**Type:**	External

genkex

UNIX Shell:	All primary shells (csh, ksh, bsh)
Function	Extracts a list of kernel extensions currently loaded onto the system and displays the address, size, and pathname for each extension.
Syntax	genkex

File Name:	genkex	**Directory:**	/usr/bin/	**Type:**	External

genkld

UNIX Shell:	All primary shells (csh, ksh, bsh)
Function	Extracts the list of shared objects currently loaded onto the system and displays the address, size, and pathname for each object.
Syntax	genkld

File Name:	genkld	**Directory:**	/usr/bin/	**Type:**	External

genld

UNIX Shell:	All primary shells (csh, ksh, bsh)
Function	Extracts a list of loaded objects for each process currently running on the system.
Syntax	genld
File Name:	genld
Directory:	/usr/bin/
Type:	External

gentun

UNIX Shell:	All primary shells (csh, ksh, bsh)
Function	Creates a definition of a tunnel between a local and a remote host.
Syntax	gentun options... [options...]

	The following three options are all required:
-s *address*	Specifies the source host or IP address.
-d *address*	Specifies the destination host or IP address.
-v *version*	Specifies the IP version for the tunnel to use: 4 or 6.
	The following options are optional:
-t *type*	Specifies the tunnel type; can be either IBM or manual.
-m *mode*	Specifies the secure packet mode: tunnel or transport.
-f *address*	Specifies the host or IP address to the firewall between the local and remote hosts.
-x *mask*	Specifies the mask for the secure network behind a firewall.
-e *algorithm*	Specifies the source packet encryption algorithm.
-a *algorithm*	Specifies the source authentication algorithm.
-p *policy*	Specifies the source policy.
-A *algorithm*	Specifies the destination authentication algorithm.
-P *policy*	Specifies the destination policy.
-k *string*	Specifies the ESP key string.
-h *string*	Specifies the source ESP key string.
-K *string*	Specifies the destination ESP key string.
-r *time*	Specifies the session key refresh overlap time.
-i *mode*	Specifies which partner will start the IBM session key negotiations; y for local and n for remote.
-n *index*	Specifies the security parameter index for the source ESP.
-u *index*	Specifies the security parameter index for the source AH.
-N *index*	Specifies the security parameter index for the destination ESP.
-U *index*	Specifies the security parameter index for the destination AH.
-b *algorithm*	Specifies the source ESP authentication algorithm.
-c *key*	Specifies the source ESP authentication key.
-B *algorithm*	Specifies the destination ESP authentication algorithm.
-C *key*	Specifies the destination ESP authentication key.
-g	Doesn't create filter rules automatically.
-z	Uses the new header format.
-E *algorithm*	Specifies the destination packet encryption algorithm.
-h *string*	The AH key string for a manual tunnel, or the MAC key string for an IBM tunnel.
-l *time*	Specifies key lifetime in minutes.
-y	Replays flags.

File Name:	gentun
Directory:	/usr/sbin/
Type:	External

get

UNIX Shell:	All primary shells (csh, ksh, bsh)
Function	Retrieves version information from the working copy of the SCCS file.
Syntax	get [options...] *files...*

-b	Used with the -e option to create a new branch. Must have the b flag set in the s.file.
-e	Allows you to edit version information by placing a lock on the s.file.
-g	Retrieves the SCCS version ID without locking the file. Used to verify SID numbers.
-k	Doesn't expand the ID keywords.
-m	Shows the SID of the delta in front of every retrieved line separated by a tab.
-n	Shows %M% ID keyword in front of every retrieved line separated by a tab.

continued

-p -s -t -l [p] -L -a*sequence* -c*date-time* -G*newname* -i *sid-list* -r { *sid* } -x *sid-list* *files...*	Lists the version information to STDOUT instead of the default setting STDERR. Suppresses all messages to STDOUT. Shows the most recent created delta. Writes a summary of delta table to file. If -lp is used, lists the summary on STDOUT. Writes a summary of delta table to STDOUT. Same as using -lp. Shows version information by delta sequence number; used by SCCS-comb. Shows version information before a specified date and time. NOTE: date-time format is yy[mm[dd[hh[mm[ss]]]]]. Uses the name specified as the name of the version. Specifies a list of SCCS deltas to be included in the retrieved version. Shows version information by SID number. Excludes version information for deltas specified by the sid-list. Specifies the input filename.

File Name:	Directory:	Type:
`get`	/usr/bin/	External

getNAME

UNIX Shell: All primary shells (csh, ksh, bsh)

Function	Captures the NAME section from a specified manual source, which can then be used for creating a table of contents or an introduction section to a manual.
Syntax	getNAME [options...] *files...*

-i	Reports information from the manual that is useful for the manual section introduction.
-t	Reports information from the manual that is useful for table of contents creation.
files...	Specifies the manual source the NAME section will be extracted from.

File Name:	Directory:	Type:
`getNAME`	/usr/lbin/	External

gettable

UNIX Shell: All primary shells (csh, ksh, bsh)

Function	Retrieves Network Information Center (NIC) format host tables from a host.
Syntax	gettable [-v] *host* { *outputfile* }

-v	Gets the version number instead of the complete host table.
host	Specifies the server that provides the host table information.
outputfile	Specifies the file to store the host table information in.

File Name:	Directory:	Type:
`gettable`	/usr/sbin/	External

getty

UNIX Shell: All primary shells (csh, ksh, bsh)

Function	Manages ports and terminal lines; not usually used on the command line.
Syntax	getty [options...] *portname*

-r	Shares the port for bi-directional usage, and waits for 1 byte of data when locked.
-u	Shares the port for bi-directional usage.
portname	Specifies the device name for the port you want to manage.

File Name:	Directory:	Type:
`getty`	/usr/sbin/	External

ghost

UNIX Shell: All primary shells (csh, ksh, bsh)

Function	Reads and reconstructs previous versions of an INed-structured file in the output file.
Syntax	ghost *oldname* [options...] { *newname* } { *date* } { *time* }

-d	Erases the .bak file when reconstructing the previous version.
-p	Includes versions earlier than, but not including, the date and time specified.
oldname	Specifies the file to be reconstructed.
newname	Specifies the new name of reconstructed file.
date	Specifies a version date for the reconstruction. Format is M/D/Y.
time	Specifies the version time for the reconstruction. Format is H:M:S.

File Name:	Directory:	Type:
`ghost`	/usr/bin/	External

glbd

UNIX Shell:	All primary shells (csh, ksh, bsh)
Function	Manages the global location broker (GLB) database, which helps clients locate servers on a network or the Internet.
Syntax	glbd [options...]

-create	Creates a replica of the GLB. The -first or -from option must also be specified, but not together.
-first	Creates the first replica. Can only be used if -create is used.
-family *name*	Specifies the address family to use for the first replica. -first must also be used.
-from *host*	Creates additional replicas of the GLB. Can only be used if -create is used.
-change_family *name*	Changes the address family of every GLB replica.
-listen *list*	Restricts the address families on which GLB listens.
-version	Shows version information.

File Name: `glbd` **Directory:** /usr/lib/ncs/bin/ **Type:** External

grap

UNIX Shell:	All primary shells (csh, ksh, bsh)
Function	Is used to typeset graphs so that they can be used with the command `pic`.
Syntax	grap [options...] [--] *{ files... }*

-l	Stops grap from looking for the `/usr/lib/dwb/grap.defines` library file.
-T*device*	Specifies the device to output commands on.
--	Indicates the end of flags.
files...	Specifies grap language files to be processed by grap.

File Name: `grap` **Directory:** /usr/bin/ **Type:** External

greek

UNIX Shell:	Bourne shell (bsh)
Function	Converts English-language output from a Teletype Model 37 workstation, reads STDIN, to output for other workstations, and writes to STDOUT.
Syntax	greek [-T *name*]

-T *name*	Specifies the workstation name.
	When omitting the -T flag, the values can be any one of the following:
300	Stands for DASI 300.
300-12	Stands for DASI 300 in 12-pitch.
300s	Stands for DASI 300s.
300s-12	Stands for DASI 300s, in 12-pitch.
450	Stands for DASI 450.
450-12	Stands for DASI 450, in 12-pitch.
2621 5	Stands for Hewlett-Packard 2621, 2640, and 264.
2640	Stands for Hewlett-Packard 2621, 2640, and 2645.
2645	Stands for Hewlett-Packard 2621, 2640, and 2645.
4014	Stands for Tektronix 4014.
hp	Stands for Hewlett-Packard 2621, 2640, and 2645.
tek	Stands for Tektronix 4014.

File Name: `greek` **Directory:** /usr/bin/ **Type:** Script

grpck

UNIX Shell:	All primary shells (csh, ksh, bsh)
Function	Verifies correctness of the group definitions in the user database by checking definitions for all or specified groups.
Syntax	grpck option *group*

-n	Reports errors but does not fix them.
-p	Fixes errors but does not report them.
-t	Reports errors and asks if they should be fixed.
-y	Reports errors and fixes them.
group	Verifies correctness for the specified group. Can be ALL to specify all groups.

File Name: `grpck` **Directory:** /usr/sbin/ **Type:** External

help

UNIX Shell:	All primary shells (csh, ksh, bsh)
Function	Shows a page with help information for new users.
Syntax	help
File Name:	help
Directory:	/usr/bin/
Type:	External

host

UNIX Shell:	All primary shells (csh, ksh, bsh)
Function	Finds hostnames for IP addresses on the Internet. The hostname information comes from DNS servers.
Syntax	host [options...] *host* { *server* }

-a	The same as -v -t any.
-c *class*	Sets the class to look in when searching non-Internet data. Use the following values: IN, CHAOS, HESIOD MIT, ANY+ wildcards or just a wildcard.
-d	Shows debug information. Shows details about network transactions.
-n	The same as the /usr/bin/hostnew command.
-r	Returns only data from its own database; doesn't ask another server.
-t *querytype*	Specifies the following querytype to show: NS, CNAME, HINFO, KEY, MINFO, MX, PTR, SIG, SOA, TXT, UINFO, WKS, or an IP address.
-v	Verbose mode. Shows more information.
-w	Waits forever for a response.
-z	Uses the new output that shows resource record information.
host	Specifies which host to look for.
server	Specifies from which server to look, default is the local computer.
File Name:	host
Directory:	/usr/bin/
Type:	External

hostent

UNIX Shell:	All primary shells (csh, ksh, bsh)
Function	Modifies hostname to IP address mapping entries in the */etc/hosts* file.
Syntax	hostent [options...]

	One of the following six options must be set first and can't be combined:
-a *address*	Adds an address-to-hostname mapping. Must be used with -h.
-d *address*	Deletes an address-to-hostname mapping.
-X	Deletes all address-to-hostname mappings.
-c *address*	Changes an address-to-hostname mapping. Must be used with -h.
-s *host*	Shows an address or hostname's mappings. Hostnames must be enclosed in quotes.
-S	Shows all address-to-hostname mappings.
-h *hosts...*	Specifies hostnames to bind the address with. Can only be used with -a and -c.
-i *address*	Specifies a new address to use when changing address-to-hostname mappings.
-Z	Shows the result in colon format. Can only be used with -s and -S.
File Name:	hostent
Directory:	/usr/bin/
Type:	External

hostid

UNIX Shell:	All primary shells (csh, ksh, bsh)
Function	Specifies or shows the hexadecimal identifier of the current local host.
Syntax	hostid { *ACTION* }

ACTION	**Select only one of the following actions:**
hexnumber	Sets a unique hexadecimal number for the current local host.
internetadress	Sets an Internet address for the current local host.
hostname	Sets a symbolic name that maps to a specified host.
File Name:	hostid
Directory:	/usr/sbin/
Type:	External

hp

UNIX Shell: All primary shells (csh, ksh, bsh)

Function	Handles special functions for the HP2640- and HP2621-series terminals.
Syntax	hp [options...]

-e	Shows characters in difference mode.
-m	Produces only one blank line for any number of successive blank lines in the text.

File Name: `hp` **Directory:** /usr/bin/ **Type:** External

hplj

UNIX Shell: All primary shells (csh, ksh, bsh)

Function	Processes the output of the troff command for output to a Hewlett-Packard Laser Jet Series printer.
Syntax	hplj [options...] *files...*

-F *directory*	Specifies the location of the font file; default is /usr/lib/font/devhplj.
-quietly	Doesn't show any nonfatal error messages.
files...	Specifies the file to processes.

File Name: `hplj` **Directory:** /usr/bin/ **Type:** External

htable

UNIX Shell: All primary shells (csh, ksh, bsh)

Function	Converts host files to the format used by network library routines.
Syntax	htable [options...] *file*

-c *ConnectedNetworks...*	Specifies a list of networks that the host is directly connected using the gateways file.
-l *LocalNetworks...*	Specifies a list of networks to treat as local.

File Name: `htable` **Directory:** /usr/sbin/ **Type:** External

hyphen

UNIX Shell: All primary shells (csh, ksh, bsh)

Function	Reads English-language files, finds all the lines ending with hyphenated words, and writes them to STDOUT.
Syntax	hyphen *{ files... }*

files...	Specifies the files to check.

File Name: `hyphen` **Directory:** /usr/bin/ **Type:** External

i4target

UNIX Shell: All primary shells (csh, ksh, bsh)

Function	Shows the target ID of your computer.
Syntax	i4target [options...]

	The following five options can't be combined:
-O	Shows the target ID of the current computer.
-V	Shows version information.
-l	Shows all target IDs of the computer.
-h	Shows help information.
-v	Verbose mode. Shows more information.

File Name: `i4target` **Directory:** /usr/opt/ifor/ls/os/aix/bin/ **Type:** External

i4tv

UNIX Shell: All primary shells (csh, ksh, bsh)

Function	Verifies if license servers are running properly.
Syntax	i4tv [options...]

-n *host*	Specifies the host to check.
-z	Enables NCS remote procedure call tracing messages.
-v	Shows progress messages during verification.
-h	Shows help information.
-p *transactions*	Specifies the number of transactions to wait for before showing performance information.

continued

-version	Shows version information.		
File Name: i4tv	**Directory:** /usr/opt/ifor/ls/os/aix/bin/	**Type:**	External

ibm3812

UNIX Shell: Korn shell (ksh)

Function	Processes the output of the troff command for output to a IBM 3812 Model 2 Pageprinter.
Syntax	ibm3812 [options...] *{ files... }*

-altpaper	Prints the file from the alternate paper drawer.
-landscape	Prints the specified file in landscape format.
-quietly	Doesn't show any nonfatal error messages.
-F*directory*	Specifies the location of the font file; default is /usr/lib/font/.
-i	Suppresses initialization of the printer that runs the PMP.init macro.
files...	Specifies the file or files to processes; if no file is given, STDIN is used.
File Name: ibm3812	**Directory:** /usr/bin/ **Type:** Script

ibm3816

UNIX Shell: All primary shells (csh, ksh, bsh)

Function	Processes the output of the troff command for output to a IBM 3816 Pageprinter.
Syntax	ibm3816 [options...] *{ files... }*

-altpaper	Prints the file from the alternate paper drawer.
-landscape	Prints the specified file in landscape format.
-quietly	Doesn't show any nonfatal error messages.
-F*directory*	Specifies the location of the font file; default is /usr/lib/font/.
-i	Suppresses initialization of the printer that runs the PMP.init macro.
files...	Specifies the file or files to processes; if no file is given, STDIN is used.
File Name: ibm3816	**Directory:** /usr/bin/ **Type:** External

ibm5585H-T

UNIX Shell: All primary shells (csh, ksh, bsh)

Function	Processes the output of the troff command for output to a IBM 5585H-T printer for traditional Chinese language.
Syntax	ibm5585H-T [-F*directory*] *{ file }*

-F*directory*	Specifies the location of the font file; default is /usr/lib/font/devibm5585H-T.
file	Specifies the file to processes, if no file is given, STDIN is used.
File Name: ibm5585H-T	**Directory:** /usr/bin/ **Type:** External

ibm5587G

UNIX Shell: All primary shells (csh, ksh, bsh)

Function	Processes the output of the troff command for output to a IBM 5587-G01, 5584-H02, 5585-H01, 5587-H01, or 5589-H01 printer.
Syntax	ibm5587G [options...] *{ files... }*

-F*directory*	Specifies the location of the font file; default is /usr/lib/font/devibm5587G.
-quietly	Doesn't show any nonfatal error messages.
files...	Specifies the file or files to processes; if no file is given, STDIN is used.
File Name: ibm5587G	**Directory:** /usr/bin/ **Type:** External

iconv

UNIX Shell: All primary shells (csh, ksh, bsh)

Function	Converts a sequence of characters in a file from one code set to another.
Syntax	iconv options... *{ files... }*

-f *inputcode*	Specifies the code set to convert from.
-t *outputcode*	Specifies the code set to convert to.
files...	Specifies the pathname of one or more files to convert code sets for.
File Name: iconv	**Directory:** /usr/bin/ **Type:** External

ike

UNIX Shell:	All primary shells (csh, ksh, bsh)
Function	Administers the use of IP Security dynamic tunnels that use the IKE protocol.
Syntax	ike cmd=3D*action* [options…]

action	**Specifies one of: activate, list, remove or log used as shown below.**
Cmd=3Dactivate	Starts the creation of an IKE tunnel.
[phase=3D *1 or 2*]	Specifies the phase to create.
[numlist=3D*numbers…*]	Specifies the numbers of the pipes to create.
[Ipaddress=3D*x,y*]	Creates a tunnel with the Ipaddresses from the local (x) to the remote (y) system.
[autostart]	Activates all tunnels created with the autostart parameter set.
Cmd=3Dlist	Shows information about the status of the tunnels.
[phase=3D *1 or 2*]	Specifies the phase to show information about.
[numlist=3D*numbers…*]	Specifies the numbers of the pipes to show information about.
[db]	Shows information about all entries in the database, not only the running ones.
[role=3D*l or r*]	Shows the information depending on initiation, l for local and r for remote.
[verbose]	Verbose mode. Shows more information about specified tunnels.
Cmd=3Dremove	Stops and removes IKE tunnels.
Phase=3D *1 or 2*	Specifies the phase to remove; must be specified.
[numlist=3D*numbers…*]	Specifies the numbers of the pipes to remove.
[all]	Removes all entries from the IKE Tunnel Definition database.
Cmd=3Dlog	Saves log information in the file specified in the /etc/isamkpd.conf file.

File Name:	ike	**Directory:**	/usr/sbin/	**Type:**	External

imake

UNIX Shell:	All primary shells (csh, ksh, bsh)
Function	Creates makefiles from a template, a set of cpp macro functions, and a per-directory file that is called Imakefile.
Syntax	imake [options…]

-D*define*	Specifies directory configurations.
-I*dir*	Specifies the directory to the imake template and configuration.
-T*template*	Specifies the name of the master template file.
-f *filename*	Specifies the per directory input file.
-C *filename*	Specifies the name of the .c file that is created, usually Imakefile.c.
-s *filename*	Specifies the name of the make description file to create.
-e	Runs the created makefile.
-v	Shows the cpp command line that is used to create the makefile.

File Name:	imake	**Directory:**	/usr/bin/X11/	**Type:**	External

imapd

UNIX Shell:	All primary shells (csh, ksh, bsh)
Function	Starts the Internet Message Access Protocol (IMAP) server process.
Syntax	imapd

File Name:	imapd	**Directory:**	/usr/sbin/	**Type:**	External

impfilt

UNIX Shell:	All primary shells (csh, ksh, bsh)
Function	Imports filter rules from text export files that are generated by the expfilt command.
Syntax	impfilt [-v 4 | 6] -f *directory* [-l *filt_id_list*]

-v 4 | 6	Specifies the IP version of the rules to be imported.
-f *directory*	Specifies the directory from which the imported text files are to be read.
-l *filt_id_list*	Shows the Ids of the filter rules to be imported.

File Name:	impfilt	**Directory:**	/usr/sbin/	**Type:**	External

importvg

UNIX Shell: Korn shell (ksh)

Function	Imports a new volume group definition to the system.
Syntax	importvg [options...] *volume*

-V *number*	Specifies the imported volume group's major number.
-y *name*	Specifies the name of the new volume group.
-f	Forces online vary of the volume group.
-c	Imports the specified group and creates it as a Concurrent Capable volume group.
-x	Used with the -c flag, sets the Concurrent Capable volume group in concurrent mode.
-L *name*	Learns about possible changes performed to the specified volume group.
-n	Causes the volume not to be varied at completion of the volume group import into system.
-F	Fast version that checks the volume group descriptor areas in same volume group.
-R	Restores ownership, group ID, and permissions of logical volume special device files.
volume	Specifies the physical volume group to import volume group definition from.

File Name:	`importvg`	**Directory:**	/usr/sbin/	**Type:**	Script

importvg -y bkvg hdisk07	Imports the volume group definition for bkvg from the disk hdisk07.

imptun

UNIX Shell: All primary shells (csh, ksh, bsh)

Function	Adds an exported tunnel definition and any user-defined filter rules associated with the tunnels to the local host.
Syntax	imptun -f *directory* [options...]

-f *directory*	Specifies the directory from which the exported files will be read.
-t *idlist*	Lists the set of tunnel IDs to be imported from the export files.
-v *version*	Specifies the IP version of the tunnel definitions, 4 or 6.
-n	Specifies that export files were generated by the IBM firewall tunnel export command.
-r	Imports the user-defined filter rules associated with the tunnels that are imported.
-g	Enables suppress of system auto-generated filter rule flag.
-l *type*	Specifies the type of the tunnels to import, ibm or manual.

File Name:	`imptun`	**Directory:**	/usr/sbin/	**Type:**	External

indent

UNIX Shell: All primary shells (csh, ksh, bsh)

Function	Inserts or erases white space in C code to make it easier to read. It can also convert from one style of C to another.
Syntax	indent *inputfile* { *outputfile* } [options...]

-bad	Inserts blank lines after declarations.
-bap	Inserts blank lines after procedure bodies.
-bbb	Inserts blank lines after block comments.
-bc	Causes `indent` to insert a new line after commas in declarations (is default).
-bl	Moves the statement braces to the line after the statement.
-br	Moves the statement braces to the same line as the statement (is default).
-c*count*	Moves comments to the column equal to count (default is 33).
-cd*count*	Moves comments that are to the right of declarations to the column equal to count.
-cdb	Puts comment delimiters on blank lines (is default).
-ce	Puts `else` directly after a preceding end brace (is default).
-ci*count*	Causes a continuation indent of *count* spaces (default is same as -i).
-cli*count*	Indents case labels count spaces (default is 0).
-d*count*	Specifies the indentation for comments not to the right of code (default is 1).
-di*count*	Moves variables to the column equal to count (default is 16).
-dj	Indents declarations more than other code.
-ei	Indents an `if` following an `else` the same as the last `if` before.
-fa	Converts old-style C code assign operators to ANSI format (is default).
-fc1	Causes `indent` to format all comments found in the first column (is default).
-i*count*	Specifies the level of indentation to count spaces (default is 8).
-ip	Indents parameter declarations (is default).

continued

-l*count*	Sets the maximum length of lines to count (default is 75).
-lp	Lines up code exceeding one row following a parentheses with continuation lines.
-npro	Stops `indent` from reading .indent.pro files containing configuration profiles.
-pcs	Inserts a space between a function call and the parentheses following it.
-ps	Puts spaces around the pointer after the -> operator.
-psl	Puts the procedure type on the line before the procedure name (is default).
-sc	Puts the * character on the left side of comments.
-slb	Causes `indent` to manage single-line comments as a block comment.
-sob	Erases all optional blank lines found in the input code.
-st	Takes input from STDIN and outputs on STDOUT.
-T*name*	Specifies typenames for the type keyword list; this is repeatable.
-troff	Formats the source for use by `troff`; by default outputs to STDOUT.
-v	Verbose mode. Shows more information.
	The following `-n` options can't be combined with their counterparts:
-nbad	Disables insertions of blank lines after declarations (is default).
-nbap	Disables insertions of blank lines after procedure bodies (is default).
-nbbb	Disables insertions blank lines after block comments (is default).
-nbc	Disables insertions of new lines after commas in declarations.
-ncdb	Disables putting comment delimiters on blank lines.
-nce	Disables putting `else` directly after a preceding end brace.
-ndj	Indents declarations as much as other code (is default).
-nei	Causes an `if` after an `else` not to be indented as the if before.
-nfa	Disables converting old-style C assign operators to ANSI format.
-nfc1	Disables formatting comments in the first column.
-nlp	Disables lining up code following a parenthesis.
-npcs	Disables inserting a space between a function call and the parentheses following it.
-nps	Disables putting spaces around the pointer after a -> operator (is default).
-npsl	Puts the procedure type on the same line as the procedure name.
-nsc	Disables putting the * character to the left of comments.
-nslb	Manages single-line comment differently from box comments.
-nv	Disables verbose mode (is default).

File Name:	`indent`	**Directory:**	/usr/ccs/bin	**Type:**	External

inetd

UNIX Shell: All primary shells (csh, ksh, bsh)

Function	Starts all services listed in the file `/etc/inetd.conf` as they are needed.
Syntax	inetd [options...] *{ file }*

-d	Outputs debug information to `syslog`.
-t *seconds*	Waits the specified number of seconds before looping.
file	Specifies what configuration file to use; default is `/etc/inetd.conf`.

File Name:	`inetd`	**Directory:**	/usr/sbin/	**Type:**	External

install_assist

UNIX Shell: All primary shells (csh, ksh, bsh)

Function	A program that helps customize your system.
Syntax	install_assist

File Name:	`install_assist`	**Directory:**	/usr/sbin/	**Type:**	External

installbsd

UNIX Shell: All primary shells (csh, ksh, bsh)

Function	The BSD version of the install command; used to install a command to the specified destination.
Syntax	installbsd [options...] *commandname destination*

-c	Copies the specified file to the specified file or directory.
-g *group*	Specifies a group for the file specified by the destination parameter.
-m *mode*	Specifies a mode for the file specified by the destination parameter.
-o *owner*	Specifies the owner for the file specified by the destination parameter.

continued

-s	Causes the file specified by the file parameter to be stripped after installation.
commandname	Specifies the command to install.
destination	Specifies the destination of the file to install.
File Name: installbsd	**Directory:** /usr/bin/ **Type:** External

install-mh

UNIX Shell: All primary shells (csh, ksh, bsh)

Function	Creates the inital setup for a first-time nmh user.
Syntax	install-mh [options...]

-auto	Queries the user for information.
-version	Shows version information.
-help	Shows help information.
File Name: install-mh	**Directory:** /usr/lib/mh/ **Type:** External

installp

UNIX Shell: All primary shells (csh, ksh, bsh)

Function	Installs and updates software products in a compatible installation package.
Syntax	installp [options...]

-A	Shows the APAR number and summary of all customer-reported problems (no installation).
-a	Installs one or more software products and/or updates.
-ac	Installs and runs a software product update.
-B	Sets the requested action to be limited to software updates.
-b	Stops the system from performing a bosboot, even if needed.
-C	Cleans up after an interrupted installation and removes incomplete pieces.
-c	Runs all specified updates that are currently applied but not yet run.
-D	Erases the installation image when the software or update is successfully installed.
-d *device*	Specifies the installation media, a tape or diskette, an installation image file, or other media.
-e *logfile*	Turns event logging on.
-F	Forces the installation of a software product even if a version already exists.
-f *file*	Reads the names of the software products from the specified file.
-g	Installs or commits any software products that are requested.
-I	Specifies the requested action should be limited to base-level filesets.
-i	Shows on STDOUT the lpp.instr, lpp.doc, lpp.README, and README files on the media.
-J	Used when the command is executed from SMIT.
-l	Shows all the software products and their separately installable options on STDOUT.
-L	Shows the contents of the media from table of contents in a colon-separated format.
-N	Disables saving of existing files that are replaced when installing or updating.
-O	Installs the specified part of the software on diskless or dataless workstations.
	The parts can be specified as follows:
r	Is used to install the root part.
s	Is used to install the /usr/share part.
u	Is used to install the /usr part.
-p	Previews an action by running all preinstallation checks.
-Q	Disables errors and warnings concerning failing to install due to installation prerequisites.
-q	Quiet mode; doesn't show the prompt for the device, except for media volume change.
-r	Rejects all specified software updates that are currently installed but not yet run.
-S	Disables multiple-volume processing if the installation device is a CD-ROM.
-s	Shows information about all software that has been installed but not run.
-t *directory*	Sets a new save directory location for files being replaced by an update.
-u	Erases a specified software product and all of its installed updates from the system.
-V *number*	Verbose option; offers four levels of detail for preinstallation output.
-v	Verifies the correct checksum value for all installed files in the fileset.
-w	Doesn't make wildcard FilesetName.
-X	Tries to expand a file system with insufficient space for the installation.
-z *size*	Sets the block size of the installation media in bytes.

continued

name	Specifies the name of the software product or installable filesets to be installed.		
level	Specifies the level of a software product or update to install.		
File Name: `installp`	**Directory:** /usr/sbin/	**Type:**	External

instfix

UNIX Shell: All primary shells (csh, ksh, bsh)

Function	Installs filesets associated with unique keywords or fixes using APAR number.
Syntax	instfix [options...]

-T	Shows the whole list of fixes present on the media.		
-s *string*	Shows fixes on media containing the specified string.		
-S	Doesn't perform multiple-volume processing if the installation device is a CD-ROM.		
-k *keyword*	Sets the APAR number or keyword to install. Multiple keywords can be entered.		
-f *file*	Specifies the input file holding keywords or fixes; get the input file format with -T.		
-p	Shows filesets related to keywords; used with the -k or -f flags.		
-d *device*	Defines the input device; needed with all flags except -i and -a.		
-i	Shows if fixes or keywords are installed.		
-t *type*	Limits searches to the specified type:		
f	Specifies a fix.		
p	Specifies preventive maintenance.		
-c	Shows colon-separated output for use with the -i flag.		
-q	Quiet mode; used with the -i flag.		
-v	Used with the -i flag to specify verbose mode.		
-F	Shows `failure` unless all filesets associated with the fix are installed.		
-a	Shows the symptom text related to a fix. Can be used with the -i, -k, or -f flags.		
File Name: `instfix`	**Directory:** /usr/sbin/	**Type:**	External
instfix -k IX38794 -d /dev/rmt0.1	Installs all filesets associated with fix IX38794 from the tape mounted on /dev/rmt0.1.		

inucp

UNIX Shell: All primary shells (csh, ksh, bsh)

Function	A simple copy program. Mostly used by the `installp` command.
Syntax	inucp -s *directory* [-e *directory*] *filename*

-s *directory*	Specifies where to find the files to copy.		
-e *directory*	Specifies where to copy the files.		
file	Specifies the file that contains a list of files, sorted by product name.		
name	Specifies the product name for the files to copy.		
File Name: `inucp`	**Directory:** /usr/sbin/	**Type:**	External

inudocm

UNIX Shell: Bourne shell (bsh)

Function	Reads the specified files and shows all supplemental information found within them.
Syntax	inudocm [options...] *name*

-d *device*	Specifies the device where the installation media is found (default is /dev/rfd0).		
-q	Quiet mode; doesn't show messages.		
name	Specifies the product name to get information from. Use all to show all products.		
File Name: `inudocm`	**Directory:** /usr/sbin/	**Type:**	Script

inurecv

UNIX Shell: All primary shells (csh, ksh, bsh)

Function	Recovers files saved by the `inusave` command.
Syntax	inurecv *name { file }*

name	Specifies the installable software product.		
file	Specifies the file that contains names of the separately installable options.		
File Name: `inurecv`	**Directory:** /usr/sbin/	**Type:**	External

inurest

UNIX Shell:	All primary shells (csh, ksh, bsh)
Function	A utility for simple archive and restore operations, used by the installp command and shell scripts.
Syntax	inurest [options...] *filename*

-d *device*	Specifies the input device (default is /dev/rfd0).
-q	Quiet mode; doesn't show messages.
file	Specifies the file that contains a list of files, sorted by product name.
name	Specifies the product name for the files to restore.

File Name: `inurest` **Directory:** /usr/sbin/ **Type:** External

inurid

UNIX Shell:	Korn shell (ksh)
Function	Deletes installation information for diskless/dataless clients from the inst_root directories of installed software.
Syntax	inurid [option]

-q	Checks if the inst_root directories have been deleted from the system.
-r	Deletes inst_root directories from the system.

File Name: `inurid` **Directory:** /usr/lib/instl/ **Type:** Script

inusave

UNIX Shell:	All primary shells (csh, ksh, bsh)
Function	Saves installed or updated files. Mostly used by the *installp* command.
Syntax	inusave *filename*

file	Specifies a file that contains files to save, sorted by product name.
name	Specifies the product name whose files will be saved.

File Name: `inusave` **Directory:** /usr/sbin/ **Type:** External

inutoc

UNIX Shell:	All primary shells (csh, ksh, bsh)
Function	Creates a .toc file for installation images in the specified directory.
Syntax	inutoc *{ directory }*

directory	Specifies the directory to put the file in and look for image files. NOTE: If no directory is specified, default is `/usr/sys/inst.images/`

File Name: `inutoc` **Directory:** /usr/sbin/ **Type:** External

inuumsg

UNIX Shell:	All primary shells (csh, ksh, bsh)
Function	Shows a pre-made error message on STDOUT.
Syntax	inuumsg *NR { arguments... }*

NR	Specifies the error number to show.
arguments...	A space-separated list of up to four arguments to use in the error message.

File Name: `inuumsg` **Directory:** /usr/sbin/ **Type:** External

ipfilter

UNIX Shell:	Korn shell (ksh)
Function	Shows specified contents from an ipreport output file.
Syntax	ipfilter [options...] *ipreport*

-d *millisec*	Shows only the call and reply pairs that have a greater value than the value specified.
-f *action*	Specifies the operations to show in ipfilter.all.
c	Shows ICMP operations.
t	Shows TCP operations.
u	Shows UDP operations.
x	Shows ipx operations.
-n	Creates an nfs.rpt file.

continued

-s *action*	Creates separate files with the specified content.
c	Adds ICMP operations.
n	Adds nfs operations.
u	Adds UDP operations.
x	Adds ipx operations.
ipreport	Specifies the ipreport file to show.
File Name: `ipfilter`	**Directory:** /usr/bin/ **Type:** Script

ipreport

UNIX Shell: All primary shells (csh, ksh, bsh)

Function	Creates a trace report from a trace file.
Syntax	ipreport [options...] *logfile*

-e	Creates the trace report in EBCDIC format.
-r	Decodes remote procedure call packets.
-n	Includes packet numbers.
-s	Shows which protocol each packet uses.
logfile	Specifies an IP trace file to create a report from.
File Name: `ipreport`	**Directory:** /usr/sbin/ **Type:** External

ipsec_convert

UNIX Shell: Korn shell (ksh)

Function	Converts an AIX IP security tunnel to either an IBM Secure Network Gateway 2.2 or IBM Firewall 3.1 tunnel.
Syntax	ipsec_convert option [-f *expdir*]

SNG22	Converts to IBM Secure Network Gateway.
FW31	Converts to IBM Firewall 3.1.
-f *expdir*	Specifies a directory to export the IPSEC files to.
File Name: `ipsec_convert`	**Directory:** /usr/samples/ipsec/ **Type:** Script

ipsecstat

UNIX Shell: All primary shells (csh, ksh, bsh)

Function	Shows the status of IP security devices, crypto algorithms, and security packets.
Syntax	ipsecstat [options...]

-c	Resets the counters.
-d	Shows the status of the IP Security devices.
-A	Shows the status of the installed authentication algorithms.
-E	Shows the status of the installed encryption algorithms.
File Name: `ipsecstat`	**Directory:** /usr/sbin/ **Type:** External

ipsectrcbuf

UNIX Shell: All primary shells (csh, ksh, bsh)

Function	Shows the tracing buffers from the IP security subsystem.
Syntax	ipsectrcbuf [options...]

-l *action*	Specifies the trace level.
0	Writes only IPSEC_ERROR trace messages to the buffer.
1	Writes IPSEC_FILTER, CAPSUL, CRYPTO, TUNNEL, and IPSEC_ERROR messages to the buffer.
2	Writes all IP Security trace messages to the buffer.
File Name: `ipsectrcbuf`	**Directory:** /usr/sbin/ **Type:** External

iptrace

UNIX Shell: All primary shells (csh, ksh, bsh)

Function	Traces incoming and outgoing IP packets.
Syntax	iptrace [options...] *logfile*

-a	Doesn't trace ARP packets.
-P *protocol*	Only records packets that use the specified protocol.
-i *interface*	Only records packets received on the specified interface.

continued

-p *port*	Only records packets that use the specified port.
-s *host*	Only records packets coming from the specified host.
-d *host*	Only records packets headed for the specified host or IP address.
-b	Uses bi-directional mode, only used with -s and -d.
logfile	Specifies where to write the trace.
File Name: iptrace	**Directory:** /usr/sbin/ **Type:** External

isakmpd

UNIX Shell: All primary shells (csh, ksh, bsh)

Function	The IKE key management daemon, used to establish security associations for authenticated and encrypted network traffic.
Syntax	isakmpd [-d*debuglevel*]

-d*debuglevel*	Specifies the debug level to limit debug printouts.
File Name: isakmpd	**Directory:** /usr/bin/ **Type:** External

istat

UNIX Shell: All primary shells (csh, ksh, bsh)

Function	Shows I-node information for a file.
Syntax	istat *file inodeNR device*

file	Specifies a file to show i-node information about; can only be used alone.
inodeNR	Specifies an i-node number to show.
device	Specifies a device; mandatory to inodeNR.
File Name: istat	**Directory:** /usr/bin/ **Type:** External

java, java_g

UNIX Shell: Korn shell (ksh)

Function	An interpreter that is used to execute Java bytecode. java_g is a non-optimized version of java used for debugging.
Syntax	java [options...] *class*

-help	Shows help information.
-version	Shows version information.
-fullversion	Shows full version information.
-verbose	Verbose mode. Shows more information.
-debug	Enables remote Java debugging.
-noasyncgc	Forbids asynchronous garbage collection.
-verbosegc	Shows a message when garbage collection occurs.
-noclassgc	Disables class garbage collection.
-cs	Checks if source is newer when loading classes.
-ss*NR*	Specifies the maximum native stack size for any thread.
-oss*NR*	Specifies the maximum Java stack size for any thread.
-ms*NR*	Specifies the initial Java heap size.
-mx*NR*	Specifies the maximum Java heap size.
-D*name=value*	Sets a system property.
-classpatch *path*	Specifies a colon-separated list of directories to look for classes in.
-prof[:*file*]	Outputs profiling data to the specified file. Default is ./java.prof.
-verify	Verifies all classes when read in.
-verifyremote	Verifies classes read in over the network.
-noverify	Doesn't verify any classes.
class	Specifies the java class to execute.
File Name: java	**Directory:** /usr/bin/ **Type:** Script

javah, javah_g

javah, javah_g	UNIX Shell:	Korn shell (ksh)

Function Creates header files used by C-language programs. javah_g is a non-optimized version of javah used for debugging.

Syntax javah [options...] *classnames...*

-help	Shows help information.
-o *outfile*	Specifies the output filename.
-d *directory*	Specifies where to save output files.
-jni	Creates a JNI-style header file.
-td *directory*	Specifies where to place temporary files.
-stubs	Creates a stubs file.
-trace	Adds tracing information to the files created with -stubs.
-v	Verbose mode. Shows more information.
-classpath *path*	Specifies the path where the system can find Java classes.
-version	Shows version information.
classnames...	Specifies either a Java class or a package to use as input.

File Name: `javah, javah_g` **Directory:** /usr/bin/ **Type:** Script

jre

jre	UNIX Shell:	Korn shell (ksh)

Function A runtime interpreter for java.

Syntax jre [options...] *classname*

-d	Shows runtime settings.
-help	Shows help information.
-verbose	Verbose mode. Shows more information.
-verbosegc	Shows a message when garbage collection occurs.
-noasyncgc	Disables asynchronous garbage collection.
-noclassgc	Disables class garbage collection.
-ss*NR*	Specifies the maximum native stack size for any thread.
-oss*NR*	Specifies the maximum Java stack size for any thread.
-ms*NR*	Specifies the initial Java heap size.
-mx*NR*	Specifies the maximum Java heap size.
-D*name=value*	Sets a system property.
-classpath *path*	Specifies the class path.
-cp *path*	Prepends the specified path to the base class path.
-verify	Verifies all classes when read in.
-verifyremote	Verifies classes read in over the network.
-noverify	Doesn't verify any classes.
-nojit	Disables the JIT compiler.
classname	Specifies the class that you want to execute.

File Name: `jre` **Directory:** /usr/bin/ **Type:** Script

just

just	UNIX Shell:	All primary shells (csh, ksh, bsh)

Function Reads text from STDINt, justifies and fills each paragraph, and writes the result to STDOUT.

Syntax just [options...] *{ requests... }*

-d	Doesn't process through the nroff formatter.
-x	Suppresses compression of multiple blanks within input text lines.
requests...	Supplies **nroff** requests.

File Name: `just` **Directory:** /usr/bin/ **Type:** External

kdb

UNIX Shell:	All primary shells (csh, ksh, bsh)
Function	Shows system images.
Syntax	kdb *{ image } { kernelfile }*
image	Specifies the image file to show.
kernelfile	Specifies a file with kernel symbol definitions.
File Name:	`kdb`
Directory:	/usr/bin/
Type:	External

keycfg

UNIX Shell:	All primary shells (csh, ksh, bsh)
Function	Shows or alters the electronic mode switch.
Syntax	keycfg option
-d	Shows the mode switch, the key mode switch, and the electronic mode switch.
-c *mode*	Changes the electronic mode switch to normal service or secure.
File Name:	`keycfg`
Directory:	/usr/sbin/
Type:	External

keycomp

UNIX Shell:	All primary shells (csh, ksh, bsh)
Function	Compiles keyboard mapping files into input method keymap files.
Syntax	keycomp *infile outfile*
infile	Specifies the file to be compiled.
outfile	Specifies the name of the keymap file to be created.
File Name:	`keycomp`
Directory:	/usr/bin/
Type:	External

keyenvoy

UNIX Shell:	All primary shells (csh, ksh, bsh)
Function	Allows some RPC calls talk to the keyserv daemon.
Syntax	keyenvoy
File Name:	`keyenvoy`
Directory:	/usr/sbin/
Type:	External

keylogin

UNIX Shell:	All primary shells (csh, ksh, bsh)
Function	Decrypts and stores the user's secret key.
Syntax	keylogin
File Name:	`keylogin`
Directory:	/usr/bin/
Type:	External

keylogout

UNIX Shell:	All primary shells (csh, ksh, bsh)
Function	Erases a user's secret key stored by the keyserv process.
Syntax	keylogout [-f]
-f	Forces the command to erase the secret key for the superuser.
File Name:	`keylogout`
Directory:	/usr/bin/
Type:	External

keymaps

UNIX Shell:	All primary shells (csh, ksh, bsh)
Function	Shows the INed command key layout for all keyboards.
Syntax	keymaps
File Name:	`keymaps`
Directory:	/usr/apache/bin/
Type:	External

keyserv

UNIX Shell:	All primary shells (csh, ksh, bsh)
Function	A server daemon that stores the private encryption keys for the currently logged in users.
Syntax	keyserv [-n]

-n	Prompts the user for a password to decrypt root's password in the public key database.
File Name: `keyserv`	**Directory:** /usr/sbin/ **Type:** External

killall

UNIX Shell:	All primary shells (csh, ksh, bsh)
Function	Cancels all active processes.
Syntax	killall [-] [-*value*]

-	Gives the processes a chance to clean up before exit.
-*value*	Specifies the signal number or signal name.
File Name: `killall`	**Directory:** /usr/sbin/ **Type:** External

krlogind

UNIX Shell:	All primary shells (csh, ksh, bsh)
Function	Provides server functions for the rlogin command.
Syntax	krlogind [options...]

-n	Turns off transport-level keep alive messages.
-s	Enables socket-level debugging.
File Name: `krlogind`	**Directory:** /usr/sbin/ **Type:** External

krshd

UNIX Shell:	All primary shells (csh, ksh, bsh)
Function	Provides server functions for remote command executions.
Syntax	krshd

File Name: `krshd`	**Directory:** /usr/sbin/ **Type:** External

ksh, sh

UNIX Shell:	Korn shell (ksh)
Function	Starts the Korn shell, which is a command interpreter and a programming language.
Syntax	ksh [options...] *{ file } { parameter }*

-a	Marks all variables for export to which an assignment is performed.
-c *command*	Runs the specified command; can't be used with the -s option.
-e	Exits immediately after receiving conditions from a command.
-f	Disables filename generation.
-h	Finds and remembers commands defined as a function in functions.
-i	Makes the shell interactive.
-k	Places all keyword parameters in the environment for a command.
-m	Creates separate processes for background jobs and shows a message when complete.
-n	Reads commands but doesn't run them.
-o *option*	Shows current settings for the option specified.
-s	Reads the commands from STDIN.
-r	Makes the shell restricted and prevents changes to the current environment.
-t	Reads and runs one command, and then exits.
-u	Exits after finding unset variables when performing variable substitution.
-v	Shows shell input lines when they are being read.
-x	Echos each command before it is executed.
	NOTE: If + is used instead of - the flag is turned off.
file	Specifies a file that contains a ksh script.
parameter	Specifies a parameter to the script.
File Name: `ksh`	**Directory:** /usr/bin/ **Type:** External

lastcomm

lastcomm		UNIX Shell:	All primary shells (csh, ksh, bsh)
Function	Shows a reverse-order list of commands executed recently.		
Syntax	lastcomm *[command*] [*user*] [*terminal*]		
command	Lists the command names that have been executed recently.		
user	Lists recently executed commands by a user.		
terminal	Lists recently executed commands from a terminal.		
File Name: `lastcomm`	**Directory:** /usr/bin/	**Type:** External	
Note:	You must run `/usr/sbin/acct/startup` first to get this command to work.		

lastlogin

lastlogin		UNIX Shell:	Bourne shell (bsh)
Function	Updates the login information in the file /var/adm/acct/sum/loginlog.		
Syntax	lastlogin		
File Name: `lastlogin`	**Directory:** /usr/sbin/acct/	**Type:** Script	

lb_admin

lb_admin		UNIX Shell:	All primary shells (csh, ksh, bsh)
Function	Manages the registration of NCS-based servers in location broker databases.		
Syntax	lb_admin [options...]		
-nq	Doesn't query for verification when unregistering.		
-version	Shows version information.		
File Name: `lb_admin`	**Directory:** /usr/lib/ncs/bin/	**Type:** External	

lb_find

lb_find		UNIX Shell:	All primary shells (csh, ksh, bsh)
Function	Shows global location broker daemons and their attributes.		
Syntax	lb_find [options...]		
-dl	Starts rpc debugging.		
-q	Queries for the global location broker servers.		
-v	Shows version information.		
File Name: `lb_find`	**Directory:** /usr/lib/ncs/bin/	**Type:** External	

leave

leave		UNIX Shell:	All primary shells (csh, ksh, bsh)
Function	Reminds you of a time to leave. Reminds you 5 minutes and 1 minute before the specified time. The time can be specified in 12- or 24- hour format, but is converted to 12-hour format.		
Syntax	leave [options...]		
HHMM	Specifies the time in hours and minutes, assumed to be in the next 12 hours.		
+HHMM	Specifies the time in hours and minutes for the alarm to go off; works like a timer.		
File Name: `leave`	**Directory:** /usr/bin/	**Type:** External	
leave +230	Sets the alarm to 2 hours and 30 minutes from now.		

line

line		UNIX Shell:	All primary shells (csh, ksh, bsh)
Function	Reads and copies one line from STDIN, and shows the line on STDOUT, which is usually the screen.		
Syntax	line		
File Name: `line`	**Directory:** /usr/bin/	**Type:** External	
line >> ucg.log	Reads a line from STDIN and appends it to ucg.log.		
who | (line;line)	Returns the first two lines of the who command.		

link

UNIX Shell:	All primary shells (csh, ksh, bsh)
Function	Links files and directories to existing files or directories; can only be used by superusers.
Syntax	link *currentfile newfile*

currentfile	Specifies which file to link to the new file or directory.
newfile	Shows the name of the just-created file.
File Name: `link`	**Directory:** /usr/sbin/ **Type:** External

lint

UNIX Shell:	All primary shells (csh, ksh, bsh)
Function	Checks a specified C program file for errors that make the file non-portable, wasteful, or buggy.
Syntax	lint [options...] *files...*

-a	Disables messages about assignments of long values to non-long variables.
-b	Disables messages about break statements that can't be reached.
-c	Creates an .ln file for every .c file specified.
-C	Enables use of the C++ libraries (/usr/lpp/xlC/lib).
-h	Disables the heuristic tests for finding bugs, improving coding, or limiting redundancy.
-l *library*	Includes the lint library `llib-llibrary.ln`.
-n	Skips the standard library compatibility check.
-o *file*	Specifies the output file. The -c flag disables this function.
-q *DBCS*	Sets the multibyte mode specified by the current locale.
-p	Checks the portability of code in the file to other C dialects.
-t	Checks for assignments that are problematic when performing a 32 to 64-bit port.
-u	Disables complaints about nondefined functions and external variables.
-v	Disables any complaint that there is an unused argument in a function.
-w *class*	Disables the specified warning class's reporting. The valid classes are:
a	Specifies non-ANSI features.
c	Specifies comparisons with unsigned values.
d	Specifies declaration consistency.
h	Specifies heuristic complaints.
k	Specifies Kernighan and Ritchie type source code.
l	Specifies assignment of long values to variables that aren't long.
n	Specifies null-effect code.
o	Specifies unknown order of evaluation.
p	Specifies various portability concerns.
r	Specifies return statement consistency.
s	Specifies storage capacity checks.
u	Specifies proper usage of variables and functions.
A	Deactivates all warnings.
C	Specifies constants occurring in conditionals.
D	Specifies external declarations that are never used.
O	Specifies obsolescent features.
P	Specifies function prototype presence.
R	Specifies detection of unreachable code.
-x	Disables reporting of unused variables that are referred to by an external declaration.
-MA	Enables the use of ANSI C language standard rules.
-Nd*Number*	Specifies the dimension table size.
-Nl*Number*	Specifies the number of type nodes.
-Nn*Number*	Specifies the size of the symbol table.
-Nt*Number*	Specifies the number of tree nodes.
-I *directory*	Specifies the directory will be added to the list of searchable directories.
-D *name* [*=def* }	Defines the name for `cpp` as if using a #define directive.
-U *name*	Removes the initial definition of the specified preprocessor name.
files...	Specifies the input file; a file ending in .c for C language and .C for C++ language.
File Name: `lint`	**Directory:** /usr/bin/ **Type:** External

listX11input

UNIX Shell:	All primary shells (csh, ksh, bsh)
Function	Shows X11 input extension records that have been entered into the ODM.
Syntax	listX11input
File Name:	`listX11input`
Directory:	/usr/bin/X11/
Type:	External

llbd

UNIX Shell:	All primary shells (csh, ksh, bsh)
Function	Manages the local location broker database.
Syntax	llbd [options...]
-family *name*	Specifies the address families to listen to.
-version	Shows version information.
File Name:	`llbd`
Directory:	/usr/lib/ncs/bin/
Type:	External

locale

UNIX Shell:	All primary shells (csh, ksh, bsh)
Function	Shows information about the current locale or all public locales.
Syntax	locale [options...] *name*
-O 64	Shows locale information as seen by a 64-bit executable.
-c	Shows the names of selected locale categories given in `name`.
-k	Shows the names and values of the selected keywords given in `name`.
	You may select one of the following two options:
-a	Shows information about all available public locales, including POSIX.
-m	Shows the names of all character maps.
name	Uses the name of a locale category, keyword, or reserved name character map.
File Name:	`locale`
Directory:	/usr/bin/
Type:	External

localedef

UNIX Shell:	All primary shells (csh, ksh, bsh)
Function	Converts locale and character set description source files to produce a locale database.
Syntax	localedef [options...] *name*
-c	Forces the creation of locale tables even if warning messages have been issued.
-f *file*	Specifies the name of a file containing a mapping of character symbols.
-i *file*	Specifies the pathname of a file containing the locale category source definitions.
-L *options*	Passes the specified link options to the ld command that is used to build the locale.
-m *file*	Specifies the method file that describes the methods to be overridden at build.
File Name:	`localedef`
Directory:	/usr/bin/
Type:	External

lock

UNIX Shell:	All primary shells (csh, ksh, bsh)
Function	Locks a terminal to a user who has verified himself with a password. The terminal stays locked until it is released by user, the timeout is reached, or a user with appropriate privileges unlocks it.
Syntax	lock [*-timeout*]
-timeout	Sets the timeout to unlock the terminal (default is 15 minutes).
File Name:	`lock`
Directory:	/usr/bin/
Type:	External

lockstat

UNIX Shell:	All primary shells (csh, ksh, bsh)
Function	Gathers and show statistics on kernel synchronization objects.
Syntax	lockstat [options...] *{ interval } { count }*
-a	Shows a list with the most requested locks.
-c *lockcount*	Specifies how many times a lock must be requested during an interval to be displayed.
-b *blockratio*	Specifies a block ratio (default is five percent).
-p *lockrate*	Shows the activity of the most requested lock in the kernel, represented as a percentage.
-t *maxlocks*	Specifies the maximum number of locks to be displayed (default is 10).

continued

interval	Specifies the amount of time in seconds between each report.		
count	Specifies the number of reports generated.		
File Name: `lockstat`	**Directory:** /usr/bin/	**Type:**	External

logform

UNIX Shell: All primary shells (csh, ksh, bsh)

Function	Formats a logical volume so that it can be used as a JFS log device.
Syntax	logform *logname*

logname	Specifies the absolute path to the logical volume to be formatted.		
File Name: `logform`	**Directory:** /usr/sbin/	**Type:**	External

lorder

UNIX Shell: All primary shells (csh, ksh, bsh)

Function	Finds ordering relation for an object or library archive, and shows a list of the pairs.
Syntax	lorder [-X *type*] *files...*

-X *type*	Specifies object file type to process.		
32	Specifies only 32-bit object types.		
64	Specifies only 64-bit object types.		
32_64	Specifies both 32-bit and 64-bit object types.		
files	Uses one or more object or library archive filenames as the input.		
File Name: `lorder`	**Directory:** /usr/bin/	**Type:**	External

lp

UNIX Shell: All primary shells (csh, ksh, bsh)

Function	Sends print request to a printer or printer queue.
Syntax	lp [options...] { *files...* }

-c	Makes a copy of the file before printing.		
-d*queue*	Specifies the printer or printer queue to use.		
-m	Sends the user a mail when printing is complete.		
-n *number*	Specifies the number of copies to print (default is one).		
-o*option*	Specifies `piobe` specific flags to pass to the backend.		
-s	Quiet mode; doesn't show messages like id information.		
-t*title*	Specifies the title for the banner page.		
-w	Shows a message when the file has been printed.		
files...	Specifies the files to use.		
File Name: `lp`	**Directory:** /usr/bin/	**Type:**	External

lpd

UNIX Shell: All primary shells (csh, ksh, bsh)

Function	Is used to start the remote print server daemon.
Syntax	lpd [options...]

-d	Sends inactive status to the log in the SRC controller and shows error messages.		
-l	Sends active status to the log in the SRC controller and then shows the job request.		
-D	Sends extensive debugging output to DebugOutputFile.		
File Name: `lpd`	**Directory:** /usr/sbin/	**Type:**	External

lppchk

UNIX Shell: All primary shells (csh, ksh, bsh)

Function	Verifies that installable software and the SoftWare Vital Product Database match.
Syntax	lppchk option [options...] { *product filelist* }

-c	Runs a checksum operation on the specified filelist.
-f	Checks that files in the filelist exist, and that file sizes match the database.
-l	Checks that symbolic links are correct in the database.
-v	Checks that software in the root file system is also in the usr file system.

continued

-m *action*	Shows error messages.
1	Shows only error messages.
2	Shows both error messages and warnings.
3	Shows information, error, and warning messages.
-O *action*	Specifies which part of the system to verify.
r	Verifies the root part, /.
s	Verifies the share part, /usr/share.
u	Verifies the usr part, /usr.
product	Specifies the name of the software to check.
filelist	Specifies the file or files to be checked.
File Name: `lppchk`	**Directory:** /usr/bin/ **Type:** External

lpstat

UNIX Shell: All primary shells (csh, ksh, bsh)

Function	Shows status information for the print service.
Syntax	lpstat [options...]

	To specify multiple units within an option, encapsulate them with quotes.
-a *printers...*	Logs the specified printers and reports if they accept requests.
-c *classes...*	Shows the specified classes and their members.
-d	Shows the default printer destination for output requests.
-o *units...*	Shows the status of output requests for the specified printers, classes, and requestIDs.
-p *printers..*	Shows the status for the specified printers.
-r	Shows the status of the LP request scheduler.
-s	Shows a short status summary.
-t	Shows all status information.
-u *userIDs...*	Shows the status of output requests for the specified users.
-v *printers...*	Shows the status of the specified printers.
-W	Shows more extensive information.
File Name: `lpstat`	**Directory:** /usr/bin/ **Type:** External

lptest

UNIX Shell: All primary shells (csh, ksh, bsh)

Function	Generates a ripple test pattern to STDOUT and shows all 96 printable ASCII characters, useful for testing printers or terminals.
Syntax	lptest *{ ;lenght number }*

;length number	Specifies the length of the output line in characters and the number of lines.
File Name: `lptest`	**Directory:** /usr/sbin/ **Type:** External

ls_admin

UNIX Shell: Korn shell (ksh)

Function	Manages the license server database.
Syntax	ls_admin *command* [options...] options...

	The following four commands can't be combined:
-a	Adds a new vendor.
-s	Shows information about the specified license server.
-d	Deletes an existing vendor.
-f	Copies a vendor specified with -v to the server specified with -n.
	One of the following two options must be specified, and must be specified last:
-v *arguments...*	Specifies the vendor to be operated upon.
-p *arguments...*	Specifies the product to be operated upon.
--	Uses X standard arguments; can't be combined with other options.
-n *node*	Specifies the server on which to find the database.
-r	Operates on a version of a product.
	The following options can't be combined with each other:
-l	Specifies the license annotation.
-z	Debug mode; shows more information.

continued

-h	Shows help information.
-version	Shows version information.
File Name: `ls_admin`	**Directory:** /usr/lib/netls/ark/bin/ **Type:** Script

ls_dpass

UNIX Shell: Korn shell (ksh)

Function	Creates passwords for customers and distributors of software products.
Syntax	ls_dpass options... [options...] *IDs...*

--	Uses X standard parameters; can't be used with other options.
	The following options are required:
-v *name*	Specifies the vendor name.
-i *ID*	Specifies the vendor ID.
-k *key*	Uses the supplier's vendor key to encode the passwords.
-p *productID*	Specifies the product ID.
-r *version*	Specifies the product revision text.
-w *type*	Specifies the password type; can either be license or compound.
-l *type*	Specifies the license type; can either be concurrent, nodelock, or useonce. NOTE: If concurrent is set, use -m to define multiple-use rules.
-n *number*	Specifies the number of licenses for all target IDs.
	The following options can only and must be specified if type (-w) is compound.
-S *date*	Specifies the license start date (format is MM/DD/YYYY).
-E *date*	Specifies the license end date (format is MM/DD/YYYY).
-D *days*	Specifies the maximum aggregate duration of all derived passwords.
	The following options are optional:
-N *name*	Specifies the product name.
-m *string*	Specifies a flag string for filtering multiple invocations. NOTE: u=same user, n=same node, g=same group, j=same job ID.
-a *annotation*	Specifies the license annotation (maximum 80 characters).
-d *days*	Specifies the password duration; can't be combined with -e.
-e *date*	Specifies the password end date; can't be combined with -d.
-s *date*	Specifies the password start date (format is M/DD/YYYY).
-t *mode*	Specifies the target type; can be domain, sun, hpux, sco, svr4, intergraph, u ltrix or any.
-u	Shows `ls_admin` command lines used to install the created passwords.
-h	Shows help information.
-version	Shows version information.
-z	Shows debug information.
IDs...	Specifies a space-separated list of target ID's to work on.
File Name: `ls_dpass`	**Directory:** /usr/lib/netls/adk/bin/ **Type:** Script

ls_rpt

UNIX Shell: All primary shells (csh, ksh, bsh)

Function	Shows information on the license server events.
Syntax	ls_rpt [options...]

-n *node*	Specifies the server node to work on.
-c	Shows data in 80-column format.
-z	Shows debug information.
	The following options can only be specified with no other options or arguments:
-h	Shows help information.
-version	Shows version information.
-a	Shows all log messages.
-l	Shows license-related events.
-e	Shows error events.
-s	Shows server start and stop events.
-m	Shows messages logged by the software product or license server.
-f	Shows fatal error events.
-d	Shows license database modification messages.

continued

-b*date*	Shows events occurred beginning at the specified date.		
date	Can be `mm/dd/yyyy` or a specified number of hours in the past.		
-t*date*	Shows events that occurred up to the specified date.		
-v *vendor*	Shows events related to the specified vendor.		
-p *product*	Shows events related to the specified product.		
-u *user*	Shows events related to the specified user.		
-r *level*	Shows license status for specified products.		
level	Specifies which level of information to show: 1or 2.		
-x*date*	Deletes log file entries written on or before the specified date.		
date	Can be `mm/dd/yyyy` or a specified number of days in the past.		
File Name: `ls_rpt`	**Directory:** /usr/lib/netls/ark/bin/	**Type:**	External

ls_stat

UNIX Shell: Korn shell (ksh)

Function	Shows the license server system status.
Syntax	ls_stat option [options...]

	One of the following options must be specified:		
--	Reads X standard arguments.		
-t	Shows a table of total license usage compared to installed licenses.		
-i	Shows installed licenses.		
-a	Shows information on all license users.		
-u *user*	Shows licenses used by the specified user.		
	The following options can't be combined with any other options:		
-h	Shows help information.		
	The following options are optional:		
-n *server*	Shows licenses located on the specified server.		
-v *vendor*	Shows licenses of the specified vendor.		
-p *product*	Shows licenses for the specified product.		
-r *version*	Shows licenses for the specified revision of a product; can't be used with -z.		
-z	Shows debug information; can't be used with -r.		
File Name: `ls_stat`	**Directory:** /usr/lib/netls/ark/bin/	**Type:**	Script

lsallq

UNIX Shell: All primary shells (csh, ksh, bsh)

Function	Shows all configured print queues.
Syntax	lsallq [-c]

-c	Shows the output in colon format inside SMIT.		
File Name: `lsallq`	**Directory:** /usr/bin/	**Type:**	External

lsallqdev

UNIX Shell: All primary shells (csh, ksh, bsh)

Function	Shows all configured plotter and printer queue device names in a specified queue.
Syntax	lsallqdev [-c] -q *name*

-c	Shows output in colon format inside SMIT.		
-q *name*	Specifies the queue name.		
File Name: `lsallqdev`	**Directory:** /usr/bin/	**Type:**	External

lsattr

UNIX Shell: All primary shells (csh, ksh, bsh)

Function	Shows attributes for devices in the system.
Syntax	lsattr option [options...]

	The following options can't be combined, but one of them must be used:
-D	Shows the default values.
-E	Shows the effective values.
-F *format*	Specifies the user-defined format.

continued

-R	Shows the range of legal values.
	The following options can be used when showing attributes:
-a *attribute*	Shows the information about the specified attributes.
-f *file*	Specifies a file to read the flags from.
-h	Shows help information.
-H	Shows the headers above the column output.
	The following option can be used only with -D or -E:
-O	Shows all the attribute names in a colon-separated list.
	The following options can be used only with -D, -F, or -R:
-l *name*	Specifies the logical name for the device.
-t *type*	Specifies the device type name.
-s *name*	Specifies the device subclass name.
-c *name*	Specifies the device class name.
File Name: `lsattr`	**Directory:** /usr/sbin/ **Type:** External
lsattr -l scsi0 -E	Shows current attributes for the scsi device scsi0.

lsauthent

UNIX Shell: All primary shells (csh, ksh, bsh)

Function	Shows all configured authentication methods in the system.
Syntax	lsauthent
File Name: `lsauthent`	**Directory:** /usr/bin/ **Type:** External

lscfg

UNIX Shell: All primary shells (csh, ksh, bsh)

Function	Shows configuration, vital product data, and diagnostic information for the system.
Syntax	lscfg [options...]
-v	Shows any VPD found in the customized VPD object class.
-p	Shows platform-specific device information.
-l *name*	Shows device information for the specified device.
-r	Shows platform-specific device information found in residual data.
File Name: `lscfg`	**Directory:** /usr/sbin **Type:** External
TIP:	This is an excellent place to find out where all of your devices are hiding.

lsclass

UNIX Shell: All primary shells (csh, ksh, bsh)

Function	Shows workload management classes.
Syntax	lsclass [options...] { *class* }
-C	Shows output in colon-separated format.
-d *confdir*	Specifies an alternative configuration directory.
-f	Shows output in stanza format.
class	Specifies the class to show.
File Name: `lsclass`	**Directory:** /usr/sbin/ **Type:** External

lsconn

UNIX Shell: All primary shells (csh, ksh, bsh)

Function	Shows which connections a device can accept.
Syntax	lsconn [options...]
-p *parentname*	Specifies the parent device's logical name; can only be used alone.
-c *parentclass*	Specifies the class name of the parent device.
-t *parenttype*	Specifies the device type the parent device.
-l *childname*	Specifies the logical name the child device.
-k *childconnkey*	Specifies the connection key of the subclass of the specified child device.
-f *file*	Reads input from a file instead of STDIN.
-F *format*	Sets the column headings for output separated by commas, or white space for a single column.
-h	Shows help information.

continued

-H		Adds headers above columns.			
File Name:	`lsconn`	**Directory:**	/usr/sbin	**Type:**	External

lscons

UNIX Shell: All primary shells (csh, ksh, bsh)

Function	Shows the device name of a console.
Syntax	lscons [options...]

-a		Shows attribute names.			
-b		Shows the pathname to the console that is used at next boot.			
-d		Shows the pathname of the current console.			
-O		Shows attributes inside SMIT.			
-s		Shows only device names, not pathnames.			
File Name:	`lscons`	**Directory:**	/usr/sbin/	**Type:**	External

lsdev

UNIX Shell: All primary shells (csh, ksh, bsh)

Function	Shows information about devices in the system.
Syntax	lsdev option [options...]

		The following two options can't be combined:			
-P		Shows device information from the predefined object class.			
-C		Shows device information from the customized object class.			
-c *class*		Specifies a device class name.			
-f *file*		Reads input from a file instead of STDIN.			
-F *format*		Specifies how to format the output.			
-H		Uses headers above columns in the output.			
-h		Shows help information.			
-l *name*		Specifies which logical name to show from the customized object class.			
-r *colname*		Shows all values in columns.			
-S *state*		Shows what state a device is in.			
-s *subclass*		Specifies a device subclass to show.			
-t *type*		Specifies a device type to show.			
File Name:	`lsdevl`	**Directory:**	/usr/sbin	**Type:**	External
Tip:	This is an excellent tool to use when you're trying to get an overview of the system. It can also be run by SMIT; use: smit lsdev.				

lsdev -Cc disk	Shows your installed drivers for your hard disks.
lsdev -Ps scsi	Shows all scsi drivers available for installation.

lsdisp

UNIX Shell: All primary shells (csh, ksh, bsh)

Function	Shows which monitors are available to the system.
Syntax	ldisp [-l]

-l		Shows no header information.			
File Name:	`lsdisp`	**Directory:**	/usr/bin	**Type:**	External

lsfilt

UNIX Shell: All primary shells (csh, ksh, bsh)

Function	Shows filter rules and their status.
Syntax	lsfilt [options...]

-a		Shows only active filter rules.			
-d		Shows dynamic filter rules used for the key exchange tunnels.			
-n *fidlist*		Specifies a list of filter IDs to show, separated with a comma or minus.			
-v 4 | 6		Specifies the IP version of the filter to show.			
File Name:	`lsfilt`	**Directory:**	/usr/sbin	**Type:**	External

lsfont

UNIX Shell: All primary shells (csh, ksh, bsh)

Function	Shows all available fonts.
Syntax	lsfont [-l]
-l	Shows no headers in output.
File Name: `lsfont`	**Directory:** /usr/bin — **Type:** External

lsfs

UNIX Shell: All primary shells (csh, ksh, bsh)

Function	Shows various file system information.
Syntax	lsfs [options...]
-a	Shows all file systems.
-c	Shows output in colon-separated format.
-l	Shows output in list format.
-q	Queries LVM for file system sizes.
-u *mountgroup*	Shows information for the file systems of a specified mount group.
-v *vfstype*	Shows information for all the file systems of a specified type.
filesystems...	Specifies the file system to show information on.
File Name: `lsfs`	**Directory:** /usr/sbin — **Type:** External

lsgroup

UNIX Shell: All primary shells (csh, ksh, bsh)

Function	Shows group attributes.
Syntax	lsgroup [options...] *{ groups... }* [ALL]
-c	Shows attributes of each specified group in a colon-separated list.
-f	Shows attributes of each specified group in an attribute=value format.
-a *list*	Specifies which attributes to show.
ALL	Shows all system groups and their attributes.
groups...	Specifies which system groups and attributes to show.
File Name: `lsgroup`	**Directory:** /usr/sbin — **Type:** External

lsitab

UNIX Shell: All primary shells (csh, ksh, bsh)

Function	Shows records from the inittab file.
Syntax	lsitab [-a] *{ identifier }*
-a	Shows all the records in the inittab file.
identifier	Shows the record of the specified object.
File Name: `lsitab`	**Directory:** /usr/sbin — **Type:** External

lskbd

UNIX Shell: All primary shells (csh, ksh, bsh)

Function	Shows which keyboard map is currently loaded.
Syntax	lskbd
File Name: `lskbd`	**Directory:** /usr/sbin — **Type:** External

lslicense

UNIX Shell: All primary shells (csh, ksh, bsh)

Function	Shows the number of fixed licenses in the system and status of the floating licenses.
Syntax	lslicense [-c]
-c	Shows output in colon-separated format.
File Name: `lslicense`	**Directory:** /usr/bin — **Type:** External

lslpp

UNIX Shell:	All primary shells (csh, ksh, bsh)
Function	Shows information about installed or updated software.
Syntax	lslpp option [options...] *identifier*

	The following eight options can't be combined:
-d	Shows which filesets are dependent on the specified software.
-f	Shows which files were installed with the specified fileset.
-h	Shows installation and update information for the specified fileset.
-i	Shows product information for the specified software.
-l	Shows the name, recent level, state, and description of the specified fileset.
-L	Shows the name, recent level, state, recent maintenance levels, and any subsystem fixes.
-p	Shows which files are required for the specified fileset.
-w	Shows which fileset the files belong to.
-a	Shows all available information about the specified fileset.
-c	Shows output in a colon-separated list.
-O *action*	Shows information about a specific part of the fileset.
r	Shows information about the root part.
s	Shows information about the \usr\share part.
u	Shows information about the \usr part.
-J	Creates an output that SMIT can use.
-q	Shows no headers for columns.
identifier	**The following fileset identifiers can be used:**
filesets...	Specifies which fileset to show.
fixids...	Specifies an AIX 3.2 formatted fileset update identifier to show.
filenames...	Specifies a file to show the fileset for.
all	Specifies to search in all filesets.

File Name:	`lslpp`	**Directory:**	/usr/bin	**Type:**	External

lslv

UNIX Shell:	All primary shells (csh, ksh, bsh)
Function	Shows status information or allocation maps for a logical volume.
Syntax	lslv [options...] *logicalvol*

-L	Doesn't wait for a lock on the volume group.
-l	Shows which physical volume the logical volume is on.
-m	Shows physical partitions and physical volume for each logical partition.
-n *physicalvol*	Shows the descriptor area of the specified physical volume.
-p *physicalvol*	Shows the logical volume allocation map for the specified physical volume.
logicalvol	Specifies the logical volume to show information about.

File Name:	`lslv`	**Directory:**	/usr/sbin	**Type:**	External

lsmaster

UNIX Shell:	All primary shells (csh, ksh, bsh)
Function	Shows the configuration for a NIS master server.
Syntax	lsmaster [options...]

-c	Shows output in colon-separated format.
-l	Shows output in list format.

File Name:	`lsmaster`	**Directory:**	/usr/sbin	**Type:**	External

lsnamsv

UNIX Shell:	All primary shells (csh, ksh, bsh)
Function	Shows name service information from the /etc/resolv.conf file.
Syntax	lsnamsv [options...]

-C	Shows all name service information.
-S *attributelist*	Shows specific attributes from the system configuration database.

continued

-Z		Shows output in colon-separated format.			
File Name:	lsnamsv	**Directory:**	/usr/sbin	**Type:**	External

lsnfsexp

UNIX Shell: All primary shells (csh, ksh, bsh)

Function	Shows information about NFS exported directories.
Syntax	lsnfsexp [options...] { *directory* }

-c		Shows output in colon-separated format.			
-l		Shows output in list format.			
-f *expfile*		Specifies an export file other tha /etc/export.			
directory		Specifies the directory to show information about.			
File Name:	lsnfsexp	**Directory:**	/usr/sbin	**Type:**	External

lsnfsmnt

UNIX Shell: Bourne shell (bsh)

Function	Shows information about NFS file systems that are available to mount.
Syntax	lsnfsmnt [options...] { *filesystem* }

-c		Shows output in a colon-separated format.			
-l		Shows output in list format.			
filesystem		Specifies the file system to show information about, if omitted, shows all file systems.			
File Name:	lsnfsmnt	**Directory:**	/usr/sbin	**Type:**	Script

lsnim

UNIX Shell: All primary shells (csh, ksh, bsh)

Function	Shows information about the Network Installation Management (NIM) environment.
Syntax	lsnim *OG1* { *OG2* } lsnim { *OG1* } { *OG3* } { *OG4* } [-Z] lsnim { *OG1* } [-a *attribute*] [-Z] lsnim -t *type* -q *operation* lsnim [-q *operation*] *objectname*

		The following options are divided into Option Groups indicated by OG.			
		The following two options must be used as OG1 and can't be combined:			
-p		Shows information predefined using default values.			
-P		Shows help information for predefined data.			
		The following two options can be used as OG2 and can't be combined:			
-c *class*		Specifies a NIM object class.			
-S		Shows a list of NIM subclasses.			
		The following three options can be used as OG3 and can't be combined:			
-c *class*		Specifies a NIM object class.			
-s *subclass*		Specifies a NIM subclass.			
-t *type*		Specifies a NIM object type.			
		The following two options can be used as OG4 and can't be combined:			
-l		Shows detailed information.			
-O		Shows the operations NIM supports.			
-a *attribute*		Shows information based on the specified attribute: operations, subclass, type, and class. NOTE: Possible attributes are: Operations, subclass, type and class.			
-L		Shows information on resources that can be accessed by a client computer.			
-q *operation*		Shows the attributes that are required for the specified operation.			
-Z		Shows information in a colon-separated format.			
		The following two options can't be combined, and only be used with AIX v4.2 or later:			
-g		Shows group objects with state information for individual members using long listing.			
-m		Applies other flags specified to group members.			
objectname		Specifies an object name.			
groupobjectname		Specifies a group object name.			
File Name:	lsnim	**Directory:**	/usr/sbin/	**Type:**	External

lsparent

lsparent	UNIX Shell:	All primary shells (csh, ksh, bsh)

Function	Shows which parent devices will accept a specified connection type or device.
Syntax	lsparent [options...]

	The following two options can't be combined:
-C	Shows device information from the Customized Devices Object Class.
-P	Shows device information from the Predefined Devices Object Class.
-f *file*	Reads flags from the specified file.
-F *format*	Shows output in a user-defined format.
-h	Shows help information.
-k *childconnkey*	Specifies a connection key to identify device subclass names for a child device.
-l *childname*	Specifies the logical name of a child device.

File Name:	`lsparent`	**Directory:**	/usr/sbin	**Type:**	External

lsprtsv

lsprtsv	UNIX Shell:	All primary shells (csh, ksh, bsh)

Function	Shows print service information from the database.
Syntax	lsprtsv [options...]

-c	Shows customized configuration information.
-h	Shows hostnames that are able to use the print server.
-p	Shows predefined configuration information
-q *qentry*	Shows specific logical print queues and their attributes.
-Z	Shows output in colon-separated format.

File Name:	`lsprtsv`	**Directory:**	/usr/sbin	**Type:**	External

lsps

lsps	UNIX Shell:	All primary shells (csh, ksh, bsh)

Function	Shows information about paging spaces.
Syntax	lsps [options...] *pagingspace*

-a	Shows paging space sizes in megabytes.
-c	Shows output in colon-separated format.
-l	Shows output in list format.
-s	Shows a summary of all paging spaces.
-t *action*	Specifies which paging space information to show.
lv	Shows information about logical volume paging space.
nfs	Shows information about NFS paging space.
pagingspace	Specifies pagingspace to show information on.

File Name:	`lsps`	**Directory:**	/usr/sbin	**Type:**	External

lspv

lspv	UNIX Shell:	All primary shells (csh, ksh, bsh)

Function	Shows information about physical volumes in the system.
Syntax	lspv [options...] *physicalvol*

-L	Doesn't wait for a lock on the volume group.
-l	Shows information about logical volumes on the physical volume.
-p	Shows physical partition information about the physical volume.
-M	Shows logical/physical partition numbers and logical/physical volume names.
-n *pvdesc*	Shows information about the descriptor area on the physical volume.
-v *vgid*	Shows information from the volume group ID variable.
physicalvol	Specifies the physical volume to show information on.

File Name:	`lspv`	**Directory:**	/usr/sbin	**Type:**	External

lsque

UNIX Shell:	All primary shells (csh, ksh, bsh)
Function	Shows queue stanza names.
Syntax	lsque [-c] -q *name*

-c	Shows output in colon-separated format.
-q *name*	Specifies which stanza queue names to show.
File Name: `lsque`	**Directory:** /usr/bin — **Type:** External

lsquedev

UNIX Shell:	All primary shells (csh, ksh, bsh)
Function	Shows queue stanza names and attributes from the /etc/qconfig file.
Syntax	lsquedev [-c] options...

-c	Shows output in colon-separated format.
-d *name*	Specifies the name of the device stanza to show.
-q *name*	Specifies the name of the device stanza queue to show.
File Name: `lsquedev`	**Directory:** /usr/bin — **Type:** External

lsresource

UNIX Shell:	All primary shells (csh, ksh, bsh)
Function	Shows a list of assigned bus resources in the system.
Syntax	lsresource [options...] -l *name*

-a	Shows allocated bus resource attributes for all devices connected to the same bus.
-r	Tries to resolve all bus resources of devices connected to the specified bus.
-d	Shows attribute text descriptions in the output.
-l *name*	Specifies the logical name of the device attributes.
File Name: `lsresource`	**Directory:** /usr/sbin — **Type:** External

lsrole

UNIX Shell:	All primary shells (csh, ksh, bsh)
Function	Shows a list of role attributes.
Syntax	lsrole [options...] *names...*

-c	Shows a list in a colon-separated format.
-f	Shows a list in stanza format.
-a *list*	Specifies which attributes to show.
names...	Specifies a role to show; to show every role use ALL.
File Name: `lsrole`	**Directory:** /usr/sbin — **Type:** External

lssec

UNIX Shell:	All primary shells (csh, ksh, bsh)
Function	Shows attributes from the security configuration files.
Syntax	lssec [options...]

-c	Shows output in colon-separated format.
-f *file*	Specifies the stanza file to show.
-s *stanza*	Specifies the stanza to show.
-a *attributes...*	Specifies the attribute to show.
File Name: `lssec`	**Directory:** /usr/bin — **Type:** External

lssrc

UNIX Shell:	All primary shells (csh, ksh, bsh)
Function	Shows the status of a subsystem or a subserver.
Syntax	lssrc [options...]

-h *host*	Specifies a remote host to show status about.
-d	Shows the default record.

continued

-g *group*	Specifies a group of subsystems to get status about.
-l	Shows the subsystem's current status in long form.
-n *notname*	Specifies a notify method; only used with the -N option.
-t *type*	Makes the subsystem send the current status of a specified subserver.
-o *object*	Passes the specified object to the subsystem as a character string.
-p *syspid*	Specifies a subsystem process ID to show status about.
-P *serverpid*	Passes the subserver process ID to the subsystem as a character string.
-s *subsystem*	Specifies which subsystem to show status about.
-S	Shows ODM records in SMIT format for the subsystem object class.
-T	Shows ODM records in SMIT format for the subserver object class.
-N	Shows ODM records in SMIT format for the notify class.
File Name: `lssrc`	**Directory:** /usr/bin **Type:** External

lstun

UNIX Shell: All primary shells (csh, ksh, bsh)

Function	Shows IP tunnel definitions.
Syntax	lstun [options...]

-v 4 | 6	Shows IP version 4 or 6 tunnels.
-t *tidlist*	Shows only the specified tunnel.
-p IBM | manual	Shows only IBM or manual tunnels.
-a	Shows only active tunnels.
File Name: `lstun`	**Directory:** /usr/sbin **Type:** External

lsuser

UNIX Shell: All primary shells (csh, ksh, bsh)

Function	Shows attributes from a user account.
Syntax	lsuser [options...] *users...*

-c	Shows output in colon-separated format.
-f	Shows output in stanza format.
-a *list*	Shows only the specified attributes.
users...	Specifies user(s) to show attributes about; to show every user use ALL.
File Name: `lsuser`	**Directory:** /usr/sbin **Type:** External

lsvfs

UNIX Shell: All primary shells (csh, ksh, bsh)

Function	Shows entries from the /etc/vfs file.
Syntax	lsvfs [-a] { *vfsname* }

-a	Shows all entries from the /etc/vfs file.
vfsname	Specifies a virtual file system to show.
File Name: `lsvfs`	**Directory:** /usr/sbin/ **Type:** External

lsvg

UNIX Shell: All primary shells (csh, ksh, bsh)

Function	Shows information about volume groups and partitions.
Syntax	lsvg [options...] *volumegroups...*

-o	Shows active volume groups only.
-n *pdescriptor*	Shows information from the descriptor area of the specified physical volume.
-i	Reads volume group names from STDIN.
-l	Shows the number of LVs, LPs, PPs and PVs in the specified volume group. NOTE: L = Logical, V = Volume, P = Primary or Partition
-M	Shows the PV name, number of PPs, LV name, number of LPs, and state of PPs.
-p	Shows the PV and state, total and free PPs and their location on disk.
volumegroups...	Specifies which volume group(s) to show information about.
File Name: `lsvg`	**Directory:** /usr/sbin **Type:** External

lsvgfs

UNIX Shell:	All primary shells (csh, ksh, bsh)
Function	Shows the file systems that are in a volume group.
Syntax	lsvgfs *volumegroup*

volumegroup	Specifies the volume group.

File Name:	lsvgfs	Directory:	/usr/sbin	Type:	External

lsvirprt

UNIX Shell:	All primary shells (csh, ksh, bsh)
Function	Shows virtual printer attributes.
Syntax	lsvirprt [options...]

-a *attribute*	Specifies the attribute to show.
-d *quedevname*	Specifies the queue device name of the virtual printer.
-D	Shows supported data streams.
-f *format*	Specifies which format to use.
-i	Uses interactive mode.
-n	Shows only attributes that have non-null values.
-s *section*	Specifies a section name to show.
-q *printqueue*	Specifies the print queue the virtual printer is assigned to.

File Name:	lsvirprt	Directory:	/usr/sbin	Type:	External

lvchkmajor

UNIX Shell:	All primary shells (csh, ksh, bsh)
Function	Shows if a device major number is in use for a specific volume group.
Syntax	lvchkmajor *majorNR volumegroup*

majorNR	Specifies the major number of the device.
volumegroup	Specifies the volume group.

File Name:	lvchkmajor	Directory:	/usr/sbin	Type:	External

lvlstmajor

UNIX Shell:	All primary shells (csh, ksh, bsh)
Function	Shows a list of device major numbers not currently in use.
Syntax	lvlstmajor

File Name:	lvlstmajor	Directory:	/usr/sbin	Type:	External

machstat

UNIX Shell:	All primary shells (csh, ksh, bsh)
Function	Shows information about the power status.
Syntax	machstat -p

-p	Shows the first four bits of the power status register.

File Name:	machstat	Directory:	/usr/sbin/	Type:	External

macref

UNIX Shell:	All primary shells (csh, ksh, bsh)
Function	Shows a cross-referenced list of macro files.
Syntax	macref [options...] *{ files... }*

-n	Shows one line for each reference to a symbol.
-s	Shows symbol-use statistics.
-t	Shows a macro table of contents.
--	Indicates the end of flags.
files...	Specifies the input files.

File Name:	macref	Directory:	/usr/bin/	Type:	External

makedev

UNIX Shell:	All primary shells (csh, ksh, bsh)
Function	Creates description files in binary format that can be read by the command `troff`.
Syntax	makedev option
DESC	Creates a font description filenamed `DESC.out` from the specified DESC file.
FontFile	Creates a font description filenamed `FontFile.out` for the font file specified.
File Name: `makedev`	**Directory:** /usr/bin/ **Type:** External

makekey

UNIX Shell:	All primary shells (csh, ksh, bsh)
Function	Creates an encryption key using ASCII characters for programs that run encryption. It generates a 13-character key from a 10-character input.
Syntax	makekey *keynumber*
keynumber	Specifies the encryption key number. This must contain ten ASCII characters.
File Name: `makekey`	**Directory:** /usr/bin/ **Type:** External

mant

UNIX Shell:	Bourne shell (bsh)
Function	Typesets man pages.
Syntax	mant [options...] *{ troffflags... } { files... }*
-M*size*	Specifies the size of the paper.
-a	Calls the -a flag of the troff command.
-c	Preprocesses the input files with the cw command.
-e	Preprocesses the input files with the eqn command.
-t	Preprocesses the input files with the tbl command.
-z	Prepares the output without the postprocessor.
-T*device*	Prepares the output for the specified printing device.
troffflags...	Specifies flags from the troff command.
files...	Specifies one or more files to read input from.
File Name: `mant`	**Directory:** /usr/bin/ **Type:** Script

mhl

UNIX Shell:	All primary shells (csh, ksh, bsh)
Function	Creates formatted message lists.
Syntax	mhl [options...]
-bell	Gives a sound signal at end of every page.
-nobell	Suppresses a sound signal at end of every page.
-clear	Clears the screen at end of every page.
-noclear	Doesn't clear the screen at end of every page (Is default).
-folder	Doesn't set the name of the folder in the "message name" field.
+folder	Sets the name of the folder in the "message name" field.
-moreproc *program*	Overrides the default moreproc and the entry in the profile.
-nomoreproc	Doesn't use moreproc. Entry as an empty value.
-form *file*	Specifies a file with an alternate output format.
-length *number*	Sets the length of the screen in lines.
-width *number*	Sets the width of the screen (default is 80).
-help	Shows the syntax, switches, and version information for the command.
File Name: `mhl`	**Directory:** /usr/lib/mhl **Type:** External

mhmail	UNIX Shell:	All primary shells (csh, ksh, bsh)	
Function	A program that reads or sends mail.		
Syntax	mhmail *users...* [options...]		
-cc *user*	Sends a carbon copy to the user.		
-from *user*	Specifies the from header of the mail.		
-body *"text"*	Specifies the content of the mail.		
-subject *"text"*	Specifies the text for the subject field of the message.		
-help	Shows syntax, available switches, and version information about the command.		
users...	Specifies the user(s) to send mail to.		
File Name: mhmail	**Directory:** /usr/bin/	**Type:** External	

mhpath	UNIX Shell:	All primary shells (csh, ksh, bsh)	
Function	Shows pathnames to folders and messages.		
Syntax	mhpath [options...] *{ msgs... }*		
-help	Shows the syntax, available switches, and version information in a list.		
+*folder*	Shows the pathname of the specified folder.		
msgs...	Specifies the messages to list pathnames for, separated with commas.		
File Name: mhpath	**Directory:** /usr/bin/	**Type:** External	

migratepv	UNIX Shell:	Korn shell (ksh)	
Function	Is used to move physical partitions from one physical volume to one or more physical volumes.		
Syntax	migratepv [options...] *sourcepv destinationpv*		
-i	Reads the destination physical volume from STDIN.		
-l *logicalvolume*	Moves only the physical partitions allocated to the specified logical volume.		
sourcepv	Specifies which partitions to move.		
destinationpv	Specifies where to move partitions.		
File Name: migratepv	**Directory:** /usr/sbin/	**Type:** Script	
migratepv hdisk1 hdisk2	Moves physical partitions from hdisk1 to hdisk2.		

mirrord	UNIX Shell:	All primary shells (csh, ksh, bsh)	
Function	Manages the mirror module for remote maintenance.		
Syntax	mirrord		
File Name: mirrord	**Directory:** /usr/sbin/	**Type:** External	

mirrorvg	UNIX Shell:	All primary shells (csh, ksh, bsh)	
Function	Mirrors all logical volumes that exist on a specified volume group.		
Syntax	mirrorvg [options...] *volumegroup { physicalvolumes... }*		
-S	Synchronizes the volume group in the background.		
-s	Doesn't synchronize anything.		
-Q	Keeps the quorum requirement from the volume group after mirroring is complete.		
-c *copies*	Specifies how many copies each volume must have after the command is completed.		
-m	Allows mirrors of logical volumes in the original physical partition order.		
volumegroup	Specifies a volume group to mirror.		
physicalvolumes...	Specifies which disks are used for mirroring; only for monitoring.		
File Name: mirrorvg	**Directory:** /usr/sbin/	**Type:** External	

mk_niscachemgr

UNIX Shell:	Korn shell (ksh)
Function	Manages how the NIS cachemgr daemons should start.
Syntax	mk_niscachemgr [options...]

-B	Uncomments entries in the /etc/rc.nfs file and starts the daemons.
-I	Uncomments entries in the /etc/rc.nfs file and starts the daemons at next boot.
-N	Starts the daemons.
File Name: `mk_niscachemgr`	Directory: /usr/sbin/ Type: Script

mk_nisd

UNIX Shell:	Korn shell (ksh)
Function	Manages how the rpc.nisd daemons should start.
Syntax	mk_nisd [options...]

-b	Makes the daemon emulate a NIS DNS resolver service.
-B	Uncomments entries in the /etc/rc.nfs file and starts the daemons.
-I	Uncomments entries in the /etc/rc.nfs file and starts the daemons at next boot.
-N	Start the daemons.
-s	Starts the rpc.nisd daemon without DES authentication.
-y	Makes the daemon emulate a NIS service.
File Name: `mk_nisd`	Directory: /usr/sbin/ Type: Script

mk_nispasswdd

UNIX Shell:	Korn shell (ksh)
Function	Manages how the rpc.nispasswdd daemons should start.
Syntax	mk_nispasswdd [options...]

-B	Uncomments entries in the /etc/rc.nfs file and starts the daemons.
-I	Uncomments entries in the /etc/rc.nfs file and starts the daemons at next boot.
-N	Starts the daemons.
File Name: `mk_nispasswdd`	Directory: /usr/sbin/ Type: Script

mkalias

UNIX Shell:	All primary shells (csh, ksh, bsh)
Function	Converts YP `mail.aliases` maps to `mail.byaddr` maps.
Syntax	mkalias *inputfile { outputfile }*

inputfile	Specifies the map to be used as input.
outputfile	Specifies the map to be used as output.
File Name: `mkalias`	Directory: /usr/sbin/ Type: External

mkboot

UNIX Shell:	All primary shells (csh, ksh, bsh)
Function	Creates a boot record, boot image, and service record. Not supported by AIX 4.2 and later.
Syntax	mkboot -d *device* [options...] -f *FileSystem*

-b	Erases save-based fields.
-d *device*	Specifies a device, which the IPL record requires.
-D	Loads the low-level debugger at startup.
-h	Disables `mkboot` from updating the boot header.
-i	Writes the normal section of the boot record.
-I	Starts the low-level debugger at startup.
	One of the following two options must be specified:
-k *kernel*	Specifies the kernel section of the boot image.
-e *expansion*	Specifies the expansion code for the kernel to create a compressed boot image file.
-l *Lvdevice*	Specifies the logical volume device in which the loadable boot code can be found.
-L	Enables lock instrumentation for systems running MP.

continued

-s	Writes the service section of the boot record.
-r	Creates a read-only storage emulation code image.
-p *address*	Specifies the address for the boot record's boot start field.
-w	Outputs the boot logical volume's first two blocks before the boot image.
-f *FileSystem*	Specifies the file system to use.
File Name: `mkboot`	**Directory:** /usr/sbin/ **Type:** External

mkcatdefs

UNIX Shell: All primary shells (csh, ksh, bsh)

Function	Prepares a message source file for input to the gencat command.
Syntax	mkcatdefs *symbolname sourcefiles...* [-h]

-h	Suppresses the generation of a SymbolName_msg.h file.
symbolname	Includes a SymbolName_msg.h file to associate the symbolic names.
sourcefiles...	Specifies the source file message file containing symbolic identifiers.
File Name: `mkcatdefs`	**Directory:** /usr/bin/ **Type:** External

mkcd

UNIX Shell: Korn shell (ksh)

Function	Creates a multi-volume CD system backup image from a mksysb, or from a user-specified volume group or previously created savevg image.
Syntax	mkcd [options...]

-d *device*	Sets the CD-R device. This flag or the -S flag is required.
-m *image*	Specifies an existing mksysb image.
-s *image*	Specifies an existing savevg image.
-v *volumegroup*	Specifies the volume group to be backed up by savevg command.
-C *dir*	Specifies the file system to use for creating the CD file system structure.
-M *target*	Specifies the directory or file system where mksysb or savevg is stored by a backup.
-V *volumegroup*	Sets which volume group to use in creating the necessary file system for the mkcd command.
-G	Creates a generic bootable mksysb CD. You must specify the -m and -p flags with -G.
-p *dir*	Specifies the directory or device containing device and kernel package images.
-B	Doesn't add non-bootable images to the CD.
-R	Doesn't remove the final CD images; stores multiple CD image sets.
-S	Doesn't write to the CD-R, but removes the final CD images.
-u *bosinst.data*	Specifies a user-supplied bosinst.data file to use instead of restoring or creating.
-i *image.data*	Specifies a user-supplied image.data file to use instead of restoring or creating.
-e	Rejects the files and directories from the backup image list.
-P	Creates a physical partition mapping during mksysb or savevg.
-l *list*	Specifies a list file with additional packages to copy to the image directory.
-b *file*	Specifies the pathname the list file of filesets to install after mksyb is restored.
-z *file*	Specifies the full pathname of the file to copy to the root directory of the CD system.
-D	Shows debug information.
File Name: `mkcd`	**Directory:** /usr/sbin/ **Type:** Script

mkcfsmnt

UNIX Shell: All primary shells (csh, ksh, bsh)

Function	Constructs an entry that is appended to the /etc/filesystems file and makes the file system available as a cache file system.
Syntax	mkcfsmnt [options...]

-d *name*	Sets the mount point for the cache directory.
-t	Specifies the file system to be cached.
nfs	Specifies that an NFS mount is backing the CacheFS file system.
cdrom	Specifies that a CD-ROM file system is backing the CacheFS file system.
-h *host*	Specifies which NFS server exports the directory.
-p *directory*	Specifies which directory is mounted on the specified pathname.
-c *cachedir*	Specifies the location of the CacheFS file system previously created by cfsadmin.
-d *directory*	Specifies the directory mounted on the specified pathname.

continued

-o *mount*	Sets a comma-separated string of options related to the backing file system type.
-b *filesystem*	Specifies a backing file system if one exists, or creates a temporary mount point to use.
-I	Adds an unmounted directory to the /etc/filesystems file.
-B	Adds an entry to the /etc/filesystems file, and tries to mount the file system.
-N	Mounts the specified directory, but doesn't modify the /etc/filesystems file.
File Name: mkcfsmnt	**Directory:** /usr/sbin/ **Type:** External

mkclass

UNIX Shell: All primary shells (csh, ksh, bsh)

Function	Creates a workload management class.
Syntax	mkclass [options...] *name*

-a *attribute=values...*	Specifies attributes and values to create the WLM class.
-d *confdir*	Uses the /etc/wlm/confdir directory as the configuration directory.
name	Specifies the name of the class.
File Name: mkclass	**Directory:** /usr/sbin/ **Type:** External

mkclient

UNIX Shell: Bourne shell (bsh)

Function	Uncomments entries in the /etc/rc.nfs file for the ypbind daemon, and starts it to configure a client.
Syntax	mkclient [options...]

-I	Uncomments starting entries for the ypbind daemon in the /etc/rc.nfs file.
-B	Uncomments starting entries in the /etc/rc.nfs file and starts the ypbind daemon.
-N	Starts the ypbind daemon.
-S *server*	Specifies the NIS server to use.
File Name: mkclient	**Directory:** /usr/sbin/ **Type:** Script

mkdev

UNIX Shell: All primary shells (csh, ksh, bsh)

Function	Adds a specified device to the system.
Syntax	mkdev [options...]

-c *class*	Sets the device class.
-s *subclass*	Sets the subclass of the device.
-t *type*	Sets the device type from the devices object class.
-l *name*	Sets the already defined device when not used with the -c, -s, and -t flags.
-a *attribute=value*	Sets one or multiple device attribute value pairs to be used instead of the defaults.
-d	Specifies a device in the Customized Devices object class; can't be used with -S.
-S	Doesn't set the device to the Available state.
-R	Configures parents of the device that have not already been configured.
-f *file*	Reads the required flags from the specified file.
-h	Shows the command usage message.
-p *name*	Specifies the parent name to assign to the device.
-q	Doesn't show the command output messages from STDOUTand STDERR.
-w *location*	Specifies the connection location on the parent.
File Name: mkdev	**Directory:** /usr/sbin/ **Type:** External

mkfile

UNIX Shell: All primary shells (csh, ksh, bsh)

Function	Creates an empty file or files that can be used as NFS-mounted or local swap areas.
Syntax	mkfile [options...] *size files...*

-n	Creates the specified file with the size reported, but without allocated blocks. NOTE: The allocated disk blocks will be created when they are needed.
-v	Shows version information.
size	Specifies the filesize; k for kilobytes, b for blocks, and m for megabytes.
files...	Specifies the name of the file to be created.
File Name: mkfile	**Directory:** /usr/lpp/nfs/sun_diskless/ **Type:** External

mkfilt

UNIX Shell:	All primary shells (csh, ksh, bsh)
Function	Activates or deactivates the filter rules.
Syntax	mkfilt [options...]

-v 4 | 6	Specifies the IP version of the rules you want to activate.
-d	Deactivates the active filter rules.
-u	Activates the filter rules in the filter rule table.
-z P | D	Sets the action of the default filter rule to permit or deny.
-g start | stop	Starts or stops the log functionality.
-i	Activates all active filter rules; only available when the -u option is used.

File Name: `mkfilt` **Directory:** /usr/sbin/ **Type:** External

mkfont

UNIX Shell:	All primary shells (csh, ksh, bsh)
Function	Adds a font pathname to the ODM.
Syntax	mkfont *{ file }*

file	Specifies the path to the font file.

File Name: `mkfont` **Directory:** /usr/bin/ **Type:** External

mkfs

UNIX Shell:	All primary shells (csh, ksh, bsh)
Function	Creates a file system on the specified disk partition.
Syntax	mkfs [options...] *device*

-b *boot*	Specifies the name of the program to install at the first block in the file system.
-l *label*	Specifies a label for the file system.
-i *NR*	Specifies how many I-nodes to create initially; not used when creating a journaled file system.
-p *name*	Sets a name of a prototype file. Command-line options override attributes in the file.
-s *size*	Sets the file system size in blocks (512-byte).
-v *label*	Specifies the label of the volume.
-V *name*	Specifies the name of the virtual file system type; must exist in /etc/vfs.
-o *options...*	**The following are specific options for the journaling file system:**
ag=*value*	Sets the allocation group size. Valid values are 8, 16, 32, or 64 in MB (default is 8).
bf=*choice*	Enables large files or not by specifying true or false (default is true).
frag=*size*	Specifies the file fragment size. Valid values are 512, 1024, 2048, or 4096 bytes.
compress=*choice*	Sets compression on or off by specifying LZ or no. Fragment size must be 2048.
nbpi=*value*	Sets the ratio of bytes per I-node. Valid values are 512, 1024, and 2048 to 131072.
device	Specifies the raw or the block device on which to make the new file system.

File Name: `mkfs` **Directory:** /usr/sbin/ **Type:** External

mkgroup

UNIX Shell:	All primary shells (csh, ksh, bsh)
Function	Creates a new group.
Syntax	mkgroup [options...] *{ attribute=value } group*

-a	Creates an administrative group.
-A	Makes the invoking user to the group administrator.
attribute=value	Initializes a group with a specific chgroup attribute; can be repeated.
group	Specifies the name of the new group.

File Name: `mkgroup` **Directory:** /usr/bin/ **Type:** External

mkhosts

UNIX Shell:	All primary shells (csh, ksh, bsh)
Function	Creates a new hosts file.
Syntax	mkhosts [-v] *hostfile*

-v	Shows each host that is added to the hosts file.
hostfile	Creates a hashed host database.

File Name: `mkhosts` **Directory:** /usr/sbin/ **Type:** External

mkitab

UNIX Shell:	All primary shells (csh, ksh, bsh)
Function	Creates records in the /etc/inittab file.
Syntax	mkitab [-i *identifier*] *format*

-i *identifier*	Specifies after which record in the /etc/inittab file to place the new record.
format	**The following four fields must be supplied with colon as separators:**
identifier	Specifies an identifier used to identify an object.
runlevel	Specifies in which run level to start the new command.
action	Specifies how init should process the specified command.
command	Specifies the command to start.
File Name: `mkitab`	**Directory:** /usr/sbin/ **Type:** External
mkitab cron:2:respawn:/usr/sbin/cron	Adds the cron daemon to the inittab file.

mkkeyserv

UNIX Shell:	All primary shells (csh, ksh, bsh)
Function	Uncomments keyserv daemon entries in the /etc/rc.nfs file and starts the daemon.
Syntax	mkkeyserv [option]

-I	Uncomments keyserv daemon entries in the /etc/rc.nfs file and restarts the daemon.
-B	Uncomments keyserv daemon entries in the /etc/rc.nfs and starts the daemon with startsrc.
-N	Doesn't alter the /etc/rc.nfs file, and uses startsrc to start the daemon.
File Name: `mkkeyserv`	**Directory:** /usr/sbin/ **Type:** External

mklost+found

UNIX Shell:	Bourne shell (bsh)
Function	Creates a lost+found directory for the fsck command.
Syntax	mklost+found
File Name: `mklost+found`	**Directory:** /usr/sbin/ **Type:** Script

mklv

UNIX Shell:	Korn shell (ksh)
Function	Creates a new logical volume.
Syntax	mklv [options...] *Group Partitions* { *Volumes...* }

-a *position*	Specifies the position of logical partitions on the physical volume as one of the following:
m	Assigns logical partitions to the outer middle part of physical volumes (is default).
c	Assigns logical partitions to the center part of physical volumes.
e	Assigns logical partitions to the outer edge part of physical volumes.
ie	Assigns logical partitions to the inner edge part of physical volumes.
im	Assigns logical partitions to the inner middle part of physical volumes.
-b *badblocks*	Specifies if bad blocks should be relocated:
y	Enables bad block relocation (is default).
n	Disables bad block relocation.
-c *copies*	Assigns 1to 3 physical partitions for each logical partition (default is 1).
-d *schedule*	Determines scheduling when several logical partitions are created:
p	Schedules `mklv` to work simultaneously (is default).
s	Schedules `mklv` to work sequentially.
-e *range*	Specifies how many physical volumes a logical volume can extend over:
x	Extends over as many physical volumes as possible.
m	Extends over as few physical volumes as possible.
	NOTE: The maximum number of physical volumes is set with the -u option.
-G *GID*	Specifies the logical volume's groupID.
-i	Specifies the `Volumes...` parameter should be read from STDIN.
-L *label*	Specifies the label of the logical volume, with a maximum size of 127 chars (default is none).
-m *PVname:PPnum*	Specifies the exact position with Physical Volume name and a Physical Partition number.
	NOTE: Several PPnums can be specified, using a dash for each after the first.

continued

-P *modes*	Determines the file modes or permissions for the logical volume.
-r *relocation*	Specifies if logical volumes can be relocated. The following values are valid:
y	Enables relocation of the logical volume when reorganizing (is default).
n	Disables relocation of logical volume. This must be set for striped logical volumes.
-s *strict*	Specifies if logical partitions can share physical volumes. The following are valid:
y	Specifies that sharing physical volumes is strictly forbidden (is default).
n	Specifies that sharing physical volumes is allowed.
s	Enables super-strict mode: not even partitions assigned to mirrors can share volumes.
-S *stripesize*	Sets the size of stripes in KB for a striped logical volume. (Valid sizes are: 4K, 8K, 16K, 32K, 64K, or 128K.)
-t *type*	Specifies type of the logical volume. Standard types are: jfs, jfslog, and paging.
-U *UID*	Specifies the userID for the special file of the logical volume.
-u *maxvolumes*	Specifies the maximum number of physical volumes for the new partitions.
-v *verify*	Specifies if all write operations should be verified. The following values are valid:
n	Disables verify-all mode for write operations on the logical volume (is default).
y	Enables verify-all mode for write operations on the logical volume.
-w *Mirrormode*	Specifies if there should be any mirror write consistency. The following are valid:
y	Enables mirror write consistency, giving data consistency in mirror copies.
n	Disables mirror write consistency.
-x *max*	Specifies the maximum number of logical partitions per logical volume (default is 512).
	The following two options can't be combined:
-y *name*	Specifies a logical volume name instead of letting the system generate one.
-Y *prefix*	Specifies a prefix instead of letting the system generate one. The maximum size is 13 characters.
Group	Specifies the volume group in which the logical volume will be created.
Partitions	Specifies the number of partitions for the logical volume.
Volumes...	Specifies physical volumes to use. If not specified, all volumes in the group are used.

File Name: `mklv` **Directory:** /usr/sbin/ **Type:** Script

mklvcopy

UNIX Shell: All primary shells (csh, ksh, bsh)

Function Creates logical volume copies.

Syntax mklvcopy [options...] *logicalvolume copiesNR { physicalvolumes... }*

-a *position*	Specifies the position of the logical partitions on the physical volume.
-e *range*	Specifies how many physical volumes to extend across.
-m *mapfile*	Uses a mapfile to specify the exact physical partitions to allocate.
-s *strict*	Specifies which strict allocation policy to use.
y	Uses a strict allocation policy.
n	Doesn't use a strict allocation policy.
s	Uses a super-strict policy.
-u *upperbound*	Specifies the maximum number of physical volumes for new allocation.
logicalvolume	Specifies the logical volume name or logical volume ID.
copiesNR	Specifies the number of copies to create.
physicalvolumes...	Specifies on which physical volume to create the copy.

File Name: `mklvcopy` **Directory:** /usr/sbin/ **Type:** External

mkmaster

UNIX Shell: Bourne shell (bsh)

Function Creates and configure a NIS master server.

Syntax mkmaster [options...]

-s *hosts...*	Specifies the slave hostnames for the master server.
-O	Overwrites any existing maps for the domain.
-o	Doesn't overwrite any existing maps for the domain.
-E	Doesn't continue if errors are encountered.
-P	Starts the yppasswdd daemon together with the ypserv daemon.
-p	Doesn't start the yppasswd daemon.
-U	Starts the ypupdated daemon together with the ypserv daemon.

continued

-u	Doesn't start the ypupdated daemon.
-C	Starts the ypbind daemon together with the ypserv daemon.
-c	Doesn't start the ypbind daemon.
-I	Alters the /etc/rc.nfs file to start the daemon on reboot.
-B	Uncomments entries in the /etc/rc.nfs file and starts the daemon.
-N	Makes the ypinit command start the appropriate daemons.
File Name: `mkmaster`	**Directory:** /usr/sbin/ **Type:** Script

mknamsv

UNIX Shell: All primary shells (csh, ksh, bsh)

Function	Adds name server addresses to the file /etc/resolv.conf.
Syntax	mknamsv option

-a *attribute=value*	Specifies the attributes to update - can be repeated.
-A *file*	Specifies the file with named daemon initialization information.
File Name: `mknamsv`	**Directory:** /usr/sbin/ **Type:** External

mknfs

UNIX Shell: All primary shells (csh, ksh, bsh)

Function	Manages NFS configuration for the system.
Syntax	mknfs [options...]

-I	Adds an entry with /etc/rc.nfs to the inittab file and starts the daemon.
-N	Adds an /etc/rc.nfs entry to the inittab file.
-B	Starts the NFS daemons immediately.
File Name: `mknfs`	**Directory:** /usr/sbin/ **Type:** External

mknfsexp

UNIX Shell: Bourne shell (bsh)

Function	Makes an NFS export of a directory to an NFS client.
Syntax	mknfsexp -d *directory* [options...]

-d *directory*	Specifies the directory to export or alter.
-f *exportfile*	Specifies an export file other than the default.
-t *type*	Specifies in which mode to export the directory:
rw	Exports in read-write mode.
ro	Exports in read-only mode.
rm	Exports in read-mostly mode.
-h *hostnames...*	Specifies the hosts that will have read-write access to the directory.
-a *uid*	Uses the specified userID as the effective userID.
-r *hostnames...*	Specifies that root users on the specified hosts will have access to the directory.
-c *hostnames...*	Specifies that all clients have mount access.
-s	Requires a more secure protocol when accessing the directory.
-n	Doesn't require a more secure protocol when accessing the directory.
-I	Adds an entry to the /etc/exports file.
-B	Adds an entry to the `/etc/exports` file and exports the file system immediately.
-N	Doesn't add an entry to the `/etc/exports` file and exports the directory.
-P	Specifies the exported directory is a public directory.
-p	Specifies the exported directory isn't a public directory.
File Name: `mknfsexp`	**Directory:** /usr/sbin/ **Type:** Script

mknfsmnt

UNIX Shell: Bourne shell (bsh)

Function	Mounts the specified directory from the specified host at the specified mounting point.
Syntax	mknfsmnt -f *mountpoint* -d *remotedirectory* -h *remotehost* [options...]

-f *mountpoint>*	Specifies a local path to use as the mount point for the remote directory.
-d *remotedirectory*	Specifies the remote directory to mount.
-h *remotehost*	Specifies the NFS remote host providing the directory.

continued

	The following two options can't be combined:
-A	Mounts the remote directory automatically at system restart.
-a	Disables mounting the remote directory automatically at system restart (is default).
	The following three options can't be combined:
-B	Mounts the file system and adds the entry to the /etc/filesystems file (is default).
-I	Disables mounting the file system but adds the entry to the /etc/filesystems file.
-N	Mounts the file system, but doesn't add the entry to the /etc/filesystems file.
-b *size*	Specifies the read buffer size in bytes.
-c *size*	Specifies the write buffer size in bytes.
	The following two options can't be combined:
-E	Enables interrupting hard mounts from the keyboard.
-e	Disables interrupting hard mounts from the keyboard (is default).
-G	Sets the group ID of all created files and directories to same as the parent directory.
-g	Disables files and directories from inheriting group ID (is default).
	The following two options can't be combined:
-H	Specifies the mount should be hard, retrying until the server responds (is default).
-S	Specifies the mount should be soft, returning an error if the server isn't responding.
	The following two options can't be combined:
-J	Enables ACLs for use on this mount.
-j	Disables ACLs from being used on this mount (is default).
-K *version*	Specifies the version of NFS. Choose one of the following:
any	Auto-detects the highest version of NFS available.
2	Sets NFS version 2.
3	Sets NFS version 3.
-k *protocol*	Specifies what transport protocol the mount should use. Choose one of the following:
any	Auto-detects an available protocol, preferring TCP.
tcp	Sets TCP protocol.
udp	Sets UDP protocol.
-m *mountype*	Mounts all unmounted file systems with type matching the specified mount type.
	The following two options can't be combined:
-n	Uses a less secure protocol (is default).
-s	Uses a more secure protocol.
-o *timeout*	Specifies the length of time in tenths of a second before the NFS times out.
-P *portnumber*	Specifies the IP port number the server should use.
-p *boidvalue*	Specifies the maximum number of biod daemons allowed on a file system (default is 6).
-Q	Requests no exchange of POSIX pathconf information when mounted as NFS Version 2.
-q	Doesn't exchange POSIX pathconf information when mounted as NFS Version 2.
-R *value*	Specifies the number of times a mount request should be retransmitted if not acknowledged.
-r *value*	Specifies the number of times to retry mounting the file system (default is 1000).
-T *value*	Sets the number of times files and directories can be accessed.
-t rw	Sets the access to the mounted directory as read-write (this is default).
-t ro	Sets the access to the mounted directory as read-only.
-U *MAXsec*	Sets the maximum number of seconds to keep cached attributes when a file is modified.
-u *MINsec*	Sets the minimum number of seconds to keep cached attributes when a file is modified.
-V *MAXsec*	Sets the maximum number of seconds to keep cached attributes when modifying a directory.
-v *MINsec*	Sets the minimum number of seconds to keep cached attributes when modifying a directory.
-w *value*	Performs the mount in the background (bg) or foreground (fg).
-X	Specifies that long device numbers will be supported (is default).
-x	Specifies that long device numbers will not be supported.
-Y	Allows the execution of `suid` and `sgid` programs in the file system.
-y	Prohibits the execution of `suid` and `sgid` programs in the file system.
-Z	Allows access to devices through the mount (is default).
-z	Prohibits access to devices through the mount (is default).

File Name:	`mknfsmnt`	**Directory:**	/usr/sbin/	**Type:**	Script

mknotify

UNIX Shell:	All primary shells (csh, ksh, bsh)
Function	Creates a notify method.
Syntax	mknotify options...

-n *notifyname*	Specifies the subsystem that the notify method belongs to.
-m *notifymethod*	Specifies a path to the notifying program.

File Name:	Directory:	Type:
mknotify	/usr/bin/	External

mkpasswd

UNIX Shell:	All primary shells (csh, ksh, bsh)
Function	Manages the user database. Creates indexes over security files that can be used by different library subroutines.
Syntax	mkpasswd [options...] *index*

-v	Reports any progress when the specified index is created.
	Choose only one of the following four:
-f	Forces the creation of all of the indexes.
-d	Erases all indexes.
-c	Checks all of the indexes and rebuilds the ones that are wrong.
index	Forces the creation of an index using the specified name.

File Name:	Directory:	Type:
mkpasswd	/usr/sbin/	External

mkproto

UNIX Shell:	Bourne shell (bsh)
Function	Creates a prototype file.
Syntax	mkproto *special prototype*

special	Specifies a block device, raw device, or a file system name.
prototype	Specifies the name of the prototype file to create.

File Name:	Directory:	Type:
mkproto	/usr/sbin/	Script

mkprtsv

UNIX Shell:	All primary shells (csh, ksh, bsh)
Function	Manages TCP/IP print services on a host.
Syntax	mkprtsv option [options...]

	The following two options can't be combined:
-c	Configures a client.
-s	Configures a server.
	The following options can be combined:
-a *attribute=values...*	Specifies attributes and values to add to the qconfig file.
-A *file*	Specifies a file with entries to add to the qconfig file.
-h *hosts...*	Specifies hosts that are allowed to print.
-H *file*	Specifies a file with hosts that allowed to print.
-q *queue*	Specifies the queue name in the qconfig file.
-S	Starts the print service.
-v *device*	Specifies the device stanza name in the qconfig file.

File Name:	Directory:	Type:
mkprtsv	/usr/sbin/	External

mkps

UNIX Shell:	All primary shells (csh, ksh, bsh)
Function	Adds paging space to the system.
Syntax	mkps [options...] -s *logicalpartitions... volumegroup { physicalvol }* mkps [options...] *serverhostname serverfilename*

-a	Configures paging space at reboot.
-n	Activates the paging space now.
-t *action*	Specifies the type of paging space to create - nfs or lv.

continued

-s *logicalpartitions...*	Specifies the size for the paging space and the logical volume.				
volumegroup	Specifies in which volume group to create the paging space.				
physicalvol	Specifies a disk in the volume group to create the paging space on.				
serverhostname	Specifies the NFS server to create a paging space on; only for NFS servers.				
serverfilename	Specifies the file to use as paging space.				
File Name:	`mkps`	**Directory:**	/usr/sbin/	**Type:**	External

mkqos

UNIX Shell: Bourne shell (bsh)

Function	Adds QoS support to the system
Syntax	mkqos [option]

-B	Adds entries to the inittab file and runs the /etc/rc.qos file.				
-I	Adds entries to the inittab file.				
-N	Starts only the daemons.				
File Name:	`mkqos`	**Directory:**	/usr/sbin/	**Type:**	Script

mkque

UNIX Shell: All primary shells (csh, ksh, bsh)

Function	Creates a print queue in the system.
Syntax	mkque [-D] -q *name* [-a *attribute=values...*]

-D	Makes the queue the default queue.				
-q *name*	Specifies the name of the queue.				
-a *attribute=values...*	Specifies attributes and values to add to the /etc/qconfig file.				
File Name:	`mkque`	**Directory:**	/usr/bin/	**Type:**	External

mkquedev

UNIX Shell: All primary shells (csh, ksh, bsh)

Function	Creates a new printer queue device in the system.
Syntax	mkquedev options...

-a *attribute=values...*	Specifies attributes and values for the `/etc/qconfig` file.				
-d *name*	Specifies the name of the print queue device.				
-q *name*	Specifies the name of printer queue.				
File Name:	`mkquedev`	**Directory:**	/usr/bin/	**Type:**	External

mkrole

UNIX Shell: All primary shells (csh, ksh, bsh)

Function	Creates a new role in the system.
Syntax	mkrole { *attribute=values...* } *name*

attribute=values...	Specifies attributes and values for the new role.				
name	Specifies the name of the new role. The name specified must be unique.				
File Name:	`mkrole`	**Directory:**	/usr/bin/	**Type:**	External

mkserver

UNIX Shell: All primary shells (csh, ksh, bsh)

Function	Creates a subserver definition in the sub server object class.
Syntax	mkserver -c *codepoint* -s *subsystem* -t *type*

-c *codepoint*	Specifies a codepoint identifier for the server.				
-s *subsystem*	Specifies a name for the subsystem that the subserver belongs to.				
-t *type*	Specifies the name of the subserver.				
File Name:	`mkserver`	**Directory:**	/usr/bin/	**Type:**	External

mkslave

UNIX Shell: Bourne shell (bsh)

Function	Configures an NIS slave server.
Syntax	mkslave [options...] *master*

-B	Runs ypinit and daemons and configures the system to start ypserv at boot.
-c	Stops on errors.
-C	Starts the ypinit command with the -n flag set.
-I	Starts ypinit immediately, but doesn't start the daemons.
-N	Starts ypinit immediately and also starts the daemons.
-o	Doesn't overwrite existing maps in the domain.
-O	Overwrites existing maps in the domain.
master	Specifies the NIS master server.

File Name:	mkslave	**Directory:**	/usr/sbin/	**Type:**	Script

mkssys

UNIX Shell: All primary shells (csh, ksh, bsh)

Function	Creates a subsystem definition in the subsystem object class.
Syntax	mkssys options... [options...]

	The following three options are required and must be used together:
-p *path*	Specifies the path to the subsystem.
-s *subsys*	Specifies the unique name of the subsystem.
-u *uid*	Specifies the user ID for the subsystem.
	The following options can be combined:
-a *arguments...*	Passes all specified arguments to the subsystem.
-d	Shows inactive subsystems with the lssrc -a command.
-D	Doesn't show inactive subsystems with the lssrc -a command.
-e *stderr*	Specifies the STDERR for the subsystem.
-E *nice*	Alters the execution priority for the subsystem.
-f *stopforce*	Specifies a signal to use to stop the subsystem by force (only when signal is used).
-G *group*	Specifies which group the subsystem belongs to.
-i *stdin*	Specifies STDIN for the subsystem.
-I *messqueue*	Uses message queues for communication.
-K	Uses sockets for communication.
-m *messtype*	Sets message type key on packets sent to the subsystem.
-n *stopnorm*	Specifies a signal to use to stop the subsystem normally (only when signal is used).
-o *stdout*	Specifies STDOUT for the subsystem.
-O	Doesn't restart if subsystem stops abnormally.
-q	Enables multiple instances.
-Q	Disables multiple instances.
-R	Restarts if subsystem stops abnormally.
-S	Uses signals for communication.
-t *synonym*	Specifies a synonym name for the subsystem.
-w *wait*	Specifies the time between SIGTERM and SIGKILL.

File Name:	mkssys	**Directory:**	/usr/bin/	**Type:**	External

mkstr

UNIX Shell: All primary shells (csh, ksh, bsh)

Function	Creates specific files containing error messages that are removed from a list of other files.
Syntax	mkstr [-] *messagefile prefix files...*

[-]	Places any error messages at the end of the message file.
messagefile	Specifies the message file to capture.
prefix	Specifies the file prefix to use for the created file.
files...	Specifies the files where the error messages will be extracted from; uses wildcards.

File Name:	mkstr	**Directory:**	/usr/ucb/	**Type:**	External

mksysb

UNIX Shell: Korn shell (ksh)

Function	Creates a bootable image of the root volume group on a tape or a file.
Syntax	mksysb [options...] *device*

-b *number*	Specifies the number of blocks to write in an output.
-e	Excludes files in the /etc/exclude.rootvg file.
	The -i and -m options may not be used together:
-i	Creates a new image.data file.
-m	Creates a new image.data file and map file.
-p	Doesn't use software packing.
-v	Verbose mode; shows more information.
-X	Expands the file system /tmp if needed.
device	Specifies either a tape device or a file to write the image to.

File Name:	`mksysb`	**Directory:**	/usr/bin/	**Type:**	Script

mksysb -i /dev/rmt0	Creates the image.data file and puts the bootimage on tape.

mkszfile

UNIX Shell: Korn shell (ksh)

Function	Updates the image.data file with new information.
Syntax	mkszfile [options...]

-m	Creates a logical-to-physical partition mapping.
-X	Expands the file system /tmp if needed.

File Name:	`mkszfile`	**Directory:**	/usr/bin/	**Type:**	Script

mktcpip

UNIX Shell: Korn shell (ksh)

Function	Configures startup values for TCP/IP on a host.
Syntax	mktcpip options... [options...]

	The following option can only be used alone:
-S *interface*	Gets information for use with SMIT.
	The following three options are required:
-h *hostname*	Specifies the hostname of the host.
-a *address*	Specifies the IP address of the host.
-i *interface*	Specifies the network interface to configure.
	The following options can be combined:
-c *subchannel*	Specifies the subchannel address for a System/370 channel adapter.
-d *domain*	Specifies the domain of the nameserver to use.
-D *destination*	Sets the destination address for a static route.
-g *gateway*	Specifies the gateway address.
-m *subnet*	Specifies the subnet mask.
-n *nsaddress*	Specifies the name server address.
-r *ringspeed*	Specifies the ring speed in token-rings networks: 4 or 16.
-s	Starts the TCP/IP daemons.
-t *cabletype*	Specifies the Ethernet cable type.

File Name:	`mktcpip`	**Directory:**	/usr/sbin/	**Type:**	Script

TIP:	Use the command `smitty tcpip` to configure your TCP/IP settings.

mktun

UNIX Shell: All primary shells (csh, ksh, bsh)

Function	Activates an IBM IP tunnel.
Syntax	mktun [options...]

-v 4 | 6	Specifies which IP version to use.
-i	Activates all tunnels that have the active flag set.
-l	Doesn't activate IBM tunnels.
-t *tidlist*	Specifies a tunnel ID to activate.

File Name:	`mktun`	**Directory:**	/usr/sbin/	**Type:**	External

mkuser

UNIX Shell:	All primary shells (csh, ksh, bsh)
Function	Creates new user accounts on the system.
Syntax	mkuser [options...] *username*

-a	Specifies the user account will have administrator privileges.
attribute=value	Specifies the attribute to change and the new value.

File Name:	`mkuser`	**Directory:**	/usr/bin/	**Type:**	External

mkvg

UNIX Shell:	Korn shell (ksh)
Function	Creates a volume group.
Syntax	mkvg [options...] *physicalvolumes...*

-B	Creates a volume group in the format big vg.
-c	Creates a volume group in the format concurrent capable.
-d *maxpvs*	Specifies the maximum number of physical volumes in the volume group (default is 32).
-f	Forces the creation of a volume group.
-G	Creates a volume group in the format big vg that will have more than 128 disks.
-i	Reads physical volumes from STDIN.
-m *maxpvsize*	Specifies the maximum size of the physical volumes.
-n	Doesn't activate the volume group automatically.
-s *size*	Specifies the size of the physical partitions in MB.
-t *factor*	Specifies the physical partition limit.
-V *majornum*	Specifies the device major number of the volume group.
-x	Will automatically vary on the volume group.
-y *volumegroup*	Specifies a name for the volume group.
physicalvolumes...	Specifies which physical volumes are in the volume group.

File Name:	`mkvg`	**Directory:**	/usr/sbin/	**Type:**	Script

mkvgdata

UNIX Shell:	Korn shell (ksh)
Function	Creates a volume group information file that can be used with the commands savevg and restvg.
Syntax	mkvgdata [options...] *vgname*

-m	Creates a logical-to-physical partition map file.
-X	Expands the file system /tmp if needed.
vgname	Specifies the volume group to create the file for.

File Name:	`mkvgdata`	**Directory:**	/usr/bin/	**Type:**	Script

mkvirprt

UNIX Shell:	All primary shells (csh, ksh, bsh)
Function	Create a virtual printer.
Syntax	mkvirprt [-A *attachmenttype*] options...

-A *attachmenttype*	Specifies the attachment type of the printer: local, remote, xstation, ASCII or file.
-d *queuedev*	Specifies the queue to assign the virtual printer to.
-n *device*	Specifies the printer device name.
-q *printqueue*	Specifies the special file for the print queue to attach to.
-s *datastream*	Specifies the printer's data stream type: asc, ps, pcl, 630, 855, gl, or kji.
-t *printertype*	Specifies the type of the printer.
-T	Specifies the printer is attached to an ASCII terminal.

File Name:	`mkvirprt`	**Directory:**	/usr/sbin/	**Type:**	External

mm

mm	UNIX Shell: Bourne shell (bsh)
Function	Prints memorandum macro-formatted documents.
Syntax	mm [options...] *files...*
-c	Calls the command col.
-e	Calls the command neqn.
-E	Calls the command nroff -e.
-M *media*	Specifies the paper size. Valid values are: A4, A5, B5, EXEC, LEGAL, or LETTER.
-t	Calls the command tbl.
-T *name*	Uses the specified workstation type.
-12	Uses a 12-pitch font.
files...	Specifies the file or files to format; use - for STDIN.
File Name: `mm`	**Directory:** /usr/bin/ **Type:** Script

mmt

mmt	UNIX Shell: Bourne shell (bsh)
Function	Typesets documents.
Syntax	mmt [options...] *file*
-a	Shows troff output in readable format.
-c	Uses cw as a preprocessor.
-D*device*	Redirects the output to the specified device.
-e	Uses eqn as a preprocessor.
-M *media*	Specifies the paper size. Valid values are: A4, A5, B5, EXEC, LEGAL, or LETTER.
-t	Uses tbl as a preprocessor.
-z	Uses no output filter.
-T*name*	Creates output for the specified troff device. **The names are: ibm3812 (Is default), ibm3816, hplj, ibm5587G, psc, X100**
file	Specifies the input file; reads from STDIN .
File Name: `mmt`	**Directory:** /usr/bin/ **Type:** Script

mmtu

mmtu	UNIX Shell: All primary shells (csh, ksh, bsh)
Function	Manages maximum transfer unit values.
Syntax	mmtu option
-a *value*	Adds the specified mtu value to a list of possible mtu values.
-d *value*	Removes the specified mtu value from the list of possible mtu values.
-s	Shows the mtu value list.
File Name: `mmtu`	**Directory:** /usr/sbin/ **Type:** External

monacct

monacct	UNIX Shell: Bourne shell (bsh)
Function	Creates accounting summary files in `/var/adm/acct/fiscal` and restarts summary files in `/var/adm/acct/sum`.
Syntax	monacct *{ NR }*
NR	Specifies the month or period to be used (default is the current month (01–12)).
File Name: `monacct`	**Directory:** /usr/sbin/acct/ **Type:** Script

monitord

monitord	UNIX Shell: All primary shells (csh, ksh, bsh)
Function	Manages licenses for each login.
Syntax	monitord [options...]
-t *minutes*	Uses a heartbeat interval of the specified number of minutes (default is 15).
-v *version*	Enables floating licenses for the specified OS version.
File Name: `monitord`	**Directory:** /usr/sbin/ **Type:** External

mosy

UNIX Shell: All primary shells (csh, ksh, bsh)

Function	Manages conversion of ASN.1, SMI, and MIB definitions to object definitions for the command snmpinfo.
Syntax	mosy -o *file* [-s] *files...*

-o *file*	Specifies the output file.
-s	Shows no output messages.
files...	Specifies the input files.

File Name: `mosy` **Directory:** /usr/bin/ **Type:** External

mpcfg

UNIX Shell: All primary shells (csh, ksh, bsh)

Function	Controls the remote maintenance service information; it only works on multi processor systems.
Syntax	mpcfg options... *index values...*

-c	Alters the values of the service information.
-d	Shows the values of the service information.
-f	Applies the -c or -d options to the diagnostic flags.
-m	Applies the -c or -d options to the site and modem configuration.
-p	Applies the -c or -d options to the remote support phone numbers.
-r	Reads service information and stores it in the NVRAM.
-s	Saves service information to an /etc/lpp/diagnostics/data/bump file.
-S	Applies the -c or -d options to the service support flags.
-w	Applies changes to a password.
index	Specifies the index to act on.
values...	Specifies the value to show or alter.

File Name: `mpcfg` **Directory:** /usr/sbin/ **Type:** External

mrouted

UNIX Shell: All primary shells (csh, ksh, bsh)

Function	Handles IP multicast routing among subnets.
Syntax	mrouted [options...]

-c *file*	Specifies an alternative configuration file for the `Config_File` variable.
-d *{ level }*	Shows the specified level of debug information.
0	Detaches itself from the terminal.
1	Sends all of the system log messages to STDERR also.
2	The same as level 1, plus sends significant events to STDERR.
3	The same as level 2, plus sends packet arrivals and departures to STDERR.
-p	Starts in non-pruning mode (default is pruning mode).
	These signals may be sent to `mrouted`:
-HUP	Restarts `mrouted` and rereads the configuration file.
-INT	Ends `mrouted` and sends good-bye messages to adjacent routers.
-TERM	The same as INT.
-USR1	Dumps the internal routing table to the file `/usr/tmp/mrouted.dump`.
-USR2	Dumps the internal cache table to the file `/usr/tmp/mrouted.cache`.
-QUIT	Dumps the internal routing table to STDERR if started with a debug level greater than 0. (To aid sending signals, mrouted writes its PID to /etc/mrouted.pid.)

File Name: `mrouted` **Directory:** /usr/sbin/ **Type:** External

msgchk

UNIX Shell: All primary shells (csh, ksh, bsh)

Function	Checks for mail for current or a specified user, and reports if the messages have been read or not.
Syntax	msgchk *users...*

users...	Specifies the user's mail box to check.

File Name: `msgchk` **Directory:** /usr/bin/ **Type:** External

msgs

msgs	UNIX Shell:	All primary shells (csh, ksh, bsh)
Function	Reads or saves system messages sent by mail.	
Syntax	msgs [options...] *{ NR }*	

-c *-days*	Cleans up any messages that are older than 21 days or the number of days specified.
-f	Disables the message `No new messages`.
-h	Prints only the first part of a message.
-l	Causes local messages to be shown.
-p	Pipes messages through a program specified by `more`.
-q	Searches to see if there are any messages.
-s	Posts a message.
m	Copies the message into a temporary mailbox and starts `mail`.
q	Quits `msgs` and picks up where it left off the next time `msgs` starts.
	The following options use the message depository `/var/msgs/bounds`:
s *{ file }*	Adds a current message to the message file in the local directory or a specified file.
s- *{ file }*	Saves the last message to the message file in the local directory or a specified file.
	Possible responses when the message doesn't fit the screen:
y	Shows the rest of the message.
n	Skips the message and goes on to the next.
RETURN	Uses the Return key on the keyboard instead of the `y` option.
-	Repeats the last message.
NR	Starts `msgs` at the specified message number not the next one.
File Name: msgs	**Directory:** /var/ **Type:** External

msh

msh	UNIX Shell:	All primary shells (csh, ksh, bsh)
Function	Creates the Message Handler Shell (MH) and executes MH mail commands within its shell.	
Syntax	msh *{ file }* [options...] *{ command }*	

	The following options are supported:
-help	Shows help information.
command -help	Shows help information for the specified MH internal command.
-prompt *string*	Prompts for the MH internal commands using the specified string.
quit	Exits the MH shell. the `Ctrl-D` key sequence also exits the shell.
	Select one of these two options, if needed, when using the internal vmh command:
-notopcur	Forces the current message to follow the center line of the vmh scan window.
-topcur	Forces the current message to follow the top line of the vmh scan window.
	The following is a list of the internal MH shell commands:
ali	Lists the mail aliases.
burst	Bursts digests into messages.
comp	Composes a message.
dist	Sends a message to other addresses.
folder	Sets or lists the current folder or message.
forw	Forwards the messages.
inc	Incorporates a new mail.
mhmail	Sends or reads mail.
msgchk	Checks for any messages.
next	Shows the next message to be viewed.
packf	Creates a single file by compressing a folder.
pick	Selects messages based on content.
prev	Shows the message just viewed.
refile	Stores the message to other folders.
repl	Replies to a message just received.
rmm	Removes one or many messages.
scan	Creates one line for every message search list.
send	Sends messages.

continued

show	Shows messages.
sortm	Sorts messages.
whatnow	Prompts the user for sending.
whom	Shows who will be sent the message.
file	Specifies the file to read.
File Name: `msh`	**Directory:** /usr/bin/ **Type:** External

mvdir

UNIX Shell: All primary shells (csh, ksh, bsh)

Function	Moves a directory within a file system.
Syntax	mvdir *directory1 directory2*

directory1	Specifies the name of the directory to be moved.
directory2	Specifies the new name of the directory.
File Name: `mvdir`	**Directory:** /usr/sbin/ **Type:** External

mvfilt

UNIX Shell: All primary shells (csh, ksh, bsh)

Function	Alters the position of a filter rule.
Syntax	mvfilt options...

-v 4 | 6	Specifies which IP version the rule applies to.
-p *pfid*	Specifies the old position of the filter rule.
-n *nfid*	Specifies the new position of the filter rule.
File Name: `mvfilt`	**Directory:** /usr/bin/ **Type:** External

mvt

UNIX Shell: Bourne shell (bsh)

Function	Typesets view graphs and slides in the English language.
Syntax	mvt [options...] *{ files... }*

-a	Shows troff output in readable format.
-c	Calls the command cw.
-e	Calls the command eqn.
-g	Calls the command grap.
-p	Calls the command pic.
-t	Calls the command tbl.
-z	Doesn't use an output filter.
-T*name*	Creates output for the specified troff device (default is ibm3816).
-D*dest*	Redirects the output to the specified device.
-	Reads input from STDIN.
files...	Specifies the file to typeset.
File Name: `mvt`	**Directory:** /usr/bin/ **Type:** Script

mwm

UNIX Shell: All primary shells (csh, ksh, bsh)

Function	The AIX Window Manager.
Syntax	mwm options...

-display *host:disp:screenID*	Specifies the host, display, and screen to open.
-xrm *string*	Specifies resources to start with the mwm.
-multiscreen	Manages all screens on the specified display.
-name *name*	Gets resources using the specified name.
-screens *names...*	Specifies the names of the screens to manage.
File Name: `mwm`	**Directory:** /usr/bin/X11/ **Type:** External

named4

UNIX Shell:	All primary shells (csh, ksh, bsh)
Function	Manages the DNS daemon. A lighter version of named8.
Syntax	named4 [options...]

-d *level*	Shows debug information, specified by values from 1 to 11; 11 shows most information.
-p *number*	Sets the port number to listen for domain requests.
-b*file*	Sets another boot file.
File Name: `named4`	**Directory:** /usr/sbin/ — **Type:** External

named8

UNIX Shell:	All primary shells (csh, ksh, bsh)
Function	A daemon that manages DNS services.
Syntax	named8 [options...]

-c *configfile*	Specifies another configuration file than the default.
-d *debuglevel*	Specifies the debug level, specified by values from 1 to 11. Higher values show more information.
-f	Runs the daemon in the foreground.
-p *portnum*	Specifies the socket where the daemon listens.
-q	Logs all name server queries.
-r	Doesn't recurse and resolve queries outside of the local database.
-t *rootdir*	Specifies a new root directory.
-w *workingdir*	Alters the working directory for the daemon.
File Name: `named8`	**Directory:** /usr/sbin/ — **Type:** External

namerslv

UNIX Shell:	All primary shells (csh, ksh, bsh)
Function	Changes the domain name server (DNS) routines in the system configuration database.
Syntax	namerslv option [options...]

	One of the following ten options must be specified:
-a	Runs the entry to the system configuration database. Must be used with the -i, -D, or -S option.
-d	Removes an entry in the system configuration database. Must be used with the -i, -n, or -l option.
-X [-l]	Removes all entries in the database.
-l	Removes all DNS entries.
-c *domainname*	Configures the domain name in the database.
-s	Shows all name and domain server entries in the configuration system database.
-b	Creates the system configuration database using the /etc/resolv.conf.sv file.
-E*filename*	Stops using a name server when it renames the system. (/etc/resolv.conf is moved, specified by the filenamevariable.)
-e	Renames the /etc/resolv.conf file to /etc/resolv.conf.sv, and stops using the DNS server.
-B*filename*	Specifies the /etc/resolv.conf file from the *filename*.
-C	Configures the search list in the /etc/resolv.conf file.
	The following options are optional:
-D	Shows the command deals with the domain name entry.
-l	Specifies the `-s` or `-X` options should print all DNS entries.
-i *ipadress*	Shows the command deals with the DNS entry. (To specify an IP address, use dotted decimal format.)
-l	Shows if the action is on the search list. Must be used with -d and -s.
-n	Specifies the operation is on the domain name. Must be used with -d and -s.
-S *searchlist*	Makes changes in the system configuration search list.
-Z	Creates colon-separated format in the output of the query. (Is used when the command is requested from the SMIT usability interface.)
File Name: `namerslv`	**Directory:** /usr/sbin/ — **Type:** External

ncheck

UNIX Shell:	All primary shells (csh, ksh, bsh)
Function	Shows a list with paths and i-node numbers for all files on a specified device.
Syntax	ncheck [options...] *{ filesystem }*

-a	Shows the . and .. names that are normally not shown.
-i *inode*	Shows only those files from the specified i-nodes.
-s	Shows only files that are special files or that have the SUID bit.
filesystem	Specifies the file system for which to show the i-node list.
File Name: `ncheck`	**Directory:** /usr/sbin/ — **Type:** External

ndp

UNIX Shell:	All primary shells (csh, ksh, bsh)
Function	Manages the IPv6-to-Ethernet or token-ring address translation tables used by IPv6 neighbor discovery protocol.
Syntax	ndp [options...] *{ host }* [temp]

-n	Shows network addresses as numbers.
-a	Shows all current ndp entries.
-d	Deletes the entry that matches the hostname parameter.
-i *interfaceindex*	Specifies the index of the interface to use when an ndp entry is added with the -s flag.
-s *host addr*	Creates an ndp entry for hostname with the hardware address addr.
temp	Specifies the entry isn't permanent; only works with -i.
host	Specifies the hostname to show.
File Name: `ndp`	**Directory:** /usr/sbin/ — **Type:** External

ndpd-host

UNIX Shell:	All primary shells (csh, ksh, bsh)
Function	Manages the Neighbor Discovery Protocol (NDP) for non-kernel activities: Router Discovery, Prefix Discovery, Parameter Discovery, and Redirects.
Syntax	ndpd-host [options...]

-d	Shows debug information.
-v	Logs all interesting events.
-t	Adds a timestamp in each log.
File Name: `ndpd-host`	**Directory:** /usr/sbin/ — **Type:** External

ndpd-router

UNIX Shell:	All primary shells (csh, ksh, bsh)
Function	Manages the NDP protocol for non-kernel activities. Provides router advertisement.
Syntax	ndpd-router [options...]

-r	Specifies that this will not be the default router in Router Advertisements.
-p	Doesn't offer prefixes from interface configuration.
-M	Sets a stateful configuration in advertisements.
-O	Sets another stateful information in advertisements.
-s	Activates the RIPng protocol.
-q	Activates the RIPng protocol, but doesn't send RIPng packets.
-g	Sends a default route in RIPng.
-n	Doesn't install routes received by RIPng.
-R	Uses split horizon without corrupting reverse for RIPng.
-S	Doesn't use any split horizon for RIPng.
-d	Activates debugging.
-t	Specifies that timestamps are added in logged messages.
-v	Logs all events from daemon.info and console.
-u *port*	Specifies the UDP port for RIPng (default is 521).
-D *max { min [/life }]*	Sends Unsolicited Router Advertisements at intervals from min to max seconds.

continued

	Valid values are as follows:
max	Ranges from 4 to 1800 seconds (default is 600).
min	Ranges from 1 to 0,75 * max (default equals max/3).
life	Specifies the lifetime from 0 to 65535 seconds (default is 10 * max).
-P *{ invlife }*/*{ deplife }*	Specifies invalid life value and deprecated life value for announced prefixes in seconds.
-T *{ reachtim }*/*{ retrans }*/*{ hlim }*	Specifies the Base Reachable Time, Retrans Time, and hop limit in seconds.
File Name: ndpd-router	**Directory:** /usr/sbin/ **Type:** External

ndx

UNIX Shell: Korn shell (ksh)

Function	Creates a subject-page index for a document.
Syntax	ndx *{ file } format*

file	Specifies a list of subjects included in the index.
format	Produces the final form of the document. Use the following syntax: formatter [flag...] file... (Format option must be closed with double quotes.)
File Name: ndx	**Directory:** /usr/bin/ **Type:** Script

neqn

UNIX Shell: All primary shells (csh, ksh, bsh)

Function	A preprocessor for the command *nroff*, used to help in equations, primarily used on terminals.
Syntax	neqn [options...] *{ files... }*

-d*xy*	Uses the character x and y as the equation delimiter.
-f*font*	Specifies the font to use.
-p*size*	Reduces subscripts and superscripts by the specified point size.
-s*size*	Specifies the point size to use.
--	Marks the end of options.
files...	Specifies the file to process. Use - to read from STDIN.
File Name: neqn	**Directory:** /usr/bin/ **Type:** External

netpmon

UNIX Shell: All primary shells (csh, ksh, bsh)

Function	Shows activity and reports network I/O statistics and network-related CPU usage.
Syntax	netpmon [options...]

-o *file*	Outputs the report to a file.
-d	Doesn't trace until the trcon command has been executed by the user.
-T *n*	Specifies the kernel's trace buffer size to n bytes.
-P	Pins text and data pages to the memory.
-t	Shows CPU reports per thread.
-v	Verbose mode; shows more information.
-O *reporttypes...*	Specifies which report type to create:
cpu	Creates a report on CPU usage.
dd	Creates a report on network device driver I/O.
so	Creates a report on internet socket call I/O.
nfs	Creates a report on NFS I/O.
all	Creates a report on cpu, dd, so, and nfs.
File Name: netpmon	**Directory:** /usr/bin/ **Type:** External

newfile

UNIX Shell: All primary shells (csh, ksh, bsh)

Function	Converts a text file into an INed structured file.
Syntax	newfile *file { newname }*

file	Specifies the file to convert.
newname	Specifies the name of the new file.
File Name: newfile	**Directory:** /usr/apache/bin/ **Type:** External

newform

UNIX Shell: All primary shells (csh, ksh, bsh)

Function	Changes the format of a text file line by line.
Syntax	newform [options...] { *files...* }

	When using these options, -s must be placed first.
-s	Cuts leading characters until the first Tab, and place them at the end of the line.
-i*tabspec*	Specifies input Tab specification, see `tabs` (default is -8).
-o*tabspec*	Specifies output Tab specification, see `tabs` (default is -8).
-p*n*	Fills with n prefix characters (see -c) to the beginning of the line.
-e*n*	Truncates the line at the end by n characters.
-a*n*	Fills up with n prefix characters (see -c) to the end of the line.
-f	Shows the format for Tab specification on STDOUT.
-c*char*	Changes the prefix characters used in the -a and -p options (default is space).
-l*n*	Sets the effective line length to n characters.
-b*n*	Truncates the line from the beginning by n characters.
files...	Specifies an input file, can be more than one.

File Name: `newform` **Directory:** /usr/bin/ **Type:** External

newgrp

UNIX Shell: All primary shells (csh, ksh, bsh)

Function	Changes a user's real and effective groupID to the specified group.
Syntax	newgrp [-] { *group* }

-	Makes the new group's environment the current environment.
group	Specifies the new group name.

File Name: `newgrp` **Directory:** /usr/bin/ **Type:** External

newkey

UNIX Shell: All primary shells (csh, ksh, bsh)

Function	Creates new Diffie-Hellman public keys needed for secure RPC or NFS services.
Syntax	newkey [options...] newkey -u *user* [option]

-h *host*	Creates new public and secret keys for a hostname, prompts for password.
-u *user*	Creates new public and secret keys for user, prompts for password.

File Name: `newkey` **Directory:** /usr/sbin/ **Type:** External

news

UNIX Shell: All primary shells (csh, ksh, bsh)

Function	Shows information about current events described in the directory /var/news.
Syntax	news [options...] { *items...* }

-a	Shows all items.
-n	Shows a short report with names of items, but not contents.
-s	Shows a short report with names of current items, but not contents.
items...	A specific news item.

File Name: `news` **Directory:** /usr/bin/ **Type:** External

nfso

UNIX Shell: All primary shells (csh, ksh, bsh)

Function	Manages the configuration of NFS network variables.
Syntax	nfso option [-c]

-a	Shows a list of all configurable options and their values.
-d *option*	Resets the specified option value.
-l *hostname*	Allows the system administrator to release NFS file locks on an NFS server.
-o *option=newval*	Shows or sets a new value to an option.

continued

-c	Shows output in a colon-separated format.		
File Name: nfso	**Directory:** /usr/sbin/	**Type:** External	

nim

UNIX Shell: All primary shells (csh, ksh, bsh)

Function	Manages configuration of NIM objects.
Syntax	nim -o *operation* [options...] *object*

-o *operation*	Specifies what operation to run on a NIM object. Possible operations are as follows:
allocate	Allocates a resource.
bosinst	Runs a BOS installation.
change	Changes the attributes of an object.
check	Checks the status of an object.
cust	Runs software customization.
deallocate	Deallocates a resource.
define	Specifies an object.
diag	Enables diagnostic boot.
dklsinit	Initializes a diskless environment.
dtlsinit	Initializes a dataless environment.
fixquery	Shows fix information for specified APARs or keywords.
lppchk	Verifies installed file sets.
lslpp	Shows licensed program information.
maint	Runs software maintenance.
remove	Erases an object.
reset	Resets an object.
syncroots	Synchronizes root directories for dataless and diskless clients.
unconfig	Unconfigures an NIM master file set.
maintboot	Enables maintenance boot mode.
showlog	Shows a NIM client installation log.
showres	Shows the content of a NIM resource.
-a *attribute=values...*	Assigns values to attributes.
-F	Doesn't run safety checks.
-t *type*	Specifies the type of NIM object to manage.
object	Specifies the object to manage.
File Name: nim	**Directory:** /usr/sbin/ **Type:** External

nimclient

UNIX Shell: All primary shells (csh, ksh, bsh)

Function	Runs NIM operations from a NIM client.
Syntax	nimclient option

-a *attribute=values...*	Passes attributes and their values to the NIM operation.
-d	Synchronizes date and time with the NIM master.
-l *lsnimparam*	Runs lsnim on the master with the specified parameters.
-o ***operation***	Specifies the operation to run.
allocate	Allocates a resource.
bos_inst	Runs a BOS installation.
change	Changes attributes for an object.
check	Checks status of a NIM object.
cust	Runs software customization.
deallocate	Deallocates a resource.
diag	Enables a host to boot a diagnostic image.
maintboot	Enables a host to boot in maintenace mode.
reset	Resets a NIM object.
showres	Shows the content of a NIM resource.
-p	Enables the NIM master to push commands.
-P	Disables the push command feature.
File Name: nimclient	**Directory:** /usr/sbin/ **Type:** External

nimconfig

UNIX Shell:	All primary shells (csh, ksh, bsh)
Function	Manages the configuration of a NIM master package.
Syntax	nimconfig option [options...]

	The following two options can't be combined:
-a *pif=pif*	Specifies the primary network interface for the NIM master server.
-a *netname=object*	Specifies a name for the NIM network.
	The following options can be combined:
-a *masterport=port*	Specifies the port number for the nemesis daemon.
-a *platform=platform*	Specifies the hardware platform of the clients.
rs6k	Specifies a microchannel-based uniprocessor model.
rs6ksmp	Specifies a microchannel-based symmetric multiprocessor model.
rspc	Specifies a PowerPC PCI bus-based uniprocessor model.
rspcsmp	Specifies a PowerPC PCI bus-based symmetric multiprocessor model.
-a *regport=port*	Specifies a portnumber for NIM client registration.
-a *ringspeed=speed*	Specifies the ring speed on token-ring networks: 4 or 16.
-a *cable=type*	Specifies the Ethernet cable type: bnc, dix, or N/A.
-r	Rebuilds the /etc/niminfo file.

File Name:	`nimconfig`	**Directory:**	/usr/sbin/	**Type:**	External

nimdef

UNIX Shell:	All primary shells (csh, ksh, bsh)
Function	Manages NIM client definitions.
Syntax	nimdef option -f *name*

-c	Creates commands using a client definition file.
-d	Defines a client using a client definition file.
-p	Shows the client definition file.
-f *name*	Specifies the client file.

File Name:	`nimdef`	**Directory:**	/usr/sbin/	**Type:**	External

niminit

UNIX Shell:	All primary shells (csh, ksh, bsh)
Function	Manages the configuration of a NIM client package.
Syntax	niminit option [options...]

	The following three options can't be combined:
-a *name=name*	Specifies a name for the workstation.
-a *pif=pif*	Specifies a network interface name for all NIM communications.
-a*master=host*	Specifies the hostname of the NIM master server.
	The following options can be combined:
-a *masterport=port*	Specifies the portnumber of the nemesis daemon.
-a *regport=port*	Specifies a portnumber to use for NIM client registration.
-a *cable=type*	Specifies the Ethernet cable type: bnc, dix, or N/A.
-a *ringspeed=speed*	Specifies the speed on a token-ring network: 4 or 16.
-a *iplrom=device*	Specifies a rom emulation image.
-a *platform=platform*	Specifies the hardware platform of the host.
rs6k	Specifies a microchannel uniprocessor model.
rs6ksmp	Specifies a microchannel symmetric multiprocessor model.
rspc	Specifies a PowerPC PCI bus-based uniprocessor model.
rspcsmp	Specifies a PowerPC PCI bus-based symmetric multiprocessor model.
-a *netbootkernel=netbootkerneltype*	Specifies which kernel to use.
-a *adapaddress=adapaddress*	Specifies the MAC address of the network interface.

File Name:	`niminit`	**Directory:**	/usr/sbin/	**Type:**	External

nis_cachemgr

UNIX Shell:	All primary shells (csh, ksh, bsh)

Function	A daemon that manages cache information about NIS+ server locations and directories.
Syntax	nis_cachemgr [options...]

-i	Flushes the cache and reinitializes.
-v	Verbose mode; shows more information.
-n	Runs the daemon in an insecure mode.

File Name:	`nis_cachemgr`	**Directory:**	/usr/sbin/	**Type:**	External

nisaddcred

UNIX Shell:	All primary shells (csh, ksh, bsh)

Function	Manages NIS+ credentials that are used for authentication.
Syntax	nisaddcred [options...] *authtype { domain }*

-p *principal*	Specifies the principal that you want to manage.
-P *nisprincipal*	Specifies that you want to manage a NIS+ principal.
-l *loginpasswd*	Uses the specified password to encrypt secret keys for the credential entry.
authtype	Specifies which authentication type you want to use: LOCAL or DES.
	The following option can be used to remove a specific NIS+ principal:
-r *principal*	Removes credentials related to the specified NIS+ principal.

File Name:	`nisaddcred`	**Directory:**	/usr/bin/	**Type:**	External

nisaddent

UNIX Shell:	All primary shells (csh, ksh, bsh)

Function	Creates NIS+ table entries using files from the /etc directory and from NIS maps.
Syntax	nisaddent [options...] *type { domain }* nisaddent [options...] -f *file type { domain }* nisaddent [options...] -y *ypdom type { domain }*

-D *defaults*	Specifies defaults to be temporarily used; uses a comma-separated list.
ttl=*time*	Specifies the default time-to-live for the created object.
owner=*ownername*	Specifies the owner of the created object.
group=*groupname*	Specifies the group owner of the created object.
access=*rights*	Specifies the access rights of the created object.
-P	Follows the cat path when performing lookups.
-a	Adds a file or a map without overwriting existing entries.
-m	Merges files and maps together with the specified NIS+ table.
-p	Processes the password fields when reading password information from a file.
-r	Replaces file or map entries from the NIS+ table.
-v	Verbose mode; shows more information.
-t *table*	Specifies the NIS+ table to work with.
-f *file*	Uses a file as input instead of the keyboard.
type	Specifies the data that is to be processed such as passwd, networks, hosts, and group.
domain	Specifies the NIS+ domain to work with.
-y *ypdom*	Uses NIS maps from the specified NIS domain as input.
-Y *map*	Uses the specified map as input.
	The following syntax options can be used to show NIS+ data:
-d	Shows the NIS+ table on the screen.
-A	Shows all data in the specified table.
-M	Runs lookup on the master server only.
-q	Dumps the table data quickly.

File Name:	`nisaddent`	**Directory:**	/usr/lib/nis/	**Type:**	External

niscat

UNIX Shell:	All primary shells (csh, ksh, bsh)
Function	Shows NIS+ tables or objects.
Syntax	niscat [options...] *tables...*

-A	Shows all data from all tables in the path.
-h	Shows header lines before table contents.
-L	Follows a linked file to its source.
-M	Uses information from the master server directly, instead of cached data.
-P	Follows the specified path.
-v	Shows binary data from the table on STDOUT.
-s *sep*	Specifies a separator character.
table...	Specifies the NIS+ table to show.
	You can use the following option instead of `table`:
-o *names...*	Searches for specific objects and shows them on STDOUT.

File Name:	`nicat`	**Directory:**	/usr/bin/	**Type:**	External

nischgrp

UNIX Shell:	All primary shells (csh, ksh, bsh)
Function	Manages group ownership of a NIS+ object.
Syntax	nischgrp [options...] *group name*

-A	Alters all table entries in the path.
-f	Tries to force execution of the command.
-L	Follows a link to its source and then alters the source.
-P	Follows the path within the specified table.
group	Specifies the NIS+ group to change to.
name	Specifies the NIS+ object to change group ownership for.

File Name:	`nischgrp`	**Directory:**	/usr/bin/	**Type:**	External

nischmod

UNIX Shell:	All primary shells (csh, ksh, bsh)
Function	Manage permission for a NIS+ object.
Syntax	nischmod [options...] *mode names...*

-A	Alters all the tables in the path.
-f	Tries to force execution of the command.
-L	Follows a linked file to its source and alters the source.
-P	Follows the path within the specified table.
mode	Specifies permissions for the NIS+ objects.
	The syntax for mode is: *who operand permission*:
	who can be one of the following:
n	Sets permissions for nobody.
o	Sets permissions for owner.
g	Sets permissions for group.
w	Sets permissions for world.
	operand can be one of the following:
+	Sets a permission.
-	Removes a permission.
=	Sets a permission explicitly.
	permission can be one or more of the following:
r	Sets read permission.
m	Sets modify permission.
c	Sets create permission.
d	Sets destroy permission.
names...	Specifies the NIS+ object to alter permissions for.

File Name:	`nischmod`	**Directory:**	/usr/bin/	**Type:**	External

nischown

UNIX Shell: All primary shells (csh, ksh, bsh)

Function	Manages the ownership of a NIS+ object.
Syntax	nischown [options...] *owner names...*

-A	Alters all table entries in the path.
-f	Tries to force execution of the command.
-L	Follows a linked file to its source and alters the source.
-P	Follows the path within a specified table.
owner	Specifies the new owner of the NIS+ object.
names...	Specifies the NIS+ object to change owner for.

File Name: nischown | **Directory:** /usr/bin/ | **Type:** External

nischttl

UNIX Shell: All primary shells (csh, ksh, bsh)

Function	Manages the time-to-live for NIS+ objects.
Syntax	nischttl [options...] *time names...*

-A	Alters all objects in the path.
-L	Follows a linked file to its source and alters the source.
-P	Follows the path within the specified table.
time	Sets the new time-to-live value in either seconds, or day, hour, minute, and second.
names...	Specifies the NIS+ object to alter.

File Name: nischttl | **Directory:** /usr/bin/ | **Type:** External

nisclient

UNIX Shell: Korn shell (ksh)

Function	A script for managing NIS+ environment for clients and users.
Syntax	nisclient option [options...] *{ client }*

	Use the following four options to specify the type. You may select only one of these:
-c	Creates NIS+ credentials.
-i	Initializes a NIS+ client.
-u	Initializes a user in NIS+ environment.
-r	Restores the network service environment.
	The following options work with all of the above types:
-x	Prints out what the command would do without actually executing the command.
-v	Verbose mode; shows more information.
	The following option only works with the -c and -i types:
-d *domain*	Points out for which NIS+ domain to create credentials for.
	The following options only work with the -c type:
-o	Forces overwrite of credentials (default is no overwrite).
-l *password*	Specifies the client network password.
-d *domain*	Specifies the NIS+ domain where to create the credentials.
client	Specifies any host or user name in the NIS+ domain. This is a required argument.
	The following options only work with the -i type:
-h *server*	Specifies hostname for the NIS+ server.
-a *address*	Gives IP address for the NIS+ server.
-k *domain*	Specifies in which key domain the credentials for root are stored.
-S *level*	Sets the authentication level: 0 for unauthenticated, or 2 for authenticated (DES).

File Name: nisclient | **Directory:** /usr/lib/nis/ | **Type:** Script

nisctl

UNIX Shell: All primary shells (csh, ksh, bsh)

Function	Shows NIS statistics and flushes NIS cache information from the NIS database.
Syntax	nisctl [options...] *domain*

-M	Shows the heap memory on the specified domain.
-s	Shows statistics in the specified domain.
-v	Verbose mode; shows more information.

continued

-f *target*	Flushes the cache of the specified target:
d	Flushes directories.
g	Flushes groups.
o	Flushes objects.
t	Flushes tables.
-n *object*	Specifies which object to flush. Can only be used when `-f o` is used.
-H *host*	Specifies the host to use.
domain	Specifies the domain.

File Name:	`nisctl`	**Directory:**	/usr/lib/nis/	**Type:**	External

nisdefaults

UNIX Shell: All primary shells (csh, ksh, bsh)

Function	Shows default values returned by NIS+ local name functions.
Syntax	nisdefaults [options...]

-a	Shows all defaults in a brief format.
-d	Shows default domain.
-g	Shows the default group.
-h	Shows the default host.
-p	Shows the default principal.
-s	Shows the default search path for directory.
-t	Shows the default TTL.
-v	Verbose mode; shows more information.

File Name:	`nisdefaults`	**Directory:**	/usr/bin/	**Type:**	External

niserror

UNIX Shell: All primary shells (csh, ksh, bsh)

Function	Shows NIS+ error messages.
Syntax	niserror *NR*

NR	Shows the NIS+ error message that has the specified status value.

File Name:	`niserror`	**Directory:**	/usr/bin/	**Type:**	External

nisgrep

UNIX Shell: All primary shells (csh, ksh, bsh)

Function	Searches for entries in a NIS+ table by using regular expression patterns.
Syntax	nisgrep [options...] *ACTION*

-A	Shows all data in all tables in the path.
-c	Shows how many entries were found.
-h	Shows a header line before matching the patterns.
-P	Follows concatenation path if the initial search is unsuccessful.
-M	Uses only information directly from the master server instead of cached information.
-o	Shows internal names of the found NIS+ objects.
-v	Verbose mode; shows more information.
-s *sep*	Specifies a column separation character.
ACTION	**You must specify only one of these two actions:**
pattern	Specifies a pattern to use for the search.
column=pattern	Specifies a column to search, for using the specified pattern.
table	Specifies the NIS+ table to search in. This must be used when specifying an action.

File Name:	`nisgrep`	**Directory:**	/usr/bin/	**Type:**	External

nisgrpadm

UNIX Shell: All primary shells (csh, ksh, bsh)

Function	Manages NIS+ groups. It can create, delete, or show groups and memberships.
Syntax	nisgrpadm option [options...] *{ principal } group*

	The following options can't be combined:
-a	Adds NIS+ principals to the specified group.

continued

-r	Deletes the list of NIS+ principals from the specified group.
-t	Shows if the principals are members in the specified group.
-d	Deletes a NIS+ group.
-d	Shows the members in the specified group.
-c	Creates a NIS+ group.
	The following options can be combined:
-s	Shows no output on screen.
-M	Uses only the master server for updates, not cached data.
group	Specifies the NIS+ group to manage.
	The following can only be used with the -a, -r, or -t options:
principal	Specifies an explicit NIS+ member.
File Name: nisgrpadm	**Directory:** /usr/bin/ **Type:** External

nisinit

UNIX Shell: All primary shells (csh, ksh, bsh)

Function	Sets up NIS+ servers or clients.
Syntax	nisinit -r nisinit -p *domain hosts...* nisinit -c [-k *keydomain*] option

-r	Sets up the server to be a NIS+ root server; can only be used alone.
-p	Sets up the root server to join the parent domain.
Y	Specifies the parent domain uses NIS version 2.
D	Specifies the parent domain uses DNS.
N	Specifies the parent domain uses NIS+.
-c	Sets up the system to be a NIS+ client.
-k *keydomain*	Specifies where root's credentials are placed.
	When using -c, you may select only one of these three options:
-H *host*	Specifies a host that is to be trusted.
-B	Uses broadcast to find NIS+ servers.
-C *file*	Sets up a NIS+ client using data from the specified file.
domain	Specifies the name of the parent domain.
hosts...	Specifies a list of servers that serve the parent domain.
File Name: nisinit	**Directory:** /usr/sbin/ **Type:** External

nisln

UNIX Shell: All primary shells (csh, ksh, bsh)

Function	Creates links between NIS+ objects and NIS+ names.
Syntax	nisln [options...] *name link*

-L	Follows a linked file to its source and alters the source.
-D	Specifies default values to use when creating a link.
name	Specifies the NIS+ object to be linked.
link	Specifies the NIS+ name to link the object to.
File Name: nisln	**Directory:** /usr/bin/ **Type:** External

nislog

UNIX Shell: All primary shells (csh, ksh, bsh)

Function	Shows the contents of the NIS+ transaction log.
Syntax	nislog [options...] *{ directories... }*

	You may select only one of the following two options:
-h *n*	Shows n transactions of the log, starting from the top. 0 shows the log header.
-t *n*	Shows n transactions of the log, starting from the bottom. 0 shows the log header.
-v	Verbose mode; shows more information.
directories...	Specifies the directories to search for logs (default is entire log).
File Name: nislog	**Directory:** /usr/sbin/ **Type:** External

nisls

nisls	UNIX Shell:	All primary shells (csh, ksh, bsh)
Function	Shows the content of a NIS+ directory.	
Syntax	nisls [options…] *{ directories… }*	

-d	Shows all directories the same way as a NIS+ object.
-g	Shows group owner instead of owner.
-l	Shows a long listing of the content.
-L	Follows linked files to their sources.
-m	Shows the last modification for the file instead of the creation.
-M	Use information from the master server directly instead of cached data.
-R	Shows all directories recursively.
Directories…	Specifies the NIS+ directory to show. Without this option, the command searches in the path.
File Name: `nisls`	**Directory:** /usr/bin/ **Type:** External

nismatch

nismatch	UNIX Shell:	All primary shells (csh, ksh, bsh)
Function	Searches for NIS+ tables.	
Syntax	nismatch [options…] *ACTIONS…*	

-A	Shows all data in the specified table.
-c	Shows a count of the entries that match the specified criteria.
-h	Shows the header line.
-M	Uses only data from the master server.
-o	Shows the internal names of the NIS+ objects.
-P	Follows the path of the object.
-v	Verbose mode; shows more information.
-s *sep*	Specifies a separator character to use between columns.
ACTIONS…	**The following actions can be used:**
key	Specifies a keyword to search for in the first column.
Colname=key	Specifies a keyword to search for in the specified column.
Table	Specifies the NIS+ table to search for.
Index	Specifies to search for an indexed name. Don't combine this with other actions.
File Name: `nismatch`	**Directory:** /usr/bin/ **Type:** External

nismkdir

nismkdir	UNIX Shell:	All primary shells (csh, ksh, bsh)
Function	Creates subdirectories in a NIS+ domain.	
Syntax	nismkdir [options…] *directory*	

-D *defaults*	Specifies default values, in a comma-separated list, for a new NIS+ directory.
Ttl=time	Specifies the time to live value for an object.
Group=name	Specifies the group owner of the object.
Access=rights	Sets permissions for the object. Uses the same values as the *nischmod* command.
	The following two options can't be combined:
-m *host*	Specifies the master server for the object.
-s *host*	Creates a replica of an existing object.
Directory	Specifies the directory to be created.
File Name: `nismkdir`	**Directory:** /usr/bin/ **Type:** External

nismkuser

nismkuser	UNIX Shell:	All primary shells (csh, ksh, bsh)
Function	Creates a new user account in the NIS+ account database.	
Syntax	nismkuser *{ attribute=values… } user*	

attribute=values…	Specifies attributes and values in the same form as the chuser command.
User	Specifies the user account to create.
File Name: `nismkuser`	**Directory:** /usr/sbin/ **Type:** External

nisping

nisping	UNIX Shell:	All primary shells (csh, ksh, bsh)
Function	Manages updates between NIS+ servers.	
Syntax	nisping [option] *{ domain }*	

-u *domain*	Shows the last time of update.
-H *host*	Contacts only the specified hostname; can be a hostname or an IP address.
-C *host*	Sends a request checkpoint instead of sending to all servers.
domain	Specifies the domain; if not specified, the local domain is used.

File Name:	nisping	Directory:	/usr/lib/nis/	Type:	External

nispopulate

nispopulate	UNIX Shell:	Korn shell (ksh)
Function	Populates NIS+ tables using files or maps.	
Syntax	nispopulate -Y [options...] -h *host* [-a *address*] -y *domain* [tables...] nispopulate -F [options...] *{ tables... }* nispopulate -C [options...] *{ ACTION }*	

	The following three options can only be used separately:
-Y	Uses NIS maps to populate the tables.
-F	Uses /etc files to populate the tables.
-p *directory*	Specifies where to get the files from; only used with the `-F` option.
-C	Populates tables using passwd and hosts tables. Used for DES authentication.
ACTION	**You may select only one of the following actions with the -C option:**
host	Uses hosts tables to populate NIS+ tables with authentication information.
passwd	Uses passwd tables to populate NIS+ tables with authentication information.
	The following options can be combined:
-x	Simulates execution.
-f	Forces population of tables.
-n	Doesn't overwrite existing files in the `/var/yp` directory.
-v	Verbose mode; shows more information.
-S *level*	Sets the authentication level, `0` for unauthenticated, and `2` for authenticated.
-d *domain*	Specifies the NIS+ domain to work with.
-h *host*	Specifies the NIS server hostname when using maps to populate tables.
-y *domain*	Specifies the NIS domain to copy maps from.
tables...	Specifies the particular tables to manage.

File Name:	nispopulate	Directory:	/usr/lib/nis/	Type:	Script

nisrm

nisrm	UNIX Shell:	All primary shells (csh, ksh, bsh)
Function	Deletes NIS+ objects.	
Syntax	nisrm [options...] *names...*	

-i	Prompts for confirmation before executing.
-f	Tries to force execution of the command.
names...	Specifies the NIS+ object to delete.

File Name:	nisrm	Directory:	/usr/bin/	Type:	External

nisrmdir

nisrmdir	UNIX Shell:	All primary shells (csh, ksh, bsh)
Function	Deletes NIS+ directories.	
Syntax	nisrmdir [options...] *directory*	

-i	Prompts for confirmation before deleting the directory.
-f	Tries to force execution of the command.
-s *host*	Deletes the specified hostname as a replica for the specified directory.
directory	Specifies the directory to delete.

File Name:	nisrmdir	Directory:	/usr/bin/	Type:	External

nisrmuser

UNIX Shell:	All primary shells (csh, ksh, bsh)
Function	Removes a user from the NIS+ user account database.
Syntax	nisrmuser *user*

user	Specifies the user to remove.

File Name:	nisrmuser	Directory:	/usr/sbin/	Type:	External

nisserver

UNIX Shell:	Korn shell (ksh)
Function	Manages the setup of a NIS+ server.
Syntax	nisserver option [options...]

	The following three options can't be combined:
-r	Sets up the server to be a root master server.
-l *password*	Specifies the password to use when creating credentials for the root master server.
-M	Sets up the server to be a master server.
-R	Sets up the server to be a replica server.
	The following options can be combined:
-x	Simulates the execution of a command without executing it.
-f	Forces a setup of a NIS+ server.
-v	Verbose mode; shows more information.
-Y	Sets up the NIS+ server in NIS compatibility mode.
-d *domain*	Specifies the domain name to use; required with the -M option.
-g *group*	Specifies the NIS+ group name for the new domain.
-h *host*	Specifies the hostname for the NIS+ server.

File Name:	nisserver	Directory:	/usr/lib/nis/	Type:	Script

nissetup

UNIX Shell:	Korn shell (ksh)
Function	Creates a NIS+ domain.
Syntax	nissetup [-Y] { *domain* }

-Y	Makes the domain compatible with both NIS and NIS+.
domain	Specifies the domain name of the NIS+ domain.

File Name:	nissetup	Directory:	/usr/lib/nis/	Type:	Script

nisshowcache

UNIX Shell:	All primary shells (csh, ksh, bsh)
Function	Shows the content of the NIS+ shared cache file.
Syntax	nisshowcache [-v]

-v	Verbose mode; shows more information, including server name and universal addresses.

File Name:	nisshowcache	Directory:	/usr/lib/nis/	Type:	External

nisstat

UNIX Shell:	All primary shells (csh, ksh, bsh)
Function	Queries a NIS+ server for statistics.
Syntax	nisstat [-H *host*] { *directory* }

-H *host*	Queries only the given host.
directory	Queries only servers holding the specified NIS+ directory.

File Name:	nisstat	Directory:	/usr/lib/nis/	Type:	External

nistbladm

UNIX Shell:	All primary shells (csh, ksh, bsh)
Function	Is used to create, delete, add, modify and remove entries from NIS+ tables.
Syntax	nistbladm option [options...] *ACTIONS... tablename* nistbladm option [options...] *ACTIONS... indexname*

	The following options are required but can't be combined:
-a	Adds entries to a NIS+ table.

continued

-c *tablename*	Creates a table called `tablename` in the namespace.
-d *tablename*	Specifies the table to remove.
-e *indexname*	Edits the entry in the table specified by `indexname`.
-r	Removes entries from a table.
-u	Updates the attributes of a table.
	The following options aren't required:
-D *defaults*	Specifies a different set of defaults when you create objects.
-p *path*	Specifies a search path when you update a table.
-s *sep*	Specifies the table separator character when you update a table.
-t *type*	Specifies the table type string when you update a table.
ACTIONS...	**The following is a list of actions that can be used:**
colname= { flags } [,access]	Specifies the column name.
	Use these options for *colname*:
flags	Specifies the different flags:
S	Specifies that a search can be done on column values.
I	Specifies that a search with `S` ignores case-sensitivity.
C	Encrypts the column values.
B	Creates column values in binary data.
X	Encrypts data in XDR format; used with `B`.
access	Specifies the access:
-A	Modifies all tables in the path that match search criteria specified in name.
-f	Forces operation and suppresses a failure.
-P	Follows the path within a named table. Used with an indexed name or with the -L option.
-L	Follows links and changes permission of the object instead of the link.
indexname	Specifies the index name.
tablename	Specifies the table name.
File Name: `nistbladm`	**Directory:** /usr/bin/ **Type:** External

nistest

UNIX Shell: All primary shells (csh, ksh, bsh)

Function	Allows shell scripts and other programs to test for NIS objects and access rights in an NIS+ database.
Syntax	nistest [options...] *object* nistest [options...] *indexed*

	The following options can be combined:
-A	Shows all data.
-L	Follows links to their sources.
-M	Uses the master server only, not cached data.
-P	Follows the initial path of the table.
	You may select one of the following two options:
-a *rights*	Checks permissions for objects or entries.
-t *type*	Tests object types. The following test conditions can be used.
D	Checks if the object is a directory object.
G	Checks if the object is a group object.
L	Checks if the object is a link object.
P	Checks if the object is a private object.
T	Checks if the object is a table object.
object	Specifies the test is to be run on an object.
indexed	Specifies the test is to be run on a specific table.
File Name: `nistest`	**Directory:** /usr/bin/ **Type:** External

nisupdkeys

UNIX Shell: All primary shells (csh, ksh, bsh)

Function	Manages public keys in a NIS+ object directory.
Syntax	nisupdkeys [options...] *{ directory }*

	The following two options can't be combined:
-a	Updates the universal addresses of the NIS+ server.

continued

-C	Removes public keys.
-H *host*	Specifies that changes can only be made to the specified host.
-s	Updates NIS+ directories on the specified server. Must be used with the option -H.
directory	Specifies the NIS+ directory to update.
File Name: `nisupdkeys`	**Directory:** /usr/bin/ **Type:** External

nl

UNIX Shell: All primary shells (csh, ksh, bsh)

Function	Reads lines from STDIN or a file, adds line numbers, and shows the result on STDOUT.
Syntax	nl [options...] { *file* }

-b*type*	Specifies the `type` of lines in the page body to be numbered.
a	Numbers all the lines.
t	Numbers only lines that contain data.
n	Doesn't use line numbering.
p*pattern*	Numbers only lines specified by the pattern variable.
-f *type*	Specifies the `type` of lines in the page header to be numbered.
-h *type*	Chooses which logical-page header lines to number.
-l *num*	Specifies the number of blank lines are treated as one line.
-d *delimiter*	Specifies the two characters used as the `delimiter` for logical page sections.
-i *inc*	Specifies the increment value to number logical page lines.
-n *format*	Specifies one of the following line numbering formats:
ln	Adjusts the format of the line number to the left and suppresses leading zeros.
rz	Adjusts the format of the line number to the right and keeps leading zeros.
-v Number	Sets the initial logical-page line number to the value specified by Number.
-w Number	Uses the value specified by *Number* as the number of characters in the line number.
-p	Doesn't reset line numbers at logical pages.
-s *?*	Specifies the character used to separate the line number and text.
file	Specifies the input file to generate line numbers for.
File Name: `nl`	**Directory:** /usr/bin/ **Type:** External

no

UNIX Shell: All primary shells (csh, ksh, bsh)

Function	Manages configuration of network attributes.
Syntax	no option

-a	Shows a list of all configurable attributes and their values.
-d *attribute*	Resets the specified attribute.
-o *attr={ newval }*	Shows or sets a new value for the specified attribute.
File Name: `no`	**Directory:** /usr/sbin/ **Type:** External

nrglbd

UNIX Shell: All primary shells (csh, ksh, bsh)

Function	Controls the global location broker database.
Syntax	nrglbd [-version]

-version	Shows which version of NCS nrglbd belongs to.
File Name: `nrglbd`	**Directory:** /usr/lib/ncs/bin/ **Type:** External

nsupdate

UNIX Shell: All primary shells (csh, ksh, bsh)

Function	Updates DNS name servers interactively or non-interactively.
Syntax	nsupdate [options...]

-a	Sets administrative mode; uses zone key instead of individual records key.
-g	Sets generation mode; generates a key pair for a primary name and a hostname.
-q	Output is turned off.
-v	Verbose mode; shows more information.
-?	Shows command line options.

continued

-k *file*	Specifies the default keyfile.
-h *hostname*	Specifies which record to update
-d *domain*	Specifies which domain to apply the update to.
-p *primary*	Sets the name or IP address of a DNS server.
-r *IPAddress*	Specifies the address of the record to update.
-s *"CommandString"*	Specifies internal commands separated by spaces or colons.

File Name: `nsupdate` **Directory:** /usr/sbin/ **Type:** External

nsupdate8

UNIX Shell: All primary shells (csh, ksh, bsh)

Function	Creates a DNS update packet readable by a BIND 8 nameserver.
Syntax	nsupdate8 [options...] { *file* }

-v	Uses a TCP connection instead of UDP.
-d	Creates additional debug information about any taken actions.
file	Specifies an input file.

File Name: `nsupdate8` **Directory:** /usr/sbin/ **Type:** External

ntpdate

UNIX Shell: All primary shells (csh, ksh, bsh)

Function	Sets the local date and time via the NTP. Gets `time` from any specified NTP servers.
Syntax	ntpdate [options...] { *servers...* }

-s	Uses `syslog` instead of STDOUT to log activities.
-b	Uses `gettimeofday` to step the time.
-d	Shows information about what will happen without actually doing it.
-a *keynumber*	Specifies a key number to authenticate transactions.
-e *delay*	Sets a delay in seconds for the authentication process. `xntpd` has more info.
-k *keyfile*	Specifies a file for the key (default is /etc/ntp.keys). `xntpd` has more info.
-o *version*	Specifies the version the program will act as: 1, 2, or 3 (default is 3).
-p *samples*	Specifies the number of required samples from the servers: 1 to 8 (default is 4).
-t *timeout*-u	Specifies the response timeout as a multiple of 0.2 (default is 1).
-u	Sends packets from an unprivileged port; useful with firewalls.
servers...	Gets the correct time by querying the specified NTP server.

File Name: `ntpdate` **Directory:** /usr/sbin/ **Type:** External

ntpq

UNIX Shell: All primary shells (csh, ksh, bsh)

Function	Sends queries to a NTP server that supports the NTP mode 6 control message format.
Syntax	ntpq [options...] { *hosts...* }

-c	Specifies an interactive-format command that would be executed on the hosts given.
-i	Uses interactive mode; puts the command on STDIN and is then shown on STDOUT.
-n	Shows output addresses as IP addresses instead of hostnames.
-p	Shows a list of known peers and a summary of their states.
hosts...	Specifies a host to query; default is localhost.
	The following commands are used when using interactive mode:
? *keyword*	Shows a list of all ntpq commands or how to use a specific command specified by the keyword.
associations	Shows a list of association IDs and status for the server's peers.
authenticate *choice*	Activates queries authentication; specify `yes` or `no`.
cl { *assocID* }	The same as clocklist.
clearvars	Removes all variables from the variable list.
clocklist { *assocID* }	Reads the clock variables in the variable list.
clockvar { *assocID* } { *name=value* }	Reads clock variables.
cooked	Gives the user the information formatted so it will be easier to read.
cv { *assocID* } { *name=value* }	The same as `clockvar`.
debug *choice*	Shows debug information in two ways: `more` or `less`. `off`=off.
delay *milliseconds*	Sets an interval in milliseconds; often used if the network is slow.

continued

help *{ command }*	Shows help on the specified command, all available commands are shown if command is specified.
host *hostname*	Specifies a hostname or an IP address where future queries will be sent.
hostnames *choice*	Information will be shown by hostname or IP address `yes`=hostname `no`=ip.
keyid *number*	Specifies a key number the server accepts for configuration requests.
keytype md5 | des	Sets the key type to use for authenticated requests.
lassociations	Shows a list of associations, including all client information.
lopeers	Gets and shows a list of all peers and clients.
lpassociations	Shows the last obtained list of associations, including client information.
lpeers	Gets and shows a list of all peers and clients.
mreadlist *assocID assocID*	Reads the peer variables in the variable list for multiple peers.
mreadvar *assocID assocID { name=value }*	Reads peer variables from multiple peers.
mrl *assocID assocID*	The same as `mreadlist`.
mrv *assocID assocID { name=value }*	The same as `mreadvar`.
ntpversion *ver*	Specifies the NTP version number the program accepts; valid versions are 1, 2, or 3.
opeers	Shows the peer list the old way (destination address rather than refid).
passociations	Shows a list of associations returned by the last association command.
passwd	Prompts the user for a password, to get the rights to perform configurations.
peers	Gets and shows a list of the server's peers.
poll *{ NR }* [verbose]	Polls an NTP server in client mode the specified number of times.
pstatus *assocID*	Shows status information returned for a peer.
quit	Exits the program.
raw	Shows all query information without filtering from the server.
readlist *{ assocID }*	Reads the peer or system variables included in the variable list.
readvar *{ assocID } { name=value }*	Reads peer or system variables.
rl *{ assocID }*	The same as `readlist`.
rmvars *names...*	Removes variables from the variable list. Separate names with commas.
rv *{ assocID } { name=value }*	The same as `readvar`.
showvars	Shows the variables in the variable list.
timeout *milliseconds*	Specifies the timeout for every query in milliseconds (default is 5000).
version	Shows version information.
writelist *{ assocID }*	Writes the peer or system variables included in the variable list.
writevar *assocID name=value*	Writes peer or system variables.
File Name: `ntpq`	**Directory:** /usr/sbin/ **Type:** External

ntptrace

UNIX Shell: All primary shells (csh, ksh, bsh)

Function	Traces the master time source. Shows where the specified server received its time.
Syntax	ntptrace [options...] *{ server }*

-d	Shows debug information.
-n	Shows IP addresses instead of hostnames for all hosts included in the trace.
-r *retries*	Specifies the number of retries for every host.
-t *timeout*	Specifies the timeout in seconds for retries (default is 2).
-v	Verbose mode; shows more information.
server	Specifies the NTP server to trace (default is local host).
File Name: `ntptrace`	**Directory:** /usr/sbin/ **Type:** External

nulladm

UNIX Shell: Bourne shell (bsh)

Function	Creates a file with the mode 644, using the owner and group `adm`.
Syntax	nulladm *files...*

files...	Specifies the name of the file or files that you want to create.
File Name: `nulladm`	**Directory:** /usr/sbin/acct/ **Type:** Script

number

UNIX Shell:	All primary shells (csh, ksh, bsh)
Function	Shows the written form of a number.
Syntax	number
File Name:	`number`
Directory:	/usr/games/
Type:	External

odmadd

UNIX Shell:	All primary shells (csh, ksh, bsh)
Function	Adds objects to object classes in the ODM.
Syntax	odmadd *{ files... }*
files...	Specifies one or more ASCII files with object data to use as input to the ODM.
File Name:	`odmadd`
Directory:	/usr/bin/
Type:	External

odmchange

UNIX Shell:	All primary shells (csh, ksh, bsh)
Function	Manages modification of a specified object class in the ODM.
Syntax	odmchange -o *class* [-q *criteria*] *{ file }*
-o *class*	Specifies the object class to manage.
-q *criteria*	Specifies the search criteria used to find the objects to modify.
file	Specifies an input file with the object to change.
File Name:	`odmchange`
Directory:	/usr/bin/
Type:	External

odmcreate

UNIX Shell:	All primary shells (csh, ksh, bsh)
Function	Creates ODM object classes.
Syntax	odmcreate [options...] *file*
-p	Runs the C preprocessor for the input file.
-h	Creates C code files and include files in the object class.
file	Specifies an input file with the object definitions.
File Name:	`odmcreate`
Directory:	/usr/bin/
Type:	External

odmdelete

UNIX Shell:	All primary shells (csh, ksh, bsh)
Function	Erases objects from object classes in the ODM.
Syntax	odmdelete -o *class* [-q *criteria*]
-o *class*	Specifies the object class to erase objects from.
-q *criteria*	Specifies the criteria used to search for objects to erase.
File Name:	`odmdelete`
Directory:	/usr/bin/
Type:	External

odmdrop

UNIX Shell:	All primary shells (csh, ksh, bsh)
Function	Erases an object class from the ODM.
Syntax	odmdrop -o *class*
-o *class*	Specifies the object class to erase from the ODM.
File Name:	`odmdrop`
Directory:	/usr/bin/
Type:	External

odmget

UNIX Shell:	All primary shells (csh, ksh, bsh)
Function	Creates an input file for odmadd by retrieving data from classes inside the ODM.
Syntax	odmget [-q *criteria*] *classes...*
-q *criteria*	Specifies the search criteria used to select objects from the object class or classes
classes...	Specifies the object class to retrieve data from.
File Name:	`odmget`
Directory:	/usr/bin
Type:	External

odmshow

UNIX Shell:	All primary shells (csh, ksh, bsh)
Function	Shows an ODM object class.
Syntax	odmshow *class*
class	Specifies the ODM object class to show.
File Name:	odmshow
Directory:	/usr/bin
Type:	External

on

UNIX Shell:	All primary shells (csh, ksh, bsh)
Function	Runs commands on other systems using the local environment.
Syntax	on [options...] *host command*
-i	Turns on special character processing and remote echoing.
-d	Shows debug information.
-n	Disables input on the remote program and will not allow data input from STDIN.
host	Specifies the remote hostname or IP address to run the command on.
command	Specifies the command and it's argument to run on the remote system.
File Name:	on
Directory:	/usr/bin
Type:	External

oslevel

UNIX Shell:	Korn shell (ksh)
Function	Shows the maintenance level of the system.
Syntax	oslevel [options...]
	The following options can't be combined:
-l *level*	Specifies an earlier maintenance level to show.
-g	Shows all filesets that were installed later than the maintenance level for the system.
-q	Shows all known maintenance levels.
File Name:	oslevel
Directory:	/usr/bin
Type:	Script

ospf_monitor

UNIX Shell:	All primary shells (csh, ksh, bsh)
Function	Shows statistics about OSPF routers.
Syntax	ospf_monitor *dbfile*
dbfile	Specifies a pathname to an OSPF records database.
File Name:	ospf_monitor
Directory:	/usr/sbin
Type:	External

pac

UNIX Shell:	All primary shells (csh, ksh, bsh)
Function	Prepares printer/plotter accounting records for each user of the selected printer or for the specified users.
Syntax	pac [options...] { *users...* }
-c	Sorts the output by cost instead of alphabetically.
-m	Ignores the hostname in the accounting file.
-p*price*	Specifies the cost in dollars (default is 0.02).
-q*file*	Specifies the queue configuration file (default is /etc/qconfig).
-r	Reverses the sorting order.
-s	Summarizes the accounting information in the summary file.
users...	Specifies the users to show statistics for.
File Name:	pac
Directory:	/usr/sbin
Type:	External

pack

UNIX Shell:	All primary shells (csh, ksh, bsh)
Function	Compresses files into .z format. Each file is compressed and replaced and retains access rights and dates.
Syntax	pack [options...] *files...*
-f	Forces packing, even if some files will not benefit.
-	Shows statistics about the files being packed.
files...	Specifies the file or files to be compressed.

continued

File Name:	pack	**Directory:**	/usr/bin	**Type:**	External
Note:	The input filename may not be larger than 253 bytes.				

packf

UNIX Shell:	All primary shells (csh, ksh, bsh)
Function	Copies and formats messages from a folder into a file.
Syntax	packf [+*folder*] { *messages...* } [-file *file*]

-file *file*	Specifies the file to put the messages in (default is msgbox).
+*folder*	Specifies the folder to find messages in (default is current message).
messages...	Specifies the messages to include (default is to include all).

File Name:	packf	**Directory:**	/usr/bin/	**Type:**	External

page

UNIX Shell:	All primary shells (csh, ksh, bsh)
Function	Shows a text file one page at a time, press Space to view the next page of the file.
Syntax	page [options...] { *files...* }

-c	Clears the screen every time a new page is shown.
-d	Shows a message about which keys to use.
-e	Exits more directly after the showing the last page in the file.
-i	Allows you to search for patterns even if the case doesn't match.
-l	Doesn't treat the usual formfeed characters as page breaks.
-N	Suppresses line numbering.
-n *number*	Specifies the number of lines per page to view.
-p *command*	Runs the page command specified when you start page.
-s	Replaces multiple blank lines with a single blank line.
-t *tagstring*	Shows a page of the file containing the tag specified.
-u	Doesn't generate escape sequences.
-v	Suppresses the graphical translation of nonprinting characters.
-w *action*	Uses the specified action as an extension.
tite	Sends the initialization and deinitialization strings (is default).
notite	Doesn't send the initialization and de-initialization strings.
-x *tabs*	Specifies the Tab stops (default is 8 columns).
-z	Shows the Tab (^I), Backspace (^H), and Return (^M) commands graphically.
files...	Specifies the file or files to show.

File Name:	page	**Directory:**	/usr/bin/	**Type:**	External

pagesize

UNIX Shell:	All primary shells (csh, ksh, bsh)
Function	Shows the page size of one page of the memory in bytes.
Syntax	pagesize

File Name:	pagesize	**Directory:**	/usr/bin/	**Type:**	External

panel20

UNIX Shell:	All primary shells (csh, ksh, bsh)
Function	Monitors activity between an HIA and the 5080 control unit.
Syntax	panel20 [option]

HIA0	Monitors HIA0 (is default).
HIA1	Monitors HIA1.
HIA2	Monitors HIA2.

File Name:	panel20	**Directory:**	/usr/bin/	**Type:**	External

pathchk

UNIX Shell:	All primary shells (csh, ksh, bsh)
Function	Is used to check if the specified path or paths are valid.
Syntax	pathchk [-p] *files...*

continued

-p	Performs pathname checks based on POSIX portability standards.
files...	Specifies the file or directory to be checked.
File Name: pathchk	**Directory:** /usr/bin **Type:** External

pax

UNIX Shell: All primary shells (csh, ksh, bsh)

Function	Manages archives. It can also copy directory structures from one location to another.
Syntax	List files: pax [options...] *{ patterns... }* Read files: pax -r [options...] *{ patterns... }* Write files: pax -w [options...] *{ files... }* Copy files: pax -r -w [options...] *{ files... } directory*

	There are 4 modes of operation: list, read, write, and copy. List requires no option.
-r	Extracts members of the pax archive read from STDIN using pattern matching.
-w	Writes file content to STDOUT or to a file in the specified archive format.
-rw	Copies file content to the destination or from STDIN.
	The following options are supported in all modes:
-d	Doesn't use subdirectories when archiving files or extracting archive members.
-v	Verbose mode; when in list mode shows table of contents, otherwise shows pathnames.
-s *oldnew*	Alters archive or file member names listed by pattern or filenames.
	oldnew follows the following format: /old/new/ [gp], where:
old	Specifies the regular expression or a string containing new line characters.
new	Contains an ampersand or a backreference \n, where n is the subpattern number.
-H	Archives the file using the symbolic link as the filename if the file is a symbolic link.
-L	Same as -H, but also checks the traversal of the file hierarchy.
-o *pairs*	Alters the archiving algorithm with a `keyword:=value pair`. Use a comma (,) between each pair.
	The following options can be used in list mode:
-c	Doesn't use archive or file members that match patterns or filenames.
-f *archive*	Specifies the archive to use as input or output instead of using STDIN or STDOUT.
	In addition to the options -c, -f, -n, and pattern, read mode supports the following:
-i	Prompts when renaming archive members or files matching the specified pattern.
-k	Doesn't overwrite files that already exist.
-o *options*	Doesn't do anything; reserved for special options.
-p *priv*	Specifies the privileges the extracted file will keep. Specify one or more of the following:
a	Doesn't save file access times.
m	Doesn't keep file modification times.
o	Keeps the user and group ID.
p	Keeps the file mode bits.
e	Keeps the user and group ID, file mode bits and the access and modification times.
-u	Skips files that are older than preexisting files or archive members.
	In addition to the options -f, -i, -o, and -u, write mode supports the following:
-a	Inserts files specified at the command line at the end of the specified archive.
-b *blocksize*	Specifies the number of bytes of information to send to each write to the archive.
-t	Resets the archived files' access times to what they had been before being read.
-x *format*	Specifies the archive format to use:
cpio	Specifies the Extended cpio Interchange Format.
ustar	Specifies the Extended tar Interchange Format.
-X	Skips directories located on other devices that have a different device IDs.
pattern	Specifies a pattern that matches at least one archive member pathname (default is all).
file	Specifies the file to use.
directory	Specifies the directory to get the files.
File Name: pax	**Directory:** /usr/bin/ **Type:** External

pcat

UNIX Shell:	All primary shells (csh, ksh, bsh)
Function	Shows the content of compressed files. pcat unpacks the file to a temporary place before showing it.
Syntax	pcat *files...*

files...	Specifies the compressed file or files to show the contents of.		
File Name: `pcat`	**Directory:** /usr/bin/	**Type:**	External

pclient

UNIX Shell:	All primary shells (csh, ksh, bsh)
Function	Opens an Xstation connection for a limited time.
Syntax	pclient options...

-a *string*	Specifies an aixterm command to initialize the X-window.		
-d *name:num*	Specifies the screen to open and the screen number.		
-l *file*	Specifies a keyboard map file.		
-m *modmap*	Specifies the xmodmap file to run.		
-p *path*	Specifies the path to the keyboard map file.		
-s *number*	Specifies how long to keep the connection open, in seconds.		
File Name: `pclient`	**Directory:** /usr/lpp/x_st_mgr/bin/	**Type:**	External

pcmciastat

UNIX Shell:	All primary shells (csh, ksh, bsh)
Function	Shows socket status for PCMCIA devices.
Syntax	pcmciastat -p *busnum* [-w *socketnum*]

-p *busnum*	Specifies the configured PCMCIA bus.		
-w *socketnum*	Specifies the socket to show status for.		
File Name: `pcmciastat`	**Directory:** /usr/sbin/	**Type:**	External

pdelay

UNIX Shell:	All primary shells (csh, ksh, bsh)
Function	Manages the availability of delayed login ports.
Syntax	pdelay [-a] *{ device }*

-a	Makes all ports enabled as delayed ports.		
device	Specifies a device to enable as delayed.		
File Name: `pdelay`	**Directory:** /usr/sbin/	**Type:**	External

pdisable

UNIX Shell:	All primary shells (csh, ksh, bsh)
Function	Disables a login port.
Syntax	pdisable [-a] *{ device }*

-a	Disable all enabled ports.		
device	Specifies a port to disable.		
File Name: `pdisable`	**Directory:** /usr/sbin	**Type:**	External

penable

UNIX Shell:	All primary shells (csh, ksh, bsh)
Function	Shows or enables a login port.
Syntax	penable [-a] *{ device }*

-a	Enables all login ports.		
device	Specifies a login port device to enable.		
File Name: `penable`	**Directory:** /usr/sbin	**Type:**	External

pg

pg	UNIX Shell:	All primary shells (csh, ksh, bsh)
Function	Shows a file's content on the screen one page at a time, and prompts for the next page.	
Syntax	pg [options...] { *files...* }	

-*NR*	Specifies another screen size than default.
-p *string*	Sets a new prompt for pg.
-c	Clears the screen between each page.
-e	Doesn't pause at the end of the file.
-f	Doesn't split lines that are too long.
-n	Automatically completes a command when the command letter is typed in.
-s	Shows all messages and the prompt in inverted mode.
+*lineNR*	Shows the page starting from the specified line number.
+/*pattern*/	Shows the page starting from a specified pattern.
files...	Specifies the file or files to be queried for content.

File Name:	Directory:	Type:
`pg`	/usr/bin	External

phold

phold	UNIX Shell:	All primary shells (csh, ksh, bsh)
Function	Holds a set of login ports so users can't log in on that port.	
Syntax	phold [-a] { *device* }	

-a	Holds all currently enabled login ports.
device	Specifies a port device to hold.

File Name:	Directory:	Type:
`phold`	/usr/sbin	External

pick

pick	UNIX Shell:	All primary shells (csh, ksh, bsh)
Function	Filters messages through specified expressions.	
Syntax	pick [+*folder*] { *msgs...* } [options...]	

-datefield *field*	Specifies the field to match the dates on (default is the `date` field).
-not	Shows the messages that don't match the next expression.
-lbrace	Handles the following options to the next -rbrace option as one expression.
-after *date*	Shows messages that have date later than the specified date.
-before *date*	Shows messages that have date earlier than the specified date.
-cc *pattern*	Shows messages containing the specified pattern in the `cc` field.
-date *pattern*	Shows all messages matching the specified date.
-from *pattern*	Shows messages matching the specified pattern in the `from` field.
-search *pattern*	Shows messages that have the specified pattern anywhere in the message.
-to *expression*	Shows messages containing the specified pattern in the `to` field.
--component *pattern*	Shows messages that have the specified pattern in to,cc,date,from,subject form.
-rbrace	Ends the expression block.
-and	Shows the messages that match both the previous and the next option expression.
-or	Shows the messages that match either the previous or the next option expression.
-sequence *name*	Sets the specified sequence name as the resulting messages.
-zero	Zeroes the sequence before adding it (is default).
-nozero	Doesn't zero the sequence before adding it.
-public	Sets the sequence as public.
-nopublic	Sets the sequence as private.
-list	Lists the messages in indexed order with one line per message (is default).
-nolist	Doesn't list the filtered files.
+*folder*	Specifies the folder to look in for the messages.
msgs...	Specifies the message files to use.

File Name:	Directory:	Type:
`pick`	/usr/bin/	External

pioattred

UNIX Shell: All primary shells (csh, ksh, bsh)

Function	Manages attributes for a virtual printer.
Syntax	pioattred options... [options...]

	The following two options are required:
-q *pqueue*	Specifies the spooler name of the print queue for the virtual printer.
-o *action*	Specifies how to manage the virtual printer definition.
0	Formats the specified attributes.
1	Formats and edits the specified attributes.
2	Edits the specified attributes.
3	Ignores any errors and save the definition.
4	Undoes any changes.
-a *attribute*	Specifies the virtual printer attribute to manage.

File Name: pioattred | **Directory:** /usr/sbin | **Type:** External

piobe

UNIX Shell: All primary shells (csh, ksh, bsh)

Function	The print job manager, a spooler backend program called by the qdaemon to process a print job.
Syntax	piobe [options...] { *files...* }

-a *level*	Sets the level of preview to one of the following values:
0	Normal print processing.
1	Shows a list of flag values and pipeline of filters to convert the input data type.
-A *level*	Sets the level of diagnostic output for errors. The values can be one of the following:
0	Ignores STDERR output produced by header, trailer, or print file pipelines.
1	Returns the STDERR output and the pipeline, and ends the print job.
2	Returns the flag values and ends the print job if an error is detected.
-d *Type*	Specifies data type of the file. The following values are examples of valid values:
a	Uses IBM extended ASCII.
p	Sends data to the printer unmodified.
s	Uses PostScript.
c	Uses PCL.
d	Uses Diablo 630.
k	Uses Kanji.
-f *Type*	Specifies the filter type. The following filter is currently available:
p	Starts the pr filter.
files...	Specifies the files to print.

File Name: piobe | **Directory:** /usr/lib/lpd/ | **Type:** External

pioburst

UNIX Shell: All primary shells (csh, ksh, bsh)

Function	Creates a burst text from the specified file, and shows it on STDOUT.
Syntax	pioburst [-H *host*] *file*

-H *host*	Replaces the default hostname with the specified one.
file	Specifies the file to read from.

File Name: pioburst | **Directory:** /usr/lib/lpd/pio/etc/ | **Type:** External

piocnvt

UNIX Shell: All primary shells (csh, ksh, bsh)

Function	Expands or compresses a virtual printer definition file.
Syntax	piocnvt [-s *state*] -i *source* [-o *destination*]

-s *state*	Specifies if the destination file is to be expanded or compressed.
+	Specifies the file is to be expanded.
!	Specifies the file is to be compressed.
-i *source*	Specifies the path to the input file; Required.

continued

-o *destination*	Specifies the path to the output file.
File Name: `piocnvt`	**Directory:** /usr/sbin **Type:** External

piodigest

UNIX Shell: All primary shells (csh, ksh, bsh)

Function	Converts a colon file to a memory image file to use with the `piobe` command.
Syntax	piodigest [options...] *file*

-s *type*	Specifies the printer data stream type.
-n *name*	Specifies the name of the printer device.
-p *directory*	Specifies the directory to put the generated file in.
-q *queue*	Specifies the name of the print queue to which the virtual printer is assigned.
-t *type*	Specifies the printer type.
-d *device*	Specifies the device name for the virtual printer.
file	Specifies file to read from. - tells the command to read from STDIN
File Name: `piodigest`	**Directory:** /usr/lib/lpd/pio/etc/ **Type:** External

piodmgr

UNIX Shell: All primary shells (csh, ksh, bsh)

Function	Compacts the Object Data Manager database.
Syntax	piodmgr option

-c	Extracts the entire database and compacts it.
-h	Compacts only information whose hostname has been changed.
File Name: `piodmgr`	**Directory:** /usr/lib/lpd/pio/etc/ **Type:** External

piofontin

UNIX Shell: Korn shell (ksh)

Function	Copies fonts from a diskette to the system.
Syntax	piofontin options... [-d *device*]

-t *ptype*	Specifies the printer type for the fonts; mandatory.
-c *codepage*	Specifies the codepage for the fonts; mandatory.
-d *device*	Specifies the device name for the diskette.
File Name: `piofontin`	**Directory:** /usr/sbin **Type:** Script

pioformat

UNIX Shell: All primary shells (csh, ksh, bsh)

Function	Initiates the printer formatter driver.
Syntax	pioformat -@ *file* [options...]

-@ *file*	Specifies the database or print queue to access.
-! *file*	Specifies the formatter to be loaded.
-# +*option*	Lets the print file pass through without formatting, if option is set to 1.
File Name: `pioformat`	**Directory:** /usr/lib//lpd/pio/etc/ **Type:** External

piofquote

UNIX Shell: All primary shells (csh, ksh, bsh)

Function	Reads data from STDIN, modifies control characters destined for PostScript printers, and writes the data to STDOUT.
Syntax	piofquote
File Name: `piofquote`	**Directory:** /usr/lib/lpd/pio/etc/ **Type:** External

piolpx

UNIX Shell: Korn shell (ksh)

Function	Adds backend printer support for printers attached to an Xstation.
Syntax	piolpx *file { flags... } files...*

file	Specifies the pseudo device file to read.
flags...	Specifies `qprt` flags to use.

continued

files...		Specifies the files to print to the virtual printer.			
File Name:	piolpx	**Directory:**	/usr/lib/lpd/pio/etc/	**Type:**	Script

piolsvp

UNIX Shell: All primary shells (csh, ksh, bsh)

Function	Shows all virtual printers and attachment types on the system.
Syntax	piolsvp option [-n*field*]

-q		Shows all queues and queue device pairs on the system.			
-v		Shows all queue device pairs for the queue that has virtual printers.			
-Q		Shows all queues on the system.			
-p		Shows all queue and queue-device pairs on the system, and shows a description on each.			
-A		Shows all attachment types and descriptions for the attachment types.			
-P *queue* [: *device*]		Specifies the queue name or queue device name to show information about.			
-P *queue*		Specifies the queue name to show information about.			
-d		Shows the queue devices associated with the specified queue.			
-N *type*		Specifies an attachment type.			
-n*field*		Specifies a field name for an attachment. (can be submit_job, add_queue, add_printer, remove_queue,) printer_conn, change_queue or change filters			
File Name:	piolsvp	**Directory:**	/usr/lib/lpd/pio/etc/	**Type:**	External

piomgpdev

UNIX Shell: All primary shells (csh, ksh, bsh)

Function	Is used to manage pseudo-devices for printer attachments.
Syntax	piomgpdev options... [-a *clauses...*]

-p *device*		Specifies the pseudo device to manage.			
-t *type*		Specifies the attachment type.			
		One of the following four must be specified:			
-A		Adds a pseudo device			
-C		Changes a pseudo device.			
-R		Removes a pseudo device.			
-D		Shows information on a pseudo device.			
-a *clauses...*		Specifies clauses to be added or changed in the file for a pseudo device.			
File Name:	piomgpdev	**Directory:**	/usr/lib/lpd/pio/etc/	**Type:**	External

piomkapqd

UNIX Shell: All primary shells (csh, ksh, bsh)

Function	Builds a SMIT dialog for a new printer and a new print queue.
Syntax	piomkapqd [options...]

-A *type*	Specifies the attachment type used to connect the printer to the data source.
	Common values for the type variable are:
local	Sets a local type.
xsta	Sets an Xstation type.
ascii	Sets an ASCII type
file	Sets the file where the data is stored.
-c *cmdexec*	Specifies the SMIT command to execute.
-d *name*	Specifies the name of the device or file to send the output to.
-e	Uses an existing print queue for the output instead of creating a new queue.
-f *name*	Specifies the file to store the output in.
-h *name*	Defines the title or header of the new SMIT dialog.
-i *disc*	Sets the discover flag used when creating a new dialog for new SMIT command scripts.
-o *objectID*	Specifies the SMIToblect ID that matches the value of the variable.
-p *printer*	Defines the type of printer as stored in the /usr/lib/lpd/pio/predef directory.
-P *port*	Specifies the port number of the Xstation where the printer is attached.
-r *adapter*	Sets the parent adapter for the printer.

continued

-s *subclass*	Sets the subclass type of the printer. Possible values are the following:
parallel	Specifies a parallel port.
rs232 or rs422	Specifies serial port standards.
-T *name*	Sets the name of the tty attached to the new printer or queue.
-v *device*	Defines the device type as stored in the ODM database.
-x *name*	Specifies the name of the Xstation.
-X *type*	Specifies the type of the Xstation.
File Name: `piomkapqd`	**Directory:** /usr/lib/lpd/ **Type:** External

piomkpq

UNIX Shell: All primary shells (csh, ksh, bsh)

Function	Creates new printer devices and print queues and virtual printers.
Syntax	piomkpq options... [options...]

-a *attribute=value*	Specifies the device attribute for a print queue and assigns it a value. **Attributes:** interface, ptop, autoconfig, speed, parity, bpc, stops, xon, dtr, and tb.
-A *type*	Specifies the type of attachment for the printer to use. The four connection types are:
local	Specifies the printer is connected locally.
xsta	Specifies the printer is connected to an X terminal.
ascii	Specifies the printer uses an ASCII connection type.
file	Specifies the location of a file that contains data.
-d *device*	Specifies the device name (such as `lp0 or tty1`) to direct the output to.
-D *datastream*	Specifies the type of datastream for the queue to use (asc for ASCII or ps for PostScript).
-p *type*	Specifies the printer type defined in the directory `/usr/lib/lpd/pio/predef`.
-q *queue*	Specifies the name of a print queue that is created.
-Q *queue*	Specifies the name of a print queue that currently exists.
-r *adapter*	Specifies the name of the parent adapter for the printer to use.
-w *port*	Specifies the port number for the printer to use.
-v *type*	Specifies the device type as it is defined in the `ODM database`.
File Name: `piomkpq`	**Directory:** /usr/lib/lpd/pio/etc/ **Type:** External

piomsg

UNIX Shell: All primary shells (csh, ksh, bsh)

Function	Recovers and sends a backend message to one or several users; started at the time a print job is performed.
Syntax	piomsg [options...] *{ MessageText }*

-a *string*	Specifies the string to be substituted into a message containing %s or %n$s subroutines. (This option is repeatable up to 10 times.)
-c *catalog*	Specifies the message catalog the message should be recovered from. Requires the -n option.
-n *number*	Specifies the number of the message. Requires the -c option.
-s *set*	Specifies the message set. Requires the -c and -n options (default is 1).
-u *userlist*	Specifies the users to which the message should be sent, separated by commas. (Node names must be preceded with an @ character.)
MessageText	Specifies the value to output if no other message is found.
File Name: `piomsg`	**Directory:** /usr/lib/lpd/pio/etc/ **Type:** External
NOTE:	If no userlist of recipients is specified, the message is sent to user who started the print job.

pioout

UNIX Shell: All primary shells (csh, ksh, bsh)

Function	Reads data from STDIN and writes it to the printer. This is the end command of a pipeline-started `piobe`.
Syntax	pioout [options...]

-A *bytes*	Specifies the number of bytes already printed for the print job.
-B *value*	Specifies the total byte size to be printed.
-C *value*	Specifies the number of times to send the cancel string when canceling (default is 3168).
-D *string*	Specifies the cancel string.
-E *mask*	Specifies one or more device-driver error-flag names.
-F *string*	Specifies the string to make the printer perform a form feed.

continued

-I *user*	Specifies the user who will handle printer intervention requests.
-K *string*	Doesn't print the message if the specified string is found within it.
-L *string*	Sends all messages containing the string to the user specified by -I.
-N *value*	Specifies the number of form-feed strings to send when the file is completed.
-O *file*	Sends the data to the specified file instead of to the printer.
-P *file*	Specifies a file whose data will be sent to the printer before the actual data.
-R *routine*	Specifies a parse routine to use on data from the printer.
-S *file*	Specifies a file whose data will be sent to the printer after the actual data.
-W +	Makes the printer wait for EOF (hex 04) before exiting.

File Name: `piooout` | **Directory:** /usr/lib/lpd/pio/etc/ | **Type:** External

piopredef

UNIX Shell: All primary shells (csh, ksh, bsh)

Function Creates a predefined printer definition using a virtual printer definition as a template.

Syntax piopredef [-r] options...

-r	Specifies the printer definition specified with -s and -t already exists.
-d *queuedev*	Specifies the queue device name for the predefined printer definition.
-q *pqueue*	Specifies the name of the print queue for the predefined printer definition.
-s *streamtype*	Specifies the stream type for the predefined printer.
asc	Specifies the data stream type is IBM extended ASCII.
gl	Specifies the data stream type is Hewlett Packard GL.
pcl	Specifies the data stream type is Hewlett Packard PCL.
ps	Specifies the data stream type is PostScript.
630	Specifies the data stream type is Diablo 630.
855	Specifies the data stream type is TI 855.
-t *ptype*	Specifies the printer type for the definition.

File Name: `piopredef` | **Directory:** /usr/sbin | **Type:** External

plotgbe

UNIX Shell: All primary shells (csh, ksh, bsh)

Function Prints HP-GL files on a plotter.

Syntax plotgbe [options...] *file*

-fr=*X*	Specifies the number of frames to plot on a multiframe drawing.
-noin	Doesn't reset plotter front panel values to their defaults.
file	Specifies the file to plot.

File Name: `plotgbe` | **Directory:** /usr/lpd/ | **Type:** External

plotlbe

UNIX Shell: All primary shells (csh, ksh, bsh)

Function Prints HP-GL files on a plotter.

Syntax plotlbe [options...] *file*

-fr=*X*	Specifies the number of frames to plot on a multiframe drawing.
-noin	Doesn't reset plotter front panel value to default.
file	Specifies the file to plot.

File Name: `plotlbe` | **Directory:** /usr/lpd/ | **Type:** External

pmctrl

UNIX Shell: All primary shells (csh, ksh, bsh)

Function Manages power management on the system.

Syntax pmctrl option [options...]

	One of the following options must be specified:
-d *{ device }* [-t]	Shows idle and standby times on the specified device, or all devices if no device is specified. (If the device is lft0, the second -t syntax is used.)
-t *{ idletime standbytime }*	Sets the idle and standby times for the specified device.
-t *{ dimtime suspendtime turnofftime }*	Sets the dim, suspend, and turnoff times for lft0.

continued

	If one of the following six options is used with -a, the setting will be set, not shown:
-e	Requests a transition to the specified state. Must be used with -a.
-c	Shows or sets system settings for Lid close.
-l	Shows or sets the system state to change to on low battery.
-p	Shows or sets the state to change to for main power switch.
-u	Shows or sets the maximum allowed state for users to change to.
-x	Shows or sets the state to change to when the system idle-timer expires.
	If mode isn't used with the following six options, the option only shows the current setting:
-b *{ mode }*	Shows or sets the current settings for beep. Mode can be either `on` or `off`.
-k *{ mode }*	Shows or sets the current settings for Low Function Terminal termination.
-r *{ mode }*	Shows or sets whether to resume from hibernation when receiving a phone call.
-s *{ mode }*	Shows or sets the current settings for sync daemon termination.
-w *{ mode }*	Shows or sets the password query.
-y *{ mode }*	Shows or sets the current settings for tty termination.
-R *{ date } { time }*	Shows or sets the date or time to resume from hibernation.
-S *{ date } { time } { mode }*	Shows or sets the date or time to change to a power-saving state.
mode	Specifies the mode to change to. Can be suspend, hibernate, or shutdown.
-t *{ time }*	Shows or sets the system idle time before changing to a power-saving state.
-g *{ time }*	Shows or sets the duration between suspend to hibernate in minutes.
-v	Shows help information.
-h	Shows help information on command usage.
-a *state*	Specifies the system state to change to. (Can only be used with -c, -l, -p, -u, -x, and must be used with -e.)

File Name:	`pmctrl`	**Directory:**	/usr/bin	**Type:**	External

pop3d

UNIX Shell: All primary shells (csh, ksh, bsh)

Function	The daemon for the post office protocol version 3.
Syntax	pop3d

File Name:	`pop3d`	**Directory:**	/usr/sbin/	**Type:**	External

portmap

UNIX Shell: All primary shells (csh, ksh, bsh)

Function	Converts RPC program numbers into DARPA protocol port numbers. Must be running to enable RPC calls.
Syntax	portmap

File Name:	`portmap`	**Directory:**	/usr/sbin	**Type:**	External

portmir

UNIX Shell: All primary shells (csh, ksh, bsh)

Function	Attaches one tty stream to another and monitor the user session on that stream.
Syntax	portmir [options...]

-c monitor	Creates a CuAt ODM database attribute to configure a port for service boot.
-d mir_modem	Sets the monitoring port for dial-in purposes.
-m *monitor*	Specifies a monitoring device.
-o	Stops monitoring and exits the command.
-q	Checks the value set with the -c option.
-s mir_modem	Used in service mode for Micro Channel Adapter SMP machines.
-t *target*	Specifies a device to monitor.

File Name:	`portmir`	**Directory:**	/usr/sbin/	**Type:**	External

post

UNIX Shell:	**All primary shells (csh, ksh, bsh)**
Function	Delivers messages to local and remote users. Must be started from another program.
Syntax	post [options...] *{ file }*

-alias *file*	Specifies the alias-file to use (default is /etc/mh/MailAliases).
-filter *file*	Specifies the file to use as a filter for the message.
-nofilter	Doesn't filter the message (is default).
-format	Formats the To: and cc: entries into standard-format entries (is default).
-noformat	Doesn't format the message.
-msgid	Adds a Message-ID: or a Resent-Message-ID to the message.
-nomsgid	Doesn't add a Message-ID: to the message (is default).
-verbose	Verbose mode; shows more information.
-noverbose	Doesn't show more information (is default).
-watch	Shows information on the progress of the delivery to local and network mail.
-nowatch	Doesn't show information on the delivery progress (is default).
-width *columns*	Specifies the width for the message headers (default is 72).
file	Specifies the message files to deliver.

File Name:	`post`	**Directory:**	/usr/lib/mh/	**Type:**	External

pppattachd

UNIX Shell:	**All primary shells (csh, ksh, bsh)**
Function	Attaches an asynchronous device stream to the PPP subsystem.
Syntax	pppattachd *TYPE* [options...] To run as a daemon: pppattachd /dev/tty*PortNR TYPE* [options...]

authenticate pap | chap	Specifies the current system as the authenticator of PAP or CHAP.
inactive *time*	Sets the time in seconds of inactivity on the link before terminating the connection.
multilink	Specifies the PPP link has a group of attachments connecting to two PPP peers.
nodaemon	Prevents the attachment process from becoming a daemon.
peer pap | chap	Sets the current system as the peer of either PAP or CHAP.
remote *name*	Defines a remote host to be used for PAP authentication.
user *name*	Defines a user entry to use for PAP authentication.
connect *program*	Sets the program to use to place the outgoing connection (only as daemon).
/dev/tty*PortNR*	Specifies the tty port to use as the outgoing connection (only as daemon).
TYPE	Set the type of subsystem connection to be bound to:
client	Sets the subsystem connection type to client.
server	Sets the subsystem connection type to server.
demand	Sets the subsystem connection type to demand.

File Name:	`pppattachd`	**Directory:**	/usr/sbin/	**Type:**	External

pppcontrold

UNIX Shell:	**All primary shells (csh, ksh, bsh)**
Function	The daemon that controls the PPP protocol.
Syntax	pppcontrold

File Name:	`pppcontrold`	**Directory:**	/usr/sbin	**Type:**	External

pppdial

UNIX Shell:	**All primary shells (csh, ksh, bsh)**
Function	Connects to a remote system using the PPP protocol.
Syntax	pppdial [options...] -f *file*

-t *timeout*	Specifies the timeout value for the session.
-v	Logs all chat activities to `syslog`.
-d *logfile*	Logs all activities to a specified file.
-f *file*	Specifies a file containing the connection dialog.

File Name:	`pppdial`	**Directory:**	/usr/sbin	**Type:**	External

pppstat

UNIX Shell:	All primary shells (csh, ksh, bsh)
Function	Monitors active PPP links.
Syntax	pppstat
File Name:	`pppstat`
Directory:	/usr/sbin/
Type:	External

pprof

UNIX Shell:	All primary shells (csh, ksh, bsh)
Function	Shows CPU usage of kernel threads.
Syntax	pprof option [options...]

	The following three options can't be combined, and one is required:
time	Specifies how long to trace the system.
-i *file*	Creates a report from a previously created pprof.flow.
-d	Waits for the user to start trcon and trcstop.
-f	Creates only the pprof.famcpu and pprof.famind reports.
-n	Creates only the pprof.namecpu report.
-p	Creates only the pprof.cpu report.
-s	Creates only the pprof.start report.
-T *bytes*	Specifies the trace kernel buffer size in bytes (default is 32000).
File Name:	`pprof`
Directory:	/usr/bin/
Type:	External

prctmp

UNIX Shell:	All primary shells (csh, ksh, bsh)
Function	Shows the session record file.
Syntax	prctmp *file*

file	Specifies a file other than `/var/adm/acct/nite/ctmp`.
File Name:	`prctmp`
Directory:	/usr/sbin/acct/
Type:	External

prdaily

UNIX Shell:	Bourne shell (bsh)
Function	A shell procedure that formats and reports previous accounting data from `/var/adm/acct/sum/rprtmmdd`.
Syntax	prdaily [options...] *{ mmdd }*

-c	Shows a report on exceptional resource usage by a command (current day's data only).
-l	Shows a report on exceptional resource usage by a login ID.
mmdd	Specifies the month and day of the report desired.
File Name:	`prdaily`
Directory:	/usr/sbin/acct/
Type:	Script

print

UNIX Shell:	Korn shell (ksh)
Function	Shows any arguments on the STDOUT.
Syntax	print [option] *{ arguments... }*

-	Shows the arguments as described by `echo`.
-n	Doesn't add new line to the output.
-R	Ignores any escape characters in the arguments (raw mode).
-r	Ignores any escape characters in the arguments (raw mode).
-p	Writes the output to a shell spawned with |&.
-s	Writes the argument to the history file.
-u*n*	A one-digit file descriptor to use as output.
arguments...	Specifies the valid arguments for the command.

prof

prof		**UNIX Shell:**	All primary shells (csh, ksh, bsh)
Function	Shows data from a profile file produced by the monitor function.		
Syntax	prof [options...] *{ prog }* [-m *mdata*]		

-g	Lists the time spent in static functions separately.
-h	Suppresses the header on the report.
-L *PathName*	Specifies a different pathname for locating shared objects.
-m *mdata*	Specifies the input profile file.
-s	Shows a summary of the monitoring parameters and statistics.
-S	Shows a summery of monitoring parameters and statistics on STDERR.
-v	Suppresses all printing and sends a graphic version to the STDOUT.
-z	Includes all symbols in the profile range.
	The following four options can't be combined:
-a	Sorts by increasing symbol address.
-c	Sorts by decreasing number of calls.
-n	Sorts lexically by symbol name.
-t	Sorts by decreasing percentage of total time
	The following two options can't be combined:
-o	Shows each symbol address and name in octal.
-x	Shows each symbol address and name in hexadecimal.
prog	Specifies the object file to use; default is `a.out`.

File Name:	`prof`	**Directory:**	/usr/bin/	**Type:**	External

proff

proff		**UNIX Shell:**	Bourne shell (bsh)
Function	Formats text for printers that use personal printer data streams.		
Syntax	proff [options...] *{ files... }*		

-L *list*	Passes the specified list as flags to the qprt command.
-P*printer*	Sends output to a specific printer.
-t	Sends output to STDOUT.
-	Uses STDIN as input instead of files.
nrofflags	Specifies nroff flags to pass to the command.
files...	Specifies the input file or files.

File Name:	`proff`	**Directory:**	/usr/bin/	**Type:**	Script

proto

proto		**UNIX Shell:**	All primary shells (csh, ksh, bsh)
Function	Creates a prototype of a file system.		
Syntax	proto *directory { prefix }*		

directory	Specifies the file system to make a prototype of.
prefix	Adds a path prefix to the directory that contains the initialization files.

File Name:	`proto`	**Directory:**	/usr/sbin/	**Type:**	External

prs

prs		**UNIX Shell:**	All primary shells (csh, ksh, bsh)
Function	Shows selected portions, all, or parts of an SCCS delta table history.		
Syntax	prs [options...] *files...*		

-a	Includes all deltas, even deltas marked as removed.
-e	Requests all information for deltas created before deltas specified with -r.
-l	Requests information for all deltas created later than deltas specified with -r.
-c*datetime*	Shows information for deltas checked in before -e, or later than -l. (The following date format is used: yy[mm[dd[hh[mm[ss]]]]].)
-d*dataspec*	Produces a report associated with the indicated data specification.
-r*sid*	Identifies the SCCS delta ID for the delta which information is requested.

continued

files...		Specifies the `s.filename` to show.			
File Name:	`prs`	**Directory:**	/usr/bin/	**Type:**	External

prtacct

UNIX Shell: All primary shells (csh, ksh, bsh)

Function	A shell procedure used to format and print TACCT (total accounting) files.
Syntax	prtacct [options...] *file* ["*heading*"]

-f *fields*		Selects fields to show.			
-v		Verbose mode; shows more information.			
"*heading*"		Specifies the header when printing the file.			
file		Specifies which file to format and print to `TACCT`.			
File Name:	`prtacct`	**Directory:**	/usr/sbin/acct/	**Type:**	External

prtty

UNIX Shell: All primary shells (csh, ksh, bsh)

Function	Prints directly to a terminal's printer port.
Syntax	prtty [-l*number*] *files...*

-l*number*		Prompts for printing and prints the specified number of lines.			
files...		Specifies the file to print.			
File Name:	`prtty`	**Directory:**	/usr/bin/	**Type:**	External

pshare

UNIX Shell: All primary shells (csh, ksh, bsh)

Function	Shows or enables shared login ports.
Syntax	pshare [-a] { *device* }

-a		Enables all ports as shared login ports.			
device		Specifies a port device to enable.			
-a		Enables all ports as shared.			
device		Use the Device parameter to specify the ports to be enabled.			
File Name:	`pshare`	**Directory:**	/usr/sbin/	**Type:**	External

pstart

UNIX Shell: All primary shells (csh, ksh, bsh)

Function	Enables login ports listed in the /etc/inittab file.
Syntax	pstart [-a] { *device* }

-a		Enables all normal, shared, and delayed ports.			
device		Specifies a login port device to enable.			
-a		Enables all ports (normal, shared, and delayed ports).			
File Name:	`pstart`	**Directory:**	/usr/sbin/	**Type:**	External

pstat

UNIX Shell: All primary shells (csh, ksh, bsh)

Function	Shows system tables on STDOUT.
Syntax	pstat [options...] { *kernel* } { *corefile* }

-a	Shows the entries in the process table.
-A	Shows the kernel thread table.
-f	Shows the open file table.
-i	Shows the i-node table and data block addresses.
-P	Shows the kernel thread table entries that are executable.
-s	Shows information about swap space usage.
-S	Shows the processor status.
-t	Shows table for terminals.
-u *procslot*	Shows the user structure in the specified slot in the process table.
-T	Shows the system variables.
-U *threadslot*	Shows the user structure in the specified thread in the kernel thread table.

continued

kernel	Specifies the kernel to use (default is /usr/lib/boot/unix).
corefile	Specifies a corefile to use.
File Name: `pstat`	**Directory:** /usr/sbin/ **Type:** External

ptx

UNIX Shell: All primary shells (csh, ksh, bsh)

Function	Reads the specified text file or STDIN, shuffles the words and phrases within it, and writes it to `outputfile`.
Syntax	ptx [options...] *{ inputfile } { outputfile }*

-f	Runs in case-insensitive mode.
-r	Performs a reference on the first field of each line.
-t	Prepares the output for the phototypesetter.
-b *file*	Uses the characters in the specified file to separate words.
-g *value*	Specifies the size of the gap column between fields.
-w *value*	Specifies the output width in columns between references.
-i *file*	Specifies the file to read the word ignore list from.
-o *file*	Specifies the file to read the word only list from.
--	Indicates the end of the options.
inputfile	Specifies the file to use; uses STDIN if no file is specified.
outputfile	Specifies the file to write to.
File Name: `ptx`	**Directory:** /usr/bin/ **Type:** External

pwdadm

UNIX Shell: All primary shells (csh, ksh, bsh)

Function	Manages user passwords.
Syntax	pwdadm [option] *user*

-f *flags...*	Specifies flag attributes for a user's password. Use commas to separate flags.
NOCHECK	Specifies that new passwords will not follow the rules for password composition.
ADMIN	Specifies that root is the only account permitted to change password information.
ADMCHG	Forces the user to change their password at next logon.
-q	Permits the root user or members of the security group to query password information.
-c	Clears all flags set in the /etc/passwd/security file.
user	Specifies the user whose password is to be managed.
File Name: `pwdadm`	**Directory:** /usr/bin/ **Type:** External

pwdck

UNIX Shell: All primary shells (csh, ksh, bsh)

Function	Verifies password information.
Syntax	pwdck option *user* | ALL

	The following options can't be combined:
-n	Reports errors, but doesn't fix them.
-p	Fixes errors, but doesn't report them.
-y	Fixes and report errors.
user	Specifies a user to check password information on.
ALL	Specifies that all entries in the password file are checked.
File Name: `pwdck`	**Directory:** /usr/bin/ **Type:** External

qadm

UNIX Shell: All primary shells (csh, ksh, bsh)

Function	Manages printers, spoolers, queues, and print jobs.
Syntax	qadm [options...]

-G	Brings down the queuing system; this option is used alone.
-D *printer*	Brings down the specified printer.
-U *printer*	Brings the printer up.
-X *printer*	Cancels all jobs for the current user on the specified printer.
File Name: `qadm`	**Directory:** /usr/bin/ **Type:** External

qcan

UNIX Shell:	All primary shells (csh, ksh, bsh)
Function	Cancels print jobs.
Syntax	qcan [options...]

-P *printer*	Specifies a printer to cancel jobs on.
-x *jobnumber*	Specifies the print job to cancel.
-X	Cancels all print jobs.

File Name:	qcan	**Directory:**	/usr/bin/	**Type:**	External

qchk

UNIX Shell:	All primary shells (csh, ksh, bsh)
Function	Shows information about a print queue.
Syntax	qchk [options...]

-A	Shows the status of all queues.
-L	Shows output in long format.
-W	Shows output in wide format.
-P *printer*	Shows the status of the specified printer.
-# *jobnumber*	Shows the status of the specified job.
-q	Shows the status of the default print queue.
-u *user*	Shows the status of all jobs sent by the specified user.
-w *seconds*	Updates status information with the specified interval in seconds.

File Name:	qchk	**Directory:**	/usr/bin/	**Type:**	External

qdaemon

UNIX Shell:	All primary shells (csh, ksh, bsh)
Function	A daemon that controls the scheduling of queued print jobs.
Syntax	qdaemon

File Name:	qdaemon	**Directory:**	/usr/sbin/	**Type:**	External

qhld

UNIX Shell:	All primary shells (csh, ksh, bsh)
Function	Manages hold and release for spooled print jobs.
Syntax	qhld [options...]

-# *jobnumber*	Specifies the print job to hold.
-P *queue*	Specifies the print queue to hold.
-r	Releases a print job or a print queue.
-u *user*	Specifies the user who owns the print job.

File Name:	qhld	**Directory:**	/usr/bin/	**Type:**	External

qmov

UNIX Shell:	All primary shells (csh, ksh, bsh)
Function	Moves spooled print jobs between queues.
Syntax	qmov [options...]

-m *newqueue*	Specifies where to move the print job.
-# *jobnumber*	Specifies the job number to move.
-P *queue*	Specifies where to move print job from.
-u *user*	Specifies the user who owns the print job.

File Name:	qmov	**Directory:**	/usr/bin/	**Type:**	External

qosstat

UNIX Shell:	All primary shells (csh, ksh, bsh)
Function	Shows the status of the Quality of Service.
Syntax	qosstat [options...]

-a	Shows all policies.
-A	Shows addresses of the QoS control block for each policy.

continued

-n	Shows network addresses and ports as numbers.		
File Name: `qosstat`	**Directory:** /usr/sbin/	**Type:**	External

qpri

UNIX Shell: All primary shells (csh, ksh, bsh)

Function	Gives priority to a job in a print queue.
Syntax	qpri [options...]

-# *jobnumber*	Specifies the job number to prioritize.		
-a *priority*	Specifies the new priority for the job.		
File Name: `qpri`	**Directory:** /usr/bin/	**Type:**	External

qprt

UNIX Shell: All primary shells (csh, ksh, bsh)

Function	Prints a specific print job.
Syntax	qprt [options...] *files...*

-#j	Shows a job number.
-#h	Queues the job in a held state.
-#v	Validates the specified printer backend flag values
-= *action*	Specifies the output bin for a job.
0	Specifies the top printer bin.
NR	Specifies high-capacity output bins (values are 1-49).
NR	Specifies printer-specific output bins (values are greater than 49).
-a *NR*	Shows parameters for a job without printing it.
0	Shows normal print processing.
1	Lists values used for converting input data to output data for the printer.
-A *level*	Specifies the level of diagnostic output (values are 0 - 3).
-b *NR*	Specifies the number of blank lines to insert at the bottom of each page.
-B *values*	Prints burst pages. Use a combination of two of the following values.
	The first character is for the header, and the second is for the trailer page.
a	Always prints the header or trailer page for each file in each job.
n	Never prints the header or trailer page.
g	Prints the header or trailer page once for each job.
-c	Makes a copy of the file and prints from the copy.
-C	Specifies to send a mail, after the job is finished.
-d *value*	Specifies the input data type. The values are:
a	Specifies extended ASCII.
c	Specifies PCL.
d	Specifies Diablo 630.
g	Specifies Hewlett Packard GL.
p	Specifies to send the file to the printer unmodified.
s	Specifies PostScript.
-D *user*	Specifies a userID or name to deliver the job to.
-E + | !	Specifies whether to use double-high print.
-F *name*	Specifies the name of X font files; only for MBCS printer queues.
-g *NR*	Starts printing at the specified page number.
-G *value*	Specifies how to print pages on a laser printer that can't print to edge of the paper.
+	Prints the whole page coordinate system.
!	Prints the page coordinate system.
-h *header*	Specifies the header text to use for the **pr** command.
-H *hostname*	Specifies the hostname on the header page.
-i *NR*	Specifies the number of spaces to indent each line.
-I *path*	Specifies the font path for files with a font alias name or a XLFD name.
-j *NR*	Initializes the printer before printing: 0=NO, 1=FULL, 2=Emulator selection only.
-J + | !	Specifies whether the printer at the end of a print job.
-k *color*	Specifies the name of the print color to use.
-K + | !	Specifies whether to use condensed print.

continued

-l *NR*	Specifies the length of the pages.
-L +	Specifies to wrap long lines to the next line.
-L !	Truncates long lines at the right margin.
-m *message*	Specifies the message to show when the job is ready to begin printing.
-M *text*	Identifies a file containing the specified text, and shows the text before printing.
-n	Reports you when the job is finished.
-N *NR*	Specifies the number of copies to print.
-O *NR*	Specifies the type of input paper: 1 for manually, 2 for continuous forms, 3 for sheet feed.
-p *NR*	Specifies the number of characters per inch.
-P *queue{ :queuedevice }*	Specifies the name of the print queue and the optional queue device name.
-q *value*	Specifies the print quality. Use one of the values 0, 1, 2, 3, 300, or 600.
-Q *value*	Specifies the size of the paper; the value is printer-dependent.
-r	Erases the print files after they have been printed.
-R *NR*	Specifies the priority of the jobs (default is 15); only for local printing.
-s *type*	Specifies the type style to use.
-S + | !	Specifies whether to use high-speed printing.
-t *NR*	Specifies the number of blank lines at the top of each page.
-T *title*	Specifies the title of the print job.
-u *value*	Specifies the paper source: 1 for primary, 2 for alternate, 3 for envelopes.
-U + | !	Specifies whether to use unidirectional printing.
-v *NR*	Specifies the number of lines per inch.
-V + | !	Specifies whether to use vertical printing.
-w *NR*	Sets the number of characters for the page width. This must include characters specified by -i.
-W + | !	Specifies whether to use double-width print.
-x *values*	Specifies automatic line feed or automatic carriage return.
0	Doesn't change anything.
1	Adds a line feed for each carriage return.
2	Adds a carriage return for each line feed and each vertical tab.
-X *name*	Specifies the code page name. The values are: **850, IBM-850, ISO8859-1to 9, BM-943, IBM-eucJP, IBM-eucKR, IBM-eucTW.**
-y + | !	Specifies whether to use double strike print.
-Y *values*	Specifies whether to use duplex (print on both sides) output. The values are: **0=Simplex, 1=Duplex, long edge binding, 2=Duplex, short edge binding.**
-z *NR*	Specifies the output. Use 0=Portrait, 1,3= Landscape right/left, 2=Upside down.
-Z + | !	Specifies whether to send a form feed command after each job is finished.
files...	Specifies the file to print. Use a - to print from STDIN.
File Name: `qprt`	**Directory:** /usr/bin/ **Type:** External

qstatus

UNIX Shell: All primary shells (csh, ksh, bsh)

Function	Shows spooling system status.
Syntax	qstatus [options...]

-# *jobnum*	Shows the status of the specified job number.
-A	Shows the status of all defined queues.
-e	Doesn't show status for queues that aren't under the qdaemons control.
-L	Verbose mode; shows more information.
-P *printer*	Shows the status of the specified printer.
-q	Shows the status of the default queue.
-u *username*	Shows the status for all jobs sent by the specified user.
-w *interval*	Shows the specified queue at the specified interval.
-W	Shows output in wide format.
File Name: `qstatus`	**Directory:** /usr/lib/lpd/ **Type:** External

quiz

UNIX Shell:	All primary shells (csh, ksh, bsh)
Function	Runs a quiz that tests knowledge in the specified subject. Shows a list of subjects if run without arguments.
Syntax	quiz [option] { *question answer* }

-t	Runs quiz in tutorial mode.
-i *file*	Specifies an index file other than the default (default is /usr/share/games/quiz.db).
question	Specifies the subject on which quiz will ask questions. Requires `answer`.
answer	Specifies the type of answer for the question. Requires `question`.

File Name:	`quiz`	**Directory:**	/usr/games/	**Type:**	External

quot

UNIX Shell:	All primary shells (csh, ksh, bsh)
Function	Shows the amount of 1024-blocks in the file system that each user currently owns and summarizes the information.
Syntax	quot [options...] *filesystems...*

-c	Shows block information about file sizes and summarizes the information in three columns.
-f	Shows the amount and space of files owned by each user. Don't use with the -v, or -c options.
-h	Estimates the number of blocks in the file.
-n	Connects names to the file list read from STDIN; must be used alone.
filesystems...	Specifies the mount-point of the file system you want to check.

File Name:	`quot`	**Directory:**	/usr/sbin/	**Type:**	External

rc

UNIX Shell:	Korn shell (ksh)
Function	Manages startup initialization of the system based upon the contents of the entries in the `/etc/inittab` file.
Syntax	rc

File Name:	`rc`	**Directory:**	/etc/	**Type:**	Script

rc.powerfail

UNIX Shell:	Korn shell (ksh)
Function	Manages system shutdown if a power failure occurs.
Syntax	rc.powerfail [options...]

-h	Shows power status information.
-s	Doesn't shut down if the system has a battery backup or fan fault.
-t *mm*	Specifies the number of minutes before shutdown if the system has a primary powerloss.

File Name:	`rc.powerfail`	**Directory:**	/etc/	**Type:**	Script

rcvdist

UNIX Shell:	All primary shells (csh, ksh, bsh)
Function	Reads mail from STDIN and forwards it to other addresses.
Syntax	rcvdist [-form *file*] *addresses...*

-form *file*	Specifies an alternative forms file.
addresses...	Specifies one or more address to forward mail to.

File Name:	`rcvdist`	**Directory:**	/usr/lib/mh/	**Type:**	External

rcvpack

UNIX Shell:	All primary shells (csh, ksh, bsh)
Function	Packs incoming messages using the **packf** command.
Syntax	rcvpack { *file* }

file	Specifies the file to save the compressed message in.

File Name:	`rcvpack`	**Directory:**	/usr/lib/mh/	**Type:**	External

rcvstore

UNIX Shell:	All primary shells (csh, ksh, bsh)
Function	Adds messages from STDIN into a mailbox folder.
Syntax	rcvstore [+*folder*] [options...]

-create	Enables creation of a folder if it doesn't exist (is default).
-nocreate	Disables creation of a folder if it doesn't exist.
-help	Shows help information.
-public	Specifies the sequences to be public.
-nopublic	Specifies the sequences to be private.
-zero	Zeroes old sequences.
-nozero	Specifies to not zero old sequences.
-sequence *name*	Adds the messages to the name of the additional sequences.
+*folder*	Specifies the mailbox folder to use (default is +INBOX).

File Name: `rcvstore` **Directory:** /usr/lib/mh/ **Type:** External

rcvtty

UNIX Shell:	All primary shells (csh, ksh, bsh)
Function	Is used to report if new mail arrives.
Syntax	rcvtty *{ command }*

command	Specifies the command to use.

File Name: `rcvtty` **Directory:** /usr/lib/mh/ **Type:** External

rdump

UNIX Shell:	All primary shells (csh, ksh, bsh)
Function	Copies files for backup from your computer to a remote computer.
Syntax	rdump [options...] *{ devicename } { directory }*

-b *blocks*	Sets the number of blocks to write in a single output operation.
-B	Stops the command without querying the user when an error occurs.
-c	Specifies the tape to be in cartridge format, not a 9-track format.
-d *density*	Specifies the tape density (default is 1600 bpi).
-f *host:file*	Specifies which file to send to the specified host; this is mandatory.
-L *length*	Specifies the length of the tape in bytes. Use one of these suffixes: b (B), k (KB), m (MB), g (GB).
-s *feet*	Sets the tape length in feet (default is 2300 feet).
-u	Updates the time, date, and level of the remote backup in the /etc/dumpdates file.
-W	Shows the file systems found in the /etc/dumpdates files.
-*level*	Sets the remote backup level (0 to 9, default is 9).
-?	Shows the usage message.
	Use only one of the following:
devicename	Specifies the physical device name (the block or raw name).
directory	Specifies the directory where the file system is normally mounted (default is root).

File Name: `rdump` **Directory:** /usr/sbin/ **Type:** External

readfile

UNIX Shell:	All primary shells (csh, ksh, bsh)
Function	Shows INed structure files.
Syntax	readfile [options...] *files...*

-d	Creates a verbose dump of the specified file.
-g	Converts control characters to printer characters.
-h	Separates output into sections with headers.
-s	Shows no error messages.
-t	Tries to illustrate the structure of the specified file with a tree diagram.
-u	Shows no output.
-?	Shows help information.
+*number*	Starts reading the file at the specified record.

continued

-*number* -o *outfile* *files...*	Sets the increment and decrement size of the indentation. Specifies an output file instead of STDOUT. Specifies the input file or files.		
File Name: `readfile`	**Directory:** /usr/bin/	**Type:**	External

readlvcopy

UNIX Shell: All primary shells (csh, ksh, bsh)

Function	Reads a mirrored copy of a logical volume.
Syntax	readlvcopy -d *device* [options...]

-d *device*	Specifies the logical volume to read from.		
	Use only one of the following three options:		
-c *copy* -b -n *numblocks* -o *outfile* -s *skip* -S *seek*	Specifies a mirrored copy to read from. Can read older copies marked as stale. Reads a mirrored copy that is marked as online backup. Specifies the number of 128K blocks to read. Specifies an output file instead of STDOUT. Specifies the number of 128K blocks to skip. Specifies the number of 128K blocks to seek.		
File Name: `readlvcopy`	**Directory:** /usr/sbin/	**Type:**	External

red

UNIX Shell: All primary shells (csh, ksh, bsh)

Function	A restricted version of the `ed` editor.
Syntax	red [options...] { *file* }

-p*string* -s *file*	Specifies the prompt indicated by string. Doesn't show character counts when using the e, r, or w commands. Specifies the input file to edit or create.		
File Name: `red`	**Directory:** /usr/bin/	**Type:**	External

redefinevg

UNIX Shell: Korn shell (ksh)

Function	Is used to redefine a volume group definition in the ODM.
Syntax	redefinevg option *volumegroup*

-d *device* -i *vgid* *volumegroup*	Specifies the volume group ID. Specifies the volume group ID number. Specifies the volume group to redefine.		
File Name: `redefinevg`	**Directory:** /usr/sbin/	**Type:**	Script

reducevg

UNIX Shell: Korn shell (ksh)

Function	Removes hard drives from a volume group.
Syntax	reducevg [options...] *volumegroup physicalvols...*

-d -f *volumegroup* *physicalvols...*	Deallocates and deletes empty logical volumes. Doesn't prompt the user for confirmation. Specifies the volume group to remove hard drives from. Specifies the hard drives to remove.		
File Name: `reducevg`	**Directory:** /usr/sbin/	**Type:**	Script
reducevg vg01 hdisk1	Removes hard drive hdisk1 from volume group vg01.		

refresh

UNIX Shell: All primary shells (csh, ksh, bsh)

Function	Refreshes daemons.
Syntax	refresh [-h *host*] option

-h *host* -g *group* -p *systemPID*	Specifies a remote host to refresh daemons on. Specifies a group of subsystems to refresh. Specifies an instance of the subsystem to refresh.

continued

-s *system*	Specifies a subsystem that you want to refresh.		
File Name: refresh	**Directory:** /usr/bin/		**Type:** External

regcmp

UNIX Shell: All primary shells (csh, ksh, bsh)

Function	Compiles regular expressions in a file and places the output in file.i.
Syntax	regcmp [-] *files...*

-	Places the output in filename.c instead of filename.i.
files...	Specifies the file to read input from.
File Name: regcmp	**Directory:** /usr/ccs/bin/regcmp **Type:** External

rembak

UNIX Shell: All primary shells (csh, ksh, bsh)

Function	Sends print jobs to a queue on a remote host.
Syntax	rembak options... [options...] *{ files... }*

	The following two options are required:
-P *queue*	Specifies the remote queue name.
-S *server*	Specifies the remote host.
-C	Sends a control file first.
-D *debugfile*	Activates debugging and outputs debug information to the specified file.
-L	Verbose mode; shows more information.
-N *filter*	Specifies the server type of the remote host.
aixshort	Specifies the remote server type is AIX.
aixv2short	Specifies the remote server type is AIX RTversion 2.
bsdshort	Specifies the remote server type is BSD based.
attshort	Specifies the remote server type is an AT&T based.
	NOTE:You must specify the path /usr/lib/lpd/ before the filters.
-q	Shows a short status report.
-o *option*	Specifies options to send to the backend of the remote system.
-R	Restarts the queue system on the remote host.
-T *timeout*	Specifies a timeout value to wait for acknowledgement (default is 90 seconds).
-u *username*	Specifies a username to cancel print jobs for.
-x	Cancels a print job request.
-X	Sends -o options even if the remote system isn't a AIX system.
-# *jobnum*	Specifies a job number to cancel.
files...	Specifies the file or files to send to a remote queue.
File Name: rembak	**Directory:** /usr/lib/lpd/ **Type:** External

remove

UNIX Shell: Bourne shell (bsh)

Function	Removes files from the directories var/adm/acct/sum and var/adm/acct/nite.
Syntax	remove
File Name: remove	**Directory:** /usr/sbin/acct/ **Type:** Script

reorgvg

UNIX Shell: All primary shells (csh, ksh, bsh)

Function	Reorganizes allocations for physical partitions in a volume group.
Syntax	reorgvg [-i] *volumegroup { logicalvols... }*

-i	Reads physical volume names from STDIN.
volumegroup	Specifies the volumegroup to work with.
logicalvols...	Reorganizes the specified logical volumes.
File Name: reorgvg	**Directory:** /etc **Type:** External

replacepv

UNIX Shell:	Korn shell (ksh)
Function	Replaces a disk in a volume group.
Syntax	replacepv [-f] *sourcedisk replacementdisk* replacepc [-R] *directory { replacementdisk }*

-f	Forces a replacement of the disk.
-R	Recovers the command if it has been interrupted; must be used with directory.
sourcedisk	Specifies the disk to be replaced.
replacementdisk	Specifies the new disk.
directory	Specifies a directory where replacepv initiated; use with the -R option.

File Name:	`replacepv`	**Directory:**	/usr/sbin/	**Type:**	Script

reset

UNIX Shell:	All primary shells (csh, ksh, bsh)
Function	A link to `tset`. Resets some default settings before it runs.
Syntax	reset [options...] *{ type }*

-	Shows the terminal type on STDOUT.
-e *char*	Specifies the erase character to use on all terminals (default is Backspace).
-i *char*	Specifies the interrupt character to use on all terminals (default is Ctrl-C).
-k *char*	Specifies the kill character to use on all terminals (default is Ctrl-U).
-l	Suppresses transmission of terminal initialization strings.
-n	Specifies that the new tty driver modes should be initialized. Applies only to BSD 4.3 tty drivers.
-Q	Suppresses printing of the erase and kill characters.
-s	Prints the sequence of csh commands that initialize the TERM environment variable.
-m *port-id { baudrate }*	Maps the terminal on the specified port.
type	Specifies a terminal type configure or to map with the -m option.
	In addition to the regular `tset` function, the following are done:
	Turns on cooked and echo modes, turns off cbreak and raw modes, turns on new line translation, and restores all special characters.

File Name:	`reset`	**Directory:**	/usr/bin/	**Type:**	External

resolve_links

UNIX Shell:	All primary shells (csh, ksh, bsh)
Function	Manages cross-book links to HTML books that aren't installed in the system.
Syntax	resolve_links [options...] *{ locales... }*

-e	Enables all-cross HTML links.
-v	Verbose mode; shows more information.
locales...	Modifies documents under the specified locale paths.

File Name:	`resolve_links`	**Directory:**	/usr/sbin/	**Type:**	External

restbase

UNIX Shell:	All primary shells (csh, ksh, bsh)
Function	Restores base-customized information from the boot image into the device configuration database during startup.
Syntax	restbase [options...]

-d *path*	Specifies the base device configuration database directory.
-o *file*	Specifies a file with base-customized data.
-v	Verbose mode; shows more output.

File Name:	`restbase`	**Directory:**	/usr/lib/boot/	**Type:**	External

restore

UNIX Shell:	All primary shells (csh, ksh, bsh)
Function	Restores files from archives created with the backup command.
Syntax	restore [options...] *{ files... }*

continued

-I	Starts the interactive mode.
	The following are the subcommands to use in interactive mode:
ls *{ directory }*	Shows directory names with a / and shows files to restore preceded with an asterisk. (In verbose mode this option also shows the i-node numbers.)
cd *directory*	Specifies a new directory to go to.
pwd	Shows the full pathname of the current directory.
add *{ file }*	Specifies the file or directory to restore, or without it restores the current directory.
delete *{ file }*	Specifies the file parameter to be ignored when extracting a list of files.
extract	Restores all files that are preceded with an asterisk.
setmodes	Sets owner, modes, and times for the files being restored.
verbose	Shows the i-node numbers of all restored files.
help	Shows help information about the subcommands.
quit	Stops the program immediately.
	The following are the options for use on the command-line:
-B	Reads the archive from STDIN.
-b *number*	Specifies the number of 512-byte blocks if the backup is done by name. Specifies the number of 1024-byte blocks if the backup is done by i-node.
-d	Restores all files in the directory if the specified filename is a directory.
-f *device*	Specifies the input device or devices.
-h	Restores only the directory named by the file parameter, not the files in it.
-M	Updates the access and modification times of restored files.
-m	Renames the restored files by i-node numbers, not filenames.
-q	Quiet mode; doesn't prompt for mounting the volume.
-R	Requests a specific volume of a multiple-volume, file system archive.
-r	Restores an entire file system. (Create an empty file system before restoring a complete file system.)
-s *number*	Specifies the backup to seek and restore on a multiple-backup tape archive.
-T	Shows information about a filename-format backup archive.
-t	Shows information about a file system-format backup archive.
-v	Verbose mode; shows more information.
-X *number*	Restores from the specified volume in a multiple-volume, file-name backup.
-x	Restores the files specified on the commandline.
-y	Suppresses the tape error messages.
?	Shows help information.
files...	Specifies the file(s) to restore.

File Name:	`restore`	**Directory:**	/usr/sbin/	**Type:**	External

restvg

UNIX Shell: Korn shell (ksh)

Function	Restores a user-defined volume group.
Syntax	restvg [options...] *{ disks... }*

-b *blocks*	Specifies how many 512-byte blocks to read in a single operation.
-f *device*	Specifies the backup device name.
-q	Doesn't show the usual prompt.
-s	Uses the smallest possible size to create logical volumes.
-n	Ignores existing maps.
-p *ppsize*	Specifies the size of the physical partitions in MB.
disks...	Specifies a disk to restore the volume group in.

File Name:	`restvg`	**Directory:**	/usr/bin/	**Type:**	Script

rev

UNIX Shell: All primary shells (csh, ksh, bsh)

Function	Reverses every line of a file, or STDIN, if no filename is given.
Syntax	rev *{ files... }*

files...	Specifies the file to reverse; if no file is specified STDIN is reversed.

File Name:	`rev`	**Directory:**	/usr/bin/	**Type:**	External

rexec

UNIX Shell: All primary shells (csh, ksh, bsh)

Function	Runs commands on a remote host.
Syntax	rexec [options...] *host command*

	Choose only one of the following two options:
-d	Shows debug information.
-n	Prompts for a user name and password, which prevents automatic login.
host	Specifies the remote host.
command	Specifies the command to run at the remote host.

File Name: `rexec` **Directory:** /usr/bin/ **Type:** External

rgb

UNIX Shell: All primary shells (csh, ksh, bsh)

Function	Creates a database containing color names. Reads from STDIN and looks for the colors red, green, and blue.
Syntax	rgb *{ database } { file }*

database	Specifies the database to create (default is /usr/lib/X11/rgb.dir).
file	Specifies the name of the input file containing colors to add.

File Name: `rgb` **Directory:** /usr/bin/X11 **Type:** External

ripquery

UNIX Shell: All primary shells (csh, ksh, bsh)

Function	Queries all routes known by a RIP gateway.
Syntax	ripquery [options...] *gateways...*

-1	Queries with a version 1 packet.
-2	Queries with a version 2 packet.
-a *password*	Uses simple authentication.
-5 *password*	Uses MD5 authentication.
-n	Doesn't lookup symbolic names.
-N *dest/mask*	Queries the specified destination and mask instead of the complete routing table.
-p	Uses the RIP POLL command to request routing data.
-r	Uses the RIP REQUEST command to request data from the gateway's routing table.
-v	Shows version information.
-w *time*	Specifies the time to wait for a response value.
gateways...	Specifies the gateways to query.

File Name: `ripquery` **Directory:** /usr/sbin/ **Type:** External

rm_niscachemgr

UNIX Shell: Bourne shell (bsh)

Function	Disables the nis_cachemgr daemon.
Syntax	rm_niscachemgr [option]

	The following options can't be combined:
-B	Comments nis_cachemgr entries in the /etc/rc.nfs file and stops the daemon.
-I	Comments nis_cachemgr entries in the /etc/rc.nfs file.
-N	Stops the daemon but doesn't make changes to the /etc/rc.nfs file.

File Name: `rm_niscachemgr` **Directory:** /usr/sbin/ **Type:** Script

rm_nisd

UNIX Shell: Bourne shell (bsh)

Function	Disables the rpc.nisd daemon.
Syntax	rm_nisd [option]

	The following options can't be combined:
-B	Comments rpc.nisd entries in the /etc/rc.nfs file and stops the daemon.
-I	Comments rpc.nisd entries in the /etc/rc.nfs file.
-N	Stops the daemon but doesn't make changes to the /etc/rc.nfs file.

File Name: `rm_nisd` **Directory:** /usr/sbin/ **Type:** Script

rm_nispasswdd

rm_nispasswdd				**UNIX Shell:**	**Bourne shell (bsh)**
Function	Disables the rpc.nispasswdd daemon.				
Syntax	rm_nispasswdd [option]				
	The following options can't be combined:				
-B	Comments the rpc.nispasswdd daemon entries in /etc/rc.nfs and stops the daemon.				
-N	Stops the daemon but doesn't make changes to the /etc/rc.nfs file.				
File Name:	`rm_nispasswdd`	**Directory:**	/usr/sbin/	**Type:**	Script

rmail

rmail				**UNIX Shell:**	**All primary shells (csh, ksh, bsh)**
Function	Administers received mail from remote hosts through Basic Networking Utilities (BNU).				
Syntax	rmail *users...*				
users...	Specifies a user or Ipaddress.				
File Name:	`rmail`	**Directory:**	/usr/bin/	**Type:**	External

rmclass

rmclass				**UNIX Shell:**	**All primary shells (csh, ksh, bsh)**
Function	Removes a workload management class from the system.				
Syntax	rmclass [-d *confdir*] *class*				
-d *confdir*	Specifies an alternative configuration directory.				
Class	Specifies the class to remove.				
File Name:	`rmclass`	**Directory:**	/usr/sbin/	**Type:**	External

rmdel

rmdel				**UNIX Shell:**	**All primary shells (csh, ksh, bsh)**
Function	Removes a delta from one or more SCCS files.				
Syntax	rmdel -r *sid sfile*				
-r *sid*	Removes the version corresponding to the indicated SID.				
Sfile	Specifies the `s.file` type to remove the SCCS delta from.				
File Name:	`rmdel`	**Directory:**	/usr/bin/	**Type:**	External

rmdev

rmdev				**UNIX Shell:**	**All primary shells (csh, ksh, bsh)**
Function	Removes a device from the system.				
Syntax	rmdev -l *name* [options...]				
-l *name*	Specifies the name in the ODM to remove.				
-d	Removes the device definition from the customized object class.				
-S	Tries to call the stop method for the device if it exists.				
-h	Shows help information.				
-q	Shows no output.				
-R	Unconfigures the children of the device.				
File Name:	`rmdev`	**Directory:**	/usr/sbin/	**Type:**	External
rmdev –dl ent0	Removes the device ent0 from the system.				

Rmfilt

Rmfilt				**UNIX Shell:**	**All primary shells (csh, ksh, bsh)**
Function	Removes a filter rule from a filter table.				
Syntax	rmfilt options... [-f]				
-v 4 | 6	Specifies the IP version of the filter to remove.				
-f	Removes auto-generated filter rules.				
File Name:	`rmfilt`	**Directory:**	/usr/sbin/	**Type:**	External

rmfs

UNIX Shell:	All primary shells (csh, ksh, bsh)
Function	Removes a file system.
Syntax	rmfs [-r] *filesystem*

-r	Removes the mount point of the file system.
Filesystem	Specifies the file system to remove.

File Name:	`rmfs`	**Directory:**	/usr/sbin/	**Type:**	External

rmgroup

UNIX Shell:	All primary shells (csh, ksh, bsh)
Function	Deletes a specified UNIX group from the system.
Syntax	rmgroup *group*

group	Specifies the name of the group to erase.

File Name:	`rmgroup`	**Directory:**	/usr/sbin/	**Type:**	External
NOTE:	You can't remove the primary group of any user.				

Rmhist

UNIX Shell:	All primary shells (csh, ksh, bsh)
Function	Removes history information from one or more Ined structured files.
Syntax	rmhist [options…] *files…*

-d	Removes the .bak file after the command completes.
-f	Shows no output.
-k *number*	Keeps the last specified number of days of history information.
Files…	Specifies the file or files to remove history information from.

File Name:	`rmhist`	**Directory:**	/usr/bin/	**Type:**	External

rmitab

UNIX Shell:	All primary shells (csh, ksh, bsh)
Function	Removes entries from the inittab file.
Syntax	rmitab *identifier*

identifier	Specifies which entry to remove from the file.

File Name:	`rmitab`	**Directory:**	/usr/sbin/	**Type:**	External

rmkeyserv

UNIX Shell:	Bourne shell (bsh)
Function	Disables the keyserv daemon.
Syntax	rmkeyserv [option]

-I	Comments the keyserv entry in the /etc/rc.nfs file.
-B	Comments the keyserv entry in the /etc/rc.nfs file and stops the keyserv daemon.
-N	Stops the keyserv daemon, but makes no changes to the /etc/rc.nfs file.

File Name:	`rmkeyserv`	**Directory:**	/usr/sbin/	**Type:**	Script

rmlv

UNIX Shell:	Korn shell (ksh)
Function	Removes a logical volume from a volume group.
Syntax	rmlv [options…] *logicalvolumes…*

-B	Runs the `chlvcopy -B -s` command for the parent's logical volume if it was created with –l.
-f	Removes the logical volume without asking for confirmation.
-p *physicalvol*	Removes logical partitions from the specified physical volume.
Logicalvolumes…	Specifies the logical volumes to remove from the volume group.

File Name:	`rmlv`	**Directory:**	/usr/sbin/	**Type:**	Script

rmlvcopy

UNIX Shell:	Korn shell (ksh)
Function	Removes copies from a logical volume.
Syntax	rmlvcopy *logicalvol copies { physicalvols... }*

logicalvol	Specifies the logical volume to remove copies from.
copies	Specifies how many copies to leave in the logical volume.
physicalvols...	Specifies that logical volumes are removed only from the specified physical volume.

File Name:	`rmlvcopy`	**Directory:**	/usr/sbin/	**Type:**	Script

rmnamsv

UNIX Shell:	All primary shells (csh, ksh, bsh)
Function	RemovesTCP/IP naming services from the system.
Syntax	rmnamsv [option]

-f	Uses the old `/etc/resolv.conf` file to rename the new file.
-F *file*	Specifies a filename to use to rename the old `/etc/resolv.conf`.

File Name:	`rmnamsv`	**Directory:**	/usr/sbin/	**Type:**	External

rmnfs

UNIX Shell:	Bourne shell (bsh)
Function	Stops NFS daemons on the system.
Syntax	rmnfs [option]

-I	Removes the entries that start the daemon from the inittab file.
-N	Stops the NFS daemons but makes no changes to the inittab file.
-B	Removes entries and stops the daemon.

File Name:	`rmnfs`	**Directory:**	/usr/sbin/	**Type:**	Script

rmnfsexp

UNIX Shell:	Bourne shell (bsh)
Function	Disables export of a directory to an NFS client.
Syntax	rmnfsexp -d *directory* [options...]

-d *directory*	Specifies the directory to disable export of.
-f *exportfile*	Specifies the path to the export file.
	Choose only one of the following three options:
-B	Removes entries from the export file and runs the exportfs command.
-N	Unexports the directory, but makes no changes to the /etc/export file.

File Name:	`rmnfsexp`	**Directory:**	/usr/sbin/	**Type:**	Script

rmnfsmnt

UNIX Shell:	Bourne shell (bsh)
Function	Removes an NFS mount from the system.
Syntax	rmnfsmnt -f *path* [option]

-f *path*	Specifies the path of the NFS file system to be removed.
-I	Deletes the specified path from the /etc/filesystems file.
-B	Deletes the specified path from the /etc/filesystems file, and unmounts the file system.
-N	Unmounts the file system, but makes no changes to the /etc/filesystems file.

File Name:	`rmnfsmnt`	**Directory:**	/usr/sbin/	**Type:**	Script

rmnotify

UNIX Shell:	All primary shells (csh, ksh, bsh)
Function	Removes a notify method from the notify object class.
Syntax	rmnotify -n *notifyname*

-n *notifyname*	Specifies the notify method to remove.

File Name:	`rmnotify`	**Directory:**	/usr/bin/	**Type:**	External

rmprtsv

UNIX Shell: All primary shells (csh, ksh, bsh)

Function	Removes a print service from a client or a server.
Syntax	rmprtsv option [options...]

	The following two options can't be combined:
-c	Removes print services for a client.
-s	Removes print services for a server.
	The following three options can't be combined:
-T	Stops the print service.
-U	Removes users from the print server.
-A	Removes the specified entries from the qconfig file.
	The following two options can't be combined:
-h *hostname*	Specifies a list of hostnames that aren't allowed to use the print server.
-H *file*	Specifies a file with hostnames that are to be left unmodified.
-q *qentry*	Specifies which entries are to be erased from the qconfig file.
-v *device*	Specifies a list of device names in the qconfig file.

File Name: `rmprtsv` **Directory:** /usr/sbin/ **Type:** External

rmps

UNIX Shell: All primary shells (csh, ksh, bsh)

Function	Removes a paging space from the system.
Syntax	rmps *pagingspace*

pagingspace	Specifies the paging space to remove.

File Name: `rmps` **Directory:** /usr/sbin/ **Type:** External

rmqos

UNIX Shell: Bourne shell (bsh)

Function	Disables the QoS support for the system.
Syntax	rmqos [option]

-B	Removes QoS entries from the inittab file and stops the daemons.
-I	Removes QoS entries from the inittab file.
-N	Turns off QoS support, but doesn't change the `initab` file.

File Name: `rmqos` **Directory:** /usr/sbin/ **Type:** Script

rmque

UNIX Shell: All primary shells (csh, ksh, bsh)

Function	Removes a print queue from the system.
Syntax	rmque -q *name*

-q *name*	Specifies the queue to remove from the system.

File Name: `rmque` **Directory:** /usr/bin/ **Type:** External

rmquedev

UNIX Shell: All primary shells (csh, ksh, bsh)

Function	Removes a printer or plotter queue from the system.
Syntax	rmquedev [options...]

-d *name*	Specifies the device stanza to remove from the configfile.
-q *name*	Specifies the device to modify in the queue stanza.

File Name: `rmquedev` **Directory:** /usr/bin/ **Type:** External

rmrole

UNIX Shell: All primary shells (csh, ksh, bsh)

Function	Removes a role from the system.
Syntax	rmrole *name*

name	Specifies the role to remove.

File Name: `rmrole` **Directory:** /usr/sbin/ **Type:** External

rmserver

rmserver	UNIX Shell:	All primary shells (csh, ksh, bsh)
Function	Removes a subserver from the object class.	
Syntax	rmserver -t *type*	

-t *type*	Specifies the subserver to remove.
File Name: rmserver	**Directory:** /usr/bin/ **Type:** External

rmss

rmss	UNIX Shell:	All primary shells (csh, ksh, bsh)
Function	Simulates the memory size in the system.	
Syntax	rmss [options...]	

-c *memsize*	Simulates a memory size to test. This option is used alone.
-r	Resets the memory settings to real memory size. This option is used alone.
-p	Shows the current memory settings. This option is used alone.
-s *memsize*	Specifies the starting memory size.
-f *memsize*	Specifies the ending memory size.
-d *memsize*	Specifies the increment between memory sizes to test.
-n *iterations*	Specifies how many times to run the command.
-o *outfile*	Specifies an output file to save the test data.
File Name: rmss	**Directory:** /usr/bin/ **Type:** External
NOTE:	You can only simulate that your system has less memory.
rmss -c 24	Simulates that the system has only 24 MB of RAM.
rmss -r	Resets the values.

rmssys

rmssys	UNIX Shell:	All primary shells (csh, ksh, bsh)
Function	Removes a subsystem from the object class.	
Syntax	rmssys -s *subsystem*	

-s *subsystem*	Specifies the subsystem to remove.
File Name: rmssys	**Directory:** /usr/bin/ **Type:** External

rmtun

rmtun	UNIX Shell:	All primary shells (csh, ksh, bsh)
Function	Erases or disables an IP tunnel.	
Syntax	rmtun options... rmtun *all* [options...]	

	The following two options are required together:
-v 4 | 6	Specifies the IP version to use.
-t *tidlist* | all	Specifies a list of tunnels to disable; all disables and erases all tunnels.
-d	Specifies that tunnels are erased from the database.
-s	Shuts down the IBM session key engine of IPv4.
File Name: rmtun	**Directory:** /usr/sbin/ **Type:** External

rmuser

rmuser	UNIX Shell:	All primary shells (csh, ksh, bsh)
Function	Erases the specified user from the system.	
Syntax	rmuser [-p] *user*	

-p	Removes user password information from the /etc/security/passwd file.
user	Specifies the name of the user to erase.
File Name: rmuser	**Directory:** /usr/sbin/ **Type:** External

rmvfs

UNIX Shell: All primary shells (csh, ksh, bsh)

Function	Removes entries from the /etc/vfs file.
Syntax	rmvfs *vfsname*

vfsname	Specifies the entries to remove.

File Name: `rmvfs` **Directory:** /usr/sbin/ **Type:** External

rmvirprt

UNIX Shell: All primary shells (csh, ksh, bsh)

Function	Removes a virtual printer from the system.
Syntax	rmvirprt [options...]

-d *queuedev*	Specifies the queue device that the virtual printer is assigned to.
-q *printqueue*	Specifies the print queue that the virtual printer is assigned to.

File Name: `rmvirprt` **Directory:** /usr/sbin/ **Type:** External

rmyp

UNIX Shell: Bourne shell (bsh)

Function	Removes NIS configurations.
Syntax	rmyp option

-s	Removes server configuration from the system.
-c	Removes client configuration from the system.

File Name: `rmyp` **Directory:** /usr/sbin/ **Type:** Script

routed

UNIX Shell: All primary shells (csh, ksh, bsh)

Function	Manages routing tables for hosts on the network and updates internetwork router hosts with copies of routing tables.
Syntax	routed [options...] option *{ file }*

-d	Enables logging of debugging information.
-g	Sets the default destination for the Internet router.
	Choose one of the following two options:
-q	Doesn't provide routing information even if the host acts as a router.
-s	Provides routing information even if the host doesn't act as a router.
-t	Logs more information to the tracefile specified or STDOUT.
file	Sends the log information to the specified file.

File Name: `routed` **Directory:** /usr/sbin/ **Type:** External

rpc.bootparamd

UNIX Shell: All primary shells (csh, ksh, bsh)

Function	Serves diskless clients with startup information at boot time.
Syntax	rpc.bootparamd [-d]

-d	Shows debug information.

File Name: `rpc.bootparamd` **Directory:** /usr/sbin/ **Type:** External

rpc.lockd

UNIX Shell: All primary shells (csh, ksh, bsh)

Function	Starts the NFS lock manager (NLM). Useful for kernels that don't do this automatically.
Syntax	rpc.lockd [options...]

-d *level*	Specifies the debug level.
-g *time*	Specifies the length of time until the file or record will be locked.
-t *time*	Specifies the length of time for which the locking service will be active.

File Name: `rpc.lockd` **Directory:** /usr/sbin/ **Type:** External

rpc.nisd

rpc.nisd	UNIX Shell:	All primary shells (csh, ksh, bsh)
Function	The NIS+ service daemon. Used to serve usernames and passwords to systems on the network.	
Syntax	rpc.nisd [options...]	

-A	Shows information about all authentications.
-C	Shows diagnostics on the console device.
-D	Shows debug information.
-F	Checkpoints the database in the server.
-h	Shows help information.
-v	Verbose mode; shows more information.
-Y	Starts the server with YP(NIS2) modules, for clients without NIS+. No authentication is used.
-c *sec*	Specifies how often to update the server's replicas, in seconds (default is 120 sec).
-d *dictionary*	Specifies an alternate dictionary used by the NIS+ database.
-L *load*	Specifies how much load the NIS+ service can use (default is 128).
-S *level*	Specifies the security level to use (default is 2).
0	Allows every client to administer the NIS database.
1	Authenticates with the AUTH_SYS and AUTH_DES credentials.
2	Allows authentications with AUTH_DES and mechanisms configured by `nisauthconf` (default).
-t *transport*	Specifies the transport to connect rpc.nisd with rpc.nisd_resolv (default is ticots).
-f	Forces registration even if a program is in use.
-T *MB*	Specifies the size of the transaction log in megabytes.

File Name:	`rpc.nisd`	**Directory:**	/usr/sbin/	**Type:**	External

rpc.nisd_resolv

rpc.nisd_resolv	UNIX Shell:	All primary shells (csh, ksh, bsh)
Function	Used as a DNS forwarder. Often used from `rpc.nisd`, can also be used from a console.	
Syntax	rpc.nisd_resolv [options...]	

-F	Runs the resolver in foreground.
-C *fd*	Specifies the fd as service export from nisd; is used with -F.
-t *transport*	Specifies the transport to use between the programs.
-p *transient*	Specifies the transient program to use.
-v	Verbose mode; shows more information in `syslog`.
-V	Verbose mode; shows more information.

File Name:	`rpc.nisd_resolv`	**Directory:**	/usr/sbin/	**Type:**	External

rpc.nispasswdd

rpc.nispasswdd	UNIX Shell:	All primary shells (csh, ksh, bsh)
Function	Updates the NIS+ password table on request from nispasswd or yppasswd.	
Syntax	rpc.nispasswdd [options...]	

-a *attempts*	Sets the maximum number of attempts to authenticate the caller.
-c *minutes*	Sets the number of minutes a failed password update is cached.
-D	Tells the daemon to run in debug mode.
-g	Creates a DES credential if the user doesn't have one.
-v	Verbose mode; sends the information to the `syslog` daemon.

File Name:	`rpc.nispasswdd`	**Directory:**	/usr/sbin/	**Type:**	External

rpc.pcnfsd

rpc.pcnfsd	UNIX Shell:	All primary shells (csh, ksh, bsh)
Function	A server for PC clients that run Sun NFS systems. It provides authentication and printing requests for PC's.	
Syntax	rpc.pcnfsd	

File Name:	`rpc.pcnfsd`	**Directory:**	/usr/sbin/	**Type:**	External

rpc.rexd

UNIX Shell: All primary shells (csh, ksh, bsh)

Function	Executes programs on remote computers.
Syntax	rpc.rexd [-s]

-s	Tells the daemon to accept only secure calls.

File Name: `rpc.rexd` **Directory:** /usr/sbin/ **Type:** External

rpc.rquotad

UNIX Shell: All primary shells (csh, ksh, bsh)

Function	Manages users of a local file system mounted with NFS by reporting quotas. Started by `rc.net`.
Syntax	rpc.rquotad

File Name: `rpc.rquotad` **Directory:** /usr/sbin/ **Type:** External

rpc.sprayd

UNIX Shell: All primary shells (csh, ksh, bsh)

Function	The server daemon for the spray command.
Syntax	rpc.sprayd

File Name: `rpc.sprayd` **Directory:** /usr/lib/netsvc/spray/ **Type:** External

rpc.statd, statd

UNIX Shell: All primary shells (csh, ksh, bsh)

Function	Is used to manage crash and recovery for locking NFS services.
Syntax	rpc.statd

File Name: `rpc.statd` **Directory:** /usr/sbin/ **Type:** External

rpc.ypupdated

UNIX Shell: All primary shells (csh, ksh, bsh)

Function	Updates information in the Network Information Service (NIS).
Syntax	rpc.ypudated [options...]

-i	Tells the daemon to accept insecure calls.
-s	Tells the daemon to accept only secure calls.

File Name: `rpc.ypupdated` **Directory:** /usr/etc/ **Type:** External

rpl

UNIX Shell: All primary shells (csh, ksh, bsh)

Function	Replaces text strings in a file.
Syntax	rpl *expression substitute*

expression	Specifies the expression that you want to replace.
substitute	Specifies the substitution for the expression.

File Name: `rpl` **Directory:** /usr/bin/ **Type:** External

rrestore

UNIX Shell: All primary shells (csh, ksh, bsh)

Function	Copies i-node backup files from a remote system to the local system.
Syntax	rrestore [options...] -f *{ filesystem } { file }*

-i	Starts the interactive mode. **The following are the subcommands to use in interactive mode:**
ls *{ directory }*	Shows directory names with a / and shows files to restore preceded with an asterisk. (When used together with -v the i-node number is also shown.)
pwd	Shows the full pathname of the current directory.
add *{ file }*	Specifies the file or directory to restore, or without it the current directory is used.
delete *{ file }*	Specifies the file parameter to be ignored during a restore.
extract	Restores all files that are preceded with an asterisk.

continued

setmodes	Sets owner, modes, and times for the files being restored.
verbose	Shows the i-node numbers of all restored files.
help	Shows help information about the subcommands.
quit	Stops the program immediately.
	The following are the options for use on the command line:
-b*number*	Specifies the number of blocks to read in a single input operation.
-h	Restores only the directory named by the file parameter, not the files in it.
-m	Restores the files by i-node number, not by the pathname.
-r	Restores an entire file system. (Create an empty file system before restoring a complete file system.)
-R	Causes a request for a specific volume in backup media when restoring file systems.
-s*number*	Specifies the backup to restore from in a multibackup medium.
-t	Shows a table of contents for the backup files.
-v	Verbose mode; shows more information.
-x	Restores individually named files.
-y	Suppresses tape error messages.
-?	Shows help information.
-f*computer:device*	Specifies the input device on the remote computer.
filesystem	Specifies the file system to put the restored files in.
file	Specifies the file or directory to restore from.

File Name:	`rrestore`	**Directory:**	/usr/sbin/	**Type:**	External

Rsh

UNIX Shell: All primary shells (csh, ksh, bsh)

Function	Invokes the restricted version of Bourne shell.
Syntax	Rsh [options...] *{ file } { parameter }*

-a	Marks all variables for export to which an assignment is performed.
-c *command*	Runs the command specified in the command variable, and no additional commands.
-e	Exits immediately after receiving conditions from a command.
-f	Disables filename generation.
-h	Finds and remembers commands in functions as the functions are defined.
-i	Makes the shell interactive.
-k	Places all keyword parameters in the environment for a command.
-n	Reads commands, but doesn't run them.
-s	Reads the commands from STDIN.
-t	Reads and runs one command, and then exits.
-u	Exits after finding unset variables when performing variable substitution.
-v	Shows shell input lines when they are being read.
-x	Echoes each command before it is executed. (If + is used instead of -, the flag is turned off.)
file	Specifies a file that contains a bsh script.
parameter	Specifies a parameter to the script.

File Name:	`Rsh`	**Directory:**	/usr/bin/	**Type:**	External

rtl_enable

UNIX Shell: Korn shell (ksh)

Function	Relinks modules so the runtime linker can use them.
Syntax	rtl_enable [options...] *file { ldFlag }* [-F *objlib*]

	Choose one of the following two options:
-R	Replaces the input file instead of creating a new file.
-o *name*	Specifies an output name other than the default.
-l	Doesn't erase import and export files.
-s	Creates a script of commands in the current directory.
-F *objlib*	Adds the specified object or library to the beginning of the created ld command.
file	Specifies the input file.
ldFlag	Copies `ld` command flags to the end of the created ld command.

File Name:	`rtl_enable`	**Directory:**	/usr/bin/	**Type:**	Script

runacct

UNIX Shell:	Bourne shell (bsh)

Function	Runs daily accounting procedures that are usually started from the cron daemon.
Syntax	runacct *{ mmdd }* *{ state }*

mmdd	Specifies which month and day to run the program.
state	**The following are the states to use in a statefile:**
SETUP	Moves active accounting files into working files.
WTMPFIX	Verifies the wtmp file, and corrects errors if necessary.
CONNECT1	Produces connect sessions information.
CONNECT2	Converts connect session records into total accounting records.
PROCESS	Converts process accounting records into tacct.h format.
MERGE	Merges the connect and process accounting information.
FEES	Converts the output of chargefee into tacct.h format.
DISK	Merges disk accounting records with connect, process, and fee accounting data.
MERGETACCT	Merges daily total accounting records in daytacct with summary totals data.
CMS	Produces command summaries.
USEREXIT	Any installation-dependent accounting programs can be included here.
CLEANUP	Cleans up temporary files and exits

File Name:	`runacct`	**Directory:**	/usr/sbin/acct/	**Type:**	Script

runcat

UNIX Shell:	Korn shell (ksh)

Function	Transfers data from the mkcatdefs command to the gencat command.
Syntax	runcat *catalog sourcefile* *{ catalogfile }*

catalog	Specifies the catalog to transfer from mkcatdefs to gencat.
sourcefile	Specifies the file with the message text and symbolic identifiers.
catalogfile	Specifies the output catalog from gencat.

File Name:	`runcat`	**Directory:**	/usr/bin/	**Type:**	Script

ruser

UNIX Shell:	All primary shells (csh, ksh, bsh)

Function	Manages entries in the remote users database.
Syntax	ruser [options...]

-a	Adds a name to the database file entry; used with either the -p, -r, or -f options.
-d	Erases a name from the database file entry; used with either the -p, -r, or -f options.
-f *user*	Specifies a user name in the /etc/ftpusers database to add or erase.
-p *host*	Specifies a hostname in the /etc/hosts.lpd file to add or erase.
-r *host*	Specifies a hostname in the /etc/hosts.equiv file to add or erase.
-X	Erases all specified names from the database, used with either the -P, -R, or -F option.
-s	Shows all entries in the database; used with either the -P, -R, or -F options.
-F	Erases or shows all entries in the /etc/ftpusers database.
-P	Erases or shows all entries in the /etc/hosts.lpd file.
-R	Erases or shows all entries in the /etc/hosts.equiv file.

File Name:	`ruser`	**Directory:**	/usr/bin/	**Type:**	External

rwall

UNIX Shell:	All primary shells (csh, ksh, bsh)

Function	Broadcasts messages to all users on the network.
Syntax	rwall [options...] *{ hosts... }*

-n *netgroup*	Specifies the network groups to send the broadcast message to.
-h *hostname*	Specifies the hostname or the IP address of the server.
hosts...	Specifies the hostname to send a message to; used alone.

File Name:	`rwall`	**Directory:**	/usr/sbin/	**Type:**	External

sa

UNIX Shell:	All primary shells (csh, ksh, bsh)
Function	Cleans up and shows information in the `/var/adm/pacct` file.
Syntax	sa [options...] *files...*

	The following options specify how output is sorted:
-b	Sorts commands by the sum of users and system time divided by the number of calls.
-d	Sorts by the average number of disk I/O operations.
-D	Sorts by the total number of disk I/O operations.
-k	Sorts by the CPU time average memory usage.
-K	Shows and sorts by the CPU-storage integral.
	Common options:
-a	Shows all command names, including those with unprintable characters.
-c	Shows the time used for each command as a percentage of the time used by all commands.
-f	Forces interactive threshold compression; used with -v only.
-i	Doesn't read the summary file.
-j	Gives seconds per call, instead of the total minutes per category.
-l	Separates system time and user time.
-m	Shows processes and CPU minutes statistics for each user.
-n	Sorts by number of calls.
-r	Reverses the sorting order.
-C	Converts the summary file to a new format and merges the accounting file into it.
-s	Merges the accounting file into the summary file.
-S *savefile*	Uses the specified file instead of the `/var/adm/savacct` file as the command summary file.
-t	Shows the ratio of real time to the sum of user and system CPU times.
-u	Shows numeric ID for user and command name for each command.
-U *userfile*	Specifies the file to accumulate per-user statistics for -m instead of `/var/adm/usracct`.
-v *number*	Shows the name of each command used the specified number of times or fewer.
files...	Specifies alternate files to use.

File Name:	`sa`	**Directory:**	/usr/sbin/	**Type:**	External

sa1

UNIX Shell:	Bourne shell (bsh)
Function	Saves system activity into the binary file `/var/adm/sa/sadd`, dd is the current day.
Syntax	sa1 *{ time amount }*

time	Specifies the number of seconds in the interval between saving samples.
amount	Specifies how many times to do a sample.

File Name:	`sa1`	**Directory:**	usr/lib/sa/	**Type:**	Script

sa2

UNIX Shell:	Bourne shell (bsh)
Function	A script that saves system activity into the file `/var/adm/sa/sar`*dd*, *dd* is the current day.
Syntax	sa2 [options...]

	Please see `sar` for the list of available options and descriptions.

File Name:	`sa2`	**Directory:**	usr/lib/sa/	**Type:**	Script

sadc

UNIX Shell:	All primary shells (csh, ksh, bsh)
Function	Saves system activity in binary format to a specified file.
Syntax	sadc *{ time } { amount } { file }*

time	Specifies the number of seconds in the interval between saving samples.
amount	Specifies how many times to sample.
file	Specifies the file to save the record (default is `/var/adm/sa/sa`*dd*). (dd is the day when the file was saved.)

File Name:	`sadc`	**Directory:**	/usr/lib/sa/	**Type:**	External

sar

UNIX Shell:	All primary shells (csh, ksh, bsh)
Function	Shows information about system utilization earlier saved in files. The files is in the directory /var/adm/sa/sadd.
Syntax	sar [options...] *{ interval } { count }*

-o *filename*	Specifies the file in which to store binary samples.
-f *file*	Specifies the file from which the data will be read (created by the -o flag).
-P *processID*	Shows statistics about children for the process given; use all for all processes.
-A	Shows all system information available.
-a	Shows how many file access system routines are used.
-b	Shows all buffer usage.
-c	Shows all calls from the system.
-e *time*	Gets data until the specified time (default is 18:00).
-i *seconds*	Updates information with the specified interval in seconds.
-k	Shows the memory allocation from the kernel.
-m	Shows the semaphore activities on the system.
-q	Shows the queue lengths average and the percentage of time they are occupied.
-r	Shows the amount of unused disk blocks and memory pages.
-s *time*	Specifies when to start analyzing data from the system (default is 08:00).
-u	Shows the CPU usage.
-V	Specifies to read the sar files created on previous versions of AIX; only used with -f.
-v	Shows processes status, the i-nodes, and file tables used.
-w	Shows the swapping and switching activity on the system.
-y	Shows the tty devices´ activities.
interval	Specifies the interval in seconds to show information for (default is 1 second).
count	Specifies the number of intervals to show information for.

File Name:	`sar`	**Directory:**	/usr/sbin/	**Type:**	External

savebase

UNIX Shell:	All primary shells (csh, ksh, bsh)
Function	Saves base customized device settings on the boot device.
Syntax	savebase [options...]

-o *path*	Specifies a directory that contains the ODM directory.
-d *file*	Specifies a device to save the information.
-v	Verbose mode; shows more information.

File Name:	`savebase`	**Directory:**	/usr/sbin/	**Type:**	External

savecore

UNIX Shell:	All primary shells (csh, ksh, bsh)
Function	Saves a crash dump of the operating system kernel (if one is created) after a system crash.
Syntax	savecore option *directory { system }*

-c	Marks the dump as invalid and causes savecore to ignore it.
-d	Copies only the core dump not the system.
directory	Saves the crash dump to the specified directory.
system	Specifies the system to use as kernel instead of default; mainly for non-UNIX dumps.

File Name:	`savecore`	**Directory:**	/usr/sbin	**Type:**	External

savevg

UNIX Shell:	Korn shell (ksh)
Function	Collects and backs up all files that belong to a specific volume group.
Syntax	savevg [options...] *vgname*

-b *blocks*	Specifies the number of 512-byte blocks to write per output.
-f *device*	Specifies the device to place the image on.
-i	Calls the mkvgdata command to create the image file.
-m	Calls the mkvgdata command to create the image file with map files.
-p	Doesn't software pack the files.
-v	Verbose mode; shows more information.

continued

-X		Automatically expands the /tmp file system if needed.			
vgname		Specifies the volume group to backup.			
File Name:	`savevg`	**Directory:**	/usr/bin	**Type:**	Script
Tip:	To make a bootable tape with the root volume group you will have to use the `mksysb` command.				

scan

UNIX Shell: All primary shells (csh, ksh, bsh)

Function	Produces a one-line-per-message listing of the specified folder or messages.
Syntax	scan [+*folder*] { *messages...* } [options...]

-clear		Clears the screen after sending the output.			
-noclear		Doesn't clear the screen after sending the output (is default).			
-form *file*		Overrides the default output format and uses the format specified in file instead.			
-format *string*		Shows the output in the format specified in the string variable.			
-header		Shows a header before showing the messages.			
-noheader		Doesn't show a header before showing the messages (is default).			
-help		Shows help information.			
-width *columns*		Specifies the width of the scan line.			
-reverse		Lists the messages in reverse order.			
-noreverse		Doesn't list the messages in reverse order (is default).			
+*folder*		Specifies the folder to scan.			
messages...		Specifies the messages to scan.			
File Name:	`scan`	**Directory:**	/usr/bin/	**Type:**	External

sccs

UNIX Shell: All primary shells (csh, ksh, bsh)

Function	A management program for the source code control system (SCCS).
Syntax	sccs [options...] *subcommand* { *file* }

-r	Uses the real user ID instead of the effective user ID.
-d*prefix*	Specifies the prefix pathname for SCCS history files (default is current directory).
-p*subdirectory*	Specifies the subdirectory where the history files are located (default is `SCCS`).
	The following are the subcommands to use with `sccs`:
admin	Changes the checksum and flags of an s.file.
cdc [options...]	Changes the commentary in the delta of an s.file.
-r*deltaID*	Specifies the ID of the delta.
-y{ *comment* }	Specifies the new comment. Without a comment, the field will be empty.
check [options...]	Searches for s.files being edited and returns an exit value greater than zero if there are any.
-b	Does not check the branches for files in progress (use with caution).
-u{ *username* }	Searches for files being edited by you or the specified user or IP address.
clean [-b]	Deletes all files in the current directory that can be retrieved from SCCS history.
-b	Does not check the branches for files in progress (use with caution).
comb	Creates scripts used to combine s.file deltas.
create	Creates an s.history file and does a `get` to show a read-only copy.
delta [options...]	Saves the changes made to an s.file in the delta.
-s	Suppresses reports on delta numbers and statistics.
-y{ *comment* }	Specifies the new comment. Without a comment, the field will be empty.
diffs [options...]	Makes a comparison between a file being edited and the history file version. (All options in the command `diff` are also supported.)
-C	Shows a list of the differences in three lines (`diff -c`).
-I	Ignores upper/lowercases of the letters (`diff -i`).
-c*time*	Compares against the most recent version before the specified time (format is yymmdd hhmmss).
-r*deltaID*	Compares against the specified delta ID.
edit	Recovers a file version for editing and locks the file for other users.
enter	Works the same way as `create`, but doesn't show the file.
fix -r*deltaID*	Deletes the specified newest version of the delta from the SCCS history.

continued

get [options...]	Shows a read-only version from the SCCS history.
-e	Same as `edit`; allows editing on the file.
-k	Shows a printable copy of the file without opening the actual file.
-m	Shows the delta ID at the beginning of each line.
-p	Shows the file on STDOUT and redirects the delta IDs and statistics to STDERR.
-s	Suppresses reports on delta numbers and statistics.
-c*time*	Compares against the most recent version before the specified time (format is yymmdd hhmmss).
-r*deltaID*	Specifies the ID of the delta.
help *{ arguments... }*	Shows help information. The command `stuck` does the same thing.
messagecode	Shows help information about the specified errorcode.
command	Shows help information about the specified SCCS command.
info [options...]	Shows a list of files in progress.
-b	Does not check the branches for files in progress (use with caution).
-u*{ user }*	Searches for files being edited by you or the specified user or IPaddress.
print	Shows all the history information about the specified file(s).
prs [options...]	Shows the delta table. The -c and -r options are also supported.
-e	Shows all delta table information before the delta specified with -r.
-l	Shows all delta table information from and after the delta specified with -r or -c.
-r*deltaID*	Specifies the ID of the delta.
-c*time*	Compares against the most recent version before the specified time (the format is yymmdd hhmmss).
rmdel -r *deltaID*	Deletes the specified delta ID; must be the newest version in the branch.
sact	Shows the activity of editing in the specified SCCS file.
sccsdiff *old new diff { options... }*	Compares the two specified versions with the `diff` command.
-r*olddeltaID*	Specifies the old version to compare.
-r*newdeltaID*	Specifies the new version to compare.
[options...]	Specifies any diff options that should be used when comparing the files.
tell [options...]	Shows a list of the files in progress.
-b	Does not check the branches for files in progress (use with caution).
-u*{ user }*	Searches for files being edited by you, or the specified user or IPaddress.
unedit	Reverses the last change made with `edit` or `get-e`.
unget	Same as `unedit`.
val	Validates the SCCS history file.
what	Shows any expanded ID keyword strings in an object or textfile.
deledit [options...]	Combines `delta` and `edit`.
-s	Suppresses reports on delta numbers and statistics.
-y*{ comment }*	Specifies a comment.
delget [options...]	Combines `delta` and `get`.
-s	Suppresses reports on delta numbers and statistics.
-y*{ comment }*	Specifies a comment.
subcommand	Specifies a command name, its options, and any operands or arguments.
file	Specifies the s.file to run the command on. SCCS history files have the prefixes.
File Name: `sccs`	**Directory:** /usr/bin/ **Type:** External

sccsdiff

UNIX Shell: Bourne shell (bsh)

Function	Compares two versions of a SCCS file.
Syntax	sccsdiff option [options...] *{ diffoptions... } file*

	You must use two -r options to specify the versions to compare:
-rSID1	Specifies the first delta of the SCCS file.
-rSID2	Specifies the second delta of the SCCS file.
-p	Shows the result through the command `pr`.
-s*NR*	Specifies the file-segment size.
diffoptions...	Specifies the options to pass to `diff`.
file	Specifies the s.file to compare versions of.
File Name: `sccsdiff`	**Directory:** /usr/bin/ **Type:** Script

sccshelp

UNIX Shell: All primary shells (csh, ksh, bsh)

Function	Shows help information about an sccs message or command.
Syntax	sccshelp *{ errorcode } { command }*

errorcode	Specifies the error code to show help information about.
command	Specifies the command to show help information about.
File Name: sccshelp	**Directory:** /usr/bin/ **Type:** External

scls

UNIX Shell: All primary shells (csh, ksh, bsh)

Function	Creates a list of modules and driver names.
Syntax	scls [option] *{ moddriv... }*

-c	Creates a list of the number of times an interface routine was called.
-l	Creates a long listing.
moddriv...	Specifies the modules or drivers to create a list of.
File Name: scls	**Directory:** /usr/sbin **Type:** External

securetcpip

UNIX Shell: Korn shell (ksh)

Function	Enables enhanced TCP/IP security for the network.
Syntax	securetcpip
File Name: securetcpip	**Directory:** /etc/ **Type:** Script

send

UNIX Shell: All primary shells (csh, ksh, bsh)

Function	Sends the specified message files to their destinations.
Syntax	send *{ files... }* [options...]

-alias *file*	Specifies the alias file to use (default is `/etc/mh/MailAliases`).
-draft	Asks whether to use the draft file, if no file is specified.
-draftfolder +*folder*	Specifies which folder in the `Mail` directory to search for the draft message.
-nodraftfolder	Uses the default draft folder (is default).
-draftmessage *message*	Specifies the message to send.
-filter *file*	Specifies the file to use as a filter for the message.
-nofilter	Doesn't filter the message (is default).
-format	Formats the To and CC entries into standard format entries (is default).
-noformat	Doesn't format the message.
-forward	Attaches the draft file to the error message if an error occurs (is default).
-noforward	Doesn't attach the draft file to the error message, if an error occurs.
-help	Shows help information.
-msgid	Adds a Message-ID: to the message.
-nomsgid	Doesn't add a Message-ID: to the message (is default).
-push	Sends the message in the background, leaving the terminal free.
-nopush	Doesn't send the message in the background (is default).
-verbose	Verbose mode. Shows information on the message delivery progress.
-noverbose	Doesn't show more information (is default).
-watch	Shows information on the progress on the delivery to local and network mail.
-nowatch	Doesn't show information of the delivery progress (is default).
files...	Specifies the message files to send.
File Name: send	**Directory:** /usr/bin/ **Type:** External

sendbug

UNIX Shell: Bourne shell (bsh)

Function	A script that sends a problem report to a specified address.
Syntax	sendbug *{ Address }*

Address	Specifies the address to send the problem report to.
File Name: sendbug	**Directory:** /usr/bin/ **Type:** Script

setclock

UNIX Shell: All primary shells (csh, ksh, bsh)

Function	Sets or shows the time and date for a host on a network.
Syntax	setclock *{ timeserver }*

timeserver	Specifies the address of a network host with time requests.

File Name: `setclock` **Directory:** /usr/bin/ **Type:** External

setgroups

UNIX Shell: All primary shells (csh, ksh, bsh)

Function	Resets a group set session.
Syntax	setgroups [options...] *{ groupset }*

-	Reinitializes the group set session.
-a *groupset*	Adds the specified group to the session.
-d *groupset*	Removes the specified group set from the session.
-r *{ group }*	Resets the real group for the current process.
groupset	Shows the current user's group set and process group set for the shell.

File Name: `setgroups` **Directory:** /usr/bin **Type:** External

setmaps

UNIX Shell: All primary shells (csh, ksh, bsh)

Function	Manages terminal and code set maps.
Syntax	setmaps [options...] option

-c	Clears all mappings on the current terminal.
-h	Shows help information.
-v	Verbose mode. Shows more information.
-d	Specifies a directory where the mapname variable is.
-D	Shows debug information.
-i *mapname*	Uses the `/usr/lib/nls/termmap/MapName.in` file as the input map.
-I *file1*	Uses the contents of the specified file1 as the input map.
-k *keyname*	Associates the specified keyname with the specified map.
-l *file2*	Loads the `/usr/lib/nls/termmap/file2` file for later use.
-L *file*	Loads the specified file for later use.
-o *mapname*	Uses the `/usr/lib/nls/termmap/MapName.out` file as the terminal output map.
-O *file*	Uses the contents of the specified file as the terminal output map.
-r	Forces a reload of the specified map.
-s	Uses any map as a code set map.
-t *mapname*	Uses the `/usr/lib/nls/termmap/mapname.in` as terminal input and `mapname.out` as output.

File Name: `setmaps` **Directory:** /usr/bin **Type:** External

setsenv

UNIX Shell: All primary shells (csh, ksh, bsh)

Function	Resets a user's protected environment.
Syntax	setsenv [-] *newenv*

-	Reinitializes the environment for the user.
newenv	Specifies the new environment.

File Name: `setsenv` **Directory:** /usr/bin **Type:** External

shell

UNIX Shell: All primary shells (csh, ksh, bsh)

Function	Starts a shell with the user's default settings.
Syntax	shell

File Name: `shell` **Directory:** /usr/bin **Type:** External

show

UNIX Shell:	All primary shells (csh, ksh, bsh)
Function	Shows specified messages or folders. This is part of the NMH package.
Syntax	show [+folder] *{ messages.. }* [options...]

-header	Shows one line of the description per message.
-noheader	Shows the entire description field.
-showproc *program*	Specifies the program to use to perform the listing.
-noshowproc	Uses the `/usr/bin/cat` command to perform the listing.
-draft	Shows the contents of the file `draft` if it exists.
-help	Shows help information.
+folder	Specifies the folder to show (default is the current folder).
messages...	Specifies the messages to show.
File Name: `show`	**Directory:** /usr/bin/ — **Type:** External

shutacct

UNIX Shell:	Bourne shell (bsh)
Function	Disables process accounting on shutdown and adds a reason record to `/var/adm/wtmp`.
Syntax	shutacct ["*reason*"]

"*reason*"	Appends a reason for the shutdown to `/var/adm/wtmp`.
File Name: `shutacct`	**Directory:** /usr/sbin/acct/ — **Type:** Script

skulker

UNIX Shell:	All primary shells (csh, ksh, bsh)
Function	Removes unwanted files like: core files, a.out files, hup files, files in /tmp, etc.
Syntax	skulker
File Name: `skulker`	**Directory:** /usr/sbin — **Type:** External

slattach

UNIX Shell:	All primary shells (csh, ksh, bsh)
Function	Attaches a network interface to a serial line.
Syntax	slattach *ttyname { baudrate dialstring } { debuglevel }*

ttyname	Specifies the tty line.
baudrate	Determines the speed of the connection (default is 9600).
dialstring	Specifies a string of expect/respond sequences with BNU/UUCP chat syntax.
debuglevel	Specifies the level of debug information: 0 for no info and 9 for the most info.
File Name: `slattach`	**Directory:** /usr/sbin — **Type:** External

slibclean

UNIX Shell:	All primary shells (csh, ksh, bsh)
Function	Removes unused modules from the kernel and library memory.
Syntax	slibclean
File Name: `slibclean`	**Directory:** /usr/sbin — **Type:** External

sliplogin

UNIX Shell:	All primary shells (csh, ksh, bsh)
Function	Turns the terminal line on STDIN into a Serial Line IP (SLIP) link to a remote host.
Syntax	sliplogin *{ user }*

user	Specifies the login name to use.
File Name: `sliplogin`	**Directory:** /usr/sbin/ — **Type:** External

slocal

slocal	UNIX Shell:	All primary shells (csh, ksh, bsh)
Function	Manages incoming messages according to actions specified in the `.maildelivery` file: started by `sendmail`.	
Syntax	slocal [options...]	

-verbose	Verbose mode. Shows more information.
-noverbose	Disables verbose mode (is default).
-debug	Shows debug information.
-help	Shows help information.
File Name: `slocal`	**Directory:** /usr/lib/mh/ — **Type:** External

smdemon.cleanu

smdemon.cleanu	UNIX Shell:	All primary shells (csh, ksh, bsh)
Function	Cleans up sendmail queues.	
Syntax	smdemon.cleanu	
File Name: `smdemon.cleanu`	**Directory:** /usr/lib/	**Type:** External

smit, smitty

smit, smitty	UNIX Shell:	All primary shells (csh, ksh, bsh)
Function	Starts the System Management Interface Tool (SMIT) to perform system management.	
Syntax	smit [options...] smitty [options...]	

-C	Starts using an ASCII interface.
-D	Shows debug information; sets the -t and -v flags.
-d *fastpath*	Identifies that fastpath is the name of a dialogue.
-f	Enables SMIT to redirect STDIN and STDOUT.
-h	Shows the command usage message.
-l *file*	Specifies to redirect the `smit.log` file to the specified file.
-M	Starts using a window-based (Motif) interface.
-m *fastpath*	Identifies that fastpath is the name of a menu.
-n *fastpath*	Identifies that fastpath is the name of a selector.
-o *directory*	Specifies a directory for SMIT objects (default is `/etc/objrepos`).
-r *mode*	Specifies the mode to run in (only in X-window version).
1	Exits `msmit` when done is clicked.
2	Exits `msmit` when OK is clicked. Shows the dialog options, but doesn't run the command.
3	Runs `msmit` silently. Shows the dialog options, but doesn't run the command.
4	Exits `msmit` when OK is clicked. Shows the command, but doesn't run the command.
-s *file*	Specifies to redirect the `smit.script` file to the specified file.
-t	Saves detailed trace information in the `smit.log` file.
-v	Saves the command string and output for intermediate and task commands.
-x	Doesn't run any command to execute, but logs them for later execution.
-X	Doesn't run any command to execute, to list, to classify, or to discover.
File Name: `smit`	**Directory:** /usr/bin — **Type:** External
NOTE:	This tool is just beautiful. You'll love it!

snap

snap	UNIX Shell:	Korn shell (ksh)
Function	Collects system configuration information, called a snapshot.	
Syntax	snap [options...] [-d *dir*] [-v *component*]	

-a	Collects all system configuration information.
-A	Collects asynchronous (tty) information.
-b	Collects SSA information.
-c	Collects a compressed tar image of all files in the specified directory.
-D	Collects dump and /unix information.
-d *dir*	Specifies an output directory.

continued

-f	Collects file system information.		
-g	Collects the output of the `lslpp -hBc` command.		
-G	Includes predefined ODM files in general information.		
-i	Collects installation debug vital product data information.		
-k	Collects kernel information.		
-l	Collects programming language information.		
-L	Collects LVM information.		
-n	Collects Network File System (NFS) information.		
-N	Doesn't check for free space.		
-o *outdevice*	Compresses the snapshot to a diskette or a tape.		
-p	Collects printer information.		
-r	Deletes any output from the `/tmp/ibmsupt` directory.		
-s	Collects Systems Network Architecture information.		
-S	Includes security files in general information.		
-t	Collects TCP/IP information.		
-v *component*	Shows the output of the command s that have been executed by `snap`.		
File Name: `snap`	**Directory:** /usr/sbin	**Type:**	Script

snmpd

UNIX Shell: All primary shells (csh, ksh, bsh)

Function	Starts the Simple Network Management Protocol (SNMP) daemon.
Syntax	snmpd [options...]

-c *file*	Specifies the config file to use for the SNMP daemon (default is `/etc/snmpd.conf`).		
-d *level*	Specifies the trace level from 0 to 3; a higher value gives more output (default is 0).		
-f *file*	Specifies the full path- and filename for the trace log file (default is no log file).		
File Name: `snmpd`	**Directory:** /usr/sbin	**Type:**	External

snmpinfo

UNIX Shell: All primary shells (csh, ksh, bsh)

Function	Manages SNMP settings for an SNMP agent.
Syntax	snmpinfo [options...] *variable.instances...*

	The following options can't be combined:		
-m *get*	Gets information about the specified MIBs.		
-m *next*	Gets information about instances that follows the specified instance.		
-m *set*	Sets a specific MIB variable.		
-m *dump*	Dumps the specified part of the MIB tree.		
	The following options can be combined:		
-c *community*	Specifies the community to use to query the SNMP agent.		
-d *level*	Sets the level for I/O debug.		
-h *hostname*	Specifies the hostname of the SNMP agent to query.		
-o *file*	Specifies the file with the MIB definitions that can be requested.		
-t *tries*	Specifies how many tries to make before terminating.		
-v	Verbose mode. Shows more information.		
variable.instances...	Specifies the variable and instance for the MIB that you want to manage.		
File Name: `snmpinfo`	**Directory:** /usr/sbin	**Type:**	External

sno

UNIX Shell: All primary shells (csh, ksh, bsh)

Function	A SNOBOL compiler.
Syntax	sno *{ files... }*

files...	Specifies the files that you want to compile.		
File Name: `sno`	**Directory:** /usr/bin	**Type:**	External

spell

UNIX Shell: Bourne shell (bsh)

Function	Is used to search for English language spelling errors.
Syntax	spell [options...] *{ files... }*

-b	Checks British spellings based on American English spellings.
-d *hashlist*	Specifies the alternative spelling list.
-h *historylist*	Specifies a file as the alternative history list.
-i	Suppresses processing of included files.
-l	Follows the chain of all included files.
-s *hashstop*	Specifies a file as the alternative stop list.
-v	Shows all words not literally in the spelling list.
-x	Shows every valid stem.
+*file*	Specifies an additional list or lists of words to use in the spelling list.
files...	Specifies the file or files to spell check. If no file is specified, STDIN is used.

File Name:	`spell`	**Directory:**	/usr/bin	**Type:**	Script

spellin

UNIX Shell: Korn shell (ksh)

Function	Combines words from STDIN and the existing spelling list and places a new spelling list on STDOUT.
Syntax	spellin *{ List } { NR }*

	Choose only one of these:
List	Specifies a list file.
NR	Specifies the number of hash codes to read from STDIN.

File Name:	`spellin`	**Directory:**	/usr/bin/	**Type:**	Script

spellout

UNIX Shell: All primary shells (csh, ksh, bsh)

Function	Checks that a specific word isn't in the spelling list.
Syntax	spellout [-d] *list*

-d	Shows words that are in the spelling list.
list	Specifies the spelling list.

File Name:	`spelltout`	**Directory:**	/usr/bin	**Type:**	External

splitlvcopy

UNIX Shell: Korn shell (ksh)

Function	Splits a logical volume copy to create a new logical volume.
Syntax	splitlvcopy [options...] *logicalvol copies { physicalvols... }*

-f	Splits open volumes without asking for confirmation.
-y *newlvname*	Specifies the name of the new logical volume.
-Y *prefix*	Specifies a prefix to use for the name of the new logical volume.
logicalvol	Specifies the logical volume to split.
copies	Specifies how many copies to save in the logical volume that is split.
physicalvols...	Specifies the physical volume to remove copies from.

File Name:	`splitlvcopy`	**Directory:**	/usr/sbin/	**Type:**	Script

splp

UNIX Shell: All primary shells (csh, ksh, bsh)

Function	Manages printer driver settings.
Syntax	splp [options...] *{ device }*

-b	Manages backspaces.
-b +	Sends backspaces to the printer.
-B *number*	Sets the speed to the specified bits per second.
-c	Manages carriage returns.
-c +	Sends carriage returns to the printer.

continued

-c !	Doesn't send carriage returns to the printer.
-C	Manages uppercase/lowercase conversion.
-C +	Converts from lowercase to uppercase.
-C !	Makes no conversion.
-e	Manages processing if errors are detected.
-e +	Shows the error.
-e !	Waits until the error is clear.
-f	Manages form feeds.
-f +	Sends a form feed to the printer.
-f !	Simulates a form feed.
-F!	Resets font status indicators.
-i *number*	Indents the specified number of columns.
-l *number*	Specifies the number of lines per page to print.
-n	Manages line feeds.
-n +	Sends a line feed to the printer.
-n !	Translates a line feed to a carriage return.
-N	Manages parity generation and detection.
-N +	Uses parity generation and detection.
-N !	Doesn't use parity generation and detection.
-p	Manages character modification.
-p +	Sends all characters unmodified to the printer.
-p !	Translates characters before sending them.
-P	Manages parity.
-P +	Uses odd parity.
-P !	Uses even parity.
-r	Manages carriage returns after line feeds.
-r +	Sends a carriage return after a line feed.
-r !	Doesn't send carriage a return after a line feed.
-s *number*	Specifies character size in bits.
-S	Manages the number of stop bits per character.
-S +	Uses two stop bits per character.
-S !	Uses one stop bit per character.
-t	Manages Tab expansion.
-t +	Doesn't expand Tabs.
-t !	Expands Tabs.
-w *number*	Specifies the number of columns to print.
-W	Manages character wrap.
-W +	Wraps characters.
-W !	Truncates characters.
device	Specifies a device to act on.

File Name:	splp	**Directory:**	/usr/bin/	**Type:**	External

spost

UNIX Shell: All primary shells (csh, ksh, bsh)

Function	Delivers a message. Other programs only start this.
Syntax	spost [options...] *file*

-filter *file*	Specifies the mail should be filtered using the specified file as filter input.
-nofilter	Specifies that no filter should be used.
-format	Specifies the mail should be formatted.
-noformat	Specifies the mail should not be formatted.
-remove	Specifies the mail should be removed.
-noremove	Specifies the mail should be kept.
-verbose	Verbose mode. Shows more information.
-noverbose	Shows less information.
-watch	Shows the transport system's handling of the message.
-nowatch	Doesn't show the transport system's handling of the message.

continued

-backup	Specifies the mail should be saved on backup.
-nobackup	Specifies the mail should not be saved on backup.
-alias *file*	Specifies a file to read aliases from.
-noalias	Specifies that no aliases should be used.
-width *columns*	Specifies the length of the header components that contain addresses.
file	Specifies the file that contains the mail.
File Name: spost	**Directory:** /usr/lib/mh/ **Type:** External

spray

UNIX Shell: All primary shells (csh, ksh, bsh)

Function	Sends a stream of packets to a host. Reports how many packets were received, and the transfer rate.
Syntax	spray *host* [options...]

-c *count*	Specifies how many packets to send.
-d *delay*	Specifies the pause between each packet, in microseconds (default is 0).
-i	Uses ICMP echo packets instead of the RPC protocol.
-l *length*	Sets the number of bytes in the packet (default is 86).
host	Specifies the host to send to.
File Name: spray	**Directory:** /usr/sbin/ **Type:** External

srcmstr

UNIX Shell: All primary shells (csh, ksh, bsh)

Function	Starts the system resource controller.
Syntax	srcmstr [options...]

-r	Accepts remote requests.
-B	Runs the daemon as an earlier release.
File Name: srcmstr	**Directory:** /usr/sbin/ **Type:** External

startsrc

UNIX Shell: All primary shells (csh, ksh, bsh)

Function	Starts a subsystem or subserver, also called a daemon.
Syntax	startsrc [options...]

-a *arg*	Specifies an argument string to pass to the subsystem on startup.
-e *env*	Specifies an environment string to pass to the subsystem on startup.
-h *host*	Specifies a remote host to start a daemon on.
-s *subsystem*	Specifies a subsystem to start.
-t *type*	Specifies that a subsystem is to be started.
-o *object*	Passes the specified subserver object to the subsystem as a character string.
-p *subsysPID*	Specifies an instance of the subsystem to start.
File Name: startsrc	**Directory:** /usr/bin/ **Type:** External

startup

UNIX Shell: Bourne shell (bsh)

Function	Turns on process accounting when the system is brought to a multi-user state.
Syntax	startup
File Name: startup	**Directory:** /usr/sbin/acct/ **Type:** Script

startx

UNIX Shell: Korn shell (ksh)

Function	Starts a single session of the X window system.
Syntax	startx [options...]

-d *display:0*	Sets the display name of the X server shown to the X clients during startup.
	The following two options can't be combinied:
-t	Starts X clients for an X terminal.
-w	Starts the X server and X clients for an X window session on a workstation.
-x *startup*	Starts an X window session using the startup script.

continued

-r *resources*	Loads the resources file if no startup script is found.
-m *manager*	Starts the specified Window Manager if no startup script is found.
-wait	Doesn't start the X session when the `xdm` command invokes `startx`.
File Name: `startx`	**Directory:** /usr/bin/X11/ **Type:** Script

stdethers

UNIX Shell: All primary shells (csh, ksh, bsh)

Function	Filters out non-YP information from a file.
Syntax	stdethers { *file* }

file	Specifies the file to act on.
File Name: `stdethers`	**Directory:** /usr/etc/yp/ **Type:** External

stdhosts

UNIX Shell: All primary shells (csh, ksh, bsh)

Function	Filters out non-YP information.
Syntax	stdhosts { *file* }

file	Specifies the file to act on.
File Name: `stdhosts`	**Directory:** /usr/etc/yp/ **Type:** External

stem

UNIX Shell: All primary shells (csh, ksh, bsh)

Function	A tool that lets the user insert instrumentation code into subroutines.
Syntax	stem option [options...]

	The following three options can't be combined:
-mf *mapfile*	Uses the specified map file as a stem map file.
-p *program*	Instruments all programs in the specified routine.
-pshm *program*	A lighter version of the -p option. Uses Stem_ShmEnter and Stem_ShmExit.
-ld_cmd	Uses the `ld_cmd` file if it exists.
-noleaf	Doesn't insert an instrument into leaf routines.
-libdir *directory*	Specifies a directory where instrument libraries are stored.
-exedir *directory*	Specifies a directory where instrumented executables are stored.
	The following options are used to manage shared memory buffers:
-on	Sets the on flag in the shared memory buffers.
-noreset	Doesn't reset the pointer to the beginning of the shared-memory buffer.
-off	Sets the off flag in the shared memory buffers.
-shm *size*	Sets the size of the shared memory buffer.
-shmkill	Erases an existing shared memory buffer.
-cg	Creates a callgraph of the shared memory.
File Name: `stem`	**Directory:** /usr/bin/ **Type:** External

stopsrc

UNIX Shell: All primary shells (csh, ksh, bsh)

Function	Stops a subsystem or subserver.
Syntax	stopsrc [-h *host*] [option] *option* stopsrc [-h *host*] [-f] -t *type* [-p *subPID*] [option]

	Syntax 1 is for stopping a subsystem. Syntax 2 is for stopping a subserver.
-h *host*	Specifies a remote host to stop a daemon on.
	You may select between these two options when stopping a subsystem:
-f	Forces a stop of the daemon.
-c	Specifies a cancelled stop request.
	You must select only one of these four options when stopping a subsystem:
-a	Stops all subsystems.
-g *group*	Specifies a group of subsystems to stop.
-s *subsystem*	Specifies which subsystem to stop.
-t *type*	Specifies that a subserver is to be stopped.

continued

	You may select between these two options when stopping a subserver:		
-P *subservPID*	Passes the subserver PID to the subsystem as a character string.		
-o *object*	Passes the subserver Object value to the subsystem as a character string.		
File Name: `stopsrc`	**Directory:** /usr/bin/	**Type:**	External

strace

UNIX Shell: All primary shells (csh, ksh, bsh)

Function	Shows streams trace messages on STDOUT. Operands can be specified multiple times, but only in triplets.
Syntax	strace *{ mid sid level }*

mid	Specifies the module or driver ID number to trace.		
sid	Specifies the sub-ID number to trace.		
level	Specifies the trace priority level. (The token all can be used to show all messages in a specified category.)		
File Name: `strace`	**Directory:** /usr/sbin/	**Type:**	External

strchg

UNIX Shell: All primary shells (csh, ksh, bsh)

Function	Alters the configurations of streams associated with the user's STDIN.
Syntax	strchg [options...]

-h *modules...*	Adds the modules to the top of the stream.		
-f *file*	Specifies a file containing a list of modules for the stream configuration.		
-p	Removes the topmost module off the stream.		
-a	Removes all modules above the topmost driver from the stream.		
-u *module*	Removes all modules above the specified module from the stream.		
File Name: `strchg`	**Directory:** /usr/sbin/	**Type:**	External

strclean

UNIX Shell: All primary shells (csh, ksh, bsh)

Function	Removes streams error logger files older than three days.
Syntax	strclean [options...]

-a *age*	Changes the maximum age for a log file, in days.		
-d *directory*	Specifies the logging directory (default is `/var/adm/streams`).		
File Name: `strclean`	**Directory:** /usr/sbin/	**Type:**	External

strconf

UNIX Shell: All primary shells (csh, ksh, bsh)

Function	Queries the configuration of a stream.
Syntax	strconf [option]

	The following options can't be combined:		
-t	Shows the topmost module only.		
-m *module*	Determines if the specified module is present on a stream.		
File Name: `strconf`	**Directory:** /usr/sbin/	**Type:**	External

strinfo

UNIX Shell: All primary shells (csh, ksh, bsh)

Function	Shows information about streams activity.
Syntax	strinfo option

-m	Shows driver and module information.		
-q	Shows information on active stream heads.		
File Name: `strinfo`	**Directory:** /usr/sbin/	**Type:**	External

stripnm

UNIX Shell:	All primary shells (csh, ksh, bsh)
Function	Shows symbol information for a specific object file.
Syntax	stripnm [options...] *file*

-x	Shows symbol address values in hexadecimal format.
-s	Shows symbol names from the traceback tables, if no symbol tables exist.
file	Specifies the object file to get symbol values from.

File Name: stripnm **Directory:** /usr/bin/ **Type:** External

strload

UNIX Shell:	All primary shells (csh, ksh, bsh)
Function	Manages the portable streams environment (PSE).
Syntax	strload [options...]

-u	Unloads extensions.
-q	Shows the load status of extensions.
-f *file*	Uses the specified file to configure PSE.
-d *devlist*	Shows PSE device drivers to load or unload.
-m *modlist*	Shows PSE modules to load or unload.

File Name: strload **Directory:** /usr/sbin/ **Type:** External

strreset

UNIX Shell:	All primary shells (csh, ksh, bsh)
Function	Resets a stream.
Syntax	strreset [options...]

-M *major*	Specifies the major number for the stream device.
-m *minor*	Specifies the minor number for the stream device.

File Name: strreset **Directory:** /usr/sbin/ **Type:** External

struct

UNIX Shell:	Bourne shell (bsh)
Function	Converts FORTRAN programs into RATFOR programs.
Syntax	struct [options...] { *file* }

-a	Disables the sequences of else-if statements into a non-RATFOR switch.
-b	Creates goto statements instead of multilevel break statements.
-c*number*	Increments labels successively in the output program.
-i	Doesn't convert computed goto statements into switches.
-n	Creates goto statements instead of multilevel next statements.
-s	Specifies that input can be in standard format.
-t*number*	Makes the specified nonzero integer the lowest-valued label in the output.
file	Specifies the program to convert.

File Name: struct **Directory:** /usr/ucb/ **Type:** Script

style

UNIX Shell:	Bourne shell (bsh)
Function	Analyzes the style of an English-language document.
Syntax	style [options...] *files...*

-a	Shows sentences with their lengths and readability index.
-e	Shows sentences that begin with an expletive.
-l *number*	Shows sentences longer than the specified number of words.
-ml	Skips lists.
-mm	Overrides the default ms macro package.
-p	Shows sentences that contain a passive verb.
-P	Shows the parts of speech of the words in the document.

continued

-r *number*		Shows sentences whose readability index is greater than the specified number.			
File Name:	style	**Directory:**	/usr/bin/	**Type:**	Script

subj

UNIX Shell: Korn shell (ksh)

Function	Creates a list of subjects from a document.
Syntax	subj *{ files... }*

files...		Specifies an English-language file as input.			
File Name:	subj	**Directory:**	/usr/bin/	**Type:**	Script

survd

UNIX Shell: All primary shells (csh, ksh, bsh)

Function	Manages the surveillance daemon.
Syntax	survd [options...]

-d *delay*		Specifies the delay period between signal sending to the bring up microprocessor.			
-h		Reboots if no signal was received.			
-r		Disables surveillance and kills the daemon.			
File Name:	survd	**Directory:**	/usr/sbin/	**Type:**	External

svmon

UNIX Shell: All primary shells (csh, ksh, bsh)

Function	Is used to take snapshots and create reports of the virtual memory.
Syntax	svmon option [options...]

		One of the following seven options is required, and they can't be combined:			
-G		Creates a global report.			
-U *logins...*		Shows statistics about memory usage for the specified login names.			
-C *commands...*		Shows statistics about memory usage for the specified command processes.			
-W *classes...*		Shows statistics about memory usage for the specified Workload Management Classes.			
-S *sids...*		Shows statistics about memory usage for the specified segment ID.			
-D *sids...*		Shows statistics about memory usage for the specified segment ID and frame, verbose mode.			
		The following options are combinable and not required:			
-i *interval times*		Shows statistics at the specified interval of seconds, and number of times.			
-z		Shows the maximum memory size that svmon allocates during execution.			
-b		Shows status for all modified bits in frames; only used with the -D option.			
-n		Includes only the non-system segments in the report.			
-w		Includes only the working segments in the report.			
-f		Includes only the persistent segments in the report.			
-c		Includes only the client segments in the report.			
-t *count*		Shows the top specified segments.			
-u		Sorts output in decreasing order by total number of pages in real memory.			
-p		Sorts output in decreasing order by total number of pinned pages.			
-g		Sorts output in decreasing order by total number of reserved pages.			
-v		Sorts output in decreasing order by total number of pages in virtual memory.			
-l		Shows which pid uses the segments.			
-d		Shows memory usage for the entity processes.			
-m		Shows source segment information.			
File Name:	svmon	**Directory:**	/usr/sbin/	**Type:**	External

swapon

UNIX Shell: All primary shells (csh, ksh, bsh)

Function	Specifies a device to start swapping or paging on.
Syntax	swapon [option] *{ devices... }*

-a		Enables all devices in the `/etc/swapspaces` file.			
devices...		Specifies a swap device.			
File Name:	swapon	**Directory:**	/usr/sbin/	**Type:**	External

swcons

UNIX Shell: All primary shells (csh, ksh, bsh)

Function	Redirects console output to another device temporarily.
Syntax	swcons [options...] *device*

-p *logfile*	Specifies the console output log file.
-s *logsize*	Specifies the size of the console output log file.
-t *tagverbose*	Specifies the verbosity level for console output tagging. Valid values are 0 to 9.
-v *logverbose*	Specifies the verbosity level for console output logging. Valid values are 0 to 9.
device	Specifies the device to use as console temporarily.

File Name: `swcons` **Directory:** /usr/sbin/ **Type:** External

synclvodm

UNIX Shell: All primary shells (csh, ksh, bsh)

Function	Synchronizes or rebuilds control blocks, ODM settings, or volume descriptor areas on a physical volume.
Syntax	synclvodm [-v] *volumegroup { logicalvols... }*

-v	Verbose mode. Shows more information.
volumegroup	Specifies the volume group to synchronize in the ODM.
logicalvols...	Works only with the specified logical volumes.

File Name: `synclvodm` **Directory:** /usr/sbin/ **Type:** External

syncvg

UNIX Shell: Korn shell (ksh)

Function	Synchronizes logical volume copies that are inconsistent.
Syntax	syncvg [options...] option *volnames...*

-f	Uses a good physical copy to synchronize with.
-i	Reads volnames from STDIN.
-H	Doesn't write to the volume until the synchronization is done.
-P *parlp*	Specifies the number of logical partitions to be synchronized in parallel.
	You must select only one of these three options:
-l	Specifies the volname is a logical volume device name.
-p	Specifies the volname is a physical volume device name.
-v	Specifies the volname is a volume group device name.
volnames...	Specifies logical volume to act on.

File Name: `syncvg` **Directory:** /usr/sbin/ **Type:** Script

syscall

UNIX Shell: All primary shells (csh, ksh, bsh)

Function	Runs a specific subroutine call.
Syntax	syscall [*-nr*] *names... { arguments... }*

-nr	Specifies the number of times to run the subroutine call.
names...	Specifies which subroutine call to run; use a colon to separate multiple subroutines.
arguments...	Specifies arguments to the subroutine.

File Name: `syscall` **Directory:** /usr/bin/ **Type:** External

syscalls

UNIX Shell: All primary shells (csh, ksh, bsh)

Function	Traces system calls.
Syntax	syscalls [options...]

-enable *bytes*	Creates the system calls buffer.
-disable	Removes the system calls buffer.
-c	Shows a summary of all system calls for all processes.
-o *file*	Prints output to a file instead of STDOUT.
-t	Shows the time associated with each system call event.
-p *pid*	Logs only the specified processes, or stops logging if -stop is used.
-start	Resets trace buffers and starts from zero.

continued

-stop	Stops logging system calls.
-x *program*	Runs a program and traces system calls to that program.
File Name: `syscalls`	**Directory:** /usr/bin/ **Type:** External

sysck

UNIX Shell: All primary shells (csh, ksh, bsh)

Function	Checks inventory information during installation or update, and updates the SoftWare Vital Product Data database.
Syntax	sysck option [options...] -f *file prodname*

	The following two options can't be combined:
-i	Checks the software products files are correctly installed.
-u	Erases file entries, and hard and symbolic links from the SWVPD.
-R *rootpath*	Specifies an alternative root path.
-N	Doesn't update the SWVPD.
-v	Checks the checksum.
-s *file*	Takes a snapshot of the VPD and saves it to the specified file.
-O *r / s / u*	Specifies which SWVPD part you want to update.
r	Updates only the root part.
s	Updates only the `/usr/share` part.
u	Updates only the `/usr` part.
-f *file*	Specifies the file with the file definitions.
prodname	Specifies which software product to check.
File Name: `sysck`	**Directory:** /usr/bin/ **Type:** External

sysdumpdev

UNIX Shell: All primary shells (csh, ksh, bsh)

Function	Manages primary and secondary dump devices in the system.
Syntax	sysdumpdev [options...]

-c	Doesn't compress dumps.
-C	Compresses all dumps from now on.
-d *directory*	Specifies a directory where the dump is copied. If the copy fails, the dump is ignored.
-D *directory*	Specifies a directory where the dump is copied to; allows a copy to an external media.
-e	Estimates the dump size of the running system.
-k	Specifies the key must be in service mode.
-K	Allows a dump with the key in normal mode, or on a system without a key switch.
-l	Shows current primary and secondary dump devices.
-L	Shows statistics about the most recent system dump.
-p *device*	Specifies a temporary primary dump device.
-q	Shows no messages on STDOUT.
-r *host:path*	Specifies a remote host and path to dump to.
-s *device*	Specifies a temporary secondary dump device.
-z	Shows if a new system dump exists.
-P	Makes the dump device specified by -p or -s flag permanent.
File Name: `sysdumpdev`	**Directory:** /usr/bin/ **Type:** External

sdumpstart

UNIX Shell: All primary shells (csh, ksh, bsh)

Function	Starts a kernel dump to a dump device.
Syntax	sysdumpstart option [-f]

-p	Starts a system dump and writes to the primary dump device.
-s	Starts a system dump and writes to the secondary dump device.
-f	Shows no prompt to make the secondary dump device ready.
File Name: `sysdumpstart`	**Directory:** /usr/bin/ **Type:** External

sysline

UNIX Shell: All primary shells (csh, ksh, bsh)

Function	Shows system status on the terminal.
Syntax	sysline [options...]

-b	Beeps on every half hour and beeps twice on every hour.
-c	Clears the status line before showing status.
-d	Shows the status line in readable format.
-D	Shows the current day and date before the time.
-e	Shows only status information and won't show control information.
-h	Shows the hostname.
-H *remote*	Shows the load average on the specified remote host.
-i	Shows the process ID of the sysline command process to STDOUT.
-j	Shows output on the left side.
-l	Shows no login names.
-m	Doesn't check mail.
-p	Doesn't show the number of processes executed.
-q	Doesn't show diagnostic messages.
-r	Doesn't use reverse video display.
-s	Shows output on the left side in short form.
-w	Shows the status of the terminal.
+N	Updates the status line every N seconds.

File Name:	`sysline`	**Directory:**	/usr/bin/	**Type:**	External

tab

UNIX Shell: All primary shells (csh, ksh, bsh)

Function	Converts spaces into tabs.
Syntax	tab [-e] *{ files... }*

-e	Converts spaces only up to the first non-space character.
files...	Specifies the input file or files.

File Name:	`tab`	**Directory:**	/usr/bin/	**Type:**	External

tabs

UNIX Shell: All primary shells (csh, ksh, bsh)

Function	Clears old settings and set new Tabs and margins on remote terminals.
Syntax	tabs [options...]

-T*type*	Specifies terminal type. Uses the values in environment var TERM if not specified.
+m*{ n }*	Moves all Tabs to the right by the number of columns specified by *n*+1.
	There are four types of Tab definitions: canned, repetitive, arbitrary, and file.
canned	The following options are the preconfigured built-in Tabs called canned:
-a	Sets Tabs to Assembler, IBM S/370, first format.
-a2	Sets Tabs to Assembler, IBM S/370, second format.
-c	Sets Tabs to COBOL, normal format.
-c2	Sets Tabs to COBOL, compact format.
-c3	Sets Tabs to COBOL, compact format with more Tabs than -c2 (recommended).
-f	Sets Tabs to FORTRAN format.
-p	Sets Tabs to PL/I format.
-s	Sets Tabs to SNOBOL format.
-u	Sets Tabs to UNIVAC 1100 Assembler format.
repetitive	Sets Tabs at every specified number of columns.
-n	Sets Tabs at 1+n, 1+2n, 1+3n, and so on, where n is a single decimal number.
arbitrary	Sets Tabs at every specified value, separated with a comma.
-n	Sets Tabs at n1, n2, n3, and so on, where n is positive decimal numbers in ascending order.
-file	Sets the Tabs from a format specification in the specified file.

File Name:	`tabs`	**Directory:**	/usr/bin/	**Type:**	External

tapechk

UNIX Shell: Korn shell (ksh)

Function	Runs a consistency check on a tape device.
Syntax	tapechk [-?] *number1 number2*

-?	Shows help information.
number1	Specifies the number of files to check.
number2	Excludes the specified files from the checklist.

File Name: tapechk **Directory:** /usr/sbin/ **Type:** Script

tapes

UNIX Shell: Korn shell (ksh)

Function	Shows any available tape devices installed in the computer.
Syntax	tapes [options...]

-r	Shows the device name of the tape device.
-p	Shows the subclass for the tape device.

File Name: tapes **Directory:** /usr/dms/scripts/ **Type:** Script

tc

UNIX Shell: All primary shells (csh, ksh, bsh)

Function	Interprets input as output from the troff command and the STDOUT.
Syntax	tc [options...] *{ file }*

-t	Specifies to not wait between pages when directing output into a file.
-e	Doesn't erase before each page.
-a*number*	Specifies the aspect ratio (default is 1.5).
-o *number*	Shows only the specified pages.
-s *number*	Doesn't show the first specified number of pages.
--	Indicates the end of the options.
-?	Shows a list of available options.
-number	Specifies the number of pages to skip backwards.
file	Specifies the file to read from. Use a dash or nothing to read from STDIN.

File Name: tc **Directory:** /usr/bin/ **Type:** External

tcbck

UNIX Shell: All primary shells (csh, ksh, bsh)

Function	Manages the security state of the system.
Syntax	tcbck option [-i] *method*

	The following four options can't be combined:
-n	Reports errors but doesn't fix them.
-p	Fixes errors but doesn't report them.
-t	Reports errors and prompts to fix them.
-y	Reports and fixes errors.
-i	Excludes any file system under the directories listed in the treeck_nodir attribute.
	The following methods can be used together. At least one is required:
ALL	Checks all file definitions in the sysck database.
tree	Checks all files in the system tree.
names...	Specifies pathnames to specific files to check.
classes...	Specifies a group of files to check.
	Use the following options to add, update, or erase file definitions:
-a	Adds or updates file definitions in the sysck database.
-d	Erases file definitions from the sysck database.
-l	Adds /dev entries to the sysck.cfg file to register them with TCB.
-f *file*	Reads file definitions from the specified file; used with the -a and -d options.
files...	Specifies the files to add, update, or erase; used with the -a and -d options.
devpath	Specifies the /dev entry to add to the sysck.cfg file; only used with the -l option.

File Name: tcbck **Directory:** /usr/bin/ **Type:** External

tcopy

UNIX Shell:	All primary shells (csh, ksh, bsh)
Function	Copies or scans a magnetic tape.
Syntax	tcopy *source { destination }*

source	Specifies the tape drive to use for input.
destination	Specifies where to copy the tape; if no destination is given, only a scan is performed.

File Name:	tcopy	**Directory:**	/usr/bin/	**Type:**	External

tcpdump

UNIX Shell:	All primary shells (csh, ksh, bsh)
Function	Shows the headers of packets on a network interface.
Syntax	tcpdump [options...] *{ expressions... }*

-c *count*	Stops after receiving count packets.
-d	Shows the compiled packet-matching code in a human-readable form and stops.
-e	Shows the link-level header on each dump line.
-f	Shows foreign Internet addresses numerically rather than symbolically.
-F *file*	Specifies a file to read filters from.
-i *interface*	Specifies the interface to use.
-l	Specifies that STDOUT should be line-buffered.
-n	Specifies that addresses should not be converted to names.
-N	Specifies that domain name-qualification of hostnames should not be shown.
-O	Specifies the packet-matching code optimizer should not be used.
-p	Specifies the interface should be put in promiscuous mode.
-q	Specifies that less information about a protocol should be shown.
-r *file*	Specifies a file to read packages from.
-s *NR*	Specifies the number of bytes to snap from each packet (default is 80).
-S	Shows absolute numbers, rather than relative numbers.
-t	Specifies that a timestamp should not be shown on each dump line.
-tt	Specifies that a timestamp should be shown on each dump line.
-v	Verbose mode. Shows more information.
-w *file*	Specifies a file to write raw package data to.
-x	Shows each package in hex format.
expressions...	**The following are the expressions that can be used:**
dst host *host*	Shows packets headers going to host.
src host *host*	Shows packet headers coming from host.
host *host*	Shows packet headers going to and coming from host.
ip host *host*	Checks each IP address for matches in cases where a host has multiple IP addresses.
dst net *network*	Shows packet headers going to network.
src net *network*	Shows packet headers coming from network.
net *net*	Shows packet headers going to and coming from network.
dst port *port*	Shows packet headers going to port.
src port *port*	Shows packet headers coming from port.
port *port*	Shows packet headers going to and coming from port. (Use tcp or udp as prependers for any port expression.)
less *length*	Shows packet headers whose length is less or equal to length.
greater *length*	Shows packet headers whose length is greater or equal to length.
ip proto *proto*	Shows packet headers that have an IP packet of type *proto.*
tcp	Specifies the TCP protocol.
udp	Specifies the UDP protocol.
icmp	Specifies the ICMP protocol.
ip broadcast	Sets to true if the packet is an IP broadcast packet.
ip multicast	Sets to true if the packet is an IP multicast packet.

continued

proto *proto*		Sets to true if the packet matches the specified protocol.			
ip		Selects the ip protocol type.			
arp		Selects the arp protocol type.			
rarp		Selects the rarp protocol type.			
File Name:	`tcpdump`	**Directory:**	/usr/sbin/	**Type:**	External
tcpdump -i en0		Listen for ip traffic on the network interface en0.			

tctl

UNIX Shell: All primary shells (csh, ksh, bsh)

Function	Controls commands to a streaming tape device.
Syntax	tctl [options...] *{ commands... }*

-b *blocksize*		Specifies the buffer size used to read and write to the tape device.			
-f *device*		Specifies a raw tape device.			
-p *buffsize*		Specifies the buffer size to be used on STDIN and STDOUT.			
-v		Verbose Mode. Shows more information.			
-n		Specifies a variable-length record to use with the read or write command.			
-B		Shows the content of the buffer when the tape is read.			
commands		**The following are commands that can be sent to the tape device:**			
eof		Specifies an end-of-file marker.			
weof		Specifies an end-of-file marker.			
fsf		Moves the tape forward the number of file marks specified by count.			
bsf		Moves the tape backwards the number of file marks specified by count.			
fsr		Moves the tape forward the number of records specified by count.			
bsr		Moves the tape backwards the number of records specified by count.			
rewind		Rewinds the tape.			
offline		Rewinds the tape and takes the tape drive offline.			
rewoffl		Rewinds the tape and takes the tape drive offline.			
erase		Erases the tape and rewinds it.			
retension		Stretches the tape.			
reset		Sends a bus device reset to the device.			
status		Shows status information about the specified tape device.			
read		Specifies to read from the tape device.			
write		Specifies to write to the tape device.			
count		Specifies a count for each operation.			
File Name:	`tctl`	**Directory:**	/usr/bin/	**Type:**	External

tdigest

UNIX Shell: All primary shells (csh, ksh, bsh)

Function	Converts term files.
Syntax	tdigest *file1 file2*

file1		Specifies a terminal description file to convert.			
file2		Specifies the converted output file.			
File Name:	`tdigest`	**Directory:**	/usr/bin/	**Type:**	External

termdef

UNIX Shell: All primary shells (csh, ksh, bsh)

Function	Queries and shows current terminal settings.
Syntax	termdef [option]

-c		Shows the current column values.			
-l		Shows the current line values.			
-t		Shows the name of the current display.			
File Name:	`termdef`	**Directory:**	/usr/bin/	**Type:**	External

tftp, utftp

UNIX Shell: All primary shells (csh, ksh, bsh)

Function	Sends files to and receives files from a remote host using the Trivial File Transfer Protocol (TFTP).
Syntax	tftp [options] *localfile Host:[Port] remotefile { netascii } { image }*

	The following options can't be combined:
-g	Gets remote data from *remotefile* from the specified host and writes to *localfile*.
-o	Overwrites an existing local file without prompting.
-p	Puts local data from *localfile* to file *remotefile*.
-r	Reads remote data from *remotefile* from the specified host and writes to *localfile*.
-w	Writes local data from *localfile* to file *remotefile*.
localfile	Specifies the local file to transfer or get data to or from.
*Host:**{ Port }***	Specifies the remote computer and port to connect to.
remotefile	Specifies the remote file to put or get data to or from.
	Use only one of the following modes:
netascii	Transfers the data as 7-bit ASCII characters in 8-bit transfer bytes.
image	Transfers the data as 8-bit binary data bytes in 8-bit transfer bytes.
	The following are internal commands that can be used in tftp or utftp:
connect	Specifies a hostname or IP address to a tftp server.
mode *{ netascii | image }*	Shows or sets the current mode used to transfer files.
put *file*	Specifies the filename of the file to transfer.
get *file*	Specifies the filename of the file to receive.
verbose	Toggles verbose mode on or off. When on, verbose mode shows more information.
trace	Toggles packet tracing during file transfer.
status	Shows the connection status, mode status, tracing status, and timeout status.
binary	Sets the transfer mode to binary; same as `mode image`.
ascii	Sets the transfer mode to ASCII; same as `mode netascii`.
timeout *value*	Specifies the timeout value for the connection.
?	Shows help information on the internal commands.

File Name:	`tftp, utftp`	**Directory:**	/usr/bin/	**Type:**	External

timed

UNIX Shell: All primary shells (csh, ksh, bsh)

Function	Synchronizes local time with other hosts.
Syntax	timed [options...]

-c	Specifies the network time is the same as the master-timed daemon.
-M	Specifies that host will become the master server if no master already exists.
-t	Traces the received messages in `/var/log/timed.log`.
-n *network*	Specifies the named network is valid; all other networks are ignored.
-i *network*	Ignores the named network; all other networks are valid.

File Name:	`timed`	**Directory:**	/usr/sbin/	**Type:**	External

timedc

UNIX Shell: All primary shells (csh, ksh, bsh)

Function	Administers the function of the `timed` program.
Syntax	timedc *{ command } { argument }*

	The following commands and their arguments are supported:
help | ? [commands...]	Shows help information about the specified commands, or all commands.
clockdiff *host others*	Shows the differences between the clock on the specified host and other systems.
election *hosts...*	Resets election timers and ensures that a timed master server is available.
quit	Exits the program.
trace on | off	Toggles the trace log of incoming messages to /var/log/timed.log.
command	Specifies the command to run.
argument	Specifies any arguments to the command.

File Name:	`timedc`	**Directory:**	/usr/sbin/	**Type:**	External

timex

UNIX Shell:	All primary shells (csh, ksh, bsh)
Function	Measures how long it takes to run a command. Shows time elapsed, user time, and system time in seconds.
Syntax	timex [options...] *command*

-o	Shows how many blocks that are read or written and characters sent by the command.
-p *{ options... }*	Shows process accounting records for the command.
f	Shows fork and exec flags and system exit status columns.
h	Shows the portion of the total available CPU time used by the process.
k	Shows the total kcore-minutes instead of the memory size.
m	Shows the mean core size (Is default).
r	Shows the CPU factor using the format `user-time/(system-time + user-time)`.
t	Shows separate user and system CPU times.
-s	Reports total system actions that occurred while the command was executed.
command	Specifies the command to be executed.
File Name: `timex`	**Directory:** /usr/bin/ **Type:** External

tip

UNIX Shell:	All primary shells (csh, ksh, bsh)
Function	Connects to a remote host with full duplex terminal connection behaving like an interactive session on a local terminal.
Syntax	tip [options...] *ACTION*

-v	Shows the execution of the commands from the file `.tiprc` as they are done.
-speed	Specifies a baud rate to use for the connection, other than the default.
ACTION	**Select one of the following actions:**
hostname	Specifies the hostname or IP address of the server to connect to.
phonenumber	Connects to a remote host using a phone number.
	The following are internal commands that are executed inside the program:
~.	Drops the connection from the remote system and exits.
~c *directory*	Specifies a name to a directory.
~!	Moves to an interactive shell on the local system.
~>	Copies files from a local system to remote system.
~<	Copies files from a remote system to a local system.
~p *from { to }*	Copies the local file specified to the remote file specified.
~t *from { to }*	Copies the remote file specified to a local file.
~|	Takes output from a remote command and uses it as input to a local command.
~C	Connects a program to a remote system.
~$	Takes output from a local command to a host or an IP address on a remote system.
~#	Sends a BREAK to the remote system.
~s	Sets a variable for normal operations.
~^Z	Stops tip when it runs under a shell that supports job control, such as the C shell.
~^Y	Stops tip only on your own system; the remote system continues.
~?	Shows a summary of ~ escape characters on the screen.
File Name: `tip`	**Directory:** /usr/bin/ **Type:** External

tn3270

UNIX Shell:	All primary shells (csh, ksh, bsh)
Function	Connects a local host with a remote host; operates in command mode and input mode.
Syntax	tn3270 [options...]

-d	Shows debug information.
-p	Maintains current tty attributes.
-n *file*	Stores network trace information in the specified file.
-e *type*	Rejects terminal-type negotiation. Values are vt 100, 3270, or none.
-f	Forwards the credentials. Can not be combined with -F.
-F	Forwards the credentials and marks them as forwardable on the remote system.
-k *realm*	Specifies the realm of the remote station if it is different from the local system's realm.
-l *user*	Specifies which remote user to log in as.
host:{ port }	Specifies the hostname or IP address and the port number to connect to.

continued

	The following are internal commands that can be used inside of the program:
close	Closes the current connection.
display	Shows operation parameters.
emulate	Emulates a vt100 or 3270 terminal.
mode	Tries to enter line-byline or character-at-a-time mode.
open	Connects to a site.
quit	Exits the program.
send	Transmits special characters.
set	Sets operating parameters.
status	Shows status information.
toggle	Toggles operation parameters.
z	Stops the program.
?	Shows help information.
File Name: `tn3270`	**Directory:** /usr/bin/ **Type:** External

tokstat

UNIX Shell: All primary shells (csh, ksh, bsh)

Function	Shows token-ring device statistics.
Syntax	tokstat [options...] *device*

-d	Shows device driver statistics.
-r	Resets all statistic values.
-t	Shows debug information.
device	Specifies the device to show statistics about.
File Name: `tokstat`	**Directory:** /usr/sbin/ **Type:** External

topas

UNIX Shell: All primary shells (csh, ksh, bsh)

Function	Shows specified local system statistics.
Syntax	topas [options...]

-d *disknum*	Specifies the maximum number of disks to show.
-h	Shows help information.
-i *interval*	Specifies the monitor interval in seconds.
-n *interfacenum*	Specifies the maximum number of network interfaces to show.
-p *processnum*	Specifies the maximum number of processes to show.
File Name: `topas`	**Directory:** /usr/bin/ **Type:** External

tprof

UNIX Shell: All primary shells (csh, ksh, bsh)

Function	Shows CPU usage statistics.
Syntax	tprof option [options...]

-d	Is only retained for compatibility purposes.
-e	Shows statistics about the kernel extension.
-k	Shows statistics about the kernel.
-i *tracefile*	Inputs trace information to a file for offline processing.
-n *gennamefile*	Specifies a generic name file to use with the -i option.
-p *program*	Shows statistics about the specified application.
-s	Shows statistics about shared libraries.
-t *pid*	Shows statistics about the specified process ID.
-v	Verbose mode. Shows more information.
-x *command.*	Allows execution of an arbitrary command.
File Name: `tprof`	**Directory:** /usr/bin/ **Type:** External

trace

UNIX Shell: All primary shells (csh, ksh, bsh)

Function	Traces specific system events.
Syntax	trace [options...]

-a	Runs the daemon in the background.
-b	Allocates memory buffers from the kernel heap.
-B	Allocates memory buffers from separate segments.
-c	Specifies to save the tracelog file.
-d	Disables automatic startup of the trace.
-f	Runs the trace in single mode.
-g	Runs the trace in a generic trace channel.
-h	Shows no header output.
-j *event*	Specifies a user-defined event to trace.
-k *event*	Specifies a user-defined event to exclude from the trace.
-l	Runs the trace in circular mode.
-m *message*	Specifies a message to show in the tracelog header.
-n	Puts additional information in the tracelog header.
-o *name*	Specifies a file other than the default to save tracelog information to.
-o-	Shows trace output on STDOUT.
-s	Stops the trace when the log file is full.
-L *size*	Overrides the default log size in MB.
-T *size*	Overrides the default trace buffer size.

File Name: `trace` **Directory:** /usr/bin/ **Type:** External

tracesoff

UNIX Shell: All primary shells (csh, ksh, bsh)

Function	Disables tracing on a subsystem or a subserver.
Syntax	tracesoff [options...]

-h *host*	Specifies a remote host to disable tracing on.
-g *group*	Specifies a group of subsystems to disable tracing on.
-p *systemPID*	Specifies a subsystem instance to disable tracing on.
-s *system*	Specifies a subsystem to disable tracing on.
-t *type*	Specifies a subserver to disable tracing on.
-o *object*	Passes a subserver object as a character string.
-P *serverPID*	Passes a server PID as a character string to the subsystem.

File Name: `tracesoff` **Directory:** /usr/bin/ **Type:** External

traceson

UNIX Shell: All primary shells (csh, ksh, bsh)

Function	Enables tracing of a subsystem or a subserver.
Syntax	traceson [options...]

-h *host*	Specifies a remote host to run a trace on.
-l	Uses a long trace.
-g *group*	Specifies that tracing is to be enabled for a group of subsystems.
-p *systemPID*	Specifies an instance to trace.
-s *system*	Specifies a subsystem to trace.
-t *type*	Specifies a subserver to trace.
-o *object*	Passes the specified subserver object as a character string.
-P *serverPID*	Passes the specified subserver PID as a character string.

File Name: `traceson` **Directory:** /usr/bin/ **Type:** External

trbsd

UNIX Shell:	All primary shells (csh, ksh, bsh)
Function	Translates characters. This is the BSD version of the command tr.
Syntax	trbsd [options...] { *strings...* }

-c	Replaces the first specified string with the second.
-d	Removes all characters found in the string from STDIN.
-s	Removes all characters except the first found in the second string.
-A	Uses ASCII collation order instead of locale collation order.
strings...	Specifies the strings to use for translation.

File Name:	trbsd	**Directory:**	/usr/bin/	**Type:**	External

trcdead

UNIX Shell:	All primary shells (csh, ksh, bsh)
Function	Extracts tracing information from a system dump image.
Syntax	trcdead [-o *file*] *dumpimage*

-o *file*	Specifies the output file.
dumpimage	Specifies the dump image to extract information from.

File Name:	trcdead	**Directory:**	/usr/bin/	**Type:**	External

trcnm

UNIX Shell:	All primary shells (csh, ksh, bsh)
Function	Creates a kernel name list.
Syntax	trcnm [options...]

	The following two options can't be used together:
-a *file*	Outputs all loader symbols to STDOUT.
-K *symbol*	Collects symbol values from the knlist system call.
file	Specifies a filename for the outputfile.

File Name:	trcnm	**Directory:**	/usr/bin/	**Type:**	External

trcrpt

UNIX Shell:	All primary shells (csh, ksh, bsh)
Function	Creates a trace report from the trace log file.
Syntax	trcrpt [options...] { *file* }

-c	Looks for syntax errors in the template file.
-d *list*	Limits the report to the specified number of IDs.
-e *date*	Ends the report on entries made on or before the specified date.
-h	Shows no header output.
-j	Shows a list of IDs.
-n *name*	Specifies a kernel name list file to interpret addresses.
-o *file*	Writes the report to a file instead of STDOUT.
-p *event*	Shows the process ID for each specified event.
-r	Shows unformatted trace entries.
-s *date*	Starts the report on entries made on or before the specified date.
-t *file*	Specifies a template file.
-T *ID*	Limits the report to the specified kernel thread ID.
-v	Verbose mode. Shows more information.
-O *options...*	Specifies options that change the content and presentation of the trcrpt command.
2line=on | off	Specifies whether to use two lines per trace event in the report.
cpuid=on | off	Specifies whether to show the cpu ID in the report.
endtime=seconds	Shows trace events recorded before the specified seconds.
exec=on | off	Specifies whether to show exec pathnames in the report.
hist=on | off	Specifies whether to log all instance numbers that each hook ID finds.
ids=on | off	Specifies whether to show the trace hook ID.
pagesize=number	Specifies the number of lines per page in the trace report.

continued

pid=on | off	Specifies whether to show the process ID in each report.
starttime=seconds	Shows trace events recorded after the specified seconds.
svc=on | off	Specifies whether to show system call values in the report.
tid=on | off	Specifies whether to show thread IDs in the report.
timestamp=*action*	Manages timestamps in the report. Action can be one of the following.
0	Returns values for the nearest nano- or microsecond.
1	Returns short elapsed time.
2	Returns microseconds.
3	Uses no timestamp.
-x	Shows exec pathnames and system call values.
file	Specifies the trace log file to make a report from.
File Name: `trcrpt`	**Directory:** /usr/bin **Type:** External

trcstop

UNIX Shell: All primary shells (csh, ksh, bsh)

Function	Turns off the trace function.
Syntax	trcstop
File Name: `trcstop`	**Directory:** /usr/bin/ **Type:** External

trcupdate

UNIX Shell: All primary shells (csh, ksh, bsh)

Function	Manages trace report format templates.
Syntax	trcupdate [options...] { *file* }
-o	Overwrites the old template with the new.
-t *file*	Specifies a template file other than the default.
-v	Verbose mode. Shows more information.
-x *idlist*	Extracts and shows the specified templates on STDOUT.
file	Specifies the new template file.
File Name: `trcupdate`	**Directory:** /usr/bin **Type:** External

trpt

UNIX Shell: All primary shells (csh, ksh, bsh)

Function	Shows information about TCP trace records on a socket marked for debugging.
Syntax	trpt [options...]
-a	Includes the source and destination addresses values for the recorded packages.
-f	Shows the information about the trace as it occurs.
-j	Shows only information about protocol control block addresses with trace records.
-p *address*	Specifies the protocol control block address. More than one `-p` may be used.
-s	Includes a detailed description of the packet sequencing information.
-t	Includes the time values for each point in the trace.
File Name: `trpt`	**Directory:** /usr/sbin **Type:** External

tsh

UNIX Shell: All primary shells (csh, ksh, bsh)

Function	A more secure command interpreter than the Korn shell. To start the shell, the user must press Ctrl-X and Ctrl-R.
Syntax	tsh
File Name: `tsh`	**Directory:** /usr/bin/ **Type:** External

tsm

UNIX Shell: All primary shells (csh, ksh, bsh)

Function	Provides terminal state management to control the ports used in the trusted path.
Syntax	tsm *port*

continued

port		**Must be invoked from inside `/etc/inittab` and have the format:** Specifies the characteristics for the port.			
File Name:	`tsm`	**Directory:**	/usr/sbin	**Type:**	External

turnacct

UNIX Shell: Bourne shell (bsh)

Function	Manages process accounting.
Syntax	turnacct option

on		Enables process accounting.			
Off		Disables process accounting.			
Switch		Changes the /var/adm/ act file into the next free name in /var/adm/pacct*incr*. (incr is a number starting with 1 that increases for each act file.)			
File Name:	`turnacct`	**Directory:**	/usr/sbin/acct/	**Type:**	Script

tvi

UNIX Shell: All primary shells (csh, ksh, bsh)

Function	A trusted version of the text editor vi.
Syntax	tvi [options…] *{ files… }*

-l		Uses the editor in LISP mode			
-R		Opens the file in read-only mode.			
-w *number*		Specifies the default window size.			
-c *command*		Specifies an ex editor subcommand to run before starting to edit the file.			
Files…		Specifies the file to edit.			
File Name:	`tvi`	**Directory:**	/usr/bin	**Type:**	External

uil

UNIX Shell: All primary shells (csh, ksh, bsh)

Function	Starts the UIL compiler, a language to describe the initial state of a users interface for a AIXwindows application.
Syntax	uil [options…] *file*

-I*pathname*		Searches for not-found include files. Searches in the specified pathname (no space).			
-m		Shows the machine code.			
-o *file*		Specifies the filename of the UID.			
-s		Configures the locale before compiling any files.			
-v *file*		Specifies a file to make a list from.			
-w		Hides all messages and warnings.			
-wmd *file*		Sets a bin widget meta-language description file to use instead of a WML description.			
File		Specifies the file to compile.			
File Name:	`uil`	**Directory:**	/usr/bin/X11	**Type:**	External

unget

UNIX Shell: All primary shells (csh, ksh, bsh)

Function	Reverses all changes in a SCCS history file made by the command `get -e`.
Syntax	unget [options…] *files…*

-n		Doesn't remove the retrieved version of the file.			
-s		Doesn't show the SCCS delta ID of the file.			
-r*SID*		Specifies which pending delta to undo when you work with multiple versions of a file.			
Files…		Specifies which s. file to undo.			
File Name:	`unget`	**Directory:**	/usr/bin/	**Type:**	External

unifdef

UNIX Shell:	All primary shells (csh, ksh, bsh)
Function	Identifies and removes lines containing an ifdef mark from a C program source, leaving the rest of the file untouched.
Syntax	unifdef [options...] { *file* }

-t	Allows the unifdef command to search in plain text.
-l	Causes removed lines to be replaced with blank lines instead of being deleted.
-c	Retains lines that would be removed or blanked and vice versa.
-D*name*	Searches for lines containing the defined symbol specified.
-U*name*	Searches for lines containing the undefined symbol specified.
-lu*name*	Searches and shows only the lines containing the undefined symbol specified.
File	Specifies the file to work on. If no file is specified, STDIN is used.

File Name: `unifdef` **Directory:** /usr/bin/ **Type:** External

units

UNIX Shell:	All primary shells (csh, ksh, bsh)
Function	Tells you interactively how to convert a unit quantity to another type, for example, from inches to centimeters.
Syntax	units [-] { *file* }

-	Lists the conversion factors.
File	Overrides the default factors in /usr/share/lib/unittab.

File Name: `units` **Directory:** /usr/bin/ **Type:** External

unlink

UNIX Shell:	All primary shells (csh, ksh, bsh)
Function	Unlinks files and directories; doesn't use any error checking.
Syntax	unlink *file*

file	Specifies the filename or directory to be unlinked.

File Name: `unlink` **Directory:** /usr/sbin **Type:** External

unloadipsec

UNIX Shell:	All primary shells (csh, ksh, bsh)
Function	Unloads a crypto module from the IP security system.
Syntax	unloadipsec -c *crmodname*

-c *crmodname*	Specifies which crypto module to unload.

File Name: `unloadipsec` **Directory:** /usr/sbin **Type:** External

unmirrorvg

UNIX Shell:	Korn shell (ksh)
Function	Breaks a mirror on a volume group.
Syntax	unmirrorvg [-c *copies*] *volumegroup* { *physicalvols...* }

-c *copies*	Specifies how many copies to leave on each logical volume.
Volumegroup	Specifies the volume group to break the mirror on.
Physicalvols...	Specifies that you want to break a mirror on a specific disk or disks.

File Name: `unmirrorvg` **Directory:** /usr/sbin **Type:** Script

unpack

UNIX Shell:	All primary shells (csh, ksh, bsh)
Function	Decompresses files created by pack. Removes the .z suffix when done.
Syntax	unpack *files...*

files...	Specifies one or more files to be unpacked.

File Name: `unpack` **Directory:** /usr/bin **Type:** External

untab

UNIX Shell:	All primary shells (csh, ksh, bsh)
Function	Converts tabs into spaces.
Syntax	untab *files...*
files...	Specifies the files to convert tabs in.
File Name: untab	**Directory:** /usr/bin — **Type:** External

update

UNIX Shell:	Bourne shell (bsh)
Function	Starts to update the file system every 30 seconds.
Syntax	update
File Name: update	**Directory:** /usr/sbin — **Type:** Script

uprintfd

UNIX Shell:	All primary shells (csh, ksh, bsh)
Function	The daemon that constructs and writes kernel messages.
Syntax	uprintfd
File Name: uprintfd	**Directory:** /usr/sbin — **Type:** External

usrck

UNIX Shell:	All primary shells (csh, ksh, bsh)
Function	Checks that a username is correct.
Syntax	usrck option *{ ALL } { user }*
-n	Shows errors but doesn't fix them.
-p	Fixes errors but doesn't show them.
-t	Shows errors and prompts the user to fix them.
-y	Fixes errors and shows them.
ALL	Checks on all users.
User	Checks only the specified user.
File Name: usrck	**Directory:** /usr/bin — **Type:** External

uucheck

UNIX Shell:	All primary shells (csh, ksh, bsh)
Function	Looks for the presence of the required **uucp** files and directories.
Syntax	uucheck [options...]
-v	Verbose mode. Shows more information.
-x *debuglevel*	Enables debugging with the levels 0 to 9; higher numbers shows most information.
File Name: uucheck	**Directory:** /usr/sbin/uucp/ — **Type:** External

uucico

UNIX Shell:	All primary shells (csh, ksh, bsh)
Function	Transfers files used by the `uucp` command to a specific location.
Syntax	uucico [options...] -s *systemname*
-r *rolenumber*	Specifies the role number: 1 for master and 0 for slave.
-x *debuglevel*	Shows debug information with the levels 0 to 9; higher levels show more information.
-s *systemname*	Specifies the system to transfer files to.
File Name: uucico	**Directory:** /usr/sbin/uucp/ — **Type:** External

uuclean

UNIX Shell:	All primary shells (csh, ksh, bsh)
Function	Removes files from the Basic Networking Utilities spooling directory.
Syntax	uuclean [options…]

-d*subdir*	Removes files from the specified subdirectory under /var/spool/uucp/.
-m	Sends a mail to each user whose files have been removed.
-n*hours*	Removes files that are older than the specified hours.
-p*prefix*	Removes files with the specified prefix.

File Name: `uuclean` **Directory:** /usr/sbin/uucp/ **Type:** External

uucleanup

UNIX Shell:	All primary shells (csh, ksh, bsh)
Function	Searches the spool directories and cleans them up.
Syntax	uucleanup [options…]

-C*time*	Removes all C. files older than the specified time in days.
-D*time*	Removes all D. files older than the specified time in days.
-m*string*	Specifies a text sting to include in the messages.
-o*time*	Erases all other files older than the specified time in days (default is 2).
-s*system*	Specifies to only execute the command on the system spool directory.
-t*time*	Erases all TM. Files older than the specified time in days (default is 7).
-W*time*	Sends a reminder about old C. files to requester (default is 1 day).
-X*time*	Removes all X. files older than the specified time in days (default is 2).

File Name: `uucleanup` **Directory:** /usr/sbin/uucp/ **Type:** External

uucp

UNIX Shell:	All primary shells (csh, ksh, bsh)
Function	Copies files from one place to another inside UNIX (uucp stands for UNIX to UNIX copy).
Syntax	uucp [options…] *sourcefile destinationfile*

-c	Specifies not to make a copy to the spool directory before transferring a file.
-C	Specifies to make a copy to the spool directory before transferring of a file.
-d	Creates all directories that the file copy needs.
-f	Specifies not to create intermediate directories for the file copy.
-g*grade*	Defines a service grade: A alphanumeric character that prioritizes the transfer.
-j	Shows the uucp job identification string on STDOUT.
-m	Reports back to the user who sent the files by mail when the copy is complete.
-n*user*	Reports to the remote system user that a file was sent.
-r	Puts the file in the queue without doing the transfer.
-s*file*	Shows the status of the transfer of the specified file.
-x*level*	Shows debug information with a level from 0 to 9; higher numbers show more information.
Sourcefile	Specifies the files that you want to copy, use the format: system-name!pathname.
destinationfile	Specifies the destination of the copy, use the format: system-name!pathname.

File Name: `uucp` **Directory:** /usr/bin/ **Type:** External

uucpadm

UNIX Shell:	All primary shells (csh, ksh, bsh)
Function	An interactive program used to manage Basic Networking Utility information.
Syntax	uucpadm

File Name: `uucpadm` **Directory:** /usr/sbin/uucp/ **Type:** External

uucpd

UNIX Shell:	All primary shells (csh, ksh, bsh)
Function	The server daemon for UUCP connections. Started by `inetd` at request.
Syntax	uucpd

File Name: `uucpd` **Directory:** /usr/sbin/ **Type:** External

uudemon.admin

uudemon.admin	UNIX Shell: Bourne shell (bsh)		
Function	Sends **uucp** status information to an administrator. It also executes the **uustat** –p and –q commands.		
Syntax	uudemon.admin		
File Name: `uudemon.admin`	Directory: /usr/sbin/uucp/	Type:	Script

uudemon.cleanu

uudemon.cleanu	UNIX Shell: All primary shells (csh, ksh, bsh)		
Function	Cleans up Basic Networking Utilities log files and spooling directories.		
Syntax	uudemon.cleanu		
File Name: `uudemon.cleanu`	Directory: /usr/sbin/uucp/	Type:	External

uudemon.hour

uudemon.hour	UNIX Shell: Bourne shell (bsh)		
Function	Starts up the commands `uusched` and `uuxqt` in the background.		
Syntax	uudemon.hour		
File Name: `uudemon.hour`	Directory: /usr/sbin/uucp/	Type:	Script

uudemon.poll

uudemon.poll	UNIX Shell: Bourne shell (bsh)		
Function	Polls remote systems by a schedule specified in `/etc/uucp/Poll`.		
Syntax	uudemon.poll		
File Name: `uudemon.poll`	Directory: /usr/sbin/uucp/	Type:	Script

uuid_gen

uuid_gen	UNIX Shell: All primary shells (csh, ksh, bsh)		
Function	Creates universal UUID's for objects, interfaces, and types.		
Syntax	uuid_gen [options…]		
-c	Creates a template with a UUID attribute for an interface definition in the C syntax.		
-C	Creates a C source-code representation of a UUID.		
-p	Creates a template with a UUID attribute for an interface definition in Pascal.		
-P	Creates a Pascal source-code representation of a UUID.		
File Name: `uuid_gen`	Directory: /usr/lib/ncs/bin/	Type:	External

uukick

uukick	UNIX Shell: All primary shells (csh, ksh, bsh)		
Function	Contacts a remote host using debug mode, and shows the information on the local system.		
Syntax	uukick [-x*debuglevel*] *sysname*		
-x*debuglevel*	Specifies the debug level from 0 to 9; higher numbers show more information (default is 5).		
Sysname	Specifies the name or address to the remote host to contact.		
File Name: `uukick`	Directory: /usr/sbin/uucp/	Type:	External

uulog

uulog	UNIX Shell: Bourne shell (bsh)		
Function	Shows information from the transaction logs of `uucp` or `uuxqt`.		
Syntax	uulog [options…]		
-x	Shows information from the file `/var/uucp/.Log/uuxqt` on the specified system.		
-*number*	Shows the specified number of lines from the end of the log file.		
-f*systems*	Shows information about file transfers involving the specified system.		
-s*system*	Shows the updates to the log information as it is created; use Ctrl-C to exit.		
File Name: `uulog`	Directory: /usr/bin	Type:	Script

uuname

uuname	UNIX Shell: All primary shells (csh, ksh, bsh)
Function	Shows a list of all the systems that are known to the `uucp` command.

continued

Syntax	uuname [option]		
-c	Shows a list of all hostnames that are known to the command `cu`.		
-l	Shows the name of your local system.		
File Name: `uuname`	**Directory:** /usr/bin/	**Type:**	External

uupick

UNIX Shell: All primary shells (csh, ksh, bsh)

Function	Searches for files sent from other systems, and prompts interactively for actions.		
Syntax	uupick [-s *system*]		
-s *system*	Works on files from the specified system only.		
File Name: `uupick`	**Directory:** /usr/bin/	**Type:**	External

uupoll

UNIX Shell: All primary shells (csh, ksh, bsh)

Function	Forces a poll of a remote Basic Networking Utilities system.		
Syntax	uupoll [options...] *sysname*		
-g *grade*	Specifies that uupoll will only send jobs with the specified grade.		
-n	Queues the null job.		
sysname	Specifies the system to poll.		
File Name: `uupoll`	**Directory:** /usr/bin/	**Type:**	External

uuq

UNIX Shell: All primary shells (csh, ksh, bsh)

Function	Shows or removes jobs from the Basic Networking Utilities queue.		
Syntax	uuq [options...]		
-l	Shows output in long format.		
-h	Shows only a summary for each system.		
-s *sysname*	Shows only jobs for the specified system.		
-u *user*	Shows only jobs for the specified user.		
-d *jobnr*	Specifies a job that you want to remove.		
-r *spooldir*	Looks for files in the specified spool directory.		
-b *baudrate*	Specifies a baud rate to use.		
File Name: `uuq`	**Directory:** /usr/bin/	**Type:**	External

uusched

UNIX Shell: All primary shells (csh, ksh, bsh)

Function	A scheduler for file transport; normally started by `cron`.		
Syntax	uusched [options..]		
-u*debuglevel*	Passes the -u debug level (0-9) option as -x debug-level to `uucico`.		
-x*debuglevel*	Shows debug messages from uusched. debuglevel is a number between 0 and 9.		
File Name: `uusched`	**Directory:** /usr/sbin/uucp/	**Type:**	External

uusend

UNIX Shell: All primary shells (csh, ksh, bsh)

Function	Sends a file to one or more remote systems.		
Syntax	uusend [options...] *sourcefile systems... remotefile*		
-m*mode*	Specifies the permission mode for the file on the remote system.		
-r	Doesn't start the uucico daemon.		
sourcefile	Specifies the file to send.		
systems...	Specifies where to send the file. Use an exclamation point as separator between systems.		
remotefile	Specifies the name of the file when it is saved on a remote system.		
File Name: `uusend`	**Directory:** /usr/bin/	**Type:**	External

uusnap

UNIX Shell:	All primary shells (csh, ksh, bsh)
Function	Shows the status of the Basic Networking Utilities.
Syntax	uusnap
File Name:	uusnap
Directory:	/usr/bin/
Type:	External

uustat

UNIX Shell:	All primary shells (csh, ksh, bsh)
Function	Shows information about the `uucp` jobs on a local or remote system.
Syntax	uustat [options...]
	The following options can't be combined:
-a	Shows a list of all jobs in the queue.
-k *jobID*	Deletes the specified jobs.
-m	Shows information about the accessibility status of all computers.
-p	Shows a full report about the status of the process IDs in the lock files.
-q	Shows a list of all the jobs in the queue for each computer.
	The following option can be combined with any options:
-n *number*	Specifies the number of computers to collect BNU status information on.
	The following options can only be combined with eachother and -n.
-s *system*	Shows status information about the `uucp` requests for the specified system.
-u *user*	Shows status on BNU requests by the specified user.
File Name:	uustat
Directory:	/usr/bin/
Type:	External

uuto

UNIX Shell:	All primary shells (csh, ksh, bsh)
Function	Uses `uucp` to send files to remote systems. Keeps access control, notifies the receiver on completion.
Syntax	uuto [options...] *sourcefile destination*
-m	Reports by mail back to the sender when the copy is complete.
-p	Makes a copy to the spool directory before the file is sent.
sourcefile	Specifies the file to copy to the remote system.
destination	Specifies the destination of the copy in the format system-name!user.
File Name:	uuto
Directory:	/usr/bin/
Type:	External

uutry

UNIX Shell:	Bourne shell (bsh)
Function	Contacts remote systems using `uucico` and stores debugging information in the file `/tmp/systemname`.
Syntax	Uutry [options...] *systemname*
-x*debuglevel*	Shows debugging information with a level of 0 to 9; higher numbers show more information.
-r	Overrides the retry time set in `/var/uucp/.Status/directory`.
systemname	Specifies the remote system to contact.
File Name:	uutry
Directory:	/usr/sbin/uucp/
Type:	Script

uux

UNIX Shell:	All primary shells (csh, ksh, bsh)
Function	Collects files from several systems, executes a command on the system specified, and sends the result to a file on the system you specify.
Syntax	uux [options...] *commandstring*
-c	Transfers the source files to the destination on the specified system.
-C	Transfers the source files to the spool directory.
-n	Prevents user notification of the success or failure of a command by mail.
-z	Notifies the user if the command completes successfully.
-	Makes STDIN to uux the standard input to the CommandString argument.
-a*name*	Replaces the user ID of the person issuing the command with the user ID specified.

continued

-b	Returns STDIN to the command if the exit status isn't zero.
-g*grade*	Specifies when the files are to be transmitted during a connection.
-j	Shows the job identification number of the process that is running the command.
-p	Uses STDIN to uux as the standard input to the CommandString argument.
-e	Enables file expansion.
-r	Prevents the starting of the spooling program that transfers files between systems.
-s*file*	Shows the status of the transfer in a file specified on the designated system.
-x*debuglevel*	Shows debugging information on the screen of the local system.
commandstring	Specifies what to do, where to do it, and where to send the result. (Quote all special shell characters, or the whole command string.)
File Name: `uux`	**Directory:** /usr/bin/ **Type:** External

uuxqt

UNIX Shell: All primary shells (csh, ksh, bsh)

Function	Executes remote requested jobs created with the `uux` command.
Syntax	uuxqt [options...]

-s*hostname*	Specifies the name of the remote system.
-x*debuglevel*	Shows debugging information with level 0 to 9; higher numbers show more information.
-e	Enables file expansion.
File Name: `uuxqt`	**Directory:** /usr/sbin/uucp/ **Type:** External

vacation

UNIX Shell: All primary shells (csh, ksh, bsh)

Function	Replies to mail automatically; useful when you are out of the office.
Syntax	vacation [options...] { *user* }

	The -I and -f options can't be combined.
-I	Initializes the $HOME/.vacation.pag and $HOME/.vacation.dir files.
-f*numberunit*	Sets the interval to send message in units: *s: sec m: min h: hours d: days w: weeks.*
user	Specifies the user.
File Name: `vacation`	**Directory:** /usr/bin/ **Type:** External

val

UNIX Shell: All primary shells (csh, ksh, bsh)

Function	Verifies an SCCS file.
Syntax	val [options...] *files...*

-s	Silent mode; suppresses the normal error or warning messages.
-m*name*	Compares name with the sccs-val.1 ID keyword in the file.
-r*SID*	Specifies SID to check if it is ambiguous, invalid, or absent from file.
-y*type*	Specifies a type to compare with the ID keyword.
-	Reads from STDIN.
files...	Specifies the input file.
File Name: `val`	**Directory:** /usr/bin/ **Type:** External

varyoffvg

UNIX Shell: Korn shell (ksh)

Function	Deactivates a volume group.
Syntax	varyoffvg [-s] *volumegroup*

-s	Deactivates the volume group and puts it into system management mode.
volumegroup	Specifies the volume group to deactivate.
File Name: `varyoffvg`	**Directory:** /usr/sbin/ **Type:** Script

varyonvg

UNIX Shell: All primary shells (csh, ksh, bsh)

Function	Activates a volume group.
Syntax	varyonvg [options...] *volumegroup*

-b	Unlocks disk reservations.
-c	Varies on the volume group in concurrent mode.
-f	Activates a volume group without quorum.
-n	Doesn't synchronize stale physical partitions.
-p	Specifies that all physical volumes must be available.
-s	Activates the volume group in system management mode only.
-u	Activates a volume group with all disks unlocked.
volumegroup	Specifies the volume group to activate.

File Name: `varyonvg` **Directory:** /usr/sbin/ **Type:** External

vc

UNIX Shell: All primary shells (csh, ksh, bsh)

Function	Copies lines from STDIN to STDOUT with arguments and control statements; used for version control.
Syntax	vc [options...] *{ keyword=value }*

-a	Replaces keywords that are surrounded by control characters.
-t	Ignores characters until the first Tab character if the control-statement is found.
-c*char*	Specifies an alternative control character to the default.
-s	Disables warning messages, but not errors.
keyword=value	Adds a value to a keyword, if it is used as an argument.
	The following are the control characters that can be used:
:dcl *keywords...*	Declares a keyword; you must declare each keyword.
:asg *keyword=value*	Adds values to a keyword.
:if *condition*	Skips lines between if and end if condition is true, see the man page for further info.
:end	Ends a statement.
::text	Replaces all keywords with their values in text; the leading colons are removed.
:on	Enables keyword replacement.
:off	Disables keyword replacement.
:ctl *char*	Specifies the control character.
:msg *message*	Specifies a diagnostic message.
:err *message*	Specifies an error message, and sends exit code 1.

File Name: `vc` **Directory:** /usr/bin/ **Type:** External

versions

UNIX Shell: All primary shells (csh, ksh, bsh)

Function	Shows the modification time of an INed structured file.
Syntax	versions *file*

file	Specifies the file to show modification time for.

File Name: `versions` **Directory:** /usr/bin/ **Type:** External

vgrind

UNIX Shell: Korn shell (ksh)

Function	Formats program source using `troff`.
Syntax	vgrind [options...] *file*

-f	Forces filter mode.
-n	Doesn't make keywords boldface.
-t	Sends the formatted text to STDOUT.
-x	Outputs the index file in a "pretty" format.
-P*printer*	Sends output to the specified printer.
-T*outputdevice*	Formats the output for the specified output device.
-d *defsfile*	Specifies an alternative language definition file.

continued

-h *header*	Specifies a header to appear on every output page.
-l*language*	Specifies the language to use. The following languages are valid:
-lc	C
-lcsh	C shell
-lp	Pascal
-lm	Model
-lsh	Shell
-lmod2	MODULA2
-lyacc	yacc
-ll	Icon
-s*n*	Specifies the point size used on output.
file	Specifies the source file to be processed.
File Name: vgrind	**Directory:** /usr/bin/ **Type:** Script

vmh

UNIX Shell: All primary shells (csh, ksh, bsh)

Function	A visual interface to the MH command.
Syntax	vmh [options...]

-prompt *string*	Specifies a new prompt to use.
-vmhproc *command*	Specifies the program to implement the client side.
-novmhproc	Runs the default vmproc without any window management protocols.
-help	Shows help information.
File Name: vmh	**Directory:** /usr/bin/ **Type:** External

watch

UNIX Shell: All primary shells (csh, ksh, bsh)

Function	Is used to monitor a program that may be unstable.
Syntax	watch [options...] *command { parameters... }*

-e *events*	Specifies the events to be audited. See the /etc/security/audit/events file.
-o *file*	Specifies the pathname of the output file.
command	Specifies the program you want to observe.
parameters...	Specifies the parameters of the specified command.
File Name: watch	**Directory:** /usr/sbin/ **Type:** External

what

UNIX Shell: All primary shells (csh, ksh, bsh)

Function	Gets SCCS version information from a file.
Syntax	what [-s] *files...*

-s	Stops after the first occurrence of the pattern.
files...	Specifies one or more files to get information from.
File Name: what	**Directory:** /usr/bin/ **Type:** External

whatnow

UNIX Shell: All primary shells (csh, ksh, bsh)

Function	A front end for the `nmh` commands to prompt the user for what to do.
Syntax	whatnow [options...] *{ file }*

-draftfolder *dir*	Specifies the draft folder.
-draftmessage *msg*	Specifies the draft messages.
-editor *editor*	Specifies the editor to use.
-noedit	Doesn't start the editor on the draft when the command is started.
-prompt *string*	Sets the prompt string (default is "What now?").
-help	Shows help information.
file	Specifies the file to use.
File Name: whatnow	**Directory:** /usr/bin/ **Type:** External

whence

UNIX Shell: Korn shell (ksh)

Function	Shows how a command will be interpreted.
Syntax	whence [options...] *names...*

-p	Searches the path even if the command is a function, a reserved word, or an alias.
-v	Verbose mode. Shows more information.
names...	Specifies the command name to show information about.

which_fileset

UNIX Shell: Korn shell (ksh)

Function	Searches through the AIX_file_list for a specific file.
Syntax	which_fileset *{ file }*

file	Specifies the file to search for.

File Name: `which_fileset` **Directory:** /usr/sbin/ **Type:** Script

wlmcntrl

UNIX Shell: All primary shells (csh, ksh, bsh)

Function	Manages workload management.
Syntax	wlmcntrl [options...]

-d *confdir*	Specifies an alternative configuration directory to use.
	Choose only one of the following:
-q	Checks if wlm is started or not.
-o	Stops workload management.
-u	Updates or loads classes.

File Name: `wlmcntrl` **Directory:** /usr/sbin/ **Type:** External

wlmstat

UNIX Shell: All primary shells (csh, ksh, bsh)

Function	Shows the status of a workload management class.
Syntax	wlmstat [options...] *{ interval count }*

-l *class*	Specifies a class name to show status for.
	Choose only one of the following two options:
-c	Shows cpu status only.
-m	Shows memory status only.
interval	Specifies the update interval.
count	Specifies how many times to run the interval.

File Name: `wlmstat` **Directory:** /usr/sbin/ **Type:** External

writesrv

UNIX Shell: All primary shells (csh, ksh, bsh)

Function	A daemon that lets the user send or receive messages from a remote system.
Syntax	writesrv

File Name: `writesrv` **Directory:** /usr/sbin/ **Type:** External

wtmpfix

UNIX Shell: All primary shells (csh, ksh, bsh)

Function	Inspects specified `wtmp`database files, corrects time, and date stamps to make the entries consistent.
Syntax	wtmpfix [*files...*]

files...	Specifies file to inspect; if no file is specified, STDIN is used.

File Name: `wtmpfix` **Directory:** /usr/sbin/acct/ **Type:** External

xdat

UNIX Shell:	All primary shells (csh, ksh, bsh)
Function	Manages date and time settings, and also schedules removes or view jobs.
Syntax	xdat [options...]

-c *operation*	Specifies a job to schedule.
-m	Starts, removes, or views scheduled jobs.

File Name:	`xdat`	**Directory:**	/usr/bin/X11/	**Type:**	External

xget

UNIX Shell:	All primary shells (csh, ksh, bsh)
Function	Receives secret mails that have been sent with the command xsend.
Syntax	xget

File Name:	`xget`	**Directory:**	/usr/bin/	**Type:**	External

xlf, xlf_r, xlf_r7, f77, xlf90, xlf90_r, xlf90_r7

UNIX Shell:	All primary shells (csh, ksh, bsh)
Function	Compiles XL FORTRAN source files, and is also used to process source and object files written in assembly language.
Syntax	xlf [option] *file*

-#	Shows a lot of information during the compile routine.
-1	If it is reached it runs DO loop once.
-B*prefix*	Creates alternate program names when added to the beginning of standard program names.
-b64	Instructs the ld command to bind with 64-bit objects (AIX 4.3 and above).
-bdynamic	Controls the processing of -l options and shared objects; links objects dynamically.
-bhalt:*error_level*>	Sets the maximum error level for the ld command to continue processing (default is 4).
-bloadmap:*name*	Saves a log of linker actions and messages in the specified file.
-bmaxstack:*bytes*	Sets the maximum space to reserve for stack segments for programs with limited regions, in bytes.
-brtl	Specifies the algorithm to use finding libraries specified with the -l option.
-bshared	The same as -bdynamic.
-bstatic	Controls processing of -l options and shared objects, links objects; to the output file.
-C	Runs runtime checking.
-c	Compiles, but doesn't call the linkage editor.
-D	Compiles lines of fixed source form FORTRAN code with a D in column 1.
-d	Doesn't delete temporary files produced by cpp.
-F[<x>][:*stanza*]	Uses an alternative configuration file as specified by stanza.
-g	Shows debug information.
-I*dir*	Searches the specified directory for INCLUDE files not starting with an absolute path.
-k	Specifies FORTRAN code as a free-source-form input format.
-L*dir*	Searches the specified directory for files specified by -l `key`.
-l*key*	Searches the specified library file and selects the file lib `key`.a.
-N*x num*	Sets storage areas for internal programs; x can be the value of -S, and num calculates the size.
-O	Optimizes compiler-generated codes.
-O2	Optimizes codes the same way as -O.
-O3	Runs -O level optimizations and additional compile-time intensive optimizations.
-O4	Optimizes the source program, and rejects additional compile time for improvements.
-o*name*	Sets a new name for the executable file instead of a.out.
-P	Starts first the -Pv preprocessor, then the compiler.
-Pv	The same as -P.
-Pk	Starts first the -Pk preprocessor, then the compiler.
-P!	Starts only the -Pv preprocessor.
-Pv!	The same as -Pv.
-Pk!	Starts only the -Pk preprocessor.
-p	Creates a simple profiling support code.
-pg	Creates a profiling support code, more extensive than -p.
-Q	Arranges all appropriate subprograms.

continued

-Q*x*	Arrange specified subprograms using one of the following values for x:
!	Doesn't arrange.
-<names>	Doesn't arrange the list of subprograms.
+<names>	Arranges the specified list of subprograms.
-S	Produces one or more .s files and shows the assembler source for each FORTRAN source.
-t*x*	Uses prefix from -B option to the specified program. <x>=one or more of the following:

Component	**-t option**	**Standard Program Name**
preprocessor	F	cpp
VAST-2 preprocessor	p	fpp
KAP preprocessor	p	fppk
compiler front end	c	xlfentry
loop optimizer	h	xlfhot
IPA processor	I	ipa
assembler	a	as
code generator	b	xlfcode
linker	l	ld
-S disassembler	d	dis
binder	z	bolt

-U	Doesn't perform lowercase folding of FORTRAN code.
-u	Defines undefined implicit data typing.
-V	Verbose mode. Shows more information on the compiler's progress in shell-executable format.
-v	Verbose mode. Shows more information on the compiler's progress.
-W<x>,*option { options... }*	Sends options to the specified component executed during compilation. Suboptions = -t.
-w	Doesn't show warning messages.
-y<x>	Sets compile-time rounding of constant floating-point expressions.
n	Rounds to the nearest (Is default).
m	Rounds toward minus infinity.
p	Rounds toward positiv infinity.
z	Rounds toward zero.
	The following file suffixes indicate the type of file to compile:
.f suffix	Indicates a FORTRAN source file.
.o suffix	Indicates an object file for the ld command.
.a suffix	Indicates an object file for the ld command.
.s suffix	Indicates an assembly source file.
.F suffix	Indicates a FORTRAN source file.
file	Specifies the source file to compile.

File Name:	`xlf`	**Directory:**	/usr/bin/	**Type:**	External

xlock

UNIX Shell: All primary shells (csh, ksh, bsh)

Function	Locks the local X screen until the user enters a password.
Syntax	xlock [options...]

-display *dsp*	Specifies the X11 display to lock.
-help	Shows help information.
-v	Verbose mode. Shows more information.
+v	Disables verbose mode.
	When you use the following options, use - to disable and + to enable:
mono	Enables or disables the monochrome override.
nolock	Enables or disables the no-password-required mode.
allowroot	Enables or disables the allow-root-password mode.
enablesaver	Enables or disables the enable X server screen saver.
allowaccess	Enables or disables the allow-new-client-access mode.
echokeys	Enables or disables the echo `?` for each password key.
usefirst	Enables or disables the first character in the password when unlocking the screen.
remote	Enables or disables the remote host access.
-mode *modename*	Specifies the animation mode.

continued

	Use these options as modes:
hop	Shows realplane fractals as described in the September 1986 issue of *Scientific American.*
life	Shows Conway's game of life.
qix	Shows spinning lines similar to the old video game by the same name.
swarm	Shows a swarm of bees.
image	Shows logos on the screen.
blank	Makes the screen blank.
-delay *usecs*	Sets the speed of an animation. A lower value makes the animation faster.
-batchcount *num*	Specifies the number of things to do per animation or batch.
-nice *priority*	Specifies the system priority for `xlock`.
-timeout *seconds*	Specifies when password screen will time out, in seconds.
-font *fontname*	Specifies the font to use for the prompt.
-fg *color*	Specifies the foreground color for the password screen.
-bg *color*	Specifies the background color for the password screen.
-username *textstring*	Specifies a text string in front of the username.
-password *textstring*	Specifies a password prompt string.
-info *textstring*	Shows a what-to-do message.
-validate *textstring*	Specifies a message that shows when validating the password.
-invalid *textstring*	Specifies text to show when the password is invalid.
File Name: `xlock`	**Directory:** /usr/bin/X11/ **Type:** External

xmodem

UNIX Shell: All primary shells (csh, ksh, bsh)

Function	Sends or receives a file using the XMODEM protocol.
Syntax	xmodem option *file*

-s	Sends data.
-r	Receives data.
file	Specifies a file to send or receive.
File Name: `xmodem`	**Directory:** /usr/bin/ **Type:** External

XNSquery

UNIX Shell: All primary shells (csh, ksh, bsh)

Function	Queries a Xerox Network System host for routing information.
Syntax	XNSquery *host*

host	Specifies the host to query.
File Name: `XNSquery`	**Directory:** /usr/sbin/ **Type:** External

XNSrouted

UNIX Shell: All primary shells (csh, ksh, bsh)

Function	Configures network routing tables for Xerox Network Systems.
Syntax	XNSrouted [options...] *{ logfile }*

-q	Doesn't route incoming XNS packets.
-s	Forces the XNS daemon to act as a router even if it is not.
-t	Shows all incoming and outgoing packets on STDOUT.
logfile	Specifies a file to log the daemon's actions.
File Name: `XNSrouted`	**Directory:** /usr/sbin/ **Type:** External

xntpd

UNIX Shell: All primary shells (csh, ksh, bsh)

Function	A daemon that controls the time of day for UNIX systems.
Syntax	xntpd [options...]

-a	Starts in authentication mode.
-b	Listens (and synchs if possible) to ntp broadcasts.
-m	Listens (and synchs if possible) for multicast messages.
-c *configfile*	Specifies a configuration file other than the default.

continued

-e *time*	Sets the time allowed to compute the ntp encryption field, in seconds.
-f *driftfile*	Specifies the drift file.
-k *keyfile*	Sets the path to the file containing ntp authentication keys.
-l *logfile*	Specifies a file to log to.
-p *file*	Specifies file to save record daemon PIDs.
-r *broadcastdelay*	Compensates for network delay between server and client, in seconds.
-s *statsdirectory*	Sets the directory to use when creating statistic files.
-t *trustedkey*	Specifies a key number to add to the trusted key list.
-v *systemvariable*	Specifies system variable to add.
-V *systemvariable*	Specifies a system variable that is listed by default.
File Name: xntpd	**Directory:** /usr/sbin/ **Type:** External

xntpdc

UNIX Shell: All primary shells (csh, ksh, bsh)

Function	Queries and control the states on the Network Time Protocol daemon called `xntpd`.
Syntax	xntpdc [options...] *hosts...*

-i	Starts in interactive command mode.
-l	Shows a list of the peers known to the servers.
-n	Shows all host addresses in dotted-decimal format (0.0.0.0).
-p	Shows a list of the peers known to the server and a summary of their states.
-s	Is like -p, but the list is shown in a different format.
-c *command*	Specifies an interactive-format command.
? *{ command }*	Shows the interactive commands, or information about the specified command.
delay *milliseconds*	Specifes that timestamps are added with the time interval specified.
host *hostname*	Specifies that queries are sent to the specified hostname or IP address.
keyid *keyid*	Specifies a key number that matches a key number on the server for authentication.
passwd	Asks for a password during authentication to complete configuration requests.
timeout *milliseconds*	Queries time out after the specified number of milliseconds.
	The following options query the states on the server:
clkbug *clockpeeraddresses...*	Shows debugging information of a reference clock driver.
clockbug *clockpeeraddresses...*	Shows debugging information of a peer clock.
dmpeers	Shows peers for which the server is maintaining state.
iostats	Shows counters that are maintained in the input-output module.
kerninfo	Shows the kernel phase-lock loop operating parameters.
loopinfo *{ action }*	Shows looped filter variables. Actions are either oneline or multiline outputs.
memstats	Shows counter statistics about memory allocation.
monlist	Shows the traffic counts that the monitor facility has.
peers	Shows peers for which the server is maintaining state, with a summary.
pstats *peeraddresses...*	Gathers per-peer statistics counters from the specified peers.
reslist	Shows the restriction list found on the server.
sysinfo	Shows local system state variables.
sysstats	Shows counter statistics from the protocol module.
timerstats	Shows counters maintained in the timer/event queue support code.
	The following options are the configuration requests available:
addpeer *peeraddress* [options...]	Adds a peer association to the server.
keyid	Specifies an integer to encrypt and send with outgoing packets to the server.
version	Specifies what version to use: 1, 2, or 3 (default is 3).
prefer	Specifies the preferred peer, when synchronizing clocks for example.
addserver *peeraddress* [options...]	The same as the addpeer comman,d but the operating mode is client.
broadcast *peeraddress* [options...]	The same as the addpeer comman,d but the operating mode is broadcast.
addtrap *address { port interface }*	Specifies a trap to add on the server.
authinfo	Shows the authentication information, such as known keys and counters.
clrtrap *address { port interface }*	Specifies a trap to delete from the server.
delrestrict *address mask { port }*	Specifies an entry to remove from the restrict list.
disable *options...*	Turns the specified server option off.
enable *options...*	Turns the specified server option on.

continued

	The following are the server options to use:
auth	Synchronizes only with authenticated, unconfigurated peers.
bclient	Listens for broadcast or multicast messages (default is off).
monitor	Uses the monitoring facility (default is on).
pll	Adjusts the server's local clock (default is on).
stats	Turns on the statistics facility filegen (default is on).
fudge *{ peeraddress } { actions... }*	Changes fudge factors for a reference clock.
time1	Specifies the starting fixed point in seconds used to calibrate time. Used with TIME2.
time2	Specifies the ending fixed point in seconds used to calibrate time. Used with TIME1.
stratum	Specifies a value (0-15) to assign a nonstandard operating stratum.
refid	Specifies an ASCII string(1-4 characters) to assign a nonstandard reference identifier.
readkeys	Purges current authentication keys and install new keys from the keys file.
restrict *address mask actions...*	Restricts the server.
ignore	Ignores all packets from the host.
limited	Specifies that hosts are subject to client limitation from the same net.
lowpriotrap	Specifies that hosts are set to lower priority.
nomodify	Ignores all NTP mode 6 and 7 packets, but allows queries.
nopeer	Specifies that hosts get time service, but no allocated peer memory resources.
noquery	Ignores all NTP mode 6 and 7 packets.
noserve	Ignores all packets that aren't NTP mode 6 or 7.
notrap	Ignores all mode 6 control message trap services.
notrust	Specifies that hosts aren't used as synchronization sources.
ntpport	Matches only the standard source port, NTP UDP (123).
unrestrict *address mask actions...*	Unrestricts an entry from the restrict list. Uses the same actions as restrict.
setprecision *number*	Sets the value (-4 to -20) of the precision for the server to advertise.
traps	Shows the traps on the server.
trustkey *keyID*	Specifies the trusted key configuration.
unconfig *peeraddresses...*	Removes the configuration from the specified peers.
untrustkey *keyID*	Specifies the untrusted key configuration.
hosts...	Specifies the servers to manage.

File Name:	xntpdc	**Directory:**	/usr/sbin/	**Type:**	External

xpcmcia

UNIX Shell: All primary shells (csh, ksh, bsh)

Function	A graphical user interface for the pcmcia utility.
Syntax	xpcmcia

File Name:	xpcmcia	**Directory:**	/usr/bin/X11/	**Type:**	External

xpowerm

UNIX Shell: All primary shells (csh, ksh, bsh)

Function	A graphical user interface for the power management system.
Syntax	xpowerm

File Name:	xpowerm	**Directory:**	/usr/lpp/X11/bin/	**Type:**	External

xpr

UNIX Shell: All primary shells (csh, ksh, bsh)

Function	Prints out X window dump information.
Syntax	xpr [options...] *{ file }*

-append *filename*	Specifies .xpr file to append to window.
-noff	When used with -append, the window shows on same page as the previous window.
-output *filename*	Specifies the output file.
-landscape	Shows a window in landscape mode.
-portrait	Prints the window in portrait mode.
-compact	Makes the presentation of the window more compact.
-cutoff *level*	Specifies the intensity level for the colors that are mapped to a printer.
-density *dpi*	Specifies the dots-per-inch to use on HP printer.

continued

-gray *scale*	Specifies grayscale conversion to a color image.
	The following options can be used with the -gray option:
2	Specifies 2x2 grayscale conversion.
3	Specifies 3x3 grayscale conversion.
4	Specifies 4x4 grayscale conversion.
-header *string*	Specifies a header string to be printed above the window.
-height *inches*	Specifies a maximum height for the page.
-left *inches*	Specifies the left margin in inches.
-noposition	Skips header, trailer, and image position for some printers.
-plane *number*	Specifies which bit plane to use in an image.
-psfig	Suppresses conversion of the PostScript picture to the center of the page.
-report	Prints statistics to STDERR about the window ImageFile parameter.
-rv	Forces the window to print in reverse video.
-scale *scale*	Specifies the size of the window on the page.
-split *number*	Specifies how many pages to split a window into.
-top *inches*	Specifies the top margin in inches for the picture. You can use fractions.
-trailer *string*	Specifies a trailer string to print below the window.
-width *inches*	Specifies a maximum width of the page.
-device *devicetype*	Specifies a device to write the dump file on.
file	Specifies the file that contains the captured bitmap of the image.
File Name: `xpr`	**Directory:** /usr/bin/X11/ **Type:** External

xsend

UNIX Shell: All primary shells (csh, ksh, bsh)

Function	Uses a secure channel to send secret mails to a user in the local system.
Syntax	xsend *user*

user	Specifies the user to send a secret mail to.
File Name: `xsend`	**Directory:** /usr/bin/ **Type:** External

xss

UNIX Shell: All primary shells (csh, ksh, bsh)

Function	An extended screen saver with screen lock.
Syntax	xss [options...]

-e *command*	Specifies a command to run when the screen saver times out or the user activates.
-timeout *sec*	Specifies the screen saver timeout value in seconds.
-v	Verbose mode. Shows more information.
-fg *color*	Specifies the foreground color for the button.
-bg *color*	Specifies the background color for the button.
-geometry *wxh+x+y*	Specifies the size and location of the client window.
File Name: `xss`	**Directory:** /usr/bin/X11/ **Type:** External

xstr

UNIX Shell: All primary shells (csh, ksh, bsh)

Function	Keeps a library of strings from component parts in large programs that can be used as shared constant strings.
Syntax	xstr *{ file }* [options...]

-c	Extracts strings from a specified file and adds them to the strings file.
-v	Verbose mode. Shows more information.
-	Reads from STDIN.
file	Specifies the file to query.
File Name: `xstr`	**Directory:** /usr/bin/ **Type:** External

yes	UNIX Shell:	All primary shells (csh, ksh, bsh)	
Function	Outputs an affirmative response repeatedly.		
Syntax	yes *{ string }*		
string	Specifies a string instead of "y".		
File Name: yes	**Directory:** /usr/bin/	**Type:**	External

yppasswd	UNIX Shell:	All primary shells (csh, ksh, bsh)	
Function	Alters the password in the NIS database.		
Syntax	yppasswd [option]		
-f *{ user }*	Alters the user's GECOS (comment) field, usually the users full name.		
-s *{ user } { shellprog }*	Alters the specified login shell for the specified user.		
File Name: yppasswd	**Directory:** /usr/bin/	**Type:**	External

ypservers	UNIX Shell:	All primary shells (csh, ksh, bsh)	
Function	Shows NIS servers.		
Syntax	ypservers [options...] *{ host }*		
-c	Provides a header for SMIT users.		
-d *domainname*	Shows servers from the specified domain.		
-m	Shows NIS master servers.		
-n	Provides verbose output for SMIT users.		
-r	Exits if no servers are found.		
-s	Shows no output.		
-t *timeout*	Specifies a timeout value for broadcast.		
host	Specifies a host to check if it is a NIS or NIS master server.		
File Name: ypservers	**Directory:** /usr/bin/	**Type:**	External

zcat	UNIX Shell:	All primary shells (csh, ksh, bsh)	
Function	Shows a compressed file on STDOUT without decompressing it.		
Syntax	zcat [options...] *{ files... }*		
-n	Doesn't show the header from the compressed file.		
-V	Writes the current version and compile options to STDERR.		
files...	Specifies the file to show.		
File Name: zcat	**Directory:** /usr/bin/	**Type:**	External

Chapter 11

Red Hat Linux Commands

The commands in this section are all of the commands from Red Hat Linux that are not listed in the Universal UNIX Commands (Chapter 9). The commands are all listed in alphabetical order by the command name.

For cross-references to other operating systems, please see the Quick Command Index (QCI) in Chapter 2.

/etc/inittab	**UNIX Shell:**	N/A
Function	Controls process dispatching. Used by `init`.	
Syntax	*id*:*rstate*:*action*:*process*	

id	Specifies a unique identifier for the entry, one to four characters.
rstate	Specifies the run level for which the entry applies.
action	Specifies how to handle the process field. The following are available:
respawn	Starts the process if it doesn't exist.
wait	Starts the process and waits for it to terminate.
once	Starts the process once.
boot	Starts the process at boot time.
bootwait	Same as `boot` but waits for process to terminate.
powerfail	Starts the process when the UPS signals that power is down.
powerwait	Same as `powerfail` but waits for process to terminate.
off	Does nothing.
ondemand	Starts the process when an ondemand run level is called. Does not change run level.
initdefault	Specifies the default run level of the system.
sysinit	Starts the process before accessing the console. Completes before continuing.
powerokwait	Starts the process when the UPS signals that power is restored.
powerfailnow	Starts the process when the UPS signals that the battery is almost empty.
ctrlaltdel	Starts the process when Ctrl+Alt+Del is pressed.
kbrequest	Starts the process when a special key combination is pressed.
process	Specifies a command.

File Name: `inittab`	**Directory:** /etc/	**Type:** Text File
id:3:initdefault:	Sets run level 3 as the default.	
ca::ctrlaltdel:/sbin/shutdown -t3 -r now	Shuts down the system if Ctrl+Alt+Del is pressed.	
1:2345:respawn:/sbin/mingetty tty1	Restarts the terminal if it dies.	

/etc/lilo.conf	UNIX Shell:	N/A
Function	The configuration file used by the Linux Loader while booting.	

	The following keywords are used in the global section:
backup=*file*	Specifies where the original boot sector should be copied.
boot=*device*	Specifies the boot device, e.g. a hard drive partition.
change-rules	Specifies changes to partition type numbers at boot.
compact	Merges read requests to speed up load time.
default=*label*	Specifies the default boot label.
delay=*time*	Specifies the delay in tenths of a second until the default image is booted.
disk=*device*	Specifies non-standard parameters for a disk.
disktab=*file*	Specifies the disk parameter table (default is `/etc/disktab`).
fix-table	Adjusts 3-D addresses in partition tables.
force-backup=*file*	Same as backup but overwrites a backup if it exists.
ignore-table	Ignores corrupt partition tables.
install=*boot-sector*	Installs the specified file as the boot sector (default is `/boot/boot.b`).
linear	Generates linear sector addresses.
lock	Records boot lines as defaults for the next boot.
map=*file*	Specifies the location of the map file (default is `/boot/map`).
message=*file*	Specifies a boot message.
nowarn	Disables warnings.
optional	Same as optional in the per-image section but applies to all images.
password=*password*	Same as password in the per-image section but applies to all images.
prompt	Forces entering the boot prompt.
restricted	Same as password in the per-image section but applies to all images.
serial=*parameters*	Enables control from a serial line.
timeout=*time*	Specifies a timeout in tenths of a second for keyboard input.
verbose=*level*	Verbose mode. Shows more information. Max level is 5.
	The following keywords are used in the per-image section:
image=*path*	Specifies the boot image.
other=*path*	Specifies an arbitrary system to boot.
range=*start-end*	Specifies a range of sectors to map. Used with `image`.
loader=*chain-loader*	Specifies the chain loader. Used with `other`.
table=*device*	Specifies the device with the partition table. Used with `other`.
unsafe	Disables sanity checks, e.g. partition table check. Used with `other`.
label=*name*	Specifies a name for the image.
alias=*name*	Specifies a second name for the image.
lock	Records boot lines as defaults for the next boot.
optional	Omits the image if it isn't available.
password=*password*	Protects the image with a password.
restricted	Requires a password only if parameters are specified on the command line.
	The following keywords are for the kernel:
append=*string*	Appends parameters are passed on to the kernel.
literal=*string*	Same as `append` but omits everything else.
ramdisk=*size*	Specifies the size of the RAM disk.
read-only	Specifies the root file system as read-only.
read-write	Specifies the root file system as read-write.
root=*device*	Specifies the device to be mounted as root.
vga=*mode*	Specifies the VGA text mode to be used during boot.

File Name:	`lilo.conf`	**Directory:**	/etc/	**Type:**	Text File

/etc/modules.conf

/etc/modules.conf		**UNIX Shell:**	All primary shells (bash, ash, tcsh)
Function	Loads modules specific options at startup.		
File Name:	`modules.conf`	**Directory:** /etc/	**Type:** Text File
alias eth0 3c59x	This line in the file specifies an alias for the 3c59x module.		

/etc/nologin

/etc/nologin		**UNIX Shell:**	Bash shell (bash)
Function	A text file that, if it exists in `/etc/`, will prevent non-root users from logging in. If a user attempts to log in, it will be shown the contents of the file, and then be disconnected.		
File Name:	`nologin`	**Directory:** /etc/	**Type:** Text File

/etc/nsswitch.conf

/etc/nsswitch.conf		**UNIX Shell:**	N/A
Function	Specifies how the lookup for different databases are performed and in what order. Lookups are done left to right.		
Syntax	*database sources... { status = success... }* *database sources... { status = success... sources... }*		

database	Specifies a database that you want to change the lookup order for.
aliases	Specifies the aliases database used by sendmail.
ethers	Specifies the database for the ethers.
group	Specifies how to look up group.
hosts	Specifies how to look up hosts.
netgroup	Specifies the database for netgroups.
networks	Specifies the database for networks.
passwd	Specifies the database to use for passwd.
protocols	Specifies the database for protocols.
publickey	Specifies the database for publickey.
rpc	Specifies the database for getrpcbyname.
shadow	Specifies the database for the shadow database.
sources...	Specifies the source to use. Search from left to right.
files	Uses the files, for example, /etc/hosts, /etc/passwd, and /etc/groups.
nis	Uses NIS to look up the names.
nisplus	Uses NIS+ to look up the names.
dns	Uses DNS to look up hostnames (may be used only for hosts).
compat	Implements + and - for groups and passwd.
db	Uses the db databases.
[status = success ...]	Specifies what to do now. Multiple pairs can be used. ([ ] must be used).
status	Specifies the current status to check.
success	Is true if the entry was found.
unavail	Is true if the source isn't responding or corrupted.
notfound	Is true if the entry was not found.
tryagain	Is true if the source is busy and may respond to retries.
action	Specifies what to do.
continue	Tries the next source in the list.
return	Returns now.

File Name:	`nsswitch.conf`	**Directory:** /etc	**Type:** Text File
hosts: files nisplus nis dns	This row in the file describes how to look up hosts.		
passwd: files nisplus nis	This row in the file describes how to look up users.		
shadow: files nisplus nis	This row in the file describes how to look up shadow.		

/etc/printcap

/etc/printcap		**UNIX Shell:**	Bash shell (bash)
Function	Describes printers and allows dynamic addition and deletion of printers by the spooling system.		
File Name:	`printcap`	**Directory:** /etc/	**Type:** Text File

/etc/sysconfig/network

/etc/sysconfig/network		UNIX Shell:	N/A
Function	Configures the system's network. Specifies hostname and gateway.		
NETWORKING="yes | no"	Specifies whether networking should be enabled or disabled.		
HOSTNAME="*hostname*"	Specifies the system's hostname.		
GATEWAY="*IP-address*"	Specifies the default router for the system.		
GATEWAYDEV="*device*"	Specifies the default router device for the system.		
FORWARD_IPV4="yes | no"	Enables or disables IPV4 forwarding for the firewall. **Below is an example of a `network` file:** NETWORKING="yes" HOSTNAME="pluto" GATEWAY="192.168.1.254" GATEWAYDEV="eth0" FORWARD_IPV4="no"		
File Name: `network`	**Directory:** /etc/sysconfig/	**Type:**	Text File

/etc/xinetd.conf

/etc/xinetd.conf		UNIX Shell:	Bash shell (bash)
Function	Contains the configuration for the extended internet services started by the `xinetd` command.		

Text syntax	service *name*
	{
	attribute operator values...
	}		

service *name*	Specifies the name of a service.		
attribute	Specifies an attribute to the service. The following attributes can be combined:		
id	Identifies a unique service. By default the id the same as the service name.		
type	Specifies the type of service. Combine any of the following:		
RPC	Specifies that this is an RPC service.		
INTERNAL	Specifies that this is a service provided by `xinetd`.		
UNLISTED	Specifies the service isn't listed in a standard system file.		
flags	Use any combination of the following:		
REUSE	Sets the SO REUSEADDR flag on the service socket.		
INTERCEPT	Specifies to verify that information is coming from accepted sources.		
NORETRY	Specifies not to attempt retry in case of a fork failure.		
IDONLY	Accepts connections only if the remote host runs an identification server.		
NAMEINARGS	Allows you to put the server name in the place for the server argument.		
NODELAY	Sets the TCP_NODELAY flag if it is a TCP server.		
DISABLE	Disables the service and overrides the enable directive.		
disable	Disables the service and overrides the enable directive.		
socket_type	Sets the socket type to one of the following:		
stream	Specifies that it is a stream-based service.		
dgram	Specifies that it is a datagram-based service.		
raw	Specifies the service needs direct IP access.		
seqpacket	Specifies the service needs reliable sequential datagram transmission.		
protocol	Specifies the protocol that the service uses. Must exist in the `/etc/protocols` file.		
wait	Specifies if the service is single- or multi-threaded.		
=yes	Sets the service to single-threaded.		
=no	Sets the service to multi-threaded.		
user	Specifies the user ID for the server process. Must exist in the `/etc/passwd` file.		
group	Specifies the group ID for the server process. Must exist in the `/etc/group` file.		
instances	Specifies the number of services that can be simultaneously active.		
=*nr*	Sets a specified number of services.		
UNLIMITED	Sets the number to unlimited (is default).		
nice	Sets the server priority. See the command `nice`.		
server	Specifies the program to run for this service.		

continued

server_args	Specifies the arguments to pass on to the server.
only_from	Specifies the remote hosts that this service is available to. **The hosts can be specified as a list in only one of the following ways:**
%d.%d.%d.%d	Numeric addresses with a zero as a wildcard. For example: 195.245.0.0.
%d.%d.%d.{%d, %d...}	Factorized addresses with the factorized part in the end.
network	Network name as found in the file `/etc/networks`.
host	The host or domain name.
IPaddress	An IP address or netmask range. Ex 1.2.3.4/32. (With no value the service will not be available to anybody.)
no_access	Specifies the remote hosts that this service isn't available to.
access_times	Specifies the time intervals that the service is available in the form h:m-h:m.
log_type	Specifies where to send the log output. There are two ways to log.
SYSLOG	Logs to a specified `syslog` with a specified level.
FILE	Logs to a specified file with a specified max volume.
log_on_success	Specifies the information to log on starts and exits for the servers. **Combine any of the following values that you want to log:**
PID	Logs the server process ID.
HOST	Logs the address of the remote host.
USERID	Logs the ID of the remote user.
EXIT	Logs all exits and the current exit status of the servers.
DURATION	Logs the time a session has been running.
log_on_failure	Logs the failed attempts to start a server.
HOST	Logs the address of the remote host.
USERID	Logs the ID of the remote user.
ATTEMPT	Logs that an attempt was made.
RECORD	Logs information from the remote end.
rpc_version	Specifies the RPC version as a single number or a range in the form nr-nr.
rpc_number	Specifies the number for an unlisted RPC service.
env	Specifies a list of strings in the form name=value to be added to the environment.
passenv	Specifies a list of environment arguments from `xinetd` to pass on to the server.
port	Specifies a service port. Must exist in the /etc/services file.
redirect	Redirects a TCP service to another host with the specified address and port number.
bind	Binds a service to an interface with a specified IP address.
interface	Same as `bind.`
banner	Writes the name of a file to a remote host when a service is opened.
banner_success38	Writes the name of a file to a remote host when a service is given access.
banner_fail	Writes the name of a file to a remote host when a service has failed to get access.
per_source	Specifies the number of instances per source IP addresses in an nr or as unlimited.
=nr	Sets a specified number of services.
UNLIMITED	Sets the number to unlimited, which also is the default.
cps	Sets the limit of the incoming connections.
nr	Specifies the max number of incoming sessions per seconds before temporary stop.
seconds	Specifies the number of seconds to wait before restart after a stop.
max_load	Sets a max average load per minute. Only supported by Linux and Solaris.
groups	Specifies the group privileges.
= yes	Runs with access to the groups that the server's effective UID has access to.
= no	Runs with no group privileges.
enabled	Enables a list of service names.
include	Includes a configuration file that is in the same form as `xinetd.conf.`
includedir	Includes a directory with configured service files. (Include operations must be specified outside a service declaration.)
operator	Specifies what to do with a certain value. Use one of the following:
=	Sets only one single assignment operator.
+=	Adds a value to a set of values for an attribute.

continued

-=	Removes a value from a set of values for an attribute. (Not all of the attributes will accept the plus / minus signs.)				
values...	Specifies the values for the attributes.				
File Name:	`xinetd.conf`	**Directory:**	/etc/	**Type:**	Text File
Note:	All assignment operators are supported by: `only_from`, `no_access`, `log_on_success`, `log_on_failure`, `passenv` & `env` (this doesn't support `-=`).				

ab

UNIX Shell: All primary shells (bash, ash, tcsh)

Function	Benchmarks your Apache server by sending requests to it.
Syntax	ab [options...] [http://] *hostname*[:*port*]/*path*

-k	Enables multiple requests in one HTTP session. This is called HTTP KeepAlive.
-i	Uses an HTTP HEAd, which replaces the GET method. Not combinable with POST.
-n *requests*	Specifies the number of requests to run in the benchmark.
-t *timelimit*	Specifies the time in seconds to use benchmarking. This sets -n to 50000.
-c *concurrency*	Specifies the number of requests to perform simultaneously, where default is 1.
-p *postfile*	Specifies a file to send in any HTTP POST requests to the Apache server.
-A *user:password*	Provides the server with Username and password entered with a : between. **Note:This is sent whether the server needs it or not, as uuencoded data.**
-P *user:password*	Runs the same procedure as the -A switch but is used with proxy servers.
-H *string*	Appends more headers to the request, usually in value:value form. Repeatable option.
-C *name=value*	Adds a cookie to the request. The option is repeatable.
-T *content-type*	Specifies the content-type header for usage with POST data.
-v *verbosity*	Specifies verbosity level. **Note:2+ warnings and info, 3+ response codes, 4+ shows header info.**
-w *output HTML*	Shows results in HTML tables. Default is two columns wide, white background.
-x *string*	Specifies the attributes for table.
-y *string*	Specifies the attributes for <tr> (table row).
-z *string*	Specifies the attributes for <td> (table data) or <th> (table header).
-V	Shows version information.
-h	Shows help information.
[http://]*hostname*:{ *port* }/*path*	Defines the URL to use when benchmarking. HTTP and port isn't required.

File Name:	`ab`	**Directory:**	/usr/sbin/	**Type:**	External
Tip:	Before you install a Web server that is heavily utilized, benchmark it to check whether it can handle the load.				

ab http://hostname:port/path	Test server on specified URL.
ab -n 5 -c 5 http://hostname:port/path	Test with five simultaneous requests per second.

access

UNIX Shell: All primary shells (bash, ash, tcsh)

Function	Checks whether a file can be accessed. Exits successfully if the file can be accessed with the specified mode.
Syntax	access -*mode file* access option

--help	Shows help information.
--version	Shows version information.
-*mode*	Specifies the mode to test. Can be one or more of r, w, or x.
file	Specifies the file to test.

File Name:	`access`	**Directory:**	/usr/bin/	**Type:**	External

access -r /etc/passwd ; echo $?	Tests whether you have read access to `/etc/passwd`. Should return 0.
access -rwx /etc/passwd ; echo $?	Tests whether you have read, write, and execute access to `/etc/passwd`. Should return 1.

actctrl

UNIX Shell: All primary shells (bash, ash, tcsh)

Function	Configures the IBM Active 2000 ISDN device driver and downloads firmware into the ISDN card.
Syntax	actctrl [-d *driverID*] *ACTION*

-d *DriverID*	Specifies the SO interface. Is required if you use multiple cards.
ACTION	**You must specify one of the following actions:**

continued

add	Enables support for an additional card in the driver.
bus	Describes the bus-type of the card. The values are 1= ISA-bus, 2= MCA, 3= PCMCIA.
port	Describes the base port in one of two ways. Use one of the following port values:
integer	Specifies the value with an integer.
auto	Enables auto probing for the base port.
	When using `port`, you may also use the following:
irq	Specifies the IRQ to use. You must use one of the following three values for irq:
integer	Specifies the value with an integer.
auto	Selects the next free IRQ automatically.
none	Enables polled mode for this card.
	When using `irq` you may also use the following:
id	Uses any string to reference the card at a later time.
dproto *protocol*	Selects the D-channel protocol and defines MSN's if it uses the Euro protocol.
1tr6	Selects the D-channel protocol.
euro	Selects the Euro protocol. You may add up to 10 MSNs:
msn0,msn9	Specifies the MSN. Use dash - for an empty entry.
load *firmware*	Downloads firmware into the card and starts operation. The filename is `bip1120.bpl`.
dump	Shows the internal driver contents on STDOUT. (Only works if the program is configured with the --enable-dump option.)
File Name: `actctrl`	**Directory:** /usr/sbin/ **Type:** External

addftinfo

UNIX Shell: All primary shells (bash, ash, tcsh)

Function	Reads troff font file and adds font metric information that is used by the groff system.
Syntax	addftinfo [option] *resolution unitwidth font*

-x-height *height*	Specifies the height of lowercase letters without ascenders such as x.
-fig-height *height*	Specifies the height of figures.
-asc-height *height*	Specifies the height of characters with ascenders, for b, d, or l.
-body-height *height*	Specifies the height of characters such as parentheses.
-cap-height *height*	Specifies the height of uppercase letters such as A.
-comma-depth *height*	Specifies the depth of a comma.
-desc-depth *height*	Specifies the depth of characters with descanters, for p, q, or y.
-body-depth *height*	Specifies the depth of characters such as parentheses.
File Name: `addftinfo`	**Directory:** /usr/bin/ **Type:** External

addr

UNIX Shell: All primary shells (bash, ash, tcsh)

Function	Shows information about network addresses. Shows you the hexadecimal format of the IP address.
Syntax	addr [options...]

-4	Input is in IPv4 format, (is default).
-6	Input is in IPv6 format.
	You must specify one of the following for the command to work:
-n *hex*	Specifies that input is given in hexadecimal format.
-p *IPaddress*	Specifies the input address.
File Name: `addr`	**Directory:** /usr/bin/ **Type:** External
addr -p 192.168.1.1	Shows information about the address 192.168.1.1.
addr -6 -p 1:1:1::1	Shows information about the address 1:1:1::1.

addr2line

UNIX Shell: All primary shells (bash, ash, tcsh)

Function	Shows filenames and line numbers for specified program addresses.
Syntax	addr2line [options...] *addresses...*

-b *bfdname*	Specifies the object code format for the object files.
-C	Converts low-level names into user-level names.
-e *file*	Specifies the executable for which addresses should be converted.
-f	Displays function names, plus file and line number information.
-s	Displays only the base of each filename.

continued

-H	Shows help information.		
-V	Shows version.		
addresses...	Specifies address.		
File Name: addr2line	**Directory:** /usr/bin/	**Type:**	External
addr2line 0x8048462	Prints line number and filename for 0x8048462 in a.out.		

adsl-connect

UNIX Shell: A shell (ash, bsh)

Function	A user-space PPPoE client. It manages an ADSL connection and reestablishes a dropped connection.
Syntax	adsl-connect *{ interface } { user } { configfile }*

interface	Specifies Ethernet interface. This overrides the configuration file setting.		
user	Specifies Ethernet username. Must be used with interface.		
configfile	Specifies file to use when PPPoE starts.		
File Name: adsl-connect	**Directory:** /usr/sbin/	**Type:**	Script

adsl-setup

UNIX Shell: A shell (ash, bsh)

Function	A PPPoE client configuration script. It is used for the adsl-start, adsl-stop and adsl-connect scripts.
Syntax	adsl-setup

File Name: adsl-setup	**Directory:** /usr/sbin/	**Type:**	Script

adsl-start

UNIX Shell: A shell (ash, bsh)

Function	Starts the Roaring Penguin user-space PPPoE client.
Syntax	adsl-start *{ interface } { user } { configfile }*

interface	Specifies the Ethernet interface. This overrides the configuration file settings.		
user	Specifies the Ethernet username. Required with interface.		
configfile	The file to use when starting the PPPoE.		
File Name: adsl-start	**Directory:** /usr/sbin/	**Type:**	Script

adsl-status

UNIX Shell: A shell (ash, bsh)

Function	Shows status of the PPPoE link that was established by the Roaring Penguin user-space PPPoE client.
Syntax	adsl-status *{ configfile }*

configfile	The file to use when checking the PPPoE (default is `/etc/ppp/pppoe.conf`).		
File Name: adsl-status	**Directory:** /usr/sbin/	**Type:**	Script

adsl-stop

UNIX Shell: A shell (ash, bsh)

Function	Stops the Roaring Penguin user-space PPPoE client.
Syntax	adsl-stop *{ configfile }*

configfile	Specifies the configuration file to use (default is `/etc/ppp/pppoe.conf`).		
File Name: adsl-stop	**Directory:** /usr/sbin/	**Type:**	Script

afm2tfm

UNIX Shell: All primary shells (bash, ash, tcsh)

Function	Used to convert an Adobe font metric file to TeX font metric format.
Syntax	afm2tfm *file1* [options...] *file2*

-e *real*	Extends the characters by a factor of REAL.
-O	Specifies the use of octal for all characters in the VPL file.
-p *encfile*	Specifies the file to read/download for the PostScript encoding.
-s *real*	Used to tilt characters by REAL.

continued

-t *encfile*	Specifies the file to read for the VPL file encoding.
-u	Used to only output characters from encodings.
-v *file*	Used to make a VPL file for conversion to VF.
-V *scfile*	Same as -v but creates small caps as lowercase.
--help	Shows help information.
--version	Shows version information.
file1	Specifies input file.
file2	Specifies output file.
File Name: `afm2tfm`	**Directory:** /usr/bin/ **Type:** External

ali

UNIX Shell: All primary shells (bash, ash, tcsh)

Function	Shows addresses for mail aliases.
Syntax	ali [options...] *{ aliases... }*

-alias *aliasfile*	Specifies file to inspect in.
-list	Shows one line per address.
-nolist	Shows multiple addresses on the same line.
-normalize	Tracks down the official hostname of the address.
-nonormalize	Disables the -normalize option.
-nouser	Doesn't show aliases.
-version	Shows version information.
-help	Shows help information.
aliases...	Specifies alias or aliases.
File Name: `ali`	**Directory:** /usr/bin/ **Type:** External
ali nisse james	Shows mail-addresses for aliases nisse and james.
ali -alias /etc/nmh/MailAliases nisse	Uses `/etc/local/aliases` as alias-file to list nisse.

allneeded

UNIX Shell: A shell (ash, bsh)

Function	Forces the calculation of all fonts that are needed to preview a set of dvi files.
Syntax	allneeded [-r] *files...*

-r	Specifies the `dvired` command to use instead of `dvips`.
files...	Specifies the location where the program should search for files.
File Name: `allneeded`	**Directory:** /usr/bin/ **Type:** Script
Note:	Doesn't recalculate existing fonts.
allneeded <texdvi file>	Shows what fonts are used when using dvips.

alloc

UNIX Shell: TC shell (tcsh)

Function	Shows how much memory is used and free.
Syntax	alloc

anacron

UNIX Shell: All primary shells (bash, ash, tcsh)

Function	Runs commands periodically.
Syntax	anacron [options...] *{ jobs... }*

-f	Forces the job to run and ignore timestamps.
-u	Updates the timestamps only; doesn't run the command.
-s	Starts no new job before the previous is ready.
-n	Runs job immediately and ignore delays. Requires the -s option.
-d	Doesn't run in background. Messages are sent to STDERR and `syslog`.
-q	Sends messages to STDERR. Used with -d option only.
-t *file*	Specifies an anacrontab file to use (default is `/etc/anacrontab`).
-V	Shows version information.
-h	Shows help information.
jobs...	Runs one or more jobs specified in the file anacrontab (default is *, means all).

continued

		The entries in the default `anacrontab` file are separated by tabs.			
days		Specifies the number of days to wait before the command is run the next time.			
minutes		Specifies the delay time for a run in minutes after waiting the number of days.			
identifier		Specifies an identifier for the job.			
command		Specifies the command to run.			
File Name:	`anacron`	**Directory:**	/usr/sbin/	**Type:**	External
anacron –u			Updates all timestamps for the jobs in the file anacrontab.		
anacron -s -t tab.new erase			Runs the job erase in the file tab.new and wait until previous job is ready.		

answer

UNIX Shell: All primary shells (bash, ash, tcsh)

Function	A utility that secretaries can use for easily creating e-mails while receiving a phone call.				
Syntax	answer [options...]				
-p		Prompts for phone slip type message fields.			
-u		Allows names that are not in the alias table.			
File Name:	`answer`	**Directory:**	/usr/bin/	**Type:**	External

apm

UNIX Shell: All primary shells (bash, ash, tcsh)

Function	Shows power status and can configure the server in standby or suspend mode.				
Syntax	apm [options...]				
-v		Shows information regarding the APM BIOS and Linux APM driver version.			
-V		Shows version information.			
-m		Shows the total minutes that remain.			
-s		Puts the workstation into suspend mode if possible.			
-S		Puts the workstation into standby mode if possible.			
File Name:	`apm`	**Directory:**	/usr/bin/	**Type:**	External
Note:	Very useful for laptops where power saving is critical.				
apm –S			Configures the workstation in standby mode.		

apmd

UNIX Shell: All primary shells (bash, ash, tcsh)

Function	A monitor daemon and works together with the APM BIOS driver in the OS kernel.
Syntax	apmd [options...]
-c *seconds*	Specifies how many seconds to block on the `/dev/apm_bios` device.
-P *proxycommand*	Specifies a command to start when certain driver events are reported.
	You can use one of the following commands for -P:
start	Starts the daemon. It configures the system wide power policy.
stop	Stops the daemon. It disables policy settings.
suspend	Enables suspend. You can use the following parameters:
bios	Conserves some power and responds fast to user activity.
user	Specifies the suspend option is a user action.
resume	Resumes the system. Following options indicate the mode it was before:
suspend	Indicates the suspend mode.
standby	Indicates the standby mode.
change power	Changes system power policy when changing from AC to battery power.
change battery	Warns when battery is low.
change capability	Changes power if device is added or removed.
-p *refresh%*	Specifies in percent how often to update the power information.
-V	Shows version information.
-v	Verbose mode. Shows more information.
-W	Uses wall to alert all users.
-w *warn%*	Specifies when to warn the user based on the percent of battery power left.
-q	Disables warnings from the -W and -w options.
-?	Shows help information.

continued

-u	Configures BIOS clock to UTC (GMT).
	The following options are hardly used - the options above are preferred:
-a *aconline*	Specifies a command to run when AC power becomes available.
-b *acoffline*	Specifies a command to run when the server operates on battery power.
-l *lowbattery*	Specifies a command to run when the APM BIOS judges that battery power is low.
-s *presuspend*	Specifies a command to run before a suspend through the driver.
-r *postresume*	Specifies a command to run after a resume through the driver.
File Name: `apmd`	**Directory:** /usr/sbin/ **Type:** External
apmd -W -w 5	Warns all users when battery level reaches 5 percent.

apmsleep

UNIX Shell: All primary shells (bash, ash, tcsh)

Function	Sets the computer in suspend or sleep mode.
Syntax	apmsleep [options...] *time*

-V	Shows version information.
-s	Suspends the computer (is default).
-S	Sets the computer in standby mode.
-w	Waits forever on an interrupt.
-n	Sets the clock and suspends the computer.
-d	Shows debug information.
[+] *time*	Sets the time to wake up in hh:mm format, plus + before will add to the current time.
File Name: `apmsleep`	**Directory:** /usr/bin/ **Type:** External
apmsleep +01:00	Suspends the computer for one hour.
apmsleep 01:00	Suspends the computer until 01:00.

appres

UNIX Shell: All primary shells (bash, ash, tcsh)

Function	Shows how much resources are used by a specific application.
Syntax	appres [options...]

class	Specifies this class name of an application.
instance	Specifies an instance name in addition to *class*.
-1	Checks a specific resource level.
toolkitoptions	Allows X toolkit options.
File Name: `appres`	**Directory:** /usr/X11R6/bin/ **Type:** External
appres xterm	Lists the resources that any xterm program uses.

arch

UNIX Shell: All primary shells (bash, ash, tcsh)

Function	Shows the hardware architecture of the current host.
Syntax	arch
File Name: `arch`	**Directory:** /bin/ **Type:** External

arping

UNIX Shell: All primary shells (bash, ash, tcsh)

Function	Pings the destination address using arp packets on the specified interface.
Syntax	arping [options...] -I *interface*

-c *NR*	Specifies the number of pings.
-w *timeout*	Specifies the stop time.
-q	Shows no messages.
-D	Specifies duplicate address detection mode. A zero is returned if successful.
-U	Automatically updates the ARP cache on destination computer.
-A	Same as -U, but uses ARP REPLY packets instead of ARP REQUEST. (In -D mode set to 0.0.0.0. In -U or -A mode set to destination address.)
-V	Shows version information.
-s *source*	Specifies the source address to use. In normal mode calculated from routing tables.

continued

-I *interface*		Specifies the interface to use.			
File Name:	`arping`	**Directory:**	/usr/sbin/	**Type:**	External
arping -I eth0 192.168.1.247		Performs an arping on the specified IP address.			
arping -U -I eth0 192.168.1.247		Updates the cache on the specified computer.			

arpsnmp

UNIX Shell: All primary shells (bash, ash, tcsh)

Function	Saves the Ethernet/IP address pairings. Logs the activity to `syslog` and sends a report of the changes by e-mail.				
Syntax	arpsnmp [options...] *files...*				
-d -f *datafile* *files...*		Enables debugging. Disables mailing the reports; it sends them to STDERR. Specifies the Ethernet/IP address database filename (default is `arp.dat`). Specifies the file to read information from.			
File Name:	`arpsnmp`	**Directory:**	/usr/sbin/	**Type:**	External
Note:	You must create an `arp.dat` file before using this command.				

arpwatch

UNIX Shell: All primary shells (bash, ash, tcsh)

Function	Saves the Ethernet/IP address pairs. Logs the activity to `syslog` and sends a report of the changes by e-mail.				
Syntax	arpwatch [options...]				
-d -f *datafile* -i *interface* -r *file*		Enables debugging. Disables forking in the background and mailing the reports. Specifies the Ethernet/IP address database filename (default is `arp.dat`). Specifies the interface to use instead of the default interface. Specifies the file to read from instead of reading from the network; it doesn't fork.			
File Name:	`arpwatch`	**Directory:**	/usr/sbin/	**Type:**	External
Note:	You must create an `arp.dat` file before using this command.				

as86

UNIX Shell: All primary shells (bash, ash, tcsh)

Function	Assembles code for the 8086 to 80386 processors.				
Syntax	as86 [options...] *file*				
-0 -1 -2 -3 -a -g -j -l *{ file }* -n *name* -o *file* -b *{ file }* -s *file* -u -w- -t NR *file*		Uses 8086 instruction and 16-bit code segment; warns for instruction >8086. Uses 80186 instruction and 16-bit code segment; warns for instruction >80186. Uses 80286 instruction and 16-bit code segment; warns for instruction >80286. Uses 80386 instruction and 32-bit segment; doesn't warn for any instruction. Enables some compatibility with Minix asld. Puts global symbols in object and symbol files. Determines whether long jumps can be replaced with short ones. Makes a list file. Place the listing in file if it specified. Specifies a name of a module. Makes an object file. Makes a raw binary file. Makes an ASCII symbol file. Assumes that undefined symbols are imported with unspecified segment. Shows warning messages. Will, in segment NR+3, move all text segment data. Specifies the source file. Use a hyphen - to read from STDIN.			
Filename:	`as86`	**Directory:**	/usr/bin	**Type:**	External

ascii-xfr

UNIX Shell: All primary shells (bash, ash, tcsh)

Function	Sends or receives files in ASCII mode.	
Syntax	ascii-xfr [options...] *file*	
 -s -r		**Select only one of the -s or -r options.** Sends the specified file. Receives a file.

continued

-d		Specifies that Ctrl-D is the End-Of-File character.			
-n		Disables the translation between CR and CRLF.			
-v		Verbose mode. Shows more information.			
-l *time*		Sets the wait time after each line transmitted in milliseconds.			
-c *time*		Sets the wait time after each character transmitted in milliseconds.			
file		Specifies the name of the file to send or receive.			
File Name:	`ascii-xfr`	**Directory:**	/usr/bin/	**Type:**	External
Warning:	No controls are made on the transferred data.				

ash, bsh

UNIX Shell: A shell (ash, bsh)

Function	A shell similar to sh with similar features as system V shell.
Syntax	ash [options...] *{ file } { arguments... }*

-c *string*		Runs the first argument from the list and passes the other arguments to `csh`.			
		The following options can also be set inside a script, using set:			
-e		If a command returns a nonzero exit status, exit the shell.			
-f		Disables filename generation.			
-I		Lets the shell ignore EOF.			
-i		Makes shell interactive.			
-j		Turns on job control.			
-n		Reads commands but not run them.			
-s		Reads commands from STDIN.			
-x		Echos each command before it is run.			
-z		Enables filename generation to generate zero files. (If + is used instead of - the flag is turned off.)			
--		Sets positional parameters with the remainder of the line.			
file		Specifies a file that contains an `ash` script.			
arguments...		Specifies arguments to the script.			
File Name:	`ash`	**Directory:**	/bin/	**Type:**	External
ash -c ls			Executes the ls command and returns to the previous shell.		

askrunlevel

UNIX Shell: All primary shells (bash, ash, tcsh)

Function	Allows selection of the operation mode at boot time.
Syntax	askrunlevel

		Select one of the following alternatives once `askrunlevel` is started:			
Press no keys at all		Starts the server operation mode boot process within 60 seconds.			
Press the Enter key		Starts the server operation mode boot process immediately.			
Press any other key		Enters the Linuxconf operation mode user interface.			
		Once into the Linuxconf operation mode, the following actions are available:			
Start		Enables three different task modes of operation: graphical, text based, and maintenance.			
Configure		Allows access to network management, boot system, control files, and status utilities.			
Select		Enables a new configuration version. Archives the original files and replaces them.			
View		Enables access to the boot logs.			
File Name:	`askrunlevel`	**Directory:**	/sbin/	**Type:**	External

aspell

UNIX Shell: All primary shells (bash, ash, tcsh)

Function	Checks for misspelled words. It has filter for e-mail, sgml, and TeX.
Syntax	aspell [options...] *command*

--conf=*file*	Specifies the main configurations file.
--conf-dir=*dir*	Specifies the directory for main configuration file.
--data-dir=*dir*	Specifies the directory for the language files.
--local-data-dir=*dir*	Specifies the directory for the local language files.
--dict-dir=*dir*	Specifies the directory for the main word list.
--add-filter=*filter*	Adds a filter.
--rem-filter=*filter*	Removes a filter.

continued

--home-dir=*dir*	Specifies the directory for personal files.
--ignore=*NR*	Ignores word with less than or equal to NR characters.
--ignore-accents	Ignores accents when checking words.
--dont-ignore-accents	Doesn't ignore accents when checking words.
--strip-accents	Strips accents from word lists.
--dont-strip-accents	Doesn't strip accents from word lists.
--ignore-case	Ignores case.
--dont-ignore-case	Doesn't ignore case.
--ignore-repl	Ignores commands to store replacement pairs.
--dont-ignore-repl	Doesn't ignore commands to store replacement pairs.
--save-repl	Saves replacement pairs on save all.
--dont-save-repl	Doesn't save replacement pairs on save all.
--lang=*lang*	Specifies the default language to use.
--master=*name*	Specifies the name of the main word list.
--mode=*mode*	Specifies filter mode.
none	Doesn't use any mode.
email	Enters e-mail mode.
sglm	Enters sgml mode.
tex	Enters TeX mode.
--per-conf=*file*	Specifies personal configuration files.
--personal=*file*	Specifies a personal word list.
--repl=*file*	Specifies a file that contains replacements list.
--run-together	Handles run-together words as legal.
--dont-run-together	Doesn't treat run-together words as legal.
--run-together-limit=*NR*	Specifies the maximum numbers that can be strung together.
--run-together-min=*NR*	Specifies the minimal length of interior words.
--sug-mode=*mode*	Specifies which suggestion mode to use (fast, normal, or bad-spellers).
--add-extra-dicts=*name*	Specifies extra dictionaries to use.
--rem-extra-dicts=*name*	Specifies dictionaries that are not currently in use to be removed.
--backup	Makes a backup file.
--dont-backup	Doesn't make a backup file.
--reverse	Shows suggest list in reverse order.
--dont-reverse	Shows suggest list in right order.
--time	Suggests time in pipe mode.
--dont-time	Doesn't suggest time in pipe mode.
--add-email-quote=*char*	Adds quote characters for e-mail filter mode.
--add-email-quote=*char*	Removes quote characters for e-mail filter mode.
--email-margin=*NR*	Specifies the number of characters that can appear before a quote character.
--add-sgml-check=*str*	Specifies sglm tag to check.
--rem-sgml-check=*str*	Specifies sgml tag not to check.
--add-sgml-extension=*str*	Adds file extensions that are recognized as an sgml file.
--rem-sgml-extension=*str*	Removes file extensions to be recognized.
--add-tex-command=*str*	Adds TeX commands to check for.
--rem-tex-command=*str*	Removes command that is not checked.
--tex-check-comments	Checks TeX comment.
--dont-tex-check-comments	Doesn't check TeX comment.
	Use one of the following commands:
--help	Shows help information.
--version	Shows version information.
-c *file*	Checks the file.
-a	Is used for compatibility with ispell and is equivalent to typing `ispell -a`.
-l	Shows a list of misspelled words.
config	Shows the current configuration.
soundslike	Shows a sounds-like equivalent for each word entered.
filter	Passes STDIN through filters.
dump *{ wordlist }*	Shows a wordlist.

continued

create *{ wordlist }*	Creates a wordlist.
merge *type { wordlist }*	Merges a master, personal, or replacement (repl) wordlist.
File Name: `aspell`	**Directory:** /usr/bin/ **Type:** External
aspell -c ucg.txt	Spell check `ucg.txt`

atd

UNIX Shell: All primary shells (bash, ash, tcsh)

Function	Runs jobs that are queued by `at`.
Syntax	atd [options...]

-l *loadfactor*	Specifies a limit load factor when batch jobs shouldn't be run.
-b *batchinterval*	Specifies minimum interval between the start of two batch jobs in seconds.
-d	Shows debug information.
-s	Processes at batch queue only once.
File Name: `atd`	**Directory:** /usr/sbin/ **Type:** External
atd -d	Runs at in debug mode.

atrun

UNIX Shell: A shell (ash, bsh)

Function	Runs jobs that are queued by the at command to run later. It is used for backward compatibility.
Syntax	atrun [options...]

-l *loadavg*	Specifies a limiting load factor. Default is 0.8 for single processor.
-d	Shows debug information.
File Name: `atrun`	**Directory:** /usr/sbin/ **Type:** Script

authconfig

UNIX Shell: All primary shells (bash, ash, tcsh)

Function	Configures `/etc/sysconfig/network` to support NIS.
Syntax	authconfig [options...]

--back	Replaces the default Cancel button with a Back button.
--test	Lets users to go trough the settings without saving any changes.
--nostart	Doesn't start `ypbind` when done with the configuration. Starts it up with system.
--authtype	Sets authorization type.
--kickstart	Disables interactive screens.
--usehadow	Uses UNIX style authentication with traditional encrypted password.
--enablemd5	Enables md5 passwords.
--enableshadow	Enables shadow passwords by default.
--disableshadow	Disables shadow passwords by default.
--disablemd5	Disables MD5 passwords by default.
--enablenis	Enables NIS.
--nisdomain *domain*	Specifies default NIS domain.
--nisserver *server*	Specifies default NIS server.
--disablenis	Disables NIS.
--enableldap	Enables ldap.
--enableldapauth	Enables ldap for authentication by default.
--disableldapauth	Disables ldap for authentication by default.
--disableldap	Disables ldap for user information by default.
--ldapserver *server*	Specifies default LDAP server.
--ldapbasedn *dn*	Specifies default LDAP base DN.
--enablekrb5	Enables Kerberos authentication by default.
--krb5kdc *server*	Specifies default Kerberos KDC.
--krb5realm *realm*	Specifies default Kerberos realm.
--krb5adminserver *server*	Specifies default Kerberos admin server.
--disablekrb5	Disables Kerberos authentication by default.
--enablehesiod	Enables hesiod for user information by default.
--hesiodlhs *lhs*	Specifies default hesiod LHS.
--hesiodrhs *rhs*	Specifies default hesiod RHS.
--disablehesiod	Disables hesiod for user information by default.

continued

File Name:	authconfig	Directory:	/usr/sbin/	Type:	External
authconfig ---useshadow			Runs authconfig, use shadow passwords.		
authconfig --authtype=nis			Runs authconfig, use NIS.		

autoexpect

UNIX Shell: Expect script

Function	Inspects your actions in a command and creates an `expect` script that re-creates your interactions.
Syntax	autoexpect *{ commands... }* [options...]

-c	Activates conservative mode. Pauses briefly before it sends each character.
-C*key*	Defines a key to toggle conservative mode.
-p	Looks for the last line of the program output, which is usually the prompt.
-P*key*	Defines a key to toggle prompt mode.
-f *name*	Specifies a filename to save the generated script into.
-quiet	Disables any created information messages.
-Q	Defines a key to use toggles literally.
commands...	Specifies a command with or without arguments, to create a script.

File Name:	autoexpect	Directory:	/usr/bin/	Type:	Script
Note:	Without arguments, autoexpect creates a new shell. Using a program and arguments, it creates that program.				
autoexpect ftp ftp.ucgbook.com			Creates an `expect` script from an FTP session.		
autoexpect rpmfind kdebase			Creates an `expect` script from an rpmfind session.		

avmcapictrl

UNIX Shell: All primary shells (bash, ash, tcsh)

Function	Configures active AVM ISA cards.
Syntax	avmcapictrl add *base irq type* avmcapictrl addcard *type base irq { memory* [*card }*] avmcapictrl trace *{ card } { action }* avmcapictrl reset *{ card }* avmcapictrl load *bootcode { card* [*protocol* [*ACTION }*]] remove *{ card }*

add *base irq type*	Adds an ISA card with the specified portbase.
addcard *base irq type*	Same as add but more generic. memory = The memory address, card = The number of the card.
reset *{ card }*	Specifies the number of the card to reset if the loading has failed.
remove *{ card }*	Specifies the card to remove.
trace	Specifies the trace for CAPI2.0 messages. You may use one of these actions:
off	Turns tracing off.
short	Shows the CAPI2.0 messages on one line and turns tracing on.
on	Turns tracing on.
full	Activates full decode tracing.
nodata	Activates full decode tracing but excludes DATA_B3_IND and DATA_B3_REQ messages.
shortnodata	Shows the CAPI2.0 (no DATA_B3_IND and DATA_B3_REQ) messages on one line, tracing on.
base	Specifies the base value to use.
irq	Specifies the IRQ to use.
type	Specifies the type, can be B1 or, T1.
bootcode	Specifies the t4-file.
card	Specifies the card to use.
protocol	Specifies the protocol to use: DSS1, CT1, VN3, AUSTEL, 5ESS, or NI1.
ACTION	**You may use one of the following actions:**
P2P	Specifies to use Point to Point Protocol.
DN1:SPID1	Specifies the 5ESS or NI1 protocols.
{ DN2:SPID2 }	Specifies a second 5ESS or NI1 protocol — the protocols must be separated with a space.

File Name:	avmcapictrl	Directory:	/usr/sbin/	Type:	External
Note:	The actual version of the t4-files you can find at ftp://ftp.avm.de/cardware/b1/linux/firmware.				

badblocks		UNIX Shell:	All primary shells (bash, ash, tcsh)
Function	Searches a device for bad blocks.		
Syntax	badblocks [options...] *device NR { block }*		

-b *block size*	Specifies block size in bytes.
-o *file*	Specifies a file to list bad blocks in. If not specified, badblocks lists on STDOUT.
-s	Shows the progress of the scan.
-v	Verbose mode. Shows more information.
-w	Initiates write mode test. Erases all data.
device	Specifies the file relating to the device.
NR	Specifies the number of blocks on the device.
block	Specifies the block to start the search at.

File Name:	`badblocks`	**Directory:**	/sbin/	**Type:**	External

badblocks /dev/hda2 1248096 -v -o bb_file	Be verbose, output to `bb_file`.
badblocks -w /dev/hda2 1248096 -o -v bb_file	As above + erase data on `/dev/hda2`.

bash, sh		UNIX Shell:	Bash shell (bash)
Function	A free version of Bourne-shell with many features from C- TC- and Korn shell.		
Syntax	bash [options...] *{ file }*		

--dump-po-strings	Is same as -D but output is in GNU portable objects format (po).
--dump-strings	Is same as -D.
--help	Shows help information.
--login	Invoked as a login shell.
--noediting	When interactive, don't read command line by reading the GNU readline library.
--noprofile	When invoked as a login shell, don't read any of the initialization files.
--norc	When interactive, don't read the personal initialization file (.bashrc).
--posix	Invoked shell to match to posix standard.
--rcfile *file*	When interactive, use file instead of the personal initialization file (.bashrc).
--restricted	Invoked as restricted shell.
--verbose	Verbose mode. Shows more information.
--version	Shows version information.
-c *string*	Reads command specified by string.
-D	Shows all double-quoted strings preceded by $ on STDOUT.
-r	Runs shell as restricted shell.
-i	Makes shell interactive.
-s	Reads commands from STDIN.
-a	Marks modified and created variables for export. (This option can also be set inside a script.)
-b	Informs the user asynchronously when a background job completes.
-e	If a command return a non-zero exit status, exit the shell.
-f	Disables filename generation.
-h	When a command is first encountered, it becomes a tracked alias.
-k	Places all keyword arguments in the environment for a command.
-m	Runs background job in separate process group. Shows a line when completed.
-n	Reads commands, but not run them.
-o *{ option }*	Sets an option. If no option is given, it shows current status. See below for option.
allexport	Same as -a.
braceexpand	Same as -B.
emacs	Uses an Emacs style in line editor for the command line.
errexit	Same as -e.
hashall	Same as -h.
histexpand	Same as -H.
history	Enables command history.
ignoreeof	Doesn't let the shell exit on EOF. The `exit` command must be used.
keyword	Same as -k.
monitor	Same as -m.

continued

noclobber	Same as -C.
noexec	Same as -n.
noglob	Same as -f.
notify	Same as -b.
nounset	Same as -u.
onecmd	Same as -t.
physical	Same as -P.
posix	Changes to POSIX standard behavior where bash differs.
privileged	Same as -p.
verbose	Same as -v.
vi	Uses a vi style in-line editor for the command line.
xtrace	Same as -x.
-p	Activates privileged mode.
-t	Runs one command and exit.
-u	When substituted, treat unset variables as an error.
-v	Shows input lines as they are read.
-x	Show commands and their arguments when they are executed.
-B	Performs brace expansion.
-C	Doesn't allow existing files to be overwritten by shell > redirection operator.
-H	Enables ! style history substitution.
-P	Uses physical directory structure instead of symbolic link structure. (If + is used instead of - the flag is turned off.)
--	Disables further option processing.
-	Turns off -x and -v flag and doesn't continue examining arguments for flag.
file	A file containing bash commands.

File Name:	bash	**Directory:**	/bin/	**Type:**	External

bash -c ls	Runs the command ls in a new bash shell.
bash –r	Starts bash in restricted mode.

bashbug

UNIX Shell: A shell (ash, bsh)

Function	Creates and sends bug reports about the bash shell to the address specified.
Syntax	bashbug *{ address }*

address	Specifies an alternate address to send the bug report (default is bug-bash@gnu.org).

File Name:	bashbug	**Directory:**	/usr/bin/	**Type:**	Script

bcc

UNIX Shell: All primary shells (bash, ash, tcsh)

Function	It is the Bruce's C compiler. A simple C compile that use K&R C syntax.
Syntax	bcc [options...] *files...*

-ansi	Allows some ANSI C to be compiled. But it's not a true ANSI C compiler.
-0	Produces 8086 code.
-3	Produces 80386 code.
-A*option*	Specifies option to the assembler.
-B*prefix*	Specifies prefix for executable search path.
-C*options*	Specifies options to the bcc-cc1.
-D*define*	Specifies definition to preprocessor.
-E	Shows preprocessor output on STDOUT.
-G	Produces GCC objects.
-I*dir*	Adds directory to the search path for include files.
-I	Doesn't use the default search path for include file.
--L*directory*	Adds directory to the search path for library files.
-L	Doesn't use the default search path for library files.
-Md	Creates MS-DOS com file.
-Mf	Creates smaller and faster code. It's not compatible with standard.
-Mc	Creates smaller and faster code.

continued

-Ms	Creates standalone Linux-86 executables.
-Ml	Creates Linux-i386 code generator and library.
-N	Creates a native a.out file.
-O	Optimizes the code.
-P	Shows preprocessor output without line numbers on STDOUT.
-Q*option*	Specifies option to `c386`.
-S	Makes an assembler file.
-T*directory*	Specifies temporary directory.
-U*undefine*	Specifies what to undefine for preprocessor.
-V	Verbose mode. Shows more information.
-X*option*	Specifies option to the linker.
-c	Creates an object file.
-e	Runs the preprocessor pass alone. This saves memory.
-o*outfile*	Specifies name for the output file.
-t1	Lets the assembler renumber the text segment for multi-segment programs.
-v	Verbose mode. Shows more information.
-w	Doesn't show any warning messages.
-W	Shows assemble warning messages.
-x	Doesn't include `crt0.o`.
files...	Specifies the file to use for input.

File Name:	`bcc`	**Directory:**	/usr/bin/	**Type:**	External

bind

UNIX Shell: Bash shell (bash)

Function	Shows or binds key sequence to readline function or macro.
Syntax	bind options...

-m *keymap*	Specifies the keymap to be affected by the subsequent bindings.
-l	Shows a list of all readline function names.
-p	Shows a list of all readline function names and bindings for readline init files.
-P	Shows a list of current readline function names and bindings.
-v	Shows a list of readline variable names and values for readline init files.
-V	Shows a list current readline variable names and values.
-s	Shows a list of readline key sequences bound to macros for readline init files.
-S	Shows a list of readline key sequences bound to macros and the strings they output.
-f *file*	Reads key bindings from file.
-q *function*	Queries which keys are bound to a function.
-u *function*	Erases all key bindings to function.
-r *keyseq*	Erases any binding for the key sequence.
-x *keyseq:function*	Assigns a function to the key sequence.

bind –v	Displays the readline variables and names.
bind -f keysequences	Load key sequences from the specified file.

bindkey

UNIX Shell: TC shell (tcsh)

Function	Binds keys to an edit command. All bindings will be shown if no options is specified.
Syntax	bindkey [options...] *{ key } { command }*

-l	Shows a short descriptions for each editor command.
-d	Sets all keybindings to default for the current editor.
-e	Sets all keybindings to standard GNU Emacs-like bindings.
-v	Sets all keybindings to standard vi-like bindings.
-a	Shows or change key-bindings.
-b	Interprets key as a control character.
-k	Interprets key as a symbolic arrow key name.
-r	Removes a key-binding.
-c	Interprets command as an internal or external command instead of an editor one.
-s	Interprets command as a string to use as input when a key is pressed.
--	Specifies the following option is a key even if it starts with -.

continued

-u	Shows help information.
key	Specifies the key to use.
command	Specifies the editor command to assign to a key.

bison

UNIX Shell: All primary shells (bash, ash, tcsh)

Function	Generates a parser program for specified grammar file.
Syntax	bison [options...] *file*

-b *file-prefix*	Uses the prefix specified for all bison output filenames.
-d	Writes macro definitions for the token type names in an extra output file.
-r	Causes bison to output bison token numbers instead.
-k	Adds a list of token names in order by token number in the name.tab.c output.
-l	Specifies the code produced in the output doesn't contain any #line constructs.
-n	Disables parser code in the output. Only shows declarations.
-o *outfile*	Specifies the output filename name for the parser file.
-p *prefix*	Uses the prefix specified for external names created by bison instead of `yy`.
-t	Compiles runtime debugging code by default generated in the parser file.
-v	Writes verbose descriptions of parser states in an extra output file.
-V	Shows the version of bison and exits.
-h	Shows help information.
-y	Imitates yacc's filename standard. Using -o `y.tab.c` has the same effect.
file	Specifies the input file containing the grammar info to create parser tables from.

File Name:	`bison`	**Directory:**	/usr/bin/	**Type:**	External

bltin

UNIX Shell: A shell (ash, bsh)

Function	Runs the internal command in the shell.
Syntax	bltin *command { argument }*

command	Specifies the internal command to run.
argument	Specifies any argument to the command.

builtin

UNIX Shell: Bash shell (bash)

Function	Forces the use of a shell that builtin commands.
Syntax	builtin *command { arguments... }*

command	Specifies a shell builtin command to run.
arguments...	Specifies arguments to command.
Tip:	This is useful when defining a function whose name is the same as a shell builtin.
builtin bind -l	Executes the internal bind command.

builtins

UNIX Shell: TC shell (tcsh)

Function	Shows all built-in commands in `tcsh`.
Syntax	builtins

bunzip2

UNIX Shell: All primary shells (bash, ash, tcsh)

Function	Decompresses bzip2 files.
Syntax	bunzip2 [options...] *{ files... }*

-k	Keeps the input files.
-f	Overwrites existing output files (default is to not overwrite)
-v	Shows more information.
-V	Shows version and license information.
-h	Shows help information.
-L	Shows software version and license.

continued

-s *files...*		Limits the amount of memory to use. Specifies a file or files to decompress.			
File Name:	bunzip2	**Directory:**	/usr/bin/	**Type:**	External
bunzip2 file.bz2		Decompresses the file specified compressed file.			

burst

UNIX Shell: All primary shells (bash, ash, tcsh)

Function	Allows a message to be split into several new messages.
Syntax	burst [+*folder*] *messages...* [options...]

+*folder*		Specifies the target folder where in the message to burst exists.			
-inplace		Replaces each digest with the "table of contents".			
-noinplace		Maintains the digest and doesn't add a table of contents (is default).			
-quiet		Disables message reporting about messages that are not in digest format.			
-noquiet		Reports nondigest format messages (is default).			
-verbose		Verbose mode. Shows more information.			
-noverbose		Disables verbose mode.			
-folder		Uses the current folder as the default burst folder.			
-version		Shows version information.			
-help		Shows help information.			
messages...		Specifies the messages to divide. This can be single or multiple messages.			
File Name:	burst	**Directory:**	/usr/bin/	**Type:**	External
burst +inbox		Bursts digest messages in the inbox.			
burst 1 2 3 5		Bursts digest messages 1, 2, 3 and 5.			

bzcat

UNIX Shell: All primary shells (bash, ash, tcsh)

Function	Decompresses a bzip2 file to STDOUT.
Syntax	bzcat [-s] { *files...* }

-s *files...*		Limits the memory amount for decompression. Specifies the file or files to decompress.			
File Name:	bzcat	**Directory:**	/usr/bin/	**Type:**	External
bzcat file.bz2		Shows the content in the specified file.			

bzip2

UNIX Shell: All primary shells (bash, ash, tcsh)

Function	Compresses, decompresses, or tests bzip2 files.
Syntax	bzip2 [options...] { *files...* }

-c		Compresses or decompresses to STDOUT.			
-d		Forces decompression.			
-f		Overwrites output files (default is to not overwrite).			
-k		Keeps the input files during compression or decompression.			
-q		Suppresses non-essential warning messages.			
-s		Limits the memory usage when compressing, decompressing, or testing.			
-t		Tests the integrity of the file or files.			
-v		Shows more information.			
-z		Forces compression.			
-V		Shows version number.			
-L		Shows license terms and conditions.			
-1 - -9		Sets the block size at 100k to 900k during compression.			
--repetitive-fast		Compresses repetitive blocks faster.			
--repetitive-best		Compresses repetitive blocks better.			
files...		Specifies the file or files to compress.			
File Name:	bzip2	**Directory:**	/usr/bin/	**Type:**	External
bzip2 file.tar		Compresses specified tar file.			
bzip2 -d file.tar.bz2		Decompresses specified bzip2 compressed file.			

bzip2recover

UNIX Shell:	All primary shells (bash, ash, tcsh)
Function	Recovers data from a damaged bzip2 compressed file.
Syntax	bzip2recover *file*

file	Specifies the file to recover.
File Name: `bzip2recover`	**Directory:** /usr/bin/ — **Type:** External
bzip2recover passwd.bz2	Recovers data from the specified bzip2 file.

c++

UNIX Shell:	All primary shells (bash, ash, tcsh)
Function	A complete compiler for C, C++, and assembler.
Syntax	c++ [options...] *files...*

-pass-exit-codes	Exits with the highest error code from a phase.
--help	Shows help information.
-dumpspecs	Shows all built in spec strings.
-dumpversion	Shows version information.
-dumpmachine	Shows the target processor for the compiler.
-print-search-dirs	Shows all search directories the compiler uses.
-print-libgcc-file-name	Shows the name of the compiler's search path.
-print-file-name=*library*	Shows the full path to the specified library.
-print-prog-name=*component*	Shows the full path to the specified compiler component.
-print-multi-directory	Shows the libgcc root directories.
-print-multi-lib	Shows mapping between command-line options and multiple library search directories.
-Wa,*options...*	Specifies assembler options to use. Must be separated by commas only.
-Wp,*options...*	Specifies preprocessor options to use. Must be separated by commas only.
-Wl,*options...*	Specifies linker options to use. Must be separated by commas only.
-Xlinker *arguments*	Specifies the arguments to pass to the linker.
-save-temps	Doesn't delete intermediate files.
-pipe	Uses pipes instead of intermediate files.
-time	Times each execution of each subprocess.
-specs=*file*	Overrides built-in specs with the contents of the specified file.
-B *directory*	Adds a directory to the compiler's search paths.
-b *machine*	Specifies the target processor.
-V *version*	Specifies the `gcc` version to use. (It must be installed.)
-v	Shows all commands executed by the compiler.
-E	Does a preprocess.
-S	Does a compile.
-c	Compiles and assembles.
-o *file*	Specifies the output file.
-x *language*	Specifies the language for the input files. Can either be C, C++, assembler, or none. **Note:"none" means like if the option has never been typed. Guesses the language.**
files...	Specifies the input files to use.
File Name: `c++`	**Directory:** /usr/bin/ — **Type:** External
Tip:	To get a list of usable sub-process options, type c++ -v --help.
c++ -o helloworld helloworld.cpp	Compiles the specified c++ file.

c++filt

UNIX Shell:	All primary shells (bash, ash, tcsh)
Function	Organizes the C++ symbols.
Syntax	c++filt [options...] *{ symbols... }*

-_	Removes the underscores in front of every name.
-s *method*	Specifies what method of mangling to use.
gnu	Decodes with the gnu method.
lucid	Decodes with the lucid method.

continued

arm --help --version *symbols...*	Decodes with the arm method. Shows help information. Shows version information. Specifies the symbols to organize. Other vice symbols are read from STDIN.		
File Name: `c++filt`	**Directory:** /usr/bin/	**Type:**	External

cancel

UNIX Shell: All primary shells (bash, ash, tcsh)

Function	Terminates a printer job.
Syntax	cancel [options...] *{ requestID }*

-P *printer* -D *options...* *requestID*	Specifies the destination printer that has the print job. Specifies a comma-separated list of debug options that are available for the program. Specifies the Identifier field vxalue or LPQ job number to cancel.		
File Name: `cancel`	**Directory:** /usr/bin/	**Type:**	External

cardctl

UNIX Shell: All primary shells (bash, ash, tcsh)

Function	Administers and controls the state of PCMCIA sockets.
Syntax	cardctl [-V] *subcommand { socket }* cardctl [options...] *scheme { name }*

-V -c *directory* -f *file* -s *file* *socket*	Shows version information. Specifies a directory containing the configuration database and scripts. Specifies a file to use for the current configuration scheme. Specifies the file to read the current configuration scheme from. Specifies the socket where the card is inserted.		
	The following are the subcommands that can be used:		
status config ident suspend resume reset eject insert scheme *{ name }*	Shows the current socket status flags. Shows the configuration information for the socket. Shows card identification information. Disables the socket and the power for that socket. Restores configuration and power to a socket. Resets the socket by a signal. Informs all client drivers that a card is ejected, and turns power off. Tells all client drivers that a card has been inserted. Shows the current configuration scheme. Specifies a new scheme and also configures for that scheme.		
File Name: `cardctl`	**Directory:** /sbin/	**Type:**	External

cardctl insert	Turns the card on.
cardctl ident	Shows the card identifications.

cardmgr

UNIX Shell: All primary shells (bash, ash, tcsh)

Function	Manages and monitors PCMCIA card sockets and does automatic installation/uninstallation.
Syntax	cardmgr [options...]

-c *directory* -d -f -q -m *directory* -o -p *file* -s *file* -v -V	Specifies the database to search for the card database and scripts. Follows the module dependencies when loading driver modules. Runs the command in the foreground until the installation is done. Doesn't beep when cards are inserted. Specifies the directory to search for loadable kernel modules in. Configures all current cards in one foreground session. Specifies a file to write the process ID of the cardmgr process to. Specifies the file to save current socket information in. Verbose mode. Shows more information. Shows version information.		
File Name: `cardmgr`	**Directory:** /sbin/	**Type:**	External

cardmgr -o	Configures all cards running in the foreground.

cc	UNIX Shell:	All primary shells (bash, ash, tcsh)
Function	The C and C++ Compiler for Linux.	
Syntax	cc [options...] *files...*	

Please see gcc for all the options.

File Name:	Directory:	Type:
cc	/usr/bin/	External

cdecl	UNIX Shell:	All primary shells (bash, ash, tcsh)
Function	Encodes or decodes C or C++ type declarations.	
Syntax	cdecl [options...] *{ files... } { statement }*	

-a	Uses the ANSI version of the C language (is default).
-p	Uses the pre-ANSI version of the C language.
-r	Uses the C version defined by the Ritchie PDP-11 compiler.
-+	Uses C++ language, not C language.
-i	Runs in interactive mode. Activates prompting, line editing, and line history.
-q	Quiets the prompt in interactive mode.
-c	Creates compatible C or C++ code as output.
-d	Shows debug information.
-D	Shows the `yacc` debug information.
-V	Shows version information and exit.
statement	Specifies a statement shown below to use, separated with a semicolon or a new line:
explain	Produces a verbose description from a C type description or cast.
declare	Composes a C type declaration from a verbose description.
cast	Composes a C type cast as might appear in an expression.
set	Enables the command line options to be set interactively.
help	Shows help information.
quit	Exits the program.
files...	Specifies the files to use.

File Name:	Directory:	Type:
cdecl	/usr/bin/	External

cdp, cdplay	UNIX Shell:	All primary shells (bash, ash, tcsh)
Function	Controls and plays audio CDs interactively or non interactively.	
Syntax	cdp [options...] [play *track*] cdplay [options...] [play *track*] [stop] [table]	

	The following are used with the non interactive version called `cdplay`:
-h	Shows help information.
-l	Waits for initiation, slow start.
-n	Disables auto play.
-s	Starts in silent mode.
play *track*	Plays from the specified track number.
stop	Stops the music.
table	Shows the CD table of contents from database.
	The following are the numpad functions for the interactive mode or `cdp`:
9	Plays the CD.
8	Pauses/resumes the CD.
7	Stops the CD.
6	Takes you to the next song on the CD.
5	Replays the CD.
4	Replays the previous song on the CD.
3	Goes forward 15 seconds.
2	Stops immediately.
1	Goes backward 15 seconds.
0	Stops slowly.
.	Shows help information.
enter	Edits the current song.

continued

a	Edits the artist name.
c	Edits the CD name.
play *track*	Plays from the specified track number.
File Name: `cdp`	**Directory:** /usr/bin/ **Type:** External

cdparanoia

UNIX Shell: All primary shells (bash, ash, tcsh)

Function	Reads audio tracks from a CD-ROM drive that is `CDDA` compatible.
Syntax	cdparanoia [options...] *span { file }*

-v	Autosenses and reads process in verbose mode.
-q	Disables process information or error information during the read process.
-e	Sends the progress information to STDERR.
-V	Shows version information.
-Q	Finds the CD-ROM and shows the CD-ROM table of contents.
-s	Finds a CD-ROM drive even if the /dev/cdrom link already exists.
-h	Shows help information.
-p	Shows raw headerless 16-bit PCM data in host byte order.
-r	Shows raw headerless 16-bit PCM data in LSB first byte order.
-R	Shows raw headerless 16-bit PCM data in MSB first byte order.
-w	Shows RIFF WAV format (LSB first byte order) (is default).
-f	Shows Apple AIFF format (MSB first byte order).
-a	Shows Apple AIFF-C format (MSB first byte order).
-B	Splits the output into multiple files at the track limits in a Cdda2wav-style batch.
-c	Handles the drive as a small endian device, ignores a CD-ROM that misreports itself.
-C	Same as -c but treats the drive as a large endian device.
-n *number*	Specifies number of sectors to read for the back-end interface to do atomic reads.
-d *device*	Forces the back-end interface to read from device instead of the first one it finds.
-g *device*	Used with -d to give total control in setting the SCSI and generic CD-ROMs separately.
-S *number*	Specifies the read rate of the CD drive (if supported).
-t *number*	Forces the entire LBA disc addressing to shift by the given amount.
-T	Corrects for CD-ROMs that attempt to incorrectly report track/sector values.
-Z	Disables all of the data correction and verification features.
-Y	Disables the intra-read data verification function.
-X	Aborts reading a track if it is corrupt or damaged.
--	Separates between a number used in the command from an option flag (see example).
span	Specifies a track number or subsections to read.
file	Specifies the output filename.
File Name: `cdparanoia`	**Directory:** /usr/bin/ **Type:** External
cdparanoia -- "-3"	Extracts the beginning of the disc up to track 3.
cdparanoia -B	Extracts the entire disk and puts each track in a different file.

cdrecord

UNIX Shell: All primary shells (bash, ash, tcsh)

Function	Records data or audio to a CD-ROM with the specified CD recorder.
Syntax	cdrecord [options...] dev=*device* [trackoptions...] *tracks...*

-v	Increases the verbose level by one.
-V	Increases the verbose level of the SCSI command transport by one.
-debug	Shows debug information.
-force	Continues to write even if some errors occurs.
-dummy	The dummy mode. Makes all the burn processes except write to the CD-ROM.
-dao	Enables the disk at once mode. Works with MMC drives that uses session at once.
-multi	Creates a multi session CD-ROM. (The CD-ROM is written in the XA mode 2 if -multi is used.)
-msinfo	Gets multisession information for `mkisofs`.
-toc	Shows the table of content of the CD-ROM.
-atip	Shows the absolute time in pregroove information of a CD recordable.
-fix	Fixates the media.
-nofix	Doesn't fixate the media when done writing the tracks.

continued

-waiti	Waits until input comes from STDIN before opening the SCSI driver.
-load	Loads the CD-ROM from a tray loading mechanism.
-eject	Ejects the CD-ROM when done.
speed=*speed*	Specifies the writing speed in numbers.
blank=*type*	Blanks a CD-RW disk with the blanking type specified. These can't be combined:
all	Erases the entire disk.
fast	Removes the PMA, the TOC and the pregap from the disk.
track	Removes a track.
unreserve	Unreserves a reserved track.
trtail	Removes the tail of a track.
unclose	Uncloses the latest session.
session	Erases the last session.
fs=*memory*	Specifies the FIFO memory size to use when buffering for real-time writes.
timeout=*seconds*	Specifies the SCSI command timeout (default is 40 seconds).
driver=*name*	Specifies what driver to use. If help is specified as the driver, drivers are listed.
driveropts=*options*	Specifies driver options on a comma-separated list. Use help option to show options.
-checkdrive	Checks whether the current drive is supported by the driver, then exits with code 0.
-prcap	Shows the SCSI-3 drive capabilities.
-inq	Shows drive information.
-scanbus	Finds SCSI devices and shows them on the screen.
-reset	Resets the CD recorder SCSI bus.
-ignsize	Doesn't care about the size of the medium.
-useinfo	Overwrites audio options with `*.inf` files.
defpregap=*gap*	Specifies the pre-gap size to use for all tracks except the first track.
-packet	Enables the packet writing mode.
pktsize=*size*	Specifies the packet size to use.
-noclose	Doesn't close track when done with it. This is used only when -packet is used.
mcn=*number*	Specifies the media catalog number to use on the CD.
	There are two ways to specify which device to use when writing:
dev=*scsibus,target,lun*	Specifies the SCSI bus, target and lun to use to get to the device.
dev=*device*	Specifies the name device to use.
	The following options are track-specific:
isrc=*number*	Specifies the International Standard Recording Number for the next track.
index=*list*	Specifies where the next track starts. Uses a comma-separated list starting with 0.
-audio	Tracks are written in CD-DA audio format.
-swab	Uses byte-swapped audio data when burning audio CD-ROMs.
-data	Tracks are written in CD-ROM mode 1 format. (The file systems ISO-9660 or Rock Ridge works with –data.)
-mode2	Tracks are written in CD-ROM mode 2 format.
-xa1	Tracks are written in CD-ROM XA mode 1 format.
-xa2	Tracks are written in CD-ROM XA mode 2 format.
-cdi	Tracks will be written in CDI format.
-isosize	Writes the next track in the ISO-9660 file system size.
-pad	Appends 15 empty sectors to the end of the tracks.
padsize=*sectors*	Specifies the number of empty sectors to add to the next track.
-nopad	Doesn't append any empty sectors to the following tracks.
-shorttrack	Disables the minimum length limit for the tracks. The minimum length is four seconds.
-noshorttrack	Enables the minimum length limit for the tracks.
pregap=*size*	Specifies a pre-gap size to use between the tracks.
-preemp	Marks any following audio tracks with a 50/15 µsec preemphasis sampled stamp.
-nopreemp	Specifies the following audio tracks have been mastered with linear data.
tsize=*size*	Specifies the next tracks raw disk size.
tracks...	Specifies tracks to write.

continued

File Name:	`cdrecord`	**Directory:**	/usr/bin/	**Type:**	External
Note:	To get IDE writing devices to work, you must compile SCSI generic support into the kernel.				

cdrecord -force speed=4 dev=0,4,0 debian-2.2.iso	Writes the specified ISO file to the device on specified SCSI bus and target.
cdrecord -v -dummy speed=8 dev=1,0,5 -data windows.iso	Fakes a write.

cfdisk

UNIX Shell: All primary shells (bash, ash, tcsh)

Function	Controls and alters partitions on hard disk drives by use of interactive menus.
Syntax	cfdisk [options...] *{ device }*

-a	Highlights the current partition with an arrow curser.
-c *number*	Specifies the number of cylinders and overrides the BIOS disk geometry information.
-g	Gets a geometry from the partition table and overrides the disk driver geometry.
-h	Specifies the number of heads and overrides the BIOS disk geometry information.
-P *format*	Shows the partition table in the specified format. Use one of the following formats:
r	Prints the raw data format just as it would be written to a disk.
s	Prints the partition table in sector order format.
t	Prints the partition table in raw format.
-s	Specifies the number of sectors and overrides the BIOS disk geometry information.
-v	Shows version information.
-z	Starts without reading the partition table — useful for repartition of the whole disk.
	The following are the command keys to use in the interactive mode:
b	Selects the primary bootable partition.
d	Deletes and converts the current partition into free space.
g	Alters the disk geometry, cylinders, heads, or sectors per track. Use with caution.
h	Shows help information.
m	Maximizes the disk usage of the current partition.
n	Creates a new partition from free space.
p	Shows the partition table in the specified format: r, s, or t, as in -P.
q	Exits without executing.
t	Alters the type of partition to create.
u	Alters the way to show the partitions: megabytes, sectors and cylinders.
device	Specifies the device name for the hard drive (default is /dev/hda).

File Name:	`cfdisk`	**Directory:**	/usr/sbin/	**Type:**	External

cfdisk –z	Starts cfdisk with no partition table.
cfdisk -P r /dev/hdb	Shows partition information in raw data format.

chage

UNIX Shell: All primary shells (bash, ash, tcsh)

Function	Alters or shows the user password expiry information for the specified user.
Syntax	chage [options...] *user*

-d *lastday*	Specifies the number of days (since Jan 1 1970) since the password was last changed.
-E *expiredate*	Specifies the number of days (since Jan 1 1970) before the password will expire. (The -d and -E options can also be specified as YYYY-MM-DD.)
-I *inactivedays*	Specifies the number of days of inactivity after expiration before the account locks.
-m *mindays*	Specifies the minimum number of days between password changes.
-M *maxdays*	Specifies the maximum number of days that the password is valid.
-W *warndays*	Specifies the number of days of warning before password expires.
-l *user*	Shows when the specified user's password or account expires.
user	Specifies the name of the user.

File Name:	`chage`	**Directory:**	/usr/bin/	**Type:**	External
Bug:	There's a Y2K bug in the program. The quick and dirty fix is to enter never instead of a proper date as argument.				

chage -l Guy	Shows when user Guy's password and account expires.
chage -I 200 Guy	Locks user Guy's account after 200 days of inactivity.

charset

UNIX Shell: A shell (ash, bsh)

Function	Changes one of the two slots for character sets.
Syntax	charset [-v] *slot charset*

-v	Verbose mode. Shows more information.
slot	Specifies the slot to use. Can be G0 or G1.
charset	Specifies the character set to use. (Available character sets are cp437, iso01, vt100, user, or an acm name.)

File Name:	`charset`	**Directory:**	/usr/bin/	**Type:**	Script

charset G1 vt100	Change character set in slot G1 to vt100.

chat

UNIX Shell: All primary shells (bash, ash, tcsh)

Function	Controls a conversation automatically between two computers over a modem connection.
Syntax	chat [options...] *{ script }*

-f *file*	Specifies a chat script file to use.
-t *timeout*	Specifies a timeout to use when waiting to receive a specified string.
-r *file*	Specifies a file to use as the reporting file where REPORT output goes to.
-e	Writes output that comes from the modem to STDERR.
-E	Allows standard environment variable substitution in chat scripts.
-v	Verbose mode. Shows more information to the `syslog`.
-V	Verbose mode. Shows more information to STDERR.
-s	Shows messages that -v produces to STDERR.
-S	Disable the use of `syslog`.
-T *phonenumber*	Specifies a phone number to use when sending a \T substitution metacharacter.
-U *phonenumber*	Specifies a phone number to use when sending a \U substitution metacharacter.
script	The chat script on one line, instead of having the script in a chat script file.

File Name:	`chat`	**Directory:**	/usr/sbin/	**Type:**	External

chattr

UNIX Shell: All primary shells (bash, ash, tcsh)

Function	Alters the file attributes on a Linux second extended file system.
Syntax	chattr [options...] *{ mode } files...*

-R	Alters the attributes recursively through the directory.
-V	Verbose mode. Shows more information.
-v *version*	Specifies the file system version name.
	The following are the different modes that can be specified:
A	Does no update to the access time when the file is altered.
S	Writes the alterations synchronously to the disk.
a	Allows only appending of data to the file, no deleting.
c	Compresses the file after the execution.
i	Blocks the file from modification of any sort, including writing to the file.
s	Writes the blocks from the deleted file back to disk.
u	Saves the contents of the deleted file.
d	Leaves the file out of a backup run with dump. (A + adds, a - deletes, and an = makes the attribute the only one.)
files...	Specifies the file or files to act upon.

File Name:	`chattr`	**Directory:**	/usr/bin/	**Type:**	External

Note:	No attributes are set when a file is created. The command `lsattr` lists file attributes.

chattr -R +c ucg_files	Makes the kernel compress directory ucg_files.
chattr =i ucg_secrets	Disables modification of file ucg_secrets, and delete all other attributes.

checkalias

UNIX Shell:	A shell (ash, bsh)
Function	Shows information about mail aliases.
Syntax	checkalias *aliases...*

aliases...	The alias or aliases to show information about, separate aliases with a comma.
File Name: `checkalias`	**Directory:** /usr/bin/ — **Type:** Script

checkpc

UNIX Shell:	All primary shells (bash, ash, tcsh)
Function	Administers information about entries in the `printcap` database.
Syntax	checkpc [options...]

-a	Specifies no accounting files should be created.
-c	Shows verbose configuration information.
-f	Creates and fix files and permissions.
-l	Doesn't create a log file.
-p	Shows verbose printcap information.
-r	Deletes junk or job files older than age specified with the -A option.
-s	Doesn't create any filter status files.
-A *date*	Shows only job files or junk older than the specified date.
-D *debugflags*	Runs in debug mode with the specified flags. See the LPRng HOWTO for details.
-V	Verbose mode. Shows more information.
-P *Printer*	Specifies a printer to run the command on.
-t *size*	Specifies the size in KB or MB to truncate log files to.
File Name: `checkpc`	**Directory:** /usr/sbin/ — **Type:** External
checkpc -t 10K	Truncates all log and accounting files to 10KB.

chfn

UNIX Shell:	All primary shells (bash, ash, tcsh)
Function	Changes your finger information.
Syntax	chfn [options...] { *user* }

-f *fullname*	Specifies your real name.
-h *phone*	Specifies your home phone number.
-o *room*	Specifies your office room number.
-p *phone*	Specifies your office phone number.
-u	Shows help information.
-v	Shows version information.
user	Specifies the user to change finger information for.
File Name: `chfn`	**Directory:** /usr/bin/ — **Type:** External
chfn	Starts the interactive mode.
chfn -f Johanna	Changes your real name.

chkconfig

UNIX Shell:	All primary shells (bash, ash, tcsh)
Function	Administers runlevel information for system services.
Syntax	chkconfig [options...] *name* [on | off | reset]

--add	Specifies a new service to add for management.
--del	Deletes the specified service from management.
--list { *name* }	Shows information about all of the specified services known by the command.
--levels *levels...*	Specifies the related run levels for an operation. [0, 1, 2, 3, 5, 6 on Red Hat].
on	Causes the specified service to start in the run levels being changed.
off	Causes the specified service to stop in the run levels being changed.
reset	Resets the startup information for the service according to the init script in use.
name	Specifies the name of the service to act upon or to add.
File Name: `chkconfig`	**Directory:** /sbin/ — **Type:** External

continued

Tip:	An excellent tool that relieves you from the tedious task of renaming the various links in the `/etc/rc.d` directory hierarchy.
chkconfig –list	Lists status of all available services.
chkconfig --level 3 ypbind on	Activates service `ypbind` in run level 3.

chkfontpath

UNIX Shell: All primary shells (bash, ash, tcsh)

Function	Configures the directories in the X font server path.				
Syntax	chkfontpath [options...]				
--add *directory*	Adds a directory to the path.				
--remove *directory*	Removes a directory from the path.				
--list	Shows current font path. Lists is also the default when no option is specified.				
--help	Shows help information.				
File Name: `chkfontpath`	**Directory:**	/usr/sbin/		**Type:**	External
chkfontpath --add /usr/share/fonts/default/TrueType	Adds the specified directory to your font path.				
chkfontpath --remove /usr/X11R6/lib/X11/fonts/Speedo	Removes the specified directory from font path.				

chpasswd

UNIX Shell: All primary shells (bash, ash, tcsh)

Function	Updates the passwords for a group of users with name and password pairs from STDIN.				
Syntax	chpasswd [-e]				
-e	Specifies the input is in encrypted form.				
File Name: `chpasswd`	**Directory:**	/usr/sbin/		**Type:**	External
Note:	The name/password pairs must be in the form username:password, where the named user already exists.				
chpasswd < passwordlist	Reads names and passwords from the file passwordlist.				
chpasswd -e < passwords	Reads names and passwords from the encrypted file passwords.				

chsh

UNIX Shell: All primary shells (bash, ash, tcsh)

Function	Changes your login shell.				
Syntax	chsh [options...] { *user* }				
-l	Shows the shells listed in `/etc/shells`.				
-s *shell*	Specifies the login shell to use - full path required.				
-u	Shows help information.				
-v	Shows version information.				
user	Specifies the user to change login shell for.				
File Name: `chsh`	**Directory:**	/usr/bin/		**Type:**	External
chsh -s /bin/csh root	Changes the shell for user root to csh.				

chvt

UNIX Shell: All primary shells (bash, ash, tcsh)

Function	Changes foreground virtual screen.				
Syntax	chvt *ttynumber*				
ttynumber	Specifies what tty that should be the foreground screen.				
File Name: `chvt`	**Directory:**	/usr/bin/		**Type:**	External
chvt 4	Makes `/dev/tty4` the foreground terminal.				

ci

UNIX Shell: All primary shells (bash, ash, tcsh)

Function	Stores revisions in the specified revision control system files.
Syntax	ci [options...] *files...*
	Doesn't put a space between the option and its value.
-r{ *revision* }	Specifies the file revision to check in. (To release a lock and remove the working file, don't specify a revision.)
-l{ *revision* }	Leaves a locked copy of the next file revision.

continued

-u{ *revision* }	Does the same things as -l does except that the working file is left read-only.
-f{ *revision* }	Creates a new revision even if there have been no changes from the one before.
-k{ *revision* }	Goes through the working file to gather file information and create a new revision.
-q{ *revision* }	Doesn't show diagnostic messages while checking a revision.
-i{ *revision* }	Creates and stores an RCS file. If the RCS file already exists, a warning will be shown.
-j{ *revision* }	Creates and stores an RCS file. If the RCS file doesn't exist, a warning will be shown.
-I{ *revision* }	Enables the interactive mode. Asks questions even when STDIN isn't a terminal.
-d{ *date* }	Specifies a date to use when storing. Or, use the time of last modification.
-M{ *revision* }	Sets the modification time for the working file to the one retrieved.
-m*message*	Specifies a message string to use with all revisions that are checked in.
-n*name*	Specifies a name to give the number of the checked-in revision.
-N*name*	Works as -n, but the previous name is overwritten.
-s*state*	Specifies a state to set to the checked-in revisions (default is Exp).
-t*file*	Overwrites the file description with the specified file.
-t-*string*	Overwrites the file description with the specified string.
-T	Uses the modification time for the latest revision when creating the RCS file.
-w*username*	Specifies what username to use in the authors field.
-V{ *version* }	Shows version information. Or specifies a version to emulate. Version can be 3,4 or 5
-x*suffixes*	The RCS files have the specified suffixes. Suffixes separated with a /.
-z*zone*	Specifies what time zone to use when setting the date format.
files...	Specifies RCS files to use.
File Name: `ci`	**Directory:** /usr/bin/ **Type:** External
ci -r2 -Nprogress none.c	Makes a revision level 2 and names that Progress.

cjpeg

UNIX Shell: All primary shells (bash, ash, tcsh)

Function	Creates a JPEG/JFIF image from a specified image file or from STDIN.
Syntax	cjpeg [options...] { *file* }

-quality *number*	Specifies the image quality, 0-100 (default is 75).
-grayscale	Takes a color input and creates a monochrome JPEG file.
-optimize	Optimizes the entropy encoding parameters.
-progressive	Creates a JPEG file in increasing (progressive) quality.
-targa	Specifies the input is in Targa format.
-dct int	Uses integer DCT method. Also (is default).
-dct fast	Uses fast integer DCT method.
-dct float	Uses floating-point DCT method.
-restart *number*	Emits a JPEG restart marker every specified MCU rows, or blocks if B is attached.
-smoot *number*	Smooths the input for dithering noise elimination, n = 1-100.
-maxmemory *number*	Specifies the max memory usage in KB or MB. 4m = 4 megabytes.
-outfile *file*	Saves the output in the specified file.
-verbose	Verbose mode. Shows more information.
-debug	Shows debug information.
-baseline	Generates baseline-compatible quantization tables.
-qtables *file*	Specifies a file with quantization tables to use.
-qslots *number*	Specifies the quantization table for each color component.
-sample *HxV*	Set JPEG sampling factors for each color component.
-scans *file*	Specifies a text file with a scan script to use.
file	Specifies the input image file.
File Name: `cjpeg`	**Directory:** /usr/bin/ **Type:** External
Note:	Supported formats are PPM, PGM, BMP, Targa, and RLE if the URT library is available.
cjpeg -quality 60 pic.ppm > pic.jpg	Compresses the PPM file foo.ppm with a quality factor of 60 and saves the output as foo.jpg.

clockdiff

UNIX Shell: All primary shells (bash, ash, tcsh)

Function	Measures clock difference between computers with the resolution of 1 msec.
Syntax	clockdiff [option] *address*

-o	Uses `ICMP ECHO` with timestamps IP option.

continued

-o1	Uses three-node timestamp.		
address	Specifies the IPaddress or hostname of the computer to compare time with.		
File Name: `clockdiff`	**Directory:** /usr/sbin/	**Type:**	External

co

UNIX Shell: All primary shells (bash, ash, tcsh)

Function	Checks out a revision from a RCS file and stores it in the corresponding working file.
Syntax	co [options...] *files...*

-r *{ revision }*	Retrieves the latest revision that is less than or equal to the specified number.		
-l *{ revision }*	Retrieves the latest revision and also locks it for the caller.		
-u *{ revision }*	Retrieves the latest revision and unlocks it if it is locked by the caller.		
-f *{ revision }*	Overwrites the working file.		
-kkv	Creates keyword strings in default form.		
-kkvl	Creates keyword strings and also inserts locker's name if the revision is locked.		
-kk	Creates only the names in keyword strings.		
-ko	Recreates the old keyword string and doesn't append the new string to the file.		
-kb	Creates a binary image of the old keyword string.		
-kv	Creates only the values for keyword strings.		
-p *{ revision }*	Shows the revision on STDOUT instead of saving it to a file.		
-q *{ revision }*	Suppresses all output of diagnostic messages.		
-I *{ revision }*	Starts the interactive mode.		
-d*date*	Stores the latest revision less than or equal to the specified date.		
-M *{ rev }*	Specifies the modification date to be the same as the revision date.		
-s*state*	Retrieves the latest revision with the specified state.		
-T	Keeps the modification time even if the file is changed.		
-w *{ login }*	Retrieves the latest revision with the specified login.		
-j*list*	Creates a new version containing the revisions in the specified list.		
-V	Shows version information.		
-V*number*	Specifies a version or RCS to emulate - 3, 4 or 5.		
-x*suffixes*	Specifies the suffixes for to characterizing the RCS files.		
-z*zone*	Specifies a time zone to show the date in (default is an empty zone).		
files...	Specifies the RCS file.		
File Name: `co`	**Directory:** /usr/bin/	**Type:**	External

codepage

UNIX Shell: All primary shells (bash, ash, tcsh)

Function	Extracts code pages from a file.
Syntax	codepage *file number* [options...]

-c	Specifies the input file is a single code page.		
-L	Shows header information.		
-l	Shows all code pages contained in the file specified.		
-a	Extract all code pages from the file.		
number	Extracts code page with number, three digits, from the file.		
file	Specifies the file that contains the code page.		
File Name: `codepage`	**Directory:** /usr/bin/	**Type:**	External
codepage ega.cpi 850	Extracts codepage 850 from `ega.cpi` and stores it in `850.cp`.		

colcrt

UNIX Shell: All primary shells (bash, ash, tcsh)

Function	Removes underlines or shows them on new lines filtering the `nroff` file for a CRT preview.
Syntax	colcrt [options...] *{ files... }*

-2	Shows all underlines lines on own rows.
-	Removes underline from input.
files...	Specifies a file to act upon.

continued

File Name:	colcrt	**Directory:**	/usr/bin/	**Type:**	External
Tip:	Use terminals that can't show underlined text.				
colcrt - nroff.file > nounderline.txt		Removes underlines from the nroff.file.			

colrm

UNIX Shell: All primary shells (bash, ash, tcsh)

Function	Deletes selected columns from a file reading from STDIN to STDOUT.
Syntax	colrm *{ startcolumn } { endcolumn }*

startcolumn	Specifies where to start in the file.
endcolumn	Specifies where to end in the file.

File Name:	colrm	**Directory:**	/usr/bin/	**Type:**	External
colrm 3 7		Deletes all columns starting with column 3 up to and including column 7 from all lines in the file.			

column

UNIX Shell: All primary shells (bash, ash, tcsh)

Function	Formats input into multiple columns.
Syntax	column [options...] *files...*

-c *count*	Formats the output for a screen with the specified number of columns.
-s *characters...*	Uses the specified set of characters as a column delimiter for the -t option.
-t	Creates a table from a determined number of columns or by use of the -s option.
-x	Fills the columns before the rows are filled.
files...	Specifies file to act on.

File Name:	column	**Directory:**	/usr/bin/	**Type:**	External
column -x -c 80 file		Fills the columns before filling the rows.			

combine

UNIX Shell: All primary shells (bash, ash, tcsh)

Function	Combines images together with new image.
Syntax	combine [options...] *image1 image2 { mask } combined*

-blend *value*	Blends two images together with a given percentage.
-cache *memory*	Specifies maximum amount of RAM memory to use (default is 80MB).
-colors *value*	Specifies the maximum number of colors in the image.
-colorspace *value*	Specifies the color space to use.
-comment *comment*	Adds comment to the image (default is the image filename).
-compose *type*	Specifies the image composition type. **Note:Type is one of: over, In, Out, Atop, Xor, Plus, Minus, Add, Subtract,** Difference, Bumpmap, Bumpmap, Replace, ReplaceRed, ReplaceGreen, ReplaceBlue and ReplaceMatte.
-compress *type*	Specifies the type of compression.
-density *WxH*	Specifies the resolution in dpi of the picture (default is 72 dpi).
-displace *HxV*	Specifies the horizontal and vertical scale for a displacement map.
-display *host:displ*	Specifies the display to use.
-dispose *method*	Specifies the GIF disposal method
-dither	Applies Floyd/Steinberg error diffusion to the image.
-font *name*	The font to use for normal text.
-geometry *WxH*	Specifies the with and height of the image.
-gravity *type*	Specifies the direction image gravitates.
-interlace *type*	Specifies the interlacing scheme.
-label *name*	Sets a label to the image.
-matte	Stores matte channel.
-monochrome	Creates a black-and-white image.
-negate	Creates a negative image.
-page *size*	Specifies the size of the image.
-quality *value*	Specifies the compression level for JPEG/MIFF/PNG.
-scene *NR*	Specifies image scene number.
-size *HxW*	Specifies the size of the image.
-stegano *offset*	Hides a watermark inside the image at offset pixel from the beginning.

continued

-stereo	Combines two images to create a stereo anaglyph.
-tile	Repeats composite operation across image.
-treedepth *value*	Sets the tree depth for the color reduction algorithm.
-verbose	Verbose mode. Shows more information.
image1	Specifies the first image to use.
image2	Specifies the second image to use.
mask	Specifies an image mask to use.
combined	Specifies the name to save the new image to.
File Name: `combine`	**Directory:** /usr/X11R6/bin/ **Type:** External

comp

UNIX Shell: All primary shells (bash, ash, tcsh)

Function	Creates a mail message with a preconfigured form.
Syntax	comp [+*folder*] { *message* } [options...]

+*folder*	Specifies a message folder containing a form to use for the new message.
-form *file*	Specifies a form file to use other than components in the nmh directory.
-noedit	Suppresses the initial edit.
-use	Tells comp to continue editing an already started message.
-file *file*	Specifies the file to use as the message draft.
-draftfolder +*folder*	Starts the nmh draft folder facility.
-draftmessage *message*	Starts the nmh draft folder facility.
-editor *editor*	Specifies the initial editor to use.
-nowhatnowproc	Disables the whatnow program.
-whatnowproc program	Prompts for confirmation to send.
-version	Shows version information.
-help	Shows help information.
message	Specifies a message containing a form to use for the new message.
File Name: `comp`	**Directory:** /usr/bin **Type:** External
comp -editor ed -file ucg_draft	Uses ucg_draft as template.

compgen

UNIX Shell: Bash shell (bash)

Function	Generates possible completion matches for the specified word according to the option.
Syntax	compgen [option] { *word* }

-a	Uses an alias for completion.
-b	Uses internal commands for completion.
-c	Uses command names for completion.
-d	Uses directory names for completion.
-f	Uses filenames for completion.
-j	Uses jobs for completion.
-k	Uses reserved keywords for completion.
-v	Uses variable names for completion.
-u	Uses usernames for completion.
-A *action*	Specifies how a completion is done.
aliases	Uses an alias for completion.
arrayvar	Uses an array variable name.
binding	Uses bindings (editor commands).
command	Uses command names.
disable	Uses name for disabled internal commands.
enable	Uses names for enabled internal commands.
export	Uses names of exported variables.
file	Uses filenames.
functions	Uses names of functions.
helptopic	Uses names of help topics.
hostnames	Uses hostnames from the file specified in the file $HOSTFILE.
job	Uses jobs.

continued

keywords	Uses reserved keywords.
running	Uses names of running jobs.
setopt	Uses valid arguments for the -o option for the set command.
shopt	Uses shell option names as used by shopt.
signal	Uses signal names.
stopped	Uses names for stopped jobs.
user	Uses usernames.
variable	Uses variable names.
-G *pattern*	Uses the pattern to generate possible completions.
-W *list*	Specifies a list of names to use for completion.
-C *command*	Specifies a command to use to generate the list of possible names.
-F *function*	Specifies a function to use to generate the list of possible names.
-X *pattern*	Specifies a pattern to use to for filename expansion.
-P *prefix*	Adds prefix to the beginning of each possible completion.
-S *suffix*	Adds suffix to the end of each possible completion.
word	Specifies the word to show completion for.

compgen -A file f	Shows any files that start with "f".

complete

UNIX Shell: Bash shell (bash), TC shell (tcsh)

Function	Declares how a command should be completed. Use the Tab key to perform the completion on the command line.
Syntax	bash: complete [option] *names...* tcsh: complete *{ command }* tcsh: complete *command word/pattern/list*[*:select*]/*{ suffix/*]

bash	
-p	Shows current complete.
-r	Removes any completion for specified names, or all if no name is specified.
-a	Uses an alias for completion.
-b	Uses internal commands for completion.
-c	Uses command names for completion.
-d	Uses directory names for completion.
-f	Uses filenames for completion.
-j	Uses jobs for completion.
-k	Uses reserved keywords for completion.
-v	Uses variable names for completion.
-u	Uses usernames for completion.
-A *action*	Specifies how a completion is done.
aliases	Uses an alias for completion.
arrayvar	Uses an array variable name.
binding	Uses bindings (editor commands).
builtin	Uses internal commands.
command	Uses command names.
directory	Uses directory names.
disable	Uses name for disabled internal commands.
enable	Uses names for enabled internal commands.
export	Uses names of exported variables.
file	Uses filenames.
functions	Uses names of functions.
helptopic	Uses names of help topics.
hostnames	Uses hostnames from the file specified in the file $HOSTFILE.
job	Uses jobs.
keywords	Uses reserved keywords.
running	Uses names of running jobs.
setopt	Uses valid arguments for the -o option for the set command.
shopt	Uses shell option names as used by shopt.
signal	Uses signal names.
stopped	Uses names for stopped jobs.

continued

User	Uses usernames.
variable	Uses variable names.
-G *pattern*	Uses the pattern to generate possible completions.
-W *list*	Specifies a list of names to use for completion.
-C *command*	Specifies a command to use to generate the list of possible names.
-F *function*	Specifies a function to use to generate the list of possible names.
-X *pattern*	Specifies a pattern to use to for filename expansion.
-P *prefix*	Adds a prefix to the beginning of each possible completion.
-S *suffix*	Adds a suffix to the end of each possible completion.
names...	Specifies a command name to make completion for the arguments.
tcsh	
command	Specifies the command to set up a completion for, or show a completion for.
word	Specifies which word that is relative to the current is to be completed.
c	Specifies that pattern must match the beginning of current word.
C	Is like c, but includes pattern when completing the word.
n	Specifies that pattern must match the beginning of previous word.
N	Is like n, but matches the beginning of the word two before the current.
p	Specifies position-dependent match. Pattern is a numeric range.
pattern	Specifies the pattern to use.
list	Specifies the possible completions.
a	Uses aliases.
b	Uses bindings (editor commands).
c	Uses commands, internal or external.
C	Uses external commands that begin with the specified path.
d	Uses directories.
D	Uses directories that begin with the specified path.
e	Uses environment variables.
f	Uses filenames.
F	Uses filenames that begin with the specified path.
g	Uses group names.
j	Uses jobs.
l	Uses limits.
n	Doesn't use anything.
s	Uses shell variables.
S	Uses signals.
t	Uses plain text files.
T	Uses plain text files that begin with the specified path.
u	Uses usernames.
x	Is like n, but shows select when list-choices is used.
X	Uses completions.
$var	Uses word from the variable $var
(...)	Uses word from the specified list.
`*command*`	Uses word from the output from the specified command.
select	Specifies an extra pattern to use as a selection for the last three option above.
suffix	Specifies a single character to add to the completion.

complete chgrp 'p/1/g/'	Completes any group specified after chgrp. (tcsh)
complete kill 'c/-/S/'	Completes the signal for kill -signal. (tcsh)

conflict

UNIX Shell: All primary shells (bash, ash, tcsh)

Function	Reports conflicts between `nmh` and the mail transport system.
Syntax	conflict [options...] [*aliasfiles...*]

-mail *username*	Specifies which user to send the results to instead of sending it to STDOUT.
-search *directory*	Specifies a directory where to check for conflicts.
-version	Shows version information.
-help	Shows help information.

continued

aliasfiles...		Checks conflicts between aliases found in the specified alias file and maildrops. (The default alias file is /etc/nmh/MailAliases.)			
File Name:	`conflict`	**Directory:**	/usr/lib/nmh/	**Type:**	External

consolechars

UNIX Shell: All primary shells (bash, ash, tcsh)

Function	Changes console screen font, screenfont map, and / or application-charset map.
Syntax	consolechars [options...]

-h	Shows help information.
-V	Shows version information.
-v	Verbose mode. Shows more information.
-n	Doesn't change console state; no write on any file.
-1	Enables the G1 charset.
--tty=*device*	Specifies a console device for `ioctls`.
-f *fontfile*	Specifies file that contains the bitmap description `glyph` of characters.
-d	Loads a default font.
-m *file*	Loads a user-defined application-charset map (ACM) - saves current ACM.
-M	Saves the previous ACM can be saved to a file.
-u *sfm*	Loads a screen font map (SFM).
--force-no-sfm	Prevents loading an SFM when loading a font that contains one.
-U file	Saves current SFM into a file.
-k file	Species the SFM file to use as an SFM fallback table, to supplement the SFM.
-F file	Saves the old font in the preferred format.
--old-font-psf-with-sfm=*file*	Saves the old font in PSF format, with corresponding SFM.
--old-font-psf=*file*	Saves the old font in PSF format (PSF mode 0 or 1).
--old-font-raw=*file*	Saves the old font in RAW format.
-H *size*	Specifies which font size to use.

File Name:	`consolechars`	**Directory:**	/bin/	**Type:**	External
consolechars –1			Loads G1 chars.		
consoleshars -H 16 -f 161.cp			Loads font 161.cp with height 16.		

consolehelper

UNIX Shell: All primary shells (bash, ash, tcsh)

Function	Authenticates users via PAM and runs the program specified including any options the command may have.
Syntax	*program { options... }*

program	Specifies the program to be executed by consolehelper.
options...	Passes any options specific to the program specified.

File Name:	`consolehelper`	**Directory:**	/usr/bin	**Type:**	External
/usr/bin/shutdown			Runs /sbin/shutdown from consolehelper.		

consoletype

UNIX Shell: All primary shells (bash, ash, tcsh)

Function	Shows the screen (console) type that is currently connected to STDIN.
Syntax	consoletype

File Name:	`consoletype`	**Directory:**	/sbin/	**Type:**	External
Note:	For returned info: vt (/dev/tty*) is virtual terminal, serial (`/dev/ttyS*`) is serial console and pty is pseudo console.				

convert

UNIX Shell: All primary shells (bash, ash, tcsh)

Function	Converts image formats, colors, sizes, creates filter effects, rotations, sequences, and more.
Syntax	convert [options...] *inputfile { subfiles... } outputfile*

-adjoin	Combines images into a single multi-image file. For JPEGs, use +adjoin.
-antialias	Takes away the pixel aliasing.
-average	Averages an image sequence.
-blur *order*	Blurs an image with an odd order value from 3 to 31.
-border *size*	Puts a colored border around the image. See `X window` for details.
-bordercolor *color*	Specifies the color of the border. See `X window` for details.

continued

-box *color*	Specifies the annotation bounding box color. See -draw and `X window`
-cache *threshold*	Sets the max memory size to the pixel cache in megabytes (default is 80MB).
-charcoal *order*	Creates a charcoal look-alike drawing with an odd order value from 3 to 31.
-coalesce	Merges a sequence of images.
-colorize *value*	Colorizes an image. Specify the red, green, and blue value with slashes as r/g/b, in percent.
-colors *value*	Specifies the preferred number of colors in the image. Please see the option -quantize.
-colorspace *type*	Sets type: GRAY, OHTA, RGB, Transparent, XYZ, YCbCr, YIQ, YPbPr, YUV, or CMYK.
-comment *string*	Annotates an image with a comment.
-compress *type*	Sets compress type: None, BZip, Fax, Group4, JPEG, LZW, RunlengthEncoded, or Zip.
-contrast	Changes the image contrast. Use a - or + sign before the option.
-crop *values...*	Crops the image by percent or specified size. See `X window` for information.
-cycle *amount*	Shifts the image color map by the specified number of positions.
-deconstruct	Takes down an image sequence into the constituent parts.
-delay *time*	Shows the next image after the specified time in 1/1000ths of a second.
-density *size*	Specifies vertical and horizontal resolution in pixels of the image.
-depth *value*	Specifies the depth of the image by the number of bits in a pixel: 8 or 16.
-despeckle	Decreases the number of speckles in an image.
-display *host:display*[.screen]	Contacts the specified X server. See `X window` for details.
-dispose *method*	Specifies the GIF disposal method: 0 to 3.
-dither	Uses Floyd/Steinberg error diffusion on the image.
-draw *string*	Adds one or more graphic primitives to the image.
-edge *order*	Detects the edges of an image with an odd order value from 3 to 31.
-emboss *order*	Embosses the image with an odd order value from 3 to 31.
-enhance	Uses a digital filter to enhance a noisy image.
-equalize	Does histogram equalization on the image.
-fill *color*	Specifies the color to use when filling in the graphic primitives in option -draw.
-filter *type*	Specifies the filter type to use on a resize of an image. See -geometry.
-flip	Reflects the image scanlines vertically to create a mirror image.
-flop	Reflects the image scanlines horizontally to create a mirror image.
-font *name*	Specifies the font to use when doing a text annotation on an image.
-frame *values...*	Frames the image with an ornamental border. See `X window` for more information.
-fuzz *distance*	Specifies the distance within which the colors are considered alike.
-gamma *value*	Specifies the level of gamma correction, 0.8 to 2.3.
-gaussian *values...*	Uses a gaussian operator with a specified width and deviation to blur the image.
-geometry *values...*	Specifies the size or location of the image when encoding.
-gravity *type*	Specifies the direction of the annotating text. See `X window` for more information.
-implode *factor*	Implodes or explodes the image with a percentage factor: 0 to 99.9 or -99.9 to 0.
-intent *type*	Specifies the rendering intent to use on the image color.
-interlace *type*	Specifies the interlacing scheme: None, Line, Plane, or Partition (default is None).
-label *name*	Assigns a name to an image.
-layer *type*	Extracts the specified type of layer from the picture: Red, Green, Blue, or Matte.
-linewidth *value*	Specifies the width of a line. See -draw for more information.
-loop *iterations*	Adds Netscape loop extension to a GIF animation with the specified count of repeats.
-map *file*	Uses a set of colors from the specified image file.
-matte	Creates an opaque matte channel or stores the matte channel from the image.
-median *order*	Uses a median filter on the image with an odd value from 3 to 31.
-modulate *value*	Alters the brightness, saturation, and hue in percentages on an image.
-monochrome	Changes the image to black and white.
-morph	Does a morph alteration on an image sequence.
-mosaic	Creates a mosaic from an image sequence.
-negate	Changes every pixel to its complementary color (white becomes black and so forth).
+negate	Changes only the grayscale pixels to their complementary color on the image.
-noise order	Adds or decreases the noise in an image.
-normalize	Alters the image to span the full range of color values.
-opaque *color*	Uses the fill color instead of the specified color. See -fill for more information.
-page *values...*	Specifies the size and location of an image canvas.
-paint *radius*	Simulates an oil painting by replacing each pixel within a specified radius.

continued

-pointsize *value*	Specifies the point size of a PostScript font.
-preview *type*	Specifies the image preview type.
-profile *file*	Adds an ICC color or an IPTC newswire information profile to image.
+profile *profile*	Removes the specified profile. ICC or IPTC.
-quality *value*	Specifies the JPEG/MIFF/PNG compression level from 0 to 100 (default is 75).
-raise *size*	Creates a 3-D effect by lightening or dimming image edges.
-region *values...*	Specifies a part of the image to run the operations on.
-roll *values...*	Moves the image around it axis vertically or horizontally.
-rotate *degrees*	Rotates the image by use of the Paeth rotation: Ex -45< or -45>.
-sample *geometry*	Uses pixel sampling to scale the image.
-scene *value*	Specifies the image scene number.
-seed *value*	Specifies the pseudo-random number generator seed value.
-segment *values...*	Analyzes the histograms of the color components to segment an image.
-shade *azimuthxelevation*	Specifies the azimuth and elevation of a distant light source to shade the image.
-sharpen *order*	Sharpens an image with an odd value from 3 to 31.
-shear *degrees...*	Shears the image along the X or Y axis by a positive or negative shear angle.
-size *values...*	Specifies the width and height and offset of an image in pixels.
-solarize *factor*	Negates all pixels above the limit level, which can be from 0 to 99.9.
-spread *amount*	Disarranges the image pixels by random inside the specified neighborhood.
-stroke *color*	Specifies the color to use when stoking a graphic primitive. See -draw.
-swirl *degrees*	Rotates the image pixels around the center in the specified tightness.
-texture *filename*	Tiles the specified texture to the background.
-threshold *value*	Specifies a limit to the image colors.
-transparency *color*	Turns the specified color transparent in the image.
-treedepth *value*	Optimizes the tree depth for the color reduction algorithm - try 2 to 8.
-units *type*	Specifies the type of image resolution: Undefined, PixelsPerInch, PixelsPerCentimeter.
-verbose	Verbose mode. Shows more information.
-view *string*	Specifies the FlashPix viewing parameters.
-wave *values...*	Alters the image along a sine wave specified with amplitude and wavelength.
inputfile	Specifies the image to use as input. A - means to use STDIN.
{ subfiles... }	Specifies any subimages to the inputfile.
outputfile	Specifies the name of the output image. A - means to use STDOUT. (The extension .Z or .gz to an in or out file decompresses or compresses it.) Prepend the infile with at (@) to get a list of images in that file.

File Name:	`convert`	**Directory:**	/usr/X11R6/bin/	**Type:**	External
convert -size 800x600 pic.bmp pic.jpg		Converts `pic.bmp` to `pic.jpg` with the resolution 800 x 600.			
convert pic.bmp -quality 100 pic.jpg		Converts `pic.bmp` to `pic.jpg` with the best quality level.			

cproto

UNIX Shell: All primary shells (bash, ash, tcsh)

Function	Creates C function prototypes and converts function definitions.
Syntax	cproto [options...] *{ files... }*

-e	Marks every created prototype or declaration that has global scope with extern.
-f *style*	Specifies how to create function prototypes. Style is from 0 to 3.
-l	Creates a comment text for lint-library usage.
-c	Is used with -f 1 and -f 2 to create comments in prototypes.
-m	Creates a macro for every prototype.
-M *name*	Specifies a name of the macro that is generated to surround prototype with the -m.
-d	Doesn't define the prototype macro with the -m option.
-o *file*	Specifies the STDOUT file (default is STDOUT).
-O *file*	Specifies the STDERR file (default is STDERR).
-p	Doesn't use old style function definitions.
-q	Disables error message when cproto can't read from specified file with #include.
-s	Causes cproto to show static declarations, plus those with global scope.
-S	Causes cproto to only show static declarations.
-T	Copies type definitions from each file.
-v	Shows declarations for variables defined in source.
-x	Doesn't show procedures and variables marked with `extern`.

continued

-a	Converts function definitions from old style to ANSI C style.				
-t	Converts function definitions from ANSI C style to old style.				
-b	Writes function definitions in two ways (ANSI C and old style).				
-B *directive*	Specifies the conditional compilation directive.				
-P *template*	Specifies the output format for generated prototypes.				
-F *template*	Specifies the output format for function definitions.				
-C *template*	Sets the output format for function definitions with parameter commands to TEMPLATE.				
-D *name*[=*value*]	Passes specified name to the preprocessor, used to define symbols.				
-U *name*	Passes specified name to the preprocessor to remove those definitions.				
-I *directory*	Passes specified directory to preprocessor where #includes are.				
-E *cpp*	Pipes input files through a preprocessor to create prototypes.				
-E 0	Disables the C preprocessor.				
-V	Shows version information.				
files...	Specifies the C file (default is STDIN).				
File Name: `cproto`	**Directory:**	/usr/bin/		**Type:**	External
cproto -e -o used.cproto used.c	Creates prototypes for the functions and marks them with extern and outputs them to used.cproto.				

createdb

UNIX Shell: A shell (ash, bsh)

Function	Creates databases on a postgres server.
Syntax	createdb [options...] *name { description }*

-h *host*	Specifies the postgres server where you want to create the database.				
-p *port*	Specifies the port to connect to on the host.				
-U *username*	Specifies the username to connect as.				
-W	Prompts you for a password to use when you connect.				
-e	Shows the information that the postgres create procedure creates.				
-q	Doesn't show any response from the `createuser`.				
-D *datadir*	Specifies an alternate database location for the database installation.				
-E *encoding*	Specifies the character encoding for the database.				
name	Specifies the name of the database you want to create.				
description	Specifies a comment to the database you want to create.				
File Name: `createdb`	**Directory:**	/usr/bin/		**Type:**	Script
createdb ucgdatabase	Creates ucgdatabase on the default postgres server.				

createlang

UNIX Shell: A shell (ash, bsh)

Function	Adds new programming languages to the specified postgres database.
Syntax	createlang [options...] *{ langname } { databasename }*

-h *host*	Specifies the Postgres server to intstall the programming language to.				
-p *port*	Specifies port to connect to on the specified host.				
-U *username*	Specifies username to connect as.				
-W	Prompts you for a password to use when you connect.				
-d *databasename*	Specifies the database where you want to install the new programming language.				
-l	Shows a list of installed programming languages.				
-e	Shows the information the postgres create procedure generates.				
langname	Specifies the programming language to add to the postgres database.				
databasename	Specifies the database.				
File Name: `createlang`	**Directory:**	/usr/bin/		**Type:**	Script
createlang -h ucgdata -U ucguser -W -d LIST pltcl	Prompts you for a password and installs programming language pltcl to your database LIST.				

createuser

UNIX Shell:	A shell (ash, bsh)
Function	Creates users in a postgres database.
Syntax	createuser [options...] { *username* }

-h *host*	Specifies `postgres` server where you want to create the user.
-p *port*	Specifies port to connect with on the host.
-e	Shows the information that the postgres create procedure creates.
-q	Doesn't show any response from the `createuser`.
-d	Enables user permission to create databases.
-D	Disables user permission to create databases.
-a	Enables user permission to add users to the database.
-A	Disables user permission to add users to the database.
-P	Prompts for a password to assign to the user.
-i *uID*	Specifies user ID to assign with the new user.
username	Specifies the username to create.

File Name:	`createuser`	**Directory:**	/usr/bin/	**Type:**	Script

createuser -h ucgdata -e -P tempuser	Creates a user on ucgdata with username tempuser, prompts for the temp user's password.
createuser -d -A dobases	Creates a user called dobases who can create databases but not add users to the databases.

csplit

UNIX Shell:	All primary shells (bash, ash, tcsh)
Function	Splits whole or parts of a file into new files.
Syntax	csplit [options...] *file ACTIONS...*

-f *prefix*	Specifies a prefix for the created files.
-b *format*	Specifies the sprintf format for the splitted files (default is "%d").
-n *number*	Specifies how many digits to use as name for created files (default is 2 digits).
-k	Doesn't remove the previously created files if an error occurs.
-z	Removes empty output files.
-s	Doesn't show messages about file sizes.
--help	Shows help information.
--version	Shows version information.
ACTIONS...	The arguments for splitting the files. Offsets must begin with a + or -.
value	Copies up to but not include the specified line number.
/REGEXP/{ *offset* }	Copies up to but not include matching lines.
%REGEXP%{ *offset* }	Skips to but not include a matching line.
{*value*}	Repeats the previous pattern a specified number of times.
{*}	Repeats the previous pattern as many times as possible.
file	Specifies the file to split.

File Name:	`csplit`	**Directory:**	/usr/bin	**Type:**	External

csplit ucg_txt 1000 {*}	Splits the file ucg_txt into as many 1,000-line files as possible.
csplit ucg_db {4}	Splits the file ucg_db in four equally large files.

ctrlaltdel

UNIX Shell:	All primary shells (bash, ash, tcsh)
Function	Sets the function of the Ctrl+Alt+Del buttons used when rebooting a computer.
Syntax	ctrlaltdel option

hard	Sets the computer to do a hard reboot, without synching the disks.
soft	Sets the computer to do a soft reset after synching the disks.

File Name:	`ctrlaltdel`	**Directory:**	/sbin	**Type:**	External

cvs	UNIX Shell:	All primary shells (bash, ash, tcsh)
Function	A version control and logging system for files or directory tree structures including any versionable files.	
Syntax	cvs [options...] *{ command }* [options...]	

	These global options may be used with most cvs commands:
-H *command*	Shows help information for cvs only, or for the specified command.
-Q	Generates output for real problems quiet mode.
-q	Outputs everything except information messages semi quiet mode.
-b *directory*	Specifies the full path to the directory that contains the RSC bind programs.
-d *directory*	Specifies the full path of the root directory for the master source repository.
-e *editor*	Specifies which editor to use to edit revision log information.
-f	Skips the `cvs` startup file `~/.cvsrc`.
-l	Executes a specified command but doesn't log it into the history.
-n	Executes a specified command but only to issue reports. Forbids file changes.
-t	Traces a programs execution step by step. Very useful when combined with -n.
-r	Sets read-only to any new working files.
-v	Shows version information.
-w	Sets read/write to any new working files (Is default).
-x	Encrypts communication between the server and client when using Kerberos.
-z *level*	Uses `gzip` with the specified compression level when transferring network files. (The global options must be listed before the command statement.)
	These command-specific options may be used with most cvs commands:
-D *date*	Uses the most recent revision that is no later than the specified ISO/Internet date.
-f	Retrieves files that would otherwise be missed if a date or tag match wasn't made.
-k *flag*	Associates a file to the specified keyword flag.
-l	Runs only in the local working directory, not in any subdirectory.
-n	Forbids the checkout, commit, tag, and update programs from running.
-P	Removes (prunes) any directories that are empty after having been updated.
-p	Pipes any files taken from the master source repository to SDTOUT.
-r *tag*	Uses the revision that is stated by the specified tag instead of the default. (The command options must be listed after the command statement.)
	The cvs commands:
add [-k *flag*] [-m *message*] *files...*	Creates a new directory or file (if created with `checkout`) in the repository.
-k *flag*	Controls the way that the file/directory is checked out by specifying the kflag.
-m *message*	Specifies which message is shown during logging.
files...	Specifies the file(s) or directory to be created. (You must use commit in order for add to take effect.)
admin [options...] *files...*	Administrates the master source repository repeatedly. Valid `rcs` options are as follows:
-i	Creates and initializes a new RCS file, but doesn't create any revision.
-a *login*	Appends the login names that appear in a comma-separated list.
-A *file*	Appends the access list of the specified old file to the access list of the RCS.
-e *login*	Erases any login names within the specified comma-separated login list.
-b *revision*	Sets the default branch to the specified revision.
-c *string*	Sets the comment leader to the specified string.
-k *string*	Sets the default keyword substitution to the specified substring.
-l *revision*	Locks the file revision to the specified revision.
-u *revision*	Unlocks the file revision to the specified revision.
-L	Sets the locking type to strict.
-U	Sets the locking type to non-strict.
-m *rev:msg*	Replaces the revisions log message with the specified revision and another message.
-M	Blocks sending a mail when breaking into somebody else's lock.
-n *name* [:rev]	Associates the specified symbolic name with the branch and any specified revision.
-N *name* [:rev]	Overrides previously set name assignments; otherwise, similar to -n.
-o *range*	Erases (outdates) the specified revisions.
-q	Doesn't show any diagnostics quiet mode.

continued

-I	Starts interactive mode.
-s *state* [:rev]	Sets the specified state attribute and any specified revision.
-t *file*	Writes the text in the specified file into the contents of the RCS file.
-t -*string*	Writes the text in the specified string into the contents of the RCS file.
-T	Preserves the modification time mark on the RCS file unless a revision is erased.
-V	Shows version information.
-x *suffix*	Uses suffixes to select out RCS files.
-z *timezone*	Uses the specified time zone as the default.
files...	Specifies the file or files to create or modify.
checkout [options...] *modules...*	Creates a working directory that has copies of source files specified by the module.
-A	Resets any sticky tags, options, or dates that have been set for example, -k options.
-j *branch*	Merges any changes between the final revision and the original revision.
-j *tag:date*	Limits the revision to a specified tag within a date. (You may combine the two -j options. Use a space in-between them.)
-c	Copies the sorted module file to STDOUT.
-s	Shows a per-module information status stored in the module files.
modules...	Specifies symbolic names for source directory collection, paths and repository files.
commit [options...] *{ files... }*	Saves changes from the working source files.
-l	Limits the effects of commit to the current directory.
-n	Doesn't allow the module program to run.
-f	Forces file commitment even if it has not changed. It also disables recursion.
-R	Reads subdirectory files and commits them if they have changed.
-r *revision*	Commits a numeric or symbolic revision of the specified files. A branch revision.
	If you want to use a different log message, select one of these two options:
-m *message*	Specifies that a log message from the command line is used.
-F *file*	Uses the contents of the argument file for the log message.
files...	Specifies the files to commit. If none, the current working directory files are used.
diff [options...] *{ files... }*	Compares working files against the revisions found in the source repository.
	The following options are `cvs diff`-specific:
-R	Forces recursive directory processing.
-l	Forces use of the local directory and isn't recursive.
-N	Includes removed and added files to the list of affected files.
-r *revision*	Specifies the revision to compare the files to.
-D *date*	Specifies the past revision to compare files with.
	The following `rcsdiff` options are supported by cvs diff:
-q	Suppresses any diagnostic output quiet mode.
-r *revision*	Selects the revision. Select two revisions by separating the -r's with a space.
-k *keyword*	Affects the keyword substitution that is specified when extracting revisions.
-T	Saves the modification time of the RCS file even if the file changes. Use carefully.
-V *num*	Imitates that the RCS version is the specified value. Values 3, 4, or 5 are valid.
-x *suffix*	Specifies the suffixes to explain RCS files.
-z *timezone*	Specifies the date output format to use for the keyword option.
files...	Specifies the files to compare. Separate each file by a space.
export [options...] *option modules...*	Copies the source of the specified module(s) without the administrative directories.
-N	Doesn't shorten the module paths.
-d *directory*	Writes the source into the specified directory.
-k *keyword*	Causes the keyword substitution to expand so that its revisions are not lost.
	You must select one of these two options:
-r *revision*	Specifies the revision tag of the source.
-D *date*	Specifies the date of the source.
modules...	Specifies the module or modules to copy. Separate each module by a space.
history [options...] *{ files... }*	Creates a global history file of every checkout, rtag, commit, update, and release done.
	These options control cvs history reports:
-c	Reports each time that `commit` is used.
-m *module*	Reports on a specified module. If more than one, split each -m module with a space.
-o	Reports on any checked-out modules.
-T	Reports on any and all tags.
-x *type*	Extracts the specified type of record from the `cvs` history.

continued

O	Specifies the record type from `checkout`.
F	Specifies the record type from `release`.
T	Specifies the record type from `rtag`.
W	Specifies the record type from `update` when the working copy is deleted.
U	Specifies the record type from `update` when the working file is copied.
G	Specifies the record type from `update` when a merge is done correctly.
C	Specifies the record type from `update` when a merge is done but has an error.
M	Specifies the record type from `commit` when a file is modified.
A	Specifies the record type from `commit` when a file is added.
R	Specifies the record type from `commit` when a file is erased.
-e	Reports on every record type.
-z *timezone*	Uses the specified time zone for record reports.
	These options constrain `cvs` history reports:
-a	Shows information for all users.
-l	Shows the last modification.
-w	Shows modification records that are in the same directory that history is run from.
-b *string*	Shows data from the module, file, or repository path that has the specified string.
-D *date*	Shows data since the specified date.
-p *store*	Shows data from the specified source repository. Separate each -p record by a space.
-r *revision*	Shows data since the specified revision in the RCS files.
-t *tag*	Shows data since the specified tag was last added to the history.
-u *user*	Shows data records from the specified username.
import [options...] *store vendor release*	Includes an entire outside source into a source repository directory.
-d	Specifies that each file's modification time is used for check-in time and date.
-b *branch*	Specifies the first-level branch instead of 1.1.1.
-I *name*	Specifies the filenames to ignore during import. Separate each -i name by a space.
store	Specifies the repository source.
vendor	Specifies the entire vendor tag branch.
release	Specifies the release tag to define the files created with import.
log [options...] *{ files... }*	Specifies log information for the specified files.
-l	Inactivates recursive mode.
	Also supports the following `rlog` options:
-L	Doesn't add the RCS files that have no lock set.
-R	Shows only the filename.
-h	Limits the output to paths, head, branch, access list, locks, symbolic, and suffix.
-t	Adds a description text to output; otherwise, the same as `-h`.
-N	Doesn't show symbolic names.
-b	Shows revision information on the branch, with the highest branch on the trunk.
-d *date*	Semicolon separated list of dates, shows information about revisions in the ranges.
-V	Shows version information.
-V *version*	Sets a specified fake RCS version when generating logs.
rdiff [options...] *modules...*	Creates a Larry Wall format `patch` between two file versions to STDOUT.
-f	Forces the use of head revision matching if a tag or date isn't found.
-l	Forces use of the local directory and isn't recursive.
-R	Forces recursive directory processing.
-V *version*	Sets the specified RCS version for keyword expansion.
	You may select one of these two options:
-r *revision*	Specifies the revision tag of the source.
-D *date*	Specifies the date of the source.
modules...	Specifies the modules that is used for the patch process.
release [options...] *modules...*	Cancels `cvs checkout` actions.
-d	Requests that working copies of source files are deleted upon successful release.
modules...	Specifies the checkout modules that are canceled.
remove [options...] *files...*	Removes files from the source repository. Use `commit` to make this take effect.
-f	Erases the file before it is removed from the repository.
-R	Activates recursive directory mode.
-l	Inactivates recursive directory mode.

continued

files...	Specifies the files that are removed.
rtag [options...] *tag modules...*	Assigns symbolic tags to specified source versions inside the repository.
-b	Forces a tag to become a branch tag, which allows separate software patch development.
-d	Removes obsolete symbolic names.
	You may select one of these two options:
-r *tag*	Specifies the revision tag of the source.
-D *date*	Specifies the date of the source.
tag	Specifies the symbolic tag that is used.
modules...	Specifies the affected modules.
status [options...] *{ files... }*	Shows a report on the present source repository status for the specified files.
-R	Activates recursive directory status report mode.
-l	Limits the search to the current directory only.
-v	Shows all symbolic tags for the RCS files as well.
files...	Specifies the reported files.
tag [options...] *tag { files... }*	Assigns symbolic tags to the closest repository version into the working resources.
-f	Forces the use of head revision matching if a tag or date isn't found.
-d	Erases the specified tag.
-F	Moves a tag if it exists.
-R	Activates recursive directory status report mode.
-l	Inactivates recursive directory status report mode.
-b	Forces a tag to become a branch tag, which allows separate software patch development.
	You may select one of these two options:
-r *tag*	Specifies the revision tag of the source.
-D *date*	Specifies the date of the source.
tag	Specifies the used tag.
files...	Specifies the working source files.
update [options...] *{ files... }*	Updates the local working source against the source repository.
-d	Builds directories similar to `checkout`.
	You may select one of these two options:
-r *tag*	Specifies the revision tag of the source.
-D *date*	Specifies the date of the source.
-k *flag*	Uses the specified RCS keyword option during checkout.
-j *revision*	Merges the changes between the current revision and the specified revision.
-I *files*	Moves the specified files to ignore. Use exclamation `!` to reset this.
	The output of `update` is a line with a prefix, where the file:
U *file*	Has been brought up-to-date in the repository.
A *file*	Was added to the working source copy only and is included at `commit`.
R *file*	Has been erased from the both sources and is included at `commit`.
M *file*	Has been modified in the working directory and merged without conflicts.
C *file*	Has been modified in the working directory and merged with conflicts.
? *file*	Is in the working directory but doesn't match the source repository.
File Name: `cvs`	**Directory:** /usr/bin/ **Type:** External

cvsbug

UNIX Shell: A shell (ash, bsh)

Function	Sends a CVS problem report to a central support site that runs GNATS.
Syntax	cvsbug *{ site }* [options...]

-f *file*	Specifies a file that contains a problem report to send.
-t *address*	Specifies the mail address to the support site that's going to receive the reports.
-P	Shows the problem report form to send. Reads the form from the variable PR_FORM.
-L	Shows the available categories.
--request-id	Sends a request for a submitter-id to the site or address specified.
-v	Shows version information.
site	Specifies a problem report site to send the reports to.
File Name: `cvsbug`	**Directory:** /usr/bin/ **Type:** Script

cytune

UNIX Shell:	All primary shells (bash, ash, tcsh)		
Function	Configures the interruption threshold for the Cyclades driver.		
Syntax	cytune [options...] *ttys...*		
-s *value*	Specifies the current threshold value.		
	Following two options can only be used one at a time:		
-t *value*	Specifies the current flush timeout value.		
-T *value*	Sets the specified value as the default timeout value.		
	Following two options can only be used one at a time:		
-g	Shows the current threshold and timeout.		
-G	Shows the default threshold and flush timeout values.		
-q	Shows information about the tty.		
-i *interval*	Logs information with the specified interval.		
ttys...	Specifies device or devices to act on.		
File Name: cytune	**Directory:** /usr/bin	**Type:**	External

dbmmanage

UNIX Shell:	Perl script		
Function	Manages DBM files with usernames and passwords to authenticate HTTP users.		
Syntax	dbmmanage *file { command } { user password }*		
	The following commands can't be combined:		
add	Adds a username and use the encrypted password.		
adduser	Asks for a password then adds a username.		
check	Finds a password and checks whether the specified username has the specified password.		
delete	Erases username from the filename.		
import	Reads username and password from STDIN and adds them to the filename.		
update	The same as adduser, but it verifies that username already exists.		
view	Shows the DBM file.		
file	Specifies the DBM file. You don't need to specify the file extension.		
user	Specifies the username to manage.		
password	Specifies an optional encrypted password to use with the username.		
File Name: dbmmanage	**Directory:** /usr/bin	**Type:**	Script
dbmmanage datafile delete user1	Erases the user user1 from the datafile.		
dbmmanage datafile import < userfile	Adds users from userfile to the datafile.		

ddate

UNIX Shell:	All primary shells (bash, ash, tcsh)
Function	Shows the date in the discordian date format.
Syntax	ddate [+*formats...*] *{ date }*
+*format*	Specifies in what format to show the dates. These options can be combined.
%A	Inserts the full name of the day.
%a	Inserts the short name of the day.
%B	Inserts the full name of the season.
%b	Inserts the short name of the season.
%d	Inserts the ordinal number of the day in the current season.
%e	Inserts the cardinal number of the day in the current season.
%H	Inserts the name of the holiday.
%N	Specifies where to stop showing the rest of the format if isn't a holiday.
%n	Inserts a line feed in the output.
%t	Appends a Tab to the output.
%X	Shows the amount of days left until the X-Day.
%{ *text* %}	Specifies text that you can have between the different formats.
date	Shows the date for the specified day month year.

continued

File Name:	ddate	**Directory:**	/usr/bin	**Type:**	External
Tip:	If you are playing with the formats, you should try `%`.				
ddate 24 12 2000			Shows the discordian date of the Gregorian date 2000/12/24.		
ddate +%{Day:%}%A%N%{and\ it is\ %}%H			Shows the current day. If it's a holiday it adds "and it is".		

deallocvt

UNIX Shell: All primary shells (bash, ash, tcsh)

Function	Disconnects the specified virtual terminal or terminals.				
Syntax	deallocvt *{ terminals... }*				
terminals...		Specifies the terminal or terminals to disconnect.			
File Name:	deallocvt	**Directory:**	/usr/bin/	**Type:**	External
deallocvt 7			Disconnects the terminal `/dev/tty7`.		

debugfs

UNIX Shell: All primary shells (bash, ash, tcsh)

Function	Debugs the ext2 file system specified.
Syntax	debugfs [options...] *{ device }*

-w	Opens the file system in read/write mode.
-f *file*	Specifies a file that contains commands for debugfs.
-R *request*	Specifies one request that is executed - when that is done, exits the program.
-V	Shows version information.
	The following commands can be used in interactive mode:
cat *inode*	Shows the contents of the specified inode.
cd *directory*	Changes the current directory to the one specified.
chroot *directory*	Specifies a directory to use as the root directory.
close	Closes the file system you are working with.
clri *file*	Clears the inode file specified.
dump [-p] *inode destination*	Outputs the contents of an inode to the specified file; -p preserves the owner information.
expand_dir *directory*	Specifies a directory to expand.
feature *{ names... }*	Specifies the features to turn on or off. A dash - in front of the name disables the feature.
find_free_block [block]	Searches for the first free block: If a block is specified, search from that.
find_free_inode [options...]	Searches for a free inode, and after that, it is allocated.
inode	Specifies the directory inode number in which the inode is to be located.
mode	Sets the specified permission mode to the new inode to be created.
freeb *block*	Specifies a block to be marked as not allocated.
freei *inode*	Specifies an inode to free.
help	Shows help information.
icheck *blocks...*	Shows you a list of the inodes that the specified block or blocks use.
initialize *device blocksize*	Creates a file system on the specified device with the specified blocksize.
kill_file *inode*	Specifies the inode to disable.
ln *inode file*	Specifies an inode to link to the specified file.
ls [-l] *directory*	Shows the contents of the directory specified. If -l is used, show long lists.
modify_inode *inode*	Specifies an inode that you want to change the content structure in.
mkdir *directory*	Specifies a directory to create.
mknod *file major minor*	Creates a special device file with the specified major and minor device numbers.
ncheck *inodes...*	Shows the pathnames to the inodes specified.
open [options...] *device*	Edits the specified file system. Options: -w = open for writing, -f = force open.
pwd	Shows the working directory.
quit	Exits the interactive mode.
rm *pathname*	Specifies a path to remove.
rmdir *directory*	Specifies a directory to remove.
setb *block*	Specifies a block to be marked as allocated.
seti *inode*	Specifies what inode to mark for use in the inode bitmap.
show_super_stats	Shows the superblock contents and the block group descriptors.
stat *inode*	Shows the inode structure contents of the specified inode.
testb *block*	Checks whether the specified block number is allocated.
testi *inode*	Checks whether the specified inode is allocated.

continued

unlink *pathname* write *source destination* *device*		Specifies a path to a link to remove. Copies the specified source file to the specified output file. Specifies the ext2 file system device to debug.			
File Name:	`debugfs`	**Directory:**	/sbin	**Type:**	External
Warning:	This command could remove data from your hard drive. Please read before applying.				
debugfs -w /dev/hda1		Edits the specified file system in read/write mode.			

depmod

UNIX Shell: All primary shells (bash, ash, tcsh)

Function	Controls dependency descriptions for loadable kernel modules.
Syntax	depmod [options...] *{ modules... }* depmod [options...] *{ kernel }*

-e		Shows unresolved symbols for every module.			
-i		Builds dependency list without checking symbol versions.			
-n		Shows the dependencies on the screen instead of putting them in `/lib/modules`.			
-s		Outputs error messages to the `syslog` daemon instead of STDERR.			
-v		Sends a notice to you with the name of every module that is being processed.			
-q		Quiet mode. Doesn't complain when missing symbols were found.			
-F *symbols*		Specifies the set of kernel symbols to use. Usually this is a copy of System.map.			
		The following options can't be used when standalone modules are specified:			
-a		Dependencies for all modules found in `/etc/modules.conf` are created.			
-A		Works as -a, but compares timestamps and only update modules that have been changed.			
-V		Shows version information.			
-r		Makes dependencies even if the module isn't owned by root. Security risk.			
-b *directory*		Specifies where to find images of the `/lib/modules` tree.			
-C *file*		Specifies a configuration file to use (default is `/etc/modules.conf`).			
kernel		Specifies the kernel version to create dependencies for.			
modules...		Specifies the loadable kernel modules to create dependencies for.			
File Name:	`depmod`	**Directory:**	/sbin	**Type:**	External
Warning:	Hackers can switch modules not owned by root. You could complete their hacks with the -r option.				
depmod -C /etc/local/modules.conf		Uses /etc/local/modules.conf as the configuration file.			
depmod -b /altroot/		Searches for modules in /altroot/lib/modules.			

dga

UNIX Shell: All primary shells (bash, ash, tcsh)

Function	Tests video modes for X-window by filling the screen with different colors each time a key is pressed.
Syntax	dga

b		Runs a benchmark by measuring the read and write speed of frame buffers.			
q		Stops the program.			
File Name:	`dga`	**Directory:**	/usr/X11R6/bin/	**Type:**	External

dhcpcd

UNIX Shell: All primary shells (bash, ash, tcsh)

Function	Manages requests for an IP address from a DHCP server.
Syntax	dhcpcd [options...] *{ interface }*

-d	Logs debug messages to `syslog`.
-k	Restarts the dhcpcd process and tell the server to release it's MAC address.
-n	Tries to receive a new IP address from the server.
-r	Uses the RFC1541 standard instead of RFC2131.
-B	Sends out a request for a broadcast response from a server.
-C	Calculates checksum on packets received from the server.
-D	Sets the domain name that the server supplies to the local computer.
-H	Sets the hostname that the server supplies to the local computer.
-R	Doesn't overwrite the current `/etc/resolv.conf` file.
-T	Asks for an IP address to use, but doesn't change any interfaces or files.
-t *seconds*	Times out after the specified amount of time when waiting for an IP address.

continued

-c *filename*	Specifies an executable file to try to execute after an interface has been configured.
-h *hostname*	Sends the hostname specified to the server when requesting an IP address.
-i *vendor*	Uses the specified vendor identifier instead of using system information to get it.
-I *client*	Uses the specified client identifier instead of using the interfaces MAC addresses.
-l *seconds*	Sends the lease time specified to the server. The server can override this.
-s *[address]*	Specifies a IP address to use when informing the DHCP server. (If no IP address is specified, dhcpcd uses the interface IP address.)
interface	Specifies what interface to use when grabbing and setting a dynamic IP address.
File Name: `dhcpcd`	**Directory:** /sbin/ **Type:** External
dhcpcd -HD eth0	Gets an IP address, hostname, and domain name from a DHCP server.

dhcrelay

UNIX Shell: All primary shells (bash, ash, tcsh)

Function	Forwards BOOTP and DHCP requests from one subnet to another subnet.
Syntax	dhcrelay [options...] *servers...*

-p *port*	Specifies the network port to listen for requests. (Default is 67.)
-d	Runs the operation in the foreground. (Default is a daemon in the background.)
-q	Minimizes information shown at startup.
-i *interface*	Specifies a network interface to forward BOOTP and DHCP requests. (Default is all.)
servers...	Specifies one or more DHCP server to forward requests to.
File Name: `dhcrelay`	**Directory:** /usr/sbin/dhcrelay **Type:** External
dhcrelay -i ep0 sun	Forwards requests to sun from interface ep0.

dialog

UNIX Shell: All primary shells (bash, ash, tcsh)

Function	Shows boxes containing questions or messages from the shell.
Syntax	dialog [options...]

	The following options can't be combined with all options:
--clear	Cleans the screen of its attributes.
--create-rc *file*	Specifies a file where a sample configuration is written.
--print-maxsize	Shows how big the dialog box can be.
--print-version	Shows version information.
	The following options alters the looks of the dialog box:
--aspect *width*	Specifies the smallest line width before doing a line wrap.
--backtitle *title*	Puts the specified title in the top of the screen.
--beep	Beeps every time the screen is refreshed.
--beep-after	Beeps when an input is interrupted.
--begin *position*	Puts the dialog box on the specified position on the screen. Position is y and x.
--cr-wrap	Makes new lines in the dialog text be a new line instead of showing all on one line.
--help	Shows help information.
--defaultno	Specifies that no is the default value if you use the yesno box.
--default-item *string*	Specifies what item in a menu box to mark as default.
--no-kill	Puts the tailboxbg box in the background and disable SIGHUP.
--no-shadow	Removes shadows around the dialog boxes.
--nocancel	Removes the Cancel button in the checklist, input, and menu boxes.
--print-size	Shows the dialog box size to STDERR.
--separate-output	Shows results from a checklist in one line without quoting.
--separate-widget *string*	Splits output on STDERR with the specified string.
--shadow	Adds a shadow the each dialog box. This is the default.
--size-err	Checks whether the size of the dialog is usable before showing the dialog.
--sleep *seconds*	Specifies the number of seconds to sleep after processing one dialog box.
--tab-correct	Changes each Tab character to one or more blank characters.
--tab-len *number*	Specifies how many blank characters to use when altering Tabs to blanks.
--title *title*	Specifies a title to use on the dialog box.

continued

	The following options always use: option, msg, H, W where: msg=text message, H=text box height, and W=text box width.
--checklist *msg H W*	Lists multiply entries which you can select among; outputs those selected to STDERR.
listheight	Specifies how many lines the visible part of the list is.
tag name status	Adds a line to the list with the specified tag, description and current status. **Note:You may add lines by using the tag name status multiple times.**
--gauge *msg H W*	Shows a percentage box. The percentage meter changes when an integer is received from STDIN.
percent	Specifies the percentage to start on.
--infobox *msg H W*	Specifies a message to show in a dialog box and then quit.
--inputbox *msg H W*	Specifies a message to show and wait for input.
{ value }	Specifies a value to use as a default input to the dialog box.
--menu *msg H W*	Lists multiple entries, that you add, that you can select one of by pressing Enter.
menuheight	Specifies how many lines the visible part of the list is.
tag name	Adds a line to the list with the specified tag and description. (You may add lines by using the tag name multiple times.)
--msgbox *msg H W*	Shows the message and waits for you to press the OK button before exiting.
--passwordbox *msg H W*	Shows the message and waits for you to input a hidden text string.
{ value }	Specifies hidden text to add automatically to the input line.
--radiolist *msg H W*	Lists multiple entries, that you add, that you can select one from.
listheight	Specifies how many lines the visible part of the list is.
tag name status	Adds a line to the list with the specified tag, description, and current status.
--yesno *msg H W*	Shows a question message and lets you answer yes or no.
	The following options show files instead of messages in the boxes:
--tailbox *file H W*	Specifies a file to continuously show contents from in a dialog box.
--tailboxbg *file H W*	Opens a dialog in the background and shows the contents of a file.
--textbox *file H W*	Specifies a text file to show in a dialog box.

File Name:	`dialog`	**Directory:**	/usr/bin	**Type:**	External

dialog --title "/etc/passwd" --textbox /etc/passwd 30 70	Shows your password file in a dialog box.
dialog --passwordbox "Enter password:" 6 40	Lets you enter a password in a dialog box.

diffstat

UNIX Shell: All primary shells (bash, ash, tcsh)

Function	Creates statistic histograms from `diff` output.
Syntax	diffstat [options...] *{ files... }*

-n *width*	Specifies the filename's minimum width.
-p *count*	Overrides the pathname strip logic.
-V	Shows version information.
-w *width*	Specifies the maximum width of the histogram.
files...	Specifies the diff output file or files that your histograms are based on. **Note: If not specified STDIN is used.**

File Name:	`diffstat`	**Directory:**	/usr/bin/	**Type:**	External

diffstat -n 20 bigpatchoutput.diff	Creates a histogram, with filenamelength of 20 and, based on bigpatchoutput.diff.

dig

UNIX Shell: All primary shells (bash, ash, tcsh)

Function	Gathers information from the DNS servers in interactive or batch mode.
Syntax	dig [*@server*] *domain* [options...]

-x *address*	Maps the specified address inversed, used when performing a reverse lookup.
-f *file*	Specifies a file that contains multiple dig queries.
-T *seconds*	Waits the specified time before performing the next dig command when using -f.
-p *port*	Specifies what port to use when connecting to a name server (default is 53).
-P	Runs `ping` to compare response times after a DNS query returns.
-t *query-type*	Specifies the type of query by using an integer or an abbreviation (mx=T_MX).
-c *query-class*	Specifies the class of query by an integer or an abbreviation (in=C_IN).
-k *directory:name*	Specifies a key name, that exists in the specified directory, to mark the query with.
-envsav	Saves the current environment to the default.

continued

-stick	Restores the environment for each line when using -f. Use `-nostick` to disable.
domain	Specifies the domain to fetch from.
+debug	Activates debugging. Use +nodebug to deactivate.
+d2	Activates extra debugging. Use +nod2 to deactivate.
+recurse	Enables recursive lookup. Use +norecurse to disable.
+retry=*count*	Specifies how many times to retry if a lookup fails.
+time=*seconds*	Specifies the timeout in seconds to use before failing a lookup.
+ko	Keeps open option. +noko will not.
+vc	Enables virtual circuit. Use +novc to disable.
+defname	Uses the default domain. +nodefname doesn't use default domain.
+search	Uses a search list. +nosearch doesn't use a search list.
+domain=*domain*	Specifies the default domain name to use.
+ignore	Ignores trunc. To use trunc, use +noignore.
+primary	Uses the primary server. Use +noprimary to not use a primary server.
+aaonly	Use only authoritative query flag; +noaaonly will not.
+cmd	Echos parsed arguments. Use +nocmd to not echo parsed arguments.
+stats	Shows query statistics. Use +nostats to hide query statistics.
+Header	Shows the basic header. Use +noHeader to hide basic headers.
+header	Shows header flags. Use +noheader to hide header flags.
+ttlid	Shows the TTL's. Use +nottlid to hide the TTLs.
+cl	Shows class information. Use +nocl to hide the class information.
+qr	Shows outgoing queries. Use +noqr to hide those.
+reply	Shows the reply. Use +noreply to hide the replies.
+ques	Shows the question section. Use +noques to hide the question sections.
+answer	Shows the answer section. Use +noanswer to hide the answer sections.
+author	Shows the authorities section. Use +noauthor to hide the authorities section.
+addit	Shows the additional section. Use +noaddit to hide the additional section.
+pfdef	Shows the default amount of output flags.
+pfmin	Shows the minimum amount of output flags.
+pfset=#	Prints flags are set to #.
+pfand=#	Prints flags with # and bitwise.
+pfor=#	Prints flags with # or bitwise. (# is a hex, octal, or a decimal number.)
server	Specifies a name server to get DNS information from.
domain	Specifies a domain name to request information about.
query-type	Specifies what DNS information you want to show.
a	Shows where an A record points.
any	Shows any information available.
mx	Shows the mail exchanger.
ns	Shows the domain name servers that the domain points to.
soa	Shows the zone of authority record.
hinfo	Shows host information.
axfr	Shows the zone transfer.
txt	Shows additional text that the DNS server have sent out.
query-class	Specifies what network class to send a request for.
in	Shows the internet class domain information.
any	Shows any class information.

File Name:	`dig`	**Directory:**	/usr/bin/	**Type:**	External

dig www.ucgbook.com a retry=3	Shows the A-record for the specified host and retries three times before quitting.
dig @ns.ucgbook.com ucgbook.com any	Shows all DNS information that exists about the specified domain at the specified server.

dip

		UNIX Shell:	All primary shells (bash, ash, tcsh)
Function	Controls dial-up or dial-in PPP connections. It dials using a specified dial-up script.		
Syntax	dip [options...] { *scriptfile* }		

-v	Verbose mode. Shows more information.
-t	Goes into the command line mode. Used for testing.
	The following two options are used when dialing out using a script file:
-m *mtu*	Specifies the maximum transfer unit to use (default is 296).

continued

-p *protocol*	Specifies what protocol to use. Can be one of the following: SLIP, CSLIP, PPP, or TERM.
	The following options handle incoming connections:
-i	Starts a login shell when receiving an incoming connection.
-a	Asks for a username and password.
	The following options disconnect existing processes:
-k	Drops the most recent connection.
-l *device*	Specifies a tty device to drop the connection on.
	The following options are used in command mode or in dial-up scripts:
beep *times*	Specifies the number of beeps to send to the terminal.
bootp	Fetches the local and remote IP addresses using the BOOTP protocol.
break	Sends a break to the session.
chatkey *keyword code*	Specifies a modem response keyword to map to a numeric code.
config *ACTION* [option] *arguments...*	Saves parameters for interface configurations. Use one of the following two actions:
interface	Specifies that interfaces are modified.
routing	Specifies that routes are modified.
	You may select only one of these four options:
pre	Applies the modification before the link comes up.
up	Applies the modification when the link is up.
down	Applies the modification when the link goes down.
post	Applies the modification when the link is down.
arguments...	Specifies what to modify in the interface or the routing table. This is required. (arguments is used as the ifconfig or route commands.)
databits *bits*	Specifies the number of databits to use. Either 7 or 8 data bits can be used.
dec $*variable value*	Decreases a variable with the specified value.
default	Uses the remote host it connected to as the default route.
dial *number { seconds }*	Dials the specified number. Aborts if no answer within the specified timeout seconds.
echo *ACTION*	Makes the modem commands visible or not. no=invisible, yes=visible.
flush	Flushes the input to the terminal.
get $*variable { ACTION }*	Receives or asks for the value of a variable. You must select one of these three.
value	Specifies a value to set for the variable or copy from another variable.
ask	Shows a prompt where you enter the value to set for the variable.
remote { value $variable }	Reads a variable value from a remote computer.
value	Specifies a timeout value to wait before giving up.
$*variable*	Specifies what variable to read.
goto *label*	Transfers control to the specified label in the dial-out script.
help	Shows help information.
if *expression* goto *label*	Checks whether expression is true, then goes to the specified label.
	The expression must have the format specified by the three lines below:
$*variable*	Specifies the variable to check.
op	Specifies what mathematical operands to use. Can be one of ==, !=, <, >, <=, or >=.
value	Specifies a value to check against the variable.
label	Specifies what label to go to if expression is true.
inc $*variable value*	Increases the specified variables number with the specified value.
init *string*	Specifies the initialization string to use.
mode *protocol*	Specifies the line protocol to use. Use one of SLIP, CSLIP, PPP, or TERM.
modem *type*	Specifies the modem type.
netmask *netmask*	Specifies the netmask to use when connection.
parity *parity*	Specifies what parity to use. Use one of E, O, or N.
password	Prompts for a password and sends it to the remote host.
proxyarp	Sends proxy ARP.
print $*variable*	Shows the specified variables contents.
psend *command { arguments... }*	Specifies a command to run and sends its output to the serial driver.
port *terminal*	Specifies the name of the terminal port to use.
quit	Exits with a nonzero exit status.
reset	Resets the modem.
send *string*	Specifies a text string to send to the serial driver.

continued

shell *command { arguments... }*	Runs the specified command through a shell with the specified arguments.
skey *{ seconds }*	Looks for an S/Key challenge. With seconds, you may say how long to wait for an answer.
sleep *seconds*	Specifies the number of seconds to wait before continuing to go through the script.
speed *bps*	Specifies the speed of the port to use (default is 38400).
stopbits *bits*	Specifies the number of bits to use. Bits are either 1 or 2.
term	Goes into terminal mode.
timeout *seconds*	Specifies the timeout in seconds.
wait *string { seconds }*	Holds until the specified text string is received. Times out after amount of seconds.
scriptfile	Specifies a chat script file to use when dialing out.
File Name: `dip`	**Directory:** /usr/sbin/ **Type:** External

diplogin

UNIX Shell: All primary shells (bash, ash, tcsh)

Function	Specifies the username to log in to the dial-in server that exists in the file `/etc/diphosts`.
Syntax	diplogin *{ user }*

user	Specifies a valid username that exists in the file `/etc/diphosts`.
File Name: `diplogin`	**Directory:** /usr/sbin/ **Type:** External

dir

UNIX Shell: All primary shells (bash, ash, tcsh)

Function	Shows files in the current directory or a specified directory.
Syntax	dir [options...] *{ directory }*

	Dir uses the same options as `ls`. See `ls` for list of all options.
directory	Specifies the complete path to the directory to view the contents of - that is, `/usr/bin`.
File Name: `dir`	**Directory:** /usr/bin/ **Type:** External
dir --color=always	Shows the contents of current directory using colors.
dir -l /boot/vmlinuz	Shows long information about `/boot/vmlinuz`.

dircolors

UNIX Shell: All primary shells (bash, ash, tcsh)

Function	Shows or sets LS_COLORS environment variable.
Syntax	dircolors [options...] *file*

-b	Outputs Bourne shell code to set LS_COLORS.
-c	Outputs C-shell code to set LS_COLORS.
-p	Outputs defaults LS_COLORS environment variable.
--help	Shows help information.
--version	Shows version information.
file	Reads the file to determine which colors to use for which file types and extensions.
File Name: `dircolors`	**Directory:** /usr/bin/ **Type:** External

dislocate

UNIX Shell: Expect script

Function	Disconnects a session without logging off to enable you to reconnect to the same session from another location.
Syntax	dislocate *{ program } { arguments... }*

Ctrl +D	Disconnects from the session and allows any processes to remain active.
Ctrl +Z	Same as Ctrl +D and exits the script and returns the console prompt.
program	Specifies the program to enable disconnect for.
arguments...	Allows for any valid argument for the process specified.
File Name: `dislocate`	**Directory:** /usr/bin/ **Type:** Script
dislocate top	Starts `top` with dislocation enabled.
dislocate	Displays all dislocated programs that you can reconnect to.

disown

UNIX Shell:	Bash shell (bash)
Function	Removes the specified job from the active job list.
Syntax	disown [options...] { *jobs...* }

-h	Doesn't remove the job from the list, but marks it so it doesn't receive any hangup.
-a	Marks all jobs in the list. Don't specify jobs.
-r	Marks all running jobs in the list. Don't specify jobs.
jobs...	Specifies job to modify. If not given, and -a or -r isn't used, use the current job.

display

UNIX Shell:	All primary shells (bash, ash, tcsh)
Function	Shows images on the screen in X-window. Multiple images can be shown.
Syntax	display [options...] *images...*

-backdrop	Shows the image on the backdrop and hides other windows.
-border *WxH*	Shows a border around the image.
-cache *memory*	Specifies maximum amount of RAM memory to use (default is 80MB).
-colormap *type*	Specifies the type of color map to use. Can be Shared or Private.
-colors *value*	Specifies the maximum number of colors in the image.
-colorspace *value*	Specifies the color space to use.
-comment *comment*	Adds comment to the image (default is the image filename).
-compress *type*	Specifies the type of compression.
-contrast	Improves the image contrast. Use +contrast to decrease contrast.
-crop *size offset*	Sets the preferred size and location.
-delay *time*	Specifies delay between images in 1/100 of a second.
-density *WxH*	Sets the resolution of the image.
-despeckle	Decreases the speckles within an image.
-display *host:displ*	Specifies the display to use.
-dispose *method*	Specifies the GIF disposal method
-dither	Uses Floyd/Steinberg error diffusion for the image.
-enhance	Improves a noisy image.
-filter *type*	Specifies filter to use when resizing an image.
-flip	Mirrors image in the vertical direction.
-flop	Mirrors image in the horizontal direction.
-frame *WxH*	Surrounds the image with an ornamental border.
-gamma *value*	Sets the gamma correction for the image.
-geometry *WxH*	Specifies the width and height of the image.
-interlace *type*	Specifies the interlace scheme.
-immutable	Prevents image from being modified.
-label *name*	Sets a label for the image.
-map *type*	Sets standard color map type to use.
-matte	Saves matte channel.
-monochrome	Creates a black and white image.
-negate	Creates a negative image.
-page *size*	Specifies the size of the image.
-quality *value*	Specifies the compression level for JPEG/MIFF/PNG.
-raise *WxH*	Creates a 3-D effect.
-remote *string*	Runs command on a remote display process.
-roll *offset*	Rolls an image vertically or horizontally.
-rotate *degrees*	Rotates the image.
-sample *geometry*	Uses geometry to scale image with pixel sampling.
-scene *NR*	Sets image scene number.
-segment *value*	Excludes clusters that are insignificant.
-sharpen *factor*	Sharpens the image. Factor can be 0.0 to 99.9 percent.
-size *WxW+offset*	Sets width and height of the image.
-texture *file*	Specifies background texture.

continued

-title *string*	Shows string as a title for the image.
-treedepth *value*	Sets the tree depth for the color reduction algorithm.
-update *time*	Specifies time in seconds to confirm an image has been updated — if so, redisplays it.
-verbose	Verbose mode. Shows more information.
-visual *type*	Shows image using this visual type.
-window *id*	Specifies target window name or ID.
-write *file*	Specifies a file to save the image in.
images...	Specifies image to show.
File Name: `display`	**Directory:** /usr/X11R6/bin/ **Type:** External

djpeg

UNIX Shell: All primary shells (bash, ash, tcsh)

Function	Decompresses the JPEG file specified and creates an image file on the STDOUT.
Syntax	djpeg [options...] *{ file }*

-colors *N*	Limits the number of colors in the image to N.
-quantize *N*	Same as -colors - quantize is for backward compatibility.
-fast	Selects fast, low-quality output with the recommended processing options.
-grayscale	Forces JPEG file to be output in grayscale even if it is in color.
-scale *M/N*	Allows the image to be scaled by a factor M/N, which must be 1/1, 1/2, 1/4, or 1/8.
-bmp	Outputs image in 24-bit BMP format. **Note: If in grayscale or -fast is set, image is in 8-bit format.**
-gif	Outputs image in 256-color GIF format.
-os2	Runs the same procedure as -bmp, but is for OS/2 1.x.
-pnm	Outputs image in PBMPLUS format, which is PPM if color or PGM if grayscale (is default).
-rle	Outputs image in RLE format, which requires the URT library.
-targa	Outputs image in Targa format.
-dct int	Enables method for DCT integer processing (is default).
-dct fast	Enables a fast but less accurate method for DCT integer processing.
-dct float	Enables method for floating-point DCT.
-dither fs	Enables dithering in color quantization using the Floyd-Steinberg method.
-dither ordered	Enables color quantization with ordered dithering. Only usable with -onepass.
-dither none	Disables dithering in color quantization.
-map *file*	Overrides -colors and -onepass by using an image file for color quantization.
-nosmooth	Enables a lower-quality but faster routine for upsampling.
-onepass	Disables two-pass color quantization by using one-pass instead.
-maxmemory *count*	Specifies limit for the memory, in KB, to use in processing large images.
-outfilename	Specifies file for the output image (default is STDOUT).
-verbose	Shows version information at startup, then shows debug information.
-debug	Same as -verbose.
file	Specifies JPEG file to decompress.
File Name: `djpeg`	**Directory:** /usr/bin/ **Type:** External
djpeg -colors 256 -bmp mo.jpg>mo.bmp	Decompresses mo.jpg and outputs it to mo.bmp.

dmesg

UNIX Shell: All primary shells (bash, ash, tcsh)

Function	Examines and controls the kernel ring buffer.
Syntax	dmesg [options...]

-c	Clears the ring buffer contents after showing the status.
-s *size*	Specifies the buffer size to query the kernel ring buffer (default is 8196).
-n *level*	Specifies which level of logging procedures to use. Disables all other options.
File Name: `dmesg`	**Directory:** /bin/ **Type:** External
Tip:	Good for debugging your bootup process and viewing hardware.
dmesg -n1	Logs panic messages only.

dnsdomainname

dnsdomainname		UNIX Shell:	All primary shells (bash, ash, tcsh)
Function	Shows the domain that you are in.		
Syntax	dnsdomainname [-v]		

-v	Verbose mode. Shows more information.
File Name: dnsdomainname	**Directory:** /bin/ **Type:** External

dnskeygen

dnskeygen		UNIX Shell:	All primary shells (bash, ash, tcsh)
Function	Creates and maintains public, private, and shared secret keys for DNS servers.		
Syntax	dnskeygen [options...] -n *name*		

-n *name*	Specifies the name of the created key.
-D *size*	Creates DSA/DSS keys. Size is 510, 576, 640, 704, 768, 832, 896, 960, or 1024.
-H *size*	Creates HMAC-MD5 keys. Size is 128 or 504.
-R *size*	Creates RSA keys. Size is 512 or 4096.
-F	Uses a large exponent for the key; only for RSA.
-z	Creates a zone key. Not used with -h or -u.
-h	Creates a host key. Not used with -z or -u.
-u	Creates a user key (email). Not used with -z or -h.
-a	Specifies the generated key can't be used for authentication.
-c	Specifies the generated key can't be used for encryption.
-p *number*	Specifies the protocol number for the generated key. 3 = dnssec, 2 = email,1 = TLS, 4 = IPSEC.
-s *number*	Specifies the strength field of the key (default is 0).
File Name: dnskeygen	**Directory:** /usr/sbin/ **Type:** External
dnskeygen -R 512 -h -n test	Creates a 512-byte big RSA key called test.
dnskeygen -D 510 -z -c -p 3 -n testone	Creates a DSA/DSS key for zone with BIND.

dnsquery

dnsquery		UNIX Shell:	All primary shells (bash, ash, tcsh)
Function	Shows information about name servers through BIND resolver library calls.		
Syntax	dnsquery [options...] *host*		

-n *name*	Specifies the name server to show information from.
-t *type*	Specifies what to show information about. Use one of the following types:
A	Shows information about host addresses.
N	Shows information about the name server.
CNAME	Shows information about the canonical names for aliases.
PTR	Shows information from the domain name pointer.
SOA	Shows the domains start of authority information.
WKS	Shows information about the supported well-known services.
HINFO	Shows information about the host CPU and system type.
MINFO	Shows mailbox or mail list information.
MX	Shows information from the mail exchanger.
RP	Shows responsible person information.
AFSDB	Shows information about AFS or DCE servers.
ANY	Shows all information.
-c class	Specifies the class to show information about. Use one of the following:
IN	Shows information about the Internet class.
HS	Shows information about the Hesiod class.
CHAOS	Shows information about the Chaos class.
ANY	Shows information about all classes.
-r *number*	Specifies the number of retries if there is no answer from the server (default is 4).
-p *time*	Specifies the period to wait before timing out (default is RES_TIMEOUT).
-d	Shows debug information.
-s	Uses TCP stream connection instead of UDP datagram packets.

continued

-v		Same as the -s option.			
host		Specifies the name or IP address of the host or the domain of interest.			
File Name:	`dnsquery`	**Directory:**	/usr/bin/	**Type:**	External
dnsquery -t MX ucg.com		Shows the mail exchange information about ucg.com.			
dnsquery -n names.ucg.com -t A ucg_main		Shows the IP address for ucg_main. Query nameserver names.ucg.com.			

doexec

UNIX Shell: All primary shells (bash, ash, tcsh)

Function	Runs a specified command showing it with another name passing the arguments provided.				
Syntax	doexec *execfilename { arguments... }*				
execfile		Specifies the file to execute.			
name		Specifies the name to camouflage the command with. Shown in the `ps`.			
arguments...		Specifies the arguments that are passed to the executable file.			
File Name:	`doexec`	**Directory:**	/bin/	**Type:**	External
doexec vi bash		Runs the program vi and shows it as running bash.			

dosfsck, fsck.msdos

UNIX Shell: All primary shells (bash, ash, tcsh)

Function	Checks a DOS file system; can also be used to fix damaged DOS file systems.				
Syntax	dosfsck [options...] *device*				
-a		Allows `dosfsck` to decide what to do if the file system needs some modification.			
-A		Enables `dosfsck` to handle Atari MS-DOS. Turns off atari mode on Ataris.			
-d*file*		Erases the specified file or the first instance, if it exists in several places.			
-f		Saves cluster chains not used to files.			
-l		Shows the whole pathname of every file being checked.			
-r		You are prompted whenever there are two ways of fixing a problem (is default).			
-t		Initiates marking of unreadable clusters as bad clusters.			
-u*file*		Initiates `dosfsck` to attempt to undelete the specified file.			
-v		Verbose mode. Shows more information.			
-V		Initiates `dosfsck` to do verification tests, twice.			
-w		Initiates dosfsck to write changes to disk immediately.			
-y		Runs the same procedure as `-a`. Exists for compatibility with other fsck tools.			
device		Specifies which device to run the file system check on.			
File Name:	`dosfsck`	**Directory:**	/sbin/	**Type:**	External
Note:	If run on Ataris don't use -A; this is default on an Atari system. When -A is used on Ataris `dosfsck` checks without the Atari mode.				
dosfsck /dev/hda1		Performs a file system check on device `/dev/hda1`. User is prompted for input if needed.			

dp

UNIX Shell: All primary shells (bash, ash, tcsh)

Function	Converts dates fitting the ARPA Internet standard (822 format).				
Syntax	dp [options...] *dates...*				
-form *file*		Specifies a file to use instead of the default output format.			
-format "*string*"		Specifies a string to be use instead of the default output format.			
-width *columns*		Specifies how many places the answer occupies on the command line.			
-version		Shows version information.			
-help		Shows help information.			
dates...		Specifies the date to parse.			
File Name:	`dp`	**Directory:**	/usr/lib/nmh	**Type:**	External

dropdb

UNIX Shell: A shell (ash, bsh)

Function	Removes a postgres database specified from the system.	
Syntax	dropdb [options...] *databasename*	
-h *host*		Specifies the host where the database exist.
-p *port*		Specifies what port `dropdb` connects to on the specified host.
-u *user id*		Connects with the User ID specified.

continued

-W		Requests a password for the username.			
-e		Causes dropdb to tell what it is writing to the postmaster server.			
-q		Reports no answer to STDOUT.			
-i		Causes droptdb to ask before doing something to the database.			
databasename		Specifies the database to be removed on the postgres database server.			
File Name:	`dropdb`	**Directory:**	/usr/bin/	**Type:**	Script
dropdb -h ucgdata -U admin -W test		This connects to server ucgdata with username admin, asks for a password, and then removes database test.			

droplang

UNIX Shell: A shell (ash, bsh)

Function	Connects to a postgres database and removes a selected programming language.
Syntax	droplang [options...] { *language* }

-d *dbname*		Specifies where to remove the language, in what databasename.			
-l		Shows a list of languages that exist in the specified database.			
-h *host*		Specifies the host where the database exist.			
-p *port*		Specifies what port `dropdb` connects to on the specified host.			
-U *userID*		Connects the user ID to connect with.			
-W		Requests a password for the username.			
language		Specifies the language to be removed on the postgres database.			
dbname		Specifies where to remove the language, in what databasename. Same as the -d option.			
File Name:	`droplang`	**Directory:**	/usr/bin/	**Type:**	Script
droplang -h ucgdata -d mydata		Connects to postgres on ucgdata, goes into database mydata, and prompts for what programming language to remove.			

dropuser

UNIX Shell: A shell (ash, bsh)

Function	Connects to a postgres database and removes the specified user.
Syntax	dropuser [options...] { *user* }

-h *host*		Specifies the host where the database exists.			
-p *port*		Specifies what port `dropdb` connects to on the specified host.			
-e		Causes dropdb to explain what it is writing to the postmaster server.			
-q		Stats quiet mode so that it doesn't show any response.			
-i		Causes droptdb to request before doing something to the database.			
user		Specifies the username that is removed on the selected postgres server.			
File Name:	`dropuser`	**Directory:**	/usr/bin/	**Type:**	Script
dropuser -h ucgdata agent1		Removes the specified user agent1 from ucgdata postgres.			

dump, rdump

UNIX Shell: All primary shells (bash, ash, tcsh)

Function	A backup program that examines files in an ext2 file system and determines if the files need to be backed up.
Syntax	dump [options...] *files...*

-*value*	Specifies the backup mode (default dump level is 9).
-0	Enables full backup mode. Backs up everything. Use this when creating a new backup.
-1	Dump level 1, incremental backup. This is the start level for incremental backups.
-2	Dump level 2, backs up files that have been changed or created since level 1 was done.
-3	Dump level 3, backs up files that have been changed or created since level 2 was done.
-4	Dump level 4, backs up files that have been changed or created since level 3 was done.
-5	Dump level 5, backs up files that have been changed or created since level 4 was done.
-6	Dump level 6, backs up files that have been changed or created since level 5 was done.
-7	Dump level 7, backs up files that have been changed or created since level 6 was done.
-8	Dump level 8, backs up files that have been changed or created since level 7 was done.
-9	Dump level 9, backs up files that have been changed or created since level 8 was done.

continued

-B *blocks*	Specifies the number of 1KB blocks to use per volume.
-a	Causes dump to write backup until the device returns an EOM (End Of Media) string.
-b *size*	Defines the amount of kilobytes to use for every dump record (default is10).
-c	Sets dump to act like it's writing to a cartridge tape drive (8000bpi and 1,700 feet).
-e *inode*	Doesn't back up the specified inode.
-h *level*	Doesn't back up files that are above or at the given level.
-d *density*	Specifies the tape density.
-f *file*	Writes a backup to a specified device or a file. Use - for STDOUT.
-F *script*	Runs a script at the end of each tapes. Checks whether the last backup was OK.
-k	Sets dump to speak Kerberos authentication with remote tape servers.
-L *label*	Specifies the label to be set on the dump backup header.
-M	Tells dump to use a multivolume feature.
-n	Notifies users in the group operator when dump requires user input.
-s *feet*	Sets the tape length to feet. If the tape is smaller, it prompts for a new tape.
-S	Checks how much space is needed to start a real dump.
-T *date*	Specifies when you want to start a dump session.
-u	Updates the file `/etc/dumpdates` after a dump.
	When showing file systems, select only one of these two options:
-W	Causes dump to show file systems and highlights those that need to be dumped.
-w	Shows only the filenames that need to be dumped. (Don't combine -w or -W with other options.)
files...	Specifies the file or files to dump.

File Name:	`dump`	**Directory:**	/sbin/	**Type:**	External

dump -0 -f /dev/st0 /home/	Creates a full backup of /home to the first SCSI tape.
dump -S -0 /	Outputs how many bytes a full dump on / is.

dumpe2fs

UNIX Shell: All primary shells (bash, ash, tcsh)

Function	Shows the superblock and blocks group information of a file system present on a device.
Syntax	dumpe2fs [options...] *device*

-b	Shows the blocks that are reserved as bad in the file system.
-ob *superblock*	Specifies backup-superblock instead of the superblock.
-oB *blocksize*	Specifies blocks of blocksize bytes when examining the file system.
-f	Forces the program to show information about a file system.
-h	Shows the superblock information.
-V	Shows version information.
device	The device to show information about.

File Name:	`dumpe2fs`	**Directory:**	/sbin/	**Type:**	External

dumpe2fs -b /dev/hda1	Shows the bad blocks for `/dev/hda1`.

dumpkeys

UNIX Shell: All primary shells (bash, ash, tcsh)

Function	Shows the contents of the keyboard translation tables on STDOUT.
Syntax	dumpkeys [options...]

-h	Shows help information.
-i	Shows a short list of the kernel's keyboard driver characteristics.
-l	Shows a long list of the kernel's keyboard driver characteristics.
-n	Shows action code values in hexadecimal instead of converting to symbolic notation.
-f	Outputs key bindings in canonical form.
-1	Outputs one modifier/keycode pair per line.
-S*shape*	Specifies the table shape for dumpkeys to use. The following shapes are valid:
1	Gives the same results as the -f option.
2	Gives the same results as the -1 option.
3	A combination between shapes 1 and 2, working as 1 until the first hole is found.
--funcs-only	Shows only the function key string definitions.
--keys-only	Shows only the key bindings.
--compose-only	Shows only the compose key combinations.

continued

-c*charset*	Specifies the character set to use. The following character sets are valid: iso-8859-1, iso-8859-2 , iso-8859-3, iso-8859-4, iso-8859-5, iso-8859-7, iso-8859-8, iso-8859-9, iso-8859-14, iso-8859-15, mazovia, koi8-r, koi8-u, iso-10646-18. (Default is iso-8859-1.)		
File Name: `dumpkeys`	**Directory:** /usr/bin/	**Type:**	External
dumpkeys --funcs-only	Shows only the function key string definitions.		
dumpkeys --keys-only	Shows only the key bindings.		

e2fsck, fsck.ext2

UNIX Shell: All primary shells (bash, ash, tcsh)

Function	Checks Linux second extended file systems.
Syntax	e2fsck [options...] *device*

-a	Acts like -p option, but with backward compatibility. (-p option recommended.)		
-b *superblock*	Uses the specified superblock instead of the normal one.		
-B *blocksize*	Specifies the block size when looking for the superblock.		
-c	Runs the `badblocks` program to check for bad blocks.		
-C *filedescriptor*	Writes completion information to the specified file descriptor.		
-d	Shows debug information.		
-f	Forces the file system to be checked, including when the clean flag is set.		
-F	Flushes the buffer cache on specified device before beginning.		
-l *file*	Adds blocks listed in specified file to the list of bad blocks.		
-L *file*	Sets blocks listed in specified file as the list of bad blocks.		
-n	Sets all questions to no, automatically. Opens file system in real-only mode.		
-p	Repairs the file system automatically without any questions.		
-r	Is provided only for backward compatibility.		
-s	Same as -S, but doesn't byte-swap when the file system already is on order.		
-S	Byteswaps the file system so it uses the normalized, standard byte order.		
-t	Shows timing statistics for e2fsck.		
-v	Verbose mode. Shows more information.		
-V	Shows version information and exits.		
-y	Answers yes to all questions.		
device	Specifies the device to use.		
File Name: `e2fsck`	**Directory:** /sbin/	**Type:**	External
Tip:	Don't overlook the -y option. It may save you a lot of time.		
e2fsck /dev/hda3	Does a file system check on the third partition on the first IDE-drive.		
e2fsck -p -y /dev/hda3	Automatically repairs; assumes a "yes" as answer to all questions.		

e2label

UNIX Shell: All primary shells (bash, ash, tcsh)

Function	Shows or changes the label of an ext2 file system.
Syntax	e2label *device { label }*

device	Shows the name for device.		
label	Sets the specified name for the device.		
File Name: `e2label`	**Directory:** /sbin/	**Type:**	External
e2label /dev/hda1 ucgdisk	Sets the name on `/dev/hda1` to ucgdisk.		

echotc

UNIX Shell: TC shell (tcsh)

Function	Exercises the terminal capabilities arguments.
Syntax	echotc [options...] *arguments...*

-s	If the argument doesn't exist, returns an empty string instead of an error messages.
-v	Verbose mode. Shows more information.
arguments...	Specifies argument from termcap. (When argument is baud, cols, lines, meta, or tabs, show the value.)
echotc cm 5 10	Moves the cursor to line 10, column 5.

ecpg

ecpg	UNIX Shell:	All primary shells (bash, ash, tcsh)
Function	A preprocessor for embedded SQL code within C and Postgres programs.	
Syntax	ecpg [options...] *files...*	

-v	Shows version information.
-t	Disables auto-transaction.
-I *path*	Specifies an include path. (Default is /usr/local/include.) (More defaults: /usr/include and for Postgres /usr/local/pgsql/lib.)
-o *outfile*	Causes `ecpg` to output info to named outfile. **Note:When not defined outfile has the same name as the processed file.**
-d	Enables debugging.
-D *name*	Specifies name.
files...	Specifies the file to process.
File Name: `ecpg`	**Directory:** /usr/bin/ **Type:** External

eiconctrl

eiconctrl	UNIX Shell:	All primary shells (bash, ash, tcsh)
Function	Configures active Eicon ISDN cards.	
Syntax	eiconctrl [-d *driverID*] *ACTION* [options...]	

-d *driverID*	Specifies the ISDN interface to use.
-v	Verbose mode. Shows more information. Requires load action.
ACTION	**The following actions can be sent to the Eicon interface:**
irq *{ interrupt }*	Specifies the interrupt to use. When none is specified, it shows current interrupt. (The irq action can only be used when it is an ISA card.)
load *protocol* [options...]	Changes the protocol into the specified one.
-l*{ channel }*	Specifies the channel to set up.
-e	Uses the CRC4 multiframe.
-t*TEI*	Uses the specified fixed TEI.
-h	Doesn't use HSCX 30 mode.
-n	Sets to NT2 mode.
-p	Uses leased line D channel.
-s*{ value }*	Specifies which value to use on LAPD layer 2 session (can either be 0, 1, or 2).
-o	Allows discovered info elements.
-z	Switches to loopback mode.
manage *{ ACTION }*	Starts the Eicon management interface.
read	Reads the present management.
exec *path*	Executes management from specified path.
xlog [cont]	Gets XLOG information from card. When cont is used, xlogs show constantly.
isdnlog on | off	Turns trace information on or off for isdnlog.
File Name: `eiconctrl`	**Directory:** /usr/sbin/ **Type:** External
eiconctrl load etsi	Loads the etsi protocol to the Eicon ISDN card found.

eject

eject	UNIX Shell:	All primary shells (bash, ash, tcsh)
Function	Ejects floppies and CDs from their drives. Works for VM managed devices and devices without eject buttons.	
Syntax	eject [options...] *{ device }*	

-h	Shows help information.
-v	Verbose mode. Shows more information.
-a on | off	Controls the autoeject mode when closing device. Only supported by some devices.
-c *slot*	Specifies which slot to eject on a CD-ROM changer.
-t	Sends a close command on the device to eject.
-n	Shows the alias name for the selected device. Does no actions on it.
-r	Tries to eject the device with the CD-ROM eject command.
-s	Tries to eject the device with SCSI commands.
-f	Tries to eject the device with a floppy disk eject command.
-q	Tries to eject the device with a tape drive offline command.
device	Specifies the device to eject.

continued

File Name:	eject	Directory:	/usr/bin/	Type:	External
eject /dev/cdrom		Ejects /dev/cdrom.			

elksemu

UNIX Shell: All primary shells (bash, ash, tcsh)

Function	Emulates 8086 ELKS programs on an i386.
Syntax	elksemu *program { arguments... }*

program	The program to be run under elksemu.
arguments...	Specifies arguments to program.

File Name:	elksemu	Directory:	/usr/bin/	Type:	External

elm

UNIX Shell: All primary shells (bash, ash, tcsh)

Function	An interactive mailer program that takes the place of mail and mailx.
Syntax	elm [options...] elm [-s *subject*] *list*

-a	Forces the arrow cursor instead of the inverse bar.
-c	Checks the given aliases only.
-d *level*	Sets debug level.
-f *folder*	Reads the specified folder (default is incoming).
-h	Shows help information.
-i *file*	Includes specified file in the edit buffer for sending.
-k	Forces knowledge of HP terminal keyboard.
-K	Enables use of soft keys on HP terminals only.
-M	Handles all folders like spool folder.
-m	Disables the menu, and gives extra lines for more message headers.
-t	Doesn't use the termcap/terminfo ti/te sequence.
-v	Shows version information.
-z	Exits the command when no mail is pending.
	The following option can't be used with any other.
-s *subject*	Specifies the subject for the message to send.
list	Specifies a list of aliases or addresses.

File Name:	elm	Directory:	/usr/bin/	Type:	External
elm -s test root		Mails root a message with subject testing; prompts you for body.			
elm -s testing root < message.txt		Mails root contents of message.txt, with subject testing.			

elmalias

UNIX Shell: All primary shells (bash, ash, tcsh)

Function	Shows information on specified elm aliases.
Syntax	elmalias [options...] *{ names... }*

-a	Shows information on an alternative output format.
-d	Shows debug information (can only be used if it was compiled with debugging enabled).
-e	Shows group aliases.
-n	Shows information on an alternative output format.
-r	Exits when a name doesn't match to a known alias.
-s	Uses the system wide alias file only (default is both files).
-u	Uses the user-specific alias file only (default is both files).
-v	Verbose mode. Shows more information on specified alias.
-V	Very verbose mode. Shows all available information on aliases.
-f *format*	Sets format. %a=alias %l=last name %n=full name %c=comment %v=address) %t=type. (The format is similar to printf; see it for more information.)
names...	Specifies the aliases to show, if they are present in the alias database.

File Name:	elmalias	Directory:	/usr/bin	Type:	External

emacs

UNIX Shell:	All primary shells (bash, ash, tcsh)
Function	Edits text files, reads and sends mail, performs outline edits, compiles and runs subshells.
Syntax	emacs [options...] *{ files... }*

-t *file*	Uses the specified file as the screen instead of using STDIN/STDOUT.
+*number*	Hops to the specified line number. Use no space between the plus + and the number.
-q	Doesn't load any `init` files.
-u *user*	Loads the specified user's `init` file.
	The following are lisp-oriented options:
-f *function*	Executes the specified lisp function.
-l *file*	Loads the lisp code from the specified file.
	Use these options when you run `emacs` as a batch editor:
-batch	Batch mode editor. Sends messages to STDERR. (You must use this option first in the argument list.)
-kill	Ends `emacs` when in batch mode.
	You may use the following options when using `emacs` under X-window:
-name *name*	Specifies the name that is assigned to the first `emacs` window.
-title *name*	Specifies the title that is used in the first X-window.
-r	Uses reverse video on the `emacs` window.
-i	Uses the bitmap icon `kitchen sink` when iconizing the `emacs` window.
-fn *font*	Specifies the emacs-compatible font to use. Fonts are /usr/lib/X11/fonts.
-ib *width*	Sets the internal border to the window to the specified pixel width (default is 1).
-geometry *width* x *height* + *Xaxis* + *Yaxis*	Sets the specific size and position of the `emacs` window.
-fg *color*	Specifies the color of text.
-bg *color*	Specifies the color of the background.
-bd *color*	Specifies the color of the border.
-cr *color*	Specifies the color of the text cursor.
-ms *color*	Specifies the color of the mouse cursor.
-d *display*	Places the `emacs` window on the specified display device.
-nw	Forbids use of the X interface.
files...	Specifies the file to edit.

File Name: `emacs`	**Directory:** /usr/bin/	**Type:**	External

emacs -geometry 80x20+5+10 README	Starts emacs in X-window with the specified geometry.

enable

UNIX Shell:	Bash shell (bash)
Function	Enables or disables internal commands.
Syntax	enable [options...] *{ names... }*

-n	Disables each name specified.
-f *filename*	Loads an internal command specified by filename.
-d	Deletes a command previous loaded with -f.
-p	Shows a list of all enabled internal commands.
-a	Shows all shell internal commands.
-s	Works on only on POSIX internal commands.
names...	Specifies names of commands to work on.

enable -n echo	Disables internal command echo; uses /bin/echo instead.

expect

UNIX Shell:	All primary shells (bash, ash, tcsh)
Function	Is used to automatically control interactive programs. It acts by reading commands from a file.
Syntax	expect [options...] *{ file } { arguments... }*

-c *command*	Executes specified command before any in the script.
-d	Shows information of what's happening while the program is running.
-D	Enables interactive debugger.
-f *file*	Specifies a file from which to read commands from. Can't be combined with the -b option.

continued

-b *file*	Reads the specified file one line at a time. Can't be combined with the -f option.		
-i	Waits for the user to type in the commands.		
-N	Doesn't source the file `$exp_library/expect.rc`.		
-n	Doesn't source the file `~/expect.rc`.		
-v	Shows version information.		
file	Specifies the file to get the commands from.		
arguments...	Specifies the arguments to send with the script. It is stored in the variable argv.		
File Name: `expect`	**Directory:** /usr/bin	**Type:**	External

expectk

UNIX Shell: All primary shells (bash, ash, tcsh)

Function	Is used to automatically control interactive programs. The same as `expect`, With `Tk` support.
Syntax	expectk [options...]

-colormap *colormap*	Specifies the color map to use for main window.		
-display *display*	Specifies the display to use.		
-geometry *geometry*	Specifies the initial geometry for the window.		
-name *name*	Specifies the name of the application.		
-sync	Uses synchronous mode for display server.		
-visual *value*	Specifies whether to be visual for main window.		
-- *arguments*	Passes all remaining arguments to script.		
-command *command*	Specifies command to execute.		
-diag	Enables diagnostics.		
-norc	Doesn't read `~/.expect.rc`.		
-NORC	Doesn't read system-wide `expect.rc`.		
-version	Shows version information.		
-Debug	Shows debug information.		
File Name: `expectk`	**Directory:** /usr/bin/	**Type:**	External

exportfs

UNIX Shell: All primary shells (bash, ash, tcsh)

Function	Controls the exported file system table for NFS.
Syntax	exportfs [options...] *{ directory }*

-a	Exports or unexports all directories.		
-o *options...*	Specifies a list of export options.		
-r	Reexports all directories. Removes non-valid export entries from the kernel.		
-u	Unexports directories.		
-v	Verbose mode. Shows more information.		
-i	Ignores the `/etc/exports` file. Only uses default and specified options.		
directory	Specifies the directory to the file system.		
File Name: `exportfs`	**Directory:** /usr/sbin/	**Type:**	External
exportfs :/home	Exports `/home` to everyone.		
exportfs workstation1:/home	Exports `/home` to the specified computer.		

extcompose

UNIX Shell: TC shell (tcsh)

Function	Creates a file containing a reference to external files on the computer.
Syntax	extcompose *file*

file	Specifies the file to make.		
File Name: `extcompose`	**Directory:** /usr/bin/	**Type:**	Script
Tip:	This is a great tool to use if you want to refer to a common program via e-mail.		

faillog

UNIX Shell:	All primary shells (bash, ash, tcsh)
Function	Manages the summary of failures in `/var/log/faillog`.
Syntax	faillog [options...]

-a	Selects all the users.
-p	Shows all the users that have ever had a login failure in a user ID order.
-u *user*	Shows the failure record on the specified user.
-t *value*	Shows only the failure records that are less than value days old.
	The following options require write access to the `/var/log/faillog` file:
-r	Resets the login failure count.
-m *value*	Sets the maximum amount of login failures.

File Name:	`faillog`	**Directory:**	/usr/bin	**Type:**	External

faillog -u root	Shows failed logins for root.

fastmail

UNIX Shell:	All primary shells (bash, ash, tcsh)
Function	Sends e-mails fast in a batch to a large group of receivers.
Syntax	fastmail [options...] *file addresses...*

-b *list*	Specifies a list of people to send blind carbon copies to.
-c *list*	Specifies a list of people to send plain carbon copies to.
-C *comment*	Specifies a text string to add to the header.
-d	Shows debug information.
-f *from*	Specifies another name as sender.
-F *address*	Specifies another from address.
-i *ID*	Specifies a message ID to refer the message to.
-r *address*	Sends the replies to the specified address.
-R *comment*	Specifies a reference text for the message.
-s *subject*	Specifies the subject of the e-mail.
file	Specifies the file to use as message or uses a - to get it from STDIN.
addresses...	Specifies the addresses of the people to send to.

File Name:	`fastmail`	**Directory:**	/usr/bin/	**Type:**	External

fastmail -s Party Invitation.txt mailing_list	Uses the file Invitation.txt as mail body.
fastmail -b [caterers_list] -s Party Invitation.txt mailing_list	Sends bcc to caterers_list.

fdisk

UNIX Shell:	All primary shells (bash, ash, tcsh)
Function	Handles partiton tables. If no arguments is specified, an interactive prompt will be used.
Syntax	fdisk [options...] *{ devices... }*

-b *sectorsize*	Specifies the sectorsize to use (either 512, 1024 or 2048).
-v	Shows version information.
-l	Shows the partitions for the specified devices and exits.
-u	Shows size in sectors instead of cylinders. Used only with -l option.
-s *partition*	Shows the specified partition size in blocks.
	The following commands are interactive commands within the program:
a	Sets the bootable flag.
b	Edits bsd disk label.
c	Sets the DOS compatibility flag.
d	Deletes a partition.
l	Shows known partition types.
m	Shows menu.
n	Creates a new partition.
o	Creates a new empty DOS partition table.
p	Shows the partition table.
q	Quits without saving changes.
s	Creates a new empty Sun disk label.
t	Changes a partition's system ID.

continued

u	Changes display/entry units.
v	Verifies the partition table.
w	Writes table to disk and exits.
x	Gives extra functionality (experts only).
b	Moves beginning of data in a partition.
e	Lists extended partitions.
c	Changes number of cylinders.
h	Changes number of heads.
s	Changes number of sectors/track.
devices...	Specifies the device or devices to use.

File Name:	fdisk	**Directory:**	/sbin/	**Type:**	External
fdisk -l /dev/hdb		Lists partitions on second IDE-drive.			

fetchmail

UNIX Shell: All primary shells (bash, ash, tcsh)

Function	Retrieves mail from POP, IMAP, or ETRN servers and forwards it to your local mail agent.
Syntax	fetchmail [options...] { *mailservers...* }

-V	Shows version information.
-c	Shows you whether there is any mail waiting without retrieving it.
-s	Suppresses all messages but actual error messages.
-v	Verbose mode. Shows more information.
-a	Retrieves all messages, both old and unread, from the mail server.
-k	Doesn't delete the retrieved messages from the mail server.
-K	Deletes the retrieved messages from the mail server.
-F	Deletes the previously saved messages from server before fetching new ones.
-p *mode*	Communicates with the mail server in the specified network protocol.
auto	When set to auto it tries IMAP, POP3, and POP2 protocols.
protocol	Other protocols to try are: apop, rpop, kpop, sdps, etrn, and imap/k4/gssa/crammd5/login.
-U	Uses UIDL; works only on POP3 servers.
-P *portID*	Specifies the TCP/IP port to use.
-t*time*	Specifies max response time in seconds.
--plugin *command*	Specifies an external program to use for connection.
--plugout *command*	Specifies an external program to use for a SMTP connection.
-r *folder*	Specifies a mail folder other than the default one. Not available with POP3 or ETRN.
--ssl	Encrypts the connection with SSL.
--sslcert *file*	Specifies the file containing client-side public SSL certificate.
--sslkey *file*	Specifies the file containing client-side private SSL key.
-S *list*	Specifies a list of addresses to forward mail to.
-D *domain*	Specifies a domain to be put in RCPT lines shipped to SMTP.
--smtpname *address*	Specifies a user and domain to be put in RCPT lines shipped to SMTP.
-Z *list*	Specifies a list of numeric SMTP errors to be interpreted as a spam-block response.
-m *command*	Passes mail to an MDA directly.
--lmtp	Delivers mail via LMTP.
--bsmtp *file*	Appends the mail to an BSMTP file.
-l *bytes*	Specifies the max size of mails to be retrieved, in bytes.
-w *seconds*	Specifies an interval in seconds between warnings about to large mails to the user.
-b *number*	Specifies the max number of mails to send to an SMTP listener before a reconnect.
-B *number*	Limits the accepted number of mails in one poll from a mail server.
-e number	Makes deletion final after the specified number of fetched messages.
-z nnn	Specifies the numeric spam errors to be interpreted.
-u *name*	Specifies the username to use as logon to the mail server.
-I *device*	Specifies the named device must be up and running before doing a poll.
-M *interface*	Monitors the specified interface for activity.
--preauth	Specifies a pre authentication type.
-f *file*	Specifies a .fetchmailrc run control file; a - specifies to read the path from STDIN.
-i *file*	Specifies a .fetchids file for to save POP3 user IDs.
-n	Disables the rewriting of headers to full addresses.

continued

-E *line* -Q *string* --configdump *mailservers...*	Changes the header. Deletes the specified string from the username in the header. Shows a configuration report on STDIN. Specifies the mail servers to get the mail from.				
File Name:	`fetchmail`	**Directory:**	/usr/bin/	**Type:**	External
Tip:	Useful when you want to use local mail and fetch external messages from an external server.				
fetchmail --flush -v -u ucg ucgmailserver	Deletes old messages on server before fetching new.				

fgconsole

UNIX Shell: All primary shells (bash, ash, tcsh)

Function	Shows you the number of the active virtual terminal.				
Syntax	fgconsole				
File Name:	`fgconsole`	**Directory:**	/usr/bin	**Type:**	External

filetest

UNIX Shell: TC shell (tcsh)

Function	Tests a file for different things.
Syntax	filetest options... *files...*

	The following options return 1 if they are true:
-r	Tests whether the file is readable.
-w	Tests whether the file is write able.
-x	Tests whether the file is executable.
-X	Tests whether the file is executable. File is in the path or a built-in.
-e	Tests whether the file exists.
-o	Tests whether the user owns the file.
-z	Tests whether the file has a zero size.
-s	Tests whether the file has a size greater than zero.
-f	Tests whether the file is a plain file.
-d	Tests whether the file is a directory.
-l	Tests whether the file is a symbolic link.
-b	Tests whether the file is a block special file.
-c	Tests whether the file is a character special file.
-p	Tests whether the file is a named pipe.
-S	Tests whether the file is socket special file.
-u	Tests whether the set-user-ID bit is set.
-g	Tests whether the set-group-ID bit is set.
-k	Tests whether the sticky bit is set.
-t	Tests whether file (must be a digit) is an open file descriptor for a terminal device.
-R	Tests whether file has been migrated.
-L	Tests where a symbolic link points, not the link itself. (The above options can be combined like this: -xy.)
	The following options return more information:
-A	Shows the last file access time, in seconds, since the epoch.
-A:	Shows the last file access time, in timestamp format.
-M	Shows the last time the file was modified, in seconds, since the epoch.
-M:	Shows the last time the file was modified, in timestamp format.
-C	Shows the last time the inode was modified, in seconds, since the epoch.
-C:	Shows the last time the inode was modified, in timestamp format.
-D	Shows the device number.
-I	Shows the inode number.
-F	Shows the composite file identifier (device:inode).
-L	Shows the name of the file to which the symbolic link points to.
-N	Shows the number of hard links.
-P	Shows the file permissions in octal without leading zero.
-P:	Shows the file permissions in octal with leading zero.
-P*mode*	Shows the file permissions in octal and with mode.
-P*mode*:	Is like -Pmode with leading zeros.
-U	Is like -Pmode with leading zeros.

continued

-U:	Shows the name of the user. When user is unknown, shows the numeric user ID.
-G	Shows the numeric group ID.
-G:	Shows the name of the group. When group is unknown, shows the numeric group ID.
-Z	Shows the size in bytes.
files...	Specifies the file to test.
filetest -rx /bin/ls	Tests whether `/bin/ls` is readable and executable.
filetest -U: /bin/ls	Shows the owner for `/etc/ls`.

findsmb

UNIX Shell: Perl script

Function	Shows information about computers on the network running MS Windows operating systems.
Syntax	findsmb *{ adress }*

-d	Shows debug information.
address	The broadcast address to use.
File Name: `findsmb`	**Directory:** /usr/bin/ **Type:** Script
findsmb	Shows information of all computers on the subnetwork.
findsmb 192.168.1.1	Shows information about 192.168.1.1.

flex, flex++, lex

UNIX Shell: All primary shells (bash, ash, tcsh)

Function	Creates a scanner program that recognizes lexical patterns in a text.
Syntax	flex [options...] *{ files... }*

-b	Creates backup information to lex.backup.
-c	Only for POSIX compliance compatibility.
-d	Causes the generated scanner to run in debug mode.
-f	Sets fast scanner, large but fast.
-h	Shows help information.
-i	Generates a case-insensitive scanner.
-l	Turns the compatibility to a maximum with the original lex.
-n	The same as -c.
-p	Creates a performance report to STDERR.
-s	Suppresses the rule that lets unmatched scanner input be echoed to STDERR.
-t	Writes the created scanner to STDOUT instead of lex.yy.c.
-v	Writes a summary of statistics to the STDERR.
-w	Doesn't show warning messages.
-B	Generates a batch scanner instead of an interactive scanner.
-F	Uses the alternative fast scanner table.
-I	Creates an interactive scanner.
-L	Tells flex not to create #line directives.
-T	Used to run in trace mode.
-V	Shows version information and exits.
-7	Creates a 7-bit scanner.
-8	Creates a 8-bit scanner.
-+	Creates a C++ scanner class.
-C*options...*	Sets the degree of table compression used. Default is -Cem.
	You can combine the following options:
a	Will trade off larger tables in the generated scanner for faster performance.
e	Constructs equivalence classes.
f	Specifies the full scanner table should be created. Doesn't compress tables.
F	Specifies that alternating the fast scanner representation should be used.
m	Creates meta-equivalence classes.
r	Causes the generated scanner to avoid use of the STDIO library for input.
-Cem	Generates equivalence classes and meta-equivalence classes.
-Cfe	Compromises between speed and size for production scanners.
-o*output*	Is used to specify output file.
-P*prefix*	Is used to specify scanner prefix.

continued

-S*skeleton_file*	Is used to specify skeleton file.				
files...	Is used to specify the input file(s). If none is given, STDIN is used.				
File Name:	`flex, flex++, lex`	**Directory:**	/usr/bin/	**Type:**	External

folder, folders

UNIX Shell: All primary shells (bash, ash, tcsh)

Function	Shows the current folder and information about the messages in it.
Syntax	folder [+*folder*] { *msg* } [options...]

+*folder*	Switches to the specified folder and makes that one the current folder.
-all	Shows an alphabetical summary for all top-level folders in the `nmh` directory
-noall	Suppresses the summaries in output.
-create	Creates new folders without any queries.
-nocreate	Suppresses the creation of non existent folders upon exit.
-fast	Shows only the folder name and doesn't read the folders.
-nofast	Shows all information and reads the folders.
-header	Shows the header information.
-noheader	Suppresses the header information.
-recurse	Shows folder information recursively.
-norecurse	Shows folder information as it is stored.
-total	Shows the total count of messages in each folder.
-nototal	Suppresses the total count of messages in folders.
-list	Shows the contents of the folder stack.
-nolist	Suppresses the showing of the folder stack.
-push	Directs folder to push the current folder onto the folder stack.
-pop	Directs folder to discard the top of the folder stack.
-pack	Compress the message names in the designated folders.
-nopack	Suppresses the compression of the message names.
-print	Shows information on STDOUT (is default).
-verbose	Verbose mode. Shows more information.
-noverbose	Suppresses the verbose information.
-version	Shows version information.
-help	Shows help information.
msg	Switches to the specified message and makes that one the current message.

File Name:	`folder`	**Directory:**	/usr/bin/	**Type:**	External
Note:	The command `folders` is the same as running the command `folder -all`.				
folder +inbox	Shows the folder inbox or creates it if nonexistent.				

fortune

UNIX Shell: All primary shells (bash, ash, tcsh)

Function	Shows an interesting or funny phrase from various people randomly each time you execute it.
Syntax	fortune [options...] [{ *percents%*] *files...* }

-a	Grabs phrases from all lists available.
-e	Uses fortune files as if they are of equal size.
-f	Shows a list of the files that would be used when grabbing phrases.
-l	Shows only long phrases.
-m *pattern*	Shows all fortunes containing the specified pattern.
-n *length*	Specifies how many characters a short phrase can contain.
-o	Shows only rude fortunes.
-s	Shows only short phrases.
-i	Disables case-sensitivity when using -m.
-w	Waits before exiting the program. Time is based on the number of characters.
percent%	Specifies the probability that a phrase is taken from the following file, for example 75%.
files...	Specifies one or more files or directories containing phrases.

continued

File Name:	`fortune`	**Directory:**	/usr/games/	**Type:**	External
Tip:	To make users know that you don't like them, put `fortune -o` in their login scripts.				
fortune 50% humorists 50% linuxcookie			Grabs a fortune from either the humorists or linuxcookie files.		
fortune -ws			Shows a short fortune and gives the reader time to read it before quitting the command. Can be used in logout scripts.		

free

UNIX Shell: All primary shells (bash, ash, tcsh)

Function	Shows the amount of free and used memory in the system.
Syntax	free [options...]

-b	Shows the amount of memory in bytes.
-k	Shows the amount of memory in kilobytes.
-m	Shows the amount of memory in megabytes.
-o	Disables the "buffer adjusted" line.
-s *seconds*	Activates continuous polling delay seconds apart.
-t	Shows a line containing the total amount of memory.
-V	Shows version information.

File Name:	`free`	**Directory:**	/usr/bin/	**Type:**	External
free -s 3			Polls every 3 seconds.		

fsck.minix

UNIX Shell: All primary shells (bash, ash, tcsh)

Function	Checks the minix file system for consistency.
Syntax	fsck.minix [options...] *device*

-l	Shows all filenames.
-a	Performs automatic repairs on the file system.
-r	Performs interactive repairs on the file system.
-v	Verbose mode Shows more information.
-s	Shows superblock information.
-m	Activates "mode not cleared" warnings.
-f	Forces file system check even if the file system is marked as valid.
device	Specifies the device to check.

File Name:	`fsck.minix`	**Directory:**	/sbin/	**Type:**	External
Warning:	Don't run this on a mounted file system.				
fsck.minix /dev/hda			Performs fsck.minix on /dev/had.		
fsck.minix -a /dev/hda			Performs automatic repairs on /dev/had.		

fsinfo

UNIX Shell: All primary shells (bash, ash, tcsh)

Function	Shows information including the capabilities about X font servers on the network.
Syntax	fsinfo [-server *host*]

-server *host*		Specifies the server, and optionally the port, to show information about.			
File Name:	`fsinfo`	**Directory:**	/usr/X11R6/bin/	**Type:**	External
Note:	To be able to see this information, you need the X font server running on target computer.				
fsinfo -server localhost:7100			Shows font server info from localhost:7100.		

fslsfonts

UNIX Shell: All primary shells (bash, ash, tcsh)

Function	Shows the fonts on the font server that match the pattern specified. Wildcards (*) can be used.
Syntax	fslsfonts [options...] [-fn *pattern*]

-server *host:port*	Specifies the X font server and port to use.
-l	Shows attributes of the font next to the font name.
-ll	Shows font parameters together with the -l option.
-lll	The same as -ll.
-m	Shows the minimum and maximum bounds for each font.
-C	Shows information in multiple columns.

continued

-1 -w *width* -n *columns* -u -fn *pattern*	Shows information in a single column. Specifies the width of the column in characters (default is 79). Specifies the number of columns to show. Doesn't sort the information. Specifies the pattern that `fslfonts` must match with.		
File Name: `fslsfonts`	**Directory:** /usr/X11R6/bin/	**Type:**	External
fslsfonts -server host:port -fn *lat*	Shows *lat* fonts on host:port.		

fstobdf

UNIX Shell: All primary shells (bash, ash, tcsh)

Function	Creates BDF fonts from an X font server. Debugs font and re-creates BDF files.
Syntax	fstobdf [-server *host*] -fn *name*

-server *host* -fn *name*	Specifies the server from which the font should be read. Specifies the font for which a BDF file should be generated.		
File Name: `fstobdf`	**Directory:** /usr/X11R6/bin/	**Type:**	External
fstobdf -fn terminal	Creates a BDF font from the terminal font from the default font server.		
fstobdf -fn terminal -server localhost:7100	Creates a BDF font from the terminal font from localhost:7100 font server.		

ftl_check

UNIX Shell: All primary shells (bash, ash, tcsh)

Function	Shows bookkeeping information for a Flash Translation Layer partition.
Syntax	ftl_check [-v] *device*

-v *device*	Verbose mode. Shows more information. Specifies the device to show information about.		
File Name: `ftl_check`	**Directory:** /sbin/	**Type:**	External
ftl_check -v /dev/mem0c0c	Shows information about `/dev/men0c0c`.		

ftl_format

UNIX Shell: All primary shells (bash, ash, tcsh)

Function	Formats a Flash Translation Layer partition on a flash memory device.
Syntax	ftl_format [options...] *device*

-q -i -s *blocks* -r *percent* -b *bootsize* *device*	Suppress the formatting statistics. Starts the interactive mode. Specifies a number of erase blocks to save as spares (default is one). Specifies the percentage to save as a reserve for efficiency (default is 5 percent). Specifies a portion on the flash card to be reserved for a boot image. Specifies the device to format.		
File Name: `ftl_format`	**Directory:** /sbin/	**Type:**	External
ftl_format -i /dev/mem0c0c	Asks for confirmation before formatting `/dev/mem0c0c`.		

ftpcount

UNIX Shell: All primary shells (bash, ash, tcsh)

Function	Shows current number of users using the FTP server.
Syntax	ftpcount [-V]

-V	Shows version information.		
File Name: `ftpcount`	**Directory:** /usr/bin/	**Type:**	External

ftprestart

UNIX Shell: All primary shells (bash, ash, tcsh)

Function	Automatically restarts shutdown FTP servers.
Syntax	ftprestart [-V]

-V	Shows version information.		
File Name: `ftprestart`	**Directory:** /usr/sbin/	**Type:**	External
ftprestart /etc/ftp/shutmsg	Restarts the FTP server with `/etc/ftp/shutmsg` information.		

ftpshut

ftpshut	UNIX Shell:	All primary shells (bash, ash, tcsh)
Function	An automatic shutdown procedure that notifies FTP users when the server is shutting down.	
Syntax	ftpshut [options...] *time { messages... }*	

-V	Shows version information.
-l *time*	Specifies the time in minutes before shutdown that access to the server is denied.
-d *time*	Specifies time in minutes before shutdown that any connections are disabled.
time	Specifies the shutdown time as now, +minutes, or HHMM.
messages...	Specifies the warning message to send to connected users.
File Name: `ftpshut`	**Directory:** /usr/sbin/ **Type:** External
ftpshut now	Shuts down the FTP server now!
ftpshut 1200 "Shutting down ftp-server at 12:00"	Shuts down the server at 12:00 and warns the users.

ftpwho

ftpwho	UNIX Shell:	All primary shells (bash, ash, tcsh)
Function	Shows information about the current processes for each FTP user.	
Syntax	ftpwho [-V]	

-V	Shows version information.
File Name: `ftpwho`	**Directory:** /usr/bin/ **Type:** External

funzip

funzip	UNIX Shell:	All primary shells (bash, ash, tcsh)
Function	Extracts the first file from a zip archive within a pipe to the standard, or specified, input.	
Syntax	funzip [*-password*] *file*	

-password	Specifies the password when the zip file is encrypted.
file	Specifies a file to use as input instead of STDIN.
File Name: `funzip`	**Directory:** /usr/bin/ **Type:** External

fuser

fuser	UNIX Shell:	All primary shells (bash, ash, tcsh)
Function	Shows all processes that are using the specified files or file systems.	
Syntax	fuser [options...] *files...*	

-a	Handles the devices as files, and, if a process uses it, shows information about it.
-s	Quiet mode. Shows less information. Can't be used with -a option.
-	Resets all options and sets the signal back to SIGKILL.
-n *space*	Specifies the name space to use.
-*signal*	Specifies the signal to use when killing processes (default is SIGKILL).
-k	Kills all processes accessing the file specified.
-i	Requests user confirmation before killing a process.
-m	Uses the `device` as a single file.
-u	Shows the process owner's username along with the process ID.
-v	Verbose mode. Shows more information.
-l	Shows all known signal names.
-V	Shows version information.
files...	Specifies the filenames to show the process ID for.
File Name: `fuser`	**Directory:** /sbin **Type:** External
fuser -m /bin/bash	Shows all processes using `/bin/bash`.
fuser -k /home	Kills all processes accessing `/home`.

g++	UNIX Shell:	All primary shells (bash, ash, tcsh)
Function	The C++ compiler version of *gcc*. It assumes that the preprocessed files `.i` are in C++.	
Syntax	g++ [options...]	

	The following options are unique to g++:
-fall-virtual	Handles all functions as though they were virtual functions.
-fenum-int-equiv	Allows conversion from `int` to `enum`.
-fhandle-signatures	Controls the recognition of signatures.
-fno-handle-signatures	Doesn't control the recognition of signatures.
-fthis-is-variable	Allows old C assignment within class members functionality.
-g	Creates debug information in the native OS format (DXB, SDB, or DWARF).
-Wenum-clash	Alerts when an attempt to convert between different enumeration types is done.
-Woverloaded-virtual	Alerts if a function has the same name as a virtual one but with unmatched signature.
-Wtemplate-debugging	Alerts if debug is unavailable when templates are in use.
+e*N*	Controls how virtual function definitions are used.
	The following options are C++ specific and are also found in `gcc`:
-c	Compiles or assembles the source files, but doesn't create a link.
-D*macro*	Determines that the specified macro uses the string "1" as its definition.
-D*macro=defn*	Allows a specific macro to be defined by the specified definition.
-E	Stops the compiler after the preprocess stage and sends it to STDOUT.
-fdollars-in-identifiers	Allows dollar signs ($) within identifiers.
-felide-constructors	Tells the compiler to use call shortcuts around constructions. Speeds up compilation.
-fexternal-templates	Creates smaller code for template declarations. Mark files with `#pragma` first.
-fno-gnu-linker	Disallows global initialization output from the GNU linker.
-fmemoize-lookups	Allows the compiler to compile faster by the use of heuristics.
-fno-default-inline	Doesn't allow member functions to be made inline by default.
-fno-strict-prototype	Causes the function that is declared with no arguments to hide its arguments.
-fnonnull-objects	Omits checks for `null`.
-I*dir*	Appends the specific directory to the list of directories that are searched.
-L*dir*	Adds the specified directory to the list of directories when looking for `-l`.
-l*library*	Uses the specified library when linking.
-nostdinc	Blocks the search of the standard system directories when looking for header files.
-nostdinc++	Same as above but allows the search.
-O	Starts compilation optimization.
-o file	Places the output into the specified file.
-S	Stops the compilation before assembly.
-traditional	Tries to support traditional C compiler aspects.
-Umacro	Undefines the specified macro.
-Wall	Shows all warnings.
-w	Blocks all warnings.

File Name:	`g++`	**Directory:**	/usr/bin/	**Type:**	External
g++ hello.cpp -o hello			Compile and link hello.cpp; produce binary file hello as output.		

g77, f77	UNIX Shell:	All primary shells (bash, ash, tcsh)
Function	The GNU Fortran compiler. This can also be started using `f77`.	
Syntax	g77 [options...] *files...*	

-c	Compiles or assembles the file. Outputs an object file.
-D*macro*	Defines a macro with the value 1.
-D*macro=value*	Defines a macro with the value.
-E	Runs the preprocessing stage. Send the preprocess source to STDOUT.
-g	Adds debugging information.
-I*directory*	Specifies directory to search for include files.
-L*directory*	Specifies directory to search for library.
-l*library*	Specifies a library to use when linking.
-nostdinc	Doesn't search standard system directories for include files.

continued

-O	Uses optimize compilation.
-o *file*	Sends the output to file.
-S	Runs the compilation but doesn't assemble. Sends the assembler code to STDOUT.
-U*macro*	Undefines the macro.
-v	Verbose mode. Shows more information.
-Wall	Activates all warning messages.
files...	Specifies the source files.

File Name:	g77	**Directory:**	/usr/bin/	**Type:**	External
Note:	Please see gcc for more options.				

gawk, awk

UNIX Shell: All primary shells (bash, ash, tcsh)

Function	A processing language from GNU built from `awk` and supports all of the options found in `awk`.
Syntax	gawk [options...] ['*scriptstr*'] files...

-F*exp*	Specifies the expression to use as field separator.
-v *variable=value*	Sets the value for the specifies variable.
-f *scriptfile*	Specifies the file that contains the specific pattern action statements to use.
-mf *value*	Sets maximum number of fields.
-mr *value*	Sets the maximum record size.
-W compat	Sets compatibility mode, `gawk` behaves identically to UNIX `awk`.
-W copyright	Shows the short version of the GNU copyright information.
-W copyleft	Shows GNU general public license.
-W help	Shows help information.
-W usage	Shows help information.
-W lint	Warns about constructs that are dubious or non portable.
-W lint-old	Warns if it isn't portable to original version UNIX `awk`.
-W posix	Uses compatibility mode.
-W re-interval	Uses interval expressions in regular expression matching.
-W source *program-text*	Specifies `awk` program source code.
-W version	Shows version information.
--	Specifies the end of options.
' *scriptstr* '	Contains the pattern action statements and must be enclosed by single quotes (').
	The following optional function is supported:
pattern { *action* }	Specifies the format for the pattern action statements specified by 'scriptstr'.
	The following arithmetic functions are supported:
atan2(*x,y*	Returns the arctan of x / y. The result is in radians.
cos(*x*)	Returns the cosine of the specified value. The value must be in radians.
exp(*x*)	Returns the exponential function of the specified value.
int(*x*	Shortens the specified value to an integer. It trims the value when x > 0.
log(*x*)	Returns the natural logarithm of the specified value.
rand()	Returns a random number between 0 and 1.
sin(*x*)	Returns the sine of the specified value. The value must be in radians.
sqrt(*x*)	Returns the square root of the specified value.
srand(*{ x }*)	Specifies a new seed for the rand function if not specified use time of day.
	The following are the supported string functions (string is indicated by s) :
gsub(*r, s* [, *t*])	Replaces all regular expression r with s in t. If t not given, use $0.
gensub(*r, s, h* [, *t*])	Same as above if h = g or G. Otherwise, h specifies the match to replace.
index(*s, sub*)	Gives the position of string *s* where the substring *sub* occurs first.
length(*s*)	Gives the total length of an argument or an entire line if there is no argument.
match(*s, re*)	Returns the position where the regular expression *re* match the string *s* .
split(*s, a, fs*)	Splits string s into an array of elements a1,a2, and separates fields with the fs exp.
sprintf(*fmt, expr...*)	Formats listed expressions with `printf` using the format specified by fmt.
sub(*r, s* [, *t*])	Same as `gsub`, but replaces only the first match.
substr(*s, m, n*)	Gives the n-character substring of the string *s* that starts at the m position.
toupper(*s*)	Returns the string with all letters uppercase.
tolower(*s*)	Returns the string with all letters lowercase.

continued

	The following are the built-in variables that can be used:
-v *var=value*	Specifies a built-in variable listed below and assign it a value.
ARGC	Defines the number of command-line arguments not counting the one to gawk.
ARGIND	Defines the index in `ARGV` of the current file being processed.
ARGV	Defines an array of command line arguments index from 0 to `ARGC` -1.
CONVFMT	Specifies the conversion format for numbers (default is %.6g).
ENVIRON	Defines an array with the environment variables.
ERRNO	Define a string containing an error description if an error occurs.
FIELDWIDTHS	Specifies a list of field widths.
FILENAME	Specifies the name of the current file being used for input.
FNR	Defines the input record number in the current input file.
FS	Defines input field separators (default is Space and Tab).
IGNORECASE	Specifies whether case is ignored. If zero (0), all function is case-sensitive.
NF	Defines number of fields in the existing file.
NR	Defines ordinal number for the current record.
OFMT	Defines output numbers in a specific format (default is %.6g).
OFS	Defines output field separators (default is blank).
ORS	Defines output record separators (default is new line).
RS	Defines input record separators (default is new line).
RSTART	Specifies index of the first character that is matched by `match()`. Returns a 0 if no match.
RLENGTH	Specifies the length of the string that is matched by `match()`. Returns a -1 if no match.
SUBSEP	Specifies the character that separates subscripts in array elements (default is \034).
	The following are control flow functions:
break	Exits from a *for*, *while*, or *do* loop.
continue	Starts the next loop cycle in a *for*, *while*, or *do* loop.
do *statement*	Executes the specified statement while the condition is true.
while (*condition*)	Is evaluated by do and runs the do statement if condition is true and exits if false.
exit *{ exp }*	Executes the end routine if exists, and exits the script with return value *exp*.
if (*condition*)	Performs the statement if the condition is true or performs the else condition.
else (*condition*)	Performs the else condition when the if condition is false.
while (*condition*)	Performs the condition as long as the condition is true.
for (*exp1; exp2 ; exp3*)	Uses three expressions (see below). Exits when any expr is false.
exp1	Sets the counter variable to an initial value, which counts the number of loops.
exp2	Defines the variable that is read and evaluated before executing the statement.
exp3	Increments each time the loop is true. (The variables exp1, exp2, and exp3 are all optional and are true if not used.)
for (*arrayvar*)	A loop that executes each variable defined in an array.
next	Reads the input line and begins a new loop or procedure.
	The following input/output functions are supported:
getline	Sets $0 into the next input record using the current input file. 1 = success, -1 = error.
print	Shows the results of the ' *scriptstr* ' and variables to STDOUT.
printf	Same as print, but also formats the output.
$*n*	Specifies the field number in the file ($1, $2, $3, and so on) and separated by FS.
$0	Uses the entire line in the file as input.
files...	Specifies the input files that are scanned for pattern matching.

File Name:	`gawk`	**Directory:**	/bin/	**Type:**	External

gcc

UNIX Shell:	All primary shells (bash, ash, tcsh)
Function	The GNU C/C++ compiler. It assumes that the preprocessed .i files are C based.
Syntax	gcc [options...] *files...*

	The following are the global options:
-x *language*	Specifies the language (C++, assembler, C, Objective-C, etc.) of the input files.
-x none	Turns off the language specification. (Is default).
-c	Compiles the source files but doesn't link them.
-S	Stops after compilation. Doesn't assemble. Outputs an assembler code file.
-E	Stops the preprocess. Doesn't run the compiler. Outputs source code to STDOUT.
-o *file*	Outputs to the specified file.

continued

-v	Verbose mode. Shows executed commands and version information.
-pipe	Uses pipes instead of temporary files when compiling.
	The following are language options:
-ansi	Supports ANSI standard C programs by turning off GNU C features that don't use ANSI.
-fno-asm	Ignores `asm`, `inline`, or `typeof` keywords. Can be used as identifiers.
-fno-builtin	Ignores functions that don't start with double underscores (_exit, abort, abs, and so on).
-fhosted	Compiles hosted environments. Assumes the `-fbuiltin` option is used.
-ffreestanding	Compiles freestanding environments. Assumes the `-fno-builtin` option is used.
-fno-strict-prototype	Handles function declarations with no arguments.
-trigraphs	Supports ANSI standard C trigraphs. Using -ansi assumes that -trigraphs are used.
-traditional	Tries to support traditional C compiler aspects.
-traditional-cpp	Tries to support traditional C preprocessor aspects.
-fdollars-in-identifiers	Allows $ within C++ identifiers. `-fnodollars-in-identifiers` forbids $.
-fexternal-templates	Creates smaller template declaration code. You must mark files with #pragma.
-fcond-mismatch	Allows for second and third argument, mismatched types, and conditional expressions.
-funsigned-char	Sets the computer type `char` to unsigned. Same as `like unsigned char`.
-fsigned-char	Sets the computer type `char` to signed. Same as `like signed char`.
-fsigned-bitfields	Sets bitfields to signed. Unsign using `-funsigned-bitfields`.
-fno-unsigned-bitfields	Sets bitfields to signed. Unsign using `-fno-signed-bitfields`. (Bitfields are signed by default unless -traditional is set.)
-fwritable-strings	Writes into string constants for old program compatibility only.
	The following are pre-processor options:
-include *file*	Processes the specified file before the regular input file.
-imacros *file*	Processes the specified file and rejects its output before processing the normal input.
-idirafter *dir*	Adds the specified directory to the second include path.
-iprefix *prefix*	Specifies the prefix for `-iwithprefix` options.
-iwithprefix *dir*	Adds the specified directory to the second include path by using `-iprefix prefix`.
-nostdinc	Ignores searching the standard system directories for header files.
-nostdinc++	Ignores searching the C++-specific standard system directories for header files.
-undef	Doesn't predefine non standard macros and architecture flags.
-E	Runs only the preprocessor.
-C	Doesn't discard comments while preprocessing.
-P	Doesn't create `#line` commands. Use with the `-E` option.
-M	Outputs a `make` rule for every source file that is preprocessed.
-MM	Same as `-m` except output uses header files added with `#include file`.
[-MG]	Handles missing header files like generated files. Use with `-M & -MM`.
-MD	Same as -M except dependency information is written to files ending with `.d`.
-MMD	Same as –MD except uses user header files.
-H	Shows each header filename that is used.
-A *question answer*	Validates an answer to a question when it is tested by a conditional like `#if`.
-D*macro*	Defines the specified macro with the definition of `1`.
-D*macro=def*	Defines the specified macro with the specified definition.
-U*macro*	Un-defines the specified macro.
-dM	Outputs only the macro definitions that are in use when preprocessing ends.
-dD	Tells the preprocessor to pass all macro definitions to the output in correct order.
-dN	Same as -dD except that macro contents and arguments are absent.
	The following are assembler options:
-Wa,*options...*	Sends the specified options (comma separated) to the assembler.
	The following are linker options:
-l*library*	Uses the specified library when linking.
-lobjc	Links an Objective C program.
-nostartfiles	Skips the standard system startup files while linking.
-nostdlib	Same as -nostartfiles but skips the standard system libraries.
-static	Stops linking with shared libraries. Works only with dynamic linking systems.
-shared	Creates a shared object that can be linked to others to create an executable.
-symbolic	Binds references to global symbols when creating a shared object.
-Xlinker *option*	Sends the specified option to the linker.

continued

-Wl, *option*	Sends the specified options (comma separated) to the linker.
-u *symbol*	Makes the specified symbol act as undefined.
	The following are directory options:
-I*dir*	Appends the specified directory to the search path.
-I-	The current directory isn't the first directory to search for the #include file.
-L*dir*	Adds the specified directory to use when searching for `-I`.
-B*prefix*	Specifies prefixes the compiler should check to find its files.
	These are the warning options:
-fsyntax-only	Checks for syntax errors but doesn't give any output.
-w	Suppresses any warnings.
-Wno-import	Suppresses any #import warnings.
-pedantic	Shows all ANSI standard C warnings and reject forbidden extensions.
-pedantic-errors	Same as -pedantic except issues errors.
-W	Shows extra warnings for various conflicts.
-Wimplicit-int	Alerts for unspecified declaration types.
-Wimplicit-function-declaration	Alerts when a function is used before it is declared.
-Wimplicit	Same as -Wimplicit-int.
-Wmain	Alerts when a suspicious declaration or definition for the main function appears.
-Wreturn-type	Alerts when a reply statement sends an unexpected no-reply value.
-Wunused-function	Alerts when a static function isn't defined but is declared.
d	Alerts when a label isn't used but is declared.
-Wunused-parameter	Alerts when a function parameter is unused.
-Wunused-variable	Alerts when a local or non constant static variable is unused.
-Wunused-value	Alerts when a statement computes a non used result.
-Wunused	Combines all of the previous -W options.
-Wswitch	Alerts when a switch statement is missing a named code case.
-Wcomment	Alerts when a comment-start `/*` sequence shows up in a comment.
-Wtrigraphs	Alerts if any trigraphs appear.
-W*format*	Verifies that proper types are used in the specified format string.
-Wchar-subscripts	Alerts when an array subscript contains the type `char`.
-Wuninitialized	Alerts when an automatic variable is utilized without being started.
-Wparentheses	Alerts when there are no parentheses in certain situations.
-Wall	Combines all of the previous -W options.
-Wtraditional	Alerts when constructs don't follow ANSI C and traditional C rules.
-Wshadow	Alerts when local variables shadow other local variables.
-Wid-clash-*len*	Alerts when two identifiers have a match in the `len` characters.
-Wpointer-arith	Alerts when anything depends upon `size of` of void or a function type.
-Wcast-qual	Alerts when a pointer is set to erase a qualifier type from a target type.
-Wcast-align	Alerts when a pointer is set to enlarge the alignment of the target type.
-Wwrite-strings	Verifies proper use of string constant types `const`. Alerts on errors.
-Wconversion	Alerts when prototype causes fixed to floating point, width, or sign conversion errors.
-Waggregate-return	Alerts when functions that report structures/unions that are already called/defined.
-Wstrict-prototypes	Alerts when a function is declared/defined without any argument types specified.
-Wmissing-prototypes	Alerts when a global function is defined without a preceding prototype declaration.
-Wmissing-declarations	Alerts when a global function is defined without a preceding declaration.
-Wredundant-decls	Alerts when anything is declared multiple times within the same scope.
-Wlong-long	Alerts if the `long` type is applied.
-Woverloaded-virtual	Alerts if a virtual function doesn't match the base class virtual type signature.
-Winline	Alerts when a function was declared inline or can't be inlined.
-Werror	Handles all warnings like errors; exits compilation after the warning.
	The following are debugging options:
-g	Shows debug information in the OS native formats: stabs, COFF, XCOFF, or DWARF.
	Use these options when GNU CC is made to handle more than one debug format:
-ggdb	Shows debug information in the native format, which includes GDB extensions if used.
-gstabs	Shows debug information in stabs format without GDB extensions. Common in BSD.
-gstabs+	Shows debug information in stabs format with GNU debugger extensions.
-gcoff	Shows debug information in COFF format. Used by SDB in pre System V systems.
-gxcoff	Shows debug information in XCOFF format. Used by DBX debugger on IBM RS/6000.

continued

-gxcoff+	Shows debug information in XCOFF format with GNU debugger extensions.
-gdwarf	Shows debug information in DWARF format. Used by SDB on System V r4 systems.
-gdwarf+	Shows debug information in DWARF format with GNU debugger extensions. (-g options using a plus (+) may make other debuggers crash or read freeze.)
	Use these six options to set debug levels: 1 = min, 3 = max (default is 2).
-g *level*	Specifies the debug information level for native formats.
-ggdb *level*	Specifies the debug information level for GDB extensions.
-gstabs *level*	Specifies the debug information level for STABS extensions.
-gcoff *level*	Specifies the debug information level for COFF extensions.
-gxcoff *level*	Specifies the debug information level for XCOFF extensions.
-gdwarf *level*	Specifies the debug information level for DWARF extensions.
-p	Generates extra code for the `prof` analysis program.
-pg	Generates extra code for the `gprof` analysis program.
-a	Generates extra code for basic blocks. Can be seen using the `tcov` program.
-ax	Generates extra code for basic block profile parameters from `bb.in`.
-d*letters*	Makes a debug dump at the specified letter time.
-dM	Dumps all macro definitions after preprocessing and creates no output.
-dN	Dumps all macro names after preprocessing.
-dD	Dumps all macro definitions after preprocessing and creates output.
-dy	Dumps debug information to STDERR while parsing.
-dr	Dumps to `file.rtl` after RTL generation.
-dx	Generates RTL for a function.
-dj	Dumps to `file.jump` after the first jump optimization.
-ds	Dumps to `file.cse` after CSE and any following jump optimization.
-dL	Dumps to `file.loop` after loop optimization.
-dt	Dumps to `file.cse2` after the second CSE pass and any following jump optimization.
-df	Dumps to `file.flow` after the flow analysis.
-dc	Dumps to `file.combine` after the instruction combination.
-dS	Dumps to `file.sched` after the first instruction schedule pass.
-dl	Dumps to `file.lreg` after the local register allocation.
-dg	Dumps to `file.greg` after the global register allocation.
-dR	Dumps to `file.sched2` after the second instruction scheduling pass.
-dJ	Dumps to `file.jump2` after the last jump optimization.
-dd	Dumps to `file.dbr` after the delayed branch scheduling.
-dk	Dumps to `file.stack` after the conversion from registers into stack.
-da	Dumps like all of the previous dump options combined.
-dm	Shows memory usage statistics to STDERR once the run is done.
-dp	Attaches a pattern type and alternative comment to the end of the assembler output.
-fpretend-float	Lets targets simulate the same floating-point format as the host.
-save-temps	Stores unusual temporary files and places them in the current directory.
-print-file-name=*library*	Shows the name of the specified library file that would be used if `gcc` were to link.
-print-libgcc-file-name	Same as `-print-file-name=libgcc.a.`
-print-prog-name=*program*	Same as `-print-file-name` except that it looks for a program.
	The following are optimization options:
-O	Optimizes code size and execution time before processing.
-O2	Optimizes more. Increases compilation time generated code performance.
-O3	Maximum optimization. Includes level 02 plus activates `-finline-functions.`
-O0	No optimization.
-ffloat-store	Doesn't save any floating-point variables in any registers.
-fsave-memoized	Uses heuristics to compile C++ faster.
-fno-default-inline	Prevents the C++ member functions inline.
-fno-defer-pop	Pops arguments to function calls as soon as the function replies.
-fforce-mem	Forces memory operands to be put into registers before calculation is done on them.
-fforce-addr	Forces memory address constants to be put into registers before calculation.
-fomit-frame-pointer	Removes the frame pointer in the registers for the functions that don't need pointers.
-finline-functions	Integrates all of the simple functions into their respective callers.
-fcaller-saves	Enables values to be assigned to registers that function calls use.

continued

-fkeep-inline-functions	Outputs a split callable run time version of the function.
-fno-function-cse	Doesn't allow function addresses to be put into registers.
-fno-peephole	Disables any host-specific peephole optimizations.
-ffast-math	Allows ANSI and IEEE rule violations to enlarge code optimizing.
	Use these options for fine-tuning optimization:
-fstrength-reduce	Performs loop strength optimization and eliminates iteration variables.
-fthread-jumps	Performs jump branch redirection optimization.
-funroll-loops	Performs loop unrolling optimization on loops that have iterations during run-time.
-funroll-all-loops	Performs loop unrolling optimization on all loops.
-fcse-follow-jumps	Scans jump instructions that otherwise are unreachable by any other paths.
-fcse-skip-blocks	Same as `-fcse-follow-jumps` but follows the jumps set by conditions like if.
-frerun-cse-after-loop	Reruns sub-expression elimination after the loop optimizations have been performed.
-felide-constructors	Initializes C++ `y` directly from the call to `foo`.
-fexpensive-optimizations	Runs a series of minor optimizations that don't necessarily improve performance.
-fdelayed-branch	Attempts to reorder any instructions in a more efficient order.
-fschedule-insn	Same as `-fschedule-insns` but requests an additional instruction pass.
	The following are target options:
-b *machine*	Specifies the host target for compilation.
-V *version*	Specifies which version of GNU CC to execute.
	The following are platform-specific options:
-m*platform*	Selects the platform specific options that are available for the specified platform.
	The following are SPARC-specific options:
-mfpu	Creates floating-point instruction output.
-mno-fpu	Creates library call output for floating point. Use with caution.
-mepilogue	Places exit code for function exits at the end of every function (smaller code).
-mno-epilogue	Places exit code for function exits at every possible exit (faster code).
-mv8	Creates SPARC v8 code.
-msparclite	Creates SPARClite code.
-mcypress	Optimizes code for the Cypress CY7C602 chip. The SparcStation/SparcServer 3xx.
-msupersparc	Optimizes code for the SuperSparc cpu. The SparcStation 10, 1000 & 2000.
	The following are IBM RS6000–specific options:
-mfp-in-toc	Sends floating-point constants to table of contents. `-mno-fp-in-toc` doesn't.
	The following are Intel-specific options:
-m486	Optimizes code for a 486. `-mno-486` doesn't.
-msoft-float	Creates library call output for floating point. Use with caution.
-mno-fp-ret-in-387	Blocks the use of FPU registers for function reply values.
	The following are Alpha station–specific options:
-msoft-float	Allows hardware floating point for floating-point operations.
-mfp-reg	Creates code that uses floating-point register set.
	The following are SYSTEM V–specific options:
-G	Passes -G to the system linker. Strictly for compatibility with different compilers.
-Qy	Identifies the compiler tool versions to an `.ident` assembler directive output.
-Qn	Blocks an `.ident` assembler directive output (is the default).
-YP,*directories...*	Searches the specified directories for libraries specified with `-l`. (You may specify more than one directory by placing colons (:) between each.)
-Ym,*directory*	Searches the specified directory for the M4 preprocessor.
	The following are code generation options:
-fnonnull-objects	Objects found with references are assumed > null. If `-fnull-objects` then null.
-fpcc-struct-return	Uses the C compiler conventions for `struct` and `union`.
-freg-struct-return	Uses the log conventions for `struct` and `union`.
-fshort-enums	Assigns an `enum` type as many bytes as it needs.
-fshort-double	Uses the same size that `float` has.
-fshared-data	Shares the non-const variables and data of this compilation.
-fno-common	Assigns unopened global variables in the `bss` part of the object file.
-fno-ident	Ignores `#indent` directive.
-fno-gnu-linker	Specifies that a non-GNU linker is used.
-finhibit-size-directive	Blocks `a.size` assembler directive output.

continued

-fverbose-asm	Adds extra commentary to the created assembly code.
-fvolatile	Marks all memory references that are used through pointers as volatile.
-fvolatile-global	Marks all memory references to `extern` global data as volatile.
-fpic	Creates position independent code for use in library that is shared.
-fPIC	Emits position-independent code for dynamic linking.
-ffixed-*reg*	Specifies the register that acts as a fixed log.
-fcall-used-*reg*	Specifies the register that acts as an allocatable log.
-fcall-saved-*reg*	Specifies the register that acts like an allocatable log that function saves.
	The following are pragmas:
#pragma interface	Allows using the header file directive to define object classes.
#pragma implementation "objects.h"	Allows included header file output and makes them globally visible.
files...	Specifies the input file(s).

File Name:	`gcc`	**Directory:**	/usr/bin/	**Type:**	External
gcc hello.c -o hello			Compiles C source file hello.c; produces binary file `hello`.		

gdb

UNIX Shell: All primary shells (bash, ash, tcsh)

Function	A debugger that can manage debugging of C, C++ and Modula-2 code. A.K.A GNU Debugger.
Syntax	gdb [options...] *{ ACTION }*

-h	Shows help information.
-s *file*	Reads the symbol table from the specified file.
-write	Allows you to edit any specified executable or core files.
-e *file*	Selects the file to execute.
-se *file*	Reads from the symbol table of the specified file and then uses it as an executable.
-c *file*	Specifies the file to use for the core dump.
-x *file*	Executes any of the GDB commands from the specified file.
-d *directory*	Adds the specified directory into the search path for source files.
-n	Ignores commands from any `.gdbinit` files.
-q	Suppresses the titles and copyright notices. Quiet mode.
-batch	Runs `gdb` in batch mode. You must use this with -x.
-cd=*directory*	Uses the specified directory as the `gdb` working directory.
-f	`Emacs` uses this option to tell `gdb` to output the file and line number.
-b*bps*	Sets the line speed baud rate to any serial interface that is used for remote debug.
-tty=*device*	Uses the specified device as the STDIN and STDOUT.
ACTION	**The type of check that the debugger will use. The following actions are valid:**
break *{ file } function*	Creates the specified function break point in the debug process or in the given file.
run *{ list }*	Starts the program with an argument list. Otherwise, just starts the program.
bt	Shows the program stack. Back trace.
print *expression*	Shows the expression values.
c	Continues to run the program after `break`.
next	Executes the next program line. It will step over any function calls.
step	Executes the next program line. It will step into any function calls.
help *{ name }*	Shows help information on the specified `gdb` command.
quit	Exits the `gdb` command.
	When using these actions, you may also select one of these two actions:
core	Specifies a core file that debug will look at.
procID	Specifies the process ID. Use this when you want to check a process that is in use.

File Name:	`gdb`	**Directory:**	/usr/bin/	**Type:**	External
gdb -nw -command=gdb.command			Runs the gdb script `gdb.command` and prints to STDOUT.		

gendiff

gendiff	UNIX Shell:	A shell (ash, bsh)
Function	Generates a `diff` file that contains the differences between two directories.	
Syntax	gendiff *directory { extension }*	

directory	Specifies the directory where the new `diff` file is made.
extension	Specifies the file extension to create. Otherwise, it's sent to STDOUT.
File Name: `gendiff`	**Directory:** /usr/bin — **Type:** Script
Note:	The file that is created by `gendiff` may later be used with the program `patch` to re-create any changes made.
gendiff /home/nisse/c++ .b > mydiff-orig.patch	Generates a diff file for all files with .b extension in `/home/nisse/c++`.

genksyms

genksyms	UNIX Shell:	All primary shells (bash, ash, tcsh)
Function	Creates a file with version information by first running `gcc -E` on it.	
Syntax	genksyms [options...] -k *version* [options...] *{ directory }*	

-w	Allows unrecognized syntax and undefined structure alerts.
-q	Disallows unrecognized syntax and undefined structure alerts. Quiet mode.
-D	Dumps any expanded symbol definitions to STDERR. Debug use only.
-d	Generates debug information. Multiple -d options means higher levels of debug output.
Level 1	The default level of debug output. Shows any actions that are done.
Level 2	Allows for parser recognition output.
Level 3	Allows for lexical analysis output.
-k *version*	Specifies the version of the kernel for output. Uses 2.1.0 as the default.
-p *string*	Adds the specified string to the front of generated CRCs. For use with SMP kernels.
directory	Specifies the output directory for .ver file; otherwise, it writes to STDOUT.
File Name: `genksyms`	**Directory:** /sbin — **Type:** External
genksyms ucgrules.c	Reads from `ucgrules.c`, and outputs to a `.ver` file.

getent

getent	UNIX Shell:	All primary shells (bash, ash, tcsh)
Function	Retrieves entries using keywords that must already exist from a system configuration file.	
Syntax	getent [options...] *file { keys... }*	

-?	Shows help information.
--usage	Shows the syntax for the command.
-V	Shows version information.
file	Specifies the configuration file to retrieve data from. Can be one of the following.
passwd	`/etc/passwd` — The system password information file.
group	`/etc/group` — The system group information file.
hosts	`/etc/hosts` — The hostname information file.
services	`/etc/services` — Contains system services and aliases.
protocols	`/etc/protocols` — Contains the system protocol database.
ether	`/etc/ethers` — Contains Ethernet address to hostname information.
network	`/etc/networks` — Contains network name information.
netmasks	`/etc/netmasks` — Contains the network mask information.
nsswitch.conf	`/etc/nsswitch.conf` — Contains DNS information.
keys...	Specifies the keyword to show entries on.
File Name: `getent`	**Directory:** /usr/bin/ — **Type:** External
getent passwd root	Shows the root entry in /etc/passwd.

getfilename

getfilename	UNIX Shell:	TC shell (tcsh)
Function	Uses a file in the specified format, then creates a copy of it using the specified filename.	
Syntax	getfilename *format file*	

format	Specifies the file format that's used to create the copy from.
file	Specifies the output file.

continued

File Name:	`getfilename`	**Directory:**	/usr/bin/	**Type:**	Script
getfilename Postscript ucg		Asks for a file in a PostScript format, then copies it to the file ucg.			

getkeycodes

UNIX Shell: All primary shells (bash, ash, tcsh)

Function	Shows kernel scan-code to key-code mapping table. Can be used to define functions of special keys.
Syntax	getkeycodes

File Name:	`getkeycodes`	**Directory:**	/usr/bin/	**Type:**	External
Tip:	Scancodes can also be shown by using `showkey -s`.				

gettext

UNIX Shell: All primary shells (bash, ash, tcsh)

Function	Gets the domain name variable from a message object made by `msgfmt`.
Syntax	gettext [options...] *{ domain } { msgid }*

-e	Enables expansion of some escape sequences.
-h	Shows help information.
-n	Suppresses trailing new line.
-V	Shows version information.
-s	Shows the `msgid` arguments to search for. Can't be used with the domain.
domain	Specifies the text domain to get messages from. Can't be use with the -s option.
msgid	Specifies the message ID to get from the domain.

File Name:	`gettext`	**Directory:**	/usr/bin/	**Type:**	External

gif2tiff

UNIX Shell: All primary shells (bash, ash, tcsh)

Function	Creates a TIFF image file from a GIF image file.
Syntax	gif2tiff [options...] *inputfile outputfile*

-c lzw	Compresses output in the default Lempel-Ziv & Welch (Compression-5) format.
-c zip	Compresses output in the default Deflate encoding format.
-c packbits	Compresses output in the default PackBits encoding format.
-c none	Creates the GIF file without any compression.
-r *size*	Specifies the size of the rows per data strip. The default is 8 kilobytes.
inputfile	Specifies the GIF87 file to use for conversion.
outputfile	Specifies the TIFF file to be created.

File Name:	`gif2tiff`	**Directory:**	/usr/bin/	**Type:**	External

gpasswd

UNIX Shell: All primary shells (bash, ash, tcsh)

Function	Administers the `/etc/group` and `/etc/gshadow` files.
Syntax	gpasswd [options...] *group*

	You may select only one of the following four options:
-a *user*	Adds users to groups. Group administrator privileges are required.
-d *user*	Removes users from groups. Group administrator privileges are required.
-R	Disables group access to the specified group through the `newgrp` command.
-r	Administrators can erase the specified group's password.
	Or, you may select a combination of these two options:
-A *users...*	Defines the specified group's administrators.
-M *users...*	Defines the specified group's members.
group	Specifies the group that's used.

File Name:	`gpasswd`	**Directory:**	/usr/bin/	**Type:**	External

gpg	UNIX Shell:	All primary shells (bash, ash, tcsh)
Function	The main security program for the GNUPG system and can check, sign, encrypt and decrypt.	
Syntax	gpg [options...] *{ command }*	

-a	Creates armored ASCII output.
-o *file*	Uses the specified file as output.
-u *userID*	Specifies the user ID to use to sign or decrypt.
--default-key *userID*	Specifies the user ID to use as the default signature.
-r *userID*	Specifies the user ID to use to encrypt.
--default-recipient *name*	Specifies the valid default receiver.
--default-recipient-self	Uses the default key as the default receiver.
--no-default-recipient	Resets the `--default-recipient` and `--default-recipient-self` options.
--encrypt-to *userID*	Specifies the user ID for the options file and may be used as encrypt-to-self.
--no-encrypt-to	Disables all of the `--encrypt-to` keys.
-v	Verbose mode. Shows more information if you use -v -v.
-q	Suppresses messages as much as possible. Quiet mode.
-z *value*	Sets the compression level. A zero disables compression (default is `zlib 6`).
-textmode	Starts standard text mode. For PGP compatibility.
-t	Starts text mode. When used with armoring and signing, enables clearsigned messages.
-n	Runs but doesn't alter anything.
-i	Prompts the user before overwriting files.
--batch	Starts batch mode. Forbids the use of interactive commands.
--no-batch	Stops batch mode.
--yes	Answers yes to most questions.
--no	Answers no to most questions.
--always-trust	Skips key validation and assumes that all used keys are trusted.
--keyserver *host*	Specifies the host to check for keys.
--honor-http-proxy	Attempts to access the key server via the proxy that was set with `http_proxy`.
--keyring *file*	Adds the specified file to the list of key rings (default is `gnupg-ring`).
--secret-keyring *file*	Adds the specified file to the list of secret key rings.
--homedir *directory*	Specifies the name of the home directory (default is `~/.gnupg`).
--charset *name*	Sets the native character set iso-8859-1 which is the default Latin 1 set.
--utf8-strings	Assumes that arguments have already been sent as UTF8 strings.
--no-utf8-strings	Assumes that the arguments have been encoded with --charset (is default). The two options above affect all of the following options:
--options *file*	Reads from a file that contains options. Ignores the file in --homedir.
--no-options	Shortcuts to --options `/dev/null`, which is read first before going to a file.
--load-extension *name§*	Loads the specified extension module.
--debug *flags*	Specifies a debug flag to use. C syntax may be used.
--debug-all	Sets all of the debug flags.
--status-fd *number*	Specifies which file descriptor the special status strings are written to.
--logger-fd *number*	Writes the log output to the specified file descriptor instead of STDERR.
--no-comment	Forbids comment packets when creating secret keys.
--comment *string*	Specifies the string to use with cleartext signatures.
--default-comment	Forces the standard comment string to be written into cleartext signatures.
--no-version	Discards the version string from the cleartext signatures.
--emit-version	Forces the version string to be written into cleartext signatures.
-N *name=value*	Sets the specified name value pair as notation data into the signature.
name	Specifies the name using alphanumeric characters. The first character can't be a number.
value	Specifies the value as any printable string that can be encoded with UTF8.
--set-policy-url *string*	Uses the specified string as the Policy URL for signatures.
--set-filename *string*	Uses the specified string as the filename, which is stored in messages.
--use-embedded-filename	Attempts to create a file from a name embedded in the data.
--completes-needed *number*	Specifies the total number of trusted users before a new key signer (default is 1).
--marginals-needed *number*	Specifies the total number of marginal users before a new key signer (default is 3).
--max-cert-depth *depth*	Sets the maximum certification chain depth (default is 5).

continued

--cipher-algo *name*	Uses the specified cipher algorithm.
--digest-algo *name*	Uses the specified message digest algorithm. This may violate the OpenPGP requirement
--s2k-cipher-algo *name*	Uses the specified cipher algorithm, which is used to protect the secret keys.
--s2k-digest-algo *name*	Uses the specified digest algorithm, which is used to mangle pass phrases.
--s2k-mode *name*	Specifies how the pass phrases are mangled.
0	Adds a plain pass phrase. Not recommended.
1	Adds a `salt` to the pass phrase. (Is default.)
3	Repeats the process.
--compress-algo *name*	Uses the specified compress algorithm (default is 2 (RFC1950 compression)).
--disable-cipher-algo *name*	Forbids the use of the specified cipher algorithm.
--disable-pubkey-algo *name*	Forbids the use of the specified public-key algorithm.
--throw-keyid	Doesn't put the key ID into any encrypted packets.
--not-dash-escaped	Alters the way cleartext signatures behave so they can be ready for patch file use.
--escape-from-lines	Handles cleartext signatures a special way when mail lines start with `From`.
--passphrase-fd *number*	Reads the pass phrase from the specified file descriptor. If 0, then STDIN is used.
--rfc1991	Attempts to be RFC1991 (PGP 2.X) compliant.
--openpgp	Resets all of the packet, digest, and cipher options to OpenPGP behavior.
--force-v3-sigs	Forces v3 signatures upon all data signatures.
--force-mdc	Forces encryption with an appended manipulation code.
--allow-non-selfsigned-uid	Allows key imports with non-self-signed user IDs. Not recommended.
--lock-once	Locks the databases when a lock request is given and doesn't unlock until termination.
--lock-multiple	Releases when a lock is no longer needed. Overrides `-lock-once`.
--no-verbose	Sets the verbose level to 0.
--no-greeting	Doesn't show the copyright message.
--no-secmem-warning	Suppresses insecure memory warning.
--no-armor	Assumes that the input isn't ASCII armored format.
--no-default-keyring	Doesn't add the default key rings to the key ring list.
--skip-verify	Skips signature verification.
--with-colons	Shows the key lists in colon format.
--with-key-data	Shows the key lists and public-key data in colon format.
--with-fingerprint	Alters the format of the output. Same as `--fingerprint`.
--fast-list-mode	Bypasses the user ID and trust information in the lists to speed up the output.
	These are the supported commands:
--clearsign	Creates a clear text signature.
-b	Creates a detached signature.
	The following two options may be combined:
-s	Creates a signature.
-e	Encrypts data.
-c	Uses symmetric cipher encryption and queries for a pass phrase.
--symmetric	Same as -c.
--store	Stores into a RFC1991 packet.
--decrypt *{ file }*	Decrypts the specified file or from STDIN if no file is specified.
--verify *{ sigfile } { signfile }*	Verifies that the signature packet is checked. With no options, STDIN is read.
sigfile	Specifies the complete or detached signature file that's read for verification.
signfile	Specifies the signed files that are read for verification.
--verify-files *{ files... }*	Verifies multiple file entries, but doesn't read detached signatures.
--list-keys *{ names... }*	Lists all of the keys of the public key ring or from those given from the command line.
--list-secret-keys *{ names... }*	Lists all of the keys of the secret key ring or from those given from the command line.
	The following three options may be combined:
--list-sigs *{ names... }*	Lists signatures of the public key ring. Otherwise the same as `--list-keys`.
--check-sigs *{ names... }*	Verifies the signatures along with doing everything that `--list-sigs` does.
--fingerprint *{ names... }*	Lists all of the keys, including their fingerprints.
--list-packets	Lists only the packet sequences. A good debug tool.
--gen-key	Creates a key pair interactively.
--edit-key *name*	Starts an interactive menu that deals with the following key-related issues:
sign	Creates a signature for the key of the username if a key isn't yet signed.
lsign	Same as `sign` but marks the signature as nonexportable.

continued

revsig	Revokes a secret-key signature.
trust	Alters the owners trust level.
disable | enable	Enables or disables a key.
adduid	Creates a different user ID.
deluid	Erases a user ID.
addkey	Adds a subkey to the key.
delkey	Erases a subkey.
revkey	Revokes a subkey.
expire	Alters the expiration time of the key.
passwd	Alters the secret key pass phrase.
uid *index*	Specifies the index number to use to toggle user ID selection. Deselects all with 0.
key *index*	Specifies the index number to use to toggle subkey selection. Deselects all with 0.
check	Checks all of the selected user IDs.
pref	Lists all of the preferences.
toggle	Toggles between secret and public key lists.
save	Saves any changes to the keyrings, then quits.
quit	Quits `gpg` without bothering to update the key rings.
--sign-key *name*	Signs the public key with the specified secret key.
--lsign-key *name*	Signs the public key with the specified secret key but makes it nonexportable.
--delete-key *name*	Erases the specified key from the public key ring.
--delete-secret-key *name*	Erases the specified secret keyring and the public one.
--gen-revoke	Creates a revoke certificate for the entire key.
--export *names...*	Exports all the keys or just the specified ones from the key rings to STDOUT.
--send-keys *names...*	Sends all of the keys, or just the specified ones to a key server.
--export-all *names...*	Exports all keys, which includes those that are not OpenPGP compatible.
--export-secret-keys *names...*	Exports all keys, but not the secret keys.
--import *files...*	Imports or merges the specified keys into the key ring.
--fast-import *files...*	Imports or merges the specified keys into the key ring but doesn't create the trustdb.
--recv-keys *keyIDs...*	Imports all of the specified key IDs from a HKP key server. Use with `-keyserver`.
--export-ownertrust	Creates a list of the assigned owner trust values into ASCII format.
--import-ownertrust *files...*	Updates the trustdb with the values stored in the specified files, or STDIN if none.
--print-md *algorithm { files... }*	Shows the message digest of the given algorithm for all of the specified STDIN files.
--gen-random *value { amount }*	Creates the specified count of random bytes at the given quality level.
value	Specifies the quality level of the byte information. Select between 0, 1, or 2.
amount	Specifies the amount of the random bytes. If 0, then an endless sequence is given.
--version	Shows version information along with all of the supported algorithms.
--warranty	Shows warranty information that is read "none" here, folks :)
-h	Shows help information.
File Name: `gpg`	**Directory:** /usr/bin/ **Type:** External

gphoto

UNIX Shell: All primary shells (bash, ash, tcsh)

Function	Administers picture handling with digital cameras. Can also be used with Web cameras and in scripts.
Syntax	gphoto [options...]

-c	Shows a summary of the camera.
-n	Shows the number of pictures on the camera.
-s *count file*	Saves the picture numbered as count as file.
-t *count file*	Saves the thumbnail numbered as count as file.
-p *file*	Takes a picture that's saved as file.
-d *count*	Erases the picture numbered as count from the camera.
-l *file*	Saves a live preview as a file.
-h	Shows help information.
File Name: `gphoto`	**Directory:** /usr/bin/ **Type:** External

gpm

gpm	UNIX Shell:	All primary shells (bash, ash, tcsh)

Function	Enables the mouse in screen mode and sets various attributes such as baud rate and mouse type.
Syntax	gpm [options...]

-a	Sets the value for acceleration when a mouse motion is longer than delta `-d`.
-A *time*	Disables mouse selection paste during startup for the specified time in seconds.
-b *baud*	Sets the mouse baud rate.
-B *sequence*	Sets the mouse button sequence 1-2-3 or other combination.
-d *delta*	Sets the motion delta value.
-D	Disables background operation entry and log alerts to STDERR.
-g *number*	Emulates the specified mouse button with tap input before -B remapping.
-h	Shows help information.
-i *time*	Sets the upper time interval between multiple mouse clicks. Use time in milliseconds.
-k	Kills the running `gpm` command.
-l *charset*	Selects the find table of `inword`.
-m *file*	Selects the mouse file that is opened (default is `/dev/mouse`).
-M	Uses two devices. Options before this control 1st mouse while those after control the 2nd mouse.
-o *options*	Calls any mouse-specific options.
-p	Forces the mouse pointer to be visible when selecting (default isn't visible).
-r *number*	Sets the mouse curser motion speed. The higher the value, the faster the response.
-R *name*	Repeater mode. Mouse data received is sent to the FIFO in the specified protocol.
-s *number*	Sets the sample rate of the mouse.
-S *command*	Activates special command options. Three of these are listed below:
left button	Reboots the system by calling the `init` process.
middle button	Executes the shutdown `/sbin/shutdown -h now`.
right button	Executes the shutdown `/sbin/shutdown -r now`.
-t *name*	Selects the mouse type.
-t help	Shows a list of valid mice types. Repeater protocols are shown using an asterisk (*).
-v *{ value }*	Verbose mode. You may select an appropriate level from 0 - 10 (default is 5).
-2	Forces two-button mode, which makes the middle button act like the right one.
-3	Forces three-button mode - not recommended for two-button mice if you need to paste.

File Name:	`gpm`	**Directory:**	/usr/sbin/	**Type:**	External
Warning:	The -A option is vital if you want to avoid having people dropping commands into the selection buffer during startup.				

gpm-root

gpm-root	UNIX Shell:	All primary shells (bash, ash, tcsh)

Function	Allows Control-Mouse events to be able to draw menus during screen mode.
Syntax	gpm-root [options...]

-m *number*	Selects what modifier (function key) to use (default is Ctrl).
-u	Denies use of anything other than `/etc/gpm-root.conf` as the configuration file.
-D	Shows debug information.
-V *{ level }*	Verbose mode. Logs more information based upon the specified level.

File Name:	`gpm-root`	**Directory:**	/usr/bin/	**Type:**	External

grodvi

grodvi	UNIX Shell:	All primary shells (bash, ash, tcsh)

Function	A `groff` driver that creates TeX dvi files that can then be printed out.
Syntax	grodvi [options...] *{ files... }*

-d	Allows horizontal and vertical line implementation but ignores all other draw commands.
-v	Shows version information.
-w *value*	Sets the line thickness to the specified value in thousandths of an `em`.
-F *directory*	Searches the specified directory for device and font description files.
Files...	Specifies the dvi file or files to create.

File Name:	`grodvi`	**Directory:**	/usr/bin/	**Type:**	External

groff

groff	UNIX Shell:	All primary shells (bash, ash, tcsh)
Function	The front end to the document formatting system used by `groff`.	
Syntax	groff [options…] *{ files… }*	

-h	Shows help information.
-e	Preprocess with the command `eqn`.
-t	Preprocess with the command `tbl`.
-p	Preprocess with the command `pic`.
-s	Preprocess with the command `soelim`.
-I *directory*	Specifies the directory to search for files. The current directory is searched first.
-R	Preprocess with the command `refer`.
-v	Shows version information for `ruff` programs.
-V	Sends piped output to STDOUT instead of executing it.
-z	Allows only error messages to be shown. Suppresses all other output.
-Z	Doesn't preprocess the output.
-P *argument*	Passes one or more arguments to the preprocessor. Use –P for each argument to pass.
-l	Sends output to the printer.
-L *argument*	Passes one or more arguments to the spooler. Use –L for each argument to pass.
-T	Prepares output for the specified device (default is `ps`).
-X	Specifies `gxditview` to preview with instead of the postprocessor.
-N	Forbids the use of new lines with `eqn` delimiters.
-S	Passes the –S option to `pic` and uses –msafer with `troff`. Safe mode.
-U	Reverts to the older type of unsafe.
	The following are a list of supported `troff` options:
-a	Creates an ASCII version of the typeset output.
-b	Prints a back trace of all of the warning and error messages.
-i	Reads from STDIN after the specified input files have been processed.
-C	Enables compatibility mode.
-E	Suppresses all error messages.
-w *name*	Enables the specified warning message.
-W *name*	Suppresses the specified warning message.
-m *name*	Reads from the specified tmac. File.
-o *list*	Outputs only the pages specified in the comma-separated list.
-r *c n*	Defines the number register c to be the integer `n`.
-F *directory*	Specifies the directory to search for DESC and font files.
-M *directory*	Specifies the directory to search for macro files before `/usr/lib/groff/tmac`.
-f *name*	Specifies the default font family.
-n *number*	Gives the first page the specified number.
Files…	Specifies the file or files to use as input.

File Name:	`groff`	**Directory:**	/usr/bin/	**Type:**	External
Tip:	This can be used to guess the correct `groff` command to use to format a file.				

Grog

Grog	UNIX Shell:	Bash shell (bash)
Function	Guesses which `groff` option is required for printing a specific file and sends this answer to STDOUT.	
Syntax	grog [options…] *{ files… }*	

	The following options specify the device types:
-ps	Specifies PostScript printers.
-dvi	Specifies TeX dvi format.
-X75	Specifies 75 dpi X11 previewer.
-X100	Specifies 100 dpi X11 previewer.
-ascii	Specifies typewriter style devices.
-latin-1	Specifies typewriter style devices that use the ISO 8859-1 character set.
-utf8	Specifies typewriter style devices that use the ISO 10646 character set.
-cp1047	Specifies typewriter style devices that use the EBCDIC code page.
-lj4	Specifies HP Laser Jet4-compatible printer.

-lbp	Specifies Canon LBP-4 and -8 style printer.

Continued

-html	Specifies HTML output.
	groff options that are suggested by grog to print the file:
-e	Preprocesses using `eqn`.
-p	Preprocesses using `pic`.
-R	Preprocesses using `refer`.
-g	Preprocesses using `grn`.
-G	Preprocesses using `grap`.
-s	Preprocesses using `soelim`.
-t	Preprocesses using `tbl`.
Files…	Specifies the file that's analyzed to determine the proper command to use.
File Name: `grog`	**Directory:** /usr/bin/ **Type:** Text File
grog –lbp paper.ms	Guesses which option that is used for the file paper.ms in order for it to print to a Canon LBP printer.

grolj4

UNIX Shell: All primary shells (bash, ash, tcsh)

Function	A `groff` driver that is used for creating output that can be printed onto an HP LaserJet 4 type printer.
Syntax	grolj4 [options…] *{ files… }*

-c *pages*	Specifies the amount of copies to print.
-l	Prints documents in landscape format.
-d *{ binding }*	Duplex mode: A 1 is for long-side binding, a 2 is for short-side binding (default is 1).
-p *size*	Sets paper size. Select letter, legal, executive, a4, com10, monarch, c5, b5, or dl.
-v	Shows version information.
-w *thickness*	Sets the default line thickness to thousandths of an em.
-F *directory*	Searches the specified directory for the device and font description file `devlj4`.
Files…	Specifies the file or files to create.
File Name: `grolj4`	**Directory:** /usr/bin/ **Type:** External
grolj4 –c4 –pa4 diploma.ps	Prints four copies of diploma.ps and use the a4 format.

grops

UNIX Shell: All primary shells (bash, ash, tcsh)

Function	Translates GNU `troff` output into PostScript.
Syntax	grops [options…] *{ files… }*

-b *level*	Works around spoolers and previewers that can't manage DSC 3.0 conventions.
	The following manage levels determine what `grops` does to its output:
0	Doesn't activate any workarounds (is default).
1	Blocks %%BeginDocumentSetup & %%EndDocumentSetup comments.
2	Blocks lines in files that have %!. This is used for Sun's Pageview previewer.
4	Blocks %%Page, %%Trailer & End-Prolog comments.
8	Forces output's first line to be %!PS-Adobe-2.0 not %!PS-Adobe-3.0.
-c *amount*	Specifies the number of copies to create of each page.
-g	Generates documents that can be printed on letter and a4 by guessing the page length.
-l	Prints the document in the landscape format.
-m	Activates the manual feed.
-w *thickness*	Specifies line thickness in thousandths of an em.
-F *directory*/dev*name*	Specifies the directory and file to search for device and font description files.
-v	Shows version information.
Files…	Specifies PostScript output file or files to create.
File Name: `grops`	**Directory:** /usr/bin/ **Type:** External
Tip:	You can use X commands with this by using the escape sequence `\X` but only those that start with a `ps:` tag.

grotty

UNIX Shell:	All primary shells (bash, ash, tcsh)
Function	Translates GNU `troff` output into a simple printer format.
Syntax	grotty [options…] *{ files… }*

-F *directory*/dev*name*	Specifies the directory and file to search for device and font description files.
-h	Lets you use horizontal tabs in the output.
-f	Lets you use form feeds in the output if the page has no output on the last line.
-b	Lets you suppress the use of over striking all bold characters.
-u	Lets you suppress the use of underlining all italic characters.
-B	Uses overstrike on all bold-italic characters.
-U	Uses underline on all bold-italic characters.
-o	Lets you suppress overstrike.
-v	Prints version information.
-d	Ignores all \D commands.
Files…	Specifies the file or files for output.

File Name:	`grotty`	**Directory:**	/usr/bin/	**Type:**	External

groupadd

UNIX Shell:	All primary shells (bash, ash, tcsh)
Function	Creates a new group definition on the system.
Syntax	groupadd [options…] *group*

-g *gid*	Assigns a specific group ID number for a new group.
-o	Allows the duplication of the specified gid.
-r	Creates the new group with a system account, with a group ID between 0 and 499.
-f	Forces the command to continue even if the group already exists.
group	Specifies the group to be created.

File Name:	`groupadd`	**Directory:**	/usr/sbin/	**Type:**	External

groupdel

UNIX Shell:	All primary shells (bash, ash, tcsh)
Function	Deletes a specified group definition in the system.
Syntax	groupdel *group*

group	Specifies the group that's deleted.

File Name:	`groupdel`	**Directory:**	/usr/sbin/	**Type:**	External
Note:	You can't delete the primary group of any existing user.				

groupmod

UNIX Shell:	All primary shells (bash, ash, tcsh)
Function	Alters a specific group definition on the system.
Syntax	groupmod [options…] *group*

-g *gid*	Specifies a new group ID to use for the specified group.
-o	Allows the new gid to be duplicated.
-n *name*	Specifies the new name for the group. This name can't exceed 8 bytes in length.
group	Specifies the group that's modified.

File Name:	`groupmod`	**Directory:**	/usr/sbin/	**Type:**	External

grpck

UNIX Shell:	All primary shells (bash, ash, tcsh)
Function	Checks the integrity of the `/etc/group` and `/etc/gshadow` files.
Syntax	grpck [-r] *{ groupfile shadowfile }*

-r	Executes in read-only mode.
groupfile	Specifies another group file than the default /etc/group.
Shadowfile	Specifies another shadow file than the default /etc/gshadow.

File Name:	`grpck`	**Directory:**	/usr/sbin/	**Type:**	External

grpconv

UNIX Shell:	All primary shells (bash, ash, tcsh)
Function	Updates the `/etc/gshadow` if the `/etc/group` file has been changed manually.
Syntax	grpconv
File Name:	`grpconv`
Directory:	/usr/sbin/
Type:	External

grpunconv

UNIX Shell:	All primary shells (bash, ash, tcsh)
Function	Creates the `/etc/group` file from the `/etc/gshadow` file, then removes the `/etc/gshadow` file.
Syntax	grpunconv
File Name:	`grpunconv`
Directory:	/usr/sbin/
Type:	External

gs

UNIX Shell:	All primary shells (bash, ash, tcsh)
Function	Starts Ghostscript and reads Adobe Systems PostScript and PDF files.
Syntax	gs [options...] *{ files... }*

-h	Shows help information.
-q	Specifies quiet startup.
-	Specifies that input comes from a pipe.
-sPAPERSIZE=*papersize*	Specifies a specific paper size – for example, a4 or letter.
-- *{ file... }*	Specifies the next argument as a file and defines arguments that remains in userdict.
-D*name{ =token }*	Specifies one name and its token in systemdict. Value is set to null without token.
-Sname=*string*	Specifies one name and its definition string in systemdict.
-g*width*x*height*	Specifies device width and device height for devices.
-r*x*x*y*	Sets X and Y resolution. When y is given only, it means both x and y.
-I*directories*	Specifies directories as search path for library files.
-sOutputFile=*file*	Specifies where to send output. Could be piped to a device or a file.
-sDEVICE=*device*	Selects a device. For a list of devices that can be used, please use the –h option.
-d*DISKFONTS*	Loads individual characters from disk the first time they are used.
-d*NOCACHE*	Sets character cache off.
-d*NOBIND*	Sets the "bind" operator off.
-d*NODISPLAY*	Sets initialization of output device off.
-d*NOPAUSE*	Sets the pause between pages off.
-d*NOPLATFONTS*	Sets the use of platform-supplied fonts off.
-d*SAFER*	Opens files in read-only mode.
-d*WRITESYSTEMDICT*	Sets systemdict writable.
Files...	Specifies the input PostScript or PDF files.

File Name:	`gs`
Directory:	/usr/bin/
Type:	External

gtbl

UNIX Shell:	All primary shells (bash, ash, tcsh)
Function	Compiles descriptions of any tables that are embedded inside `troff` files.
Syntax	gtbl [options...] *{ files... }*

-C	Finds .TS and .TE even if not followed by a space or a new line.
-v	Shows version information.
Files...	Specifies the output file or files that are created. If none, then STDOUT is used

File Name:	`gtbl`
Directory:	/usr/bin/
Type:	External

gunzip

UNIX Shell:	All primary shells (bash, ash, tcsh)
Function	Extracts files created by `gzip`, `zip`, `compress` or `pack`.
Syntax	gunzip [options...] *{ names... }*

-a	Is ASCII text mode, converts end-of-lines. Supported only for some non-UNIX systems.
-c	Doesn't change the file and write to STDOUT.
-f	Forces decompression.
-h	Shows help information.
-l	Shows information about compressed file.

continued

-L	Shows information about license, then quits.
-n	Doesn't restore filename if present (is default).
-N	Restores filename if it exists.
-q	Suppresses all warnings.
-r	Decompresses recursive.
-S *.ext*	Specifies suffix of the output file.
-t	Tests the file integrity.
-v	Verbose mode. Shows more information.
-V	Shows version information.
names...	Specifies the files to decompress.

File Name: gunzip | **Directory:** /bin/ | **Type:** External

gv

UNIX Shell: All primary shells (bash, ash, tcsh)

Function: Allows you to view PostScript and PDF documents.

Syntax: gv [options...] *{ files... }*

-ad *file*	Uses any additional resources from the specified resource file.
-antialias	Activates antialiasing. Otherwise, use -noantialias.
-arguments *argument*	Starts the viewer with any additional options that are specified by the argument.
-center	Centers the page automatically. -nocenter doesn't.
-dsc	Accepts DSC comments. -nodsc ignores them.
-eof	Allows the PS scanner to recognize EOF markers.-noef ignores EOFs.
-pixmap	Manages obscured parts of the page by use of a larger pixmap.
-nopixmap	Specifies the X server manages obscured parts of the page.
-v	Shows version information, then exits.
-h	Shows standard help information.
-help	Shows verbose help information.
-scale *value*	Specifies the scale relative to the value 1.0.
-scalebase *value*	Specifies the scale base value.
-monochrome	Sets the color palette to monochrome.
-grayscale	Sets the color palette to grayscale.
-color	Sets the color palette to color.
-media *size*	Selects the paper size. Uses X-Y coordinate values.
-page *label*	Shows the page with the specified label.
-portrait	Sets the orientation to portrait.
-landscape	Sets the orientation to landscape.
-seascape	Sets the orientation to seascape.
-upsidedown	Sets the orientation to upside down.
-quiet	Starts Ghostscript with the -dQUIET option. -noquiet doesn't.
-resize	Automatically fits the window to the page size. -noresize doesn't.
-safer	Starts Ghostscript with the -dSAFER option. -nosafer doesn't.
-spartan	Shortcuts to -style gv_spartan.dat.
-style *file*	Uses additional resources from the specified file.
-swap	Swaps the meanings between landscape and seascape. -noswap does the opposite.
-watch	Checks for changes in the document and automatically shows the recent version.
-nowatch	Doesn't check for changes in the document.
files...	Specifies the file or files to view.

File Name: gv | **Directory:** /usr/X11R6/bin/ | **Type:** External

gzexe

UNIX Shell: All primary shells (bash, ash, tcsh)

Function: Compresses executable files into a self extracting archive.

Syntax: gzexe [-d] *{ files... }*

-d	Decompresses the specified file or files.
files...	Specifies the file or files to compress.

File Name: gzexe | **Directory:** /usr/bin/ | **Type:** External

gzip

UNIX Shell:	All primary shells (bash, ash, tcsh)
Function	Compresses files with Lempel Ziv-coding.
Syntax	gzip [options...] *{ files... }*

-a	Is ASCII text mode, converts end-of-lines. Supported only for some non-UNIX systems.
-c	Doesn't change file only write to STDOUT.
-d	Decompresses the file. This is the same as using the gunzip command.
-f	Forces compression.
-h	Shows help information.
-l	Shows information about compressed file.
-L	Shows information about license and quits.
-n	Doesn't save name and timestamp.
-N	Saves name and timestamp.
-q	Suppresses all warnings.
-r	Compresses all files in subdirectories, recursively.
-S *.ext*	Specifies the suffix.
-t	Tests integrity of the file.
-v	Verbose mode. Shows more information.
-V	Shows version information.
-*number*	Specifies the compression rate. 1 is fast but least compressed and 9 is slow but most compressed.
--fast	Uses the fast but least compression rate. Same as -1.
--best	Uses the slow but most compression rate. Same as -9.
files...	Specifies the file or files to be compressed.

File Name:	`gzip`	**Directory:**	/bin/	**Type:**	External

h2ph

UNIX Shell:	Perl script
Function	Converts the specified C header files into Perl header file format.
Syntax	h2ph [options...] *{ files... }*

-d *path*	Specifies a directory to save the converted filename to.
	The following two options can't be combined:
-r	Runs on all files in all subdirectories.
-a	Runs on the filenames and all `.h` files that they include.
-l	Replicates all links into the specified directory.
-h	Creates hints into the Perl file to make it easier to troubleshoot the script.
-D	Takes code from .h file and adds that as comments to the .ph file. Used for debuging.
-Q	Doesn't show names of converted files. Quiet mode.
files...	Specifies the header files to convert.

File Name:	`h2ph`	**Directory:**	/usr/bin/	**Type:**	Script

h2xs

UNIX Shell:	Perl script
Function	Creates Perl extensions from C header files.
Syntax	h2xs [options...] *{ files... directories... }*

-A	Skips all auto loaded values and disables the autoloader in the .pm file.
-C	Doesn't create the changes file, and adds a HISTORY section to POD template.
-F	Specifies flags for C preprocessor to find function parameters in header. (Use the -x option with -F.)
-M *expression*	Specifies macros or functions to process.
-O	Overwrites directories if they already exist.
-P	Skips the stub POD section.
-X	Skips the XS portion. Creates templates for non- XS-based modules.
-a	Creates accessory method for each method of struts and unions.
-c	Skips constants in the `.as` file and matching autoload in the `.pm` file.
-d	Shows debug information.

continued

-f	Creates an extension for a header.
-h	Shows help information.
-k	Skips the const attribute in the XS code.
-m	Creates a Perl variable for each corresponding variable in the header file.
-n *module*	Specifies name to use for extension.
-o *expression*	Specifies `opaque` data. (When you use -o you must use the -x option.)
-p *prefix*	Specifies prefix to remove from the Perl function names.
-s *sub1,sub2*	Creates subroutines for the specified macros.
-v *version*	Specifies the version number for this extension.
-x	Creates XSUBs from function declarations in the header file.
files...	Specifies header file or files.
directories...	Specifies the extra directories that have C header files.
File Name: `h2xs`	**Directory:** /usr/bin/ **Type:** Script

hdparm

UNIX Shell: All primary shells (bash, ash, tcsh)

Function	Sets or retrieves hard drive parameters.
Syntax	hdparm [options...] *device*

-a	Sets or retrieves the sector count for the read-ahead of the file system.
-A	Toggles between enabling and disabling the IDE read-lookahead feature (default is enable).
-c *value*	Enables or disables (E)IDE 32-bit I/O support for data transfers on the PCI/VLB bus.
0	Disables 32-bit support.
1	Enables 32-bit transfers.
3	Enables 32-bit transfers with special synchronization for chipsets.
-C	Checks the current power mode status of the IDE.
-d	Toggles between enabling and disabling of the using_dma option for the drive.
-D	Enables or disables defect management for the drive.
-E *xspeed*	Sets the CD-ROM speed to the specified amount - 2, 4, 6, and so forth.
-f	Synchronizes and flush the cache for the device buffer on exit.
-g	Shows the drive geometry such as number of heads, sectors, and so on.
-h	Shows help information.
-i	Shows information about the drive that was available at boot time.
-I	Shows information about the drive that is available now.
-k	Toggles the keep_settings_over_reset option for the drive (default is off).
-K	Sets the keep_features_over_reset option for the drive. Same as using -APSWXZ.
-L	Sets the doorlock option for the drive.
-m	Sets the multiple sector I/O sector count for the drive.
0	Disables multiple sector I/O sector count.
2-64	Sets sector count values using the specified factors of two (2, 4, 8, 16, 32, and 64).
-n *flag*	Sets or shows the ignore-write-errors flag. Valid flags are 0 and 1.
-p *mode*	Attempts to program the IDE interface chipset to the specified PIO mode. Modes 0 - 5.
-P	Sets the sector count for the internal prefetch mechanism of the drive to maximum.
-q	Suppress the output of the following option. Doesn't work for -i, -v, -t, or -T.
-r	Toggles the read-only option of the device.
-R	Registers the IDE interface. Use with caution.
-S	Sets the spindown timeout for the drive.
0	Turns the spindown timeout off.
1-240	Specifies multiples of 5-second intervals. Minimum is 5 seconds, max is 20 minutes.
241-251	Specifies multiples of 30-minute intervals. Minimum is 30 minutes, max is 5.5 hours.
252	Specifies a spindown timeout of 21 minutes.
253	Specifies the vendor pre-defined timeout.
255	Specifies a spindown timeout of 21 minutes and 15 seconds.
-T	Shows the speed of the Linux buffer cache without disk access.
-t	Shows the speed of the buffer cache read on an empty cache buffer.
-u *value*	Sets the `interrupt-unmask` option of the drive to the specified value.
-U	Un-registers the IDE interface. Use with caution.
-v	Shows all of the drives current settings except -i.
-W	Toggles between enabling and disabling of the IDE write-caching feature.

continued

-X *value*	Sets the IDE transfer mode for (E)IDE/ATA2 drives.
34	Selects multiword mode2 DMA transfers.
66	Selects UltraDMA mode2 transfers.
-y	Forces the IDE drive to enter standby mode.
-Y	Forces the IDE drive to enter sleep or shutdown mode.
-Z	Disables the power-saving features of Seagate ST3xxx series drives.
File Name: `hdparm`	**Directory:** /sbin/ **Type:** External

help

UNIX Shell: Bash shell (bash)

Function	Shows help information about internal commands.
Syntax	help [-s] *{ name }*

-s	Shows only a short descriptions.
name	Specifies the name of the internal command to get information about.

hexdump

UNIX Shell: All primary shells (bash, ash, tcsh)

Function	Dumps a file in hexadecimal format on the screen.
Syntax	hexdump [options...] *{ files... }*

-b	Shows the output as 1-byte octal format.
-c	Shows the output as 2-byte character format.
-d	Shows the output as 2-byte decimal format.
-o	Shows the output as 2-byte octal format.
-x	Shows the output as 2-byte hexadecimal format.
-v	Shows every line of output. Otherwise, equal lines are only shown with a single *.
-e *string*	Specifies a format string to use.
-f *file*	Specifies a file containing format information.
-n *NR*	Shows the first NR bytes of a file.
-s *NR*	Skips NR bytes in the file.
files...	Specifies files to dump. If not specified, it reads from STDIN.
File Name: `hexdump`	**Directory:** /usr/bin/ **Type:** External

hisaxctrl

UNIX Shell: All primary shells (bash, ash, tcsh)

Function	Sets up the HiSax-ISDN device driver, if you are using the HiSax driver.
Syntax	hisaxctrl *driverID command parameters...*

driverID	Specifies the card to use when you have several.
command	Specifies the setup category, use one of the following integers:
0	Shows card information.
1	Uses generic debugging.
11	Uses layer 1 development debugging.
13	Uses layer 3 development debugging.
2	Sets the B channel ON delay to parameter.
5	Sets the B channel in leased mode.
6	Sets the B channel in testloop mode.
7	Sets or resets card in Point To Point mode.
8	Sets card in fixed TEI mode.
9	Loads DSP cards firmware.
10	Specifies the B-channel usage limit to 1 or 2 channels.
12	Sets echo logging mode. B-channel usage limit should be 1 if enabled.
parameters...	Specifies a bitmask that turn different debug facilities on.
	Bitmasks to use with generic debugging selected:
0x001	Sets link-level <--> hardware-level communication.
0x002	Sets top state machine.
0x004	Sets D-channel Q.931 (call control messages).
0x008	Sets D-channel Q.921.

continued

0x010	Sets B-channel X.75.
0x020	Sets D-channel l2.
0x040	Sets B-channel l2.
0x080	Sets D-channel link state debugging.
0x100	Sets B-channel link state debugging.
0x200	Sets TEI debug.
0x400	Sets LOCK debug in `callc.c`.
0x800	Sets more debug in `callc.c` (not for normal use).
	Bitmasks to use with layer 1 development debugging selected:
0x001	Warnings (default is on).
0x002	Sets IRQ status.
0x004	Sets ISAC.
0x008	Sets ISAC FIFO.
0x010	Sets HSCX.
0x020	Sets HSCX FIFO (attention: full B-Channel output!).
0x040	Sets D-Channel LAPD frame types.
	Bitmasks to use with layer 3 development debugging selected:
0x001	Warnings (default is on).
0x002	Sets l3 protocol descriptor errors.
0x004	Sets l3 state machine.
0x008	Sets charge info debugging (1TR6).

File Name: `hisaxctrl` **Directory:** /usr/sbin/ **Type:** External

host

UNIX Shell: All primary shells (bash, ash, tcsh)

Function Looks up hostnames or IP-addresses using name servers.

Syntax host [options...] *host { server }*

-w	Waits forever for a response.
-v	Verbose mode. Shows more information.
-r	Returns only data from its own database. Doesn't ask another server.
-d	Shows debug information. Shows details about network transactions.
-t *querytype*	Specifies the following query type to show: a, ns, md, mf, cname, soa, mb, mg, mr, null, wks, ptr, hinfo, minfo, mx, uinfo, uid, gid, unspec. Wildcards can be used.
-c *class*	Specifies a query class for non-Internet data.
-a	This is a synonym for -v -t any.
-l	Shows a complete domain.
host	Specifies which host to look for.
server	Specifies from which server to look from (default is the local computer).

File Name: `host` **Directory:** /usr/bin/ **Type:** External

hostid

UNIX Shell: All primary shells (bash, ash, tcsh)

Function Shows an identifier for the current host in hexadecimal format.

Syntax hostid [options...]

--version	Shows version information.
--help	Shows help information.

File Name: `hostid` **Directory:** /usr/bin/ **Type:** External

hpftodit

UNIX Shell: All primary shells (bash, ash, tcsh)

Function Uses an HP tagged font metric file and creates a font file for use with `groff -Tlj4`.

Syntax hpftodit [options...] *HPfile fontfile outfile*

-v	Shows version information.
-i *count*	Generates an italic correction for each character with the specified number of units.
-s	Specifies that a font is special and adds it to the font file.
HPfile	Specifies the HP tagged font metric file to use as input.

continued

fontfile	Specifies a file containing the `groff` names for characters in the font.		
outfile	Specifies the name of the file containing the output `groff` font file.		
File Name: `hpftodit`	**Directory:** /usr/bin/		**Type:** External

htdigest

UNIX Shell: All primary shells (bash, ash, tcsh)

Function	Manages HTTP user authentication files.
Syntax	htdigest [-c] *file realm user*

-c	Creates a password file, even if it already exists.
file	Specifies the file that holds password, realm, and username information.
realm	Specifies the realm where the user belongs.
user	Specifies the username that you want to manage.
File Name: `htdigest`	**Directory:** /usr/bin/ **Type:** External

htpasswd

UNIX Shell: All primary shells (bash, ash, tcsh)

Function	Manages HTTP user authentication.
Syntax	htpasswd [options...] *passwordfile username { password }*

-b	Uses the command line to get the password.
-c	Creates a password file even if it exists.
	The following four encryption methods can't be combined:
-m	Uses the MD5 algorithm for passwords.
-d	Uses crypt for passwords.
-s	Uses the SHA encryption for passwords.
-p	Uses plain text passwords.
passwordfile	Specifies the file that holds password username information.
username	Specifies the username to work with.
password	Specifies the password to encrypt with -m, d, s, or p. Only used with the -b option.
File Name: `htpasswd`	**Directory:** /usr/bin/ **Type:** External
htpasswd -c .htpasswd speed	Creates `.htpasswd` and adds user speed.

httpd

UNIX Shell: All primary shells (bash, ash, tcsh)

Function	The Apache Internet Web server.
Syntax	httpd [options...]

-X	Runs the server in single-process mode.
-R *libexecdir*	Specifies where the server puts dynamic shared object files.
-d *serverroot*	Sets the root directory for the server.
-f *config*	Specifies a config file with startup commands.
-C *bconfig*	Runs the specified configuration before reading the config file.
-c *aconfig*	Runs the specified configuration after reading the config file.
-D *params*	Specifies parameters to use with IfDefine tags.
	The following options can't be combined with those above:
-h	Shows help information.
-l	Shows a list of compiled modules.
-L	Shows a list of directives and attributes.
-v	Shows version information.
-V	Shows version and build information.
-S	Shows the settings that are in the config file.
-t	Runs a configuration file test.
-T	Runs a configuration file test without checking the document root.
File Name: `httpd`	**Directory:** /usr/sbin/ **Type:** External

hup

hup	UNIX Shell:	TC shell (tcsh)
Function	Allows a command to catch a hangup signal. This is the opposite of `nohup`.	
Syntax	hup *{ command }*	

command	Specifies the command to run.

hwclock, clock

hwclock, clock	UNIX Shell:	All primary shells (bash, ash, tcsh)
Function	Shows and configures the hardware clock.	
Syntax	hwclock [options...]	

-r	Shows the hardware clock time on the screen.
--set	Configures the hardware clock together with other options.
-s	Synchronizes the system time from hardware clock.
-w	Synchronizes the hardware clock time from system time.
-a	Adds or removes time from hwclock for systematic drift since last adjustment.
--getepoch	Shows kernel hwclock epoch value. This is only used on Alpha systems.
--setepoch	Specifies the epoch value of the hwclock.
-v	Shows version information.
--date=*date*	Specifies the time to configure the hardware clock.
--epoch=*year*	Specifies the year to begin the hardware clock epoch.
--localtime	Indicates that hwcock is kept in coordinated universal time or local time.
--directisa	Uses I/O instructions to access hardware clock.
--badyear	Stores years outside range of 1994–1999.
-F	Uses UF bit instead of UIP bit in hwclock to find time transition. Only on Alpha systems.
-J	Specifies that you are running on a Jensen model. Only on Alpha systems.
-A	Uses epoch 1980 in its hwclock. Only on Alpha systems.
-S	Specifies that your system runs on epoch 1900. Only on Alpha systems.
--test	Doesn't update the hardware clock or anything else, but does everything else.
--debug	Shows debug information.

File Name:	`hwclock`	**Directory:**	/sbin/	**Type:**	External

ibench

ibench	UNIX Shell:	All primary shells (bash, ash, tcsh)
Function	Shows how many connections the daemon can manage during a specified time. Also identifies users.	
Syntax	ibench [options...] *{ seconds } { port } { user }*	

-i	Ignores ident reports.
-r*address*	Specifies a remote computer to run a reverse lookup against.
-h	Shows help information.
seconds	Specifies how long the test will be (default is 60 seconds).
port	Specifies the port to use when connecting to an ident daemon (default is 113).
user	Specifies the user to run the test as.

File Name:	`ibench`	**Directory:**	/usr/sbin/	**Type:**	External

iceauth

iceauth	UNIX Shell:	All primary shells (bash, ash, tcsh)
Function	Modifies or shows authorization information to connect with ICE.	
Syntax	iceauth [options...] *{ commands... }*	

-f *file*	Specifies the authority file.
-v	Enables extra messages.
-q	Disables extra messages.
-i	Ignores locks on authority file.
-b	Breaks locks on authority file.
commands...	**Here are the commands to use in the ICE program:**
add	Adds an entry.
exit	Saves changes and exits program.
extract	Extracts entries into file.

continued

help	Shows help information.		
info	Shows information about entries.		
list	Shows entries.		
merge	Merges entries from files.		
quit	Aborts changes and exit program.		
remove	Erases entries.		
source	Reads commands from file.		
?	Shows help information.		
File Name: iceauth	**Directory:** /usr/X11R6/bin/	**Type:** External	

ident

UNIX Shell: All primary shells (bash, ash, tcsh)

Function	Searches for RCS keyword strings in files.
Syntax	ident [options...] *files...*

-q	Suppresses warning messages.
-V	Shows version information.
files...	Specifies files to search in.
File Name: ident	**Directory:** /usr/bin/ **Type:** External

ifcfg

UNIX Shell: Bash shell (bash)

Function	Configures the Ethernet interfaces.
Syntax	ifcfg *interface ACTION*

interface	Specifies the network interface.
ACTION	**You may select one of the following three actions:**
stop	Flushes the device, removes all the addresses from it.
add	Adds the address to the device.
del	Removes the address from the device.
	The following may be used with either add or del:
address	Specifies the address to add or delete.
/length	Specifies the network length.
gateway	Specifies a default router to add.
File Name: ifcfg	**Directory:** /sbin/ **Type:** Script
ifcfg eth0 add 192.168.1.1/24	Adds address 192.168.1.1 to device eth0 with network length 24.

ifdown

UNIX Shell: A shell (ash, bsh)

Function	Deactivates a network interface.
Syntax	ifdown *interface*

interface	Specifies the name of the interface to deactivate.
File Name: ifdown	**Directory:** /sbin/ **Type:** Script

ifport

UNIX Shell: All primary shells (bash, ash, tcsh)

Function	Set or views the transceiver type for the network interface.
Syntax	ifport *interface { type }*

type	Specifies what type of transceiver to use. The different type are shown below:
auto	Sets the transceiver to autodetect the type.
10baseT	Sets the transceiver type to 10BaseT.
10base2	Sets the transceiver type to 10Base2.
aui	Sets the transceiver type to AUI.
100baseT	Sets the transceiver type to 100BaseT.
interface	Specifies the interface to use.

continued

File Name: ifport	**Directory:** /sbin/	**Type:** External	
ifport eth0 10baseT	Sets the transceiver type for eth0 to 10BaseT.		

ifup

UNIX Shell: Bash shell (bash)

Function	Activates a network interface.
Syntax	ifup *interface*

interface	Specifies the name of the interface to activate.	
File Name: ifup	**Directory:** /sbin/	**Type:** Script

ifuser

UNIX Shell: All primary shells (bash, ash, tcsh)

Function	Shows whether any of the specified hosts are routed through the specified interface.
Syntax	ifuser [-v] *interface { hosts... }*

-v	Verbose mode. Shows more information.	
interface	Specifies the network interface to query.	
hosts...	Specifies host addresses to query. Both IP address and name can be used.	
File Name: ifuser	**Directory:** /sbin/	**Type:** External
ifuser -v eth0 pluto sun	Shows whether the hosts pluto and sun are routed through eth0.	

igawk

UNIX Shell: A shell (ash, bsh)

Function	Adds the ability to have include files in `gawk`. It accepts all `gawk` options. Gawk also includes additional options from Bell Labs and GNU-specific options.
Syntax	igawk [options...] [' *scriptstr* '] [-v *var=value*] *{ files... }* igawk [options...] [-f *scriptfile*] [-v *var=value*] *{ files... }*

File Name: igawk	**Directory:** /bin/	**Type:** Script

imon

UNIX Shell: All primary shells (bash, ash, tcsh)

Function	Monitors your ISDN activities.
Syntax	imon [options...]

-q	Disables the use of q to quit the program. Use this in rc scripts.	
-p *phonebook*	Specifies a phonebook file. The format is: nr – Tab - description.	
File Name: imon	**Directory:** /usr/sbin/	**Type:** External

imontty

UNIX Shell: All primary shells (bash, ash, tcsh)

Function	Shows the status of all ISDN lines.
Syntax	imontty *{ phonebook }*

phonebook	Specifies a phonebook file. The format for each line is: number – Tab - name.	
File Name: imontty	**Directory:** /usr/sbin/	**Type:** External

import

UNIX Shell: All primary shells (bash, ash, tcsh)

Function	Captures some or all of an X server screen and saves it to a file.
Syntax	import [options...] *{ file }*

-adjoin	Saves images in separate files.
+adjoin	Joins images into a single multi-image file.
-border	Includes image borders in the output image.
-cache *value*	Specifies the available megabytes of memory to the pixel cache.
-colorspace *value*	Specifies the type of color space.
-comment *string*	Adds string to the output filename.
-compress *type*	Specifies the compression type.
-crop *withxheight*	Specifies the preferred size and location of the cropped image.
-delay *millisecond*[x*seconds*]	Shows the next image after pausing milliseconds.
seconds	Specifies the number of seconds to wait before repeating your animation sequence.

continued

-density *withxheight*	Specifies the vertical and horizontal resolution in pixel of the image.
-descend	Obtains image by descending window hierarchy.
-display *host:display[.screen*]	Specifies the X server to contact.
-dispose *method*	Specifies GIF disposal method.
-dither	Applies Floyd/Steinberg error diffusions to the image.
-frame	Includes window manager frame.
-geometry *widthxheight*	Specifies the width and height of the image.
-interlace *type*	Specifies the type of interlacing scheme.
-monochrome	Makes the image black and white.
-negate	Replaces every pixel with its complementary color.
-page *widthxheight*	Specifies the preferred size and location of an image canvas.
-pointsize	Specifies the point size of the PostScript font.
-quality *value*	Specifies the JPEG, MIFF, and PNG compression level.
-rotate *degrees{ ACTION }*	Specifies the image should be rotated.
	The following ACTIONS can be used:
<	Specifies the image should only be rotated if its width is less than the height.
>	Specifies the image should only be rotated if its width exceeds the height.
-scene *value*	Specifies the number of screen snapshots.
-screen	Captures the root window, not the specified window.
-silent	Operates silently.
-transparency *color*	Specifies the color that should be transparent.
-treedepth *value*	Specifies the color depth of the image.
-verbose	Shows detailed information about the image.
-window *value*	Selects window with this ID or name.
file	Specifies the image to save the capture to.

File Name:	`import`	**Directory:**	/usr/bin/X11/	**Type:**	External

import -window root root.jpeg	Captures the whole X window and saves it in `root.jpeg`.

in.identd, identd

UNIX Shell: All primary shells (bash, ash, tcsh)

Function	Returns user information about the owner of a connection to a remote computer.
Syntax	identd [options...] in.identd [options...]

-h	Shows help information.
-V	Shows version information.
-d	Shows debug information.
-C*file*	Specifies an additional config file to use.
-i	Starts in identd nowait mode.
-w	Used when starting the daemon by `inetd` with the "wait" option.
-I	Starts in init mode.
-b	Starts in standalone mode.
-l	Writes a log message to `syslog` at startup.
-t*time*	Specifies the request timeout limit.
-p*port*	Specifies a port to listen for connection on (default is 113).
-g*group*	Specifies a group to run the daemon as.
-u*user*	Specifies a username to run the daemon as.
-P*file*	Specifies a file to write process number information to.
-K*threads*	Specifies number of threads to use for kernel lookups.
-L*facility*	Specifies the `syslog` facility to use instead of daemon.
-o	Returns OTHER instead of Linux.
-E	Enables DES encryption of the returned data.
-n	Returns user numbers instead of usernames.
-N	Checks for `.noident` file in user's home dir. If found, lookup is disabled.
-e	Enables protocol extensions.
-m	Enables multiple requests to be processed per session.

File Name:	`in.identd`	**Directory:**	/usr/sbin/	**Type:**	External

indent	UNIX Shell:	All primary shells (bash, ash, tcsh)
Function	Inserts or erases white space in C code to make it easier to read. Converts from one C style to another.	
Syntax	indent [options...] *{ inputfiles... }* indent [options...] *{ inputfile }* [-o *outputfile*]	

-bad	Inserts blank lines after declarations.
-bap	Inserts blank lines after procedure bodies.
-bbb	Inserts blank lines after block comments.
-bbo	Splits long lines before Boolean operators, not after.
-bc	Causes `indent` to insert a new line after commas in declarations.
-bl	Moves the statement braces to the line after the statement.
-bli*count*	Indents braces count spaces.
-bls	Moves braces to the line following a struct declaration.
-br	Moves the statement braces to the same line as the statement.
-brs	Moves braces to the same line as the struct declaration line.
-bs	Inserts a space between sizeof and the argument following it.
-c*count*	Moves comments that are to the right of code to the column equal to count.
-cbi*count*	Indents braces following a case label count spaces.
-cd*count*	Moves comments that are to the right of declarations to the column equal to count.
-cdb	Puts comment delimiters on blank lines.
-ce	Puts `else` directly after a preceding end brace.
-ci*count*	Causes a continuation indent of *count* spaces.
-cli*count*	Indents case labels count spaces.
-cp*count*	Moves comments that are to the right of #else and #endif statements to column count.
-cs	Inserts a space after a cast operator.
-d*count*	Specifies the indentation for comments not to the right of code to count spaces.
-di*count*	Moves variables to the column equal to count.
-fc1	Causes `indent` to format all comments found in the first column.
-fca	Enables formatting of comments.
-gnu	Enables indenting according to GNU coding style (is default).
-hnl	Causes `indent` to try and break long lines at new lines in the input.
-i*count*	Specifies the level of indentation to count spaces.
-ip*count*	Indents old-style function definition parameter types by count spaces.
-kr	Enables indenting according to Kernighan & Ritchie coding style.
-l*count*	Specifies the maximum length of lines to count. This doesn't affect comment lines.
-lc*count*	Set maximum line length for comment formatting to n.
-lp	Lines up code exceeding one row following a parentheses with continuation lines.
-lps	Doesn't erase space between preprocessor directives and the #.
-nbad	Disables insertions of blank lines after declarations.
-nbap	Disables insertions of blank lines after procedure bodies.
-nbbo	Disables splitting of long lines before Boolean operators, not after.
-nbc	Disables insertions of new lines after commas in declarations.
-ncdb	Disables putting comment delimiters on blank lines.
-nce	Disables putting `else` directly after a preceding end brace.
-ncs	Disables insertions of a space after cast operators.
-nfca	Disables all formatting of comments.
-nhnl	Disables splitting long lines at new lines found in code.
-nip	Disables all parameter indentation.
-nlp	Disables lining up code following a parentheses.
-npcs	Disables inserting a space between a function call and the parentheses following it.
-nprs	Disables putting a space before and after code inside parentheses.
-npsl	Puts procedure type on the same line as the procedure name.
-nsc	Disables putting the * character to the left of comments.
-nsob	Disables erasing optional blank lines found in the input code.
-nss	Disables inserting a space between certain statements and it's semicolon.
-nv	Disables verbose mode.
-orig	Enables indenting according to the Berkeley coding style.

-npro	Stops `indent` from reading .indent.pro files containing configuration profiles.

continued

-pcs	Inserts a space between a function call and the parentheses following it.
-pi*count*	Specifies the extra indentation on broken statements.
-pmt	Maintains output file access and modification times.
-prs	Inserts a space before and after code inside parentheses.
-psl	Puts procedure type on the line before the procedure name.
-sbi*count*	Indents struct's, union's or enum's braces count spaces.
-sc	Puts the * character on the left side of comments.
-sob	Erases all optional blank lines found in the input code.
-ss	Inserts a space before the semicolon in one-line for and while statements.
-st	Outputs the results of the infile to STDOUT. Is usable only with one inputfile.
-T *typename*	Specifies typenames for indent.
-ts*count*	Specifies the size of tabs to count spaces.
-v	Verbose mode. Shows more information.
-version	Shows version information.
-o *outpufile*	Specifies the output file.
inputfile	Specifies one input file and is usable with the -o option and the -st option.
inputfiles...	Specifies the input files to indent. (Backups are created and the files are replaced with the output.)
File Name: `indent`	**Directory:** /usr/bin/ **Type:** External
Tip:	It is possible to turn of indentation for specific sections of the code by placing /* *INDENT-OFF/ON* */ around the section.

info

UNIX Shell: All primary shells (bash, ash, tcsh)

Function	Reads hypertext info nodes. Info nodes fill the same function on as man pages.
Syntax	info [options...] { *menuitem* }

--apropos=*subject*	Finds specified subject in all indices of all manuals.
--directory=*dir*	Adds dir to `infopath`.
--dribble=*file*	Remembers user key strokes in specified filename.
--file=*file*	Specifies the info file to show.
--help	Shows help information.
--node=*nodename*	Specifies nodes in first visited info file.
--index-search=*string*	Specifies string to find that entry.
--output=*file*	Specifies filename to save selected nodes.
--restore=*file*	Reads initial key strokes from specified file.
--usage	Shows command-line options node information.
--subnodes	Recursively output menu items.
--vi-keys	Uses vi-like and less-like key bindings.
--version	Shows version information.
menuitem	Specifies what item to show information about.
File Name: `info`	**Directory:** /usr/bin/ **Type:** External
info bash	Shows the info node for bash.
info --apropos=emacs	Searches all info nodes for string emacs and shows the results briefly.

infotocap

UNIX Shell: All primary shells (bash, ash, tcsh)

Function	Reads the specified file and converts found `terminfo` descriptions to `termcap` descriptions. The converted descriptions is shown on STDOUT.
Syntax	infotocap [options...] *file*

-v *level*	Verbose mode. Shows more information. Level specifies the verbose Level to use.
-V	Shows version information.
-1	Does only one field per line.
-w *width*	Changes the output to specified width of characters.
file	Specifies the terminfo file to convert.
File Name: `infotocap`	**Directory:** /usr/bin/ **Type:** External

initdb

UNIX Shell: A shell (ash, bsh)

Function	Creates a new Postgres database system.
Syntax	initdb [options...]

-D *dbdir*	Specifies the location for the database.
-i *sysID*	Specifies the system ID for the database superuser.
-E *encoding*	Specifies the default multibyte encoding of the template database.
-W	Prompts for a password of the database superuser.
-L *libdir*	Specifies where to find the input files.
-n	Doesn't clean up after errors.
-d	Shows debug information.
-t	Reinitializes template database only.

File Name: `initdb` **Directory:** /usr/bin/ **Type:** Script

initlocation

UNIX Shell: A shell (ash, bsh)

Function	Creates another Postgres secondary database storage area.
Syntax	initlocation *directory*

directory	Specifies where to put the alternate database.

File Name: `initlocation` **Directory:** /usr/bin/ **Type:** Script

initlog

UNIX Shell: All primary shells (bash, ash, tcsh)

Function	Sends log messages to the system logging facility.
Syntax	initlog [options...]

-c *command*	Runs the specified program and outputs all program messages to the logger.
-e *number*	Specifies an event to log. The following events are valid for number:
1	Logs when the action was completed successfully.
2	Logs when the action failed.
3	Logs when the action was cancelled by the user.
4	Logs when the action failed by the system.
-f *facility*	Specifies a facility to use as a logger (default is daemon).
-n *name*	Specifies the name of the log event.
-p *priority*	Specifies what `syslog` priority to log (default is notice).
-r *command*	Runs the specified program and allows the program to pass back commands.
-s *string*	The specified string is logged.
-conf=*file*	Specifies a configuration file to use (default is `/etc/initlog.conf`).

File Name: `initlog` **Directory:** /sbin/ **Type:** External

insmod

UNIX Shell: All primary shells (bash, ash, tcsh)

Function	Installs loadable kernel modules (device drivers) in the running kernel.
Syntax	insmod [options...] *module { symbol=values... }*

-f	Loads the module even if there is a version conflict with the present module.
-k	Auto-cleans and erase modules that have not been utilized in one minute.
-m	Shows a load map to ease up the debug.
-o *modulename*	Specifies internal module name.
-L	Prevents modules from being loaded several times.
-p	Checks whether the module can be successfully loaded.
-q	Hides unresolved symbols and doesn't complain about version mismatch.
-r	Hides error and allows root to load modules that are not owned by root.
-s	Shows information in `syslog` instead of screen.
-v	Verbose mode. Shows more information.
-x	Disables export all of the module's external symbols.
-X	Exports all of the module's external symbols.
-Y	Adds ksymoops symbols to ksyms.
-y	Doesn't add ksymoops symbols to ksyms.
-P *prefix*	Extracts the prefix, which must exist in any kernel that supports modules.

continued

module	Specifies module to use.		
symbol=values...	Specifies parameter value to module.		
File Name: `insmod`	**Directory:** /sbin/	**Type:**	External
Note:	The modules are located in `/lib/modules` and subdirectories. They have names like `sound.o`.		
insmod sb io=0x220 irq=5 dma=1 dma16=3	Inserts the Soundblaster module with the specified arguments.		
insmod -f 3c509	Forces loading of module.		
insmod -m soundcore 1 > soundcore.debug	Shows debug information and redirects output to file soundcore.debug.		

install-info

UNIX Shell: All primary shells (bash, ash, tcsh)

Function	Installs or erases menu entries in `info` directory files.
Syntax	install-info [options...] *{ file1 } { file2 }*

--delete	Erases the entries that exist in file from the directory.
-d *name*	Specifies the info directory file. This is the same as using the argument dir-file.
-e *name*	Names the menu item corresponding to the info directory entry.
-h	Shows help information.
-i *file*	Installs info from specified file into the directory file. Same as the file argument.
-D*dir*	Runs the same procedure as the `-d name` option.
--item=*name*	Runs the same procedure as the `-e name` option.
--quiet	Disables warnings.
-r	Runs the same procedure as the `--delete` option.
-s *section*	Installs the menu entries in the specified section of the directory file.
-V	Shows version information.
file1	Specifies the file that contains the menu entries to update the directory file with.
file2	Specifies the directory file in which the entries are to be installed or erased.

File Name: `install-info` | **Directory:** /sbin/ | **Type:** External

install-mh

UNIX Shell: All primary shells (bash, ash, tcsh)

Function	Creates the initial setup for a first-time nmh user.
Syntax	install-mh [options...]

-auto	Queries the user for information.
-version	Shows version information.
-help	Shows help information.

File Name: `install-mh` | **Directory:** /usr/lib/nmh/ | **Type:** External

ipcalc

UNIX Shell: All primary shells (bash, ash, tcsh)

Function	Calculates IP address information.
Syntax	ipcalc [options] *ipaddress { netmask }*

--hostname	Shows the hostname for the given IP address.
--broadcast	Shows the broadcast address for the given IP address.
--network	Shows the network address for the given IP address.
--netmask	Shows the default netmask for the given IP address.
--silent	Doesn't show error messages.
ipaddress	Specifies an IP address to use as a base for the calculation.
netmask	Specifies a netmask to use as a base for the calculation.

File Name: `ipcalc` | **Directory:** /bin/ | **Type:** External

ipcclean

UNIX Shell: A shell (ash, bsh)

Function	Cleans up shared memory and semaphores from aborted back-ends.
Syntax	ipcclean

File Name: `ipcclean` | **Directory:** /usr/bin/ | **Type:** Script

ipchains		UNIX Shell:	All primary shells (bash, ash, tcsh)
Function	Manages IP firewall rules in the Linux 2.2 kernel.		
Syntax	ipchains *command* [options...]		

	These are the commands that can be used. They can't be combined.
-A *chain rule*	Adds a rule specification to the end of the specified chain.
-D *chain rule*	Removes specified rule number or rule specification from selected chain.
-R *chain rulenumber rule*	Replaces the specified rule number with the specified rule.
-I *chain { rulenumber } rule*	Inserts a rule specification to the first line in a chain or on the specified line.
-L *{ chain }*	Shows the rules inside all chains or only in the specified chain.
-F *{ chain }*	Deletes rules in all chains, or only in the specified chain.
-Z *{ chain }*	Resets byte counters in the specified in all chains or in the specified chain.
-N *chain*	Creates one more chain of the specified name.
-X *chain*	Removes the specified user-defined chains. The chain must be empty first.
-P *chain policy*	Sets policy for the specified chain to the specified policy: DENY, REJECT, or ACCEPT.
-M *action*	Sets or shows masquerading options and connections.
-L	Shows the currently masqueraded connections.
-S	Sets the kernel masquerading parameters.
-S *tcp tcpfin udp*	Changes masquerade timeout values for TCP, TCPFIN, and UDP packets.
-C *chain rule*	Checks packets against the selected chain.
	These options match packets. The exclamation ! excludes the option.
-p [!] *protocol*	Specifies the protocol.
-s [!] *address*	Specifies the source address.
[*/netmask*]	Specifies a netmask to use with the source address specified.
[i] *{ port }*	Specifies a port from the source address.
[*:port*]	Specifies a last port to use in a port range from the first port specified.
-d [!] *address*	Specifies the destination address.
[*/netmask*]	Specifies a netmask to use with the destination address specified.
[i] *{ port }*	Specifies a port on the destination address.
[*:port*]	Specifies a last port to use in a port range from the first port specified.
--source-port [!] *{ port }* [*:port*]	Specifies a source port to match.
--destination-port [!] *{ port }* [*:port*]	Specifies a destination port to match. (To specify a port range, use a colon (:) between the first port and the last port.)
--icmp-type [!] *typename*	Specifies the ICMP type to use.
-j *target*	Specifies what to do with the matched packet. Often, ACCEPT, DENY, or MASQ is used.
-i [!] *interface*	Specifies the interface to use.
-f	The rule only refers to a second or further fragments of fragmented packets.
-b	Enables the rule to go both ways - for example, allowing packets from source to source.
-v	Verbose mode.
-n	Shows IP addresses instead of hostnames.
-l	Enables logging.
-o *{ maxsize }*	Causes packets that match to be copied to userspace device.
-m *value*	Marks packets that match the rule - for example, useful when using `ipmasqadm mfw`.
-t *andmask xormask*	Changes the TOS field in IP headers.
-x	Shows exact numbers. Only used with -L.
[!) -y	Checks TCP packets that have the SYN bit set.
--line-numbers	Shows line numbers on rules.
--no-warnings	Suppresses all warning messages.

File Name:	`ipchains`	**Directory:**	/sbin/	**Type:**	External
Note:	When using IP forwarding, remember to put a 1 in the `/proc/sys/net/ipv4/ip_forward` file.				

ipchains -A forward -j MASQ -s 192.168.1.0/24 --destination-port 20:80	Masquerades the internal network 192.168.1.0/24 and allows access to port 20 trough 80.
ipchains -I input -j DENY -p icmp	Rejects all IMCP packets going into this system.
ipchains -A forward -j ACCEPT -s 192.168.40.64/192 -i eth2	Accepts packets from 192.168.40.64 network from eth2 to be routed through this computer.

ipchains-restore

UNIX Shell:	Bash shell (bash)				
Function	Restores IP firewall chains from STDIN.				
Syntax	ipchains-restore [options...]				
-f	Removes chains without asking.				
-v	Shows every rule.				
-p	Creates referred-to chain that doesn't exist.				
File Name:	`ipchains-restore`	**Directory:**	/sbin/	**Type:**	Script
Tip:	When managing ipchains rules, `ipchains-save/restore` is perfect.				
ipchains-restore < saved_ipchainsrules	Restores ipchains rules from `saved_ipchainsrules`.				

ipchains-save

UNIX Shell:	Bash shell (bash)				
Function	Shows the firewall chains on the screen.				
Syntax	ipchains-save *{ chain }* [-v]				
-v	Shows every rule.				
chain	Specifies chain to save.				
File Name:	`ipchains-save`	**Directory:**	/sbin/	**Type:**	Script
Tip:	When managing ipchains rules, ipchains-save/restore is perfect.				
ipchains-save > saved_ipchainsrules	Store ipchains rules to saved_ipchainsrules.				

ipppd

UNIX Shell:	All primary shells (bash, ash, tcsh)
Function	A modified `pppd` that provides synchronous PPP support for ISDN connections.
Syntax	ipppd [options...] *{ device }*
local:remote	Specifies the local and/or remote interface IP addresses.
-ac	Disables address/control compression.
-all	Specifies that nonrequest or allow negotiation should be used.
auth	Specifies the peer must authenticate itself.
bsdcomp *number,total*	Specifies the compression level for the peer to send using BSD compression.
-bsdcomp	Disables BSD compression.
noccp	Disables the compression control protocol, same as -ccp.
+chap	Requires the peer to authenticate itself using CHAP.
-chap	Disables authentication using CHAP.
chap-interval *number*	Specifies rechallenge of the peer every number of seconds.
chap-max-challenge *number*	Specifies the maximum number of CHAP challenge transmission to number (default is 10).
chap-restart *number*	Specifies the CHAP retransmission timeout for challenges to number seconds.
debug	Specifies that connection debugging should be done, same as -d.
defaultroute	Adds a default route to the system routing tables.
-detach	Specifies the program shouldn't be forked to the background.
domain *domain*	Adds domain to the local hostname for authentication.
file *file*	Specifies a file to read option from.
-ip	Disables IP address negotiation.
+ip-protocol	Enables the IPCP and IP protocols.
-ip-protocol	Disables the IPCP and IP protocols.
+ipx-protocol	Enables the IPXCP and IPX protocols.
-ipx-protocol	Disables the IPXCP and IPX protocols.
ipcp-accept-local	Specifies the peer's idea of our local IP address is accepted.
ipcp-accept-remote	Specifies the peer's idea of our remote IP address is accepted.
ipcp-max-configure *number*	Specifies the maximum number of IPCP configure requests to be sent (default is 10).
ipcp-max-failure *number*	Specifies the maximum number of IPCP NAKs returned before sending rejects.
ipcp-max-terminate *number*	Specifies the maximum number of IPCP terminate requests (default is 3).
ipcp-restart *number*	Specifies the IPCP restart interval to number seconds (default is 3).
ipparam *string*	Specifies an extra parameter to the `ip-up` and `ip-down` scripts.
ipx-network *number*	Specifies the IPX network number in the IPXCP configure request frame.
ipx-node *number:number*	Specifies the IPX local node number and the peer's node number.

continued

ipx-router-name *{ string }*	Specifies the name of the IPX router.
ipx-routing *number*	Specifies the routing protocol to be received by this option.
ipxcp-accept-local	Accepts peer's NAK for the node number.
ipxcp-accept-network	Accepts peer's NAK for the network number.
ipxcp-accept-remote	Specifies the peer's network number specified in the configure request frame.
ipxcp-max-configure *number*	Specifies the maximum number of IPXCP configure request frames.
ipxcp-max-failure *number*	Specifies the maximum number of IPXCP NAK frames.
ipxcp-max-terminate *number*	Specifies the maximum number of IPXCP terminate request frames.
kdebug *number*	Specifies the number for debugging the PPP driver in the kernel.
lcp-echo-failure *number*	Specifies the number of LCP echo request frames before assuming the peer is dead.
lcp-echo-interval *number*	Specifies that LCP echo-requests should be sent every number seconds.
lcp-max-configure *number*	Specifies the maximum number of LCP configure-request transmissions (default is 10).
lcp-max-failure *number*	Specifies the maximum number of LCP NAKs returned before sending rejects.
lcp-max-terminate *number*	Specifies the maximum number of LCP terminate-request transmission (default is 3).
lcp-restart *number*	Specifies the LCP retransmission timeout to number seconds (default is 3).
lock	Creates a UUCP-style lock file for the serial device.
login	Uses the system password database for authenticating.
-mn	Disables magic number negotiation.
+mp	Enables MPPP negotiation
mru *number*	Specifies the MRU number.
-mru	Disables MRU negotiation.
ms-get-dns	Obtains one or two DNS addresses.
ms-get-wins	Obtains one or two WINS addresses.
mtu *number*	Specifies the MTU number.
name *name*	Specifies the name of the local system for authentication purposes.
netmask *address*	Specifies a netmask to the interfaces.
noipdefault	Specifies the default behavior when no local IP address is specified.
passive	Specifies that it should be passive until it gets a valid LCP packet and not exit.
-p	Same as the passive option.
+pap	Queries the peer to authenticate itself using PAP.
-pap	Disables PAP authentication.
papcrypt	Indicates that all secrets in the `/etc/ppp/pap-secrets` file are encrypted.
pap-max-authreq *number*	Specifies the maximum number of PAP authenticate-request transmissions (default is 10).
pap-restart *number*	Specifies the PAP retransmission timeout to number seconds (default is 3).
pap-timeout *number*	Specifies the maximum time to wait for the peer to authenticate itself with PAP.
-pc	Disables protocol field compression negotiation.
pidfile *file*	Uses file instead of `/var/run/ipppd.pid`.
pred1comp	Enables Predictor-1 compression.
-pred1comp	Disables Predictor-1 compression.
proxyarp	Adds an entry to this system's ARP.
-proxyarp	Disables that an entry to this system's ARP should be added.
remotename *name*	Specifies the remote system name for authentication purposes.
set_userip	Reads defined IPs in `/etc/ppp/useriptab`.
silent	Specifies that LCP packets shouldn't be sent to initiate a connection.
+ua *file*	Enables PAP authentication and read passwords from file.
usefirstip	Gets the remote address from the first entry in the auth file.
usehostname	Specifies enforcing of the hostname.
usepeerdns	Asks the peer for up to two DNS server addresses.
username	Specifies the name used for authenticating the local system to the peer.
useifip	Gets the IP address for the negotiation from the attached network interface.
-vj	Disables negotiation of Van Jacobson-style TCP/IP header compression.
-vjccomp	Disables the connection-ID compression option in VJ style TCP/IP header compression.
vj-max-slots *number*	Specifies the number slots to use by the Van Jacobson TCP/IP header compression.
device	Specifies the PPP device to use.

File Name:	`ipppd`	**Directory:**	/usr/sbin/	**Type:**	External

ipppstats		UNIX Shell:	All primary shells (bash, ash, tcsh)
Function	Shows PPP-related statistics.		
Syntax	ipppstats [options...] *{ unit }*		

-v	Shows statistics like the number of packets tossed.
-r	Shows the overall packet compression rate. The rate is between 0 – 1.
-c	Specifies screen mode to show packet compression statistics.
-i *secs*	Sets the interval between printouts. (Default is 5 seconds.)
unit	Specifies the interface to use to gather statistics.
File Name: ipppstats	**Directory:** /usr/sbin/ **Type:** External

iprofd		UNIX Shell:	All primary shells (bash, ash, tcsh)
Function	Creates the modem register of the ISDN-ttys AT-emulator permanent.		
Syntax	iprofd *{ registerfile }*		

registerfile	Specifies the file where the register should be saved.
File Name: iprofd	**Directory:** /usr/sbin/ **Type:** External

iptables		UNIX Shell:	All primary shells (bash, ash, tcsh)
Function	Manages IP firewall rules in the Linux 2.4 kernel.		
Syntax	iptables [-t] *command* [options...]		

-t *table*	Specifies which one of the three tables to use (default is filter).
filter	Controls packets going into, from, and through the firewall itself.
nat	Controls packets that open new connections and directs them where to go.
mangle	Controls special packet alterations.
	These are the commands that can be used. They can't be combined.
-A *chain rule*	Adds a rule specification to the end of the specified chain.
-D *chain rule*	Removes specified rule number or rule specification from selected chain.
-R *chain rulenumber rule*	Replaces the specified rule number with the specified rule.
-I *chain { rulenumber } rule*	Inserts a rule specification to the first line in a chain or on the specified line.
-L *{ chain }*	Shows the rules inside all chains or only in the specified chain.
-F *{ chain }*	Deletes rules in all chains, or only in the specified chain.
-Z *{ chain }*	Resets the byte counters all chains, or in the chain specified.
-N *chain*	Creates one more chains of the specified name.
-X *chain*	Removes the specified user-defined chains. The chain must be empty first.
-P *chain policy*	Sets policy for the specified chain to the specified policy: DENY, REJECT, or ACCEPT.
-E *chain newchain*	Renames the chain specified to the new name.
-h	Shows help information.
	The following options match packets:
-p [!] *protocol*	Specifies the protocol. Protocols are: UDP, TCP, ICMP or all.
-s [!] *address*	Specifies the source address to use.
[*/netmask*]	Specifies a netmask to use with the address specified.
-d [!] *address*	Specifies the destination address to use.
4 [*/netmask*]	Specifies a netmask to use with the address specified.
-i [!] *{ interface }*	Specifies an interface to use for packets coming into the system.
-o [!] *{ interface }*	Specifies an interface to use for packets going from the system.
[!] -f	Creates the rule to refer only to the second or further fragments of packets.
--source-port [!] *{ port }* [*:port*]	Specifies a source port to match.
--destination-port [!] *{ port }* [*:port*]	Specifies a destination port to match. (To specify a port range use a colon (:) between the start port and the end port.)
--port *{ port }*	Matches the rule if the port is the in the same source and destination. (To specify several ports, you may split them with a comma.)
--tcp-flags [!] *examineflags useflags*	Inspects the TCP flags specified and matches packets that have the wanted TCP flags. (The TCP flags are SYN, ACK, FIN, RST, URG, PSH, ALL, or NONE.)

continued

[!] --syn	Checks only packets that is marked with the SYN flag and the ACK and FIN cleared.
--tcp-option [!] *number*	Matches if the TCP option is set for the packet.
--icmp-type [!] *type*	Specifies the ICMP type to use.
-v	Verbose mode. Shows more information.
-n	Shows IP addresses instead of hostnames.
-x	Shows the exact packet and byte count.
--line-numbers	Shows the rule number to the left when listing the rules.
--mac-source [!] *address*	Specifies a MAC address to match.
--limit *rate*	Specifies a maximum average matching rate (default is 3/hour).
--limit-burst *number*	Specifies a maximum initial count of packets to match (default is 5).
--mark *value*	Specifies a mark value to match.
--uid-owner *userID*	Matches the packet if it was created by the specified user ID.
--gid-owner *groupID*	Matches the packet if it was created by a user in the specified group ID.
--pid-owner *processID*	Matches the packet if it was created by the specified process ID.
--sid-owner *sessionID*	Matches the packet if it was created by the specified session group ID.
--state *state*	Specifies a connection state to match. Multiple states are separated by commas.
--tos *tos*	Specifies a Type of Service name or number to match.
-j *target*	Specifies what to do with the matched packet. Most used is ACCEPT or REJECT.
	The following are the targets and their module options that you can use:
ACCEPT	Allows the matched packet.
DROP	Stops the matched packet and doesn't look back.
QUEUE	Puts the matched packet into user space.
RETURN	Jumps from the current chain to the previous chain that called the current chain.
LOG	Logs the matched packets. The following are log options used with this target.
--log-level *level*	Specifies at what `syslog` level to log.
--log-prefix *message*	Specifies a message to put before the log messages that goes to the `syslog`.
--log-tcp-sequence	Logs TCP sequence numbers to `syslog`.
--log-tcp-options	Logs TCP packet header options.
--log-ip-options	Logs IP packet header options.
MARK	Sets the netfilter mark to the packet. Used only in the mangle table.
--set-mark *mark*	Specifies the mark to set.
REJECT	Stops the matched packet and reports an error message.
--reject-with *type*	Specifies a reject type to report to the sender.
TOS	Sets the Type of Service field to the IP header.
--set-tos	Specifies a Type of Service name or number to set.
MIRROR	Switches the source and destination fields in the IP header.
SNAT	Changes the source address in the packet.
--to-source *address*	Specifies a new source IP address for the packet matched.
[*-address*]	Specifies an IP range to use. Range is from the first IP specified to the last.
[*:port-port*]	Specifies what port range to use.
DNAT	Alters the destination address in the packet.
--to-destination *address*	Specifies a new destination IP address for the packet matched.
[*-address*]	Specifies a IP range to use. Range is from the first IP specified to the last.
[*:port-port*]	Specifies what port range to use.
MASQUERADE	Sets the IP address to the packet going from the interface specified.
--to-ports *port* [*-port*]	Specifies a source port or port range to use.
REDIRECT	Alters the destination IP address of the matched packet.
--to-ports *port* [*-port*]	Specifies a destination port or port range to use.
DIAGNOSTICS	Shows error messages on STDERR.

File Name:	`iptables`	**Directory:**	/sbin/	**Type:**	External
Note:	To exclude the specified modifier from a rule, use the exclamation ! sign. For example, -p ! *protocol* uses all except the specified protocol.				

iptables -t nat -A POSTROUTING -s 192.168.1.0/24 -d 0/0 -j MASQUERADE	Lets the specified source to connect through using masquerading.
iptables -n –L	Lists all rules in the filter table.

iptunnel

iptunnel	UNIX Shell:	All primary shells (bash, ash, tcsh)
Function	Configures various types of IP tunnels.	
Syntax	iptunnel *ACTION { name } { mode }* [remote *IPaddress*] [local *IPaddress*] [options...]	

-V	Shows version information.
ttl *value*	Specifies the TTL value.
tos *value*	Specifies the TOS value.
nopmtudisc	Disable path MTU discovery.
dev *device*	Specifies the device to use.
	The following options only work with GRE tunnels:
key *value*	Specifies same key for both incoming and outgoing packets.
ikey *value*	Specifies a key for incoming packets.
okey *value*	Specifies a key for outgoing packets.
csum	Combines the icsum and ocsum options.
icsum	Requires incoming packets to have the correct checksum.
ocsum	Checksums outgoing packets.
seq	Combines the iseq and oseq options.
iseq	Requires incoming packets to be serialized.
oseq	Serializes outgoing packets.
name	Specifies the name of the tunnel.
mode	The following modes can be used:
ipip	Uses IP in IP tunnel mode.
gre	Specifies that GRE tunnel mode should be used.
sit	Uses SIT tunnel mode.
IPaddress	Specifies an IP address for the local and remote computer.
ACTION	**The following actions can be used:**
show	Shows tunnel configuration.
add	Adds a tunnel.
change	Modifies a tunnel.
del	Deletes a tunnel.

File Name:	`iptunnel`	**Directory:**	/sbin/	**Type:**	External

iptunnel add work ipip remote 10.0.0.1 local 10.0.0.2	Adds tunnel to IP address 10.0.0.1 and uses 10.0.0.2 as the local IP address.

ipx_cmd

ipx_cmd	UNIX Shell:	All primary shells (bash, ash, tcsh)
Function	A bridge between local IPX network and Novell's SCMD driver.	
Syntax	ipx_cmd -A *host* [-l *interface*]	

-A *host*	Specifies the IP address — DNS or dotted quad server address is also allowed.
-l *interface*	Specifies the IP address for the client side of the CMD driver.

File Name:	`ipx_cmd`	**Directory:**	/usr/bin/	**Type:**	External

ipx_configure

ipx_configure	UNIX Shell:	All primary shells (bash, ash, tcsh)
Function	Queries or configures IPX behavior with respect to automatic IPX interface detection.	
Syntax	ipx_configure [options...]	

-help	Shows help information.
-auto_interface=*action*	Enables or disables to automatically create an interface (actions = on or off).
-auto_primary=*action*	Enables or disables to automatically select a primary interface (actions = on or off).

File Name:	`ipx_configure`	**Directory:**	/sbin/	**Type:**	External

ipx_interface

ipx_interface	UNIX Shell:	All primary shells (bash, ash, tcsh)
Function	Manages IPX interfaces.	
Syntax	ipx_interface [option] *{ device } { frame }*	

add *device frame*	Creates a specific IPX interface.
-p	The IPX interface is made primary.
networkNR	Specifies the network number.
nodeNR	Specifies the node number.
del *device frame*	Removes the specified IPX interface.
check *device frame*	Shows the device, frame type, and network number of an IPX interface.
delall	Removes all IPX interfaces.
help	Shows help information.
device	Specifies the IPX interface.
frame	Specifies the correct IEEE frame type.

File Name:	`ipx_interface`	**Directory:**	/sbin/	**Type:**	External
ipx_interface add -p Eth0 802.2		Adds eth0 as primary IPX-interface with frame 802.2.			

ipx_internal_net

ipx_internal_net	UNIX Shell:	All primary shells (bash, ash, tcsh)
Function	Adds or removes the IPX internal network.	
Syntax	ipx_internal_net option	

add *networkNR*	Creates the IPX internal network with a specification of a network number.
nodeNR	Specifies the Ethernet address.
del	Removes the IPX internal network.

File Name:	`ipx_internal_net`	**Directory:**	/sbin/	**Type:**	External
ipx_internal_net add 0x00ABCDEF		Creates internal IPX network 0x00ABCDEF.			

ipx_route

ipx_route	UNIX Shell:	All primary shells (bash, ash, tcsh)
Function	Adds or removes an IPX route.	
Syntax	ipx_route add *destination_net netNR*[:*MACaddress*] ipx_route del *destination_net*	

add	Creates the route to a target network.
del	Removes the route to a target network.
destination_net	Specifies the network number to route to.
netNR	Specifies the network to route.
MACaddress	Specifies MACaddress of the IPX router.

File Name:	`ipx_route`	**Directory:**	/usr/bin/	**Type:**	External
Note:	The kernel IPX stores only one route per target network.				
ipx_route del 0x00ABCDEF		Removes the route to network 0x00ABCDEF.			

isapnp

isapnp	UNIX Shell:	All primary shells (bash, ash, tcsh)
Function	Reads the configuration file to configure ISA PnP cards.	
Syntax	isapnp [option] *file*	

-h	Shows help information.
-v	Shows version information.
file	Specifies the configuration file (default is `/etc/isapnp.conf`).

File Name:	`isapnp`	**Directory:**	/sbin/	**Type:**	External

isdnconf

UNIX Shell: All primary shells (bash, ash, tcsh)

Function	Manipulates or reads ISDN phone number config files.
Syntax	isdnconf [options...]

-A	Adds a new entry, which is read from STDIO.
-D	Deletes one or more entries that match the data options given.
-V	Shows version information.
-n *number*	Specifies the number to match, can contain wildcards.
-a *alias*	Specifies the alias name to match, can contain wildcards.
-t *value*	Specifies the service indicator to match.
-c *code*	Specifies the area code of the phone number.
-i	Specifies ignore case for the -n and -a options.
-w *word*	Specifies the parameters for -n and -a must match the whole value.
-d	Specifies that AND should be used instead of OR.
-q	Enables quiet mode.
-m	Creates a new MSN entry.
-s	Shows only alias and the number.
-l	Shows the programs to run.
-f *filename*	Specifies the config file to use (default is `/etc/isdn/callerid.conf`).
-g	Edits `/etc/isdn/callerid.conf` instead of `~/.isdn`.
-1	Shows or deletes only the first entry.
-M	Used internally by `isdnmon` to get alias info.

File Name:	`isdnconf`	**Directory:**	/usr/bin/	**Type:**	External

isdnctrl

UNIX Shell: All primary shells (bash, ash, tcsh)

Function	Configures ISDN device information.
Syntax	isdnctrl *ACTION devices...*

ACTION	**The following actions can be used:**
addif *name*	Adds a new ISDN interface name to the kernel.
delif *name* [force]	Removes the ISDN interface name from the kernel; force executes ifconfig down.
reset [force]	Removes all ISDN interfaces from the kernel; force executes ifconfig down.
ifdefaults *name*	Resets the interface name to some reasonable defaults.
dialmode *name { mode }*	**Sets the dial mode of the interface to one of the following:**
off	Specifies that no connection can be made, an existing connection is terminated.
manual	Specifies manual dialing and hangup.
auto	Specifies autodial mode.
addphone *name* out *number*	Adds the phone number to the list of incoming number of the ISDN interface name.
delphone *name mode number*	Removes phone number from the incoming or outgoing phone list; mode can be in or out.
eaz *name { number }*	Specifies the EAZ (German) or MSN (Europe) for ISDN interface name to number.
huptimeout *name { seconds }*	Sets the hangup timeout for ISDN interface name to seconds.
cbdelay *name { seconds }*	Sets the callback delay for ISDN interface name to seconds.
dialmax *name { number }*	Sets the number of dial attempts for ISDN interface name.
ihup *name* [on | off]	Turns on or off the hangup timeout for incoming calls on interface name.
chargehup *name* [on | off]	Turns on or off hangup before next charge info for interface name.
chargeint *name { seconds }*	Sets the charge interval for the given interface name if seconds are given.
secure *name* [on | off]	Turns on or off the security feature for interface name.
callback *name { mode }*	Sets callback mode for interface name to mode.
cbhup *name* [on | off]	Turns on or off hangup for interface name before starting callback.
encap *name { encapsulation }*	Sets the encapsulation mode for interface name.
l2_prot *name { protocol }*	Sets the layer-2 protocol for interface name. Values: x75i, x75ui, x75bui, and hdl.
l3_prot *name { protocol }*	Sets the layer-3 protocol for interface name. At the moment, only trans is supported.
list *name*	Lists all parameters and the charge info for interface name.
status *name*	Shows the connection status for interface name.

continued

verbose *number*	Sets the verbosity level to number.
hangup *name*	The connection of interface name is closed immediately.
bind *name driverId,channel { exclusive }*	Binds an interface name to a physical channel.
unbind *name*	Unbinds a bound interface name.
pppbind *name { number }*	Binds the interface name to an IPPP device.
pppunbind *name*	Unbinds the previously bound interface name.
busreject *driverId* [on | off]	Rejects incoming calls instead of ignoring them.
addslave *name slave*	Adds a slave interface named slave to interface name for raw channel bundling.
sdelay *name number*	Sets delay for slave dialing to interface name.
trigger *name number*	Sets trigger level for slave dialing to interface name.
addlink *name*	Adds a slave interface to the existing connection for MPPP.
removelink *name*	Removes a slave interface from the existing connection for MPPP.
dial *name*	Forces dialing of interface name.
mapping *driverId arguments...*	Installs a mapping table for MSD to EAZ mapping.
device	Specifies the device to act on.

File Name:	`isdnctrl`	**Directory:**	/usr/sbin/	**Type:**	External

isdnlog

UNIX Shell: All primary shells (bash, ash, tcsh)

Function	Shows decoded information from the ISDN card.
Syntax	isdnlog [options...] *device { file }*

-V	Shows version information.
-f*file*	Reads options from the config file.
-A*value*	Sets digits necessary to get an outside line when connecting through a PABX.
-B*value*	Sets the provider preselection to the given value.
-R*prefix*	Sets the preselected provider to value.
-0*value:value*	Suppresses leading digits.
-i*value*	Considers numbers shorter than value to be internal numbers.
-o	Specifies that normally causes are not shown for other connected ISDN devices.
-u*value*	Ignores housekeeping frames.
-U*value*	Ignores COLP/CLIP frames.
-2*value*	Enables dual mode.
-1	Specifies that an HFC-based card is used for echo mode.
-r	Replays a debug file.
-n	Shows throughput messages on the same line.
-W*value*	Limits all messages to value character per line.
-v*value*	Specifies that all information is to be copied to /tmp/DEVICE.
-s	Specifies the debug file `/tmp/DEVICE` is flushed after each access.
-P	Copies the debug information to STDOUT.
-D	Starts as a daemon.
-T	Activates trace mode.
-K	Shows every pressed key; can't be combined with -d option.
-b	Specifies that a bilingual network terminator is used.
-m*value*	Logs to STDERR.
-O*value*	Logs to value instead of STDERR.
-C *value*	Logs to console value instead of STDERR.
-M	Generates output for monitor programs.
-l*value*	Logs to `syslog`, values specifies the log code.
-x*value*	Passes information to x11 client.
-p*value*	Passes information to x11 clients on this port value.
-c*value*	Saves the last value calls and passes this information to an x11 client.
-L*value*	Saves the last value messages and passes this information to an x11 client.
-w*values*	Enables throughput logging every value seconds.
-I*value:value*	Specifies interval for showing charge messages.
-d*value*	Specifies a bitmap to use.
-t*value*	Sets the local system time to the time transmitted by ISDN service provider.
-h*value*	Specifies the kernel should hang up a few seconds before the next charge signal.
-S	Activates the "START" feature.

continued

device	Specifies the ISDN device to use.		
file	Specifies a file to read options from.		
File Name: isdnlog	**Directory:** /usr/sbin/	**Type:** External	

isdnrate

UNIX Shell: All primary shells (bash, ash, tcsh)

Function	Shows telephone rates and various info from rate files.
Syntax	isdnrate [options...] *NRs...*

-b*value*	Shows only value providers (default is all).
-d*day*	Calculates rates for day.
-f*from*	Specifies caller's location.
-h*time*	Specifies time of call (default is now).
-l*length*	Specifies length of call in seconds (default is 153).
-o	Shows only booked providers listed in `rate.conf`.
-p*provider...*	Shows only info for given providers, separated with comma.
-s	Considers number as the name of a service and shows all numbers or providers.
-t*value*	Shows only providers that have calculation impulses smaller or equal to value.
-v*level*	Sets the verbose level.
-x *providers...*	Specifies providers to exclude; values are separated with commas.
-C	Connects to a running `isdnrate` daemon.
-D	Starts as a daemon and waits for a connection from a client.
-D2	Starts as a daemon and goes to the background.
-CD3	Stops a running daemon.
-G*number*	Shows raw data for connection-number can be 97, 98, or 99.
-H	Shows header.
-L	Shows a semicolon-separated list.
-N	Shows information about following numbers.
-O*file*	Writes socket to given file on start of daemon (default is `/tmp/isdnrate`).
-P*directory*	Writes own PID to `directory/isdnrate.pid` on start of daemon.
-S*sort*	Sorts the output. The sort value can be v for VBN or n for provider name (default is by charge).
-T	Shows a table of charges for day times, weekdays, or weekends.
-V	Shows version information.
-X*value*	Shows additional information for charge or from ratefile.
-Z	Shows info for LCR.
NRs...	Specifies a number to show ratings for.
File Name: isdnrate	**Directory:** /usr/bin/ **Type:** External

isdnrep

UNIX Shell: All primary shells (bash, ash, tcsh)

Function	Shows ISDN activity.
Syntax	isdnrep [options...]

-V	Shows version information.
-a	Shows all connections registered.
-h	Shows no header for each day.
-n	Shows numbers instead of the aliases for those numbers.
-f*file*	Specifies the file to write the report to, default is `/var/log/isdn.log`.
-t *time*	Specifies a time span covered by the log file.
-d *time*	Deletes entries from the log file up to the specified time.
-E	Shows all connections and connection attempts.
-v	Verbose mode. Shows more information.
-p *numbers...*	Shows only the selected phone numbers; values are separated with comma.
-i	Shows only incoming connections.
-o	Shows only outgoing connections.
-u	Shows all numbers not aliased in `callerid.conf` or `~/.isdn` at end.
-w*value*	Shows output in HTML format - values: 0 (HTML header is suppressed), 1 (complete HTML).
-s*value*	Specifies format for the output generated for each connection.

continued

-F*values*	Specifies a format string in `isdn.conf`.
File Name: `isdnrep`	**Directory:** /usr/bin/ **Type:** External

isoinfo

UNIX Shell: All primary shells (bash, ash, tcsh)

Function	Does directory-like listings of iso9660 images.
Syntax	isoinfo [options...]

-h	Shows help information.
	The following two options can't be used together:
-f	Creates an output that looks like as the `find . -print` command had been used.
-l	Creates an output that looks like as the `ls -lR` command had been used.
-d	Shows the primary volume descriptor information.
-i *image*	Specifies the path to the image to use.
-N *sector*	Specifies the sector number where ISO image should start on a disk when saving.
-p	Shows path table information.
-R	Shows information from Rock Ridge extensions.
-J	Shows information from Joliet extensions.
-T *sector*	Specifies the section number on a disk where the image is that is to be examined.
-x *path*	Shows the specified image file on STDOUT.
File Name: `isoinfo`	**Directory:** /usr/bin/ **Type:** External

isovfy

UNIX Shell: All primary shells (bash, ash, tcsh)

Function	Checks an iso9660 image for errors.
Syntax	isovfy *isoimage*

isoimage	Specifies the iso9660 image to check.
File Name: `isovfy`	**Directory:** /usr/bin/ **Type:** External

ispell

UNIX Shell: A shell (ash, bsh)

Function	A compatibility script for the `aspell` spell checker.
Syntax	ispell [options...] { *file* }

	Please see `aspell` for options.
file	Specifies a file to spell check.
File Name: `ispell`	**Directory:** /usr/bin/ **Type:** Script

jobid

UNIX Shell: A shell (ash, bsh)

Function	Shows the process id for the job or for the current job if not given.
Syntax	jobid { *jobid* }

jobid	Specifies job ID.

jpegtran

UNIX Shell: All primary shells (bash, ash, tcsh)

Function	Converts JPEG from one compression to another.
Syntax	jpegtran [options...] { *file* }

-optimize	Optimizes the entropy encoding parameters.
-progressive	Creates a JPEG in progressive format.
-restart *n*	Sends a JPEG restart marker with an interval of `n` MCU rows.
-scans *file*	Uses the specified scan script.
-flip *horizontal*	Horizontally mirrors the image.
-flip *vertical*	Vertically mirrors the image.
-rotate *90*	Rotates the image 90 degrees.
-rotate *180*	Rotates the image 180 degrees.
-rotate *270*	Rotates the image 270 degrees.
-transpose	Flips the image from upper left to lower right.
-transverse	Flips the image from upper right to lower left.

continued

-grayscale	Makes a grayscale output.
-copy *none*	Doesn't copy extra markers from the source file.
-copy *comments*	Copies comment markers.
-copy *all*	Copies all markers.
-maxmemory *n*	Sets the amount of memory used to process the file conversion.
-outfilename	Specifies the output file.
-verbose	Verbose mode. Shows more information.
-debug	Shows debug information.
file	Specifies input file.
File Name: `jpegtran`	**Directory:** /usr/bin/ **Type:** External

kbd_mode

UNIX Shell: All primary shells (bash, ash, tcsh)

Function	Changes the keyboard translation mode. Useful when a program doesn't restore the translation mode.
Syntax	kbd_mode [option]

-s	Sets keyboard to scancode mode.
-k	Sets keyboard to keycode mode.
-a	Sets keyboard to ASCII mode.
-u	Sets keyboard to Utf-8, Unicode mode.
File Name: `kbd_mode`	**Directory:** /usr/bin/ **Type:** External

kbdconfig

UNIX Shell: All primary shells (bash, ash, tcsh)

Function	Configures the keyboard.
Syntax	kbdconfig [options...]

--back	Shows a Back button instead of a Cancel button.
--test	Enables non-root users to run the command.
File Name: `kbdconfig`	**Directory:** /usr/sbin/ **Type:** External

kbdrate

UNIX Shell: All primary shells (bash, ash, tcsh)

Function	Changes keyboard configurations.
Syntax	kbdrate [options...]

-s	Shows no output.
-r *rate*	Alters the keyboard repeat rate in characters per seconds.
-d *delay*	Alters the keyboard delay rate in milliseconds.
-V	Shows version information.
File Name: `kbdrate`	**Directory:** /sbin/ **Type:** External

kernelversion

UNIX Shell: A shell (ash, bsh)

Function	Shows the major version of the kernel.
Syntax	kernelversion
File Name: `kernelversion`	**Directory:** /sbin/ **Type:** Script

kibitz

UNIX Shell: Expect script

Function	Allows multiple interactions to one shell.
Syntax	kibitz [options...] *user { program arguments... }*

-noproc	Runs the command as standalone without any child processes.
-noescape	Disables the escape character.
-escape *char*	Sets a new escape character.
-silent	Shows no output.
-tty *ttyname*	Specifies the tty device to use.

continued

	Users can be one of the following:
user	Specifies a user on the local system.
user@host	Specifies a user on a remote system.
program	Specifies any `expect` or `tcl` program to run in the shell.
arguments...	Specifies options to `expect` or `tcl`.
File Name: `kibitz`	**Directory:** /usr/bin **Type:** Script

killall

UNIX Shell: All primary shells (bash, ash, tcsh)

Function	Kills all processes running the specified commands.
Syntax	killall [options...] [-*signal*] *commands...*

-e	Requires an exact match for long names.
-g	Kills the process group to which the process belongs.
-i	Asks for confirmation before killing a process.
-q	Quiet mode. Doesn't produce any output if nothing is killed.
-v	Shows if the signal was successfully sent.
-V	Shows version information.
-w	Waits for all the killed processes to die.
-l	Shows a list of available signals.
signal	Specifies the signal to send to the process (default is SIGTERM).
commands...	Specifies the commands to be killed. (If a filename is given, processes executing that file are killed.)
File Name: `killall`	**Directory:** /usr/bin/ **Type:** External
killall -HUP xinetd	Sends a SIGHUP to the Internet daemon.

killall5

UNIX Shell: All primary shells (bash, ash, tcsh)

Function	Kills all processes but the ones in it's own session. Same as the System V `killall` command.
Syntax	killall5 [-*signalNR*]

signalNR	Specifies the signal to send.
File Name: `killall5`	**Directory:** /sbin/ **Type:** External

klogd

UNIX Shell: All primary shells (bash, ash, tcsh)

Function	A daemon that is used to log kernel messages.
Syntax	klogd [options...]

-c *n*	Sets the default log level.
-d	Shows debug information.
-f *file*	Specifies a file to log messages to.
-i	Reloads kernel module symbols.
-I	Reloads kernel module symbols.
-n	Doesn't run daemon in background.
-o	Reads all messages in the kernel message buffers.
-p	Logs kernel module symbols if any oops strings are found.
-s	Uses the system call interface to log kernel symbols.
-k *file*	Specifies a kernel symbol file.
-v	Shows version information.
-x	Doesn't read the `system.map` file.
File Name: `klogd`	**Directory:** /sbin/ **Type:** External

ksymoops

UNIX Shell: All primary shells (bash, ash, tcsh)

Function	Decodes Linux kernel Oops.
Syntax	ksymoops [options...] *{ files... }*

-v *vmlinux*	Specifies the vmlinux file to read.
-V	Doesn't use any vmlinux file (is default).
-k *ksym*	Specifies where to find kernel symbols (default is `/proc/ksyms`).

continued

-K	Doesn't use any kernel symbols.
-l *lsmod*	Specifies where the list of loaded modules is (default is `/proc/modules`).
-L	Doesn't read any list of modules.
-r *object*	Specifies where to find objects for modules (default is `/lib/modules/*r/`).
-R	Doesn't read any objects.
-m *system.map*	Specifies where the system map file is (default is `/usr/src/linux/System.map`).
-M	Doesn't use the system map file.
-s *save.map*	Specifies a file to store the system map in (default isn't to).
-S	Specifies that long output lines can be used.
-e	Toggles between native and reverse endian-ness.
-x	Shows offset and length in decimal.
-1	Runs ksymoops in one-shot mode.
-d	Increases the debugging level each time specified.
-h	Shows help information, and current configuration.
-t *target*	Specifies the target to use. Use `ksymoops -t '?'` for list.
-a *arch*	Specifies architecture to use. Use `ksymoops -a '?'` for list.
files...	Specifies one or more files containing oops text.

File Name:	`ksymoops`	**Directory:**	/usr/bin/	**Type:**	External

ksyms

UNIX Shell: All primary shells (bash, ash, tcsh)

Function	Shows kernel symbols that have been exported.
Syntax	ksyms [options...]

-a	Shows all symbols
-h	Shows no header output.
-m	Shows information about the kernel module.

File Name:	`ksyms`	**Directory:**	/sbin/	**Type:**	External

kudzu

UNIX Shell: All primary shells (bash, ash, tcsh)

Function	Checks the hardware. If there are some changes in the system, it gives the opportunity to configure the hardware.
Syntax	kudzu [options...]

-q	Quiet mode. Configures without user inputs.
-s	Inspects in a way that doesn't disturb hardware.
-t *seconds*	Specifies the timeout in seconds.
-?	Shows help information.
--usage	Shows the usage message.
-f *file*	Specifies the file to read hardware info from.

File Name:	`kudzu`	**Directory:**	/usr/sbin/	**Type:**	External

lastb

UNIX Shell: All primary shells (bash, ash, tcsh)

Function	Shows all bad login attempts.
Syntax	lastb [options...] *{ user } { tty }*

-R	Suppresses the hostname field.
-*lines*	Specifies how many lines to show.
-n *lines*	The same as -lines.
-a	Shows the hostname in the last column.
-d	Stores hostname and IP address and translates IP to hostname of non local login.
-i	Same as -d, but it displays IP in dotted-decimal notation.
-o	Reads an old-type wtmp file.
-x	Shows the system shutdown entries and run level.
-f *file*	Specifies log file, other than `/var/log/wtmp`.
user	Specifies a username to find.
tty	Specifies a tty to find.

continued

File Name:	lastb	**Directory:**	/usr/bin/	**Type:**	External
Note:	A great way to look for hackers.				

lastlog

UNIX Shell: All primary shells (bash, ash, tcsh)

Function	Shows the contents of the last login log. The information includes login name, port, and last login time.
Syntax	lastlog [options...]
-u *user*	Specifies the user to show lastlog entries for.
-t *days*	Specifies days to show entries that are more recent.
File Name: lastlog	**Directory:** /usr/bin/ **Type:** External

lc

UNIX Shell: A shell (ash, bsh)

Function	Runs the last function specified by function or the last command entered.
Syntax	lc *{ function }*
function	Specifies a function to use.

ld86

UNIX Shell: All primary shells (bash, ash, tcsh)

Function	Links object files produced by the as86 assembler into I&D executables.
Syntax	ld86 [options...] *files...*
-0	Creates a header with 16-bit magic.
-3	Creates a header with 32-bit magic.
-d	Erases the header from the output file.
-C*file*	Adds file libdir-from-search/crtx.o to the list of files linked.
-D	Specifies that a data base address follows in a format suitable for strtoul.
-H	Specifies the initial stack address in a format suitable for strtoul.
-L*directory*	Adds the specified directory to the search list of library directories.
-M	Shows symbols linked on STDOUT.
-N	Creates a native Linux OMAGIC output file.
-O*directory*	Adds library libdir-from-search/directory to the list of files linked.
-T	Specifies that a text base address follows in a format suitable for `strtoul`.
-i	Separates the I&D output.
-lx	Adds library libdir-from-search/libx.a to list of files linked.
-m	Shows the modules linked on STDOUT.
-o	Specifies the name of the output file follows.
-s	Strips symbols.
-r	Creates a relocatable object from one source object.
-t	Specifies the trace modules being looked at on STDOUT.
-y	Allows `elks` executables to store more than eight characters in labels.
-z	Creates an unmapped zero page or QMAGIC executables.
-	Turn off all the options not taking an argument by pending the option with a dash.
	The following are predefined labels that can be imported to user programs:
__etext	The standard C variable for the end of the text segment.
__edata	The standard C variable for the end of the initialized data.
__end	The standard C variable for the end of the bss area.
__segoff	The setoff between the text and data segment in 16-byte segments.
__segXDL	The lowest address with data in segment X.
__segXDH	The top segment X's data area.
__segXCL	The bottom segment X's common data area.
__segXCH	The top segment X's common data area.
__segXSO	The adjusted offset from segment 0 in the start of segment X in paragraphs.
files...	Specifies input files.
File Name: ld86	**Directory:** /usr/bin/ **Type:** External

ldconfig

UNIX Shell: All primary shells (bash, ash, tcsh)

Function	It is used to configure run time bindings for the dynamic linker.
Syntax	ldconfig [options...]

-c *format*	Specifies the format to use (one of new, old, or compat).
-C *file*	Specifies a cache file.
-f *file*	Specifies a configuration file.
-l	Links individual libraries manually.
-n	Processes directories specified on the command line. Doesn't create cache.
-N	Doesn't create cache.
-p	Shows cache.
-r *directory*	Uses directory as the root directory.
-v	Verbose mode. Shows more information.
--help	Shows help information.
--version	Shows version information.
--usage	Shows a short usage descriptions.

File Name: `ldconfig` **Directory:** /sbin/ **Type:** External

ldd

UNIX Shell: All primary shells (bash, ash, tcsh)

Function	Shows a list of executable files and their dynamic dependencies or shared objects.
Syntax	ldd [options...] *file*

-d	Is used to check references to data objects.
-r	Checks Data objects and functions in one operation.
-v	Verbose mode. Shows more information.
file	Specifies the filename and checks for compatibility.

File Name: `ldd` **Directory:** /usr/bin/ **Type:** External

less

UNIX Shell: All primary shells (bash, ash, tcsh)

Function	A text pager for UNIX system, used to show ASCII files.
Syntax	less [options...] *{ files... }*

+*command*	Specifies an internal command to perform when showing new files.
-?	Shows help information.
-a	Performs no search on lines shown on the screen; instead, does search on lines under.
-b*buffers*	Sets the amount of buffers to use for each file. (One buffer is 1K).
-B	Doesn't automatically assign buffers when needed. Uses amount specified with -bn.
-c	Shows full screen lines from the top down instead of appending from the bottom.
-C	Is used as -c except that screen is cleared before a new page is shown.
-d	Doesn't show error messages if the terminal can't do what it's supposed to.
-D*xcolor*	Sets the text's type and color of it. Color is a value.value pair (MS-DOS only). (The text type x is n = normal, s = standout, d = bold, u = underlined, k = blink.)
-e	Quits the second time less reaches a EOF instead of just give a warning.
-E	Quits directly when the EOF is reached.
-f	Opens all files - mot only those that are regular.
-F	Shows the file and if it's only one page, quits.
-g	Specifies that only the last search string found is highlighted.
-G	Doesn't highlight strings found by the search commands.
-h*lines*	Specifies the number of lines that can be shown by scrolling back.
-i	Isn't case-sensitive when matching patterns.
-I	The same as -i but won't be case-sensitive even when pattern contains uppercase.
-j*line*	Marks a screen line as the line on the screen where the search begins.
-J	Shows a status column on the screen. Is used only with the -w or -W option.
-k*filename*	Specifies a filename to open as a lesskey file. Is repeatable.
-m	Makes verbose prompts with percentages of the file instead of colons.

continued

-M	Makes prompts look even more verbose than with -m.
-n	Doesn't use line numbers.
-N	Shows line numbers at the beginning of the lines.
-o*filename*	Specifies a file to put the input from STDIN in when showing it on the screen.
-O*filename*	Does the same as -o except that it overwrites the specified file.
-p*pattern*	Shows the specified file from the first line containing the specified pattern.
-P*prompt*	Specifies another prompt to use instead of the default.
-q	Sets quiet mode. Never rings the bell when the EOF has been reached.
-Q	Sets very quiet mode. Never ring the bell.
-r	Shows control characters that could create screen problems.
-R	Does the same as -r except that it tries to keep the correct screen appearance.
-s	Combines multiple blank lines into one blank line.
-S	Chops lines longer than the screen width.
-t*tag*	Shows the file containing tag. For this to work, `ctags` must have been run.
-T*tagsfile*	Is used with the -t option. Specifies another tags file to use instead of the default.
-u	Shows backspaces and new line characters as usual characters.
-U	Handles Tabs, backspaces, and newlines as control characters.
-V	Shows version information.
-w	Highlights the first new line when a full page movement has been done.
-W	The same a -w, but highlights when more than one line of movement is performed.
-x*NR*	Uses the NR to specify where to set the Tab stops (default is 8).
-X	Disables sending termcap initialization and deinitialization strings to the screen.
-y*NR*	Uses the NR to specify the maximum number of lines to scroll forward.
-[z]*NR*	Uses NR to specify default scrolling window lines (default is one screen full).
-" *charchar*	Specifies the start and end quote characters to use instead of using quotes.
-~	Enables lines after EOF to be shown as blank lines.
-*NR*	Specifies the horizontal scrolling length for the left and right arrow commands.
--	Specifies the end of options. After this, everything is taken as filenames.
	Commands invoked from within less:
m*letter*	Marks position with specified lowercase letter.
'*letter*	Goes to the earlier marked letter, or with ^ or $, it goes to beginning or end of file.
Space	Scrolls down one screen. You can also use Ctrl+V, Ctrl+F, or f.
{ *NR* } z	The same as Space. NR also sets the size of the screen.
Esc+Space	The same as Space, but scrolls down one screen even if you reach the EOF.
{ *NR* } Return	Scrolls down one line or number of lines. You can also use Ctrl+J, Ctrl+E, f, or j.
{ *NR* } d	Scrolls down half a screen or the specified number of lines. You can also use Ctrl+D.
{ *NR* } Esc+v	Scrolls up one screen or the specified number of lines. You can also use Ctrl+B or b.
{ *NR* } w	The same as Esc+V. Number also sets the default size of the screen.
{ *NR* } y	Scrolls up the number of lines. You can also use Ctrl+Y, Ctrl+P, Ctrl+K, or k.
{ *NR* } u	Scrolls down half a screen or the specified number of lines. You can also use Ctrl+U.
{ *NR* } Esc+)	Scrolls right the number of characters (default is 8). You can also use right arrow.
{ *NR* } Esc+(	Scrolls left the number of characters (default is 8). You can also use left arrow.
r	Repaints the screen. You can also use Ctrl+R or Ctrl+L.
R	The same as r, but discards buffered input.
F	Scrolls forward, even if the EOF is reached.
{ *NR* } g	Goes to line number in the file (default is 1). You can also use < or Esc-<.
{ *NR* } G	Goes to line number in the file (default last line). You can also use > or Esc->.
NR p	Specifies in percent where to start reading in the file. You can also use %.
	Number specifies which one to use, if there is more than one on the top line.
{ *NR* } {	Goes to the matching } if a { is shown in the top line.
{ *NR* } }	Goes to the matching { if a } is shown at the bottom line.
{ *NR* } [	Goes to the matching] if a [is shown in the top line.
{ *NR* }]	Goes to the matching [if a] is shown at the bottom line.
{ *NR* } (	Goes to the matching) if a (is shown in the top line.
{ *NR* })	Goes to the matching (if a) is shown at the bottom line.
ESC-ctrl+F *charchar*	The same as {. Handles the characters as opening and closing brackets.
ESC-ctrl+B *charchar*	The same as }. Handles the characters as opening and closing brackets.
/*pattern*	Searches the file for lines containing the pattern.

continued

/!*pattern*	Searches the file for lines which don't match the pattern.
/**pattern*	Continues to the next file in the command-line list if the pattern isn't found.
/@*pattern*	Starts the search at the first file in the command-line list.
/ctlr+K*pattern*	Highlights found words on the screen, but keeps current cursor position.
/ctrl+R*pattern*	Creates a simple textual comparison.
?*pattern*	Searches the file backwards for lines containing the pattern.
?!*pattern*	Searches the file backwards for lines which don't match the pattern.
?**pattern*	Searches backward in multiple files. Searches in previous file if no match is found.
?@*pattern*	Starts the backward search at last line of the last file in the command-line list.
/ctlr+K?*pattern*	Highlights found words in a backward search, but keeps current cursor position.
/ctrl+R?*pattern*	Creates a simple textual comparison in a backward search.
n	Repeats previous search.
N	Repeats previous search but in reverse direction.
ESC-n	Repeats previous search over files on the command list.
ESC-N	Repeats previous search but in reverse direction over files on the command list.
ESC-u	Turns off search highlighting.
:e *filename*	Inspects a new file.
E *filename*	The same as :e.
:n*{ NR }*	Inspects the next file in the command-line list. Number specifies the NRth next file.
:p*{ NR }*	Inspects previous file in command-line list. Number specifies the NRth previous file.
:x*{ NR }*	Inspects the first file in the command-line list. Number specifies the NRth file.
:d	Erases the current file from the list of files.
=	Shows some information about the file.
V	Shows version information.
q	Quits less. You can also use Q, :q, :Q, or ZZ.
	The next four options don't work on all installations.
v	Starts an editor to edit the current file being shown.
! *Shellcmd*	Invokes a shell to run the specified Shellcmd.
! *letter Shellcmd*	Invokes shell, pipes section between current position and earlier marked letter. (The letter is marked with m letter, ^ and $ works as specified.)
s *file*	Saves the input in a file. The input must be a pipe.
-+option	Resets the specified command-line option to its default.
-!option	Sets the specified command-line option to opposite of its default.
_option	Shows the specified command-line option's current value.
-option	Changes the settings of specified command line option and shows a message of changes. (If the option has an operand, its settings can be changed as well.)
files...	Specifies one or more files to open.

File Name:	`less`	**Directory:**	/usr/bin/	**Type:**	External
Note:	`more` gives less and `less` gives more.				

less +14 /etc/inittab	Shows inittab and go to line 14.
less -ce /etc/services	Shows services and repaint screen for every new page; quits on EOF.
less -p ucgbook ~/books.txt	Scrolls down to the first ucgbook match.

lesskey

UNIX Shell:	All primary shells (bash, ash, tcsh)
Function	Manages key bindings for less.
Syntax	lesskey [options...] *{ file }*

-V	Shows version information.
-o *output*	Specifies the output file.
-	Reads input from STDIN instead of from a file.
file	Specifies an input file with key binding information.

File Name:	`lesskey`	**Directory:**	/usr/bin/	**Type:**	External

let

UNIX Shell:	Bash shell (bash)
Function	Performs arithmetic calculations using the arguments specified; can be used in advanced shell scripts.
Syntax	let arg *{ arguments... }*

arguments...	An arithmetic expression. Please see `expr` for mathematical expressions.

let a=a*3	Sets variable a to variable a multiple with 3.
let i=i+1	Set var i to 1, added to var i.

lilo

UNIX Shell:	All primary shells (bash, ash, tcsh)
Function	Allows you to have several operating systems installed and boot into any of them at startup.
Syntax	lilo [options...]

	The following are the four standalone ways of operation:
-q	Shows a list of the currently mapped files in `/boot/map`.
-R *command*	Specifies a command for the boot loader to run in next execution (once only command).
-I *label*	Shows the corresponding pathname to the label of the running kernel.
-u *device*	Uninstalls lilo, a timestamp is also checked. Use -U if you don't want the timestamp.
	The following are the options to use:
-c	Enables map compaction, merges read requests from adjacent sectors = faster boot.
-C *file*	Specifies a nondefault config file to use (default is `/etc/lilo.conf`).
-d *time*	Specifies the wait time in deciseconds before the first choice is picked for boot.
-D *label*	Specifies the kernel to use as default boot device.
-f *disktab*	Specifies disk geometry parameter file (default is `/etc/disk-tab`).
-i *file*	Specifies a new boot sector file (default is `/boot/boot.b`).
-l	Creates linear sector addresses instead of sector/head/cylinder addresses.
-m *file*	Specifies a map file to use instead of the default.
-P *action*	Fixes or ignores corrupt partition tables. Valid actions are fix or ignore.
-r *directory*	Does a `chroot` to the specified directory before execute to fix a setup.
-s *file*	Specifies an alternate save file for old boot sector or with -u restore from the file.
-S *file*	Allows the command to overwrite an old existing save file.
-t	Tests the new boot loader but doesn't execute the changes.
-v	Verbose mode. Shows more information. More v's gives more information.
-V	Shows debug information.

File Name:	`lilo`	**Directory:**	/sbin/	**Type:**	External
Tip:	If you compile the kernel with the options `make zlilo` or `make bzlilo`, `lilo` is automatically invoked.				

links

UNIX Shell:	All primary shells (bash, ash, tcsh)
Function	A simple command-line URL browser.
Syntax	links [options...] *url*

-async-dns 1 | 0	Selects if the ansync DNS resolver is off (0) or on (1).
-max-connections *value*	Specifies the maximum number of connections (default is 10).
-max-connections-to-host *value*	Specifies the maximum number of connections to a host (default is 2).
-retries *value*	Specifies the number of retries that are allowed (default is 3).
-receive-timeout *seconds*	Selects the receive timeout (default is 120 seconds).
-unrestartable-receive-timeout *seconds*	Selects the nonrestartable connection timeout (default is 600 seconds).
-format-cache-size *size*	Specifies the number of document pages that can be cached (default is 5).
-memory-cache-size *size*	Selects the size of the cache memory in kilobytes (default is 1024kb).
-http-proxy *host:port*	Specifies the host and port number of the HTTP proxy.
-ftp-proxy *host:port*	Specifies the host and port number of the FTP proxy.
-download-dir *path*	Selects the default directory to use for download (default is current directory).
-assume-codepage *page*	Specifies code page to use if the Web page doesn't have one (default is ISO 8859-1).
-anonymous	Limits the program to run on an anonymous account.
-no-connect	Runs the program like a separate instance.

continued

-version	Shows version information.
-help	Shows help information.
	The following quick key strokes are also supported:
ESC	Shows the menu.
^C	Quits.
^P	Scrolls up.
^N	Scrolls down.
[	Scrolls to the left.
]	Scrolls to the right.
arrow up	Selects the link above.
arrow down	Selects the link below.
arrow right	Follows the link.
arrow left	Goes back one step.
g	Goes to the URL.
G	Goes to the URL that is based upon the current URL name.
/	Searches forwards.
?	Searches backwards.
n	Finds the next selection.
N	Finds the previous selection.
=	Specifies the document information.
\	Specifies the document source.
d	Downloads.
q	Quits.
URL	Specifies the URL that's used.

File Name:	`links`	**Directory:**	/usr/bin/	**Type:**	External
links -retries 2			Specifies that only two retries are allowed.		
links -async-dns 1			Activates the async DNS resolver.		

linuxconf

UNIX Shell: All primary shells (bash, ash, tcsh)

Function	An interactive menu configuration program.
Syntax	linuxconf [options...]

--archive *{ systems... }*	Stores the configuration files for the current system profile or specified subsystems.
--diff *{ systems... }*	Compares current and last revisions of the configuration file or specified subsystem.
--extract *{ systems... }*	Extracts the latest copy of the current configuration file or a list of subsystems.
--history *{ systems... }*	Shows the current system profile archive log or a list of subsystems.
--gui	Starts the GUI menu.
--guiproto	Informs `linuxconf` that was started from a GUI front end.
--help	Starts the GUI help section for command-line options.
--helpfile	Shows the location of all of the available help files in `/usr/lib/linuxconf/`.
--listconfig	Shows a complete list of all of the configuration settings.
--setmod *module*	Registers the specified module. Doesn't change any disabled modules.
--shutdown	Goes directly to the system shutdown dialog.
--status	Lists items that are required to make the current configuration up-to-date.
--text	Operates in text mode even when running X11.
--mono	Operates the GUI in black and white.
--unsetmod *module*	Unregisters the specified module.
--update	Initiates the Linux update routine, which does what it takes to update the system.
--vdb	Adds, deletes, gets, or replaces the config file `modules.conf`.
--version	Shows version information.

File Name:	`linuxconf`	**Directory:**	/sbin/	**Type:**	External
http://localhost:98/			Access linuxconf from the net with this address.		

listalias

listalias	UNIX Shell:	A shell (ash, bsh)
Function	Shows user and system mail aliases in the system. This is one part of the elm mailer.	
Syntax	listalias [option] *{ expression }*	

-s	Shows the system aliases.
-u	Shows the user aliases.
expression	Specifies a regular expression to show aliases for.

File Name:	`listalias`	**Directory:**	/usr/bin/	**Type:**	Script
listalias [gG]uy		Shows aliases that match regular expression [gG]uy - that is guy or Guy.			

listres

listres	UNIX Shell:	All primary shells (bash, ash, tcsh)
Function	Creates a list of widget's names and classes.	
Syntax	listres [options...]	

-all	Shows information for all widgets and objects.
-nosuper	Doesn't show resources inherited from a superclass.
-variable	Defines widgets by the names of the class record variables.
-top *name*	Specifies the name of the widget to be treated as the top of the hierarchy.
-format *printf-string*	Specifies the string to show such data as name and class.

File Name:	`listres`	**Directory:**	/usr/X11R6/bin/	**Type:**	External

lkbib

lkbib	UNIX Shell:	All primary shells (bash, ash, tcsh)
Function	Finds references in the bibliographic database that contain the specified keyword.	
Syntax	lkbib [options...] *keywords...*	

-v	Shows version information.
-i*string*	Specifies string to ignore matches for.
-p*file*	Specifies filename to inspect. It can be used multiple times.
-t*NR*	Specifies how many characters of keyword to match (default is 6).
keywords...	Specifies the keyword to search for.

File Name:	`lkbib`	**Directory:**	/usr/bin/	**Type:**	External

lndir

lndir	UNIX Shell:	All primary shells (bash, ash, tcsh)
Function	Makes a shadow directory tree from fromdir with symbolic links.	
Syntax	lndir [options...] *directory1 { directory2 }*	

-silent	Runs in silent mode, doesn't show each subdirectory.
-ignorelinks	Links to the symbolic link in fromdir instead of what it's pointing to.
directory1	Specifies the directory to link to.
directory2	Specifies the directory to make links in (default is the current directory).

File Name:	`lndir`	**Directory:**	/usr/X11R6/bin/	**Type:**	External

loadkeys

loadkeys	UNIX Shell:	All primary shells (bash, ash, tcsh)
Function	Reads and modifies the keyboard translation tables.	
Syntax	loadkeys [options...] *file*	

-c	Erases the kernel's accent table, if accent key definitions exist.
-d	Loads a default keymap (default is defkeymap.map).
-h	Shows help information.
-m	Shows a file that may be used as default keymap.
-q	Sets quiet mode, disabling the showing of standard messages.
-s	Erases the kernel string table instead of replacing or adding strings in it.
-v	Verbose mode. Shows more information. More v's give more information.

File Name:	`loadkeys`	**Directory:**	/bin/	**Type:**	External
loadkeys /usr/lib/kbd/keymaps/i386/qwerty/se-latin1.kmap.gz		Loads Swedish keymap.			

local

UNIX Shell:	Bash shell (bash)

Function	Creates a local variable within a function and set variable's attribute.
Syntax	local [options...] *{ name[=value] }*

-p	Shows names and values of each variable and function.
-F	Shows function names and attributes, not the function definitions. Implies -f.
-a	Sets name to be an array variable.
-f	Sets name to be a function.
-i	Handles the variable as an integer.
-r	Makes name readonly.
-x	Exports name to the environment. (Use + instead of - to turn off the attribute (not for -a).)
name[=value]	Assigns value to name. If value isn't given, it shows the current value.
Note:	Must be used inside a function.

locale

UNIX Shell:	All primary shells (bash, ash, tcsh)

Function	Shows locale-specific information.
Syntax	locale [option] *{ name }*

-a	Writes information about all available public locales including POSIX.
-c	Writes the names of selected locale categories. Can be combined with the -k option.
-k	Writes the names and values of selected keywords, see operand.
-m	Writes names of all character maps.
name	Use the name of a locale category, keyword or reserved name character map.

File Name:	`locale`	**Directory:**	/usr/bin/locale	**Type:**	External

localedef

UNIX Shell:	All primary shells (bash, ash, tcsh)

Function	Compiles or creates locale specifications.
Syntax	localedef [options...] *name*

--charmap=*file*	Looks for symbolic character name definitions in the specified file.
--inputfile=*file*	Looks for the source definitions in the specified file.
--repertoire-map=*file*	Specifies the file that contains mapping from symbolic names to UCS4 values.
--force	Forces creating output even if warning messages occur.
--old-style	Uses old-style tables.
--posix	Is strictly POSIX conforming.
--prefix=*string*	Specifies output file prefix.
--quiet	Quiet mode. Shows less information.
--verbose	Verbose mode. Shows more information.
--help	Shows help information.
--version	Shows version information.
--usage	Shows a brief usage description.
name	Specifies the locale environment.

File Name:	`localedef`	**Directory:**	/usr/bin/	**Type:**	External

lockfile

UNIX Shell:	All primary shells (bash, ash, tcsh)

Function	Creates semaphore files used to limit the access so that only one program is allowed to access the file or files.
Syntax	lockfile [options...] *files...*

-*sleeptime*	Waits the specified time in seconds after an error, then tries again.
-r *count*	Specifies the max count of retries before returning an error.
-l *time*	Deletes any lockfiles after specified time in seconds since last update.
-s*time*	Specifies the number of seconds to suspend use after a removal.
-!	Inverts the output value.
-ml	Locks your mailbox.
-mu	Unlocks your mailbox.
-h	Shows command-line help information.

continued

-v		Shows version information.			
files...		Specifies the filename. (Several ! toggles the output value back and forth.)			
File Name:	`lockfile`	**Directory:** /usr/bin/		**Type:**	External
Note:	All the files created are as read-only. To remove them, use the command `rm -f`.				

logresolve

UNIX Shell: All primary shells (bash, ash, tcsh)

Function	Resolves IP addresses in Apache's access log files. This is to reduce the impact for the name server.
Syntax	logresolve [options...] < *accesslog* > *newaccesslog*

-s *file*		Specifies the filename for the log file.			
-c		Verifies IP addresses to names with DNS.			
accesslog		Specifies the Apache accesslog to run lookups on.			
newaccesslog		Specifies an output file.			
File Name:	`logresolve`	**Directory:** /usr/sbin/		**Type:**	External
Tip:	Good when Apache is configured with Hostname Lookups Off and you want a clean log file.				

logrotate

UNIX Shell: All primary shells (bash, ash, tcsh)

Function	Administrates log files by rotating, compressing, removing, and mailing the log files.
Syntax	logrotate [options...] *files...*

-d	Shows debug information and also implies the verbose mode.
-v	Verbose mode. Shows more information.
-f	Executes a rotation even if it isn't necessary.
-s *file*	Specifies an alternate state file to use (default is `/var/lib/logrotate.status`).
--usage	Shows usage information.
file	Specifies the configuration file to use (default is `/etc/logrotate.conf`).
	The following are the directives that can be used in the configuration files:
compress	Compresses the old log files with `gzip`.
copytruncate	Truncates the original log file in place after a copy is made.
create *attributes*	Specifies the mode, owner, and group attributes for the new file after a rotation.
daily	Rotates logs daily.
delaycompress	Waits till the next execution to compress the old log file.
errors *address*	Sends any errors by mail to the specified address.
extension *text*	Specifies an extension to append to the log files after rotation.
ifempty	Forces the rotation even if the file is empty.
include *path*	Handles the specified file or directory as if it were included.
mail *address*	Sends the log file that is no longer in use to the specified address.
mailfirst	Sends the new file instead of the oldest file to the specified address.
maillast	Sends the oldest file to the specified address. (Is default.)
missingok	Continues with the next file if the intended file is missing without error messages.
monthly	Rotates log files the first time in the month the command is executed.
nocompress	Doesn't compress the old log files.
nocopytruncate	Doesn't truncate the original log file in place after a copy is made.
nocreate	Doesn't create a new file after rotation.
nodelaycompress	Compresses the old rotated without delay.
nomail	Doesn't send any old log files.
nomissingok	Shows an error message if a log file doen't exist.
noolddir	Rotates log files in the same directory as they exist.
nosharedscripts	Executes `prerotate` and `postrotate` scripts for every rotated script.
notifempty	Doesn't rotate an empty log file.
olddir *directory*	Specifies a directory to use for rotation.
postrotate	Executes the lines between `postrotate` and `endscript` after a rotation.
prerotate	Executes the lines between `postrotate` and `endscript` before a rotation.
endscript	Ends the part of lines to execute with `postrotate` and `endscript`.
rotate *count*	Specifies the number of rotations before the file are sent or removed.
size *size*	Specifies the max size of a file before rotation. Append a "M" to specified size to use megabytes.

continued

sharedscripts	Runs the `prerotate` and `postrotate` scripts only once.
tabooext [+] *list*	Changes the current taboo extension file.
weekly	Executes a rotate if the log was not rotated within a week.
File Name: `logrotate`	**Directory:** /usr/sbin/ **Type:** External

loopctrl

UNIX Shell: All primary shells (bash, ash, tcsh)

Function	Configures the isdnloop ISDN driver.
Syntax	loopctrl [-d *DriverID*] *ACTION*

-d *DriverID*	Specifies the driver ID to use if there is more than one.
ACTION	**The following are the actions that can be specified on the command line:**
add *{ cardID }*	Adds a card with an ID created by the system or the specified ID.
leased on | off	Shifts to leased-line mode when set to on and dial-up when set to off.
start *arguments...*	Specifies the D-channel protocol and one or more phonenumbers and starts driver.
dump	Dumps the internal driver variables to STDOUT, if configured with --enable-dump.
File Name: `loopctrl`	**Directory:** /usr/sbin/ **Type:** External

losetup

UNIX Shell: All primary shells (bash, ash, tcsh)

Function	Administers and controls loop devices.
Syntax	losetup [-d] *device* losetup [options...] *device file*

-d *device*	Removes the file or device associated with the specified loop device.
-e *type*	Enables data encryption as NONE, XOR, or DES encryption types.
-o *offset*	Moves the data start to the specified number of bytes into the file or device.
device	Specifies the block device.
file	Specifies the file.
File Name: `losetup`	**Directory:** /sbin/ **Type:** External
losetup /dev/loop0	Shows the status of loop device loop0.
losetup -e des /dev/loop0 /pr.raw	Enables DES encryption for pr.raw on loop0.

lp

UNIX Shell: All primary shells (bash, ash, tcsh)

Function	Sends print request to a printer or printer queue.
Syntax	lp [options...] *{ files... }*

-A	Uses authenticated transfer.
-c	Makes a copy of the file before printing.
-m	Sends the user a mail after done printing.
-s	Quiet mode. Doesn't show messages like ID information.
-w	Shows a message when the files have been printed.
-d *printer*	Specifies the printer or printer queue to use.
-f *name*	Specifies the form name to use as the form when printing.
-n *number*	Specifies the number of copies to print (default is 1).
-o *ACTION*	Specifies printer-dependent options. Can be one of the following.
nobanner	Doesn't print a banner page.
width=*value*	Specifies the page width.
-q *level*	Specifies the priority level for the files (0 is highest, 25 is lowest).
-S *method*	Prints the request using the specified character set or print wheel.
-t *title*	Specifies the title for the banner page.
-T *type*	Prints on a printer that can support the specified content type.
-y *list*	Specifies the printing mode to use.
-D *options...*	Specifies the debug options to use.
files...	Specifies the files to use.
File Name: `lp`	**Directory:** /usr/bin/ **Type:** External

lpbanner	UNIX Shell:	All primary shells (bash, ash, tcsh)
Function	Shows a banner on a fixed-size font printer.	
Syntax	lpbanner [options...]	

-w*width*	Sets the page width in characters (default is 132).
-l*length*	Sets the page length in lines (default is 60).
-P*printer*	Specifies the printer queue for banner information.
-L*bannername*	Specifies the bannername used as main name.
-n*loginname*	Specifies the loginname.
-h*host*	Specifies the hostname.
-J*jobtitle*	Specifies the string used on banner as main title.
-C*class*	Specifies the class string.
-?*Value*	Ignores all other options and arguments provided by LPRng.
all	Uses all options for `lpbanner`.
File Name: `lpbanner`	**Directory:** /usr/libexec/filters/ **Type:** External

lpc	UNIX Shell:	All primary shells (bash, ash, tcsh)
Function	Used by the system administrator to control the operation of the line printer system.	
Syntax	lpc [options...] *{ ACTIONS... }*	

-A	Uses the AUTH environment variable as authentication.
-P*printer*	Specifies the printer spool queue to operate on.
-a	Operates on all printer spool queues.
-S*server*	Specifies the server to send the commands to, instead of specifying a printer.
-V	Shows version information.
-U*user*	Specifies the username for request.
-D*options*	Specifies the debug options to use, separated by commas (type "-D=" for debug help).
ACTIONS...	**Specifies the built-in commands to use.**
active *{ pr@[host }*]	Makes a connection to the LPD server for the specified printer.
abort *printer*	Kills the active job and disables unspooling for the specified printer. Can use "all".
class *printer mode*	Controls the class of jobs currently being printed.
defaultq	Shows the default queue for the LPC program.
defaults	Shows default values for the configuration information.
debug *printer { string }*	Sets the debugging string for the specified printer.
disable *printer*	Disables spooling for the specified printer.
down *printer*	Disables both queuing and printing for specified printer.
enable *printer*	Enables spooling for the specified printer.
hold *printer jobID*	Holds the specified printer job in queue.
holdall *printer*	Activates automatic job holding of new jobs.
kill *printer*	Resets the specified printer.
client *printer*	Shows LPRng client configuration and printcap information on the local host.
lpd *{ pr@[host }*]	Determines if LPD daemon process on print server is running, and gets the PID.
lpq *printer* [options]	Runs lpq from inside the `lpc` program.
lprm *printer jobIDs*	Runs lprm from inside the `lpc` program.
move *printer { jobID } destprinter*	Sends specified jobs to destination printer and removes them from the printer queue.
msg *printer message string*	Updates the specified status message for the specified printer.
noholdall *printer*	Turns off automatic job holding.
redirect *{ printer } { destprinter }*	Redirects jobs in printer queue to another printer.
redo *printer jobID*	Reprints the selected job.
release *printer jobID*	Releases the selected job for printing.
reread *{ pr@[host }*]	Makes the specified printer to reread configuration and printcap information.
server *printer*	Shows printcap entries for printer as the LPD server would use them.
start *printer*	Starts the printer.
status *printer*	Shows the status of daemons and queues on the local computer.
stop *printer*	Shows any further unspooling after the current job completes.
topq *printer jobID*	Places the selected job at the top of the printer queue.

continued

up *printer* ? exit		Enables queuing and printing for the specified printer. Shows help information. Exits the command.			
File Name:	`lpc`	**Directory:**	/usr/sbin/	**Type:**	External
Tip:	Learn the internal command hold - this can make your boss go crazy.				
lpc redirect ljet4a bigprinter		Redirects the queue for ljet4a to bigprinter.			

lpd

UNIX Shell: All primary shells (bash, ash, tcsh)

Function	Starts the printer server.				
Syntax	lpd [options...]				
-L*logfile* -F -V -D*debugoption*		Specifies an alternate file to write log information to (default is `syslog`). Forces the program to foreground mode. Shows version information. Enables debugging mode.			
File Name:	`lpd`	**Directory:**	/usr/sbin/	**Type:**	External

lpf

UNIX Shell: All primary shells (bash, ash, tcsh)

Function	Is used as a general printer filter. It is often used in the printcap file as a filter.				
Syntax	lpf options... *{ file }*				
 -P*printer* -w*width* -l*length* -x*width* -y*width* -K*file* -L*name* -n*user* -h*host* -F*format* -Z*options* -c -i*indent* -C*name* -J*name* -R*file* -D*level* -Tcrlf -T*NR* *file*		**Specify one of the following options:** Specifies the name of the printer. Specifies the width of the paper in characters. Specifies the length of the paper in lines. Specifies the width of the paper in pixels. Specifies the length of the paper in pixels. Specifies a control file to use. Specifies the name of the banner. Specifies the user's login name. Specifies the host from which the job was submitted. Specifies the format for the job. Passed from the -F option for `lpr`. **The following options are optional:** Specifies more options passed from the -Z option for `lpr`. Ignores control character. Specifies the indentation amount. Specifies the class name. Specifies the job name. Specifies the accounting file. Sets the debug level. Turns off translation of `LF` to `CR/LF`. Specifies an integer number to add at the end of each line. NR is in C format. The file to use as input.			
File Name:	`lpf`	**Directory:**	/usr/libexec/filters/	**Type:**	External
Note:	This command is called by line printer daemon (lpd).				

lpraccnt

UNIX Shell: All primary shells (bash, ash, tcsh)

Function	A printer accounting program template. It opens a specified TCP port to send information.				
Syntax	lpraccnt [options...]				
-p *port* -D *level*		Opens a connections on the specified port (default is port 3000). Shows debug information with the specified level.			
File Name:	`lpraccnt`	**Directory:**	/usr/sbin/	**Type:**	External

lpstat

UNIX Shell:	All primary shells (bash, ash, tcsh)
Function	Shows status information on a printer or printer queue.
Syntax	lpstat [options...] *{ printers... }*

	To specify multiple units within an option, encapsulate them with quotes ".
-A	Uses the AUTH environment variable as authentication.
-a *printers...*	Logs the specified printers and reports if they accept requests.
-c *classes...*	Shows the specified classes and their members.
-d	Shows default printer destination for output requests.
-f *forms...*	Shows all printers supporting the specified forms.
-o *units...*	Shows the status of output requests for the specified printers, classes, and requestID.
-p *printers...*	Shows the status for the specified printers.
-r	Shows the status of the LP request scheduler.
-s	Shows a short status summary.
-t	Shows all status information.
-u *userIDs...*	Shows the status of output requests for the specified users.
-T*options...*	Specifies the debug options to use, separated by commas (type "-D=" for debug help).
printers...	Specifies the printer or printers to show information about.
File Name: `lpstat`	**Directory:** /usr/bin/ **Type:** External

lpunlock

UNIX Shell:	Expect script
Function	Unlocks a printer that is waiting for lock.
Syntax	lpunlock *printer { server }*

printer	Specifies the printer to unlock.
server	Specifies the server where the printer is located.
File Name: `lpunlock`	**Directory:** /usr/bin/ **Type:** Script

lsattr

UNIX Shell:	All primary shells (bash, ash, tcsh)
Function	Shows the file attributes on a Linux second extended file system.
Syntax	lsattr [options...] *files...*

-a	Shows all files in directories.
-d	Shows directories like other files instead of showing their contents.
-v	Shows the files version.
-V	Shows version information.
-R	Shows the attributes recursively from the directories.
files...	Specifies the file to show attributes on.
File Name: `lsattr`	**Directory:** /usr/bin/ **Type:** External

ls-F

UNIX Shell:	TC shell (tcsh)
Function	Lists files like `ls -F`. It's much faster than ls.
Syntax	ls-F [options...] *files...*

options...	Sends these options to the `ls` command.
files...	Specifies files to show. Wildcards can be used.

lsmod

UNIX Shell:	All primary shells (bash, ash, tcsh)
Function	Shows information about the loaded modules.
Syntax	lsmod

-h	Shows help information.
-V	Shows version information.
File Name: `lsmod`	**Directory:** /sbin/ **Type:** External

lsof

UNIX Shell:	All primary shells (bash, ash, tcsh)

Function	Shows a listing of open files.
Syntax	lsof [options...] [--] *{ names... }*

-h	Shows help information.
-a	Specifies the listing should be ANDed.
-A *name*	Specifies an alternate name list file; only available on systems with AFS.
-b	Avoids kernel functions that might block lstat(), readlink(), and stat().
-c *value*	Specifies that only files with value as part of name are shown, can be used multiple times.
-C	Disables the reporting of any pathname components from the kernel's name cache.
+d *directory*	Searches for all open instances of directory and its contents.
-d *value*	Shows files whose file descriptors are in the comma-separated sets.
+D *directory*	Searches for all open instances of directory and it's contents, symlinks are ignored.
-D *parameter*	Indicates the device cache file will be used.
	One of the following parameters may be used:
?	Shows device cache file paths.
b	Builds the device cache file.
i	Ignores the device cache file.
r	Reads the device cache file.
u	Reads and updates the device cache file.
+f *parameter*	Specifies that all pathname arguments are taken as file system names.
-f *parameter*	Specifies that all pathname arguments are taken to be simple files.
	The following parameters can be used but are not available in all versions of Linux:
c	Specifies file structures use count.
f	Specifies file structures' addresses.
g	Specifies file flags' abbreviations.
G	Specifies file flags in hexadecimal.
n	Specifies file structures node addresses.
-F *list*	Specifies a character list that selects the fields to be outputted.
-g *{ list }*	Selects the listing of files for the processes whose optional process group ID list.
-i *{ address }*	Shows files matching Internet addresses or, if address is specified, the one matching.
-k *file*	Specifies a kernel name list file.
-l	Converts user ID numbers to login names.
+L *{ number }*	Shows all files with link counts or files with a link count less than the number, if specified.
-L	Doesn't show files with link counts.
-m *file*	Specifies a kernel memory file.
+M	Enables the reporting of port mapper registration for local TCP and UDP ports.
-M	Disables the reporting of port mapper registration for local TCP and UDP ports.
-n	Converts network hostnames to network numbers.
-N	Lists NFS files.
-o	Shows file offsets at all times.
-o *value*	Specifies the number of decimal digits to be shown after the file.
-O	Bypasses the strategy to avoid being blocked by some kernel operations.
-p *list*	Shows files for the processes whose ID numbers are in the list.
-P	Converts network port names to port numbers.
+r *{ seconds }*	Enables repeat mode, seconds is the time to pause between reruns.
-r *{ seconds }*	Enables endless repeat mode, seconds is the time to pause between reruns.
-R	Shows the parent process identification number in the PPID column.
-s	Shows file size at all times.
-S *{ number }*	Specifies an optional timeout (seconds) value for kernel functions (minimum is 2).
-T *{ parameter }*	Shows some TCP/IP information.
	The following parameters can be used:
q	Specifies queue length reporting.
s	Specifies state reporting.
w	Specifies window size reporting, only works in Solaris.

continued

-t	Specifies terse output including process identifiers without including any header information.
-u *value*	Shows files for user. Value can be username or user ID, comma separates values.
-U	Shows UNIX domain socket files.
-v	Shows version information.
-V	Shows the items it could not find but was asked for.
+w	Enables warning messages.
-w	Disables warning messages.
--	Specifies the end of the options.
name	Specifies files to show information about.

File Name: `lsof` **Directory:** /usr/sbin/ **Type:** External

lspci

UNIX Shell: All primary shells (bash, ash, tcsh)

Function: Shows information about all PCI buses in the system and all devices connected to them.

Syntax: lspci [options...]

-v	Verbose mode. Shows more information.
-vv	Verbose mode. Shows even more information.
-n	Shows the device codes and PCI vendor as numbers.
-x	Shows a dump in hexadecimal of first 64 bytes in PCI configuration space.
-xxx	Shows a dump in hexadecimal of the whole PCI configuration space.
-b	Shows all IRQ numbers as seen by the PCI bus cards instead of as seen by the kernel.
-t	Shows a diagram tree containing all buses, bridges, devices, and connections.
-s [arguments...]	Shows devices in specified bus, slots and function. Uses hexadecimal.
-d [arguments...]	Shows only devices with specified vendor and device ID. Uses hexadecimal.
-i *file*	Specifies a PCI ID database to use instead of /usr/share/pci.ids.
-p *dir*	Specifies a directory containing PCI bus information instead of /proc/bus/pci.
-m	Uses machine-readable form to dump PCI device data in for easy parsing by scripts.
-M	Scans the bus extensively to find all devices.
--version	Shows version information.
	The following options are control parameters of the PCI library:
-P *directory*	Access to the specified directory with Linux 2.1 instead of /proc/bus/pci.
-S	Uses PCI access syscalls. (Linux on Alpha and UltraSparc only).
-F *file*	Specifies a file containing the output of `lspci -x`to use for information.
-G	Specifies higher level of debug information.
	The following options works for i386 and compatible only:
-H1	Access direct hardware via Intel configuration mechanism 1.
-H2	Access direct hardware via Intel configuration mechanism 2.

File Name: `lspci` **Directory:** /sbin/ **Type:** External

Tip: In the -s and -d options you can use '*' -- it means any value.

ltrace

UNIX Shell: All primary shells (bash, ash, tcsh)

Function: Traces library calls of a given program.

Syntax:
ltrace [options...] *{ command }*
ltrace [options...] *{ command arguments... }*

-d	Shows debug information.
-f	Follows forks.
-i	Shows instruction pointer at time of library call.
-L	Doesn't show library calls.
-S	Shows system calls.
-r	Shows relative timestamps.
-t	Shows absolute timestamps.
-tt	Shows absolute timestamps and includes microseconds.
-ttt	Shows absolute timestamps and includes microseconds and number of seconds since epoch.
-C	Decodes low-level symbol names into user-level names.
-a *number*	Aligns return values in a specific column (default is 50).
-s *length*	Specifies the maximum string size to show.
-o file	Writes the trace output to file.

continued

-u *user*	Runs command with the user ID and group ID of user.
-p *number*	Attaches to the process with the process ID (PID).
-e *expression*	Modifies which events to trace.
-h	Shows help information.
-V	Shows version information.
command	Specifies the command to execute.
arguments...	Specifies one or more arguments to the command to execute.
File Name: `ltrace`	**Directory:** /usr/bin/ **Type:** External

lynx

UNIX Shell: All primary shells (bash, ash, tcsh)

Function	A fully featured, text-only WWW browser. Shows HTML documents with links to files on the local system and for remote hosts running HTTP, FTP, NNTP, WAIS, and Gopher.
Syntax	lynx [options...] { *url* }

-locexec	Enables local program execution from local files only.
-	Expects arguments from STDIN.
?	Shows help information inside of `lynx`.
-accept_all_cookies	Accepts all received cookies.
-anonymous	Applies limitations for nameless accounts.
-assume_charset=*name*	Specifies a MIME character set for documents that don't specify one.
-assume_local_charset=*namename*	Assumes a MIME character set for the local host.
-assume_unrec_charset=*name*	Specifies a MIME character set instead of unrecognized charsets.
-auth=*ID*:*password*	Sets the ID and password for documents at startup.
-base	Adds a BASE tag and a requested URL comment to the output of `-source` dump.
-blink	Forces high-intensity background colors when in color mode.
-book	Uses the bookmark page instead of the default as the start file.
-buried_news	Activates buried reference search for new articles and converts them to links.
-cache=*number*	Specifies the number of documents that are cached into memory. (default is 10).
-case	Enables case-sensitive string search.
-cfg=*file*	Specifies the configuration file for `lynx` instead of lynx.cfg.
-child	Disables saves to disk and enables left-arrow exit in the start file.
-cmd_log=*file*	Copies keystroke commands to the file that is specified.
-cmd_script=*file*	Reads keystroke commands from the file that is specified.
-color	Forces color mode if it is available.
-cookies	Allows Set-Cookie headers.
-cookie_file=*file*	Specifies a file to dump the cookies into.
-connect_timeout=*time*	Specifies the connection timeout in seconds.
-core	Forces core dumps when fatal errors happen.
-crawl	Sends a page to a file with -traverse, sends to STDOUT with -dump.
-debug_partial	Shows stages of debug with MessageSecs delay.
-display=*display*	Sets the display variable for X Window reexecuted programs.
-dont_wrap_pre	Blocks text wrap when dumping lines.
-dump	Dumps default or specified document output to STDOUT.
-editor=*editor*	Uses the specified editor for external editing.
-emacskeys	Enables key movement similar to Emacs.
-enable_scrollback	Allows scroll-back key compatibility with communication programs.
-error_file=*file*	Specifies the file to put HTTP access codes.
-exec	Allows for local program execution.
-fileversions	Stores all file versions in the local VMS directory list.
-force_empty_hrefless_a	Causes `A` elements that lack HREF to be empty.
-force_html	Forces the first document to be considered an HTML document.
-force_secure	Toggles forced SSL secure flag cookies.
-forms_options	Toggles between key or form-based Options menu.
-from	Toggles the transmission of `From` headers.
-ftp	Disables access of FTTP.
-get_data	Sends data from STDIN by use of the GET method and dumps result.
-head	Sends a HEAD request for any MIME headers.
-help	Shows help information from the command line.

continued

-hiddenlinks=*option*	Controls how hidden links are shown.
merge	Links are shown in numbered brackets.
listonly	Shows only hidden links for `L`, `P`, and `-dump`.
ignore	Suppresses hidden link appearance.
-historical	Toggles terminator comment markers > or -->.
-homepage=*URL*	Specifies the home page to be separated from the start page.
-image_links	Toggles link inclusion for all images.
-index=*URL*	Sets the index file default to the specified site.
-ismap	Toggles ISMAP link inclusion when MAPs are present.
-justify	Sets justification format to text.
-link=*start*	Specifies the start count for any `lnk#.dat` files created by `-crawl`.
-localhost	Disables any URLs that point to a remote host.
-locexec	Enables local program file execution only.
-mime_header	Shows the MIME header along with its source for any fetched document.
-minimal	Toggles between valid or minimal comment parsing.
-newschunksize=*articles*	Specifies the number of articles that are chunked into news lists.
-newsmaxchunk=*articles*	Specifies the maximum number of news articles before you `chunk` them.
-nobold	Disables the bold-video attribute.
-nobrowse	Disables the browse function for directories.
-nocc	Disables the `cc:` prompts.
-nocolor	Forces black and white (color off) and overrides any screen settings.
-noexec	Disables local program execution.
-nofilereferer	Disables `Refer` header transmission for any file URLs.
-nolist	Disables link-list features within dumps.
-nolog	Prevents error messages from being mailed to document owners.
-nonrestarting_sigwinch	Speeds up window changes when applied within an `xterm`.
-nopause	Prevents the automatic status line pause from working.
-noprint	Disables most of the print functions.
-noredir	Prevents the automatic redirection of a site and shows a link to the URL instead.
-noreferer	Disables all `Refer` header transmissions.
-noreverse	Disables the reverse-video attribute.
-nosocks	Blocks `SOCKS` proxy usage.
-nostatus	Disables any messages that show retrieval status.
-nounderline	Disables the underline-video attribute.
-number_fields	Forces links and form input fields to be numbered.
-number_links	Forces links to be numbered.
-partial	Toggles partial page view when loading.
-partial_thres=*linecount*	Specifies the number of lines to create before screen repaint.
-pauth=*ID:password*	Sets the ID and password for a proxy server under startup.
-popup	Toggles single-choice SELECT option handling by use of popup windows.
-post_data	Reads from STDIN and is then sent to a form. The input line must end with three dashes (---).
-preparsed	Shows the HTML source reformatted when `-source` is in use.
-prettysrc	Shows the HTML source view in a pretty color format.
-print	Enables the print function.
-pseudo_inlines	Toggles semi-ALTs for the input lines that have no ALTstring.
-raw	Toggles between 8-bit character translation or CJK mode settings.
-realm	Prevents access to any URLs within the starting realm.
-reload	Flushes cache memory on a proxy server.
-restrictions=[options...]	Specifies which services that are disabled. You can combine any of these options:
all	Blocks all of the following options.
bookmark	Forbids changing the bookmark file location.
bookmark_exec	Blocks link start via the bookmark file.
change_exec_perms	Blocks execute permission changes to files.
default	Same as `-anonymous` -that is it disables default services.
dired_support	Forbids local file management.
disk_save	Prevents a save when in the download or print menus.
dotfiles	Forbids access and creation of hidden files.
download	Omits use of some downloads within the download menu.

continued

editor	Forbids external editing.
exec	Disables script execution.
exec_frozen	Blocks the capability to alter the local execution option.
externals	Ignores external configuration lines when URLs are passed to external commands.
file_url	Forbids the use of goto, bookmarks for file URLs and served links.
goto	Disables the g option.
inside_ftp	Prohibits FTP access from users in the domain.
inside_news	Forbids use of USENET news from users in the domain.
inside_rlogin	Forbids use of rlogin from users in the domain.
inside_telnet	Forbids use of telnet from users in the domain.
jump	Disables the j option.
multibook	Forbids use of multiple bookmarks.
mail	Prohibits mail.
news_post	Forbids use of USENET news posting service.
options_save	Prohibits saving any options to .lynxrc.
outside_ftp	Prohibits FTP access from users outside the domain.
outside_news	Forbids use of USENET news from users outside the domain.
outside_rlogin	Forbids use of rlogin from users outside the domain.
outside_telnet	Forbids use of telnet from users outside the domain.
print	Prohibits most printer options.
shell	Prohibits the use of shell escapes and lynx exec and prog goto.
suspend	Forbids Ctrl-Z suspend actions.
telnet_port	Forbids port specification within telnet gotos.
useragent	Blocks any changes to the UserAgent header.
-resubmit_posts	Toggles between no-cache resubmissions of forms from PREV_DOC or history list.
-rlogin	Inhibits detection of rlogin commands.
-selective	Forces files that are browsable to browse directories.
-short_url	Replaces the ends of long URLs with dots ... on the status line.
-show_cursor	Places the curser at the beginning of the selected link.
-source	Same as -dump but outputs in HTML instead of text.
-stack_dump	Disables the SIGINT cleanup handler.
-startfile_ok	Permits a non-HTTP homepage and startfile with `-validate`.
-stdin	Uses STDIN to read the startfile.
-tagsoup	Uses Tag Soup DTD instead of SortaSGML to start the parser.
-telnet	Disables any detection of `telnet` commands.
-term=*term*	Specifies which screen to use for external use of `lynx`.
-timeout=*sec*	Sets the win32 network timeout in seconds.
-tlog	Toggles between a lynx trace log or STDERR for trace output of the session.
-tna	Activates Textfields Need Activation mode.
-trace	Activates trace mode. The destination depends upon `-tlog`.
-traversal	Navigates all of the HTTP links that come from the start file into an indexable output.
-underscore	Toggles the underline format in dumps.
-use_mouse	Activates mouse support if lynx was compiled with `ncurses` or `slang`.
-useragent=*name*	Specifies an alternate User-Agent header.
-validate	Allows HTTP URLs.
-verbose	Toggles between IMAGE, LINK, and INLINE comments.
-version	Shows version information.
-vikeys	Emulates `vi` key movement.
-wdebug	Enables Waterloo TCP/IP debug packets for WATTCP/WATT-32 compiled DOS.
-width=*columns*	Specifies the number of columns for the dump format. The default is 80.
-with_backspaces	Puts backspaces into the output if -crawl or -dump is used.
	Any of the following Internal commands (one keystroke) can be used:
Up arrow	Scrolls upward through the list of hypertext links.
Down arrow	Scrolls downward through the list of hypertext links.
Right arrow	Goes to the hypertext link that is highlighted.
Left arrow	Backs up one page.
K	Shows a list of the current keystroke map.

continued

a	Adds what ever is highlighted to your bookmark list.
b	Views the previous page of the document, similar to left arrow.
c	Sends a comment to the current document's author.
C	Changes the current directory.
d	Downloads the current link.
e	Edits the current document.
E	Edits the current URL or ACTION link, then goes to it.
f	Shows a menu of various file operations.
g	Goes to the document that is specified by the URL.
G	Edits the URL of the current document, then goes to it.
h	Shows help information on browser usage.
i	Shows an index of documents that may come in handy.
j	Goes straight to a target action or document.
k	Shows the key map.
l	Shows the references and links of the current document.
m	Returns to the home page.
n	Searches for the next appearance of the word, phrase, or page.
o	Shows and changes the option settings.
p	Shows printing choices for the current document.
q	Quits `lynx` and asks whether you are sure.
Q	Quits `lynx` without unnecessary questions.
r	Deletes from your personal bookmark list.
s	Allows for the search of an index.
t	Tags a directory or a file for later action.
u	Goes back to the last document. Similar to left arrow.
v	Shows your list of bookmarks.
V	Shows all of the links that have been visited during the session.
x	Forces submission of link or form with `no-cache`. See also `-resubmit_posts`.
z	Interrupts the network connection.
^H	Shows the stack of currently suspended documents.
TAB	Goes to the next link or text area.
^K	Looks into the cookie jar (where the cookies are kept).
^L	Refreshes the screen.
return	Goes to the document that is behind the current link.
^N	Goes forward in the document by two lines.
^P	Goes backward in the document by two lines.
^R	Reloads (refreshes) the current document.
^T	Toggles the tracing of browser operations on or off.
^V	Toggles between the two ways of parsing HTML.
space	Goes to the next page of the `lynx` help or the active document.
#	Toggles between soft vs. valid double-quote parses.
$	Goes to the toolbar or banner of the current document.
'	Forces the last link listed on the line to be the current one.
(	Toggles between valid/minimal vs. historical comment parses.
)	Goes back half a page within the document.
*	Goes forward half a page within the document.
+ | ,	Toggles between the use of images or links.
.	Runs an external program with the URL.
/	Searches inside the current document.
0	Starts the `Follow link number` prompt.
:	Prompts for, then executes, a command.
;	Shows the trace log if it is started in the current session.
<	Goes to a previous link.
=	Shows information about the current document and its link.
>	Goes to the next link.
@	Toggles between CJK mode or raw 8-bit translations.
`	Toggles between pseudo-ALTs for inlines or not.
[	Toggles between source or presentation of the current document.

continued

\	Sends a HEAD request to the link or current document.
]	Makes the first found link on the line the current one.
^	Removes all authorization information for the session.
_	Toggles between valid vs. minimal comment parsing.
delete	Shows the stack that contains the currently suspended documents.
Page Down	Shows the next page.
Page Up	Shows the previous page.
Home	Goes to the start of the document.
End	Goes to the end of the document.
F1	Shows context-related help.
Do Key	Goes to the document that is attached to the current link.
Insert Key	Goes backward in the document by two lines.
Remove Key	Goes forward in the document by two lines.
Back Tab	Goes to the last link or text area.
URL	Loads the specified local file or remote URL.

File Name: `lynx` | **Directory:** /usr/bin/ | **Type:** External

mailto

UNIX Shell: All primary shells (bash, ash, tcsh)

Function	Sends multimedia mail in MIME format. It can only be used to send mail.
Syntax	mailto [options...] *{ recipient }*

-a *charset*	Specifies an alternate character set.
-c *name*	Specifies a name to send carbon copies of message to.
-s *subject*	Sets a subject for the mail. Uses double quotes " to make a sentence.
-r *replyid*	Sets replyid.
recipient	Specifies the mail address to send to.

File Name: `mailto` | **Directory:** /usr/bin/ | **Type:** External

make_smbcodepage

UNIX Shell: All primary shells (bash, ash, tcsh)

Function	Creates a codepage for use with Samba.
Syntax	make_smbcodepage [option] *codepage inputfile outputfile*

	The following two options can't be used together:
-c	Compiles a text codepage to binary format.
-d	Decompiles a binary file to text format.
codepage	Specifies the codepage to process.
inputfile	Specifies the input file. It can be either a text file or a binary file.
outputfile	Specifies the output file.

File Name: `make_smbcodepage` | **Directory:** /usr/bin/ | **Type:** External

MAKEDEV

UNIX Shell: All primary shells (bash, ash, tcsh)

Function	Creates device entries in the /dev directory.
Syntax	MAKEDEV [options...] *devices...*

-V	Shows version information.
-d *directory*	Specifies the directory in which to create the devices.
-c *confdir*	Specifies a directory where configuration files are stored.
-m *maxdev*	Specifies the maximum number of devices that can be created.
-n	Simulates execution.
-v	Verbose mode. Shows more information.
-i	Shows no error output when reading configuration files.
devices...	Specifies the device to create.

File Name: `MAKEDEV` | **Directory:** /dev/ | **Type:** External

makeg

UNIX Shell:	A shell (ash, bsh)
Function	Makes an executable file that can be used for debug operations.
Syntax	makeg [options...] *{ file }*

	Please see `make` for options.
file	Specifies the output file.

File Name:	`makeg`	**Directory:**	/usr/X11R6/bin/	**Type:**	Script

makeinfo

UNIX Shell:	All primary shells (bash, ash, tcsh)
Function	Converts Texinfo files to plain text, HTML or info files for online reading.
Syntax	makeinfo [options...] *files...*

--commands-in-node-names	Specifies that @ commands in node names are allowed.
-D *variable*	Defines a variable, as with @set.
--macro-expand *file*	Writes macro-expanded source to file.
--error-limit=*number*	Exits after number of errors are encountered (default is 100).
--fill-column=*number*	Break info lines at number characters (default is 72).
--footnote-style=*style*	Outputs footnotes according to style.
--force	Forces output even if error occurs.
--help	Shows help information.
--html	Outputs HTML instead of `Info` format.
-I *directory*	Appends directory to the @include search path.
--ifhtml	Processes @ifhtml and @html text when not generating HTML.
--ifinfo	Processes @ifinfo text when generating HTML.
--iftex	Processes @iftex and @tex text.
--no-headers	Specifies that `Info` node separators and Node: lines shouldn't be output.
--no-ifhtml	Specifies that @ifhtml @html text shouldn't be processed.
--no-ifinfo	Specifies that @ifinfo text shouldn't be processed.
--no-iftex	Specifies that @iftex and @tex text shouldn't be processed.
--no-split	Disables splitting of large `Info` files or generation of one HTML file per node.
--no-validate	Disables node cross-reference validation.
--no-warn	Disables suppress warnings.
--number-sections	Includes such numbers as chapter and section in output.
--output=*file*	Writes output to file. Ignore @setfilename.
-P *directory*	Prepends directory to the @include search path.
--paragraph-indent=*value*	Indents `Info` paragraphs by value spaces (default is 3).
--reference-limit=*number*	Shows warnings about at most number references (default is 1000).
-U *variable*	Undefines a variable; same as @clear.
--verbose	Verbose mode. Shows more information.
--version	Shows version information.
files...	Specifies the TexInfo filename to create.

File Name:	`makeinfo`	**Directory:**	/usr/bin/	**Type:**	External

makemap

UNIX Shell:	All primary shells (bash, ash, tcsh)
Function	Uses the keyed map lookups in `sendmail` and creates the database map by reading from STDIN.
Syntax	makemap [options...] *type name*

-N	Adds the null byte that terminates the strings in the specified map.
-d	Allows duplicate keys in the specified map. Works with B-tree format maps.
-f	Disables uppercase letters from being forced into lowercase (default is uppercase).
-o	Appends to a previously existing file.
-r	Allows for repeating existing keys. Default gives an error if repeated keys exist.
-s	Disables the safety check on the map being created.
-u	Outputs the contents of the database to STDOUT.
-v	Verbose mode. Shows more information.

continued

name	Specifies the map name of the map database being created.		
type	Specifies the specific database map format. Only one of the following may be used:		
btree	Forces the map to follow B-tree format rules.		
hash	Forces the map to follow hash format rules.		
File Name: `makemap`	**Directory:** /usr/bin/	**Type:**	External
makemap -d btree newmap	Allows duplicate keys in the B-tree formatted map.		

makepsres

UNIX Shell: All primary shells (bash, ash, tcsh)

Function	Creates an PostScript language database file that contains the resources in the specified pathnames.
Syntax	makepsres [options...] *directories...*

-o *file*	Writes output to the specified file. Type "-" as file to send to STDOUT.		
-f *file*	Uses the resource database formatted file information to aid in resource typing.		
-dir *dir*	Specifies the given directory is a directory, not a file.		
-d	Discard mode. Doesn't use entries from the input file. Uses command-line entries.		
-e	Makes the `PSres.upr` file exclusive to improve search performance.		
-i	Starts interactive query mode, which asks for the resource type of any unknown files.		
-k	Keep mode. Uses all resource entries in the input database files for the output file.		
-nb	No backup mode. If the file exists, it isn't backed up.		
-nr	Non-recursive mode. Doesn't look into subdirectories when finding resource files.		
-p	Specifies the search doesn't look for a common directory prefix.		
-q	Ignores all files that can't be identified, instead of giving a warning. Quiet mode.		
-s	Ends with an error if it finds a file that can't be identified. Strict mode.		
directories...	Specifies the paths that contain the resource files. (Type "-" as the file to read from STDIN.)		
File Name: `makepsres`	**Directory:** /usr/X11R6/bin/	**Type:**	External

makestrs

UNIX Shell: All primary shells (bash, ash, tcsh)

Function	Creates string table C source files and headers and outputs them on STDOUT.
Syntax	makestrs [options...]

-f *file*	Specifies the file to read source from.		
-sparcabi	Used on the SPARC platforms.		
-intelabi	Used on Intel platforms.		
-earlyR6abi	Maintains binary compatibility between X11R6 public-patch 11 and patch 12.		
-functionabi	Generates a functional `ABI` to the string table.		
-arrayperabi	Generates a separate array for each string.		
-defaultabi	Forces the generation of the normal string table.		
File Name: `makestrs`	**Directory:** /usr/bin/X11/	**Type:**	External

man2html

UNIX Shell: All primary shells (bash, ash, tcsh)

Function	Converts manual pages to HTML format.
Syntax	man2html [options...] *{ file }*

-D *path*	Takes away the last two parts from the pathname.		
-E *string*	Specifies a string to use for error messages.		
-h	Sets the method:cgipath to http://localhost.		
-H *host.dom:port*	Sets the method:cgipath to http://host.domain:port.		
-l	Sets the method:cgipath to lynxcgi:/home/httpd.		
-L *directory*	Sets the method:cgipath to ynxcgi:directory.		
-M *path*	Sets the man2html path.		
-p	Uses a slash (/) as the separator character.		
-q	Uses a question mark (?) as the separator character.		
file	Specifies the manual page to convert.		
File Name: `man2html`	**Directory:** /usr/bin/	**Type:**	External

manpath

manpath	UNIX Shell:	All primary shells (bash, ash, tcsh)

Function	Shows search paths for man pages.
Syntax	manpath [options...] *{ names... }*

-a	Shows all found search paths.
-c	Formats the output to fit the screen size.
-d	Shows debug information.
-D	Shows search paths and debug information.
-f	Makes a search using whatis.
-h	Shows help information.
-k	Uses keywords.
-K	Searches the whole system.
-t	Formats output using groff.
-w	Shows the source directory of the man pages.
-W	Shows the source directory and filenames of the man pages.
-C *file*	Specifies the manual page configuration file to use.
-M *path*	Specifies a list of directories where to search for manual page directories.
-P *pager*	Specifies which pager to use.
-S *list*	Specifies a list of manual sections to search for.
-m *system*	Specifies another set of manual pages than the default to search for.
-p *pp*	Specifies which preprocessor to run the output through.
e	Uses egn.
p	Uses pic.
t	Uses tbl.
g	Uses grap
r	Uses refer.
v	Uses vgrind.
names...	Specifies a manual page to show paths for.

File Name:	`manpath`	**Directory:**	/usr/bin/	**Type:**	External

mattrib

mattrib	UNIX Shell:	All primary shells (bash, ash, tcsh)

Function	Changes file attributes for MS-DOS files.
Syntax	mattrib [options...] *files...*

	The following four options are used with either a + or a - sign.
a	Sets or unsets the archive bit.
h	Sets or unsets the hidden bit.
r	Sets or unsets the read-only bit.
s	Sets or unsets the system bit.
-/	Does a recursive listing of all file attributes in all subdirectories.
-X	Shows only the file attributes, not the filenames.
-p	Resets the attributes on a file system to default after running the tar command.
files...	Specifies the files that you want to show attributes for. Wildcards are allowed.

File Name:	`mattrib`	**Directory:**	/usr/bin/	**Type:**	External

mbadblocks

mbadblocks	UNIX Shell:	All primary shells (bash, ash, tcsh)

Function	Tests a floppy disk for bad blocks and marks them in the file allocation table.
Syntax	mbadblocks *device*

device	Specifies the device that you want to test. Usually A: is the floppy drive in MS-DOS.

File Name:	`mbadblocks`	**Directory:**	/usr/bin/	**Type:**	External

mc

mc	UNIX Shell:	All primary shells (bash, ash, tcsh)

Function	A file manager used to browse directories and files.
Syntax	mc [options...] *{ directories... }* [-v *file*]

-a	Doesn't use graphic characters.
-b	Doesn't use color.
-c	Uses colors.
-C *cset*	Specifies a different color set to use.
-d	Doesn't use mouse support.
-f	Shows compiled search paths for mc.
-h	Shows help information.
-k	Sets softkeys to default values.
-l *file*	Saves an FTP dialog in a specific file.
-P	Show the last working directory when the program ends.
-s	Enables slow terminal mode.
-t	Uses values from TERMCAP instead of the systems terminal database.
-u	Doesn't use concurrent shell.
-U	Uses concurrent shell.
-v *file*	Specifies a file that you want to view.
-V	Shows version information.
-x	Uses xterm settings.
directories...	Shows the specified directories from left to right.

File Name:	`mc`	**Directory:**	/usr/bin/	**Type:**	External

mcat

mcat	UNIX Shell:	All primary shells (bash, ash, tcsh)

Function	Copies a disk image to or from a floppy disk.
Syntax	mcat [-w] *device*

-w	Reads the disk image from STDIN.
device	Specifies the device where to write the output or to read the input.

File Name:	`mcat`	**Directory:**	/usr/bin/	**Type:**	External

mcd

mcd	UNIX Shell:	All primary shells (bash, ash, tcsh)

Function	Changes directory in a MS-DOS directory structure.
Syntax	mcd *{ directory }*

directory	The directory to change to.

File Name:	`mcd`	**Directory:**	/usr/bin/	**Type:**	External

mcd D:	Changes to drive D:.

mcedit

mcedit	UNIX Shell:	All primary shells (bash, ash, tcsh)

Function	Edits file. It starts Midnight Commander (mc) in edit mode.
Syntax	mcedit *{ +line } { file }* [options...]

+*line*	Starts the edit on the line specified.
-b	Specifies that a black and white screen is used.
-c	Specifies that a color screen is used.
-C *cset*	Specifies a different color set to use.
-d	Doesn't use mouse support.
-f	Shows compiled search paths for mc.
-t	Uses values from termcap instead of the systems terminal database.
-V	Shows version information.
-x	Uses xterm settings.
-s	Enables slow terminal mode.

continued

-?	Shows help information.
file	Specifies the file to edit.
File Name: `mcedit`	**Directory:** /usr/bin/ **Type:** External

mcookie

UNIX Shell: All primary shells (bash, ash, tcsh)

Function	Creates a magic cookie that works with the command xauth.
Syntax	mcookie [options...]

-v	Verbose mode. Shows more information.
-f *file*	Specifies an input file to use to create the magic cookie.
File Name: `mcookie`	**Directory:** /usr/bin/ **Type:** External

mcopy

UNIX Shell: All primary shells (bash, ash, tcsh)

Function	Copies MS-DOS files to or from a UNIX system.
Syntax	mcopy [options...] *sources... { destination }*

-b	Runs in batch mode.
-s	Makes a recursive copy.
-p	Doesn't change file attributes.
-Q	Quits as soon as an error occurs.
-a	Copies all files as text.
-n	Overwrites UNIX files without asking.
-m	Keeps the modification time of the files.
-v	Verbose mode. Shows more information.
	The following options overwrite, skip, or rename files that exist:
-D o	Overwrites primary names.
-D O	Overwrites secondary names.
-D r	Renames primary names.
-D R	Renames secondary names.
-D a	Autorenames primary names.
-D A	Autorenames secondary manes.
-D s	Skips primary names.
-D S	Skips secondary names.
-D m	Asks what to do with primary names.
-D M	Asks what to do with secondary names.
sources...	Specifies the source to copy from.
destination	Specifies where to copy to.
File Name: `mcopy`	**Directory:** /usr/bin/ **Type:** External

md5sum

UNIX Shell: All primary shells (bash, ash, tcsh)

Function	Verifies MD5 checksums.
Syntax	md5sum [options...] *{ files... }*

-b	Handles all input files as binary files.
--help	Shows help information.
-t	Handles all input files as text files.
-v	Verbose mode. Shows more information.
-V	Shows version information.
-c *list*	Checks the checksum against the specified list.
--status	Shows no output.
-w	Warns for not properly formatted checksum lines.
files...	Specifies the file to check or print.
File Name: `md5sum`	**Directory:** /usr/bin/ **Type:** External

mdel

UNIX Shell: All primary shells (bash, ash, tcsh)

Function	Deletes a file in an MS-DOS file system.
Syntax	mdel [-v] *files...*

-v	Shows version information.
files...	Specifies the files that you want to delete.

File Name: `mdel` **Directory:** /usr/bin/ **Type:** External

mdeltree

UNIX Shell: All primary shells (bash, ash, tcsh)

Function	Deletes a directory from an MS-DOS file system.
Syntax	mdeltree [-v] *directories...*

-v	Prints the version information.
directories...	Specifies the directory or directories to delete.

File Name: `mdeltree` **Directory:** /usr/bin/ **Type:** External

mdir

UNIX Shell: All primary shells (bash, ash, tcsh)

Function	Shows files in an MSDOS directory.
Syntax	mdir [options...] *files...*

-/	Shows a recursive output.
-w	Shows output wide over the screen.
-a	Shows hidden files.
-f	Shows all files fast, doesn't calculate free space on the disk.
-b	Shows a short list of all files.
files...	Specifies the files that you want to list.

File Name: `mdir` **Directory:** /usr/bin/ **Type:** External

mdu

UNIX Shell: All primary shells (bash, ash, tcsh)

Function	Shows disk usage for a specific file or files on an MS-DOS file system.
Syntax	mdu [options...] *{ files... }*

-a	Shows disk usage for all files.
-s	Shows only the total space.
files...	Specifies the files that you want to show disk usage for.

File Name: `mdu` **Directory:** /usr/bin/ **Type:** External

merge

UNIX Shell: All primary shells (bash, ash, tcsh)

Function	Merges three files together. It merges the changes between input file 2 and 3 into input file number 1.
Syntax	merge [options...] *file1 file2 file3*

-A	Verbose mode. Shows more information.
-E	Shows no error messages.
-e	Shows no error messages.
-L *label*	Specifies a label to use instead of filenames in conflict reports.
-p	Shows output on the screen.
-q	Shows no output.
file1 file2 file3	Specifies the files to merge.

File Name: `merge` **Directory:** /usr/bin/ **Type:** External

messages

messages	UNIX Shell:	A shell (ash, bsh)
Function	Shows how many messages you have in your mailbox or folder.	
Syntax	messages *{ folder }*	

folder	Specifies the folder to look in.

File Name:	`messages`	**Directory:**	/usr/bin/	**Type:**	Script

metamail

metamail	UNIX Shell:	All primary shells (bash, ash, tcsh)
Function	Manages how to show mails that are non text-based.	
Syntax	metamail [options...] *{ file }*	

-b	Indicates that the mail isn't RFC 822 formatted.
-B	Shows messages in the background.
-c *contenttype*	Uses the specified content type instead of the content type found in the header.
-d	Doesn't prompt for any questions.
-e	Takes away leading new lines in the messages body.
-f *address*	Specifies the sender name for the message.
-h	Shows a message.
-m *mailername*	Specifies the mail program that's called metamail.
-p	Shows output one page at a time.
-P	Shows output one page at a time and prompts the user to press a button for next page.
-q	Shows no output.
-r	Specifies the command can be run as root.
-s *subject*	Sets a subject for the mail.
-w	Decodes the file and writes it in binary format.
-x	Specifies the command isn't run on a terminal even if it is.
-y	Yanks a MIME-format message from the body of the message.
-z	Deletes the input file when done.
file	Specifies the input file.

File Name:	`metamail`	**Directory:**	/usr/bin/	**Type:**	External

metasend

metasend	UNIX Shell:	All primary shells (bash, ash, tcsh)
Function	Sends non-text mails.	
Syntax	metasend [options...]	

-b	Uses the non interactive mode.
-c *cc*	Specifies the carbon copy address.
-F *from*	Sets the sender address.
-e *encoding*	Sets the encoding type.
-f *file*	Specifies the file to send.
-m *mimetype*	Sets the MIME-type.
-s *subject*	Specifies the subject of the mail.
-S *splitsize*	Specifies the maximum file size before splitting the files.
-t *address*	Specifies where to send the mail.
-z	Specifies that temporary files are deleted.
-n	Attaches a file to the mail.
-D *description*	Specifies a content description.
-o *outputfile*	Sends output to a file instead of sending it as a mail.
-/ subtype	Specifies a MIME multipart subtype.
-E	Specifies the file being included already has an entry.
-P *preamblefile*	Specifies a file with preamble data to put in the preamble area of the mail.
-i *contentid*	Specifies a content ID for the MIME entity.
-I *contentid*	Specifies a content ID for the multipart entity.

File Name:	`metasend`	**Directory:**	/usr/bin/	**Type:**	External

metasend -e base64	Uses base64 encoding.

mformat

UNIX Shell:	All primary shells (bash, ash, tcsh)
Function	Formats MS-DOS floppy disks.
Syntax	mformat [options...] *drive:*

-v *volname*	Adds a volume label to the disk.
-f *size*	Specifies the size of the floppy disk. Use 160,180,320,360,720,1200,1440, or 2880.
-t *tracks*	Specifies the number of tracks to write to the disk.
-h *heads*	Specifies the number of heads of the disk.
-n *sectors*	Specifies the number of sectors per track.
-1	Formats only one side.
-4	Formats 360K double sided.
-8	Formats the disk with eight sectors per track.
-F	Formats with FAT32.
-S *sizecode*	Sets sector size code.
-X	Formats as an XDF disk.
-2 *sectors*	Specifies the number of sectors on track 0.
-3	Doesn't use specified number of sectors on track 0.
-0 *rate*	Specifies the transfer rate on track 0.
-A *rate*	Specifies the transfer rate on other tracks than 0.
-M *size*	Specifies the software sector size.
-N *serialnumber*	Specifies a serial number.
-a	Specifies Atari-style serial numbers.
-C	Creates disk images.
-H *sectors*	Specifies the number of hidden sectors.
-I *version*	Specifies the version ID for FAT32.
-c *clustersize*	Specifies cluster sector size.
-r *size*	Specifies the root directory size.
-L *length*	Specifies the length of the file allocation table.
-B *bootsector*	Uses the specified boot sector.
-k	Keeps the boot sector.
drive:	Specifies the drive that you want to format.

File Name:	`mformat`	**Directory:**	/usr/bin/	**Type:**	External
mformat a:			Formats a floppy in the drive A:.		

mhl

UNIX Shell:	All primary shells (bash, ash, tcsh)
Function	Shows and filters text messages in New Messages Handling System (NMH).
Syntax	mhl [options...] *{ files... }*

-help	Shows debug information.
-version	Shows version information.
-bell	Gives a sound signal at end of every page (is default).
-nobell	Doesn't give a sound signal at end of every page.
-clear	Clears the screen at the end of every page.
-noclear	Doesn't clear the screen at end of every page (is default).
-moreproc *program*	Overrides the default moreproc and the entry in the profile.
-nomoreproc	Doesn't use moreproc.
-length *lines*	Sets in lines the length of the screen (default is 40).
-width *columns*	Sets in columns the width of the screen (default is 80).
-form *file*	Specifies another type of format file other than the default `mhl.format`.
+folder	Sets the name of the folder in the "messagename" field.
-folder	Doesn't set the name of the folder in the "messagename" field.
files...	Specifies a message file.

File Name:	`mhl`	**Directory:**	/usr/lib/nmh/	**Type:**	External

mhmail

UNIX Shell:	All primary shells (bash, ash, tcsh)
Function	Reads or sends mail.
Syntax	mhmail *{ addresses... }* [options...]

-subject *subject*	Specifies a subject for the message.
-body *text*	Specifies the contents of mail.
-from *address*	Specifies the from header of the mail.
-cc *addresses*	Sends carbon copy to addresses.
-version	Shows version information.
-help	Shows help information.
addresses...	Specifies where to send mail.
File Name: `mhmail`	**Directory:** /usr/bin/ **Type:** External

mhpath

UNIX Shell:	All primary shells (bash, ash, tcsh)
Function	Shows pathnames to folders and mailboxes.
Syntax	mhpath [options...] *{ msg }*

+folder	Shows pathname of the specified folder.
-version	Shows version information.
-help	Shows help information.
msg	Specifies a mail message to show pathname for.
File Name: `mhpath`	**Directory:** /usr/bin/ **Type:** External

mikmod

UNIX Shell:	All primary shells (bash, ash, tcsh)
Function	Plays modules on a UNIX system.
Syntax	mikmod [options...] [modules...]

-d *n*	Specifies a device to use.
-o *output*	Specifies output: 8 or 16-bit in stereo or mono - 8s, 8m, 16s, or 16m.
-f *freq*	Specifies the mixing frequency in hertz.
-nointerpolate	Doesn't use interpolated mixing.
-hq	Uses the high-quality software mixer.
--nohqmixer	Doesn't use the high-quality software mixer.
-s	Uses surround mixing.
--nosurround	Doesn't use surround mixing.
-r *n*	Specifies reverb: 0 = no reverb and 15 = full reverb.
-i	Uses interpolated mixing.
-v *volume*	Specifies the volume in percent.
-F	Fades volume at the end of each module.
--nofadeout	Doesn't fade volume at the end of each module.
-l	Uses in-module backward loops.
--noloops	Doesn't use in-module backward loops.
-a	Uses panning effects.
--nopanning	Doesn't use panning effects.
-x	Uses the protracker extended speed effects.
--noprotracker	Doesn't use the ProTracker extended speed effects.
-c	Checks for hidden patterns in module.
--nocurious	Doesn't check for hidden patterns in module.
-p *n*	Specifies play list options to use. N can be one of the following:
0	Loops the current module.
1	Plays the play list one time.
2	Loops the play list.
3	Plays the play list in random mode.
-t	Skips a module if it can't be read.
--notolerant	Halts if a module can't be read.
	Need root for this.

continued

-s *action*	Sets renice value to -20. Action can be yes or no.
--norenice	Doesn't renice to -20-
-S *action*	Increases real-time priority. Action can be yes or no.
--norealtime	Doesn't increase real-time priority.
-q	Shows no output.
-te	Shows a stripped version of mikmod 2.
-n	Shows known drivers and modules.
-V	Shows version information.
-h	Shows help information.
--norc	Doesn't read the `.mikmodrc` configuration file.
modules...	Specifies a modules or a list of modules to play.
File Name: `mikmod`	**Directory:** /usr/bin/ **Type:** External

mimencode

UNIX Shell: All primary shells (bash, ash, tcsh)

Function	Converts or deconverts any standard mail-encoding formats defined by MIME.
Syntax	mimencode [options...] *{ file }* [-o outputfile]

-u	Decodes STDIN.
-b	Uses base64 encoding.
-q	Uses the quoted-printable encoding.
-p	Converts decoded CR + LF sequences into the local new line conventions.
-o *outputfile*	Specifies an output file instead of STDOUT.
file	Specifies input file.
File Name: `mimencode`	**Directory:** /usr/bin **Type:** External

mingetty

UNIX Shell: All primary shells (bash, ash, tcsh)

Function	A smaller getty that works with virtual consoles.
Syntax	mingetty [options...] *tty*

--noclear	Doesn't clear the screen before prompting for the login name.
--long-hostname	Shows the full hostname.
tty	Specifies the device to use.
File Name: `mingetty`	**Directory:** /sbin/ **Type:** External

minicom

UNIX Shell: All primary shells (bash, ash, tcsh)

Function	A text-based window serial communication program.
Syntax	minicom [options...] *{ file }*

-s	Edits the system configuration file /etc/minirc.dfl and starts the cfg. menu.
-o	Doesn't run initialization code.
-m	Uses the Alt or Meta key as the command key.
-M	Same as `-m` but assumes that the eighth bit of the character is set.
-z	Specifies the screen status line is to be used.
-l	Doesn't try to convert the IBM line characters.
-a on | off	Sets the use of attributes.
-t *term*	Specifies the screen type to use.
-c on | off	Specifies whether to use color.
-S *script*	Runs the script at startup and before -d.
-d *entry*	Dials a number from the dialing directory specified by entry.
-p *dev*	Specifies pseudo-screen to use.
-C *file*	Saves all activity to the capture file.
-8	Passes through 8-bit characters without modification.
file	Specifies the cfg. file `minirc.configuration` not the default `minirc.dfl`. (Start the configuration menu for all of the advanced functions of minicom.)
File Name: `minicom`	**Directory:** /usr/bin/ **Type:** External

mkbootdisk

UNIX Shell:	Bash shell (bash)
Function	Creates a boot floppy for the running system.
Syntax	mkbootdisk [options...] *kernelversion*

--version	Shows version information.
--noprompt	Shows no prompt.
--verbose	Shows verbose information.
--mkinitrdargs *args*	Passes arguments to `mkinitrd`.
--device *file*	Specifies the device where to create the boot file.
--compact	Uses the `lilo` compact option.
kernelversion	Specifies which version of the kernel that the boot floppy should have.

File Name:	`mkbootdisk`	**Directory:**	/sbin/	**Type:**	Script

mkdep

UNIX Shell:	All primary shells (bash, ash, tcsh)
Function	Creates makefile dependency lines for a specified source file.
Syntax	mkdep *file*

file	Specifies a filename to the source code to create dependencies for.

File Name:	`mkdep`	**Directory:**	/usr/src/linux/scripts/	**Type:**	External
Note:	This is a command that comes with the Linux kernel source and is used mainly by the system.				

mkdosfs, mkfs.msdos

UNIX Shell:	All primary shells (bash, ash, tcsh)
Function	Creates an MS-DOS file system in Linux.
Syntax	mkdosfs [options...] *device { blockNR }*

-A	Uses the file system in Atari mode.
-b *backupsecset*	Sets the location of the backup boot sector for FAT32.
-c	Checks the device for bad blocks before creating the file system.
-C	Creates the file given as device on the command line.
-f *fatnumb*	Sets the number of file allocation tables.
-F *fatsize*	Specifies the file allocation table type. Use 12, 16, or 32.
-i *volumeid*	Sets the volume ID of the file system.
-I	Forces mkdosfs to ignore problems.
-l *file*	Reads a bad block list from the specified file.
-m *message*	Sets a boot message file.
-n *volname*	Specifies a volume label for the file system.
-r *rootent*	Specifies the number root directory entries to be available.
-R *reservsec*	Specifies the number of reserved sectors.
-s *clustersec*	Specifies the number of sectors per cluster.
-S *sectorsize*	Specifies the logical sector size.
-v	Verbose mode. Shows more information.
device	Specifies where to create the MS-DOS file system.
blockNR	Specifies the number of blocks on the device.

File Name:	`mkdosfs`	**Directory:**		**Type:**	External

mke2fs, mkfs.ext2

UNIX Shell:	All primary shells (bash, ash, tcsh)
Function	Creates a second extended file system.
Syntax	mke2fs [options...] *device { blocks }*

-l *filename*	Specifies a file containing a list of bad blocks.
-b *blocksize*	Specifies the block size in bytes.
-f *fragsize*	Specifies the fragment size in bytes.
-i *bytesperinode*	Specifies the bytes per inode to use.
-N *numberofinodes*	Specifies the number of inodes to reserve for the file system.
-m *resblockspercent*	Specifies the percentage of blocks to reserve for the root user.
-o	Overrides the default values of creator OS.
-O *features...*	Specifies a list of features to use to create the file system.
-r *fsrevlevel*	Specifies revision of the new file system.

continued

-R *raidoptions*	Specifies RAID related options to the file system.
-s *action*	Sets the sparse super flag. Action can be 1 = on or 0 = off.
-c	Checks the specified device for bad blocks.
-q	Shows no output.
-v	Shows verbose information.
-F	Runs the command even if the file system mounted.
-L	Specifies a volume label for the file system.
-M	Sets the file system's last mounted directory.
-S	Writes superblock and group descriptors only.
-V	Shows version information.
-T *fstype*	Specifies the file system type. Currently, only news is supported.
-n	Simulates the execution.
device	Specifies the device to create a file system on.
blocks	Specifies the number of blocks on the device.
File Name: `mke2fs`	**Directory:** /sbin/ **Type:** External
Warning:	Be careful when using this command; double-check device name.
mke2fs /dev/hda2	Creates a file system on the second partition on the first IDE drive.

mkfs

UNIX Shell: All primary shells (bash, ash, tcsh)

Function	Creates a Linux file system on the specified device.
Syntax	mkfs [-V] [-t *FSType*] [options...] *device { blocks }*

-V	Verbose mode. Shows more information. (Disables file system commands from being run if set more than once.)
-t *FSType*	Specifies which FSType file system to create (default is ext2fs).
	The next three options are passed to the FS builder and work with most system builders.
-c	Checks the device for bad blocks before creating the file system.
-l *filename*	Specifies the file to read the bad blocks list from.
-v	Verbose mode. Shows more information.
device	Specifies either the device or the mount point for the file system.
blocks	Specifies the number of blocks to use for the file system.
File Name: `mkfs`	**Directory:** /sbin/ **Type:** External
Note:	This is just a front end to the real file-system builders - `mkfs.minix` and so forth.
mkfs -t minix /dev/fd0	Creates a minix floppy.

mkfs.minix

UNIX Shell: All primary shells (bash, ash, tcsh)

Function	Creates a minix file system.
Syntax	mkfs.minix [options...] *device { blocks }*

-c	Checks the specified device for bad blocks.
-l *filename*	Reads a list of bad blocks from filename.
-n *namelenght*	Specifies the maximum length for filenames.
-i *inodecount*	Specifies the number of inodes that the file system can use.
-v	Creates a minix version 2 file system.
device	Specifies the device where to create the file system.
blocks	Specifies the file system size in blocks.
File Name: `mkfs.minix`	**Directory:** /sbin/ **Type:** External

mkinitrd

UNIX Shell: Bash shell (bash)

Function	Creates a ramdisk to preload modules to gain access to the root file system.
Syntax	mkinitrd [options...] *image kernelversion*

-f	Overwrites any existing image files.
-v	Shows verbose information.
--fstab=*fstab*	Uses `/etc/fstab` to determine the file system type for the root device.

continued

--omit-raid-modules	Doesn't load any raid modules.
--omit-scsi-modules	Doesn't load any scsi modules.
--preload=*module*	Specifies a module to load in the ramdisk.
--version	Shows version information.
--with=*module*	Specifies a module to load in the ramdisk.
--ifneeded	Builds the image only if there are modules that need to be loaded during boot.
image	Specifies the name of the boot image.
kernelversion	Specifies the version of the kernel.
File Name: `mkinitrd`	**Directory:** /sbin/ **Type:** Script

mkisofs

UNIX Shell: All primary shells (bash, ash, tcsh)

Function	Creates an ISO9660, Joliet, or HFS file system that is used on CDs and handles Rock Ridge attributes.
Syntax	mkisofs [options...] -o *file directories...*

-abstract *file*	Specifies an abstract filename.
-A *ID*	Specifies text to be written into the application volume header (max 128 characters).
-allow-lowercase	Allows lowercase characters in the `ISO9660` filenames. (Violates ISO9660 standard but works on some systems.)
-allow-multidot	Allows several dots to exist in `ISO9660` filenames. Violates `ISO9660` standard.
-biblio *file*	Specifies the name of the bibliographic file.
-b *file*	Specifies path- and filename to a boot image. Must be 1.2, 1.44, or a 2.88 MB size.
-eltorito-alt-boot	Enables several different boot images to be created (up to 63 per CD).
-B *imglist*	Specifies a comma-separated list of boot images — for creating a bootable CD for SPARC.
-G *gfile*	Specifies path- and filename to generic boot image — for creating a generic bootable CD.
-hard-disk-boot	Specifies the `El-Torito` boot image is a hard drive image.
-no-emul-boot	Specifies the `El-Torito` boot image isn't an emulation image.
-no-boot	Marks the `El-Torito` cd as not bootable.
-boot-load-seg *address*	Specifies the boot image's load segment address for no-emulation `El-Torito` cd's.
-boot-load-size *sector*	Sets the number of virtual (512-byte) sectors to load when in non emulation mode.
-boot-info-table	Uses a 56-byte CD-ROM information table to patch at offset 8 in the boot file.
-C *sector,sector*	Creates an additional image on a CD containing images to create a multisession CD-ROM. **Note:First value = First sector, last session. Second value=start sector, new session.**
-c *file*	Sets the filename and its path to the boot catalog, for creating an `El-Torito` boot CD.
-check-oldnames	Compares every filename imported from an old session for `ISO9660` compliance:
-copyright *file*	Sets copyright on the specified file. Can be set in the `.mkisofsrc` file.
-d	Excludes a trailing period from files that lack a period. Use this with caution.
-D	Packs the directory as it is seen. Doesn't use deep directory relocation.
-f	Generates the file system by following symbolic links.
-gui	Switches to GUI behavior and makes the output more verbose.
-graft-points	Allows graft points for filenames.
-hide *glob*	Selects a file containing a list of `globs` to be covered.
-hide-list *file*	Selects a file containing a list of `globs` to be hidden.
-hidden *glob*	Adds the hidden `ISO9660` directory attribute for the specified `glob`.
-hidden-list *file*	Specifies a file that holds a list of `globs` that hidden attributes are fetched from.
-hide-joliet *glob*	Hides the specified `glob` from the Joliet directory.
-hide-joliet-list *file*	Specifies a file that contains a list of `globs` that are hidden from the Joliet.
-hide-joliet-trans-tbl	Hides `trans.tbl` files from the Joliet tree.
-hide-rr-moved	Renames the Rock Ridge tree directory `RR_MOVED` to `.rr_moved`.
-l	Allows for full 31-character filenames. Use with caution.
-is-level *level*	Specifies the `ISO9660` conformance level. Valid levels are 1–3.
1	Files are allowed to only contain one section and filenames no more than 8.3 characters.
2	Files are allowed to only contain one section.
3	Specifies no restrictions.
-J	Creates regular `ISO9660` filenames and Joliet directory records.
-jcharset *set*	Specifies the character set that converts filenames into Joliet records.
-L	Allows `ISO9660` filenames that begin with a period.
-log-file *file*	Writes all warning and errors to the specified log file instead of STDERR.

continued

-m *glob*	Excludes the specified `glob` from being written to CD-ROM.
-exclude-list *file*	Specifies a file that contains a list of `globs` that are excluded from CD-ROM.
-max-iso9660-filenames	Allows a maximum of 37 characters for `ISO9660` filenames.
-M *device*	Specifies the SCSI device using the syntax: `dev=cdrecord`.
-M *path*	Specifies the path to an `ISO9660` image that is merged.
-N	Excludes version numbers from `ISO9660` filenames.
-nobak	Doesn't include any backup files on the `ISO9660` file system.
-no-bak	Doesn't include files that contain ~ or #, or end with `.bak`.
-no-rr	Doesn't allow Rock Ridge attributes from any previous session.
-no-split-symlink-components	Doesn't split the SL components; instead begins a new continuation area (CE).
-no-split-symlink-fields	Doesn't split the SL fields; instead begins a new continuation area (CE).
-o *file*	Specifies the name of the file to which the `ISO9660` file system image should be written.
-pad	Adds the end of the `ISO9660` file by 16 sectors (23KB).
-path-list *file*	Specifies the pathspec file to be added to the `ISO9660` file system.
-P *publD*	Sets a text string that's written into the volume publisher header.
-p *prepID*	Sets a text string that is written into volume preparer header.
-print-size	Prints the estimated size of the file system.
-quiet	Enables quiet mode. No progress output is shown.
-R	Creates SUSP & RR records with Rock Ridge protocol to describe `ISO9660` files.
-r	The same as -R except file ownership and modes are set to other values.
-relaxed-filenames	Includes digits in `ISO9660` files, uppercase chart, and other 7-bit ASCII characters.
-sort *sort file*	Uses the specified file and the sort information for positioning files on the media.
-sysid *ID*	Specifies the system ID to use. Same as parameter SYSI=system_id in `.mkisofsrc`.
-T	Creates the TRANS.TBL file in each directory on the CD-ROM.
-table-name *table*	Specifies an alternate translation table filename to use. Assumes `-T` is active.
-ucs-level *level*	Sets the Unicode conformity level in the Joliet SVD. Levels are 1-3 (default is 3).
-use-fileversion	Uses the version numbers given in the files instead of starting with version 1.
-U	Allows untranslated filenames. This violates `ISO9660` standards.
-no-iso-translate	Forbids translating ~ and #. Violates `ISO9660` but works on many systems.
-V *ID*	Specifies the volume ID that is written to the master block.
-volset *ID*	Specifies the volume set ID to use.
-volset-size *NR*	Specifies the number of CDs that are in the CD set.
-volset-seqno *NR*	Sets the number to the volume set sequence which is the index number of the CD.
-v	Verbose mode. Shows more information.
-x *paths...*	Excludes the specified path from be written to the CD-ROM. Separate paths by a space.
-z	Creates SUSP records for compressed files that are transparent.
	The following are HFS-specific options:
-hfs	Creates a `HFS/ISO9660` CD hybrid volume. Should be used with `-map`.
-apple	Creates an `ISO9660`. CD with the Apple extensions.
-map *file*	Uses the specified map file to set the creator and type information for a file.
-magic *file*	Sets the creator and type information using the specified magic number.
-hfs-creator *creator*	Sets the creator default for all of the files. Must contain exactly four characters.
-hfs-type *type*	Sets the type default for all of the files. Must contain exactly four characters.
-probe	Searches the contents of all files for any known Apple/UNIX file formats.
-no-desktop	Forbids the creation of empty desktop files.
-mac-name	Uses HFS filenames as a starting point for Joliet, `ISO9660`, and Rock Ridge filenames.
-boot-hfs-file *file*	Installs the specified file that's used to create the bootable Macintosh CD.
-part	Creates an HFS partition table.
-auto *file*	Specifies the file that's started on the HFS CD using QuickTime 2.0 autostart.
-cluster-size *size*	Sets the cluster or allocation unit size of PC Exchange files in bytes.
-hide-hfs *glob*	Hides the specified `glob` from the HFS volume, yet still exist in the `ISO9660/Joliet`.
-hide-hfs-list *file*	Uses the specified file to receive a list of globs that are hidden from the HFS.
-hfs-volid *ID*	Specifies the volume name for the HFS partition. Replaces any -V option in use.
-icon-position	Uses the Icon position information from an Apple/UNIX file if it exists.
-root-info *file*	Specifies the file that sets such values as size, folder view, and location for the root.
-prep-boot *files...*	Specifies up to four PReP boot image files to use.
--cap	Searches for AUFS CAP Macintosh file formats.

continued

--netatalk	Searches for NETATALK Macintosh file formats.
--double	Searches for AppleDouble Macintosh file formats.
--ethershare	Searches for Helios EtherShare Macintosh file formats.
--ushare	Searches for IPT UShare Macintosh file formats.
--exchange	Searches for PC Exchange Macintosh file formats.
--sgi	Searches for SGI Macintosh file formats.
--xinet	Searches for XINET Macintosh file formats.
--macbin	Searches for MacBinary Macintosh file formats.
--single	Searches for AppleSingle Macintosh file formats.
--dave	Searches for Thursby Software Systems DAVE Macintosh file formats.
--sfm	Searches for Microsoft's NT Service Macintosh file formats.
directories...	Specifies the directory to create a `ISO-9660` file system from.
File Name: `mkisofs`	**Directory:** /usr/bin/ **Type:** External
mkisofs -o image.iso image_dir	Creates a ISO-9660 file system image specified by file `image.iso` in the specified directory.

mklost+found

UNIX Shell: All primary shells (bash, ash, tcsh)

Function	Creates a lost+found directory.
Syntax	mklost+found
File Name: `mklost+found`	**Directory:** /usr/sbin/ **Type:** External

mkmanifest

UNIX Shell: All primary shells (bash, ash, tcsh)

Function	Creates a shell script that restores UNIX filenames that has been shortened by MS-DOS file systems.
Syntax	mkmanifest *files...*
files...	Specifies the files that you want to put in the script.
File Name: `mkmanifest`	**Directory:** /usr/bin/ **Type:** External

mkpasswd

UNIX Shell: Expect script

Function	Generates a new password and assigns it to a user if you specify one.
Syntax	mkpassword [options...] *{ user }*
-l *length*	Sets the length of the password (default is 9).
-d *number*	Defines the minimum number of digits (default is 2).
-c *number*	The minimum number of lowercase alphabetic characters (default is 2).
-C *number*	The minimum number of uppercase alphabetic characters (default is 2).
-p *program*	Specifies a program to set the password.
-2	Causes characters to be chosen so that they alternate between right and left hands.
-v	Causes the password-setting interaction to be visible.
user	The user to assign a password to.
File Name: `mkpasswd`	**Directory:** /usr/bin/ **Type:** Script

mkraid

UNIX Shell: All primary shells (bash, ash, tcsh)

Function	Manages RAID arrays.
Syntax	mkraid [options...] *devices...*
-c *filename*	Uses another configuration file than the default `/etc/raidtab`.
-f	Initializes the RAID even if there are existing data.
-h	Shows help information.
-o	Upgrades the RAID array to the current kernels version.
-V	Shows version information.
devices...	Specifies the RAID array device. (usually `/dev/md`).
File Name: `mkraid`	**Directory:** /usr/sbin/ **Type:** External

mkswap

UNIX Shell:	All primary shells (bash, ash, tcsh)
Function	Creates a swap area in Linux.
Syntax	mkswap [options...] *device { size }*

-c	Checks for bad blocks.
-f	Forces the creation of the swap area.
-v*action*	Specifies the swap area style. Action is 0 for old and 1 for a new-style swap area.
-p *pagesize*	Specifies the page size to use.
device	Specifies the device where to create the swap area.
size	Specifies the wanted swap area size in 1,024 blocks. This isn't in use.

File Name:	Directory:	Type:
`mkswap`	/sbin/	External

mktemp

UNIX Shell:	All primary shells (bash, ash, tcsh)
Function	Creates a temporary filename using another filename as a template.
Syntax	mktemp [options...] *file*

-d	Creates a directory instead of a file.
-q	Shows no output on errors.
-u	Unlinks the file before mktemp exits.
file	Specifies the file to use as a template.

File Name:	Directory:	Type:
`mktemp`	/bin/	External

mktexlsr

UNIX Shell:	A shell (ash, bsh)
Function	Manages ls-R databases.
Syntax	mktexlsr [options...] *directories...*

--help	Shows help information.
--version	Shows version information.
directories...	Specifies the directories to be in the ls-R databases.

File Name:	Directory:	Type:
`mktexlsr`	/usr/bin/	Script

mkxauth

UNIX Shell:	All primary shells (bash, ash, tcsh)
Function	Manages .Xauthority files.
Syntax	mkxauth [options...] -m *login* mkxauth [options...] option *host* [-l *login*] mkxauth [options...] -c *{ host }*

-q	Shows no output.
-u *login*	Specifies a user whose `.Xauthority` file you want to manage.
-l *login*	Logs in as a different user. Only with the -r and -z options.
	The following options can't be combined:
-c	Creates an .Xauthority file.
-f	Merges the local .Xauthority file with a remote .Xauthority file via FTP.
-m	Merges the local .Xauthority file with another local user's .Xauthority file.
-r	Merges the local .Xauthority file with a remote .Xauthority file via rsh.
-z	Will gzip the file before transfer over a network if the .Xauthority file is too large
host	Specifies a remote host to contact - only with -c, -f, -r, or -z.
login	Specifies a login name to use with the -m option.

File Name:	Directory:	Type:
`mkxauth`	/usr/X11R6/bin/	External

mlabel	UNIX Shell:	All primary shells (bash, ash, tcsh)
Function	Creates a volume label on MS-DOS file systems.	
Syntax	mlabel [options...] *drive:label*	

-v	Verbose mode. Shows more information.
-c	Deletes the existing volume label.
-s	Shows the existing volume label.
-n	Creates a random serial number for the disk.
-N *sn*	Specifies a serial number for the disk.
drive:label	Specifies the drive and its label.
File Name: `mlabel`	**Directory:** /usr/bin/ **Type:** External

mmd	UNIX Shell:	All primary shells (bash, ash, tcsh)
Function	Create directories on MS-DOS file systems.	
Syntax	mmd [options...] *directories...*	

	The following options overwrite, skip, or rename existing files:
-D o	Overwrites the specified directory only.
-D O	Overwrites all directories, including subdirectories.
-D r	Renames the specified directory only.
-D R	Renames all directories including subdirectories.
-D a	Autorenames the specified directory only.
-D A	Autorenames all directories, including subdirectories.
-D s	Skips the specified directory only.
-D S	Skips all directories, including subdirectories.
-D m	Prompts the user if primary name exists.
-D M	Prompts the user if secondary names exist.
directories...	Specifies the directory or directories to create.
File Name: `mmd`	**Directory:** /usr/bin/ **Type:** External

mmount	UNIX Shell:	All primary shells (bash, ash, tcsh)
Function	Mounts a MS-DOS file system in Linux.	
Syntax	mmount [options...] *device { mountopt }*	

-h	Shows help information.
-V	Shows version information.
drive:	Specifies the MS-DOS drive to mount.
mountopt	Specifies mount options to pass to the command.
File Name: `mmount`	**Directory:** /usr/bin/ **Type:** External

mmove	UNIX Shell:	All primary shells (bash, ash, tcsh)
Function	Moves files on MS-DOS file systems.	
Syntax	mmove [options...] *files... directory*	

-h	Shows help information.
-V	Shows version information.
	The following options overwrite, skip, or rename existing files:
-D o	Overwrites the specified directory, only if it exists.
-D O	Overwrites all directories including subdirectories if they exist.
-D r	Renames the specified directory, only if it exists.
-D R	Renames all directories, including subdirectories if they exist.
-D a	Autorenames the specified directory, only if it exists.
-D A	Autorenames all directories, including subdirectories if they exist.
-D s	Skips the specified directory, only if it exists.
-D S	Skips all directories including subdirectories if they exist.
-D m	Prompts the user if primary name exists.

continued

-D M	Prompts the user if secondary names exist.
files...	Specifies the source to move files from.
directory	Specifies where to move files.
File Name: `mmove`	**Directory:** /usr/bin/ **Type:** External

modinfo

UNIX Shell: All primary shells (bash, ash, tcsh)

Function	Shows information about the specified kernel module.
Syntax	modinfo [options...] *module*

-a	Shows the author of the module.
-d	Shows the description of the module.
-f*string*	Specifies a random format string that gathers information from specified module.
-p	Shows parameters supported by the module.
-h	Shows help information.
-V	Shows version information.
module	Specifies the kernel module object file without the `.o` extension.
File Name: `modinfo`	**Directory:** /sbin/ **Type:** External

modprobe

UNIX Shell: All primary shells (bash, ash, tcsh)

Function	Probes for modules in Linux.
Syntax	modprobe [options...] *module { pattern }*

-a	Loads all matching modules.
-c	Shows the current configuration.
-d	Shows information about the stack of modules.
-k	Uses autoclean on loaded modules.
-l	Shows all matching modules.
-n	Simulates the command.
-q	Shows no output on errors.
-r	Removes a module.
-s	Sends messages to `syslog` instead of STDERR.
-t *type*	Only probes for the specified module type.
-v	Verbose mode. Shows more information.
-V	Shows version information.
module	Specifies a module to probe.
pattern	Specifies a pattern to probe for.
File Name: `modprobe`	**Directory:** /sbin/ **Type:** External

mogrify

UNIX Shell: All primary shells (bash, ash, tcsh)

Function	Modifies images by scaling, rotating, twisting and cropping. It also converts image files.
Syntax	mogrify [options...] *file*

-antialias	Erases pixel aliases.
-blur *factor*	Creates a blurry image. Factor is an odd number between 3 and 31.
-border *width* x *height*	Specifies a border to use with the image.
-bordercolor *color*	Specifies the border color.
-box *color*	Specifies the color to use for the bounding box.
-charcoal *factor*	Converts the image to charcoal. Factor is an odd number between 3 and 31.
-colorize *value*	Colorizes the image. Value is in percent.
-colors *value*	Specifies the number of colors to use to colorize the image.
-colorspace *value*	Specifies the colorspace type. gray, xyz, ohta, rgb, ycbcr, cmyk, and so forth.
-comment *string*	Supplies a comment to an image.
-compress *type*	Specifies the compression. Select BZip, Fax, Group4, JPEG, LZW, ZIP, or None.
-contrast	Sets the contrast.

continued

-crop *width* x *height xoffset yoffset*	Crops the image. A percentage factor can be used instead (for example, factor 10%).
-cycle *amount*	Shows the color map for the image.
-delay *seconds*	Shows next image after a pause. Use values in terms of 1/100ths of a second.
-density *width* x *height*	Sets image density.
-depth *value*	Specifies the depth of the image. Value is either 8 or 16.
-despeckle	Lowers the speckles in the image.
-display *host:display*	Specifies an X server to connect to.
-dispose *method*	Specifies a GIF disposal method to use.
0	Uses no disposal.
1	Doesn't dispose between frames.
2	Overwrites frame with background color.
3	Overwrites frame with previous frame.
-dither	Uses FS error diffusion on the image. `+dither` blocks text and graphic alias.
-draw *string*	Supplies a graphic primitives to an image.
-edge *factor*	Finds edges in an image.
-emboss *order*	Embosses the image.
-enhance	Uses a digital filter to enhance image.
-equalize	Equalizes the histogram of the image.
-fill *color*	Specifies a color filling for graphic primitives.
-filter *value*	Specifies a filter to use to resize the image (default is Lanczos).
-flip	Flips image vertically.
-flop	Flips image horizontally.
-format *type*	Specifies the image format.
-font *name*	Specifies a font to use for annotation. Use an @ in front of TrueType font types.
-frame *width* x *height* + *outerbevel* + *innerbevel*	Uses an ornamental frame around the image when inner and outer bevel width is set.
-fuzz *distance*	Specifies which colors should be considered equal.
-gamma *value*	Specifies gamma correction value.
-gaussian *width* x *sigma*	Gausses the image.
-geometry *width* x *height xoffset yoffset*	Sets height and width of the image.
-gravity *type*	Specifies where to place text in the image.
-implode *factor*	Implodes the image.
-interlace *type*	Specifies interlacing type.
-layer *type*	Specifies the type of layer to use.
-linewidth *value*	Specifies the width of a line.
-loop *iteration*	Uses Netscape loop extensions for GIF images.
-map *file*	Specifies a color map to use.
-matte	Saves matte channels.
-median *order*	Uses a median filter on the image.
-modulate *value*	Sets saturation and brightness for the image.
-monochrome	Shows the image in monochrome mode.
-negate	Shows the image in inverted colors.
-noise *value*	Alters noise for the image.
-normalize	Uses all available colors in image.
-opaque *color*	Specifies fill color for the image.
-page *width* x *height xoffset yoffset*	Specifies the size for the image canvas in dots per inch or page type in pixels.
-paint *radius*	Shows the image as an oil painting.
-pointsize *value*	Specifies point size for PostScript font.
-quality *value*	Specifies compression and image values for JPEG, MIFF and PNG images. (You select between level 0 worst to 100 best (default is 75).)
-raise *width* x *height*	Lightens or darkens the edges of the image to create 3D raised edge effects. (Use +raise for regular edge shading.)
-region *width* x *height xoffset yoffset*	Allows portions of the image to be affected by any following options.
-roll *xoffset xoffset*	Rolls the image vertically or horizontally.
-rotate *degrees*	Rotates the image to the right `degrees>` or left `degrees`.
-sample *geometry*	Scales the image using the selected pixel geometry.
-scene *value*	Specifies the number for the scene.
-seed *value*	Specifies the value for the seed random number generator output.

continued

-segment *cluster* x *smoothing*	Segments the image by cluster and smoothing threshold values.
-shade *azimuth* x *elevation*	Adds shade to the image by specifying a distant light source.
-sharpen *factor*	Sharpens the image. Uses an odd number scale factor from 3 to 31.
-shear *xdegrees* x *ydegrees*	Cuts and slides the image along an X-Y axis.
-size *width* x *height* + *offset*	Specifies the size of any unknown image size - for example gray, RGB and CMYK.
-solarize *threshold*	Suppresses all pixels above the specified threshold. `factor%` can also be used.
-spread *value*	Swaps pixels at random amounts within a local area that is specified by `value`.
-stroke *color*	Specifies the color to use when you need to stroke a primitive.
-swirl *degrees*	Swirls the image around its center.
-texture *file*	Specifies the texture file to tile into the background of the image.
-threshold *value*	Suppresses pixel intensity that exceeds the specified threshold.
-transparency *color*	Specifies which color is be made transparent.
-treedepth *value*	Specifies the color reduction by selection of a tree depth value from 0 to 8.
-units *type*	Specifies the type of image resolution: Undefined, Pixels/inch, or Pixels/cm.
-verbose	Verbose mode. Shows more information about the image.
-view *string*	Specifies the FlashPix parameters.
-wave *amplitude* x *wavelength*	Alters the image along the specified sine wave.
file	Specifies image to act on.

File Name:	`mogrify`	**Directory:**	/usr/X11R6/bin	**Type:**	External

mouseconfig

UNIX Shell: All primary shells (bash, ash, tcsh)

Function	Manages mouse configuration.
Syntax	mouseconfig [options...] *{ mousetype }*

--help	Shows help information.
--back	Shows a Back-button.
--expert	Starts the configuration in expert mode.
--noprobe	Doesn't probe for the mouse.
--kickstart	Probes the mouse to automatically configure it.
--device *device*	Specifies the device where the mouse is.
--emulthree	Emulates a three-button mouse.
--test	Tests the new configuration.
mousetype	Specifies the mouse type.

File Name:	`Mouseconfig`	**Directory:**	/usr/sbin/	**Type:**	External

mpage

UNIX Shell: All primary shells (bash, ash, tcsh)

Function	Prints several pages on one sheet of paper. The input files can be either plain text or PostScript.
Syntax	mpage [options...] *files...*

-8	Prints eight pages per sheet.
-4	Prints four pages per sheet. (Is default.)
-2	Prints two pages per sheet.
-1	Prints one page per sheet.
-0	Prints two pages per sheet Only print the first and fourth page of every set of four pages.
-E	Prints two pages per sheet. Only print the second and third page of every set of four pages.
-p *{ prprog }*	Specifies a program to use as a filter before sending the output to the printer.
-c	Prints several files on each page.
-C *encoding*	Specifies the character encoding.
-D *dateformat*	Sets the date format to use.
-o	Doesn't print outlines around each reduced page.
-v	Prints the total number of sheets of paper used.
-f	Prints folding lines that are longer than the page width.
-F *font*	Specifies the font to use (default is courier).
-l	Prints in landscape mode.
-R	Switching from left to right mode.
-B*{ NR*[*lrtb* *]*]	Specifies the thickness for text box margins and line.
-m*{ NR*[*lrtb* *]*]	Specifies margin for the sheet.

continued

-M{ *NR*[*lrtb*]}	Specifies margin for logical page.
	Use at least one of the following for `lrtb`:
l	Means the left margin.
r	Means the right margin.
t	Means the top margin.
b	Means the bottom margin.
-a	Specifies that successively numbered pages run down the sheet.
-da	Assumes that input is a text file.
-dp	Assumes that input is a PostScript file.
-A	Specifies A4-sized paper.
-U	Specifies US letter-sized paper.
-b *papersize*	Specifies paper size. Can be A3, A4, letter, or legal.
-S	Allows non square page reduction.
-I *NR*	Indents the text NR characters.
-j*f*[-*l*][%*i*]	Prints every i page between page f and l (default is 1 for l and last page for l).
-k	Ignores the %%TRailer and %%PSTRailer in PostScript file.
-P { *printer* }	Specifies the printer to use. If no printer given, use the default printer.
-r	Prints the pages in reverse order.
-R	Prints the first page on left bottom corner.
-t	Prints on both sides of the paper.
-T	In duplex mode tumbles every second page.
-W *width*	Specifies page width in characters.
-L *lines*	Sets the number of lines per page.
-x	Shows help information and default settings.
-X { *header* }	Prints header on each physical page. If no header given, show the filename.
-z *printcmd*	Specifies the command to use to print the page (default is `lpr`).
-Z{ *options* }	Specifies options for the print command specified with -z.
-s *tabstop*	Sets the width of Tab stop (default is 8-eight characters).
-h *header*	Specifies the header to use with -H.
-H	Shows a header for each logical page. The header can be specified with -h.
files...	Specifies the files to print.
File Name: `mpage`	**Directory:** /usr/bin/ **Type:** External

mpartition

UNIX Shell: All primary shells (bash, ash, tcsh)

Function	Partitions an MS-DOS hard disk, to create an MS-DOS file system.
Syntax	mpartition options...

	Use one of the following options:
-p *drive*	Shows the partition information for drive.
-r *drive*	Removes the partition described by drive.
-I *drive*	Removes all partition by initializing the partitions table.
-a *drive*	Makes the partition bootable.
-d *drive*	Makes the partition not bootable.
-c *drive*	Creates a new partition.
	The following options are used together with -c:
s *sectors*	Specifies the sector count.
-h *heads*	Specifies the head count.
-t *cylinders*	Specifies the cylinder count.
b *offset*	Specifies the offset where the partition starts.
-l *length*	Specifies the length of the partition.
	The following option is used together with -I and -c:
-B *file*	Specifies a file where the template for the master boot record is.
	The following options are used together with -r, -I, -a, -d, and -c:
-f	Forces an update even if there are some inconsistencies.
	The following options can be used together with every command:
-v	Verbose mode. Shows more information.
-vv	Very verbose mode. Shows even more information.
File Name: `mpartition`	**Directory:** /usr/bin/ **Type:** External

mpg123

UNIX Shell:	All primary shells (bash, ash, tcsh)
Function	Reads files or URLs and plays them on the audio device or outputs them to STDOUT.
Syntax	mpg123 [options...] *{ source }*

-t	Tests the file without output it to the audio device.
-s	Sends the output to STDOUT instead of the audio device.
-c	Checks for filter range violations, and shows them for each frame if any occur.
-v	Verbose mode. Shows more information.
-q	Suppresses diagnostic messages.
-y	Tries to resynch and continue decoding if an error occurs.
-0	Decodes only channel 0 (left).
-1	Decodes only channel 1 (right).
-m	Mixes both channels.
-2	Performs a downsampling of ratio 2:1 (22 kHz).
-4	Performs a downsampling of ratio 4:1 (11kHz).
-b size	Uses an audio output buffer of size KB.
-k num	Skips first num frames.
-n num	Decodes only num frames.
-f factor	Alters scale factor (default is 32768).
-r rate	Sets sample rate (default is automatic).
-g gain	Sets audio hardware output gain (default is don't change).
-a dev	Specifies the audio device to use (default is /dev/dsp).
-o s	Directs audio output to the speaker.
-o h	Directs audio output to headphone connector.
-o l	Directs audio output to the line-out connector.
-d n	Plays every n'th frame only.
-h n	Plays each frame n times.
-p URL:port	Specifies the proxy to use for HTTP requests.
-u auth	HTTP authentication to use when receiving files via HTTP.
-@ file	Specifies a playlist file.
-z	Plays random song from playlist.
--stereo	Forces stereo output.
--reopen	Forces reopening of the audio device after every song.
--8bit	Forces 8-bit output.
-Z	Specifies full random play.
source	Specifies the file or URL to play. If - is used, it reads input from STDIN.

File Name:	`mpg123`	**Directory:**	/usr/bin/	**Type:**	External

mrd

UNIX Shell:	All primary shells (bash, ash, tcsh)
Function	Deletes an MS-DOS directory.
Syntax	mrd [-v] *directories...*

-v	Shows version information.
directories...	Specifies the directory or directories to delete.

File Name:	`mrd`	**Directory:**	/usr/bin/	**Type:**	External

mren

UNIX Shell:	All primary shells (bash, ash, tcsh)
Function	Renames or moves MS-DOS files.
Syntax	mren [options...] *source destination*

-h	Shows help information.
-V	Shows version information
-v	Verbose mode. Shows more information.
	The following options overwrite, skip, or rename existing files:
-D o	Overwrites the specified files, only if they exist.
-D O	Overwrites all files.

continued

-D r	Renames the specified files, only if they exist.
-D R	Renames all files.
-D a	Autorenames the specified files, only if they exist.
-D A	Autorenames all files.
-D s	Skips the specified files, only if they exist.
-D S	Skips all files.
-D m	Prompts the user if primary name exists.
-D M	Prompts the user if secondary names exist.
source	Specifies the file to rename.
destination	Specifies what you want to rename files to.

File Name: `mren` **Directory:** /usr/bin/ **Type:** External

msgchk

UNIX Shell: All primary shells (bash, ash, tcsh)

Function Checks maildrops for new incoming mail messages.

Syntax msgchk [options...] *{ users... }*

-date	Shows messages sorted by date.
-nodate	Shows messages unsorted.
-notify *action*	Reports status. Action can be all, mail, or nomail.
-nonotify *action*	Don't report status. Action can be all, mail, or nomail.
-version	Shows version information.
-help	Shows help information.
users...	Specifies the user or users to check messages for.

File Name: `msgchk` **Directory:** /usr/bin/ **Type:** External

msgfmt

UNIX Shell: All primary shells (bash, ash, tcsh)

Function Creates message object files from portable object files. It doesn't change the portable object files.

Syntax msgfmt [options...] *files...*

-a *value*	Aligns strings to specified number of bytes (default is 1).
-c	Does language-dependent checks on strings.
-D *directory*	Adds the specified directory to the list of directories for input files.
-f	Uses fuzzy entries in output.
-h	Shows help information.
-o *file*	Specifies the output filename.
-v	Verbose mode. Shows more information.
-V	Shows version information.
--no-hash	Doesn't include the hash table within the binary file.
--statistics	Shows translation statistics.
--strict	Enables strict Uniforum mode.
files...	Specifies the input files. The filename extension must be `.po`.

File Name: `msgfmt` **Directory:** /usr/bin/ **Type:** External

msh

UNIX Shell: All primary shells (bash, ash, tcsh)

Function Reads a usual mail message file or a message file compressed with `packf`.

Syntax msh [options...] *{ command } { file }*

-prompt *string*	Sets the prompt string.
-quit	Quits the program and asks the user whether any changes should be saved.
-noscan	Discards all of the messages.
-version	Shows version information.
-help	Shows help information.
-exit	Exits the program.
	These commands are available when `msh` is started from `bbc`:
-scan	Scans the BBoard for new items on start up.
-mark	Erases all of the messages from the BBoard that you are in.
-quit	Turns management from `msh` over to `bbc`.

continued

-exit	Exits from everything and marks all of the messages as read.
	These commands are available when msh is started from vmh:
-topcur	Causes the current message to track the top line of the vmh window.
-notopcur	Causes the current message to track the center of the vmh window.
	msh supports the following nmh commands as well:
ali	Lists the mail aliases.
burst	Bursts digests into messages.
comp	Composes a message.
dist	Sends a message to other addresses.
folder	Sets or lists the current folder or message.
forw	Forwards the messages.
inc	Incorporates a new mail.
mark	Marks messages.
mhmail	Sends or reads mail.
mhn	Shows, lists, caches, or stores MIME messages.
msgchk	Checks for any messages.
next	Shows the next message to be viewed.
packf	Creates a single file by compressing a folder.
pick	Selects messages based upon content.
prev	Shows the message just viewed.
refile	Stores the message into other folders.
repl	Replies to a message just received.
rmm	Removes one or many messages.
scan	Creates one line for every message search list.
send	Sends messages.
show	Shows messages.
sortm	Sorts messages.
whatnow	Prompts the user for sending.
whom	Shows who receives the message.
file	Specifies the file to read.

File Name:	msh	**Directory:**	/usr/bin/	**Type:**	External

mshowfat

UNIX Shell: All primary shells (bash, ash, tcsh)

Function	Shows file allocation table entries for an MS-DOS file.
Syntax	mshowfat *files...*

files...	Specifies the files you want to show FAT entries for.

File Name:	mshowfat	**Directory:**	/usr/bin/	**Type:**	External

mtools

UNIX Shell: All primary shells (bash, ash, tcsh)

Function	Shows all the programs in the mtools package which are used for accessing DOS FAT volumes.
Syntax	mtools

File Name:	mtools	**Directory:**	/usr/bin/	**Type:**	External

mtype

UNIX Shell: All primary shells (bash, ash, tcsh)

Function	Shows the content of an MS-DOS file.
Syntax	mtype [options...] *files...*

-s	Strips the high bit from the data.
-t	Views the file as a text file.
files...	Specifies the files to view.

File Name:	mtype	**Directory:**	/usr/bin/	**Type:**	External

mutt	UNIX Shell:	All primary shells (bash, ash, tcsh)
Function	Manages mail boxes. Sends and reads e-mails.	
Syntax	mutt [options...] *{ address }*	

-a *file*	Attaches a file to the e-mail.
-b *address*	Specifies a blind carbon copy address.
-c *address*	Specifies a carbon copy address.
-e *command*	Specifies a configuration to use after the command startup scripts.
-f *mailbox*	Specifies the mailbox to load.
-F *muttrc*	Specifies an alternative run control script to run.
-h	Shows help information.
-H *draft*	Specifies a draft e-mail to use as template.
-i *include*	Specifies a file to be included in the e-mail body.
-m *type*	Specifies the mailbox type.
-n	Doesn't use the system's configuration files.
-p	Resumes an e-mail.
-R	Starts a mailbox in read only mode.
-s "*subject*"	Specifies a subject to the e-mail.
-v	Shows version information.
-x	Uses the mailx compose mode.
-y	Shows all specified mailboxes.
-z	Doesn't start the program if the mailbox is empty.
-Z	Opens the first specified mailbox that contains a new e-mail.
address	Specifies the mail address to send to.

File Name:	Directory:	Type:
`mutt`	/usr/bin/	External

mzip	UNIX Shell:	All primary shells (bash, ash, tcsh)
Function	Sends commands to an Iomega ZIP drive.	
Syntax	mzip [options...]	

-e	Ejects the disk.
-f	Ejects the disk even if it is mounted.
-r	Writes protects the disk.
-w	Removes write protection.
-p	Sets password write protection.
-x	Sets password protection.
-u	Sets the disk to be unprotected until ejected.
-q	Shows status information.
-V	Shows version information.

File Name:	Directory:	Type:
`mzip`	/usr/bin/	External

named-xfer	UNIX Shell:	All primary shells (bash, ash, tcsh)
Function	Handles inbound zone transfer. Is used by `named` and should not be used directly.	
Syntax	named-xfer options... [options...] *nameservers... { ACTION }*	

	The following options are required:
-z *transferzone*	Specifies the zone that you want to transfer.
-f *file*	Specifies the file where to put the zone that is received from the name servers.
-s *serialno*	Specifies the serial number of the zone.
	The following options are optional:
-d *level*	Shows debug information. Debug level can be between 1 and 10.
-l *logfile*	Specifies where to put debug messages.
-i *file*	Specifies the file to put zone changes from incremental zone transfer.
-t *tracefile*	Specifies a protocol trace file for debugging the zone transfer.
-p *port*	Sets a new port number to use instead of the default.
-S	Transfers only SOA, NS, and A records.

continued

nameservers...	Specifies the name server or servers to run a zone transfer on.
ACTION	**Specifies the type of zone transfer to perform.**
ixfr	Does a full zone transfer.
axfr	Does an incremental zone transfer.
File Name: `named-xfer`	**Directory:** /usr/sbin/ — **Type:** External

namei

UNIX Shell: All primary shells (bash, ash, tcsh)

Function	Shows which kind of file each part of a pathname is. Follows symbolic links until they stop in a proper file.
Syntax	namei [options...] *paths...*

-x	Shows mount point directories with a D, instead of a d.
-m	Shows the mode bits of each file type in the style of `ls` for example, `rwxr-xr-x`.
paths...	Specifies the path to use.
File Name: `namei`	**Directory:** /usr/bin/ — **Type:** External

ncftp

UNIX Shell: All primary shells (bash, ash, tcsh)

Function	A browser program for the Internet FTP service.
Syntax	ncftp [-u *user*] { *host* }

-u *user*	Specifies the user to connect with.
host	Connects to the specified host. Can also be a URL.
File Name: `ncftp`	**Directory:** /usr/bin/ — **Type:** External

ncftpbatch

UNIX Shell: All primary shells (bash, ash, tcsh)

Function	Processes FTP requests added by the `ncftp` program.
Syntax	ncftpbatch [option]

-d	Starts background processing of FTP jobs in the current user's directory.
-D	Same as -d except that the process doesn't become a daemon.
-l	Shows the contents of the user's job queue.
File Name: `ncftpbatch`	**Directory:** /usr/bin/ — **Type:** External

ncftpget

UNIX Shell: All primary shells (bash, ash, tcsh)

Function	Transfers files from the command line or shell scripts instead of using interactive FTP programs.
Syntax	ncftpget [options...] *remotehost localdirectory remotefiles...* ncftpget [options...] *URL*

-u *username*	Specifies your username.
-p *password*	Specifies the password to use with the username.
-P *port*	Specifies port number instead of the default FTP service port.
-j *account*	Specifies account in supplement to the username and password (deprecated).
-d *file*	Specifies the file for debug logging.
-a	Uses ASCII transfer type instead of binary.
-t *time*	Specifies the seconds to do a timeout.
-v	Uses progress meters (is default if the output stream is a tty).
-V	Doesn't use progress meters.
-f *file*	Reads the file for host, user, and password information.
-A	Attaches to local files instead of overwriting them.
-z	Tries to resume transfers (is default).
-Z	Doesn't try to resume transfers.
-E	Uses regular (PORT) data connections.
-F	Uses passive (PASV) data connections (is default).
-DD	Erases remote file after completely downloading it.
-R	Recursive mode. Copies whole directory trees.
-r *NR*	Specifies the maximum number of times to redial the remote FTP server.
-T	Doesn't use on-the-fly TAR mode when downloading whole directory trees.

continued

-b	Runs in the background (by submitting a job to ncftpbatch).
-B *bytes*	Specifies the TCP/IP socket buffer size in bytes.
remotehost	Specifies the hostname or the IP address of the computer to connect to.
localdirectory	The local directory to place the transferred files.
remotefiles	Specifies the remote files to copy. Multiple files are separated by a space.
URL	Specifies the complete FTP URL.
File Name: `Ncftpget`	**Directory:** /usr/bin/ **Type:** External
ncftpget -u ucg -p imroot ftp://server/info.txt	Apply username and password on command prompt.

ncftpls

UNIX Shell: All primary shells (bash, ash, tcsh)

Function	Creates remote directories listings without using interactive FTP programs.
Syntax	ncftpls [options...] *URL*

-1	Uses most basic format, one item per line.
-l	Uses long list format
-x -*flags*	Specifies `ls` flags to pass on to the server.
-u *username*	Specifies your username.
-p *password*	Specifies the password to use with the username.
-P *port*	Specifies port number instead of the default FTP service port.
-d *file*	Specifies the file for debug logging.
-t *time*	Specifies the seconds to do a timeout.
-F	Uses passive (PASV) data connections (is default).
-E	Uses regular (PORT) data connections.
-r *NR*	Specifies the maximum number of times to redial the remote FTP server.
URL	Specifies the complete FTP `URL` including the path- and filename.
File Name: `ncftpls`	**Directory:** /usr/bin/ **Type:** External

ncftpput

UNIX Shell: All primary shells (bash, ash, tcsh)

Function	Transfers files from the command line or shell scripts instead of using interactive FTP programs.
Syntax	ncftpput [options...] *host directory files...* ncftpput -c *host directory*

-u *username*	Specifies the username to use (default is anonymous).
-p *password*	Specifies the password to use on the username.
-P *port*	Specifies the port to use (default is 21).
-j *account*	Inserts the specified account with the username.
-d *file*	Writes debug information into the specified file.
-a	Uses ASCII transfer type instead of binary.
-m	Creates the remote destination before copying.
-t *time*	Specifies the time to wait before doing a timeout.
-U *value*	Specifies the value for the umask.
-v	Shows progress meters (is default if the output stream is a tty).
-V	Doesn't show progress meters.
-f *file*	Reads the specified file for host, user, and password information.
-A	Appends remote files if they already exist (default is to overwrite).
-T *prefix*	Uploads into temporary files with the specified prefix.
-S *suffix*	Uploads into temporary files with the specified suffix.
-R	Copies whole directory trees (recursive mode).
-r *NR*	Specifies the maximum number of times to redial the remote FTP server.
-z	Resumes transfers (is default).
-Z	Doesn't resume transfers.
-E	Uses regular data connections.
-F	Uses passive data connections (is default).
-DD	Erases local files after completely uploading them.
-y	Tries to use "SITE UTIME" to preserve timestamps on remote host.
-b	Runs the command in the background.
-B *size*	Sets the TCP/IP socket buffer size to the specified size.

continued

-c	Reads the files to copy from STDIN.
host	Specifies the hostname or the IP address of the computer to connect to.
directory	The remote directory to place the transferred files.
files...	Specifies the local files to copy. Multiple files are separated by a space.
File Name: `ncftpput`	**Directory:** /usr/bin/ **Type:** External
ncftpput -R -u ucg -p imroot -m server /lux /lux/	Puts files in /lux/ onto server in directory /lux.

ncopy

UNIX Shell: All primary shells (bash, ash, tcsh)

Function	Copies files over the NetWare network.
Syntax	ncopy [options...] *files... destination*

-m	Copies Macintosh resource fork with data fork.
-M	Copies Macintosh resource fork to or from a non-Mac file system.
-n	Sleeps a second between copying blocks.
-s *amount*	Specifies how many 100K blocks to copy before sleeping (default is 10).
-p	Maintains file attributes and date/time during copy.
-pp	Same as -p but does also maintain the owner name (not user ID) of files during copy.
-t	Maintain strustees during copy. Trustee name is maintained, not ID.
-v	Shows the name of every file copied and the percentage completed.
-V	Shows version information.
files...	Specifies which file(s) to copy.
destination	Specifies where to copy the file; it should be a filename or a directory.
File Name: `ncopy`	**Directory:** /usr/bin/ **Type:** External
Tip:	Doesn't use the network as a normal cp would do, so if you have NetWare mounts, you should use this command.

ncpmount

UNIX Shell: All primary shells (bash, ash, tcsh)

Function	Mounts volumes on a NetWare file server.
Syntax	ncpmount [options...] *mountpoint*

-S *server*	Specifies the NetWare file server to use.
-h	Shows help information.
-C	Turns off the conversion to uppercase for password.
-n	Specifies that no password is used, required when no password is required.
-P *password*	Specifies the password to use for the NetWare user ID.
-U *username*	Specifies the NetWare user ID to use when logging into the server.
-m	Mounts more than one connection with the same username.
-u *userID*	Specifies which user ID to use when assigning to files on the NetWare mount.
-g *groupID*	Specifies which group ID to use when assigning to files on the NetWare mount.
-c *username*	Specifies the username of the owner of the connection.
-f *file*	Specifies which permission should be assigned to files on the Netware mount.
-d *directory*	Specifies which permission should be assigned to directories on the Netware mount.
-V *volume*	Mounts only the specified volume.
-t *time*	Specifies the time for the server to wait to answer the request (default is 60/100 s).
-r *NR*	Specifies the number of times to send a packet to the server (default is 5).
-y *iorcharset*	Converts names from Unicode with the specified charset name (for example, iso-8859-1).
-p *codepage*	Converts Unicode to NetWare with the specified codepage name (for example, cp437).
-b	Connects to NetWare 4 or 5 through bindery emulation instead of NDS.
-i *level*	Uses packet signing. Levels: 0 = disable, 1 = if needed, 2 = if allowed, 3 = always.
-v	Shows version information.
-A *DNS server*	Switches to UDP mode and uses the specified DNS server.
-N *namespace*	Ignores specified namespaces in NFS, LONG(OS/2), and DOS on NetWare volumes.
-2	Use `ncpfs` interface version 2. Used in kernel 2.0.x.
-3	Use `ncpfs` interface version 3. Used in kernel 2.2.x.
-s	Allows deletion of a read-only file from a NetWare file system.
passwdfile=file	Specifies password and doesn't store it into world-readable `/etc/fstab`.
mountpoint	Specifies the directory that the file system is mounted over.

continued

File Name:	`ncpmount`	**Directory:**	/usr/bin/	**Type:**	External
Tip:	If you use -V to specify one volume, you are able to export this mountpoint over NFS.				
ncpmount -S srv01 -U ucg -V /home /mnt	Mount your home directory to `/mnt`; prompt for the password.				

ncpumount

UNIX Shell: All primary shells (bash, ash, tcsh)

Function	Unmounts a NetWare file system that was previously mounted with the `ncpmount`.
Syntax	ncpumount *mountpoint*

mountpoint	Specifies the directory to unmount.

File Name:	`ncpumount`	**Directory:**	/usr/bin/	**Type:**	External

ndc

UNIX Shell: All primary shells (bash, ash, tcsh)

Function	Administers and manages the operations of a name server.
Syntax	ndc [options...] *{ commands... }*

-c *channel*	Specifies which control channel to use (default is `/var/run/ndc`). (To specify the control channel as a TCP/IP socket, it is ipaddress/port.)
-l *localsock*	Specifies an address to bind the client's control channel to.
-p *pidfile*	Specifies a pidfile to use when using UNIX signals for control communications.
-d	Shows debug information.
-q	Causes `ndc` not to output any prompt or result text on the screen.
-s	Causes `ndc` to output only fatal error message
-t	Enables tracing of protocols and system status.
commands...	Specifies the in-built commands to use. If not specified, interactive mode will start.

File Name:	`ndc`	**Directory:**	/usr/sbin/	**Type:**	External

neqn

UNIX Shell: A shell (ash, bsh)

Function	A preprocessor for the command *nroff* and is used to help out in equations.
Syntax	neqn [options...] *{ files... }*

-r	Does only a one-size reduction.
-v	Shows version information.
-C	Recognizes all .EQ and .EN sentences, not only those preceded by a space.
-N	Forbids new lines within delimiters.
-R	Doesn't load `eqnrc`.
-d*xy*	Uses the characters `x` and `y` as the equation delimiters.
-T*name*	Specifies the name of the output device.
-M*directory*	Searches the specified directory for eqnrc before the default directories.
-f*font*	Specifies the font to use.
-s*size*	Specifies the point size to use.
-p*size*	Reduces subscripts and superscripts by the specified point size.
-m*size*	Specifies the minimum point size to use.
files...	Specifies the file to process.

File Name:	`neqn`	**Directory:**	/usr/bin/	**Type:**	Script

netconf

UNIX Shell: All primary shells (bash, ash, tcsh)

Function	An interactive user interface that allows configuration of a TCP/IP network.
Syntax	netconf [options...]

	May be accessed by the GUI or the following command-line options:
--bootrc *path { oldpath }*	Specifies the new `rc` directory path.
oldpath	Specifies the old path to replace.
--connect *site* [--fore]	Specifies the PPP site to connect using the pppsetup option of Linuxconf.
--fore	Forces the connection to be kept in the foreground.
--dialctl	Shows a list of PPP/Slip dialout configurations and their status.
--disconnect *site*	Specifies the PPP site to disconnect.
--initnet	Initiates the existing Ethernet network.

continued

--postconnect *site device*	Post-connects the specified Linux configuration site and specified PPP device.
--predisconnect *site device*	Pre-disconnects the specified Linux configuration site and specified PPP device.
site	Specifies the dial-in or dial-out site for pre-connection or post-connection.
device	Specifies the PPP device to use for pre-connection or post-connection.
--resetfw	Turns the packet firewall off.
--runlevel	Specifies the operation mode to run.
local	Uses local mode.
client	Uses client mode.
server	Uses client mode.
--setdevdef	Sets up the dial device.
--setgateway *address*	Specifies the IP gateway address.
--setupdaild *setup options...*	Sets up the dial device using a combination of parameters.
--status	Shows what's needed to bring the current configuration up to synch.
--update	Initiates the checks listed below and refreshes the configuration file:
	Checks the kernel's modules.
	Mounts all local volumes.
	Checks file permissions.
	Checks the lilo.
	Runs `Sysv` initiation scripts.

File Name: `netconf` **Directory:** /sbin/ **Type:** External

netconfig

UNIX Shell: All primary shells (bash, ash, tcsh)

Function	Configures the network on the command line or in interactive mode.
Syntax	netconfig [options...]

--bootproto=*value*	Specifies the boot protocol. Values are dhcp, bootp, or none.
--gateway=*host*	Specifies the gateway to use.
--ip=*address*	Specifies the IP address to use.
--nameserver=*address*	Specifies the name server to use
--netmask=*address*	Specifies the netmask to use.
--hostname=*host*	Specifies the hostname.
--domain=*domain*	Specifies the domain name.
--device=*device*	Specifies the network interface to configure.
--help	Shows help information.
--usage	Shows short usage message.

File Name: `netconfig` **Directory:** /usr/sbin/ **Type:** External

netconfig --ip=192.168.1.2 --gateway=192.18.1.1 --device=eth0	Configures eth0 with address 192.168.1.2 and gateway 192.168.1.1.

netreport

UNIX Shell: All primary shells (bash, ash, tcsh)

Function	Requests network management scripts send a SIGIO signal when network interface changes occur.
Syntax	netreport [-r]

-r	Erase the current request for the calling process.

File Name: `netreport` **Directory:** /sbin/ **Type:** External

netscape

UNIX Shell: A shell (ash, bsh)

Function	A graphic based Web browser.
Syntax	netscape *{ ACTION }* [*-option*]

ACTION	**Use one of the following actions:**
+news	Shows Collabra discussion groups.
+mail	Shows the mail inbox.
+edit	Opens the composer window.
+addr	Opens the address book.
+hist	Shows the history window.

continued

+book	Shows the bookmarks.
+mailto	Opens an empty e-mail.
+component-bar	Shows the component launch bar.
-option	Passes the option directly to the Netscape binary code.
File Name: `netscape`	**Directory:** /usr/bin/ **Type:** Script

newalias

UNIX Shell: All primary shells (bash, ash, tcsh)

Function	Installs new `elm` aliases for system and/or user.
Syntax	newalias [-g]

-g	Updates the systems databases. Global flag.
File Name: `newalias`	**Directory:** /usr/bin/ **Type:** External

newer

UNIX Shell: All primary shells (bash, ash, tcsh)

Function	Compares modification times of two files and exits successfully if file1 is at least as old as file2.
Syntax	newer [option] *file1 file2*

--help	Shows help information and exits.
--version	Shows version information and exits.
file1	Specifies the file to use.
file2	Specifies the file to compare with.
File Name: `newer`	**Directory:** /usr/bin/ **Type:** External

newgrp

UNIX Shell: All primary shells (bash, ash, tcsh)

Function	Changes a user's real and effective group ID to the specified group.
Syntax	newgrp *{ group }*

group	Specifies the new group name.
File Name: `newgrp`	**Directory:** /usr/bin/ **Type:** External

newusers

UNIX Shell: All primary shells (bash, ash, tcsh)

Function	Updates and creates new users in batch. User information is taken from the specified file.
Syntax	newusers *{ newusers }*

newusers	Creates a new user.
File Name: `newusers`	**Directory:** /usr/sbin/ **Type:** External

nhfsstone

UNIX Shell: All primary shells (bash, ash, tcsh)

Function	Benchmarks Network File System (NFS).
Syntax	nhfsstone [options...] *{ directories... }*

-v	Verbose mode. Shows more information.
-t *seconds*	Sets calls based on the given running time and the load.
-c *number*	Specifies the total number of NFS calls to generate (default is 5000).
-l *number*	Specifies the load to generate in NFS calls per second (default is 30).
-p *number*	Specifies the number of load-generating sub processes to fork (default is 7).
-m *file*	Specifies the file to read mix of NFS operations from.
directories...	Specifies one or more mount points of the NFS system to check.
File Name: `nhfsstone`	**Directory:** /usr/sbin/ **Type:** External

nisdomainname

nisdomainname	UNIX Shell:	All primary shells (bash, ash, tcsh)
Function	Shows or sets system's NIS domain name.	
Syntax	nisdomainname [-v] *{ domainname }*	

-v	Verbose mode. Shows more information.
domainname	Sets the `nisdomainname` to the specified domain name. Must be at root for this.
File Name: `nisdomainname`	**Directory:** /bin **Type:** External

nl

nl	UNIX Shell:	All primary shells (bash, ash, tcsh)
Function	Reads lines from STDIN or a file, adds line numbers, and shows the result to STDOUT.	
Syntax	nl [options...] *{ file }*	

-d *??*	Specifies the two characters used as the delimiter for logical page sections.
-i *inc*	Line number increments at each line.
-l *num*	Specifies the number of blank lines that are treated as a one.
-b=*style*	Specifies the `style` of lines in page body to be numbered.
-f *style*	Specifies the `style` of lines in page footer to be numbered.
-h *style*	Specifies the `style` of lines in page header to be numbered.
	You can use one of the following for style:
a	Numbers all lines.
t	Numbers only the lines that contain data.
n	Doesn't use line numbering.
-n *format*	Specifies the format of line numbers, uses the formats supplied below:
ln	Adjusts the format of line numbers to the left and suppresses leading zeros.
rn	Adjusts the format of line numbers to the right and suppresses leading zeros.
rz	Adjusts the format of line numbers to the right and keeps leading zeros.
-i *inc*	Specifies the increment value to number logical page lines.
-l *num*	Specifies the number of blank lines that are treated as a one.
-p *num*	Doesn't reset line numbers at logical pages.
-s *?*	Specifies the character used to separate the line number and text.
-v *startnum*	Specifies the first line number on each logical page.
-w *num*	Specifies the number of characters used for the column width (default is 6).
--help	Shows help information.
--version	Shows version information.
file	The input file used to generate line numbers for.
File Name: `nl`	**Directory:** /usr/bin/ **Type:** External

nmbd

nmbd	UNIX Shell:	All primary shells (bash, ash, tcsh)
Function	A server that replies to NetBIOS over IP name service requests from a Windows client.	
Syntax	nmbd [options...]	

-D	Operates as a daemon.
-a	Each new connection attaches a log message to the log file.
-h	Shows help information.
-o	Overwrites the log file when opened.
-V	Shows version information.
-H *lmhosts file*	Uses the specified NetBIOS lmhosts file.
-d *debuglevel*	Sets the debug level to an integer between 0 and 10 (default is 0).
-l *logfile*	Specifies a path and base filename from the running nmbd server that is logged.
-n *primary NETBIOS name*	Overrides the NETBIOS name that Samba uses for itself.
-p *port number*	Changes the UDP port number to respond to queries on (default is 137).
-s *configuration file*	Uses specified configuration file.
File Name: `nmbd`	**Directory:** /usr/sbin/ **Type:** External

nmblookup	**UNIX Shell:**	All primary shells (bash, ash, tcsh)

Function	Requests NetBIOS names and maps them to IP addresses.
Syntax	nmblookup [options...] *name*

-M	Searches for a master browser.
-R	Makes a recursive lookup. Used with WINS servers.
-S	Does a node status query after the name query has returned an IP address.
-r	Tries to bind to UDP port 137 to send and receive UDP datagrams.
-A	Converts a **name** to an IP address and do a node status query on this address.
-h	Shows help information.
-B *broadcast address*	Sends the query to the given broadcast address.
-U *unicast address*	Does a unicast query to the given unicast address. Used with WINS servers.
-d *debuglevel*	Sets debug level to an integer from 0 to 10 (default is 0).
-s *smb config file*	Specify the pathname to the Samba configuration file.
-i *scope*	Specifies the NetBIOS scope to communicate with when creating NetBIOS names.
-T	Shows the DNS name first.
name	Specifies the NetBIOS name or IP address to query.

File Name:	`nmblookup`	**Directory:**	/usr/bin/	**Type:**	External

nprint	**UNIX Shell:**	All primary shells (bash, ash, tcsh)

Function	Prints files to print queues located on a NetWare file server.
Syntax	nprint [options...] *file*

-S *server*	Specifies the server that you want to use.
-U *username*	Specifies the username to use for the print request at the server.
-P *password*	Specifies password to use for the print request at the server.
-n	Is used if no password is required for the print request.
-C	Converts passwords to uppercase. Disable this conversion by -C.
-q *QUEUENAME*	Specifies the queue to use. You must specify uppercase letters.
-d *jobdescription*	Specifies a description for the print job.
-p *path*	Specifies a pathname to print on the banner page. You may use up to 12 characters.
-f *filename*	Specifies text to append to the top of the banner.
-l *lines*	Specifies number of lines to print per page.
-r *rows*	Specifies number of rows to print per page (default is 80 lines).
-c *copies*	Specifies number of copies of a document (default is 1).
-t *tabs*	Specifies number of spaces for one Tab character (default is 8).
-T	Expands Tab character and uses eight spaces.
-N	Disables form feeds on the print server.
-F *formnumber*	Specifies the form number to send to the printer.
-h	Shows help information.
file	Specifies the file to print.

File Name:	`nprint`	**Directory:**	/usr/bin/	**Type:**	External

nsend	**UNIX Shell:**	All primary shells (bash, ash, tcsh)

Function	Sends messages to NetWare users or user groups.
Syntax	nsend [options...] -i *userID* nsend -c *number* nsend [-t *type*] *ACTION message*

-h	Shows help information.
-S *server*	Specifies the server to use.
-U *username*	Reports your NetWare username to the server.
	Specify one of these two options. (If neither is given, then `nsend` prompts.)
-P *password*	Specifies a password if required by the server.
-n	Is used if the user doesn't have a password.
-C	Forbids conversion of passwords to uppercase.

continued

-a	Suppresses the `From...` start text on a message.
-i *userID*	Specifies the recipient object ID.
-c *number*	Specifies connection numbers of recipients.
-t *type*	Specifies the recipient type.
ACTION	**Specify either one of these two actions:**
-o *name*	Specifies recipient's name. Specifies user or group.
name	Specifies the user or group to receive the message.
message	Specifies the message to send.
File Name: `nsend`	**Directory:** /usr/bin/ **Type:** External

nsupdate

UNIX Shell: All primary shells (bash, ash, tcsh)

Function	Updates DNS name servers interactively or non-interactively.
Syntax	nsupdate [options...] *{ file }*

-k *keyname*	Marks updates with TSIG.
-d	Shows debug information.
-v	Uses TCP for updates instead of UDP.
file	Specifies a name of the file containing the update data.
File Name: `nsupdate`	**Directory:** /usr/bin/ **Type:** External

ntsysv

UNIX Shell: All primary shells (bash, ash, tcsh)

Function	Configures run levels to set what services that should be started or stopped.
Syntax	ntsysv [options...]

--back	Makes a Back (instead of Cancel) button appear.
--level *LEVEL*	Specifies level. Only 0, 1, 2, 3, 5, or 6 are available.
File Name: `ntsysv`	**Directory:** /usr/sbin/ **Type:** External
Note:	This program actually creates links from the scripts in `/etc/init.d` to the `/etc/rc*.d` directories.

nwauth

UNIX Shell: All primary shells (bash, ash, tcsh)

Function	Logs in to a NetWare server. If no arguments are given, the user's `.nvclient` file is used.
Syntax	nwauth [options...]

-h	Shows help information.
-S *server*	Specifies which server to use.
-U *username*	Tells the server about your NetWare username.
-P *password*	Specifies which password to use.
-n	Specifies that no password is used — should be used if no password is required.
File Name: `nwauth`	**Directory:** /usr/bin/ **Type:** External

nwbocreate

UNIX Shell: All primary shells (bash, ash, tcsh)

Function	Creates a NetWare bindery object.
Syntax	nwbocreate [options...]

-h	Shows help information.
-S *server*	Specifies the server you want to use.
-U *username*	Specifies the username to login with.
-P *password*	Specifies the password to use for log in.
-n	Use this if no password is required to log in.
-C	Converts passwords to uppercase. Disables this conversion with -C.
-o *objectname*	Specifies name of object to create.
-t *type*	Specifies type of the object.
-r *readflag*	Specifies the read security.
-w *writeflag*	Specifies the write security.

continued

	You may use these values for the -r and -w options:
ANYONE	Specifies that anyone may access the object.
LOGGED	Specifies that anyone who is logged in may access the object.
OBJECT	Enables logged in as the object or supervisor equivalent to access the object.
SUPERVISOR	Enables anyone logged in as a supervisor equivalent to access the object.
NETWARE	Enables only the bindery to access the object
File Name: `nwbocreate`	**Directory:** /usr/bin/ **Type:** External

nwbols

UNIX Shell: All primary shells (bash, ash, tcsh)

Function	Shows specified NetWare bindery objects that are visible for the user.
Syntax	nwbols [options...]

-h	Shows help information.
-S *server*	Specifies the server to use.
-U *user*	Specifies the user to use for login.
-P *password*	Specifies password to use for login.
-n	Is used if no password is required for the login.
-C	Converts passwords to uppercase. You can disable this conversion with -C.
-t *type*	Specifies type of the object to show. Use a decimal number as the type.
-o *pattern*	Specifies a pattern to restrict how objects are shown.
-v	Verbose mode. Shows more information.
File Name: `nwbols`	**Directory:** /usr/bin/ **Type:** External

nwboprops

UNIX Shell: All primary shells (bash, ash, tcsh)

Function	Shows all the properties of the specified NetWare bindery objects.
Syntax	nwboprops [options...]

-h	Shows help information.
-S *server*	Specifies which server to use.
-U *user*	Specifies the username to use.
-P *password*	Specifies the password to use.
-n	Specifies that no password is used — should be used if no password is required.
-C	Turns off the conversion to uppercase for the password.
-o *object name*	Specifies which object is be inspected.
-t *type*	Specifies the object type as decimal value (1 - user, 2 - group, 3 -printer queue).
-v	Verbose mode. Shows more information.
File Name: `nwboprops`	**Directory:** /usr/bin/ **Type:** External

nwborm

UNIX Shell: All primary shells (bash, ash, tcsh)

Function	Removes a NetWare bindery object.
Syntax	nwborm [options...]

-h	Shows help information.
-S *server*	Specifies the name of the server you want to use.
-U *user*	Specifies the username to use for login.
-P *password*	Specifies the password to use for login.
-n	Is used if no password is required for the login.
-C	Converts passwords to uppercase. You can disable this conversion with -C.
-o *objectname*	Specifies the name of the object to remove.
-t *objecttype*	Specifies type of the object. It must be a decimal value (for example, 1, 2, 3).
File Name: `nwborm`	**Directory:** /usr/bin/ **Type:** External

nwbpadd

nwbpadd	UNIX Shell:	All primary shells (bash, ash, tcsh)
Function	Specifies the value of a NetWare bindery property.	
Syntax	nwbpadd [options...] *value*	

-h	Shows help information.
-S *server*	Specifies the name of the server you want to use.
-U *user*	Specifies the username to use for login.
-P *password*	Specifies the password to use for login.
-C	Doesn't make passwords uppercase before sending them to the server.
-o *objectname*	Specifies the name of the object to touch.
-t *type*	Specifies the type of the object.
-p *property*	Specifies the name of the property to set.
value	Specifies an object ID in hexadecimal notation.

File Name:	nwbpadd	**Directory:**	/usr/bin/	**Type:**	External

nwbpcreate

nwbpcreate	UNIX Shell:	All primary shells (bash, ash, tcsh)
Function	Creates the specified NetWare property.	
Syntax	nwbpcreate [options...]	

-h	Shows help information.
-S *server*	Specifies the name of the server you want to use.
-U *user*	Specifies the username to log in with.
-P *password*	Specifies the password to log in with.
-n	Is used if no password is required for the login.
-C	Converts passwords to uppercase. You may disable this conversion with -C.
-o *objectname*	Specifies the name of the object to touch.
-t *objecttype*	Specifies type of the object. It must be a decimal value (for example, 1, 2, or 3).
-p *property*	Specifies the name of the property to remove.
-s	Creates property of type SET instead of type ITEM.
-r *flag*	Specifies read security.
-w *flag*	Specifies write security.
flag:	**flag can be one of the following:**
ANYONE	Specifies that anyone can access the property.
LOGGED	Specifies that anyone that is logged in can access the property.
OBJECT	Specifies that anyone that is logged in as object or supervisor can access the property.
SUPERVISOR	Specifies that anyone logged in as supervisor can access the property.
NETWARE	Specifies that only bindery can access the property.

File Name:	nwbpcreate	**Directory:**	/usr/bin/	**Type:**	External

nwbprm

nwbprm	UNIX Shell:	All primary shells (bash, ash, tcsh)
Function	Removes the specified NetWare bindery property.	
Syntax	nwbprm [options...]	

-h	Shows help information.
-S *server*	Specifies the name of the server you want to use.
-U *user*	Specifies the username to log in with.
-P *password*	Specifies the password to log in with.
-n	Is used if no password is required for the login.
-C	Converts passwords to uppercase. You may disable this conversion with -C.
-o *objectname*	Specifies the name of the object to touch.
-t *objecttype*	Specifies type of the object. It must be a decimal value (for example, 1, 2, or 3).
-p *property*	Specifies the name of the property to remove.

File Name:	nwbprm	**Directory:**	/usr/bin/	**Type:**	External

nwbpset

nwbpset	UNIX Shell:	All primary shells (bash, ash, tcsh)

Function	Creates a Bindery property or configures the values.
Syntax	nwbpset [options...]

-h	Shows help information.
-S *server*	Specifies the name of the server you want to use.
-P *password*	Specifies the password to use for login.
-n	Is used if no password is required for login.
-U *username*	Specifies the username to log in with.
-C	Converts passwords to uppercase. You may disable this conversion with -C.

File Name:	`nwbpset`	**Directory:**	/usr/bin/	**Type:**	External

nwbpvalues

nwbpvalues	UNIX Shell:	All primary shells (bash, ash, tcsh)

Function	Shows NetWare bindery property's contents.
Syntax	nwbpvalues [options...]

-h	Shows help information.
-S *server*	Specifies the name of the server you want to use.
-U *user*	Specifies the username to use for login.
-P *password*	Specifies the password to use with login.
-n	Is used if no password is required to log in.
-C	Converts passwords to uppercase. You may disable this conversion with -C.
-o *objectname*	Specifies the name of the object to look up.
-t *objecttype*	Specifies type of the object. This is specified as a decimal value.
-p *property*	Specifies the property to show.
-v	Verbose mode. Shows more information.
-c	Uses canonical output, to use with `nwbpset`.

File Name:	`nwbpvalues`	**Directory:**	/usr/bin/	**Type:**	External

nwdir

nwdir	UNIX Shell:	All primary shells (bash, ash, tcsh)

Function	Shows files, directories, and their attributes from a NetWare directory.
Syntax	nwdir [options...] *{ directory }*

-h	Shows help information.
-v	Verbose mode. Shows more information.
-l	Shows name space information.
-t	Shows all file information also in hexadecimal numbers.
-d	Shows directories like other files, instead of showing their contents.
directory	Specifies the path to show. No wildcards are allowed.

File Name:	`nwdir`	**Directory:**	/usr/bin/	**Type:**	External

nwfsctrl

nwfsctrl	UNIX Shell:	All primary shells (bash, ash, tcsh)

Function	Performs commands remotely on a NetWare server.
Syntax	nwfsctrl *options... { servercommands }*

-h	Shows help information.
-S *server*	Specifies which server to use.
-U *user*	Specifies the username to use.
-P *password*	Specifies the password to use.
-n	Specifies that no password is used — should be used if no password is required.
-C	Turns off the conversion to uppercase for passwords.
-o	Opens bindery.
-c	Closes bindery.
-d	Takes the server down. Complains if there are open files.
-fd	Takes the server down. Doesn't complain if there are open files.

continued

	The following server command can be used (not with -o and -c):
load *module options...*	Loads the module on the server. Options are for the module.
unload *module*	Unloads the module form the server.
mount *volume*	Mounts the volume.
dismount *volume*	Unmounts the volume.
set *variable* = *value*	Sets the variable to value.
open bindery	Opens bindery.
close bindery	Closes bindery.
enable login	Enables login to the server.
disable login	Disables login to the server
enable tts	Enables tts.
disable tts	Disables tts.
File Name: `nwfsctrl`	**Directory:** /usr/bin/ — **Type:** External

nwfsinfo

UNIX Shell: All primary shells (bash, ash, tcsh)

Function	Shows some information about a NetWare server without logging in.
Syntax	nwfsinfo [options...]

-h	Shows help information.
-S *server*	Specify which server to use.
-t	Shows the file server's current time.
-d	Shows the file server description strings.
-i	Shows extended file server information.
File Name: `nwfsinfo`	**Directory:** /usr/bin/ — **Type:** External

nwfstime

UNIX Shell: All primary shells (bash, ash, tcsh)

Function	Shows or sets a NetWare server's date and time.
Syntax	nwfstime [options...]

-h	Shows help information.
-S *server*	Specifies which server to use.
-U *user*	Specifies the username to use.
-P *password*	Specifies the password to use.
-n	Specifies that no password is used — should be used if no password is required.
-C	Turns off the conversion to uppercase for passwords.
-s	Uses the local time and date.
File Name: `nwfstime`	**Directory:** /usr/bin/ — **Type:** External

nwgrant

UNIX Shell: All primary shells (bash, ash, tcsh)

Function	Adds a bindery object with the matching trustee rights to a directory.
Syntax	nwgrant [options...] *directory*

-h	Shows help information.
-S *server*	Specifies which server to use.
-U *user*	Specifies the username to use.
-P *password*	Specifies the password to use.
-n	Specifies that no password is used — should be used if no password is required.
-C	Turns off the conversion to uppercase for password.
-o *objectname*	Specifies the name of the object to add as trustee.
-t *objecttype*	Specifies the type of the object. This is specified as a decimal value.
-r *rights*	Specifies the rights to grant to the bindery objects.
directory	Specifies the directory wherein to add the object as trustee.
File Name: `nwgrant`	**Directory:** /usr/bin/ — **Type:** External
Warning:	Beware — the permissions access of the $HOME/.nwclient must be 600.

nwmsg

UNIX Shell:	All primary shells (bash, ash, tcsh)
Function	Is called using kerneld when a NetWare server sends a broadcast message.
Syntax	nwmsg *mountpoint*

mountpoint	Specifies the mount point to use.

File Name:	`nwmsg`	**Directory:**	/usr/sbin/	**Type:**	External

nwpasswd

UNIX Shell:	All primary shells (bash, ash, tcsh)
Function	Changes a user's password.
Syntax	nwpasswd [options...]

-h	Shows help information.
-S *server*	Specifies which server to use.
-U *username*	Specifies the name of the bindery object that's changed.
-O *objectname*	Specifies the name of any other users that are changed. Only for supervisors.
-t *objecttype*	Specifies the type of the object that are changed.

File Name:	`nwpasswd`	**Directory:**	/usr/bin/	**Type:**	External

nwpurge

UNIX Shell:	All primary shells (bash, ash, tcsh)
Function	Permanently erases previously erased files.
Syntax	nwpurge [options...] *{ directory }*

-h	Shows help information.
-a	Specifies the subdirectories are also erased.
-s	Doesn't show files — only total is shown.
-l	Disables purge. Files are only shown.
directory	Specifies the directory to purge. Must be in Linux format — not in NetWare.

File Name:	`nwpurge`	**Directory:**	/usr/bin/	**Type:**	External

nwrevoke

UNIX Shell:	All primary shells (bash, ash, tcsh)
Function	Revokes the specified NetWare bindery object with corresponding trustee rights from the directory.
Syntax	nwrevoke [options...] *directory*

-h	Shows help information.
-S *server*	Specifies which server to use.
-U *user*	Specifies the username to use.
-P *password*	Specifies the password to use.
-n	Specifies that no password is used — should be used if no password is required.
-C	Turns off the conversion to uppercase for passwords.
-o *object name*	Specifies the object name to be added as trustee.
-t *type*	Specify the object type as decimal value (1 - user, 2 - group, 3 - printer queue).
-r *rights*	Specifies the rights to revoke.
directory	Specifies the directory from which to erase the object as trustee.

File Name:	`nwrevoke`	**Directory:**	/usr/bin/	**Type:**	External
Note:	The access permissions of `$HOME/.nwclient` must be 600 for security reasons.				

nwrights

UNIX Shell:	All primary shells (bash, ash, tcsh)
Function	Asks a NetWare server for the effective rights in a file or directory for the user.
Syntax	nwrights [-h] *file*

-h	Shows help information.
file	Specifies the file or directory to ask information about.

File Name:	`nwrights`	**Directory:**	/usr/bin/	**Type:**	External

nwsfind

UNIX Shell:	All primary shells (bash, ash, tcsh)
Function	Searches for a NetWare server and locates a route to the server.
Syntax	nwsfind [-t *type*] { *name* }

-t *type*	Searches for a type of server other then a file server. Type is an integer.
name	Specifies which server to find.

File Name:	`nwsfind`	**Directory:**	/usr/bin/	**Type:**	External

nwtrustee

UNIX Shell:	All primary shells (bash, ash, tcsh)
Function	Shows the trustee directories' assignments that a user has on a volume.
Syntax	nwtrustee [options...]

-h	Shows help information.
-S *server*	Specifies which server to use.
-U *user*	Specifies the username to use.
-P *password*	Specifies the password to use.
-n	Specifies that no password is used — should be used if no password is required.
-C	Turns off the conversion to uppercase for passwords.
-O *objectID*	Specifies the bindery object ID of the user to show.
-o *objectname*	Specifies the name of the user to show.
-t *objecttype*	Specifies type of the object. This is specified as an integer (default is 1 = user).
-v	Verbose mode. Shows more information.
-l *volume number*	Specifies the number of the volume to show.

File Name:	`nwtrustee`	**Directory:**	/usr/bin/	**Type:**	External

nwuserlist

UNIX Shell:	All primary shells (bash, ash, tcsh)
Function	Shows information about the users logged in to a NetWare server.
Syntax	nwuserlist [options...]

-h	Shows help information.
-S *server*	Specifies which server to use.
-U *user*	Specifies the username to use.
-P *password*	Specifies the password to use.
-n	Specifies that no password is used — should be used if no password is required.
-C	Turns off the conversion to uppercase for passwords.
-a	Shows the IPX address.
-q	Shows the object ID in addition to username.

File Name:	`nwuserlist`	**Directory:**	/usr/bin/	**Type:**	External

nwvolinfo

UNIX Shell:	All primary shells (bash, ash, tcsh)
Function	Shows information on a NetWare server volume.
Syntax	nwvolinfo [options...]

-h	Shows help information.
-S *server*	Specifies which server to use.
-U *user*	Specifies the username to use.
-P *password*	Specifies the password to use.
-n	Specifies that no password is used — should be used if no password is required.
-C	Turn off the conversion to uppercase for passwords.
-v *volume*	Specifies the volume name to use.
-N	Shows information only in numerical format for use in a pipe.

File Name:	`nwvolinfo`	**Directory:**	/usr/bin/	**Type:**	External

objcopy

UNIX Shell:	All primary shells (bash, ash, tcsh)

Function	Copies object files using the GNU BFD Library.
Syntax	objcopy [options...] *inputfile* { *outputfile* }

-I *bfdname*	Reads input file, assuming it is in the object format specified in bfdname.
-O *bfdname*	Writes the output file using the object format specified in bfdname.
-F *bfdname*	Uses the object format specified in bfdname for both input and output files.
-j *section*	Copies only the named section from the input file to the output file.
-R *section*	Erases the named section from the output file.
-S	Doesn't copy information about relocation and symbols from source file.
-g	Skips debugging symbols when copying from the source file.
--strip-unneeded	Erases unneeded symbols.
-K *symbolname*	Keeps only the symbol specified in symbolname when copying the source file.
-N *symbolname*	Erases symbol specified in symbolname when copying from the source file.
-L *symbolname*	Changes symbol specified in symbolname to local, which makes it invisible.
-W *symbolname*	Changes symbol specified in symbolname to weak.
-x	Copies only global symbols from the source file.
-X	Skips copying compiler-generated local symbols.
-b *count*	Copies only every count byte of data of the input source file.
-i *interleave*	Allows copying one of every interleave bytes, set by -b (default is 4).
-p	Copies access and modification dates from the input file to the output file.
--debugging	Converts debug information, if this is possible.
--gap-fill=*value*	Uses specified value to fill gaps in the load address between sections.
--pad-to=*address*	Fills out the output file to address by adding to the last section. (The value used for this is specified in --gap-fill (default is 0).)
--set-start=*value*	Specifies value to set the start address of new file to.
--change-start=*incr*	Adds the specified incr to the start address. Not supported by all file formats.
--change-addresses=*incr*	Alters all sections address by adding incr. Not supported by all file formats.
--change-section-address *section action value*	Alters LMA and VMA address where action is either =, +, or - with value.
--change-section-lma *section action value*	Alters LMA address where action is either =, +, or - with value.
--change-section-vma *section action value*	Alters VMA address where action is either =, +, or - with value.
--change-warnings	Gives out a warning when --change fails (is default).
--no-change-warnings	Disables warnings when --change fails.
--set-section-flags *section=flags*	Specifies the flags to set for the specified section.
--add-section *name=file*	Adds a new section with specified name containing information from specified file.
--change-leading-char	Alters the special character defined in the object file format when copying. (Doesn't work if both file formats use the same special characters.)
--remove-leading-char	Erases the special characters on global symbols.
--redefine-sym *old=new*	Alters the name of symbol from old to new.
--weaken	Alters all the files global symbols to weak.
-v	Verbose mode. Shows more information about files modified.
-V	Shows version information and exits.
--help	Shows help information and exits.
inputfile	Specifies the source file to use.
outputfile	The output file and is created automatically using input filename if not specified.

File Name:	`objcopy`	**Directory:**	/usr/bin/	**Type:**	External

objdump

UNIX Shell:	All primary shells (bash, ash, tcsh)

Function	Shows information about object files.
Syntax	objdump [options...] *objectfiles...*

-a	Shows archive header information, if any object file is an archive file.
--adjust-vma=*offset*	Adds offset before section addresses in dump information.
-b *bfdname*	Sets the object-code format to bfdname for object files. Please see -i option for formats.
-C	Changes low-level into user-level names, and removes underscores added by the system.
--debugging	Shows debug information.

continued

-d	Shows the assembler instructions in the object file — for instruction sections only.
-D	Shows the assembler instructions in the object file — for all sections.
--prefix-addresses	Shows information in an older format, a complete address at every line.
--disassemble-zeroes	Shows disassembly information even for blocks of zeroes.
-EB	Specifies that big endian is in use when disassemble.
-EL	Specifies that little endian is in use when disassemble.
-f	Shows all information of the overall header summary for each object file.
-h	Shows for each object file a summary of the section header.
--help	Shows help information.
-i	Shows all architectures and object formats to use with -b and -m options.
-j *name*	Specifies the name of the section to show information for.
-l	Labels the display if used with the -d, -D, or -r options.
-m *architecture*	Sets the architecture when disassemble object files. Please see -i option for formats.
-p	Shows specific information for object file format.
-r	Shows the relocation entries for the object file.
-R	Shows the dynamic relocation entries for the object file.
-s	Shows all contents for any section.
-S	Shows disassembly information in the source code, when possible.
--show-raw-insn	Shows the instructions in HEX and symbolic form when disassembling instructions.
--no-show-raw-insn	Suppresses output of the instruction bytes when disassembling instructions.
--stabs	Shows the content in .stab sections in an ELF object file.
--start-address=*address*	Specifies the address to start showing data from.
--stop-address=*address*	Specifies the address to stop showing data from.
-t	Shows the symbol table entries in the object file.
-T	Shows the dynamic symbol table entries in the object file.
--version	Shows version information.
-x	Shows all header information, with the symbol table and relocation entries.
objectfiles...	Specifies the object files to examine.
File Name: `objdump`	**Directory:** /usr/bin/ — **Type:** External

odvitype

UNIX Shell: All primary shells (bash, ash, tcsh)

Function	Checks and translate DVI files to human-readable form.
Syntax	odvitype [options...] *file*

-dpi=*value*	Sets the resolution to value pixels per inch (default is 300.0).
-magnification=*number*	Overrides existing magnification with number.
-max-pages=*number*	Processes number pages (default is one million).
-output-level=*number*	Specifies the verbosity level, from 0 to 4 (default is 4).
-page-start=*value*	Specifies the page to start on.
-show-opcodes	Shows numeric opcodes.
-help	Shows help information.
-version	Shows version information.
file	Specifies a DVI file to convert.
File Name: `odvitype`	**Directory:** /usr/bin/ — **Type:** External

oldps

UNIX Shell: All primary shells (bash, ash, tcsh)

Function	Shows process status information.
Syntax	oldps [options...] *processIDs...*

--sort:*key...*	Sorts the output given by one or more key.
key	**The following keys can be used:**
user	Sorts by username, same as -Ou.
uid	Sorts by user ID, same as -OU.
ppid	Sorts by ppid, same as -OP.
session	Sorts by session, same as -Oo.
tpgid	Sorts by tpgid, same as -OG.
stime	Sorts by stime, same as -OK.

continued

cstime	Sorts by cstime, same as -OJ.
start_time	Sorts by start time, same as -OT.
min_flt	Sorts by minor flt, same as -Om.
maj_flt	Sorts by major flt, same as -OM.
vsize	Sorts by vsize, same as -Ov.
pcpu	Sorts by pcpu, same as -OC.
resident	Sorts by resident, same as -OR.
cmd	Sorts by command, same as -Oc.
pid	Sorts by pid, same as -Op.
pgrp	Sorts by pgrp, same as -Og.
tty	Sorts by tty, same as -Ot.
utime	Sorts by utime, same as -Ok.
cutime	Sorts by cutime, same as -Oj.
priority	Sorts by priority, same as -Oy.
flags	Sorts by flags, same as -Of.
cmin_flt	Sorts by cmin_flt, same as -On.
cmaj_flt	Sorts by cmaj_flt, same as -ON.
rss	Sorts by rss, same as -Or.
size	Sorts by size, same as -Os.
share	Sorts by share, same as -OS.
--help	Shows help information.
--version	Shows version information.
processIDs...	Specifies one or more processes to show information about.
File Name: `oldps`	**Directory:** /usr/bin/ **Type:** External

omega, iniomega, viromega

UNIX Shell: All primary shells (bash, ash, tcsh)

Function	Converts extended Unicode TeX.
Syntax	omega [options...] { *commands...* }

--fmt *format*	Specifies the format as the name of the format to use.
--help	Shows help information.
--ini	Dumps formats. Same as executing the `iniomega`.
--interaction *mode*	Sets the interaction mode: batch mode, nonstop mode, scroll mode, and errorstop mode.
--ipc	Sends DVI output to a socket, the usual output file.
--ipc-start	Starts the ipc server at the other end as well.
--kpathsea-debug *bitmask*	Sets path searching debugging flags according to the bitmask.
--maketex *format*	Enables `mktexfmt`, where format must be one of tex or tfm.
--no-maketex *format*	Disables `mktexfmt`, where format must be one of tex or tfm.
--output-comment *string*	Uses the string for the DVI file comment instead of the data.
--progname *name*	Pretends to be program name.
--shell-escape	Enables the \write18{command} construct.
--version	Shows version information.
commands...	Specifies the commands to run.
File Name: `omega`	**Directory:** /usr/bin/ **Type:** External

openssl

UNIX Shell: All primary shells (bash, ash, tcsh)

Function	Performs various cryptographic functions from the shell and can create certificates.
Syntax	openssl *command* [command options...] { *command arguments...* } openssl [list-*command*] openssl no-*command*

list-*command*	Shows a list of commands that are supported by the installed OpenSSL utility.
standard-commands	Shows a list of standard commands.
message-digest-commands	Shows a list of message digest commands.
cipher-commands	Shows a list of cipher commands.
no-*command*	Tests to check whether the specified command is available for use and outputs to STDOUT.

continued

	These are the standard commands:
asn1parse	The parse tool. Sends an ASN.1 sequence.
ca	Initiates certificate authority (CA) management.
CA.pl	The more user-friendly version of CA management.
ciphers	Starts the SSL cipher list and display tool.
crl	The certificate revocation list (CRL) management tool.
crl2pkcs7	Converts CRL and certificates into a PKCS#7 structure.
dgst	Starts message digest calculation.
dh	Initiates Diffie-Hellman (DH) data key management.
dhparam	The DH parameter management tool.
dsa	The DSA digital signature algorithm management tool.
dsaparam	The DSA parameter management tool.
enc	Starts symmetric cipher routines.
errstr	Converts error numbers into error strings.
gendh	Creates Diffie-Hellman parameters.
gendsa	Creates DSA private keys.
genrsa	Creates RSA private keys.
nseq	Creates and explores a Netscape certificate sequence.
passwd	Creates hashed passwords and updates a user's authentication token.
pkcs12	The PKCS#12 file management utility.
pkcs7	The PKCS#7 utility.
pkcs8	The PKCS#8 private key management utility.
rand	Generates a series of random bytes.
req	Starts X.509 certificate signing request (CSR) management.
rsa	Starts RSA public key management tool.
s_client	Initiates the SSL/TLS generic client.
s_server	Starts the SSL/TLS generic server.
s_time	Starts the SSL connection timer.
sess_id	Initiates SSL session handling utility.
smime	Starts S/MIME mail processing
speed	Initiates algorithm speed measurement for testing the speed of the library.
spkac	Starts the SPKAC print and create utility.
verify	Verifies X.509 certificates.
version	Shows version information.
x509	Starts X.509 certificate management utility.
	These are the message digest commands:
md2	The message digest for hash functions.
md5	The `perl` interface for the message digest algorithm.
mdc2	The MDC message digest.
rmd160	The RMD-160 digest.
sha	The `perl` interface for the NIST secure hash algorithm.
sha1	The `perl` interface for the NIST secure hash-1 algorithm.
	This is the cipher and encoding command for Base64:
base64	Selects Base64 encoding and decoding depending upon its encryption flag.
	These are the cipher and encoding commands for Blowfish:
bf	128-bit key encryption. Other types: bf-cbc, bf-cfb, bf-ecb, and bf-ofb.
	These are the cipher and encoding commands for CAST:
cast	56-bit encryption. Other types: cast-cbc, cast5-cbc, cast5-cfb, cast5-ecb, and cast5-ofb.
	These are the cipher and encoding commands for DES:
des	56-bit key encryption. Other types: des-cbc, des-cfb, and des-ecb.
	These are the cipher and encoding commands for EDE-DES:
des_ede	112-bit key encryption. Other types: des-ede-cbc, des-ede-cfb, and des-ede-ofb.
	These are the cipher and encoding commands for Triple DES:
des_ede3	168-bit key encryption. Other types: des-ede3-cbc, des-ede3-cfb, and des-ede3-ofb.
	These are the cipher and encoding commands for RC2:
rc2	128-bit encryption. Other types: rc2-40-cbc, rc2-64-cbc, rc2-cbc, rc2-cfb, rc2-ecb, and rc2-ofb.

continued

	These are the cipher and encoding commands for RC4:
rc4	128-bit key encryption. Other types: rc4-40.
	These are the cipher and encoding commands for RC5:
rc5	XXX-bit key encryption. Other types: rc5-cbc, rc5-cfb, rc5-ecb and rc5-ofb.
	Many of the commands accept the following arguments for -passin and -passout:
password:password	Sets the -passin and -passout to the specified passwords.
environment:variable	Sets the -passin to the specified environment and -passout to the specified variable.
file:path	Sets the -passin to the specified file/device and -passout to the first line of the path.
descriptor:number	Sets the -passin to the specified file descriptor and -passout to the specified number.
STDIN	Reads the password that is given from STDIN.
File Name: `openssl`	**Directory:** /usr/bin/ **Type:** External

openvt

UNIX Shell: All primary shells (bash, ash, tcsh)

Function	Opens a new virtual terminal and runs the specified command with the arguments specified.
Syntax	openvt [options...] *{ command } { arguments... }*

-c *vtnumber*	Opens VT number instead of the first available.
-s	Runs the command in the new VT, which is considered the current VT.
-u	Uses the owner of the current VT to log in into the new one.
-l	Runs the command as a login shell if a - is added at the beginning of the command.
-v	Verbose mode. Shows more information.
-w	Waits for the command to finish.
--	Defines the end of `openvt's` options. Required when the command has options.
command	Specifies the command to be run in the new VT. If no command is given, use $SHELL.
arguments...	Specifies the arguments to pass to the command.
File Name: `openvt`	**Directory:** /usr/bin/ **Type:** External

pack

UNIX Shell: All primary shells (bash, ash, tcsh)

Function	A packing tool used for maintaining a packing list.
Syntax	pack *ACTION* pack *slaves...*

ACTION	**The following actions can't be used together:**
configure *slaves... options...*	Configures and manages specified slaves by use of option modifiers.
slaves...	Specifies the slave or slaves that are managed by one of these options:
-after *other*	Switches active master to the `other` master and moves all slaves after other.
-anchor *anchor*	Positions slaves in the specified anchor position in the parcel (default is center).
-before *other*	Switches active master to the `other` master and move all slaves before other.
-expand *expression*	Toggles slave expansion by any valid boolean expression (default is 0).
-fill *style*	Stretches the slave to fill the parcel. Uses one of the following style values:
none	Expands the slave to the required dimensions plus any padding requests (is default).
x	Stretches the slave to fit the width of the parcel, plus any external padding.
y	Stretches the slave to fit the height of the parcel, plus any external padding.
both	Stretches the slave to fit both the width and the height.
-in *other*	Inserts slaves at the very end of the packing order for the master of `other`.
-ipadx *padlevel*	Specifies how much internal horizontal padding to put on each side of the slave.
-ipady *padlevel*	Specifies how much internal vertical padding to put on each side of the slave. (Use a valid screen padding distance like 2 (default is 0).)
-padx *padlevel*	Specifies how much external horizontal padding to put on each side of the slave.
.pady *padlevel*	Specifies how much external vertical padding to put on each side of the slave.
-side *placement*	Specifies which side the slaves are packed on the master. (Select placement between top, bottom, right, or left [default is top].)
forget *slaves...*	Erases the specified slaves from the packing list and no longer manages them.
info *slave*	Shows the current configuration state of the specified slave.
propagate *master expression*	Toggles copy use for the specified master by using a valid boolean expression.
	Note:If expression = true it activates. If it is false it deactivates.

continued

Slaves *master*	Shows a list of all of the slaves that are in the specified masters packing order.		
slaves...	Packs the specified slaves around the master. (If a window name is used for slave, pack processes like configure.)		
File Name: `pack`	**Directory:** /usr/lib/tkX8.2/help/tk/control/	**Type:**	External

packf

UNIX Shell: All primary shells (bash, ash, tcsh)

Function	Copies and formats messages from a folder into a file.
Syntax	packf [+*folder*] { *msg* } [options...]

-mbox	Uses mbox (UUCP) style delimiter as separator for the messages (is default).		
-mmdf	Uses mmdf style delimiters as separator for the messages.		
-*filename*	Specifies the name of the file (default is msgbox).		
+*folder*	Specifies the folder (default is current folder).		
-version	Shows version information.		
-help	Shows help information.		
msg	Specify messages (default is all).		
File Name: `packf`	**Directory:** /usr/bin/	**Type:**	External
Tip:	Messages that are packed by packf can be unpacked using inc.		

passmass

UNIX Shell: Expect script

Function	Lets you change passwords on many computers.
Syntax	passmass [options...] { *hosts...* }

	The following options are used with a host argument:		
-user	Specifies the user whose password is changed (default is current user).		
-rlogin	Specifies rlogin for host access (is default).		
-slogin	Specifies slogin for host access.		
-telnet	Specifies telnet for host access.		
-program *program*	Specifies program to use to change password (default is passwd).		
-prompt *suffix*	Sets the system prompt for script to use (default is # for root and % for user).		
-timeout *timeout*	Sets timeout in seconds when waiting for host response (default is 30).		
-su *n*	Specifies if root password is changed or not. Type 1 to change, 0 to not change.		
hosts...	Specifies the host to change password onto. At least one host is required.		
File Name: `passmass`	**Directory:** /usr/bin	**Type:**	Script

patch-metamail

UNIX Shell: TC shell (tcsh)

Function	Attempts to retrieve a patch from a server via FTP and install in the local metamail installation directory.
Syntax	patch-metamail *sourceroot patchNR* { *host directory prefix* }

sourceroot	Specifies the source directory for the local metamail installation.		
patchNR	Specifies the number of the patch.		
host	Specifies the FTP host to get patch (default is thumper.bellcore.com).		
directory	Specifies directory to get patch (default is pub/nsb).		
prefix	Specifies patch name prefix (default is mm).		
File Name: `patch-metamail`	**Directory:** /usr/bin/	**Type:**	Script

pathchk

UNIX Shell: All primary shells (bash, ash, tcsh)

Function	Checks whether the file or files specified are valid or portable.
Syntax	pathchk [options...] *files...*

-p	Checks for all POSIX systems, not only this one.		
--help	Shows help information.		
--version	Shows version information.		
files...	Specifies the file to check.		
File Name: `pathchk`	**Directory:** /usr/bin/	**Type:**	External

pcinitrd

UNIX Shell:	A shell (ash, bsh)
Function	Creates an initrd RAM disk image, which can be useful to boot the system from a PCMCIA device.
Syntax	pcinitrd [options...] *image { modules... }*

-v	Verbose mode. Shows more information.
-a	Installs all drivers for various devices to use when managing packages.
-d *path*	Specifies a search patch where the initrd image files are.
-r *kernel*	Specifies the version of kernel. (that is, 2.2.16) (default is the kernel in use).
-s *size*	Sets the image size in 1K blocks to create (default is 1440).
-u	Updates `cardmgr` and kernel modules in an initrd image.
image	Specifies the image file to create.
modules...	Specifies extra modules to include. The pcmcia/pcmcia_core and pcmcia/ds are default.

File Name:	`pcinitrd`	**Directory:**	/sbin/	**Type:**	Script

pclbanner

UNIX Shell:	All primary shells (bash, ash, tcsh)
Function	Prints a PCL banner on a fixed-size font printer.
Syntax	pclbanner [options...]

-w*width*	Sets the page width in characters (default is 132).
-l*length*	Sets the page length in lines (default is 60).
-P*printer*	Specifies the printer queue for banner information.
-L*bannername*	Specifies the bannername used as main name.
-n*loginname*	Specifies the login name.
-h*host*	Specifies the hostname.
-J*jobtitle*	Specifies the string used on banner as main title.
-C*class*	Specifies the class string.
-?*value*	Ignores all other options and arguments provided by LPRng.
all	Uses all options for `pclbanner`.

File Name:	`pclbanner`	**Directory:**	/usr/libexec/filters/	**Type:**	External

perlbug

UNIX Shell:	Perl script
Function	Creates bug reports for `perl`.
Syntax	perlbug [options...] *{ ACTION }*

-a *address*	Specifies the address to send the bug report to (default is perlbug@perl.com).
-s *subject*	Specifies a subject for the bug report.
-b *body*	Specifies a body for the bug report.
-f *infile*	Specifies a file with the body report already written.
-F *outfile*	Specifies an output file instead of sending the bug report by email.
-r *returnaddress*	Specifies the return address.
-e *editor*	Specifies the editor that's used.
-c *adminaddress*	Specifies an address where to send a copy of the bug report.
-C	Doesn't send any copies of the bug report to the administrator.
-S	Sends the bug report without waiting for confirmation.
-t	Runs the command in test mode.
-d	Shows your configuration data.
-h	Shows help information.
-v	Verbose mode. Shows more information.
ACTION	**The following actions can't be combined:**
-ok	Reports successful builds on the system.
-okay	Reports successful builds on older systems.
-nok	Reports unsuccessful builds on the system.
-nokay	Reports unsuccessful builds for older systems.

File Name:	`perlbug`	**Directory:**	/usr/bin/	**Type:**	Script

perldoc

UNIX Shell: Perl script

Function	Finds and shows Perl documentation from inside installations trees or scripts.
Syntax	perldoc [options...] *{ items... }*

-q *expr*	Specifies a regular expression to search the perlfaq for matching entries.
-v	Shows verbose information.
-t	Shows documents in plain text.
-u	Finds the documents, but doesn't show them.
-m	Shows the whole module.
-l	Shows the filename of the module.
-F	Considers arguments as filenames.
-X	Looks for an entry base name that matches the name on the command line.
-f *function*	Shows the man page for the perl function specified.
-h	Shows help information.
items...	Items can be one of these: page name, module name, or program name.

File Name: `perldoc` **Directory:** /usr/bin/ **Type:** Script

pfbtops

UNIX Shell: All primary shells (bash, ash, tcsh)

Function	Converts a PostScript font in .pfb format into ASCII format.
Syntax	pfbtops *{ pfbfile }*

pfbfile	Specifies the .pfb file to convert.

File Name: `pfbtops` **Directory:** /usr/bin/ **Type:** External

pg_ctl

UNIX Shell: A shell (ash, bsh)

Function	Starst, stops, or restarts the postmaster.
Syntax	pg_ctl [options...] *ACTION*

ACTION	**Select only one of the following actions:**
start	Initiates the postmaster.
-p *path*	Gives the path to the postmaster image.
stop	Deactivates the postmaster.
restart	Cycles the postmaster from stop to start.
status	Shows the current postmaster state.
	This option may be used with every action:
-D *directory*	Specifies the directory to read databases from.
	This option only works with `start` and `restart`:
-o *options*	Specifies the options that are passed directly to the postmaster.
	This option only works with `start`, `stop`, and `restart`:
-w	Waits for the database server to start by watching for creation of the pid file.
	This option only works with `stop` and `restart`:
-m *mode*	Specifies the shutdown mode. Select only one of these three options:
s	Waits until all of the clients have logged off. This is default. Smart mode.
f	Sends the SIGTERM to the back end and active transactions are rolled back. Fast mode.
i	Sends SIGUSR1 to the back end, and requires a database recovery on startup. Immediate mode

File Name: `pg_ctl` **Directory:** /usr/bin/ **Type:** Script

pg_dump

UNIX Shell: All primary shells (bash, ash, tcsh)

Function	Extracts a Postgres database into a script file.
Syntax	pg_dump [options...] *{ database }*

-a	Dumps out only the data, no schema.
-c	Cleans schema before create.
-d	Dumps data as proper insert strings.
-D	Dumps data as inserts with attribute names.

continued

-i	Ignores version mismatch between the program and the database server.
-n	Suppresses double quotes around identifiers unless necessary.
-N	Includes double quotes around identifiers.
-o	Dumps objects identifiers for every table.
-s	Dumps out only the schema, no data.
-t *value*	Dumps data for table value only.
-u	Uses password authentication. Prompts for username and password.
-v	Verbose mode. Shows more information.
-x	Prevents dumping of ACLs and table ownership information.
-h *host*	Specifies the hostname or IP address of the server to connect to.
-p *port*	Specifies the port to use when connecting.
database	Specifies the database to dump to STDOUT.

File Name: `pg_dump` **Directory:** /usr/bin/ **Type:** External

pg_dumpall

UNIX Shell: A shell (ash, bsh)

Function	Extracts all Postgres databases into a script file.
Syntax	pg_dumpall [options...]

-a	Dumps out only the data, no schema.
-d	Dumps data as proper insert strings.
-D	Dumps data as inserts with attribute names.
-n	Suppresses double quotes around identifiers unless necessary.
-o	Dumps objects identifiers for every table.
-s	Dumps out only the schema, no data.
-u	Uses password authentication. Prompts for username and password.
-v	Verbose mode. Shows more information.
-x	Prevents dumping of ACLs and table ownership information.
-h *host*	Specifies the hostname or IP address of the server to connect to.
-p *port*	Specifies the port to use when connecting.

File Name: `pg_dumpall` **Directory:** /usr/bin/ **Type:** Script

pg_passwd

UNIX Shell: All primary shells (bash, ash, tcsh)

Function	Manipulates the flat password file for Postgres.
Syntax	pg_passwd *file*

file	Specifies the password file to use.

File Name: `pg_passwd` **Directory:** /usr/bin/ **Type:** External

pg_upgrade

UNIX Shell: A shell (ash, bsh)

Function	Allows upgrade from a previous release without reloading data.
Syntax	pg_upgrade [-f] *directory*

-f *file*	Specifies the file with the old database or databases in it.
directory	Specifies the old data directory to use.

File Name: `pg_upgrade` **Directory:** /usr/bin/ **Type:** Script

pgrep

UNIX Shell: All primary shells (bash, ash, tcsh)

Function	Searches for specific processes by using different criteria.
Syntax	pgrep [options...] *{ pattern }*

-f	Specifies that `pattern` has to match the full process argument string.
-l	Shows output in long format.
-n	Matches against the most newly created processes.
-v	Checks all processes except the ones specified.
-x	Makes an exact match.
-d *delimiter*	Sets a new delimiter string to use between process IDs.
-P *ppidlist*	Finds processes that are in the specified list.
-g *pgrplist*	Finds processes that have the same process group ID as in the specified list.

continued

-s *sidlist*	Finds processes that have the same session ID as in the specified list.
-u *euidlist*	Finds processes that have the same effective user ID as in the specified list.
-U *uidlist*	Finds processes that have the same real user ID as in the specified list.
-G *gidlist*	Finds processes that have the same real group ID as in the specified list.
-t *termlist*	Finds processes that are related to a certain terminal in the specified list..
pattern	Specifies an extended regular expression used to find a specific process.
File Name: `pgrep`	**Directory:** /usr/bin/ **Type:** External

pick

UNIX Shell: All primary shells (bash, ash, tcsh)

Function	Filters messages through specified expressions.
Syntax	pick [+*folder*] { *msgs...* } [options...]

-and	Shows the messages that match both the previous and the next option expression.
-or	Shows the messages that match either the previous or the next option expression.
-not	Shows the messages that don't match the next expression.
-lbrace	Handles the following options to the next -rbrace option as one expression.
-rbrace	Ends the expression block.
--component *pattern*	Shows messages that have the specified pattern in To, CC, Date, From, Subject form.
-cc *pattern*	Shows messages containing the specified pattern in the `CC` field.
-date *pattern*	Shows all messages matching the specified date.
-from *pattern*	Shows messages matching the specified pattern in the `From` field.
-search *pattern*	Shows messages that have the specified pattern anywhere in the message.
-subject *expression*	Shows messages containing the specified pattern in the `Subject` field.
-to *expression*	Shows messages containing the specified pattern in the `To` field.
-after *date*	Shows messages that have a newer date than the specified date.
-before *date*	Shows messages that have an older date than the specified date.
-datefield *field*	Specifies the field to match the dates on (default is the `date` field).
-sequence *name*	Sets the specified sequence name as the resulting messages.
-public	Sets the sequence as public.
-nopublic	Sets the sequence as private.
-zero	Zeroes the sequence before adding it (is default).
-nozero	Doesn't zero the sequence before adding it.
-list	Lists the messages in indexed order and with one line per message (is default).
-nolist	Doesn't list the filtered files.
-version	Shows version information.
-help	Shows help information.
+*folder*	Specifies the folder in which to look for the messages.
msgs...	Specifies the message files to use.
File Name: `pick`	**Directory:** /usr/bin/ **Type:** External

pinky

UNIX Shell: All primary shells (bash, ash, tcsh)

Function	Shows information about users. Similar to `finger`.
Syntax	pinky [options...] { *users...* }

--help	Shows help information.
---version	Shows version information.
-l	Shows output in long format.
-d	Doesn't show user's home directory in long format output.
-h	Doesn't show user's project file in long format output.
-p	Doesn't show user's plan file in long format output
-s	Shows output in short format (is default).
-f	Doesn't show columns header in short format output.
-w	Doesn't show user's full name in short format output.
-i	Doesn't show user's full name and remote host in short format output.
-q	Doesn't show user's full name, remote host, and idle time in short format output.

continued

users...		Specifies one or more users.			
File Name:	`pinky`	**Directory:**	/usr/bin/	**Type:**	External

pkill

UNIX Shell: All primary shells (bash, ash, tcsh)

Function	Finds and kilsl processes by signaling it with the kill command.
Syntax	pkill [options...] *{ pattern }*

-*signal*		Specifies which kill signal should be sent to the process (default is SIGTERM).			
-f		Specifies that `pattern` has to match the full process argument string.			
-n		Checks against the most newly created processes.			
-v		Kills all processes except the ones specified.			
-x		Makes an exact match.			
-P *ppidlist*		Kills processes that are in the specified list.			
-g *pgrplist*		Kills processes that have the same process group ID as in the specified list.			
-s *sidlist*		Kills processes that have the same session ID as in the specified list.			
-u *euidlist*		Kills processes that have the same effective user ID as in the specified list.			
-U *uidlist*		Kills processes that have the same real user ID as in the specified list.			
-G *gidlist*		Kills processes that have the same real group ID as in the specified list.			
-t *termlist*		Kills processes that are related to a certain terminal in the specified list.			
pattern		Specifies an extended regular expression used to find a specific process.			
File Name:	`pkill`	**Directory:**	/usr/bin/	**Type:**	External
pkill -9 -n xterm			Kills the latest `xterm` process with signal 9.		

pl2pm

UNIX Shell: Perl script

Function	Converts perl4 files to perl5 modules.
Syntax	pl2pm *files...*

files...		Specifies the files to convert.			
File Name:	`pl2pm`	**Directory:**	/usr/bin/	**Type:**	Script

pmake

UNIX Shell: All primary shells (bash, ash, tcsh)

Function	Compiles files depending on other files based on a makefile, and it does this in parallel mode.
Syntax	pmake [options...] *{ variables... } { files... }*

-B	Acts like `make`.
-C	Has no compatibility at all.
-D*var*	Defines the specified variable and set the its value to 1.
-I *path*	Specifies the search path for include files used in the makefile.
-J *number*	Specifies the number of jobs to be run simultaneously on all computers.
-L *number*	Specifies the number of jobs to be run simultaneously locally.
-M	Acts like `make`, with no parallel mode.
-P	Doesn't use pipes.
-R *when*	Checks targets again. Can either be always, never, or locals.
-S	Stops when an error occur. Overrides the -k option.
-V	Uses old-style variable expansion.
-W	Doesn't show warning messages
-X	Doesn't export commands. Shouldn't be used with -x option.
-Z *c*	Uses c as the prefix for directives like #include.
-d *flags*	Shows debug information. Flags specifies which modules will debug.
a	Shows debug information on archive searching.
c	Shows debug information on conditional evaluation.
d	Shows debug information on directory searching.
j	Shows debug information on job scheduling.
m	Shows debug information on make dependencies.
p	Shows debug information on makefile parsing.
q	Shows debug information on job queue maintenance.
r	Shows debug information on remote execution.

continued

s	Shows debug information on suffix processing.
t	Shows debug information on target list maintenance.
v	Shows debug information on variable assignments.
*	Shows debug information on all modules specified above.
-e	Uses environment variables instead of the one defined in the makefile.
-f *file*	Specifies the makefile to use (default is `makefile`).
-h	Show help information.
-i	Ignores errors from commands.
-k	Continues to process the commands that don't depend on an error from another command.
-l	Toggles the directory lock mode.
-n	Doesn't execute any command - just show which would have been executed.
-p *number*	Tells pmake when to show the output graph (1 - before, 2 - after).
-q	Queries the status of a target and returns 0 if it's up-to-date.
-r	Doesn't use the built-in rules.
-s	Doesn't show any command echoes when they are executed.
-t	Uses touch instead of executing the commands to create the target.
-x	Forces export of commands in compatibility mode.
-v	Uses system V compatibility mode.
variables...	Presets specified variables. The format is like "`variable=value`".
files...	Specifies the files to use.

File Name:	Directory:	Type:
`pmake`	/usr/bin/	External

pmap_set

UNIX Shell: All primary shells (bash, ash, tcsh)

Function	Restarts a running portmapper or sets the list of registered RPC programs on the local host. For restarting the portmapper you must redirect the output of `pmap_dump` to a file.
Syntax	pmap_set

File Name:	Directory:	Type:
`pmap_set`	/usr/sbin/	External

pnpdump

UNIX Shell: All primary shells (bash, ash, tcsh)

Function	Dumps ISA Plug-and-Play device resource information to a specified file or STDOUT.
Syntax	pnpdump [options...] *{ parameter }*

-c	Tries to find the safe settings for the PnP devices.
-d	Dumps all of the standard configuration registers for each board.
-D	Outputs extra information.
-i	Ignores any checksum errors when it verifies that the readport address is valid.
-m	Shows any valid interrupts and DMA channels in binary bitmask format.
-o=*file*	Sends output to the specified file (default is STDOUT).
-r	Resets any PnP boards that are in use by the kernel.
-s=*file*	Writes a shell script to the specified file that contains PnP board settings.
-t=*time*	Sets real-time priority for the process to the specified time length.
0	Disables the timeout (default timeout is 5).
-v	Shows version information.
	These parameters skip the default isolation process of `pnpdump`:
devs	Specifies how many PnP cards that BIOS has found that have isolated and allocated CSNs.
readport	Specifies the read port address to use for PnP access.

File Name:	Directory:	Type:
`pnpdump`	/sbin/	External

Tip:	After using this command, edit `/etc/isapnp.conf` to see that everything went well before using `isapnpconfig /etc/isapnp.conf`.
pnpdump > /etc/isapnp.conf	Outputs `isapnp.conf` information to `/etc/isapnp.conf`.

pnpprobe

UNIX Shell:	All primary shells (bash, ash, tcsh)
Function	Searches the ISA bus for Plug and Play sound cards.
Syntax	pnpprobe
File Name:	pnpprobe
Directory:	/usr/sbin/
Type:	External

portmap

UNIX Shell:	All primary shells (bash, ash, tcsh)
Function	Converts RPC program numbers into DARPA protocol port numbers.
Syntax	portmap [options...]
-d	Debug mode. Shows debug information on STDERR.
-v	Verbose mode. Shows more information.
File Name:	portmap
Directory:	/sbin/
Type:	External
Note:	Remember, every RPC program needs this to run.

post

UNIX Shell:	All primary shells (bash, ash, tcsh)
Function	Delivers messages to local and remote users. The default program for `send` to use.
Syntax	post [options...] *{ file }*
-alias *file*	Specifies the alias file to use (default is /etc/mnh/MailAliases).
-filter *file*	Specifies the file to use as a filter for the message.
-nofilter	Doesn't filter the message (is default).
-format	Formats the To and CC entries into standard format entries (is default).
-noformat	Doesn't format the message.
-mime	Formats the message to MIME rules.
-nomime	Doesn't format the message to MIME rules (is default).
-msgid	Adds a message ID or a resent message ID to the message.
-nomsgid	Doesn't add a Message ID to the message (is default).
-verbose	Verbose mode. Shows more information.
-noverbose	Doesn't show more information (is default).
-watch	Shows information on the progress on the delivery to local and network mail.
-nowatch	Doesn't show information on the delivery progress (is default).
-width *columns*	Specifies the width for the message headers (default is 72).
-version	Shows version information.
-help	Shows help information.
file	Specifies the message files to deliver.
File Name:	post
Directory:	/usr/lib/nmh/
Type:	External

postgres

UNIX Shell:	All primary shells (bash, ash, tcsh)
Function	Runs a Postgres single-user back-end.
Syntax	postgres [options...] *{ database }*
-B *size*	Specifies the size of the shared-memory buffers.
-C	Specifies the server version number shouldn't be shown.
-D *directory*	Specifies the directory to use as the root of the tree of databases.
-E	Echoes all queries.
-F	Disables an automatic fsync() call after each transaction.
-O	Overrides restrictions, so system table structures can be modified.
-P	Ignores system indexes to scan or update system tuples.
-Q	Uses quiet mode.
-S *value*	Specifies the amount of memory internal sorts and hashes can use.
-d *{ value }*	Specifies debug mode and the optional level of the output to be shown.
-e	Specifies that dates passed to and from the front end be in European format.
-o *file*	Sends all debugging and error output to file.
-s	Shows time information and other statistics at the end of each query.
-v value	Specifies the number of font- or back-end protocols to use for this session.

continued

	The following options are for Postgres system developers only:
-A	Shows a tremendous amount of output.
-L	Turns off the locking system.
-N	Disables use of new line as a query delimiter.
-f	Forbids the use of particular scan and join methods.
-i	Prevents query execution, but shows the plan tree.
-p *database*	Specifies the back-end server has been started by a postmaster.
-t	Shows timing statistics for each query in relation to each of the major system modules.
database	Specifies the database to use.

File Name: `postgres` **Directory:** /usr/bin/ **Type:** External

postgresql-dump

UNIX Shell: A shell (ash, bsh)

Function Administers PostgreSQL when the database format is incompatible with an old version.

Syntax postgresql-dump [options...]

-c	Dumps the database, then copies it to the screen.
-d	Destroys the database files after dumping the database.
-i	Creates a new database with inidb. The -d option is required.
-l	Loads the dump into a new database. The -i option is required.
-p *directory*	Moves the database files to directory instead of deleting them. Only works with -d.
-t *target*	Specifies where the dump should be written. This option is always required.
-u	Uses the program `pg_upgrade` to upgrade.
-v	Verbose mode. Shows more information.
-x	Disables dumping the old database, forces the -c option.

File Name: `postgresql-dump` **Directory:** /usr/bin/ **Type:** Script

postmaster

UNIX Shell: All primary shells (bash, ash, tcsh)

Function Runs the Postgres multiuser back-end.

Syntax postmaster [options...]

-B *size*	Specifies the size of the shared-memory buffers.
-D *directory*	Specifies the directory to use as the root of the tree of databases.
-N *number*	Sets the maximum number of back-end server processes.
-S	Specifies the postmaster process should start up in silent mode.
-d *{ value }*	Specifies debug mode and the optional level of the output to be shown.
-i	Allows clients to connect via TCP/IP connections.
-l	Enables secure connections using SSL.
-o *options*	Passes options to all back-end server processes started.
-p *port*	Specifies the TCP/IP port to local UNIX domain socket file extension.
-n	Specifies that shared data structures shouldn't be reinitialized.
-s	Stops all other back-end processes by sending the signal SIGSTOP.

File Name: `postmaster` **Directory:** /usr/bin/ **Type:** External

poweroff

UNIX Shell: All primary shells (bash, ash, tcsh)

Function Writes pending information to disk, stops the processing and powers off the computer.

Syntax poweroff [options...]

-n	Doesn't run a synch before shutting down.
-w	Writes only to `wtmp`. No shutdown is executed.
-d	Shuts down but doesn't write to `wtmp`.
-f	Forces a shut down.
-i	Keeps network interfaces running until the last action has completed.

File Name: `poweroff` **Directory:** /usr/bin/ **Type:** External

pppd	**UNIX Shell:**	All primary shells (bash, ash, tcsh)

Function	Starts the Point to Point Protocol daemon.
Syntax	pppd *{ tty }* *{ speed }* [options...]

local:remote	Specifies the local and/or remote interface IP addresses.
ipv6 *local:remote*	Specifies the local and/or remote 64-bit interface identifier.
active-filter *expression*	Specifies a packet filter to be applied to data packets to detect link activity.
allow-ip *addresses...*	Specifies one or more IP address or subnet that peers are allowed to use.
asyncmap *map*	Specifies an async character map.
auth	Specifies the peer must authenticate itself.
bsdcomp *number,total*	Specifies the compression level for the peer to send using BSD compression.
call *script*	Specifies a file in `/etc/ppp/peers/name` to read options from.
cdtrcts	Uses a non standard hardware flow control.
chap-interval *number*	Specifies rechallenge of the peer every number of seconds.
chap-max-challenge *number*	Specifies the maximum number of CHAP challenge transmission to number (default is 10).
chap-restart *number*	Specifies the CHAP retransmission timeout for challenges to number seconds.
connect *script*	Specifies a script to set up the serial line.
connect-delay *number*	Waits up to number of milliseconds for a valid PPP packet on script end.
crtscts	Uses hardware flow control on the serial port.
debug	Specifies that connection debugging should be done.
default-asyncmap	Disables async map negotiation.
default-mru	Disables MRU negotiation.
defaultroute	Adds a default route to the system routing tables.
deflate *number:total*	Specifies the compression level for the peer to send using deflate scheme.
demand	Initiates the link only when data traffic is present.
disconnect *script*	Specifies a script to run when the link is terminated.
domain *domain*	Adds domain to the local hostname for authentication.
escape *characters*	Specifies that certain characters should be escaped on transmission.
file *file*	Specifies a file to read option from.
hide-password	Hides the password in the log files.
holdoff *number*	Specifies the number of seconds before reinitiating the link after it terminates.
idle *number*	Closes the link if the link is idle for number seconds.
init *script*	Specifies a script to execute when initializing the serial line.
ipcp-accept-local	Specifies the peer's idea of our local IP address is accepted.
ipcp-accept-remote	Specifies the peer's idea of our remote IP address is accepted.
ipcp-max-configure *number*	Specifies the maximum number of IPCP configurerequest to be sent (default is 10).
ipcp-max-failure *number*	Specifies the maximum number of IPCP NAKs returned before sending rejects.
ipcp-max-terminate *number*	Specifies the maximum number of IPCP terminaterequests (default is 3).
ipcp-restart *number*	Specifies the IPCP restart interval to number seconds (default is 3).
ipparam *string*	Specifies an extra parameter to the `ip-up` and `ip-down` scripts.
ipv6cp-max-configure *number*	Specifies the maximum number of IPv6CP configure-request transmissions (default is 10).
ipv6cp-max-failure *number*	Specifies the maximum number of IPv6CP configure NAKs returned (default is 10).
ipv6cp-max-terminate *number*	Specifies the maximum number of IPv6CP terminate request transmission (default is 3).
ipv6cp-restart *number*	Specifies the IPv6CP restart interval to number seconds (default is 3).
ipx	Enables the IPXCP and IPX protocols.
ipx-network *number*	Specifies the IPX network number in the IPXCP configure request frame.
ipx-node *number:number*	Specifies the IPX local node number and the peer's node number.
ipx-router-name *{ string }*	Specifies the name of the IPX router.
ipx-routing *number*	Specifies the routing protocol to be received by this option.
ipxcp-accept-local	Accepts peer's NAK for the node number.
ipxcp-accept-network	Accepts peer's NAK for the network number.
ipxcp-accept-remote	Specifies the peer's network number specified in the configure request frame.
ipxcp-max-configure *number*	Specifies the maximum number of IPXCP configure request frames.
ipxcp-max-failure *number*	Specifies the maximum number of IPXCP NAK frames.
ipxcp-max-terminate *number*	Specifies the maximum number of IPXCP terminate request frames.
kdebug *number*	Specifies the number for debugging the PPP driver in the kernel.

continued

ktune	Specifies that kernel settings can be altered as appropriate.
lcp-echo-failure *number*	Specifies the number of LCP echo-request frame before assuming the peer is dead.
lcp-echo-interval *number*	Sends LCP echo request every number seconds.
lcp-max-configure *number*	Specifies the maximum number of LCP configure request transmissions (default is 10).
lcp-max-failure *number*	Specifies the maximum number of LCP NAKs returned before sending rejects.
lcp-max-terminate *number*	Specifies the maximum number of LCP terminate request transmissions (default is 3).
lcp-restart *number*	Specifies the LCP retransmission timeout to number seconds (default is 3).
linkname *name*	Specifies the name of the link.
local	Specifies the modem control lines shouldn't be used.
lock	Creates a UUCP-style lock file for the serial device.
logfd *number*	Specifies a file descriptor to send log messages to.
logfile *file*	Specifies a file to append log messages to.
login	Uses the system password database for authenticating.
maxconnect *number*	Specifies the number of seconds to wait before terminate the connection.
maxfail *number*	Specifies the maximum number of failed connection attempts before terminating the link.
modem	Uses the modem control lines (is default).
mru *number*	Specifies the MRU number.
ms-dns *address*	Specifies a DNS address for a Microsoft Windows client. Can be used twice.
ms-wins *address*	Specifies a WINS address for a Microsoft Windows client. Can be used twice.
mtu *number*	Specifies the MTU number.
name *name*	Specifies the name of the local system for authentication purposes.
netmask *address*	Specifies a netmask to the interface.
noaccomp	Disables address/control compression.
noauth	Specifies the peer don't need to authenticate itself. This option is privileged.
nobsdcomp	Disables BSD compression.
noccp	Disables compression control protocol.
nocrtscts	Disables hardware flow control. Same as nodtrcts.
nodtrcts	Disables hardware flow control. Same as nocrtscts.
nodefaultroute	Disables defaultroute option.
nodeflate	Disables deflate scheme.
nodetach	Disables detaching from the controlling terminal.
noip	Disables IPCP negotiation and IP communication.
noipv6	Disables IPv6CP negotiation and IPv6 communication.
noipdefault	Specifies the default behavior when no local IP address is specified.
noipx	Specifies the IPXCP and IPX protocol should be disabled.
noktune	Specifies that changing system settings are disabled.
nolog	Specifies that send log messages to a file or file descriptor is disabled.
nopcomp	Disables the field compression negotiation protocol.
nopersist	Specifies that once a connection has been made it should be terminated.
nopredictor1	Disables Predictor-1 compression.
noproxyarp	Disables proxyarp option.
notty	Uses a pseudo-tty master/slave terminal.
novj	Disables Van Jacobson-style TCP/IP header compression.
novjccomp	Disables Van Jacobson connection-ID compression.
papcrypt	Indicates that all secrets in the `/etc/ppp/pap-secrets` file are encrypted.
pap-max-authreq *number*	Specifies the maximum number or PAP authenticate-request transmission (default is 10).
pap-restart *number*	Specifies the PAP retransmission timeout to number seconds (default is 3).
pap-timeout *number*	Specifies the maximum time to wait for the peer to authenticate itself with PAP.
passive	Specifies that it should be passive until it gets a valid LCP packet and not exit.
pass-filter *expression*	Specifies a packet filter to apply to data packets being sent or received.
persist	Reopens a terminated connection.
plugin *file*	Specifies a share library object file to load as a plug-in.
predictor1	Uses Predictor-1 compression.
privgroup *group*	Specifies that all members of a group can use privileged options.
proxyarp	Adds an entry to this system's ARP.
pty *script*	Specifies a command script to use instead of a specific terminal device.
receive-all	Accepts all control characters from the peer.

continued

record *file*	Saves all characters sent and received in file.
remotename *name*	Specifies the remote system name for authentication purposes.
refuse-chap	Specifies that CHAP authentication is disabled.
refuse-pap	Specifies that PAP authentication is disabled.
require-chap	Specifies that CHAP authentication is required.
require-pap	Specifies that PAP authentication is required.
show-password	Shows password in the log messages.
silent	Specifies that LCP packets should not be sent to initiate a connection.
sync	Uses synchronous serial encoding instead of asynchronous.
updetach	Specifies the program detaches from its controlling terminal.
usehostname	Specifies enforcing of the hostname.
usepeerdns	Asks the peer for up to two DNS server addresses.
username	Specifies the name used for authenticating the local system to the peer.
vj-max-slots *number*	Specifies the number of slots used by the Van Jacobson TCP/IP header compression.
welcome *script*	Specifies a script to execute before initiating PPP negotiation.
xonxoff	Uses software flow control.
tty	Specifies the device to communicate over.
speed	Specifies the baud rate to use.
File Name: pppd	**Directory:** /usr/sbin/ **Type:** External

pppdump

UNIX Shell: All primary shells (bash, ash, tcsh)

Function Converts PPP record file to readable format.

Syntax pppdump [options...] *{ files... }*

-h	Shows the bytes sent and received in hexadecimal.
-p	Collects the bytes sent and received into PPP packets.
-d	Used with the -p option; this causes decompression of compressed packets.
-r	Reverses the direction of the packages.
-m *value*	Specifies the MRU to show for sent and received packages.
files...	Specifies one or more files to read PPP records from.
File Name: pppdump	**Directory:** /usr/sbin/ **Type:** External

pppoe

UNIX Shell: All primary shells (bash, ash, tcsh)

Function Runs the user-space PPPoE client.

Syntax pppoe -A [options...]

-I *interface*	Specifies the Ethernet interface to use.
-T *timeout*	Specifies the program should exit if no session traffic is detected for timeout.
-D *file*	Dumps every packet to the specified file.
-V	Shows version information.
-A	Sends a PADI packet.
-S *name*	Specifies the service name.
-C *value*	Specifies which name to report as the access concentrator name.
-U	Inserts Host-Uniq tag in the discovery packets.
-s	Uses synchronous PPP encapsulation.
-m *value*	Causes the program to clamp the TCP maximum segment size at the specified value.
-p *file*	Specifies a file to write process ID information to.
-e *session:mac*	Skips discovery phase and move to the session phase.
-k	Causes terminations of an existing session by sending a PADT to it.
-d	Performs a discovery and then exit.
-f *disc:session*	Specifies the Ethernet frame types for PPPoE discovery and session frames.
-h	Shows help information.
File Name: pppoe	**Directory:** /usr/sbin/ **Type:** External

pppoe-server

UNIX Shell: All primary shells (bash, ash, tcsh)

Function	Starts the user-space server for PPPoE.
Syntax	pppoe-server [options...]

-F	Specifies the program shouldn't be forked and become a daemon.
-I *interface*	Specifies the Ethernet interface to use.
-T *timeout*	Specifies the program should exit if no session traffic is detected for timeout.
-C *value*	Specifies which name to report as the access concentrator name.
-m *value*	Causes the program to clamp the TCP maximum segment size at the specified value.
-L *address*	Specifies the local IP address.
-R *address*	Specifies the remote IP address.
-N *number*	Allows at most number concurrent PPPoE sessions (default is 64).
-f *disc:session*	Specifies the Ethernet frame types for PPPoE discovery and session frames.
-h	Shows help information.

File Name: `pppoe-server` **Directory:** /usr/sbin/ **Type:** External

pppoe-sniff

UNIX Shell: All primary shells (bash, ash, tcsh)

Function	Examines network for non-standard PPPoE frames.
Syntax	pppoe-sniff [options...]

-I *interface*	Specifies the Ethernet interface to use.
-V	Shows version information.

File Name: `pppoe-sniff` **Directory:** /usr/sbin/ **Type:** External

pppstats

UNIX Shell: All primary shells (bash, ash, tcsh)

Function	Shows PPP-related statistics for a PPP-interface. The statistics are shown since the last report.
Syntax	pppstats [options...] { *interface* }

-a	Shows absolute values instead of deltas. Shown since the link was initiated.
-c *count*	Specifies the number of times the statistics are shown (default is 1).
-r	Shows statistics about compression ratio of the packet compression algorithm in use.
-v	Shows statistics related to the Van Jacobson TCP header compression algorithm.
-w *time*	Specifies the time between updates of the screen (default is 5 sec).
-z	Shows statistics indicating the performance of the packet compression algorithm in use.
interface	Specifies the interface to use (default is ppp0).

File Name: `pppstats` **Directory:** /usr/sbin/ **Type:** External

ppp-watch

UNIX Shell: All primary shells (bash, ash, tcsh)

Function	Runs from within an `ifup-ppp` script that allows PPP interfaces to act like other interfaces.
Syntax	ppp-watch *interface interface* [boot]

boot	Calls ppp-watch during boot time and times out if no PPP connection is found.
interface	Specifies the PPP interface to start up.

File Name: `ppp-watch` **Directory:** /sbin/ **Type:** External

pqlist

UNIX Shell: All primary shells (bash, ash, tcsh)

Function	Shows print queues on a NetWare server.
Syntax	pqlist [options...] { *pattern* }

-C	Turns off the conversion to uppercase for passwords.
-h	Shows help information.
-P *password*	Specifies the password to use.
-n	Specifies that no password is used — should be used if no password is required.
-S *server*	Specifies the NetWare file server to use.

continued

-U *username*	Specifies the NetWare username to use when logging into the server.		
pattern	Shows only specified queues.		
File Name: `pqlist`	**Directory:** /usr/bin/	**Type:**	External

pqrm

UNIX Shell: All primary shells (bash, ash, tcsh)

Function	Removes print requests from a NetWare print queue.
Syntax	pqrm [options...] *queue requests...*

-C	Sets password conversion to uppercase off.		
-h	Shows help information.		
-n	Specifies the share doesn't require a password.		
-P *password*	Sets the password to use.		
-S *server*	Sets the name of the server to use.		
-U *username*	Sets the username to use to connect to NetWare server if other than UNIX username.		
queue	Specifies the queue to use. Wildcards are not valid.		
request	Specifies the print request to remove.		
File Name: `pqrm`	**Directory:** /usr/bin/	**Type:**	External
pqrm -S printserver -U ucg workqueue 3	Deletes job 3 in queue workqueue - this prompts for the password.		

pqstat

UNIX Shell: All primary shells (bash, ash, tcsh)

Function	Shows the specified NetWare print queue, showing the jobs being processed.
Syntax	pqstat [options...] *queue { count }*

-C	Disables password conversion to uppercase. Most servers require uppercase.		
-h	Shows help information.		
-n	Mounts shares not requiring a password to login. Requests a password.		
-P *password*	Specifies the password on the command line instead of in a script.		
-S *server*	Specifies the server on which to find the print queue.		
-U *userID*	Specifies your NetWare user ID. Not required if your UNIX and NetWare User IDs match.		
queue	Specifies the print queue to show.		
count	Specifies the amount of entries to show (defaul is to show all entries).		
File Name: `pqstat`	**Directory:** /usr/bin/	**Type:**	External

praliases

UNIX Shell: All primary shells (bash, ash, tcsh)

Function	Shows system mail aliases. If no key is specified all keys and their values are shown.
Syntax	praliases [options...] *{ keys... }*

-f *file*	Reads specified alias file instead of the default sendmail system alias file.		
-C *file*	Reads specified file instead of the sendmail alias file.		
keys...	Finds a specific alias key.		
File Name: `praliases`	**Directory:** /usr/sbin/	**Type:**	External

printmail

UNIX Shell: A shell (ash, bsh)

Function	Shows all mails in your mailbox.
Syntax	printmail [-p] *{ file }*

-p	Messages are separated by a form feed instead of a line of dashes.		
file	Specifies the file to use instead of the default mailbox.		
File Name: `printmail`	**Directory:** /usr/bin/	**Type:**	Script

privatepw

UNIX Shell: All primary shells (bash, ash, tcsh)

Function	Administers WU-FTPD group access file information.
Syntax	privatepw [options...] *{ group }*

-c	Creates a new ftpgroups file.
-d	Deletes the specified access group's information from the group file.
-g *group*	Sets the real system group to group specified.

continued

-f *file*	Specifies the file to use for all updates.
-l	Shows the contents of the appropriate group file.
-?	Shows help information.
-V	Shows version and copyright information.
group	Specifies group to act on.
File Name: `privatepw`	**Directory:** /usr/sbin/ — **Type:** External

ps2ascii

UNIX Shell: A shell (ash, bsh)

Function	A Ghostscript converter from PostScript or PDF to ASCII format.
Syntax	ps2ascii { *input.ps* } { *output.txt* } ps2ascii *input.pdf* { *output.txt* }

input.ps	Specifies the PostScript file to convert.
input.pdf	Specifies the PDF file to convert.
output.txt	Specifies the output file.
File Name: `ps2ascii`	**Directory:** /usr/bin/ — **Type:** Script

ps2epsi

UNIX Shell: A shell (ash, bsh)

Function	Converts a PostScript file and creates a new file in Adobe's Encapsulated PostScript Interchange format.
Syntax	ps2epsi *input.ps* { *outputfile* }

infile	Specifies which PostScript file to convert.
outfile	Specifies the output file use .epsi for UNIX and .epi for DOS.
File Name: `ps2epsi`	**Directory:** /usr/bin/ — **Type:** Script

ps2pdf

UNIX Shell: A shell (ash, bsh)

Function	Converts a PostScript file into a file in Adobe Portable Document Format.
Syntax	ps2pdf [options...] *infile.ps outfile.pdf*

-dCompatibilityLevel=1.1	Specifies the output to be in PDF 1.1 format and compatible with Acrobat 2.x. Please see `gs` for other options.
infile	Specifies the PostScript file to convert.
outfile	Specifies the output file.
File Name: `ps2pdf`	**Directory:** /usr/bin/ — **Type:** Script

psbanner

UNIX Shell: All primary shells (bash, ash, tcsh)

Function	Prints a PostScript banner on a fixed-size font printer.
Syntax	psbanner [options...]

-w*width*	Sets the page width in characters (default is 132).
-l*length*	Sets the page length in lines (default is 60).
-P*printer*	Specifies the printer queue for banner information.
-L*bannername*	Specifies the banner name used as the main name.
-n*loginname*	Specifies the login name.
-h*host*	Specifies the hostname.
-J*jobtitle*	Specifies the string used on the banner as the main title.
-C*class*	Specifies the class string.
-?*value*	Ignores all other options and arguments provided by LPRng.
all	Uses all options for `psbanner`.
File Name: `psbanner`	**Directory:** /usr/libexec/filters/ — **Type:** External

pserver

UNIX Shell:	All primary shells (bash, ash, tcsh)
Function	Connects to a NetWare server's print queues and sends the incoming print jobs to the Linux printing system.
Syntax	pserver [options...]

-h	Shows help information.
-S *server*	Specifies which server to use.
-U *user*	Specifies the print server name at the print server you want to use at the moment.
-P *password*	Specifies the password to use for the print server at the server.
-n	Specifies that no password is used — should be used if no password is required.
-C	Turns off the conversion to uppercase for passwords.
-q *queue name*	Specifies the name of the print queue you want to service.
-c *command*	Specifies the command that is run for each job (default is `lpr`).
-j *job type*	Specifies the number of the form the job should be printed on (default is 1).
-d	Doesn't daemonize (go to sleep).
-t *time*	Specifies the time for the server to wait between two requests (default is 30 sec).

File Name:	`pserver`	**Directory:**	/usr/bin/	**Type:**	External

psql

UNIX Shell:	All primary shells (bash, ash, tcsh)
Function	Starts Postgres interactive terminal.
Syntax	psql [options...] *{ database } { user }*

-a	Shows all the lines to the screen as they are read.
-A	Switches to unaligned output mode.
-c *query*	Specifies a query string to execute.
-d *database*	Specifies the database to connect to.
-e	Shows all queries that are sent to the back end.
-E	Shows the actual queries generated by \d and other backslash commands.
-f *file*	Uses the file as the source of queries instead of reading queries interactively.
-F *separator*	Uses the separator as the field separator.
-h *host*	Specifies the host to connect to.
-H	Activates HTML tabular output.
-l	Shows all available databases.
-o *file*	Puts all query output into file.
-p *port*	Specifies the port to connect to.
-P *value*	Allows specifying printing options in the style of \pset on the command line.
-q	Uses the quiet mode.
-R *separator*	Uses separator as the record separator.
-s	Runs in single-step mode.
-S	Runs in single-line mode where a new line terminates a query, as a semicolon does.
-t	Turns of showing of column names and result row count footers and so forth.
-T *options*	Allows specifying options to be placed within the HTML table tag.
-u	Prompts for username and password.
-U *user*	Specifies the user to connect as.
-v *assignment*	Performs a variable assignment.
-V	Shows version information.
-W	Prompts for a password.
-x	Activates extended row format mode.
-X	Specifies the `~/.psqlrc` file shouldn't be read.
-?	Shows help information.
database	Specifies the database to use.
user	Specifies the user to log in as.

File Name:	`psql`	**Directory:**	/usr/bin/	**Type:**	External

pstree

UNIX Shell:	All primary shells (bash, ash, tcsh)
Function	Shows the current processes in a tree format.
Syntax	pstree [options...] *{ root }*

-a	Shows the command-line arguments.
-c	Doesn't show identical subtrees in a short format.
-G	Sets VT100 terminal line-drawing characters.
-h	Highlights the current process.
-H*PID*	Highlights the specified process.
-l	Shows long lines.
-n	Sorts processes by PID instead of by name.
-p	Shows the PIDs.
-u	Shows the UIDs when they change.
-U	Sets UTF-8 line-drawing characters.
-V	Shows version information.
root	Specifies the root of the tree — can be a PID or a username (default is `init`).

File Name:	Directory:	Type:
`pstree`	/usr/bin/	External

pstree	Shows the whole process tree.

pstruct, c2ph

UNIX Shell:	All primary shells (bash, ash, tcsh)
Function	Translates C to Perl code (union and structure declarations).
Syntax	c2ph [options...] [variable=*value*] *{ files... }*

-w	Wide format, equals type_width = 45, member_width = 35, offset = 8.
-x	Hexadecimal format, equals offset_fmt = x, offset_width = 08, size_fmt = x, size_width = 04.
-n	Doesn't generate perl code. This is the default when started as `pstruct`.
-p	Generates Perl code.
-v	Same as -p except that it uses C declarations for comments.
-i	Doesn't recompute sizes for intrinsic data types.
-a	Dumps information on intrinsics also.
-t	Traces executions.
-d	Verbose mode. Shows more debug information.
-slist	Specifies a list of structures in a comma-separated list.
variable=*value*	Transfers values.
files...	Specifies file to cat on.

File Name:	Directory:	Type:
`pstruct`	/usr/bin/	External

pswrap

UNIX Shell:	All primary shells (bash, ash, tcsh)
Function	Creates wraps that send PostScript language code to the PostScript Interpreter.
Syntax	pswrap [options...] *{ file }*

-a	Creates ANSI C prototypes for procedure definitions.
-p	Makes every string passed by wraps padded so data objects start on 4-byte boundary.
-h *file*	Creates a file that contains extern declarations for non-static wraps.
-o *file*	Specifies the file wherein to put the created wrap procedures.
-r	Enables the wraps to be called recursively or by more than one thread.
-s *length*	Specifies the max length of a PostScript string.
file	Specifies the input file to use.

File Name:	Directory:	Type:
`pswrap`	/usr/X11R6/bin/	External

ptx

ptx	UNIX Shell:	All primary shells (bash, ash, tcsh)
Function	Makes a permuted index of the specified file's contents.	
Syntax	ptx [options...] *{ inputfile } { outputfile }*	

-A	Shows automatically generated references.
-C	Shows copyright and copying conditions.
-G	Behaves like the System V's `ptx` command.
-F *string*	Specifies the string for flagging line truncations.
-M *name*	Specifies the macro name to use (default is "xx").
-O	Generates as `roff` directives.
-R	Puts the references at the right side.
-S *expression*	Specifies the regular expression for end of lines or end of sentences.
-T	Generates as `TeX` directives.
-W *expression*	Uses the specified regular expression to match each keyword.
-b *file*	Puts word break characters in the specified file.
-f	Runs in no case-sensitive mode.
-g *size*	Specifies the gap column size between fields.
-i *file*	Specifies the file to read word-ignore list from.
-o *file*	Specifies the file to read word-read list from.
-r	Does a reference on the first field of each line.
-w *size*	Specifies the output width in columns between references.
--help	Shows help information.
--version	Shows version information.
inputfile	Specifies the file to use. Uses STDIN if typed "-" or not used at all.
outputfile	Specifies the file to write to. Can only be used when using the -G option.
File Name: `ptx`	**Directory:** /usr/bin/ **Type:** External

pump

pump	UNIX Shell:	All primary shells (bash, ash, tcsh)
Function	A network interface manager daemon working with the DHCP or BOOTP protocol.	
Syntax	pump [options...]	

-c *file*	Specifies the configuration file to use. If not specified, pump uses `/etc/pump.conf`.
-h *host*	Specifies hostname to request.
-i *interface*	Specifies the interface to configure.
-k	Disables all interfaces and stops the daemon.
-l *count*	Specifies the length of time in hours to have the address.
-r	Frees the interface.
-R	Initiates immediate lease renewal.
-s	Shows the status of the interface.
-d	Disable updating `resolve.conf`.
--lookup-hostname	Enables hostname and domain lookup in DNS.
-?	Shows help information.
--usage	Shows short help information.
	The following options are used in a configuration file specified by -c:
device *device*	Specifies options for the specified device.
	Note:The list of options must start with { and end with }.
domainsearch *path*	Specifies the DNS search path.
nonisdomain	Disables setting a new NIS domain. This only works within `device`.
nodns	Disables creation of a new `/etc/resolv.conf`. This only works within `device`.
retries *count*	Retries the DHCP phases count times.
timeout *count*	Specifies the timelimit for each phase to count seconds.
script *executable file*	Runs the file specified when events occur, with arguments depending on the situation .
File Name: `pump`	**Directory:** /sbin/ **Type:** External

pwck

pwck	UNIX Shell:	All primary shells (bash, ash, tcsh)

Function	Verifies the integrity of password files.				
Syntax	pwck [-r] { *password shadow* }				
-r	Sets read-only mode — all questions about changes are silently answered no.				
password	Specifies an optional file instead of the default `/etc/passwd`.				
shadow	Specifies an optional file instead of the default `/etc/shadow`.				
File Name:	`pwck`	**Directory:**	/usr/sbin/	**Type:**	External

pwconv

pwconv	UNIX Shell:	All primary shells (bash, ash, tcsh)

Function	Modifies or creates the shadow password file `/etc/shadow` from the `passwd` password file.				
Syntax	pwconv				
File Name:	`pwconv`	**Directory:**	/usr/sbin/	**Type:**	External

pwunconv

pwunconv	UNIX Shell:	All primary shells (bash, ash, tcsh)

Function	Converts from shadow password file to standard passwd file.				
Syntax	pwunconv				
File Name:	`pwunconv`	**Directory:**	/usr/sbin/	**Type:**	External
Warning:	This isn't recommended because the system is less secure.				

raid0run

raid0run	UNIX Shell:	All primary shells (bash, ash, tcsh)

Function	Starts up old RAID0 or LINEAR arrays.				
Syntax	raid0run [options...] *devices...*				
-c *file*	Specifies the configuration file to use (default is `/etc/raidtab`).				
-a	Starts up all nonpersistent RAID0 and LINEAR arrays defined in the config file.				
-v	Shows version information.				
-h	Shows help information.				
devices...	Specifies the RAID device to run `/dev/md?`.				
File Name:	`raid0run`	**Directory:**	/sbin/	**Type:**	External
raid0run /dev/md0	Starts `/dev/md0` RAID device.				

raidstart

raidstart	UNIX Shell:	All primary shells (bash, ash, tcsh)

Function	Starts existing RAID devices.				
Syntax	raidstart [options...] *raiddevices...*				
-a	Starts all devices in the configuration file.				
-c *file*	Specifies the configuration file (default is `/etc/raidtab`).				
-h	Shows help information.				
-V	Shows version information.				
raiddevices...	Specifies the device to start. Can't be used with -a.				
File Name:	`raidstart`	**Directory:**	/sbin/	**Type:**	External
raidstart /dev/md2	Starts the RAID device `/dev/md2`.				

raidstop

raidstop	UNIX Shell:	All primary shells (bash, ash, tcsh)

Function	Stops an existing RAID device.
Syntax	raidstop [options...] *raiddevices...*
-a	Stops all active RAID devices in the configuration file.
-c *file*	Specifies the configuration file (default is `/etc/raidtab`).
-h	Shows help information.

continued

-V	Shows version information.
raiddevices...	Specifies the device to stop. Can't be used with -a.
File Name: `raidstop`	**Directory:** /sbin/ **Type:** External

ramsize

UNIX Shell: All primary shells (bash, ash, tcsh)

Function	Sets the RAM disk size for the system, and is equivalent to `rdev -r`.
Syntax	ramsize [-o *value*] { *image size offset* }

-o *value*	Specifies the byte offset.
image	Specifies a bootable Linux kernel image.
size	Specifies the RAM disk size in kilobytes.
offset	Specifies an offset for the kernel image.
File Name: `ramsize`	**Directory:** /usr/sbin/ **Type:** External

random

UNIX Shell: A shell (ash, bsh)

Function	Snapshots a random state, then reloads that state at boot time a random number generator.
Syntax	random { *ACTION* }

ACTION	**Select only one of the following actions:**
start	Starts the generator.
stop	Stops the generator and saves the random state.
status	Shows if the random state exists.
restart	Restarts the system with the new state.
reload	Reloads the random state.
File Name: `random`	**Directory:** /etc/rc.d/init.d/ **Type:** Script

rarp

UNIX Shell: All primary shells (bash, ash, tcsh)

Function	Alters the information in the kernels RARP table.
Syntax	rarp -a rarp -d rarp [-t] –s

-a	Shows all current entries in the RARP table.
-d *hostname*	Erases all RARP entries for the specified host.
-s *hostname hardwareadress*	Creates a RARP address map with the specified address for the specified host.
-t *class*	Specifies the class of entries to check or set (default is ether).
	The verbose mode can be used together with both the -d and -s options.
-v	Verbose mode. Shows more information.
-V	Shows version information.
-h	Shows help information.
File Name: `rarp`	**Directory:** /sbin/ **Type:** External

raw

UNIX Shell: All primary shells (bash, ash, tcsh)

Function	Binds a Linux raw character device.
Syntax	raw *rawdevice major minor* raw *rawdevice blockdevice* raw options... { *rawdevice* }

-q	Queries an existing binding instead of setting a new one.
-a	Queries all bound raw devices, if used with -q option.
-h	Shows help information.
rawdevice	Specifies the raw device to use
major	Specifies the major number of the raw device.
minor	Specifies the minor number of the raw device.
blockdevice	Specifies the block device to use.
File Name: `raw`	**Directory:** /usr/bin/ **Type:** External

rb

UNIX Shell:	All primary shells (bash, ash, tcsh)
Function	Receives files using YMODEM, XMODEM, and ZMODEM protocols.
Syntax	rb [options...]

-+	Appends received data to an existing file.
-a	Converts files to UNIX conventions by stripping carriage returns.
-b	Uses binary transfers.
-c	Uses 16-bit CRC over XMODEM.
-C	Allows the execution of commands remotely.
-e	Enables the use of escape control characters over ZMODEM.
-E	Renames any existing files.
-p	Protects any existing files with the same name.
-q	Uses quiet mode.
-r	Resumes interrupted file transfers.
-R	Enters more restricted mode.
-t *timeout*	Changes the timeout to timeout.
-U	Turns off restricted mode.
-v	Verbose mode shows more information.
-B *size*	Specifies the buffer size.
-D	Outputs file data to `/dev/null`.
--delay-startup *seconds*	Waits seconds before doing anything.
-E	Renames incoming files if the files exist.
-h	Shows help information.
-m *number*	Stops transmission if BPS rate drops down under number.
-M *number*	Stops transmission if number of seconds specified is exceeded.
--o-sync	Opens output files in synchronous write mode.
-s *value*	Stops transmission at value of time (format is HH:MM).
-S	Requests time synch packet from the sender.
--syslog[=off]	Turns `syslog` on or off.
--tcp-client *host:port*	Acts as a TCP/IP client and connects to host or IP address and port.
--tcp-server	Acts as a TCP/IP server.
-w*value*	Sets window size to value.
-X	Uses the XMODEM protocol for file transfers.
-y	Overwrites an existing file.
--ymodem	Uses the YMODEM protocol for file transfers.
-Z	Uses the ZMODEM protocol for file transfers.

File Name:	`rb`	**Directory:**	/usr/bin/	**Type:**	External

rc

UNIX Shell:	Bash shell (bash)
Function	Starts and stops services when the system runlevel changes.
Syntax	rc *currentlevel newlevel*

currentlevel	Specifies the current runlevel on the system.
newlevel	Specifies the run level to change to.

File Name:	`rc`	**Directory:**	/etc/	**Type:**	Script
Note:	This script should normally not be used by users.				

rcs

UNIX Shell:	All primary shells (bash, ash, tcsh)
Function	Creates and or changes the attributes of RCS files.
Syntax	rcs options... *files...*

-i	Creates and initializes a new RCS file, but doesn't create any revision.
-a *login*	Appends the login names that appear in a comma-separated list.
-A *file*	Appends the access list of the specified old file to the access list of the RCS.
-e *login*	Erases any login names within the specified comma-separated login list.
-b *revision*	Sets the default branch to the specified revision.
-c *string*	Sets the comment leader to the specified string.

continued

-k *string*	Sets the default keyword substitution to the specified sub string.
-l *revision*	Locks the file revision to the specified revision.
-u *revision*	Unlocks the file revision to the specified revision.
-L	Sets the locking type to `strict`.
-U	Sets the locking type to `non-strict`.
-m *rev:msg*	Replaces the revisions log message with the specified revision and another message.
-M	Blocks sending a mail when breaking into somebody else's lock.
-n *name* [:rev]	Associates the specified symbolic name with the branch and any specified revision.
-N *name* [:rev]	Same as `-n` except overrides previously set name assignments.
-o *range*	Erases specified revision's. Range is specified with startrevision:stoprevision.
-q	Doesn't print any diagnostics. Quiet mode.
-I	Interactive mode.
-s *state* [:rev]	Sets the specified state attribute and any specified revision.
-t *file*	Writes the text in the specified file into the contents of the RCS file.
-t *-string*	Writes the text in the specified string into the contents of the RCS file.
-T	Preserves the modification time stamp on the RCS file unless a revision is erased.
-V	Shows version information.
-V *n*	Emulates the specified RCS version.
-x *suffix*	Uses suffixes to select out RCS files.
-z *timezone*	Uses the specified time zone as the default.
files...	Specifies the file or files that is created or modified.

File Name:	`rcs`	**Directory:**	/usr/bin/	**Type:**	External
Note:	A system crash may leave a RCS trash file. Remove this file if you receive the warning that the RCS file is in use.				

rcsclean

UNIX Shell: All primary shells (bash, ash, tcsh)

Function	Removes files based upon revision differences. If there is no difference, it removes the working file.
Syntax	rcsclean [options...] *{ files... }*

-k *keyword*	Uses keyword substitution when the comparison for revision is captured.
-n *{ revision }*	Shows what the program, at the set revision level, would have done.
-q *{ revision }*	Activates quiet mode. Shows less information for the set revision level.
-r *{ revision }*	Specifies the revision to use for comparison.
-T	Keeps the modification time of the RCS file even if the file changes.
-u *{ revision }*	Unlocks the specified revision if there is no revision difference found.
-V	Shows version information.
-V*version*	Emulates the specified RCS version.
-x *suffix*	Characterizes the files with the specified suffixes.
-z *timezone*	Specifies the date output format to use for the keyword option.
files...	Specifies the files to use.

File Name:	`rcsclean`	**Directory:**	/usr/bin/	**Type:**	External

rcsdiff

UNIX Shell: All primary shells (bash, ash, tcsh)

Function	Compares different versions of RCS files using the `diff` command.
Syntax	rcsdiff [options...] *files...*

-q	Suppresses any diagnostic output. Quiet mode.
-r*revision*	Selects the revision. Select two revisions by separating the -rs with a space.
-k*keyword*	Affects the keyword substitution that is specified when extracting revisions.
-T	Saves the modification time of the RCS file even if the file changes. Use carefully.
-V*num*	Imitates that the RCS version is the specified value. Values 3, 4, or 5 are valid.
-x*suffix*	Specifies the suffixes to explain RCS files.
-z*timezone*	Specifies the date output format to use for the keyword option.
	Note: `rcsdiff` also supports all of the `diff` command options.
files...	Specifies the RCS files that are compared. Separate these by a space.

File Name:	`rcsdiff`	**Directory:**	/usr/bin/	**Type:**	External
rcsdiff -r2 -r3 multiple			Compares the specified file.		

rcsmerge

UNIX Shell:	All primary shells (bash, ash, tcsh)
Function	Merges two RCS files by finding the differences between them, then creating a new file.
Syntax	rcsmerge [options...] *file1* { *file2* } { *file3* }

-A	Merges changes from file1 to file2 and stores it in file3. Outputs `diff3`-type conflicts.
-E	Shows conflicts in less verbose mode than -A (is default).
-e	Disables warnings about conflicts totally.
-k*keyword*	Uses the specified keyword substitution when compare and merge takes place.
	You must specify at least one, at the most two, of these three options:
-p*revision*	Sends results to STDIN instead of overwriting the working file of the set revision.
-q*revision*	Runs quietly. Doesn't show any diagnostics at all about the specified revision.
-r*revision*	Merges with respect to the specified revision — if none is specified, then the latest revision.
-T	Is for compatibility with other RCS commands only.
-V	Shows version information.
-V*version*	Emulates the specified RCS version.
-x*suffix*	Specifies the suffix to be used to explain RCS files.
-z*timezone*	Specifies the date output format to use for the keyword substitution.
file1	Specifies the file that is checked for changes before producing an output file
file2	Specifies a second source file that is compared to the first before a merge.
file3	Specifies a third source file that is compared to the others before a merge.

File Name:	`rcsmerge`	**Directory:**	/usr/bin/	**Type:**	External

rcsmerge -p -r2.8 -r3.4 ucg_rules.txt	Compares and merges the different versions of ucg_rules.txt and overwrites the file with the new information.

rcvdist

UNIX Shell:	All primary shells (bash, ash, tcsh)
Function	Forwards mail to other addresses. It reads mail from STDIN.
Syntax	rcvdist [options...] [postprocoptions...] *addresses...*

-form *file*	Specifies an alternative forms file.
-version	Shows version information.
-help	Shows help information.
postprocoptions...	Specifies options for `postproc`.
addresses...	Is one or more address to forward mail to.

File Name:	`rcvdist`	**Directory:**	/usr/lib/nmh/	**Type:**	External

rcvpack

UNIX Shell:	All primary shells (bash, ash, tcsh)
Function	Creates a copy of the message and saves it in the specified file.
Syntax	rcvpack *file* [option]

-mbox	Specifies the messages are separated using mbox-style delimiters (is default).
-mmdf	Specifies the messages are separated using mmdf-style delimiters.
-version	Shows version information.
-help	Shows help information.
file	Specifies the file to use.

File Name:	`rcvpack`	**Directory:**	/usr/lib/nmh/	**Type:**	External

rcvstore

UNIX Shell:	All primary shells (bash, ash, tcsh)
Function	Adds messages from STDIN into a mailbox folder.
Syntax	rcvstore [+*folder*] [options...]

-create	Enables creation of a folder if it doesn't exist.
-nocreate	Disables creation for non-existing folders.
-unseen	Adds a messages to each sequence where the profile is named as Unseen-Sequence.
-nounseen	Disables the unseen option.
-zero	Zeroes old sequences.
-nozero	Doesn't zero old sequences.
-public	Specifies the sequences to be public.

continued

-nopublic	Specifies the sequences to be private.		
-sequence *names...*	Adds the messages to the name of the additional sequences.		
-version	Shows version information.		
-help	Shows help information.		
+*folder*	Specifies the mailbox folder to use.		
File Name: `rcvstore`	**Directory:** /usr/lib/nmh/	**Type:**	External

rcvtty

UNIX Shell: All primary shells (bash, ash, tcsh)

Function	Reports a new mail. Runs a command with the message as its STDIN, and shows the results on the screen.
Syntax	rcvtty *{ command } { options... }*

-form *file*	Overrides the default output format and uses the format specified in file instead.		
-format *string*	Overrides the default output format and uses the format specified in string instead.		
-width *columns*	Specifies the width of the scan line.		
-bell	Activates the terminal bell after output (is default).		
-nobell	Turns off the terminal bell after output.		
-newline	Adds a new line before the message output (is default).		
-nonewline	Turns off the new line before the message output.		
-biff	Uses the notification status set by the command `biff`.		
-version	Shows version information.		
-help	Shows help information.		
command	Specifies the command to use.		
File Name: `rcvtty`	**Directory:** /usr/lib/nmh/	**Type:**	External

rdate

UNIX Shell: All primary shells (bash, ash, tcsh)

Function	Gets the time from a specified remote system and sets or shows it on the local system.
Syntax	rdate [option] *{ hosts... }*

-p	Shows the time from the other system.		
-s	Sets the time on the local system.		
hosts...	Specifies the name or IP address of the remote system.		
File Name: `rdate`	**Directory:** /usr/bin/	**Type:**	External

rdev

UNIX Shell: All primary shells (bash, ash, tcsh)

Function	Shows or sets the root device for bootable Linux kernel images.
Syntax	rdev [options...] *{ image }* rdev [options...] *image { value } { offset }* rdev [options...] *image { device } { offset }*

-r	Enables `rdev` to act as the command `ramsize`.		
-R	Enables `rdev` to act as the command `rootflags`.		
-s	Enables `rdev` to act as the command `swapdev`.		
-v	Enables `rdev` to act as the command `vidmode`.		
-h	Shows help information.		
-o *value*	Specifies the byte offset.		
image	Specifies a bootable Linux kernel image. You may select one of these two options:		
value	Specifies the settings of the specified image.		
device	Specifies the root device to set to the image.		
offset	Specifies an offset for the kernel image.		
File Name: `rdev`	**Directory:** /usr/sbin/	**Type:**	External

rdev vmlinuz-2.2.17	Shows what root device the specified kernel image has.
rdev vmlinuz-2.2.17 /dev/hda1	Specifies that /dev/hda1 should be the root device for the specified kernel.

rdistd

rdistd	UNIX Shell:	All primary shells (bash, ash, tcsh)

Function	Is used by the `rdist` command as a remote file distribution server program.
Syntax	rdistd [options...]

-S	Specifies the `rdistd` isn't accidentally started. Required.
-D	Shows debug information. Messages are logged via `syslog`.
-V	Shows version information. With this option, you don't need the -S option.

File Name:	`rdistd`	**Directory:**	/sbin/	**Type:**	External

rdjpgcom

rdjpgcom	UNIX Shell:	All primary shells (bash, ash, tcsh)

Function	Shows the embedded comments in JPEG files.
Syntax	rdjpgcom [-verbose] { *file* }

-verbose	Verbose mode. Shows more information.
file	Specifies the file to use.

File Name:	`rdjpgcom`	**Directory:**	/usr/bin/	**Type:**	External

readlink

readlink	UNIX Shell:	All primary shells (bash, ash, tcsh)

Function	Shows the destination name of a symbolic link.
Syntax	readlink [option] { *file* }

--help	Shows help information.
--version	Shows version information.
file	Specifies the pathname to the symbolic link.

File Name:	`readlink`	**Directory:**	/usr/bin/	**Type:**	External

readprofile

readprofile	UNIX Shell:	All primary shells (bash, ash, tcsh)

Function	Shows kernel profile information to STDOUT in a three-column table if the profile buffer exists.
Syntax	readprofile [options...]

-m *mapfile*	Specifies a system mapfile to use (default is `/usr/src/linux/System.map`).
-p *profile*	Specifies another profiling buffer (default is `/proc/profile`).
-i	Shows information about the resolution of the profiling buffer only.
-t	Cleans up the output. Shows only decimal number.
-a	Shows all symbols even if there are zero report ticks in the mapfile.
-r	Specifies a reset of the profiling buffer. For root only.
-v	Verbose mode. Shows more information.
-V	Shows version information.

File Name:	`readprofile`	**Directory:**	/usr/sbin/	**Type:**	External

rec

rec	UNIX Shell:	All primary shells (bash, ash, tcsh)

Function	Records audio.
Syntax	rec [options...] *file*

-c *NR*	Specifies the number of channels are recorded into the output file.
-d *device*	Defines a device to play the output file to.
-f *format*	Specifies the bit format to use for the sample.
s	Specifies the bit format is signed linear.
u	Specifies the bit format is unsigned linear.
U	Specifies the bit format is U-law (U.S. logarithmic telephone sound compression).
A	Specifies the bit format is A-law (same as U-law but International standard).
a	Specifies the bit format is ADPCM (average sound compression/decode time).
g	Specifies the bit format is GSM (European telephone sound compression).
-r *rate*	Specifies the sample rate for the audio data.

continued

-s *size*	Interprets the size of the sample.		
b	Specifies the sample data will be in bytes.		
w	Specifies the sample data will be in 16-bit words.		
l	Specifies the sample data will be in 32-bit longwords.		
f	Specifies the sample data will be in 32-bit floats (native machine format).		
d	Specifies the sample data will be in 64-bit double floats (native machine format)		
D	Specifies the sample data will be in 80-bit IEEE floats (native machine format).		
-t *type*	Specifies which type of audio format to use.		
-v *volume*	Changes the level (amplitude) of the audio volume (<1.0 decreases, >1.0 increases).		
-x	Reverses the order of the byte sample. This only works with 16 & 32-bit data samples.		
-h	Shows help information.		
--version	Shows version information.		
file	Specifies the file to create that will contain the sound recording.		
File Name: `rec`	**Directory:** /usr/bin/	**Type:**	External
rec -f g -t wav ucgsong.wav	Records the ucgsong into wav formatted file using GSM sound compression.		

red

UNIX Shell: All primary shells (bash, ash, tcsh)

Function	A restricted version of `ed` and is often used to edit files automatically in a script.
Syntax	red [options...] *file*

	Uses same options as the command `ed`.		
File Name: `red`	**Directory:** /bin/	**Type:**	External
red filfan	The file filfan is edited.		

rename

UNIX Shell: All primary shells (bash, ash, tcsh)

Function	Renames multiple files by replacing strings.
Syntax	rename *string1 string2 files...*

string1	Specifies the string to be replaced.		
string2	Specifies the string that replaces string1.		
files...	Specifies the files to use.		
File Name: `rename`	**Directory:** /usr/bin/	**Type:**	External
rename .jpeg .jpg *.jpeg	Renames all your .jpeg files to .jpg.		

reset

UNIX Shell: All primary shells (bash, ash, tcsh)

Function	Restores a session's runtime parameters to default values.
Syntax	reset *variable*

variable	Specifies the variable to reset to default values.		
File Name: `reset`	**Directory:** /usr/bin/	**Type:**	External

resize2fs

UNIX Shell: All primary shells (bash, ash, tcsh)

Function	Resizes an ext2 file system on specified device altering the amount of blocks to size.
Syntax	resize2fs [options...] *device { size }*

-d *flags...*	Sets debug flag, 1 = Disk I/O, 2 = blocks moved, 8 = inodes moved, 16 = inode tables moved.		
-f	Overrides safety checks, continuing with file system resize operation.		
-F	Frees the buffer caches in the file system before starting.		
-p	Shows percentage completion bars for the operations.		
device	Specifies the device where the file system to resize exists.		
size	Sets the size of the blocks of the file system. This can't be larger than the partition.		
File Name: `resize2fs`	**Directory:** /sbin/	**Type:**	External
resize2fs /dev/hdb1	Maximizes the specified file system.		

restore, rrestore

restore, rrestore	UNIX Shell: All primary shells (bash, ash, tcsh)
Function	Restores files or file systems from a dump backup.
Syntax	restore option [options…] *{ files… }*

	The following options can't be combined:
-C	Compares the files from a dump with the files on the disk.
-i	Opens an interactive shell that allows you to use the following commands:
add *directory*	Specifies a directory to restore later on.
cd *directory*	Specifies a directory to use as current working directory.
delete *directory*	Specifies a directory not to restore later on.
extract	Restores all the directories specified with the add command.
help	Shows help information.
ls *{ directory }*	Shows the contents of the current directory or the directory specified.
pwd	Shows the current working directory.
quit	Exits the interactive shell directly without dealing with the extraction list.
setmodes	Sets the directories owner, modes, and times.
verbose	Shows `ls` output with inode numbers and shows file information when restoring.
-R	Continues a full restore that has been interrupted.
-r	Restores the file system to the current directory that is an empty file system.
-t	Lists files specified as they are on the backup.
-x	Restores the specified directory recursively. (If no file is specified for the two options above use the root as a file.)
	The following options can be combined and are used with the options above:
-b *blocksize*	Specifies the number of kilobytes to use for each dump record.
-c	Allows only old format dumps to restore from.
-D *filesystem*	Specifies the file system to use when using the –C option to validate the backup.
-f *file*	Specifies a file to use as backup. File could be a device or a dash – for STDIN.
-k	Authentication to remote tape servers is done with the Kerberos authentication module.
-h	Restores the directory instead of the files inside of it.
-m	Restores the files by their inode numbers instead of their filenames.
-M	Uses the multivolume feature.
-N	Shows a list of files that are restored. This doesn't perform a restore.
-s *fileNR*	Specifies a file number to start reading from in a backup.
-T *directory*	Specifies a directory to use as the temporary storage place.
-u	Removes old entries on the file system before restoring the ones on backup.
-v	Verbose mode. Shows more information.
-X *files…*	Specifies a file that contains the files to be restored. Works with –t or –x.
-y	Automatically answer yes if there is a bad block and restore wants to skip it.

File Name:	`restore`	**Directory:**	/sbin/	**Type:**	External

restore –C –D /dev/hda1 –f /dev/st0	Performs a backup check on the specified device from the specified tape device.
restore –r –f /dev/st0	Restores the dump backup on the specified device to the current working directory.
restore –t –f /dev/st0 /etc/passwd /etc/shadow	Shows where the specified files are on the backup.

rev

rev	UNIX Shell: All primary shells (bash, ash, tcsh)
Function	Reverses every line of a file or STDIN.
Syntax	rev *{ file }*

file	Specifies the file to reverse.

File Name:	`rev`	**Directory:**	/usr/bin/	**Type:**	External

revpath

revpath	UNIX Shell: All primary shells (bash, ash, tcsh)
Function	Generates a relative path.
Syntax	revpath *directory*

directory	Specifies the path to generate relative path information from.

File Name:	`revpath`	**Directory:**	/usr/bin/X11/	**Type:**	External

rexec

rexec		**UNIX Shell:**	All primary shells (bash, ash, tcsh)
Function	Runs commands on a remote host.		
Syntax	rexec [options…] *host command*		

-a	Doesn't set up an external channel for STDERR.
-b	Handles signals similar to the BSD `rsh` command.
-c	Doesn't turn off remote STDIN as the local closes.
-d	Shows debug information.
-h	Shows help information.
-n	Prevents automatic login.
-s	Prevents sending signals to remote process.
-l *username*	Specifies the username at the remote host (not with –n).
-p *password*	Specifies the password for the username at the remote host (not with –n).
host	Specifies the remote host.
command	Specifies the command to run at the remote host.

File Name:	`rexec`	**Directory:**	/usr/bin/	**Type:**	External

rlog

rlog		**UNIX Shell:**	All primary shells (bash, ash, tcsh)
Function	Shows information about RCS files and log messages.		
Syntax	rlog [options…] *files…*		

-L	Doesn't include the RCS files that have no locks set.
-R	Shows only the filename.
-h	Limits the output to paths, head, branch, access list, locks, symbolics, and suffix.
-t	Same as –h but also adds description text to output.
-N	Doesn't show symbolic names.
-b	Shows revision information on the branch, with the highest branch on the trunk.
-d*DATES*	Semicolon-separated list of ranges of dates, shows information about revisions in the ranges.
-l *{ LOCKERS }*	Shows information about locked revisions. Lockers is a comma-separated list of users.
-r *{ REVISIONS }*	Shows information about revisions in the comma-separated list of revisions.
-s *STATES*	Shows information about revisions if the state matches one in the list of states.
-w *{ LOGINS }*	Shows information about revisions if the logins match one in the list of logins.
-x *SUFFIXES*	Specifies the suffix to characterize RCS files.
-z *{ ZONE }*	Sets the timezone to use for dates. LT=local time, empty (is default) or +01.30.
-V	Shows version information.
-V *N*	Sets a fake RCS version N when generating logs.
files…	Specifies file(s) to act on.

File Name:	`rlog`	**Directory:**	/usr/bin/	**Type:**	External

rmail

rmail		**UNIX Shell:**	All primary shells (bash, ash, tcsh)
Function	Administers received mail from remote hosts through basic networking utilities.		
Syntax	rmail *users…*		

users…	Specifies a user or IP address.

File Name:	`rmail`	**Directory:**	/usr/bin/	**Type:**	External

rmmod

rmmod		**UNIX Shell:**	All primary shells (bash, ash, tcsh)
Function	Unloads specified loadable modules as long as they are not in use and not referred to by other modules.		
Syntax	rmmod [options…] *modules…*		

-a	Unloads all modules that can be automatically unloaded and are not in use.
-r	Unloads a stack of modules, requiring that the top module be specified.
-s	Disables all output to terminal by redirecting it to `syslog` instead.
modules…	Specifies the modules to unload.

File Name:	`rmmod`	**Directory:**	/sbin/	**Type:**	External

rootflags

UNIX Shell:	All primary shells (bash, ash, tcsh)
Function	Sets the flags used when mounting the root file system. The same as `rdev -R`.
Syntax	rootflags [-o *value*] { *image* } { *flags...* } { *offset* }
-o *value*	Specifies the byte offset.
image	Specifies a bootable Linux kernel image.
flags...	Mounts root file system in read-only if set to other than 0.
offset	Specifies an offset for the kernel image.
rootflags /vmlinux 1	Sets read-only status on `vmlinux`.

rotatelogs

UNIX Shell:	All primary shells (bash, ash, tcsh)
Function	Starts a new log file and saves the old.
Syntax	rotatelogs *logfile rotationtime*
logfile	Specifies the log file that you want to rotate.
rotationtime	Specifies the rotation time in seconds for the log file.
File Name: `rotatelogs`	**Directory:** /usr/sbin/ **Type:** External
rotatelogs accesslog 86400	Rotates the log named accesslog every 24 hours.

rpc.lockd

UNIX Shell:	All primary shells (bash, ash, tcsh)
Function	Starts the NFS lock manager (NLM). Useful for kernels that don't do this automatically.
Syntax	rpc.lockd
File Name: `rpc.lockd`	**Directory:** /sbin/ **Type:** External

rpc.rquotad

UNIX Shell:	All primary shells (bash, ash, tcsh)
Function	An RPC server that manages users of a local file system mounted over the NFS by reporting quotas.
Syntax	rpc.rquotad
File Name: `rpc.rquotad`	**Directory:** /usr/sbin/ **Type:** External
Note:	To show the quotas generated by `rpc.rquotad`, the command `quota` is used.

rpc.statd

UNIX Shell:	All primary shells (bash, ash, tcsh)
Function	Performs passive monitoring of the server and implements the reboot notification service used by rpc.lockd that performs file lock recovery functions in the event the server is rebooted.
Syntax	rpc.statd [-F]
-F	Runs in foreground (default is background).
File Name: `rpc.statd`	**Directory:** /usr/sbin/ **Type:** External

rpc.ypxfrd

UNIX Shell:	All primary shells (bash, ash, tcsh)
Function	Transfers NIS maps from the master server to the slave server.
Syntax	rpc.ypxfrd [options...]
--debug	Shows debug information.
-d *directory*	Specifies the directory to use (default is `/var/yp`).
-p *port*	Specifies the port to use.
--version	Shows version information.
File Name: `rpc.ypxfrd`	**Directory:** /usr/sbin/ **Type:** External

rpm		UNIX Shell:	All primary shells (bash, ash, tcsh)
Function	Adds and removes software on a system. It's also used to create software packages.		
Syntax	rpm [options...] *{ packages... }*		

--help	Shows help information.
--version	Shows version information.
-v	Verbose mode. Shows more information.
-vv	Verbose mode. Shows even more information.
--quiet	Quiet mode. Shows as little as possible - only error messages.
--rcfile *filelist*	A list of configurations files.
--root *directory*	Uses directory as the root directory for all operations.
--dbpath *directory*	Uses the RPM database in directory.
--justdb	Updates the database, not the file system.
--ftpproxy *host*	Uses host as an FTP proxy host.
--httpproxy *host*	Uses host as an HTTP proxy host.
--fptport *port*	The port for the FTP proxy host.
--httpport *port*	The port for the HTTP proxy host.
--pipe *command*	Sends the output from RPM to command.
-i	Installs a package.
-U	Upgrades or installs a package.
-F	Upgrades a package only if an older version exist.
	The following option works with -i, -U, and -F:.
--force	The same as --replacepkgs, --replacefiles, and --oldpackage.
-h	Shows 50 hash marks while the package is unpacked.
--oldpackage	Allows an upgrade to replace a newer package with older one.
--percent	Shows percentage while the package is unpacked.
--replacefiles	Allows an upgrade to replace files from other packages.
--replacepkgs	Installs a package even if it's already installed.
--allfiles	Installs all files even if they exist.
--nodeps	Doesn't do any dependency check.
--noscripts	Doesn't run any scripts.
--notriggers	Doesn't run any scripts that are triggered by this installation.
--ignoresize	Doesn't check whether it has sufficient disk space left before installing.
--excludepath *path*	Doesn't install files beginning with path.
--excludedocs	Doesn't install any documentation.
--includedocs	Installs documentation (is default).
--test	Checks whether the packed can be installed. Don't install it.
--ignorearch	Installs the package even if the architectures don't match.
--ignoreos	Installs the package even if it's the wrong OS.
--prefix *path*	Adds path to packages that can be relocated.
--relocate *oldpath=newpath*	Relocates a package from the old path to the new path if it can be relocated.
--badreloc	Is used together with --relocate to force relocation for packages that don't allow it.
--noorder	Doesn't reorder the package before installation.
-q	Queries package.
	The following options select package to query:
-a	Queries all installed packages.
--whatrequires *cap*	Queries packages that require cap capability.
--whatprovides *cap*	Queries packages that provides cap capability.
-f *file*	Shows all package that own file.
-g *group*	Shows all package that belong to group.
-p *packagefile*	Queries an uninstalled package in packagefile.
--specfile *specfile*	Queries specfile like a package.
--querybynumber *NR*	Shows entry NR in the database.
--triggeredby *pkg*	Shows packages that are trigged by package pkg.

continued

	The following options specify witch information to show:
-i	Shows package information.
-R	Shows all dependencies for this package.
--provides	Shows what capabilities a package has.
--changelog	Shows the change log for this package.
-l	Shows all files in the package.
-s	Shows the state for each file in the package.
-d	Shows only documentations files.
-c	Shows only configuration files.
--scripts	Shows all scripts that are used during installation and uninstallation.
--triggers	Shows any trigger scripts that exist.
--dump	Shows file information.
--last	Orders the output with the last installed package first.
--filesbypkg	Shows all files in each package.
--triggerscripts	The same as --triggers.
-V	Verifies a package.
--nofiles	Ignores any missing files.
--nomd5	Doesn't check the MD5 checksum.
--nopgp	Doesn't do any PGP check
--noscripts	Doesn't run any verify scripts.
--checksig *files...*	Checks the signature with PGP for package file.
-e	Uninstalls a package.
--allmatches	Removes all versions of a package that match.
--noscripts	Doesn't run any uninstallations scripts.
--notriggers	Doesn't run any scripts that are trigged by this script.
--nodeps	Doesn't check for any dependencies.
--test	Checks whether a removal is possible.
-b*option*	Builds a package using a spec file.
-t*option*	Builds a package using a spec file inside a compressed tar file.
	The following options can be used with either the -b or -t options shown above:
p	Runs the %prep stage.
l	Checks whether all the files exist.
c	Runs the %build stage.
i	Runs the %install stage.
b	Builds a binary package.
s	Builds the source package.
a	Builds both a binary and a source package.
	The following options can also be used:
--short-circuit	Skips all stages leading to a specified stage.
--timecheck *sec*	Includes files newer than sec (use 0 to disable).
--clean	Removes the build tree after the package is finished.
--rmsource	Removes the source after the package is finished.
--test	Is used for testing spec files.
--sign	Adds a PGP signature to the file.
--buildroot *dir*	Overrides BuildRoot with directory dir.
--target *platform*	Uses platform as the target platform.
--recompile *srcpkgs...*	Installs a source package, then compiles and installs it.
--rebuild *srcpkgs...*	The same as --recompile except that it also builds a binary package.
--resign *binpkgs...*	Generates a new signature for the packages.
--addsign *binpkgs...*	Generates a signature for the packages.
--rebuilddb	Rebuilds an RPM database.
--initdb	Creates a new RPM database.
--showrc	Shows options set in the configuration file.
packages...	Specifies one or more package to use.

continued

File Name:	rpm	Directory:	/bin/	Type:	External
rpm -i package.rpm			Installs the specified package.		
rpm -q -i package.rpm			Shows information about the `rpm` package		
rpm -V -vv package.rpm			Verifies the `rpm` package and show lots of information.		

rpm2cpio

UNIX Shell: All primary shells (bash, ash, tcsh)

Function	Converts a Red Hat Package (RPM) file to a cpio archive on STDOUT.
Syntax	rpm2cpio *{ file }*

file		Specifies the `RPM` file to convert. If none given, STDIN is used.			
File Name:	`rpm2cpio`	**Directory:**	/usr/bin/	**Type:**	External
rpm2cpio rpm-1.1-1.i386.rpm > rpm.cpio			Converts the RPM package to a cpio archive named `rpm.cpio`.		

rstart

UNIX Shell: A shell (ash, bsh)

Function	Executes programs on a remote computer using the Remote Execution Protocol.
Syntax	rstart [options...] *host command arguments...*

-c *context*	Specifies which environment to use. The default context is X window.
-g	Allows common commands to be started as generic commands.
-l *user*	Starts the command as the specified user. This option is passed to `rsh`.
-v	Verbose mode. Gives more information without disconnecting the program.
host	Specifies the hostname or IP address.
command	Specifies the command that is used.
arguments...	Specifies the valid arguments that are available for the command.

File Name:	`rstart`	**Directory:**	/usr/bin/X11/	**Type:**	Script
Tip:	For security reasons, I recommend you not to run `rsh/rstart` - please see `ssh` instead.				

rstartd

UNIX Shell: A shell (ash, bsh)

Function	A script that helps the use of working with a remote shell.
Syntax	rstartd

File Name:	`rstartd`	**Directory:**	/usr/X11R6/bin/	**Type:**	Script

rsync

UNIX Shell: All primary shells (bash, ash, tcsh)

Function	Copies files from or to a remote site.
Syntax	rsync [options...] *source host:destination* rsync [options...] *host:source destination*

-v	Verbose mode. Shows more information.
-q	Quiet mode. Shows less information.
-I	Synchs all files even if they have the same time-stamp and are the same size.
--size-only	Synchs all files except those having the same size.
-C	Checksums all files before sending.
-a	Preserves everything and uses recursion when sending.
-r	Copies directories recursively. Should be used when copying directories.
-R	Sends the whole path to the remote computer instead of only the file it points to.
-b	Will backup existing files that are to be overwritten and assign them a ~ extension.
--backup-dir=*directory*	Specifies a directory where the backups are placed.
--suffix=*suffix*	Specifies a backup suffix to use (default is ~).
-u	Updates files that exist on the remote computer that are older than the source.
-l	Takes the symbolic links and implements them on the remote computer.
-L	Copies symbolic links to the remote computer like ordinary files.
--copy-unsafe-links	Copies symbolic links that point outside of the source tree like ordinary files.
--safe-links	Ignores all the symbolic links that point outside of the source tree.
-H	Copies hard links to the remote computer as they are.
-W	Sends the whole file as it is, instead of using the incremental rsync algorithm.
-p	Updates the permissions on the remote computer to match the local file permissions.

continued

-o	Updates the owner of the files on the remote computer to match the local owner.
-g	Updates the file group on the remote computer to match the local group.
-D	Sends character and block device information so the remote computer can create these.
-t	Attaches the modification times to the files and updates them on the remote system.
-n	Reports what would have been done - no transfers. Run in dummy mode.
-S	Sparses files to the remote computer.
-x	Doesn't go to another file system when using -r.
--existing	Updates only the files that exists on the remote computer. Doesn't create new ones.
--max-delete=*number*	Specifies a maximum number of directories to remove.
--delete	Removes extra files that only exist on the remote computer.
--delete-excluded	Removes files that are excluded on the remote computer.
--delete-after	Doesn't remove existing files before the file transfer has been completed.
--force	Removes directories even if they are not empty.
-B *blocksize*	Specifies the block size to use in the rsync algorithm.
-e *command*	Specifies a program to use when transferring data (default is rsh).
--rsync-path=*path*	Specifies the path to rsync on the remote computer.
--exclude=*pattern*	Specifies files that aren't be sent to the remote computer.
--exclude-from=*file*	Specifies a file that contains a list of files that should be skipped.
--include=*pattern*	Specifies files that should be included when sending.
--include-from=*file*	Specifies a file that contains a list of files that should be sent.
-C	Ignores files the in the same algorithm as CVS uses.
--csum-length=*bytes*	Specifies the checksum bytes to use (default is 16 — which is the maximum).
-T *directory*	Specifies a directory on the remote computer, where temporary files are stored.
--compare-dest=*directory*	Specifies the directory to use when comparing files when doing transfers.
-z	Compresses files before sending them to the remote computer.
--numeric-ids	Transfers files using group and user IDs instead of group and usernames.
--timeout=*seconds*	Times out if no data is sent before the specified time in seconds.
--daemon	Starts as a daemon and waits for input from a socket, usually from `inetd`.
--address	Reads a specific IP address to bind the daemon to.
--config=*file*	The config file to use if running as a daemon (default is `/etc/rsyncd.conf`).
--port=*port*	Specifies a port number to bind to (default is 873).
--log-format=*format*	Specifies what logs to send to STDOUT.
--stats	Shows statistics over the file transfer.
--partial	Removes unfinished files if a transfer is interrupted.
--progress	Shows the transfer progress.
-P	Does the same as --partial and --progress together.
--password-file	Prompts you for a password to use when connecting to a remote computer.
--bwlimit=*kbps*	Limits the transfer rate to the specified number of kilobytes per second.
source	Specifies the source files to send.
host	Specifies the hostname to send them to or from.
destination	Specifies the destination.

File Name:	`rsync`	**Directory:**	/usr/bin/	**Type:**	External

rsync -av ucgbook.com:book/ /	Transfers the book directory from ucgbook.com.

runlevel

UNIX Shell: All primary shells (bash, ash, tcsh)

Function	Shows the previous and current system runlevel.
Syntax	runlevel *{ file }*

file	Specifies a different system `utmp` (default is `/var/run/utmp`).

File Name:	`runlevel`	**Directory:**	/sbin/	**Type:**	External

rx	**UNIX Shell:**	All primary shells (bash, ash, tcsh)

Function	Receives files using XMODEM protocol.
Syntax	rx [options...] *file*

-a	Converts files to UNIX conventions by stripping carriage returns.
-b	Uses binary transfers.
-q	Uses quiet mode.
-R	Enters more restricted mode.
-t *timeout*	Changes the timeout to timeout.
-U	Turns off restricted mode.
-v	Verbose mode shows more information.
-B *size*	Specifies the buffer size.
-C	Allows remote command execution.
-D	Outputs file data to `/dev/null`.
--delay-startup *seconds*	Waits seconds before doing anything.
-E	Renames incoming files if the files exist.
-h	Shows help information.
-m *number*	Stops transmission if BPS rate drops down under number.
-M *number*	Stops transmission if number of seconds exceeds number.
--o-sync	Opens output files in synchronous write mode.
-s *value*	Stops transmission at value of time (format is HH:MM).
-S	Requests time synch packet from the sender.
--syslog[=off]	Turns `syslog` on or off.
--tcp-client *host:post*	Acts as a TCP/IP client connects to host and port.
--tcp-server	Acts as a TCP/IP server.
--version	Shows version information.
-w*value*	Sets window size to value.
-X	Uses the XMODEM protocol for file transfers.
--ymodem	Uses the YMODEM protocol for file transfers.
-Z	Uses the ZMODEM protocol for file transfers.
-e	Forces sender to escape all control characters.
-c	Uses 16-bit CRC.
file	Specifies the file that stores the data.

File Name:	`rx`	**Directory:**	/usr/bin/	**Type:**	External

rz	**UNIX Shell:**	All primary shells (bash, ash, tcsh)

Function	Receives files using ZMODEM protocol.
Syntax	rz [options...]

-a	Converts files to UNIX conventions by stripping carriage returns.
-b	Uses binary transfers.
-q	Uses quiet mode.
-R	Enters more restricted mode.
-t *timeout*	Changes the timeout to timeout.
-U	Turns off restricted mode.
-v	Verbose mode. Shows more information.
-B *size*	Specifies the buffer size.
-C	Allows remote command execution.
-D	Outputs file data to `/dev/null`.
--delay-startup *seconds*	Waits seconds before doing anything.
-E	Renames incoming files if the files exist.
-h	Shows help information.
-m *number*	Stops transmission if BPS rate drops down under number.
-M *number*	Stops transmission if number of seconds exceeds number.
--o-sync	Opens output files in synchronous write mode.
-r	Resumes interrupted file transfers.

continued

-s *value*	Stops transmission at value of time (format is HH:MM).
-S	Requests time synch packet from the sender.
--syslog[=off]	Turns `syslog` on or off.
--tcp-client *host:post*	Acts as a TCP/IP Client connects to host and port.
--tcp-server	Acts as a TCP/IP server.
--version	Shows version information.
-w*value*	Sets window size to value.
-+	Appends received data to an existing file.
-X	Uses the XMODEM protocol for file transfers.
--ymodem	Uses the YMODEM protocol for file transfers.
-Z	Uses the ZMODEM protocol for file transfers.
-y	Overwrites an existing file.
-e	Forces sender to escape all control characters.
File Name: `rz`	**Directory:** /usr/bin/ **Type:** External

s2p

UNIX Shell: Perl script

Function	Converts a `sed` script to a `perl` script. The converted script will be shown on STDOUT.
Syntax	s2p [options...] { *file* }

-D*number*	Specifies which debug flags to use.
-n	Handles the script as if it were always executed with the `sed` -n option.
-p	Handles the script as if it were never executed with the `sed` -n option.
file	The `sed` script file to convert. If not specified, STDIN will be used.
File Name: `s2p`	**Directory:** /usr/bin/ **Type:** Script

sa1

UNIX Shell: A shell (ash, bsh)

Function	Saves system activity into the binary file `/var/log/sa/sadd`, where dd is the current day.
Syntax	sa1 { *time* } { *amount* }

time	Specifies the number of seconds in the interval between saving samples.
amount	Specifies how many times it does a sample.
File Name: `sa1`	**Directory:** /usr/lib/sa/ **Type:** Script

sa2

UNIX Shell: A shell (ash, bsh)

Function	Saves system activity into the file `/var/adm/sa/sardd` where `dd` is the current day.
Syntax	sa2 [options...]

	Please see `sar` for options.
File Name: `sa2`	**Directory:** /usr/lib/sa/ **Type:** Script
sa2	Creates a report file about today in `/var/adm/sa`.

sadc

UNIX Shell: All primary shells (bash, ash, tcsh)

Function	Saves system activity in binary format to a specified file.
Syntax	sadc [options...] { *time* } { *amount* } { *file* }

-I	Reports statistics for all system interrupts, not only the total number.
-V	Shows version information.
-x *pid*	Specifies the process ID to report statistics on.
-X *pid*	Reports statistics on the specified process ID and all its child processes.
time	Specifies the number of seconds in the interval between saving samples.
amount	Specifies how many times it will sample.
file	Specifies the file to save the record (default is `/var/adm/sa/sadd`). (dd is the day when the file was saved.)
File Name: `sadc`	**Directory:** /usr/lib/sa/ **Type:** External
sadc 30 4 sarfile	Creates four samples with a 30-second interval into `sarfile`.

samba

samba	UNIX Shell:	A shell (ash, bsh)
Function	Manages samba `smbd` and `nmdb` daemons.	
Syntax	samba *ACTION*	

ACTION	**Select one of the following actions:**
start	Starts the samba daemons.
stop	Stops the samba daemons.
restart	Restarts the samba daemons. This is the same as doing stop and then start.
reload	Reloads the `smb.conf` file.
status	Shows status on the `smbd` and `nmdb` daemons.
condrestart	Restarts the conditions for samba.

File Name:	Directory:	Type:
`samba`	/usr/sbin/	Script

sar

sar	UNIX Shell:	All primary shells (bash, ash, tcsh)
Function	Shows system utilization information earlier saved in files. Please see `sadc` to set up data collection.	
Syntax	sar [options...] *{ interval } { count }*	

-A	Shows all system information available.
-b	Shows statistics about I/O.
-B	Shows statistics about paging.
-c	Shows processes started per second.
-e *time*	Gets data until the specified time (default is 18:00:00).
-f *file*	Specifies the file from which the data is read.
-i *seconds*	Updates information with the specified interval in seconds.
-I *source*	Shows statistics for the source specified.
irq	Specifies the interrupt number.
SUM	Specifies all interrupts per second.
ALL	Specifies the first 16 interrupts.
XALL	Specifies all interrupts and includes interrupts from APIC sources.
PROC	Specifies interrupts by CPU.
-n *source*	Shows statistics for the network source specified.
DEV	Specifies information about network traffic over an interface.
EDEV	Specifies information about network failures.
SOCK	Specifies information about sockets.
FULL	Specifies information about all statistics.
-r	Shows swap statistics.
-R	Shows memory statistics.
-o *filename*	Specifies the file where to store binary samples.
-s *time*	Specifies when to start analyzing data from the system (default is 08:00:00).
-u	Shows the CPU utilization.
-U *cpu*	Specifies a specific CPU to show utilization for. Valid values are ALL or a number.
-v	Shows processes' status — the i-nodes and file tables used.
-V	Shows version information.
-w	Shows the switch activity on the system.
-W	Shows the swap activity on the system.
-x *process*	Shows statistics for the process given — is ignored with -o option.
PID	Specifies a process ID.
SELF	Specifies the command process itself.
SUM	Specifies the system faults.
ALL	Specifies all system processes.
-X *process*	Shows statistics about children for the process given. Is ignored with -o option.
PID	Specifies a process ID.
SELF	Specifies the command process itself.
ALL	Specifies all system processes.
-y	Shows the tty devices statistics.
interval	Specifies the interval in seconds to show information for.
count	Specifies the number of intervals to show information for.
Sap-o/var/lug/sa/graph 505	Reports activity every 50 seconds five times, to file graph.

File Name:	Directory:	Type:
`sar`	/usr/bin/	External

sash

UNIX Shell:	All primary shells (bash, ash, tcsh)
Function	A standalone shell with many extra built-in commands.
Syntax	sash [options...] { *script* }

-c *command*	Executes the next argument as a command.
-p *prompt*	Takes the next argument as the prompt string to be used when prompting for commands.
-q	Starts quiet mode.
-a	Creates aliases for the built-in commands so that they replace the regular commands.
script	Allows scripts to use sash as their script interpreter
	The following are internal built-in commands. The dash - must be used:
-ar	Creates and updates library files. It combines files into a single archive file.
-chattr	Is used to alter the file attributes on a Linux second extended file system.
-chgrp	Sets or changes the group ID for the file or files specified.
-chmod	Is used to alter or assign permissions to a file.
-chown	Alters the ownership ID of files and sets the group ID if it is specified.
-cmp	Compares two files and shows line numbers where the files are not the same.
-cp	Copies files and directories to a new destination.
-dd	Copies and converts an input file to an output file.
-echo	Copies the written string to the screen.
-ed	A line-based text editor.
-grep	Searches files for a specified pattern or string and shows the result to STDOUT.
-file	Determines the file type of a file.
-find	Finds files in directories and subdirectories using Boolean expressions.
-gunzip	Extracts files that are created by gzip, zip compress, compress -H, and `pack`.
-mknod	Creates a directory entry for a specified special file.
-more	Shows a text file one page at a time and continues when the Space is pressed.
-mount	Mounts a file system to a directory.
-mv	Moves files from a source to a destination.
-gzip	Compresses one or more files.
-kill	Sends a signal to the process ID.
-losetup	Associates loopback devices to system files.
-ln	Links files from a source to a destination.
-ls	Shows a list of filenames.
-lsattr	Shows specified file attributes for the ext2 file system.
-mkdir	Creates directories.
-printenv	Shows current environment variable values.
-pwd	Shows the current work directory.
-rm	Removes files.
-rmdir	Removes directories.
-sum	Calculates file checksums.
-sync	Forces a system synchronization.
-tar	Extracts, lists or creates `tar` files.
-touch	Alters the modify dates and times of files.
-umount	Unmounts a file system.
-where	Shows all of the paths in the PATH variable.

File Name:	`sash`	**Directory:**	/sbin/	**Type:**	External

sasldblistusers

UNIX Shell:	All primary shells (bash, ash, tcsh)
Function	Shows the users in the SASL password database (usually `/etc/sasldb`).
Syntax	sasldblistusers

File Name:	`sasldblistusers`	**Directory:**	/usr/sbin/	**Type:**	External

saslpasswd

saslpasswd	UNIX Shell:	All primary shells (bash, ash, tcsh)
Function	Sets the SASL password for server programs.	
Syntax	saslpasswd [options...] *user*	

-p	Doesn't prompt or verify the password that was entered correctly.
-c	Creates an entry for the user if the user doesn't exist.
-d	Deletes the entry for the user.
-u *domain*	Uses the specified domain for the user.
-a *appname*	Sets the application name for the user.
user	Specifies the user to use.
File Name: saslpasswd	**Directory:** /usr/sbin/ **Type:** External

sb

sb	UNIX Shell:	All primary shells (bash, ash, tcsh)
Function	Sends files in batch using YMODEM or ZMODEM protocol.	
Syntax	sb [options...] *{ files... }*	

-2	Uses two stop bits while communicating. Be careful with this.
-a	Converts NL characters to CR/LF.
-B *size*	Specifies the size of the read buffer in bytes (default is 16384 bytes).
-c *command*	Sends the specified command to the receiver to be executed.
-C *tries*	Specifies how many times to retry sending the command (default is 11).
-d	Alters all dots . to slashes / in the pathname.
--delay-startup *seconds*	Sets a specified delay time before anything is allowed to start.
-e	Escapes all of the control characters. Forces the sender to rename the new file.
-f	Sends the full pathname during transmission.
-h	Shows help information.
-i *command*	Sends the specified command to the receiver and returns immediately after success.
-k	Sends files using 1024 byte blocks.
-m *rate*	Stops the transmission if the BPS rate falls below the specified amount.
-M *rate*	Sets the minimum transmission rate in BPS (default is 120 seconds).
-l *length*	Causes the receiver to answer correct data for the specified length of characters.
-O	Disables the timeout handling for read requests.
-q	Suppresses verbose. Quiet mode.
-R	Sets restricted mode. Restricts current directory pathnames and PUBDIR.
-s *HH:MM*	Stops the transmission at the specified time.
-S	Enables support for the time synch protocol - incompatible with ZMODEM.
--syslog *=off*	Turns system logging on or off.
-t *time*	Alters the timeout to the specified time in tenths of a second.
-T	Ignores certain characters during transmission: ^P, ^P|0x80 and [CR + @]. Turbo mode.
--tcp	Tries to start a TCP/IP connection. All handshaking is done by the ZMODEM program.
--tcp-client *address:port*	Acts as the TCP/IP client by connecting to the specified address:port.
--tcp-server	Acts as a server.
-u	Unlinks the file once a successful transmission has taken place.
-U	Turns restricted mode off.
-v	Verbose mode. Shows more information.
--ymodem	Uses the YMODEM protocol for everything.
File Name: sb	**Directory:** /usr/bin/ **Type:** External

scan

scan	UNIX Shell:	All primary shells (bash, ash, tcsh)
Function	Gives a brief description of messages stored in the specified folder, or default folder if not specified.	
Syntax	scan [*+folder*] *{ messages... }* [options...]	

-clear	Makes a new line before exiting.
-noclear	Doesn't make a new line before exiting (is default).
-form *file*	Overrides the default output format and uses the format specified in file instead.
-header	Shows a header before showing the messages.

continued

-noheader	Doesn't show a header before showing the messages (is default).
-width *columns*	Specifies the width of the scan line.
-reverse	Lists the messages in reverse order.
-noreverse	Doesn't list the messages in reverse order (is default).
-file *filename*	Shows a list of messages in the specified file. This file is produced by `packf`.
-version	Shows version information.
-help	Shows help information.
+*folder*	Specifies the folder to scan.
messages...	Specifies the messages to scan (default folder is ~/Mail/inbox).
File Name: `scan`	**Directory:** /usr/bin/ **Type:** External

scanpci

UNIX Shell: All primary shells (bash, ash, tcsh)

Function	Shows information about your PCI bus.
Syntax	scanpci [options...]

-v	Shows config space.
-1	Specifies config type 1.
-2	Specifies config type 2.
-O	Enables OS config support.
-f	Forces a config type.
-V	Specifies the level of verbosity messages.
File Name: `scanpci`	**Directory:** /usr/bin/X11/ **Type:** External

sched

UNIX Shell: TC shell (tcsh)

Function	A simple scheduler used to run commands at a later time.
Syntax	sched [option] sched *time command*

-*n*	Removes event n.
time	Specifies the time to run command — can be 24-hour or 12-hour format.
command	Specifies the command to run.

sclient

UNIX Shell: All primary shells (bash, ash, tcsh)

Function	A Kerberos client. When connected to Kerberos server it returns a Kerberos authentication.
Syntax	sclient *host*

host	Specifies the server to connect to.
File Name: `sclient`	**Directory:** /usr/kerberos/bin/ **Type:** External

scp

UNIX Shell: All primary shells (bash, ash, tcsh)

Function	Copies files in a secure way with all network traffic encrypted by `ssh`.
Syntax	scp [options...] *source destination*

-c *cipher*	Specifies the cipher to use for encryption - for example, `3des` or `blowfish`.
-i *identityfile*	Specifies where the private key is located (default is `$HOME/.ssh/identity`).
-p	Preserves times and modes of copied files.
-r	Copies whole directories recursively.
-v	Verbose mode. Shows more information.
-B	Batch mode. Doesn't ask for passwords.
-q	Quiet mode. No progress meter.
-C	Enables compression.
-P *port*	Specifies the port to use for connecting.
-4	Specifies IP version 4 only.
-6	Specifies IP version 6 only.

.continued

source	Specifies one or more files to use as the source. (If more than one file is specified, destination must be a directory.)		
destination	Specifies a file or directory to use as destination.		
File Name: `scp`	**Directory:** /usr/bin/	**Type:**	External
Note:	Source and destination can be specified as `file`, `host:file` or `user@host:file`.		
scp /etc/passwd ucg@pluto:/tmp	Copies the local file `/etc/passwd` to the host pluto as user ucg into /tmp.		
scp /etc/passwd pluto:	Copies the local file `/etc/passwd` as current user to the home directory on the host pluto.		
scp ucg@pluto:/etc/passwd .	Copies the remote file `/etc/passwd` from the host pluto as user ucg to current directory.		

screen

UNIX Shell: All primary shells (bash, ash, tcsh)

Function	Runs many programs on one terminal. Makes programs detached so they can be attached somewhere else.
Syntax	screen [options...] *{ command }* screen -r *session*

-a	Includes all capabilities in the new screen.
-A	Applies the current screen size on all screens.
-c *file*	Specifies a config file other than the default `$HOME/.screenrc`.
-d *{ session }*	Disconnects the screen session running.
-r *{ session }*	Reopens a session - if it is already running, it disconnects it first.
-R *{ session }*	Creates, disconnects, and reopens a session.
-RR	Does the same as a -d -R but on the first session.
-D *{ session }*	Disconnects the screen session running and remotely logs out.
-r *{ session }*	Reopens a session - if one is already attached, it's disconnected.
-R *{ session }*	Starts a session right where you are, reopens an attached session if found.
-RR	Does the same as -D -R.
-e*characters*	Alters the command characters to be used as Ctrl+A a (default is ^Aa). (On a new or multiuser session, it sets the default characters.)
-f	Sets the flow control to on.
-fn	Sets the flow control to off.
-fa	Sets the flow control to automatic switching mode.
-h *lines*	Specifies how many lines to remember in the scrollback buffer.
-i	Sets the interrupt key to do an interrupt immediately when flow control is on.
-l	Sets the login mode to on.
-ln	Sets the login mode to off.
-ls	Shows a list of all running, multi, disconnected, and dead sessions.
-list	Does the same as -ls.
-L	Specifies the screen has a writable last position.
-m	Ignores the $STY environment variable.
-d	Creates the new session in disconnected mode.
-D	Does the same as -m -d but doesn't fork a new process.
-O	Alters the mode to a more optimal output for the screen.
-q	Suppresses error messages.
-R	Tries to restart the first disconnected session.
-s	Specifies another default shell than that in the environment variable $SHELL. (The default shell for new sessions is /bin/sh (Bourneshell).)
-S*sessionname*	Specifies a name for the new session. Can be used as identifier to the -r function.
-t *name*	Specifies the title for the default shell or the specified session.
-w *{ session }*	Removes the specified sessions or, if no session is specified, all the dead ones.
-x	Lets you in on an already started session that becomes a multi-user session.
	The -r option can only be used alone or together with -d and -D:
-r *{ session }*	Reopens a disconnected session at the specified session or process ID.
	The following are the screen commands that you can use inside a session: (The Ctrl-A combination specifies that a key command will follow.)
Ctrl+A '	Lets you select a session to go to from a prompt.
Ctrl+A *number*	Switches to the specified session number or to the blank session with a -.
Ctrl+A Tab	Switches the focus of the input to the next region.
Ctrl+A Ctrl-A	Toggles between the current and the previous session.

continued

Ctrl+A a	Sends the Ctrl+A keys to another screen attached inside the current screen.
Ctrl+A A	Prompts for a name to the current session.
Ctrl+A b	Breaks the session.
Ctrl+A B	Restarts the communication line and sends a break to the session.
Ctrl+A c	Opens a new window inside the current attached screen.
Ctrl+A C	Clears the screen.
Ctrl+A d	Makes screen run in the background. It will be "detached".
Ctrl+A D D	Detaches the session and logs out.
Ctrl+A f	Toggles the flow control on, off, or auto.
Ctrl+A F	Alters the sizes to the current region size.
Ctrl+A C-g	Toggles the mode of the visual bell on or off.
Ctrl+A h	Saves a hard copy of the current screen to the file `hardcopy.n`.
Ctrl+A H	Toggles the log of the current session on or off. The log is saved in `screenlog.n`.
Ctrl+A i	Shows information about the current screen.
Ctrl+A k	Kills the current window.
Ctrl+A l	Restarts the current session from the beginning.
Ctrl+A L	Toggles the current session's login slot.
Ctrl+A m	Shows the last message from the message line again.
Ctrl+A M	Toggles the monitoring of the current session on or off.
Ctrl+A Space	Switches to the next window.
Ctrl+A N	Shows the current session's number and title.
Ctrl+A Backspace	Switches to the previous session.
Ctrl+A q	Sends the Ctrl-Q (starts the flow) character to the session.
Ctrl+A Q	Kills all regions but the current one.
Ctrl+A r	Toggles the current sessions line-wrap setting on or off.
Ctrl+A s	Sends a Ctrl-S (halts the flow) to the session.
Ctrl+A S	Splits the current session into two new sessions.
Ctrl+A t	Shows information about the system.
Ctrl+A v	Shows version information.
Ctrl+A Ctrl+V	Enters the digraph.
Ctrl+A w	Shows a list of all sessions.
Ctrl+A W	Toggles the column width between 80 and 132 characters.
Ctrl+A x	Puts a lock on the session.
Ctrl+A X	Kills the current region.
Ctrl+A z	Suspends the screen if your system supports BSD job control.
Ctrl+A Z	Resets the values to initial state.
Ctrl+A .	Shows a `termcap` file.
Ctrl+A ?	Shows help information about the key commands.
Ctrl+A \	Kills all windows, including the current screen.
Ctrl+A :	Gives you the command line.
Ctrl+A [	Enters the copy / scrollback mode.
Ctrl+A]	Pastes the copied information into the current session.
Ctrl+A {	Copies the previous command line.
Ctrl+A }	Pastes the previous command line.
Ctrl+A >	Saves the copied information to a file.
Ctrl+A <	Puts the information from the save file into the paste buffer.
Ctrl+A =	Deletes the information in the save file.
Ctrl+A ,	Shows license information.
Ctrl+A _	Toggles the monitoring for inactivity on or off.
Ctrl+A *	Shows a list of all attached screens.

File Name:	`screen`	**Directory:**	/usr/bin/	**Type:**	External
Tip:	Useful if you want to run a long-term process on a remote computer and don't want to be connected to that computer.				

screen lynx	Starts a new screen with lynx in it using the same size.
Ctrl-A c	Internal. Creates a new screen in the screen session.
Ctrl-A Space	Internal. Switches to the next screen inside of that screen session.

screendump

UNIX Shell:	All primary shells (bash, ash, tcsh)
Function	Dumps the contents of the screen to STDOUT.
Syntax	screendump [options...]

-s=*screen*	Dumps the contents of specified screen.
-h	Shows help information.
-V	Shows version information.

File Name:	`screendump`	**Directory:**	/usr/bin/	**Type:**	External

scsi

UNIX Shell:	A shell (ash, bsh)
Function	Administers PCMCIA SCSI adapters.
Syntax	scsi *ACTION device*

ACTION	Specifies the action to perform on the device.
start	Starts the device.
check	Checks the device's status.
stop	Stops the device.
suspend	Suspends the device.
resume	Resumes the device.
device	Specifies the device to use.

File Name:	`scsi`	**Directory:**	/etc/pcmcia/ ; /usr/src/linux-2.2.16/pcmcia-cs-3.1.19/etc/	**Type:**	Script

scsi_info

UNIX Shell:	All primary shells (bash, ash, tcsh)
Function	Shows information about SCSI-devices, such as address parameters, device vendor information, etc.
Syntax	scsi_info *device*

device	Gets SCSI address parameters from specified SCSI device.

File Name:	`scsi_info`	**Directory:**	/sbin/	**Type:**	External

scsi_info /dev/sda	Displays information about the first SCSI disk.
scsi_info /dev/st0	Displays information about the first SCSI tape device.

send

UNIX Shell:	All primary shells (bash, ash, tcsh)
Function	Sends the specified letter files to it's destinations, defined in the message.
Syntax	send [options...] *{ files... }*

-alias *file*	Specifies the alias file to use (default is `/etc/mnh/MailAliases`).
-draft	Doesn't ask whether to use the draft file, if no file is specified.
-draftfolder +*folder*	Specifies which folder in the `Mail` directory to search for the draft message.
-nodraftfolder	Uses the default draft folder (is default).
-draftmessage *file*	Specifies the draft file to use.
-filter *file*	Specifies the file to use as filter for the message.
-nofilter	Doesn't filter the message (is default).
-format	Formats the To and CC entries into standard format entries (is default).
-noformat	Doesn't format the message.
-forward	Attaches the draft file to the error message if an error occurs (is default).
-noforward	Doesn't attach the draft file to the error message, if an error occurred.
-mime	Formats the message to MIME rules.
-nomime	Doesn't format the message to MIME rules (is default).
-msgid	Adds a "Message-ID:" to the message.
-nomsgid	Doesn't add a "Message-ID:" to the message (is default).
-push	Sends the message in the background, leaving the terminal free.
-nopush	Doesn't send the message in the background (is default).
-split *seconds*	Splits the message and sends all the parts, with specified intervals between.
-verbose	Verbose mode. Shows information on the progress before the delivery.
-noverbose	Doesn't show more information (is default).
-watch	Shows information on the progress on the delivery to local and network mail.
-nowatch	Doesn't show information on the delivery progress (is default).
-width *columns*	Specifies the width for the message headers (default is 72).

continued

-version	Shows version information.
-help	Shows help information.
files...	Specified the message files to send.
File Name: send	**Directory:** /usr/bin/ — **Type:** External

sendfiles

UNIX Shell: A shell (ash, bsh)

Function	Sends multiple files via a MIME message.
Syntax	sendfiles [*-seconds*] *mailaddr subject files...*

-seconds	Specifies number of seconds to sleep between each mail.
mailaddr	Specifies the address to send the mail to.
subject	Specifies the subject of the mail.
files...	Specifies one or more files to include in the mail.
File Name: sendfiles	**Directory:** /usr/bin/ — **Type:** Script

setclock

UNIX Shell: All primary shells (bash, ash, tcsh)

Function	Sets the time for the hardware clock.
Syntax	setclock
File Name: setclock	**Directory:** /usr/sbin/ — **Type:** External

setfdprm

UNIX Shell: All primary shells (bash, ash, tcsh)

Function	A utility to set and change parameters on auto-detecting floppy devices.
Syntax	setfdprm [option] *device* setfdprm -p *device name* setfdprm -p *device size sectors heads tracks rate*

-p	Loads the parameter set permanently for the device. (It can either be physically be set, or as a name in /etc/fdprm.)
-c *device*	Clears the specified device for it's parameter set.
-y *device*	Enables format detection for the specified device.
-n *device*	Disables format detection messages for the specified device.
device	Specifies the floppy device to use.
name	Specifies the name of the floppy device as found in `/etc/fdprmis`.
size	Specifies the size in kbytes.
sectors	Specifies the sectors per track.
heads	Specifies the number of cylinder heads.
tracks	Specifies the number of tracks.
rate	Specifies the transfer rate.
File Name: setfdprm	**Directory:** /usr/bin/ — **Type:** External

setleds

UNIX Shell: All primary shells (bash, ash, tcsh)

Function	Sets the status flags for the keyboard LED's. Shows current status if no option is specified.
Syntax	setleds [options...] *{ ACTIONS... }*

-v	Verbose mode. Shows more information.
-L	Changes the LEDs, not the actual flags.
-D	Makes the specified flags default settings.
-F	Changes the flags only.
ACTIONS...	**The following actions can either have a - or + sign before it to set or clear the flag:**
num	Sets or clears Num lock.
caps	Sets or clears Caps lock.
scroll	Sets or clears Scroll lock.
File Name: setleds	**Directory:** /usr/bin/ — **Type:** External
Bug:	When using the -F option, it may change the LEDs as well.
setleds +caps	Turns Cap locks and the Cap locks LEDS on.

setpci

UNIX Shell: All primary shells (bash, ash, tcsh)

Function	Is used to query and configure PCI devices. All numbers are entered in hexadecimal values.
Syntax	setpci [options...] option *operations...*

-v	Verbose mode. Shows more information.
-f	Sends error message if no proper device is specified.
-D	Simulates configuration space access, doesn't use the real one.
--version	Shows version information.
	One of the following options must be specified. They can't be combined.
-s *{ bus*:] [*slot }* [*.function*]	Selects devices in specified bus, slot, and function. A wildcard "*" can be used.
-d *{ vendor }* [*:device*]	Selects devices with specified vendor and device ID.
operations...	Specifies the operations to set. (operation=the value to set.) (Can also use the register address, following .B, .W, .L ([byte, word, long].)
File Name: `setpci`	**Directory:** /sbin/ — **Type:** External

setquota

UNIX Shell: All primary shells (bash, ash, tcsh)

Function	Sets the specified quota for a user or a group from the command line.
Syntax	setquota [options...] *name filesystem { ACTION }*

-n	Edits the quota on remote computers using `rpc.rquotad`.
-p *prototype*	Specifies a user or group to use as a prototype when setting the quotas.
	One of these two options should be used. They can't be combined.
-u	Sets the quotas for the specified user.
-g	Sets the quotas for the specified group.
name	Specifies a username or a group to edit quotas for.
filesystem	Specifies the filename wherein to set the quotas for the specified user or group.
ACTION	**Use one of the following actions when not using a prototype specified with the -p option:**
blocksoft	Specifies the soft block to set.
blockhard	Specifies the hard block to set.
inodesoft	Specifies the soft limit of files to set.
inodehard	Specifies the hard limit of files to set.
File Name: `setquota`	**Directory:** /usr/sbin/ — **Type:** External
setquota -u ucg /home 15000 17000 0 0	Sets a 15MB quota limit on `/home` for the user ucg.
setquota -p ucg -u speed /home	Receives the quota limits from the user ucg and copies them to the user speed.

setserial

UNIX Shell: All primary shells (bash, ash, tcsh)

Function	Sets or retrieve serial port information.
Syntax	setserial [options...] *device { ACTIONS... }* setserial -g [options...] *devices...*

-a	Shows all available information when reporting the configuration of a serial device.
-b	Shows a summary of the device's configuration.
-v	Verbose mode. Shows more information.
-g	Shows the characteristics for all the specified devices.
	The following option can only be combined with the -g option:
-G	Shows information in a format that can be fed back to setserial.
	The following options can't be combined with the -g option:
-V	Shows version information.
-W	Does wild interrupt initialization and exit.
-z	Sets all flags to zero before starting to set them.
-q	Quiet mode. Shows less information.
device	Specifies the serial device to configure or read information from.
ACTIONS...	**The value for the parameters is in decimal unless a 0x is typed (hexadecimal).**
port *value*	Sets the I/O port.
irq *value*	Sets hardware IRQ.
uart *type*	Sets the UART type. (Type none to disable the device.)

continued

autoconfig	Tries to set the UART type automatically. The I/O port must first be set.
baud_rate *value*	Sets the baud rate. The highest baud rate is 115,200.
spd_hi	Uses 57.6KB when the application requests 38.4KB.
spd_vhi	Uses 115KB when the application requests 38.4KB.
spd_shi	Uses 230KB when the application requests 38.4KB.
spd_warp	Uses 460KB when the application requests 38.4KB.
spd_cust	Uses the baud rate divided by divisor when the application requests 38.4KB.
spd_normal	Uses 38.4KB when the application requests 38.4KB.
divisor *value*	Sets the custom division.
close_delay *value*	Specifies the time between closing and raising the DTR (in hundreds of seconds).
closing_wait *value*	Specifies the time the kernel waits for data when the port gets closed.
	For the following options: If you specify a ^, it disables the sentence:
[^]auto_irq	Tries to set the IRQ automatically during autoconfiguration.
[^]skip_test	Skips the UART test during autoconfiguration.
[^]sak	Uses the secure attention key as the break key.
[^]fourport	Configures the port as an AST Fourport card.
[^]session_lockout	Allows only one process at a time to have access to specified device session.
[^]pgrp_lockout	Allows only one process at a time to have access to specified device callout port.
[^]hup_notify	Notifies the process if it is blocked when opening a dial-in line.
[^]split_termios	Separates the termios settings for callout and dial-in devices.
[^]callout_nohup	Doesn't hang up the tty when carrier detect is dropped if device is opened as a callout.
[^]low_latency	Makes the device's receive latency minimal.

File Name:	`setserial`	**Directory:**	/bin/	**Type:**	External

setserial /dev/ttyS1 uart 16550A port 0x02f8 irq 3 baud_base 115200 spd_vhi skip_test	Sets specified values for `/dev/ttyS1`.

setsid

UNIX Shell: All primary shells (bash, ash, tcsh)

Function	Runs the specified program in a new session.
Syntax	setsid *command { arguments... }*

command	Specifies the command to run.
arguments...	The arguments for the command.

File Name:	`setsid`	**Directory:**	/usr/bin/	**Type:**	External

settc

UNIX Shell: TC shell (tcsh)

Function	Makes the shell believe that the terminal capability has the specified value.
Syntax	settc *cap value*

cap	Specifies the terminal capability to set (defined in `termcap`).
value	Specifies the value to use.

setterm

UNIX Shell: All primary shells (bash, ash, tcsh)

Function	Sets terminal attributes.
Syntax	setterm [options...]

-term *name*	Specifies the terminal name.
-reset	Resets the terminal.
-initialize	Shows the terminal startup string used by the terminal.
-cursor on | off	Sets cursor mode application on or off.
-repeat on | off	Sets keyboard repeat on or off.
-appcursorkeys on | off	Sets `Cursor Key Application Mode` on or off.
-linewrap on | off	Sets automatic line wrapping on or off.
-default	The terminal renders the default option value.
-foreground *color*	Specifies the foreground text color.
-background *color*	Specifies the background text color.
-ulcolor *colors*	Specifies the color for underlined characters.

continued

-hbcolor *colors*	Specifies the color for half-bright characters.
-inversescreen on | off	Invert the screen colors.
-bold on | off	Sets bold mode on or off.
-half-bright on | off	Sets dim mode on or off.
-blink on | off	Sets the blink mode on or off.
-reverse on | off	Sets reverse video mode on or off.
-underline on | off	Sets underline mode on or off.
-store	Specifies the default options should be saved as defaults.
-clear *{ ACTION: }*	**The following actions can be used:**
all	Clear the screen (default if no argument is specified).
rest	Clears from the current cursor position to the end of the screen.
-tabs *{ tabs }*	Sets Tab stops at the given horizontal cursor position (range is 1 to 160).
-clrtabs *{ tabs }*	Clears Tab stops from the given horizontal cursor positions (range is 1 to 160).
-regtabs *{ tabs }*	Clears all Tab stops, then sets a regular Tab stop pattern.
-blank *{ minutes }*	Specifies after how many minutes the file is to go blank (with no argument, 0 is used).
-dump *{ number }*	Specifies that log files should be overwritten, not appended; overrides `-append`.
-append *{ number }*	Specifies that log files should be appended, not overwritten. Won't work with -dump.
number	Specifies a number between 1 and however many consoles you have.
-file *file*	Specifies the snapshot filename for any -dump or -append options.
-msg on | off	Enables or disables kernel printk() messages.
-msglevel *number*	Specifies the console logging level for kernel printk() messages. (Range is 1 to 8.)
-powersave *ACTION*	**The following actions can be used:**
on | vsync	Puts the monitor into VESA vsync suspend mode.
off	Sets off monitor VESA power saving features.
hsync	Puts the monitor into VESA hsync suspend mode.
powerdown	Puts the monitor into VESA power down mode.
-powerdown *{ number }*	Specifies the VESA power down interval in minutes (range is 0 to 60).
-blength *{ number }*	Specifies the bell duration in milliseconds (range is 0 to 2000).
-bfreq *{ number }*	Specifies the bell frequency in Hz (with no arguments, 0 is used).

File Name:	Directory:	Type:
`setterm`	/usr/bin/	External

setty

UNIX Shell: TC shell (tcsh)

Function	Sets which tty modes the shell allows to be changed.
Syntax	setty [options...]

	The options -d, -q, and -x can't be combined.
-d	Lets setty act on the edit set of tty modes.
-q	Lets setty act on the quote set of tty modes.
-x	Lets setty act on the execute set of tty modes (is the default).
-a	Shows all tty modes for the chosen set.
+*mode*	Fixes the mode on.
-mode	Fixes the mode off.
mode	Removes control for mode in the current set.

setup

UNIX Shell: All primary shells (bash, ash, tcsh)

Function	Configures the system in interactive mode.
Syntax	setup

File Name:	Directory:	Type:
`setup`	/usr/sbin/	External

setvar

UNIX Shell: A shell (ash)

Function	Sets variable to value.
Syntax	setvar *variable value*

variable	Specifies the variable.
value	Specifies the value to set the variable to.
setvar ucgbook best	Sets variable ucgbook to best.

setxkbmap

setxkbmap	UNIX Shell:	All primary shells (bash, ash, tcsh)
Function	Sets the keyboard layout by means of the X keyboard extension.	
Syntax	setxkbmap [options...]	

-help	Shows help information.
-compat *name*	Specifies compatibility map for the keyboard layout construction.
-config *file*	Specifies the file containing keyboard configuration information.
-display *display*	Updates the display specified with the new keyboard layout.
-geometry *name*	Specifies the geometry component for the keyboard layout construction.
-keymap *name*	Specifies the key map for the keyboard layout construction.
-layout *name*	Uses the layout specified to choose components for the keyboard description.
-variant *name*	Specifies a variant of the layout specified.
-option *name*	Specifies an option for the layout specified. This option is repeatable.
-model *name*	Uses the model specified to choose components for the keyboard description.
-rules *file*	Uses the rules file specified to interpret the components chosen in the layout and model.
-symbols *name*	Uses the symbols component specified for a keyboard layout construction.
-synch	Synchronizes X requests.
-types *name*	Uses the type component specified for a keyboard layout construction.

File Name:	`setxkbmap`	**Directory:**	/usr/X11R6/bin/	**Type:**	External

sfdisk

sfdisk	UNIX Shell:	All primary shells (bash, ash, tcsh)
Function	Administers partition tables.	
Syntax	sfdisk [options...] *device*	

-v	Shows version information.
-?	Shows help information.
-T	Shows the system IDs that have been recognized.
-s *{ partition }*	Shows the size of the specified partition.
-g	Shows estimated size of the specified disk.
-l	Shows all partitions on the specified device.
-d	Dumps the partition information so it can be used as arguments for `sfdisk`.
-V	Tests the partitions to verify that they are correct.
-i	Sets all first indexes as 1 instead of 0.
-N*number*	Changes the specified partition on the specified device.
-A*number*	Specifies the partition to make active. All other partitions are set to inactive.
-c *number { ID }*	Sets the ID for the partition or, if no ID is specified, shows the current ID.
-u*type*	Accepts or reports in units of sectors (S), blocks (B), cylinders (C), or megabytes (M).
-x	Shows non-primary extended partitions, and is expecting descriptions for them on input.
-C *value*	Specifies the cylinder amount, instead of using the suggested value from the kernel.
-H *value*	Specifies the head amount, instead of using the suggested value from the kernel.
-S *value*	Specifies the sector amount, instead of using the suggested value from the kernel.
-f	Uses force mode. Does what it is told, even if it makes no sense.
-q	Uses quiet mode. Shows no warning messages.
-L	Doesn't complain even if it's irrelevant for Linux.
-D	Spares the first track in DOS partitions, leaving some space for disk managers.
-E	Uses the start of DOS inner extended partitions as a link to the end of the outer ones.
--IBM	Leaves the last sector unallocated.
-n	Tests the procedures, doesn't actually write to the disk.
-R	Makes the kernel re-read the partition table.
--no-reread	Checks whether the disk is mounted before repartitioning it. If so, it doesn't continue.
-O *file*	Writes the sectors are overwritten to the specified file.
-I *file*	Restores the file system by reading the sectors from the file created by the -O option.
device	Specifies the device to use.

File Name:	`sfdisk`	**Directory:**	/sbin/	**Type:**	External

sfdisk -l /dev/hda	Shows the partitions of `/dev/hda`.

shar

shar	UNIX Shell:	All primary shells (bash, ash, tcsh)
Function	Converts binary files to a text friendly archive.	
Syntax	shar [options...] *files...*	

--help	Shows help information.
--version	Shows version information.
--quiet	Doesn't show verbose messages when producing the archive.
-p	Allows positional parameter options.
-S	Reads the files from STDIN, rather than som the command line.
-o *file*	Saves the archive to the file with she suffix ".01" and so on.
-l *size*	Limits the size of output files without splitting input files. -o option must be set.
-L *size*	Limits the size of output files by splitting the input files. -o option must be set.
-n *name*	Specifies the name of an archive to include in the header. -a option must be set.
-s *who@where*	Sets the submitter name instead of determining it automatically.
-a	Creates the archive header automatically.
-c	Adds the line `Cut here` at the start of each output file.
-M	Determines if the files are text or binary and archives them correctly (is default).
-T	Handles all files as text.
-B	Handles all files as binary and uses `uuencode` before packing.
-z	Uses `gzip` and `uuencode` before packing.
-g *level*	Specifies the compression level to use when using -z option (default is 9).
-Z	Compresses and uses `uuencode` on all files before packing.
-b *BITS*	Specifies how many bits per code to use when doing compression.
-w	Doesn't do a character count after unpacking (default is to count).
-D	Doesn't verify the unpacked files with `md5sum` (default is to verify).
-F	Adds the prefix character at the beginning of all lines.
-d *string*	Uses the string at the end of all files in the shar file, instead of "SHAR_EOF".
-V	Produces `vanilla shar` that only needs `sed` and `echo` to work.
-P	Uses temporary files instead of pipes.
-x	Overwrites files without questions.
-X	Overwrites files if the user confirms it.
-m	Keeps the existing dates for the files instead of updating them at unpack.
-Q	Doesn't show comment's inclusion when the archive is unpacked.
-f	Restores by filename, not by path.
--no-i18n	Uses default English messages when creating the archive.
--print-text-domain-dir	Shows the directory that `shar` uses to find message files for different languages.
files...	Specifies the files to compress.

File Name:	`shar`	**Directory:**	/usr/bin/	**Type:**	External
Note:	Good feature for making binary files readable as plain text. Is also self-extracted through `/bin/sh`.				

shar file.c > file.shar	Compresses file.c into file.shar.
/bin/sh file.shar	Decompresses the specified file.

shopt

shopt	UNIX Shell:	Bash shell (bash)
Function	Alters optional shell variables controlling the behavior of the shell.	
Syntax	shopt [options...] *optnames...*	

-p	Shows current status of all options.
-s	Enables the option.
-u	Disables the option.
-q	Doesn't show normal output. Checks the status of an option.
-o	Restricts the option names to those defended by the -o option for set.
optnames...	Specifies the option to set.
cdable_vars	Specifies that input to CD can be a variable name instead of a directory.
cdspell	Specifies that options to CD are spell checked and correct.
chekhash	First checks the internal hash table for the command.
checkwinsize	Checks the window size after each command and update lines and columns.
cmdhist	Specifies that multiple-line commands are saved in one history entry.
dotglob	Specifies that filenames beginning with `.` are taken in the filename expansion.

continued

execfail	Doesn't exit if an exec command fails in a non interactive shell.
expand_aliases	Expands aliases.
extglob	Uses extended pattern matching for filename expansion.
histappend	Appends the history list to the file specified by HISTFILE variable.
hsitreedit	Specifies that `readline` can be used to edit failed history substitution.
histverify	Uses `readline` to edit the resulting history substitution.
huponexit	Sends `nohup` to all processes on exit from the shell.
interactive_comments	Allows lines be a commented (begin with #).
lithist	Saves multiline commands with new line instead of `;` in the history list.
mailwarn	Checks for mail.
no_empty_cmd_completion	Searches the PATH for possible command completion
nocaseglod	Matches filename in a case-insensitive fashion.
nullglob	Allows pattern controlled searches, that don't match any files, to expand to a null string.
progcomp	Enables programmable completion facilities.
promptvars	Performs variable and parameter expansion on prompt strings.
restricted_shell	Specifies the shell is restricted (read only).
shift_verbose	Specifies that shift should report any error.
sourcepath	Specifies the `.` command should use the PATH to search for the command.
xpg_echo	Specifies the internal echo should expand backslash-escape sequences.

show

UNIX Shell: All primary shells (bash, ash, tcsh)

Function	Shows specified messages or folders. This is part of the NMH package.
Syntax	show [+folder] *{ messages.. }* [options...] *{ arguments... }*

+folder	Specifies the folder under the directory `~/Mail` (default is inbox).
-header	Shows one line of the description per message.
-noheader	Shows the entire description field.
-checkmime	Checks whether the messages are non-text messages.
-nocheckmime	Doesn't test if the messages are non-text messages.
-form *formatfile*	Shows the contents with the format specified in the file.
-moreproc *program*	Specifies the program to add information to the message.
-nomoreproc	Doesn't add information on the messages.
-length *value*	Shows the specified amount of lines, starting from the bottom up.
-width *value*	Specifies the width of the messages.
-showproc *program*	Filters the messages through the specified program, instead of `mhl`.
-showmimeproc *program*	Filters non-text messages through the specified program, instead of `mhshow`.
-noshowproc	Doesn't filter the messages.
-draft	Shows the contents of the file `draft`, if it exists.
-version	Shows version information.
-help	Shows help information.
messages...	Specifies the messages to show.
arguments...	Specifies the arguments to use for the -showproc or -showmimeproc options.

File Name:	`show`	**Directory:**	/usr/bin/	**Type:**	External

showaudio

UNIX Shell: All primary shells (bash, ash, tcsh)

Function	Plays an audio email message on your workstation.
Syntax	showaudio *files...*

files...	Specifies audio files to play.

File Name:	`showaudio`	**Directory:**	/usr/bin/	**Type:**	External
Note:	Currently plays audio on Sun & Sony workstations with `rshell`.				

showfont

UNIX Shell:	All primary shells (bash, ash, tcsh)		
Function	Shows information from the X font server about a specified font.		
Syntax	showfont [options...] -fn *font*		

-server *host:port*	Connects to the specified X font server.
-fn *font*	Specifies the font to show information about.
-lsb	Sets the bit order of the font to be least significant bit first.
-msb	Sets the bit order of the font to be most significant bit first.
-LSB	Sets the byte order of the font to be least significant byte first.
-MSB	Sets the byte order of the font to be most significant byte first.
-ext	Shows only the extents of the font.
-start*number*	Shows a range of characters from the number specified.
-end*number*	Shows a range of characters up to the number specified.
-unit*number*	Sets the fonts scanline unit. The values are 8, 16, 32, or 64.
-pad*number*	Sets the fonts scanpad unit. The values are 8, 16, 32, or 64.
-b*number*	Specifies the fonts bitmap padding unit. The values are 0, 1, or 2.

File Name:	`showfont`	**Directory:**	/usr/X11R6/bin/	**Type:**	External

showrgb

UNIX Shell:	All primary shells (bash, ash, tcsh)
Function	Converts a compiled RGB color name database back to the original form.
Syntax	showrgb *{ database }*

database	Specifies the database to be converted.

File Name:	`showrgb`	**Directory:**	/usr/X11R6/bin/	**Type:**	External

shred

UNIX Shell:	All primary shells (bash, ash, tcsh)
Function	Erases files by overwriting them repeatedly. Which makes it very hard to restore the information.
Syntax	shred [options...] *files...*

-f	Force mode. If lack of permissions, permissions are set to allow writing.
-n *value*	Overwrites data specified number of times (default is 25).
-s *value*	Specifies the size to shred (k, M, and G suffixes could be used).
-u	Removes and truncates after shredding.
-v	Verbose mode. Shows more information.
-x	Prevents the rounding of file size to next full block.
-z	Makes the last write contain only zero bits.
-	Shreds to STDOUT.
--help	Shows help information.
--version	Shows version information.
files...	Specifies the file to act on.

File Name:	`shred`	**Directory:**	/usr/bin/	**Type:**	External
Warning:	Be aware that shredded files are data files and can't be read by the `more` command.				

skill

UNIX Shell:	All primary shells (bash, ash, tcsh)
Function	Kills processes. Combines features from `kill` and `killall`.
Syntax	skill *{ signal }* [options...] *processes...*

-f	Sets to fast mode. This option isn't functional at this time.
-i	Asks to approve each action.
-v	Verbose mode. Shows more information about the selected processes.
-w	Enables warnings. This option isn't functional at this time.
-n	Shows the process ID only.
-l	Lists all signals that can be used.
-t	Specifies the next argument is a terminal.
-u	Specifies the next argument is a username.

continued

-p	Specifies the next argument is a process ID number.		
-c	Specifies the next argument is a command name.		
signal	Specifies the signal to send (default is TERM).		
processes...	Specifies the process to modify.		
File Name: skill	**Directory:** /usr/bin/	**Type:**	External
skill -9 top	Kills the process top with signal 9 (SIGKILL).		

slattach

UNIX Shell: All primary shells (bash, ash, tcsh)

Function	Transfers a serial line connection to a network interface.
Syntax	slattach [options...] { *tty* }

-d	Shows debug information.		
-e	Exits after initializing. Doesn't wait for the line to hang up.		
-h	Exits when the carrier is lost.		
-l	Creates a lockfile for the device in `/var/lock`, using the UUCP style.		
-L	Sets the terminal to `CLOCAL` mode and disables carrier watching.		
-m	Doesn't initialize the line into 8 bits raw mode.		
-n	Sets the terminal to read-only mode.		
-q	Sets to quiet mode. Shows no messages.		
-v	Verbose mode. Shows more information.		
-c *command*	Starts the command when the line is hung up.		
-p *protocol*	Specifies what kind of protocol to use - CSLIP, SLIP, PPP, or KISS.		
-s *speed*	Specifies the line speed. Overrides the default value.		
tty	Specifies the terminal to use.		
File Name: slattach	**Directory:** /sbin/	**Type:**	External

slist

UNIX Shell: All primary shells (bash, ash, tcsh)

Function	Shows all NetWare servers present on the network.
Syntax	slist { *pattern* }

pattern	Shows only the servers that matches the specified pattern.		
File Name: slist	**Directory:** /usr/bin/	**Type:**	External
slist "n*"	Matches specified regular expression (all names beginning with an `n`).		

slocal

UNIX Shell: All primary shells (bash, ash, tcsh)

Function	Processes inbound messages according to a selection criterion.
Syntax	slocal { *address info sender* } [options...]

-addr *address*	Specifies the sender's address.		
-info *arguments*	Specifies arguments to sub-processes.		
-sender *user*	Specifies the username of the sender.		
-user *user*	Specifies the user that delivers mail.		
-mailbox *maildrop*	Specifies the name of the maildrop file.		
-file *file*	Specifies a file to read messages from (default is STDIN).		
-maildelivery *file*	Specifies file to read message selection criteria from.		
-verbose	Verbose mode. Shows more information.		
-noverbose	Disables verbose mode.		
-suppressdup	Enables check for duplicate messages.		
-nosuppressdup	Disables check for duplicate messages.		
-debug	Shows debug information.		
-version	Shows version information.		
-help	Shows help information.		
address	Specifies the sender's address.		
info	Specifies arguments to the subprocesses.		
sender	Specifies the username of the sender.		
File Name: slocal	**Directory:** /usr/lib/nmh/	**Type:**	External

slocate, locate

UNIX Shell:	All primary shells (bash, ash, tcsh)
Function	Looks quickly in a database to find files.
Syntax	slocate [options...] *{ string }*

-q	Sets the command into quiet mode. Shows no error messages.
-d *path*	Specifies the path in the database to search in.
-i	Does a case-insensitive search.
-r *expression*	Searches the database using the specified regular expression.
-v	Verbose mode. Shows more information.
-o *file*	Creates the database in the specified file.
-e *directories...*	Skips the specified directories when searching.
-f *fstypes...*	Skips the specified file systems when searching.
-l *level*	Specifies the security level (0 means no security check, (default is 1).
-c	Gets information from `/etc/updatedb.conf` when updating the database.
-U *directory*	Creates the database, starting at specified directory.
-u	Creates the database, starting at root directory.
-V	Shows version information.
-h	Shows help information.
-n *value*	Specifies the maximum amount of hits.
string	Specifies the string to search for.

File Name:	`slocate`	**Directory:**	/usr/bin/	**Type:**	External
Note:	Use the command `updatedb` to update the locate database.				

smbadduser

UNIX Shell:	TC shell (tcsh)
Function	Adds users to SMB's password file.
Syntax	smbadduser *unixusername:ntusername*

unixusername	Specifies the username on the UNIX computer.
ntusername	Specifies the username on the NT computer.

File Name:	`smbadduser`	**Directory:**	/usr/bin/	**Type:**	Script

smbclient

UNIX Shell:	All primary shells (bash, ash, tcsh)
Function	Connects to a remote service using SMB.
Syntax	smbclient *service { password }* [options...]

-s *path*	Specifies the pathname to `smb.conf` file.
-O *options*	Specifies socket options to use.
-R *name*	Specifies resolve order.
-M *hostname*	Specifies a hostname to send a window popup message to.
-i *scope*	Specifies the NetBIOS scope.
-N	Specifies that a password shouldn't be asked for.
-n *name*	Specifies the NetBIOS name to use.
-d *level*	Specifies the debug level.
-P	Specifies the remote service is a printer.
-p *port*	Specifies a port to connect to.
-l *basename*	Specifies the base name for log and debug files.
-h	Shows help information.
-I *address*	Specifies the address to connect to.
-E	Shows messages on STDERR instead of STDOUT.
-U *user*	Specifies the username to connect as.
-L *host*	Shows a list of shares available on host.
-t *code*	Specifies the terminal I/O code; can be sjis, euc, jis7, jis8, junet, or hex.
-m *level*	Specifies the max protocol level.
-W *workgroup*	Specifies the workgroup name.
-T*modeflags*	Specifies command-line `tar`. Mode can be c or x, flags can be: I, X, F, q, g, b, N, a, or n.
-D	Specifies the directory to start from.
-c *command*	Specifies a command string to execute. Commands must be separated using semicolons.
-b *buffer*	Changes the transmit and send buffer (default is 65520).

continued

service		Specifies the service to connect to.			
password		Specifies a password to use when connecting.			
File Name:	`smbclient`	**Directory:**	/usr/bin/	**Type:**	External
smbclient '\\ucg\directory'		Connects to service ucg and the share directory.			

smbd

UNIX Shell: All primary shells (bash, ash, tcsh)

Function	Starts the Samba daemon that handles SMB/CIFF requests.
Syntax	smbd [options...]

-D	Specifies that it should be run as a daemon (this isn't default).
-a	Specifies that each new connection appends log messages to the log file (is default).
-o	Specifies the log files will be overwritten when opened (default is to append).
-P	Specifies that no network traffic should be sent. Is used for debugging.
-h	Shows help information.
-V	Shows version information.
-d *debuglevel*	Specifies the debug level, from 0 to 10. The higher the number, the more that is shown.
-l *filename*	Specifies the file to log messages to.
-p *port*	Specifies the port to listen on.
-O *socket*	Specifies the socket options to control the networking layer.
-s *filename*	Specifies the config file to read options from.

File Name:	`smbd`	**Directory:**	/usr/sbin/	**Type:**	External

smbmnt

UNIX Shell: All primary shells (bash, ash, tcsh)

Function	Mounts SMB file system shares. Checks if a user has write permissions on the mount point before mounting.
Syntax	smbmnt *directory* [options...]

-r	Mounts the file system as read-only.
-u *uid*	Specifies the owner of the files by the UID.
-g *gid*	Specifies the owner of the files by the GID.
-f *mask*	Specifies the octal file mask applied.
-d *mask*	Specifies the octal directory mask applied.
-s *name*	Specifies the share name on the server.
directory	The directory to share.

File Name:	`smbmnt`	**Directory:**	/usr/bin/	**Type:**	External
Note:	The `smbmnt` program is normally invoked by `smbmount` and shouldn't be used directly.				

smbmount

UNIX Shell: All primary shells (bash, ash, tcsh)

Function	Mounts an SMB file system.
Syntax	smbmount *service mountpoint* [-o *options...*]

-o	**The following options can be used, but they must be separated by commas:**
username=*user*	Specifies a user to connect as.
password=*password*	Specifies a password to connect with.
netbiosname=*name*	Specifies a NetBIOS name (default is the local hostname).
uid=*number*	Specifies a user ID to mount as.
gid=*number*	Specifies a group ID to mount as.
port=*number*	Specifies a port to connect to.
fmask=*octal*	Specifies the file mask (default is based on current umask).
dmask=*octal*	Specifies the directory mask (default is based on current umask).
debug=*level*	Specifies a debug level.
ip=*address*	Specifies the remote IP to connect to.
workgroup=*name*	Specifies the workgroup on the destination.
sockopt=*argument*	Specifies the TCP socket options.
scope=*argument*	Specifies the NetBIOS scope.
guest	Doesn't prompt the user for a password.
ro	Specifies that it should be mounted as read-only.

continued

rw	Specifies that it should be mounted as read and write.		
service	Specifies a service to mount.		
mountpoint	Specifies a mount point where the service is mounted.		
File Name: `smbmount`	**Directory:** /usr/bin/	**Type:**	External
smbmount \\ucg /mnt	Mounts service \\ucg in `/mnt`.		
smbmount \\ucg /mnt -o username=uk,ro	Mounts service \\ucg in `/mnt` with user `uk` and as read-only.		

smbpasswd

UNIX Shell: All primary shells (bash, ash, tcsh)

Function	Changes the user's SMB password.
Syntax	smbpasswd [options...] *user*

-a	Creates a new user using the specified name. Can only be used by root.
-x	Deletes the specified user from the user list. Can only be used by root.
-d	Disables the specified user. Can only be used by root.
.	Enables the specified user. Can only be used by root.
-D *debuglevel*	Sets the debugging level, must be between 0-10 (default is 0).
-n	Sets the password to a blank line. Can only be used by root.
-r *computer*	Sets the computer NetBIOS name you want to change the password on.
-R *name*	Specifies the resolution services to use when trying to connect by a NetBIOS name.
lmhosts	Searches the IP address in the Samba `lmhosts` file.
host	Searches the IP address from the file `/etc/hosts` or by NIS or DNS lookups.
wins	Resolves hostname IP address using WINS. Must specify WINS server in `smb.conf`.
bcast	Performs a broadcast on each known local interface specified in `smb.conf`.
-m	Specifies the account is a computer account. Can only be used by root.
-j DOMAIN	Adds a SMB server into a Windows NT domain. Can only be used by root.
-U *username*	Specifies the username to change on the remote connection. Can only be used with -r.
-h	Shows help information.
-s	Silent mode. Reads the password from STDIN instead of prompting it.
user	Specifies the username to change the password on.
File Name: `smbpasswd`	**Directory:** /usr/bin/ **Type:** External

smbspool

UNIX Shell: All primary shells (bash, ash, tcsh)

Function	Sends a print file to an SMB printer.
Syntax	smbspool *job user title copies options... { file }*

job	Specifies the job ID. Currently not used, but must be specified.
user	Specifies the username. Currently not used, but must be specified.
title	Specifies the title of the job. The remote print filename sets this.
copies	Specifies the number of copies to make. Only used if a file is specified. (Even if the file isn't specified, you must specify the copies argument.)
options...	Specifies print options. Currently not used, but must be specified.
file	Specifies the file to print. If not specified, STDIN is used.
File Name: `smbspool`	**Directory:** /usr/bin/ **Type:** External

smbstatus

UNIX Shell: All primary shells (bash, ash, tcsh)

Function	Shows the current Samba connections.
Syntax	smbstatus [options...]

-P	Shows the contents of the profiling shared memory area only.
-b	Gives brief output.
-d	Verbose mode. Shows more information.
-L	Shows locks only.
-p	Shows a list of smbd processes.
-S	Shows shares only.
-s *config-file*	Specifies configuration file to use, other than the default `/etc/smb.conf`.

continued

-u *username*		Shows information relevant to username only.			
File Name:	smbstatus	**Directory:**	/usr/bin/	**Type:**	External

smbtar

UNIX Shell: Bourne shell (sh)

Function	This command script is a utility that dumps SMB shares into a tape device.
Syntax	smbtar -s *server* [options...] *files...*

-s *server*		Specifies the SMB/CIFS server that provides the share.			
-x *name*		Specifies the share name on the server (default is backup).			
-X		Excludes filenames from `tar` create or restore.			
-p *password*		Specifies the password on the share.			
-d *directory*		Changes to specified directory before restoring or backing up files.			
-u *userID*		Specifies the user ID to log in with (default is the current login name).			
-t *device*		Specifies the tape device. Can also be a path to a file.			
-b *size*		Specifies the block size, which is multiplied by 512 (default is 20).			
-N *file*		Backs only up files newer than the specified file.			
-i		Backs up `tar` files if they have the archive bit set.			
-r		Restores files from the tar file.			
-l *level*		Specifies the log level (is between 0 and 10 when 0 is no logging).			
-v		Verbose mode. Shows more information.			
-a		Resets the archive bit.			
files...		Specifies file to act on.			
File Name:	smbtar	**Directory:**	/usr/bin/	**Type:**	Script

smbtar -s host -t tarfile docs	Backs up files in directory `docs` at `host` into tarfile.
smbtar -s host -x share -r -t tarfile	Restores files from tarfile into `share` at `host`.
smbtar -s host -p passwd -t tarfile	Backs up files from `host` to tarfile with passwd as `password`.

smbumount

UNIX Shell: All primary shells (bash, ash, tcsh)

Function	Lets users unmount their SMB mounted directories. The directory must have the SUID set to root.
Syntax	smbumount *directory*

directory		Specifies the mounted directory to unmount.			
File Name:	smbumount	**Directory:**	/usr/bin/	**Type:**	External

smproxy

UNIX Shell: All primary shells (bash, ash, tcsh)

Function	Works as an X application proxy and allows the application to use an X11R6 session.
Syntax	smproxy [options...]

-clientId *clientID*		Specifies the session ID that was used in the previous session.			
-restore *file*		Specifies the file that was used to save the state in from the previous session.			
File Name:	smproxy	**Directory:**	/usr/X11R6/bin/	**Type:**	External

smrsh

UNIX Shell: All primary shells (bash, ash, tcsh)

Function	Restricts users to only be able to run certain sendmail commands in a shell.
Syntax	smrsh -c *command*

-c *command*		Specifies a valid command to run.			
File Name:	smrsh	**Directory:**	/usr/sbin/	**Type:**	External

sndAppleSingle

UNIX Shell:	A shell (ash, bsh)				
Function	Allows the user to send Macintosh files stored inside a UNIX file system with the CAP AUFS program.				
Syntax	sndAppleSingle *file*				
file	Specifies the Macintosh file that's sent.				
File Name:	sndAppleSingle	**Directory:**	/usr/bin/	**Type:**	Script
Note:	Works only if the CAP package has been installed and the cvt2apple program is available (converts CAP to AppleSingle format).				

sndconfig

UNIX Shell:	All primary shells (bash, ash, tcsh)				
Function	A graphic interface program that configures sound cards to work with a Linux kernel module.				
Syntax	sndconfig [options...]				
--help	Shows help information.				
--noprobe	Doesn't search for, or run, any changes to PnP cards.				
--noautoconfig	Doesn't run any autconfiguration on PnP cards. It prompts for settings.				
File Name:	sndconfig	**Directory:**	/usr/sbin/	**Type:**	External

snice

UNIX Shell:	All primary shells (bash, ash, tcsh)				
Function	Shows process status and sets new priorities for processes.				
Syntax	snice *{ priority }* [options...] *processes...*				
-f	Sets to fast mode. This is unavailable at this moment.				
-i	Asks for approval for each action.				
-v	Shows information about selected processes.				
-w	Enables warnings. This is unavailable at the moment.				
-n	Shows the process ID only.				
-t	Specifies the next argument is a terminal.				
-u	Specifies the next argument is a username.				
-p	Specifies the next argument is a process ID.				
-c	Specifies the next argument is a command name.				
priority	Specifies the priority to set (is between -20 and 20, where -20 is the highest).				
processes...	Specifies the processes to modify.				
File Name:	snice	**Directory:**	/usr/bin/	**Type:**	External
snice +7 netscape	Slows down Netscape.				
snice -17 root bash	Gives a very high priority to the root's shell.				

snmpbulkget

UNIX Shell:	All primary shells (bash, ash, tcsh)
Function	Communicates with a network entity using SNMP BULK requests.
Syntax	snmpbulkget [options...] *host { community } { objectID }*
-h	Shows help information.
-H	Shows configuration file directives understood.
-V	Shows version information.
-v *version*	Specifies the SNMP version to use; values are 1, 2c, or 3.
	The following option is version 1- or 2c-specific:
-c *number*	Specifies the community name, values are v1 or v2c.
	The following options are version 3-specific:
-Z *argument*	Specifies the destination engine boots and time.
-e *argument*	Specifies the security engine ID.
-E *argument*	Specifies the context engine ID.
-n *argument*	Specifies the context name.
-u *argument*	Specifies the security name.
-l *argument*	Specifies the security level - values are noAuthNoPriv, authNoPriv, or authPriv.

continued

-a *argument*	Specifies the authentication protocol - values are MD5 or SHA.
-A *argument*	Specifies the authentication protocol pass phrase.
-x *argument*	Specifies the privacy protocol values as DES.
-X *argument*	Specifies the privacy protocol pass phrase.
	The following options are general for all protocol versions:
-p *port*	Specifies the port to use.
-T *layer*	Specifies the layer for the network — values are UDP or TCP.
-t *number*	Specifies the request timeout.
-r *number*	Specifies the number of retries.
-d	Shows input and output packets.
-D *argument*	Specifies debugging for some or all tokens - values are all or the name of the token.
-m *argument*	Specifies the MIBs to use, or if argument is all, then all is used to listen for.
-M *argument*	Specifies the directory to search for MIBs.
-P *argument*	Toggles various defaults controlling MIB parsing.
-O *argument*	Toggles various defaults controlling output display.
-I *argument*	Toggles various defaults controlling input parsing.
-B *number number*	Specifies the nonrepeaters and maximum repetitions over the remainder.
host	Specifies the host to connect to.
community	Specifies the community to connect as.
objectID	Specifies the object ID to ask for.

File Name:	snmpbulkget	Directory:	/usr/bin/	Type:	External

snmpbulkwalk

UNIX Shell:	All primary shells (bash, ash, tcsh)
Function	Communicates with a network entity using SNMP BULK requests.
Syntax	snmpbulkwalk [options...] *host { community } { objectID }*

-h	Shows help information.
-H	Shows configuration file directives understood.
-V	Shows version information.
-v *version*	Specifies the SNMP version to use — values are 1, 2c, or 3.
	The following option is version 1- or 2c-specific:
-c *number*	Specifies the community name — values are v1 or v2c.
	The following options are version 3-specific:
-Z *argument*	Specifies the destination engine boots or time.
-e *argument*	Specifies the security engine ID.
-E *argument*	Specifies the context engine ID.
-n *argument*	Specifies the context name.
-u *argument*	Specifies the security name.
-l *argument*	Specifies the security level — values are noAuthNoPriv, authNoPriv, or authPriv.
-a *argument*	Specifies the authentication protocol values are MD5 or SHA.
-A *argument*	Specifies the authentication protocol pass phrase.
-x *argument*	Specifies the privacy protocol, values as DES.
-X *argument*	Specifies the privacy protocol pass phrase.
	The following options are general for all protocol versions:
-p *port*	Specifies the port to use.
-T *layer*	Specifies the layer for the network — values are UDP or TCP.
-t *number*	Specifies the request timeout.
-r *number*	Specifies the number of retries.
-d	Shows input and output packets.
-D *argument*	Specifies debugging for some or all tokens — values are all or the name of the token.
-m *argument*	Specifies the MIBs to use or if argument is all then all is used to listen for.
-M *argument*	Specifies the directory to search for MIBs.
-P *argument*	Toggles various defaults controlling MIB parsing.
-O *argument*	Toggles various defaults controlling output display.
-I *argument*	Toggles various defaults controlling input parsing.
host	Specifies the host to connect to.

continued

community	Specifies the community to connect as.		
objectID	Specifies the object ID to ask for.		
File Name: `snmpbulkwalk`	**Directory:** /usr/bin/	**Type:**	External

snmpd

UNIX Shell: All primary shells (bash, ash, tcsh)

Function	An agent that responds to SNMP request packets. Monitors networks.
Syntax	snmpd [options...]

-a	Writes the addresses that connects to the SNMP agent to STDERR or the log file.
-V	Shows the agents protocol transaction.
-d	Dumps sent and received UDP packets to STDERR or the log file.
-q	Quiet mode. Shows less information.
-D	Shows debug information.
-p *port*	Specifies the port to open on (default is 161).
-f	Doesn't fork from the calling shell.
-l *file*	Dumps all information to the specified log file.
-L	Dumps all information to STDOUT and STDERR.
-A	Appends the log file, instead of truncating it.
-c *file*	Reads the configuration from the specified file.
-C	Doesn't use any configuration files, except the one -c specifies.
-r	Doesn't exit if it can't open certain files. Lets non-root users use this command.
-v	Shows version information.
-x	Listens for the specified AgentX connections not `/var/agentx/master`.

File Name: `snmpd`	**Directory:** /usr/sbin/	**Type:**	External
Tip:	This is useful when you have big networks and want to be able to run software on one computer to check whether anything goes down or just check status on agents.		

snmpdelta

UNIX Shell: All primary shells (bash, ash, tcsh)

Function	Monitors deltas of integer-valued SNMP variables.
Syntax	snmpdelta [options...] *host { community } { objectID } oids...*

-h	Shows help information.
-H	Shows configuration file directives understood.
-V	Shows version information.
-v *version*	Specifies the SNMP version to use - values are 1, 2c, or 3.
	The following option is version 1- or 2c-specific:
-c *number*	Specifies the community name — values are v1 or v2c.
	The following options are version 3-specific:
-Z *argument*	Specifies the destination engine boots and time.
-e *argument*	Specifies the security engine ID.
-E *argument*	Specifies the context engine ID.
-n *argument*	Specifies the context name.
-u *argument*	Specifies the security name.
-l *argument*	Specifies the security level - values are noAuthNoPriv, authNoPriv, or authPriv.
-a *argument*	Specifies the authentication protocol — values are MD5 or SHA.
-A *argument*	Specifies the authentication protocol pass phrase.
-x *argument*	Specifies the privacy protocol values as DES.
-X *argument*	Specifies the privacy protocol pass phrase.
	The following options are general for all protocol versions:
-p *port*	Specifies the port to use.
-T *layer*	Specifies the layer for the network — values are UDP or TCP.
-t *number*	Specifies the request timeout.
-r *number*	Specifies the number of retries.
-d	Shows input and output packets.
-D *argument*	Specifies debugging for some or all tokens — values are all or the name of the token.
-m *argument*	Specifies the MIBs to use, or if argument is all, then all is used to listen for.
-M *argument*	Specifies the directory to search for MIBs.
-P *argument*	Toggles various defaults controlling MIB parsing.

continued

-O *argument*	Toggles various defaults controlling output display.
-I *argument*	Toggles various defaults controlling input parsing.
-Cf	Don't fix errors or retry the request.
-l	Writes configurations to file.
-f *file*	Loads configurations from file.
-p *number*	Specifies the poll period.
-P *peaks*	Specifies the reporting period in poll periods.
-v *number*	Specifies number of variables per packet.
-k	Keeps seconds in output time.
-m	Shows max values.
-S	Logs to a sum file.
-s	Shows timestamps.
-t	Gets timing from agent.
-T	Show output in tabular form.
-L *file*	Specifies the sum file.
host	Specifies the host to connect to.
community	Specifies the community to connect as.
objectID	Specifies the object ID to ask for.
oids...	Specifies the integer value or values to monitor and reports changes made to them.

File Name:	`snmpdelta`	**Directory:**	/usr/bin/	**Type:**	External

snmpget

UNIX Shell: All primary shells (bash, ash, tcsh)

Function	Communicates with a network entity using SNMP GET requests.
Syntax	snmpget [options...] *host { community } { objectID }*

-h	Shows help information.
-H	Shows configuration file directives understood.
-V	Shows version information.
-v *version*	Specifies the SNMP version to use — values are 1, 2c, or 3.
	The following option is version 1- or 2c-specific:
-c *number*	Specifies the community name, values are v1 or v2c.
	The following options are version 3-specific:
-Z *argument*	Specifies the destination engine boots and time.
-e *argument*	Specifies the security engine ID.
-E *argument*	Specifies the context engine ID.
-n *argument*	Specifies the context name.
-u *argument*	Specifies the security name.
-l *argument*	Specifies the security level — values are noAuthNoPriv, authNoPriv, or authPriv.
-a *argument*	Specifies the authentication protocol — values are MD5 or SHA.
-A *argument*	Specifies the authentication protocol pass phrase.
-x *argument*	Specifies the privacy protocol values as DES.
-X *argument*	Specifies the privacy protocol pass phrase.
	The following options are general for all protocol versions:
-p *port*	Specifies the port to use.
-T *layer*	Specifies the layer for the network — values are UDP or TCP.
-t *number*	Specifies the request timeout.
-r *number*	Specifies the number of retries.
-d	Shows input and output packets.
-D *argument*	Specifies debugging for some or all tokens — values are all or the name of the token.
-m *argument*	Specifies the MIBs to use, or if argument is all, then all is used to listen for.
-M *argument*	Specifies the directory to search for MIBs.
-P *argument*	Toggles various defaults controlling MIB parsing.
-O *argument*	Toggles various defaults controlling output display.
-I *argument*	Toggles various defaults controlling input parsing.
-Cf	Don't fix errors or retry the request.
host	Specifies the host to connect to.
community	Specifies the community to connect as.

continued

objectID	Specifies the object ID to ask for.		
File Name: `snmpget`	**Directory:** /usr/bin/	**Type:**	External

snmpgetnext

UNIX Shell: All primary shells (bash, ash, tcsh)

Function	Communicates with a network entity using SNMP GET NEXT requests.
Syntax	snmpgetnext [options...] *host { community } { objectID }*

-h	Shows help information.
-H	Shows configuration file directives understood.
-V	Shows version information.
-v *version*	Specifies the SNMP version to use — values are 1, 2c, or 3.
	The following option is version 1- or 2c-specific:
-c *number*	Specifies the community name — values are v1 or v2c.
	The following options are version 3-specific:
-Z *argument*	Specifies the destination engine boots and time.
-e *argument*	Specifies the security engine ID.
-E *argument*	Specifies the context engine ID.
-n *argument*	Specifies the context name.
-u *argument*	Specifies the security name.
-l *argument*	Specifies the security level — values are noAuthNoPriv, authNoPriv, or authPriv.
-a *argument*	Specifies the authentication protocol — values are MD5 or SHA.
-A *argument*	Specifies the authentication protocol pass phrase.
-x *argument*	Specifies the privacy protocol — values as DES.
-X *argument*	Specifies the privacy protocol pass phrase.
	The following options are general for all protocol versions:
-p *port*	Specifies the port to use.
-T *layer*	Specifies the layer for the network — values are UDP or TCP.
-t *number*	Specifies the request timeout.
-r *number*	Specifies the number of retries.
-d	Shows input and output packets.
-D *argument*	Specifies debugging for some or all tokens — values are all or the name of the token.
-m *argument*	Specifies the MIBs to use or if argument is all then all is used to listen for.
-M *argument*	Specifies the directory to search for MIBs.
-P *argument*	Toggles various defaults controlling MIB parsing.
-O *argument*	Toggles various defaults controlling output display.
-I *argument*	Toggles various defaults controlling input parsing.
-Cf	Don't fix errors or retry the request.
host	Specifies the host to connect to.
community	Specifies the community to connect as.
objectID	Specifies the object ID to ask for.
File Name: `snmpgetnext`	**Directory:** /usr/bin/ **Type:** External

snmpnetstat

UNIX Shell: All primary shells (bash, ash, tcsh)

Function	Shows network status using SNMP.
Syntax	snmpnetstat [options...] *host { community } { interval }*

-v *version*	Specifies the SNMP version — values are 1 or 2c.
-V	Shows version information.
-p *port*	Specifies the port to connect with.
-c *community*	Specifies the community name.
-t *number*	Specifies the SNMP packet timeout in seconds.
-i	Shows interfaces with packet counters.
-o	Shows interfaces with octet counters.
-s	Shows general statistics.
-n	Shows IP addresses, not names.
-a	Shows sockets in `listen` mode.
-P *protocol*	Shows only this protocol.
-I *interface*	Specifies the interface to show information on.

continued

-d	Dumps packets.
-D*debugspec*	Specifies the debug specifications.
host	Specifies the host to connect to.
community	Specifies the community to connect as.
interval	Specifies the interval to check for values.
File Name: `snmpnetstat`	**Directory:** /usr/bin/ **Type:** External

snmpset

UNIX Shell: All primary shells (bash, ash, tcsh)

Function	Communicates with a network entity using SNMP SET requests.
Syntax	snmpset [options...] *host { community } { objectID type value }*

-h	Shows help information.
-H	Shows configuration file directives understood.
-V	Shows version information.
-v *version*	Specifies the SNMP version to use — values are 1, 2c, or 3.
	The following option is version 1- or 2c-specific:
-c *number*	Specifies the community name — values are v1 or v2c.
	The following options are version 3-specific:
-Z *argument*	Specifies the destination engine boots and time.
-e *argument*	Specifies the security engine ID.
-E *argument*	Specifies the context engine ID.
-n *argument*	Specifies the context name.
-u *argument*	Specifies the security name.
-l *argument*	Specifies the security level — values are noAuthNoPriv, authNoPriv, or authPriv.
-a *argument*	Specifies the authentication protocol — values are MD5 or SHA.
-A *argument*	Specifies the authentication protocol pass phrase.
-x *argument*	Specifies the privacy protocol values as DES.
-X *argument*	Specifies the privacy protocol pass phrase.
	The following options are general for all protocol versions:
-p *port*	Specifies the port to use.
-T *layer*	Specifies the layer for the network — values are UDP or TCP.
-t *number*	Specifies the request timeout.
-r *number*	Specifies the number of retries.
-d	Shows input and output packets.
-D *argument*	Specifies debugging for some or all tokens — values are all or the name of the token.
-m *argument*	Specifies the MIBs to use or if argument is all then all is used to listen for.
-M *argument*	Specifies the directory to look for MIBs in.
-P *argument*	Toggles defaults that control MIB parsing.
-O *argument*	Toggles defaults that control output display.
-I *argument*	Toggles defaults that control input parsing.
host	Specifies the host to connect to.
community	Specifies the community to connect as.
objectID	Specifies the object ID to ask for.
type	Specifies the type of the object ID.
value	Specifies the value to set to the object ID.
File Name: `snmpset`	**Directory:** /usr/bin/ **Type:** External

snmpstatus

UNIX Shell: All primary shells (bash, ash, tcsh)

Function	Retrieves important information from a network host.
Syntax	snmpstatus [options...] *hostname { community }*

-h	Shows help information.
-H	Shows configuration file directives understood.
-V	Shows version information.
-v *version*	Specifies the SNMP version to use — values are 1, 2c, or 3.
	The following option is version 1- or 2c-specific:
-c *number*	Specifies the community name — values are v1 or v2c.

continued

	The following options are version 3-specific:
-Z *argument*	Specifies the destination engine boots and time.
-e *argument*	Specifies the security engine ID.
-E *argument*	Specifies the context engine ID.
-n *argument*	Specifies the context name.
-u *argument*	Specifies the security name.
-l *argument*	Specifies the security level — values are noAuthNoPriv, authNoPriv, or authPriv.
-a *argument*	Specifies the authentication protocol — values are MD5 or SHA.
-A *argument*	Specifies the authentication protocol pass phrase.
-x *argument*	Specifies the privacy protocol values as DES.
-X *argument*	Specifies the privacy protocol pass phrase.
	The following options are general for all protocol versions:
-p *port*	Specifies the port to use.
-T *layer*	Specifies the layer for the network — values are UDP or TCP.
-t *number*	Specifies the request timeout.
-r *number*	Specifies the number of retries.
-d	Shows input and output packets.
-D *argument*	Specifies debugging for some or all tokens — values are all or the name of the token.
-m *argument*	Specifies the MIBs to use or, if argument is all, then all is used to listen for.
-M *argument*	Specifies the directory to search for MIBs.
-P *argument*	Toggles various defaults controlling MIB parsing.
-O *argument*	Toggles various defaults controlling output display.
-I *argument*	Toggles various defaults controlling input parsing.
-Cf	Don't fix errors or retry the request.
host	Specifies the host to connect to.
community	Specifies the community to connect as.

File Name:	`snmpstatus`	**Directory:**	/usr/bin/	**Type:**	External

snmptable

UNIX Shell:	All primary shells (bash, ash, tcsh)
Function	Shows SNMP tables after retrieving them.
Syntax	snmptable [options...] *host { community } objectID*

-h	Shows help information.
-H	Shows configuration file directives understood.
-V	Shows version information.
-v *version*	Specifies the SNMP version to use — values are 1, 2c, or 3.
	The following option is version 1- or 2c-specific:
-c *number*	Specifies the community name — values are v1 or v2c.
	The following options are version 3-specific:
-Z *argument*	Specifies the destination engine boots and time.
-e *argument*	Specifies the security engine ID.
-E *argument*	Specifies the context engine ID.
-n *argument*	Specifies the context name.
-u *argument*	Specifies the security name.
-l *argument*	Specifies the security level — values are noAuthNoPriv, authNoPriv, or authPriv.
-a *argument*	Specifies the authentication protocol - values are MD5 or SHA.
-A *argument*	Specifies the authentication protocol pass phrase.
-x *argument*	Specifies the privacy protocol values as DES.
-X *argument*	Specifies the privacy protocol pass phrase.
	The following options are general for all protocol versions:
-p *port*	Specifies the port to use.
-T *layer*	Specifies the layer for the network — values are UDP or TCP.
-t *number*	Specifies the request timeout.
-r *number*	Specifies the number of retries.
-d	Shows input and output packets.
-D *argument*	Specifies debugging for some or all tokens — values are all or the name of the token.
-m *argument*	Specifies the MIBs to use or, if argument is all, then all is used to listen for.
-M *argument*	Specifies the directory to search for MIBs.

continued

-P *argument*	Toggles various defaults controlling MIB parsing.
-O *argument*	Toggles various defaults controlling output display.
-I *argument*	Toggles various defaults controlling input parsing.
-Cw *width*	Shows tables in parts of width characters.
-Cf *number*	Shows a number-delimited table.
-Cb	Shows brief field names.
-Ci	Shows index values.
-Ch	Shows only the column headers.
-CH	Shows no column headers.
host	Specifies the host to connect to.
community	Specifies the community to connect as.
objectID	Specifies the object ID to ask for.
File Name: `snmptable`	**Directory:** /usr/bin/ **Type:** External

snmptest

UNIX Shell: All primary shells (bash, ash, tcsh)

Function	Communicates with a network entity using SNMP requests.
Syntax	snmptest [options...] *host { community }*

-h	Shows help information.
-H	Shows configuration file directives understood.
-V	Shows version information.
-v *version*	Specifies the SNMP version to use — values are 1, 2c, or 3.
	The following option is version 1- or 2c-specific:
-c *number*	Specifies the community name — values are v1 or v2c.
	The following options are version 3-specific:
-Z *argument*	Specifies the destination engine boots and time.
-e *argument*	Specifies the security engine ID.
-E *argument*	Specifies the context engine ID.
-n *argument*	Specifies the context name.
-u *argument*	Specifies the security name.
-l *argument*	Specifies the security level — values are noAuthNoPriv, authNoPriv, or authPriv.
-a *argument*	Specifies the authentication protocol — values are MD5 or SHA.
-A *argument*	Specifies the authentication protocol pass phrase.
-x *argument*	Specifies the privacy protocol values as DES.
-X *argument*	Specifies the privacy protocol pass phrase.
	The following options are general for all protocol versions:
-p *port*	Specifies the port to use.
-T *layer*	Specifies the layer for the network — values are UDP or TCP.
-t *number*	Specifies the request timeout.
-r *number*	Specifies the number of retries.
-d	Shows input and output packets.
-D *argument*	Specifies debugging for some or all tokens — values are all or the name of the token.
-m *argument*	Specifies the MIBs to use or, if argument is all, then all is used to listen for.
-M *argument*	Specifies the directory to search for MIBs.
-P *argument*	Toggles various defaults controlling MIB parsing.
-O *argument*	Toggles various defaults controlling output display.
-I *argument*	Toggles various defaults controlling input parsing.
host	Specifies the host to connect to.
community	Specifies the community to connect as.
File Name: `snmptest`	**Directory:** /usr/bin/ **Type:** External

snmptranslate

UNIX Shell: All primary shells (bash, ash, tcsh)

Function	Translates SNMP objects into more useful information.
Syntax	snmptranslate [options...] *{ objectID }*

-h	Shows help information.
-V	Shows version information.

continued

-m *argument*	Specifies the MIBs to use, or if argument is all, then all is used to listen for.
-D	Enables snmplib debugging messages.
-M *argument*	Specifies the directory to search for MIBs.
-w *width*	Specifies the width of the tree output.
-T *arguments*	Shows one or more MIB symbol reports.
-P *argument*	Toggles various defaults controlling MIB parsing.
-O *argument*	Toggles various defaults controlling output display.
-I *argument*	Toggles various defaults controlling input parsing.
objectID	Specifies the object ID to ask for.
File Name: `snmptranslate`	**Directory:** /usr/bin/ **Type:** External

snmptrap

UNIX Shell: All primary shells (bash, ash, tcsh)

Function	Sends an SNMP TRAP to a manager.
Syntax	snmptrap [options...] *host { community } { parameters... }*

-h	Shows help information.
-H	Shows configuration file directives understood.
-V	Shows version information.
-v *version*	Specifies the SNMP version to use — values are 1, 2c, or 3.
	The following options are version 1- or 2c-specific:
-c *number*	Specifies the community name — values are v1 or v2c.
	The following options are version 3-specific:
-Z *argument*	Specifies the destination engine boots and time.
-e *argument*	Specifies the security engine ID.
-E *argument*	Specifies the context engine ID.
-n *argument*	Specifies the context name.
-u *argument*	Specifies the security name.
-l *argument*	Specifies the security level — values are noAuthNoPriv, authNoPriv, or authPriv.
-a *argument*	Specifies the authentication protocol — values are MD5 or SHA.
-A *argument*	Specifies the authentication protocol pass phrase.
-x *argument*	Specifies the privacy protocol values as DES.
-X *argument*	Specifies the privacy protocol pass phrase.
	The following options are general for all protocol versions:
-p *port*	Specifies the port to use.
-T *layer*	Specifies the layer for the network — values are UDP or TCP.
-t *number*	Specifies the request timeout.
-r *number*	Specifies the number of retries.
-d	Shows input and output packets.
-D *argument*	Specifies debugging for some or all tokens — values are all or the name of the token.
-m *argument*	Specifies the MIBs to use or, if argument is all, then all is used to listen for.
-M *argument*	Specifies the directory to search for MIBs.
-P *argument*	Toggles various defaults controlling MIB parsing.
-O *argument*	Toggles various defaults controlling output display.
-I *argument*	Toggles various defaults controlling input parsing.
host	Specifies the host to connect to.
community	Specifies the community to connect as.
parameters...	Specifies one or more trap parameters to send.
File Name: `snmptrap`	**Directory:** /usr/bin/ **Type:** External

snmptrapd

UNIX Shell: All primary shells (bash, ash, tcsh)

Function	Receives and logs SNMP trap messages.
Syntax	snmptrapd [options...]

-h	Shows help information.
-H	Shows what can be in the configuration file.
-V	Shows version information.
-q	Quickly shows mib display.
-D*{ token... }*	Activates on debugging output.

continued

-p *port*	Specifies the port to listen on.
-P	Shows output on STDOUT.
-u *file*	Creates file with process ID information.
-e	Shows events.
-s	Logs to `syslog`
-f	Specifies the program should be in foreground.
-l *{ daemonnumber }*	Specifies the `syslog` facility to log daemon — number can be in range of 0 to 7.
-d	Dumps input and output packets.
-n	Outputs numeric IP addresses.
-a	Ignores authentication failure traps.
-c *file*	Specifies the config file to read options from.
-C	Don't use the config file.
-m *argument*	Specifies the MIBs to use, or if argument is all, then all is used to listen for.
-M *argument*	Specifies the directory to search for MIBs.
-O *argument*	Toggles various defaults controlling output display.
File Name: `snmptrapd`	**Directory:** /usr/sbin/ **Type:** External

snmpusm

UNIX Shell: All primary shells (bash, ash, tcsh)

Function	Administers SNMPv3 users on a remote entity.
Syntax	snmpusm [options...] *host { community } command*

-h	Shows help information.
-H	Shows configuration file directives understood.
-V	Shows version information.
-v *version*	Specifies the SNMP version to use — values are 1, 2c, or 3.
	The following option is version 1- or 2c-specific:
-c *number*	Specifies the community name — values are v1 or v2c.
	The following options are version 3-specific:
-Z *argument*	Specifies the destination engine boots and time.
-e *argument*	Specifies the security engine ID.
-E *argument*	Specifies the context engine ID.
-n *argument*	Specifies the context name.
-u *argument*	Specifies the security name.
-l *argument*	Specifies the security level — values are noAuthNoPriv, authNoPriv, or authPriv.
-a *argument*	Specifies the authentication protocol — values are MD5 or SHA.
-A *argument*	Specifies the authentication protocol pass phrase.
-x *argument*	Specifies the privacy protocol values as DES.
-X *argument*	Specifies the privacy protocol pass phrase.
	The following options are general for all protocol versions:
-p *port*	Specifies the port to use.
-T *layer*	Specifies the layer for the network — values are UDP or TCP.
-t *number*	Specifies the request timeout.
-r *number*	Specifies the number of retries.
-d	Shows input and output packets.
-D *argument*	Specifies debugging for some or all tokens — values are all or the name of the token.
-m *argument*	Specifies the MIBs to use, or if argument is all, then all is used to listen for.
-M *argument*	Specifies the directory to search for MIBs.
-P *argument*	Toggles various defaults MIB parsing.
-O *argument*	Toggles various defaults controlling output display.
-I *argument*	Toggles various defaults controlling input parsing.
host	Specifies the host to connect to.
community	Specifies the community to connect as.
command	**The following commands can be used:**
create *user { from }*	Creates a user, if `from` is specified, the user is cloned from the specified entity.
delete *user*	Deletes a user.
4 cloneFrom *user from*	Clones user from another entity.
passwd [options...] *old new*	Specifies the old and new pass phrase.

continued

	The following options can be used:
-Co	Uses the ownKeyChange objects.
-Cx	Changes the privacy key.
-Ca	Changes the authentication key.
File Name: snmpusm	**Directory:** /usr/bin/ **Type:** External

snmpwalk

UNIX Shell: All primary shells (bash, ash, tcsh)

Function	Communicates with a network entity using SNMP GET next requests.
Syntax	snmpwalk [options...] *host { community } { objectID }*

-h	Shows help information.
-H	Shows configuration file directives understood.
-V	Shows version information.
-v *version*	Specifies the SNMP version to use — values are 1, 2c, or 3.
	The following option is version 1- or 2c-specific:
-c *number*	Specifies the community name — values are v1 or v2c.
	The following options are version 3-specific:
-Z *argument*	Specifies the destination engine boots and time.
-e *argument*	Specifies the security engine ID.
-E *argument*	Specifies the context engine ID.
-n *argument*	Specifies the context name.
-u *argument*	Specifies the security name.
-l *argument*	Specifies the security level — values are noAuthNoPriv, authNoPriv, or authPriv.
-a *argument*	Specifies the authentication protocol — values are MD5 or SHA.
-A *argument*	Specifies the authentication protocol pass phrase.
-x *argument*	Specifies the privacy protocol values as DES.
-X *argument*	Specifies the privacy protocol pass phrase.
	The following options are general for all protocol versions:
-p *port*	Specifies the port to use.
-T *layer*	Specifies the layer for the network — values are UDP or TCP.
-t *number*	Specifies the request timeout.
-r *number*	Specifies the number of retries.
-d	Shows input and output packets.
-D *argument*	Specifies debugging for some or all tokens — values are all or the name of the token.
-m *argument*	Specifies the MIBs to use, or if argument is all, then all is used to listen for.
-M *argument*	Specifies the directory to look for MIBs in.
-P *argument*	Toggles various defaults controlling MIB parsing.
-O *argument*	Toggles various defaults controlling output display.
-I *argument*	Toggles various defaults controlling input parsing.
-C *argument*	Toggles various application-specific behavior.
host	Specifies the host to connect to.
community	Specifies the community to connect as.
objectID	Specifies the object ID to ask for.
File Name: snmpwalk	**Directory:** /usr/bin/ **Type:** External

spell

UNIX Shell: A shell (ash, bsh)

Function	A capability script for the `aspell` spell checker.
Syntax	spell [options...] *{ file }*

options...	Please see `aspell` for options.
file	Specifies a file to spell check.
File Name: spell	**Directory:** /usr/bin/ **Type:** Script

splitmail

splitmail	UNIX Shell:	All primary shells (bash, ash, tcsh)
Function	Splits an e-mail into smaller pieces according to proposed Internet standard for multimedia mail formats.	
Syntax	splitmail [options...] *{ file }*	

-d	Delivers the mail after splitting, using `sendmail`.
-v	Verbose mode. Shows more information.
-s *size*	Specifies the size for the split files (default is 250000).
-p *prefix*	Specifies the prefix for the splitted files (default is `/tmp/split`).
-i *suffix*	Sets the files' message ID as similar. Specifies the suffix for the split files.
file	Specifies the file to split. If not specified, STDIN is used.

File Name:	`splitmail`	**Directory:**	/usr/bin/	**Type:**	External

spost

spost	UNIX Shell:	All primary shells (bash, ash, tcsh)
Function	Delivers a message.	
Syntax	spost [options...] *file*	

-filter *file*	Filters the mail using file as filter input.
-nofilter	Specifies that no filter should be used.
-format	Formats the mail.
-noformat	Don't formats the mail.
-remove	Removes the mail.
-noremove	Keeps the mail.
-verbose	Verbose mode. Shows more information.
-noverbose	Shows less information.
-watch	Shows the transport system's handling of the message.
-nowatch	Don't show the transport system's handling of the message.
-backup	Saves the mail on backup.
-nobackup	Does not save the mail on backup.
-alias *file*	Specifies a file to read aliases from.
-noalias	Don't use aliases.
-width *columns*	Specifies the length of the header components that contain addresses.
-version	Shows version information.
-help	Shows help information
file	Specifies the file that contains the mail.

File Name:	`spost`	**Directory:**	/usr/lib/nmh	**Type:**	External

sserver

sserver	UNIX Shell:	All primary shells (bash, ash, tcsh)
Function	A Kerberos server application. When there is a connection it, returns a Kerberos principal.	
Syntax	sserver [options..] *{ port }*	

-p port	Specifies the TCP client port, not the port specified during installation.
-S *keytab*	Specifies a different `keytab` not the default one.
port	Specifies the server port.

File Name:	`sserver`	**Directory:**	/usr/kerberos/sbin/	**Type:**	External

ssh, slogin

ssh, slogin	UNIX Shell:	All primary shells (bash, ash, tcsh)
Function	Logins secure to a remote computer. It's intended to replace `rlogin`.	
Syntax	ssh [options...] *hostname { command }*	

-a	Disables forwarding of the authentication agent connection.
-A	Enables forwarding of the authentication agent connection.
-c *encryption*	Specifies the encryption type to use. Types are `3des` and `blowfish` (default is 3des).
-e	Specifies the escape character (default is ~).
-f	Runs in the background before command execution.

continued

-g	Specifies that remote hosts are allowed to connect to local forwarded ports.
-i *filename*	Specifies the identity for RSA authentication is read.
-k	Disables forwarding of Kerberos tickets and AFS tokens.
-l *username*	Specifies the username to login as.
-n	Redirects STDIN from `/dev/null`. Must be used when it runs in the background.
-N	Disables execution of remote commands. Only available in protocol version 2.
-o *option*	Gives options in the format used in the configuration file.
-p *port*	Specifies the port to connect to on the remote computer.
-P	Uses a non-privileged port for outgoing connections.
-q	Disables error and warnings messages — it only shows fatal.
-t	Forces pseudo-tty allocation.
-T	Disables pseudo-tty allocation. Only available in protocol version 2.
-v	Verbose mode. Shows more information.
-x	Disables X11 forwarding.
-X	Enables X11 forwarding.
-C	Compresses all data.
-L *port:host:port*	Forwards the port on the local computer to host and port remotely.
-R *port:host:port*	Forwards the port on the remote computer to host and port locally.
-2	Forces to try protocol version 2 only.
-4	Forces to use IPv4 addresses only
-6	Forces to use IPv6 addresses only
hostname	Specifies the hostname to connect to.
command	Specifies the command to execute on the remote computer.

File Name:	`ssh`	**Directory:**	/usr/bin/	**Type:**	External

ssh -l ucg shell.ucgbook.com	Connects securely to shell.ucgbook.com with user ucg.
ssh -C -l ucg shell.ucgbook.com	Connects securely to shell.ucgbook.com with user ucg using compression.

ssh-add

UNIX Shell: All primary shells (bash, ash, tcsh)

Function	Administrates RSA identities for the SSH authentication agent.
Syntax	ssh-add [options...] *{ files... }*

-l	Shows fingerprints of all identities used by the authentication agent.
-L	Shows public-key parameters of all identities used by the authentication agent.
-d	Removes the identity from the authentication agent instead of adding it.
-D	Removes all identities from the authentication agent.
files...	Is one or more alternative files to write authentication information to.

File Name:	`ssh-add`	**Directory:**	/usr/bin/	**Type:**	External

ssh-agent

UNIX Shell: All primary shells (bash, ash, tcsh)

Function	Holds private keys for RSA authentication.
Syntax	ssh-agent [options...] *{ command arguments... }*

-c	Generates C-shell commands on STDOUT.
-s	Generates Bourne shell commands on STDOUT.
-k	Stops the current agent.
command	Runs the command after starting the agent.
arguments...	Specifies the arguments to use with the command.

File Name:	`ssh-agent`	**Directory:**	/usr/bin/	**Type:**	External

sshd

UNIX Shell: All primary shells (bash, ash, tcsh)

Function	The secure shell daemon that allows `ssh` clients access the computer.
Syntax	sshd [options...]

-b *bits*	Specifies the length of the server key (default is 768).
-d	Shows debug information.
-f *configfile*	Specifies the configuration file (default is `/etc/ssh/sshd_config`).
-g *logingracetime*	Specifies the time a client has to authenticate before being disconnected.

continued

-h *hostkeyfile*	Specifies the RSA host key file.
-i	Specifies that sshd is run from `xinetd`.
-k *keygentime*	Specifies the time between regenerating the server key (default is every hour).
-p *port*	Specifies the port to use for connections (default is 22).
-q	Specifies quiet mode — doesn't log anything.
-Q	Doesn't show an error message if RSA support is missing.
-V *clientprotocolid*	Assumes that the client uses the specified protocol.
-4	Specifies IP version 4 only.
-6	Specifies IP version 6 only.
File Name: `sshd`	**Directory:** /usr/sbin/ — **Type:** External

ssh-keygen

UNIX Shell: All primary shells (bash, ash, tcsh)

Function	Is used it create public and private SSH keys.
Syntax	ssh-keygen [options...]

-d	Creates DSA Keys instead of RSA keys.
-q	Specifies silent mode.
-b *bits*	Specifies the number of bits to use (default is 1024).
-c	Changes the comment in a private and a public key.
-f *file*	Specifies the key file.
-l	Shows the fingerprint for the specified public or private key.
-p	Requests a new pass phrase.
-N *passphrase*	Specifies a new pass phrase.
-P *passphrase*	Specifies the old pass phrase.
-C *comment*	Provides a comment.
-x	Reads a private open SSH DSA key and outputs a public SSH2 key.
-X	Reads a private SSH2 key and outputs a public open SSH DSA key.
-y	Reads a private open SSH DSA key and outputs a public open SSH DSA key.
-R	Checks whether RSA support exists. Exits with exit code 0 if so; otherwise, 1.
File Name: `ssh-keygen`	**Directory:** /usr/bin/ — **Type:** External

startx

UNIX Shell: A shell (ash, bsh)

Function	Starts a single session of the X-window system. A front end to `xinit`.
Syntax	startx *{ client }* [options...] [-- *server*] [options...]

options...	Specifies the options to use for the specified client or server.
client	Specifies the client to use.
-- *server*	Specifies the server to use.
File Name: `startx`	**Directory:** /usr/X11R6/bin/ — **Type:** Script

stat

UNIX Shell: All primary shells (bash, ash, tcsh)

Function	Shows information on the specified files of file systems.
Syntax	stat [options...] *files...*

-l	Traces the links and shows the information about the destination.
-f	Shows the information about the file system the file is stored in.
-v	Shows version information.
-t	Shows the information in terse form, making it suitable for parsing by other programs.
files...	Specifies file(s) to act on.
File Name: `stat`	**Directory:** /usr/bin/ — **Type:** External

statserial

statserial	UNIX Shell:	All primary shells (bash, ash, tcsh)
Function	Shows information about the specified serial port. Useful to debug modems and ports.	
Syntax	statserial [options...] *device*	

-n	Disables the continuous loop function.
-d	Shows the modem status as a decimal number.
-x	Shows the modem status as a hexadecimal number.
device	Specifies port to show information on.
File Name: `statserial`	**Directory:** /usr/bin/ **Type:** External

stinit

stinit	UNIX Shell:	All primary shells (bash, ash, tcsh)
Function	Initializes SCSI magnetic tape drives.	
Syntax	stinit [options...] *{ devices... }*	

-f *file*	Specifies the file to read the definitions for the tape drive types from. (The default file is stinit.def, either in current dir or /etc/.)
-h	Shows help information.
-p	Parses the definition file, but doesn't initialize.
-r	Rewinds all devices being initialized.
-v	Verbose mode. Shows more information. Two -v options shows even more information.
devices...	Specifies the devices to initialize.
File Name: `stinit`	**Directory:** /sbin/ **Type:** External

strace

strace	UNIX Shell:	All primary shells (bash, ash, tcsh)
Function	Records all system calls sent and received by the processes within the specified command.	
Syntax	strace [options...] *{ command } { arguments... }*	

-c	Shows a summary of time, calls, and errors for each system call when exiting.
-e *expression*	Specifies an expression that filters which calls to trace.
expression	Format is `qualifier=[ ! ]values...`. Values must be separated with commas. (Qualifier is either trace, abbrev, verbose, raw, signal, read, or write.)
	The following options can't be combined with the -c option:
-d	Shows debug information on STDERR.
-f	Traces child processes also.
-F	Traces child processes created by `vfork` also.
-ff	Splits all PIDs into separate files with the PID as suffix. Only usable with `-o`.
-h	Shows help information.
-i	Shows the instruction pointer at the time of the system call.
-q	Suppresses messages about attaching, detaching, and so on. Quite mode.
-r	Shows the interval between system calls.
-t	Begins all trace lines with the time it was executed.
-tt	Includes also microseconds.
-ttt	Include also the number of seconds since the epoch.
-T	Shows the time spent in system calls.
-v	Shows full versions of the various calls that have been invoked.
-V	Shows version information.
-x	Shows non-ASCII strings in hexadecimal form.
-xx	Shows all strings in hexadecimal form.
-a *height*	Specifies the column height to align the return values to (default is 40).
-o *file*	Writes the information to the specified file instead of STDOUT.
-p *PID*	Attaches to the specified process and begin tracing.
-s *size*	Specifies the maximum string size to show (default is 32).
-u *user*	Specifies the username to run the command in.
	The following options can only be combined with the `-c` option:
-O *microseconds*	Sets the overhead for tracing system calls to the specified microseconds.

continued

-S *mode*	Specifies what to sort by when using the -c option. (Mode can either be time, calls, name, or nothing ([default is time]).)		
command	Specifies the command to trace.		
arguments...	Specifies the arguments for the command.		
File Name: strace	**Directory:** /usr/bin/	**Type:**	External

strfile

UNIX Shell: All primary shells (bash, ash, tcsh)

Function	Creates a random access file for saving strings. Lines are separated by the delimiting character.
Syntax	strfile [options...] *sourcefile { outputfile }*

-c *char*	Specifies a delimiting character (default is %).		
-i	Ignores case when ordering the strings.		
-o	Orders strings in alphabetical order. The offset table is sorted.		
-r	Does the entries in the offset table in a random order.		
-s	Runs silent and doesn't give a summary message when finished.		
-x	Sets the STR_ROTATED bit in the header `str_flags` fields.		
sourcefile	Specifies the file to use.		
outputfile	Specifies the outputfile (default is `sourcefile.dat`).		
File Name: strfile	**Directory:** /usr/sbin/	**Type:**	External

stunnel

UNIX Shell: All primary shells (bash, ash, tcsh)

Function	Makes it possible to use SSL-enabled connections between two computers, using non-SSL-enabled daemons.
Syntax	stunnel [options...]

-c	Uses client mode (default is server mode).		
-T	Runs as a transparent proxy if supported by hosts.		
-p *pemfile*	Specifies the certificate file. Clients don't use a pemfile. **Note: Default pemfile is `/usr/share/ssl/certs/stunnel.pem`.**		
-v *level*	Verifies peer certificate (1 = if present, 2 = verify, 3 = use locally installed).		
-a *directory*	Specifies the directory when using -v 3 (default is `/usr/share/ssl/certs/trusted`).		
-t *timeout*	Specifies the timeout time for the session cache (default is 300sec.).		
-u *user*	Specifies user checking with IDENT (RFC 1413).		
-n *protocol*	Negotiates for an SSL connection with the specified protocol (only SMTP is supported).		
-d [ip:]port	Uses daemon mode (default is `inet` mode, IP defaults to INADDR_ANY).		
-f	Runs `stunnel` in foreground mode (default is running as a daemon in background mode).		
-l *program* [-- args]	Runs the specified local inetd-type program.		
-L *program* [-- args]	Runs the specified program and opens a local PTY.		
-s *username*	Sets the setuid() to username in daemon mode.		
-g *groupname*	Clears all other groups and makes a setgid() to groupname in daemon mode.		
-r [ip:]port	Connects to a remote service (IP defaults to INADDR_LOOPBACK).		
File Name: stunnel	**Directory:** /usr/sbin/	**Type:**	External
stunnel -d 993 -l /usr/sbin/imapd -- imapd	Provides an SSL encapsulation to your local `imapd` service.		
stunnel -d 2020 -L /usr/sbin/pppd -- pppd local	Provides tunneling to your `pppd` daemon on port 2020.		

suexec

UNIX Shell: All primary shells (bash, ash, tcsh)

Function	Switches the user when executing an external application through programs that are used internally by Apache.
Syntax	suexec

File Name: suexec	**Directory:** /usr/sbin/	**Type:**	External
Tip:	For more information about this command, see `http://www.apache.org`.		

suidperl

suidperl	UNIX Shell:	All primary shells (bash, ash, tcsh)

Function	Executes a Perl script in suID mode.
Syntax	suidperl [options...] [--] *{ file } { arguments... }*

-0*{ octal }*	Specifies record separator (default is "\0").
-a	Activates autosplit mode. Must be combined either with -n or -p options.
-C	Enables native wide character system interfaces.
-c	Checks the syntax of the script without running it.
-d [:*debugger*]	Specifies the module to run as debugger for the script.
-D*{ flags }*	Specifies debugging flags.
-e '*command*'	Runs the specified command. Doesn't look for a script filename.
-F*pattern*	Specifies an expression to split on. Must be combined with -a option.
-i *{ suffix }*	Edits the files in its actual places in the construct processor.
-I*dir*	Specifies the directory to search for include files. Must be combined with -p option.
-l*octal*	Specifies line terminator and enables line ending processing.
-m[-]*module*[=*argument*]	Runs the specified module before the script.
[-]	Doesn't run the specified module.
argument	Specifies the argument for the operand.
-n	Assumes an input loop around the script. Doesn't show the input lines.
-p	Assumes an input loop around the script. Shows the input lines.
-P	Runs the C preprocessor before compile.
-s	Changes the arguments to variable switches that can be invoked in the program.
-S	Uses the PATH environment variable to search for the script.
-T	Forces taint checks.
-u	Dumps the core after compile.
-U	Allows unsafe operations.
-v	Shows version information.
-V	Shows perl configuration values and the current value of @INC.
-w	Shows warnings on spelling errors and other error-prone constructs in the script.
-W	Enables that all warnings.
-X	Disables that all warnings.
-x*directory*	Ignores trash text before the actual script.
--	Tells to load script from STDIN, and takes all following operands as parameters.
file	Specifies program file to run.
arguments...	Specifies the arguments for the script program.

File Name:	`suidperl`	**Directory:**	/usr/bin/	**Type:**	External

suidperl -e 'print "UCG\n"'	Shows "UCG" on the screen.

sulogin

sulogin	UNIX Shell:	All primary shells (bash, ash, tcsh)

Function	Prompts for the root password to enter single-user mode, or to press Ctrl-D to proceed with normal startup.
Syntax	sulogin [options...] *{ tty-device }*

-t *timeout*	Specifies the timeout.
-p	Starts the shell as a login shell, instead of a single user shell (default is not).
tty-device	Specifies a tty device (default is `/dev/console`).

File Name:	`sulogin`	**Directory:**	/sbin/	**Type:**	External

SuperProbe

SuperProbe	UNIX Shell:	All primary shells (bash, ash, tcsh)

Function	Finds installed video hardware, used by some X11 configuration software to determine configurations.
Syntax	SuperProbe [options...]

-verbose	Verbose mode. Shows more information.
-no16	Doesn't use any ports that use 16-bit I/O address decoding.
-excl *list*	Specifies the list of I/O ports that aren't included from the automatic inspect.
-mask10	The port addresses are masked to 10-bit. Used with -excl option.
-order *list*	Specifies the chipset names that will tested.

continued

-noprobe *list*		Specifies the chipset names that aren't tested.			
-bios *base*		Specifies the base address to the graphic-hardware BIOS.			
-no_bios		Doesn't read from video BIOS and assumes it is an EGA, VGA, or SVGA.			
-no_dac		Stops inspecting of RAMDAC type when an (S)VGA is identified.			
-no_mem		Stops inspecting the installed video memory.			
-info		Shows a list of cards that can be identified.			
File Name:	SuperProbe	**Directory:**	/usr/X11R6/bin/	**Type:**	External
Note:	Not all vendors are supported and can be identified.				

swapdev

UNIX Shell: All primary shells (bash, ash, tcsh)

Function	Sets the kernel's swap device. Shows usage information if run without parameters. The equivalent of `rdev -s`.				
Syntax	swapdev [-o *value*] { *image* } { *device* } { *offset* }				
-o *value*		Specifies the byte offset.			
image		Specifies a bootable Linux kernel image.			
device		Specifies the swap device.			
offset		Specifies an offset for the kernel image.			
File Name:	swapdev	**Directory:**	/usr/sbin/	**Type:**	External
swapdev /vmlinux /dev/hda5			Sets /dev/hda5 to be the swap device in the kernel.		

swapoff

UNIX Shell: All primary shells (bash, ash, tcsh)

Function	Disables swapping on the specified devices.				
Syntax	swapoff [options...] { *swapdevices...* }				
-V		Shows version information.			
-h		Shows help information.			
-a		Disables swapping for all swap partitions in `/etc/fstab`.			
-s		Shows information about the current swap devices.			
swapdevices...		Specifies the swap device to disable.			
File Name:	swapoff	**Directory:**	/sbin/	**Type:**	External

swapon

UNIX Shell: All primary shells (bash, ash, tcsh)

Function	Specifies a device to start swap or page on.				
Syntax	swapon [options...] { *devices...* }				
-a		Starts all devices marked as swap devices in `/etc/fstab`.			
-p *priority*		Specifies priority for swapping (value between 0 and 32767).			
-s		Shows swap usage summary by device.			
-h		Shows help information.			
-V		Shows version information			
devices...		Specifies swap device.			
File Name:	swapon	**Directory:**	/sbin/	**Type:**	External

swat

UNIX Shell: All primary shells (bash, ash, tcsh)

Function	Configures Samba over the web. Short for Samba Web Administration Tool. Is run from `xinetd`.				
Syntax	swat [options...]				
-s *configfile*		Specifies the configuration file to use (default is `/etc/samba/smb.conf`).			
-a		Disables authentication. Everyone can modify `smb.conf`. **Note:This is very insecure!**			
File Name:	swat	**Directory:**	/usr/sbin/	**Type:**	External
lynx http://localhost:901			Goes to the swat Web configuration page.		

switchdesk

UNIX Shell: A shell (ash, bsh)

Function	Is used to switch between various desktop environments like GNOME, KDE and AnotherLevel.
Syntax	switchdesk *{ name }*

name	Specifies the name of the new desktop to use.

File Name: switchdesk **Directory:** /usr/bin/ **Type:** Script

switchdesk-helper

UNIX Shell: All primary shells (bash, ash, tcsh)

Function	Specifies what window manager to run when starting X.
Syntax	switchdesk-helper *name*

name	Specifies the desktop name to make as default X manager.

File Name: switchdesk-helper **Directory:** /usr/bin/ **Type:** External

sx

UNIX Shell: All primary shells (bash, ash, tcsh)

Function	Sends files using XMODEM protocol.
Syntax	sx [options...] *{ files... }*

-2	Uses two stop bits while communicating. Be careful with this.
-a	Converts NL characters to CR/LF sender started (X & YMODEM) recover started (ZMODEM).
-B *size*	Specifies the size of the read buffer in bytes (default is 16384 bytes).
-c *command*	Sends the specified command to the receiver to be executed.
-C *tries*	Specifies how many times to retry sending the command (default is 11).
-d	Alters all dots `.` to slashes `/` in the pathname.
--delay-startup *seconds*	Sets a specified delay time before anything is allowed to start.
-e	Escapes all of the control characters. Forces the sender to rename the new file.
-f	Sends the full pathname during transmission.
-h	Shows help information.
-i *command*	Sends the specified command to the receiver and returns immediately after success.
-k	Sends files using 1,024 byte blocks. X & YMODEM only. ZMODEM sends what it can.
-m *rate*	Stops the transmission if the BPS rate falls below the specified amount.
-M *rate*	Sets the minimum transmission rate in BPS (default is 120 seconds).
-l *length*	Causes the receiver to answer correct data for the specified length of characters.
-N	Sends and overwrites the destination file if the source file is newer or longer.
-O	Disables the timeout handling for read requests.
-q	Suppresses verbose. Quiet mode.
-R	Sets restricted mode. Restricts current directory pathnames and PUBDIR.
-s *HH:MM*	Stops the transmission at the specified time.
-S	Enables support for the timesync protocol. Incompatible with ZMODEM.
--syslog *=off*	Turns the logging to `syslog` on or off.
-t *time*	Alters the timeout to the specified time in tenths of a second.
-T	Ignores certain characters during transmission: ^P, ^P|0x80 and [CR + @]. Turbo mode.
--tcp	Tries to start a TCP/IP connection. All handshaking is done by the ZMODEM program.
--tcp-client *address:port*	Acts as the TCP/IP client by connecting to the specified address:port.
--tcp-server	Acts as a server. You must start `lsz` with the --tcp-client option first.
-u	Unlinks the file once a successful transmission has taken place.
-U	Turns restricted mode off.
-v	Verbose mode. Shows more information.
-X	Uses the XMODEM protocol.
--ymodem	Uses the YMODEM protocol.
-Z	Uses the ZMODEM protocol.

File Name: sx **Directory:** /usr/bin/ **Type:** External

sysctl

UNIX Shell: All primary shells (bash, ash, tcsh)

Function	Configures kernel parameters at runtime — the parameters are listed in `/proc/sys/`.
Syntax	sysctl [options...] { *variable* }

-n	Disables showing the key name when showing values.
	The following options can't be combined:
-w *key=value*	Changes the settings for the specified key to the specified value.
-p *filename*	Specifies the settings file (default is `/etc/sysctl.conf`).
-a	Shows the currently available values.
-A	Shows the currently available values in table form.
variable	Specifies the key to read from.

File Name:	`sysctl`	**Directory:**	/sbin/	**Type:**	External

sysctl -w kernel.domainname=ucgbook.com	Sets kernel.domainname to ucgbook.com.
sysctl -p /etc/perfectctl.conf	Load settings from `perfectctl.conf`.

sysklogd

UNIX Shell: All primary shells (bash, ash, tcsh)

Function	A system logging utility.
Syntax	sysklogd [options...]

-a *socket*	Specifies any additional sockets to listen to.
-d	Starts in debug mode.
-f *config_file*	Specifies a different configuration file to use instead of the default.
-h	Forwards any remote messages to the defined forwarding hosts.
-l *hostlist*	Specifies a list of hostnames that only should be logged with their simple hostnames.
-m *interval*	Logs a mark timestamp regularly (default interval is 20 minutes).
-n	Avoids auto-backgrounding.
-p *socket*	Specifies a different UNIX domain socket.
-r	Receives message from the network using an Internet domain socket.
-s *domainlist*	Specifies a list of domain names that should be stripped off before logging.
-v	Shows version information.

File Name:	`sysklogd`	**Directory:**	/usr/sbin/	**Type:**	External

sys-unconfig

UNIX Shell: A shell (ash, bsh)

Function	Resets the system configuration. The file /.unconfigured tells the system to run the programs to configure system.
Syntax	sys-unconfig

File Name:	`sys-unconfig`	**Directory:**	/usr/sbin/	**Type:**	Script

sz

UNIX Shell: All primary shells (bash, ash, tcsh)

Function	Sends files using ZMODEM protocol.
Syntax	sz [options...] { *files...* }

-+	Instructs the receiver to attach the sent data to an existing file.
-2	Uses two stop bits while communicating. Be careful with this.
-8	Attempts to use 8KB block size while communicating. Good for BBS.
--start-8k	Starts with a 8KB block size.
-a	Converts NL characters to CR/LF.
-b	Transfers a file without any translation.
-B *size*	Specifies the size of the read buffer in bytes (default is 16384 bytes).
-c *command*	Sends the specified command to the receiver to be executed.
-C *tries*	Specifies how many times to retry sending the command (default is 11).
-d	Alters all dots `.` to slashes `/` in the pathname.
--delay-startup *seconds*	Sets a specified delay time before any thing is allowed to start.
-e	Escapes all of the control characters. Forces the sender to rename the new file.

continued

-f	Sends the full pathname during transmission.
-h	Shows help information.
-i *command*	Sends the specified command to the receiver and returns immediately after success.
-L *length*	Uses the specified subpacket lengths.
-m *rate*	Stops the transmission if the BPS rate falls below the specified amount.
-M *rate*	Sets the minimum transmission rate in BPS (default is 120 seconds).
-l *length*	Causes the receiver to answer correct data for the specified length of characters.
-n	Sends and overwrites the destination file if the source file is newer.
-N	Sends and overwrites the destination file if the source file is newer or longer.
-o	Disables the automatic selection of 32-bit CRC.
-O	Disables the timeout handling for read requests.
-p	Protects the destination file from being overwritten by skipping the send.
-q	Suppresses verbose. Quiet mode.
-R	Sets restricted mode. Restricts current directory pathnames and PUBDIR.
-r	Resumes any interrupted file transfers.
-s *HH:MM*	Stops the transmission at the specified time.
-S	Enables support for the timesync protocol. Incompatible with ZMODEM.
--syslog *=off*	Turns the logging to `syslog` on or off.
-t *time*	Alters the timeout to the specified time in tenths of a second.
-T	Ignores certain characters during transmission: ^P, ^P|0x80 and [CR + @]. Turbo mode.
--tcp	Tries to start a TCP/IP connection. All handshaking is done by the ZMODEM program.
--tcp-client *address:port*	Acts as the TCP/IP client by connecting to the specified address:port.
--tcp-server	Acts as a server. You must start `lsz` with the --tcp-client option first.
-u	Unlinks the file once a successful transmission has taken place.
-U	Turns restricted mode off.
-w *size*	Limits the transmission window to the specified size in bytes.
-v	Verbose mode. Shows more information.
-y	Tells the receiver to overwrite any existing file with the same name.
-Y	Same as `-y` except it skips source files that have matching pathnames.
--ymodem	Uses YMODEM protocol.
-Z	Uses ZMODEM protocol.
-X	Uses XMODEM protocol.

File Name:	`sz`	**Directory:**	/usr/bin/	**Type:**	External

tac

UNIX Shell: All primary shells (bash, ash, tcsh)

Function	Shows files in reverse order. The opposite of cat.
Syntax	tac [options...] *files...*

--before	Insert the separator before, instead of after.
--regex	Interprets the separator as a regular expression.
--separator=*string*	Specifies the separator to use instead of newline.
--help	Shows help information.
--version	Shows version information.
files...	Specifies the file(s) to use.

File Name:	`tac`	**Directory:**	/usr/bin/	**Type:**	External

tailf

UNIX Shell: All primary shells (bash, ash, tcsh)

Function	Shows the growth of a file.
Syntax	tailf *file*

file	Specifies the file to monitor.

File Name:	`tailf`	**Directory:**	/usr/bin/	**Type:**	External

tangle

UNIX Shell: All primary shells (bash, ash, tcsh)

Function	Converts a WEB file to Pascal.
Syntax	tangle *webfile* { *changefile* }

webfile	Specifies the WEB file to convert.
changefile	Specifies a changefile that overrides parts of the WEB file.

File Name: `tangle` **Directory:** /usr/bin/ **Type:** External

tc

UNIX Shell: All primary shells (bash, ash, tcsh)

Function	Creates and associate queues with output devices.
Syntax	tc [options...] *object* { *ACTION* }

	If using options, select only one of these three:
-s	Shows the finished object statistics.
-d	Shows details of the finished object.
-r	Shows the finished object in raw format.
	When specifying an object, select only one of these three:
qdisc	Specifies that a queuing discipline is created.
class	Specifies that a class is created.
filter	Specifies that a filter is created.
ACTION	**When using an object, select one of these two actions:**
commands...	Specifies which command(s) (including options) create the object.
help	Shows help information for the selected object.

File Name: `tc` **Directory:** /sbin/ **Type:** External

tc filter add dev eth1 parent 1:0 protocol ip prior 50 route	Installs a route classifier that is attached to a CBQ tree root that defines IP packets and assigns the priority to 50.

tclsh

UNIX Shell: All primary shells (bash, ash, tcsh)

Function	The Tool command language (Tcl) shell.
Syntax	tclsh { *file* } tclsh { *file options...* }

file	Specifies a Tcl script to run.
options...	Specifies options to the Tcl script.

File Name: `tclsh` **Directory:** /usr/bin/ **Type:** External

tcpd

UNIX Shell: All primary shells (bash, ash, tcsh)

Function	Controls and logs incoming requests for Internet services. Used from `inetd`.
Syntax	tcpd

File Name: `tcpd` **Directory:** /usr/sbin/ **Type:** External

tcpdchk

UNIX Shell: All primary shells (bash, ash, tcsh)

Function	Checks your TCP wrapper configuration and reports all potential problems it can find.
Syntax	tcpdchk [options...]

-a	Shows access control rules that permit access without an explicit ALLOW keyword.
-d	Examines `hosts.allow` and `hosts.deny` files in the current directory.
-i *filename*	Specifies where `inetd.conf` or `tlid.conf` can be found if not found.
-v	Verbose mode. Shows the contents of each access control rule.

File Name: `tcpdchk` **Directory:** /usr/sbin/ **Type:** External

tcpdmatch		UNIX Shell:	All primary shells (bash, ash, tcsh)
Function	Predicts how the TCP wrapper would handle a specific request for service.		
Syntax	tcpdmatch [options...] *daemon*[@*server*] { *username*@]*client*		

-d	Examines `host.allow` and `host.deny` files in current directory.
-i *filename*	Specifies where your `inetd.conf` or `tlid.conf` files are if not found.
daemon	Specifies a daemon process name.
server	Specifies a hostname or network address.
username	Specifies a user identifier (default is unknown).
client	Specifies a hostname or network address.
File Name: `tcpdmatch`	Directory: /usr/sbin/ — Type: External
tcpdmatch in.telnetd localhost	Checks whether localhost is granted access to `in.telnetd`.

tcpdump		UNIX Shell:	All primary shells (bash, ash, tcsh)
Function	Shows the headers of packets on a network interface.		
Syntax	tcpdump [options...] [*expressions...*]		

-a	Shows captured data in ASCII format.
-b *protocol*	Specifies what protocol to capture.
-c *count*	Stops when specified amount of packets has passed.
-d	Shows the compiled packet-matching code in a human-readable form.
-dd	Shows the compiled packet-matching code in C program fragments.
-ddd	Shows the compiled packet-matching code in decimal numbers.
-e	Shows the link-level header on each dump line.
-f	Shows "foreign" Internet addresses numerically, not symbolically.
-F *filename*	Specifies a file to read filters from.
-i *interface*	Specifies the interface to use.
-l	Specifies that STDOUT should be line buffered.
-n	Specifies that addresses shouldn't be converted to names.
-nn	Specifies that port numbers shouldn't be converted to service names.
-N	Specifies that domain name qualification of hostnames shouldn't be shown.
-O	The packet-matching code optimizer shouldn't be used.
-p	Puts the interface in promiscuous mode.
-q	Shows less information about a protocol.
-r *filename*	Specifies a file to read packages from.
-R	Uses RAW socket interface.
-s *number*	Specifies the numbers of bytes to snap from each packet (default is 68).
-T *type*	Forces packets selected by expression to be interpreted the specified type.
-S	Shows absolute, not relative numbers.
-t	Specifies that a timestamp shouldn't be showed on each dump line.
-tt	Shows an unformatted timestamp on each dump line.
-v	Verbose mode. Shows more information.
-vv	Verbose mode. Shows more information than -v does.
-w *filename*	Specifies a file to write raw package data to.
-x	Shows each package in hex format.
-X	Uses packet socket interface (is the default mode).
expressions...	Specifies which packet to dump. If no expression is given, all packets will dump.
	An expression must contain at least one of these primitives:
dst host *host*	Shows packet headers going to host.
src host *host*	Shows packet headers going from host.
host *host*	Shows packet headers from and to host.
ether dst *host*	Shows packet headers going to MAC address host.
ether src *host*	Shows packet headers coming from MAC address host.
ether host *host*	Shows packet headers coming from and to MAC address host.
gateway *host*	Shows packet headers if they were going to the gateway.
dst net *network*	Shows packet headers going to network.

continued

src net *network*	Shows packet headers coming from network.
net *network*	Shows packet headers from or to the network.
net *network* mask *netmask*	Shows packet headers from or to network with netmask.
net *network*/ *length*	Shows packet headers from or to network with netmask length.
dst port *port*	Shows packet headers going to port.
src port *port*	Shows packet headers coming from port.
port *port*	Shows packet headers from or to the port.
less *length*	Shows packet headers with a packet length less than or equal to length.
greater *length*	Shows packet headers with a packet length greater than or equal to length.
ip proto *protocol*	Shows packet headers matching protocol.
ether broadcast	Shows packet headers if it is an Ethernet broadcast.
ip broadcast	Shows packet headers if it is an IP broadcast.
ether multicast	Shows packet headers if it is an Ethernet multicast.
ip multicast	Shows packet headers if it is an IP multicast.
ether proto *protocol*	Shows packet headers if it is an ether and matches protocol.
decnet src *host*	Shows packet headers from host if it is a DECNET.
decnet dst *host*	Shows packet headers to host if the DECNET destination is the specified host.
decnet host *host*	Shows packet headers if the DECNET source or destination is the specified host.
ip	A shortcut that can be used instead of using `ether proto ip`.
arp	A shortcut that can be used instead of using `ether proto arp`.
rarp	A shortcut that can be used instead of using `ether proto rarp`.
decnet	A shortcut that can be used instead of using `ether proto decnet`.
	These shortcuts can't be parsed by `tcpdump`:
lat	A shortcut that can be used instead of using `ether proto lat`.
moprc	A shortcut that can be used instead of using `ether proto moprc`.
mopdl	A shortcut that can be used instead of using `ether proto mopdl`.
tcp	A shortcut that can be used instead of using `ip proto tcp`.
udp	A shortcut that can be used instead of using `ip proto udp`.
icmp	A shortcut that can be used instead of using `ip proto icmp`.
proto { expression:size }	Allows access to data inside a packet. proto=ETHER,FDDI,IP,ARP,RARP,TCP,UDP, or ICMP.
expression	Specifies the byte offset respective to the protocol layer.
size	Specifies the size of the field of interest in bytes. Select 1–4 bytes (default is 1).
	Each primitive is usually followed by at least one of these qualifiers:
type	Specifies the object that the primitive refers to. Select between host, net or port.
direction	Specifies the transfer direction. Select between src, dst, src or dst & src and dst.
proto	Restricts the match to a protocol (see below for the list of valid ones). (Protocols:ETHER,FDDI,IP,ARP,RARP,DECNET,LAT,SCA,MOPRC,MOPDL,TCP & UDP.)

File Name:	`tcpdump`	**Directory:**	/usr/sbin/	**Type:**	External

tcpdump ip and not net localnet	Shows IP packets passing your computer, but not packets on the local net.

tcsh

UNIX Shell: TC shell (tcsh)

Function	An enchanced version of the C-shell that is completely compatible.
Syntax	tcsh *{ options... } { arguments... }* tcsh -l

-b	Lets the rest of options to be passed directly to the scripts.
-c	Runs the first argument from the list and places the other in argv shell variable.
-d	Loads the directory stack from `~/.cshdirs`.
-D *name*[=*value*]	Sets the environment variable name to value.
-e	Exits on nonzero exit status or other abnormally terminations.
-f	Is used for fast start. Doesn't run `.cshrc` and `.login`.
-F	Uses fork instead of vfork to spawn processes.
-i	Forces the command prompt on any sort of terminal for interactive use.
-l	Starts the shell as a login shell. Must be used alone.
-m	Loads `~/.tcshrc` even if it doesn't belong to the user.
-n	Interprets but doesn't run the commands, used for debugging scripts.

continued

-q	Lets the shell accept SIGQUIT		
-s	Reads STDIN to get the commands.		
-t	Runs a single command line.		
-v	Verbose mode. Shows more information. Sets verbose after reading `.cshrc`.		
-V	Verbose mode. Shows more information. Sets verbose before reading `.cshrc`.		
-x	Echoes each command before it is run. Sets echo after reading `.cshrc`.		
-X	Echoes each command before it is run. Sets echo before reading `.cshrc`.		
arguments...	Specifies arguments to command.		
File Name: `tcsh`	**Directory:** /bin/	**Type:**	External

telesctrl

UNIX Shell: All primary shells (bash, ash, tcsh)

Function	Configures the log level of the HiSax-ISDN device driver. Log information is stored in `/dev/isdnctrl`.
Syntax	telesctrl *driverid debugcmd debugflags*

driverid	Specifies driver ID if you use more than one passive card.		
debugcmd	Specifies debugging level. Values are 1, 11, or 13.		
debugflags	Specifies the value for the bitmask it changes debug facility on or off for.		
File Name: `telesctrl`	**Directory:** /usr/sbin/	**Type:**	External
telesctrl HiSax 1 0x3ff	Enables full generic debugging.		

telltc

UNIX Shell: TC shell (tcsh)

Function	Shows the current values of all terminal capabilities.
Syntax	telltc

testparm

UNIX Shell: All primary shells (bash, ash, tcsh)

Function	Reads a Samba configuration file to check whether it is correct.
Syntax	testparm [options...] *{ file } { host }*

-s	Doesn't wait for a carriage return after the name of the service to check.		
-L *server*	Specifies the value of the %L macro for testing include files.		
-h	Shows help information.		
file	Specifies the configuration file to use (default is `/etc/samba/smb.conf`).		
host	Specifies a hostname and IP address and checks whether the host is allowed access. (If a hostname is specified, an IP address must follow.)		
File Name: `testparm`	**Directory:** /usr/bin/	**Type:**	External
Note:	If anything is wrong with the config file, the exit status equals 1; if not, then exit status equals 0.		

testprns

UNIX Shell: All primary shells (bash, ash, tcsh)

Function	Checks whether a given printer name is valid to use with `smbd`.
Syntax	testprns *printername { printcapname }*

printername	Specifies the printer name to check.		
printcapname	Specifies the printercap file to search for the printername in.		
File Name: `testprns`	**Directory:** /usr/bin/	**Type:**	External

tex, initex, virtex

UNIX Shell: All primary shells (bash, ash, tcsh)

Function	Formats text and typesetting.
Syntax	tex [options...] *{ commands... }*

--fmt *format*	Specifies the format as the name of the format to use.
--help	Shows help information.
--ini	Dumps formats. Same as executing the `initex`.
--interaction *mode*	Sets the interaction mode: batchmode, nonstopmode, scrollmode and errorstopmode.
--ipc	Sends DVI output to a socket, plus the usual output file.
--ipc-start	Starts the IPC server at the other end as well.
--kpathsea-debugbitmaks	Sets path searching debugging flags according to the bitmask.

continued

--maketex *format*	Enables mktexfmt, where format must be one of tex or tfm.
--mltex	Enables MLTeX extensions.
--no-maketex *format*	Disables mktexfmt, where format must be one of tex or tfm.
--output-comment *string*	Uses the string for the DVI file comment instead of the data.
--progname *name*	Pretends to be program name.
--shell-escape	Enables the \write18{command} construct.
--translate-filename	Uses the name translation table.
--version	Shows version information.
commands...	Specifies the commands to run.
File Name: tex	**Directory:** /usr/bin/ **Type:** External

texindex

UNIX Shell: All primary shells (bash, ash, tcsh)

Function	Creates an index for a TeX output file.
Syntax	texindex [options...] *files...*

-k	Keeps the temporary files after the command is run.
--no-keep	Deletes the temporary files after the command is run, which also is the default.
-o *file*	Specifies a file to save the output in.
-h	Shows help information.
--version	Shows version information.
files...	Specifies the input file to use.
File Name: texindex	**Directory:** /usr/bin/ **Type:** External

tfmtodit

UNIX Shell: All primary shells (bash, ash, tcsh)

Function	Creates groff font files to use with groff -Tdvi.
Syntax	tfmtodit [options..] *tfmFile mapFile font*

-v	Shows version information.
-s	Indicates the font as special.
-k *NR*	Indicates the skewchar is at position NR in this font.
-g *file*	Specifies the .gf file produced by metafont to use.
tfmFile	Specifies the name of TeX metric font file.
mapFile	Specifies the name of a map file giving groff names for characters.
font	Specifies the name of the groff font file.
File Name: tfmtodit	**Directory:** /usr/bin/ **Type:** External

thumbnail

UNIX Shell: All primary shells (bash, ash, tcsh)

Function	Creates a TIFF image file with thumbnail images.
Syntax	thumbnail [options...] *inputfile outputfile*

-w *width*	Specifies the width of the thumbnail image.
-h *height*	Specifies the height of the thumbnail image.
-c *curve*	Specifies a contrast curve to use when generating the thumbnail images.
inputfile	Specifies the input TIFF image file to use.
outputfile	Specifies the output TIFF image file to use.
File Name: thumbnail	**Directory:** /usr/bin/ **Type:** External

tie

UNIX Shell: All primary shells (bash, ash, tcsh)

Function	Merges or applies WEB system change files.
Syntax	tie [options...] *outputfile masterfile changefiles...*

-c	Creates a single file from the specified change files.
-m	Creates a new master file by using the specified change file.
outputfile	Specifies the file where to save the new merged file or the patched master file.
masterfile	Specifies the file to apply patches to.
changefiles...	Specifies the file or files to merge, up to 9 nine files are allowed.
File Name: tie	**Directory:** /usr/bin/ **Type:** External

tiff2bw

tiff2bw	UNIX Shell:	All primary shells (bash, ash, tcsh)
Function	Converts a color TIFF image to grayscale.	
Syntax	tiff2bw [options...] *inputfile outputfile*	

-c *name*	Specifies the compression to use. (Available compressions are: none, packbits, zip, g3, g4, or lzw.)
-r *number*	Specifies the output data to be number of rows per strip.
-R *number*	Specifies the percentage of the red channel to use (default is 28).
-G *number*	Specifies the percentage of the green channel to use (default is 59).
-B *number*	Specifies the percentage of the blue channel to use (default is 11).
inputfile	Specifies the input file.
outputfile	Specifies the output file.
File Name: `tiff2bw`	**Directory:** /usr/bin/ **Type:** External

tiff2ps

tiff2ps	UNIX Shell:	All primary shells (bash, ash, tcsh)
Function	Converts TIFF images to PostScript format.	
Syntax	tiff2ps [options...] *files...*	

-1	Generates PostScript Level 1. (Is default.)
-2	Generates PostScript Level 2.
-a	Generates output for all IFDs in the input file.
-d *directory*	Specifies the initial TIFF directory to the specified directory number.
-e	Forces the generation of encapsulated PostScript.
-h *size*	Specifies the vertical size of the print area in inches.
-o	Specifies the initial TIFF directory to the IFDs at the file offset.
-p	Forces the generation of non encapsulated PostScript.
-s	Generates output for a single IFD in the input file.
-w *size*	Specifies the horizontal size of the print area in inches.
-z	Uses the whole page. Has no effect with PostScript Level 1.
files...	Specifies one or more TIFF images to convert.
File Name: `tiff2ps`	**Directory:** /usr/bin/ **Type:** External

tiffcmp

tiffcmp	UNIX Shell:	All primary shells (bash, ash, tcsh)
Function	Compares two TIFF files.	
Syntax	tiffcmp [options...] *file1 file2*	

-l	Shows each byte of image data that differs between the files.
-t	Ignores any differences in directory tags.
file1 file2	Specifies the two files to compare.
File Name: `tiffcmp`	**Directory:** /usr/bin/ **Type:** External

tiffcp

tiffcp	UNIX Shell:	All primary shells (bash, ash, tcsh)
Function	Merges TIFF images together into a single multi-image file.	
Syntax	tiffcp [options...] *infiles... outfile*	

-B	Uses Big-Endian byte order in the output.
-C	Doesn't use `strip chopping on uncompressed data.
-c *style*	Specifies the compression style to use. (Styles: none, packbits, lzw (value), jpeg, zip, g3 (1d, 2d, fill), g4.)
-f *fillorder*	Specifies a bit fill order for the output. Fill orders are: lsb2msb or msb2lsb.
-l *number*	Sets the length of a tile in pixels.
-L	Uses the Little-Endian byte order in the output.
-M	Doesn't use memory-mapped files from the images.
-p *style*	Sets a planar configuration: config = multi-sample, separate = separate planes.
-r *rows*	Sets the number of rows in an output data strip.
-s	Writes output in strips instead of tiles.
-t	Writes output in tiles instead of strips.
-w *pixels*	Sets the width in pixels of a tile.

continued

infiles...		Specifies input file.			
outfile		Specifies output file.			
File Name:	`tiffcp`	**Directory:**	/usr/bin/	**Type:**	External

tiffdither

UNIX Shell: All primary shells (bash, ash, tcsh)

Function	Converts an 8-bit grayscale TIFF image to a bilevel TIFF image.
Syntax	tiffdither [options...] *input output*

-c		Specifies the compression to use for the output file.			
-f		Specifies the bit fill order to use.			
-t *value*		Specifies the threshold value for dithering (default is 128).			
input		Specifies the input file.			
output		Specifies the output file.			
File Name:	`tiffdither`	**Directory:**	/usr/bin/	**Type:**	External

tiffinfo

UNIX Shell: All primary shells (bash, ash, tcsh)

Function	Shows information about TIFF files.
Syntax	tiffinfo [options...] *files...*

-c		Shows the color map and color/gray response curves, if present.			
-D		Decompresses all data in the image files without showing it.			
-d		Shows each byte of decompressed data in hexadecimal.			
-j		Shows any JPEG-related tags that are present.			
-o		Specifies the initial TIFF directory according to the file offset.			
-s		Shows the offset and byte counts for each data strip in a directory.			
-*directory*		Specifies the initial TIFF directory.			
files...		Specifies the filename to show information about.			
File Name:	`tiffinfo`	**Directory:**	/usr/bin/	**Type:**	External

tiffsplit

UNIX Shell: All primary shells (bash, ash, tcsh)

Function	Creates single-image files from a multi-image TIFF file.
Syntax	tiffsplit *infile prefix*

infile		Specifies the multi-image file that is to be split.			
prefix		Specifies the prefix to the created single files.			
File Name:	`tiffsplit`	**Directory:**	/usr/bin/	**Type:**	External

timeconfig

UNIX Shell: All primary shells (bash, ash, tcsh)

Function	Configures the computer time in a ncurses-based environment.
Syntax	timeconfig [options...] { *timezone* }

--utc		Sets computer clock to universal time.			
--arc		Stores the computer clock in ARC platform format, ALPHA computers only.			
--back		Specifies that a Back button should be present instead of a cancel button.			
--test		Doesn't make changes to the computer.			
timezone		Specifies the time zone to use.			
File Name:	`timeconfig`	**Directory:**	/usr/sbin/	**Type:**	External

tin

UNIX Shell: All primary shells (bash, ash, tcsh)

Function	A Usenet news reader, which can read locally or remotely via an NNTP server.
Syntax	tin [options...] { *newsgroups...* }

-a	Activates ANSI colors.
-A	Uses authentication on connect.
-c	Create/updates index files for groups found in `~/.newsrc` and marks them read.
-d	Doesn't show newsgroups descriptions.

continued

-D *level*	Specifies the debug level. (1 = NNTP, 2 = all).
-f *file*	Specifies the file to use instead of ~/ .newsrc.
-g *server*	Specifies the server to use.
-G *NR*	Specifies the number of articles to retrieve from the server.
-I *dir*	Specifies the directory where to save newsgroup index files.
-l	Receives number of articles per group from an active file.
-m *dir*	Specifies which mail directory to use (default is ~/Mail).
-M *user*	Mails unread articles to user.
-n	Loads only groups that are subscribed to in ~/.newsrc.
-N	Mails unread articles to yourself.
-o	Starts and mail postponed articles and quit.
-p *port*	Specifies the port to use to connect to nntpservers (default is 119).
-q	Doesn't check for new newsgroups.
-Q	Runs as fast as possible.
-r	Reads news from a remote server specified in /etc/nntpserver.
-R	Reads news saved with the -S option.
-s *dir*	Specifies the directoryin which to save and read news (default is ~/News).
-S	Saves unread articles for later reading.
-u	Creates/updates index files for groups found in ~/.newsrc (doesn't work for an NNTP server).
-U	Updates index files in the background while reading news in the foreground.
-v	Verbose mode. Shows more information for the options -c, -M, -S, -u, and -Z.
-w	Enables quick mode to just start and post an article and then quit.
-X	Starts in read-only mode. It won't overwrite ~/.newsrc or ~/.tin.
-z	Checks whether there are any new unread articles then starts;otherwice, exits directly.
-V	Shows version and date information.
newsgroups...	Specifies the newsgroup or newsgroups to enter.
File Name: tin	**Directory:** /usr/bin/ **Type:** External

tload

UNIX Shell: All primary shells (bash, ash, tcsh)

Function	Shows system load as a graph.
Syntax	tload [options...] { *tty* }

-V	Shows version information.
-s *scale*	Specifies a vertical scale.
-d *delay*	Specifies the delay between graph updates in seconds.
tty	Specifies the tty to show the graph on.
File Name: tload	**Directory:** /usr/bin/ **Type:** External

tmpwatch

UNIX Shell: All primary shells (bash, ash, tcsh)

Function	Erases files that haven't been accessed for a specified number of hours.
Syntax	tmpwatch [options...] *hours directories...*

-a	Erases all file types.
-f	Erases files even if root doesn't have write access.
-q	Runs in background
-v	Verbose mode. Shows more information. Use it two times to get the most information.
-t	Goes through the motions of erasing without erasing the files (implies -v).
-s	Runs command fuser to check whether a file is open before erasing it.
-u	Erases a file based on the file's access time.
-m	Erases a file based on the file's modification time.
-c	Erases a file based on the file's inode change time.
hours	Specifies the access time for erasing a file.
directories...	Specifies the directories to erase files from.
File Name: tmpwatch	**Directory:** /usr/sbin/ **Type:** External
tmpwatch -a 20 /var/tmp	This erases all files that haven't been used in 20 hours.

toe

UNIX Shell:	All primary shells (bash, ash, tcsh)
Function	Shows a list of all available terminal types by primary name with their descriptions.
Syntax	toe [options...] *{ directory }*

-h	Makes a directory header when each directory is entered.
-u *file*	Makes a report on dependencies in the specified file.
-U *file*	Makes a report on reverse dependencies in the specified file.
-V	Shows version information.
-v*{ NR }*	Verbose mode. Shows more information. Specify the level using 1–10.
directory	Specifies the directory to search.
File Name: toe	**Directory:** /usr/bin/ **Type:** External
toe /usr/share/terminfo/l	Shows all terminal types that begins with "l".

top

UNIX Shell:	All primary shells (bash, ash, tcsh)
Function	Shows a list of the most active CPU processes.
Syntax	top [options...]

-d *delay*	Specifies the time between screen updates (default is 5 seconds).
-p *pID*	Shows only processes with the specified process ID.
-q	Updates without any delay.
-S	Uses cumulative mode where CPU time includes dead children.
-s	Uses secure mode with some dangerous interactive commands disabled.
-i	Ignores any idle or zombie processes.
-C	Shows total CPU states in addition to individual CPUs (only in SMP system).
-c	Shows full command line instead of only the command name.
-n *NR*	Specify number of iterations before top exits.
-b	Uses batch mode.
File Name: top	**Directory:** /usr/bin/ **Type:** External

tracepath

UNIX Shell:	All primary shells (bash, ash, tcsh)
Function	Shows the path, and the MTU that is found on the way, to the specified destination.
Syntax	tracepath *destination port*

destination	Specifies the destination host or IPaddress of the trace.
port	Specifies the UDP port to use for the trace.
File Name: tracepath	**Directory:** /usr/sbin/ **Type:** External

tune2fs

UNIX Shell:	All primary shells (bash, ash, tcsh)
Function	Alters tunable file system parameters on second extended file systems.
Syntax	tune2fs [options...] *device*

-l	Shows superblock contents for the file system.
-c *NR*	Alters the maximum number of mounts between file system checks.
-e *errors-behavior*	Changes what the kernel does when an error is detected.
-i *time*	Alters the maximum time between file system checks.
-m *percentage*	Alters the percentage of reversed space on a file system.
-r *NR*	Alters the number of reserved blocks on a file system
-s *flag*	Alters the sparse superblock flag.
-u *user*	Sets user who can use the reserved blocks.
-g *group*	Sets group that can use the reserved blocks.
-C *NR*	Sets how many times the file system has been mounted.
-L *label*	Alters the volume label of the file system.
-M *directory*	Alters the last mounted directory for the file system.
-O *feature*	Sets or clears file system features.
-U *UUID*	Alters the file system UUID.

continued

device		Specifies the file system device to tune.			
File Name:	`tune2fs`	**Directory:**	/sbin/	**Type:**	External
Warning:	Running this on a read-write file system could wreck it. Remount to read-only before using this command.				
tune2fs -l /dev/hda1		Shows information about the file system on `/dev/hda1`.			
tune2fs -u ucguser /dev/hda1		Lets specified user use the reserved blocks on `/dev/hda1`.			
tune2fs -L ucgdisk /dev/hda3		Labels the `hda3` partition as ucgdisk.			

tunelp

UNIX Shell: All primary shells (bash, ash, tcsh)

Function	Configures various parameters for the lp device.
Syntax	tunelp *device* [options...]

-t *timeout*		Specifies the timeout time for the printer.			
-c *number*		Specifies the number of times to try to output a character to the printer.			
-w *number*		Specifies the number of microseconds we wait while using the strobe signal.			
-a yes | no		Specifies if the printer should abort when an error occurs.			
-o yes | no		Checks the device if it's online or not.			
-C yes | no		Uses extra error checking or not.			
-s		Shows current printer status.			
-T yes | no		Specifies whether the `lp` device should trust the IRQ.			
-r		Resets the printer port.			
-q yes | no		Shows the current IRQ setting.			
-i *irq*		Specifies the IRQ of the parallel port.			
device		Specifies the device to configure.			
File Name:	`tunelp`	**Directory:**	/usr/sbin/	**Type:**	External
tunelp /dev/lp0 -C on		Disables the errors that the printer produces.			

twm

UNIX Shell: Bash-shell (bash)

Function	A X-window manager that provides icon management, macros, key bindings, title bars, and shaped windows.
Syntax	twm [options...]

-display *display*		Specifies the X display to use.			
-s		Manages only the default screen.			
-f *file*		Specifies the startup file to use (default is `~/.twmrc`).			
-v		Prints found error messages directly.			
File Name:	`twm`	**Directory:**	/usr/X11R6/bin/	**Type:**	External

tzselect

UNIX Shell: A shell (ash, bsh)

Function	Configures the time zone in an interactive mode.
Syntax	tzselect

File Name:	`tzselect`	**Directory:**	/usr/bin/	**Type:**	Script

unbuffer

UNIX Shell: Expect script

Function	Disables the output buffering when the specified program is redirected.
Syntax	unbuffer *program { arguments... }*

program		Specifies any program and its options.			
arguments...		Specifies the argument on the needed redirect or saves the output.			
File Name:	`unbuffer`	**Directory:**	/usr/bin/	**Type:**	Script

uncomplete

UNIX Shell: TC shell (tcsh)

Function	Removes any pattern specified with complete.
Syntax	uncomplete *pattern*

pattern	Specifies a pattern to remove.

unicode_start

UNIX Shell:	A shell (ash, bsh)
Function	Sets Unicode mode to the screen and keyboard.
Syntax	unicode_start *{ font } { map }*

font	Specifies the font to load.
map	Specifies the screen-font-map to load.

File Name:	`unicode_start`	Directory:	/usr/bin/	Type:	Script

unicode_stop

UNIX Shell:	A shell (ash, bsh)
Function	Takes screen and keyboard out of Unicode mode and into 8-bit mode.
Syntax	unicode_stop

File Name:	`unicode_stop`	Directory:	/usr/bin/	Type:	Script

unshar

UNIX Shell:	All primary shells (bash, ash, tcsh)
Function	Searches mail messages for shell archives, unpacks them, and saves them in a single file.
Syntax	unshar [options...] *{ file }*

-c	Overwrites existing files.
-d *Directory*	Specifies the directory to unpack in.
-e	Unpacks shell archives into a single mail folder, using the exit 0 separation string.
-E *String*	Works like -e, but allows you to specify the file separation string.
-f	Same as -c.
--version	Shows version information.
--help	Shows help information.
file	Specifies the file to where the shell archives are unpacked.

File Name:	`unshar`	Directory:	/usr/bin/	Type:	External

unshar -d /unshared/ /root/text.shar	Unpacks text.shar into directory /unshared/.

unstr

UNIX Shell:	All primary shells (bash, ash, tcsh)
Function	Shows the strings from a file created by the `strfile` command.
Syntax	unstr [options...] *infile { outfile }*

-c*character*	Specifies a new separation character.
-i	Ignores uppercase and lowercase when sorting the strings.
-o	Shows the strings in alphabetical order.
-r	Shows the strings in randomize order.
-s	Suppresses summary messages.
-x	Rotates characters in a simple Caesar cipher.
infile	Specifies the file created by the `strfile` command.
outfile	Specifies an output file to save the output to instead of writing to STDOUT.

File Name:	`unstr`	Directory:	/usr/sbin/	Type:	External

unzip

UNIX Shell:	All primary shells (bash, ash, tcsh)
Function	Uncompress, list, test, or show the compressed files from a zip archive.
Syntax	unzip [options...] *{ files... }*

-Z	Causes the options to be interpreted as `zipinfo` options.
-A	Shows extended help for the DLL's programming interface on OS/2 and UNIX.
-c	Uncompresses files and shows them on STDOUT like they were stored.
-f	Updates the files on a disk, uncompresses the newest version of the files on the disk.
-l	Shows archive files in a short form list, sizes, modification dates and print times.
-p	Shows the file data on STDOUT and sends uncompressed files to a pipe.
-t	Tests archive files to check whether the files have changed.
-T	Marks all archives with the same timestamp as the newest file.
-u	Works like the -f option, but also creates new files if they don't exist.
-v	Verbose mode. Shows more information.

continued

-z	Shows only the archive comment.
-a	Specifies that text files are identified as in text format.
-b	Specifies that all files are treated as binary on a non-VMS, equal to ---a.
-b	Alters all files to a 512-byte record format on a VMS.
-bb	Uncompresses all files in a 512-byte record format.
-B	Saves a backup copy with a tilde (~) appendix of all overwritten files.
-C	Doesn't take any notice about uppercase and lowercase letters in filenames.
-E	Shows the content in the Mac OS extra field. Mac OS only.
-F	Keeps the NFS type extensions in a uncompress operation. Acorn only.
-F	Translates and appends Acorn to NFS extensions. Acorn compiled UNIX only.
-i	Ignores the names stored in the Mac OS extra field. Mac OS only.
-j	Puts all files in specified archive without keeping the original archive structure.
-J	Restores only the data in a BeOS file, not the attributes.
-J	Ignores all Mac OS extra fields skipping all information.
-L	Alters filenames made on uppercase-only systems to lowercase filenames.
-M	Pipes all the output through an internal pager.
-n	Doesn't overwrite existing files.
-o	Is used when you want to overwrite files without any prompt questions.
-P	Specifies a password to use when a file has a protection against uncompression.
-q	Quiet mode, suppresses most error messages. Two q's (qq) gives even more effect.
-s	Creates underscores instead of spaces in filenames (OS/2, NT, MS-DOS).
-U	Leaves all filenames in uppercase as they are (obsolete, please see -L).
-V	Keeps all VMS file version numbers.
-X	Restores all group and user information in UNIX or protection/owner info in VMS.
-$	Restores the volume label if the file is uncompressed from a removable medium.
-/	Overrides the list of extensions in Unzip$Ext environment. Acorn only.
files...	Specifies the compressed zip file or files to uncompress.
File Name: `unzip`	**Directory:** /usr/bin/ **Type:** External

unzipsfx

UNIX Shell: All primary shells (bash, ash, tcsh)

Function	Creates self-extracting zip archives. A binary stub to be added to existing zip archives.
Syntax	unzipsfx *{ zipfile } selfextractingzipfile* [options...] *{ files... }*

-x *files...*	Specifies files not to extract. All common wildcards are accepted.
-d *directory*	Specifies a directory to extract the files into. Works only if SFX_EXDIR is defined.
	The following `unzip` modifiers and options are supported:
-a	Recognizes and extracts all text files as text.
-n	Doesn't overwrite existing files.
-o	Overwrites existing files without any questions.
-q	Suppresses most of the error messages.
-C	Doesn't take any notice about uppercase and lowercase letters in filenames.
-L	Alters filenames made on uppercase-only systems to lowercase filenames.
-j	Puts all files in the original archive without keeping the archive structure.
-V	Shows version information.
-X	Restores the VMS owner and protection information.
-s	Alters the spaces in the filename from DOS, OS/2, and NT to underscores.
-$	Restores the volume labels from DOS, OS/2, NT, and Amiga files.
-c	Uncompresses the files and shows them on STDOUT like they were stored.
-p	Shows only the file data on STDOUT and sends the uncompressed files to a pipe.
-f	Updates the files on a disk, uncompresses the newest version of the files on the disk.
-u	Works like the -f option but also creates new files if they don't exist.
-z	Shows only the archive comment.
-t	Tests archive files to check whether they have been changed.
zipfile	Specifies the file and the name of the zip archive.
selfextractingzipfile	Specifies the name of the self extracting file to create.
files...	Specifies files in the zip archive that is handled during extraction or creation.
File Name: `unzipsfx`	**Directory:** /usr/bin/ **Type:** External
unzipsfx uggbook.zip > ucgbook.bin	Creates a self-extracting file called `ucgbook.bih`.

up2date

UNIX Shell:	Python script
Function	Updates packets installed on your computer.
Syntax	up2date [options...] { *packages...* }

--allpackages	Makes all packages available, not just those on your system.
--list	Shows a list of packages available for download.
--help	Shows help information.
--nosig	Specifies that GPG shouldn't be used to check package signatures.
--register	Registers as an anonymous user with Red Hat Network.
--version	Shows version information.
packages...	Specifies one or more installed packages to upgrade.

File Name:	**Directory:**	**Type:**
up2date	/usr/sbin/	Script

update

UNIX Shell:	All primary shells (bash, ash, tcsh)
Function	Tells the kernel daemon to flush dirty buffers back to disk (also known as bdflush).
Syntax	update [options...]

-d	Shows the kernel parameters without starting the daemon.
-s *time*	Specifies the time in seconds between synchronization calls (default is 30).
-f *time*	Specifies the time in seconds between flush calls (default is 5).
-0 *count*	Specifies the max fraction of LRU list to examine for dirty blocks.
-1 *count*	Specifies the max number of dirty blocks to write each time activated.
-2 *count*	Specifies the count of clean buffers to be loaded onto free list.
-3 *count*	Specifies the dirty block threshold for to activate the command.
-4 *count*	Specifies the percentage of cache to scan for free clusters.
-5 *count*	Specifies the time for data buffers to age before flushing.
-6 *count*	Specifies the time for nondata (dir ,bitmap, and so forth) buffers to age before flushing.
-7 *count*	Sets the time buffer cache load average constant.
-8 *count*	Sets the LAV ratio (used to determine threshold for buffer fratricide).
-h	Shows help information.

File Name:	**Directory:**	**Type:**
update	/sbin/	External

updatedb

UNIX Shell:	All primary shells (bash, ash, tcsh)
Function	A utility to update the slocate database.
Syntax	updatedb [options...]

-u	Creates the slocate database from the root directory.
-U *path*	Specifies the slocate database to be created starting at path.
-e *dirs*	Specifies a comma-separated list of directories to exclude from the slocate database.
-f *fstypes*	Specifies a comma-separated list of file systems to exclude from the slocate database
-l *num*	Sets the security level. (-l 0 to turn security checks off and -l 1 to turn them on.)
-q	Shows no error messages.
-v	Shows files indexed when creating a database.
--help	Shows help information.
--version	Shows version information.

File Name:	**Directory:**	**Type:**
updatedb	/usr/bin/	External

updatedb -e /home	This creates a database of all files except for those that exist under `/home`.

urlview

UNIX Shell:	All primary shells (bash, ash, tcsh)
Function	Reads all URLs it can find in a file and shows them in an interactive menu.
Syntax	urlview *files...*

files...	Specifies one or more files to read URL information from.

File Name:	**Directory:**	**Type:**
urlview	urlview	External

useradd, adduser

UNIX Shell:	All primary shells (bash, ash, tcsh)				
Function	Creates a new user or updates default new user information.				
Syntax	useradd [options...] *username*				
-c *comment*	Specifies a text about the user. Usually the full name of the user.				
-d *directory*	Specifies the new user's home directory.				
-G *group*	Defines the secondary group membership for the user.				
-m	Is used to create the home directory for the new user if it doesn't exist.				
-k *directory*	Specifies a directory that contains reconfigured information such as `.profile`.				
-M	Doesn't create a home directory for the user while adding. Causes -m not to work.				
-n	Doesn't add a group named as the username when adding.				
-r	Adds a system user with UID lower than the user minimum and without a home.				
-o	Allows duplicates of the user IDs.				
-p *password*	Specifies an encrypted password to set for the user.				
-u *userID*	Specifies the ID for the new user.				
-g *group*	Defines the primary group membership for the user. Also used as the default.				
-f *days*	Specifies the maximum days the login can be unused before it becomes invalid.				
-e *date*	Specifies the date when the login becomes invalid.				
-s *shell*	Specifies a full pathname of the program to use as the default shell for the user.				
-D	Shows or sets default values for the user.				
-b *directory*	Specifies the default base directory for the system. (Other options to set default values are: -g, -f, -e, and -s.)				
username	Specifies a username to create.				
File Name:	`useradd`	**Directory:**	/usr/sbin/	**Type:**	External
Warning:	BEWARE!! Adding users could be dangerous for your network!				
useradd -c "Ove" -d /home/ove -g 100 -m -s /bin/bash -u 550 ove	Creates the user ove with specified settings.				
useradd -D -g users	Sets the default group to users.				

userconf

UNIX Shell:	All primary shells (bash, ash, tcsh)				
Function	Configures system accounts and groups interactively or on the command line.				
Syntax	userconf [options...]				
--adduser *user group gecos shell*	Adds a new user.				
--deluser *user*	Deletes a user.				
--addgroup *group*	Adds a new group to the system.				
--delgroup *group*	Deletes a group.				
--help	Shows help information.				
File Name:	`userconf`	**Directory:**	/sbin/	**Type:**	External
userconf --adduser uk users Joachim /bin/bash	Adds user uk with group users and comment Joachim and shell `/bin/bash`.				

userdel

UNIX Shell:	All primary shells (bash, ash, tcsh)				
Function	Erases a user's account from the system.				
Syntax	userdel [-r] *user*				
-r	Erases the user's home directory.				
user	Specifies the user to erase from the system.				
File Name:	`userdel`	**Directory:**	/usr/sbin/	**Type:**	External
Tip:	Great way to eliminate user problems. Just delete the user's account and the problem is gone!				

userhelper

UNIX Shell:	All primary shells (bash, ash, tcsh)
Function	An interface to `pam` that is used to alter the user's shell, password, and GECOS information.
Syntax	userhelper [options...] *{ user }*

	The following are the command line options:
-w *command*	Specifies a program and its arguments to run.
-d *descriptors...*	Specifies three descriptors that are to be reattached to the handles before execution.
-t	Uses text mode authentication instead of the message numbers.
-c	Changes the current users password. Cannot be used with any of the other options.
-f *name*	Alters to a new full name.
-o *office*	Alters to a new office.
-p *officephone*	Alters to a new office phone number.
-h *homephone*	Alters to a new home phone number.
-s	Alters to a new shell.
user	Specifies the name of the user.
	The `userhelper` output is sent to STDOUT in the format <number> <string>:
<number>	Shows the type of prompt given by `pamlib`.
1	A visible input prompt.
2	An invisible input prompt.
3	An informational message.
4	An error message.
5	A count of the messages that have been sent in this block up till now.
6	Specifies the name of the used service.
7	Sends a yes or no to run if authentication fails.
8	Specifies the name of the user being authenticated.
<string>	Specifies the prompt that is given to the user.

File Name:	Directory:	Type:
`userhelper`	/usr/sbin/	External

userinfo

UNIX Shell:	All primary shells (bash, ash, tcsh)
Function	Alters the user's finger information just like the command `chfn`, but does so interactively.
Syntax	userinfo

File Name:	Directory:	Type:
`userinfo`	/usr/bin/	External

usermod

UNIX Shell:	All primary shells (bash, ash, tcsh)
Function	Alters a specified user's login account permissions and memberships on the system.
Syntax	usermod [options...] *user*

-c *comment*	Specifies a new text about the user. Usually the full name of the user.
-d *directory*	Specifies the users new home directory.
-m	Moves the user to the new home directory specified with -d.
-e *expire*	Specifies the new date when the login becomes invalid.
-f *inactive*	Specifies the maximum numberr of days the login can be unused before it becomes invalid.
-g *group*	Defines the new primary group membership for the user.
-G *group*	Defines the new secondary group membership for the user.
-l *loginname*	Specifies the new login name of the user.
-p *password*	Specifies the encrypted password.
-s *shell*	Specifies a full pathname of the new program to use as the default shell for the user.
-u *userID*	Specifies the new ID for the user.
-o	Allows duplicates of the user's ID.
-L	Locks a user's password. This option can't be used with -p or -U.
-U	Unlocks a user's password. This option can't be used with -p or -L.
user	Specifies the username to act on.

File Name:	Directory:	Type:
`usermod`	/usr/sbin/	External

usermod -l ucg ucg_account	Changes the username of ucg_account to ucg.

usermount

usermount	UNIX Shell:	All primary shells (bash, ash, tcsh)
Function	Starts a graphical tool to mount, unmount, and format file systems.	
Syntax	usermount	
File Name: usermount	Directory: /usr/bin/	Type: External

usernetctl

usernetctl	UNIX Shell:	All primary shells (bash, ash, tcsh)
Function	Changes the status of the specified network interface.	
Syntax	usernetctl *interface* option	

up	Brings interface up.
down	Brings interface down.
report	Shows whether the user is allowed to bring the network interface up or down.
interface	Specifies the name of the network interface.

File Name: usernetctl	Directory: /usr/sbin/	Type: External

userpasswd

userpasswd	UNIX Shell:	All primary shells (bash, ash, tcsh)
Function	A graphical tool that lets users change their passwords.	
Syntax	userpasswd	
File Name: userpasswd	Directory: /usr/bin/	Type: External

usleep

usleep	UNIX Shell:	All primary shells (bash, ash, tcsh)
Function	Sleeps for some number of microseconds.	
Syntax	usleep [options...] *{ number }*	

--usage	Shows the syntax of the command.
--help	Shows help information.
--version	Shows version information
--oot	Shows "oot says hey!".
number	Specifies the number of microseconds to sleep.

File Name: usleep	Directory: /bin/	Type: External

usleep 10000000	Sleeps for 10 seconds.

uuidgen

uuidgen	UNIX Shell:	All primary shells (bash, ash, tcsh)
Function	Creates a new UUID value.	
Syntax	uuidgen [options...]	

-r	Generates a random-based UUID (is default).
-t	Generates a time-based UUID, based on system clock and Ethernet hardware address.

File Name: uuidgen	Directory: /usr/bin/	Type: External

vacuumdb

vacuumdb	UNIX Shell:	A shell (ash, bsh)
Function	Cleans your Postgres database. The Postgres query optimizer uses it to generate internal statistics.	
Syntax	vacuumdb [options...]	

-d	Specifies the database to clean or analyze.
-z	Calculates stats on the database for use by the optimizer.
-a	Vacuums all databases.
-v	Verbose mode. Shows more information.
-t *table*] *{ column.. }*	Cleans or analyzes only table. Columns only work with -z option.
-h *hostname*	Specifies the database server host.
-p *port*	Specifies the database server port.
-e	Shows the command being sent to the back-end.
-q	Doesn't show any output.
-U *username*	Specifies the username to login with.
-W *password*	Specifies the password to login with.

File Name: vacuumdb	Directory: /usr/bin	Type: External

vdir

UNIX Shell:	All primary shells (bash, ash, tcsh)
Function	Shows information about the current or the specified directory.
Syntax	vdir [options...] *{ directory }*

-a	Shows all information, including hidden entries that start with a dot.
-A	Shows everything but hidden entries started with a dot and a double dot.
-b	Shows the octal escapes for nongraphic characters.
-B	Shows all but the backup files that are entries ending with a tilde sign (~).
--block-size=*size*	Specifies the block size in bytes.
-c	Shows the information sorted by last modification (ctime) time if used with -lt. Shows the information sorted by name and also shows the ctime with -l.
-C	Shows the entries in columns.
--color *when*	Sets when colors are to be used in information: never, always, or auto.
-d	Shows directory entries instead of contents.
-D	Creates output designed for Emacs dired mode.
-f	Doesn't sort the information.
-F	Appends an indicator to the entries (one of / = @ |).
--format=*format*	Specifies the way to show information (across and horizontal = -x, commas = -m, long and verbose = -l, single column = -1, vertical = -C).
--full-time	Shows both full time and date.
-G	Doesn't show any information about groups.
-h	Shows sizes in 1K, 234M, 2G, and so on. This is called human-readable sizes.
-H	Prints sizes like above, but use 1K = 1000 instead of 1K = 1024.
-i	Shows the file's index number.
-I *string*	Doesn't show any information about entries matching the specified string.
-k	Synonym for --block-size=1024.
-l	Shows the information in a long format.
-L	Shows information about entries pointed to by symbolic links.
-m	Shows the information with a comma-separated list of entries.
-n	Shows numeric user IDs and group IDs, not the names.
-N	Shows the raw entry names.
-o	Shows a long listing format with no group info.
-p	Appends an indicator to the entries (one of / = @ |).
-q	Shows a ? instead of control characters.
--show-control-chars	Shows all control characters as they are.
-Q	Puts the entry names inside double quotes.
--quoting-style=*style*	Specifies a quoting style for entry names: literal, locale, shell, c, or escape.
-r	Shows the information in reversed order.
-R	Shows the subdirectories recursively.
-s	Shows the size of each file in blocks.
-S	Shows the information sorted by file size.
--sort=*style*	Specifies the way to sort the information (extension = -X; none = -U; size = -S; time = -t; version = -v; status = -c; time = -t; atime, access, and use = -u).
--time=*style*	Shows time as atime, access, use, ctime, or status instead of the modification time.
-t	Shows the information sorted by modification time.
-T *count*	Specifies tabstops at the specified interval instead of 8.
-u	Shows the information sorted by access time with -lt and with -l by name.
-U	Shows the information sorted in the same order as the directories.
-v	Shows the information sorted in version order.
-w *count*	Specifies another screen width than the current.
-x	Shows the information sorted by lines instead of by columns.
-X	Shows the information sorted alphabetically by entry extension.
-1	Shows the information one file per line.
--help	Shows help information.
--version	Shows version information.
directory	Specifies directory to act on (default is current directory).

File Name:	vdir	**Directory:**	/usr/bin/	**Type:**	External

vidmode

UNIX Shell: All primary shells (bash, ash, tcsh)

Function	Sets video mode for a kernel image. Is equivalent to `rdev -v`.
Syntax	vidmode [-o *value*] { *image* }

-o *value*	Specifies the byte offset.
image	Specifies a bootable Linux kernel image.
mode	Sets the video mode with one of the following:
-3	Causes command to prompt for mode.
-2	Enables extended VGA.
-1	Enables normal VGA.
	Note:If mode isn't specified, the image is queried for the video mode setting.
offset	Specifies an offset for the kernel image.

File Name:	`vidmode`	**Directory:**	/usr/sbin/	**Type:**	External

vidmode /vmlinux -2	Sets the video mode to extended VGA.

viewres

UNIX Shell: All primary shells (bash, ash, tcsh)

Function	Shows a tree structure of the widget class hierarchy of the Athena Widget Set.
Syntax	viewres [options...]

-top *name*	Shows the name of the highest widget in the hierarchy.
-variable	Shows the widget variable names in nodes instead of class name.
-vertical	Shows the widget tree top to bottom instead of left to right.

File Name:	`viewres`	**Directory:**	/usr/X11R6/bin/	**Type:**	External

vigr

UNIX Shell: All primary shells (bash, ash, tcsh)

Function	Is used to edit the `/etc/group` file.
Syntax	vigr [-V]

-V	Shows version information.

File Name:	`vigr`	**Directory:**	/usr/sbin/	**Type:**	External

vimtutor

UNIX Shell: A shell (ash, bsh)

Function	Shows a help page on how to start using the very powerful editor `vim` in Linux.
Syntax	vimtutor

	Note:To exit the vi program without any savings, type Esc:q!.

File Name:	`vimtutor`	**Directory:**	/usr/bin/	**Type:**	Script

vipw

UNIX Shell: All primary shells (bash, ash, tcsh)

Function	Edits the `/etc/passwd` file.
Syntax	vipw [-V]

-V	Shows version information.

File Name:	`vipw`	**Directory:**	/usr/sbin/	**Type:**	External

vt-is-UTF8

UNIX Shell: All primary shells (bash, ash, tcsh)

Function	Checks whether current VT is in UTF8- or byte mode.
Syntax	vt-is-UTF8 [options...]

-h	Shows help information.
-V	Shows version information.
-q	Makes the program quiet. Exit status are, 1 = UTF8 mode; 0 = byte mode.

File Name:	`vt-is-UTF8`	**Directory:**	/usr/bin/	**Type:**	External

watch

UNIX Shell:	All primary shells (bash, ash, tcsh)
Function	Runs a specified command several times to show the change of the output.
Syntax	watch [options...] *command*

-d[=cumulative]	Highlights all that is different in output between the runs.
=cumulative	Makes the highlighted changes stay on screen.
-h	Shows help information.
-n *time*	Specifies the interval between runs in seconds (default is 2).
-v	Shows version information.
command	Specifies the command to run.

File Name: watch | **Directory:** /usr/bin/ | **Type:** External

weave

UNIX Shell:	All primary shells (bash, ash, tcsh)
Function	Translates a file from .web style to a TeX style file.
Syntax	weave [-x] *webfile { Texfile }*

-x	Suppresses the index, module name list, and table of contents pages.
webfile	Specifies the .web file.
Texfile	Specifies the name of the file to save the output in.

File Name: weave | **Directory:** /usr/bin/ | **Type:** External

whatnow

UNIX Shell:	All primary shells (bash, ash, tcsh)
Function	Is used as a front end for the nmh commands to prompt the user of what to do.
Syntax	whatnow

-draftfolder *dir*	Specifies the draft folder.
-draftmessage *msg*	Specifies the draft messages.
-nodraftfolder	Doesn't use any draft folders.
-editor *editor*	Specifies the editor to use.
-noedit	Doesn't start the editor on the draft when the command is started.
-prompt *string*	Sets the prompt string (default is What now?).
-version	Shows version information.
-help	Shows help information.

File Name: whatnow | **Directory:** /usr/bin/ | **Type:** External

where

UNIX Shell:	TC shell (tcsh)
Function	Shows where a command is located, including alias, Internal, and in the path.
Syntax	where *command*

command	Specifies a command to show information about.

wish

UNIX Shell:	All primary shells (bash, ash, tcsh)
Function	Specifies the Tool command language with a graphic tool kit (Tcl/Tk) used to run Tcl/Tk scripts in graphic mode.
Syntax	wish *{ file }* [options...]

-colormap *new*	Specifies a new color map to use.
-display *display*	Specifies the display to use.
-geometry *geometry*	Specifies the initial geometry to use for the main window.
-name *name*	Specifies the name of the window.
-sync	Runs all X server commands synchronously.
-use *id*	Specifies the ID of the window to use.
-visual *visual*	Specifies the visual for the window.
--	Passes the remaining options to the Tcl script.
file	Specifies options to the Tcl script containing toolkit commands.

wnewmail

UNIX Shell: All primary shells (bash, ash, tcsh)

Function	Alerts you when a new mail arrives.
Syntax	wnewmail [options...] *mailboxes...*

-d	Shows debug information.
-i *seconds*	Specifies how often to check for mail (default is 60 seconds).
mailboxes...	Specifies the mailbox or mailboxes to check for new mails.

File Name:	`wnewmail`	**Directory:**	/usr/bin/	**Type:**	External

word-list-compress

UNIX Shell: All primary shells (bash, ash, tcsh)

Function	Compresses or decompresses word list files read from STDIN and output on STDOUT.
Syntax	word-list-compress options...

c	Compresses wordlist read from STDIN.
d	Decompresses wordlist read from STDIN.

File Name:	`word-list-compress`	**Directory:**	/usr/bin/	**Type:**	External

writevt

UNIX Shell: All primary shells (bash, ash, tcsh)

Function	Inserts a text string in a terminal's input buffer.
Syntax	writevt [options...]

-t*terminal*	Specifies the terminal device to insert the text to.
-T*text*	Specifies the text to insert.
-h	Shows help information.
-V	Shows version information.

File Name:	`writevt`	**Directory:**	/usr/bin/	**Type:**	External

wrjpgcom

UNIX Shell: All primary shells (bash, ash, tcsh)

Function	Inserts text information into a JPEG picture.
Syntax	wrjpgcom [options...] *file*

-replace	Deletes any existing COM blocks in the picture file.
-comment *text*	Specifies the comment to insert into the picture.
-cfile *filename*	Reads comments from `filename`.
file	Specifies the picture file to use.

File Name:	`wrjpgcom`	**Directory:**	/usr/bin/	**Type:**	External

wvdial

UNIX Shell: All primary shells (bash, ash, tcsh)

Function	Dials a modem and initiates PPP. Configured from command line or from the file `/etc/wvdial.conf`.
Syntax	wvdial [options...] *{ sections... }*

	You must select between these three options:
--chat	Runs command from within `pppd`, then starts `pppd`.
--help	Shows help information.
--version	Shows version information.
--remotename	Specifies the remote name to send to `pppd`.
sections...	Specifies the sections in the `/etc/wvdial.conf` file. (List the sections using a space between each one.)

File Name:	`wvdial`	**Directory:**	/usr/bin/	**Type:**	External

wvdialconf

UNIX Shell: All primary shells (bash, ash, tcsh)

Function	Detects your modem and its attributes, then updates the `/etc/wvdial.conf` file.
Syntax	wvdialconf *file*

file	Specifies the configuration file to update. (Default is `/etc/wvdial.conf`)

File Name:	`wvdialconf`	**Directory:**	/usr/bin/	**Type:**	External
Note:	You may must manually edit the `/etc/wvdial.conf` file to specify your phone number, password, and login name for your Internet account.				

x11perf

UNIX Shell: All primary shells (bash, ash, tcsh)

Function	Measures the performance of an X server.
Syntax	x11perf [options...]

-display *host:disp*	Specifies the display to use.
-sync	Runs the test in synchronous mode.
-pack	Packs rectangles right next to each other in the rectangles test.
-repeat *NR*	Repeats every test NR times.
-time *time*	Specifies how long each test should be run (default is 5).
-all	Runs all tests.
-range *test1[,test2]*	Specifies a range of tests to run.
-labels	Generates descriptive labels for each test.
-fg *color*	Specifies the foreground color to use.
-bg *color*	Specifies the background color to use.
-clips *NR*	Specifies default number of clip windows.
-ddbg *NR*	Specifies the second color to use for double dashed line or arc.
-rop *list*	Specifies a list of specified raster ops to use.
-pm	Specifies a list of specified plane masks to use.
-depth *depth*	Specifies the visual planes per pixel to use.
-vclass *vclass*	Specifies vclass type: StaticGray, GrayScale, StaticColor, PseudoColor, TrueColor, or DirectColor.
-reps *NR*	Sets the repletion count.
-subs *list*	Specifies a list of number of subwindows to use.
-v1.2	Runs only x11pref V1.2 tests.
-v1.3	Runs only x11pref V1.3 tests.
-su	Sets the save under window attribute to True.
-bs *backingStoreHint*	Sets the backing store hint.
-*testname*	Specifies the test. Use x11pref by its own to see a list (there are about 270 of them).

File Name:	`x11perf`	**Directory:**	/usr/X11R6/bin/	**Type:**	External

x11perfcomp

UNIX Shell: All primary shells (bash, ash, tcsh)

Function	Compares and shows the difference between x11servers.
Syntax	x11perfcomp [options...] *files...*

-r	Shows server performance relative to the first server also.
-ro	Shows only performance to the first server.
-l *file*	Specifies a label file containing tests. Please see `x11perf -label`.
files...	Specifies the files to get the test results from on each server.

File Name:	`x11perfcomp`	**Directory:**	/usr/X11R6/bin/	**Type:**	External

Xconfigurator

UNIX Shell: All primary shells (bash, ash, tcsh)

Function	Configures the XFree86 server.
Syntax	Xconfigurator [options...]

--help	Shows help information.
--expert	Gains more control over some parameters that normally are automatic.
--kick start	Autoprobes for all needed information.
--server *server*	Specifies the server to use in kick start mode.
--card *card*	Specifies the card type to use in kick start mode.
--monitor *monitor*	Specifies the monitor type to use in kick start mode.
--hsync	Specifies the horizontal sync ranges for the monitor.
--vsync	Specifies the vertical sync ranges for the monitor.
--noddcprobe	Disables probe on the monitor.
--nodri	Disables DRI on XFree 4 servers.
--preferxf3	Uses the XFree 3.3.x server if available.

continued

--preferxf4		Uses the XFree 4 server if available.			
File Name:	Xconfigurator	**Directory:**	/usr/X11R6/bin/	**Type:**	External

xconsole

UNIX Shell: All primary shells (bash, ash, tcsh)

Function	Shows console messages with X.
Syntax	xconsole [options...]

-file *file*	Specifies the device to monitor (default is `/dev/console`).
-notify	Enables notification of new messages. Icon name changes so you will notice.
-nonotify	Disables message notification. The icon won't change when things happen.
-daemon	Runs in the background as a daemon.
-verbose	Verbose mode. Shows more information.
-exitOnFail	Exits if it is unable to retrieve output from the device.

File Name:	xconsole	**Directory:**	/usr/X11R6/bin/	**Type:**	External

xf86config

UNIX Shell: All primary shells (bash, ash, tcsh)

Function	A console-based application to configure the XF86Config file.
Syntax	xf86config

File Name:	xf86config	**Directory:**	/usr/X11R6/bin/	**Type:**	External
Tip:	I prefer this application when configuring my X instead of other graphical apps like XF86Setup.				

XFree86

UNIX Shell: All primary shells (bash, ash, tcsh)

Function	A free X server that is delivered with several Linux distributions.
Syntax	XFree86 *{ screen }* [options...]

vt*dev*	Sets the virtual terminal device number that the X server use.
-crt	Does the same as vt, but functions with the native SCO X server.
-probeonly	Probes the devices but doesn't run.
-quiet	Doesn't show all information text on the startup.
-depth *count*	Specifies the default color depth to 8, 15, 16, or 24.
-fbbpp *bits*	Specifies the count of frame buffer bits per pixel: 8, 16, 24, or 32. Use with caution.
-weight *count*	Specifies RGB weighting only on servers that supports 16 BPP (default is 565).
-flipPixels	Inverts the black and white colors.
-disableVidMode	Stops `xvidtune` clients from to alter VidModes.
-allowNonLocalXvidtune	Enables a `xvidtune` client to connect from another host.
-disableModInDev	Forbids dynamic modification alterations to input devices.
-allowNonLocalModInDev	Enables remote users to alter keyboard and mouse settings.
-allowMouseOpenFail	Starts the X server even if a mouse isn't present.
-gamma *count*	Specifies the gamma correction to use, from 0.1 to 10 (default is 1).
-rgamma *count*	Specifies the red gamma correction to use, from 0.1 to 10 (default is 1).
-ggamma *count*	Specifies the green gamma correction to use, from 0.1 to 10 (default is 1).
-bgamma *count*	Specifies the blue gamma correction to use, from 0.1 to 10 (default is 1).
-showconfig	Shows version and server configuration information.
-verbose	Verbose mode. Shows more information on STDERR.
-version	Shows version and server configuration information.
-xf86config *file*	Specifies an X server configuration file to read.
-keeptty	Doesn't detach the server from its initial screen. Useful on a debug session.
	The following key sequences are supported in the XFree86 server:
Ctrl+Alt+Backspace	Causes XFree86 to quit immediately.
Ctrl+Alt+Keypad-Plus	Increases the video resolution order to the next one specified in configuration.
Ctrl+Alt+Keypad-Minus	Decreases the video resolution order to the previous one specified in configuration.
Ctrl+Alt+F1...F12	Switches between the text consoles and the different X servers. (F1 = virtual terminal 1).
screen	Specifies the screen number and host to run the X server on.

File Name:	XFree86	**Directory:**	/usr/X11R6/bin	**Type:**	External

XFree86 :1 -xf86config ~/myXFfile &	Starts the X server on the next free virtual console on display number 1, uses myXFfile as configuration file.

xfwp

UNIX Shell:	All primary shells (bash, ash, tcsh)
Function	An X firewall proxy. Provides an application layer firewall for X traffic.
Syntax	xfwp [options...]

-cdt *time*	Sets closing time for inactive xfwp client connections in secs (default is 604800).
-clt *time*	Sets closing time for inactive xfwp client listen ports in secs (default is 86400).
-pdt *time*	Sets closing time for inactive proxy manager connections in secs (default is 3600).
-config *filename*	Specifies the filename for the configuration file.
-pmport *port*	Sets port address for proxy manager connections (default is 4444).
-verify	Shows what role in the configuration that matched the service request.
-logfile *filename*	Specifies a name of the audit information log file.
-loglevel *n*	Sets the log level, where 0 is all and 1 is unsuccessful connections.
-max_pm_conns *num*	Specifies max number of connections to the proxy manager (default is 10).
-max_pm_conns *num*	Specifies max number of connections to the X server (default is 100).

File Name:	`xfwp`	**Directory:**	/usr/X11R6/bin/	**Type:**	External

xgetfile

UNIX Shell:	All primary shells (bash, ash, tcsh)
Function	A file manager based on X-window.
Syntax	xgetfile [options...]

-display *screen*	Specifies the screen on which to show the control window.
-fn *font*	Specifies another font to use than the default.
-title *title*	Shows the given title in the title bar.
-path *path*	Specifies a default search path.
-pattern *string*	Shows only the files that match the specified string.
-file *file*	Specifies a file to show the user as the default selection.
-popup	Pops up the window as temporary directly under the pointer.
-quote	Quotes the filename on exit.
-exec *command*	Executes the specified command when a file is chosen.
-queue	Allows you to specify a new file even if the command is still not executed.

File Name:	`xgetfile`	**Directory:**	/usr/X11R6/bin/	**Type:**	External

xgetfile -exec "mpg123 %s" -queue	When you select the file, it'll start playing.

xgettext

UNIX Shell:	All primary shells (bash, ash, tcsh)
Function	Creates portable message files that contain copies of C strings that are found in ANSI C source code.
Syntax	xgettext [options...] *files...*

-a	Extracts all strings.
-c *commandtag*	Marks the beginning of the comment.
-C	Uses the programming language C++.
--debug	Shows debug information.
-d *name*	Specifies the name of the output file - .po is appended to the filename.
-D *directory*	Specifies a directory from where to search for input files.
-e	Disables the C escape output.
-E	Enables the C escape output.
-f *file*	Reads the list of input files from the specified file.
--force-po	Writes the PO file even if it's empty.
--foreign-user	Doesn't output FSF copyright to foreign user.
-F	Sorts the output by file location.
-h	Shows help information.
-i	Uses the indented style to write the PO file.
-j	Joins messages with existing message files.
-k *keyword*	Specifies one more keyword to grep for.
-l *number*	Specifies the string length limit (default is 900).
-L *name*	Specifies what programming language to use of the following: C, C++, or PO.
-m *prefix*	Fills in the msgstr with prefix. This is useful for debug.
-M *suffix*	Fills in the msgstr with suffix. This is useful for debug.

continued

--no-location	Doesn't show filename and line number.
-n	Adds comment lines to the output file. Shows filename and line number.
--omit-header	Doesn't write header with message ID.
-o *file*	Specifies which output file to use.
-p *directory*	Specifies the directory in which to place the output files.
-s	Creates a list sorted by message IDs with all double message IDs removed.
--strict	Outputs a strict Uniforum conforming PO file.
-T	Accepts ANSI C trigraphs as input.
-V	Shows version information.
-w *number*	Specifies the page width.
-x *file*	Specifies a PO file that contains a list of message IDs that aren't extracted.
files...	Specifies the input files to use.

File Name: `xgettext` **Directory:** /usr/bin/ **Type:** External

xinetd

UNIX Shell: Bash shell (bash)

Function	Monitors service ports and starts the required services when the requests come.
Syntax	xinetd [options...]

-d	Shows debug information.
-syslog *name*	Starts `syslog` logging of the messages. Use `daemon, auth, user, or local.`
-filelog *file*	Specifies a file to save the messages in.
-f *file*	Specifies the file to use as config file instead of the default `/etc/xinetd.conf`.
-pidfile *file*	Specifies a file to write the process ID in.
-loop*count*	Specifies the max number of servers per second that can be forked (defaults is 10).
-reuse	Allows binding of a socket Internet address even if there are programs that use it.
-limit *count*	Limits the number of simultaneously running processes started by the command.
-logprocs *count*	Limits the number of simultaneously running servers for remote user ID acquisition.
-shutdownprocs *count*	Limits the number of simultaneously running servers for service shutdown.
-cc *time*	Specifies the interval in seconds for a periodic internal consistency checks.

File Name: `xinetd` **Directory:** /usr/sbin/ **Type:** External

xisdnload

UNIX Shell: All primary shells (bash, ash, tcsh)

Function	Shows periodically updated information about the ISDN load average.
Syntax	xisdnload [options...]

-hl	Sets the color of the scale lines.
-online *color*	Sets the background color when one or more ISDN channels are online.
-active *color*	Sets the background color for a route directed to an ISDN or ippp interface.
-trying *color*	Sets the background color, when one attempt to set up a connection is waiting.
-jumpscroll *count*	Specifies the number of pixels to jump to the left when the right border is reached.
-label *string*	Specifies a string of information to show in the label when online.
-nolabel	Suppress the label.
-scale *count*	Sets the minimum number of tick marks in the histogram (default is one).
-update *time*	Sets the update interval for the screen in seconds (default is 10 seconds).
-activate *command*	Executes the specified startup command if dial-on-demand isn't active.
-deactivate *command*	Executes the specified shutdown command when dial-on-demand is active.
-number *expression*	Specifies a regular expression used to limit the set numbers to be observed.

File Name: `xisdnload` **Directory:** /usr/X11R6/bin/ **Type:** External

Note: All standard X toolkit command-line options are accepted.

xkbevd

UNIX Shell: All primary shells (bash, ash, tcsh)

Function	Monitors for XKB events and runs the requested commands when they occur.
Syntax	xkbevd [options...]

-cfg *file*	Reads the specified configuration file or `~/.xkb/xkbevd.cf` or $(LIBDIR)/xkb/xkbevd.cf. (The configuration file is a list of event/action pairs and variables.)
-sc *cmd*	Uses the specified command to play sounds.

continued

-sd *directory*	Specifies the root directory for the sound files.		
-display *screen*	Specifies another screen to use if the one in $DISPLAY won't be used.		
-bg	Forks the command and runs it in the background.		
-synch	Synchronizes all X requests.		
-v	Verbose mode. Shows more information.		
-help	Shows help information.		
File Name: `xkbevd`	**Directory:** /usr/X11R6/bin/	**Type:**	External

xkibitz

UNIX Shell: Expect script

Function	Allows many people to interact with each others' programs.
Syntax	xkibitz [options...] { *program arguments...* }

-escape *character*	Changes the escape character (default is ^]).		
-display *display*	Adds a display to the session. Same as + in the interactive mode.		
program	Specifies the program to run.		
arguments...	Specifies the arguments to the program.		
File Name: `xkibitz`	**Directory:** /usr/bin/	**Type:**	Script

xkill

UNIX Shell: All primary shells (bash, ash, tcsh)

Function	Kills an X client. Useful for removing problematic programs.
Syntax	xkill [options...]

-display *displayname*	Specifies the X server to contact.		
-id *resource*	Specifies the X identifier on resource to abort.		
-button *number*	Specifies the number of pointer buttons to use when you select a window to kill.		
-frame	Ignores standard conventions to find top-level client windows.		
-all	Kills all clients with top-level windows on the screen.		
File Name: `xkill`	**Directory:** /usr/X11R6/bin/	**Type:**	External

xload

UNIX Shell: All primary shells (bash, ash, tcsh)

Function	Shows a histogram over the average system load.
Syntax	xload [options...]

-scale *integer*	Specifies the minimum tick marks to use in the histogram.		
-update *seconds*	Sets the interval to update the histogram.		
-hl *color*	Sets the color of the scale lines.		
-highlight *color*	Same as -hl.		
-jumpscroll *pixels*	Sets the number of pixels to move the scale line to the left when it reaches the end.		
-label *string*	Sets a label over the scale.		
-nolabel	Shows no labels.		
-lights	Uses keyboard LEDs to show the current load average.		
File Name: `xload`	**Directory:** /usr/X11R6/bin/	**Type:**	External

xlsatoms

UNIX Shell: All primary shells (bash, ash, tcsh)

Function	Shows the specified interned atoms on the server.
Syntax	xlsatoms [options...]

-display *dpy*	Specifies the X server to contact.		
-format *string*	Specifies printf-style string of how to show each atom.		
-range { *low* }-{ *high* }	Specifies the range of atoms to check. If low isn't given, 1 is used. (If high isn't given, xlsatoms continues until the first undefined atom.)		
-name *string*	Specifies an atom to show.		
File Name: `xlsatoms`	**Directory:** /usr/X11R6/bin/	**Type:**	External

xlsclients

UNIX Shell:	All primary shells (bash, ash, tcsh)
Function	Shows client applications that run on a screen.
Syntax	xlsclients [options...]

-display *displayname*	Specifies the X server to contact.
-a	Shows clients from all screens.
-l	Shows a long listing.
-m *maxcmdlen*	Specifies the maximum number of characters in a command to show (default is 10000).

File Name:	`xlsclients`	**Directory:**	/usr/X11R6/bin/	**Type:**	External

xmag

UNIX Shell:	All primary shells (bash, ash, tcsh)
Function	Enlarges parts of the screen.
Syntax	xmag [options...]

-mag *factor*	Specifies the magnification to use (default is 5).
-source *geom*	Specifies size and/or location of the source region on the screen.
-*toolkitoptions...*	Specifies additional standard X Toolkit command-line options.

File Name:	`xmag`	**Directory:**	/usr/X11R6/bin/	**Type:**	External

xman

UNIX Shell:	All primary shells (bash, ash, tcsh)
Function	Shows man pages in a browser when running X.
Syntax	xman [options...]

-helpfile *file*	Uses another help file than the default.
-bothshown	Shows both manual page and directory on screen at the same time.
-notopbox	Starts the browser without the top menu.
-geometry *W*H+X+Y*	Specifies the size and location of the top menu.
-pagesize *W*H+X+Y*	Specifies the size and location for the manual pages.

File Name:	`xman`	**Directory:**	/usr/X11R6/bin/	**Type:**	External

xmonisdn

UNIX Shell:	All primary shells (bash, ash, tcsh)
Function	Shows the status of ISDN network connections and enables the starting or stopping of subsystems.
Syntax	xmonisdn [options...]

-help	Shows help information on STDERR.
-update *time*	Updates the screen with the specified time in tenths of a second (default is 5).
-file *file*	Specifies the file that is to be monitored (default is /dev/isdninfo).
-volume *count*	Specifies the volume of the bell in percent when important information shows.
-shape	Shapes the X Window if masks for the images are given.
	The following are standard X Toolkit command-line arguments to the command:
-display *name*	Contacts the specified X server.
-geometry *size*	Sets the position and size of the window.
-bg *color*	Specifies the background color.
-bd *color*	Specifies the border color.
-bw *count*	Specifies the border width in pixels.
-fg *color*	Specifies the foreground color.
-rv	Changes the back and foreground color and simulates reverse video.
-xrm *string*	Specifies a resource string.

File Name:	`xmonisdn`	**Directory:**	/usr/X11R6/bin/	**Type:**	External

xmorph

UNIX Shell: All primary shells (bash, ash, tcsh)

Function	Morphs images in an X window environment.
Syntax	xmorph [options...]

-start *srcimgfile*	Uses `srcimgfile` as source image file.
-finish *dstimgfile*	Uses `dstimgfile` as destination image file.
-src *srcmeshfile*	Uses `srcmeshfile` as source mesh file.
-dst *dstmeshfile*	Uses `dstmeshfile` as destination mesh file.
-help	Shows help information.
-out *outimgfile*	Writes the output image to `outimgfile`.
-mt *morphtween*	Changes the shape of the output. Values are 0 = source mesh and 1 = destination mesh.
-dt *dissolvetween*	Changes the dissolve value to use.

File Name: `xmorph` **Directory:** /usr/X11R6/bin/ **Type:** External

xon

UNIX Shell: A shell (ash, bsh)

Function	Executes the specified command on the specified remote host.
Syntax	xon *host* [options...] { *command* }

-access	Adds the remote host to the access list in the local X server.
-debug	Shows debug information.
-name *name*	Sets a different window title and application name than the default `xterm`.
-nols	Disables the use of the -ls option to the remote `xterm`.
-screen *screen*	Specifies the screen number to the DISPLAY variable on the remote command.
-user *user*	Specifies alternate username or IP address.
host	Specifies the remote server to start process on.
command	Specifies command to run on remote computer.

File Name: `xon` **Directory:** /usr/X11R6/bin/ **Type:** Script

xplaycd

UNIX Shell: All primary shells (bash, ash, tcsh)

Function	Plays audio CD-ROMs interactively.
Syntax	xplaycd [options...]

-mixer	Uses the `/dev/mixer` device to adjust playback volume.
-nomixer	Controls the volume with the drive directly.
-emptypoll	Detects if a CD-ROM was inserted to the drive.
-display *display*	Specifies the X display to use.
-fn *font*	Specifies the font to use.
-v	Shows version information.

File Name: `xplaycd` **Directory:** /usr/X11R6/bin/ **Type:** External

xrefresh

UNIX Shell: All primary shells (bash, ash, tcsh)

Function	Refreshes all or part of an X screen.
Syntax	xrefresh [options...]

-white	Uses white background.
-black	Uses black background.
-solid *color*	Specifies a color to create a background of.
-root	Uses the root window background.
-none	Refreshes all of the window (is default).
-display *displayname*	Specifies a server and screen to refresh.
-geometry *Width**Height+X+Y*	Specifies the part of screen to refresh.

File Name: `xrefresh` **Directory:** /usr/X11R6/bin/ **Type:** External

xsetmode

UNIX Shell: All primary shells (bash, ash, tcsh)

Function	Sets the mode for an input device under X window.
Syntax	xsetmode *device* option

ABSOLUTE	Specifies absolute mode.
RELATIVE	Specifies relative mode.
device	Specifies an X input device.

File Name: `xsetmode` **Directory:** /usr/X11R6/bin/ **Type:** External

xsetpointer

UNIX Shell: All primary shells (bash, ash, tcsh)

Function	Sets the main pointer for X window.
Syntax	xsetpointer [-l] *{ device }*

-l	Lists all available devices.
device	Specifies the X input device to use.

File Name: `xsetpointer` **Directory:** /usr/X11R6/bin/ **Type:** External

xsm

UNIX Shell: All primary shells (bash, ash, tcsh)

Function	Manages X sessions. Allows applications to run and lets them become part of the session.
Syntax	xsm [options...]

-display *name*	Specifies an X screen to connect to.
-session *name*	Specifies a session to load.
-verbose	Verbose mode. Shows more information.
	The following are operations to use inside the session:
Load Session	Loads the selected session.
Delete Session	Deletes the selected session.
Default/Fail Safe	Starts with a set of default applications.
Cancel	Cancels a delete operation or to exit the manager from the session.
	The following are options to use in the main window:
Client List	Shows a list of clients in the session in a new window and allows operations on them.
Session Log	Shows log information about the session.
Checkpoint	Saves the state of all applications that are running in the session.
Shutdown	Saves the state and exits the session.

File Name: `xsm` **Directory:** /usr/X11R6/bin/ **Type:** External

xwininfo

UNIX Shell: All primary shells (bash, ash, tcsh)

Function	Shows information about windows.
Syntax	xwininfo [options...]

-help	Shows help information.
-id *id*	Specifies a target window ID.
-root	Designates X root window as the target.
-name *name*	Specifies the window named `name` as the target window.
-int	Shows all X window IDs as integer values.
-children	Shows the root, children, and parent windows ID.
-tree	Shows all children recursively.
-stats	Shows statistical information about the window.
-bits	Shows bit information about the window.
-size	Shows size information about the window.
-wm	Shows the selected window's windows manager hints.
-frame	Causes windows manager frames to look in when selecting windows.
-all	Queries everything.
-metric	Shows metric information about the window.
-display *display*	Specifies the server that you want to connect to.
-events	Shows the selected windows event masks.

continued

-shape		Shows the selected window's window and border shape extents.			
-english		Shows all geometric values in inches.			
File Name:	xwininfo	**Directory:**	/usr/X11R6/bin/	**Type:**	External

xxd

UNIX Shell: All primary shells (bash, ash, tcsh)

Function	Converts binary files or STDIN to a hexadecimal file, or vice versa.
Syntax	xxd [options...] *{ infile }* *{ outfile }*

-a		Sets auto skip on or off.			
-b		Does a binary digits dump instead of hex dump.			
-c *count*		Specifies the count of octets per line (default is 16; max is 256).			
-E		Uses EBCDIC character encoding in the right column instead of ASCII.			
-g *bytes*		Creates a white space every specified count of bytes to split the output.			
-h		Shows help information.			
-i		Includes the file style and complete static array definition in the created file.			
-l *count*		Stops writing after the specified count of octets.			
-p		Produces a PostScript (plain) hex dump.			
-r		Reverses the function, creates a binary of a hex dump. Use first in command line.			
-seek*count*		Adds the specified count as offset to the file positions on a reverse conversion.			
-s *count*		Specifies the start position relative to the current position with a + or - .			
-u		Enables uppercase hexadecimal letters, (default is lowercase).			
-v		Shows version information.			
infile		Specifies the file to convert from.			
outfile		Specifies the file to save the output in.			
File Name:	xxd	**Directory:**	/usr/bin/	**Type:**	External

yes

UNIX Shell: All primary shells (bash, ash, tcsh)

Function	Shows the command-line arguments, separated by spaces and new lines forever.
Syntax	yes [option] *{ string }*

--help		Shows help information.			
--version		Shows version information.			
string		The string to repeat.			
File Name:	yes	**Directory:**	/usr/bin/	**Type:**	External

ypchfn

UNIX Shell: All primary shells (bash, ash, tcsh)

Function	Changes the users GECOS field, where full name and user-related information exist.
Syntax	ypchfn *{ user }*

user		Specifies user to change the GECOS field for.			
File Name:	ypchfn	**Directory:**	/usr/bin/	**Type:**	External

ypchsh

UNIX Shell: All primary shells (bash, ash, tcsh)

Function	Alters the users default shell in the NIS database.
Syntax	ypchsh *{ user }*

user		Specifies user to alter the default shell for.			
File Name:	ypchsh	**Directory:**	/usr/bin/	**Type:**	External

ypdomainname

UNIX Shell: All primary shells (bash, ash, tcsh)

Function	Shows or sets the system's NIS/YP domain name.
Syntax	ypdomainname [-v]

-v		Verbose mode. Shows more information.			
File Name:	ypdomainname	**Directory:**	/bin/	**Type:**	External

yppasswd

yppasswd	UNIX Shell:	All primary shells (bash, ash, tcsh)
Function	Alters the yellow pages password in the NIS database.	
Syntax	yppasswd [options...] *{ user }*	

-f	Changes the user's GECOS (comment) field - usually the user's full name.
-l	Changes the user's login shell.
-p	Changes the user's NIS password.
user	Specifies which user's password to change.

File Name:	`yppasswd`	**Directory:**	/usr/bin/	**Type:**	External

yppasswdd

yppasswdd	UNIX Shell:	A shell (ash, bsh)
Function	A script that executes the `rpc.yppasswdd` that makes it easier to control the daemon.	
Syntax	yppasswdd options...	

start	Starts the `rpc.yppasswdd` daemon.
stop	Stops the `rpc.yppasswdd` daemon.
status	Shows the current status of the `rpc.yppasswdd` daemon.
restart	Restarts the `rpc.yppasswdd` daemon.
reload	Stops, then restarts the `rpc.yppasswdd` daemon.
condrestart	Restarts only the `rpc.yppasswdd` only if it is currently running.

File Name:	`yppasswdd`	**Directory:**	/etc/rc.d/init.d/	**Type:**	Script

zcat

zcat	UNIX Shell:	All primary shells (bash, ash, tcsh)
Function	Uncompresses a list of files from the command line or STDIN, then writes to STDOUT.	
Syntax	zcat [options...] *files...*	

-c	Writes to STDOUT
-d	Decompresses the file.
-f	Forces file decompression - that is, forces `zcat` to act like `cat`.
-h	Shows help information.
-l	Shows the contents of a compressed file.
-L	Shows license information, then exits.
-n	Doesn't save or restore the original name and timestamp of the file.
-N	Saves or restores the original name and timestamp of the file.
-q	Doesn't show warning messages.
-r	Compresses files recursively in directories and subdirectories.
-S *suffix*	Uses the specified suffix for the compressed file.
-t	Tests the integrity of the compressed file.
-v	Verbose mode. Shows more information.
-V	Shows version information.
-1	Performs faster compression
-9	Performs better compression
files...	Specifies the file or a list of files that are used.

File Name:	`zcat`	**Directory:**	/bin/	**Type:**	External

zcat file.gz	Uncompresses file.gz to STDOUT.

zcmp

zcmp	UNIX Shell:	A shell (ash, bsh)
Function	Compares two compressed files. Return status is 0 = identical, 1 = different, 1 < error.	
Syntax	zcmp [options...] *file1 { file2 }*	

-l	Shows the byte number (dec) and the byte value (oct) for each difference.
-s	Shows nothing.
file1	Specifies the first file.
file2	Specifies the second file. If not given, use the uncompressed file with same name.

File Name:	`zcmp`	**Directory:**	/usr/bin/	**Type:**	Script

zdiff

UNIX Shell: A shell (ash, bsh)

Function	Compares compressed files. It uses the command `diff` to run the comparison.
Syntax	zdiff [options...] *file1* { *file2* }

Please see `diff` for all of the `zdiff` options.

File Name:	`zdiff`	**Directory:**	/usr/bin/	**Type:**	Script

zdump

UNIX Shell: All primary shells (bash, ash, tcsh)

Function	Shows the current date and time for the time zones that you specify on the command line.
Syntax	zdump [options...] { *timezones...* }

-v	Verbose mode. Shows more information.
-c *cutoffyear*	Limits the verbose output to just before the year that you specify.
timezones...	Specifies which time zone to dump. If a wrong time zone is given, GMT is shown.

File Name:	`zdump`	**Directory:**	/usr/sbin/	**Type:**	External

zforce

UNIX Shell: A shell (ash, bsh)

Function	Adds a .gz extension to a compressed (gzip) file. Useful for files with names truncated after a file transfer.
Syntax	zforce { *files...* }

files...	Specifies one or more compressed files to add .gz extension to.

File Name:	`zforce`	**Directory:**	/usr/bin/	**Type:**	Script

zgrep, zfgrep, zegrep

UNIX Shell: A shell (ash, bsh)

Function	Searches for text strings inside compressed files.
Syntax	zgrep [options...] *pattern files...*

options...	Specifies options from the `grep`, `egrep`, or `fgrep` commands.
pattern	Specifies pattern to search for.
files...	Specifies one or more files to search in.

File Name:	`zgrep`	**Directory:**	/usr/bin/	**Type:**	Script

zgrep myzip /ucg_examples/*gz	Search for string "myzip" in the gzipped files in the specified directory.
zgrep [Mm][Yy][Zz][Ii][Pp] /ucg_examples/*gz	Searches for string "myzip", ignoring cases.

zic

UNIX Shell: All primary shells (bash, ash, tcsh)

Function	Creates files that can be used for time conversion.
Syntax	zic [options...] { *files...* }

-v	Prompts if the year in the input file is out of range.
-d *directory*	Creates time conversion files in the specified directory.
-l *localtime*	Uses the specified time zone as local time.
-p *timerules*	Uses the rules from the specified time zone to manage posix time zone variables.
-L *file*	Reads leap second information from the specified file.
-s	Limits the time values in the output files.
-y *yeartype*	Checks how years are to be written.
-	Reads time conversion information from STDIN.
files...	Specifies a file with time conversion information.

File Name:	`zic`	**Directory:**	/usr/sbin/	**Type:**	External

zip

UNIX Shell: All primary shells (bash, ash, tcsh)

Function	Compresses files.
Syntax	zip [options...] { *zipfiles...* } [-ix *files...*]

-a	Translates file to ASCII format.
-A	Adjusts self-extracting executable archive.
-B	Forces file to be read binary (default is text).

continued

-Bn	Sets edit/enscribe formatting options with n defined as bit.
-c	Adds a comment to an archive file.
-df	Only includes data fork of files zipped into the archive.
-d	Removes directories or files from an archive file.
-D	Doesn't create directory entries in the archive file.
-e	Specifies a password for the archive file.
-E	Uses the .LONGNAME Extended Attribute as the filename.
-i *files...*	Includes only the specified files. Can't be used together with -x.
-f	Replaces an existing entry in the zip archive.
-F	Tries to repair an archive file. It can't fix bad CRC.
-g	Appends specified files to an existing archive.
-h	Displays the zip help information.
-j	Stores just the name of a saved file, and doesn't store directory names.
-jj	Records the full path including volume name.
-J	Strips pretended data from the archive.
-k	Converts pathnames and names to MS-DOS format.
-ll	Translates MS-DOS end-of-line characters to UNIX end-of-line characters.
-l	Doesn't scan image files.
-L	Displays the zip license.
-m	Moves the specified files into the zip archive.
-N	Uses Amiga file notes as comments for the archive file.
-o	Sets the "last modified" time of the zip archive to the latest time in the zip archive.
-P	Encrypts zip files with a password.
-q	Quiet mode.
-Qn	Stores information about the file in the file header.
-r	Travels the directory structure recursively.
-R	Travels the directory structure recursively starting at the current directory.
-S	Includes system and hidden files.
-T	Tests the integrity of the new zip file.
-u	Updates an existing entry in the zip archive.
-v	Verbose mode.
-V	Saves VMS file attributes.
-w	Appends version number of the files to the name, including multiple versions of files.
-x *files...*	Excludes files from the archive. Can't be used together with -i.
-X	Doesn't save extra file attributes.
-y	Stores symbolic links as such in the zip archive instead of compressing and storing.
-z	Prompts for a multiline comment for the entire zip archive.
-#	Sets compression level (1 = low and 9 = high).
-!	Uses privileges to obtain all aspects of WinNT security.
-@	Takes the list of input files from STDIN.
-$	Includes the volume label for the drive holding the first file to be compressed.
-b\ *path*	Uses the specified path for the temporary zip archive.
-n\ *suffixes*	Doesn't attempt to compress files named with the given suffixes.
-t\ *mmddyyyy*	Doesn't operate on files modified before the specified date.
-tt *mmddyyyy*	Doesn't operate on files modified after or at the specified date.
zipfiles...	Specifies the files that you want to compress.

File Name: `zip`	**Directory:** /usr/bin/	**Type:** External

zip myzip.zip *	Compresses all files in current directory into archive myzip.
zip -m myzip.zip *.dat	Moves files with extension *.dat into archive myzip.zip.
zip -r myzip.zip /usr	Operates recursively; includes all files under the directory /usr in the archive myzip.zip.

zipcloak

zipcloak	UNIX Shell:	All primary shells (bash, ash, tcsh)
Function	Is used for encryption or decryption of a compressed file.	
Syntax	zipcloak [options...] *file*	

-d	Erases directories or files from an archive file.
-h	Shows help information.
-L	Shows license information.
-v	Shows version information.
-b *path*	Specifies a directory where to put temporary zip archives.
file	Specifies the zip file that you want to work with.

File Name:	`zipcloak`	**Directory:**	/usr/sbin/	**Type:**	External

zipgrep

zipgrep	UNIX Shell:	A shell (ash, bsh)
Function	Searches for text strings inside zip archive files.	
Syntax	zipgrep [options...] *pattern zipfile { files... }* [-x *files...*]	

	Please see `egrep` for more options.
-x *files...*	Identifies files to be excluded in the search. Could be useful when using wildcards.
pattern	Specifies the pattern to be located in the zip file.
zipfile	Specifies the zipfile to search in.
files...	A list of archive members to search in. Wildcards may be used.

File Name:	`zipgrep`	**Directory:**	/usr/bin/	**Type:**	Script

zipinfo

zipinfo	UNIX Shell:	All primary shells (bash, ash, tcsh)
Function	Shows technical information about a zip archive.	
Syntax	zipinfo [options...] *zipfile { files... }* [-x *files...*]	

-1	Shows filenames. Skips headers, trailers, and comments. Good for shell scripts.
-2	Shows filenames one per line and allows headers, trailers, and comments.
-s	Shows information in short UNIX format.
-m	Shows information in medium UNIX format.
-l	Shows information in long UNIX format.
-v	Verbose mode. Shows more information.
-h	Shows header line, archive name, actual size, and total number of files.
-M	Pipes all output to an internal pager. Looks like `--more--`.
-t	Shows the totals for the listed files or for all the files.
-T	Shows the specified file, date, and time in the format `yymmdd.hhmmss`.
-z	Adds the archive comment in the listing.
-x *files...*	Files in the zip archive that aren't processed.
zipfile	Specifies a path to the zip archive.
files...	Files in the zip archive that are processed.

File Name:	`zipinfo`	**Directory:**	/usr/bin/	**Type:**	External

zipnote

zipnote	UNIX Shell:	All primary shells (bash, ash, tcsh)
Function	Inserts notes and comments into zip files.	
Syntax	zipnote [options...] *file*	

-b path	Specifies the path to the file to work with.
-w	Writes comments from STDIN.
-h	Shows help information.
-v	Shows version information.
-L	Shows license information.
file	Specifies the zip file to work with.

File Name:	`zipnote`	**Directory:**	/usr/bin/	**Type:**	External

zipsplit

UNIX Shell:	All primary shells (bash, ash, tcsh)
Function	Splits one zip file into many zip files.
Syntax	zipsplit [options...] *file*

-t	Reports how many zip files the original zip file is split to
-i	Makes an index file and count its size against first zip file.
-n *size*	Sets the size of the new zip files.
-r *room*	Leaves some space on the first disk.
-b *path*	Sets the path where the zip files will go.
-p	Pauses between output zip files.
-s	Uses a sequential split even if it takes more zip files.
-h	Shows help information.
-v	Shows version information.
-L	Shows software license.
file	Specifies the zip file to process.

File Name:	`zipsplit`	**Directory:**	/usr/bin/	**Type:**	External

zless

UNIX Shell:	A shell (ash, bsh)
Function	Enables compressed text files to be inspected one full screen at a time.
Syntax	zless *{ files... }*

files...	Specifies one or more compressed text files to be inspected.

File Name:	`zless`	**Directory:**	/usr/bin/	**Type:**	Script

zmore

UNIX Shell:	A shell (ash, bsh)
Function	Shows compressed text files one screen at a time.
Syntax	zmore *{ files... }*

files...	Specifies one or more files to show.

File Name:	`zmore`	**Directory:**	/usr/bin/	**Type:**	Script

znew

UNIX Shell:	A shell (ash, bsh)
Function	Recompresses a .Z compressed file to a .gz file.
Syntax	znew [options...] *{ files... }*

-f	Forces recompression even if the .gz file already exists.
-t	Checks the new file before deleting the originals.
-v	Verbose mode. Shows more information.
-9	Uses the most powerful compression method.
-P	Uses pipes to convert the file to reduce disk space usage.
-K	Keeps the .Z file if it's smaller than the .gz file.
files...	Specifies file to recompress.

File Name:	`znew`	**Directory:**	/usr/bin/	**Type:**	Script

Bug:	znew doesn't maintain the timestamp with the -P option if cpmod(1) isn't available and touch(1) doesn't support the -r option.

znew myzip.Z	Recompress myzip.Z to myzip.gz.

Chapter 12

OpenBSD Commands

The commands in this section are all of the commands from OpenBSD that are not listed in the Universal UNIX Commands (Chapter 9). The commands are all listed in alphabetical order by the command name.

For cross-references to other operating systems, please see Chapter 1, the "Quick Command Index."

/etc/inetd.conf

/etc/inetd.conf	UNIX Shell:	N/A
Function	The Internet server database ASCII file that contains a list of available servers. Is invoked by `inetd` when it gets an Internet request via a socket.	
Syntax	inetd.conf	

The fields are as follows:	**The database file must follow the following format separated by Space or Tab:** **service endpoint protocol status uid program arguments**
service	Specifies the name of a service that is found in the services file.
endpoint	Specifies the endpoint type, which can be only one of the following:
stream	Specifies a stream socket.
dgram	Specifies a datagram socket.
raw	Specifies a raw socket.
seqpacket	Specifies a sequenced packet socket.
tli	Specifies all tli endpoints.
protocol	Specifies a valid protocol that is found in the `/etc/inet/protocols` file.
status	Activates nowait mode for all datagram servers except those that are single-threaded.
uid	Specifies the user ID that the servers should run under.
program	Specifies the server program to be started by `inetd`. Specify pathname.
arguments	Invokes a server from the command line using a list of no more than five arguments.

File Name:	`inetd.conf`	**Directory:**	/etc/	**Type:**	Text File
ftp stream TCP nowait root /usr/libexec/ftpd ftpd -US			This is the line for the FTP service.		

/etc/mygate

/etc/mygate	UNIX Shell:	N/A
Function	Defines the systems default router or gateway.	
Syntax	None	

The following is an example of a `defaultrouter` file:

```
# This is the default router
192.168.1.254
```

File Name:	`mygate`	**Directory:**	/etc/	**Type:**	Text File

/etc/myname

/etc/myname	UNIX Shell:	N/A
Function	Specifies the real hostname for the system.	
Syntax	None	

Below is the contents of `myname`, which assigns the hostname mercury:

```
mercury
```

File Name:	`myname`	**Directory:**	/etc/	**Type:**	Text File

/etc/printcap

/etc/printcap	UNIX Shell:	N/A
Function	Describes printers and allows dynamic addition and deletion of printers by the spooling system.	
Syntax	printcap	

File Name:	`printcap`	**Directory:**	/etc/	**Type:**	Text File

/etc/rc.conf

/etc/rc.conf	UNIX Shell:	N/A
Function	A configuration file used to configure the system daemons. It has three sections, the first turns features on or off, the second turns daemons on or off, and the third sets parameters for the daemons in use.	
Syntax	*daemon=flags*	

daemon	Specifies the daemon to configure, enable, or disable.
flags	Specifies configuration parameters for the daemon.

File Name:	`rc.conf`	**Directory:**	/etc/	**Type:**	Text File

sendmail_flags="-bd"	Example for the first section, if set to NO sendmail would not start.
sshd=YES	Example for the second section, only ON or OFF are allowed.
ipfilter_rules=/etc/ipf.rules	Example for the third section, only parameters to daemons started in the first two sections are allowed.

ab

ab	UNIX Shell:	All primary shells (csh, ksh, sh)
Function	Benchmarks your Apache server by sending requests to it.	
Syntax	ab [options...] [http://]*hostname*[:*port*]/*path*	

-k	Enables multiple requests in one HTTP session. This is called HTTP KeepAlive.
-n *requests*	Specifies the number of requests to run in the benchmark.
-t *timelimit*	Specifies the time in seconds to use benchmarking. This sets -n to 50000.
-c *concurrency*	Specifies the amount of requests to perform simultaneously. (Default is 1.)
-p *postfile*	Specifies a file to send in any HTTP POST requests to the Apache server.
-A *user:password*	Provides the server with username and password entered with a `:` between. (This will be sent whether the server needs it or not, as uuencoded data.)
-P *user:password*	Runs the same procedure as the -A switch, but is used with proxy servers.
-C *name=value*	Adds a cookie to the request. The option is repeatable.
-T *content-type*	Specifies the content-type header for usage with POST data.
-v *verbosity*	Specifies verbosity level. (2+ warnings and info, 3+ response codes, 4+ shows header info.)
-w *output HTML*	Shows results in HTML tables (default is two columns wide, white background).
-H *string*	Appends more headers to the request. The argument is usually in value:value form.
-x *string*	Specifies the attributes for `table`.
-y *string*	Specifies the attributes for `tr`.
-z *string*	Specifies the attributes for `td` or `th`.
-V	Shows version information.
-h	Shows help information.
[http://]*hostname*:{ *port* }/*path*	Defines the URL to use when benchmarking. `Http` and `port` aren't required.

File Name:	`ab`	**Directory:**	/usr/sbin/	**Type:**	External

ac

ac	UNIX Shell:	All primary shells (csh, ksh, sh)
Function	Counts how long a user or users have been using their accounts.	
Syntax	ac [options...] *users...*	

-d	Shows a list of the time for each day the user has been logged in.
-p	Shows the total login time for each individual user.
-t *tty*	Specifies the ttys only to show time on. Can be used multiple times. (To exclude a tty, put a ! before typing it. Wildcards can also be used.)
-w *file*	Reads the time account from specified file, instead of default `/var/log/wtmp`.
users...	Specifies the users to show login time on. If none are specified, all users will be used.
File Name: `ac`	**Directory:** /usr/sbin/ **Type:** External
ac -p -t ttyp*	Shows login time about users from ttyp*.
ac -p -t !ttyp*	Shows login time about users not from ttyp*.

accton

accton	UNIX Shell:	All primary shells (csh, ksh, sh)
Function	Outputs process accounting to the specified file. Without file, process accounting will be turned off.	
Syntax	accton *{ file }*	

file	Specifies an existing file where the kernel stores process accounting records.
File Name: `accton`	**Directory:** /usr/sbin/ **Type:** External
accton /var/account/acct	Exports system accounting information to the `acct` file.

addftinfo

addftinfo	UNIX Shell:	All primary shells (csh, ksh, sh)
Function	Reads `troff` font file and adds font metric information that is used by the `groff` system.	
Syntax	addftinfo [options...] *res unitwidth font*	

-x-height *height*	Specifies the height of lowercase letters without ascenders, such as x.
-fig-height *height*	Specifies the height of figures.
-asc-height *height*	Specifies the height of characters with ascenders for b, d, or l.
-body-height *height*	Specifies the height of characters such as parentheses.
-cap-height *height*	Specifies the height of uppercase letters such as A.
-comma-depth *height*	Specifies the depth of a comma.
-desc-depth *height*	Specifies the depth of characters with descenders for p, q, or y.
-body-depth *height*	Specifies the depth of characters such as parentheses.
res	Same as the corresponding parameters in the DESC file.
uniwidth	Same as the corresponding parameters in the DESC file.
font	Specifies the name of a file describing the font.
File Name: `addftinfo`	**Directory:** /usr/bin/ **Type:** External

adduser

adduser	UNIX Shell:	All primary shells (csh, ksh, sh)
Function	Adds a user to the system. Asks for required additional data that has not been specified on the command line.	
Syntax	adduser [options...]	

-batch *user { groups... } { name } { passwd }*	Specifies multiple users on the command line in a compact format. (Separate multiple groups with commas.)
-check_only	Checks the consistency in password, group, and shell databases.
-config_create	Creates or edits default configuration information and message file.
-dotdir *directory*	Copies the contents in the specified directory to the new user's home directory.
-e *method*	Specifies the encryption method to use on the password.
-group login_group	Specifies the default login group.
-h	Shows help information.
-home *device*	Specifies the partition where all user's home directories are located.

continued

-message *file*	Sends a welcome message, specified in file, to new users.
-noconfig	Doesn't read the default configuration file.
-shell *shell*	Specifies the default shell for the new users.
-s	Silent mode. Shows less information.
-uid *value*	Specifies the lowest UID to generate when creating UIDs for the new users.
-uid_start *value*	Specifies the lowest UID to generate when creating UIDs for the new users.
-uid_end *value*	Specifies the highest UID to generate when creating UIDs for the new users.
-v	Verbose mode. Shows more information.
-unencrypted	Doesn't encrypt the password for the new user.
File Name: adduser	**Directory:** /usr/sbin/ **Type:** External

afslog

UNIX Shell: All primary shells (csh, ksh, sh)

Function Is used to gather AFS tokens for specified cells.

Syntax afslog [options...] *{ arguments... }*

-d	Shows debug information.
-c *cell*	Specifies the cell to use.
-k *realm*	Specifies the Kerberos realm to use.
-p *directory*	Specifies the directory to find the cell.
-unlog	Removes all tokens and ignores all following arguments.
-createuser	Tries to create a remote user principal in another cell.
arguments...	Is either a name of a cell or a pathname of a file in the cell to get tokens for.
File Name: afslog	**Directory:** /usr/bin/ **Type:** External

amd

UNIX Shell: All primary shells (csh, ksh, sh)

Function Tries to automount a file system whenever a directory or file within it is accessed.

Syntax amd [options...] *{ directories... } { files... }*

-n	Translates alias names into official hostnames.
-p	Shows the process ID for the command.
-r	Restarts existing mounts as automounts.
-v	Shows version and configuration information.
-a *directory*	Specifies an alternative directory for the mount points (default is /a).
-c *value*	Specifies the duration in seconds to cache a looked-up name (default is 5 minutes).
-d domain	Specifies the local domain name.
-k *architecture*	Specifies the kernel architecture.
-l *file*	Specifies the file to put log records to.
-t *interval.interval*	Specifies the interval, in tenths of a second, between NFS/RCP/UDP retries. (The interval after the dot is the retransmit counter.)
-w *value*	Specifies the interval to wait to dismount the system, after exceeding the cache time.
-x *options...*	Specifies what to log in run-time. multiple options must be separated by commas. (The options are: fatal, error, user, warn, info, map, stats, all.)
-y YP-domain	Specifies an alternative NIS domain from which to fetch the NIS maps.
-C *cluster*	Specifies the cluster service name.
-D *options...*	Specifies what to debug.
directories...	Specifies the directory to attach itself.
files...	Specifies the map name file which determines how to resolve the lookup.
File Name: amd	**Directory:** /usr/sbin/ **Type:** External

amq

UNIX Shell: All primary shells (csh, ksh, sh)

Function	Is used to determine the current state of the `amd` program.
Syntax	amq [options...] *{ directories... }*

-f	Makes the program to flush the internal caches.
-h *host*	Specifies the hostname to query (default is localhost).
-m	Gets a list of mounted file systems and any errors that occurred while mounting.
-s	Gets system-wide mount statistics from the automounter.
-u	Tries to unmount the specified mount directories.
-v	Shows version information on the automounter.
directories...	Uses the specific mounted directories. If none is specified, all mount points are used.

File Name: `amq` **Directory:** /usr/sbin/ **Type:** External

apm

UNIX Shell: All primary shells (csh, ksh, sh)

Function	Shows the current power status or puts the system in standby or suspend mode.
Syntax	apm [options...]

-z	Puts the system in suspend mode.
-S	Puts the system in standby mode.
-l	Shows information about estimated battery lifetime in percent.
-m	Shows information about estimated battery lifetime in minutes.
-b	Shows the status of the battery. 0 = high, 1 = low, 2 = critical, 3 = charging, 4 = absent, 255 = unknown.
-a	Shows the status of the external charger. 0 = disconnected, 1 = connected, 2 = backup source, 255 = unknown.
-f *socket*	Specifies a socket to connect to `apmd` through.
-v	Verbose mode. Shows more information.

File Name: `apm` **Directory:** /usr/sbin/ **Type:** External

apmd

UNIX Shell: All primary shells (csh, ksh, sh)

Function	Monitors the APM pseudo-device and executes the actions requested by the `apm` command.
Syntax	apmd [options...]

-d	Starts debug mode.
-s	Shows the current battery statistics via `syslog`.
-a	Ignores all BIOS-initiated suspend or standby requests when not running on battery.
-q	Suppresses the sound signaling on suspend and standby requests.
-e	Enables power status messages.
-p	Shows only battery power messages when the expected lifetime changes.
-m	Disables all messages coming from the APM driver.
-t *seconds*	Specifies the time between information polls (default is 600 seconds).
-S *socket*	Specifies an alternative socket for communication with the `apm` command.
-f *device*	Specifies an alternative device to control the APM kernel driver.

File Name: `apmd` **Directory:** /usr/sbin/ **Type:** External

apply

UNIX Shell: All primary shells (csh, ksh, sh)

Function	Runs the specified command once for every argument specified. A magic character followed by a number will be replaced by the remaining argument matching the number index.
Syntax	apply [options...] *command arguments...*

-a*character*	Specifies the character to use as the magic character (default is %).
-*value*	Specifies the number of arguments to be passed to the command each time.

continued

command		Specifies the command.			
arguments...		Specifies the arguments for the command.			
File Name:	`apply`	**Directory:**	/usr/bin/	**Type:**	External

apply -2 ls -l -F -m -F	Runs first ls -l -F, then ls -m -F.
apply -2 "echo %2 %1" world! Hello "are you?" How	Shows "Hello world!" and then "How are you?"

appres

UNIX Shell: All primary shells (csh, ksh, sh)

Function	Is used to show how many resources will be used by a specific application.
Syntax	appres *{ class } { instance }* [-1] *{ toolkitoptions }*

class		Is used to specify the class name of an application.			
instance		Is used to specify an instance name in addition to `class`.			
-1		Matches a specific resource level.			
toolkitoptions		Allows the use of X toolkit options.			
File Name:	`appres`	**Directory:**	/usr/X11R6/bin/	**Type:**	External

arch

UNIX Shell: All primary shells (csh, ksh, sh)

Function	Is used to show the computer's architecture.
Syntax	arch [option]

		You can only use one of the following options and they can't be combined:			
-k		Shows the kernel architecture — for example, `sun4m` and `sun4c`.			
-s		Shows the architecture without the system prefix.			
File Name:	`arch`	**Directory:**	/usr/bin/	**Type:**	External

arithmetic

UNIX Shell: All primary shells (csh, ksh, sh)

Function	A simple math game that keeps track of progress and shows results after every 20 questions.
Syntax	arithmetic [options...]

-o *type*		Specifies the type of math problem to be tested on.			
+		Uses addition problems.			
-		Uses subtraction problems.			
x		Uses multiplication problems.			
/		Uses division problems.			
-r *range*		Specifies the range of numbers to be used in the game (default is 10).			
File Name:	`arithmetic`	**Directory:**	/usr/games/	**Type:**	External

asa, fpr

UNIX Shell: All primary shells (csh, ksh, sh)

Function	Converts Fortran carriage control output to a printable format and sends it to STDOUT.
Syntax	asa *{ files... }* fpr *{ files... }*

files...		Specifies the pathname and a text file to be used for input.			
		The following characters are interpreted as below:			
<SPACE>		Outputs the rest of the line without changes.			
0		Outputs a new line before printing the rest of the line.			
1		Outputs a form feed before printing the rest of the line.			
+		The previous new line is replaced by a carriage return before printing the rest of the line.			
File Name:	`asa, fpr`	**Directory:**	/usr/bin/	**Type:**	External

atactl

UNIX Shell:	All primary shells (csh, ksh, sh)
Function	Is used to control standard IDE and ATA controller devices.
Syntax	atactl *device ACTION*

ACTION	**The following actions may be used on IDE and ATA devices:**
identify	Shows information about the device.
idle	Sets the device to idle mode.
standby	Sets the device to standby mode.
sleep	Sets the device to sleep mode. Must then be reset to resume operation.
setidle *value*	Sets the device to idle mode and sets the standby timer, specified in seconds.
setstandby *value*	Sets the device to standby mode and sets the standby timer, specified in seconds.
checkpower	Shows which mode the device is in — active, idle, or standby.
device	Specifies the device to manipulate.

File Name:	**Directory:**	**Type:**
`atactl`	/usr/bin/	External

atactl /dev/wd0a identify	Gets information about the device.

atrun

UNIX Shell:	All primary shells (csh, ksh, sh)
Function	Runs jobs that are queued by the at command to run later.
Syntax	atrun [options...]

-l *load_avg*	Specifies a limiting load factor (default is 0.8 for single processor).
-d	Shows debug information.

File Name:	**Directory:**	**Type:**
`atrun`	/usr/libexec/	External

audioctl

UNIX Shell:	All primary shells (csh, ksh, sh)
Function	Shows and sets driver variables for various audio systems.
Syntax	audioctl [options...] *{ names.... }*

-f *file*	Uses an alternative audio control device instead of `/dev/audioctl`.
-n	Suppress printing the variable name.
-a	Prints all variables for the device.
-w *variable=value*	Sets the specified variables to the given values. Multiple variables may be used.
names....	Specifies the device name.

File Name:	**Directory:**	**Type:**
`audioctl`	/usr/bin/	External

audioctl -w play.sample_rate=11025	Sets the playing sampling rate to 11025.

bad144

UNIX Shell:	All primary shells (csh, ksh, sh)
Function	Shows or writes hard disk bad sector information in standard DEC 144 format.
Syntax	bad144 [options...] *disk { serial } { sectors... }*

-a	Adds new bad sectors to an existing list. The sectors have to be in order.
-c	Tries to copy the old sector to the replacement.
-f	Formats the new sectors as bad. Required if the sectors are not marked already.
-v	Verbose mode. Shows more information.
disk	Specifies hard disk device name.
serial	Specifies the serial number of disk pack, a device to handle many hard disks.
sectors...	Specifies one or more sectors to add or show information for.

File Name:	**Directory:**	**Type:**
`bad144`	/usr/sbin/	External

badsect

UNIX Shell: All primary shells (csh, ksh, sh)

Function	Creates files over the bad sectors so that no other files can use the bad sectors.
Syntax	badsect *directory sectors...*

directory	Specifies an existing directory for bad sector files.
sectors...	Specifies bad sectors to add to files. These are found in error messages.

File Name:	`badsect`	**Directory:**	/sbin/	**Type:**	External

bdes

UNIX Shell: All primary shells (csh, ksh, sh)

Function	Encrypts or decrypts from STDIN to STDOUT. It uses the Data Encryption Standard (DES).
Syntax	bdes [options...]

-a	Interprets initialization vector strings and key as ASCII.
-b	Sets mode to electronic code book.
-d	Decrypts encrypted input.
-p	Doesn't convert the parity bit to odd. Use with ASCII key only.
-F *n*	Sets n as alternative cipher feedback mode (is between 7 and 56 as a multiple of 7).
-f *n*	Specifies n as cipher feedback mode (is between 8 and 64 as a multiple of 8).
-k *key*	Specifies the cryptographic key.
-m *n*	Specifies n as the bits to use for input to calculate the MAC (is between 1 and 64).
-o *n*	Specifies n as output feedback mode (is between 8 and 64 as a multiple of 8).
-v *string*	Specifies vector string to use when initializing.

File Name:	`bdes`	**Directory:**	/usr/bin/	**Type:**	External

cat file1| bdes > file2	Encrypts file1 and results in file2. It will prompt for a key.
cat file2 | bdes -d > file3	Decrypts input file file2 and encrypts into the file3.

biff

UNIX Shell: All primary shells (csh, ksh, sh)

Function	Enables or disables mail notification. If no arguments are used, it will show the current status.
Syntax	biff [option]

n	Disables mail notification.
y	Enables mail notification.

File Name:	`biff`	**Directory:**	/usr/bin/	**Type:**	External

boot

UNIX Shell: All primary shells (csh, ksh, sh)

Function	Loads the system kernel, sets console baud rate, and runs various machine-dependent commands.
Syntax	boot

	The following commands may be run from the boot prompt:
boot { *image* [options...] }	Boots the specified kernel image with any options, where image = `device:file`.
echo { *arguments...* }	Shows the specified arguments.
help	Shows a list of available machine-dependent or other types of commands.
machine { *command* }	Starts one of the following i386 architecture, machine-dependent commands:
diskinfo	Shows hard disk information, which includes BIOS device numbers and geometry.
memory { *arguments...* }	Shows the memory configuration allowed by BIOS routines. Arguments may be used.
arguments...	Uses any argument(s) that add or remove memory. (The valid argument format is [+ or -]size@address.)
regs	Shows the contents of the DEBUG compiled processor registers.
-ls *directory*	Shows the contents of the specified directory using the long format.
reboot	Reboots the system using the warm-boot procedure.
set { *variable* [*value* }]	Shows a list of variables and any values if variable and value are not specified.

continued

variable	Shows the contents of the specified variable.
value	Alters the value of the specified variable when used together with `variable`.
addr	Specifies the address that the kernel will be loaded at.
howto	Shows which options may be sent to the loaded kernel.
debug	Sets the debug flag if `boot` was compiled with DEBUG defined.
device	Specifies the boot device name — for example, `fd0a, sd0a`.
tty	Specifies the device name for the console device.
image	Specifies the file that contains the kernel image.
stty *{ device* [*rate }*]	Shows the baud rate for the console device if no device or rate is given.
device	Specifies the console device to alter the baud rate of.
rate	Specifies the baud rate for the device. (default is 9600).
time	Shows the time and date of the system.
File Name: `boot`	**Directory:** /usr/mdec/, / **Type:** External

bootpd

UNIX Shell: All primary shells (csh, ksh, sh)

Function	The Internet Bootstrap Protocol server.
Syntax	bootpd [options...] *{ cfgfile } { dumpfile }*

-i	Forces `inetd` mode.
-s	Forces the standalone mode. For backward compatibility only.
-t *timeout*	Specifies the timeout for a BOOTP packet.
-d *level*	Sets the debug level.
-c *path*	Sets the current directory for checking client boot files.
cfgfile	Specifies the configuration file to load the database holding client options.
dumpfile	Specifies the file that the internal database will be dumped into during a SIGUSR1.
File Name: `bootpd`	**Directory:** /usr/sbin/ **Type:** External

bootpef

UNIX Shell: All primary shells (csh, ksh, sh)

Function	Builds BOOTP extension files.
Syntax	bootpef [options...] *{ clients... }*

-c *directory*	Specifies the directory to use as current while creating files.
-d *n*	Specifies n as debug level.
-f *name*	Specifies the name of the configuration file for client data option.
clients...	Sets the names of the clients to compile extensions for.
File Name: `bootpef`	**Directory:** /usr/sbin/ **Type:** External
bootpef pluto	Compiles an extension file for the client pluto.
bootpef -c /tftpboot pluto	Compiles an extension file for the client pluto and uses directory /tftpboot.

bootpgw

UNIX Shell: All primary shells (csh, ksh, sh)

Function	Acts as a gateway between subnets and forwards BOOTP requests and replies.
Syntax	bootpgw [options...] *server*

-i	Starts service in `inetd` mode, listens for boot requests.
-s	Starts service in standalone mode, which means starts it from a shell.
-t *timeout*	Specifies the timeout value in minutes to wait between BOOTP packet (default is 15).
-d *n*	Specifies n as the debug level to use.
server	Specifies the server name to forward boot requests to. **The next line must be put into the `/etc/inetd.conf` file:** bootps dgram udp wait root /usr/sbin/bootpgw bootpgw server
File Name: `bootpgw`	**Directory:** /usr/sbin/ **Type:** External
bootpgw sun	Starts the bootpgw service and listens for BOOTP requests to forward to the server sun.

bootptest

UNIX Shell: All primary shells (csh, ksh, sh)

Function	Tests a BOOTP server. It listens for responses on the requests sent.
Syntax	bootptest [options...] *server { template }*

-f *bootfile*	Specifies the name of the boot file.
-h	Identifies the client on its Ethernet address.
-m *magicNR*	Specifies the magic number to initialize the first word in the vendor options field.
server	Specifies the server to contact
template	Specifies a binary file to initialize the options in the request packet.
File Name: `bootptest`	**Directory:** /usr/sbin/ **Type:** External
bootptest sun	Sends BOOT requests and tests the server sun.

brconfig

UNIX Shell: All primary shells (csh, ksh, sh)

Function	Shows and controls bridge interfaces.
Syntax	brconfig *bridge commands...* brconfig -a

-a	Shows status information for all bridges.
bridge	Specifies the name of the bridge to manage.
	These are the available commands:
up	Starts the bridge and forward packets.
down	Halts the bridge and stops forward packets.
addr	Shows the addresses that the bridge knows about.
add *interface*	Specifies a new interface name to be a bridge member.
delete *interface*	Specifies an interface name to remove as a bridge member.
maxaddr *size*	Specifies the address cache size (default is 100).
timeout *time*	Specifies the address cache timeout in seconds (default is 240).
static *interface address*	Sets an address as a static pointer to an interface in the address cache.
deladdr *address*	Removes an address from the cache.
flush	Removes all non-static addresses from the cache.
flushall	Remove all addresses from the cache.
	For the next commands, a minus (-) placed before the command means "do not":
blocknonip *interface*	Marks an interface so that packets that aren't IPv4, IPv6, ARP or rARP are accepted.
-blocknonip *interface*	Does the opposite of blocknoip.
discover *interface*	Sets an interface name in discover mode. It forwards packets for unknown destinations.
learn *interface*	Sets an interface name in learn mode. It adds source addresses into cache.
link0	Stops forward of all non-IP multicast packets by the bridge.
link1	Stops forward of all IP multicast packets by the bridge.
rule *{ rulespec }*	Adds a filtering rule to an interface.
rulefile *filename*	Loads a set of rules from a file.
File Name: `brconfig`	**Directory:** /sbin/ **Type:** External
brconfig bridge0 flushall	Removes all addresses in cache for the bridge bridge0.
brconfig bridge0 up -learn le0	Starts the bridge bridge0 and sets the interface le0 to not add addresses to cache.

c++

UNIX Shell: All primary shells (csh, ksh, sh)

Function	A complete compiler for C, C++, and Assembler.
Syntax	c++ [options...] *files...*

-dumpspecs	Shows all built-in spec strings.
-dumpversion	Shows version information.
-dumpmachine	Shows the target processor for the compiler.
-print-search-dirs	Shows all search directories the compiler uses.
-print-libgcc-file-name	Shows the name of the compiler's companion library.
-print-file-name=*library*	Shows the full path to the specified compiler component.
-print-multi-directory	Shows the libgcc root directories.

continued

-print-multi-lib	Shows mapping between command-line options and multiple library search directories.
-Wa,*options...*	Specifies assembler options to use. Must be separated by commas.
-Wp,*options...*	Specifies preprocessor options to use. Must be separated by commas.
-Wl,*options...*	Specifies linker options to use. Must be separated by commas.
-Xlinker *arguments*	Specifies the arguments to pass to the linker.
-save-temps	Doesn't delete intermediate files.
-pipe	Uses pipes instead of intermediate files.
-specs=*file*	The content of the specified file will override the built-in specs.
-std=*standard*	Assumes that the given standard is the input source.
-B *directory*	Adds the specified directory to the compiler's search paths.
-b *host*	Runs gcc for target <host>.
-V *version*	Specifies the `gcc` version to use (it must be installed).
-v	Shows the programs executed by the compiler.
-E	Preprocesses.
-S	Compiles.
-c	Compiles and assembles.
-o *file*	Specifies the output file.
-x *language*	Specifies the language for the input files. Can either be C, C++, Assembler, or none. ("none" means as if the option had never been typed. Guesses the language.)
files...	Specifies the input files to use.

File Name: `c++` **Directory:** /usr/bin/ **Type:** External

c++filt

UNIX Shell: All primary shells (csh, ksh, sh)

Function	Organizes the C++ symbols.
Syntax	c++filt [options...] *{ symbols... }*

-_	Removes the underscores in front of every name.
-n	Doesn't remove the underscores in front of every name.
-s *method*	Specifies what method of mangling to use.
gnu	Decodes with the gnu method.
lucid	Decodes with the lucid method.
arm	Decodes with the arm method.
hp	Decodes with the HP method.
edg	Decodes with the edg method.
--help	Shows help information.
--version	Shows version information.
symbols...	Specifies the arguments to organize. Other vice arguments are read from STDIN.

File Name: `c++filt` **Directory:** /usr/bin/ **Type:** External

c2ph, pstruct

UNIX Shell: Perl script

Function	Translates C code to Perl code.
Syntax	c2ph [options...] [variable=*value*] *{ files... }*

-w	Specifies wide format: type_width = 45, member_width = 35, offset = 8.
-x	Specifies hexadecimal format: offset_fmt = x, offset_width = 08, size_fmt = x, size_width = 04.
-n	Doesn't generate perl code.
-p	Generates perl code.
-v	Same as -p except that it uses C declarations for comments.
-i	Does not recalculate sizes for inherent data types.
-a	Shows information about inherent data types.
-t	Traces execution.
variable=*value*	Specifies values to transfer to perl.
files...	Specifies C code to translate.

File Name: `c2ph, pstruct` **Directory:** /usr/bin/ **Type:** Script

caesar

UNIX Shell: All primary shells (csh, ksh, sh)

Function	Is used to decipher caesar crypto by reading from STDIN and showing the results to STDOUT.
Syntax	caesar *{ rotation }*

{ rotation	Specifies a letter rotation value to use.

File Name:	`caesar`	**Directory:**	/usr/games/	**Type:**	External

calendar

UNIX Shell: All primary shells (csh, ksh, sh)

Function	Reads from the default calendar file or from a specified one and shows any scheduled events.
Syntax	calendar [options...]

-a	Processes every user's calendar file and mails the results to them.
-A *days*	Shows information from today and the specified number of days in the future.
-B *days*	Shows information from today and the specified number of days in the past.
-t *date*	Uses the specified date as today's date. Date format is: [cc][yy][mm][dd].
-f *file*	Uses the specified file as the default calendar file.

File Name:	`calendar`	**Directory:**	/usr/bin/	**Type:**	External

Tip:	Specifies the local national code table of your country in the calendar file by inserting `LANG=locale_name`.

calendar -a	Processes and mails all calendar files to all users.
calendar -A 10	Shows all calendar entries from today and 10 days into the future.
calendar -B 10	Shows all calendar entries from today and 10 days in the past.

cap_mkdb

UNIX Shell: All primary shells (csh, ksh, sh)

Function	Creates a hashed capability database out of the `termcap` or `terminfo` logical databases.
Syntax	cap_mkdb [options...] *files...*

-i	Parses the capability records into `terminfo` format.
-f *file*	Uses an alternate database base name.
-v	Prints out the number of capability records in the database.
files...	Specifies the `termcap` or `terminfo` databases to use.

File Name:	`cap_mkdb`	**Directory:**	/usr/bin	**Type:**	External

cc

UNIX Shell: All primary shells (csh, ksh, sh)

Function	The C and C++ compiler for BSD. See `gcc` or `g++` for complete information.
Syntax	cc

File Name:	`cc`	**Directory:**	/usr/bin/	**Type:**	External

cccp

UNIX Shell: All primary shells (csh, ksh, sh)

Function	A macro processor used to transform a program before compilation. Mainly used by the C compiler.
Syntax	cccp [options...] *infile outfile*

-$	Doesn't allow the use of $ characters in identifiers.
-A *name*(*value*)	Asserts the specified name with the token list value.
-C	Passes the comments to the output file.
-D*name { =definition }*	Defines the name as a macro with the specified definition (or 1 if none is specified).
-dD	Shows a list of #define directives for macros defined during the execution.
-dM	Shows a list of #define directives for all macros.
-I *directory*	Adds the specified directory to search for header files.
-I-	Makes all the directories specified by –I only to be searched by local includes.
-H	Shows the name of all used header files.
-imacros *file*	Reads the specified file and uses all the macros on the main process.
-include *file*	Reads the specified file and uses all the includes in the main process.
-idirafter *directory*	Searches the directory if no include file is found in main search directories.

continued

-iprefix *prefix*	Specifies the prefix to use with the -iwithprefix directories.
-iwithprefix *directory*	Searches the directory if no include file is found in main search directories.
-lang-c	Specifies the source language as pure C code.
-lang-c++	Specifies the source language as C++ code.
-lang-objc	Specifies the source language as objective C code.
-langobjc++	Specifies the source language as objective C++ code.
-lint	Looks for lint commands in comments and sets them in "#pragma lint" sentences.
-M [-MG]	Shows a `make` suitable description containing the object and include files.
-MM [-MG]	Is like -M, but only shows local include files (#include " ").
-MG	Assumes missing include files to be in the same directory as the source code. (Can only be combined with -M or -MM.)
-MD *file*	Is like -M, but writes the information on the specified file.
-MMD *file*	Is like -MD, but writes the information on the specified file.
-nostdinc	Doesn't use the standard system directories to look for include files.
-nostdinc++	Doesn't use the c++ standard system directories to look for include files.
-P	Doesn't let # lines to pass through the preprocessor.
-pedantic	Shows warnings if required by ANSI C standard.
-pedantic-errors	Shows warnings by ANSI C standard as errors.
-traditional	Tries to imitate the behavior of old-fashioned C.
-trigraphs	Converts to ANSI standard trigraph sequences.
-U*name*	Doesn't predefine the specified name.
-undef	Doesn't predefine nonstandard macros.
-Wtrigraphs	Warns if any trigraphs are encountered.
-Wcomment	Warns if a comment's start sequence "/*" appears in a comment.
-Wall	The same as -Wtrigraphs and -Wcomments.
-Wtraditional	Warns if a construct differs from traditional and ANSI C.
infile	Specifies the file to use.
outfile	Specifies the file to be created.
File Name: `cccp`	**Directory:** /usr/bin/ **Type:** External

ccdconfig

UNIX Shell: All primary shells (csh, ksh, sh)

Function	Configures concatenated disk devices.
Syntax	ccdconfig [options...] *{ ccd }* ccdconfig [-v] *ccd ileave flags device*

-v	Verbose mode. Shows more information. Cannot be used with -g option.
-f *file*	Specifies the config file to use (default is `/etc/ccd.conf`).
-M *core*	Gets name list values from a core file. Used with -g option.
-N *system*	Gets the name list from system. Used with -g option (default is `/bsd`).
	The following options can't be combined:
-C	Configures all the ccd devices listed in the ccd configuration file.
-g	Dumps the current configuration for the specified ccds in configuration file format.
-u	Unconfigures the specified ccds.
-U	Unconfigures all ccds listed in the configuration file.
ccd	Specifies the ccd to use. Is only required with -u option and optional with -g option.
ileave	Specifies the ileave number for the ccd.
flags	Specifies the flags for the ccd.
device	Specifies the device for the ccd.
File Name: `ccdconfig`	**Directory:** /sbin **Type:** External

cdio

UNIX Shell: All primary shells (csh, ksh, sh)

Function	A CD audio player.
Syntax	cdio [options...] *{ ACTION }*

-s	Silent mode. Shows less information.
-v	Verbose mode. Shows more information.
-f *device*	Specifies the CD device to use.

continued

ACTION	**Select one of the following three actions:**
play *starttrack { endtrack }*	Plays from the start track to the end track.
play *startm:starts:startf* [endm:ends.endf]	Plays from minute:second.frame to minute:second.frame.
play *{ startblock } { length }*	Plays from specified block to the given length of blocks.
pause	Pauses the playing.
next	Plays the next track.
previous	Plays the previous track.
replay	Plays the current track once more.
resume	Resumes playing from the place where you issued the pause command.
stop	Stops playing.
eject	Opens the CD tray.
close	Closes the CD tray.
volume *leftchannel rightchannel*	Sets the volume on the left and the right channels (is between 0 and 255).
volume mute	Turns the sound off.
volume mono	Sets to mono mode.
volume stereo	Sets to stereo mode.
volume left	Plays the left subtrack on both left and right channels.
volume right	Plays the right subtrack on both left and right channels.
info	Shows the table of contents.
status	Shows current status on the disc; current playing status and position, and so forth.
help	Shows help information about the commands.
debug on	Turns the debugging on the CD-ROM driver on.
debug off	Turns the debugging on the CD-ROM driver off.
device *device*	Changes the default CD-ROM device to the device specified.
reset	Resets the CD device's hardware.
set msf	Sets mode to minute-second-frame `ioctl` (is default).
set lba	Sets mode to LBA `ioctl`.
quit	Quits the program.
File Name: `cdio`	**Directory:** /usr/bin **Type:** External
cdio -s play 1 5	Starts cdio in silent mode any play from track 1 to 5.
cdio pause	Pauses the CD.

certpatch

UNIX Shell: All primary shells (csh, ksh, sh)

Function	Adds subjectAltname to a PEM certificate. Signs the certificate with the signing key after the addition.
Syntax	certpatch [-t] options... *infile outfile*

-t *type*	Specifies the type of the given identity. Can be ip, fqdn, or ufqdn.
-i *identity*	Specifies the identity for the subjectAltname to insert into the certificate.
-k *key*	Specifies the CA signing key to use when signing the certificate.
infile	Specifies the certificate to use.
outfile	Specifies where to write the new certificate.
File Name: `certpatch`	**Directory:** /usr/sbin/ **Type:** External

chat

UNIX Shell: All primary shells (csh, ksh, sh)

Function	An automated chat program doing conversational exchange between the computer and the modem.
Syntax	chat [options...] *{ script }*

-f *file*	Reads the chat script from the specified file.
-t *timeout*	Sets the timeout for the expected string to be received.
-r *file*	Writes the report strings to the specified file.
-e	Sets the echo option to on.
-v	Runs the chat script in verbose mode.
-V	Runs the chat script in verbose mode and sends all verbose text to STDERR.
-s	Sends all log and error messages to STDERR.
-S	Doesn't send error messages to `syslog`.

continued

-T *phonenumber*	Uses the phone number as a replacement for \T substitution metacharacter.		
-U *phone number 2*	Uses the phone number as a replacement for \U substitution metacharacter.		
script	Specifies the script in the form of parameters, if a script file was not specified.		
File Name: `chat`	**Directory:** /usr/sbin/	**Type:**	External

checknr

UNIX Shell: All primary shells (csh, ksh, sh)

Function	Checks `nroff` or `troff` files for errors such as missing delimiters and unknown commands.
Syntax	checknr [options...] *file*

-a *.x.y*	Adds macro pairs to the list of pairs to check.		
-c *x.y*	Defines commands that otherwise would create error messages.		
-f	Ignores the changes to \f fonts.		
-s	Ignores the changes to \f fonts.		
file	The name of the file to verify (default is STDIN).		
File Name: `checknr`	**Directory:** /usr/bin/	**Type:**	External

checknr -f /var/adm/messages	Checks and ignores font changes.
checknr -s /var/adm/messages	Checks and ignores size changes.
checknr -a.BS.ES	Defines the macro pair BS and ES.

chflags

UNIX Shell: All primary shells (csh, ksh, sh)

Function	Changes the flags/attributes for the specified files.
Syntax	chflags [options...] *flags... files...*

-R	Changes the flags for all files in subdirectories.		
	The following options can only be used with the -R option:		
-H	Allows symbolic links on the command line.		
-L	Follows all symbolic links.		
-P	Follows no symbolic links.		
flags...	Specifies the flags, separated by commas, to set on the files.		
	The following are the flags to set. To disable the flag, put "no" before it.		
arch	Sets the archived flag.		
opaque	Sets the opaque flag.		
nodump	Sets the nodump flag.		
sappnd	Sets the system append-only flag.		
schg	Sets the system immutable flag.		
uappnd	Sets the user append-only flag.		
uchg	Sets the user immutable flag.		
files...	Specifies the files to set the flags on.		
File Name: `chflags`	**Directory:** /usr/bin/	**Type:**	External

chio

UNIX Shell: All primary shells (csh, ksh, sh)

Function	A tool for controlling medium changers.
Syntax	chio [-f] *ACTION*

-f *device*	Specifies the device changer, rather than the default `/dev/ch0`.
ACTION	**Select one of the following actions:**
move *fromET fromEU toET toEU* [inv]	Moves the media unit from and to the specified ET/EU.
inv	Inverts the media before moving it.
exchange *sET sEU d1ET d1EU { d2ET d2EU } { i1 i2 }*	Exchanges a media unit.
sET, sEU	Specifies the source ET/EU.
d1ET,d1EU	Specifies the destination ET/EU.
d2ET,d2EU	Specifies the second destination ET/EU to store the old destination ET/EU.
i1	Inverts the exchange from source to destination.
i2	Inverts the exchange from destination to destination2.

continued

position *toET toEU* [inv]	Sets the picker in front of the element specified.
inv	Inverts before insertion.
params	Shows information on the changer, like slots, drivers, pickers, and portals.
getpicker	Shows which picker is set to be used by the changer.
setpicker *unit*	Specifies the picker to be used by the changer.
status *{ type }*	Shows the status of all elements in the changer.
type	Specifies the element type to show information on. Can be one of the following:
FULL	Specifies all elements containing a media unit.
IMPEXP	Specifies all elements deposited by an outside human operator.
EXCEPT	Specifies all elements that are in an abnormal state.
ACCESS	Specifies all elements accessible by a picker.
EXENAB	Specifies all elements that support exporting to an outside human operator.
INENAB	Specifies all elements that support importing from an outside human operator.
File Name: chio	**Directory:** /bin/ **Type:** External

chpass, chfn, chsh

UNIX Shell: All primary shells (csh, ksh, sh)

Function	Manages user databases, allowing editing of the information within.
Syntax	chpass [options...] *{ username }*

-a *list*	Adds a new user entry in the database as a colon-separated list of all user fields. (Available only to the superuser and isn't supported in a YP environment.)
-l	Alters local information instead of the information in the YP.
-s *newshell*	Changes, if possible, the user's shell to the new shell specified.
-y	Alters information in the YP instead of the local information.
username	Specifies which user's information to edit (default is the current user).
File Name: chpass	**Directory:** /usr/bin/ **Type:** External

ci

UNIX Shell: All primary shells (csh, ksh, sh)

Function	Creates and stores revisions in the specified revision control system files.
Syntax	ci [options...] *files...*

This is the same command as the one found in Linux. Please see ci in the Linux chapter for all the options.

File Name: ci	**Directory:** /usr/bin/ **Type:** External

clri

UNIX Shell: All primary shells (csh, ksh, sh)

Function	Is used to clear inodes by writing zeros as the inode number.
Syntax	clri *device inodes...*

device	Specifies the file system to clear on.
inodes...	Specifies the inodes to clear.
File Name: clri	**Directory:** /sbin/ **Type:** External
Note:	Has been made obsolete by the fsck command.

co

UNIX Shell: All primary shells (csh, ksh, sh)

Function	Checks out a revision from a RCS file and stores it in the corresponding working file.
Syntax	co [options...] *files...*

This is the same command as the one found in Linux. Please see co in the Linux chapter for all the options.

File Name: co	**Directory:** /usr/bin/ **Type:** External

colcrt

colcrt	UNIX Shell:	All primary shells (csh, ksh, sh)
Function	Removes underlines or shows them on new lines filtering the `nroff` file for a CRT preview.	
Syntax	colcrt [options...] *{ files... }*	

-	Removes underline from input.
-2	Shows all underline lines on own rows.
files...	Specifies a file to act upon.

File Name:	Directory:	Type:
`colcrt`	/usr/bin/	External

colcrt - nroff.file > nounderline.txt	Removes underlines from the nroff file
colcrt -2 nroff.file > ownunderlines.txt	Shows output with separate underline lines.

colrm

colrm	UNIX Shell:	All primary shells (csh, ksh, sh)
Function	Deletes selected columns from a file reading from STDIN to STDOUT.	
Syntax	colrm *{ startcolumn } { endcolumn }*	

startcolumn	Specifies where to start in the file.
endcolumn	Specifies where to end in the file.

File Name:	Directory:	Type:
`colrm`	/usr/bin/	External

colrm 3	Deletes all columns starting with column 3 from all lines in the file.
colrm 3 7	Deletes all columns starting with column 3 up to and including column 7 from all lines in the file.

column

column	UNIX Shell:	All primary shells (csh, ksh, sh)
Function	Formats input into multiple columns.	
Syntax	column [options...] *files...*	

-c *count*	Formats the output for a screen with the specified number of columns.
-s *characters...*	Uses the specified set of characters as a column delimiter for the -t option.
-t	Creates a table from a determined number of columns or by use of the -s option.
-x	Fills the columns before the rows are filled.
files...	Specifies file to act on.

File Name:	Directory:	Type:
`column`	/usr/bin/	External

compile_et

compile_et	UNIX Shell:	All primary shells (csh, ksh, sh)
Function	Compiles error tables, converting them to a C source file usable with the `com_err` library.	
Syntax	compile_et *file*	

file	Specifies the file containing the error table to compile. Must have the suffix .et.

File Name:	Directory:	Type:
`compile_et`	/usr/bin/	External

compile_et file.et	Converts file.et to a C source file.

comsat

comsat	UNIX Shell:	All primary shells (csh, ksh, sh)
Function	The daemon that listens to the datagram port for any reports of incoming mail and notifies users.	
Syntax	comsat	

File Name:	Directory:	Type:
`comsat`	/usr/libexec/	External

config

config	UNIX Shell:	All primary shells (csh, ksh, sh)
Function	Creates kernel compilation directories and allows kernel configuration.	
Syntax	config [options...] *configfile* config [options...] *kernel*	

	The following options can be used only if you specify a config file:
-b *builddir*	Creates the specified build directory rather than the default /compile/configfile.
-p	Configures the kernel for usage with a system including profiling code.

continued

-s *srcdir*	Specifies the top-level kernel source directory to use instead of the default. (Default is four directories above the build directory.)
	The following options can be used only if you specify a kernel:
-e	Enables editing the configuration of the kernel's devices.
-u	Checks for boot-time kernel configuration changes, compares with kernel specified. (If boot kernel is the same as specified kernel, the changes are applied.)
	Choose between the two following options:
-f	Causes `config` to overwrite the kernel specified with the altered kernel.
-o *outfile*	Specifies the kernel outfile.
configfile	Specifies the kernel configuration file to create the kernel build directory from.
kernel	Specifies the kernel to configure.
	The following are internal commands:
add *device*	Adds a device by copying the device specified.
base *count*	Changes the base of numbers entered and shown to 8, 10, or 16.
change	Configures one or several devices. The following arguments are valid:
number	Specifies the device number of the device to configure.
device	Specifies the device to configure.
disable	Disables one or several devices. The following arguments are valid:
attribute value	Specifies a common attribute and disables all port devices.
number	Specifies the device number of the device to disable.
device	Specifies the device to disable.
enable	Enables one or several devices. The following arguments are valid:
attribute value	Specifies a common attribute and enables all port devices.
number	Specifies the device number of the device to enable.
device	Specifies the device to enable.
exit	Exits without saving changes.
find	Finds one or several devices. The following arguments are valid:
number	Specifies the device number of the device to find.
device	Specifies the device to find.
help	Shows help information.
list	Shows all the devices that are known, one screen at a time.
lines *count*	Specifies the number of rows per page.
quit	Exits and saves changes.
show *attribute value*	Shows all devices with the attribute and attribute value specified.

File Name:	`config`	**Directory:**	/usr/sbin/	**Type:**	External

csh

UNIX Shell: C shell (csh)

Function	The C-shell command interpreter that uses a syntax similar to the C language.
Syntax	csh [-l] [options...] *{ arguments... }*

-	When used as the first argument, a complete login to the shell is done.
-b	Lets the rest of the options pass directly to the scripts.
-c	Runs the first argument from the list and passes the other arguments to csh.
-e	Exits on nonzero exit status or other abnormal terminations.
-f	Does a fast start. Doesn't run .cshrc and .login.
-i	Forces the command prompt on any type of terminal for interactive use.
-n	Interprets but doesn't run the commands, used for debugging scripts.
-m	Reads .cshrc, regardless of its own and group's. Dangerous, should only be used as root.
-s	Takes command input from the STDIN.
-t	Runs a single command line.
-v	Verbose mode. Shows more information. Sets verbose after reading .cshrc.
-V	Verbose mode. Shows more information. Sets verbose before reading .cshrc.
-x	Echoes each command before it is run. Sets echo after reading .cshrc.
-X	Echoes each command before it is run. Sets echo before reading .cshrc.
	The -l option can only be used alone:
-l	Runs the complete login to the shell.
arguments...	Specifies one or more argument to the command.

continued

File Name:	csh	Directory:	/bin/	Type:	External
csh			Start C shell.		
csh -t			Reads and executes a single command line.		
csh -c "ls -l"			Execute ls -l in csh.		

ctm

UNIX Shell: All primary shells (csh, ksh, sh)

Function	Creates backup files by creating a delta between two directories.
Syntax	ctm [options...] *files...*

-c	Checks the current directory delta without altering anything.
-F	Force mode. Does the changes no matter what.
-k	Keeps backup files even if the original is deleted.
-l	Shows the files processed by the command, and the actions being taken on them.
-q	Quiet mode. Shows less information.
-u	Stores file modification time to the CTM delta creation time.
-v	Verbose mode. Shows more information.
-b *directory*	Sets the specified directory before every file.
-t *command*	Replaces tar with the specified command. Can only be used with the -B option. (Use a "%s" to specify the name of the backup file.)
-T *directory*	Specifies the directory to put the temporary files in.
-B *file*	Backs up all files specified by the command to the specified file.
-e *expression*	Processes the files matching the specified regular expression.
-V *level*	Verbose mode. Shows more information, based on the level specified.
-x *expression*	Processes the files not matching the specified regular expression.
files...	Specifies backup file.

File Name:	ctm	Directory:	/usr/sbin/	Type:	External

ctm_dequeue

UNIX Shell: All primary shells (csh, ksh, sh)

Function	Sends all messages in the specified queue directory.
Syntax	ctm_dequeue [options...] *directory*

-l *file*	Writes all information to the specified file.
-n *value*	Limits the number of mail messages to be sent each time.
directory	Specified the queue directory to use.

File Name:	ctm_dequeue	Directory:	/usr/sbin/	Type:	External
Tip:	Also see ctm				
ctm_dequeue -n 1			Limits the number of messages to send to 1.		

ctm_rmail

UNIX Shell: All primary shells (csh, ksh, sh)

Function	Decodes and reassembles delta files from mail files. Is used to send and receive *ctm* deltas via mail.
Syntax	ctm_rmail [options...] *{ files... }*

-l *file*	Writes all information verbose to the specified log file.
-p *directory*	Specifies the directory to collect delta mail pieces from.
-d *directory*	Specifies the directory to collect complete deltas from.
-b *directory*	Specifies the directory to apply the completed deltas in.
-D	Erases deltas after successful application by ctm.
-f	Sets the command to run in the background.
-u	Sets the -u flag when executing ctm.
-v	Makes ctm run in verbose mode.
files...	Specifies file to act on.

File Name:	ctm_rmail	Directory:	/usr/sbin/	Type:	External
ctm_rmail -p ~/pieces			Collects pieces of deltas in this directory.		

ctm_smail

UNIX Shell:	All primary shells (csh, ksh, sh)
Function	Splits the specified delta file into multiple mail files. Is used to send and receive `ctm` deltas via mail.
Syntax	ctm_smail [options...] *deltafile mailfile*

-l *file*	Writes all information verbose to specified log file.
-m *size*	Limits the maximum size for the mail message to be sent (default is 64,000 bytes).
-c *size*	Limits the maximum size for the delta to be sent (default is no limit).
-q *directory*	Stores the split mail files in the specified directory, instead of sending them.
deltafile	Specifies the delta file to split.
mailfile	Specifies the name for the split files.

File Name:	`ctm_smail`	**Directory:**	/usr/sbin/	**Type:**	External

ctm_smail -m 1000 delta deltamail	Sets the split files to be smaller than 1,000 bytes.

cu

UNIX Shell:	All primary shells (csh, ksh, sh)
Function	Connects you to a remote computer or acts as a dial-in terminal.
Syntax	cu [options...] *command ACTION*

-e	Uses the even parity when sending data.
-o	Uses the odd parity when sending data.
--parity=none	Doesn't use any parity.
-h	Uses half-duplex communication mode.
--nostop	Stops the XON/XOFF handling (default is ON).
-E *character*	Sets the escape character to the one specified (default is ~).
-z *system*	Specifies the system to call up.
-c *number*	Specifies a telephone number to dial.
-p *port*	Specifies the name of the port to use.
-a *port*	The same as -p.
-l *line*	Specifies a device to use for communication, overrides the default search.
-s *speed*	Sets the transmission baud rate to use.
-n	Asks for a telephone number to dial.
-d	Shows debugging information.
-x *type*	Specifies what debugging types to use. Multiple types are separated with commas.
-I *file*	Specifies a configuration file to use.
-v	Shows version information and exits.
--help	Shows help information.
	The following are internal commands to control the program. (This is documented with the default escape character ~.)
~.	Terminates the connection.
~p *from to*	Sends a file to a remote UNIX system.
~t *from to*	Receives a file from a remote UNIX system
~! *command*	Runs the specified command in a shell.
~$ *command*	Runs the specified command and sends the STDOUT to the remote site.
~| *command*	Runs the specified command and takes the STDIN from the remote site.
~+ *command*	Sends the STDOUT and receives the STDIN from the remote site.
~#	Sends a break signal to the port.
~c *directory*	Changes to the specified local directory.
~> *file*	Sends the specified file to the remote site.
~<	Asks for a local filename and a remote command and receives a file.
~s *variable value*	Specifies a value to set to the specified variable (default is true).
~! *variable*	Specifies a variable to set to false.
~z	Suspends the current session.
~%nostop	Stops the XON/XOFF handling.
~%stop	Starts the XON/XOFF handling.
~v	Shows a list of values of all variables available.

continued

~?	Shows help information.
ACTION	**You may use one of the following actions to connect. Cannot be combined.**
dir	Connects directly to the port specified.
system	Specifies system name or hostname to contact.
number	Specifies the telephone number to call.
File Name: cu	**Directory:** /usr/bin/ **Type:** External
cu 7147359611	Connects to the telephone number specified.

cursor

UNIX Shell: All primary shells (csh, ksh, sh)

Function	Sets the cursor shape in a console virtual screen system.
Syntax	cursor [options...]

-d *device*	Sets the shape on the cursor for the specified device.
-n *screen*	Specifies what screen number to set the parameters on.
-s *line*	Sets the starting scan line to use for the cursor.
-e *line*	Sets the last scan line to use for the cursor.
File Name: cursor	**Directory:** /usr/sbin/ **Type:** External

cvs

UNIX Shell: All primary shells (csh, ksh, sh)

Function	A version control and logging system for files or directory tree structures including any versionable files.
Syntax	cvs [options...] *{ command }* [options...]

This is the same command as the one found in Linux. Please see cvs in the Linux chapter for all of the options.

File Name: cvs	**Directory:** /usr/bin/	**Type:** External

cvsbug

UNIX Shell: Bourne shell (sh)

Function	Sends a CVS problem report to a central support site that runs GNATS.
Syntax	cvsbug *{ site }* [options...]

-f *file*	Specifies a file that contains a problem report to send.
-t *address*	Specifies the mail address to the support site that's going to receive the reports.
-P	Shows the problem report form to send. Reads the form from the variable PR_FORM.
-L	Shows the available categories.
--request-id	Sends a request for a submitter ID to the site or address specified.
-v	Shows version information.
site	Specifies a problem report site to send the reports to.
File Name: cvsbug	**Directory:** /usr/bin/ **Type:** Script
cvsbug -f report -t reports@ucgbook.com	Reports the problem found in file report to the specified e-mail address.

dbmmanage

UNIX Shell: Perl script

Function	Manages DBM files with usernames and passwords to authenticate HTTP users.
Syntax	dbmmanage *file { command } { user } { password }*

	The following commands can't be combined:
add	Adds a username and uses the encrypted password.
adduser	Asks for a password then adds a username.
check	Finds a password and checks if the specified username has the specified password.
delete	Removes username from the filename.
import	Reads username and password from STDIN and adds them to the filename.
update	The same as adduser, but it verifies that the username already exists.
view	Shows the DBM file.
file	Specifies the DBM file. You don't need to specify the file extension.
user	Specifies the username to manage.
password	Specifies an optional encrypted password to use with the username.
File Name: dbmmanage	**Directory:** /usr/bin/ **Type:** Script
dbmmanage datafile add user1 F4Az\4z	Adds the user user1 F4Az\4z to datafile.

deroff

UNIX Shell: All primary shells (csh, ksh, sh)

Function	Removes macro calls, requests, table descriptions, and backslashes from `nroff`, `troff`, `tbl`, `eqn`, or text files.
Syntax	deroff [-w] *files...*

-w	Shows a word-by-word list.
files...	Specifies the files to work on.

File Name:	`deroff`	**Directory:**	/usr/bin/	**Type:**	External

deroff -w /etc/passwd	Shows one word per line of the /etc/passwd file.

dev_mkdb

UNIX Shell: All primary shells (csh, ksh, sh)

Function	Creates the /dev directory from the database /var/run/dev.db.
Syntax	dev_mkdb

File Name:	`dev_mkdb`	**Directory:**	/usr/sbin/	**Type:**	External

dev_mkdb	Rebuilds the /dev directory.

dga

UNIX Shell: All primary shells (csh, ksh, sh)

Function	Tests video modes for X-window by filling the screen with different colors each time a key is pressed.
Syntax	dga

b	Runs a benchmark by measuring the read and write speed of framebuffers.
q	Stops the program.

File Name:	`dga`	**Directory:**	/usr/X11R6/bin/	**Type:**	External

dga	Starts the program. After that, press the b key to start the benchmark if wanted.

dhclient

UNIX Shell: All primary shells (csh, ksh, sh)

Function	Configures network interfaces to use DHCP.
Syntax	dhclient [options...] *{ interfaces... }*

-1	Exits if the interface configuration fails.
-d	Runs in foreground even after configuration is ready.
-p *port*	Specifies the network port to listen for BOOT replies (default is UDP 68).
interface	Specifies a network interface to configure (default is all).

File Name:	`dhclient`	**Directory:**	/sbin/	**Type:**	External

dhclient -1	Starts dhclient and forces it to exit if it fails.
dhclient ep1	Starts dhclient and tries to configure the network interface ep1.
dhclient -p 69	Starts dhclient and listens to UDP port 69.

dhcpd

UNIX Shell: All primary shells (csh, ksh, sh)

Function	It is a DHCP server that serves hosts with IP addresses on the network.
Syntax	dhcpd [options...] *{ interfaces... }*

-p	Specifies the network port to listen for request (default is 67).
-f	Runs in foreground (default is a daemon in the background).
-d	Specifies to send all log activity to STDERR.
-q	Minimizes information shown at startup.
-cf *configuration*	Specifies a configuration filename (default is `/etc/dhcpd.conf`).
-lf *lease*	Specifies a lease filename (default is `/var/db/dhcpd.leases`).
interface	Specifies network interface to listen for broadcasts (default is all interfaces).

File Name:	`dhcpd`	**Directory:**	/usr/sbin/	**Type:**	External

dhcpd -q	Starts up without so much information on the screen.
dhcpd -lf /tmp/dhcpd.conf	Starts up with the alternative configuration file `/tmp/dhcpd.conf`.

dhcrelay

UNIX Shell:	All primary shells (csh, ksh, sh)
Function	Forwards BOOTP/DHCP requests from a subnet without a DHCP server to a subnet that has a DHCP server.
Syntax	dhcrelay [options...] *servers...*

-p *port*	Specifies the network port to listen for requests (default is 67).
-d	Runs in foreground only (default is a daemon in the background).
-q	Minimizes information shown at startup.
-i *interface*	Specifies a network interface to forward BOOTP and DHCP requests (default is all).
servers...	Specifies one or more DHCP servers to forward requests to.

File Name:	`dhcrelay`	**Directory:**	/usr/sbin/	**Type:**	External

dhcrelay -q sun	Forwards requests to sun and minimizes the information at startup.
dhcrelay -i ep0 sun	Forwards requests to sun from interface ep0.

dig

UNIX Shell:	All primary shells (csh, ksh, sh)
Function	Gathers information from the DNS servers in interactive or batch mode.
Syntax	dig [*@server*] *domain* [options...]

-f *file*	Specifies a file that contains multiple dig queries.
-T *seconds*	Waits the specified time before performing the next dig command when using -f.
-p *port*	Specifies what port to use when connecting to a name server (default is 53).
-P *ping*	Runs `ping` to compare response times after a DNS query returns.
-t *query-type*	DNS query type. The following types can be used:
a	Specifies the network address.
any	Specifies all or any information about the specified domain.
mx	Specifies the mail exchanger for the domain.
ns	Specifies name servers.
soa	Specifies the zone of authority record.
hinfo	Specifies the host information.
axfr	Specifies the zone transfer.
txt	Specifies arbitrary number of strings.
-c *query-class*	Specifies the network class requested in the query. The following classes can be specified:
in	Specifies the Internet class domain.
any	Specifies all or any class information.
-envsav	Saves the current environment to the default.
-envset	Same as envsav, but for batch files.
-stick	Restores dig environment before each query line in a dig batch file.
-nostick	Do not restore dig environment before each query line in a dig batch file.
+keyword=value	Specifies an option to change in the query packet or to change dig output specifics.
%comment	Includes an argument not to be parsed.
-x dot-notation-address	Inverses address mapping.
@server	Specifies the server to query.
domain	Specifies the domain to request information from.

File Name:	`dig`	**Directory:**	/usr/sbin/	**Type:**	External

disklabel

UNIX Shell:	All primary shells (csh, ksh, sh)
Function	Shows, installs, or modifies a hard disk label. Information in the disk label is used by the operating system.
Syntax	disklabel [foption] [options...] *ACTION*

	The following function options (foption) control the function:
-w	Sets a label of standard format.
-e	Edits a disk label with the editor vi if the environment variable EDITOR isn't set.
-E	Edits a disk label with the built-in simple editor.
-R	Restores an earlier overwritten label that is stored in a file.

continued

-B	Installs bootstrap code. To use with -w or -R.
	The following options are regular options:
-N	Denies writes to the pack label area.
-W	Allows writes to the pack label area.
-n	Changes nothing on the system, only shows what it's doing.
-v	Verbose mode. Shows more information.
-r	Reads or writes directly to disk without use of the system's copy of the label.
-b *boot*	Sets the boot program of the system. The single level or the primary boot.
-s *boot*	Uses the secondary boot program if the system has a two-level bootstrap.
-d	Ignores all disk partitions that exist and uses the default disk label. Not with -r.
-c	Updates the system copy of the disk label with the one in the disk. Not with -r.
-t	Specifies the label in a format the `disktab` recognizes.
-f *tempfile*	Writes to tempfile, mount point info for partitions in `fstab` format.
	The following are commands used in the editor that starts with the -e option:
? *{ command }*	Shows help information for all commands or for one specified.
M	Shows a manual page.
u	Reverses changes. First time, change is removed; next time, it is restored.
p	Shows the existing label.
{ unit }	Specifies output format as unit, b, c, k, m, or g for bytes, cylinders, KB, MB, and GB.
e	Sets parameters for the disk.
b	Specifies where to permit changes on the disk.
r	Recalculates the hard disk free space.
a *{ partition }*	Specifies a partition to add. System will ask if no partition is specified.
c *{ partition }*	Resizes a partition. System will ask if no partition is specified.
d *{ partition }*	Deletes a partition. System will ask if no partition is specified.
g	Specifies which configuration for disk geometry to use.
{ configuration }	Choices for configuration are d for disk, b for BIOS, and u for user.
m *{ partition }*	Alters the parameters for a partition. System will ask if no partition is specified.
n *{ partition }*	Specifies partition mount point. System will ask if no partition is specified.
s *{ file }*	Stores the label to a file. System will ask if no file with directory is specified.
w	Sets the changes to the on-disk label permanent.
q	Exits the editor and the system asks to save changes.
x	Exits the editor and the system will not save changes.
X	Toggles export mode, allows the use of some settings available only in this mode.
ACTION	**Select one of the following actions:**
disk	Specifies the hard disk to use.
disktype	Specifies the disk type. Is required with -w and optional with -B and -R foptions.
protofile	Specifies the protofile. Is required with -R foption.
packid	Specifies the pack ID. Is optionally used with -w foption.

File Name:	`disklabel`	**Directory:**	/sbin/	**Type:**	External
Warning:	Data may be lost if this isn't used with care.				

disklabel /dev/wd0a	Shows the disk label on the disk /dev/wd0a.

dmesg

UNIX Shell: All primary shells (csh, ksh, sh)

Function	A tool for viewing the contents of the system message buffer.
Syntax	dmesg [options...]

-M *core*	Extracts values from the name list from the specified core (default is `/dev/kmem`).
-N *system*	Extracts the name list from the specified system (default is `/bsd`).

File Name:	`dmesg`	**Directory:**	/sbin/	**Type:**	External

dmesg | grep cpu	Extracts CPU information from the buffer.

dnsquery

dnsquery	UNIX Shell:	All primary shells (csh, ksh, sh)
Function	Shows information about nameservers through BIND resolver library calls.	
Syntax	dnsquery [options...] *host*	

This is the same command as the one found in Linux. Please see dnsquery in the Linux chapter for all the options.

File Name:	`dnsquery`	**Directory:**	/usr/sbin/	**Type:**	External

dump, rdump

dump, rdump	UNIX Shell:	All primary shells (csh, ksh, sh)
Function	A backup program that examines your ext2 file system and determines which files to be backed up.	
Syntax	dump [options...] *files...*	

-*value*	Specifies the backup mode (dump level 9 is default).
-0	Enables full backup mode. Backs up everything. Use this when creating a new backup.
-1	Dump level 1, incremental backup. This is the start level for incremental backups.
-2	Dump level 2, backs up files that have been changed or created since level 1 was done.
-3	Dump level 3, backs up files that have been changed or created since level 2 was done.
-4	Dump level 4, backs up files that have been changed or created since level 3 was done.
-5	Dump level 5, backs up files that have been changed or created since level 4 was done.
-6	Dump level 6, backs up files that have been changed or created since level 5 was done.
-7	Dump level 7, backs up files that have been changed or created since level 6 was done.
-8	Dump level 8, backs up files that have been changed or created since level 7 was done.
-9	Dump level 9, backs up files that have been changed or created since level 8 was done.
-a	Causes dump to write backup until the device returns an EOM (end of media) string.
-c	Sets dump to act like it's writing to a cartridge tape drive. (8000bpi and 1700).
-n	Notifies users in the group `operator` when dump requires user input.
-u	Updates the file /etc/dumpdates after a successful dump.
-B *blocks*	Specifies the number of 1KB blocks to use per volume.
-b *size*	Defines the number of kilobytes to use for every dump record (10 is the default).
-d *density*	Specifies the tape density.
-f *file*	Writes a backup to a specified device or a file. Use – for STDOUT.
-h *level*	Doesn't backup files that are above or at the given level.
-s *feet*	Sets the tape length to feet. If the tape is smaller, it will prompt for a new tape.
-T *date*	Specifies when you want to start a dump session.
	When showing file systems, select only one of these two options:
-w	Shows only the filenames that need to be dumped.
-W	Causes dump to show file systems and highlight those that need to be dumped. (Don't combine -w or -W with other options.)
files...	Specifies the file or files to dump.

File Name:	`dump`	**Directory:**	/sbin/	**Type:**	External

dump -0 -u -f homedump /home/*	Conducts a full backup, sends it to homedump and then updates the file `/etc/dumpdates`.
dump -S -0 /	Outputs how many bytes a full dump on / will be.

dumpfs

dumpfs	UNIX Shell:	All primary shells (csh, ksh, sh)
Function	Shows information about a device or a file system specified.	
Syntax	dumpfs *{ filesystem } { device }*	

	The following can't be combined:
filesystem	Shows the information about the specified file system.
device	Shows the information about the specified device.

File Name:	`dumpfs`	**Directory:**	/sbin/	**Type:**	External

dumpfs /usr/home	Shows information about the home file system.

eject

eject	UNIX Shell:	All primary shells (csh, ksh, sh)
Function	Ejects a magnetic tape.	
Syntax	eject [-f]	

-f *tapename*	Specifies the tape to eject. Can either be a device or address to a remote computer.		
File Name: `eject`	**Directory:** /bin/	**Type:**	External
Note:	This command is actually an alias for `mt -f` *`device`* `offline`.		
eject -f /dev/rst0	Ejects rst0.		

elf2olf

elf2olf	UNIX Shell:	All primary shells (csh, ksh, sh)
Function	Converts the specified ELF version module into the default OLF object module format.	
Syntax	elf2olf [options...] *module*	

-v	Verbose mode. Shows more information.
-o *system*	Uses the OLF tag for the operating system specified below.
openbsd	OpenBSD.
netbsd	NetBSD.
freebsd	FreeBSD.
44bsd	4.4BSD.
linux	Linux.
svr4	AT&T System V Release 4.
esix	esix UNIX.
solaris	Solaris.
irix	SGI IRIX.
sco	SCO UNIX.
dell	DELL SVR4.
ncr	NCR SVR4.
module	Specifies a ELF module to convert.
File Name: `elf2olf`	**Directory:** /usr/bin/ **Type:** External

encrypt

encrypt	UNIX Shell:	All primary shells (csh, ksh, sh)
Function	Shows the encrypted form of the string to the STDOUT.	
Syntax	encrypt [options...] { *string* }	

-k	Specifies to be in makekey-compatible mode.
-b *rounds*	Specifies to use Blowfish hashing for encrypting, with the specified rounds.
-m	Specifies to use MD5 when encrypting the string.
-s *salt*	Specifies to use DES when encrypting, with the specified salt.
-p	Prompts for a single string with no echo.
string	Specifies the string to encrypt.
File Name: `encrypt`	**Directory:** /usr/bin/ **Type:** External

error

error	UNIX Shell:	All primary shells (csh, ksh, sh)
Function	Is used to insert compiler error messages into a source file.	
Syntax	error [options...] { *file* }	

-n	Does not modify any files, but shows all error messages.
-q	Asks if the error should be inserted into the file — respond with a y or n.
-s	Shows statistics regarding the error categorization.
-v	Runs the `vi` program on all touched files to edit the errors.
-t *suffixlist*	Specifies a suffix list for the files to modify.
-I *ignorefile*	Specifies names of functions to ignore, instead of .errors from the home directory.
file	Specifies a file to use error messages from instead of STDIN.
File Name: `error`	**Directory:** /usr/sbin/ **Type:** External

ext_srvtab

UNIX Shell: All primary shells (csh, ksh, sh)

Function	Reads service key files from Kerberos key distribution center database.
Syntax	ext_srvtab [options...] *{ host... }*

-n	Specifies to read the master key from the master key cache file.
-r *realm*	Specifies the realm fields in the extracted file match the specified realm.
host...	Creates service key file for the specified host.

File Name: `ext_srvtab` **Directory:** /usr/sbin/ **Type:** External

fdisk

UNIX Shell: All primary shells (csh, ksh, sh)

Function	A utility for handling DOS partitions.
Syntax	fdisk [options...] *device*

-i	Initializes the MBR sector.
-e	Edits existing MBR sectors.
-f *file*	Specifies an alternate MBR template file.
-c	Specifies the number of cylinders to use.
-h	Specifies the number of headers to use.
-s	Specifies the number of sectors to use.
device	Specifies the device to work on.
	Following is a list of commands to use within the program:
help	Shows help information.
manual	Shows the manual for `fdisk`.
reinit	Re-initializes the current selected partition with the boot block.
disk	Shows the current disk's geometry.
edit	Edits parts of the current boot block.
flag	Sets the current partition as bootable.
update	Updates the actual boot block with the newly edited block.
select	Selects and loads the boot block into memory.
print	Shows the selected in-memory boot block and its tables.
write	Writes the in-memory boot block to disk.
exit	Exits the current level, or the program, if in the topmost level.
quit	Like exit, but will write the modified block out.
abort	Exits the program without saving changes.

File Name: `fdisk` **Directory:** /sbin/ **Type:** External

file2c

UNIX Shell: All primary shells (csh, ksh, sh)

Function	Decompiles binary or other files into C-source.
Syntax	file2c *{ string1 } { string2 }*

string1	Shows the specified string before the output data.
string2	Shows the specified string after the output data.

File Name: `file2c` **Directory:** /usr/bin/ **Type:** External

flex, flex++

UNIX Shell: All primary shells (csh, ksh, sh)

Function	Is used to create a scanner program that recognizes lexical patterns in a text.
Syntax	flex [options...] *{ files... }*

This is the same command as the one found in Linux. Please see flex in the Linux chapter for all the options.

File Name: `flex` **Directory:** /usr/bin/ **Type:** External

fortune

UNIX Shell: All primary shells (csh, ksh, sh)

Function	Shows an interesting or funny phrase from various files randomly each time you execute it.
Syntax	fortune [options...] [*{ percents%*] *files... }*

-a	Grabs phrases from all lists available.
-e	Uses fortune files as if they were of equal size.

continued

-f	Shows a list of the files that would be used when grabbing phrases.		
-l	Shows only long phrases.		
-m *pattern*	Shows all fortunes containing the specified pattern.		
-o	Shows only rude fortunes.		
-s	Shows only short phrases.		
-i	Disables case-sensitivity when using -m.		
-w	Waits before exiting the program. Time is based on the number of characters.		
percents%	Specifies the probability that a phrase is taken from the following file — for example, 75%.		
files...	Specifies one or more files or directories containing phrases.		
File Name: `fortune`	**Directory:** /usr/games/	**Type:**	External
fortune 50% humorists 50% linuxcookie	Grabs a fortune from either the humorists or linuxcookie files.		
fortune -l drugs	Grabs a long fortune from the drugs file.		

fpr, asa

UNIX Shell: All primary shells (csh, ksh, sh)

Function	Interprets Fortran carriage-control characters into line printer control characters.
Syntax	fpr { *files...* }

files...	Specifies one or more input files.		
File Name: `fpr`	**Directory:** /usr/bin/	**Type:**	External
ucgprog | fpr | lpr	Converts the output from the Fortran program and sends it to the printer.		

from

UNIX Shell: All primary shells (csh, ksh, sh)

Function	Shows headers for mail sent by the specified sender.
Syntax	from [options...] { *username* }

-s *sender*	Shows headers for mail sent by sender.		
-f *file*	Reads from the specified file instead of the default mailbox.		
username	Specifies the username to check on. If not specified, current user is used.		
File Name: `from`	**Directory:** /usr/bin/	**Type:**	External
from	Shows all users that have sent mail to the user.		
from -s ucg	Shows a header for all mail sent by ucg.		

fsck_ext2fs

UNIX Shell: All primary shells (csh, ksh, sh)

Function	Makes an interactive file system consistency check and repairs the specified file systems.
Syntax	fsck_ext2fs [options...] *filesystems...*

-b *number*	Specifies the number of the superblock for the file system.		
-d	Shows debug information.		
-f	Forces checking of file systems.		
-m *octal*	Specifies the permissions bits, in octal , when creating the lost+found directory.		
-p	Specifies to be in preen mode. Limited inconsistent correction.		
-y	Specifies to do a yes response to all questions asked.		
-n	Specifies to do a no response to all questions asked, except for CONTINUE.		
filesystems...	Specifies the file system to repair.		
File Name: `fsck_ext2fs`	**Directory:** /sbin/	**Type:**	External
fsck_ext2fs /dev/wd0e	Performs file system check on Linux file system `/dev/wd0e`.		
fsck_ext2fs -f /dev/wd0e	Forces check, ignores the "clean" flag.		
fsck_ext2fs -y /dev/wd0e	Performs file system check, and assumes that you would answer yes on all questions.		

fsck_ffs

UNIX Shell: All primary shells (csh, ksh, sh)

Function	Makes a fast file system consistency check and interactive repair for the specified file system.
Syntax	fsck_ffs [options...] { *filesystems...* }

-p	Specifies to be in preen mode. Limited inconsistent correction.
-f	Forces checking of file systems.
-m *octal*	Specifies the permissions bits, in octal , when creating the lost+found directory.

continued

-b *number* -c *level* -y -n *filesystems...*	Specifies the number of the superblock for the file system. Changes the file system to level (0-3). The level can only be raised. Specifies to do a yes response to all questions asked. Specifies to do a no response to all questions asked, except for CONTINUE. Specifies the file system to repair.
File Name: `fsck_ffs`	**Directory:** /sbin/ **Type:** External
fsck_ffs /dev/wd0a	Performs file system check on BSD file system `/dev/wd0a`.
fsck_ffs -f /dev/wd0a	Forces check, ignores the "clean" flag.
fsck_ffs -y /dev/wd0a	Performs file system check, and assumes that you would answer yes on all questions.

fsck_msdos

UNIX Shell: All primary shells (csh, ksh, sh)

Function	Makes a DOS/Windows (FAT) file system consistency check and repairs the specified file systems.
Syntax	fsck_msdos [options...] *filesystems...*

-p -f -n -y *filesystems...*	Specifies to be in preen mode. Limited inconsistent correction. Present only for compatibility reasons. Specifies to do a no response to all questions asked, except for CONTINUE. Specifies to do a yes response to all questions asked. Specifies the file system to check and repair.
File Name: `fsck_msdos`	**Directory:** /sbin/ **Type:** External
fsck_msdos /dev/fd0	Performs a file system check on MS-DOS file system `/dev/fd0`.
fsck_msdos -y /dev/fd0	Performs file system check, and assumes that you would answer yes on all questions.

fsdb

UNIX Shell: All primary shells (csh, ksh, sh)

Function	A tool for debugging and editing file system inode data.
Syntax	fsdb [-d] -f *partition*

-d -f *partition*	Shows more debug information. Specifies the partition to edit or debug.
File Name: `fsdb`	**Directory:** /sbin/ **Type:** External

fsinfo

UNIX Shell: All primary shells (csh, ksh, sh)

Function	Shows information, including the capabilities about X font servers on the network.
Syntax	fsinfo [-server *hostname*]

-server *hostname*	Is used to specify the server, and optionally the port, to show information about.
File Name: `fsinfo`	**Directory:** /usr/sbin/ **Type:** External
fsinfo -server localhost:7100	Shows font server info from localhost:7100.

fsirand

UNIX Shell: All primary shells (csh, ksh, sh)

Function	Creates random inode generation numbers on all inodes on the specified device. It also creates a file system ID in the superblock.
Syntax	fsirand [options...] *device*

-b -f -p *device*	Defaults to the 512KB block size instead of what's gathered from the disklabel. Forces command to run even on unclean file systems. Shows the generation numbers for all inodes. Specifies the special device that holds the inodes.
File Name: `fsirand`	**Directory:** /sbin/ **Type:** External

fslsfonts

UNIX Shell: All primary shells (csh, ksh, sh)

Function	Shows the fonts on the font server that match the pattern specified. Wildcards * can be used.
Syntax	fslsfonts [options...]

-server *host:port* -l	Specifies the X font server and port to use. Shows attributes of the font next to the font name.

continued

-ll	Shows font parameters together with the -l option.		
-lll	The same as -ll.		
-m	Shows the minimum and maximum bounds for each font.		
-C	Shows information in multiple columns.		
-1	Shows information in a single column.		
-w width	Is used to specify the width of the column in characters (default is 79).		
-n columns	Is used to specify the number of columns to show.		
-u	Doesn't sort the information.		
-fn *pattern*	Specifies the pattern that fslfonts must match with.		
File Name: `fslsfonts`	**Directory:** /usr/X11R6/bin/	**Type:**	External
fslsfonts -u	Runs fslsfonts and leaves all output unsorted.		

fsplit

UNIX Shell: All primary shells (csh, ksh, sh)

Function	Reads Fortran source code from a file or STDIN and splits the input into separated routine files.
Syntax	fsplit -e *subprograms...* { *file* }

-e *subprograms...*	Specifies the subprogram units that only will be split into separated files.		
file	Specifies the Fortran file to split.		
File Name: `fsplit`	**Directory:** /usr/bin/	**Type:**	External
fsplit -e readit -e doit prog.f	Splits readit and doit into separated files.		

fstat

UNIX Shell: All primary shells (csh, ksh, sh)

Function	Identifies and shows all open files in the system.
Syntax	fstat [options...] { *files...* }

-f	Restricts the examination of files to the specified file.		
-n	Specifies to be in numerical format.		
-v	Verbose mode. Shows more information.		
-M *core*	Reads values associated with the specified core list instead of the default `/dev/kmem`.		
-N *system*	Reads the name list from the specified system (default is `/bsd`).		
-p *PID*	Shows all files open with the specified PID.		
-u *user*	Shows all files open by the specified user.		
files...	Specifies the file to restrict your reports to.		
File Name: `fstat`	**Directory:** /usr/bin/	**Type:**	External
fstat -p 9386	Shows all files opened by process 9386.		
fstat -u ucg	Shows all files opened by user ucg.		

fstobdf

UNIX Shell: All primary shells (csh, ksh, sh)

Function	Creates BDF fonts from an X font server. It is used to debug fonts and re-create BDF files.
Syntax	fstobdf [-server *hostname*] -fn *name*

-server *hostname*	Specifies the server to read the font from.		
-fn *name*	Specifies the font to create a BDF file for.		
File Name: `fstobdf`	**Directory:** /usr/X11R6/bin/	**Type:**	External
fstobdf -fn terminal	Creates a BDF font from the terminal font from the default font server.		
fstobdf -fn terminal -server localhost:7100	Creates a BDF font from the terminal font from localhost:7100 font server.		

fvwm

UNIX Shell: All primary shells (csh, ksh, sh)

Function	A window manager for X11. Is used to minimize memory consumption, provide a 3-D look to window frames.
Syntax	fvwm [options...]

-f *configfile*	Reads the specified config file as its initialization file (default is `.fvwm2rc`).
-cmd *initcmd*	Specifies the initialization command to use instead of read `.fvwm2rc`.
-debug	Shows debug information. Slows things down, but guarantees the error messages are right.

continued

-d d*display* -s -version	Specifies to use display instead of the name from the environment variable $DISPLAY. Runs only on the screen named in $DISPLAY or the display specified in the -d option. Prints the version to STDERR.				
File Name:	`fvwm`	**Directory:**	/usr/X11R6/bin/	**Type:**	External
Tip:	The -f and -cmd options can be used 10 times and they will be executed in the order specified.				

g++

UNIX Shell: All primary shells (csh, ksh, sh)

Function	The C++ compiler version of `gcc`.				
Syntax	g++ [options...]				
This is the same command as the one found in Linux. Please see g++ in the Linux chapter for all the options.					
File Name:	`g++`	**Directory:**	/usr/bin/	**Type:**	External
g++ hello.cpp -o hello	Compiles and links hello.cpp; produces binary file hello as output.				

g77, f77

UNIX Shell: All primary shells (csh, ksh, sh)

Function	The GNU Fortran compiler. This can also be started using `f77`.				
Syntax	g77 [options...] *files...*				
-c	Compiles or assembles the file. Outputs an object file.				
-D*macro*	Defines a macro with the value 1.				
-D*macro=value*	Defines a macro with the specified value.				
-E	Runs the preprocessing stage. Sends the preprocess source to STDOUT.				
-g	Adds debugging information.				
-I*directory*	Specifies directory to search for include files.				
-L*directory*	Specifies directory to search for library.				
-l*library*	Specifies a library to use when linking.				
-nostdinc	Doesn't search standard system directories for include files.				
-O	Uses optimize compilation.				
-o *file*	Sends the output to file.				
-S	Runs the compilation, but doesn't assemble. Sends the assembler code to STDOUT.				
-U*macro*	Undefines the macro.				
-v	Verbose mode. Shows more information.				
-Wall	Turns on all warning messages.				
files...	Specifies the source files.				
File Name:	`g77, f77`	**Directory:**	/usr/bin/	**Type:**	External
g77 -S	Stops after the stage of compilation proper, doesn't assemble.				

gcc, cc

UNIX Shell: All primary shells (csh, ksh, sh)

Function	The GNU project C and C++ compiler.				
Syntax	gcc [options...] *files...*				
This is the same command as the one found in Linux. Please see gcc in the Linux chapter for all the options.					
File Name:	`gcc, cc`	**Directory:**	/usr/bin/	**Type:**	External

gdb

UNIX Shell: All primary shells (csh, ksh, sh)

Function	A debugger that can manage debugging of C, C++, and Modula-2 code. A.K.A. GNU Debugger.				
Syntax	gdb [options...] *{ ACTION }*				
This is the same command as the one found in Linux. Please see gdb in the Linux chapter for all the options.					
File Name:	`gdb`	**Directory:**	/usr/bin/	**Type:**	External
gdb -nw -command=gdb.command	Runs the gdb script `gdb.command` and prints to STDOUT.				

gencat

UNIX Shell:	All primary shells (csh, ksh, sh)
Function	Formats text from a message file and merges the information into the formatted message database called a cat file.
Syntax	gencat *outputfile inputfiles...*

outputfile	Specifies the database file to create.
inputfiles...	Specifies the message files to read from.

File Name:	`gencat`	**Directory:**	/usr/bin/	**Type:**	External

getNAME

UNIX Shell:	All primary shells (csh, ksh, sh)
Function	Captures NAME sections from manual sources, and can be used to create manual introduction sections or a TOC.
Syntax	getNAME [options...] *files...*

-i	Reports information from the manual that is useful for manual section introduction.
-t	Reports information from the manual that is useful for table of contents creation.
-w	Determines if traditional, new, or unknown formats exist.
files...	Specifies the manual source that the NAME section will be extracted from.

File Name:	`getNAME`	**Directory:**	/usr/libexec/	**Type:**	External

getNAME /usr/man/man1/*	Shows the name section of the man files in `/usr/man/man1/*`.

getty

UNIX Shell:	All primary shells (csh, ksh, sh)
Function	Is used to manage ports and terminal lines. Is not usually used on the command line.
Syntax	getty option

type	Is used to specify a line configuration found in `/etc/gettytab`.
tty	Specifies the tty device name found in `/dev`.

File Name:	`getty`	**Directory:**	/usr/libexec/	**Type:**	External

gnubc

UNIX Shell:	All primary shells (csh, ksh, sh)
Function	Is used to calculate arbitrary precision numbers. Statements will be read from a file specified or from STDIN.
Syntax	gnubc [options] *{ file }*

-l	Uses the standard math library.
-w	Shows POSIX warning extensions.
-s	Uses the POSIX bc language.
-q	Doesn't show the welcome message.
-v	Shows version information.
file	Specifies a file that contains statements to calculate.

File Name:	`gnubc`	**Directory:**	/usr/bin/	**Type:**	External

grodvi

UNIX Shell:	All primary shells (csh, ksh, sh)
Function	A `groff` driver that creates TeX dvi files that can then be printed out.
Syntax	grodvi [options...] *{ files... }*

-d	Allows horizontal and vertical line implementation, but ignores all other draw commands.
-v	Shows version information.
-w *value*	Sets the line thickness to the specified value in thousandths of an `em`.
-F *directory*	Searches the specified directory for device and font description files.
files...	Specifies the dvi file or files to create.

File Name:	`grodvi`	**Directory:**	/usr/bin/	**Type:**	External

groff

groff	UNIX Shell:	All primary shells (csh, ksh, sh)
Function	The front end to the document formatting system used by `groff`.	
Syntax	groff [options...] *{ files... }*	

This is the same command as the one found in Linux. Please see groff in the Linux chapter for all the options.

File Name:	**Directory:**	**Type:**
`groff`	/usr/bin/	External

grog

grog	UNIX Shell:	All primary shells (csh, ksh, sh)
Function	Guesses which `groff` option is required for printing a specific file and sends this answer to STDOUT.	
Syntax	grog [options...] *{ files... }*	

This is the same command as the one found in Linux. Please see grog in the Linux chapter for all the options.

File Name:	**Directory:**	**Type:**
`grog`	/usr/bin/	External

grolj4

grolj4	UNIX Shell:	All primary shells (csh, ksh, sh)
Function	A `groff` driver that is used for creating output that can be printed onto an HP LaserJet 4-type printer.	
Syntax	grolj4 [options...] *{ files... }*	

-c *pages*	Specifies the number of copies to print.
-l	Prints documents in landscape format.
-p *size*	Sets paper size. Select letter, legal, executive, a4, com10, monarch, c5, b5, or dl.
-v	Shows version information.
-n *{ number }*	Uses duplex mode: 1- long side binding (is default), 2- short side binding.
-w *thickness*	Sets the default line thickness to thousandths of an `em`.
-F *directory*	Searches the specified directory for the device and font description file `devlj4`.
files...	Specifies the file or files to create.

File Name:	**Directory:**	**Type:**
`grolj4`	/usr/bin/	External

grolj4 -c4 -pa4 diploma.ps	Prints four copies of diploma.ps and uses the a4 format.

grops

grops	UNIX Shell:	All primary shells (csh, ksh, sh)
Function	Translates GNU `troff` output into PostScript. Usually started by `groff -Tps`.	
Syntax	grops [options...] *{ files... }*	

-b *level*	Works around spoolers and previewers that can't manage DSC 3.0 conventions. **The following manage levels determine what will be done to the output:**
0	Does not activate any workarounds (is default).
1	Blocks %%BeginDocumentSetup and %%EndDocumentSetup comments.
2	Blocks lines in files that have %!. This is used for Sun's Pageview previewer.
4	Blocks %%Page, %%Trailer, and End-Prolog comments.
8	Forces output's first line to be %!PS-Adobe-2.0, not %!PS-Adobe-3.0.
-c *amount*	Specifies the number of copies to create of each page.
-g	Generates documents that can be printed on letter and a4 by guessing the page length.
-l	Prints out the document in the landscape format.
-m	Turns on the manual feed.
-w *thickness*	Specifies line thickness in thousandths of an em.
-F *directory*/dev*name*	Specifies the directory and file to search for device and font description files.
-v	Shows version information.
files...	Specifies the PostScript output file or files to create.

File Name:	**Directory:**	**Type:**
`grops`	/usr/bin/	External

grops -g ucgcontract.ps	Prints the document ucgcontract.ps on either a4 or letter paper format.
grops -g -l ucgcontract.ps	Prints the document ucgcontract.ps on either a4 or letter but using the landscape format.

grotty

UNIX Shell: All primary shells (csh, ksh, sh)

Function	Translates GNU `troff` output into a simple printer format. Usually started from `groff`.
Syntax	grotty [options...] *{ files... }*

-F *directory*/dev*name*	Specifies the directory and file to search for device and font description files.
-h	Puts horizontal tabs every eight columns in the output.
-f	Puts form feeds in the output if the page has no output on the last line.
-b	Suppresses the use of overstriking all bold characters.
-u	Suppresses the use of underlining all italic characters.
-B	Allows only overstrike on bold-italic characters.
-U	Allows only underline on bold-italic characters.
-o	Suppresses overstrike on other than bold or underlined characters.
-d	Ignores all \D commands.
-v	Shows version information.
files...	Specifies the file or files for output.

File Name:	`grotty`	**Directory:**	/usr/bin/	**Type:**	External

groupadd

UNIX Shell: All primary shells (csh, ksh, sh)

Function	Creates a new group and adds it to the system.
Syntax	groupadd [options...] *group*

-g *GID*	Assigns a specific GID number to the new group.
-o	Allows the duplication of the GID.
-v	Verbose mode. Shows more information.
group	Specifies the name of the new group.

File Name:	`groupadd`	**Directory:**	/usr/sbin/	**Type:**	External

groupadd ucg	Adds the group ucg to the system.
groupadd -g 101 ucg	Adds the group ucg to the system with a GID of 101.

gunzip

UNIX Shell: All primary shells (csh, ksh, sh)

Function	Extracts files created by `gzip`, `zip`, `compress`, or `pack`.
Syntax	gunzip [options...] *{ names... }*

-a	Is ASCII text mode, converts end-of-lines. Supported only for some non-UNIX systems.
-c	Doesn't change the file and write to STDOUT.
-f	Forces decompression.
-h	Shows help information.
-l	Shows information about compressed file.
-L	Shows information about license and then quits.
-n	Doesn't restore filenames if present (is default).
-N	Restores filename if it exists.
-r	Decompresses recursive.
-S *.ext*	Specifies suffix of the output file.
-q	Uses quiet mode.
-t	Tests the file integrity.
-v	Verbose mode. Shows more information.
-V	Shows version information.
names...	Specifies one or more files to decompress.

File Name:	`gunzip`	**Directory:**	/usr/bin/	**Type:**	External

gunzip ucg.gz	Extracts the file ucg.gz to ucg.
gunzip -l -v ucg.gz ucg.Z	Shows information about ucg.gz and ucg.Z.

gzcat

UNIX Shell:	All primary shells (csh, ksh, sh)
Function	Uncompresses a list of files from the command line or STDIN and writes the uncompressed data to STDOUT.
Syntax	gzcat [options...] *files...*

-f	Forces compression or decompression.
-h	Shows help information.
-L	Shows information about license.
-V	Shows version information.
files...	Specifies the input file(s).

File Name:	`gzcat`	**Directory:**	/usr/bin/	**Type:**	External
Note:	Is sometimes used instead of `zcat` to preserve the original link to `compress`.				

gzcat -L	Shows the gzip license and then quits.

gzexe

UNIX Shell:	All primary shells (csh, ksh, sh)
Function	Compresses executable files into a self-extracting archive.
Syntax	gzexe [option] *{ files... }*

-d	Decompresses the specified file or files.
files...	Specifies the file or files to compress.

File Name:	`gzexe`	**Directory:**	/usr/bin/	**Type:**	External
Note:	Performance will suffer from use of this command — recommended only on small disks.				

gzexe ls	Compresses the command ls. It will expand on the fly when used.
gzexe -d ls	Decompress ls to original size.

gzip

UNIX Shell:	All primary shells (csh, ksh, sh)
Function	Compresses files with Lempel-Ziv-coding.
Syntax	gzip [options...] *{ files... }*

-a	Is ASCII text mode, converts end-of-lines. Supported only for some non-UNIX systems.
-c	Doesn't change file, only writes to STDOUT.
-d	Decompresses the file. This is the same as using the `gunzip` command.
-f	Forces compression.
-h	Shows help information.
-l	Shows information about compressed file.
-L	Shows information about license and quits.
-n	Doesn't save name and timestamp.
-N	Saves name and timestamp.
-q	Suppresses all warnings.
-r	Compresses all files in subdirectories, recursively.
-S *.ext*	Specifies the suffix.
-t	Tests integrity of the file.
-v	Verbose mode. Shows more information.
-V	Shows version information.
-*number*	Specifies the compression rate 1 is fast but least compressed, and 9 is slow but most compressed.
--fast	Specifies to use the fast but least compression rate. The same as -1.
--best	Specifies to use the slow but most compression rate. The same as -9.
files...	Specifies one or more files to compress.

File Name:	`gzip`	**Directory:**	/usr/bin/	**Type:**	External

gzip ucg.filename	Compresses the file ucg.filename.
gzip -9 -r ucgdir	Compresses all files in the directory ucgdir with maximum compression.

h2ph

UNIX Shell:	Perl script
Function	Converts the specified C header files into Perl header file format.
Syntax	h2ph [options...] *{ files... }*

-d *path*	Specifies a directory to save the converted filename to.
	The -r and -a options can't be combined.
-r	Runs on all files in all subdirectories.
-a	Runs on the filenames and all .h files that they include.
-l	Replicates all links into the specified directory.
-h	Creates hints into the Perl file to make it easier to troubleshoot the script.
-D	Takes code from the .h file and adds that as comments to the .ph file. Used for debug.
-Q	The quiet mode. Doesn't show names of converted files.
files...	Specifies the header files to convert.

File Name:	`h2ph`	**Directory:**	/usr/bin/	**Type:**	Script

h2xs

UNIX Shell:	Perl script
Function	Creates Perl extensions from C header files.
Syntax	h2xs [options...] *{ files... directories... }*

-A	Skips all autoloaded values and disables the autoloader in the .pm file.
-C	Doesn't create the changes file, and adds a HISTORY section to POD template.
-F	Specifies flags for C preprocessor to find function parameters in header. (You need to use the -x option with -F.)
-M *expression*	Specifies macros or functions to process.
-O	Overwrites directories if they already exist.
-P	Skips the stub POD section.
-X	Skips the XS portion. Used to create templates for non-XS-based modules.
-a	Creates accessory method for each method of struts and unions.
-c	Skips constants in the `.as` file and matching autoloads in the .pm file.
-d	Shows debug information.
-f	Creates an extension for a header.
-h	Shows help information.
-k	Skips the const attribute in the XS code.
-m	Creates a perl variable for each corresponding variable in the header file.
-n *module*	Specifies name to use for extension.
-o *expression*	Specifies `opaque` data. (When you use -o you have to use the -x option.)
-p *prefix*	Specifies prefix to remove from the Perl function names.
-s *sub1,sub2*	Creates subroutines for the specified macros.
-v *version*	Specifies the version number for this extension.
-x	Creates XSUBs from function declarations in the header file.
files...	Specifies header file or files.
directories...	Specifies the extra directories that have C header files.

File Name:	`h2xs`	**Directory:**	/usr/bin/	**Type:**	Script

help

UNIX Shell:	All primary shells (csh, ksh, sh)
Function	Assists the user and system administrators in the use of OpenBSD.
Syntax	help *{ command }*

command	Shows help information for the specified command name.

File Name:	`help`	**Directory:**	/usr/bin/	**Type:**	External

Note: This is interchangeable with the command `man`.

help	Shows a general help for new users.
help ls	Shops help information for ls.
help find	Shows help information for find.

hexdump

hexdump	UNIX Shell:	All primary shells (csh, ksh, sh)
Function	Shows files in ASCII, hexadecimal, decimal, or octal format on STDOUT.	
Syntax	hexdump [options...] *{ files... }*	

-b	Shows the output as 1-byte octal format.
-c	Shows the output as 1-byte character format.
-d	Shows the output as 2-byte decimal format.
-o	Shows the output as 2-byte octal format.
-v	Shows every line of output. Otherwise, equal lines are only shown with a single *.
-x	Shows the output as 2-byte hexadecimal format.
-e *string*	Specifies a format string to use.
-f *file*	Specifies a file containing format information.
-n *count*	Shows only the specified length of input.
-s *count*	Skips the specified number of bytes from the beginning of the input.
files...	Specifies one or more files to show. If not specified, STDIN is read.

File Name:	hexdump	**Directory:**	/usr/bin/	**Type:**	External

host

host	UNIX Shell:	All primary shells (csh, ksh, sh)
Function	Looks up hostnames or IP addresses using name servers.	
Syntax	host [options...] *name { server } { zone }* host [options...] option *names...* host [options...] option *zone*	

-w	Waits forever for a response.
-v	Verbose mode. Shows more information.
-r	Returns only data from its own database. Doesn't ask another server.
-d	Shows debug information. Shows details about network transactions.
-t *querytype*	Specifies the query type.
-a	This is a synonym for -v -t any.
-l *zone*	Shows a complete domain from the specified zone.
-H	Shows the count of unique hostnames encountered within the zone.
-G	Implies -H, but shows the names of gateway hosts.
-E	Implies -H, but shows the names of extra zone hosts.
-D	Implies -H, but shows the names of duplicate hosts.
-C	Initiates the SOA records for the used zone to be compared as found at each server.
-A	Specifies that it is to be in a special address mode.
-L *level*	Specifies the level to recursively create zone listings.
-S	Shows statistics about the types of resource records found during zone listings.
-p	Contacts only the primary name server for zone transfers during zone listings.
-P *server*	Prioritizes the specified server residing in domains given in a comma-separated list.
-N *skipzone*	Stops zone transfers for the zones specified in a comma-separated list.
-f *logfile*	Saves the resource record output to the specified file and shows it also on STDOUT.
-F *logfile*	Same as -f, but all STDOUT goes to the log file.
-I *chars*	Specifies a character to avoid warning messages about illegal domain names.
-i	Creates a query for the reverse mapping inaddr.arpa domain.
-n	Creates a query for the reverse mapping nsap.int domain.
-q	Specifies to be in quit mode.
-T	Shows the time-to-leave values.
-Z	Shows the chosen resource record output in full zone file format.
-c *class*	Sets the class to look in when searching non-Internet data.
-e	Excludes information about names not residing in the specified zone during listings.
-m	Same as -t MAILB.
-o	Stops the resource record output to STDOUT.
-r	Turns off the name server recursion in the request.
-R	Specifies that normally query name should be fully qualified.
-s *seconds*	Specifies the timeout value for a new name server.
-u	Uses virtual circuits (TCP) instead of datagrams (UDP) when doing name server queries.

continued

-x	Allows multiple arguments on the command line.		
-X *server*	Specifies an explicit server to use. Implies the -x option.		
name	Specifies the hostname or IP address to search for.		
server	Specifies a server to query.		
zone	Specifies a domain zone name to query.		
File Name: `host`	**Directory:** /usr/sbin/	**Type:** External	
Tip:	host is better than nslookup but dig is better than host.		
host -l ucgbook.com	Shows all hosts under ucgbook.com.		
host -a ucgbook.com	Shows any available info about the domain.		

hpftodit

UNIX Shell: All primary shells (csh, ksh, sh)

Function	Uses an HP tagged font metric file and creates a font file for use with `groff -Tlj4`.
Syntax	hpftodit [options...] *HPfile fontfile outfile*

-s	Specifies that a font is special and adds it to the font file.
-v	Shows version information.
-in	Generates an italic correction for each character with the specified number of units.
HPfile	Specifies the HP tagged font metric file to use as input.
fontfile	Specifies a file containing the `groff` names for characters in the font.
outfile	Specifies the name of the file containing the output `groff` font file.
File Name: `hpftodit`	**Directory:** /usr/bin/ **Type:** External

htdigest

UNIX Shell: All primary shells (csh, ksh, sh)

Function	Manages HTTP user authentication files.
Syntax	htdigest [-c] *file realm user*

-c	Is used to create a password file, even if it exists.
file	Specifies the file that holds password, realm, and username information.
realm	Specifies the realm where the user belongs.
user	Specifies the username that you want to manage.
File Name: `htdigest`	**Directory:** /usr/bin/ **Type:** External
htdigest -c pass Home Scarloc	Creates pass and adds the user Scarloc to the realm Home.

htpasswd

UNIX Shell: All primary shells (csh, ksh, sh)

Function	Manages HTTP user authentication.
Syntax	htpasswd [options...] *passwordfile user { password }*

-b	Uses the command line to get the password.
-c	Creates a password file even if it exists.
	The following four encryption methods can't be combined:
-m	Uses the MD5 algorithm for passwords.
-d	Uses crypt for passwords.
-s	Uses the SHA encryption for passwords.
-p	Uses plain text passwords.
passwordfile	Specifies the file that holds password username information.
user	Specifies the username to work with.
password	Specifies the password to encrypt with -m, d, s, or p. Only used with the -b option.
File Name: `htpasswd`	**Directory:** /usr/bin/ **Type:** External

httpd

UNIX Shell: All primary shells (csh, ksh, sh)

Function	The Apache Internet Web server.
Syntax	httpd [options...]

-X	Runs the server in single-process mode.
-R *libexecdir*	Specifies where the server will put dynamic shared object files.
-d *serverroot*	Is used to set the root directory for the server.

continued

-f *config*		Specifies a config file with startup commands.			
-C *bconfig*		Runs the specified configuration before reading the config file.			
-c *aconfig*		Runs the specified configuration after reading the config file.			
-D *params*		Is used to specify parameters to be used with IfDefine tags.			
		The following options can't be combined with those above:			
-h		Shows help information.			
-l		Shows a list of compiled modules.			
-L		Shows a list of directives and attributes.			
-v		Shows version information.			
-V		Shows version and build information.			
-S		Shows the settings that are in the config file.			
File Name:	`httpd`	**Directory:**	/usr/sbin/	**Type:**	External

iceauth

UNIX Shell: All primary shells (csh, ksh, sh)

Function	Modifies or shows authorization information to connect with ICE.
Syntax	iceauth [-f *file*] [options...] *{ commands... }*

-f *file*		Specifies the authority file.			
-v		Enables extra messages.			
-q		Disables extra messages.			
-i		Ignores locks on authority file.			
-b		Breaks locks on authority file.			
commands...		**Here are the commands to use in the ICE program:**			
add		Adds an entry.			
exit		Saves changes and exits program.			
extract		Extracts entries into file.			
help		Shows help information.			
info		Shows information about entries.			
list		Shows entries.			
merge		Merges entries from files.			
quit		Aborts changes and exits program.			
remove		Erases entries.			
source		Reads commands from file.			
?		Shows help information.			
File Name:	`iceauth`	**Directory:**	/usr/X11R6/bin/	**Type:**	External
iceauth info			Shows information about auth entries.		

ident

UNIX Shell: All primary shells (csh, ksh, sh)

Function	Searches for RCS keyword strings in files.
Syntax	ident [options...] *files...*

-q		Suppresses warning messages.			
-V		Shows version information.			
files...		Specifies the files to search in.			
File Name:	`ident`	**Directory:**	/usr/bin/	**Type:**	External
Note:	The strings are normally inserted from the RCS command `co`, but can also be inserted manually.				

identd

UNIX Shell: All primary shells (csh, ksh, sh)

Function	Searches TCP/IP connections and shows the usernames that own the connections.
Syntax	identd [options...]

	The following three options are not to be combined:
-i	Runs as if started from `inetd` with the nowait option.
-w	Runs as if started from `inetd` with the wait option.
-b	Runs as a stand alone daemon.

continued

	All the following options can be combined with any mode of operation.
-h	Shows the username as an opaque token in the log for later examination.
-t *time*	Specifies the timeout in seconds when running in wait mode (default is none).
-u *userID*	Specifies the user to switch to after connection, if run as a standalone daemon.
-g *groupID*	Specifies the group to switch to after connection, if run as a standalone daemon.
-p *port*	Specifies an alternative service or port, if run as a standalone daemon.
-a *address*	Specifies an IP address in dotted quad format, if run as a standalone daemon.
-V	Shows version information.
-l	Logs all information in with the `syslogd` command.
-v	Logs all information to `syslog` if -l is set.
-o	Hides the real operating system type and shows OTHER instead.
-e	Returns the message UNKNOWN ERROR instead of NO-USER and INVALID-PORT.
-c *characters*	Specifies an optional character set to use in replies.
-n	Returns the user as ID number instead of name.
-N	Checks for the file .noident and returns HIDDEN-USER if it is accessible.
-m	Allows the process of multiple requests per session.
-d	Shows debug information.
File Name: `identd`	**Directory:** /usr/libexec **Type:** External

imake

UNIX Shell: All primary shells (csh, ksh, sh)

Function	Creates Makefiles from a template, a set of cpp macro functions, and a per-directory file that is called Imakefile.
Syntax	imake [options...]

-D*define*	Specifies directory configurations.
-I*dir*	Specifies directory to the imake template and configuration.
-U*define*	Specifies variables to unset when debugging imake configuration files.
-T*template*	Specifies the name of the master template file.
-f *filename*	Specifies the per-directory input file.
-C *filename*	Specifies the name of the .c file that is created — usually Imakefile.c.
-s *filename*	Specifies the name of the make description file to create.
-e	Runs the created Makefile.
-v	Shows the cpp command line that is used to create Makefile.
File Name: `imake`	**Directory:** /usr/X11R6/bin/ **Type:** External
imake -v	Shows the cpp command line.

indent

UNIX Shell: All primary shells (csh, ksh, sh)

Function	Inserts or erases whitespace in C code to make it easier to read. Converts from one C style to another.
Syntax	indent [options...] *{ inputfile } { outputfile }*

-bad	Inserts blank lines after declarations.
-bap	Inserts blank lines after procedure bodies.
-bbb	Inserts blank lines after block comments.
-bc	Causes `indent` to insert a new line after commas in declarations (is default).
-bl	Moves the statement braces to the line after the statement.
-br	Moves the statement braces to the same line as the statement (is default).
-c*count*	Moves comments to the column equal to count (default is 33).
-cd*count*	Moves comments that are to the right of declarations to the column equal to count.
-cdb	Is used to put comment delimiters on blank lines (is the default).
-ce	Puts `else` directly after a preceding end brace (is default).
-ci*count*	Causes a continuation indent of *count* spaces (default is same as -i).
-cli*count*	Indents case labels count spaces (default is 0).
-d*count*	Specifies the indentation for comments not to the right of code (default is 1).
-di*count*	Moves variables to the column equal to count (default is 16).
-dj	Indents declarations more than other code.
-ei	Indents an `if` following an `else` the same as the last if before.
-fc1	Causes `indent` to format all comments found in the first column (is default).
-i*count*	Specifies the level of indentation to count spaces (default is 8).

continued

-ip	Indents parameter declarations (is default).
-l*count*	Specifies the maximum length of lines to count (default is 75).
-lp	Lines up code exceeding one row following a parentheses with continuation lines.
-npro	Stops `indent` from reading .indent.pro files containing configuration profiles.
-pcs	Inserts a space between a function call and the parentheses following it.
-psl	Puts procedure type on the line before the procedure name (is default).
-sc	Puts the * character on the left side of comments.
-sob	Erases all optional blank lines found in the input code.
-st	Takes input from STDIN and outputs on STDOUT.
-T*name*	Specifies type names for the type keyword list. Is repeatable.
-troff	Formats the source for usage by `troff` and by default outputs to STDOUT.
-v	Verbose mode. Shows more information.
	The following `-n` options can't be combined with their counterparts:
-nbad	Disables insertions of blank lines after declarations (is default).
-nbap	Disables insertions of blank lines after procedure bodies (is default).
-nbbb	Disables insertions of blank lines after block comments (is default)
-nbc	Disables insertions of new lines after commas in declarations.
-ncdb	Disables putting comment delimiters on blank lines.
-nce	Disables putting else directly after a preceding end brace.
-nei	Causes an if after an else not to be indented as the if before.
-ndj	Indents declarations as much as other code (is default).
-nfc1	Disables formatting comments in the first column.
-nlp	Disables lining up code following a parentheses.
-npcs	Disables inserting a space between a function call and the parentheses following it.
-npsl	Puts procedure type on the same line as the procedure name.
-nsc	Disables putting the * character to the left of comments.
-nsob	Disables erasing optional blank lines found in the input code (is default).
-nv	Disables verbose mode (is default).
inputfile	Specifies file to act on.
outputfile	Specifies filename on the result.

File Name:	`indent`	**Directory:**	/usr/bin/	**Type:**	External

indent HelloWorld.c	Indents HelloWorld.c according to defaults.
indent HelloWorld.c -bad -bbb	Indents HelloWorld.c with blank lines after declarations and procedure bodies.
indent Helloworld.c -i12 -npro	Indents Helloworld.c by 12 spaces instead of 8 and skips profile reading.

inetd

UNIX Shell: All primary shells (csh, ksh, sh)

Function	Manages startup of all services listed in the file `/etc/inetd.conf`.
Syntax	inetd [options...] *{ file }*

-d	Shows debug information.
-R *times*	Limits the number of times one service can be called during one minute.
file	Specifies what configuration file to use (default is `/etc/inetd.conf`).

File Name:	`inetd`	**Directory:**	/usr/sbin/	**Type:**	External

inetd	Starts looking for connections on the services specified in the default configuration file.
inetd -R 10	Starts and limits the number of times a service can be accessed during one minute to the specified number of times.

info

UNIX Shell: All primary shells (csh, ksh, sh)

Function	Shows hypertext info nodes. Info nodes fill the same function as man pages.
Syntax	info [options...] *{ file } { item }*

--directory *directory*	Adds the specified directory to the `infopath`.
--apropos=*subject*	Looks up subject in all indices of all manuals.
--index-search=*string*	Goes to node pointed to by string.
--vi-keys	Use vi-like and less-like key bindings.
--dribble *file*	Remembers the user's keystrokes in the specified file.
--file *file*	Specifies an info file to show directly.
--node *name*	Specifies nodes in the first visited info file.

--output *file* --restore *file* --subnodes --help --version *file* *item*	Saves the selected nodes in the specified file. Reads initial keystrokes from the specified file. Shows the menu items recursively. Shows help information. Shows version information. Specifies the info file to show. Specifies an item, or node, in the info file to show.

File Name:	`info`	**Directory:**	/usr/bin/	**Type:**	External

info emacs	Shows the `emacs` node from the top level.
info emacs buffers	Shows the node `buffers` in the `emacs` manual.
info -f ./foo.info	Shows the file /foo.info.

infotocap

UNIX Shell: All primary shells (csh, ksh, sh)

Function	Reads the specified file and converts found `terminfo` descriptions to `termcap` descriptions.
Syntax	infotocap [options...] *files...*

-v *level* -V -1 -w *width* *files...*	Verbose mode. Shows more information. Level specifies the verbose level to use. Shows version information. Does one field per line. Changes the output to specified width of characters. Specifies the terminfo file to convert.

File Name:	`infotocap`	**Directory:**	/usr/bin/	**Type:**	External
Note:	This is actually a symbolic link to `tic`. Please see `tic` for more available options.				

infotocap infofile	Converts the info file to termcap format.

installboot

UNIX Shell: All primary shells (csh, ksh, sh)

Function	Installs a first stage boot program to the boot area of an ffs disk partition.
Syntax	installboot [options...] *boot biosboot disk*

-n -v -s *value* -h *value* *boot* *biosboot* *disk*	Does everything, but writes nothing to the disk. Verbose mode. Shows more information. Specifies the number of sectors per track, works if sector translation is activated. Specifies the number of tracks per cylinder, works if sector translation is activated. Specifies where the second-stage boot program is installed as a full pathname. Specifies the name of the first-stage prototype file, usually /usr/mdec/biosboot. Specifies the disk on which to install the new boot program.

File Name:	`installboot`	**Directory:**	/usr/mdec	**Type:**	External

install-info

UNIX Shell: All primary shells (csh, ksh, sh)

Function	Erases or installs specified entries in the info files.
Syntax	install-info [options...] *{ file } { directory }*

--delete --dir-file=*file* --entry=*text* --help --info-file=*file* --info-dir=*file* --item=*text* --quiet --remove --section=*section* --version	Erases the specified entries, doesn't install anything. Specifies the name of the info directory file. Same as the argument directory. Adds the specified text as an info file. Shows help information. Specifies the name of the info file. Same as the argument file. Same as --dir-file. Same as --entry. Suppresses all warnings. Same as --delete. Puts the info file in the specified section of the info files. Shows version information.

continued

file	Specifies the info file to install or erase.
directory	Specifies the info directory file in which the entries are to be installed or erased.
File Name: `install-info`	**Directory:** /usr/bin/ **Type:** External

ipf

UNIX Shell: All primary shells (csh, ksh, sh)

Function	Manages IP firewall and filter rules in the kernel.
Syntax	ipf [options...]

-A	Changes will be made to the active ruleset.
-P	Adds rules as temporary entries in the authorization rule table.
-I	Changes will be made to the inactive ruleset.
-D	Disables the filter.
-E	Enables the filter.
-F	Flushes entries. Below are the two valid flushing arguments:
list	Flushes filter list.
table	Flushes entries from the state tables.
-d	Shows debug information.
-f *filename*	Specifies a file that contains rules that should be read.
-l *category*	Logs the category specified.
-n	Changes will not be made.
-o	Inserts or removes rules in the output list instead of the input list.
-s	Changes the active and inactive set of rules.
-r	Ignores matching filter rules instead of adding them to the in-kernel lists.
-V	Shows version information.
-v	Verbose mode. Shows more information.
-y	Modifies the filter lists to use the current network interface IP address.
-z	Shows each rule and its statistics. The rule counters will then be set to 0 again.
-Z	Resets statistics for all the kernel filters.
File Name: `ipf`	**Directory:** /sbin **Type:** External
Note:	Makes sure ipfilter is enabled in `/etc/rc.conf`, IP forwarding is enabled in `/etc/sysctl.conf`, and uses a correct kernel.
ipf -I -Fa -f /ucg_examples/ipf.rules	Flushes rules and installs the ones found in the specified rules file.
ipf -s	Changes the inactive rules with the active rules.

ipfstat

UNIX Shell: All primary shells (csh, ksh, sh)

Function	Shows packet filter statistics and filter lists.
Syntax	ipfstat [options...]

-a	Shows the accounting filter list and bytes counted against each rule. Used with -i, -h.
-A	Shows packet authentication statistics.
-d *device*	Specifies to use device instead of `/dev/ipl` for interfacing with the kernel.
-f	Shows fragment and held state information.
-h	Shows the number of times there is a hit for each rule. Used with -i, -o.
-i	Shows the filter list of rules used for the input side of the kernel IP processing.
-o	Shows the filter list of rules used for the output side of the kernel IP processing.
-I	Switches between retrieving inactive and active filter list details. Used with -h.
-n	Specifies to show the rule number for each rule.
-M *device*	Specifies the device to use for extraction of values associated with the name list.
-s	Shows packet/flow and held state information.
-v	Verbose mode. Shows more information.
File Name: `ipfstat`	**Directory:** /sbin **Type:** External

ipftest

ipftest	UNIX Shell:	All primary shells (csh, ksh, sh)

Function	Sends test packets through an ipf filter rule set found in a specified ruleset file.
Syntax	ipftest [options...] -r *file* [-i *file*]

-v	Verbose mode. Shows more information about packets that pass and those that fail.
-d	Shows debug information.
-b	Shows the result of each packet. Results can be pass, block, or no match.
-I *interface*	Specifies the interface name to bind a packet to. Used with -P, -S, and -E.
-P	Reads the input file as a binary file created by libpcap.
-S	Reads the input file as a snoop file.
-T	Reads the input file as a tcpdump output file.
-H	Reads the input file as hex digits.
-X	Reads the input file as text descriptions of packets.
-E	Reads the input file as an etherfind output file.
-i *file*	Reads the input from the specified file (default is STDIN).
-r *file*	Uses the filter rules found in the specified file.

File Name:	`ipftest`	**Directory:**	/usr/sbin/	**Type:**	External

Tip:	Use this to test your filter rules instead of trying them on real packets.

ipftest -v -H -i packets -r /etc/ipf.rules	Reads the specified hex digits contained in the file specified and matches them against `/etc/ipf.rules` and shows what happens to the packets.

ipmon

ipmon	UNIX Shell:	All primary shells (csh, ksh, sh)

Function	Shows the logged packets going through the IP packet log device.
Syntax	ipmon [options...] { *file* }

-a	Shows all log messages from the device log files.
-f *device*	Uses the specified device or file to use as the log device (default is `/dev/ipl`).
-D	Goes into background.
-F	Resets the packet log buffer and shows how many bytes have gone through.
-N *file*	Uses the specified log file to read NAT log messages from.
-n	Shows hostnames instead of IP addresses and service names instead of ports.
-o	Reads messages from the log files represented by a letter that can be combined.
S	Shows state log messages.
N	Shows NAT log messages.
I	Shows normal IP log messages.
-O	Does the same thing as -o, except that it will not show the log files specified.
S	Doesn't show state log messages.
N	Doesn't show NAT log messages.
I	Doesn't show normal IP log messages.
-s	Writes the packet information to `syslog`.
-S	Handles the log file like a state log record.
device	Specifies which device will be opened to read state logs from.
-v	Shows the TCP window and the ACK and sequence fields.
-x	Shows packet data in hex.
-X	Shows the log header record data in hex.
file	Outputs all messages to a file (default is STDOUT).

File Name:	`ipmon`	**Directory:**	/usr/sbin/	**Type:**	External

ipmon -o N	Shows the logged packets going through NAT.
ipmon -a -D network.log	Writes all log messages to network.log while being in the background.
ipmon -o S -s	Writes state messages to `syslog`.

ipnat

UNIX Shell:	**All primary shells (csh, ksh, sh)**
Function	Is used to configure IP network address translation rules. NAT is used to hide private networks.
Syntax	ipnat [options...]

-C	Removes all NAT rules.
-F	Removes the mappings in the NAT table.
-l	Shows the current rules and mappings.
-n	Doesn't change the NAT table.
-r	Removes the rules specified in the file.
-s	Shows statistics.
-v	Verbose mode. Shows more information.
-f *file*	Reads the NAT rules from the specified file (default is `/etc/ipnat.rules`).

File Name:	`ipnat`	**Directory:**	/sbin/	**Type:**	External

Tip:	Use network address translation to let computers on the LAN access the internet.
ipnat -l	Lists the current NAT rules.
ipnat -f /etc/ipnat.rules	Adds the NAT rules found in the specified file.

ipresend

UNIX Shell:	**All primary shells (csh, ksh, sh)**
Function	Sends out captured packets to the network.
Syntax	ipresend [options...]

-E	Reads the input file as an etherfind output file.
-H	Reads the input file as hex digits.
-P	Reads the input file as a binary file created by libpcap.
-R	Sends the packets in RAW format.
-S	Reads the input file as a snoop file.
-T	Reads the input file as a tcpdump output file.
-X	Reads the input file as text descriptions of packets.
-d *interface*	Specifies the interface name to bind a packet to. Used with -P, -S, and -E.
-g *gateway*	Uses the specified gateway to send the packets through.
-m *mtu*	Fakes the MTU to send.
-r *file*	Reads input from the specified file (default is STDIN).

File Name:	`ipresend`	**Directory:**	/usr/sbin/	**Type:**	External

ipsecadm

UNIX Shell:	**All primary shells (csh, ksh, sh)**
Function	Configures the security associations (SA) in the kernel to use IPSec.
Syntax	ipsecadm *{ command } modifiers...*

	The following are available commands:
new esp	Sets the new esp as transform when the SA is set up (is the default).
old esp	Sets the old esp as transform when the SA is set up.
new ah	Sets the new ah as transform when the SA is set up.
old ah	Sets the old ah as transform when the SA is set up.
ip4	Specifies use of the IP-in-IP encapsulation protocol.
delspi	Deletes the SA.
group	Creates a group of two SAs.
flow	Creates a flow to see which SA routes which packet.
bind	Specifies an association between an incoming and an outgoing SA.
flush	Removes SAs with its routes and flows.
	The following are modifiers:
-src	Specifies the source IP address.
-dst	Specifies the destination address for the SA.
-proxy	Checks this IP address against the inner IP address when tunneling into a firewall.
-spi	Sets the security parameter index.
-tunnel	Has been stripped down to be similar to the -forcetunnel option.
-newpadding	This option is no longer supported.

continued

-forcetunnel	Forces IP-inside-IP encapsulation before ESP or AH processing is done on outpackets
-enc	Specifies an encryption algorithm to use with the SA.
des	Encrypts using DES. This is an older type of encryption that should be avoided.
3des	Encrypts using 3DES. Is safer than DES due to its use of larger encryption keys.
blf	Encrypts using Blowfish. Is available only with the newer esp.
cast	Encrypts using CAST. Is available only with the newer esp.
skipjack	Encrypts using SKIPJACK. Is faster than 3DES and was developed by the NSA.
-auth	Specifies the SA authentication algorithm that is used.
md5	Works with both older and newer ah and the newer esp.
sha1	Works with both older and newer ah and the newer esp.
rmd160	Works with both the newer ah and the newer esp.
-key *key*	Specifies the secret key for encryption. Hexadecimal digits only.
-authkey	Specifies the secret key material for the newer esp mode if needed.
-iv	Has been stripped down to be similar to the -halfiv option.
-halfiv	Permits use of a 4-byte IV, which means that it may only be used with old esp.
-proto	Specifies the security protocol needed by flow, delspi, group, or bind.
50	Specifies the IPPROTO_ESP security protocol.
51	Specifies the IPPROTO_AH security protocol.
4	Specifies the IPPROTO_IP security protocol.
symbolicname	Specifies the esp, ah, or ip4 security protocols.
-chain	Deletes the entire SPI chain or the specified SPI.
-dst2	Specifies the second IP destination used by group.
-spi2	Specifies the second SPI used by group.
-proto2	Specifies the second security protocol that is used by group.
50	Specifies the IPPROTO_ESP security protocol.
4	Specifies the IPPROTO_IP security protocol.
symbolicname	Specifies the esp, ah, or ip4 security protocols.
-addr	Specifies source address, network mask, and destination addresses for security packets.
-transport	Specifies the protocol number that is used for packet security matching.
-sport	Specifies the source port that must match the packets. Use a number or service name.
-dport	Creates a flow that matches local packets. Same as 0.0.0.0/255.255.255.255.
-delete	Deletes an existing flow instead of creating one.
-ah	Supports only flush SAs of the type ah.
-esp	Supports only flush SAs of the type esp.
-oldah	Supports only flush SAs of the type oldah.
-oldesp	Supports only flush SAs of the type oldesp.
-ip4	Supports only flush SAs of the type ip4.

File Name:	`ipsecadm`	**Directory:**	/sbin/	**Type:**	External

ipsecadm flush -esp	Removes esp SAs with its routes and flows.
ipsecadm new ah -forcetunnel	Forces IP-inside-IP encapsulation before ESP or AH processing is done on out packets.
ipsecadm ip4 -spi	Sets the security parameter index for IP-in-IP encapsulation protocol.

ipsend

UNIX Shell: All primary shells (csh, ksh, sh)

Function	Sends IP packets to a destination host.
Syntax	ipsend [options...] *{ destination } { flags... }*

-d	Shows debug information.
-v	Verbose mode. Shows more information.
-f *offset*	Specifies any decimal or hexadecimal value in the IP offset field.
-g *gateway*	Specifies the name of the host to use as gateway between networks.
-i *interface*	Sets the name of the interface to use on the network.
-m *MTU*	Specifies the maximum transmitting unit (MTU) manually. The total data packet length.
-o *option*	Specifies additional IP header options.
-s *source*	Specifies an IP address or a hostname to include in the packet as a source address.
-t *NR*	Sets the destination port number.
-w *size*	Specifies the size of the TCP packet window.

continued

-I	Uses the ICMP protocol.		
-T	Uses the TCP protocol.		
-U	Uses the UDP protocol.		
-P *protocol*	Specifies a name of a protocol to use that exists in the `/etc/protocols` file.		
destination	Specifies the destination host.		
flags...	Specifies TCP flags to use.		
File Name: `ipsend`	**Directory:** /usr/sbin/	**Type:**	External

iptest

UNIX Shell: All primary shells (csh, ksh, sh)

Function	Tests the IP's functions by generating packets and sending them to specified destinations.
Syntax	iptest [options...] *destination*

-1	Tests IP headers. Point tests that can be set with the -p option are as follows:
1	ip_hl < ip_len.
2	ip_hl > ip_len.
3	ip_v < 4.
4	ip_v > 4.
5	ip_len < packetsize, long packets.
6	ip_len > packetsize, short packets.
7	Zero-length fragments.
8	Packet > 64K after reassembly.
9	IP offset with MSB set.
10	TTL variations.
-2	Tests IP options. Point tests are as follows:
1	Option length > packet length.
2	Option length = 0.
-3	Tests the ICMP. Point tests are as follows:
1	ICMP types 0-31 and 255.
2	Type 3 and codes 0-31.
3	Type 4 and codes 0, 127, 128, 255.
4	Type 5 and codes 0, 127, 128, 255.
5	Types 8-10, 13-18 with codes 0, 127, 128, and 255.
6	Type 12 and codes 0, 127, 128, 129, 255.
7	Type 3 and codes 9, 10, 13, 14; and 17, 18 — shortened packets.
-4	Tests the UDP. Point tests are as follows:
1	UDP length > packetsize.
2	UDP length < packetsize.
3	Sport = 0, 1, 32767, 32768, 65535.
4	Dport = 0, 1, 32767, 32768, 65535.
5	sizeof(struct ip) <= MTU <= sizeof(struct udphdr) + sizeof(struct ip).
-5	Tests the TCP. Point tests are as follows:
1	TCP flags variations, all combinations.
2	Seq = 0, 0x7fffffff, 0x8000000, 0xa0000000, 0xffffffff.
3	Ack = 0, 0x7fffffff, 0x8000000, 0xa0000000, 0xffffffff.
4	SYN packet with window of 0, 32768, 65535.
5	Sets urgent pointer to 1, 0x7fff, 0x8000, 0xffff.
6	Data offset.
7	Sport = 0, 1, 32767, 32768, 65535.
8	Dport = 0, 1, 32767, 32768, 65535.
-6	Tests overlapping fragments by trying to exhaust the network holding packets buffers.
-7	Tests the IP with random packets.
-d *device*	Specifies the interface device (default is lan0). (Lan0 doesn't normally exist in OpenBSD, and so it should be specified.)
-g *gateway*	Specifies the gateway to route packets through.
-m *mtu*	Specifies MTU to use allowing network interfaces with a small MTU to be simulated.
-p *pointtest*	Specifies the point test to run on specified group.

continued

-s *src*	Specifies the IP packets source address.		
destination	Specifies where to send packets.		
File Name: `iptest`	**Directory:** /usr/sbin/	**Type:** External	

isakmpd

UNIX Shell: All primary shells (csh, ksh, sh)

Function	The IKE key management daemon that establishes security associations for authenticated/encrypted network traffic.
Syntax	isakmpd [options...]

-c *file*	Specifies a configuration file to use instead of `/etc/isakmpd/isakmpd.conf`.
-d	Runs the daemon in the foreground and logs to STDERR.
-D *class=level*	Specifies the debug class and the debug level to limit debug printouts.
-f *fifo*	Specifies the named pipe (FIFO) that the daemon will listen to for requests.
-	Specifies that STDIN will be used for input.
-n	Blocks the kernel from negotiating.
-p *port*	Specifies the port that `isakmpd` will be bound to.
-P *port*	Specifies the port that `isakmpd` will bind its local end to.
-r *seed*	Specifies a number sequence for internal use. Used for regression tests.
-R *file*	Specifies a file to save internal state reports instead of the default.
File Name: `isakmpd`	**Directory:** /sbin/ **Type:** External

ispcvt

UNIX Shell: All primary shells (csh, ksh, sh)

Function	Verifies whether the current video driver installed in the kernel is a PCVT driver.
Syntax	ispcvt [options...]

-c	Shows all options for the PCVT driver used when the kernel was compiled.
-d *device*	Specifies the device to check.
-v	Verbose mode. Shows more information.
File Name: `ispcvt`	**Directory:** /usr/sbin/ **Type:** External

jot

UNIX Shell: All primary shells (csh, ksh, sh)

Function	Creates a sequence of numbers, characters or words, according to the operands specified in the parameters.
Syntax	jot [options...] *{ repetitions } { start } { end } { step }*

-c	Shows the numbers as characters.
-n	Doesn't do a new line on the last generated value.
-r	Generates random data instead of sequels. Generates values from 1 to 100.
-b *word*	Shows the specified word specified number of times.
-w *word*	Handles the word like printf format and uses the generated values on it.
-s *string*	Specifies the string to insert between the values (default is new line).
-p *decimals*	Sets the number of decimals to show the values on (default is 0).
repetitions	Specifies how many values to generate.
start	Specifies the starting value or character.
end	Specifies the end value or character.
step	Specifies the change of each value. Can be decimal and negative.
File Name: `jot`	**Directory:** /usr/bin/ **Type:** External

jot 10 0 0 -1	Does a countdown from 9 to 0.
jot -s ", " 100	Creates values from 1 to 100 with a comma between them, instead of a new line.
jot -w "%i green bottles hanging on the wall..." 100 100 1 -1	Creates the text for a very famous song.

kadmin

UNIX Shell: All primary shells (csh, ksh, sh)

Function	The interactive Kerberos database administration program.
Syntax	kadmin [options..]

-u *user*	Specifies the user to act as when using the program (default is current user).
-p *principal*	Specifies the default principal.

continued

-T timeout	Sets timeout. -m equals -T 0.		
-x	Uses existing tickets.		
-r *realm*	Specifies the default realm for transactions (default is the local realm).		
-m	Doesn't allow any other users to be logged in as the administrator while on it.		
File Name: `kadmin`	**Directory:** /usr/sbin/	**Type:**	External
Note:	This command can be used over the network, but the master database computer must then have kadmind running.		

kadmind

UNIX Shell: All primary shells (csh, ksh, sh)

Function	The daemon for the Kerberos network database administrator program.
Syntax	kadmind [options...]

-n	Takes the master key from the master key cache file, instead of asking for it.		
-h	Shows status on the permissible control arguments.		
-i *address*	Listens only on that address.		
-m	Prompts the user to enter master key.		
-r *realm*	Pretends that the specified realm is the local realm, instead of the real realm.		
-f *file*	Specifies the file to use on log information.		
-d *name*	Specifies the database name to use.		
-a *acldirectory*	Searches for access control lists in the specified directory.		
File Name: `kadmind`	**Directory:** /usr/libexec/	**Type:**	External

kauth

UNIX Shell: All primary shells (csh, ksh, sh)

Function	A login utility for the Kerberos database program.
Syntax	kauth [options...] *{ commands... }*

-n *name*	Specifies the principal to get tickets for.		
-r *user*	Specifies the remote host user that should own the ticket file.		
-t *host ticket file*	Specifies the ticket file on the remote host.		
-h *hosts...*	Specifies the remote hosts to obtain tickets for.		
-l *lifetime*	Specifies the tickets lifetime.		
-f *srvtab*	Specifies the srvtab to get service keys from (default is `/etc/kerberosIV/srvtab`).		
-c *cell*	The AFS cell to get tokens for (default is local cell).		
commands...	Specifies the commands to execute.		
File Name: `kauth`	**Directory:** /usr/bin/	**Type:**	External

kauthd

UNIX Shell: All primary shells (csh, ksh, sh)

Function	A remote login daemon for the Kerberos database program.
Syntax	kauthd [-i]

-i	Runs the command in interactive mode. Doesn't expect to be started by `inetd`.		
File Name: `kauthd`	**Directory:** /usr/libexec/	**Type:**	External

kbd

UNIX Shell: All primary shells (csh, ksh, sh)

Function	Is used to show or change the keyboard's values.
Syntax	kbd -l kbd [-q] *name*

-l	Shows all available keyboard encoding.		
-q	Sets quiet mode until an error occurs.		
name	Sets the keyboard encoding to name.		
File Name: `kbd`	**Directory:** /sbin/	**Type:**	External
kbd -l	Shows all available keyboard values.		

kcon

UNIX Shell: All primary shells (csh, ksh, sh)

Function	A keyboard configuration utility for the PCVT video driver.
Syntax	kcon [options...]

-d *delay*	The delay to start to repeat strokes. The delay is 250 + delay * 250 milliseconds.
-m *map*	Specifies the keyboard mapping to use, if found in the `keycap` database.
-l	Shows the keyboard map currently used by the driver.
	The following three options can only be use with the -l option:
-o	Shows the keyboard map in octal.
-x	Shows the keyboard map in hexadecimal (is default).
-p	Doesn't show associated names on certain characters, only the values.
-r *rate*	Specifies the rate of strokes per seconds is between 0 to 31.
-R	Resets the keyboard.
-s	Shows delay and rate values on repeating keystrokes.
-t *mode*	Enables or disables repetition on keystrokes (+ = enables, - = disables).
File Name: `kcon`	**Directory:** /usr/bsbin/ **Type:** External
kcon -l	Shows current keyboard mapping.
kcon -d 3 -r 30	Configures the keyboard to start repeating after 1 second, and then strike 30 times per second.
kcon -t -	Disables the autorepeat feature.

kdb_destroy

UNIX Shell: All primary shells (csh, ksh, sh)

Function	Deletes a Kerberos key distribution center database. Prompts the user for verification before actually doing it.
Syntax	kdb_destroy
File Name: `kdb_destroy`	**Directory:** /usr/sbin/ **Type:** External

kdb_edit

UNIX Shell: All primary shells (csh, ksh, sh)

Function	Creates or changes principals stored in the Kerberos key distribution center database.
Syntax	kdb_edit [-n]

-n	Gets the master key from the master key cache file, instead of asking for it.
File Name: `kdb_edit`	**Directory:** /usr/sbin/ **Type:** External

kdb_init

UNIX Shell: All primary shells (csh, ksh, sh)

Function	Initializes a Kerberos key distribution center database and creates the necessary principals.
Syntax	kdb_init { *realm* }

realm	Specifies the realm to create. Asks for the realm if not specified.
File Name: `kdb_init`	**Directory:** /usr/sbin/ **Type:** External

kdb_util

UNIX Shell: All primary shells (csh, ksh, sh)

Function	Performs utility functions on the Kerberos key distribution center database.
Syntax	kdb_util *ACTION file*

ACTION	**Specifies the action to perform on the database.**
load	Initializes the database with the records contained in the specified file.
merge	Merges entries from file into database.
dump	Dumps the database to the specified file.
slave_dump	Is like dump, but also creates a semaphore file signaling that an update has occurred.
new_master_key	Dumps the database encrypted by the new master key, asked by the program.
convert_old_db	Dumps the old database and encrypts it with the new master key, asked by the program.
file	Specifies the file to use.
File Name: `kdb_util`	**Directory:** /usr/sbin/ **Type:** External

kdestroy

UNIX Shell:	All primary shells (csh, ksh, sh)
Function	Writes zeros to the files containing the user's Kerberos authorization tickets, to destroy them.
Syntax	kdestroy [options...]

-f	Doesn't display any status message.
-q	Doesn't beep you if operation fails.
-t	Destroys only tickets, keeps AFS tokens.
-u	Unlogs (removes tokens, leaves tickets).
File Name: `kdestroy`	**Directory:** /usr/bin/ **Type:** External
kdestroy	Destroys the Kerberos tickets for the current user.

kdump

UNIX Shell:	All primary shells (csh, ksh, sh)
Function	Converts kernel trace files produced with `ktrace` to readable format. Shows it on STDOUT.
Syntax	kdump [options...]

-d	Shows all numbers in decimal.
-e *emulation*	Specifies the emulation name to use instead of "bsd."
-f *file*	Specifies the file to use (default is ktrace.out).
-l	Reads to the end of the file, and then waits for further data (infinite loop).
-m *amount*	Specifies the max amount of bytes when decoding I/O.
-n	Doesn't do ad hoc translations.
-R	Shows relative timestamps.
-T	Shows absolute timestamps.
-t *string*	Specifies the kernel trace points. Can be one of the following or combined:
c	Translates system calls.
e	Translates emulation changes.
n	Translates name translations.
i	Translates I/O.
s	Translates signal processing.
File Name: `kdump`	**Directory:** /usr/bin/ **Type:** External

keynote

UNIX Shell:	All primary shells (csh, ksh, sh)
Function	Handles keynote operations. The function is described by the first identifier.
Syntax	keynote keygen *algorithm size public private { offset } { length }* keynote sign -v *algorithm assertion private* keynote sigver *{ assertion }* keynote verify [options...] *{ files... }*

keygen	Creates a private and a public key pair.
sign	Creates a signature for assertion information.
sigver	Verifies the public-key signature.
verify	Verifies one assertion in the given files.
-v	Verifies the new signature (to use with the sign identifier).
-h	Shows help information.
-e *file...*	Specifies files with environment variables (format is var = "value" required).
-l *files...*	Specifies files with trusted signatures. No verification on signature (required).
-r *list*	Specifies a comma-separated list of values to return, lowest value first (required).
-k *file*	Specifies a file that contains a key to add in the action authorizers (required).
algorithm	Specifies a name of an algorithm to use, for example, sig-dsa-sha1-hex.
size	Specifies the size of the key in bits (values are 512, 1,048 or 2,048).
public	Sets the name of the file that stores the public key.
private	Sets the name of the file that stores the private key.
offset	Specifies the offset where the printout of the key will start.
length	Specifies how many characters to print out.
assertion	Sets the name of the file that contains assertion information.
files...	Specifies the files to verify.
File Name: `keynote`	**Directory:** /usr/bin/ **Type:** External

kgmon

UNIX Shell: All primary shells (csh, ksh, sh)

Function	The monitor for kernel profiling.
Syntax	kgmon [options...]

-b	Starts kernel profiling.
-h	Stops kernel profiling.
-p	Dumps the kernel profiling buffers to a gmon.out file.
-r	Resets the kernel profiling buffers.
-M *file*	Specifies a core file to read values from (default is `/dev/kmem`).
-N *kernel*	Specifies a system kernel to read names from (default is `/bsd`).

File Name:	`kgmon`	**Directory:**	/usr/sbin/	**Type:**	External

kinit

UNIX Shell: All primary shells (csh, ksh, sh)

Function	Logs in to a Kerberos authentication system.
Syntax	kinit [options...] *{ name }*

-i	Requests a Kerberos instance.
-r	Requests a Kerberos realm to use when connecting to a remote Kerberos server.
-v	Verbose mode. Shows more information.
-l	Requests a time in minutes, how long the ticket should be activated.
-p	Acquires a ticket for changepw.kerberos.
name	Specifies a Kerberos initialization name to use.

File Name:	`kinit`	**Directory:**	/usr/bin/	**Type:**	External
Warning:	Remember to use `kdestroy` to remove your ticket before logout.				

klist

UNIX Shell: All primary shells (csh, ksh, sh)

Function	Shows you information listed in the ticket file about current Kerberos tickets held.
Syntax	klist [options...]

-s	Doesn't show ticket filename, owner name, or information on issue and expire times.
-t	Exits with status 0 if there are any valid tickets and 1 if there are not.
-file *file*	Specifies the file to use as the ticket file.
-srvtab	Uses the ticket file as a service key file and shows all of the keys it contains. (If no ticket file is specified -srvtab uses /etc/srvtab by default.)

File Name:	`klist`	**Directory:**	/usr/bin/	**Type:**	External

kprop

UNIX Shell: All primary shells (csh, ksh, sh)

Function	Propagates the Kerberos database to the Kerberos slaves.
Syntax	kprop *database slavefile* [options...]

-realm	Uses the specified realm instead of the default.
-force	Forces propagation to slaves even if there have been no recent changes to the master.
database	Specifies the file to extract data from.
slavefile	Specifies the file on the Kerberos master that lists the Kerberos slaves.

File Name:	`kprop`	**Directory:**	/usr/sbin/	**Type:**	External

kpropd

UNIX Shell: All primary shells (csh, ksh, sh)

Function	Receives the Kerberos database propagated from a kprop process on a Kerberos master.
Syntax	kpropd [options...] *file*

-r *realm*	Specifies the receiver realm for which data is accepted.
-s *srvtab*	Specifies the service table file from which to read the password of the daemon.
-d *file*	Specifies the primary Kerberos database file of a Kerberos slave.
-i	Runs in standalone mode.
-l *file*	Specifies the name of the log file to use.
-p *kdb_util_path*	Specifies the full path to the program `kdb_util`.

continued

-P *kdb_util_path*	Same as option -p.		
file	Specifies the file to write incoming data to.		
File Name: `kpropd`	**Directory:** /usr/libexec/	**Type:**	External

ksh, rksh

UNIX Shell: Korn shell (ksh)

Function	The Korn shell, a standard/restricted command and programming language.
Syntax	ksh [options...] *{ arguments... }* ksh -c [options...] *command { arguments... }* rksh [options...] *{ arguments... }* rksh -c [options...] *command { arguments... }*

	These options may only be used from the command line:
-c *command*	Specifies the command to read.
-i	Makes the shell interactive. TERMINATE, INTERRUPT, and QUIT are ignored.
-l	Starts the login shell.
-r	Runs the shell in restricted shell (same as rksh).
-s	Reads commands from STDIN.
	The following options can be changed with the set command in a script:
-A	Sets the array parameter elements to the specified arguments.
-a allexport	Is used to automatically export any parameters that are defined.
-b notify	Sends print job notification asynchronously.
-C noclobber	Protects files from being overwritten by shell > redirection.
-e errexit	Runs the ERR tarp and exits if a command returns a non-zero exit status.
-f noglob	Doesn't enlarge filename patterns.
-h trackall	Tracks encountered commands as aliases.
-i interactive	Makes the shell interactive. Works only if the shell is already active.
-k keyword	Puts all keyword arguments in the environment for a command.
-l login	Sets the shell as the login shell. Works only if the shell is already active.
-m monitor	Enables job control.
-n -lc -noexec	Reads commands, but will not run them.
-p privileged	Sets the shell if the UID or GID doesn't match the EUID or the EGID.
-r restricted	Starts restricted mode.
-s stdin	Reads commands from STDIN. Is set automatically if the shell starts without arguments.
-u nounset	Handles an unset parameter as an error unless the – or + is used.
-v verbose	Sends the shell input lines to STDERR as they are read.
-x xtrace	Shows commands and their arguments when they are executed.
-X markdirs	Marks the directories with a trailing / during a file rename.
bgnice	Runs background jobs with a lower priority.
braceexpand	Activates brace expansion (alteration).
emacs	Activates command editing with a BRL Emacs-like editor.
gmacs	Activates command editing with a Gmacs-like editor.
ignoreeof	Prevents exiting when an EOF marker is read.
nohup	Doesn't stop jobs with an HUP signal.
nolog	Does not do anything. Backward compatibility only.
physical	Forces the `cd` and `pwd` commands to use physical directories.
posix	Activates POSIX mode.
vi	Activates vi-like editing from the command line.
viraw	Does not do anything. Backward compatibility only.
vi-esccomplete	Allows command and filename completion when escape `^[` is called in command mode.
vi-show8	Prefixes characters using an eighth bit set with `M-`.
vi-tabcomplete	Allows command and filename completion when Tab `^I` is called in insert mode.
arguments...	Specifies additional arguments to the shell or a script.
File Name: `ksh, rksh`	**Directory:** /bin/ **Type:** External
rksh	Switch to restricted Korn shell.
ksh -r	Switch to restricted Korn shell.

ksrvutil

UNIX Shell: All primary shells (csh, ksh, sh)

Function	Manipulates host Kerberos key files.
Syntax	ksrvutil *operation* [options...]

-k	Shows the old and new keys.
-i	Prompts for yes or no before changing any key.
-a	Specifies the AFS string-to-key function should be used.
-f *filename*	Specifies the file to read keys from.
operation	**The following operations can be used:**
list	Shows the keys in the key file.
change	Changes all the keys in the key file.
add	Adds a key to the key file.

File Name:	`ksrvutil`	**Directory:**	/usr/sbin/	**Type:**	External

kstash

UNIX Shell: All primary shells (csh, ksh, sh)

Function	Saves the Kerberos key distribution center database master key in the master key file.
Syntax	kstash

File Name:	`kstash`	**Directory:**	/usr/sbin/	**Type:**	External

ktrace

UNIX Shell: All primary shells (csh, ksh, sh)

Function	Does log the kernel trace of the specified process.
Syntax	ktrace [options...] *command*

-a	Appends the existing trace file instead of overwriting it.
-C	Doesn't trace processes if they are owned by the user.
-c	Clears the trace points associated with the specified file or processes.
-d	Traces child processes for the specified process.
-f *file*	Specifies the file to put log information to (default is `ktrace.out`).
-g *gpid*	Enables tracing on all processes in the process group.
-i	Passes the trace flags to all future children of the designated processes.
-p *pid*	Enables tracing on the indiced process ID.
-t *string*	Specifies the kernel trace points to trace. Can be one of the following, or combined:
c	Traces system calls.
e	Traces emulation changes.
n	Traces name translations.
i	Traces I/O.
s	Traces signal processing.
command	Specifies the process to trace.

File Name:	`ktrace`	**Directory:**	/usr/bin/	**Type:**	External

kvm_mkdb

UNIX Shell: All primary shells (csh, ksh, sh)

Function	Creates kernel databases.
Syntax	kvm_mkdb [-v] *{ file }*

-v	Verbose mode. Shows more information.
file	Specifies the name of the file to create.

File Name:	`kvm_mkdb`	**Directory:**	/usr/sbin/	**Type:**	External

kx

kx	UNIX Shell:	All primary shells (csh, ksh, sh)
Function	Forwards X connections from a remote client to a local screen through an authenticated and encrypted stream.	
Syntax	kx [options...] *host*	

-l *username*	Specifies the username to use for login.
-k	Disables keep-alive on the TCP connections.
-d	Specifies the program should not fork.
-t	Listens on both TCP and UNIX sockets.
-p *port*	Specifies the port to use.
-P	Forces passive mode.
host	Specifies hostname to connect to.

File Name:	`kx`	**Directory:**	/usr/X11R6/bin/	**Type:**	External

kxd

kxd	UNIX Shell:	All primary shells (csh, ksh, sh)
Function	Forwards X connections securely.	
Syntax	kxd [options...]	

-t	Specifies that UNIX sockets should not be used.
-i	Starts in interactive mode.
-p *port*	Specifies the port to listen on.

File Name:	`kxd`	**Directory:**	/usr/X11R6/bin/	**Type:**	External

lam

lam	UNIX Shell:	All primary shells (csh, ksh, sh)
Function	Copies specified files parallel to STDOUT.	
Syntax	lam [options...] *files...*	

-f *min.max*	Shows fragments of line specified by the format string of the width.
-p *min.max*	Like -f, but pads the specific file when end of file is reached.
-s *sepstring*	Shows specified string before showing line fragments from next file.
-t*c*	Specifies the input terminator instead of a new-line.
files...	Specifies which file to copy.

File Name:	`lam`	**Directory:**	/usr/bin/	**Type:**	External

lastcomm

lastcomm	UNIX Shell:	All primary shells (csh, ksh, sh)
Function	Shows a reverse order list of commands executed last.	
Syntax	lastcomm [-f *file*] *{ command } { user } { terminal }*	

-f *file*	Specifies an accounting file to use.
command	Lists the command names that have been executed recently.
user	Lists recently executed commands by a user.
terminal	Lists recently executed commands from a terminal.

File Name:	`lastcomm`	**Directory:**	/usr/bin/	**Type:**	External

ldconfig

ldconfig	UNIX Shell:	All primary shells (csh, ksh, sh)
Function	Scans built-in and specified system directories and stores any information about shared libraries in /var/run/ld.	
Syntax	ldconfig [options...]	

-m	Merges information to the /var/run/ld file instead of rebuilding it.
-r	Shows the content of the file /var/run/ld on STDOUT.
-s	Leaves out the built-in library /usr/lib when a scan is made.
-v	Verbose mode. Shows more information.

File Name:	`ldconfig`	**Directory:**	/sbin/	**Type:**	External
Note:	The command is usually run as a boot sequence.				

ldd

UNIX Shell:	All primary shells (csh, ksh, sh)
Function	Shows all shared objects that are required to run the specified program.
Syntax	ldd [-f *format*] *program*

-f *format*	Specifies a format string that is passed to rtld, which customizes ldd's output. (This option is repeatable up to two times.)
-v	Verbose mode. Shows more information.
program	Specifies the program to show requirements for.

File Name:	`ldd`	**Directory:**	/usr/bin/	**Type:**	External

leave

UNIX Shell:	All primary shells (csh, ksh, sh)
Function	Reminds you of a time to leave. Reminds you 5 minutes and 1 minute before the specified time.
Syntax	leave [options...]

HHMM	Specifies the time in hours and minutes. Assumes to be in the next 12 hours.
+HHMM	Specifies the time in hours and minutes for the alarm to go off. It is like a timer.

File Name:	`leave`	**Directory:**	/usr/bin/	**Type:**	External

leave	Asks for the time when you have to leave.
leave 1100	Sets the alarm to 11:00.
leave +230	Sets the alarm to 2 hours and 30 minutes from now.

less, page

UNIX Shell:	All primary shells (csh, ksh, sh)
Function	A text pager for UNIX system, used to show ASCII files.
Syntax	less [options...] *filenames...*

+*command*	Specifies an internal command to perform when showing new files.
-?	Shows help information.
-a	Performs no search on lines shown on the screen; instead, does a search on lines under.
-b*buffers*	Sets the number of buffers to use for each file (one buffer is 1K).
-B	Doesn't automatically assign buffers when needed. Use amount specified with -bn.
-c	Shows full screen lines from the top down instead of appending from the bottom.
-C	Is used as -c, except that screen will be cleared before a new page is shown.
-d	Doesn't show error messages if the terminal can't do what it's supposed to.
-D*xcolor*	Sets the text's type and color. Color is a value.value pair (MS-DOS only). (The text type x is n = normal, s = standout, d = bold, u = underlined, and k = blink.)
-e	Quits the second time less reaches an EOF instead of just giving a warning.
-E	Quits directly when the EOF is reached.
-f	Opens all files not only those who are regular.
-F	Shows the file, and if it's only one page, quits.
-g	Specifies that only the last search string found will be highlighted.
-G	Doesn't highlight strings found by the search commands.
-h*lines*	Specifies the number of lines that can be shown by scrolling back.
-i	Isn't case-sensitive when matching patterns.
-I	The same as -i, but won't be case-sensitive even when pattern contains uppercase.
-j*line*	Marks a screen line as the line on the screen where the search begins.
-J	Shows a status column on the screen. Is used only with the -w or -W option.
-k*filename*	Specifies a filename to open as a lesskey file. Is repeatable.
-m	Makes verbose prompts with percentages of the file instead of colons.
-M	Makes prompts look even more verbose than with -m.
-n	Doesn't use line numbers.
-N	Shows line numbers at the beginning of the lines.
-o*filename*	Specifies a file where to put the input from STDIN when showing it on the screen.
-O*filename*	Does the same thing as -o, except that it will overwrite the specified file.
-p*pattern*	Shows the specified file from the first line containing the specified pattern.
-P*prompt*	Specifies another prompt to use instead of the default.

continued

-q	Sets quiet mode. Won't ring the bell when the EOF has been reached.
-Q	Sets very quiet mode. Never rings the bell.
-r	Shows control characters that could create screen problems.
-R	Does the same as -r, except that it tries to keep the correct screen appearance.
-s	Combines multiple blank lines into one blank line.
-S	Chops lines longer than the screen width.
-t*tag*	Shows the file containing tag. For this to work, `ctags` must have been run.
-T*tagsfile*	Is used with the -t option. Specifies another tags file to use instead of the default.
-u	Shows backspaces and new line characters as usual characters.
-U	Handles Tabs, backspaces, and new lines as control characters.
-V	Shows version information.
-w	Highlights the first new line when a full page movement has been done.
-W	The same as -w, but highlights when more than one line of movement is performed.
-x*NR*	Uses the NR to specify where to set the Tab stops (default is 8).
-X	Disables sending termcap initialization and deinitialization strings to the screen.
-y*NR*	Uses the NR to specify the maximum number of lines to scroll forward.
-[z]*NR*	Uses NR to specify default scrolling window lines (default is one full screen).
-" *charchar*	Specifies the start and end quote characters to use instead of using quotes.
-~	Enables lines after EOF to be shown as blank lines.
-*NR*	Specifies the horizontal scrolling length for the left and right arrow command.
--	Specifies the end of options. After this, everything is taken as filenames.
	Commands invoked from within less:
m*letter*	Marks position with specified lowercase letter.
'*letter*	Goes to the earlier marked letter, or with ^ or $ it goes to beginning or end of file.
Space	Scrolls down one full screen. You can also use Ctrl+V, Ctrl+F, or f.
{ NR } z	The same as Space. NR also sets the size of the screen.
Esc+Space	The same as Space, but scrolls down one full screen even if you reach the EOF.
{ NR } Return	Scrolls down one line or number of lines. You can also use Ctrl+J, Ctrl+E, f, or j.
{ NR } d	Scrolls down half a screen or the specified number of lines. You can also use Ctrl+D.
{ NR } Esc+v	Scrolls up one screen or the specified number of lines. You can also use Ctrl+B or b.
{ NR } w	The same as Esc+V. Number also sets the default size of the screen.
{ NR } y	Scrolls up the number of lines. You can also use Ctrl+Y, Ctrl+P, Ctrl+K, or k.
{ NR } u	Scrolls down half a screen or the specified number of lines. You can also use Ctrl+U.
{ NR } Esc+)	Scrolls right the number of characters (default is 8). You can also use right arrow.
{ NR } Esc+(	Scrolls left the number of characters (default is 8). You can also use left arrow.
r	Repaints the screen. You can also use Ctrl+R or Ctrl+L.
R	The same as r, but discards buffered input.
F	Scrolls forward, even if the EOF is reached.
{ NR } g	Goes to line number in the file (default is 1). You can also use < or Esc+<.
{ NR } G	Goes to line number in the file (default last line). You can also use > or Esc+>.
NR p	Specifies in percent where to start reading in the file. You can also use %.
	Number specifies which one to use, if there is more than one on the top line:
{ NR } {	Goes to the matching } if a { is shown in the top line.
{ NR } }	Goes to the matching { if a } is shown at the bottom line.
{ NR } [	Goes to the matching] if a [is shown in the top line.
{ NR }]	Goes to the matching [if a] is shown at the bottom line.
{ NR } (	Goes to the matching) if a (is shown in the top line.
{ NR })	Goes to the matching (if a) is shown at the bottom line.
ESC-ctrl+F *charchar*	The same as {. Handles the characters as opening and closing brackets.
ESC-ctrl+B *charchar*	The same as }. Handles the characters as opening and closing brackets.
/*pattern*	Searches the file for lines containing pattern.
/!*pattern*	Searches the file for lines that don't match the pattern.
/* *pattern*	Continues to the next file in the command line list if the pattern isn't found.
/@*pattern*	Starts the search at the first file in the command line list.
/ctlr+K*pattern*	Highlights found words on the screen, but keeps current cursor position.
/ctrl+R*pattern*	Creates a simple textual comparison.
?*pattern*	Searches the file backwards for lines containing pattern.
?!*pattern*	Searches the file backwards for lines that don't match the pattern.

continued

?**pattern*	Searches backward in multiple files. Searching in previous file if no match found.
?@*pattern*	Starts the backward search at last line of the last file in the command-line list.
/ctlr+K?*pattern*	Highlights found words in a backward search, but keeps current cursor position.
/ctrl+R?*pattern*	Creates a simple textual comparison in a backward search.
n	Repeats previous search.
N	Repeats previous search, but in reverse direction.
ESC-n	Repeats previous search over files on the command list.
ESC-N	Repeats previous search, but in reverse direction over files on the command list.
ESC-u	Turns off search highlighting.
:e *filename*	Inspects a new file.
E *filename*	The same as :e.
:n*{ NR }*	Inspects the next file in the command line list. Number specifies the NRth next file.
:p*{ NR }*	Inspects previous file in command line list. Number specifies the NRth previous file.
:x*{ NR }*	Inspects the first file in the command line list. Number specifies the NRth file.
:d	Erases the current file from the list of files.
:t	Goes to the tag given.
=	Shows some information about the file.
V	Shows version information.
q	Quits less. You can also use Q, :q, :Q, or ZZ.
	The next four options don't work on all installations:
v	Starts an editor to edit the current file being shown.
! *Shellcmd*	Invokes a shell to run the specified Shellcmd.
! *letter Shellcmd*	Invokes shell, pipes section between current position and earlier marked letter. (The letter is marked with m letter, ^ and $ work as specified.)
s *file*	Specifies to save the input in a file. The input must be a pipe.
-+option	Resets the specified command-line option to its default.
-!option	Sets the specified command-line option to opposite of its default.
_option	Shows the specified command-line option's current value.
-option	Changes the settings of specified command-line option and shows a message of changes. (If the option has an operand, its settings can be changed as well.)
filenames...	Specifies file to show.

File Name:	`less`	**Directory:**	/usr/bin/	**Type:**	External
Note:	`less` is `more`, `more` is use-`less`.				

less -N /etc/passwd	Shows `/etc/passwd` with a line number at the beginning of each line.
less -h10 /etc/passwd	Shows `/etc/passwd`; when Space is pressed displays the next 10 lines instead of the next full screen.
less -p ucgbook ~/books.txt	Scrolls down to the first ucgbook match.

lesskey

UNIX Shell: All primary shells (csh, ksh, sh)

Function	Is used to manage key bindings for less.
Syntax	lesskey [options...] *{ file }*

-V	Shows version information.
-o *output*	Is used to specify the output file.
-	Is used to read input from STDIN instead of from a file.
file	Specifies an input file with key binding information.

File Name:	`lesskey`	**Directory:**	/usr/bin/	**Type:**	External

lint

UNIX Shell: All primary shells (csh, ksh, sh)

Function	Is used to check a specified C program file for errors that leave it nonportable, wasteful, or buggy.
Syntax	lint [options...] *files...*

-a	Reports if long values are assigned to short variables.
-aa	Is like -a, but reports integer value assignments that cause poor conversions.
-b	Shows any break statements that can't be reached.
-c	Reports about casts with questionable portability.

continued

-e	Reports about unusual enum- and integer-type operations.
-g	Suppresses warnings for extensions of `gcc` to the C language.
-h	Starts a series of heuristic tests to find bugs, improve coding, or limit redundancy.
-i	Creates a `.ln` file for every `.c` file from the command line.
-n	Skips the standard library compatibility check.
-p	Checks the portability of code within the file to other C dialects.
-r	Reports the position of a previous declaration if there is a redeclaration.
-s	Checks if code is following ANSI C rules and gives errors or warnings if not.
-t	Checks if code is following traditional C rules and gives errors or warnings if not.
-v	Suppresses any complaint that there is an unused argument in a function.
-x	Reports if there is an unused variable that is referred to by an external declaration.
-z	Complains about undefined structures.
-C *library*	Creates a library called `llib-llibrary.ln`.
-D *name* [=*def*]	Defines the name for `cpp` as if using a #define directive.
-I *directory*	Specifies that this directory will be added to the list of searchable directories.
-L *directory*	Searches for lint libraries in the specified directory first.
-F	Shows file pathnames.
-H	Shows the name of the included file if an error comes from an included file.
-o *file*	Specifies the output file.
-U *name*	Removes the initial definition of the specified preprocessor name.
-V	Shows all the command lines created by the controller program.
files...	Specifies file to act on.

File Name:	`lint`	**Directory:**	/usr/bin/	**Type:**	External

Note: Routines that don't give any return, like `exit`, will not be understood by `lint`, which may cause incorrect reporting.

lint -I ucg	Specifies that ucg will be added to the list of searchable directories.

listres

UNIX Shell: All primary shells (csh, ksh, sh)

Function	Generates a list of a widget's resource database.
Syntax	listres [options...]

-all	Shows information for all widgets and objects.
-nosuper	Doesn't show resources inherited from a super class.
-variable	Defines widgets by the names of the class record variables.
-top *name*	Specifies the name of the widget to be treated as the top of the hierarchy.
-format *printf-string*	Specifies the string to be used to show the name, class and so forth.

File Name:	`listres`	**Directory:**	/usr/X11R6/bin/	**Type:**	External

listres -all	Lists all known widgets and objects.

lkbib

UNIX Shell: All primary shells (csh, ksh, sh)

Function	Searches for references in bibliographic databases that contains the specified keyword. Shows result on STDOUT.
Syntax	lkbib [options...] *keywords...*

-v	Shows version information.
-i*string*	Ignores the specified strings when searching the database.
-p*file*	Specifies filename to inspect. It can be used multiple times.
-t*number*	Specifies how many of the first characters that must match (default is 6).
keywords...	Specifies the keyword to search for.

File Name:	`lkbib`	**Directory:**	/usr/bin/	**Type:**	External

lndir

UNIX Shell: All primary shells (csh, ksh, sh)

Function	Creates a shadow of the current or specified directory containing only symbolic links to the parent directory.
Syntax	lndir [options...] *{ directory1 } { directory2 }*

-e *file*	Adds the specified file to a list of files to be excluded from the shadow directory.
-s	Suppresses all normal error messages in operation.

continued

-i	Creates symbolic links to the parent directories' symbolic links (not recommended).		
directory1	Specifies the parent directory.		
directory2	Specifies the shadow directory to create.		
File Name: `lndir`	**Directory:** /usr/bin/	**Type:**	External

locate

UNIX Shell: All primary shells (csh, ksh, sh)

Function	Finds files in a database. The script /usr/libexec/locate.updatedb, usually run by `cron` daily, lists all files on the system and builds /var/db/locate.database.
Syntax	locate [options...] *pattern*

-S	Shows statistics about the database and exit.
-c	Specifies to show a count of matching filenames.
-d *database*	Searches the specified database instead of default. Use colon to specify multiple databases.
-i	Ignores case distinctions in both the database and the pattern.
-l *number*	Limits the number of output files and exit.
-m	Specifies to use mmap(2) instead of the STDIO(3) library (is the default).
-s	Specifies to use STDIO(3) instead of default.
pattern	Specifies the pattern to search for.
File Name: `locate`	**Directory:** /usr/bin/ **Type:** External
Tip:	Note that you won't find files that were created or renamed after /usr/libexec/locate.updatedb was last run.
locate .jpg	Find files whose names contain string .jpg.
locate make | grep bin	Looks for commands containing string make; extracts the files that contain the string bin.
locate -i .JPG	Searches for files whose names contain the string .JPG; ignores case. This also searches for files containing the string .jpg.

locate.updatedb

UNIX Shell: All primary shells (csh, ksh, sh)

Function	Updates the `locate` database. This is usually updated using the `/etc/weekly` script.
Syntax	locate.updatedb [options...]

--tmpdir=*directory*	Sets the temporary directory for the files.
--fcodes=*file*	Uses the specified file as the find codes database.
--searchpaths=*directories...*	Adds the specified directory paths into the database.
--prunepaths=*directories...*	Specifies a list of directories that will not be included into the database.
--filesystems=*types...*	Specifies which file system types are navigated by the `find` command.
File Name: `locate.updatedb`	**Directory:** /usr/libexec/ **Type:** External
locate.updatedb --tmpdir=/ucgtemp	Sets the temporary directory to UCGtemp.

lock

UNIX Shell: All primary shells (csh, ksh, sh)

Function	Locks a terminal to a user with password. It stays locked until it's released by a user or timed out.
Syntax	lock [options...]

-n	Disables the timeout function.
-p	Uses the user's login name or s/key instead of a password.
-t *time*	Specifies the timeout limit in minutes (default is 15).
File Name: `lock`	**Directory:** /usr/bin/ **Type:** External
lock	Locks the terminal until 15 minutes has passed or the password is entered.
lock -p -t 60	Locks the terminal for 60 minutes, doesn't ask for password when invoked; instead, login password is used.
lock -n	Asks for a password twice, then locks the terminal until that password is entered again.

lockspool

UNIX Shell: All primary shells (csh, ksh, sh)

Function	Locks user's system mailbox.
Syntax	lockspool *{ user }*

user	Specifies the username to lock the mailbox for.

File Name: `lockspool` **Directory:** /usr/libexec/ **Type:** External

logresolve

UNIX Shell: All primary shells (csh, ksh, sh)

Function	Resolves IP-addresses in Apache's access log files. This is to reduce the impact for the name server.
Syntax	logresolve [options...] *accesslog newaccesslog*

-s *file*	Specifies the filename for the log file.
-c	Verifies IP addresses to names with DNS.
accesslog	Specifies the Apache access log to run lookups on.
newaccesslog	Specifies an output file.

File Name: `logresolve` **Directory:** /usr/sbin/ **Type:** External

lorder

UNIX Shell: Bourne shell (sh)

Function	Finds ordering relation for an object or library archive and shows a list of the pairs.
Syntax	lorder *filenames...*

filenames...	Can use one or more object or library archive filenames as the input.

File Name: `lorder` **Directory:** /usr/bin/ **Type:** Script

lpc

UNIX Shell: All primary shells (csh, ksh, sh)

Function	Is used by the system administrator to control the operation of the line printer system.
Syntax	lpc *{ ACTION }*

ACTION	**Select one of the following actions:**
? *{ commands... }*	Shows a short description of each command specified in the argument list.
abort *printer*	Kills the active job and disables unspooling for the specified printer. Can use "all."
clean *printer*	Removes any temporary files, data files, and control files that can't be printed.
disable *printer*	Disables spooling for the specified printer.
down *printer*	Disables both queuing and printing for the specified printer.
enable *printer*	Enables spooling for the specified printer.
exit	Exits the command.
restart *printer*	Attempts to start a new printer daemon.
start *printer*	Starts the printer.
status *printer*	Shows the status of daemons and queues on the local computer.
stop *printer*	Shows any further unspooling after the current job completes.
topq *printer jobID*	Places the selected job at the top of the printer queue.
up *printer*	Enables queuing and printing for the specified printer.
quit	Quits program.
help	Shows help information.

File Name: `lpc` **Directory:** /usr/sbin/ **Type:** External

lpc start ljet4a	Starts the printer ljet4a.

lpd

UNIX Shell: All primary shells (csh, ksh, sh)

Function	A print daemon.
Syntax	lpd *{ -l }*

-l	Logs valid requests from the network.

File Name: `lpd` **Directory:** /usr/sbin/ **Type:** External

lpf

UNIX Shell: All primary shells (csh, ksh, sh)

Function	Is used by `lpd` in the printcap file to filter printouts.
Syntax	lpf options... [options...]

	The following options must be specified. This is done by `lpd`.
-P*printer*	Specifies what printer to use.
-w*chars*	Specifies the width of the page in chars.
-l*lines*	Specifies the length of the page in lines.
-x*pixels*	Specifies the width of the page in pixels.
-y*pixels*	Specifies the length of the page in pixels.
-K*file*	Specifies the control file to use.
-L*banner*	Specifies the banner name.
-n*user*	Specifies the username.
-h*host*	Specifies the host the job came from.
-F*format*	Specifies the job format.
	The following option isn't needed, but if used it is set through `lpd`:
-Z*option*	Specifies extra options directly to lpf taken from the `lpr` command line.
	The following options are used mainly from the printcap file but also from lpr:
-c	Ignores control characters. Set with lpr -b or lpr -l.
-i*indent*	Specifies which indentation amount. Set with lpr -i indent.
-C*class*	Specifies the class name. Set with lpr -C class.
-J*job*	Specifies the job name. Set with lpr -J job.
-R*file*	Specifies the accounting file.
-D*number*	Specifies the debugging level number to use.
-Tcrlf	Turns off CR/LF translation.
-T*number*	Adds the corresponding character for the integer specified to the end of the line.

File Name:	`lpf`	**Directory:**	/usr/libexec/lpr/	**Type:**	External

lptest

UNIX Shell: All primary shells (csh, ksh, sh)

Function	Creates a ripple test pattern to STDOUT and shows all 96 printable ASCII characters useful for testing.
Syntax	lptest *{ length number }*

length -+number	Specifies the length of the output line in characters and the number of lines.

File Name:	`lptest`	**Directory:**	/usr/sbin/	**Type:**	External

lptest	Displays a test with 79 columns and 200 lines.
lptest 60 50	Displays a test with 60 columns and 50 lines.

lynx

UNIX Shell: All primary shells (csh, ksh, sh)

Function	A fully featured, text only Web browser.
Syntax	lynx [options...] *{ url }*

This is the same command as the one found in Linux. Please see lynx in the Linux chapter for all the options.

File Name:	`lynx`	**Directory:**	/usr/bin/	**Type:**	External

lynx -cookies http://www.ucgbook.com/	Starts lynx and goes to the URL `http://www.ucgbook.com`.
lynx -color http://www.ucgbook.com	Starts lynx with colors and goes to the URL `http://www.ucgbook.com`.

machine

UNIX Shell: All primary shells (csh, ksh, sh)

Function	Shows the kernel or application architecture.
Syntax	machine [-a]

-a	Shows the application architecture.

File Name:	`machine`	**Directory:**	/usr/bin/	**Type:**	External

machine	Returns the kernel architecture, for example, "i386."
machine -a	Returns the application architecture, for example, "i386."

mail.local

UNIX Shell:	All primary shells (csh, ksh, sh)			
Function	Reads from STDIN and appends the information to the specified user's mail file.			
Syntax	mail.local [options...] *users...*			
-f *name*	Specifies the sender's name.			
-l	Requests that files ending with `.lock` be used for locking (is the default).			
-L	Does not create a lock file when locking the spool.			
users...	Specifies the user mailbox that is appended.			
File Name:	`mail.local`	**Directory:** /usr/libexec/	**Type:**	External
Warning:	When running disk quotas on `/var/mail`, you must unset the `m` mail option for the local mailer.			

mailwrapper

UNIX Shell:	All primary shells (csh, ksh, sh)			
Function	Starts appropriate MTA software based on configuration information in `/etc/mailer.conf`. It is designed to replace `usr/sbin/sendmail`.			
Syntax	mailwrapper			
File Name:	`mailwrapper`	**Directory:** /usr/sbin/	**Type:**	External

MAKEDEV

UNIX Shell:	Bourne shell (sh)			
Function	Create system and device special files. This script is run at installation, but can be run later.			
Syntax	MAKEDEV *names...*			
names...	Specifies device name.			
File Name:	`MAKEDEV`	**Directory:** /dev/	**Type:**	Script
/dev/MAKEDEV all	Makes all devices.			
/dev/MAKEDEV st1	Makes device st1 (SCSII tapes).			
/dev/MAKEDEV std	Makes all the standard devices for the specific architecture.			

makeg

UNIX Shell:	Bourne shell (sh)			
Function	Is used to make an executable file that can be used for debug operations.			
Syntax	makeg [options...] *{ file }*			
	The command will take any `make` options.			
file	Specifies the output file.			
File Name:	`makeg`	**Directory:** /usr/X11R6/bin/	**Type:**	Script
makeg program	If a target program is specified in the makefile, a debuggable executable program is made.			

makeinfo

UNIX Shell:	All primary shells (csh, ksh, sh)			
Function	Converts TeX info files to plain text, HTML or info files for online reading.			
Syntax	makeinfo [options...] *files...*			
This is the same command as the one found in Linux. Please see makeinfo in the Linux chapter for all the options.				
File Name:	`makeinfo`	**Directory:** /usr/bin/	**Type:**	External

makekey

UNIX Shell:	All primary shells (csh, ksh, sh)			
Function	Creates an encryption key using ASCII characters for programs that run encryption.			
Syntax	makekey *options...*			
-k	Runs makekey in compatible mode.			
-b *rounds*	Encrypts the string using Blowfish hashing with the specified rounds.			
-m	Encrypts the string using MD5.			
-p	Prompts for a single string with the echo turned off.			
-s *salt*	Encrypts the string using DES, with the specified salt.			
File Name:	`makekey`	**Directory:** /usr/libexec/	**Type:**	External

makemap

UNIX Shell: All primary shells (csh, ksh, sh)

Function	Uses the keyed map lookups in `sendmail` to create the specified type of database map. Reads from STDIN and writes to the specified new map name.
Syntax	makemap [options...] *type name*

-N	Adds the null byte that will terminate the strings in the specified map.
-d	Allows the use of duplicate keys in the specified map. Works with B-tree format maps.
-f	Disables uppercase letters from being forced into lowercase (default is uppercase).
-o	Appends to a previously existing file.
-r	Allows for repeating existing keys. Default gives an error if repeated keys exist.
-s	Disables the safety check on the map being created.
-v	Verbose mode. Shows more information.
name	Specifies the map name of the map database being created.
type	Specifies the specific database map format. Only one of the following may be used:
dbm	Specifies the map will follow DMB format rules.
btree	Specifies the map will follow B-Tree format rules.
hash	Specifies the map will follow hash format rules.

File Name:	`makemap`	**Directory:**	/usr/sbin/	**Type:**	External

makemap -d btree newmap	Allows the use of duplicate keys in the B-tree formatted map.

map-mbone

UNIX Shell: All primary shells (csh, ksh, sh)

Function	Shows all multicast routers that are available from the specified multicast router startingrouter.
Syntax	map-mbone [options...] *{ router }*

-d *level*	Specify the debug level to 0-3 (default is 0).
-f	Initiates a recursive search. Always done if no starting router is specified.
-g	Specifies the graphing format to GraphEd format.
-n	Disables DNS lookup for the names of the multicast routers.
-r *number*	Specifies the number of neighbor query retries (default is 1).
-t *seconds*	Sets the seconds to wait for a neighbor query reply before retrying (default is 2).
router	Specifies which starting router to begin with (default is local host).

File Name:	`map-bone`	**Directory:**	/usr/sbin/	**Type:**	External

md5

UNIX Shell: All primary shells (csh, ksh, sh)

Function	An algorithm used for digital signature applications to create a 128-bit message-digest fingerprint.
Syntax	md5 [options...] *{ file }*

-s *string*	Shows a checksum of the specified string.
-p	Echoes the STDIN to STDOUT and appends the `md5` sum to STDOUT.
-t	Runs a built-in time trial.
-x	Runs a built-in test script.
file	Specifies the file to calculate on.

File Name:	`md5`	**Directory:**	/bin/	**Type:**	External

merge

UNIX Shell: All primary shells (csh, ksh, sh)

Function	Merges three files together. It merges the changes between input files two and three into input file number one.
Syntax	merge [options...] *file1 file2 file3*

-A	Verbose mode. Shows more information.
-e	Shows no error or conflict messages.
-E	Shows no error messages (is the default).
-L *label*	Specifies a label to use instead of filenames in conflict reports.
-p	Shows output on the screen.
-q	Shows no output.

continued

-V	Shows version information.		
file1 file2 file3	Specifies the files to merge.		
File Name: `merge`	**Directory:** /usr/bin/	**Type:** External	

midiplay

UNIX Shell: All primary shells (csh, ksh, sh)

Function	Is used to play MIDI files.
Syntax	midiplay [options...] *{ files... }*

-d *number*	Specifies the device number to use for MIDI output (default is 0).
-f *device*	Specifies the sequencers device.
-l	Shows the possible MIDI output devices without playing anything.
-m	Shows MIDI file meta events.
-t *tempo*	Specifies the tempo (default is 100).
-v	Verbose mode. Shows more information. If repeated, the verbosity increases.
-x	Plays a small sample sound.
files...	Specifies the MIDI file to play.

File Name: `midiplay`	**Directory:** /usr/bin/	**Type:** External
midiplay -t 150 techno.mid	Plays the file techno.mid in tempo 150.	

mkalias

UNIX Shell: All primary shells (csh, ksh, sh)

Function	Converts YP `mail.aliases` maps to `mail.byaddr` maps.
Syntax	mkalias [options...] *inputfile { outputfile }*

-v	Verbose mode. Shows more information.
-e	Verifies that the host exists.
-E	Verifies that the host exists, and that a valid MX-record exists.
-d	Assumes that the domain names are valid. Use with the -e option.
-u	Assumes that the UUCP names are valid. Use with the -e option.
-n	Adds capital letters to each name. Changes ucgbook.com to Ucgbook.Com.
inputfile	Specifies the map to be used as input.
outputfile	Specifies the map to be used as output.

File Name: `mkalias`	**Directory:** /usr/sbin/	**Type:** External

mk-amd-map

UNIX Shell: All primary shells (csh, ksh, sh)

Function	Creates database maps for Amd.
Syntax	mk-amd-map [-p] *mapname*

-p	Shows the map on STDOUT instead of creating a database.
mapname	Specifies the map name of the database map to create.

File Name: `mk-amd-map`	**Directory:** /usr/sbin/	**Type:** External

mkdep

UNIX Shell: Bourne shell (sh)

Function	Creates Makefile dependency lines for a specified source file.
Syntax	mkdep [options...] *{ files... }*

-a	Allows multiple mkdeps to run from a single Makefile by appending to the output file.
-p	Makes mkdep to produce dependencies from the form: program: program.c
-f *file*	Specifies a file to write the include file dependencies to.
flags	List of flags for the C compiler.
files...	Specify input file(s).

File Name: `mkdep`	**Directory:** /usr/bin/	**Type:** Script
mkdep input.c	Creates dependency lines for the specified source file.	

mkisofs

mkisofs	UNIX Shell:	All primary shells (csh, ksh, sh)
Function	Creates an ISO9660 file system. Uses the specified directory tree to create a ISO9660 file system copy.	
Syntax	mkisofs [options...] -o *file directory*	

-a	Includes all ISO9660 files and backup files that use ~ or #.
-A *ID*	Specifies text to be written into the application volume header (max 128 characters).
-b *file*	Specifies path- and filename to a boot image. Must be 1.2, 1.44, or 2.88 MB in size.
-c *directory*	Specifies a boot directory to use when creating a bootable CD.
-d	Excludes a trailing period from files that lack a period. Use this with caution.
-D	Packs the directory as it is seen. Does not use deep directory relocation.
-f	Generates the file system by following symbolic links.
-i *list*	Specifies the file to be used to create a list of files to add to the directory.
-l	Enables the use of 32-character filenames.
-L	Permits the use of filenames that begin with a period.
-m *glob*	Specifies a glob to ignore when writing to a CD.
-M *path*	Specifies a path to an ISO-9660 image that needs to be merged.
-N	Doesn't put ISO-9660 version numbers in the filenames.
-o *file*	Specifies the name of a file to write the file system image to.
-P *ID*	Specifies publisher info text to be written into volume header (max 128 characters).
-p *ID*	Specifies prepared info text to be written into the volume header (max 128 characters).
-R	Creates SUSP and RR records to explain the created files.
-r	Similar to -R, but with more user-friendly values to show nodes and ownership.
-T	Creates a TRANS.TBL file in each directory on the CD-ROM.
-V *ID*	Specifies the volume ID to be written into the master block.
-v	Verbose mode. Shows more information.
-x *paths...*	Excludes the specified path from being written to the CD-ROM. Separate paths by a space.
-z	Creates SUSP records for compressed files that are transparent.
directory	Specifies the directory to create an ISO-9660 file system of.

File Name:	`mkisofs`	**Directory:**	/usr/sbin/	**Type:**	External
Note:	Options -d and -D don't follow ISO9660 rules.				

mkisofs -o rom -m '*.x' -m ucg -m rules	Excludes all files ending with `.x` and that are called `ucg` or `rules` to be copied to CD-ROM.
mkisofs -o cd -x /local/ucgbook	Does not write files from the directory /local/ucgbook to the CD-ROM.

mkstr

mkstr	UNIX Shell:	All primary shells (csh, ksh, sh)
Function	Creates specific files containing error messages that are extruded from a list of other files.	
Syntax	mkstr [-] *messagefile prefix files...*	

[-]	Places any error messages at the end of the message file.
messagefile	Specifies the message file to be captured.
prefix	Specifies the file prefix to use for the created file.
files...	Specifies the files where the error messages will be extracted from. Use wildcards.

File Name:	`mkstr`	**Directory:**	/usr/bin/	**Type:**	External
Note:	mkstr was intended for the limited architecture of the PDP 11 family, so very few programs actually use it. The Pascal interpreter, pi(1), and the editor, ex(1), are two programs that are similar.				

mkstr pistrings processed *.c	Places the error messages from C source files into the file `pistrings` and places them in files with a prefix of processed.

mktemp

UNIX Shell:	All primary shells (csh, ksh, sh)
Function	Creates a temporary filename using another filename as a template.
Syntax	mktemp [options...] *file*

-d	Creates a directory instead of a file.
-q	Quiet mode. Fails silently if an error occurs.
-u	Unlinks the file before mktemp exits.
file	Specifies the file to use as a template.

File Name:	`mktemp`	**Directory:**	/usr/bin/	**Type:**	External

modload

UNIX Shell:	All primary shells (csh, ksh, sh)
Function	Loads a loadable kernel module into a running system where the input file in the syntax is an object file (.o file).
Syntax	modload [options...] [-o *outputfile*] *inputfile*

-d	Shows debug information about modload itself.
-q	Sets quiet mode.
-u	Erases the output file of the loaded module after loading.
-v	Verbose mode. Shows more information.
-A *kernel*	Specifies kernel's symbol file used to resolve module references to external symbols. (If specified file is other than running kernel's, it can crash the system.)
-e *entry*	Specifies the entry point of the module (default is xxxinit).
-p *exec*	Specifies a shell script or program that is executed on successful module load.
-o *outputfile*	Specifies the output file. If not specified, a file modulename.out is created in /tmp.
inputfile	Specifies the name of the module object file to load.

File Name:	`modload`	**Directory:**	/sbin/	**Type:**	External

modstat

UNIX Shell:	All primary shells (csh, ksh, sh)
Function	Shows the status of any loadable kernel modules present in the kernel.
Syntax	modstat [options...]

-i *ID*	Shows the status of the module with the ID.
-n *name*	Shows the status of the module with the name.

File Name:	`modstat`	**Directory:**	/usr/bin/	**Type:**	External

modunload

UNIX Shell:	All primary shells (csh, ksh, sh)
Function	Unloads a previously loaded module from a running system.
Syntax	modunload [options...]

-i *moduleID*	Unloads the module with the specified ID.
-n *name*	Unloads the module with the specified name.

File Name:	`modunload`	**Directory:**	/sbin/	**Type:**	External

Note: The modunload command was designed to be similar in functionality to the corresponding command in SunOS 4.1.3.

modunload -i 14	Unloads module 14.

mopchk

UNIX Shell:	All primary shells (csh, ksh, sh)
Function	Shows information about MOP images.
Syntax	mopchk [options...] *{ file }*

-a	Shows all the Ethernets connected to the system.
-v	Shows version information of `mopprobe`.
file	Specifies the file to read the MOP-images information from — it reads from the header.

File Name:	`mopchk`	**Directory:**	/usr/sbin/	**Type:**	External

Bug: In some implementations, the same interface can occur more than once.

mopd

UNIX Shell: All primary shells (csh, ksh, sh)

Function	A MOP loader daemon that services MOP load requests on the Ethernet connected to one or all interfaces.
Syntax	mopd [options...] { *interface* }

-a	Listens on all the Ethernets connected to the system.
-d	Runs in debug mode in the foreground, with all the output to STDOUT.
-f	Specifies to run in the foreground.
interface	Specifies which interface to use. Must be specified if there is no -a.

File Name:	`mopd`	**Directory:**	/usr/sbin/	**Type:**	External
Note:	Supports two kinds of files. The file is first checked to see if it is in a.out format. If not, a few of Digital's formats are checked. Anomalies and errors are reported via `syslog`.				

mopprobe

UNIX Shell: All primary shells (csh, ksh, sh)

Function	Shows Ethernet address and node name for DEC servers 100/200/250/300 connected to one or all interfaces.
Syntax	mopprobe [options...] { *interface* }

-a	Listens on all the Ethernets connected to the system.
-3	Ignores all MOP V3 messages (Ethernet II).
-4	Ignores all MOP V4 messages (Ethernet 802.3).
-o	Shows a node just once.
-v	Shows all nodes sending MOP/RC SID messages.
interface	Specifies which interface to use. Must be specified if there is no -a.

File Name:	`mopprobe`	**Directory:**	/usr/sbin/	**Type:**	External

moptrace

UNIX Shell: All primary shells (csh, ksh, sh)

Function	Shows the contents of MOP packages on the Ethernet connected to one or all interfaces.
Syntax	moptrace [options...] { *interface* }

-a	Listens on all the Ethernets connected to the system.
-3	Ignores all MOP V3 messages (Ethernet II).
-4	Ignores all MOP V4 messages (Ethernet 802.3).
-d	Runs in debug mode, with all the output to STDERR.
interface	Specifies which interface to use. Must be specified if there is no -a.

File Name:	`moptrace`	**Directory:**	/usr/sbin/	**Type:**	External

mount_ados

UNIX Shell: All primary shells (csh, ksh, sh)

Function	Is used to mount an Amiga DOS file system.
Syntax	mount_ados [options...] *device path*

-o *options*	Specifies the mount options, as described in the `mount` command.
-u *UID*	Specifies the owner of the files in the file system.
-g *GID*	Specifies the group of the files in the file system.
-m *mask*	Specifies the default file permissions for files in the file system.
device	Specifies where the file system resides.
path	Specifies where to mount the file system.

File Name:	`mount_ados`	**Directory:**	/sbin/	**Type:**	External

mount_ados /dev/wd1a /mnt	Mounts the Amiga DOS file system from `/dev/wd1a` in `/mnt`.
mount_ados -u 0 -m 700 /dev/wd1a /mnt	Same as above, but makes root owner of all files and sets full permissions for root and none for all others.

mount_cd9660

mount_cd9660	UNIX Shell:	All primary shells (csh, ksh, sh)

Function	Mounts an ISO-9660 file system found on the specified device to the specified mount point path.
Syntax	mount_cd9660 [options...] *device directory*

-e	Uses extended attributes.
-g	Doesn't remove the version numbers of the files.
-j	Disables the Joliet extensions on the file system.
-o *options...*	Specifies options to use when mounting. Multiple options are separated with a comma.
-R	Disables the Rock ridge extensions on the file system.
-v	Verbose mode. Shows more information.
device	Specifies a special device to use as the source when mounting.
directory	Specifies a directory to use as the destination when mounting.

File Name:	`mount_cd9660`	**Directory:**	/sbin/	**Type:**	External

mount_cd9660 /dev/cd0a /mnt	Mounts the CD-ROM found in `/dev/cd0a` to `/mnt`.
mount_cd9660 -e /dev/cd0a /mnt	Mounts and disables the Joliet extensions.

mount_ext2fs

mount_ext2fs	UNIX Shell:	All primary shells (csh, ksh, sh)

Function	Mounts an extended2 file system found on the specified device and attaches that to the specified destination directory.
Syntax	mount_ext2fs [options...] *device directory*

-o *options...*	Specifies options to use when mounting. Multiple options are separated with a comma.
device	Specifies a special device to use as the source when mounting.
directory	Specifies a directory to use as the destination when mounting.

File Name:	`mount_ext2fs`	**Directory:**	/sbin/	**Type:**	External

mount_ext2fs /dev/wd0d /linux	Mounts the specified partition to `/linux`.

mount_fdesc

mount_fdesc	UNIX Shell:	All primary shells (csh, ksh, sh)

Function	Mounts an instance of the per-process file descriptor namespace to the file system.
Syntax	mount_fdesc [-o] *mountpoint*

-o *options*	Specifies a comma-separated list of any `mount` options.
mountpoint	Specifies the contents of the mount point options as follows:
fd	A directory's contents that appear as a list of numbered files.
stderr	Appears as symlinks to the relevant entry in the `/dev/fd` subdirectory.
stdin	Appears as symlinks to the relevant entry in the `/dev/fd` subdirectory.
stdout	Appears as symlinks to the relevant entry in the `/dev/fd` subdirectory.
tty	An indirect reference to the current process's controlling terminal.

File Name:	`mount_fdesc`	**Directory:**	/sbin/	**Type:**	External

mount_ffs

mount_ffs	UNIX Shell:	All primary shells (csh, ksh, sh)

Function	Mounts a Berkeley Fast File System on the specified device and node.
Syntax	mount ffs [-o] *device node*

-o *options*	Specifies a comma-separated list of any `mount` options.
device	Specifies the special device the file system will be mounted in.
node	Specifies the node the file system will be mounted to.

File Name:	`mount_ffs`	**Directory:**	/sbin/	**Type:**	External

mount_kernfs

mount_kernfs	UNIX Shell:	All primary shells (csh, ksh, sh)

Function	Mounts an instance of the kernel parameter namespace to the global file system.
Syntax	mount kernfs [-o] *mountpoint*

-o *options*	Specifies a comma-separated list of any `mount` options.
mountpoint	Specifies the Kern file system mount point.

File Name:	`mount_kernfs`	**Directory:**	/sbin/	**Type:**	External

mount_mfs

UNIX Shell:	All primary shells (csh, ksh, sh)
Function	Creates a file system in the virtual memory and then mounts it on the specified node.
Syntax	mount [options...] *file node*

-o *options*	Specifies a comma-separated list of any `mount` options.
-N	Shows the parameters, but doesn't create the files.
-a *count*	Specifies the maximum number of blocks laid out before a rotational delay (default is 8).
-b *size*	Specifies the block size of the file system in bytes.
-c *count*	Specifies the number of cylinders per cylinder group in a file system (default is 16).
-d *time*	Specifies the expected time in milliseconds for a transfer completion / initialization.
-e *count*	Specifies the maximum number of blocks any file can allocate in a cylinder group.
-f *size*	Specifies the fragment size in bytes.
-i *count*	Specifies the file systems inode density in bytes (default is 4096).
-m *count*	Specifies the space reserved from normal users in percent (default is 5).
-n *number*	Specifies the number of distinguished rotational partitions.
-s *size*	Specifies the size of the file system in sectors.
file	Specifies the special file to read for parameters.
node	Specifies the mount node.

File Name:	Directory:	Type:
`mount_mfs`	/sbin/	External

mount_msdos

UNIX Shell:	All primary shells (csh, ksh, sh)
Function	Mounts an MS-DOS file system to the specified special device at the specified node.
Syntax	mount [options...] *device node*

-o *options*	Specifies a comma-separated list of any `mount` options.
-u *user*	Specifies the name of the owner to the file system.
-g *group*	Specifies the name of the group owner.
-m *mask*	Specifies the file's permissions in octal numbers.
-s	Disables Windows 95/98 long filenames.
-l	Enables Windows 95/98 long filenames.
-9	Ignores the special Windows 95/98 directory entries even if deleted. Forces -s flag.
-G	Interprets the file system as an Atari Gemdos file system.
device	Specifies device to mount at.
node	Specifies node at the specified device.

File Name:	Directory:	Type:
`mount_msdos`	/sbin/	External

Warning: The -9 flag could result in damaged file systems. Default handling for -s and -l will result in empty file systems to be populated with short filenames only.

mount_nfs

UNIX Shell:	All primary shells (csh, ksh, sh)
Function	Mounts the NFS directory located on the computer specified to the mount point.
Syntax	mount_nfs *{ options... } hostname:sourcepath mountpoint*

-2	Uses version 2 of NFS.
-3	Uses version 3 of NFS.
-D *threshold*	Specifies the dead server threshold to set with the `NQNFS`.
-I *size*	Specifies the read size to set on the readdir.
-K	Uses Kerberos authentications with client-to-server mapping.
-L *seconds*	Specifies the lease term in seconds.
-P	For compatibility only.
-R *tries*	Specifies the amount of tries to mount before giving up.
-T	Disables the use of UDP and uses only TCP for transport.
-U	Disables the use of TCP and uses only UTP for transport.
-a *number*	Specifies how many blocks will be read before a large file is being read.
-b	Tries to connect to the NFS server even if the contact failed.
-c	Sends UTP requests to an NFS server without sending a TCP connect.
-d	Disables the retransmit timeout estimator.

continued

-g *groups*	Specifies how many groups a user can be a member of.
-i	Interrupts a mount when a server stops responding.
-l	Uses cache to make the RPC traffic faster.
-m *realm*	Specifies the Kerberos realm to use.
-o *options...*	Specifies options to use when mounting. Multiple options are separated with a comma.
port=*number*	Specifies a port to connect to on the NFS server. (There are other standard options that can be sent.)
-q	Uses the NFS version 3 leasing extensions.
-r *size*	Specifies what read data size to use.
-s	Performs a soft mount.
-t *seconds*	Specifies the retransmit timeout to use.
-w *size*	Specifies what write data size to use.
-x *number*	Specifies how many retries to use when mounting soft.
hostname	Specifies the NFS server's hostname.
sourcepath	Specifies the pathname to the shared directory on the NFS server.
mountpoint	Specifies the place to mount the NFS.
File Name: `mount_nfs`	**Directory:** /sbin/ **Type:** External
Tip:	NFS is perfect if you have several computers and want to share the same home file system.
mount_nfs ucgbook.com:/home/nfs /ucg	Mounts the remote directory `/home/nfs` to the local directory `/mnt`.

mount_null

UNIX Shell: All primary shells (csh, ksh, sh)

Function	Duplicates a subtree of the file system namespace and creates a null file system layer.
Syntax	mount_null [-o] *{ mountpoint }*

-o *options*	Specifies a comma-separated list of any `mount` options.
mountpoint	Specifies the mount point of the null file system layer.
File Name: `mount_null`	**Directory:** /sbin/ **Type:** External
Tip:	Two good reasons for a null layer: A good demo to use when teaching "how to build a layer" and a good prototype layer, because it has all the necessary layer framework that you need.

mount_portal

UNIX Shell: All primary shells (csh, ksh, sh)

Function	Mounts an instance of the portal daemon to the global file system namespace.
Syntax	mount_portal [-o] *mountpoint*

-o *options*	Specifies a comma-separated list of any `mount` options.
mountpoint	Specifies the mount point.
File Name: `mount_portal`	**Directory:** /sbin/ **Type:** External

mount_procfs

UNIX Shell: All primary shells (csh, ksh, sh)

Function	Mounts an instance of the process namespace to the global file system namespace.
Syntax	mount_procfs [-o] *mountpoint*

-o *options*	Specifies a comma-separated list of any `mount` options.
mountpoint	Specifies the mount point.
File Name: `mount_procfs`	**Directory:** /sbin/ **Type:** External

mount_ufs

UNIX Shell: All primary shells (csh, ksh, sh)

Function	Mounts a Berkeley Fast File System on the specified device to the specified mount point.
Syntax	mount ufs [options...] *device node*

-o *options*	Specifies a comma-separated list of any `mount` options.
device	Specifies the special device the file system will be mounted in.
node	Specifies the node the file system will be mounted to.
File Name: `mount_ufs`	**Directory:** /sbin/ **Type:** External

mount_umap

UNIX Shell: All primary shells (csh, ksh, sh)

Function	Mounts a subtree of a file system with a different set of UIDs and GIDs than the local system.
Syntax	mount umap [options...] *target mountpoint*

-o *options*	Specifies a comma-separated list of any `mount` options.
-u *file*	Specifies the file containing the UID mappings to be made between the identifiers.
-g *file*	Specifies the file containing the GID mapping to be made between the identifiers.
target	Specifies the current location of the subtree.
mountpoint	Specifies a directory where the mapped subtree is to be placed.

File Name:	`mount_umap`	**Directory:**	/sbin/	**Type:**	External

Note: The layer created by this command is meant to serve as an example of file system layering, so this is a good template or a training tool.

mount_union

UNIX Shell: All primary shells (csh, ksh, sh)

Function	Mounts a directory above uniondir and makes the contents of both directories visible.
Syntax	mount union [options...] *directory unioundirectory*

-o options	Specifies a comma-separated list of any `mount` options.
-b	Inverts the layer positions to make the new directory the lower one.
-r	Hides the lower layer.
directory	Specifies the union directory that is the lower layer.
uniondirectory	Specifies the union directory that is the upper layer.

File Name:	`mount_union`	**Directory:**	/sbin/	**Type:**	External

mount_xfs

UNIX Shell: All primary shells (csh, ksh, sh)

Function	Mounts one of the xfs character devices.
Syntax	mount_xfs [-o *list*] *device mountpoint*

-o *list*	Specifies a comma-separated list of any `mount` options.
device	Specifies a device to use for communication.
mountpoint	Specifies the mount point of the xfs character device.

File Name:	`mount_xfs`	**Directory:**	/sbin/	**Type:**	External

mrinfo

UNIX Shell: All primary shells (csh, ksh, sh)

Function	Shows the configuration information from a multicast router. Must be run as `root`.
Syntax	mrinfo [options...] *{ multicastrouter }*

-d *evell*	Specify the debug level to 0-3 (default is 0).
-t *seconds*	Sets the seconds to wait for a neighbor query reply before retrying (default is 4).
-r *number*	Specifies the number of neighbor query retries (default is 3).
multicastrouter	Specifies which multicastrouter to query.

File Name:	`mrinfo`	**Directory:**	/usr/sbin/	**Type:**	External

mrouted

UNIX Shell: All primary shells (csh, ksh, sh)

Function	Handles IP multicast routing among subnets.
Syntax	mrouted [options...]

-c *file*	Specifies a filename for the overriding configuration commands.
-d *{ level }*	Shows debug information with the specified level of 0-3.
-p	Starts in nonpruning mode.

File Name:	`mrouted`	**Directory:**	/usr/sbin/	**Type:**	External

Tip: The tunneling mechanism allows mrouted to establish a virtual Internet, for the purpose of multicasting only which is independent of the physical Internet and which may span multiple autonomous systems.

mset

UNIX Shell:	All primary shells (csh, ksh, sh)
Function	Retrieves mapping information for the ASCII keyboard to an IBM 3270 terminal.
Syntax	mset [options...] { *name* }

-picky	Shows warnings about all unknown entries.
-shell	Breaks the entries to fit in the shell environment.
name	Specifies a keyboard to take the mapping from.

File Name:	`mset`	**Directory:**	/usr/bin/	**Type:**	External

mset -picky	Shows all warning messages.

msgs

UNIX Shell:	All primary shells (csh, ksh, sh)
Function	Is used to read or save system messages sent by mail.
Syntax	msgs [options...] { *position* }

-f	Disables the message `No new messages`.
-q	Searches to see if there are any messages.
-h	Prints only the first part of a message.
-r	Deactivates the ability to do a message save or enter the mailer.
-l	Causes local messages to be shown.
-p	Pipes messages through a program specified by `pager` or with `more`.
-s	Prepares message posting and must be put into `/etc/aliases` to work.
	Possible responses when the message is longer than the screen:
y	Shows the rest of the message.
RETURN	Uses the Return key on the keyboard instead of the `y` option.
n	Skips the message and goes on to the next.
-	Repeats the last message.
q	Quits `msgs` and picks up where it left off the next time `msgs` starts.
m	Copies the message into a temporary mailbox and starts `mail`.
s { *file* }	Adds a current message to the message file in the local directory or a specified file.
s- { *file* }	Saves the last message to the message file in the local directory or a specified file.
position	Specifies the position (integer) in `.msgsrc` to start reading messages from.
-position	Specifies the position (integer) in `.msgsrc` to read messages backwards from.

File Name:	`msgs`	**Directory:**	/usr/bin/	**Type:**	External

msgs -h 1	Shows the beginning of all of the messages available in the `.msgsrc`, starting from the first one.
msgs -20	Shows all of the messages available in the `.msgsrc`, starting from the 20th one and going backward to the first one.
msgs -f	Disables the `No new messages` message.

mtrace

UNIX Shell:	All primary shells (csh, ksh, sh)
Function	Shows trace information about IP multicast traffic.
Syntax	mtrace [options...] *source* { *receiver* } { *group* }

-g *name*	Sends the trace unicast directly to the specified multicast router.
-e *number*	Tries to trace past a non-responding router the specified number of times.
-i *address*	Specifies the local and also default receiver address.
-l	Runs the trace as a loop and show information every ten seconds.
-M	Uses multicast to send responses only.
-m *count*	Specifies the maximum number of hops to trace.
-n	Shows hop addresses numerically only.
-q *count*	Specifies the maximum number of query attempts for a hop (default is 3).
-p	Listens passively to multicast responses from traces started by others.
-r *destinationt*	Sends the response to the specified destination.
-s	Shows only the multicast path as output.
-S *time*	Specifies the interval between traces in seconds (default is10).
-t *time*	Specifies the maximum number of hops (TTL) for a multicast trace (default is 64).
-v	Verbose mode. Shows more information.
-w *time*	Specifies the time to wait for a trace response in seconds (default is 3).

continued

source	Specifies the source of the query.		
receiver	Specifies the receiver of the query. The default is the host that is running mtrace.		
group	Specifies the multicast group. Default group is MBone Audio (224.2.0.1).		
File Name: mtrace	**Directory:** /usr/sbin/	**Type:**	External
Warning:	Ver. 3.3 and 3.5 will crash if a trace query is received via a unicast packet without a route for the source address.		

mtree

UNIX Shell: All primary shells (csh, ksh, sh)

Function	Shows the difference between a rooted directory and a specification on STDIN.
Syntax	mtree [options...]

-c	Shows a specification of the file hierarchy on STDOUT.
-d	Shows only directory type files.
-e	Ignores any error messages from files in the file hierarchy, but not the specification.
-f *file*	Specifies a file to read the specification from instead of STDIN.
-i	Indents with four spaces each time a directory level is descended, only when -c is used.
-K *words*	Adds the specified (whitespace or comma-separated) keywords to the current set.
-k *words*	Uses the specified and the type keywords instead of the current set.
-n	Does not emit pathname comments when a specification is created.
-p *path*	Specifies a different file hierarchy to use instead of the current directory.
-q	Quiet mode. Does not show error messages about missing directories.
-r	Deletes all files in the hierarchy that are not described in the specification.
-t	Updates the timestamps to match the specification time.
-s *value*	Shows a single checksum of the files, seeded with the specified value.
-U	Modifies the owner, group, and permissions to match the specification.
-u	Same as -U, except that status 2 is returned if the file hierarchy did not match.
-x	Does not descend below mount points in the directory.

File Name: mtree	**Directory:** /usr/sbin/	**Type:** External

named.reload

UNIX Shell: All primary shells (csh, ksh, sh)

Function	Initiates the name server to synchronize its database. It sends a SIGHUP to the running name server.
Syntax	named.reload

File Name: named.reload	**Directory:** /usr/sbin/	**Type:** External

named.restart

UNIX Shell: All primary shells (csh, ksh, sh)

Function	Stops the running name server by sending a SIGKILL signal and starts a new name server.
Syntax	named.restart

File Name: named.restart	**Directory:** /usr/sbin/	**Type:** External
Warning:	Does not wait after killing the old server before starting a new one. Does not check whether the name server is actually running.	

named-xfer

UNIX Shell: All primary shells (csh, ksh, sh)

Function	A program that is used to run inbound zone transfers.
Syntax	named-xfer options... [options...] *nameservers... { ACTION }*

	The following options are required:
-z *transferzone*	Is used to specify the zone that you want to transfer.
-f *file*	Specifies the file where to put the zone that is received from the name servers.
-s *serialno*	Is used to specify the serial number of the zone.
	The following options are optional:
-d *level*	Shows debug information. Debug level can be between 1 and 10.
-l *logfile*	Specifies where to put debug messages.
-t *tracefile*	Specifies a protocol trace file for debugging the zone transfer.
-p *port*	Sets a new port number to use instead of the default.
-S	Transfers only SOA, NS, and A records.

continued

nameservers...	Specifies the name server or servers to run a zone transfer on.		
ACTION	**Specifies the type of zone transfer to perform.**		
ixfr	Does a full zone transfer.		
axfr	Does an incremental zone transfer.		
File Name: `named-xfer`	**Directory:** /var/named/	**Type:**	External

nawk, awk

UNIX Shell: All primary shells (csh, ksh, sh)

Function	Scans each input file for lines that match any of a set of patterns specified as a string.
Syntax	nawk/awk [options...] ['*scriptstr*'] { *files...* }

-F *expression*	Specifies the expression to use as field separator.
-safe	Disables file output and access to the environment.
-mr *value*	Sets the maximum record size.
-mf *value*	Sets maximum number of fields.
' *scriptstr* '	Contains the pattern action statements and must be enclosed by singles quotes (').
	The following arithmetic functions are supported:
pattern { *action* }	The format for the pattern action statements specified by ' scriptstr '.
	The following arithmetic functions are supported:
atan2(*x,y*)	Returns the arctan of x / y. The result is in radians.
cos(*x*)	Returns the cosine of the specified value. The value must be in radians.
exp(*x*)	Returns the exponential function of the specified value.
int(*x*)	Shortens the specified value to an integer. It trims the value when x > 0.
log(*x*)	Returns the natural logarithm of the specified value.
rand( )	Returns a random number between 0 and 1.
sin(*x*)	Returns the sine of the specified value. The value must be in radians.
sqrt(*x*)	Returns the square root of the specified value.
srand({ *x* })	Specifies a new seed for the rand function; if not specified, use time of day.
	The following are the supported string functions (string is indicated by s):
gsub(*r, s* [, *t*])	Replaces all regular expression r with s in t. If t not given, use $0.
gensub(*r, s, h* [, *t*])	Is same as above if h = g or G. Otherwise, h specifies the match to replace.
index(*s, sub*)	Gives the position of string *s* where the substring sub occurs first.
length(*s*)	Gives the total length of an argument or an entire line if there is no argument.
match(*s, re*)	Returns the position where the regular expression re matches the string s.
split(*s, a, fs*)	Splits string s into an array of elements a1, a2, and separates fields with the fs exp.
sprintf(*fmt, expr...*)	Formats listed expressions with printf using the format specified by fmt.
sub(*r, s* [, *t*])	The same as gsub, but replaces only the first match.
substr(*s, m, n*)	Gives the n-character substring of the string s that starts at the m position.
toupper(*s*)	Returns the string with all letters uppercase.
tolower(*s*)	Returns the string with all letters lowercase.
	The following are the built-in variables that can be used:
-v *var=value*	Is used to specify a built-in variable listed below and assign it a value.
ARGC	Defines the number of command-line arguments, not counting the one to gawk.
ARGIND	Defines the index in ARGV of the current file being processed.
ARGV	Defines an array of command-line arguments index from 0 to ARGC-1.
CONVFMT	Specifies the conversion format for numbers (default is %.6g).
ENVIRON	Defines an array with the environment variables.
ERRNO	Define a string containing error description if an error occurs.
FIELDWIDTHS	Specifies a list of field widths.
FILENAME	Specifies the name of the current file being used for input.
FNR	Defines the input record number in the current input file.
FS	Defines input field separators (default is Space and Tab).
IGNORECASE	Specifies if case will be ignored. If zero (0), all function is case-sensitive.
NF	Defines number of fields in the existing file.
NR	Defines ordinal number for the current record.
OFMT	Defines output numbers in a specific format (default is %.6g).
OFS	Defines output field separators (default is blank).
ORS	Defines output record separators (default is new line).
RS	Defines input record separators (default is new line).

continued

RSTART	Specifies index of the first character match by match(); 0 if no match.
RLENGTH	Specifies the length of the string that matched by match(); -1 is no match.
SUBSEP	Specifies the character that separates subscripts in array elements (default is \034).
	The following are control flow functions:
break	Is used to exit from a for, while, or do loop.
continue	Starts the next loop cycle in a for, while, or do loop.
do *statement*	A loop that executes the specified statement while the condition is true.
while (*condition*)	Is evaluated by do and runs the do statement if the condition is true and exits if false.
exit *{ exp }*	Executes the end routine if it exists, and exits the script with return value exp.
if (*condition*)	Performs the statement if the condition is true or will perform the else condition.
else (*condition*)	Performs the else condition when the if condition is false.
while (*condition*)	Performs the condition as long as the condition is true.
for (*exp1; exp2 ; exp3*)	A loop that uses three expressions (see below). Exit when any expression is false.
exp1	Sets the counter variable an initial value that counts the number of loops.
exp2	Defines the variable that is read and evaluated before executing the statement.
exp3	A counter that increments each time the loop is true. (The variables exp1, exp2, exp3 are all optional and are true if not used.)
for (*arrayvar*)	A loop that executes each variable defined in an array.
next	Reads the input line and begins a new loop or procedure.
	The following input/output functions are supported:
getline	Sets $0 into the next input record using the current input file. (1 = success, –1 = error.)
print	Shows the results of the ' *scriptstr* ' and variables to STDOUT.
printf	Same as print, but also formats the output.
$*n*	Specifies the field number in the file ($1, $2, $3, and so forth) and separated by FS.
$0	Specifies to use the entire line in the file as input.
files...	Specifies the input files that are scanned for pattern matching.
File Name: `nawk`	**Directory:** /usr/bin/ **Type:** External

nc

UNIX Shell: All primary shells (csh, ksh, sh)

Function	Is used for TCP and UDP connections and listens.
Syntax	nc [options...]

-e *command*	Runs the specified command.
-g *host*	Specifies a chain in a loose source-routed path. Can be used several times.
-G *pointer*	Is used to position the hop counter in the list of hosts. Must be a multiple of 4.
-i *seconds*	Specifies the time interval between lines of text sent and received.
-l	Listens to incoming connection. Doesn't start a connection.
-n	Doesn't use DNS lookup.
-o *filename*	Creates a log file of transfer information in hexadecimal format.
-p *port*	Specifies the port to use.
-r	Uses semirandom ports for source and destination.
-s *ip-adress*	Specifies the IP address for the interface to use. Can be specified with the name.
-t	Uses RFC854 Don't and won't response to DO and WILL request.
-u	Uses UDP, not TCP.
-v	Verbose mode. Shows more information.
-w timeout	Specifies the timeout for nc. After the timeout, nc will end.
-z	Scans for listening daemons, without sending any data to them.
File Name: `nc`	**Directory:** /usr/bin/ **Type:** External
nc -p 31337 example.host 42	Opens a TCP connection to port 42 of example.host, and uses port 31337 as the source port.
nc -w 5 example.host 42	Opens a TCP connection to port 42 of example.host, and times out after five seconds while attempting to connect.
nc -u example.host 53	Sends any data from STDIN to UDP port 53 of example.host, and shows any data returned.

ncheck_ffs, ncheck

ncheck_ffs, ncheck	UNIX Shell:	All primary shells (csh, ksh, sh)
Function	Creates a list of filenames and inode numbers for the given file system.	
Syntax	ncheck_ffs [options...] *filesystem*	

-i *numbers*	Shows only those files whose inode numbers follow.
-a	Shows the filenames dot (.) and double dot (..), which are ordinarily skipped.
-m	Verbose mode. Shows more information about inodes.
-s	Shows only special files and files with set-user ID or set-group ID set.
filesystem	Specifies which file system to use.
File Name: `ncheck_ffs`	Directory: /sbin/ Type: External
Tip:	-s is a great way of finding hidden violations of security policies.

ndc

ndc	UNIX Shell:	Bourne shell (sh)
Function	Allows the administrator of the name server to send commands to the name server.	
Syntax	ndc *{ ACTIONS... }*	

ACTIONS...	**Select one or more of the following actions:**
status	Shows the status of the name server.
dumpdb	Dumps the name server database and cache to /var/named/namedb/named_dump.db.
reload	Checks the name server serial numbers of the primary/secondary zones and loads changes.
stats	Dumps the name server statistics to `/var/named/namedb/named.stats`.
trace	Increases the name server's tracing level by one. Find it at `/var/named/namedb/named.run`.
notrace	Causes named to set tracing level to 0 and closes /var/named/namedb/named.run if open.
querylog	Toggles query logging, which starts a `syslog` of queries.
start	Starts the name server as long as it isn't already active.
stop	Stops the name server as long as it is active.
restart	Stops and then starts the name server.
File Name: `ndc`	Directory: /usr/sbin/ Type: Script
Tip:	Query logging consumes a lot of file space and any arguments that are sent to the name server are not saved by `restart`.
ndc status	Shows the status of the name server.
ndc stats	Dumps the name server statistics to `/var/named/namedb/named.stats`.

netgroup_mkdb

netgroup_mkdb	UNIX Shell:	All primary shells (csh, ksh, sh)
Function	Creates netgroup databases (`/etc/netgroup.db`) from the `/etc/netgroup` file and saves it in `/etc/netgroup.db`.	
Syntax	netgroup_mkdb [-o *database*] *{ file }*	

-o *database*	Uses the specified database instead of /etc/netgroup.db.
file	Specifies a different file than /etc/netgroup to use as input.
File Name: `netgroup_mkdb`	Directory: /usr/sbin/ Type: External

newfs

newfs	UNIX Shell:	All primary shells (csh, ksh, sh)
Function	Creates a new file system using defaults based on the disk label created by `disklabel`.	
Syntax	newfs [options...]	

-N	Shows what the command would do, but doesn't execute.
-O	Creates an older boot ROMs compatible 4.3-BSD format file system.
-a *value*	Specifies the maximum contiguous blocks before forcing a rotational delay (default is 8).
-b *bsize*	Specifies the logical block size in bytes when you create a file system.
-c *cgsize*	Specifies the number of cylinders to use per cylinder group (default is 16).
-d *gap*	Specifies the time a service can take to initiate a new transfer if it's interrupted. (The time is specified in milliseconds, (default is 0).)
-e *value*	Specifies the max amount of blocks per cylinder group a file may use.

continued

-f *fragsize*	Specifies the fragment size in bytes to use on the new file system.
-i *idensity*	Specifies the inode density in the file system (default is 1 inode per 4096 bytes).
-m *free*	Specifies the minimum percentage of free space to be available (default is 5%).
-n *nrpos*	Specifies the number of rotational positions per cylinder group (default is 1).
-o *opt*	Minimizes time spent allocating time or minimizing fragments space.
-q	Sets quiet mode.
-s *size*	Specifies the size of the file system in sectors.
	The following options skip the defaults, for creating an FS for other disks:
-S *size*	Specifies the size of sectors in bytes (often 512 bytes).
-k *value*	Used to describe problems in the media format to compensate for slow controllers.
-l hardware sector interleave	Used to describe problems in the media format to compensate for slow controllers.
-p sector(s)	Spares sectors per track. This is often used to spare bad sectors.
-r revolutions per minute	Shows the speed of the disk in revolutions per minute.
-z #tracks/cylinder	The number of tracks/cylinders available for data allocation by the file system.
-t filesystemtype	Sets the file system type of the file system you wish to create, like `newfs_fstype`.
-u sectors per track	The number of sectors per track available for data allocation by the file system.
-x sector(s)	Spares sectors per cylinders. This is often used to spare bad sectors.
File Name: `newfs3`	**Directory:** /sbin/ **Type:** External

newfs_msdos

UNIX Shell: All primary shells (csh, ksh, sh)

Function	Creates a new MS-DOS file system on the device.
Syntax	newfs_msdos [options...] *device*

-s *kilobytes*	Specifies the size in kilobytes (can be 360, 720, 1200, or 1440).
-L *label*	Specifies the label of the disk (default is 4.4-BSD).
device	Specifies the device to use.
File Name: `newfs_msdos`	**Directory:** /sbin/ **Type:** External
newfs_msdos /dev/wd1a	Creates a new MS-DOS file system on `/dev/wd1a`.
newfs_msdos -s 1440 /dev/fd/0	Creates a new MS-DOS file system on a 1.44MB floppy.

newsyslog

UNIX Shell: All primary shells (csh, ksh, sh)

Function	Archives system log files at intervals or when log file exceeds a specified size.
Syntax	newsyslog [options...]

-v	Verbose mode. Shows more information.
-m	Runs `newsyslog` in monitoring mode. (Only entries marked with an M in flags are processed.)
-n	Outputs what `newsyslog` would do with the log file, but does nothing.
-r	Enables `newsyslog` to run without being root. Mainly for debugging.
-f [config file]	Uses the specified configuration file (default is `/etc/newsyslog.conf`).
	The following fields exists in the configuration file:
logfile name	Specifies full pathname to the system log file.
owner.group of archives	Specifies the owner and the group for the archives (is optional).
mode of logfile &archives	Specifies the octal mode of created archives and log files.
number of archives	Specifies how many archives to keep, except the original log file.
	To skip any of the two following insert an * in that field:
size of archives	Specifies the size of the log file at which it will be archived.
archive interval	Specifies the interval in hours at which the log file will be archived.
flags	Enables special processing (is optional). The following flags are valid:
Z	Compresses the archive using gzip or compress.
B	Assumes the file is a binary file.
M	Handles the log file as monitored.
monitor notification	Specifies an account to send messages to when a log file is monitored (is optional).
pid file	Specifies a PID file to send the SIGHUP signal (is optional). (Default is /var/run/syslog.pid.)
File Name: `newsyslog`	**Directory:** /usr/bin/ **Type:** External
newsyslog -v -f mypersonalsyslog.conf	Runs `newsyslog` in verbose mode and uses the specified config file.

nfsiod

UNIX Shell:	All primary shells (csh, ksh, sh)
Function	Improves performance for NFS asynchronous I/O requests for its server.
Syntax	nfsiod [-n *number*]

-n *number*	Specifies the number of servers that are started (max 20).				
File Name:	`nfsiod`	**Directory:**	/sbin/	**Type:**	External

nologin

UNIX Shell:	All primary shells (csh, ksh, sh)
Function	A shell used only to deny a user to login. Shows the user the contents of `/etc/nologin.txt`.
Syntax	nologin

File Name:	`nologin`	**Directory:**	/sbin/	**Type:**	External
Tip:	I use this when I want to reject an abusive user from the system for a short time instead of removing the user.				

objdump

UNIX Shell:	All primary shells (csh, ksh, sh)
Function	Shows information about object files. Information shown is controlled by given options.
Syntax	objdump [options...] *objectfiles...*

-a	Shows archive header information if any object file is an archive file.
-b *bfdname*	Sets the object-code format to bfdname for object files. Please see -i option for formats.
--debugging	Shows debug information.
-d	Shows the assembler instructions in the object file for instruction sections only.
-D	Shows the assembler instructions in the object file for all sections.
--prefix-addresses	Shows information in an older format, a complete address at every line.
-EB	Specifies that big endian is in use when disassembled.
-EL	Specifies that little endian is in use when disassembled.
-f	Shows all information of the overall header summary for each object file.
-h	Shows a summary of the section header for each object file.
--help	Shows help information.
-i	Shows all architectures and object formats to use with -b and -m options.
-j *name*	Specifies the name of the section to show information for.
-l	Labels the display if used with the -d, -D, or -r options.
-m *architecture*	Sets the architecture when disassembling object files. See -i option for formats.
-r	Shows the relocation entries for the object file.
-R	Shows the dynamic relocation entries for the object file.
-s	Shows all contents for any section.
-S	Shows disassembly information in the source code when possible.
--show-raw-insn	Shows the instructions in HEX and symbolic form when disassembling instructions.
--noshow-raw-insn	Doesn't show the instruction bytes.
--stabs	Shows the content in .stab sections in an ELF object file.
--start-address=*address*	Specifies the address to start showing data.
--stop-address=*address*	Specifies the address to stop showing data.
-t	Shows the symbol table entries in the object file.
-T	Shows the dynamic symbol table entries in the object file.
--version	Shows version information.
-x	Shows all header information, with the symbol table and relocation entries.
objectfiles...	Specifies the object files to examine.

File Name:	`objdump`	**Directory:**	/usr/bin/	**Type:**	External
objdump -f hello.o		Shows overall header summary information for object hello.o.			

oldrdist

UNIX Shell:	All primary shells (csh, ksh, sh)
Function	A file distribution program that remotely maintains copies of files over multiple hosts.
Syntax	oldrdist [options...] [-f *file*] [-d *var=value*] [-m *host*] *{ names... }* rdist [options...] -c *names... { user@] host [:destination }*

	The following options are valid for both syntax formats:
-b	Compares binary differences between files.

continued

-d *var=value*	Forces a specified variable to have a specific value.
-h	Follows any symbolic links by copying the file that the link points to.
-i	Ignores any unresolved links.
-m *host*	Limits which hosts will be updated. Use more `m's` for more hosts.
-n	Shows the commands, but will not run them.
-q	Starts quiet mode. Any file modification information is suppressed.
-R	Removes any extra files while a directory is being updated.
-v	Verifies that the host files are up-to-date. Any out-of-date files will be shown.
-w	Starts whole mode — that is, the entire filename is appended to the destination directory.
-y	Starts younger mode. Forbids the updates of files that are newer than the master copy.
	This option works only with the first syntax:
-f *file*	Specifies which distfile to use. If a hyphen - is used then STDIN is the input.
	This option works only with the second syntax:
-c *names...*	Specifies the distfile that is used.
user@host [*:destination*]	Forces `oldrdist` to interpret these arguments as an additional distfile.
user	Specifies the login ID.
host	Specifies the host to use.
destination	Specifies the file destination.
File Name: `oldrdist`	**Directory:** /usr/bin/ — **Type:** External

olf2elf

UNIX Shell: All primary shells (csh, ksh, sh)

Function	Converts from OLF to ELF object module format.
Syntax	olf2elf [-v] *files...*

-v	Verbose mode. Shows more information.
files...	Specifies the files to convert.
File Name: `olf2elf`	**Directory:** /usr/bin/ — **Type:** External

openssl

UNIX Shell: All primary shells (csh, ksh, sh)

Function	Performs various cryptographic functions from the shell and can create certificates.
Syntax	openssl *command* [command options...] *{ command arguments... }* openssl [list-*command*] openssl no-*command*

This is the same command as the one found in Linux. Please see openssl in the Linux chapter for all the options.

File Name: `openssl`	**Directory:** /usr/sbin/ — **Type:** External
openssl list-standard-commands	Shows the complete list of standard commands that are available.

otp-md4

UNIX Shell: All primary shells (csh, ksh, sh)

Function	Creates one-time passwords to authenticate access to a computer system with the MD4 hash algorithm.
Syntax	otp-md4 [options...] *NR key*

-x	Shows the string in hexadecimal instead of ASCII.
-4,-5	Selects MD4 or MD5, respectively, as the response generation algorithm.
-n *value*	Specifies how many one-time passwords to show.
-p *password*	Specifies the password to use. if not specified, the command will ask for it.
NR	Specifies a sequence number to use.
key	Specifies the key to use.
File Name: `otp-md4`	**Directory:** /usr/bin/ — **Type:** External
otp-md4 954 shagul1	Generates a password string.

otp-md5

otp-md5	UNIX Shell:	All primary shells (csh, ksh, sh)
Function	Creates one-time passwords to authenticate access to a computer system with the MD5 hash algorithm.	
Syntax	otp-md5 [options...] *NR key*	

-x	Shows the string in hexadecimal instead of ASCII.
-n *value*	Specifies how many one-time passwords to show.
-p *password*	Specifies the password to use. If not specified, the command will ask for it.
NR	Specifies a sequence number to use.
key	Specifies the key to use.

File Name:	`otp-md5`	**Directory:**	/usr/bin/	**Type:**	External
otp-md5 873 ksjdur		Generates a password string.			

otp-rmd160

otp-rmd160	UNIX Shell:	All primary shells (csh, ksh, sh)
Function	Creates one-time passwords to authenticate access to a computer system with the rmd160 hash algorithm.	
Syntax	otp-rmd160 [options...] *NR key*	

-x	Shows the string in hexadecimal instead of ASCII.
-n *value*	Specifies how many one-time passwords to show.
-p *password*	Specifies the password to use. If not specified, the command will ask for it.
NR	Specifies a sequence number to use.
key	Specifies the key to use.

File Name:	`otp-rmd160`	**Directory:**	/usr/bin/	**Type:**	External
otp-rmd160 99 shagul1		Generates a password string.			

otp-sha1

otp-sha1	UNIX Shell:	All primary shells (csh, ksh, sh)
Function	Creates one-time passwords to authenticate access to a computer system with the sha1 hash algorithm.	
Syntax	otp-sha1 [options...] *NR key*	

-x	Shows the string in hexadecimal instead of ASCII.
-n *value*	Specifies how many one-time passwords to show.
-p *password*	Specifies the password to use. If not specified, the command will ask for it.
NR	Specifies a sequence number to use.
key	Specifies the key to use.

File Name:	`otp-sha1`	**Directory:**	/usr/bin/	**Type:**	External
otp-sha1 99 shagul1		Generates a password string.			

pac

pac	UNIX Shell:	All primary shells (csh, ksh, sh)
Function	Shows you general statistics about a printer or a plotter.	
Syntax	pac [options...] *{ users... }*	

-P*printer*	Shows the account file for the specified printer.
-c	Makes the output be sorted by cost, instead of sorting alphabetically.
-m	Ignores the hostname in the accounting file.
-p*price*	Specifies the cost in dollars (default is 0.02 or what's in `/etc/printcap`).
-r	Reverses the sorting order.
-s	Summarizes the accounting information in the summary file.
users...	Specifies the users to show statistics for.

File Name:	`pac`	**Directory:**	/usr/sbin/	**Type:**	External
pac -Pprinter1 -c		Shows statistics about printer1 sorted by cost.			

pagesize

pagesize	UNIX Shell:	All primary shells (csh, ksh, sh)
Function	Shows the page size of memory.	
Syntax	pagesize	

File Name:	`pagesize`	**Directory:**	/usr/bin/	**Type:**	External

pax	UNIX Shell:	All primary shells (csh, ksh, sh)

Function	Administers archives. Lists member; extracts archives and archive files.
Syntax	pax -r [options...] *{ patterns... }* pax -w [options...] *{ files... }* pax -r -w [options...] *{ files... } directory* pax [options...] *{ patterns... }*

	Select one of these modes of operation:
-r	Extracts members of the pax archive read from STDIN using pattern matching.
-w	Writes the file content to STDOUT or to a file in the specified archive format.
-rw	Copies the file content to the destination or from STDIN.
	The following options are supported in all modes:
-d	Doesn't use subdirectories when archiving files or extracting archive members.
-v	Verbose mode. When in list mode, shows table of contents; otherwise, pathnames.
-s *oldnew*	Alters archive or file member names listed by pattern or filenames. (oldnew follows the following format: /old/new/ [gp] where:.)
old	Specifies the regular expression or a string containing new line characters.
new	Contains ampersand and/or a back reference \n, where n = subpattern number.
g	Applies the replacement globally.
p	Causes successful replacements to be written to STDERR.
-U *user*	Selects a file based on its username or user ID if it starts with "#."
-G *group*	Selects a file based on its group name or group ID if it starts with "#."
-T*{ fromdate }* [*,todate*] [/] [c] [m]	Selects files changed between the specified time range.
fromdate	Specifies the start date.
todate	Specifies the end date.
c	Uses the inode change time for comparison. Can only be used in write or copy mode.
m	Uses the modification change time for comparison. Can only be used in w or c mode.
	The following options are only available in a mode if the first letter appears: L = list, R = read, W = write, C = copy:
-c	(LR) Doesn't use archive or file members that match patterns or filenames.
-n	(LRC) Uses the first archive member for every specified pattern.
-z	(LRW) Compresses or decompresses the file. Cannot be used with -a option.
-f *file*	(LRW) Specifies the file of the input or output archive, instead of STDIN or STDOUT.
-i	(RWC) Prompts when renaming archive members or files matching the specified pattern.
-k	(RC) Doesn't overwrite files that already exist.
-u	(RWC) Skips files that are older than preexisting files or archive members.
-D	(RC) Is like -u, but will check the inode change time, instead of modification time.
-Y	(RC) Is like -D, but will check the pathname created after file modifications are done.
-Z	(RC) Is like -u, but will check the pathname created after file modifications are done.
-o *options*	(RW) Specifies how to modify the algorithm for extracting or writing archive files.
options	Modifies the algorithm with the format name = value.
-p *priv*	(RC) Specifies the privileges that the extracted file will keep.
a	Doesn't save file access times.
m	Doesn't keep the file modification times.
o	Keeps the user and group IDs.
p	Keeps the file mode bits.
e	Keeps the user and group IDs, file mode bits, and the access and modification times.
-E *limit*	(R) Specifies how many read faults to accept before stopping the operation.
-t	(WC) Resets the archived files' access times to what they had before being read.
-H	(WC) Follows command-line symbolic links while doing a physical FS traversal.
-L	(WC) Follows all symbolic links to perform a logical file system traversal.
-P	(WC) Doesn't follow symbolic links.
-X	(WC) Doesn't include subdirectories if they don't match parent device ID.
-b *blocksize*	Specifies the number of bytes per write to the archive file. Must be a multiple of 512.
-a	(W) Appends the specified files to the end of the archive. (Can only be used with the -f option.)
-x	(W) Specifies the archive format to use. Can be one of the following:
cpio	Specifies the extended cpio interchange format.

continued

bcpio	Specifies the old binary cpio format.
sv4cpio	Specifies the system V release 4 cpio.
sv4crc	Specifies the system V release 4 cpio with file crc checksums.
tar	Specifies the old BSD tar format.
ustar	Specifies the extended tar interchange format.
-B *bytes*	(W) Limits the number of bytes that can be written to a single archive volume. (Can have a suffix for multiple. m=1,048,576,k = 1,024, b = 512.)
-l	(C) Makes hard links between src and dst file hierarchies whenever possible.
patterns...	Specifies files of archive members
File Name: `pax`	**Directory:** /bin/ **Type:** External

pctr

UNIX Shell: All primary shells (csh, ksh, sh)

Function	Shows the current values of TSC and can access the pctr pseudo device on i386-compatible computers.
Syntax	pctr [-l *value*]

-l 5 or 6	Lists vendor-specific counters (5 or 6 specify which family to show).
File Name: `pctr`	**Directory:** /usr/bin/ **Type:** External

perlbug

UNIX Shell: All primary shells (csh, ksh, sh)

Function	Is used to create bug reports for `perl`.
Syntax	perlbug [options...] *{ ACTION }*

-a *address*	Specifies the address to send the bug report to. Default is perlbug@perl.com.
-s *subject*	Specifies a subject for the bug report.
-b *body*	Specifies a body for the bug report.
-f *infile*	Specifies a file with the body report already written.
-F *outfile*	Specifies an output file instead of sending the bug report by e-mail.
-r *returnaddress*	Specifies the return address.
-e *editor*	Specifies the editor that is used.
-c *adminaddress*	Specifies an address where to send a copy of the bug report.
-C	Sends any copies of the bug report to the administrator.
-S	Sends the bug report without waiting for confirmation.
-t	Runs the command in test mode.
-d	Shows your configuration data.
-h	Shows help information.
-v	Verbose mode. Shows more information.
ACTION	**The following actions can't be combined:**
-ok	Reports successful builds on the system.
-okay	Reports successful builds on older systems.
-nok	Reports unsuccessful builds on the system.
-nokay	Reports unsuccessful builds for older systems.
File Name: `perlbug`	**Directory:** /usr/bin/ **Type:** External

perlbug -ok	Reports on any successful binds on the system.
perlbug -t	Runs perlbug in test mode.
perlbug -d	Shows configuration data.

perldoc

UNIX Shell: Perl script

Function	Is used to find and show Perl documentation from inside installation's trees or scripts.
Syntax	perldoc [options...] *item*

-h	Shows help information.
-v	Shows verbose information.
-t	Shows documents in plain text instead of `nroff`.
-u	Finds the documents, but doesn't show them.
-m	Shows the whole module.
-l	Shows the filename of the module.
-F	Takes all arguments as filenames, not directories.

continued

-X		Uses an index, if available.	
-f *function*		Uses a perl function to pick out function-specific information.	
-q *expr*		Specifies a regular expression to search the perlfaq for matching entries.	
		The following items can be searched for:	
page		Specifies a page to search for.	
module		Specifies a module to search for.	
program		Specifies a program to search for.	
File Name:	`perldoc`	**Directory:** /usr/bin/	**Type:** Script

pfbtops

UNIX Shell: All primary shells (csh, ksh, sh)

Function	Converts a PostScript font in .pfb format into ASCII format.
Syntax	pfbtops *{ pfbfile }*

pfbfile		Specifies the .pfb file to convert.	
File Name:	`pfbtops`	**Directory:** /usr/bin/	**Type:** External

photurisd

UNIX Shell: All primary shells (csh, ksh, sh)

Function	It is a daemon used for IPSec key management.
Syntax	photurisd [options...]

-c		Forces a primality check of the bootstrapped module.	
-v		Starts photurisd in VPN mode.	
-i		Ignores the photuris.startup file.	
-d *directory*		Specifies the directory where the startup file is.	
-p *port*		Specifies the local port to use.	
File Name:	`photurisd`	**Directory:** /sbin/	**Type:** External

pkg_add

UNIX Shell: All primary shells (csh, ksh, sh)

Function	Installs software package distributions.
Syntax	pkg_add [options...] *pkgnames...*

-v		Verbose mode. Shows more information.	
-I		Doesn't run any installation script that exists.	
-n		Doesn't install the package, only shows the steps.	
-f		Is used to force an installation even if some requirements are not met.	
-R		Doesn't record any information about the packet. Packet cannot be uninstalled.	
-M		Runs pkg_add in MASTER mode.	
-S		Runs pkg_add in SLAVE mode.	
-t *template*		Specifies a template to be used by `mktemp`.	
-p *directory*		Specifies the directory to look in for the package.	
pkgnames...		Specifies the package to install - . (dot) searches in current directory.	
File Name:	`pkg_add`	**Directory:** /usr/sbin/	**Type:** External

pkg_add .	Search for package from the current directory.
pkg_add -v newpackage	Add newpackage in verbose mode.

pkg_create

UNIX Shell: All primary shells (csh, ksh, sh)

Function	Utility for creating software package distributions.
Syntax	pkg_create [options...] *pkgname*

-f *packlist*	Uses pack list as the packing list for the package.
-c *file*	Specifies a file that contains a one-line description for the package.
-c *-description*	Specifies a description of the package.
-d *file*	Specifies a file that contains a long description for the package.
-d *-description*	Specifies a long description of the package.
-Y	Uses yes as the answer for all questions.
-N	Uses no as the answer for all questions.

continued

-O	Uses packing list only mode.
-v	Verbose mode. Shows more information.
-h	Makes tar follow symbolic links.
-i *script*	Specifies an installation script.
-P *pkgs...*	Specifies a list of dependency packages.
-C *pkgs...*	Specifies a list of conflicts packages.
-p *directory*	Specifies the directory to start to build the package from.
-k *script*	Specifies a deinstallation script.
-r *script*	Specifies a script to check for requirements.
-t template	Specifies the template for mktemp (default is `/tmp/instmp.XXXXXX`).
-X *excludefile*	Specifies a list of files to exclude in the package.
-D *file*	Specifies a file to be shown with more after the installation.
-m *mtreefile*	Runs `mtree` with mtreefile before the package is installed.
pkgname	Specifies the name of the package to create.
File Name: `pkg_create`	**Directory:** /usr/sbin/ **Type:** External

pkg_delete

UNIX Shell: All primary shells (csh, ksh, sh)

Function	It is used to remove previously installed software packages from the system.
Syntax	pkg_delete [options...] *pkgnames...*

-v	Verbose mode. Shows more information.
-D	Doesn't run any deinstallation scripts.
-n	Doesn't deinstall the package, only shows the steps.
-p *directory*	Specifies a directory where to start deleting files. Normally, this isn't used.
-d	Removes empty directories.
-f	Forces a removal of the package.
pkgnames...	Specifies the name of the package to be removed.
File Name: `pkg_delete`	**Directory:** /usr/sbin/ **Type:** External
pkg_delete softpack	Delete the package softpack.

pkg_info

UNIX Shell: All primary shells (csh, ksh, sh)

Function	Is used to show information about software packages, both installed and not installed.
Syntax	pkg_info [options...] *pkgnames..*

-a	Shows information for all packages.
-c	Shows the one-line comment.
-D	Shows the install message file (if any).
-d	Show the long description.
-e *pkgname*	Tests if the package is installed. If so, returns 0.
-f	Shows the packing list instructions.
-I	Shows the index entry.
-i	Shows the install script (if any).
-k	Shows the de-install script (if any).
-L	Shows the files in the package with a full path.
-l *prefix*	Sets a prefix for the information category header shown.
-m	Shows the mtree file (if any).
-p	Shows the installation prefix.
-q	Doesn't show any report headers. Shows only the raw information.
-R	Shows the required packages for the package.
-r	Shows the requirements script (if any).
-v	Verbose mode. Shows more information.
-h	Shows help information.
pkgnames...	Specifies package to show information about. Can be a file or an installed package.
File Name: `pkg_info`	**Directory:** /usr/sbin/ **Type:** External
pkg_info -a	Shows information about all installed packages.

pl2pm

UNIX Shell: Perl script

Function	Is used to convert perl4 .pl files to perl5 .pm modules.				
Syntax	pl2pm *files...*				
files...	Specifies the files to convert.				
File Name:	`pl2pm`	**Directory:**	/usr/bin/	**Type:**	Script
pl2pm module.pl	Converts the file to module.pm.				

pom

UNIX Shell: All primary shells (csh, ksh, sh)

Function	Shows the current moon phase.				
Syntax	pom *datetime*				
datetime	Specifies the date and time using the following format: ccyymmddHH.				
File Name:	`pom`	**Directory:**	usr/games/pom	**Type:**	External

portmap

UNIX Shell: All primary shells (csh, ksh, sh)

Function	Converts RPC program numbers into DARPA protocol port numbers.				
Syntax	portmap [-d]				
-d	Debug mode. Shows debug information on STDERR.				
File Name:	`portmap`	**Directory:**	/usr/sbin/	**Type:**	External
portmap -d	Runs a debug and shows the result without starting the daemon.				

ppp

UNIX Shell: All primary shells (csh, ksh, sh)

Function	Creates user PPP links over the tunnel device.				
Syntax	ppp [options...] *{ systems... }*				
-alias	Enables packet aliasing features.				
-auto	Configures the interface automatically.				
-background	Attempts to establish a connection with the peer immediately.				
-direct	Receives incoming connections.				
-dedicated	Keeps the device open and never uses any configure chat scripts.				
-ddial	Brings the link back up any time it's dropped for any reason.				
-interactive	Starts the interactive mode.				
systems...	Specifies one or more systems defined in `/etc/ppp/ppp.conf`.				
File Name:	`ppp`	**Directory:**	/usr/sbin/	**Type:**	External

pppctl

UNIX Shell: All primary shells (csh, ksh, sh)

Function	Is used to control the PPP daemon.				
Syntax	pppctl [options...] *socket { commands... }*				
-v	Verbose mode. Shows more information.				
-t *sec*	Specifies the timeout in seconds (default is 2 seconds).				
-p *passwd*	Specifies the password used. If not given, pppctl will ask for one.				
socket	Specifies the socket to connect to. It can be one of the following syntaxes:				
*{ host: }*port	Specifies a local port to use, or a port on host.				
localsocket	Specifies a localsocket to use.				
commands...	Specifies commands to send to the PPP daemon.				
File Name:	`pppctl`	**Directory:**	/usr/sbin/	**Type:**	External

pppd	UNIX Shell:	All primary shells (csh, ksh, sh)
Function	Starts the Point-to-Point Protocol daemon.	
Syntax	pppd *{ tty }* *{ speed }* [options...]	

active-filter *expression*	Specifies a packet filter to be applied to data packets to detect link activity.
asyncmap *map*	Specifies an async character map.
auth	Specifies the peer must authenticate itself.
bsdcomp *number,total*	Specifies the compression level for the peer to send using BSD compression.
call *script*	Specifies a file in `/etc/ppp/peers/name` to read options from.
chap-interval *number*	Specifies rechallenge of the peer every number of seconds.
chap-max-challenge *number*	Specifies maximum number of CHAP challenge transmission to number (default is 10).
chap-restart *number*	Specifies the CHAP retransmission timeout for challenges to number seconds.
connect *script*	Specifies a script to set up the serial line.
crtscts	Specifies that hardware flow control should be used on the serial port.
debug	Specifies that connection debugging should be done.
default-asyncmap	Specifies that asyncmap negotiation should be disabled.
default-mru	Specifies that MRU negotiation should be disabled.
defaultroute	Specifies that a default route should be added to the system routing tables.
deflate *number:total*	Specifies the compression level for the peer to send using a deflate scheme.
demand	Specifies the link only should be initiated when data traffic is present.
disconnect *script*	Specifies a script to run when the link is terminated.
domain *domain*	Specifies that domain should be added to the local hostname for authentication.
escape *characters*	Specifies that certain characters should be escaped on transmission.
file *file*	Specifies a file to read option from.
holdoff *number*	Specifies the number of seconds before reinitiating the link after it terminates.
idle *number*	Specifies the link should be closed if the link is idle for number of seconds.
ipcp-accept-local	Specifies the peer's idea of our local IP address is accepted.
ipcp-accept-remote	Specifies the peer's idea of our remote IP address is accepted.
ipcp-max-configure *number*	Specifies maximum number of IPCP configure requests to be sent (default is 10).
ipcp-max-failure *number*	Specifies the maximum number of IPCP NAKs returned before sending rejects.
ipcp-max-terminate *number*	Specifies maximum number of IPCP terminate requests (default is 3).
ipcp-restart *number*	Specifies IPCP restart interval to number seconds (default is 3).
ipparam *string*	Specifies an extra parameter to the ip-up and ip-down scripts.
ipx	Specifies the IPXCP and IPX protocols should be enabled.
ipx-network *number*	Specifies the IPX network number in the IPXCP configure request frame.
ipx-node *number:number*	Specifies the IPX local node number and the peer's node number.
ipx-router-name *{ string }*	Specifies the name of the IPX router.
ipx-routing *number*	Specifies the routing protocol to be received by this option.
ipxcp-accept-local	Specifies that peer's NAK should be accepted for the node number.
ipxcp-accept-network	Specifies that peer's NAK should be accepted for the network number.
ipxcp-accept-remote	Specifies the peer's network number specified in the configure request frame.
ipxcp-max-configure *number*	Specifies the maximum number of IPXCP configure request frames.
ipxcp-max-failure *number*	Specifies the maximum number of IPXCP NAK frames.
ipxcp-max-terminate *number*	Specifies the maximum number of IPXCP terminate request frames.
kdebug *number*	Specifies the number for debugging the PPP driver in the kernel.
lcp-echo-failure *number*	Specifies the number of LCP echo-request frames before assuming the peer is dead.
lcp-echo-interval *number*	Specifies that LCP echo-request should be sent every number of seconds.
lcp-max-configure *number*	Specifies the maximum number of LCP configure-request transmissions (default is 10).
lcp-max-failure *number*	Specifies the maximum number of LCP NAKs returned before sending rejects.
lcp-max-terminate *number*	Specifies the maximum number of LCP terminate-request transmissions (default is 3).
lcp-restart *number*	Specifies the LCP retransmission timeout to number seconds (default is 3).
local	Specifies the modem control lines should not be used.
lock	Specifies that a UUCP-style lock file for the serial device should be created.
login	Specifies the system password database should be used for authenticating.
maxconnect *number*	Specifies the number of seconds to wait before terminating the connection.
modem	Specifies the modem control lines should be used (is the default).

continued

modem_chat	Enables usage of the modem control lines when running chat scripts. For cua devices.
mru *number*	Specifies the MRU number.
ms-dns *address*	Specifies a DNS address for a Microsoft Windows client. Can be used twice.
ms-wins *address*	Specifies a WINS address for a Microsoft Windows client. Can be used twice.
mtu *number*	Specifies the MTU number.
name *name*	Specifies the name of the local system for authentication purposes.
netmask *address*	Specifies a netmask to the interface.
noaccomp	Specifies that address/control compression should be disabled.
noauth	Specifies the peer doesn't need to authenticate itself. This option is privileged.
nobsdcomp	Specifies that BSD compression should be disabled.
noccp	Specifies that compression control protocol should be disabled.
nocrtscts	Specifies that hardware flow control should be disabled.
nodefaultroute	Specifies the defaultroute option should be disabled.
nodeflate	Specifies that deflate scheme should be disabled.
nodetach	Specifies that detaching from the controlling terminal should be disabled.
noip	Specifies that IPCP negotiation and IP communication should be disabled.
noipdefault	Specifies the default behavior when no local IP address is specified.
noipx	Specifies the IPXCP and IPX protocol should be disabled.
nomagic	Disables detections of looped back lines by disabling magic number negotiations.
nopcomp	Specifies the field compression negotiation protocol should be disabled.
nopersist	Specifies that once a connection has been made, it should be terminated.
nopredictor1	Specifies that Predictor-1 compression should be disabled.
noproxyarp	Specifies that proxyarp option should be disabled.
novj	Specifies that Van Jacobson-style TCP/IP header compression should be disabled.
novjccomp	Specifies that Van Jacobson connection-ID compression should be disabled.
papcrypt	Indicates that all secrets in the /etc/ppp/pap-secrets file are be encrypted.
pap-max-authreq *number*	Specifies maximum number of PAP authenticate-request transmissions (default is 10).
pap-restart *number*	Specifies the PAP retransmission timeout to number of seconds (default is 3).
pap-timeout *number*	Specifies the maximum time to wait for the peer to authenticate itself with PAP.
passive	Specifies that it should be passive until it gets a valid LCP packet, and not to exit.
pass-filter *expression*	Specifies a packet filter to apply to data packets being sent or received.
persist	Specifies that a terminated connection should be reopened.
predictor1	Specifies that Predictor-1 compression should be used.
proxyarp	Specifies that an entry to this system's ARP should be added.
remotename *name*	Specifies the remote system name for authentication purposes.
refuse-chap	Specifies that CHAP authentication is disabled.
refuse-pap	Specifies that PAP authentication is disabled.
require-chap	Specifies that CHAP authentication is required.
require-pap	Specifies that PAP authentication is required.
silent	Specifies that LCP packets should not be sent to initiate a connection.
usehostname	Specifies enforcing of the hostname.
username	Specifies the name used for authenticating the local system to the peer.
vj-max-slots *number*	Specifies the number of slots to be used by the Van Jacobson TCP/IP header compression.
welcome *script*	Specifies a script to execute before initiating PPP negotiation.
xonxoff	Specifies that software flow control should be used.
local:remote	Specifies the local and/or remote interface IP addresses.
tty	Specifies the device to communicate over.
speed	Specifies the baud rate to use.

File Name:	pppd	**Directory:**	/usr/sbin/	**Type:**	External

pppstats

UNIX Shell: All primary shells (csh, ksh, sh)

Function	Shows PPP-related statistics for a PPP interface. The statistics are shown since the last report.
Syntax	pppstats [options...] *{ interface }*

-a	Shows absolute values instead of deltas. Shown since the link was initiated.
-c *count*	Specifies the number of times the statistics will be shown.
-d	Shows values in terms of data rate (KB/s) rather than in bytes.

continued

-r		Shows statistics about compression ratio of the packet compression algorithm in use.			
-v		Shows statistics related to the Van Jacobson TCP header compression algorithm.			
-w *time*		Specifies the time between updates of the screen.			
-z		Show statistics indicating the performance of the packet compression algorithm in use.			
interface		Specifies the interface to use (default is ppp0).			
File Name:	`pppstats`	**Directory:**	/usr/sbin/	**Type:**	External

praliases

UNIX Shell: All primary shells (csh, ksh, sh)

Function	Shows system mail aliases.
Syntax	praliases [-f *file*]

-f *file*		Reads specified alias file instead of the default sendmail system alias file.			
File Name:	`praliases`	**Directory:**	/usr/sbin/	**Type:**	External

primes

UNIX Shell: All primary shells (csh, ksh, sh)

Function	Shows primes, one per line, in ascending order.
Syntax	primes *{ start } { stop }*

start		The value must be at least 0 and can't be greater than stop.			
stop		The value cannot be greater than 4,294,967,295.			
File Name:	`primes`	**Directory:**	usr/games/primes	**Type:**	External

print

UNIX Shell: Kornshell (ksh)

Function	Is used to show any arguments on the STDOUT.
Syntax	print [option] *{ arguments... }*

-	Is used to show the arguments as describe by `echo`.
-n	Doesn't add new line to the output.
-R	Ignores any escape characters in the arguments (raw mode).
-e	Processes \ sequences when using the -R option.
-n	Same as option -e, but will also suppress trailing new lines.
-r	Ignores any escape characters in the arguments (raw mode).
-p	Writes the output to a shell spawned with |&.
-s	Writes the argument to the history file.
-u*n*	A one-digit file descriptor to use as output.
arguments...	Specifies the valid arguments that are used with the command.

print UCG-book	Shows UCG-book on the screen
print -n Prompt:	Shows Prompt: with no new line.

psbb

UNIX Shell: All primary shells (csh, ksh, sh)

Function	Shows the bounding box information from PostScript documents.
Syntax	psbb *file*

file		Specifies the PostScript document to use.			
File Name:	`psbb`	**Directory:**	/usr/bin/	**Type:**	External
psbb ucgpsfile		Shows the bounding box from ucgpsfile.			

pstat

UNIX Shell: All primary shells (csh, ksh, sh)

Function	Shows open file entries, swap space utilization, terminal state, and vnode data structure information.
Syntax	pstat [options...]

-T	Shows the number of used and free slots for open files, used vnodes, and swap space.
-f	Shows the open file table with various headings.
-k	Specifies that 1KB blocks should be used.
-n	Shows devices by major and minor number rather than by name.
-s	Shows information about swap space usage on areas compiled into the kernel.

continued

-t		Shows table for terminals with various headings.			
-v		Shows the active vnodes.			
-M *core*		Specifies a core to search in.			
-N *system*		Specifies a namelist to search in (default is `/bsd`).			
File Name:	`pstat`	**Directory:**	/usr/sbin/	**Type:**	External
pstat -f		Shows the open file table.			

pts

UNIX Shell: All primary shells (csh, ksh, sh)

Function	Administers AFS users and groups.
Syntax	pts [options...]

adduser		Adds a user to a group.			
chown		Changes owner of user or group.			
creategroup		Creates a group.			
createuser		Creates a user.			
dump		Dumps databases.			
delete		Deletes entries.			
examine		Shows information about a user or group.			
help		Shows help information.			
listmax		Shows largest UID and GID.			
listowned		Shows groups owned by a user or group, or orphaned groups.			
membership		Shows group or user membership.			
removeuser		Removes user from group.			
rename		Renames user or group.			
syncdb		Syncs ptsdb with `/etc/passwd`.			
File Name:	`pts`	**Directory:**	/usr/sbin/	**Type:**	External

pwd_mkdb

UNIX Shell: All primary shells (csh, ksh, sh)

Function	Creates a secured or unsecured database for the specified file and installs it into `/etc/master.passwd`.
Syntax	pwd_mkdb [options...] *file*

-c		Checks whether the password file is in the right format.			
-p		Creates a version 7-style password and installs it into /etc/passwd.			
-d *directory*		Operates in the specified directory rather than the default `/etc`.			
file		Specifies the absolute path to a file using the master.passwd format.			
File Name:	`pwd_mkdb`	**Directory:**	/usr/sbin/	**Type:**	External
pwd_mkdb -p		Creates a password and places it into /etc/passwd.			

quiz

UNIX Shell: All primary shells (csh, ksh, sh)

Function	Runs a quiz that tests knowledge in the specified subject. Shows a list of subjects if run without arguments.
Syntax	quiz [options...] *{ question } { answer }*

-t		Runs quiz in tutorial mode.			
-f *file*		Specifies an index file other than the default (default is `/usr/share/games/quiz.db`).			
question		Specifies the subject on which quiz will ask questions. Requires `answer`.			
answer		Specifies the type of answer for the question. Requires `question`.			
File Name:	`quiz`	**Directory:**	/usr/games/	**Type:**	External
quiz Asian capital		Tests your knowledge on Asian capitals by naming an Asian country, and expects a city name as answer.			

quot

UNIX Shell: All primary shells (csh, ksh, sh)

Function	Shows the number of blocks in the file system that each user currently owns and summarizes the information.
Syntax	quot [options...] *filesystem*

-a	Creates a report for file systems that are currently mounted.
-c	Shows block information about file sizes and summarizes the information in three columns.

continued

-f	Shows the number and space of files owned by each user (Do not use with -v, -c).
-h	Is used to estimate the number of blocks in the file.
-k	Causes the numbers to be reported in kilobytes instead of BLOCKSIZE environment variable value.
-n	Connects names to the file list read from STDIN (must be used alone).
-v	Shows information about blocks not accessed for the last 30, 60, and 90 days.
filesystem	The mount point of the file system you want to check.
File Name: quot	**Directory:** /usr/sbin/ **Type:** External
quot -a	Creates a report of all currently mounted file systems.
quot -a -f -k	Shows disk space and number of files occupied by each user.
quot -a -k -v	Same as above, but adds files not accessed within 30, 60, and 90 days.

raidctl

UNIX Shell: All primary shells (csh, ksh, sh)

Function	Configures RAID frame disk drivers.
Syntax	raidctl [options...]

-a *component device*	Makes the specified component to a spare for the specified device.
-B *device*	Starts a copyback of reconstructed data to the original disk from a spare disk.
-c *file device*	Uses the specified config file to configure the specified RAID device.
-C *file device*	Works as -c, but forces the configuration, disregarding any error messages.
-f *component device*	Marks the component specified as failed.
-F *component device*	Works as -f, but also begins a reconstruction onto a hot spare.
-g *component device*	Shows the label of the specified component.
-i *device*	Rewrites the parity on the specified device.
-I *serialnumber device*	Sets the component labels on each component of the device.
-p *device*	Checks the status of the parity on the RAID set.
-P *device*	Same as -p, but rewrites the parity if the parity isn't up-to-date.
-r *component device*	Removes the specified spare disk from the set of spare components.
-R *component device*	Marks the specified component as failed and begins a reconstruction.
-s *device*	Shows the status of the RAID frame device for each component and spares.
-S *device*	Checks component reconstruction status.
-u *device*	Unconfigures the specified RAID frame device.
-v	Verbose mode. Shows more information.
File Name: `raidctl`	**Directory:** /sbin/ **Type:** External

random

UNIX Shell: All primary shells (csh, ksh, sh)

Function	Copies lines it reads from the STDINT to the STDOUT with a probability of 1/value.
Syntax	random [options...] *{ value }*

-e	Causes `random` to return a randomized exit code between 0 and value -1.
-r	Causes all `random` output to be unbuffered.
value	Specifies a value (default is 2).
File Name: `random`	**Directory:** /usr/games/ **Type:** External
random -e 7	Randomizes a value between 0 and 6, shows it on standard output and exits.

rarpd

UNIX Shell: All primary shells (csh, ksh, sh)

Function	Provides MAC-address-to-IP-address resolution to workstations at startup.
Syntax	rarpd [options...] *{ interface }*

-a	Listens to all interfaces on the system. If not given, interface must be specified.
-d	Shows debug information on STDERR.
-f	Runs `rarpd` in the foreground.
-l	Logs all requests to `syslog`.
interface	Specifies the interface to listen on.
File Name: `rarpd`	**Directory:** /usr/sbin/ **Type:** External
rarpd -a	Starts `rarpd` on every interface.

rbootd

UNIX Shell: All primary shells (csh, ksh, sh)

Function	A server for Hewlett-Packard workstations on a local network.
Syntax	rbootd [options...] *{ file }*

-a	Ignores the configuration file and responds to boot requests from any system.
-d	Starts the debug mode and shows packet information.
-i *interface*	Specifies the interface to use for boot requests.
file	Specifies a configuration file to use if not the default.

File Name: `rbootd` **Directory:** /usr/sbin/ **Type:** External

rc

UNIX Shell: Bourne shell (sh)

Function	Runs system housekeeping and starts up system daemons.
Syntax	rc

	`rc` runs through the following sequences:
fsck -p	Auto-checks and repairs disks.
rc.conf	Asks for config. variables, mounts file systems, and sets what daemons and services to run.
[netstart]	If system daemons runs, netstart defines the server name, alters network interfaces.
[rc.securelevel]	Starts daemons that must run before it alters level to values specified by rc.conf.
rc.local	Holds commands and daemons not being part of the stock installation.

File Name: `rc` **Directory:** /etc/rc **Type:** Script

rcs

UNIX Shell: All primary shells (csh, ksh, sh)

Function	Creates and/or changes the attributes of RCS files.
Syntax	rcs [options...] *files...*

This is the same command as the one found in Linux. Please see rcs in the Linux chapter for all the options.

File Name: `rcs` **Directory:** /usr/bin/ **Type:** External

rcsclean

UNIX Shell: All primary shells (csh, ksh, sh)

Function	Erases files based upon revision differences.
Syntax	rcsclean [options...] *{ files... }*

-n*{ revision }*	Shows what the program, at the set revision level, would have done.
-q*{ revision }*	Activates quiet mode. Shows less information for the set revision level.
-r*{ revision }*	Specifies the revision to use for comparison.
-T	Saves the modification time of the RCS file even if the file changes. Use carefully.
-u*{ revision }*	Unlocks the specified revision if there is no revision difference found.
-V	Shows version information.
-k*keyword*	Specifies the keyword to use when the comparison for revision is captured.
-V*{ version }*	Emulates the specified RCS version.
-x*suffix*	Characterizes the files with the specified suffixes.
-z*timezone*	Specifies the date output format to use for the keyword option.
files...	Specifies the files to use.

File Name: `rcsclean` **Directory:** /usr/bin/ **Type:** External

rcsdiff

UNIX Shell: All primary shells (csh, ksh, sh)

Function	Compares different versions of RCS files using the `diff` command.
Syntax	rcsdiff [options...] *files...*

-q	Suppresses any diagnostic output. Quiet mode.
-r*{ revision }*	Selects the revision. Select two revisions by separating the -r's with a space.
-k*keyword*	Affects the keyword substitution that is specified when extracting revisions.
-T	Saves the modification time of the RCS file even if the file changes. Use carefully.
-V*{ num }*	Imitates that the RCS version is the specified value. Values 3, 4, or 5 are valid.
-x*suffix*	Specifies the suffixes to explain RCS files.

continued

-z*timezone*	Specifies the date output format to use for the keyword option. (rcsdiff also supports all of the diff command options.)
-v	Shows version information.
files...	Specifies the RCS files that are compared. Separate these by a space.
File Name: `rcsdiff`	**Directory:** /usr/bin/ **Type:** External

rcsfreeze

UNIX Shell: Bourne shell (sh)

Function	Assigns a unique revision number (freeze) to all RCS files that are checked in.
Syntax	rcsfreeze *name*

name	Specifies a symbolic name of the configuration.
File Name: `rcsfreeze`	**Directory:** /usr/bin/ **Type:** Script

rcsmerge

UNIX Shell: All primary shells (csh, ksh, sh)

Function	Merges two RCS files by first comparing the differences between them, and then creates a new file.
Syntax	rcsmerge [options...] *file*

-A	Merges changes from file1 to file2 and stores it in file3. Outputs diff3 type conflicts.
-E	Shows conflicts in less verbose mode than -A (is default).
-e	Same as -E, but disables warnings about conflicts totally.
-k*keyword*	Uses the specified keyword substitution when "compare and merge" takes place.
	You must specify at least one, at the most two, of these `rev` options:
-p*{ revision }*	Sends results to STDIN instead of overwriting the working file of the set revision.
-q*{ revision }*	Runs quietly. Doesn't show any diagnostics at all about the specified revision.
-r*{ revision }*	Merges with respect to the specified revision — if none, then the latest revision.
-T	Is for compatibility with other RCS commands only. Doesn't do a thing otherwise.
-V	Shows version information.
-V*version*	Emulates the specified RCS version.
-x*suffix*	Specifies the suffix to be used to explain RCS files.
-z*timezone*	Specifies the date output format to use for the keyword substitution.
file	Specifies the file to use.
File Name: `rcsmerge`	**Directory:** /usr/bin/ **Type:** External
rcsmerge -p -r2.8 -r3.4 ucg_rules.txt	Compares and merges the different versions of ucg_rules.txt and overwrites the file with the new information.

rdate

UNIX Shell: All primary shells (csh, ksh, sh)

Function	Gets the time from a specified remote system and sets or shows it on the local system.
Syntax	rdate [options...] *hostname*

-p	Show the time from the other system.
-s	Sets the time on the local system.
-a	Changes the time on the local system gradually to the remote system time.
hostname	Specifies the name or IP address of the remote system.
File Name: `rdate`	**Directory:** /usr/sbin/ **Type:** External
rdate -p pluto	Shows the time on pluto.
rdate -s pluto	Sets the time to that of pluto, without any output.
rdate -a pluto	Changes your local time gradually to that of pluto.

rdconfig

UNIX Shell: All primary shells (csh, ksh, sh)

Function	Configures RAM disk devices.
Syntax	rdconfig *file block*

file	Specifies a range of user virtual memory.
block	Specifies the size of user space memory.
File Name: `rdconfig`	**Directory:** /usr/sbin/ **Type:** External
Tip:	Should be run in the background.

rdistd

UNIX Shell:	All primary shells (csh, ksh, sh)
Function	Is used by the `rdist` command as a remote file distribution server program.
Syntax	rdistd [options...]

-S	Specifies that the `rdistd` isn't accidentally started. Must be used.
-V	Shows version information. With this option, you don't need the -S option.
-D	Shows debug information. Messages are logged in `syslog`.
File Name: `rdistd`	**Directory:** /usr/bin/ **Type:** External

readlink

UNIX Shell:	All primary shells (csh, ksh, sh)
Function	Shows the destination name of a symbolic link.
Syntax	readlink [options...] *file*

-f	Shows the full path to the target recursively.
-n	Does not show the trailing new line characters.
file	Specifies the pathname to the symbolic link.
File Name: `readlink`	**Directory:** /usr/bin/ **Type:** External
readlink ucg	If ucg is a link, it returns the target. If not, nothing is returned.
readlink -f ucg	Shows full path of target to ucg.

reconfig

UNIX Shell:	All primary shells (csh, ksh, sh)
Function	Converts the older Xconfig file format to the XF86config file format.
Syntax	reconfig < *Xconfig* > *XF86config*

Xconfig	Specifies file to convert.
XF86config	Specifies the name of the converted file.
File Name: `reconfig`	**Directory:** /usr/X11R6/bin/ **Type:** External

reset

UNIX Shell:	All primary shells (csh, ksh, sh)
Function	Links to the `tset` command that determines and configures terminals.
Syntax	reset [options...] *{ type }>*

-	Shows the terminal type on STDOUT.
-e *char*	Specifies the erase character to use on all terminals (default is Backspace).
-i *char*	Specifies the interrupt character to use on all terminals (default is Ctrl +C).
-k *char*	Specifies the kill character to use on all terminals (default is Ctrl +U).
-I	Suppresses transmission of terminal initialization strings.
-n	Specifies the new tty driver modes should be initialized. For BSD 4.3 tty driver.
-Q	Suppresses printing of the erase, interrupt, and line kill characters.
-q	Shows the terminal type on STDOUT, but doesn't initialize it.
-r	Prints the terminal type on STDERR.
-S	Shows the terminal type and the termcap entry on STDOUT.
-s	Prints the sequence of csh commands that initialize the TERM environment variable.
-m *port-id { baudrate }*	Maps the terminal on the specified port.
type	Specifies a terminal type configure or to map with the -m option. (In addition to the regular tset function, the following is done): Turns on cooked and echo modes. Turns off cbreak and raw modes. Turns on newline translation. Restores all special characters.
File Name: `reset`	**Directory:** /usr/bin/ **Type:** External

restore, rrestore

UNIX Shell: All primary shells (csh, ksh, sh)

Function	Restores files or file systems from backups made with dump.
Syntax	restore *{ ACTION }* [options...] *{ files... }*

ACTION	**Use one of the following five actions:**
-i	Sets interactive restoration of files from a dump — use one of the following commands:
add *arg*	Adds the current directory or the specified argument to the extraction list.
cd *arg*	Changes the working directory to the specified argument.
delete *directory*	Deletes the current directory or the specified argument to the extraction list.
extract	Extracts all files in the extraction list from the dump.
help	Shows a list of the available commands.
ls *{ arg }*	Lists current or specified directory.
pwd	Shows the pathname of the working directory.
quit	Exits directly without dealing with the extraction list.
setmodes	Sets the directory's owner, modes, and times.
verbose	Shows ls output with inode numbers and shows file information when restoring.
-R	Requests a tape of a multivolume set to restart a full restore.
-r	Rebuilds a file system.
-t	Lists files if they occur on the backup.
-x	Reads the named files from the given media.
	These options are combinable:
-c	Reads the dump in the old format.
-h	Extracts the actual directory.
-m	Extracts by inode numbers.
-v	Verbose mode. Types the name and file type of each file it treats.
-y	Skips over bad blocks and continues to restore in the event of an error.
-b *blocksize*	Sets the number of kilobytes per dump record.
-f *file*	Specifies a file to use as backup.
-s *fileno*	Reads from the specified file number on a multifile tape.
files...	Specifies the file or files that are to be restored.

File Name:	`restore, rrestore`	**Directory:**	/sbin/	**Type:**	External

restore -f ucg.bak	Reads the backup from ucg.bak.

rev

UNIX Shell: All primary shells (csh, ksh, sh)

Function	Reverses every line of a file or STDIN if no filename is given.
Syntax	rev *{ file }*

file	The file to reverse. If not specified, STDIN is reversed.

File Name:	`rev`	**Directory:**	/usr/bin/	**Type:**	External

rev	Reverses every line you type.
rev ucg1 > ucg2	Reverses ucg1 to ucg2.

rlog

UNIX Shell: All primary shells (csh, ksh, sh)

Function	Shows information about RCS files and log messages.
Syntax	rlog [options...] *files...*

-L	Doesn't include the RCS files that have no lock set.
-R	Shows only the filename.
-h	Limits the output to paths, head, branch, access list, locks, symbolics, and suffix.
-v *{ string }*	Shows only working path and tip-revision. Optional string is prepended to the output line.
-t	Same as -h, but also adds description text to output.
-N	Doesn't show symbolic names.
-b	Shows revision information on the branch, with the highest branch on the trunk.
-d *dates*	Shows information about revisions checking the date-time, dates - range of dates.
-T	Has no effect — for compatibility only.
-V	Shows RCS version number.

continued

-l *{ lockers }*	Prints information about locked revisions only.
-r *{ revisions }*	Shows information about revisions in the comma-separated list of revisions.
-w *{ logins }*	Shows information about revisions checked in by users in a comma-separated list.
-Vn	Simulates RCS version "n" when generating logs.
-s*states*	Shows information about revisions if the state matches one in the list of states.
-x*suffixes*	Specifies the suffix to characterize RCS files.
-z*zone*	Sets the date output format.
-d*dates*	Shows information about revisions within specified dates.
files...	Specifies file(s) to act on.
File Name: `rlog`	**Directory:** /usr/bin/ **Type:** External
rlog -L -R RCS/*	Shows information for files in the RCS directory.

rmail

UNIX Shell: All primary shells (csh, ksh, sh)

Function	Administer received mail from remote hosts through basic networking utilities (BNU).
Syntax	rmail *users...*
users...	Specifies users or IPaddresses.
File Name: `rmail`	**Directory:** /bin/ **Type:** External
Note:	This command is for use with `uucp` and `sendmail` only.

rmd160

UNIX Shell: All primary shells (csh, ksh, sh)

Function	Shows a calculated checksum of the specified files.
Syntax	rmd160 [options...] *{ files... }*
-p	Appends the sum to STDOUT echoing from STDIN.
-t	Runs a time trial.
-x	Runs a test script.
-s *string*	Shows a checksum of the given string.
files...	Specifies the file to act on.
File Name: `rmd160`	**Directory:** /bin/ **Type:** External

rmgroup

UNIX Shell: Bourne shell (sh)

Function	Deletes a specified UNIX group from the system.
Syntax	rmgroup *group*
group	Specifies the name of the group to erase.
File Name: `rmgroup`	**Directory:** /usr/sbin/ **Type:** Script
rmgroup ucg	Deletes the group ucg from the system.

rmuser

UNIX Shell: Perl script

Function	A perl script that will erase the specified user from the system.
Syntax	rmuser *{ user }*
user	Specifies the name of the user to erase.
File Name: `rmuser`	**Directory:** /usr/sbin/ **Type:** Script
rmuser	Prompts you for the user to remove.
rmuser ucg1	Removes ucg1 from the system.

rotatelogs

UNIX Shell: All primary shells (csh, ksh, sh)

Function	Starts a new log file and saves the old. Only for Apache Web server.
Syntax	rotatelogs *logfile rotationtime*
logfile	Specifies the log file that you want to rotate.
rotationtime	Specifies the rotation time in seconds for the log file.

continued

File Name:	`rotatelogs`	**Directory:**	/usr/sbin/	**Type:**	External
rotatelogs accesslog 86400		Rotates the log named accesslog every 24 hours.			

routed

UNIX Shell: All primary shells (csh, ksh, sh)

Function	Manages and provides network routing tables for hosts on the network.
Syntax	routed [options...]

-s	Provides routing information even if the host doesn't act as a router.
-q	Doesn't provide routing information, even if the host acts as a router.
-d	Runs in the foreground. Meant for interactive use.
-g	Sets the default destination for the Internet router.
-h	Specifies that hosts or point-to-point routes will not be advertised.
-m	Specifies that hosts or point-to-point routes will be advertised.
-A	Does not ignore RIPv2 authentication.
-t	Logs more information to the trace file specified with -T or STDOUT.
-T *file*	Increases the debug level and sends the information to the specified file.
-F *net { mask }*	Minimizes transmission routes on interfaces specified.
{ hops. }	Makes a fake default route to the specified system with the specified number of hops.
-P *parameters*	Adds the specified parameters to the `/etc/gateways` file.

File Name:	`routed`	**Directory:**	/sbin/	**Type:**	External

rpc.bootparamd

UNIX Shell: All primary shells (csh, ksh, sh)

Function	Serves diskless clients with startup information at boot time.
Syntax	rpc.bootparamd [options...]

-d	Shows debug information.
-s	Sends debugging to `syslog`.
-r *router*	Specifies the router to use.
-f *file*	Specifies which file to read boot parameters from (default is `/etc/bootparams`).

File Name:	`rpc.bootparamd`	**Directory:**	/usr/sbin/	**Type:**	External
rpc.bootparamd -r 192.168.1.1		Starts the daemon and uses the specified router.			
rpc.bootparamd -d -s		Shows debugging information to `syslog`.			
rpc.bootparamd -f /boot/param/bootparam		Uses the specified bootparam files.			

rpc.lockd

UNIX Shell: All primary shells (csh, ksh, sh)

Function	Starts the NFS lock manager (NLM). Useful for kernels who do this automatically.
Syntax	rpc.lockd [-d *level*]

-d *level*	Specifies level of debugging. The higher the level, the more debug information (default is 1).

File Name:	`rpc.lockd`	**Directory:**	/usr/libexec/	**Type:**	External
rpc.lockd -d		Shows one line of debug information per protocol operation.			
rpc.lockd -d 4		Shows more debug information, such as operation arguments and internal operations.			

rpc.pcnfsd

UNIX Shell: All primary shells (csh, ksh, sh)

Function	Provides authentication and printing requests to and from different PCs.
Syntax	rpc.pcnfsd

File Name:	`rpc.pcnfsd`	**Directory:**	/usr/sbin/	**Type:**	External
Warning:	This program doesn't provide any high security at all.				

rpc.rquotad

UNIX Shell: All primary shells (csh, ksh, sh)

Function	An RPC server that manages users of a local file system mounted over the NFS by reporting quotas.
Syntax	rpc.rquotad

File Name:	`rpc.rquotad`	**Directory:**	/usr/libexec/	**Type:**	External

rpc.sprayd

UNIX Shell: All primary shells (csh, ksh, sh)

Function	The server daemon for the spray command.
Syntax	rpc.sprayd

File Name:	`rpc.sprayd`	**Directory:**	/usr/libexec/	**Type:**	External

rs

UNIX Shell: All primary shells (csh, ksh, sh)

Function	Converts lines from STDIN to columns on STDOUT.
Syntax	rs [options...] *{ rows... } { columns... }*

-c*character*	Uses the specified character (or ^I) as the delimiter of the input columns.
-s*count*	Uses the specified number of strings as delimiter of the input.
-C*character*	Uses the specified character (or ^I) as the delimiter of the output columns.
-S*count*	Uses the specified number of padded strings as delimiter of the output.
-t	Uses the columns from the input to fill the rows in the output.
-T	Shows the pure transpose of the input.
-k*count*	Specifies the number of rows to ignore from the beginning of the input.
-K*count*	Works like -k, but shows the ignored lines from the input.
-g*count*	Specifies the gutter width.
-G*count*	Adds the specified percent of maximum column width to the gutter.
-e	Handles each line of input as an array entry.
-n	Uses null entries to pad out lines if they are shorter than the first line.
-y	Pads the output by recycling the input from the beginning instead of blanks.
-h	Shows only the shape of the input array and does nothing else.
-H	Works like -h, but also shows the line length.
-j	Adjusts columns to the right side.
w*count*	Specifies the width of the screen.
-m	Does not erase excess delimiters from the ends of the output array.
-z	Adjusts the column width to the largest string.
rows...	Specifies the number of rows.
columns...	Specifies the number of columns.

File Name:	`rs`	**Directory:**	/usr/bin/	**Type:**	External

rstart

UNIX Shell: Bourne shell (sh)

Function	A simple example of the remote start client. This script relies upon `rsh`.
Syntax	rstart [options...] *host command arguments...*

-c *context*	Specifies which environment to use. The default context is X-window.
-g	Allows common commands to be started as generic commands.
-l *user*	Starts the command as the specified user. This option is passed to `rsh`.
-v	Verbose mode. Gives more information without disconnecting the program.
host	Specifies the hostname or IP address.
command	Specifies the command that is used.
arguments...	Specifies the valid arguments that are available for the command.

File Name:	`rstart`	**Directory:**	/usr/X11R6/bin/	**Type:**	Script

rstartd

UNIX Shell: Bourne shell (sh)

Function	A script that helps the use of working with a remote shell.
Syntax	rstartd

File Name:	`rstartd`	**Directory:**	/usr/X11R6/bin/	**Type:**	Script

rstartd &	Runs the script in the background.

rtquery

rtquery	UNIX Shell: All primary shells (csh, ksh, sh)
Function	Shows information about the routing tables of the daemons `routed` or `gated`.
Syntax	rtquery [options...] *hosts...*

-n	Shows only the numeric information, not symbolic.
-p	Uses the poll command to get information from `gated`.
-1	Uses RIP version 1 instead of RIP version 2 when information is gathered.
-w *time*	Specifies the time for hosts to answer in seconds (default is 15).
-r *address*	Shows information about the route to the specified address.
-t *operation*	Changes the behavior of `routed` to one of the following operations:
on=*tracefile*	Starts trace and logs information into the specified file, mostly `/etc/routed.trace`.
more	Shows debug information.
off	Turns off the trace.
dump	Saves the routing table of `routed` to the current trace file.
hosts...	Specifies host or hosts to gather information from.
File Name: `rtquery`	**Directory:** /sbin/ **Type:** External

rwall

rwall	UNIX Shell: All primary shells (csh, ksh, sh)
Function	Send an message to all users on a network.
Syntax	rwall *host { file }*

host	Sends a message to the users logged into the specified host.
file	Specifies the file to read from instead of STDIN.
File Name: `rwall`	**Directory:** /usr/bin/ **Type:** External
rwall 192.168.1.1 hello	Sends the message "hello" to all users logged on to 192.168.1.1

rxtelnet

rxtelnet	UNIX Shell: Bourne shell (sh)
Function	Starts an `xterm` telnet window on a specified host and enables X connections.
Syntax	rxtelnet [options...] *hostname port*

-l username	Specifies the name to use as login to the remote host.
-k	Specifies not to use keep-alives.
-t *arguments*	Sends the specified arguments to telnet.
-x *arguments*	Sends the specified arguments to the `xterm` command.
-w *emulator*	Specifies the emulator to use instead of `xterm`.
hostname	Specifies the hostname or IP address of the system to start the window on.
port	Specifies the port to use instead of the default.
File Name: `rxtelnet`	**Directory:** /usr/X11R6/bin/ **Type:** Script

rxterm

rxterm	UNIX Shell: Bourne shell (sh)
Function	Starts an `xterm` window on a remote system.
Syntax	rxterm [options...] *hostname port*

-l *username*	Specifies the name to use as login to the remote host.
-k	Specifies not to use keep-alives.
-r *arguments*	Sends the specified arguments to the `rsh` command.
-x *arguments*	Sends the specified arguments to the `xterm` command.
-w *emulator*	Specifies the emulator to use instead of `xterm`.
hostname	Specifies the hostname or IP address of the system to start the window on.
port	Specifies the port to use instead of the default.
File Name: `rxterm`	**Directory:** /usr/X11R6/bin/ **Type:** Script

s2p

UNIX Shell:	Perl script
Function	Converts a `sed` script to a `perl` script. The converted script will be shown on STDOUT.
Syntax	s2p [options...] *{ file }*

-D*value*	Specifies the number of debug flags.
-n	Specifies the sed script was always started with the -n option.
-p	Specifies the sed script was never started with the -n option.
file	The sed script file to convert.

File Name: `s2p`	**Directory:** /usr/bin/	**Type:**	Script

Tip: One of the perl-to-other tools. See also a2p, which converts perl scripts from awk scripts, and `perlcc`, which compiles C-binaries from perl source code.

s2p sedscript	Converts sedscript to a perl script and shows result on STDOUT.
s2p sedscript > perlscript	Writes the created perl script to file perlscript.

sa

UNIX Shell:	All primary shells (csh, ksh, sh)
Function	Administers accounting files. Cleans up and shows information in the `/var/account/acct` file.
Syntax	sa [options...] *files...*

-a	Shows all commands typed by the users.
-b	Sorts commands by the sum of users and system time divided by the number of calls.
-c	Shows percentage of the total overall command.
-d	Sorts by the average number of disk I/O operations.
-D	Sorts by the total number of disk I/O operations.
-f	Forces the threshold comparison with the -v option to be in noninteractive mode.
-i	Doesn't read in summary files.
-j	Gives seconds per call, instead of the total minutes per category.
-k	Sorts average memory usage by the CPU time.
-K	Shows and sorts by the CPU storage integral.
-l	Separates system and user time.
-m	Shows per-user statistics rather than per-command statistics.
-n	Sorts by number of calls
-q	Quiet mode. Only shows errors.
-r	Reverses the sorting order.
-s	Truncates the accounting files when done and merges their data into the summary files.
-t	Shows the ratio of real time to the sum of user and system CPU times.
-u	Supercedes all other flags.
-v *value*	If a command is used fewer times than value, asks if it would go to *junk* category.
files...	Specifies an alternate file to use.

File Name: `sa`	**Directory:** /usr/sbin/	**Type:**	External

savecore

UNIX Shell:	All primary shells (csh, ksh, sh)
Function	Saves a crash dump of the operating system kernel (if one is created) after a system crash.
Syntax	savecore [-c] savecore [options...] *directory*

-c	Clears the crash dump. Cannot be combined with other options.
-f	Causes savecore to force a dump to be taken even if there isn't enough disk space.
-v	Verbose mode. Shows more information.
-z	Compresses the kernel and core dump.
-N *system*	Specifies the system to use as kernel instead of default (default is `/bsd`).
directory	Saves the crash dump to the specified directory.

File Name: `savecore`	**Directory:** /sbin/	**Type:**	External

savecore -f -v /dumps	Forces a verbose dump into directory /dumps.

scan_ffs

scan_ffs	UNIX Shell:	All primary shells (csh, ksh, sh)
Function	Finds any UFS/FFS partitions on the specified disk.	
Syntax	scan_ffs [options...] *device*	

-l	Converts and shows a `disklabel`-friendly input string.
-s	Doesn't scan partitions for superblocks.
-v	Verbose mode. Shows more information.
-b *value*	Specifies which partition number to begin searching for file systems.
-e *value*	Specifies which partition number to stop searching for file systems.
device	Specifies the device to look for file systems.
File Name: `scan_ffs`	**Directory:** /sbin/ **Type:** External

scanpci

scanpci	UNIX Shell:	All primary shells (csh, ksh, sh)
Function	Shows information about the PCI bus.	
Syntax	scanpci [options...]	

-v	Shows config space.
-1	Specifies config type 1.
-2	Specifies config type 2.
File Name: `scanpci`	**Directory:** /usr/X11R6/bin/ **Type:** External

scon

scon	UNIX Shell:	All primary shells (csh, ksh, sh)
Function	Configures the pcvt VT220 video driver.	
Syntax	scon [options...]	

-a	Shows what video adapter is found.
-b *number*	Specifies how many pages of scroll back buffer there should be.
-c *screen*	Changes from the current screen to the specified.
-d *device*	Changes will be made on the specified device.
-f on | off	Turns full VT220 support on or off. On is 24 lines and off is 25 lines.
-h	Shows help information.
-l	Shows the settings that are changeable during runtime.
-m	Shows what type of screen is found.
-v	Verbose mode. Shows more information.
-V	Makes the current screen a pure VT220 screen.
-H	Makes the current screen a HP/VT220 screen.
-o	Changes the old pcvt mode to a traditional PC mode.
-s *number*	Specifies how many characters one line could contain — could be 25, 28, 35, 40, 43, or 50.
-p *palette*	Specifies what VGA palette to use.
default	Uses the default color palette.
list	Shows the VGA DAC palettes that can be used.
entry,red,green,blue	Specifies what palette to change and to what RGB color.
-t *seconds*	Specifies how many seconds to wait before the screen saver is activated.
	When altering screen column widths, select only one of these options:
-1	Uses 132 columns — used only by VGA adaptors.
-8	Uses 80 columns.
File Name: `scon`	**Directory:** /usr/sbin/ **Type:** External
scon -o	Changes the old pcvt mode to a traditional PC mode.
scon -p black,0,0,0 -p white,255,255,255	Shows pure black-and-white text and text background.

scp

UNIX Shell:	All primary shells (csh, ksh, sh)
Function	Copies files in a secure way with all network traffic encrypted by `SSH`.
Syntax	scp [options] *source destination*

-p	Preserves times and modes of copied files.
-B	Selects batch mode.
-4	Forces to use IPv4 addresses only.
-6	Forces to use IPv6 addresses only.
-q	Quiet mode. No progress meter.
-r	Copies whole directories recursively.
-v	Verbose mode. Shows more information.
-C	Enables compression.
-P *port*	Specifies the port to use for connecting.
-c *cipher*	Specifies the cipher to use for encryption — for example 3des or blowfish.
-i *identityfile*	Specifies where the private key is located (default is `$HOME/.ssh/identity`).
source	Specifies one or more files to use as the source. (If more than one file is specified, destination must be a directory.)
destination	Specifies a file or directory to use as the destination.

File Name:	Directory:	Type:
`scp`	/usr/bin/	External

scp /etc/passwd ucg@pluto:/tmp	Copies the local file /etc/passwd to the host pluto as user ucg into /tmp.
scp /etc/passwd pluto:	Copies the local file /etc/passwd as current user to the home directory on the host pluto.
scp ucg@pluto:/etc/passwd .	Copies the remote file /etc/passwd from the host pluto as user ucg to current directory.

scsi

UNIX Shell:	All primary shells (csh, ksh, sh)
Function	Sends commands to or probes a specified SCSI device.
Syntax	scsi -f *device* [options...] [option] scsi -f *device* [-v] [-s *seconds*] -c *format { arguments... }* -o *size format { arguments... }* -i *size format*

-f *device*	Specifies the SCSI device that is opened.
	Select only one of these six options. They can't be combined:
-d *level*	Sets the debug level of the SCSI kernel.
-z *time*	Halts the activity on all SCSI busses for the specified time in seconds.
-v	Sends a `BEL` character to STDOUT at the start and end of the bus freeze. (When using this -v option, it must be placed before the -z.)
-m *page*	Reads a specified device mode page.
-P *value*	Specifies the value of a page control field, which must be one of the following:
0	Uses the current values field.
1	Uses the changeable values field.
2	Uses the default values field.
3	Uses the saved values field.
-e	Allows field edits.
	When probing SCSI devices, select only one of these two options:
-p	Inspects devices with the specified SCSI lun on the given SCSI bus.
-r	Restarts an inspection at the specific SCSI device at a given bus, target, and lun.
-b *bus*	Specifies the bus to use for probing.
-t *target*	Specifies the target. This can only be used with the `-r` option.
-l *lun*	Specifies the lun to use for probing.
-c *format { arguments... }*	Sends user-level SCSI commands and arguments specified on the command line to a device.
-v	Verbose mode. Shows more information.
-s seconds	Sets the command timeout to seconds.
-o *size format { arguments... }*	Sends data from the system to the device in the given byte size and format arguments.
-i *size format*	Reads data from the system into the device with the specified byte size and format.

File Name:	Directory:	Type:
`scsi`	/sbin/	External

scsi -f /dev/rsd2c -m 1 -e -P 3	Conducts an inquiry to /dev/rsd2c.

sendbug

UNIX Shell:	Bourne shell (sh)		
Function	A script that sends problem reports to a central support site, using the `vi` editor.		
Syntax	sendbug [options...]		

-P	Shows the form specified by the PR_FORM environment variable. Sends no mail.
-L	Shows a list of available categories. Sends no mail.
-V	Shows version information. Sends no mail.

File Name:	`sendbug`	**Directory:**	/usr/bin/	**Type:**	Script

sendbug -P	Starts `vi` with the form specified in PR_FORM.

setxkbmap

UNIX Shell:	All primary shells (csh, ksh, sh)
Function	Sets the keyboard layout by means of the X keyboard extension.
Syntax	setxkbmap [options...]

-help	Prints a message describing the valid input.
-compat *name*	Specifies compatibility map for the keyboard layout construction.
-config *file*	Specifies the file containing configuration info for the keyboard to use.
-display *display*	Updates the display specified with the new keyboard layout.
-geometry *name*	Specifies the geometry component for the keyboard layout construction.
-keymap *name*	Specifies the key map for the keyboard layout construction.
-layout *name*	Uses the layout specified to choose components for the keyboard description.
-variant *name*	Specifies variant of the layout specified.
-option *name*	Specifies an option for the layout specified. This option is repeatable.
-model *name*	Uses the model specified to choose components for the keyboard description.
-rules *file*	Uses the rules file specified to interpret the components chosen in layout and model.
-symbols *name*	Uses the symbols component specified for a keyboard layout construction.
-synch	Synchronizes X requests.
-types *name*	Uses the type component specified for a keyboard layout construction.

File Name:	`setxkbmap`	**Directory:**	/usr/X11R6/bin/	**Type:**	External

sh

UNIX Shell:	Bourne shell (sh)
Function	The Bourne shell command interpreter.
Syntax	sh [options...] *{ file } { arguments... }*

-c *string*	Reads commands to execute from string.
-s	Reads commands from STDIN. `file` will be ignored.
	Replace the - to + to disable the following options:
-a	Marks modified and created variables for export.
-b	Shows job notifications asynchronously, rather than just before the prompt.
-C	Prevents redirections from overwriting existing files.
-e	Exits immediately with a nonzero exit status.
-h	Locates and remembers function commands when they are defined.
-i	Makes the shell interactive. TERMINATE, INTERRUPT and QUIT are ignored.
-k	Places all keyword arguments in the environment for a command.
-l	Makes the shell as a login shell.
-m	Enables job control.
-n	Reads commands but does not run them.
-p	Sets automatically if the read UID or GID doesn't match the effective UID.
-r	Enables restricted mode.
-u	Handles unset variables as an error if it is a substitute.
-v	Shows input lines as they are read.
-x	Shows commands and their arguments when they are executed.
-X	Marks directories with a trailing / during filename generation.
-o *name*	Enables an option based on its long name.
file	Specifies the file the shell reads commands from.
arguments...	Specifies arguments to commands.

File Name:	`sh`	**Directory:**	/bin/	**Type:**	External

shar

shar	UNIX Shell:	Bourne shell (sh)

Function	Creates a shell archive of files.
Syntax	shar *files...*

files...		Specifies the name of the archive.			
File Name:	shar	**Directory:**	/usr/bin/	**Type:**	Script

showfont

showfont	UNIX Shell:	All primary shells (csh, ksh, sh)

Function	Shows information from the X font server about a specified font.
Syntax	showfont [options...]

-server *host:port*		Connects to the specified X font server.			
-fn *font*		Specifies the font to show information about.			
-lsb		Sets the bit order of the font to be least significant bit first.			
-msb		Sets the bit order of the font to be most significant bit first.			
-LSB		Sets the byte order of the font to be least significant byte first.			
-MSB		Sets the byte order of the font to be most significant byte first.			
-ext		Shows only the extents of the font.			
-start *number*		Shows a range of characters from the number specified.			
-end *number*		Shows a range of characters up to the number specified.			
-unit *number*		Sets the font's scan line unit. The values are 8, 16, 32, or 64.			
-pad *number*		Sets the font's scan pad unit. The values are 8, 16, 32, or 64.			
-b *number*		Specifies the font's bitmap padding unit. The values are 0, 1, or 2.			
-noprops		Specifies not to show the font properties.			
File Name:	showfont	**Directory:**	/usr/X11R6/bin/	**Type:**	External

showrgb

showrgb	UNIX Shell:	All primary shells (csh, ksh, sh)

Function	Converts a compiled RGB color name database back to the original form.
Syntax	showrgb *{ database }*

database		Specifies the database to be converted.			
File Name:	showrgb	**Directory:**	/usr/X11R6/bin/	**Type:**	External
showrgb			Converts the default color database.		

skey

skey	UNIX Shell:	All primary shells (csh, ksh, sh)

Function	Generates an encrypted string by getting a password key and sequence number.
Syntax	skey [options...] *sequence key*

-x		Shows the string in hexadecimal instead of ASCII.			
-n *value*		Specifies how many one-time passwords to show.			
-p *password*		Specifies the password to use. If not specified, the command will ask for it.			
		The following options can't be combined:			
-md4		Selects MD4 as the hash algorithm.			
-md5		Selects MD5 as the hash algorithm.			
-sha1		Selects SHA-1 (NIST Secure Hash Algorithm Revision 1) as the hash algorithm.			
-rmd160		Selects RMD-160 (160-bit Ripe Message Digest) as the hash algorithm.			
sequence		Specifies which algorithm to use.			
key		A six-character-long key to use as the decryption key.			
File Name:	skey	**Directory:**	/usr/bin/	**Type:**	External
skey -md4 -n 10 -p sitbobosit 44 gooddog			Shows generated string sequences from 34-44 with the password sitbobosit and the key gooddog.		
skey 100 abcdef			Asks for the password and uses abcdef as the key. Only shows the 100th generated word.		
skey -x -p hello 10 abcdef			Shows the generated string in hexadecimal format.		

skeyaudit

UNIX Shell:	All primary shells (csh, ksh, sh)
Function	Notifies users that have a low number of one-time passwords.
Syntax	skeyaudit [options...]
-a	Checks all keys in `/etc/skeykeys`. Can only be used by root.
-i	Runs the command in interactive mode. Shows only information doesn't send it.
-l *value*	Notifies the user if the user has fewer passwords left than specified (default is 12).
File Name: `skeyaudit`	**Directory:** /usr/bin/ **Type:** External
skeyaudit -i	Doesn't send notifications, just shows them on the screen.
skeyaudit -l 5	Notifies all users that have fewer than five passwords left.

skeyinfo

UNIX Shell:	All primary shells (csh, ksh, sh)
Function	Shows the specified user's next S/key challenge. Current user will be used if no user is specified.
Syntax	skeyinfo [-v] { *user* }
-v	Shows the hash algorithm.
user	Shows the next S/Key challenge for the specified user.
File Name: `skeyinfo`	**Directory:** /usr/bin/ **Type:** External
skeyinfo -v	Shows which hash algorithm is used.

skeyinit

UNIX Shell:	All primary shells (csh, ksh, sh)
Function	Administers the user's S/Key authentications.
Syntax	skeyinit [options...] { *user* }
-x	Shows the password phrase in hexadecimal, not ASCII.
-s	Specifies that you are working on a secure system.
-z	Allows the user to erase their password.
-n *count*	Starts the `skey` sequence at the specified count (default is 100).
-md4	Uses MD4 as the hash algorithm.
-md5	Uses MD5 as the hash algorithm.
-sha1	Uses SHA (NIST Secure Hash Algorithm Revision 1) as the hash algorithm.
-rmd160	Uses RMD-160 (160-bit Ripe Message Digest) as the hash algorithm.
user	Specifies the username that is to be changed or added.
File Name: `skeyinit`	**Directory:** /usr/bin/ **Type:** External

skeyprune

UNIX Shell:	Perl script
Function	Erases old and zeroed entries in the `/etc/skeykeys` file.
Syntax	skeyprune { *days* }
days	Specifies the number of days of inactivity before it will be erased.
File Name: `skeyprune`	**Directory:** /usr/bin/ **Type:** Script
skeyprune	Removes commented out entries.
skeyprune 100	Removes commented out entries and entries not modified in 100 days.

slattach

UNIX Shell:	All primary shells (csh, ksh, sh)
Function	Assigns tty lines to a network interface.
Syntax	slattach [options...] { *ttyname* }
-h	Turns the RTC/CTS flow control on (default is off).
-m	Maintains the modem control signals after closing line — this disables the HUPCL.
-s *baudrate*	Determines the speed of the connection (default is 9600).
ttyname	Specifies the tty device.
File Name: `slattach`	**Directory:** /sbin/ **Type:** External

sliplogin

sliplogin	UNIX Shell:	All primary shells (csh, ksh, sh)	
Function	Turns the terminal line on STDIN into a serial line IP (SLIP) link to a remote host.		
Syntax	sliplogin *{ user }*		
user	Specifies the login name to use.		
File Name: `sliplogin`	**Directory:** /usr/sbin/	**Type:** External	
sliplogin ucg	Reads `/etc/sliphome/slip.hosts` for the user ucg and then connects to the remote host specified in the configuration file.		

slstats

slstats	UNIX Shell:	All primary shells (csh, ksh, sh)	
Function	Shows statistic information for a slip interface.		
Syntax	slstats [options...] *NR*		
-v	Verbose mode. Shows more information.		
-i *interval*	Specifies the time between reports (default is 5 sec).		
-N *system*	Shows the name list for the specified system (default is bsd).		
-M *core*	Extracts values associated with the name list from the specified.		
NR	Specifies the unit number for the sl interface (default is 0).		
File Name: `slstats`	**Directory:** /usr/sbin/	**Type:** External	
slstats -v	Shows more information about interface 0.		
slstats 1	Shows information about interface 1.		

smproxy

smproxy	UNIX Shell:	All primary shells (csh, ksh, sh)	
Function	Works as a proxy for an X application that doesn't support X11R6 management.		
Syntax	smproxy [options...]		
-clientId *clientID*	Specifies the session ID that was used in the previous session.		
-restore *file*	Specifies the file that was used to save the state in from the previous session.		
File Name: `smproxy`	**Directory:** /usr/X11R6/bin/	**Type:** External	

smrsh

smrsh	UNIX Shell:	All primary shells (csh, ksh, sh)	
Function	Restricts a shell for users to only be able to run certain commands.		
Syntax	smrsh [-c *command*]		
-c *command*	Specifies a valid command to run.		
File Name: `smrsh`	**Directory:** /usr/sbin/	**Type:** External	

smtpd

smtpd	UNIX Shell:	All primary shells (csh, ksh, sh)
Function	Is used to receive mails from other SMTP servers, will put messages in the spool directory.	
Syntax	smtpd [options...]	
-H	Doesn't check if the host connected is valid against a DNS.	
-P	Stops the connection if the hostname looks strange.	
-D	Starts as a daemon and listens to port 25.	
-L	Doesn't let children of the daemon write to `syslog`.	
-q	Quiet mode. Sends fewer messages to the `syslog`.	
-c *directory*	Specifies a directory to chroot into when starting up.	
-d *directory*	Specifies where to put the spool messages.	
-u *user*	Runs the program as the specified user, who needs to be able to run sendmail -f.	
-g *group*	Runs the program as the specified group.	
-m *hostname*	Specifies what hostname the daemon should use.	
-s *bytes*	Specifies how big the messages are allowed to be.	
-l *address*	Specifies what IP address to listen on.	
-p *port*	Specifies what TCP port to listen on.	

continued

-i *file*	Specifies a process ID file to use.		
File Name: smtpd	**Directory:** /usr/libexec/	**Type:**	External

smtpfwdd

UNIX Shell: All primary shells (csh, ksh, sh)

Function	Forwards SMTPFWDD emails from a spool directory to their destinations.
Syntax	smtpfwdd [options...]

-d *directory*	Specifies a spool directory and should be the same directory as for `smtpd`.
-g *group*	Specifies a group that is run.
-M *children*	Specifies the maximum number of children to create during delivery (default is 10).
-P *time*	Specifies the polling interval for the spool directory, in seconds (default is 10 sec).
-q	Starts quiet mode. Shows only one log message line per message exchange.
-s *program*	Specifies the mail program to use instead of the default `/usr/sbin/sendmail`.
-u *user*	Specifies which user to run `smtpfwdd` as. Does not have to be root.
File Name: smtpfwdd	**Directory:** /usr/libexec/ **Type:** External

spray

UNIX Shell: All primary shells (csh, ksh, sh)

Function	Sends a stream of packets to a host. Reports how many were received and the transfer rate.
Syntax	spray [options...] *host*

-c *count*	Specifies how many packets to send.
-d *delay*	Specifies in microseconds the pause between each packet (default is 0).
-l *length*	Sets the number of bytes in the packet (default is 86).
host	Specifies the host to send to.
File Name: spray	**Directory:** /usr/sbin/ **Type:** External
spray sun	Sends packets to the host sun.
spray -c 50 sun	Sends 50 packets.
spray -c 20 -d 1000000 sun	Sends 20 packets with a 1-second pause between each.

ssh, slogin

UNIX Shell: All primary shells (csh, ksh, sh)

Function	Logins securely to a remote computer. Intended to replace rlogin.
Syntax	ssh [options...] *host* { *command* }

This is the same command as the one found in Linux. Please see ssh, slogin in the Linux chapter for all the options.

File Name: ssh	**Directory:** /usr/bin/ **Type:** External
Tip:	Use ssh instead of telnet — it's so much more secure.
ssh -l uk newstyledata.net	Connects securely to newstyledata.net with user uk.
ssh -C -l uk newstyledata.net	Connects securely to newstyledata.net with user uk using compression.

ssh-add

UNIX Shell: All primary shells (csh, ksh, sh)

Function	Administrates RSA identities for the SSH authentication agent.
Syntax	ssh-add [options...] { *files...* }

-l	Shows fingerprints of all identities used by the authentication agent.
-d	Erases the identity from the authentication agent instead of adding it.
-D	Erases all identities from the authentication agent.
files...	Is one or more alternative files to write authentication information to.
File Name: ssh-add	**Directory:** /usr/bin/ **Type:** External
ssh-add -l	Shows all identities fingerprints.
ssh-add -D	Erases all identities.

ssh-agent

ssh-agent	UNIX Shell:	All primary shells (csh, ksh, sh)
Function	Holds private keys for RSA authentication.	
Syntax	ssh-agent *command*	

-c	Generates C-shell commands on stdout (is default).
-s	Generates Bourne-shell commands on STDOUT.
-k	Kills the current agent.
command	Runs the command and exits.
File Name: ssh-agent	**Directory:** /usr/bin/ **Type:** External

sshd

sshd	UNIX Shell:	All primary shells (csh, ksh, sh)
Function	Listens for secure connections from ssh clients.	
Syntax	sshd [options...]	

-d	Shows debug information.
-i	Specifies that sshd is run from inetd.
-q	Specifies quiet mode. Doesn't log anything.
-Q	Doesn't show error messages if RSA support is missing.
-v *client-protocol-id*	Stops the protocol Version identification exchange.
-4	Uses IPv4 addresses only.
-6	Uses IPv6 addresses only.
-b *bits*	Specifies the length of the server key (default is 768).
-f *configfile*	Specifies the configuration file (default is /etc/sshd_config).
-g *logingracetime*	Specifies the time a client has to authenticate before being disconnected.
-h *hostkeyfile*	Specifies the RSA host key file (default is /etc/ssh_host_key).
-k *keygentime*	Specifies the time between regenerating the server key (default is every hour).
-p *port*	Specifies the port to use for connections (default is 22).
File Name: sshd	**Directory:** /usr/sbin/ **Type:** External

ssh-keygen

ssh-keygen	UNIX Shell:	All primary shells (csh, ksh, sh)
Function	Creates public and private SSH keys.	
Syntax	ssh-keygen [options...]	

-q	Specifies silent mode.
-f *filename*	Specifies the filename of the key file.
-R	Exits with code 0 if RSA support is working; else it exits with 1.
-y	Reads a private open SSH DSA format file and prints an OpenSSH DSA public key to STDOUT.
-x	Reads and prints an SSH2-compatible public key to STDOUT.
-l	Shows fingerprint of specified public or private key file.
-b *bits*	Specifies the number of bits to use (default is 1024).
-N *passphrase*	Specifies a new pass phrase.
-C *comment*	Provides a comment.
-p	Requests a new pass phrase.
-P *passphrase*	Specifies the old pass phrase.
-c	Changes the comment in a private and a public key.
File Name: ssh-keygen	**Directory:** /usr/bin/ **Type:** External
Tip:	Tired of entering a password every time? Add an empty pass phrase. This is a security risk.
ssh-keygen	Creates an authentication key for the current user.
ssh-keygen -p -P oldie -N ucgworld	Changes pass phrase.

startkey

UNIX Shell: All primary shells (csh, ksh, sh)

Function	Is used to initialize a key exchange with the `photurisd` daemon.
Syntax	startkey [-d *directory*] options...

-d *directory*	Specifies a directory where `photurisd` looks for startup files.
dst=*ip-address*	Specifies the IP address where the server is.
port=*number*	Specifies the port number to use.
options=*opt*	Specifies the options used in the exchange (opt can be enc or auth).
tsrc=*ip-address/netmask*	Is used together with tdst to set up an IP tunnel.
tdst=*ip-address/netmask*	Is used together with tsrc to set up an IP tunnel.
exchange_lifetime=*time*	Specifies the lifetime of the exchange (default is 1800 sec).
spi_lifetime=*time*	Specifies the lifetime for each created SPI.
user=*name*	Specifies the username for whom the key shall be done.
File Name: `startkey`	**Directory:** /sbin/ **Type:** External

startx

UNIX Shell: Bourne shell (sh)

Function	Starts a session of the X-window system. A front end to `xinit`. Usually run without arguments.
Syntax	startx { *client* } { *options...* } [--] { *server* } { *options...* }

--	Is used only when specifying color depth for a specified program server.
client	Specifies the hostname or IP address of the client to use.
options...	Specifies the options to use for the specified client.
server	Specifies the hostname or IP address of the server to use.
options...	Specifies the options to use for the specified server.
File Name: `startx`	**Directory:** /usr/X11R6/bin/ **Type:** Script

stdethers

UNIX Shell: All primary shells (csh, ksh, sh)

Function	Deletes unwanted information in a file.
Syntax	stdethers { *file* }

file	Specifies file to act in.
File Name: `stdethers`	**Directory:** /usr/sbin/ **Type:** External

stdhosts

UNIX Shell: All primary shells (csh, ksh, sh)

Function	Is used to get rid of unwanted information.
Syntax	stdhosts { *file* }

file	Specifies file to act in.
File Name: `stdhosts`	**Directory:** /usr/sbin/ **Type:** External
stdhosts > ucghost	Filters what you type into a clean host filenamed ucghost.
stdhosts ucghosts1 > ucghosts2	Filters ucghosts1 and outputs the result to ucghosts2.

sudo

UNIX Shell: All primary shells (csh, ksh, sh)

Function	Allows a permitted user to execute a command as the super user.
Syntax	sudo [options...] *command*

-V	Shows version information.
-L	Lists parameters that may be set in a defaults line + short description.
-K	Removes the user's timestamp.
-S	Reads the password from STDIN.
-h	Shows help information.
-l	Shows what commands the user can run and can't run.
-v	Resets the timeout counter that allows the user to run without a password. (If the timeout limit is reached, the user needs to specify his or her password.)
-k	Removes the timeout counter and make the user specify his or her password.

continued

-s	Runs a shell found in the SHELL environment variable.				
-H	Changes the HOME environment variable to the super user home directory.				
-b	Runs the specified command in the background.				
-r *realm*	Lets the user specify other Kerberos realm than the system default.				
-p *prompt*	Specifies other password prompt than the default.				
-u *username*	Specifies a username to run the command as instead of root.				
--	Stops processing command-line arguments.				
command	Specifies what command to run.				
File Name:	`sudo`	**Directory:**	/usr/bin/	**Type:**	External
sudo adduser	Runs `adduser` as root.				

suexec

UNIX Shell: All primary shells (csh, ksh, sh)

Function	Switches user when executing an external application through programs that is used internally by Apache.				
Syntax	suexec				
File Name:	`suexec`	**Directory:**	/usr/sbin/	**Type:**	External
Tip:	Without Apache, this won't do anything.				

sup

UNIX Shell: All primary shells (csh, ksh, sh)

Function	Upgrades files or programs by acting like a client and then talks to a file server process.
Syntax	sup [options...] *{ file } { ACTION }*

	These options affect all specified collections and may not be combined:
-t	Shows the time that each collection was upgraded. Doesn't start an upgrade.
-N	Traces any network messages sent and received by the `sup` network protocol.
-P	Uses nonprivileged network ports otherwise reserved for debugging.
	These options affect all collections unless over-ridden by another option:
-a	Copies all the files in the collection from the repository no matter what the status.
-b	Saves the contents of the local files before overwriting them.
-B	Overrides and disables the -b option.
-d	Erases any files left in the collection that are left over from a previous `sup`.
-D	Overrides and disables the -d option.
-e	Starts commands that should be run when a file is being upgraded. (If no -e is given, sup specifies which command.)
-E	Overrides and disables the -e option.
-f	Upgrades only lists and shows what would happen if an upgrade was done.
-k	Checks the local file modification times before updating. Newer local files are kept.
-K	Overrides and disables the `-k` option.
-l	Upgrades collections even if the repository is a local one.
-m	Sends mail to the `suo` user or the user specified by the notify supfile option.
-o	Checks all collection files for changes instead of just the new ones.
-O	Overrides and disables the `-o` option.
-z	Compresses, sends, and decompresses a file over the network and restores its attributes.
-Z	Overrides and disables the `-z` option.
-v	Shows messages while `sup` is running.
-s	Uses the system sup file instead of a specified one.
ACTION	**The following actions may be used in the specified sup file:**
release=*release*	Specifies which particular release is needed for upgrading.
base=*directory*	Specifies another base directory to use for a collection.
prefix=*directory*	Specifies another base directory to use for a collection's file content.
host=*host*	Specifies a host containing private collections to be upgraded.
login=*ID*	Specifies a different account ID for the file server.
password=*password*	Specifies a different password for the file server.
crypt=*key*	Specifies an encryption key to use for network transmission.
notify=*address*	Sends the log messages by mail to another netmail address.
backup	The same as the -b option.

continued

delete	The same as the -d option.
execute	The same as the -e option.
keep	The same as the -k option.
old	The same as the -o option.
use-rel-suffix	Uses the release name as a suffix for the first and last files in the collection.
	You must select -s or specify the sup file for `sup` to work.
-s	Uses the system sup file instead of the specified one.
file	Specifies the `sup` file that is used.
File Name: `sup`	**Directory:** /usr/bin/ **Type:** External

SuperProbe

UNIX Shell: All primary shells (csh, ksh, sh)

Function	Finds installed video hardware, used by some X11 configuration software to determine configurations.
Syntax	SuperProbe [options...]

-verbose	Verbose mode. Shows more information.
-no16	Specifies to not use any ports that use 16-bit I/O address decoding.
-excl *list*	Specifies the list of I/O ports that will not be included from the automatic inspect.
-mask10	Specifies the port addresses will be masked to 10 bits. Used with -excl option.
-order *list*	Specifies the chipset names that will be tested.
-noprobe *list*	Specifies the chipset names that will not be be tested.
-bios *base*	Specifies the base address to the graphic-hardware BIOS.
-no_bios	Specifies to not read from video BIOS and assumes it is an EGA, VGA, or SVGA.
-no_dac	Stops inspecting of RAMDAC type if an (S)VGA is identified.
-no_mem	Stops inspecting the installed video memory.
-info	Shows a list of cards that can be identified.
File Name: `SuperProbe`	**Directory:** /usr/X11R6/bin/ **Type:** External
SuperProbe	The most usual way of running SuperProbe, it will do much automatically.
SuperProbe -verbose -no_dac	Enables verbose mode and doesn't try to find any ramdac.

supfilesrv

UNIX Shell: All primary shells (csh, ksh, sh)

Function	The software upgrade protocol server to serve client upgrades.
Syntax	supfilesrv [options...]

-l	Waits for a connection and handles it.
-q	Quiet mode. Doesn't show log messages.
-N	Shows more information about the network communications.
-P	Shows more information about the nonprivileged TCP port that is used.
-O *directory*	Specifies a lock directory to use. IP addresses will be looked up in this directory. (Connections will be refused if there is no file named as the IP address.)
-C *maxrequests*	Specifies the amount of requests the server will respond to.
File Name: `supfilesrv`	**Directory:** /usr/sbin/ **Type:** External
supfilesrv -l	Waits for a request from a client.
supfilesrv -C 5 -l	Changes the number of clients to accept and waits for them.

supscan

UNIX Shell: All primary shells (csh, ksh, sh)

Function	Creates a list of the files on the sup server. This speeds up the service if there is a large number of files.
Syntax	supscan [options...] *{ collection } { basedirectory }*

-v	Verbose mode. Shows more information while finding files.
-s	Scans all the system collections.
collection	Specifies what collection to create a list of.
basedirectory	Specifies the base directory of the collection to create a list of.
File Name: `supscan`	**Directory:** /usr/sbin/ **Type:** External

swapctl

UNIX Shell: All primary shells (csh, ksh, sh)

Function	Controls the swap devices and files. Adds, removes, or prioritizes the swap.
Syntax	swapctl option [options...]

	The following options can't be combined:
-A	Makes all the devices marked as an sw in `/etc/fstab`to swap devices.
-a *path*	Specifies a path to be added to the kernel list of swap devices.
-c *path*	Specifies what priority to set for the specified swap device or file.
-d *path*	Removes the specified path from kernel list of swap devices or files.
-l	Lists all the swap devices and files used now.
-s	Shows one line of the current swap statistics.
	The following options can be used with some of the above ones:
-p *priority*	Specifies what priority to set for swap devices or files. Used with -A, -a, and -c.
-k	Uses blocks of 1024 bytes instead of the default 512 bytes. Used with -l and -s.
-t	Specifies what types of devices to add. Used only with -A.
blk	Uses all block devices.
noblk	Uses all nonblock devices.

File Name:	`swapctl`	**Directory:**	/sbin/	**Type:**	External

swapctl -A	Uses all swap devices.
swapctl -s	Shows the statistics about the swap.

swapon

UNIX Shell: All primary shells (csh, ksh, sh)

Function	Manages swap devices and files for the system.
Syntax	swapon -a [option] swapon *path*

-a	Makes all the devices marked as an sw in `/etc/fstab` swap devices.
-t	Specifies what types of devices to add. Used only with -A.
blk	Uses all block devices.
noblk	Uses all nonblock devices.
path	Specifies a path to be added to the kernel list of swap devices.

File Name:	`swapon`	**Directory:**	/sbin/	**Type:**	External

swapon -a	Makes the swap devices going.

sysctl

UNIX Shell: All primary shells (csh, ksh, sh)

Function	Retrieves and allows the configuring of kernel states.
Syntax	sysctl [options...] *{ variable }*

-n	Disables showing the variable's name when showing values.
	The following options and variables can't be combined:
-a	Shows the currently available values.
-A	Shows the currently available values in table form.
-w *variable=value*	Changes the settings for the specified key to the specified value.
variable	Specifies the variable to read from.

File Name:	`sysctl`	**Directory:**	/usr/sbin/	**Type:**	External

sysctl kern.osrelease	Retrieves the OS release information.
sysctl -w kern.maxproc=2000	Sets max processes to 2,000.

systat

UNIX Shell:	All primary shells (csh, ksh, sh)
Function	A statistics showing program, showing the current load and the programs consuming much CPU.
Syntax	systat [options...] *{ display } { refresh }*

-M *core*	Uses the specified core to extract values (default is `/dev/kmem`).
-N *system*	Uses the specified system (default is `/bsd`).
-w *seconds*	Specifies how many seconds there should be before a screen update.
display	Specifies what to show statistics on. Can be one of the following:
pigs	Shows the processes that are consuming the greatest amount of CPU.
iostat	Shows the CPU and disk activity statistics.
swap	Shows the swap statistics.
mbufs	Shows how many mbufs are allocated for the different uses.
vmstat	Shows statistics for memory, interrupts, disk, CPU usage, and process scheduling.
netstat	Shows statistics for the network connections.
refresh	Acts exactly like -w. Is used for compatibility reasons.

File Name:	`systat`	**Directory:**	/usr/bin/	**Type:**	External

systat -w 1 iostat	Shows input/output statistics with 1-second update rate.

tcopy

UNIX Shell:	All primary shells (csh, ksh, sh)
Function	Copies or scans a magnetic tape.
Syntax	tcopy [options...] *{ source } { destination }*

-c	Verifies the tapes after they have been copied.
-v	Verifies the two tapes specified as source and destination.
-x	Shows messages on STDERR.
-s *size*	Sets the maximum block size.
source	Specifies tape drive to use for input (default is `/dev/rst0`).
destination	Specifies where to copy the tape. If not given, only a scan is performed.

File Name:	`tcopy`	**Directory:**	/usr/bin/	**Type:**	External

tcpd

UNIX Shell:	All primary shells (csh, ksh, sh)
Function	Controls and logs incoming requests for Internet services. Use from inetd-like programs.
Syntax	tcpd

File Name:	`tcpd`	**Directory:**	/usr/libexec/	**Type:**	External

tcpdchk

UNIX Shell:	All primary shells (csh, ksh, sh)
Function	Checks your TCP wrapper configuration and reports all potential problems it can find.
Syntax	tcpdchk [options...]

-a	Shows access control rules that permit access without an explicit ALLOW keyword.
-d	Checks current directory for `hosts.allow`/`hosts.deny` and examines them.
-i *filename*	If `inetd.conf` or `tlid.conf` can't be found, specify path here.
-v	Shows content of each access control rule (verbose mode).

File Name:	`tcpdchk`	**Directory:**	/usr/sbin/	**Type:**	External

tcpdchk -v	Shows all access control rules.

tcpdmatch

UNIX Shell:	All primary shells (csh, ksh, sh)
Function	Predicts how the tcpwrapper would handle a specific request for service.
Syntax	tcpdmatch [options...] *daemon*[*@server*] *{ username@ }client*

-d	Examines `host.allow` and `host.deny` files in current directory.
-i *filename*	Specifies where your `inetd.conf` file exists.
daemon	Specifies a daemon process name.
server	Specifies a hostname or network address.

continued

username	Specifies a user identifier (default is unknown).
client	Specifies a hostname or network address.
File Name: `tcpdmatch`	**Directory:** /usr/sbin/ **Type:** External

tcpdump

UNIX Shell: All primary shells (csh, ksh, sh)

Function	Shows the headers of packets matching the specified expression, on a network interface.
Syntax	tcpdump [options...] *{ expressions... }*

-a	Converts network and broadcast addresses to names.
-c *count*	Stops after receiving count packets.
-d	Shows the compiled packet-matching code in a human-readable form and stops.
-dd	Shows the compiled packet-matching code in C program fragment.
-ddd	Shows the compiled packet-matching code in decimal numbers.
-e	Shows the link-level header on each dump line.
-f	Shows "foreign" Internet addresses numerically rather than symbolically.
-F *filename*	Specifies a file to read filters from.
-i *interface*	Specifies the interface to use.
-l	Specifies that STDOUT should be line buffered.
-n	Specifies that addresses should not be converted to names.
-N	Specifies that domain name qualification of hostnames should not be shown.
-O	Specifies the packet-matching code optimizer should not be used.
-p	Specifies the interface should be put in promiscuous mode.
-q	Specifies that less information about a protocol should be shown.
-r *filename*	Specifies a file to read packages from.
-s *number*	Specifies the number of bytes to snap from each packet (default is 68).
-T *type*	Specifies packets selected by expression to be interpreted as specified type.
-S	Shows absolute, rather than relative, numbers.
-t	Specifies that a timestamp should not be shown on each dump line.
-tt	Specifies that a timestamp should be shown on each dump line.
-v	Verbose mode. Shows more information.
-vv	Verbose mode. Shows more information than -v does.
-vvv	Verbose mode. Shows more information than -vv does.
-w *filename*	Specifies a file to write raw package data to.
-x	Shows each package in hex format.
-X	Same as -x, but dumps the packet in Emacs-hexl-like format.
expressions...	**The following are the expressions that can be used:**
dst host *host*	Shows packets headers going to host.
src host *host*	Shows packet headers going from host.
host *host*	Shows packet headers from and to host.
ether dst *host*	Shows packet headers going to MAC address host.
ether src *host*	Shows packet headers coming from MAC address host.
ether host *host*	Shows packet headers coming from and to MAC address host.
gateway *gateway*	Shows packet headers if they were going to the gateway.
dst net *network*	Shows packet headers going to network.
src net *network*	Shows packet headers coming from network.
net *net*	Shows packet headers coming from and to network.
dst port *port*	Shows packet headers coming to port.
src port *port*	Shows packet headers coming from port.
port *port*	Shows packet headers coming from and to port. (Use tcp or udp as prependers to any port expression to match only TCP packets whose source port is port.)
less *length*	Shows packet headers whose length is less than or equal to length. (Is equivalent to: len <= length.)
greater *length*	Shows packet headers whose length is greater than or equal to length. (Is equivalent to: len >= length)

continued

ip proto *proto*	Shows packet headers that are an IP packet of type *proto.*
tcp	A protocol.
udp	A protocol.
icmp	A protocol.
ether broadcast	Sets true if the packet is an Ethernet broadcast packet.
ip broadcast	Sets true if the packet is an IP broadcast packet.
ether multicast	Sets true if the packet is an Ethernet multicast packet.
ip multicast	Sets true if the packet is an IP multicast packet.
ether proto *proto*	Sets true if the packet is the specified proto type.
ip	Selects the IP proto type.
arp	Selects the ARP proto type.
rarp	Selects the RARP proto type.
decnet	Selects the DECNET proto type.
lat	Selects the lat proto type.
moprc	Selects the moprc proto type.
mopdl	Selects the mopdl proto type.
decnet src *host*	Sets true if the DECNET source address matches the specified host.
decnet dst *host*	Sets true if the DECNET destination address matches the specified host.
decnet host *host*	Sets true if the DECNET source or destination address matches the specified host.
File Name: `tcpdump`	**Directory:** /usr/sbin/ **Type:** External
tcpdump host 192.168.1.1	Shows packets heading to or from 192.168.1.1.
tcpdump ip and not net localnet	Shows IP packets passing your computer, but not packets on the local net.

tenletxr

UNIX Shell: Bourne shell (sh)

Function	Forwards X connections from your host to the specified host.
Syntax	tenletxr [options...] *host { port }*

-l *user*	Logs in as the specified user.
-k	Disables keep-alive.
host	Specifies the host to connect to.
port	Specifies the port to use.
File Name: `tenletxr`	**Directory:** /usr/X11R6/bin/ **Type:** Script
tenletxr pluto	Logs in to the host pluto and shows the X-window on pluto.

texindex

UNIX Shell: All primary shells (csh, ksh, sh)

Function	Creates an index for a TeX output file.
Syntax	texindex [option] *file*

-k	Specifies to keep the temporary files after the command is run.
--no-keep	Deletes the temporary files after the command is run, which also is the default.
-o *file*	Specifies a file to save the output in.
-h	Shows help information.
--version	Shows version information.
file	Specifies the input file to use.
File Name: `texindex`	**Directory:** /usr/bin/ **Type:** External

tfmtodit

UNIX Shell: All primary shells (csh, ksh, sh)

Function	Is used to create `groff` font files to be used with `groff` -Tdvi.
Syntax	tfmtodit [options..] *tfmFile mapFile font*

-s	Specifies the font is special.
-v	Shows version information.
-k*NR*	Specifies the skew char is at position NR in this font.
-g*file*	Specifies a gf file produced by metafont to use.
tfmFile	The name of TeX metric font file.
mapFile	The name of a map file giving groff names for characters.

continued

font	The name of the groff font file		
File Name: `tfmtodit`	**Directory:** /usr/bin/	**Type:**	External

tftp

UNIX Shell: All primary shells (csh, ksh, sh)

Function	Sends files to and from a remote host using the Trivial File Transfer Protocol (TFTP).
Syntax	tftp *{ host }*

host	Specifies host to connect to.
	Below are the commands you can use after starting tftp:
get *filename...*	Takes file or files from the remote host.
verbose	Verbose mode. Shows more information.
trace	Toggles tracing of packet.
status	Shows status.
rexmt	Sets timeout in seconds for retransmission of per-packet.
timeout	Sets timeout in seconds for total transmission.
ascii	Is used to specify ASCII mode.
binary	Is used to specify binary mode.
?	Shows help information.
quit	Quits the tftp session.
put *filename...*	Sends a file or files to the remote host.
File Name: `tftp`	**Directory:** /usr/bin/ **Type:** External
tftp ucg_main	Starts a tftp connection to ucg_main.

timed

UNIX Shell: All primary shells (csh, ksh, sh)

Function	Is used to synchronize local time with other hosts.
Syntax	timed [options...]

-M	Host will become master server if no master already exists or if the master fails.
-t	Traces the received messages in `/var/log/timed.log`.
-d	Debug mode. Does not run the daemon in the background.
-i *network*	Ignores the named network. All other networks are valid.
-n *network*	The named network is valid. All other networks are ignored.
-F *hosts...*	Specifies the trusted hosts.
-t	Enables tracing of received messages and log to `/var/log/timed.log`.
File Name: `timed`	**Directory:** /usr/sbin/ **Type:** External
timed -M	Runs as master server if needed.

timedc

UNIX Shell: All primary shells (csh, ksh, sh)

Function	Administers the function of the `timed` program.
Syntax	timedc *{ command } { argument }*

	The following commands and their arguments are supported:
help | ? [commands...]	Shows help information about all of the specified commands.
clockdiff *host others*	Shows the differences between the clock on the specified host and other systems.
msite *hosts...*	Shows the master time server for specified host or hosts.
trace on | off	Toggles the trace log to /var/log/timed.log of incoming messages.
election *host*	Tries to reset the target host's election timers.
quit	Exits the program.
command	Specifies the command to run.
argument	Specifies any arguments to the command.
File Name: `timedc`	**Directory:** /usr/sbin/ **Type:** External

tip

tip	UNIX Shell:	All primary shells (csh, ksh, sh)

Function	Connects to a remote host.
Syntax	tip [options...] *ACTION*

-v	Shows the execution of the commands from the file `.tiprc` as they are done.
-n	Disables the escape ~ character.
-*speed*	Specifies a baud rate to use for the connection other than the default.
ACTION	**Select one of the following two actions:**
hostname	Specifies the hostname or IP address of the server to connect to.
phonenumber	Connects to a remote host using a phone number.
	The following are internal commands that are executed inside the program:
~.	Drops the connection from the remote system and exits.
~c *directory*	Specifies a name to a directory.
~!	Moves you to an interactive shell on the local system.
~>	Copies a file from a local system to a remote system.
~<	Copies a file from a remote system to a local system.
~p *from { to }*	Copies the local file specified to the remote file specified.
~t *from { to }*	Copies the remote file specified to a local file.
~|	Takes output from a remote command and uses it as input to a local command.
~C	Connects a program to a remote system.
~D	Drops connection and exits.
~$	Takes output from a local command to a host or an IP address on a remote system.
~#	Sends a BREAK to the remote system.
~s	Sets a variable for normal operations.
~^Z	Stops tip when it runs under a shell that supports job control, such as C-shell.
~^Y	Stops tip only on your own system — the remote system continues.
~?	Shows a summary of tilde escape characters on the screen.

File Name:	`tip`	**Directory:**	/usr/bin/	**Type:**	External

tn3270

tn3270	UNIX Shell:	All primary shells (csh, ksh, sh)

Function	Is used to remotely log in to IBM computers with full screen and full duplex. Emulates the IBM 3270 terminal.
Syntax	tn3270 [options...] *{ host [port }]*

-d	Enables socket-level tracing. Only for the superuser.
-n*file*	Specifies a file for network trace data output.
-t*command*	Specifies a command to process received IBM 4994 transparent mode data.
host	Specifies the remote system to connect to.
port	Specifies the port to connect to (default is 23).

File Name:	`tn3270`	**Directory:**	/usr/bin/	**Type:**	External

tn3270	Starts the command in interactive mode. Type `?` for help information.
tn3270 bigcomputer	Connects to the host bigcomputer.

top

top	UNIX Shell:	All primary shells (csh, ksh, sh)

Function	Shows and updates information about the top CPU processes.
Syntax	top [options...] *{ NR }*

-S	Shows also the system processes.
-b	Runs the command in batch mode, ignoring all terminal commands except interrupt.
-i	Runs the command in interactive mode.
-I	Does not show idle processes.
-n	Runs the command in noninteractive mode. This is the same as batch mode.
-q	Runs the command as `nice` = 20 so that it will run faster (only as root).
-u	Shows only the user ID numbers, not the usernames.
-d *NR*	Shows the result with the specified numbers of updates before exit.
-s *time*	Specifies the delay between screen updates in seconds (default is 5).

continued

-o *field*	Shows the process area with the specified field as the primary key. Supported fields are: cpu, size, res, time, and pri.
-U *username*	Shows only the processes owned by the specified user.
	The following commands are supported in interactive mode:
Ctrl+L	Re-creates the screen.
h | ?	Shows help information.
q	Quits the program.
d	Changes the number of screen updates.
n | #	Changes the number of processes to show.
s	Changes the delay between screen updates.
k	Sends a signal to processes (default is TERM).
r	Changes the priority of processes.
u	Shows only processes belonging to a specified user.
e	Shows a list of any generated errors from the k or r action.
i | I	Turns the display of idle processes on or off.
NR	Shows information about the processes with the specified number.

File Name:	`top`	**Directory:**	/usr/bin/	**Type:**	External

top -U root	Shows only root's processes.
top -d 2	Shows only first and second updates.

trpt

UNIX Shell: All primary shells (csh, ksh, sh)

Function	Shows information about TCP trace records on a socket marked for debugging.
Syntax	trpt [options...]

-a	Includes the source and destination addresses values for the recorded packages.
-f	Shows the information of the trace as it occurs.
-j	Shows only information about protocol control block addresses with trace records.
-p *address*	Shows only information associated with the given hexadecimal address.
-s	Includes a detailed description of the packet sequencing information.
-t	Includes the time values for each point in the trace.
-M *core*	Shows information associated with the name list in the specified core.
-N *system*	Shows information associated with the name list in the specified system.

File Name:	`trpt`	**Directory:**	/usr/sbin/	**Type:**	External

trsp

UNIX Shell: All primary shells (csh, ksh, sh)

Function	Shows information about SPP trace records on a socket marked for debugging.
Syntax	trsp [options...]

-a	Includes the source and destination addresses values for the recorded packages.
-j	Shows only information about protocol control block addresses with trace records.
-p *address*	Shows only information associated with the given hexadecimal address.
-s	Includes a detailed description of the packet sequencing information.
-t	Includes the time values for each point in the trace.
-z	Empties the debugging buffers in the kernel.
-M *core*	Shows information associated to the name list in the specified core.
-N *system*	Shows information associated to the name list in the specified system.

File Name:	`trsp`	**Directory:**	/usr/sbin/	**Type:**	External

ttyflags

UNIX Shell: All primary shells (csh, ksh, sh)

Function	Is used to set device-specific flags for terminals.
Syntax	ttyflags [options...] *ttys...*

-a	Uses the file /etc/ttys and sets the flags for all terminals found in the file.
-p	Shows only information about the flags without changing anything.
-v	Verbose mode. Shows more information.

continued

ttys...	Specifies terminal to act on.		
File Name: `ttyflags`	**Directory:** /sbin/	**Type:**	External

tunefs

UNIX Shell: All primary shells (csh, ksh, sh)

Function	Changes the dynamic parameters of an unmounted file system that exists in `/etc/vfstab`.
Syntax	tunefs [options...] *filesystem*

-a *maxcontig*	Sets the max number of contiguous blocks to write before forcing a rotational delay.
-A	All backups will be modified as well as the primary superblock. Use with caution.
-d *rotdelay*	Specifies time in milliseconds for a transfer completion/initiation on the same disk.
-e *maxbpg*	Sets maximum number of blocks a file can use in a cylinder group before using other cylinders.
-m *minfree*	Sets the percent of space that isn't available for normal users.
-o	Specifies the file system's optimization strategy.
{ space }	Optimizes the file system to conserve space.
{ time }	Optimizes the file system to minimize access time.
-p	Shows a summary of the current tunable settings on the selected file system.
-s *enable* | *disable*	Enables or disables soft updates on the file system.
filesystem	Specifies the unmounted file system to modify.
File Name: `tunefs`	**Directory:** /sbin/ **Type:** External

unifdef

UNIX Shell: All primary shells (csh, ksh, sh)

Function	Identifies and removes lines containing an ifdef mark from a C program source.
Syntax	unifdef [options...] *{ file }*

-c	Retains lines that would be removed or blanked, and vice versa.
-l	Replaces removed lines with blank lines instead of deleting them.
-t	Disables parsing for C comments and quotes.
-Dsym | -Usym	Specifies which symbols to define or undefine.
-iDsym | -iUsym	Ignores ifdefs.
file	Specifies the file to work upon. If no file is specified, STDIN will be used.
File Name: `unifdef`	**Directory:** /usr/bin/ **Type:** External

units

UNIX Shell: All primary shells (csh, ksh, sh)

Function	Converts a unit quantity to another type — for example, from inch to centimeter.
Syntax	units *{ options... }*

-f *filename*	Specifies the unit file to load.
-q	Suppresses prompting for units and the statistics about number of units loaded.
-v	Shows the version number.
FROM *unit*	The unit to convert from.
TO *unit*	The unit to convert to.
File Name: `units`	**Directory:** /usr/bin/ **Type:** External

units	Interactively asks for units to convert between and displays factors to and from.
units -q	Same as above, but no prompts.
units mm inch	Returns "* 0.039, / 25.4".

unvis

UNIX Shell: All primary shells (csh, ksh, sh)

Function	Alters the result of the command `vis` on a file back to nonvisible characters.
Syntax	unvis *file*

file	Specifies the changed file to alter back to original form.
File Name: `unvis`	**Directory:** /usr/bin/ **Type:** External

uucico

UNIX Shell:	All primary shells (csh, ksh, sh)
Function	Transfers files used by the `uucp` command to a specific location.
Syntax	uucico [options...]

-r1	Starts in master mode.
-r0	Starts in slave mode (is the default).
-s *systemname*	Specifies the system to transfer files to.
-S *systemname*	Calls the named system, ignoring any required wait.
-f	Forces the execution even if the maximum number of uucicos are reached.
-l	Prompts for login name and password.
-p *port*	Specifies a port to call out on or to listen to.
-e	Enters an endless loop of login and password prompts.
-w	Enters an endless loop after calling out.
-q	Disables start of the `uuxqt` daemon when finished.
-c	Disables so no error message is shown.

File Name:	Directory:	Type:
`uucico`	/usr/libexec/uucp/	External

uuconv

UNIX Shell:	All primary shells (csh, ksh, sh)
Function	Is used to convert UUCP configuration files from one type to another.
Syntax	uuconv options... [options...]

	The following two options are mandatory:
-i *input*	Specifies one of three input types: taylor, v2, or hdb.
-o *output*	Specifies one of three output types: taylor, v2, or hdb.
-p *program*	Specifies the program that is converted — for example, `uucp` or `cu`.
-I *file*	Specifies the Taylor UUCP configuration file that is used.
-v	Shows version information and then exits.
--help	Shows help information.

File Name:	Directory:	Type:
`uuconv`	/usr/libexec/uucp/	External

uucp

UNIX Shell:	All primary shells (csh, ksh, sh)
Function	Copies files from one place to another inside UNIX (UNIX-to-UNIX copy).
Syntax	uucp [options...] *sourcefile destinationfile*

-c	Specifies not to make a copy to the spool directory before the transfer of a file.
-C	Specifies to make a copy to the spool directory before the transfer of a file.
-d	Creates all directories that the file copy needs.
-f	Specifies not to create intermediate directories for the file copy.
-g*grade*	Defines a service grade, single letter, number, or a string of alphanumeric characters.
-j	Shows the uucp job identification string on STDOUT.
-I *file*	Specifies a configuration file to use.
-m	Reports back to the user that sent the files by mail when the copy is complete.
-n*user*	Reports to the remote system user that a file was sent.
-r	Puts the file in queue without doing the transfer.
-R	Copies recursively to the destination directory.
-t	Calls by the `uuto` shell script.
-v	Shows version information.
-W	Disables pretend remote relative path names with the current directory.
-x*level*	Shows debug information with a level from 0 to 9 (higher level = more information).
--help	Shows help information.
sourcefile	Specifies the files that you want to copy, uses the format: system-name!pathname.
destinationfile	Specifies the destination of the copy, uses the format: system-name!pathname.

File Name:	Directory:	Type:
`uucp`	/usr/bin/	External

uucpd

UNIX Shell:	All primary shells (csh, ksh, sh)
Function	The server daemon for UUCP connections. Invoked by `inetd` at request.
Syntax	uucpd

File Name:	Directory:	Type:
`uucpd`	/usr/libexec/	External

uulog

UNIX Shell:	All primary shells (csh, ksh, sh)
Function	Shows information from the transaction logs of `uucp` or `uuxqt`.
Syntax	uulog [options...]

-n *number*	Shows given number of lines from end of log.
-s *system*	Shows information about file transfers involving the specified system.
-f *systems*	Shows the updates to the log information as it is created. Use Ctrl+C to exit.
-u *user*	Shows entries for the specified user.
-F	Follows entries for any system.
-S	Shows statistics file.
-D	Shows debugging file.
-X *level*	Specifies the debugging level.
-I *file*	Specifies a configuration file to use.
-v	Shows version information.
--help	Shows help information.

File Name:	Directory:	Type:
`uulog`	/usr/bin/	External

uuname

UNIX Shell:	All primary shells (csh, ksh, sh)
Function	Shows a list of all the systems that are known to the `uucp` command.
Syntax	uuname [options...]

-a	Shows all aliases.
-l	Shows the name of your local system.
-I *file*	Specifies the config file to use.
-v	Shows version information and exits.
-help	Shows help and exits.

File Name:	Directory:	Type:
`uuname`	/usr/bin/	External

uupick

UNIX Shell:	All primary shells (csh, ksh, sh)
Function	Searches for files sent from other systems and prompts interactively for action.
Syntax	uupick [options...]

-s *system*	Works on files from the specified system.
-x *level*	Shows debug information. Level indicates the debugging level.
-I *file*	Specifies the configuration file to use.
-v	Shows version information.
--help	Shows help information.

File Name:	Directory:	Type:
`uupick`	/usr/bin/	External

uustat

UNIX Shell:	All primary shells (csh, ksh, sh)
Function	Shows information about the UUCP jobs on a local or remote system.
Syntax	uustat [options...]

-a	Shows all queued file transfer requests.
-e	Shows all queued execution requests.
-s *system*	Shows all jobs queued for the specified system.
-S *system*	Shows all jobs not queued for the specified system.
-u *user*	Shows status information about the UUCP requests from the specified user.
-U *user*	Shows status information about the UUCP requests not from the specified user.

continued

-c *command*	Shows all jobs requesting the execution of the specified command.
-C *command*	Shows all jobs not requesting the execution of the specified command.
-o *hours*	Shows all queued jobs older than the specified number of hours.
-y *hours*	Shows all queued jobs younger than the specified number of hours.
-k *jobid*	Kills the specified job.
-r *jobid*	Resets the specified job's queue time.
-q	Shows command, execution, and conversation status for all remote systems.
-m	Shows conversation status for all remote systems.
-p	Shows status on all processes holding UUCP locks on systems or ports.
-i	Does a prompt on all jobs whether to kill it or not.
-K	Kills all jobs.
-R	Resets all job's queue times.
-M	Sends a mail to the UUCP administrator for each job in the system.
-N	Sends a mail for each job in the system to the user who requested the specified job.
-W *comment*	Specifies a comment to send with the mail when using -M and -N options.
-B *lines*	Specifies the number of lines in the mail to read from STDIN for each job.
-Q	Quiet mode. Doesn't show anything on STDOUT.
-x *type*	Shows debug information. (Type can be abnormal, config, spooldir, or execute.)
-I *file*	Specifies the configuration file to use.
-v	Shows version information.
--help	Shows help information.
File Name: `uustat`	**Directory:** /usr/bin/ **Type:** External

uux

UNIX Shell: All primary shells (csh, ksh, sh)

Function	Executes a command on a remote UNIX-based system and still enables the user to work locally.
Syntax	uux [options...] *commandstring*

-a *address*	Reports job status to the specified e-mail address.
-c	Does not copy local files to the spool directory.
-C	Copies local files to the spool directory.
-g *grade*	Sets the grade of the file transfer command.
-I *file*	Sets configuration file to use.
-j	Shows job IDs on STDOUT.
-l	Links local files into the spool directory.
-n	Doesn't send mail about the status of the job, even if it fails.
-r	Doesn't start the `uucico` daemon immediately.
-v	Shows version information.
-x *type*	Turns on particular debugging types.
-z	Sends mail about the status of the job if an error occurs.
-	Reads STDIN and uses it as the standard for commands input.
-p	Same as option -.
commandstring	Specifies what to do, where to do it, and where to send the result. (Quote all special shell characters or the whole command string.)
File Name: `uux`	**Directory:** /usr/bin/ **Type:** External

uuxqt

UNIX Shell: All primary shells (csh, ksh, sh)

Function	Is used to execute remote requested jobs created with the `uux` command.
Syntax	uuxqt [options...]

-s*hostname*	Specifies the name of the remote system.
-x*debuglevel*	Shows debugging information with level 0-9. Higher level gives more information.
-c *command*	Executes requests for the specified command.
-I *file*	Specifies the configuration file to use.
-v	Shows version information.
--help	Shows help information.

continued

File Name:	uuxqt	**Directory:**	/usr/libexec/uucp/	**Type:**	External
uuxqt			Executes all remote requests.		
uuxqt -s192.168.1.1			Executes requests from 192.168.1.1.		
uuxqt -command rmail			Executes only requests to the program `rmail`.		

vacation

UNIX Shell: All primary shells (csh, ksh, sh)

Function	Replies to mail automatically. Useful when you are out of the office.
Syntax	vacation [options...] *{ login }*

-a *alias*	Specifies alias to also reply from.
-i	Initializes the vacation database files.
-r *days*	Sets the reply interval to days (default is one week).
login	Specifies login.

File Name:	vacation	**Directory:**	/usr/bin/	**Type:**	External

vgrind

UNIX Shell: C shell (csh)

Function	Formats the program source using `troff`.
Syntax	vgrind [options...] *file*

-d *defsfile*	Specifies alternative language definition file.
-f	Forces filter mode.
-h *header*	Is used to specify a header to appear on every output page.
-l*language*	Is used to specify the language to use. The following languages are valid:
-lsh	Bourne shell
-lc	C
-lc++	C++
-lcsh	C-shell
-lml	Emacs MLisp
-lf	FORTRAN
-lI	Icon
-i	ISP
-lLDL	LDL
-lm	Model
-lp	Pascal
-lr	RATFOR
-n	Doesn't make keywords boldface.
-s*n*	Specifies the point size used on output.
-t	Sends the formatted text to STDOUT.
-W	Forces the output to wide printer instead of narrow.
-x	Outputs the index file in a "pretty" format.
-	Takes input from STDIN.
file	Specifies the source file to be processed.

File Name:	vgrind	**Directory:**	/usr/bin/	**Type:**	Script

viewres

UNIX Shell: All primary shells (csh, ksh, sh)

Function	Shows a tree structure of the widget class hierarchy of the Athena Widget Set.
Syntax	viewres [options...]

-top *name*	Shows the name of the highest widget in the hierarchy.
-variable	Shows the widget variable names in nodes instead of the class name.
-vertical	Shows the widget tree top to bottom instead of left to right.

File Name:	viewres	**Directory:**	/usr/X11R6/bin/	**Type:**	External
viewres -vertical			Shows tree from top to bottom.		

vipw	UNIX Shell:	All primary shells (csh, ksh, sh)	
Function	Is used to edit the password file, `/etc/passwd`.		
Syntax	vipw		
File Name: `vipw`	**Directory:** /usr/bin/	**Type:** External	

vis	UNIX Shell:	All primary shells (csh, ksh, sh)
Function	Converts and shows nonprintable characters in visible format.	
Syntax	vis [options...] *file*	
-b	Converts the file with a minimum of change to the original. Similar to `cat -v`.	
-c	Shows nonprintable characters with C-style backslash sequences.	
-F *foldwidth*	Folds the output in the specified width.	
-f	Same as -F.	
-l	Adds a \$ sign to all new lines.	
-n	Disables encoding.	
-o	Shows non-printable characters with octal numbers.	
-s	Converts only characters that are considered unsafe to send as they are to a terminal.	
-t	Converts tabs also.	
-w	Converts white spaces.	
file	Specifies a file containing non-printable characters.	
File Name: `vis`	**Directory:** /usr/bin/	**Type:** External

visudo	UNIX Shell:	All primary shells (csh, ksh, sh)
Function	Checks and edits the `/etc/sudoers` file and makes sure that it is correct, without any errors.	
Syntax	visudo [options...]	
-V	Shows version information.	
-s	Enables strict checking of `sudoers` file.	
File Name: `visudo`	**Directory:** /usr/sbin/	**Type:** External
Note:	Opens the editor of your choice, if you have specified it in your EDITOR variable.	

vnconfig	UNIX Shell:	All primary shells (csh, ksh, sh)
Function	Allows a regular file to be used as if it is a disk. Use it as a swap file or mount it with a file system.	
Syntax	vnconfig -c [-v] *device file* vnconfig -u [-v] *device*	
-c	Associates the specified device with the specified file.	
-u	Takes away the association from the specified device.	
-v	Verbose mode. Shows more information.	
device	Specifies the special device.	
file	Specifies the regular file.	
File Name: `vnconfig`	**Directory:** /usr/sbin/	**Type:** External

vos	UNIX Shell:	All primary shells (csh, ksh, sh)
Function	Administers AFS volumes in interactive mode.	
Syntax	vos *{ command } { arguments... }*	
command	Specifies the command that is applied to the AFS volume. **Any of the following commands are available in the interactive mode:**	
apropos	Does an apropos.	
create	Creates a volume.	
createentry	Creates a vldb entry.	
dump	Dumps a volume.	

continued

endtrans	Ends a transaction.
examine	Shows information about a volume, same as volinfo.
volinfo	Shows information about a volume, same as examine.
help	Shows help information, same as ?.
?	Shows help information, same as help.
listpart	Shows partitions on a server.
listvldb	Shows volumes in the volume-location-database.
listvol	Shows volumes on a server.
partinfo	Shows partition information on a server.
status	Shows volume server transactions.
syncsite	Shows the sync site.
quit	Exits the interactive mode.
arguments...	Applies any accompanying arguments to the specified commands.

File Name: `vos` | **Directory:** /usr/sbin/ | **Type:** External

vt220keys

UNIX Shell: All primary shells (csh, ksh, sh)

Function	Defines SHIFTED function keys on VT220 terminals.
Syntax	vt220keys [options...] *{ keyname keystring }*

-c	Clears all SHIFTED function keys before setting them to user-defined strings.
-i	Reads the `.vt220rc` file in the user's home directory for SHIFTED function keys.
-l	Locks the function keys from further definition.
keyname	Specifies the key to define.
keystring	Specifies the function to bind to the specified key.

File Name: `vt220keys` | **Directory:** /usr/sbin/ | **Type:** External

vttest

UNIX Shell: All primary shells (csh, ksh, sh)

Function	Is used to test the functionality of VT100 -type terminals, and is menu driven.
Syntax	vttest

File Name: `vttest` | **Directory:** /usr/sbin/ | **Type:** External

what

UNIX Shell: All primary shells (csh, ksh, sh)

Function	Shows version information of object modules.
Syntax	what *file*

file	Specifies file to get information from.

File Name: `what` | **Directory:** /usr/bin/ | **Type:** External

what /lib/libcrypt.so	Gets version information about the file `/lib/libcrypt.so`.

whence

UNIX Shell: Kornshell (ksh)

Function	Shows how a command will be interpreted.
Syntax	whence [options...] *names...*

-p	Searches the path even if the command is a function, a reserved word, or an alias.
-v	Verbose mode. Shows more information.
names...	Specifies the command name or names to interpret.

whence ls	Searches the path even if the command is a function, a reserved word, or an alias.
whence -v ftp	Shows where the FTP is.

wicontrol

UNIX Shell: All primary shells (csh, ksh, sh)

Function	Configures and controls WaveLAN/IEEE wireless network devices using the `wi` driver.
Syntax	wicontrol *interface* [options...]

-e *value*	Enables or disables Web encryption, 0 = disable, 1 = enable.
-k *key*	Sets Web encryption keys, key can be 1 to 4.

continued

-T *value*	Specifies which key to use for packet transmission encryption, value can be 1 to 4.
-o	Shows the statistic counters as opposed to the card settings.
-t *rate*	Specifies the rate of transmission for the specified interface. Select one of these:
1	Sets fixed low rate (1 Mbps).
2	Sets fixed standard (2 Mbps).
3	Sets auto rate Selected (High) (is default).
4	Sets fixed medium rate (4 Mbps).
5	Sets fixed high rate (6 Mbps).
6	Sets auto rate Selected (Standard).
7	Sets auto rate Selected (Medium).
-n *network*	Specifies the service set (IBSS) name that this station will join.
-s *station*	Specifies the station name for the interface.
-c *action*	Permits IBSS creation if a one (1) is used. Block creation with a zero (0).
-q *SSID*	Sets the name for the IBSS or SSID that is created on the interface.
-p *port*	Specifies the port type for the specified interface.
1	Requires that a host relate with a IBSS that is controlled via an access point.
3	Communicates directly to any stations within direct radio range (is default).
-a *density*	Sets the access point density for the specified interface.
1	Sets low density.
2	Sets medium density.
3	Sets high density.
-m *MAC*	Specifies the MAC station address for the interface. Hexadecimal separated by colons.
-d *length*	Sets the maximum transmit and receive frame size. Valid values are 350 to 2,304.
-r *threshold*	Specifies the RTS/CTS threshold for the interface. Valid values are 0 to 2,047.
-f *frequency*	Specifies the radio frequency of the specified interface in the form of a channel ID.
-P 0 or 1	Enables or disables interface power management — 0 = off, 1 = on (default is 0).
-S *duration*	Specifies the interface sleep interval in milliseconds (default is 100).
interface	Specifies the WaveLAN/IEEE device that is used.

File Name:	`wicontrol`	**Directory:**	/sbin/	**Type:**	External

window

UNIX Shell: All primary shells (csh, ksh, sh)

Function	Creates and starts windows on ASCII terminals.
Syntax	window [options...]

-t	Starts terse mode.
-f	Does a fast start without any startup action.
-d	Creates the two default windows without caring about the .windowrc file.
-e *character*	Uses the specified character as an escape character.
-c *command*	Specifies a command to run before anything else is done.

File Name:	`window`	**Directory:**	/usr/bin/	**Type:**	External

wm2

UNIX Shell: All primary shells (csh, ksh, sh)

Function	A nonconfigurable window manager for X.
Syntax	wm2

File Name:	`wm2`	**Directory:**	/usr/X11R6/bin/	**Type:**	External
Note:	The X server must support the shape extension or else the command will not work.				

x11perf

UNIX Shell: All primary shells (csh, ksh, sh)

Function	Is used to measure the performance of an X server.
Syntax	x11perf [options...]

This is the same command as the one found in Linux. Please see x11perf in the Linux chapter for all the options.

File Name:	`x11perf`	**Directory:**	/usr/X11R6/bin/	**Type:**	External

x11perfcomp

UNIX Shell:	All primary shells (csh, ksh, sh)
Function	Compares and shows the difference between x11servers.
Syntax	x11perfcomp [options...] *files...*

-r	Shows server performance relative to the first server also.
-ro	Shows only performance to the first server.
-l *file*	Specifies a label file containing tests. Please see the `x11perf -label`.
files...	Specifies the files to get the test results from on each server.

File Name:	`x11perfcomp`	**Directory:**	/usr/X11R6/bin/	**Type:**	External

xautolock

UNIX Shell:	All primary shells (csh, ksh, sh)
Function	Is used to either lock the X Window or start a program when a specified amount of time has expired.
Syntax	xautolock [options...]

-help	Shows help information.
-version	Shows version information.
-time *interval*	Sets the timeout interval to the specified amount (default is 10 minutes).
-locker *lock*	Specifies the type of lock to use. This may be a program.
-killtime *interval*	Specifies the secondary timeout after the locker starts (default is 20 minutes).
-killer *killaction*	Specifies the type of killer to use (default is none).
-notify *margin*	Warns the user before locking. Specify the notification margin in seconds.
-notifier *notice*	Specifies the type of notice to use.
-bell *level*	Sets the loudness level for the notification (default is 40%).
-corners *action*	Sets any special actions to be taken when the mouse enters one of the window corners.
-cornerdelay *delay*	Sets the delay before an action, when the mouse enters a + corner.
-cornerredelay *delay*	Sets the delay before an action, when a lock exits before the mouse leaves a corner.
-cornersize *pixels*	Sets the corner area pixel size (default is 10).
-resetsaver	Resets the X screen saver once the locker has been started.
-secure true | false	Runs secure mode, which ignores -enable, -disable, -toggle, and -exit (default is false).
-nocloseerr	Does not allow STDERR to close.
-noclose	Does not allow STDERR and STDOUT to close.
-disable	Disables any process that is active.
-enable	Enables any process that is active.
-toggle	Toggles a process that is active between enable and disable.
-exit	Forces an exit from any process that is active.
-locknow	Forces a window lock while a process is active.
-unlocknow	Unlocks a window lock while a process is active.
-nowlocker *lock*	Specifies the type of lock to use if the -unlocknow option is used.

File Name:	`xautolock`	**Directory:**	/usr/X11R6/bin/	**Type:**	External

Tip:	When using locker, killer, and notifier, specify the PATH to use `/bin/sh`. This means that most ~ expansions won't work.

xautolock -killtime 30	Specifies the secondary timeout after the locker starts.
xautolock -cornerredelay 2	Sets the delay to 2 seconds before an action, when a lock exits before the mouse leaves a corner.
xautolock -exit	Forces an exit from any process that is active.

xconsole

UNIX Shell:	All primary shells (csh, ksh, sh)
Function	Shows console messages with X.
Syntax	xconsole [options...]

-file *file*	Specifies the device to monitor (default is `/dev/console`).
-notify	Enables notification of new messages. Icon name will change so you will notice.
-nonotify	Disables message notification. The icon won't change when things happen.
-daemon	Runs in the background, as a daemon.
-verbose	Verbose mode. Shows more information.
-exitOnFail	Exits if it is unable to retrieve output from the device.

continued

File Name:	xconsole	Directory:	/usr/X11R6/bin/	Type:	External
xconsole -daemon			Used in Xinit scripts to run xconsole in the background.		
xconsole -nonotify			Runs xconsole and doesn't change the icon if xconsole is iconified.		

xf86config

UNIX Shell: All primary shells (csh, ksh, sh)

Function	A console-based application to configure the XF86Config file.
Syntax	xf86config

File Name:	xf86config	Directory:	/usr/X11R6/bin/	Type:	External

XF86Setup

UNIX Shell: All primary shells (csh, ksh, sh)

Function	Configures the XFree86 server in GUI mode.
Syntax	XF86Setup [options...] *{ file }* [-- *arguments...*] XF86Setup [options...] *{ file }* *{ arguments... }*

-sync	Activates synchronization for X server communication.
-name *application*	Specifies the application name to use for the window name.
	The following options are only available when a file is specified:
-display *display*	Specifies the display that is communicated with.
-geometry *geomspec*	Specifies the starting geometry for the window.
-notk	Specifies that no connection to the X server should be made.
-script	Tries to find the specified file in the script's directory.
	The following option is only available when no file is specified:
-nodialog	Prohibits the use of the dialog program.
file	Specifies the file to be used and is interpreted as if it were a Tcl/TK script file.
arguments...	Specifies argument to send to the script.

File Name:	XF86Setup	Directory:	/usr/X11R6/bin/	Type:	External

xfwp

UNIX Shell: All primary shells (csh, ksh, sh)

Function	An X firewall proxy. Provides an application layer firewall for X traffic.
Syntax	xfwp [options...]

-pdt *time*	Sets closing time for inactive proxy manager connections in seconds (default is 3600).
-clt *time*	Sets closing time for inactive `xfwp` client listen ports in seconds (default is 86400).
-cdt *time*	Sets closing time for inactive `xfwp` client connections in seconds (default is 604800).
-pmport *port*	Sets port address for proxy manager connections (default is 4444).
-config *filename*	Specifies the filename for the configuration file.
-verify	Displays the configuration file rule matched for each service request.

File Name:	xfwp	Directory:	/usr/X11R6/bin/	Type:	External

xkbevd

UNIX Shell: All primary shells (csh, ksh, sh)

Function	Monitors for XKB events and runs the requested commands when they occur.
Syntax	xkbevd [options...]

-cfg *file*	Reads the specified configuration file or ~/.xkb/xkbevd.cf or $(LIBDIR)/xkb/xkbevd.cf. (The configuration file is a list of events/action pairs and variables.)
-sc *cmd*	Uses the specified command to play sounds.
-sd *directory*	Gets the soundfiles from the specified directory.
-display *screen*	Specifies another screen to use if not the one in $DISPLAY.
-bg	Forks the command and runs it in the background.
-synch	Synchronizes all X requests.
-v	Verbose mode. Shows more information. More -v's gives more information.
-help	Shows help information.

File Name:	xkbevd	Directory:	/usr/X11R6/bin/	Type:	External
Note:	This is only a prototype program for developers — not intended for end users.				

xkill

UNIX Shell: All primary shells (csh, ksh, sh)

Function	Kills an X client. Useful for removing problematic programs.
Syntax	xkill [options...]

-display *displayname*	Specifies the X server to contact.
-id *resource*	Specifies the X identifier on resource to abort.
-button *number*	Specifies the number of pointer buttons to use when you select a window to kill.
-frame	Ignores standard conventions to find top-level client windows.
-all	Kills all clients with top-level window on the screen.

File Name:	`xkill`	**Directory:**	/usr/X11R6/bin	**Type:**	External

xkill	Lets you select the window to kill by pointing at it.

xload

UNIX Shell: All primary shells (csh, ksh, sh)

Function	Is used to show a histogram over the average system load.
Syntax	xload [options...]

-scale *integer*	Specifies the minimum tick marks to use in the histogram.
-update *seconds*	Sets the interval to update the histogram.
-hl *color*	Sets the color of the scale lines.
-highlight *color*	Same as -hl.
-jumpscroll *pixels*	Sets the number of pixels to move the scale line to the left when it reaches the end.
-label *string*	Sets a label over the scale.
-nolabel	Shows no labels.
-lights	Use keyboard LEDs to show the current load average.

File Name:	`xload`	**Directory:**	/usr/X11R6/bin	**Type:**	External

xload -label myaverage	Start xload using myaverage as the label above the load average.

xlock

UNIX Shell: All primary shells (csh, ksh, sh)

Function	Locks the local X screen until the user enters a password.
Syntax	xlock [options...]

-display *dsp*	Specifies the X display to lock.
-help	Shows help information.
-name *resource-name*	Specifies a resource to use instead of XLock.
-mode *modename*	Specifies the animation mode. There are over 90 different modes.
-delay *usecs*	This is used to set the speed of an animation. A lower value makes animation faster.
-version	Shows version information.
-resources	Shows default resource file on STDOUT.
-visual *visual*	Specifies the screen's visual. Use default to set the root window; otherwise use these: StaticGray, GrayScale, StaticColor, PseudoColor, TrueColor, DirectColor.
-name *resource-name*	Specifies a resource to use instead of XLock.
-count *num*	Specifies number of things to do per animation or batch.
-batchcount *num*	If it is working, it is the same as count.
-cycles *num*	Specifies the number of cycles for modename until it does a timeout.
-size *num*	Specifies the maximum size of an object in modename.
-ncolors *num*	Specifies the maximum number of colors to use.
-saturation *value*	Specifies saturation value (0 is grayscale and 1 is a very rich color).
-erasemode *name*	Specifies the name of the erase mode. There are different names.
-erasedelay *time*	Specifies the time in microseconds for steps of the erase mode.
-vtlock *modename*	Manages the VT switching on an XFree86 system. Use one of these four options as the mode:
off	Specifies no locking.
switch	Switches to Xlock VT when activated.
restore	Switches to Xlock VT when activated, and switches back to previous VT when deactivated.
noswitch	Specifies to do a VT switch locking only when Xlock VT is active.
-nice *nicelevel*	Specifies the so-called system nicelevel of Xlock.
-lockdelay *time*	Specifies the time in seconds before the screen needs a password to be unlocked.

continued

-timeout *seconds*	Specifies when password screen will time out, in seconds.
-font *fontname*	Specifies the font to use on the prompt.
-planfont *fontname*	Specifies the font name to use for the text in the lower part of the password screen.
-fg *color*	Specifies foreground color for the password screen.
-bg *color*	Specifies background color for the password screen.
-username *textstring*	Specifies a text string in front of the username.
-password *textstring*	Specifies a password prompt string.
-info *textstring*	Shows a "what to do" message.
-validate *textstring*	Specifies a message that shows when validating the password.
-invalid *textstring*	Specifies a text to show when password is invalid.
-geometry *geom*	Specifies the size and offset of the lock window (use format 25x25).
-icongeometry *geom*	Specifies the size of the icons (default is 64x64).
-glgeometry *geom*	Specifies the size of the screen in g1 mode.
-delta3d *value*	Specifies the space between the center of your two eyes for 3-D mode.
-none3d *color*	Specifies the color to use for empty size in 3-D mode.
-right3d *color*	Specifies the color to use for right eye in 3-D mode.
-left3d *color*	Specifies the color to use for left eye in 3-D mode.
-both3d *color*	Specifies the color to use for overlapping images for left and right eyes in 3-D mode.
-program *programname*	Specifies the program to use as the fortune generator (only in marquee and nose modes).
-messagesfile *formatted-filename*	Specifies the file to use as the fortune generator (only in marquee and nose modes).
-message *textstring*	Specifies the text to show in a mode (only in flag, marquee, and nose modes).
-messagefont *fontname*	Specifies the font name to use in a mode (only in flag, marquee, and nose modes).
-bitmap *filename*	Shows the xbm, xpm or ras file for flag, life(1d), maze, eyes, pacman, or puzzle mode.
-neighbors *num*	Specifies the numbers of neighbors of a cell.
	When you use these options, use - minus to disable and + plus to enable:
mono	Enables or disables the monochrome override.
nolock	Enables or disables the no password required mode.
allowaccess	Enables or disables the allow new client access.
remote	Enables or disables the remote host access.
inwindow	Enables or disables the running in a window.
inroot	Enables or disables the running in the root window.

File Name:	`xlock`	**Directory:**	/usr/X11R6/bin/	**Type:**	External

xlsatoms

UNIX Shell: All primary shells (csh, ksh, sh)

Function	Shows the specified interned atoms on the server.
Syntax	xlsatoms [options...]

-display *dpy*	Specifies the X server to contact.
-format *string*	Specifies printf-style string of how to show each atom.
-range *{ low }-{ high }*	Specifies the range of atoms to check. If low isn't given, 1 is used. (If high isn't given, xlsatoms continues until the first undefined atom.)
-name *string*	Is used to specify an atom to show.

File Name:	`xlsatoms`	**Directory:**	/usr/X11R6/bin/	**Type:**	External

xlsclients

UNIX Shell: All primary shells (csh, ksh, sh)

Function	Is used to show client applications that run on a screen.
Syntax	xlsclients [options...]

-display *displayname*	Specifies the X server to contact.
-a	Shows clients from all screens.
-l	Shows a long listing.
-m *maxcmdlen*	Specifies the maximum number of characters in a command to show (default is 10000).

File Name:	`xlsclients`	**Directory:**	/usr/X11R6/bin/	**Type:**	External

xlsclients -display monza	Shows the applications running on the screen monza.

xmag

UNIX Shell:	All primary shells (csh, ksh, sh)
Function	Is used to enlarge parts of the screen.
Syntax	xmag [options...]

-mag *factor*	Specifies the magnification to use (default is 5).
-source *geom*	Specifies size and/or location of the source region on the screen.
-*toolkitoptions...*	Specifies additional standard X Toolkit command-line options.

File Name:	`xmag`	**Directory:**	/usr/X11R6/bin/	**Type:**	External

xman

UNIX Shell:	All primary shells (csh, ksh, sh)
Function	Is used to show man pages in a browser when running X.
Syntax	xman [options...]

-helpfile *file*	Uses help file other than the default.
-bothshown	Shows both manual page and directory on the screen at the same time.
-notopbox	Starts the browser without the top menu.
-geometry *W*H+X+Y*	Specifies the size and location of the top menu.
-pagesize *W*H+X+Y*	Specifies the size and location for the manual pages.

File Name:	`xman`	**Directory:**	/usr/X11R6/bin/	**Type:**	External

xman xman	Shows the man page for the command xman.

Xnest

UNIX Shell:	All primary shells (csh, ksh, sh)
Function	Opens a new window X server that will nest inside of the real X server.
Syntax	Xnest [options...]

-display *display*	Specifies the display address to the real X server to connect to.
-sync	Synchronizes the window and graphics operation with the real X server.
-full	Generates the real X server objects and opens a new connection to the X server.
-class *class*	Sets the visual class on the nested server.
-depth *depth*	Sets the visual depth of the nested server.
-sss	Activates the screen saver.
-geometry *geometry*	Specifies where to place the top-level windows on the real X server. (Geometry is specified like width + height + x + y. Each value is in pixels.)
-bw *pixels*	Specifies the Xnest window border width in pixels.
-name *name*	Specifies the Xnest window name.
-scrns *number*	Creates the specified number of screens in the nested server.
-install	Skips the real X server's color map installation and uses its own.
-parent *windowID*	Specifies the root window to use instead of creating a new window.

File Name:	`Xnest`	**Directory:**	/usr/X11R6/bin/	**Type:**	External
Note:	One cool way of running two or more window managers at the same time.				

Xnest -display :0	Starts a nested X server on the first X server on localhost.
Xnest -display workstation:0	Starts a nested X server on the first X server on the workstation.

xon

UNIX Shell:	Bourne shell (sh)
Function	Executes the specified command on the specified remote host.
Syntax	xon *host* [options...] { *commands...* }

-access	Adds the remote host to the access list in the local X server.
-debug	Shows debug information.
-name *name*	Sets a different window title and application name than the default `xterm`.
-nols	Disables the use of the -ls option to the remote `xterm`.
-screen *screen*	Specifies the screen number to the DISPLAY variable on remote command.
-user *user*	Specifies alternate username or IP address.
host	Specifies the remote server to start process on.
commands...	Specifies command to run on remote computer.

continued

File Name:	xon	Directory:	/usr/X11R6/bin/	Type:	Script
xon monza		Runs an xterm -ls on the host monza.			
xon monza -access		Adds monza to the access list in the local X server.			

xrefresh

UNIX Shell: All primary shells (csh, ksh, sh)

Function	Is used to refresh all or part of an X screen.
Syntax	xrefresh [options...]

-white	Uses white background.
-black	Uses black background.
-solid *color*	Specifies a color to create a background of.
-root	Uses the root window background.
-none	Refreshes all of the window (is the default).
-display *displayname*	Specifies a server and screen to refresh.
-geometry *Width**Height+X+Y*	Specifies the part of screen to refresh.

File Name:	xrefresh	Directory:	/usr/X11R6/bin	Type:	External

xsetmode

UNIX Shell: All primary shells (csh, ksh, sh)

Function	Is used to set the mode for an input device under X-window.
Syntax	xsetmode *device* option

ABSOLUTE	Specifies absolute mode.
RELATIVE	Specifies relative mode.
device	Specifies an X input device.

File Name:	xsetmode	Directory:	/usr/X11R6/bin	Type:	External

xsetpointer

UNIX Shell: All primary shells (csh, ksh, sh)

Function	Is used to set the main pointer for X-window.
Syntax	xsetpointer [-l] *{ device }*

-l	Lists all available devices.
device	Specifies the X input device to use.

File Name:	xsetpointer	Directory:	/usr/X11R6/bin/	Type:	External

xsm

UNIX Shell: All primary shells (csh, ksh, sh)

Function	Manages X sessions. Runs applications and lets them become part of the session.
Syntax	xsm [options...]

-display *name*	Causes xsm to connect to the specified X display.
-session *name*	Specifies a session to load.
-verbose	Verbose mode. Shows more information.
	The following are operations to use inside the session:
Load Session	Loads the selected session.
Delete Session	Deletes the selected session.
Default/Fail Safe	Starts with a set of default applications.
Cancel	Is used to cancel a delete operation or to exit the manager from the session.
	The following are options to use in the main window:
Client List	Shows a list of clients in the session in a new window and allows operations on them.
Session Log	Shows log information about the session.
Checkpoint	Saves the state of all applications that are running in the session.
Shutdown	Saves the state and exits the session.

File Name:	xsm	Directory:	/usr/X11R6/bin/	Type:	External

xstr

UNIX Shell:	All primary shells (csh, ksh, sh)
Function	Keeps a library of string from component parts in large programs that can be used as shared constant strings.
Syntax	xstr *{ file }* [options...]

-	Makes xstr to read from the STDIN.
-c *filename*	Specifies a file with C source text.
-l *array*	Specifies a program reference array.
file	Specifies the file to query.
File Name: `xstr`	**Directory:** /usr/bin/ — **Type:** External
xstr -c ucgfile	Extracts the strings from the C source `ucgfile`.

Xvfb

UNIX Shell:	All primary shells (csh, ksh, sh)
Function	A virtual X server that uses virtual memory to emulate a frame buffer for X-window version 11.
Syntax	Xvfb [options...]

	Supports all of the X server options along with the following ones:
-screen *number WxHxD*	Creates a screen with the specified number and sets it to the given size.
-pixdepths *list*	Specifies the pixel map depth list that is supported (valid values in the list 1-32).
-shmem	Places the frame buffer into shared memory. Works only with System V shared memory.
-linebias *value*	Adjusts the way thin lines are pixelized. The specified value is the bitmask size.
-blackpixel *value*	Specifies the black pixel value that the server will use.
-whitepixel *value*	Specifies the white pixel value that the server will use.
File Name: `Xvfb`	**Directory:** /usr/X11R6/bin/ — **Type:** External

xwininfo

UNIX Shell:	All primary shells (csh, ksh, sh)
Function	Is used to show information about X-window.
Syntax	xwininfo [options...]

-help	Shows help information.
-id *id*	Specifies a target window ID.
-root	Specifies that X root window is the target.
-name *name*	Specifies the window named `name` as the target window.
-int	Shows all X-window IDs as integer values.
-children	Shows the root, children, and parent windows' IDs.
-tree	Shows all children recursively.
-stats	Shows statistical information about the window.
-bits	Shows bit information about the window.
-events	Shows window event mask information.
-size	Shows size information about the window.
-wm	Shows the selected window's window manager hints.
-shape	Shows the window manager border shape information.
-frame	Causes windows manager frames to look in when selecting windows.
-metric	Shows metric information about the window.
-english	Shows lengths in Anglo-Saxon units — for example, yards, miles, and feet.
-all	Queries everything.
-display *display*	Specifies the X server that you want to connect to.
File Name: `xwininfo`	**Directory:** /usr/X11R6/bin — **Type:** External
xwininfo -size	Shows sizes of the selected window.
xwininfo -display localhost:1	Shows the information on the specified X server.
xwininfo -all	Shows all available information about the windows.

yes

yes	UNIX Shell:	All primary shells (csh, ksh, sh)
Function	Outputs a string or "y" forever.	
Syntax	yes *{ string }*	

string		You can enter a string instead of "y."			
File Name:	`yes`	**Directory:**	/usr/bin/	**Type:**	External
yes | rm -i ucg*		Enters a "y" to every question from rm.			
yes yes | rm -i ucg*		Enters a "yes" to every question from rm.			

yptest

yptest	UNIX Shell:	All primary shells (csh, ksh, sh)
Function	Checks a series of YP functions to see if the YP server is working properly.	
Syntax	yptest	

File Name:	`yptest`	**Directory:**	/usr/sbin/	**Type:**	External
NIS	The following tests are run: YP match, YP first, YP next, YP master, YP order, YP maplist, and YP all.				

yyfix

yyfix	UNIX Shell:	Bourne shell (sh)
Function	This script will extract tables from the `yacc` generated file `y.tab.c`.	
Syntax	yyfix *file { tables... }*	

file		Specifies the file that is used to save the extracted tables into.			
tables...		Specifies the list of tables to be extracted from `y.tab.c`.			
File Name:	`yyfix`	**Directory:**	/usr/bin	**Type:**	Script

zcmp

zcmp	UNIX Shell:	Bourne shell (sh)
Function	Compares two compressed files. Return status is 0 = identical, 1 = different, 1 < error.	
Syntax	zcmp [options...] *file1 { file2 }*	

-l		Shows the byte number (dec) and the byte value (oct) for each difference.			
-s		Shows nothing for differing files.			
file1		Specifies the first file.			
file2		Specifies the second file. If not given, use the uncompressed file with same name.			
File Name:	`zcmp`	**Directory:**	/usr/bin	**Type:**	Script
zcmp a.Z b.Z		Compares a.Z and b.z; reports where b.Z differs from a.Z.			
zcmp a.Z a.gz		Compares compressed file a.Z with gzipped file a.gz.			
zcmp -l a.Z a.gz		Shows number and the differing byte values.			

zdiff

zdiff	UNIX Shell:	All primary shells (csh, ksh, sh)
Function	Compares compressed files. It uses the command `diff` to run the comparison.	
Syntax	zdiff [options...] *file1 { file2 }*	

		Please see the command `diff` for the options.			
File Name:	`zdiff`	**Directory:**	/usr/bin/	**Type:**	External
zdiff -y myzip2.Z myzip2.1.Z		Compares the file myzip2.Z with myzip.gz and shows the differences side by side.			

zdump

zdump	UNIX Shell:	All primary shells (csh, ksh, sh)
Function	Shows the current date and time for the time zones that you specify on the command line.	
Syntax	zdump [options...] *{ timezones... }*	

-v	Verbose mode. Shows more information.
-c *cutoffyear*	Limits the verbose output to just before the year that you specify.
timezones...	Specifies which time zone to dump. If a wrong time zone is given, GMT is shown.

continued

File Name:	zdump	**Directory:**	/usr/sbin/	**Type:**	External
zdump -v Europe			Shows European time in verbose mode.		
zdump -v -c 1999			Doesn't show years after 1999.		

zforce

UNIX Shell: All primary shells (csh, ksh, sh)

Function	Adds a .gz extension to a compressed (gzip) file.
Syntax	zforce *{ files... }*

files...		Specifies file to add the extension to.			
File Name:	zforce	**Directory:**	/usr/bin/	**Type:**	External
zforce RFC9999			If RFC9999 is a gzipped file, RFC9999 is renamed RFC9999.gz.		

zgrep, zfgrep, zegrep

UNIX Shell: Bourne shell (sh)

Function	Is used to search for text strings inside compressed files.
Syntax	zgrep [options...] *pattern files...*

options...		Specifies options from the `grep`, `egrep`, or `fgrep` command .			
pattern		Specifies pattern to search for.			
files...		Specifies one or more files to search in.			
File Name:	zgrep	**Directory:**	/usr/bin/	**Type:**	Script
zgrep ISDN rfc44444.gz			Searches for string ISDN in the gzipped file rfc44444.gz.		
zgrep -v ISDN rfc4444.Z			Searches for lines not containing string ISDN in compressed file RFC4444.Z.		

zic

UNIX Shell: All primary shells (csh, ksh, sh)

Function	Is used to set time conversion.
Syntax	zic [options...] *{ files... }*

-d *directory*		Creates time conversion files in the specified directory.			
-l *localtime*		Uses the specified time zone as the local time.			
-p *timerules*		Uses the rules from the specified time zone to manage posix time zone variables.			
-L *file*		Reads leap second information from the specified file.			
-v		Prompts if the year in the input file is out of range.			
-s		Limits time values stored in output files to values that are same.			
-y *yeartype*		Checks how years are to be written.			
-		Reads time conversion information from STDIN.			
files...		Specifies a file with time conversion information.			
File Name:	zic	**Directory:**	/usr/sbin/	**Type:**	External

zmore

UNIX Shell: Bourne shell (sh)

Function	Shows compressed text files one screen at a time.
Syntax	zmore *{ files... }*

files...		Specifies one or more files to show.			
File Name:	zmore	**Directory:**	/usr/bin/	**Type:**	Script
zmore RFC1001.gz			Shows the compressed file one page at the time.		

znew

UNIX Shell: All primary shells (csh, ksh, sh)

Function	Converts a .Z file to a .gz file.
Syntax	znew [options...] *{ filenames... }*

-f	Forces recompression even if the .gz file already exists.
-t	Checks the new file before deleting the originals.
-v	Verbose mode. Shows more information.
-9	Specifies to use the most powerful compression method.
-P	Uses pipes to convert the file to reduce disk space usage.

continued

-K *filenames...*		Keeps the .Z file if it's smaller than the .gz file. Specifies the file to recompress.			
File Name:	znew	**Directory:**	/usr/bin/	**Type:**	External
znew ucg_secrets.Z		Produces the gzipped ucg_secrets.gz.			
znew -K ucg_secrets.Z		Keeps ucg_secrets.Z if it is smaller than ucg_secrets.gz			
znew -9 ucg_secrets.Z		Uses the most powerful compression method.			

zzz

UNIX Shell: All primary shells (csh, ksh, sh)

Function	Places the system into one of two modes of advanced power management (APM) suspension.				
Syntax	zzz [options...]				
-S -z -f *socket*		Suspends the system. Places the system into stand-by. Specifies the socket that is used to manage who has access to APM.			
File Name:	zzz	**Directory:**	/usr/sbin/	**Type:**	External
zzz		Places the system directly into suspension.			
zzz -z		Places the system into stand-by.			

Chapter 13

Solaris 8 Commands

The commands in this section are all of the commands from Solaris 8 that are not listed in the Universal UNIX Commands (Chapter 9) or shared with Solaris 7 (Chapter 14). These exclusive commands are all listed in alphabetical order by the command name.

For cross-references to other operating systems, please see Chapter 1, the "Quick Command Index."

ab	**UNIX Shell:**	All shells (bash, tcsh, sh, ksh, csh, zsh)
Function	Benchmarks your Apache server by sending requests to it.	
Syntax	ab [options...] [http://] *hostname*[:*port*]/*path*	

-k	Enables multiple requests in one HTTP session. This is called HTTP KeepAlive.
-i	Uses an HTTP HEAD, which replaces the GET method. Not combinable with POST.
-n *requests*	Specifies the number of requests to run in the benchmark.
-t *timelimit*	Specifies the time in seconds to use benchmarking. This sets -n to 50,000.
-c *concurrency*	Specifies the number of requests to perform simultaneously where default is 1.
-p *postfile*	Specifies a file to send in any HTTP POST requests to the Apache server.
-A *user:password*	Provides the server with user name and password, entered with a colon between. (Sent, whether the server needs it or not, as uuencoded data.)
-p *user:password*	Runs the same procedure as the -A switch, but is used with proxy servers.
-C *name=value*	Adds a "Cookie:" to the request. The option is repeatable.
-p *string*	Appends more headers to the request. The argument is usually in value:value form.
-T *content-type*	Specifies the content-type header for usage with POST data.
-v *verbosity*	Specifies verbosity level.
-w *output HTML*	Shows results in HTML tables. (Default is two columns wide, white background.)
-x *string*	Specifies the attributes for `table`.
-y *string*	Specifies the attributes for `tr`.
-z *string*	Specifies the attributes for `td` or `th`.
-V	Shows version information.
-h	Shows help information.
-H *attribute*	Adds arbitrary header line. The option is repeatable.
[http://]*hostname*:{ *port* }/*path*	Defines the URL to use when benchmarking. `Http` and `port` aren't required.

File Name:	`ab`	**Directory:**	/usr/apache/bin	**Type:**	External

alloc	**UNIX Shell:**	TC shell (tcsh)
Function	Shows how much memory is used and is free.	
Syntax	alloc	

apptrace

UNIX Shell:	All shells (bash, tcsh, sh, ksh, csh, zsh)
Function	Traces function calls that a specific program makes to shared libraries.
Syntax	apptrace [options...] *command { command arguments... }*

-f	Follows any child processes created by fork and shows trace output for each process.
-o *outfile*	Specifies an output file instead of STDERR.
	An exclamation point (!) before the argument removes the argument from the trace:
-F [!]*tracefrom*	Traces calls from a list of shared objects.
-T [!]*traceto*	Traces calls to a list of shared objects.
-t [!]*call*	Traces function calls.
-v [!]*call*	Shows call traces in verbose format.
command	Specifies the command that you want to trace.
arguments...	Is used to specify options to the command.

File Name:	`apptrace`	**Directory:**	/usr/bin/	**Type:**	External

autoload

UNIX Shell:	Z shell (zsh)
Function	Marks the function for auto loading.
Syntax	autoload *function*

function	Specifies the function to be marked for auto loading.

bash

UNIX Shell:	Bash shell (bash)
Function	The GNU Bourne-again shell. It's compatible with the Bourne shell, with additional functions from Korn and C-shell.
Syntax	bash [options...] *{ file }*

--dump-po-strings	Is same as -D, but output is in GNU portable objects format (po).
--dump-strings	Is same as -D.
--help	Shows help information.
--login	Invoked as a login shell.
--noediting	Doesn't read command line by reading the GNU readline library.
--noprofile	Doesn't read any of the initialization files when invoked as a login shell.
--norc	Doesn't read the personal initialization file (.bashrc).
--posix	Invokes shell to match to POSIX standard.
--rcfile *file*	Uses the specified file instead of the personal initialization file (.bashrc).
--restricted	Invokes as restricted shell.
--verbose	Verbose mode. Shows more information.
--version	Shows version information.
-c *string*	Reads command specified by string.
-D	Shows all double-quoted strings preceded by $ on STDOUT.
-r	Runs shell as restricted shell.
-i	Makes shell interactive.
-s	Reads commands from STDIN.
-a	Marks modified and created variables for export. (This option can also be set inside a script.)
-b	Informs the user asynchronously when a background job completes.
-e	Exits the shell if a command returns a non-zero exit status.
-f	Disables filename generation.
-h	Tracks aliases for the first encountered command.
-k	Places all keywords arguments in the environment for a command.
-m	Runs background job in separate process group. Shows a line when completed.
-n	Reads commands, but doesn't run them.
-o *{ option }*	Is used to set option. If no option is given, shows current status. See below for option.
allexport	The same as -a.
braceexpand	The same as -B.

continued

emacs	Uses an Emacs style inline editor for the command line.
errexit	The same as -e.
hashall	The same as -h.
histexpand	The same as -H.
history	Enables command history.
ignoreeof	Doesn't let the shell exit on EOF. The `exit` command must be used.
keyword	The same as -k.
monitor	The same as -m.
noclobber	The same as -C.
noexec	The same as -n.
noglob	The same as -f.
notify	The same as -b.
nounset	The same as -u.
onecmd	The same as -t.
physical	The same as -P.
posix	Changes to POSIX standard behavior where bash differs.
privileged	The same as -p.
verbose	The same as -v.
vi	Uses a vi-style inline editor for the command line.
xtrace	The same as -x.
-p	Turns on privileged mode.
-t	Runs one command and exits.
-u	Substitutes, treats unset variables as an error.
-v	Shows input lines as they are read.
-x	Show commands and their arguments when they are executed.
-B	Performs brace expansion.
-C	Forbids existing files to be overwritten by shell > redirection operator.
-H	Enables ! style history substitution.
-P	Uses physical directory structure instead of symbolic link structure. (If + is used instead of –, the flag is turned off.)
--	Sets positional parameters with the remaining of the line.
-	Turns off -x and -v flags and doesn't continue to examining arguments for flags.
file	A file containing bash commands.

File Name:	`bash`	**Directory:**	/usr/bin/	**Type:**	External

bind

UNIX Shell: Bash shell (bash)

Function	Shows or binds key sequences to a readline function or macro.
Syntax	bind options...

-m *keymap*	Specifies the keymap to be affected by the subsequent bindings.
-l	Shows a list of all readline function names.
-p	Shows a list of all readline function names and bindings for readline init files.
-P	Shows a list of current readline function names and bindings.
-v	Shows a list of readline variable names and values for readline init files.
-V	Shows a list of current readline variable names and values.
-s	Shows a list of readline key sequences bound to macros for readline init files.
-S	Shows a list of readline key sequences bound to macros and the strings they output.
-f *file*	Reads key bindings from file.
-q *function*	Queries which keys are bound to a function.
-u *function*	Erases all key bindings to function.
-r *keyseq*	Erases any binding for the key sequence.
-x *keyseq:function*	Assigns function to the key sequence.

bindkey

bindkey	UNIX Shell:	TC shell (tcsh)
Function	Binds keys to an edit command in the shell. Without any options, shows all bindings.	
Syntax	bindkey [options...] *{ key } { command }*	

-l	Shows a short description for each editor command.
-d	Sets all key bindings to default for the current editor.
-e	Sets all key bindings to standard GNU Emacs-like bindings.
-v	Sets all key bindings to standard vi-like bindings.
-a	Shows or changes key bindings.
-b	Interprets a key as a control character.
-k	Interprets a key as a symbolic arrow key name.
-r	Removes a key binding.
-c	Interprets a command as an internal or external command instead of an editor one.
-s	Interprets a command as a string to use as input when a key is pressed.
--	Specifies that the following option is a key even if it starts with -.
-u	Shows help information.
key	Specifies the key to use.
command	Specifies the editor command to assign to a key.

builtin

builtin	UNIX Shell:	Bash shell (bash), Z shell (zsh)
Function	Forces the use of a shell built-in command.	
Syntax	builtin *command { arguments... }*	

command	Specifies a shell builtin command to run.
arguments...	Specifies arguments to command.

builtins

builtins	UNIX Shell:	TC shell (tcsh)
Function	Shows all built-in commands in tcsh.	
Syntax	builtins	

bunzip2

bunzip2	UNIX Shell:	All shells (bash, tcsh, sh, ksh, csh, zsh)
Function	Decompresses bzip2 compressed files.	
Syntax	bunzip2 [options...] *{ filenames... }*	

-k	Keeps the input files.		
-f	Overwrites existing output files (default is no overwrite).		
-v	Shows more information.		
-V	Shows version and license information.		
-L	Shows software version and license.		
-s	Is used to limit the amount of memory to use.		
filenames...	Specifies a file or files to decompress.		
File Name: `bunzip2`	**Directory:** /usr/bin/	**Type:**	External

busstat

busstat	UNIX Shell:	All shells (bash, tcsh, sh, ksh, csh, zsh)
Function	Collects statistics and shows bus-performance counters.	
Syntax	busstat option busstat [options...] *{ interval count }*	

	The following options can't be combined:
-e *device*	Shows a list of events that are supported by the specified device.

continued

-l	Shows a list of devices that support performance counters.
	The following options can be combined:
-a	Shows only absolute counter values.
-n	Shows no output title.
-w *device*	Specifies the device to write counters for.
picnr=events...	Specifies the counters and events to show; uses a comma-separated list.
-r *device*	Specifies a device to read and show values for.
interval	Specifies an interval for collecting data.
count	Specifies how many times to collect data.
File Name: `busstat`	**Directory:** /usr/bin/ **Type:** External

bye

UNIX Shell: Z shell (zsh)

Function	Leaves the shell. It's the same as exit.
Syntax	bye

bzcat

UNIX Shell: All shells (bash, tcsh, sh, ksh, csh, zsh)

Function	Decompresses a bzip2 compressed file to STDOUT.
Syntax	bzcat [-s] *{ files... }*

-s	Is used to limit the memory amount allowed for decompression.
file...	The file or files to decompress.
File Name: `bzcat`	**Directory:** /usr/bin/ **Type:** External

bzip2

UNIX Shell: All shells (bash, tcsh, sh, ksh, csh, zsh)

Function	Is used to compress, decompress, or test bzip2 files.
Syntax	bzip2 [options...] *{ filenames... }*

-c	Compresses or decompresses to STDOUT.
-d	Forces decompression.
-f	Overwrites output files (default is no overwrite).
-k	Is used to keep the input files during compression or decompression.
-s	Is used to limit the memory usage when compressing, decompressing, or testing.
-t	Tests the integrity on the file or files.
-v	Shows more information.
-z	Forces compression.
-L	Shows license terms and conditions.
-1 - -9	Is used to set the block size at 100K to 900K during compression.
--repetitive-fast	Compresses repetitive blocks faster.
--repetitive-best	Compresses repetitive blocks better.
filenames...	Specifies the file or files to compress.
File Name: `bzip2`	**Directory:** /usr/bin/ **Type:** External

bzip2recover

UNIX Shell: All shells (bash, tcsh, sh, ksh, csh, zsh)

Function	Recovers data from a damaged bzip2 compressed file.
Syntax	bzip2recover *filename*

`filename`	Specifies the file to recover.
File Name: `bzip2recover`	**Directory:** /usr/bin/ **Type:** External

clinfo

UNIX Shell:	All shells (bash, tcsh, sh, ksh, csh, zsh)
Function	Shows information about the cluster configuration of the node on which the command was executed.
Syntax	clinfo [options...]

-h	Shows the highest node number in the cluster configuration.
-n	Shows the number of the node where clinfo was executed.

File Name:	`clinfo`	**Directory:**	/usr/sbin/	**Type:**	External

complete

UNIX Shell:	TC shell (tcsh)
Function	Declares how a command should be completed.
Syntax	complete *{ command }* complete *command word/pattern/list*[*:select*]/*{ suffix/ }*

command	Specifies the command to set up a completion for, or to show a completion for.
word	Specifies which word, relative to the current, is to be completed.
c	Specifies the pattern that must match the beginning of the current word.
C	Includes pattern when completing the word.
n	Specifies the pattern that must match the beginning of previous word.
N	Specifies the pattern that must match the word previous to the previous word (2 words previous).
p	Specifies position-dependent match. Pattern is a numeric range.
pattern	Specifies the pattern to use.
list	Specifies the possible completions.
a	Uses aliases.
b	Uses bindings (editor commands).
c	Uses internal or external commands.
C	Uses external commands that begin with the specified path.
d	Uses directories.
D	Uses directories that begin with the specified path.
e	Uses environment variables.
f	Uses filenames.
F	Uses filenames that begin with the specified path.
g	Uses group names.
j	Uses jobs.
l	Uses limits.
n	Doesn't use anything.
s	Uses shell variables.
S	Uses signals.
t	Uses plain text files.
T	Uses plain text files that begin with the specified path.
v	Uses any variables.
u	Uses usernames.
x	Shows select when list-choices is used.
X	Uses completions.
$var	Uses word from the variable $var
(...)	Uses word from the specified list.
`command`	Uses word from the output from the specified command.
select	Specifies an extra pattern to use as a selection for the last three options above.
suffix	Specifies a single character to add to the completion.

consadm

UNIX Shell:	**All shells (bash, tcsh, sh, ksh, csh, zsh)**
Function	Shows console messages to the terminal or screen specified. Can show messages on many screens at one time.
Syntax	consadm [options...]

-a *device*	Adds the device specified to the list of screen devices to receive console messages.
-d *device*	Erases the device from the list of screen devices and stops showing console messages.
-p	Shows list of screen devices that will receive messages even when server is rebooted.

File Name:	`consadm`	**Directory:**	/usr/sbin/	**Type:**	External

coreadm

UNIX Shell:	**All shells (bash, tcsh, sh, ksh, csh, zsh)**
Function	Manages the core files in the system.
Syntax	coreadm [options...] { *pids...* }

-g *pattern*	Specifies location and filename of global core files.
-i *pattern*	Specifies location and filename of core files. Used in init while starting up.
-e *actions...*	Is used to enable specific core file actions.
-d *actions...*	Is used to disable specific core file actions.
	The following actions are used with the -e and -d options:
global	Allows core dumps using the global core pattern.
process	Allows core dumps using the preprocess core pattern.
globalsetid	Allows set ID core dumps using the global core pattern.
procsetid	Allows set ID core dumps using the per-process pattern.
log	Creates a `syslog` message when a global core file is created.
-p *pattern*	Is used to set a per-process core filename pattern for each specified PID.
-u	Updates the system-wide core file from the /etc/coreadm.conf; used alone.
pids...	Specifies a process ID; only used with the -p option.

File Name:	`coreadm`	**Directory:**	/usr/bin/	**Type:**	External

cpustat

UNIX Shell:	**All shells (bash, tcsh, sh, ksh, csh, zsh)**
Function	Collects CPU statistics and shows performance counters.
Syntax	cpustat [options...] { *interval* }

-c *events...*	Specifies a set of events for the CPU performance counters to show.
-n	Removes all header information.
-t	Tracks processor cycles and shows the output in column format.
-D	Shows debug information.
interval	Specifies an interval in seconds to collect samples.
count	Specifies the number of times to collect sample values.

File Name:	`cpustat`	**Directory:**	/usr/sbin/	**Type:**	External

cputrack

UNIX Shell:	**All shells (bash, tcsh, sh, ksh, csh, zsh)**
Function	Uses CPU counters to monitor how a process behaves on the system.
Syntax	cputrack -c [options...] { *command* }

-c *eventspec*	Specifies the events that you want to monitor. Uses -h options to see valid events.
-D	Starts debug mode.
-e	Monitors and follows all `exec` and `execve` calls to not lose the track.
-f	Follows all child processes that are created by `fork`, `fork1`, or `vfork`.
-h	Shows a help message on how to use the options and how to specify events.
-n	Suppresses header output.
-N *amount*	Sets the number of monitor samples to do before exit.
-o *file*	Specifies the file to save the output in.
-p *processID*	Specifies a process ID to monitor.

continued

-t	Shows the processor cycle counts, if possible.
-T *interval*	Sets the interval between CPU counter samples (default is 1 second).
-v	Verbose mode. Shows more information.
command	Specifies a command to monitor the behavior of.
argument	Specifies arguments to the command.
File Name: `cputrack`	**Directory:** /usr/bin/ — **Type:** External

crle

UNIX Shell: All shells (bash, tcsh, sh, ksh, csh, zsh)

Function	Creates and displays runtime linking configuration files. If used with no or the -c option, it displays the configuration file.
Syntax	crle [options...]

-64	Processes 64-bit object instead of the default 32-bit.
-a *name*	Specifies an alternative name to add to the configuration file.
-c *conf*	Used to specify the name of the configuration file.
-f *flags*	Provides symbolic flag arguments to `dldumb` calls.
-i *name*	Specifies an individual name to be added to the configuration cache.
-g *name*	Specifies a group name to be added to the configuration cache.
-G *name*	Same as -g, and any shared objects have alternatives created via `dldump`.
-l *dir*	Specifies a new default search directory for standard AOUT or ELF objects.
-o *dir*	Specifies the directory in which alternate objects will be created.
-s *dir*	Specifies a new default search directory for secure AOUT or ELF objects.
-t *type*	Toggles object type relevant to the -l or -s option. Valid types are AOUT or ELF.
-v	Verbose mode. Shows more information.
File Name: `crle`	**Directory:** /usr/bin/ — **Type:** External

dbmmanage

UNIX Shell: N/A

Function	Manages DBM files with usernames and passwords to authenticate HTTP users.
Syntax	dbmmanage *file { command } { user password }*

	The following commands can't be combined:
add	Adds a username and uses the encrypted password.
adduser	Asks for a password then adds a username.
check	Finds a password and checks if the specified username has the specified password.
delete	Removes username from the filename.
import	Reads username and password from STDIN and adds them to the filename.
update	Verifies that username already exists.
view	Shows the DBM file.
file	Specifies the DBM file. You don't need to specify the file extension.
user	Specifies the username to manage.
password	Specifies an optional encrypted password to use with the username.
File Name: `dbmmanage`	**Directory:** /usr/bin/ — **Type:** Script

devfsadm

UNIX Shell: All shells (bash, tcsh, sh, ksh, csh, zsh)

Function	Is used to create, update, and configure any /dev or /devices entries in the system.
Syntax	devfsadm [options...]

-C	Cleans up unwanted logical links.
-c *deviceclass*	Runs on specified device classes only; can be disk, tape, port, audio, or pseudo.
-i *drivername*	Configures the devices with the specified driver.
-n	Doesn't add drivers or nodes to the kernel tree.
-s	Doesn't make changes to /dev or /devices, simulates execution.
-t *tablefile*	Specifies devlink.tab file other than the default.
-r *rootdir*	Specifies a new root directory for /dev and /devices.
-v	Verbose mode. Shows more information.
File Name: `Devsadm`	**Directory:** /usr/sbin — **Type:** External

devfsadmd

devfsadmd	UNIX Shell:	All shells (bash, tcsh, sh, ksh, csh, zsh)
Function	Manages any device configuration done by the command `devfsadm`.	
Syntax	devfsadmd	
File Name: `devfsadmd`	**Directory:** /usr/lib/devfsadm/	**Type:** External

devfseventd

devfseventd	UNIX Shell:	All shells (bash, tcsh, sh, ksh, csh, zsh)
Function	Manages services for kernel event notification used by the `devfsadmd` command.	
Syntax	devfseventd	
File Name: `devfseventd`	**Directory:** /usr/lib/devfsadm/	**Type:** External

dhcpmgr

dhcpmgr	UNIX Shell:	All shells (bash, tcsh, sh, ksh, csh, zsh)
Function	A graphical user interface used to manage the DHCP service on the local system.	
Syntax	dhcpmgr	

	The following tasks can be performed after starting the program:
DHCP	Configures the system as a DHCP server.
BOOTP	Configures the system as a BOOTP relay.
DHCP or BOOTP	Starts, stops, enables, disables, or unconfigures the service.
DHCP addresses	Adds, modifies, or deletes IP addresses leased by the DHCP service.
DHCP macros	Adds, modifies, or deletes macros that supply configuration parameters to the client.
DHCP options	Adds, modifies, or deletes options that define parameters delivered through DHCP.
File Name: `dhcpmgr`	**Directory:** /usr/sadm/admin/bin/ **Type:** External

disable

disable	UNIX Shell:	Z shell (zsh)
Function	Disables names in the hash table. If no option is given, shows all disabled names.	
Syntax	disable [option] *{ names... }*	

-a	Is used to disable an alias name.
-f	Is used to disable a function.
-r	Is used to disable a reversed word.
-m	Specifies the name is a pattern. Use quotes around the name.
names...	Specifies names to disable.

disown

disown	UNIX Shell:	Bash shell (bash), Z shell (zsh)
Function	Removes the specified job from the active job list.	
Syntax	bash: disown [options...] *{ jobs... }* zsh: disown *{ jobs... }*	

jobs...	Specifies job to modify. If not given and -a or -r isn't used, use the current job.
bash	
-h	Doesn't remove the job from the list, but marks it so it will not receive any hang-up.
-a	Marks all jobs in the list. Doesn't specify jobs.
-r	Marks all running jobs in the list. Doesn't specify jobs.

echotc

echotc	UNIX Shell:	TC shell (tcsh)
Function	Is used to exercise the terminal capabilities arguments.	
Syntax	echotc [options...] *arguments...*	

-s	Shows an empty string instead of an error message, if argument doesn't exist.
-v	Verbose mode. Shows more information.
arguments...	Specifies argument from termcap. (If argument is one of baud, cols, lines, meta, or tabs, shows the value.)

emulate

UNIX Shell:	Z shell (zsh)
Function	Emulates other shells with Z-shell. C-shell will not be fully emulated.
Syntax	emulate [options...] *{ shell }*

-L	Uses the options LOCAL_OPTIONS and LOCAL_TRAP.
-R	Resets all options to the default values.
shell	Specifies the shell to emulate. Can be zsh, sh, ksh, or csh.

enable

UNIX Shell:	Bash shell (bash), Z shell (zsh)
Function	Enables or disables `bash` internal commands.
Syntax	enable [options...] *{ names... }*

	These options are used by Z-shell (zsh):
-a	Enables an alias name.
-f	Enables a function.
-r	Enables a reversed word.
-m	Specifies the name is a pattern. Uses quotes around the name.
names...	Specifies name to enable.
	These options are used by Bash shell (bash):
-n	Disables each name specified.
-f	Loads a built-in command specified by the name dynamic.
-d	Erases a command previously loaded with -f.
-p	Shows a list of enabled shell built-ins.
-a	Shows all shell built-ins.
-s	Works only on POSIX built-ins.
names...	Specifies name of commands to work on.

fbconfig

UNIX Shell:	All shells (bash, tcsh, sh, ksh, csh, zsh)
Function	Configures frame buffer attributes and shows information about them.
Syntax	fbconfig [options...] fbconfig [options...] *{ devoptions... }*

	Select between these two options for more device dependent information:
-list	Shows a list of installed frame buffers and device-specific configuration routines.
	The following options may be combined when configuring a frame buffer:
-dev *{ name }*	Specifies the device to configure. The default is `/dev/fbs/ffb0`.
-prconf	Shows hardware configuration information.
-propt	Shows current software option settings.
-res *mode*	Specifies the video mode to use on the device.
\?	Shows a list of available video modes.
devoptions...	Specifies any device-specific options.

File Name:	`fbconfig`	**Directory:**	/usr/sbin/	**Type:**	External

filetest

UNIX Shell:	TC shell (tcsh)
Function	Tests a file for different things.
Syntax	filetest options... *files...*

	The following options return 1 if they are true:
-r	Tests whether the file is readable.
-w	Tests whether the file is writable.
-x	Tests whether the file is executable.
-X	Tests whether the file is executable. File is in the path or a built-in.
-e	Tests whether the file exists.
-o	Tests whether the user owns the file.

continued

-z	Tests whether the file has a zero size.
-s	Tests whether the file has a size greater than zero.
-f	Tests whether the file is a plain file.
-d	Tests whether the file is a directory.
-l	Tests whether the file is a symbolic link.
-b	Tests whether the file is a block special file.
-c	Tests whether the file is a character special file.
-p	Tests whether the file is a named pipe.
-S	Tests whether the file is a socket special file.
-u	Tests whether the set-user-ID bit is set.
-g	Tests whether the set-group-ID bit is set.
-k	Tests whether the sticky bit is set.
-t	Tests whether the file (must be a digit) is an open file descriptor for a terminal device.
-R	Tests whether the file has been migrated.
-L	Tests what a symbolic link points to rather than the link itself. (The above options can be combined like this: -xy.)
	The following options will return more information:
-A	Shows the last file access time in seconds since the epoch.
-A:	Shows the last file access time in timestamp format.
-M	Shows the last time the file was modified in seconds since the epoch.
-M:	Shows the last time the file was modified in timestamp format.
-C	Shows the last time the inode was modified in seconds since the epoch.
-C:	Shows the last time the inode was modified in timestamp format.
-D	Shows the device number.
-I	Shows the inode number.
-F	Shows the composite file identifier (device:inode).
-L	Shows the name of the file to which the symbolic link points.
-N	Shows the number of hard links.
-P	Shows the file permissions in octal without leading zero.
-P:	Shows the file permissions in octal with leading zero.
-P*mode*	Shows the file permissions in octal and with mode.
-P*mode*:	Shows the file permissions in octal, with leading zeros.
-U	Shows the numeric user ID.
-U:	Shows the name of the user. If user is unknown, shows the numeric user ID.
-G	Shows the numeric group ID.
-G:	Shows the name of the group. If group is unknown, shows the numeric group ID.
-Z	Shows the size in bytes.
files...	Specifies the file to test.

functions

UNIX Shell: Z shell (zsh)

Function	Shows or sets attribute for shell functions.
Syntax	functions [options...] *{ names... }*

-t	Turns on execution trace on this function.
-u	Marks the function for auto loading.
-m	Specifies that the name is a pattern to use to select functions. (If the prefix for the option is + instead of –, the option is turned off.)
names...	Specifies the functions to use.

geniconvtbl

UNIX Shell: All shells (bash, tcsh, sh, ksh, csh, zsh)

Function	Creates binary code conversion tables for iconv using text files.
Syntax	geniconvtbl [options...] *{ files... }*

-f	Overwrites any existing output file or files.
-n	Doesn't create any output file.
-q	Doesn't show any error messages.

continued

-p *preprocessor*	Specifies preprocessor to use other than the default CPP.
-W *arg*	Passes arguments to the preprocessor. The following can be used:
-D*name*	Adds a definition.
-D*name=def*	Adds a define directive.
-I*directory*	Inserts a directory into the search path.
-U*name*	Removes name definitions.
files...	Specifies the input file or files.

File Name:	`geniconvtbl`	**Directory:**	/usr/bin/	**Type:**	External

genlayouttbl

UNIX Shell: All shells (bash, tcsh, sh, ksh, csh, zsh)

Function	Creates a binary layout table from a locale.
Syntax	genlayouttbl [-o *outfile*] *file*

-o *outfile*	Specifies an output file to put the binary layout table in.
file	Specifies an input file instead of STDIN.

File Name:	`genlayouttbl`	**Directory:**	/usr/bin/	**Type:**	External

getln

UNIX Shell: Z shell (zsh)

Function	Reads a line from the command stack and doesn't treat a \ at the end of a row in any special way.
Syntax	getln [options...] *variables...*

-A	Specifies the first variable is an array to assign values to.
-c	Reads word of the current command (used inside a function).
-l	Assigns the line as a scalar (used inside a function).
-nc	Gives the number of the word the cursor is on.
-nl	Gives the index of the character the cursor is on.
-e	Echoes the output to STDOUT, doesn't assign any variables.
-E	Echoes the output to STDOUT.
variables...	Specifies the variables to use.

gpatch

UNIX Shell: All shells (bash, tcsh, sh, ksh, csh, zsh)

Function	Applies changes from the patch file to the original file. The patch file is made by the `diff` command.
Syntax	gpatch [options...] { *origfile patchfile* }

--backup	Takes a backup of all files before patching the files.
--backup-if-mismatch	Takes a backup if the patch doesn't match exactly.
--no-backup-if-mismatch	Doesn't take a backup if the patch doesn't match exactly.
--prefix=*pref*	Puts a prefix to the backup file, the prefix can be a directory.
--binary	Works in binary mode.
--context	Looks at the patch file as an ordinary context diff.
--directory=*dir*	Changes directory before running the command.
--ifdef=*define*	Uses specified #ifdef tags to mark any changes.
--dry-run	Simulates patch execution.
--ed	Takes the patch file to be an ed script.
--remove-empty-files	Removes any empty output files after patching.
--force	Forces execution without asking for confirmation.
--fuzz=*num*	Sets the maximum fuzz-factor value.
--get=*num*	Manages the commands actions if the file is under RCS or SCCS control.
--input=*patchfile*	Specifies a file that holds the patch information.
--ignore-whitespace	Patterns don't have to match exactly.
--normal	Looks at the patch file as a normal diff.
--forward	Doesn't patch if patches already have been applied.
--output=*outfile*	Sends output to a file instead of patching.
--strip=*num*	Strips the specified number of prefixes from each file in the patch file.

continued

--posix	Uses strictly POSIX standard.
--quoting-style=*word*	Uses predefined words to output names differently.
literal	Shows names as they are.
shell	Shows shell output names that normally would cause garbage output.
shell-always	Shows all names as the shell would show them.
c	Shows names as C language strings.
escape	Shows names as C language strings without double-quote characters.
--reject-file=*rejectfile*	Specifies where to put a reject file.
--reverse	Does a reverse operation if you have mixed old and new versions.
--silent	Shows no output.
--batch	Asks no questions.
--set-time	Sets access and modification times of the patch file.
--unified	Looks at the patch file as a unified context diff.
--version-control=*method*	Specifies which method to use to find out backup filenames.
existing	Numbers the backup files that already have been numbered.
numbered	Always number the backup files.
simple	Makes simple backups.
--verbose	Shows verbose information.
--debug=*num*	Sets internal debug flags.
--basename-prefix=*pref*	Appends a prefix to the base name of the file when creating simple backup filenames.
--suffix=*suffix*	Sets suffix for simple backups.
--set-utc	Uses context diff headers to set access and modification times for the patch files.
origfile	Specifies the file that is to be patched.
patchfile	Specifies the patch file.

File Name:	gpatch	**Directory:**	/usr/bin/	**Type:**	External

gunzip

UNIX Shell: All shells (bash,tcsh,sh,ksh,csh,zsh)

Function	Extracts files. Support files that are created by gzip, zip compress, compress -H and pack.
Syntax	gunzip [options...] *{ names... }*

-a	Specifies ASCII text mode.
--ascii	The same as -a.
-c	Doesn't change the file; writes to STDOUT.
--stdout	The same as -c.
--to-stdout	The same as -c.
--decompress	Decompresses.
--uncompress	Uncompresses.
-f	Forces decompression.
--force	The same as -f.
-l	Shows information about compressed files.
--list	The same as -l.
-L	Shows information about licenses and then quits.
--license	The same as -L.
-n	Doesn't restore filename if present (is default).
--no-name	The same as -n.
-N	Restores filename if it exists.
--name	The same as -N.
-r	Decompresses recursive.
--recursive	The same as -r.
-t	Tests the file integrity.
--test	The same as -t.
-v	Verbose mode. Shows more information.
--verbose	The same as -v.
-q	Suppresses all warnings.
--quiet	The same as -q.
-s.ext	Specifies suffix to the output file.

continued

--suffix *.ext*	The same as -S.
-*number*	Specifies the compression rate (1 is least compression and 9 is highest).
--fast	The fastest, and least compression (is the same as -1).
--best	The slowest, and best compression (is the same as -9).
name	Specifies the file to decompress.
File Name: gunzip	**Directory:** /usr/bin/ **Type:** External

gzcat

UNIX Shell: All shells (bash, tcsh, sh, ksh, csh, zsh)

Function	Shows (concatenates) the content of a compressed file on the screen.
Syntax	gzcat [options...] *{ files... }*

-f	Forces compression or decompression.
--force	The same as -f.
-L	Shows information about license.
--license	The same as -L.
files...	Specifies the input file.
File Name: gzcat	**Directory:** /usr/bin/ **Type:** External

gzcmp

UNIX Shell: Bourne shell (sh)

Function	Compares the difference between compressed files.
Syntax	gzcmp [options...] *file1 { file2 }*

-l	Shows the byte (dec) number and the differing bytes (oct) for all non-matches.
-s	Reports the exit status from the compare.
file1	Compares the first file with an uncompressed version of it.
file2	Is used when you want to compare two files.
File Name: gzcmp	**Directory:** /usr/bin/ **Type:** Script

gzdiff

UNIX Shell: Bash shell (bash)

Function	Runs the diff program on compressed files.
Syntax	gzdiff [options...] *file1 { file2 }*

options...	See the command `diff` for option description.
file1	Specifies the files that you want to compare against the compressed same file.
file2	Specifies that you want to compare file1 against file2.
File Name: gzdiff	**Directory:** /usr/bin/ **Type:** Script

gzforce

UNIX Shell: Bourne shell (sh)

Function	Adds a .gz extension to a file compressed with gzip if the extension was lost (during a file copy, for example).
Syntax	gzforce *{ names... }*

names...	Specifies the file or files to add the .gz extension to.
File Name: gzforce	**Directory:** /bin **Type:** Script

gzgrep

UNIX Shell: All shells (bash, tcsh, sh, ksh, csh, zsh)

Function	Starts the grep on compressed or gzipped files. Options specified are passed to grep.
Syntax	gzgrep [options...] *pattern files...*

options...	Please see the command `grep` for a list of options.
-e *pattern-list*	Specifies a list of patterns to search for.
pattern	Specifies a pattern to search for.
files...	Specifies a filename. If no filename is specified, STDIN is decompressed and used.
File Name: gzgrep	**Directory:** /usr/bin/ **Type:** External

gzip		UNIX Shell:	All shells (bash, tcsh, sh, ksh, csh, zsh)
Function	Compresses files with Lempel-Ziv coding. If it is possible, the file is replaced by one with the .gz extension.		
Syntax	gzip [options...] *{ files... }*		

-a	ASCII text mode, converts end-of-lines. Supported only for some non-UNIX systems.
--ascii	The same as -a.
-c	Doesn't change file; only writes to STDOUT.
--stdout	The same as -c.
--to-stdout	The same as -c.
-d	Decompresses the file. This is the same as using the gunzip command.
--decompress	The same as -d.
--uncompress	The same as -d.
-f	Forces compression.
--force	The same as -f.
-l	Shows information about compressed file.
--list	The same as -l.
-L	Shows information about license and quit.
--license	The same as -L.
-n	Doesn't save name and timestamp.
--no-name	The same as -n.
-N	Saves name and timestamp.
--name	The same as -N.
-r	Compresses all files in subdirectories, recursively.
--recursive	The same as -r.
-t	Tests integrity of the file.
--test	The same as -t.
-v	Verbose mode. Shows more information.
--verbose	The same as -v.
-*number*	Specifies the compression rate (1 is fast but least compressed, and 9 is slow but most compressed).
--fast	Specifies to use the fast but least compression rate (is the same as -1).
--best	Specifies to use the slow but most compression rate (is the same as -9).
-q	Suppresses all warnings.
--quiet	The same as -q.
-S *.ext*	Specifies the suffix.
files...	Specifies the file to decompress.
File Name: `gzip`	**Directory:** /usr/bin/ **Type:** External

gzmore		UNIX Shell:	Bash shell (bash)
Function	Shows compressed files with a suffix of .gz, .z, or .Z, one screen at a time.		
Syntax	gzmore *{ files... }*		

files...	Specifies the file or files that you want to show on the screen.
File Name: `gzmore`	**Directory:** /usr/bin/ **Type:** Script

gznew		UNIX Shell:	Bourne shell (sh)
Function	Compresses files with `compress` (*.Z) even more and gives them a .gz extension.		
Syntax	gznew [options...] *{ files... }*		

-f	Recompresses a .Z file to a .gz file even if a .gz file with the same name exists.
-t	Is used to test the new file to see if it works before deleting the original.
-v	Shows the old filename, the percentage it decreased, and the new filename.

continued

-9	Uses the optimal compression method, which makes it a bit slower.
-P	Reduces disk space usage for the conversion with the use of pipes.
-K	Is used to keep a .Z file when it is smaller than the .gz file.
files...	Specifies the name of the .Z file.
File Name: `gznew`	**Directory:** /usr/bin/ **Type:** Script

h2ph

UNIX Shell: N/A

Function	Converts the specified C header files into Perl header file format.
Syntax	h2ph [options...] { *files...* }

-d *path*	Specifies a directory to save the converted filename to. **The -r and -a options can't be combined.**
-r	Runs on all files in all subdirectories.
-a	Runs on the filename and all `.h` files that it includes.
-l	Replicates all links into the specified directory.
-h	Creates hints into the Perl file to make it easier to troubleshoot the script.
-D	Takes code from .h file and adds that as comments to the .ph file. Used for debug.
-Q	Quiet mode. Doesn't show names of converted files.
files...	Specifies the header files to convert.
File Name: `h2ph`	**Directory:** /usr/bin/ **Type:** Script

h2xs

UNIX Shell: N/A

Function	Creates Perl extensions from C header files.
Syntax	h2xs [options...] { *files... directories...* }

-A	Skips all auto loaded values and disables the autoloader in the .pm file
-F	Specifies flags for C preprocessor to find function parameters in header. (You need to use the -x option with -F.)
-M *regularexpression*	Specifies macros or functions to process.
-O	Overwrites directories if they already exist.
-P	Skips the stub POD section.
-X	Skips the XS portion. Used to create templates for non-XS-based modules.
-a	Creates accessory method for each method of struts and unions.
-c	Skips constants in the `.as` file and matching auto load in the `.pm` file.
-d	Shows debug information.
-f	Creates an extension for a header.
-h	Shows help information.
-k	Skips the const attribute in the XS code.
-m	Creates a Perl variable for each corresponding variable in the header file.
-n *module*	Specifies name to use for extension.
-o *regularexpression*	Specifies `opaque` data. (When you use -o, you have to use the -x option.)
-p *prefix*	Specifies prefix to remove from the Perl function names.
-s *sub1,sub2*	Creates subroutines for the specified macros.
-v *version*	Specifies the version number for this extension.
-x	Creates XSUBs from function declarations in the header file.
files...	Specifies header file or files.
directories...	Specifies the extra directories that have C header files.
File Name: `h2xs`	**Directory:** /usr/bin/ **Type:** Script

help

UNIX Shell: Bash shell (bash)

Function	Shows information about internal commands. With no option, shows a short description about internal commands.
Syntax	help [-s] { *name* }

-s	Shows only a short description.
name	Specifies the name of the internal command to get information about.

htdigest

UNIX Shell:	All shells (bash, tcsh, sh, ksh, csh, zsh)
Function	Manages HTTP user authentication files.
Syntax	htdigest [-c] *file realm username*

-c	Is used to create a password file, even if it exists.
file	Specifies the file that holds password, realm, and user name information.
realm	Specifies the realm where the user belongs.
username	Specifies the user name that you want to manage.

File Name:	`htdigest`	**Directory:**	/usr/apache/bin/	**Type:**	External

htpasswd

UNIX Shell:	All shells (bash, tcsh, sh, ksh, csh, zsh)
Function	Manages HTTP user authentication.
Syntax	htpasswd [options...] *passwordfile username { password }*

-b	Uses the command line to get the password.
-c	Creates a password file even if it exists.
	The following four encryption methods can't be combined:
-m	Uses the MD5 algorithm for passwords.
-d	Uses crypt encryption for passwords.
-s	Uses the SHA encryption for passwords.
-p	Uses plain text passwords.
passwordfile	Specifies the file that holds password username information.
username	Specifies the username to work with.
password	Specifies the password to encrypt with -m, d, s, or p. Only used with the -b option.

File Name:	`htpasswd`	**Directory:**	/usr/apache/bin/	**Type:**	External

httpd

UNIX Shell:	All shells (bash, tcsh, sh, ksh, csh, zsh)
Function	The Apache Internet Web server.
Syntax	httpd [options...]

-X	Runs the server in single-process mode.
-R *libexecdir*	Specifies where the server will put dynamic shared object files.
-d *serverroot*	Sets the root directory for the server.
-f *config*	Specifies a configuration file with startup commands.
-C *bconfig*	Runs the specified configuration before reading the configuration file.
-c *aconfig*	Runs the specified configuration after reading the configuration file.
-D *params*	Specifies parameters to be used with IfDefine tags.
	The following options can't be combined with those above.
-h	Shows help information.
-l	Shows a list of compiled modules.
-L	Shows a list of directives and attributes.
-v	Shows version information.
-V	Shows version and build information.
-S	Shows the settings that are in the configuration file.
-t	Runs a configuration file test.
-T	Runs a configuration file test without checking the document root.

File Name:	`httpd`	**Directory:**	/usr/apache/bin/	**Type:**	External

hup

UNIX Shell:	TC shell (tcsh)
Function	Allows a command to catch a hang-up signal. This is the opposite of `nohup`.
Syntax	hup *{ command }*

command	Specifies the command to run.

in.ndpd

in.ndpd	UNIX Shell:	All shells (bash, tcsh, sh, ksh, csh, zsh)
Function	Makes auto-configurations for hosts and routers of Neighbor Discovery and Address Auto configuration for IPv6.	
Syntax	in.ndpd [options...]	

-a	Disables stateless address auto configuration.
-d	Enables debugging output on STDOUT.
-t	Enables tracing to show all outgoing and incoming packets.
-f config_file	Specifies the config file instead of information from /etc/inet/ndpd.conf.

File Name:	Directory:	Type:
in.ndpd	/usr/sbin/	External

in.ripngd

in.ripngd	UNIX Shell:	All shells (bash, tcsh, sh, ksh, csh, zsh)
Function	Manages network routing tables for the IPv6 Routing Information Protocol.	
Syntax	in.ripngd [options...] *{ file }*	

-q	Doesn't supply routing information.
-s	Forces the daemon to supply routing information.
-p *number*	Specifies the UDP port number to send and receive routing packets.
-P	Disables "Poison Reverse."
-t	Prints all sent and received packets to STDOUT.
-v	Prints all routing updates with time information.
file	Specifies the log file.

File Name:	Directory:	Type:
in.ripngd	/usr/lib/inet/	External

install_conduit

install_conduit	UNIX Shell:	Bourne shell (sh)
Function	A script that allows users to install Java-based pipes for synchronization with a Palm Pilot.	
Syntax	install_conduit [-delete] -creator *creatorID* -remote *rdbname* [options...] *file*	

-delete	Erases a specific pipe.
-creator *creatorID*	Specifies the creator ID of the database to synchronize with.
-remote *rdbname*	Specifies the name of the database to synchronize with.
-classname *classname*	Specifies the Java class name of the pipe.
-registry *action*	Specifies in which registry to install pipe. Action can be either system or personal.
system	Installs conduit in the system registry.
personal	Installs conduit in the personal registry of the user.
-classpath *classpath*	Sets the class path for the jar file.
-directory *datadir*	Specifies the directory wherein to put the pipe's data.
-file0 *condatafile*	Specifies the data file that the pipe is going to synchronize.
-name *conduit*	Sets pipe name to show in the PDASync interface.
-priority *prioritynr*	Sets priority level for the pipe.
file	Specifies the jar file containing the pipe to install (default is conduit.jar).

File Name:	Directory:	Type:
install_conduit	/usr/dt/bin/	Script

integer

integer	UNIX Shell:	Z shell (zsh)
Function	Shows or sets attribute for integer variables.	
Syntax	integer [options...] *{ name [=value] }*	

-g	Doesn't restrict any resulting parameters to local scope.
-l	Converts uppercase to lowercase.
-r	Sets the variable to read-only.
-t	Tags the variable.
-u	Converts lowercase to uppercase.
-x	Exports the variables to the environment.
name	Specifies the variable.
=value	Specifies the value to assign to the variable.

ipsecconf

ipsecconf		**UNIX Shell:**	All shells (bash, tcsh, sh, ksh, csh, zsh)
Function	Manages IP security policies.		
Syntax	ipsecconf [options...]		

	The options -a, -d, -f, and -l can't be used at the same time.
-a *file*	Adds an IP security policy to the system using an IP security configuration file.
-d *policy*	Erases the specified policy.
-f	Flushes all policies.
-l	Shows all entries in the policy.
-n	Shows ports, addresses, and protocols. Can only be used with the -l option.
-q	Doesn't show error messages. Can only be used with the -a option.
File Name: `ipsecconf`	**Directory:** /usr/sbin/ **Type:** External

ipseckey

ipseckey		**UNIX Shell:**	All shells (bash, tcsh, sh, ksh, csh, zsh)
Function	Manages the security association database for the network security services `ipsecah` and `ipsecesp` manually.		
Syntax	ipseckey [options...] ipseckey [options...] *ACTION { SAtype } { extension }*		

-n	Prevents printing of symbolic host and network names in reports.
-v	Verbose mode. Shows more information.
-p	Prevents printing of all material regarding keys.
-f *file*	Reads actions from a file.
-s *file*	Directs output to a file or to STDOUT if '-' is specified.
ACTION	**The following are actions to use; some use SA and extensions:**
add	Adds an SA. Only in interactive mode.
update	Updates the SA lifetime and key materials. Only in interactive mode.
delete	Erases a specific SA entry from an SADB. Requires an SA type and an extension.
get	Shows a specific SA from a specified SADB. Requires an SA type and an extension.
flush	Removes all SAs for all or a specified SA type.
monitor	Reports continuously PF_KEY messages using the SADB_X_PROMISC message.
pmonitor	Reports continuously PF_KEY messages without using the SADB_X_PROMISC message.
dump	Shows all SA for all or a specified SA type.
save	Takes a snapshot of a specified SA type.
help	Shows help information.
	These are valid SA types:
all	Specifies all types, only used with the actions dump and flush.
ah	Specifies the IPsec authentication header.
esp	Specifies the IPsec encapsulating security payload.
	These are the valid extensions:
spi *num*	Specifies an index for the security parameters.
replay *num*	Specifies the size num of the window for replay (default is zero).
state *state*	Specifies the SA state where state is a value (larval, mature, dying, dead, or a num).
authalg *authalg*	Specifies authentication algorithm used where authalg is a value, number, or a string.
	The strings used with authalg: `md5, hmac-md5, sha, sha-1, hmac-sha1, hmac-sha.`
encralg *encralg*	Specifies the algorithm for encryption. A numeric value or an algorithm name.
srcaddr *address*	Specifies the source address for the SA (default is unspecified).
dstaddr *address*	Specifies the destination address for the SA (default is unspecified).
proxyaddr *addr*	Specifies the proxy addr for an SA. A source addr of an inner protocol header.
authkey *string*	Specifies the key to authenticate this SA (is a hexadecimal string).
encrkey *string*	Specifies the key for encryption of this SA (is a hexadecimal string).
	These are the valid lifetime extensions:
softbytes *number*	Specifies what this SA can protect (is a number of bytes; default is zero).
hardbytes *number*	Same as soft; when expired, this is removed while softbytes gets state dying.
softaddtime *number*	Sets the time in seconds that this SA exists, after update.
hardaddtime *number*	Sets as soft; when expired, this is removed while softaddtime gets state dying.

continued

softusetime number	Sets the time in seconds that this SA exists, after it has been used for the first time.
hardusetime *number*	Same as soft; when expired, this is removed while softusetime gets state dying.
srcidtype *type, value*	Specifies the identity of the certificate for this SA.
dstidtype *type, value*	Specifies the identity of the destination certificate for this SA.
	These are the types used in srcidtype and dstidtype:
prefix	Specifies that the type is an address prefix.
mailbox	Specifies a user in the form user@domain.
domain	Specifies that type is a fully qualified domain name.
user_fqdn	Specifies a user in the form user@fqdn.
	The value in srcidtype and dstidtype identifies the certificate.
File Name: `ipseckey`	**Directory:** /usr/sbin/ **Type:** External

jarsigner

UNIX Shell: Korn shell (ksh)

Function	Creates passwords and verifies the signatures of jar files.
Syntax	jarsigner [options...] *file alias* jarsigner -verify [options...] *file*

-keystore *url*	Is used to specify the key store location.
-storepass *password*	Specifies the password for key store reliability.
-storetype *type*	Is used to specify the type of key store that is used.
-keypass *password*	Specifies the password for the private key if it is different than the key store.
-sigfile *file*	Specifies the name of the .SF/.DSA file that is used.
-signedjar *file*	Specifies the name of the signed jar file.
-verify	Verifies the specified signed jar file.
-verbose	Verbose mode. Shows more information during signing and verifying.
-certs	Shows certificates in `verbose` and `verify` modes.
-internalsf	Includes the `.SF` file within the signature block.
-sectionsonly	Skips the hash computation of the manifest.
file	Specifies a jar file.
alias	Specifies an alias name.
File Name: `jarsigner`	**Directory:** /usr/bin/ **Type:** Script

kstat

UNIX Shell: Bourne shell (sh)

Function	Examines the current available kernel statistics.
Syntax	kstat [options...] *{ interval NR }*

-c *class*	Shows only kstats that match the specified class.
-i *instance*	Shows kstats that match the specified instance.
-l	Shows names that match kstat without displaying values.
-m *module*	Shows only kstats that match the specified module.
-n *name*	Shows only kstats that match the specified name.
-p	Shows the output in an easier-to-read format.
-q	Returns appropriate exit status for matches against given criteria.
-s *statistic*	Shows only kstats that match the specified statistic.
-T *action*	Shows a timestamp before each statistics block.
d	Shows in ctime format.
u	Shows alphanumeric representation returned by the time command.
mod:inst:name:stat	Specifies module, instance, name, or statistics. This is an alternative method.
interval	Specifies interval between reports in seconds.
NR	Specifies number of reports to print.
File Name: `kstat`	**Directory:** /usr/bin/ **Type:** Script

ldap_cachemgr

ldap_cachemgr	UNIX Shell: All shells (bash, tcsh, sh ,ksh, csh, zsh)
Function	Updates the configuration cache for the LDAP naming services.
Syntax	ldap_cachemgr [options...]

-g	Shows the current configuration and statistics.
-l *log-file*	Specifies an alternative log file.
-r *revalidate-interval*	Specifies the refresh interval in seconds.
File Name: `ldap_cachemgr`	**Directory:** /usr/lib/ldap/ **Type:** External

ldap_gen_profile

ldap_gen_profile	UNIX Shell: All shells (bash, tcsh, sh ,ksh, csh, zsh)
Function	Creates an LDIF file to be loaded into an LDAP server. This file can later be downloaded by an LDAP client.
Syntax	ldap_gen_profile -P *profilename* [options...] *host*

-a *method*	Specifies authentication method. Multiple values can be entered with commas. **The following method may be used for -a:**
none	Disables authentication.
simple	Specifies the simple authentication mode. Use this with the -w option.
cram_md5	Specifies the cram_md5 authentication mode. Use this with the -w option.
-b *baseDN*	Specifies the search baseDN (for example, dc = eng, dc = sun, dc = com).
-B *alternateSearchDN*	Specifies alternative searches for baseDN and LDAP.
-d *domainname*	Specifies the domain name.
-D *BindDN*	Specifies the bind distinguished name. Examples for -D: cn = proxyagent, ou = profile, cd = eng, dc = sun, dc = com.
-e *clientTTL*	Specifies the TTL value for the client information.
-o *timeoutvalue*	Specifies LDAP operation timeout value (default is 3 minutes).
-p *serverpreference*	Specifies the server preference list.
-r *searchreferrals*	Finds referral option - either followref or ornoref.
-w *clientPassword*	Specifies the client password for the simple and cram_md5 authentication modes.
-P *profilename*	Specifies profile to download from server and autoconfigures all entries.
-O	Informs client to contact servers only on the preferred list.
host	Specifies the LDAP server IP address.
File Name: `ldap_gen_profile`	**Directory:** /usr/sbin/ **Type:** External

ldapclient

ldapclient	UNIX Shell: All shells (bash, tcsh, sh ,ksh, csh, zsh)
Function	Configures an LDAP client machine.
Syntax	ldapclient [options...] *{ host }*

-a *method*	Specifies the authentication method. Multiple methods can be specified, separated with commas. **These are the methods to use with -a:**
none	Disables authentication (is the default).
simple	Specifies the simple authentication mode. Requires the -w option.
cram_md5	Specifies the cram_md5 authentication mode. Requires the -w option.
-b *baseDN*	Specifies baseDN to search.
-B *alternatesearchDN*	Specifies an alternative baseDN to search.
-d *domainname*	Specifies the default domain for the machine.
-D *BindDN*	Specifies the bind distinguished name.
-e *clientTTL*	Specifies Time To Live for client information.
-i	Enables client (initialize).
-l	Shows cache of an LDAP client.
-m	Sets or resets the parameters in the configuration file.
-o *timeoutvalue*	Specifies timeout value for LDAP operations.
-O	Contacts servers only in the preferred list.
-p *serverpreference*	Specifies the preference list for servers.

-P *profilename*	Downloads the client profile from the server.
-r *followreferals*	Specifies followref or noref as search referral option (default is followref).
-u	Disables LDAP client (uninitialize).
-v	Verbose mode. Shows more information.
-w *clientpassword*	Specifies client password for the `simple or cram_md5` authentication modes.
host	Specifies LDAP server IP address and port number separated by a colon (:).
File Name: `ldapclient`	**Directory:** /usr/sbin/ **Type:** External

ldaplist

UNIX Shell: All shells (bash, tcsh, sh ,ksh, csh, zsh)

Function	Shows a list of naming information from an LDAP directory service file.
Syntax	ldaplist [options...] *{ database } { keys... }*

-h	Shows a list of the database mapping. Works only as a single option.
-d	Shows the list of attributes, not the entries, for the specified database.
-l	Shows a list of information on the specified objects in the `key` argument.
-v	Verbose mode. Shows more information.
database	Specifies the database to show information about.
keys...	Specifies the object. `my*` will list any strings that start with `my`.
File Name: `ldaplist`	**Directory:** /usr/bin/ **Type:** External

less

UNIX Shell: All shells (bash, tcsh, sh ,ksh, csh, zsh)

Function	A text pager for UNIX systems, used to displays ASCII files.
Syntax	less [options...] *filenames...*

+*command*	Specifies an internal command to perform when showing new files.
-?	Shows help information.
-a	Performs no search on lines shown on the screen — instead, searches on lines under.
-bn *buffers*	Sets the amount of buffers to use for each file (one buffer is 1K).
-B	Doesn't automatically assign buffers when needed. Uses amount specified with -bn.
-c	Shows full screen lines from the top down instead of appending from the bottom.
-C	Is used as -c, except that screen will be cleared before a new page is shown.
-d	Doesn't show error messages if the terminal can't do what it's supposed to.
-e	Quits the second time less reaches an EOF instead of just giving a warning.
-E	Quits directly when the EOF is reached.
-f	Opens all files — not only those that are regular.
-F	Shows the file, and if it's only one page, then quits.
-g	Specifies that only the last search string found will be highlighted.
-G	Doesn't highlight strings found by the search commands.
-h*lines*	Specifies the number of lines that can be shown by scrolling back.
-i	When matching patterns, don't be case-sensitive.
-I	When matching patterns, don't be case-sensitive even when patterns contain uppercase.
-j*line*	Marks a screen line as the line on the screen where the search begins.
-k*filename*	Specifies a filename to open as a lesskey file.
-m	Makes verbose prompts with percentages of the file instead of colons.
-M	Makes prompts look even more verbose than with -m.
-n	Doesn't use line numbers.
-N	Shows line numbers at the beginning of the lines.
-o*filename*	Specifies a file in which to put the input from STDIN when showing it on the screen.
-O*filename*	Does the same thing as -o, except that it will overwrite the specified file.
-p*pattern*	Shows the specified file from the first line containing the specified pattern.
-P*prompt*	Specifies another prompt to use instead of the default.
-q	Silent mode. Won't ring the bell when the EOF has been reached.
-Q	Silent mode. Never rings the bell.
-r	Shows control characters that could create screen problems.
-R	Does the same thing as -r, except that it tries to keep the correct screen appearance.

continued

-S	Chops lines longer than the screen width.
-s	Combines multiple blank lines into one blank line.
-t*tag*	Shows the file containing tag. For this to work, ctags must have been run.
-T*tagsfile*	Is used with the -t option. Specifies another tags file to use instead of the default.
-u	Shows backspaces and new line characters as usual characters.
-U	Handles tabs, backspaces, and newlines as control characters.
-w	When a full page movement has been done, highlights the first new line.
-W	When a full line movement has been done, highlights the first new line.
-x*NR*	Uses the NR to specify where to set the Tab stops (default is 8).
-X	Disables sending termcap initialization and deinitialization strings to the screen.
-y*NR*	Uses the NR to specify the maximum number of lines to scroll forward.
-[z]*NR*	Uses NR to specify default scrolling window lines (default is one full screen).
-"se	Specifies the start and end quote characters to use instead of using double quotes.
-~	Initiates lines after EOF to be shown as blank lines.
m*letter*	Marks position with specified lowercase letter.
'*letter*	A single quota makes it go to the position that is marked with lowercase letter.
--help	Shows help information.
--version	Shows version information.
--	Specifies the end of options. After this, everything is taken as filenames.
	Commands invoked from within less:
Space	Scroll down one full screen. You can also use Ctrl+V, Ctrl+F, or f.
{ NR } z	Same as Space. NR also sets the size of the screen.
Esc+Space	Same as Space, but scrolls down one full screen, even if you reach the EOF.
{ NR } Return	Scroll down one line or the number of lines. You can also use Ctrl+J, Ctrl+E, f, or j.
{ NR } d	Scroll down half a screen or the specified number of lines. You can also use Ctrl+D.
{ NR } Esc-v	Scrolls up one screen or the specified number of lines. You can also use Ctrl+B or b.
{ NR } w	Same as Esc+V. Number also sets the default size of the screen.
{ NR } y	Scrolls up the number of lines. You can also use Ctrl+Y, Ctrl+P, Ctrl+K, or k.
{ NR } u	Scrolls down half a screen or the specified number of lines. You can also use Ctrl+U.
{ NR } Esc+)	Scrolls right the number of characters (default is 8). You can also use right arrow.
{ NR } Esc+(	Scrolls left the number of characters (default is 8). You can also use left arrow.
r	Repaint the screen. You can also use Ctrl+R or Ctrl+L.
R	Same as r, but discards buffered input.
F	Scrolls forward, even if the EOF is reached.
{ NR } g	Goes to line number in the file (default is 1). You can also use < or Esc+<.
{ NR } G	Goes to line number in the file (default is the last line). You can also use > or Esc->.+>.
NR p	Specifies the number in percent where to start reading in the file. You can also use %.
	Number specifies which one to use, if there is more than one on the top line.
{ NR } {	If a { is shown in top line, go to the matching }.
{ NR } }	If a } is shown in top line, go to the matching }.
{ NR } [	If a [is shown in top line, go to the matching [.
{ NR }]	If a] is shown in top line, go to the matching].
{ NR } (	If a (is shown in top line, go to the matching (.
{ NR })	If a) is shown in top line, go to the matching).
Esc-Ctrl+F xy	Same as {. Handles x and y as opening and closing brackets.
Esc-Ctrl+B xy	Same as }. Handles x and y as opening and closing brackets.
/*pattern*	Searches the file for lines containing pattern.
/!*pattern*	Searches the file for lines that don't match the pattern.
/**pattern*	If pattern isn't found, continues to the next file in the command-line list.
/@*pattern*	Starts the search at the first file in the command-line list.
/ctlr+K*pattern*	Highlights found words on the screen, but keeps current cursor position.
/ctrl+R*pattern*	Makes a simple textual comparison.
?*pattern*	Searches the file backward for lines containing pattern.
?!*pattern*	Searches the file for lines that don't match the pattern.
?**pattern*	Searches backward in multiple files, searching in previous file if no match is found.
?@*pattern*	Starts the search at the last line of the last file in the command-line list.

continued

/ctlr+K?*pattern*	Highlights found words on the screen, but keeps current cursor position.
/ctrl+R?*pattern*	Makes a simple textual comparison.
n	Repeats previous search.
N	Repeats previous search, but in reverse direction.
Esc-n	Repeats previous search over files on the command list.
Esc-N	Repeats previous search, but in reverse direction over files on the command list.
Esc-u	Turn off search highlighting.
:e *filename*	Inspects a new file.
E *filename*	Same as :e.
:n*{ NR }*	Inspects the next file in the command-line list. Number specifies which file.
:p*{ NR }*	Inspects the previous file in the command-line list. Number specifies which file.
:x*{ NR }*	Inspects the first file in the command-line list. Number specifies which file.
:d	Erases the current file from the list of files.
=	Shows some information about the file.
V	Shows version information.
q	Quits less. You can also use Q, :q, :Q, or ZZ.
	The next three options may not work — it depends on your installation.
v	Starts an editor to edit the current file being shown.
! *Shellcmd*	Invokes a shell to run the specified Shellcmd.
s *file*	Specifies to save the input in a file. The input must be a pipe.
-+ option	Resets that option to its default.
-! option	Resets that option to opposite of its default.
_ option	Shows that option's current value.
File Name: less	**Directory:** /usr/bin/ **Type:** External

lesskey

UNIX Shell: All shells (bash, tcsh, sh, ksh, csh, zsh)

Function	Manages key bindings for less.
Syntax	lesskey [options...] *{ file }*

-V	Shows version information.
-o *output*	Is used to specify the output file.
-	Is used to read input from STDIN instead of from a file.
file	Specifies an input file with key binding information.
File Name: lesskey	**Directory:** /usr/bin/ **Type:** External

local

UNIX Shell: Bash shell (bash), Z shell (zsh)

Function	Creates a local variable within a function and sets the variable's attribute.
Syntax	local [options...] *{ name[=value] }*

-a	Sets the name to be an array variable.
-r	Makes the name read-only. (Use + instead of - to turn off the attribute for all options except –a.)
name[=value]	Is used to assign value to name. If value isn't given, it shows the current value.
bash:	
-p	Shows name and values of each variable and function.
-F	Shows function name and attributes, not the function definitions. Implies -f.
-f	Sets the name to be a function.
-i	Handles the variable as an integer.
-x	Exports the name to the environment.
zsh	
-A	Specifies that the name is an associative array.
-L*{ n }*	Left-justifies value by removing leading space.
-R*{ n }*	Right-justifies value by adding space in the beginning.
-U	Keeps only the first occurrence of duplicated values in an array.
-Z*{ n }*	Right-justifies value by adding 0 in the beginning, if first character is a digit.

continued

-i{ *n* }	Is used for integer. If n isn't zero, it's the base for the value.
-l	Converts uppercase to lowercase.
-t	Tags the variable.
-u	Converts lowercase to uppercase.

lofiadm

UNIX Shell: All shells (bash, tcsh, sh ,ksh, csh, zsh)

Function	Administers the loopback file driver and associates a file to a block device.
Syntax	lofiadm *{ option } { file } { device }*

-a	Sets an association between the specified file and, optionally, the device.
-d	Removes the association connected to the specified file or device.
file	Shows the block device associated with the specified file.
device	Shows the filename associated with the specified block device.

File Name: `lofiadm` **Directory:** /usr/sbin/ **Type:** External

log

UNIX Shell: TC shell (tcsh), Z shell (zsh)

Function	Lists all users that are logged in and affected by the watch parameter.
Syntax	log

logresolve

UNIX Shell: All shells (bash, tcsh, sh ,ksh, csh, zsh)

Function	Resolves IP addresses in Apache's access log files. This is to reduce the impact for the name server.
Syntax	logresolve [options...] *accesslog newaccesslog*

-s *file*	Specifies the filename for the log file.
-c	Verifies IP addresses to names with DNS.
accesslog	Specifies the Apache access log to run lookups on.
newaccesslog	Specifies an output file.

File Name: `logresolve` **Directory:** /usr/sbin/ **Type:** External

ls-F

UNIX Shell: TC shell (tcsh)

Function	Lists files like `ls -F`. It's much faster than ls.
Syntax	ls-F [options...] *files...*

options...	Sends these options to the `ls` command.
files...	Specifies files to show. Wildcards can be used.

mdb

UNIX Shell: All shells (bash,tcsh,sh,ksh,csh,zsh)

Function	A low-level modular debugger used to operate crash dumps, processes, core dumps, and so forth.
Syntax	mdb [options...] *{ ACTION }*

-A	Disables automatic module loading.
-F	Forces takeover of specified user process.
-I *path*	Specifies location path for macro files.
-L *path*	Sets the location path for debugger modules.
%i	Expands the ISA name `sparc`, `i386`, or `sparcv9`.
%o	Expands the older value of the path that is modified.
%p	Expands to the string of the current platform.
%r	Expands to the root directory pathname.
%t	Expands to the current target name.
-k	Forces debug in kernel mode. Assumes that object and core files are OS crash dump files.
-m	Skips processing the kernel module list and doesn't provide a per-module symbol table.
-M	Loads all of the kernel module symbols during startup.
-o *option*	Specifies a debugger option to use. A `+o` will disable the specified option.
adb	Enables a restrictive `adb` compatibility.

continued

follow_child	Follows any child process if a `fork` system call appears.
ignoreeof	Skips exit if an EOF `^D` sequence is made from the screen.
pager	Enables the output pager.
repeatlast	Repeats the previous command if a new line is entered as the complete command.
-p *pID*	Specifies a process ID to attach to and stops.
-P *prompt*	Specifies command prompt (default is >).
-R *directory*	Specifies the root directory path for pathname expansion.
-s *distance*	Specifies the distance for symbol matching used for address/symbol name conversions. (The default distance is 0, which starts smart-match mode.)
-S	Does not read the users `~/.mdbrc` macro file.
-u	Forces debug mode. Assumes that object and core files are not OS crash dump files.
-V *Dver*	Specifies the disassembler version to use.
-w	Enables the ability to write to object and core files.
-y	Enables screen initialization sequence use.
ACTION	**When specifying a load source, you must select one of these three actions:**
object	Specifies the object to load. This may be a base name, executable, or shared library.
core	Specifies a process core file for the object.
core	Specifies a process core file to inspect.
suffix	Specifies a numerical suffix for a pair of OS crash dump files.

File Name:	`mdb`	**Directory:**	/usr/bin/	**Type:**	External

mkisofs

UNIX Shell: All shells (bash, tcsh, sh ,ksh, csh, zsh)

Function	Creates an ISO9660 images file that is used to burn CDs.
Syntax	mkisofs [options...] -o *file directory*

-a	Creates a file system, which includes backup files that use ~ or #.
-abstract *file*	Specifies an abstract filename.
-A *ID*	Specifies text to be written into the application volume header, (max 128 characters).
-biblio *file*	Specifies the name of the bibliographic file.
-b *file*	Specifies path- and filename to a boot image. Must be 1.2, 1.44, or 2.88 MB in size.
-C *sector,sector*	Creates an additional image on a CD containing an image to create a multisession CD-ROM. (First value = First sector, last session. Second value=start sector, new session.)
-c *directory*	Specifies a boot directory to use when creating a bootable CD.
-copyright *file*	Specifies the name of a copyright file. This can also be done with `.mkisofsrc`.
-d	Removes trailing period from files that don't have a period. Use this with caution.
-D	Packs directories in the way that they are seen. Caution — violates ISO-9660, but works.
-f	Creates the file system and follows symbolic links.
-hide *glob*	Hides files that contain a glob pattern in its name on an ISO-9660 directory.
-hide-joliet *glob*	Hides files that contain a glob pattern in its name on a Joliet directory.
-l	Enables the use of 32-character filenames.
-J	Creates ISO-9660 filenames and Joliet directory records.
-L	Permits the use of filenames that begin with a period.
-log-file *file*	Shows all warnings and error messages to the specified file instead of to STDERR.
-m *glob*	Specifies a glob to ignore when writing to a CD.
-M *path*	Specifies a path to an ISO-9660 image that you want to merge. Use with -C only.
-N	Does not put ISO-9660 version numbers in the filenames.
-no-split-symlink-components	Begins a new continuation area instead of splitting the symlink components.
-no-split-symlink-fields	Begins a new continuation area instead of splitting the symlink fields.
-o *file*	Specifies the name of a file to write the file system image to.
-P *ID*	Specifies publisher info text to be written into volume header (max 128 characters).
-p *ID*	Specifies prepared info text to be written into the volume header (max 128 characters).
-print-size	Shows the estimated size of the file system.
-R	Creates SUSP and RR records to explain the created files.
-r	Similar to -R, but with more user-friendly values to show nodes and ownership.
-sysid *ID*	Specifies the system ID.

continued

-T	Creates a TRANS.TBL file in each directory on the CD-ROM.
-v	Verbose mode. Shows more information.
-V *ID*	Specifies the volume ID to be written into the master block.
-volset *ID*	Specifies the volume set ID.
-volset-size *size*	Specifies the size of the volume set.
-volset-seqno *number*	Specifies sequence number on the volume set.
-x *path*	Does not write files from the specified path to CD-ROM.
-z	Creates special SUSP records for transparently compressed files.
directory	Specifies the directory to create an ISO-9660 file system of.

File Name:	`mkisofs`	**Directory:**	/usr/bin/	**Type:**	External

mofcomp

UNIX Shell: Bourne shell (sh)

Function	Compiles MOF files to CIM classes. These files can also be converted to Java.
Syntax	mofcomp [options...] *file*

-c *cimomhostname*	Specifies the host system that runs the SIM Object Manager.
-h	Shows the arguments to the mofcomp utility.
-p *password*	Specifies a password to connect to the CIM Object Manager.
-sc	Compiles with the specified class.
-si	Compiles with the specified instance.
-sq	Compiles with the specified qualifier type.
-u *username*	Specifies user name to connect to the CIM Object Manager.
-v	Verbose mode. Shows more information.
-version	Shows version information.
file	Specifies the name and path of file to compile.

File Name:	`mofcomp`	**Directory:**	/usr/sadm/bin/	**Type:**	Script

msgid

UNIX Shell: All shells (bash, tcsh, sh ,ksh, csh, zsh)

Function	Creates a unique message identifier.
Syntax	msgid

File Name:	`msgid`	**Directory:**	/usr/sbin/	**Type:**	External

ncab2clf

UNIX Shell: All shells (bash, tcsh, sh ,ksh, csh, zsh)

Function	Converts the binary log files from the Solaris Network Cache and Accelerator to Common Log File format.
Syntax	ncab2clf [options...]

-b	Specifies the block size in the binary file (default is 64KB).
-D	Disables the direct I/O.
-i *inputfile*	Specifies the file to convert. (Default is STDIN.)
-o *outputfile*	Specifies the file to save the result in. (Default is STDOUT.)
-h	Shows help information.
-v	Verbose mode. Shows more information.

File Name:	`ncab2clf`	**Directory:**	/usr/bin/	**Type:**	External

nfslogd

UNIX Shell: All shells (bash, tcsh, sh ,ksh, csh, zsh)

Function	Creates the activity log with information from the RPC operations that were processed by the NFS server.
Syntax	nfslogd

File Name:	`nfslogd`	**Directory:**	/usr/lib/nfs/	**Type:**	External

nisopaccess

UNIX Shell:	All shells (bash, tcsh, sh ,ksh, csh, zsh)
Function	Administration tool to configure the access for NIS+ operations.
Syntax	nisopaccess [options...] *directory { operation } { rights }*

-l	Shows the access granted for a specified operation or for all operations.
-r	Deletes the access control for a specified operation on a specified directory.
-v	Verbose mode. Shows more information.
	The following arguments can be used where they are appropriate:
directory	Specifies an NIS+ directory.
operation	Specifies the operation to set the access for.
rights	Sets the permissions for the specified operation - read, modify, or delete.
	The following are the operations that the command can alter:
NIS_CHECKPOINT	Is used in the command `nisping -c`.
NIS_CPTIME	Is used in the command `nisping rpc.nisd`.
NIS_MKDIR	Is used in the command `nismkdir`.
NIS_PING	Is used in the command `nisping rpc.nisd`.
NIS_RMDIR	Is used in the command `nisrmdir`.
NIS_SERVSTATE	Is used in the command `nisbackup nisrestore`.
NIS_STATUS	Is used in the command `nisstat rpc.nispasswdd`.

File Name:	`nisopaccess`	**Directory:**	/usr/lib/nis/	**Type:**	External

noglob

UNIX Shell:	Z shell (zsh)
Function	Turns off file globing for the command. No filename will be expanded.
Syntax	noglob *command*

command	Specifies the command with options.

ocfserv

UNIX Shell:	All shells (bash, tcsh, sh ,ksh, csh, zsh)
Function	A central communication point for smartcards that are connected to the host.
Syntax	ocfserv *ACTION*

start	Starts the daemon.
stop	Stops the daemon.

File Name:	`ocfserv`	**Directory:**	/usr/sbin/	**Type:**	External

perlbug

UNIX Shell:	Bash shell (bash)
Function	Creates bug reports for Perl.
Syntax	perlbug [options...]

-v	Shows verbose information.
-a *address*	Specifies the address to which to send the bug report.
-s *subject*	Specifies a subject for the bug report.
-b *body*	Specifies a body for the bug report.
-f *infile*	Specifies a file with the body report already written.
-F *outfile*	Specifies an output file instead of sending the bug report by e-mail.
-r *returnaddress*	Specifies the return address.
-e *editor*	Specifies the editor that you want to use.
-c *adminaddress*	Specifies an address to which to send a copy of the bug report.
-C	Doesn't send any copies of the bug report.
-S	Sends the bug report without waiting for confirmation.
-t	Runs the command in test mode.
-d	Shows your configuration data.
-h	Shows help information.

continued

	The following options can't be combined:
-ok	Reports successful builds on the system.
-okay	Reports successful builds for older systems.
-nok	Reports unsuccessful builds on the system.
-nokay	Reports unsuccessful builds for older systems.
File Name: `perlbug`	**Directory:** /usr/perl5/5.00503/bin/ **Type:** Script

perldoc

UNIX Shell: Bash shell (bash)

Function	Finds and shows perl documentation from inside installations trees or scripts.
Syntax	perldoc [options...] *item*

-v	Shows verbose information.
-t	Shows documents in plain text.
-u	Finds the documents, but doesn't show them.
-m	Shows the whole module.
-l	Shows the filename of the module.
-F	Takes all arguments as filenames, not directories.
-X	Uses an index if available.
-f *function*	Uses a Perl function to pick out function-specific information.
-q *expr*	Specifies a regular expression to search the perlfaq for matching entries.
	The following items can be searched for:
page	Specifies a page to search for.
module	Specifies a module to search for.
program	Specifies a program to search for.
File Name: `perldoc`	**Directory:** /usr/perl5/5.00503/bin/ **Type:** Script

pfexec, pfsh, pfcsh, pfksh

UNIX Shell: Bash shell (bash)

Function	Runs a command with a specific profile like user ID, group ID, and so forth.
Syntax	pfexec *command*

command	Specifies the command to run.
pfsh	The profiling Bourne shell.
pfcsh	The profiling C-shell.
pfksh	The profiling Korn shell.
File Name: `pfexec`	**Directory:** /usr/bin/ **Type:** Internal

pl2pm

UNIX Shell: Bash shell (bash)

Function	Converts perl4 files to perl5 modules.
Syntax	pl2pm *files...*

files...	Specifies the files that you want to convert.
File Name: `pl2pm`	**Directory:** /usr/perl5/5.00503/bin/ **Type:** Script

praliases

UNIX Shell: All shells (bash, tcsh, sh ,ksh, csh, zsh)

Function	Shows system mail aliases. If no key is specified, all keys and their values will be shown.
Syntax	praliases [options...] *{ key }*

-c *configfile*	Specifies a sendmail configuration file.
-f *aliasfile*	Reads specified aliasfile instead of the default sendmail system alias file.
key	Finds a specific alias key.
File Name: `praliases`	**Directory:** /usr/bin/ **Type:** External

printmgr

printmgr	UNIX Shell:	Bourne shell (sh)
Function	Manages local and remote printer access in a network using X-window.	
Syntax	printmgr	

	When using the print manager, the following tasks are available:
Select a Name Service	Is used to select a name service for recovering or altering printer information.
Add Access to a Printer	Adds printer access on a printer client.
Add an Attached Printer	Installs a local printer and makes it available for printing.
Add a Network Printer	Installs a remote printer and makes it available for printing.
Modify Printer Properties	Alters printer attributes.
Delete a Printer	Deletes printer access from a client or printer from the server or the name service.

File Name:	`printmgr`	Directory:	/usr/sadm/admin/bin/	Type:	Script

profiles

profiles	UNIX Shell:	All shells (bash, tcsh, sh ,ksh, csh, zsh)
Function	Shows execution profiles for the user specified with process attributes used when started using a privileged command interpreter such as: pfcsh, pfksh, and pfexec.	
Syntax	profiles [-l] { *users...* }	

-l	Shows commands in each profile along with the attributes such as GID, UID, and so forth.
users...	Specifies the user whose profile you want to show.

File Name:	`profiles`	Directory:	/usr/bin/	Type:	External

prstat

prstat	UNIX Shell:	All shells (bash, tcsh, sh ,ksh, csh, zsh)
Function	Shows statistics about active processes according to selected sort order and output mode.	
Syntax	prstat [options...] { *number count* }	

-a	Shows information about processes and users.
-c	Appends reports to previous report instead of overwriting.
-C *list*	Specifies a list that contains processor sets that bind processes or LWPs.
-L	Shows statistics for each LWP.
-m	Shows statistics about microstate process accounting.
-n *lines*	Specifies the number of process or LWPs lines to report.
,lines	Specifies the number of user stats to report if -a or -t are used.
-p *PID*	Shows processes whose process IDs are found in the specified list.
-P *list*	Shows the most recently used process or LWPs on a CPU found in the specified list.
-R	Enables real-time scheduling.
-s *key*	**Sorts by the specified keyword. You must select one of the following keys:**
cpu	Sorts by process CPU usage (default).
time	Sorts by process execution time.
size	Sorts by size of process image.
rss	Sorts by resident set size.
pri	Sorts by process priority.
-S *key*	Sorts by keywords in ascending order. Uses the same keywords as `-s`.
-t	Shows total usage for each user.
-u *list*	Shows processes whose effective user ID is found in the specified list.
-U *list*	Shows processes whose real user ID is found in the specified list.
-v	Verbose mode. Shows more information.
interval	Specifies the sample rate interval in seconds.
count	Specifies how many times the statistics will be repeated.

File Name:	`prstat`	Directory:	/usr/bin/	Type:	External

pstruct, c2ph

UNIX Shell: Bourne shell (sh)

Function	Translates C to Perl code. It takes .c, .h, or .s files and shows the C program structure.
Syntax	pstruct [options...] [variable=*value*] *{ files... }*

-w	Wide format, equals the following: type_width = 45, member_width = 35, offset = 8.
-x	Hexadecimal format, equals: offset_fmt = x, offset_width = 08, size_fmt = x, size_width = 04.
-n	Does not generate Perl code. This is the default when started as pstruct.
-p	Generates Perl code. This is the default when started as c2ph.
-v	Same as -p, except that it uses C declarations for comments.
-i	Does not recalculate sizes for inherent datatypes.
-a	Shows information about inherent datatypes.
-t	Traces execution.
-d	Verbose mode. Shows more debug information.
-slist	Specifies a list of structures in a comma-separated list.
	These are the variables with their default values:
CC=cc	Specifies the compiler to call.
CFLAGS=-g -S	Specifies how to generate *.s files with stabs.
DEFINES=	Defines extra cflags or cpp defines.
type_width=20	Specifies the width of the type field (column 1).
member_width=20	Specifies the width of the member field (column 2).
offset_width=6	Specifies the width of the offset field (column 3).
size_width=5	Specifies the width of the size field (column 4).
offset_fmt=d	Specifies the sprintf format type for offset.
size_fmt=d	Specifies the sprintf format type for size.
indent=2	Specifies how far to indent each nesting level.
files...	Specifies the files to use.

File Name:	pstruct	**Directory:**	/usr/perl5/5.00503/bin/	**Type:**	Script

pushln

UNIX Shell: Z shell (zsh)

Function	Pushes a string to the editor buffer stack.
Syntax	pushln *{ strings... }*

strings...	Specifies strings to push to the editor buffer stack.

r

UNIX Shell: Z shell (zsh)

Function	Reruns the last command.
Syntax	r

roleadd

UNIX Shell: All shells (bash, tcsh, sh ,ksh, csh, zsh)

Function	Manages new role accounts.
Syntax	roleadd [options...] *role* roleadd -D [options...]

-A *authorization*	Specifies authorizations in a comma-separated list for the new role account.
-c *comment*	Specifies a description for the new role account.
-d *dir*	Specifies home directory for the new role account.
-e *expire*	Specifies expiration date for the new role account.
-f *inactive*	Specifies the maximum inactive days before the account is locked out.
-g *group*	Specifies primary group membership for the new role account.
-G *groups...*	Specifies secondary group memberships for the new role account.
-k *skeleton*	Specifies a directory that contains templates for the new role account.
-m	Creates a new home directory for the account if it doesn't exist.
-o	Specifies the UID can be duplicated.
-s *shell*	Specifies a login shell for the new role account.

continued

-u *uid*	Specifies the UID for the new role account.				
-b *rootdir*	Specifies a new root directory for the command to use.				
-P *profile*	Specifies a profile for the new role account.				
	The -D option can only be used with the -b, -e, -f, -g, -A, and -P options.				
-D	Shows loginshell, rootdir, expiredate, skeleton directory, groupID, and inactivetime.				
role	Specifies the role that you want to add to the system.				
File Name:	roleadd	**Directory:**	/usr/sbin/	**Type:**	External

roledel

UNIX Shell: All shells (bash, tcsh, sh ,ksh, csh, zsh)

Function	Removes a role account and its login from the system.
Syntax	roledel [-r] *role*

-r	Removes the role's home directory.				
role	Specifies which role to remove.				
File Name:	roledel	**Directory:**	/usr/sbin/	**Type:**	External

rolemod

UNIX Shell: All shells (bash, tcsh, sh ,ksh, csh, zsh)

Function	Modifies the information about a role login on the system.
Syntax	rolemod [options...] *role*

-A *authorization*	Specifies one or more authorizations by use of a comma-separated list.				
-c *comment*	Specifies a description text string as comment.				
-d *dir*	Specifies a home directory for the specified role.				
-m	Moves the home directory to the location specified by -d.				
-e *expire*	Specifies an expiration date for a specified role.				
-f *inactive*	Specifies maximum days between use of a loginID before it becomes invalid.				
-g *ID*	Specifies the group ID for the specified role.				
-G *IDs...*	Specifies one or more group IDs for the role by use of a comma-separated list.				
-l *name*	Specifies a new login name for the specified role.				
-P *profile*	Specifies one or more execution profiles by use of a comma-separated list.				
-s *shell*	Specifies new login shell for the specified role.				
-u *ID*	Specifies a new UID for the specified role.				
-o	Allows the UID in -u to be duplicated.				
role	Specifies the role to modify.				
File Name:	rolemod	**Directory:**	/usr/sbin/	**Type:**	External

roles

UNIX Shell: All shells (bash, tcsh, sh ,ksh, csh, zsh)

Function	Shows the roles that are granted to specified user.
Syntax	roles *{ users... }*

users...	Specifies the user or users.				
File Name:	roles	**Directory:**	/usr/sbin/	**Type:**	External

rotatelogs

UNIX Shell: All shells (bash, tcsh, sh, ksh, csh, zsh)

Function	Starts a new log file and save the old.
Syntax	rotatelogs *logfile rotationtime*

logfile	Specifies the log file that you want to rotate.				
rotationtime	Specifies the rotation time in seconds for the log file.				
File Name:	rotaelogs	**Directory:**	/usr/apachel/bin	**Type:**	External

rpm2cpio

UNIX Shell: Bourne shell (sh)

Function	Converts a Red Hat Package (RPM) file to a cpio archive on STDOUT.
Syntax	rpm2cpio *{ file }*

file	Specifies the .rpm file to convert. If none is given, STDIN is used.

File Name: `rpm2cpio` **Directory:** /usr/bin/ **Type:** Script

rstart

UNIX Shell: Bourne shell (sh)

Function	A simple example of the remote start client (Remote Execution Protocol).
Syntax	rstart [options...] *host command arguments...*

-c *context*	Specifies which environment to use. The default context is X-window.
-g	Allows common commands to be started as generic commands.
-l *user*	Starts the command as the specified user. This option is passed to `rsh`.
-v	Verbose mode. Gives more information without disconnecting the program.
host	Specifies the hostname or IP address.
command	Specifies the command that is used.
arguments...	Specifies the valid arguments that are available for the command.

File Name: `rstart` **Directory:** /usr/openwin/bin/ **Type:** Script

rstartd

UNIX Shell: Bourne shell (sh)

Function	A script that helps the use of working with a remote shell.
Syntax	rstartd

File Name: `rstartd` **Directory:** /usr/bin/ **Type:** Script

s2p

UNIX Shell: Bourne shell (sh)

Function	Takes a sed script specified on the command line and produces a comparable Perl script on the STDOUT.
Syntax	s2p [options...] *{ file }*

-D*number*	Specifies the number of debug flags.
-n	Specifies the sed script was always started with a sed -n.
-p	Specifies the sed script was always started with a sed -p.
file	The sed script file to convert. (Default is to read from STDIN.)

File Name: `s2p` **Directory:** /usr/perl5/5.00503/bin **Type:** Script

sched

UNIX Shell: TC shell (tcsh)

Function	Schedules commands to be executed at a later time from the shell. Note that it is the shell that runs the commands.
Syntax	sched [option] sched *time command*

-n	Removes event n.
time	Specifies the time to run command. Can be 24-hour or 12-hour format.
command	Specifies the command to run.

sdtpdasync

UNIX Shell: Korn shell (ksh)

Function	Starts the utility PDASync, which is a Java-based application that synchronizes handheld Palm devices with CDE.
Syntax	sdtpdasync [-debug *NR*]

-debug *NR*	Specifies a debug level to use. Valid level is 0-5, where 0 gives most information.

File Name: `sdtpdasync` **Directory:** /usr/dt/bin/ **Type:** Script

sdtrlogin

UNIX Shell:	Korn shell (ksh)
Function	Parses a URL string and connects to a computer.
Syntax	sdtrlogin telnet://{ *username*[:*password*]@]{ *hostname*[:*port*]] sdtrlogin rlogin://{ *username*[:*password*]@]{ *hostname*[:*port*]]

username	The username to log in with.
password	The password to log in with.
hostname	The hostname to connect to.
port	The port to connect to.
File Name: `sdtrlogin`	**Directory:** /usr/dt/bin/ **Type:** Script

setopt

UNIX Shell:	Z shell (zsh)
Function	Sets the shell's options. Please see `zsh` for all options.
Syntax	setopt [option] { *argument* }

option	Please see `zsh` for options.
argument	The argument to use for any option.

settc

UNIX Shell:	TC shell (tcsh)
Function	Makes the shell believe that the terminal capability has the specified value.
Syntax	settc *cap value*

cap	Specifies the terminal capability to set (defined in `termcap`).
value	Specifies the value to use.

setty

UNIX Shell:	TC shell (tcsh)
Function	Sets which tty modes the shell allows to change.
Syntax	setty [options...]

	The options -d, -q, and -x can't be combined.
-d	Lets setty act on the edit set of tty modes.
-q	Lets setty act on the quote set of tty modes.
-x	Lets setty act on the execute set of tty modes (default).
-a	Shows all tty modes for the chosen set.
+*mode*	Fixes the mode on.
-*mode*	Fixes the mode off.
mode	Removes control for mode in the current set.

shopt

UNIX Shell:	Bash shell (bash)
Function	Changes optional shell variables controlling the behavior of the shell.
Syntax	shopt [options...] *optnames...*

-p	Shows current status of all options.
-s	Enables the option.
-u	Disables the option.
-q	Doesn't show normal output. Used to check the status of an option.
-o	Restricts the option names to those defined by the -o option for `set`.
optnames...	Specifies the option to `set`.
cdable_vars	Specifies that input to cd can be a variable name instead of a directory.
cdspell	Specifies that options to cd will be spell-checked and corrected.
chekhash	First checks in the internal hash table for the command.
checkwinsize	Checks the window size after each command and updates lines and columns.
cmdhist	Specifies that multiple lines command will be saved in one history entry.
dotglob	Specifies that filename beginning with period (.) will be taken in the filename expansion.

continued

execfail	Doesn't exit if an exec command fails in a noninteractive shell.
expand_aliases	Expands aliases.
extglob	Specifies that extended pattern matching should be used for filename expansion.
histappend	Appends the history list to the file specified by HISTFILE variable.
hsitreedit	Specifies that readline can be used to edit failed history substitution.
histverify	Uses readline to edit the resulting history substitution.
huponexit	Sends nohup to all processes on exit from the shell.
interactive_comments	Allows lines to be a comment (begin with #).
lithist	Saves multiline commands with new line instead of semicolon (;) in the history list.
mailwarn	Checks for mail.
no_empty_cmd_completion	Searches the PATH for possible command completion.
nocaseglob	Specifies to match filename in a case-insensitive fashion.
nullglob	Specifies that patterns that match no file should expand to a null string.
progcomp	Enables programmable completion facilities.
promptvars	Performs variable and parameter expansion on prompt strings.
restricted_shell	Specifies that the shell is restricted (read-only).
shift_verbose	Specifies that shift should report any error.
sourcepath	Specifies that the period (.) command should use the PATH to search for the command.
xpg_echo	Specifies the internal echo should expand backslash-escape sequences.

smartcard

UNIX Shell: Bash shell (bash)

Function	Configures and administers a smart card.
Syntax	smartcard -c *subcommand* [options...]

-c *subcommand*	Specifies the subcommand that you want to use.
	The following are the subcommands and their options:
admin [options...]	Lists and modifies the OCF properties.
[-a *application*]	Specifies the application name for the configuration parameter (default is OCF).
{ OFCproperty }	**Specifies the OCF property. The following are the four properties:**
defaultcard	Specifies the default card for an application.
defaultreader	Specifies the default reader for an application.
authmechanism	Validation mechanism.
validcards	Shows a list of valid cards for an application.
admin [options...]	Modifies the properties.
[-a *application*]	Specifies the application name for the configuration parameter (default is OCF).
[-x*action*]	Specifies what to do, add, delete, or modify.
{ property=value }	Specifies the property value.
admin options...	Administers the property specified with -t.
-t *service*	Updates the card service provider details.
-j *classname*	Specifies the class name.
-x*action*	Specifies what to do, add, delete, or modify.
admin [options...]	Administers the property specified with -t.
-t *terminal*	Updates the card reader provider details.
-j *classname*	Specifies the classname.
-d *device*	Specifies which device the reader is connected to.
-r *name*	Specifies the user-defined name of the reader where the card is inserted.
-n *name*	Specifies the name of the reader as required by the driver.
-x*action*	Specifies what to do, add, delete, or modify.
[-R]	Restarts the OCF server.
admin options...	Administers the property specified with -t.
-t debug	Changes the OFC trace level.
-j *classname*	Specifies the class name.
-l *level*	Sets the debug level, 0-9 (higher level gives more information).
-x*action*	Specifies what to do, add, delete, or modify.
admin options...	Administers the property specified with -t.
-t override	Overrides a system property with the same name.
-x*action*	Specifies what to do, add, delete, or modify.

continued

property=value	Specifies the property value.
admin options...	Administers the keys.
-I	Imports keys from the file specified with -i.
-k *keytype*	Specifies the key type.
-i *file*	Specifies the input filename.
admin options...	Administers the keys.
-E	Exports the keys to the file specified with -o.
-k *keytype*	Specifies the key type.
-o *file*	Specifies the output file.
load [options...]	Loads applets to the card.
-A *alpha ID*	Sets a unique alphanumeric string that identifies the applet (min 5, max 16 characters).
[-r *name*]	Specifies the user-defined name of the reader where the card is inserted.
-P *pin*	Specifies the pin that is used to validate to the card.
[-s *slot*]	Specifies the slot number that is used for initialization.
[-i *file*]	Specifies the input filename.
[-p *file*]	Specifies the filename where to find the properties.
[-v]	Verbose mode. Shows more information.
property=value	Specifies the property value.
load -u [options...]	Unloads applets from the card.
-u	Unloads the applet specified by the ID on the card (no ID = all applets).
-P *pin*	Specifies the pin that is used to validate to the card.
[-A *alphaID*]	Sets a unique alphanumeric string that identifies the applet (min 5, max 16 characters).
[-r *name*]	Specifies the user-defined name of reader where the card is inserted.
[-s *slot*]	Specifies the slot number that is used for initialization.
[-v]	Verbose mode. Shows more information.
bin2capx [options...]	Converts a card applet in Java to a capx format before downloading it to the card.
-T *cardname*	Specifies the name of the card.
[-i *file*]	Specifies the input filename.
-o *file*	Specifies the output filename.
[-p *file*]	Specifies the filename where to find the properties.
[-I*file*]	Imports from the specified capx file.
[-v]	Verbose mode. Shows more information.
property	Specifies the property value.
init [options...]	Specifies personal user information that is required on the card.
-A *alphaID*	Sets a unique alphanumeric string that identifies the applet (min 5, max 16 characters).
[-r *name*]	Specifies the user-defined name of the reader where the card is inserted.
[-s *slot*]	Specifies the slot number that is used for initialization.
[-L]	Shows a list of all configurable properties in an applet.
init [options...]	Specifies personal user information that is required on the card.
-A *alphaID*	Sets a unique alphanumeric string that identifies the applet (min 5, max 16 characters).
[-r *name*]	Specifies the user-defined name of the reader where the card is inserted.
-P *pin*	Specifies the pin that is used to validate to the card.
[-s *slot*]	Specifies the slot number that is used for initialization.
property	Specifies the property value.
enable	Enables the host for the card.
disable	Disables the host for the card.

File Name:	`smartcard`	**Directory:**	/usr/bin/	**Type:**	Script

smrsh

UNIX Shell: All shells (bash, tcsh, sh, ksh, csh, zsh)

Function	A restricted shell used together with sendmail. It only allows certain commands to be run.
Syntax	smrsh [-c *command*]

-c *command*	Specifies a valid command to run.

File Name:	`smrsh`	**Directory:**	/usr/lib/	**Type:**	External

tcsh

UNIX Shell:	TC shell (tcsh)
Function	The enhanced version of the UNIX C shell `csh`.
Syntax	tcsh [options...] *{ arguments... }*

	Use these for argument list processing:
-	Specifies a login shell if used as the first argument to the shell.
-b	Forces an option process stop so that a shell argument isn't treated as shell option.
-c	Commands will be read from the specified argument. All other arguments go to argv.
-d	Loads the directory stack from `~/.cshdirs`.
-e	Preserves the shell if a command abnormally terminates or gives a nonzero status.
-f	Ignores `~/.tcshrc` so that the shell starts faster.
-F	Uses the command `fork` instead of `vfork` to create processes.
-i	Forces the shell to go interactive and then prompts the user for its top-level input.
-l	Specifies a login shell if used as the only argument when starting the shell.
-m	Loads `~/.tcshrc` even if the user is different.
-q	Forces the shell to allow SIGQUIT, which makes it act like it is used by a debugger.
-s	Accepts command input from STDIN.
-t	Reads and starts from a single line of input. Uses \ to escape the new line.
-v	Activates the verbose shell variable so that any command input is echoed.
-x	Activates the echo shell variable so that any commands are echoed before starting.
-V	Activates the verbose shell variable before starting `~/.tcshrc`.
-X	Activates the echo shell variable before starting `~/.tcshrc`.
-n	Parses the commands from the shell, but will not start them.
-D*name=value*	Sets the specified environment variable to the new value (only domain/OS).
arguments...	Specifies arguments to command.

File Name:	`tcsh`	**Directory:**	/usr/bin/	**Type:**	External

telltc

UNIX Shell:	TC shell (tcsh)
Function	Shows the current values of all terminal capabilities.
Syntax	telltc

ttyctl

UNIX Shell:	Z shell (zsh)
Function	Freezes and unfreezes the tty. With no option, it shows the current status.
Syntax	ttyctl [option]

-f	Freezes the ttl.
-u	Unfreezes the ttl.

uncomplete

UNIX Shell:	TC shell (tcsh)
Function	Removes any patterns specified with the command complete.
Syntax	uncomplete *pattern*

pattern	Specifies a pattern to remove.

unfunction

UNIX Shell:	Z shell (zsh)
Function	Removes functions.
Syntax	unfunction *name*

name	Specifies the name of the function to remove.

unsetopt	UNIX Shell:	Z shell (zsh)
Function	Unsets any of the shell variables. Please see `zsh` for all options.	
Syntax	unsetopt [option] { *argument* }	

-m	Handles any arguments as a pattern.
option	Please see `zsh` for options.
argument	The argument to use for any option.

where	UNIX Shell:	TC shell (tcsh), Z shell (zsh)
Function	Shows where a command is located, including alias, internal, and in the path.	
Syntax	where [options...] *command*	

command	Specifies a command to show information about.
zsh:	
-w	Shows if a name is alias, built-in, command, function, hashed, reserved, or none.
-p	Searches the path even if the command is a function, a reserved word, or an alias.
-m	Uses the argument as a pattern and shows all matching commands.
-s	Shows also the symlink-free pathname if the pathname contains symlinks.

xfwp	UNIX Shell:	All shells (bash, tcsh, sh, ksh, csh, zsh)
Function	An X firewall proxy. Provides an application layer firewall for X traffic.	
Syntax	xfwp [options...]	

-cdt *time*	Sets closing time for inactive xfwp client connections in seconds (default is 604,800).
-clt *time*	Sets closing time for inactive xfwp client listen ports in seconds (default is 86,400).
-pdt *time*	Sets closing time for inactive proxy manager connections in seconds (default is 3,600).
-config *filename*	Specifies the filename for the configuration file.
-pmport *port*	Sets port address for proxy manager connections (default is 4444).
-verify	Shows what role in the configuration matches the service request.
-logfile *filename*	Specifies a name of the audit information log file.
-loglevel *n*	Sets the log level, where 0 is all and 1 is unsuccessful connections.
-max_pm_conns *num*	Specifies maximum number of connections to the proxy manager (default is 10).
-max_pm_conns *num*	Specifies maximum number of connections to the X server (default is 100).
	This is the command in the config file for the firewall with the following syntax:
Syntax	access source sourcemask [destination destinationmask] [operator service]
access	
permit	Specifies access. Access will be allowed.
deny	Specifies access. Access will be denied.
source	Specifies source. The IP address of the host where request originated.
sourcemask	Specifies source. The subnet mask of the host where request originated.
destination	Specifies destination. The target IP address for the request.
destinationmask	Specifies destination. The target subnet mask for the request.
	These two commands are used together and only when destination is specified:
operator	Specifies operator. Is always eq.
service	Specifies service. Is pm if proxy manager, fp if xfindproxy and cd if client data.
	This is the configuration command for the target X server. It uses this syntax:
Syntax	requirement policy [policystring...]
requirement	
require	Specifies requirement. At least one site policy must be configured.
disallow	Specifies requirement. No site policy should be configured.
policy	Specifies a keyword that is required.
policystring	Specifies any string that corresponds to a policy.

File Name:	Directory:	Type:
`xfwp`	/usr/openwin/bin	External

xntpdc	UNIX Shell:	All shells (bash, tcsh, sh, ksh, csh, zsh)
Function	Queries and controls the states on the Network Time Protocol daemon called `xntpd`.	
Syntax	xntpdc [options...] *hosts...*	

-i	Starts up in interactive command mode.
-l	Shows a list of the peers known to the servers.
-n	Shows all host addresses in dotted decimal format (0.0.0.0).
-p	Shows a list of the peers known to the server and a summary of their state.
-s	Like -p, but the list is shown in a different format.
-c *command*	Specifies an interactive format command.
? *{ command }*	Shows the interactive commands. Shows information about command specified.
delay *milliseconds*	Timestamps will be added in the time interval specified.
host *hostname*	Queries will be sent to the specified hostname or IP address.
hostnames *yes/no*	Hostnames will either be shown in hostnames (yes) or IP addresses (no).
keyid *keyid*	Specifies a key number that matches a key number on the server for authentication.
passwd	Asks for a password during authentication to complete configuration requests.
timeout *milliseconds*	Queries will timeout after the specified amount of milliseconds.
	The following options will query the states on the server:
clkbug	Shows debugging information from a clock driver. Does not work with all clock drivers.
clockinfo *hostname*	Shows information about the specified peer clock hostname.
dmpeers	Shows peers that the server is maintaining state.
iostats	Shows counters that are maintained in the input/output module.
kerninfo	Shows the kernel phase-lock loop operating parameters.
listpeers	Shows a short list of peers that the server is maintaining state.
loopinfo *{ action }*	Shows looped filter variables. Actions are either one-line or multiline outputs.
memstats	Shows counter statistics about memory allocation.
monlist	Shows the traffic counts that the monitor facility has.
peers	Shows peers with a summary that the server is maintaining state.
pstats *peer_addresses...*	Gathers per-peer statistics counters from the specified peers.
reslist	Shows the restriction list found on the server.
showpeer *peer_addresses*	Lists peer variables in a detailed way.
sysinfo	Shows local system state variables.
sysstats	Shows counter statistics from the protocol module.
timerstats	Shows counters that are maintained in the timer/event queue support code.
	The following options are the configuration requests available:
addpeer *peer_address* [options...]	Adds a peer association to the server.
keyid	Specifies an integer to encrypt and send with outgoing packets to the server.
version	Specifies what version to use — can be one of 1, 2, or 3 (default is 3).
prefer	Specifies the preferred peer when, for example, synchronizing clocks.
addserver *peer_address* [options...]	Does the same thing as addpeer command, but operating mode will be client.
broadcast *peer_address* [options...]	Does the same thing as addpeer command, but operating mode will be broadcast.
addtrap *address { port interface }*	Specifies a trap to add on the server.
authinfo	Shows you the authentication information such as known keys and counters.
clrtrap *address { port interface }*	Specifies a trap to delete on the server.
delrestrict *address mask { port }*	Specifies an entry to remove from the restrict list.
fudge *peer_address*	Changes fudge factors for a reference clock.
readkeys	Purges current authentication keys and installs new keys from the keys file.
restrict *address mask flag*	Restricts the server.
reset	Resets the counters in the modules on the server.
traps	Shows the traps on the server.
trustkey *keyID*	Specifies the trusted key configuration.

continued

untrustkey *keyID*	Specifies the untrusted key configuration.
unconfig *peer_address*	Removes configuration from the specified peers.
unrestrict *address mask flag*	Unrestricts an entry from the restrict list.
hosts...	Specifies the servers to manage.
File Name: xntpdc	**Directory:** /usr/sbin/ **Type:** External

Xprt

UNIX Shell: All shells (bash, tcsh, sh, ksh, csh, zsh)

Function	An X print server for Solaris
Syntax	Xprt [options...]

-ac	Gives access to any host and lets them change the access list.
-audit *level*	**The following options can be used to set audit level:**
0	Disables audit trail.
1	Reports only on rejected connections.
2	Reports only successful connections
4	Enables security messages.
-auth *file*	Specifies a file containing authorized users.
-bs	Doesn't use backing store support on any screen.
-help	Shows help information.
-I	Ignores any following command-line arguments.
-ld *kilobytes*	Specifies the maximum number of kilobytes of data space the server can use.
-lf *files...*	Specifies how many open files you can have on the server.
-ls *kilobytes*	Specifies the maximum number of kilobytes of stack space the server can use.
-sp *file*	Specifies a security policy file that Xprt will read to set up security policies.
-terminate	Tells Xprt not to continue going when a server reset is made.
File Name: Xprt	**Directory:** /usr/openwin/bin/ **Type:** External

zip

UNIX Shell: All shells (bash, tcsh, sh, ksh, csh, zsh)

Function	Compresses files.
Syntax	zip [options...] *{ zipfiles... }* [-ix *files...*]

-A	Adjusts the SFX entries that are added to the self-extracting archive file.
-b *path*	Specifies a directory in which to put temporary zip archives.
-c	Is used to add a comment to an archive file.
-d	Removes directories or files from an archive file.
-D	Doesn't create directory entries in the archive file.
-e	Specifies a password for the archive file.
-f	Is used to replace entries in the archive file.
-F	Tries to repair an archive file. It can't fix bad CRC.
-FF	Scans for signatures to identify break points between files when fixing the archive.
-g	Appends specified files to an existing archive.
-h	Shows help information.
-i *files...*	Includes only the specified files. Can't be used with -x.
-I	Doesn't scan image files.
-j	Doesn't save pathnames.
-J	Strips off any preamble data from the archive file.
-k	Converts pathnames and names to MSDOS format.
-l	Translates UNIX end-of-line characters to MS-DOS end-of-line characters.
-ll	Translates MS-DOS end-of-line characters to MS-DOS end-of-line characters.
-L	Shows license information.
-m	Moves the specified files into the archive file.
-n *suffixes*	Doesn't archive files that have the specified suffix.
-N	Uses Amiga file notes as comments for the archive file.
-o	Changes the last modified time to the oldest modification time.
-r	Includes everything, even subdirectories, in zip archive.
-R	Descends into the directory structure recursively starting at the current directory.

continued

-t *mmddyyyy*	Doesn't use files that are equal to or newer than the specified time.
-tt *mmddyyyy*	Doesn't use files that are equal to or older than the specified time.
-T	Tests the archive file.
-u	Updates the archive only if the new file has been modified more recently.
-v	Verbose mode. Shows more information.
-V	Is used to save VMS file attributes.
-w	Shows version information.
-x *files...*	Excludes files from the archive. Can't be used with -i.
-X	Doesn't save extended file attributes from OS/2 or UNIX.
-y	Saves symbolic links.
-z	Prompts to add a comment line.
-#	Sets compression level (1 = low and 9 = high).
-@	Uses STDIN to define input files.
-$	Includes the volume label in the archive file.
zipfiles...	Specifies the files that you want to compress.

File Name:	`zip`	**Directory:**	/usr/bin/	**Type:**	External

zipcloak

UNIX Shell: All shells (bash, tcsh, sh, ksh, csh, zsh)

Function	Encrypts or decrypts a compressed file.
Syntax	zipcloak [options...] *file*

-d	Erases directories or files from an archive file.
-L	Shows license information.
-b *path*	Specifies a directory inwhich to put temporary zip archives.
file	Specifies the zip file that you want to work with.

File Name:	`zipcloak`	**Directory:**	/usr/bin/	**Type:**	External

zipnote

UNIX Shell: All shells (bash, tcsh, sh, ksh, csh, zsh)

Function	Inserts notes and comments into zip files.
Syntax	zipnote [options...] *file*

-b path	Is used to specify the path to the file to work with.
-w	Is used to write comments from STDIN.
-L	Shows license information.
file	The zip file to work with.

File Name:	`zipnote`	**Directory:**	/usr/bin/	**Type:**	External

zipsplit

UNIX Shell: All shells (bash, tcsh, sh, ksh, csh, zsh)

Function	Splits one zip file into many zip files.
Syntax	zipsplit [options...] *file*

-t	Reports how many zip files the original zip file will be split into.
-i	Is used to make an index file and count its size against first zip file.
-n *size*	Is used to set the size of the new zip files.
-r *room*	Is used to leave some space on the first disk.
-b *path*	Is used to set the path where the zip files will end up.
-p	Is used to pause between output zip files.
-s	Is used to do a sequential split even if it takes more zip files.
-L	Shows software license.
file	The zip file to process.

File Name:	`zipsplit`	**Directory:**	/usr/bin/	**Type:**	External

zsh	UNIX Shell:	Z shell (zsh)
Function	An interactive login shell and shell script command processor.	
Syntax	zsh [options...]	

-c *string*	Reads the commands listed in the specified string.
-i	Forces the shell to go into interactive mode.
-s	Forces the shell to read commands from STDIN.
	The following are the single-letter options for `zsh`:
-0	Tries to correct any command misspellings.
-1	Shows the exit value of any programs that have a nonzero exit status.
+2	Shows an error message if a filename pattern is generated poorly.
+3	Shows an error message if a filename pattern has no matches.
-4	Matches a filename without needing to have a leading period (.).
-5	Immediately reports the status of a background job.
-6	Runs the background jobs with a lower priority (default).
-7	Doesn't exit when an EOF appears. Forces the use of `exit` or `logout`.
-8	Adds a trailing slash (/) to the directories that were created during globbing.
-9	Shows the user a list of selections when a confusing completion is made.
-A	Is used by `set` for array setting.
+B	Beeps.
+C	Allows the redirections > `&` >> file truncation and creation.
-D	Forces `pushd` without arguments to act like `pushd $HOME`.
-E	Suppresses the directory stack from showing after `pushd` or `popd`.
+F	Starts filename generation.
-G	Erases a pattern form an argument list if a filename generation pattern doesn't match.
-H	Doesn't query the user before running `rm*` or `rm path/*`.
-I	Prohibits brace expansion.
-J	Does a `cd` on the directory if a command is missing from the hash table.
+K	Starts the textual history substitution.
-L	Ignores any trailing backquotes (`) if there is an odd number of them in a line.
-M	Starts single-line editing mode.
-N	Forces `cd` to push the old directory into the directory stack.
-O	Tries to correct for spelling errors in all of the arguments on a line.
-P	Replaces foo${xx}bar with fooabar foobbar foocbar when a-b-c is valid.
-Q	Initiates a path search on command names including those with slashes (/).
-R	Shows jobs using the long format by default.
-S	Forces recognition of exact matches during completion even if they don't make sense.
-T	Expands the expression if a `cd` command isn't a directory.
-U	Shows a warning message if the mail file has been accessed since the last shell check.
+V	Prints a carriage return before showing a prompt at the line editor.
-W	Handles a single word command as a continuation of an existing job.
-X	Shows the file types of all files that are possible completions.
-Y	Inserts the first match when a vague completion happens.
-Z	Allows the use of the `zsh` line editor.
-a	Exports all defined parameters automatically.
-c	Specifies a single command from the command line.
-e	Runs the ZERR trap when a command has a nonzero exit status.
+f	Sources `/etc/zshrc, .zshrc, /etc/zlogin, .zlogin, and .zlogout` at startup.
-g	Stops putting command lines in the history list if a command line starts with a blank.
-h	Stops putting command lines in the history list if they are event duplicates.
-I	Starts the interactive shell if STDIN is a tty and commands are read from STDIN.
-k	Allows the use of comments in the interactive shells.
-l	The login shell.

continued

-m	Allows for job control. Is automatically set by default when an interactive shell stars.		
+n	Executes the commands. Without this option, commands are read but not run.		
-o	Allows the use of long option names.		
-p	Starts privileged mode.		
-s	Reads commands from STDIN.		
-t	Forces the shell to exit once a single command has been run from STDIN.		
+u	Handles any unset parameters like they were empty during substitution.		
-v	Verbose mode. Shows more information.		
-w	Converts symbolic links into their true values.		
-x	Prints commands and their arguments while they are executing.		
	The following options are used when `zsh` emulates `sh` and `ksh`:		
-a	The same as `zsh` -a.		
-b	The same as `zsh` +5.		
+C	The same as `zsh` +C.		
-e	The same as `zsh` -e.		
+f	The same as `zsh` +F.		
-i	The same as `zsh` -i.		
-l	The same as `zsh` -l.		
-m	The same as `zsh` -m.		
+n	The same as `zsh` +n.		
-p	The same as `zsh` -p.		
-s	The same as `zsh` -s.		
-t	The same as `zsh` -t.		
+u	The same as `zsh` +u.		
-v	The same as `zsh` -v.		
-x	The same as `zsh` -x.		
-X	The same as `zsh` -8.		
File Name: `zsh`	**Directory:** /usr/bin/	**Type:**	External

Chapter 14

Solaris 7 Commands

The commands in this section are all of the commands shared by Solaris 7 and Solaris 8 that are not listed in the Universal UNIX Commands (Chapter 9). The commands are all listed in alphabetical order by the command name.

For cross-references to other operating systems, please see the Quick Command Index (QCI) in Chapter 1.

/etc/defaultrouter

/etc/defaultrouter		**UNIX Shell:**	N/A
Function	Defines the system's default routers. Values must be separated with whitespace, # can be used for comments.		
	The following is an example of a `defaultrouter` file. # This is the default router 192.168.1.254		
File Name:	`defaultrouter`	**Directory:** /etc/	**Type:** Text File

/etc/hostname.*interface*

/etc/hostname.*interface*		**UNIX Shell:**	N/A
Function	Contains the hostname of the system and should match the hostname defined in the `/etc/hosts` file. The file is named with the interface name, such as hostname.hme0 or hostname.le0.		
	Below is the content of a hostname.hme0 file and assigns the hostname sun. sun		
File Name:	`hostname.hme0`	**Directory:** /etc/	**Type:** Text File

/etc/inetd.conf

/etc/inetd.conf		**UNIX Shell:**	N/A
Function	The Internet server database, used by the `inetd` daemon, which contains a list of available network services.		
The fields are:	**The database file must follow the following format separated by space or Tab:** **service endpoint protocol status uid program arguments**		
service	Specifies the name of a service that is found in the services file.		
endpoint	Specifies the endpoint type, which can be only one of the following:		
stream	Specifies a stream socket.		
dgram	Specifies a datagram socket.		
raw	Specifies a raw socket.		
seqpacket	Specifies a sequenced packet socket.		
tli	Specifies all tli endpoints.		
protocol	Specifies a valid protocol that is found in the `/etc/inet/protocols` file.		
status	Activates nowait mode for all datagram servers except those that are single threaded.		
uid	Specifies the user ID that the servers should run under.		
program	Specifies the server program to be started by `inetd`. Specifies pathname.		
arguments	Invokes a server from the command line by using a list of no more than five arguments.		
File Name:	`inetd.conf`	**Directory:** /etc/inet/	**Type:** Text File
Warning:	Don't configure UDP services as nowait (status option); it causes a race condition and slows down the server.		
ftp stream TCP nowait root /usr/sbin/in.ftpd in.ftpd	This is the line for the FTP service.		

/etc/inittab

/etc/inittab		UNIX Shell:	N/A
Function	A script used by `init`. Controls process dispatching.		
Syntax	*id:rstate:action:process*		

id	Specifies a unique identifier for the entry. One or two characters.
rstate	Specifies the run level for which the entry applies.
action	**Specifies how to handle the process field. The following actions are available:**
respawn	Starts the process if it doesn't exist.
wait	Starts the process and waits for it to terminate.
once	Starts the process once.
boot	Starts the process at boot time.
bootwait	Same as `boot` but waits for process to terminate.
powerfail	Starts the process when the power fail signal (SIGPWR) is received.
powerwait	Same as `powerfail` but waits for process to terminate.
off	Sends the process a SIGTERM signal, waits 5 seconds and then sends SIGKILL.
ondemand	Same as `respawn` but for run levels a, b, and c.
initdefault	Specifies the default run level of the system.
sysinit	Starts the process before accessing the console. Completes before continuing.
process	Specifies a command.

File Name:	`inittab`	**Directory:**	/etc/	**Type:**	Text File

is:3:initdefault:	Sets run level 3 as the default.
sc:234:respawn:/usr/lib/saf/sac -t 300	Restarts the service access controller if it isn't running.

/etc/nodename

/etc/nodename		UNIX Shell:	N/A
Function	Specifies the real hostname for the system.		

	Below is the content of `nodename` which assigns the hostname orion. orion

File Name:	`nodename`	**Directory:**	/etc	**Type:**	Text File

/etc/nologin

/etc/nologin		UNIX Shell:	N/A
Function	A text file message that is shown to the user who tries to log on during a system shutdown process. After the message appears, the log on procedure ends.		

File Name:	`nologin`	**Directory:**	/etc/	**Type:**	Text File
Note:	Superuser logons are not affected. For the message to work, it has to be placed in the `/etc/` directory.				

/etc/nsswitch.conf

/etc/nsswitch.conf		UNIX Shell:	N/A
Function	Specifies how the lookup for different databases is done and in what order.		
Syntax	*database sources... { status = success ... }* *database sources... { status = success ... sources... }*		

database	Specifies a database to the lookup order.
aliases	Specifies the aliases database used by sendmail.
automount	Specifies the database for automount.
bootparams	Specifies the database for rpc.bootparams
ethers	Specifies the database for the ethers.
group	Specifies how to look up group.
hosts	Specifies how to look up hosts.
netgroup	Specifies the database for netgroups.
netmasks	Specifies the database for netmasks
networks	Specifies the database for networks.
passwd	Specifies the database to use for passwd.

continued

protocols	Specifies the database for protocols.
publickey	Specifies the database for publickey.
rpc	Specifies the database for getrpcbyname.
sendmailvars	Specifies the database used by sendmail.
services	Specifies the database for getservicebyname.
sources...	Specifies the source to use. Searches from left to right.
files	Uses the files; for example, `/etc/hosts /etc/passwd` ...
nis	Uses NIS to look up the names.
nisplus	Uses NIS+ to look up the names.
dns	Uses DNS to look up hostnames (may be used only for hosts).
compat	Implements + and - for group and passwd.
[status = success ...]	Specifies what to do now. Multiple pair can be used. ([ ] must be used.)
status	Specifies the current status to check.
SUCCESS	Is true if the entry was found.
UNAVAIL	Is true if the source isn't responding or is corrupted.
NOTFOUND	Is true if the entry was not found.
TRYAGAIN	Is true if the source is busy and may respond to retries.
action	Specifies what to do.
continue	Tries the next source in the list.
return	Returns now.
	Below is a sample `nsswitch.conf` file. passwd: files nis group: files nis # Consults NIS first, then dns, and finally the /etc "files." hosts: nis [NOTFOUND=return] DNS files networks: nis dns [NOTFOUND=return] files

File Name:	`nsswitch.conf`	**Directory:**	/etc	**Type:**	Text File
Note:	There are several prototype files in /etc for different naming systems (nis, nisplus, etc...).				

ab_admin

UNIX Shell: All primary shells (csh, ksh, sh)

Function	Manages an `AnswerBook` card catalog database through a shell-level interface.
Syntax	ab_admin option [options...]

-listpaths	Shows the fully qualified pathnames of all card catalogs you have available.
-file *file*	Manages the card catalog that you specify; required with all options.
-merge *file*	Merges entries from the catalog file you specify into another catalog file.
-convert *file*	Creates a new card catalog entry from the information in a bookinfo file.
-add *id attribute*	Creates a new card catalog entry for the AnswerBook.
-remove *id*	Erases the AnswerBook entry that you specify.
-match *id*	Shows the contents of the AnswerBook entry that you specify.
-modify *id attribute*	Alters the fields of the AnswerBook entry that you specify.
-verify *id*	Verifies the AnswerBook entry that you specify exists and is ready for use.
-list	Shows all entries in the card catalog you specify.

File Name:	`ab_admin`	**Directory:**	/usr/openwin/bin/	**Type:**	External
Tip:	A creative way to add your own network documentation.				

ab_admin -listpaths	Lists pathnames of the card catalogs you have access to.

accept

UNIX Shell: Bourne shell (sh)

Function	Enables the printer queue specified to receive print requests.
Syntax	accept *printers...*

printers...	Specifies the names of printer queues or class of printers to accept print requests.

File Name:	`accept`	**Directory:**	/usr/sbin/	**Type:**	Script
Tip:	To see if the printer will accept or reject requests type `lpstat -a`				

accept printer	Allows print requests to the printer printer.
accept hplj5	Allows print requests to the printer hplj5.

accessx

UNIX Shell:	All primary shells (csh, ksh, sh)
Function	Configures the keyboard for use by people with disabilities. Requires OpenWindows version 3.4 or later.
Syntax	accessx [options...]

-o	Uses the system's current settings instead of the user's default settings.
-i	Shows the user interface as an icon at startup.
-a	Automatically opens pop ups for `Sticky Keys`.

File Name:	`accessx`	**Directory:**	/usr/openwin/bin/	**Type:**	External

accessx -i	Starts the application as an icon.
accessx -a	Starts the application and opens `Sticky Keys` automatically.

acctcms

UNIX Shell:	All primary shells (csh, ksh, sh)
Function	Reads files, adds the records for processes that execute commands with the same name, and then shows a summary.
Syntax	acctcms [options...] *file { files... }*

-a	Shows output in ASCII format.
-o	Shows non-working-hours command summary.
-p	Shows working-hours command summary.
-t	Processes all collected records as total accounting records.
-c	Shows total CPU time.
-j	Shows all commands invoked only once under the column `***other`.
-n	Sorts commands by number of invocations.
-s	Files from this point on are in internal summary format already.
file	Requires one file as input.
files...	Reads more files as input.

File Name:	`acctcms`	**Directory:**	/usr/lib/acct/	**Type:**	External

acctcms -a /var/adm/pacct	Shows a total command summary.
acctcms -ap /var/adm/pacct	Shows a working hours command summary.

acctcom

UNIX Shell:	All primary shells (csh, ksh, sh)
Function	Searches for account information in files, STDIN, or `/var/adm/pacct`. Shows output as described by `acct`.
Syntax	acctcom [options...] *{ files... }*

-a	Is used to show the average statistics about the selected processes.
-b	Shows the most recent commands first.
-f	Shows the system exit status columns and `fork/exec` flag in octal format.
-h	Shows the portion of the total available CPU time used by the process.
-i	Prints the columns that contain the I/O counts in the output.
-k	Shows the total kcore-minutes instead of the memory size.
-m	Shows the mean core size. This is the default.
-q	Does not print the output record, just the statistics.
-r	Shows the CPU factor using the format `user-time/(system-time + user-time)`.
-t	Shows separate user and system CPU times.
-v	Excludes the column titles from the output.
-e *time*	Selects the processes that exist before or at time.
-E *time*	Selects processes that end before or at time.
-g *group*	Shows the processes that belong to group. Uses group ID or a group name.
-H *factor*	Shows the processes that exceed the used CPU time factor.
-I *chars*	Shows the processes that have more characters than the number shown in chars.
-l *line*	Shows the processes which belong to terminal `/dev/term/line`.
-n *pattern*	Shows the commands that match `pattern`.
-o *output-file*	Copies the selected records in the input data format to a specified output file.
-O *sec*	Shows the processes which the CPU system time exceeds `sec` seconds.
-s *time*	Selects the processes that exist at or after time. Uses the format hr[:min[:sec]].
-S *time*	Selects processes starting before or at time.

continued

-u *user* -C *sec* *files...*		Shows the processes that belong to the user. User ID, username or ? are allowed. Shows the processes for which the CPU system plus user time exceeds `sec` seconds. Specifies the input file(s) other than the STDIN or `/var/adm/pacct`.			
File Name:	`acctcom`	**Directory:**	/usr/bin/	**Type:**	External
Tip:	This command only reports processes that have ended; you can use `ps` if you want to see active processes.				
acctcom -u root /var/adm/wtmpx		Prints root user access history from /var/adm/wtmpx.			
acctcom -i /var/adm/wtmpx		Prints I/O for user access/administration history.			

acctcon

UNIX Shell: All primary shells (csh, ksh, sh)

Function	Reads login/logoff records from STDIN and converts them to total accounting records.				
Syntax	acctcon [options...]				
-l *lineuse* -o *reboot*		Creates a summary file containing information about user activities. Shows a record of the accounting period including usage, reboot, and date changes.			
File Name:	`acctcon`	**Directory:**	/usr/lib/acct/	**Type:**	External
Tip:	Comes in handy for tracking line usage, for finding bad lines, and for identifying software and hardware issues.				
cat /vad/adm/utmp | accton -l infofile		Creates `infofile` with user activites information.			

acctcon1

UNIX Shell: All primary shells (csh, ksh, sh)

Function	Converts login/logoff records into ASCII. It reads from STDIN or the wtmp file in `/var/adm/`.				
Syntax	acctcon1 [options...]				
-p -t -l *lineuse* -o *reboot*		Shows line name, login name, and time in numeric and date/time format. Uses the last time found the file instead of the current time for the ending time. Shows summary of line usage. Tracks line usage and identifies bad lines. Gives information on start/end times, date changes, and number of reboots.			
File Name:	`acctcon1`	**Directory:**	/usr/lib/acct/	**Type:**	External
acctcon1 < /var/adm/wtmp		Shows login and logoff records in the file `/var/adm/wtmp`.			

acctcon2

UNIX Shell: All primary shells (csh, ksh, sh)

Function	Reads the ASCII records created by `acctcon1` and converts them into total accounting (tacct) records.				
Syntax	acctcon2				
File Name:	`acctcon2`	**Directory:**	/usr/lib/acct	**Type:**	External
acctcon2 < acctcon1.input > tacct.output		Creates total accounting records from the file acctcon1.input into `tacct.output`.			

acctdisk

UNIX Shell: All primary shells (csh, ksh, sh)

Function	Converts information regarding transferred disk blocks by userID or login name by reading the accounting file (usually /var/adm/pacct) and then creates total accounting records.				
Syntax	acctdisk				
File Name:	`acctdisk`	**Directory:**	/usr/lib/acct/	**Type:**	External

acctdusg

UNIX Shell: All primary shells (csh, ksh, sh)

Function	Calculates disk resource consumption for users. Reads from STDIN.				
Syntax	acctdusg [options...]				
-u *file* -p *file*		Creates a `No charge` file that specifies which files no one will be charged for. Specifies a password file. Isn't used if the file is `/etc/passwd`.			
File Name:	`acctdusg`	**Directory:**	/usr/lib/acct	**Type:**	External
find . -print | /usr/lib/acct/acctdusg		Makes a summary and shows disk resource usage.			

acctmerg		UNIX Shell:	All primary shells (csh, ksh, sh)
Function	Merges or adds accounting files in the total accounting (tacct) or ASCII format.		
Syntax	acctmerg [options...] *{ file }*		
-a	Creates output of an ASCII version of tacct file.		
-i	Specifies the input file is in ASCII format.		
-p	Shows the input without performing any processing.		
-t	Creates a single record that totals all input.		
-u	Summarizes by userID only instead of by both user ID and username.		
-v	Verbose mode. Shows more information.		
file	Specifies the total accounting (tacct) or ASCII file to merge or add.		
File Name: `acctmerg`	**Directory:** /usr/lib/acct/	**Type:** External	

accton		UNIX Shell:	All primary shells (csh, ksh, sh)
Function	Outputs process accounting to the specified file. If no filename is given, will turn process accounting off.		
Syntax	accton *{ file }*		
file	Specifies the existing file in which the kernel stores process accounting records.		
File Name: `accton`	**Directory:** /usr/lib/acct/	**Type:** External	
accton	Turns off process accounting.		
accton /var/adm/pacct	Turns on process accounting and uses the specified accounting file.		

acctprc1		UNIX Shell:	All primary shells (csh, ksh, sh)
Function	Converts information created with `acct` and adds the login names that correspond with the user IDs.		
Syntax	acctprc1 *{ ctlmp }*		
ctmp	Supplies a list of sessions sorted by user IDs and their login name.		
File Name: `acctprc1`	**Directory:** /usr/lib/acct/	**Type:** External	
Note:	The *ctmp* list helps to sort the sessions when several usernames share the same user ID.		
cat /var/adm/pacct | acctprc1	Creates a list with resource usage by user ID and login name.		

acctprc2		UNIX Shell:	All primary shells (csh, ksh, sh)
Function	Reads records from STDIN in the `acctprc1` format and sorts them by ID and name. Result is shown to STDOUT.		
Syntax	acctprc2		
File Name: `acctprc2`	**Directory:** /usr/lib/acct/	**Type:** External	

acctwtmp		UNIX Shell:	All primary shells (csh, ksh, sh)
Function	Writes a UTMP record with the current time and a string of characters that describe the reason, into specified file.		
Syntax	acctwtmp *reason file*		
reason	Specifies the reason to put in the record. Cannot be longer than 11 characters.		
file	Specifies the file to write the record in.		
File Name: `acctwtmp`	**Directory:** /usr/lib/acct/	**Type:** External	
acctwtmp "Shutdown" /var/adm/wtmp	Writes "Shutdown" as reason in the file `/var/adm/wtmp`.		

adb		UNIX Shell:	All primary shells (csh, ksh, sh)
Function	Provides a controlled environment to examine files. An interactive debugger to examine core files.		
Syntax	adb [options...] [files...]		
-k	Performs kernel memory mapping on a system crash corefile, swap file, or on `/dev/mem`.		
-w	Creates an objectfile and a corefile, if needed, and opens them for use by `adb`.		
-I *dir*	Specifies a list of directories that are read and that are colon-separated.		

continued

-P *prompt*	Changes the prompt inside of `adb`.		
-V *mode*	Disassembles and registers display modes. 1 = v8, 2 = v9 (generic), 4 = v9 (UltraSPARC).		
	The following files may be used and can be combined.		
objectfile	Specifies the executable program file that should contain the symbol table.		
corefile	Specifies the corefile image file produced from objectfile.		
swapfile	Specifies the image of the swap device. Can only be used with the -k option.		
File Name: `adb`	**Directory:** /usr/bin/	**Type:** External	
adb -k /dev/ksyms /dev/mem	Start adb on the running kernel.		
adb -P "Dugging:"	Change the prompt for adb.		

add_drv

UNIX Shell: All primary shells (csh, ksh, sh)

Function	Installs new device drivers in the computer and assigns device names.
Syntax	add_drv [options...] *driver*

-b *basedir*	Installs the driver into the root directory specified by `basedir`.		
-c *class*	Exports the class of the driver that is being installed to the system.		
-i *identify*	Lists the aliases names for the driver `driver`.		
-m *permission*	Specifies the device nodes permissions for the file system.		
-n	Modifies the configuration files without loading the device driver.		
-f	Forces add_drv to add the driver even if a reconfiguration boot is required.		
-v	Verbose mode. Shows more information.		
driver	Specifies the device driver to add to the system.		
File Name: `add_drv`	**Directory:** /usr/sbin/	**Type:** External	
Note:	Device drivers are usually bundled and installed in packages.		
add_drv -f audio	Adds the driver audio by force if reconfigure boot is needed.		

addbib

UNIX Shell: All primary shells (csh, ksh, sh)

Function	Creates, modifies, or updates a library database of information.
Syntax	addbib [options...] *database*

-a	Doesn't prompt for a summary.	
-p *file*	Uses another step-by-step prompting scheme other then the default.	
database	Specifies the database to create, modify, or update.	
File Name: `addbib`	**Directory:** /usr/bin/	**Type:** External
addbib ucgbook.db	Creates your own book database.	
addbib -a ucgbook.db	Doesn't prompt for a summary.	

admin, sccs-admin

UNIX Shell: All primary shells (csh, ksh, sh)

Function	Manages SCCS history files. SCCS history files have the form `s.filename`.
Syntax	admin [options...] *file*

-b	Forces binary encoding even if the file isn't recognized as a binary file.
-h	Checks structure of the old file and compares the checksum with the new s.file.
-n	Creates a new history file.
-z	Recalculates the file checksum and stores it in the first line of history file.
-a *username*	Gives permissions for a specified user to change deltas.
-a *groupID*	Gives permissions for a specified group to change deltas.
-d *flag*	Erases a specific flag from the history file.
-e *username*	Takes away the ability to make deltas for a specific user.
-e *groupID*	Takes away the ability to make deltas for a specific group.
-f *flag* [values...]	Sets values to the specified history file flag. These are the flags that can be used.
b	When the b flag is set it will allow the SCCS-get command to create branch deltas.
c*ceil*	Limits the number of releases that can be checked out.
f*floor*	Sets a limit or a floor for the number of releases that can be checked out.
d*sid*	Specifies the default SID that is the delta number that is used by `SCCS-get`.
i	Handles the message `No id keywords (ge6)` as an error instead of as a warning.

continued

j	Allows multiple simultaneous updates.
la	Locks all releases against deltas. The `SCCS-get` command will not work.
l *release*[releases...]	Locks only the release or releases specified against deltas.
n	Creates an empty release or empty delta when a release is skipped over.
q*value*	Specifies the value to expand when a read-only version is retrieved.
m*module*	Specifies the module name to use. The default name is the SCCS file with no leading s.
t*type*	Specifies the module type that you want to expand.
v*{ program }*	Specifies verification program to use when verifying the MR numbers in a new delta.
-i *file*	Uses text from input file to start a new history file.
-m *mr-list*	Puts modification request numbers to the comments for the first version.
-r *release*	Sets release level for the delta.
-t *desc-file*	Adds additional text for description into the delta from a specified file.
-y *comment*	Adds additional text for comments into the comment field of the delta.
file	Specifies a file to create or manage.
File Name: `admin`	**Directory:** /usr/ccs/bin/ **Type:** External
admin -n s.sccshist	Creates a new SCCS history file.
admin -h s.sccshist	Checks the structure of a SCCS history file.

admintool

UNIX Shell: All primary shells (csh, ksh, sh)

Function	Manages users, groups, printers, and software in an X-window environment.
Syntax	admintool

	The following are the tasks you can perform using admintool.
Group Management	Creates, deletes, or modifies group accounts. Automatically updates the /etc/groups file.
Host Management	Deletes, adds, or modifies hosts. Automatically updates the /etc/hosts file.
Port Management	Disables or enables serial port services to use with a modem or a terminal.
Printer Management	Adds or removes access to a printer or modifies a system's access to a printer.
Software Management	Adds or removes software. Can add software from a product CD or from a hard disk.
User Managment	Creates, deletes, or modifies user accounts. Automatically updates the /etc/passwd file.
File Name: `admintool`	**Directory:** /usr/bin/ **Type:** External
Tip:	Easy to use, but remember to specify a home directory such as `/export/home/username`.

afbconfig

UNIX Shell: All primary shells (csh, ksh, sh)

Function	Configures AFB Graphics Accelerators and some X11 window defaults.
Syntax	afbconfig [options...]

-dev *file*	Specifies the special device AFB file. The default device is `/dev/fbs/afb0`.
-file *{ client }*	Updates the OWconfig file that is specific to the computer.
-file *{ system }*	Updates the global OWconfig file.
-res *videomode { ACTION }*	Specifies the video mode for the monitor and can optionally use an ACTION listed below.
	When specifying the video mode you can use the following syntax:
widthxheightxrate	Where width and height are pixels and rate is the vertical frequency of the refresh.
	Or you can use any of the following symbolic names:
svga	Sets the resolution to 1024x768x60.
1152	Sets the resolution to 1152x900x76.
1280	Sets the resolution to 1280x1024x76.
stereo	Sets the resolution to 960x680x112s stereo video mode.
ntsc	Sets the resolution to 640x480x60i interlaced video.
pal	Sets the resolution to 768x575x50i interlaced video.
none	Selects what's presently being used by the device.
ACTION	**When you set videomode you can select one of the following actions:**
now	Updates the OWconfig file and show the video mode at once.
try	Shows the video mode and prompts the user for confirmation.
	When using try you can select between two actions:
noconfirm	Forces the confirmation of the video mode.

continued

nocheck	Bypasses error checking and shows the video mode regardless of the monitor type.
-defoverlay *{ action }*	Specifies whether the PseudoColor visual will be used as default.
true	Uses the PseudoColor overlay as default.
false	Uses the closest matching visual defaults from defdepth, defclass, and so on.
-linearorder *{ order }*	Selects in which order the linear visuals appear on the X11screen list.
first	Shows linear visuals before the nonlinear ones.
last	Shows linear visuals after the nonlinear ones.
-overlayorder *{ order }*	Selects in which order the Overlay visual will appear on the X11visual list.
first	Shows overlay visuals before the non-overlay visual.
last	Shows overlay visuals after the non-overlay visual.
-expvis *{ action }*	Specifies if OpenGL Visual Expansion will be used.
enable	Enables OpenGL Visual Expansion to be used.
disable	Deactivates OpenGL Visual Expansions.
-sov *{ action }*	Specifies if the SERVER_OVERLAY_VISUALS will be exported or not.
enable	Exports SOV visuals.
disable	Doesn't export SOV visuals.
-maxwids n	Specifies the maximum number of pixel values to be reserved for window IDs. **Only the values 1, 2, 4, 8, 16, 32, and 64 are valid.**
-extovl *{ action }*	Specifies whether extended overlay will be available.
enable	Enables extended overlays.
disable	Disables extended overlays.
-g *gcvalue*	Changes the gamma correction value. Default is 2.22. A value of 0 or less is invalid.
-gfile *gcfile*	Loads the specified RGB gamma correction table from a file.
-defaults	Resets all option values to default.
-propt	Shows current AFB configuration with values from -file and -dev.
-help	Shows help information.
-prconf	Shows the hardware configuration of the AFB device.

File Name:	`afbconfig`	**Directory:**	/usr/sbin/	**Type:**	External

afbconfig -props	Shows current configuration settings.
afbconfig -res 1280 try	Sets resolution to 1280x1024x76 and prompts for confirmation.

aliasadm

UNIX Shell:	All primary shells (csh, ksh, sh)
Function	Manages NIS+ aliases maps.
Syntax	aliasadm option *alias expansion { options comments }* aliasadm [options...]

	The following options can't be combined:
-a	Adds an NIS+ alias.
-c	Alters an NIS+ alias.
-d	Deletes an NIS+ alias.
-e	Edits the NIS+ alias map.
-l	Lists the NIS+ alias map.
-m	Shows or matches an NIS+ alias.
alias	Specifies the alias name to be configured.
expansion	Sets the alias value that will appear in the `/etc/aliases` file.
options	Sets additional options to the alias, currently only CANON is supported.
CANON	Is used when an inverse alias lookup is made. It will show CANON first.
comments	Adds comments to the alias, which is then read by the `sendmail` command.
	The following options can be combined.
-I	Starts the NIS+ alias database.
-D *domainname*	Alters the aliases map in a domain other than the current domain.
-f *file*	Uses file instead of an editor to list or edit the aliases database.
-M *mapname*	Alters the specified map name instead of an alias.

File Name:	`aliasadm`	**Directory:**	/usr/bin/	**Type:**	External

allocate

UNIX Shell: All primary shells (csh, ksh, sh)

Function	Assigns and manages device allocation and ensures that each given device is used by only one user at a time.				
Syntax	allocate [options...] *{ device }*				
-s		Is Silent mode. Doesn't show diagnostic output.			
-U *uname*		Specifies the user ID `uname` as a replacement for the userID.			
		You must choose one of the following devices.			
device		Specifies the device to be managed.			
-g *devtype*		Assigns an unassigned device to the device type specified.			
-F *device*		Reassigns a device from one user to another user. Superuser only.			
File Name:	`allocate`	**Directory:**	/usr/sbin/	**Type:**	External
Note:	This works only if the Basic Security Module (/etc/security/bsmconv) is enabled.				
allocate /dev/audio		Assigns the device `/dev/audio` to current user.			
allocate -s /dev/audio		Assigns `/dev/audio` to current user silently.			

answerbook

UNIX Shell: Bourne shell (sh)

Function	Starts the AnswerBook browser where you can search for information online.				
Syntax	answerbook [options...]				
-b *library-file*		Specifies a library file to use other than the default `$HOME/.ab_library`.			
-c *card-catalog*		Specifies the card catalog files to use to find Answerbooks.			
File Name:	`answerbook`	**Directory:**	/usr/openwin/bin/	**Type:**	Script
Tip:	There is also great documentation on Sun's Web site, `http://docs.sun.com`.				

answerbook2

UNIX Shell: All primary shells (csh, ksh, sh)

Function	Starts up a browser and shows online documentation from an AnswerBook2 server.				
Syntax	answerbook2 [-h]				
-h		Shows help information.			
File Name:	`answerbook2`	**Directory:**	/usr/dt/bin/	**Type:**	External

answerbook2_admin

UNIX Shell: All primary shells (csh, ksh, sh)

Function	Starts the Answerbook administration GUI interface in your default Web browser.				
Syntax	answerbook2_admin [-h]				
-h		Shows a usage statement.			
File Name:	`answerbook2_admin`	**Directory:**	/usr/dt/bin/	**Type:**	External
Tip:	A great way to make your own online personalized documentation.				

appletviewer

UNIX Shell: Korn shell (ksh)

Function	Executes Java applets outside the browser and shows them in a separate window.				
Syntax	appletviewer [options...] *url...*				
-debug		Shows debug information.			
-encoding *name*		Specifies the name of the HTML input file.			
-J *string*		Passes the string as an argument to Java for compilation.			
url...		Specifies URLs to connect to. A URL can be a local HTML document.			
File Name:	`appletviewer`	**Directory:**	/usr/bin/	**Type:**	Script
appletviewer -debug my.html		Starts applet viewer for debugging `my.html`.			
appletviewer my.html		Runs applet `my.html` in a separate window.			

appres

appres	**UNIX Shell:**	All primary shells (csh, ksh, sh)
Function	Shows how much resources a specific application will use.	
Syntax	appres [options...]	

class	Specifies the class name of an application.
instance	Specifies an instance name in addition to *class*.
-1	Matches a specific resource level.
toolkitoptions	Allows the use of X toolkit options.

File Name:	`appres`	**Directory:**	/usr/openwin/bin/	**Type:**	External
Note:	Helps programmers make applications more efficient.				

appres xterm	Lists resources that xterm will load.

arch

arch	**UNIX Shell:**	Bourne shell (sh)
Function	Shows the hardware architecture of the current host. All SunOs 5.x SPARC-based systems report as `sun4`.	
Syntax	arch [-k] { *archname* }	

	You can only use one of the following options and they can't be combined.
-k	Shows the kernel architecture, for example `sun4m` and `sun4c`.
archname	Checks whether the host system is compatible with the application architecture.

File Name:	`arch`	**Directory:**	/usr/bin/	**Type:**	Script
Note:	This is used for backward compatibility only. Use `uname` instead.				

arch -k	Shows the kernel architecture of host.

asa

asa	**UNIX Shell:**	All primary shells (csh, ksh, sh)
Function	Converts FORTRAN carriage control output to a printable format.	
Syntax	asa [-f] { *files...* }	

-f	Starts every file on a different page.
files...	Specifies the pathname and a text file to be used for input.
-	Uses STDIN for input.

File Name:	`asa`	**Directory:**	/usr/bin/	**Type:**	External

aset

aset	**UNIX Shell:**	All primary shells (csh, ksh, sh)
Function	A set of utilities used for security administration named ASET. Analyzes system files for permissions and attributes.	
Syntax	aset [options...]	

-p	Adds an entry to the crontab file to automatically run the ASET program periodically.
-d *asetDir*	Specifies a different working directory for ASET (default is `/usr/aset`).
-l *seclevel*	Specifies a security level of either `high`, `med`, or `low` for ASET to use.
-n *user@host*	Sends error logs to the user on the specified host (default for error log is STDOUT).
-u *userlist*	Specifies a filename containing a list of users ASET will run security checks for.

File Name:	`aset`	**Directory:**	/usr/aset	**Type:**	External

aset -l med	Sets the security level to medium.
aset -p	Specifies to run periodically. The file /usr/aset/asetenv sets the time.

aset.restore

aset.restore	**UNIX Shell:**	Bourne shell (sh)
Function	Resets system files to the same state as they were before ASET was installed.	
Syntax	aset.restore [-d *directory*]	

-d *directory*	Sets the ASET working directory (default is `/usr/aset/`).

File Name:	`aset.restore`	**Directory:**	/usr/aset/	**Type:**	Script

aspppd

UNIX Shell:	All primary shells (csh, ksh, sh)

Function	Provides PPP services to connect to remote hosts. Automatically starts the connection when a PPP request is made.				
Syntax	aspppd [-d *debuglevel*]				
-d *debuglevel*	Specifies debug level between 0 and 9; 9 shows the most detailed information.				
File Name:	`aspppd`	**Directory:**	/usr/sbin/	**Type:**	External

aspppls

UNIX Shell:	All primary shells (csh, ksh, sh)

Function	Initiates the link manager to allow incoming calls. This connects the incoming clients to `aspppd` on the host server.				
Syntax	aspppls				
File Name:	`aspppls`	**Directory:**	/usr/sbin/	**Type:**	External
Note:	It is started at boot time if the configuration file `/etc/asppp.cf` is present.				

audioplay

UNIX Shell:	All primary shells (csh, ksh, sh)

Function	Plays audio files and can copy a specified audio file to an audio device.				
Syntax	audioplay [options...] *files...*				
-i	Exits and shows an error message if the audio device is busy.				
-V	Sends any messages to STDERR when waiting for audio device access.				
-v *vol*	Specifies the volume level. It must be a value from 0 to 100.				
-b *bal*	Specifies the balance level. Range is -100 (left) to 100 (right). Middle is set at zero.				
-p *option*	Specifies the output port.				
speaker	Uses the built-in speaker.				
headphone	Uses the headphone jack.				
line	Uses the line out.				
-d *dev*	Specifies an audio device to send its output to.				
files...	Specifies one or more files to play in a sequential order.				
-\?	Shows help information.				
File Name:	`audioplay`	**Directory:**	/usr/bin/	**Type:**	External
audioplay -d /dev/audio music.au	Plays music.au on device /dev/audio.				
audioplay stairway_to_heaven.au	Plays stairway_to_heaven.au.				

audiotool

UNIX Shell:	All Primary shells (sh, ksh, csh)

Function	Records, plays, and edits audio data. Used only in X-window.				
Syntax	audiotool [options...] *{ arguments... } files...*				
-p	Allows you to use the prompt for the application.				
-d *device*	Specifies an audio device to use.				
arguments...	Specifies any device options.				
files...	Specifies the audio files to play.				
File Name:	`audiotool`	**Directory:**	/usr/openwin/bin/	**Type:**	External
audiotool &	Opens a graphic audiotool in an X-window.				

audit

UNIX Shell:	All primary shells (csh, ksh, sh)

Function	Manages the behavior of the audit daemon `auditd`.				
Syntax	audit option				
	The following options must be used separately and can't be combined.				
-n	Disables the current audit file and opens a new one.				
-s	Rereads the audit file.				
-t	Stops auditing and kills the daemon.				
File Name:	`audit`	**Directory:**	/usr/sbin/	**Type:**	External

auditconfig

auditconfig	UNIX Shell:	All primary shells (csh, ksh, sh)
Function	Configures the audit parameters used by the kernel to use auditing.	
Syntax	auditconfig options...	

	The following options must be used separately and can't be combined.
-chkconf	Checks the consistency between kernel audit events and class mappings.
-conf	Configures mappings between audit events and classes.
-getfsize	Shows the maximum and current size of the audit file.
-setfsize *size*	Sets the maximum size in bytes of the audit file.
-getcond	Shows the state of the kernels audit.
-setcond *auditing*	Enables auditing.
-setcond *noaudit*	Disables auditing.
-lsevent	Shows information about currently configured auditing.
-getpinfo *pid*	Shows audit information about the specified process.
-setpmask *pid*	Is used to specify the pre-selection mask for the given process.
-setsmask *asid*	Is used to specify the pre-selection mask for the given audit session.
-setumask *auid*	Is used to specify the pre-selection mask for the given audit.
-lspolicy	Shows the kernel's audit policies.
-getclass *event*	Shows the pre-selection mask that is mapped to the specified audit event.
-setclass *event audit_flag*	Configures mappings between audit events and classes.
-getpolicy	Shows the policy of the kernel audit.
-getstat	Shows statistics about the kernel.
-setpolicy + *policy*	Sets a new kernel audit policy.
-setpolicy - *policy*	Removes a kernel audit policy.
	The following policies can be used:
arge	Adds environment arguments from `execv` to the audit record.
argv	Adds parameter arguments from `execv` to the audit record.
cnt	Drops audit records if resources are low.
group	Adds the group token to the audit record.
path	Adds the path token to the audit record.
trail	Adds the trailer token to the audit record.
seq	Adds the sequence token to the audit record.

File Name:	`auditconfig`	**Directory:**	/usr/sbin/	**Type:**	External

auditconfig -getpolicy	Shows the kernel audit policy.
auditconfig -getcond	Shows the kernel audit condition.

auditd

auditd	UNIX Shell:	All primary shells (csh, ksh, sh)
Function	The daemon that manages auditing and uses the audit control file to set working environment.	
Syntax	auditd	

File Name:	`auditd`	**Directory:**	/usr/sbin/	**Type:**	External

auditreduce

auditreduce	UNIX Shell:	All primary shells (csh, ksh, sh)
Function	Selects and merges audit records collected from audit trail files.	
Syntax	auditreduce [options...] *{ files... }*	

-A	Selects all records from the input file.
-C	Processes files that are not currently in use.
-D *suffix*	Deletes files when they have been processed.
-M *machine*	Selects only the files that have the suffix *machine*.
-O *suffix*	Puts output to a file and names it with a *suffix*.
-Q	Shows no errors.
-R *pathname*	Sets a new root directory for audit.
-S *server*	Collects audit trail files from other location than the default.
-V	Verbose mode. Shows more information.
-a *datetime*	Collects records that were created at or later than *datetime*.

continued

-b *datetime*	Selects records that were created before *datetime*.
-c *audit-classes*	Selects records that match the specified audit class.
-d *datetime*	Selects records that were created on a specific day.
-e *effective-user*	Selects records that match the specified user.
-f *effective-group*	Selects records that match the specified effective group.
-g *real-group*	Selects records that match the specified real group.
-j *pid*	Selects records that match the specified process ID.
-m *event*	Selects records that match the specified event.
-o objecttype=*objectID*	Selects objects where types and IDs match.
	The following object types and objectIDs are valid:
file=*pathname*	Selects audit records from files with the specified pathname.
msgqid=*ID*	Selects records that match the specified message queue ID.
pid=*ID*	Selects records that match the specified process ID.
semid=*ID*	Selects records that match the specified semaphore ID.
shmid=*ID*	Selects records that match the specified shared memoryID.
sock=*port*	Selects records that match the specified port number.
sock=*computer*	Selects records matching the specified computer name defined in `etc/hosts`.
-r *real-user*	Selects records that match the specified real user.
-u *audit-user*	Selects records that match the specified audit user.
files...	Specifies the audit trail file or files that you want to manage.

File Name:	`auditreduce`	**Directory:**	/usr/sbin/	**Type:**	External
Tip:	Use with `praudit` to be able to read and show audit trail files.				

auditstat

UNIX Shell: All primary shells (csh, ksh, sh)

Function	Shows kernel audit statistics as well as other useful information about the kernel.
Syntax	auditstat [options...]

-c *count*	Shows statistics count times.
-n *numlines*	Shows a header for every numlines of statistics.
-i *interval*	Shows the statistics every interval in seconds.
-n	Shows the number of configured kernel audit events on the computer.
-v	Shows version information.
	The following are the possible fields shown by auditstat and their meaning:
aud	Totals the number of records that audit has processed.
ctl	Is no longer used.
drop	Totals the number of audit records that have not been processed.
enq	Totals the number of queued audit records.
gen	Totals the number of created audit records.
kern	Totals the number of audit records created by user processes.
mem	Totals the amount of memory that the kernel uses for auditing.
nona	Totals the number of audit records that are not set for a specific user.
rblk	Totals the number of blocks for which `auditsvc` has been waiting to process data.
tot	Totals the amount of data that has been written to the audit trail file.
wblk	Totals the number of times that a user process blocked the audit queue at upperlimit.
wrtn	Totals the number of audit records that have been written.

File Name:	`auditstat`	**Directory:**	/usr/sbin/	**Type:**	External

auditstat -i 5	Shows kernel stats every 5 seconds.

automount

UNIX Shell: All primary shells (csh, ksh, sh)

Function	Installs mount points automatically upon user requests. It associates automount maps to an installed mount point.
Syntax	automount [options...]

-t *duration*	Specifies timeout for a mount point that isn't in use (default is 10 minutes).
-v	Verbose mode. Shows more information.

continued

File Name:	automount	**Directory:**	/usr/sbin/	**Type:**	External
automount -t 1200			Specifies to unmount filesystems not accessed for 20 minutes.		

automountd

UNIX Shell: All primary shells (csh, ksh, sh)

Function	The daemon that manages mount and unmount requests made by `autofs`.
Syntax	automountd [options...]

-T	Gives trace information of each RPC call.
-v	Verbose mode. Shows more information.
-n	Disables all `autofs` mount points.
-D *name=value*	Sets additional values to the automount map.

File Name:	automountd	**Directory:**	/usr/lib/autofs/	**Type:**	External

autopush

UNIX Shell: All primary shells (csh, ksh, sh)

Function	Configures a list of modules that are automatically streamed when a device is opened.
Syntax	autopush [options...]

	The following three options must be used separately and can't be combined.
-f *file*	Creates the autopush configuration for a driver based upon the file.
	Requires a text file that is made up of four or more columns separated by spaces.
Example file	minor major last-minor moduleA moduleB moduleC
-g -M*major* -m*minor*	Gets the current setting of the specified major and minor devices.
-r -M*major* -m*minor*	Removes the configuration setting of the specified major and minor devices.

File Name:	autopush	**Directory:**	/sbin/	**Type:**	External

awk

UNIX Shell: All primary shells (csh, ksh, sh)

Function	Scans the input file or files for lines that match the specified pattern in '*scriptstr*' or from a file.
Syntax	awk [options...] [' *scriptstr* '] [-v *var=value*] { *files...* } awk [options...] [-f *scriptfile*] [-v *var=value*] { *files...* }

-f *scriptfile*	Specifies the file that contains the specific pattern action statements to be used.
-F*exp*	Specifies the expression to use as a field separator.
' *scriptstr* '	Contains the pattern action statements and must be enclosed by single quotes (').
	The pattern action statements must follow the format: pattern { action }.
pattern { *action* }	Formats the pattern action statement string specified by ' *scriptstr* '.
	The following arithmetic functions are supported:
cos(*x*)	Returns the cosine of the specified value. The value must be in radians.
sin(*x*)	Returns the sine of the specified value. The value must be in radians.
exp(*x*)	Returns the exponential function of the specified value.
log(*x*)	Returns the natural logarithm of the specified value.
sqrt(*x*)	Returns the square root of the specified value.
int(*x*)	Shortens the specified value to an integer. It trims the value when x > 0.
	The following are the supported string functions: String is indicated by s.
index(*s, sub*)	Gives the position of string *s* where the substring *sub* occurs first.
int(*s*)	Trims *s* to an integer. If no *s* is shown, then $0 will be used.
length(*s*)	Gives the total length of an argument or an entire line if there is no argument.
match(*s, re*)	Returns the position where the regular expression *re* matches the string *s*.
split(*s, a, fs*)	Splits string s into an array of elements a1,a2, and separates fields with the fs expression.
sprintf(*fmt, expr...*)	Formats listed expressions with `printf`using the format specified by fmt.
substr(*s, m, n*)	Gives the n-character substring of the string s that starts at the m position.
	The following are the built-in variables that can be used:
-v *var=value*	Specifies a built-in variable listed below and assigns it a value.
FILENAME	Specifies the name of the current file being used for input.
FS	Defines input field separators (default is space and Tab).
NF	Defines number of fields in the existing file.
NR	Defines ordinal number for the current record.

continued

OFMT	Defines output numbers in a specific format (default is %.6g).
OFS	Defines output field separators (default is blank).
ORS	Defines output record separators (default is new-line).
RS	Defines input record separators (default is new-line).
	The following are control flow functions:
break	Exits from a *for*, *while*, or *do* loop.
continue	Starts the next loop cycle in a *for*, *while*, or *do* loop.
do *statement*	A loop that executes the specified statement while the condition is true.
while (*condition*)	Is evaluated by do and runs the do statement if condition is true; exits if false.
exit *{ exp }*	Executes the end routine if it exists, and exits the script with return value *exp*.
if (*condition*)	Performs the statement if the condition is true or will perform the else condition.
else (*condition*)	Performs the else condition when the if condition is false.
while (*condition*)	Performs the condition as long as the condition is true.
for (*exp1; exp2 ; exp3*)	A loop that uses three expressions (see below). Exits when any expression is false.
exp1	Sets the counter variable to an initial value that counts the number of loops.
exp2	Defines the variable that is read and evaluated before executing the statement.
exp3	A counter that increments each time the loop is true. (The variables exp1, exp2, and exp3 are all optional and are true if not used.)
for (*arrayvar*)	A loop that executes each variable defined in an array.
next	Reads the input line and begins a new loop or procedure.
	The following input/output functions are supported:
getline	Sets $0 into the next input record using the current input file. 1 = success, -1 = error.
print	Shows the results of the ' *scriptstr* ' and variables to STDOUT.
printf	Same as print but also formats the output.
$*n*	Specifies the field numbers in the file ($1, $2, $3,...) and are separated by FS.
$0	Specifies to use the entire line in the file as input.
files...	Specifies the input files that are scanned for pattern matching.

File Name:	`awk`	**Directory:**	/usr/bin/	**Type:**	External

awk -F: '{print $1}' /etc/passwd | sort	Shows the first field (username) in the /etc/passwd file and sorts it.
who | awk '{print $6}'	Shows the IP addresses for all users logged in.

bdconfig

UNIX Shell: All primary shells (csh, ksh, sh)

Function	Configures the SunButtons and SunDials stream, autopush facility, and the serial device to use with the stream.
Syntax	bdconfig [options...] *{ term }* [options...]

startup	Uses the last known configuration before the system went down.
off	Reconfigures the device for `tty` use.
on	Reconfigures the device for SunButtons and SunDials use.
term	Specifies the serial device for SunButtons and SunDials use.
status	Shows the current configuration.
verbose	Verbose mode. Shows more information.

File Name:	`bdconfig`	**Directory:**	/usr/sbin/	**Type:**	External

bdconfig status	Shows the status of the SunButtons and SunDials configuration.
bdconfig on	Reconfigures the device to be used with SunButtons and SunDials.

bdiff

UNIX Shell: All primary shells (csh, ksh, sh)

Function	Compares files that are too large for the command `diff`.
Syntax	bdiff *file1 file2 { NR }* [-s]

file1	The first file to be compared.
file2	The second file to be compared.
NR	Sets the number of line segments (default is 3500).
-s	Is silent mode; will not show diagnostics.

continued

File Name:	bdiff1	Directory:	/usr/bin/	Type:	External
bdiff bigfile biggerfile -s			Compare bigfile with biggerfile in silent mode.		
bdiff bigfile biggerfile 5000			Compare bigfile with biggerfile.		

bfs

UNIX Shell: All primary shells (csh, ksh, sh)

Function	Scans big files to identify sections and can be used like `ed`. Default will show the size of the file.
Syntax	bfs [-] *file*

-	Doesn't show sizes.
file	Specifies the file to scan.

File Name:	bfs1	Directory:	/usr/bin/	Type:	External
bfs myfile			Scans myfile.		
bfs - myfile			Scans myfile and doesn't show file sizes.		

biff

UNIX Shell: All primary shells (csh, ksh, sh)

Function	Enables or disables mail notification. If no arguments are used, shows the current status.
Syntax	biff [option]

y	Enables mail notification.
n	Disables mail notification.

File Name:	biff1	Directory:	/usr/ucb/	Type:	External
biff y			Enables mail notification.		
biff n			Disables mail notification.		

binder

UNIX Shell: All primary shells (csh, ksh, sh)

Function	Binds applications, print methods, icons, colors, or open methods to files.
Syntax	binder [option]

-user	Modifies the database bindings for a user.
-system	Modifies the database bindings for the system. Must be a superuser to execute it.
-network	Modifies the database bindings for the network. Requires root access to server.

File Name:	binder1	Directory:	/usr/openwin/bin/	Type:	External
binder -user			Starts the GUI and modifies your bindings.		
binder -system			Starts the GUI and modifies the system's bindings.		

cachefslog

UNIX Shell: All primary shells (csh, ksh, sh)

Function	Shows where the statistics for `CacheFS` are logged. Can also redirect the log or stop logging altogether.
Syntax	cachefslog [option] *mount-point*

-f *logfile*	Sets the log file where you want to log the statistics.
-h	Stops the logging.
mount-point	Specifies the mount point of a cache file system; all files under the point will be logged.

File Name:	cachef1slog	Directory:	/usr/sbin/	Type:	External
Note:	Remember that it's illegal to specify a path within a cache file system.				
cachefslog /cache/home			Checks whether the directory `/cache/home` is logged.		
cachefslog -f /cache/log /cache/home			Alters the log file for the directory `/cache/home`.		

cachefspack

UNIX Shell: All primary shells (csh, ksh, sh)

Function	Compresses or decompresses files and file systems located in cache.
Syntax	cachefspack [options...] *{ files... }*

-f *packing-list*	Specifies a file that contains a list of files and directories to be compressed.
	The following three options can't be combined:
-i	Shows information about the compressed files.
-p	Specifies to compress file or files (default).

continued

-u	Specifies to decompress file or files.
-U *cache-directory*	Decompresses all files in the specified cache directory.
-h	Shows help information.
-d	Shows selected filenames.
-v	Verbose mode. Shows more information.
-r	Interprets strings in LIST rules as regular expressions.
-s	Takes away the `./` from the beginning of a pattern name.
file...	Specifies the pathname to the file or files to be compressed or decompressed.
File Name: `cachefspack`	**Directory:** /usr/bin/ **Type:** External
cachefspack -p /home/ucg/ucg_examples	Compresses file ucg_examples into cache.
cachefspack -u /cache/ucg_examples	Decompresses file ucg_examples from cache.

cachefsstat

UNIX Shell: All primary shells (csh, ksh, sh)

Function	Shows various cache statistics like hits and misses about a cache file system that is mounted on a path.
Syntax	cachefsstat [-z] *{ paths... }*

-z	Reinitializes cache statistics. Use this before running `cachefsstat` again.
paths...	Specifies the mount point for the cache file system.
File Name: `cachefsstat`	**Directory:** /usr/bin/ **Type:** External
Note:	Uses `cachefswssize` to show the `cachefs` workspace size.
cachefsstat /home/cache	Shows statistics for the `/home/cache` CacheFS.
cachefsstat -z /home/cache	Reinitializes the statistics for the `/home/cache` CacheFS.

cachefswssize

UNIX Shell: All primary shells (csh, ksh, sh)

Function	Shows the workspace size and the total cache size statistics for the specified cache log file.
Syntax	cachefswssize *logfile*

logfile	Specifies the name of the CacheFS log file to show statistics for.
File Name: `cachefswssize`	**Directory:** /usr/sbin/ **Type:** External
cachefswssize /var/tmp/logfile	Shows the end size and highwater size for the specified log file.

calctool

UNIX Shell: All primary shells (csh, ksh, sh)

Function	A graphic desktop calculator that you can use with the mouse or the keyboard.
Syntax	calctool [options...]

-2	Starts the calculator in 2D mode (is default).
-3	Starts the calculator in 3D mode.
-a *number*	Sets the accuracy level of the calculator. 0 to 9 decimal places (default is 2 decimal places).
-c	Shows the calculator in color.
-l	Starts the left-handed version.
-m	Shows the calculator in monochrome even on a color screen.
-r	Starts the right-handed version.
-v	Shows version information.
-Wn	Starts without title line.
+Wn	Starts with title line.
-name *app-name*	Specifies the name of the application from which you want to receive resources.
-?	Same as -v. You must use Ctrl+C to exit this if you are using C shell.
File Name: `calctool`	**Directory:** /usr/openwin/bin/ **Type:** External
calctool -3	Starts in 3D mode.
calctool -l	Starts the left-hand version.

calendar

calendar	UNIX Shell:	Bourne shell (sh)
Function	Reads your calendar file and shows any notes that you have entered for today and tomorrow.	
Syntax	calendar [-]	
-	Reads the calendar file in everyone's login directory and sends a mail.	
File Name: calendar	**Directory:** /usr/bin/	**Type:** Script
calendar -	Reads everyone's calendar and sends a mail.	

cancel

cancel	UNIX Shell:	All primary shells (csh, ksh, sh)
Function	Removes print requests to printers or printer pools. Stops all print requests for the user or a specific print request.	
Syntax	cancel *{ request-ID } { destination }* cancel -u *users... { destinations... }*	
-u *user*	Cancels the print requests for the username. Must be your own username.	
request-ID	Specifies the LP-style request-ID to cancel.	
destination	Specifies the printer or class of printers to cancel.	
File Name: cancel	**Directory:** /usr/bin/	**Type:** External
Warning:	If you don't specify a destination, then all destinations are canceled.	
cancel printer1	Stops jobs on the printer1 printer.	
cancel <request-ID> printer1	Stops request-IDs on printer1.	

catman

catman	UNIX Shell:	All primary shells (csh, ksh, sh)
Function	Creates and manages the manual pages and the windex database that contains short command descriptions.	
Syntax	catman [options...] *{ sections... }*	
-c	Creates the manpages from the SGML sources.	
-n	Does not allow the `windex` database to be created or re-created.	
-p	Shows what would be done, but doesn't execute the changes.	
-t	Creates `troff` entries in the `fmt` subdirectories.	
-w	Creates the windex database used by `whatis` and `man -f, -k` only.	
-M *directory*	Updates the manual pages located in this directory.	
-T *macro-package*	Uses macro-package instead of the standard manual page macros.	
sections...	Updates the manpage section specified. Uses whole numbers 1, 2, 3, ...	
File Name: catman	**Directory:** /usr/bin/	**Type:** External
Tip:	If you want to use `apropos`, `whatis`, `man -k`, or `man -f`, you must use `catman -w` first!	
catman 1 4 6	Updates sections 1, 4, and 6.	
catman -n	Does not allow updating or creating of the windex database.	

cc

cc	UNIX Shell:	Bourne shell (sh)
Function	An interface for the BSD Compatibility Package C compiler. Works only if the SPROcc package is installed.	
Syntax	cc [options...] *files...*	
-c	Suppresses loading and saves any produced object files.	
-D *name* (= *def*)	Sets the #define directive to 1, or specifies it to be `def`.	
-E	Runs only the macro processor, and shows the result on STDOUT.	
-g	Creates symbol-table information to use for debugging.	
-I*dir*	Searches the specified directory for include files that don't begin with a slash (/).	
-l*name*	Links the specified file to the library files.	
-L*dir*	Adds the directory to the list of directories to be searched for in the libraries.	
-o*file*	Sends the output to the specified file.	
-O	Optimizes the object code.	
-p	Generates a code to count routine calls and to log it to a file called /mon.out.	
-P	Runs only the preprocessor and saves the result in the file (file.i).	
-S	Compiles and saves the result in the file (file.s) but doesn't assemble or load.	

continued

-U*name* -Y P, *directory*	Removes the definition of the specified name. Alters the default directory that you use for searching libraries.				
File Name:	`cc`	**Directory:**	/usr/ucb/	**Type:**	Script
Note:	There is no C compiler installed by default. Download it from `http://www.sunfreeware.com`.				
cc file_with_c_code.c	Compiles `file_with_c_code.c`.				

cdc, sccs-cdc

UNIX Shell: All primary shells (csh, ksh, sh)

Function	Alters the delta commentary of an SCCS delta. It can also be used to explain the commentary.
Syntax	cdc -r*SID* [options...] *files...*

-r*SID*	Specifies the SID (SCCS deltaID) of the delta to change.				
-m*MR-list*	Modifies, adds, or erases one or more MR numbers specified in the list. (Place a ! before mr-list to erase the MR numbers.) The v flag must be set in the s.file to enable prompting of MR numbers.				
-y ["*comment*"]	Makes a comment as an explanation in the delta commentary.				
-	Uses STDIN as the input instead of a filename.				
files...	Specifies the input file or directories.				
File Name:	`cdc`	**Directory:**	/usr/ccs/bin/	**Type:**	External
Note:	If using - as the input for an SCCS history, you must use the -m and -y options.				
cdc -r1.6 -y "This is a test" s.program.c	Adds the comment "This is a test" to the delta 1.6 in s.program.c.				

cfsadmin

UNIX Shell: All primary shells (csh, ksh, sh)

Function	A disk space administration utility for use with the Cache File System (CacheFS).
Syntax	cfsadmin option [options...] *cachedir* cfsadmin -s *action*

	The following options can't be combined.				
-c	Creates a cache directory under the specified directory.				
-d *option*	Removes a cache directory. The options can be one of the following two.				
cacheID	Removes the cache directory that has the specified cacheID.				
all	Removes all file systems in the cache directory.				
-l	Shows the file systems that are in the cache directory.				
-s *action*	Runs a consistency check on mounted file system. Action can be one of the following.				
mountpoint	Runs a consistency check on the specified mountpoint only.				
all	Runs a consistency check on all cache file systems.				
-u	Updates resource parameters for the specified cache directory.				
	The following options are file system-specific and are only used with -c and -u.				
-o *fstype-specific*	File system-specific options can be used together if separated by a comma.				
maxblocks=*n*	Specifies the maximum space that cacheFS can use in percent.				
minblocks=*n*	Specifies the minimum space that cacheFS can use in percent.				
threshblocks=*n*	Specifies the maximum number of blocks that cacheFS can use in the front file system.				
maxfiles=*n*	Specifies the maximum number of files that cacheFS can use in percentage of inodes.				
minfiles=*n*	Specifies the minimum number of files that cacheFS can use in percentage of inodes.				
threshfiles=*n*	Specifies the maximum number of inodes that cacheFS can use in the front file system.				
maxfilesize=*n*	Sets the largest allowed file size for the cache directory.				
	The following can be used together with the -c, -d, -l, and -u options.				
cachedir	Specifies the cache directory that you want to manage.				
File Name:	`cfsadmin`	**Directory:**	/usr/sbin/	**Type:**	External
cfsadmin -c /ucgcache	Creates a cache under `/ucgcache`.				
cfsadmin -l /ucgcache	Shows the contents and statistics of the cache directory.				

chargefee

UNIX Shell:	Bourne shell (sh)		
Function	An accounting command that is used to charge units to a login.		
Syntax	chargefee *user num*		
user	Specifies the login name to charge units from.		
num	Specifies the number of units to charge.		
File Name: `chargefee`	**Directory:** /usr/lib/acct	**Type:**	Script
chargefee ucg 100	Charge 100 units to ucg.		

checkeq

UNIX Shell:	All primary shells (csh, ksh, sh)		
Function	Creates a report of wrong or lost delimiters and equation start/end markers (EQ/EN).		
Syntax	checkeq *{ files... }*		
files...	Specifies the name of the file that you want to verify.		
File Name: `checkeq`	**Directory:** /usr/bin/	**Type:**	External
Tip:	Use it to check whether you have the proper delimiters after you have used `eqn` or `neqn`.		
checkeq ucgfile	Checks the file for improper delimiters or EQ/EN pairs.		

check-hostname

UNIX Shell:	Bourne shell (sh)		
Function	Checks whether the host has a fully qualified hostname, which is needed by `sendmail`.		
Syntax	check-hostname		
File Name: `check-hostname`	**Directory:** /usr/lib/mail/sh/	**Type:**	Script

checknr

UNIX Shell:	All primary shells (csh, ksh, sh)		
Function	Checks `nroff and troff` files for errors such as missing delimiters and unknown commands.		
Syntax	checknr [options...] *{ files... }*		
-f	Ignores the changes to \f fonts.		
-s	Ignores the changes to \s size.		
-a .x1.y1...	Adds macro pairs to the list of pairs to check. (Example -a.BS.ES)		
-c .c1.c2...	Defines commands that otherwise would create error messages.		
files...	The name of the file or files to verify. The default is STDIN.		
File Name: `checknr`	**Directory:** /usr/bin/	**Type:**	External
checknr -f /var/adm/messages	Checks and ignores font changes.		
checknr -s /var/adm/messages	Checks and ignores size changes.		

check-permissions

UNIX Shell:	Bourne shell (sh)		
Function	Checks permissions on `sendmail` files. Warns if permissions are not safe.		
Syntax	check-permissions *{ users... }*		
users...	Specifies users whose home directories are to be checked (default is current user). (Use ALL to check all users' home directories.)		
File Name: `check-permissions`	**Directory:** /usr/lib/mail/sh/	**Type:**	Script
check-permissions ucg	Checks the home directory of the ucg user.		
check-permissions ALL	Checks the home directories of all users.		

chkey

UNIX Shell:	All primary shells (csh, ksh, sh)
Function	Alters a user's secret key pair and secure RPC public key.
Syntax	chkey [options...]
-p	Uses the user login password to re-encrypt the secret key.
-s *nisplus*	Updates the NIS+ database.

continued

-s *nis*	Updates the NIS database.		
-s *files*	Updates the files database.		
-m *mechanism*	Changes or re-encrypts the secret key for the specified mechanism.		
	The following mechanisms are supported:		
des	Authentication flavor for this mechanism is `AUTH_DES`.		
dh640-0	Authentication flavor for this mechanism is `RPCSEC_GSS`.		
dh1024-0	Authentication flavor for this mechanism is `RPCSEC_GSS`.		
File Name: `chkey`	**Directory:** /usr/bin/	**Type:**	External
Note:	Uses the 192-bit Diffie-Hellman cryptographic key.		
chkey -p	Re-encrypts the existing secret key.		
chkey -s nis	Updates the NIS database.		

ckdate

UNIX Shell: All primary shells (csh, ksh, sh)

Function	Prompts the user for a date format and then verifies the response.
Syntax	ckdate [options...]

-Q	Does not allow `quit` as an answer.		
-W *width*	Specifies the width to show messages.		
-d *default*	Sets the default value.		
-h *help*	Sets the text for the help message.		
-e *error*	Sets the text for the error message.		
-p *prompt*	Sets the text for the prompt.		
-k *PID*	Sends a signal to this process ID when the user exits.		
-s *signal*	Specifies the signal to send to the process specified with the -k option.		
-f *format*	Specifies the date format to be used.		
	The following formats are supported:		
%b	Uses abbreviated months: Jan, Feb, Mar...		
%B	Uses the full month and day: 01 to 31.		
%D	Uses the date: %m/%d/%y (default).		
%e	Uses the shortened day with the month: 1 to 31. A space must follow any single digit.		
%h	Same as %b.		
%m	Uses the number of the month: 01, 02, 03, ...		
%y	Uses the last two numbers of the full year: 99, 00, 01, ...		
%Y	Uses the full year: 2001, 2002, 2003, ...		
File Name: `ckdate`	**Directory:** /usr/bin/	**Type:**	External
ckdate -h "use the format mmddyy"	Sets the help text to: use the format mmddyy.		
ckdate -p myprompt	Sets the prompt message text to myprompt.		

ckgid

UNIX Shell: All primary shells (csh, ksh, sh)

Function	Prompts the user for a group ID and verifies the answer.
Syntax	ckgid [options...]

-Q	Does not allow `quit` as an answer.		
-W *width*	Specifies the width to show messages. Stops auto formatting.		
-m	Shows all groups to select from when the user needs help.		
-d *default*	Sets the default value.		
-h *help*	Sets the text for the help message.		
-e *error*	Sets the text for the error message.		
-p *prompt*	Sets the text for the prompt.		
-k *PID*	Sends a signal to this process ID when the user exits.		
-s *signal*	Specifies the signal to send to the process specified with the -k option.		
File Name: `ckgid`	**Directory:** /usr/bin/	**Type:**	External
ckgid -Q	Specifies that quit isn't a valid response.		
ckgid -h "enter the name of an existing group"	Sets the help text to: enter the name of an existing group.		

ckint

ckint	UNIX Shell:	All primary shells (csh, ksh, sh)
Function	Prompts the user for an integer and then verifies the answer.	
Syntax	ckint [options...]	

-Q	Does not allow `quit` as an answer.
-W *width*	Specifies the width to show messages.
-b *base*	Sets the base for the input, 2-36. Default is 10.
-d *default*	Sets the default value.
-h *help*	Sets the text for the help message.
-e *error*	Sets the text for the error message.
-p *prompt*	Sets the text for the prompt.
-k *PID*	Sends a signal to this process ID when the user exits.
-s *signal*	Specifies the signal to send to the process specified with the -k option.

File Name:	`ckint`	**Directory:**	/usr/bin/	**Type:**	External

ckint -Q	Sets `quit` as an invalid response.
ckint -e Wrong	Sets error message to be `wrong`.

ckitem

ckitem	UNIX Shell:	All primary shells (csh, ksh, sh)
Function	Creates a menu and then prompts the user to select a menu option that will then be verified. Use this to define prompt, help, and error messages, and to define a default value.	
Syntax	ckitem [options...] *{ choices... }*	

-f *file*	Specifies a file that contains a list of items to show as the menu.
-Q	Does not allow `quit` as an answer.
-W *width*	Specifies the width to show messages.
-u	Shows the menu items as an unnumbered list.
-n	Shows the menu items in alphabetic order.
-o	Returns only one menu token.
-l *label*	Sets a text line to use as a label to the menu.
-i *invis*	Sets invisible choices that will not be shown in the menu.
-m *max*	Sets the max number of menu items you can use (default is 1).
-d *default*	Sets the default value.
-h *help*	Sets the text for the help message.
-e *error*	Sets the text for the error message.
-p *prompt*	Sets the text for the prompt.
-k *PID*	Sends a signal to this process ID when the user exits.
-s *signal*	Specifies the signal to send to the process specified with the -k option.
choices...	Specifies the menu items that the user can select from. Separates items using spaces.

File Name:	`ckitem`	**Directory:**	/usr/bin/	**Type:**	External
Note:	There are two visual tools that are linked to this command: `erritem` and `helpitem`.				

ckitem -m 5	Specifies the user have five menu items to select from.
ckitem -u TheMenu	Specifies the choices will be shown as an unnumbered list.

ckkeywd

ckkeywd	UNIX Shell:	All primary shells (csh, ksh, sh)
Function	Prompts the user for a keyword and then verifies the response.	
Syntax	ckkeywd [options...] *{ keywords... }*	

-Q	Does not allow `quit` as an answer.
-W *width*	Specifies the width to show messages.
-d *default*	Sets the default value.
-h *help*	Sets the text for the help message.
-e *error*	Sets the text for the error message.
-p *prompt*	Sets the text for the prompt.
-k *PID*	Sends a signal to this process ID when the user exits.
-s *signal*	Specifies the signal to send to the process specified with the -k option.
keywords...	Specifies the keywords that the user can select.

continued

File Name:	`ckkeywd`	**Directory:**	/usr/bin/	**Type:**	External
Tip:	When you use a tilde at the start or end of a custom message, the default message will be inserted.				
ckkeywd not			Sets the keyword to not.		
ckkeywd -e "wrong word" Yes No			Sets the error message to wrong word and keywords to Yes and No.		

ckpacct

UNIX Shell: All primary shells (csh, ksh, sh)

Function	Sets the maximum file size for the process accounting file.				
Syntax	ckpacct *{ size }*				
size		Specifies the maximum size in blocks of the accounting file `/var/adm/pacct`.			
File Name:	`ckpacck`	**Directory:**	/usr/lib/acct/	**Type:**	External
Note:	This function also turns the accounting off if free space in `/var` is too small.				

ckpath

UNIX Shell: All primary shells (csh, ksh, sh)

Function	Prompts the user for a path and verifies the answer.				
Syntax	ckpath [options...]				
-Q		Does not allow `quit` as an answer.			
-W *width*		Specifies the width to show messages.			
-a		Specifies the pathname must be an absolute path.			
-l		Specifies the pathname must be a relative path.			
-b		Specifies the pathname must be a block special file.			
-c		Specifies the pathname must be a character special file.			
-f		Specifies the pathname must be a regular file.			
-y		Specifies the pathname must be a directory.			
-n		Specifies the pathname is a new name.			
-o		Specifies the pathname is old; that is existing.			
-z		Specifies the pathname must contain a file larger than zero bytes.			
-r		Specifies the pathname must allow read access.			
-t		Creates pathname if it doesn't exist.			
-w		Specifies the pathname must allow write access.			
-x		Specifies the pathname must be executable.			
-d *default*		Sets the default value.			
-e *error*		Sets the text for the error message.			
-h *help*		Sets the text for the help message.			
-p *prompt*		Sets the text for the prompt.			
-k *processID*		Sends a signal to this process ID when the user exits.			
-s *signal*		Specifies the signal to send to the process specified with the -k option.			
File Name:	`ckpath`	**Directory:**	/usr/bin/	**Type:**	External
ckpath -y			Specifies the given path must be a directory.		
ckpath -x			Specifies the given path must be executable.		

ckstr

UNIX Shell: All primary shells (csh, ksh, sh)

Function	Prompts the user for a response and verifies the answer.	
Syntax	ckstr [options...]	
-Q		Does not allow `quit` as an answer.
-W *width*		Specifies the width to show messages.
-r *regexp*		Sets the regular expression that is verified against the input.
-l *length*		Sets the maximum length of the input.
-d *default*		Sets the default value.
-h *help*		Sets the text for the help message.
-e *error*		Sets the text for the error message.
-p *prompt*		Sets the text for the prompt.

continued

-k *PID* -s *signal*		Sends a signal to this process ID when the user exits. Specifies the signal to send to the process specified with the -k option.			
File Name:	`ckstr`	**Directory:**	/usr/bin/	**Type:**	External
ckstr -l 100			Specifies the input string maximum as 100 characters.		
ckstr -p "Enter a string"			Sets the prompt to be Enter a string.		

cktime

UNIX Shell: All primary shells (csh, ksh, sh)

Function	Prompts the user for a time format and then verifies the response.
Syntax	cktime [options...]

-Q	Does not allow `quit` as an answer.
-W *width*	Specifies the width to show messages.
-d *default*	Sets the default value.
-h *help*	Sets the text for the help message.
-e *error*	Sets the text for the error message.
-p *prompt*	Sets the text for the prompt.
-k *PID*	Sends a signal to this process ID when the user exits.
-s *signal*	Specifies the signal to send to the process specified with the -k option.
-f *format*	Specifies the format against which the input will be verified.
	The following time formats are supported:
%H	Specifies standard 24 hour as 00 to 23.
%I	Specifies standard 12 hour as 00 to 12.
%M	Specifies minutes as 00 to 59.
%p	Specifies PM instead of AM.
%r	Specifies time as %I:%M:%S %p%R instead of the default %H%M.
%S	Specifies seconds as 00 to 59.
%T	Specifies time as %H:%M:%S.

File Name:	`cktime`	**Directory:**	/usr/bin/	**Type:**	External
cktime -p "Give a time"			Sets the prompt to be `Give a time`.		
cktime -e "Wrong time"			Sets the error message to be `Wrong time`.		

ckuid

UNIX Shell: All primary shells (csh, ksh, sh)

Function	Prompts the user for a valid username and verifies the answer.
Syntax	ckuid [options...]

-Q	Does not allow `quit` as an answer.
-W *width*	Specifies the width to show messages.
-m	Shows a list of all user logins if the user needs help.
-d *default*	Sets the default value.
-h *help*	Sets the text for the help message.
-e *error*	Sets the text for the error message.
-p *prompt*	Sets the text for the prompt.
-k *PID*	Sends a signal to this process ID when the user exits.
-s *signal*	Specifies the signal to send to the process specified with the -k option.

File Name:	`ckuid`	**Directory:**	/usr/bin/	**Type:**	External
ckuid -p "Type a user"			Sets the prompt to be Type a user.		
ckuid -e "Use a valid name"			Sets the error message to be Use a valid name.		

ckyorn

UNIX Shell: All primary shells (csh, ksh, sh)

Function	Prompts the user for a yes or a no and verifies the answer.
Syntax	ckyorn [options...]

-Q	Does not allow `quit` as an answer.
-W *width*	Specifies the width to show messages.
-d *default*	Sets the default value.
-h *help*	Sets the text for the help message.

continued

-e *error*	Sets the text for the error message.
-p *prompt*	Sets the text for the prompt.
-k *PID*	Sends a signal to this process ID when the user exits.
-s *signal*	Specifies the signal to send to the process specified with the -k option.
File Name: `ckyorn`	**Directory:** /usr/bin/ — **Type:** External
ckyorn -Q	Specifies that `quit` isn't allowed as answer.
ckyorn -p "YES or NO"	Sets the prompt to be `YES or NO`.

clear_locks

UNIX Shell: All primary shells (csh, ksh, sh)

Function	Removes file, record, and share locks that were made by an NFS client.
Syntax	clear_locks [-s] *hostname*

-s	Removes all locks made on the local computer as well as those locks held on the specified server.
hostname	Specifies the hostname or the IP address of the client or server.
File Name: `clear_locks`	**Directory:** /usr/sbin/ — **Type:** External
Tip:	Useful when an NFS client has crashed. You must be a superuser to use this command.
clear_locks host1	Removes all file, record, and share locks used by host1.

closewtmp

UNIX Shell: All primary shells (csh, ksh, sh)

Function	Places a false DEAD_PROCESS record into the file `/var/adm/wtmp` for each user logged in. It is then used by the command `runacct` to track each user's connection time.
Syntax	closewtmp

File Name: `closewtmp`	**Directory:** /usr/lib/acct/ — **Type:** External
Note:	The `wtmp` file contains logon/logoff information.

clri, dcopy

UNIX Shell: All primary shells (csh, ksh, sh)

Function	Clears inodes by writing zeros on the specified inode number.
Syntax	clri [options...] *device inode*

-F *Fstype*	The file system type to operate on.
-V	Echos the command line for verification but doesn't execute it.
device	The special device where the file system containing the inode to clear is located.
inode	Specifies the inode number to write zeros to.
File Name: `clri`	**Directory:** /usr/sbin/ — **Type:** External
Note:	Primarily used to remove a file that doesn't appear in a directory.
clri -F ufs /dev/rdsk/c0t0d0s0 125125	Clears the inode 125125 on `/dev/rdsk/c0t0d0s0`.

cm

UNIX Shell: All primary shells (csh, ksh, sh)

Function	The OpenWindows calendar manager. Useful in many ways as a reminder and scheduler.
Syntax	cm *arguments...* [options...]

-c *calendar*	Specifies a calendar different from the default calendar.
-i *2*	Selects the OpenWindows version 2 icons that show the current month.
-i *3*	Selects the OpenWindows version 3 icons that show the current date.
arguments...	Specifies any OpenWindows generic tool argument.
File Name: `cm`	**Directory:** /usr/openwin/bin/ — **Type:** External
cm -c anders.cal	Starts the Anders calendar.
cm -i 2	Starts the calendar in Open Windows version 2 style.

cm_delete

UNIX Shell:	All primary shells (csh, ksh, sh)
Function	Removes appointments from the `cm` Calendar Manager.
Syntax	cm_delete [options...]

-c *calendar*	Specifies a calendar other than the default calendar.
-d *date*	Specifies a specific date to delete appointments from; format = mm/dd/yy.
-v *view*	Shows all appointments for a specified time span; day, week, or month.
File Name: `cm_delete`	**Directory:** /usr/openwin/bin/ **Type:** External
cm_delete -d 04/04/01	Lets you interactively choose from appointments for April 4, 2001.

cm_insert

UNIX Shell:	All primary shells (csh, ksh, sh)
Function	Inserts an appointment into the `cm` Calendar Manager.
Syntax	cm_insert [options...]

-c *calendar*	Specifies the name of a calendar other than the default calendar.
-d *date*	Specifies the date for the appointment you want to insert; format = mm/dd/yy.
-s *start*	Specifies the appointment start time.
-e *end*	Specifies the appointment ending time.
-v *view*	Specifies a time span to show; day, week, or month.
-w *what*	Specifies the appointment subject.
File Name: `cm_insert`	**Directory:** /usr/openwin/bin/ **Type:** External
cm_insert -s 11:30 am -e 12:30 pm -d 04/04/01 -w lunch	Adds a lunch appointment for 11:30-12:30 April 4 2001.

cm_lookup

UNIX Shell:	All primary shells (csh, ksh, sh)
Function	Finds your appointments in the `cm` Calendar Manager.
Syntax	cm_lookup [options...]

-c *calendar*	Specifies a calendar other than the default calendar.
-d *date*	Specifies the date for the appointment that you want to show; format = mm/dd/yy.
-v *view*	Specifies the time span you want to show; day, week, or month.
File Name: `cm_lookup`	**Directory:** /usr/openwin/bin/ **Type:** External
cm_lookup -c anders@wks1	Shows you the appointments for the user Anders at the host wks1.

cmap_alloc

UNIX Shell:	All primary shells (csh, ksh, sh)
Function	Creates custom color maps for X11 clients that need to run programs that cannot use the default color map.
Syntax	cmap_alloc [options...]

-display *display:n.screen*	Specifies the X11 server to use. Default is the DISPLAY environment variable.
-force	Always creates the color maps, even if they already exist.
-allscreens	Creates empty colormaps for all screens, not only the default screen.
-depth *n*	Creates colormaps that are to be used together with the specified depth only.
-visual *class*	Creates colormaps that are to be used together with the specified class only. **The following classes are supported: GrayScale, PseudoColor, and DirectColor.**
-verbose	Verbose mode. Shows more information.
-help	Shows help information.
File Name: `cmap_alloc`	**Directory:** /usr/openwin/bin/ **Type:** External
cmap_alloc -verbose	Creates color maps for the current display only and shows the debugging information.
cmap_alloc -allscreens	Creates color maps for all screens instead of just the default one.

cmap_compact

cmap_compact	UNIX Shell:	All primary shells (csh, ksh, sh)
Function	Reduces color map flashing by assigning color values towards the high end of 255 in the default color map.	
Syntax	cmap_compact [operation] [-display *displayname*]	

	The following operations can be used:
save	Saves the read-only colors from the default color maps of all active screens.
init	Reads the saved colors and assigns them as read-only to the high end.
discard	Deletes the file ~/.owcolors.
dealloc	Resets the assigned colors created by init back to normal.
show	Prints all the saved RGB values for each screen.
name	Specifies the X11 screen to use (default is 0).
-display *displayname*	Specifies which X11 display to use (default is ':0').

File Name:	`cmap_compact`	**Directory:**	/usr/openwin/bin/	**Type:**	External

Note: The colors are saved in the file `~/.owcolors.`

cmap_compact save	Saves the color values to the file "~/.owcolors."
cmap_compact show	Shows all saved color values for each screen.

cmdtool

cmdtool	UNIX Shell:	All primary shells (csh, ksh, sh)
Function	Opens an enhanced terminal window that is used to run programs or shells.	
Syntax	cmdtool [options...] *{ program }* cmdtool [options...] *{ program arguments }*	

-C	Sends system screen output to the window.
-M *bytes*	Overwrites the log from the beginning after this number of bytes (default is 100 KB).
-P *countv*	Creates log checkpoints after this many operations.
-B *style*	Specifies the style used to show bold text in the window.
-I *command*	Sends the commands to the shell for execution.
program { arguments }	Specifies the program that you want to run in the terminal window.

File Name:	`cmdtool`	**Directory:**	/usr/openwin/bin/	**Type:**	External

Tip: You have `cmdtool`, `xterm` and `terminal` to choose from if you need a terminal window.

cmdtool -C	Redirects the system console to the window.
cmdtool -I "ls -l"	Passes the `ls` command to the command window.

colorchooser

colorchooser	UNIX Shell:	All primary shells (csh, ksh, sh)
Function	Allows you to change colors of icons for use in an X window environment.	
Syntax	colorchooser	

File Name:	`colorchooser`	**Directory:**	/usr/openwin/bin/	**Type:**	External

comb, sccs-comb

comb, sccs-comb	UNIX Shell:	All primary shells (csh, ksh, sh)
Function	Creates a script that re-creates and combines older versions of SCCS files, `s.files`. All changes are saved in deltas, together with a version identification line (SID).	
Syntax	comb [options...] *files...* comb [options...] *directory*	

-o	Allows you to access the new version `delta` that is to be created.
-s	Does not combine deltas but does create scripts to show how much space would be saved.
-c*sidlist*	Specifies a list of delta identifiers `(SIDs)` to combine.
-p*SID*	Specifies the SID of the oldest delta to keep a copy of.
files...	Specifies the `s.files...` that are to be re-created.
directory	Creates scripts for all `s.files...` found in that directory. (Use sccs-get -lp to show a delta table log to STDOUT.)

continued

File Name:	comb	**Directory:**	/usr/ccs/bin/	**Type:**	External
Bug:	Comb may change the shape of the delta tree and may actually increase the size of the delta.				
comb s.UCG			Creates a script to use on the s.UCG file.		
comb -s s.UCG			Shows you the changes that would be created on s.UCG.		

comsat, in.comsat

UNIX Shell: All primary shells (csh, ksh, sh)

Function	Listens for incoming mail and notifies users that have asked to be told when new mail comes (`biff y`).				
Syntax	in.comsat				
File Name:	in.comsat	**Directory:**	/usr/sbin/	**Type:**	External

constype

UNIX Shell: All primary shells (csh, ksh, sh)

Function	Shows the type of Sun console you are using by showing the Sun code.
Syntax	constype

	The following is a list of valid Sun codes:
bw?	Black-and-White screen.
cg?	Color Graphics screen.
gp2	Optional Graphics Processor board.
gx	Sun GX (cg6) Graphics Accelerator.
gt	Sun GT Graphics Accelerator.
ns?	Not Sun display.
sx	Sun SX (cg14) Graphics Accelerator.
zx	Sun ZX (leo) Graphics Accelerator.
SUNWffb	Sun FFB Graphics Accelerator.

File Name:	constype	**Directory:**	/usr/openwin/bin/	**Type:**	External

conv_lp

UNIX Shell: Bourne shell (sh)

Function	Converts line printer configuration from a directory to an output file.
Syntax	conv_lp [options...]

-d *directory*	Specifies the directory from which LP configuration is read (default is `/`).
-f *file*	Specifies the output file (default is `/etc/printers.conf`).

File Name:	conv_lp	**Directory:**	/usr/lib/print/	**Type:**	Script
conv_lp -d /export/home/ucg			Converts LP configuration from /export/home/ucg/ to /etc/printers.conf.		

conv_lpd

UNIX Shell: Bourne shell (sh)

Function	Converts `LPD` configuration files between the `printers.conf` and the `printcap` formats.
Syntax	conv_lpd [options...] *file*

-c *printers*	Specifies the output should be a printers.conf file (default).
-c *printcap*	Specifies the output should be a printcap file.
-n	Maintains all names during conversion.
file	Specifies the `printers.conf` or the `printcap` file to be converted.

File Name:	conv_lpd	**Directory:**	/usr/lib/print/	**Type:**	Script
conv_lpd /etc/printcap			Converts /etc/printcap to a printers.conf file.		

crash

UNIX Shell: All primary shells (csh, ksh, sh)

Function	Examines the image of the system memory of a currently running or crashed system.
Syntax	crash [options...] For crashed system: crash [options...] function [arguments...]

	The following three ways specify how the command will work:
-d *dumpfile*	Specifies the file to use when saving the system image (default is `/dev/mem`).
-n *namelist*	Specifies the file with the image symbol table information (default is `/dev/ksyms`).

continued

-w *outputfile*	Logs the crash session to this file instead of to STDOUT.
	The following are the functions and their options to use on a crashed system:
?	Creates a list of available functions.
!*command*	Exits to the shell and executes the specified command.
base *number*	Shows the `number` in binary, octal, decimal, and hexadecimal format. 0b = binary, 0 = octal, 0x = hexadecimal.
buffer *format*	Shows the content of a buffer in the specified format (default is hexadecimal). -b = byte, -c = character, -d = decimal, -x = hexadecimal, -o = octal, and -i = inode.
bufferslot	Specifies the slot for the buffer.
startaddress	Specifies the start address for the buffer.
bufhdr *tableentry*	Shows you all headers for the system buffer.
callout	Shows the callout table.
class *tableentry*	Shows information about the process scheduler classes.
help *function*	Shows help information on the given function, including syntax and aliases.
kmastat	Shows kernel memory allocator statistics.
kmausers *[cachenames...]*	Shows information of recent, medium, and large users of the kernel memory allocator.
cachenames...	Limits the information to the specified cache name or names (default is all names).
lck *lockaddress*	Shows record locking information. No address = shows locks relative to UFS inodes.
mblk *argument*	Shows allocated streams message block and data block headers.
mount *tableentry*	Shows information about all mounted filename systems.
nm *symbol*	Shows the type and value of the given symbol.
od *startaddress { count }*	Shows `count` values from the specified start address.
-format	Shows the result in one of the following formats (default is ASCII): -c = character, -d = decimal, -x = hexadecimal, -o = octal, -a = ASCII, -h = -c and -x.
mode	Shows the result in one of the following modes: -l = long, -t = short, -b = byte.
proc *PID*	Shows the process table. Any table entry and process ID may be used. **All process IDs specified must have the prefix #.**
-r	Specifies table information for runnable processes.
snode *tableentry*	Shows information about open special filenames.
strstat	Shows STREAMS statistics.
tsdptbl *tableentry*	Shows the time-sharing dispatcher parameter table.
uinode [-r]	Shows the UFS inode table. Displays all free UFS inodes with -r.
var	Shows the tunable system parameters.
vfs *addresses...*	Shows information about the mounted filename systems.
vfssw *tableentry*	Shows information about configured filename system types.
vnode *addresses...*	Show information about vnodes.
vtop *startaddress*	Show the physical address translation of the virtual address.
	The following options work with most of the functions:
-e	Shows all entries in the table.
-f	Shows the full structure.
-l	Show all related locking information.
-p	Reads all address arguments as physical addresses.
-s *process*	Specifies process slot other than the default.
-w *filename*	Redirects the output of a function to the specified file.
tableentry	Specifies slot number, address, symbol, range, or expression.
startaddress...	Specifies an address, symbol, or expression. (Examine Kernel core dumps on the same platform as they were created on.)

File Name: `crash`	**Directory:** /usr/sbin/	**Type:** External
crash -d /dev/mem	Examines the system image; use ? to see options.	
crash -n /dev/ksyms	Examines the system namelist.	

crypt	UNIX Shell:	All primary shells (csh, ksh, sh)
Function	Encrypts or decrypts a file. Uses STDIN and STDOUT.	
Syntax	crypt *password* < *cleartextfile* > *newfile*	

password	Specifies the password needed to encrypt/decrypt the file.		
cleartextfile	Specifies the name of the unencrypted file you intend to encrypt.		
newfile	Specifies the name of the encrypted version of the file.		
File Name: `crypt`	**Directory:** /usr/bin/	**Type:**	External
crypt secretpassword < cleartext > encrypted	Encrypts the file `cleartext` into a filenamed `encrypted`.		
crypt secretpassword < encrypted > cleartext	Decrypts the file encrypted into a filenamed cleartext.		

csh	UNIX Shell:	C shell (csh)
Function	The C shell command interpreter, which uses a syntax similar to the C language.	
Syntax	csh [options...] *{ arguments... }*	

-b	Lets the rest of the options be passed directly to the scripts.		
-c	Runs the first argument from the list and passes the other arguments to csh.		
-e	Exits on nonzero exit status or other abnormal terminations.		
-f	Performs a fast start. Doesn't run .cshrc and .login.		
-i	Forces the command prompt on any type of terminal for interactive use.		
-n	Interprets but doesn't run the commands; used for debugging scripts.		
-s	Reads STDIN to get the commands.		
-t	Runs a single command line.		
-v	Verbose mode. Shows more information. Sets verbose after reading .cshrc.		
-V	Verbose mode. Shows more information. Sets verbose before reading .cshrc.		
-x	Echos each command before it is run. Sets echo after reading .cshrc.		
-X	Echos each command before it is run. Sets echo before reading .cshrc.		
arguments...	Specifies one or more arguments for the command.		
File Name: `csh`	**Directory:** /usr/bin/	**Type:**	External
csh -c "ls -l"	Execute `ls -l` in csh.		

csplit	UNIX Shell:	All primary shells (csh, ksh, sh)
Function	Splits all or part of a file into other files in the way specified by your arguments.	
Syntax	csplit [options...] *file arguments...*	

-f *prefix*	Specifies a prefix for the created files.		
-k	Does not remove the previously created files if an error occurs.		
-n *number*	Specifies how many digits to use as name for created files (default = 2 digits).		
-s	Does not show messages about file sizes.		
file	Name and path of the file to split.		
arguments	Arguments to set the function of csplit.		
	The following arguments are supported:		
/rexp/	Creates a file from the current line to the line before the regular expression.		
offset	Sets a positive or negative line number value to use.		
{num}	Repeats the argument this many times.		
%rexp%	Does not create a file from the current line to the line before the regular expression.		
offset	Sets a positive or negative line number value to use.		
{num}	Repeats the argument this many times.		
lineno	Creates a file from the current line to the line before this line number.		
{num}	Splits the file with the line number this many times.		
File Name: `csplit`	**Directory:** /usr/bin/	**Type:**	External
csplit -k orgfil 5 {2}	Splits `orgfil` into pieces.		

ct

UNIX Shell:	All primary shells (csh, ksh, sh)
Function	Dials a phone number to a terminal modem and initiates a login process to that terminal.
Syntax	ct [options...] *phoneNR*

-h	Does not hang up and wait for process to stop before returning control to the user.
-s*baudrate*	Sets data baud rate (default is 1200 baud).
-v	Verbose mode; sends information to STDERR.
-w*n*	Waits this many minutes for a line if no line is available at the moment.
-x*n*	Sets debug mode with a number from 1 to 9; higher number gives you more details.
phoneNR	Specifies the telephone number to dial.

File Name:	`ct`	**Directory:**	/usr/bin/	**Type:**	External

ct -s 9600 800-456-1234	Dials the number 800-456-1234 with the speed 9600 baud.
ct -s 9600 -h 714-765-9876	Dials up with the speed 9600 baud and doesn't hang up the line.

ctlmp

UNIX Shell:	All primary shells (csh, ksh, sh)
Function	Generates a PostScript format version from text files. Use it when you want to print text files.
Syntax	ctlmp [options...] *files...*

-A4	Formats the text in A4 paper size.
-C	Uses the value of the Content-Length mail header to mark the start of a new mail.
-F	Shows who the mail is from in the header. Default is to show who the mail is to.
-L *localename*	Specifies the locale of the file to print.
-O *orientation*	Specifies the text orientation; rtl (right to left) ltr (left to right) and context.
-PS	Specifies that PostScript files be printed as text.
-US	Formats the text in US paper size. This is the default size.
-a	Formats the file to look like a newspaper article.
-c *chars*	Sets the max number of characters to extract from the GECOS field in `/etc/passwd`.
-d	Shows the file as a summary.
-e	Specifies the ELM mail front-end intermediate file format.
-ff	Formats the file to be used with a Filofax personal organizer.
-FP	Formats the file to be used with a Franklin Planner personal organizer.
-l	Formats the output to be landscape-oriented.
-m	Formats the file to look like a mail folder with several messages.
-o	Formats the file to be an ordinary ASCII file.
-p *file*	Uses the specified file's prologue as the PostScript prologue file.
-s *subject*	Uses the specified subject as the new subject for the printout.
-tm	Formats the file to be used with a Time Manager personal organizer.
-ts	Formats the file to be used with a Time System International personal organizer.
-v	Shows version information.
-w *words*	Sets maximum number of words to extract from the GECOS field in `/etc/passwd`.
-?	Shows usage information. Use escape to quit when you are in `C shell`.
files...	Specifies the input file or files to format for printing.

File Name:	`ctlmp`	**Directory:**	/usr/openwin/bin/	**Type:**	External

ctlmp ucg.txt | lp	Prints ucg.txt on a PostScript printer.

cu

UNIX Shell:	All primary shells (csh, ksh, sh)
Function	Connects to a terminal on another UNIX system or even a non-UNIX system
Syntax	cu [options...] *ACTION command*

-c *device*	Uses only the entries in the /etc/uucp/Devices file `type` field.
-l *line*	Specifies a device to use for communication; overrides the default search.
-s *speed*	Sets the transmission baud rate; default is the line speed set in `/etc/uucp/Devices`.
-b *bits*	Sets transmission to either 7 or 8 bits for communication between different systems.

continued

-h	Uses half duplex communication mode.
-n	Prompts for a telephone number to dial.
-t	Uses appropriate carriage mapping when dialing an autoanswer terminal.
-d	Shows the diagnostic traces.
-o	Uses the odd parity when sending data.
-e	Uses the even parity when sending data.
-L	Uses the login chat sequence file specified in the /etc/uucp/Systems file.
-H	Ignores the first hangup.
-C *command*	Specifies the command to run on the remote host.
ACTION	**You may use one of the following actions; they may not be combined:**
systemname	Specifies system name or hostname to contact.
phoneNR	Specifies the telephone number to call.

File Name:	`cu`	**Directory:**	/usr/bin/	**Type:**	External

cu -l /dev/term/b -s 9600	Calls a system with the speed 9600 and /dev/term/b.
cu -H -l /dev/tty/b	Ignores the first hang up and connects through /dev/term/b.

deallocate

UNIX Shell: All primary shells (csh, ksh, sh)

Function	Disables access of a device for a user.
Syntax	deallocate [options...] *{ device }*

-s	Doesn't show diagnostic information.
device	Specifies a file for the device to disable; `superuser` only.
-F *device*	Specifies a file for the device to be disabled using force.
	This option can be used alone or with the `-s` option:
-I	Disables access to all available devices by force; `superuser` only.

File Name:	`deallocate`	**Directory:**	/usr/sbin/	**Type:**	External

deallocate /dev/audio	Disables access to the device /dev/audio.

delta, sccs-delta

UNIX Shell: All primary shells (csh, ksh, sh)

Function	Saves the changes made to an original SCCS file and creates a new deltaID for that version. The SCCS utilities are a programming feature that helps to keep track of changes and versions.
Syntax	delta [options...] *s.files...*

-d	Uses `diff` when comparing the old/new files instead of `bdiff`.
-n	Keeps the edited file on screen instead of removing it.
-p	Shows the differences line-by-line on the STDOUT in `diff` format.
-s	Does not show any warnings and confirmation messages.
-g *deltaIDs...*	Excludes deltaIDs from being used. DeltaIDs are separated by a comma, or a dash for a range.
-m *mrlist*	Specifies one or more modification request numbers for the new delta.
-r *deltaID*	Specifies the version to save when two or more versions are checked out.
-y *comment*	Specifies a text string to save as a comment to the version file.
files...	Specifies the file to save and create the delta for.

File Name:	`delta`	**Directory:**	/usr/ccs/bin/, /usr/xpg4/bin/	**Type:**	External
Note:	The original file must be created with the -v flag set to use the -m option.				

deroff

UNIX Shell: All primary shells (csh, ksh, sh)

Function	Removes macro calls, requests, table descriptions, and backslash constructs from the specified nroff, troff, tbl, eqn, or text files and shows the result to STDOUT.
Syntax	deroff [options...] *files...*

-mm	Disregards the text in macro lines and shows the plain text of the file to STDOUT.
-ml	The same as -mm but also deletes all lists associated with -mm macros.
-w	Shows a column containing one word per line
-i	Ignores `.so` `.nx` commands.
files...	Specifies the file or files to read and process.

continued

File Name:	deroff	Directory:	/usr/bin/	Type:	External
deroff -w /etc/passwd			Shows one word per line of the /etc/passwd file.		

devattr

UNIX Shell: All primary shells (csh, ksh, sh)

Function	Shows the attribute values for a device.
Syntax	devattr [-v] *device { attributes... }*

-v	Verbose mode. Shows attribute = value format.
device	Shows the attribute of the chosen device.
attribute	Defines the attribute that you want to see the values for. Please see the command putdev for the attributes that can be used.

File Name:	devattr	Directory:	/usr/bin/	Type:	External
devattr /dev/dsk/c0t0d0s0			Shows device attributes for s0.		
devattr -v /dev/dsk/c0t0d0s0			Shows verbose information for s0.		

devfree

UNIX Shell: All primary shells (csh, ksh, sh)

Function	Frees a device from exclusive use that was assigned exclusive use by the devreserv command.
Syntax	devfree *key { devices... }*

key	Specifies the reservation key of a device.
devices...	Specifies the device to erase the reservation from.

File Name:	devfree	Directory:	/usr/bin/	Type:	External
devfree 2222			Releases device that was reserved with key 2222.		

devinfo

UNIX Shell: All primary shells (csh, ksh, sh)

Function	Is used to show device specific and device partition information.
Syntax	devinfo option *device*

	Use only one of the following options; they can't be combined:
-i	Shows device name, drive ID, blocks per cylinder, bytes per block, and software version.
-p	Shows partition information, including the device name and partition starting block.
device	Specifies the device name to get information about.

File Name:	devinfo	Directory:	/usr/sbin/	Type:	External
devinfo -p /dev/rdsk/c0t0d0s0			Shows partition information about the raw device c0t0d0s0.		
devinfo -i /dev/rdsk/c0t0d0s0			Shows device information about the raw device c0t0d0s0.		

devlinks

UNIX Shell: All primary shells (csh, ksh, sh)

Function	Creates /dev entries for various devices by creating symbolic links between the /dev directory tree and the device nodes in the /devices tree.
Syntax	devlinks [options...]

-d	Shows debug information and specifies what links would be created.
-r *directory*	Specifies the root directory of /dev and /devices.
-t *file*	Specifies an ASCII table file to use when creating device links (default is /etc/devlink.tab).

File Name:	devlinks	Directory:	/usr/sbin/	Type:	External
devlinks -d | more			Shows debug information and sends STDOUT to more.		

devnm

UNIX Shell: All primary shells (csh, ksh, sh)

Function	Shows the location where the device is mounted.
Syntax	devnm *name { names... }*

name	Specifies a device to show information about.
names...	Specifies devices to show information about. Separate multiple devices with a space.

continued

File Name:	devnm	**Directory:**	/usr/sbin/	**Type:**	External
devnm /usr		Shows on which device /usr is mounted.			
devnm /var		Shows on which device /var is mounted.			

devreserv

UNIX Shell: All primary shells (csh, ksh, sh)

Function	Reserves devices for exclusive use. To remove the reservation, use the devfree command.
Syntax	devreserv *{ key } { lists... }*

key		Specifies a reservation key.			
lists...		Specifies a list of devices to reserve.			
File Name:	devreserv	**Directory:**	/usr/bin/	**Type:**	External
devreserv 2222 /dev/dsk/c0t0d0s0		Reserves device /dev/dsk/c0t0d0s0with key 2222.			

dfmounts

UNIX Shell: All primary shells (csh, ksh, sh)

Function	Shows information about mounted devices.
Syntax	dfmounts [options...] *{ restrictions... }*

-F *FSType*		Specifies file system type.			
-h		Suppresses header line in output.			
-o*FSoptions*		Specifies options specific to the file system available with the -F option.			
restrictions...		Restricts printout to specified NFS servers.			
File Name:	dfmounts	**Directory:**	/usr/sbin/	**Type:**	External

dfshares

UNIX Shell: All primary shells (csh, ksh, sh)

Function	Shows list of shared resources available from remote or local systems.
Syntax	dfshares [options...] [servers...]

-F *FSType*		Specifies the file system type.			
-h		Suppresses header line in output.			
-o*FSoptions*		Specifies options specific to the file system available with -F.			
server		Shows the available resources on local or remote systems.			
File Name:	dfshares	**Directory:**	/usr/sbin/	**Type:**	External
dfshares sun		Shows distributed file systems on server sun.			

dhcpagent

UNIX Shell: All primary shells (csh, ksh, sh)

Function	The client daemon for the Dynamic Host Configuration Protocol (DHCP).
Syntax	dhcpagent [options...]

-d*debug*		Specifies debug level, and enables log messages.			
-f		Runs in the foreground instead of as a daemon process.			
-l*logwarning*		Specifies warning n > 0 or log n > 1 messages.			
File Name:	dhcpagent	**Directory:**	/sbin/	**Type:**	External
dhcpagent -f		Runs dhcpagent in foreground.			

dhcpconfig

UNIX Shell: Korn shell (ksh)

Function	Starts the DHCP service configuration utility.
Syntax	dhcpconfig

File Name:	dhcpconfig	**Directory:**	/usr/sbin/	**Type:**	Script

dhcpinfo

UNIX Shell:	All primary shells (csh, ksh, sh)

Function	Shows DHCP information that is configured on your host and your network interfaces.
Syntax	dhcpinfo [options...] *ACTION*

-i *interface*	Specifies the interface to show information about.
-n *limit*	Limits number of tags to show.
ACTION	**The following actions can't be used together:**
identifier	Specifies an identifier to show information about.
name	Specifies a long name to show information about.
tag	Specifies the tag number to show information about.

File Name:	`dhcpinfo`	**Directory:**	/sbin/	**Type:**	External
Note:	You must have the dhcpagent running.				

dhcpinfo NetMask	Shows data with identifier NetMask.
dhcpinfo Subnet mask	Shows data with long name.

dhtadm

UNIX Shell:	All primary shells (csh, ksh, sh)

Function	Manages the DHCP configuration table.
Syntax	dhtadm option [options...]

-C	Creates the DHCP service configuration table, dhcptab.
-A	Creates a symbol or macro definition to the dhcptab table.
	The following options are used with –A:
-m *macroname*	Specifies a macro to create.
-d *definition*	Specifies a macro -m or symbol -s definition.
-s *symbolname*	Specifies a symbol name to create.
-D	Removes a symbol or macro definition.
	The following options are used with –D:
-m *macroname*	Specifies a macro to erase.
-s *symbolname*	Specifies a symbol to erase.
-M	Modifies symbol or macro definition.
	The following options are used with –M:
-d *definition*	Specifies a macro -m or symbol -s definition.
-e *symbol=value*	Specifies the symbol definition to create or erase.
-m *macroname*	Specifies the macro name.
-n *newname*	Specifies a new macro name.
-s *symbolname*	Specifies a symbol
-P	Shows dhcptab table.
-R	Erases the dhcptab table.
-r *resource*	Specifies the resource type to modify the `/etc/default/dhcp` configuration value.
-p *path*	Specifies the resource path to modify the `/etc/default/dhcp` configuration value.

File Name:	`dhtadm`	**Directory:**	/usr/sbin/	**Type:**	External

dhtadm -P	Shows the dhcptab table.
dhtadm -C	Creates the dhcptab table.

diffmk

UNIX Shell:	Bourne shell (sh)

Function	Compares two versions of a troff input file and then creates a third file.
Syntax	diffmk *originalfile modifiedfile comparedfile*

originalfile	Specifies the original version of the file.
modifiedfile	Specifies the modified version of the file.
comparedfile	Specifies the comparison file that is created with the changed mark request.

File Name:	`diffmk`	**Directory:**	/usr/bin/	**Type:**	Script

diffmk file1 file2 diffout	Compares file1 and file2 and outputs the differences into diffout.

dircmp

dircmp	UNIX Shell:	Korn shell (ksh)
Function	Compares two directories and shows a file list of the differences between them (unique files).	
Syntax	dircmp [options...] *path1 path2*	

-d	Compares files/directories and shows a list of changes needed to make them identical.
-s	Suppresses messages about identical files.
-w *width*	Specifies how many characters wide the list will be.
path1	Specifies the first pathname to be compared.
path2	Specifies the second pathname to compare against first pathname.
File Name: `dircmp`	**Directory:** /usr/bin/ **Type:** Script
dircmp -d /ucg_examples /ucg1	Compares directories and shows a list of changes needed.

dis

dis	UNIX Shell:	All primary shells (csh, ksh, sh)
Function	Reads an object file and creates a list of assembly statements. The binary data is shown in octal or hexadecimal.	
Syntax	dis [options...] *files...*	

-C	Shows demangled C++ symbol names in the disassembly.
-o	Shows numbers in octal values.
-V	Shows version information.
-L	Starts a search of C-language source labels in the symbol table.
-d *sec*	Specifies the section to show balance of the data.
-D *sec*	Specifies the section in which to show the address of the data.
-F *function*	Specifies the function to disassemble in each object file.
-l *string*	Specifies a string in the archive file to disassemble.
-t *sec*	Specifies a section to disassemble.
files...	Specifies an object file or an archive.
File Name: `dis`	**Directory:** /usr/ccs/bin/ **Type:** External
dis 3c90x.o	Uses dis on 3com driver.
dis /usr/bin/passwd >dispass.txt	Runs dis on binary passwd and redirects to a file.

disable

disable	UNIX Shell:	Bourne shell (sh)
Function	Disables the printer specified from receiving additional print jobs sent by using the `lp`command.	
Syntax	disable [options...] *printers...*	

-c	Cancels print requests that are currently printing. Can't be used with -w option.
-W	Waits so that any current print job can finish. Can't be used with -c option.
-r *{ reason }*	Sets the reason the printer was disabled that shows when typing `lpstat -p`.
printer	Specifies the name of printer to disable print requests for.
File Name: `disable`	**Directory:** /usr/bin/ **Type:** Script
disable print01	Disables the printer print01 to receive requests.

disks

disks	UNIX Shell:	All primary shells (csh, ksh, sh)
Function	Creates /dev entries for hard disks attached to the system.	
Syntax	disks [options...]	

-C	Removes invalid links after adding entries to `/dev/dsk` and `/dev/rdsk`.
-r *rootdir*	Sets new root directory for `/dev/dsk, /dev/rdsk`, and `/devices`.
File Name: `disks`	**Directory:** /usr/sbin **Type:** External
Tip:	First run drvconfig to ensure that /devices is consistent with the current device configuration.

dispadmin

dispadmin	UNIX Shell:	All primary shells (csh, ksh, sh)
Function	Shows or changes the parameters of the process scheduler on a running system.	
Syntax	dispadmin -l dispadmin -c *class* -g [-r *res*] dispadmin -c *class* -s *file*	

continued

-l -c *class* -s *file* -g -r *res*	Shows currently configured scheduler classes in the system. Specifies the class parameters to show or change . Valid values are: RT, TS, and IA. Uses the values in file to set scheduler parameters for the specified class. Takes and writes the parameters for the specified class to STDOUT. Specifies the resolution to be used for the time quantum values to the output.
File Name: `dispadmin`	**Directory:** /usr/sbin/ **Type:** External
Warning:	Be careful when changing scheduler parameters; it could affect the performance of the system.
dispadmin -c RT -g -r 1000000	Retrieves parameters for real-time class from kernel.
dispadmin -c TS -g	Retrieves parameters for the time-sharing class.

dispgid

UNIX Shell: All primary shells (csh, ksh, sh)

Function	Shows a list of all the available groups that are defined on the system, one group per line.
Syntax	dispgid
File Name: `dispgid`	**Directory:** /usr/bin/ **Type:** External

dispuid

UNIX Shell: All primary shells (csh, ksh, sh)

Function	Shows a simple list of all valid usernames on the system, one line per name.
Syntax	dispuid
File Name: `dispuid`	**Directory:** /usr/bin/ **Type:** External

dmesg

UNIX Shell: All primary shells (csh, ksh, sh)

Function	Shows diagnostic messages on STDOUT.
Syntax	dmesg [-]
-	Only shows new messages since the last time dmesg was run.
File Name: `dmesg`	**Directory:** /usr/bin/ **Type:** External

dminfo

UNIX Shell: All primary shells (csh, ksh, sh)

Function	Shows updates and information about a device in the `device_maps` file.
Syntax	dminfo [options...] option
-v -a -f *pathname* -n *dev-name* -d *dev-path* -t *dev-type* -u *dm-entry*	Verbose mode. Shows more information. Works only if the requested entries are found. Uses a device_maps file with pathname instead of `/etc/security/device_maps`. **The following options can't be combined:** Specifies device name to find in `device_maps`. Specifies pathname to find in `device_maps`. Specifies device type to find in `device_maps`. Specifies the `device_maps` file to update.
File Name: `dminfo`	**Directory:** /usr/sbin/ **Type:** External
Note:	You have to enable the Basic Security Module (BSM).

docviewer

UNIX Shell: All primary shells (csh, ksh, sh)

Function	An X window application used to view Answer Book online documentation.
Syntax	docviewer -d *document-name* -p *tooltalk-procid* [-c *card-catalog-file*]
-d *document-name* -p *tooltalk-procID* -c *card-catalog-file*	Specifies the name of the document to be viewed. Specifies the tooltalk process ID executing the docviewer. Specifies the filename for the card catalog file that is needed to find AnswerBooks.
File Name: `docviewer`	**Directory:** /usr/openwin/bin/ **Type:** External

dodisk

dodisk	UNIX Shell: All primary shells (csh, ksh, sh)
Function	Runs disk accounting functions and is normally started by the `cron` command.
Syntax	dodisk -o *{ files... }*
-o	Uses the `acctdusg` to perform accounting on the login directory (slower).
files...	Runs accounting on the specified file systems only.
File Name: `dodisk`	**Directory:** /usr/lib/acct — **Type:** External
dodisk /usr/ucg	Specifies the /usr/ucg directory to be used for disk accounting.

dos2unix

dos2unix	UNIX Shell: All primary shells (csh, ksh, sh)
Function	Converts text files from DOS format into the ISO standard format. With this you can import your old DOS textfiles.
Syntax	dos2unix [options...] *file1 file2*
-ascii	Removes extra carriage returns and converts EOF characters from DOS to SunOS.
-iso	Converts DOS extended character set to the match the ISO.
-7	Converts 8-bit DOS graphics characters to 7-bit space characters.
file1	Specifies the text file in the DOS format.
file2	Specifies the name of the converted file.
File Name: `dos2unix`	**Directory:** /usr/sbin/ — **Type:** External
dos2unix dosfile ISOfile	Converts dosfile to an ISO standard file.

download

download	UNIX Shell: All primary shells (csh, ksh, sh)
Function	Adds host resident fonts to files, and shows results on the STDOUT.
Syntax	download [options...] *{ files... }*
-f	Forces a scan to be completed; ignores comments in input file.
-p *printer*	Checks for printer-resident fonts in `/etc/lp/printers/printer/residentfonts`.
-m *name*	Specifies the font map table.
-H *directory*	Specifies the host font directory. Default is `/usr/lib/lp/postscript.`
files...	Specifies pathname of the host resident fonts.
File Name: `download`	**Directory:** /usr/lib/lp/postscript/ — **Type:** External

dpost

dpost	UNIX Shell: All primary shells (csh, ksh, sh)
Function	Converts files that have been created by `troff` into PostScript files and shows the result on STDOUT.
Syntax	dpost [options...] *{ files... }*
-c *num*	Specifies how many copies you want of each page.
-e *num*	Specifies the encoding level.
-m *num*	Specifies the magnify factor to use on each logical page.
-n *num*	Specifies how many logical pages to show on each piece of paper.
-o *list*	Specifies pages to print, in a comma-separated list.
-p *mode*	Prints files in portrait or landscape mode.
-w *num*	Specifies line width for `troff` graphics.
-x *num*	Moves the origin position to the specified inch distance along the positive x-axis.
-y *num*	Moves the origin position to the specified inch distance along the positive y-axis.
-F *dir*	Specifies the font directory.
-H *dir*	Specifies the host-resident font directory.
-L *file*	Specifies the PostScript prologue.
-O	Suppresses PostScript picture inclusion.
-T *name*	Specifies font files as description of PostScript fonts.
files...	Specifies `troff` files to convert into PostScript.
File Name: `dpost`	**Directory:** /usr/lib/lp/postscript/ — **Type:** External
Note:	Output files don't usually conform to Adobe's file structuring conventions.

drvconfig

UNIX Shell: All primary shells (csh, ksh, sh)

Function	Configures the /devices directory.
Syntax	drvconfig [options...]

-b	Adds a new major number to name binding in the kernel.
-n	Doesn't load or attach any drivers.
-a *alias*	Adds an alias to the driver.
-c *class*	The driver being added to the system exports the specified class.
-i *driver*	Only configures the devices for the specified driver.
-m *major*	Specifies major number for driver to add to the kernel's name_to_major binding.
-r *rootdir*	Builds the device tree under the specified path instead of /devices.

File Name: `drvconfig` **Directory:** /usr/sbin/ **Type:** External

Tip: Often used before the command `disks` to add disks without reboot.

ds_server_init

UNIX Shell: All primary shells (csh, ksh, sh)

Function	Reduces color map flashing within applications that require colors by restricting applications to use colors.
Syntax	ds_server_init [options...]

-f *filename*	Specifies the filename that contains the colors.
-a	Forces the allocation of the DeskSet colors at the time ds_server_init starts.

File Name: `ds_server_init` **Directory:** /usr/openwin/bin/ **Type:** External

Note: $OPENWINHOME/share/xnews/client/ds_server_init/ds_colors.txt contains DeskSet colors.

dsdm

UNIX Shell: All primary shells (csh, ksh, sh)

Function	Manages drag-and-drop operations in an X window environment for databases.
Syntax	dsdm [-x]

-x	Stops managing the database and sets the owner of the _SUN_DRAGDROP_DSDM to None.

File Name: `dsdm` **Directory:** /usr/openwin/bin/ **Type:** External

dtaction

UNIX Shell: All primary shells (csh, ksh, sh)

Function	Allows non-CDE applications and shell scripts to be run in the X window environment.
Syntax	dtaction [options...] *actionname { actionargs... }*

-contextDir *dir*	Specifies the current working directory for the application or script.
-execHost *hostname*	Specifies the hostname or IP address for the server that will run the application.
-termOpts *argument*	Specifies any necessary arguments for the application or script.
-user *username*	Specifies the username to run the application. Runs as current user by default.
actionname	Specifies an action to use. Described in the `dtactionfile manual page.`
actionargs...	Specifies arguments to the action. Described in the `dtactionfile manual page.`

File Name: `dtaction` **Directory:** /usr/dt/bin/ **Type:** External

dtbuilder

UNIX Shell: All primary shells (csh, ksh, sh)

Function	Makes it easier for developers to create applications that work well in the CDE.
Syntax	dtbuilder *{ projectfile }*

projectfile	Specifies the project file to load and edit.

File Name: `dtbuilder` **Directory:** /usr/dt/bin/ **Type:** External

dtchooser

UNIX Shell: All primary shells (csh, ksh, sh)

Function	Allows the user to choose host to login to. Is used by `dtlogin` and isn't intended to run manually.
Syntax	dtchooser

File Name: `dtchooser` **Directory:** /usr/dt/bin/ **Type:** External

dtcodegen

UNIX Shell:	All primary shells (csh, ksh, sh)
Function	Creates C, Motif, and CDE source code files from Builder Interface Language (BIL) files.
Syntax	dtcodegen [options...] *files...*

-changed	Creates only source code for the modules that have been changed since last run.
-help	Shows help information.
-main	Keeps the application's main routine and its associated files.
-merge	Merges created files with the existing files.
-nomerge	Does not merge old and new files.
-module *module*	Creates code for specified module; which is expected to be defined in *module*.bil.
-p *project*	Creates code for specified project; which is expected to be defined in *project*.bip.
-noproject	Ignores the project file and uses default project settings instead.
-showall	Shows all application windows at startup, even those that are set invisible.
-noshowall	Shows only the application windows that are visible by default at startup.
-s	Works silently. Only shows error messages when creating source code.
-v	Verbose mode. Shows more information.
files...	Specifies the module or project file.

File Name:	`dtcodegen`	**Directory:**	/usr/dt/bin/	**Type:**	External

dtconfig

UNIX Shell:	Korn shell (ksh)
Function	Integrates CDE with the operating system.
Syntax	dtconfig [option]

-d	Disables desktop auto-start.
-e	Enables desktop auto-start.
-kill	Stops desktop login process and any user sessions associated with it.
-reset	Reads configuration files to add any changes.
-p	Creates printer actions for any known printer on platform.
-inetd	Adds `/usr/dt/bin daemons` to the `/etc/inetd.conf` file.
-inetd.ow	Changes the tooltalk and calendar manager daemons start lines in `/etc/inetd.conf` back to the older `/usr/openwin/bin` area.

File Name:	`dtconfig`	**Directory:**	/usr/dt/bin/	**Type:**	Script

dtconvertvf

UNIX Shell:	Korn shell (ksh)
Function	Converts VUE 3.0 action file-type database files into CDE 1.0 format. For the files to be recognized by CDE, the files must be named with .dt extension.
Syntax	dtconvertvf

File Name:	`dtconvertvf`	**Directory:**	/usr/dt/bin/	**Type:**	Script

cat file.vf | dtconvertvf > file.dt	Converts file.vf to the new file.dt.

dtcreate

UNIX Shell:	All primary shells (csh, ksh, sh)
Function	Creates actions and data types used to integrate applications into the CDE.
Syntax	dtcreate [option]

	The following options can't be combined:
-help	Shows help information.
-session *sessionfile*	Specifies the session file to execute.
file	Specifies filename to modify in `dtcreate`.

File Name:	`dtcreate`	**Directory:**	/usr/dt/bin/	**Type:**	External

dterror.ds

UNIX Shell:	Korn shell (ksh)
Function	Shows error messages from applications or actions that can't be shown in the context of the executable program.
Syntax	dterror.ds *messagetext messagetext buttonlabel*

messagetext	Specifies text to show in the dialog box.

continued

dialogtitle *buttonlabel*		Specifies text on the title bar. Specifies text on the button.			
File Name:	dterror.ds	**Directory:**	/usr/dt/bin/	**Type:**	Script
Note:	This script is used by several system actions to display error dialogs or event notices.				
dterror.ds "System crash" WARNING OK			Shows a dialogue box with System crash.		
dterror.ds "Universal Command Guide"			Shows a dialogue box with Universal Command Guide.		

dtexec

UNIX Shell: All primary shells (csh, ksh, sh)

Function	Executes command actions. Is mostly used by the CDE and should not be started by users.
Syntax	dtexec [options...] *command { commandargs... }*

-open *suboption*		Specifies whether action should continue to run or exit after the command terminates.			
-1		Continues to execute after the command stops (default).			
0		Exits when the command stops.			
seconds		Continues if the command stops before specified seconds.			
-ttprocid *PID*		Specifies the PID to send status messages to, which is usually the program that executed it.			
-tmp *file*		Specifies a temporary file that is removed when the command stops.			
command		Specifies the command to execute.			
commndargs...		Specifies the arguments for the command to execute.			
File Name:	dtexec	**Directory:**	/usr/dt/bin/	**Type:**	External

dtfile

UNIX Shell: All primary shells (csh, ksh, sh)

Function	The CDE file manager. It is used to view and manage the file system.
Syntax	dtfile [options...]

-noview	The Server mode. Shows a window only when client wants to show a folder.
-standalone	Runs with process attributes that are different from the server that run -noview.
-session *sessionfile*	Specifies a session file to run with.
-folder *folders...*	Specifies folders separated by commas to show a window for each folder.
-dir *folder*	The same as -folder.
-restricted	Doesn't show folders above the restricted folder.
-reuse	Opens new windows for the specified folders.
-grid *action*	Specifies the grid; action is on or off
-tree *action*	Specifies the tree; action is on or off.
-title *title*	Specifies the title bar.
-help_volume *helpvolumename*	Specifies help volume to use with File Manager.
-tree_files *action*	Specifies if files will be shown in the folder tree mode.
	Here are the 3 available actions:
never	Never shows files.
always	Always shows files.
choose	Enables user to choose if files are to be shown.
-order *ordertype*	Specifies the order to show files.
	Here are the available types to show files:
alphabetical	Shows files alphabetically.
file_type	Show files by file types together.
date	Show files in order that is based on date files were last modified.
size	Shows files in order by their size.
-view *viewtype*	Shows files in specified format.
	Here are the view types to specify with -view:
no_icon	Shows files by their name.
large_icon	Shows files by name and with a large icon (default).
small_icon	Shows files by name and with a small icon.
attributes	Shows files by their attributes.
-direction *direction*	Specifies the direction to show files in.

continued

	Then use these values as directions:
ascending	Shows files in the ascending direction (default).
descending	Shows files in the descending direction.
-small_icon_width *size*	Specifies the small icon height in pixels (default is 24 pixels).
-large_icon_width *size*	Specifies the large icon width in pixels (default is 38 pixels).
-large_icon_height *size*	Specifies the large icon height in pixels (default is 38 pixels).
File Name: dtfile	**Directory:** /usr/dt/bin/ **Type:** External

dtfile_copy

UNIX Shell: All primary shells (csh, ksh, sh)

Function	Copies folders and subfolders with their content to the target folder. It deletes a file in the target folder if that file doesn't exist in the source folder.
Syntax	dtfile_copy [options...] *sourcedir targetdir*

-dontDoIt	Writes description of the actions that would be done but doesn't modify.
-keepNew	Does not replace the target if it exists.
-keepOld	Renames target if it exists.
-dontDelete	Keeps object if it exists in target folder but not in source folder.
-dontAdd	Keeps object if it exists in source folder but not in target folder.
-dontReplace	Does not replace object if it exists in both target and source folders.
-dontRecur	Works only with files in the source folders and ignores the subdirectories.
-keepLinks	Keeps link if it is a symbolic link.
-keepCopies	Keeps the target file if it is a symbolic link.
-forceCopies	Copies source object even if the same target object exists.
-linkFolders	Creates a symbolic link in target directory that points to the source directory.
-linkFiles	Creates a symbolic link of the source file in the target destination.
-copyFolders	Copies the source folder that a link refers to instead of copying the link.
-copyFiles	Copies the source file that a link refers to instead of copying the link.
-copyTop	Creates target folder.
-move	Moves the source folder to the target folder.
-confirmReplace	Shows a dialog of a choice if the source and target object exist.
-confirmErrors	Prompts the user for a choice if an error occurs during the operation.
-popDown	Removes the dialog after specified delay option.
-delay	Specifies in microseconds how long to show dialog after operation is done.
-slow	Pauses between each file operation.
sourcedir	Specifies the directory to copy.
targetdir	Specifies where to copy the directory.
File Name: dtfile_copy	**Directory:** /usr/dt/bin/ **Type:** External
dtfile_copy /etc /etc_new	Creates a copy of the contents in /etc named /etc_new.

dtfile_error

UNIX Shell: Korn shell (ksh)

Function	Shows an error dialog based on the specified message.
Syntax	dtfile_error *message*

message	Specifies the message to show in the dialog.
File Name: dtfile_error	**Directory:** /usr/dt/bin/ **Type:** Script
Tip:	Perfect for debugging and error messages in applications or scripts, no additional code is needed.
dtfile_error File not found.	Shows a dialog with an OK button and the message "File not found."

dtksh

UNIX Shell: Korn shell (ksh)

Function	This is a CDE-extended version of the Korn shell. It gives access to many X, Xt, Xm, and CDE functions.
Syntax	dtksh [options...] *{ arguments... }*

-i	Makes the shell interactive. TERMINATE, INTERRUPT, and QUIT are ignored.
-s	Reads commands from STDIN.

continued

	The following options can also be modified with the set command in a script:
-a	Marks modified and created variables for export.
-b	Informs the user asynchronously when a background job completes.
-C	Does not allow existing files to be overwritten by shell > redirection operator.
-e	If a command returns a non-zero exit status, then run the ERR trap and exit.
-f	Disables filename generation.
-h	When a command is first encountered, it becomes a tracked alias.
-k	Places all keywords arguments in the environment for a command.
-m	Runs background job in separate process group. Shows a line when completed.
-n	Reads commands but doesn't run them.
-p	Does not process $HOME/.profile.
-u	Handles parameters currently unset as an error when replacing variables.
-v	Shows input lines as they are read.
-x	Shows commands and their arguments when they are executed.
-o *{ option }*	Sets one of the following flags:
allexport	The same as -a.
errexit	The same as -e.
bgnice	Runs background job at lower priority. This is the default.
emacs	Uses an emacs style in-line editor for the command line.
gmacs	Uses a gmacs style in-line editor for the command line.
ignoreeof	Does not let the shell exit on EOF. The `exit` command must be used.
keyword	The same as -k.
markdirs	Marks all directories with a trailing / for result from a filename generation.
monitor	The same as -m.
noclobber	The same as -C.
noexec	The same as -n.
noglob	The same as -f.
nolog	Does not save function definition in the history file.
notify	Is equivalent to -b.
nounset	The same as -u.
privileged	The same as -p.
verbose	The same as -v.
trackall	The same as -h.
vi	Uses a vi style in-line editor for the command line.
viraw	Processes each character as it is typed in vi mode.
xtrace	The same as –x.
-	Turns off -x and -v flags and doesn't continue to examine arguments for flags.
--	Does not change any flags. (If + is used instead of - the flag is turned on.)
arguments...	Specifies additional arguments for the shell or a script with arguments to run.

File Name:	`dtksh`	**Directory:**	/usr/dt/bin/	**Type:**	External

dtlp

UNIX Shell: Korn shell (ksh)

Function	Prints out a file specified. A command-line front-end to `lp`.
Syntax	dtlp [options...] *{ file }*

-b *bannertitle*	Specifies the banner on the title page.
-d *lpdest*	Specifies printer destination for a file.
-n *copycount*	Specifies number of copies to print (default is 1).
-m *printcommand*	Specifies a pathname for the lp command (default is lp).
-u *userfilename*	Specifies how the filename appears in dialog or the print output.
-a	Formats the file with the man command.
-e	Removes file after it is printed.
-h	Shows help information.
-r	Formats the file before printing it.
-s	Specifies silent mode. Prints the file and suppresses dialog when done.

continued

-v -w -o *options...* *file*		Verbose mode. Shows more information. Sends raw output to the printer. Passes other options directly to the print command. For advanced users. Specifies the file to save to.			
File Name:	`dtlp`	**Directory:**	/usr/dt/bin/	**Type:**	Script
dtlp -n 2 doc1			Prints out two copies of doc1 to the default printer.		

dtmail

UNIX Shell: All primary shells (csh, ksh, sh)

Function	A mail utility to read, send, and manage mail. It supports MIME and Sun Mail Tool message formats, as well as IMAP4, to access remote mailboxes.
Syntax	dtmail [options...]

-c -h -f *{ server: } { mailfile }* -l *deadletter* -a *file1...fileN* -T *address*		Opens a new `Compose` window. Shows help information. Specifies the mail file to load with the utility. Specifies an incomplete letter to load when opening the Compose window. Specifies file1 through fileN as attachments to a Compose window. Specifies the address to send to when opening a Compose window.			
File Name:	`dtmail`	**Directory:**	/usr/dt/bin/	**Type:**	External

dtpad

UNIX Shell: All primary shells (csh, ksh, sh)

Function	Edits text files in the CDE environment.
Syntax	dtpad [options...] *{ file }*

-saveOnClose -missingFileWarning -noReadOnlyWarning -noNameChange -viewOnly -statusLine -wrapToFit -workspaceList *workspacelist...* -session *sessionfile* -standAlone -noBlocking -server -exitOnLastClose *file*		Saves changes when exiting. Shows a warning if a specified file doesn't exist. Disables warning if a specified file has read-only permission. Does not change default filename when text is saved under a different filename. Enables read-only mode. Shows a status line at the bottom of the editor. Enables the on wrap-to-fit mode. Specifies workspace(s) to start the edit window with. Restores settings to all editing windows from previous CDE shutdown. Forces the editor to do text processing in its own window. Stops the editor request if the text editor server can handle the edit request. Starts a text editor server to process all edits for the screen. Stops the text editor server when all edit windows for the screen are closed. Specifies a file to edit.			
File Name:	`dtpad`	**Directory:**	/usr/dt/bin/	**Type:**	External

dtpower

UNIX Shell: All primary shells (csh, ksh, sh)

Function	Manages system power.
Syntax	dtpower [options...]

toolarguments -nobell -sampletime *n* -st *n*		Accepts any xview generic tool arguments. Turns off the signal. **The following options can't be combined:** Sets the battery check interval in seconds. Sets the battery check interval in seconds.			
File Name:	`dtpower`	**Directory:**	/usr/dt/bin/	**Type:**	External

dtprintinfo

UNIX Shell: All primary shells (csh, ksh, sh)

Function	Shows the print queue and print job status.
Syntax	dtprintinfo [options...]
-p *printer*	Shows the information for a specified printer.

continued

-all	Shows the information for all printers.
-populate	Creates the default events for all printers in `/etc/dt/appconfig/types/LANG`.
-help	Shows help information.
-session *session file*	Specifies which file to save your settings to.

File Name:	`dtprintinfo`	**Directory:**	/usr/dt/bin/	**Type:**	External

dtprintinfo -p lp0	Shows the status of the print queue called `lp0`.
dtprintinfo -all	Shows the status of all print queues.

dtscreen

UNIX Shell: All primary shells (csh, ksh, sh)

Function	The CDE screen saver utility.
Syntax	dtscreen [options...]

-display *dsp*	Specifies the screen on which to animate the screen saver.
-delay *usecs*	Specifies the speed of a screen saver animation.
-batchcount *num*	Specifies number of things to do per batch.
-saturation *value*	Specifies the color span; 0 = grayscale, 1 = very rich color.
-nice *nicelevel*	Specifies the priority level of the process.
-create	Creates its own window ID for the process.
-help	Shows help information.
-resources	Shows the default values of the main resources for customizing.
-mode *mode*	Sets which animation to use.
hop	Shows hopalong iterated fractals.
life	Shows `Conway's game of life.`
qix	Shows spinning lines.
image	Shows random bouncing image.
swarm	Shows a swarm of bees.
rotor	Shows a rotor.
pyro	Shows fireworks.
flame	Shows `Cosmic Flame Fractals.`
worm	Shows `Wiggly Worms.`
random	Shows random animations.

File Name:	`dtscreen`	**Directory:**	/usr/dt/bin/	**Type:**	External

dtscreen -mode qix -create	Starts screensaver in qix mode.

dtsearchpath

UNIX Shell: All primary shells (csh, ksh, sh)

Function	Sets the search paths for where the desktop is to look for application manager groups, file types, and action definitions.
Syntax	dtsearchpath [options...]

-u *username*	Reports the search path for the specified username.
-v	Verbose mode. Shows more information.
-o	Forces it to add a path to the search path even if there is no existing path.
-csh	Shows the search values used by a C-shell script.
-ksh	Shows the search values used by a Korn- or Bourne-shell script (the default).

File Name:	`dtsearchpath`	**Directory:**	/usr/dt/bin/	**Type:**	External

dtsearchpath -u root	Returns root's search path.

dtstyle

UNIX Shell: All primary shells (csh, ksh, sh)

Function	Manages desktop styles.
Syntax	dtstyle

File Name:	`dtstyle`	**Directory:**	/usr/dt/bin/	**Type:**	External

dtterm

UNIX Shell:	All primary shells (csh, ksh, sh)
Function	Emulates a screen window. *VALUE* is always a minus (-) or a plus (+) symbol. Default is always the plus symbol except when using the -aw, -J, or -sb option.
Syntax	dtterm [options...]

*VALUE*132	Allows/disallows DECCOLM escape sequence to switch between 80- and 132-column mode.
*VALUE*aw	Allows (default) or disallows auto-wraparound.
-bg *color*	Specifies the standard background color for the screen.
-background *color*	The same as -bg.
*VALUE*bs	Uses or doesn't use the Motif select color for the background color.
-C	Redirects output from /dev/console to this screen.
-display *display name*	Specifies which X11 server to connect to.
-e *program args*	Specifies a program and its arguments to execute in the terminal.
-fb *fontset*	Specifies the Motif fontset to be used as bold font; supports only character fonts.
-fg *color*	Sets the standard foreground color for the screen.
-fn *fontset*	Specifies the Motif fontset to be used for normal output.
-geometry *geometry string*	Sets the preferred size of the screen in lines and columns (default is 24/80).
-help	Shows help information.
*VALUE*iconic	Shows or doesn't show the screen in iconified state.
*VALUE*j	Does (default) or doesn't enable jump scrolling.
*VALUE*kshMode	Enables or disables use of ksh style extended key mode; mostly used by emacs.
*VALUE*l	Enables or disables (default) output logging.
-lf *filename*	Specifies logfile for output logging; a pipe can be used to specify piping to a command.
*VALUE*ls	Reads or doesn't read system and user profile and/or login files (login shell mode).
*VALUE*map	Does or doesn't de-iconify screens on screen output.
*VALUE*mb	Does or doesn't sound the bell when the user nears the right margin of the screen.
-ms *color*	Specifies a color for the mouse pointer within the screen.
-name *string*	Specifies the X11 name of the screen.
-nb *number*	Specifies the number of characters for the right margin in the -mb option.
*VALUE*rw	Enables or disables reverse-wraparound.
-S*ccn*	Uses the last two characters of the pty device for `cc` and `n` is the descriptor number.
-S*c.n*	Uses the last component of the pty device name for `c` and `n` is the descriptor number.
*VALUE*sb	Enables (default) or disables scroll bar.
*VALUE*sf	Uses or doesn't use Sun escape sequences instead of ANSI escape sequences.
-sl *length*[s]	Specifies the length of buffer beyond the screen. The s specifies it to be length +1.
-ti *screen type*	Specifies the screen type; valid values are vt100, vt101, vt102, and vt220 (default).
-title *string*	Specifies the title of the X11 screen.
-tm *settings*	Specifies the settings of the screen; overrides the standard settings.
-tn *name*	Specifies the TERM variable within the screen (default is dtterm).
-usage	Shows a usage message.
*VALUE*vb	Uses or doesn't use a visual bell.
-xrm string	Specifies an X11 resource manager string on the command line.

File Name:	`dtterm`	**Directory:**	/usr/dt/bin/	**Type:**	External
Note:	Expert mind required, mere mortals would simply use: dtterm -sb -sl 1000.				

dtterm -sb -sl 1000	Opens a dtterm with a scroll bar and good-size scroll buffer.
dtterm -fg white -bg black	Sets the text to white and the background to black.

dtwm

UNIX Shell:	All primary shells (csh, ksh, sh)
Function	The CDE Window manager, which is based on the OSF/Motif window manager mwm.
Syntax	dtwm [options...]

-display *display*	Specifies the display to use.
-xrm *string*	Specifies a resource string to use.
-multiscreen	Manages all screens on the display.
-name name	Retrieves its named resources.

continued

-screens *names...*	Specifies the resource name or names to use for the screens.			
File Name:	`dtwm`	**Directory:** /usr/dt/bin/	**Type:**	External
Note:	This command is normally started by `dtsession`, and should not be typed in manually.			

dump

UNIX Shell: All primary shells (csh, ksh, sh)

Function	Takes selected parts of the object file arguments and dumps them.
Syntax	dump [options...] *file*

-a	Specifies to dump the archive header of each archive member.
-c	Dumps the string table.
-C	Specifies to dump the decoded C++ symbol table names.
-D	Dumps debugging information.
-f	Dumps the file header for each file.
-g	Dumps the global symbols in the archive symbol table.
-h	Dumps the section headers.
-l	Dumps line number information.
-L	Dumps static shared library information and dynamic linking information.
-o	Dumps each program's execution headers.
-r	Dumps relocation information.
-s	Dumps section contents in hexadecimal.
-t	Dumps symbol table entries.
-T *index*	Dumps specified symbol table entries.
-T *index1,index2*	Dumps a range of specified symbol table entries.
-V	Shows version information.
	The following options can be used with the above options to alter their capabilities.
-d *number*	Dumps the section number.
-d *number1,number2*	Dumps the range of section numbers, begins and ends with the numbers given.
-n *name*	Specifies the entity in which the information pertaining to that entity should be dumped.
-p	Represses the showing of the headings.
-v	Specifies to dump in symbolic representation instead of numeric.
file	Specifies the filename to dump to.

File Name:	`dump`	**Directory:** /usr/ccs/bin/	**Type:**	External
Note:	The dump attempts to format the information it dumps in a meaningful way.			

/usr/ccs/bin/dump -h /bin/ls	Shows section headers for ls.
/usr/ccs/bin/dump -o /bin/find	Shows the execution header for find.

dumpadm

UNIX Shell: All primary shells (csh, ksh, sh)

Function	Configures the crash dump of the operating system.
Syntax	dumpadm [options...]

-n	Does not run savecore on reboot.
-u	Updates the kernel dump configuration in /etc/dumpadm.conf.
-y	Enables savecore to run on reboot.
-c *contenttype*	Specifies dump content to add. Content type can be either kernel or all.
kernel	Dumps kernel memory pages.
all	Adds all memory pages.
-d *dumpdevice*	Specifies which dump device to use. It can be either a device or swap.
device	Specifies a pathname to a dump device.
swap	Uses swap as the dump device.
-m *space ACTION*	Specifies a minimum of free space that the system can use to save core files.
ACTION	**The following actions can be used to set minimum free space.**
k	Creates free space with kilobytes of free space.
m	Creates free space with megabytes of free space.
%	Creates free space with percentage of free space.

continued

-r *rootdir* -s *savedir*		Specifies an alternate rootdir where dumpfile is created. Specifies directory where to save savecore files.			
File Name:	dumpadm	**Directory:**	/usr/sbin/	**Type:**	External
Note:	This is useful if the system crashes.				
dumpadm -y		Runs savecore automatically on reboot			
dumpadm -n		Does not run savecore automatically on reboot.			

dumpcs

UNIX Shell: All primary shells (csh, ksh, sh)

Function	Shows the printable characters of the current locale.
Syntax	dumpcs [options...]

-0 -1 -2 -3 -v -w		Shows ASCII codeset. Shows EUC codeset 1. Shows EUC codeset 2. Shows EUC codeset 3. Verbose mode. Shows more information. Replaces code values with the corresponding wide character values.			
File Name:	dumpcs	**Directory:**	/usr/bin/	**Type:**	External
dumpcs -0		Shows the ASCII codeset.			

dumpkeys

UNIX Shell: All primary shells (csh, ksh, sh)

Function	Shows the contents of the keyboard translation tables on STDOUT.
Syntax	dumpkeys

File Name:	dumpkeys	**Directory:**	/usr/bin/	**Type:**	External

edit

UNIX Shell: All primary shells (csh, ksh, sh)

Function	A line-based text editor for casual users. It works like `ex` with novice, report, and showmode set to `on`.
Syntax	edit [options...] *file*

-s -l -L -R -r *file* -t *tag* -v -V -x -w*n* -C -c *command*		Suppresses all interactive user feedback. Useful in scripts. Edits LISP programs. Shows the name of all files saved as the result of an editor or system crash. Starts in read-only mode. Prevents overwriting a file by accident. Opens filename in the editor after an editor or system crash. Opens the file and positions the editor at the position for tag. Uses the vi editor. Verbose mode. Shows more information. Uses encryption and attempts to determine whether or not the file is encrypted. Sets the default window size to `n`. Uses encryption but assumes that the text is encrypted. Executes the editor command after the file is read.			
File Name:	edit	**Directory:**	/usr/bin/	**Type:**	External
edit -v /etc/hosts		Edits the /etc/hosts file in vi mode.			
edit -v -R /etc/passwd		Opens the /etc/passwd in vi mode and as read-only.			

eeprom

UNIX Shell: Bourne shell (sh)

Function	Shows or changes the values of parameters in the EEPROM.
Syntax	eeprom [options...] [parameter [=value]]

- -f *device* -I *mmu-modlist*	Reads parameters and values from STDIN. Specifies the device to use as the EEPROM device. Initializes boot properties; only used on x86-based systems. Creates a list of modules that manage memory for `x86` systems.

continued

	The following are `OpenBoot` NVRAM configuration parameters:
auto-boot?	Boots the system automatically after power-on or reset (default is true).
ansi-terminal?	Defines whether the terminal emulator interprets ANSI escape sequences (default is true).
boot-command	Specifies the command executed if auto-boot? is true (default is boot).
boot-device	Specifies which device to boot from (default is disk net).
boot-file	Specifies the file to boot (default is empty string).
boot-from	Specifies the boot device and file. Used only in OpenBoot 1.x (default is vmunix).
boot-from-diag	Specifies the diagnostic boot device and filename (default is le()unix).
com*X*-noprobe	Prevents device probing on serial port specified by `X`.
diag-device	Specifies the device for the diagnostic boot device (default is network).
diag-file	Specifies the boot file to execute when booting in diagnostic mode.
diag-level	Specifies diagnostic level. Possible values are: include off, min, max, and menus.
diag-switch?	Specifies to run in the diagnostic mode if value is set to true (default is true).
fcode-debug?	Includes the parameter names for plug-in device FCodes (default is false).
hardware-revision	Shows system version information.
input-device	Specifies input device to be used when turning the system on (default is keyboard).
keyboard-click?	Enables or disables keyboard click sound. If true, click is enabled (default is false).
keymap	Specifies a customized keyboard mapping.
last-hardware-update	Shows the last time the hardware was updated.
load-base	Defines the default loading address that client programs use (default is 16384).
local-mac-address?	Specifies whether network card drivers use their own MAC address (default is false).
mfg-mode	Specifies manufacturing mode argument off, chamber for POST (default is off).
mfg-switch?	Repeats self tests on system until interrupted with STOP-A (default is false).
nvramrc	Specifies the contents of NVRAMRC (default is empty).
oem-banner	Specifies a customized OEM banner (default is empty string).
oem-banner?	Shows the OEM banner if there is one (default is false).
oem-logo	Specifies a customized byte array; OEM logo shown in hexadecimal format.
oem-logo?	Shows the custom OEM logo if it exists (default is false).
output-device	Specifies the default output device used when powered on (default is screen). (These configuration parameters are dependent on the PROM version.)
sbus-probe-list	Specifies the SBus slots to probe as well as the order (default is 0123).
screen-#columns	Specifies the number of columns that appear on the screen (default is 80).
screen-#rows	Specifies the number of rows that appear on the screen (default is 34).
scsi-initiator-id	Configures the SCSI bus address for the host adapter. The range is 0 to 7 (default is 7).
sd-targets	Maps SCSI disk units' `OpenBoot ver 1.x only` (default is 31204567).
security-#badlogins	Shows the number of failed login attempts.
security-mode	Specifies firmware security level of none, command, or full (default is none).
security-password	Specifies the firmware password if security mode is set to command or full.
selftest-#megs	Specifies the MB of RAM to test. Ignored if diag-switch? is true (default is 1).
skip-vme-loopback?	Specifies whether POST should perform VMEbus loopback tests (default is false).
st-targets	Maps SCSI tape units `OpenBoot ver 1.x only` (default is 45670123).
sunmon-compat?	Shows the restricted monitor prompt `(>)` (default is false).
testarea	Creates a 1-byte working area for read-and-write tests (default is 0).
tpe-link-test?	Enables the link test for the built-in 10baseT Ethernet adapter. (default is true).
ttya-mode	Defines `baud rate, # of bits, parity, # of stops, and handshake` (default is 9600,8,n,1,-).
ttyb-mode	Defines `baud rate, # of bits, parity, # of stops, and handshake` (default is 9600,8,n,1,-).
ttya-ignore-cd	Specifies the OS will ignore carrier detect on ttya (default is true).
ttyb-ignore-cd	Specifies the OS will ignore carrier detect on ttyb (default is true).
ttya-rts-dtr-off	Specifies the OS will not declare DTR and RTS on ttya (default is false).
ttyb-rts-dtr-off	Specifies the OS will not declare DTR and RTS on ttyb (default is false).
use-nvramrc?	Executes commands in NVRAMRC when system is started (default is false).
version2?	Specifies the hybrid (1.x/2.x) PROM is set to 2.x (default is true).
watchdog-reboot?	Reboots after a watchdog reset if set to true (default is false).

continued

File Name:	eeprom	Directory:	/usr/sbin/	Type:	Script
eeprom auto-boot?=true			Sets system to boot automatically after reboot.		
eeprom			Lists current settings.		

eject

UNIX Shell: All primary shells (csh, ksh, sh)

Function	Ejects floppies and CDs from their drives. Only works for VM-managed devices and devices without eject buttons.
Syntax	eject [options...] *{ device }*

-d	Shows the default device name.
-f	Forces the device to be ejected even if the drive is busy.
-n	Shows the alias names.
-p	Does not try to call the eject_popup program.
-q	Checks to see whether there is media in the drive.
	The following device names are supported:
device	The device name that is specified in the directory /dev or by nickname.
	The following are the list of device nicknames and their paths:
fd	/dev/rdiskette
fd0	/dev/rdiskette
fd1	/dev/rdiskette1
diskette	/dev/rdiskette
diskette0	/dev/rdiskette0
diskette1	/dev/rdiskette1
rdiskette	/dev/rdiskette
rdiskette0	/dev/rdiskette0
rdiskette1	/dev/rdiskette1
floppy	/dev/rdiskette
floppy0	/dev/rdiskette0
floppy1	/dev/rdiskette1

File Name:	eject	Directory:	/usr/bin/	Type:	External
Note:	Useful if you don't want to eject your CD-ROM with a paper clip.				

elfdump

UNIX Shell: All primary shells (csh, ksh, sh)

Function	Shows information from selected parts of an object file.
Syntax	elfdump [options...] *files...*

-c	Shows the section header.
-d	Shows the contents of the .dynamic section.
-e	Shows the elf header.
-i	Shows the contents of the .interp section.
-h	Shows the contents of the .hash section.
-n	Shows the contents of the .note section.
-p	Shows the program headers.
-r	Shows the contents of the relocation sections.
-s	Shows the contents of the symbol table sections.
-v	Shows the contents of the version sections.
-G	Shows the contents of the .got section.
-N *name*	Shows an option with a specific name.
-w *file*	Writes the contents of a specified section to the named file.
files...	Writes the contents to the given file.

File Name:	elfdump	Directory:	/usr/ccs/bin/	Type:	External
elfdump test.o			Shows all information of object file test.o on the screen.		
elfdump -p test.o			Shows the program header from test.o on the screen.		

enable

enable	UNIX Shell:	Bourne shell (sh)
Function	Enables printers to print requests from the lp command. Runs only on the print server.	
Syntax	enable *printers...*	

printers...	Specifies one or more printers to enable.
File Name: `enable`	**Directory:** /usr/bin/ — **Type:** Script
enable ucglaser	Enables the printer ucglaser.

erritem

erritem	UNIX Shell:	All primary shells (csh, ksh, sh)
Function	Shows error messages that are used with the command `ckitem`.	
Syntax	erritem [options...] *{ choices... }*	

-W *width*	Sets width for the error message.
-e *error*	Defines the error message.
choices...	Specifies the available menu choices.
File Name: `erritem`	**Directory:** /usr/sadm/bin/ — **Type:** External

error

error	UNIX Shell:	All primary shells (csh, ksh, sh)
Function	Inserts compiler error messages into a source file.	
Syntax	error [options...] *{ file }*	

-n	Does not modify any files, all error messages are shown on the screen.
-q	Asks whether the error should be inserted into the file; response is `y` or `n`.
-s	Shows statistics regarding the error categorization.
-v	Starts the vi editor with the files modified after the command finish.
-t *suffixlist*	Specifies a suffix list for the files to modify.
-I *ignorefile*	Specifies names of functions to ignore instead of .errors from the home directory.
file	Uses error messages from file instead from STDIN.
File Name: `error`	**Directory:** /usr/ccs/bin/ — **Type:** External
cc -c any.c |& error	Compile `any.c` and update it with error messages.

exportfs

exportfs	UNIX Shell:	All primary shells (csh, ksh, sh)
Function	Translates `exportfs` options to share/unshare commands. Without options it shows all shared NFS file systems.	
Syntax	exportfs [options...] *{ path }*	

-a	Uses shareall to share all file system files in `/etc/dfs/dfstab.`
-i	Ignores any options in `/etc/dfs/dfstab.`
-u	Uses unshare on the given path. When used with -a `unshareall` is used.
-v	Verbose mode. Shows more information.
-o *list*	Specifies options for the share; for example, access permissions (rw, ro, rw=host, ro=host).
path	Specifies the path to the file system.
File Name: `exportfs`	**Directory:** /usr/sbin/ — **Type:** External
Note:	Solaris uses `share` to export the file system via NFS. This command is used for compatibility with BSD systems.
exportfs -a -v	Does a share all and shows output verbosely.

exstr

exstr	UNIX Shell:	All primary shells (csh, ksh, sh)
Function	Extracts strings from source files written in the C language surrounded by `double quotes.`	
Syntax	exstr [options...] *files...*	

-e	Shows a list of strings from the C-source files. Don't use with -r or -d.
file	Specifies the name of the source file.
line	Specifies the line number in the file.
position	Specifies the character position in the line.

continued

msgfile	Specifies the file that contains the text strings to be replaced.		
msgnum	Specifies the sequence number.		
string	Specifies the extracted text string.		
-r	Replaces strings in the source files.		
-d	Shows the string if the string was not found; used only with -r option.		
File Name: `exstr`	**Directory:** /usr/bin/	**Type:**	External
exstr -e truss.c >truss.strout	Extracts strings from truss.c to truss.strout.		
exstr -r truss.c <truss.strin >newtruss.c	Replaces string in truss.c with data from truss.strin.		

face

UNIX Shell: All primary shells (csh, ksh, sh)

Function	Shows your files and folders on the screen. It uses a system of menus and forms.
Syntax	face [options...] *{ files... }*

-a *aliasfile*	Specifies the alias file.		
-c *commandfile*	Specifies the command file.		
-i *initialfile*	Specifies the initial file.		
files...	Specifies the path to the initial filename(s).		
File Name: `face`	**Directory:** /usr/vmsys/bin	**Type:**	External
Note:	You must be set up as a FACE user to do this.		
face Menu.start	Opens menu screen `Menu.start`.		
face -i start.conf Menu.start	Opens the menu with initial configuration.		

fastboot

UNIX Shell: Bourne shell (sh)

Function	Restarts the system but doesn't take the time to write data in memory to the disks.
Syntax	fastboot [options...]

-d	Dumps the system core before restarting the system.		
-l	Does not send a message to the system log daemon about who rebooted the system.		
-n	Does not sync the disks. Can cause file system damage!		
-q	Performs quick and ungraceful shutdown by not shutting down running processes first.		
File Name: `fastboot`	**Directory:** /usr/ucb/	**Type:**	Script
Note:	For compatibility only. Rather use `shutdown` or `init`.		

fasthalt

UNIX Shell: Bourne shell (sh)

Function	Stops the system immediately.
Syntax	fasthalt [options...]

-l	Suppresses message to the system log daemon about who executed halt.		
-n	Prevents sync before stopping.		
-q	Does a quick halt.		
-y	Halts the system even if a dialup terminal is used.		
File Name: `fasthalt`	**Directory:** /usr/ucb/	**Type:**	Script
Note:	For compatibility only. Rather use `shutdown` or `init`.		

fdisk

UNIX Shell: All primary shells (csh, ksh, sh)

Function	Creates or alters the disk partition table on your internal hard drive. You must specify `rdevice`, which is the raw device to a fixed disk.
Syntax	fdisk [options...] *device*

-o *offset*	Specifies block offset from start of disk. Can only be used with -P, -r, and -w.
-s *size*	Specifies the number of blocks to operate on.
-P *fill_patt*	Fills disk with this given pattern, decimal or hexadecimal.
-S *geom-file*	Sets the label geometry to the content of the file.
-w	Writes to disk information from STDIN, see the -o and -s options.
-r	Reverses; reads from disk to STDOUT.

continued

-d	Verbose mode. Don't use with the -F option.
-n	Does not update fdisk table (just writes MBR to disk) unless explicitly specified.
-I	Creates a file image of what would be on the disk; must use with the -S option.
-B	Is default to one Solaris partition that uses the whole disk.
-t	Changes incorrect slice table entries so that they don't cross partition table boundaries.
-T	Erases incorrect slice table entries that cross partition table boundaries.
-g	Shows the label geometry for the disk on STDOUT.
-G	Shows the physical geometry or the disk on STDOUT.
-R	Handles disk as read only. For testing purposes.
-F *fdisk_file*	Uses the `fdisk_file` to initialize table. This zeros out the VTOC.
-v	Shows the HBA geometry dimensions. Must use with -F.
-W *fdisk_file* | -	Writes the disk table to the `fdisk_file` or to STDOUT if a dash (-) is used.
-h	Shows help information.
-b *masterboot*	Specifies the file to use as the master boot program; only on x86.
-A	Adds a partition. The following arguments are used with -A:
id	Specifies the type of partition, the correct numeric values may be found in fdisk.h .
act	Activates partition flag; 0 means not active and 128 means active.
bhead	Specifies the head where the partition starts. If set to 0, fdisk fills this.
bsect	Specifies the sector where the partition starts. If set to 0, fdisk fills this.
bcyl	Specifies the cylinder where the partition starts. If set to 0, fdisk fills this.
ehead	Specifies the head where the partition ends. If set to 0, fdisk fills this.
esect	Specifies the sector where the partition ends. If set to 0, fdisk fills this.
ecyl	Specifies the cylinder where the partition ends. If set to 0, fdisk fills this.
rsect	Specifies the relative sector from the beginning of disk where the partition starts.
numsect	Specifies the size in sectors of the disk partition.
-D	Erases a partition; uses the same syntax as with the -A option.
device	Specifies the raw device to operate on; for example `/dev/rdsk/c0t0d0s0`.
File Name: `fdisk`	**Directory:** /usr/sbin/ **Type:** External
Note:	Disks must support fixed disk partition tables.
fdisk -R /dev/rdsk/c0t0d0s0	Runs fdisk on the device in read-only mode.

fdl

UNIX Shell: Korn shell (ksh)

Function	Manages font information on printers connected to Solaris hosts. It also allows users to manage printer maintenance.
Syntax	fdl

The File menu	
Exit	Ends the script. Can be started using `Alt-X`.
The Edit menu	
Font Bundle	Starts the Font Bundle editor. Can be started using `Alt-B`.
The Printer menu	
Add	Adds a printer to the list of printers. Can be started using `Alt-Insert`.
Delete	Removes a printer from the list. Can be started using `Alt-Delete`.
Properties	Shows the properties of the selected printer. Can be started using `Alt-E`.
Reset	Resets the selected printer to the default. Can be started using `Alt-R`.
The Download menu	
Font	Selects the font to download to the printer. Can be started using `Ctrl-S`.
Bundle	Creates, modifies or downloads font bundles. Can be started using `Ctrl-B`.
The Help menu	
About	Opens the Help interface.
File Name: `fdl`	**Directory:** /usr/dt/bin/ **Type:** Script

ff

ff	UNIX Shell:	All primary shells (csh, ksh, sh)

Function	Shows filenames and statistics for a file system.
Syntax	ff [options...] *devices...*

-F *FSType*	Specifies the file system type.
-V	Echos the complete command line, but doesn't execute the command.
-I	Does not print any i-node numbers after each pathname.
-l	Creates an extended list of pathnames for multiple-linked files.
-p *prefix*	Adds a prefix to each of the new pathnames.
-s	Shows the file size, in bytes, after each of the pathnames.
-u	Shows the owner's login name after each of the pathnames.
-a *n*	Selects whether the file has been accessed during the past n days.
-m *n*	Selects whether the file has been written or created during the past n days.
-c *n*	Selects whether file's status has been changed during the past n days.
-n *file*	Selects whether the file has been modified more recently than the argument file.
-i *inode- list*	Generates names for i-nodes that are specified in i-node-list.
-o *specific_options*	Specifies `FSType` specific options using a comma-separated list.
devices...	Specifies a special device.

File Name:	`ff`	**Directory:**	/usr/sbin/	**Type:**	External
Note:	This may not be supported on all file systems.				

ff /dev/dsk/c0t0d0s1	Lists filenames for the file system `/dev/dsk/c0t0d0s1`.
ff -a -3 /dev/dsk/c0t0d0s1	Lists all files that have been accessed within the last three days.

ffbconfig, SUNWffb_config

ffbconfig, SUNWffb_config	UNIX Shell:	All primary shells (csh, ksh, sh)

Function	Configures the FFB Graphics Accelerator.
Syntax	ffbconfig [options...]

-dev *file*	Specifies the device file that is associated with the FFB graphic card.
-res *videomode*	Sets video mode. You can use any of the following modes:
1024x768x60	Sets video to 1024 x 768 with a 60 hertz refresh rate.
1024x768x70	Sets video to 1024 x 768 with a 70 hertz refresh rate.
1024x768x75	Sets video to 1024 x 768 with a 75 hertz refresh rate.
1024x768x77	Sets video to 1024 x 768 with a 77 hertz refresh rate.
1024x800x84	Sets video to 1024 x 800 with an 84 hertz refresh rate.
1152x900x66	Sets video to 1152 x 900 with a 66 hertz refresh rate.
1152x900x76	Sets video to 1152 x 900 with a 76 hertz refresh rate.
1280x800x76	Sets video to 1280 x 800 with a 76 hertz refresh rate.
1280x1024x60	Sets video to 1280 x 1024 with a 60 hertz refresh rate.
1280x1024x67	Sets video to 1280 x 1024 with a 67 hertz refresh rate.
1280x1024x76	Sets video to 1280 x 1024 with a 76 hertz refresh rate.
960x680x112s	Sets video to 960 x 680 with a 112 hertz stereo refresh rate.
960x680x108s	Sets video to 960 x 680 with a 108 hertz stereo refresh rate.
640x480x60	Sets video to 640 x 480 with a 60 hertz refresh rate.
640x480x60i	Sets video to 640 x 480 with a 60 hertz interlaced refresh rate.
768x575x50i	Sets video to 768 x 575 with a 50 hertz interlaced refresh rate.
1440x900x76	Sets video to 1440 x 900 with a 76 hertz refresh rate.
1600x1000x66	Sets video to 1600 x 1000 with a 66 hertz refresh rate.
1600x1000x76i	Sets video to 1600 x 1000 with a 76 hertz interlaced refresh rate.
1600x1280x76	Sets video to 1600 x 1280 with a 76 hertz refresh rate.
1920x1080x72	Sets video to 1920 x 1080 with a 72 hertz refresh rate.
1920x1200x70	Sets video to 1920 x 1200 with a 70 hertz refresh rate.
now	Shows the videomode directly.
try	Prompts the user for confirmation to use the new videomode.
noconfirm	Forces the new videomode.

continued

nocheck	Forces the new videomode regardless of monitor type.
-file *action*	Updates the OWconfig file. Action can be `system` for global or `machine`.
-deflinear *action*	Sets linear mode. Action can be either `linear` or `nonlinear`.
-defoverlay *action*	Sets overlay visual. Action can be either `true` or `false`.
-linearorder *action*	Sets linear order. Action can be either `first` or `last`.
-overlayorder *action*	Sets the order for overlayvisuals. Action can be `first` or `last`.
-expvis *action*	Activates OpenGL visuals. Actions can be `enable` or `disable`.
-sov *action*	Broadcasts root windows SOV. Action are `enable` or `disable`.
-maxwids *n*	Sets the maximum reserved pixels for windowIDs. n=1, 2, 4, 8, 16, or 32.
-extovl *action*	Sets extended overlay. Actions are enable or disable. Only works with FFB2+ graphic card.
-g *gamma*	Alters the gamma correction value.
-gfile *gammacorrfile*	Uses gamma correction values from a file.
-propt	Shows the current values from the OWconfig file.
-prconf	Shows the hardware configuration of the FFB graphics accelerator.
-defaults	Resets all values to default values.
-help	Shows help information.
-res *?*	Shows allowed videomodes.
File Name: `ffbconfig`	**Directory:** /usr/sbin/ — **Type:** External

filemgr

UNIX Shell: All primary shells (csh, ksh, sh)

Function	A GUI-based file management application. Alters file permissions and creates folders in your file system.
Syntax	filemgr [options...]

-a	Forces filemgr to check for modify times on folders and files.
-C	Shows only generic, folder, and application icon file types.
-c	Shows file pane items by columns instead of by rows.
-d *directory*	Specifies the path where the file manager will start.
-i *secs*	Sets the timer to monitor file and folder modification times every x seconds.
-M	Uses only the foreground and background colors, even on color screens.
-name *app-name*	Uses the specified application resource in $HOME/.desksetfdefaults file.
-nomedia	Suppresses the floppy or CD-ROM window pop-up.
-r	Shows file pane items by rows.
-v	Shows version information.
-?	Shows help information.
File Name: `filemgr`	**Directory:** /usr/openwin/bin/ — **Type:** External

filesync

UNIX Shell: All primary shells (csh, ksh, sh)

Function	Synchronizes files between different computers.
Syntax	filesync [options...] [-r*directory*] filesync [options...] -s *source* -d *destination files...*

-a	Forces a check of the Access Control Lists and tries to synchronize the permissions.
-e	Marks the differences between the files.
-h	Halts if an error occurs.
-m	Checks the modification times to be sure they are the same.
-n	Determines the needed changes but doesn't actually synchronize the files.
-q	Runs in quiet mode by suppressing messages.
-v	Shows file comparison information about each file.
-y	Avoids safety check prompts.
-d *destination*	Specifies the destination directory on the system you are copying to.
-o src	Favors the source file over the destination file and forces a one-way reconciliation.
-o dst	Favors the destination file over the source file and forces a one-way reconciliation.
-f src	Favors the source file over the destination file when determining conflicting changes.
-f dst	Favors the destination file over the source file when determining conflicting changes.
-f old	Favors the old file over the new file when determining conflicting changes.

continued

-f new -r *directory* -s *source* *files...*	Favors the new file over the old file when determining conflicting changes. Limits the reconciliation to the specified directory. Specifies the source directory on the system you are copying from. Specifies the ordinary file, directory, symbolic link, or special file to be synchronized.				
File Name:	`Filesync`	**Directory:**	/usr/bin/	**Type:**	External
Tip:	Use this to synchronize to your laptop computer from a server.				
filesync -s server:/etc -d /etc	Synchronize /etc between server and local host.				
filesync -s /home/guy -d /home/anders	Synchronize two home directories with each other.				

firewall

UNIX Shell: Bourne shell (sh)

Function	Turns off IP forwarding and prevents route information from being visible by starting `/usr/etc/in.routed.asetoriginal` with the -q flag.
Syntax	firewall

	This script performs these functions: Turns ip_forwarding off, which tells the firewall not to pass on IP packets. Moves /usr/etc/in.routed to /usr/etc/in.routed.asetoriginal. Creates a script in the name of /usr/etc/in.routed that calls in.routed.asetoriginal.				
File Name:	`Fire1wall`	**Directory:**	/usr/aset/tasks/	**Type:**	Script

fmgc

UNIX Shell: All primary shells (csh, ksh, sh)

Function	Manages the garbage collection and hierarchy information for users. These hierarchy files are created by the program `filemgr` and store information about directories visited by users.
Syntax	fmgc [options...] *{ directories... }*

-l *limit* -u *username* -v -V -? *directories...*	Limits the garbage file size (default size is 1.5 megabytes). Specifies the users that will have their `~/.fm` directory garbage collected. Shows version information. Verbose mode. Shows more information. Shows help information. Specifies a directory or directories to clean up.				
File Name:	`Fmgc`	**Directory:**	/usr/openwin/bin/	**Type:**	External
fmgc -u ucg	Starts `fmgc` for the user ucg.				

fmli

UNIX Shell: All primary shells (csh, ksh, sh)

Function	Starts the form and menu language translator. It opens the frames that are specified by the filename argument.
Syntax	fmli [options...] *files...*

-a *aliasfile* -c *commandfile* -i *initfile* *files...*	Specifies the file to make alias on paths in fmli scripts. Specifies the file to disable standard fmli commands and to add custom commands. Specifies an initialize file to start with. The file containing the frame definitions.				
File Name:	`fmli`	**Directory:**	/usr/bin/	**Type:**	External
fmli Form.first	Opens a form using the Form.first file as the initial frame definition file.				
fmli -i init.app Form.first	Opens a form using the Form.first file as the initial frame and the init.app file for application characteristics.				

fmthard

UNIX Shell: All primary shells (csh, ksh, sh)

Function	Updates the Volume Table of Contents (VTOC) on hard disks.
Syntax	fmthard option [i] */dev/rdsk/c? [t] d?s2*

	The options -d, -n, and -s can't be combined.
-d *data*	Signifies the information for a partition in the current VTOC.
-n *volumename*	Specifies the volume name up to eight characters long.
-s *datafile*	Specifies a datafile made by a user to give instructions to VTOC.

continued

-i	Creates the VTOC but shows on STDOUT instead of modifying VTOC.		
/dev/rdsk/c?t?d?s2	Specifies the device on which to install the VTOC.		
File Name: fmthard	**Directory:** /usr/sbin/	**Type:**	External
fmthard -n myvolume /dev/rdsk/c0d0t3s2	Specifies the volume name `myvolume` on the disk.		

fmtmsg

UNIX Shell: All primary shells (csh, ksh, sh)

Function	Writes a message to STDERR or system console.
Syntax	fmtmsg [options...] *text*

-u *subclass*	Specifies a list of keywords that define the message.
appl	Specifies whether the condition started in an application.
util	Specifies whether the condition started in a utility.
opsys	Specifies whether the condition started in the kernel.
recov	Specifies the application will recover from the condition.
nrecov	Specifies the application will not recover from the condition.
print	Shows the message to the standard error stream STDERR.
console	Writes the message to the system console.
-l *label*	Identifies the source of the message.
-s *severity*	Indicates how critical an error is; keywords are info, warn, error, and halt.
info	Specifies the level to informational.
warn	Specifies the level to warning.
error	Specifies the level to error.
halt	Specifies the level to halt.
-c *class*	Describes the source of the message. Uses one of the options below:
soft	Explains that it is software.
firm	Explains that it is firmware.
hard	Explains that it is hardware.
-a *action*	Describes the first step of the error recovery process.
text	Specifies a text string to describe the condition.
-t *tag*	Specifies an identifier for the message.
File Name: fmtmsg	**Directory:** /usr/bin/ **Type:** External
Tip:	Cool to confuse users with error messages that are not understandable. Wait a minute . . . they already are!
fmtmsg -u print -s error -a Aspirin You	Shows an error message to STDERR.

fnattr

UNIX Shell: All primary shells (csh, ksh, sh)

Function	Manages the attributes of FNS (Federated Naming Service) objects.
Syntax	fnattr [options...] *compositename* [options...]

-L	Does not manipulate the XFN links that are associated by its attributes.
-A	Consults the authoritative source to get attribute information.
compositename	Specifies an FNS object.
	When you use these options you can't combine them:
-d *identifiervalue*	Deletes an attribute associated with object composite name.
-m *identifier oldvalue newvalue*	Modifies an attribute associated to composite name.
-a *identifiervalue*	Adds an attribute to the attribute associated with object composite name.
	The FN_ID_STRING form can be modified by these three options:
-s	Replaces or adds attributes by the new value. Used only with the -a option.
-O	Translates the identifier as an ASN.1 string.
-U	Translates the identifier as a DCE UUID string.
File Name: fnattr	**Directory:** /usr/bin/ **Type:** External
fnattr user/antw	Lists attributes associated with object user/antw.
fnattr user/antw -as age 27	Replaces attribute age associated with object user/antw with value 27.

fnbind

UNIX Shell: All primary shells (csh, ksh, sh)

Function	Associates a resource to an FNS name, or binds a reference specified on the command line to an FNS name.
Syntax	fnbind [options...] *name newname* fnbind -r [options...] *newname*

-s	Binds to `newname` even if it is already bound.
-v	Shows the reference that is bound to `newname`.
-L	Creates an XFN link and binds a name to `newname`.
-r	Creates reference from the command line, excluding name option in this case.
reftype	Specifies type of reference, this is specified as an FN_ID_STRING.
addrtype	Specifies type of address, this is specified as an FN_ID_STRING.
addrcontents	Specifies the contents of address, which are stored in XDR encoding.
-U	Translates reftype as a DCE UUID string.
-O	Translates reftype as an ASN.1 string.
-x	Specifies a hexadecimal string; stored as hexadecimal.
-c	Modifies to store in the specified type.
-O	Translates reftype as an ASN.1 string.
-U	Translates reftype as a DCE UUID string.
name	Specifies the resource to bind.
newname	Specifies the new resource name to bind to.

File Name:	`fnbind`	**Directory:**	/usr/bin/	**Type:**	External

fnbind user/antw user/aw	Binds the name user/aw to the reference user/antw.
fnbind -v user/antw user/aw	Binds the name user/aw to reference user/antw and shows the contents of the reference.

fncheck

UNIX Shell: Bourne shell (sh)

Function	Checks for consistency between FNS (Federated Naming Service) data and NIS+ data.
Syntax	fncheck [options...] *{ domain }*

-r	Shows items that appear in the FNS context but not in the NIS+ table
-s	Shows terms that appear in the NIS+ table but not in the FNS table.
-u	Updates the FNS context based on information in the NIS+ table.
-t *type*	Specifies the type of context to check, can be either hostname or username.
domain	Specifies the NIS+ domain name.

File Name:	`fncheck`	**Directory:**	/usr/sbin/	**Type:**	Script

fncheck -r ucgbook.com	Shows items from the FNS context missing from NIS+ domain ucgbook.com.
fncheck -u -t username ucgbook.com	Updates the FNS context for usernames from the NIS+ domain ucgbook.com.

fncopy

UNIX Shell: All primary shells (csh, ksh, sh)

Function	Copies FNS (Federated Naming Service) contexts from one naming service to another.
Syntax	fncopy [options...] *oldfns newfns*

-f *filename*	Specifies filename with FNS context to copy.
-i *oldnamingservice*	Specifies the source naming service.
-o *newnamingservice*	Specifies the target naming service.
oldfns	Specifies the current FNS context.
newfns	Specifies the new FNS context.

File Name:	`fncopy`	**Directory:**	/usr/sbin/	**Type:**	External

fncopy ucg.com ucg.net	Copy context ucg.com to new context ucg.net in the default naming service.
fncopy -i nis ucg.com ucg.net	Copy NIS context ucg.com to ucg.net context in the default naming service.

fncreate

UNIX Shell:	All primary shells (csh, ksh, sh)
Function	Creates an FNS (Federated Naming Service) context.
Syntax	fncreate -t *type* [options ...] *compositename*

-t *type*	Specifies the context type to create. The available types are listed below.
org	Creates the organization context.
hostname	Creates the hostname context.
host	Creates the host context for a specific host.
username	Creates a username context.
user	Creates the user context for a specific user.
service	Creates a service context.
fs	Creates a file system context.
site	Creates a site context.
nsid	Creates a namespace context.
generic	Creates a generic context.
-r *referencetype*	References the generic context that is created.
-s	Creates the context and binds it in to ignore any existing bindings to a composite.
-o	Creates context of compositename and doesn't create sub contexts.
-v	Verbose mode. Shows more information.
-f *inputfile*	Specifies inputfile of users and hosts to create the context.
compositename	Specifies an FNS named object.
-D	Shows information about each context that is created.

File Name:	`fncreate`	**Directory:**	/usr/sbin/	**Type:**	External

fncreate -t username ucg/test/user/antw	Creates a username context `antw` in the sub organization `test.`

fncreate_fs

UNIX Shell:	All primary shells (csh, ksh, sh)
Function	Creates File System contexts within the FNS (Federated Naming Service) namespace.
Syntax	fncreate_fs [options...] -f *inputfile* *compositename*

-r	Replaces the bindings in the context specified by `compositename.`
-v	Verbose mode. Shows more information.
-f *inputfile*	Reads input from inputfile if hyphenated – then reads from STDIN.
compositename	Specifies an FNS named object.

File Name:	`fncreate_fs`	**Directory:**	/usr/sbin/	**Type:**	External

fncreate_fs ucg/test/fs/apps -ro venus:/export/apps	Creates an apps fs context in the ucg/test/fs context, mounting as read-only from server venus.

fncreate_printer

UNIX Shell:	All primary shells (csh, ksh, sh)
Function	Creates a new printer in the FNS (Federated Naming Service) namespace.
Syntax	fncreate_printer [options...] *compositename printername printeraddress* fncreate_printer [options...] [-f*filename*] *compositename*

-s	Makes new address ignore an address that exists with the same address type.
-v	Verbose mode. Shows more information.
-f *filename*	Specifies file with printer context; excludes printer name and printer address.
compositename	The FNS name for the organization, host, user, or site.
printername	Specifies name of the new printer context.
printeraddress	Specifies an address to be associated with the printer context name.

File Name:	`fncreate_printer`	**Directory:**	/usr/bin/	**Type:**	External

fncreate_printer -s ucg/test	Creates printers in the ucg/test context from the entries in `/etc/printers.conf.`

fndestroy

UNIX Shell: All primary shells (csh, ksh, sh)

Function	Removes an FNS (Federated Naming Service) context from the specified name.				
Syntax	fndestroy *compositename*				
compositename	Specifies the name of the FNS context to be removed.				
File Name:	`fndestroy`	**Directory:**	/usr/sbin/	**Type:**	External
fndestroy user/ucg	Removes the bindings from the context named by user/ucg/.				

fnlist

UNIX Shell: All primary shells (csh, ksh, sh)

Function	Shows the name and reference bound in an FNS (Federated Naming Service) context.				
Syntax	fnlist [options...] { *compositename* }				
-A	Looks in the authoritative source for information.				
-l	Shows the references and the names bound in the context `compositename.`				
-v	Verbose mode. Shows more information.				
compositename	Specifies an FNS named object.				
File Name:	`fnlist`	**Directory:**	/usr/bin/	**Type:**	External
fnlist ucg/test	Shows names bound in context ucg/test.				
fnlist -l ucg/test	Shows names and references bound in context ucg/test.				

fnlookup

UNIX Shell: All primary shells (csh, ksh, sh)

Function	Shows the binding of an FNS (Federated Naming Service) name that you specify.				
Syntax	fnlookup [options...] *compositename*				
-A	Looks in the authoritative source for information.				
-L	Shows the resource that the composite name is bound to.				
-v	Verbose mode. Shows more information.				
compositename	Specifies an FNS named object.				
File Name:	`fnlookup`	**Directory:**	/usr/bin/	**Type:**	External
fnlookup user/antw/service	Shows the reference bound to the name user/antw/service.				

fnrename

UNIX Shell: All primary shells (csh, ksh, sh)

Function	Renames the binding of an FNS (Federated Naming Service) name.				
Syntax	fnrename [options...] *contextname oldname newname*				
-s	Overwrites any references that are already bound to newname.				
-v	Shows bindings that are renamed.				
contextname	Specifies the context to rename.				
oldname	Specifies name to rename.				
newname	Specifies the new name.				
File Name:	`fnrename`	**Directory:**	/usr/bin/	**Type:**	External
fnrename user/antw/service/ enail e-mail	Binds e-mail to the reference bound to enail then unbinds enail within the context user/antw/service/.				

fnsearch

UNIX Shell: All primary shells (csh, ksh, sh)

Function	Searches for FNS (Federated Naming Service) objects with specified attributes and/or values.
Syntax	fnsearch [options...] *name* [options...] *expression { arguments... }*
-A	Looks in the authoritative sources for information.
-l	Shows the reference of each object that matche the filter expression.
-L	Follows XFN links during the search.
-v	Shows detailed reference of objects that match filter expression.
-n *max*	Specifies maximum number of objects to show.
-s *scope*	Sets the scope of the search, object, context, or sub-tree.

continued

name	Is used to specify an FNS named object.
-a *identifiers...*	Shows attribute of each object that matches the filter expression.
-O	Translates the filter expression into ASN.1 dot-separated integer list.
-U	Translates the filter expression into DCE UUID in string form.
expression	Sets a filter expression to use for searching objects.
arguments...	Specifies the filter argument.
	Then use these options as the filter argument:
%a	Specifies attribute.
%s	Specifies string.
%i	Specifies identifier.
%v	Specifies attribute value.
File Name: `fnsearch`	**Directory:** /usr/bin/ **Type:** External
fnsearch ucg/ "e-mail"	Shows all objects with an e-mail attribute.
fnsearch ucg/user/ "age > 35"	Shows all objects in ucg/user/ context who have attribute age with a value greater than 35.

fnselect

UNIX Shell: All primary shells (csh, ksh, sh)

Function	Selects a naming service to use for the FNS (Federated Naming Service) initial context creation.
Syntax	fnselect [-D] *{ namingservice }*

-D	Shows the actual naming service used to create the FNS initial context.
namingservice	Sets naming service to use.
	Then use these options with naming service:
default	Uses the default algorithm to determine naming service.
nisplus	Uses NIS+ as the naming service.
nis	Uses NIS as the naming service.
files	Uses /etc files as the target naming service.
File Name: `fnselect`	**Directory:** /usr/sbin/ **Type:** External
fnselect nis	Sets initial context creation to use NIS.

fnsypd

UNIX Shell: All primary shells (csh, ksh, sh)

Function	A daemon used by NIS clients to update the FNS context on a NIS master server.
Syntax	fnsypd
File Name:	`fnsypd` **Directory:** /usr/sbin/ **Type:** External
Note:	Daemon should be run at system boot to service NIS client requests.

fnunbind

UNIX Shell: All primary shells (csh, ksh, sh)

Function	Unbinds the resource from a FNS (Federated Naming Service) name.
Syntax	fnunbind *name*

name	Specifies the composite name to be unbound.
File Name: `fnunbind`	**Directory:** /usr/bin/ **Type:** External
Note:	Be sure to use `fndestroy` on a context first, or this command will fail.
fnunbind ucg/user/antw/	Unbinds a previously destroyed context name.

format

UNIX Shell: All primary shells (csh, ksh, sh)

Function	Partitions, labels, repairs, and analyzes disks on the system. Without options, the interactive tool starts.
Syntax	format [options...] *{ list }*

-d *diskname*	Specifies which disk will be made current upon entry into the program.
-e	Enables SCSI expert menu.
-f *commandfile*	Takes command input from the command file.
-l *logfile*	Specifies a log file to log transcript from the format session.
-m	Enables extended messages.

continued

-M		Enables extended and diagnostic messages.			
-p *partitionname*		Specifies the partition table that is current upon entry into the program.			
-t *disktype*		Specifies the type of disk that is current upon entry into the program.			
-s		Specifies silent mode.			
-x *datafile*		Specifies to use a data file that contains a list of disks.			
list		Specifies a list of disks to edit.			
File Name:	`format`	**Directory:**	/usr/sbin/	**Type:**	External
Warning:	Use the interactive utility (format) but be careful because you can destroy data.				

format_floppy

UNIX Shell: All primary shells (csh, ksh, sh)

Function	Formats floppy disks. Mainly the file manager uses it.				
Syntax	format_floppy options... [options...]				
		The following two options are required:			
-d *device*		Specifies the raw device file of the floppy drive.			
-m *mountpoint*		Specifies the mount point of the floppy disk.			
		The following options are not required and can be combined:			
-h		Shows help information.			
-n *name*		Specifies a name for the floppy that you want to format.			
-p *popup*		Specifies the pop-up menu. The pop-up menu can be formated, unformatted, or unlabeled.			
-r		Specifies the floppy can be renamed using the -n option.			
-x *xpos*		Specifies the x coordinate position for the pop-up menu.			
-y *ypos*		Specifies the y coordinate position for the pop-up menu.			
File Name:	`format_floppy`	**Directory:**	/usr/openwin/bin/	**Type:**	External

from

UNIX Shell: All primary shells (csh, ksh, sh)

Function	Shows sender and date of newly arrived mail messages.				
Syntax	from [-s *sender*] { *username* }				
-s *sender*		Shows headers for mail sent by sender.			
username		Inspects the mailbox for the specified user.			
File Name:	`from`	**Directory:**	/usr/ucb/	**Type:**	External
from -s root			Shows headers for mail sent by root.		

fsadmin

UNIX Shell: All primary shells (csh, ksh, sh)

Function	Controls whether the font server is or isn't started automatically by `inetd`.				
Syntax	fsadmin [option]				
		The following options can't be combined:			
-e		Enables `inetd` to start font server automatically.			
-d		Disables `inetd` so that it can't start font server automatically.			
-usage		Shows help information.			
File Name:	`fsadmin`	**Directory:**	/usr/openwin/bin/	**Type:**	External
Warning:	Don't enable the fs service on a secure server.				
fsadmin -e			Enables font server in `inetd.conf`.		
fsadmin -d			Disables font server in `inetd.conf`.		

fsdb

UNIX Shell: All primary shells (csh, ksh, sh)

Function	Debugs a file system after a crash.	
Syntax	fsdb [options...] *device*	
-F *fstype*		Specifies the file system type.
-V		Simulates command, but doesn't execute.
-o		Specifies options that are specific to the file system you want to debug.
device		Specifies the device where the file system resides.

continued

File Name:	fsdb	**Directory:**	/usr/sbin/	**Type:**	External
Note:	It might not be supported for all file system types.				
fsdb -F ufs /dev/dsk/c0t0d0s0		Starts debug mode for the c0t0d0s0 disk.			

fsinfo

UNIX Shell: All primary shells (csh, ksh, sh)

Function	Shows information including the capabilities about X font servers on the network.
Syntax	fsinfo [-server *hostname*]

-server *hostname*		Specifies the server and, optionally, the port to show information about.			
File Name:	fsinfo	**Directory:**	/usr/openwin/bin/	**Type:**	External
Note:	The default font server is specified in the FONTSERVER environment variable.				
fsinfo -server localhost:7100		Shows font server info from localhost:7100.			

fsirand

UNIX Shell: All primary shells (csh, ksh, sh)

Function	Creates random inode generation numbers to increase security for NFS file systems. It also creates a file system ID in the superblock.
Syntax	fsirand [-p] *device*

-p		Shows the generation numbers for all inodes.			
device		Specifies the special device that holds the inodes.			
File Name:	fsirand	**Directory:**	/usr/sbin/	**Type:**	External
Warning:	Don't use this on mounted file system.				

fslsfonts

UNIX Shell: All primary shells (csh, ksh, sh)

Function	Shows the fonts on the font server that match the pattern specified. Wildcards * can be used.
Syntax	fslsfonts [options...] [-fn *pattern*]

-server *host:port*		Specifies the X font server and port to use.			
-l		Shows attributes of the font next to the font name.			
-ll		Shows font parameters together with the -l option.			
-lll		The same as -ll.			
-C		Shows information in multiple columns.			
-1		Shows information in a single column.			
-w *width*		Specifies the width of the column in characters (default is 79).			
-n *columns*		Specifies the number of columns to show.			
-u		Does not sort the information.			
-fn *pattern*		Specifies the pattern that fslfonts must match.			
-m		Shows the minimum and maximum bounds for each font.			
File Name:	fslsfonts	**Directory:**	/usr/openwin/bin/	**Type:**	External
Note:	The default font server is set in the FONTSERVER environment variable.				
fslsfonts -server localhost:7100		Shows fonts from the font server that run on the local host.			
fslsfonts -fn terminal*		Shows fonts that start with terminal from the default font server.			

fstobdf

UNIX Shell: All primary shells (csh, ksh, sh)

Function	Creates BDF fonts from an X font server. It is used to debug font and re-create BDF files.
Syntax	fstobdf [-server *hostname*] -fn *name*

-server *hostname*		Specifies the server to read the font from.			
-fn *name*		Specifies the font to create a BDF file for.			
File Name:	fstobdf	**Directory:**	/usr/openwin/bin/	**Type:**	External
Note:	The default font server is set in the FONTSERVER environment variable.				
fstobdf -fn terminal		Creates a BDF font from the terminal font from the default font server.			
fstobdf -fn terminal -server localhost:7100		Creates a BDF font from the terminal font from localhost:7100 font server.			

fstyp

UNIX Shell: Bourne shell (sh)

Function	Determines the file system type for unmounted file systems.
Syntax	fstyp [-v] *file*

-v	Verbose mode. Shows more information.
file	Specifies a file to determine file system type on.

File Name:	`fstyp`	**Directory:**	/usr/sbin/	**Type:**	Script

Tip:	Useful if you do not know which fstyp an unmounted file system is.

fstyp /dev/rdsk/c0t3d0s2	Shows the file system type.
fstyp -v /dev/dsk/c0t3d0s2	Shows the file system in verbose mode.

fuser

UNIX Shell: All primary shells (csh, ksh, sh)

Function	Shows process IDs of files that are specified.
Syntax	fuser [options...] *files...*

-c	Shows files that are mount points for file systems.
-f	Shows a report.
-k	Sends a SIGKILL signal to each process.
-u	Shows the user login name in parentheses after the process ID.
files...	Specifies the filenames to show the process ID for.

File Name:	`fuser`	**Directory:**	/usr/sbin/	**Type:**	External

Tip:	This command is useful if you can't open the CD-ROM because someone else is using it.

fuser /tmp	Checks if someone uses the catalog `/tmp`.

fwtmp

UNIX Shell: All primary shells (csh, ksh, sh)

Function	Converts binary records in `wtmp` to readable text records. Reads from STDIN and writes to STDOUT.
Syntax	fwtmp [-ic]

-ic	Specifies that input is readable text and output is binary.

File Name:	`fwtmp`	**Directory:**	/usr/lib/acct/	**Type:**	External

cat /var/adm/wtmp | fwtmp > textfile	Converts the binary records and saves them to a text file.

gcore

UNIX Shell: All primary shells (csh, ksh, sh)

Function	Creates a core file image for the process you specify. The default image filename will be `core.processID`.
Syntax	gcore [-o *file*] *processIDs...*

-o *file*	Creates your own output filename instead of the default `core.processID`.
processIDs...	Specifies the process ID to create a core image for.

File Name:	`gcore`	**Directory:**	/usr/bin/	**Type:**	External

gcore 18453	Creates an image file for the process with ID 18453.

gencat

UNIX Shell: All primary shells (csh, ksh, sh)

Function	Formats text from a message file and merges the information into the formatted message database called a catfile.
Syntax	gencat *catfile msgfiles...*

catfile	Specifies the name of the formatted message database.
msgfiles...	Specifies the name of the message text source file.
	To format the message file you must use the following format.
$set n comment	Assigns a set number for the message catalog specified by `n`.
$delset n comment	Removes a set number for the message catalog specified by `n`.
$ comment	Specifies a comment when there is a $ symbol followed by a space.
m message-text	The `m` assigns the message an ID and is followed by the message text.
$quote c	Specifies quote characters are to be used to surround the message text. This is optional.

continued

	The following special characters and escape sequences can be used:
NL(LF)	Used for a new line. The escape sequence is *\n*.
HT	Used for a horizontal tab. The escape sequence is *\t*.
VT	Used for a vertical tab. The escape sequence is *\v*.
BS	Used for a backspace. The escape sequence is *\b*.
CR	Used for a carriage return. The escape sequence is *\r*.
FF	Used for a form feed. The escape sequence is *\f*.
\	Used for a backslash. The escape sequence is \\.
ddd	Used for a bit pattern. The escape sequence is *ddd* and ddd is any three characters.
File Name: gencat	**Directory:** /usr/bin/ **Type:** External
gencat UCGdb newcommand	Merges a new command into the UCG database.

genmsg

UNIX Shell: All primary shells (csh, ksh, sh)

Function	Creates message source files by extracting the messages from other source files.
Syntax	genmsg [options...] *files...*

-a	Appends the message output into the message file specified with the –o option.
-b	Extracts comments and places them in the output file.
-c *message-tag*	Extracts comments from messages that have a message-tag defined.
-d	Includes the text of the original message with its translations as a comment.
-f	Overwrites input and project files when used with options –l or –r.
-g *project-file*	Generates a project-file containing a list of set numbers and maximum message numbers.
-l *project-file*	Replaces numbers using the calculated numbers from the project-file.
-m *prefix*	Fills in the message by using what's specified by the prefix. Used for testing.
-M *suffix*	Fills in the message by using what's specified by the suffix. Used for testing.
-n	Adds comments to specify line numbers and filename for input files.
-o *message-file*	Writes the output to the message-file specified.
-p *preprocessor*	Starts the preprocessor to preprocess define statements and macros for catgets calls.
-r	Replaces the message numbers with –1 and is the reverse of the –l option.
-s *set-tag*	Extracts set number comment tags in input files to an output file using $ as prefix.
-t	Creates a message three times longer then original message for testing purposes.
-x	Suppresses all warnings regarding range checks and conflicts.
files...	Specifies the source filenames to extract the messages from.
File Name: genmsg	**Directory:** /usr/bin/ **Type:** External

get, sccs-get

UNIX Shell: All primary shells (csh, ksh, sh)

Function	Retrieves version information from the working copy of the SCCS file.
Syntax	get [options...] *files...*

-b	Is used with the –e option to create a new branch. Must have b flag set in s.file.
-e	Allows you to edit version information by placing a lock on the s.file.
-g	Retrieves the SCCS version ID without locking the file. Used to verify SID numbers.
-k	Does not expand the ID keywords.
-m	Shows the SID of the delta in front of every retrieved line separated by a Tab.
-n	Shows %M% ID keyword in front of every retrieved line separated by a Tab.
-p	Shows the version information to STDOUT instead of to the default setting STDERR.
-s	Suppresses all messages to STDOUT.
-t	Shows the most recently created delta.
-l [p]	Writes summary of delta table to file. If –lp is used, shows summary on STDOUT.
-a*sequence*	Shows version information by delta sequence number. Used by SCCS-comb
-c*date-time*	Shows version information before a certain date and time specified by date-time. (Date-time format is yy[mm[dd[hh[mm[ss]]]]].)
-G*newname*	Uses the name specified by newname as the name of the version.
-i *sid-list*	Specifies list of SCCS deltas to be included in the retrieved version.

continued

-r *{ sid }* -x *sid-list* *files...*		Shows version information by SID number. Excludes version information for deltas specified by the SID-list. Specifies the input filename.			
File Name:	`get`	**Directory:**	/usr/ccs/bin/	**Type:**	External
get s.filename		Get SCCS information about the file s.filename.			

getdev

UNIX Shell: All primary shells (csh, ksh, sh)

Function	Creates a device list that matches the criteria specified.
Syntax	getdev [options...] *{ criteria... } { device... }*

-a -e *criteria...* attribute=value attribute!=value attribute:* attribute!:* *device...*		Shows only devices that match ALL criteria specified. Excludes devices that match the criteria specified. Defines the criteria for the device you want included in the list. Selects and shows devices that are defined and that equal the value specified. Selects and shows devices that are defined but do not equal the value specified. Selects and shows devices that have the requested attribute defined. Selects and shows devices that do not have the requested attribute defined. Specifies the device alias or device pathname that should be included in the list.			
File Name:	`getdev`	**Directory:**	/usr/bin/	**Type:**	External
Note:	The device file is located in `/etc/device.tab`.				
getdev -a disk1		Lists disk1.			
getdev -e disk2		Lists all the devices except disk2.			

getdgrp

UNIX Shell: All primary shells (csh, ksh, sh)

Function	Creates a list of device groups that match the specified criteria.
Syntax	getdgrp [options...] *{ criterias... } { dgroups... }*

-a -e -l *criterias...* attribute=value attribute!=value attribute:* attribute!:* *dgroups...*		Shows only devices that match ALL criteria specified. Excludes device groups that match the criteria specified. Shows all device groups even if there are no valid device members. Defines the criteria for the device group you want included in the list. Selects and shows device groups that are defined and that equal the value specified. Selects and shows device groups that are defined but do not equal the value specified. Selects and shows device groups that have the requested attribute defined. Selects and shows device groups that do not have the requested attribute defined Specifies the set of device groups that should be included or excluded in the list.			
File Name:	`getdgrp`	**Directory:**	/usr/bin/	**Type:**	External
getdgrp -l		Shows all device groups.			
getdgrp -a disk		Shows device group disk.			

getent

UNIX Shell: All primary shells (csh, ksh, sh)

Function	Retrieves entries from system database files using keywords that exist in the database.
Syntax	getent *file { keys... }*

file	Specifies the configuration file to retrieve data from. The list of files used is
passwd	`/etc/passwd` — The system password information file.
group	`/etc/group` — The system group information file.
hosts	`/etc/hosts` — The hostname information file.
services	`/etc/services` — Contains system services and aliases.
protocols	`/etc/protocols` — Contains the system protocol database.
ether	`/etc/ethers` — Contains Ethernet address to hostname information.
network	`/etc/networks` — Contains network name information.
netmasks	`/etc/netmasks` — Contains the network mask information.
nsswitch.conf	`/etc/nsswitch.conf` — Contains DNS information.

continued

keys...		The key words are specific to the configuration file used.			
File Name:	getent	**Directory:**	/usr/bin/	**Type:**	External
Note:	You may also use cat or more on these files instead.				
getent passwd root			Shows the root entry in /etc/passwd.		
getent services tftp			Lists the tftp entry in /etc/services.		

getfacl

UNIX Shell: All primary shells (csh, ksh, sh)

Function	Shows the Access Control List (ACL), the owner, and the group for the specified file.				
Syntax	getfacl [options...] *files...*				
-a		Shows the filename, the file owner, the group owner, and the ACL of the file.			
-d		Shows the filename, the file owner, the group owner, and the default ACL of the file.			
files...		Specifies the file that you want to retrieve ACL information about.			
File Name:	getfacl	**Directory:**	/usr/bin/	**Type:**	External
getfacl /usr/bin/getfacl			Shows the settings and the ACL of the file.		
getfacl -d /usr/bin/getfacl			Shows the settings and the default ACL of the file.		

getNAME

UNIX Shell: All primary shells (csh, ksh, sh)

Function	Captures the NAME section from a specified manual source, which can then be used for creating a table of contents or an introduction section to a manual.				
Syntax	getNAME [options...] *files...*				
-i		Reports information from the manual that is useful for manual section introduction.			
-t		Reports information from the manual that is useful for table of contents creation.			
files...		Specifies the manual source that the NAME section will be extracted from.			
File Name:	getNAME	**Directory:**	/usr/lib/	**Type:**	External
getNAME /usr/man/man1/*			Shows the name section of the manfiles in /usr/man/man1/*.		

gettable

UNIX Shell: All primary shells (csh, ksh, sh)

Function	Gets the DoD Internet host table via the TCP port connection of a specified host server.				
Syntax	gettable *hostname*				
hostname		Specifies the hostname to obtain a table from.			
File Name:	gettable	**Directory:**	/usr/sbin/	**Type:**	External
Note:	Obsoleted by DNS for the majority of available servers, but is useful for some non-DNS sites.				
gettable hs.ucg.com			Gets the host table from hs.ucg.com.		

gettext

UNIX Shell: All primary shells (csh, ksh, sh)

Function	Gets domain name variable from a message object created by msgfmt that matches the specified id.				
Syntax	gettext *{ domain } msgid*				
domain		Specifies the text domain message object.			
msgid		Specifies the message ID that you want to get.			
File Name:	gettext	**Directory:**	/usr/bin/	**Type:**	External

gettxt

UNIX Shell: All primary shells (csh, ksh, sh)

Function	Gets a text string from a specific message file database found in the directory. /usr/lib/locale/locale/LC_MESSAGES, where the locale name corresponds to the string language.				
Syntax	gettxt *msgfile:msgnum { string }*				
msgfile		Specifies the message file that is searched.			
msgnum		Specifies the sequence number of the string to get from the msgfile.			
string		Specifies the default text to display if gettxt fails.			
File Name:	gettxt	**Directory:**	/usr/bin/	**Type:**	External

getty

getty	UNIX Shell: All primary shells (csh, ksh, sh)
Function	Defines the terminal settings, including the line speed and terminal behavior.
Syntax	getty [options...] *line* { *speed* } ttymon -c *file*

-h	Does not force a hangup when modifying the line speed.
-t *timeout*	Specifies the period of time of inactivity before `getty` exits.
-c *file*	No longer supported. The command /usr/sbin/sttydefs -l will verify the /etc/ttydefs file.
line	Specifies the name of the tty name to connect to (that is, `/dev/ttya`).
speed	Sets the baud rate that is defined in the file `/etc/ttydefs` (default is 300).
File Name: `getty`	**Directory:** /etc/ **Type:** External
Note:	Only provided for compatibility reasons because some applications may still call getty directly.
getty -h ttya	Sets ttya to not hang up when modifying the line speed.

getvol

getvol	UNIX Shell: All primary shells (csh, ksh, sh)
Function	Verifies that the device specified is available and that the proper media is inserted and ready for use.
Syntax	getvol [options...] *device*

-f	Formats and creates a volume when inserting new media.
-F	Formats and creates a volume and then creates a file system when inserting new media.
-n	Executes getvol in non-interactive mode and assumes that there is media already inserted.
-o	Gives the administrator the permission to override a label check.
-w	Gives the administrator the permission to write a new label on the device.
-l *label*	Specifies a required label that must exist on device when inserting new media.
-x *label*	The same as -l but shows a message prompting for the correct volume name.
device	Specifies the device that you want to verify the accessibility for.
File Name: `getvol`	**Directory:** /usr/bin/ **Type:** External
getvol /dev/fd	Checks device `/dev/fd`.

groupadd

groupadd	UNIX Shell: All primary shells (csh, ksh, sh)
Function	Creates a new group definition on the system by editing the `/etc/group` file.
Syntax	groupadd [options...] *group*

-g *gid*	Assigns a specific group ID number to a new group.
-o	Allows the duplication of the specified gid.
group	Specifies a new group definition.
File Name: `groupadd`	**Directory:** /usr/sbin/ **Type:** External
Note:	Adds definitions only to the local `/etc/group` file; it doesn't change information on a NIS/NIS+ server.
groupadd ucg	Adds the group ucg to the system.
groupadd -g 101 ucg	Adds the group ucg to the system with a gid of 101.

groupdel

groupdel	UNIX Shell: All primary shells (csh, ksh, sh)
Function	Deletes a specified group definition in the system that resides in the `/etc/group` file.
Syntax	groupdel *group*

group	Specifies the group that is deleted.
File Name: `groupdel`	**Directory:** /usr/sbin/ **Type:** External
Note:	Deletes group definitions from the local `/etc/group`, but not from a NIS/NIS+ server.
groupdel ucg	Erases the group ucg from the system.

groupmod

UNIX Shell: All primary shells (csh, ksh, sh)

Function	Alters a specific group definition on the system using the `/etc/group` file.
Syntax	groupmod [options...] *group*

-g *gid*	Specifies a new group ID to use for the specified group.
-o	Allows the new gid to be duplicated.
-n *name*	Specifies the new name for the group. This name cannot exceed 8 bytes in length.
group	Specifies the group that is modified.

File Name:	`groupmod`	**Directory:**	/usr/sbin/	**Type:**	External

Note: Modifies only the local `/etc/group` file, and not the file on the NIS/NIS+ server.

groupmod -n ucg1 ucg	Renames the group `ucg` to `ucg1`.
groupmod -g 101 ucg1	Gives the group `ucg1` the groupID `101`.

grpck

UNIX Shell: All primary shells (csh, ksh, sh)

Function	Verifies the entries in the group file.
Syntax	grpck *{ file }*

file	Specifies a group file other than the default `/etc/group`.

File Name:	`grpck`	**Directory:**	/usr/sbin/	**Type:**	External

Tip: Use this to check the number of fields, that users exists in /etc/passwd, and more.

gsscred

UNIX Shell: All primary shells (csh, ksh, sh)

Function	Manages table entries that are used on servers to find the UID of clients connected by RPCSEC_GSS.
Syntax	gsscred [options...]

-n *user*	Specifies the principal name.
-o *oid*	Specifies the object identifier that denotes the name type of the user.
-c *comment*	Inserts a specific comment about the table entry.
-u *uid*	Specifies the UID when it isn't a local user.
-m *mech*	Specifies the mechanism to be translated.
-a	Adds a table entry for the specified mechanism.
-r	Removes the specified entry from the table.
-l	Searches the table for the specified entry.

File Name:	`gssscred`	**Directory:**	/usr/sbin/	**Type:**	External

gzexe

UNIX Shell: All primary shells (csh, ksh, sh)

Function	Compresses executable files into a self-extracting archive.
Syntax	gzexe *{ files... }*

files...	Specifies the file or files to compress.
-d	Decompresses the specified file or files.

File Name:	`gzexe`	**Directory:**	/usr/local/bin/	**Type:**	External

Tip: Very useful command if you have small disks and need to save space.

gzexe /usr/bin/passwd	Compresses the file `/usr/bin/passwd`.
gzexe -d /usr/bin/passwd	Uncompresses the file `/usr/bin/passwd`.

helpitem

UNIX Shell: All primary shells (csh, ksh, sh)

Function	Is used to format and show help messages for the command `ckitem`.
Syntax	helpitem [options...] *{ choices... }*

-W *width*	Specifies the line width for the help message.
-h *help*	Specifies the help message.

continued

choices...		Specifies which menu choices the user has.			
File Name:	`helpitem`	**Directory:**	/usr/sadm/bin/	**Type:**	External

hostconfig

UNIX Shell: All primary shells (csh, ksh, sh)

Function	Configures host parameters automatically, like hostname and domain name for a system using. `bootp`.
Syntax	hostconfig -p *protocol* [options...]

-p *protocol*		Specifies which protocol to use. Use bootparams or bootp.			
-d		Shows debug information.			
-n		Does the request, but doesn't change the parameters.			
-v		Verbose mode. Shows more information.			
-i *interface*		Uses only the specified network interface.			
-f *hostname*		Executes the protocol chosen as if the server's name is what's specified by hostname.			
File Name:	`hostconfig`	**Directory:**	/usr/sbin/	**Type:**	External
hostconfig -p bootparams -n -v			Shows what parameters would be set.		
hostconfig -p bootparams -v			Configures a server's host parameters.		

hostid

UNIX Shell: All primary shells (csh, ksh, sh)

Function	Shows the hexadecimal identifier of the current computer.
Syntax	hostid

File Name:	`hostid`	**Directory:**	/usr/bin/	**Type:**	External

htable

UNIX Shell: All primary shells (csh, ksh, sh)

Function	Converts a host's tables to network library routines from the older RFC 952 format.
Syntax	htable *file*

file		Specifies the file to convert.			
File Name:	`htable`	**Directory:**	/usr/sbin/	**Type:**	External
htable hosts			Convert host's tables to network library routines format.		

iceauth

UNIX Shell: All primary shells (csh, ksh, sh)

Function	Edits and shows authorization information to connect with ICE. Reads authorization data from one host and adds the information to another.
Syntax	iceauth [-f *file*] [options...] *{ commands }*

-f *file*		Specifies the authority file.			
-v		Enables extra messages.			
-q		Disables extra messages.			
-i		Ignores locks on authority file.			
-b		Breaks locks on authority file.			
Commands		**The commands to use in the ICE program are:**			
add		Adds an entry.			
exit		Saves changes and exits program.			
extract		Extracts entries into file.			
help		Shows help information.			
info		Shows information about entries.			
list		Shows entries.			
merge		Merges entries from files.			
quit		Aborts changes and exits program.			
remove		Erases entries.			
source		Reads commands from file.			
?		Shows help information.			
File Name:	`iceauth`	**Directory:**	/usr/openwin/bin/	**Type:**	External
iceauth info			Shows information about auth entries.		

iconv

UNIX Shell: All primary shells (csh, ksh, sh)

Function	Converts characters from one code set to another.
Syntax	iconv options... *{ files... }*

-f *inputcode*	Specifies the code set to convert from.
-t *outputcode*	Specifies the code set to convert to.
files...	Specifies the pathname of one or more files to convert code sets for.

File Name:	`iconv`	**Directory:**	/usr/bin/	**Type:**	External

imagetool

UNIX Shell: All primary shells (csh, ksh, sh)

Function	A GUI that is used to show gif, tiff, jpeg, and PostScript images.
Syntax	imagetool [options...]

-usage	Shows valid command-line options.
-v	Shows the current version of imagetool.
-verbose	Shows lots of debugging information.
-timeout seconds	Sets the timeout value for the display PostScript server.
imagefile	Specifies the file to show.

File Name:	`imagetool`	**Directory:**	/usr/openwin/bin/	**Type:**	External

imagetool myimage.jpg	Starts the imagetool GUI and loads the jpeg image myimage.jpg.

imake

UNIX Shell: All primary shells (csh, ksh, sh)

Function	Creates Makefiles from a template, a set of cpp macro functions, and a per-directory file that is called Imakefile.
Syntax	imake [options...]

-D*define*	Specifies directory configurations.
-I*dir*	Specifies directory to the imake template and configuration.
-T*template*	Specifies the name of the master template file.
-f *filename*	Specifies the per-directory input file.
-C *filename*	Specifies the name of the .c file that is created, usually Imakefile.c.
-s *filename*	Specifies the name of the make description file to create.
-e	Runs the created makefile.
-v	Shows the cpp command line that is used to create makefile.

File Name:	`imake`	**Directory:**	/usr/openwin/bin/	**Type:**	External

in.dhcpd

UNIX Shell: All primary shells (csh, ksh, sh)

Function	Configures the DHCP. It is used to forward or respond to DHCP or BOOTP protocol requests.
Syntax	in.dhcpd [options...]

	The following options are used when configured in BOOTP Server mode:
-d	Shows debug information.
-n	Disables automatic duplicate IP address detection.
-v	Verbose mode. Shows more information.
-b *mode*	Enables DHCP server to respond to BOOTP clients.
automatic	Automatically allocates IP addresses to BOOTP clients.
manual	Allocates IP addresses to registered BOOTP clients in server's database.
-h *relayhops*	Specifies the maximum number of relay hops before it drops the DHCP/BOOTP datagram.
-i *interface*	Specifies network interfaces and shows DHCP/BOOTP datagrams.
-o *DHCP-offer-Time-to-Live*	Specifies how long the DHCP server will hold the clients' requests.
-t *dhcptab-rescan-interval*	Specifies interval to read the dhcptab information.
	The following options are used when configured in BOOTP relay agent mode:
-r *relaylist*	Specifies a list of IP addresses or hostnames of DHCP or BOOTP server to relay requests for.
IPaddresses...	Specifies IP address of DHCP or BOOTP server to forward BOOTP requests.
hostnames...	Specifies hostname of DHCP or BOOTP server to forward BOOTP requests. (The relay list of servers must be specified in a comma-separated list.)
-d	Shows debug information.

continued

-v -h *relayhops* -i *interface*	Verbose mode. Shows more information. Specifies the maximum number of relay hops before it drops the DHCP/BOOTP datagram. Specifies network interfaces and shows DHCP/BOOTP datagrams.		
File Name: `in.dhcpd`	**Directory:** /usr/lib/inet/	**Type:**	External

in.rarpd, rarpd

UNIX Shell: All primary shells (csh, ksh, sh)

Function	Provides MAC-address to IP-address resolution to workstations at startup.
Syntax	in.rarpd [-d] -a in.rarpd [-d] *device { NR }*

-d -a *device* *NR*	Shows debug information. Starts a RARP daemon on all network interfaces that are running IP. Starts a RARP daemon for the device that you specify. Specifies the instance number of the device that you want to start.		
File Name: `in.rarpd`	**Directory:** /usr/sbin/	**Type:**	External

in.rdisc

UNIX Shell: All primary shells (csh, ksh, sh)

Function	Finds default routes on the network or broadcasts that your host is a router.
Syntax	in.rdisc [options...] *{ router } { host }*

 -a -f -s -r -p *preference* -T *interval* *router* *host*	**The following options can only be used with hosts:** Accepts all routers and puts them in the routing table in the kernel. Does not stop in.rdisc even if no routers are found. Sends three messages at startup to find routers. **The following options can only be used with routers:** Makes the host act as a router. Sets the preference level of the router to send to hosts. Specifies the send interval in seconds. **The following operands can be used with hosts and routers:** Sends messages to the multicast router address 224.0.0.2. Receives messages to the multicast host address 224.0.0.1.		
File Name: `in.rdisc`	**Directory:** /usr/sbin/	**Type:**	External

in.routed, routed

UNIX Shell: All primary shells (csh, ksh, sh)

Function	Provides network routing tables for hosts on the network. Also updates hosts acting as routers.
Syntax	in.routed [options...]

-g -q -s -S -t -v *file*	Sets the default destination for the Internet router. Does not provide routing information even if the host acts as a router. Provides routing information even if the host doesn't act as a router. Makes the host act as an Internet router. Shows all incoming and outgoing packets on STDOUT. Creates a log file with information about changes in the routing table.		
File Name: `in.routed`	**Directory:** /usr/sbin/	**Type:**	External

in.uucpd, uucpd

UNIX Shell: All primary shells (csh, ksh, sh)

Function	The server daemon for UUCP connections. Invoked by `inetd` upon request.
Syntax	in.uucpd [-n]

-n	Does not log the username in `wtmp`, `utmp`, and `lastlog`.		
File Name: `in.uucpd`	**Directory:** /usr/sbin/	**Type:**	External

inetd

UNIX Shell: All primary shells (csh, ksh, sh)

Function	Starts all services listed in the file `/etc/inetd.conf` It starts all Internet standard services such as FTP, telnet, SMTP, and HTTP, and is normally started during bootup.
Syntax	inetd [options...] *{ file }*

-d	Shows debug information.
-s	Runs inetd outside the control of the Service Access Facility.
-t	Logs all incoming IP addresses and port numbers to the system log.
-r	Finds and stops all connections to a UDP service that are lost.
-r *count interval*	Tries to start all lost connections, count = times and interval = seconds.
file	Specifies another inetd configuration file other than the default `/etc/inetd.conf`.

File Name:	`inetd`	**Directory:**	/usr/sbin/	**Type:**	External
Tip:	The `/etc/inetd.conf` file can be used to turn off some services such as FTP and telnet.				

installboot

UNIX Shell: Bourne shell (sh)

Function	Installs a bootblock in a partition to make it bootable.
Syntax	SPARC: installboot *bootblock device* x86: installboot *pboot bootblock device*

bootblock	Specifies the bootblock code to install on device.
device	Specifies the device to install a bootblock on; it must be a raw device.
pboot	Specifies the name of the partition boot file.

File Name:	`installboot`	**Directory:**	/usr/sbin/	**Type:**	Script

installboot /usr/platform/`uname -i`/lib/fs/ufs/bootblk /dev/rdsk/c0t0d0s3	Installs a bootblock on c0t0d0s3 on a SPARC computer.

installf

UNIX Shell: All primary shells (csh, ksh, sh)

Function	Maintains and updates the database that holds information about installed software.
Syntax	installf [options...] *package-instance { pathname }*

-c *class*	Specifies the class associations for the installed software.
-f	Specifies the installation is complete.
-M	Does not use the /etc/vfstab file to determine mount points for hosts.
-R *rootpath*	Specifies a new rootpath to use.
-V *file*	Specifies another vfstab file other than the default.
package-instance	Specifies the package-instance to associate with the pathname.
pathname	Specifies the pathname that is updated.
	The following operands are used with `pathname` only:
ftype	Specifies the file type: b = block, c = character, d = directory, and so on.
major	Specifies the major device number.
minor	Specifies the minor device number.
mode	Specifies the mode of the file in octal.
owner	Specifies the owner of the file.
group	Specifies which group the file belongs to.

File Name:	`installf`	**Directory:**	/usr/sbin/	**Type:**	External

isainfo

UNIX Shell: All primary shells (csh, ksh, sh)

Function	Shows the architecture and instruction set of the kernel.
Syntax	isainfo [options...]

-v	Verbose mode. Shows more information.
-k	Shows the instruction set used by the system.
-n	Shows the name of the instruction set.

continued

-b		Shows whether it is a 32- or 64-bit instruction set.			
File Name:	`isainfo`	**Directory:**	/usr/bin/	**Type:**	External
isainfo –k			Shows the instruction set used by the kernel.		

isalist

UNIX Shell: All primary shells (csh, ksh, sh)

Function	Shows all instruction sets that can run on the system to STDOUT.
Syntax	isalist

File Name:	`isalist`	**Directory:**	/usr/bin/	**Type:**	External

jar

UNIX Shell: Korn shell (ksh)

Function	Compresses multiple files into a single JAR file. Can also compress files in `ZIP` and `ZLIB` formats.
Syntax	jar [options...] *{ manifestfile } destinationfile inputfiles...*

-c	Creates a new archive.
-f	Specifies the name of the jar file to process.
-M	Does not create a manifest file.
-m	Includes patent information from the manifest file.
-o	Stores the file without compressing it.
-t	Lists the table of contents from STDOUT.
-v	Verbose mode. Shows more information.
-x *{ files... }*	Extracts all files; or just the specified files from STDIN.
manifestfile	Specifies the manifest file.
destinationfile	Specifies the destination file.
inputfiles...	Specifies the input file or files.

File Name:	`jar`	**Directory:**	/usr/bin/	**Type:**	Script
jar -cvf jarfile.jar *.sh			Creates a compressed jar file of all .sh files.		
jar -tvf jarfile.jar			Lists all files in jarfile.jar.		

java

UNIX Shell: Korn shell (ksh)

Function	Executes Java programs.
Syntax	java [options...] *classname*

-cs	Compares modification time of the class bytecode and the class source.
-checksource	Compares modification time of the class bytecode and the class source.
-classpathpath	Specifies the path to the Java classes.
-D*property=newvalue*	Sets new property values.
-debug	Starts debugging.
-fullversion	Shows the full version of Java.
-noclassgc	Disables garbage collection.
-noverify	Disables verification.
-ossx	Sets the maximum stack size for Java code.
-prof	Enables Java profiling.
-prof*file*	Enables Java profiling with a specific output file.
-ssx	Sets the maximum stack size for C code.
-t	Traces which instructions are being executed.
-v	Verbose mode. Shows more information.
-verbose	Verbose mode. Shows more information.
-verbosegc	Makes the garbage collector show free memory.
-verify	Verifies all code.
-verifyremote	Verifies all code loaded via a classloader.
-version	Shows the build version information.
-help	Shows help information.
-msx	Sets the startup size of the memory allocation pool.
-mxx	Sets the maximum memory allocation pool that can be used.
-noasyncgc	Does not use asynchronous garbage collection.

continued

classname	Specifies the Java class to execute.				
File Name:	`java`	**Directory:**	/usr/bin/	**Type:**	Script

java_g

UNIX Shell: Korn shell (ksh)

Function	A non-optimized Java version that can be used with debuggers.
Syntax	java_g [options...] *classname*

-checksource	Compares timestamp with the source file and updates if it is newer.
-classpath*path*	Specifies path to the class files.
-D*property=value*	Sets a new value for a property.
-debug	Shows debug information. It uses the jdb program.
-fullversion	Shows full version information.
-help	Shows help information.
-ms*x*	Sets the memory allocation startup size in bytes.
-mx*x*	Sets the maximum pool size for memory allocation.
-noasyncgc	Disables asynchronous garbage collection.
-noclassgc	Disable garbage collection for Java classes.
-noverify	Disables verification.
-oss*x*	Sets the maximum stack size that can be used by Java code in a single thread.
-prof	Enables Java profiling.
-prof*file*	Enables Java profiling with a specified output file.
-ss*x*	Sets the maximum stack size that can be used by C-code in a single thread.
-t	Shows trace information.
-v	Verbose mode. Shows more information.
-verbose	Verbose mode. Shows more information.
-verbosegc	Shows messages when it frees up memory.
-verify	Enables verification on all code.
-verifyremote	Verifies all code that has been loaded by a classloader.
-version	Shows version information.
classname	Specifies the class to be executed.

File Name:	`java_g`	**Directory:**	/usr/bin/	**Type:**	Script

javac

UNIX Shell: All primary shells (csh, ksh, sh)

Function	Compiles Java code into Java bytecode.
Syntax	javac [options...] *files...*

-classpath *path*	Specifies the path to the Java classes.
-d *directory*	Specifies where to put compiled Java classes.
-depend	Recompiles classes that have other class files as source.
-deprecation	Warns for the use of every code line that has the @deprecated tag.
-encoding *encname*	Specifies the encoding name of the source file.
-g	Creates debugging tables.
-J*javaoption*	Passes any given Java options along to the Java interpreter.
-nowarn	Disables warning messages.
-O	Optimizes the Java code and makes it run faster. However, the .class files are larger.
-verbose	Verbose mode. Shows more information.
files...	Specifies file or files that contains Java source code.

File Name:	`javac`	**Directory:**	/usr/bin/	**Type:**	External

javadoc

UNIX Shell: Korn shell (ksh)

Function	Manages documentation about classes, interfaces, methods, and the like in HTML format.
Syntax	javadoc [options...] *{ file }*

-author	Includes @author tags.
-classpath *path*	Specifies path to the Java class files.

continued

-d *directory*	Specifies where to put the HTML output files.
-docencoding *name*	Specifies the encoding name of the output files.
-encoding *name*	Specifies the encoding name of the source files.
-J *flag*	Passes options directly to the runtime system.
-nodeprecated	Excludes @deprecated tags.
-noindex	Disables package indexing.
-notree	Disables class and interface hierarchy.
-package	Shows package, protected, and public classes and their members.
-private	Shows all classes and their members.
-protected	Shows public and protected classes and their members.
-public	Shows public classes and their members.
-sourcepath *path*	Specifies path to the Java source files.
-verbose	Verbose mode. Shows more information in the output.
-version	Includes @version tags.
file	Specifies a java package or source file about which to generate an HTML description.

File Name:	`javadoc`	**Directory:**	/usr/bin/	**Type:**	Script

javadoc -d /my/public_html/doc java.lang	Creates documentation for java.lang in doc.
javadoc -sourcepath /my/java/lang	Specifies the path to the Java source files.

javah

UNIX Shell: Korn shell (ksh)

Function	Creates header files for use by C-language compilers.
Syntax	javah [options...] *classnames...*

-classpath *path*	Specifies the path where the system can find Java classes.
-d *directory*	Specifies where to save output files.
-help	Shows help information.
-jni	Outputs prototypes with JNI native methods.
-o *outfile*	Outputs a list of headers and source files to an output file.
-stubs	Creates C declarations from Java object files.
-td *directory*	Specifies where to place temporary files.
-trace	Adds tracing information to the files created with -stubs.
-v	Verbose mode. Shows more information.
-version	Shows version information.
classnames...	Specifies either a Java class or a package to use as input.

File Name:	`javah`	**Directory:**	/usr/bin/	**Type:**	Script

javakey

UNIX Shell: All primary shells (csh, ksh, sh)

Function	A security tool that generates digital signatures for Java archive files.
Syntax	javakey [options...]

	Options to `javakey` can't be combined.
-c *username { action }*	Creates an identity with a specific username. Action can be one of the following.
true	Specifies that username is trusted.
false	Specifies that username isn't trusted.
-cs *username { action }*	Creates a signer with a specific username. Action can be one of the following.
true	Specifies that signer is trusted.
false	Specifies that signer isn't trusted.
-dc *certfile*	Shows the certificates that are stored in the specified file.
-ec *user certnum outfile*	Exports a specific certificate from a specific signer or identity.
user	Specifies a signer or an identity.
certnum	Specifies a certificate.
outfile	Specifies the outputfile.
-ek *user pubfile [privfile]*	Exports a public key for a specific identity or signer.
user	Specifies a signer or an identity.
pubfile	Specifies the public key file.
{ private }	Specifies the private key for a specific signer.

continued

-g *signer algorithm keysize [pubfile] [privfile]*	Creates a key pair for a signer. You can also use -gk.
signer	Specifies the signer.
algorithm	Specifies the algorithm to use when creating a key pair.
keysize	Specifies the size in bits for the keys.
{ pubfile }	Specifies the public key file to write information to.
{ private }	Specifies where to write private key information.
-gc *file*	Uses the specified file to create a certificate.
-gs *file jarfile*	Uses information from the specified file to sign a Java archive file.
-ic *user certfile*	Imports a public key certificate and associated it with a signer or identity.
user	Specifies a signer or identity.
certfile	Specifies a file that contains a certificate.
-ii *user*	Supplies information for the specified user.
-ik *identity keyfile*	Associates an identity with a public key.
-ikp *signer pubfile privfile*	Associates a public and private key to a specific signer.
-l	Shows the usernames of all signers and identities.
-ld	Verbose mode. Shows more information about all signers and identities.
-li *user*	Shows verbose information about the specified signer or identity.
-r *user*	Removes the specified signer or identity.
-t *user { action }*	Specifies trust level for a signer or an identity. Action can be true or false.
true	Sets the trust level.
false	Removes the trust level.
File Name: `javakey`	**Directory:** /usr/bin/ **Type:** External

javald

UNIX Shell: Korn shell (ksh)

Function	Captures the environment needed to run a Java application specified by class name.
Syntax	javald [options...] *name*

-C *path*	Specifies where to search for classes. Adds to CLASSPATH.
-H *dir*	Sets JAVA_HOME to the specified directory.
-j *optionlist*	Passes a set of options.
-o *outfile*	Puts the wrapper in outfile.
-R *path*	Specifies where to search for native methods. Adds to LD_LIBRARY_PATH.
name	A Java application.
File Name: `javald`	**Directory:** /usr/bin **Type:** Script
javald -o /opt/ucg/bin/ucgapp1 ucgapp1	Creates a wrapper for ucgapp1 in /opt/ucg/bin.

javap

UNIX Shell: Korn shell (ksh)

Function	Disassembles Java class files.
Syntax	javap [options...] *classes...*

-b	Uses backward compatibility.
-c	Shows disassembled code for methods in the class file.
-classpath*path*	Sets the class path for `javap`.
-h	Creates C header file code.
-J *flag*	Passes options directly to the runtime system.
-l	Shows the tables of local and line variables.
-package	Shows protected, public, and package classes and their members.
-private	Shows all classes and their members.
-protected	Shows public and protected classes and their members.
-public	Shows public classes and their members.
-s	Shows the internal type signs.
-verbose	Verbose mode. Shows more information.
-verify	Starts the verifier.
-version	Shows version information.
classes...	Specifies the Java class files to disassemble.

continued

File Name:	javap	Directory:	/usr/bin/	Type:	Script

jdb

UNIX Shell: Korn shell (ksh)

Function	Debugs Java classes with a command-line interface similar to dbx using Java debugger APIs.
Syntax	jdb [options...] *{ name }*

-host *hostname*	Specifies the hostname or IP address of the computer to connect to.
-password *password*	Specifies the password shown when the Java interpreter is started with the -debug option.
name	Specifies the Java class name to debug.

File Name:	jdb	Directory:	/usr/bin/	Type:	Script

jdb my_classname	Starts the Java debugger with class my_classname.

jre

UNIX Shell: Korn shell (ksh)

Function	A runtime interpreter for Java.
Syntax	jre [options...] *name*

-classpath *path*	Sets class path for `jre`.
-cp *path*	Sets additional class paths to the base class path.
-D*property=value*	Sets a new property value.
-help	Shows help information.
-mx*x*	Sets the memory allocation startup size in bytes.
-ms*x*	Sets the maximum memory allocation pool size in bytes.
-noasyncgc	Disables asynchronous garbage collection.
-noclassgc	Disables garbage collection of class files.
-nojit	Disables the use of JIT compilers.
-noverify	Disables verification.
-oss*x*	Sets the maximum stack size per thread for Java code.
-ss*x*	Sets the maximum stack size per thread for C code.
-v	Verbose mode. Shows more information.
-verbose	Verbose mode. Shows more information.
-verbosegc	Shows a message when garbage collection frees up memory.
-verify	Verifies bytecode for the specified class file.
-verifyremote	Runs verification on all code that has been loaded via a class loader.
name	Specifies the class that you want to execute.

File Name:	jre	Directory:	/usr/bin/	Type:	Script

jsh

UNIX Shell: Bourne shell (sh)

Function	The Job control shell and command interpreter. It has similar functions as Bourne shell (sh), with job control.
Syntax	jsh [options...] *arguments...*

-c *string*	Reads commands form string.
-i	Makes the shell interactive. TERMINATE, INTERRUPT, and QUIT are ignored.
-p	Does not set the effective user and group IDs to the real user and group IDs.
-r	Runs the shell in restricted shell (same as rsh).
-s	Reads commands from STDIN.
	The following options can also be changed by using the set command in a script.
-a	Marks modified and created variables for export.
-e	Exits immediately with a non-zero exit status.
-f	Disabled filename generation.
-h	Locates and remembers function commands when they are defined.
-k	Places all keyword arguments in the environment for a command.
-n	Reads commands but doesn't run them.
-t	Runs one command and exits.
-u	When substituting, treats unset variables as an error.
-v	Shows input lines as they are read.

continued

-x	Shows commands and their arguments when they are executed.		
--	Does not change any flags. (If + is used instead of -, the flag is turned off.)		
arguments...	Specifies additional arguments to the shell or a script with arguments to run.		
File Name: jsh	**Directory:** /usr/bin/	**Type:**	External

kbd

UNIX Shell: All primary shells (csh, ksh, sh)

Function	Manipulates, shows, or changes the keyboard's values.
Syntax	kbd [options...]

-i	Reads and sets the default keyboard settings. If used with -d it reads and processes from the specified device.		
-r	Resets the keyboard.		
-t	Shows you the keyboard version.		
-c *on off*	Turns the keyboard clicking on or off.		
-a *enable disable*	Enables or disables the keyboard abort keys.		
-d *keyboard device*	Specifies the keyboard device to use; default is /dev/kbd.		
File Name: kbd	**Directory:** /usr/bin/	**Type:**	External
kbd -t	Shows the keyboard setting.		
kbd -c on	Turns keyboard clicking on.		

kbd_mode

UNIX Shell: All primary shells (csh, ksh, sh)

Function	Changes the keyboard translation mode.
Syntax	kbd_mode [option]

	The following options can't be combined		
-a	Creates simple ASCII characters.		
-n	Creates unencoded bytes.		
-e	Creates SunWindows input events with ASCII characters in the value field.		
-u	Creates input events with unencoded bytes in the value field.		
File Name: kbd_mode	**Directory:** /usr/openwin/bin	**Type:**	External
kbd_mode -a	Creates ASCII characters for the keyboard.		

kdestroy

UNIX Shell: All primary shells (csh, ksh, sh)

Function	Writes zeros to the user's Kerberos authorization tickets so as to destroy the file.
Syntax	kdestroy [options...]

-f	Does not display any status message.		
-n	Does not invalidate the kernel's NFS credentials.		
-q	Does not beep if operation fails.		
File Name: kdestroy	**Directory:** /usr/bin/	**Type:**	External
Note:	All of the user's tickets are not kept in the same place.		
kdestroy -q	Destroys Kerberos tickets for current user in silent mode.		
kdestroy -n	Destroys the tickets but not the NFS credentials.		

kerbd

UNIX Shell: All primary shells (csh, ksh, sh)

Function	Generates and validates the Kerberos tickets for the kernel RPC.
Syntax	kerbd [options...]

-d	Shows debug information.		
-g	Includes only each user's group in the mapped credentials.		
File Name: kerbd	**Directory:** /usr/sbin/	**Type:**	External

keylogin		UNIX Shell:	All primary shells (csh, ksh, sh)		
Function	Decrypts and stores a user's secret key, which is used in requests to any secure RPC service such as NIS+.				
Syntax	keylogin [-r]				
-r		Updates the `/etc/.rootkey` file and can only be used by superuser.			
File Name:	`keylogin`	**Directory:**	/usr/bin/	**Type:**	External
Tip:	New users would use the command *newkey* to generate their secret keys.				
keylogin -r		Starts keylogin and updates the /etc/.rootkey file.			

keylogout		UNIX Shell:	All primary shells (csh, ksh, sh)		
Function	Erases a user's secret key that is stored by the `keyserv` process.				
Syntax	keylogout [-f]				
-f		Forces the command to erase the secret key for the superuser.			
File Name:	`keylogout`	**Directory:**	/usr/bin/	**Type:**	External
Note:	This is used only for NIS+.				
keylogout -f		Forces the command to erase the key for the superuser.			

keyserv		UNIX Shell:	All primary shells (csh, ksh, sh)		
Function	A server daemon that stores the private encryption keys for the currently logged-in users.				
Syntax	keyserv [options...]				
-c		Specifies not to use the disk caches.			
-d		Disables the use of default keys for nobody.			
-D		Starts debug mode and logs all requests to the command.			
-n		Prompts the user for a password to decrypt root's password in the public key database. (Stores the root password in the /etc/.rootkey file after decryption.)			
-s		Specifies the size of the common key disk caches in one of the following formats.			
mechtype=size		Specifies the max number of entries, or max size in MB; for example, 2 MB.			
size		Uses the specified size on all caches.			
File Name:	`keyserv`	**Directory:**	/usr/sbin/	**Type:**	External
Note:	You must have a secure RPC domain configured. Set up the domain by using `/usr/bin/domainname`.				

kgmon		UNIX Shell:	All primary shells (csh, ksh, sh)		
Function	Monitors kernel profiling.				
Syntax	kgmon [options...]				
-i		Starts profiling buffers.			
-b		Starts kernel profiling.			
-h		Stops kernel profiling.			
-r		Resets the kernel profiling buffers.			
-p		Dumps the kernel profiling buffers.			
-d		Deallocates the kernel profiling buffers.			
-D		Shows debug information.			
File Name:	`kgmon`	**Directory:**	/usr/bin/	**Type:**	External
kgmon -b		Starts kernel profiling.			
kgmon -h		Stops kernel profiling.			

killall

killall		UNIX Shell:	All primary shells (csh, ksh, sh)
Function	Stops all active processes. Only a superuser can run this command.		
Syntax	killall *{ signal }*		

signal	Specifies the signal to send to each process. Default is signal 15.

File Name:	`killall`	**Directory:**	/usr/sbin/	**Type:**	External
Note:	It actually kills itself.				

kinit

kinit		UNIX Shell:	All primary shells (csh, ksh, sh)
Function	Logs in to the Kerberos authentication system.		
Syntax	kinit [options...] *user*		

-i	Prompts you to log in and start another session.
-l	Sets number of minutes that the ticket will live to between 5–1275 minutes (default is 480 minutes).
-r	Specifies to log in to a remote server.
-v	Verbose mode. Shows more information.
user	Specifies the username to use to log in.

File Name:	`kinit`	**Directory:**	/usr/bin/	**Type:**	External

klist

klist		UNIX Shell:	All primary shells (csh, ksh, sh)
Function	Shows you information listed in the ticket file about current Kerberos tickets held.		
Syntax	klist [options...]		

-s	Doesn't show ticket filename, owner name, or information on issue and expire times.
-t	Exits with status 0 if there are any valid tickets and with status 1 if there are no valid tickets.
-file *file*	Specifies the file to use as the ticket file.
-srvtab	Uses the ticket file as a service key file and shows all of the keys that it contains. (If no ticket file is specified, -srvtab uses /etc/srvtab by default.)

File Name:	`klist`	**Directory:**	/usr/bin/	**Type:**	External

ksh, rksh

ksh, rksh		UNIX Shell:	Korn shell (ksh)
Function	The Korn shell, a standard/restricted command and programming language.		
Syntax	ksh [options...] *{ arguments... }* ksh -c [options...] *command { arguments... }* rksh [options...] *{ arguments... }* rksh -c [options...] *command { arguments... }*		

-c *command*	Specifies the command to read.
-s	Reads commands from STDIN.
-i	Makes the shell interactive. TERMINATE, INTERRUPT, and QUIT are ignored.
-r	Runs the shell in restricted shell (same as rksh).
	The following options can be changed by using the `set` command in a script:
-a	Exports defined variables automatically.
-b	Informs the user asynchronously when a background job completes.
-C	Doesn't allow existing files to be overwritten by the shell redirection (>) operator.
-e	Runs the ERR tarp and exits if a command returns a non-zero exit status.
-f	Disables filename generation.
-h	When a command is first encountered, it becomes a tracked alias.
-k	Places all keyword arguments in the environment for a command.
-m	Runs background job in separate process group. Shows a line when completed.
-n	Reads commands but doesn't run them.

continued

-o *{ option }*	Sets option. If no option given, shows current status. See below for options.
allexport	The same as -a.
errexit	The same as -e.
bgnice	Runs background job at a lower priority. This is the default.
emacs	Uses an emacs-style in-line editor for the command line.
gmacs	Uses a gmacs-style in-line editor for the command line.
ignoreeof	Doesn't let the shell exit on EOF. The `exit` command must be used.
keyword	The same as -k.
markdirs	Marks all directories with a trailing / for result from a filename generation.
monitor	The same as -m.
noclobber	The same as -C.
noexec	The same as -n.
noglob	The same as -f.
nolog	Doesn't save function definition in the history file.
notify	The same to -b.
nounset	The same as -u.
privileged	The same as -p.
verbose	The same as -v.
trackall	The same as -h.
vi	Uses a vi-style in-line editor for the command line.
viraw	Processes each character as it is typed in vi mode.
xtrace	The same as -x.
-p	Doesn't process $HOME/.profile.
-s	Sorts the positional parameters lexicographically.
-t	Runs one command and exits.
-u	Handles parameters currently unset as an error when replacing variables.
-v	Shows input lines as they are read.
-x	Shows commands and their arguments when they are executed.
-	Turns off -x and -v flags and doesn't continue examining arguments for flags.
--	Doesn't change any flags. (If + is used instead of -, the flag is turned off.)
arguments...	Specifies additional arguments to the shell or a script with arguments to run.
File Name: `ksh`	**Directory:** /usr/bin/ **Type:** External

ksrvtgt

UNIX Shell: All primary shells (csh, ksh, sh)

Function	Manages Kerberos ticket-granting tickets.
Syntax	ksrvtgt *name instance* [*{ service } key*]
name	Specifies the username.
instance	Specifies the system name.
service	Specifies the Kerberos authentication service.
key	Specifies a service key to use for decryption.
File Name: `ksrvtgt`	**Directory:** /usr/bin/ **Type:** External

labelit

UNIX Shell: All primary shells (csh, ksh, sh)

Function	Writes or shows the label of an unmounted file system.
Syntax	labelit [options...] *device { filesystem }*
-F *fstype*	Specifies the file system type to run the command on.
-V	Simulates the command but doesn't execute it.
device	Specifies the raw device where the file system is.
filesystem	Specifies file system specific operands to either ufs or hsfs.
File Name: `labelit`	**Directory:** /usr/sbin/ **Type:** External

lastcomm

lastcomm	UNIX Shell: All primary shells (csh, ksh, sh)
Function	Shows the last commands executed, in reverse order.
Syntax	lastcomm *{ commandnames... } { usernames... } { terminalnames... }*

	The following arguments either can be combined or used separately.
commandnames...	Lists recently executed command names.
usernames...	Lists recently executed commands by a user.
terminalnames...	Lists recently executed commands from a terminal.
File Name: `lastcomm`	**Directory:** /usr/bin/ — **Type:** External
Tip:	A good way to find your terminal number is by using the command `who am i`.
lastcomm root	Lists if root has executed commands.
lastcomm halt root pts/1	Checks whether halt was executed by root on terminal 1.

lastlogin

lastlogin	UNIX Shell: Bourne shell (sh)
Function	Updates the login information in the file `/var/adm/acct/sum/loginlog`.
Syntax	lastlogin
File Name: `lastlogin`	**Directory:** /usr/lib/acct/ — **Type:** Script

ldapadd

ldapadd	UNIX Shell: All primary shells (csh, ksh, sh)
Function	Adds new entries to the LDAP server. Rejects duplicate attributes for same entry.
Syntax	ldapadd [options...]

-b	Assumes that any value that starts with a / is the pathname.
-c	Continues even if errors are reported. Default is exit after an error is found.
-n	Is used to preview modifications. Doesn't change existing entries.
-v	Verbose mode. Shows more information.
-F	Forces all changes regardless of content.
-d *debuglevel*	Sets the LDAP debugging level.
The debug levels are:	**You may combine or add debug levels together (for example 34 = debug filters and packets).**
1	Debugs trace only.
2	Debugs packets.
4	Debugs arguments only.
32	Debugs filters.
128	Debugs access control.
-D *binddn*	Uses the name specified in `binddn` and binds it to the directory.
-w *passwd*	Creates a password that is needed for authentication to the directory.
-h *ldaphost*	Specifies the server that is running LDAP.
-p *ldapport*	Specifies the TCP port that the `slapd` server is listening on.
-f *file*	Reads the modified entries from file instead of from STDIN.
-l *connections*	Defines the number of connections to process and modify in a directory (default is 1).
File Name: `ldapadd`	**Directory:** /usr/bin/ — **Type:** External

ldapdelete

ldapdelete	UNIX Shell: All primary shells (csh, ksh, sh)
Function	Erases one or multiple entries from an LDAP server.
Syntax	ldapdelete [options...] *{ names... }*

-n	Shows what will be done but will not erase any entries.
-v	Verbose mode. Shows more information.
-c	Continues even if errors are reported. Default is to exit after finding an error.
-d *debuglevel*	Sets the LDAP debugging level.

continued

The debug levels are:	**You may combine or add debug levels together (for example, 34 = debug filters and packets).**
1	Debugs trace only.
2	Debugs packets.
4	Debugs arguments only.
32	Debugs filters.
128	Debugs access control.
-f *file*	Reads information about deleted entries from the specified file.
-D *ibinddn*	Uses the name specified in `binddn` and binds it to the directory.
-w *passwd*	Creates a password that is needed for authentication to the directory.
-h *ldaphost*	Specifies the server that is running LDAP.
-M *authentication*	Binds the directory by using the specified authentication mechanism.
-p l*ldapport*	Specifies the TCP port that the LDAP sever is listening on.
names...	Specifies which distinguished entry names to delete.
File Name: `ldapdelete`	**Directory:** /usr/bin/ **Type:** External

ldapmodify

UNIX Shell: All primary shells (csh, ksh, sh)

Function	Binds, modifies, or adds entries to the LDAP server; rejects duplicates for the same entry.
Syntax	ldapmodify [options...]

-a	Adds new entries.
-b	Assumes that any value that starts with a / is the pathname.
-c	Continues even if errors are reported. Default is to exit after finding an error.
-r	Replaces existing value with a specified value.
-n	Shows what will be done but will not erase any entries.
-v	Verbose mode. Shows more information.
-F	Forces application of all changes regardless of the content of input lines.
-d *debuglevel*	Sets the LDAP debugging level.
The debug levels are:	**You may combine or add debug levels together (for example, 34 = debug filters and packets).**
1	Sets the LDAP debugging level.
2	Debugs packets.
4	Debugs arguments only.
32	Debugs filters.
128	Debugs access control.
-f *file*	Reads the modified entries from file.
-D *binddn*	Uses the name specified in `binddn` and binds it to the directory.
-w *passwd*	Creates a password that is needed for authentication to the directory.
-h *ldaphost*	Specifies the server that is running LDAP.
-M *authentication*	Binds the directory by using the specified authentication mechanism.
-p l*ldapport*	Specifies the TCP port that the LDAP sever is listening on.
-l *connections*	Specifies the number of connections to process and modify in a directory (default is 1).
File Name: `ldapmodify`	**Directory:** /usr/bin/ **Type:** External

ldapmodrdn

UNIX Shell: All primary shells (csh, ksh, sh)

Function	Connects to the LDAP server and modifies the RDN entries.
Syntax	ldapmodrdn [options...] *{ dn rdn }*

-r	Overrules the default by erasing old RDN values from entries.
-n	Shows what will be done but will not erase any entries.
-v	Verbose mode. Shows more information.
-c	Continues even if errors are reported. Default is to exit after finding an error.
-d *debuglevel*	Sets the LDAP debugging level.

continued

The debug levels are:	You may combine or add debug levels together (for example, 34 = debug filters and packets).		
1	Sets the LDAP debugging level.		
2	Debugs packets.		
4	Debugs arguments only.		
32	Debugs filters.		
128	Debugs access control.		
-f *file*	Reads the modified entries from file.		
-D *binddn*	Uses the name specified in `binddn` and binds it to the directory.		
-w *passwd*	Creates a password that is needed for authentication to the directory.		
-h *ldaphost*	Specifies the server that is running LDAP.		
-M *authentication*	Binds the directory by using the specified authentication mechanism (for example, CRAM-MD5).		
-p l*ldapport*	Specifies the TCP port that the LDAP server is listening on.		
dn rdn	Specifies the DN and RDN pair names. Separate multiple pairs by adding a space.		
File Name: `ldapmodrdn`	**Directory:** /usr/bin/	**Type:**	External

ldapsearch

UNIX Shell: All primary shells (csh, ksh, sh)

Function	Makes a connection to an LDAP server, performs searches by using the specified filter.
Syntax	ldapsearch [options...] *filter { attributes... }*

-n	Shows how, but doesn't form the search.
-u	Includes, in the form of the Distinguished Name (DN), the user-friendly form.
-v	Verbose mode. Shows more information.
-t	Writes retrieved values to a set of temporary files. Useful with non-ASCII.
-A	Retrieves attributes only without values.
-B	Doesn't display non-ASCII values. Automatically set by the -L option.
-L	Shows search results in modified format. Ignores the -F option.
-F *sep*	Separates fields between attribute names and values (default is =).
-S *attribute*	Sorts the returned entries by attribute.
-d *debuglevel*	Specifies debug level for the LDAP server.
-f *file*	Makes an LDAP search for each line in the file.
-D *binddn*	Specifies name to bind to.
-w *passwd*	Specifies password to the directory.
-h *ldaphost*	Specifies an alternative host for the slapd server to run on.
-M *authentication*	Sets the mechanism used to bind to the directory. The bind DN and password are mandatory.
-p *ldapport*	Specifies an alternate TCP port where the slapd server is listening.
-b *searchbase*	Specifies `searchbase` as starting point for the search.
-s *scope*	Specifies the scope of the search. Values are: base, one, or sub (default is sub).
-a *deref*	Specifies how alias dereferencing is done.
-l *timelimit*	Specifies maximum time limit in seconds for a search to be done.
-z *sizelimit*	Specifies the maximum size limit entries for a search to be done.

File Name: `ldapsearch`	**Directory:** /usr/bin/	**Type:**	External
Note:	It works like an SQL query.		
ldapsearch "cn=mark smith" cn telephoneNumber	The CommonName and telephoneNumber values are displayed.		

ldd

UNIX Shell: All primary shells (csh, ksh, sh)

Function	Lists executable files and their dynamic dependencies or shared objects. Also lists the pathnames of all shared objects that are needed when file is executed.
Syntax	ldd [options...] *file*

-d	Checks references to data objects.
-r	Data objects and functions are checked in one operation.
-f	Forces a check on insecure executable files.
-i	Shows the initialization order of execution.
-l	Forces the processing of all filters and their dependencies.

continued

-s -v *file*		Shows the search path to locate shared object dependencies. Shows all dependency relationships caused by processing `filename`. Specifies the filename and checks for compatibility.			
File Name:	ldd	**Directory:**	/usr/bin/	**Type:**	External
Warning:	Using the -d or -r option with shared objects can give misleading results.				
ldd /usr/bin/passwd			Lists the dynamic dependencies of the file passwd.		
ldd -i /usr/bin/finger			Displays init sections execution order for finger.		

line

UNIX Shell: All primary shells (csh, ksh, sh)

Function	Reads and copies one line from STDIN and shows the line on STDOUT, usually the screen.				
Syntax	line				
File Name:	line	**Directory:**	/usr/bin/	**Type:**	External
Note:	Very often used inside shell files or scripts to read from the user's terminal.				

link

UNIX Shell: All primary shells (csh, ksh, sh)

Function	Links files and directories to existing files or directories. Only superusers can use it.				
Syntax	link *currentfile newfile*				
currentfile *newfile*		Specifies which file to link to the new file or directory. Shows the name of the just created file.			
File Name:	link	**Directory:**	/usr/sbin/	**Type:**	External
Warning:	You should use `ln` instead.				
link /usr/java1.1 /usr/java			Makes a link (java) to directory java1.1.		
link /export/home/ucg /ucg			Makes a link to ucg home directory.		

lint

UNIX Shell: Bourne shell (sh)

Function	Finds the link to `/usr/ccs/bin/ucblint`; it is used by the C program verifier to find libraries.				
Syntax	lint [options...]				
-I *dir* -L *dir* -Y P *dir*		First searches the directory specified for filenames not starting with a slash `/`. Adds the directory specified to a list of directories searched by `/usr/ccs/bin/ucblint`. Modifies the default directory used to find libraries.			
File Name:	`lint`	**Directory:**	/usr/ucb/	**Type:**	Script
Note:	The program verifier `/usr/ccs/bin/ucblint` is only available with the SPROcc package.				

list_devices

UNIX Shell: All primary shells (csh, ksh, sh)

Function	Lists assigned devices in the system and checks their association with current processes.				
Syntax	list_devices [options...] *{ device }*				
 -l *{ device }* -n *{ device }* -u *{ device }* -s -U *uid*		**At least one of the following options is needed and can't be combined:** Shows device pathnames of special files associated with device and current process. Same as -l except shows devices currently not allocated to a process. Shows device pathnames of special files a device allocated to owner of process. **The following options can be combined and used with any of the above options:** Specifies silent mode. Uses the user ID `uid` to run the operation. Only superuser can use it.			
File Name:	`list_devices`	**Directory:**	/usr/sbin/	**Type:**	External
Note:	Available only if the Basic Security Module has been enabled.				
list_devices -l			Shows assigned devices in the system.		

listdgrp

listdgrp	UNIX Shell:	All primary shells (csh, ksh, sh)
Function	Shows members of the device group list specified by `dgroup`.	
Syntax	listdgrp *dgroups...*	

dgroups...	Specifies the device group.		
File Name: `listdgrp`	**Directory:** /usr/bin/	**Type:**	External
Note:	The file `/etc/dgroup.tab` stores the device group table.		
listdgrp dpart	Shows the dpart device group members.		
listdgrp disk	Shows the disk device group members.		

listres

listres	UNIX Shell:	All primary shells (csh, ksh, sh)
Function	Creates a list of widget's names and classes.	
Syntax	listres [options...]	

-all	Shows information for all widgets and objects.		
-nosuper	Doesn't show resources inherited from a super class.		
-variable	Defines widgets by the names of the class record variables.		
-top *name*	Specifies the name of the widget to be treated as the top of the hierarchy.		
-format *printf-string*	Specifies the string to be used to show the name, class, and so on.		
File Name: `listres`	**Directory:** /usr/openwin/bin/	**Type:**	External
listres -all	Lists all known widgets and objects.		

listusers

listusers	UNIX Shell:	All primary shells (csh, ksh, sh)
Function	Lists all user logins and shows the login ID and account field value from specified database.	
Syntax	listusers [options...]	

-g *groups*	Lists and sorts all user logins from specified group by login.		
-l *logins*	Lists and sorts specified user logins by login.		
File Name: `listusers`	**Directory:** /usr/bin/	**Type:**	External
Note:	A user login is one that has a UID of 100 or greater.		
listusers -g ucg1	Lists all users in the group ucg1.		

loadkeys

loadkeys	UNIX Shell:	All primary shells (csh, ksh, sh)
Function	Reads and modifies the keyboard translation tables.	
Syntax	loadkeys *{ filename }*	

filename	Specifies the keyboard layout filename.		
File Name: `loadkeys`	**Directory:** /usr/bin/	**Type:**	External

locale

locale	UNIX Shell:	All primary shells (csh, ksh, sh)
Function	Shows locale-specific information.	
Syntax	locale [option] *name*	

-a	Writes information about all available public locales, including POSIX.		
-c	Writes the names of selected locale categories. Can be combined with the -k option.		
-k	Writes the names and values of selected keywords, see `operand`.		
-m	Writes the names of all character maps.		
name	Uses the name of a locale category, keyword, or reserved name character map.		
File Name: `locale`	**Directory:** /usr/bin/	**Type:**	External
Tip:	Using `locale` without options shows the current locale settings.		
locale LC_TIME	Shows the locale LC_TIME on STDOUT.		
locale -a	Lists all available public locales.		

localedef

UNIX Shell: All primary shells (csh, ksh, sh)

Function	Defines the locale definition format.
Syntax	localedef [options...] *localename*

-c	Creates output even if warning is given.
-C *compiler options*	Sends compiler options to the C compiler.
-f *charmap*	Specifies a different character mapping than the default.
-i *sourcefile*	Defines the source file.
-L *linker option*	Passes the linker option to the C compiler (old option; same as -W cc. arg).
-m *model*	Specifies whether `localedef` will generate a 64-bit or a 32-bit locale object.
-W *cc,arg*	Passes `arg` options to the C compiler; separate arguments with comma.
-x *extensions file*	Specifies in which extension file various `localedef` options are listed.
localename	Defines the locale to be processed.

File Name:	`localedef`	**Directory:**	/usr/bin/	**Type:**	External

lockd

UNIX Shell: All primary shells (csh, ksh, sh)

Function	Performs record locking on NFS files.
Syntax	lockd [options...] *{ threads }*

-g *graceperiod*	Time a client has to reclaim a lock after a server reboot (default is 45 seconds).
-t *timeout*	Time to wait before sending another lock request (default is 15 seconds).
threads	Specifies the maximum number of concurrent threads (default is 20).

File Name:	`lockd`	**Directory:**	/usr/lib/nfs/	**Type:**	External

lockfs

UNIX Shell: All primary shells (csh, ksh, sh)

Function	Reports and changes the status of the file system locks. It unlocks file systems that were improperly locked by an application.
Syntax	lockfs [options...] *{ filesystems... }*

-a	Applies command to all mounted, UFS-type file systems.
-c *string*	Specifies a comment field.
-d	Delete-lock (`dlock`) suspends access that could remove directory entries.
-e	Error-lock (`elock`) blocks all local access to the locked file system.
-f	Flushes the log and writes the transactions to the file system.
	The following are transactions to the master file system:
-h	Hard-locks the specified file system. It can't be unlocked.
-n	Name-locks (`nlock`) the specified file system.
-u	Unlocks (`ulock`) the specified file system.
-w	Write-locks (`wlock`) the specified file system.
filesystems...	Specifies the file system or file systems. Separated by blank space.

File Name:	`lockfs`	**Directory:**	/usr/sbin/	**Type:**	External

lockfs -a	Shows the lockfs output.

lockstat

UNIX Shell: All primary shells (csh, ksh, sh)

Function	Gathers and shows statistics on kernel synchronization objects.
Syntax	lockstat [options...] *command { arguments... }*

-A	Monitors all events. -A is same as -CEH.
-C	Monitors conflicts; active by default.
-E	Monitors error events; active by default.
-H	Monitors hold events; off by default.
-e *event list*	Only monitors the specified events. Event list is comma-separated.
-b	Monitors basic statistics: lock, caller, number of events.
-t	Monitors timing: basic plus timing for all events, which is the default.
-h	Monitors histogram: timing plus time distribution histograms.
-s *depth*	Stacks trace: monitors histogram plus stack traces of events.

continued

-n *nlocks*		Defines the maximum number of locks to watch.			
-l *lock*[,*size*]		Only monitors lock. Can be specified as a symbolic name or hex address.			
-d *duration*		Monitors only events longer than duration.			
-T		Traces events. Default is off.			
-c		Merges lock data for lock arrays.			
-w		Discerns events by `lock` not by `caller`.			
-W		Discerns events by `caller` not by `lock`.			
-R		Shows rates rather than counts.			
-p		Creates a parsable output format.			
-D *count*		Shows only the top count events of each type.			
-o *filename*		Directs output to filename.			
command		Gathers kernel-locking statistics until the specified command completes.			
arguments...		Specifies any arguments to the specified command.			
File Name:	`lockstat`	**Directory:**	/usr/sbin/	**Type:**	External
lockstat -A ls -lia			Shows lockstat for `ls -lia`.		

logins

UNIX Shell: All primary shells (csh, ksh, sh)

Function	Shows a list of logins on a system. Information is shown about both user and system logins.				
Syntax	logins [options...]				
-a		Shows the password's expiration day and the number of days it can be unused.			
-d		Shows only logins with duplicate user ids.			
-m		Shows group memberships for all logins.			
-o		Shows the output in one colon-separated line.			
-p		Shows the logins that have no passwords.			
-s		Shows all system logins.			
-t		Sorts the output by login.			
-u		Shows all user logins.			
-x		Shows more information: home directory, login shell, and password information.			
-g *groups...*		Shows users in a specified group. For multiple groups, lists them comma-separated.			
-l *logins...*		Shows a specified login. For multiple logins, lists them comma-separated.			
File Name:	`logins`	**Directory:**	/usr/bin/	**Type:**	External
Tip:	Used for example when you want to know who doesn't have a password.				
logins -a -l root,joe,lisa			Shows information about these users with password aging.		
logins -x -l joe			Shows extended information about the user joe.		

lorder

UNIX Shell: Bourne shell (sh)

Function	Finds ordering relation for an object or library archive and shows a list of the pairs.				
Syntax	lorder *filenames...*				
filenames...		Can use one or more objects or library archive filenames as the input.			
File Name:	`lorder`	**Directory:**	/usr/ccs/bin/	**Type:**	Script

lp

UNIX Shell: All primary shells (csh, ksh, sh)

Function	Sends print requests to a destination.	
Syntax	lp [options...] *{ files... }* lp -i *requestID* [options...]	
-c		Copies file before showing.
-m		Sends mail when the file is shown.
-p		Allows a notice when the print request ends. (Needs additional software to run.)
-s		Doesn't show messages sent from the command.
-w		Sends a message on the user's terminal or a mail when the files are printed.
-d *destination*		Prints file on a specified destination — a printer or a class of printers.
-f *form-name*		Prints file on the form name. Ensures that the form is mounted on the printer.

continued

-H *special-handling*	Prints the request according to specified special handling. **The following values are accepted with special handling:**
hold	Holds the print request until notified. Stops a print job.
resume	Continues a held print request.
immediate	Prints the most recent request next if more than one request is assigned.
-m	Sends mail when print file is completed.
-n *number*	Prints copies of file as specified by number. Number is specified by digits.
-o *options...*	Specifies printer-dependent options.
nobanner	Doesn't print a banner page. The LP administrator can disallow this option.
nofilebreak	Doesn't insert a form feed between multiple print requests.
length=*numberi*	Specifies length in inches. Uses number to specify how many inches.
length=*numberc*	Specifies length in centimeters.
length=*number*	Specifies length in lines.
width=*numberi*	Specifies the width in inches.
width=*numberc*	Specifies the width in centimeters.
width=*number*	Specifies the width in columns. (The length options may not be used with the -f option.)
lpi=*number*	Prints request with the line pitch set to inch; number specifies lines in an inch. (The above option may not be used with the -f option.)
cpi=*n*	Specifies how many characters per inch will be printed.
cpi=*pica*	Sets 10 characters per inch.
cpi=*elite*	Sets 12 characters per inch.
cpi=*compressed*	Sets pitch to as many characters as the printer can handle.
stty=*list*	Prints according to the `stty` options specified in the list below:
-a	Writes all of the option settings for the terminal to the `STDOUT`.
-g	Reports current settings as an argument that can be used by another `ssty` command. (If the list contains blanks, you must use single quotes: '-a -g')
-P *page-list*	Prints a specified list of pages in ascending order.
-p	Allows a notice when the print request ends. (Needs additional software to run.)
-q *priority-level*	Assigns a priority of 0 to 39 to the print request. Use 0 to specify the highest priority.
-s	Suppresses the messages sent from `lp`.
-S *character-set*	Prints the request with the specified character set.
-S *print-wheel*	Prints the request with the specified printwheel.
-t *title*	Prints a title instead of the name of the file on the banner page.
-T *content-type* [-r]	Specifies the content type to use. Uses a filter if type not supported by printer.
-r	Specifies that a filter will not be used to convert the type to an acceptable format.
-w	Sends a message on the user's terminal or a mail when the files are printed.
-y *mode-list*	Specifies the mode-list to use. Uses a filter if mode isn't supported by printer.
-i *requestID*	Specifies the requestID of what you would like to print. (RequestID can only be used with LP version 2.6 or a compatible version.)
files...	Specifies the filename(s), including the path of the file to print.

File Name:	`lp`	**Directory:**	/usr/bin/	**Type:**	External
Tip:	`$HOME/.printers` holds the user-configurable printer database.				

lp /etc/hosts	Prints host file to default printer.
lp -m /etc/hosts	Prints host file to default printer and notifies by mail.

lpadmin

UNIX Shell: Bourne shell (sh)

Function	Manages print services.
Syntax	lpadmin [options...]

-p *printer-options*	Configures a new printer or changes the configuration of an existing printer. (When creating a new printer, use one of the options -v, -U, or -s.)
-x *dest*	Removes a printer destination.
-d *dest*	Sets/changes the system default destination. No other option can be used with -d.
-S *print-wheel*	Mounts the printwheel on a given printer. Only used with the option -M.
-A *alert-type*	Defines an alert that informs the administrator when a printer fault is detected.

continued

mail	Sends the alert message to the administrator by mail.
write	Writes the message to the terminal where the administrator is logged in.
quiet	Doesn't send messages for the current condition.
showfault	Runs a fault handler on each system that has a print job in the queue if it can. (Showfault is invoked with printer name, date, and filename.)
none	Doesn't send messages; removes the existing alert definition for the printer.
shell-command	Runs the shell command every time the alert needs to be sent.
list	Shows the type of alert for the printer fault without making changes.
-W *minutes*	Sets the interval for sending alerts.
-Q *requests*	Alerts are sent when a certain number of print requests are waiting.
-M	Mounts one of the following: (for example, `-M, -f, form-name`)
-f *form-name*	Mounts the form on a given printer.
-a	Prints alignment pattern without banner page.
-o *filebreak*	Inserts a form feed between each copy of the alignment pattern.
-t *tray-number*	Uses printer tray number.
-c *class*	Inserts printer into the specified class.
-D *comment*	Saves the comment to show whether a user asked for a full description of printer.
-e *printer*	Copies interface program of existing printer to another printer. Don't use -i or -m.
-F *fault-recovery*	Specifies the recovery to use for print request stopped because of a printer fault.
	Fault-recovery can be one of the following:
continue	Continues printing from where it stopped. Requires a filter to wait for the fault to clear.
beginning	Starts printing the request again from the beginning.
wait	Stops printing and waits for the administrator or a user to start printing again.
-f allow/deny:*form-list*	Allows or denies the forms to be printed on a new printer.
-h	Specifies the device associated with the printer is hardwired.
-I *content-type-list*	Allows printer to handle print requests using the content-type list.
-i *interface*	Creates a new interface program for printer. Specifies pathname for the interface. (You can not use -e and -m together with –i.)
-l	Specifies the associated device is a login terminal.
-m *model*	Selects model interface program for printer. Cannot be used with -e and -i.
-P *paper-name*	Specifies list of paper type that is supported by the printer.
-r *class*	Removes printer from the specified class.
-S *list*	Specifies a list of printwheels or character sets to be used on the printer.
-s *system-name*[!*printer-name*]	Creates a remote printer (via remote host). Specifies printer name or IP address.
-T *printer-type-list*	Sets printer type; types are found in the term info.
-t *number-of-trays*	Sets the number of trays when creating the printer.
-u allow/deny:*ACTION*	Allows or denies access to printer for users in the login ID list.
login-ID	Specifies a user on any system.
system-name!*login-ID*	Specifies a system and a user.
system-name!all	Specifies a system and all its users.
all!*login-ID*	Specifies user on all systems.
-all	Specifies all users on all systems.
-list	Allows or denies the users specified by login ID list access to the printer.
-U *dial-info*	Gives print service permission to access a remote printer.
-v device	Relates a pathname with one or several printers.

File Name:	`lpadmin`	**Directory:**	/usr/sbin/	**Type:**	Script
Tip:	Remember to run `accept` on request cue and to enable the printer.				

lpadmin -p hp -v /dev/null	Installs printer hp.
lpadmin -p hp -s 192.168.1.200	Assigns IP address to printer hp.

lpc

lpc			**UNIX Shell:**	All primary shells (csh, ksh, sh)
Function	Controls line printers.			
Syntax	lpc *{ command }* *{ parameters... }*			

command	Specifies an internal command.
	These commands can be used from the `lpc` prompt or directly after the command.
quit	Exits from lpc.
restart [all | printers ...]	Starts at least one or all printer daemons.
status [all | printer ...]	Shows the status of at least one or all print daemons and print queues.
	Only a superuser can execute the following `lpc` commands:
abort [all | printer ...]	Stops all or specific print files from print queue.
clean [all | printer ...]	Removes one or all print spool files from the print queue.
disable [all | printer ...]	Turns off the print queue for at least one or all printers.
down [all | printer] mess	Turns print queue off, disables printing, and inserts message to printer status file.
enable [all | printer ...]	Enables `lpr` to add new jobs on all or on specified printers in the spool queue.
start [all | printer ...]	Starts spooling daemon for all or for specified printers.
stop [all | printer ...]	Stops spooling daemon for all or specified printers when the current job is complete.
up [all | printer ...]	Turns all or specific printer queues on. Undoes the effects of down.
topq *printer { operands... }*	Moves print jobs or a request-ID from a user on a printer to the start of the queue.
	One or both identifiers can be used, but only in this order:
request-ID...	Specifies which request-ID or print job will be moved.
user...	Specifies the user's job or request that is moved. Uses the login name.

File Name:	`lpc`	**Directory:**	/usr/ucb/	**Type:**	External

lpc status	Shows status on default printer.
lpc up all	Turns queue on for all printers.

lpfilter

lpfilter			**UNIX Shell:**	All primary shells (csh, ksh, sh)
Function	Makes the file content compatible for a printer. Specific filters will assist to convert the file into the proper format.			
Syntax	lpfilter -f *filter* option			

-f *filter*	Selects the name of the filter that is added, changed, deleted, listed, or reset.
	You must use only one of the following options:
-	Adds or changes the settings of a filter by using `STDIN`.
-F *file*	Specifies a file and its path that is used to add or change a filter.
	File must contain at least one of the types below, separated by commas:
Input types:	Specifies the content types that are used by the filter (default is any).
Output types:	Specifies the content types that are produced from an input type (default is any).
Printer types:	Specifies the printer types that can be used by the printer (default is any).
Printers:	Specifies the printers that the filter can be used with (default is any).
Filter type:	Specifies a `slow` or `fast` filter type: slow = remote printer, fast = local.
Command:	Specifies the shell command that starts the filter. Includes path and any options.
Options:	Specifies a list of templates that are used to create filter characteristics.
-i	Resets the specified filter to its default.
-x	Deletes the specified filter.
-l	Shows the description on a filter.
all	Specifies that all filters will be affected. This is foolish in some cases.

File Name:	`lpfilter`	**Directory:**	/usr/sbin/	**Type:**	External
Note:	You must use either the -F *file* or the – to add or change a filter.				

lpforms

UNIX Shell:	All primary shells (csh, ksh, sh)
Function	Manages forms to use with the LP print service.
Syntax	lpforms -f *form-name* option [options...]

-f *formname*	Specifies the form.
	The first form of `lpforms` requires one of the following options to be used:
-F *pathname*	Adds or changes the form name specified by the information in pathname.
-	Adds new form or changes the form name.
-x	Deletes the form name. Must use this option separately.
-l	Lists the attributes of the form name.
	The second form of `lpforms` requires one of the following options to be used:
-f *formname*	Same as -f.
-A *Alert-type*	Specifies alert to mount the form when there are queued jobs that need it.
-P *paper-name* [-d]	Specifies paper name on the form. If -d is used, this paper is default.
-Q *requests*	Specifies number of print requests waiting before sending an alert.
-W *minutes*	Specifies interval in minutes to send an alert.

File Name:	`lpforms`	**Directory:**	/usr/sbin/	**Type:**	External

lpforms -f olducgform	Loads a form called olducgform.
lpform -F newucgform	Creates a new form called newucgform.

lpget

UNIX Shell:	All primary shells (csh, ksh, sh)
Function	Shows a printing configuration report.
Syntax	lpget [-k] *{ destinations... } { list }*

-k *key*	Shows a configuration report for the defined key.
destinations...	Shows a configuration report for a printer or class of printers.
list	Shows a report of all configured destinations.

File Name:	`lpget`	**Directory:**	/usr/bin/	**Type:**	External

lpget list	Shows all available printer configurations.
lpget storhp	Shows configurations for the printer storhp.

lpmove

UNIX Shell:	All primary shells (csh, ksh, sh)
Function	Moves queued print requests between destinations on the local system.
Syntax	lpmove *requestID destination* lpmove *destination1 destination2*

	Moves specific print requests to a specific destination:
requestID	Specifies the print request to be moved.
destination	Specifies the name of the printer or printers to which to move the print request.
	Then uses these options to move from one destination to another:
destination1	Specifies the name of the destination from which lpmove moves all print requests.
destination2	Specifies the name of the destination to which lpmove moves all print requests.

File Name:	`lpmove`	**Directory:**	/usr/sbin/	**Type:**	External
Tip:	Use lpstat to get the request-IDs. All destination options can use the POSIX-style server: destination or FNS names.				

lpmove hp-4 hplaser	Move print request with ID 4 to hplaser.
lpmove hpcolor hplaser	Move print requests from hpcolor to hplaser.

lpsched

UNIX Shell:	All primary shells (csh, ksh, sh)
Function	Starts or restarts the LP print service.
Syntax	lpsched [options...]

continued

-f *filters* -n *notifiers* -p *fd* -r *fd*		Number of concurrent slow filters (default is 1). Number of concurrent notification processes (default is 1). File descriptor limit (default is 4096). Number of reserved file descriptors for internal use (default is 2).			
File Name:	`lpsched`	**Directory:**	/usr/lib/lp/	**Type:**	External
lpsched -p 8192			Assigns more file descriptors for print servers with a heavy load.		

lpset

UNIX Shell: All primary shells (csh, ksh, sh)

Function	Creates and updates printing configuration in the system configuration databases.
Syntax	lpset [options...] *{ destination }*

-n system -n fns -x -a *key=value* -d *key* *destination*		Updates the configuration information in `/etc/printers.conf` file. Updates the configuration information using the FNS naming context. Removes all configurations for the destination. Configures the specified key=value pair for the destination. Deletes the configuration option specified by key for the destination entry. Specifies the entry in which to create or modify information.			
File Name:	`lpset`	**Directory:**	/usr/bin/	**Type:**	External
Note:	POSIX-style destination names are not acceptable.				
lpset -x hplaser			Removes all configuration information for hplaser.		

lpshut

UNIX Shell: All primary shells (csh, ksh, sh)

Function	Stops the LP print service.
Syntax	lpshut

File Name:	`lpshut`	**Directory:**	/usr/sbin/	**Type:**	External
Tip:	Use `lpsched` to restart printers.				

lpstat

UNIX Shell: All primary shells (csh, ksh, sh)

Function	Shows status information of the print service.
Syntax	lpstat [options...]

-d	Shows the default print queue for print requests.
-r	Shows the status of the LP request scheduler.
-R	Shows the position number of each request in the print queue.
-s	Shows status of LP scheduler, default destination, and list of printers and devices.
-t	Shows all status information including all information received with the -s option.
-o *list*	Shows the status of output requests. Lists printers, class names, and requestIDs.
-c *list*	Shows names of all classes and their members. List gives a list of class names.
-f *list*	Shows verification that forms are recognized by the LP print service.
-l	Lists the form descriptions.
-p list	Shows the status of printers. Lists printers. Can be used with the following options:
-l	Returns a full description of each printer's configuration and the interface used.
-D	Shows a brief description for each printer in list.
-S *list*	Verifies that the character sets or print wheels specified are recognized by LP service.
-l	Shows mounted print wheels or character sets; specifies the built-in character sets.
-u *options...*	Shows the status of output requests for users. You can use the following options:
login-ID	Specifies a user on any system.
system name!*Login*	Specifies a user on system `system name`.
system name!All	Specifies all users on system `system name`.
all!*loginID*	Specifies a user on all systems.
all	Specifies all users on all systems.
-a *list*	Reports that print destination accepts the request.
list	Shows a merged list of printer names and class names.

File Name:	`lpstat`	**Directory:**	/usr/bin/	**Type:**	External
Tip:	You can also use the command `/usr/ucb/lpc`.				
lpstat -t			Shows status information about all printers.		
lpstat -r			Shows whether the scheduler is running.		

lptest

UNIX Shell: All primary shells (csh, ksh, sh)

Function	Generates a ripple test pattern to STDOUT and shows all 96 printable ASCII characters; useful for testing printers.
Syntax	lptest *{ length number }*

length *number*		Determines the length of each test line (default is 79). Determines the number of test lines to print.			
File Name:	`lptest`	**Directory:**	/usr/ucb/	**Type:**	External
lptest 40 500			Writes 40 characters in width and 500 lines.		

lpusers

UNIX Shell: All primary shells (csh, ksh, sh)

Function	Sets printing queue priorities. Can be assigned to jobs sent by users of LP print service.
Syntax	lpusers [options...]

-d *priority-level* -l -q *priority-level* -u *login-ID-list*		Sets the system-wide priority default to priority level (0 to 39 where 0 is high). Lists the default priority level and the priority limits assigned to users. **The options -q and -u can be used together or by themselves.** Sets highest priority level for users not explicitly covered. Removes priority levels for specified users granted explicit access.			
File Name:	`lpusers`	**Directory:**	/usr/sbin/	**Type:**	External
lpusers -l			Lists default priority level and limits.		
lpusers -d 5			Sets default priority level to 5.		

luxadm

UNIX Shell: All primary shells (csh, ksh, sh)

Function	Manages RSM, SENA, and SPARCstorage Array subsystem and individual FC AL devices.
Syntax	luxadm [options ...] *subcommand* [options ...] *ACTION*

pathname	Specifies the logical and physical paths to the device or controller.
	The following path types and formats are used:
SENA	For a SENA device use a complete physical, logical, or WWN pathname.
SPARC	For a SPARCstorage Array or RSM controller, use `cN` where N = controller number.
enclosure	When specifying an enclosure, use one of these formats:
box [,f*n*]	Where box = SENA enclosure name, ,f = front slot, and n = slot number 0-6 or 0-10.
box [,r*n*]	Where box = SENA enclosure name, ,r = rear slot, and n = slot number 0-6 or 0-10.
subcommand	Most subcommands follow the syntax subcommand [option] *{ ACTION }* where:
download	Downloads the prom image specified by file path to the specified SENA or SPARC object.
	You may select one of these options:
-s	Saves the downloaded firmware into the FEPROM. Use with caution!
-w *WWN*	Changes the WWN of the SPARCstorage Array controller.
-f *path*	Specifies the path and name of the prom image file. (If no filepath is given, then the following defaults apply:)
	SPARC = usr/lib/firmware/ssa/ssafirmware, SENA = usr/lib/locale/C/LC_MESSAGES.
ACTION	**Specifies the type of enclosure.**
enclosure	Alters a name of one or more enclosures. Works only on SENA.
	You must specify one of the following:
newname enclosure	Applies a new name (less than 17 characters) to the object `enclosure`.
newname pathname	Applies a new name (less than 17 characters) to the object `pathname`.
fc_s_download	Downloads fcode from the fcodefile into any FC/S Sbus Cards. Single-user mode only.
-F	Forces an fcode download.
-f *file*	Specifies the file that fcode will be taken from. Default = current FC Sbus version.
fcal_s_download	Downloads fcode from the fcode file into any FC100/S Sbus Cards. Single-user mode only.
-f *file*	Specifies the file that fcode will be taken from. Default = current FC100 bus version.

continued

power_off	Starts power-save mode for SENA or SPARC objects.
	Uses the syntax power_off *pathname ACTION* where:
-F	Attempts to power off even those devices that are busy.
tray	Specifies the controller tray.
port	Specifies the enclosure port. (If a SENA is addressed, the SENA drive becomes unavailable.) If an Enclosure Services card in SPARC is addressed, the RSM tray is turned off.
probe	Searches and shows attached SENA subsystem information.
-p	Shows the physical pathname.
release *pathname*	Frees any reservation put on the specified disk.
replace_device	Replaces new devices or device chains by hot removing. Works only on RSM.
	Uses the syntax replacedevice [-F] *pathname* where:
-F	Forces hot plugging one or more devices even if they are being used.
reserve *pathname*	Reserves the specified disk to be used by the delivering host.
set_boot_dev	Sets system PROM boot device variable to the physical device name to *pathname*.
	Uses the syntax set_boot_dev [-y *pathname*] where:
-y *pathname*	Runs the subcommand in non-interactive mode.
start	Spins every disk that is specified. SPARCstorage Array only.
	Uses the syntax start [-t *tray*] *pathname* where:
-t *tray*	Spins all of the disks on the specified tray number.
stop	Spins down every disk that is specified. SPARCstorage Array only.
	Uses the syntax stop [-t *tray*] *pathname* where:
-t *tray*	Spins down all of the disks on the specified tray number.
	The following sub options use the ACTION: `pathname` OR `enclosure`
remove_device	Removes new devices or device chains by hot removing. Works only on SENA or RSM.
-F	Forces hot plugging one or more devices even if they are being used.
display	Shows device or enclosure-specific sense and status information, including any disks.
	Select one of the following when specifying an option:
-p	Shows device or subsystem performance information.
-r	Shows device-specific error information as specified by ACTION. SENA only.
-v	Shows data in verbose mode. This also includes mode sense data.
inquiry	Shows the device specific inquiry information specified by ACTION.
insert_device	Inserts new devices or device chains by hot hotplugging. Works only on SENA or RSM.
led	Shows the current LED state of the related disk specified by ACTION.
led_blink	Blinks the LED related to the disk specified by ACTION.
led_off	Disables the LED related to the disk specified by ACTION. SENA state may alter off.
led_on	Enables the LED related to the disk specified by ACTION.
power_on	Forces the SENA out of power-save mode. Sets devices to their normal startup state.
	These options are for subcommands only:
-e	Initiates expert mode.
-v	Verbose mode. Shows more information.

File Name:	`luxadm`	**Directory:**	/usr/sbin/	**Type:**	External
Warning:	Beware of the subcommand removedevice or replacedevice -F option.				

luxadm probe	Shows any SENAs on the system.
luxadm display 2200002037001246	Shows a SENA enclosure or disk using a WWN.

m64config

m64config	**UNIX Shell:**	**All primary shells (csh, ksh, sh)**

Function	Configures the M64 Graphics Accelerator and can also alter some of the X11 window defaults for the M64.
Syntax	m64config [options...]

-dev *file*	Specifies the special device M64 file. The default device is /dev/fbs/m640.
-file *{ client }*	Updates the OWconfig file that is specific to the computer.
-file *{ system }*	Updates the global OWconfig file.
-res *videomode { ACTION }*	Specifies the video mode for the monitor and can optionally use an ACTION listed below.
-res *'?'*	Shows valid video modes. You must use single quotes around the question mark.
	When specifying the video mode, you can use the following syntax:
widthxheightxrate	Where width and height are pixels and rate is the vertical frequency of the refresh.

continued

	Or you can use any of the following Symbolic names:
svga	Sets the resolution to 1024x768x60.
1152	Sets the resolution to 1152x900x76.
1280	Sets the resolution to 1280x1024x76.
none	Selects what's presently being used by the device.
ACTION	**When setting video mode, you can select one of the following actions:**
now	Updates the OWconfig file and shows the video mode NOW.
try	Shows the video mode and prompts the user for confirmation.
	When using try, you can select between two actions:
noconfirm	Forces the confirmation of the video mode.
nocheck	Bypasses error checking and shows the video mode regardless of the monitor type.
-depth *value*	Sets the color depth to either 8 or 24 bits.
-defaults	Resets everything to the default values.
-propt	Shows the current values in the configuration file.
-prconf	Shows the current hardware configuration.
-help	Shows help information.

File Name:	`m64config`	**Directory:**	/usr/sbin/	**Type:**	External
Note:	The set configuration file values may differ from the current hardware configuration until the system is rebooted.				

m64config -prconf	Shows the current hardware configuration.
m64config -depth 24	Sets the color depth to 24-bit true color.

mach

UNIX Shell: All primary shells (csh, ksh, sh)

Function	Shows what processor your computer is running on.
Syntax	mach

File Name:	`mach`	**Directory:**	/usr/bin/	**Type:**	External
Note:	Use uname -p instead; mach is provided for compatibility reason.				

mail.local

UNIX Shell: All primary shells (csh, ksh, sh)

Function	A local mail delivery agent for `sendmail`.
Syntax	mail.local [options...] *mailbox*

-f *sender*	Specifies the `envelope from address` and should be used every time.
-d	Used for backward compatibility. Use no space between this option and the operand.
mailbox	Specifies the receiver of the mail message.

File Name:	`mail.local`	**Directory:**	/usr/lib/	**Type:**	External
Note:	Reads from STDIN and appends the message to the specified user's mailbox found in the `/var/mail` directory.				

mailcompat

UNIX Shell: All primary shells (csh, ksh, sh)

Function	Makes the Solaris mailbox format compatible with SunOS 4.x clients.
Syntax	mailcompat

File Name:	`mailcompat`	**Directory:**	/usr/bin/	**Type:**	External

mailprint

UNIX Shell: All primary shells (csh, ksh, sh)

Function	Erases any attachments from the specified mail file and adds a line to inform how many were removed.
Syntax	mailprint [-b] *{ mailfile }*

-b	Adds a formfeed at the end of every message.
mailfile	Specifies the file that contains one or more mail messages.

File Name:	`mailprint`	**Directory:**	/usr/openwin/bin/	**Type:**	External
Tip:	The `printtool` gives the same functionality.				

makekey

makekey	UNIX Shell:	All primary shells (csh, ksh, sh)
Function	Creates an encryption key using ASCII characters for programs that run encryption. It generates a 13-character key from a 10-character input.	
Syntax	makekey *keynumber*	

keynumber	Specifies the encryption key number. This must contain 10 ASCII characters.		
File Name: `makekey`	**Directory:** /usr/lib/	**Type:**	External
makekey 7578392067	Creates the encryption key `75gIM0WaLjZJE#`.		

makemap

makemap	UNIX Shell:	All primary shells (csh, ksh, sh)
Function	Uses the keyed map lookups in `sendmail` and creates the specified type of database map by reading from STDIN and writes to the specified new map name.	
Syntax	makemap [options...] *type name*	

-N	Adds the null byte that will terminate the strings in the specified map.		
-d	Allows the use of duplicate keys in the specified map. Works with B-tree format maps.		
-f	Disables uppercase letters from being forced into lowercase. Default is uppercase.		
-o	Appends to a previously existing file.		
-r	Allows for repeating existing keys. Default gives an error if repeated keys exist.		
-s	Disables the safety check on the map being created.		
-v	Verbose mode. Shows more information.		
name	Specifies the map name of the map database being created.		
type	Specifies the specific database map format. Only one of the following may be used:		
dbm	Specifies the map will follow DMB format rules.		
btree	Specifies the map will follow B-Tree format rules.		
hash	Specifies the map will follow hash format rules.		
File Name: `makemap`	**Directory:** /usr/sbin/	**Type:**	External
Note:	In order for the -N option to work, it must match the K line in `sendmail.cf` specified by its -N option.		
makemap -d btree newmap	Allows the use of duplicate keys in the btree formatted map.		
makemap -r dbm newmap	Allows for repeating existing keys in the DBM formatted map.		

makepsres

makepsres	UNIX Shell:	All primary shells (csh, ksh, sh)
Function	Creates an Adobe PostScript language database file called `PSres.upr`.	
Syntax	makepsres [options...] *directories...*	

-o *file*	Writes output to the specified file.		
-	Sends the output to STDOUT instead of a file.		
-f *file*	Uses the resource database formatted file information to aid in resource typing.		
-dir *dir*	Specifies the given directory is a directory, not a file.		
-d	Discard mode. Doesn't use entries from the input file. Uses command line entries.		
-e	Makes the `PSres.upr` file exclusive to improve search performance.		
-i	Starts interactive query mode, which asks for the resource type of any unknown files.		
-k	Keep mode. Uses all resource entries in the input database files for the output file.		
-nb	No Backup mode. If the file exists, it will not be backed up.		
-nr	Nonrecursive mode. Does not look into subdirectories when finding resource files.		
-p	Specifies the search will not look for a common directory prefix.		
-pfb	Recognizes binary PostScript .pfb fonts along with the normal .pfa fonts.		
-q	Ignores all files that can't be identified instead of giving a warning. Quiet mode.		
-s	Ends with an error if it finds a file that can't be identified. Strict mode.		
directories...	Specifies the paths that contain the resource files.		
-	Reads from STDIN. If no entry is made at all, the current directory is used.		
File Name: `makepsres`	**Directory:** /usr/openwin/bin/	**Type:**	External
makepsres -i -o local.upr /usr/local/lib/ps/fonts	Runs in interactive mode and creates a resource db file called local.upr in the directory /usr/local/lib/ps/fonts.		

mconnect

UNIX Shell:	All primary shells (csh, ksh, sh)
Function	Connects you to the specified remote SMTP mail server socket, or to the local host if no remote host is specified.
Syntax	mconnect [options...] *{ hostname }*

-p *port*	Specifies a port number for SMTP other than the default (default port is 25).
-r	Enables `RAW mode` by disabling input handling and line buffering.
hostname	Specifies the hostname or IP address of the server to connect to.
File Name: `mconnect`	**Directory:** /usr/bin/ **Type:** External
mconnect smtpserver	Opens an SMTP connection to server smtpserver.
mconnect -p 11111 smtpserver	Opens an SMTP connection on smtpserver port 11111.

mcs

UNIX Shell:	All primary shells (csh, ksh, sh)
Function	Adds, erases, shows, and compresses the contents in the comment section of an ELF object file.
Syntax	mcs option *files...*

-c	Compresses the comment section contents of the specified ELF files.
-d	Deletes the comment section contents of the specified ELF files.
-p	Shows the comment section contents of the specified ELF files to STDOUT.
-V	Shows version information on STDERR.
-a *string*	Appends the specified text string to the comment section or sections.
-n *name*	Specifies a comment section other than the default `.comment`.
files...	Specifies the object files to alter.
File Name: `mcs`	**Directory:** /usr/ccs/bin/ **Type:** External
Note:	Archives are treated as a list of individual files to alter.
mcs -a updated object.so	Adds the text updated to the file object.so.

mibiisa

UNIX Shell:	All primary shells (csh, ksh, sh)
Function	Is Sun's RFC 1157-compliant SNMP agent.
Syntax	mibiisa [options...]

-a	Disables generation of the authentication traps.
-r	Starts the read-only mode.
-c *directory*	Specifies the directory for the snmpd.conf file (default is `/etc/snmp/conf`).
-d *level*	Sets the debug level from 0 to 3; 0 gives no debug output, whereas 3 is maximum output (default is 0).
-p *port*	Specifies which UDP port to use (default is port 161).
File Name: `mibiisa`	**Directory:** /usr/lib/snmp/ **Type:** External
mibiisa -d 3	Starts the agent using maximum debug output.

mkalias

UNIX Shell:	All primary shells (csh, ksh, sh)
Function	Converts YP `mail.aliases` maps to `mail.byaddr` maps.
Syntax	mkalias [options...] *inputfile { outputfile }*

-e	Verifies that the host exists.
-u	Assumes that the UUCP names are valid. Use with the -e option.
-d	Assumes that the Domain names are valid. Use with the -e option.
-v	Verbose mode. Shows more information.
-s	No information found on this option.
-n	Adds capital letters to each name. Changes `ucgbook.com` to `Ucgbook.Com`.
inputfile	Specifies the map to be used as input.
outputfile	Specifies the map to be used as output.
File Name: `mkalias`	**Directory:** /usr/lib/netsvc/yp/ **Type:** External

mkfile

mkfile	UNIX Shell:	All primary shells (csh, ksh, sh)
Function	Creates an empty file or files that can be used as NFS-mounted or local swap areas.	
Syntax	mkfile [options...] *size filename*	

-n	Creates the specified file with the size reported but without allocated blocks. (The allocated disk blocks are created when they are needed.)
-v	Shows version information.
size	Specifies the file size. k = kilobytes; b = blocks; m = megabytes.
filename	Specifies the name of the file to be created.
File Name: `mkfile`	**Directory:** /usr/sbin/ **Type:** External
mkfile 1m megfile	Creates a 1-MB file called megfile.
mkfile -n 1m emptyfile	Creates a 1-MB file called emptyfile without allocated blocks.

mkfs

mkfs	UNIX Shell:	All primary shells (csh, ksh, sh)
Function	Creates a file system on the specified disk partition `rawdevicefile` by calling upon the default FS or the specific one that is given by the `-F FSType` option.	
Syntax	mkfs [options...] *rawdevicefile*	

-F *FSType*	Specifies which FSType file system to create.
-V	Repeats the command line input without executing the command.
-m	Shows the command line that was used to create the file system.
-o *options*	Specifies the ufs type-specific options below. Must be separated by commas.
N	Shows the file system parameters without creating the file system.
nsect=*n*	Specifies sectors per track. Default is 32.
ntrack=*n*	Specifies tracks per cylinder. Default is 16.
bsize=*n*	Specifies logical block size; either 4096 or 8192 is valid. Default is 8192.
fragsize=*n*	Specifies the smallest disk space for a file. Valid sizes: 512, 1024, 2048, and 4096 bytes.
cgsize=*n*	Specifies cylinders per group. Default is 16.
free=*n*	Specifies the minimum percent of free space to leave in the file system. Default is 10 percent.
rps=*n*	Specifies the rotation speed of the disk. Default is 60 rpm.
nbpi=*n*	Specifies the inode density in the file system in bytes. Default is 2048.
opt=*value*	Specifies optimization of space `s` or of time `t`. Default is `t`.
apc=*n*	Specifies alternate per cylinder to reserve for SCSI device bad block replacement.
gap=*n*	Specifies the rotational spacing to use between successive blocks in the file in msec.
nrpos=*n*	Specifies how many rotational positions to divide a cylinder group into. Default is 8.
maxcontig=*n*	Specifies the number of blocks for each file before inserting a rotational delay. (The default for a 4K file system is 14 blocks. The default for an 8K file system is 7.)
rawdevicefile	Specifies the disk partition to be written to.
File Name: `mkfs`	**Directory:** /usr/sbin/ **Type:** External
Tip:	The option -m is good to use when trying to determine how an existing file system was created.
mkfs -m /dev/dsk/c0t0d0s0	Shows the command line to create `/dev/dsk/c0t0d0s0.`

mkmsgs

mkmsgs	UNIX Shell:	All primary shells (csh, ksh, sh)
Function	Creates a file of text strings that is accessible with the text retrieval tools `gettxt, srchtxt and exstr.` The input is a file of text strings for a specified geographic locale.	
Syntax	mkmsgs [options...] *inputstrings msgfile*	

-o	Overwrites an existing msgfile.
-i *locale*	Installs the msgfile in the /usr/lib/locale/locale/LC_MESSAGE directory.
inputstrings	Specifies the file that contains the original text strings.
msgfile	Specifies where to save the created msgfile.
File Name: `mkmsgs`	**Directory:** /usr/bin/ **Type:** External
mkmsgs /etc/passwd passtxt	Creates file passtxt from passwd.

mkstr

mkstr	UNIX Shell:	All primary shells (csh, ksh, sh)
Function	Creates specific files containing error messages that are extruded from a list of other files.	
Syntax	mkstr [-] *messagefile prefix files...*	

[-]	Places any error messages at the end of the message file.
messagefile	Specifies the messagefile to be captured.
prefix	Specifies the file prefix to use for the created file.
files...	Specifies the files where the error messages will be extracted from; uses wildcards.

File Name:	`mkstr`	**Directory:**	/usr/ucb/	**Type:**	External

mkstr pistrings processed *.c	Places the error messages from C source files into the file `pistrings` and places them in files with a prefix of processed.

modinfo

modinfo	UNIX Shell:	All primary shells (csh, ksh, sh)
Function	Shows you information about loaded kernel modules.	
Syntax	modinfo [-i]	

-i *moduleID*	Shows information about the specified module.

File Name:	`modinfo`	**Directory:**	/usr/sbin/	**Type:**	External

modinfo -i 33	Shows you information about module with ID 33.

modload

modload	UNIX Shell:	All primary shells (csh, ksh, sh)
Function	Loads a specified loadable kernel module into the running system.	
Syntax	modload [options...] *file*	

-p	Sets the search path for the module to be the kernel's internal modpath variable.
-e *file*	Specifies a shell script or executable image to execute after the module is loaded.
file	Specifies an object file produced by `ld -r` to load.

File Name:	`modload`	**Directory:**	/usr/sbin/	**Type:**	External
Tip:	Use `add_drv` to add device drivers to the system.				

modload /mods/3c5x9	Loads module 3c5x9 to the system.

modunload

modunload	UNIX Shell:	All primary shells (csh, ksh, sh)
Function	Unloads a previous loaded module from a running system.	
Syntax	modunload -i [-e]	

-i *moduleID*	Unloads the specified module. (All autoloaded unloadable modules are unloaded with the moduleID 0.)
-e *file*	Executes the specified script or image file before the module is unloaded.

File Name:	`modunload`	**Directory:**	/usr/sbin/	**Type:**	External
Tip:	Use `modinfo` to find the module IDs.				

modunload -i 0	Unloads all autoloaded modules that are unloadable, but not modules loaded by modload.
modunload -i 89 -e modulescript.sh	Executes a script before the module is unloaded.

monacct

monacct	UNIX Shell:	Bourne shell (sh)
Function	Creates accounting summary files and places them into `/var/adm/acct/fiscal`. Also restarts summary files in `/var/adm/acct/sum`.	
Syntax	monacct *{ period }*	

period	Specifies the month or period to be used. Default is the current month (01 to 12).

File Name:	`monacct`	**Directory:**	/usr/lib/acct/	**Type:**	Script

mountall

UNIX Shell:	Bourne shell (sh)
Function	Mounts all file systems from the file system table.
Syntax	mountall [options...] *{ filesystemtable }*

-F *fstype*	Specifies the type of file systems to be mounted.
	Only one of the two options below may be used:
-l	Only local file systems may be mounted.
-r	Only remote file systems may be mounted.
filesystemtable	An optional file system table instead of the default /etc/vfstab.
File Name: `mountall`	**Directory:** /usr/sbin/ — **Type:** Script
Tip:	Often used without options as a quick way to mount all file systems in /etc/vfstab.

mpstat

UNIX Shell:	All primary shells (csh, ksh, sh)
Function	Shows statistics for each processor in tabular form. Each row is for one processor activity only.
Syntax	mpstat *{ interval } { count }*

interval	Sets the interval time for reports in seconds.
count	Shows only the number of reports, specified by count.
File Name: `mpstat`	**Directory:** /usr/bin/ — **Type:** External
mpstat 30	Shows a snapshot every 30 seconds.

msgfmt

UNIX Shell:	All primary shells (csh, ksh, sh)
Function	Creates message object files from portable object files. It doesn't change the portable object files.
Syntax	msgfmt [options...] *filename.po*

-v	Verbose mode. Shows more information.
-o *output*	Specifies the output file.
filename.po	Specifies the input files. The filename extension must be .po.
File Name: `msgfmt`	**Directory:** /usr/bin/ — **Type:** External
msgfmt -o hello.mo module1.po module2.po	Produces the output file hello.mo.

mvdir

UNIX Shell:	All primary shells (csh, ksh, sh)
Function	Moves a directory within a file system.
Syntax	mvdir *directory name*

directory	Specifies the directory to move.
name	Specifies the destination name for the directory to be moved into.
File Name: `mvdir`	**Directory:** /usr/sbin/ — **Type:** External
mvdir /export/home/anders /user	Moves the user anders home directory to /user.

named-bootconf

UNIX Shell:	Korn shell (ksh)
Function	Converts named.boot configuration files used by BIND 4.9 or older to newer versions used by BIND 8.1.1 or later.
Syntax	named-bootconf [options...]

-i *inputfile*	Specifies the location of the input file if it is other than `/etc/named.boot`.
-o *outputfile*	Specifies the location for the output file if it is other than `/etc/named.conf`.
File Name: `named-bootconf`	**Directory:** /usr/sbin/ — **Type:** Script
named-bootconf -i bind4 -o bind8	Converts the file `BIND4` to the file `BIND8`.

named-xfer

UNIX Shell: All primary shells (csh, ksh, sh)

Function	Runs inbound zone transfers. It is used by `in.named` but can be used directly for debugging purposes.
Syntax	named-xfer options... [options...] *nameservers...*

	The following options are required:
-z *transferzone*	Specifies the zone that you want to transfer.
-f *file*	Specifies the file in which to put the zone that is received from the name servers.
-s *serialno*	Specifies the serial number of the zone.
	The following options are optional:
-d *level*	Shows debug information. Debug level can be between 1 and 10.
-l *logfile*	Specifies where to put debug messages.
-t *tracefile*	Specifies a protocol tracefile for debugging the zone transfer.
-p *portnr*	Sets a new port number to use instead of the default.
-S	Transfers only SOA, NS, and A records.
nameservers...	Specifies the nameserver or servers to run a zone transfer on.

File Name:	`named-xfer`	**Directory:**	/usr/sbin/	**Type:**	External

native2ascii

UNIX Shell: Korn shell (ksh)

Function	Converts files into Latin-1 and Unicode-encoded characters if they contain other character encoding.
Syntax	native2ascii [options...] *{ inputfile } { outputfile }*

-encoding *name*	Specifies a name for the conversion.
-reverse	Converts a file in reverse order, from Latin-1 or Unicode into a native-encoded file.
inputfile	Specifies an input file other than STDIN.
outputfile	Specifies an output file other than STDOUT.

File Name:	`native2ascii`	**Directory:**	/usr/bin/	**Type:**	Script

navigator

UNIX Shell: All primary shells (csh, ksh, sh)

Function	Shows the AnswerBook on-line documentation.
Syntax	navigator [options..]

-b *library-file*	Enables you to load a specific AnswerBook library.
-c *card-catalog*	Locates AnswerBooks by specifying the name of a card catalog file.

File Name:	`navigator`	**Directory:**	/usr/openwin/bin/	**Type:**	External

nawk

UNIX Shell: All primary shells (csh, ksh, sh)

Function	A newer version of `awk`. It is usually used to search for patterns specified by ' *scriptstr* '.
Syntax	nawk [options...] [' *scriptstr* '] [-v *var=value*] *{ files... }* nawk [options...] [-f *scriptfile*] [-v *var=value*] *{ files... }*

-f *scriptfile*	Specifies the file that contains the specific pattern action statements to be used.
-F*expression*	Uses a regular expression as a field separator. (Appendix A has list of expressions.)
' *scriptstr* '	Contains the pattern action statements and must be enclosed by singles quotes ('). (The pattern action statements must follow the format pattern { action }.)
pattern { *action* }	The format for the pattern action statements specified by *' scriptstr '*.
	The following are supported arithmetic functions:
atan2(*y,x*)	Returns the arctangent of y and x.
cos(*x*)	Returns the cosine of the specified value. The value must be in radians.
sin(*x*)	Returns the sine of the specified value. The value must be in radians.
exp(*x*)	Returns the exponential function of the specified value.
log(*x*)	Returns the natural logarithm of the specified value.
sqrt(*x*)	Returns the square root of the specified value.
int(*x*)	Shortens the specified value to an integer. It trims the value when x > 0.

continued

rand()	Generates a random number between 0 and 1.
srand(*{ expr }*)	Sets a new seed number for rand.
	The following string functions are supported (string is indicated by s):
index(*s, sub*)	Gives the position of string *s* where the substring *sub*occurs first.
length[(*{ s }*)]	Gives the total length of an argument or an entire line if there is no argument.
match(*s, re*)	Gives the string s the position of the regular expression re when it occurs.
split (*s,aa*[*,fs*])	Splits string s into an array of elements a1, a2, and separates fields with the fs expression.
sprintf(*fmt, expr...*)	Formats listed expressions with `printf` by using the format specified by fmt.
sub(*EXP,SUB,{ STR }*)	Substitutes the value specified by SUB with EXP when a match is found in STR.
EXP	The expression that you want to search and substitute for the value of SUB.
SUB	The value used as the replacement value when a match is found in STR.
(&)	Replaces the ampersand (&) with the value in STR that matches the value in EXP.
(\)	Uses the characters following the backslash \ symbol literally.
STR	The string or the argument that is searched.
gsub(*EXP,SUB,{ STR }*)	Same as sub but will globally replace ALL occurrences of the expression STR.
substr(*s,pos*[*,len*])	Shows substring *s* starting at *pos* to the length specified by *len*.
tolower(*s*)	Converts uppercase characters specified in string *s* to lowercase.
toupper(*s*)	Converts lowercase characters specified in string *s* to uppercase.
	The following built-in variables can be used.
-v *var=value*	Specifies a built-in variable listed below and assigns it a value.
ARGC	Defines the number of command-line arguments the ARGV array will use.
ARGV	Takes command arguments from ARGC and creates an index from zero to variable ARGC-1.
CONVFMT	Converts numbers to strings using the printf format (default is %.6g).
ENVIRON	Shows the current nawk environment.
FILENAME	Specifies the name of the current file being used for input.
FNR	Defines ordinal numbers for the current file.
FS	Defines input field separators (defaults are space and Tab).
NF	Defines number of fields in the existing file.
NR	Defines ordinal number for the current record.
OFMT	Defines output numbers in a specific format (default is %.6g).
OFS	Defines output field separators (default is blank).
ORS	Defines output record separators (default is new-line).
LENGTH	Defines the size of the string to be matched by the match ( ) function.
RS	Defines input record separators (default is new-line).
RSTART	The first position in the string that is matched by the match ( ) function.
SUBSEP	The subscript separator string used with multidimensional arrays (default is 1).
	The following are control flow functions:
break	Exits from a `for`, `while`, or `do` loop.
continue	Starts the next loop cycle in a `for`, `while`, or `do` loop.
delete array [arg]	Deletes an argument from an array. All arguments are removed if no arg is specified.
do *statement*	A loop that executes the specified statement while the condition is true.
while (*condition*)	Evaluated by do. Runs the do statement if the condition is true, and exits if it is false.
exit *{ exp }*	Executes the end routine if it exists, and exits the script with return value *exp*.
if (*condition*)	Performs the statement if the condition is true, or will perform the else condition.
else (*condition*)	Performs the else condition when the if condition is false.
while (*condition*)	Performs the condition as long as the condition is true.
for (*exp1; exp2 ; exp3*)	A loop that uses three expressions (see below). Exits when any expression is false.
exp1	Sets the counter variable to an initial value that counts the number of loops.
exp2	Defines the variable that is read and evaluated before executing the statement.
exp3	A counter that increments each time the loop is true. (The variables exp1, exp2, and exp3 are all optional and are true if not used.)
for (*arrayvar*)	A loop that executes each variable defined in an array.
next	Reads the input line and begins a new loop or procedure.
return *{ exp }*	Returns the value of *exp* and exits a user-defined function.
	The following input/output functions are supported:
close (*expr*)	Closes files or a pipe opened by print, printf, or getline with specified expr.
command*{ var }*	Takes the result of the command and sets $0 and NF, or sets *var* if specified.

continued

getline	Sets $0 as next input and sets variables NR, NF, and FNR by using the current input file.
getline *var*	Reads the next line from the input file and sets variables *var*, FNR, and NR.
getline *{ var } expr*	Same as above but uses the string *expr* as the full path to the file.
print	Shows the results of the ' *scriptstr* ' and variables to STDOUT.
printf	Same as print but also formats the output.
$*n*	Specifies the field numbers in the file ($1, $2, $3, and so on), which are separated by FS.
$0	Specifies to use the entire line in the file as input.
system(*cmd*]	Runs the command specified by *cmd*.
function name(args...) { statements }	Creates a function that uses `awk`.
files...	Specifies the input files that are scanned for pattern matching.
	The following escape sequences can be used: `\a` = alert; `\b` = backspace; `\f` = form feed; `\n` = new line; `\r` = carriage return; `\t` = tab; `\v` = vertical tab; `\\`=backslash; `\"` = double quotes; `\/` = forward slash; `\ooo` = octal number; `\hhh` = hexadecimal value

File Name:	`nawk`	**Directory:**	/usr/bin/	**Type:**	External
Tip:	Nawk is a wonderful way to process text files in scripts.				

nawk -F: '{print $1}' /etc/passwd | sort	Shows the first field (username) in the `/etc/passwd` file and sorts it.
who | nawk '{print $6}'	Shows the IP addresses for all logged in users.

ncheck

UNIX Shell: All primary shells (csh, ksh, sh)

Function	Shows a list with paths and inode numbers for all files on a specified device.
Syntax	ncheck [options...] *{ devices... }*

-F *FStype*	Specifies the FSType where you want to run the command.
-V	Shows what the command would do if it was executed.
	The following three options are generic to FSType:
-i *inodelist*	Reports only on the files that are in the specified inodelist.
-a	Shows names that are normally suppressed.
-s	Shows only files that are special files or that have the SUID bit.
-o *attributes*	Specifies FSType-specific attributes.
devices...	Specifies the device or devices that you want to run ncheck on.

File Name:	`ncheck`	**Directory:**	/usr/sbin/	**Type:**	External
Note:	It may not be supported for all FSTypes.				

ndd

UNIX Shell: All primary shells (csh, ksh, sh)

Function	Modifies configuration parameters, but currently only for the TCP/IP protocol family.
Syntax	ndd [-set] *driver parameter { value }*

-set	Passes parameter values to the driver. Default is to get values from driver. (When you use the -set option, you also need to use the value option.)
driver	Specifies the driver to set or get information about.
parameter	Sets new parameter or shows named parameter.
value	The parameter value to be used with the parameter option.

File Name:	`ndd`	**Directory:**	/usr/sbin/	**Type:**	External
Warning:	Use the set option carefully.				

ndd /dev/tcp tcp_debug	Shows parameter value for `tcp_debug`.
ndd -set /dev/tcp tcp_debug 1	Passes the `tcp_debug` parameter the value 1.
ndd /dev/udp \?	Shows all parameters for the `/dev/udp`.

neqn	UNIX Shell:	All primary shells (csh, ksh, sh)
Function	A preprocessor for the command `nroff`. It helps when writing equations and is primarily used with terminals.	
Syntax	neqn *files...*	

files...	Specifies an `nroff` file or files.
File Name: `neqn`	**Directory:** /usr/bin/ **Type:** External

newform	UNIX Shell:	All primary shells (csh, ksh, sh)
Function	Changes format of a text file line by line.	
Syntax	newform [options...] *{ filenames... }*	

	When using these options, -s must be placed first.
-s	Cuts leading characters until first Tab, and places them at the end of the line.
-i*tabspec*	Specifies input Tab specification; see Tabs (default is -8).
-o*tabspec*	Specifies output Tab specification; see Tabs (default is -8).
-p*n*	Fills up with n prefix characters (see -cchar) to the beginning of the line.
-e*n*	Truncates the line at the end by n characters.
-a*n*	Fills up with n prefix characters (see -cchar) to the end of the line.
-f	Shows the format for Tab specification on STDOUT.
-c*char*	Changes the prefix char used in -a and -p options (default is space).
-l*n*	Sets the effective line length to n characters.
-b*n*	Truncates the line from the beginning by n characters.
inputfile	An input file; could be more than one.
File Name: `newform`	**Directory:** /usr/bin/ **Type:** External
newform -f	Outputs the Tab format.
newform -cb -a4 textfile1	Adds four b characters at the end of all not full lines.

newfs	UNIX Shell:	All primary shells (csh, ksh, sh)
Function	Creates a new file system with the FSType UFS.	
Syntax	newfs [options...] *rawdevice*	

-N	Shows what the command would do, but doesn't execute.
-v	Verbose mode. Shows more information.
	The following options are `mkfs` options that can be used by newfs:
-a *apc*	Specifies the number of blocks to use for bad blocks on a SCSI drive.
-b *bsize*	Specifies the logical block size to use when you create a file system.
-c *cgsize*	Specifies the number of cylinders to use per cylinder group.
-d *gap*	Specifies the time a service can take to initiate a new transfer if it's interrupted.
-f *fragsize*	Specifies the fragment size to use on the new file system.
-i *nbpi*	Specifies the number of inodes to use on the new file system.
-m *free*	Specifies the minimum percentage of free space to be available on the new FS.
-n *nrpos*	Specifies the number of rotational positions per cylinder group.
-o *opt*	Minimizes time spent allocating `time` or minimizing fragment `space`.
-r *rpm*	Specifies the speed of the hard drive.
-s *size*	Specifies the size of the file system in sectors.
-t *ntrack*	Specifies the number of tracks per cylinder.
-C *maxcontig*	Specifies the maximum number of blocks that can be used by one file.
rawdevice	Specifies where to create the new file system. Rawdevices are in `/dev/rdsk`.
File Name: `newfs`	**Directory:** /usr/sbin/ **Type:** External
Note:	Superusers can use this command, but a user can only use it in on a floppy.
newfs /dev/rdsk/c0t1d0s0	Creates a new file system on the disk `/dev/rdsk/c0t1d0s0`.

newgrp

UNIX Shell: All primary shells (csh, ksh, sh)

Function	Changes a user's real and effective group ID to group.
Syntax	newgrp [-l] *{ group }*

-l	Changes the environment to what it would be if the user logged in.
group	Specifies the new groupname.

File Name:	`newgrp`	**Directory:**	/usr/bin/	**Type:**	External

newgrp - sys	Logs in to the group sys and changes the environment.
newgrp staff	Logs in to the group staff.

newkey

UNIX Shell: All primary shells (csh, ksh, sh)

Function	Creates new Diffie-Hellman public keys that are needed for secure RPC or NFS services.
Syntax	newkey -h *hostname* [option] newkey -u *user* [option]

-h *hostname*	Creates new public and secret keys for a hostname; prompts for password.
-u *user*	Creates new public and secret keys for a user; prompts for password.
	When there are multiple name services, choose one of these options:
-s nisplus	Specifies NIS+.
-s nis	Specifies NIS.
-s files	Specifies files.

File Name:	`newkey`	**Directory:**	/usr/sbin/	**Type:**	External

newkey -h moon -s nisplus	Changes NIS+ keypair for the host moon.
newkey -u steve	Changes keypair for the default naming service.
newkey -h moon -s nis	Changes NIS keypair for the host moon, invoked on NIS master server.

news

UNIX Shell: All primary shells (csh, ksh, sh)

Function	Informs about current events described in directory `/var/news`.
Syntax	news [options...] *{ items... }*

-a	Prints all items.
-n	Creates a report of all current items without showing the contents.
-s	Creates a report of the number of items without showing the contents.
items...	Specifies news items to show.

File Name:	`news`	**Directory:**	/usr/bin/	**Type:**	External

news -s	Shows how many current items exist.
news -a	Shows all items.

newsyslog

UNIX Shell: Bourne shell (sh)

Function	Saves the old log file `messages` and starts with a new, empty log file.
Syntax	newsyslog

File Name:	`newsyslog`	**Directory:**	/usr/lib	**Type:**	Script
Note:	By default, this command is started in crontab once per week.				

nis_cachemgr

UNIX Shell: All primary shells (csh, ksh, sh)

Function	A daemon that manages cache information about NIS+ server locations and directories.
Syntax	nis_cachemgr [options...]

-i	Flushes the cache and reinitializes.
-v	Verbose mode. Shows more information.

File Name:	`nis_cachemgr`	**Directory:**	/usr/sbin/	**Type:**	External

nis_cachemgr -i	Flushes the cache and reinitializes it.

nisaddcred

UNIX Shell: All primary shells (csh, ksh, sh)

Function	Manages NIS+ credentials that are used for authentication.
Syntax	nisaddcred [options...] *authtype { domain }*

-p *principal*	Specifies the principal that you want to manage.
-P *nisprincipal*	Specifies that you want to manage a NIS+ principal.
-l *loginpasswd*	Uses the specified password to encrypt secret keys for the credential entry.
authtype	Specifies which authentication type you want to use — `LOCAL` or `DES`.
domain	Specifies in which NIS+ domain you want to operate.
	The following option can be used to remove a specific NIS+ principal:
-r *principal*	Removes credentials that are related to the specified NIS+ principal.

File Name:	`nisaddcred`	**Directory:**	/usr/bin/	**Type:**	External

nisaddent

UNIX Shell: All primary shells (csh, ksh, sh)

Function	Creates NIS+ table entries by using files from the `/etc` directory and from NIS maps.
Syntax	nisaddent [options...] *type { domain }* nisaddent [options...] -f *file type { domain }* nisaddent [options...] -y *ypdom type { domain }*

-D *defaults*	Specifies defaults to be temporarily used. Uses a comma-separated list.
ttl=*time*	Specifies the default time-to-live for the created object.
owner=*ownername*	Specifies the owner of the created object.
group=*groupname*	Specifies the group owner of the created object.
access=*rights*	Specifies the access rights of the created object.
-P	Follows the cat path when performing lookups.
-a	Adds a file or a map without writing over existing entries.
-m	Merges files and maps together with the specified NIS+ table.
-o	Suppresses warning messages about missing authentication algorithm fields.
-p	Processes the password fields when reading password information from a file.
-r	Replaces file or map entries from the NIS+ table.
-v	Verbose mode. Shows more information.
-t *table*	Specifies the NIS+ table to work with.
-f *file*	Uses a file instead of the keyboard as input.
type	Specifies the data that is to be processed: passwd, networks, hosts, group, and so on.
domain	Specifies the NIS+ domain to work with.
-y *ypdom*	Uses NIS maps from the specified NIS domain as input.
-Y *map*	Uses the specified map as input.
	The following syntax options can be used to show NIS+ data:
-d	Shows the NIS+ table on the screen.
-A	Shows all data that are in the specified table.
-M	Runs lookup on the master server only.
-q	Quickly dumps the table data.

File Name:	`nisaddent`	**Directory:**	/usr/lib/nis/	**Type:**	External

nisaddent -rv -f /etc/passwd passwd	Updates the passwd table with information from `/etc/passwd`.
nisaddent -d passwd	Shows content of the passwd table on the screen.

nisauthconf

UNIX Shell: All primary shells (csh, ksh, sh)

Function	Manages security authentication in NIS+.
Syntax	nisauthconf [-v] *{ authmech }*

-v	Verbose mode. Shows more information.
authmech	Specifies the authentication mechanism that you want to use on the system.

File Name:	`nisauthconf`	**Directory:**	/usr/lib/nis/	**Type:**	External

nisbackup

UNIX Shell: All primary shells (csh, ksh, sh)

Function	Manages backups of NIS+ directory objects on a NIS+ master server.
Syntax	nisbackup [-v] *backupdir directories...* nisbackup [-v] -a *backupdir*

-v	Verbose mode. Shows more information.
-a	Creates a backup of all directories on the server. (When using -a, directories can't be specified.)
backupdir	Specifies the directory in which you want to place the backup copy.
directories...	Specifies the NIS+ directory that you want to make a backup of.

File Name: `nisbackup` **Directory:** /usr/sbin/ **Type:** External

niscat

UNIX Shell: All primary shells (csh, ksh, sh)

Function	Shows NIS+ tables or objects.
Syntax	niscat [options...] *tables...*

-A	Shows all data from all tables in the path.
-h	Shows header lines before table contents.
-L	Follows a linked file to its source.
-M	Uses information from the master server directly, instead of cached data.
-P	Follows the specified path.
-v	Shows binary data from the table on STDOUT.
-s *sep*	Specifies a separator character.
table...	Specifies which NIS+ table to show.
	You can use the following option instead of `table`:
-o *names...*	Searches for specific objects and shows them on STDOUT.

File Name: `niscat` **Directory:** /usr/bin/ **Type:** External

nischgrp

UNIX Shell: All primary shells (csh, ksh, sh)

Function	Manages group ownership of a NIS+ object.
Syntax	nischgrp [options...] *group names...*

-A	Alters all table entries that are in the path.
-f	Tries to force the execution of the command.
-L	Follows a link to its source and then alters the source.
-P	Follows the path within the specified table.
group	Specifies the NIS+ group to change to.
names...	Specifies the NIS+ object to change group ownership for.

File Name: `nischgrp` **Directory:** /usr/bin/ **Type:** External

nischmod

UNIX Shell: All primary shells (csh, ksh, sh)

Function	Manages permission for a NIS+ object.
Syntax	nischmod [options...] *mode names...*

-A	Alters all the tables in the path.
-f	Tries to force the execution of the command.
-L	Follows a linked file to its source and alters the source.
-P	Follows the path within the specified table.
mode	Specifies permissions for the NIS+ objects.
	Valid mode syntax is: *who operand permission* where:
	Who can be one of the following:
n	Sets permissions for nobody.

continued

o	Sets permissions for owner.
g	Sets permissions for group.
w	Sets permissions for world.
a	Sets permissions for all.
	Operand can be one of the following:
+	Sets a permission.
-	Removes a permission.
=	Sets a permission explicitly.
	Permission can be one or more of the following:
r	Sets read permission.
m	Sets modify permission.
c	Sets create permission.
d	Sets destroy permission.
names...	Specifies the NIS+ object to alter permissions for.
File Name: `nischmod`	**Directory:** /usr/bin/ **Type:** External

nischown

UNIX Shell: All primary shells (csh, ksh, sh)

Function	Manages the ownership of a NIS+ object.
Syntax	nischown [options...] *owner names...*

-A	Alters all table entries in the path.
-f	Tries to force the execution of the command.
-L	Follows a linked file to its source and alters the source.
-P	Follows the path within a specified table.
owner	Specifies the new owner of the NIS+ object.
names...	Specifies the NIS+ object to change owner for.
File Name: `nischown`	**Directory:** /usr/bin/ **Type:** External

nischttl

UNIX Shell: All primary shells (csh, ksh, sh)

Function	Manages the time-to-live for NIS+ objects.
Syntax	nischttl [options...] *time names...*

-A	Alters all objects in the path.
-f	Tries to force the execution of the command.
-L	Follows a linked file to its source and alters the source.
-P	Follows the path within the specified table.
time	Sets the new time-to-live value in either seconds or day, hour, minute, and second.
names...	Specifies the NIS+ object to alter.
File Name: `nischttl`	**Directory:** /usr/bin/ **Type:** External

nisclient

UNIX Shell: Bourne shell (sh)

Function	Initializes NIS+ environment for clients and users.
Syntax	nisclient option [options...] *{ client }*

	Use these four options to specify the type. You may select only one of these:
-c	Creates NIS+ credentials.
-i	Initializes a NIS+ client.
-u	Initializes a user in NIS+ environment.
-r	Restores the network service environment.
	These options work with all of the above types:
-x	Prints out what the command would do without actually executing the command.
-v	Verbose mode. Shows more information.
	This option works only with the -c and -i types:
-d *domain*	Points out for which NIS+ domain to create credentials for.
	These options work only with the -c type:
-o	Forces overwrite of credentials (default is no overwrite).

continued

-l *password*		Specifies the client network password.			
-d *domain*		Specifies the NIS+ domain in which to create the credentials.			
client		Specifies any host or username in the NIS+ domain. This is a required argument.			
		These options work only in -i type:			
-h *server*		Specifies hostname for the NIS+ server. This is required with -c option.			
-a *address*		Gives IP address for the NIS+ server.			
-k *domain*		Specifies in which keydomain the credentials for root are stored.			
-S *level*		Sets the authentication level: 0 = unauthenticated; 2 = authenticated (DES).			
File Name:	`nisclient`	**Directory:**	/usr/lib/nis/	**Type:**	Script
nisclient -u		Initializes the current (logged in) user.			
nisclient -i -h nisserver moon		Initializes the current client/server to the default domain; NIS+ master is nisserver.			

nisctl

UNIX Shell: All primary shells (csh, ksh, sh)

Function	Shows NIS statistics and flushes NIS cache information from the NIS database.
Syntax	nisctl [options...] *domain*

-M		Shows the heap memory on specified domain.			
-s		Shows statistics in the specified domain.			
-v		Verbose mode. Shows more information.			
-f *target*		Flushes the cache of the specified target, listed below.			
d		Flushes directories.			
g		Flushes groups.			
o		Flushes objects.			
t		Flushes tables.			
-n *object*		Specifies which object to flush. Can only be used when `-f o` is used.			
-H *host*		Specifies the host to use.			
domain		Specifies the domain.			
File Name:	`nisctl`	**Directory:**	/usr/lib/nis/	**Type:**	External

nisdefaults

UNIX Shell: All primary shells (csh, ksh, sh)

Function	A utility that shows default values returned by NIS+ local name functions.
Syntax	nisdefaults [options...]

-a		Shows all defaults in a brief format.			
-d		Shows default domain.			
-g		Shows default group.			
-h		Shows default host.			
-p		Shows default principal.			
-r		Shows default access rights that new objects will receive.			
-s		Shows the default search path for directory.			
-t		Prints the default TTL.			
-v		Verbose mode. Shows more information.			
File Name:	`nisdefaults`	**Directory:**	/usr/bin/	**Type:**	External
nisdefaults -t		Prints the default time-to-live value.			
nisdefaults -d		Prints the default domain name.			

niserror

UNIX Shell: All primary shells (csh, ksh, sh)

Function	Shows NIS+ error messages from error codes.
Syntax	niserror *n*

n		Shows the NIS+ error message that has the specified status value.			
File Name:	`niserror`	**Directory:**	/usr/bin/	**Type:**	External
niserror 0		Returns Success.			
niserror 5		Returns NIS+ servers unreachable.			
niserror 2		Returns Not found.			

nisgrep

UNIX Shell: All primary shells (csh, ksh, sh)

Function	Searches for entries in a NIS+ table by using regular expression patterns.
Syntax	nisgrep [options...] *ACTION*

-A	Shows all data in all tables that are in the path.
-c	Shows how many entries were found.
-h	Shows a header line before matching the patterns.
-i	Makes no distinction between uppercase and lowercase letters.
-M	Uses information directly from the master server; doesn't use cached information.
-o	Shows internal names of the found NIS+ objects.
-v	Verbose mode. Shows more information.
-s *sep*	Specifies a column separation character.
ACTION	**You must specify only one of these two actions:**
pattern	Specifies a pattern to use for the search.
column=pattern	Specifies a column to search for using the specified pattern.
table	Specifies the NIS+ table to search in. This must be used when specifying an action.

File Name:	nisgrep	**Directory:**	/usr/bin/	**Type:**	External

nisgrpadm

UNIX Shell: All primary shells (csh, ksh, sh)

Function	Manages NIS+ groups. It can create, delete, or show groups and memberships.
Syntax	nisgrpadm option [options...] *group*

	The following options can't be combined:
-a	Adds NIS+ principals to the specified group.
-r	Deletes the list of NIS+ principals from the specified group.
-t	Shows whether the principals are members of the specified group.
-d	Deletes a NIS+ group.
-l	Shows the members of the specified group.
-c	Creates a NIS+ group.
	The following options can be combined:
-s	Shows no output on-screen.
-M	Uses only the master server for updates; doesn't use cached data.
-D *defaults*	Specifies default values to use temporarily. It uses a comma-separated list.
ttl=*time*	Specifies the time-to-live value for the created objects.
owner=*owner*	Specifies the owner of the created object.
group=*group*	Specifies the group owner of the created object.
access=*rights*	Specifies access permissions for the created object.
group	Specifies the NIS+ group to manage.
	The following can only be used together with the -a, -r, or -t option.
principal	Specifies an explicit NIS+ member.

File Name:	nisgrpadm	**Directory:**	/usr/bin/	**Type:**	External

nisinit

UNIX Shell: All primary shells (csh, ksh, sh)

Function	Sets up NIS+ servers or clients.
Syntax	nisinit -r nisinit -p *domain hosts...* nisinit -c [-k *keydomain*] option

-r	Sets up server to be a NIS+ root server. Can only be used alone.
-p	Sets up the root server to join the parent domain.
Y	Specifies the parent domain uses NIS version 2.
D	Specifies the parent domain uses DNS.
N	Specifies the parent domain uses NIS+.
-c	Sets up the system to be a NIS+ client.
-k *keydomain*	Specifies where root's credentials are placed.

continued

	When using -c you may select only one of these three options:
-H *host*	Specifies a host that is to be trusted.
-B	Uses broadcast to find NIS+ servers.
-C *file*	Sets up a NIS+ client using data from the specified file.
domain	Specifies the name of the parent domain.
hosts...	Specifies a list of servers that serves the parent domain.
File Name: nisinit	**Directory:** /usr/sbin/ **Type:** External
nisinit -r	Sets up the server as a NIS+ root server.

nisln

UNIX Shell: All primary shells (csh, ksh, sh)

Function	Creates links between NIS+ objects and NIS+ names.
Syntax	nisln [options...] *name link*

-L	Follows a linked file to its source and alters the source.
-D *defaults*	Specifies default values to use when creating a link.
name	Specifies the NIS+ object to be linked.
link	Specifies the NIS+ name to link the object to.
File Name: nisln	**Directory:** /usr/bin/ **Type:** External

nislog

UNIX Shell: All primary shells (csh, ksh, sh)

Function	Shows the contents of the NIS+ transaction log.
Syntax	nislog [options...] *{ directories... }*

	You may select only one of these two options:
-h *n*	Shows n transactions of the log starting from the top; 0 displays the header.
-t *n*	Shows n transactions of the log from the bottom; 0 displays the header.
-v	Verbose mode. Shows more information.
directories...	Specifies the directories to search for logs (default is entire log).
File Name: nislog	**Directory:** /usr/sbin/ **Type:** External
nislog -h 20	Returns the first 20 transactions in all logs.
nislog -t 20	Returns the last 20 transactions in all logs.

nisls

UNIX Shell: All primary shells (csh, ksh, sh)

Function	Show a NIS+ directory content.
Syntax	nisls [options...] *{ names... }*

-d	Shows all directories the same way as a NIS+ object.
-g	Shows group owner instead of owner.
-l	Shows a long listing of the content.
-L	Follows linked files to their sources.
-m	Shows the last modification for the file instead of the creation.
-M	Uses information from the master server directly instead of cached data.
-R	Shows all directories recursively.
names...	Specifies the NIS+ directory to show. Without this option it searches in the path.
File Name: nisls	**Directory:** /usr/bin/ **Type:** External
nisls -l	Shows a long listing of the first directory that is in the path.

nismatch

UNIX Shell: All primary shells (csh, ksh, sh)

Function	Searches for NIS+ tables.
Syntax	nismatch [options...] *ACTIONS...*

-A	Shows all data in the specified table.
-c	Shows a count of the entries that matched the specified criteria.
-h	Shows the header line.
-M	Use only data from the master server.

continued

-o	Shows the internal names of the NIS+ objects.
-P	Follows the path of the object.
-v	Verbose mode. Shows more information.
-s *sep*	Specifies a separator character to use between columns.
ACTIONS...	**The following actions can be used:**
key	Specifies a keyword to use for searching in the first column.
colname=key	Specifies a keyword to use for searching in the specified column.
table	Specifies the NIS+ table to search for.
index	Specifies to search for an indexed name. Don't combine with other actions.
File Name: `nismatch`	**Directory:** /usr/bin/ **Type:** External

nismkdir

UNIX Shell: All primary shells (csh, ksh, sh)

Function	Creates a new NIS+ directory within an existing domain. Creates replicated directories and also subdirectories that have the same master.
Syntax	nismkdir [options...] *directory*

-D *defaults*	Specifies default values, comma-separated, for a new NIS+ directory.
ttl=time	Specifies the time-to-live value for an object.
owner=name	Specifies the owner of the object.
group=name	Specifies the group owner of the object.
access=rights	Sets permissions for the object. Uses the same values as the `nischmod` command.
-m *host*	Specifies the master serve for the object.
-s *host*	Creates a replica of an existing object.
directory	Specifies the directory to be created.
File Name: `nismkdir`	**Directory:** /usr/bin/ **Type:** External

nispasswd

UNIX Shell: All primary shells (csh, ksh, sh)

Function	Manages NIS+ passwords.
Syntax	nispasswd [options...] *user*

-g	Alters the finger information.
-h	Alters home directory for the specified user.
-s	Alters login shell for the specified user.
-D *domain*	Specifies the domain to get password information from.
-d *user*	Shows password data for the specified user.
-l	Locks password for the specified user.
-f	Expires the password so that the specified user must change it at next login.
-n *min*	Sets minimum number of days between password changes.
-x *max*	Sets maximum days that the password is valid.
-w *warn*	Warns the user the specified number of days before the password expires.
-a	Shows password data for all entries. This option must be used alone.
user	Specifies the user whose password data you want to manage.
File Name: `nispasswd`	**Directory:** /usr/bin/ **Type:** External
nispasswd ucg	Alters the password for the user ucg.

nisping

UNIX Shell: All primary shells (csh, ksh, sh)

Function	Manages updates between NIS+ servers.
Syntax	nisping [options...] *{ ACTION }* nisping -C [options...] *{ directory }*

-u	Shows the last time of update.
-f	Forces update.
-H *host*	Contacts only the specified hostname. It can be a hostname or an IPaddress.
-C	Sends a request checkpoint instead of sending to all servers.
-a	Checkpoints all directories on the server.

continued

ACTION	**The following two actions cannot be combined:**
-r	Updates root objects from root servers.
directory	Specifies the directory to get update information from.
File Name: `nisping`	**Directory:** /usr/lib/nis/ **Type:** External
nisping -C ucgbook.com	Sends a request to ucgbook.com.

nispopulate

UNIX Shell: Bourne shell (sh)

Function	Populates NIS+ tables by using files or maps.
Syntax	nispopulate -Y [options...] -h *host* [-a *address*] -y *domain* [tables...] nispopulate -F [options...] *{ tables... }* nispopulate -C [options...] *{ ACTION }*

	The following three options can only be used separately:
-Y	Uses NIS maps to populate the tables.
-F	Uses `/etc` files to populate tables.
-p *directory*	Specifies where to get files from. Only used with the `-F` option.
-C	Populates tables using passwd and host tables. Used for DES authentication.
ACTION	**You may select only one of the following actions with the -C option:**
host	Uses hosts tables to populate NIS+ tables with authentication information.
passwd	Uses passwd tables to populate NIS+ tables with authentication information.
	The following options can be combined:
-x	Simulates execution.
-f	Forces population of tables.
-n	Does not overwrite existing files in the `/var/yp` directory.
-u	Updates tables using files or maps.
-v	Verbose mode. Shows more information.
-S *level*	Sets authentication level: 0 = unauthenticated and 2 = authenticated.
-l *password*	Specifies a network password to use for the operation.
-d *domain*	Specifies the NIS+ domain to work with.
-h *host*	Specifies the NIS server hostname when you are using maps to populate tables.
-a *address*	Specifies the NIS server ipaddress when using maps to populate tables.
-y *domain*	Specifies the NIS domain to copy maps from.
tables...	Specifies the particular tables to manage.
File Name: `nispopulate`	**Directory:** /usr/lib/nis/ **Type:** Script
nispopulate -F -p /etc	Populates the NIS+ tables using `/etc` files.

nisprefadm

UNIX Shell: All primary shells (csh, ksh, sh)

Function	Manages NIS+ server preferences for NIS+ clients.
Syntax	nisprefadm option *{ ACTION }* [options...] *server*

	The following options cannot be combined:
-a	Adds a server to the list of preferred servers.
-r	Removes a server from the list of preferred servers.
-u	Clears the list of preferred servers before updating it.
-m	Manages the list of preferred servers.
-x	Removes the list of preferred servers.
-l	Shows the list of preferred servers.
-F	Makes `nis_cachemgr` update the selected server. Use this option alone.
ACTION	**One of the following two actions must be used with the -a, -r, -u, -m, -x, and -l options:**
-L	Specifies that you want to save the preferred server list locally.
-G	Specifies that you want to save the preferred server list globally.
	The following options can be combined:
-C *client*	Associates a preferred server to a client.
-d *domain*	Specifies the domain to work with.

continued

-o *action*	Specifies preferred server options. Actions are `all` or `pref_only`.
server	Specifies the server to manage preferences for.
old=new	Replaces preferences for an old server with a new server.
File Name: `nisprefadm`	**Directory:** /usr/bin/ **Type:** External

nisrestore

UNIX Shell: All primary shells (csh, ksh, sh)

Function	Restores a NIS+ directory from an existing backup.
Syntax	nisrestore [options...] *backupdir* nisrestore *object*

-f	Tries to force restore of the directory without asking the server first.
-v	Verbose mode. Shows more information.
	The following two options can't be used together:
-a	Restores all objects from the backup directory.
-t	Shows all objects from the backup directory.
backupdir	Specifies the directory holding the backup copy.
object	Specifies a single object in the directory that you want to restore.
File Name: `nisrestore`	**Directory:** /usr/sbin/ **Type:** External

nisrm

UNIX Shell: All primary shells (csh, ksh, sh)

Function	Deletes NIS+ objects.
Syntax	nisrm [options...] *names...*

-i	Prompts for confirmation before executing.
-f	Tries to force execution of the command.
names...	Specifies the NIS+ object to delete.
File Name: `nisrm`	**Directory:** /usr/bin/ **Type:** External

nisrmdir

UNIX Shell: All primary shells (csh, ksh, sh)

Function	Deletes NIS+ directories.
Syntax	nisrmdir [options...] *directory*

-i	Prompts for confirmation before deleting the directory.
-f	Tries to force execution of the command.
-s *host*	Deletes the specified hostname as a replica for the specified directory.
directory	Specifies the directory to delete.
File Name: `nisrmdir`	**Directory:** /usr/bin/ **Type:** External

nisserver

UNIX Shell: Bourne shell (sh)

Function	Manages the setup of a NIS+ server.
Syntax	nisserver option [options...]

	The following three options can't be combined:
-r	Sets up the server to be a root master server.
-l *password*	Specifies the password to use when creating credentials for the root master server.
-M	Sets up the server to be a master server.
-R	Sets up the server to be a replica server.
	The following options can be combined:
-x	Simulates the execution of a command without executing it.
-f	Forces a setup of a NIS+ server.
-v	Verbose mode. Shows more information.
-Y	Sets up NIS+ server in NIS compatibility mode.
-d *domain*	Specifies the domain name to use. Required with the -M option.
-g *group*	Specifies the NIS+ group name for the new domain.
-h *host*	Specifies the hostname for the NIS+ server.

continued

File Name:	`nisserver`	**Directory:**	/usr/lib/nis/	**Type:**	Script
nisserver -r -d ucgbook.com			Sets up a NIS+ root master server for the domain ucgbook.com.		

nissetup

UNIX Shell: Bourne shell (sh)

Function	Creates a NIS+ domain.
Syntax	nissetup [-Y] *{ domain }*

-Y	Makes the domain compatible with both NIS and NIS+.
domain	Specifies the domain name of the NIS+ domain.

File Name:	`nissetup`	**Directory:**	/usr/lib/nis/	**Type:**	Script
nissetup ucg			Creates a NIS+ domain called ucg.		

nisshowcache

UNIX Shell: All primary shells (csh, ksh, sh)

Function	Shows the content of the NIS+ shared cache file.
Syntax	nisshowcache [-v]

-v	Verbose mode. Shows more information, including server name and universal addresses.

File Name:	`nisshowcache`	**Directory:**	/usr/lib/nis/	**Type:**	External

nisstat

UNIX Shell: All primary shells (csh, ksh, sh)

Function	Queries a NIS+ server for statistics.
Syntax	nisstat [-H *host*] *{ directory }*

-H *host*	Queries only the given host.
directory	Queries only servers holding the specified NIS+ directory.

File Name:	`nisstat`	**Directory:**	/usr/lib/nis/	**Type:**	External

nistbladm

UNIX Shell: All primary shells (csh, ksh, sh)

Function	Creates, deletes, adds, modifies, and removes entries from NIS+ tables.
Syntax	nistbladm option [options...] *ACTIONS...*

	The following options are required but can't be combined:
-a	Adds entries to a NIS+ table.
-A	The same as -a but adds the entry even if it already exists.
-c	Creates a table called `tablename` in the namespace.
-d *tablename*	Specifies tablename to remove.
-e	Edits the entry in the table that is specified by `indexname`.
-E	The same as -e but forces the modification.
-m	The same as -E.
-r	Removes entries from a table.
-R	The same as -r but forces removal if there is more than one entry.
-u	Updates the attributes of a table.
	These options are not required:
-D *defaults*	Specifies a different set of defaults when you create objects.
-p *path*	Specifies a search path when you update a table.
-s *sep*	Specifies the table separator character when you update a table.
-t *type*	Specifies the table type string when you update a table.
ACTION	**The following actions can be used:**
colname= { flags } [,access]	Specifies the column name.
	Use these options for *colname*:
flags	Specifies the different flags. Below are the possible choices:
S	Specifies that a search can be done on column values.
I	Specifies that a search with `S` will ignore case-sensitivity.
C	Encrypts the column values.
B	Creates column values in binary data.
X	Encrypts data in XDR format. Use this with `B`.

continued

access	Specifies the access.
-A	Modifies all tables in the path that match search criteria specified in name.
-f	Forces operation and suppresses a failure.
-P	Follows path within a named table. Used with indexed name or with -L option.
-L	Follows links and changes permission of object instead of the link.
indexname	Specifies the index name.
tablename	Specifies the table name.
File Name: `nistbladm`	**Directory:** /usr/bin/ — **Type:** External

nistest

UNIX Shell: All primary shells (csh, ksh, sh)

Function	Tests NIS+ permissions, entries, types, and the like.
Syntax	nistest [options...] *object* nistest [options...] *indexed* nistest -c *dir1 expression dir2*

	The following options can be combined:
-A	Shows all data.
-L	Follows links to their sources.
-M	Uses master server only; no cached data.
-P	Follows the initial path of the table.
	You may select one of these two options:
-a *rights*	Checks permissions for objects or entries.
-t *type*	Is used to test object types. The following test conditions can be used.
D	Checks whether the object is a directory object.
G	Checks whether the object is a group object.
L	Checks whether the object is a link object.
P	Checks whether the object is a private object.
T	Checks whether the object is a table object.
	The following syntax options compare directory relations:
-c *dir1 expression dir2*	Compares the specified relationship between two specified directories.
dir1	Specifies the first directory.
dir2	Specifies the second directory.
expression	Specifies the expression to use between dir1 and dir2.
<	Is less than.
lt	Is less than.
<=	Is less than or equal to.
le	Is less than or equal to.
=	Is equal to.
eq	Is equal to.
>	Is greater than.
ht	Is greater than.
gt	Is greater than.
>=	Is greater than or equal to.
he	Is greater than or equal to.
ge	Is greater than or equal to.
!=	Is not equal to.
ne	Is not equal to.
ns	Is not sequential.
object	Specifies the test is to be run on an object.
indexed	Specifies the test is to be run on a specific table.
File Name: `nistest`	**Directory:** /usr/bin/ — **Type:** External
Note:	Commonly used by shell scripts.

nisupdkeys

nisupdkeys	UNIX Shell:	All primary shells (csh, ksh, sh)

Function	Manages public keys in a NIS+ object directory.
Syntax	nisupdkeys [options...] *{ directory }* nisupdkeys -s [option] -H *host*

	The following two options can't be combined:
-a	Updates the universal addresses of the NIS+ server.
-C	Removes public keys.
-H *host*	Changes can only be made to the specified host.
-s	Updates NIS+ directories in the specified server. Must be used with the option -H.
directory	Specifies the NIS+ directory to update.

File Name:	`nisupdkeys`	**Directory:**	/usr/lib/nis/	**Type:**	External

nisupdkeys -s -H sun.ucgbook.com	Updates all objects served by sun.ucgbook.com.

nl

nl	UNIX Shell:	All primary shells (csh, ksh, sh)

Function	Reads lines from STDIN or a file, adds line numbers, and shows the result to STDOUT.
Syntax	nl [options...] *{ file }*

-p	When a logical page delimiter is found, the line numbering will not restart.
-b*type*	Specifies the `type` of lines in page body to be numbered (default is t).
-f*type*	Specifies the `type` of lines in page footer to be numbered (default is n).
-h*type*	Specifies the `type` of lines in page header to be numbered (default is n).
a	Numbers all lines.
t	Only numbers lines that contain data.
n	Does not use line numbering.
p*exp*	Only numbers lines that match the specified pattern.
-n*format*	Specifies the format of line number, use the formats supplied (default is rn).
ln	Adjusts the format of line number to the left and suppresses leading zeros.
rn	Adjusts the format of line number to the right and suppresses leading zeros.
rz	Adjusts the format of line number to the right and keeps leading zeros.
-d*??*	Specifies the two characters used as the `delimiter` for logical page sections.
-i*inc*	Specifies the increment value to number logical page lines (default is 1).
-l*num*	Specifies the number of blank lines that are treated as one (default is 1).
-s*?*	Specifies the character used to separate the line number and text (default is Tab).
-v*startnum*	Specifies the starting number.
-w*num*	Specifies the number of characters used for the column width (default is 6).
file	The input file used to generate line numbers for.

File Name:	`nl`	**Directory:**	/usr/bin/	**Type:**	External

Tip:	If you just want to make a quick line count, you could use the command `wc` instead.
nl -v10 -i10 /etc/passwd	Numbers lines in passwd starting from 10 and by using an interval of 10.
nl /etc/passwd	Numbers lines in passwd using default settings.

nlsadmin

nlsadmin	UNIX Shell:	All primary shells (csh, ksh, sh)

Function	Manages the network listener processes, which are configured individually.
Syntax	nlsadmin [options...] *process* nlsadmin [options...] -N *pmtag*

	The following options can be used with `process` or with the -N option:
-a *service*	Adds a new service to the listener specified by `process` in the options.
	The following sub options are used with the `-a` option:
-p *modules*	Pushes the specified STREAM modules before starting service (optional).
-w *user*	Specifies the username to act as owner for the listener service (optional).
-c *cmd*	Specifies the command to start when the service is accessed (optional).

continued

-y *comment*	Specifies a comment to use for reports (required).
-q	Shows exit codes for the specified listener `process`.
-v	Shows report for servers specified by `process`.
-s	Starts the listener process for the specified network.
-k	Kills the listener process for the specified network.
-i	Initializes a network listener instance specified by `process`.
-e *service*	Enables the service specified by `servicecode` for the specified network.
-d *service*	Disables the service specified by `servicecode` for the specified network.
-r *service*	Removes the entry for the *servicecode* from that listener's list of services.
-z *service*	Shows report for servers specified by `servicecode`.
-q -z *service*	Shows report for services specified by `servicecode`.
-l *address*	Manages the transport address that the listener listens to.
-t *address*	Manages the address for the terminal service request listener.
-N *pmtag*	Specifies the instance tag to identify the listener in the SAF.
	The following options can be used alone with `nlsadmin`:
-V	Shows version information.
-x	Shows the status for all listener processes.
	Use the following syntax to pass arguments to `pmadm`:
-c *cmd*	Specifies the command to start when the service is accessed (required).
-o *streamname*	Specifies a path of a FIFO file or a STREAM where the server receives a connection.
-p *modules*	Pushes the specified STREAM modules before starting service.
-A address	Interprets address as the server's private address.
-D	Assigns the service a private address dynamically.
-R *prog:vers*	Registers the server's program and version number for the RPC service.
process	Specifies the listener process that you want to manage.

File Name:	`nlsadmin`	**Directory:**	/usr/sbin/	**Type:**	External

nlsadmin –x	Reports the status of any installed listener services.

nscd

UNIX Shell: All primary shells (csh, ksh, sh)

Function	Provides cache for name services. It is a daemon process that caches `passwd`, `hosts`, and `groups` databases.
Syntax	nscd [options...]

-f *conf-file*	Specifies the configuration file (default is `/etc/nscd.conf`).
-g	Shows statistics and information about configuration.
-d *debuglevel*	Specifies the debug level (default is 0).
-l *logfilename*	Specifies the log filename (default is `/var/adm/nscd.log`).
-i *cachename*	Invalidates the cache that is specified.
	The following options need a database name (db) to cache and a parameter:
-e *db,choice*	Enables cache (after the cachename): yes = enable, no = disable.
-s *db,num*	Specifies the suggested size (default is 211).
-o *db,choice*	Specifies whether the old data is treated as OK (default is no).
-c *db,choice*	Specifies if the files will be checked, yes or no (default is yes).
-h *db,num*	Specifies the number of hot-count to keep (default is 20).
-p *db,TTL*	Specifies the positive Time-to-Live (TTL) value (default is 3600).
-n *db,TTL*	Specifies the negative Time-to-Live (TTL) value (default is 5). (The databases normally used are passwd, groups, and hosts.)

File Name:	`nacd`	**Directory:**	/usr/sbin/	**Type:**	External

nstest

UNIX Shell: All primary shells (csh, ksh, sh)

Function	Tests DNS queries interactively in a shell environment. The result is shown to STDOUT.
Syntax	nstest [options...] *{ ipaddress }*

-d	Writes binary copies on every packet into a filenamed `ns_packet.dump`.
-i	Sets the flag `RES_IGNTC` for completed queries.
-r	Sets the flag `RES_RECURSE` to off for completed queries.
-v	Sets the flags `RES_USEVC and RES_STAYOPE` to on when res_send calls are completed.

continued

-p *port*	Specifies a port to use other than the default port for the name server.
ipaddress	Specifies the IP address for the DNS server to use.
logfile	A log file to write all queries and replies to. Only used with the ipaddress option.
File Name: `nstest`	**Directory:** /usr/sbin/ — **Type:** External
Tip:	Type `?` inside `nstest` to get the valid keyletters that can be used when querying.
nstest 192.168.1.254	Starts on the server 192.168.1.254.
nstest -d 192.168.1.254	Starts and creates a file `ns_packet.dump` to store copies of all raw packets.

nsupdate

UNIX Shell: All primary shells (csh, ksh, sh)

Function	Updates DNS name servers interactively or non-interactively.
Syntax	nsupdate [options...] *{ file }*

-d	Shows debug information.
-v	Uses TCP for updates instead of UDP.
file	Specifies a name of the file containing the update data.
	Shows content and should be used in this order and with space separators:
class	Specifies the `opcodes`: update, zone, or prereq.
section	Specifies the `opcodes`: add, delete, nxdomain, yxdomain, nxrrset, or yxrrset.
name	Specifies the name of the added entry.
TTL	Specifies the TTL value for the entry.
type	Specifies the RR type to use: a, cname, ns, mx, ptr, or txt.
rdata	Specifies the update data for the RR type.
File Name: `nsupdate`	**Directory:** /usr/sbin/ — **Type:** External
nsupdate updatefile	Runs nsupdate in non-interactive mode.

ntpdate

UNIX Shell: All primary shells (csh, ksh, sh)

Function	Sets the local date and time via the NTP. Gets time from any specified NTP servers.
Syntax	ntpdate [options...] *{ servers... }*

-s	Uses `syslog` instead of STDOUT to log activities.
-b	Uses `gettimeofday` to step the time.
-d	Shows information about what will happen without actually doing it.
-a *keynumber*	Specifies a key number to authenticate transactions.
-e *delay*	Sets a delay in seconds for the authentication process; `xntpd` has more information.
-k *keyfile*	Specifies a file for the key (default is `/etc/ntp.keys`); `xntpd` has more information.
-m	Uses the server argument as a multicast group to join (default is 224.0.0.1).
-w	Stands until it's able to join groups and synchronize.
-o *version*	Specifies the version the program will act as: 1, 2, or 3 (default is 3).
-p *samples*	Specifies the number of required samples from the servers: 1 to 8 (default is 4).
-t *timeout*	Specifies the response timeout. The value is a multiple of 0.2 (default is 1).
-u	Sends packets from an unprivileged port; useful with firewalls.
server...	Gets the correct time by querying the specified NTP server.
File Name: `ntpdate`	**Directory:** /usr/sbin/ — **Type:** External
ntpdate timer.sunet.se	Uses the server timer.sunet.se to update time and date.
ntpdate –d timer.sunet.se	Uses the server specified, but without actually updating.

ntpq

UNIX Shell: All primary shells (csh, ksh, sh)

Function	Queries a NTP server that supports the NTP mode 6 control message format by the command line or interactively.
Syntax	ntpq [options...] *{ hosts... }*

-c	Specifies an interactive format command that would be executed on the hosts given.
-i	Uses interactive mode. Puts command on STDIN and is then shown on STDOUT.
-n	Shows output address as ipnumber instead of hostnames.
-p	Shows a list of known peers and a summary of their state.
hosts...	Specifies a host to query; default is localhost.

continued

	These commands are used when using interactive mode:
? *keyword*	Gives information about all commands or how to use the command specified by keyword.
addvars *name*[=*value*]	Adds variables to the variable list or changes their values.
associations	Shows a list of association IDs and status for the server's peers.
authenticate *choice*	Activates queries authentication: yes = yes, no = no.
cl *{ assocID }*	Reads the clock variables in the variable list.
clearvars	Removes all variables from the variable list.
clocklist *{ assocID }*	Reads the clock variables in the variable list.
clockvar *{ assocID } { name=value }*	Reads clock variables.
cooked	Gives the user the information formatted so it is more easily read.
cv *{ assocID } { name=value }*	Same as clockvar.
debug *choice*	Shows debug information in two ways: more or less; off = off.
delay *milliseconds*	Sets an interval in milliseconds; often used if the network is slow.
help *{ command }*	Shows help on specified command; all available commands are shown if used alone.
host *hostname*	Specifies a hostname or an IP address where future queries will be sent.
hostnames *choice*	Information is shown by hostname or IP address; yes = hostname, no = ip.
keyid *number*	Specifies a key number that the server accepts for configuration requests.
keytype md5 | des	Sets the key type to use for authenticated requests.
lassociations	Shows a list of associations including all client information.
lopeers	Is used to get and show a list of all peers and clients.
lpassociations	Shows the last obtained list of associations including client information.
lpeers	Gets and shows a list of all peers and clients.
mreadlist *assocID assocID*	Reads the peer variables in the variable list for multiple peers.
mreadvar *assocID assocID { name=value }*	Reads peer variables from multiple peers.
mrl *assocID assocID*	Same as mreadlist.
mrv *assocID assocID { name=value }*	Same as mreadvar.
ntpversion *ver*	Specifies the NTP version number the program accepts; valid versions are 1, 2, or 3.
opeers	Shows the peer list the old way (destination address rather than refid).
passociations	Shows a list of associations returned by the last association command.
passwd	Prompts the user for a password to get the rights to perform configurations.
peers	Gets and shows a list of the server's peers.
poll *{ NR }* [verbose]	Polls an NTP server in client mode the specified number of times.
pstatus *assocID*	Shows status information returned for a peer.
quit	Leaves the program.
raw	Shows all query information without filtering from the server.
readlist *{ assocID }*	Reads the peer or system variables included in the variable list.
readvar *{ assocID } { name=value }*	Reads peer or system variables.
rl *{ assocID }*	Same as `readlist`.
rmvars *names...*	Removes variables from the variable list. Separate with comma.
rv *{ assocID } { name=value }*	Same as `readvar`.
showvars	Shows the variables in the variable list.
timeout *milliseconds*	Specifies the timeout in milliseconds for every query (default is 5000).
version	Shows version information.
writelist *{ assocID }*	Writes the peer or system variables included in the variable list.
writevar *assocID name=value*	Writes peer or system variables.

File Name:	`ntpq`	**Directory:**	/usr/sbin/	**Type:**	External
ntpq -p ntpserver			Prints a list of peers known to the ntpserver.		

ntptrace

UNIX Shell:	All primary shells (csh, ksh, sh)
Function	Traces the master time source. Shows where the specified server received its time.
Syntax	ntptrace [options...] *{ server }*

-d	Shows debug information.
-n	Shows IP addresses instead of hostnames for all hosts included in the trace.
-r *retries*	Specifies the number of retries for every host.

continued

-t *timeout*	Specifies the timeout in seconds for retries (default is 2).		
-v	Verbose mode. Shows more information.		
server	Specifies the NTP server to find where it received its time (default is local host).		
File Name: `ntptrace`	**Directory:** /usr/sbin/	**Type:**	External
ntptrace 192.168.1.254	Shows where the host with IP address 192.168.1.254 got its time.		

nulladm

UNIX Shell: All primary shells (csh, ksh, sh)

Function	Creates a file with the mode 644, by using the owner and group `adm`.
Syntax	nulladm *files...*

files...	Specifies the name of the file or files that you want to create.		
File Name: `nulladm`	**Directory:** /usr/lib/acct/	**Type:**	External

on

UNIX Shell: All primary shells (csh, ksh, sh)

Function	Runs commands on other systems by using the local environment.
Syntax	on [options...] *host command*

-i	Turns on special character processing and remote echoing.		
-d	Shows debug information.		
-n	Initiates the remote program to not accept data from STDIN.		
host	Specifies the remote hostname or IP address to run the command on.		
command	Specifies the command and its argument to run on the remote system.		
File Name: `on`	**Directory:** /usr/bin/	**Type:**	External
Note:	Can't be used by root. Ctrl-Z hangs the window if the working directory is remotely mounted over NFS.		
on appserver backup.sh	Executes backup.sh on the remote appserver.		

openwin

UNIX Shell: Bourne shell (sh)

Function	A script that helps you start OpenWindow the correct way.
Syntax	openwin [options...]

-server *xserver*	Specifies the X server binary to run. Default is Xsun.		
-noauth	Uses user-specific authorization system, instead of host. This is a security risk.		
-auth *protocol-name*	Specifies the authentication protocol to use when user clients connect.		
-includedemo	Adds the demo path to the user's path.		
-wm *wm*	Specifies the window manager to use. Default is olwm.		
-dev *device*	Specifies the name of framebuffer device to use.		
-display *display*	Specifies the name of the X server display.		
File Name: `openwin`	**Directory:** /usr/openwin/bin/	**Type:**	Script
Tip:	This is used if you find OpenWindow more attractive than CDE.		
openwin -display :1	Runs OpenWindow on display :1 on localhost.		

optisa

UNIX Shell: All primary shells (csh, ksh, sh)

Function	Asks `isalist` for the best instruction set to use.
Syntax	optisa *instructionsets...*

instructionsets...	A list of instruction sets to choose from.
	To show SPARC instruction sets you can specify these:
sparc	Indicates the SPARC V8 instruction.
sparcv7	Indicates the SPARC V8 that has been compiled with xarch to be V7 instruction.
sparcv8-fsmuld	Indicates that the SPARC V8 instruction integer multiply and divide is calculated in hardware.
sparcv8	Indicates SPARC V8-fsmuld but that the fsmuld will be calculated in hardware.
sparcv8plus	Shows the SPARC V8 and V9 instruction.
sparcv8plus+vis	Indicates SPARC V8 and V9 and UltraSPARC I visualization instruction.
sparcv8plus+fmuladd	Shows SPARC V8 and V9 and the Hal SPARC64 instruction.

continued

sparcv9 *sparcv9+vis* *sparcv9+fmuladd* *i386* *i486* *pentium* *pentium+mmx* *pentium_pro* *pentium_pro+mmx*	Indicates SPARC V9 instruction. Indicates Sparc V9 and UltraSPARC I visualization instruction. Shows Sparc V9 and the Hal SPARC64 instruction. **To show Intel instruction sets you can specify these:** Indicates Intel 80386 instruction. Indicates Intel 80486 instruction. Indicates Intel Pentium instruction. Indicates Intel Pentium and MMX instruction. Indicates the Intel Pentium Pro instruction. Indicates Intel Pentium Pro and MMX instruction.
File Name: optisa	**Directory:** /usr/bin/ **Type:** External
optisa sparcv7 sparcv8 sparcv8plus+vis	Determines optimal variant instruction set.

owplaces

UNIX Shell: All primary shells (csh, ksh, sh)

Function	Shows on a specified screen what applications clients are running.
Syntax	owplaces [options...]

-display *string*	Specifies the screen that you want to monitor.
-timeout *secs*	Specifies timeout value to wait for clients to update the command line.
-single	Searches only the default screen of specified display for clients.
-multi	Searches all screens of the specified display for clients (default).
-pointer	Prints the client selected by clicking the mouse in the desired window.
-all	Prints clients on all hosts (default).
-local	Allows printing from local clients only.
-remote	Allows printing from remote clients.
-host *hostname*	Allows printing from hostname only. (If multi also is specified, the script can handle multiple screens.)
-script	Shows Bourne shell script to use as a start file.
-output *file*	Specifies a filename to direct output. Specifies a filename to direct the output.
-ampersand	Sets an ampersand character to end a command line.
-tw	Prepends the command toolwait to each client.
-silent	Suppresses error messages.
File Name: owplaces	**Directory:** /usr/openwin/bin/owplaces **Type:** External

pack

UNIX Shell: All primary shells (csh, ksh, sh)

Function	Compresses files into .z format. Each file is compressed and replaced.
Syntax	pack [options...] *files...*

-f	Compresses files even if there will be problems compressing them.
-	Compresses on a byte-by-byte basis.
files...	The file or files to be compressed.
File Name: pack	**Directory:** /usr/bin/ **Type:** External
Warning:	Removes the original file if the compress was successful.
pack -f database	Compresses the file database even if errors occur.

page

UNIX Shell: All primary shells (csh, ksh, sh)

Function	Shows a text file one page at a time.
Syntax	page [options...] *{ files... }*

-c	Clears the screen every time a new page is to be shown.
-d	Shows error messages on the screen instead of ringing the terminal bell.
-s	Replaces multiple blank lines with a single blank line.
-f	Prints lines containing nonprinting characters or escape sequences.
-l	Does not treat usual formfeed characters as page breaks.
-r	Shows the control characters found in document.

continued

-u	Does not generate escape sequences that might be created for underlining and so on.
-w	Doesn't quit until a key is pressed when page comes to the end of the file.
-*lines*	Shows the count of lines specified as one page.
+ *linenumber*	Starts showing text at the specified line.
+/*pattern*	Starts showing text from two lines above the line containing the pattern.
files...	The file or files to show.

File Name:	`page`	**Directory:**	/usr/bin/	**Type:**	External
Note:	The only difference between `more` and `page` is that `page` clears the screen before the next page.				

page -c /var/adm/messages	Clears screen and shows messages.
page -s /var/adm/messages	Shows messages and skips repeated empty lines.

pagesize

UNIX Shell: All primary shells (csh, ksh, sh)

Function	Shows the page size of memory.
Syntax	pagesize

File Name:	`pagesize`	**Directory:**	/usr/bin/	**Type:**	External
Tip:	Useful when constructing portable shell scripts.				

passmgmt

UNIX Shell: All primary shells (csh, ksh, sh)

Function	Adds, deletes, or modifies data in the password files `/etc/passwd` and `/etc/shadow`.
Syntax	passmgmt option [options...] *user*

-a	Adds a user.
-m	Alters information for the user.
-d	Erases a user from the password files.
	To add or modify users you can use the following options:
-c *comment*	The field where the user's real name and other information about the user is stored.
-h *homedir*	Specifies the home directory for the user.
-u *uid*	Specifies the user ID for the user.
-o	Used when the user will share a user ID with another user. Used only with -u.
-g *gid*	Specifies the group ID for the user.
-s *shell*	The shell for the user.
-l *newname*	Changes the username to the specified username. Used only with -m.
user	The username to add, modify, or delete.

File Name:	`passmgmt`	**Directory:**	/usr/sbin/	**Type:**	External
Note:	Doesn't create a homedir for the user; account will be active when password is changed.				

passmgmt -a -c "Ucg user" -s /usr/bin/ksh ucg	Adds the user ucg with real name Ucg user and ksh as shell.
passmgmt -d admin	Removes the user admin from the password files.

patchadd

UNIX Shell: Korn shell (ksh)

Function	Installs patches and updates system files. Patches can be installed from a directory or one by one.
Syntax	patchadd [options...] *{ patch }*

-d	Doesn't back up the destination files that patch will affect.
-p	Shows the patches that already have been installed. Used with -C, -R, or -S.
-u	Unconditionally applies patches to destination files without validating the file.
-R *pathname*	Specifies the path where the patch files are stored. Cannot be used with -S.
-B *directory*	Specifies the directory in which to store backout data.
-S *service*	Selects an alternate service other then the default. Cannot be used with -R.
-M *patchdir patchlist*	Installs all patches written in the patch list from the directory specified.
-M *patchdir patchID*	Installs patches specified by patchID. You can specify multiple patchIDs together.
-C *netimage*	Installs patches to a net install image (a.k.a. mini root) used by other hosts.
patch	Specifies the path and patchID to the patch that is installed.
patchID	Specifies the patchID to be installed. A patch ID may look similar to 106945-02.

continued

File Name:	`patchadd`	**Directory:**	/usr/sbin/	**Type:**	Script
patchadd /usr/share/patch/106945-02		Adds the patch 104945-02 to the system.			
patchadd -u /usr/share/patch/106945-02		Installs the patch 104945-02 even if it is already installed.			

patchrm

UNIX Shell: Korn shell (ksh)

Function	Restores saved original files that existed before a patch was installed.
Syntax	patchrm [options...] *patch*

-f	Removes patch even if the patched files were replaced by patches installed later.
-B *directory*	Specifies the directory in which to look for backout data for patch.
-R *pathname*	Specifies the path to client directory where the patch files are stored.
-S *service*	Specifies an alternate service other than the default.
-C *netimage*	Removes patches from a net image.
patch	Specifies the patchID to the patch that is erased.

File Name:	`patchrm`	**Directory:**	/usr/sbin/	**Type:**	Script
Note:	Doesn't work with Solaris 1 patches.				
patchrm 1415545-03		Erases the patch 1415545-03.			
patchrm -f 1415545-03		Forces removal of the patch 1415545-03.			

pathchk

UNIX Shell: All primary shells (csh, ksh, sh)

Function	Checks whether the path or paths specified are valid.
Syntax	pathchk [-p] *paths...*

-p	Shows information about the paths with non-portable characters.
paths...	The path or paths to be checked.

File Name:	`pathchk`	**Directory:**	/usr/bin/	**Type:**	External
Tip:	Use it to verify that a path can be used to create files or directories.				
pathchk /usr/local/bin		Checks the path specified.			
Pathchk -p /		Shows that is it not a valid path because it contains non-portable characters.			

Pax

UNIX Shell: All primary shells (csh, ksh, sh)

Function	Administers archives. Lists archive members, extracts archives and archive files, and copies directory structures.
Syntax	pax –r [options…] *{ patterns… }* pax –w [options…] *{ files… }* pax –r –w [options…] *{ files… } directory*

	There are four modes of operation: list, read, write, and copy. Select only one mode.
-r	Extracts members of the pax archive read from STDIN using pattern matching.
-w	Writes file content to STDOUT or to a file in the specified archive format.
-rw	Copies file content to the destination or from STDIN.
	The following options are supported in all modes:
-d	Doesn't use subdirectories when archiving files or extracting archive members.
-v	Verbose mode. When in list mode, shows table of contents; otherwise shows pathnames.
-s *oldnew*	Alters archive or file member names listed by pattern or filenames.
	Oldnew follows the following format /old/new/ [gp]
old	Specifies the regular expression or a string containing new line characters.
New	Contains ampersand (&) or a backreference (\n), where n = subpattern number.
G	Applies the replacement globally.
P	Causes successful replacements to be written to STDERR.
	The following options can be used in list mode:
-c	Doesn't use archive or file members that match patterns or filenames.
-f *archive*	Specifies the archive to use as input or output, instead of using STDIN or STDOUT.
-n	Uses the first archive member for every specified pattern.

continued

	Besides the options c, f, n, and pattern, read mode supports the following:				
-i	Prompts when renaming archive members or files matching the specified pattern.				
-k	Doesn't overwrite files that already exist.				
-o *options*	Doesn't do anything. Reserved for special options.				
-p *priv*	Specifies the privileges that the extracted file will keep. Specifies one or more:				
a	Doesn't save file access times.				
m	Doesn't keep the file modification times.				
o	Keeps the user and group ID.				
p	Keeps the file mode bits.				
e	Keeps the user and group ID, file mode bits, and the access and modification times.				
-u	Skips files that are older than preexisting files or archive members.				
	In addition to the options f, i, o, and u, write mode supports the following:				
-a	Inserts files specified at the command line at the end of the specified archive.				
-b *blocksize*	Specifies the number of bytes of information to send to each write to the archive.				
-t	Resets the archived files' access time to what they had before being read.				
-x *format*	Specifies the archive format to use. Can be either of the following.				
cpio	Specifies the Extended cpio Interchange Format.				
ustar	Specifies the Extended tar Interchange Format.				
-X	Skips directories located on other devices that have different device IDs.				
-l	Makes hard links from source to destination when copying directories.				
pattern	Specifies a pattern that matches at least one archive member pathname. Default = all.				
file	Specifies the file to use.				
directory	Specifies the directory to get the files.				
File Name:	`pax`	**Directory:**	/usr/bin/	**Type:**	External
Note:	If no -r or -w option is specified, then list mode is activated. Lists pax archive contents.				
pax -w -d -f /dev/rmt/1m /project/	Writes the project directory without subdirectories to `/dev/rmt/1m`.				

pbind

UNIX Shell: All primary shells (csh, ksh, sh)

Function	Manages the bindings between processes and processors.				
Syntax	pbind option *pids...*				
-b *processorid*	Binds all lightweight processes to a specific processor.				
-q	Shows all bindings of the specified process.				
-u	Deletes all lightweight processes with a specific process ID.				
pids...	Specifies a process ID or process IDs to manage.				
File Name:	`pbind`	**Directory:**	/usr/sbin/	**Type:**	External
pbind -b 2 204 223	Binds pid 204 and 223 to processor 2.				
pbind -u 204	Deletes bindings for pid 204.				

pcat

UNIX Shell: All primary shells (csh, ksh, sh)

Function	Shows content of files that are compressed. Unpacks file to a temporary place before showing it.				
Syntax	pcat [options...] *files...*				
-f	Forces packing of file.				
-	Uses Huffman code as compressor method. Can only be used with -f option.				
files...	The name of the compressed file or files that you want to show the contents of.				
File Name:	`pcat`	**Directory:**	/usr/bin/	**Type:**	External
Note:	Use this command on files compressed with the pack command, which has file-ending .z.				
pcat /ucg_examples/file1.z	Shows the content of the packed file.				
pcat file1.z file2.z	Shows the content of the two packed files.				

perfmeter

perfmeter	UNIX Shell:	All primary shells (csh, ksh, sh)
Function	Monitors performance statistics in either strip charts or meter dials.	
Syntax	perfmeter [options...] *{ hostname }*	

-a	Shows all performance statistics at the same time.
-d	Starts the perfmeter in meter dials mode.
-g	Starts the perfmeter in strip charts mode.
-h *hhi*	Sets new interval in seconds for the hour hand meter.
-l	Logs perfmeter sample statistics to a file.
-m *mhi*	Sets new interval in seconds for the minute hand meter.
-n *samplefile*	Specifies the file in which to save perfmeter statistics samples.
-name *application*	Specifies an application to run performance tests on.
-p *plength*	Sets the page length for saved samples.
-s *sampletime*	Sets the time for collection of samples, in seconds.
-t *value*	Specifies which performance values you want to monitor.
cpu	Shows CPU utilization in percent.
kts	Shows sent Ethernet packets per seconds.
page	Shows memory paging statistics and number of pages occurring in memory per second.
swap	Shows the number of jobs swapped out to disk per second.
intr	Shows device interrupts per second.
disk	Shows disk transfers per second.
cntxt	Shows context switches per second.
load	Shows the average load over the last minute.
colls	Shows Ethernet packet collisions per second.
errs	Shows received Ethernet packet collisions per seconds.
-v	Shows version information.
-C *chartlimit*	Sets a high-water mark for the strip chart.
-H	Starts with multiple strip charts or meter dials horizontally.
-L	Shows strip charts in line mode.
-M *chart start min max*	Sets maximum start value and minimum and maximum values.
-S	Shows strip charts in solid-fill mode.
-V	Starts with multiple strip charts or meter dials vertically.
-W*n*	Starts the perfmeter without title line.
+W*n*	Starts the perfmeter with title line.
hostname	Specifies host other than the current one to monitor.

File Name:	Directory:	Type:
`perfmeter`	/usr/openwin/bin/	External

pfinstall

pfinstall	UNIX Shell:	All primary shells (csh, ksh, sh)
Function	Tests an installation profile to check the action before using it to install or upgrade.	
Syntax	pfinstall [options...] *profile*	

	One of the two following options must be specified. They can't be combined.
-D	Uses the system's disk configuration to test the profile.
-d *diskconfig*	Uses the disk configuration file to test the profile.
-c *Cdpath*	Sets the path to the Solaris installation image; required if the CD-ROM isn't mounted.
profile	Specifies the filename of the profile to test.

File Name:	Directory:	Type:
`pfinstall`	/usr/sbin/install.d/	External

Warning: The -d or -D option must be specified or an installation is performed and data is overwritten.

pfinstall -D -c /cdrom/cdrom0/s0 basic.prof	This example tests the basic.prof profile against the disk configuration.

pg

pg	UNIX Shell:	All primary shells (csh, ksh, sh)
Function	Shows a file's content on the screen one page at a time and prompts for the next page.	
Syntax	pg [options...] *{ files... }*	

-*number*	Specifies a screen size other than the default.
-p *string*	Sets a new prompt for pg.
-c	Clears the screen between each page.
-e	Doesn't pause at the end of the file.
-f	Doesn't split lines that are too long.
-n	Automatically ends a command when the command letter is typed in.
-r	Uses restricted shell mode; pg escape isn't allowed.
-s	Shows all messages and the prompt in inverted mode.
+ *linenumber*	Shows the page starting from a specific line number.
+/ *pattern* /	Shows the page starting from a specified pattern.
files...	Specifies the file or files that are queried for content.

File Name:	`pg`	**Directory:**	/usr/bin/	**Type:**	External

pg + 200 /var/adm/messages	Shows messages from /var/adm/messages starting at line 200.
pg -c /var/adm/messages	Shows messages and clears screen between messages.

pgrep

pgrep	UNIX Shell:	All primary shells (csh, ksh, sh)
Function	Searches for specific processes by using different criteria.	
Syntax	pgrep [options...] *{ pattern }*	

-f	Specifies that `pattern` has to match the full process argument string.
-l	Shows output in long format.
-n	Matches against the most newly created processes.
-v	Matches all processes except the ones specified.
-x	Makes an exact match.
-d *delimiter*	Sets a new delimiter string to be used between process IDs.
-P *ppidlist*	Finds processes that are in the specified list.
-g *pgrplist*	Finds processes that have the same process groupID as in the specified list.
-s *sidlist*	Finds processes that have the same sessionID as in the specified list.
-u *euidlist*	Finds processes that have the same effective userID as in the specified list.
-U *uidlist*	Finds processes that have the same real userID as in the specified list.
-G *gidlist*	Finds processes that have the same real groupID as in the specified list.
-t *termlist*	Finds processes that are related to a certain terminal in the specified list.
pattern	Specifies an extended regular expression used to find a specific process.

File Name:	`pgrep`	**Directory:**	/usr/bin/	**Type:**	External
Note:	This command is like `ps` and `grep` combined into one.				

pgrep -l -d / -u root	Lists processes and their PIDs for the user root, delimited by a `/`.
pgrep -n -G 0	Shows the PID of the newest created process with groupID is 0.

pkgadd

pkgadd	UNIX Shell:	All primary shells (csh, ksh, sh)
Function	Installs or spools software packages into the system.	
Syntax	pkgadd [options...] *{ instances... }*	

-a *admin*	Defines a full pathname to an administration file to use for installation.
-d *device*	Defines a full pathname to a directory or device that contains packages to install.
-M	Doesn't use the `$root_path/etc/vfstab` to identify the client's mount point.
-v	Traces all scripts executed by pkgadd, is used to debug scripts.
-n	Creates a non-interactive installation.
-r *response*	Provides a full pathname of a file or directory from a previous `pkgask` session.
-R *path*	Defines the complete pathname from the root (when installing from server to client).

continued

-s *spool* -v -V *file* *instances...*	Writes the package into spool directory but doesn't install it. Traces all scripts executed by pkgadd, located in `/pkginst/install directory`. Specifies a substitute fs file to map file systems of the client. Specifies which package instance or list of instances to install.		
File Name: `pkgadd`	**Directory:** /usr/sbin/	**Type:** External	
Tip:	The easiest way to use this is with the -d option and a path to the package.		
pkgadd -d /cdrom/cdrom0/s0/Solaris_7.0/SUNWman	Installs the package SUNWman from a Solaris CD.		
pkgadd -d /export/home/SUNWopt	Installs the package SUNWopt in `/export/home`.		

pkgask

UNIX Shell: All primary shells (csh, ksh, sh)

Function	Creates an answer file, which can then be used as input to questions at installation time.
Syntax	pkgask [options...] -r*response instances...*

-d *device* -R *rootpath* -r *response* *instances...*	Specifies the request script for a package to run on device. Defines the full name of a directory as the root path. Specifies a file or directory to create, which will contain package communication. Specifies which package instance or list of instances to install.	
File Name: `pkgask`	**Directory:** /usr/sbin/	**Type:** External
Tip:	Useful if you want to create installation scripts.	

pkgchk

UNIX Shell: All primary shells (csh, ksh, sh)

Function	Checks the accuracy of installed files and shows package files information.
Syntax	pkgchk [options...] *{ instances... }*

-a	Checks only the file attributes, not the contents (default is to check both).	
-c	Checks only the contents, not the file attributes (default is to check both).	
-d *device*	Specifies a directory or device where a spooled package exists.	
-e *envfile*	Requests that envfile be used to resolve parameters given in the mapfile.	
-f	Tries to correct file attributes.	
-i *file*	Compares files containing pathnames against the installation software database.	
-l	Lists information about the specified files that make a package. (-l can not be used with -a, -c, -f, -g, or –v.)	
-m *pkgmap*	Checks the package against the specified package map file.	
-M	Doesn't use `$root path/etc/vfstab` to determine client's mount points.	
-n	Doesn't check unstable or editable files. Use for post-installation checking.	
-p *path*	Checks that the path is accurate. Path can be several pathnames separated by commas.	
-q	Silent mode; doesn't report missing files.	
-R *rootpath*	Specifies a directory's full name as the root path to use.	
-v	Verbose mode. Shows more information.	
-V *file*	Specifies a substitute fs file to map the file system of the client.	
-x	Searches for files that doesn't exist in the software database or the pkgmap file.	
instances...	Specifies which package instances or list of instances to check.	
File Name: `pkgchk`	**Directory:** /usr/sbin/	**Type:** External
pkgchk -l | more	Lists files that make a package and pipes to `more`.	
pkgchk -vf | more	Corrects file attributes in verbose mode.	

pkginfo

UNIX Shell: All primary shells (csh, ksh, sh)

Function	Shows one line of information about each package that is installed on the system.
Syntax	pkginfo [options...] *{ instances... }*

	You must select one of these two options:
-p	Shows only information for partially installed packages.
-i	Shows only information for fully installed packages.
-r	Shows the installation base for relocatable packages.
-d *device*	Specifies a directory or device pathname to package.
-R *root path*	Specifies which directory's full pathname to use as the root path.

continued

	You can only select one of these three options:
-q	Doesn't show any information. Uses inside program to check whether package is installed.
-x	Assigns an extracted list of available package information.
-l	Long listing; shows all available information about the assigned packages.
-a *arch*	Specifies the architecture of the package.
-v *version*	Specifies the version parameters of the package.
-c *category*	Shows package parameters matching the category.
instances...	Specifies a package designation by its instance.
File Name: `pkginfo`	**Directory:** /usr/bin/ **Type:** External
pkginfo -l SUNWarc	Long listing of the packet SUNWarc.
pkginfo -l -i	Shows all information of fully installed packages.

pkgmk

UNIX Shell: All primary shells (csh, ksh, sh)

Function	Creates an installable package to use as the input into the command `pkgadd`.
Syntax	pkgmk [options...] *{ variable=value } { instance }*

-o	Overwrites a package instance if it exists.
-a *arch*	Specifies an architecture to use instead of what's in `pkginfo`.
-b *base sourcedir*	Adds the pathname to the relocatable objects on the server.
-d *device*	Specifies the directory or device where to create the package.
-f *prototype*	Uses the prototype file as the input.
-l *limit*	Limits the output device to a maximum size of 512 byte blocks.
-p *pstamp*	Overrides the production stamp in the `pkginfo` file with the specified stamp.
-r *rootpath*	Ignores the destination path in the prototype file and uses this rootpath instead.
-v *version*	Overrides version information in `pkginfo` with the specified version.
variable=value...	Places the specified variable in the package environment.
instance	Identifies a package by its instance.
File Name: `pkgmk`	**Directory:** /usr/bin/ **Type:** External

pkgparam

UNIX Shell: All primary shells (csh, ksh, sh)

Function	Shows the value of the package parameters; values are stored in the `pkginfo-file` for `pkginst`.
Syntax	pkgparam [options...] *{ instance } { parameters... }*

-v	Verbose mode. Shows more information.
-d *device*	Specifies a directory or device where to find the `pkginst`.
-R *path*	Define a full pathname to a directory to use as the root path.
	You must select one of these two parameter value sources:
-f *file*	Specifies the file that contains the parameter values.
instance	Specifies the package instance that contains the parameter values.
parameters...	Specifies which parameter values to show.
File Name: `pkgparam`	**Directory:** /usr/bin/ **Type:** External
Tip:	This is another way of getting information about a package instead of by using `pkginfo`.
pkgparam -v SUNWypu	Gives detailed information about an installed package.
pkgparam SUNWypu	Shows only the values of parameters, not their names for a package.

pkgproto

UNIX Shell: All primary shells (csh, ksh, sh)

Function	Creates prototype file entries to be used as input to the `pkgmk` command.
Syntax	pkgproto [options...] *{ paths... }* pkgproto [options...] *{ path1=path2 }*

-i	Ignores symbolic links and saves the path as a file.
-c *class*	Specifies which class should be used.
path1	Specifies the path where objects are found.
path2	Specifies path2 as the output for path1. (When using path2 the following format is used: path1 = path2.)

continued

File Name:	pkgproto	**Directory:**	/usr/bin/	**Type:**	External
Tip:	A good help when you want to create packages to install by using pkgadd.				
pkgproto /usr/bin > protofile			Creates a prototype file from what's in /usr/bin.		
pkgproto -i /usr/bin > protofile			Same as above but ignores symbolic links.		

pkgrm

UNIX Shell: All primary shells (csh, ksh, sh)

Function	Erases a package from the system or from a spooling area.
Syntax	pkgrm [options...] *{ instances... }*

-n	Specifies noninteractive mode.
-v	Traces all scripts that are being executed by the command.
-a *admin*	Specifies an alternative installation administration file.
	Before use of the -R option, one of these options can be selected:
-A	Removes the package absolutely, even if it has dependencies.
-M	Doesn't use $rootpath/etc/vfstab file to determine client's mountpoints.
-R *root path*	Specifies the complete pathname of a directory to use as root path.
-V *fs file*	Sets another fs file to map client's file systems (default is root_path/etc/vfstab).
-s *spool*	Specifies the directory to erase spooled packages from (default is /var/sadm/pkg).
instances...	Specifies the package instance(s) to be erased.

File Name:	pkgrm	**Directory:**	/usr/sbin/	**Type:**	External
Tip:	Use the pkginfo utility to find the package's name.				
pkgrm SUNWman			Erases SUNWman if there are no dependencies.		
pkgrm -A SUNWman			Erases SUNWman disregarding dependencies.		

pkgtrans

UNIX Shell: All primary shells (csh, ksh, sh)

Function	Converts installable packages from file system format to datastream and reverse, or from one file system to another.
Syntax	pkgtrans [options...] *device1 device2 { instances... }*

-i	Only copies pkginfo and pkgmap files.
-n	Updates the instance of this package on the destination.
-o	Overwrites the instance on the destination device if it already exists.
-s	Writes package to device2 as datastream instead of as a file system format.
device1	Specifies the source device to translate from.
device2	Specifies the destination device to translate to.
instances...	Specifies package instance on device1 to be translated. Use all for all instances.

File Name:	pkgtrans	**Directory:**	/usr/bin/	**Type:**	External
Tip:	Use with -i option and see pkgmap and pkginfo files for information on the package before installing.				
pkgtrans gzip-sparc-local /var/spool/pkg			Converts the gzip package into /var/spool/pkg.		
pkgtrans gzip-sparc-local . all			Converts all instances to the current directory.		

pkill

UNIX Shell: All primary shells (csh, ksh, sh)

Function	Finds and kills processes by signaling it with the kill command.
Syntax	pkill [options...] *{ pattern }*

-signal	Specifies which kill signal should be sent to the process (default is SIGTERM).
-f	Specifies that *pattern* has to match the full process argument string.
-n	Matches against the most newly created processes.
-v	Matches all processes except the ones specified.
-x	Makes an exact match.
-P *ppidlist*	Finds processes that are in the specified list.
-g *pgrplist*	Finds processes that have the same process group ID as in the specified list.
-s *sidlist*	Finds processes that have the same sessionID as in the specified list.
-u *euidlist*	Finds processes that have the same effective userID as in the specified list.
-U *uidlist*	Finds processes that have the same real userID as in the specified list.
-G *gidlist*	Finds processes that have the same real groupID as in the specified list.

continued

-t *termlist* *pattern*		Finds processes that are related to a certain terminal in the specified list. Specifies an extended regular expression used to find a specific process.			
File Name:	`pkill`	**Directory:**	/usr/bin/	**Type:**	External
Note:	If you use the `signal` option, it must be listed first.				
pkill -n xterm			Kills the newest created `xterm` process.		
pkill -9 -n xterm			Kills the newest created `xterm` process with signal 9.		

plimit

UNIX Shell: All primary shells (csh, ksh, sh)

Function	Sets or gets the resource limits of a running process identified by process ID list. Only the owner of a process or a superuser is permitted to modify the limits.
Syntax	plimit [-km] *PIDs...* plimit [option] *PIDs...*

-k	Shows file sizes in kilobytes to output.
-m	Shows file and memory sizes in megabytes to output.
	The following options accept the form soft = current limit or hard = maximum limit.
-c *soft,hard*	Sets the limits of the core file size (default unit is 512-byte blocks).
-d *soft,hard*	Sets the limits of data segment size (default unit is kilobytes).
-f *soft,hard*	Sets the limits of file size (default unit is 512-byte blocks).
-n *soft,hard*	Sets the limits of file descriptor.
-s *soft,hard*	Sets the limits of stack segment size (default unit is kilobytes).
-t *soft,hard*	Sets the limits of CPU time (default unit is seconds).
-v *soft,hard*	Sets the limits of virtual memory size (default unit is kilobytes).
PIDs...	Specifies the ID of the process. You can use ps -ef to list all current process IDs. (You may use these suffixes with the above options.)
k	Kilobytes.
m	Megabytes.
h	Hours.
mm:ss	Minutes and seconds, for CPU time only.

File Name:	`plimit`	**Directory:**	/usr/bin/	**Type:**	External

pmadm

UNIX Shell: All primary shells (csh, ksh, sh)

Function	Manages port monitor services on the system.
Syntax	pmadm -a [option] options... [options...] pmadm options... pmadm option [options...]

	The following options refer to the first syntax:
-a	Adds a service as an entry to the port monitor's administrative file.
-p *pmtag*	Specifies the tag associated with the port monitor; can't be used with the -t option.
-t *type*	Specifies the type of the port monitor; can't be used with the -p option.
-s *svctag*	Specifies the service tag to the port monitor's administrative file.
-i *ID*	Specifies the identity to be assigned to svctag; ID must be an entry in `/etc/passwd`.
-m *pmspecific*	Specifies port monitor specific file entries for the service.
-v*ver*	Specifies the version number of the port monitor administration file.
-f *action*	Specifies flags to include in the administrative file. Actions can be x and u.
x	Doesn't enable service svctag.
u	Creates a utmp entry for svctag.
-y *comment*	Adds a comment to the service entry in the administrative file.
-z *script*	Specifies the per-service configuration script.
	The following options refer to the second syntax:
-r	Removes a service. Must be used with the -p and -s options.
-e	Enables a service. Must be used with the -p and -s options.
-d	Disables a service. Must be used with the -p and -s options.

continued

	The following option must be used with the -p, -s or the -s, -t, and -z options:
-g	Shows, installs, or replaces the per-service configuration script.
	The following options refers to the third syntax:
-l	Shows all services on the system. Can be used with the -t or -p and -s options.
-L	Shows all services on the system in condensed format.
File Name: pmadm	**Directory:** /usr/sbin/ **Type:** External

pmconfig

UNIX Shell: All primary shells (csh, ksh, sh)

Function	Activates the power management system by reading a configuration file called `power.conf`.
Syntax	pmconfig [-r]

-r	Resets all power-managed devices.
File Name: pmconfig	**Directory:** /usr/sbin/ **Type:** External
pmconfig -r	Resets power to the managed devices.

pntadm

UNIX Shell: All primary shells (csh, ksh, sh)

Function	Manages the DHCP network table by, for example, adding, removing, or commenting hostnames or IP addresses.
Syntax	pntadm option [options...] *network*

-C	Creates DHCP network table for the specified network.
-A *name*	Specifies hostname or IP address of client to add.
	You may use these sub options:
-c *comment*	Specifies a comment.
-e *date*	Specifies an absolute lease period. The format is MM/DD/YYYY.
-f *actions*	Specifies a flag.
DYNAMIC	Enables the server to manage leases.
PERMANENT	Makes this entry permanent.
MANUAL	The administrator manages assignments.
UNUSABLE	Makes this entry invalid.
BOOTP	Reserves this entry for BOOTP hosts.
-h *hostname*	Specifies the client hostname.
-i *clientID*	Specifies the client identifier.
-a	Specifies that client name is in ASCII format.
-m *dhcptab*	Shows information of a macro name.
macro	Specifies the macro name.
-y	Verifies the macro name.
-s *server*	Specifies the name or IP address of the server.
-D *name*	Removes the client entry with hostname or IP address.
-y	Removes associated entry in the host table.
-M *name*	Specifies hostname or IP address to modify the entry. (-M has the same subcommands as described in -A.)
-P	Shows the DHCP network table that is specified.
-v	Verbose mode. Shows more information.
-R	Removes DHCP network table that is specified.
	The following options can be combined and are optional:
-p *path*	Specifies alternative DHCP configuration path.
-r *resources*	Overrides the default DHCP configuration values.
network	Specifies network name or address for the DHCP network table.
File Name: pntadm	**Directory:** /usr/sbin/ **Type:** External
pntadm -P -v ucgdomain	Shows network DHCP table in verbose mode.

ports

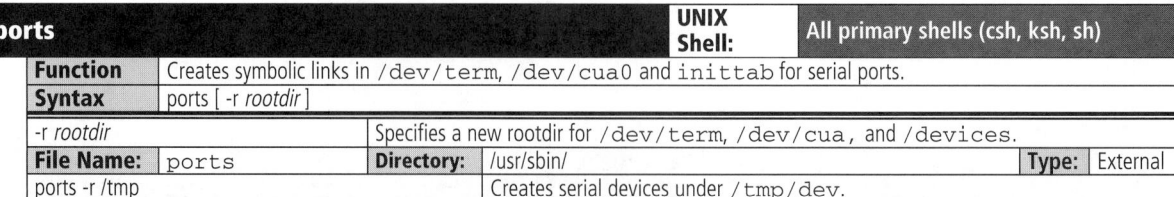

ports	UNIX Shell:	All primary shells (csh, ksh, sh)
Function	Creates symbolic links in /dev/term, /dev/cua0 and inittab for serial ports.	
Syntax	ports [-r *rootdir*]	

-r *rootdir*	Specifies a new rootdir for /dev/term, /dev/cua, and /devices.
File Name: ports	**Directory:** /usr/sbin/ **Type:** External
ports -r /tmp	Creates serial devices under /tmp/dev.

postio

postio	UNIX Shell:	All primary shells (csh, ksh, sh)
Function	Sends files via the serial interface to a PostScript printer.	
Syntax	postio -l *line* [options...] { *files...* }	

-D	Shows debug information.
-q	Prevents status queries while files are sent to the printer.
-b *speed*	Specifies the baud rate for transmitting over the line (default is 9600 baud).
-B *num*	Specifies the internal buffer size for processing files.
-l *line*	Connects to the printer attached to line.
-L *file*	Saves data received on line in a file.
-P *string*	Sends string to the printer before any output file.
-R *num*	Runs either as a single process (1) or as a separate read and write process (2).
-i	Runs the program in interactive mode.
-t	Writes data not recognized as printer or status information to STDOUT.
	Use the following option if all else fails. It provides a reliable connection.
-S	Slows the transmission of data to the printer and runs as a single process.
files...	Specifies the files that are sent.
File Name: postio	**Directory:** /usr/lib/lp/postscript/ **Type:** External
postio -l /dev/tty01file1 file2	Sends file1 and file2 to the printer attached to /dev/tty01 at 9600 baud.

postprint

postprint	UNIX Shell:	All primary shells (csh, ksh, sh)
Function	Translates text files into PostScript and writes to STDOUT.	
Syntax	postprint [options...] { *files...* }	

-c *num*	Specifies the number of copies to print of each page (default is 1 copy).
-f *name*	Specifies font to use when printing (default is Courier).
-l *num*	Specifies the length of page by number of lines (default is 66 lines).
-m *num*	Magnifies each page by the factor num, pages are scaled uniformly (default is 1.0).
-n *num*	Specifies number of pages printed on each piece of paper (default is 1).
-o *list*	Specifies that a comma-separated list of pages be printed.
-p *mode*	Specifies portrait or landscape mode by using the first character of the mode.
-r *num*	Specifies carriage return behavior: 0 = ignore, 1 = return to column, 2 = newline.
-s *num*	Specifies scaling point size. Increasing point size also increases virtual image size.
-t *num*	Sets tabs every specified number of columns.
-x *num*	Moves the origin the specified number of inches along the positive x axis to the right.
-y *num*	Moves the origin the specified number of inches down the positive y axis.
files...	Specifies the text file to use.
File Name: postprint	**Directory:** /usr/lib/lp/postscript/ **Type:** External
Note:	Unprintable ASCII characters are ignored.
postprint /etc/passwd	Translates passwd into PostScript.
postprint -pland /etc/inetd.conf	Translates and prints the file inetd.conf into landscape mode.

postreverse

UNIX Shell: All primary shells (csh, ksh, sh)

Function	Reverses the page order in a PostScript file of Adobe's Version 1.0 or 2.0 format.
Syntax	postreverse [options...] *{ file }*

-o *list*	Specifies a comma-separated list from which the page numbers are read.
-r	Doesn't reverse the pages.
file	Specifies the PostScript file to use.

File Name:	`postreverse`	**Directory:**	/usr/lib/lp/postscript/	**Type:**	External
Note:	The STDIN is read if no file is specified.				

postreverse -o1-100 file	This selects pages 1 to 100 from file and reverses the pages.

powerd

UNIX Shell: All primary shells (csh, ksh, sh)

Function	A power daemon that manages two types of system shutdown: automatic or low power.
Syntax	powerd [-n]

-n	Silently shuts down the system without notifying `syslogd`. **The power management configuration information file is /etc/power.conf**

File Name:	`powerd`	**Directory:**	/usr/lib/power/	**Type:**	External

poweroff

UNIX Shell: All primary shells (csh, ksh, sh)

Function	Writes pending information to disk, stops the processing, and powers off the computer.
Syntax	poweroff [options...]

-l	Does not send a message to the system log. Default is to log the event.
-n	Does not run the sync command before shutting down.
-q	Does a quick halt.
-y	Halts the system even if you are on a dialup terminal.

File Name:	`poweroff`	**Directory:**	/usr/sbin/	**Type:**	External
Warning:	If you use the -n option, your disks may become corrupted.				

poweroff -l	Does not send a message to `syslogd`.
poweroff -q	Does a quick halt.

praudit

UNIX Shell: All primary shells (csh, ksh, sh)

Function	Reads files or STDIN and shows the specified data as audit trail records.
Syntax	praudit [options...] *{ files... }*

-l	Shows one line per record in short form.
-r	Shows RAW records such as Times, UIDs, GIDs, record types, and events as integers.
-s	Shows records in short form. (The -r and -s options should not be used together.)
-d*del*	Specifies a new delimiter instead of the default comma (,).
files...	Specifies audit trail file(s).

File Name:	`praudit`	**Directory:**	/usr/sbin/	**Type:**	External

praudit -l /auditfile	Shows the contents in the file with one line per record.
praudit -s -d# /auditfile	Shows the records in their short form and replaces the delimiter with a #.

prctmp

UNIX Shell: All primary shells (csh, ksh, sh)

Function	Shows the session record file that is created by `acctcon1`.
Syntax	prctmp *file*

file	Specifies a file other than `/var/adm/acct/nite/ctmp`.

File Name:	`prctmp`	**Directory:**	/usr/lib/acct/	**Type:**	External

prdaily

prdaily	UNIX Shell:	Bourne shell (sh)

Function	Formats and reports the previous day's accounting data from `/var/adm/acct/sum/rprt/mmdd`.
Syntax	prdaily [options...] *{ mmdd }*

-c	Shows a report on exceptional resource usage by a command (current day's data only).
-l	Shows a report on exceptional resource usage by a login ID.
mmdd	Specifies month and day of the report desired.

File Name:	`prdaily`	**Directory:**	/usr/lib/acct/	**Type:**	Script

prdaily -c	Prints a report on exceptional resource usage by a command.

prex

prex	UNIX Shell:	All primary shells (csh, ksh, sh)

Function	An interface to control, manipulate, or debug a process or the kernel.
Syntax	prex [options...] *command { arguments... }* prex [options...] -p *pid* prex -k [-s *kbsize*]

-s *kbsize*	Specifies the maximum size of the output trace file in kilobytes.
-o *tracefile*	Specifies file to use for the trace output in the current working directory of prex.
-l *libraries*	Specifies library to link into the target application.
-p *pid*	Specifies the Process ID for a program.
-k	Sets kernel mode, which defines additional commands.
arguments...	Specifies the applications to be started by prex.
command	Specifies the command arguments to the application.

File Name:	`prex`	**Directory:**	/usr/bin/	**Type:**	External

print

print	UNIX Shell:	Korn shell (ksh)

Function	Shows any arguments on the STDOUT.
Syntax	print [option] *{ arguments... }*

-	Shows the arguments as described by `echo`.
-n	Doesn't add new line to the output.
-R	Ignores any escape characters in the arguments (Raw mode).
-r	Ignores any escape characters in the arguments (Raw mode).
-p	Writes the output to a shell spawned with `|&`.
-s	Writes the argument to the history file.
-u*n*	A one-digit file descriptor to use as output.
arguments...	Specifies the valid arguments that are used with the command.
zsh:	
-b	Recognizes all escape sequences as defined for the `bindkey` command.
-m	Uses the first argument as a pattern to remove the arguments that match.
-l	Shows arguments separated by a new line instead of a space.
-N	Shows arguments separated by a NULL character.
-o	Shows arguments sorted in order.
-O	Shows arguments sorted in reverse order.
-i	Specifies the sort will be performed without regard to case.
-c	Shows the arguments in columns.
-z	Pushes the arguments to the editing buffer stack.
-D	Handles the arguments as directories.
-P	Performs prompt expansion.

print -n Prompt:	Shows Prompt: with no new line.

printtool

printtool	UNIX Shell:	All primary shells (csh, ksh, sh)

Function	An OpenWindow GUI-tool for printing files.		
Syntax	printtool [options...]		
-P *printer*	Specifies which printer to use.		
-v	Shows version number and usage messages.		
-?	The same as -v option.		
File Name: printtool	**Directory:** /usr/openwin/bin/	**Type:** External	
Note:	Printtool is usually started inside OpenWindow.		
printtool -P laser	Starts printtool and uses the printer laser.		

priocntl

priocntl	UNIX Shell:	All primary shells (csh, ksh, sh)

Function	Manages scheduling parameters for processes. There are four main ways to use it; specified by the first option.
Syntax	priocntl -l priocntl -d [-i *type*] *{ idlist }* priocntl -s [options...] *{ idlist }* priocntl -e [options...] *command { arguments... }*
	The following four options cannot be combined:
-l	Shows a list of classes with specific information configured on the system.
-d	Shows the parameter settings for a set of processes.
-s	Sets parameters for a set of processes
-e	Executes a command with the parameter settings specified.
-c *class*	Sets a class. Sub options depend on the value. Valid values are RT, TS, and IA.
	These are the available options when RT (real-time) is specified in the class field:
-p *pri*	Specifies the process priority to pri in the range 0 to x; see -l option.
-t *tqntm*	Specifies the amount of the process cycle time for tqntm to use for the processes.
[-r *res*]	Sets resolution to 1/res seconds (default is 1000 which is milliseconds).
	These are the available options when TS (time-sharing) is specified in the class field:
-m *prilim*	Specifies the limit to prilim for the user priority of specified processes.
-p *pri*	Specifies the user priority to pri for processes.
	These are the available options when IA (inter-active) is specified in the class field:
-m *prilim*	Specifies the user priority limit to prilim for processes.
-p *pri*	Specifies the user priority to pri for processes.
	The following options may only be used with the -c class or the -d option:
-i *type*	Explains to the system which process type was used. Could be one of the following.
pid	Specifies the following list contains PIDs.
ppid	Specifies the following list contains parent PIDs.
pgid	Specifies the following list contains process group IDs.
sid	Specifies the following list contains session IDs
class	Specifies the following list contains a class name.
uid	Specifies the following list contains user IDs.
gid	Specifies the following list contains group IDs.
all	Specifies all processes. When this type is used no idlist should be specified.
{ idlist }	Specifies the list of IDs that is required in addition to a type.
command	Executes the specified command. Must be used with -e.
arguments...	Specifies any needed arguments that are available to the command specified.
File Name: priocntl	**Directory:** /usr/bin/ **Type:** External

prof

UNIX Shell: All primary shells (csh, ksh, sh)

Function	Shows data from a profile file produced by the monitor function.
Syntax	prof [options...] { *prog* }

-C	Organizes C++ symbol names before printing.
-h	Suppresses header on the report.
-s	Shows a summary of the monitoring parameters and statistics.
-V	Shows prof version information.
-z	Includes all symbols in the profile range.
	The following options can't be combined:
-a	Sorts by increasing symbol address.
-c	Sorts by decreasing number of calls.
-n	Sorts lexically by symbol name.
-t	Sorts by decreasing percentage of total time.
	The following options can't be combined:
-o	Shows each symbol address and name in octal.
-x	Shows each symbol address and name in hexadecimal.
	The following options can't be combined:
-g	Separately lists the time spent in static functions.
-l	Suppresses printing statically declared functions (the opposite of -g).
-m *mdata*	Specifies the input profile file.

File Name:	`prof`	**Directory:**	/usr/ccs/bin/	**Type:**	External

prs, sccs-prs

UNIX Shell: All primary shells (csh, ksh, sh)

Function	Shows selected portions, all, or parts of an SCCS delta table history.
Syntax	prs [options...] *files...*

-a	Includes all deltas, even deltas marked as removed.
-e	Requests all information for deltas created before deltas specified with -r or -c.
-l	Requests information for all deltas created later than deltas specified with -r or -c.
-c*datetime*	Shows information for deltas checked in before -e, or later than -l. (The following date format is used: yy[mm[dd[hh[mm[ss]]]]].)
-d*dataspec*	Produces a report associated to the indicated data specification.
-r*sid*	Identifies the SCCS delta ID for the delta about which information is requested.
files...	Specifies `s.filename` to show.

File Name:	`prs`	**Directory:**	/usr/ccs/bin/	**Type:**	External

prt

UNIX Shell: All primary shells (csh, ksh, sh)

Function	Shows selected delta table information of an SCCS file.
Syntax	prt [options...] *files...*

-a	Shows all delta log entries, even those marked as removed.
-b	Shows the body of the source file.
-d	Shows the entries for delta tables (default).
-e	Shows everything (same as -d, -i, -u, -f, and -t).
-f	Shows the flags of each specified source file.
-i	Shows the serial numbers of all deltas.
-s	Shows only the first line of entries, up to the statistics.
-t	Shows the descriptive text of the `s.file`.
-u	Shows the user-names and/or numerical group IDs of users allowed to make deltas.
-c*datetime*	Excludes delta table entries specified by cutoff date and time.
-r*datetime*	Excludes delta table entries created later than specified cutoff date and time.
-y*sid*	Excludes the delta table entries made before the specified SID.

continued

files...		Specifies from which source file to take information.			
File Name:	`prt`	**Directory:**	/usr/ccs/bin/	**Type:**	External

prtacct

UNIX Shell: All primary shells (csh, ksh, sh)

Function	A shell procedure used to format and print TACCT (total accounting) files.
Syntax	prtacct *file* ["*heading*"]

"*heading*"		Specifies the header when printing the file. Use quotes " for multiple words.			
file		Specifies which file to format and print to `TACCT`.			
File Name:	`prtacct`	**Directory:**	/usr/lib/acct/	**Type:**	External
prtacct /var/adm/wtmp 'Page Number:'			Shows a logon/logoff history file with the header Page Number.		

prtconf

UNIX Shell: All primary shells (csh, ksh, sh)

Function	Shows system configuration information.
Syntax	prtconf option [options...]

		The following options can't be combined:			
-V		Shows platform-dependent version information: SPARC = PROM, x86 = boot system.			
-F		Returns the device pathname of the console frame buffer if it exists.			
-x		Reports whether the firmware on the system is 64-bit ready.			
		The following options can be combined:			
-v		Verbose mode. Shows more information.			
-p		Shows information from the device tree.			
-P		Adds information about pseudo devices.			
-D		Shows each device driver used to manage each peripheral.			
File Name:	`prtconf`	**Directory:**	/usr/sbin/	**Type:**	External
Note:	The -F option is used only for SPARC.				

prtdiag

UNIX Shell: All primary shells (csh, ksh, sh)

Function	Shows information about the system and diagnostic information.
Syntax	prtdiag [options...]

-v		Verbose mode. Shows more information.			
-l		Logs error information to `syslogd`.			
File Name:	`prtdiag`	**Directory:**	/usr/platform/platform-name/sbin	**Type:**	External
Tip:	The active platform name in the path can be found with the command `uname -i`, for example, sun4u.				

prtvtoc

UNIX Shell: All primary shells (csh, ksh, sh)

Function	Reads the VTOC to show disk geometry and partitioning.
Syntax	prtvtoc [options...] *device*

-f		Reports free disk space.			
-h		Shows no headers in output.			
-s		Shows only column header in output.			
-t *vfstab*		Uses vfstab for file system defaults instead of `/etc/vfstab`.			
-m *mnttab*		Uses mnttab for mounted file systems instead of `/etc/mnttab`.			
device		Specifies a device to display VTOC information from.			
File Name:	`prtvtoc`	**Directory:**	/usr/sbin/	**Type:**	External
Tip:	You can also use the `format` command.				
prtvtoc /dev/rdsk/c0t0d0s2			Shows the VTOC of disk c0t0d0s2.		
prtvtoc -f /dev/rdsk/c0t0d0s2			Reports free space on disk c0t0d0s2.		

psradm

UNIX Shell:	All primary shells (csh, ksh, sh)
Function	Changes the operational status of one or more processors.
Syntax	psradm [-a] [option] [-v] *{ cpuids... }*

-a	Alters the status on as many processors as possible.
	You must select one of the following three options:
-f	Sets processor to off-line.
-i	Sets processor to no interrupts.
-n	Sets processor to online.
-v	Verbose mode. Shows more information.
cpuids...	Specifies which processor or processors to manipulate. Must be set if -a isn't used.

File Name:	psradm	**Directory:**	/usr/sbin/	**Type:**	External

psradm -f 2	Sets processor 2 off-line.
psradm -n 1 2	Sets processors 1 and 2 online.

psrinfo

UNIX Shell:	All primary shells (csh, ksh, sh)
Function	Shows processor information. Shows online/off-line status, powered on/off status and when the status was last modified.
Syntax	psrinfo [option] *{ cpuid }*

-v	Verbose mode. Shows more information.
-s *cpuid*	Sets silent mode; only shows information about whether a processor is or isn't online.
cpuid	Specifies which processor to view.

File Name:	psrinfo	**Directory:**	/usr/sbin/	**Type:**	External

psrinfo -s 0	Shows 0 if processor 0 is down and 1 if it is up.

pswrap

UNIX Shell:	All primary shells (csh, ksh, sh)
Function	Creates wraps by sending segments of PostScript language code from the specified file to the PostScript Interpreter.
Syntax	pswrap [options...] *{ file }*

-a	Creates ANSI C prototypes for procedure definitions.
-p	Pads strings so that each data object starts on the long-word boundary (4-byte).
-h *file*	Creates a file that contains extern declarations for nonstatic wraps.
-o *file*	Specifies the file in which to put the created wrap procedures.
-r	Enables the wraps to be called recursively or by more than one thread.
-s *length*	Specifies maximum length of a PostScript string.
file	Specifies the input file to use.

File Name:	pswrap	**Directory:**	/usr/openwin/bin/	**Type:**	External

putdev

UNIX Shell:	All primary shells (csh, ksh, sh)
Function	Adds, removes, or modifies a device in the device table.
Syntax	putdev [option] *device { attributes... }*

	The following options can not be used together:
-a	Specifies alias name for device to be added. Can also be used with attributes.
-m	Adds specified attribute if undefined or alters a current device attribute if existing.
-d	Removes specified device if undefined or deletes the specified attribute.
Attributes	**Here are some additional attributes that you can use with this command:**
type	The type of device (for example, 9-track, ctape, directory, diskette, disk, dbart, qtape).
dparttype	Specifies the type of disk partition for this device.
	These attributes can only be used if type = dpart and dparttype = fs.
nblocks	Specifies the number of blocks for the file system on this partition.
ninodes	Specifies the number of inodes for the file system on this partition.
dpartlist	Lists the disk partitions for the device; device aliases must have mtype = dpart.
mountpt	Specifies the mount point for the device; used only if the device is mountable.

continued

fsname	Specifies the file system name on this partition.
volname	Specifies the volume name on the file system on this partition.
	These attributes are not dependent on the type and dparttype attributes:
alias	Specifies the unique name by which a device is known (alphanumeric, 14 characters).
bdevice	Specifies the pathname to the block device; must be unique (for example `/dev/rdsk/rmt2`).
capacity	Specifies the capacity of the device or of the typical volume.
cdevice	Specifies the pathname to the character device; must be unique (for example `/dev/dsk/rmt2`).
cyl	Used by the command specified in the `mkfscmd` attribute.
desc	Describes any instance of a volume associated with the device (for example "Tape drive").
erasecmd	Specifies the command string that will erase the device.
fmtcmd	Specifies the command string that will format the device.
mkfscmd	Specifies the command that will place a file system on an earlier formatted device.
variable	A variable used by the command specified by the mkfscmd attribute if needed.
norewind	Doesn't rewind the device when it is opened.
pathname	Defines the pathname to a device, such as directories.
volume	Text string that describes the volume on the device. For removable devices.
	You can also use one of the following to specify the device to work with:
alias	Specifies the name or the alias of the device to add. Used with -a option.
device	Add, modifies, or removes attributes from the device name or device path specified.

File Name:	`putdev`	**Directory:**	/usr/bin/	**Type:**	External
Tip:	Your devices are listed in the `/etc/device.tab` file.				

putdev -a backup /var/adm:desc="Backup device"	The device backup `/var/adm` is added.
putdev -d backup	Deletes the device backup.

putdgrp

UNIX Shell: All primary shells (csh, ksh, sh)

Function	Manages the device group table.
Syntax	putdgrp [-d] *group { device }*

-d	Erases the specified group or device.
group	Specifies the device group name to add or erase.
device	Specifies the pathname or alias of the device that is to be added or erased.

File Name:	`putdgrp`	**Directory:**	/usr/bin/	**Type:**	External
Tip:	Use this if you have connected a new type of device.				

putdgrp floppy diskette	Creates the device alias diskette in device group floppy.
putdgrp -d floppy	Deletes device group floppy and all of its devices.

pvs

UNIX Shell: All primary shells (csh, ksh, sh)

Function	Shows internal version information contained within an executable file.
Syntax	pvs [options...] *files...*

-d	Shows version definition information.
-l	When used with -s shows symbols that have been demoted from global to local bind.
-n	Shows only the head of each version definition within the object.
-o	Shows one-line version definition.
-r	Shows version dependency information.
-s	Shows the symbols related with each version definition.
-v	Verbose mode. Shows more information.
-N*name*	Shows only the information for the specified version definition name.
files...	Specifies one or more input files.

File Name:	`pvs`	**Directory:**	/usr/bin/	**Type:**	External
Tip:	Definitions may be quite long, so you could effectively send output to a file for later use.				

pvs -d /usr/lib/libelf.so.1	Prints the version definition for the file `libelf.so.1`.
pvs -ds /usr/lib/libelf.so.1	Prints the version definition and symbols for `libelf.so.1`.

pwck

UNIX Shell: All primary shells (csh, ksh, sh)

Function	Searches the password file for field number validation, user and group IDs, login names, and the like.				
Syntax	pwck *{ file }*				
file	Specifies another password file (default is `/etc/passwd`).				
File Name:	`pwck`	**Directory:**	/usr/sbin/	**Type:**	External
Tip:	Useful when looking for problems within the password file.				

pwconv

UNIX Shell: All primary shells (csh, ksh, sh)

Function	Modifies or creates the file `/etc/shadow` from the standard `/etc/passwd` file.				
Syntax	pwconv				
File Name:	`pwconv`	**Directory:**	/usr/sbin/	**Type:**	External
Tip:	It is more secure to store passwords in `/etc/shadow` than in `/etc/passwd`.				

quot

UNIX Shell: All primary shells (csh, ksh, sh)

Function	Shows the amount of blocks (1024 bytes) in the file system that each user currently owns and summarizes the information.				
Syntax	quot [options...] *filesystem*				
-a	Creates a report for file systems that are currently mounted.				
-c	Shows block information about file sizes and summarizes the information in 3 columns.				
-f	Shows the amount and space of files owned by each user (do not use with -v, -c).				
-h	Estimates the number of blocks in the file.				
-n	Connects names to the file list read from STDIN (must be used alone).				
-v	Shows information about blocks not accessed for the last 30, 60, and 90 days.				
filesystem	The mount-point of the file system you want to check.				
File Name:	`quot`	**Directory:**	/usr/sbin/	**Type:**	External
quot -a	Creates a report of all currently mounted file systems.				

rdate

UNIX Shell: All primary shells (csh, ksh, sh)

Function	Sets system date and time from a remote host.				
Syntax	rdate *hostname*				
hostname	Specifies server to use for system date.				
File Name:	`rdate`	**Directory:**	/usr/bin/	**Type:**	External

red

UNIX Shell: All primary shells (csh, ksh, sh)

Function	A text editor similar to the `ed` utility but is a restricted version. Only allows editing of files in current directory and doesn't allow the use of shell commands by using the !.				
Syntax	red [options...] *{ file }*				
	You may select only one of the two options below:				
-s	Does not show character counts when using e, r, and w commands.				
-;	Shows all counts.				
-p *string*	Specifies the prompt indicated by string.				
-x	An encryption option.				
-C	Assumes that the text has already been encrypted.				
file	Specifies the input file to edit or create.				
File Name:	`red`	**Directory:**	/usr/bin/	**Type:**	External
Tip:	You could use the great `vi` editor instead.				

regcmp

UNIX Shell:	All primary shells (csh, ksh, sh)
Function	Compiles the regular expressions in a file and places the output in file.i.
Syntax	regcmp [-] *files...*

-	Places the output in filename.c instead of filename.i.
files...	The file to read input from.

File Name:	`regcmp`	**Directory:**	/usr/ccs/bin/	**Type:**	External

reject

UNIX Shell:	All primary shells (csh, ksh, sh)
Function	Rejects print queue requests to the specified destination.
Syntax	reject [-r] *destinations...*

-r *reason*	Writes a note to show why the destination printer is rejecting print queue requests.
destinations...	The destination name of the queue. The names are found in the printers.conf file.

File Name:	`reject`	**Directory:**	/usr/sbin/	**Type:**	External
Note:	Only affects queuing on the print server's spooling system.				

reject printserver	Rejects print requests on server printserver.

rem_drv

UNIX Shell:	All primary shells (csh, ksh, sh)
Function	Reports to the system that the device driver is invalid. It will unload the device driver from memory if possible, and it will also update the system driver configuration files.
Syntax	rem_drv [-b] *{ driver }*

-b basedir	Specifies the path to the root directory of the diskless client.
driver	Specifies the device driver to be removed.

File Name:	`rem_drv`	**Directory:**	/usr/sbin/	**Type:**	External
Note:	System automatically performs a reconfiguration at next reboot if rem_drv has been executed.				

rem_drv sd	Removes device driver sd from the system.

removef

UNIX Shell:	All primary shells (csh, ksh, sh)
Function	Removes a file from the software database. The output is a list of erasable pathnames that may be safely erased.
Syntax	removef [options...] *pkginst path* removef [options...] *pkg*

-M	Instructs to not use the `$rootpath/etc/vfstab` file on the client.
-R *rootpath*	Specifies the complete pathname to the directory to use as the root path.
-V *fsfile*	Specifies the filename that is used to map the client's file system.
-f *pkginst*	Use this option after the erase phase to specify that the operation is completed.
path	The name of the path you want to erase.
pkg	Specifies the name of the package to be erased from the specified path.

File Name:	`removef`	**Directory:**	/usr/sbin/	**Type:**	External

reset

UNIX Shell:	All primary shells (csh, ksh, sh)
Function	Resets the terminal to default values.
Syntax	reset [options...] *{ type }*

-	Shows the terminal type on STDOUT.
-e*char*	Specifies the erase character to use on all terminals. (default is Backspace.)
-i*char*	Specifies the interrupt character to use on all terminals. (default is Ctrl+C.)
-k*char*	Specifies the kill character to use on all terminals. (default is Ctrl+U.)
-I	Suppresses transmission of terminal initialization strings.
-n	Specifies the new tty driver modes should be initialized. For BSD 4.3 tty driver.
-Q	Suppresses printing of the erase and kill characters.
-r	Shows the terminal type in addition to all other actions.

continued

-s -m *port-id { baudrate }* *type*	Prints the sequence of csh commands that initialize the TERM environment variable. Maps the terminal on the specified port. Specifies a terminal type configure or to map with the -m option. (In addition to the regular tset function the following is done:) Turns on Cooked and Echo modes. Turns off cbreak and Raw modes. Turns on new-line translation. Restores all special characters.
File Name: `reset`	**Directory:** /usr/ucb/ **Type:** External

rgb

UNIX Shell: All primary shells (csh, ksh, sh)

Function	Creates a database containing color names. Finds decimals for the colors followed by the color name in STDIN.
Syntax	rgb *database*

database	Specifies the database to create. (`default is /usr/openwin/lib/X11/rgb.dir`).
File Name: `rgb`	**Directory:** /usr/openwin/bin/ **Type:** External
echo "0 0 139 BLUE" | rgb blue.dir	Creates a color database named blue that contains one color.
rgb colors.dir < /usr/openwin/lib/X11/rgb.dir	Creates a database with all common colors.

rmail

UNIX Shell: All primary shells (csh, ksh, sh)

Function	Sends messages in text format as mail to users, reads from STDIN or a terminal. Recipient must be a user.
Syntax	rmail [options...] *recipients...*

-t	Adds a To: line to the message header for every recipient.
-w	Sends the message without waiting for a reply from the remote transfer program.
-m *messagetype*	Specifies the Message Type: line to send with the message.
recipients...	Specifies the e-mail address or addresses that should receive the message.
File Name: `rmail`	**Directory:** /usr/bin/ **Type:** External
rmail info@ucgbook.com	Starts rmail with the recipient specified.

rmdel, sccs-rmdel

UNIX Shell: All primary shells (csh, ksh, sh)

Function	Removes a delta from one or more SCCS files.
Syntax	rmdel [-r] *sfile*

-r*sid*	Removes the version corresponding to the indicated SID.
sfile	Specifies the `s.file` type to remove SCCS delta from.
File Name: `rmdel`	**Directory:** /usr/ccs/bin/ **Type:** External

rmic

UNIX Shell: All primary shells (csh, ksh, sh)

Function	A compiler that creates skeleton and stub class files for use with remote objects from compiled Java classes.
Syntax	rmic [options...] *class-name*

-classpath *path*	Specifies the path to look up classes. Separates directories by colons (.:/classes).
-d *directory*	Specifies the directories of the class hierarchy or the stub and skeleton files.
-depend	Initiates the compiler to recompile classes referenced by other classes.
-g	Specifies debugging to contain information about local variables.
-keepgenerated	Retains the created .java source files for the stubs and skeletons.
-nowarn	Does not show a warning message.
-O	Optimizes compiled code by inlining static, final, and private methods.
-show	Shows the Graphical User Interface for the compiler.
-verbose	Verbose mode. Shows more information.
class-names	Specifies a class name and must be compiled successfully with the `javac` program.
File Name: `rmic`	**Directory:** /usr/bin/ **Type:** External

rmiregistry

UNIX Shell: All primary shells (csh, ksh, sh)

Function	Starts and creates a Java remote object registry. It creates no output because it is run in the background.
Syntax	rmiregistry *{ port }*

port	Specifies the port number on the current host (default is 1099).

File Name: `rmiregistry` **Directory:** /usr/bin/ **Type:** External

rmmount

UNIX Shell: All primary shells (csh, ksh, sh)

Function	Mounts removable media. The Volume Manager uses it to mount the device when a new media is inserted.
Syntax	rmmount [-D]

-D	Shows debug information.

File Name: `rmmount` **Directory:** /usr/sbin/ **Type:** External

Note: You should configure your /etc/rmmount.conf after your needs.

roffbib

UNIX Shell: All primary shells (csh, ksh, sh)

Function	Shows records in a bibliographic database in bibliography format, not as footnotes or endnotes.
Syntax	roffbib [options...] *{ filenames... }*

-e	Uses the whole screen width when producing output.
-h	Replaces sequences of blanks with tabs.
-m *macro*	Specifies macro files to be used instead of the default macros.
-n*number*	Specifies the number of what to number the first page as (default is 1).
-o*first-last*	Shows pages between the specified page numbers separated by a dash.
-last	Shows pages from the first page to the specified page to stop on.
first-	Shows pages from the specified page number and continues to the last page.
-r*aN*	Sets register `a` to `N`.
-s*number*	Specifies the amount of pages to be shown before taking a pause.
-T*terminal*	Specifies the terminal type to use.
-V	Outputs to Versatec and sets page offset to one inch.
-x	Formats comments into paragraphs.
-Q	Queues output to the phototypesetter and sets page offset to one inch.
filenames...	Specifies the filename or filenames to use.

File Name: `roffbib` **Directory:** /usr/bin/ **Type:** External

Note: Roffbib is often used with sortbib.

rpc.bootparamd

UNIX Shell: All primary shells (csh, ksh, sh)

Function	Serves diskless clients with startup information at boot time.
Syntax	rpc.bootparamd [-d]

-d	Shows debug information.

File Name: `rpc.bootparamd` **Directory:** /usr/sbin/ **Type:** External

rpc.nisd

UNIX Shell: All primary shells (csh, ksh, sh)

Function	The daemon for the NIS+ service.
Syntax	rpc.nisd [options...]

-A	Shows information about all authentications.
-C	Shows diagnostics on the console device.
-D	Shows debug information.
-F	Checkpoints the database in the server.
-h	Shows help information.
-v	Shows version information.
-Y	Starts server with YP(NIS2) modules for clients without NIS+. No authentication is used.

continued

-B	Starts server with DNS forwarding; used when resolving NIS hosts for clients.
-t *transport*	Specifies the transport to connect rpc.nisd with rpc.nisd_resolv. Default is ticots.
-d *dictionary*	Specifies an alternate dictionary used by the NIS+ database.
-L *load*	Specifies how much load the NIS+ service can use.
-S *level*	Specifies the security level to use:
0	Lets every client administer the NIS database.
1	Authenticates with the AUTH_SYS and AUTH_DES credentials.
2	Allows authentications with AUTH_DES and mechanisms configured by `nisauthconf`.

File Name:	`rpc.nisd`	**Directory:**	/usr/sbin/	**Type:**	External
Note:	The NIS+ service is much more secure than the standard NIS service.				

rpc.nisd -A -S 0	Enables verbose mode on authentications and lets everyone use the database.
rpc.nisd -Y	Enables the NIS (YP) service. Lets clients that are using the standard NIS service grab information.

rpc.nisd_resolv

UNIX Shell: All primary shells (csh, ksh, sh)

Function	Is used by NIS hosts as a DNS forwarder. It is often used from `rpc.nisd`, but can also be used from the console.
Syntax	rpc.nisd_resolv [options...]

-F	Runs the resolver in foreground.
-C *fd*	Specifies the fd as service export from nisd. It is used with -F.
-t *transport*	Specifies the transport to use between the programs.
-p *transient*	Specifies the transient program to use.
-v	Verbose mode. Shows more information in `syslog`.
-V	Verbose mode. Shows more information.

File Name:	`rpc.nisd_resolv`	**Directory:**	/usr/sbin/	**Type:**	External

rpc.nisd_resolv -F	Runs the resolver in the foreground.
rpc.nisd_resolv -t ticots	Uses transport ticots.

rpc.nispasswdd

UNIX Shell: All primary shells (csh, ksh, sh)

Function	Updates the NIS+ password table on request from nispasswd or yppasswd.
Syntax	rpc.nispasswdd [options...]

-a *attempts*	Sets the maximum attempts to authenticate the caller.
-c *minutes*	Sets number of minutes a failed password update is cached.
-D	Tells the daemon to run in debug mode.
-g	Creates a DES credential if the user doesn't have one.
-v	Verbose mode. Sends the information to the `syslog` daemon.

File Name:	`rpc.nispasswdd`	**Directory:**	/usr/sbin/	**Type:**	External

rpc.nispasswdd -a 5 -c 60	Tells the daemon that users have five attempts to identify themselves. Users cannot try for another hour if they fail.

rpc.rexd

UNIX Shell: All primary shells (csh, ksh, sh)

Function	Is used for program execution on remote computers.
Syntax	rpc.rexd [-s]

-s	Tells the daemon to only accept secure calls.

File Name:	`rpc.rexd`	**Directory:**	/usr/sbin/	**Type:**	External

rpc.sprayd

UNIX Shell: All primary shells (csh, ksh, sh)

Function	The server daemon for the spray command.
Syntax	rpc.sprayd

File Name:	`rpc.sprayd`	**Directory:**	/usr/lib/netsvc/spray/	**Type:**	External
Note:	Spray isn't very reliable as a benchmark and may overload the network.				

rpc.ypupdated

UNIX Shell:	All primary shells (csh, ksh, sh)
Function	Updates information in the Network Information Service (NIS).
Syntax	rpc.ypudated [options...]

-i	Tells the daemon to accept insecure calls.
-s	Tells the daemon to only accept secure calls.

File Name:	`rpc.ypupdated`	Directory:	/usr/lib/netsvc/yp/	Type:	External

rpcbind

UNIX Shell:	All primary shells (csh, ksh, sh)
Function	Creates universal addresses by converting RPC program numbers.
Syntax	rpcbind [options...]

-d	Shows debug information.
-w	Does a warm start.

File Name:	`rpcbind`	Directory:	/usr/sbin/	Type:	External
Note:	Normally, rpcbind starts at system startup.				

rpld

UNIX Shell:	All primary shells (csh, ksh, sh)
Function	Provides network booting support for clients running on the x86 (Intel-compatible) platform.
Syntax	rpld [options...] *interface* rpld -a [options...]

-f *config-file*	Specifies a configuration file (default is /var/spool/rpld.log).
-d *debug-level*	Specifies a debug level between 0 and 9 where 9 is full debugging (default is 0).
-D *debug-dest*	Specifies debug information destination: 0 = STDOUT, 1 = `syslogd`, 2 = log file (is default).
-M *maximum clients*	Defines the maximum number of simultaneous clients to be served.
-b *mode*	Specifies the mode the server will run in: 0 = foreground, 1 = background.
-l *file*	Creates a new log file for the debug destination or the config file.
-g *delay granularity*	Adjusts delay count for client if retransmission occurs.
-z *frame size*	Sets the size of the data frames.
-s *start delay count*	Specifies the delay time between outgoing data (default is 20).
-a	Starts one daemon for each network interface found.
interface	Specifies the network interface to monitor for requests. Cannot be specified with -a.

File Name:	`rpld`	Directory:	/usr/sbin/	Type:	External
Tip:	If you specify the -D option or a config file to write to the STDOUT, the server will not run in background mode.				

rpld -a	Starts the rpld daemon for each Network Interface Card (NIC) found.
rpld /dev/le0	Starts the rpld daemon for the le0 NIC.

runacct

UNIX Shell:	Bourne shell (sh)
Function	Runs daily accounting procedures that are usually started from the cron daemon.
Syntax	runacct *{ mmdd } { state }*

mmdd	Specifies which month and day to run the program.
state	**The following are the states to use in a state file:**
SETUP	Moves active accounting files into working files.
WTMPFIX	Verifies the wtmp file. Corrects errors if necessary.
CONNECT	Produces connect sessions information.
PROCESS	Converts process accounting records into tacct.h format.
MERGE	Merges the connect and process accounting information.
FEES	Converts output of chargefee into tacct.h format.
DISK	Merges disk accounting records with connect, process, and fee accounting data.
MERGETACCT	Merges daily total accounting records in daytacct with summary totals data.
CMS	Produces command summaries.
USEREXIT	Any installation-dependent accounting programs can be included here.

continued

CLEANUP		Cleans up temporary files and exits.			
File Name:	`runacct`	**Directory:**	/usr/lib/acct	**Type:**	Script

rusage

UNIX Shell: All primary shells (csh, ksh, sh)

Function	Shows the resource usage for a command (CPU time, wall clock, System CPU, and so on).
Syntax	rusage *command*

command		Specifies a command to run.			
File Name:	`rusage`	**Directory:**	/usr/ucb/	**Type:**	External
Tip:	This helps you know how much of your system resources are used when running a command.				
rusage ps -ef			Prints out all processes running followed by resources used.		
rusage ls			Prints out all files in current directory followed by resources used.		

rwall

UNIX Shell: All primary shells (csh, ksh, sh)

Function	Reads a message from STDIN and sends it as a broadcast message to the users logged on to the specified host.
Syntax	rwall [options...]

-n *netgroup*		Specifies the network groups to send the broadcast message to.			
-h *hostname*		Specifies the hostname or the IP address of the server.			
File Name:	`rwall`	**Directory:**	/usr/sbin/	**Type:**	External
Tip:	Useful if you want to write to all users.				
rwall -h sun			Starts the interactive utility on server sun.		

sa1

UNIX Shell: Bourne shell (sh)

Function	Saves system activity into the binary file `/var/adm/sa/saDD`, where DD is the current day.
Syntax	sa1 *{ time } { amount }*

time		Specifies the number of seconds in the interval between saving samples.			
amount		Specifies how many times it will do a sample.			
File Name:	`sa1`	**Directory:**	/usr/lib/sa	**Type:**	Script
Tip:	Run this script from `crontab` for automatic samples.				
sa1 1200 3			Takes three samples with an interval of 20 minutes between samples.		

sa2

UNIX Shell: Bourne shell (sh)

Function	A script that saves system activity into the file `/var/adm/sa/saDD` where `DD` is the current day. This is similar to sar and it uses the same options.
Syntax	sa2 [options...]

		Please see `sar` for the list of available options and descriptions.			
File Name:	`sa2`	**Directory:**	/usr/lib/sa	**Type:**	Script
sa2 -f sarfile			Creates a report from the file `sarfile`.		
sa2 -d -f sarfile			Creates a report from the file `sarfile` and shows block devices.		

sacadm

UNIX Shell: All primary shells (csh, ksh, sh)

Function	The port monitor administration tool. It is used to add/remove, enable/disable, start/stop a port monitor.
Syntax	sacadm option [options...]

-p *pmtag*	Specifies the tag associated with the port monitor.
-t *type*	Specifies port monitor type. Can only be used with -a, -l, and -L.
-c *cmd*	Runs the command string cmd to start a port monitor. Only used with the -a option.
-v *ver*	Specifies version number of the port monitor. Only used with the -a option.
-f *character*	Does not enable (d) or start (x) the new port monitor.
-n *count*	Specifies count to restart. Only used with the -a option.
-y *comment*	Adds comment in the _sactab entry for the pmtag. Only used with the -a option.

continued

-z *script*	Specifies the configuration script. Only used with the -a, -g, or -G options.		
-p pmtag*italics*	Specifies which port monitor to manipulate. Not used with the -G option.		
	The following options can only be combined with -p, if nothing else is specified.		
-a	Adds a port monitor. Requires -p, -t, -c, and -v options: -f, -n, -y, and -z are optional.		
-r	Removes a port monitor; -p is required.		
-s	Starts a port monitor; -p is required.		
-k	Stops a port monitor; -p is required.		
-e	Enables a port monitor; -p is required.		
-d	Disables a port monitor; -p is required.		
-l	Shows port monitor information; can either have -p, -t, or no additional options.		
-L	The same as -l except the output is shown in a condensed format.		
-g	Requests output or installs or replaces per-port monitor configuration script.		
-G	Requests output or installs per-system configuration script; -z can be combined.		
-x	Reads the database file. With -p option, pmtag will read its administrative file.		
File Name: `sacadm`	**Directory:** /usr/sbin/	**Type:**	External

sact, sccs-sact

UNIX Shell: All primary shells (csh, ksh, sh)

Function	Informs the user that the s.file is checked out for editing by somebody else.
Syntax	sact *files...*

files...	Specifies the file(s) that is in progress.		
File Name: `sact`	**Directory:** /usr/ccs/bin/	**Type:**	External

sadc

UNIX Shell: All primary shells (csh, ksh, sh)

Function	Saves system activity in binary format to a specified file.
Syntax	sadc *{ time } { amount } { file }*

time	Specifies the number of seconds in the interval between saving samples.		
amount	Specifies how many times it will sample.		
file	Specifies the file to save the record to (default is `/var/adm/sa/sa`*dd*). (dd is the day when the file was saved.)		
File Name: `sadc`	**Directory:** /usr/lib/sa	**Type:**	External
Tip:	Do not use this command; instead, use the script sa1 to collect system activity information.		
sadc 30 4 sarfile	Creates four samples, with a 30-second-interval between samples, into a `sarfile`.		

sag

UNIX Shell: All primary shells (csh, ksh, sh)

Function	Shows a graph of the system activity data from the binary datafile created by a run of `sar`.
Syntax	sag [options...]

-e *time*	Shows data up to a specified time (default is 18:00).		
-f *file*	Specifies a data source file.		
-i *sec*	Specifies the data selection interval in seconds.		
-s *time*	Shows data from the specified time (default is 08:00).		
-T *term*	Creates an output that is suitable for the specified terminal (default is $TERM).		
-x *spec*	Specifies the xaxis. The `spec` value should be in the following format:		
name	Specifies a single text string matching a column header in the `sar` report.		
{ dev }	Specifies an optional device to go into the name string.		
{ lo hi }	Specifies the low and high numeric scale limits.		
-y *spec*	Specifies a text string like -x. Specifies up to 5 strings. (Default string is -y"%usr0100;%usr+%sys0100;%usr+%sys+%wio0100.")		
File Name: `sag`	**Directory:** /usr/bin/	**Type:**	External

sar

sar	UNIX Shell:	All primary shells (csh, ksh, sh)
Function	Shows information about system use for a specified period of time.	
Syntax	sar [options...] *time { amount }* sar [options...]	

-a	Shows how many file access system routines are used.
-A	Shows all system information available.
-b	Shows all buffer usage.
-c	Shows all calls from the system.
-d	Shows the block devices activities.
-g	Shows the page-out activities.
-k	Shows the memory allocation from the kernel.
-m	Shows the semaphore activities on the system.
-p	Shows the page-in activities.
-q	Shows the queue lengths average and percent of time it is occupied.
-r	Gives you the amount of unused disk blocks and memory pages.
-u	Shows the CPU use.
-v	Shows processes status, the i-nodes, and file tables used.
-w	Shows the swapping and switching activity on the system.
-y	Shows the tty devices activities.
	To increase sample activity counters for the system you can use:
-o *filename*	Specifies the file where to store samples.
time	Specifies the amount of seconds to wait until a new sample is about to be added.
amount	Specifies the amount of times that the system states will be stored.
	To read system information from a previously recorded file you can use:
-e *time*	Gets data until the specified time (default is 18:00).
-f *file*	Specifies the file from which the data will be read.
-i *seconds*	Updates information with the specified interval in seconds.
-s *time*	Specifies when to start analyzing data from the system (default is 08:00).

File Name:	`sar`	**Directory:**	/usr/sbin/	**Type:**	External
Note:	A good way to collect system data is to use the `sadc` report package.				

sar -o graph 50 5	Reports activity every 50 seconds 5 times to file graph.
sar -A	Reports all data saved for today in `/var/adm/sa/sadd`.

savecore

savecore	UNIX Shell:	All primary shells (csh, ksh, sh)
Function	Saves a crash dump of the operating system kernel (if one is created) after a system crash.	
Syntax	savecore [options...] *directory*	

-L	Saves a crash dump without a reboot or system alteration.
-v	Verbose mode. Shows more information.
-d	Ignores the dump header valid flag and forces a crash dump save.
-f *file*	Saves a crash dump from the specified file instead of the system's dump device.
directory	Saves the crash dump to the specified directory.

File Name:	`savecore`	**Directory:**	/usr/bin/	**Type:**	External
Note:	By default, savecore automatically runs at boot time by the `/etc/init.d/savecore` script.				

savecore -f /dump/crash	Saves a crash dump from the file `/dump/crash`.
savecore -d	Saves a crash dump even if a dump already exists.

sccs	UNIX Shell:	All primary shells (csh, ksh, sh)
Function	Executes subcommands on SCCS history files or directories. SCCS = Source Code Control System.	
Syntax	sccs [options...] *subcommand { file }*	

-r	Uses the real userID instead of the effective userID.
-d*prefix*	Specifies the prefix pathname for SCCS history files (default is current directory).
-p*subdirectory*	Specifies the subdirectory where to find the history files (default is `SCCS`).
subcommand	Specifies a command name, its options, and any operands/arguments.
file	Specifies the s.file to run the command on. SCCS history files have the prefix s.
	The following are the subcommands to use with `sccs`:
admin	Changes the checksum and flags of an s.file.
cdc [options...]	Changes the commentary in the delta of an s.file.
-r*deltaID*	Specifies the ID of the delta.
-y*{ comment }*	Specifies the new comment. Without comment ,the field is empty.
check [options...]	Searches for `s.files` being edited and returns a NR larger than zero if there are.
-b	Does not check the branches for files in progress (use with caution).
-u*{ username }*	Searches for files being edited by yourself or by the specified user or IPaddress.
clean [-b]	Deletes all files in the current directory that can be retrieved from SCCS history.
-b	Does not check the branches for files in progress (use with caution).
comb	Creates scripts that combine s.file deltas.
create	Creates an s.history file and does a `get` to show a read-only copy.
delta [options...]	Saves the changes made to an s.file in the delta.
-s	Suppresses reports on delta numbers and statistics.
-y*{ comment }*	Specifies the new comment. Without comment, the field is empty.
diffs [options...]	Makes a comparison between a file being edited and the history file version. (All options in the command diff are also supported.)
-C	Shows a list of the differences in three lines (`diff -c`).
-I	Ignores upper-/lowercases of the letters (`diff -i`).
-c*time*	Compares against the version closest to but before the specified time (yymmdd hhmmss).
-r*deltaID*	Compares against the specified deltaID.
edit	Recovers a file version for editing and locks the file from other users.
enter	Works the same way as `create` but doesn't show the file.
fix -r*deltaID*	Deletes the specified newest version of the delta from the SCCS history.
get [options...]	Shows a read-only version from the SCCS history.
-e	Same as `edit`. Allows editing on the file.
-k	Shows a printable copy of the file without opening the actual file.
-m	Shows the deltaID in the beginning of each line.
-p	Shows the file on STDOUT and redirects the deltaIDs and statistics to STDERR.
-s	Suppresses reports on delta numbers and statistics.
-c*time*	Compares against the version closest to but before the specified time (yymmdd hhmmss).
-r*deltaID*	Specifies the ID of the delta.
help *{ argument... }*	Shows help information. The word `stuck` does the same thing.
messagecode	Shows help information about the specified error code.
command	Shows help information about the specified SCCS command.
info [options...]	Shows a list of files in progress.
-b	Does not check the branches for files in progress (use with caution).
-u*{ username }*	Searches for files being edited by yourself or the specified user or IPaddress.
print	Shows all the history information about the specified file(s).
prs [options...]	Shows the delta table. The -c and -r options are also supported.
-e	Shows all delta table information previous to the delta specified with -r.
-l	Shows all delta table information from and after the delta specified with -r or -c.
-r*deltaID*	Specifies the ID of the delta.
-c*time*	Compares against the version closest to but before the specified time (yymmdd hhmmss).
prt [-y]	Shows the delta table without the MR field.
-y	Shows the latest delta in the table.

continued

rmdel -r *deltaID*	Deletes the specified deltaID. Must be the newest version in the branch.
sact	Shows the activity of editing in the specified SCCS file.
sccsdiff *old new diff { options... }*	Compares the two specified versions with the `diff` command.
-r*olddeltaID*	Specifies the old version to compare.
-r*newdeltaID*	Specifies the new version to compare.
[options...]	Specifies any diff options that should be used when comparing the files.
tell [options...]	Shows a list of the files in progress.
-b	Does not check the branches for files in progress (use with caution).
-u*{ username }*	Searches for files being edited by yourself or the specified user or IPaddress.
unedit	Undoes the last change made with `edit` or `get-e`.
unget	Does the same thing as `unedit`.
val	Validates the SCCS history file.
what	Shows any expanded ID keyword strings in an object or text file.
deledit [options...]	Combines `delta` and `edit`.
-s	Suppresses reports on delta numbers and statistics.
-y*{ comment }*	Specifies a comment.
delget [options...]	Combines `delta` and `get`.
-s	Suppresses reports on delta numbers and statistics.
-y*{ comment }*	Specifies a comment.
File Name: `sccs`	**Directory:** /usr/ccs/bin/ **Type:** External
Note:	If no file is specified, all files in the directory are affected.

sccsdiff, sccs-sscsdiff

UNIX Shell: Bourne shell (sh)

Function	Is used to compare two versions of a SCCS file and show the differences.
Syntax	sccsdiff [options...] -r -r *{ diff options... } file*

-p	Shows the result through the command `pr`.
-g	Uses `get` in the directory from which it was run, instead of default directory.
	You must use -r twice to specify the versions to compare.
-r*deltaID*	Specifies the deltaID for the version of the s.file.
diff options	Specifies options to pass to `diff`.
file	Specifies the s.file to compare the versions of.
File Name: `sccsdiff`	**Directory:** /usr/ccs/bin/ **Type:** Script

sccs-help, help

UNIX Shell: All primary shells (csh, ksh, sh)

Function	Shows help on error or warning messages from Source Code Control System (SCCS)
Syntax	help *{ errorID }*

errorID	Specifies an error message number, or an SCCS command name.
File Name: `help`	**Directory:** /usr/ccs/bin/ **Type:** External
help stuck	Shows a little help about SCCS.

serialver

UNIX Shell: Korn shell (ksh)

Function	Reports the serial version UID for at least one class; output is in an evolving class format.
Syntax	serialver [-show] *{ classname }*

	You may select one of the following but not both:
-show	Shows a simple user interface.
classname	Specifies the class that is reported.
File Name: `serialver`	**Directory:** /usr/bin/ **Type:** Script
Note:	This script and Java will not run under SUNOS4.X (SOLARIS 1.X).
serialver javaclass	Shows serial version UID for javaclass.

server_upgrade		**UNIX Shell:**	**Bourne shell (sh)**		
Function	Upgrades various clients (Intel- or SPARC-based) from the server.				
Syntax	server_upgrade -d *installdir* [-p]				
-d *installdir*		Specifies the path and directory where the installation image resides.			
-p *profile*		Specifies the path to a custom JumpStart profile.			
File Name:	`server_upgrade`	**Directory:**	/usr/sbin/	**Type:**	Script
server_upgrade -d /cdrom/cdrom0		Upgrades the shared services using the CD-ROM.			
server_upgrade -d /cdrom/cdrom0 -p myprofile		Uses a JumpStart profile when upgrading.			

setfacl		**UNIX Shell:**	**All primary shells (csh, ksh, sh)**		
Function	Is used to manage the Access Control List for one or more files.				
Syntax	setfacl [options...] *{ file }* setfacl [-r] -f *ACLfile file*				
-r		Recalculates permissions for the ACL mask entry.			
		The following options cannot be combined.			
-s *ACLentries*		Sets a file's ACL. Erases and overwrites the old ACL entries.			
-m *ACLentries*		Adds new ACL entries to the file. If the entry exists, the old will be replaced.			
-d *ACLentries*		Deletes specified entry or entries on the file.			
-f *ACLfile*		Sets a file's ACL by reading the entries from the specified file.			
file		Specifies the file to modify using the -s, -m, and -d options.			
File Name:	`setfacl`	**Directory:**	/usr/bin/	**Type:**	External
Note:	Sets ACL for a file for user, group, other, and mask entries. Use `getfacl` to check a file's ACL.				
setfacl -m user:anders:rwx anders.txt		Sets full access to user anders to the file anders.txt.			
getfacl file1 | setfacl -f - file2		Uses `getfacl` to give file2 the same ACL as file1.			

setmnt		**UNIX Shell:**	**All primary shells (csh, ksh, sh)**		
Function	Allows you to re-create /etc/mnttab file line by line.				
Syntax	setmnt				
		The following options are used in the program:			
filesystem mountpoint		Specifies the file system and the mountpoint.			
Enter Ctrl-D		Exits the program.			
File Name:	`setmnt`	**Directory:**	/usr/sbin/	**Type:**	External
Warning:	Be careful when you run this program because it overwrites the existing `/etc/mnttab`.				
setmnt		Starts the setmnt utility. After executing, see examples 2 and 3.			
/dev/dsk/c0t0d0s3 /ucg		Specifies the file system and mount point.			
Enter Ctrl-D		Exits the program.			

settime		**UNIX Shell:**	**All primary shells (csh, ksh, sh)**		
Function	Alters the file access and modification times. This command is equal to `touch -c`.				
Syntax	settime [-f *timefile*] *file*				
-f *timefile*		Uses the times of the specified file instead of current time.			
file		Specifies the file to alter.			
File Name:	`settime`	**Directory:**	/usr/bin/	**Type:**	External
Tip:	You can also use the command `touch`. It performs the same tasks as settime, but has more options.				
settime /ucg_examples/settime.testfile		Sets the times to current time.			
settime -f /var/adm/messages.0 /ucg_examples/settime.testfile		Sets the time and uses the time from the /var/adm/messages.0 file instead of current time.			

setuname

UNIX Shell:	All primary shells (csh, ksh, sh)
Function	Manages parameter values for the system and node name.
Syntax	setuname [options...]

-t	Makes a temporary change only.
	One or both of the -n and -s options must be specified.
-n name	Changes the node name.
-s name	Changes the system name.
File Name: `setuname`	**Directory:** /usr/bin/ **Type:** External
Warning:	The system may place requirements on the size of the system and node name. If so, the command shows a warning message. If the requirement isn't met, the command shows an error message.
setuname -t -n sun2	Changes the node name temporarily to sun2.
setuname -t -s Solaris	Changes the system name temporarily to Solaris.

sh, rsh

UNIX Shell:	Bourne shell (sh)
Function	The Bourne shell command interpreter and rsh is a restricted version of the Bourne shell.
Syntax	sh [options...] *{ arguments... }* rsh [options...] *{ arguments... }*

-c *string*	Reads commands from string.
-i	Makes the shell interactive. TERMINATE, INTERRUPT, and QUIT are ignored.
-p	Doesn't set the effective user and group IDs to the real user and group IDs.
-r	Runs the shell in restricted shell (same as rsh).
-s	Reads commands from STDIN.
	The following options can be changed with the `set` command in a script:
-a	Marks modified and created variables for export.
-e	Exits immediately with a nonzero exit status.
-f	Disables filename generation.
-h	Locates and remembers function commands when they are defined.
-k	Places all keyword arguments in the environment for a command.
-n	Reads commands but doesn't run them.
-t	Runs one command and exits.
-u	When substituting, treats unset variables as an error.
-v	Shows input lines as they are read.
-x	Shows commands and their arguments when they are executed.
--	Doesn't change any flags. (If + is used instead of -, the flag is turned off.)
arguments...	Additional arguments to the shell or a script with arguments to run.
File Name: `sh` `rsh`	**Directory:** /usr/bin/ /usr/lib/ **Type:** External
Note:	This shell is the same as Job control shell (jsh), but without jobcontrol.

share

UNIX Shell:	All primary shells (csh, ksh, sh)
Function	Makes local resources available to remote hosts.
Syntax	share [options...] *{ pathname }*

-F fstype	Specifies the type of file system to share; for example, nfs.
-o options	Specifies options for the share; for example, access permissions (rw, ro, rw=host, ro=host).
-d description	Describes the share.
pathname	Specifies the directory to be shared.
File Name: `share`	**Directory:** /usr/sbin/ **Type:** External
share -F nfs /export/ucg	Shares a Network File System.
share -o ro=pluto:moon /export/ucg	Shares /export/ucg read only to the hosts pluto and moon.

shareall

UNIX Shell:	Bourne shell (sh)
Function	Shares the resources in a file; for example, /etc/dfs/dfstab.
Syntax	shareall [options...]

-F *fstype...*	Specifies the type of file systems, default is the first entry in /etc/dfs/fstypes.
	Only one of the following options can be used:
-	Receives the share commands from STDIN.
file	Receives the share commands from a file, default is `/etc/dfs/dfstab`.
File Name: `shareall`	**Directory:** /usr/sbin/ **Type:** Script

showfont

UNIX Shell:	All primary shells (csh, ksh, sh)
Function	Shows information from the X font server about a specific font.
Syntax	showfont [options...]

-server *host:port*	Connects to the specified X font server.
-l	Sets the bit order of the font to be least significant bit first.
-m	Sets the bit order of the font to be most significant bit first.
-L	Sets the byte order of the font to be least significant byte first.
-M	Sets the byte order of the font to be most significant byte first.
-extents_only	Shows only the extents of the font.
-start*number*	Shows a range of characters from the number specified.
-end*number*	Shows a range of characters up to the number specified.
-unit*number*	Sets the fonts scanline unit. The values are 1, 2, 4, or 8.
-pad*number*	Sets the fonts scanpad unit. The values are 1, 2, 4, or 8.
-bitmap_pad*number*	Specifies the fonts bitmap padding unit. The values are 0, 1, or 2.
-fn *font*	Specifies the fontname to show information about.
File Name: `showfont`	**Directory:** /usr/openwin/bin/ **Type:** External

showrev

UNIX Shell:	All primary shells (csh, ksh, sh)
Function	Shows revision information for the hardware and software.
Syntax	showrev [options...]

-a	Shows all information available.
-p	Only shows information about patches.
-w	Only shows information about OpenWindows.
-c command	Shows the revision information for the specified command.
-s hostname	Runs showrev on the specified host.
File Name: `showrev`	**Directory:** /usr/bin/ **Type:** External
showrev -p | grep 106597	Lets you see whether patch 106597 is installed or not.

showrgb

UNIX Shell:	All primary shells (csh, ksh, sh)
Function	Converts a compiled rgb color name database back to the original form.
Syntax	showrgb *{ database }*

database	Specifies the database to be converted.
File Name: `showrgb`	**Directory:** /usr/openwin/bin/ **Type:** External

showsnf

UNIX Shell:	All primary shells (csh, ksh, sh)
Function	Shows the content of font files in the SNF format or converts glyphs into arrays of characters.
Syntax	showsnf [options...]

-v	Shows character bearings and sizes.
-g	Shows character glyph bitmaps.
-m	Sets most significant bit first to be the order for the font.
-M	Sets most significant byte first to be the order for the font.

continued

-l	Sets least significant bit first to be the order for the font.
-L	Sets least significant byte first to be the order for the font.
-p*number*	Specifies the glyph padding of the font.
-u*number*	Specifies the scanline unit of the font.
File Name: `showsnf`	**Directory:** /usr/openwin/bin/ **Type:** External

shutacct

UNIX Shell: Bourne shell (sh)

Function	Disables process accounting on shutdown and adds a reason record to `/var/adm/wtmp`.
Syntax	shutacct *{ reason }*
reason	Appends a reason for the shutdown to /var/adm/wtmp.
File Name: `shutacct`	**Directory:** /usr/lib/acct/ **Type:** Script

snapshot

UNIX Shell: All primary shells (csh, ksh, sh)

Function	Takes a snapshot of the screen, or a part of the screen, and saves it to a raster file.
Syntax	snapshot [options...]
-d *directory*	Specifies the default directory for saving and loading operations.
-f *file*	Specifies the default filename to use for saving and loading operations.
-g	Shows color images using a grayscale ramp.
-l *file*	Specifies the image file to automatically load and view on startup.
-n	Overwrites previously loaded images or snapshot without confirmation from user.
-v	Shows version information.
File Name: `snapshot`	**Directory:** /usr/openwin/bin/ **Type:** External

snoop

UNIX Shell: All primary shells (csh, ksh, sh)

Function	Grabs packets from the network and shows information about the content.
Syntax	snoop [options...] *{ expression }*
-a	Sends packet information to /dev/audio.
-C	Shows generated text that comes from the kernel filter or snoops own filter.
-D	Shows the amount of dropped packets on the summary line.
-N	Reads a specified capture file and creates a new file containing IPaddress and host.
-P	Doesn't enable promiscuous mode, grabs only packets addressed to current system.
-S	Shows the Ethernet frame size in bytes on the summary line.
-v	Verbose mode. Shows more information.
-V	Verbose summary mode. Shows more information on the summary line.
-t	Defines when to time stamp packets.
r	Gives the time since the first packet got captured until the current packet.
a	Timestamps the packets with the current time.
d	Gives the time between the current and the previous packet.
-c *count*	Exits after receiving the specified amount of packets.
-d *device*	Specifies the interface to use for receiving packets.
-i *filename*	Uses the specified file to read captured packets from.
-n *filename*	Specifies the file to use as IPaddress to hostname mapping; used like /etc/hosts.
-o *filename*	Stores packets in the specified output file.
-s *bytes*	Skips the rest of the packet if it reaches the specified bytes.
-p *first*	Specifies the first packet to show from a capture file.
[, *last*]	Specifies the last packet to show from a capture file.
-x *offset*	Shows the received packets in hexadecimal and in ASCII format. Shows from offset.
[, length]	Shows the packet until it reaches length; if not specified, shows whole packet.
{ expression }	Specifies an expression to match the packets to show information about.
host *hostname*	Matches source or destination host.
IPaddress or *MACaddress*	Matches either IPaddress or MACaddress.
from or src	Matches only source address, port, or the RPC reply.

continued

to or dst	Matches only destination address, port, or the RPC call.
ether	Resolves hosts to Ethernet addresses.
ethertype *number*	Matches packet if the Ethernet type is as specified.
ip	Matches ip packets.
arp	Matches arp packets.
rarp	Matches rarp packets.
broadcast	Matches if the packet is a broadcast.
multicast	Matches if the packet is a multicast.
apple	Matches if the packet is an apple Ethertalk packet.
decnet	Matches if the packet is a decnet packet.
greater *length*	Matches if the packet is longer than the length in bytes specified.
less *length*	Matches if the packet is shorter than the length in bytes specified.
utp	Matches UTP protocol packets.
tcp	Matches TCP protocol packets.
icmp	Matches ICMP protocol packets.
net *netaddress*	Matches packets with the source or destination network address as specified.
port *port*	Matches packets with the source or destination port specified.
rpc *protocol*	Matches packets with the rpc protocol specified.
gateway *hostname*	Matches packets that are going through the specified gateway.
nofrag	Shows packets that are unfragmented or the first packet in a series of fragments.

File Name:	`snoop`	**Directory:**	/usr/sbin/	**Type:**	External
Tip:	Perfect for learning what you should reject or accept on your firewall.				

snoop -d hme0 host sunbox	Grabs the packets on network interface hme0 that contains the host sunbox.
snoop -t a -c 200 -o network	Shows the time when the packets ran through the network; quits after 200 packets and prints them to the file network.

soconfig

UNIX Shell: All primary shells (csh, ksh, sh)

Function	Alters the transport provider driver used with sockets.
Syntax	soconfig [-f] *family type protocol { path }*

-f *file*	Sets the configuration by reading from specified file.
	The following operands are expressed as a value:
family	Specifies the protocol family, which is defined in `/usr/include/sys/socket.h`.
type	Specified the socket type, which is defined in `/usr/include/sys/socket.h`.
protocol	Specifies the protocol number, which is specified in the family specific include file.
path	Specifies the pathname of the device that corresponds to the transport provider.

File Name:	`soconfig`	**Directory:**	/sbin/	**Type:**	External

solregis

UNIX Shell: All primary shells (csh, ksh, sh)

Function	Starts the Solaris user registration procedure.
Syntax	solregis [options...]

-d	Waits until the X display is properly set, and then shows the initial screen.
-c	Changes the command to conditional mode. Doesn't show information on exit.

File Name:	`solregis`	**Directory:**	/usr/dt/bin/	**Type:**	External

sortbib

UNIX Shell: All primary shells (csh, ksh, sh)

Function	Sorts the specified bibliographic database, based on the sorting keys.
Syntax	sortbib [-s] *databases...*

-s *characters...*	Tells the command how to sort the database; specified by the character symbols.
	The following are the characters and their meaning that can be specified.
%A	Sorts by Author's name (is default).
%B	Sorts by Book containing article referenced.
%C	Sorts by Place of publication.
%D	Sorts by Date of publication (is default).

continued

%E	Sorts by Editor of book containing article referenced.		
%F	Sorts by Footnote number or label.		
%G	Sorts by Government order number.		
%H	Sorts by Header commentary.		
%I	Sorts by Publisher.		
%J	Sorts by Journal containing article.		
%K	Sorts by Keywords to use in locating reference.		
%L	Sorts by Label field; used by -k option of reference.		
%M	Sorts by Bell Labs Memorandum.		
%N	Sorts by Number within volume.		
%O	Sorts by Other commentary; printed at end of reference.		
%P	Sorts by Page number.		
%Q	Sorts by Corporate or Foreign Author.		
%R	Sorts by Report, paper, or thesis.		
%S	Sorts by Series title.		
%T	Sorts by Title of article or book.		
%V	Sorts by Volume number.		
%X	Sorts by Abstract.		
database	Specifies the database to read through.		
File Name: `sortbib`	**Directory:** /usr/bin/	**Type:**	External
Tip:	Records with missing author fields should probably be sorted by title.		

sotruss

UNIX Shell: Korn shell (ksh)

Function	Traces dynamic library calls made by the command specified and shows them on STDOUT.
Syntax	sotruss [options...] *command*

-f	Also traces children created by `fork`.		
-F *list*	Also traces calls from the specified libraries in the list.		
-T *list*	Traces only calls from the command to specified libraries in the list.		
-o *file*	Tells the command to save the output in the specified file instead of the screen.		
command	Specifies the command to trace.		
File Name: `sotruss`	**Directory:** /usr/bin/	**Type:**	Script

sotruss printf "hello world!\n"	Runs sotruss on the command printf.
sotruss -o sotruss.txt printf "Hello world!\n"	Runs sotruss on printf and directs output to sotruss.txt.

speckeysd

UNIX Shell: All primary shells (csh, ksh, sh)

Function	A `CDE/OpenWindows` daemon that detects special keys on Type 5/Compact 1 keyboards.		
Syntax	speckeysd		
File Name: `speckeysd`	**Directory:** /usr/openwin/bin/	**Type:**	External

spell

UNIX Shell: Korn shell (ksh)

Function	Collects words from specified file or files and looks them up in a spelling list. If the word doesn't exist, it will report it. It uses `deroff` to follow chains of included files.
Syntax	spell [options...] *{ files... }*

-b	Checks British spelling.		
-i	Causes deroff to ignore .so and .nx commands.		
-l	Follows the chains of all included files.		
-v	Shows all words not literally in the spelling list.		
-x	Shows every valid stem.		
+file	Specifies an additional list or lists of words to use in the spelling list.		
files...	Specifies the file or files to spell check. If not specified, STDIN is used.		
File Name: `spell`	**Directory:** /usr/bin/	**Type:**	Script

spell -b cleartext.txt	Checks the file cleartext.txt for British spelling.

spellin	UNIX Shell:	All primary shells (csh, ksh, sh)
Function	Reads a specified amount of hash codes from STDIN and shows a compressed spelling list.	
Syntax	spellin *amount*	

amount	Specifies how many codes to read.			
File Name: `spellin`	**Directory:**	/usr/lib/spell	**Type:**	External

spray	UNIX Shell:	All primary shells (csh, ksh, sh)
Function	Sends a stream of packets to a host. Reports how many were received and the transfer rate.	
Syntax	spray [options...] *host*	

-c *count*	Specifies how many packets to send.			
-d *delay*	Specifies in microseconds the pause between each packet (default is 0).			
-l *length*	Sets the number of bytes in the packet (default is 86).			
-t *nettype*	Specifies the class of transport (default is netpath).			
host	Specifies the host to send to.			
File Name: `spray`	**Directory:**	/usr/sbin/	**Type:**	External
Warning:	Spray isn't very reliable as a benchmark and may overload the network.			
spray -c 50 sun	Sends 50 packets.			
spray -c 20 -d 1000000 sun	Sends 20 packets with a one second pause between each.			

srchtxt	UNIX Shell:	All primary shells (csh, ksh, sh)
Function	Shows the content of a message database or searches for a match to the text string specified.	
Syntax	srchtxt [options...] *{ text }*	

-s	Doesn't show the sequence numbers of the messages.			
-l *directory*	Accesses files in the directory `/usr/lib/locale/directory/LC_MESSAGES`.			
-m *files...*	Accesses specified files, separated by commas, as the message files.			
text	Specifies text string to search for. If not specified, all messages show.			
File Name: `srchtxt`	**Directory:**	/usr/bin/	**Type:**	External

ssaadm	UNIX Shell:	All primary shells (csh, ksh, sh)
Function	Administers SPARC storage Arrays and SPARC storage RSM disk systems.	
Syntax	ssaadm [options...] *subcommand*	

-v	Verbose mode. Shows more information.
-e	Expert mode. Enables additional subcommands.
subcommand	Specifies a subcommand. Almost all subcommands end with a pathname.
pathname	Specifies the SPARCstorage system controller or a disk in the SPARCstorage system.
	The following are the subcommands and their options:
display [-p] *pathname*	Shows configuration information for the specified unit or units.
-p	Shows performance information for the specified controller.
download [options...] *pathname*	Downloads an image to the specified controller.
-f *file*	Downloads the prom image from the specified file to the specified controller. (When the download is complete, the SPARCstorage array must be reset.)
-w *wwn*	Changes the specified controller's World Wide Name, which is a 12-digit hex number.
fast_write [-s] option *pathname*	Enables/disables the use of NVRAM to enhance the performance of writes in the array.
-s	Saves the requested state that so it will persist across power cycles.
-c	Enables fast writes for synchronous writes only.
-e	Enables fast writes.
-d	Disables fast writes.
fc_s_download [-f]	Shows current version of the fcode in each FC/S Sbus card.
-f *file*	Downloads the fcode in the specified file into all the FC/S Sbus Cards.
insert_device *pathname*	Shows a guide how to go through a hot insertion of a disk device.

continued

perf_statistics option *pathname*	Enables/disables the accumulation of performance statistics for specified controller.
-e	Enables the accumulation of performance statistics.
-d	Disables the accumulation of performance statistics.
purge *pathname*	Erases any fast write data from NVRAM for specified disk or controller array.
reserve *pathname*	Assigns the specified controller or disk for exclusive use by the issuing host.
release *pathname*	Releases specified disk or controller if it is assigned for exclusive use.
remove_device *pathname*	Shows a guide how to go through a hot removal of a disk device.
replace_device *pathname*	Shows a guide how to go through a hot replacement of a disk device.
set_boot_dev [-y] *pathname*	Sets the boot device variable in the PROM to the physical device name specified.
-y	Sets the boot device without any confirmation requested or required.
start [-t] *pathname*	Spins up the specified disk or all disks in the array if a controller is specified.
-t *tray number*	Spins up all disks in the tray specified. A controller must be specified.
stop [-t] *pathname*	Spins down specified disk or all disks in the array if a controller is specified.
-t *tray number*	Spins down all disks in the tray specified. A controller must be specified.
sync_cache *pathname*	Moves all outstanding writes for the specified disk or array from NVRAM to the media.
	The following commands can either refer to a disk, a controller, or a tray number:
env_display *pathname*	Shows the environmental information for the specified unit.
alarm *pathname*	Shows current state of the audible alarm.
alarm_on *pathname*	Enables the audible alarm for specified device.
alarm_off *pathname*	Disables the audible alarm for specified device.
alarm_set *pathname seconds*	Sets specified device's alarm setting to specified seconds.
led *pathname*	Shows current state of the led for the specified disk.
led_on *pathname*	Enables the led for specified disk.
led_off *pathname*	Disables the led for specified disk.
power_off *pathname*	Powers down specified RSM array.
	The following commands are available only with the -e option:
bus_getstate *pathname*	Gets and shows the state of the specified bus.
bus_quiesce *pathname*	Sets specified bus into a passive state.
bus_reset *pathname*	Resets specified bus.
bus_resetall *pathname*	Resets specified bus and all devices on that bus.
bus_unquiesce *pathname*	Sets specified bus into an active state.
dev_getstate *pathname*	Shows whether the specified device is online or offline.
dev_reset *pathname*	Resets specified device.
offline *pathname*	Sets the specified device offline.
online *pathname*	Sets the specified device online.

File Name:	ssaadm	**Directory:**	/usr/sbin/	**Type:**	External
Warning:	When updating the prom images, all activity on the interface must be stopped.				

startup

UNIX Shell:	Bourne shell (sh)				
Function	Turns the process accounting on when the system is brought to a multi-user state.				
Syntax	startup				
File Name:	startup	**Directory:**	/usr/lib/acct/	**Type:**	Script

stdethers

UNIX Shell:	All primary shells (csh, ksh, sh)				
Function	Is used to erase NIS information from the specified file or STDIN.				
Syntax	stdethers *{ file }*				
File Name:	stdethers	**Directory:**	/usr/lib/netsvc/yp	**Type:**	External

stdhosts

UNIX Shell:	All primary shells (csh, ksh, sh)				
Function	Is used to erase NIS information from the specified file or STDIN.				
Syntax	stdhosts *{ file }*				
File Name:	stdhosts	**Directory:**	/usr/lib/netsvc/yp	**Type:**	External

strace

strace	UNIX Shell:	All primary shells (csh, ksh, sh)
Function	Shows STREAMS trace messages on STDOUT. Operands can be specified multiple times, but only in triplets.	
Syntax	strace *{ mid sid level }*	

mid	Specifies the module or driver ID number to trace.
sid	Specifies the sub ID number to trace.
level	Specifies the trace priority level. (The token all can be used to show all messages in that category.)

File Name:	`strace`	**Directory:**	/usr/bin/	**Type:**	External

strchg

strchg	UNIX Shell:	All primary shells (csh, ksh, sh)
Function	Adds or removes topmost modules of the stream associated with the user's STDIN.	
Syntax	strchg [options...]	

-h *modules...*	Adds the modules onto the top of the stream. This option can't be combined.
-f *file*	Specifies a file containing a list of modules for stream configuration.
-p	Removes topmost module off the stream.
-a	Removes all modules above topmost driver off the stream.
-u *module*	Removes all modules above specified module off the stream.

File Name:	`strchg`	**Directory:**	/usr/bin/	**Type:**	External
Note:	In a more specific way, this command pushes and pops modules into and out of the stream.				

strchg -p -u ldterm	Removes all modules above `ldterm`.

strclean

strclean	UNIX Shell:	All primary shells (csh, ksh, sh)
Function	Removes STREAMS error logger files older than 3 days.	
Syntax	strclean [options...]	

-a *age*	Changes the maximum age in days for a log file.
-d *directory*	Specifies logging directory; default is `/var/adm/streams`.

File Name:	`strclean`	**Directory:**	/usr/sbin/	**Type:**	External
Tip:	A good way to make this program run well is to schedule it. See `cron` and `crontab` for examples.				

strclean -a 5	Erases all `error.*` files older than 5 days.

strconf

strconf	UNIX Shell:	All primary shells (csh, ksh, sh)
Function	Manages the configuration of a stream.	
Syntax	strconf [option]	

-m *module*	Determines whether the specified module is present on a stream.
-t	Shows the topmost module only.

File Name:	`strconf`	**Directory:**	/usr/bin/	**Type:**	External

sttydefs

sttydefs	UNIX Shell:	All primary shells (csh, ksh, sh)
Function	Maintains the `/etc/ttydefs` file, which is used for controlling the tty port hunt sequences and for line settings.	
Syntax	sttydefs [option] [options...]	

-a *label*	Adds a record, with the specified tty label, to the ttydefs file.
-b	Autobaud mode. Permits setting the line speed of a tty port to its connected device.
-f *finalflags*	Specifies the value in the final flags field of the `/etc/ttydefs`.
-i *initialflags*	Specifies the value in the initial flags field of the `/etc/ttydefs`.
-n *nextlabel*	Specifies the value in the next label field of the `/etc/ttydefs`.
-l	Shows the entire record of `/etc/ttydefs`.
label	Shows a record from `/etc/ttydefs` that contains the specified tty label.
-r *label*	Removes a record from `/etc/ttydefs` with the specified tty label.

continued

File Name:	sttydefs	**Directory:**	/usr/sbin/	**Type:**	External
Note:	Only a superuser can use the flags -a and -r.				
sttydefs -l 9600			Displays the entire record that contains the label 9600.		
sttydefs -a newtty -b			Adds the label newtty and activates autobaud mode.		

sulogin

UNIX Shell: All primary shells (csh, ksh, sh)

Function	Asks the user to type in root password and go to single-user mode, or to press Ctrl+D to precede a normal startup.
Syntax	sulogin

File Name:	sulogin	**Directory:**	/sbin/	**Type:**	External
Note:	Sulogin should never be directly invoked by the user.				

swap

UNIX Shell: All primary shells (csh, ksh, sh)

Function	Manages the systems swap areas that are used by the memory manager.
Syntax	swap option *{ swaplow } { swaplen }*

-a *swapname*	Adds the specified swap area. Can only be done by the superuser.
-d *swapname*	Deletes the specified swap area. Can only be done by the superuser.
-l	Lists the status of all the swap areas.
-s	Shows information about total swap space usage and availability.
swaplow	Tells the offset to add or remove the swap area. The offset is in 512-byte blocks.
swaplen	Tells the length of the swap area in 512-byte blocks.

File Name:	swap	**Directory:**	/usr/sbin/	**Type:**	External
swap -a /dev/dsk/c0t3d0s4			Adds swap area on device c0t3d0s4.		
swap -l			Lists the status of all the swap areas.		

swmtool

UNIX Shell: All primary shells (csh, ksh, sh)

Function	A tool for installing, upgrading, and removing software packages.
Syntax	swmtool [-d]

-d *directory*		Specifies the directory where the software installation is located.			
File Name:	swmtool	**Directory:**	/usr/sbin/	**Type:**	External

syncinit

UNIX Shell: All primary shells (csh, ksh, sh)

Function	Sets interface operating parameters for a serial line.
Syntax	syncinit *device { baudrate }* [options...]

device	Specifies the device to operate on.
baudrate	Sets the baud rate to specified bits per second.
echo=yes	Makes the port operate in auto-echo mode.
echo=no	Disables auto-echo mode.
nrzi=yes	Makes the port operate with NRZI data encoding.
nrzi=no	Makes the port operate with NRZ data encoding.
txc=txc	Sets the TxC signal as the transmit clock source (pin 15).
txc=rxc	Sets the RxC signal as the transmit clock source (pin 17).
txc=baud	Sets the internal baud rate generator as the transmit clock source.
txc=pll	Sets the output of the DPLL circuit as the transmit clock source.
rxc=txc	Sets the TxC signal as the receive clock source (pin 15).
rxc=rxc	Sets the RxC signal as the receive clock source (pin 17).
rxc=baud	Sets the internal baud rate generator as the receive clock source.
rxc=pll	Sets the output of the DPLL circuit as the receive clock source.
loop=yes	Makes the port to operate in internal loopback mode.
loop=no	Disables the internal loopback mode.

continued

File Name:	`syncinit`	**Directory:**	/usr/sbin/	**Type:**	External
syncinit zsh0 9600 loop=yes	Sets the first CPU port to loop internally, to use clocking, and to operate at 9600 baud.				

syncloop

UNIX Shell: All primary shells (csh, ksh, sh)

Function	A program for testing synchronous serial loopback.
Syntax	syncloop [options...] *device*

-c *packetcount*	Specifies the packet amount sent in the multiple-packet phase.
-d *bytes*	Specifies the command will fill each packet with the value of specified bytes.
-l *packetsize*	Specifies the packet length, in bytes.
-s *linespeed*	Specifies bit rate in bits per seconds.
-v	Verbose mode. Shows more information.
-t *mode*	Specifies, in numbers 1 to 4, which test to perform.
device	Specifies the device to run loopback test on.
	Here is a description on what the different test modes do:
1	Runs an internal loopback test.
2	Runs an external loopback test with internal transmit and receive clock sources.
3	Runs an external loopback test with external transmit and receive clock sources.
4	Runs a test using predefined parameters. Uses the `syncinit` command.

File Name:	`syncloop`	**Directory:**	/usr/sbin/	**Type:**	External
Note:	Run this command on a port that isn't in use at the test moment.				
syncloop -t 1 -s 56000 -c 5000 zsh0	Performs an internal loopback test on the first CPU port, using 5000 packets with 56K bitrate.				

syncstat

UNIX Shell: All primary shells (csh, ksh, sh)

Function	Shows driver statistics from a synchronous serial link.
Syntax	syncstat [-c] *device { interval }*

-c	Clears the accumulative statistics for the device.
device	Specifies the name of a serial device. No device directory is needed. See example.
interval	Shows the difference on the statistics between the interval of specified seconds.

File Name:	`syncstat`	**Directory:**	/usr/sbin/	**Type:**	External
syncstat -c zsh0	Runs syncstat on zsh0 with cleared stats.				

sysdef

UNIX Shell: All primary shells (csh, ksh, sh)

Function	Shows definition on all devices, modules, etc. on the computer.
Syntax	sysdef [options...]

-n *namelist*	Specifies a name list other than `/dev/kmem`, which is the default.
-h	Shows, in hexadecimal, the host identifier.
-d	Shows the configuration of system peripheral, formatted as a device tree.
-D	Displays the name of the device driver used to manage the peripheral.

File Name:	`sysdef`	**Directory:**	/usr/sbin/	**Type:**	External
Tip:	Pipe through more or redirect to a file because there is a lot of information.				
sysdef -D	Shows the name of the device driver used to manage the peripheral.				

sysidconfig

UNIX Shell: All primary shells (csh, ksh, sh)

Function	Is used to manage definition and execution of system configuration applications.
Syntax	sysidconfig [options...]

-a *application*	Specifies the application name to add to the list of defined applications.
-b *basedir*	Specifies the root directory when listing, deleting, adding, or running applications.
-l	Shows a list of applications currently defined in the order in which they will be executed.
-r *application*	Removes the application specified from the list of defined applications.
-v	Verbose mode. Shows more information.

continued

File Name:	sysidconfig	**Directory:**	/usr/sbin/	**Type:**	External
Note:	Sysidconfig program's activity can be found in /var/log/sysidconfig.log.				

sysidtool

UNIX Shell: All primary shells (csh, ksh, sh)

Function	A bundle of five programs that manages configuration and reconfiguration of a system.
Syntax	*Program Name*

	The following programs are used by *sysidtool*:
sysidnet	Sets the system's default locale, console type, hostname, and IP address.
sysidnis	Sets naming service, NIS, NIS+, DNS, or None as well as domain, hostname, and IP address.
sysidsys	Sets subnet mask, time zone, and date and time for the system.
sysidroot	Sets a new root password.
sysidpm	Is used for power management.

File Name:	sysidtool	**Directory:**	/usr/sbin/	**Type:**	External
Note:	The sysidtool programs run automatically at system installation.				

sys-suspend

UNIX Shell: All primary shells (csh, ksh, sh)

Function	Suspends, shuts down, or powers off the computer.
Syntax	sys-suspend [options...]

-f	Forces suspend and all processes to stop. Use with care.
-n	Disables the selection pop-up dialog at the start time.
-x	Disables the execution of lockscreen at resume time (like xlock).
-h	Changes the default from suspend to shut down.
-d displayname	Connects to the X server specified.

File Name:	sys-suspend	**Directory:**	/usr/openwin/bin/	**Type:**	External
Note:	/etc/default/sys-suspend is a file for setting a default value for the PERMS variable.				

sys-suspend -fh	Forces the system to shut down.

sys-unconfig

UNIX Shell: All primary shells (csh, ksh, sh)

Function	Resets the system configuration to the standard state.
Syntax	sys-unconfig

File Name:	sys-unconfig	**Directory:**	/usr/sbin/	**Type:**	External
Note:	Sys-unconfig isn't available on diskless clients.				

tabs

UNIX Shell: All primary shells (csh, ksh, sh)

Function	Clears old settings and sets new Tabs and margins on remote terminals.
Syntax	tabs [options...]

-T *type*	Specifies terminal type. Uses the values in environment var TERM if not specified.
+m*{ n }*	Moves all Tabs to the right by the number of columns specified by *n*+1.
	There are four types of Tab definitions: (canned, repetitive, arbitrary, and file)
Canned definitions	The following options are the pre-configured built-in Tabs called canned.
-a	Sets Tabs to Assembler, IBM S/370, first format.
-a2	Sets Tabs to Assembler, IBM S/370, second format.
-c	Sets Tabs to COBOL, normal format.
-c2	Sets Tabs to COBOL compact format.
-c3	Sets tabs to COBOL compact format with more Tabs than -c2 (recommended).
-f	Sets Tabs to FORTRAN format.
-p	Sets Tabs to PL/I format.
-s	Sets Tabs to SNOBOL format.
-u	Sets Tabs to UNIVAC 1100 Assembler format.

continued

Repetitive definition -n **Arbitrary definition** -n **File definition** *-file*	Sets Tabs at every specified number of columns. 1+n, 1+2n, 1+3n, and so on, where n is a single decimal number. Sets Tabs every specified value separated with a comma. n1, n2, n3, and so on where n is positive decimal numbers in ascending order. Sets the Tabs from a format specification in the specified file.			
File Name: tabs	**Directory:**	/usr/bin/	**Type:**	External

tapes

UNIX Shell: All primary shells (csh, ksh, sh)

Function	Creates /dev/rmt entries for tape drives connected to the system.
Syntax	tapes [-r]

-r *rootdir*	Specifies the root directory for /dev/rmt (default is /).			
File Name: tapes	**Directory:**	/usr/sbin/	**Type:**	External
Tip:	Use `drvconfig` before `tapes`.			
tapes -r /ucgdevices	Creates entries in /ucgdevices/dev/rmt.			

tcopy

UNIX Shell: All primary shells (csh, ksh, sh)

Function	Copies or scans a magnetic tape.
Syntax	tcopy *source { destination }*

source *destination*	Specifies tape drive to use for input. Specifies where to copy the tape; if not given, then only a scan is performed.			
File Name: tcopy	**Directory:**	/usr/bin/	**Type:**	External
tcopy /dev/rmt/0 /dev/rmt/1	Copies the tape in device 0 to device 1.			
tcopy /dev/rmt/0	Scans the tape in device 0 and displays sizes and files.			

timex

UNIX Shell: All primary shells (csh, ksh, sh)

Function	Measures how much time it takes to run a command. It shows elapsed, user, and system time in seconds.
Syntax	timex [options...] *command*

-o -p f h k m r t -s *command*	Shows how many blocks are read or written and how many characters are sent by the command. Shows process accounting records for the command. Shows fork and exec flags plus system exit status columns. Shows parts of total available CPU time inspired by the process. Shows the total kcore minutes instead of memory size. Shows mean core size (is default). Shows the CPU factor. Shows split system and user CPU times. Reports total system action that occurred while command executed. Specifies the command to be executed.			
File Name: timex	**Directory:**	/usr/bin/	**Type:**	External
Note:	You must install the process accounting software.			
timex -o sleep 5	Shows total number of blocks read, written, and transferred.			
timex -s who	Shows total system activity for the command who.			

tip

UNIX Shell: All primary shells (csh, ksh, sh)

Function	Connects to a remote host with full-duplex terminal connection creating an interactive session on a local terminal.
Syntax	tip [options...] *ACTION*

-v *-speedentry*	Shows the execution of the commands from the file `.tiprc` as they are done. Specifies a baud rate to use for the connection other than the default.

continued

ACTION	**Select one of the following actions:**
hostname	Specifies the hostname or IP address of the server to connect to.
phonenumber	Connects to a remote host using a phone number.
device	Connects to a remote host using a device.
	The following are internal commands that are executed inside the program:
~.	Drops the connection from the remote system and exits.
~c *{ directory }*	Specifies a name to a directory.
~!	Moves you to an interactive shell on the local system.
~>	Copies file from a local system to remote system.
~<	Copies file from a remote system to a local system.
~p from [to]	Sends file to a hostname or an IP address on a remote system.
~t from [to]	Takes file from a hostname or IP address on a remote system.
~|	Takes output from a remote command to use as input to a local command.
~C	Connects a program to a remote system.
~$	Takes output from a local command to a host or an IP address on a remote system.
~#	Sends a BREAK to the remote system.
~s	Sets a variable for normal operations.
~^Z	Stops tip when it runs under a shell that supports job control, such as C shell.
~^Y	Stops tip only on your own system; the remote system continues.
~?	Shows a summary of tilde escape characters on the screen.
File Name: `tip`	**Directory:** /usr/bin/ **Type:** External
tip 192.168.1.250	Connects to 192.168.1.250.

tnfdump

UNIX Shell: All primary shells (csh, ksh, sh)

Function	Converts TNF files to ASCII to make it suitable to analyze.
Syntax	tnfdump [-r] *{ TNFfiles... }*

-r	Converts TNF files to ASCII format.
TNFfiles...	Specifies the binary files to convert to ASCII.
File Name: `tnfdump`	**Directory:** /usr/bin/ **Type:** External
tnfdump /tmp/trace-2130	Converts the binary file /tmp/trace-2130 to ASCII

tnfxtract

UNIX Shell: All primary shells (csh, ksh, sh)

Function	Collects and extracts kernel trace information into a trace file.
Syntax	tnfxtract [options...] *{ tnf-file }*

	You must use the options -d and -n together.
-d *dumpfile*	Specifies the dumpfile as the system memory image.
-n *namelist*	Specifies the name list that contains symbol table information for the provided dump file.
tnf-file	Specifies the output file.
File Name: `tnfxtract`	**Directory:** /usr/bin/ **Type:** External
Note:	If neither the -d nor -n option is specified, trace output is extracted from the running kernel.
tnfxtract tracefile.out	Shows information from the tracefile.out file.

truss

UNIX Shell: All primary shells (csh, ksh, sh)

Function	Is used to manage tracing of specific system calls and signals.
Syntax	truss [options...] *{ command }*

-f	Shows information about child processes created by `fork` or `vfork`.
-c	Shows a count on the traces made instead of all the information.
-a	Adds the argument strings that are used in each `exec` system call.
-e	Adds the environment strings that are used in each `exec` system call.
-i	Doesn't show interruptible sleeping system calls until they are complete.
-l	Shows the lightweight process ID in each output line.
-d	Shows the elapsed time from the start for each trace line in output.

continued

-D	Shows the elapsed time from the previous trace line in output.
-t *syscall*	Specifies what system calls to trace (default is -tall).
-T *syscall*	Specifies system calls to halt the process (default is -T!all).
-v *syscall*	Shows verbose information about the specified system calls (default is -v!all).
-x *syscall*	Shows the arguments to the specified system calls in raw (hexadecimal) form.
-s *signal*	Specifies what system signals to trace (default is -sall).
-S *signal*	Specifies system calls to halt the process (default is -S!all).
-m *fault*	Specifies what server faults to trace (default is -mall and -m!fltpage).
-M *fault*	Specifies server faults to stop the process (default is -M!all).
-r *filedescriptor*	Shows the full I/O buffer contents for each `read` (default is -r!all).
-w *filedescriptor*	Shows the full I/O buffer contents for each `write` (default is -w!all).
-u *library:function*	Shows information about the user-level function calls specified.
-U *library:function*	Specifies user-level function calls to halt the process.
-o *outfile*	Specifies the file in which to save the output (default is STDERR).
-p *processIDs*	When used instead of a command, it traces the specified, existing processes.
[!]	When used before an option operand, it reverses the function; for example, include becomes exclude.
command	Specifies the command to execute and trace.

File Name:	`truss`	**Directory:**	/usr/bin/	**Type:**	External

Note: Not all possible structures passed in all possible system calls are displayed with the -v option.

truss find . -print >find.out	Saves the trace of the find command to the file find.out

ttyadm

UNIX Shell: All primary shells (csh, ksh, sh)

Function	Manages port monitor specific data.
Syntax	ttyadm [options...] options...

-b	Specifies the port is to be bi-directional.
-c	Specifies the port is to start a service when a connection is received.
-h	Specifies the port will not hang up.
-I	Starts the specified service only once.
-r *count*	Specifies the port waits *count* lines before it shows the prompt.
-i *msg*	Specifies a message to use if the port is unavailable.
-m *modules*	Specifies a list of STREAMS modules to push before start of the service.
-p *prompt*	Sets a new prompt message.
-t *timeout*	Shuts down the port if no data is received in *timeout* seconds.
-S *action*	Sets the software carrier value: yes = on or no = off.
-T *termtype*	Specifies the terminal type to use.
-d *device*	Specifies the path to a tty device file. Required if -V isn't used.
-l *ttylabel*	Specifies the ttylabel to use with the tty. Required if -V isn't used.
-s *service*	Specifies the service to use with the tty. Required if -V isn't used.
-V	Shows version information.

File Name:	`ttyadm`	**Directory:**	/usr/sbin/	**Type:**	External

ttymon

UNIX Shell: All primary shells (csh, ksh, sh)

Function	Is used to manage port settings for terminal ports.
Syntax	ttymon -g [options...]

-g	Sets baud rate and terminal settings on a port. This is a required option.
-d *devicedevice*	Shows the name of the port to which ttymon is to attach.
-h	Hangs up the line if not specified by setting the speed to zero.
-l *ttylabel*	Specifies the speed in baud ttymon will run with (default is 9600 baud).
-m *modules*	Shows all modules on the port and then pushes modules in the order specified.
-p *prompt*	Permits a user to specify a prompt string (default prompt is Login:).
-t *timeout*	Enters timeout seconds after the prompt is sent.
-T *termtype*	Sets the TERM environment variable to termtype.

File Name:	`ttymon`	**Directory:**	/usr/lib/saf/	**Type:**	External

Tunefs

UNIX Shell: All primary shells (csh, ksh, sh)

Function	Changes the dynamic parameters of an unmounted file system that exists in `/etc/vfstab`.
Syntax	tunefs [options...] *filesystem*

-a *maxcontig*	Sets the max number of contiguous blocks to write before forcing a rotational delay.
-d *rotdelay*	Specifies time in milliseconds for a transfer completion/initiation on the same disk.
-e *maxbpg*	Sets the maximum number of blocks a file can use in a cyl group before using other cylinders.
-m *minfree*	Sets the percent of space that is unavailable to normal users.
-o	Specifies the file system's optimization strategy.
{ space }	Optimizes the file system to conserve space.
{ time }	Optimizes the file system to minimize access time.
filesystem	Specifies the unmounted file system to modify.

File Name:	`tunefs`	**Directory:**	/usr/sbin/	**Type:**	External

turnacct

UNIX Shell: Bourne shell (sh)

Function	Manages process accounting.
Syntax	turnacct option

	One of the following options is required:
on	Enables process accounting.
off	Disables process accounting.
switch	Changes the `/var/adm/pacct` file to the next free name in /var/adm/pacct*incr*. (incr is a number starting with 1 that increases for each pacct file.)

File Name:	`turnacct`	**Directory:**	/usr/lib/acct/	**Type:**	Script
Note:	Is useful if you want to keep track on the usage of the resources.				

ucblinks

UNIX Shell: All primary shells (csh, ksh, sh)

Function	Is used to add compatibility for SunOS 4.x devices to a SunOS 5.x system. Adds /dev entries.
Syntax	ucblinks [options...]

-e *rulebase*	Specifies a nawk rule-base file containing nawk pattern-action statements. (The default nawk rule-base is found in /usr/ucblib/ucblinks.awk.)
-r *rootdir*	Specifies the directory in which to find the dev and devices files. Default is root, /.

File Name:	`ucblinks`	**Directory:**	/usr/ucb	**Type:**	External
Note:	This is a SunOS/BSD Compatibility Package Command.				

ucblinks -e /altroot	Sets an alternative rootdir for /dev and /devices.

ufsdump

UNIX Shell: All primary shells (csh, ksh, sh)

Function	Creates a backup of all specified files or file systems to a hard drive, floppy disk, or tape.
Syntax	ufsdump [options...] *{ arguments... } files...*

	All options must be written as a one-letter string without arguments.
NR	Specifies the backup level to perform. You may choose any level you wish (range is 0-9).
0	Backs up the entire file system to the backup media.
1-9	Backs up changes that occurred since a lower, or equal number, backup was performed. (Same number means incremental backup.)
a *archivefile*	Creates the specified file on the media with a table of contents of all the files.
b *factor*	Sets the blocking factor in 512-byte blocks when writing to a tape.
c	Specifies the blocking factor and tape density to be the default for cartridges.
d *bpi*	Specifies the tape density.
D	Specifies the backup is to be made to a floppy disk.
f *dumpfile*	Specifies a file to save the backup to instead of /dev/rmt/0. A — saves on STDOUT.
l	Does a 2-minute wait at the end of tape to give an autoloader a chance to switch tapes.
n	Sends a message to all users in the group that a backup is being made.
o	Takes the tape drive offline when the backup is complete.

continued

s *size*	Specifies the backup volume in feet for tapes and in 1024-byte blocks for floppy disks.
S	Shows you the space that would be used without doing the actual backup.
t *tracks*	Specifies the number of tracks on a cartridge tape.
u	Updates the dump records in /etc/dumpdates for the created backup.
v	Verifies the backup by comparing the result with the original files.
w	Warns you about file system that has not been backed up within a day.
W	Is similar to w but with more information and it also highlights the file systems.
arguments...	Specifies argument to the option(s), which must be in the same order as the option(s).
files...	Specifies the files or the file system to create a backup from.
Example:	ufsdump 0fv /dev/rnt/1 /dev/rdsk/c0t3d0s0 where /dev/rnt/1 is the argument to f.

File Name:	`ufsdump`	**Directory:**	/usr/sbin/	**Type:**	External

ufsdump 0cfu /dev/rmt/0 /dev/rdsk/c0t3d0s0	Creates a full dump of a root file system on c0t3d0, on a 150-MB cartridge tape unit.
ufsdump 5fuv /dev/rmt/1 /dev/rdsk/c0t3d0s6	Verifies an incremental dump at level 5 of the usr partition of c0t3d0, on a 1/2-inch reel tape.

ufsrestore

UNIX Shell: All primary shells (csh, ksh, sh)

Function	Restores backup files created with `ufsdump` from backup media. Restore is placed in current directory.
Syntax	ufsrestore option [options...] *{ arguments... } { files... }*

	You must specify one, and only one, of the following functions:
i	Starts the interactive interface and allows you to select files from the backup.
r	Restores all backup files from the media into the current directory.
R	Resumes restoring from a checkpoint when interrupted while doing a full restore.
t	Lists all files in the table of contents, useful for determining whether the file is on the media.
x	Restores the specified files from the backup media. Default is the root directory.
	The following function modifiers must be written as a string with no arguments:
a *archivefile*	Specifies the table of contents file, not the backup media. Use with t, i, or x.
b *factor*	Specifies the blocking factor to use when reading tapes.
c	Takes a media in 4.1bsd and converts it to the new ufs file system format.
d	Shows debug information.
f *dumpfile*	Restores from the specified file instead of from /dev/rmt/0.
h	Restores or lists only the actual directory, not the complete subtrees, from the file.
m	Uses the inode numbers when doing a restore instead of the complete filenames.
s *n*	Starts a restore from the file number specified in a media or dumpfile.
v	Verbose mode. Displays the inode number, name, and file type of each restored file.
y	Doesn't show any questions when a tape error occurs; just skips the bad block(s).
arguments...	Specifies argument to the option(s), which must be in the same order as the option(s).
Example:	`ufsrestore fv /dev/rmt/1` where `/dev/rmt/1` is the argument to f.
	The following are interactive i mode commands. Default is current directory.
add *file*	Adds the specified file or directory to the list of files to restore.
cd *directory*	Takes you to the specified directory inside the media or file system.
delete *file*	Erases the file or directory from the list of files to restore.
extract	Executes the command on the files in the list.
help	Shows help information about the interactive commands.
ls *directory*	Lists all files in the specified or current directory.
pwd	Tells you where you are in the file system by showing you the full pathname.
quit	Exits the interactive mode without executing anything.
setmodes	Sets the owner/mode for the period ".". Type y to set the mode, type n to leave it unchanged.
verbose	Toggles the `v` function on or off.
what	Shows you the backup header from the media.
files...	Specifies the name of the files or directories to restore.

File Name:	`ufsrestore`	**Directory:**	/usr/sbin/	**Type:**	External

ufsrestore rfv /dev/rmt/1	Restores the files from `/dev/rmt/1` to the current directory.

Uil

UNIX Shell: All primary shells (csh, ksh, sh)

Function	Starts the UIL compiler. A language to describe the initial state of a user interface for a Motif application.
Syntax	uil [options…] *file*

-I*pathname*	Searches for not found include files. Searches in the specified pathname (no space).
-m	Shows the machine code. A description of records added to the UID.
-o *file*	Specifies filename of the UID.
-s	Configures the locale before compiling any files.
-v *file*	Specifies a file to make a list from.
-w	Hides all messages and warnings.
-wmd *file*	Sets a bin widget meta-language description file to use instead of a WML description.
File	Specifies the file to compile.

File Name:	`uil`	**Directory:**	/usr/dt/bin/	**Type:**	External
Warning:	In the –I option, you should not use a space before you type the pathname.				

Umountall

UNIX Shell: Bourne shell (sh)

Function	Unmounts all mounted filesystems except root, /proc, /var, and /usr.
Syntax	umountall [options…]

-k	Sends the SIGKILL signal to the processes using the file system.
-s	Specifies not to perform the `umount` operation in parallel.
-h *host*	Unmounts all file systems in `/etc/mnttab` that are remote mounted from the specified host.
	Specify only one of the following two options:
-l	Umounts local file systems only.
-r	Umounts remote file systems only.
-F *FSType*	Specifies the file system type to unmount.

File Name:	`umountall`	**Directory:**	/usr/sbin/	**Type:**	Script
Warning:	The effect of the –k option isn't guaranteed to work on live file systems.				

Unget, sccs-unget

UNIX Shell: All primary shells (csh, ksh, sh)

Function	Undoes all changes in a SCCS history file that was made by the command `get -e`.
Syntax	unget [options…] *files…*

-n	Doesn't remove the retrieved version of the file.
-s	Doesn't show the SCCS delta ID of the file.
-rsid	Specifies which pending delta to undo when you work with multiple versions of a file.
files…	Specifies which s.file to undo.

File Name:	`unget`	**Directory:**	/usr/ccs/bin/	**Type:**	External
Note:	If a directory name is used in place of the s.filename, unget applies to all s.files in that directory.				

Unifdef

UNIX Shell: All primary shells (csh, ksh, sh)

Function	Identifies and removes lines containing an ifdef mark from a C program source, leaving the rest of the file untouched.
Syntax	unifdef [options…] *{ filename }*

-c	Retains lines that would be removed or blanked and vice versa.
-l	Puts blank lines in the places of the removed lines.
-t	Doesn't search for comment and single or double quotes, only for plain text.
-D*name*	Searches for lines containing the defined symbol specified.
-U*name*	Searches for lines containing the undefined symbol specified.
-iD*name*	Searches and shows only the lines containing the defined symbol specified.
IU*name*	Searches and shows only the lines containing the undefined symbol specified.
Filename	Specifies the file to work upon. If no file is specified, STDIN is used.

File Name:	`unifdef`	**Directory:**	/usr/ccs/bin/	**Type:**	External

units

units	UNIX Shell:	All primary shells (csh, ksh, sh)
Function	Tells you interactively how to convert a unit quantity to another type, for example, from inches to centimeters.	
Syntax	units	

Note: The file /usr/share/lib/unittab shows you a complete list of unit types.

File Name:	units	**Directory:**	/usr/bin/	**Type:**	External

unix2dos

UNIX Shell: All primary shells (csh, ksh, sh)

Function	Converts the ISO standard characters in a file to match with the DOS format.
Syntax	unix2dos [options…] *inputfile outputfile*

-ascii	Adds to a SunOS file the end-of-file and carriage returns that are used by DOS.
-iso	Converts the ISO standard characters to the corresponding DOS (is default).
-7	Creates a 7-bit DOS character file from an 8-bit SunOS character file.
inputfile	Specifies the name of a UNIX inputfile.
outputfile	Specifies the name of the converted DOS file.

File Name:	unix2dos	**Directory:**	/usr/bin/	**Type:**	External

Tip: You can use it from a DOS client as well, if the filename works in a DOS environment.

Unix2dos unixfile dosfile	Converts the input ISO text file to a DOS text file.

unlink

UNIX Shell: All primary shells (csh, ksh, sh)

Function	Unlinks files and directories. Does not use any error checking.
Syntax	unlink *file*

file	Specifies the filename or directory to be unlinked.

File Name:	unlink	**Directory:**	/usr/sbin/	**Type:**	External

Tip: Can be used to remove problem files and directories that can't be removed with `rm` and `rmdir`.

unpack

UNIX Shell: All primary shells (csh, ksh, sh)

Function	Decompresses files created by pack. Removes the .z suffix when done.
Syntax	unpack *files…*

files…	Specifies one or more files to be unpacked.

File Name:	unpack	**Directory:**	/usr/bin/	**Type:**	External

unpack ucg.z	Decompresses the file ucg.z into ucg.

nshare

UNIX Shell: All primary shells (csh, ksh, sh)

Function	Makes the shared local resource unavailable for mounting from remote systems.
Syntax	unshare [options…] *{ ACTION }*

-F *FSType*	Specifies the file system type.
-o *options*	Specifies options that are specific to the file system specified with –F.
ACTION	**You must select only one of the following actions:**
path	Specifies the pathname to the local resource you want to unshare.
resource	Specifies the name of the local resource you want to unshare.

File Name:	nshared	**Directory:**	/usr/sbin/	**Type:**	External

Tip: Use unshareall if you want to unshare all distributed file systems on the system.

unshare /export/home/ucg	Unshares the directory /export/home/ucg.

unshareall

UNIX Shell: Bourne shell (sh)

Function	Unassigns the shared resources on the specified File System Types.
Syntax	unshareall [-F *FSTypes…*]

-F *FSTypes…*	Unassigns the specified file system type. (If FSType is omitted, it defaults to the first entry in /etc/dfs/fstypes.)

File Name:	unshareall	**Directory:**	/usr/sbin/	**Type:**	Script

Note: Without the –F option, it unassigns all the resources specified in the `/etc/dfs/sharetab` file.

unzip

unzip	UNIX Shell:	All primary shells (csh, ksh, sh)

Function	Is used to uncompress and show the compressed files from a zip archive. It also shows or tests compressed files.
Syntax	unzip [options…] *{ files… }*

-Z	Causes the following options to be interpreted as `zipinfo` options.
-A	Shows extended help for the DLL's programming interface on OS/2 and UNIX.
-c	Uncompresses files and shows them on STDOUT like they were stored.
-f	Updates the files on a disk and uncompresses the newest version of the files on the disk.
-l	Shows archive files in a short form; lists sizes, modification dates, and print times.
-p	Shows only the file data on STDOUT and sends uncompressed files to a pipe.
-t	Tests archive files to check whether the files have changed.
-T	Marks all archives with the same timestamp as the newest file.
-u	Works like the –f option but also creates new files if they don't exist.
-v	Verbose mode. Shows more information.
-z	Shows only the archive comment.
-a	Specifies that text files will be identified as in text format.
-b	Specifies that all files will be treated as binary on a non-VMS, equal to ---a.
-b	Alters all files to a 512-byte record format on a VMS.
-bb	Uncompresses all files in a 512-byte record format.
-B	Saves a backup copy with a tilde (~) appendix of all overwritten files.
-C	Disregards whether letters in filenames are uppercase or lowercase.
-j	Puts all files in specified archive without keeping the original archive structure.
-L	Alters filenames made on uppercase-only systems to lowercase filenames.
-M	Pipes all output through an internal pager.
-n	Specifies that newer files are to overwrite existing files.
-N	Uncompresses file comments as Amiga file notes.
-o	Overwrites files without any prompt questions.
-x *files…*	Excludes the specified files in the list from uncompressing.
-d *directory*	Specifies a directory for the uncompressed files.
-q	Quiet mode; suppresses most error messages.
files…	Specifies the path and filename to the zip file to uncompress. (Wildcards in the filename are accepted but not in the path.)

File Name:	`unzip`	**Directory:**	/usr/sbin/	**Type:**	External
Note:	Multi-part archives are not yet supported.				

Unzip zipfile.zip	Unzips the file zipfile.zip.
unzip –n zipfile.zip	Unzips the zipfile.zip but doesn't overwrite files.

useradd

useradd	UNIX Shell:	All primary shells (csh, ksh, sh)

Function	Creates an account for a new user with permissions and memberships set.
Syntax	useradd [options…] *loginname*

-c *comment*	Specifies a text for the user. Usually the full name of the user.
-d *directory*	Specifies the new user's home directory.
-G *group*	Defines the secondary group membership for the user.
-k *directory*	Specifies a directory that contains reconfigured information such as `.profile`.
-m	Creates the home directory for the new user if it doesn't exist.
-s *shell*	Specifies a full pathname of the program to use as the default shell for the user.
-u *useID*	Specifies the ID for the new user.
-o	Allows duplicates of the user's ID.
-D	Shows the current default values for the user.
	The following options, when used with the –D option, will set the default:
-b *directory*	Specifies the default base directory for the system.
-e *expire*	Specifies the date when the login becomes invalid.
-f *inactive*	Specifies the maximum number of days the login can be unused before it becomes invalid.

continued

-g *group*		Defines the primary group membership for the user. Also used as default.			
loginname		Specifies the login name of the new user.			
		The following options are added in Solaris 8:			
-A *authorization*		Specifies one or more authorizations to assign to the user.			
-P *profile*		Specifies one or more execution profiles to assign to the user.			
-R *role*		Specifies one or more execution profiles to assign to the user.			
File Name:	`useradd`	**Directory:**	/usr/bin/	**Type:**	External
Tip:	Add a user and then use `passwd` to give the user a login password.				

userdel

UNIX Shell: All primary shells (csh, ksh, sh)

Function	Erases a user's account from the system.
Syntax	userdel [-r] *user*

-r		Erases the user's home directory.			
user		Specifies the user to erase from the system.			
File Name:	`userdel`	**Directory:**	/usr/sbin/	**Type:**	External
Note:	Only works with local accounts.				

userdel -r ucg	Erases user ucg and the user's associated home directory.
userdel ucg	Erases ucg's user account.

usermod

UNIX Shell: All primary shells (csh, ksh, sh)

Function	Alters a specified user's login account permissions and memberships on the system.
Syntax	usermod [options...] *loginname*

-u *userID*		Specifies the new ID for the user.			
-o		Allows duplicates of the user's ID.			
-g *group*		Defines the new primary group membership for the user.			
-G *group*		Defines the new secondary group membership for the user.			
-d *directory*		Specifies the user's new home directory.			
-m		Moves the user to the new home directory specified with -d.			
-s *shell*		Specifies a full pathname of the new program to use as the default shell for the user.			
-c *comment*		Specifies a new text about the user. Usually the full name of the user.			
-l *loginname*		Specifies the new login name of the user.			
-e *expire*		Specifies the new date when the login becomes invalid.			
-f *inactive*		Specifies the maximum nr of days the login can be unused before it becomes invalid.			
loginname		Specifies the loginname of the account to alter.			
		The following options are added in Solaris 8:			
-A *authorization*		Specifies one or more authorizations to assign to the user.			
-P *profile*		Specifies one or more execution profiles to assign to the user.			
-R *role*		Specifies one or more execution profiles to assign to the user.			
File Name:	`usermod`	**Directory:**	/usr/sbin/	**Type:**	External

usermod -u 855 anders	Sets the new userID for user anders.
usermod -d /anders -m anders	Sets the new home directory and moves anders there.

utmp2wtmp

UNIX Shell: All primary shells (csh, ksh, sh)

Function	Is used by *runacct* to create an entry in the file /var/adm/wtmp for every user logged on to the system.
Syntax	utmp2wtmp

File Name:	`utmp2wtmp`	**Directory:**	/usr/lib/acct/	**Type:**	External

utmpd

utmpd	UNIX Shell:	All primary shells (csh, ksh, sh)

Function	Monitors `/var/adm/utmp` and `/var/adm/utmpx` files and fixes them if they are not correct.
Syntax	utmpd [-debug]

-debug		Writes debugging information to STDOUT.			
File Name:	`utmpd`	**Directory:**	/usr/lib/	**Type:**	External

uucheck

uucheck	UNIX Shell:	All primary shells (csh, ksh, sh)

Function	Is used to monitor uucp directories and permissions files.
Syntax	uucheck [options...]

-v		Verbose mode. Shows more information.			
-x *debuglevel*		Enables debugging with the levels 0 to 9. Highest number shows most information.			
File Name:	`uucheck`	**Directory:**	/usr/lib/uucp	**Type:**	External

uucico

uucico	UNIX Shell:	All primary shells (csh, ksh, sh)

Function	Transfers files used by the `uucp` command to a specific location.
Syntax	uucico [options...]

-f		Forces the execution even if the maximum number of uucicos is reached.			
-c *type*		Uses only the entries in type field that match the user-specified type.			
-d *spooldirectory*		Specifies the directory containing the files to transfer.			
-i *interface*		Specifies the interface to use: TLI or TLIS.			
-r *rolenumber*		Specifies the role number: 1 for master, 0 for slave.			
-s *systemname*		Specifies the system to transfer files to.			
-x *debuglevel*		Shows debug information with level 0 to 9. Higher level shows more information.			
File Name:	`uucico`	**Directory:**	/usr/lib/uucp/	**Type:**	External

uucleanup

uucleanup	UNIX Shell:	All primary shells (csh, ksh, sh)

Function	Searches the spool directories and cleans them up.
Syntax	uucleanup [options...]

-C *time*		Removes all C. files that are older than the specified time in days.			
-D *time*		Removes all D. files that are older than the specified time in days.			
-m *string*		Specifies a text sting to include in the messages.			
-o *time*		Deletes all other files that are older than the specified time in days (default is 2).			
-s *system*		Specifies to only execute on the system spool directory.			
-W *time*		Sends a reminder about old C. files to requester (default is 1 day).			
-x *debuglevel*		Shows debugging information with level 0 to 9. Higher level shows more information.			
-X *time*		Removes all X. files that are older than the specified time in days (default is 2).			
File Name:	`uucleanup`	**Directory:**	/usr/lib/uucp	**Type:**	External

uucleanup -x0	Executes with the lowest debug output.
uucleanup -D4	Removes D. files older than 4 days.

uucp

uucp	UNIX Shell:	All primary shells (csh, ksh, sh)

Function	Copies files from one place to another inside UNIX (UNIX to UNIX copy).
Syntax	uucp [options...] *sourcefile destinationfile*

-c	Specifies not to make a copy to the spool directory before the transfer of a file.
-C	Specifies to make a copy to the spool directory before the transfer of a file.
-d	Creates all directories that the file copy needs.
-f	Specifies not to create intermediate directories for the file copy.
-g*grade*	Defines a service grade, single letter, number, or a string of alphanumeric characters.

continued

-j		Shows the uucp job identification string on STDOUT.			
-m		Reports back to the user that sent the files by mail when the copy is complete.			
-n*user*		Reports to the remote system user that a file was sent.			
-r		Puts the file in queue without doing the transfer.			
-s*file*		Ignored; for compatibility only.			
-x*level*		Shows debug information with a level from 0 to 9. Higher level shows more information.			
sourcefile		Specifies the files that you want to copy, uses the format: system-name!pathname.			
destinationfile		Specifies the destination of the copy; uses the format: system-name!pathname.			
File Name:	`uucp`	**Directory:**	/usr/bin/	**Type:**	External
Note:	All files received by uucp will be owned by uucp.				

uudemon.admin

UNIX Shell: Bourne shell (sh)

Function	Sends uucp status information to an administrator.				
Syntax	uudemon.admin				
File Name:	`uudemon.admin`	**Directory:**	/usr/lib/uucp/	**Type:**	Script

uudemon.hour

UNIX Shell: Bourne shell (sh)

Function	Starts the commands `uusched` and `uuxqt` in the background.				
Syntax	uudemon.hour				
File Name:	`uudemon.hour`	**Directory:**	/usr/lib/uucp/	**Type:**	Script

uudemon.poll

UNIX Shell: All primary shells (csh, ksh, sh)

Function	Polls remote systems by a schedule specified in `/etc/uucp/Poll`				
Syntax	uudemon.poll				
File Name:	`uudemon.poll`	**Directory:**	/usr/lib/uucp/	**Type:**	External

uuglist

UNIX Shell: All primary shells (csh, ksh, sh)

Function	Shows you a list of available service grades on the system.				
Syntax	uuglist [-u]				
-u		Shows a list of the service grades that is available to the current user.			
File Name:	`uuglist`	**Directory:**	/usr/bin/	**Type:**	External
Note:	The file /etc/uucp/Grades contains the list of service grades.				

uulog

UNIX Shell: Bourne shell (sh)

Function	Shows information from the transaction logs of `uucp` or `uuxqt`.				
Syntax	uulog [options...] *system*				
-s *system*		Shows information about file transfers involving the specified system.			
-f *systems*		Shows the updates to the log information as it is created. Use Ctrl+C to exit.			
-x		Shows information from the file /var/uucp/.Log/uuxqt on the specified system.			
-*number*		Shows this many lines from the end of the log file.			
system		Specifies the host where the log file is.			
File Name:	`uulog`	**Directory:**	/usr/bin/	**Type:**	Script

uuname

UNIX Shell: All primary shells (csh, ksh, sh)

Function	Shows a list of all the systems that are known to the `uucp` command.				
Syntax	uuname [option]				
-c		Shows a list of all hostnames that are known to the command `cu`.			
-l		Shows the name of your local system.			
File Name:	`uuname`	**Directory:**	/usr/bin/	**Type:**	External

uupick

UNIX Shell:	Bourne shell (sh)
Function	Searches for files sent to you from other systems and prompts you for action.
Syntax	uupick [-s *system*]

-s *system*	Search for files in PUBDIR from the specified system only.

File Name:	`uupick`	**Directory:**	/usr/bin/	**Type:**	Script
Note:	PUBDIR is the /var/spool/uucppublic public directory.				

uusched

UNIX Shell:	All primary shells (csh, ksh, sh)
Function	A scheduler for file transport and is normally started by `cron`.
Syntax	uusched [options..]

-u	Passes the –u debug-level option as -x debug level.
-x	Shows debug messages from uusched.

File Name:	`uusched`	**Directory:**	/usr/lib/uucp/	**Type:**	External

uustat

UNIX Shell:	All primary shells (csh, ksh, sh)
Function	Shows information about the `uucp` jobs on a local or remote system.
Syntax	uustat [options...]

	The following options cannot be combined:
-m	Shows information about accessibility status of all machines.
-p	Shows a full report about the status of the process IDs in the lock files.
-q	Shows a list of all the jobs in queue for each machine.
-k *jobid*	Deletes the specified jobs.
-r *jobid*	Updates the specified jobID to the current time to prevent it from being deleted.
	The following option can be used with the -k and the -r options:
-n	Does not show anything on STDOUT but sends information to STDERR.
-a	Shows a list of all jobs in queue.
	When using -a, the following four options can be used:
-s *system*	Shows status information about the `uucp` requests for the specified system.
-j	Shows a list of the total number of jobs on the display.
-u *user*	Shows status information about the `uucp` requests from the specified user.
-S *qric*	Shows the jobs state: q = queued, r = running, i = interrupted, and c = completed jobs.
-t *system*	Shows information about the specified remote system for the past 60 minutes.
	When using -t, the following options can be used:
-c	Shows information about average queue time instead of average transfer rate.
-d *number*	Shows information for the past specified number of minutes.

File Name:	`uustat`	**Directory:**	/usr/bin/	**Type:**	External
Note:	The -t option shows no message when the data needed for the calculations are not being recorded.				

uuto

UNIX Shell:	Bourne shell (sh)
Function	Uses `uucp` to send files to remote systems. Keeps access control, notifies the receiver on completion.
Syntax	uuto [options...] *sourcefile destination*

-m	Reports by mail back to the sender when the copy is complete.
-p	Makes a copy to the spool directory before the file is sent.
sourcefile	Specifies the file to copy to the remote system.
destination	Specifies the destination of the copy in the format system-name!user.

File Name:	`uuto`	**Directory:**	/usr/bin/	**Type:**	Script

Uutry

Uutry	UNIX Shell:	Bourne shell (sh)
Function	Contacts remote systems using `uucico` and stores debugging information in `/tmp/systemname`.	
Syntax	Uutry [options...] *systemname*	

-r	Overrides the retry time that is set in `/var/uucp/.Status/systemname`.
-c *type*	Uses only entries in the type field that match the user-specified type.
-x *debuglevel*	Shows debugging information with a level of 0 to 9. Higher level shows more information.
systemname	Specifies the remote system to contact.
File Name: `Uutry`	**Directory:** /usr/lib/uucp/ **Type:** Script

uux

uux	UNIX Shell:	All primary shells (csh, ksh, sh)
Function	Is used to execute a command on a remote UNIX-based system and still enable the user to work locally.	
Syntax	uux [options...] *commandstring*	

-	Sets the STDIN for `uux` to be the STDIN for the `command string`.
-a*name*	Replaces the initiator user ID with the specified user job identification name.
-b	Returns the received result even if an error occurred.
-c	Specifies to not copy the local file to the spool directory before transfer.
-C	Specifies to copy the local file to the spool directory before transfer.
-g*grade*	Specifies a service grade — a letter, number, or an alphanumeric string.
-j	Show the job ID string on STDOUT.
-n	Doesn't show any messages if an error occurs.
-p	Same as the - option.
-r	Puts the job in queue but doesn't execute.
-s*file*	Ignored; for compatibility only.
-x*level*	Shows debug information, level from 0 to 9. Higher level gives more information.
-z	Notifies the user when executed successfully.
commandstring	Specifies what to do, where to do it, and where to send the result.
File Name: `uux`	**Directory:** /usr/bin/ **Type:** External

uuxqt

uuxqt	UNIX Shell:	All primary shells (csh, ksh, sh)
Function	Executes remote requested jobs created by using the `uux` command.	
Syntax	uuxqt [options...]	

-s *hostname*	Specifies the name of the remote system.
-x *debuglevel*	Shows debugging information with level 0 to 9. Higher level gives more information.
File Name: `uuxqt`	**Directory:** /usr/lib/uucp/ **Type:** External
uuxqt -s192.168.1.1	Executes requests from 192.168.1.1.

vacation

vacation	UNIX Shell:	All primary shells (csh, ksh, sh)
Function	Replies to mail automatically. Useful when you are out of the office.	
Syntax	vacation [options...] *{ user }*	

-I	Clears and reinitializes the log files and deletes previous list of senders. (Option -I must be used alone.)
-j	Doesn't check whether the recipient appears in the To: or the Cc: line.
-a *alias*	Specifies alias to also reply from.
-t*time*	Specifies to repeat the reply to the same sender (default is 1 week).
user	Sends one copy of incoming message to username and one to vacation.
File Name: `vacation`	**Directory:** /usr/bin/ **Type:** External
Note:	Disable by deleting or renaming the .forward file.

val, sccs-val

val, sccs-val	UNIX Shell:	All primary shells (csh, ksh, sh)
Function	Verifies an SCCS file.	
Syntax	val [options...] *files...*	

-s	The silent mode. Suppresses the normal error or warning messages.
-m *name*	Compares name with the sccs-val.1 ID keyword in the file.
-r*SID*	Specifies SID to check whether it is ambiguous, invalid, or absent from file.
-y *type*	Specifies a type to compare with the ID keyword.
-	Reads from STDIN.
files...	Specifies input file.
File Name: `val`	**Directory:** /usr/ccs/bin/ **Type:** External

valyorn

valyorn	UNIX Shell:	All primary shells (csh, ksh, sh)
Function	Validates a response; used with `ckyorn`.	
Syntax	valyorn *value*	

value	Specifies the value to validate; for example, y, n, yes, or no.
File Name: `valyorn`	**Directory:** /usr/sadm/bin/ **Type:** External
Note:	Values other than yes or no are considered a failure.
valyorn y ; echo $?	Shows 0 (success).
valyorn ucg ; echo $?	Shows 1 (failure).

vc

vc	UNIX Shell:	All primary shells (csh, ksh, sh)
Function	Copies lines from STDIN to STDOUT with arguments and control statements. Used for version control.	
Syntax	vc [options...] *{ keyword=value }*	

-a	Replaces keywords that are surrounded by control characters.
-t	Ignores characters until first Tab character if the control statement is found.
-c*char*	Specifies alternative control character to the default.
-s	Disables warning messages, but not errors.
keyword=value	Adds a value to a keyword, if it is used as an argument.
	The following are the control characters that can be used:
:dcl *keywords...*	Declares a keyword. You must declare each keyword.
:asg *keyword=value*	Adds values to keyword.
:if *condition*	Skips lines between if and end if condition is true; see man page for further information.
:end	End statement.
::text	Replaces all keywords by their values in a text, the leading :: are removed.
:on	Enables keyword replacement.
:off	Disables keyword replacement.
:ctl *char*	Specifies the control character.
:msg *message*	Specifies a diagnostic message.
:err *message*	Specifies an error message and sends exit code 1.
File Name: `vc`	**Directory:** /usr/ccs/bin/ **Type:** External

vedit

vedit	UNIX Shell:	All primary shells (csh, ksh, sh)
Function	The `vi` editor for beginners, it sets the report flags to 1 and turns showmode and novice flags on.	
Syntax	vedit [options...] *files...*	

	Please see the `vi` command for options and examples.
File Name: `vedit`	**Directory:** /usr/bin/ **Type:** External

vgrind

vgrind	UNIX Shell:	C shell (csh)
Function	Formats program source using `troff` to make it easier to read.	
Syntax	vgrind [options...] *file*	

-2	Creates two-column output.
-f	Forces filter mode.
-n	Doesn't make keywords boldface.
-t	Sends the formatted text to STDOUT.
-w	Replaces Tab characters with four columns instead of eight columns.
-W	Forces the output to wide printer instead of to a narrow printer.
-x	Outputs the index file in a "pretty" format.
-d *defsfile*	Specifies an alternative language definition file.
-h *header*	Specifies a header to appear on every output page.
-l*language*	Specifies the language to use. See below.
-lsh	Bourne shell
-lc	C
-lc++	C++
-lcsh	C shell
-lml	emacs MLisp
-lf	FORTRAN
-lI	Icon
-i	ISP
-lLDL	LDL
-lm	Model
-lp	Pascal
-lr	RATFOR
-s*n*	Specifies the point size used on output.
-o*pagelist*	Only prints the pages specified in the comma-separated pagelist.
-P*printer*	Sends output to the specified printer.
-T*outputdevice*	Formats the output for the specified output device.
file	Specifies the source file to be processed.

File Name:	Directory:	Type:
`vgrind`	/usr/bin/	Script

viewres

viewres	UNIX Shell:	All primary shells (csh, ksh, sh)
Function	Shows the tree structure of the widget class hierarchy of the Athena Widget Set.	
Syntax	viewres [options...]	

-top *name*	Shows the name of the highest widget in the hierarchy.
-variable	Shows the widget variable names in nodes instead of class name.
-vertical	Shows the widget tree top to bottom instead of left to right.

File Name:	Directory:	Type:
`viewres`	/usr/openwin/bin/	External

viewres -vertical	Displays tree from top to bottom.

vipw

vipw	UNIX Shell:	All primary shells (csh, ksh, sh)
Function	Edits the password file `/etc/passwd`.	
Syntax	vipw	

File Name:	Directory:	Type:
`vipw`	/usr/ucb/	External

Note:	This is more secure than editing manually because it adds several security features.

volcheck

UNIX Shell: All primary shells (csh, ksh, sh)

Function	Checks whether any new media has been inserted into any removable media device.
Syntax	volcheck [options...] *pathname*

-v	Verbose mode. Shows more information.
-i *secs*	Specifies how often the drive check will be done.
-t *secs*	Specifies in seconds when to do the next check of the named devices.
pathname	Specifies pathname of a media device.

File Name:	`volcheck`	**Directory:**	/usr/bin/	**Type:**	External

volcheck -v /dev/floppy	Checks whether there is any media in the floppy device.
volcheck -i 3 -t 300 /dev/diskette	Performs the check every 30 seconds for 3 seconds.

volcopy

UNIX Shell: All primary shells (csh, ksh, sh)

Function	Makes an image copy of the file system.
Syntax	volcopy [options...] *device*

-F *fstype*	Specifies the file system type to operate on.
-V	Shows the command line but does not execute.
-a	Prompts the user to respond `yes` or `no` before copying file system.
-s	Starts the DEL if it is the wrong verification sequence.
-o *fstypeoptions...*	Specifies file-system type-specific options in a comma-separated list.
device	Specifies the device to operate on.

File Name:	`volcopy`	**Directory:**	/usr/sbin/	**Type:**	External
Note:	This command may not be supported for all file systems.				

Vold

UNIX Shell: All primary shells (csh, ksh, sh)

Function	The volume management daemon that manages CD-ROM and floppy devices.
Syntax	vold [options...]

-n	Updates media labels with unique information. Never writeback.
-t	Copies the NFS trace information to log file.
-v	Verbose mode. Shows more information.
-f *configfile*	Specifies alternative configuration file (default is /etc/vold.conf).
-l *logfile*	Specifies alternative log file (default is /var/adm/vold.log).
-d*rootdir*	Specifies alternative rootdirectory (default is /vol).
-L *debuglevel*	Specifies debug level for the log information. Values are 0 to 99.

File Name:	`vold`	**Directory:**	/usr/sbin/	**Type:**	External

volrmmount

UNIX Shell: All primary shells (csh, ksh, sh)

Function	Used to mount or unmount media. To do this, it uses `rmmount`.
Syntax	volrmmount [option] *{ name }*

-i	Simulates insertion of media.
-e	Simulates ejection of media.
-d	Shows the name of the default device that volrmmount will use.
name	Specifies a device name or device nickname to use with Volume Management.

File Name:	`volrmmount`	**Directory:**	/usr/bin/	**Type:**	External

vsig

UNIX Shell: All primary shells (csh, ksh, sh)

Function	Synchronizes a co-process with its controlling FMLI application. To synchronize, it signals to the FMLI process.
Syntax	vsig

File Name:	`vsig`	**Directory:**	/usr/bin/	**Type:**	External

what

what	UNIX Shell:	All primary shells (csh, ksh, sh)

Function	Gets SCCS version information from a file.
Syntax	what [-s] *files...*

-s	Stops after the first occurrence of the pattern.
files...	Specifies one or more files to get information from.

File Name:	`what`	**Directory:**	/usr/ccs/bin/	**Type:**	External

what /lib/libcrypt.so	Gets version information about the file `/lib/libcrypt.so`.

whence

whence	UNIX Shell:	Korn shell (ksh)

Function	Shows how a command will be interpreted.
Syntax	whence [options...] *names...*

-p	Searches the path even if the command is a function, a reserved word, or an alias.
-v	Verbose mode. Shows more information.
names...	Specifies the command name to show information about.
zsh	
-c	Shows the result in csh-like format.
-w	Shows whether a name is an alias, built-in, command, function, hashed, reserved, or none.
-f	Shows the content of a function.
-a	Searches for all occurrences of name.
-m	Uses the argument as a pattern and shows all matching commands.
-s	Shows the symlink-free pathname if the pathname contains symlinks.

whence ls	Shows `/usr/bin/ls`.
whence -v ftp	Shows `ftp is /usr/bin/ftp`.

whocalls

whocalls	UNIX Shell:	Korn shell (ksh)

Function	Tracks procedure calls.
Syntax	whocalls [-l *wholib*] *funcname executable*

-s	Inspects -symtab for local symbols when showing a stack trace.
-l	Specifies an alternative who.so to use.
funcname	Specifies the function to trace calls to.
executables	Specifies the program that makes the calls.

File Name:	`whocalls`	**Directory:**	/usr/bin/	**Type:**	Script

whodo

whodo	UNIX Shell:	All primary shells (csh, ksh, sh)

Function	Shows who is doing what on the system.
Syntax	whodo [options...] *{ user }*

-h	Doesn't show a header.
-l	Verbose mode. Shows more information.
user	Specifies user to show information about.

File Name:	`whodo`	**Directory:**	/usr/sbin/	**Type:**	External

whodo -l	Shows output in long format.
whodo -l ucg	Shows output for the user ucg in long format.

winsysck

winsysck	UNIX Shell:	All primary shells (csh, ksh, sh)

Function	Checks which window system protocols are available.
Syntax	winsysck [options...] *protocol*

-v	Shows name of the first available protocol.
-a	Continues checking of available protocols even after determining if one is available.
-display *string*	Specifies display string when determining available x11protocols.
-timeout *secs*	Sets timeout for winsysck in seconds.

continued

protocol		Specifies the protocol to use. **Use these as protocol values:**			
x11		Specifies the `x11` protocol.			
news		Specifies the `news` protocol.			
x11news		Specifies the `x11news` protocol.			
sunview		Specifies the `sunview` protocol.			
File Name:	`winsysck`	**Directory:**	/usr/openwin/bin/	**Type:**	External
Note:	Exit status is 0 if protocol is available, 1 if not, and 2 if an error occurred.				
winsysck x11			Checks whether x11 is available.		

wsinfo

UNIX Shell: All primary shells (csh, ksh, sh)

Function	A GUI that shows name, type, host ID, IP address, domain, memory, OS version, and more about the system.				
Syntax	wsinfo				
File Name:	`wsinfo`	**Directory:**	/usr/openwin/bin/	**Type:**	External

wtmpfix

UNIX Shell: All primary shells (csh, ksh, sh)

Function	Inspects specified `wtmp`database files; corrects the time-and-date stamps to make the entries consistent.				
Syntax	wtmpfix *{ files... }*				
files		Specifies the files to check. If no files are given, STDIN is used.			
File Name:	`wtmpfix`	**Directory:**	/usr/lib/acct/	**Type:**	External

xconsole

UNIX Shell: All primary shells (csh, ksh, sh)

Function	Shows console messages with X.				
Syntax	xconsole [options...]				
-file *file*		Specifies the device to monitor (default is /dev/console).			
-notify		Enables notification of new messages. Icon name changes so you will notice.			
-nonotify		Disables message notification. The icon won't change when something happens.			
-daemon		Runs in the background as a daemon.			
-verbose		Verbose mode. Shows more information.			
-exitOnFail		Exits if it is unable to retrieve output from the device.			
File Name:	`xconsole`	**Directory:**	/usr/openwin/bin/	**Type:**	External
Note:	Use this program to get console messages that you would see if you were in text console mode.				
xconsole -daemon			Used in Xinit scripts to run xconsole in the background.		
xconsole -nonotify			Runs xconsole and doesn't change the icon if xconsole is iconified.		

xgettext

UNIX Shell: All primary shells (csh, ksh, sh)

Function	Creates portable message files that contain copies of C string that are found in ANSI C source code.	
Syntax	xgettext [options...] *files...*	
-n		Adds comment lines to the output file. Shows filename and line number.
-s		Creates list sorted by msgids with all duplicate msgids removed.
-a		Extracts all strings.
-c *comment-tag*		Marks the beginning of the comment.
-d *default-domain*		Specifies the default domain to rename output file from `messages.po`.
-j		Joins messages with existing message files.
-m *prefix*		Fills in the `msgstr` with a prefix. This is useful for debugging.
-M *suffix*		Fills in the `msgstr` with a suffix. This is useful for debugging.
-p *pathname*		Specifies the directory to place the output files.
-x *exclude-file*		Specifies a .po file that contains a list of msgids that will not be extracted.
-h		Shows help information.
files...		Specifies file to use.

continued

File Name:	`xgettext`	**Directory:**	/usr/bin	**Type:**	External
Note:	By default, xgettext creates a .po file in the current working directory.				

xkill

UNIX Shell: All primary shells (csh, ksh, sh)

Function	Kills an X client. Useful for removing problematic programs.
Syntax	xkill [options...]

-display *displayname*	Specifies the X server to contact.
-id *resource*	Specifies the X identifier on resource to abort.
-button *number*	Specifies the number of pointer buttons to use when you select a window to kill.
-frame	Ignores standard conventions to find top-level client windows.
-all	Kills all clients with top-level windows on the screen.

File Name:	`xkill`	**Directory:**	/usr/openwin/bin/	**Type:**	External
Tip:	If no -id is given, a cursor is displayed so you can point on the window to kill.				

xload

UNIX Shell: All primary shells (csh, ksh, sh)

Function	Shows a histogram over the average system load.
Syntax	xload [options...]

-scale *integer*	Specifies the minimum tick marks to use in the histogram.
-update *seconds*	Sets the interval to update the histogram.
-hl *color*	Sets the color of the scale lines.
-highlight *color*	Same as -hl.
-jumpscroll *pixels*	Sets the number of pixels to move the scale line to the left when it reaches the end.
-label *string*	Sets a label over the scale.
-nolabel	Shows no labels.
-lights	Uses keyboard LEDs to show the current load average.

File Name:	`xload`	**Directory:**	/usr/openwin/bin/	**Type:**	External
xload -label myaverage			Start xload by using myaverage as the label above the load average.		

xlock

UNIX Shell: All primary shells (csh, ksh, sh)

Function	Locks the local X screen until the user enters a password.
Syntax	xlock [options...]

-display *dsp*	Specifies the X display to lock.
-help	Shows help information.
-name *resource-name*	Specifies a resource to use instead of XLock.
-v	Verbose mode. Shows more information.
	When you use these options, use - (minus) to disable and + (plus) to enable:
mono	Enables or disables the monochrome override.
nolock	Enables or disables the no password required mode.
allowroot	Enables or disables the allow root password mode.
enablesaver	Enables or disables the enable X server screen saver.
allowaccess	Enables or disables the allow new client access.
echokeys	Enables or disables the echo `?` for each password key.
usefirst	Enables or disables using the first character typed in password.
remote	Enables or disables the remote host access.
-mode *modename*	Specifies the animation mode.
	Then use these options as modes:
hop	Shows real plane fractals as described in the September 1986 issue of Scientific American.
life	Shows Conway's game of life.
qix	Shows the spinning lines similar to the old video game by the same name.
image	Shows sun logos on the screen.
swarm	Shows a swarm of bees.
rotor	Shows a swirling rotor-like thing.
pyro	Shows fireworks.

continued

flame	Shows strange fractals.
blank	Makes the screen blank.
random	Chooses randomly among the above modes except the blank mode.
-delay *usecs*	Sets the speed of an animation. A lower value makes animation faster.
-batchcount *num*	Specifies number of things to do per animation or batch.
-nice *nicelevel*	Specifies the so-called system nicelevel of xlock.
-timeout *seconds*	Specifies when password screen will time out in seconds.
-saturation *value*	Specifies saturation value: 0 is grayscale and 1 is very rich color.
-font *fontname*	Specifies the font to use on the prompt.
-fg *color*	Specifies foreground color for the password screen.
-bg *color*	Specifies background color for the password screen.
-username *textstring*	Specifies a text string in front of username.
-password *textstring*	Specifies a password prompt string.
-info *textstring*	Shows a what-to-do message.
-validate *textstring*	Specifies a message to show when validating the password.
-invalid *textstring*	Specifies text to show when password is invalid.
-resources	Shows default resource file on STDOUT.
File Name: `xlock`	**Directory:** /usr/openwin/bin/ **Type:** External

xlsatoms

UNIX Shell: All primary shells (csh, ksh, sh)

Function	Shows the specified interned atoms on the server.
Syntax	xlsatoms [options...]

-display *dpy*	Specifies the X server to contact.
-format *string*	Specifies printf-style string of how to show each atom.
-range *{ low }-{ high }*	Specifies the range of atoms to check. If low isn't given, 1 is used. (If high isn't given, xlsatoms continues until the first undefined atom.)
-name *string*	Specifies an atom to show.
File Name: `xlsatoms`	**Directory:** /usr/openwin/bin/ **Type:** External

xlsclients

UNIX Shell: All primary shells (csh, ksh, sh)

Function	Shows client applications that run on a screen.
Syntax	xlsclients [options...]

-display *displayname*	Specifies the X server to contact.
-a	Shows clients from all screens.
-l	Shows a long listing of applications.
-m *maxcmdlen*	Specifies the maximum number of characters in a command to show (default is 10000).
File Name: `xlsclients`	**Directory:** /usr/openwin/bin/ **Type:** External

xlswins

UNIX Shell: All primary shells (csh, ksh, sh)

Function	Shows a window tree for X.
Syntax	xlswins [options...] *{ windowid }*

-display *displayname*	Specifies which X server to contact.
-l	Shows a long list for each window.
-format *radix*	Specifies the radix to use when showing windows' IDs.
-indent *number*	Specifies number of spaces to be indented for each level in the window tree.
windowid	Specifies a new starting point.
File Name: `xlswins`	**Directory:** /usr/openwin/bin/ **Type:** External

xmag

xmag	UNIX Shell:	All primary shells (csh, ksh, sh)

Function	Enlarges parts of the screen.
Syntax	xmag [options...]

-mag *factor*	Specifies the magnification to use. Default is 5.
-source *geom*	Specifies size and or location of the source region on the screen.
-*toolkitoptions...*	Specifies additional standard X Toolkit command-line options.

File Name:	`xmag`	**Directory:**	/usr/openwin/bin/	**Type:**	External

xman

xman	UNIX Shell:	All primary shells (csh, ksh, sh)

Function	Shows man pages in a browser when running X.
Syntax	xman [options...]

-helpfile *file*	Uses a help file other than the default.
-bothshown	Shows both manual page and directory on-screen at the same time.
-notopbox	Starts the browser without the top menu.
-geometry *W*H+X+Y*	Specifies the size and location of the top menu.
-pagesize *W*H+X+Y*	Specifies the size and location for the manual pages.

File Name:	`xman`	**Directory:**	/usr/openwin/bin/	**Type:**	External

xman xman	Shows the man page for the command xman.

xntpd

xntpd	UNIX Shell:	All primary shells (csh, ksh, sh)

Function	A daemon that controls the time of day for UNIX systems.
Syntax	xntpd [options...]

-a	Starts in authentication mode.
-b	Listens (and synchronizes if possible) to ntp broadcasts.
-c	Specifies a configuration file other than the default.
-d	Shows debug information.
-e	Sets time allowed to compute ntp encryption field (in seconds).
-f *driftfile*	Specifies the drift file.
-k	Sets the path to the file containing ntp authentication keys.
-l *logfile*	Specifies a file to log to.
-m	Listens (and synchronizes if possible) for multicast messages.
-p *file*	Specifies file to save record daemon PIDs.
-r	Compensates for network delay between server and client.
-s	Sets directory to use when creating statistic files.
-t *trustedkey*	Specifies a key number to add to the trustedkey list.
-v	Specifies system variable to add.
-V	Specifies a system variable that is listed by default.

File Name:	`xntpd`	**Directory:**	/usr/lib/inet/	**Type:**	External
Note:	The configuration file is /etc/inet/ntp.conf.				

xpr

xpr	UNIX Shell:	All primary shells (csh, ksh, sh)

Function	Prints out X window dump information.
Syntax	xpr [options...] *{ filename }*

-device *devicetype*	Specifies a device to write dump file on.
-scale *scale*	Specifies size of the window on the page.
-height *inches*	Specifies a maximum height of the page.
-width *inches*	Specifies a maximum width of the page.
-top *inches*	Specifies top margin in inches for the picture. You can use fractions.
-header *string*	Specifies a header string to be printed above the window.
-trailer *string*	Specifies a trailer string to print below the window.

continued

-plane *number*	Specifies which bit plane to use in an image.
-landscape	Shows a window in landscape mode.
-gray *scale*	Specifies the grayscale conversion on the color image.
	The following options can be used with the -gray option:
2	Specifies 2x2 grayscale conversion.
3	Specifies 3x3 grayscale conversion.
4	Specifies 4x4 grayscale conversion.
-portrait	Prints the window in portrait mode.
-rv	Prints the window in reverse video.
-append *filename*	Specifies .xpr file to append to window.
-split *number*	Specifies how many pages to split a window.
-slide	Allows overhead transparencies to be printed by using PaintJet printers.
-noff	When used with -append, window shows on same page as previous window.
-psfig	Suppresses conversion of the PostScript picture to the center of the page.
-density *dpi*	Specifies dot-per-inch to use on HP printer.
-compact	Makes the presentation of the window more compact.
-output *filename*	Specifies output filename.
-cutoff *level*	Specifies the intensity level for the colors that are mapped to a printer.
-noposition	Skips header, trailer, and image position for some printers.
-gamma *correction*	Specifies intensity of colors on PaintJet XL printer. The range is 0.00 to 3.00.
-render *algorithm*	Specifies the image quality on a PaintJet XL printer.
filename	Specifies the file to be printed.

File Name:	`xpr`	**Directory:**	/usr/openwin/bin/	**Type:**	External
Note:	The -split option isn't supported for HP printers.				

xrefresh

UNIX Shell: All primary shells (csh, ksh, sh)

Function	Refreshes all or part of an X screen.
Syntax	xrefresh [options...]

-white	Uses white background.
-black	Uses black background.
-solid *color*	Specifies a color to create a background of.
-root	Uses the root window background.
-none	Refreshes all of the window; this is the default.
-display *displayname*	Specifies a server and screen to refresh.
-geometry *Width*Heigth+X+Y*	Specifies the part of screen to refresh.

File Name:	`xrefresh`	**Directory:**	/usr/openwin/bin/	**Type:**	External

xstr

UNIX Shell: All primary shells (csh, ksh, sh)

Function	Keeps a library of strings from component parts in large programs that can be used as shared constant strings.
Syntax	xstr *{ file }* [options...]

-c *filename*	Specifies a file with C source text.
-v	Verbose mode. Shows more information.
-l *array*	Specifies a program reference array.
file	Specifies the file to query.

File Name:	`xstr`	**Directory:**	/usr/bin/	**Type:**	External
xstr -c ucgfile		Extracts the strings from the C source `ucgfile`.			

xwininfo

UNIX Shell: All primary shells (csh, ksh, sh)

Function	Shows X window information on the X server.
Syntax	xwininfo [options...]

-help	Shows help information.
-id *id*	Specifies a target windowID.

continued

-root		Specifies that X root window is the target.			
-name *name*		Specifies the window named `name` as the target window.			
-int		Shows all X window IDs as integer values.			
-children		Shows the root, children, and parent windows ID.			
-tree		Shows all children recursively.			
-stats		Shows statistical information about the window.			
-bits		Shows bit information about the window.			
-events		Shows the window's event masks.			
-size		Shows size information about the window.			
-wm		Shows the selected window's window manager hints.			
-shape		Shows the window and border shape extends.			
-frame		Causes windows manager frames to look in when selecting windows.			
-english		Shows height, width, x, and y in inches.			
-metric		Shows metric information about the window.			
-all		Queries everything.			
-display *display*		Specifies the server that you want to connect to.			
File Name:	`xwininfo`	**Directory:**	/usr/openwin/bin/	**Type:**	External

yppasswd

UNIX Shell: All primary shells (csh, ksh, sh)

Function	Alters the password in the NIS database.				
Syntax	yppasswd *{ user }*				
user		Specifies the user for which you want to change the password.			
File Name:	`yppasswd`	**Directory:**	/usr/bin/	**Type:**	External
yppasswd ucg			Alters the password for the user ucg.		

ypstart

UNIX Shell: Bourne shell (sh)

Function	Starts NIS (Network Information Service). Use `ypstop` to stop it.				
Syntax	ypstart				
File Name:	`ypstart`	**Directory:**	/usr/lib/netsvc/yp/	**Type:**	Script

ypstop

UNIX Shell: Bourne shell (sh)

Function	Stops NIS (Network Information Service). Use `ypstart` to start it.				
Syntax	ypstop				
File Name:	`ypstop`	**Directory:**	/usr/lib/netsvc/yp	**Type:**	Script

ypxfrd

UNIX Shell: All primary shells (csh, ksh, sh)

Function	Efficiently transfers entire NIS maps. Should be run from the master server.				
Syntax	ypxfrd				
File Name:	`ypxfrd`	**Directory:**	/usr/lib/netsvc/yp	**Type:**	External

zcat

UNIX Shell: All primary shells (csh, ksh, sh)

Function	Decompresses and shows the specified files without altering them.				
Syntax	zcat *{ files... }*				
files...		Specifies one or more files to use as input to zcat instead of STDIN.			
File Name:	`zcat`	**Directory:**	/usr/bin/	**Type:**	External
Note:	This is the same command as `uncompress -c`.				
zcat ucg.Z			Shows the uncompressed contents of the file ucg.Z.		
zcat ucg1.Z ucg2.Z			Shows the uncompressed contents of ucg1.Z and ucg2.Z.		

zdump

zdump	UNIX Shell:	All primary shells (csh, ksh, sh)
Function	Shows the current date and time for the time zones that you specify on the command line.	
Syntax	zdump [options...] *{ timezones... }*	

-v	Verbose mode. Shows more information.
-c *cutoffyear*	Limits the verbose output to just before the year that you specify.
timezones...	Specifies which time zone to dump. If a wrong time zone is given, then GMT is shown.
File Name: `zdump`	**Directory:** /usr/sbin/ **Type:** External
Note:	/usr/share/lib/zoneinfo is the standard time zone information directory.
zdump -v europe	Shows European time in verbose mode.
zdump -v CET	Shows information about Central European Time.

zic

zic	UNIX Shell:	All primary shells (csh, ksh, sh)
Function	Creates files that can be used for time conversion.	
Syntax	zic [options...] *{ files... }*	

-s	Limits the time values in the output files.
-v	Prompts if the year in the input file is out of range.
-l *localtime*	Uses the specified time zone as local time.
-p *timerules*	Uses the rules from the specified time zone to manage posix time zone variables.
-d *directory*	Creates time conversion files in the specified directory.
-y *yeartype*	Checks how years are to be written.
files...	Specifies a file with time conversion information.
-	Reads time conversion information from STDIN.
File Name: `zic`	**Directory:** /usr/sbin/ **Type:** External

zipinfo

zipinfo	UNIX Shell:	All primary shells (csh, ksh, sh)
Function	Shows information about a zip archive, permissions, compression type, encryption, OS, version type, and more.	
Syntax	zipinfo [options...] *zipfile { files... }* [-x *files...*]	

-1	Shows filenames. Skips headers, trailers, and comments. Good for shell scripts.
-2	Shows filenames, one per line, and allows headers, trailers, and comments.
-s	Shows information in short UNIX format.
-m	Shows information in medium UNIX format.
-l	Shows information in long UNIX format.
-v	Verbose mode. Shows more information.
-h	Shows header line, archive name, actual size, and total number of files.
-M	Pipes all output to an internal pager. Looks like `--more--`.
-t	Shows the totals for the listed files or for all the files.
-T	Shows the specified file date and time in the format `yymmdd.hhmmss`.
-z	Adds the archive comment in the listing.
zipfile	Specifies a path to the zip archive.
files...	Files in the zip archive that are processed.
-x *files...*	Files in the zip archive that will not be processed.
File Name: `zipinfo`	**Directory:** /usr/bin/ **Type:** External
zipinfo -1 ucg.zip	Shows one filename per line.
zipinfo -h ucg.zip	Shows the header line, name, size, and number of files.

In This Part

Chapter 15
Macintosh Commands

This part shows you the commands of the Macintosh OS, the powerful and enduring operating system that is still the first choice for most graphics-intensive work.

Chapter 15

Macintosh Commands

The commands in this section cover all of the commands from Macintosh. The commands are all listed in alphabetical order by the command name.

When using the Macintosh command, special considerations should be given when executing the command. The Syntax field will often direct you to make a series of mouse movements and double-clicks in order to perform a specific task. A series of these types of actions are shown by placing a ">" in-between each action. Sometimes key-combinations are used in parallel with mouse clicks. When this needs to be done, each keystroke will be clearly specified and will be separated by a "+" symbol.

Anytime you see bold text in the options field, this indicates that this is a window menu or sub-menu heading, so you will have to click on it in order to find the listed sub-functions.

About This Computer

Description:	Shows system version, size of built-in memory, size of virtual memory, the largest unused memory blocks and how much memory application uses.
Syntax:	Apple Menu > About This Computer

Apple menu > About this computer	Shows how much memory application uses.

Appearance Control Panel

Description:	Sets themes, fonts, desktop pictures, sounds, and appearance options for Finder.
Syntax:	Apple Menu > Control Panels > Appearance *selections...* control + click on desktop > change desktop background *selections...*

Themes	Sets predefined appearance schemes for the Finder.
Appearance	
Appearance	Sets appearance for menus, icons, windows, and controls.
Highlight Color	Sets highlight color for selected text.
Variation	Sets color for menus and controls.
Fonts	
Large System Font	Sets font for menus and headings.
Small System Font	Sets font for explanatory text and labels.
View Font	Sets font and size for lists and icons.
Smooth all fonts on screen	Uses anti-aliasing on fonts larger or equal to the selected size.
Desktop	Sets pattern or pictures to the desktop.
Sound	Sets the sound for menus, windows, controls, and Finder.
Options	
Smart Scrolling	Places scroll arrows at the bottom of the window and sizes scrollbar after content.
Double-Click title bar to collapse windows	Closes windows by just double-clicking the title bar.

File Name:	`appearance`	**Directory:**	HD: System Folder: Control Panels:	**Type:**	External

Apple Menu > Control Panels > Appearance> Desktop	Here you can change your background picture.
Apple Menu > Control Panels > Appearance > Variation	Here you can change the color for the menus.

Apple System Profiler

Description:	Shows system information about memory, hardware, network, devices, volumes, control panels, extensions, applications, and the system folder.
Syntax:	Apple Menu > Apple System Profiler

System profile	
Software overview	Shows system and application versions.
Memory overview	Shows virtual and built-in memory, and volume.
Hardware overview	Shows Machine ID, model names, keyboard type, processor info, and computer speed.
Network overview	Shows Ethernet, open transport, AppleTalk, and TCP/IP information.
Printer overview	Shows information about the printer.
Production information	Shows ROM revision.
Devices and volumes	Shows information about all connected devices and volumes.
Control panel	Shows name, version, size, and creator for control panels and whether it's enabled.
Extensions	Shows name, version, size, and creator for extensions and whether it's enabled.
Applications	Shows name, version, size, and creator for installed applications.
System folder	Shows name and location for the active system folder.

File Name:	`apple system profiler`	**Directory:**	HD: System Folder: Apple Menu Items:	**Type:**	External

Apple menu > Apple system profiler > Network overview	Shows information about network card.
Apple menu > Apple system profiler > Applications	Shows information about all applications.

AppleCD Audio Player

Description:	Plays music from the CD drive.
Syntax:	Double-click the AppleCD Audio Player icon.

File Name:	`applecd audio player`	**Directory:**	HD: Applications: AppleCD Audio Player:	**Type:**	External

AppleTalk Control Panel

Description:	Configures whether AppleTalk connects via Ethernet, modem port, printer port, or remote only. Also allows user to see Macintosh, hardware, and router addresses.
Syntax:	Apple Menu > Control Panels > AppleTalk *selections...*

Connect via	
Ethernet	Connects AppleTalk via Ethernet.
Modem port	Connects AppleTalk via the modem port.
Printer port	Connects AppleTalk via the printer port.
Remote only	Connects via remote only.
	The following options are only available in Advanced or Administrator mode.
AppleTalk address:	Specifies whether the AppleTalk node and network should be user-defined.
Node:	Shows or sets the node.
Network:	Shows or sets the network.
Network range:	Shows the network range.
Info	Shows Macintosh, hardware, and router addresses and Open Transport, AppleTalk version.
Options...	Allows user to make AppleTalk active or inactive.

File Name:	`appletalk`	**Directory:**	HD: System Folder: Control Panels: AppleTalk	**Type:**	External
Note:	Changes user mode by selecting User Mode under Edit menu.				

Apple Menu > Control Panels > AppleTalk > Ethernet	Here you can change the modem connection to Ethernet.

Arrange

Description:	Arranges files and folders by name, date, size, kind, and label.
Syntax:	View > Arrange > *selections...*

by Name	Arranges files and folders in an alphabetic order.
by Date Modified	Arranges files and folders after date modified.
by Date Created	Arranges files and folders after date created.
by Size	Arranges files and folders by size.
by Kind	Arranges files and folders by kind
by Label	Arranges files and folders by label.
Tip:	Use mouse: Control + click in window > Arrange > *selections...*

As Buttons

Description:	Shows all files and folders as buttons in a window.
Syntax:	View > As Buttons
Tip:	This is good for kids.
View > As Buttons	Views files and folders as buttons. You only click once to open them.

As Icons

Description:	Shows all files and folders as icons in a window.
Syntax:	View > As Icons control + Click in window > View > As icons

As List

Description:	Shows all files and folders as a list in a window.
Syntax:	View > As List control + click i window > View > As List

As Pop-up Window

Description:	Changes the active window to a pop-up window. A pop-up window places itself as a tab at the bottom of the screen.
Syntax:	View > As Pop-up Window control + click in window > View > As Pop-up Window

As Windows

Description:	Changes the active pop-up window to an ordinary window.
Syntax:	View > As Window control + click in window > View > As Window
Tip:	The easiest way to convert a pop-up window to a window is by dragging it to the desktop.

Boot from a CD

Description:	Starts the computer from a bootable CD.
Syntax:	Hold down the key c during startup.
Note:	Standard procedure when the installed system fails.
Hold down the key c during startup.	Installs a new system from a CD.

Boot from a specified partition

Description:	Enables the computer to boot from a specified partition on your hard drive.
Syntax:	Hold down the keys `Command + Alt + E + N` during startup.

Boot from a specified SCSI-number

Description:	Boots the computer from an SCSI disk with the specified SCSI-ID.
Syntax:	Hold down the keys `Command + Alt + Shift + Delete + the SCSI-ID` during startup.

Boot from internal disk

Description:	Boots from the internal disk when the default startup disk is set to something else.
Syntax:	Hold down the key `d` during startup.

Boot from network

Description:	Boots from a network.
Syntax:	Hold down the key `n` during startup.
Note:	Only works on iMac and later models.

Boot from other disk

Description:	Boots the computer from the next disk in the SCSI chain.
Syntax:	Hold down the keys `Command + Alt + Shift + Delete` during startup.

Boot from Zip

Description:	Boots the computer from an internal Zip-drive.
Syntax:	Hold down the key `z` during startup.

Calculator

Description:	Is a simple graphical calculator.
Syntax:	Apple Menu > Calculator

File Name:	`calculator`	**Directory:**	HD: System Folder: Apple Menu Items	**Type:**	External

Cancel Operation

Description:	Cancels current operation.
Syntax:	Command + Dot

Command + Dot	Cancels current process.

Change Name

Description:	Renames disks, files, and folders.
Syntax:	Click the icon's title bar once, wait until text is selected, then type the new text.

Chooser

Description:	Selects a printer or other output device and creates a desktop printer icon for it. Is also used to browse shared disks, folders, and the local network.
Syntax:	Apple Menu > Chooser *selections...*

	The following option only works when AppleShare icon is selected.
Server IP address	Enters the IP address.
	The following two options only work when LaserWriter 8 icon is selected.
Select a PostScript printer:	Selects a specific network printer.
Setup:	Shows printer info, lets you configure and select PPD for your printer.
	The following three options only work when a printer icon is selected.
Connect to:	Selects a port for your personal printer.
Setup:	Logs printer usage and shares your printer.
Background printing:	Enables you to print in the background while working with other applications.
AppleTalk Active/Inactive	Activates and inactivates AppleTalk.

File Name:	`chooser`	**Directory:**	HD: System Folder: Apple Menu Items:	**Type:**	External

Apple menu > Chooser > Select a printer	Choose a printer to use.

Clean Up

Description:	Aligns files and folders into rows and columns.
Syntax:	View > Clean up Command + Drag file and drop

Close all open windows

Description:	Closes all open windows, including pop up windows.
Syntax:	Command + Alt + Shift + W

Close Finder windows during startup

Description:	Closes all open windows when Finder starts up.
Syntax:	Hold down the key `Alt` during startup.

Close foremost window

Description:	Closes the top window or collapses a pop-up window to its tab state at the bottom of the screen.
Syntax:	Command + W

Close pop-up window

Description:	Closes a pop-up window.
Syntax:	Command + Shift + W

Close Window

Description:	Closes the active window.
Syntax:	Command + W Click the close window box.

Collapse content in list view

Description:	Collapses the contents of the selected folder in a list view.
Syntax:	Command + left arrow Click the arrow left of the folder.

Collapse folders in list view

Description:	Collapses the marked folder and all folders contained within it in a list view.
Syntax:	Alt + Click the arrow left of the folder Alt + command + left arrow

Collapse/Expand all windows

Description:	Collapses or expands all open windows.
Syntax:	Alt + Double-click the title bar Alt + Click the windowshade box
Tip:	Useful to reach the desktop when many windows are open.

Copy File

Description:	Makes an exact copy of a file.
Syntax:	Alt + Drag a file

Copy Text

Description:	Copies marked text for later pasting.
Syntax:	Command + C Edit > Copy

Create New Folder

Description:	Creates a new empty folder.
Syntax:	Command + N File > New Folder

Cut

Description:	Cuts out highlighted text.
Syntax:	Command + X Edit > Cut

Date & Time Control Panel

Description:	Sets time and date. Also sets time zone and whether a network time server should be used. You can also activate the menu bar clock.
Syntax:	Apple Menu > Control Panels > Date & Time *selections...*

Date Formats	Sets the date to different regions.
Time Formats	Runs the clock in 12-hour or 24-hour format.
Time Zone	Sets the properties of Daylight Saving Time.
Set Time Zone	Sets time zone to use.
Use a Network Time Server	Sets the use of a time server.
Server Options	Sets which time server to use and when to update the time.

continued

Menu Bar Clock Clock Options	Sets whether the clock appears in the Menu Bar. Set the apperance and functions of the clock.				
File Name:	`date & time`	**Directory:**	HD: System Folder: Control Panels: Date & time	**Type:**	External

Disk Copy

Description:	Creates and mounts disk images.				
Syntax:	Double-click the Disk Copy icon.				
File Name:	`disk copy`	**Directory:**	HD: Applications: Utilities:	**Type:**	External
Tip:	Useful to make a copy of a CD to your desktop.				

Disk First Aid

Description:	Verifies and repairs disks.				
Syntax:	Double-click the Disk First Aid icon.				
File Name:	`disk first aid`	**Directory:**	HD: Applications: Utilities:	**Type:**	External
Tip:	If you have problems with your disk, check it with this application.				

Drag background window

Description:	Drags the background window without making it active.
Syntax:	Command + Click and drag background window.

Drive Setup

Description:	Formats and divides disks into multiple partitions.				
Syntax:	Double-click the Drive Setup icon.				
File Name:	`drive setup`	**Directory:**	HD: Applications: Utilities: Drive Setup	**Type:**	External

Dropdown Path

Description:	Shows a dropdown list with the path to the active window.
Syntax:	Command + click the name in title bar.
Command + click the name in the title bar.	Returns to an earlier directory.

Duplicate

Description:	Creates an exact copy of marked files and folders.
Syntax:	Command + D File > Duplicate

Eject Disks

Description:	Is used to ejects disks.
Syntax:	Select disk + Special > Eject Command + E Drag disk icon to the trash. File > Put away Command + Y Control + Click disk icon > Eject Command + Shift + 1

Empty Trash

Description:	Deletes all files in the trashcan.
Syntax:	Shift + Command + Delete Special > Empty Trash
Warning:	You really delete your files when you perform this command.

Energy Saver Control Panel

Description:	Sets time and date when the computer should sleep or shut down.
Syntax:	Apple Menu > Control Panels > Energy Saver *selections...*

Sleep Setup	Sets the time range before the computer is put to sleep.
Schedule	
Start up the computer	Sets date and time when the computer starts.
Shut down the computer	Sets date and time when the computer shuts down.
Notification	
Scheduled Shutdown	Sets how long time before schedules shutdown.
Wakeup	Sets a wakeup sound.
Advanced Settings	Mutes sound when the computer is asleep and auto restarts after power failure.

File Name:	`energy saver`	**Directory:**	HD: System Folder: Control Panels:	**Type:**	External

Enlarge a window

Description:	Enlarges a window to full screen size.
Syntax:	Alt + click zoom box

Erase Disk

Description:	Erases disks after selected format.
Syntax:	Special > Erase Disk *selections...*

Name	Enters the name of the disk.
Format	
Mac OS Standard	Formats the disk to Mac OS Standard.
Mac OS Extended	Formats the disk to Mac OS Extended.
Dos	Formats the disk to MS-DOS.
Pro Dos	Formats the disk to Pro-DOS.

Expand Content

Description:	Expands the contents of the selected folder in a list view.
Syntax:	Command + right arrow Click the arrows left of the folder.

Expand folders in list view

Description:	Expands the marked folder and all folders contained within it in a list view.
Syntax:	Alt + click the arrow left of the folder Alt + Command + right arrow

Alt + click the arrow left of the folder Alt + command + right arrow	Expands a folder and all folders within it in list view.

Extension Manager

Description:	Enables and disables system extensions, control panels, and other items in the system folder.
Syntax:	Apple Menu > Control Panels > Extensions Manager *selections...*

Selected set:					
Mac Os 9.1 All		Uses all startup items.			
Mac Os 9.1 Base		Uses only the most essential startup items.			
My settings		Activates selected settings.			
File Name:	`extension manager`	**Directory:**	HD: System Folder: Control Panels:	**Type:**	External

File Sharing Control Panel

Description:	Manages file sharing and program linking. Shows connected users and shared items. Creates new users and groups.
Syntax:	Apple Menu > Control Panels > File Sharing *selections...*

Start/Stop					
Network identity		Enters name, password, and computer name.			
File sharing Start/Stop		Starts and stops file sharing.			
File Sharing check box		Lets clients connect over TCP/IP.			
Program linking Start/Stop		Starts and stops program linking.			
Program linking check box		Connects over TCP/IP.			
Activity Monitor					
Disconnect		Disconnects selected user.			
Privileges		Shows the privileges for a shared item.			
Users & Groups					
New User					
Identity		Sets name and password for new user.			
Sharing		Allows user to use program linking and connect to your computer.			
Remote access		Allows user to dial in to the computer.			
New Group		Creates a new group.			
Open		Opens a new user or group.			
Duplicate		Duplicates a user or group.			
Delete		Deletes a user or group.			
File Name:	`file sharing`	**Directory:**	HD: System Folder: Control Panels:	**Type:**	External
Tip:	This command is good for sharing files with other computers.				

Find File

Description:	Searches the Internet, network, or drive.
Syntax:	Command + F File > Find

Finder Preferences

Description:	Configures general Finder settings and sets which view to use in Finder. Also allows user to use Simple Finder.
Syntax:	Edit > Preferences *selections...*

General	
Simple Finder	Removes commands from the menus to make it easier.
Spring-loaded folders	Opens a folder when the user holds an icon over it.
Grind spacing	
Tight	Arranges icons tighter.
Wide	Arranges icons wider.

continued

Views	Standard view options for List.
Use relative date	Uses Today or Yesterday when applicable, otherwise it will show the actual date.
Calculate folder sizes	Calculates folder size.
Icon size	
Small	Shows small icons.
Medium	Shows medium icons.
Big	Shows big icons.
Show columns:	
Date modified	Shows the date when it was last modified.
Date created	Shows the date when it was created.
Size	Shows the size of a file.
Kind	Shows what kind of file it is.
Label	Shows the label of the file if the file has a label.
Comments	Shows comments for the file.
Version	Shows version information.
	The following are standard view options for buttons and icons.
Button/Icon arrangement:	
None	Doesn't arrange the Icons or buttons
Always snap to grid	Arranges the Icons or buttons to grid.
Keep arranged	Arranges the Icons or buttons. (The following options can only be used when Keep arranged is selected.)
by Name	Arranges the Icons or buttons by name.
by Date modified	Arranges the Icons or buttons by modified date.
by Date created	Arranges the Icons or buttons by created date.
by Size	Arranges the Icons or buttons by size.
by Kind	Arranges the Icons or buttons by kind.
by Label	Arranges the Icons or buttons by label.
Button/Icon Size:	
Small	Makes the button or icon small.
Big	Makes the button or icon big.
Labels	Selects icon colors.

Force Quit

Description:	Quits an application or operation that has frozen.
Syntax:	Command + Alt + Esc

Force Restart

Description:	Forces the computer to restart.
Syntax:	Command + Control + power button

command + control + power button	If your computer has frozen, you can restart it with this shortcut.

Forced Shut Down

Description:	Forces the computer to shut down.
Syntax:	Control + Command + Alt + power button

General Controls Control Panel

Description:	Activates desktop hiding, adjusts blinking rate for cursors and menus, and specifies default folder that appears in save dialog box.
Syntax:	Apple Menu > Control Panels > General Controls

File Name:	`general controls`	**Directory:**	HD: System Folder: Control Panels:	**Type:**	External

Get Info

Description:	Shows type, size, and version information of file. Allows user to change the memory requirements for an application.
Syntax:	Select icon > Command + I Select icon > File > Get Info Control + Click file or folder + Get Info + General Information *selections...*

General Information	Shows type, size, and version.
Label	Gives the file or folder different colors for easier recognition.
Locked	Prevents file from being changed.
Sharing	Allows or prevents file and program sharing.
Memory	Checks and changes memory requirements.
Minimum Size	Shows the recommended minimum memory requirements for the application.
Preferred Size	Sets maximum memory delivery for the application.
Locked	Prevents file from being changed. (The folder[s] isn't shown when you get info on folder[s].)

Note:	Can also share files and folders and configure the memory requirements.

Hide Others

Description:	Hides every open application except the active one.
Syntax:	Application Menu > Hide Others
Tip:	Useful to clear the screen and hide the other applications.

Hide windows from previous program

Description:	Hides the active application and brings the selected one to the front.
Syntax:	Alt + Application Menu > Choose application Alt + Click window in another application.
Tip:	Many windows open? Hide the unused applications.

Internet Control Panel

Description:	Configures e-mail, web, news, and personal Internet settings.
Syntax:	Apple Menu > Control Panels > Internet *selections...*

Personal	
Identity:	Configures name, e-mail address, and organization.
Other Information:	Is used to type in other information.
Signature:	Creates a signature for the end of mails.
E-mail	
E-mail Account information	Configures account ID, incoming and outgoing mail server, and password.
E-mail Notification	Sets a flashing icon, display dialog, or a sound when messages arrive.
Default E-mail Application	Sets your default e-mail application.
Web	
Default pages:	Sets default home and search page.
Download files to:	Selects a download folder.
Colors & Links	Sets colors for links.
Default web browser:	Sets default web browser.
News	
News server settings:	Configures news server and connects as a guest or a registered user.
Default news application	Sets default news application.
Advanced	
File transfer	Sets default server for Archie server, Info-Mac server, and UMich server.
Helper Apps	Adds, removes, or changes helper applications.
Fonts	Selects size and font for list font, screen font, and printer font.
File mapping	Adds, removes, or changes file extension mappings.

continued

Firewalls Messages Hosts		Configures Firewall settings. Adds text to all outgoing news and mail messages. Sets address to different hosts.			
File Name:	`internet`	**Directory:**	HD: System Folder: Control Panels:	**Type:**	External

Internet Setup Assistant

Description:	Helps user to set up the computer for Internet.				
Syntax:	Double-click the Internet Setup Assistant icon.				
File Name:	`internet setup assistant`	**Directory:**	HD: Applications: Utilities: Assistants: Internet Setup	**Type:**	External

Key Caps

Description:	Shows all characters in each installed font and how to enter the character from your keyboard.				
Syntax:	Apple Menu > Key Caps				
File Name:	`key caps`	**Directory:**	HD: System Folder: Apple Menu Items:	**Type:**	External
Note:	If you don't know how to enter a character, check here.				

Keyboard Control Panel

Description:	Selects keyboard layouts and adjusts the way keys repeat. You can also set keyboard shortcuts here.				
Syntax:	Apple Menu > Control Panels > Keyboard				
File Name:	`keyboard`	**Directory:**	HD: System Folder: Control Panels:	**Type:**	External

Mac Help

Description:	Opens the Mac Help application.
Syntax:	Command + ? Help > Mac Help
Tip:	Really useful for beginners.

Make Alias

Description:	Creates a shortcut to the selected file or folder.
Syntax:	Command + M Alt + Command + Drag the file or folder to make an alias of.

Memory Control Panel

Description:	Configures memory setting for cache, virtual memory, and RAM disk. User can activate virtual memory and RAM disk.				
Syntax:	Apple Menu > Control Panels > Memory *selections...*				
Select Hard disk Use Default		Chooses a disk to take space from. Sets every memory setting to default.			
File Name:	`memory`	**Directory:**	HD: System Folder: Control Panels:	**Type:**	External

Modem Control Panel

Description:	Configures modem settings. Chooses which modem to use and whether the modem should use sound. Chooses whether the modem should dial with tone or pulse.				
Syntax:	Apple Menu > Control Panels > Modem *selections...*				
Connect via:		Chooses either modem or printer port.			
Modem:		Chooses modem in the list.			
Sound:		Switches modem sound on or off.			
Dialing:		Configures modem dialing with tone, pulse or ignore.			
Ignore dial tone		Controls whether modem should wait for dial tone before dialing.			
File Name:	`modem`	**Directory:**	HD: System Folder: Control Panels:	**Type:**	External

Monitors Control Panel

Description:	Configures color depth, resolution, and other settings depending on which monitor is connected.				
Syntax:	Apple Menu > Control Panels > Monitors *selections...*				
Monitor		Opens menu for general options for the monitor.			
Color depth		Sets the color depth (how many colosr to use).			
Resolution		Sets resolution to use.			
Contrast		Controls the contrast of the colors with a slide bar.			
Brightness		Controls the brightness of the monitor with a slide bar.			
Color		Controls which color sync profile to use. (This panel changes for the specific monitors it controls.)			
File Name:	`monitors`	**Directory:**	HD: System Folder: Control Panels:	**Type:**	External
Note:	New control panel tabs could appear depending on the type of monitor that is connected.				
Apple Menu > Control Panels > Monitors > Monitor		Changes your resolution.			

Mouse Control Panel

Description:	Configures mouse tracking speed and double-clicking speed.				
Syntax:	Apple Menu > Control Panels > Mouse				
File Name:	`mouse`	**Directory:**	HD: System Folder: Control Panels:	**Type:**	External
Apple Menu > Control Panels > Mouse			Adjusts arrow's speed.		

Move File

Description:	Moves files and folders.
Syntax:	Select file or folder > Drag the file or folder

Move From Trash

Description:	Moves files and folders from the trashcan.
Syntax:	Double-click trashcan and drag the files or folders to the desktop.

Move To Trash

Description:	Moves an item to the trashcan.
Syntax:	Command + Backspace Drag selected files or folders to trashcan. Control click on file or folder > Move to trash
command + Backspace	For deleting files or folders.

Multiple Users Control Panel

Description:	Allows multiple users with different accounts on your computer.
Syntax:	Apple Menu > Control Panels > Multiple Users *selections...*

New User	Creates a new user and opens the option window for the user.
Username:	Enters username for the user.
Password:	Gives the user a password to login on your computer.
Kind of User Account:	
Normal	Gives user normal access to most features in Finder.
Limited	Limits access to Finder.
Panels	Simplifies and limits access to Finder.
User Info:	
User Picture:	Selects a picture for the user.
User can change password	Enables the user to change his own password.
Can log in	Enables you to disable user without deleting.
Can manage user accounts	Enables user to manage user accounts.
Access by others to user's documents:	Controls how other users view this user's documents.
Applications:	Selects applications that users with limited or panels accounts can use.
Privileges	
Allow access to	
CD/DVD-ROMs	Prevents user from accessing CD-ROM or DVD-ROM drive.
Other removable media	Gives user access to other removable media such as floppy drives and zip drives.
Shared folder	Gives users access to shared folder.
Chooser and network browser	Gives users access to chooser and network browser.
Control Panels	Gives users access to the control panel.
Other Apple menu items	Gives users access to the Apple system profiler, calculator, scrapbook, and stickies.
User can print	Gives users access to print on any printer or on a specified printer.
Alternate password	
This user uses the alternate password	Gives users voice verification.
Allow this user to change his or her voiceprint.	Allows the user to change the voiceprint.
Open	Edit existing user settings.
Duplicate	Creates a copy of an existing user account.
Delete	Removes a user.
Option	
Login	Edits login settings and sets welcome message.
CD/DVD-ROM Access	Manages which CD/DVD titles a restricted user can use.
Other	Manages additional properties for login accounts.

File Name:	`multiple users`	**Directory:**	HD: System Folder: Control Panels:	**Type:**	External

Network Browser

Description:	Shows and connects to shared disks and folders on your network.
Syntax:	Apple Menu > Network Browser

File Name:	`network browser`	**Directory:**	HD: Applications:	**Type:**	External
Tip:	Use shortcut icons for quick access to file servers on TCP/IP or AppleTalk network.				

Numbers Control Panel

Description:	Changes decimal, thousands separator, and symbol to show currency.
Syntax:	Apple Menu > Control Panels > Numbers

File Name:	`numbers`	**Directory:**	HD: System Folder: Control Panels:	**Type:**	External

Open

Description:	Opens either a file or a folder.
Syntax:	Command + O Control click on file or folder > open File > Open Double-click on a file.

command + o	Open a text document.
Double-click	Open an application.

Open Extension Manager when startup

Description:	Opens Extension Manager during the startup process. Use the Extension Manager to control which extension and control panels to use on the computer.
Syntax:	Hold down the key `Space` during startup *selections...*

Selected set:	
MacOS 9.1 All	Uses all startup items.
MacOS 9.1 Base	Uses only essential startup items.
My settings	Settings users can switch on and off.
Hold down the key `Space` during startup.	Changes the extension setup when you start the computer.

Outlook Express

Description:	Is used to read and send e-mail messages. It can also be used to access newsgroups.
Syntax:	Double-click on the Outlook Express icon.

File Name:	`outlook express`	**Directory:**	HD: Applications: Outlook Express	**Type:**	External

Paste

Description:	Pastes what has been copied.
Syntax:	Command + V Edit > Paste

command + v	Paste copied text fields.
Edit > Paste	Paste copied file.

Print

Description:	Opens the print window where user selects which pages to print and how many. Also allows user to choose a printer.
Syntax:	Command + P File > Print

command + p	Print a text document.

PrintMonitor

Description:	Monitors print jobs and allows user to cancel print jobs being sent to printer.
Syntax:	Application Menu > PrintMonitor

File Name:	`PrintMonitor`	**Directory:**	HD: System Folder: Extensions	**Type:**	External
Note:	The PrintMonitor appears automatically when a file is being printed.				

Put Away

Description:	Returns a disc, file, or folder to it's original position.
Syntax:	Command + Y File > Put Away

command + y	Ejects a CD.
command + y	Ejects a floppy disk.

QuickTime PictureViewer

Description:	Shows pictures in various formats.
Syntax:	Double-click the Picture Viewer icon.

File Name:	`pictureviewer`	**Directory:**	HD: Applications: Quicktime:	**Type:**	External

QuickTime Player

Description:	Plays video, animations, sound, music, text, pictures, interactive images, and 3-D graphics.
Syntax:	Double-click the QuickTime Player icon.

File Name:	`quicktime player`	**Directory:**	HD: Applications: Quicktime:	**Type:**	External

Quit

Description:	Quits the active application.
Syntax:	Command + Q File > Quit

Rebuild Desktopfile

Description:	Rebuilds the desktop file.
Syntax:	Hold down the keys `Alt + Command` during startup.
Tip:	To rebuild the desktop file for a floppy disk or other removable media, hold command + option when inserting disk.

Hold down the keys `alt + command` during startup.	Fix corrupted information in the desktop file.

Remote Access Control Panel

Description:	Configures all remote connections.
Syntax:	Apple Menu > Control Panel > Remote Access *selections...*

Name	Enters your username.
Password	Enters your password.
Number	Enters the phone number of the server.
options...	
Redialing	Configures whether Remote Access should redial when there is no answer.
Connection	
Use verbose logging	Shows extra details in the connections log.
Launch Status application when connecting	Sets the behavior of connection reminders.
Flash icon in menu bar while connected	Controls the icon above the Apple menu icon when the user is online.
Prompt every X minutes to maintain connection	Shows a dialog box every *X* minutes and disconnects if no response is received.
Disconnect if idle for X minutes	Disconnects if no activity has taken place within X minutes.

continued

Protocol	
Use protocol:	
Automatic	Lets the Remote Access pick an appropriate protocol.
PPP	Connects to an ISP or remote TCP/IP network.
ARAP	Connects to a network server using the Apple Remote Access Protocol.
Connect automatically when starting TCP/IP applications	Connects automatically when starting TCP/IP applications.
Allow error correction and compression in modem	Allows modem hardware to compress sent data and check for errors in transmission.
Use TCP header compression	Determines whether the TCP header is compressed.
Connect to a command-line host:	Provides account and password information when the connection requires it.

File Name:	`remote access`	**Directory:**	HD: System Folder: Control Panels:	**Type:**	External

Replace File

Description:	Automatically prompts to replace a file when two files have the same name in the same folder or on the desktop.

Reset Column Position

Description:	Resets the columns in a list view.
Syntax:	View > Reset column position

View > Reset column position	If you have moved columns, you can reset them with this command.

Reset PRAM

Description:	Resets the Chooser and control panel settings stored in parameter RAM.
Syntax:	Hold down the keys `Command + Alt + P + R` during startup.

Hold down the keys `Command + Alt + p + r` during startup.	Resets your settings for a number of control panels, such as memory, monitors, and sound.

Scrapbook

Description:	Is used to store pictures, sounds, movies, text, and 3-D objects for easy and fast access.
Syntax:	Apple Menu > Scrapbook

File Name:	`scrapbook`	**Directory:**	HD: System Folder: Apple Menu Items:	**Type:**	External

Screen Shot

Description:	Makes a screen shot of the screen with Command + shift +3, and takes a screen shot of a part of the screen with Command + Shift + 4.
Syntax:	Command + Shift + 3 Command + Shift + 4

Screen shot of window

Description:	Takes a screen shot of selected window.
Syntax:	Caps Lock: on + Command + Shift + 4 + click in window

Note:	Caps Lock must be on!

Search Internet

Description:	Starts Sherlock 2 in search Internet mode.
Syntax:	Command + H File > Search Internet

Select All

Description:	Selects everything in the active window.
Syntax:	Command + A Edit > Select All

command + a	Selects all text in an open document.

Show All

Description:	Shows all open windows in all open applications.
Syntax:	Application Menu > Show All

Show Clipboard

Description:	Shows what was copied.
Syntax:	Edit > Show Clipboard

Show Original

Description:	Finds the shortcut's original.
Syntax:	Select shortcut icon > Command + R. File > Show original

Select shortcut icon > command + r.	If you have forgotten where the original file is, mark the alias and press command + r.

Shut Down

Description:	Stops the computer.
Syntax:	Power Button > Shut Down Special > Shut Down

SimpleText

Description:	Is a simple text editor for Mac.
Syntax:	Double-click the Simple Text icon.

File Name:	`SimpleText`	**Directory:**	HD: Applications:	**Type:**	External

Sound Control Panel

Description:	Selects input, output source, and alert sound, and configures speaker sound.
Syntax:	Apple Menu > Control Panels > Sound

File Name:	`sound`	**Directory:**	HD: System Folder: Control Panels:	**Type:**	External

Speech Control Panel

Description:	Allows users with visual or physical disabilities to control the computer with their voice.
Syntax:	Apple Menu > Control Panels > Speech

Voice	
Voice:	Specifies a voice for the computer to use.
Rate:	Specifies the speed of the voice.
Listening	
Key(s)	Specifies a key that must be held down for the computer to listen.
Methods:	
Listen only while key(s) are pressed	Makes the computer listen only when the specified key is held down.
Key(s) toggle listening on and off	Turns the key(s) toggle listening on or off.
Microphone:	Specifies a sound source.
Feedback	
Character	Specifies a character to use.
Speak text feedback	Displays only text when the computer gives feedback.
Recognized	Plays a recognize sound before the message.
Speakable Items	
Speakable items are	Allows user to open files located in the Speakable Items Folder by saying their names.
Recognize buttons such as "OK" and "Cancel"	Recognizes buttons as OK or Cancel when user speaks.
Talking Alerts	
Speak the phrase	Specifies a phrase to speak when an alert appears.
Speak the alert text	Speaks the text in the alert message.
Wait before speaking	Specifies the time in seconds to wait before speaking the alert text.

File Name:	`speech`	**Directory:**	HD: System Folder: Control Panels	**Type:**	External

Start Internet Explorer

Description:	Starts Internet Explorer.
Syntax:	Double-click the Internet Explorer icon.

File Name:	`internet explorer`	**Directory:**	HD: Applications: Internet Explorer:	**Type:**	External

Start without extensions

Description:	Turns off all extensions on your computer.
Syntax:	Hold down the key `Shift` during startup.
Note:	Can be used when troubleshooting your computer.

Start without virtual memory

Description:	Starts the computer without using virtual memory. Some applications perform better without virtual memory.
Syntax:	Hold down the key `Command` during startup.

Hold down the key `command` during startup.	Starts the computer without virtual memory.

Startup Disk Control Panel

Description:	Selects which drive the computer boots from.
Syntax:	Apple Menu > Control Panels > Startup Disk

File Name:	`startup disk`	**Directory:**	HD: System Folder: Control Panels:	**Type:**	External

StuffIt Expander

Description:	Decompresses .sit, .zip, .gz, tgz., .hqx, .bin, .uu, .uue, .pf, and ShrinkWrap disk images files.
Syntax:	Double-click the StuffIt Expander icon.

File Name:	`stuffIt expander`	**Directory:**	HD: Applications: Internet Utilities: Alladin Folder: Stuffit Expander:	**Type:**	External

TCP/IP Control Panel

Description:	Configures the TCP/IP protocol. You can set the IP address, subnet mask, router address, and DNS server information. for the computer manually or configure the computer to use DHCP.
Syntax:	Apple Menu > Control Panel > TCP/IP *selections...*

Connect via:	
AppleTalk (Mac IP)	Connects via MacIP.
Ethernet	Connects via Ethernet.
PPP	Connects via PPP.
Configure:	
Manually	Configures TCP/IP manually.
Using BootP Server	Configures TCP/IP using BootP Server.
Using DHCP Server	Configures TCP/IP using DHCP Server.
Using RARP Server	Configures TCP/IP using RARP Server.
IP Address:	User's IP number (is provided automatically by most configuration methods).
Subnet mask:	User's subnet mask (is provided automatically by most configuration methods).
Router Address:	User's router address (provided automatically by most configuration methods).
Name server address:	User's DNS (provided automatically by most configuration methods).
Search domains	Specifies the hostname of the DNS server.

File Name:	`TCP/IP`	**Directory:**	HD: System Folder: Control Panels:	**Type:**	External

Undo

Description:	Cancels and repairs last operation if possible.
Syntax:	Command + Z Edit > Undo

command + z	Undo what you did wrong, if possible.

View Options

Description:	Shows all the options for viewing files and folders.
Syntax:	View > View Options... *selections...* command + j Control + click in window > View Options *selections...*

Icon Arrangement:	
None	Shows No icon arrangement.
Always snap to grind	Snaps icons to a grid.
Keep arrangement:	
by Name	Arranges icons by name.
by Date Modified	Arranges icons by date modified.
by Date Created	Arranges icons by date created.
by Size	Arranges icons by size.
by Kind	Arranges icons by kind.
by Label	Arranges icons by label.
Set to standard views	Sets the options to the setting in the preferences.
	The following options can only be used when folders and icons are in list view.
Use relative date	Shows the relative date for files and folders.
Calculate folder sizes	Calculates folder size.

continued

Icon sizes	
Small	Shows small icons.
Medium	Shows medium icons.
Big	Shows big icons.
Show Columns:	
Date Modified	Shows the date when it was last modified.
Date Created	Shows the date when it was created.
Size	Shows the size of a file.
Kind	Shows what kind of file it is.
Label	Shows the label of the file when the file has a label.
Comments	Shows comments for the file.
Version	Shows the version of the file.
Set to standard views	Sets the options to the settings in the preferences.

Web Sharing Control Panel

Description:	Creates a personal Web server.
Syntax:	Apple Menu > Control Panels > Web Sharing *selections...*

My Address:	Shows users address when Web sharing is active.
Web Folder:	
Select	Selects a folder.
Home Page:	
Select	Selects the user's home page.
Start/stop	Activates and deactivates Web sharing.
Give everyone read-only access	Gives everyone read-only access.
Use File Sharing to control user access	Activates the user and password control that the user sets up in Users and Groups.

File Name:	`web sharing`	**Directory:**	HD: System Folder: Control Panels:	**Type:**	External

WhatRoute

Description:	Traces route to a specified target.
Syntax:	Double-click on the WhatRoute icon.

File Name:	`whatroute`	**Directory:**	HD: Applications: Utillities	**Type:**	External

Appendix

About the CD-Rom

The CD-ROM at the back of this book contains useful applications, team biographies, authorial thanks, UCG facts, and lots of other useful and funny things.

After you insert the CD-ROM into your computer, you get an automatic introduction to usher you into the *Universal Command Guide for Operating Systems.* Make sure you have your sound volume turned up far enough to hear it.

System Requirements

You need *at least* the following hardware and software to use the CD:

- A PC with a 486 processor or better
- Microsoft Windows, Macintosh 9+
- At least 32 MB of RAM
- A CD-ROM drive
- A sound card
- An SVGA monitor
- An Internet connection (to use the links)

Using the CD

To install the items from the CD to your hard drive, follow these steps:

To install the items from the CD to your hard drive, follow these steps:

1. Insert the CD into your computer's CD-ROM drive.
2. Click Start➡Run.
3. Type **X:\index.html** in the text box labeled Open, where *X* is letter of your CD-ROM drive.
4. Click OK.
5. To bypass the Introduction, click Skip Intro at the top of the screen.
6. To install the UCG Finder, click the Finder link on the right hand side, then click Click Here to Install. Note: This is a Windows-only component.
7. To view the items for an operating system, click Software.
8. For more information about a program, click the www link to go to that program's home page.
9. If you would like to install the program, click the appropriate Install button.

What You'll Find

UCG Team

In this section you can find out about the people who made this book possible and the UCG story about how the book was written. All team members have included some personal information, along with some of their favorite links. The author would also like to thank you (the reader) for reading this book, so please take some time and read this section of the CD-ROM.

FindIT

FindIT, the UCG Finder, was developed to complement the *Universal Command Guide for Operating Systems* and make it even easier to find the command you need, when you need it. You can quickly find the commands you need by typing the keywords relating to the task you want to accomplish. With FindIT, you can save and manage your own searches. FindIT also supports appended queries. If you need a command, go FindIT and then ReadIT in the *Universal Command Guide for Operating Systems.*

Software and Freeware

This section provides the user with an easy interface to install the most popular software and freeware today. Some of the following applications are included in the CD-ROM; others may be downloaded from the application home page:

- **ACDsee** is a picture & graphics viewer and manager for Windows and Macintosh.
- **Acrobat Reader** allows you to view and print Adobe Portable Document Format (PDF) files. Available for AIX, Linux, Windows, and Macintosh.
- **Apache Web Server** is, because of its stability, one of the most-used Web servers on the Internet. It's available for AIX, BSD, Linux, Solaris, and Windows.
- **Default Folder** will make the files on a Macintosh computer easier to manage.
- **Directx** is an advanced suite of multimedia APIs for Microsoft Windows systems.
- **Disinfectant** is an excellent (and free) antivirus program for the Macintosh.
- **Domain Name Analyzer** helps you to select a perfect domain name.
- **Drop Stuff** is a compression tool for Windows and Macintosh computers.
- **Fetch** is an easy-to-use FTP client for Macintosh computers.
- **FlashFXP** is a popular FTP and FXP client for Microsoft Windows.
- **Foldey** prevents folders from opening automatically when you start your computer (handy in environments that must limit automatic functions).
- **iMedia** is a Macintosh database program that keeps track of your various media collections (such as VHS and DVD movies).
- **iPassword** keeps track of your passwords and online information for your Macintosh.
- **Kaspersky AVP** is antivirus software for Linux and Windows.
- **Knowatch** gives you status of the network in NetWare.
- **Lan Clean** removes unused accounts, print queues, and files from NetWare servers.
- **Lan Test** measures and tests performance of AppleShare services.
- **ListMaster Pro** manages mailing lists in an easy way.
- **Litestep** makes your Windows desktop look a little like a Linux X-window desktop.
- **MacPing** is a Macintosh tool for testing IP and AppleTalk networks.

- **MI/X** is a handy X-window server for Windows or Macintosh computers.
- **MySQL** is the most popular Open Source SQL database product out there; it's available for AIX, BSD, Linux, Solaris and Windows.
- **Netstat Live** (for Macintosh) informs you about transfers on the Internet.
- **OpenGL** is an Application Program Interface (API) for 3-D games.
- **Ownerfix** changes the registered owner and company for Microsoft Windows.
- **Perl** is a high-level programming language.
- **Perl Studio** makes it easier for you to manage your Perl scripts.
- **PHP** is an HTML embedded scripting language.
- **Putty** is an outstanding telnet and SSH client used by the UCG Team during the development of the *Universal Command Guide for Operating Systems.*
- **Registry Toolkit** will make the Windows Registry easier to manage.
- **ResetID** allows users to reset passwords (and do other useful tasks) on NetWare servers.
- **Ruby** is the interpreted scripting language for quick and easy object-oriented programming.
- **Search and Replace** finds text strings in files.
- **Shrink Wrap** creates copies of disks, floppies, or CDs to disk images on a Macintosh.
- **StuffIt** makes Internet e-mail communication seamless and hassle-free.
- **Synchro** monitors changes in NDS user accounts and system login scripts on NetWare servers.
- **Sysey** is a system-information program.
- **Syslogd** is a system-logging utility.
- **TNTlite** is software for geospatial data analysis.
- **Tweak-ME** is a tweaker for optimizing memory on systems running Windows ME, 95, and 98.
- **Tweak-XP** is a tweaker for optimizing memory on systems running Windows XP.
- **Ultimate Boot Disk** helps you to install, troubleshoot, and fix Microsoft Windows.
- **Ultraedit** is a great editor for text, hex, HTML, and programming (and it's made for Microsoft Windows).
- **VMware Workstation** lets you run multiple operating systems on one computer.
- **VNC Remote Control** enables you to access desktops from anywhere. It's for Linux, Solaris, and Windows computers.
- **What Route** finds the names of routers that an IP packet passes. For Macintosh.
- **WhoIs Ultra** checks domain registrations from your Microsoft Windows system.
- **Winbatch** assigns Windows tasks to simple menu selections or hotkeys.
- **WinRAR** is a compression utility for Microsoft Windows.
- **WinTasks** is a task manager that improves your control over tasks running on Windows.
- **WinZIP** is a compression utility for Microsoft Windows.
- **WS_FTP Pro** is a file-transfer application for Microsoft Windows.
- **X-Win32** allows Windows users to connect to Linux/UNIX X-servers.
- **Ziney** is a newsletter editor.
- **Ziney Pro** is a newsletter editor and then some.
- **Zipey Pro** is a compression utility for Microsoft Windows.

Fun and Cool Stuff

These sections contain games, wallpapers, quotes, links, team stats, and some comedy.

Games and Stuff

Here you can find some games made by a UCG team member. There are also some beautiful UCG wallpapers for decorating your desktop.

Computer Quotes

Read some interesting quotes by computer people for computer people.

Useful and Funny Links

Contains very useful documentation and other help for AIX, Citrix, NetWare, MacOS, Open BSD, Red Hat, Solaris, and Windows. You can also find cool and funny links here.

Cool Stats

This is a list of statistics from the book project. For example, how many cups of coffee we drank, how many bags of chips we ate, and lots more. (Burp!)

Comedy

Sound clips from Three Dead Trolls in a Baggie. We think you will find this very amusing and funny. We have had some great laughs while listening to these guys. Thank you trolls, we needed it!

If You Have Problems

In the event you have problems with any of the programs on the CD, you might try the following troubleshooting steps.

- Disable any antivirus software.
- Close any running programs.
- Try loading/running the program through Windows Explorer instead of using the CD interface.

If you still have trouble with the CD, please call the Hungry Minds Customer Care phone number: (800) 762-2974. Outside the United States, call 1 (317) 572-3994. You also can contact Hungry Minds Customer Service by e-mail at techsupdum@wiley.com. Hungry Minds will provide technical support only for installation and other general quality control items; for technical support on the applications themselves, consult the program's vendor or author.

Index

A

B

C

D

G

H

K

L

M

N

O

P

Q

T

U

V

W

X

Z

Hungry Minds, Inc.
End-User License Agreement

READ THIS. You should carefully read these terms and conditions before opening the software packet(s) included with this book ("Book"). This is a license agreement ("Agreement") between you and Hungry Minds, Inc. ("HMI"). By opening the accompanying software packet(s), you acknowledge that you have read and accept the following terms and conditions. If you do not agree and do not want to be bound by such terms and conditions, promptly return the Book and the unopened software packet(s) to the place you obtained them for a full refund.

1. **License Grant.** HMI grants to you (either an individual or entity) a nonexclusive license to use one copy of the enclosed software program(s) (collectively, the "Software") solely for your own personal or business purposes on a single computer (whether a standard computer or a workstation component of a multi-user network). The Software is in use on a computer when it is loaded into temporary memory (RAM) or installed into permanent memory (hard disk, CD-ROM, or other storage device). HMI reserves all rights not expressly granted herein.

2. **Ownership.** HMI is the owner of all right, title, and interest, including copyright, in and to the compilation of the Software recorded on the disk(s) or CD-ROM ("Software Media"). Copyright to the individual programs recorded on the Software Media is owned by the author or other authorized copyright owner of each program. Ownership of the Software and all proprietary rights relating thereto remain with HMI and its licensers.

3. **Restrictions on Use and Transfer.**

   (a) You may only (i) make one copy of the Software for backup or archival purposes, or (ii) transfer the Software to a single hard disk, provided that you keep the original for backup or archival purposes. You may not (i) rent or lease the Software, (ii) copy or reproduce the Software through a LAN or other network system or through any computer subscriber system or bulletin-board system, or (iii) modify, adapt, or create derivative works based on the Software.

   (b) You may not reverse engineer, decompile, or disassemble the Software. You may transfer the Software and user documentation on a permanent basis, provided that the transferee agrees to accept the terms and conditions of this Agreement and you retain no copies. If the Software is an update or has been updated, any transfer must include the most recent update and all prior versions.

4. **Restrictions on Use of Individual Programs.** You must follow the individual requirements and restrictions detailed for each individual program in the Appendix of this Book. These limitations are also contained in the individual license agreements recorded on the Software Media. These limitations may include a requirement that after using the program for a specified period of time, the user must pay a registration fee or discontinue use. By opening the Software packet(s), you will be agreeing to abide by the licenses and restrictions for these individual programs that are detailed in the Appendix and on the Software Media. None of the material on this Software Media or listed in this Book may ever be redistributed, in original or modified form, for commercial purposes.

5. **Limited Warranty.**

(a) HMI warrants that the Software and Software Media are free from defects in materials and workmanship under normal use for a period of sixty (60) days from the date of purchase of this Book. If HMI receives notification within the warranty period of defects in materials or workmanship, HMI will replace the defective Software Media.

(b) **HMI AND THE AUTHOR OF THE BOOK DISCLAIM ALL OTHER WARRANTIES, EXPRESS OR IMPLIED, INCLUDING WITHOUT LIMITATION IMPLIED WARRANTIES OF MERCHANTABILITY AND FITNESS FOR A PARTICULAR PURPOSE, WITH RESPECT TO THE SOFTWARE, THE PROGRAMS, THE SOURCE CODE CONTAINED THEREIN, AND/OR THE TECHNIQUES DESCRIBED IN THIS BOOK. HMI DOES NOT WARRANT THAT THE FUNCTIONS CONTAINED IN THE SOFTWARE WILL MEET YOUR REQUIREMENTS OR THAT THE OPERATION OF THE SOFTWARE WILL BE ERROR FREE.**

(c) This limited warranty gives you specific legal rights, and you may have other rights that vary from jurisdiction to jurisdiction.

6. **Remedies.**

(a) HMI's entire liability and your exclusive remedy for defects in materials and workmanship shall be limited to replacement of the Software Media, which may be returned to HMI with a copy of your receipt at the following address: Software Media Fulfillment Department, Attn.: *Universal Command Guide for Operating Systems*, Hungry Minds, Inc., 10475 Crosspoint Blvd., Indianapolis, IN 46256, or call 1-800-762-2974. Please allow four to six weeks for delivery. This Limited Warranty is void if failure of the Software Media has resulted from accident, abuse, or misapplication. Any replacement Software Media will be warranted for the remainder of the original warranty period or thirty (30) days, whichever is longer.

(b) In no event shall HMI or the author be liable for any damages whatsoever (including without limitation damages for loss of business profits, business interruption, loss of business information, or any other pecuniary loss) arising from the use of or inability to use the Book or the Software, even if HMI has been advised of the possibility of such damages.

(c) Because some jurisdictions do not allow the exclusion or limitation of liability for consequential or incidental damages, the above limitation or exclusion may not apply to you.

7. **U.S. Government Restricted Rights.** Use, duplication, or disclosure of the Software for or on behalf of the United States of America, its agencies and/or instrumentalities (the "U.S. Government") is subject to restrictions as stated in paragraph (c)(1)(ii) of the Rights in Technical Data and Computer Software clause of DFARS 252.227-7013, or subparagraphs (c) (1) and (2) of the Commercial Computer Software-Restricted Rights clause at FAR 52.227-19, and in similar clauses in the NASA FAR supplement, as applicable.

8. **General.** This Agreement constitutes the entire understanding of the parties and revokes and supersedes all prior agreements, oral or written, between them and may not be modified or amended except in a writing signed by both parties hereto that specifically refers to this Agreement. This Agreement shall take precedence over any other documents that may be in conflict herewith. If any one or more provisions contained in this Agreement are held by any court or tribunal to be invalid, illegal, or otherwise unenforceable, each and every other provision shall remain in full force and effect.